1992-93 TEXAS ALMANAC

AND STATE INDUSTRIAL GUIDE

Published By

The Dallas Morning News

ISBN   0-914511-14-9   *(hardback)*
ISBN   0-914511-15-7   *(paperback)*
Library of Congress Card No. 10-3390
Copyright 1991, A.H. Belo Corp., P.O. Box 655237, Communications Center,
Dallas, TX 75265

Distributed by
Gulf Publishing Co.
P.O. Box 2608
Houston, TX 77252-2608
(713) 520-4444
FAX (713) 520-4438

1992-93 TEXAS ALMANAC

TABLE OF CONTENTS

Mike Kingston, *Editor*
Mary G. Crawford, *Associate Editor*

Steve Chambers, *Art Director*   Grayson Moody, *Production*
Sue Ellen Brown, *Cover Illustration*   Virginia Gardner, *Production*

Roseate Spoonbill   Brown-crested Flycatcher

Birdwatching in Texas

by Judith M. Garrett

Texas is the richest state in the union for birdwatching, providing birders the possibility to see more than three-fourths of all bird species found in the United States. The great abundance is possible because of the variety of habitats that exist within the state's diverse geography. From the vast coastline of the Gulf of Mexico, to the mountains of West Texas, and from the upland prairies to the Chihuahuan desert, Texas is home during some part of the year to **more species of birds than any other state.**

The **Texas Ornithological Society** has documented 570 species in Texas, and it acknowledges another 34 species that might be seen here. Of that large number, only 24 species are recognized to be common throughout most of the state. Each region has its own distinct bird life, in both seasonal visitors and year-round residents.

To further complicate and enrich the life of birdwatchers, Texas spans the division between the eastern and western United States. Most publishers of field guides, in order to keep the book sizes manageable, divide the birds of North America between east and west. Thus, birds found in the eastern part of Texas are generally listed in one field guide, and those found in the western part are listed in a different one. Birdwatching in Texas requires a small library of bird books, to cover all the possibilities.

In addition to the birds that nest in the state, a great many other species of birds travel the length of Texas, stopping along the way during both the **spring and fall migrations.** The migrations last for several weeks or even months. During those times, even inland birders might catch sight of spiraling flights of 50 to 100 American White Pelicans traveling together, or large formations of honking geese. A fairly common but always thrilling sight in the winter is the dormant grain field in Central Texas covered with **Canada and Snow Geese.**

In the spring, Texas provides birders with some of the best opportunities in the country to see the brilliantly colorful warblers. All species of **North American warblers** have been seen during their migrations through Texas. During the peak of the migration, birders along the coast can easily spot and watch at great length the exhausted warblers resting in dense, lo[...] brush after flying across the water. Warblers pa[...] through in the fall, as well, and truly serious birders te[...] their identification skills by trying to distinguish the[...] from each other in their fairly uniform, olive-yellow fa[...] plumage.

Winter is the best birding time along the Texa[...] coast, and the farther south, the better it gets. Along th[...] central coast, the rare **Whooping Crane** winters on th[...] **Aransas National Wildlife Refuge,** and in the Lower R[...] Grande Valley, the elegant **Osprey,** or "fish eagle,"[...] spends the winter fishing in the resacas and shallo[...] bays. Every body of water along the length of the Gu[...] coast is winter home to some species of waterfowl. Bir[...] ers can see everything from **American Wigeons** to **Vi[...] ginia Rails,** from **Common Loons** to **Ruddy Turnstones.**

Another winter visitor to South Texas is the **Sandh[...] Crane.** Large flocks can easily be observed makin[...] early morning and late evening flights from th[...] plowed fields where they congregate to the marsh[...] areas around the bays where they feed.

Winter birdwatching can be eventful even in Nor[...] and Central Texas, as large flocks of migrating duc[...] and other waterfowl stop over in area lakes. Som[...] such as the **Double-Crested Cormorant** and **Rudd[...] Ducks,** among others, stay all winter in city lakes.

Drawn by the exotic avian visitors from Mexi[...] and further south, thousands of birders travel to Te[...] as every year to see birds that enter the United Stat[...] only in subtropical south Texas. From the **Crested Ca[...] acara** to the **Plain Chachalaca,** from the **Groove-bill[...] Ani** to the **Great Kiskadee,** the **Lower Rio Grande Vall[...]** is a birdwatcher's paradise in the areas where habit[...] has been preserved.

Year-round near the coast in the Lower Rio Grand[...] Valley, it is not unusual at sunset to see a flock[...] glowing pink **Roseate Spoonbills** flying overhead fr[...] the shallow bays to their roosting areas inland.

The key word in Texas birdwatching is possibilit[...]

More on Page [...]

THE RIGHT RUG CAN MAKE A ROOM COME TO LIFE. *Suddenly, the setting is reborn. Awakening the senses. The only requirement, an authentic hand-woven Oriental or Persian rug. One made with craftsmanship of the highest investment quality. Selected from the right source.*

F E I Z Y

323 WORLD TRADE CENTER DALLAS 214 651 0877
HIGH POINT CHICAGO CINCINNATI DENVER ORLANDO

Texas Birds (clockwise from upper left): White-tailed Hawk, Hooded Oriole, Altamira Oriole, Buff-bellied Hummingbird, Tricolored Heron, Yellow-crowned Night-Heron, Black-crowned Night-Heron, Least Bittern. Photos by Mike Krzywonski, Laguna Vista, TX.

More Texas Birds (clockwise from upper left): Crested Caracara, White-winged Dove, Great Kiskadee, Red-billed Pigeon, Mangrove Warbler, Green Jay, Black-bellied Whistling-Duck, Plain Chachalaca. Photos by Mike Krzywonski, Laguna Vista, TX.

Northern Beardless-Tyrannulet

Black-necked Stilt

Continued from Page 6.

which is a driving force for most birders. While no one can be guaranteed a sighting of any one bird species, the possibilities are greater in Texas than anywhere else that birders will be rewarded in their efforts to add another species to their life lists or to have another look at some special favorite.

In addition to many small local preserves maintained around the state by regional chapters of the **Audubon Society,** the State maintains more than 30 **wildlife management areas** containing more than 200,000 acres. Most of the national, state, county and city parks are protected areas for birds, and Texas' 14 national wildlife refuges incorporate more than 250,000 acres of land where birds and birders are seasonally abundant. But all of the protected areas add up to less than 2 percent of the land mass of Texas.

Birders know that in Texas often the only movement required to view interesting birds is a simple raising of the chin, to look up into the trees overhead, even in city backyards. Within every community, no matter the size, birds are drawn to water, whether it is in a backyard bird bath, a lake, or the local sewage treatment plant. Find water, and you usually find birds.

Most communities have local birding organizations, most of which are affiliated with the **National Audubon Society.** The local groups organize outings, which are usually announced in newsletters, and they welcome everyone interested in bird life, from novice to expert.

Attesting the state's great birding possibilities, Texas is the only state in the union with its own **Peterson Field Guide,** a handy reference for anyone who sets out to identify birds in the state, whether the focus is on a neighborhood back yard in Texarkana or the mountains of Big Bend.

The following bibliography is a sampling of field guides and other reference books that are helpful for birdwatching in Texas. Some of the books listed, particularly those with a smaller regional focus, may be difficult to find except in large bookstores or by special order. Local chapters of the Audubon Society can be helpful in finding the best reference materials for each locale.

Bull, John and Farrand, John, Jr., *The Audubon Society Field Guide to North American Birds, Eastern Region,* New York: Alfred A. Knopf, Inc., 1977.

Ehrlich, Paul R., Dobkin, David S., and Whey Darryl, *The Birder's Handbook: A Field Guide to t Natural History of North American Birds,* New Yor Simon & Schuster, Inc., 1988.

Jones, John Oliver, *Where The Birds Are: A Gui to All 50 States and Canada,* New York: Willia Morrow and Co., Inc., 1990.

Kutac, Edward A., *Birder's Guide to Texas,* Hou ton: Gulf Publishing, 1989.

Lane, James A., *A Birder's Guide to the R Grande Valley of Texas,* Sacramento: L & P Photogr phy, 1978.

Lane, James A., and Tveten, John, *A Birde Guide to the Texas Coast,* Sacramento: L & P Photc raphy, 1980.

National Geographic Society, *Field Guide to Bir of North America,* Second Edition, Washington: N tional Geographic Society, 1987.

Oberholser, Harry C. and Kincaid, Edgar B., J *The Bird Life of Texas,* Austin: University of Tex Press, 1974.

Peterson, Roger Tory, *A Field Guide to the Bir of Texas and Adjacent States,* Boston: Houghton M flin Co., 1963.

Peterson, Roger Tory, *A Field Guide to the We ern Birds,* Second Revised Edition, Boston: Hought Mifflin Co., 1961.

Peterson, Roger Tory, *A Field Guide to the Bir* Fourth Edition, Boston: Houghton Mifflin Co., 1973.

Pulich, Warren M., *The Birds of North Cent Texas,* College Station: Texas A & M University Pre 1988.

Rappole, John H. and Blacklock, Gene W., *Birds the Texas Coastal Bend: Abundance and Distributi* College Station: Texas A & M University Press, 1985.

Robbins, Chandler S., et al., *Birds of North Ame ca: A Guide to Field Identification,* Expanded, Revis Edition, New York: Golden Press, 1983.

Udvardy, Miklas D. F., *The Audubon Society Fi Guide to North American Birds: Western Region,* N York: Alfred A. Knopf, Inc., 1977.

Wauer, Roland H., *Birds of Big Bend National Pa and Vicinity,* Austin: Texas Monthly Press, 1985.

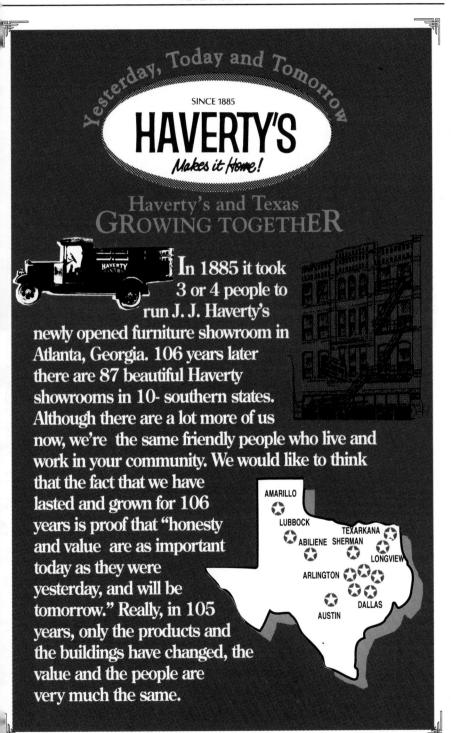

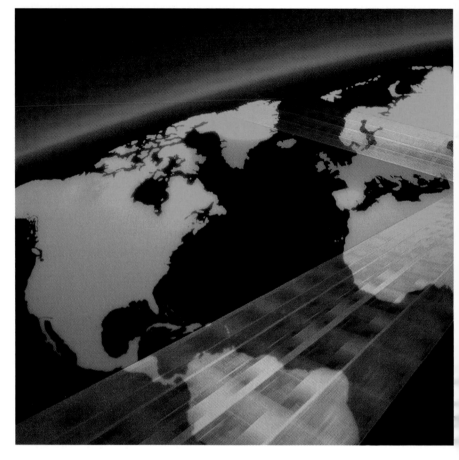

How to get to where your future is taking you.

The world is changing. Overnight. Evolving every day. And with it so are the needs and opportunities of catalogers, publishers and many other users of information.

To help you reach your goals and the world you serve, we work hard to learn your markets. Anticipate your needs. Customize our services to fit your requirements. Target products to attract your consumers and advertisers. Apply our technology and expertise to help ensure your competitive advantage.

As a result, we've become a global company. With facilities that go across the country, around the globe and into the skies. So we can help you get where your future is taking you--better and faster than you might get there otherwise.

R.R. DONNELLEY & SONS COMPANY

ADDING EFFICIENCY TO RETAIL ADVERTISING
708/574-3840

The Birds of Texas

The following is a generally recognized list of birds found in Texas, using their common names only. The illustrations accompanying the text provide a sampling of some of the state's most beautiful birds.

Anhinga
Groove-billed Ani
American Avocet
Rose-throated Becard
American Bittern
Least Bittern
Brewer's Blackbird
Red-Winged Blackbird
Rusty Blackbird
Yellow-headed Blackbird
Eastern Bluebird
Mountain Bluebird
Western Bluebird
Bobolink
Northern Bobwhite
Blue-faced Booby
Brown Booby
Red-footed Booby
Brant
Bufflehead
Indigo Bunting
Lark Bunting
Lazuli Bunting
Painted Bunting
Varied Bunting
Bushtit
Canvasback
Crested Caracara
Northern Cardinal
Gray Catbird
Plain Chachalaca
Yellow-breasted Chat
Black-capped Chickadee
Carolina Chickadee
Mountain Chickadee
Chuck-will's-widow
American Coot
Double-crested Cormorant
Olivaceous Cormorant
Bronzed Cowbird
Brown-headed Cowbird
Sandhill Crane
Whooping Crane
Brown Creeper
Red Crossbill
American Crow
Fish Crow
Mexican Crow
Black-billed Cuckoo
Yellow-billed Cuckoo
Long-billed Curlew
Dickcissel
American Dipper
Ground Dove
Inca Dove
Mourning Dove
Ringed Turtle-Dove
Rock Dove
Ruddy Ground Dove
White-fronted Dove
White-winged Dove
Long-billed Dowitcher
Short-billed Dowitcher
American Black Duck
Harlequin Duck
Masked Duck
Mottled Duck
Muscovy Duck
Ring-necked Duck
Ruddy Duck
Black-bellied Whistling-Duck
Fulvous Whistling-Duck
Wood Duck
Dunlin
Bald Eagle
Golden Eagle
Cattle Egret
Great Egret
Reddish Egret
Snowy Egret
Common Eider
Aplomado Falcon
Peregrine Falcon
Prairie Falcon
Cassin's Finch
House Finch
Purple Finch

Greater Flamingo
Northern Flicker
Acadian Flycatcher
Ash-throated Flycatcher
Brown-crested Flycatcher
Dusky Flycatcher
Dusky-capped Flycatcher
Fork-tailed Flycatcher
Gray Flycatcher
Great Crested Flycatcher
Hammond's Flycatcher
Least Flycatcher
Olive-sided Flycatcher
Scissor-tailed Flycatcher
Sulphur-bellied Flycatcher
Vermilion Flycatcher
Western Flycatcher
Yellow-bellied Flycatcher
Magnificent Frigatebird
Gadwall
Purple Gallinule
Northern Gannet
Black-tailed Gnatcatcher
Blue-gray Gnatcatcher
Hudsonian Godwit
Marbled Godwit
Barrow's Goldeneye
Common Goldeneye
American Goldfinch
Lawrence's Goldfinch
Lesser Goldfinch
Barnacle Goose
Blue Goose
Canada Goose
Greater White-fronted Goose
Ross' Goose
Snow Goose
Northern Goshawk
Boat-tailed Grackle
Common Grackle
Great-tailed Grackle
Eared Grebe
Horned Grebe
Least Grebe
Pied-billed Grebe
Red-necked Grebe
Western Grebe
Black-headed Grosbeak
Blue Grosbeak
Evening Grosbeak
Pine Grosbeak
Rose-breasted Grosbeak
Bonaparte's Gull
California Gull
Franklin's Gull
Glaucous Gull
Great Black-backed Gull
Herring Gull
Laughing Gull
Lesser Black-backed Gull
Ring-billed Gull
Sabine's Gull
Northern Harrier
Broad-winged Hawk
Common Black-Hawk
Cooper's Hawk
Ferruginous Hawk
Gray Hawk
Harris' Hawk
Red-shouldered Hawk
Red-tailed Hawk
Roadside Hawk
Rough-legged Hawk
Sharp-shinned Hawk
Short-tailed Hawk
Swainson's Hawk
White-tailed Hawk
Zone-tailed Hawk
Black-crowned Night-Heron
Great Blue Heron
Green-backed Heron
Little Blue Heron
Tricolored Heron
Yellow-crowned Night-Heron
Allen's Hummingbird
Anna's Hummingbird
Black-chinned Hummingbird

Blue-throated Hummingbird
Broad-billed Hummingbird
Broad-tailed Hummingbird
Buff-bellied Hummingbird
Calliope Hummingbird
Costa's Hummingbird
Lucifer Hummingbird
Ruby-throated Hummingbird
Rufous Hummingbird
Rufous-tailed Hummingbird
White-eared Hummingbird
Glossy Ibis
Scarlet Ibis
White Ibis
White-faced Ibis
Northern Jacana
Parasitic Jaeger
Pomarine Jaeger
Blue Jay
Brown Jay
Green Jay
Pinyon Jay
Scrub Jay
Steller's Jay
Dark-eyed Junco
Yellow-eyed Junco
American Kestrel
Killdeer
Cassin's Kingbird
Couch's Kingbird
Eastern Kingbird
Gray Kingbird
Tropical Kingbird
Western Kingbird
Belted Kingfisher
Green Kingfisher
Ringed Kingfisher
Golden-crowned Kinglet
Ruby-crowned Kinglet
Great Kiskadee
Black-shouldered Kite
Hook-billed Kite
Mississippi Kite
Black-legged Kittiwake
Red Knot
Horned Lark
Limpkin
Chestnut-collared Longspur
Lapland Longspur
McCown's Longspur
Smith's Longspur
Arctic Loon
Common Loon
Red-throated Loon
Black-billed Magpie
Mallard
Gray-breasted Martin
Purple Martin
Eastern Meadowlark
Western Meadowlark
Common Merganser
Hooded Merganser
Red-breasted Merganser
Merlin
Northern Mockingbird
Common Moorhen
Rufous Mourner
Common Nighthawk
Lesser Nighthawk
Clark's Nutcracker
Brown-headed Nuthatch
Pygmy Nuthatch
Red-breasted Nuthatch
White-breasted Nuthatch
Oldsquaw
Altamira Oriole
Audubon's Oriole
Hooded Oriole
Northern Oriole
Orchard Oriole
Scott's Oriole
Osprey
Ovenbird
Barn Owl
Barred Owl
Burrowing Owl
Elf Owl

Flammulated Owl
Great Horned Owl
Long-eared Owl
Ferruginous Pygmy-Owl
Northern Pygmy-Owl
Northern Saw-whet Owl
Eastern Screech-Owl
Western Screech-Owl
Short-eared Owl
Snowy Owl
Spotted Owl
American Oystercatcher
Yellow-headed Parrot
Northern Parula
Tropical Parula
Common Pauraque
American White Pelican
Brown Pelican
Band-rumped Storm-Petrel
Leach's Storm-Petrel
Greater Pewee
Eastern Wood-Pewee
Western Wood-Pewee
Phainopepla
Red Phalarope
Red-necked Phalarope
Wilson's Phalarope
Ring-necked Pheasant
Black Phoebe
Eastern Phoebe
Say's Phoebe
Band-tailed Pigeon
Red-billed Pigeon
Northern Pintail
White-cheeked Pintail
Sprague's Pipit
Water Pipit
Black-bellied Plover
Lesser Golden-Plover
Mountain Plover
Piping Plover
Semipalmated Plover
Snowy Plover
Wilson's Plover
Common Poorwill
Greater Prairie-Chicken
Lesser Prairie-Chicken
Pyrrhuloxia
Gambel's Quail
Montezuma Quail
Scaled Quail
Black Rail
Clapper Rail
King Rail
Virginia Rail
Yellow Rail
Chihuahuan Raven
Common Raven
Redhead
Common Redpoll
American Redstart
Painted Redstart
Greater Roadrunner
American Robin
Clay-colored Robin
Sanderling
Baird's Sandpiper
Buff-breasted Sandpiper
Curlew Sandpiper
Least Sandpiper
Pectoral Sandpiper
Purple Sandpiper
Semipalmated Sandpiper
Sharp-tailed Sandpiper
Solitary Sandpiper
Spotted Sandpiper
Stilt Sandpiper
Western Sandpiper
White-rumped Sandpiper
Williamson's Sapsucker
Yellow-bellied Sapsucker
Greater Scaup
Lesser Scaup
Black Scoter
Surf Scoter
White-winged Scoter
White-collared Seedeater
Audubon's Shearwater
Sooty Shearwater
Northern Shoveler
Loggerhead Shrike
Northern Shrike

Gray Silky-Flycatcher
Pine Siskin
Black Skimmer
Common Snipe
Townsend's Solitaire
Sora
Bachman's Sparrow
Baird's Sparrow
Black-chinned Sparrow
Black-throated Sparrow
Botteri's Sparrow
Brewer's Sparrow
Cassin's Sparrow
Chipping Sparrow
Clay-colored Sparrow
Field Sparrow
Fox Sparrow
Golden-crowned Sparrow
Grasshopper Sparrow
Harris' Sparrow
Henslow's Sparrow
House Sparrow
Lark Sparrow
LeConte's Sparrow
Lincoln's Sparrow
Olive Sparrow
Rufous-crowned Sparrow
Sage Sparrow
Savannah Sparrow
Seaside Sparrow
Sharp-tailed Sparrow
Song Sparrow
Swamp Sparrow
Vesper Sparrow
White-crowned Sparrow
White-throated Sparrow
Roseate Spoonbill
European Starling
Black-necked Stilt
Wood Stork
Surfbird
Bank Swallow
Barn Swallow
Cave Swallow
Cliff Swallow
Northern Rough-winged Swallow
Tree Swallow
Violet-green Swallow
Tundra Swan
Black Swift
Chimney Swift
Vaux's Swift
White-throated Swift
Hepatic Tanager
Scarlet Tanager
Summer Tanager
Western Tanager
Blue-winged Teal
Cinnamon Teal
Green-winged Teal
Arctic Tern
Black Tern
Caspian Tern
Common Tern
Elegant Tern
Forster's Tern
Gull-billed Tern
Least Tern
Roseate Tern
Royal Tern
Sandwich Tern
Sooty Tern
Bendire's Thrasher
Brown Thrasher
Crissal Thrasher
Curve-billed Thrasher
Long-billed Thrasher
Sage Thrasher
Gray-cheeked Thrush
Hermit Thrush
Swainson Thrush
Varied Thrush
Wood Thrush
Bridled Titmouse
Plain Titmouse
Tufted Titmouse
Brown Towhee
Green-tailed Towhee
Rufous-sided Towhee
Elegant Trogon
Red-billed Tropicbird
White-tailed Tropicbird
Wild Turkey

Ruddy Turnstone
Northern Beardless-Tyrannulet
Veery
Verdin
Bell's Vireo
Black-capped Vireo
Gray Vireo
Hutton's Vireo
Philadelphia Vireo
Red-eyed Vireo
Solitary Vireo
Warbling Vireo
White-eyed Vireo
Yellow-green Vireo
Yellow-throated Vireo
Black Vulture
Turkey Vulture
Bachman's Warbler
Bay-breasted Warbler
Black-and-White Warbler
Blackburnian Warbler
Blackpoll Warbler
Black-throated Blue Warbler
Black-throated Gray Warbler
Black-throated Green Warbler
Blue-winged Warbler
Canada Warbler
Cape May Warbler
Cerulean Warbler
Chestnut-sided Warbler
Colima Warbler
Connecticut Warbler
Golden-cheeked Warbler
Golden-crowned Warbler
Golden-winged Warbler
Grace's Warbler
Hermit Warbler
Hooded Warbler
Kentucky Warbler
Lucy's Warbler
MacGillivray's Warbler
Magnolia Warbler
Mourning Warbler
Nashville Warbler
Olive Warbler
Orange-crowned Warbler
Palm Warbler
Pine Warbler
Prairie Warbler
Prothonotary Warbler
Red- faced Warbler
Swainson's Warbler
Tennessee Warbler
Townsend's Warbler
Virignia's Warbler
Wilson's Warbler
Worm-eating Warbler
Yellow Warbler
Yellow-rumped Warbler
Yellow-throated Warbler
Louisiana Waterthrush
Northern Waterthrush
Bohemian Waxwing
Cedar Waxwing
Whimbrel
Whip-poor-will
American Wigeon
Eurasian Wigeon
Willet
American Woodcock
Acorn Woodpecker
Downy Woodpecker
Golden- fronted Woodpecker
Hairy Woodpecker
Ivory-billed Woodpecker
Ladder-backed Woodpecker
Lewis' Woodpecker
Pileated Woodpecker
Red-bellied Woodpecker
Red-cockaded Woodpecker
Red-headed Woodpecker
Bewick's Wren
Cactus Wren
Canyon Wren
Carolina Wren
House Wren
Marsh Wren
Rock Wren
Winter Wren
Greater Yellowlegs
Lesser Yellowlegs
Common Yellowthroat
Gray-crowned Yellowthroat

This Tenontosaur once roamed ancient North Texas. Its skeleton, reconstructed by the Dallas Museum of Natural History, was found in Wise County. It is the only mounted Texas dinosaur specimen on display at this time. (See sketch, page 24.) Photo courtesy Dallas Museum of Natural History.

Texas Dinosaurs

The following article was prepared especially for this edition of the Almanac by Georg Zappler of Smithville.

Among Texas' numerous fossil finds are 16 of the approximately 300 kinds of dinosaurs known worldwide. (A "kind" of dinosaur as used here is the scientific category of the genus, such as *Tyrannosaurus*. Each genus contains one or more related species. *Tyrannosaurus rex*, for example, is one of several species of *Tyrannosaurus*. The vast majority of dinosaur genera contain only a single species.)

The dinosaurs that once roamed the land now called Texas can be arranged into three "batches" in terms of the geological time frames within which their preserved bones and footprints are found.

Dinosaurs

The earliest batch dates to about 225 million years ago and comes from a fossil-bearing, late Triassic formation exposed along the brakes and escarpments of the Panhandle High Plains. The time represented by these sedimentary deposits marks the first appearance of the two major categories of dinosaurs: the saurischians, or "lizard-hips," and the ornithischians, or "bird-hips." ("Lizard-hips" include all the carnivorous dinosaurs, small and large, as well as the giant herbivorous brontosaurlike sauropods. "Bird-hips" include only plant-eaters, among them the duckbills and the horned, armored and plated dinosaurs.) Finds from late-Triassic Texas include one early, small-sized representative from each dinosaur category:

Coelophysis was a lightly built, two-legged, sharp-toothed lizard-hip. About eight feet long, three feet high at the hips and weighing over 100 pounds, this early dinosaur is well known from dozens of complete skeletons found in New Mexico; Texas remains are fragmentary.

Technosaurus was named after Texas Tech, since it was discovered near Lubbock. Only a distinctive jaw fragment with small, leaf-shaped teeth identifies this dinosaur as belonging to a stem group of plant-eating bird-hips best known from South Africa. About four feet long, slight and light-boned, it ran on its hind legs and probably afforded many a meal to flesh-eating *Coelophysis*.

The environment in which these dinosaurs lived was a tropical inland basin surrounded by mountains. Dense stands of archaic, 50- to 100-foot-high conifers formed a closed canopy across well-drained bottomlands, and fern- and cycad-covered swamps bordered numerous streams and ponds. In the waters lived small and large primitive fishes (including a lobefin and a lungfish), huge, pancake-shaped amphibians and crocodilelike archaic reptiles. Sharing the land with the two dinosaurs were heavily armored and spiked, now extinct, reptiles, as well as the earliest known representatives of modern lizards, snakes and birds.

The second batch of Texas dinosaurs are world-famous by virtue of the hundreds of well-preserved footprints left in what then were tidal flats bordering the Gulf of Mexico of about 105 million years ago during early Cretaceous times. The rocks preserving this ancient, fluctuating shoreline are now exposed through much of Central and North Central Texas. Complementing three distinctive kinds of tracks are partial fossil skeletons, found in the same or contemporary deposits, that permit educated guesses as to the identity of the track-makers. Discovered fossil bones belong to five different dinosaurs:

Acrocanthosaurus was a 30-foot-long, dagger-toothed lizard-hip with elongated spines enclosed in a ridge of muscle, along the back. Weighing about three tons, this powerful hunter is thought to be the originator of the most common kinds of tracks: 12- to 14-inch-long, birdlike, three-toed imprints, with a stride ranging from almost four to over five feet. Fossils of this dinosaur include a partial skull from Texas and several incomplete skeletons from Oklahoma.

Pleurocoelus, was a giant, up-to-50-foot-long, 40-ton sauropod, or brontosauruslike, plant-eating lizard-hip. It had a relatively short tail, which it probably used as a

Acrocanthosaurus (30 ft. long)

Acknowledgements

The beautiful sketches of dinosaurs in this section are presented through the courtesy of the Texas Department of Parks and Wildlife, Interpretation and Exhibits Branch. The artist is G. Aaron Morris, a former Texas resident now living in North Carolina.

Tyrannosaurus (40 feet long, 18 feet high)

prop while browsing from the top branches of the conifers growing beyond the marshes bordering the tidal flats. The largest tracks, consisting of coupled saucer-shaped and crescent-shaped depressions, were almost certainly made by the elephantine hind feet and sheathed, hooflike front feet of this dinosaur. Some of these tracks are three feet long and two feet wide, with stride lengths of from seven to 10 feet. In some locations, sauropod trackways accounting for several dozen of these dinosaurs traveling as a herd have been described. At Dinosaur Valley State Park in Glen Rose, two parallel trackways record the dramatic chase and possible attack of a *Pleurocoelus* by an *Acrocanthosaurus*. Several partial skeletons of *Pleurocoelus* have been found in Texas; it is also known from Maryland.

Tenontosaurus, a 15- to 20-foot-long, relatively small-headed, stout-bodied bird-hip, had a tail that accounted for half its length. Recessed behind bone-framed cheek pouches was a powerful battery of wide grinding teeth

for tough plant food. A number of fairly complete skeletons have been found in North Central Texas and adjoining states. *Tenontosaurus* has been proposed as a maker of the third kind of tracks — three-toed like those of *Acrocanthosaurus*, but more stubby in front and rounder-heeled in outline. However, since this plant-eater had four toes behind and five in front, it makes an unsatisfactory candidate.

Iguanodon, a 20- to 30-foot-long, four- to five-ton, plant-eating bird-hip, is known from most continents. Recent discoveries of *Iguanodon* fragments in early-Cretaceous deposits of Texas confirm its presence here. *Iguanodon* is a more likely choice for the originator of the blunt-toed, round-heeled footprints, since, unlike four-toed *Tenontosaurus*, its hind feet had three toes ending in stubby, hooflike claws. *Iguanodon* is thought to have traveled mostly on its hind legs,
More on Page 22.

Chasmosaurus (17 feet long)

Edmontosaurus (42 feet long, 15 feet tall)

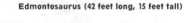

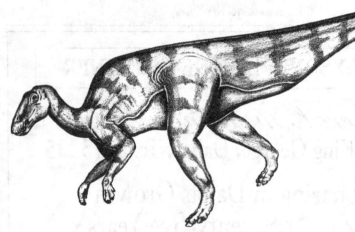

Pleurocoelus (50 feet long)

occasionally sinking down on its four-toed front feet, which were armed with spiked thumbs for defense.

Deinonychus, 10 feet long, weighing 175 pounds and standing on two legs, was a swift and fearsome predator with a straight, stiff tail. It was armed with impressive claws, especially the five-inch movable sickle blades carried on the second toe of each hind foot, which were used for disemboweling prey. One such blade has been found in early Cretaceous Texas deposits, confirming the presence of this carnivore, well-known from other western states. As far as we know, none of its footprints were preserved.

The dinosaurs of the tidal flats and adjoining marshes and uplands of the Texas Gulf Coast of 105 million years ago shared their environment with crocodiles, turtles and flying reptiles. Also present, and indicative of the future, were the earliest marsupial mammal and the earliest placental mammal known to science.

The remaining and largest batch of Texas dinosaurs is found in late-Cretaceous rocks, of between 75 and 65 million years ago, located in the Big Bend region. These dinosaurs mostly belong to the last flowering of certain dinosaur families (as the duckbills and horned dinosaurs) just before the extinction of dinosaurs as a whole. The Big Bend country of late Cretaceous times lay to the west of an inland sea that cut across North America from the Gulf of Mexico to Alaska. The dinosaur bones were buried in sedimentary deposits laid down by rivers on their eastward course toward the inland sea. Nine kinds of dinosaurs have been identified:

Alamosaurus was a 70-foot-long, 30-ton sauropod of relatively slender build. It was one of the few of its kind to survive into late Cretaceous times, most sauropods **More on Page 24.**

The Lone Star Champion

Champion International Corporation is today one of the world's largest paper companies. And we're one of the biggest companies in Texas, to boot.

Champion now manages 1.1 million acres of timberlands in Texas. Those trees support two major paper mills, two plywood plants, a paperboard milk and juice carton plant, and three paper distribution warehouses. Together, these operations employ more than 3,000 Texans — more Champions than in any other state.

Our mills in Lufkin and Sheldon make newsprint for your daily paper as well as directory paper used in telephone books. Our other plants and offices are spread across the state in Arlington, Camden, Corrigan, Dallas, Fort Worth, Houston, Huntsville, and San Antonio.

Champion has been a Texas company for half a century; and we're proud to have grown with the Lone Star State. Champion's long tradition of excellence — effectively managing our natural resources and hiring the best people to make high-quality products efficiently — fits right in with the Texas way of doing things.

We're proud to be Champions. And we're proud to be Texans.

Champion
Champion International Corporation

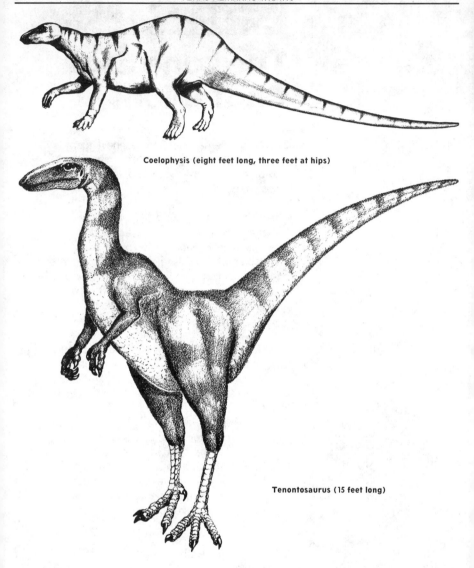

Coelophysis (eight feet long, three feet at hips)

Tenontosaurus (15 feet long)

dying out tens of millions of years before. Leg and pelvis bones have been found in Texas; other remains are known from New Mexico, Utah and Montana.

Tyrannosaurus was one of the largest of the two-legged, meat-eating lizard-hips. It measured 40 feet from head to tail tip, and its huge skull was lined with serrated teeth up to seven inches long. Its arms were disproportionately small, but built for efficient grappling. Texas has some skull fragments of this dinosaur, known from most of western North America and from China.

Chasmosaurus, a relatively small, four-legged horned dinosaur of the plant-eating, bird-hipped clan, carried a long frill jutting out from the skull and covering its neck and shoulders. The 17-foot-long, two-and-a-half-ton dinosaur had a small nose horn and two larger horns above the brows. Known from fragmentary Texas material, skeletons of *Chasmosaurus* have been found in New Mexico and Alberta, Canada.

Torosaurus was the largest of the horned dinosaur family. The three-horned skull accounted for nine feet of its 25-foot overall length. The nine-ton beast ranged from Montana to Texas, where fragmentary remains authenticate its presence.

Edmontosaurus was one of the largest of the duck-bills, a family of plant-eating bird-hips. It moved mainly on its hind legs and had the broad, toothless beak, with batteries of grinding teeth further back in the jaws, characteristic of the group. Loose skin around the nose area could be blown up to help make bellowing calls. It is best known from Alberta, Canada, and also from fragmentary New Jersey and Texas remains.

Hadrosaurus (Kritosaurus), a 30-foot-long, three-ton duckbill, had a deep, narrow face, a hump in front of the eyes and a soft frill along the back. Standing some 10 feet high at the hips, it moved mainly by balancing **More on Page 25.**

Alamosaurus (70 feet long)

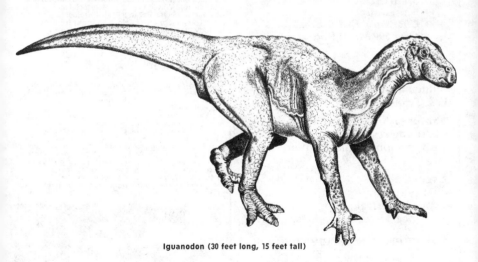

Iguanodon (30 feet long, 15 feet tall)

its body on powerful hind legs, sometimes sinking down on all fours. The Texas material is fragmentary; good skeletons are known from New Jersey, New Mexico and Alberta, Canada.

Ornithomimus was one of the ostrich dinosaurs, a family of predaceous lizard-hips, resembling tall flightless birds. Moving on long legs and counterbalanced by its long tail, toothless *Ornithomimus* preyed on small reptiles and insects and also dug up eggs. It is known from western North America and from Tibet. Texas has some of this dinosaur's hand and foot bones.

Stegoceras, a small member of the bone-headed dinosaur family of plant-eating bird-hips, was characterized by thick-domed skulls. This dinosaur, weighing up to 120 pounds and measuring six-and-a-half feet in length, also had a frill of bony bumps around the back of its head. Its unusually sharp teeth may indicate insect-

eating habits in addition to a plant diet. *Stegoceras* remains are known from several western states and northwest China. The Texas fossils are fragmentary.

Panoplosaurus was one of the last of the armored dinosaurs, a family of plant-eating bird-hips characterized by bony armor plating on the back and skull. This 23-foot-long, four-ton dinosaur also had long spines along its flanks. Its fossils are found throughout western North America. Texas has some distinctive bony fragments.

Contemporaries of the Big Bend dinosaurs included a giant flying reptile with a 40-foot wingspread and a gigantic crocodile with a six-foot-long skull. The environment, however, would appear quite modern to a time traveler. Flowering plants had replaced the ancient conifers, cycads and ferns of previous ages, and the dinosaurs roamed forests of oak, fig and elm trees.

This colorful crayfish was discovered in the Parkhill Prairie area of Collin County in 1990.

Newly Discovered Species Found in Texas

Two newly discovered species — one a **North Central Texas crayfish**, the other a far **West Texas yellow violet** — were announced during 1990. So far, both have been found only in Texas.

The **crayfish** discovery was made by Ken Steigman, curator of natural sciences at the Heard Natural Science Museum and Wildlife Sanctuary in McKinney. Steigman was working in the **Parkhill Prairie** area of Collin County, a protected tallgrass prairie, on a grant from the county to study the prairie's animal life. The crayfish (*Procambarus girardiella steigmani*) was caught in one of Steigman's snake traps. Crayfish resemble miniature lobsters, and the male of this particular species has a red body with blue sides, rough-textured pincers and an unusual pattern of teeth. The zoologist emeritus of the Smithsonian Institution in Washington, D.C., verified that the new mudbug was indeed a never-before-known species. The tallgrass prairie where the crayfish lives benefits from the tiny crustacean's burrowing, which aerates the soil.

The **yellow violet** was discovered in the **Guadalupe Mountains National Park** near El Paso by Park Ranger Brent Wauer in 1987. The plant, whose scientific name is *Viola guadalupensis*, has been described as "small, beautiful and tough as a boot." Admirers of Stormie Jones, who was the world's first heart and liver transplant patient, say that the West Texas girl exhibited those same characteristics during her seven-year fight to survive. After Stormie's death on Nov. 11, 1990, at the age of 13, they campaigned successfully to give the plant the common name of "the Stormie Jones violet."

The Guadalupe Mountains National Park in far West Texas is home to this newly discovered yellow violet.

Origins of American Indians

Debate on the origins of American Indians, as discussed in a related article on this page, is not new. It began a bit after Columbus' contact with the New World.

Columbus, of course, thought he had reached the Indies. Consequently, there was no mystery about the natives' origins. They were Asiatic, an idea supported by their oriental appearance.

It became apparent that the New World was not the Orient, however. Scholars and theologians began to seriously ponder the origin of these strange new people. Early speculation had to be consistent with the teachings of the church at the time and had to have origins confirmed in the Bible. That required an explanation based on Noah's family, the only eight humans to have survived the great flood.

Most early thought held that ancestors of the natives were descendent of Carthaginians, the greatest of ancient mariners. Or, surprisingly, some thought the inhabitants were survivors of the doomed continent of Atlantis, as revealed in Plato's writings. In Mexico, where the missionaries heard the Aztec legends of migration, speculation often centered on the possibility that the natives were descendents of the Lost Tribes of Israel.

In 1589, Joseph de Acosta did the first comprehensive review of American origins, and the first book devoted to the subject was published in 1607.

No great controversy arose on origins of the inhabitants before 1550 because of Columbus' assumption. Some surprisingly modern notions began to develop, however. Bartoleme de las Casas, a vigorous defender of the New World inhabitants, acknowledged the principal of stratification. In his history of the Indies, de las Casas described visiting mines in which strata could be seen that held burned wood and ashes that looked to be only a few days old. He acknowledged that water washed over the fire pits burying them in silt and that the process took many years to build the strata over them. From this observation, he concluded that man had been in the New World from very ancient times.

Most attempts at determining the origins of the na-

Ancient Texans

How did the first human beings get to Texas? How did they live? What record of their existence did they leave behind? So go the questions about Texas' prehistoric past. These are not new queries. When applied to the New World, the speculations go back to the earliest days of the Spanish conquest. (See previous article.)

Some bits of bone dredged from Texas coastal waters have opened a new avenue of inquiry about the state's earliest settlers and, indeed, about the entire settlement process in the New World.

The question has been raised that maybe, the people of the Clovis culture, long thought to be the first Texans, were actually descendants of an earlier populace. Why, then, have we not found evidence of the earlier inhabitants? The answer is complicated.

The standard theory is that the earliest immigrants got to North America about 11,500 years ago. These big-game hunters lived off large animals, such as mammoths, mastodons and giant bison that roamed the

Archaeology

prairies and woodlands of the period. Settlers of Texas, according to this scenario, were either immigrants from Northeast Asia or the successors of those who first ventured across the Bering Strait during recent ice ages.

These nomads left major diagnostic artifacts across Texas' prehistoric landscape. The most notable is the Clovis point. (See pictures on page 29.) This is a large, bifaced, fluted projectile point. Usually between three and six inches long, this point is thought to have been used on spears to kill these huge beasts. The point also could have been hafted and used as a knife for butchering. Often shortened versions of the points, obviously resharpened by chipping, are found at butchering sites. A tallow buildup on the edge of the point during the butchering of an animal would have required frequent sharpening.

Texas apparently was a friendly hunting ground for these prehistoric immigrants. More than 300 Clovis points have been found across the state, mostly on the South Plains and on the beaches of Jefferson County in Southeast Texas. They were scattered across more than 95 counties, according to a survey by Dr. David Meltzer of Southern Methodist University. These results may be deceiving, however, since they represent pieces found in public collections and in holdings of reputable amateur archaeologists. The number of points in unreported private collections cannot even be estimated. To an extent, the distribution of the artifacts reflects the archaeological activity in the counties in which they are found. Also a dearth of the points in a broad band just east of the Caprock does not mean that Clovis man was not in the area. But more than 30 feet of dirt now covers the land on which the ancient hunters would have walked. There-fore the points, if there are any, are probably several feet underground.

Texas has long figured in the debate over the arrival and presence of man in the New World. Actually, one of the first so-called Clovis points was found in the state before the site near Clovis, N. Mex., was excavated. A man and a boy walking along Wolf Creek near Colorado City in Mitchell County in 1923 found the bones of an ancient bison sticking out of the embankment. The skeleton was excavated by workers who thought they were only retrieving the skeleton of an ancient beast. Then three projectile points were found within the rib cage, indicating that the animal had been killed by humans. Unfortunately, the points were discovered long after proper scientific protection for the dig had been ignored. The site could not be used to prove that man had been in North America much longer than thought at the time. (This missed opportunity did prompt Cyrus Ray, an Abilene physician, to organize what became the Texas Archeological Society in 1928, launching the modern era of archaeology in the state.)

A Clovis point found near Lake Lewisville in Denton County in the 1950s sparked one of the state's longest standing archaeological controversies. Initial radiocarbon dating of material found with the point indicated an age of more than 30,000 years. That threw scientifically accepted calculations about the presence of humans in the New World out of kilter. A second excavation of the site in the late 1970s, however, caused a revision of the projected age. It probably is in the 10,000-11,000 year range. In the original dig, some of the dated material apparently was contaminated with lignite, which looks much like charcoal, but, of course, is much older. The presence of lignite in the test sample would have given a false reading.

A second Clovis site was found below the dam at Lake Ray Roberts also in Denton County. About 20 miles north of the Lake Lewisville find, this site, discovered in the December 1988, may be one of the largest ever found, covering several acres. Archaeologist Reid Ferring and his eight-year-old son, Taylor, came upon the site while looking for fossils. The site was secretly excavated by North Texas State University under contract to the Fort Worth District Army Corps of Engineers for more than a year to avoid the threat of vandalism.

What has been uncovered are two campsites about 120 yards apart along the old bed of the river. They may be parts of the same campsite that could cover up to five or six acres, although today much of it is under 25 feet of dirt.

Bones of several types of animals, large and small, have been discovered, many with apparent butchering marks on them. Various tasks also have been identified with specific locations within the camp. Areas where tools were made have been found, separate from the butchering operations and from the cooking area.

More on Page 29.

tives centered on cultural comparisons of speech, dress, manner and religion with known Old-World cultures and speculating on a method of transporting them to the New World.

Joseph de Acosta in 1589 took an approach close to scientific in analyzing the problem. He doubted the Americans' ancestors sailed to the New World in ancient times because the lodestone or compass was not in use at the time. Therefore, they could not have crossed the Atlantic.

There was also the problem of New-World animals that appeared closely related to beasts in the Old World. They could not have been transported by boat.

Consequently, both man and beast must have reached the New World by land, Acosta thought. No known land route between Europe and America existed in the 16th century nor was any known of in ancient times. Acosta speculated a land bridge existed to the west and connected with Asia. Along this route, the New-World inhabitants had made their way into the new homeland. The migration took place in small groups over a considerable length of time, not a major, massive movement of people in a short period.

Although there had been earlier speculation about a land bridge, Acosta was the first to postulate one not connected with European legend.

Acosta was the first writer to set ground rules about how the migration took place. His works were widely read after 1590, and his careful analysis gives him the distinction of providing the first "scientific" approach to the solving the problem. The work was first published in English in 1607.

The debate on the origins moved into northern Europe in the 17th century. Between 1640 and 1675, dozens of academic dissertations on American Indians appeared in the universities of the region.

Rumors of the Russian expedition of 1728 that discovered the Bering Strait confirmed the speculations of a possible land bridge and the close proximity of Asia and the New World. Acosta's theory of 140 years earlier was exonerated.

Today's debates accept the Bering land route a priori, and the major question revolves around "when" not "how" the early migrants made their way to the New World. Texas in many ways is right in the middle of the research and debate in the current scientific studies. It remains to be seen if a new Acosta is emerging whose theory on timing will one day be embraced as perceptive and correct.

FOR FURTHER READING: Huddleston, Lee Eldridge, **Origins of American Indians: European Concepts, 1492-1729;** University of Texas Press, Austin and London, 1967, 1972.

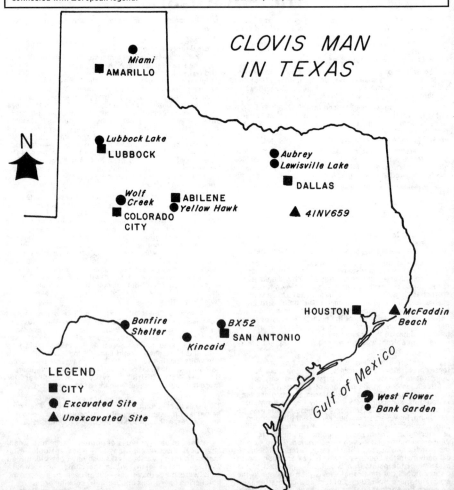

CLOVIS MAN IN TEXAS

N

- Miami
- ■ AMARILLO
- Lubbock Lake
- ■ LUBBOCK
- Aubrey
- Lewisville Lake
- ■ DALLAS
- Wolf Creek
- ■ ABILENE
- Yellow Hawk
- ■ COLORADO CITY
- ▲ 41NV659
- Bonfire Shelter
- BX52
- ■ SAN ANTONIO
- Kincaid
- HOUSTON ■
- ▲ McFaddin Beach
- Gulf of Mexico

LEGEND
- ■ CITY
- ● Excavated Site
- ▲ Unexcavated Site

- ? West Flower
- ● Bank Garden

This distinctive artifact (each side shown) found across Texas is a Clovis point. Both sides of the point have been fluted to fit on the end of a shaft. It could be used as a projectile point or as a knife for butchering game. This point, found by Fern Rater Fry near Prospect, Rains County, in 1926, is new, showing no evidence of sharpening. Photo courtesy of Larry Banks.

From Page 27.

According to Dr. Ferring, the campsites are in pristine condition, appearing to have been used only once and for a short period of time, probably less than a season. The people came, harvested animals and possibly wild nuts and berries and left, never to return. One thing for certain, they left nothing of value, only the daily refuse of a Stone-Age society.

The stone used for making tools was imported from the Alibates Quarry on the Canadian River and from other places in West Texas. The Alibates flint was popular among prehistoric people, being found across Texas and beyond. It is tough to chip and has to be fired to remove moisture and become malleable, a feature apparently appreciated by early stone nappers.

Several different environmental studies have been conducted on the site, which will probably give archaeologists the best picture yet of a period of prehistoric life in North Central Texas.

Fewer than 10 Clovis sites have been excavated in Texas. One site initially thought to be much younger was re-evaluated as a Clovis site based on the presence of another diagnostic artifact, the so-called Clovis blade (see sketch on page 30). The blades were recognized as a Clovis technology in 1963 by F.E. Green of Texas Tech University at the time. Though not as good a marker as the projectile points, within the proper setting the blades are useful in identifying Clovis sites.

Using these blades as a diagnostic tool, Dr. Michael Collins, a research associate at the Texas Archeological Laboratory at the University of Texas at Austin, determined that the Kinkaid site in Uvalde County, excavated in 1948 and 1953, was a Clovis site. It is a young one, however, dating only about 10,000 years old.

The site gave a broader view of the Clovis culture than that of the typical nomadic hunter-gatherer. At Kinkaid, occupants had moved more than two tons of stone into a rock shelter to fill a low spot and paved the floor to provide additional living space. It was the oldest evidence of "anything approaching architecture" in Texas, Dr. Collins says.

Until this site was determined to be from the Clovis culture, archaeologists had thought these hunters did not use rock shelters. The site also laid aside another theory: that the Clovis people hunted big game exclusively. Bones of several small- and medium-sized animals were found in the shelter, indicating the hunters took a wide range of game. The Kincaid site also provided an intimate view of the stone-working technology of the Clovis culture, both points and blades.

Clovis blades also have been found in Navarro and Taylor counties. In Navarro County, a bulldozer turned up a cache of several blades. Since the surrounding earth had been disturbed, no analysis could be made of the site. But apparently the blades had been buried for later use.

At the Yellow Hawk site in Taylor County, some blades and points were found near an ancient quarry.

Most surprising of the locales where Clovis points turn up is McFaddin Beach in Jefferson County where more than 25 of the artifacts have been found in recent years. Authorities, like Dr. Meltzer and Larry Banks, archaeologist for the U.S. Army Corps of Engineers in Dallas, think the points are eroding out of sites now under the Gulf and washing onto the beach. The artifacts are not smooth and rounded as they would be expected to be if they had been moved a great distance by water across sand.

As interesting have turned up bone fragments that have turned up in material dredged from the floor of the Gulf. The pieces of bone show evidence of having been butchered, indicating again that humans probably inhabited the Gulf plain of Texas. In the Pleistocene Epoch at the end of the last great Ice Age, these plains extended up to 100 miles farther south when the formation of huge glaciers dropped sea levels nearly 400 feet.

The whole theory of Clovis man's appearance in the New World fits together rather neatly and has been in vogue for half a century. No evidence of Clovis has been found south of Panama and very little below the Rio Grande. But troubling sites keep turning up in Mexico and South America, indicating the presence of man earlier than the 11,500-year threshold embraced in the Clovis theory.

Dates of most of the sites in Mexico and South America have been challenged for one reason or another and are still subject to debate. Dr. Tom Dellihay of the University of Illinois (and a graduate of the University of Texas at Austin) has excavated a site in southern Chile known as Monte Verde. Radiocarbon reading from material in an upper stratum at this site dates 13,000 years old, well older than the Clovis sites in North America. Material from another lower stratum has radiocarbon dated to be more than 30,000 years old and doubtless will be challenged by demanding critics. Still, the 13,000-year dating of the upper stratum deflates the Clovis theory.

Chances are that other sites in South America and Mexico also may prove to be much older than normally accepted. So the entire Clovis theory could be shaky.

Or is it? Banks thinks the evidence is accumulating to support another hypothesis: Clovis was a secondary culture. It developed when climatic changes at the end of the last Ice Age raised sea levels and forced early humans to change their life styles.

The earliest immigrants in Banks' scenario would have been a sea coast people who settled on the west coasts of North and South America, moving southward rapidly after first contact. The population would have been supplemented by later migrations of people across the Bering land bridge. That probably was be-

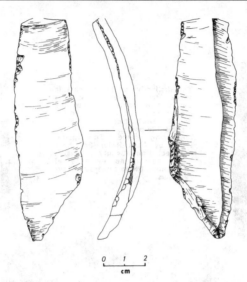

0   1   2
cm

A Clovis blade, sketched by Pam Headrick.

tween 20,000 to 15,000 years ago when a pathway between two major North American glaciers would have been open.

However, the first settlers would have adapted their sea-oriented culture to the coasts of the New World, supplementing fishing with hunting and gathering inland. Perhaps this culture lasted thousands of years.

When the climate changed, the temperature rose and the glaciers receded. The ancient coasts were flooded by the rising sea levels, destroying the environment that supported these first Americans. Although the process would have taken decades, no trace of the early culture would remain, for any artifacts would be under water, far under in some cases, and also covered by sediments.

As human beings usually do, the sea-dependent peoples would have adjusted their life styles to the new realities. Rising sea levels would have pushed the coastal inhabitants farther inland than they previously ventured. This movement put them in contact with the mammoth, mastodon, bison and other large animals. The people would have turned to hunting the big beasts, or perhaps scavenging the meat after the animals died.

From their experience, the new inlanders would fashion adequate tools for killing and butchering their new prey. Hence, the development of the Clovis point. (By the way, no evidence of a Clovis-type culture has been found on the west side of the Bering Strait. If the people of Clovis were immigrants, would not they have left some evidence at the beginning of their trek across the strait?)

Maybe the people making the transition from sea-dependency to hunting-gathering were more sophisticated than we realize. Clovis man left few artifacts, mostly projectile points and other tools fashioned from stone. Perhaps his tool kit was more comprehensive than the archaeological record reflects.

The Windover site in Florida reveals why early man may be underestimated by his modern counterparts. This 8,000-year-old wetlands site produced 168 burials. Among the artifacts were undergarments of the quality of modern T-shirts but woven from plant fibers. Fishing nets of several gauges were found in the graves with wooden tools. What few stone tools they used were primitive. Many of the corpses recovered from this peat-bog like site still had brain material intact.

If this culture once had existed on the Texas coast, few artifacts would have survived the hostile physical environment. The evidence of the sophistication of the culture would not be available. Probably all that would be found would be the primitive stone tools. And from them probably would have come a mistaken evaluation of the culture.

Nevertheless, Banks would like to see some potential underwater Clovis sites identified and investigated. Con-

sidering the fact that Texas' Gulf Coast would have been tens of miles farther south 20,000 years ago, that would be a big job.

One intriguing site might be near the West Flower Bank Gardens, the coral structures that are to be protected by the federal government. The coral built the impressive structures on top of what was a nice sized hill on the Pleistocene landscape, a landmark that might have attracted ancient Texans.

Banks may have a problem getting his theory of Clovis as a secondary culture accepted, for archaeologists fiercely defend the current thesis. So fiercely, in fact, that some contemporaries claim a double standard is used in judging sites that do not fit into the general Clovis theory.

And well it should be, for scientific theories should be well-founded and changes embraced only after most exacting criteria are met. Dr. Meltzer thinks the first site significantly older than the generally accepted 11,500 years must meet three criteria: The artifacts must be good, the geology must be excellent and the dating of the artifacts must be unassailable. That is a tall order, but one that Dr. Dellihay may have fulfilled in at least the upper level of the Monte Verde site in Chile.

As impassioned as the debate gets, what difference does it make if early man reached the New World 11,500 or 20,000 years ago?

Not much, according to Dr. Meltzer. If earlier sites are found, "it just means we were wrong by a few centuries," he says.

Of course, if it turns out that man reached the New World 100,000 to 200,000 years ago, as Louis Leakey, the renowned paleontologist, asserted several years ago after viewing a site in California, well, that is a different story. That is an age before homo sapien sapien (modern man) came on the scene. But no evidence of any type human other than modern man has been found in the New World. And certainly, no trace of Neanderthal man, the modern human's predecessor in Europe, Africa and Asia, has been found in North or South America. The presence of earlier men would call into question present theories on the pace of evolution and on the migratory patterns of humans.

That is all well ahead of the present state of archaeological discovery in Texas and the Western Hemisphere. The 11,500-year barrier has not yet been acceptably breached, and until it is, man in the New World must be considered only the younger cousin of those elsewhere in the world.

If Banks' ideas prove out, however, it may be that the Clovis people were actually native Texans, whose forebears had made the difficult journey from northern Asia then along the coasts of the Pacific, the Atlantic, and the Gulf of Mexico to the plains of Texas thousands of years before it is thought possible today.

Central Texas:
A History
Acknowledgements

Mary G. Crawford, associate editor of the Texas Almanac, prepared this brief history of Central Texas. She wishes to thank the following historians for their help in presenting this material accurately: T. Lindsay Baker, curator, Gov. Bill and Vara Daniel Historic Village, Strecker Museum, Baylor University, Waco; Walter L. Buenger, Ph.D., associate professor of history, Texas A&M University, College Station; Bob Calvert, Ph.D., associate professor of history, Texas A&M University, College Station; Randolph B. "Mike" Campbell, Ph.D., professor of history, University of North Texas, Denton; Donald E. Chipman, Ph.D., professor of history, University of North Texas, Denton; Thomas R. Hester, Ph.D., director, Texas Archeological Research Laboratory, Balcones Research Center, Austin; Paul Lack, Ph.D., professor of history, McMurry College, Abilene; Robert S. Weddle, Bonham; Frank Weir, Ph.D., State Department of Highways and Public Transportation, Austin; and Ralph Wooster, Ph.D., Regents Professor of History, Lamar University, Beaumont.

Introduction

The mild climate, gently rolling terrain and dependable water supplies of Central Texas attracted immigrants of many different nationalities. Central Texas still shows the influence of these different cultures, prominent among them American Indians, Spanish, French, Mexicans, English, Scots, Germans, Czechs, Poles and Italians, and, to a smaller extent, Belgians, Chinese, Alsatians and Irish. The most common ethnic footprints visible in Central Texas today are the names of cities, towns and topographic features: Osage and Keechi from the Indian; San Antonio and Lampasas, to name just two of hundreds from the Spanish; Westphalia and Weimar from the German.

Some Central Texas communities exhibit ties with the homelands of their founding families beyond mere place names — the German architecture, foods and traditions of Germany in Fredericksburg and New Braunfels; the Czech foods and fraternal organizations in West, McLennan County. The central region of the Lone Star State, then, is not exactly a melting pot; it is more like a stew pot, with clearly recognizable parts, each contributing flavor to the whole dish that is Central Texas. What follows is the recipe for that "stew" — the ingredients that went into the making of present-day Central Texas.

The Earliest Central Texans

We do not know exactly when the first humans arrived in Texas. Since they were nomadic and left few concentrations of artifacts, there is but scarce evidence of their existence. But several archaeological sites have yielded up faint whispers of human habitation in Central Texas at the end of the last Ice Age.

Paleo-Indians migrated to the Western Hemisphere across land bridges over the Bering Sea. The bridges, which are under water most of the time, were exposed during the Ice Ages of the Pleistocene era when the amount of ocean water tied up in ice caused a drop in sea level.

In January 1982, professional archaeologists with the State Department of Highways and Public Transportation began investigating the Wilson-Leonard site in Williamson County, north of Austin. Since 1970, Texas law has required that an archaeological impact statement be completed before any highway construction. From 1970 to late 1982, the archaeology section of the highway department excavated more than 60 of the 600 prehistoric sites that had been found during preparations for road construction.

The Wilson-Leonard dig was routine until archaeologist Wayne Young uncovered three skeletal fingers on Dec. 29, 1982. Two inches away was the skull. Excavation of the prehistoric burial pit revealed the skeleton of a woman between 5 feet 2 inches and 5 feet 4 inches tall, who died between 25 and 35 years of age. She was lying on her right side, with her legs drawn up toward her chest and her head resting on her hands. Grave goods, including a granitic sandstone grinding stone with a cutting edge, and a fossil shark tooth, which may have been part of a necklace, indicated a possible ceremonial burial.

Most important was the age of the site. Radiocarbon dating indicates that the burial occurred between 9,000 and 10,000 years ago. Wilson-Leonard contains one of the longest records of continual occupation in prehistoric Texas. State Archeologist Robert Mallouf says that the site is one of the three or four intact grave sites in North America. Since the site was near the town of Leander, the skeleton was nicknamed "Leann" by archaeologists.

Not long after the Leander discovery, amateur archaeologists made public the discovery of two complete skeletons in a rock shelter in Bosque County near Waco. Protected from the elements by the rock overhang, the skeletons were well preserved. The Horn Shelter site was discovered on Aug. 15, 1970, by amateur archaeologists Al Redder and the late Frank Watt, both with the Central Texas Archeological Society (CTAS). The discovery was kept confidential while the site was being excavated to protect it from vandals. The excavation was done with painstaking care over a 15-year-period by amateur archaeologists from the CTAS using scientific methods.

The skeletons were of a man between 30 and 40 years of age and a 12-year-old child of undetermined sex. Each was buried in a flexed position, much as "Leann," but on their left sides, with their heads, which were resting on turtle shells, to the south and their feet to the north. Their bodies, except for the skulls, were completely covered with limestone slabs. This site, too, was about 10,000 years of age. Artifacts found with the bodies included seashells, apparently from the Gulf Coast, as well as flint that may be from the Alibates quarry in the High Plains, suggesting that these people participated in a broad trade network. Many seashell beads were found, along with projectile points and other stone tools, a small-eyed, curved bone needle and a shaft straightener made of deer antler. Artifacts found in strata above the double burial indicate seasonal, regular habitation of the shelter.

The culture of early human inhabitants of Central Texas is divided into three basic periods: the Paleo-Indian (from about 11,200 years ago to 8,000 years ago), Archaic (about 8,000 years ago to A.D. 700) and the Late Prehistoric (1,000 years ago to the time of European contact). Radiocarbon dating places the Wilson-Leonard and Horn Rock Shelter sites in the Paleo-Indian period.

Many archaeological sites of later periods have been excavated in Central Texas, indicating that the lush vegetation, clear streams and plentiful game have lured humans to the area for thousands of years prior to European settlement.

Beginning of the Historic Period

When the Spanish arrived in Texas in the 16th century, they found it inhabited by scattered bands of Indians. In Central Texas, the numerous Tonkawas were concentrated along the streams and rivers, living in small groups. These typical Southern Plains Indians were hunters-gatherers with little or no agriculture. Until the Spanish introduced horses, the Tonkawas used dogs for pack animals as they followed the bison herds that were the mainstay of their existence.

The name Tonkawa is taken from the Waco Indian word for the tribe — "tonkaweya," meaning "they all stay together." The Tonkawas' name for themselves was "tickanwatic," meaning roughly "the most human of people."

Both men and women painted and tattooed their bodies and wore earrings and necklaces of shell, bone and feathers. Men wore long breechclouts, skin shirts and buckskin or bisonhide moccasins and leggings. The principal garment worn by Tonkawa women was a short skin skirt.

Unstable relations with other tribes, war and diseases brought by the Spanish greatly reduced the Tonkawa population in the 17th and 18th centuries. By early in the 19th century, they had gathered their tattered remnants together as an identifiable tribe, but their troubles were far from over. Bison were not as numerous in Central Texas as they were on the Southern Plains to the west. As the bisons' range receded westward in the mid-1800s, the Tonkawas were unable to follow, because the more powerful Comanches controlled the region. Thereafter, the Tonkawas relied more on deer, fish and small game.

The Tawakonis and the Wacos, the other principal Indians groups living in Central Texas when the Spanish came, were subgroups of the Wichitas. The Wichitas had migrated south into the Texas area in the 17th and 18th centuries. The Tawakonis and Wacos settled on the Brazos River at the present town of Waco and on the Trinity upstream from present Palestine by 1772. By 1779, the Trinity site had been abandoned and members of that group joined those on the Brazos.

The Comanches descended to the Southern Plains by the 18th century in a number of family bands at different times. More than any other Indian group, they used the horse to the greatest advantage. On foot, this loosely affiliated group of crudely equipped hunters-gatherers appeared short, squat and ungraceful. On horseback, the fierce Comanches dominated the Southern Plains for more than a century.

The word "Comanche" originated from the Ute word "Komantcia," meaning enemy. But the Comanches called themselves "The People." The Comanches did not live in Central Texas, but raided the region, and they were greatly feared by the white settlers.

A lesser force in Central Texas, but still one to be reckoned with, was he Lipan-Apache tribe. They were forced out of their traditional hunting areas by the fierce Comanches as they made their way onto the Southern Plains.

As the Europeans spread their settlements across the face of Texas, they appropriated for their own the lands of the agrarian Indians. The newcomers planted their houses and corn cribs on the nomadic Indians' hunting grounds. The clash of cultures that followed was inevitable.

Three Centuries of Spain

The Spanish were the first Europeans to have prolonged contact with the Texas Indians, and the result was frustrating — and sometimes deadly — to both. Initially lured by tales of the wealth of the legendary Seven Cities of Cibola and Gran Quivira, the Spanish first visited the area that became Texas in 1519. In that year, Alonso Alvarez de Pineda mapped the Gulf Coast from Florida to Veracruz.

Francisco Vazquez de Coronado, governor of New Galicia, was appointed by the Spanish king to lead an expedition to explore the American Southwest in 1540. His report to King Charles V, after a fruitless trek across the High Plains, Oklahoma and Kansas, recommended that Spain drop efforts to further explore and colonize the northern interior of New Spain.

Except for missionary activity in the El Paso area, Spanish interest in Texas waned until the French explorer Rene Robert Cavalier, Sieur de la Salle, landed at Matagorda Bay in February 1685. His men built Fort St. Louis on Garcitas Creek near present Vanderbilt. Indians soon destroyed the fort and La Salle was murdered by one of his own men in 1687. Word of French activities on the coast threw the Spanish into a frenzy. In 1689, Alonso de Leon, governor of Coahuila, found the ruins of Fort St. Louis. To prevent future French incursions into what the Spanish considered "their" territory, the Spanish founded two missions in East Texas in 1690.

To facilitate travel between the East Texas missions and the provincial capital in Mexico, Domingo Teran de los Rios, the first provincial governor of Texas, blazed El Camino Real (the King's Highway) in 1691. Later known as the Old San Antonio Road, the route was actually a network of roads. The principal stem was for many years the main route between Nacogdoches and San Antonio.

Meandering for 540 miles through what is today Texas, the route of El Camino Real passed through the present-day counties of Sabine, San Augustine, Nacogdoches, Cherokee and Houston to the Trinity River. Between the Trinity and the Brazos, it formed the boundary between Madison and Leon counties and between Robertson and Brazos counties. Continuing west, it traversed Burleson, Lee and Bastrop counties and became the boundary between Hays and Caldwell counties. Then the road cut through Comal, Bexar, Atascosa, Frio, La Salle, Dimmit and Maverick counties to Paso de Francia or Paso de los Pacuaches below present Eagle Pass on the Rio Grande, terminating at the Mexican town of Guerrero. Through Central Texas, the route crossed the Leon, Rogers, Wheelock, Cobb and String prairies of Central Texas.

The Indians in the East Texas missions had no immunity to European diseases and were hit by an epidemic that wiped out great numbers of potential converts. Many survivors resisted efforts to separate them from their traditional religious practices. After one mission was destroyed by flood, the other was abandoned in 1693.

In 1716, the Spanish government responsded to a new French threat by re-establishing missions in East Texas. As early as 1709, Fray Antonio de San Buenaventura y Olivares, a Franciscan missionary of the College of Santa Cruz de Queretaro, sought permission to establish a mission in Texas, preferably at San Pedro Springs in today's San Antonio. He was impressed by the Indians of the region, the climate and the plentiful water supply afforded by the river there. His initial request was denied. But when the East Texas missions were re-established, the Spanish government recognized the need for a way station between East Texas and northern Mexico. Fray Olivares received permission to found his mission. Don Martin de Alarcon, captain general and governor of the province of Texas and leader of the military group that accompanied Olivares' missionaries, took official possession of San Antonio in the name of the King of Spain on May 5, 1718. Fray Olivares founded the Mission San Antonio de Valero, later known as the Alamo. "San Antonio " was in honor of Saint Anthony, while "de Valero" was to honor the viceroy of Mexico at the time, the Marques de Valero. Alarcon established the presidio San Antonio de Bexar south of San Pedro Springs. The name honors the viceroy's half brother, the Duke of Bexar, a Spanish military hero.

By January 1719, there were enough Indians in the mission for the Spaniards to organize an informal pueblo government. That month was also spent constructing irrigation ditches for the fields, which were later planted with watermelon, pumpkins, chiles, melons, corn, beans and grains. Vine and fig-tree cuttings from Coahuila were also planted, and herds of cattle, sheep and goats were acquired.

The new mission was first housed in a temporary

structure of brush, mud and straw located a short distance downstream from the presidio. About a year later, the mission was moved to the other side of the river near the present site of the Alamo.

The East Texas missionaries, driven out by the French in the summer of 1719, took refuge in this second location of the San Antonio mission and remained there until March 1721. While in exile, one of the East Texas friars, Fray Antonio Margil de Jesus, founded Mission San Jose y San Miguel de Aguayo near the Valero mission in February 1720.

The Indians at San Jose worked cattle and kept large herds of sheep and goats for wool. They raised cotton, corn, various vegetables, sugar cane and fruits. They wove their own cloth and blankets and made their clothes in the mission's tailor shop. There were also a carpenter shop, a granary, a workshop and a mill where loaf sugar and molasses were processed. The present church building was built between 1768 and 1777.

When the Marques de San Miguel de Aguayo took command of the military detachment in March 1721, he moved the garrison from its original location to the present Military Plaza and built an adobe presidio.

Aguayo established the mission San Francisco Xavier de Najera on March 12, 1722, one league south of Valero to fulfill a promise the marques had made to Chief Juan Rodriguez of the Coahuiltecan Ervipiame Indians. The mission was little more than a name, however, and in 1726, it merged with Valero.

During the 1720s, there were about 200 Spaniards at San Antonio: 53 officers and soldiers and their families, plus four civilians and their families. There were about 600 Indians in the two missions.

San Antonio de Valero, which at the time consisted of some huts and a small stone tower, was destroyed by a fierce storm in 1724. The mission was rebuilt on the site of what is now Alamo Plaza.

By 1727, 273 Indians were in residence. Construction had started on a stone convent, but there was no chapel. Services were held in a temporary hut. Much of the energy of the mission's residents had gone into construction of a two-and-a-half-mile-long irrigation ditch, now known as the Alamo Ditch, to provide water for the fields and gardens.

The Spanish government, realizing that permanent settlers were needed to legitimize its claims to the area, recruited immigrants from the Canary Islands to settle in San Antonio. Fifty-five islanders arrived on March 9, 1731, after a problem-plagued sea journey and a difficult overland trek. They became the first permanent civilian settlers in present-day Texas (see article, "The Canary Islanders").

In 1730, economic troubles forced Spain to move three of the East Texas missions — Nuestra Senora de la Purisima Concepcion de los Hainai, San Francisco de los Neches, and San Jose de los Nazonis — to a temporary home on the Colorado River near Barton Springs in present-day Austin. Just before the Canary Islanders arrived, the missions were moved again, re-established near San Antonio de Bexar and renamed Nuestra Senora de la Purisima Concepcion de Acuna (commonly called Concepcion), San Francisco de la Espada (called Espada) and San Juan Capistrano (called San Juan).

It took approximately 20 years to build the Mission Concepcion church: It was dedicated on Dec. 8, 1755. Constructed of local limestone, the building had twin towers, a handsome dome and carved doorways. The facade was covered with quatrefoils and squares in brilliant shades of red, blue, orange and yellow. All the colors except the blue were made from pulverized stones; the blue was supplied by native wild indigo plants.

The chapel of Mission San Juan Capistrano was built some time between 1745 and 1756. Surmounted by a pierced belfry containing three bells, the chapel adjoined a granary and a convent.

Mission Espada was distinguished by its elaborate irrigation and water-supply system built between 1731 and 1745, consisting of a dam and an aqueduct, including a double span to lift the water over Piedras Creek. The chapel of the mission proper was built about 1745.

Smallpox and measles struck the missions' residents in 1739, killing many Indians and frightening others away.

Indian raids were a constant threat to the San Antonio missions. Apaches were fond of striking while the settlers or the mission Indians were working in the fields away from protection. The Canary Islanders became dissatisfied with their grazing rights. The settlers' only way of making a living was by cattle ranching. Since the missionaries had pre-empted all the

The Canary Islanders

In 1719, the Council of the Indies, the governing body of the colonies, recommended to the Spanish crown that families from the Canary Islands be recruited to populate Texas. The Canaries are a group of 13 islands, seven of them inhabited, in the Atlantic Ocean about 60 miles off the coast of northwest Africa. The original inhabitants were the Guanches, a tall, blond people thought to be of Berber extraction. But the islands had been colonized by Spain in the 15th century, and the Guanches had been absorbed into the Spanish population. The council reasoned that a Spanish civilian colony on the Texas coast would

History Highlights

firmly establish Spain's claim to the territory and would block the French from westward expansion.

At the urging of the Marques de Aguayo, the king finally granted permission in July 1723 for 200 volunteer families to be recruited. By September 19, the 200 families had signed on. But there followed years of governmental bickering over the best location for the new colony, the optimum number of families to send at one time, financing of the group and many other details. The colony's location was finally fixed at San Antonio, and the first group of 55 people, led by Juan Leal Goraz, arrived on March 9, 1731, after a difficult ocean voyage and a grueling overland march. It is not known how many actually started out from the islands, but when the land portion of the trip began, there were 10 families. By the time it arrived at San Antonio, the group comprised 15 families because of marriages along the way. The trip was harder on the horses than on the people: From the records, it appears that at least four people died on the trip

through Mexico; 125 horses were lost to fatigue and exhaustion. Fifty-five Canary Islanders formed the nucleus of San Fernando de Bexar, the civilian component of the settlement on the San Antonio River. The King of Spain declared them all to be Hidalgos, a title of minor nobility roughly equivalent to the British designation of Gentleman.

Although the original plan called for 200 families eventually to populate the settlement, the scheme was scrapped before the first 15 families had reached San Fernando, and no more Canary Islanders made the trip.

Captain Juan Antonio de Almazan urged the settlers to become self sufficient as quickly as possible. He apportioned the arable lands around the settlement among the arriving families, urging them to plant as much as possible. The families were housed temporarily in troop quarters in the presidio. After the harvest in early July, the captain and his men helped the Canary Islanders lay out San Fernando and begin building houses. Capt. Almazan, appointed officials of the new civilian government of San Fernando on July 20, 1731, with the group's unofficial leader, Juan Leal Goraz, named the first regidor or councilman. In all, Almazan appointed six regidores, an alguacil mayor (sheriff), and a mayordomo de los propios (administrator of public lands). The first election in Texas was held on August 1, 1731, when the recently appointed officials were called together to elect the first two alcaldes ordinarios (justices of the peace). Records of all the appointments and the results of the history-making election were sent to the viceroy, who granted his official approval of the proceedings on October 24, 1731. The first official permanent civilian settlement in Texas was born.

land close to the missions, the only pastures available to the newcomers were to the west and north, making them particularly vulnerable to raids. Some relief came in 1749, when the Apaches, feeling pressure from the encroaching Comanches, made peace with the Spaniards. A formal ceremony held on August 16 included Roman Catholic rites (Mass was celebrated in the San Fernando church) and American Indian ceremony (a live horse was buried, along with a tomahawk, a lance and six arrows).

Still, the missions' populations continued to shrink. By 1785, the Valero mission contained only 52 Indians; Concepcion, 71; San Jose, 138; San Juan, 58; and Espada, 57. And the numbers continued to decline. In 1793, Valero was the first San Antonio mission to be secularized. The others were closed one after the other, with the last, San Jose, shutting its doors for the last time in 1824.

Central Texas was also home, though briefly, to three missions and their accompanying presidio on the San Gabriel (San Xavier) River. Remnants of several bands of Tonkawas and related tribes lived there during the first half of the 18th century. Franciscan missionaries established the San Xavier missions in 1749 in response to a request by four chiefs.

Because of internal discord and unfavorable conditions, the San Xavier missions were moved in 1755. San Francisco Xavier de Horcasitas was renamed Nuestra Senora de Guadalupe and temporarily moved to the Guadalupe River, while the other two — Nuestra Senora de la Candelaria and San Ildefonso — and the presidio were sent temporarily to the San Marcos River. In 1757, the properties of the San Xavier missions were transferred to the authority of Fray Alonso Giraldo de Terreros for use in a mission that was established on the San Saba River in present Menard County by June of that year. When a horde of Comanches and their allies descended on the San Saba mission in March 1758, killing many of the inhabitants, looting the buildings and burning what they could not carry away, Spanish expansion in Texas virtually ceased.

In 1762, France ceded Louisiana to Spain as compensation for helping in the Seven Years War in Europe, easing Spain's fears about the threat on her eastern border.

But not all of Spain's troubles were French in origin; internal troubles in New Spain (Mexico) were increasing. Realizing that drastic measures were necessary, the Bourbon king, Charles III, sent the Marques de Rubi to the New World in 1766 to survey frontier defenses from the Gulf of California to Louisiana. He reported that the widely separated Texas missions could not be adequately maintained with the resources available.

The royal order that resulted, on Sept. 10, 1772, called for abandoning settlements in Texas except La Bahia, near Goliad in Southeast Texas, and San Antonio; moving settlers from East Texas and what is now west Louisiana to San Antonio; and a new Indian

policy calling for extermination of the Apaches and friendly relations with the northern tribes, to be cemented by periodic gift-giving.

The Baron de Ripperda came to Texas as governor in 1770. He appointed as lieutenant governor Athanase de Mezieres, a Frenchman with years of service in Louisiana as soldier, planter and Indian trader, and assigned him to deal with the Indians. Mezieres established friendly relations with some of the tribes. By 1771, he had reached agreements with the Taovayas on the Red River and with other Wichitas. He visited the Tawakoni villages near present-day Waco, continuing up the Brazos for 100 miles and returning to San Antonio.

But the Comanches made life miserable for most of the Texas settlements, and Mezieres was never able to pacify them. The campaign against the Apaches was largely ineffective.

With fewer than 200 troops scattered among three or four presidios to furnish escorts for travelers and to supply guards for the missions, there were never enough to go around. Ripperda asked for more troops. A few were sent, but never enough. And he discovered that giving gifts to the Indians did not stop their raids.

In 1777, San Antonio and its missions had a population of 2,060 (excluding Indians) and La Bahia had 696. By this time, there were also scattered ranches along the San Antonio River from San Antonio to La Bahia. Threats to Spain's claims to her Texas territory came from a new source shortly after the beginning of the 19th century. In the Treaty of San Ildefonso in 1800, Napoleon persuaded Spain to cede Louisiana back to France. Three years later, Napoleon sold the Louisiana territory to the United States. The United States quickly planted settlers in Louisiana and looked longingly into Texas.

Of all of Spain's attempts to pacify and convert the Indians and to populate the Texas area, San Antonio was its greatest success. But Spain's traditional administrative methods, which worked well among the highly civilized, settled Indians of the Valley of Mexico, were not particularly effective among the mobile, fragmented tribes of Texas. The Spanish government's shifting colonial policy and priorities also affected its pacification efforts.

Spain's attempts to preserve and exploit her New World territories were finally ended in 1821 with Mexico's successful fight for independence.

Spain was a physical presence in Texas for about three hundred years. Spain was the first European culture to establish a presence in Texas, and our language and customs still bear her mark. Spain's influence, which is mingled with Mexico's, is still seen in our many Spanish place names; in the cattle industry and the use of horses; in the law, particularly pertaining to property rights for women and to mineral rights; and in some remaining examples of elegant Spanish architecture.

The Mexican Period

The ferment in Mexico against the Spanish government was brought to a head on Sept. 16, 1810. That day, Father Miguel Hidalgo y Costilla and his followers, intent at the time on reform, not revolution, began an uprising at the Mexican town of Dolores.

Mexico's battle for independence spilled over into Central Texas several times. Filibusters, Anglo-American adventurers who were attempting to take control of the colonial government, were very busy during this uneasy time. One of the earliest was Philip Nolan, an Irish native and sometime horse trader. Known in Texas by 1791, Nolan, with Spanish permission, rounded up horses and took them out of the country on more than one occasion. But when he returned in the fall of 1800 with 17 armed followers, the Spanish tried to arrest him. In a fight near present-day Waco, Nolan was killed, and most of his followers were arrested.

In early 1812, Jose Bernardo Gutierrez de Lara, diplomatic agent of the Mexican revolutionaries, initiated a filibustering expedition in Nachitoches, La., with the help of U.S. agents. With 130 men, Gutierrez selected West Point graduate Augustus W. Magee as commander. Magee led Gutierrez's Republican Army of the North across the Sabine into Texas on Aug. 8, 1812. The insurgents easily took Nacogdoches; La Bahia fell to

them in November. When Magee died on Feb. 6, 1813, Samuel Kemper of Virginia assumed command. Advancing on San Antonio, Kemper and about 800 filibusters defeated about 1,200 royalists at the Battle of Rosalis, and Gov. Manuel Maria de Salcedo surrendered San Antonio on April 1. Raising the Green Flag of the Republican Army of the North, sometimes called the seventh flag over Texas, Gutierrez and his followers declared the first Republic of Texas. Two days later, Gutierrez permitted the execution of 14 Spanish officers, including Salcedo. A disgusted Kemper led more than 100 troops back to Louisiana. Gutierrez, undaunted, set up a provisional government — a seven-man junta with himself as chairman — and, by April 17, drafted a constitution.

Royalist Col. Ignacio Elizondo besieged San Antonio with about 990 men. Reuben Ross, successor to Kemper, advised retreat and left, but the others refused to follow. Henry Perry, taking Ross' place, defeated Elizondo's troops in the Battle of Alazan on June 20, 1813. The increasing hostility of his own troops prompted Gutierrez to return to Louisiana. On Aug. 18, 1813, the remaining filibusters were ambushed and thoroughly defeated by about 4,000 men led by Gen. Joaquin de Arredondo in the Battle of Medina River, about 14 miles south of San Antonio. About 300 of the filibusters were taken prisoner

In late 1813, the desperate Spanish Cortes (legislature) approved a plan to populate Texas with loyalists. Empresarios introducing settlers into Texas would be rewarded with large land grants, but two-thirds of the newcomers were to be Spaniards, and all were required to be Catholics. The Cortes was dissolved in 1814 with the defeat of Napoleon and the return of Ferdinand VII to the throne of Spain, and the plan died.

San Antonio barely survived the year 1819. A long drought, followed by an epidemic, followed by flood dealt a near-death blow.

With Spain's hold on Mexico loosening, the Cortes issued a decree in September 1820 opening all Spanish dominions to any foreigners, the only stipulation being that they respect the Spanish constitution and the laws of the land. In December, Moses Austin requested permission to settle Americans in Spanish Texas. A Connecticut native, Moses Austin had lived in Missouri in 1799 when it was part of Spanish Louisiana. He came to San Antonio in late 1820 and received approval to settle 300 families in East Texas. He returned to Missouri, where he died in June 1821, before fulfilling his contract.

Austin's 27-year-old son, Stephen Fuller Austin, was granted authority to carry out his father's plan and became the first great empresario of Texas. In 1821, Mexico declared itself finally free of Spain, and Austin reaffirmed his empresario contract with the Mexican government. Between 1821 and 1824, Austin recruited 300 families to settle in his colony, earning those families the nickname of "The Old Three Hundred."

Austin's colony extended from the Gulf Coast to Central Texas and included parts of the present-day Central Texas counties of Bastrop, Brazos, Burleson and Lee. Each family could obtain a *sitio*, or square league (about 4,428 acres), of grazing land and a labor (about 177 acres) of farming land. They paid surveying and administrative fees as low as $50, payable in six years, with no down payment required. For their services, empresarios received five *sitios* and five labors of land for each 100 families settled. The settlers also enjoyed a 10-year tax exemption on their land. It was a bright, shiny carrot of opportunity for land-hungry Anglo-Americans.

Austin was given almost complete responsibility for his colony, and he managed it to the letter of the contract with Mexico. He was well aware of the mistrust with which many Mexican authorities regarded American settlers. In 1825, Austin was granted the right to bring in 900 more families, and, in partnership with Samuel Williams, he agreed to settle 800 Mexican and European families in a colony north and west of his original one. The Austin and Williams grant covered a large area of Central and North Central Texas.

Second only to Austin's colony in size, the Robertson Colony originated in 1822 as the Texas Association at Nashville, Tenn. By 1825, Robert Leftwich, agent for the group, had obtained the right to settle 800 families in Texas. Leftwich transferred the contract to the association with the stipulation that it be named "Leftwich's Grant." The transfer was approved in 1827 by the Mexican government, who replaced Leftwich with Hosea H. League as empresario and expanded the boundaries of the colony to an area 100 miles wide and 200 miles long. Included were all or parts of 30 present Texas counties. Those in the Central Texas area were Bastrop, Bell, Brazos, Burleson, Burnet, Coryell, Falls, Lampasas, Lee, McLennan, Milam, Mills, Robertson and Williamson. Through an error, the contract used the name "Nashville Company" instead of "Texas Association."

In 1825, Green De Witt, a Missourian of Dutch ancestry, was granted the right to settle 400 families on the Guadalupe, San Marcos and Lavaca rivers. Included were parts of present-day Caldwell, DeWitt, Fayette, Gonzales, Guadalupe, Jackson, Lavaca and Victoria counties. De Witt's colony, which adjoined Austin's on the west, was more exposed to Indian harassment and did not gain population as fast as Austin's. It had about 82 residents in 1828, 531 in 1832 and more than 1,200 in 1834.

The governing body of the state of Coahuila y Texas passed a generous colonization law on March 24, 1825. Each family brought in by an empresario could, for a fee of $30, buy a *sitio* of land for $62.50, or $87.50 for irrigated land. Empresarios were rewarded for their services with five leagues and five labors of land for each 100 families. Compensation was forfeited if at least 100 families had not been settled in each colony by the end of the contract.

The Texas region was allowed two representatives on the 12-member legislature of Coahuila y Texas. The administrator for the Texas region, who lived in San Antonio, was responsible for law enforcement, command of the militia and the administration of justice.

Ayuntamientos (town councils), elected by citizens in each town, were responsible for collecting taxes, taking census counts, maintaining roads and public buildings and overseeing public health, charity, public safety and police services. Money was scarce in the Texas province, and the *ayuntamientos* allowed residents to pay two-thirds of their local taxes in goods or livestock, with a cow and a calf equal to $10. Barter was widely used to acquire goods.

In 1830, the Mexican government established Fort Tenoxtitlan on the west side of the Brazos River 12 miles below the crossing of the Camino Real in present-day Burleson County. Named in honor of the Aztec capitol of Mexico, Fort Tenoxtitlan was used to guard transfers of funds from Bexar to Nacogdoches until 1832. After that, Anglo settlers used the fort as a supply center and mustering point for expeditions against Indians. Five signers of the Texas Declaration of Independence, an Alamo martyr and seven soldiers in the Battle of San Jacinto once lived there. It was abandoned in 1841 after numerous Indian raids.

For many Anglo settlers, one of the major sticking points in the Mexican laws governing colonization was that slavery was prohibited. To get around the law, some slave-owners called their slaves "indentured servants."

Much immigration into Central Texas was not organized through empresarios. Many Anglos simply drifted across the border into Texas and squatted on vacant land. The growing numbers of Anglo-Americans made Mexican officials more and more uneasy. To the Anglos, the bright promise of cheap land was dimmed by a government struggling to adjust to the change from an absolutist monarchy to a federal republic. Taxation and trade were other Anglo concerns. When the colonists' requests for more ports and legal status for foreign ships were ignored, smuggling became common.

Finally, the Mexican government, in the Law of April 6, 1830, banned settlement of "citizens of foreign countries lying adjacent to the Mexican territory," i.e., the United States. The ban on further legal American immigration alarmed and angered the Anglo-Texans.

Parts of the Nashville Company grant adjoined Austin's colony, leading to disputes over land titles. Then Austin and his colleague, Samuel M. Williams, convinced the Mexican officials that the Nashville Company had not settled enough families to fulfill its contract and were granted the disputed territory. In 1834, Sterling Clack Robertson, then agent for the Nashville Company, took his protest to Mexican authorities, claiming that the required 100 families had been settled before the Law of April 6, 1830. Robertson's claim was upheld. He was named empresario, and the colony became "Robertson's Colony." Robertson established the capital of the colony, Sarahville de Viesca, about six miles east of present-day Marlin at the falls on the Brazos. The name honored Robertson's mother, Sara Maclin Robertson, and Agustin Viesca, governor of the province of Coahuila y Texas. A fort bearing the same name was established at that site in 1834. It was renamed Fort Milam in December 1835, and a ranging company was based there to protect colonists from Indians. In May 1835, the legislature of Coahuila y Texas decided that the requisite number of families had *not* been settled in time and again awarded the land to Austin and Williams.

The Anglo colonists had pledged to become faithful Mexican citizens, expecting to live under the republican form of government provided for in the Constitution of 1824. Such repressive measures as the Law of April 6 went against the grain.

Gen. Antonio Lopez de Santa Anna, who was to play a leading role in the drama of Texas' fight for independence, surfaced in Mexico. He was leading an attempt to overthrow Gen. Bustamante, who had himself attained the office of president in 1828 in a coup. Appearing to espouse the republican cause, Santa Anna won the backing of the Texans.

In their traditional Anglo-American method of petitioning the government for redress of grievances, the colonists met in convention at San Felipe, the capital of Austin's colony, in October 1832. Austin served as president of the convention. The delegates wanted government separate from Coahuila, title to their lands in East Texas, an end to encroachment on Indian lands, a militia to protect them from Indian raids, and government-provided land for public schools.

The Mexican officials considered the convention illegal. Under their system, the method for approaching the government was on the local level, through the *ayuntamientos.* They refused to consider the petitioners' requests.

One result of the convention was the organization of a "committee of safety and correspondence" in each district to established a communications network among the colonies. Small, local committees of safety and correspondence already existed in several Anglo communities, mainly to organize defense against Indian raids. Their number increased as the dissatisfaction with Mexican rule spread. On May 8, 1835, Mina became the first town to form a committee of safety and correspondence in response to the Mexican government's unrest. Other communities soon followed. Mina, later renamed Bastrop, was established in 1825 near the site of Puesta del Colorado, a Spanish fort located on the Camino Real. It was named for Mexican revolutionary leader Xavier Mina.

Despite the government's objections, a second convention met in April 1833, which called for repeal of the Law of April 6, 1830, and separation from Coahuila. The delegates even framed and approved a state constitution. Stephen F. Austin took the demands of the convention to Mexico City. After long delays, President Santa Anna appeared to agree to many of the reforms. However, Austin was arrested in Saltillo on his return trip and was sent to prison in Mexico City, further infuriating the Anglos.

Santa Anna began centralizing the federalist government, and those who opposed him were brutally repressed. However, he did repeal the Law of April 6, 1830, in 1834. With this victory, colonists were encouraged to continue fighting for a more responsive government. A new convention, called a "consultation" to avoid upsetting the suspicious Mexican officials, was scheduled for October 1835 at Washington-on-the-Brazos. Its purpose was "to secure peace if it is to be obtained on constitutional terms, and to prepare for war, if war be inevitable." Austin had returned from prison in Mexico convinced that war was the only means by which the colonists could gain their rights under the Constitution of 1824. Delegates to the consultation, which was postponed until November, created a provisional government and named Henry Smith governor.

Santa Anna sent his brother-in-law, Gen. Martin Perfecto de Cos, to bolster the military presence in Texas. Cos headed for Bexar with about 400 troops, with more to follow. Col. Domingo Ugartechea, at San Antonio, ordered Lt. Francisco Castaneda and 100 troops to retrieve a cannon from Gonales — a six-pounder lent to the residents to protect them from Indian raids. The colonists refused to give it up. Arriving at Gonzales on Oct. 2, 1835, Mexican troops were confronted with a banner flying over the cannon bearing the words "Come and Take It." The defiant officials at Gonzales stuffed the barrel with chains and scrap iron and fired. After a brief skirmish, the Mexicans retreated. As battles go, it was minor. But the first shots of the Texas revolution had been fired.

Revolution

Santa Anna, the self-proclaimed "Napoleon of the West" had pushed his way to the top of the Mexican political ladder. The ambitious general shifted positions with every change in the political wind.

Santa Anna began his military career in the Spanish empire, serving under Gen. Arredondo in the bloody Green Flag revolt of 1813. He fought on the republican side in the Mexican Revolution of 1821, but soon parted company with its leader, Agustin de Iturbide. By 1833, he was supreme leader of Mexico. In his career, he was ruler of Mexico 11 times and was exiled five times. He was, first and foremost, a survivor.

While the Texans at Gonzales had protected their cannon, Gen. Cos entered San Antonio and barricaded the streets. The Mexican forces at Gonzales moved west to join him.

The consultation at Washington-on-the-Brazos named Stephen F. Austin commander in chief, and he marched for San Antonio on Oct. 12, 1835, along with James Bowie, James W. Fannin Jr. and 90 men. The Texans made camp on the evening of Oct. 27 about a mile from the Concepcion mission. The Mexican force of about 400 that attacked the next morning was defeated by the 93 Texans in a 30-minute battle. The Texans lost only one man; the Mexicans lost 60.

The consultation that met on Nov. 3 in San Felipe faced a fundamental question: Were the colonists supporting the Mexican Constitution of 1824 or fighting for independence? The delegates compromised by calling for a provisional government under the Constitution of 1824. The delegates elected Sam Houston commander in chief. The provisional government included a governor, lieutenant governor and a general council with one delegate from each municipality.

Houston sent appeals for help to all corners of the United States. Unable to offer pay, he offered land. Money for the Texas cause was collected at gatherings as far afield as Mobile, Ala., Macon, Ga., and at Tammany Hall in New York.

In New Orleans, two separate groups of men, both called the New Orleans Greys, signed up as volunteers and marched for Texas. A girl presented the first group with a banner of azure blue fringed with gold, with the words "First Company of Texan Volunteers! From New-Orleans." In the center of the flag was an eagle with the legend "God and Liberty." Some historians claim that the flag that flew over the Alamo was a modified Mexican flag, with the central eagle removed and the number 1824 in its place, signifying the Texans' wish to return to the Mexican Constitution of 1824. There is no evidence of such a banner, however. The only flag that was captured by the Mexican army at the Alamo was that of the New Orleans Greys. The second company of New Orleans Greys went to Goliad to serve under Fannin.

On they came, lured by the promise of adventure and action: the Kentucky Mustangs, the Red Rovers of Alabama, the Mobile Greys. If near-hysterical fervor and ardent patriotism could win battles, the outcome at the Alamo would have been different.

The main Texas army now joined the victorious Concepcion battle participants in a siege of San Antonio, their numbers increased by the out-of-state recruits. The siege lasted more than a month; the Texans, new and old, became restless and bored. On Dec. 5, Ben Milam, tired of waiting, led the assault on Cos and his troops with a special force of 300. After five days of house-to-house fighting, Cos capitulated and marched his remaining men toward Laredo, promising not to interfere in the restoration of the provisions of the Constitution of 1824. The Texans now held San Antonio.

Believing that seizure of the town of Matamoros, the Mexican town at the mouth of the Rio Grande, would be beneficial to the cause of constitutional government, the council sent an attack force to the border city. Commander Frank W. Johnson and James Grant stripped the garrison at San Antonio of supplies for the expedition. They took horses, blankets, food, arms, ammunition, clothing and medicines and headed south. Fannin raised a force of about 400 volunteers for the effort, then settled in at Goliad, fortifying the site and drilling the troops as he waited.

Meeting Johnson and Grant and their force of about 500 men near Refugio, Sam Houston persuaded most of them that the Matamoros project was futile. He then washed his hands of the affair and left for East Texas. With only about 150 troops left, Johnson's group was wiped out almost to a man in early 1836 by the Mexican cavalry advancing north under Jose Urrea.

The garrison at San Antonio was dwindling fast. The ill-fated Matamoros expedition had taken a large number of men. With few clothing and no enemy to fight — and when the paymaster did not arrive in January — many simply left and went home to their families. By mid-January 1836, the commander, Col. James C. Neill, was left with only about 80 men.

On Jan. 17, Gen. Houston sent 40-year-old Col. James Bowie and between 25 and 30 men from Goliad to San Antonio with instructions to dismantle the fortifica-

More on Page 38

The Alamo

The building called the Alamo originally was built as the chapel of the Mission San Antonio de Valero. Like all Spanish missions, Valero was a combination religious and industrial trade school for Indians. For several years, the mission consisted of several huts and a small stone tower, which were destroyed by a storm in 1724. Mass was celebrated in temporary quarters until the first stone church building was constructed about 1744. This building collapsed about 1756. The second stone chapel, begun about 1758 and never finished, stands today in Alamo Plaza.

Cruciform in shape and 35 Spanish varas (more than 90 feet) long, the chapel has a large nave and a broad transept. The walls, built of local limestone blocks, are more than 3.5 feet thick. The floor was probably paved with flagstones.

The mission complex once covered up to four acres of ground and contained not only the church, but also the *convento*, or priests' quarters, a granary, workrooms, storerooms and Indian housing, all surrounded by an outer wall.

Epidemics depopulated the missions to the point that by 1778, not enough Indians were left to work the fields. In 1793, Valero was converted into a self-supporting parish church.

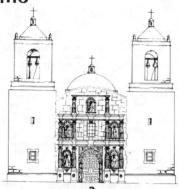

a

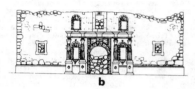

b

c

a. The Alamo as planned but not completed; b. Alamo at the time of the 1836 battle; c. The Alamo today, with alterations made by the U.S. Army in 1849. Illustration courtesy Jack D. Eaton and the Center for Archaeological Research, UT-San Antonio.

History Highlights

After the conversion, the still-unfinished Valero chapel was stripped of usable doors, windows and hardware. It served at times as a parish church for soldiers who were stationed there, and it became San Antonio's first hospital from 1806 to 1812.

The Valero mission building came to be known as the "Alamo" when a company of cavalry — called the *Segunda Compania Volante de San Jose y Santiago del Alamo de Parras* (Second Flying Company of San Jose and Santiago of the Alamo of Parras) — was stationed there for more than 10 years, beginning in 1801 or 1802. The town of San Jose y Santiago del Alamo de Parras in the Mexican state of Coahuila was where, in the 1780s, the unit had been recruited. As tradition dictated, the company was identified by the full name of the town. "Alamo" is the Spanish word for "cottonwood." "Alamo" in the town's name is thought to refer to a landmark cottonwood tree growing on a ranch near Parras. The mission chapel is still called the Alamo; the town of Parras, however, is now called Viesca.

To Texans, of course, the most important use of the Alamo was as a fort during the Texas revolution. Mexican Gen. Martin Perfecto de Cos used the Alamo as his headquarters in San Antonio. In preparation for the Texan assault in late 1835, Cos tore down the chapel's arches to use as ramps for hauling cannon to the tops of the walls. And the climactic 13-day siege and battle of the Alamo in 1836 was all-important in turning the tide of the Texas revolution.

The signature scalloped roof line of the Alamo was not part of the building until 1849. It was added by the U.S. Army when it leased the former chapel from the Roman Catholic Church to use for storing hay and grain. The two outer windows on the upper level also were added at that time. Many representations of the building in paintings, drawings and movies wrongly show these late additions as part of the building during the 1836 battle. An army artist who sketched the Alamo compound in 1849 after the remodeling commented that the chapel had been topped with "a ridiculous scroll, giving the building the appearance of the headboard of a bedstead." Of the present Alamo building, probably only the bottom 23 feet of wall are part of the original.

The Alamo changed hands at least 16 times among Spanish, Mexican, Texan, Union and Confederate forces between 1810 and the end of the Civil War. During the early 1840s, stones from the Alamo were hauled away by scavengers. Development began creeping onto the mission grounds in the 1850s.

When a supply depot was built at Fort Sam Houston in 1878, the army left the Alamo compound, and merchant Hugo Grenet purchased the convent (also called the long barracks) from the church, remodeling the property to house a retail store. He leased the chapel for use as a warehouse. Grenet's renovations gave the convent the appearance of a medieval castle.

After Grenet died in 1882, the mercantile firm of Hugo & Schmeltzer purchased the convent; the chapel reverted to the church, which sold it to the state in 1883.

In the 1890s, Adina de Zavala, granddaughter of Mexican-born Texas patriot Lorenzo de Zavala and first vice president of the Daughters of the Republic of Texas (DRT), extracted a promise from merchant Gaston Schmeltzer that he would sell her the convent building for $75,000. But her fund raising stalled short of the goal. In February 1904, Clara Driscoll, from a wealthy San Antonio family, advanced at no interest the $25,000 needed to hold the convent until the Legislature appropriated the purchase price. She was reimbursed by the state in 1905, and the Legislature entrusted both convent and chapel to the DRT. Although Driscoll is called the "Savior of the Alamo,"

More on Next Page

From Page 36

tions, remove the artillery, and take the munitions to Gonzales and Copano.

Bowie has been characterized by one writer as "game hunter, fortune hunter, alligator wrestler, horse tamer, gambler and, above all, knife fighter." He had even smuggled slaves with French pirate Jean Lafitte. The Bowie who arrived at the Alamo with his men on Jan. 19 was also grief-stricken by the recent loss of his wife, children and parents-in-law, who died in a cholera epidemic in Mexico. Col. Neill refused to carry out Houston's orders, saying that there were not enough draft animals left to move the artillery. There were undoubtedly other reasons: San Antonio was a political capital, and was seen as the linchpin to all of Texas. Also, keeping the Mexicans busy in Central Texas kept them away fom the settlements in East Texas. The other men voted to stay, so Bowie stayed with them, sending out a plea for men and supplies. Col. William Barret Travis and 30 men answered his appeal, arriving on Feb. 3. The 26-year-old Travis, described by some as egocentric and supercilious, had persuaded Gov. Smith to give him a commission. A native of South Carolina, Travis had come to Texas and settled in San Felipe de Austin to practice law.

On Feb. 8, the Alamo troops were joined by 50-year-old David Crockett of Tennessee, who brought 12 men with him. The well-known frontiersman and former U.S. representative from Tennessee has been described thus: "At his best he was honest, brave, noble, resourceful, blessed with abundant 'horse sense,' independent to a fault and able to tell a good story; at his worst, uneducated, crude, violent, boastful, drunken, and even clownish." When Travis offered him a high rank, he demurred, saying he preferred to be a "high private."

Three days later, Col. Neill left, placing Travis in charge. The volunteers held an election and voted to follow only Bowie. Bowie and Travis signed a letter on Feb. 14 agreeing that Col. Bowie would command the volunteers of the garrison, while Travis commanded the regulars.

Travis badly miscalculated the situation on at least two crucial points: He expected the Mexican troops to wait until spring to move north. And he expected Fannin to arrive from Goliad at any moment with 400 men.

But Santa Anna marched his troops northward through the bitter winter weather. The Mexican army was a duke's mixture of professional soldiers, presidial soldiers, militia, impressed convicts and one battalion of Mayan Indians who didn't speak Spanish and had never been out of the tropics.

Among the Texans, boredom was rampant. Travis sent out a steady stream of appeals for more men and arms. He had sent several desperate pleas to Col. Fannin at Goliad, all of which had been turned down. Travis finally sent James Bonham to persuade Fannin. Bowie and many of the other men were ill. By mid-February, there were about 150 fighting men in the Alamo.

Some of the men ransacked nearby houses for grain and herded the cattle they found into a corral on the east side of the Alamo compound.

The Alamo

From Previous Page

the Alamo itself already belonged to the state. What Driscoll saved was the convent.

De Zavala and Driscoll fought over the best way to preserve the site. De Zavala wanted both chapel and convent restored to demonstrate the site's use as a mission. Ironically, Driscoll, who had saved the convent, wanted it demolished, so that the chapel's role in the Texas revolution would be emphasized. A public hearing was held in December 1911, during which de Zavala offered documentation as to the importance of the convent. The convent was saved.

In its almost 300-year existence, the Alamo has been many things to many people. It has served as the chapel of a Spanish mission; quarters for troops; housing for Indians, Tejanos and squatters; hospital; army supply depot; Masonic lodge; jail; commercial store and warehouse; public park; tourist attraction; movie set; and historic site. To Texans, however, it will always be "The Alamo — Shrine of Texas Liberty."

Most defenders of the Alamo were relatively new to Texas; most had not even been in Texas when the fighting first started in the fall of 1835. They came from 18 different states and several European countries.

Santa Anna crossed the Rio Grande on Feb. 18 and, by pushing his troops to their utmost, led about 1,500 men into Alamo Plaza on Feb. 23. Other units of the Mexican army were on their way to join him. San Antonio's civilian residents who had not already left scrambled into the Alamo compound for protection.

Raising the red flag of no quarter from the top of San Fernando parish church on Main Plaza, Santa Anna sent an emissary to give Travis the chance to surrender. Travis answered with a cannon shot. Also on Feb. 23, Bonham returned from Goliad with Fannin's latest refusal of aid.

Fannin finally started for San Antonio on the Feb. 26 with 400 men, four pieces of artillery and a number of wagons. A wagon broke down and he turned back. He remained at Goliad, drilling his troops. Bonham left the Alamo yet again on Feb. 27 with what would be Travis' final appeal to Fannin.

The men in the Alamo were slightly cheered by the arrival on March 1 of 32 men from Gonzales, who had eluded the Mexican patrols. The Gonzales reinforcements must have known that death was almost certain. But they also understood that keeping Santa Anna busy at San Antonio would buy time for the rest of the Texas army.

Meanwhile, on March 2 at Washington-on-the-Brazos, the convention delegates signed the Texas Declaration of Independence from Mexico, a document that echoed the United States Declaration of Independence that preceded it by 60 years.

Travis sent his last appeal for help out of the Alamo on March 3 . . . the same day that Bonham dashed back into the fort with the news that Fannin had once more refused to come to San Antonio. According to the lone adult Anglo survivor, Mrs. Susannah Dickinson, Travis called his men together on the evening of March 5 during a lull in the Mexican cannonade. He explained the futility of their situation, and told them that if they did not wish to stay, they could take their chances on leaving. Only one man, Moses Rose, left.

There were probably between 18 and 21 cannon inside the Alamo compound, but not enough cannonballs to sustain a long battle. When a cannonball was not available, the men stuffed the barrel with jagged pieces of broken rock and metal, creating a large shotgun. The effects were devastating on massed infantry. But there were not enough soldiers to keep them all firing at the same time.

Most of the Alamo defenders were armed with hunting rifles, most often Kentucky or long rifles. These weapons were slow to load, but very accurate to fire. The *escopetas* of the Mexican army, on the other hand, were 3rd model Brown Bess muskets purchased as surplus from the British East India Company. They were faster to load and fire, but their accuracy was marginal.

No one knows why Santa Anna did not simply wait out the Alamo defenders. But about dawn on March 6, Santa Anna ordered his troops to attack. The Mexican forces, numbering about 4,000 with the arrival of reinforcements, twice charged the Alamo compound, and twice were repulsed. Then they breached the north wall. In an hour and a half, the battle was over. Mexican soldiers tore down the flag of the New Orleans Greys and raised the Mexican tricolor.

All the fighting men of the Alamo died. Those who had been too sick to participate or were wounded were killed on the spot. Santa Anna ordered the bodies piled up and burned. After the Texan victory at San Jacinto a month and a half later, remnants of the Texas army buried the remains of the Alamo defenders, but no one knows where.

About 600 Mexican troops were killed or wounded. At least 14 of the Alamo's non-combatants survived, among them Susannah Dickinson, wife of Capt. Almeron Dickinson, and their 15-month-old daughter, Angelina; Travis' black slave, Joe; and a number of Hispanic women and children — residents of San Antonio who had sought protection in the Alamo.

As the Mexican army advanced to the east, Houston's strategy was to pull back. As the army retreated, the civilians along the way desperately packed up and moved out, too, in a headlong rush that became known as the Runaway Scrape. Houston had sent orders to Fannin to pull back, also, and be prepared to cooperate. Once again, Fannin waited too long. Starting out on March 19, his men were soon surrounded by Gen. Urrea's troops. The 400 men were marched back to Goliad and imprisoned for a week. On Palm Sunday, they were led into the woods and shot. Many escaped.

Retreating toward the coast, Houston and his army of about 900 cut Santa Anna off from his only means of escape. At about 4 p.m. on April 21, while Santa Anna napped, Houston ordered the attack. The Texans surged forward, partially screened by trees and rolling terrain, shouting "Remember the Alamo! Remember Goliad!" Eighteen minutes later, it was over. The Texans lost nine men, and 34 were wounded.

Santa Anna was found in hiding the next day and was captured.

The freedom of the new nation had been bought at great price. But for the next nine years, the republic's leaders spent much time and effort to lose that freedom — to the United States. Annexation became the goal of the Texas government.

The Reluctant Republic

Was there ever so reluctant a nation as the Republic of Texas? In the same Sept. 1836 election in which the first elected officials of the republic were chosen and the constitution was ratified, the voters overwhelmingly approved a proposal to request annexation to the United States.

The new republic had a massive debt and few assets except land. Land was used to pay veterans of the revolution and to lure homesteaders to settle. Heads of families could receive a first-class headright, which was a league and a labor of land (4,605 acres). Single men over 17 could receive 1/3 league (1,476 acres). An additional bounty of 320 acres was available for each three months of military service, up to two sections.

Several forts were built in Central Texas during the days of the republic for protection from sporadic Indian raids. Some of them were set up by individual settlers and others were built as ranger camps. These forts included Fort Colorado, also called Coleman's Fort, a ranger post established on Walnut Creek about seven miles east of Austin in June 1836; Little River Fort, also called Fort Griffin or Smith's Fort, built for a company of rangers on the Leon River in present Bell County in Nov. 1836; Fort Fisher, a temporary ranger post on Waco Springs in 1837; Kenney's Fort, built in 1839 on the south side of Brushy Creek at its juncture with Dyer's Creek in present Williamson County for protection of the Kenney family; Fort Burleson, set up for protection of settlers on the falls of the Brazos in present Falls County in Aug. 1839; and Fort Boggy, the headquarters of the Boggy and Trinity Rangers, built in 1840 five miles south of present-day Centerville, Leon County, and serving as protection for about 77 people.

In 1837, the town of Mina and the county of the same name were incorporated and changed their names to Bastrop to honor a friend of Moses Austin who called himself the Baron de Bastrop. A Dutchman with a scandal-tainted background, Bastrop had settled in San Antonio about 1806, where he ran a freighting business. He served as second alcalde of San Antonio in 1810 and was a prime negotiator with the Mexican government for Austin's colony.

In 1839, the Texas Congress authorized a commission to select a site for a permanent capital north of the Old San Antonio Road between the Trinity and Colorado rivers. It was to be on major north-south and east-west trade routes and near the center of the state. The commission selected a site near Waterloo, an outpost on the Colorado, about 80 miles northeast of San Antonio. The location was enhanced by a mild climate and plentiful water from nearby springs.

The town was laid out between Shoal and Waller creeks under the direction of Judge Edwin Waller, a signer of the Texas Declaration of Independence, with the assistance of $113,000 in Republic of Texas scrip and 200 laborers. Initially it was a mile-square crosshatch of streets and cabins. Sites were selected for the capitol, an armory, a hospital, a university, an academy, a penitentiary and four public squares. The new capital was named in honor of Stephen F. Austin. The first sale of town lots was held on Aug. 1, 1839; 301 lots were sold for a total of $182,585, which practically paid for the government buildings under construction at the time. Houston opposed the new capital, preferring to stay in his namesake city on the Gulf Coast. But the seat of government was moved to Austin in 1840.

The executive offices were housed in a double log cabin (dog-trot cabin) at first. Pine lumber from the "Lost Pines" near Bastrop was used in many early Austin buildings. The president's house, called the White House, was on a hill, with small slave cabins dotting the grounds. Lamar and Houston lived there before it burned in 1847.

Hope of some relief from Indian raids was raised in January 1840, when three headmen of the Penateka Comanches appeared in San Antonio requesting a peace talk in March. They promised to return all their white prisoners, numbering between 15 and 20, at that time. Texas officials agreed. On March 19, about 65 Comanches arrived at the Council House in San Antonio, led by a dozen chiefs and followed by many women and children. But they brought only one prisoner — 15-year-old Matilda Lockhart, who had clearly been tortured. She reported that at least 15 other whites were captive, and the Comanches planned to release the prisoners individually in order to get more ransom goods. Indian Commissioner Hugh McLeod announced that the chiefs would be held captive until all prisoners were returned as promised. When the Comanches attempted to break out of the Council House, the carnage that ensued left seven Texans and 35 Comanches dead, including all of the chiefs. The rest of the Indians were imprisoned. A chief's widow took word back that the captives must be released. The Penatekas responded to the whites' treachery by executing their white captives.

But the angry Indians saved their major retaliatory strike for August, when they swept across Central Texas following the only remaining chief, the one called Buffalo Hump by the whites. About 400-500 warriors participated, and there were about 500 family members plus 3,000 horses and many wagons and pack animals in the raiding party.

The Comanches plunged down the Guadalupe Valley, drawing the first blood on Aug. 5 near the site of present-day Hallettsville. They thundered through Victoria on Aug. 6, killing both whites and slaves. Their headlong rush took them all the way to Linnville on Lavaca Bay in present Calhoun County, far beyond their usual range. They killed several people and took others captive. Then they looted stores and warehouses. The raiders loaded their wagons and pack animals with plunder and turned back toward home, foolishly retracing their steps.

Texas Ranger Ben McCulloch called every available man together at Good's Crossing on Plum Creek. The Comanches, slowed by heavily loaded wagons that often became mired in the boggy ground and with their party strung out across the prairie, were met by about 200 Texans on Comanche Flats, five miles southeast of present Lockhart. The Texans were joined by more than a dozen unmounted Tonkawas, who wore white armbands to distinguish themselves from the raiders.

The fighting ranged over 10 or 12 miles before the Penatekas abandoned their loot and fled for their lives. Texan casualties were light; about 80 Comanches were killed. The once-horseless Tonkawas went home well-mounted and completely equipped from the spoils.

After a Ranger expedition deep into the Comanches' own territory the following October that killed 50 more Indians, no more raids struck deeply into Central Texas. However, Indians continued to harass the new capital on the Colorado.

In 1841, President Houston, who was cutting costs wherever possible, renewed his efforts to negotiate a $5 million loan from France. But the Texans' side was weakened by the Pig War.

France's first representative to the Republic of Texas, Charge D'Affaires Jean Peter Isidore Alphonse Dubois de Saligny, became embroiled in a dispute with hotel keeper Richard Bullock. Bullock's pigs occasionally invaded de Saligny's property next door, ruining his garden and eating his papers. De Saligny complained, but Bullock refused to corral his swine. The Frenchman ordered his servant to kill any marauding porkers. Bullock, angry that de Saligny was protected by diplomatic immunity, thrashed the servant. The "Pig War" ended when de Saligny broke off diplomatic relations and left in a huff for Louisiana, conveniently evading a host of unpaid creditors.

A kinsman of de Saligny was representing France in the loan negotiations. Was it simply coincidence that the Texas government's loan request was denied?

De Saligny returned to Texas in 1842 and periodically served as charge d'affaires. When he departed in 1845, he left behind the charming Louisiana bayou-style French Legation building. Built of hand-sawn Bastrop pine with French fittings, it is today the oldest original structure in Austin.

Mexico tried to reassert its claims to Texas in 1842. Gen. Rafael Vasquez and about 500 Mexican troops raided San Antonio on March 5. They withdrew within two days, but President Houston, perhaps glad for an excuse, ordered the government moved to his namesake city.

Although full diplomatic recognition was granted to Texas by England, the Netherlands and Belgium, the republic's financial problems continued. Texas' debt was one roadblock to annexation. Another was that slaves made up just over a quarter of the population of Texas by the mid-1840s. The abolitionists in the U.S. Congress didn't want another slave-holding state admitted to the Union.

In September 1842, 1,400 Mexican soldiers, commanded by Gen. Adrian Woll, captured San Antonio. About 200 Texas volunteers led by Col. Mathew Caldwell and Capt. John C. "Jack" Hays lured the invaders to a spot on Salado Creek, about six miles out of the city, and defeated the Mexican forces with the loss of but one man.

A detachment of Mexican cavalry encountered Capt. Nicholas Dawson and about 53 volunteers from La Grange, who were coming to help defend San Antonio, about a mile and a half from the fighting on the Salado. Outgunned, Dawson tried to surrender, but the Mexicans kept firing, killing 35 Texans including Dawson. Fifteen were captured, marched to Mexico and thrown into prison. The remains of Capt. Dawson and his men were returned to La Grange, were they were buried together at what is today called Monument Hill.

When the Texas troops returned, only a few families remained in Austin. Many were moving east for protection. In December, President Houston ordered the government archives removed to Houston. A local "archive committee" buried them at Austin instead. Twenty-six of Houston's men slipped into Austin on the night of Dec. 29 with three wagons to spirit the archives away, but they were discovered by Mrs. Angelina Eberly. The innkeeper fired the city's cannon to warn Austin's citizens. Houston's men were intercepted by a posse on Brushy Creek near Kenney's Fort on Dec. 31. The citizens took the archives back to Austin, thus ensuring that the seat of government would return to Austin when the Mexican menace was eliminated.

Both San Antonio and Austin were desolate, dreary towns during the days of the republic. In San Antonio, hardly any immigrants arrived and little building was done. Austin's population dropped to about 24 families. Few of the log houses were occupied. Doors and windows hung open. Even the president's house was full of bats, lizards and stray cattle. The government moved back to Austin in 1845, but at the time of annexation in 1846, fewer than 250 people called Austin home.

What may have been the first retail store "chain" in Texas was established by John F. Torrey and Company in 1843. The Torrey Trading Houses were set up at Austin, San Antonio and New Braunfels to do business with the Indians, with branch stores located on the Navasota River and near the falls of the Brazos. Post No. 2, on a tributary of Tehuacana Creek just below Waco, was officially authorized as an Indian trading station by the Republic of Texas on Jan. 14, 1843. Post manager George Barnard purchased the store from the Torreys in 1848 and moved it to Waco in 1849.

In September 1844, a new empresario added yet another ingredient to the Central Texas ethnic stew. Henri Castro, a Frenchman of Portugese decent, negotiated an empresario contract with the Republic of Texas in 1842 to settle a colony on the Medina River. Castro had been active in the republic's ill-fated negotiations for a loan from France, and he had become interested in Texas at that time. Castro recruited his colonists principally from Alsace, a French province on the border with Germany, where the residents spoke a German dialect. After many delays and great expense, the first 35 settlers of Castro's colony arrived in present-day Medina County on Sept. 3, 1844. By 1847, Castro had brought 2,134 settlers to the new colony, including 485 families and 457 single men. Castro also founded the nearby towns of Quihi in 1845, Vandenburg in 1846 and D'Hanis in 1847.

Anson Jones assumed the presidency in December 1844, and the government offices were moved back to Austin in 1845. During Jones' administration, a bill to annex Texas finally passed the U.S. Congress, providing for full statehood and for Texas to retain her public lands and her public debt. The Texas Congress accepted the offer and drew up a state constitution. Texans approved annexation in an October election, and the U.S. Congress accepted the constitution. On Dec. 19, 1845, U.S. President James K. Polk signed the resolution of acceptance.

The end of the reluctant republic was punctuated by President Jones' moving speech on Feb. 16, 1846, to the first meeting of the first legislature of the newest state in the Union. Jones ended his speech with these words: "The Lone Star of Texas . . . has passed on and become fixed forever in that glorious constellation which all freemen and lovers of freedom in the world must reverence and adore — the American Union. . . The first act in the great drama is now performed. The Republic of Texas is no more."

The Twenty-Eighth Star

When Texas entered the Union, Central Texas was on the verge of a wave of immigration that would leave an indelible imprint of many cultures and traditions. The stability afforded by annexation and Texas' liberal land policy were irresistible lures to settlers. Texas' population grew almost 50 percent between 1847 and 1850.

Surveyors were hired by homesteaders to locate their land and survey it. Payment for their services and for the risks of the job was one-third of the total acreage. Indians recognized surveying instruments, referring to them as "the thing that stole the land," and they attacked surveyors whenever possible.

As new immigrants from many different countries and ethnic bakgrounds were attracted to Texas, the mostly Anglo-American and Mexican-American population evolved into one more complex and flavorful.

A few Irish settled in San Antonio by 1842. Many others came to Texas serving as sutlers and teamsters with the U.S. Army during the war with Mexico. They settled near the Alamo, then being used as a quartermaster's depot, in an area that was known as Irish Flat. Some of the San Antonio Irish remained with the army, while others were artisans, merchants and politicians.

Germans were among the first to settle in the new state. In their homeland, they had little voice in government. Food was scarce, and overpopulation exacerbated the hunger and unemployment. Opportunities for the young were limited. So great was German fascination with Texas that a group of German noblemen in 1842 organized the Adelsverein, an association whose sole purpose was to settle German immigrants in Texas.

The Adelsverein purchased rights to the Fisher-Miller grant, which consisted of more than 3 million acres on the southern banks of the Colorado River between the Llano and San Saba rivers about 100 miles west of Austin. Present-day counties either partially or wholly within the Fisher-Miller grant were Concho, Kimble, Llano, McCulloch, Mason, Menard and San Saba. However, the Fisher-Miller land was unsuitable for farming, and it was roamed by Indians who reacted violently when settlers entered their traditional hunting grounds. With time running short and with hundreds of immigrants waiting on the Gulf Coast, Commissioner General Prince Carl of Solms Braunfels purchased 1,300 acres on the Guadalupe River on March 14, 1845, and the first settlers arrived a week later. The new community was named New Braunfels.

The Germans faced several serious problems during their first years in Texas. Most immediate was a series of epidemics, including dysentery, malaria, cholera, typhoid and yellow fever. Finances of the new settlement were in dreadful disarray. And the Germans had trouble adapting to farming in arid Texas. They considered drought abnormal, and they were slow to change from crop-oriented agriculture to livestock ranching.

Prince Carl, though a nobleman in the German court, was a miserable failure as a businessman and frontiersman in Texas. Leaving the finances of the new settlement in a shambles, Prince Carl returned to Germany without waiting for his replacement. Baron Ottfried Hans Freiherr von Meusebach arrived in 1845. He, too, was a nobleman, but his training was broad and well-suited to managing the fledgling settlement. Meusebach's background included mining engineering, forestry, political science, finance, jurisprudence, state economy and civil service. He read five languages and spoke English fluently. Dropping his title upon arrival in Texas, he became plain John O. Meusebach.

Meusebach soon had the affairs of New Braunfels in hand. He then founded Fredericksburg about 80 miles to the northwest for the next wave of German immigrants, who arrived on May 8, 1846. Determined to use the Fisher-Miller lands, Meusebach negotiated a treaty with the Comanches the following March. It was one of the few treaties in Texas history that were honored by both sides. Several small communities were established in the Fisher-Miller territory, but none was as successful as New Braunfels and Fredericksburg.

By 1850, Texans of German birth or parentage outnumbered Mexican-Americans. Ten years later, Germans were in the majority in three counties in the Austin-San Antonio area and were a substantial minority of six others. Immigration from Germany continued through the century and left a band of German communities from the Gulf Coast into the Hill Country west of San Antonio, with concentrations in Gillespie, Comal, Kendall, Austin and Washington counties.

While some immigrants came to Texas for economic and political reasons, others came for religious freedom. In 1854, a group of 588 Wends migrated to Texas from Germany to escape government interference with their faith. Led by John Kilian, they settled in what is today Lee County. About six miles south of present-day Giddings on the Smithville-Houston Oxcart Road, these Slavic descendants of the Serbs established the town of Serbin. Other pockets of Wends settled in the present-day Central Texas counties of Fayette, Williamson, Coryell and Bell.

Immigrant groups from Czechoslovakia began arriving in Texas in the 1850s, fleeing government repression after an unsuccessful revolution in 1848. Czech families established the town of Hostyn in Fayette County about seven miles southwest of La Grange in 1850, making it one of the first Czech settlements in Texas. Some of the early Czech migrants also settled in what was originally the predominantly German town of Fayetteville.

Many Poles immigrated to Texas because of the influence of a Polish Franciscan priest, Leopold Moczygemba. He came to Texas in 1851 to serve the Germans in New Braunfels. His glowing letters to friends in Poland urged them to join him in Texas. The first Polish village in Central Texas was St. Hedwig, established near San Antonio in 1857. First named Martinez, it was renamed for the patron saint of Silesia. There was also a well-defined Polish neighborhood in San Antonio, which comprised 200 families by 1860.

The Houston and Texas Central Railroad started laying track westward out of Houston toward Central Texas in 1856. But its slow expansion halted completely during the Civil War.

Before railroads came to Central Texas, freight moved by ox- or mule-drawn wagons over routes that were little more than trails. Heavy wagons often bogged down when roads were muddy. Passengers moved on horseback or stagecoach, and families used wagons. Stage lines charged 10 cents a mile, but the price could double in bad weather. Most towns had a wagon yard — usually next to a hotel — which was a large enclosure with sheds for sheltering the teams. Wealthier travelers slept in the hotel; others bedded down in their wagons.

In the 1850s, scheduled stagecoaches transported passengers and mail from Austin to the Gulf Coast; from San Antonio to the Gulf Coast and to Eagle Pass; and from Waco to Nacogdoches. By 1857, a semimonthly mail and passenger service was operating between San Antonio and San Diego, Calif., a trip taking 30 days and costing $200.

The major roads at this time were primarily old military roads first blazed by the Spanish or by Texans during the days of the republic. Preston Road was laid out in 1841, following an old Indian trail, just after Fort Preston was built on the Red River in present Grayson County. It connected Fort Preston to Austin by way of Dallas and Waco. The Old San Antonio Road from San Antonio to Nacogdoches through Bastrop and Crockett was still used, as was the road from Indianola to San Antonio, a principal route for cargo to and from Gulf ports.

The frontier settlements were still being raided by Indians, so the U.S. Army built a line of forts for protection. Westward expansion was so fast, however, that these were active for only two or three years. Among these short-lived posts was Fort Croghan, established on Hamilton Creek about three miles south of present-day Burnet on March 13, 1849. It was first called Camp Croghan in honor of Col. George Croghan. It was moved to a site three and a half miles farther north in October. The post was occupied by the 2nd Dragoons in 1852, but was abandoned except for a token guard the following year.

Fort Gates was built on the north bank of the Leon River above Coryell Creek, about five miles east of present Gatesville, on Oct. 26, 1849. Named for Brevet Maj. Collinson Reed Gates, a veteran of the war with Mexico, Fort Gates was abandoned in March 1852.

A third Central Texas fort was established on March 27, 1849, on the east bank of the Brazos River at the old Waco Indian village near the newly founded town of Waco Village. Fort Graham was named for William M. Graham, a veteran of the battle of Molino del Rey in 1847. The troops were withdrawn in 1853.

The first sale of lots in Waco Village, named for the area's earlier Indian inhabitants, took place on March 1, 1849, just before Fort Graham was established. Town lots sold for $5, with farming lots selling for $2 to $3 an acre. McLennan County, created Jan. 22, 1850, and organized the following August, was named for an early settler in the area, Scotsman Neil McLennan, and Waco Village was chosen the county seat in 1850. When officially incorporated in 1856, the town's name was changed to Waco.

On March 4, 1850, an election was held to determine the permanent seat of the state government. Austin won over a number of contenders, including Palestine, Washington, Huntsville and Tehuacana (spelled "Tywackanah" on some county election returns).

Austin during the early 1850s experienced a building boom, with many new business buildings being constructed of bricks from the brickworks at the mouth of Shoal Creek. Log structures were being replaced by buildings of dressed lumber and native stone.

The first brick capitol was built in March 1852. The Governor's Mansion was built in 1855-1856 near the capitol, and was first occupied by Gov. Elisha M. Pease, who selected the site and the Greek-Revival style. Abner Cook, pioneer architect and contractor, who designed and built many fine homes and buildings throughout Austin, supervised the construction. The six massive Ionic columns across the front were carved from Bastrop pine. Austin-made bricks were used.

In 1856, the 6th Legislature provided $40,000 for a new land office on the southeast corner of the capitol grounds, and the deed records were moved into the building the following year. Since land was the state's greatest resource, security of land records was of highest priority. Designed in Romanesque Revival style by Conrad C. Stremme, a German immigrant, the structure was two-and-a-half stories of stuccoed stone and brick.

One of the earliest artesian well experiments in the state began on the capitol grounds in April 1857. Using a cable tool rig, drillers worked slowly. They reached a depth of 1,160 feet in early 1862, when the cable broke and the drilling tools were irretrievably lost in the bottom of the well. The Civil War forced abandonment of the effort. But the drillers had struck mineral water at the 323-foot level, and a small stream of water eventually reached the surface. The watering hole became a popular retreat. When the current capitol was built in 1882-1888, it covered the old well, but the flow was conducted to a small stone grotto outside the building by a special pipe. It was finally covered over and sealed in the 1950s.

San Antonio in the 1850s began to grow again. The

first post office was established in 1850. Catholic orders headquartered in France established Ursuline Academy for girls in 1851 and St. Mary's for boys in 1852. Four public schools opened in San Antonio in 1853, one for boys and one for girls on either side of the river. Streets, which were practically impassable in wet weather, received some improvements in 1857, including the installation of several bridges. Gas lights were installed in 1860.

The Menger Hotel, two-and-a half stories high and constructed of fine cut stone, opened in 1859 on Alamo Plaza. The hotel, with an on-premises brewery, was famous for wild game dinners, which sometimes included turtles plucked straight from the San Antonio River.

The threat of Indian raids was greatly diminished by the establishment in 1854 of two Indian reservations: one in Young County near the town of Graham, and the other about 40 miles away in Throckmorton County on the Clear Fork of the Brazos. There were still raids, but they were infrequent in Central Texas, and they mostly struck at the least-protected frontier outposts.

In 1860, the population of Austin was 3,493; Travis County had 8,080 residents. San Antonio's population was 8,235; Bexar County totaled 14,454 residents, more than double the 6,052 who lived there in 1850. McLennan County was home to 6,206. Altogether, the counties that make up Central Texas were home to 98,919 people in 1860. The population of the entire state was 604,215, with the foreign-born making up approximately three-quarters of the total and representing almost every country of Western Europe.

During the 1850s, most Texans were small farmers, and most owned no slaves. Cotton and corn were leading crops, however, and as cotton grew more profitable, slavery increased. By 1860, the statewide production of cotton reached 431,000 bales.

As the clouds of war gathered in the East, Texas slave-holders became more uneasy. Their personal finances were on the line, since considerable money was invested in slaves. In the German areas of Central Texas, sentiment was overwhelmingly against slavery and, therefore, pro-Union.

The number of slaves in the state had increased from 443 owned by 69 slaveholders in Austin's colony in 1825 to 182,566 owned by 21,878 slaveholders in 1860. While the vast majority of slaveholders were white, a few free blacks also owned slaves.

Most Texas slaves lived along the Gulf Coast or in the river valleys of East Texas, providing labor on large plantations whose principal crops were cotton, corn and sugar. But about half the slaves in Texas lived on smaller farms, as was the case in much of Central Texas, where there was some breakdown in class barriers as slaves and owners worked together in the fields.

Baptist and Methodists sent missionaries to conduct church services for slaves. But white ministers had little understanding of the slaves' condition or feelings. Homer Thrall, a Methodist, expressed the beliefs of most white Protestant ministers when he said, "Slavery is not only innocent but scriptural and right and . . . it is our imperative duty to protect and perpetuate this institution as a blessing to both races" because "a state of bondage is the normal state of the African race." Slaves often held their own services on the sly at night.

In addition to the rural slaves in Central Texas, several hundred lived in Austin, San Antonio and other large towns. Most urban slaves were house servants, but some worked as cooks and waiters, in the construction trades, as barbers, teamsters, or coachmen. Some had jobs in flour mills, sawmills, brickyards and other factories.

Generally, slaves who broke the law suffered harsher penalties than did free men. But even those who were not abused were subject to the inhuman cruelty inherent in the very idea of one human's ownership of another. When life within the "peculiar institution" became unbearable, many escaped, or attempted to escape. In Texas, Mexico was a popular destination since that country was known to abhor slavery. Others fled to the comparative safety of the anti-slavery state north of the Mason-Dixon Line.

In the Deep South, the talk of secession turned to action on Dec. 20, 1860, when South Carolina left the Union. Texas soon followed the rush to leave the Union despite opposition by Gov. Sam Houston. When Houston refused to take the oath of allegiance to the Confederate States of America that was required of all officials, the office of governor was declared vacant and Lt. Gov. Edward Clark assumed the governorship. The commander of federal forces in Texas, Maj. Gen. D. E. Twiggs, a Southerner by birth and a Confederate sympathizer, surrendered the federal posts and forts and about 2,700 troops to state authorities.

On March 2, 1861, 25 years to the day that Texas declared her independence from Mexico, the official proclamation was read. Texas had cast her lot with the Confederacy for better or worse.

The Confederate Years

Although the fighting never reached Central Texas, the Civil War affected almost every aspect of the residents' lives. Texas was vital to the Confederate cause, serving as the link to the ports in Mexico. With Union troops blockading ports in the Confederate states, cotton, the most available item of value in the state, was exported through Mexico.

Cotton from the Brazos Valley and North Texas was taken to Millican near present-day Bryan in Brazos County, the northernmost railroad terminus when the war began. From there it was shipped by rail to Houston, where it was transported over the "Cotton Road" by wagons to Brownsville. It was then moved across the Rio Grande to the Mexican port of Bagdad and loaded onto ships. The return trip brought back military supplies and merchandise for distribution across the Confederate states.

More than 60,000 Texans wore Confederate gray; military companies were organized in practically every county. The Central Texas county of Robertson was typical: Five troop companies were organized as soon as secession was approved. Commanders included W. P. Townsend, a Mexican War veteran, with a company of 70 men. Townsend's troops became Company C of the 4th Texas Regiment, which in turn became part of the legendary Hood's Texas Brigade. Company B of the 4th Texas came from Travis County, while Company F was raised in Bexar County. Hood's Brigade fought with Robert E. Lee's army at the battles of Chickamauga, Gettysburg and Wilderness and the second battle of Manassas. After observing the 4th Texas in battle, Hood had high praise for their bravery, saying, "I could double-quick the Fourth Texas to the gates of Hell and never break their line." Also in Hood's Brigade were Cos. C and G of the 5th Texas from Leon and Milam counties,

respectively. Of the 4,500 Texans who served in Hood' Brigade, only some 550 survived.

The Robertson County war effort included establishing a mill to make flour, cotton and wool cloth. Cotton cards, medicines, flour, bacon and salt were furnished to soldiers' families, also.

Salado, Bell County, was the headquarters of the 27th Brigade, Texas State Troops, under the command of the former empresario, Brig. Gen. Sterling Clack Robertson. The Texas Lancers were organized in Bell County in April 1862. The 27th Brigade moved to Camer on in 1863, with Brig. Gen. H. P. Hale commanding. In all, Bell County sent 12 troop companies into the fighting. Goods were supplied to the war effort from Bell County flour mills, a hat factory, a tanyard, leather works, blacksmith shops, a cabinet shop and beef slaughter pens in the county.

The Milam County Guards were organized in May 1861, followed by the San Andres Light Horse Company and the Milam Guards in June. The previously mentioned Co. G of the 5th Texas Regiment was originally organized as the Milam County Grays.

When Brig. Gen. Henry H. Sibley raised a Confederate force in San Antonio in 1861 to drive the Union forces out of New Mexico, two companies from Milam County and one each from Falls, Comal, Travis and Williamson counties joined, along with others from across the state. Sibley's Brigade won the battle of Valverde on Feb. 21, 1862, then took Albuquerque without a fight. But, after winning a Pyrrhic victory at Glorieta Pass on March 28 after furious, bloody hand-to-hand fighting, Sibley was forced to retreat back to Texas after Union forces captured the Confederate supply train. When Sibley's Brigade got to Texas in July, had 1,000 fewer men: About five hundred had been killed and a like number had been taken prisoner.

In addition to the troops that volunteered for the Confederate army from Waco, six Confederate generals called Waco home: Thomas Harrison, L. S. Ross, H. C. Granbury, Allison Nelson, James E. Harrison and W. H. Parsons. Waco also produced five Civil War colonels: E. J. Gurley, Richard Coke, J. W. Speight, P. F. Ross and W. A. Taylor.

In the outlying communities, there were similar contributions to the war effort. There were two sewing machines in Cameron at the outbreak of the war; they were moved to the Baptist Church, where the women of Cameron gathered to sew uniforms. All over the state, school girls knitted socks for the soldiers. Farmers were asked to share produce with the Confederate forces. Scarce foods were replaced by substitutes: Ersatz coffee was made at home from parched corn, rye or potatoes.

The Texas Military Board was set up in Austin to obtain arms and munitions for the 33 militia districts in the state. A city arsenal was set up on Waller Creek. The Land Office building on the capitol grounds housed a gun-cap factory that produced 14,000 shells a day. A foundry turned out guns and cannon. Other Austin factories manufactured shoes and gunpowder. Gunpowder was also manufactured and stored in the Longhorn Caverns near Burnet during the war. In the basement of the capitol a sewing room was set up to make clothing for the Confederate Army.

Communications from the state capital to the outside world were maintained by five stage lines that linked Austin to the railhead at Brenham. Hotels in Austin rented rooms only to people paying in gold, silver or scarce, easily bartered goods, such as tobacco or nails. As a result, some lawmakers were reduced to sleeping in their wagons and cooking over campfires.

Although Travis County voted against secession, the Tom Green Rifles, originally called the Austin City Light Infantry, and the Travis Rifles organized and went to war. Only about one-third of Travis County's volunteers returned. The Travis Rifles became Company G, 6th Infantry; the Tom Green Rifles became Company B of the 4th Texas Infantry.

Many of the anti-secessionists in the hills west of Austin held regular military drills and set up their own spy network. In Austin itself, Unionists organized a Home Guard that marched and drilled.

At the outbreak of hostilities, the U.S. Army's Department of Texas was headquartered in an unfinished arsenal in San Antonio. After transfer to Confederate hands, the limestone building was completed. The arsenal supplied the Confederacy with arms for South Texas and for frontier defense.

By 1863, the Confederate government was sending agents to Texas to buy cattle to supply the army with meat.

Crops were good during the war years, but labor was scarce. Salt was in short supply. A salt works was set up between Tow Valley and Old Bluffton 15 miles northeast of Lampasas. Brine, trapped in sand and rock strata during the Cambrian period 500 million years ago when the area was covered by sea water, was boiled in 250-gallon iron kettles. Twenty to 30 bushels of salt were produced each day to be used as table salt and for curing meat and hides and feeding cavalry horses.

Paper was especially scarce, and most newspapers cut their size and frequency. Small, one-sheet issues were common by the end of the war, and some papers went out of business entirely.

The Civil War in Texas ended when Kirby Smith surrendered the Trans-Mississippi forces to the Union on June 2, 1865. The emancipation of the slaves was not announced in Texas until June 19, when Union Gen. Gordon Granger arrived at Galveston with his occupation forces. The holiday of Juneteenth, unique to Texas, is a commemoration of that date. The shooting war was over, and the occupation was about to begin. It was called Reconstruction.

Reconstruction

Originally, presidential Reconstruction was to heal the wounds and re-form the Union with as little rancor as possible. A.J. Hamilton, a former congressman from Texas and Union army veteran, was appointed provisional governor of Texas on June 17, 1865, by President Andrew Johnson. Abraham Lincoln devised a reconstruction plan before his assassination. President Johnson attempted to follow Lincoln's moderate plan, which called for amnesty for almost all who served in the Confederate army if they swore an oath of allegiance to the Union. Appointive offices were to be filled with Unionists whenever possible, but when impossible, with secessionists known to be capable and trustworthy. Civil governments were to be re-established in each state when 10 percent of the 1860 electorate took the prescribed loyalty oath.

Conflict and suspicion soon surfaced, both between former Confederates and Unionists and between conservative and radical factions in the Unionist ranks.

Some Confederate soldiers looted government warehouses on their way home, feeling that the property of the Confederacy was now theirs. They usually left private property alone.

When Gen. Gordon Granger landed in Galveston on June 19, 1865, and declared slaves to be free, he assumed command of all military forces in Texas. Most Union troops in Texas were sent to the Rio Grande to guard the border against the French, who were fighting or control of Mexico. With few soldiers to maintain order, lawlessness and banditry were widespread. Texans were fearful of the newly freed blacks and of the reconstruction to be imposed upon them by the Union.

The number of slaves in Texas, which had been 182,-66 at the beginning of the war, had grown as slaveowners in other southern states sent their bondsmen to the relative safety of Texas during the fighting. Many former slaves were unprepared for freedom, having no money, no education, no homes and limited job skills. Believing that they could get help in the city — food, shelter, and the protection afforded by the presence of Union troops — freedmen flocked to the urban areas of the state just after emancipation. They found limited services and a flooded job market. By fall, disillusioned, many were back in rural Texas. A widely circulated rumor led them to believe that each freedman would receive "40 acres and a mule" when the plantations were confiscated and divided among former slaves on Christmas Day 1865. When it didn't happen, many blacks became bitter.

Congress created the Bureau of Refugees, Freedmen and Abandoned Lands, commonly known as the Freedmen's Bureau, in March 1865 to provide relief services for destitute former slaves and war refugees. Congress expanded the bureau's jurisdiction in 1866 to include establishing its own courts to hear racial discrimination cases. The bureau also operated night schools and supervised work contracts to protect blacks from exploitation.

Unionists who had actively opposed secession or who had refused to serve in the Confederate army were considered traitors in some parts of the state. They were harassed by vigilance committees, which formed after the war theoretically to bring some semblance of law and order to areas with scant military protection. Some vigilance committees were in reality only a couple of steps above lynch mobs. Some confederate diehards chose to leave the state rather than submit to Northern occupation.

The U.S. Civil Rights Act of 1866 guaranteed citizenship to all persons born in the United States and gave them the right to sue, to testify in court, to own property and to enjoy equal protection under the law.

Delegates to the Texas constitutional convention, called by Gov. Hamilton for Feb. 7, 1866, approved a constitution that granted blacks the same right to appear before court as whites, but blacks could not testify in court except in cases involving other blacks. It required them to ride in separate railroad cars from whites. It also canceled the state debt incurred during the war, an action that the United States required of all former Confederate states, thereby punishing those who had financed the war effort.

J.W. Throckmorton was elected governor in the summer of 1866. Throckmorton had been one of only eight delegates to the Secession Convention to vote against secession. However, when secession was approved, he was one of the first men in Texas to swear allegiance to the Confederacy. He had served as commander of the Third Military District of Texas, as brigadier general commanding the Frontier District and as Confederate commissioner to the Indians. He had also presided over the Constitutional Convention of February 1866.

The 11th Legislature, the first elected under the new constitution, passed legislation to allow blacks to testify only in court cases involving other blacks; to segregate blacks on public transportation; to prohibit blacks from holding public office, serving on juries or voting; and to prohibit blacks from marrying whites. Radical Republicans gained control of Congress in the November 1866 election, and Reconstruction began to take a serious turn.

Dissatisfied with the moderate provisions of presidential Reconstruction, Congress imposed military rule on the Southern states. Congress nullified all state governments except Tennessee's and divided the former Confederacy into five military districts, giving the commanding general of each district total power over state laws and officials. Gen. Philip Sheridan was in charge of the 5th Military District, which included Texas.

Seeking their political rights, blacks began to organize chapters of the Loyal Union League in major cities in the spring of 1867 with the help of Republicans, who saw the chance for a coalition to gain control of state government.

Gen. Charles Griffin, first military commander of the subdistrict of Texas under Gen. Sheridan, tightened the restrictions for jury service and voter qualifications in a way that enfranchised thousands of blacks and disenfranchised about 10,000 whites. Gov. Throckmorton protested. On July 30, 1867, Gen. Sheridan replaced Throckmorton with Elisha M. Pease. In the next four months, the military commanders replaced 500 Democratic officeholders with Republicans.

An election was held in February 1868 on whether to hold another constitutional convention. In Webberville, near Austin, a black man carrying an American flag and armed with a saber led the town's black voters to the polls. Republicans in some county seats gave shelter to blacks who came into town from surrounding farms to vote. Statewide, only 32 percent of the whites voted; 82 percent of the blacks turned out to approve another convention.

The 1868 convention was consumed by bickering. Besides the differences between conservative Democrats and Republicans, there was, within the Republican party, an ever-deepening division between moderates and radicals.

The convention produced no constitution, nor did a second late in the year. In February 1869, a coalition of moderate Republicans and Democrats gained control of the convention, turned the incomplete constitution over to military authorities and adjourned. The final constitution was written by a three-man committee appointed by Gen. Joseph J. Reynolds, Griffin's successor as commander of the subdistrict of Texas. It pleased no one. Only half of the 90 delegates signed the Constitution of 1869.

The governor's race in the election held between Nov. 30 and Dec. 3 pitted radical Republican E.J. Davis against moderate Republican A.J. Hamilton. The vote count was so close that the military impounded the ballots and awarded the office to Davis.

After the Legislature ratified the 14th and 15th amendments to the U.S. Constitution and elected two radicals to the U.S. Senate, Texas was formally readmitted to the Union. Military rule ended on April 16, 1870.

The infamous Ku Klux Klan first appeared in Texas about 1868. What began as an effort to frighten blacks, so that they would leave town or would not vote, escalated into mindless violence. The organization's name became synonymous with arson, assassination and lynching. In Bastrop, a group of masked white men lynched two delegates to the state convention of the Union League. In Burleson and Brazos counties, prominent black politicians were assassinated. When a black posse formed by a local minister attempted to arrest Klan leaders in Brazos County, up to 100 blacks were killed in a four-day battle before federal troops stepped in to stop the massacre. Whites pursued the survivors and hanged the minister.

The 12th Legislature convened on April 28, 1870, and promptly postponed the next elections, thereby increasing legislators' terms of office. In the senate, when a group of Democrats and conservative Republicans blocked some of their pet legislation, the radicals had the dissenters arrested and temporarily removed.

Speaker of the House Ira H. Evans, was removed from office in May 1871 for opposing certain measures.

In the name of law and order, the Legislature gave the governor the power to declare martial law in any county, and it authorized creation of a militia and a state police force. Critics claimed the state police force was poorly trained and poorly supervised. Some officers were accused of brutality and abuse of power. Although some critics admitted that the force was effective, the fact that 40 percent of the 258-man force was black was enough to provoke fear and hatred among the conservatives.

Even though the 12th Legislature provided the beginnings of a public road system, enacted a homestead law, supplemented frontier defense forces with state troops, and established a compulsory, free public school system, its program and its use of law enforcement personnel were bitterly resented.

The pendulum began its return swing when a special election was held in October 1871 to fill four congressional seats. Amid violence and voting irregularities, the four seats were won by Democrats. In the regular election in 1872, the Democrats won all congressional seats and gained a majority in the Legislature.

The conservative majority in the 13th Legislature dismantled the structure of Reconstruction as quickly as it could. The lawmakers did away with the state police, established one-day elections, and stripped the governor of the power to declare martial law. But they also threw out the radicals' attempts to create an effective public school system.

When Democrat Richard Coke was elected governor in December 1873, Gov. Davis tried to have the election invalidated. The state Supreme Court sided with Davis, but the voters ignored the decisions. When Davis was not supported by the federal government, he gave up.

Texas' finances were in ruins. The radicals' programs had been expensive, and the public debt had increased by more than $2 million. Land values were down. Cotton had dropped to less than half its 1866 value.

A sharecropping system started replacing slave labor shortly after the war ended. A landowner supplied his workers with houses and equipment in return for half to two-thirds of the crop. In 1873, Texas produced more cotton than it had before the war and went on to become a leading cotton producer.

The first cattle drives from Texas on the legendary Chisholm Trail headed north out of DeWitt County in 1866, crossing Central Texas toward the markets and railheads in Kansas. The trail was named for Indian trader Jesse Chisholm, who blazed a cattle trail in 1865 between the North Canadian and Arkansas rivers. That initial trail was expanded north and south by other drovers. The trail was not one fixed route. As one historian remarked, "trails originated wherever a herd was shaped up and ended wherever a market was found. A thousand minor trails fed the main routes."

Roughly, the trail went from the Rio Grande near Brownsville through Cameron, Willacy, Kleberg, Nueces, San Patricio, Bee, Karnes, Wilson, Guadalupe, Hays, Travis, Williamson, Bell, McLennan, Bosque, Hill, Johnson, Tarrant, Wise and Montague counties. It crossed the Red River and continued to Dodge City and Abilene, Kans. Another popular route approximately paralleled the main trail, but lay farther east. Fixed points on the trail, which all the drives on the Chisholm Trail used, were the crossing on the Colorado River near Austin; Brushy Creek near Round Rock; Kimball Bend on the Brazos River; and the Trinity Ford in Fort Worth below the junction of the Clear and West forks.

Peak year on the Chisholm Trail was 1871. After interstate railroads came to Texas in the mid-1870s, trailing cattle to the Midwest became unnecessary. The Chisholm Trail was virtually shut down by the 1884 season.

In Waco, politics and reconstruction were forgotten for a few days as the first bridge over the Brazos River and the first suspension bridge in the state, was opened with great fanfare. The first tolls were collected on Jan. 1, 1870, and a gala celebration was held on January (see article, "The Waco Suspension Bridge").

Reconstruction had been nine years of confusion and uncertainty, fear and hatred, economic disaster and racial violence. The day that E.J. Davis left office Jan. 15, 1874, Reconstruction was over in the Lone Star State. But the aftertaste lingered for a century.

The original, medieval-style design of the Waco bridge towers shown here was changed during a major reconstruction in 1913-14. Photo courtesy The Texas Collection, Baylor University.

The Waco Suspension Bridge

Until the late 1860s, the only way to cross the Brazos River at Waco was by ferry or by fording the river when the water was low. Capt. Shapley Ross had operated a primitive ferry across the river at Waco since 1849. But the Brazos could be treacherous after a rain and sometimes was impassable for days at a time.

Waco business leaders received a charter from the state in 1866 to build a permanent toll bridge over the Brazos. Even with money scarce and interest rates high during Reconstruction, the Waco Bridge Company sold all its stock. In mid-1868, the company chose to work with John A. Roebling and Son of Trenton, New Jersey, in designing and building a new suspension-type bridge. Roebling designed and built New York's Brooklyn Bridge, which opened in 1883, using the same technique and style. Civil engineer Thomas M. Griffith, a Roebling employee who had worked

History Highlights

with similar bridges, was the actual designer and construction supervisor.

Work began in September 1868. At that time, Waco had no machine shops or any artisans with the skills to build a bridge of this magnitude, and the nearest railroad was 100 miles away. The woven wire cables and other components were shipped to Galveston by steamer, transferred by rail to Bryan, then taken by ox wagons on a rutted, dusty road to Waco.

Construction began with the excavation for the footings of the twin double towers that would anchor the span. The towers, which required 2.7 million locally produced bricks to construct, were topped with crenelated ornamentation resembling a medieval castle. Workmen carried wires across the river to form the massive cables that would support the wooden roadway. The span was completed in late December

1869, and the first tolls were collected on January 1, 1870. The $141,000 structure — the first bridge across the Brazos — was dedicated five days later. The main span was so wide that two stagecoaches could pass each other, and it was 475 feet long.

Not only did the bridge company charge people to cross, but it also collected five cents per head from cattle drovers "for each loose animal of the cattle kind" that used the span. Since the Chisholm Trail went through Waco, a large number of cattle lumbered across, which helped the bridge company to retire its debt. Most drovers, however, still chose the cheaper alternative of swimming their herds across the Brazos.

The Waco Suspension Bridge triggered Waco's transformation from frontier outpost to city. The waves of immigrants heading west after the Civil War used this easy way across the Brazos. These travelers also needed supplies and equipment of all kinds, repairs for their harness and fresh horses and mules. Waco met their demands, and it prospered and grew. The year the bridge opened, there were slightly more than 3,000 people in Waco. Ten years later, the population had more than doubled to 7,295.

The bridge operated as a toll bridge from 1870 to 1889, when it was sold to McLennan County. The county turned it over to the City of Waco to operate as a free bridge. Major reconstruction was done in 1913-1914. The pier towers were rebuilt and stuccoed, with the medieval crenelations supplanted by a much plainer design. Stronger steel cables replaced the original ones. Steel trusses were added on both sides to enable the span to carry heavier loads and to provide walkways. The bridge reopened in 1914 and was used by vehicular traffic until 1971, when it was retired to the rank of historical monument.

Today it is open for pedestrian traffic in a park just east of the Waco central business district near the site of the original Waco Springs. The Waco Suspension Bridge is on the National Register of Historic Places and has a Texas historical medallion.

Iron Horses and Cotton Bolls

Cotton and railroads rolled across Central Texas in tandem following Reconstruction.

Cotton was growing wild in Texas when the Spanish first explored the area in the 16th century. Spanish missionaries cultivated the plant, and in 1745, the missions in San Antonio were producing several thousand pounds annually. The first hybrid, improved cotton was introduced into Texas by one of Stephen F. Austin's Old Three Hundred, Col. Jared Groce. For his pioneering work, Groce is called the father of the Texas cotton industry.

In 1846, Texas exported about 27,000 bales of cotton, and cotton farming spread slowly across the eastern third of the state. In 1853, exporter Francis Moreau of New Braunfels shipped nine bales of locally grown cotton to New Orleans via Indianola. Cotton was being cultivated in Castroville in 1854. The cotton gin owner there sold the seed to farmers in order to promote business.

Cotton farming increased after the Civil War and began to spread rapidly through the river valleys of Central Texas. Soon textile mills were operating in the area. By 1868, the Bastrop Manufacturing Company, the oldest textile mill in the state, had 1,100 spindles producing 1,000 yards of cloth per day. The Waco Manufacturing Company had 1,000 spindles, with an 800-yard capacity. The water-powered cotton mill at New Braunfels employed girls and children, working long hours for low wages. Although he never heated the mill, the owner bragged, he did not shut down for cold weather more than three or four days each winter. In 1878, a woolen mill at New Braunfels, said to be the most profitable textile mill in the state, netted $81,000.

The first commercial cottonseed-oil mill in Texas was built in High Hill, Fayette County, in 1867. At that time, cottonseed oil was primarily burned in lamps for light, although some was used in the manufacture of soap and paints and for lubrication. Not until 1879 was a method developed to refine cottonseed oil so it could be used in foods, and there was little growth in the industry until the turn of the century.

Cotton was too bulky to ship as lint, and many small neighborhood cotton gins sprang up around the Central Texas cotton-growing regions. But even after it was stripped of seeds and baled, cotton was awkward to handle. Cotton compresses reduced the size of the bale by about half, making it easier to handle. Before the Civil War, however, the only compress in Texas was in Galveston. Shortly after the railroads came, cotton compresses were built in every important railroad shipping point.

Railroads had inched into the edges of Central Texas just before the Civil War. The Houston and Texas Central (H&TC), laying rails to the northwest out of Houston, reached Millican, Brazos County, in 1860. Construction halted there until the war was over. The rails reached the town of Bryan in 1867. Bryan had been in existence since 1855, and an official townsite was donated by Joel Bryan in 1865 as the railroad was approaching. The county seat was moved to Bryan from Boonville, several miles east, the following year in anticipation of the railroad's arrival.

The H&TC advanced to Hearne in 1868. Two years later, it had stretched to Groesbeck and beyond. The H&TC also began building in 1870 from Brenham toward Austin, reaching the capital city in 1871.

To persuade the railroads to build through their towns, officials offered incentives, often consisting of a donation of land for the right of way through the county plus a cash bonus. There were also liberal land grants from the state, usually 16 sections per mile of track constructed. About 41 railroad companies received state land grants before the Legislature discovered in 1881 that it had promised to give away more land than was available. Lawmakers repealed the land grant act the following year. More than 32 million acres of land, an area slightly larger than the state of New York, were given away to encourage railroad building in Texas.

Before railroads were built, farm families had little incentive to grow more food crops than they could use themselves. The freight charges for shipping products by wagon equalled or exceeded the market prices of the commodities. Families grew their own wheat, which was ground into flour at small local mills. After the railroads came, flour shipped in from large commercial flour mills in the north was cheaper, so local wheat growing declined. Cotton farming increased as freight

rates declined, helping to change the character of Central Texas agriculture from subsistence farming to a commercial agricultural system. The popular cash crop was planted everywhere — plains and prairies, bottomlands and uplands.

To help small farmers obtain credit after the Civil War, the crop-lien system was developed. Merchants extended credit to hard-pressed farmers in exchange for a lien on their crop. Since cotton was the major cash crop, many farmers were discouraged from planting anything else, adding to the concentration of cotton.

Agricultural leaders, agriculture teachers, newspaper editors and others were alarmed by this overwhelming plunge into cotton farming. They preached diversification of crops. Farmers responded by planting more cotton. Bell County was typical: In 1879, Bell County farmers produced 84,267 bushels of wheat and 9,217 bales of cotton. The railroad arrived in Bell County in 1881. By 1889, the county was producing one quarter of the wheat it had grown in 1879, but more than four times more cotton. Although cotton farming lacked the romance of cattle ranching, it rose to the top in economic importance to the state.

With the H&TC moving toward the northwest out of Bryan, Lum Hearne offered railroad officials land for a right of way. Settlers began moving in. A general store and a private bank were among the first of many businesses to be drawn to the new town of Hearne. Then the International Railroad Company was lured to Hearne with a donation of 700 acres of land.

Hearne took on boom-town characteristics common to all such early railroad towns with large payrolls. Gamblers and con men abounded. The two railroads crossed north of the original depot, so the town's businesses moved themselves to the intersection.

The H&TC reached Calvert, Robertson County, in June 1869. For a period of time Calvert was a railhead, which gave it, too, a boom-town atmosphere. By Jan. 1, 1870, Calvert had 104 businesses, some of which were open 24 hours a day, seven days a week. General stores stocked whiskey in barrels and sold it by the gallon. The jail was said to be the largest building in town, although con men, prostitutes and gamblers operated with little interference from the law. Calvert was named for Judge Robert Calvert, who donated the townsite.

Trains connected at Calvert with stage lines to Waco via Marlin, continuing to Dallas and, to Houston and Galveston. People from North, Northeast and Northwest Texas came to Calvert in wagons, on horseback and afoot to meet the trains. Lodgings were in short supply. To house the multitude, hotels were supplemented with tents, covered wagons and temporary buildings. The resulting unsanitary conditions probably contributed to an outbreak of yellow fever in 1873 that killed several hundred people.

In 1869, about 300 Chinese laborers were recruited in California by the H&TC to grade the right of way north out of Calvert. After six months, the exotic railroad workers encountered labor problems, and their contract was terminated. A number of them returned to Calvert and surrounding towns to settle; others joined them from China. Although the total number of Chinese who came to Texas during this time is not available, at least 150 people of Chinese origin were registered to vote in Hearne in 1874.

Other Chinese, who worked on the Southern Pacific line through West Texas, settled in San Antonio after the railroad was completed. By 1890, about 50 Chinese were living there and working mostly as laundrymen, truck farmers and restaurant workers.

Bremond, also in Robertson County, blossomed overnight when the H&TC reached the site in 1870. The town was founded by three of the principal stockholders of the railroad, Abraham Groesbeck, William Robinson Baker and William Marsh Rice, as a private speculation. They named it for Paul Bremond of Houston, the principal promoter of the H&TC.

At first, Bremond comprised several long, two-story buildings, with businesses occupying the ground floors and living quarters upstairs. When the rails moved north, the structures, which had sprung up like mushrooms, were torn down just as fast and moved north with the railroad. Some residents stayed; more settlers arrived. Stock raising and farming became Bremond's primary economic base.

Waco's first train was the Waco & Northwestern, also called the Waco Tap, built from Bremond in 1871 to connect to the H&TC. The H&TC was completed between Brenham and Austin in 1871. The town of Giddings, named for Jabez D. Giddings of Washington County, a Texas transportation pioneer, was established in Lee County as a shipping point. Many of the early settlers of Giddings were Wends from nearby Serbin.

The International and Great Northern (I&GN), which some wags called "the Insignificant and Good for Nothing," reached Rockdale in 1874 and stretched to Georgetown and Austin by 1876. By 1875, the H&TC and the Texas & Pacific Railway (T&P) reached Dallas. The International Railroad laid tracks north out of Hearne, extending across Robertson County the same year. San Antonio welcomed its first train, the Galveston, Harrisburg and San Antonio line, also called the Sunset Line, on February 19, 1877. In 1881, the I&GN reached San Antonio.

The tracks of the Gulf, Colorado and Santa Fe Railway Co., (GC&SF) originating in Galveston, reached Cameron, Milam County, and Belton in 1881. Where its tracks crossed those of the I&GN, the town of Milano Junction, now Milano, Milam County, developed.

The GC&SF also finished the stretch of tracks between Temple and Fort Worth in 1881. The same year, the I&GN extended from Austin to Laredo, and the Texas & St. Louis of Texas connected Corsicana with Waco.

Even after railroads linked most of the larger towns in Central Texas, stagecoaches transported passengers and freight from outlying areas to the rail stops. A typical rural stage stop was the limestone structure built by Marsden Ogletree southwest of Gatesville at present-day Copperas Cove in 1878. It served not only as a stop on the Lampasas-to-Belton stagecoach line, but also as family home, feed store and, from 1879, post office.

Stagecoaches and trains were popular targets for bandits such as Sam Bass. Originally from Indiana, Bass worked as a teamster around Denton. He went north to Nebraska with a cattle drive and fell in with a group of outlaws. After the gang held up a Union Pacific train in the fall of 1877, Bass returned to North Texas. He planned to rob a bank in Round Rock, just north of Austin, in 1878, but one of the gang members alerted the Texas Rangers. When the Bass gang rode into Round Rock on July 19, Rangers confronted them. In the ensuing gunfire, Bass was mortally wounded.

While cotton and railroads surged across Texas, immigration continued to add new flavors to the Central Texas stew. During the 1860s, two Texans, Travis Shaw and John Hester, journeyed to Denmark to recruit Danes to settle in Central Texas. More than 20 Danish families followed the men back to Texas and settled about eight miles west of Lexington in present-day Lee County. So many other Danes joined them in the next two decades, the northern part of Lee County was called "Little Denmark." There is no longer a recognizable Danish colony in Lee County; it was gradually absorbed into the surrounding community.

The first Polish immigrant to settle in Bremond was Joseph Bartula, who arrived with his family in 1875 from Galveston. More Polish families followed, and the Bremond area soon became the focus of a major wave of Polish immigration. By 1877, Bremond was home to about 50 Polish families. Polish settlers also were living in Marlin, Falls County, as early as 1870.

Bryan first welcomed Polish immigrants in 1873. The influx of Polish families, coming either from other Polish communities in Texas or directly from Poland, continued for three decades.

As the H&TC laid tracks out of Millican after the Civil War, Isaac, Lehman and Philip Sanger were right behind it. The brothers followed the H&TC from Bryan to Hearne, then to Calvert, Bremond, Kosse, Groesbeck and Corsicana, opening stores one after the other. By 1872, the Sangers were in Dallas. (Prior to the war, they had opened stores in McKinney, Decatur and Weatherford.) Later they opened branches in Waco, Sherman, Fort Worth and Clarendon.

Farmers, encouraged by the drop in freight rates with the coming of the railroads, were becoming increasingly restive. Rates were now going up, commodity prices were decreasing and land was getting more expensive. Feeling the economic pinch, many farmers

blamed big business, particularly big railroads, and penurious bankers.

The Patrons of Husbandry, better known as the Grange, organized its first Texas chapter at Salado, about 40 miles north of Austin in Bell County, in 1873. By 1877, they claimed 50,000 members statewide. The group's aims were to buy less, sell more and make their farms self-sufficient. They urged crop diversification and discontinuation of the credit system. However, their goals were contrary to the trends in the economy, and the farms were often too small to support a family. What were needed were larger farms, fewer farmers and more machinery to increase efficiency. The Grange planned to establish a network of stores, mills and factories that could charge members lower prices than most retail stores through cooperative buying and selling agreements. The gins, warehouses and tanneries they established were poorly managed and undercapitalized, and they overextended the granting of credit. Farmers, not merchants, were installed as managers, and they made many disastrous mistakes. By 1879, there were only 4,000 members left.

The Grange did, however, give voice to the farmers' frustrations at being at the mercy of big business, although its spokesmen tended not to distinguish between corporations and monopolies. As many as half the delegates to the Constitutional Convention of 1876 were Grangers. They pressed for restraints on corporate actions, particularly railroads; denying state agencies the power to charter banks; reduction of taxes; lower salaries for public officials; biennial legislative sessions rather than annual; and a homestead law protecting a certain portion of property from forced sale. The constitution they helped create is basically the one governing Texas today, although in a considerably amended version. The Grange also influenced the development of agricultural experiment stations. And it paved the way for the Farmer's Alliance and the Populist political movement.

The Grand State Farmers' Alliance, founded in 1875 in Lampasas County, was reorganized in Poolville, Parker County, in 1879. By 1886, it had become a national organization with more than 3,000 chapters. Its basic purposes, as with the Grange, were improving the welfare of the farmer and promoting agriculture. The alliance's co-op stores suffered the same fate as those of the Grange, and for the same reasons. In 1887 it merged with another national farm organization.

Opportunities for higher education in Central Texas expanded following Reconstruction. Southwestern University, Georgetown, was formed in 1873 by five Texas Conferences of the Methodist Episcopal Church, South, from a merger of Rutersville College, Fayette County; Wesleyan College, San Augustine; McKenzie College, Clarksville; and Soule University, Chappell Hill. The new university, initially named Texas University, enrolled 63 men by its second year. The name was changed to Southwestern University on Feb. 6, 1875. After the I&GN reached Georgetown in 1875, enrollment increased to 109. A Female Department was added in 1878, enrolling 52 women. By 1900, total enrollment reached 417.

Southwestern joined Baylor University, founded in Waco in 1849, and St. Mary's University, which had been operating in San Antonio since 1852.

The first public college in the state was founded near Bryan in 1876. Named the Agricultural and Mechanical College, it evolved into today's Texas A&M University (see article, "The University of Texas and Texas A&M").

San Antonio was a colorful crossroads in the decades following Reconstruction. Poet Sidney Lanier described the view from the Commerce Street bridge over the San Antonio River in the early 1870s — canvas-covered "bathing houses"; covered freight wagons drawn by 14-mule teams; burros bearing cargos of mesquite firewood; and many odd and distinctive characters.

Construction began in San Antonio in 1876 on a permanent military post, called at first "Post of San Antonio," later renamed in honor of Sam Houston. The fort's first building, the Quadrangle, opened in December 1879. A hospital and officers' quarters, begun in 1881, opened in 1886. The 4th Cavalry brought a famous "guest" to Fort Sam Houston in 1886: Apache chief Geronimo and his followers, including wives and children, camped there for about a month as prisoners.

San Antonio's first water system was completed in 1878, using water pumped from the San Antonio River. Later an artesian well was added to the system.

Also in 1878, mule-drawn streetcars began operating from Alamo Plaza to San Pedro Springs. The railway later switched to electric power. By 1881, gaslights were operating in many prosperous citizens' homes. The first telephone exchange in the Alamo City began operating in 1882 and soon had 200 subscribers. The first electric street lights, also installed in 1882, sputtered badly. Not until the first successful light plant was put into operation in 1887 did they work well.

Ice plants were built in many towns across Central Texas. In 1879, Austin had two plants; the resulting competition led to a price war. Belton had a small ice plant charging 10 cents a pound delivered.

In the years following the Civil War, Central Texas experienced growth in many directions: railroads, cotton farming, continuing immigration from Europe and Mexico, and the construction and development of services, utilities and infrastructure in the larger towns. This was but an introduction to the development that was to follow.

The Century Ends

The last 20 years of the century were busy in Central Texas.

Austin

In Austin, the old capitol burned on Nov. 9, 1881. To some it was not such a great loss. Not only had the government outgrown the old capitol, built in the early 1850s, but critics complained that it resembled a "large-size corn crib with a pumpkin for a dome."

The Constitutional Convention of 1876 had reserved 3 million acres of public domain to pay for a new capitol, plus 50,000 acres to cover the cost of surveying. Successful bidder for construction of the new capitol, the fourth in Austin, was Mattheas Schnell of Rock Island, Ill. In May 1882, he transferred his interest to John V. and Charles B. Farwell, Abner Taylor and Amos G. Babcock of Taylor, Babcock & Co. of Chicago, also called the Capitol Syndicate. The public lands exchanged for the building of the capitol, located in all or parts of nine Panhandle counties, were developed into the famed XIT Ranch.

Architect Elijah E. Myers of Detroit won a national design competition with his Renaissance Revival-style plan in the shape of a Greek cross 200 yards long and 100 yards across. The building originally was to be built of limestone quarried by prison labor at Convict Hill nearby. But the limestone was plagued by streaks caused by naturally occurring iron pyrites. Owners of Granite Mountain, 45 miles northwest near Marble Falls in Burnet County, could not afford to develop a quarry on their own. They offered the state all the pink granite needed for the capitol in exchange for development of a quarry. The state also agreed to furnish convict labor to cut the stone, to construct a narrow-gauge railway from Burnet to the quarry, and to rebuild the wagon road between Burnet and Austin.

Because of the use of convict labor, the International Association of Granite Cutters called for a boycott of the project. The syndicate imported 62 Scottish stoneworkers, triggering a suit by the Knights of Labor charging violation of the federal law against importation of contract labor.

Despite the boycot, more than 15,000 carloads of stone were shipped from Granite Mountain to Burnet on the narrow-gauge line and on to Austin on the Austin and Northwestern railroad. The Capitol's beautifully detailed interior used 114 cases of acid-etched glass panels from Britain in doors and transoms and thousands of square feet of carved wainscotting of Texas ash, cedar, cherry, mahogany, oak, pine and walnut. The dome was made in Belgium of cast iron; height to its peak is 309 feet, seven feet higher than the capitol in Washington, D.C. It is surmounted by the Goddess of Liberty, a statue then called "Old Hatchet Face" because of the strong planes of her facial features. The 26-acre grounds are surrounded by a black wrought-iron fence studded with stars.

The lights were turned on in the new capitol on April 20, 1888. The week-long dedication and celebration featured parades and military drill teams from all over the state. The capitol officially opened on May 16, 1888, with Sam Houston's youngest son, Temple Houston, as a special guest.

During the 1880s, Austin's economy was boosted by the construction of both the capitol and the University of Texas. The long-delayed university opened in Austin in Sept. 15, 1883, although some classes were held in the temporary capitol for several months until the west wing of the main building was finished (see article, "The University of Texas and Texas A&M").

Tillotson Collegiate and Normal Institute, a senior college for African-Americans, opened in Austin with 250 students in 1881. The school was named for George Jeffrey Tillotson, who selected the site and raised $16,000 for its construction. The institute's sponsor was the American Missionary Association of the Congregational Church of New York. Tillotson merged in 1951 with Samuel Huston College to become Huston-Tillotson College.

William Sydney Porter, a native of North Carolina, arrived in Austin in the spring of 1884. He worked as a clerk and bookkeeper, then as a draftsman at the General Land Office. From 1891 to 1894, he was a teller in the First National Bank, a job from which he resigned to publish *The Rolling Stone*, a humorous weekly. When the publication failed, he moved to Houston to write for the Houston *Post*. When Austin bank officials discovered a shortage of more than $4,000 that had occurred while Porter was a teller, he was tried for embezzlement and convicted. Although the charges were technical, he refused to implicate bank officials. While serving his five-year sentence in a federal penitentiary in Ohio, he wrote many short stories, and he continued to write after his release. Porter wrote more than 400 short stories in all, many of them under the pen name, "O. Henry." Forty of his stories had Texas settings.

Recreation in Austin in mid-1880s included Tyrolean concerts at Scholz Garten, performances at Millett's Opera House, and moonlight boat rides on the

This 1888 photo shows the statue of the Goddess of Liberty just before it was hoisted to the top of the new state capitol. Photo courtesy the Texas State Library.

Belle of Austin steamboat or the Ben Hur, a three-decked sidewheel steamer.

Austin was turned on its ear by the arrival in 1892 of 59-year-old German-born sculptress Elisabet Ney. A former confidante of European nobility, she and her husband, Dr. Edmund Montgomery, had lived near Hempstead since 1873. Contrary to the traditions of the day, Ney retained her maiden name. Texans' eyebrows were raised by such eccentricities as her wearing bloomer-type slacks and, when one of her children died, cremating his remains in her fireplace. In her limestone studio and home in Austin, she created statues of noted Texas figures. Her marble statues of Stephen F. Austin and Sam Houston stand in the Texas Capitol; duplicates were placed in Statuary Hall in the national capitol in Washington, D.C.

An innovative street-lighting system was installed in Austin in 1894-1895. Each of the 31 towers held a cluster of arc lights atop a triangular cast-and wrought-iron tower with a framework 150 feet high on a 15-foot iron base supported by heavy steel-cable guy wires. The tower lights were designed to produce a circle of light bright enough that the time could be read on the average watch on the darkest night. First lighted May 6, 1895, the "moonlight towers" required a city employee to ascend each tower each night to turn them on. A switch was installed at the base of each tower in 1936, and in 1942, the controls were centralized.

San Antonio

Until about 1890, Military Plaza in San Antonio was perhaps the most colorful spot in Central Texas. It was part open-air supermarket, part short-order cafe, part flea market — and all floor show. The "chili queens" cooked all night over charcoal braziers on the plaza's south side and served their spicy wares during the day. Fresh vegetables, eggs and poultry were sold on the east side. And on the west were vendors of hay, wool, hides, songbirds and other commodities — an al fresco variety store. After the new city hall was built in the middle of the plaza, although some vendors remained, the chili queens moved to Alamo Plaza.

William Gebhardt, a German-born New Braunfels restauranteur, sold the first commercial chili powder in 1894. Before that, chili was a seasonal dish, served only when fresh chili peppers were available. By 1896, there was enough demand for the eye-watering spice that Gebhardt established a factory in San Antonio. Gebhardt added the nation's first canned chili con carne and canned tamales to his offerings in 1911.

Recruiting troops for the First Volunteer Cavalry for the Spanish-American War brought Teddy Roosevelt to San Antonio in 1898. Called the Rough Riders, it was an elite group, chiefly from Arizona, New Mexico, Texas and Indian Territory. Legend says that Roosevelt did much of his Texas recruiting in the bar of the Menger Hotel. The recruits' civilian occupations ranged from dancer to football player, from gourmet to oarsman, plus policeman, cowboy, "down-and-outer," musician and "bad man." There were several full-blooded Indians and one ex-marshal of Dodge City, as well as a sprinkling of "swells" from Harvard and Yale. Despite the disparity in their origins, however, the Rough Riders became, as one writer said, "one homogeneous mass of patriotism and pluck." Col. Leonard Wood, an army surgeon, was the group's commander, chosen for the post by Roosevelt because of his superior military experience. So popular were the Rough Riders with San Antonio's residents that guards had to be posted to keep the civilians from overrunning the fairgrounds where the troops were drilling. On May 29, more than 1,000 of "Teddy's Terrors" left for Florida. Less than a month later, they were in Cuba. Because of supply and transportation snags, however, their horses remained in Florida. The Rough Riders fought valiantly, but many were killed or wounded. The survivors were mustered out at Long Island after barely three months' service. In all, Texas contributed about 10,000 recruits to the Spanish-American War effort.

Waco

Waco was a lively place in the last 15 years of the century. The popular soft drink, Dr Pepper, was first served at the Old Corner Drug Store in Waco in 1885 by druggist Charles C. Alderton. The formula was acquired from Alderton by druggist Wade B. Morrison, who named the drink after a friend, Dr. Charles K. Pepper of Rural Retreat, Va. Morrison and Robert S. Lazenby, a Waco beverage chemist who was already bottling and distributing his own brand of ginger ale, organized the Artesian Manufacturing and Bottling Company in 1891 to manufacture and market Dr Pepper. The headquarters moved to Dallas in 1922.

Baylor University, which had been chartered at Independence, Washington County, by the Republic of Texas in 1845, and Waco University, founded in 1861, consolidated at Waco in 1886, retaining the Baylor name. The female department of Baylor, named Baylor Female College in 1866, moved to Belton in 1886. In 1934, the name was changed to Mary Hardin-Baylor to honor philanthropist Mrs. Mary Hardin.

The Slayden-Kerksey Woolen mill, which made fabric for men's suits, was built in Waco in 1885. Historian T. Lindsay Baker calls it the most successful Texas textile mill of all time.

The controversial journalist William Cowper Brann, an Illinois native, lived for short periods in Galveston and Houston from 1886 to 1891, when he moved to Austin. There he founded and published The Iconoclast, which soon failed. He became editor of the San Antonio Express in 1892, then editor of the Waco Morning News in 1894. Citing a desire to combat hypocrisy and intolerance, he revived the monthly Iconoclast, which increased in circulation from 3,000 to 98,000 within three years. His vitriolic attacks on the administrators of Baylor University earned him many enemies. One such enemy, T. E. Davis, met Brann on a Waco street on April 1, 1898. The exchange of gunfire left both Brann and Davis mortally wounded; they died the next day.

Waco built the Cotton Palace in Padgitt Park in 1894 for holding fairs and expositions. The first fair was held that year, but just before the second could be held in 1895, the main building burned. The site remained dormant until, in 1909, the Waco Young Men's Business League rebuilt five exhibit buildings and the 10,000-seat Coliseum, a replica of the Coliseum in Washington, D.C. The Cotton Palace was also the site of grand opera performances and debutante balls. The buildings were abandoned in 1932 because of the Depression, and they were sold or demolished.

The eyes of Central Texans, as well as others across the state, were all on a point slightly south of the town of West in McLennan County on Sept. 15, 1896. In a publicity stunt billed as "The Crash at Crush," two trains of the Katy line were deliberately crashed head-on. The stunt had been tried successfully in Ohio several months before. The elaborate preparations were supervised by Katy Passenger Agent William G. Crush, whose idea the event was and for whom the site was named. The stunt attracted an estimated 30,000 spectators brought in by dozens of special trains. Engines 999 and 1001, each pulling six cars, rolled toward each other about 5 p.m. with whistles blowing repeatedly. Each locomotive reached a speed of about 45 miles an hour just before the crash, producing a collision force equivalent to hitting a stationary, solid object at 90 miles per hour. Despite precautions, both boilers exploded on impact, hurling jagged pieces of iron and steel into the crowd. Two were killed, and many were injured. The railroad settled all claims with dispatch.

Lampasas was the site of the founding of the Texas Bankers Association in 1885. The Park Hotel, the newest, most luxurious resort in Central Texas, was built around one of the many mineral springs found near Lampasas. The bankers were so pleased with their first meeting in the highly-touted, glamorous resort that they held their meeting there again the following year.

The ethnic stew of Central Texas added another ingredient in the 1880s as a wave of Italian immigrants moved into the Brazos Valley, mostly from Bryan northward. They were motivated to immigrate by overpopulation, epidemics of malaria and cholera and a series of earthquakes in their home country. In the mid-1870s, after businessmen from the lower Brazos Valley advertised in European newspapers for immigrants in an attempt to spur the local economy, a few Italians responded, moving into the Bryan area. Most farmed the fertile, though flood-prone, river bottoms along the Brazos River between Hearne and Bryan. By the 1890s, Brazos County had one of the largest concentrations of Italian farmers in the United States. Other Italians worked on the railroads or in the coal mines at Thurber, Erath County. By 1910, Burleson and Robertson counties also had significant numbers of

St. Paul Lutheran Church in Serbin, Lee County, was built in 1868-71 by Wends, who migrated from Germany to Texas in 1854 seeking freedom from religious persecution. Texas Almanac staff photo.

loads of wool being brought to town and stored in vacant houses. The West Texas Co-operative Marketing Association was formed in San Saba when it was the terminus of stagecoach lines to the west. When the Santa Fe laid tracks to San Angelo, the wool markets moved there.

A different kind of agricultural history was made in the cotton fields of Central Texas starting about 1895. The boll weevil first appeared in the Lower Rio Grande Valley from Mexico in 1893. By 1895, it had advanced as far north as San

Italian immigrants. Statewide, the number of Italian-born residents jumped from 186 in 1870 to 2,107 in 1890 and to 8,024 in 1920.

Foreign-born settlers were so numerous in Texas near the turn of the century that several towns had locally published foreign-language newspapers. German newspapers were published in Austin, Giddings, La Grange, Lockhart, San Antonio and Temple. Czech newspapers were distributed from La Grange and Taylor, and Swedish from Austin.

Severe droughts in 1886-1887 were disastrous to Central Texas farmers. George Tyler in Bell County reported that there was no rain in the winter and spring of 1886. The corn failed, but a late summer shower saved some of the cotton. The first substantial rain was on June 4, 1887, too late to save the corn, but early enough to make a somewhat better cotton crop than the previous year.

A few barbed-wire fences had been strung in Texas by 1880, and the wire, which was first patented by J.F. Glidden in DeKalb, Ill., in 1873, was widely used by 1883. Free-range cattlemen, accustomed to running their cattle across unfenced lands at will, were enraged to find fences blocking their way across private property. The fence-cutting wars that ensued prompted legislation in 1884 making fence cutting a felony and requiring gates in fences every three miles.

The last two decades of the 19th century were marked by a series of epidemics in Central Texas. Smallpox hit Robertson County in 1883; the Austin area in 1886; the area around San Gabriel, Milam County, in 1891; and the Taylor area of Williamson County in 1895.

Agriculture history was made in San Saba County in 1888 with the development of papershell pecans by the West Texas Pecan Nursery. Pecans are very much a part of San Saba's history: Fossil pecans have been found there that date from prehistoric times. San Saba also developed into a major wool market, with wagon-

Antonio. The U.S. Department of Agriculture recommended to the Texas Legislature that it require farmers to plow up their cotton stalks, where the insects lived, as soon as the harvest was complete. The Legislature dragged its feet; the voracious insect quickly spread across the state and throughout the South.

The financial Panic of 1893 brought several years of relative depression in both the rural and urban sectors. Farmers continued to be plagued by high freight rates, monopolies, depressions and declining prices despite the gains made by farmers' organizations.

In James Stephen Hogg, who served as governor from 1891 to 1895, the farmers found a champion. Hogg established the Texas Railroad Commission to regulate freight rates and to establish rules for railroad operations within the state. Railroad Commission Chairman John H. Reagan, who resigned from the U.S. Senate to take the post, claimed that lower cotton rates saved Texas farmers $800,000 in 1897.

By 1900, about half the farms in Texas were tenant-operated. The shift from self-contained to commercialized agriculture was widespread. But cotton was no longer the only commercial crop. It had been joined by wheat and hay and, in South Texas, sugar cane and rice. Poultry and eggs also were added. In 1870, the most important industry in Texas was flour milling. But by 1900, lumbering, mostly confined to the East Texas Piney Woods, was first in value of output, followed by cottonseed oil and cake, with flour milling third.

Then the oil well known as Spindletop blew in near Beaumont on Jan. 10, 1901, and Texas' economy turned from agriculture toward manufacturing. In 20 years, industrial output exceeded the value of agricultural products, and the disparity continued to increase. Texas was on the verge of its own industrial revolution.

The Early Twentieth Century

The first decade of the 20th century was fairly prosperous, especially coming after the great industrial panic of 1893 to 1897.

In 1900, only 17 percent of Texans lived in cities, but urbanization was increasing at a greater rate than the growth in total population. San Antonio was the largest city in the state, with a population of 53,321; Austin and Waco were sixth and seventh with 22,258 and 20,686 residents, while Temple was twentieth with 7,065.

The backbone of communications within the growing state was newspapers. Many publications were started in the mid-1800s, but lasted only a few years and had only limited local influence. Others survived and flourished into the new century, among them the *San Antonio Express*, started in 1865; the *Austin Statesman*, founded in 1871; and the *San Antonio Light*, dating from 1881. Statewide, 985 different publication were printed in 1912.

Texas took a giant step backward in 1902, when the Legislature required voters to pay an annual poll tax of $1.50 to $1.75 to be eligible to vote. As expected, poor blacks and whites were excluded from voting. Poll taxes remained a requirement for voting until 1966.

Texas made gains in education during the early 1900s. During the first 15 years of the new century, the Legislature made changes that encouraged construction of badly needed school buildings and increased local funding of smaller school districts. The first compulsory school attendance law became effective in 1916, and a constitutional amendment in 1918 provided for free textbooks. Black schools, however, continued to be separate. Their buildings, equipment and books were generally hand-me-downs, and black teachers were paid only one-third the salaries of white teachers.

Library construction throughout the state was boosted by the philanthropy of Andrew Carnegie, "the Santa Claus of Texas Public Libraries." Carnegie, a Scottish steel magnate in Pennsylvania, donated millions worldwide to build libraries and other public facilities. Between 1898 and 1917, Carnegie provided 34 grants in the Lone Star State to fund 30 public libraries, one college library, two branch libraries and one lecture hall. In the Central Texas region, Carnegie libraries were built in Belton, Bryan, Franklin, San Antonio and Temple. The Belton, Bryan and Franklin buildings are still standing: The Belton Carnegie is now used for a museum; Bryan's is a historic monument; and the Franklin building houses the Robertson County Library upstairs and a community center downstairs.

A few automobiles were in use in Texas by 1900. By 1907, there were enough motorized vehicles on the roads that the first traffic laws were passed, limiting speed to 18 miles per hour and requiring that autos stop when meeting horse-drawn vehicles. Each vehicle had to be registered in the owner's home county. The state collected license fees for cars beginning in 1915. Railway and bus stations maintained two waiting rooms — one for whites and one for "colored" — and most public buildings had segregated water fountains and restroom facilities as well. Not until the Civil Rights Act of 1964 became law did this situation change.

Central Texas farmers suffered setbacks in 1908, 1911 and again in 1914 when cotton prices fell sharply after 10 years of comparative prosperity. A public warehouse system was created to help prop up the commodity. Prices rose in 1916, spurred by the war in Europe. The same wartime inflation helped to double the value of farmland between 1910 and 1920, followed by a sharp drop in 1921.

Electrical power was produced locally in Texas until 1913, when a Texas Power and Light Company high-voltage transmission line was completed from Waco to Fort Worth, with a branch from Hillsboro through Waxahachie to Ferris, where it branched again — north to Dallas and south to Corsicana.

The Central Texas town of Temple was the location chosen by Dr. Arthur Carroll Scott and Dr. Raleigh R. White for a hospital in 1904. First established in a converted house, the institution was originally called Temple Sanitarium. The hospital moved to a former Catholic convent where it stayed for 59 years, adding buildings as the need arose, until it comprised 31 buildings. In 1923 the name was changed to Scott and White

Hospital, by which it became internationally known. Scott and White moved to its present plant in 1963, and by the 1970s, it was serving more than 100,000 patients annually.

The Amicable Building was erected in Waco in 1910-1911. When it was new, the 22-story steel-frame building was said to be the tallest building in the South. The Amicable had its own electrical plant and artesian well, and its own shallow oil wells supplied fuel for its steam heating system.

The year 1910 also marked the start of electric interurban service between Bryan and College Station. The railway provided service over a seven-mile track between Bryan and Texas A&M until 1923. An interurban linked Waco with Dallas and the towns between the two cities beginning in 1912.

Military aviation history was made in San Antonio in February 1910, when Lt. Benjamin Foulois arrived at Fort Sam Houston with 17 crates full of airplanes, accompanied by a number of student mechanics. Foulois, assigned to the Aviation Section of the U.S. Army Signal Corps, had taken three flying lessons with Wilbur Wright. Because of the winter weather at the Signal Corps facility at College Park, Md., flight training was shifted to Fort Sam Houston. Foulois had orders to put the plane together, learn to fly it and train others to fly it.

The aircraft was a Wright brothers biplane with a wingspan of 36 feet, 4 inches, and an overall length of 32 feet, 10 inches. The power plant was a four-cylinder, water-cooled 30.6 horsepower Wright engine. Instead of wheels, the plane was equipped with sleigh-like runners. Take-off was aided by a sort of catapult. The plane was ready to fly by March 1. By the outbreak of World War I in 1917, the U.S. Army Signal Corps had 35 trained pilots and 200 training planes. Foulois proved that aviation could be a vital part of military operations and helped establish Texas as a major military aviation center. He rose to the rank of major general and became chief of the Air Corps before he retired in 1935.

A quiet Austin businessman and planter named Edward M. House became the first Texan to exert influence in national politics. He had guided the election campaigns of governors Hogg, Culberson, Sayers and Lanham, and he effectively controlled the 40 Texas delegates to the Democratic convention in Baltimore in 1912. He served Woodrow Wilson as an informal advisor, but resisted an official position and title, preferring to work behind the scenes.

President Wilson appointed two Austin residents to high posts in his administration. Thomas Watt Gregory served as Attorney General, while Albert Sidney Burleson was Postmaster General.

When the United States entered World War I, Texans were distracted by the controversies surrounding the Ferguson administration. Jim Ferguson was a Temple banker who won the gubernatorial election in 1914 by assuming a country-boy demeanor that belied his education and intelligence. Called "Farmer Jim" by some, he appealed to the tenant farmers of Texas by promising them protection from unreasonable rents. The time-honored rental agreement — with the landlord taking one-fourth of the cotton and one-third of the other crops — was ignored in some areas with the richest farmlands. Ferguson proposed a law making one-fourth and one-third mandatory. That won the hearts of the tenants, who managed 62.6 percent of Texas farms in 1910, but the law, passed in 1915, was declared unconstitutional in 1921. Despite his popularity with farmers, however, certain of his questionable financial shenanigans were exposed. Ferguson was impeached after a year and a half in office, but he resigned the day before the judgement was announced. He managed his wife's two successful gubernatorial campaigns in 1924 and 1932. Miriam "Ma" Ferguson's campaign slogan, indicating that Farmer Jim would be calling the shots, was, "Two governors for the price of one."

Central Texans participated in the "War to End All Wars" in several ways. The area sent its share of young people into the armed services. Statewide, almost one million Texans registered for service; about 200,000, including 31,000 blacks, actually served in the military forces. More than 5,000 lost their lives. About 450 Texas women served as military nurses.

Two large army training camps were established in

Central Texas: Camp MacArthur in Waco and Camp Travis in San Antonio. In addition, the Leon Springs First Officers Training Camp was built at Leon Springs, Bexar County, in May 1917. About 1,500 volunteers graduated from the Leon Springs camp and were commissioned with ranks from lieutenant to major.

Construction also began at Kelly Field, first called Camp Kelly, in San Antonio in May 1917; within five months it was the largest flight training school in the world. Kelly Field was named for George E. M. Kelly, the first army aviator to lose his life while piloting a military aircraft. The fatal crash occurred at Fort Sam Houston in May 1911. Virtually all air force commanders who won their pilot wings before World War II trained at Kelly. Jimmy Doolittle was stationed at Kelly when he made his "dawn to dusk" flight in 1922, the first to span the continent during daylight hours. Such aviation luminaries as Billy Mitchell and Hap Arnold were Kelly alumni. Kelly Air Force Base is today the oldest continuously used military aviation base in Texas.

At the outbreak of World War I, San Antonio offered an 873-acre tract of land south of the city for a pilot-training facility. Brooks Field, which opened in December 1917, was named for Cadet Sidney J. Brooks Jr., who was killed earlier in 1917 in a training flight originating at Kelly Field. Brooks was the site, on April 28, 1929, of the first mass parachute drop in the world. Among those training at one time or another at Brooks Field, later Brooks Air Force Base, were Charles Lindbergh; Elwood Quesada, who pioneered mid-flight refueling and was later chief administrator of the Federal Aviation Administration; and Hoyt Vandenberg, Nathan Twining, Thomas D. White and Curtis LeMay, all later chiefs of staff of the Air Force. One of the flight instructors at Brooks was Claire Chennault, leader of the famed World War II Flying Tigers.

Camp Mabry in Austin, which had been a Texas Volunteer Guard summer encampment since 1890, was converted into a federal military post for the duration of the hostilities.

Those Central Texans who stayed home did their parts for the war effort by buying Victory and Liberty bonds and War Savings Stamps. Wheatless Mondays and Wednesdays, meatless Tuesdays and porkless Thursdays and Saturdays aided the wartime food conservation effort. War gardens were popular.

Patriotism during the period reached new heights in some cases, new depths in others. Anti-German propaganda fueled hate and mistrust of all Germans, at times even German-Texans who were loyal citizens. Gov. William P. Hobby even vetoed appropriations for the German Department at The University of Texas in 1919.

The war ended in November 1918, allowing Central Texans to turn their concentration once more to the diverse problems at home.

Between the Wars

Public spending in Texas had increased greatly during the war — from $13 million in 1913 to $27 million in 1919. The movement toward woman suffrage also grew during the early 1900s. Although the Legislature allowed women to vote in primaries beginning in 1918, Texas voters rejected a woman suffrage amendment to the state constitution in 1919. However, the Legislature ratified the 19th amendment to the Constitution of the United States, which provided for woman suffrage, effective August 1920.

Farmers sought greater control over their economic and physical lives in the 1920s and 1930s. The Texas Farm Bureau was organized in 1920 as the state arm of the national Farm Bureau Federation, which was established in 1919. The Farm Bureau worked for better rural living conditions and for the improvement of agricultural education and research and of animal health laws. They lobbied for better farm-to-market roads, for better and more efficient production and distribution of farm products, for eventual phase-out of crop controls and price supports, and against minimum wage for farm workers. The Texas Farm Bureau grew rapidly to about 40,000 members in 1922; the failure of a cotton pool among its members wiped it out in 1926. However, the Farmer's Protective Committee organized in 1933, later becoming the Texas Agricultural Association, which affiliated in 1936 with the American Farm Bureau Federation. The resurrected Texas Farm Bureau is still active today.

The Ku Klux Klan reappeared in Texas about 1921. It was a new organization tailored on and using the same name as one that formed in the Southern states during Reconstruction, and it resurfaced first in Atlanta, Ga., about 1915. On a wave of anti-foreign agitation that grew out of the World War, KKK members terrorized, sometimes lynched, anyone who believed or looked different from themselves — usually blacks, Catholics and Jews. The white-sheeted night riders also targeted anyone appearing to be friendly to those groups. The burning crosses of the Klan symbolized hate and bigotry, not Christianity. The excesses of the Klan disgusted those who had joined the organization in support of its political activities. Anti-Klan sentiment grew among the general public, spurred by the Klan's increasing terrorism and violence, during the political campaigns of 1922 and 1924. After the Klan's candidate for governor was defeated in 1924, the organization began to decline, and Klan terrorists were vigorously prosecuted by a number of district attorneys across the state. The Klan finally died out except for a few lunatic-fringe white supremacists who, using the name of the Klan, still occasionally parade around in their sheets.

Waco lawyer Pat Neff, a graduate of the University of Texas law school, served two terms as Texas' governor from 1921 to 1925. Neff had been a state legislator, and he served as Speaker of the Texas House of Representatives from 1903 to 1905. Neff was president of Baylor University from 1932 to 1947.

Air passenger service in the state began in 1928 when Texas Air Transport initiated service linking Dallas, San Antonio, Fort Worth and Galveston. Air service expanded rapidly with additional lines and routes.

The Great Depression started with the stock market crash on Oct. 29, 1929. But the effects were felt well beyond Wall Street. The federal government inaugurated the most ambitious social and economic programs in U.S. history. In an unemployment census in 1933, Texas listed 105,045 families on relief statewide, or 7.1 percent, which, though unacceptably high, was not as severe as the national rate of 10.3 percent. During Gov. Miriam "Ma" Ferguson's second administration (1933-1935), voters approved $20 million in "bread bonds" to augment federal relief efforts. They also approved a $3,000 homestead exemption to protect property owners who risked losing their homes because they could not pay their taxes. Unfortunately, these actions also worsened the state's financial troubles.

The Civilian Conservation Corps, inaugurated by the federal government in 1933, provided jobs by constructing 510 public buildings, laying 998.7 miles of new highway pavement and making improvements in 135 parks and playgrounds across the state. President Franklin D. Roosevelt's administration spawned many other agencies, such as the National Youth Administration and the Works Projects Administration, that were designed to employ as many out-of-work Americans as possible.

One such agency, the Treasury Section of Painting and Sculpture, employed out-of-work artists to paint decorative murals in post offices. Central Texas post offices that were decorated with New Deal art included Elgin, Gatesville, Lampasas, Lockhart, Rockdale, San Antonio and Smithville.

One of the projects assigned to the National Youth Administration in 1939 was the renovation of La Villita, an area of San Antonio containing early Spanish buildings, into an arts-and-crafts center. The San Antonio missions were restored with WPA funds. Also undertaken about the same time was the beautification of the banks of the San Antonio River through the middle of San Antonio. This project marked the beginnings of today's charming and popular Paseo del Rio, also called the River Walk. Earlier, some San Antonio businessmen wanted to convert the downtown section of the river into a sewer and build a street on top of it.

Bastrop State Park was constructed as a Civilian Conservation Corp project. The Tower of The University of Texas at Austin was also made possible by New Deal employment programs.

When cotton prices dropped from 18 cents a pound

Cotton, which was growing wild in Texas in the 16th century when the Spanish arrived, became the major cash crop of Central Texas by the later 1800s. This ready-to-be harvested cotton was photographed in Falls County. Texas Almanac staff photo.

in 1929 to less than six cents a pound in 1931 and to five cents in 1932, the warnings voiced in the 1880s urging farmers not to specialize in cotton farming but to diversify came back to haunt Central Texas farmers. Farm workers and tenant farmers migrated to the cities to find work. What they found was city-dwellers also looking for work. Both groups were forced to fall back on relief and public works projects. A cotton-acreage limitation bill was passed by the Legislature in 1931 in an attempt to cut the cotton surplus and increase prices, but the law was declared unconstitutional in 1932.

The New Deal farm program was elaborate and far-reaching. To eliminate agricultural surpluses that caused prices to drop, the federal government restricted production and held surpluses off the market. The Agricultural Adjustment Acts of 1933 and 1938 also instituted soil conservation programs and made credit easier for farmers to obtain. The cotton program aimed to take 10 million acres of cotton land out of production. Since the 1933 AAA went into effect in mid-summer, farmers had to plow under growing crops. The deliberate destruction of crops, plus a later livestock program that called for shooting cattle on the range and leaving them to rot, left a bad taste in many Texas mouths. But not farming was proving more profitable than farming, and in four races for the presidency, Franklin D. Roose-

velt carried the agricultural vote in Texas by not less than 82 percent.

When the government started paying farmers to idle their land by designating it for the soil "bank," the land idled was usually the marginally productive acreage. The best soil was still in production. And, ironically, improvement in farming techniques, greater mechanization of farm work and the development of higher-yielding strains of crops led to greater production from less acreage. The result was that, even though the government was paying farmers to idle their acreage, it had to buy up an increasing amount of surplus commodities. While this strange farce was being played out, the average farm was increasing in size and the number of Texans employed in agriculture was decreasing. The number of tenant farmers dropped statewide from 301,660 in 1930 to 23,218 in 1982, and the trend continued. In 1940, one in three Texans lived on farms. Now 80.5 percent of the population lives in urban areas.

Texas strengthened its status as a primary military aviation center when Randolph Field opened in 1930. The multi-million-dollar "West Point of the Air," named for Capt. William M. Randolph, who was killed in a crash while stationed at Kelly Field in 1928, was built on a 2,300-acre tract of land 18 miles northeast of San Antonio. Randolph-trained pilots formed the nucleus of the air force's cadre of flight officers for World War II and the Korean War.

Flood control and dependable water supplies were Central Texas problems in the late 1920s and early 1930s. In 1929, the Brazos River Conservation and Reclamation District (name changed in 1953 to Brazos River Authority) was formed to control the river and its watershed, making it the oldest such district in Texas. It is also the largest, covering about one-sixth of the area of the state. The authority completed its first dam, the Morris Sheppard Dam impounding Possum Kingdom Lake, in March 1941. Possum Kingdom extends into Jack, Stephens and Young counties. Farther downstream are Lake Granbury in Hood County and Whitney Lake in Johnson, Hill and Bosque counties. Waco Lake on the Bosque River and Belton Lake on the Leon River are two tributary lakes within the authority's jurisdiction.

The Colorado River bisects Central Texas on its way from Dawson County near the New Mexico border to Matagorda Bay on the Gulf of Mexico. For years, the Colorado regularly flooded thousands of acres from West Texas to the coastal plains, causing loss of life and millions of dollars in property and crop damage. The Lower Colorado River Authority (LCRA) was approved in 1934 by the 43rd Texas Legislature to manage the waters of the Colorado.

Buchanan Dam, impounding Lake Buchanan, was the first water-control project on the Colorado, and it is the uppermost of the six dams that were eventually built on the river. Buchanan generated its first electric power in Jan. 1938. Inks Dam, 12 miles west of Burnet, was completed later the same year. Other LCRA reservoirs include Lyndon B. Johnson Lake, Marble Falls Lake, Lake Travis and Lake Austin. Counties within the LCRA's jurisdiction include Bastrop, Blanco, Burnet, Colorado, Fayette, Llano, Matagorda, San Saba, Travis and Wharton.

The World War of 1917-1918 suddenly became World War I when the Japanese bombed the American naval base at Pearl Harbor in the Territory of Hawaii on Dec. 7, 1941, and plunged the United States into World War II.

World War II and Beyond

The economic hardship of the Depression was finally eased by the federal government's massive spending on World War II. Central Texas received its share of expenditures in Texas. Of some 100 army and army air force installations in the state during World War II, 23 were in Central Texas. Camp Swift, located at Bastrop, was an infantry training camp activated in January 1942. The 97th and 102nd infantry divisions trained at Camp Swift, as well as the 5th Headquarters Special Troops of the Third Army. The 116th and 120th tank destroyer battalions trained at Camp Swift before being transferred to Camp Hood. Camp Swift also housed German prisoners of war for a time.

Camp Hood, established on 160,000 acres between Killeen and Gatesville, was first occupied in March 1942. Named for Confederate General John Bell Hood, the post was primarily a training center for tank de-

stroyers. By late June 1943, troop capacity was more than 95,000. Some prisoners of war were also interned at Camp Hood. The facility shrank considerably after the war, with only 10,000 troops in residence by January 1946. During a reorganization the same year, Camp Hood was renamed Fort Hood and became the permanent home of the 2nd Armored Division, which was nicknamed "Hell on Wheels." Today it is also the home of the II Armored Mobile Corps. It is the largest armored installation in the free world and is known throughout the U.S. Army as "The Great Place."

Waco was home to the Waco Army Airfield, renamed Connally Air Force Base in 1949, and the Blackland Army Airfield.

The McCloskey General Hospital in Temple opened in June 1942. It was one of the army's largest general hospitals, at its peak serving more than 5,000 patients. It became a Veterans Administration hospital at the close of the war.

Camp Mabry in Austin, originally established in the 19th century and transformed into a federal facility during World War I, was reactivated during World War II as a supply and replacement depot.

U.S. Army Air Force stations in Central Texas included the Bryan, Hondo, San Marcos and Waco army air fields, Bergstrom Field at Austin and Blackland in Waco.

San Antonio was home to the largest collection of armed services posts in the state, including the army's Fort Sam Houston, Fort Bullis, the San Antonio Arsenal, the San Antonio Army Service Forces and Adjutant General depots and Brooke General Hospital. Military aviation facilities in San Antonio included Brooks, Kelly, Randolph and Stinson fields and the San Antonio Aviation Cadet Center, which became Lackland Army Air Field in 1946.

About a million and a quarter men trained for military service in Texas during World War II: 20 combat divisions had been trained in Texas by the end of 1944. About 750,000 Texas men served in the military. More than 8,000 Texas women enlisted in the Women's Army Corps (WACs), and 4,200 served in the WAVES (Women Accepted for Voluntary Emergency Service). Smaller numbers signed up for the SPARS (women's branch of the Coast Guard) and the women's branch of the Marines.

Twenty-one prisoner-of-war base camps and more than 20 branch camps were established in Texas during the war, housing German, Japanese and Italian prisoners, and several were in Central Texas (see article, "Prisoner-of-War Camps").

World War II brought full employment, high wages and high prices. It also brought austerity, with government-imposed rationing of sugar, meats, fats, canned goods, coffee, shoes, gasoline, tires — everything needed to keep the military services supplied. Scrap-metal drives were organized in towns all across the state to collect metal of all kinds to be recycled into supplies and equipment vital to the war effort. Rents and wages were frozen during the war, and price increases were discouraged. War-bond drives and air-raid drills were experienced by all Texans.

After the war's end in 1945, Texas' prosperity continued into the 1950s and 1960s. Peacetime saw Central Texas, as well as the rest of the state, enjoying relatively prosperous times, although per capita income was below the national average. The Texas economy expanded, ensuring the continuation of high employment, wages and prices. Those returning from World War II found jobs in the expanding industrial sector.

Lyndon Baines Johnson, a Central Texas native, was elected to the U.S. Senate in 1948 in one of the most controversial elections in Texas history. Johnson, who was born near Stonewall, Gillespie County, in 1908, attended Southwest Texas State Teachers College (now Southwest Texas State University) in San Marcos. He first went to Washington as a congressman in 1937, elected to fill the unexpired term of the late James Paul Buchanan. His squeaker of a victory over Coke Stevenson in 1948, an 87-vote margin out of almost 1 million cast, earned Johnson the nickname of "Landslide Lyndon." Selected as John F. Kennedy's running mate in 1960, he succeeded to the presidency upon Kennedy's assassination in Dallas on Nov. 22, 1963. Johnson was elected to his own four-year term in 1964. He retired to his ranch outside Stonewall in 1968, where he died of a heart attack on Jan. 22, 1973.

Texas was forced to take a reluctant giant step toward integration in 1950 when a black student, H. M. Sweatt, was admitted to the University of Texas law school because of a U.S. Supreme Court ruling. However, even though they had gained the right to attend classes on the University campus by the mid-1950s, blacks could not share living space there with white students. They had to live many blocks away in dormitories at predominantly black Huston-Tillotson College.

In 1954, the Supreme Court declared public-school segregation unconstitutional, and, though it was slow and sometimes painful, integration in Central Texas schools was accomplished over the next decade.

Nature struck Central Texas with a vengeance on May 11, 1953. A tornado ripped through Waco, killing 114 and injuring 597. It was one of the two most disastrous tornadoes ever to hit the state. The twister destroyed 150 homes and 185 other buildings; 900 houses and 500 other structures in the city were damaged. The cost of the destruction was estimated at more than $41 million.

The number of state agencies increased rapidly in the 1950s and 1960s, along with state expenditures. In 1965 alone, the Legislature added 17 agencies to the 70 already existing. State spending increased from more than $103 million in 1930 to almost $2 billion in 1966 and $15 billion in 1986.

In honor of its 250th anniversary in 1968, San Antonio held a world's fair, called the HemisFair. Ninety-two acres of slums were virtually razed near the Alamo and replaced by fair buildings centered by the Tower of the Americas, a 750-foot-high structure topped by a revolving restaurant and observation deck. Some of the neighborhood's older buildings were incorporated into the fairgrounds. Today the site includes museums, the Institute of Texan Cultures, a branch of the National University of Mexico, a convention center and many amusements.

During the 1970s, Austin became a major western music center. Singer Willie Nelson's move from Nashville to Austin in 1972 brought such music spots as the Armadillo World Headquarters to international prominence.

Although the bulk of Texas' oil production and related industry is in East and West Texas, the oil "tail" tends to wag the entire state. Beginning in the late 1950s, the United States imported more and more oil. When the Arab-dominated Organization of Petroleum Exporting Countries (OPEC) began flooding the market with cheap Middle-Eastern crude, the price of domestic oil dropped. Then OPEC instituted an embargo in 1973 on shipments to the United States and several other countries that supported Israel, and the value of Texas crude increased dramatically. Wildcatters were soon drilling anything that didn't move.

The embargo was lifted in 1974, but oil prices continued to rise. Lending institutions supported the boom with generous infusions of cash. But the nation's economic slump of the early 1980s could not be ignored for long. The petroleum industry was most directly affected, but the economy of the entire state eventually suffered the effects of lower oil prices. Banks and savings-and-loan associations across the state collapsed as the oil patch's problems became everyone's problems, and the real estate market began a parallel nosedive.

High technology joined the twin economc mainstays of government and the University in Austin in the 1980s. Already home to several semiconductor-based companies, Austin beat out more than 50 other U.S. cities in attracting Microelectronics and Computer Technology Corporation (MCC) in 1983. The private research consortium, which comprised 21 companies by mid-1986, was established to bring the brightest scientific minds of the member companies together to solve common electronic problems in competition with the Japanese. Fields in which research was being conducted in 1986 included semiconductor packaging, software technology, computer-aided design (CAD), artificial intelligence, parallel processing and human factors technology.

Austin followed the MCC coup with another, when in early 1988 Sematech, a semiconductor-manufacturing joint research venture, chose Austin for its headquarters also. Unlike privately funded MCC, Sematech depends on the federal government for about half its budget and on its private-business members for the balance. As of early 1988, there were 12 industry members. The presence of MCC and Sematech has persuaded more private firms in semiconductor and related fields to locate in Austin. There has also been high growth in the Bryan-College Station area in high-technology industry during the 1980s.

The population of Central Texas cities has mushroomed since the end of World War II: 132,459 residents in 1950 to 507,462 in 1988; San Antonio more than doubled from 408,442 in 1950 to 994,292 in 1988; Bryan tripled from 18,102 to 58,120 in the same time period; Temple almost doubled from 25,467 to 50,373, and Waco increased more than 30 percent from 84,706 to 112,861.

As the decade of the 1980s ended, water problems in Central Texas were once more of concern. This time the problem was not too much water in the flooding Brazos and Colorado rivers, it was the diminishing quality and quantity of water in the Edwards Aquifer, which underlies much of the Central Texas area. Serious studies of how to keep a safe, plentiful water supply for the increasing population of Central Texas will probably continue well into the next-to-last decade of the 20th century.

Bibliography

Books

Ashcraft, Allan C., **Texas in the Civil War;** Texas Civil War Centennial Comm., 1862.

Ashford, Gerald, **Spanish Texas: Yesterday and Today;** Jenkins Publishing Co., Austin, 1971.

Baker, T. Lindsay, **Building the Lone Star: An Illustrated Guide to Historic Sites;** Texas A&M University Press, College Station, 1986.

Baker, T. Lindsay, **The Polish Texans;** Institute of Texan Cultures, San Antonio, 1982.

Banks, Jimmy and John E. Babcock, **Corralling the Colorado: The First Fifty Years of the Lower Colorado River Authority;** Eakin Press, Austin, 1988.

Bannon, John Francis, **The Spanish Borderlands Frontier, 1513-1821;** University of New Mexico Press, Albuquerque, 1974.

Barkley, Mary Starr, **History of Travis County and Austin, 1839-1899;** Texian Press, Waco, 1963.

Barnhill, J. Herschel, **From Surplus to Substitution: Energy in Texas;** American Press, Boston, 1983.

Barr, Alwyn, **Black Texans: A History of Negroes in Texas, 1528-1971;** Jenkins Publishing Co., The Pemberton Press, Austin, 1973.

Batte, Lelia M., **History of Milam County, Texas;** The Naylor Company, San Antonio, 1956.

Belfiglio, Cav. Valentine J., **The Italian Experience in Texas;** Eakin Press, Austin, 1983.

Benthul, Herman F., **Wording Your Way Through Texas;** Eakin Press, Burnet, 1981.

Berry, Margaret C., **The University of Texas: A Pictorial Account of Its First Century;** University of Texas Press, Austin, 1980.

Biesele, Rudolph Leopold, **The History of the German Settlements in Texas, 1831-1861;** German-Texan Heritage Society, San Marcos, 1987 (first printed 1930).

Binkley, William C., **The Texas Revolution;** Louisiana State University Press, 1952 (reprint, Texas State Historical Assn., Austin, 1979).

Bolton, Herbert Eugene, **Texas in the Middle Eighteenth Century;** University of California Press, Berkeley, 1915.

Buenger, Walter L., **Secession and the Union in Texas;** University of Texas Press, Austin, 1984.

Carroll, H. Bailey, **The Texan Santa Fe Trail;** Panhandle-Plains Historical Society, Canyon, 1951.

Carver, Charles, **Brann & the Iconoclast;** University of Texas Press, Austin, 1957.

Castaneda, Carlos E., **Our Catholic Heritage in Texas, Vols. 1-4;** Von Boeckmann-Jones Co., Austin, 1933-38.

Chabot, Frederick C., **The Alamo, Altar of Texas Liberty;** 1931.

Conger, Roger N., **Highlights of Waco History;** Roger Conger, Waco, 1945.

Curtis, Albert, **Fabulous San Antonio;** The Naylor Co., San Antonio, 1955.

Davis, John L., **The Danish Texans;** The Institute of Texan Cultures, San Antonio, 1979.

Day, James M., compiler, **The Texas Almanac, 1857-1873: A Compendium of Texas History;** Texian Press, Waco, 1967.

Dethloff, Henry C., **A Centennial History of Texas A&M University, 1876-1976;** Texas A&M University Press, College Station, 1975.

Dooley, Clyde and Betty, **Why Stop? A Guide to Texas Historical Roadside Markers, 2nd ed.;** Lone Star Books Div., Gulf Publishing Co., Houston, 1985.

Eaton, Jack D., **Excavations at the Alamo Shrine: Special Report #10;** Center for Archaeological Research, UT-San Antonio, San Antonio, 1980.

Ellis, Harry E., **Dr Pepper: King of Beverages;** Dr Pepper Co., Dallas, 1979.

Encyclopedia Americana, International Edition; Grolier, Inc., Danbury, 1985.

Flannery, John Brendan, **The Irish Texans;** University of Texas Insitute of Texan Cultures, San Antonio, 1980.

Foster, Nancy H. & Ben Fairbank Jr., **San Antonio, 2nd ed.;** Texas Monthly Press, Inc., San Antonio, 1988.

Gard, Wayne, **The Chisholm Trail;** University of Oklahoma Press, Norman, 1954.

Gatton, T. Harry, **The Texas Bankers Association: The First Century, 1885-1985;** The Texas Bankers Association, Austin, 1984.

Goodwyn, Lawrence, **The Populist Movement: A Short History of the Agrarian Revolt in America;** Oxford University Press, Oxford, 1978.

Haley, J. Evetts, **The Alamo Mission Bell;** Encino Press, Austin, 1974.

Haley, James L., **Texas: An Album of History;** Doubleday & Company, Inc., Garden City, NY, 1985.

Hamrick, Alma Ward, **The Call of the San Saba;** The Naylor Company, San Antonio, 1941.

Institute of Texan Cultures, **The Chinese Texans;** The University of Texas, San Antonio, 1981.

Institute of Texan Cultures, **The Czech Texans;** The University of Texas, San Antonio, 1973.

Institute of Texan Cultures, **The German Texans;** The University of Texas, San Antonio, 1970.

Institute of Texan Cultures, **The Indian Texans;** The University of Texas, San Antonio, 1970.

Institute of Texan Cultures, **The Italian Texans;** The University of Texas, San Antonio, 1973.

Institute of Texan Cultures, **The Polish Texans;** The University of Texas, San Antonio, 1972.

Institute of Texan Cultures, **The Swiss Texans;** The University of Texas, San Antonio, 1981.

Jordan, Terry G., **Environment and Environmental Perceptions in Texas;** American Press, Boston, 1980.

Jordan, Terry G., **German Seed in Texas Soil: Immigrant Farmers in Nineteenth-Century Texas;** University of Texas Press, Austin, 1966.

Jordan, Terry G., **Immigration to Texas;** American Press, Boston, 1980.

Kendall, George Wilkins, **Kendall's Narrative of the Santa Fe Expedition, Vols. I & II;** Wiley & Putnam, London, 1844 (reprint, The Steck Co., Austin, 1935).

Kingston, Michael T., ed., **The Texas Almanac, 1984-85;** A. H. Belo Corp., Dallas, 1983.

Kingston, Mike, ed., **The Texas Almanac, 1986-87;** A. H. Belo Corp., Dallas, 1985.

Kingston, Mike, ed., **The Texas Almanac, 1990-91;** A. H. Belo Corp., Dallas, 1989.

Krammer, Arnold, **Nazi Prisoners of War in America;** Stein & Day, New York, 1979.

Lampasas Springs and Environs; Poole Bros. Printers and Engravers, Chicago, ca.1889 (reprinted from Lampasas Spring-Ho Festival, 1972).

Lich, Glen E., **The German Texans;** University of Texas Institute of Texan Cultures, San Antonio, 1981.

Lich, Glen E. and Dona B. Reeves, **German Culture in Texas;** Twayne Publishers, Boston, 1980.

Lord, Walter, **A Time to Stand: The Epic of the Alamo;** University of Nebraska Press, Lincoln, 1961.

Lukes, Edward A., **De Witt Colony of Texas;** Jenkins Publishing Company, Austin, 1976.

McComb, David G., **Texas: A Modern History;** University of Texas Press, Austin, 1989.

McDonald, Archie P., **The Republic of Texas;** American Press, Boston, 1981.

Newcomb, W. W. Jr., **The Indians of Texas;** University of Texas Press, Austin, 1961.

Nunn, W.C., **Texas Under the Carpetbaggers;** University of Texas Press, Austin, 1962.

Ornish, Natalie, **Pioneer Jewish Texans;** Texas Heritage Press, Dallas, 1989.

Parker, Richard Denny, **Historical Recollections of Robertson County Texas;** The Anson Jones Press, Salado, 1955.

Pass, Fred, ed., **The Texas Almanac, 1980-1981;** A. H. Belo Corp., Dallas, 1979.

Ramsdell, Charles, **San Antonio, A Historical and Pictorial Guide, 2nd Rev. Ed.;** University of Texas Press, Austin, 1985.

Reed, S. G., **A History of the Texas Railroads;** St. Clair Publishing Co., Houston, 1941.

Richardson, R.N. and Ernest Wallace, **Texas: The Lone Star State;** Prentice-Hall, Inc., Englewood Cliffs, NJ, 1970.

Schoelwer, Susan P., **Alamo Images: Changing Perceptions of a Texas Experience;** De Golyer Library and SMU Press, Dallas, 1985.

Simmons, Frank E., **History of Coryell County;** Coryell County News, Coryell County, 1936.

Smyrl, Frank H., **Texas in Gray: The Civil War Years, 1861-1865;** American Press, Boston, 1983.

Smyrl, Frank H., **The Twenty-Eighth Star: Texas During the Period of Early Statehood, 1846-1861;** American Press, Boston, 1983.

Spratt, John Stricklin, **The Road to Spindletop: Economic Change in Texas 1875-1901;** SMU Press, Dallas, 1955 (reprint, University of Texas Press, Austin, 1983).

Steely, James Wright, compiler, **A Catalog of Texas**

The pink granite capitol today appears dwarfed by the modern office towers lining Congress Avenue. The skyscrapers share Austin's major thoroughfare with many restored 19th-century commercial buildings. Texas Almanac staff photo.

Properties in the National Register; The Texas Historical Commission, Austin, 1984.

Stephens, A. Ray and William M. Holmes, **Historical Atlas of Texas**; University of Oklahoma Press, Norman, 1989.

Taylor, T. U., **The Chisholm Trail and Other Routes**; Frontier Times, Bandera, printed by The Naylor Company, San Antonio, 1936.

Timmons, W. H., **The Anglo-American Advance into Texas, 1810-1830**; American Press, Boston, 1981.

Tinkle, Lon, **13 Days to Glory**; McGraw-Hill Book Co., Inc., New York, 1958.

Vigness, David M., **Spanish Texas, 1519-1810**; American Press, Boston, 1983.

Webb, Walter Prescott, ed., **The Handbook of Texas, Vols. 1, 2 & 3**; The Texas State Historical Association, Austin, 1952.

Weber, David J., **The Mexican Frontier, 1821-1856: The American Southwest Under Mexico**; University of New Mexico Press, Albuquerque, 1979.

Williams, Lyle W., **Ranches and Ranching in Spanish Texas**; American Press, Boston, 1982.

Wintz, Cary D., **Reconstruction in Texas**; American Press, Boston, 1983.

World Almanac and Book of Facts, 1986; Newspaper Enterprise Assn., Inc., New York, 1985.

Zelade, Richard, **Austin**; Texas Monthly Press, Austin, 1988.

Zlatkovich, Charles P., **Texas Railroads: A Record of Construction and Abandonment**; Bureau of Business Research, University of Texas at Austin, Austin, 1981.

Articles and Manuscripts

Bacarisse, Charles A., **"Baron de Bastrop"**; South-western Historical Quarterly (SHQ), Texas State Historical Assn. (TSHA), Vol. LVIII, No. 3, Jan. 1955.

Carlisle, John C., **"Our Post Office Art"**; Texas Highways, July 1984.

Conger, Roger N., **"Waco: Cotton and Culture on the Brazos"**; SHQ, TSHA, Vol. LXXV, No. 1, July 1971, Austin.

Fitzhugh, Newton, **History of Dallas County** (unpublished historic narrative); Dallas County Historical Commission, Dallas, 1986.

Krammer, Arnold P., **"When the Afrika Korps Came to Texas"**; SHQ, TSHA, Vol. LXXX, No. 3, Jan. 1977, Austin.

Leal, John (Bexar County archivist), Phone Interview, June 27, 1990.

McCallum, Henry D., **"Barbed Wire in Texas"**; SHQ, TSHA, Vol. LXI, No. 2, Oct. 1957.

Persons, Billie, **"Secular Life in the San Antonio Missions"**; SHQ, TSHA, Vol. LXII, No. 1, July 1958, Austin.

Pool, William C., **"The Origin of Military Aviation in Texas, 1910-1913"**; SHQ, TSHA, Vol. LVIII, No. 3, Jan. 1955, Austin.

Redder, Albert J. and John W. Fox, **"Excavation and Positioning of the Horn Shelter's Burial and Grave Goods"**; Central Texas Archeologist, No. 11, Baylor University Press, Waco, Spring 1988.

The Dallas Morning News, **"Is over at last: Head-end collision is a thing of the past"**; Sept. 16, 1896.

The Dallas Morning News, **"The Crash at Crush"**; Sept. 15, 1896.

The Dallas Morning News, **"They are all ready: Arrangements for the great head-end have all been made."**; Sept. 14, 1896.

Belo Corp. Marks 150th Anniversary

A. H. Belo Corporation, publisher of **The Dallas Morning News** and the **Texas Almanac,** has a history parallel to that of Texas itself. Pioneered in 1842 as the one-page Galveston News, Belo has grown to become a leading southwestern media company, encompassing both newspaper publishing and network-affiliated television broadcasting operations across the country.

Celebrating its 150th anniversary in 1992, A. H. Belo Corporation is the oldest continuously operating business in Texas. Founded by Samuel Bangs, a transplanted publisher from Boston, the company was in the publishing business three years before the Republic of Texas achieved statehood. Bangs sold the business within a year of its founding to Wilbur F. Cherry and Michael Cronican, and Cherry soon acquired sole ownership.

Another Massachusetts emigre, Willard Richardson, became editor of the paper a few years later. He campaigned editorially for annexation, fiscal responsibility and railroads. Soon after his campaign began, Texas was annexed to the United States. In 1857, Richardson conceived and founded the **Texas Almanac,** which he hoped would help attract settlers to the new state. Eight years later, he hired A. H. Belo, for whom the company was eventually named.

A. H. Belo, a former Confederate colonel from North Carolina, joined the company as bookkeeper. He was made a full partner in the growing company after only three months and carved out a new life for himself in the Southwest.

Nine years later, George Bannerman Dealey, a 15-year-old English emigrant, was hired as an office boy. Dealey, like A. H. Belo, was full of enthusiasm and energy. He, too, quickly moved up in the company. Working tirelessly, Dealey made his way from office boy to business manager and then to publisher of **The Dallas Morning News.** It was Dealey who chose the then-small settlement of Dallas as a site for a sister publication. Dealey and several other members of the Galveston News' staff relocated in Dallas, and the company prospered and grew.

The Dallas Morning News began publication on October 1, 1885, with a circulation of 5,000 subscribers. After being in operation only two months, **The Dallas Morning News** acquired its first competitor, the **Dallas Herald** (not to be confused with the current **Dallas Times Herald**). Rather than compete with each other for subscribers, the two newspapers combined, keeping the name of **The Dallas Morning News,** but dating itself with the volume number of the former **Dallas Herald.**

In 1906, on the 21st anniversary of **The Dallas Morning News,** Dealey gave a speech that became the motto for the company: "Build The News upon the rock of truth and righteousness. Conduct it always upon the lines of fairness and integrity. Acknowledge the right of the people to get from the newspaper both sides of every important question." Today these words are carved in a three-story-high space above the entrance to **The Dallas Morning News.** The News building, a long-standing dream of Dealey, was completed in 1949, three years after his death.

Belo also was a pioneer in radio in Texas. It began operating a 50-watt radio station, WFAA-AM, on June 26, 1922, which was the first network station in the state. The company sold the last of its radio properties in 1987.

While Belo has grown into a multi-faceted media entity, **The Dallas Morning News** remains the flagship of its newspaper business. Growing from that original one-page newspaper in Galveston, **The Dallas Morning News** now has a total daily circulation of more than 412,000. It is the leading newspaper in the Dallas-Fort Worth area, and its growth is evident in the opening in 1985 of its satellite printing plant in Plano, Texas.

In 1963, Belo purchased six daily newspapers — the **Arlington Daily News, Garland Daily News, Grand Prairie Daily News, Irving Daily News, Mid-Cities Daily News** and **Richardson Daily News** — and the weekly **Suburban News,** since renamed **Metrocrest News,** which together form the wholly-owned subsidiary Dallas-Fort Worth Suburban Newspapers, Inc.

Belo entered the television broadcasting business in 1950 with the acquisition of its principal station WFAA-TV, Channel 8, the ABC affiliate in Dallas-Fort Worth. The station had begun broadcasting five months earlier as KBTV-TV.

December 1981 marked the beginning of a new era in A. H. Belo Corporation's history. In that month, the company became a publicly held entity, and its common stock is now traded on the New York Stock Exchange. In May 1987, A. H. Belo Corporation re-incorporated in the State of Delaware, although its headquarters and operations did not move.

In 1984 Belo purchased four television stations from Dun & Bradstreet. The company acquired VHF stations KHOU-TV in Houston, KXTV in Sacramento, California, KOTV in Tulsa, Oklahoma and WVEC-TV in Hampton-Norfolk, Virginia.

Officers and Directors

Officers of A. H. Belo Corporation are Robert W. Decherd, chairman of the board and chief executive officer; James P. Sheehan, president and chief operating officer; Ward L. Huey Jr., vice chairman of the board and president/broadcast division; Michael J. McCarthy, senior vice president, secretary and general counsel; and Michael D. Perry, senior vice president and chief financial officer.

The following are members of the A. H. Belo Corporation board of directors: John W. Bassett Jr., Joe M. Dealey, Robert W. Decherd, Dealey D. Herndon, Ward L. Huey Jr., Lester A. Levy, James M. Moroney Jr., Burl Osborne, Reece A. Overcash Jr., Hugh G. Robinson, William H. Seay, James P. Sheehan, William T. Solomon, Thomas B. Walker Jr. and J. McDonald Williams.

Officers of **The Dallas Morning News** are Burl Osborne, publisher and editor; Jeremy L. Halbreich, president and general manager; Harry M. Stanley Jr., senior vice president/sales and marketing; J. William Cox, senior vice president/administration and finance; Ralph Langer, senior vice president and executive editor; Harold F. Gaar Jr., vice president/marketing; Grover D. Livingston, vice president/information management; Frank McKnight, vice president/circulation; Barry Peckham, vice president and controller; Rena Pederson, vice president and editorial page editor; and Richard Starks, vice president/advertising.

The principal executives of the five television operating companies are as follows: David T. Lane, senior vice president of The Belo Broadcast Division and president and general manager, WFAA-TV, Dallas-Fort Worth, Texas; James A. Parham, vice president and station manager, WFAA-TV; Allan Howard, president and general manager, KHOU-TV, Houston, Texas; James G. Saunders, president and general manager, KXTV, Sacramento, California; J. William Beindorf, president and general manager, WVEC-TV, Hampton-Norfolk, Virginia; and Lee R. Salzberger, president and general manager, KOTV, Tulsa, Oklahoma.

Officers of Dallas-Fort Worth Suburban Newspapers, Inc. are Daniel L. Crowe, president and chief executive officer; J. Randall Chandler, vice president/operations; Banks Dishmon Jr., vice president/circulation; Shawnya L. McPherson, vice president/controller.

Robert W. Decherd

Robert W. Decherd is chairman of the board and chief executive officer of A. H. Belo Corporation and has been a member of the company's board of directors since 1976. He is the son of the late H. Ben Decherd, who served as chairman of the board until his death in 1972.

After graduating from St. Mark's School of Texas in Dallas, Mr. Decherd entered Harvard University. While at Harvard, he became the first Texan to be elected president of The Harvard Crimson, the university's daily student newspaper. Mr. Decherd had worked previously at Dallas-Fort Worth Suburban Newspapers, Inc., and was a stringer for The New York Times. He graduated cum laude from Harvard in 1973. He was elected class orator for the class of 1973 and received the David McCord Award for literary contributions in addition to an honorary freshman scholarship.

Returning to Dallas, Mr. Decherd joined the management training program at **The News** in September 1973. After holding a series of staff positions at The News and Belo, he was elected vice president, corporate administration in 1979.

In February 1980, Mr. Decherd was named executive vice president of **The News,** a position he held until January 1982. Subsequently he was elected executive vice president of A. H. Belo Corporation, chief operating officer and president. He became chairman of the board and chief executive officer effective Jan. 1, 1987.

Ward L. Huey Jr.

Ward L. Huey Jr., vice chairman of the board and president, broadcast division, A. H. Belo Corporation, has an extensive background in broadcast operations and management.

A graduate of Southern Methodist University, Huey joined the WFAA-TV production department in 1960. He rose rapidly through the management ranks, and on Jan. 1, 1975, Huey was named vice president and general manager of Belo Broadcasting Corporation with management responsibilities for all Belo radio and television properties and was also elected to its board of directors. Huey became president and chief executive officer of Belo Broadcasting Corporation on April 27, 1981, and was elected to the board of directors of A. H. Belo Corporation on April 20, 1982. In 1987, he was elected vice chairman of the board and president of the broadcast division of A. H. Belo Corporation. He serves on the A. H. Belo Corporation management committee.

A native of Dallas, Huey is a past chairman of the ABC Television Affiliates Board of Governors, a past member of the board of directors of the Television Bureau of Advertising, vice chairman of the board of directors of the Maximum Service Telecasters, and past chairman of the board of directors of the Television Operators Caucus. He also is involved in a variety of other professional and civic organizations.

James P. Sheehan

James P. Sheehan joined A. H. Belo Corporation as senior vice president and chief financial officer in February 1982 and was elected to the Board of Directors in April 1982. He became executive vice president of Belo in 1984, and in January 1987 he became president and chief operating officer.

Prior to joining Belo, he spent eight years with United Technologies Corporation and most recently was vice president and controller of the Pratt and Whitney Manufacturing Division.

He received a B.S. from Seton Hall University and an M.B.A. in finance from Wayne State University. From 1967 to 1969 he served in the U.S. Navy.

Mr. Sheehan serves on the University of Texas at Dallas Development Board, Dallas Citizens Council, St. Paul Medical Center Foundation and is active in numerous industry organizations.

Burl Osborne

Burl Osborne joined **The Dallas Morning News** as executive editor in October 1980 and added the title of vice president in 1981. In 1983, he was named senior vice president and editor; in 1985, he became president and editor; and he was elected to the board of directors in May 1987 and was named publisher of **The Morning News** in 1991.

Mr. Osborne came to **The News** after 20 years with the Associated Press, where he started as a correspondent and editor-reporter, served in a variety of management positions and became managing editor in 1977.

He holds a bachelor's degree in journalism and mathematics from Marshall University, West Virginia, and a master's degree in business from Long Island University.

He is chairman of the American Press Institute, director and former president of the American Society of Newspaper Editors and a director of the Foundation for American Communications, among others. He is a member of the Pulitzer Prize Board and the Advisory Council of the University of Texas at Austin, College of Communications Foundation.

James M. Moroney

James M. Moroney Jr. is the son of the late James M. Moroney and the late Maidie Dealey Moroney. He was born in Dallas, attended Highland Park School and St. John's Military Academy in Delafield, Wis. He graduated from the University of Texas at Austin in 1943. During summer vacations, he worked part-time at radio and television stations WFAA and **The Dallas Morning News**.

During World War II, he entered the U.S. Navy, rising to the rank of lieutenant (jg). He saw much action, including the D-Day landing in Normandy. He was released from active duty in 1946.

More on Page 62.

Architecture
Space Planning/Interior Design
Master Planning

**Corgan
Associates
Architects**

501 Elm Street
Suite 500
Dallas, Texas 75202
Tel 214 748 2000
Fax 214 653 8281

Recently we introduced a new firm identity program. The new "mark" symbolizes teamwork and collaboration with a wide range of people, firms, groups, and cultures as the best way to make great Architecture. Optimism and a positive approach are our traditional firm values.

WFAA-TV aired many live remote broadcasts during the "Golden Age of Television," such as this early 1950s cooking show from the State Fair of Texas.

George Bannerman Dealey was named president of *The Dallas Morning News* in 1920. Upon his death in 1946, Dealey had completed 72 years of service to the organization.

A.H. BELO CORPORATION

The Dallas Morning News published its first edition in this building in 1885.

The first issue of *The Dallas Morning News* was printed on this Bullock press. G. B. Dealey is at far left.

1842 1992

A broadcast sponsor is feted in this 1951 WFAA photo.

From Page 58.

Mr. Moroney joined **The News** as a reporter, served as an advertising salesman and worked in the promotion and circulation departments before becoming assistant to the business manager in 1950. He also spent a year at the radio and television stations.

He progressed to assistant treasurer of the corporation and was elected to the board of directors in 1952. In 1955, he was named treasurer, elevated to vice president and treasurer in 1960 and became executive vice president in 1970. In 1973, Mr. Moroney was named president and chief executive officer of Belo Broadcasting Corporation and in 1974 became chairman of the board of that corporation.

In 1980, he was elected to president and chief executive officer of **The Dallas Morning News** and president and chief operating officer of A. H. Belo Corporation.

He was promoted to the position of president and chief executive officer of A. H. Belo Corporation January 1983. In April 1984, he was elected to the additional position of chairman of the board. In January 1985 he relinquished the title of president.

Mr. Moroney retired as an active operating officer of A. H. Belo on Dec. 31, 1986. He currently is a consultant to the corporation and holds the title of chairman of the executive committee.

Joe M. Dealey

Joe M. Dealey, past chairman of the board of the A. H. Belo Corporation, is the son of the late E. M. (Ted) Dealey and the late Clara MacDonald Dealey. A native of Dallas, he graduated from Highland Park High School and, in 1941, from the University of Texas at Austin. By attending the Southwest School of Printing, he learned to operate mechanical equipment in the printing industry. He also worked in the mailing room and photographic laboratory of **The Dallas Morning News.** His permanent employment began Jan. 4, 1942, as a reporter.

In May 1942, Mr. Dealey joined the U. S. Air Force, serving two years as an aircraft mechanic. After attending Officers Training School, he was graduated in 1944 as a second lieutenant. He served as aircraft maintenance officer in the United States and in Berlin until his discharge from service in 1946.

Returning to his previous job as a reporter on **The News,** Mr. Dealey later served as assistant business news editor and assistant to the managing editor. He joined the executive department as assistant secretary in 1950 and was elected to the board of directors in 1952. From 1955 until 1960, he was secretary of the corporation and then president until 1980 when he was named chairman and chief executive officer, following an internal reorganization of the company. On Dec. 31, 1982, he became chairman of the board and held that title until April 1984.

John W. Bassett Jr.

John W. Bassett Jr. is a native of Roswell, N.M., where he practices law. After graduating from Roswell High School, he attended Stanford University, where he majored in economics and received a bachelor's degree in 1960.

Following graduation, he was commissioned as a second lieutenant in the Army and entered active duty at Fort Benning, Ga. He served in the Second Infantry Division there and in the Army Reserves, where he was advanced to first lieutenant.

Mr. Bassett attended the University of Texas School of Law and became an associate editor of The Texas Law Review. Upon graduating with honors in June 1964, he was awarded a bachelor of law degree and became a member of the Order of the Coif, a legal honorary organization.

After passing the Texas and New Mexico Bar examinations in 1964, he practiced law in Roswell.

In 1966, Mr. Bassett was selected as a White House Fellow and for a year served as a special assistant to the attorney general of the United States.

In October 1967, Mr. Bassett returned to private practice with the law firm of Atwood, Malone, Mann and Turner, P.A., in Roswell.

Mr. Bassett was elected to the board of directors of A. H. Belo Corporation in 1979. He also serves as a member of the Board of Education for the State of New Mexico, is a Rotarian and is a member of several boards of directors of local charitable institutions in Roswell.

More on Page 64.

From Page 62.

Dealey D. Herndon

Dealey D. Herndon of Austin was elected to the Board of Directors in 1986. She was born in Dallas and is the daughter of the late H. Ben Decherd and Isabelle Thomason Decherd. She is an honors graduate of Hockaday School and the University of Texas at Austin. She was administrator of Friends of the Governor's Mansion from 1983 to 1984.

Mrs. Herndon has lived in El Paso, Dallas and Austin, where she has been active in civic and non-profit activities for the past eight years. In Dallas, she served on the board of the Dallas County Heritage Society. In Austin, she has been a board member of the Austin Junior League, West Austin Youth Association, the Seton Hospital Development Board and the Pebble Project, a child abuse prevention agency. She served as president of the Austin History Center Association Board. She was treasurer of the St. Andrew's Episcopal School board of trustees and chairman of the Austin High School Excellence Fund.

She is president and a director of the Friends of the Governor's Mansion in Austin, Texas, and the executive director of the State Preservation Board of the State of Texas.

Lester A. Levy

Lester A. Levy was born and educated in Dallas. He attended the University of Texas at Austin until early 1943, at which time he entered the Air Force. He received his license to practice law during 1943 while in the service. After an honorable discharge in 1946, he joined his father's company, now known as NCH Corporation, while awaiting a semester change in order to take refresher courses at the University of Texas. His father's untimely death caused him to remain with the company, where he is presently chairman of the board of directors.

Mr. Levy was elected to the board of directors of A. H. Belo Corporation in 1985. He has served on the boards of the University of Dallas, Greenhill School, Baylor College of Dentistry, the Lamplighter School, and was co-founder and director of the Winston School. He has also served as a trustee for Temple Emanu-El, Golden Acres Home for the Aged and Special Care and Career Center (formerly Special Care School for Handicapped Children).

Reece A. Overcash

Reece A. Overcash Jr. was elected to the board of directors of A. H. Belo Corpoiration in 1983. He is chairman of the board of directors and chief executive officer of Associates of North America, a consumer/commercial finance company, having joined The Associates in April 1975 as president and chief operating officer.

Mr. Overcash was born and reared in Charlotte, N.C., where he was named as "Man of the Year" in 1972. He earned a degree in commerce from the University of North Carolina and served in the infantry during World War II.

He is active in many professional, civic and community organizations and serves as director of Duke Power Company, Aancor Holdings, Inc., and a number of other organizations.

Hugh G. Robinson

Hugh G. Robinson was elected to the board of directors of A. H. Belo Corporation in 1989. He is chief executive officer of The Tetra Group, a construction management firm. For more than five years prior to that, Mr. Robinson was president of Cityplace Development Corporation, a real estate development subsidiary of The Southland Corporation, and vice president of The Southland Corporation.

Mr. Robinson was born in Washington, D.C., and graduated from the U.S. Military Academy, West Point, in 1954. He earned a master's degree in civil engineering from M.I.T. in 1959, and he holds the Honorary Doctor of Laws degree from Williams College.

He entered the U.S. Army in 1954, following his graduation from West Point, and served until his retirement in 1983 with the rank of Major General. He received numerous military awards, including the Distinguished Service Medal. He is chairman of the board of directors of the Federal Reserve Bank of Dallas and a member of the boards of directors of Lomas Mortgage Securities Fund, Inc. and TU Electric Company, among others.

William H. Seay

William H. Seay is retired chairman of the board and chief executive officer of Southwestern Life Insurance Company, which is one of the nation's 10 largest stock life insurance companies.

Mr. Seay was born and reared in Dallas. He holds a degree in business administration from the University of Texas and served during World War II as an infantry captain in the Army.

In 1948, he became a partner in the Dallas investment banking firm of Henry, Seay and Black. Eleven years later he joined Universal Life and Accident Insurance Company as vice president, advancing in 1961 to president.

Universal was acquired by Southwestern Life Insurance Company in September 1968, and four months later Mr. Seay was named president and chief executive officer of the parent firm. He continued in that capacity until the transition to a holding-company concept in late 1972.

Mr. Seay is active in many professional, civic and community organizations and serves as director of numerous Dallas-based business firms. He was elected to the board of directors of A. H. Belo Corporation on March 27, 1973.

William T. Solomon

William T. Solomon is chairman, president and chief executive officer of Austin Industries Inc., which is the largest general contractor in Dallas and one of the five largest contractors in the southern half of the United States. Austin Industries is the only major contractor in its markets that is completely employee-owned.

Born and reared in Dallas, Mr. Solomon holds a civil engineering degree from Southern Methodist University and an M.B.A. from Harvard Graduate School of Business.

Mr. Solomon joined Austin full-time in 1967, becoming president and chief executive officer in 1970. The title of chairman was added in 1987.

Mr. Solomon is a member of the board of directors of Fidelity Union Life Insurance Company and serves on the board of trustees of Southern Methodist University. He is a past chairman of the Dallas Chamber of Commerce and serves on the boards of directors of numerous other civic and community organizations. He was elected to the board of directors of A. H. Belo Corporation in 1983.

Thomas B. Walker Jr.

Thomas B. Walker Jr. has been a partner, either general or limited, in Goldman, Sachs & Co., investment bankers, since 1968. He was elected to the board of directors of A. H. Belo Corporation in 1982.

Mr. Walker is a native of Nashville, Tennessee and is a Phi Beta Kappa graduate of Vanderbilt University. During World War II, he sered as a lieutenant in the U.S. Navy operating in the Mediterranean, Atlantic and South Pacific areas.

After the war, Mr. Walker joined the Equitable Securities Corporation and moved to Dallas in 1950. He served as senior vice president and director, Equitable Securities (American Express Company) until 1968.

He is also a member of the boards of directors of NCH Corporation, SYSCO Corporation, Central and Southwest Corporation and Kleinwort Benson International Equity Fund.

J. McDonald Williams

J. McDonald (Don) Williams is a native of Roswell, N.M. He graduated from Abilene Christian University in 1963 and from George Washington University Law School in 1966, both with honors.

He practiced law in Dallas seven years until he joined the Trammell Crow Company in May 1973. He entered the firm as the partner responsible for overseas developments and then was named managing partner in 1977.

Mr. Williams was elected to the board of directors of A. H. Belo Corporation in 1985. He also is a member of the boards of directors of Fidelity Union Life Insurance Company, and he serves on the boards of Abilene Christian University, George Washington University, Pepperdine University and Southwestern Christian College.

ENVIRONMENT

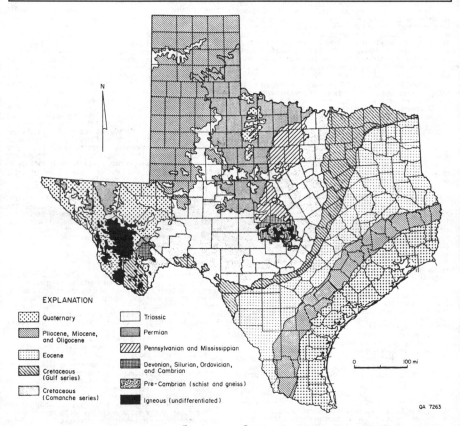

EXPLANATION

- Quaternary
- Pliocene, Miocene, and Oligocene
- Eocene
- Cretaceous (Gulf series)
- Cretaceous (Comanche series)
- Triassic
- Permian
- Pennsylvanian and Mississippian
- Devonian, Silurian, Ordovician, and Cambrian
- Pre-Cambrian (schist and gneiss)
- Igneous (undifferentiated)

0   100 mi

QA 7263

Geology of Texas

This article on the geology of Texas was prepared by the Bureau of Economic Geology at The University of Texas at Austin.

History in the Rocks

The fascinating geologic history of Texas is recorded in rocks — both those exposed at the surface and those penetrated by holes drilled in search of oil and natural gas. The rocks reveal a dynamic, ever-changing earth — ancient mountains, seas, volcanoes, earthquake belts, rivers, hurricanes and winds. Today, the volcanoes and great earthquake belts are no longer active, but rivers and streams, wind and rain, and the slow, inexorable alterations of rocks at or near the surface continue to change the face of Texas. The geologic history of Texas, as documented by the rocks, began more than a billion years ago; its legacy is the mineral wealth and varied land forms of modern Texas.

Geologic Time Travel

The story preserved in the rocks requires an understanding of the origin of the strata and how they have been deformed. **Stratigraphy** is the study of the composition, sequence and origin of the rocks: of what the rocks are made, how they were formed and the order in which the layers were formed. Structural geology reveals the architecture of the rocks: the locations of the mountains, volcanoes, sedimentary basins and earthquake belts. The map above shows the rocks of various geologic ages at the surface of Texas today.

History concerns events through time, but geologic time is such a grandiose concept that most of us find it difficult to comprehend. So, geologists have named the various chapters of earth history.

Precambrian Eon

Precambrian rocks, more than 600 million years old, are exposed at the surface in the Llano Uplift of Central Texas and in scattered outcrops in West Texas, around and north of Van Horn and near El Paso. These rocks, some more than a billion years old, include complexly deformed rocks that were originally formed by cooling from a liquid state as well as rocks that were altered from pre-existing rocks.

Precambrian rocks, often called the "basement

complex," are thought to form the foundation of continental masses. Precambrian rocks underlie all of Texas, and the outcrop in Central Texas is only the exposed part of the Texas Craton, which is primarily buried by younger rocks.

Paleozoic Era

During the early part of the **Paleozoic Era** (approximately 600 million to 350 million years ago), broad, relatively shallow seas repeatedly inundated the Texas Craton and much of North and West Texas. The evidence for these events is the sandstones, shales and limestones, similar to sediments that form in seas today, and fossils of animals, similar to modern crustaceans — the brachiopods, clams, snails and related organisms that live in modern marine environments. Early Paleozoic rocks are now exposed around the Llano Uplift and in far West Texas near Van Horn and El Paso and exist in the subsurface over most of West and North Texas.

By late Paleozoic (approximately 350 million to 240 million years ago), the Texas Craton was bordered on the east and south by a long, deep marine basin, called the Ouachita Trough. Sediments slowly accumulated in this trough until late in the Paleozoic Era. Plate-tectonic theory postulates that the collision of the North American Plate (upon which the Texas Craton is located) with the European and African-South American plates uplifted the thick sediments that had accumulated in the trough to form the Ouachita Mountains, which at that time extended across Texas. Today, in Texas that old mountain range is entirely buried by younger rocks and all that remains at the surface of the once majestic Ouachita Mountain chain is exposed only in southeastern Oklahoma and southwestern Arkansas.

During the **Pennsylvanian Period,** however, the Ouachita Mountains bordered the eastern margin of shallow inland seas that covered most of West Texas. Rivers flowed westward from the mountains to the sea bringing sediment to form deltas along an ever-changing coastline, and the sediments were then reworked by waves and currents of the inland sea. Today, these fluvial, delta and shallow marine deposits compose the late Paleozoic rocks that crop out and underlie the surface of North Central Texas.

Broad marine shelves divided the West Texas seas into several sub-basins, or deeper areas that received more sediments than accumulated on the limestone shelves. Limestone reefs rimmed the deeper basins. Today, these reef limestones are important oil reservoirs in West Texas. These seas gradually withdrew from Texas, and by the late **Permian Period,** all that was left in West Texas were shallow basins and wide tidal flats in which salt, gypsum and red muds accumulated in a hot, arid land. Strata deposited during the Permian Period are exposed today along the edge of the Panhandle as far east as Wichita Falls and south to Concho County and in the Trans-Pecos.

Mesozoic Era

Approximately 240 million years ago, the major geologic events in Texas shifted from West Texas to East and Southeast Texas. The European and African-South American plates, which had collided with the North American plate to form the Ouachita Mountains, began to separate from North America. A series of faulted basins, or rifts, extending from Mexico to Nova Scotia were formed. These rifted basins received sediments from adjacent uplifts, and as Europe and the southern continents continued to drift away from North America, the Texas basins were eventually buried beneath thick deposits of marine salt within the newly formed East Texas and Gulf Coast basins. Jurassic and Cretaceous rocks in East and Southeast Texas document a sequence of broad limestone shelves at the edge of the developing Gulf of Mexico. From time to time, the shelves were buried beneath deltaic sandstones and shales, which built the northwestern margin of the widening Gulf of Mexico to the south and southeast. As the underlying salt was buried more deeply by dense sediments, the salt became unstable and moved toward areas of least pressure. As the salt moved, it arched or pierced overlying sediments forming, in some cases, columns known as "salt domes." In some cases, these salt domes moved to the surface; others remain beneath a sedimentary overburden. This mobile salt formed numerous structures that would serve to trap oil and natural gas.

By the early **Cretaceous** (approximately 140 million years ago), the shallow Mesozoic seas covered a large part of Texas, eventually extending west to the Trans-Pecos area and north almost to the present-day state boundaries. Today, the limestones deposited in those

seas are exposed in the walls of the magnificent canyons of the Rio Grande in the Big Bend National Park area and in the canyons and headwaters of streams that drain the Edwards Plateau, as well as in Central Texas from San Antonio to Dallas.

Animals of many types lived in the shallow Mesozoic seas, tidal pools and coastal swamps. Today these lower Cretaceous rocks are some of the most fossiliferous in the state. Tracks of dinosaurs occur in several localities, and remains of terrestrial, aquatic and flying reptiles have been collected from Cretaceous rocks in many parts of Texas.

During most of the late Cretaceous, much of Texas lay beneath marine waters that were deeper than those of the early Cretaceous seas, except where rivers, deltas and shallow marine shelves existed. River delta and strandline sandstones are the reservoir rocks for the most prolific oil field in Texas. When discovered in 1930, this East Texas oil field contained recoverable reserves estimated at 5.6 billion barrels. The chalky rock that we now call the "Austin Chalk" was deposited when the Texas seas became deeper. Today, the chalk (and other Upper Cretaceous rocks) crops out in a wide band that extends from near Eagle Pass on the Rio Grande, east to San Antonio, north to Dallas and eastward to the Texarkana area. The Austin Chalk and other upper Cretaceous rocks dip southeastward beneath the East Texas and Gulf Coast basins. The late Cretaceous was the time of the last major seaway across Texas, because mountains were forming in the western United States that influenced areas as far away as Texas.

A chain of volcanoes formed beneth the late Cretaceous seas in an area roughly parallel to and south and east of the old, buried Ouachita Mountains. The eruptions of these volcanoes were primarily on the sea floor and great clouds of steam and ash likely accompanied them. Between eruptions, invertebrate marine animals built reefs on the shallow volcanic cones. Pilot Knob, located southeast of Austin, is one of these old volcanoes that is now exposed at the surface.

Cenozoic Era

At the dawn of the **Cenozoic Era,** approximately 65 million years ago, the northern and northwestern margins of the East Texas Basin were sites of deltas fed by rivers flowing eastward that drained areas to the north and west. Although there were minor incursions of the seas, the Cenozoic rocks principally document extensive seaward building by broad deltas, marshy lagoons, sandy barrier islands and embayments. Thick vegetation covered the levees and areas between the streams. Coastal plains were taking shape, under the same processes still at work today.

The Mesozoic marine salt became buried by thick sediments in the coastal plain area, and the salt began to form ridges and domes in the Houston and Rio Grande areas. The heavy load of sand, silt and mud deposited by the deltas eventually caused some areas of the coast to subside and form large fault systems, essentially parallel to the coast. Many of these coastal faults moved slowly and probably generated little earthquake activity. However, movement along the Balcones and Luling-Mexia-Talco Zones, a complex system of faults along the western and northern edge of the basins, likely generated large earthquakes millions of years ago.

Predecessors of modern animals roamed the Texas Cenozoic coastal plains and woodlands. Bones and teeth of horses, camels, sloths, giant armadillos, mammoths, mastodons, bats, rats, large cats and other modern or extinct mammals have been dug from coastal plain deposits. Vegetation in the area included varieties of plants and trees both similar and dissimilar to modern ones. Fossil palmwood, the Texas "state stone," is found in sediments of early Cenozoic age.

The Cenozoic Era in Trans-Pecos Texas was entirely different. There extensive volcanic eruptions formed great calderas and lava flows. These eruptions ejected great clouds of volcanic ash and rock particles into the air — many times the amount of material ejected by the Mount St. Helens eruption. Ash from the eruptions drifted eastward and is found in many of the sand-and-siltstones of the Gulf Coastal Plains. Lava flowed over the older Paleozoic and Mesozoic rocks, and igneous intrusions melted their way upward into the crustal rocks. These volcanic and intrusive igneous rocks are well exposed in the arid areas of Trans-Pecos Texas today.

In the Texas Panhandle, streams originating in the recently elevated southern Rocky Mountains brought floods of gravel and sand into Texas and formed great alluvial fans as the braided streams crisscrossed the area. These fans were deposited on the older Paleozoic and Mesozoic rocks and occur from northwestern Texas into Nebraska. Between 1 million and 2 million years ago, the streams of the Texas Panhandle were isolated from their Rocky Mountain source, and the eastern edge of this sheet of alluvial material began to retreat westward, forming the caprock of the modern High Plains of Texas.

During the latter part of the Cenozoic Era, a great Ice Age descended upon the northern part of the North American continent. For more than 2 million years, there were successive advances and retreats of the thick sheets of glacial ice. Four periods of extensive glaciation were separated by warmer interglacial pe-riods. Although the glaciers never reached as far south as Texas, the state's climate and sea level underwent major changes with each period of glacial advance and retreat. Sea level during times of glacial advance was 300 to 450 feet lower than during the warmer interglacial periods because so much sea water was captured in the ice sheets. The climate was both more humid and cooler than today, and the major Texas rivers carried more water and more sand and gravel to the sea. These deposits underlie the outer 50 miles or more of the Gulf Coastal Plain.

Approximately 3,000 years ago, sea level reached its modern position, and the rivers, deltas, lagoons, beaches and barrier islands that we know as coastal Texas have formed since that time.

Mineral Wealth
Fuel Minerals

Oil and natural gas are the most valuable minerals produced in Texas, contributing 28 percent of the oil production and 33 percent of the gas production in the United States in 1984. Oil and gas have been produced from most areas of Texas and from rocks of all geologic eras except the Precambrian. All of the major sedimentary basins of Texas, have produced some oil or gas. The well-known Permian Basin of West Texas has yielded large quantities of oil since 1921, and it is an area of considerable . promise for future production as well. Although large quantities of petroleum have been produced from rocks of Permian age, production in the area also occurs from older Paleozoic rocks. Production from rocks of Paleozoic age occurs primarily from North Central Texas westward to New Mexico and southwestward to the Rio Grande (Paleozoic outcrop area and west on map), but there is also significant Paleozoic production in North Texas in Tarrant, Grayson and Cooke counties.

Mesozoic rocks are the primary hydrocarbon reservoirs of the East Texas Basin and the area south and east of the Balcones Fault Zone. Cenozoic sandstones are the main reservoirs along the Gulf Coast and offshore state waters.

Coal and lignite occur in rocks of Pennsylvanian, Cretaceous and Tertiary ages. Coal was produced in Texas from about 1850 to the 1940s, when petroleum became the common fuel. Significant production of coal did not resume until the mid-1970s. Most of the pre-1940 production was bituminous coal from North Central Texas, an area near Eagle Pass or from near Laredo. North Central Texas production was from Pennsylvanian rocks. Thurber, Newcastle and Bridgeport all had viable coal industries in the early 1900s. As early as 1850, soldiers from Fort Duncan near Eagle Pass are reported to have mined coal from the Cretaceous rocks. Commercial mining of coal from Eocene rocks near Laredo began in 1881. In addition to the commercial mining, small amounts of coal occurring in the Trans-Pecos were used to roast the ore in mercury mining districts in the Big Bend.

Small amounts of "brown coal" or lignite have been produced throughout the history of the state. It was mined by many early settlers for family and small industry use, and it was used to generate "coal gas" or "producer gas" for Texas cities around the turn of the century. Today, Texas ranks sixth nationally in coal production, and lignite accounts for most of this. Almost all of the lignite is consumed by mine-mouth electrical generating plants. Approximately 20 percent of the electricity generated in the state in 1986 was from plants fired by Texas lignite.

Uranium occurs in several widely separated Texas localities, but production has been limited to the Cenozoic sandstones along the coastal plains of south-central Texas, roughly from Karnes County southwest to Webb County. The surface mines, active from 1959 to the mid-1970s, have largely been abandoned and reclaimed, and production today is all from in-situ leaching. This re-quires the injection of a leaching fluid into the uranium-bearing strata, reaction of the fluid with the uranium ore and return of the fluid to the surface for stripping of the uranium. The fluid is then re-used.

Non-Fuel Minerals

In 1985, the value of non-fuel minerals produced was more than $1.9 billion dollars, ranking Texas second nationally. The non-fuel minerals found in Texas are summarized below in terms of geologic setting:

Igneous and metamorphic rocks are favorable sites for mineralization and the outcrops of Precambrian rocks provide occurrences of many metals and some rare earths. There is no mining of these at this time. The area around Llano has occurrences of several metals and is commonly referred to as the "Central Mineral Region," reflecting a history of complex mineralization. In the past, the Central Mineral Region had commercial production of such minerals as graphite and vermiculite, and it has enough varied mineral occurrences to make it a hunting ground for gem and mineral collectors. The Precambrian rocks of the Trans-Pecos also have complex mineralization suites. Copper and other metals have been produced from this area.

Igneous rocks occur primarily in Llano and adjacent counties and in the Trans-Pecos area. The Precambrian granites of the Llano area long have been utilized as dimension stones. Our state capitol and capitol-complex office buildings are built of this stone, which is shipped nationally. The Cenozoic igneous activity in the Trans-Pecos provided solutions rich with many metals, and metals now occur in host rocks of several different geologic time periods. Most of the gold and silver production recorded for the state was from this region. Other metals, including mercury and some lead and zinc, were produced from this area.

Most of the value of Texas non-fuel minerals is in the non-metallics. Crushed stone and sand and gravel are mixed with cement for all types of construction and, in addition, provide the roadbed for highways. Stone also is stacked to provide rip-rap for dams and jetties, and some is used to face buildings. There are numerous other uses of crushed stone, such as pigments, fillers, carriers, ceramics and bricks. Crushed limestone is used to manufacture cement and to produce lime. It is also used in agriculture and in the abatement of acidic gases produced by the burning of some fossil fuels. Limestone constitutes more than 95 percent of all the crushed stone produced in Texas and comes primarily from rocks of Cretaceous age. Outcrops of Paleozoic limestones and Cenozoic limestones and caliche also provide some crushed stone.

The rocks deposited in West and North Central Texas by the vanishing Permian seas left vast deposits of evaporitic rocks, such as gypsum, anhydrite and rock salt. The gypsum is now an important source material for the manufacture of wallboard. Gypsum also occurs in the area around Fredericksburg, in the Finlay Mountains east of El Paso, and overlying many salt domes as a "caprock."

The Permian salt beds and the salt domes of East and Gulf Coast Texas are a source of brine, produced primarily for use in the oil industry, but it also has other industrial and manufacturing applications. Rock salt is mined from two salt domes.

The clays of Texas, particularly those of the Pennsylvanian and Tertiary periods, have a number of uses including ceramics, bricks and refractory products. Some clays and shales expand when subjected to heat and are used as lightweight aggregate.

Texas is one of the few states that produce significant quantities of helium. The gas is produced in the Panhandle from Permian rocks, but the source of the helium is considered to be from Precambrian igneous rocks.

Native sulfur occurs in caprock over some of the Gulf Coast salt domes, and in bedded Permian rocks of far West Texas. Some crude oils and gases contain substantial amounts of sulfur, which is removed during processing. Texas is an important source of this secondary sulfur.

Physiography of Texas

Mountains, seas, coastal plains, rocky plateaus, high plains, forests — all this physiographic variety in Texas is controlled by the varied rocks and structures that underlie and crop out in Texas. State and national parks set aside glimpses of this variation so that Texans and visitors may enjoy the beauty of our state. Parks and the physical features of Texas are discussed elsewhere in this volume.

Vegetational Areas

(Editor's note: This article was updated for this edition of The Texas Almanac by **Stephan L. Hatch, Curator, S.M. Tracy Herbarium** and **Professor, Dept. of Rangeland Ecology and Management, Texas A&M University.**)

Difference in amount and frequency of rainfall, in soils and in frost-free days gives Texas a great variety of vegetation. From the forests of East Texas to the deserts of West Texas, from the grassy plains of North Texas to the semi-arid brushlands of South Texas, plant species change continuously.

The following discussion of Texas' 10 vegetational areas (see map) and rangeland resources was prepared for the Texas Almanac by authorities at Texas A&M University.

Sideoats grama, which occurs on more different soils in Texas than any other native grass, was officially designated as the **state grass of Texas** by the Texas Legislature in 1971.

The 10 principal plant life areas of Texas, starting in the east, are:

1. **Piney Woods.** Most of this area of some 16 million acres ranges from about 50 to 700 feet above sea level and receives 40 to 56 inches of rain yearly. Many rivers, creeks and bayous drain the region. Nearly all of Texas' commercial timber comes from this area. **Pine** is the principal timber. There are three native species — the **longleaf, shortleaf** and **loblolly pine.** An introduced species, the **slash pine,** also is widely grown. Hardwoods include a variety of **oaks, elm, hickory, magnolia, sweet** and **black gum, tupelo** and others.

The area is interspersed with native and improved grasslands. Cattle are the primary grazing animals. Deer and quail are abundant in properly managed localities. Primary forage plants, under proper grazing management, include species of the **bluestems, rossettegrass, panicums, paspalums, blackseed needlegrass, Canada** and

Virginia **wildryes, purpletop, broadleaf** and **spike woodoats, switchcane, lovegrasses, indiangrass** and legume species.

Highly disturbed areas have understory and overstory of undesirable woody plants that suppress growth of pine and desirable grasses. The primary forage grasses have been reduced and the grasslands invaded by **threeawns, annual grasses, weeds, broomsedge bluestem, red lovegrass** and shrubby woody species.

2. **Gulf Prairies and Marshes.** The Gulf Prairies and Marshes cover approximately 10 million acres. There are two subunits: (a) The **marsh** and **salt grasses** immediately at tidewater, and (b) a little farther inland, a strip of **bluestems** and **tall grasses,** with some **gramas** in the western part. These grasses, except **salt** and **marsh grasses,** make excellent grazing. **Oaks, elm** and other hardwoods grow to some extent, especially along streams, and the area has some **post oak** and brushy extensions along its borders. Much of the Gulf Prairies is fertile farmland. The area is well suited for cattle.

Principal grasses of the Gulf Prairies are **tall bunchgrasses,** including **big bluestem, little bluestem, seacoast bluestem, indiangrass, eastern gamagrass, Texas wintergrass, switchgrass** and **gulf cordgrass. Seashore saltgrass** occurs on moist saline sites. Heavy grazing has changed the range vegetation in many cases so that the predominant grasses are the less desirable **broomsedge bluestem, smutgrass, threeawns, tumblegrass** and many other inferior grasses. The other plants that have invaded the productive grasslands include **oak underbrush, Macartney rose, huisache, mesquite, prickly pear, ragweed, bitter sneezeweed, broomweed** and others.

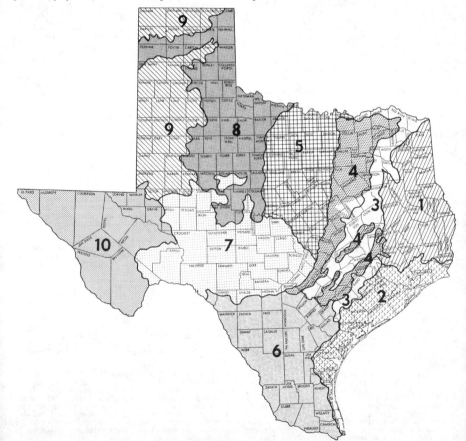

Vegetation of the Gulf Marshes consists primarily of sedges, bullrush, flat-sedges, beakrush and other rushes, smooth cordgrass, marshhay cordgrass, marsh millet and maidencane. The marshes are grazed best during winter.

3. Post Oak Savannah. This secondary forest region, also called the **Post Oak Belt**, covers some 7 million acres. It is immediately west of the primary forest region, with less annual rainfall and a little higher elevation. Principal trees are **post oak, blackjack oak** and **elm**. Along streams are growths of **pecans, walnuts** and other kinds of water-demanding trees. The southwestern extension of this belt is often poorly defined, with large areas of prairie.

The upland soils are sandy and sandy loam, while the bottomlands are sandy loams and clays.

The original vegetation consisted mainly of **little bluestem, big bluestem, indiangrass, switchgrass, purpletop, silver bluestem, Texas wintergrass, spike woodoats, longleaf woodoats, post oak** and **blackjack oak.** The area is still largely native or improved grasslands, with small farms located throughout. Intensive grazing has caused much of this area to degenerate to dense stands of a woody understory of **yaupon, greenbriar** and **oak brush. Mesquite** has become a serious problem. Good forage plants have been replaced by such inferior plants as **splitbeard bluestem, red lovegrass, broomsedge bluestem, broomweed, bullnettle** and **western ragweed.**

4. Blackland Prairies. This area of about 12 million acres, while called a "prairie," has much timber along the streams, including a variety of **oaks, pecan, elm, horse-apple (bois d'arc)** and **mesquite.** In its native state it was largely a grassy plain — the first native grassland in the westward extension of the Southern Forest Region.

Most of this fertile area has been cultivated, and only small acreages of meadowland remain in original vegetation. In heavily grazed pastures, the **tall bunchgrass** has been replaced by **buffalograss, Texas grama** and other less productive grasses. **Mesquite, lotebush** and other woody plants have invaded the grasslands.

The original grass vegetation was **big** and **little bluestem, indiangrass, switchgrass, sideoats grama, hairy grama, tall dropseed, Texas wintergrass** and **buffalograss.** Nongrass vegetation is largely legumes and composites.

5. Cross Timbers and Prairies. Approximately 15 million acres of alternating woodlands, often called the West Cross Timbers, and prairies constitute this region. Sharp changes in the vegetational cover are associated with different soils and topography, but the grass composition is rather uniform.

The prairie-type grasses are **big bluestem, little bluestem, indiangrass, switchgrass, Canada wildrye, sideoats grama, hairy grama, tall grama, tall dropseed, Texas wintergrass, blue grama** and **buffalograss.**

On the Cross Timbers soils, the grasses are composed of **big bluestem, little bluestem, hooded windmill-grass, sand lovegrass, indiangrass, switchgrass** and many species of **legumes.** The woody vegetation includes **shinnery, blackjack, post** and **live oaks.**

The entire area has been invaded heavily by woody brush plants of **oaks, mesquite, juniper** and other unpalatable plants that furnish little forage for livestock.

6. South Texas Plains. South of San Antonio, between the coast and the Rio Grande, are some 21 million acres of subtropical dryland vegetation, consisting of small trees, shrubs, cactus, weeds and grasses. The area is noteworthy for extensive brushlands, known as the **brush country,** or the Spanish equivalents of **chaparral** or **monte.** Principal plants are **mesquite, small live oak, post oak, prickly pear (Opuntia) cactus, catclaw, blackbrush, whitebrush, guajillo, huisache, cenizo** and others which often grow very densely. The original vegetation was mainly perennial warm-season **bunchgrasses** in post oak, live oak and mesquite savannahs. Other brush species form dense thickets on the ridges and along streams. Long-continued grazing caused the region to be densely covered with a mixture of brush. Most of the desirable grasses have persisted under the protection of brush and cacti.

There are distinct differences in the original plant communities on various soils. Dominant grasses on the sandy loam soils are **seacoast bluestem, bristlegrass, paspalum, windmillgrass, chloris, silver bluestem, big sandbur** and **tanglehead.** Dominant grasses on the clay and clay loams are **silver bluestem, Arizona cottontop, buffalograss, common curlymesquite, bristlegrass, pappusgrass, gramas, plains lovegrass, Texas cupgrass, vine-mesquite,** other **panicums** and **Texas wintergrass.** Low saline areas are characterized by **gulf cordgrass, seashore saltgrass, alkali sacaton** and **switchgrass.** In the post oak and live oak savannahs, the grasses are mainly **seacoast bluestem, indiangrass, switchgrass, crinkleawn, paspalums** and **panicums.** Today much of the area has been reseeded to **buffelgrass.**

7. Edwards Plateau. These 25 million acres are rolling to mountainous, with woodlands in the seastern part and grassy prairies in the west. There is a good deal of brushy growth in the central and eastern parts. The combination of grasses, weeds and small trees is ideal for cattle, sheep, goats, deer and wild turkey.

This limestone-based area is characterized by the large number of springfed, perennially flowing streams which originate in its interior and flow across the **Balcones Escarpment,** which bounds it on the south and east. The soils are shallow, ranging from sands to clays and are calcareous in reaction. This area is predominantly rangeland, with cultivation confined to the deeper soils.

In the east central portion is the well-marked **Central Basin** centering in Mason, Llano and Burnet counties, with a mixture of granitic and sandy soils. The western portion of the area comprises the semi-arid **Stockton Plateau.**

Noteworthy is the growth of **cypress** along the perennially flowing streams. Separated by many miles from cypress growth of the moist Southern Forest Belt, they constitute one of Texas' several "islands" of vegetation. These trees grow to stately proportions and, in the past, have been commercialized.

The principal grasses of the clay soils are **cane bluestem, silver bluestem, little bluestem, sideoats grama, hairy grama, indiangrass, common curlymesquite, buffalograss, fall witchgrass, plains lovegrass, wildryes** and **Texas wintergrass.**

The rocky areas support tall or mid-grasses with an overstory of **live oak, shinnery oak, cedar** and **mesquite.** The heavy clay soils have a mixture of **tobosagrass, buffalograss, sideoats grama** and **mesquite.**

Throughout the Edwards Plateau, **live oak, shinnery oak, mesquite** and **cedar** dominate the woody vegetation. Woody plants have invaded to the degree that they should be controlled before range forage plants can reestablish.

8. Rolling Plains. This is a region of approximately 24 million acres of alternating woodlands and prairies. The area is half mesquite woodland and half prairie. **Mesquite trees** have steadily invaded and increased in the grasslands for many years, despite constant control efforts.

Soils range from coarse sands along outwash terraces adjacent to streams to tight or compact clays on redbed clays and shales. Rough broken lands on steep slopes are found in the western portion. About two-thirds of the area is rangeland. But cultivation is important in certain localities.

The original vegetation includes **big, little, sand** and **silver bluestems, Texas wintergrass, indiangrass, switchgrass, sideoats** and **blue gramas, wildryes, tobosagrass** and **buffalograss** on the clay soils.

The sandy soils support **tall bunchgrasses,** mainly **sand bluestem. Sand shinnery oak, sand sagebrush** and **mesquite** are the dominant woody plants.

Continued heavy grazing causes increase in woody plants, low-value grasses such as **red grama, red lovegrass, tumblegrass, gummy lovegrass, Texas grama, sand dropseed** and **sand bur;** and **western ragweed, croton** and many other weeds. **Yucca** is a problem plant on certain rangelands.

9. High Plains. The High Plains, some 19 million treeless acres, are an extension of the **Great Plains** to the north. The level nature and porous soils prevent drainage over wide areas. The relatively light rainfall flows into the numerous shallow "playa" lakes or sinks into the ground to feed the great underground aquifer that is the source of water for the countless wells that irrigate the surface of the plains. A large part of this area is under irrigated farming, but native grassland remains in about one-half of the High Plains.

Blue grama and **buffalograss** comprise the principal vegetation on the clay and clay loam "hardland" soils. Important grasses on the sandy loam "sandy land" soils are **little bluestem, western wheatgrass, indiangrass, switchgrass** and **sand reedgrass. Sand shinnery oak, sand sagebrush, mesquite** and **yucca** are conspicuous invading brushy plants.

10. Trans-Pecos, Mountains and Basins. With as little as eight inches of annual rainfall, long hot summers and usually cloudless skies to encourage evaporation, this 18-million-acre area produces only drouth-resistant vegetation without irrigation. Grass is usually short and sparse. The principal growth consists of **lechuguilla, ocotillo, yucca, cenizo** and other arid land plants. In the more arid areas, **yeso, chino** and **tobosagrass** prevail. There is some **mesquite.** The vegetation includes creosote-tarbush, desert shrub, grama grassland, yucca and juniper savannahs, pine oak forest and saline flats.

The mountains are 3,000 to 8,751 feet in elevation and support **pinon pine, juniper** and some **ponderosa pine** and other forest vegetation on a few of the higher slopes.

The grass vegetation, especially on the higher mountain slopes, includes many southwestern and Rocky Mountain species not present elsewhere in Texas. On the desert flats, **black grama, burrograss** and **fluffgrass** are frequent. More productive sites have numerous species of **grama, muhly, Arizona cottontop, dropseed** and perennial **threeawn grasses.** At the higher elevations, **plains bristlegrass, little bluestem, Texas bluestem, sideoats grama, chino grama, blue grama, pinon ricegrass, wolftail** and several species of needlegrass are frequent.

The common invaders on all depleted ranges are **woody plants, burrograss, fluffgrass, hairy erioneuron, ear muhly, sand muhly, red grama, broom snakeweed, croton, cacti** and several poisonous plants.

Range Resources

More than 100 million acres of Texas are devoted to providing grazing for domestic and wild animals. This is the largest single use for land in the state. Primary range uses include: watershed for streams, springs, lakes; food and cover for wildlife; forage for domestic livestock; and recreation for man.

The **Piney Woods,** primarily valued for timber, also provide significant grazing. More than 80 percent of the acreage is devoted to range in the **Edwards Plateau, Cross Timbers and Prairies, South Texas Plains** and **Trans-Pecos Mountains and Basins.**

Because it is perennial, range is a renewable resource. Range management seeks to perpetuate plants and methods which yield maximum returns, while controlling or eliminating competitive, undesirable plants.

FOR FURTHER READING — Hatch, S. L., K. N. Gandhi and L. E. Brown, **Checklist of the Vascular Plants of Texas;** MP1655, Texas Agricultural Experiment Station, College Station, 1990.

Soil Conservation and Use

The following discussion was prepared especially for the Texas Almanac by the **Soil Conservation Service,** U. S. Department of Agriculture, Temple, Texas. Additional information may be obtained from that source.

The vast expanse of Texas soils encouraged wasteful use of soil and water throughout much of the state's history. Some **1,100 different soils series** are recognized in the state. Settlers were attracted by these rich soils and the abundant water of the eastern half of the region, used them to build an agriculture and agribusiness of vast proportions, then found their abuse had created critical problems.

In the 1930s, interest in soil and water conservation began to mount. In 1935, the Soil Conservation Service was created in the U. S. Department of Agriculture. In 1939, the **Texas Soil Conservation Law** made it possible for landowners to organize local soil and water conservation districts.

The state as of Jan. 1, 1991, had **211 conservation districts** which manage the various conservation functions within the district. A subdivision of state government, each district is governed by a board of five elected landowners. Technical assistance in planning and applying conservation work is provided through the USDA Soil Conservation Service. State funds for districts are administered through the **Texas State Soil and Water Conservation Board.** (See Index.)

The 1987 National Resources Inventory showed that more than twice as much soil is being lost to wind erosion each year than to sheet and rill erosion. The inventory also showed that about 21 percent of all land in Texas is "prime farmland."

Soil Subdivisions

Most authorities divide Texas into 20 major subdivisions that have similar or related soils, vegetation, topography, climate and land uses. These are called Major Land Resource Areas. Brief descriptions of these subdivisions follow.

1. TRANS-PECOS SOILS

The 18.7 million acres of the Trans-Pecos, mostly west of the Pecos River, are diverse plains and valleys intermixed with mountains — quite different from other Texas areas. (See also section on physiography.)

Upland soils are light reddish brown to brown clay loams, clays and sands, (mostly high in lime, some saline) and many areas of shallow soils and rock lands. Main series: Hoban, Reeves, Reagan (lower basins); Brewster, Lozier, Verhalen, Musquiz (mountains and valleys); Hueco, Wink, Kermit (sandy soils); Orla (gypsic soils). Bottomland soils are dark grayish brown to reddish brown, silt loams to clayey, alluvial soils (some saline). Main series: Harkey, Glendale (Rio Grande); Pecos, Arno (Pecos River).

Rainfall is sparse, and vegetative cover is as thin and variable as the topography, soils and drainage conditions. In general it is of two types: short grasses and shrubs on the flat soils of the basins and valleys, and a mixture of mid and short grasses and species of oak, pine, juniper and semiarid plants and shrubs on the rough and mountainous lands. Alkali sacaton and other salt-tolerant plants occur in the basin.

2. HIGH PLAINS SOILS

The High Plains area comprises the vast high plateau of more than 19.4 million acres in Northwestern Texas. It lies in the southern part of the Great Plains province that includes large similar areas in Oklahoma and New Mexico. The flat, nearly level surface of very large areas has few streams of any dissection to cause local relief. However, several major rivers originate in the High Plains or cross the area. The largest is the Canadian River which has cut a deep valley across the Panhandle section.

Playas, small intermittent lakes scattered through the area, lie up to 20 feet below the surrounding flat plains. Early estimates were that playas numbered 37,000; a 1965 survey indicated more than 19,000 in 44 counties, occupying some 340,000 acres. They received most of the runoff, with less than 10 percent of this water percolating back to the aquifer.

Soils are brown to reddish, mostly deep, clay loams, sandy loams and sands. Free lime is present under many soils at various depths. Main series: Pullman, Olton, Sherm (hardlands); Amarillo, Portales (mixed lands); Brownfield, Tivoli (sandy lands); Potter (loamy soils, shallow over caliche). The Guadalupe, Spur and Bippus series are the main soils of bottomlands, but are minor in extent.

The soils are moderately productive and the flat surface encourages irrigation and mechanization. Limited rainfall and constant danger of wind erosion are handicaps; but the region is Texas' leading producer of three most important crops — cotton, grain sor-ghums and wheat.

The native vegetation is of three distinct kinds. In the northern part and on the fine-textured soils south of the Canadian River, the vegetation is short grasses, mainly **buffalo** with some **grama.** In the southern part on the sandy loam soils it is largely **grama** and **threeawn.** On the deep sands it is mainly **little bluestem, sand dropseed, sideoats grama** and **threeawn grasses.** In places these sands support a thick growth of **shinoak** and **sand sage** (Artemisia).

3. ROLLING PLAINS SOILS

The Rolling Plains comprise an eastern section of the Great Plains in Northwestern Texas. The area lies west of the North Central Prairies and extends from the edge of the Edwards Plateau in Tom Green County northward into Oklahoma. It includes about 21.7 million acres. The **Red Beds** and associated reddish soils led to use of the name **Red Plains** by some.

Upland soils are pale brown through reddish brown to dark grayish brown sandy loams, clay loams and clays. Most soils have free lime in the lower part and are saline in places; some are shallow and stony; some are deep sands. Main series: Miles, Woodward, Springer, Vernon, Tillman (northern two-thirds); Abilene, Rowena, Mereta, Lueders (southern one-third).

Bottomland soils include minor areas of reddish brown, sandy to clayey, alluvial soils. Main series: Lincoln, Yahola, Guadalupe, Clairemont, Spur, Bippus and Mangum.

The native vegetation varies with soils and surface conditions. On the finer-textured soils **curly mesquite, buffalo** and **grama grasses** are dominant, with some scattered shrubs in places. On the coarser-textured soils the principal grasses are **little bluestem, sideoats** grama and **threeawn grasses** with **sand sage** and **shinnery** on areas of deep sand.

4. ROLLING RED PRAIRIES SOILS

The Rolling Red Prairies occupy about 1 million acres in North Central Texas adjoining Oklahoma. The area is dominantly prairie. The principal soils are of the Anocon, Bluegrove, Kamay, Kirkland and Stoneburg series. Bottomland soils are of the Gaddy, Yomont and Mangum series.

Native vegetation is mainly **little bluestem, sideoats, hairy** and **blue grama, Indiangrass** and **buffalograss**. The area is mainly used for cattle ranching and growing small grains.

5. NORTH CENTRAL PRAIRIE SOILS

The North Central Prairies occupy about 7 million acres in Central North Texas. The area lies between the Western Cross Timbers and Rolling Plains and was heretofore often referred to as the Reddish Prairie. The area is dominantly prairie, but numerous small wooded areas are intermixed. The principal soils are of the Truce, Thurber, Bonti and Owens series. Narrow strips of alluvial soils, mainly of the Bosque and Frio series, occur in the flood plains of local streams. Small areas of other soils similar to those of the West Cross Timbers and Grand Prairie are intermixed. They are best suited for growing small grains and native grasses.

Native vegetation is mainly **little bluestem, sideoats, hairy** and **blue grama, Indian** and **buffalo grass.** Scrubby trees and shrubs, mainly **post oak** and **mesquite,** and **cacti** grow rather thickly in places.

6. EDWARDS PLATEAU SOILS

The 22.7 million acres of the Edwards Plateau are on an extensive tableland of Southwest Texas. Many of the soils are shallow over limestone, and streams have cut many valleys and canyons. Upland soils are dark, calcareous clays and clay loams, mostly gravelly and stony. Some deeper, less stony soils occur on the flat divides. Main series: Tarrant, Eckrant, Brackett and Tobosa (eastern two-thirds); Ector, Upton, Reagan (western one-third). Bottomland soils include minor areas of dark, calcareous, clayey alluvial soils. Main series: Frio, Oakalla and Dev.

This is principally a livestock, ranching region, the center of Texas' and the nation's mohair and wool production. Except where there is limited irrigation, cropping is largely confined to such drought-resistant crops as grain sorghums and grasses. Grasses, shrubs and scrubby trees dominate the native vegetation. There are many **cedar brakes.**

7. CENTRAL BASIN SOILS

The Central Basin, also known as the **Llano Basin,** occupies a relatively small area in Central Texas. It includes parts or all of Llano, Mason, Gillespie and adjoining counties. The total area is about 1.6 million acres.

Upland soils are reddish brown to brown, mostly gravelly and stony, sandy loams shallow over granite, limestone, gneiss and schist; deeper, less stony, sandy loam soils in the valleys. Main series: Pontotoc, Pedernales, Ligon, Castell, Katemcy, Hensley and Voca. Bottomland soils are minor areas of dark gray, alluvial soils. Main series: Frio and Oakalla.

The native vegetation consists of grass and small **oak** and **mesquite trees.** On some rocky slopes, **juniper** forms the principal growth. Ranching is the main enterprise, with some farms producing peaches, grain sorghum and wheat.

8. NORTHERN RIO GRANDE PLAIN SOILS

The Northern Rio Grande Plain comprises about 6.3 million acres in an area of Southern Texas extending from Uvalde to Beeville. The main soils are deep, reddish brown or dark grayish brown, loamy, and of the Clareville, Elmendorf, Floresville, Miguel and Webb series in the eastern part. Native range is grassland, thorny brush and cacti. Most of the area is range grazed by beef cattle. Grain sorghum, cotton, corn, flax and small grain are grown in the eastern part. Irrigated cropland is in the Winter Garden area of the western part and produces corn, cotton, grain sorghum and truck crops such as spinach, carrots and cabbage.

9. WESTERN RIO GRANDE PLAIN SOILS

The Western Rio Grande Plain comprises about 5.3 million acres in an area of Southwestern Texas from Del Rio to Rio Grande City. The main upland soils are clayey, saline and of the Catarina and Montell series. The vegetation is mid and short grasses with low thorny brush and **cacti.** Soils along the Rio Grande are mainly the Laredo, Rio Grande and Zalla series. Most of the soils along the river are used for growing vegetables and

sorghums. The upland soils are used for grazing beef cattle.

10. CENTRAL RIO GRANDE PLAIN SOILS

The Central Rio Grande Plain comprises about 5.9 million acres in an area of Southern Texas from Live Oak to Hidalgo County. The main soils are Nueces and Sarita series (sandy); Delfina, Delmita and Duval (loamy); Randado and Zapata series (shallow). The vegetation is tall and mid grasses with scattered trees and shrubs. Much of the area is in large ranches used for raising beef cattle. A few areas are used for growing grain sorghum, cotton and small grain.

11. LOWER RIO GRANDE VALLEY SOILS

The Lower Rio Grande Valley comprises about 2.1 million acres in extreme Southern Texas. The main soils are deep, loamy and clayey, and of the Brennan, Hidalgo, Harlingen, Raymondville and Rio Grande series. Most of the soils are used for growing irrigated vegetables and citrus, along with cotton, grain sorghum and sugar cane. Some areas are in range and used for growing beef cattle.

12. WEST CROSS TIMBERS SOILS

The West Cross Timbers comprises a total of about 2.6 million acres. The area includes the wooded section west of the Grand Prairie and extends from the Red River southward to the north edge of Brown County. Small areas also occur intermixed or interlaced with soils of the western part of the Grand Prairie. The principal series are Windthorst, Nimrod and Duffau. Narrow areas of alluvial soils, mainly of the Gowen series, occur in the flood plains of local streams. Soils of the Ships, Yahola and Weswood series occur in the flood plains of the through-flowing rivers.

The native vegetation is mainly **shinnery oak** and **post oak** trees and a few other hardwoods. The trees are scrubby, of small size and unsuited for most uses other than **firewood** or **fence posts.** In places, grasses, including **little bluestem, grama** and **threeawn,** and scattered **mesquite** trees form a thick ground cover where the oak overstory is thin. Rangeland and pastures are used for grazing beef and dairy cattle. Crops are peanuts, grain sorghum, small grains, peaches, pecans and vegetables.

13. EAST CROSS TIMBERS SOILS

The East Cross Timbers includes a long narrow strip of wooded soils that separates the northern parts of the Blackland Prairie and Grand Prairie. This strip is only a few miles wide and extends from the Red River southward into Hill County and includes a total area of about 1 million acres. The soils are mainly of the Callisburg, Crosstell, Silstid and Gasil series.

The native vegetation is mainly **post oak** trees and a few other hardwoods. The trees are scrubby, of small size and unsuited for most uses other than firewood or fence posts. In places, grasses, including **little bluestem, grama** and **threeawn,** and scattered **mesquite** trees form a thick ground cover where the oak overstory is thin. Rangelands and pastures are used for grazing beef and dairy cattle. Crops are peanuts, grain sorghums, small grains, peaches, pecans and vegetables.

14. GRAND PRAIRIE SOILS

The Grand Prairie includes the prairie just west of the Blackland Prairie in North Central Texas. It extends south from the Red River to about the Colorado River and comprises about 6.3 million acres.

The principal soils of the Grand Prairie are of the Eckrant, Slidell and Denton series. Small areas of soils of the Crawford, Brackett, Krum and Lewisville series occur also on the uplands. Alluvial soils, mainly of the Frio and Bosque series, occur in the flood plains of streams.

The native vegetation is mainly short grasses with some mid and tall grasses on the deeper soils. **Buffalo** and **grama grasses, little bluestem** and **Indian grass** are the most widespread. In many places, especially on rocky slopes of shallow soils, small **oak** and **juniper trees** form a thick cover, and scattered **mesquite trees** occur throughout the area. The area is mainly used for grazing beef cattle. Some small grain, grain sorghum and corn are grown.

15. BLACKLAND PRAIRIE SOILS

An almost treeless area, the Blackland Prairies consist of about 12.6 million acres of East Central Texas extending southwesterly from the Red River to Bexar County. There are smaller, similar areas to the southeast.

The soils of the greater portion of the Blackland Prairie proper are mainly of the Houston Black, Heiden and Austin series with smaller areas of Lewisville, Altoga and Eddy soils. Bottomland soils are mainly Tinn and Trinity clays.

The native vegetation consists of bunch and short grasses. The main species are little and big **bluestems, grama, Indian, buffalo** and **threeawn grasses.** In places, scattered **mesquite trees, cacti** and other shrubs form a rather thick cover. Hardwood trees — mainly **elm, hackberry** and **pecan** — occur in stream bottoms. The main crops are grain sorghum, wheat, cotton, corn and hay. Pastures are used for beef and dairy cattle.

16. CLAYPAN AREA SOILS

The Claypan Area is a nearly level to gently rolling moderately dissected woodland savannah to brushy area **(Post Oak Belt)** with moderate surface drainage. The area is more than 6.1 million acres.

Upland soils are sandy loams, commonly thin over gray, mottled or red, firm, clayey subsoils. Some deep, sandy soils with less clayey subsoils exist. Main series: Lufkin, Axtell, Tabor (thin-surface claypan soils); Freestone and Padina (thick-surface sandy and loamy soils). Bottomlands are reddish brown to dark gray, to loamy to clayey alluvial soils. Main series: Ships, Weswood (Brazos and Colorado Rivers); Kaufman, Trinity, Gladewater, Nahatche (Trinity River and other smaller streams).

Vegetation consists of scattered stands of **post oak** and **blackjack oak** with tall bunchgrasses in the uplands; **yaupon** and other underbrush prevalent in places. In the bottomlands, hardwoods are predominant but **pecans** occur in some areas. The land is woodland and brushy range. A few areas are used for tame pasture and cool-season forage crops.

17. EAST TEXAS TIMBERLAND SOILS

The East Texas Timberlands comprise the forested eastern part of the state, about 16.1 million acres.

The principal soil series are the Woodtell, Kirvin, Cuthbert, Bowie, Lilbert and Tonkawa soils in the northern and central parts; Nacogdoches and Elrose soils in the "Redland" section; and Diboll, Kisatche, Rayburn, Tehran, Doucette, Pinetucky and Shankler soils in the southern part of the area. Alluvial soils, mainly Mantachie, Iuka, Severn and Estes are on flood plains of streams.

The native vegetation is a pine-hardwood forest. It is mainly **loblolly pine, shortleaf pine, sweetgum** and **red oak trees** with an understory of grasses and shrubs. Forestry and pastures are the main uses.

18. COAST PRAIRIE SOILS

The Coast Prairie includes the nearly flat strip that is near the Gulf Coast in Southeast Texas in the humid and subhumid zones. It ranges from 30 to 80 miles in width and parallels the coast from the Sabine River in Orange County to Baffin Bay in Kleberg County. Total area of the Coast Prairie is about 8.7 million acres. The principal soils in the eastern portion from about the San Antonio River to the Sabine River are Lake Charles, Bernard, Edna, Morey and Beaumont soils near the coast, comprising more than 4 million acres.

The more inland soils in the eastern section are Hockley, Katy and Crowley series, comprising nearly 2 million acres. The portions west and south of the San Antonio River are Victoria, Orelia, Papalote and Clareville soils, comprising some 2 million acres. Other important soils, which occur in the bottomlands, are Brazoria, Norwood, Pledger, Kaman and Urbo. The nearly level topography and productive soils encourage farming. Rice, grain sorghum, cotton and soybeans are main crops. The native vegetation is tall prairie grasses, mainly species of **andropogon, paspalum** and **panicum,** with a narrow fringe of trees along the streams.

19. COAST SALINE PRAIRIES SOILS

The Coast Saline Prairies include a narrow strip of wet lowlands adjacent to the coast and the barrier islands that extend from Mexico to Louisiana. The surface is at or only a few feet above sea level and it ranges from 3 to 20 miles wide. The total area is about 3.2 million acres. Important soil series are the Harris, Tatton, Veston and Galveston series in the eastern part, and the Mustang, Aransas, Placedo, Francitas, Barrada and Galveston in the southern part. Cattle grazing is the chief economic use of the various salt tolerant **cordgrasses** and **sedges.** Recreation is an important use of the barrier islands.

20. FLATWOODS SOILS

The Flatwoods area includes the flat, rather poorly drained forested area in humid Southeast Texas. Total area is about 2.5 million acres. Most soils have a water table near the surface at least part of the year. Soils are mainly fine sandy loam with loamy or clayey subsoils. Important soil series are the Segno, Sorter, Splendora, Kirbyville, Malbis and Evadale.

The land is mainly used for forest. The typical vegetation is a pine-hardwood forest that is mainly **longleaf pine, loblolly pine, sweetgum** and various **oak** species.

Physical Features

Texas is at the crossroads of five major physiographic regions of North America: the **Gulf Coastal Plain;** the **Great Plains;** the **Interior Lowlands;** the **Rocky Mountain System;** and the **Basin and Range Province.**

A special thanks to Dr. William M. Holmes, chairman of the Department of Geography at North Texas State University, for his assistance in revising this section.

Physical Regions

Principal physical regions of Texas usually are listed as follows: (See also Plant Life and Soils.)

THE GULF COASTAL PLAINS

Texas' Gulf Coastal Plains are the western extension of the coastal plain extending from the Atlantic to beyond the Rio Grande. Its characteristic rolling to hilly surface covered with a heavy growth of pine and hardwoods extends into East Texas, but in the increasingly arid west its forests become secondary in nature, consisting largely of post oaks and, farther west, prairies and brush lands.

The interior limit of the Gulf Coastal Plains in Texas is the line of the **Balcones Fault** and **Escarpment.** This geologic fault or shearing of underground strata extends eastward from a point on the Rio Grande near Del Rio. It extends to the northwestern part of Bexar County where it turns northeastward and extends through Comal, Hays and Travis counties, intersecting the Colorado River immediately above Austin. The fault line is a single, definite geologic feature, accompanied by a line of southward- and eastward-facing hills. The resemblance of the hills to balconies when viewed from the plain below accounts for the Spanish name, balcones. North of Waco, features of the fault zone are sufficiently inconspicuous that the interior boundary of the Coastal Plain follows the traditional geologic contact between upper and lower Cretaceous rocks. This contact is along the western edge of the Eastern Cross Timbers.

This fault line is usually accepted as the boundary between lowland and upland Texas. Below this fault line the surface is characteristically coastal plains. Above the Balcones Fault the surface is characteristically interior rolling plains.

Pine Belt or "Piney Woods"

The Pine Belt (often called locally the "Piney Woods") extends into Texas from the east 75 to 125 miles. From north to south it extends from the Red River to within about 25 miles of the Gulf Coast. Interspersed among the pines are some hardwood timbers, usually in valleys of rivers and creeks. This area is the source of practically all of Texas' large commercial timber production. (See index for chapter on forest resources.) It was settled early in Texas history and is an older farming area of the state. This area's soils and climate are adaptable to production of a variety of fruit and vegetable crops. Cattle raising has increased greatly, accompanied by the development of pastures planted to improved grasses. Lumber production is the principal manufacturing industry. There is a large iron and steel industry near Daingerfield in Morris County based on nearby iron deposits. Iron deposits are also worked in Rusk and one or two other counties.

A great oil field discovered in Gregg, Rusk and Smith counties in 1931 has done more than anything else to contribute to the economic growth of the area. This area has a variety of clays, lignite and other minerals as potentials for development.

Post Oak Belt

The main Post Oak Belt of Texas is wedged between the Pine Belt on the east, Blacklands on the west, and the Coastal Prairies on the south, covering a consider-

NATURAL REGIONS OF TEXAS

able area in East Central Texas. Principal industry is diversified farming and livestock raising.

Throughout, it is spotty in character with some insular areas of blackland soil, and some that closely resemble those of the Pine Belt. There is a small isolated area of pines in Bastrop County known as the **Lost Pines.** The Post Oak Belt has lignite, commercial clays and some other minerals.

Blackland Belt

The Blackland Belt stretches from the Rio Grande to the Red River, lying just below the line of the Balcones Fault, and varying in width from 15 to 70 miles. It is narrowest below the segment of the Balcones Fault from the Rio Grande to Bexar County and gradually widens as it runs northeast to the Red River. Its rolling prairie, easily turned by the plow, developed rapidly as a farming area until the 1930s and was the principal cotton-producing area of Texas. Now, however, other Texas irrigated, mechanized areas lead in farming. Because of the early growth, the Blackland Belt is still the most thickly populated area in the state and contains within it and along its border more of the state's large and middle-sized cities than any other area. Primarily because of this concentration of population, this belt has the most diversified manufacturing industry of the state.

Coastal Prairies

The Texas Coastal Prairies extend westward along the coast from the Sabine River, reaching inland 30 to 60 miles. Between the Sabine and Galveston Bay the line of demarcation between the prairies and the Pine Belt forests to the north is very distinct. The Coastal Prairie in varying character extends along the Gulf from the Sabine to the Lower Rio Grande Valley. The eastern half is covered with a heavy growth of grass; the western half, in a more arid area, is covered with short grass, and in

some places with small timber and brush. The soil is heavy clay. Grass supports the densest cattle population in Texas, and cattle ranching is the principal agricultural industry. Rice is a major crop, grown under irrigation from wells and rivers. Cotton, grain sorghum and truck crops are grown.

Coastal Prairie areas have seen the greatest industrial development in Texas history since World War II. Chief concentration has been from Orange and Beaumont to Houston, and much of the development has been in **petrochemicals,** or chemicals derived from petroleum.

Corpus Christi, and the surrounding **Coastal Bend** region, and, south of the coastal plains, Brownsville, with its adjacent **Lower Rio Grande Valley** area, are rapidly developing seaports, agricultural and industrial sections. Cotton, grain, vegetables and citrus fruits are the principal crops. Cattle production is significant, with the famed **King Ranch** and other large ranches located here.

Lower Rio Grande Valley

The deep alluvial soils and distinctive economy cause the Lower Rio Grande Valley to be classified as a subregion of the Gulf Coastal Plain. Here is concentrated Texas' greatest citrus-winter vegetable area because of the normal absence of freezing weather and the rich delta soils of the Rio Grande. Despite occasional **damaging freezes,** as in 1951 and 1961, the Lower Valley ranks high among the nation's intensified fruit-and-truck regions. Much of the acreage is irrigated from the Rio Grande, although dryland farming also is practiced.

Rio Grande Plain

This may be roughly defined as lying south of San Antonio and between the Rio Grande and the Gulf Coast. The Rio Grande Plain shows characteristics of both the Texas Gulf Coastal Plain and the North Mexico Plains because there is similarity of topography, climate and plant life all the way from the Balcones Escarpment in Texas to the Sierra Madre Oriental in Mexico, which runs past Monterrey about 160 miles south of Laredo.

The Rio Grande Plain is part prairie, but much of it is covered with a dense growth of **prickly pear, cactus, mesquite, dwarf oak, catclaw, guajillo, huisache, blackbrush, cenizo** and other wild shrubs. This country is devoted primarily to raising cattle, sheep and goats. The Texas Angora goat and mohair industry centers in this area and on the Edwards Plateau, which borders it on the north. San Antonio and Laredo are its chief commercial centers, with San Antonio dominating trade.

There is some farming and the **Winter Garden,** centering in Dimmit and Zavala counties north of Laredo, is irrigated from wells and streams to produce vegetables in late winter and early spring. Primarily, however, the central and western part of the Rio Grande Plain is devoted to livestock raising. The rainfall is less than 25 inches annually and the hot summers bring heavy evaporation so that cultivation without irrigation is limited. Over a large area in the central and western parts of the Rio Grande Plain, the growth of **small oaks, mesquite, prickly pear (Opuntia) cactus** and a variety of wild shrubs is very dense and it is often called the **Brush Country.** It is also referred to as the **Chaparral** or the **monte.** (Monte is a Spanish word meaning mountain, also heavy forest or dense brush.)

INTERIOR LOWLAND

The North Central Plains of Texas are a southwestern extension into Texas of the interior lowlands that extend northward to the Canadian border, paralleling the Great Plains to the west. The North Central Plains of Texas extend from the Blackland Belt on the east to the **Cap Rock Escarpment** on the west. From north to south they extend from the Red River to the Colorado.

West Texas Rolling Plains

The West Texas Rolling Plains, approximately the western two-thirds of the North Central Plains in Texas, rise from east to west in altitude from about 750 feet to 2,000 feet at the base of the Cap Rock Escarpment. Annual rainfall ranges from about 30 inches on the east to 20 on the west. Temperature varies rather widely between summer's heat and winter's cold.

This area still has a large cattle-raising industry with many of the state's largest ranches. However, there is much level cultivable land.

Grand Prairie

Near the eastern edge of the North Central Plains is the Grand Prairie, extending south from the Red River in an irregular band through Cooke, Montague, Wise, Denton, Tarrant, Parker, Hood, Johnson, Bosque, Coryell and some adjacent counties. It is a limestone-based area, usually treeless except along the numerous streams, and adapted primarily to livestock raising and staple crop growing.

Sometimes called the **Fort Worth Prairie,** it has an agricultural economy and largely rural population, with no large cities except Fort Worth on its eastern boundary.

East and West Cross Timbers

Hanging over the top of the Grand Prairie and dropping down on each side are the East and West Cross Timbers. The two southward-extending bands are connected by a narrow strip along the Red River. The East Cross Timbers extend southward from the Red River through eastern Denton County and along the Dallas-Tarrant County boundary, then through Johnson County to the Brazos River and into Hill County. The much larger **West Cross Timbers** extend from the Red River south through Clay, Montague, Jack, Wise, Parker, Palo Pinto, Hood, Erath, Eastland, Comanche, Brown and Mills counties to the Colorado, where they meet the Edwards Plateau. Their soils are adapted to fruit and vegetable crops, which reach considerable commercial production in some areas in Parker, Erath, Eastland and Comanche counties.

GREAT PLAINS

The Great Plains which lie to the east of the base of the Rocky Mountains extend into Northwest Texas. This Texas area, known as the **Staked Plains** or the Spanish equivalent, **Llano Estacado,*** is a vast, flat high plain covered with thick layers of alluvial material.

---

*Historians differ as to the origin of this name. Some think that it came from the fact that the Coronado expedition, crossing the trackless sea of grass, staked its route so that it would be guided on its return trip. Others think that the "estacado" refers to the palisaded appearance of the Caprock in many places, especially the west-facing escarpment in New Mexico.

The **Caprock Escarpment** is the dividing line between the High Plains and the Lower Rolling Plains of West Texas. Like the Balcones Escarpment, the Caprock Escarpment is an outstanding natural boundary line. Unlike the Balcones Escarpment, the Caprock Escarpment is caused by surface erosion. In many places this escarpment is a striking physical feature, rising abruptly 200, 500 and in some places almost 1,000 feet above the plains at its base. Where rivers issue from the eastern face of this escarpment there frequently are notable canyons, such as the **Palo Duro Canyon** on the Prairie Dog Town Fork (main channel) of the Red Riv-

---

Area of Texas

Texas occupies about 7 percent of the total water and land area of the United States. **Second in size** among the states, Texas, according to the revised 1980 U.S. Census Bureau figures, has a land and water area of 266,807 square miles as compared with Alaska's 591,004 square miles. California, third largest state, has 158,706 square miles. Texas is as large as all of New England, New York, Pennsylvania, Ohio and Illinois combined.

The state's area consists of 262,017 square miles of land and 4,790 square miles of inland water, or 167,-690,880 acres of land area and 3,065,600 acres of inland water.

The area given here differs from that given by the State Land Office in the chapter on State Government.

LENGTH AND BREADTH

The longest straight-line distance in a general north-south direction is 801 miles from the northwest corner of the Panhandle to the extreme southern tip of Texas on the Rio Grande below Brownsville. The greatest east-west distance is 773 miles from the extreme eastward bend in the Sabine River in Newton County to the extreme western bulge of the Rio Grande just above El Paso. The **geographic center** of Texas is southwest of Mercury in the northern portion of McCulloch County.

LATITUDE, LONGITUDE—ELEVATION

The extremes of latitude and longitude are as follows: From Latitude 25° 50′ N. at the extreme southern turn of the Rio Grande on the south line of Cameron County to Latitude 36° 30′ N. along the north line of the Panhandle, and from Longitude 93° 31′ W. at the extreme eastern point on the Sabine River on the east line of Newton County to Longitude 106° 38′ W. on the extreme westward point on the Rio Grande above El Paso.

In elevation the surface of the state varies from sea level along the Gulf Coast to 8,749 feet at the summit of Guadalupe Mountain in Culberson County.

TEXAS BOUNDARY LINE

The boundary of Texas by segments, including only larger river bends and only the great arc of the coast line, is as follows:

	Miles
Rio Grande	889.0
Coast line	367.0
Sabine River, Lake and Pass	180.0
Sabine River to Red River	106.5
Red River	480.0
East Panhandle line	133.6
North Panhandle line	167.0
West Panhandle line	310.2
Along 32nd parallel	209.0
Total	2,842.3

Following the smaller meanderings of the rivers and the tidewater coast line, the following are the boundary measurements:

Rio Grande	1,248
Coast line (tidewater)	624
Sabine River, Lake and Pass	292
Red River	726
The five line segments given above	926
Total, including line segments given in table above	3,816

For Further Reading: "Texas: A Geography," by Terry G. Jordan with John L. Bean Jr. and William M. Holmes; Westview Press, Boulder and London, 1984.

er and the breaks along the Canadian as it crosses the Panhandle north of Amarillo.

Along the eastern edge of the Panhandle there is a gradual descent of the earth's surface from high to low plains, but at the Red River the Caprock Escarpment becomes a striking surface feature. It continues as an east-facing wall south through Briscoe, Floyd, Motley, Dickens, Crosby, Garza and Borden counties, gradually decreasing in elevation. South of Borden County the escarpment is less obvious, and the boundary between the High Plains and the Edwards Plateau occurs where the alluvial cover of the High Plains disappears.

Stretching over the largest level plain of its kind in the United States, the High Plains rise gradually from about 2,700 feet on the east to more than 4,000 feet in spots along the New Mexico border.

Chiefly because of climate and the resultant agriculture, subdivisions are called the **North Plains** and **South Plains.** The North Plains, from Hale County north, has primarily wheat and grain sorghum farming, but with significant ranching and petroleum developments. Amarillo is the largest city, with Plainview on the south and Borger on the north as important commercial centers. The South Plains, also a leading grain sorghum region, leads Texas in cotton production. Lubbock is the principal city, and Lubbock County is the state's largest cotton producer. Irrigation from underground reservoirs, centered around Lubbock and Plainview, waters much of the crop acreage.

Edwards Plateau

Geographers usually consider the Great Plains at the foot of the Rocky Mountains continuing southward from the High Plains of Northwest Texas to the Rio Grande and the Balcones Escarpment. This southern and lower extension of the Great Plains in Texas is known as the Edwards Plateau.

It lies between the Rio Grande and the Colorado River. Its southeastern border is the Balcones Escarpment from the Rio Grande at Del Rio eastward to San Antonio and thence to Austin on the Colorado. Its upper boundary is the Pecos River, though the Stockton Plateau is geologically and topographically classed with the Edwards Plateau. The Edwards Plateau varies from about 750 feet high at its southern and eastern borders to about 2,700 feet in places. Almost the entire surface is a thin, limestone-based soil covered with a medium to thick growth of cedar, small oak and mesquite with a varying growth of prickly pear. Grass for cattle, weeds for sheep and tree foliage for the browsing goats, support three industries—cattle, goat and sheep raising—upon which the area's economy depends. It is the nation's leading Angora goat and mohair producing region and one of the nation's leading sheep and wool areas. A few crops are grown.

Toyah Basin

To the northwest of the Edwards and Stockton plateaus is the Toyah Basin, a broad, flat remnant of an old sea floor that occupied the region as recently as Quaternary time.

Located in the Pecos River Valley, this region, in relatively recent time, has become important for many agricultural products as a result of irrigation. Additional economic activity is afforded by local oil fields.

The Hill Country

The Hill Country is a popular name for an area of hills and spring-fed streams along the edge of the Balcones Escarpment. It is popular with tourists who visit the dude ranches and other attractions. Notable large springs include **Barton Springs** at Austin, **San Marcos Springs** at San Marcos, **Comal Springs** at New Braunfels, several springs at San Antonio, and a number of others.

The Llano Basin

The Llano Basin lies at the junction of the Colorado and Llano rivers in Burnet and Llano counties. Earlier this was known as the "Central Mineral Region," because of the evidence there of a large number of minerals.

On the Colorado River in this area a succession of dams impounds two large and four small reservoirs. Uppermost is **Lake Buchanan**, one of the two large reservoirs, between Burnet and Llano counties. Below it in the western part of Travis County is **Lake Travis.** Between these two large reservoirs are three smaller ones, **Inks, L. B. Johnson** (formerly **Granite Shoals**) and **Marble Falls** reservoirs, used primarily for maintaining heads to produce electric power from the overflow from Lake Buchanan. **Lake Austin** is just above the city of Austin. Still another small lake is formed by a low-water dam in Austin.

A name for this recreational area is the **Highland Lakes Country.** Geologically this is an interesting area with Precambrian and Paleozoic rocks found on the surface.

BASIN AND RANGE PROVINCE

The Basin and Range province, with its center in Nevada, surrounds the Colorado Plateau on the west and south and enters far West Texas from southern New Mexico. It consists of broad interior drainage basins interspersed with scattered fault-block mountain ranges. Although this is the only part of Texas regarded as mountainous, these should not be confused with the Rockies. Of all the independent ranges in West Texas, only the Davis Mountains resemble the Rockies, and there is much debate about this.

Texas west of the Edwards Plateau is bounded on the north by New Mexico and on the south by the Rio Grande is distinctive in its physical and economic conditions. Traversed from north to south by an eastern range of the Rockies, it contains all of Texas' true mountains and also is very interesting geologically.

Highest of the Trans-Pecos Mountains is the **Guadalupe Range,** which enters the state from New Mexico. It comes to an abrupt end about 20 miles south of the boundary line, where are situated **Guadalupe Peak,** (8,749 feet, highest in Texas) and **El Capitan** (8,085 feet), which, because of perspective, appears to the observer on the plain below to be higher than Guadalupe and was for many years thought to be the highest mountain in Texas. Lying just west of the Guadalupe range and extending to the **Hueco Mountains** a short distance east of El Paso is the **Diablo Plateau** or basin. It has no drainage outlet to the sea. The runoff from the scant rain that falls on its surface drains into a series of salt lakes that lie just west of the Guadalupe Mountains. These lakes

---

Texas' Highs, Lows

Though most of Texas is located on flat plains or rolling prairies, there are substantial mountains in the Trans-Pecos region of far West Texas. The highest point in the state is **Guadalupe Peak** at 8,749 feet above sea level. Its twin, **El Capitan** stands at 8,085 feet and also is located in Culberson County near the New Mexico state line. Both are in the **Guadalupe Mountains National Park,** which includes scenic **McKittrick Canyon.** These elevations and the others in this article have been determined by the U.S. Geological Survey, unless otherwise noted.

In addition to Guadalupe and El Capitan, other peaks standing more than 8,000 feet above sea level include: **Shumard,** 8,615; **Bartlett,** 8,508; **Bush Mountain,** 8,631; **Hunter Peak** (also known as **Pine Top Mountain**), 8,368; **Baldy Peak,** 8,378, and **Mount Livermore,** 8,206. **Emory Peak** in the Chisos Mountains at 7,825 feet is another well-known elevation.

Fort Davis in Jeff Davis County is the **highest town of any size** in Texas at 5,050 feet, and the county has the highest average elevation. The **highest state highway point** also is in the county at McDonald Observatory at the end of a tap from State Highway 118 on Mount Locke. The observatory stands at 6,781 feet, as determined by the Texas Department of Highways and Public Transportation.

The **highest railway point** is **Paisano** on the Southern Pacific in Presidio County.

Sea level is the lowest elevation determined in Texas, and it can be found in all the coastal counties. No point in the state has been found by the geological survey to be below sea level.

The following is a list of the 10 highest peaks in Texas and their locations:

The 10 Highest Peaks in Texas

Name	County	Elevation
Guadalupe Peak	Culberson	8,749
Bush Mountain	Culberson	8,631
Shumard Peak	Culberson	8,615
Bartlett Peak	Culberson	8,508
Baldy Peak	Jeff Davis	8,378
Hunter Peak (Pine Top Mtn.)	Culberson	8,368
Mount Livermore	Jeff Davis	8,206
El Capitan	Culberson	8,085
Lost Peak	Culberson	7,830
Emory Peak	Brewster	7,825

are entirely dry during periods of low rainfall, exposing bottoms of solid salt, and for years they were a source of commercial salt.

Davis Mountains

The **Davis Mountains** are principally in Jeff Davis County. The highest peak, **Mount Livermore,** (8,206 feet) is one of the highest in Texas. There are a number of mountains more than 7,000 feet high. These mountains intercept the moisture-bearing winds and receive more precipitation than elsewhere in the Trans-Pecos. They are greener with the growth of grass and forest trees than the other Trans-Pecos mountains. Noteworthy are the **San Solomon Springs** at the northern base of these mountains.

Big Bend

South of the Davis Mountains lies the **Big Bend** country, so called because it is encompassed on three sides by a great southward swing of the Rio Grande. It is a mountainous country of scant rainfall and sparse population. Its principal mountains, the **Chisos,** rise to 7,825 feet in **Mount Emory.** Along the Rio Grande are the **Santa Elena, Mariscal** and **Boquillas** canyons with rim elevations of 3,500 to 3,775 feet. They are among the noteworthy canyons of the North American continent. Because of its remarkable topography, and plant and animal life, the southern part of this region along the Rio Grande is home to the **Big Bend National Park,** with headquarters in a deep valley in the Chisos Mountains. It is a favorite recreation area.

Upper Rio Grande Valley

The Upper Rio Grande (El Paso) Valley is a narrow strip of irrigated land running down the river from El Paso for a distance of 75 miles or more. In this area are the historic towns and missions of **Ysleta, Socorro** and **San Elizario** , oldest in Texas. Cotton is the chief product of the valley, much of it long-staple variety. This limited area has a dense urban and rural population in marked contrast to the territory surrounding it.

Texas Wildlife

Texas has many native animals and birds, plus species introduced on game preserves.

More than 540 species of **birds** — about three fourths of all different species found in the United States — have been identified in Texas. (See the special feature on birdwatching, including a list of Texas birds, elsewhere in this edition.)

Some 142 species of **animals,** including some that today are extremely rare, are found in Texas.

Through efforts of the **Texas Parks and Wildlife Department** and many individual landowners involved in conservation practices, our wildlife should be a permanent resource.

Mammals

A few of the leading native mammals of Texas are described here. More complete information is found in "The Mammals of Texas," by William B. Davis, Bulletin 41 of the Texas Parks and Wildlife Department, Austin.

ARMADILLO—The **nine-banded armadillo** (Dasypus novemcinctus) is one of Texas' most interesting mammals. It has migrated north and east and is now common as far north and east as Oklahoma and Mississippi. There has been limited commercialization of the armadillo's shell in the manufacture of curios.

BADGER—The badger (Taxidea taxus) is found through West Texas, but in greatly reduced numbers since wholesale eradication of the prairie dog on which the badger preyed. It is a predator, but its pelt is valuable. The range of the badger includes the Texas Panhandle and South Texas, where it is common.

BAT—Thirty-two species of these winged mammals have been found in Texas, more than in any other state in the United States. Of these, 27 species are known residents, though they are seldom seen by the casual observer. The **Mexican free-tailed bat** (Tadarida brasiliensis) and the **cave myotis** (Myotis velifer) constitute most of the cave-dwelling bats of Southwest and West Texas. They have some economic value for their deposits of nitrogen-rich **guano.** Some commercial guano has been produced from Mason Bat Cave, Mason County; Beaver Creek Cavern, Burnet County; and from large deposits in other caves including Devil's Sink Hole in Edwards County, Blowout Cave in Blanco County and Bandera Bat Cave, Bandera County. The **big brown bat** (Eptesicus fuscus), the **red bat** (Lasiurus borealis) and the **evening bat** (Nycticeius humeralis) are found in East and Southeast Texas. The evening and big brown bats are forest and woodland dwelling mammals. Most of the rarer species of Texas bats have been found along the Rio Grande and in the Trans-Pecos. Bats can be observed at dusk near a water source, and many species may also be found foraging on insects attracted to street lights. Everywhere bats occur, they are the main predators of night-flying insects, including mosquitoes and many crop pests.

BEAR—The black bear (Ursus americanus) was formerly common throughout most of the state. It is now almost extinct, with only small pockets of animals surviving in the inaccessible river bottoms of eastern Texas and in the higher portions of the Trans-Pecos.

BEAVER—Two subspecies of beaver are found in Texas, the **Mexican beaver** (Castor canadensis mexicanus) ranging along the Rio Grande and Devils River and the **Texas beaver** (Castor canadensis texensis) which has been brought back from the verge of extinction to abundance through restocking.

BIGHORN—(See **Sheep.**)

BISON—The largest of native terrestrial wild mammals of North America, the **American bison,** or **buffalo** (Bison bison) is found today on a few ranches and in zoos. This fine animal became rare about 1885 as the result of slaughter for hides, reaching a peak about the year 1875. Estimates of the number of buffalo hides vary, but as many as 200,000 hides sold in Fort Worth at a two-day sale. Except for the interest of the late **Col. Charles Goodnight** and a few other forevisioned men, the bison might be extinct.

CAT—The jaguar (Felis onca) is probably now extinct in Texas and, along with the **ocelot, jaguarundi and margay,** is listed as rare and endangered by both federal and state wildlife agencies. The **cougar** (Felis concolor), which is also known as **mountain lion, puma, panther, Mexican cougar,** etc., is found occasionally in the broken country of the Edwards Plateau and in the Trans-Pecos Mountains and the South Texas brush country. The former **panther** of the East Texas forest, which was closely related, may be extinct in Texas but still exists in a few areas of Southeastern U.S. The **ocelot** (Felis pardalis), also known as the **leopard cat,** is found usually along the border. The **red-and-gray cat,** or **jaguarundi** (Felis yagouaroundi Geoffroy) is found in extreme South Texas. The **margay** (Felis wiedii) was reported in 1884 near Eagle Pass. The **bobcat** (Felis rufus) is found over the state in large numbers. The **feral housecat** has become a destroyer of game in many parts of Texas.

CHIPMUNK—The **gray-footed chipmunk** (Tamias canipes) is found at high altitudes in the Guadalupe and Sierra Diablo ranges of the Trans-Pecos. (See "Ground Squirrel," with which it is often confused in public reference.)

COATI—The **coati** (Nasua narica), a relative of the raccoon, is occasionally found in southern Texas. It inhabits woodland areas and feeds both on the ground and in trees. The species is also found occasionally in Big Bend National Park.

COYOTE—The **coyote** (Canis latrans), great in number, is the most destructive Texas predator of livestock. On the other hand, it is probably the most valuable predator in the balance of nature. It is a protection to crops and range lands by its control of rodents, rabbits, etc. It is found throughout the state, but is most numerous in the brush country of Southwest Texas.

DEER—The **white-tailed deer** (Odocoileus virginianus) is an important Texas game animal. Its number in Texas is estimated at 3 million. It thrives best in the wooded and broken areas of the Edwards Plateau and south of San Antonio where it often competes for feed with domestic animals. Texas Parks and Wildlife Department has had success in **transplanting** deer. In East Texas, the timbered sections of North Central Texas, and even in the thinly populated areas of Northwest Texas, the white-tailed deer population has increased greatly. The **mule deer,** (Odocoileus hemionus) is found principally in the Trans-Pecos and in smaller numbers in the less thickly settled parts of the Staked Plains. It has increased in number in recent years. The little **Del Carmen deer** (white-tailed subspecies) is found in limit-

ed numbers in the high valleys of the Chisos Mountains in the Big Bend. The **American elk** (Cervus canadensis), though not the original subspecies found in Texas, has been introduced into the Guadalupe and Davis mountains.

FERRET—The **black-footed ferret** (Mustela nigripes) was formerly found widely ranging through the West Texas country of the prairie dog on which it preyed. It is now considered extinct in Texas. It is of the same genus as the weasel and the mink.

FOX—Most common is the **gray fox** (Urocyon cinereoargenteus) found in the forested area of East Texas and throughout most of the state where there is cover, notably in the broken parts of the Edwards Plateau and the rough country at the foot of the Staked Plains. The **kit** or **Swift fox** (Vulpes velox) is found in the plains country of Northwest Texas. A second species of **kit fox** (Vulpes macrotis) is found in the Trans-Pecos and is fairly numerous in some localities. The **red fox** (Vulpes vulpes) is not a native but was introduced for sport.

GOPHER—Six species of pocket gophers occur in Texas. The **Botta's pocket gopher** (Thomomys bottae) is found in West Texas south of the High Plains, notably along the Rio Grande. The **plains pocket gopher** (Geomys bursarius) is found in the Panhandle and throughout North Central and East Texas. The **desert pocket gopher** (Geomys arenarius) and the **yellow-faced pocket gopher** (Pappogeomys castanops) are found in the Trans-Pecos. The **Texas pocket gopher** (Geomys personatus) is found in the sandy soils of the lower coastal region.

GROUND SQUIRREL—There are five or more species, living usually in the western part of the state. The **rock squirrel** (Spermophilus variegatus) is found throughout the Edwards Plateau and Trans-Pecos. The **Mexican ground squirrel** (Spermophilus mexicanus) is found in the Mexican border country from Brownsville to the Davis Mountains. The **spotted ground squirrel** (Spermophilus spilosoma) is found generally in favorable localities throughout the western half of the state. The **thirteen-lined ground squirrel** (Spermophilus tridecemlineatus) is found in the Panhandle and in a narrow strip from Red River to the Gulf between Dallas and Corpus Christi. The **Texas antelope squirrel** (Ammospermophilus interpres) is found along the Rio Grande from El Paso to Val Verde County.

JAVELINA—The javelina or **collared peccary** (Tayassu tajacu) is found in the border country of Southwest Texas. It is fairly numerous. Its meat is edible if properly prepared, and there is limited use of its hide for the manufacture of gloves and other leather articles. Hunting it with dogs is a favorite sport of that region. A scrappy animal, it is the subject of many tall tales.

MINK—The **mink** (Mustela vison) is found in East Texas and along the Coastal Belt, usually in forested river bottoms. It yields a considerable fur crop. It is akin to the otter and weasel. Mink farming, partly with native and partly with introduced species, is found on a limited scale, usually in East Texas.

MOLE—The **mole** (Scalopus aquaticus) is found generally throughout the eastern half of the state.

MUSKRAT—There are three subspecies of muskrat in Texas, the **muskrat** (Ondatra zibethica rivalicia), which is found in Southeast Texas near Beaumont where it is commercially produced on muskrat ranges; the **Pecos River muskrat** (Ondatra zibethica ripensis) of Western Texas; and the **Great Plains muskrat** (Ondatra zibethica cinnamonia) of the Panhandle region. The muskrat is one of the most valuable of Texas' fur-bearing animals. Production of pelts comes largely from the coastal area near Beaumont.

NUTRIA—This introduced species (Myocastor coypus) is found in Texas, except the Panhandle and extreme western portions. The fur is not valued too highly and, since they are in competition with muskrats, their spread is discouraged. They are used widely in Texas as a cure-all for ponds choked with vegetation.

OPOSSUM—This Texas marsupial, the Virginia opossum (Didelphis virginiana) is found in nearly all parts of the state. The opossum has economic value for its pelt, and its meat is considered a delicacy by some. It is one of the chief contributors to the Texas fur crop.

OTTER—A few **river otter** (Lutra canadensis) are found along East Texas rivers and coastal marshes. Although it is a prized fur-bearing animal, there is no evidence that the river otter can be considered either rare or endangered. The species is numerous in Liberty County where biologists have determined that its numbers have increased in recent years. While excess pop-

ulations of this species, like other forms of wildlife, can be harvested with no danger to the species, loss of habitat through encroaching civilization presents the most formidable threat to its continued existence.

PORCUPINE—The **yellow-haired porcupine** (Erethizon dorsatum) is found in small numbers in higher mountain ranges of the Trans-Pecos and has recently moved into the eastern portion of the Panhandle along the Caprock.

PRAIRIE DOG—Until recent years probably no sight was so universal in West Texas as the **black-tailed prairie dog** (Cynomys ludovicianus) and its burrow. Naturalists estimated its population in the hundreds of millions. Its destruction of range grasses, plus its peculiar susceptibility to eradication (usually by the introduction of the fumes of carbon disulphide into its burrow) have caused a great reduction in its numbers over its past range. However, it is making a comeback. **Prairie dog towns** often covered many acres with thickly spaced burrows or **prairie dog holes**. It is being propagated in several public zoos, notably in the prairie dog town in **Mackenzie Park** at Lubbock. It has been accorded its monument in Texas in the name of the **Prairie Dog Town Fork** of the Red River, along one segment of which is located the beautiful Palo Duro Canyon.

PRONGHORN—The **Pronghorn** (Antilocapra americana) is primarily a plains animal. It almost became extinct, but a continuous closed season and a sound management program raised its numbers. There have been limited open seasons since 1944. Specifically, these animals inhabit the plains and basin regions of Brewster, Presidio, Jeff Davis, Culberson and Hudspeth counties. They have also sufficiently increased in numbers in the Permian Basin and Panhandle to permit open seasons in recent years.

RABBIT—The **black-tailed jack rabbit** (Lepus californicus) is found throughout Texas except in the East Texas forest area. It breeds rapidly, and its long hind legs make it one of the world's faster-running animals. The **Eastern cottontail** (Sylvilagus floridanus) is found throughout Texas except in Trans-Pecos region. The **desert cottontail** (Sylvilagus auduboni) is found in South and West Texas, usually on the open range. The **swamp rabbit** (Sylvilagus aquaticus) is found in East Texas and the coastal area.

RACCOON—The **raccoon** (Procyon lotor) is found along streams throughout Texas.

RATS AND MICE—There are 40 or 50 species of rats and mice in Texas of varying characteristics, habitats and economic destructiveness. The **Norway rat** (Rattus norvegicus) and the **black rat** (Rattus rattus) are probably the most common and the most destructive. Some of the species are native, and others, notably the Norway rat, are invaders. The common **house mouse** (Mus musculis) is estimated in the hundreds of millions annually. The rare **Guadalupe Mountain vole** (Microtus mexicanus guadalupensis) is found only in the **Guadalupe Mountains National Park** and just over the border into New Mexico.

RINGTAIL—The **ringtail** (Bassariscus astutus) is found generally in wooded areas west of the Trinity and in the broken sections of the Edwards Plateau. It is a valuable fur-bearing mammal.

SHEEP—The barbary, or **Aoudad, sheep** (Ammotragus lervia), first introduced to the Palo Duro Canyon area in 1957-58, have become firmly established. Barbary sheep have been introduced into many areas of Texas, but are designated as game animals in only eight counties of the Panhandle surrounding Palo Duro Canyon. Efforts are now under way by the Texas Parks and Wildlife Department to establish the **desert bighorn** (Ovis canadensis) in range formerly occupied.

SHREW—Three species are found in Texas, the **northern short-tailed shrew** (Blarina brevicauda), the **least shrew** (Cryptotis parva) and the **desert shrew** (Notiosorex crawfordi). The first-mentioned is rarer, occurring in the Big Thicket. The least shrew is found generally in South Central and East Texas. The gray shrew is found in very limited numbers in the semiarid areas of West Texas and along the border.

SKUNK—There are six species of skunk in Texas. The **Eastern spotted skunk** (Spilogale putorius) is found throughout North Texas. A small skunk, it is often erroneously called civet cat. This skunk also is found in East Texas and the Gulf area. The **Western spotted skunk** (Spilogale gracilis) is found in the central, western and southern parts of the state. The **long-tailed**, or **broad-striped skunk** (Mephitis mephitis) is found in many parts of the state, usually along streams or in wooded areas. The **hooded skunk** (Mephitis macroura) is found in limited numbers in the Trans-Pecos mountains. The **Gulf Coast hog-nosed skunk** (Conepatus leuconotus), found in the Brownsville area, ranges southward into Mexico. The **mountain hog-nosed skunk** (Conepatus mesoleucus) is found in sparsely timbered areas of Edwards Plateau, Central Texas, Trans-Pecos.

SQUIRREL—The **fox squirrel** (Sciurus niger) is found throughout East, Central and West Central Texas. The **gray,** or **cat, squirrel** (Sciurus carolinensis) is found generally in the eastern third of the state. The **flying squirrel** (Glaucomys volans) is widely distributed in the Piney Woods and the East Texas Post Oak Belt.

WEASEL—The **brindled** or **long-tailed weasel** (Mustela frenata), akin to the mink, is found in the Panhandle-Plains and South Texas.

WOLF—The **red wolf** (Canis rufus) was once found over a wide range in Eastern and Central Texas. It is now considered extirpated from the wild, with the only known remnants of the population now in captive propagation. The **gray wolf** (Canis lupus) once had a wide range over Central, Southern and Western Texas. It has been reduced almost to extinction. The **red wolf** and **gray wolf** are listed on the federal and state rare and endangered species lists; the few **gray wolves** which may be encountered in Texas are believed to be occasional individuals crossing over from Mexico.

Reptiles and Arachnids

Most of the more than 100 species of **snakes** found in Texas are beneficial as also are other reptiles. There are **15 poisonous species** and subspecies and there are more cases of snakebite reported in Texas than any other state. Principal **poisonous reptiles** include three kinds of **copperheads** (Southern, Broadbanded and Trans-Pecos); one kind of **cottonmouth;** 10 kinds of **rattlesnakes** (western massasauga, desert massasauga, western pigmy, western diamondback, timber, banded rock, mottled rock, blacktailed, Mojave and prairie); and the **Texas coral snake.**

Also noteworthy are the **horned lizard; the vinegarroon,** a type of **whip scorpion; tarantulas,** a hairy spider; and **alligators.**

State Wildlife Areas

In addition to national wildlife refuges in the state of Texas, there are **two public lands programs** administered by the Texas Parks and Wildlife Department. A brief description of each program is given below. For further information concerning public use opportunities on state public lands, write to **Texas Parks and Wildlife,** 4200 Smith School Rd., Austin 78744, or call 1-800-792-1112.

Type II public lands are lands leased and managed by the Department to provide public hunting and recreation opportunities. Access to Type II properties is by one of two types of permits: consumptive use permit (hunting and fishing allowed) and limited use permit (may not hunt or fish). Since there are more than 80 of these Type II lands and most are small, they will not be described here. A Parks and Wildlife Department map booklet detailing the areas, rules and regulations is issued with the purchase of a permit.

Type I public lands are wildlife management areas (WMAs) where research is conducted concerning the conservation, management and wise use of wildlife resources and habitats. Hunting is regulated by one of three permit systems: permission by registration (no cost), regular permit (nominal daily fee) and special permit (permit fee assessed for successfully drawn applicants). A brief description of each Type I area is given below:

Candy Cain Abshier WMA (Chambers County) is a 207-acre tract managed primarily for non-game wildlife. Located on Smith Point, approximately 25 miles south of Anahuac, the area is popular with birdwatchers during the spring and fall. No public facilities are available on the area but commercial facilities are nearby.

Atkinson Island WMA (Harris County) consists of 151 acres of wading shorebird habitat adjacent to the Houston Ship Channel. The area is accessible only by boat and there are no public use facilities on the island.

Brazos Bend State Park (Fort Bend County) consists of 4,900 acres approximately 20 miles southeast of Richmond, mostly in the Brazos River floodplain. Plantlife includes oaks, pecan and numerous species of shrubs and vines. Waterproof footwear recommended.

Walter Buck WMA (Kimble County) includes 2,123 acres on the South Fork of the Llano River approximately three miles southwest of Junction. The gently rolling terrain is punctuated by canyons with dense stands of ashe juniper, elm and live oak. White-tailed deer are numerous, along with some feral Spanish goats and free-ranging axis and sika deer. Wild turkey are seasonally abundant. No camping or fires are permitted on the area, but camping is permitted at South Llano River State Park nearby; commercial facilities are available in Junction.

Chaparral WMA (La Salle and Dimmit counties), consisting of 15,200 acres eight miles west of Artesia Wells, is vegetated by plant life representative of South Texas brush country: thorny brush, or "chaparral," includes mesquite, pricklypear cactus, granjeno, blackbrush and leatherstem. The terrain is flat to gently rolling. The deer population is moderate; native javelina and feral hogs are numerous; quail and mourning doves are seasonally abundant; Western diamondback rattlesnakes are common. A primitive campground is available for hunters; commercial facilities can be found nearby.

Colorado Bend State Park (San Saba and Lampasas counties) consists of 4,592 acres on the Colorado River, approximately 10 miles above Lake Buchanan. The flat to gently rolling terrain is cut by Gorman and Spicewood creeks. Uplands support ashe juniper and live oak, and there are numerous white-tailed deer. Primitive camping is permitted; open campfires are prohibited. There is no electricity available; drinking water and chemical toilets are provided.

Dam B WMA (Jasper and Tyler counties) is located on the upper reaches of B. A. Steinhagen Lake. Its 13,445 acres of land and water are generally flat with many sloughs separated by low ridges. Waterproof footwear, preferably knee-length, is recommended. Trees include oaks and hickories, cedar elm, American hornbeam, black and sweet gums, greenbriers, holly and hawthorn. Common near water are cypress, tupelo, water elm and buttonbush. Good populations of white-tailed deer, gray and fox squirrels, cottontail and swamp rabbits and waterfowl are found on the area. Access is by boat only; airboats are prohibited on the Angelina-Neches Scientific Area of the WMA. Permits are required for camping.

James E. Daughtrey WMA (Live Oak and McMullen counties) is located between Three Rivers and Tilden. Approximately 8,000 acres surrounding Choke Canyon Reservoir are available for public hunting. The rolling terrain is covered with thorny brush dominated by mesquite, blackbrush and cacti. Wildlife on the area includes a large deer population along with javelina, turkey, quail, mourning dove, waterfowl and feral hogs. Roads are primitive.

Elephant Mountain WMA (Brewster County) consists of 23,000 acres approximately 26 miles south of Alpine. Vegetation consists of juniper, pinyon, Spanish oak, mesquite, sotol, yucca, lechuguilla and cacti. There is a well-established deer population and a small herd of pronghorn. Other game includes javelina, quail and doves. Desert bighorn sheep were released on the area in 1987 and are slowly increasing. Primitive camping is allowed; campfires are permitted, but wood must be brought in. Water facilities are unreliable; hunters should bring all water.

Gus Engeling WMA (Anderson County) comprises 10,941 acres northwest of Palestine and 32 miles southeast of Corsicana. Wildlife research station operated by Parks and Wildlife for the Post Oak Savannah Ecological Region of East Texas. The flat to gently rolling post-oak woodlands, include dense stands of oak-hickory overstory, along with yaupon, greenbrier, dogwood, hawthorn, elm and huckleberry. Wildlife includes numerous deer, feral hogs, squirrels, quail, mourning dove, waterfowl and turkey.

Granger WMA (Williamson County), located three miles southeast of Granger, comprises 11,116 acres of upland grassland with some bottomland hardwoods. The gently rolling terrain supports wildlife including mourning dove, quail, fox squirrel, rabbits, pheasant and migrant waterfowl. Only shotguns are allowed on the area. There is no camping on the area, but Corps of

Engineer campgrounds are available around Granger Lake.

Guadalupe Delta WMA (Calhoun County), consisting of 4,669 acres of marsh 3.5 miles northeast of Tivoli is managed primarily for waterfowl and migratory shore birds, alligators and other wetland wildlife.

Hill Country Natural Area (Bandera and Medina counties) is a 4,753-acre tract located southwest of Bandera. Gently rolling to hilly terrain supports vegetation that is primarily live oak grassland. White-tailed deer are numerous. Camping permitted only in designated primitive camping area; no groundfires are permitted, but containerized fuel stoves can be used. All water and other supplies must be brought in. Water in area is unusable even after boiling and treatment.

Gene Howe WMA (Hemphill County) consists of 5,821 acres of rolling sandhills with large natural meadows

Hunting, Fishing Licenses

A hunting license is required of Texas residents and nonresidents of Texas who hunt any bird or animal. Hunting licenses and stamps are valid during the period September 1 through the following August 31 of each year, except those issued for a specific number of days and lifetime licenses. A hunting license (except the nonresident special hunting license and non-resident 5-day special hunting license) is valid for taking all legal species of wildlife in Texas including deer, turkey, javelina, antelope, aoudad sheep and all small game and migratory game birds. Special licenses and tags are required for taking alligators, and a trapper's license is required to hunt fur-bearing animals.

All sport fishing licenses and stamps are valid only during the period September 1 through August 31, except those issued for a specific number of days and lifetime licenses.

In addition to sports hunting and fishing licenses, hunting/fishing stamps are required for special hunting/fishing privileges.

Detailed information concerning licenses, stamps, seasons, regulations and related information can be obtained from: Texas Parks and Wildlife Department, 4200 Smith School Road, Austin, Texas 78744 (1-800-792-1112).

The Texas Parks and Wildlife Department reported revenue of $33.7 million from sales of all licenses during fiscal 1990, a decrease of some $26,000 over fiscal 1988. In excess of 3 million licenses were sold. Various types of sports hunting and fishing licenses with fees and number sold during fiscal year 1990 are listed below.

Licenses Sold During FY 1990

Type of License	Fee (FY 1990)	Number Sold
Resident Hunting	$10.00	272,924
Special Resident Hunting (Exempt)	6.00	159,523
Resident Lifetime Hunting	300.00	420
Resident Comb. Hunting & Fishing	15.00	671,028
Resident Lifetime Comb. Hunting & Fishing	500.00	750
Resident Alligator Hunter's	35.00	908
Resident Trapper's	10.75	14,134
Nonresident General Hunting	200.00	14,704
Nonresident Special Hunting (Small Game)	75.00	1,712
Non-resident 5-Day Special Hunting (Small Game)	$25.00	16,764
White-Winged Dove Stamp	6.00	39,068
Archery Hunting Stamp	6.00	80,495
Texas Waterfowl Stamp	5.00	111,162
Resident Fishing	8.00	1,047,997
Temporary Resident Fishing (14-Day)	5.00	40,329
Special Resident Fishing	1.50	5,925
Nonresident Fishing	15.00	48,202
Temporary Nonresident Fishing (5-Day)	8.00	62,536
Freshwater Trout Stamp	5.00	33,088
Saltwater Sportfishing Stamp	5.00	580,388

There were **477,000 white-tailed deer killed** in the 1989-90 hunting season, compared to 475,000 in the 1988-89 season. **Wild turkey killed** in 1989-90 estimated at 87,403. There were 6,800 mule deer killed in 1989-90, compared to 7,300 the previous season. The **javelina** harvest was 18,500 in 1988-89 and 21,300 in 1989-90.

along the north bank of the Canadian River. Woody cover is provided by sumac, plum and sagebrush; riparian habitat along the river is primarily persimmon, cottonwood and buttonbush. There are well-established populations of deer, turkey, quail and mourning dove. Open fires are not permitted; hunters may use gas camp stoves. Water is available. High-clearance or four-wheel drive vehicles are recommended.

Keechi Creek WMA (Leon County), a waterfowl management area, consists of 1,500 acres approximately 10 miles south of Oakwood. The terrain is principally bottomland intersected with creek drainages containing numerous standing-water sloughs; vegetation includes willow, water and overcup oaks, elm and sweetgum. Principal wildlife species are eastern turkey, deer, squirrels, feral hogs and woodland waterfowl. Camping is not allowed on the area; commercial facilities are available nearby. Waterproof footwear, preferably knee-length, is recommended.

Kerr WMA (Kerr County), 6,493 acres located on the headwaters of the North Fork of the Guadalupe River 12 miles west of Hunt, is typical of the Edwards Plateau, with rolling hills, fresh water springs, dense cedar brakes and live oak-shin oak thickets. Wildlife includes Rio Grande turkey, mourning dove, quail, javelina, armadillo, fox, gray squirrels, threatened black-capped vireo and golden-cheeked warbler. No camping or fires are allowed on the area. Camping is available at Kerrville-Schreiner State Park; commercial facilities can be found nearby.

Kickapoo Cavern Park Site (Kinney and Edwards counties) is located 22 miles north of Brackettville in the southernmost extension of the Edwards Plateau. Vegetation consists of a mixture of live oak, ashe juniper, mountain laurel, mesquite and pinyon pine. Good populations of white-tailed deer and Rio Grande turkey, plus white-winged doves, Meam's quail, black-capped vireos and golden-cheeked warblers are found in the area. The site is undeveloped; there are no facilities. Camping is not permitted and no open fires are allowed. All water, food and other supplies must be brought in. Commercial facilities available close by.

Las Palomas WMA (Cameron, Hidalgo, Starr, Willacy and Presidio counties) comprises 16 units, more than 3,900 acres in all, most covered by native brush vegetation, some open farmland, and some wetlands, which is managed primarily as habitat for white-winged doves. Other wildlife includes black-bellied tree ducks, chachalacas, mourning doves, javelina, scaled quail, mule deer, ocelot and jaguarundi. Camping is permitted on some units, not on others. Check with Department of Parks and Wildlife for details.

Lower Neches WMA (Orange County) consists of 5,591 acres of coastal marsh located near the upper end of Sabine Lake. The area is managed primarily for wintering waterfowl, migratory shore birds and alligators. Hunting is permitted on specified days during the season. A boat launching ramp is available near the south end of the area, but no other public facilities have been developed.

Mad Island WMA (Matagorda County), located five miles west of the town of Matagorda, consists of 5,700 acres of marsh, surrounded by extensive agricultural and native pasture uplands. Water diversion and control structures are being developed to reduce the amount of saltwater intrusion into fresh-water marshlands caused by the Gulf Intracoastal Waterway. Mad Island is the winter home of a wide assortment of puddle and diver ducks, sandhill cranes, snow, Canada and white-fronted geese. There is a substantial alligator population, along with mottled duck, raccoon, river otter, mink, armadillo, white-tailed deer, bobcat, gray fox and cottontail, jack and swamp rabbits.

Matagorda Island WMA (Calhoun County) contains 7,000 acres used as a conservation park unit and 36,900 acres comprising the WMA. The island, which is approximately 35 miles long, averaging two miles wide, is located 5.5 miles off the mainland coast. Access is by boat only; aircraft are not allowed to land on island. The terrain is primarily sand dunes and barrier flats vegetated by cordgrass, sunflowers, grass bur, vetch, daisy and bermuda grass. Bayside marshes are habitat for endangered whooping crane and many varieties of waterfowl. Only primitive camping is allowed; all water and other supplies must be brought in. No telephone, electricity or other public utilities are available.

Old Tunnel WMA (Kendall County) consists of 10.5 acres of Hill Country habitat and includes an abandoned railroad tunnel, which serves as a summer roost site for bats. There are no public use facilities on the area, but facilities are available 13 miles away at Comfort.

Pat Mayse WMA (Lamar County), located 12 miles northwest of Paris, consists of 8,925 acres of land and water adjacent to and including part of Pat Mayse Reservoir. The terrain is primarily upland oak woodlands with some bottomland hardwood habitat vegetated primarily by post and blackjack oak, pecan, hackberry, cottonwood and Osage orange, with open savannahs containing many tall grasses. Camping is allowed in designated areas.

J.D. Murphree WMA (Jefferson County) is approximately 13,250 acres of water marsh along the upper Texas coast, divided into three units. It is managed primarily for preservation and enhancement of the marsh complex for wintering and resident waterfowl and associated wildlife. Airboats are restricted to certain areas. All supplies must be brought in; commercial facilities are available nearby.

Peach Point WMA (Brazoria County) is located five miles west of Freeport, containing 10,312 acres of upland hardwood, upland prairie, fresh and saltwater marshes. Vegetation is dominated by live oak, elm and pecan; also Chinese tallow, baccharis and elm, sea ox-eye and shortgrass. Peach Point is home to waterfowl, rails, gallinules, mourning doves, quail, squirrel and white-tailed deer, cottontail rabbits, armadillo, feral hogs, alligators and various shore birds. No camping or open fires are allowed. Commercial facilities are available nearby.

Pedernales Falls State Park (Blanco County) contains 4,860 acres approximately nine miles east of Johnson City. The terrain is flat to rolling, vegetated with live oak and ashe juniper. White-tailed and exotic deer are common. Camping facilities are available.

Playa Lakes WMA (Moore, Castro and Hartley counties) consists of three tracts in the Panhandle totalling 2,-240 acres, managed for waterfowl and other wildlife species associated with playa lakes. At present no hunting is permitted on these areas.

Sea Rim State Park (Jefferson County) consists of 15,109 acres of Gulf coast beach and marshland about 10 miles west of Sabine Pass. Its marsh estuarine system is an important nursery ground for marine life and is part of the most important waterfowl wintering area in the Central Flyway. No camping is permitted; food and other supplies must be brought in. Commercial facilities are available nearby.

Sierra Diablo WMA (Hudspeth and Culberson counties), located in the mountain range of same name, consists of 10,991 acres approximately 32 miles northnorthwest of Van Horn. Rough, rugged hills and steep canyons make up most of the area, with an average elevation of 6,200 feet, breaking sharply to desert floor to east. There is a well-established desert mule deer population. The WMA is used for bighorn sheep broodstock production and there are free-ranging bighorns on the area. Only primitive camping is allowed on area; all water and other supplies must be brought in. The nearest commercial facilites are one-and-one-half hours away.

Somerville State Recreation Area (Burleson and Lee counties) contains approximately 5,000 acres of post oak, hickory, blackjack oak and water oak with dense stands of yaupon. The terrain is flat to gently rolling. Whitetailed deer are numerous. Camping is permitted on area.

Somerville WMA (Burleson and Lee counties), located 12 miles west southwest of Somerville, comprises 3,180 acres of Post Oak Savannah habitat with post, water and blackjack oak and hickory, along with yaupon, coralberry, American beautyberry, greenbrier and grape. The terrain is flat to gently rolling and wildlife on the area includes white-tailed deer, squirrel, rabbit and migrant waterfowl. Camping is permitted on the area.

Welder Flats Coastal Preserve (Calhoun County) consists of 1,480 acres of submerged coastal wetlands managed to perpetuate and enhance the natural resources thereon and to provide recreational opportunities that are compatible with these purposes. Numerous species of wading and shore birds use the preserve, with the most distinctive being the whooping crane. Hunting and fishing are permitted in conformance with general regulations for Calhoun County.

Texas Endangered and Threatened Species

The following species of Texas flora and fauna are either endangered or threatened as of June 1, 1991, according to the Texas Parks and Wildlife Department. Strict laws protect species identified as endangered or threatened, and it is generally unlawful to take, possess, transport, export, process, sell or offer for sale, or ship any species of fish or wildlife within the state or sell or offer for sale any goods made from the fish and wildlife in this list not born or raised in captivity. Any questions about the wildlife and plants in the following lists and the laws covering them should be directed to the **Endangered Resources Branch, Texas Department of Parks and Wildlife, 4200 Smith School Road, Austin 78744, or call 1-800-792-1112.**

Endangered Species
Animals
Mammals: Bat, Mexican long-nosed; Bear, black; Coati; Ferret, black-footed; Jaguar; Jaguarundi; Manatee; Margay; Ocelot; Whale — black right, blue, fin, sperm; Wolf — gray, red.

Birds: Crane, whooping; Curlew, Eskimo; Eagle, bald; Falcon — American peregrine, Aplomado; Pelican, brown; Prairie-chicken, Attwater's greater; Tern, interior least; Vireo, black-capped; Woodpecker — Ivorybilled, Red-cockaded.

Reptiles: Snakes: Racer, speckled; Snake — Concho water, Louisiana pine, Northern cat-eyed, Western smooth green. Turtles: Big Bend mud; Hawksbill, Atlantic; Leatherback; Loggerhead; Ridley, Atlantic.

Amphibians: Frog, white-lipped; Newt, blackspotted; Salamander — Blanco blind, Texas blind; Siren, Rio Grande lesser; Toad, Houston.

Fishes: Darter, fountain; Gambusia — Big Bend, blotched, Clear Creek, Pecos, San Marcos; Goby, blackfin; Paddlefish; Pupfish — Comanche Springs, Leon Springs; Shiner — bluntnose, phantom; Sturgeon, shovelnose.

Invertebrates: Ground beetle, Tooth Cave; Harvestman, Bee Creek Cave; Mold beetle, Kretschmar Cave; Pseudoscorpion, Tooth Cave; Spider, Tooth Cave.

Plants
Cacti: Cactus — black lace, Lloyd's hedgehog, Nellie cory, Sneed pincushion, Tobusch fishhook; Pitaya, Davis' green.

Grasses and Grass-like Plants: Wild-rice, Texas.

Orchids: Navasota ladies'-tresses.

Trees, Shrubs and Sub-Shrubs: Frankenia, Johnston's; Snowbells, Texas.

Wildflowers: Bladderpod, white; Dogweed, ashy; Poppy-mallow, Texas; Prairie dawn; Rush-pea, slender; Verbena, large-fruited sand.

Threatened Species
Animals
Mammals: Bat — Rafinesque's big-eared, Southern yellow, Spotted; Dolphin — Atlantic spotted, Roughtoothed; Mouse, Palo Duro; Rat — Coues' rice, Texas kangaroo; Whale — Dwarf sperm, False killer, Gervais' beaked, Goose-beaked, Killer, Pygmy killer, Pygmy sperm, Short-finned pilot.

Birds: Becard, rose-throated; Egret, reddish; Falcon, Arctic peregrine; Hawk — Common black, Gray, Whitetailed, Zone-tailed; Ibis, white-faced; Kite, American swallow-tailed; Owl, ferruginous pygmy; Parula, tropical; Plover, piping; Sparrow — Bachman's, Botteri's; Stork, wood; Tern, sooty; Tyrannulet, northern beardless; Warbler, golden- cheeked.

Reptiles: Turtles: Tortoise, Texas; Turtle — Alligator snapping, Atlantic green. Lizards: Gecko, reticulated; Lizard — Mountain short-horned, Reticulate collared, Texas horned. Snakes: Rattlesnake, timber; Snake — Big Bend blackhead, Black-striped, Brazos water, Northern scarlet, Texas indigo, Texas lyre, Texas scarlet.

Amphibians: Frog, sheep; Salamander — Cascade Caverns, Comal blind, San Marcos; Toad, Mexican burrowing; Treefrog, Mexican.

Fishes: Blindcat — Toothless, Widemouth; Chub, Rio Grande; Chubsucker, creek; Darter — Blackside, Rio Grande; Goby, river; Minnow, Devils River; Pipefish, opossum; Pupfish — Conchos, Pecos; Shiner — Bluehead, Chihuahua, Proserpine; Stoneroller, Mexican; Sucker, blue.

Plants
Cacti: Bunched cory, Chisos Mountain, Lloyd's mariposa.

Trees: Oak, Hinckley's.

Wildflowers: Pennyroyal, McKittrick.

National Wildlife Refuges

In addition to the many state and national parks that can be reached from most major cities in Texas, there are 14 national wildlife refuges that may be visited at different times of the year for bird watching and wildlife viewing. It is best to write before visiting to check on facilities available and to be sure the refuge is open to visitors at that time. Addresses are given at the end of the description of each refuge.

Texas has more than 250,000 acres set aside in its 14 national wildlife refuges. Short sketches of each are given below from information supplied by the **U.S. Fish and Wildlife Service**, U.S. Department of the Interior.

Anahuac

The more than 28,000 acres of this refuge are located along the upper Texas Gulf Coast in Chambers County. The fresh and saltwater marshes and miles of beautiful, sweeping coastal prairie provide wintering habitat for large concentrations of **geese** and other waterfowl. The **peregrine falcon** and **bald eagle**, both endangered species, also find protection on the refuge. Other species of interest include the **alligator, mottled duck, wood stork** and **least tern**. Fishing, bird watching and waterfowl hunting are available. Address: Box 278, Anahuac 77514. Phone (409)267-3337.

Aransas

Located midway between Rockport and Port Lavaca on the Gulf Coast eight miles southeast of Austwell, this refuge comprises 58,763 acres of oak woodlands, fresh and saltwater marshes and coastal grasslands. Besides providing wintering grounds for the endangered **whooping crane**, the refuge is home to **deer, javelina, alligator** and many other species of wildlife. Bird life abounds from late fall to early May. A visitor center, open daily from 7:30 a.m. to 4:30 p.m., offers information and interpretive exhibits. Other facilities include an observation tower, picnic area, paved auto tour route and walking trails. Entrance fee. Address: Box 100, Austwell 77950. Phone (512)286-3559. Information about the opportunities available at nearby **Matagorda Island**, a coastal barrier island managed jointly with the Texas Parks and Wildlife Department, can also be obtained from this address.

Attwater Prairie Chicken

Established on July 1, 1972, to preserve habitat for the endangered **Attwater's prairie chicken**, the refuge comprises 7,980 acres of land consisting of native prairie, potholes, sandy knolls and some wooded areas. A 12-mile auto tour route is available year-round, and 350 acres of marsh are accessible for fall and winter birding. Blind and guided tours are available to observe the prairie chickens from February 1 through April 30. Hours of access to the refuge vary by season. Address: Box 518, Eagle Lake 77434. Phone (409)234-3021.

Big Boggy

This refuge was established on 4,377 acres of coastal prairie and salt marsh along East Matagorda Bay on the Gulf Coast for the benefit of wintering waterfowl, attracting thousands of ducks and geese to its ponds and potholes. The refuge is generally closed, and visitors are encouraged to visit nearby San Bernard or Brazoria refuges. Waterfowl hunting is permitted in season. Address: Box 1088, Angleton 77515. Phone (409)849-6062.

Brazoria

The almost 40,854 acres of this refuge, located along the Gulf coast in Brazoria County, serve as nesting area for **mottled ducks**. The refuge also supports many marsh and water birds, from **roseate spoonbills** and **great blue herons** to **white ibis** and **sandhill cranes**. Brazoria Refuge is within the Freeport Christmas Bird Count circle, which frequently achieves the highest number of species seen in a 24-hour period. The refuge has an open house the first weekend of every month throughout the year, when visitors can drive the refuge tour route to observe wildlife in a coastal environment. Fishing is permitted, as well as waterfowl hunting in season; however, access for these activities is by boat only. Address: Box 1088, Angleton 77515. Phone (409)849-6062.

Buffalo Lake

Comprising about 8,000 acres in Randall County in the Panhandle, this refuge has been one of the major waterfowl refuges in the Central Flyway. At present, the lake is dry, with the dam and spillway needing major rehabilitation. When water is available in this semi-arid environment, the refuge's marshes and lake provide a resting and feeding area for migrating waterfowl. Activities available include picnicking, sightseeing, birding, nature study, photography and camping. Entrance fee. Address: Box 228, Umbarger 79091. Phone (806)499-3382.

Hagerman

Hagerman National Wildlife Refuge lies on the Big Mineral arm of Texoma Lake in Grayson County. The 11,320 acres provide a feeding and resting place for migrating waterfowl. The refuge includes 3,000 acres of marsh and water and 8,000 acres of farmland, grassland and woodlands. Bird watching and fishing are the most popular activities. Hunting is permitted during limited seasons in designated areas. Address: Rt. 3, Box 123, Sherman 75090-9564. Phone (214)786-2826.

Laguna Atascosa

Established in 1946 as southernmost waterfowl refuge in the Central Flyway, this refuge contains more than 45,000 acres fronting on the Laguna Madre in the Lower Rio Grande Valley. Its open lagoons, coastal prairies, salt flats and brushlands support large numbers of wintering **ducks**, including the United States' largest concentration of wintering **redheads**. **White-tailed deer, javelina, armadillo** and **Texas tortoise** can be found, along with the rare **ocelot**. Bird watching and nature study are popular, with migratory birds present in the winter and **exotic Mexican birds** year-round. Saltwater fishing is permitted in the Harlingen Ship Channel. Bow and rifle hunts are held most years for deer and feral hogs. Entrance fee. Address: Box 450, Rio Hondo 78583. Phone (512)748-3607.

Lower Rio Grande Valley

The U.S. Fish and Wildlife Service is slowly acquiring land in the Lower Rio Grande Valley for a new national refuge, which will encompass some 107,500 acres within the four-county area of Cameron, Hidalgo, Starr and Willacy counties. Area acquired for the refuge will include 10 different habitat types, including sabal palm forest, tidal flats, coastal brushland, mid-delta thorn forest, woodland potholes and basins, upland thorn scrub, flood forest, barretal, riparian woodland and Chihuahuan thorn forest. At least 115 unique vertebrate species that are listed as endangered, threatened, or which occur at the periphery of their range call the area home. Funds to purchase lands for the refuge come from the Federal Land and Water Conservation Fund, whose monies come from sale of Outer Continental Shelf oil and gas leases, taxes on motorboat fuels and the sale of certain surplus federal lands. For more information, contact Santa Ana/ Lower Rio Grande Valley National Wildlife Refuges, Rt. 2, Box 202A, Alamo 78516. Phone (512)787-7861.

McFaddin

Purchased in 1979 and 1980 with duck stamp revenues, this refuge's 42,955 acres are of great importance to wintering populations of migratory waterfowl. The endangered **southern bald eagle** and **peregrine falcon** are rare visitors, but may occasionally be seen during peak fall and spring migrations. One of the densest populations of **alligators** in Texas is found here. Activities on the refuge include wildlife observation, waterfowl hunting, fishing, crabbing, swimming, camping and picnicking. Address: Box 609, Sabine Pass 77655. Phone (409)971-2909.

Muleshoe

Oldest of national refuges in Texas, Muleshoe provides winter habitat for waterfowl and the continent's largest wintering population of **sandhill cranes**. Comprising 5,809 acres in the high plains of Bailey County, the refuge consists of three playa lakes, marsh areas, caliche outcroppings and native grasslands. Tour roads are available as well as a **prairie dog town**, nature trail, campground and picnic area. Address: Box 549, Muleshoe 79347. Phone (806)946-3341.

San Bernard

Located on the Gulf of Mexico near Freeport, this refuge's nearly 25,000 acres attract migrating waterfowl, including thousands of **snow geese**, which spend the winter on the refuge. Habitats consist of coastal prairies, salt/mud flats and saltwater and freshwater ponds and potholes. Visitors enjoy photography and bird watching; fishing is permitted, as well as waterfowl hunting in season. A special permit waterfowl hunt is conducted three days per week. Contact refuge office for details. Address: Box 1088, Angleton 77515. Phone: (409)849-6062.

Santa Ana

Established in 1943 and referred to as "**gem of the National Wildlife Refuge System**," Santa Ana's more than 2,000 acres of subtropical forest and native brushland provide habitat for many unusual birds. Located on the north bank of the Rio Grande in Hidalgo County, the refuge attracts many birders who come from across the United States to view many species of **Mexican birds** as they reach the northern edge of their ranges in South Texas. Also finding sanctuary on this refuge are **ocelot** and **jaguarundi**, endangered members of the cat family.

Address: Rt. 2, Box 202A, Alamo 78516. Phone (512)787-3079.

Texas Point

Purchased in 1979 with duck stamp revenues, Texas Point's 8,952 acres are located on the Upper Gulf Coast, where they serve a large wintering population of waterfowl as well as migratory birds. The endangered **southern bald eagle** and **peregrine falcon** may occasionally be seen during peak fall and spring migrations. **Alligators** are commonly observed during the spring, summer and fall months. Activities include wildlife observation, waterfowl hunting, fishing and crabbing. Access to the refuge is by boat and on foot only. Address: Box 609, Sabine Pass 77655. Phone (409)971-2909.

The 1991 Waterfowl Stamp features the wood duck as painted by artist Daniel Smith. Photo courtesy Collectors Covey.

Wildlife Stamps and Prints

Information in the following article was furnished by the Texas Parks and Wildlife Dept., 4200 Smith School Road, Austin, TX 78744, and Collectors Covey, Box 57306, Dallas, TX 75207.

Since 1981, the Texas Parks and Wildlife Department has funded some of its acquisition, development and management of natural areas with the sale of wildlife stamps and matching art prints, designed by leading wildlife artists. There are currently three types of state-issued wildlife stamps, as described below. (There are various other stamps issued and sold by non-profit organizations for the benefit of wildlife habitats. Because of space limitations, only the state-authorized stamps and prints are discussed here.)

Waterfowl Stamp: Commonly called a "Duck Stamp," the waterfowl stamp has been required of all waterfowl hunters since Fiscal Year 1982. Funds from the sale of waterfowl stamps and prints may be used for research, management and protection of waterfowl, for the acquisition, lease or development of waterfowl habitats in the state and for grants to international non-profit organizations for the purpose of acquiring, developing and maintaining waterfowl propagation areas in Canada. Subjects of waterfowl stamp artwork and artists are: 1981, mallards, Larry Hayden; 1982, pintails, Ken Carlson; 1983, American widgeons, Maynard Reece; 1984, wood ducks, David Maass; 1985, lesser snow geese, John P. Cowan; 1986, green-winged teal, Herb Booth; 1987, white-fronted geese, Gary Moss; 1988, pintails, John P. Cowan; 1989, mallards, David Maass; 1990, American wigeon, Robert Bateman; 1991, wood duck, Daniel Smith.

Saltwater Stamp: Funds from the saltwater stamp, which has been required of all saltwater fishermen since 1986, may be used for coastal fisheries and management. In 1986, the featured fish was the redfish as depicted by artist John P. Cowan; in 1987, the spotted seatrout, by Al Barnes; 1988, redfish, Herb Booth; 1989, speckled trout, John P. Cowan; 1990, redfish, John Dearman; 1991, speckled trout, Al Agnew.

Non-game and Endangered Species Stamp: A non-game and endangered species stamp, the only one of the three wildlife stamps that is not a user stamp, was offered for the first time in 1985. Funds from sale of the non-game stamps and art prints are used for acquisition and development of habitats for, surveys of, research and management of, protection and restoration of, and dissemination of information about non-game and endangered species. The 1985 non-game stamp and art subject was the whooping crane by artist Ken Carlson; 1986, Attwater's prairie chicken by John P. Cowan; 1987, the bald eagle by artist Bob Kuhn; 1988, kestrels, Charles Beckendorf; 1989, ocelot, Al Agnew; 1990, Mearn's quail, Sherrie Russell Meline; 1991, white-tailed hawk, Pamela Davis-King.

The white-tailed hawk is the subject of the 1991 Non-game and Endangered Species Stamp design by artist Pamela Davis-King. Photo courtesy Collectors Covey.

Research Facilities, Fish Hatcheries

The **Texas Parks and Wildlife Department** (TP&WD)operates a number of fish hatcheries and two research facilities to support the conservation and management of fishery resources.

In the list below, the field stations and fish hatcheries have no public facilities, but scheduled tours of hatcheries are available by letter request for groups of 20 or more at no charge. Write to individual hatchery for information.

INLAND FISHERIES BRANCH

The Inland Fisheries Branch of the TP&WD operates 14 field stations around the state. Most of the facilities are leased from private owners for office space and equipment storage. From these facilities, state fisheries biologists conduct research and management activities on the state's vast and varied freshwater fisheries.

Research Facility

Heart of the Hills — Junction Star Route, Box 62, Ingram. Fishery management techniques that will enhance the conservation and management of freshwater reservoirs and streams are tested in the laboratory and pond facilities. Sophisticated laboratory and data analysis equipment provides fishery scientists with the capability to investigate most fishery problems.

Field Offices

The state of Texas is divided into three regions containing 16 management districts. Each district contains a crew of several fisheries biologists and technicians. These personnel are responsible for management activities in all public reservoirs and streams within their district boundaries. Responsibilities include surveying and making recommendations to improve or maintain quality fishing. Consultation by phone or printed material is provided for these waters on private land.

Region I: West Texas. Office address: 3407 South Chadbourne, San Angelo 76904.

District IA — Box 835, Canyon 79015. Major responsibilities include lakes Meredith and Greenbelt and Mackenzie Reservoir.

District IB — 5325 N. 3rd, Abilene 79603. Lakes Brownwood and Fort Phantom Hill and Hubbard Creek Reservoir.

District IC — 4002 N. Chadbourne, San Angelo 76903. E. V. Spence and Twin Buttes reservoirs and Coleman Lake.

District ID — 134 Braniff, San Antonio 78216. Amistad and Falcon reservoirs.

District IE — Box 116, Mathis 78368. Choke Canyon Reservoir.

Region II: North Central, Central and East Central Texas. Office Address: 1601 E. Crest Dr. Waco 76705.

District IIA — Rt. 4, Box 157, Denison 75020. Texoma, Ray Roberts and Lavon lakes.

District IIB — 4110 New Corsicana Hwy., Waco 76705. Whitney, Granbury and Stillhouse Hollow lakes.

District IIC — Box 947, San Marcos 78667-0947. Buchanan and Canyon lakes and Fayette County.

District IID — 6200 Hatchery Rd., Fort Worth 76114. Lewisville, Eagle Mountain and Arlington lakes.

District IIE — 1004 E. 26th, Bryan 77803. Conroe and Limestone lakes.

District IIF — Rt. 5, Box 402, Huntsville 77340. Livingston Reservoir.

Region III: East Texas. Office Address: Rt. 10, Box 1043, Tyler 75707.

District IIIA — 3802 East End Blvd. South, Marshall 75670. Wright Patman and Murvaul lakes and Lake O' the Pines.

District IIIB — 2122 Old Henderson Hwy., Tyler 75701. Tawakoni and Pat Mayse lakes and Lake Fork Reservoir.

District IIIC — Rt. 10, Box 1043, Tyler 75707. Richland/Chambers and Cedar Creek reservoirs and Lake Palestine.

District IIID — Jasper State Fish Hatchery, Jasper 75951. Rayburn and Toledo Bend reservoirs.

District IIIE — Jasper Aquatic Habitat Enhancement, Rt. 5, Box II-2, Jasper 75951. B. A. Steinhagen Reservoir.

Fish Hatcheries

Dundee — Archer County below the dam on Lake Diversion. Total acreage 141; pond acreage 78. Consists of 94 earthen ponds; fishes raised include striped bass, hybrid striped bass and smallmouth and largemouth bass.

Huntsville — Walker County off State 19. Total acreage 247; pond acreage 32.51. Consists of 39 earthen ponds; presently decommissioned.

Jasper — Jasper County off State 63. Total acreage 227; pond acreage 64. Consists of 63 earthen ponds. Fishes raised include Florida largemouth bass, Kemp's largemouth bass, blue catfish and crappie.

GCCA/CPL Marine Development Center — Nueces County near Corpus Christi. Total area 64 acres with 40 acres of ponds. Red drum, common snook and spotted seatrout fry and fingerlings are raised for stocking Texas bays. Facility, the only one of its kind in the world, resulted from cooperative effort by TP&WD, Gulf Coast Conservation Association and Central Power & Light Co. of Corpus Christi.

Possum Kingdom — Palo Pinto County below Possum Kingdom Reservoir Dam on State 16. Total acreage 103; pond acreage 28.98. Consists of 44 earthen ponds; fishes raised are striped bass and hybrid striped bass.

A.E. Wood — Hays County south of San Marcos. The facility produces smallmouth bass, Florida bass, channel catfish, blue catfish, sunfish, paddlefish and grow-out rainbow trout.

Tyler — Smith County off State 31. Total acreage 42; pond acreage 15. Consists of 35 earthen ponds; fishes produced are Kemp's largemouth bass and Florida largemouth bass.

COASTAL FISHERIES BRANCH
Research Facility

Perry R. Bass Marine Fisheries Research Station — Calhoun County off State Hwy. 35 on Wells Point Rd. (FR3280). Has 21 ponds, total acreage 40; pond acreage 22.8. Experimental marine research.

Field Stations

There are no public facilities.

Corpus Christi — Nueces County in Corpus Christi. Headquarters for personnel assigned to Corpus Christi Bay and upper Laguna Madre research programs.

Olmito — Cameron County, 3 mi. N. of Brownsville. Headquarters for personnel assigned to lower Laguna Madre and Gulf of Mexico research programs.

Palacios — Calhoun County in Palacios. Headquarters for personnel assigned to research programs in East Matagorda, Matagorda and Lavaca Bay areas.

Port Arthur — Jefferson County on Pleasure Island. Serves as area headquarters for personnel assigned to Sabine Lake and Gulf of Mexico fishery programs.

Port O'Connor — Calhoun County in Port O'Connor. Area headquarters for personnel assigned to San Antonio Bay system and Gulf of Mexico programs.

Marine Laboratories

Rockport — Aransas County, on Rockport boat basin. Headquarters for field program administrators and personnel assigned to Aransas Bay, Corpus Christi Bay and Gulf of Mexico research programs. Complete marine way and repair facility for department vessels and vehicles.

Seabrook — Harris County, on Seabrook waterfront. Headquarters for Coastal Fisheries research on Galveston Bay and Gulf of Mexico and Resource Protection Division chemist and biologist.

National Fish Hatcheries

The Fish and Wildlife Service of the U.S. Department of the interior operates three national fish hatcheries in Texas:

Inks Dam NFH — (Burnet County) Total acreage 84.7; pond acreage 25. Twenty-eight ponds; produces approximately 400,000 channel catfish and largemouth and striped bass annually. Has visitor facilities. Access is from Highway 29, then six miles south on Park Road 4. Address: Ft. 2, Burnet 78611. Phone (512) 793-2474.

San Marcos NFH and Technology Center — (Hays County) Total acreage 116 acres; pond acreage four in forty ponds and eight raceways. Fish production is secondary to research into numerous fish species. Two laboratory buildings house many tanks and aquaria managed by highly skilled research staff. Address: Rt. 1, Box 159-D, San Marcos 78666. Phone (512) 353-0011.

Uvalde NFH — (Uvalde County) Total acreage 100; pond acreage 62. Forty-nine ponds produce approximately 2 million channel catfish and largemouth and striped bass. Has visitor facilities. Access is gained from Highway 90 west of Uvalde. Address: Box 708, Uvalde 78801. Phone (512) 278-2419.

Freshwater Fishing

During the 1989-90 fiscal year an estimated 2.5 million Texas fishermen spent more than 41 million days fishing on our 1.7 million acres of public impoundments and 80,000 miles of rivers, streams and bayous. These anglers fished for sport and food, avidly seeking such longtime favorites as largemouth bass, crappie, white bass, sunfish and the various species of catfish. Considerable time was spent seeking introduced species such as smallmouth bass, walleye, striped bass and the striped/white bass hybrid.

Freshwater recreational fishing is big business in Texas. During the fiscal year, these fishermen, both residents and visitors, spent an estimated $4.9 billion on the purchase of goods and services related to recreational fishing, according to Texas Parks and Wildlife Department officials.

The year 1988 marked the beginning of a new era of freshwater fishing in Texas. New, more restrictive regulations on the two most popular sport fishes, largemouth bass and crappie, reflected the state's commitment to maintaining and improving the quality of fishing in Texas.

The increasing number of fishermen is straining some fishery resources. New and better fishing equipment is adding to this increased pressure. Catch-and-release fishing has emerged on the Texas scene as the conservation theme of fishermen who desire continued quality fishing.

TP&WD has continued its programs of stocking fish in public waters to increase fish numbers and species diversity. Among the most successful introductions are:

• **Florida bass,** a subspecies of largemouth bass, grows heavier than native bass. The Florida bass has been stocked in almost every Texas reservoir and has forever changed the face of bass fishing in Texas. The 17-pound, 10-ounce bass caught in Texas in 1986 is among the 10 largest bass ever captured in the United States and places Texas among the top states in trophy bass fishing. Eight- to 12-pound bass, once a rare catch anywhere, are now commonly taken in Texas. All of the top 50 largemouth bass ever caught in Texas have been caught since the introduction of Florida bass in 1972.

• **Striped bass** were once native to Texas' coastal areas, and efforts to re-establish the species on the coast are underway. They also have been introduced successfully in fresh water. Reproducing populations have been established in Lakes Whitney and Texoma, and excellent striper fishing can be found at Lakes Buchanan, E. V. Spence, Possum Kingdom, Amistad and Livingston. A hybrid between the striped bass and white bass has added another sport fish for many smaller Texas reservoirs.

• **Walleyes,** native to the northern United States, have been stocked in many Texas reservoirs in the western half of the state. They adapt well to clear, rocky lakes that provide only sparse habitat for largemouth bass. Lake Meredith is noted for its walleye fishery.

• **Smallmouth bass** also are doing well in many reservoirs in the western half of the state, where they have built sustained populations through natural reproduction. The state record smallmouth bass, caught in 1988 at Lake Whitney, weighed 7 pounds, 11.5 ounces, and many lakes have produced smallmouths weighing more than five pounds.

• **Saltwater red drum** have been introduced into some Texas freshwater reservoirs, and they are doing especially well in Lake Braunig at San Antonio. Other lakes supporting good numbers of these fish are Fairfield, Tradinghouse Creek and Colorado City.

In addition, rainbow trout are stocked during the winter months on a put-and-take basis at more than 50 locations, including the Guadalupe River below Canyon Reservoir Dam, the Brazos River below the Morris Sheppard Dam, Possum Kingdom Lake, Foster County Park at San Angelo, Boykin Springs in Angelina County, the San Gabriel River below Lake Georgetown, the Clear Fork of the Trinity River in Fort Worth, and in dozens of small lakes in state and city parks.

Saltwater Fishing

The Coastal Fisheries Branch is responsible for making management recommendations regarding the state's saltwater fishery resources within the bays and estuaries and out to nine nautical miles into the Gulf of Mexico. The coastal fisheries conducted in Texas' 4 million acres of salt water by about 20,000 commercial fishermen and an estimated 1.6 million recreational fishermen have an economic impact of about $1.9 billion annually.

The objectives of the Costal Fisheries Branch are to:

(1) Assess annually the status of finfish, shrimp, crab and oyster populations and associated environmental variables in the coastal waters.

(2) Seek the best scientific information and approaches available in making management assessments of the fishery by consulting the scientific literature, other resource management agencies and resource users and by publishing and presenting results of scientific studies.

(3) Prepare long-range management plans that determine optimum yield for brown shrimp, white shrimp, blue crab, red drum, spotted seatrout, Southern flounder, black drum and Eastern oyster to provide maximum economic benefits to the fishermen while protecting the resource.

(4) Enhance existing fishery populations by stocking red drum, spotted seatrout, striped bass, snook, tarpon and white shrimp in Texas bays and assessing the impacts of stocking on present populations and existing fisheries.

(5) Enhance fishery habitat and economic benefits by revitalizing 500 acres of reefs.

(6) Determine annually the demand for, utilization of and economic value of fishery resources, and the motivations, management attitudes and satisfaction of resource users.

(7) Inform fishermen and consumers on seafood utilization to the maximum extent possible through improved communications with users of the resources.

(8) Prepare fishery plans and manage coastal resources through participation in the Gulf of Mexico Fishery Management Council and other entities.

(9) Develop mariculture techniques for the commercial production of black drum and spotted seatrout and provide information to the commercial mariculturist in Texas.

(10) Implement the artificial reef management plan to provide for orderly and effective use of this management tool to ensure maximum economic benefit and fisheries enhancement for the State of Texas.

The **Perry R. Bass Marine Fisheries Research Station** at Palacios provides information and techniques necessary for the improvement of Texas fisheries management plans. Research is directed toward methods for spawning and rearing marine fish and shellfish. Once developed, such techniques will be used to provide animals for stocking coastal bays and freshwater reservoirs, and information on techniques will be made available to commercial mariculturists in Texas. Coastal fisheries personnel exchange information with their counterparts in other states.

As directed by the Texas Legislature, the **Seafood Marketing Program** was initiated to increase the utilization and value of seafood products. This charge is aimed at all functional levels within the marketing channel. The Seafood Marketing Program functions through an inter-agency contract with Texas A&M University, the Texas Agricultural Extension Service, the Sea Grant College Program's Marine Advisory Service and the Texas Department of Agriculture. Several fisheries development foundations nationwide have also supported various work completed by the Seafood Marketing Program.

Activities in Fiscal 1990

• The closure period for Gulf shrimping in state waters was coordinated with the National Marine Fisheries Service (NMFS) for closure of the Exclusive Economic Zone to increase yield and value for the shrimping industry.

• More than 8,000 biological samples and associated water and weather data were collected.

• The Texas Shrimp Fishery Management Plan and Economic Impact Statement was adopted, and a Shrimp Advisory Committee was created and appointed.

• The most comprehensive shrimp management regulations since the Shrimp Conservation Act of 1959 was enacted were adopted.

• Regulations were modified to prevent depletion of spotted seatrout damaged by freezing weather by placing a 15-inch minimum size to increase spawning potential. Size and bag limits were also modified for gafftopsail catfish, Florida pompano, snook, red snapper and blue crabs.

• Crab trap gear tags were made valid for 30 days to prevent waste caused by abandoned traps.

• Harmful or potentially harmful exotic fish, shellfish and aquatic plants were defined and rules for their importation, sale, purchase, propagation, possession or release into Texas public waters were adopted.

• Sharks were defined as gamefish, making the pole and line the only legal means for their capture. Sharks are in danger of depletion.

• It was made unlawful for any person to use game fish as bait.

• Snagging and jerking of fish was better defined to prevent the taking of fish stunned by cold weather.

• A definition of "legal shrimping operations" was adopted to ensure against possible abuse of the provision allowing for the retention of fish (except red drum and spotted seatrout) caught in shrimp trawls.

• Snapper traps and trotlines were prohibited in the Gulf of Mexico in compliance with federal government rules to protect red snapper and red drum, which are in danger of depletion.

• Development of an artificial reef management plan was completed.

• Coastal Fisheries staff was mobilized to assess the fish kill caused by freezing temperatures in December. Almost 6 million fishes were killed.

• 1,540 survey-days were spent to estimate landings and pressure of sport-boat fishermen.

• A one-year survey of shore-based fishermen was started to reassess the relative contribution of these recreational fishermen to the total saltwater recreational fishery.

• Gulf of Mexico waters from Alabama to the Rio Grande were sampled to a depth of 270 feet during June-July and October-November with other Gulf states and the NMFS. This effort was coordinated by the Gulf States Marine Fisheries Commission through SEAMAP. Results of sampling were used by the NMFS to evaluate the closure of Gulf waters to shrimping.

• A statewide mail survey of holders of the saltwater sport fishing stamp was conducted. The survey examines species preference, participation and socio-economic aspects of saltwater fishermen in Texas.

• Routine collection of commercial landings data continued through a formal cooperative statistics agreement with NMFS. TP&WD collected commercial landings statistics on crabs, oysters and finfishes, while NMFS continued to gather landings statistics on shrimp.

• Studies of spotted seatrout, tarpon and snook culture and reproduction continued. Methods for artificially inducing sexual maturity and spawning in these species were examined. Pond-cultured fry and fingerling of several fish species were stocked in Texas bays and inland reservoirs.

Commercial Fisheries

Shrimp made up 84 percent of the pounds landed and 94 percent of the value of all reported commercial marine products during 1989.

Commercial Landings
(Jan. 1, 1989 to Dec. 31, 1989)
Source: Texas Parks and Wildlife Department

Species	Pounds	Value
Finfish		
Drum, Black..............	610,900	$474,600
Flounder	154,200	187,100
Sheepshead	42,000	12,600
Snapper................	589,100	1,185,300
Other..................	1,069,800	1,168,700
Total Finfish...........	2,466,000	$3,028,300
Shellfish		
Shrimp (Heads On):	62,453,900	$119,761,700
Brown and Pink........	10,850,300	22,325,700
White	3,807,600	2,018,200
Other	9,066,200	3,946,300
Crabs.................	1,979,900	4,903,900
Other.................	202,000	132,000
Total Shellfish	88,360,000	$153,087,800
Grand Total............	90,826,000	$156,116,100

Water Supplies and Needs

The 69th Legislature separated the state's single water agency, the Texas Department of Water Resources, into two agencies: the Texas Water Commission and the Texas Water Development Board. In addition, the three-member Texas Water Commission was retained to handle judicial matters, and a six-member Texas Water Development Board was retained to establish board policy.

Texas, through its river authorities, municipalities, water districts and state-level agencies, exercises the dominant role in development of municipal and industrial water supplies. Approximately 80 percent of the money invested in the state's water projects has been provided by Texas entities of government.

Ground-Water Supplies and Use

Aquifers underlie about 76 percent of the area of Texas. This ground water has long been the principal source of municipal supplies, but cities now increasingly depend upon surface reservoirs due to depletion of water in aquifer storage. More than half of Texas' total agricultural crop value is produced utilizing **ground water** for irrigation, mainly from the **High Plains (Ogallala) aquifer,** which underlies most of the Panhandle.

Declining water levels, mining and exhaustion of ground water, coupled with increasing energy costs, are major problems facing the state's water managers today.

Major aquifers in Texas follow (see map):

High Plains (Ogallala) — This formation furnishes practically the only usable quality water on the High Plains. It is composed of unconsolidated, fine- to coarse-grained, gray to red sand, clay, silt and gravel. Effective recharge from precipitation is small, averaging less than one-quarter inch yearly, whereas ground-water pumping is heavy, averaging about 8.9 million acre-feet yearly (1984). Depletion at the present pumping rate threatens this as a water source for irrigation. The High Plains (Ogallala) aquifer supplies Texas' largest irrigated farming region, which produces most of Texas' cotton, grain sorghum and other crops.

Alluvium and Bolson Deposits — These water-bearing deposits are scattered throughout many areas in the state. They include the **Hueco and Mesilla Bolsons,** the **Cenozoic Alluvium** of West Texas, the alluviums of North Central Texas, the **Leona Alluvium** of Tom Green County and the **Brazos River Alluvium** of Southeast Texas. These deposits consist generally of sand, gravel, silt and clay. The quality of the water can range from fresh to saline.

In the westernmost Texas region, the Mesilla and Hueco Bolsons are the primary source of water supply for the **El Paso area,** where serious problems exist regarding ground-water depletion and quality degradation. Other sources of ground-water supply are from the **Salt Bolson (Wildhorse Draw, Michigan Flat, Lobo Flat** and **Ryan Flat** areas), the **Red Light Draw Bolson,** the **Green River Valley Bolson** and the **Presidio** and **Redford Bolsons.** In the Cenozoic Alluvium region, the **Coyonosa** area of northwest Pecos and northeast Reeves counties and northeastern Ward County are the most productive areas of usable quality ground water. Supplies are produced from the **Seymour aquifer** in North Central Texas.

Edwards-Trinity (Plateau) — This aquifer underlies the **Edwards Plateau region** of Southwest Texas. It consists of saturated sediments of the **Lower Cretaceous Comanchean Series** made up of sand, sandstone, gravel and conglomerate of the **Trinity Group (Antlers Sand);** and cherty, gypsiferous, argillaceous, cavernous lime-and dolomites of the **Comanche Peak, Edwards and Georgetown formations.** The ground water generally flows southeasterly, and near the edge of the Plateau, movement is toward the main streams where the water issues from springs. The water ranges in quality from fresh to slightly saline and is hard. Most of the municipalities on the Plateau depend on this aquifer for their water supply. Where the land is arable and yield from wells is sufficient, irrigated farming is possible. Problems exist in those areas where development has exceeded the capabilities of the aquifer.

Edwards (Balcones Fault Zone) — Ground water occurs in fractures, honeycomb zones and solution channels in this aquifer that underlies an area along the **Balcones Fault Zone** from **Kinney County** on the west through **Bexar County** to **Bell County** on the north. Geologically, it is made up of the **Edwards and associated limestones** of Cretaceous age and consists of massive to thin-bedded, nodular, cherty, gypsiferous, argillaceous, white to gray limestone and dolomite of the **Comanche Peak, Edwards** and **Georgetown formations,** which have been downthrown from the Edwards Plateau due to faulting. The aquifer is recharged rapidly by water discharged from springs along the edge of the Edwards Plateau, which then flows in streams that traverse the many faults along the Balcones. The ground water moves through the aquifer generally in an easterly, northeasterly direction to points of discharge, notable of which are **Leona, San Antonio, San Pedro, Comal, San Marcos, Barton** and **Salado springs,** plus numerous smaller springs. In **Bexar County,** wells pumping from this aquifer are among the world's largest. The water is generally of good quality and it is used for public supply, irrigation, industrial, domestic and livestock watering purposes. Hydrologically, the aquifer is unique and is one of the state's most valuable natural resources. In the past, the aquifer was adequate to meet **San Antonio's** water needs, but increased growth and development in this area necessitate additional surface water supplies.

Trinity Group — These basal Cretaceous-age rocks extend over a large area of North and Central Texas and are composed primarily of sand with interbedded clays, limestone, dolomite, gravel and conglomerates. The Trinity Group is made up of the **Twin Mountains, Glen Rose** and **Paluxy formations;** however, to the west and north where the Glen Rose Formation thins or pinches out, the **Twin Mountains** and **Paluxy formations** coalesce and are called the **Antlers Formation.** The water quality is acceptable for most municipal and industrial purposes. Extensive irrigation occurs in **Comanche, Eastland** and **Erath counties.** The aquifer has been overdeveloped in the **Dallas-Fort Worth metropolitan** area and in the vicinity of **Waco,** where wa-

ter levels have declined to near 1,200 feet below the land surface.

Carrizo-Wilcox — This aquifer of Eocene age is one of the most extensive water-bearing formations in Texas geograpically, and it furnishes water to wells in a wide belt extending from the Rio Grande northeastward into Arkansas and Louisiana. It consists of hydrologically connected ferruginous, cross-bedded sand with clay, sandstone, silt, lignite and gravel of the **Wilcox Group** and overlying **Carrizo Formation.** Throughout most of Texas, the Carrizo-Wilcox aquifer yields fresh to slightly saline water which is acceptable for most irrigation, public supply and industrial uses. Because of excessive pumping, the water levels have been significantly lowered, particularly in the **Winter Garden District** of **Dimmit** and **Zavala counties** and in the municipal and industrial areas located north of **Lufkin** in **Angelina** and **Nacogdoches counties.** However, water-level declines in the Winter Garden area have been significantly arrested during the past 10 years.

Gulf Coast Aquifer — Geologically, the Gulf Coast aquifer ranges in age from Miocene to Holocene, and it is collectively composed of the **Catahoula, Oakville, Lagarto, Goliad, Willis, Lissie** and **Beaumont formations.** Lithologically, it consists of alternating beds of clay, silt, sand and gravel which are hydrologically connected. The principal water-bearing units are the Goliad, Willis and Lissie formations. It parallels the Texas Gulf Coast from Mexico to Louisiana. Normally, fresh to slightly saline ground water occurs in the aquifer from the San Antonio River basin northeastward to Louisiana. In this area, large quantities are pumped for municipal, industrial and irrigation use. Ground-water quality tends to deteriorate in the San Antonio River basin and southwestward to Mexico, where there are areas in which no appreciable amounts of fresh to slightly saline water can be found. Problems of land-surface subsidence in the Houston area are well documented. Additionally, withdrawal of ground water from the Gulf Coast aquifer can cause increased chloride content, especially in the southwest portion, and salt-water encroachment along the coast. Therefore, management of future withdrawals from the aquifer is necessary in order to alleviate serious ground-water problems.

Streams and Drainage Basins

Some 11,247 named streams are identified in the **U.S. Geological Survey Geographic Names Information System.** Their combined length is about 80,000 miles, and they drain 263,513 square miles within Texas. The following discussion describes 13 major rivers.

Rio Grande

The Pueblo Indians called this river **P'osoge,** "river of great water." In 1582, Antonio de Espejo of Nueva Vizcaya, Mexico, followed the course of the Rio Conchos to its confluence with a great river, which Espejo named **Rio de Norte** (River of the North). The name **Rio Grande** was first given the stream apparently by the explorer Juan de Oñate, who arrived on its banks near present day El Paso in 1598.

Thereafter the names were often consolidated, as **Rio Grande del Norte.** (It has its counterpart in the Portuguese Rio Grande do Sul in the state of that name in Brazil.) It was shown also on early Spanish maps as **Rio San Buenaventura** and **Rio Ganapetuan.** In its lower course it early acquired the name **Rio Bravo,** and it is called by that name today by many Mexicans living in its valley. At times it has also been known as **Rio Turbio,** probably because of its appearance during its frequent rises.

From source to mouth, the Rio Grande drops 12,000 feet to sea level as a snow-fed mountain torrent, carver of canyons, desert stream and meandering coastal river. Along its banks and in its valley Indian civilizations developed, and the white man made some of his first North American settlements.

This river rises in Colorado, flows the north-south length of New Mexico and forms the boundary of Texas and international U.S.-Mexican boundary for 889 to 1,248 miles, depending upon method of measurement. (See Texas Boundary Line.) The length of the Rio

Grande, as of other rivers, depends on method of measurement and varies yearly as its course changes. Latest International Boundary and Water Commission figure is 1,896 miles, which is considerably below the 2,200-mile figure often used. Depending upon methods of measurement, the Rio Grande is the fourth- or fifth-longest North American river, exceeded only by the Missouri-Mississippi, McKenzie-Peace, St. Lawrence and possibly Yukon. Since all of these except the Missouri-Mississippi are partly in Canada, the Rio Grande is the second-longest river entirely within or bordering the United States. It is Texas' longest river.

The snow-fed flow of the Rio Grande is used for irrigation in Colorado below the San Juan Mountains, where the river rises at the Continental Divide. Turning south, it flows through a canyon in northern New Mexico and again irrigates a broad valley of central New Mexico. Dating from the 1600s, this is the oldest irrigated area of the United States, where Spanish missionaries encouraged Indian irrigation. Southern New Mexico impounds Rio Grande waters in Elephant Butte Reservoir for irrigation for 150 miles of valley above and below El Paso. Here is the oldest irrigated area in Texas and one of the oldest in the United States. Extensive irrigation practically exhausts the water supply. In this valley are situated the three oldest towns in Texas — Ysleta, Socorro and San Elizario. At the lower end of the El Paso irrigated valley, the upper Rio Grande, a snow-fed mountain stream, virtually ends except in seasons of above-normal flow.

It starts as a perennially flowing stream again where the Rio Conchos of Mexico flows into it at Presidio-Ojinaga. Through the Big Bend the Rio Grande flows through three successive canyons, the **Santa Elena,** the **Mariscal** and the **Boquillas.** The Santa Elena has a river bed elevation of 2,145 feet and a canyon rim elevation of 3,661. Corresponding figures for the Mariscal are 1,925 and 3,625, those for the Boquillas, 1,850 and 3,490. The river here flows around the base of the great Chisos Mountains. For about 100 miles the river is the southern boundary of the **Big Bend National Park**.

Below the Big Bend, the Rio Grande gradually emerges from mountains onto the Coastal Plains. At the confluence of the Rio Grande and the Devils River, the U.S. and Mexico have built **Amistad Dam,** to impound 3,-383,900 acre-feet of water, of which Texas' share is 56.2 percent. **Falcon Reservoir,** also an international project, impounds 2,667,600 acre-feet of water, of which Texas' share in Zapata and Starr counties is 58.6 percent. Finally, the Rio Grande has created a fertile delta where it joins the Gulf of Mexico, called the **Lower Rio Grande Valley,** that is a major vegetable-fruit area.

The Rio Grande drains over 40,000 square miles of Texas.

Principal tributaries flowing from the Texas side of the Rio Grande are the Pecos and the Devils rivers. On the Mexican side are the **Rio Conchos,** the **Rio Salado** and the **Rio San Juan.** About three-fourths of the water running into the Rio Grande below El Paso comes from the Mexican side.

Nueces River

The Nueces River rises in Edwards County and flows 315 miles to Nueces Bay on the Gulf near Corpus Christi. Draining 17,000 square miles, it is a beautiful, spring-fed stream flowing through canyons until it issues from the Balcones Escarpment onto the Coastal Plain in northern Uvalde County. Alonso de Leon, in 1689, gave it its name. (Nueces, plural of nuez, means nuts in Spanish.) Much earlier, Cabeza de Vaca had referred to a Rio de las Nueces in this region, probably the same stream. Its original Indian name seems to have been Chotilapacquen. Crossing Texas in 1691, Teran de los Rios named the river San Diego. The Nueces was the boundary line between the Spanish provinces of Texas and Nuevo Santander. After the Revolution of 1836, both Texas and Mexico claimed the territory between the Nueces and the Rio Grande, a dispute which was settled by the Treaty of Guadalupe Hidalgo in 1848, which fixed the international boundary at the Rio Grande. Nueces runoff is about 620,000 acre-feet a year in its lower course. Principal water conservation projects are **Lake Corpus Christi and Choke Canyon Reservoir.** Principal tributaries of the Nueces are the **Frio** and the **Atascosa.**

San Antonio River

The San Antonio River has its source in large springs within and near the corporate limits of San Antonio. It flows 180 miles across the Coastal Plain to a junction with the Guadalupe near the Gulf Coast. Its channel through San Antonio has been developed into a parkway. Its principal tributaries are the **Medina River** and **Cibolo Creek,** both spring-fed streams and this, with its own origin in springs, gives it a remarkably steady flow of clear water.

This stream was first named the Leon by Alonso de Leon during his trip across Texas in 1689. (De Leon was not naming the stream for himself, but called it "lion" because its channel was filled with a rampaging flood.)

Because of its limited and rather arid drainage area (4,200 square miles) the average runoff of the San Antonio River is relatively small, about 350,000 acre-feet annually near its mouth, but its flow, because of its springs, is one of the steadiest of Texas rivers.

Guadalupe River

The Guadalupe rises in its north and south prongs in the west-central part of Kerr County. A spring-fed stream, it flows eastward through the Hill Country until it issues from the Balcones Escarpment near New Braunfels. It then meanders across the Coastal Plain to San Antonio Bay. Its total length is about 250 miles, and its drainage area is about 6,000 square miles. Its principal tributaries are the **San Marcos,** another spring-fed stream, which flows into it in Gonzales County, the **San Antonio,** which flows into it just above its mouth on San Antonio Bay and the **Comal,** which joins it at New Braunfels. The **Comal River** has its source in large springs within the city limits of New Braunfels and flows only about 2.5 miles to the Guadalupe. It is the **shortest river in Texas** and also the shortest river in the United States carrying an equivalent amount of water. There has been power development on the Guadalupe near

Gonzales and Cuero for many years. There is now also power generation at Canyon Reservoir. Because of its springs, and its considerable drainage area, it has an annual runoff of more than 1 million acre-feet in its lower course.

The name Guadalupe is derived from Nuestra Senora de Guadalupe, the name given the stream by Alonso de Leon.

Lavaca River

The Lavaca is considered a primary stream in the Texas Basin because it flows directly into the Gulf, through Lavaca Bay. Without a spring water source and with only a small watershed, including that of its principal tributary, the **Navidad,** its flow is intermittent. The Spanish called it the Lavaca (cow) River because of the numerous bison they found. It is the principal stream running to the Gulf between the Guadalupe and the Colorado. The principal lake on the Nueces is Lake Texana. Runoff averages about 600,000 acre-feet yearly into the Gulf.

Colorado River

Measured by length and drainage area, the Colorado is the largest river wholly in Texas. (This comparison excludes the Brazos, whose drainage basin extends into New Mexico.) Rising in Dawson County, the Colorado flows about 600 miles to Matagorda Bay on the Gulf. Its drainage area is 39,900 square miles. Its runoff reaches a volume of more than 2 million acre-feet near the Gulf. Its name is a Spanish word meaning "reddish." There is evidence that the name, Colorado, was given originally by Spanish explorers to the muddy Brazos, and Spanish mapmakers later transposed the two names. The river flows through a rolling, usually prairie terrain to the vicinity of San Saba County, where it enters the rugged Hill Country and Burnet-Llano Basin. It passes through a picturesque series of canyons until it issues from the Balcones Escarpment at Austin and flows across the Coastal Plain to the Gulf. In this area the most remarkable series of reservoirs in Texas has been built. There are two large reservoirs, **Lake Buchanan** in Burnet and Llano counties and **Lake Travis** in Travis County. Between these, in Burnet County, are three smaller reservoirs: **Inks, Johnson** (formerly **Granite Shoals**) and **Marble Falls,** built to aid power production from water running over the Buchanan Lake spillway. Below Lake Travis is the older **Lake Austin,** largely filled with silt, whose dam maintains a head for production of power from waters flowing down from the lakes above. Town Lake is in the city of Austin. This area is known as the **Highland Lakes Country.**

As early as the 1820s, Anglo-Americans settled on the banks of the lower Colorado, and in 1839 the **Capital Commission** of the Republic of Texas chose the picturesque area where the river flows from the Balcones Escarpment as the site of a new capital of the Republic — now **Austin,** capital of the state. The early colonists encouraged navigation along the lower channel with some success and boats occasionally ventured as far upstream as Austin. However, a natural log "raft" in the channel near the Gulf blocked river traffic. Conservation and utilization of the waters of the Colorado are under jurisdiction of three agencies created by the state Legislature, the **Lower, Central** and **Upper Colorado River Authorities.**

The principal tributaries of the Colorado are the several prongs of the **Concho River** on its upper course, the **Pecan Bayou** (farthest west "bayou" in the United States) and the Llano, San Saba and Pedernales rivers. All except the Pecan Bayou flow into the Colorado from the Edwards Plateau and are spring-fed, perennially flowing. In the numerous mussels found along these streams occasional pearls have been found. The Middle Concho was designated on early Spanish maps as **Rio de las Perlas.**

Brazos River

The Brazos is the largest river between the Rio Grande and the Red River and is third in size of all rivers in Texas. It rises in three upper forks, the **Double Mountain, Salt** and **Clear forks** of the Brazos. The Brazos River proper is considered as beginning where the Double Mountain and Salt Forks flow together in Stonewall County. The Clear Fork joins this main stream in Young County, just above Lake Possum Kingdom. The Brazos crosses most of the main physiographic regions of

Texas — High Plains, West Texas Lower Rolling Plains, West Cross Timbers, Grand Prairie and Gulf Coastal Plain.

The total length from the source of its longest upper prong, the Double Mountain Fork, to the mouth of the main stream at the Gulf, is about 840 miles, and the drainage area is about 42,800 square miles.

It flows directly into the Gulf near Freeport. Its annual runoff at places along its lower channel exceeds 5 million acre-feet.

The original name of this river was **Brazos de Dios**, meaning **"Arms of God."** There are several legends as to why. One is that the Coronado expedition, wandering on the trackless Llano Estacado, exhausted its water and was threatened with death from thirst. Arriving at the bank of the river they gave it the name of Brazos de Dios in thankfulness. Another is that a ship exhausted its water supply and its crew was saved when they found the mouth of the Brazos. Still another story is that miners on the San Saba were forced by drouth to seek water near present-day Waco and called it Brazos de Dios in thankfulness. There is also the theory that the early Spanish cartographers called the river "Arms of God" because of the great spread of its tributaries.

Much early Anglo-American colonization of Texas took place in the Brazos Valley. Along its channel were **San Felipe de Austin,** capital of Austin's colony, **Washington-on-the-Brazos,** where Texans declared independence, and other historic settlements. There was some navigation of the lower channel of the Brazos in this period. Near its mouth it intersects the Gulf Intracoastal Waterway, which provides connection with the commerce on the Mississippi.

Most of the Brazos Valley lies within the boundaries of the **Brazos River Authority,** which conducts a multipurpose program for development. A large reservoir on the Brazos is **Whitney Lake** (622,800 acre-feet capacity) on the main channel, where it is the boundary line between Hill and Bosque counties. Another large reservoir is **Possum Kingdom Lake** in Palo Pinto, Stephens, Young and Jack counties. **Waco Lake** on the Bosque and **Belton Lake** on the Leon are among the principal reservoirs on its tributaries. In addition to its three upper forks, other chief tributaries are the **Paluxy, Little** and **Navasota rivers.**

San Jacinto River

A short river with a drainage basin of 3,976 square miles and nearly 2 million acre-feet runoff, the San Jacinto runs directly to the Gulf through Galveston Bay. It is formed by the junction of its East and West forks in the northeastern part of Harris County. Its total length, including the East Fork, is about 85 miles. There are two stories of the origin of its name. One is that when early explorers discovered it, its channel was choked with hyacinth ("Jacinto" is the Spanish word for hyacinth). The other is that it was discovered on Aug. 17, St. Hyacinth's Day. Through the lower course of the San Jacinto and its tributary, Buffalo Bayou, runs the Houston Ship Channel connecting the Port of Houston with the Gulf. On the shore of the San Jacinto was fought the **Battle of San Jacinto,** April 21, 1836, in which Texas won its independence from Mexico. The **San Jacinto State Park and monument** are there.

Trinity River

The Trinity rises in its East Fork, Elm Fork, West Fork and Clear Fork in Grayson, Montague, Archer and Parker counties, respectively. The main stream begins with the junction of the Elm and West forks at Dallas. Its length is 550 river miles and its drainage area, 17,969 square miles. Because of moderate to heavy rainfall over its drainage area, it has a flow of 5,800,000 acre-feet near its mouth on the Gulf, exceeded only by the Neches, Red and Sabine River basins.

The Trinity derives its name from the Spanish "Trinidad." Alonso de Leon named it **La Santisima Trinidad** (the Most Holy Trinity).

Navigation was developed along its lower course with several riverport towns, such as **Sebastopol** in Trinity County. For many years there has been a basin-wide movement for navigation, conservation and utilization of its water. The **Trinity River Authority** is a state agency and the **Trinity Improvement Association** is a publicly supported nonprofit organization advocating its development.

The Trinity has in its valley more large cities, greater population and more industrial development than any other river basin in Texas. On the Lower Coastal Plain there is large use of its waters for rice irrigation. Largest reservoir on the Elm Fork is **Lewisville Lake** (formerly **Garza-Little Elm** and **Lake Dallas**). There are four reservoirs above Fort Worth—**Lake Worth, Eagle Mountain** and **Bridgeport** on the West Fork and **Benbrook Lake** on the Clear Fork. **Lavon Lake** in southeast Collin County and **Lake Ray Hubbard** in Collin-Dallas-Kaufman-Rockwall counties are on the East Fork.

Neches River

The Neches is in East Texas with total length of about 416 miles and drainage area of 10,011 square miles. Abundant rainfall over its entire basin gives it a flow near the Gulf of about 6 million acre-feet a year. The river takes its name from the Neches Indians that the early Spanish explorers found living along its banks. Principal tributary of the Neches, and comparable with the Neches in length and flow above their confluence, is the **Angelina River,** so named from **Angelina (Little Angel),** a Hainai **Indian girl** who converted to Christianity and played an important role in the early development of this region.

Both the Neches and the Angelina run most of their courses in the Piney Woods and there was much settlement along them as early as the 1820s. **Sam Rayburn (McGee Bend) Reservoir,** near Jasper on the Angelina River, was completed and dedicated in 1965.

Sabine River

The Sabine River is formed by three forks rising in Collin and Hunt counties. From its sources to its mouth on **Sabine Lake,** it flows approximately 360 miles and drains 9,733 square miles. Sabine comes from the Spanish word for cypress, as does the name of the Sabinal River, which flows into the Frio in Southwest Texas. The Sabine has the largest water discharge (6,800,000 acrefeet) at its mouth of any Texas river. Throughout most of Texas history the lower Sabine has been the eastern Texas boundary line, though for a while there was doubt as to whether the Sabine or the Arroyo Hondo, east of the Sabine in Louisiana, was the boundary. For a number of years the outlaw-infested **neutral ground** lay between them. There was also a boundary dispute in which it was alleged that the Neches was really the Sabine and, therefore, the boundary.

Travelers over the Camino Real, or Old San Antonio Road, crossed the Sabine at the famous **Gaines Ferry,** and there were famous crossings for the **Atascosito Road** and other travel and trade routes of that day.

Two of Texas' larger man-made reservoirs have been created by dams constructed on the Sabine River. The first of these is **Lake Tawakoni,** in Hunt, Rains and Van Zandt counties, with a capacity of 936,200 acre-feet. **Toledo Bend Reservoir** impounds 4,472,900 acre-feet of water on the Sabine in Newton, Panola, Sabine and Shelby counties. This is a joint project of Texas and Louisiana, through the Sabine River Authority.

Red River

The Red River (1,360 miles) is exceeded in length only by the Rio Grande among rivers associated with Texas. Its original source is water in Curry County, New Mexico, near the Texas boundary, forming a definite channel as it crosses Deaf Smith County, Texas, in tributaries that flow into **Prairie Dog Town Fork of the Red River.** These waters carve the spectacular **Palo Duro Canyon** of the High Plains before the Red River leaves the Caprock Escarpment, flowing eastward.

Where the Red River crosses the 100th meridian, the river becomes the Texas-Oklahoma boundary and is soon joined by the **Salt Fork** to form the main channel. Its length across the Panhandle is about 200 miles and, from the Panhandle east, it is the Texas-Oklahoma boundary line for 440 miles and thereafter the Texas-Arkansas boundary for 40 miles before it flows into Arkansas, where it swings south to flow through Louisiana. The Red River is a part of the Mississippi drainage basin, and at one time it emptied all of its water into the Mississippi. In recent years, however, part of its water, especially at flood stage, has flowed to the Gulf via the Atchafalaya. The Red River takes its name from the red color of the current. This caused every explorer who came to its banks to call it "red" regardless of the language he spoke — **Rio Rojo** or **Rio Roxo** in Spanish, **Riviere Rouge** in French and Red River in English. The Spanish and French names were often found on maps until the middle of the last century when the English, Red River, came to be generally accepted. At an early date, the river became the axis for French advance from Louisiana northwestward as far as present-day Montague County. There was consistent early navigation of the river from its mouth on the Mississippi to Shreveport, above which navigation was blocked by a natural **log raft.** A number of important gateways into Texas from the North were established along the stream such as **Pecan Point** and **Jonesborough** in Red River County, **Colbert's Ferry** and **Preston** in Grayson County and, later, **Doan's Store Crossing** in Wilbarger County. The river was a menace to the early traveler because of both its variable current and its **quicksands** which brought disaster to many a trail herd cow as well as ox team and covered wagon.

The largest water conservation project on the Red River is **Texoma Lake,** which is the largest lake lying wholly or partly in Texas and the tenth largest reservoir (in capacity) in the United States. Its capacity is 5,382,000 acre feet. Texas' share is 2,722,000.

Red River water's high content of salt and other minerals limits its usefulness along its upper reaches. Ten salt springs and tributaries in Texas and Oklahoma contribute most of these minerals.

The uppermost tributary of the Red River in Texas is the Tierra Blanca Creek, which rises in Curry County, N.M., and flows easterly across Deaf Smith and Randall counties to become the Prairie Dog Town Fork a few miles east of Canyon. Other principal tributaries in Texas are the Pease and the Wichita in North Central Texas and the Sulphur in Northeast Texas, which flows into the Red River after it has crossed the boundary line into Arkansas. From Oklahoma the principal tributary is the **Washita.** The **Ouachita,** a river with the same pronunciation of its name, though spelled differently, is the principal tributary to its lower course.

Canadian River

The Canadian River heads near Raton Pass in northern New Mexico near the Colorado boundary line and flows into Texas on the west line of Oldham County. It crosses the Texas Panhandle into Oklahoma and there flows into the Arkansas. Most of its course across the Panhandle is in a deep gorge. A tributary dips into Texas' North Panhandle and then flows to a confluence with the main channel in Oklahoma. One of several theories as to how the Canadian got its name is that some early explorers thought it flowed into Canada. **Lake Meredith,** formed by **Sanford Dam** on the Canadian, provides water for 11 Panhandle cities.

Because of the deep gorge and the **quicksand** at many places, the Canadian has been a peculiarly difficult stream to bridge. It is known especially in its lower course in Oklahoma as outstanding among the streams of the country for great amount of quicksand in its channel.

Lakes and Reservoirs

The large increase in the number of reservoirs in Texas during the past half-century has greatly improved water conservation and supplies. As late as 1913, Texas had only eight major reservoirs with a total storage capacity of 376,000 acre-feet. Most of this capacity was in **Medina Lake,** with 254,000 acre-feet capacity, created by a dam completed in May 1913.

By 1920, Texas had 11 major reservoirs with combined storage capacity of 449,710 acre-feet. The state water agency reported 32 reservoirs and 1,284,520 acre-feet capacity in 1930; 47 reservoirs with 5,369,550 acre-feet capacity in 1940; 66 with 9,623,870 acre-feet capacity by 1950; 105 with total capacity of 22,746,200 in 1960; 149 with total capacity of 51,086,200 in 1970; 168 with total capacity of 53,302,400 in 1980. In January 1983, Texas had 189 major reservoirs existing or under construction, with a total capacity near 58.6 million acre-feet, of which 38.4 million acre-feet was conservation storage, 17.8 million acre-feet was flood control storage and 2.4 million acre-feet was considered inactive.

According to the U.S. Statistical Abstract of 1987, Texas ranks second behind Minnesota in inland water area among the continental states. Texas has 4,790 square miles of inland water, according to this survey, compared to Minnesota's 4,854 square miles.

The following table lists reservoirs in Texas having more than 5,000 acre-feet capacity. A few locally significant reservoirs of less capacity are not included. With few exceptions, the listed reservoirs are those that were completed by Jan. 1, 1987, and in use. An asterisk (*) indicates those that are under construction.

There are about 5,700 reservoirs in Texas with surface areas of 10 acres or larger; however, conservation water storage capacity in the listed reservoirs represents about 97 percent of total conservation water storage capacity in all Texas reservoirs.

Conservation storage capacity is used in the table below; the **surface area** used is that area at conservation elevation only. (Different methods of computing capacity are used; detailed information may be obtained from Texas Water Development Board, Austin; U.S. Army Corps of Engineers or local sources.) Also, it should be noted that boundary reservoir capacities include water designated for Texas use and non-Texas water.

In the list below, information is given in the following order: (1) Name of lake or reservoir; (2) county or counties in which located; (3) river or creek on which located; (4) location with respect to some city or town; (5) purpose of reservoir; (6) owner of reservoir. Some of these items, when not listed, are not available. For the larger lakes and reservoirs, the dam impounding water to form the lake bears the same name, unless otherwise indicated. Abbreviations in list below are as follows: L., lake; R., river; Co., county; Cr., creek; (C) conservation; (FC) flood control; (R) recreation; (P) power; (M) municipal; (D) domestic; (Ir.) irrigation; (In.) industry; (Mi.) mining including oil production; (FH) fish hatchery; USAE, United States Army Corps of Engineers; WC&ID, Water Control and Improvement District; WID, Water Improvement District; USBR, United States Bureau of Reclamation.

Lakes and Reservoirs	Conservation Surface Area (Acres)	Conservation Storage Capacity (Acre-Ft.)
Abilene L.—Taylor Co.; Elm Cr.; 6 mi. NW Tuscola; (M-In.-R); City of Abilene	595	7,900
Addicks Reservoir—Harris Co.; S. Mayde and Langham Crs.; 1 mi. E. Addicks; (for flood control only); USAE	0	0
Alcoa L.—Milam Co.; Sandy Cr.; 7 mi. SW Rockdale; (In.-R); Aluminum Co. of America	880	14,750
Amistad Reservoir—Val Verde Co.; Rio Grande, dam between Del Rio and confluence of Rio Grande and Devils River; an international project of the U.S. and Mexico; 12 mi. NW Del Rio; (C-R-Ir.-P-FC); International Boundary and Water Com. (Texas' share of conservation capacity is 56.2 percent.)	64,900	3,383,900
Amon G. Carter, L.—Montague Co.; Big Sandy Cr.; 6 mi. S Bowie; (M-In.); City of Bowie	1,540	20,050
Anahuac L.—Chambers Co.; Turtle Bayou; near Anahuac; (Ir.-In.-Mi.); Chambers-Liberty counties Navigation District.	5,300	35,300
***Applewhite Reservoir**—Bexar Co.; Medina R.	0	0
Aquilla L.—Hill Co.; Aquilla Cr.; 10.2 mi. SW of Hillsboro; (FC-M-Ir.-In.-R); USAE-Brazos R. Auth.	3,280	52,400
Arlington L.—Tarrant Co.; Village Cr.; 7 mi. W Arlington; (M-In.); City of Arlington	2,275	45,710

Arrowhead, L.—Clay Co.; Little Wichita R.; 13 mi. SE Wichita Falls; (M); City of Wichita Falls . . . . 16,200 | 262,100

Athens, L.—Henderson Co.; 8 mi. E Athens; (M-FC-R); Athens Mun. Water Authority (formerly **Flat Creek Reservoir**) . . . . 1,520 | 32,690

Aubrey L.—(See **Ray Roberts L.**)

Austin, L.—Travis Co.; Colorado R.; W Austin city limits; (M-In.-P); City of Austin, leased to LCRA (impounded by **Tom Miller Dam**) . . . . 1,830 | 21,000

Balmorhea, L.—Reeves Co.; Sandia Cr.; 3 mi. SE Balmorhea; (Ir.); Reeves Co. WID No. 1 573 | 6,350

Bardwell L.—Ellis Co.; Waxahachie Cr.; 3 mi. SE Bardwell; (FC-C-R); USAE . . . . 3,570 | 53,580

Barker R.—Harris-Fort Bend counties; Buffalo Bayou; 1 mi. S Addicks; (for flood control only); USAE . . . . 0 | 0

Barney M. Davis Cooling Reservoir—Nueces Co.; off-channel storage reservoir of Laguna Madre arm of Gulf; 14 mi. SE Corpus Christi; (In.); Central Power & Light Co. . . 1,100 | 6,600

Bastrop, L.—Bastrop Co.; Spicer Cr.; 3 mi. NE Bastrop; (In.); LCRA . . . . 906 | 16,590

Baylor Creek Lake—Childress Co.; 10 mi. NW Childress; (M-R); City of Childress . . . . . . 610 | 9,220

Belton L.—Bell-Coryell counties; Leon R.; 3 mi. N. Belton; (M-FC-In.-Ir.); USAE-Brazos R. Auth . . . . 12,300 | 457,300

Benbrook L.—Tarrant Co.; Clear Fk. Trinity R.; 10 mi. SW Fort Worth; (FC-R); USAE . . 3,770 | 88,200

Big Brown Creek Reservoir—Freestone Co. (See **Fairfield L.**)

Big Hill Reservoir—Jefferson Co. (See **Valley Area Impoundments.**). . . . .

Bivins L.—Randall Co.; Palo Duro Cr.; 8 mi. NW Canyon; (M); Amarillo (also known as **Amarillo City Lake**); City of Amarillo. . . . . 379 | 5,120

Blackburn Crossing L.—(See **Lake Palestine.**)

Bonham, L.—Fannin Co.; Timber Cr.; 5 mi. NE Bonham; (M); Bonham Mun. Water Auth.. . . . . 1,020 | 12,000

Bowie L.—(See **Amon G. Carter, L.**) . . . .

Brady Creek Reservoir—McCulloch Co.; Brady Cr.; 3 mi. W Brady; (M-In.); City of Brady 2,020 | 29,110

Brandy Branch Reservoir—Harrison Co.; Brandy Br.; 10 mi. SW Marshall; (In.); Southwestern Electric Power Co. . . . . 1,240 | 29,500

Brazoria Reservoir—Brazoria Co.; off-channel reservoir; 1 mi. NE Brazoria; (In.); Dow Chemical Co.. . . . . 1,865 | 21,970

Bridgeport, L.—Wise-Jack counties; W. Fk. of Trinity R.; 4 mi. W Bridgeport; (M-In.-FC-R); Tarrant Co. WC&ID Dist. No. 1 . . . . 13,000 | 386,420

Brownwood, L.—Brown Co.; Pecan Bayou; 8 mi. N Brownwood; (M-In.-Ir.); Brown Co. WC&ID No. 1 . . . . 7,300 | 143,400

Brushy Creek Reservoir—(See **Valley L.**)

Bryan Utilities L.—Brazos Co.; unnamed stream; 6 mi. NW Bryan; (R-In.); City of Bryan 829 | 15,227

Buchanan, L.—Burnet-Llano-San Saba counties; Colorado R.; 13 mi. W Burnet; (M-Ir.-Mi.-P); LCRA . . . . 23,060 | 955,200

Buffalo L.—Randall Co.; Tierra Blanca Cr.; 2 mi. S Umbarger; (R); U.S. Fish & Wildlife Service (impounded by **Umbarger Dam**). . . . . 1,900 | 18,150

Buffalo Springs L.—Lubbock Co.; Double Mtn.Fk. Brazos R.; 9 mi. SE Lubbock; (M-In.-R); Lubbock Co. WC & ID No. 1; (impounded by **W. G. McMillan Sr. Dam**) . . . . 200 | 3,950

Caddo L.—Harrison-Marion counties, Texas and Caddo Parish, La. An original natural lake, whose surface and capacity were increased by the construction of a dam on Cypress Creek near Mooringsport, La. . . . . 25,400 | 59,800

Calaveras L.—Bexar Co.; Calaveras Cr.; 15 mi. SE San Antonio; (In.); City Public Service Bd. of San Antonio . . . . 3,450 | 61,800

Camp Creek L.—Robertson Co.; 13 mi. E Franklin; (R); Camp Creek Water Co. . . . . 750 | 8,550

Canyon L.—Comal Co.; Guadalupe R.; 12 mi. NW New Braunfels; (M-In.-P-FC); Guadalupe-Blanco R. Authority & USAE. . . . . 8,240 | 385,600

Casa Blanca L.—Webb Co.; Chacon Cr.; 3 mi. NE Laredo; (R); Webb County (impounded by **Country Club Dam**) . . . . 1,656 | 20,000

Cedar Bayou Cooling Reservoir—Chambers Co.; Cedar Bayou; 15 mi. SW Anahuac; (In.); Houston Lighting & Power Co. . . . . 2,600 | 20,000

Cedar Creek Reservoir—Henderson-Kaufman counties; Cedar Cr.; 3 mi. NE Trinidad; (sometimes called **Joe B. Hogsett L.**); (M-R); Tarrant Co. WC&ID No. 1. . . . . 33,750 | 679,200

Cedar Creek Reservoir—Fayette Co.; Cedar Cr.; 8.5 mi. E. La Grange; (In.); LCRA. . . . . 2,420 | 71,400

Champion Creek Reservoir—Mitchell Co.; 7 mi. S. Colorado City; (M-In.); Tex. Elec. Service Co. . . . . 1,560 | 41,600

Cherokee L.—Gregg-Rusk counties; Cherokee Bayou; 12 mi. SE Longview; (M-In.-R); Cherokee Water Co. . . . . 3,987 | 46,700

Choke Canyon Reservoir—Live Oak-McMullen counties; Frio R.; 4 mi. W Three Rivers; (M-In.-R-FC); City of Corpus Christi-USBR. . . . . 26,000 | 690,400

Cisco, L.—Eastland Co.; Sandy Cr.; 4 mi. N. Cisco; (M); City of Cisco (impounded by **Williamson Dam**) . . . . 445 | 8,800

Cleburne, L. Pat—Johnson Co.; Nolan R.; 4 mi. S. Cleburne; (M); City of Cleburne . . . . . 1,550 | 25,300

Clyde, L.—Callahan Co.; N. Prong Pecan Bayou; 6 mi. S. Clyde; (M); City of Clyde and USDA Soil Conservation Service. . . . . 449 | 5,748

Coffee Mill L.—Fannin Co.; Coffee Mill Cr.; 12 mi. NW Honey Grove; (R); U.S. Forest Service . . . . 650 | 8,000

Coleman L.—Coleman Co.; Jim Ned Cr.; 14 mi. N. Coleman; (M-In.); City of Coleman . . . 2,000 | 40,000

Coleto Creek Reservoir—Goliad-Victoria counties; Coleto Cr.; 12 mi. SW Victoria; (In); Guadalupe-Blanco River Auth.. . . . . 3,100 | 35,080

Colorado City, L.—Mitchell Co.; Morgan Cr.; 4 mi. SW Colorado City; (M-In.-P); Texas Elec. Service Co. . . . . 1,612 | 30,800

Conroe, L.—Montgomery-Walker counties; W. Fk. San Jacinto R.; 7 mi. NW Conroe; (M-In.-Mi.); San Jacinto River Authority, City of Houston and Texas Water Dev. Bd. . . 20,985 | 429,900

*Cooper L.—Delta-Hopkins counties; Sulphur R.; 3 mi. SE Cooper; (FC-M-R); USAE . . . 19,305 | 310,000

Corpus Christi, L.—Live Oak-San Patricio-Jim Wells counties; Nueces R.; 4 mi. SW Mathis; (P-M-In.-Ir.-Mi.-R.); Lower Nueces River WSD (impounded by **Wesley E. Seale Dam**) . . . . 19,336 | 269,900

Crook, L.—Lamar Co.; Pine Cr.; 5 Mi. N. Paris; (M); City of Paris . . . . 1,226 | 9,964

Cypress Springs, L.—Franklin Co.; Big Cypress Cr.; 8 mi. SE Mount Vernon; (In-M); Franklin Co. WD and Texas Water Development Board (formerly **Franklin Co. L**); impounded by **Franklin Co. Dam**. . . . . 3,400 | 66,800

Dallas L.—(See **Lewisville L.**)

Dam B Reservoir—(See **Steinhagen L., B.A.**)

Daniel, L.—Stephens Co.; Gunsolus Cr.; 7 mi. S Breckenridge; (M-In.); City of Breckenridge; (impounded by **Gunsolus Creek Dam**) . . . . 924　9,515
Davis L.—Knox Co.; Double Dutchman Cr.; 5 mi. SE Benjamin; (Ir.); League Ranch . . . . 585　5,395
Decker L.—(See **Walter E. Long, Lake.**)
DeCordova Bend Reservoir—(See **Lake Granbury.**)
Delta Lake Res. Units 1 and 2—Hidalgo Co.; Rio Grande (off channel); 4 mi. N. Monte Alto; (Ir.); Hidalgo-Willacy counties WC&ID No. 1 (formerly **Monte Alto Reservoir**). . . 2,371　25,000
Diablo Reservoir—(See **Amistad Reservoir.**)
Diversion, L.—Archer-Baylor counties; Wichita R.; 14 mi. W Holliday; (M-In.); City of Wichita Falls and Wichita Co. WID No. 2 . . . . 3,419　40,000
Dunlap, L.—Guadalupe Co.; Guadalupe R.; 9 mi. NW Seguin; (P); Guadalupe-Blanco R. Authority; (impounded by **TP-1 Dam**) . . . . 410　3,550
Eagle L.—Colorado Co.; Colorado R. (off channel); in Eagle Lake; (Ir.); Lakeside Irrigation Co. . . . . 1,200　9,600
Eagle Mountain Lake—Tarrant-Wise counties; W. Fk. Trinity R.; 14 mi. NW Fort Worth; (M-In.-Ir.); Tarrant Co. WC&ID No. 1 . . . . 9,200　190,300
East L.—(See **Victor Braunig Lake.**)
Eddleman L.—(See **Lake Graham.**)
Electra City L.—Wilbarger Co.; Camp Cr. and Beaver Cr.; 7 mi. SW Electra; (In.-M); City of Electra . . . . 660　8,055
Ellison Creek Reservoir—Morris Co.; Ellison Cr.; 8 mi. S. Daingerfield; (P-In.); Lone Star Steel . . . . 1,516　24,700
Fairfield L.—Freestone Co.; Big Brown Cr.; 11 mi. NE Fairfield; (In.); TP&L, Texas Elec. Service Co., DP&L and Industrial Generating Co. (formerly **Big Brown Creek Reservoir**) . . . . 2,350　50,600
Falcon Reservoir—Starr-Zapata counties; Rio Grande; (International—U.S.-Mexico); 3 mi. W Falcon Heights; (M-In.-Ir.-FC-P-R); International Boundary and Water Com.; (Texas' share of total conservation capacity is 58.6 per cent) . . . . 87,210　2,667,600
Farmers Creek Reservoir—Montague Co.; 8 mi. NE Nocona; (M-In.-Mi.) N Montague County Water Supply District (also known as **Lake Nocona**) . . . . 1,470　25,400
Ferrell's Bridge Dam Reservoir—(See **Lake O' the Pines.**)
Flat Creek Reservoir—(See **Athens Lake.**)
Forest Grove Reservoir—Henderson Co.; Caney Cr.; 7 mi. NW Athens; (In.); Texas Utilities Services, Inc., Agent . . . . 1,502　20,038
Forney Reservoir—(See **Ray Hubbard Lake.**)
Fort Phantom Hill, Lake—Jones Co.; Elm Cr.; 5 mi. S. Nugent; (M-R); City of Abilene . . . 4,246　74,300
Franklin County L.—(See **Cypress Springs Lake.**)
Galveston County Industrial Water Reservoir—Galveston Co.; off-channel storage Dickinson Bayou; 16 mi. S La Porte; (In.-M.); Galveston Co. Water Auth. . . . . 812　7,308
Garza-Little Elm—(See **Lewisville L.**)
Georgetown, L.—Williamson Co.; N. Fk. San Gabriel R.; 3.5 mi. W Georgetown; (FC-M-In.); USAE (formerly **North Fork L.**) . . . . 1,310　37,050
Gibbons Creek Reservoir—Grimes Co.; Gibbons Cr.; 9.5 mi NW Anderson; (In.); Texas Mun. Power Agency . . . . 2,490　26,824
Gladewater, L.—Upshur Co.; Glade Cr.; in Gladewater; (M-R); City of Gladewater . . . . 800　6,950
Graham L.—Young Co.; Flint and Salt Creeks; 2 mi. NW Graham; (M-In.); City of Graham . . . . 2,550　45,000
Granbury L.—Hood-Parker counties; Brazos R.; 8 mi. SE Granbury; (M-In.-Ir.-P); Brazos River Authority (impounded by **DeCordova Bend Dam**) . . . . 8,700　151,300
Granger L.—Williamson Co.; San Gabriel R.; 10 mi. NE Taylor; (FC-M-In.); USAE (formerly **Laneport Lake**) . . . . 4,400　64,540
Granite Shoals L.—(See **Johnson L.**)
Grapevine L.—Tarrant-Denton counties; Denton Cr.; 2 mi. NE Grapevine; (M-FC-In.-R.); USAE . . . . 7,380　187,700
Greenbelt L.—Donley Co.; Salt Fk. Red R.; 5 mi. N Clarendon; (M-In.); Greenbelt M&I Water Auth. . . . . 1,990　58,200
H-4 Reservoir—Gonzales Co.; Guadalupe R.; 4.5 mi. SE Belmont; (P); Guadalupe-Blanco R. Auth. (also called **Guadalupe River H-4**) . . . . 696　5,200
Halbert, L.—Navarro Co.; Elm Cr.; 4 mi. SE Corsicana; (M-In-R); City of Corsicana . . . . 650　7,420
Harris Reservoir—Brazoria Co.; off-channel between Brazos R. and Oyster Cr.; 8 mi. NW Angleton; (In.); Dow Chemical Co. . . . . 1,663　12,000
Hawkins, L.—Wood Co.; Little Sandy Cr.; 3 mi. NW Hawkins; (FC-R); Wood County; (impounded by **Wood Co. Dam No. 3**) . . . . 776　11,570
Holbrook L.—Wood Co.; Keys Cr.; 4 mi. NW Mineola; (FC-R); Wood County; (impounded by **Wood Co. Dam No. 2**) . . . . 653　7,770
Honea Reservoir—(See **Conroe Lake.**)
Hords Creek L.—Coleman Co.; Hords Cr.; 5 mi. NW Valera; (M-FC); City of Coleman and USAE . . . . 510　8,600
Houston County L.—Houston Co.; Little Elkhart Cr.; 10 mi. NW Crockett; (M-In.); Houston Co. WC&ID No. 1 . . . . 1,282　19,500
Houston, L.—Harris Co.; San Jacinto R.; 4 mi. N Sheldon; (M-In.-Ir.-Mi.-R); City of Houston; (impounded by **Lake Houston Dam**) . . . . 12,240　140,500
Hubbard Creek Reservoir—Stephens Co.; 6 mi. NW Breckenridge; (M-In.-Mi.); West Central Texas Mun. Water Authority . . . . 15,250　317,800
Imperial Reservoir—Reeves-Pecos counties; Pecos R.; 35 mi. N Fort Stockton; (Ir.); Pecos County WC&ID No. 2. . . . . 1,530　6,000
Inks L.—Burnet-Llano counties; Colorado R.; 12 mi. W Burnet; (M-Ir.-Mi.-P); Lower Colorado River Authority . . . . 803　17,540
Iron Bridge Dam L.—(See **Lake Tawakoni.**)
Jacksonville, L.—Cherokee Co.; Gum Cr.; 5 mi. SW Jacksonville; (M-R); City of Jacksonville; (impounded by **Buckner Dam**) . . . . 1,320　30,500
J. B. Thomas, L.—Scurry-Borden counties; Colorado R.; 16 mi. SW Snyder; (M-In.-R); Colorado River Mun. Water Dist.; (impounded by **Colorado R. Dam**) . . . . 7,820　202,300
J. D. Murphree Wildlife Management Area Impoundments—Jefferson Co.; off-channel reservoirs between Big Hill and Taylor Bayous; at Port Acres; (FH-R); State Park & Wildlife Dept. (formerly **Big Hill Reservoir**) . . . . 6,881　13,500
Joe B. Hogsett, L.—(See **Cedar Creek Reservoir.**)
Joe Pool Reservoir—Dallas-Tarrant-Ellis counties; Mountain Cr.; 14 mi. SW Dallas; (FC-M-R); USAE-Trinity River Auth. . . . . 7,470　176,900

Johnson Creek Reservoir—Marion Co.; 13 mi. NW Jefferson; (In.); Southwestern Electric Co. ... 650   10,100
Johnson L., Lyndon B.—Burnet-Llano counties; (formerly Granite Shoals L.); Colorado R.; 5 mi. SW Marble Falls; (P); LCRA; (impounded by Alvin Wirtz Dam) ... 6,375   138,500
Kemp, L—Baylor Co.; Wichita R.; 6 mi. N Mabelle; (M-P-Ir.); City of Wichita Falls; Wichita Co. WID No. 2 ... 16,540   319,600
Kemp Diversion Dam—(See Diversion Lake.)
Kickapoo, L.—Archer Co.; N. Fk. Little Wichita R.; 10 mi. NW Archer City; (M); City of Wichita Falls ... 6,200   106,000
Kiowa, L.—Cooke Co.; Indian Cr.; 8 mi. SE Gainesville; (R); Lake Kiowa, Inc. ... 560   7,000
Kirby L.—Taylor Co.; Cedar Cr.; 5 mi. S. Abilene; (M); City of Abilene. ... 740   7,620
Kurth, L.—Angelina Co.; off-channel reservoir; 8 mi. N Lufkin; (In.); Southland Paper Mills, Inc. ... 770   16,200
Lake Creek L.—McLennan Co.; Manos Cr.; 4 mi. SW Riesel; (In.); Texas P&L Co. ... 550   8,400
Lake Fork Reservoir—Wood-Rains counties; Lake Fork Cr.; 5 mi. W Quitman; (M-In.); SRA ... 27,690   635,200
Lake O' the Pines—Marion-Upshur-Harrison-Morris-Camp counties; Cypress Cr.; 9 mi. W Jefferson; (FC-C-R-In.-M); USAE. (Lake impounded by Ferrell's Bridge Dam.) ... 18,700   252,000
Lakeview L.—(See Joe Pool Reservoir.)
Lampasas Reservoir—(See Stillhouse Hollow Reservoir.)
Laneport L.—(See Granger Lake.)
Lavon L. (Enlargement)—Collin Co.; East Fk. Trinity R.; 2 mi. W Lavon; (M-FC-In.); USAE ... 21,400   443,800
Leon, Lake—Eastland Co.; Leon R.; 7 mi. S Ranger; (M-In.); Eastland Co. Water Supply Dist. ... 1,590   26,420
Lewis Creek Reservoir—Montgomery Co.; Lewis Cr.; 10 mi. NW Conroe; (In.) Gulf States Utilities Co. ... 1,010   16,400
Lewisville L.—Denton Co.; Elm Fk. Trinity R.; 2 mi. NE Lewisville; (M-FC-In.-R); USAE; (called also Lake Dallas and Garza-Little Elm) ... 23,280   464,500
Limestone, L.—Leon-Limestone-Robertson counties; Navasota R.; 7 mi. NW Marquez; (M-In.-Ir.); BRA ... 14,200   225,400
Livingston L.—Polk-San Jacinto-Trinity-Walker counties; Trinity R.; 6 mi. SW Livingston; (M-In.-Ir.); City of Houston and Trinity River Authority ... 82,600   1,750,000
Loma Alta Lake—Cameron Co.; off-channel Rio Grande; 8 mi. NE Brownsville; (M-In.); Brownsville Navigation Dist. ... 2,490   26,500
Lone Star Reservoir—(See Ellison Creek Lake.)
Los Fresnos, Resaca de—(See Resacas.)
*Lost Creek Reservoir—Jack Co.; Lost Cr.; 4 mi. NE Jacksboro; (M); City of Jacksboro . 360   11,960
McGee Bend Reservoir—(See Sam Rayburn Reservoir.)
McQueeney, L.—Guadalupe Co.; Guadalupe R.; 5 mi. W Seguin; (P); Guadalupe-Blanco R. Authority; (impounded by Abbott Dam) ... 396   5,000
Mackenzie Reservoir—Briscoe Co.; Tule Cr.; 9 mi. NW Silverton; (M); Mackenzie Mun. Water Auth ... 910   46,250
Marble Falls L.—Burnet County; Colorado R.; (impounded by Max Starcke Dam); 1.25 mi. SE Marble Falls; (P); LCRA ... 780   8,760
Martin L.—Rusk-Panola counties; Martin Cr.; 17 mi. NE Henderson; (P); Texas Utilities Service Co., Inc. ... 5,020   77,620
Max Starcke Dam—(See Marble Falls Lake.)
Medina L.—Medina-Bandera counties; Medina R.; 8 mi. W Rio Medina; (Ir.); Bexar-Medina-Atascosa Co. WID No. 1 ... 5,575   254,000
Meredith, L.—Moore-Potter-Hutchinson counties; Canadian R.; 10 mi. NW Borger; (M-In.-FC-R); cooperative project for municipal water supply by Amarillo, Lubbock and other High Plains Cities. Canadian R. Municipal Water Authority-USBR; (impounded by Sanford Dam) ... 16,504   821,300
Mexia, L.—Limestone Co.; Navasota R.; 7 mi. SW Mexia; (M-In) Bistone Mun. Water Dist.; (impounded by Bistone Dam) ... 1,200   10,000
Millers Creek Reservoir—Baylor Co.; Millers Cr.; 9 mi. SE Goree; (M); No. Central Tex. Mun. Water Auth. and Texas Water Development Board ... 2,350   30,700
Mineral Wells L.—Parker Co.; Rock Cr.; 4 mi. E Mineral Wells; (M); Palo Pinto Co. Mun. WD No. 1 ... 646   6,760
Monte Alto Reservoir—(See Delta Lake Res. Units 1 and 2.)
Monticello Reservoir—Titus Co.; Blundell Cr.; 2.5 mi. E. Monticello; (In.); Industrial Generating Co. ... 2,000   40,100
Moss L., Hubert H.—Cooke Co.; Fish Cr.; 10 mi. NW Gainesville; (M-In.); City of Gainesville ... 1,125   23,210
Mountain Creek L.—Dallas Co.; Mountain Cr.; 4 mi. SE Grand Prairie; (In.); Dallas P&L Co. ... 2,710   22,840
Mud Creek Dam L.—(See Tyler Lake, East.)
Murphree, J. D. Area Impoundments.—(See J. D. Murphree.)
Murvaul L.—Panola Co.; Murvaul Bayou; 10 mi. SW Carthage; (M-In.-R); Panola Co. Fresh Water Supply Dist. No. 1 ... 3,820   45,815
Nacogdoches, L.—Nacogdoches Co.; Bayo Loco Cr.; 10 mi. W Nacogdoches; (M); City of Nacogdoches ... 2,210   41,140
Nasworthy, L.—Tom Green Co.; S Concho R.; 6 mi. SW San Angelo; (M-In.-Ir); City of San Angelo ... 1,596   12,390
Navarro Mills L.—Navarro-Hill counties; Richland Cr.; 16 mi. SW Corsicana; (M-FC); USAE ... 5,070   60,900
Nocona L.—(See Farmers Creek Reservoir.)
North Fk. Buffalo Creek Reservoir—Wichita Co.; 5 mi. NW Iowa Park; (M); Wichita Co. WC&ID No. 3 ... 1,500   15,400
North Fork L.—(See Georgetown L.)
North L.—Dallas Co.; S. Fork Grapevine Cr.; 2 mi. SE Coppell; (In.); Dallas P&L Co. ... 800   17,000
Oak Creek Reservoir—Coke Co.; 5 mi. SE Blackwell; (M-In.); City of Sweetwater ... 2,375   39,360
O. C. Fisher L.—Tom Green Co.; N. Concho R.; 3 mi. NW San Angelo (M-FC-C-Ir.-R-In.-Mi); USAE — Upper Colo. Auth. (formerly San Angelo L.) ... 5,440   119,200
O. H. Ivie Reservoir—Coleman-Concho-Runnels counties; 24 mi. SE Ballinger; (M-In.), Colorado R. Mun. Water Dist. ... 19,150   554,340
Olmos Reservoir—Bexar Co.; Olmos Cr.; in San Antonio city limits; (exclusively for flood control); maximum capacity 12,600 acre-feet; City of San Antonio ... 0   0

Palestine, L.—Anderson-Cherokee-Henderson-Smith counties; Neches R.; 4 mi. E Frankston; (M-In.-R); Upper Neches R. MWA (impounded by **Blackburn Crossing Dam**) 25,560 411,300
Palmetto Bend Reservoir—(See **Texana, L.**)
Palo Alto Resaca—(See **Resacas** in this list.)
***Palo Duro Reservoir**—Hansford Co.; Palo Duro Cr.; 12 mi. N Spearman; (M-R); Palo Duro River Auth. 2,410 60,900
Palo Pinto, L.—Palo Pinto Co.; 15 mi. SW Mineral Wells; (M-In.); Palo Pinto Co. Municipal Water Dist. No. 1 . . . . 2,661 42,200
Panola L.—(See **Murvaul L.**)
Pat Mayse L.—Lamar Co.; Sanders Cr.; 2 mi. SW Arthur City; (M-In.-FC); USAE 5,993 124,500
Pinkston Reservoir—Shelby Co.; Sandy Cr.; 12.5 mi. SW Center; (M); City of Center; (formerly **Sandy Creek Reservoir**). 523 7,380
Possum Kingdom L.—Palo Pinto-Young-Stephens-Jack counties; Brazos R.; 11 mi. SW Graford; (M-In.-Ir.-Mi.-P-R); Brazos R. Authority; (impounded by **Morris Sheppard Dam**) 17,700 569,380
Proctor L.—Comanche Co.; Leon R.; 9 mi. NE Comanche; (M-In.-Ir.-FC); USAE-Brazos River Authority. 4,610 59,300
Quarters Resaca.—(See **Resacas.**)
Quitman, L.—Wood Co.; Dry Cr.; 4 mi. N Quitman; (FC-R); Wood County (impounded by **Wood Co. Dam No.** 1) 814 7,440
Randall, L.—Grayson Co.; Shawnee Cr.; 4 mi. NW Denison; (M); City of Denison 311 6,290
Ray Hubbard, L.—Collin-Dallas-Kaufman-Rockwall counties; (formerly called **Forney Reservoir**); E. Fk. Trinity R.; 15 mi. E Dallas; (M); City of Dallas 22,745 490,000
Ray Roberts L.—Denton-Cooke-Grayson counties; Elm Fk. Trinity R.; 11 mi. NE Denton; (FC-M-D); City of Denton, Dallas, USAE; (also known as **Aubrey Reservior**) 29,350 799,600
Red Bluff Reservoir—Loving-Reeves counties, Texas; and Eddy Co.; N.M.; Pecos R.; 5 mi. N Orla; (Ir.-P); Red Bluff Water Power Control District 11,700 307,000
Resacas—Cameron-Hidalgo-Willacy counties; Rio Grande; these reservoirs are primarily for storage of water during periods of normal or above-normal flow in the river for use when the river's water volume is low. Some of these are old loops and bends in the river that have been isolated by the river's changing its channel. They are known by the Spanish name of resacas. Also a number of reservoirs have been constructed and connected with the main channel of the river by ditches through which the reservoirs are filled either by gravity flow or by pumping. This is reserve irrigation water for use during periods of low flow in the river channel. Most of these reservoirs are near the main channel of the river, but some of them are 20 or 25 miles distant . . . .
Reservoir No. 1 & No. 2—Cameron Co.; off-channel Rio Grande R.; 7 mi. SW San Benito; (Ir.-M-In.); Cameron Co. WID No. 2 . . . . 900 14,200
Rita Blanca L.—Hartley Co.; Rita Blanca Cr.; 2 mi. S Dalhart; (R) City of Dalhart 524 12,100
River Crest L.—Red River County; off-channel reservoir; 7 mi. SE Bogata; (In.); Texas P&L 555 7,000
Robert Lee Reservoir.—(See **Spence Reservoir.**).
Salt Creek L.—(See **Graham L.**).
Sam Rayburn Reservoir—Jasper-Angelina-Sabine-Nacogdoches-San Augustine counties; Angelina R.; (formerly **McGee Bend**); (FC-P-M-In.-Ir.-R); USAE 114,500 2,876,300
San Angelo L.—(See **O. C. Fisher L.**)
Sandlin, L. Bob—Titus-Wood-Camp-Franklin counties; Big Cypress Cr.; 5 mi. SW Mount Pleasant; (In.-M-R); Titus Co. FWSD No. 1 (impounded by **Fort Sherman Dam**). 9,460 202,300
Sandow L.—(See **Alcoa Lake.**)
Sandy Creek Reservoir.—(See **Pinkston Reservoir.**)
San Estaban L.—Presidio Co.; Alamito Cr.; 10 mi. S Marfa; (R); Wm. B. Blakemore 762 18,770
Sanford Reservoir.—(See **Meredith Lake.**)
Santa Rosa L.—Wilbarger Co.; Beaver Cr.; 15 mi. S Vernon; (Mi.); W. T. Waggoner Estate 1,500 11,570
Sheldon Reservoir—Harris Co.; Carpenters Bayou; 2 mi. SW Sheldon; (R-FH); State Parks & Wildlife Com. 1,700 5,420
Smithers L.—Fort Bend Co.; Dry Creek; 10 mi. SE Richmond; (In.); Houston Lighting & Power Co. 2,480 18,700
Somerville L.—Burleson-Washington counties; Yegua Cr.; 2 mi. S Somerville; (M-In.-Ir.-FC); USAE-Brazos River Authority 11,460 160,100
Southland Paper Mills Reservoir.—(See **Kurth Lake.**)
South Texas Project Reservoir—Matagorda Co.; off-channel Colorado R.; 16 mi. S Bay City; (In.); Houston Lighting & Power. 7,000 187,000
Spence Reservoir, E. V.—Coke Co.; Colorado R.; 2 mi. W. Robert Lee; (M-In.-Mi.) Colorado R. Mun. Water Dist.; (impounded by **Robert Lee Dam**). 14,950 484,800
Squaw Creek Reservoir—Somervell-Hood counties; Squaw Cr.; 4.5 mi. N Glen Rose; (In.); Texas Utilities Services, Inc. 3,228 151,047
Stacy Reservoir—(See **O. H. Ivie Reservoir.**)
Stamford, L.—Haskell Co.; Paint Cr.; 10 mi. SE Haskell; (M-In.); City of Stamford 4,690 52,700
Steinhagen L., B. A.—(Also called **Town Bluff Reservoir** and **Dam B. Reservoir**); Tyler-Jasper counties; Neches R.; 1/2 mi. N Town Bluff; (FC-R-C); (impounded by **Town Bluff Dam**). 13,700 94,200
Stillhouse Hollow L.—Bell Co.; Lampasas R.; 5 mi. SW Belton; (M-In.-Ir.-FC); USAE-Brazos R. Authority; (sometimes called **Lampasas Reservoir**) 6,430 234,900
Striker Creek Reservoir—Rusk-Cherokee counties; Striker Cr.; 18 mi. SW Henderson; (M-In.); Angelina-Nacogdoches WC&ID No. 1 . . . . 2,400 26,960
Sulphur Springs L.—Hopkins Co.; White Oak Cr.; 2 mi. N Sulphur Springs; (M); Sulphur Springs WD; (impounded by **Lake Sulphur Springs Dam** and formerly called **White Oak Creek Reservoir**) 1,910 17,710
Swauano Creek Reservoir—(See **Welsh Reservoir.**)
Sweetwater L.—Nolan Co.; Bitter and Cottonwood Creeks; 6 mi. SE Sweetwater; (M-In.); City of Sweetwater. 630 11,900
Tawakoni, L.—Rains-Van Zandt-Hunt counties; Sabine R.; 9 mi. NE Wills Point; (M-In.-Ir.-R); Sabine River Authority; (impounded by **Iron Bridge Dam**). 36,700 936,200
Terrell City L., New—Kaufman Co.; Muddy Cedar Cr.; 6 mi. E Terrell; (M-R); City of Terrell 830 8,712
Texana, L.—Jackson Co.; Navidad R. and Sandy Cr.; 6.8 mi. SE Edna; (M-Ir); USBR, Lavaca-Navidad R. Auth., Texas Water Dev. Bd.; (formerly **Palmetto Bend Reservoir**) 11,000 157,900

The natural serenity of Town Lake is conveniently close to the urban action of downtown Austin, making it a popular spot for joggers, walkers and nature lovers. Almanac Staff Photo.

Texarkana L.—(See **Wright Patman Lake**.)

Texoma L.—Grayson-Cooke counties, Texas; Bryan-Marshall-Love counties, Okla.; impounded by **Denison Dam** on Red R. short distance below confluence of Red and Washita Rivers; (P-FC-C-R); USAE .... 89,000 | 2,722,000

Thomas L.—(See **J. B. Thomas L.**)

Toledo Bend Reservoir—Newton-Panola-Sabine-Shelby counties; Sabine R.; 14 mi. NE Burkeville; (M-In.-Ir.-PR); Sabine River Authority. (Texas' share of capacity is half amount shown.) .... 181,600 | 4,472,900

Town Bluff Reservoir—(See **Steinhagen, Lake B. A.**)

Tradinghouse Creek Reservoir—McLennan Co.; Tradinghouse Cr.; 9 mi. E Waco; (In.); Texas P&L .... 2,010 | 35,124

Travis, L.—Travis-Burnet counties; Colorado R.; 13 mi. NW Austin; (M-In.-Ir.-Mi.-P-FC-R); LCRA: (impounded by **Mansfield Dam**) .... 18,930 | 1,144,100

Trinidad L.—Henderson Co.; off-channel reservoir Trinity R.; 2 mi. S. Trinidad; (P); Texas P&L Co. .... 740 | 7,450

Truscott Brine L.—Knox Co.; Bluff Cr.; 26 mi. NNW Knox City; (Chlorine Control); Red River Auth. of Texas .... 2,978 | 107,000

Turtle Bayou Reservoir—(See **Anahuac Lake.**)

Twin Buttes Reservoir—Tom Green Co.; Concho R.; 8 mi. SW San Angelo; (M-In.-FC-Ir.-R.); City of San Angelo-USBR-Tom Green Co. WC&ID No. 1 .... 9,080 | 177,800

Twin Oaks Reservoir—Robertson Co.; Duck Cr.; 12 mi. N. Franklin; (In) Texas P&L ...... 2,300 | 30,319

Tyler L.—Smith Co.; Prairie and Mud Crs.; 12 mi. SE Tyler; (M-In); City of Tyler; (impounded by **Whitehouse and Mud Creek Dams**) .... 4,800 | 73,700

Upper Nueces Reservoir—Zavala Co.; Nueces R.; 6 mi. N Crystal City; (Ir.); Zavala-Dimmit Co. WID No. 1 .... 316 | 7,590

Valley Acres Reservoir—Hidalgo Co.; off-channel Rio Grande; 7 mi. N Mercedes; (Ir-M-FC); Valley Acres Water Dist .... 906 | 7,840

Valley L.—Fannin-Grayson counties; 2.5 mi. N Savoy; (P); TP&L; (formerly **Brushy Creek Reservoir**) .... 1,080 | 16,400

Victor Braunig L.—Bexar Co.; Arroyo Seco; 15 mi. SE San Antonio; (In.); City Public Service Bd. of San Antonio .... 1,350 | 26,500

Waco L.—McLennan Co.; Bosque R.; 2 mi. W Waco; (M-FC-C-R); City of Waco-USAE-Brazos River Authority .... 7,270 | 151,900

*Wallisville L.—Liberty-Chambers counties; Trinity R.; 2 mi. S Wallisville; (M-In.-Ir.); USAE .... 19,700 | 58,000

Walter E. Long L.—Travis Co.; Decker Cr.; 9 mi. E of capital, Austin; (M-In.-R); City of Austin; (formerly **Decker Lake**) .... 1,269 | 33,940

Waxahachie L.—Ellis Co.; S Prong Waxahachie Cr.; 4 mi. SE Waxahachie; (M-In); Ellis County WC&ID No. 1; (impounded by **S. Prong Dam**) .... 690 | 13,500

Weatherford L.—Parker Co.; Clear Fork Trinity River; 7 mi. E Weatherford; (M-In.); City of Weatherford. .... 1,210 | 19,470

Welsh Reservoir—Titus Co.; Swauano Cr.; 11 mi. SE Mount Pleasant; (R-In.); Southwestern Electric Power Co.; (formerly **Swauano Creek Reservoir.**) .... 1,365 | 23,587

White Oak Creek Reservoir—(See **Sulphur Springs Lake.**)

White River L.—Crosby Co.; 16 mi. SE Crosbyton; (M-In.-Mi.); White River Municipal Water Dist. .... 2,020 | 44,300

White Rock L.—Dallas Co.; White Rock Cr.; within NE Dallas city limits; (R); City of Dallas. .... 1,119 | 10,740

Whitney L.—Hill-Bosque-Johnson counties; Brazos R.; 5.5 mi. SW Whitney; (FC-P); USAE .... 23,560 | 622,800

Wichita, L.—Wichita Co.; Holliday Cr.; 6 mi. SW Wichita Falls; (M-P-R); City of Wichita Falls. .... 2,200 | 9,000

Winnsboro, L.—Wood Co.; Big Sandy Cr.; 6 mi. SW Winnsboro; (FC-R); Wood County; (impounded by **Wood Co. Dam No. 4**) .... 806 | 8,100

Winters L.—Runnels Co.; Elm Cr.; 4.5 mi. E. Winters; (M); City of Winters .... 640 | 8,370

Worth, L.—Tarrant Co.; W. Fk. Trinity R.; in NW Fort Worth; (M); City of Fort Worth ... 3,560 | 38,130

Wright Patman L.—Bowie-Cass-Morris-Titus-Red River counties; Sulphur R.; 8 mi. SW Texarkana; (FC-M); USAE; (formerly **Texarkana Lake**) .... 20,300 | 142,700

*Reservoir under construction.

The "Lost Pines" near Bastrop were so named because they are found about 100 miles west of East Texas' Piney Woods area, where the state's major conifer forests are located.

Texas Forest Resources

This information was compiled and prepared by Sam D. Logan, director of Information and Education for the Texas Forest Service, a part of the Texas A&M University System.

Forests in Texas may be one of the Lone Star State's best kept secrets yet are a most important natural resource, and trees, unlike petroleum, are a renewable resource.

The popular stereotype of Texas — likely fostered by generations of Hollywood-produced movies — is that "Texas is mostly plains, sand, oil wells and cactus . . ."

There are several reasons for the popular misconception that there are few trees in Texas. First, Texas is the third most populous state of the 50 United States, yet fully 80 percent of the population lives in several large metropolitan cities, only two of which (Houston and Beaumont) are located in the primary timber region. Of this 80 percent, an estimated one-third have lived in Texas less than 10 years. The large majority of these urbanites simply have little or no knowledge of, nor contact with, Texas' forests.

Second, Texas, the second-largest state geographically, has only 14 percent of its land area in forests. What many people don't realize is that this 14 percent is about the size of the state of Indiana.

Third, there is confusion as to just where "forests" fit into our compulsion to categorize everything. Are forests a renewable natural resource to be conserved for beauty and habitat for wildlife, or are they an agricultural crop to be harvested and replanted? Actually they are both.

Finally, there is the factor often called the "supermarket syndrome," a term coined after a school child wrote a paper stating that we no longer need farmers and cows because his mother buys milk at the supermarket.

It isn't any wonder then that too few Texans realize the size and importance of forestry in the Lone Star State.

Let's consider the economic impact of timber as both a raw material and as manufactured products:

• Texas' wood-based industry is the ninth largest in the nation and fourth largest in the South, with sales of $5.6 billion and a value-added contribution of $2.3 billion.

• Texas is one of the top 10 states in the United States in primary wood-based manufacturing. Texas ranks third in plywood production, seventh in pulpwood consumption, and 12th in lumber production.

• Timber is the most valuable agricultural crop in the South. In Texas, timber consistently ranks among the top four cash crops, with an annual delivered value of approximately $500 million.

• Timber grown in East Texas is processed into primary wood-based products that had a sales value of $1.6 billion and a value-added contribution of $550 million in 1984.

• The wood-based industry provides more than one-fourth of the manufacturing employment opportunities in rural East Texas.

• A one-percent increase in the output of the primary manufacturing sector of the industry — lumber and plywood, and pulp and paper — will produce a statewide impact of almost $50 million.

• The forest-products industry in Texas manufactures wood-based products such as lumber, plywood, poles, railroad cross-ties, furniture, pulp, paper, shakes, shingles and a host of other products from the timber grown in Texas forests. This wood-based industry is a vital part of Texas' diverse economy. As unbelievable as it may sound, Texas is one of the top producers of forest products in the nation.

• In 1990, Texas also ranked second only to Florida among the 50 states in having the largest number of national champion big trees, with more than 80 species that have been crowned national champs or co-champs.

Future of Texas'
Forest Resources and Industry

Much public concern has been exhibited recently over the trend toward global warming, or so-called "greenhouse effect," and the planting of trees by both groups and individuals has been encouraged around the world.

Some Texans have a good record for **reforestation**, but others need improvement.

The five largest timber industries in Texas are doing a creditable job, maintaining their own tree nurseries, growing and planting 133 million tree seedlings every year. Logic would dictate that these forest industries would never allow their lands to become barren.

The **Texas Forest Service** maintains two nurseries and produces an average of 25 million seedlings per year (27 million in 1989), which are sold at cost to small, private, non-industrial landowners for reforestation and wind and erosion control.

Perhaps Texas' greatest future problem lies in the fact that the private non-industrial landowners are currently replanting only one acre for every nine acres harvested. There are advantages to growing trees for harvest. You don't have to feed them like cattle, nor till them like row crops, and they are profitable. But there are risks, such as fire, insects, flood and drought.

The biggest problem, and the reason that many do not replant after harvest, is lack of incentive. It takes 20 or more years to produce a crop of trees, and many small landowners simply can't wait that long for a return on their investment.

There are some incentives for replanting forest lands available (discussed later in this section), but most foresters and landowners agree that reinstatement of the federal government's capital gains tax allowance would be a major step toward growing more trees in Texas.

The 22,032,000 acres of forests in Texas — an area larger than the states of Massachusetts, Connecticut, New Hampshire, Rhode Island and Vermont combined — form the land base for this important renewable resource. There are two timber-producing counties in East Texas (Harris and Houston) that are each larger than the entire state of Rhode Island.

Besides the economic impacts and market values discussed earlier, recreational opportunities in forests have been expanded. The **Texas Forestry Association's Woodlands Trails** program provides public hiking through designated scenic portions of privately owned timberland. (See Recreation section in this Almanac. Additional information is available from Texas Forestry Association, Box 1488, Lufkin 75902-1488; the Texas Dept. of Highways and Public Transportation and other sources.) State and national forests in East Texas also are being improved for recreational purposes and to provide habitat and forage for wildlife. Trees are also valuable for prevention and control of pollution and erosion.

The following information is supplied largely by the **Texas Forest Service**, the **Texas Forestry Association** and federal agencies. Texas' forested areas stretch over an estimated 22.032 million acres. The principal forest and woodlands regions are: pine-hardwood, 10,901,500 acres; post oak, 2,993,600; East and West Cross Timbers, 2,226,310; cedar brakes, 4,561,053; costal forests, 575,071; and miscellaneous, 774,442 acres.

The most important forest area of the state, producing nearly all of the commercial timber, is the East Texas pine-hardwood region known as the **Piney Woods**. It extends over all or parts of 43 of Texas' 254 counties.

Forest Conservation

Many agencies, companies, associations and others cooperate in the **conservation of Texas forest resources**. Among them are federal and state agencies, district, city and county governments, timber producers and processors, and wood product manufacturers. Only a few major programs can be listed here.

Texas Reforestation Foundation

One of the most successful programs is the **Texas Reforestation Foundation** (TRe), which is a landowner-assistance, forestry-incentives program designed to help reforest and improve Texas' timberlands. Unlike other assistance programs, TRe is wholly financed by private interests through voluntary contributions. The money is distributed to private, non-industrial Texas landowners on a matching basis, with operations directed from the Texas Forestry Association office in Lufkin, with technical assistance from the Texas Forest Service. TRe is a non-profit foundation, operating with its own elected board of directors.

Since TRe began in 1981, more than $3.5 million in cost-share funds from the foundation have helped to reforest nearly 70,000 acres of Texas land.

Tree Farms

A tree farm is a privately owned, taxpaying woodland dedicated to continuing growth of forest crops and officially recognized by the **Texas Forestry Association** in cooperation with the **American Forest Council**, the national sponsor. Tree farmers agree to manage their timber for the growth and harvest of forest products, and to protect their timber from fires, insects, disease and destructive overgrazing. Any landowner with 10 or more acres of forest land on which the trees are more than one year of age or land with a stand of viable tree seedlings may qualify.

On January 1, 1990, there were 3,479 officially recognized tree farms in Texas, according to the Texas Forestry Association. Total area was 4,527,063 acres. Texas ranked fifth in the nation in number of tree farms and ninth in number of acres.

Texas Forest Service

In 1915, the Legislature created a **State Department of Forestry** and placed it under the direction of the **Agricultural & Mechanical College of Texas**. In 1926, it was reorganized as the **Texas Forest Service** (TFS) under the board of **A&M College**. Today the office of the director, the **Forest Management Department, Reforestation Department, Forest Genetics Laboratory** and the **Information and Education Section** are located on the campus of **Texas A&M University** in College Station.

The **Forest Fire Control Department, Forest Products Laboratory** and **Forest Pest Control Section** are located in the **Cudlipp Forestry Center** at Lufkin. Five area offices and 13 districts are located throughout East Texas, with area offices headquartered at Linden, Henderson, Lufkin, Woodville and Conroe.

In 1971, a staff silviculturist was stationed in Lubbock to assist landowners in establishing and maintaining windbreaks to protect their homesteads and fields from the high, drying winds in that region. In 1973, an urban forestry program was established to assist the public and city governments with developing land to maintain the urban forests, with TFS foresters in Fort Worth, Dallas, Houston, Galveston, San Antonio and Austin.

Protecting Forests From Pests

Insects and diseases affecting forest trees cost landowners millions of dollars annually. The **TFS Pest Control Section**, established in 1962, is responsible for monitoring pest activity on 12 million acres of state and private forest lands in East Texas. The section also conducts applied research on major insect and disease pests of pine-seed orchards, plantations and natural forest stands. The major insect pest of Texas forests is the **southern pine beetle**. Other important insect pests include **seed- and cone-destroying insects, leaf-cutting ants, pine tip moths** and **pine sawflies**. The most important disease in East Texas pine forests is **fusiform rust**. In Central Texas, a disease known as **oak wilt** is causing significant oak mortality in 43 counties.

In the South, southern pine beetles kill more timber annually than forest fires. The Texas Forest Service coordinates all beetle-control activity in Texas, which includes detecting infestations from the air, notifying landowners and assisting them in controlling the infestations. The most severe outbreak of southern pine beetles known in Texas occurred in 1985 when an estimated 78.7 million cubic feet of timber was killed. The Pest Control Section is conducting applied research on a new control tactic that uses non-toxic "chemical messages" to confuse beetles and prevent them from attacking and killing more trees.

Valuable seeds carrying superior genetic qualities must be protected from insect pests in southern pine seed orchards. Without control measures, insects will usually reduce potential seed crops by more than 50 percent. **Coneworms** and **seedbugs** are the major insect pests in southern pine seed orchards. The TFS is involved in a research program directed toward developing improved measures for controlling these insect pests.

Pests of young pine plantations are increasing in importance with the acceleration of reforestation in East Texas. Texas **leaf-cutting ants** often cause serious mortality when present in or near newly planted pine plantations. These ants prefer deep, sandy soils, and they damage pine seedlings by removing needles and buds, particularly in the winter when other green vegetation is unavailable. This insect pest must be controlled in new plantations to prevent economic losses. TFS entomologists are testing toxic baits for control of these ants. Several experimental baits are quite effective, and one may soon be registered for ant control by the Environmental Protection Agency. Other pests in pine plantations include **pine tip moth, pine sawflies, gophers** and **rabbits.**

Fusiform rust has been recognized for many years as a severe problem on both slash and loblolly pines in the southeastern United States. The disease has its greatest impact in young pine plantations. The TFS has been involved in periodic surveys, initiated in Texas in 1969, which have indicated that fusiform rust is most severe in slash pine plantations in southeast Texas. Loblolly pine is not seriously damaged. The severity of the disease increased dramatically between 1969-1980, but appears to have increased only slightly since 1980. The TFS also is evaluating forest management practices and producing rust-resistant seedlings that will reduce losses caused by the disease.

Public concern is increasing over the extensive mortality of oaks in the Hill Country of Central Texas. The vascular wilt organism, **"oak wilt,"** is the major causal agent of live oak mortality in Central Texas.

In 1988 the Texas Forest Service, Texas A&M University, USDA-Forest Service, Texas Agricultural Extension Service and City of Austin initiated a cooperative oak wilt suppression project to combat the disease in Texas. A concerted education and information campaign was launched. Also cost-share funds are available through the Texas Forest Service for establishing control treatments of this disease on private lands.

Texas Forest Service entomologists are also asked to evaluate insect and disease problems in other areas of the state. Assistance has been provided regarding windbreak trees in the High Plains area and problems in coniferous forests in the mountains of West Texas.

The **gypsy moth** has been a serious defoliator of hardwood trees in the northeast United States for many years. In the past decade this insect pest has been transported to many other areas of the country, including the West Coast, the Great Lakes area and various parts of the South. During the summer of 1984, male gypsy moths were trapped for the first time in Texas. Since then a few moths have been trapped each summer. To date, no established gypsy moth populations are known to occur in Texas, but summer trapping programs continue. A task force of leading entomologists in the state has been formed to coordinate trapping efforts in Texas and prevent the gypsy moth from becoming a serious tree pest in Texas.

Forest Fire Protection

Organized fire protection is provided by the TFS with some financial assistance from the federal government and from landowners. Texas first qualified for federal assistance in protection against forest fires in 1916. A division of forest protection, now the **Forest Fire Control Department,** was established at Lufkin in 1925.

From 1925 through 1990, **174,573 forest fires** were reported and suppressed in East Texas by TFS. In 1990, 1,577 fires burned 27,644 acres, averaging 17.5 acres per fire. For the past five years, the average annual acreage loss to wildfire was 0.15 percent of the area protected.

Causes of the 1,577 fires in 1990 were: debris burning, 48 percent; incendiary, 34 percent; smokers, 2 percent; campfires, 2 percent; and lightning, miscellaneous, equipment use, railroads and children amounted to 14 percent.

For 57 years, from 1916 to 1975, basic rural fire-fighting responsibility was confined to 48 counties, or the commercial forest area of East Texas. Since 1975 however, TFS has used its wildfire suppression expertise to assist with major wildland fires anywhere in the state, and under a mutual aid compact, TFS also lent its help several times in other states, including the California Fire Siege of 1987 and the Yellowstone fires of 1988. In March 1988, the Texas Forest Service organized the effort that controlled the largest wildfire in modern Texas history. Known as the "Big Country Fire," it burned 300,000 acres in Shackelford and parts of two adjacent

Total Timber Production and Value by County in Texas, 1989

County	Pine	Hardwood	Total	Stumpage Value	Delivered Value
		Cubic feet		Thousand dollars	
Anderson	6,029,200	1,077,776	7,106,976	$3,878	$6,300
Angelina	29,981,605	3,470,003	33,451,608	16,076	28,058
Bowie	6,558,615	3,085,292	9,643,907	3,008	6,775
Camp	1,302,092	455,544	1,757,635	830	1,454
Cass	17,978,828	9,999,046	27,977,874	8,247	19,573
Chambers	2,153,204	526,080	2,679,284	1,425	2,359
Cherokee	21,665,841	5,037,238	26,703,079	11,947	21,573
Franklin	31,185	576,584	607,769	136	376
Gregg	1,940,610	1,683,142	3,623,752	1,251	2,627
Grimes	4,015,178	15,280	4,030,458	2,241	3,624
Hardin	28,961,667	13,068,380	42,030,047	16,321	32,087
Harris	6,146,445	119,228	6,265,673	3,761	5,846
Harrison	13,253,924	5,119,515	18,373,439	5,740	12,969
Houston	17,403,838	1,497,462	18,901,300	9,677	16,339
Jasper	27,847,797	5,537,664	33,385,461	14,666	26,866
Jefferson	1,522,229	1,662,880	3,185,109	1,024	2,263
Leon	307,074	108,326	415,400	215	357
Liberty	20,314,807	6,481,127	26,795,933	11,958	21,679
Marion	7,431,502	3,024,927	10,456,429	3,547	7,557
Montgomery	20,638,901	1,198,028	21,836,928	10,741	18,515
Morris	4,347,560	2,189,088	6,536,648	1,929	4,504
Nacogdoches	17,982,562	4,162,352	22,144,914	9,482	17,610
Newton	24,382,747	4,560,466	28,943,213	12,520	23,170
Orange	7,466,232	1,856,033	9,322,266	4,113	7,511
Panola	7,444,286	1,948,687	9,392,972	3,603	7,168
Polk	28,740,622	4,112,906	32,853,528	14,614	26,577
Red River	1,017,234	294,110	1,311,344	630	1,104
Rusk	9,887,241	3,810,873	13,698,113	5,977	10,929
Sabine	12,674,120	1,484,364	14,158,485	7,921	12,739
San Augustine	14,832,548	4,127,818	18,960,367	8,692	15,559
San Jacinto	13,471,107	327,259	13,798,366	6,873	11,768
Shelby	17,238,223	3,656,504	20,894,726	7,779	15,678
Smith	4,534,892	1,987,972	6,522,865	2,237	4,714
Titus	526,519	570,077	1,096,596	269	711
Trinity	17,417,449	99,979	17,517,429	9,342	15,420
Tyler	19,497,325	2,064,988	21,562,312	9,823	17,842
Upshur	8,818,278	2,088,679	10,906,958	4,371	8,439
Walker	10,735,455	171,888	10,907,343	5,405	9,268
Waller	1,212,237	0	1,212,237	655	1,079
Wood	1,873,055	203,654	2,076,709	1,183	1,883
Other Counties	2,572,854	1,315,833	3,888,687	1,266	2,773
Totals	462,157,091	104,777,048	566,934,140	$245,374	$453,314

counties. More than 400 personnel (from 47 fire departments and other agencies) and $400,000 in costs were required to suppress this blaze.

The backbone of the TFS fire operations is a two-man fire crew with a crawler tractor equipped with a fire plow. This unit and its transport vehicle are both equipped with two-way radios. There are 70 such units in the 48-county area. These crewmen are trained at the **Texas Forest Service Ground Cover Training Facility** in Lufkin.

In 1973, the TFS was given the responsibility in the state legislature for rural wildland fire defense in the entire state. The legislation authorized the TFS to develop rural fire protection plans and to provide training and equipment to volunteer firefighters and organized groups throughout the state. It did not expand the operational area of the TFS fire units beyond the 48 counties of East Texas.

Rural Fire Protection in Texas

Of the huge loss annually caused by fire in the United States, much occurs in towns and villages with fewer than 10,000 residents. In general, most of these towns cannot afford the fire equipment necessary for their protection. The **Rural Community Fire Protection Program** (RCFP), administered in Texas through the Texas Forest Service, is helping meet this need.

Based on data collected by the Texas Forest Service from towns under 10,000 population, there are more than 38,000 rural fires annually. Twenty thousand of these are ground-cover fires, which burn an estimated one million acres each year. The next two highest categories of rural fires are single-story residence and vehicular, which account for 7,100 and 5,300 fires respectively.

Some counties have received increased requests for operating funds from local communities whose main fire business has been in areas outside of corporate limits. There is an understandable but unfortunate tendency for city fire departments to refuse to make rural runs, and the smaller communities with established, well-organized departments are finding it increasingly expensive to take up the slack.

TFS began, in September 1973, an equipment development and testing program to assist rural communities in acquiring basic fire trucks at affordable prices. Testimony to the unqualified popularity of this equipment phase is that TFS has, through 1990, modified and delivered more than 1,200 complete rural fire trucks to small communities all over the state — with more than 100 active requests on hand at all times.

TFS has developed a new type of suppression equipment that is evolving into a family of systems with wide applicability and effectiveness. The system is basically an air-injection, foam-generating unit that combines a foaming agent in water under pressure. Expansion rates vary from 5-to-1 as high as 20-to-1, depending upon equipment and operating characteristics. The equipment has practical use on standard tractor-plow units for safety and tractor-operator protection. On pumper units used by volunteer fire departments, it greatly extends pumping time and effectiveness.

The TFS established courses to provide basic, intermediate and advanced training to VFD cooperators and to other interested groups. The courses comprise segments on equipment operation and maintenance, fire behavior, tactics, wildland fire organization and safety.

In 1976, the original training team included a chief training officer and two assistants. Inordinate travel costs and difficult scheduling problems for the team quickly necessitated a different approach. Contractual arrangements have been made with eight certified fire trainers in various regions of Texas to deliver the standard courses to local volunteers. All Texas Forest Service training is certified by the Texas Firemen's and Fire Marshal's Association and counts toward firefighter certification.

As of December 1990, the Texas Forest Service trainers have conducted more than 3,000 classes and trained 45,000 firefighters. Plans are to continue to offer the courses at the request of local fire departments.

Tree Seedlings Production
(East Texas Nursery)

Pine seedlings are used in many areas of the state as the preferred method of reforestation. The **Indian Mound Nursery** near Alto, Cherokee County, is operated by the Texas Forest Service for the purpose of providing seedlings to non-industrial forest landowners. The nursery has an area of 120 acres and produces approximately 22 million pine seedlings annually. Seedlings are sold at cost. Application for seedling purchase can be obtained from the Texas Forest Service, county agricultural extension agents and Soil Conservation Service district offices. It is recommended that applications for purchase be submitted to the TFS by January 1.

Virtually all seedlings are raised from genetically improved seed produced by TFS orchards. Sources available include both loblolly and shortleaf pine selected for growth rate and form, loblolly pine selected for drought resistance, slash pine selected for resistance to fusiform rust, Virginia pine selected for Christmas tree characteristics and longleaf pine. The nursery also raises a number of hardwood species for use in windbreaks to help prevent wind and water erosion of soil.

(West Texas Nursery)

Conifer and hardwood windbreak seedlings are grown at the **West Texas Nursery** in Lubbock. Two crops of containerized conifer seedlings are grown in a climate-controlled greenhouse and shipped to planters in about 105 counties each spring. A variety of bare-root hardwood seedlings is also produced in a 5-acre field nursery. Distribution is made through **Soil and Water Conservation Districts**.

State Forests

The first state forest, now known as the **E.O. Siecke State Forest** in Newton County, was purchased by the state in 1924. It contains 1,722 acres of pine land. An additional 100 acres were added by a 99-year lease in 1946.

The **W. Goodrich Jones State Forest**, south of Conroe in Montgomery County, containing 1,725 acres, was purchased in 1926. A 20-acre adjunct was given to the state in 1969.

The **I.D. Fairchild State Forest**, Texas' largest, is located west of Rusk in Cherokee County. This forest was transferred from the state prison system in 1925. An additional 536 acres were added to the original 2,360 acres in 1963 from the Texas State Hospitals and Special Schools, bringing the combined acreage total to 2,896.

The **John Henry Kirby State Forest** of 626 acres was donated by the late lumberman, John Henry Kirby, in 1929, and later donors. Revenue from this forest is given to the **Association of Former Students of Texas A&M Uni-**

Annual Growth and Annual Harvest of Growing Stock in East Texas 1975-1989

Year	Species	Growth (Millions Cu. Ft.)	Harvest (Millions Cu. Ft.)	Harvest Percent of Growth
1975	Pine........	452.1	389.3	86
	Hardwood	162.2	72.6	45
1976	Pine........	454.4	432.8	95
	Hardwood	165.6	80.6	49
1977	Pine........	455.1	453.9	100
	Hardwood	168.8	89.1	53
1978	Pine........	454.2	475.4	105
	Hardwood	171.6	103.1	60
1979	Pine........	453.6	465.1	103
	Hardwood	174.4	102.4	59
1980	Pine........	453.5	446.8	99
	Hardwood	177.1	109.6	62
1981	Pine........	454.7	418.3	92
	Hardwood	180.0	99.6	55
1982	Pine........	457.3	397.9	87
	Hardwood	183.4	89.2	49
1983	Pine........	459.1	455.8	99
	Hardwood	186.3	130.1	70
1984	Pine........	460.1	426.8	93
	Hardwood	188.7	118.2	63
1985	Pine........	461.8	434.0	94
	Hardwood	191.6	117.5	61
1986	Pine........	438.9	458.9	105
	Hardwood	177.3	115.1	65
1987	Pine........	436.4	499.5	114
	Hardwood	179.6	119.6	67
1988	Pine........	435.6	481.8	111
	Hardwood	182.0	120.8	66
1988	Pine........	432.3	484.5	112
	Hardwood	184.2	130.2	71

versity for student loan purposes. All of the state forests are used primarily for demonstration and research.

The newest state forest, the **Paul N. Masterson Memorial Forest** of 520 acres, was donated in the fall of 1984. Mrs. Leonora O'Neal Masterson of Beaumont donated the land in Jasper County in honor of her husband, an active member of the Texas Forestry Association and a tree farmer.

Forest Industry and Harvest Trends

Timber is the second most valuable agricultural crop in the state and provides the raw materials for the ninth largest manufacturing industry. The timber-producing region of Texas, known as the Piney Woods, is in the eastern portion of the state. There are about 40 counties from which large amounts of timber are harvested. These trees are principally used to make paper products, lumber and plywood.

Texas' forest industry ranks third in the South in payroll, at $1.0 billion, and annually ships $5.6 billion in products.

The 1989 Harvest

Timber harvesting in East Texas increased for the fifth straight year, reaching a record 614.0 million cubic feet. Included in this harvest estimate are removals for industrial use and an estimate of removals for fuelwood, logging residue, and miscellaneous removals. The gain from 1988 was just under 2 percent. Pine harvesting rose less than 1 percent to 462.2 million cubic feet. The hardwood harvest showed a more dramatic gain, increasing 9 percent to 104.8 million cubic feet. Most of the increase was pulpwood material.

The largest timber-producing counties were Hardin, Angelina, Jasper and Polk. Each produced over 30 million cubic feet and together provided one-quarter of the East Texas harvest. In terms of cubic-foot harvest per acre of timberland, however, Morris, Hardin, Chambers and Angelina counties received the most intensive harvesting pressure.

The value of the timber harvest on the stump was $245.4 million, based on average statewide stumpage prices as reported in the Texas Forest Service bimonthly timber market report. This represented an increase of 7 percent from the 1988 harvest. The value of the harvest delivered to the first point of processing was $453.3 million, 9 percent above the 1988 value.

The sawlog harvest was up 3 percent to 1.3 billion board feet. The pine sawlog harvest rose by over 3 percent, while hardwood sawlog removals remained about the same as for 1988. On a cubic-foot basis, sawlogs represented one-third of the total harvest. The harvest of veneer and panel roundwood dipped slightly in 1989, to 140.7 million cubic feet compared to 142.6 million feet used in 1988. Pine used for this purpose declined by 1 percent, while hardwood use declined 14 percent. This product category comprised 23 percent of the total harvest. More Texas timber is harvested for conversion into pulp and paper products than for any other product category. Thirty-five percent of the 1989 timber harvest ended up at pulp and paper mills. Roundwood utilized in the production of pulp and paper products increased by nearly 8 percent in 1989. Pine roundwood pulpwood gained 4 percent to reach 1.8 million cords. Hardwood round pulpwood increased to 0.9 million cords, a gain of 14 percent. Hardin and Cass counties were the largest producers of pulpwood. Total pulpwood utilization, including roundwood and mill residues, was up 6 percent, reaching 4.8 million cords.

Primary Forest Products

An estimated 1.2 billion board feet of lumber and ties were produced in Texas during 1989, representing a gain of 7 percent. This was the highest level of lumber output in 25 years, although Texas Forest Service historical records show that similar levels of production were common in the 1940-1955 time period as well as between 1900 and 1929. Eighty-seven percent of the production was from softwood species. Pine-lumber production surged past the 1 billion-board-foot mark, increasing by nearly 8 percent to reach 1.1 billion board-feet.

Structural-panel production at Texas' 11 panel mills declined by 9 percent. This was the first decline since 1984, and probably reflects the downturn in the housing industry nationwide. Production was 2.1 billion square feet, or 8 percent of the total U.S. production.

Texas paper and paperboard production also showed a decline in 1989. A total of 2.8 million tons was produced, including 1.1 million tons of paper and 1.7 million tons of paperboard. Paper production dropped 6 percent and paperboard production was off by 2 percent. The net decline was nearly 4 percent.

Growth-Harvest

For the fourth consecutive year, removals of pine timber exceeded the estimated annual growth in East Texas. Total pine removals were 484.5 million cubic feet, 12 percent above the predicted growth of 432.3 million cubic feet. Over the 1980-1989 period, harvests have represented 99.6 percent of growth. Hardwood growth continues to exceed harvests by a substantial margin. The harvest, 130.2 million cubic feet, was 71 percent of the estimated 184.2 million cubic feet of growth.

Tree planting on nonindustrial private land holdings increased significantly; however, reforestation on industrial tracts was down. In total, 135,023 acres were planted or seeded in 1989, down by 25,000 acres from the previous year. Nonindustrial private landowners took advantage of $1.2 million in cost-share assistance funds available through federal and state incentive programs. The Forestry Incentives Program is a federal program administered by the Texas Forest Service and ASCS. The Texas Reforestation Foundation also funds cost-share payments through voluntary contributions from forest-products companies in Texas.

Texas Lumber Production, 1975-1989

Year	*Lumber production Pine	Hardwood	Tie production Pine	Hardwood
	Thd. bd. ft.		Thd. pieces	
1975	704,572	147,359	352	978
1976	844,253	146,333	502	878
1977	848,253	191,686	259	1,366
1978	867,759	214,118	297	1,314
1979	845,830	204,536	305	1,214
1980	755,078	292,221	173	1,475
1981	707,311	275,591	172	1,756
1982	752,727	160,235	154	971
1983	862,378	152,350	155	866
1984	898,212	165,460	337	1,001
1985	856,157	175,254	101	926
1986	944,465	176,322	120	772
1987	902,987	163,271	112	587
1988	990,118	154,440	61	604
1989	1,067,458	154,726	31	600

*Includes tie volumes.

Texas Structural Panel Production, 1975-1989

Year	Pine	Year	Pine
	Thd. sq. ft.		Thd. sq. ft.
1975	959,649	1983	1,898,556
1976	1,225,513	1984	1,881,071
1977	1,352,527	1985	1,985,699
1978	1,455,139	1986	2,082,659
1979	1,299,282	1987	2,250,279
1980	1,481,944	1988	2,343,241
1981	1,553,345	1989	2,130,575
1982	1,604,102		

Texas Pulpwood Production, 1975-1989

Year	Roundwood Pine	Hardwood	Chips & Sawdust Pine	Hardwood	All Species Total Pulpwood Production
	Thousand cords				
1975 . .	2,051	295	1,114	89	3,549
1976 . .	1,982	404	1,088	111	3,585
1977 . .	2,028	401	1,115	86	3,630
1978 . .	2,068	458	1,118	185	3,829
1979 . .	2,128	453	1,131	128	3,868
1980 . .	2,196	473	1,378	183	4,230
1981 . .	2,114	395	1,329	177	4,016
1982 . .	1,900	495	1,445	135	3,975
1983 . .	2,053	913	1,772	262	4,982
1984 . .	1,890	731	1,567	228	4,416
1985 . .	1,901	716	1,591	462	4,670
1986 . .	1,623	715	1,517	570	4,426
1987 . .	1,650	782	1,456	578	4,466
1988 . .	1,695	819	1,562	492	4,568
1989 . .	1,769	935	1,625	518	4,847

National Forests in Texas

There are four national forests and all or part of five national grasslands in Texas. These federally owned lands are administered by the U.S. Department of Agriculture-Forest Service. These units cover 782,681 acres in parts of 18 Texas counties, as follows:

ANGELINA NATIONAL FOREST—Angelina County, 58,475 acres; Jasper, 20,910; Nacogdoches, 9,238; San Augustine, 64,278. Total, 152,883.

DAVY CROCKETT NATIONAL FOREST—Houston County, 94,990 acres; Trinity, 68,130. Total, 163,120.

SABINE NATIONAL FOREST—Jasper County, 64 acres; Sabine, 93,430; San Augustine, 4,317; Shelby, 58,911; Newton, 1,781. Total, 158,503.

SAM HOUSTON NATIONAL FOREST—Montgomery County, 47,608 acres; San Jacinto, 59,639; Walker, 54,023. Total, 161,370.

BLACK KETTLE NATIONAL GRASSLAND—Hemphill County, 576 acres; Roger Mills County, Okla., 31,000 acres. Total, 31,576.

CADDO NATIONAL GRASSLAND—Fannin County, 17,785 acres. Total, 17,785.

LYNDON B. JOHNSON NATIONAL GRASSLAND—Montague County, 61 acres; Wise, 20,254. Total, 20,315.

McCLELLAN CREEK NATIONAL GRASSLAND—Gray County, 1,449 acres. Total, 1,449.

RITA BLANCA NATIONAL GRASSLAND—Dallam County, 78,027 acres; Cimarron County, Okla., 15,736 acres. Total, 93,763.

Administrative Units

The four National Forests and two National Grasslands (Caddo and Lyndon B. Johnson) in East Texas are administered by the Forest Supervisor with headquarters in Lufkin. This division is known as the National Forests in Texas and is locally administered by eight District Rangers, as follows:

Angelina National Forest, Angelina District at Lufkin. Sabine National Forest, Tenaha District at San Augustine; Yellowpine District at Hemphill. Davy Crockett National Forest, Neches District at Crockett; Trinity District at Apple Springs. Sam Houston National Forest, Raven District at New Waverly; San Jacinto District at Cleveland. Caddo-Lyndon B. Johnson District at Decatur. The three National Grasslands (Black Kettle, McClellan Creek and Rita Blanca) in West Texas are administered by the Forest Supervisor in Albuquerque, New Mexico, as units of the Cibola National Forest. The Black Kettle and McClellan Creek National Grasslands are administered locally by a District Ranger in Cheyenne, Okla., and the Rita Blanca by a District Ranger at Texline.

National Forests in Texas were established by invitation of the Texas Legislature by an Act of 1933, authorizing the purchase of lands in Texas for the establishment of national forests. President Franklin D. Roosevelt proclaimed these purchases of national forests on Oct. 15, 1936. Acquisition authority for purchase of the National Grasslands are primarily the Bankhead-Jones Farm Tenant Act (1937).

Timber Management

Each national forest constitutes a timber management working circle. All work is done under a detailed prescription prepared by a trained forester. Over 80,000 acres have been reforested artificially and thousands of additional acres have been treated to increase the quantity and quality of the timber.

Sales of sawtimber, pulpwood and other forest products are made at regular intervals.

The estimated net growth is over 200 million board feet per year and is valued at $20 million. About one-third of this growth is removed by cutting. The balance is left to grow. By the year 2000, growth is expected to exceed 300 million board feet per year.

Fire Protection

U.S. Forest Service cooperates with the Texas Forest Service in the protection of private and forest service lands inside the national forest boundaries. Detection of forest fires is done from airplanes.

Grazing Permits

Permits to graze cattle on national forests and national grasslands are granted to local residents for an annual fee. Approximately 4,700 head of cattle are grazed on national forests and 2,000 head of cattle are grazed on the Caddo-Lyndon B. Johnson area annually. On the Rita Blanca NG, 5,417 cattle are grazed each year, most of them in Texas.

Recreation Facilities

An estimated 2 million people visited the national forests in Texas for recreation in 1990. Many of these used established recreation areas. These areas are primarily for the purpose of picnicking, swimming, fishing, camping, boating and nature enjoyment and are: **Ratcliff Lake**, 25 miles west of Lufkin on Highway 7, has a 45-acre lake and facilities for picnicking, swimming, boating, fishing, camping and a 250-seat capacity campfire theater. Also, electrical hookups are available. **Double Lake**, 3 miles south of Coldspring on FM Road 2025, has a 30-acre lake and facilities for picnicking, camping, swimming and fishing. **Stubblefield Lake**, 15 miles west-northwest of New Waverly on the shores of Lake Conroe, has facilities for camping, picnicking and fishing. **Scotts Ridge Boat Ramp**, 8 miles west of Willis, provides a boat ramp and parking lot on **Lake Conroe**. **Boykin Springs**, 15 miles southeast of Zavalla, has a 6-acre lake and facilities for swimming, picnicking, fishing and camping. **Red Hills Lake**, 4 miles north of Milam on Highway 87, has a 17-acre lake and facilities for fishing, swimming, camping and picnicking. Electrical hookups are available. **Bouton Lake**, 7 miles southeast of Zavalla off Texas Highway 63, has a 9-acre natural lake with facilities for camping, picnicking and fishing.

Several areas have been built on the shores of **Sam Rayburn Reservoir**, which has 100 miles of national forest shoreline. These areas provide camping, picnicking, nature enjoyment, boating and fishing. Recreation areas are: **Sandy Creek** on Forest Service Road 333, 25 miles northwest of Jasper; **Caney Creek**, 10 miles southeast of Zavalla off FM 2743, in addition to the facilities mentioned above, has a 500-seat capacity campfire theater for evening campfire programs; **Harvey Creek**, 10 miles south of Broaddus on FM 2390, and **Townsend**, 7 miles north off FM 1277.

The recreational areas at **Toledo Bend Reservoir** include the following: **Willow Oak Recreation Area**, located 14 miles south of Hemphill off State Highway 87, has facilities for picnicking and camping and a boat ramp; **Indian Mounds Recreation Area**, accessible by FM 83 and FM 3382 a total distance of 15 miles east of Hemphill, has camping facilities and a boat launch ramp; **Ragtown**, 25 miles southeast of Center and accessible by State Highways 87 and 139, County Highway 3184 and Forest Service Road 132, has facilities for camping and boat launching; **Lakeview**, a primitive campground 12 miles southeast of Hemphill, can be reached via State Highway 87, County Highway 2928 and Forest Service Road 120.

Hiking Trails in National Forests

The **Lone Star Hiking Trail**, approximately 140 miles long, is located in the **Sam Houston National Forest** in Montgomery, Walker and San Jacinto counties. Twenty-six miles of the trail in San Jacinto County has been designated as **national recreation trail**.

The **4Cs National Recreation Trail** is 19 miles long and goes from **Ratcliff Recreation Area** to the Neches Bluff overlook in the **Davy Crockett National Forest**.

The **Saw Mill Trail** is 5½ miles long and goes from the old Aldrich Saw Mill site to **Boykin Springs Recreation Area** in the **Angelina National Forest**.

Equestrian Trail

The **Piney Creek Horse Trail**, 50 miles long, is located on the Davy Crockett National Forest approximately three miles south of Kennard off F.S. Road 525. There is a 30-unit horse camp at this location, but it does not have drinking water available.

National Grasslands

The submarginal Dust Bowl project lands, purchased by the federal government under the Bankhead-Jones Farm Tenant Act, are today well covered with grasses and native shrubs. They are administered much like the national forests under a policy of multiple use for range, watershed, recreation and wildlife.

Recreation on the National Grasslands

Lake Davy Crockett Recreation Area, 11 miles north of Honey Grove on FM 100, has a boat launch ramp and camping sites on a 450-acre lake. **Coffee Mill Lake Recreation Area** has camping and picnic facilities on a 750-acre lake. This area is 4 miles west of Lake Davy Crockett Recreation Area. **Black Creek Lake Picnic Area** is located 8 miles southeast of Alvord. It has camping and picnic facilities and a boat launch ramp. This site is on a 30-acre lake.

Lake McClellan in Gray County and **Lake Marvin**, which is part of the Black Kettle National Grassland in Hemphill County, provide for flood control and recreation, receive over 28,000 recreation visitors annually. These lake areas provide camping, picnicking, fishing and boating facilities. Concessionaires operate facilities at both lakes and a nominal fee is charged for use of the areas. A limited amount of wildlife provides for public hunting under state game laws. At the **Rita Blanca National Grassland**, about 4,500 visitors a year enjoy picnicking and hunting.

Calendar For 1992 and 1993

The subsequent calendars were calculated principally from basic data in the U.S. Naval Observatory's publication, **Astronomical Phenomena.** Data were adapted for use in Texas on the basis of **Central Standard Time,** except for the period from 2 a.m. on the first Sunday in April until 2 a.m. on the last Sunday in October, when **Daylight Saving Time,** which is one hour later than Central Standard Time, is in effect.

All of Texas is in the Central Time Zone except El Paso and Hudspeth counties and the northwest corner of Culberson County, which observe **Mountain Time.** See accompanying map. Mountain Time is one hour earlier than Central Time.

All times here are figured for the intersection of meridian 99° 10′ West and parallel 31° 23′ North, which is about 15 miles northeast of Brady, McCulloch County. This point is the approximate geographical center of the state.

To get the time of sunrise or sunset, moonrise or moonset for any point in Texas, apply the following rules: Add to the time given in this calendar four minutes for each degree of longitude that any given place lies west of the 99th meridian, and subtract four minutes for each degree of longitude such place lies east of the 99th meridian.

At times there will also be considerable variation for distances north and south of the line of latitude 31 degrees 23 minutes north, but the rule for calculating it would be complicated. Procedure given above will get sufficiently close results.

An accompanying map shows the intersection for which all time is calculated, with some Texas major cities and their longitudes. These make it convenient to calculate time at any given point.

Planetary Configurations and Phenomena

In the center column of the calendar on following pages are given the phenomena and planetary configurations of heavens for 1992 and 1993. Below is an explanation of the signs of the Sun, Moon and planets, and symbols used in the tables:

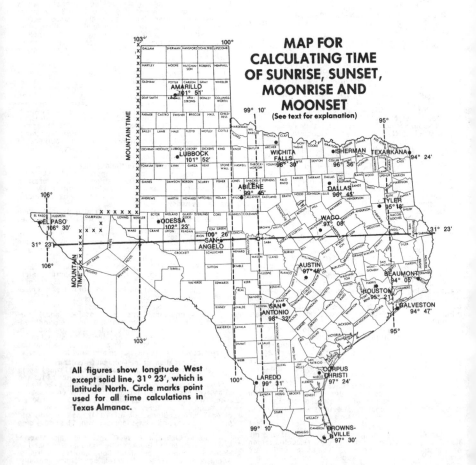

MAP FOR CALCULATING TIME OF SUNRISE, SUNSET, MOONRISE AND MOONSET
(See text for explanation)

All figures show longitude West except solid line, 31° 23′, which is latitude North. Circle marks point used for all time calculations in Texas Almanac.

☉ The Sun.	⊕ The Earth.	♅ Uranus.
☾ The Moon.	♂ Mars.	♆ Neptune.
☿ Mercury.	♃ Jupiter.	♇ Pluto.
♀ Venus.	♄ Saturn.	

Aspects

☌ This symbol appearing before the symbols for heavenly bodies means they are "in conjunction," that is having the same longitude as applies to the sky and appearing near each other.

☍ This symbol means that the two heavenly bodies are in "opposition," or differ by 180 degrees of longitude.

Common Astronomical Terms

Aphelion — Point at which a planet's orbit is farthest from the sun.

Perihelion — Point at which a planet's orbit is nearest the sun.

Apogee — That point of the moon's orbit farthest from the earth.

Perigee — That point of the moon's orbit nearest the earth.

Aspect — Apparent situation of a planet with respect to another body.

Eclipses, 1992 and 1993
1992

There will be five eclipses during 1992, three of the Sun and two of the Moon, as follows:

Jan. 4-5 — Annular eclipse of the Sun, visible in Oceania, Philippines, Japan, extreme coast of northeast Asia, northern Australia, western coast of North America.

June 15 — Partial eclipse of the Moon, visible in Antarctica, east Africa, southern tip of Greenland, South America, North America except northwest, Central America and eastern New Zealand.

June 30 — Total eclipse of the Sun, visible in central South America and southwest Africa.

December 9-10 — Total eclipse of the Moon, visible in Asia, except extreme eastern part; Europe, including the British Isles; Africa; Iceland; Greenland; South America, except southern part; Central America; and North America except western coast.

December 23-24 — Partial eclipse of the Sun, visible in eastern China, Korea, Japan, extreme eastern part of Soviet Union and southwest Alaska.

1993

There will be four eclipses in 1993, two of the Sun and two of the Moon, as follows:

May 21 — Partial eclipse of the Sun, visible in North America except the southeast, Arctic regions, Greenland, Iceland, Northern Europe including northern British Isles, and northwestern part of Soviet Union.

June 4 — Total eclipse of the Moon, visible on the tip of South America, western coast of North America, Antarctica, Australasia and southeastern Asia.

Nov. 13 — Partial eclipse of the Sun, visible from the tip of South America, Antarctica, New Zealand, and southern Australia.

Nov. 29 — Total eclipse of the Moon, visible throughout most of Europe, including the British Isles; western Africa; Iceland; Greenland; Arctic region; the Americas and northeastern Asia.

Chronological Eras and Cycles, 1992 and 1993

The year 1992 of the Christian era comprises the latter part of the 216th and the beginning of the 217th year of the independence of the United States of America, and corresponds to the year 6705 of the Julian period.

Jan. 1, 1992, Julian calendar, corresponds to Jan. 14, 1992, Gregorian calendar.

The year 7501 of the Byzantine era begins on Sept. 14, 1992, Gregorian calendar.

The year 5753 of the Jewish era begins at sunset on Sept. 27, 1992, Gregorian calendar.

The year 4629 of the Chinese era begins Feb. 4, 1992.

The year 2745 since the foundation of Rome, according to VARRO, begins on Jan. 14, 1992, Gregorian calendar.

The year 2741 of the era of NABONASSAR begins on April 25, 1992, Gregorian calendar.

The year 2304 of the Grecian era, or the era of the SELEUCIDAE, begins in the present-day usage of the Syrians on Oct. 14, 1992, or on Sept. 14, 1992, Gregorian calendar, according to different sects.

The year 1709 of the era of DIOCLETIAN begins on Sept. 11, 1992, Gregorian calendar.

The year 1413 of the Islamic era, or the era of the Hegira, begins at sunset on July 1, 1992, Gregorian calendar.

The year 1914 of the Saka era begins on March 21, 1992, Gregorian calendar, in the reformed Indian calendar.

The year 2652 of the Japanese era begins on Jan. 1, 1992, Gregorian calendar.

CHRONOLOGICAL CYCLES, 1992

Dominical Letter	ED	Julian Period	6705
Epact	25	Roman Indiction	15
Golden Number or		Solar Cycle	13
Lunar Cycle	XVII		

CHRONOLOGICAL ERAS, 1993

The year 1993 of the Christian era comprises the latter part of the 217th and the beginning of the 218th year of the independence of the United States of America, and corresponds to the year 6706 of the Julian period.

Jan. 1, 1993, Julian calendar, corresponds to Jan. 14, 1993, Gregorian calendar.

The year 7502 of the Byzantine era begins on Sept. 14, 1993, Gregorian calendar.

The year 5754 of the Jewish era begins at sunset on Sept. 15, 1993, Gregorian calendar.

The year 4630 of the Chinese era begins Jan. 23, 1993.

The year 2746 since the foundation of Rome, according to VARRO, begins on Jan. 14, 1993, Gregorian calendar.

The year 2742 of the era of NABONASSAR begins on April 25, 1993, Gregorian calendar.

The year 2305 of the Grecian era, or the era of the SELEUCIDAE, begins in the present-day usage of the Syrians on Sept. 14 (or Oct. 14), 1993, Gregorian calendar, according to different sects.

The year 1710 of the era of DIOCLETIAN begins on Sept. 11, 1993, Gregorian calendar.

The year 1414 of the Islamic era, or the era of the Hegira, begins at sunset on Jan. 20, 1993, Gregorian calendar.

The year 1915 of the Saka era begins on March 22, 1993, Gregorian calendar, in the reformed Indian calendar.

The year 2653 of the Japanese era begins on Jan. 1, 1993, Gregorian calendar.

CHRONOLOGICAL CYCLES, 1993

Dominical Letter	C	Julian Period	6706
Epact	6	Roman Indiction	1
Golden Number or		Solar Cycle	14
Lunar Cycle	XVIII		

The Seasons, 1992 and 1993
1992

The seasons of 1992 begin as follows: **Spring,** March 20, 2:48 a.m. (CST); **Summer,** June 20, 10:14 p.m. (CDT); **Fall,** Sept. 22, 1:43 p.m. (CDT); **Winter,** Dec. 21, 8:43 a.m. (CST).

1993

The seasons of 1993 begin as follows: **Spring,** March 20, 8:41 a.m. (CST); **Summer,** June 21, 4:00 a.m. (CDT); **Fall,** Sept. 22, 7:22 p.m. (CDT); **Winter,** Dec. 21, 2:26 p.m. (CST).

Morning and Evening Stars, 1992 and 1993
Morning Stars, 1992

Venus — Jan. 1-May 7.

Mars — Jan. 1-Dec. 31.

Jupiter — Jan. 1-Feb. 29; Oct. 1-Dec. 31.

Saturn — Feb. 16-Aug. 7.

Evening Stars, 1992

Venus — July 20-Dec. 31.

Jupiter — Feb. 29-Sept. 4.

Saturn — Jan. 1-Jan. 13; Aug. 7-Dec. 31.

Morning Stars, 1993

Venus — April 6-Dec. 6.

Mars — Jan. 1-Jan. 7.

Jupiter — Jan. 1-March 30; Nov. 1-Dec. 31.

Saturn — Feb. 27-Aug. 19.

Evening Stars, 1993

Venus — Jan. 1-March 28.

Mars — Jan. 7-Nov. 2.

Jupiter — March 30- Oct. 5.

Saturn — Jan. 1-Jan. 23; Aug. 19-Dec. 31.

Holidays, Anniversaries and Festivals, 1992 and 1993

Bank Holidays — By act of the Sixty-second Legislature, 1971, legally prescribed (compulsory) bank holidays in Texas, in addition to Sundays, are New Year's Day, Washington's Birthday, Memorial Day, Independence Day, Labor Day, Columbus Day, Veterans Day, Thanksgiving and Christmas. The 69th Legislature, 1985-1986, established Martin Luther King's birthday as an official bank holiday; the 72nd Legislature in 1991 made it an official state holiday and dropped Columbus Day. Should New Year's Day, Independence Day or Christmas fall on Saturday, banks close the preceding Friday. Should any of the three fall on Sunday banks close the next Monday. At their option, banks may close one day a week besides Sunday, usually Saturday, but on any day selected by individual banks. Prior to this act, permitting a 5-day banking week, bank holidays included all holidays in the list below marked with asterisk (*), double asterisk (**) or dagger (†).

1992		1993	
*New Year's Day	Wednesday, Jan. 1	*New Year's Day	Friday, Jan. 1
Epiphany	Monday, Jan. 6	Epiphany	Wednesday, Jan. 6
Sam Rayburn Day	Monday, Jan. 6	Sam Rayburn Day	Wednesday, Jan. 6
**Confederate Heroes Day	Monday, Jan. 20	**Confederate Heroes Day	Monday, Jan. 18
‡Martin Luther King's Birthday	Monday, Jan. 20	‡Martin Luther King's Birthday	Monday, Jan. 18
*Lincoln's Birthday	Wednesday, Feb. 12	Inauguration Day	Wednesday, Jan. 20
‡Washington's Birthday	Monday, Feb. 17	*Lincoln's Birthday	Friday, Feb. 12
†Texas Independence Day	Monday, March 2	‡Washington's Birthday	Monday, Feb. 15
‡Sam Houston Day	Monday, March 2	§§First Day of Ramadan (Tabular)	Tuesday, Feb. 23
‡Texas Flag Day	Monday, March 2	Ash Wednesday	Wednesday, Feb. 24
Ash Wednesday	Wednesday, March 4	†Texas Independence Day	Tuesday, March 2
§§First Day of Ramadan (Tabular)	Thursday, March 5	‡Sam Houston Day	Tuesday, March 2
Palm Sunday	Sunday, April 12	‡Texas Flag Day	Tuesday, March 2
Good Friday	Friday, April 17	Palm Sunday	Sunday, April 4
¶First Day of Passover (Pesach)	Saturday, April 18	¶First Day of Passover (Pesach)	Tuesday, April 6
Easter Day	Sunday, April 19	Good Friday	Friday, April 9
†San Jacinto Day	Tuesday, April 21	Easter Day	Sunday, April 11
§Arbor Day	Friday, April 24	†San Jacinto Day	Wednesday, April 21
Loyalty Day	Friday, May 1	§Arbor Day	Friday, April 30
Primary Election Day	Saturday, May 2	Loyalty Day	Saturday, May 1
Armed Forces Day	Saturday, May 16	Primary Election Day	Saturday, May 1
‡Memorial Day	Monday, May 25	Armed Forces Day	Saturday, May 15
Ascension Day	Thursday, May 28	Ascension Day	Thursday, May 20
¶Feast of Weeks (Shavuot)	Sunday, June 7	¶Feast of Weeks (Shavuot)	Wednesday, May 26
Whit Sunday (Pentecost)	Sunday, June 7	Whit Sunday (Pentecost)	Sunday, May 30
Trinity Sunday	Sunday, June 14	‡Memorial Day	Monday, May 31
†Emancipation Day in Texas	Friday, June 19	Trinity Sunday	Sunday, June 6
§§Islamic New Year (Tabular)	Thursday, July 2	†Emancipation Day in Texas	Saturday, June 19
*Independence Day	Saturday, July 4	§§Islamic New Year (Tabular)	Monday, June 21
‡Texas Pioneers' Day	Wednesday, Aug. 12	*Independence Day	Sunday, July 4
†Lyndon B. Johnson's Birthday	Thursday, Aug. 27	‡Texas Pioneers' Day	Thursday, Aug. 12
*Labor Day	Monday, Sept. 7	†Lyndon B. Johnson's Birthday	Friday, Aug. 27
Constitution and Citizenship Day	Thursday, Sept. 17	*Labor Day	Monday, Sept. 6
¶Jewish New Year (Rosh Hashanah)	Monday, Sept. 28	¶Jewish New Year (Rosh Hashanah)	Thursday, Sept. 16
¶Day of Atonement (Yom Kippur)	Wednesday, Oct. 7	Constitution and Citizenship Day	Friday, Sept. 17
¶First Day of Tabernacles (Succoth)	Monday, Oct. 12	¶Day of Atonement (Yom Kippur)	Saturday, Sept. 25
‡Columbus Day	Monday, Oct. 12	¶First Day of Tabernacles (Succoth)	Thursday, Sept. 30
‡§Poetry Day	Thursday, Oct. 15	‡Columbus Day	Monday, Oct. 11
*General Election Day	Tuesday, Nov. 3	‡§Poetry Day	Friday, Oct. 15
‡Father of Texas Day	Tuesday, Nov. 3	‡Father of Texas Day	Wednesday, Nov. 3
*Veterans Day	Wednesday, Nov. 11	*Veterans Day	Thursday, Nov. 11
*Thanksgiving Day	Thursday, Nov. 26	*Thanksgiving Day	Thursday, Nov. 25
First Sunday in Advent	Sunday, Nov. 29	First Sunday in Advent	Sunday, Nov. 28
*Christmas Day	Friday, Dec. 25	*Christmas Day	Saturday, Dec. 25

In these tables, the Jewish (¶) and Islamic (§§) dates, are tabular dates, which begin at sunset on the previous evening and end at sunset on the date listed above.

*National holidays which are also state holidays by act of the Texas Legislature, except Lincoln's Birthday, Feb. 12, which was exclusively a bank holiday, until the number of bank holidays was restricted by state law in 1955, providing a 5-day week and restricting the number of bank holidays.

†Legal holiday in Texas only.

‡"Special observance days," set aside by Texas Legislature. They are not legal holidays, though two of them fall on March 2, which is otherwise designated as a state legal holiday, except for bank closing.

§A "special observance day" by resolution of the Texas Legislature but also observed by legislative enactment in many other states.

In 1973, the Texas Legislature made Lyndon B. Johnson's Birthday, Aug. 27, a state holiday and made Jan. 19 **Confederate Heroes Day, combining the birthdays of Robert E. Lee (Jan. 19) and Jefferson Davis (June 3).

††THANKSGIVING DAY IN TEXAS was designated as the "fourth Thursday in November" by the Fifty-fifth Legislature, 1957. This made the state Thanksgiving coincide with the national holiday in all years. Prior to that Texas had, beginning with 1939, celebrated separate national and state Thanksgiving Days in all Novembers having five Thursdays. Texas, first by governor's proclamation, and by legislative resolution after 1951, continued to observe the last Thursday, until changed in 1957 to coincide in all years with the national holiday.

‡Starting in 1971, these changes were made in official holidays by the U.S. and Texas governments to give employees 3-day holiday weekends: Columbus Day made national holiday and set for second Monday in October; Washington's Birthday will be observed on third Monday in February; Memorial Day will be observed on last Monday in May. The addition of Martin Luther King Jr's. birthday to this list was effective in 1986 (bank holiday only in Texas until 1992, when it became an official state holiday).

Texas Special Observance Weeks, 1992 and 1993

Texas Week in 1992 will be the week of Sunday, March 1 to Saturday, March 7, inclusive; in 1993, it will be observed the week of Monday, March 1 to Sunday, March 7, inclusive. This week includes **Texas Independence Day,** March 2.

Texas Conservation and Beautification Week includes the period beginning two days before **San Jacinto Day,** April 21, and ending two days after **National Wildflower Day,** April 24.

Calendar For 1992

Time given in this calendar is according to **Central Standard Time,** except for the period from April 5 to Oct. 25, during which **Daylight Saving Time** is observed. See page 102 for explanation of how to get exact time at any certain Texas point. (Boldface figures for moonrise and moonset indicate p.m.) Times are figured for the point 99° 10′ West and 31° 23′ North, the approximate geographic center of the state.

1st Month JANUARY, 1992 31 Days

Moon's Phases—New, Jan. 4, 5:10 p.m.; First Qtr., Jan. 12, 8:32 p.m.; Full, Jan. 19, 3:28 p.m.; Last Qtr., Jan. 26, 9:27 a.m.

Day of Year	Day of Month	Day of Week	Planetary Configurations —Phenomena	*Hour of Sunrise	*Hour of Sunset	*Hour of Moonrise	*Hour of Moonset
1	1	We.	♀☌☾	7:36	5:44	4:55	**3:05**
2	2	Th.	. . . .	7:36	5:45	5:50	**3:55**
3	3	Fr.	⊕ at Perihelion. . .	7:36	5:46	6:40	**4:47**
4	4	Sa.	♅☌☉	7:36	5:47	7:25	**5:42**
5	5	Su.	. . . .	7:36	5:47	8:06	**6:38**
6	6	Mo.	☾ at Apogee	7:37	5:48	8:42	**7:33**
7	7	Tu.	♆☌☉	7:37	5:49	9:14	**8:28**
8	8	We.	. . . .	7:37	5:50	9:44	**9:22**
9	9	Th.	. . . .	7:37	5:50	10:12	**10:16**
10	10	Fr.	☿☌♂	7:37	5:51	10:40	**11:11**
11	11	Sa.	. . . .	7:37	5:52	11:09	. . .
12	12	Su.	. . . .	7:37	5:53	11:40	12:07
13	13	Mo.	. . . .	7:36	5:54	**12:15**	1:06
14	14	Tu.	. . . .	7:36	5:55	**12:55**	2:08
15	15	We.	. . . .	7:36	5:56	**1:43**	3:10
16	16	Th.	. . . .	7:36	5:56	**2:20**	4:18
17	17	Fr.	. . . .	7:36	5:57	**3:44**	5:22
18	18	Sa.	. . . .	7:36	5:58	**4:55**	6:22
19	19	Su.	☾ at Perigee	7:35	5:59	**6:09**	7:15
20	20	Mo.	. . . .	7:35	6:00	**7:21**	8:02
21	21	Tu.	☿☌♆.	7:35	6:01	**8:32**	8:42
22	22	We.	♃☌☾.	7:34	6:02	**9:40**	9:19
23	23	Th.	. . . .	7:34	6:03	**10:45**	9:54
24	24	Fr.	. . . .	7:34	6:04	**11:48**	10:28
25	25	Sa.	. . . .	7:33	6:05	. . .	11:02
26	26	Su.	. . . .	7:33	6:05	12:51	11:39
27	27	Mo.	. . . .	7:32	6:06	1:51	**12:19**
28	28	Tu.	. . . .	7:32	6:07	2:50	**1:03**
29	29	We.	♄☌☉	7:31	6:09	3:46	**1:51**
30	30	Th.	. . . .	7:31	6:09	4:37	**2:43**
31	31	Fr.	. . . .	7:30	6:10	5:23	**3:37**

2nd Month FEBRUARY, 1992 29 Days

Moon's Phases—New, Feb. 3, 1:00 p.m.; First Qtr., 10:15 a.m.; Full, Feb. 18, 2:04 a.m.; Last Qtr., Feb. 25, 1:56 a.m.

Day of Year	Day of Month	Day of Week	Planetary Configurations —Phenomena	*Hour of Sunrise	*Hour of Sunset	*Hour of Moonrise	*Hour of Moonset
32	1	Sa.	♂☌☾	7:29	6:11	6:05	**4:32**
33	2	Su.	☾ at Apogee	7:29	6:12	6:43	**5:27**
34	3	Mo.	. . . .	7:28	6:13	7:16	**6:22**
35	4	Tu.	. . . .	7:27	6:14	7:47	**7:17**
36	5	We.	. . . .	7:27	6:14	8:16	**8:11**
37	6	Th.	. . . .	7:26	6:15	8:44	**9:05**
38	7	Fr.	. . . .	7:25	6:16	9:12	**10:01**
39	8	Sa.	♀☌♆	7:24	6:17	9:42	**10:58**
40	9	Su.	. . . .	7:24	6:18	10:15	**11:58**
41	10	Mo.	. . . .	7:23	6:19	10:52	. . .
42	11	Tu.	. . . .	7:22	6:20	11:36	12:59
43	12	We.	☿ Superior	7:21	6:21	**12:26**	2:02
44	13	Th.	. . . .	7:20	6:21	**1:25**	3:05
45	14	Fr.	. . . .	7:19	6:22	**2:31**	4:05
46	15	Sa.	. . . .	7:18	6:23	**3:41**	5:00
47	16	Su.	. . . .	7:17	6:24	**4:54**	5:49
48	17	Mo.	☾ at Perigee	7:17	6:25	**6:05**	6:32
49	18	Tu.	. . . .	7:16	6:26	**7:15**	7:11
50	19	We.	♃☌☾	7:15	6:26	**8:23**	7:48
51	20	Th.	. . . .	7:14	6:27	**9:30**	8:23
52	21	Fr.	. . . .	7:13	6:28	**10:35**	8:59
53	22	Sa.	. . . .	7:12	6:29	**11:38**	9:36
54	23	Su.	. . . .	7:10	6:30	. . .	10:16
55	24	Mo.	. . . .	7:09	6:30	12:40	10:59
56	25	Tu.	. . . .	7:08	6:31	1:38	11:47
57	26	We.	. . . .	7:07	6:32	2:31	**12:38**
58	27	Th.	♇ Stationary	7:06	6:33	3:20	**1:31**
59	28	Fr.	♃☍	7:05	6:33	4:03	**2:26**
60	29	Sa.	☾ at Apogee	7:04	6:34	4:42	**3:21**

*See text before January calendar for explanation.

3rd Month MARCH, 1992 31 Days

Moon's Phases—New, March 4, 7:22 a.m.; First Qtr., March 11, 8:36 p.m.; Full, March 18, 12:18 p.m.; Last Qtr., March 25, 8:30 p.m.

Day of Year	Day of Month	Day of Week	Planetary Configurations —Phenomena	*Hour of Sunrise	*Hour of Sunset	*Hour of Moonrise	*Hour of Moonset
61	1	Su.	♂☌☾	7:03	6:35	5:17	**4:16**
62	2	Mo.	. . . .	7:02	6:36	5:49	**5:10**
63	3	Tu.	. . . .	7:00	6:36	6:19	**6:05**
64	4	We.	. . . .	6:59	6:37	6:47	**7:00**
65	5	Th.	. . . .	6:58	6:38	7:16	**7:56**
66	6	Fr.	♂☌♄	6:57	6:39	7:46	**8:53**
67	7	Sa.	. . . .	6:56	6:39	8:18	**9:52**
68	8	Su.	. . . .	6:55	6:40	8:54	**10:53**
69	9	Mo.	♂ Gr. elong. E. . . .	6:53	6:41	9:35	**11:55**
70	10	Tu.	. . . .	6:52	6:42	10:22	. . .
71	11	We.	. . . .	6:51	6:42	11:17	12:56
72	12	Th.	. . . .	6:50	6:43	**12:18**	1:55
73	13	Fr.	. . . .	6:48	6:43	**1:24**	2:50
74	14	Sa.	. . . .	6:47	6:44	**2:33**	3:39
75	15	Su.	. . . .	6:46	6:45	**3:43**	4:24
76	16	Mo.	☾ at Perigee	6:45	6:45	**4:52**	5:04
77	17	Tu.	. . . .	6:43	6:46	**6:00**	5:41
78	18	We.	. . . .	6:42	6:47	**7:07**	6:17
79	19	Th.	. . . .	6:41	6:48	**8:13**	6:52
80	20	Fr.	Spring Begins . . .	6:40	6:48	**9:19**	7:30
81	21	Sa.	. . . .	6:38	6:49	**10:23**	8:09
82	22	Su.	. . . .	6:37	6:50	**11:24**	8:52
83	23	Mo.	. . . .	6:36	6:50	. . .	9:39
84	24	Tu.	. . . .	6:35	6:51	12:21	10:30
85	25	We.	. . . .	6:33	6:51	1:13	11:23
86	26	Th.	♂ Inferior	6:32	6:52	1:59	**12:17**
87	27	Fr.	. . . .	6:31	6:53	2:40	**1:13**
88	28	Sa.	☾ at Apogee	6:30	6:53	3:16	**2:08**
89	29	Su.	♄☌☾	6:28	6:54	3:49	**3:02**
90	30	Mo.	♂☌☾	6:27	6:55	4:19	**3:57**
91	31	Tu.	. . . .	6:26	6:55	4:49	**4:52**

4th Month APRIL, 1992 30 Days

Moon's Phases—New, Apr. 2, 11:01 p.m.; First Qtr., Apr. 10, 5:06 a.m.; Full, Apr. 16, 11:42 p.m.; Last Qtr., Apr. 24, 4:40 p.m.

Day of Year	Day of Month	Day of Week	Planetary Configurations —Phenomena	*Hour of Sunrise	*Hour of Sunset	*Hour of Moonrise	*Hour of Moonset
92	1	We.	♀☌☾	6:25	6:56	5:18	**5:47**
93	2	Th.	☿☌☾	6:23	6:57	5:48	**6:44**
94	3	Fr.	. . . .	6:22	6:57	6:20	**7:44**
95	4	Sa.	. . . .	6:21	6:58	6:55	**8:45**
96	5	†Su.	☿☌♀	7:20	7:59	8:35	**10:48**
97	6	Mo.	. . . .	7:18	7:59	9:21	**11:50**
98	7	Tu.	♂ Stationary	7:17	8:00	10:15	. . .
99	8	We.	. . . .	7:16	8:01	11:12	12:50
100	9	Th.	. . . .	7:15	8:01	**12:16**	1:46
101	10	Fr.	. . . .	7:14	8:02	**1:23**	2:36
102	11	Sa.	. . . .	7:12	8:03	**2:30**	3:20
103	12	Su.	. . . .	7:11	8:03	**3:37**	4:00
104	13	Mo.	☾ at Perigee	7:10	8:04	**4:43**	4:37
105	14	Tu.	. . . .	7:09	8:05	**5:49**	5:13
106	15	We.	. . . .	7:08	8:05	**6:54**	5:48
107	16	Th.	. . . .	7:07	8:06	**7:59**	6:24
108	17	Fr.	. . . .	7:05	8:07	**8:04**	7:02
109	18	Sa.	. . . .	7:04	8:07	**10:07**	7:44
110	19	Su.	. . . .	7:03	8:08	**11:07**	8:29
111	20	Mo.	♆ Stationary	7:02	8:09	. . .	9:19
112	21	Tu.	♅ Stationary	7:01	8:09	12:02	10:12
113	22	We.	. . . .	7:00	8:10	12:51	11:07
114	23	Th.	♂ Gr. elong. W. . . .	6:59	8:11	1:35	**12:03**
115	24	Fr.	. . . .	6:58	8:11	2:13	**12:58**
116	25	Sa.	☾ at Apogee	6:57	8:12	2:47	**1:53**
117	26	Su.	. . . .	6:56	8:13	3:19	**2:47**
118	27	Mo.	. . . .	6:55	8:13	3:48	**3:41**
119	28	Tu.	. . . .	6:54	8:14	4:17	**4:36**
120	29	We.	♂☌☾	6:53	8:15	4:47	**5:33**
121	30	Th.	☿☌☾	6:52	8:16	5:18	**6:31**

†Daylight Saving Time begins at 2 a.m.

Calendar For 1992

5th Month **MAY, 1992** **31 Days**

Moon's Phases—New, May 2, 12:44 p.m.; First Qtr., May 9, 10:43 a.m.; Full, May 16, 11:03 a.m.; Last Qtr., May 24, 10:53 a.m.; New, May 31, 10:57 p.m.

Day of Year	Day of Month	Day of Week	Planetary Configurations —Phenomena	*Hour of Sunrise	*Hour of Sunset	*Hour of Moonrise	*Hour of Moonset
122	1	Fr.	. . . .	6:51	8:13	5:52	**7:32**
123	2	Sa.	. . . .	6:50	8:14	6:31	**8:35**
124	3	Sa.	. . . .	6:49	8:15	7:16	**9:39**
125	4	Mo.	. . . .	6:48	8:15	8:07	**10:42**
126	5	Tu.	. . . .	6:47	8:16	9:05	**11:40**
127	6	We.	. . . .	6:47	8:17	10:09	. . .
128	7	Th.	. . . .	6:46	8:18	11:16	12:33
129	8	Fr.	☾ at Perigee	6:45	8:18	**12:23**	1:20
130	9	Sa.	. . . .	6:44	8:19	**1:29**	2:01
131	10	Su.	♃☌☾	6:44	8:20	**2:34**	2:38
132	11	Mo.	♇☍	6:43	8:21	**3:38**	3:13
133	12	Tu.	. . . .	6:42	8:22	**4:42**	3:47
134	13	We.	. . . .	6:41	8:23	**5:46**	4:21
135	14	Th.	. . . .	6:41	8:23	**6:49**	4:58
136	15	Fr.	. . . .	6:40	8:24	**7:53**	5:38
137	16	Sa.	. . . .	6:39	8:24	**8:54**	6:21
138	17	Su.	. . . .	6:39	8:25	**9:51**	7:10
139	18	Mo.	. . . .	6:38	8:25	**10:43**	8:02
140	19	Tu.	. . . .	6:38	8:26	**11:29**	8:56
141	20	We.	♅☌☾	6:37	8:26	. . .	9:52
142	21	Th.	. . . .	6:37	8:27	12:09	10:48
143	22	Fr.	☾ at Apogee	6:36	8:28	12:45	11:43
144	23	Sa.	♄☌☾	6:36	8:29	1:18	**12:38**
145	24	Su.	. . . .	6:35	8:30	1:48	**1:31**
146	25	Mo.	. . . .	6:35	8:30	2:17	**2:25**
147	26	Tu.	. . . .	6:34	8:31	2:45	**3:20**
148	27	We.	. . . .	6:34	8:32	3:15	**4:17**
149	28	Th.	♂☌☾	6:34	8:32	3:48	**5:16**
150	29	Fr.	. . . .	6:33	8:33	4:24	**6:18**
151	30	Sa.	. . . .	6:33	8:33	5:06	**7:23**
152	31	Su.	☿ Superior	6:33	8:34	5:55	**8:27**

6th Month **JUNE, 1992** **30 Days**

Moon's Phases—First Qtr., June 7, 3:47 p.m.; Full, June 14, 11:50 p.m.; Last Qtr., June 23, 3:11 a.m.; New, June 30, 7:18 a.m.

Day of Year	Day of Month	Day of Week	Planetary Configurations —Phenomena	*Hour of Sunrise	*Hour of Sunset	*Hour of Moonrise	*Hour of Moonset
153	1	Mo.	. . . .	6:33	8:36	6:52	**9:29**
154	2	Tu.	. . . .	6:32	8:37	7:55	**10:25**
155	3	We.	☾ at Perigee	6:32	8:37	9:03	**11:16**
156	4	Th.	. . . .	6:32	8:38	10:13	**11:59**
157	5	Fr.	. . . .	6:32	8:38	11:21	. . .
158	6	Sa.	. . . .	6:32	8:39	**12:27**	12:39
159	7	Su.	♃☌☾.	6:32	8:39	**1:32**	1:15
160	8	Mo.	. . . .	6:32	8:40	**2:36**	1:49
161	9	Tu.	. . . .	6:31	8:40	**3:38**	2:23
162	10	We.	. . . .	6:31	8:41	**4:41**	2:58
163	11	Th.	. . . .	6:31	8:41	**5:43**	3:36
164	12	Fr.	. . . .	6:31	8:42	**6:44**	4:18
165	13	Sa.	♀ Superior	6:32	8:42	**7:42**	5:04
166	14	Su.	. . . .	6:32	8:42	**8:36**	5:54
167	15	Mo.	. . . .	6:32	8:43	**9:24**	6:47
168	16	Tu.	♅☌☾	6:32	8:43	**10:06**	7:43
169	17	We.	. . . .	6:32	8:43	**10:44**	8:39
170	18	Th.	. . . .	6:32	8:43	**11:18**	9:34
171	19	Fr.	☾ at Apogee	6:32	8:44	**11:48**	10:29
172	20	Sa.	Summer Begins . .	6:32	8:44	. . .	11:23
173	21	Su.	. . . .	6:33	8:44	12:17	**12:16**
174	22	Mo.	. . . .	6:33	8:44	12:46	**1:10**
175	23	Tu.	. . . .	6:33	8:45	1:15	**2:05**
176	24	We.	. . . .	6:33	8:45	1:45	**3:02**
177	25	Th.	. . . .	6:34	8:45	2:19	**4:02**
178	26	Fr.	♂☌☾	6:34	8:45	2:58	**5:04**
179	27	Sa.	. . . .	6:34	8:45	3:43	**6:08**
180	28	Su.	. . . .	6:35	8:45	4:35	**7:11**
181	29	Mo.	. . . .	6:35	8:45	5:36	**8:11**
182	30	Tu.	. . . .	6:35	8:45	6:43	**9:05**

*See text before January calendar for explanation.

7th Month **JULY, 1992** **31 Days**

Moon's Phases—First Qtr., July 6, 9:43 p.m.; Full, July 14, 2:06 p.m.; Last Qtr., July 22, 5:12 p.m.; New, July 29, 2:35 p.m.

Day of Year	Day of Month	Day of Week	Planetary Configurations —Phenomena	*Hour of Sunrise	*Hour of Sunset	*Hour of Moonrise	*Hour of Moonset
183	1	We.	☾ at Perigee	6:36	8:45	7:53	**9:53**
184	2	Th.	☿☌☾.	6:36	8:45	9:05	**10:36**
185	3	Fr.	⊕ at Aphelion	6:37	8:45	10:14	**11:14**
186	4	Sa.	♃☌☾	6:37	8:45	11:22	**11:50**
187	5	Su.	☿ Gr. elong. E. . . .	6:38	8:45	**12:27**	. . .
188	6	Mo.	. . . .	6:38	8:45	**1:32**	12:24
189	7	Tu.	♅☍	6:39	8:44	**2:35**	1:00
190	8	We.	. . . .	6:39	8:44	**3:37**	1:37
191	9	Th.	♆☍	6:40	8:44	**4:38**	2:17
192	10	Fr.	. . . .	6:40	8:44	**5:37**	3:01
193	11	Sa.	. . . .	6:41	8:44	**6:31**	3:50
194	12	Su.	. . . .	6:41	8:43	**7:20**	4:42
195	13	Mo.	. . . .	6:42	8:43	**8:05**	5:36
196	14	Tu.	♅☌☾	6:42	8:43	**8:44**	6:32
197	15	We.	. . . .	6:43	8:42	**9:19**	7:27
198	16	Th.	♄☌☾	6:43	8:42	**9:51**	8:22
199	17	Fr.	☾ at Apogee	6:44	8:41	**10:20**	9:16
200	18	Sa.	☿ Stationary	6:45	8:41	**10:48**	10:10
201	19	Su.	. . . .	6:45	8:40	**11:17**	11:03
202	20	Mo.	. . . .	6:46	8:40	**11:46**	11:57
203	21	Tu.	. . . .	6:46	8:39	. . .	**12:52**
204	22	We.	. . . .	6:47	8:39	12:18	**1:49**
205	23	Th.	. . . .	6:48	8:38	12:53	**2:48**
206	24	Fr.	♂☌☾	6:48	8:38	1:34	**3:50**
207	25	Sa.	☿☌♀	6:49	8:37	2:21	**4:52**
208	26	Su.	. . . .	6:50	8:37	3:17	**5:53**
209	27	Mo.	. . . .	6:50	8:36	4:20	**6:50**
210	28	Tu.	. . . .	6:51	8:35	5:29	**7:41**
211	29	We.	. . . .	6:51	8:34	6:40	**8:27**
212	30	Th.	☾ at Perigee	6:52	8:34	7:52	**9:08**
213	31	Fr.	. . . .	6:53	8:33	9:03	**9:47**

8th Month **AUGUST, 1992** **31 Days**

Moon's Phases—First Qtr., Aug. 5, 5:58 a.m.; Full, Aug. 13, 5:27 a.m.; Last Qtr., Aug. 21, 5:01 a.m.; New, Aug. 27, 9:42 p.m.

Day of Year	Day of Month	Day of Week	Planetary Configurations —Phenomena	*Hour of Sunrise	*Hour of Sunset	*Hour of Moonrise	*Hour of Moonset
214	1	Sa.	♃☌☾	6:53	8:32	10:12	**10:23**
215	2	Su.	☿ Inferior	6:54	8:31	11:19	**10:59**
216	3	Mo.	. . . .	6:55	8:31	**12:24**	**11:37**
217	4	Tu.	♇ Stationary	6:55	8:30	**1:29**	. . .
218	5	We.	. . . .	6:56	8:29	**2:32**	12:17
219	6	Th.	. . . .	6:57	8:28	**3:31**	1:00
220	7	Fr.	♄☍	6:57	8:27	**4:27**	1:47
221	8	Sa.	. . . .	6:58	8:26	**5:18**	2:38
222	9	Su.	. . . .	6:59	8:25	**6:04**	3:32
223	10	Mo.	♅☌☾	6:59	8:24	**6:44**	4:27
224	11	Tu.	. . . .	7:00	8:23	**7:20**	5:22
225	12	We.	☿ Stationary	7:00	8:23	**7:53**	6:17
226	13	Th.	☾ at Apogee	7:01	8:22	**8:24**	7:11
227	14	Fr.	. . . .	7:02	8:20	**8:52**	8:05
228	15	Sa.	. . . .	7:02	8:19	**9:21**	8:58
229	16	Su.	. . . .	7:03	8:18	**9:49**	9:52
230	17	Mo.	. . . .	7:04	8:17	**10:20**	10:46
231	18	Tu.	. . . .	7:04	8:16	**10:53**	11:42
232	19	We.	. . . .	7:05	8:15	**11:31**	**12:39**
233	20	Th.	☿ Gr. elong. W. . . .	7:05	8:14	. . .	**1:38**
234	21	Fr.	. . . .	7:06	8:13	12:15	**2:38**
235	22	Sa.	♂☌☾	7:07	8:12	1:05	**3:38**
236	23	Su.	. . . .	7:07	8:11	2:03	**4:35**
237	24	Mo.	. . . .	7:08	8:10	3:07	**5:28**
238	25	Tu.	. . . .	7:09	8:08	4:16	**6:15**
239	26	We.	☿☌☾	7:09	8:07	5:27	**6:59**
240	27	Th.	☾ at Perigee	7:10	8:06	6:38	**7:39**
241	28	Fr.	. . . .	7:10	8:05	7:48	**8:17**
242	29	Su.	♀☌☾.	7:11	8:04	8:57	**8:54**
243	30	Su.	. . . .	7:12	8:02	10:06	**9:32**
244	31	Mo.	. . . .	7:12	8:01	11:13	**10:13**

Calendar For 1992

9th Month SEPTEMBER, 1992 30 Days

Moon's Phases—First Qtr., Sept. 3, 5:39 p.m.; Full, Sept. 11, 9:17 p.m.; Last Qtr., Sept. 19, 2:53 p.m.; New, Sept. 26, 5:40 a.m.

Day of			Planetary Configurations —Phenomena	*Hour of			
Year	Month	Week		Sunrise	Sunset	Moonrise	Moonset
245	1	Tu.		7:13	8:00	**12:19**	**10:56**
246	2	We.		7:13	7:59	**1:22**	**11:43**
247	3	Th.		7:14	7:58	**2:20**	...
248	4	Fr.		7:15	7:56	**3:14**	12:34
249	5	Sa.		7:15	7:55	**4:01**	1:27
250	6	Su.	♂☌☾	7:16	7:54	**4:43**	2:22
251	7	Mo.		7:16	7:52	**5:21**	3:17
252	8	Tu.	♄☌☾	7:17	7:51	**5:55**	4:12
253	9	We.	☾at Apogee	7:18	7:50	**6:26**	5:06
254	10	Th.		7:18	7:49	**6:56**	6:00
255	11	Fr.		7:19	7:47	**7:24**	6:54
256	12	Sa.		7:19	7:46	**7:53**	7:47
257	13	Su.		7:20	7:45	**8:24**	8:41
258	14	Mo.	☿Superior	7:20	7:43	**8:56**	9:37
259	15	Tu.		7:21	7:42	**9:33**	10:34
260	16	We.		7:22	7:41	**10:14**	11:32
261	17	Th.	♃☌☉	7:22	7:40	**11:01**	**12:31**
262	18	Fr.		7:23	7:38	**11:54**	**1:29**
263	19	Sa.		7:23	7:37	...	**2:25**
264	20	Su.		7:24	7:36	12:54	**3:18**
265	21	Mo.		7:25	7:34	1:58	**4:06**
266	22	Tu.	Fall Begins	7:25	7:33	3:06	**4:50**
267	23	We.		7:26	7:32	4:15	**5:30**
268	24	Th.	☾at Perigee	7:26	7:30	5:24	**6:09**
269	25	Fr.		7:27	7:29	6:33	**6:46**
270	26	Sa.		7:28	7:28	7:42	**7:25**
271	27	Su.	♆ Stationary	7:28	7:27	8:51	**8:05**
272	28	Mo.	♀☌☾	7:29	7:25	9:59	**8:48**
273	29	Tu.		7:29	7:24	11:05	**9:34**
274	30	We.		7:30	7:23	**12:07**	**10:25**

10th Month OCTOBER, 1992 31 Days

Moon's Phases—First Qtr., Oct. 3, 9:12 a.m.; Full, Oct. 11, 1:03 p.m.; Last Qtr., Oct. 18, 11:12 p.m.; New, Oct. 25, 2:34 p.m.

Day of			Planetary Configurations —Phenomena	*Hour of			
Year	Month	Week		Sunrise	Sunset	Moonrise	Moonset
275	1	Th.		7:31	7:21	**1:04**	**11:19**
276	2	Fr.		7:31	7:20	**1:55**	...
277	3	Sa.	♂☌☾	7:32	7:19	**2:40**	12:14
278	4	Su.		7:33	7:18	**3:20**	1:10
279	5	Mo.		7:33	7:16	**3:55**	2:06
280	6	Tu.	♄☌☾	7:34	7:15	**4:27**	3:00
281	7	We.	☾at Apogee	7:35	7:14	**4:57**	3:54
282	8	Th.		7:35	7:13	**5:26**	4:47
283	9	Fr.		7:36	7:12	**5:55**	5:41
284	10	Sa.		7:37	7:10	**6:26**	6:35
285	11	Su.		7:37	7:09	**6:58**	7:30
286	12	Mo.		7:38	7:08	**7:34**	8:27
287	13	Tu.		7:39	7:07	**8:14**	9:26
288	14	We.		7:39	7:06	**8:59**	10:25
289	15	Th.		7:40	7:05	**9:51**	11:24
290	16	Fr.	♄Stationary	7:41	7:03	**10:48**	**12:21**
291	17	Sa.		7:41	7:02	**11:50**	**1:14**
292	18	Su.	♂☌☾	7:42	7:01	...	**2:02**
293	19	Mo.		7:43	7:00	12:55	**2:46**
294	20	Tu.		7:44	6:59	2:01	**3:26**
295	21	We.		7:44	6:58	3:08	**4:04**
296	22	Th.	☾at Perigee	7:45	6:57	4:14	**4:40**
297	23	Fr.		7:46	6:56	5:21	**5:17**
298	24	Sa.		7:47	6:55	6:21	**5:56**
299	25	†Su.		6:47	5:54	6:36	**5:37**
300	26	Mo.		6:48	5:53	7:43	**6:23**
301	27	Tu.	☿☌☾	6:49	5:52	8:48	**7:13**
302	28	We.	♀☌☾	6:50	5:51	9:49	**8:06**
303	29	Th.		6:51	5:50	10:44	**9:02**
304	30	Fr.		6:51	5:49	11:33	**9:59**
305	31	Sa.	☿Gr. elong. E.	6:52	5:48	**12:15**	**10:56**

†Daylight Saving Time ends at 2 a.m. *See text before January calendar for explanation.

11th Month NOVEMBER, 1992 30 Days

Moon's Phases—First Qtr., Nov. 2, 3:11 a.m., Full, Nov. 10, 3:20 a.m.; Last Qtr., Nov. 17, 5:39 a.m.; New, Nov. 24, 3:11 a.m.

Day of			Planetary Configurations —Phenomena	*Hour of			
Year	Month	Week		Sunrise	Sunset	Moonrise	Moonset
306	1	Su.		6:53	5:48	**12:53**	**11:51**
307	2	Mo.	♄☌☾	6:54	5:47	**1:26**	...
308	3	Tu.	☾at Apogee	6:55	5:46	**1:57**	12:45
309	4	We.		6:55	5:45	**2:26**	1:39
310	5	Th.		6:56	5:44	**2:55**	2:32
311	6	Fr.		6:57	5:44	**3:25**	3:26
312	7	Sa.		6:58	5:43	**3:57**	4:21
313	8	Su.		6:59	5:42	**4:32**	5:17
314	9	Mo.		7:00	5:41	**5:11**	6:16
315	10	Tu.		7:00	5:41	**5:55**	7:16
316	11	We.	☿Stationary	7:01	5:40	**6:46**	8:16
317	12	Th.		7:02	5:40	**7:43**	9:15
318	13	Fr.		7:03	5:39	**8:44**	10:10
319	14	Sa.	♇☌☉	7:04	5:38	**9:49**	11:00
320	15	Su.	♂☌☾	7:05	5:38	**10:54**	11:46
321	16	Mo.		7:06	5:37	**11:59**	**12:26**
322	17	Tu.		7:06	5:37	...	**1:04**
323	18	We.	☾at Perigee	7:07	5:37	1:04	**1:39**
324	19	Th.		7:08	5:36	2:09	**2:15**
325	20	Fr.	♃☌☾	7:09	5:36	3:14	**2:52**
326	21	Sa.	☿Inferior	7:10	5:35	4:19	**3:31**
327	22	Su.		7:11	5:35	5:25	**4:14**
328	23	Mo.		7:12	5:35	6:30	**5:01**
329	24	Tu.		7:13	5:34	7:33	**5:53**
330	25	We.		7:13	5:34	8:31	**6:48**
331	26	Th.	♀☌♂	7:14	5:34	9:23	**7:45**
332	27	Fr.	♀☌☾	7:15	5:34	10:09	**8:43**
333	28	Sa.		7:16	5:34	10:49	**9:40**
334	29	Su.	♂Stationary	7:17	5:34	11:24	**10:35**
335	30	Mo.		7:18	5:33	11:56	**11:29**

12th Month DECEMBER, 1992 31 Days

Moon's Phases—First Qtr., Dec. 2, 12:17 a.m.; Full, Dec. 9, 5:41 p.m.; Last Qtr., Dec. 16, 1:13 p.m.; New, Dec. 23, 6:43 p.m.; First Qtr., Dec. 31, 9:38 p.m.

Day of			Planetary Configurations —Phenomena	*Hour of			
Year	Month	Week		Sunrise	Sunset	Moonrise	Moonset
336	1	Tu.	☾at Apogee	7:18	5:33	**12:26**	...
337	2	We.		7:19	5:33	**12:55**	12:22
338	3	Th.		7:20	5:33	**1:24**	1:15
339	4	Fr.		7:21	5:33	**1:55**	2:09
340	5	Sa.		7:22	5:33	**2:27**	3:04
341	6	Su.		7:22	5:33	**3:04**	4:01
342	7	Mo.		7:23	5:34	**3:47**	5:01
343	8	Tu.		7:24	5:34	**4:35**	6:02
344	9	We.	☿Gr. elong. W.	7:25	5:34	**5:30**	7:02
345	10	Th.		7:25	5:34	**6:32**	8:01
346	11	Fr.		7:26	5:34	**7:38**	8:54
347	12	Sa.	♂☌☾	7:27	5:35	**8:45**	9:43
348	13	Su.	☾at Perigee	7:27	5:35	**9:52**	10:26
349	14	Mo.		7:28	5:35	**10:58**	11:05
350	15	Tu.		7:29	5:35	...	11:40
351	16	We.		7:29	5:36	12:03	**12:25**
352	17	Th.	♃☌☾	7:30	5:36	1:07	**12:52**
353	18	Fr.		7:30	5:37	2:11	**1:30**
354	19	Sa.		7:31	5:37	3:15	**2:10**
355	20	Su.		7:31	5:38	4:19	**2:54**
356	21	Mo.	Winter Begins	7:32	5:38	5:21	**3:43**
357	22	Tu.	☿☌☾	7:32	5:39	6:20	**4:37**
358	23	We.		7:33	5:39	7:14	**5:33**
359	24	Th.		7:33	5:40	8:02	**6:30**
360	25	Fr.		7:34	5:40	8:44	**7:28**
361	26	Sa.		7:34	5:41	9:22	**8:24**
362	27	Su.	♄☌☾	7:34	5:41	9:55	**9:19**
363	28	Mo.	♀☌☾	7:35	5:42	10:26	**10:12**
364	29	Tu.	☾at Apogee	7:35	5:43	10:55	**11:05**
365	30	We.		7:35	5:43	11:24	**11:58**
366	31	Th.		7:36	5:44	11:53	...

Calendar For 1993

Time given in this calendar is according to **Central Standard Time**, except for the period from April 4 to Oct. 31, during which **Daylight Saving Time** is observed. See page 102 for explanation of how to get exact time at any certain Texas point. (Boldface figures for moonrise and moonset indicate p.m.) Times are figured for the point 99° 10' West and 31° 23' North, the approximate geographic center of the state.

1st Month   JANUARY, 1993   31 Days
Moon's Phases—Full, Jan. 8, 6:37 a.m.; Last Qtr., Jan. 14, 10:01 p.m.; New, Jan. 22, 12:27 p.m.; First Qtr., Jan. 30, 5:20 p.m.

Year	Month	Week	Planetary Configurations —Phenomena	Sunrise	Sunset	Moonrise	Moonset
1	1	Fr.	. . . .	7:36	5:45	**12:25**	12:52
2	2	Sa.	. . . .	7:36	5:46	**12:59**	1:47
3	3	Su.	⊕ at Perihelion	7:36	5:46	**1:38**	2:45
4	4	Mo.	. . . .	7:36	5:47	**2:22**	3:44
5	5	Tu.	. . . .	7:36	5:48	**3:14**	4:44
6	6	We.	. . . .	7:37	5:49	**4:13**	5:44
7	7	Th.	♂ ☍	7:37	5:49	**5:18**	6:40
8	8	Fr.	☌ ☾	7:37	5:50	**6:26**	7:33
9	9	Sa.	. . . .	7:37	5:51	**7:36**	8:20
10	10	Su.	☾ at Perigee	7:37	5:52	**8:45**	9:02
11	11	Mo.	. . . .	7:37	5:53	**9:52**	9:41
12	12	Tu.	. . . .	7:36	5:54	**10:59**	10:18
13	13	We.	. . . .	7:36	5:54	. . .	10:54
14	14	Th.	♃ ☌ ☾	7:36	5:55	12:04	11:31
15	15	Fr.	. . . .	7:36	5:56	1:09	**12:11**
16	16	Sa.	. . . .	7:36	5:57	2:13	**12:54**
17	17	Su.	. . . .	7:36	5:58	3:14	**1:40**
18	18	Mo.	. . . .	7:35	6:00	4:13	**2:31**
19	19	Tu.	♀ Gr. elong. E.	7:35	6:00	5:08	**3:25**
20	20	We.	. . . .	7:35	6:01	5:57	**4:22**
21	21	Th.	. . . .	7:34	6:02	6:41	5:19
22	22	Fr.	. . . .	7:34	6:02	7:21	6:15
23	23	Sa.	☿ Superior	7:34	6:03	7:55	7:10
24	24	Su.	. . . .	7:33	6:04	8:27	8:04
25	25	Mo.	☌ ♆	7:33	6:05	8:57	8:57
26	26	Tu.	☾ at Apogee	7:32	6:06	9:26	9:50
27	27	We.	. . . .	7:32	6:07	9:55	10:43
28	28	Th.	. . . .	7:31	6:08	10:25	11:37
29	29	Fr.	♃ Stationary	7:31	6:09	10:57	. . .
30	30	Sa.	. . . .	7:30	6:10	11:33	12:33
31	31	Su.	. . . .	7:30	6:11	**12:14**	1:29

3rd Month   MARCH, 1993   31 Days
Moon's Phases—First Qtr., March 1, 9:46 a.m.; Full, March 8, 3:46 a.m.; Last Qtr., March 14, 10:16 p.m.; New, March 23, 1:14 a.m.

Year	Month	Week	Planetary Configurations —Phenomena	Sunrise	Sunset	Moonrise	Moonset
60	1	Mo.	☿ Stationary	7:03	6:35	11:44	1:14
61	2	Tu.	. . . .	7:02	6:35	**12:40**	2:10
62	3	We.	☌ ☾	7:01	6:36	**1:41**	3:03
63	4	Th.	. . . .	7:00	6:37	**2:41**	3:54
64	5	Fr.	. . . .	6:58	6:38	**3:55**	4:40
65	6	Sa.	. . . .	6:57	6:38	**5:05**	5:23
66	7	Su.	. . . .	6:56	6:39	**6:15**	6:04
67	8	Mo.	☾ at Perigee	6:55	6:40	**7:25**	6:43
68	9	Tu.	♀ Stationary	6:54	6:40	**8:35**	7:22
69	10	We.	. . . .	6:52	6:41	**9:45**	8:03
70	11	Th.	. . . .	6:51	6:42	**10:52**	8:46
71	12	Fr.	. . . .	6:50	6:43	**11:57**	9:33
72	13	Sa.	. . . .	6:49	6:43	. . .	10:23
73	14	Su.	. . . .	6:47	6:44	12:57	11:17
74	15	Mo.	. . . .	6:46	6:45	1:51	**12:12**
75	16	Tu.	. . . .	6:45	6:45	2:38	**1:08**
76	17	We.	♆ ☌ ☾	6:44	6:46	3:20	**2:04**
77	18	Th.	. . . .	6:42	6:47	3:57	**2:59**
78	19	Fr.	. . . .	6:41	6:47	4:31	**3:53**
79	20	Sa.	Spring Begins	6:40	6:48	5:02	**4:47**
80	21	Su.	☾ at Apogee	6:39	6:49	5:32	**5:39**
81	22	Mo.	. . . .	6:37	6:49	6:01	**6:32**
82	23	Tu.	. . . .	6:36	6:50	6:31	**7:26**
83	24	We.	☌ ☾	6:35	6:51	7:02	**8:20**
84	25	Th.	. . . .	6:34	6:51	7:35	**9:15**
85	26	Fr.	. . . .	6:32	6:52	8:12	**10:12**
86	27	Sa.	. . . .	6:31	6:53	8:54	**11:08**
87	28	Su.	. . . .	6:30	6:53	9:40	. . .
88	29	Mo.	. . . .	6:29	6:54	10:33	12:03
89	30	Tu.	♃ ☍	6:27	6:55	11:30	12:56
90	31	We.	☌ ☾	6:26	6:55	**12:32**	1:46

2nd Month   FEBRUARY, 1993   28 Days
Moon's Phases—Full, Feb. 6, 5:55 p.m.; Last Qtr., Feb. 13, 8:57 a.m.; New, Feb. 21, 7:05 a.m.

Year	Month	Week	Planetary Configurations —Phenomena	Sunrise	Sunset	Moonrise	Moonset
32	1	Mo.	. . . .	7:29	6:12	**1:01**	2:28
33	2	Tu.	. . . .	7:28	6:12	**1:55**	3:26
34	3	We.	. . . .	7:28	6:13	**2:55**	4:32
35	4	Th.	☌ ☾	7:27	6:14	**4:01**	5:17
36	5	Fr.	. . . .	7:26	6:15	**5:11**	6:07
37	6	Sa.	. . . .	7:25	6:16	**6:21**	6:52
38	7	Su.	☾ at Perigee	7:25	6:17	**7:32**	7:34
39	8	Mo.	. . . .	7:24	6:18	**8:41**	8:13
40	9	Tu.	♄ ☌ ☉	7:23	6:19	**9:49**	8:51
41	10	We.	♃ ☌ ☾	7:22	6:19	**10:57**	9:30
42	11	Th.	. . . .	7:21	6:20	. . .	10:10
43	12	Fr.	. . . .	7:20	6:21	12:03	10:52
44	13	Sa.	. . . .	7:19	6:22	1:07	11:39
45	14	Su.	. . . .	7:19	6:23	2:08	**12:29**
46	15	Mo.	♂ Stationary	7:18	6:24	3:04	**1:22**
47	16	Tu.	. . . .	7:17	6:25	3:55	**2:17**
48	17	We.	♆ ☌ ☾	7:16	6:25	4:40	**3:13**
49	18	Th.	. . . .	7:15	6:26	5:20	**4:09**
50	19	Fr.	. . . .	7:14	6:27	5:56	**5:04**
51	20	Sa.	. . . .	7:13	6:28	6:29	**5:58**
52	21	Su.	☿ Gr. elong. E. . . .	7:12	6:29	7:00	**6:51**
53	22	Mo.	☾ at Apogee	7:11	6:29	7:29	**7:44**
54	23	Tu.	☌ ☾	7:10	6:30	7:58	**8:37**
55	24	We.	♀ Gr. Brilliancy . . .	7:09	6:31	8:28	**9:31**
56	25	Th.	. . . .	7:08	6:32	8:59	**10:25**
57	26	Fr.	. . . .	7:06	6:32	9:33	**11:21**
58	27	Sa.	☿ Stationary	7:05	6:33	10:11	. . .
59	28	Su.	. . . .	7:04	6:34	10:55	12:17

4th Month   APRIL, 1993   30 Days
Moon's Phases—Full, April 6, 1:43 p.m.; Last Qtr., April 13, 2:39 p.m.; New, April 21, 6:49 p.m.; First Qtr., April 29, 7:40 a.m.

Year	Month	Week	Planetary Configurations —Phenomena	Sunrise	Sunset	Moonrise	Moonset
91	1	Th.	♀ Inferior	6:25	6:56	**1:37**	2:32
92	2	Fr.	. . . .	6:24	6:57	**2:44**	3:15
93	3	Sa.	. . . .	6:22	6:57	**3:51**	3:55
94	4	†Su.	. . . .	7:21	7:58	**6:00**	5:34
95	5	Mo.	☾ at Perigee	7:20	7:59	**7:09**	6:13
96	6	Tu.	♃ ☌ ☾	7:19	7:59	**8:19**	6:53
97	7	We.	. . . .	7:17	8:00	**9:29**	7:35
98	8	Th.	. . . .	7:16	8:01	**10:37**	8:21
99	9	Fr.	. . . .	7:15	8:01	**11:41**	9:11
100	10	Sa.	. . . .	7:14	8:02	. . .	10:05
101	11	Su.	. . . .	7:13	8:02	12:40	11:02
102	12	Mo.	. . . .	7:11	8:03	1:31	11:59
103	13	Tu.	♆ ☌ ☾	7:10	8:04	2:17	**12:57**
104	14	We.	. . . .	7:09	8:04	2:56	**1:53**
105	15	Th.	. . . .	7:08	8:05	3:31	**2:48**
106	16	Fr.	♄ ☌ ☾	7:07	8:06	4:03	**3:41**
107	17	Sa.	. . . .	7:06	8:06	4:34	**4:34**
108	18	Su.	☾ at Apogee	7:05	8:07	5:03	**5:27**
109	19	Mo.	♀ ☌ ☾; ☿ ☌ ☾	7:03	8:08	5:33	**6:20**
110	20	Tu.	. . . .	7:02	8:09	6:04	**7:14**
111	21	We.	. . . .	7:01	8:09	6:37	**8:09**
112	22	Th.	♆ Stationary	7:00	8:10	7:13	**9:06**
113	23	Fr.	. . . .	6:59	8:11	7:53	**10:03**
114	24	Sa.	. . . .	6:58	8:11	8:39	**10:58**
115	25	Su.	. . . .	6:57	8:12	9:30	**11:52**
116	26	Mo.	♂ Stationary	6:56	8:13	10:25	. . .
117	27	Tu.	. . . .	6:55	8:13	11:25	12:42
118	28	We.	☌ ☾	6:54	8:14	**12:28**	1:28
119	29	Th.	. . . .	6:53	8:15	**1:32**	2:13
120	30	Fr.	. . . .	6:52	8:15	**2:37**	2:57

*See text before January calendar for explanation.   †Daylight Saving Time begins at 2 a.m.

Calendar For 1993

5th Month **MAY, 1993** **31 Days**

Moon's Phases—Full, May 5, 10:34 p.m.; Last Qtr., May 13, 7:20 a.m.; New, May 21, 9:06 a.m.; First Qtr., May 28, 1:21 p.m.

Day of			Planetary Configurations —Phenomena	*Hour of			
Year	Month	Week		Sunrise	Sunset	Moonrise	Moonset
121	1	Sa.		6:51	8:16	**3:42**	3:30
122	2	Su.		6:50	8:17	**4:49**	4:07
123	3	Mo.	☾at Perigee	6:49	8:17	**5:57**	4:45
124	4	Tu.		6:49	8:18	**7:06**	5:26
125	5	We.		6:48	8:19	**8:14**	6:09
126	6	Th.	♀Gr. Brilliancy	6:47	8:19	**9:21**	6:57
127	7	Fr.		6:46	8:20	**10:24**	7:50
128	8	Sa.		6:45	8:21	**11:20**	8:47
129	9	Su.		6:44	8:22	...	9:45
130	10	Mo.	♆☌☾	6:44	8:22	12:09	10:45
131	11	Tu.		6:43	8:23	12:52	11:43
132	12	We.		6:42	8:24	1:29	**12:39**
133	13	Th.		6:42	8:24	2:03	**1:33**
134	14	Fr.	♄☌☾	6:41	8:25	2:34	**2:27**
135	15	Sa.	☾at Apogee	6:40	8:26	3:04	**3:20**
136	16	Su.		6:40	8:26	3:34	**4:12**
137	17	Mo.	♀☌☾	6:39	8:27	4:04	**5:06**
138	18	Tu.		6:38	8:28	4:36	**6:01**
139	19	We.		6:38	8:28	5:11	**6:57**
140	20	Th.		6:37	8:29	5:50	**7:54**
141	21	Fr.	Eclipse ☉	6:37	8:30	6:35	**8:52**
142	22	Sa.		6:36	8:30	7:24	**9:47**
143	23	Su.		6:36	8:31	8:20	**10:39**
144	24	Mo.		6:35	8:32	9:19	**11:28**
145	25	Tu.		6:35	8:32	10:22	...
146	26	We.		6:35	8:33	11:25	12:12
147	27	Th.	♂☌☾	6:34	8:33	**12:29**	12:52
148	28	Fr.		6:34	8:34	**1:34**	1:30
149	29	Sa.		6:33	8:35	**2:38**	2:07
150	30	Su.	♃☌☾	6:33	8:35	**3:43**	2:43
151	31	Mo.	☾at Perigee	6:33	8:36	**4:50**	3:21

6th Month **JUNE, 1993** **30 Days**

Moon's Phases—Full, June 4, 8:02 a.m.; Last Qtr., June 12, 12:36 a.m.; New, June 19, 8:52 p.m.; First Qtr., June 26, 5:43 p.m.

Day of			Planetary Configurations —Phenomena	*Hour of			
Year	Month	Week		Sunrise	Sunset	Moonrise	Moonset
152	1	Tu.	♃Stationary	6:33	8:36	**5:56**	4:02
153	2	We.		6:32	8:37	**7:03**	4:47
154	3	Th.		6:32	8:37	**8:07**	5:37
155	4	Fr.	Eclipse ☾	6:32	8:38	**9:06**	6:31
156	5	Sa.		6:32	8:38	**9:59**	7:30
157	6	Su.		6:32	8:39	**10:45**	8:29
158	7	Mo.	♆☌☾	6:32	8:39	**11:25**	9:29
159	8	Tu.		6:32	8:40	...	10:27
160	9	We.		6:32	8:40	12:01	11:23
161	10	Th.	♄☌☾	6:31	8:41	12:34	**12:18**
162	11	Fr.		6:31	8:41	1:04	**1:11**
163	12	Sa.	☾at Apogee	6:31	8:41	1:34	**2:04**
164	13	Su.		6:32	8:42	2:04	**2:57**
165	14	Mo.		6:32	8:42	2:35	**3:51**
166	15	Tu.		6:32	8:43	3:09	**4:46**
167	16	We.	♀☌☾	6:32	8:43	3:46	**5:43**
168	17	Th.	☿Gr. elong. E.	6:32	8:43	4:28	**6:40**
169	18	Fr.		6:32	8:43	5:16	**7:37**
170	19	Sa.		6:32	8:44	6:09	**8:32**
171	20	Su.		6:32	8:44	7:08	**9:23**
172	21	Mo.	Summer Begins	6:33	8:44	8:11	**10:10**
173	22	Tu.		6:33	8:44	9:16	**10:52**
174	23	We.		6:33	8:45	10:22	**11:31**
175	24	Th.	♂☌☾	6:33	8:45	11:27	...
176	25	Fr.	☾at Perigee	6:34	8:45	**12:31**	12:08
177	26	Sa.	♃☌☾	6:34	8:45	**1:36**	12:45
178	27	Su.		6:34	8:45	**2:41**	1:22
179	28	Mo.		6:35	8:45	**3:46**	2:01
180	29	Tu.		6:35	8:45	**4:51**	2:43
181	30	We.	☿Stationary	6:35	8:45	**5:55**	3:30

*See text before January calendar for explanation

7th Month **JULY, 1993** **31 Days**

Moon's Phases—Full, July 3, 6:45 p.m.; Last Qtr., July 11, 5:49 p.m.; New, July 19, 6:24 a.m.; First Qtr., July 25, 10:25 p.m.

Day of			Planetary Configurations —Phenomena	*Hour of			
Year	Month	Week		Sunrise	Sunset	Moonrise	Moonset
182	1	Th.		6:36	8:45	**6:55**	4:22
183	2	Fr.		6:36	8:45	**7:49**	5:17
184	3	Sa.		6:37	8:45	**8:38**	6:16
185	4	Su.	⊕at Aphelion	6:37	8:45	**9:21**	7:16
186	5	Mo.		6:38	8:45	**9:59**	8:14
187	6	Tu.		6:38	8:45	**10:33**	9:12
188	7	We.	♄☌☾	6:39	8:45	**11:05**	10:07
189	8	Th.		6:39	8:44	**11:35**	11:01
190	9	Fr.		6:40	8:44	...	11:55
191	10	Sa.	☾at Apogee	6:40	8:44	12:04	**12:48**
192	11	Su.	♆☍	6:41	8:44	12:35	**1:41**
193	12	Mo.	♅☍	6:41	8:43	1:07	**2:35**
194	13	Tu.		6:42	8:43	1:42	**3:31**
195	14	We.	☿Inferior	6:42	8:43	2:21	**4:27**
196	15	Th.	♀☌☾	6:43	8:42	3:06	**5:24**
197	16	Fr.		6:43	8:42	3:57	**6:19**
198	17	Sa.		6:44	8:41	4:53	**7:12**
199	18	Su.		6:45	8:41	5:55	**8:02**
200	19	Mo.		6:45	8:41	7:00	**8:47**
201	20	Tu.		6:46	8:40	8:07	**9:29**
202	21	We.		6:46	8:40	9:14	**10:08**
203	22	Th.	☾at Perigee	6:47	8:39	10:21	**10:46**
204	23	Fr.		6:48	8:39	11:27	**11:23**
205	24	Sa.	♃☌☾	6:48	8:38	**12:33**	...
206	25	Su.	☿Stationary	6:49	8:37	**1:39**	12:02
207	26	Mo.		6:49	8:37	**2:44**	12:43
208	27	Tu.		6:50	8:36	**3:48**	1:28
209	28	We.		6:51	8:35	**4:48**	2:18
210	29	Th.		6:51	8:35	**5:43**	3:11
211	30	Fr.		6:52	8:34	**6:33**	4:08
212	31	Sa.	♆☌☾	6:53	8:33	**7:18**	5:06

8th Month **AUGUST, 1993** **31 Days**

Moon's Phases—Full, Aug. 2, 7:10 a.m.; Last Qtr., Aug. 10, 10:19 a.m.; New, Aug. 17, 2:28 p.m.; First Qtr., Aug. 24, 4:57 a.m.; Full, Aug. 31, 9:33 p.m.

Day of			Planetary Configurations —Phenomena	*Hour of			
Year	Month	Week		Sunrise	Sunset	Moonrise	Moonset
213	1	Su.		6:53	8:32	**7:57**	6:05
214	2	Mo.		6:54	8:32	**8:33**	7:02
215	3	Tu.	♄☌☾	6:55	8:31	**9:06**	7:58
216	4	We.		6:55	8:30	**9:36**	8:53
217	5	Th.		6:56	8:29	**10:06**	9:46
218	6	Fr.	☾at Apogee	6:56	8:28	**10:36**	10:39
219	7	Sa.		6:57	8:27	**11:07**	11:32
220	8	Su.		6:58	8:27	**11:41**	**12:26**
221	9	Mo.		6:58	8:26	...	**1:20**
222	10	Tu.		6:59	8:25	12:18	**2:15**
223	11	We.		7:00	8:24	12:59	**3:11**
224	12	Th.		7:00	8:23	1:46	**4:06**
225	13	Fr.		7:01	8:22	2:39	**4:59**
226	14	Sa.	♀☌☾	7:02	8:21	3:37	**5:50**
227	15	Su.		7:02	8:20	4:40	**6:37**
228	16	Mo.		7:03	8:19	5:46	**7:21**
229	17	Tu.		7:03	8:18	6:54	**8:02**
230	18	We.		7:04	8:17	8:03	**8:42**
231	19	Th.	☾at Perigee	7:05	8:15	9:11	**9:21**
232	20	Fr.	♃☌☾; ♂☌☾	7:05	8:14	10:20	**10:00**
233	21	Sa.		7:06	8:13	11:28	**10:42**
234	22	Su.		7:07	8:12	**12:35**	**11:27**
235	23	Mo.		7:07	8:11	**1:40**	...
236	24	Tu.		7:08	8:10	**2:42**	12:16
237	25	We.		7:08	8:09	**3:39**	1:08
238	26	Th.		7:09	8:08	**4:31**	2:04
239	27	Fr.	♆☌☾	7:10	8:06	**5:16**	3:01
240	28	Sa.		7:10	8:05	**5:57**	3:59
241	29	Su.	☿Superior	7:11	8:04	**6:34**	4:56
242	30	Mo.		7:11	8:03	**7:07**	5:52
243	31	Tu.	♄☌☾	7:12	8:02	**7:38**	6:46

Calendar For 1993

9th Month   **SEPTEMBER, 1993**   30 Days
Moon's Phases—Last Qtr., Sept. 9, 1:26 a.m.; New, Sept. 15, 10:10 p.m.; First Qtr., Sept. 22, 2:52 p.m.; Full, Sept. 30, 1:54 p.m.

Year	Month	Week	Planetary Configurations —Phenomena	Sunrise	Sunset	Moonrise	Moonset
244	1	We.	....	7:13	8:00	8:09	7:40
245	2	Th.	....	7:13	7:59	8:39	8:33
246	3	Fr.	ℂ at Apogee	7:14	7:58	9:09	9:26
247	4	Sa.	....	7:14	7:57	9:42	10:19
248	5	Su.	....	7:15	7:55	10:17	11:13
249	6	Mo.	♂♂♃	7:16	7:54	10:56	12:07
250	7	Tu.	....	7:16	7:53	11:40	1:01
251	8	We.	....	7:17	7:52	...	1:55
252	9	Th.	....	7:17	7:50	12:29	2:48
253	10	Fr.	....	7:18	7:49	1:23	3:38
254	11	Sa.	....	7:19	7:48	2:22	4:46
255	12	Su.	....	7:19	7:46	3:26	5:11
256	13	Mo.	♀♂ℂ	7:20	7:45	4:31	5:53
257	14	Tu.	....	7:20	7:44	5:39	6:33
258	15	We.	....	7:21	7:42	6:48	7:13
259	16	Th.	ℂ at Perigee	7:21	7:41	7:57	7:53
260	17	Fr.	♃♂ℂ	7:22	7:40	9:07	8:35
261	18	Sa.	♂♂ℂ	7:23	7:39	10:17	9:20
262	19	Su.	....	7:23	7:37	11:26	10:09
263	20	Mo.	....	7:24	7:36	12:32	11:02
264	21	Tu.	....	7:24	7:35	1:32	11:58
265	22	We.	Fall Begins	7:25	7:33	2:27	...
266	23	Th.	....	7:26	7:32	3:15	12:56
267	24	Fr.	♆♂ℂ	7:26	7:31	3:57	1:54
268	25	Sa.	....	7:27	7:29	4:34	2:51
269	26	Su.	....	7:27	7:28	5:09	3:47
270	27	Mo.	♄♂ℂ	7:28	7:27	5:40	4:42
271	28	Tu.	....	7:29	7:26	6:11	5:35
272	29	We.	♆ Stationary	7:29	7:24	6:41	6:28
273	30	Th.	ℂ at Apogee	7:30	7:23	7:12	7:21

10th Month   **OCTOBER, 1993**   31 Days
Moon's Phases—Last Qtr., Oct. 8, 2:35 p.m.; New, Oct. 15, 6:36 a.m.; First Qtr., Oct. 22, 3:52 a.m.; Full, Oct. 30, 7:38 a.m.

Year	Month	Week	Planetary Configurations —Phenomena	Sunrise	Sunset	Moonrise	Moonset
274	1	Fr.	....	7:31	7:22	7:44	8:14
275	2	Sa.	....	7:31	7:21	8:19	9:08
276	3	Su.	....	7:32	7:19	8:56	10:02
277	4	Mo.	....	7:32	7:18	9:38	10:56
278	5	Tu.	....	7:33	7:17	10:25	11:49
279	6	We.	♀♂♂	7:34	7:16	11:16	12:41
280	7	Th.	....	7:34	7:14	...	1:31
281	8	Fr.	....	7:35	7:13	12:12	2:18
282	9	Sa.	....	7:36	7:12	1:11	3:03
283	10	Su.	....	7:36	7:11	2:14	3:44
284	11	Mo.	....	7:37	7:09	3:18	4:24
285	12	Tu.	....	7:38	7:08	4:24	5:03
286	13	We.	♀♂ℂ	7:38	7:07	5:32	5:43
287	14	Th.	ℂ at Perigee	7:39	7:06	6:41	6:24
288	15	Fr.	....	7:40	7:05	7:52	7:08
289	16	Sa.	♂♂ℂ	7:41	7:04	9:03	7:56
290	17	Su.	♀♂ℂ	7:41	7:03	10:12	8:49
291	18	Mo.	♃♂⊙	7:42	7:01	11:17	9:46
292	19	Tu.	....	7:43	7:00	12:17	10:45
293	20	We.	....	7:43	6:59	1:09	11:45
294	21	Th.	♆♂ℂ	7:44	6:58	1:54	...
295	22	Fr.	....	7:45	6:57	2:34	12:44
296	23	Sa.	....	7:46	6:56	3:09	1:41
297	24	Su.	♄♂ℂ	7:46	6:55	3:42	2:37
298	25	Mo.	♀ Stationary	7:47	6:54	4:13	3:31
299	26	Tu.	....	7:48	6:53	4:43	4:24
300	27	We.	ℂ at Apogee	7:49	6:52	5:14	5:16
301	28	Th.	♀♂♂	7:50	6:51	5:46	6:09
302	29	Fr.	....	7:50	6:50	6:20	7:02
303	30	Sa.	....	7:51	6:49	6:57	7:56
304	31	†Su.	....	6:52	5:49	6:38	7:51

11th Month   **NOVEMBER, 1993**   30 Days
Moon's Phases—Last Qtr., Nov. 7, 12:36 a.m.; New, Nov. 13, 3:34 p.m.; First Qtr., Nov. 20, 8:03 p.m.; Full, Nov. 29, 12:31 a.m.

Year	Month	Week	Planetary Configurations —Phenomena	Sunrise	Sunset	Moonrise	Moonset
305	1	Mo.	....	6:53	5:48	7:23	8:45
306	2	Tu.	....	6:54	5:47	8:13	9:38
307	3	We.	....	6:54	5:46	9:07	10:28
308	4	Th.	....	6:55	5:45	10:05	11:16
309	5	Fr.	♀ Inferior	6:56	5:44	11:04	11:59
310	6	Sa.	....	6:57	5:44	...	12:41
311	7	Su.	....	6:58	5:43	12:06	1:20
312	8	Mo.	♀♂♃	6:59	5:42	1:09	1:58
313	9	Tu.	....	6:59	5:42	2:13	2:36
314	10	We.	....	7:00	5:41	3:19	3:15
315	11	Th.	....	7:01	5:40	4:27	3:56
316	12	Fr.	ℂ at Perigee	7:02	5:40	5:37	4:42
317	13	Sa.	Eclipse ⊙	7:03	5:39	6:47	5:32
318	14	Su.	♀♂♀	7:04	5:39	7:55	6:28
319	15	Mo.	....	7:05	5:38	8:59	7:28
320	16	Tu.	....	7:05	5:38	9:56	8:29
321	17	We.	♂♂ℂ	7:06	5:37	10:46	9:31
322	18	Th.	....	7:07	5:37	11:30	10:30
323	19	Fr.	....	7:08	5:36	12:08	11:28
324	20	Sa.	♆♂ℂ	7:09	5:36	12:42	...
325	21	Su.	....	7:10	5:35	1:14	12:23
326	22	Mo.	♀ Gr. elong. W.	7:11	5:35	1:44	1:17
327	23	Tu.	....	7:11	5:35	2:15	2:10
328	24	We.	ℂ at Apogee	7:12	5:35	2:46	3:02
329	25	Th.	....	7:13	5:34	3:19	3:55
330	26	Fr.	....	7:14	5:34	3:55	4:49
331	27	Sa.	....	7:15	5:34	4:35	5:44
332	28	Su.	....	7:16	5:34	5:19	6:39
333	29	Mo.	Eclipse ℂ	7:17	5:34	6:08	7:33
334	30	Tu.	....	7:17	5:33	7:02	8:25

12th Month   **DECEMBER, 1993**   31 Days
Moon's Phases—Last Qtr., Dec. 6, 9:49 a.m.; New, Dec. 13, 3:27 a.m.; First Qtr., Dec. 20, 4:26 p.m.; Full, Dec. 28, 5:05 p.m.

Year	Month	Week	Planetary Configurations —Phenomena	Sunrise	Sunset	Moonrise	Moonset
335	1	We.	....	7:18	5:33	7:59	9:14
336	2	Th.	....	7:19	5:33	8:59	10:00
337	3	Fr.	....	7:20	5:33	10:00	10:42
338	4	Sa.	....	7:21	5:33	11:02	11:21
339	5	Su.	....	7:21	5:33	...	11:59
340	6	Mo.	....	7:22	5:33	12:04	12:35
341	7	Tu.	....	7:23	5:34	1:07	1:12
342	8	We.	....	7:24	5:34	2:12	1:51
343	9	Th.	....	7:24	5:34	3:18	2:33
344	10	Fr.	ℂ at Perigee	7:25	5:34	4:26	3:20
345	11	Sa.	....	7:26	5:34	5:33	4:11
346	12	Su.	....	7:26	5:35	6:39	5:09
347	13	Mo.	....	7:27	5:35	7:39	6:09
348	14	Tu.	....	7:28	5:35	8:33	7:12
349	15	We.	♆♂ℂ	7:28	5:35	9:21	8:14
350	16	Th.	....	7:29	5:36	10:03	9:14
351	17	Fr.	....	7:30	5:36	10:39	10:11
352	18	Sa.	♄♂ℂ	7:30	5:37	11:13	11:07
353	19	Su.	....	7:31	5:37	11:44	...
354	20	Mo.	....	7:31	5:37	12:15	12:01
355	21	Tu.	Winter Begins	7:32	5:38	12:46	12:53
356	22	We.	ℂ at Apogee	7:32	5:38	1:18	1:46
357	23	Th.	....	7:33	5:39	1:53	2:40
358	24	Fr.	....	7:33	5:40	2:31	3:34
359	25	Sa.	....	7:34	5:40	3:13	4:29
360	26	Su.	♂♂⊙	7:34	5:41	4:00	5:23
361	27	Mo.	....	7:34	5:41	4:53	6:17
362	28	Tu.	....	7:35	5:42	5:50	7:08
363	29	We.	....	7:35	5:43	6:50	7:56
364	30	Th.	....	7:36	5:43	7:52	8:41
365	31	Fr.	....	7:36	5:44	8:55	9:22

†Daylight Saving Time ends at 2 a.m. *See text before January calendar for explanation.

249-YEAR CALENDAR, 1752-2000, A.D., INCLUSIVE

By this calendar one may ascertain the day of week for any day of month and year for the period 1752-2000, inclusive. The calendar covers the period beginning with †1752, the year of the adoption by England of the New Style, or Gregorian calendar.

To ascertain any day of the week, first look in the table for the year required, and under the months are figures which refer to the corresponding figures at the head of the columns of days below. For example: To know on what day of the week Aug. 4 fell in the year 1914, in the table of years look for 1914, and in a parallel line under Aug., is Fig. 6, which directs to Col. 6, in which it will be seen that Aug. 4 fell on Tuesday.

COMMON YEARS, 1753 TO 1999

											Jan.	Feb.	Mar.	Apr.	May	June	July	Aug.	Sept.	Oct.	Nov.	Dec.
1761	1767	1778	1789	1795	....	....	....	....	....	....												
1801	1807	1818	1829	1835	1846	1857	1863	1874	1885	1891	4	7	7	3	5	1	3	6	2	4	7	2
1903	1914	1925	1931	1942	1953	1959	1970	1981	1987	1998												
1762	1773	1779	1790	....	....	....	....	....	....	....												
1802	1813	1819	1830	1841	1847	1858	1869	1875	1886	1897	5	1	1	4	6	2	4	7	3	5	1	3
1909	1915	1926	1937	1943	1954	1965	1971	1982	1993	1999												
1757	1763	1774	1785	1791	....	....	....	....	....	....												
1803	1814	1825	1831	1842	1853	1859	1870	1881	1887	1898	6	2	2	5	7	3	5	1	4	6	2	4
1910	1921	1927	1938	1949	1955	1966	1977	1983	1994	....												
1754	1765	1771	1782	1793	1799	....	....	....	....	....												
1805	1811	1822	1833	1839	1850	1861	1867	1889	1895	....	2	5	5	1	3	6	1	4	7	2	5	7
1901	1907	1918	1929	1935	1946	1957	1963	1974	1985	1991												
1755	1766	1777	1783	1794	1800	....	....	....	....	....												
1806	1817	1823	1834	1845	1851	1862	1873	1879	1890	....	3	6	6	2	4	7	2	5	1	3	6	1
1902	1913	1919	1930	1941	1947	1958	1969	1975	1986	1997												
1758	1769	1775	1786	1797	....	....	....	....	....	....												
1809	1815	1826	1837	1843	1854	1865	1871	1882	1893	1899	7	3	3	6	1	4	6	2	5	7	3	5
1905	1911	1922	1933	1939	1950	1961	1967	1978	1989	1995												
1753	1759	1770	1781	1787	1798	....	....	....	....	....												
1810	1821	1827	1838	1849	1855	1866	1877	1883	1894	1900	1	4	4	7	2	5	7	3	6	1	4	6
1906	1917	1923	1934	1945	1951	1962	1973	1979	1990	....												

LEAP YEARS, 1976 TO 2000 (Feb. = 29)

										Jan.	Feb.	Mar.	Apr.	May	June	July	Aug.	Sept.	Oct.	Nov.	Dec.
1764	1792	1804	1832	1860	1888	....	1928	1956	1984	7	3	4	7	2	5	7	3	6	1	4	6
1768	1796	1808	1836	1864	1892	1904	1932	1960	1988	5	1	2	5	7	3	5	1	4	6	2	4
1772	....	1812	1840	1868	1896	1908	1936	1964	1992	3	6	7	3	5	1	3	6	2	4	7	2
1776	....	1816	1844	1872	....	1912	1940	1968	1996	1	4	5	1	3	6	1	4	7	2	5	7
1780	....	1820	1848	1876	....	1916	1944	1972	2000	6	2	3	6	1	4	6	2	5	7	3	5
1756	1784	1824	1852	1880	....	1920	1948	1976	....	4	7	1	4	6	2	4	7	3	5	1	3
1760	1788	1828	1856	1884	....	1924	1952	1980	....	2	5	6	2	4	7	2	5	1	3	6	1

1	2	3	4	5	6	7
Mon......1	Tues......1	Wed......1	Thurs......1	Fri......1	Sat......1	SUN......1
Tues......2	Wed......2	Thurs......2	Fri......2	Sat......2	SUN......2	Mon......2
Wed......3	Thurs......3	Fri......3	Sat......3	SUN......3	Mon......3	Tues......3
Thurs......4	Fri......4	Sat......4	SUN......4	Mon......4	Tues......4	Wed......4
Fri......5	Sat......5	SUN......5	Mon......5	Tues......5	Wed......5	Thurs......5
Sat......6	SUN......6	Mon......6	Tues......6	Wed......6	Thurs......6	Fri......6
SUN......7	Mon......7	Tues......7	Wed......7	Thurs......7	Fri......7	Sat......7
Mon......8	Tues......8	Wed......8	Thurs......8	Fri......8	Sat......8	SUN......8
Tues......9	Wed......9	Thurs......9	Fri......9	Sat......9	SUN......9	Mon......9
Wed......10	Thurs......10	Fri......10	Sat......10	SUN......10	Mon......10	Tues......10
Thurs......11	Fri......11	Sat......11	SUN......11	Mon......11	Tues......11	Wed......11
Fri......12	Sat......12	SUN......12	Mon......12	Tues......12	Wed......12	Thurs......12
Sat......13	SUN......13	Mon......13	Tues......13	Wed......13	Thurs......13	Fri......13
SUN......14	Mon......14	Tues......14	Wed......14	Thurs......14	Fri......14	Sat......14
Mon......15	Tues......15	Wed......15	Thurs......15	Fri......15	Sat......15	SUN......15
Tues......16	Wed......16	Thurs......16	Fri......16	Sat......16	SUN......16	Mon......16
Wed......17	Thurs......17	Fri......17	Sat......17	SUN......17	Mon......17	Tues......17
Thurs......18	Fri......18	Sat......18	SUN......18	Mon......18	Tues......18	Wed......18
Fri......19	Sat......19	SUN......19	Mon......19	Tues......19	Wed......19	Thurs......19
Sat......20	SUN......20	Mon......20	Tues......20	Wed......20	Thurs......20	Fri......20
SUN......21	Mon......21	Tues......21	Wed......21	Thurs......21	Fri......21	Sat......21
Mon......22	Tues......22	Wed......22	Thurs......22	Fri......22	Sat......22	SUN......22
Tues......23	Wed......23	Thurs......23	Fri......23	Sat......23	SUN......23	Mon......23
Wed......24	Thurs......24	Fri......24	Sat......24	SUN......24	Mon......24	Tues......24
Thurs......25	Fri......25	Sat......25	SUN......25	Mon......25	Tues......25	Wed......25
Fri......26	Sat......26	SUN......26	Mon......26	Tues......26	Wed......26	Thurs......26
Sat......27	SUN......27	Mon......27	Tues......27	Wed......27	Thurs......27	Fri......27
SUN......28	Mon......28	Tues......28	Wed......28	Thurs......28	Fri......28	Sat......28
Mon......29	Tues......29	Wed......29	Thurs......29	Fri......29	Sat......29	SUN......29
Tues......30	Wed......30	Thurs......30	Fri......30	Sat......30	SUN......30	Mon......30
Wed......31	Thurs......31	Fri......31	Sat......31	SUN......31	Mon......31	Tues......31

†Days of the week can be calculated for 1752 as follows: 1752 is the same as 1772 from Jan. 1 to Sept. 2, inclusive. It is the same as 1780 from Sept. 14 to Dec. 31. (Note that 1752, 1772 and 1780 are leap years.) Sept. 3 to 13, inclusive, were omitted in the change from Old Style to New Style (Julian to Gregorian) calendar.

BEGINNING OF YEAR

The Athenians began the year in June, the Macedonians in September, the Romans first in March and afterward in January, the Persians on Aug. 11, the ancient Mexicans on Feb. 23. The Chinese year, which begins late in January or early in February, is similar to the Mohammedan year in having twelve months of twenty-nine and thirty days alternating, while in every nineteen years there are seven months which have thirteen months. This is not quite commensurate with planetary movements, hence the Chinese have formed a cycle of sixty years in which period twenty-two intercalary months occur.

Weather Highlights, 1989 and 1990

The following summary was prepared for the Texas Almanac by John F. Griffiths and Jon W. Zeitler, Office of the Texas State Climatologist, Department of Meteorology, Texas A&M University.

Feb. 2-7, 1989: Approximately one inch of sleet and freezing rain fell across the eastern two-thirds of Texas, bringing most of the state's transportation to a near halt. Six people died in automobile accidents and the extreme cold that followed the storm as it moved southeast.

March 28-29, 1989: Rainfall amounts such as 13.25 inches at Longview, Rusk County, 11.05 inches at Henderson, Rusk County, and 8.92 inches at Atlanta, Cass County, caused severe flooding throughout Northeast

Weather

Texas. Seventy bridges were washed out temporarily or destroyed by raging flood waters. Numerous homes had to be evacuated as the flood waters approached. One person was killed and total damage of $10 million-$15 million resulted from the storms.

May 17, 1989: A tornado hit Jarrell, Williamson County, destroying approximately two-thirds of the town of 700. Thirty-five homes and 12 mobile homes were either severely damaged or destroyed. One person was killed and 28 people were injured by the tornado, although most of the injuries only required short hospital visits.

May 16-29, 1989: Up to 15 inches of rain fell in many locations of the Upper Coast and North Central divisions of Texas during this span of time, causing some of the worst flooding in recent history. In North Texas, Lake Benbrook, Tarrant County, went over the emergency spillway for only the second time in history, while the Trinity River in Dallas, Dallas County, was at its fifth highest stage ever. In Southwest Texas, 10.36 inches of rain fell at Houston Intercontinental Airport on May 17-18 alone, while approximately 15 inches fell at

Spring, Harris County. The widespread rains caused the floodgates at the Toledo Bend Dam, Sabine County, to be opened for the first time ever. Around 1,200 homes in the state were severely flooded by the storms in North and Southeast Texas, with total damage running near $50 million. Five people died statewide as a result of the floods.

June 26-30, 1989: Tropical Storm Allison made landfall near Freeport, Brazoria County, on the 26th, bringing with it sustained winds of 45 mph and seas of 3 feet-5 feet above normal. Over the next five days, Allison and her remnants dumped rains of 10 inches-15 inches in the coastal areas from Houston to Beaumont, Jefferson County. The severe flooding that resulted from Allison and lingering thunderstorms caused an estimated $60 million in damage, while total damage from the storm including hail and wind effects topped $110 million in Texas and Louisiana. No deaths were directly attributed to the storm and injuries were kept to a minimum due in part to advance warnings.

July 2, 1989: A downburst in the northern portions of Texas created widespread damage on the 2nd. In Allen, Collin County, $3 million-5 million in damage occurred from a combination of baseball-size hail and strong winds. In Dallas, Dallas County, winds were estimated at 95 mph in the Pleasant Grove section. Power outages affected over 100,000 residents, and tree damage was estimated between $5 million-7 million to city parks and golf courses.

August 1-4, 1989: The first few days of August were tension-filled for many Texans along the Upper Coast and in East Texas as Hurricane Chantal made landfall near High Island, Chambers County, around 8 a.m. on the 1st. Chantal was only a Category 1 hurricane, as the maximum wind gust of 82 mph at Galveston was well below the Category 2 threshold of 96 mph. Despite being

Meteorological Data

Source: NOAA, Environmental Data Service, Local Climatological Data.

Additional data for these locations are listed in the table of Texas temperature, freeze, growing season, and precipitation records, by counties.

| | Temperature | | | | | | Precipitation | | | | | Relative Humidity | | Wind | | | |
	Record Highest	Month and Yr.	Record Lowest	Month and Yr.	No. Days Max. 90° and Above	No. Days Min. 32° and Below	Maximum in 24 Hours	Month and Year	Snowfall Mean Annual	Max. Snowfall in 24 Hours	Month and Year	6:00 A.M. CST	Noon CST	Speed, MPH Mean Annual	Highest Miles Per Hour	Month and Year	Percent Possible Sunshine
Abilene	110	7-78	−9	1-47	96.6	53.6	6.70	9-61	4.9	7.5	1-73	74	51	12.1	46	9-84	70
Amarillo	108	6-90	−14	2-51	63.8	110.7	6.75	5-51	14.9	13.5	2-71	73	46	13.6	58	9-79	73
Austin	109	7-54	−2	1-49	105.0	21.1	7.22	10-60	1.1	7.0	1-44	83	56	9.2	52	9-87	60
Brownsville	106	3-84	16	12-89	117.3	2.2	12.19	9-67	T	0.0	—	89	60	11.5	48	8-80	60
Corpus Christi	104	7-39	13	12-89	101.9	6.6	8.92	8-80	0.1	1.1	2-73	90	62	12.0	55	8-80	62
Dallas-Fort Worth . .	113	6-80	−1	12-89	96.2	40.9	5.91	10-59	3.2	12.1	1-64	82	56	10.9	73	8-59	64
Del Rio	112	6-88	10	12-89	124.2	17.3	7.60	10-84	0.9	8.6	1-85	79	54	9.9	60	8-70	70
El Paso	112	7-79	−8	1-62	104.0	65.0	2.63	7-68	5.4	16.8	12-87	35	28	8.9	48	2-77	83
Galveston	101	7-32	8	2-99	12.2	3.6	14.35	7-00	0.2	15.4	2-95	83	72	11.0	*100	9-00	62
***Houston	107	8-80	7	12-89	94.2	21.2	10.36	5-89	0.4	2.0	1-73	90	59	7.8	51	8-83	56
Lubbock	110	6-90	−16	1-63	78.6	94.6	5.82	10-83	10.5	16.3	1-83	74	47	12.4	70	3-52	72
Midland-Odessa. . . .	112	7-89	−11	2-85	96.2	64.7	5.99	7-61	4.1	6.8	1-74	74	43	11.0	67	2-60	74
Prt. Arthur-Beaumont	107	8-62	12	12-89	81.2	16.3	17.16	9-80	0.4	4.4	2-60	91	64	9.8	55	6-86	58
San Angelo	111	7-60	−4	12-89	106.8	53.9	6.25	9-80	3.3	7.4	1-78	78	49	10.4	75	4-69	73
San Antonio	108	8-86	0	1-49	110.8	22.7	7.28	9-73	0.8	13.2	1-85	83	55	9.3	48	7-79	60
Victoria.	107	8-62	9	12-89	102.7	12.1	9.30	6-77	0.2	2.1	1-85	89	60	10.0	99	7-63	62
Waco	112	8-69	−5	1-49	108.5	35.2	7.18	5-53	1.5	7.0	1-49	83	57	11.3	69	6-61	63
Wichita Falls	117	6-80	−8	2-85	105.9	68.1	6.22	9-80	6.0	8.1	1-85	82	51	11.7	60	6-54	68
**Shreveport, LA . . .	112	8-62	3	1-62	89.4	37.3	7.17	4-53	1.3	5.6	1-82	87	58	8.4	52	4-75	63

*100 mph recorded at 6:15 p.m. Sept. 8 just before anemometer blew away. Maximum velocity estimated 120 mph from NE between 7:30 p.m. and 8:30 p.m.

**This station is included because it is near the boundary line and its data can be considered representative of the eastern border of Texas.

††Measured at Orange, Texas, near Port Arthur.

‡Trace, an amount too small to measure.

***The official Houston station was moved from near downtown to Intercontinental Airport, located 12 miles north of the old station.

relatively weak, Chantal still managed to dump up to 9 inches of rain in the Hobby Airport-Friendswood area, Harris-Galveston Counties, which is somewhat unusual as these areas were covered by the south and west sides of the storm, which typically experience less rain than areas covered by the northeast side of the storm. At least four tornadoes were reported with the storm, however, no major damage from the twisters resulted. Three persons were killed in Texas due to Chantal, while total damage was estimated in the tens of millions of dollars.

October 15-17, 1989: At 7:18 p.m. on the 15th, Hurricane Jerry made landfall on West Galveston Island, Galveston County, packing sustained winds of 85 mph, tides 5 feet-7 feet above normal, and 6 tornadoes. Rainfall amounts of 4 inches-8 inches were confined primarily to the area between Hobby Airport, Harris County, and Galveston. Despite being a weak hurricane, Jerry still managed to do an estimated $8 million in damage and caused one death.

December 19-24, 1989: One of the strongest cold outbreaks ever to hit the state brought freezing rain and snow over North Central and East Texas, causing numerous accidents. Snowfall was recorded at 1 foot to 3 feet as far south as Houston, the first for a few years. By the 23rd, the core of the cold air was centered over the state, causing temperature records to be broken at many stations. At College Station, Brazos County, the 2 degree F minimum was the lowest temperature ever recorded in a December, beating the previous record low by 9 degrees F. Many stations' average temperatures were 6 degrees F-8 degrees F below average. Total losses in agriculture and water damage were estimated at $125 million for North Central and East Texas. However, total damage from the severe cold in South Texas

was estimated to be near $1 billion. In the Lower Rio Grande Valley alone, $300 million-400 million damage was done to the citrus fruit and trees. The Upper Coast had estimated damage of $300 million-500 million. Three deaths due to hypothermia were reported in the area.

February 15, 1990: Strong westerly gradient winds blew across the High Plains and Trans-Pecos divisions. A peak gust of 61 mph was measured at Lubbock International Airport, Lubbock County. Wind speeds as high as 80 mph were reported in the Guadalupe Pass, Culberson County, while stations recorded average wind speeds of 45 mph in response to a developing low pressure area over northern Mexico.

February 20, 1990: Heavy snow was reported in the northern half of the Panhandle, with areas receiving from 6 inches-12 inches. Approximately 9 inches of snow fell at Dalhart, Hartley County, and 12 inches at Perryton, Ochiltree County.

March 14, 1990: Thunderstorms brought large rainfall amounts and high winds to much of North Central Texas. In Rogers, Bell County, an estimated $120,000 in damage occurred when a downburst damaged the roof of a department store. A weak tornado also touched down in Hill County, while approximately 12,000 homes were affected by power outages.

April 14-16, 1990: Strong thunderstorms developed in North Central Texas as a warm frontal boundary moved north bringing winds up to 64 mph to Denison, Grayson County, while softball-sized hail fell 5 miles northwest of Rotan, Fisher County. Golfball-sized hail accumulated up to a depth of 4 inches at Bells, Grayson

More on Page 605.

Weather Summary—1989

This can be characterized as a year in which a good portion of the rainfall came in short bursts, which slowed the agricultural industry's recovery from the dry conditions in 1988. In January mean temperatures around the state ran 4 degrees F-6 degrees F above average, while in February mean temperatures were 3 degrees F-5 degrees F below average. Despite the difference, both months had periods of temperatures in the 70s and 80s in South Central and Southern Texas, which broke some daily records. Northern sections of Texas had above-average precipitation during January and February, while the High Plans were quite dry. Icy conditions caused by freezing rain were prevalent across East Texas and the Upper Coast on February 5th and 6th, causing numerous automobile accidents, and closing many businesses and schools.

March temperatures were near average, while precipitation was near normal except for Southern Texas, Trans-Pecos, and Panhandle regions. In East Texas, thunderstorms on the 27th and 29th brought 13.25 inches to Longview, Rusk County, 11.05 inches to Henderson, Rusk County, and 8.92 inches to Atlanta, Cass County. At least two people died when their cars were swept off flooded roads. April and May were generally warm, with temperatures nearing 90 degrees F statewide in April and 100 degrees F in early May. Precipitation was below average across Texas except for the Lower Rio Grande Valley in April, while the Upper Coast was the only above-average area in May.

Another round of heavy thunderstorms on the 17th and 18th brought a tornado to Jarrell, Williamson County, which destroyed two-thirds of the town and caused 29 casualties. As the storms moved east, their movement slowed, which caused them to remain over the Houston-Port Arthur, Harris and Jefferson counties, area. Rainfall amounts of greater than 10 inches fell in Harris County where Intercontinental Airport received 10.35 inches and Spring over 15 inches. The combined effect of the runoff from the earlier rains in North Central Texas with the new rain caused some of the most extensive flooding ever along the Upper Coast.

June was generally wet except for the Trans-Pecos, and temperatures were at or below normal statewide. A brief blast of warm, dry air from Mexico caused temperatures to soar above 100 degrees F across western portions of Texas. Meanwhile, Tropical Storm Allison made landfall near Freeport on the 26th, bringing winds of 45 mph and seas 3 feet-5 feet above normal. Rains of 10 inches-15 inches fell from Houston to Port Arthur. July temperatures were near average while precipitation was below average in the Edwards Plateau and Low Rolling Plains. August temperatures were also near average, while rainfall amounts varied widely from station to sta-

tion. Hurricane Chantal made landfall near High Island, Chambers County, on the 1st, but the strong winds and heavy rains were primarily limited to the area around Galveston Bay.

The first half of September brought the only major heat wave of the summer as the summer as temperatures topped 100 degrees F at most stations. Much cooler temperatures prevailed over the state during the final week of the month. Precipitation was once again light in North Central Texas, but near average elsewhere. October was a dry month, as only South Central Texas received above-average precipitation at most locations. Hurricane Jerry made landfall on Galveston Island, Galveston County, bringing 4 inches-8 inches of rain and sustained winds of 85 mph. Like Chantal, Jerry's effects were primarily limited to the coastal areas around Houston.

November was warm and dry as temperatures ran 2 degrees F-3 degrees F above average. Precipitation amounts were below average at many locations. December was one of the coldest months ever on record at many stations, with mean monthly temperatures running 7 degrees F-11 degrees F below average. Some minimum temperatures, such as 2 degrees F at College Station, Brazos County, on the 23rd, broke daily, monthly and seasonal records.

Weather Summary—1990

The last year of the climatic decade was very similar to its predecessor, 1989. Spring floods in North Central, East Texas and the Upper Coast were more severe

IS IT NORMAL OR AVERAGE?

Confusion often occurs when climate summaries refer to the "normal" or "average" of a climate variable. The term "normal" indicates calculations based upon data from the most recent 30-year period ending with a year containing a zero for the last digit. The 1951-1980 period is the current 30-year "normal," however 1961-1990 will become the new "normal" period when calculations are finished in 1992. 1901-1930 was selected as the first International Standard Period for Normals. Because of the overlap from one normal period to the next, since 20 years are common to both, some authorities recommend the distinct 30-year periods, such as 1901-1930, 1931-1960, and 1961-1990, making this new period especially important.

The "average" refers to calculations based upon the complete period of record. Usually this is from the first complete year on record to the most recent entire year of record. Therefore, the "normal" and "average" values usually differ to some degree.

in 1990 than in 1989. December 1990 brought an outbreak of cold air that broke some of the records set in the 1989 cold outbreak.

January's maximum temperatures averaged in the 60s for most of Texas, a welcome occurrence after the bitterly cold conditions of December 1989. Precipitation was well above average in North Central and East Texas. In particular, Dallas, Dallas County, received 275 percent of its average January precipitation. However, many of the Southern, Lower Rio Grande Valley, and High Plains stations recorded below-average precipitation. The pattern of mild temperatures continued in February, with maximum temperatures averaging 3 degrees F-5 degrees F above normal. A strong winter storm system moved across the state at mid-month, providing 6 inches-10 inches of snow in parts of the High Plains. The storm moved eastward and brought rainfalls of 2 inches-3 inches to most of North Central, East Texas, and the Upper Coast. Except for those stations in the Lower Valley and Trans-Pecos divisions, most stations recorded 150 percent-250 percent of normal for February precipitation. Above-average precipitation amounts continued in March and April in the North Central and East Texas divisions. Dallas/Fort Worth, Dallas and Tarrant Counties, received 12.79 inches during the two-month period, more than double the average March-April precipitation of 6.05 inches. Other incredible rainfall amounts were 13.50 Inches at Caldwell, Burleson County, on April 25, 11.49 inches at Brownwood, Brown County, on April 26, and 14.96 degrees at De Leon, Comanche County, on April 25-26. Temperatures were near average at most locations for the two-month period.

The culmination of runoff from heavy rains in April and additional rainfall amounts of 7 inches-17 inches in May caused extensive flooding of the Trinity River and Red River, along with many smaller creeks and streams. The East Texas division received 2.99 inches of rain above average in May. Lufkin 7 NW (7 miles to the northwest), Angelina County, received 17.28 inches during the month. Dallas/Fort Worth recorded 27.17 inches from January 1 through May 24, 17.5 inches above average. The Trinity River set a new depth record of 29.9 feet at Liberty, Liberty County, while 30,000 sandbags had to be used along the Red River in Texarkana, Bowie County. Besides the flooding, maximum temperatures reached the 90 degrees F-100 degrees F range during the last half of May. The combination of flood waters and heat brought dreadful conditions to those in East Texas.

The wet pattern dominating the state in April and May abated in June. For many locations, June 1990 was one of the warmest, driest Junes on record. The High Plains and Trans-Pecos had temperature departures of + 4.9 degrees F and + 5.4 degrees F respectively, while other divisions were 2 degrees F-4 degrees F above average. Maximum temperatures from 95 degrees F-105

degrees F were common over most of Texas. For precipitation, the Southern division received only 5 percent of average precipitation for June. The remaining divisions also recorded below-average precipitation for the month.

The hot, dry conditions of June persisted into early July, as maximum temperatures once again rose to near 100 degrees F. A strong cold front brought relief at mid-month, dropping maximum temperatures into the low 80s for many locations. The South Central division received 295 percent of average precipitation, while Victoria, Victoria County, received 13.59 inches for the month, 527 percent of average. August was almost the opposite of July, with mild conditions during the first two weeks and hot conditions the final two weeks. North Central Texas was the hot spot, where Waco, McClennan County, had an average maximum temperature of 100.1 degrees F. Precipitation was light along the Upper Coast, with Houston, Harris County, receiving 8 percent of average and Galveston, Galveston County, receiving 4 percent of average. Other divisions generally recorded below-average precipitation, however; some stations such as El Paso, El Paso County, and Wichita Falls, Wichita County, received above-average amounts.

Despite unseasonably warm maximum temperatures in the 90s during the first few days of October, only Austin, Travis County, Lubbock, Lubbock County, and Wichita Falls, Wichita County, recorded above-average mean temperatures for the entire month for first order stations. Stations in the High Plains, Low Rolling Plains and Trans-Pecos recorded the first fall freezing temperatures during mid-October. Precipitation was generally near average to slightly below average. Of first order stations, Amarillo, Potter County, reported 0.29 inches, only 33 percent of the month's average precipitation.

November and December were very similar months. Mild temperatures in the 60s and 70s prevailed during the first days of each month. However, a strong cold front in mid-November dropped maximum temperatures into the 30s and 40s in the High Plains. A warming trend followed to provide mild December conditions until a major outbreak of cold Arctic air hit the Lone Star State on the 21st. Numerous minimum temperature records were broken with minimums below 0 degrees F in the High Plains.

Precipitation was above average at most locations in November, and below average in December. A snowfall of 4.3 inches was recorded at El Paso, El Paso County, on November 7-8. Freezing rain and snow accompanied the cold-air surge in December, causing hazardous driving conditions in North Central and East Texas. The year ended with another blast of cold air that dropped minimum temperatures into single digits in northern sections of the state.

Destructive Weather

This list of exceptionally destructive weather in Texas since 1766 is compiled from ESSA-Weather Bureau information:

Sept., 4, 1766: **Hurricane. Galveston Bay.** A mission destroyed.

Sept. 12, 1818: **Hurricane. Galveston Island.** Salt water flowed four feet deep. Only six buildings remained habitable. Of the six vessels and two barges in the harbor, even the two not seriously damaged were reduced to dis-masted hulks. Pirate **Jean Lafitte** moved to one hulk so his **Red House** might serve as a hospital.

Aug. 6, 1844: **Hurricane.** Mouth of Rio Grande. All houses destroyed at the mouth of the river and at **Brazos Santiago,** eight miles north; 70 lives lost.

Sept. 16, 1875: **Hurricane.** Struck **Indianola,** Calhoun County. Three-fourths of town swept away; 176 lives lost. Flooding from the bay caused nearly all destruction.

Aug. 19-21, 1886: **Hurricane. Indianola.** Every house destroyed or damaged. Indianola never rebuilt.

June 27-July 1, 1899: **Rainstorm.** A storm, centered over the Brazos River watershed, precipitated an average of 17 inches over an area of 7,000 square miles. At **Hearne** the gage overflowed at 24 inches, and there was an estimated total rainfall of 30 inches. At **Turnersville,** Coryell County, 33 inches were recorded in three days. This rain caused the worst **Brazos River** flood on record. Between 30 and 35 lives were lost. Property damage was estimated at $9 million.

Sept. 8-9, 1900: **Hurricane. Galveston.** The **Great Galveston Storm** was the worst natural disaster in U.S. histo-

ry. Loss of life at Galveston has been estimated at 6,000 to 8,000, but the exact number has never been definitely ascertained. The island was completely inundated, and not a single structure escaped damage. Most of the loss of life was due to drowning by storm tides that reached 15 feet or more. The anemometer blew away when the wind reached 100 miles per hour at 6:15 p.m. on the 8th. Wind reached an estimated maximum velocity of 120 miles per hour between 7:30 and 8:30 p.m. Property damage has been estimated at $30 to $40 million.

May 22-25, 1908: **Rainstorm;** unique because it originated on the Pacific Coast. It moved first into North Texas and southern Oklahoma and thence to Central Texas, precipitating as much as 10 inches. Heaviest floods were in the upper Trinity basin, but flooding was general as far south as the Nueces. Property damage exceeded $5 million and 11 lives were lost in the Dallas vicinity.

July 21, 1909: **Hurricane. Velasco,** Brazoria County. One-half of town destroyed, 41 lives lost; damage $2,000,000.

Dec. 1-5, 1913: **Rainstorm.** This caused the second major **Brazos River flood,** and caused more deaths than the storm of 1899. It formed over Central Texas and spread both southwest and northeast with precipitation of 15 inches at **San Marcos** and 11 inches at **Kaufman.** Floods caused loss of 177 lives and $8,541,000 damage.

April 20-26, 1915: **Rainstorm.** Originated over Central Texas and spread into North and East Texas with precipitation up to 17 inches, causing floods in Trinity, Brazos, Colorado, and Guadalupe rivers. More than 40 lives lost and $2,330,000 damage.

Aug. 16-19, 1915: Hurricane. Galveston. Peak wind gusts of 120 miles recorded at **Galveston;** tide ranged 9.5 to 14.3 feet above mean sea level in the city, and up to 16.1 feet near the causeway. Business section flooded with 5 to 6 feet of water. At least 275 lives lost, damage $56 million. A new seawall prevented a repetition of the 1900 disaster.

Aug. 18, 1916: Hurricane. Corpus Christi. Maximum wind speed 100 miles per hour. 20 Lives lost; damage $1,600,000.

Jan. 10-12, 1918: Blizzard. This was the most severe since that of February, 1899; it was accompanied by zero degree temperature in North Texas and temperatures from 7° to 12° below freezing along the lower coast.

Sept. 14, 1919: Hurricane. Near Corpus Christi. Center moved inland south of **Corpus Christi;** tides 16 feet above normal in that area and 8.8 feet above normal at **Galveston.** Extreme wind at Corpus Christi measured at 110 miles per hour; 284 lives lost; damage $20,272,000.

Sept. 8-10, 1921: Rainstorm. Probably the **greatest rainstorm in Texas history,** it entered Mexico as a hurricane from the Gulf. Torrential rains fell as the storm moved northeasterly across Texas. Record floods occurred in **Bexar, Travis, Williamson, Bell** and **Milam counties,** killing 215 persons, with property losses over $19 million. Five to nine feet of water stood in downtown San Antonio. A total of 23.98 inches was measured at the U.S. Weather Bureau station at **Taylor** during a period of 35 hours, with a 24-hour maximum of 23.11 on September 9-10. The **greatest rainfall recorded in United States history** during 18 consecutive hours fell at Thrall, Williamson County, 36.40 inches fell on Sept. 9.

April 23-28, 1922: Rainstorm. An exceptional storm that entered Texas from the west and moved from the Panhandle to North Central and East Texas. Rains up to 12.6 inches over **Parker, Tarrant,** and **Dallas counties** caused severe floods in the Upper Trinity at **Fort Worth;** 11 lives lost; damage was estimated at $1 million.

April 12, 1927: Tornado. Edwards, Real and **Uvalde counties;** 74 killed, 205 injured; damage $1,230,000. Most of damage was in Rocksprings where 72 deaths occurred and town was practically destroyed.

May 9, 1927: Tornado. Garland; eleven killed; damage $100,000.

May 9, 1927: Tornado. Nevada, Collin County; **Wolfe City,** Hunt County; and **Tigertown,** Lamar County; 28 killed, over 200 injured; damage $900,000.

May 6, 1930: Tornado. Bynum, Irene and Mertens in Hill County; **Ennis,** Ellis County; and **Frost,** Navarro County; 41 killed; damage $2,100,000.

Aug. 13, 1932: Hurricane. Near Freeport, Brazoria County. Wind speed at **East Columbia** estimated at 100 miles per hour; 40 lives lost, 200 injured; damage $7,500,000.

July 22-25, 1933: Tropical Storm. One of the greatest U.S. storms in area and general rainfall. The storm

reached the vicinity of **Freeport** late on July 22 and moved very slowly overland across eastern Texas, July 22-25. The storm center moved into northern Louisiana on the 25th. Rainfall averaged 12.50 inches over an area of about 25,000 square miles. Twenty inches or more fell in a small area of eastern Texas and western Louisiana surrounding **Logansport, La.** The 4-day total at Logansport was 22.30 inches. Property damage was estimated at $1,114,790.

July 25, 1934: Hurricane. Near **Seadrift,** Calhoun County, 19 lives lost, many minor injuries; damage $4.5 million. About 85 percent of damage was in crops.

April 28, 1942: Tornado. Crowell, Foard County; 11 killed, 250 injured; damage $1,500,000.

July 27, 1943: Hurricane. Near **Galveston.** Center moved inland across Bolivar Peninsula and Trinity Bay. A wind gust of 104 miles per hour was recorded at **Texas City;** 19 lives lost; damage estimated at $16,550,000.

Jan. 4, 1946: Tornado. Near Lufkin, Angelina County and Nacogdoches, Nacogdoches County; 13 killed, 250 injured; damage $2,050,000.

April 9, 1947: Tornado. White Deer, Carson County; **Glazier,** Hemphill County; and **Higgins,** Lipscomb County; 68 killed, 201 injured; damage $1,550,000. Glazier completely destroyed. One of the largest tornadoes on record. Width of path, 1½ miles at Higgins; length of path, 221 miles across portions of Texas, Oklahoma and Kansas. This tornado also struck **Woodward, Okla.**

May 15, 1949: Tornado. Amarillo and vicinity; six killed, 83 injured. Total damage from tornado, wind and hail, $5,310,000. Total destruction over one-block by three-block area in southern part of city; airport and 45 airplanes damaged; 28 railroad boxcars blown off track.

May 11, 1953: Tornado. Near **San Angelo,** Tom Green County; eleven killed, 159 injured; damage $3,239,000.

May 11, 1953: Tornado. Waco, McLennan County; 114 killed, 597 injured; damage $41,150,000. One of two most disastrous tornadoes; 150 homes destroyed, 900 homes damaged; 185 other buildings destroyed; 500 other buildings damaged.

April 2, 1957: Tornado. Dallas, Dallas County; 10 killed, 200 injured; damage $4 million. Moving through Oak Cliff and West Dallas, it damaged 574 buildings, largely homes.

June 27, 1957: Hurricane Audrey. Center crossed the Gulf coast near the Texas-Louisiana line. **Orange** was in the western portion of the eye between 9 and 10 a.m. In Texas, nine lives were lost, 450 persons injured; property damage was $8 million. Damage was extensive in Jefferson and Orange counties, with less in Chambers and Galveston counties. Maximum wind reported in Texas, 85 m.p.h. at Sabine Pass, with gusts to 100 m.p.h.

Oct. 28, 1960: Rainstorm. Rains of 7-10 inches fell in South Central Texas; 11 died from drowning in flash floods. In Austin about 300 families were driven from their homes. Damage in Austin was estimated at $2.5 million.

Sept. 8-14, 1961: Hurricane Carla. Port O'Connor;

Extreme Texas Weather Records

NOAA Environmental Data Service lists the following recorded extremes of weather in Texas:

TEMPERATURE

Lowest—Tulia, February 12, 1899		−23° F
Seminole, February 8, 1933		−23° F
Highest—Seymour, August 12, 1936		120° F
Coldest Winter		1898-1899

RAINFALL

Wettest year—entire state	1941	42.62 in.
Driest year—entire state	1917	14.30 in.
Greatest annual—Clarksville	1873	109.38 in.
Least annual—Wink	1956	1.76 in.
†Greatest in 24 hours—Thrall		
September 9-10, 1921		38.20 in.

SNOWFALL

Greatest seasonal—Romero 1923-1924	65.0 in.
Greatest monthly—Hale Center	
February, 1956	36.0 in.
Greatest single storm—Hale Center	
Feb. 2-5, 1956	33.0 in.
Greatest in 24 Hours—Plainview	
Feb. 3-4, 1956	24.0 in.
Maximum depth on ground—Hale Center	
Feb. 5, 1956	33.0 in.

1989 Weather Extremes

Lowest Temp.—Lipscomb, Lipscomb County	
Quanah 5 SE, Hardeman County	
Glen Rose 2 W, Somervell County	
Dec. 23	−15° F
Highest Temp.—Boquillas Ranger Station,	
Brewster County May 25	116° F
24-hr. Precip.—Antelope, Jack County	
May 16	11.18″
Monthly Precip.—Orange 9 N, Orange County	
June	20.14″
Least Annual Precip.—La Tuna 1 S	
El Paso County	4.42″
Greatest Annual Precip.—Orange, 9 N	
Orange County	72.43″

1990 Weather Extremes

Lowest Temp.—Bravo, Hartley County	
Dec. 23	−12° F
Highest Temp.—Red Bluff Dam, Reeves County	
Ysleta, El Paso County,	
June 26 +	114° F
24-hr. Precip.—Caldwell, Burleson County	
Apr. 25	13.50″
Monthly Precip.—Goliad 1 SE, Goliad County	
July	19.20″
Least Annual Precip.—Odessa, Ector County	8.64″
Greatest Annual Precip.—Dekalb, Bowie County	79.87″

maximum wind gust at **Port Lavaca** estimated at 175 miles per hour. Highest tide was 18.5 feet at **Port Lavaca.** Most damage was to coastal counties between **Corpus Christi** and **Port Arthur** and inland Jackson, Harris and Wharton counties. In Texas, 34 persons died; seven in a tornado that swept across Galveston Island; 465 persons were injured. Property and crop damage conservatively estimated at $300 million. The evacuation of an estimated 250,000 persons kept loss of life low. Hurricane Carla was the **largest hurricane** of record.

April 3, 1964: **Tornado.** Wichita Falls. Seven killed, 111 injured; damage $15 million; 225 homes destroyed, 50 with major damage, and 200 with minor damage. Sixteen other buildings received major damage.

April 22-29, 1966: **Flooding.** Northeast Texas. Twenty to 26 inches of rain fell in portions of Wood, Smith, Morris, Upshur, Gregg, Marion and Harrison counties. Nineteen persons drowned in the rampaging rivers and creeks that swept away bridges, roads and dams, and caused an estimated $12 million damage.

April 28, 1966: Dallas County. **Flash flooding** from torrential rains in Dallas County resulted in 14 persons drowned and property losses estimated at $15 million.

Sept. 18-23, 1967: **Hurricane Beulah.** Near **Brownsville.** The third largest hurricane of record, Hurricane Beulah moved inland near the mouth of the Rio Grande on the 20th. Wind gusts of 136 miles per hour were reported during Beulah's passage. Rains 10 to 20 inches over much of the area south of San Antonio resulted in record-breaking floods. An unofficial gaging station at Falfurrias registered the highest accumulated rainfall, 36 inches. The resultant stream overflow and surface runoff inundated 1.4 million acres. Beulah spawned 115 tornadoes, all in Texas; the greatest number on record for any hurricane. Hurricane Beulah caused 13 deaths and 37 injuries, of which five deaths and 34 injuries were attributed to tornadoes. Property losses were estimated at $100 million and crop losses at $50 million.

April 18, 1970: **Tornado.** Near **Clarendon,** Donley County. Seventeen killed, 42 injured; damage $2,100,000. Fourteen persons were killed at a resort community at Green Belt Reservoir, 7½ miles north of Clarendon.

May 11, 1970: **Tornado.** Lubbock, Lubbock County. Twenty-six killed, 500 injured; damage $135 million. Fifteen square miles, almost one-quarter of the city of Lubbock, suffered damage.

Aug. 3-5, 1970: **Hurricane Celia. Corpus Christi.** Hurricane Celia was a unique but severe storm. Measured in dollars, it was the costliest in the state's history to that time. Sustained wind speeds reached 130 miles per hour, but it was great bursts of kinetic energy of short duration that appeared to cause the severe damage. Wind gusts of 161 miles per hour were measured at the Corpus Christi National Weather Service Office. At Aransas Pass, peak wind gusts were estimated as high as 180 miles per hour, after the wind equipment had

More on Page 605.

Tornadoes

An average of 118 tornadoes touch Texas soil each year. The annual total varies considerably, and certain areas are struck more often than others. Tornadoes occur with greatest frequency in the Red River Valley.

While tornadoes may occur in any month, and at

More on Page 606.

Texas Annual Average Precipitation, 1892-1990

Source: State Climatologist for Texas

Year	Inches	Year	Inches
1892	26.32	1942	30.68
1893	18.50	1943	24.28
1894	25.61	1944	34.08
1895	29.83	1945	30.06
1896	25.15	1946	35.16
1897	24.21	1947	24.75
1898	24.56	1948	21.79
1899	27.57	1949	35.08
1900	36.87	1950	24.48
1901	20.13	1951	21.99
1902	28.28	1952	23.27
1903	29.64	1953	24.76
1904	26.78	1954	19.03
1905	35.98	1955	23.59
1906	29.19	1956	16.17
1907	28.51	1957	36.93
1908	29.06	1958	32.71
1909	21.58	1959	31.29
1910	19.52	1960	33.78
1911	26.83	1961	30.20
1912	24.92	1962	24.05
1913	33.25	1963	20.95
1914	35.19	1964	24.11
1915	28.79	1965	27.55
1916	23.05	1966	28.68
*1917	14.30	1967	28.44
1918	26.03	1968	34.54
1919	42.15	1969	29.85
1920	29.90	1970	26.36
1921	25.18	1971	29.58
1922	29.83	1972	28.73
1923	37.24	1973	38.37
1924	22.32	1974	32.78
1925	25.37	1975	29.07
1926	32.97	1976	33.37
1927	24.32	1977	24.04
1928	27.56	1978	27.00
1929	29.47	1979	31.43
1930	28.44	1980	24.49
1931	28.37	1981	32.65
1932	32.76	1982	26.97
1933	26.15	1983	25.75
1934	25.59	1984	26.08
1935	35.80	1985	29.97
1936	30.32	1986	34.11
1937	25.89	1987	30.49
1938	25.35	1988	21.01
1939	23.52	1989	25.59
1940	32.70	1990	31.77
**1941	42.62		

103-year mean 27.86 inches.

*Driest year, 1917.

**Wettest year, 1941.

Number Texas Tornadoes 1951-1989

Source: State Climatologist for Texas

Year	Jan.	Feb.	Mar.	April	May	June	July	Aug.	Sept.	Oct.	Nov.	Dec.	Annual
1951	0	0	1	1	5	7	1	0	0	0	0	0	15
1952	0	1	3	4	2	1	0	1	0	0	0	1	13
1953	0	2	2	3	6	2	3	5	0	2	1	6	32
1954	0	3	1	23	21	14	5	1	4	5	0	0	77
1955	0	0	7	15	42	32	1	5	2	0	0	0	104
1956	0	3	5	3	17	5	6	4	2	9	2	0	56
1957	0	1	21	69	33	5	0	3	2	6	5	0	145
1958	2	0	7	12	15	13	10	7	0	0	8	0	74
1959	0	0	8	4	32	14	10	3	4	5	6	0	86
1960	4	1	0	8	29	14	3	4	2	11	1	0	77
1961	0	1	21	15	24	30	9	2	12	0	10	0	124
1962	0	4	12	9	25	56	12	15	7	2	0	1	143
1963	0	0	3	9	19	24	8	4	6	4	5	0	82
1964	0	1	6	22	15	11	9	7	3	1	3	0	78
1965	2	5	3	7	43	24	2	9	4	6	0	3	108
1966	0	4	1	21	22	15	3	8	3	0	0	0	77
1967	0	2	11	17	34	22	10	5	124	2	0	5	232
1968	2	1	3	13	47	21	4	8	5	8	11	16	139
1969	0	1	1	6	65	16	6	7	6	8	1	0	127
1970	1	3	5	23	23	9	5	20	9	20	0	3	121
1971	0	20	10	24	27	33	7	20	7	16	4	23	191
1972	1	0	19	13	43	12	19	13	8	9	7	0	144
1973	14	1	29	25	21	24	4	8	5	3	9	4	147
1974	2	1	8	19	18	26	3	9	6	22	2	0	116
1975	5	2	9	12	50	18	10	3	3	3	1	1	117
1976	1	1	8	53	63	11	16	6	13	4	0	0	176
1977	0	0	3	34	50	4	5	5	12	0	6	4	123
1978	0	0	0	34	45	10	13	6	6	1	2	0	137
1979	1	2	24	33	39	14	12	10	4	15	3	0	157
1980	0	2	7	26	44	21	2	34	10	5	0	2	153
1981	0	7	7	9	71	26	5	20	5	23	3	0	176
1982	0	0	6	27	123	36	4	0	3	0	3	1	203
1983	5	7	24	1	62	35	4	22	5	0	7	14	186
1984	0	13	9	18	19	19	0	4	1	5	2	5	95
1985	0	1	6	7	25	8	3	1	1	3	1	2	90
1986	0	12	4	21	50	24	3	5	4	7	1	0	131
1987	1	1	7	0	54	19	11	3	8	0	16	4	124
1988	0	0	0	11	7	7	6	2	42	4	10	0	89
1989	3	0	5	3	70	63	0	6	3	6	1	0	160
Total	44	102	305	698	1,423	742	234	295	341	215	131	95	4,625

TEXAS TEMPERATURE, FREEZE, GROWING SEASON AND PRECIPITATION RECORDS, BY COUNTIES

Data in the table below are from the office of the State Climatologist for Texas, College Station. Because of the small change in averages, data are revised only at intervals of several years. Data below are the latest compilations, as of Jan. 1, 1989.

Table shows temperature, freeze, growing season and precipitation for each county in Texas. Data for counties where a National Weather Service Station has not been maintained long enough to establish a reliable measure are interpolated from isoline charts prepared from mean values from stations with long-established records. Mean maximum temperature for July is computed from the sum of the daily maxima. Mean minimum January is computed from the sum of the daily minima. Mean monthly temperature for July is the sum of mean maximum and mean minimum (for July) divided by 2. For stations where precipitation "Length of Record" are designated with an "N," data are based on the 30-year normal period 1951-80. Stations which have a specified precipitation "Length of Record" are based on data mainly from the period 1931-60.

County and Station	Temperature Length of Record (Yr.)	Mean Max. July (°F.)	Mean Min. January (°F.)	Record Highest (°F.)	Record Lowest (°F.)	Average Freeze Dates: Last in Spring	First in Fall	Growing Season* Days	Length of Record (Yr.)	Normal Total Precipitation (In.): January	February	March	April	May	June	July	August	September	October	November	December	Annual
Anderson, Palestine	N	95	35	114	−6	Mar. 8	Nov. 27	264	N	3.1	3.0	3.6	4.5	4.8	3.8	2.1	2.8	3.8	3.6	3.5	3.4	41.7
Andrews, Andrews	19	95	29	111	−6	Apr. 6	Nov. 5	213	N	0.4	0.4	0.6	0.8	1.8	2.0	2.4	1.8	2.2	1.5	0.5	0.3	14.1
Angelina, Lufkin	N	94	38	108	−2	Mar. 14	Nov. 13	244	N	3.6	3.1	3.7	4.3	4.3	3.4	2.6	2.5	2.9	3.6	3.6	3.9	41.5
Aransas, Austwell	N	92	45	103	10	Feb. 7	Dec. 16	312	Z	2.2	1.7	1.7	2.6	3.9	3.7	2.8	4.3	5.7	4.0	2.7	2.7	36.9
Archer, Archer	17	98	28	114	−10	Mar. 31	Nov. 6	220	Z	1.0	1.3	1.7	2.9	3.9	2.6	2.1	2.3	4.1	2.7	1.8	1.2	27.7
Armstrong, Claude	18	92	27	108	−7	Apr. 6	Nov. 5	213	Z	0.4	0.6	0.8	1.5	3.1	3.1	2.6	2.7	2.0	2.0	0.9	0.6	20.6
Atascosa, Poteet	N	97	39	110	−1	Apr. 6	Dec. 2	282	Z	1.3	1.9	1.1	2.5	4.1	2.8	2.4	2.4	3.7	2.8	1.9	1.4	27.8
Austin, Sealy	N	94	43	110	0	Feb. 25	Dec. 2	282	N	3.0	3.2	3.0	3.5	4.5	4.4	2.8	2.9	4.0	3.7	2.9	3.7	40.4
Bailey, Muleshoe	15	91	20	110	−21	Apr. 22	Oct. 20	181	15	0.5	0.5	0.6	0.9	1.9	2.4	2.8	2.4	1.8	1.4	0.7	0.4	16.1
Bandera, Medina	N	96	31	109	−5	Mar. 26	Nov. 16	235	N	1.7	1.8	1.6	2.3	4.0	3.7	2.5	2.6	4.4	2.9	1.8	1.8	35.1
Bastrop, Smithville	N	96	38	116	6	Mar. 7	Nov. 30	268	N	1.8	2.2	1.8	3.3	4.1	3.7	1.9	2.3	3.7	2.9	2.3	2.4	36.5
Baylor, Seymour	N	98	26	116	−14	Mar. 7	Nov. 3	214	Z	0.9	1.1	1.4	2.4	4.0	3.3	2.1	2.6	2.9	2.8	1.7	1.7	25.7
Bee, Beeville	N	95	41	109	9	Feb. 22	Dec. 4	285	N	1.8	1.4	1.4	2.0	3.6	3.0	1.9	2.5	5.5	3.3	2.0	1.7	33.8
Bell, Temple	N	96	36	112	−9	Mar. 9	Nov. 24	260	Z	1.9	2.1	2.0	3.6	4.7	3.0	1.9	1.9	3.6	3.0	2.3	2.4	29.1
Bexar, San Antonio	N	95	41	108	0	Mar. 6	Nov. 26	265	N	1.5	1.9	1.3	2.5	3.7	3.5	2.2	2.6	3.4	3.3	2.0	2.0	34.7
Blanco, Blanco	17	95	33	109	−6	Mar. 15	Nov. 15	234	Z	1.5	1.9	0.8	1.7	3.8	3.0	2.3	2.2	2.9	2.9	2.3	0.6	18.7
Borden, Gail	18	95	35	113	−3	Mar. 26	Nov. 6	214	18	0.5	0.6	1.1	2.0	2.7	2.5	2.1	2.2	1.6	2.0	0.7	0.6	18.7
Bosque, Lake Whitney	N	97	33	111	10	Mar. 23	Nov. 21	243	18	0.5	0.8	0.8	1.1	3.5	3.5	2.3	3.2	3.6	2.7	2.8	0.6	31.6
Bowie, Texarkana	N	93	32	105	−3	Mar. 21	Nov. 11	235	Z	3.6	3.7	4.2	5.1	4.4	3.9	3.1	2.3	3.5	3.5	4.2	3.9	45.3
Brazoria, Angleton	N	92	45	106	−9	Mar. 5	Nov. 28	274	Z	3.6	2.5	2.4	3.2	4.6	5.5	4.5	5.0	6.9	3.4	3.0	3.0	39.1
Brazos, College Station	N	95	41	108	−3	Apr. 5	Nov. 30	223	Z	3.5	0.6	0.4	1.0	4.9	3.2	1.5	2.3	1.2	1.6	0.6	0.5	14.8
Brewster, Alpine	19	86	32	103	−11	Apr. 7	Nov. 8	223	Z	0.5	0.4	0.4	0.4	1.0	2.0	2.2	2.6	2.7	2.4	0.7	1.1	16.7
Brewster, Chisos Basin	N	86	31	108	0	Mar. 31	Nov. 9	214	Z	0.5	0.6	0.4	0.7	1.4	1.9	1.7	3.0	2.3	2.9	2.8	2.8	20.4
Briscoe, Silverton	N	91	28	110	−16	Apr. 7	Nov. 5	303	16	0.5	0.6	0.7	1.4	3.1	3.6	2.9	2.8	2.7	2.4	1.3	1.1	25.8
Brooks, Falfurrias	N	98	44	110	−10	Feb. 10	Dec. 1	242	16	1.4	1.4	1.5	2.7	2.9	2.9	1.7	2.4	4.9	2.4	1.5	2.8	26.1
Brown, Brownwood	N	97	31	111	−1	Mar. 22	Nov. 19	275	Z	1.4	1.8	1.8	2.7	4.4	2.5	1.6	2.2	3.6	2.9	1.7	1.9	30.4
Burleson, Somerville	N	98	37	105	3	Mar. 29	Dec. 1	230	Z	2.7	2.1	1.8	3.9	5.1	3.3	1.6	2.4	3.5	3.4	2.9	2.8	34.7
Burnet, Burnet	27	97	44	108	8	Mar. 1	Dec. 1	275	16	1.6	2.5	1.8	3.3	4.4	3.8	1.9	2.2	7.3	3.5	3.1	1.9	42.2
Caldwell, Luling	N	93	37	107	−4	Feb. 19	Dec. 16	300	Z	2.0	2.7	1.8	3.0	5.5	2.5	1.6	2.4	5.2	4.1	2.0	2.6	24.5
Calhoun, Port Lavaca	17	96	45	108	11	Feb. 28	Nov. 28	228	Z	2.8	2.7	1.8	2.6	4.4	2.5	2.6	2.8	5.0	3.5	2.8	1.0	25.4
Callahan, Putnam	N	94	31	110	0	Mar. 21	Dec. 12	341	Z	1.3	2.1	1.6	2.8	3.3	2.5	1.5	2.2	4.2	2.7	1.4	1.2	43.3
Cameron, Brownsville	N	94	39	109	−10	Mar. 17	Nov. 21	238	Z	1.6	1.2	0.5	1.2	2.2	3.4	2.5	2.8	5.4	3.5	1.4	3.5	19.7
Camp, Pittsburg	N	93	21	103	8	Apr. 17	Oct. 25	191	22	3.3	3.3	4.1	5.4	4.6	3.9	2.5	2.8	1.7	3.2	4.0	3.5	46.3
Carson, Panhandle	19	91	19	107	−8	Apr. 17	Nov. 25	237	Z	0.7	0.7	1.1	1.2	3.1	3.3	2.5	2.8	1.9	3.0	0.7	0.5	16.6
Cass, Linden	12	91	41	107	8	Mar. 19	Oct. 25	193	Z	0.4	3.6	0.7	4.3	1.7	4.6	2.5	3.0	3.9	3.0	4.1	4.1	46.3
Castro, Dimmitt	N	94	37	107	−7	Mar. 6	Nov. 20	261	Z	3.6	3.9	3.6	4.0	4.7	3.6	2.4	2.4	3.6	3.6	0.7	0.5	51.6
Cherokee, Rusk	N	92	35	108	−8	Mar. 3	Nov. 20	258	Z	3.8	3.9	3.6	4.0	4.4	3.6	2.7	2.4	3.6	3.4	3.5	4.0	44.6
Childress, Childress	N	91	35	110	−7	Apr. 6	Nov. 6	217	Z	0.6	0.7	1.1	1.8	3.6	3.5	1.9	2.4	2.4	2.0	0.8	0.7	19.9
Clay, Henrietta	N	96	26	115	−8	Apr. 3	Nov. 14	232	Z	1.3	1.3	2.1	2.9	4.6	2.6	2.1	2.5	3.7	2.9	1.7	1.4	30.1
Cochran, Morton	17	91	22	110	−12	Apr. 18	Oct. 24	189	Z	0.4	0.5	0.5	0.9	1.8	2.4	2.3	2.9	2.6	1.6	0.5	0.3	16.6

Texas Temperature, Frost, Growing Season and Precipitation Records, by Counties — (continued)

County and Station	Temp †Length of Record (Yr.)	July Mean Max (°F.)	January Mean Min (°F.)	Record Highest (°F.)	Record Lowest (°F.)	Last in Spring	First in Fall	*Growing Season (Days)	Precip †Length of Record (Yr.)	Jan. (In.)	Feb. (In.)	Mar. (In.)	Apr. (In.)	May (In.)	June (In.)	July (In.)	Aug. (In.)	Sept. (In.)	Oct. (In.)	Nov. (In.)	Dec. (In.)	Annual (In.)
Coke, Robert Lee	18	97	28	110	-2	Mar. 31	Nov. 12	226	N	0.7	0.9	0.9	2.0	2.8	2.2	1.6	1.7	3.3	2.6	1.1	0.8	20.7
Coleman, Coleman	N	96	32	114	-2	Mar. 26	Nov. 16	235	N	1.3	1.3	1.2	2.3	4.3	3.2	1.9	2.2	3.7	2.9	1.6	1.1	26.9
Collin, McKinney	N	96	33	118	-7	Mar. 26	Nov. 3	230	N	1.9	2.3	3.1	4.5	5.0	3.2	2.2	2.2	4.5	2.9	2.1	2.1	36.9
Collingsworth, Wellington	21	96	23	111	-6	Apr. 5	Nov. 3	212	N	0.5	0.7	1.1	2.1	3.1	3.2	1.8	2.2	2.5	2.1	0.8	0.6	21.2
Colorado, Columbus	18	96	39	108	4	Mar. 1	Dec. 6	280	N	2.9	3.0	2.3	4.0	5.3	4.1	2.7	2.8	5.1	3.3	3.0	3.0	41.4
Comal, New Braunfels	N	96	38	108	2	Mar. 12	Nov. 26	261	N	1.9	1.9	1.6	3.1	4.5	3.2	2.0	2.5	4.3	3.5	2.1	1.4	33.6
Comanche, Proctor Reservoir	17	95	30	111	-8	Mar. 27	Nov. 20	238	17	1.8	1.9	2.1	3.5	4.5	1.7	1.4	2.5	4.3	3.0	1.7	0.9	29.3
Concho, Eden	N	96	33	108	-7	Mar. 27	Nov. 8	226	N	1.0	1.3	1.1	1.9	3.4	2.4	1.8	2.4	3.7	2.3	1.4	0.7	23.3
Cooke, Gainesville	N	97	33	111	-7	Mar. 29	Nov. 10	226	N	1.7	2.0	2.7	3.4	4.3	3.1	2.2	2.0	3.7	3.2	2.2	1.7	33.0
Coryell, Gatesville	N	96	34	112	-6	Mar. 25	Nov. 21	241	N	1.8	2.5	1.9	3.3	4.3	3.1	2.0	2.3	3.7	3.2	2.2	1.9	32.5
Cottle, Paducah	26	97	28	112	-7	Apr. 2	Nov. 7	219	N	0.7	1.1	1.2	2.4	3.6	3.0	2.0	2.3	2.6	2.1	0.9	0.8	22.0
Crane, Crane	N	96	31	109	3	Mar. 31	Nov. 11	225	N	0.6	0.6	0.7	0.9	1.6	1.2	1.3	1.7	2.1	1.1	0.6	0.5	12.0
Crockett, Ozona	27	96	29	109	4	Mar. 26	Nov. 14	233	N	0.6	0.8	0.7	1.4	2.3	2.6	1.8	2.0	2.8	2.0	1.0	0.5	18.2
Crosby, Crosbyton	N	93	24	110	-6	Apr. 2	Nov. 2	206	N	0.5	0.6	1.0	1.2	3.0	2.9	2.1	2.1	2.7	2.0	0.8	0.7	20.5
Culberson, Van Horn	40	95	30	107	-21	Apr. 10	Nov. 10	224	N	0.5	0.3	0.7	0.9	0.6	1.2	1.8	2.4	1.3	1.1	0.6	0.4	11.1
Dallam, Dalhart	N	91	18	113	-12	Apr. 23	Oct. 18	178	N	0.3	0.4	0.7	1.3	2.3	2.9	2.4	2.4	1.7	1.0	0.6	0.4	16.5
Dallas, Dallas	N	96	36	110	-17	Mar. 18	Nov. 8	235	N	2.0	2.7	2.1	3.5	4.9	2.8	2.3	3.4	4.5	3.6	2.6	2.3	35.9
Dawson, Lamesa	N	95	25	108	-10	Apr. 3	Oct. 29	210	N	0.5	0.4	0.7	1.0	2.1	3.8	2.2	2.4	1.6	1.5	0.6	0.4	16.2
De Witt, Yoakum	N	95	42	110	6	Mar. 8	Nov. 28	270	N	2.2	2.5	1.7	3.5	1.9	3.9	2.2	2.2	4.5	3.6	2.6	2.6	36.2
Deaf Smith, Hereford	N	90	21	104	-10	Apr. 16	Oct. 8	195	N	0.4	0.5	0.7	0.7	1.2	3.9	2.2	2.2	1.6	1.5	0.6	0.4	16.0
Delta, Cooper	N	94	30	110	-3	Mar. 25	Nov. 13	233	N	2.4	2.9	3.6	4.8	5.0	3.9	2.1	2.8	4.5	3.6	3.3	3.4	42.7
Denton, Denton	N	96	32	110	-2	Mar. 27	Nov. 8	226	N	2.6	2.0	2.2	4.1	4.7	2.6	2.1	2.3	3.3	3.2	2.2	0.7	33.5
Dickens, Dickens	15	100	27	114	-8	Apr. 4	Nov. 6	217	N	0.9	0.6	0.8	1.2	1.2	2.6	1.2	2.3	3.3	2.8	0.7	0.9	20.7
Dimmit, Carrizo Springs	N	95	41	111	11	Feb. 19	Dec. 6	290	N	1.2	1.2	0.8	1.9	3.4	3.4	1.2	2.4	2.1	2.5	0.9	0.9	21.5
Donley, Clarendon	N	95	26	111	-9	Apr. 9	Nov. 1	206	N	0.5	0.7	0.7	1.6	2.7	2.7	1.2	2.4	2.1	1.7	0.6	0.6	21.5
Duval, Freer	N	95	41	109	16	Feb. 16	Dec. 11	298	N	1.4	1.3	1.5	1.6	2.9	2.7	2.0	2.7	4.8	2.7	1.4	1.1	24.4
Eastland, Rising Star	18	97	30	109	-4	Mar. 27	Nov. 11	229	N	2.1	2.8	2.8	2.9	4.1	2.8	2.5	2.7	3.7	3.0	1.7	1.6	27.2
Ector, Penwell	N	95	28	112	0	Apr. 3	Nov. 6	217	N	0.2	0.5	0.4	0.7	1.3	1.6	1.6	2.0	3.5	1.2	0.4	0.4	12.7
Edwards, Carta Valley	17	95	35	110	-7	Mar. 9	Nov. 14	250	17	0.6	0.4	0.9	2.7	2.9	2.1	1.6	2.7	1.4	0.5	1.1	0.4	23.6
El Paso, El Paso	N	97	30	109	-8	Mar. 20	Nov. 12	248	N	0.4	0.5	0.3	0.3	0.2	0.6	1.8	1.2	4.2	0.7	0.3	0.4	7.8
Ellis, Waxahachie	N	95	33	110	3	Mar. 20	Nov. 21	246	N	1.9	2.4	2.7	4.6	5.0	4.1	1.8	2.5	3.3	3.5	2.6	2.5	36.3
Erath, Dublin	N	97	31	110	-9	Mar. 27	Nov. 18	238	N	2.0	1.7	2.6	3.6	4.7	2.8	1.9	2.4	3.6	3.5	2.6	1.5	30.1
Falls, Marlin	N	97	36	114	-7	Mar. 13	Nov. 25	257	N	2.1	2.5	2.6	4.2	5.1	4.1	2.0	2.4	4.8	3.3	3.0	2.7	36.0
Fannin, Bonham	N	95	31	110	-7	Mar. 27	Nov. 4	228	39	2.3	2.7	3.6	4.8	5.1	2.6	1.8	2.4	5.2	3.5	2.8	2.8	41.6
Fayette, Flatonia	18	93	41	112	3	Mar. 2	Dec. 4	277	N	2.3	2.8	1.6	4.0	3.4	3.2	1.9	2.4	3.4	3.5	2.8	2.8	37.4
Fisher, Rotan	N	97	30	114	-9	Apr. 7	Nov. 6	218	N	0.4	0.9	0.7	1.9	2.8	2.5	2.3	1.9	2.4	1.7	0.7	0.5	22.5
Floyd, Floydada	N	93	24	106	-7	Apr. 2	Nov. 7	213	N	0.7	0.6	0.9	1.2	2.8	2.3	1.3	2.2	3.1	2.7	1.0	0.8	19.0
Foard, Crowell	N	97	41	105	-6	Apr. 7	Nov. 12	219	N	0.9	1.1	0.8	2.0	4.1	4.1	3.4	2.4	3.1	2.7	1.2	0.8	23.9
Fort Bend, Sugar Land	18	93	33	109	-1	Feb. 14	Dec. 7	296	18	2.8	3.3	2.6	3.5	4.3	2.6	3.4	1.9	4.9	3.9	3.7	4.8	43.9
Franklin, Mount Vernon	N	93	33	111	-9	Mar. 23	Nov. 12	234	N	2.8	3.3	3.4	4.5	4.7	2.6	1.3	2.5	4.9	2.6	3.7	3.1	46.8
Freestone, Fairfield	19	98	35	113	-9	Mar. 11	Dec. 2	263	N	2.1	2.7	2.1	4.5	4.6	1.8	3.4	2.4	3.6	3.7	3.2	3.2	38.3
Frio, Dilley	N	95	39	108	8	Feb. 23	Dec. 4	291	N	1.1	1.4	1.4	2.0	3.7	3.5	1.3	2.4	3.6	2.6	1.4	1.7	23.9
Gaines, Seminole	N	95	25	113	-9	Apr. 4	Nov. 4	210	N	0.6	0.6	0.7	1.0	3.3	3.0	2.1	2.4	2.3	1.6	0.6	0.6	15.8
Galveston, Galveston	N	87	48	101	8	Jan. 24	Dec. 25	335	N	3.0	2.3	2.1	2.6	3.3	2.8	3.8	4.4	5.8	1.8	3.2	3.6	40.2
Garza, Post	18	95	26	109	-1	Apr. 2	Nov. 7	216	N	0.6	0.7	0.6	1.3	2.7	3.2	2.4	2.4	2.5	1.8	0.8	0.5	19.4
Gillespie, Fredericksburg	N	95	36	109	-5	Apr. 1	Nov. 6	219	N	1.2	1.7	1.4	2.7	3.8	2.9	1.8	2.9	4.0	3.2	1.7	1.3	28.7

Texas Temperature, Frost, Growing Season and Precipitation Records, by Counties — (continued)

County and Station	Temperature — Length of Record (Yr.)	Mean Max. July (°F.)	Mean Min. January (°F.)	Highest Record (°F.)	Lowest Record (°F.)	Avg. Freeze — Last in Spring	Avg. Freeze — First in Fall	Growing Season (Days)	Precip. — Length of Record (Yr.)	January (In.)	February (In.)	March (In.)	April (In.)	May (In.)	June (In.)	July (In.)	August (In.)	September (In.)	October (In.)	November (In.)	December (In.)	Annual (In.)
Glasscock, Garden City	16	93	21	109	0	Apr. 2	Nov. 10	222	N	0.5	0.6	0.6	1.2	2.1	1.6	2.0	1.7	2.5	1.8	0.7	0.5	15.8
Goliad, Goliad	N	96	43	112	7	Feb. 24	Dec. 6	285	N	2.0	2.2	1.5	3.0	4.3	3.3	2.2	3.4	5.8	3.5	2.3	2.2	36.8
Gonzales, Nixon	N	97	41	113	−3	Feb. 28	Dec. 1	276	N	1.9	2.5	1.4	3.3	3.9	3.3	1.6	2.4	4.9	3.5	2.4	1.8	32.6
Gray, Pampa	44	95	30	111	−12	Apr. 15	Oct. 27	195	N	0.5	0.8	1.4	1.8	3.1	3.5	2.5	2.5	1.9	1.5	0.8	0.5	19.6
Grayson, Sherman	N	95	35	110	−2	Mar. 16	Nov. 9	227	N	1.7	2.5	3.1	4.6	5.3	3.5	3.0	2.2	4.8	3.2	2.8	2.1	38.2
Gregg, Longview	N	94	40	108	−1	Mar. 16	Nov. 15	247	N	3.8	3.3	3.7	5.2	4.9	4.2	3.0	2.8	4.5	3.0	3.9	4.1	46.5
Grimes, Anderson	9	96	40	109	4	Mar. 6	Dec. 9	278	13	3.1	3.3	2.8	4.3	4.3	3.1	1.8	2.0	4.1	3.1	3.4	3.4	40.4
Guadalupe, Seguin	N	96	40	109	−7	Mar. 6	Nov. 28	267	N	1.8	2.5	1.8	3.2	4.3	3.1	2.6	2.0	4.1	3.4	0.6	1.7	31.4
Hale, Plainview	N	92	25	109	−17	Apr. 10	Nov. 4	211	N	0.5	0.7	0.8	1.2	2.6	2.3	2.2	2.0	2.2	1.6	0.7	0.5	19.0
Hall, Memphis	N	97	35	117	0	Apr. 10	Nov. 6	213	N	0.8	0.9	1.1	2.6	3.8	2.6	3.0	2.5	2.2	1.6	0.7	0.6	20.3
Hamilton, Hico	N	95	26	107	−7	Apr. 4	Nov. 6	239	N	1.8	1.9	1.9	2.6	4.0	2.6	2.3	2.4	3.1	1.2	1.6	1.6	29.8
Hansford, Spearman	N	97	24	114	−22	Apr. 27	Oct. 25	186	N	0.5	0.9	1.2	1.1	3.2	3.3	3.0	2.5	1.7	1.2	0.9	0.8	19.2
Hardeman, Quanah	12	93	38	102	−15	Apr. 22	Nov. 14	221	N	0.7	4.1	1.2	1.9	3.9	2.3	2.3	2.4	3.1	1.2	1.0	0.8	23.4
Hardin, Evadale	N	93	46	107	12	Mar. 31	Nov. 14	300	N	5.0	3.7	3.6	5.2	4.6	4.5	4.9	4.2	5.6	3.7	4.6	5.2	55.4
Harris, Houston	N	94	33	108	7	Feb. 14	Dec. 11	245	N	3.3	1.0	3.6	5.1	4.9	3.7	3.3	2.4	4.8	3.4	3.4	3.2	42.6
Harrison, Marshall	13	92	28	113	−2	Mar. 1	Oct. 19	180	N	4.1	2.7	4.0	5.1	2.2	2.8	2.4	2.8	4.1	3.2	3.7	4.1	46.4
Hartley, Channing	N	92	36	110	−6	Apr. 28	Oct. 19	232	N	0.4	0.8	0.7	2.0	3.8	3.0	1.8	2.4	1.9	1.3	0.7	0.2	16.1
Haskell, Haskell	N	95	36	109	−14	Mar. 14	Nov. 16	254	N	0.8	1.1	1.2	1.5	4.4	3.4	1.6	2.8	3.3	3.5	1.2	0.9	24.1
Hays, San Marcos	N	95	35	106	−2	Mar. 14	Oct. 30	204	N	1.9	3.1	1.6	3.5	4.4	2.9	2.2	2.3	4.4	3.8	2.8	2.1	34.3
Hemphill, Canadian	47	96	27	113	−16	Apr. 11	Nov. 6	260	N	0.4	0.8	0.6	1.6	2.1	2.8	1.9	2.4	2.1	1.3	0.7	0.7	20.1
Henderson, Athens	27	92	36	110	−1	Mar. 11	Nov. 26	327	N	2.6	2.8	3.0	4.0	4.8	3.0	1.8	1.8	4.2	3.2	3.4	3.3	39.4
Hidalgo, McAllen	N	97	41	110	21	—	—	250	N	1.3	0.9	0.6	2.2	2.2	2.8	1.6	2.6	4.1	1.3	1.2	1.0	23.0
Hill, Hillsboro	N	96	33	110	−16	Mar. 13	Nov. 18	196	N	1.9	2.0	2.4	3.9	4.9	2.9	2.5	2.7	3.2	3.6	2.6	3.3	34.2
Hockley, Levelland	N	93	33	107	−6	Apr. 15	Oct. 28	232	N	0.4	0.9	0.7	1.0	2.2	3.4	1.8	2.4	2.5	2.0	0.5	0.4	18.1
Hood, Granbury	28	97	33	111	−4	Mar. 26	Nov. 13	238	N	1.9	2.0	1.7	3.9	4.9	3.7	2.7	1.8	2.9	2.9	2.1	1.5	30.9
Hopkins, Sulphur Springs	N	94	33	107	0	Mar. 23	Nov. 16	265	N	2.7	2.8	3.6	4.7	5.4	4.0	3.1	2.5	4.4	3.7	3.5	3.4	44.2
Houston, Crockett	N	94	37	108	21	Mar. 23	Nov. 26	217	N	3.4	3.1	2.8	4.7	5.1	3.8	1.8	2.8	4.4	3.7	3.8	3.5	42.2
Howard, Big Spring	N	95	41	113	−3	Apr. 4	Nov. 11	231	N	0.6	0.3	0.8	0.3	1.4	2.8	1.9	2.3	2.9	1.5	0.3	0.6	17.7
Hudspeth, Salt Flat	N	93	31	105	−4	Apr. 4	Nov. 13	237	N	0.5	0.3	0.8	0.2	0.9	0.9	1.8	3.4	1.8	0.9	0.6	0.4	8.0
Hunt, Greenville	22	95	30	102	−4	Mar. 21	Oct. 24	187	N	2.3	2.8	3.4	4.7	4.5	2.7	1.7	4.1	4.5	3.7	3.7	2.8	40.4
Hutchinson, Borger	N	95	32	104	−10	Mar. 23	Nov. 1	232	N	0.5	0.8	0.8	1.7	4.0	2.7	1.3	2.2	1.6	1.3	0.7	0.5	19.3
Irion, Mertzon	17	97	42	107	12	Apr. 7	Nov. 18	218	N	0.6	0.9	0.8	1.5	3.7	2.9	2.7	2.4	2.8	1.8	1.1	0.7	18.0
Jack, Jacksboro	N	94	38	109	−4	Mar. 13	Nov. 13	290	N	1.4	1.1	1.8	2.8	3.2	2.9	3.1	2.7	3.4	2.9	2.8	1.2	28.0
Jackson, Edna	N	93	42	114	7	Feb. 19	Nov. 5	229	N	2.2	2.8	1.7	2.8	4.0	3.8	2.5	3.0	5.7	3.7	4.6	2.5	40.9
Jasper, Evadale	8	83	42	112	−12	Mar. 11	Dec. 6	—	16	5.0	4.1	3.6	4.1	4.8	2.9	4.9	3.4	3.0	3.6	4.3	5.5	55.4
Jeff Davis, Mount Locke	12	93	42	112	−10	Apr. 11	Oct. 16	250	N	0.6	0.5	0.4	0.3	0.9	2.1	5.4	4.1	6.1	2.1	1.6	0.8	18.9
Jefferson, Port Arthur	27	93	43	105	12	Feb. 15	Dec. 15	303	23	4.2	3.7	2.9	4.1	5.5	4.6	5.4	4.1	6.4	3.6	4.3	4.6	52.8
Jim Hogg, Hebbronville	23	97	33	111	12	Feb. 18	Dec. 18	289	N	1.1	1.3	0.8	1.7	2.2	2.1	1.8	2.2	6.4	2.2	1.6	0.8	22.4
Jim Wells, Alice	N	98	41	110	−7	Feb. 14	Nov. 4	233	N	1.8	2.0	1.1	2.0	3.7	3.3	2.0	2.4	5.3	3.2	1.6	1.1	28.5
Johnson, Cleburne	22	93	31	107	−3	Mar. 31	Nov. 9	281	N	1.1	2.4	2.7	4.2	4.7	3.2	2.3	2.7	3.8	3.2	1.2	1.8	32.4
Jones, Anson	N	97	32	111	−14	Feb. 24	Nov. 21	248	N	1.1	2.9	1.1	2.2	3.2	2.4	2.5	3.0	3.4	2.4	1.2	1.0	25.3
Karnes, Kenedy	17	97	35	110	−5	Mar. 4	Dec. 2	236	N	2.3	2.1	1.8	2.1	4.0	2.7	1.6	3.1	4.3	4.6	2.3	1.8	33.2
Kaufman, Kaufman	N	96	45	107	−3	Mar. 18	Nov. 21	281	N	2.4	2.4	2.7	4.8	4.8	2.9	2.1	3.1	4.6	3.7	2.3	3.1	38.2
Kendall, Boerne	N	93	24	110	14	Mar. 25	Nov. 18	319	14	1.6	2.9	1.8	4.8	3.9	2.9	1.6	3.2	6.4	3.9	1.3	1.8	32.2
Kenedy, Armstrong	14	95	45	110	14	Feb. 25	Dec. 18	319	N	1.2	1.7	0.5	4.7	4.4	3.4	2.1	3.2	6.4	2.9	1.8	1.3	29.7
Kent, Jayton	18	97	24	110	−5	Apr. 4	Nov. 6	216	N	0.6	0.9	1.1	1.5	2.8	2.3	1.6	3.2	3.3	1.8	0.8	0.7	20.6

Texas Temperature, Frost, Growing Season and Precipitation Records, by Counties — (continued)

County and Station	Temperature †Length of Record Yr.	Mean Max. July °F	Mean Min. January °F	Record Highest °F	Record Lowest °F	Last in Spring	First in Fall	Growing Season* Days	Precip. †Length of Record Yr.	Jan. In.	Feb. In.	Mar. In.	Apr. In.	May In.	June In.	July In.	Aug. In.	Sept. In.	Oct. In.	Nov. In.	Dec. In.	Annual In.
Kerr, Kerrville		94	32	110	−7	Apr. 6	Nov. 6	216		1.6	2.2	2.0	3.1	3.8	2.6	1.7	2.1	4.0	3.6	1.6	1.6	29.8
Kimble, Junction		97	32	110	−11	Apr. 3	Nov. 3	213		1.0	1.4	1.7	2.1	3.8	2.3	1.5	2.6	2.7	2.4	1.0	1.0	22.5
King, Guthrie	17	97	26	114	−10	Apr. 3	Nov. 8	219		0.7	0.9	0.9	1.7	3.5	2.6	1.9	2.3	3.1	2.2	1.0	0.6	21.5
Kinney, Brackettville		96	36	109	10	Mar. 26	Nov. 26	270	45	0.8	1.1	0.9	2.0	3.1	3.0	1.4	2.6	3.1	3.0	1.0	0.8	21.1
Kleberg, Kingsville	13	95	46	108	9	Feb. 16	Dec. 16	314		1.5	1.6	1.0	2.0	3.5	3.2	2.0	2.9	5.0	3.0	1.3	1.1	27.5
Knox, Munday		98	29	116	−7	Apr. 1	Nov. 6	217		0.8	1.0	1.1	2.0	3.1	3.2	1.1	2.6	2.8	2.8	1.3	1.0	23.1
La Salle, Cotulla		99	42	111	7	Mar. 20	Dec. 6	288		0.9	1.1	0.8	1.9	3.1	2.2	2.1	2.7	2.3	2.8	1.0	1.0	21.6
Lamar, Paris		92	30	111	−1	Mar. 14	Nov. 14	235		3.4	3.0	3.7	4.8	5.1	3.3	3.5	2.4	3.2	4.0	3.4	3.4	45.0
Lamb, Littlefield		92	23	111	−14	Apr. 16	Oct. 27	194		0.4	0.5	0.6	1.2	2.7	3.3	2.5	2.4	2.3	1.7	0.5	0.4	18.6
Lampasas, Lampasas	24	96	31	111	−12	Apr. 1	Nov. 10	223		1.5	2.6	1.8	2.9	4.2	3.3	1.8	2.3	3.3	3.1	2.9	1.8	29.5
Lavaca, Hallettsville	29	94	41	111	−5	Mar. 1	Dec. 6	280		2.4	2.7	2.3	3.4	5.2	3.8	2.4	2.8	5.3	2.8	2.9	2.5	38.4
Lee, Lexington		94	34	104	−1	Mar. 1	Nov. 29	273	18	2.4	3.2	2.7	3.4	5.0	3.0	1.7	2.2	3.9	3.7	2.8	2.4	35.1
Leon, Centerville		94	35	111	−3	Mar. 6	Nov. 1	270		2.9	3.9	2.8	4.7	5.0	3.9	2.4	2.6	5.3	4.2	3.0	3.0	39.3
Liberty, Liberty		93	40	107	−7	Mar. 3	Nov. 19	261		4.0	2.8	2.7	4.4	4.7	4.5	4.6	3.8	4.9	4.5	3.6	4.8	50.7
Limestone, Mexia		95	34	110	−5	Mar. 15	Nov. 26	255		2.7	3.5	3.9	4.4	4.7	3.2	2.1	2.1	5.3	4.5	2.8	2.8	38.3
Lipscomb, Follett		96	20	110	−12	Apr. 10	Oct. 29	202		0.6	0.6	0.8	1.9	3.6	2.9	2.7	2.8	1.8	1.3	0.6	0.6	21.3
Live Oak, George West	25	97	41	110	−1	Feb. 20	Dec. 6	289		1.7	1.7	1.4	2.2	3.9	2.3	1.5	2.9	4.7	2.8	1.4	1.4	27.6
Llano, Llano	32	96	32	113	−6	Mar. 29	Nov. 13	222		1.1	1.8	1.4	2.5	3.9	2.8	1.8	2.4	3.5	3.1	1.6	1.3	26.6
Loving, Mentone		92	28	114	−16	Apr. 1	Nov. 8	229		0.4	0.5	0.3	0.8	0.9	0.9	1.5	1.4	2.1	0.8	0.4	0.3	9.1
Lubbock, Lubbock		92	24	111	−17	Apr. 9	Nov. 3	208		0.4	0.5	0.6	1.3	2.6	2.8	1.8	2.0	2.1	1.6	0.7	0.7	17.8
Lynn, Tahoka	25	92	24	107	−11	Apr. 5	Nov. 6	217	33	0.4	0.7	0.7	1.3	2.6	2.9	2.3	2.0	2.6	1.8	0.7	0.4	18.3
Madison, Madisonville	32	94	39	109	−8	Mar. 18	Nov. 26	272		3.1	3.5	2.8	4.8	4.6	3.4	2.4	2.7	4.6	3.5	3.7	3.1	41.1
Marion, Jefferson		94	30	109	9	Apr. 1	Nov. 9	236	23	3.9	3.9	3.9	5.3	4.6	3.4	3.1	2.5	3.0	4.2	3.8	4.1	44.7
Martin, Lenorah		96	30	109	10	Apr. 13	Nov. 6	215		0.8	0.8	0.5	1.2	2.3	1.6	1.7	1.7	2.6	1.6	0.6	0.6	17.2
Mason, Mason	14	94	32	102	−5	Mar. 13	Nov. 6	217	24	1.5	2.5	1.7	2.9	4.0	2.3	1.8	2.0	3.3	2.4	1.5	1.1	24.8
Matagorda, Matagorda	24	91	46	109	−1	Feb. 17	Dec. 10	296		3.1	2.5	2.1	2.9	4.8	4.0	4.1	4.1	7.3	3.4	2.9	2.9	43.2
Maverick, Eagle Pass	29	99	38	115	−2	Feb. 31	Dec. 3	285	25	0.6	0.8	0.5	1.7	3.6	2.2	1.7	2.4	2.9	2.5	0.9	0.7	21.0
McCulloch, Brady	18	97	30	110	−7	Mar. 16	Nov. 12	226	42	1.1	1.4	1.5	2.3	4.0	2.4	1.7	2.0	3.2	2.5	1.1	1.1	24.7
McLennan, Waco		96	36	112	−2	Mar. 19	Nov. 24	253		1.7	2.7	2.0	3.8	4.7	2.6	1.9	2.0	3.4	3.1	2.2	1.9	31.0
McMullen, Tilden		97	36	109	−7	Feb. 19	Dec. 7	291		1.3	1.5	1.5	2.3	3.7	2.1	1.8	2.4	3.9	2.1	1.5	1.2	24.4
Medina, Hondo	23	95	39	107	−11	Mar. 11	Nov. 6	263		1.7	2.3	1.5	2.8	3.1	2.9	2.1	2.4	4.2	3.5	1.4	1.5	28.5
Menard, Menard		95	30	112	−18	Apr. 13	Nov. 6	220		0.9	1.1	0.9	2.0	3.7	2.4	1.6	2.2	3.1	2.0	0.6	0.8	22.2
Midland, Midland		96	29	109	−4	Mar. 23	Nov. 24	218	27	0.5	0.6	0.4	0.8	1.9	1.4	1.9	1.8	2.1	1.4	0.5	0.5	13.7
Milam, Cameron	27	96	34	110	−5	Apr. 4	Nov. 16	256		2.7	2.5	2.2	3.9	4.4	2.7	1.8	2.1	4.5	3.4	2.6	2.6	34.3
Mills, Goldthwaite		96	34	111	−1	Apr. 2	Nov. 5	230		1.7	2.7	2.1	2.9	4.8	2.9	1.7	2.3	3.4	2.1	1.3	1.3	28.5
Mitchell, Colorado City		97	31	111	−7	Mar. 31	Nov. 11	217		0.6	0.7	0.9	1.6	3.2	2.9	1.8	1.8	2.9	1.8	0.7	0.7	19.8
Montague, Bowie		95	31	115	−11	Mar. 30	Nov. 26	229		1.6	1.9	2.5	3.4	4.9	3.9	2.3	2.3	4.9	3.8	1.9	1.9	32.3
Montgomery, Conroe		93	38	107	−18	Apr. 21	Dec. 22	270	42	3.5	3.4	2.9	4.9	4.7	4.5	3.4	3.6	4.9	3.8	3.8	4.2	46.6
Moore, Dumas		90	19	109	−4	Apr. 30	Nov. 12	185	23	0.5	0.5	1.1	1.3	2.7	2.7	3.4	2.3	1.6	1.2	0.6	0.6	18.5
Morris, Daingerfield		95	35	112	−5	Apr. 1	Nov. 7	236		3.2	3.4	2.9	5.4	4.5	3.1	3.0	2.5	3.9	3.3	4.1	4.2	44.2
Motley, Matador		95	27	111	−10	Apr. 16	Nov. 12	218		0.5	0.6	0.9	1.4	3.1	3.2	2.4	2.5	3.8	2.4	0.8	0.7	20.4
Nacogdoches, Nacogdoches	34	94	36	113	−1	Mar. 16	Nov. 9	243		4.2	3.9	3.7	4.8	5.5	3.9	2.9	2.5	3.8	3.7	3.8	4.7	47.5
Navarro, Corsicana	27	96	34	110	−7	Mar. 24	Nov. 5	253		4.8	4.3	3.6	4.6	5.3	2.8	2.1	2.1	5.1	3.8	4.7	2.9	36.6
Newton, Kirbyville Forest Service		93	40	110	−11	Mar. 24	Nov. 20	228		4.8	4.3	2.7	4.6	5.3	4.6	5.3	3.7	4.0	2.4	1.2	6.0	56.0
Nolan, Roscoe		95	30	110	−5	Apr. 4	Nov. 9	221		0.9	1.0	1.2	2.2	2.9	2.6	2.0	2.1	4.0	2.4	1.2	0.9	23.4
Nueces, Corpus Christi		94	46	104	13	Feb. 9	Dec. 15	309		1.6	1.6	0.8	2.0	3.1	3.4	2.0	3.5	6.2	3.2	1.6	1.4	30.2

Texas Temperature, Frost, Growing Season and Precipitation Records, by Counties — (continued)

County and Station	Temperature Length of Record (Yr.)	July Mean Max. (°F.)	January Mean Min. (°F.)	Record Highest (°F.)	Record Lowest (°F.)	Last in Spring	First in Fall	Growing Season (Days*)	Precip. Length of Record (Yr.†)	January (In.)	February (In.)	March (In.)	April (In.)	May (In.)	June (In.)	July (In.)	August (In.)	September (In.)	October (In.)	November (In.)	December (In.)	Annual (In.)
Ochiltree, Perryton	16	94	16	110	-8	Apr. 18	Oct. 26	191	N	0.5	0.6	1.2	1.2	3.5	2.9	3.0	2.6	1.6	1.2	1.0	0.5	19.6
Oldham, Vega	N	91	19	108	-17	Apr. 19	Oct. 21	186	N	0.5	0.6	0.9	1.1	2.8	2.8	2.8	2.5	1.6	1.2	0.7	0.5	17.4
Orange, Orange	17	91	40	104	10	Mar. 16	Nov. 11	240	17	5.5	3.4	3.8	4.2	6.0	4.7	6.0	5.4	5.8	4.9	4.8	5.4	59.2
Palo Pinto, Mineral Wells	N	97	32	114	3	Mar. 31	Nov. 7	221	N	1.7	1.7	2.0	3.4	4.1	2.6	2.3	2.2	3.3	2.9	1.8	1.4	29.3
Panola, Carthage	25	95	37	108	1	Mar. 16	Nov. 11	240	N	4.2	3.6	4.0	4.7	4.1	3.5	2.3	2.5	3.4	3.0	4.1	4.5	46.2
Parker, Weatherford	N	97	31	119	-10	Mar. 29	Nov. 9	225	N	1.7	1.8	2.5	3.9	4.2	2.7	1.9	2.6	3.4	3.2	1.8	1.6	31.1
Parmer, Friona	18	95	21	108	-10	Apr. 20	Oct. 20	183	N	0.4	0.5	0.4	0.9	1.6	1.4	1.3	1.4	1.1	1.2	0.8	0.4	15.3
Pecos, Fort Stockton	N	97	30	111	3	Mar. 31	Nov. 10	224	18	0.4	0.6	0.5	0.5	1.8	1.8	1.3	3.0	2.1	1.2	0.8	0.4	12.2
Polk, Livingston	N	95	37	112	14	Mar. 11	Nov. 16	250	N	4.0	3.7	3.9	4.7	4.8	3.5	2.7	3.0	4.9	3.7	4.2	4.4	48.0
Potter, Amarillo	22	91	22	108	-14	Apr. 17	Oct. 24	190	N	0.4	0.6	0.3	1.1	2.8	3.5	2.4	1.6	1.7	1.4	0.6	0.5	19.1
Presidio, Marfa	N	102	25	106	-4	Mar. 20	Nov. 13	238	N	0.4	0.5	0.3	0.4	0.9	1.9	2.5	1.6	1.7	0.8	0.4	0.3	14.8
Presidio, Presidio	19	95	33	110	14	Mar. 20	Nov. 13	238	22	0.4	0.5	0.2	0.3	0.5	1.3	2.4	2.9	3.9	1.6	0.6	0.3	9.3
Rains, Emory	N	92	31	110	7	Mar. 21	Nov. 18	242	N	2.8	3.3	3.8	5.1	5.1	3.4	2.4	2.3	2.7	4.0	3.6	3.3	42.2
Randall, Canyon	N	94	23	107	-14	Apr. 15	Oct. 27	195	N	0.5	0.6	0.5	1.7	2.0	3.1	2.5	2.5	2.7	1.6	0.6	0.4	18.4
Reagan, Big Lake	9	93	31	112	0	Mar. 28	Nov. 17	236	17	1.0	0.9	0.8	1.7	2.0	1.7	2.4	3.6	4.1	2.3	1.1	0.6	19.5
Real, Prade Ranch	N	93	38	106	-5	Mar. 26	Nov. 17	236	9	1.0	0.9	1.4	2.7	5.0	2.1	1.7	3.6	1.8	3.2	1.7	1.0	25.7
Red River, Clarksville	16	100	37	111	9	Mar. 23	Nov. 11	226	N	2.7	3.1	4.0	5.0	5.4	3.5	3.7	2.4	7.8	3.9	3.9	3.4	44.1
Reeves, Balmorhea	N	94	31	110	-5	Apr. 1	Nov. 11	226	N	0.3	0.4	0.3	0.5	1.0	1.0	1.3	1.2	1.8	1.1	0.5	0.3	12.7
Reeves, Pecos	N	94	31	110	-7	Feb. 16	Nov. 14	234	N	0.4	0.5	0.3	0.4	1.0	1.3	1.3	1.7	1.5	1.5	0.9	1.9	9.6
Refugio, Refugio	19	96	43	114	15	Apr. 1	Dec. 15	304	16	1.9	2.3	1.1	2.6	3.7	3.9	2.7	2.5	3.8	4.0	2.5	0.6	38.8
Roberts, Miami	N	94	19	106	-15	Apr. 16	Oct. 25	192	N	0.4	0.4	1.1	0.4	1.6	2.8	2.6	2.2	1.5	1.5	1.5	3.2	20.7
Robertson, Franklin	16	96	37	104	7	Mar. 6	Nov. 29	268	16	3.1	2.8	2.3	1.7	4.7	3.1	2.4	2.0	3.8	4.2	3.5	3.2	39.3
Rockwall, Rockwall	N	96	33	110	7	Mar. 23	Nov. 14	236	N	3.1	2.4	3.8	4.3	4.7	3.1	2.4	2.0	3.9	3.3	3.5	2.9	36.9
Runnels, Ballinger	N	96	30	111	-9	Mar. 30	Nov. 13	228	N	1.0	1.1	0.8	1.7	2.7	2.2	1.5	2.3	3.9	2.3	4.0	0.9	22.1
Rusk, Henderson	6	93	35	108	9	Mar. 11	Nov. 16	250	N	3.7	3.5	5.7	4.7	5.1	3.8	2.0	2.7	3.8	3.3	3.8	3.8	44.7
Sabine, Hemphill	14	93	36	105	8	Mar. 21	Nov. 12	236	14	5.2	3.7	3.7	4.9	4.5	4.5	4.0	3.0	3.8	4.5	3.8	4.5	52.5
San Augustine, Jackson Hill	17	94	35	104	8	Mar. 17	Nov. 12	238	N	3.8	3.7	3.5	4.9	4.7	3.7	3.1	3.0	5.1	3.4	3.8	5.3	46.3
San Jacinto, Coldspring	N	94	35	105	11	Mar. 5	Nov. 21	261	N	3.8	3.4	2.7	4.8	4.7	4.8	3.1	3.2	4.9	4.2	4.7	4.7	48.0
San Patricio, Sinton	23	94	44	107	11	Feb. 14	Dec. 14	303	25	2.0	2.0	1.0	4.1	4.7	4.8	1.6	3.2	5.1	4.2	1.9	1.2	34.4
San Saba, San Saba	17	96	32	112	10	Mar. 14	Nov. 14	227	N	1.1	1.5	1.3	2.2	3.9	3.2	1.6	2.3	3.1	2.7	0.9	0.6	25.9
Schleicher, Eldorado	15	96	28	107	-10	Apr. 4	Nov. 12	229	N	0.7	0.8	0.8	1.7	2.5	1.9	1.6	2.4	3.1	2.1	1.0	0.6	19.0
Scurry, Snyder	N	95	26	115	-7	Apr. 4	Nov. 4	224	N	0.5	0.9	0.7	1.7	3.7	2.5	1.3	3.1	3.1	2.4	1.0	1.0	20.3
Shackelford, Albany	29	98	29	110	-8	Mar. 30	Nov. 9	214	N	1.3	1.4	1.1	2.9	2.7	3.9	3.6	4.0	3.1	2.9	4.0	4.4	27.1
Shelby, Center	N	93	34	108	8	Mar. 17	Nov. 12	240	N	4.4	3.8	4.3	4.9	4.4	3.3	3.6	4.0	4.5	2.9	0.8	0.3	49.7
Sherman, Stratford	18	94	18	114	-19	Apr. 23	Oct. 21	182	N	0.3	0.4	0.8	1.2	2.7	2.3	2.8	2.5	1.5	1.0	1.0	3.7	16.9
Smith, Tyler	17	94	33	108	10	Mar. 17	Nov. 21	259	N	3.0	3.3	3.5	4.9	4.4	2.5	2.8	2.5	3.3	3.3	3.2	1.9	43.1
Somervell, Glen Rose	N	98	32	110	2	Mar. 25	Nov. 7	236	N	1.8	2.1	2.7	4.1	4.0	2.5	1.8	1.9	3.0	3.2	1.8	0.7	32.2
Starr, Rio Grande City	19	99	44	111	15	Feb. 5	Dec. 6	314	N	0.9	0.9	0.5	1.5	1.3	2.7	1.7	2.2	3.2	2.5	0.7	1.3	20.6
Stephens, Breckenridge	N	97	32	111	-7	Apr. 1	Nov. 11	222	N	1.4	1.5	1.3	2.4	3.4	2.6	1.8	1.9	3.2	2.5	1.3	0.7	26.4
Sterling, Sterling City	N	98	30	114	-11	Apr. 1	Nov. 10	224	N	0.6	0.8	1.1	1.6	2.7	2.6	2.0	1.8	1.9	2.6	1.6	0.5	18.6
Stonewall, Aspermont	N	98	31	109	-7	Mar. 31	Nov. 16	220	N	0.7	1.1	0.8	1.7	3.4	3.0	2.0	2.3	2.5	2.4	1.2	0.5	22.2
Sutton, Sonora	N	95	32	108	-2	Apr. 2	Nov. 11	235	N	0.7	1.0	1.1	2.0	2.7	2.5	1.9	2.0	2.5	2.4	0.7	2.4	22.4
Swisher, Tulia	17	92	27	108	-10	Apr. 26	Oct. 26	205	19	0.6	0.5	0.8	1.1	2.7	2.6	1.8	1.7	2.5	2.6	1.3	0.9	20.7
Tarrant, Fort Worth	18	96	32	110	9	Mar. 26	Nov. 26	230	19	2.0	2.2	2.5	3.6	4.6	3.0	1.7	2.5	2.6	2.6	2.3	2.4	31.3
Taylor, Abilene	N	95	32	111	-8	Mar. 26	Nov. 11	225	27	1.0	1.0	1.3	2.4	3.0	2.5	1.9	2.1	2.5	2.3	0.9	0.9	23.3
Terrell, Sanderson	27	93	31	110	-11	Mar. 26	Nov. 11	237	N	0.4	0.5	0.8	0.9	1.3	1.6	2.4	2.1	2.5	1.4	0.6	0.3	12.8
Terry, Brownfield	N	93	28	110	-8	Apr. 10	Nov. 2	206	N	0.4	0.6	0.8	1.0	2.3	2.6	2.4	2.1	2.5	1.8	0.6	0.4	17.5
Throckmorton, Throckmorton	N	97	28	113	-11	Mar. 31	Nov. 6	220	N	1.0	1.2	1.3	2.5	3.4	2.5	2.0	2.4	4.1	2.4	1.2	1.0	25.0

Texas Temperature, Frost, Growing Season and Precipitation Records, by Counties — (continued)

County and Station	Temperature — Length of Record (Yr.)	July Mean Max. (°F.)	January Mean Min. (°F.)	Record Highest (°F.)	Record Lowest (°F.)	Last in Spring	First in Fall	Growing Season (Days)	Precip. Length of Record (Yr.)	January (In.)	February (In.)	March (In.)	April (In.)	May (In.)	June (In.)	July (In.)	August (In.)	September (In.)	October (In.)	November (In.)	December (In.)	Annual (In.)
Titus, Mount Pleasant	N	95	30	111	−12	Mar. 23	Nov. 12	233	N	3.1	3.4	3.9	5.2	4.5	3.7	3.3	2.7	4.4	3.6	4.1	3.6	45.5
Tom Green, San Angelo	N	97	32	111	−4	Mar. 25	Nov. 15	235	N	0.6	0.8	0.8	1.8	2.5	1.9	1.2	1.9	3.0	2.1	1.0	0.6	18.2
Travis, Austin	N	95	39	109	−2	Mar. 3	Nov. 28	270	N	1.6	2.5	1.7	3.1	4.2	3.1	1.9	2.2	3.6	3.6	2.1	2.1	31.5
Trinity, Groveton	13	94	38	108	1	Mar. 6	Nov. 21	260	13	3.2	2.7	3.3	4.0	5.3	4.5	4.1	3.2	4.5	3.5	3.8	3.9	46.9
Tyler, Warren	20	94	38	106	6	Mar. 17	Nov. 16	241	N	4.4	4.4	3.3	4.9	5.1	4.3	4.1	3.4	4.5	3.9	4.4	5.2	52.0
Upshur, Gilmer	N	94	32	109	−4	Mar. 16	Nov. 12	245	N	4.4	3.4	3.3	6.0	4.8	3.6	3.0	2.4	2.3	3.9	4.0	3.8	45.1
Upton, McCamey	N	96	31	111	−2	Mar. 26	Nov. 21	232	N	0.4	0.6	0.5	0.7	1.8	1.3	1.3	1.6	2.7	1.5	0.7	0.4	12.7
Uvalde, Uvalde	N	96	37	111	6	Feb. 10	Dec. 9	255	N	1.0	1.3	0.9	2.2	3.0	2.8	1.7	2.9	2.7	3.1	1.2	1.0	24.1
Val Verde, Del Rio	N	98	38	112	10	Mar. 10	Nov. 21	300	N	0.5	0.9	0.6	1.9	2.0	1.7	1.7	1.6	2.7	2.2	0.8	0.6	17.2
Van Zandt, Wills Point	N	97	38	107	−2	Mar. 16	Dec. 6	250	N	2.9	2.1	3.1	5.8	4.5	3.7	1.7	2.1	2.2	3.3	3.3	3.3	42.4
Victoria, Victoria	N	94	43	113	9	Feb. 16	Nov. 27	290	N	1.9	2.2	1.3	3.7	4.7	4.5	3.3	3.3	6.2	3.9	2.2	2.1	36.9
Walker, Huntsville	N	95	38	107	−2	Feb. 19	Dec. 4	265	23	3.2	3.4	2.8	4.6	4.7	3.6	2.0	3.1	5.0	3.3	3.5	3.0	44.2
Waller, Hempstead	N	95	39	107	13	Mar. 7	Nov. 10	283	21	3.2	2.9	2.1	3.9	4.7	3.6	2.3	2.4	4.6	4.0	3.2	3.5	38.2
Ward, Monahans	N	96	29	113	−9	Feb. 28	Dec. 26	223	N	0.3	0.5	0.4	0.7	1.7	1.7	1.1	2.6	2.3	1.1	0.6	0.6	13.7
Washington, Brenham	15	96	45	110	13	Apr. 1	Dec. 26	277	N	2.7	3.0	2.1	4.0	4.6	3.6	1.7	2.7	3.5	3.5	3.8	3.2	39.7
Webb, Laredo	21	99	44	110	−8	Mar. 7	Nov. 1	322	N	0.7	1.1	0.4	1.2	2.5	2.7	1.1	4.3	5.8	1.8	0.9	0.9	20.1
Wharton, Danevang	N	93	22	108	−8	Feb. 7	Dec. 26	266	N	2.8	2.8	1.2	2.9	4.0	4.7	2.4	4.3	5.8	3.5	2.9	2.6	41.3
Wheeler, Shamrock	17	96	28	113	−8	Mar. 5	Nov. 7	208	N	0.5	1.0	1.0	2.9	3.9	3.2	2.4	2.1	2.4	1.8	0.9	0.6	22.6
Wichita, Wichita Falls	N	99	28	117	14	Apr. 27	Dec. 11	229	N	0.9	1.0	1.2	3.0	4.6	2.9	2.1	2.0	2.9	2.8	1.3	1.2	26.7
Wilbarger, Vernon	N	99	28	119	−5	Mar. 27	Nov. 24	221	N	0.9	1.0	1.5	2.4	4.6	3.5	1.7	2.1	2.7	2.7	1.3	1.0	25.3
Willacy, Raymondville	N	96	47	107	24	Mar. 31	Dec. 8	331	N	1.4	1.3	0.6	1.6	3.0	2.9	1.6	3.1	4.4	3.5	1.6	1.6	27.5
Williamson, Taylor	N	97	35	107	−14	Feb. 6	Nov. 8	258	N	1.4	2.8	1.8	3.6	4.0	2.9	2.1	2.1	4.1	3.1	2.7	2.4	34.2
Wilson, Floresville	18	97	28	108	−8	Mar. 24	Nov. 6	280	N	2.7	0.4	1.5	2.8	3.9	2.9	1.6	1.2	4.9	3.5	2.1	1.6	29.4
Winkler, Wink	N	100	28	114	−12	Feb. 5	Nov. 18	219	14	0.4	0.4	0.4	0.7	1.4	1.4	1.2	1.7	1.9	1.3	0.4	0.3	11.0
Wise, Bridgeport	N	98	29	115	−8	Feb. 24	Nov. 31	220	N	1.6	3.0	2.0	3.2	4.3	3.4	2.5	2.5	3.3	2.9	1.9	1.5	28.9
Wood, Mineola	14	92	31	107	−2	Mar. 31	Nov. 18	246	N	3.1	1.6	4.0	4.7	4.9	3.4	3.0	2.4	3.2	2.9	3.7	3.6	45.0
Yoakum, Plains	N	92	23	108	−12	Apr. 15	Oct. 4	199	N	0.6	1.4	0.6	1.0	1.9	1.9	2.0	2.3	2.9	2.6	0.5	0.4	16.2
Young, Graham	N	97	23	112	−8	Apr. 2	Dec. 4	216	17	1.3	1.0	0.5	3.1	2.8	2.8	2.5	2.3	2.9	2.6	1.2	1.2	28.0
Zapata, Zapata	17	97	45	112	16	Apr. 2	Dec. 15	304	N	0.7	1.0	0.5	1.2	2.6	2.3	1.5	1.9	5.5	1.7	1.0	0.9	19.8
Zavala, Crystal City	N	98	41	109	11	Feb. 14	Dec. 1	280	N	0.8	1.1	0.7	1.7	3.4	2.5	1.5	2.4	2.8	2.7	1.0	0.8	21.3

More weather information available on Pages 605-608, including temperature and precipitation by region for 1989 and 1990.

Texas State Parks

Texas' expanding system of state parks attracted 21,-111,659 visitors in fiscal 1990. The parks offer contrasting attractions, mountains and canyons, forests, spring-fed streams, sandy dunes and saltwater surf.

Most of these parks are listed here. **Texas Parks and Wildlife Department** provided the information. Additional information is available from the Department's Austin headquarters (4200 Smith School Rd., Austin 78744; 1-800-792-1112 within Texas, (512) 389-4890 outside the state), personnel at individual parks or other sources of tourist information.

Abilene State Park, 19 miles southwest of Abilene in Taylor County, 621.4 acres. The land was deeded by the city of Abilene in 1933. A part of the official **Texas long-horn herd** is located in the park. In addition to **Lake Abilene, Buffalo Gap,** the original Taylor County seat (1878) and one of the early frontier settlements, is nearby. Buffalo Gap was on the **Western,** or **Dodge City, Trail,** over which pioneer Texas cattlemen drove herds to Kansas.

Acton State Historical Park is a .006-acre cemetery plot where **Davy Crockett's** second wife, Elizabeth, was buried in 1860. It is six miles east of Granbury in Hood County.

Recreation

Adm. Nimitz Museum Historical Park is 4.52 acres in Fredericksburg featuring **Nimitz Steamboat Hotel,** which is now museum; named for **Adm. Chester W. Nimitz** of World War II fame. Nearby is **Kerrville State Park.**

Atlanta State Park is 1,475 acres located 11 miles northwest of Atlanta in Cass County; adjacent to **Wright Patman Dam and Lake.** Texas acquired the land from the U.S. Army in 1954.

Balmorhea State Park is 45.9 acres four miles southwest of Balmorhea in Reeves County, deeded in 1935 by private owners. Swimming pool fed by natural spring **(San Solomon Springs);** also provides water to **pupfish refuge** located in park. Nearby are city of **Pecos, Fort Davis National Historic Site,** scenic loop drive through **Davis Mountains** and **Davis Mountains State Park.**

Bastrop State Park is 3,503.7 acres. The park was acquired by deeds from the city of Bastrop and private owners during 1933 to 1935. Site of famous **"Lost Pines,"** isolated timbered region of loblolly pine and hardwoods. Nearby **Lake Bastrop** offers good fishing. **State capitol** at Austin 30 miles away; 13-mile drive through forest leads to **Buescher State Park.**

Battleship Texas State Historic Site, located in Harris County, eight miles southeast of Houston on U.S. 78 and IH-45 to Texas 225, then east on Texas 225 for 12 miles to Texas 134 for three miles to Park Road 1836. The U.S.S. Texas was moored in the Houston Ship Channel at the **San Jacinto Battleground** on San Jacinto Day, 1948, and is the only survivor of the dreadnought class, a veteran of two world wars and many campaigns. The Battleship is open. Admission charged.

Bentsen-Rio Grande Valley State Park, a scenic park, is along the Rio Grande in Hidalgo County. The 587 acres were acquired from private owners in 1944. Park is excellent base from which to tour Rio Grande Valley of Texas and adjacent Mexico; most attractions within 1½ hours' drive. Three miles of hiking trail lead to Rio Grande; provides chance to study unique plants, animals and birds of park. Many species of birds unique to southern United States found here, including **Lichtenstein's oriole, pauraque, groove-billed ani, green jay, Kiskadee flycatcher, red-billed pigeon, elf owl** and **chachalaca.** Park also one of last natural refuges in Texas for cats such as **ocelot** and **jaguarundi.**

Big Bend Ranch State Natural Area, 221,536.3 acres of wilderness in **Brewster** and **Presidio** counties, was purchased from Humble Oil and Gas Co. in 1988. The purchase almost doubled the size of the state park system, which had at that time a total of 220,000 acres. The wilderness area, which includes an **extinct volcano,** several waterfalls, two **mountain ranges,** at least 11 **rare species of plants and animals,** and 90 major **archaeological sites,** has been designated by the U.S. Government as an **international biosphere reserve,** a natural area recognized under a United Nations program. At this time, there is no development, but the area is available to backpackers and wilderness campers.

Big Spring State Park is 381.99 acres located in Howard County. It was named for a natural spring that was replaced by an artificial spring. The park was deeded by the city of Big Spring in 1934 and 1935. Drive to top of Scenic Mountain provides panoramic view of surrounding country. The "big spring" nearby provided watering place for herds of bison, antelope and wild horses. Used extensively also as campsite for early Indians, explorers and settlers. **Prairie dog colony** on mountain.

Blanco State Park is 104.6 acres along the Blanco River in Blanco County. The land was deeded in 1936 by private owners. The land was used as campsite by early explorers and settlers. **LBJ Ranch** and **LBJ State Historical Park** located less than 30 miles away.

Bonham State Park is a 261-acre park located near Bonham in Fannin County. It includes a 65-acre lake. The land was acquired in 1933 and 1934 from the city of Bonham. **Sam Rayburn Memorial Library** in Bonham. **Sam Rayburn Home** and **Valley Lake** nearby.

Brazos Bend State Park in Fort Bend County, seven miles west of Rosharon on FM 762 (approximately 28 miles south of Houston). Total acreage, 4,897. Acquired from private landowners in 1976. Includes **George Observatory.**

Bryan Beach State Park is 878 acres near Freeport. Acquired by purchase in 1973 from private sources. (No developed facilities in 1987.)

Buescher State Park, a scenic area, is 1,016.68 acres near Smithville in Bastrop County. The state was deeded the park by the city of Smithville between 1933 and 1936. **El Camino Real** (King's Highway) once ran near park; road connected **San Antonio de Bexar** with Spanish missions in East Texas and generally followed pres-ent-day Texas State Highway 21 and **Old San Antonio Road.** Parkland included in Stephen F. Austin's colonial grant. Scenic park road connects **Buescher State Park** with **Bastrop State Park.**

Caddo Lake State Park, one mile west of Karnack in Harrison County, consists of 483.8 acres along **Cypress Bayou,** which runs into **Caddo Lake.** A scenic area, it was acquired from private owners in 1933-37. Nearby Karnack is childhood home of **Mrs. Lyndon B. Johnson.** Close by is old city of **Jefferson,** famous as commercial center of Northeast Texas during last half of 19th century. Caddo Indian legend attributes formation of **Caddo Lake** to earthquake. Lake originally a natural lake, but dam added in 1914 for flood control; new dam replaced old one in 1971.

Caddoan Mounds State Historical Park in Cherokee County near Alto. Total of 93.8 acres acquired in 1975 by condemnation.

Caprock Canyons State Park, 3.5 miles north of Quitaque off Texas 86 in Briscoe County, has 13,960.6 acres. Purchased in 1975.

Cassells Boykin State Park, Angelina County, seven miles northeast of Zavalla on **Sam Rayburn Reservoir.** Total acreage, 265. Acquired in October 1982, by lease from the Department of the Army. Facilities include boat ramp, two-pit toilets, 20 picnic sites, 16 campsites, water well and dump station. No fees are charged.

Cedar Hill State Park is an urban park located on 1,810.57 acres 10 miles southwest of Dallas on Joe Pool Reservoir. Most campsites have electricity and water and are located in wooded areas; reservations are recommended. Fishing from two lighted jettys and a perch pond for children. Swimming beach (no lifeguard), two boat ramps, picnic sites with tables and grills. Animals include bobcats, coyote, fox squirrels, armadillos and raccoons. Trees are mostly cedar elm, honey locust, mesquite and juniper. Several sections of **tall-grass prairie** exist in the park. Structures from **19th-century Penn Farm** currently undergoing renovation.

Choke Canyon State Park consists of two units located on 26,000-acre Choke Canyon reservoir, a water supply for Corpus Christi. The park was acquired in 1981 in a 50-year cooperative agreement among the Bureau of Reclamation, the city of Corpus Christi and the Nueces River Authority. The 385-acre South Shore Unit is located in Live Oak County four miles west of Tree Rivers on State Highway 72. The Calliham Unit, containing 1,100 acres, is located in McMullen County 11 miles west of Three Rivers, also on State Highway 72. Each unit provides picnic sites, restrooms, showers, a trailer dump station, campsites with and without electricity, a group shelter, playground and boat ramp. Fishing and water skiing are allowed, but no facilities are provided. The Calliham Unit also has a swimming pool, boats to rent, a hiking trail and a grocery store (seasonal).

Christmas Bay State Park, located on Follet's Island seven miles northeast of Freeport on San Louis Pass Road, contains 484.8 acres, including 1½ miles of Gulf beach. The park site is open to the public, but no facilities are provided.

Cleburne State Park is a 528.8-acre park located in Johnson County with 116-acre lake; acquired from the city of Cleburne, Johnson County and private owners in 1935 and 1936. Glen Rose **dinosaur tracks** found on Paluxy River may be seen at nearby **Dinosaur Valley State Park.**

Colorado Bend State Park, a 5,328.3-acre facility, is located 32 miles west of Lampasas. Access is via a 6-mile gravel road south of the community of Bend on Farm Road 580. The park site was purchased partly in 1984, with the balance acquired in 1987. Public use is primitive at this time. Plans for the park include restoration of parts of it to its natural condition. Overnight camping is permitted only in designated areas. Campfires are not permitted; cooking is allowed only on contained fuel stoves or portable grills. Breakable container not permitted. Camping is available. Drinking water is provided at two locations; chemical toilets are provided. Access road is subject to flooding.

Confederate Reunion Grounds State Historical Park, located in Limestone County on the Navasota River where it is joined by Jack's Creek, is 74.1 acres in size. The park may be reached by going 6 miles south of Mexia on State Highway 14, then 2.5 miles west on FM 2705.

Copano Bay State Fishing Pier, a 5.9-acre park with fishing pier, is located five miles north of Rockport in Aransas County. Operated by leased concession.

Copper Breaks State Park, 12 miles south of Quanah on Texas 6, was acquired in 1970. Recreation park features rugged scenic beauty on 1,888.7 acres and has a 70-acre lake. Medicine Mounds were important ceremonial sites of Comanche Indians. Nearby **Pease River** was site of battle, 1860, in which **Cynthia Ann Parker** was recovered from Comanches. Portion of official **Texas longhorn herd** maintained at park.

Daingerfield State Park in Morris County is a 550.89-acre recreational area which includes an 80-surface-acre lake; deeded in 1935 by private owners. This area center of iron industry in Texas; nearby is **Lone Star Steel Co.** On grounds of company is old blast furnace that helped in manufacturing guns and other metal objects for Civil War.

Davis Mountains State Park is 1,320.78 acres in Jeff Davis County. The scenic area, near Fort Davis, was deeded over many years by private owners. First European, **Antonio de Espejo,** came to area in 1583. Nearby points of interest include **Fort Davis National Historic Site, McDonald Observatory** and scenic loop through **Davis Mountains.** Davis Mountains State Park located halfway between **Carlsbad Caverns** and **Big Bend National Park.** Nearby are scenic **Limpia, Madera, Musquiz** and **Keesey** canyons; **Camino del Rio;** ghost town of **Shafter; Capote Falls; Sul Ross State University** in Alpine; and **Fort Leaton State Historic Site.** Indian Lodge, built by the Civilian Conservation Corps during the early 1930s, has 39 rooms, a restaurant and a swimming pool.

Dinosaur Valley State Park, located near Glen Rose in Somervell County, is a 1,274.1-acre scenic park. Land was acquired from private owners in 1969 and 1973. Dinosaur tracks and two full-scale dinosaur models on display. There is **longhorn herd** in park.

Eisenhower State Park, 457.3 acres located in Grayson County, was acquired by an Army lease in 1954 and named for the 34th U.S. president, Dwight David Eisenhower. Park located on shores of **Lake Texoma.** First Anglo settlers came to area in 1835 and 1836; **Fort Johnson** was established in area in 1840; **Colbert's Ferry** established on Red River in 1853 and operated until 1931.

Eisenhower Birthplace State Historical Park is 3 acres, including the birthplace of **Dwight David Eisenhower,** in Denison, Grayson County. The property was acquired in 1958 from the Sid Richardson Foundation. Restoration of home complete, with furnishings of period and some personal effects of Gen. Eisenhower. His history of World Wars I and II is here. Also crank-type telephone with personal greetings from "Ike." Town of **Denison** established on **Butterfield Mail Route** in 1858.

Enchanted Rock State Natural Area is 1,643.5 acres on Big Sandy Creek 18 miles north of Fredericksburg on FM 965. Acquired in 1978 from Texas Nature Conservancy. **Enchanted Rock** is huge granite boulder rising 500 feet above ground and covering 640 acres. Indians be-

lieved ghost fires flickered at top and were awed by weird creaking and groaning geologists now say resulted from rock's heating by day and contracting in cool night.

Fairfield Lake State Park is 1,460 acres, six miles northeast of the city of Fairfield in Freestone County. Now open for overnight use, the park is leased from Texas Utilities. Surrounding woods predominantly oak and offer sanctuary for many species of birds and wildlife.

Falcon State Park is 572.6 acres located at southern end of **Falcon Lake** at Falcon Heights in Starr and Zapata counties. The park was leased from the International Boundary and Water Commission in 1954. Nearby are Mexico and **Fort Ringgold** in Rio Grande City; **Bentsen-Rio Grande Valley State Park** is 65 miles away.

Fannin Battleground State Historical Park, 9 miles east of Goliad in Goliad County. The 13.6-acre park was acquired by legislative enactment in 1965. At this site on March 20, 1836, **Col. J. W. Fannin** surrendered to Mexican **Gen. Jose Urrea** after **Battle of Coleto;** 342 massacred and 28 escaped near what is now **Goliad State Historical Park.** Near Fannin site is **Gen. Zaragoza's Birthplace** and partially restored **Mission Nuestra Senora del Espiritu Santo de Zuniga.** (See also **Goliad State Historical Park** in this list.)

Fanthorp Inn State Historical Park includes a historic structure and 1.4 acres at Anderson in Grimes County; acquired by purchase in 1977 from Edward Buffington. Inn records report visits from many prominent civic and military leaders, including Sam Houston, Anson Jones, Ulysses S. Grant and generals Robert E. Lee and Stonewall Jackson. It is the only authentically restored stagecoach inn of the 1850s in the state.

Fort Griffin State Historical Park is 506.20 acres 15 miles north of Albany in Shackelford County. The state was deeded the land by the county in 1935. A herd of **Texas longhorns** resides on the park range. On bluff overlooking townsite of Fort Griffin and Clear Fork of Brazos River valley are ruins of **Old Fort Griffin,** restored bakery, replicas of enlisted men's huts. (Townsite is not in park boundaries.) Fort constructed in 1867, deactivated 1881; crumbling ruins of various structures still may be seen. Albany annually holds **"Fandangle"** in commemoration of frontier times.

Fort Lancaster State Historical Park, 81.6-acres located about 33 miles west of Ozona on U.S. 290 in Crockett County, acquired in 1968 by deed from Crockett County; Henry Meadows donated 41 acres in 1975. **Fort Lancaster** established Aug. 20, 1855, to guard San Antonio-El Paso Road and protect movement of supplies and immigrants from Indian hostilities; fort abandoned March 19, 1861, after Texas seceded from Union.

Fort Leaton State Historical Park, four miles east of Presidio in Presidio County on FM 170, was acquired in 1967 from private owners. Consists of 17.5 acres, 5 of which are on site of pioneer trading post. In 1848, **Ben Leaton** built fortified trading post known as **Fort Leaton** near present Presidio. Ben Leaton died in 1851. Partial reconstruction of fort begun in early 1930\$ and in 1936, Texas Centennial Commission placed marker at site.

Fort McKavett State Historical Park, 81.94 acres acquired in 1967 and 1968 in part from Fort McKavett Restoration, Inc., and Menard County, is located 17 miles west of Menard. Fort built for protection of settlers against Indians in 1852. Originally called **Camp San Saba,** built by War Department as protection for frontier settlers. Camp later renamed for **Capt. Henry McKavett,** killed at Battle of Monterrey, Sept. 21, 1846. Fort abandoned March 1859; reoccupied April 1, 1868; after **Gen. Ranald S. Mackenzie** subdued Indians, fort no longer needed, abandoned June 30, 1883.

Fort Parker State Park includes 1,458.78 acres south of Mexia in Limestone County. Named for the former fort located near the present park, the site was acquired by deeds from private owners between 1935 and 1937. Nearby point of interest is **Old Fort Parker State Historic Site,** replica of fort erected in 1834 for protection from Indians. Daughter of founder, **Cynthia Ann Parker,** captured by Indians May 19, 1836. She married **Chief Peta Nocona** and mothered **Quanah Parker,** last great Comanche chief, involved in **Battle of Palo Duro.**

Fort Richardson State Historical Park, located one-half mile south of Jacksboro in Jack County, contains 396.1 acres. Acquired in 1968 from City of Jacksboro. Fort founded in summer of 1866; named **Fort Jacksboro** at that time. April 1867 it was abandoned for site 20 miles farther north; on Nov. 19, 1867, made permanent post at Jacksboro and named for **Israel Richardson. Fort Richardson** part of defensive system against Indians. Expeditions sent from Fort Richardson arrested Indians responsible for **Salt Creek Massacre** in 1871 and fought Comanches in Palo Duro Canyon. Fort abandoned again in May 1878.

Franklin Mountains State Park, created by an act of the legislature in 1979 to protect the mountain range as a wilderness preserve, comprises 23,122.54 acres in El Paso County. Pedestrian access for day-use activities such as hiking, nature study and picnicking is permitted. The site is undeveloped, with no facilities or utilities, and vehicular traffic is prohibited.

Fulton Mansion State Historic Structure is 3.4 miles north of Rockport in Aransas County. Total acreage of 2.3 acquired by purchase from private owner in 1976. Three-story wooden structure, built in 1871-1876, was home of George W. Fulton, prominent in South Texas for economic and commercial influence; mansion derives significance from its innovative construction and Victorian design.

Galveston Island State Park, located approximately six miles southwest of Galveston on FM 3005, is a 1,950.01-acre site acquired in 1970 from private owners. Offers camping, nature study and fishing amid sand dunes and grassland.

Garner State Park is 1,419.8 acres of recreational facilities in northern Uvalde County. Named for **John Nance Garner,** U.S. Vice President, 1933-1941, the park was deeded in 1934 by private owners. Nearby is **John Nance "Cactus Jack" Garner Museum** in Uvalde. Nearby also are historic ruins of **Mission Nuestra Senora de la Candelaria del Canon,** founded in 1749; **Camp Sabinal** (a U.S. Cavalry post and later Texas Ranger camp) established 1856; **Fort Inge,** established 1849.

Goliad State Historical Park is 187.33 acres along the San Antonio River in Goliad County. The land was deeded in 1931 by the city and county of Goliad. Nearby are the sites of several battles in the Texas fight for independence from Mexico. The park includes a replica of **Mission Nuestra Senora del Espiritu Santo de Zuniga,** originally established 1722 and settled at its present site in 1749. Park unit contains **Gen. Zaragoza's Birthplace** which is located at **Presidio la Bahia.** He was Mexican national hero who led troops against French at historic Battle of Puebla. Park property also contains ruins of **Mission Nuestra Senora del Rosario,** established 1754, located four miles west of Goliad on U.S. 59. Other nearby points of historical interest are restored **Presidio Nuestra Senora de Loreto de la Bahia,** established 1722 and settled on site in 1749; it is located ¼ mile south of **Goliad State Historical Perk** on U.S. 183. Goliad memorial shaft marking common burial site of **Fannin** and victims of **Goliad massacre** (1836) is near Presidio la Bahia. (See also **Fannin Battleground State Historic Site,** above.)

Goose Island State Park in Aransas County is 314 acres; it was deeded by private owners in 1931-1935. Located here is the tree estimated to be 2,000 years old and listed by American Forestry Association as the **national co-champion live oak;** certified largest live oak in Texas in 1969. **Aransas Wildlife Refuge,** wintering ground for rare and endangered **whooping cranes,** just across St. Charles Bay.

Gov. Hogg Shrine State Historical Park is a 26.7-acre tract in Quitman, Wood County. Named for **James Stephen Hogg,** first native-born governor of Texas, the park includes a museum housing items which belonged to Hogg. Seventeen acres deeded by the Wood County Old Settlers Reunion Association in 1946; 4.74 acres gift of Miss Ima Hogg in 1970; 3 acres purchased. Old Settlers Reunion held annually in August in this park. **Gov. James Stephen Hogg Memorial Shrine** created in 1941. Gov. Hogg's wedding held in **Stinson Home; Miss Ima Hogg Museum** houses both park headquarters and display of representative history of entire Northeast Texas area.

Guadalupe River State Park in Kendall and Comal counties, 13 miles east of Boerne on Texas 46. Total acreage 1,938.1 on Guadalupe River. Acquired by deed from private owners in 1975. Park has four miles of river frontage with several white-water rapids and is located in middle of 20-mile stretch of Guadalupe River noted for canoeing. It has picnic areas, and campsites with restroom and shower facilities.

Hill Country State Natural Area (Louise Merrick Unit) in Bandera and Medina counties, nine miles west of Bandera on FM 1077. Total acreage 5,369.8 acquired by gift and purchase in 1976. Park is located in typical Texas Hill Country on West Verde Creek and contains several spring-fed streams.

Honey Creek State Natural Area consists of 2,293.7 acres adjacent to Guadalupe River State Park (above). It was acquired from the Texas Nature Conservancy in 1985. Entrance is in Guadalupe River SP. Open on Saturdays only for guided naturalist tours starting about 9 a.m.

Hueco Tanks State Historical Park, located 32 miles northeast of El Paso in El Paso County, was obtained from the county in 1969. Featured in this 860.3-acre park are large natural rock basins and site of last great Indian battle in county. Apaches, Kiowas, Comanches and earlier Indian tribesmen camped here and left behind **pictographs** telling of their adventures. Tanks served as watering place for **Butterfield Overland Mail Route.**

Huntsville State Park is 2,083.2-acre recreational area in Walker County, acquired by deeds from private owners in 1934. **Sam Houston State University** located at nearby Huntsville. **Texas Department of Corrections** also located in Huntsville. At Huntsville is old homestead of Sam Houston **(Steamboat House)** and his grave; homestead contains personal effects of Houston. Park adjoins **Sam Houston National Forest** and encloses **Lake Raven.** Approximately 50 miles away is **Alabama-Coushatta Indian Reservation** in Polk County.

Inks Lake State Park is 1,201.7 acres of recreational facilities along Inks Lake, on the Colorado River, in Burnet County. The park was acquired by deeds from the Lower Colorado River Authority and private owners in 1940. Nearby are **Longhorn Cavern State Park, LBJ Ranch, LBJ State Historical Park, Pedernales Falls State Park** and **Enchanted Rock State Natural Area. Granite Mountain** and quarry at nearby Marble Falls furnished material for Texas **state capitol.** Deer, turkey and other wildlife abundant. **Buchanan Dam,** largest multi-arch dam in world, located six miles from park.

Jim Hogg State Historical Park is 178.17 acres in **East Texas Piney Woods** in Cherokee County. A memorial to the state's first native-born governor, **James Stephen Hogg,** the property was deeded by the city of Rusk in 1941.

Jose Antonio Navarro State Historical Park, on .6 acre in downtown San Antonio, was acquired by donation from San Antonio Conservation Society Foundation in 1975. Has furnished Navarro House complex built about 1848.

Kerrville-Schreiner State Park is a 517.2-acre area along the Guadalupe River in Kerr County. The land was deeded by the city of Kerrville in 1934. Near the park is the site of **Camp Verde,** scene of an experiment involving the use of **camels** for transportation; the camp was active from 1855 to 1869. **Bandera Pass,** 12 miles south of Kerrville, noted gap in chain of mountains through which passed **camel** caravans, wagon trains, Spanish conquistadors, immigrant trains. In nearby Fredericksburg is atmosphere of old country of Germany and famous **Nimitz Hotel.** (See **Admiral Nimitz Museum Historical Park.**)

Kreische Brewery State Historical Park, located adjacent to **Monument Hill State Historical Park** in LaGrange, Fayette County, is 36 acres, acquired by purchase from private owners. Contains Kreische Brewery and house complex built between 1850-1855 on Colorado River; probably first commercial brewery in state. Brewery closed in 1888; it now consists of several intact structures surrounded by ruins in various stages of deterioration. Various out-buildings located on site were associated with brewery and family. Tours on weekends and by special request.

Lake Arrowhead State Park consists of 524 acres in Clay County, about eight miles south of Wichita Falls on U.S. 281 to Farm Road 1954, then six miles to park. The area was acquired in 1970 from the city of Wichita Falls. Lake Arrowhead is a reservoir on the Little Wichita River and covers approximately 13,500 surface acres with 106 miles of shoreline. The land surrounding the lake is generally semiarid, gently rolling prairie, much of which has been invaded by mesquite in recent decades.

Lake Bob Sandlin State Park, on the wooded shoreline of 9,400-acre Lake Bob Sandlin, is located 12 miles southwest of Mount Pleasant off FM 21 in Titus County. Facilities in the 640.8-acre park include picnic sites, a group picnic shelter, screened shelters, multi-use campsites, primitive camping, trails, a two-lane boat ramp and a fishing pier. Oak, hickory and pine abound, and the reservoir is stocked with largemouth bass, catfish and crappie.

Lake Brownwood State Park in Brown County is 537.5 acres acquired from the Brown County Water Improvement District No. 1 in 1934. Park situated on **Lake Brownwood** near **geographical center** of Texas.

Lake Colorado City State Park, 500 acres leased for 50 years from a utility company. It is located in Mitchell County 11 miles southwest of Colorado City.

Lake Corpus Christi State Park, a 288 land-acre park located in San Patricio, Jim Wells and Live Oak counties, was leased from city of Corpus Christi in 1934. Lake noted for big blue, channel and yellow catfish. Sunfish, bass and crappie also taken. City of Corpus Christi and **Padre Island National Seashore** are nearby.

Lake Lewisville State Park is a 721-acre park located on the reservoir's east central shore and was developed as the result of a 50-year lease agreement with the Corps of Engineers. Located north of Dallas in Denton County, the park has campsites, screened shelters, boat ramps, park store and swimming. Geology of Lake Lewisville directly affects the soils, thus the vegetation. Underlying the east side of the lake is the Eagle Ford Formation, a dark gray to tan shale with marine fossils deposited about 100 million years ago. Lake Lewisville State Park is located on what is called an upland terrace, where silts were deposited on top of shale by the ancient Trinity River.

Lake Livingston State Park, in Polk County, six miles southwest of Livingston on FM 3126, contains 635.5 acres along Lake Livingston. Acquired by deed from private landowners in 1971. Near ghost town of **Swartwout,** steamboat landing on Trinity River in 1830s and 1840s. Polk County's first commissioners court met there before voters selected Livingston as county seat.

Lake Mineral Wells State Park, located four miles east of the city of Mineral Wells on Highway 180 in Parker County, consists of 2,905 acres encompassing **Lake Mineral Wells.** The city of Mineral Wells donated 1,095 land acres and the 646-acre lake to Texas Parks and Wildlife Department in 1976. Some of the remaining acreage was transferred from **Fort Wolters Army Post** by the U.S. Government to the State of Texas for use as park land.

Lake Somerville State Park, in Lee and Burleson counties, was leased from the federal government in 1969. The 5,520-acre park includes many recreational facilities. Many species of wild game observed at park; white-tailed deer, fox, coyote, raccoon, rabbit and quail abundant. Various park areas feature sandy or grassy shallow shorelines ideal for wading or swimming.

Lake Texana State Park is 575 acres, seven miles east of Edna on State Highway 111, with camping, boating, fishing, picnicking facilities. It was acquired by a 50-year lease agreement with the Bureau of Reclamation in 1977.

Lake Whitney State Park is 955 acres along the east shore of **Lake Whitney** in Hill County. Acquired in 1954 by a Department of the Army lease, the state has control until 2003. Located on **Lake Whitney** near ruins of **Towash,** early Texas settlement inundated by Lake Whitney. Towash Village named for chief of Hainai Indians that moved into area in 1835. Park noted for bluebonnets in spring.

Landmark Inn State Historical Park 4.7 acres in Castroville acquired through donation by Miss Ruth Lawler in 1974. **Castroville,** known as **Little Alsace of Texas,** headquarters for group of Alsatian farmers settled there in 1840s. **Landmark Inn** built about 1844 as residence and store for Caesar Monad, mayor of Castroville 1851-1864.

Lipantitlan State Historical Park is five acres east of Orange Grove in Nueces County. The property was deeded by private owners in 1937. Fort constructed here in 1833 by Mexican government; fort fell to Texas forces in 1835. **Lake Corpus Christi State Recreation Area** is nearby.

Lockhart State Park is 263.7 acres near Lockhart in Caldwell County. The land was deeded by private owners between 1934 and 1937. **Emanuel Episcopal Church** in Lockhart is one of **oldest Protestant churches** in continuous use in Texas. After Comanche **raid at Linnville, Battle of Plum Creek** (1840) was fought in area.

Longhorn Cavern State Park in Burnet County is 639 acres classified as a scenic park. It was acquired in 1932-1937 from private owners. The cave has been used as a shelter since prehistoric times. Among legends about the cave is one that the outlaw Sam Bass hid a $2 million cache of stolen money. Another legend is that the defenders of the Confederacy made gunpowder in the cave during the Civil War, and another story states Gen. Robert E. Lee, while stationed in Texas before the Civil War, chased some Indians into the cave but lost their trail. **Inks Lake State Park** and federal fish hatchery located nearby. Park operated by concession agreement.

Lost Maples State Natural Area consists of 2,174.2 scenic acres in Bandera County, four miles north of Vanderpool on Ranch Road 187. Acquired by purchase from private owners in 1973. Outstanding example of Edwards Plateau flora and fauna, features isolated stand of uncommon Uvalde **bigtooth maple. Golden-cheeked warbler** and **black-capped vireo** have been sighted in park.

Lubbock Lake Landmark State Historical Park is a 308.6-acre archaeological site on the northwest edge of the city of Lubbock near intersection of Loop 239 and Clovis Road (U.S. 84). The site was leased from the city of Lubbock for 50 years in 1986. **Evidence of human habitation from 12,000 years ago** to the recent past has been uncovered. Only known site in North America containing deposits related to all cultures known to have existed on the Southern Plains. Interpretive center, three interpretive trails, three rest areas. Ongong excavation can be viewed.

Lyndon B. Johnson State Historical Park, in Gillespie County near Stonewall, contains 732.75 acres. Acquired in 1967 with private donations. Statue of **Johnson** unveiled in 1974 ceremonies. Home of **Lyndon B. Johnson** located north bank of Pedernales River across Ranch Road 1 from park; portion of official Texas **longhorn herd** maintained at park. Wildlife exhibit includes turkey, deer and buffalo. Living history demonstrations in progress at restored **Sauer-Beckmann house.** Reconstruction of **Johnson birthplace,** located east of ranch house at end of Park Road 49, open to public. Nearby is family cemetery where former president and relatives are buried. In Johnson City is boyhood home of President Johnson. Near outskirts of Johnson City is cluster of stone barns and buildings constructed by his grandfather, Sam Ealy Johnson Sr., and his brother Tom. (See also **National Parks.**)

McKinney Falls State Park in Travis County east of Interstate 35 and near Bergstrom AFB is a 640.6-acre park acquired in 1970 from private donation. The headquarters of the **Parks and Wildlife Department** are at this location.

Mackenzie State Park in Lubbock County is a 542.2-acre park acquired in 1935 from the city of Lubbock, then leased to that city until 2037. The park was named for Gen. Ranald S. Mackenzie, famous for his campaigns against Indians in West Texas. One of the main features is a colony of native Texas **prairie dogs;** a section is called **"Prairie Dog Town."** (Not operated by parks department.)

Magoffin Home State Historical Park, in El Paso County in the city of El Paso; total acreage, 1.5. Purchased jointly by the state of Texas and the city of El Paso in 1976, it is operated by the Texas Parks and Wildlife Department. The Magoffin Home was built in 1875 by pioneer El Pasoan Joseph Magoffin and displays a regional architectural style developed in the Southwest between 1865 and 1880.

Martin Creek Lake State Park is located 4 miles south of Tatum off State Highway 43 in Rusk County. Total acreage 286.9 acres, deeded to the Parks and Wildlife Department by the Texas Utilities Generating Company in 1976. The area provides 20 primitive campsites, 60 campsites with water and electricity, 21 screened shelters, 48 picnic sites, a pavillion and a boat ramp.

Martin Dies Jr. State Park, until 1965 the **Dam B State Park,** is 705-acre recreational area in Jasper and Tyler counties. The land was acquired from the U.S. Army Corps of Engineers by lease in 1964. Park located at edge of **Big Thicket.** In spring, Dogwood Festival is held at Woodville. Park approximately 30 miles from **Alabama-Coushatta Indian Reservation.**

Matagorda Island State Park and Wildlife Management Area: Separated from the mainland by San Antonio and Espiritu Santo bays, Matagorda Island is one of the barrier islands that border the Gulf and protect the mainland from the great tides and strong wave action of the open ocean. The southwestern tip of the island, consisting of 11,500 acres, is privately owned, and the remainder, which extends approximately 24 miles to the northeast, consists of 24,893 acres of state land and 19,000 acres of federal land. Under a cooperative agreement between the U.S. Department of the Interior and the State of Texas approved in 1983, the entire area of public lands is managed by the Texas Parks and Wildlife Department. The park occupies abut 7,325 acres of the total.

Matagorda Peninsula State Park, 6,255.2 acres of undeveloped Gulf Beach, is located south of the town of Matagorda on FM 2031. Day use only; access only by **four-wheel-drive vehicles.** Fishing, swimming and picnicking are allowed, but no facilities of any kind are provided.

Meridian State Park in Bosque County is a 502.4-acre park including a 73-acre lake. The land was acquired from private owners in 1933-1935. **Tonkawa Indians** lived in surrounding area before coming of white man; **Tawakoni Indians** also occupied area prior to 1841. **Texan-Santa Fe expedition** of 1841 passed through Bosque County near present site of park. Park located on Bee Creek in Bosque Valley is very popular for bream, crappie, catfish and bass fishing. **Golden-cheeked warblers** nest here annually.

Mission Tejas State Historical Park is a 118-acre park in Houston County. Situated in the **Davy Crockett National Forest**, the park was acquired from the Texas Forest Service in 1957 by legislative enactment. In the park is a replica of the **Mission San Francisco de los Tejas,** which was established in 1690; was first mission in East Texas; abandoned due to Indians; re-established 1716 but again abandoned 1719. In 1721, third attempt made and was successful for a while but was abandoned for third and final time in 1730 and moved to San Antonio; renamed **San Francisco de la Espada** and is today one of four historic mission sites included in the **San Antonio Missions National Historical Park.**

Monahans Sandhills State Park consists of 3,840 acres of sand dunes in Ward and Winkler counties. The land is leased by the state until 2056. Because water was readily available, dunes used as meeting place by raiding Indians. Burial site of prehistoric Indians in exhibit building adjacent to interpretive center. **Odessa meteor crater** is nearby.

Monument Hill State Historical Park consists of 4.4 acres southwest of La Grange in Fayette County adjacent to Kreische Brewery State Historic Site. The land was acquired in two parcels — monument and tomb area transferred from Board of Control in 1949; the rest from the Archbishop of San Antonio in 1956. The hill, a historical site, bears a memorial shaft dedicated to **Capt. Nicholas Dawson** and his men, who fought at **Salado Creek** in 1842, in Mexican Gen. Woll's invasion of Texas, and to the men of the **"black bean lottery"** (1843) of the **Mier Expedition.** Bodies of these heroes were brought to Monument Hill for reburial in 1848. In La Grange, old tree under which Captain Dawson recruited ill-fated expedition still stands.

Mother Neff State Park was **the first official state park** in Texas. It originated with six acres designated for park purposes by the will of Mrs. I.E. Neff, mother of **Pat M. Neff,** Governor of Texas from 1921 to 1925. The park now contains 259 acres along the Leon River in Coryell County. The additional land was deeded to the state in 1934 by private owners.

Mustang Island State Park is 3,703.58 acres on Gulf of Mexico in Nueces County, 14 miles south of Port Aransas; acquired from private owners in 1972. Mustang Island has a unique and complicated ecosystem, dependent upon the sand dune. The seemingly sterile dunes are the product of wind-deposited sand held in place by stabilizing drought-resistant vegetation. The foundation plants of the dunes are sea oats, beach panic grass and soilbind morning glory. Studies have shown that plants and their progeny can collect enough sand to build a 15-foot dune in three years. The dunes are capable of reducing the destructive might of hurricane-driven waves and protecting bay and mainland areas.

Old Fort Parker State Historical Park, a 37.5-acre park in Limestone County, was deeded by private owners in 1933. In the park is a replica of **Fort Parker** stockade, built in 1834 and was site of abduction of **Cynthia Ann Parker** on May 19, 1836, by Comanche and Kiowa Indians.

Palmetto State Park, a scenic park, is 267.72 acres along the San Marcos River in Gonzales County. The land was deeded in 1934-1937 by private owners. Artesian wells produce distinctive, sulphur-laden water. Nearby Gonzales and Ottine important in early Texas history. Gonzales settled 1825 as center of **Green DeWitt's colonies.** Nearby is site of **Elks' Hospital** and **Texas Rehabilitation Center.**

Palo Duro Canyon State Park, the state's largest, consists of 16,402.1 acres in Armstrong and Randall counties. The land was deeded by private owners in 1933 and is the scene of the annual production of the drama, **Texas.** Scenic canyon one million years old and exposes rocks spanning about 200 million years of geological time. **Coronado** may have visited canyon in 1541. Canyon officially discovered by **Capt. R. B. Marcy** in 1852. Scene of decisive battle in 1874 between Comanche and Kiowa Indians and U.S. Army troops under **Gen. Ranald Mackenzie.** Also scene of early ranch undertaking started by **Charles Goodnight** in 1876. Part of **state longhorn herd** is kept here.

Pedernales Falls State Park, 4,860 acres in Blanco County about 14 miles east of Johnson City. Acquired from private owners in 1970 along banks of scenic Pedernales River. This area typifies Edwards Plateau with live oaks, deer, turkey and stone hills. **Golden-cheeked warbler** nests here.

Port Isabel Lighthouse State Historical Park consists of .6 acre in Port Isabel in Cameron County. It was acquired by purchase from private owners in 1950 and includes a **lighthouse** constructed in 1852; near battle site of **Palmito Ranch** (1865); lighthouse remodeled 1952 and is still used. Resort facilities available across Queen Isabella Causeway at **South Padre Island.**

Port Lavaca State Fishing Pier is a recreational area, acquired by transfer of authority from Texas Highway Department in 1963. It is 1.8 acres on Lavaca Bay in Calhoun County. Main attraction is a 3,200-foot fishing pier made from the former causeway across the bay. Port Lavaca City Park is at base of the pier and offers a boat ramp and picnicking facilities. Operated by leased concession.

Possum Kingdom State Park in Palo Pinto County is 1,528.7 acres adjacent to **Possum Kingdom Lake,** in Palo Pinto Mountains and Brazos River Valley. Numerous deer, other wildlife and some cattle of official **Texas longhorn herd** live in park. The area was acquired from the Brazos River Authority in 1940.

Purtis Creek State Park is located in Henderson and Van Zandt counties, three miles north of Eustace on FM 316. Total acreage 1,566 acquired in 1976 from private owners. The park has 40 picnic sites and 59 campsites with water and electricity.

Rusk/Palestine State Park. Rusk unit located adjacent to Texas State Railroad Rusk Depot with total acreage of 136. Palestine unit located adjacent to Texas State Railroad Palestine Depot with 26 acres. (See also **Texas State Railroad State Historical Park.**)

Sabine Pass Battleground State Historical Park in Jefferson County, southeast of Sabine Pass, contains 56.3 acres, acquired by deed from Kountze County Trust in 1971. **Richard W. Dowling,** with small Confederate force, repelled an attempted 1863 invasion of Texas by Union naval gunboats during Civil War.

Sam Bell Maxey House State Historical Park in Paris, Lamar County, donated by city of Paris in 1976. Consists of .4 acre. Most of furnishings accumulated by Maxey family included. In March 1971, the Maxey House was officially listed on the National Register of Historic Places.

San Jacinto Battleground State Historical Park is 1,002.82 acres on which is situated the 570-foot-tall monument erected in honor of Texans who defeated Mexican **Gen. Antonio Lopez de Santa Anna** on April 21, 1836. The site, classified a historical park, is in east Harris County. The 59th Legislature transferred the park to the Texas Parks and Wildlife Department. **The U.S.S. Texas** is moored in the park.

San Jose Mission is currently operated as part of San Antonio Missions National Historical Park.

Sea Rim State Park in Jefferson County, 10 miles west of Sabine Pass, contains 15,094.19 acres of marshland with five miles of Gulf beach shoreline, acquired from private owners in 1972. It is prime wintering area for waterfowl; also home of endangered **red wolf,** American **alligator,** rare **river otter** and muskrat.

Sebastopol House State Historical Park in Seguin, Guadalupe County, was acquired by purchase in 1976 from Seguin Conservation Society, approximately 2.2 acres. Built about 1854 by Col. Joshua W. Young of limecrete, concrete made from local gravel and lime, the Greek Revival-style house was restored to its 1870-1880 appearance by the TP&WD. Open and tours available Wednesday through Sunday.

Seminole Canyon State Historical Park in Val Verde County, nine miles west of Comstock, contains 2,172.5 acres; acquired by purchase from private owners in 1973. Canyon area contains several important prehistoric **Indian pictograph sites.** Historic interpretive center open.

Sheldon Wildlife Management Area and Park Site, Harris County on Carpenter's Bayou 20 miles northeast of downtown Houston just north of US 90. Total acreage, 2,503. Acquired by purchase in 1952 from the city of Houston. Facilities include two boat ramps with parking areas and restrooms; five T-head fishing piers and 5.5 miles of levees. Activities include nature study of coastal marshland habitat, bird watching of primarily waterfowl and marsh birds, and fishing with free access to all public facilities during the prescribed mid-February through September fishing season. No rates or charges.

South Llano River State Park adjoins Walter Buck State Wildlife Management Area five miles south of Junction in Kimble County off U.S. 377 on Park Road 73. The 2,640.8-acre site was donated to the TP&WD by Walter Buck in 1977. Wooded bottomland along the winding South Llano River is **largest and oldest winter roosting site for the Rio Grande Turkey** in Central Texas. Other animals include wood ducks, white-tailed deer, squirrels, jack rabbits, javelina, fox, beaver, bobcat, cottontails and armadillos. Campsites include those with water and electricity with restrooms and showers nearby, walk-in sites with picnic tables and fire rings, and primitive campsites for backpackers. Picnic tables near river. Canoeing, tubing, swimming and fishing allowed. Hiking trails cross into adjacent wildlife management area. Parts of park may be closed during flooding or for wildlife management activities.

Starr Mansion State Historical Park, 3.1 acres in Marshall, Harrison County. Mansion was home to five generations of Starr family, powerful and economically influential Texans. Acquired by gift in 1976. Additional land acquired in 1982.

Stephen F. Austin State Historical Park, is 667.4 acres along the Brazos River in Austin County, named for the "Father of Texas." The area was deeded by the San Felipe de Austin Corporation and the San Felipe Park Association in 1940. Site of township of **San Felipe** was seat of government where conventions of 1832 and 1833 and **Consultation of 1835** held. These led to **Texas Declaration of Independence.** San Felipe was home of **Stephen F. Austin** and other famous early Texans; home of Texas' first Anglo newspaper (the **Texas Gazette**) founded in 1829; postal system of Texas originated here; beginning of **Texas Rangers.**

Texas State Railroad State Historical Park, Anderson and Cherokee counties, between the cities of Palestine and Rusk, adjacent to US 84. Total acreage, 499. Acquired by Legislative Act in 1971. See local Parks and Wildlife office for schedules. The railroad was built by the State of Texas to support the state-owned iron works at Rusk. Begun in 1896, the railroad was gradually extended until it reached Palestine in 1909 and established regular rail service between the towns. (See also **Rusk/Palestine State Park.**)

Tips State Park, 31.3 acres of recreational facilities, is on the Frio River in Live Oak County. The park, a mile west of Three Rivers, was deeded by private owners in 1925 and then leased for 99 years to Three Rivers. Park near site of **first glass factory** in Texas.

Tyler State Park is 985.5 acres north of Tyler in Smith County, includes a 64-acre lake. The land was deeded by private owners in 1934 and 1935. Nearby Tyler famous as **rose capital of world;** there are located **Tyler Junior College** and **planetarium, Tyler Rose Garden, Caldwell Children's Zoo** and the **Goodman Museum.** Tyler is home of the **Tyler Rose Festival** each fall. **Morton salt mines** in Grand Saline, 40 miles from park.

Varner-Hogg Plantation State Historical Park is 65.7 acres along Varner Creek east of West Columbia in Brazoria County. The land originally was owned by Martin Varner, a member of Stephen F. Austin's "Old Three Hundred" colony, but became a later home of Texas governor **James Stephen Hogg.** The state acquired the property in 1956 by a deed from Miss Ima Hogg, daughter of the former governor. First rum distillery in Texas established in 1829 by Varner.

Washington-on-the-Brazos State Historical Park, consists of 240.12 acres southwest of Navasota in Washington County. The land was deeded by private owners in 1916. The land includes the site of the signing in 1836 of the Texas **Declaration of Independence** from Mexico, as well as the site of the later signing of the **Constitution of the Republic of Texas.** In 1842 and 1845, the land included the **capitol of the Republic;** it also included the home of **Anson Jones,** last president of the Republic of Texas.

Future Parks

The following parks were in the planning stage when this edition of the Texas Almanac went to press: Arroyo Colorado Site SP, near Harlingen; Davis Hill Site SP, Beaumont; Devils River SNA; Devil's Sinkhole SNA, Rocksprings; Eagle Mountain Lake SP, Fort Worth; Elephant Mountain Ranch SP, Alpine; Fort Boggy SP, Leona; Gorman Falls SP, Bend; Kickapoo Caverns SP, Brackettville; Lake Bastrop SP; Lake Houston SP, La Porte; Lake Tawakoni SP; Rancho de las Cabras SHP, FLoresville; Resaca de la Palma SP, Brownsville; and Village Creek SP, Lumberton.

State Park Trails

Below are listed the recreational trails in Texas state parks, along with notations on which activities are provided for on each park's trails: hiking, nature study/pleasure walking, backpacking (includes trail camping), bicycling, jogging, camping, motorbiking, horseback riding and equestrian camping. Total trail miles may not be available for all uses. For easy reference, those parks that offer horseback riding are designated with an * before the name. Visitors must bring their own horses, except at Palo Duro Canyon State Park, where horses can be rented. For more information contact **Texas Parks and Wildlife Dept.,** 4200 Smith School Rd., Austin 78744.

Atlanta State Park, Cass County; FM 1154 northwest of Atlanta on Lake Wright Patman; 5.0 total trail miles. Hiking, motorbiking, nature study/pleasure walking, camping.

Bastrop State Park, Lost Pines Hiking Trail, Bastrop County; Hwy. 21 east of Bastrop; 8.5 trail miles through Lost Pines. Backpacking, hiking, nature study/pleasure walking, camping.

Bentsen-Rio Grande Valley State Park, Hidalgo County; P43 southwest of McAllen; 3.3 trail miles through South Texas brushland. Hiking, nature study/pleasure walking, camping.

Brazos Bend State Park, Fort Bend County; FM 1462 southeast of Richmond; 16.1 trail miles. Backpacking, bicycling, hiking, jogging, nature study/pleasure walking, camping.

Buescher State Park, Bastrop County; Hwys. 71/95 and FM2104 north of Smithville; 7.8 trail miles through Lost Pines.

Caddo Lake State Park, Harrison County; FM 134 northeast of Marshall on Caddo Lake; 4.0 trail miles through East Texas forests. Hiking, nature study/pleasure walking, camping.

*****Caprock Canyons State Park,** Briscoe County; Hwy. 86 northwest of Quitaque; 14.0 trail miles through scenic canyons. Backpacking, hiking, nature study, camping and designated equestrian camping.

*****Copper Breaks State Park,** Hardeman County; Hwy. 6 south of Quanah on Lake Copper Breaks; 2.5 trail miles. Hiking, nature study/pleasure walking; 320 acres trail area; horseback riding, camping, but horses must be kept in trailers.

Davis Mountains State Park, Jeff Davis County; Hwy. 118 northwest of Fort Davis; 4.0 trail miles. Hiking, nature study/pleasure walking, camping.

Dinosaur Valley State Park, Somervell County; Hwy. 201 northwest of Glen Rose; 5.5 trail miles take you past some of the best-preserved dinosaur fossil footprints in Texas. Backpacking, hiking, nature study/pleasure walking, camping.

Eisenhower State Park, Grayson County; FM 1310 northwest of Denison on Lake Texoma; 4.2 trail miles. Hiking, nature study/pleasure walking, 10 acres trail area; motorbiking, camping.

Enchanted Rock State Natural Area, Gillespie and Llano counties; RR 965 north of Fredericksburg; 8.0 trail miles give opportunities for rock climbing. Backpacking, hiking, nature study/pleasure walking.

Fairfield Lake State Park, Freestone County; FM 3285 northeast of Fairfield on Fairfield Lake; 3.5 trail miles. Backpacking, hiking, nature study/pleasure walking, camping.

Galveston Island State Park, Galveston County; FM 3005 southwest of Galveston seawall on Gulf of Mexico; 4.0 trail miles. Hiking, nature study/pleasure walking, camping.

*****Hill Country State Natural Area,** Bandera and Medina counties; FM 1077 southwest of Bandera. Park use by advance registration only. Backpacking, hiking, horseback riding, nature study.

Hueco Tanks State Historical Park, El Paso County; RR 2775 east of El Paso; 300 acres trail area, 1.5 trail miles with views of Chihuahuan Desert scrub vegetation; caves and rock formations displaying Indian rock art. Hiking, nature study/pleasure walking.

Huntsville State Park, Walker County; I-45 south of Huntsville on Lake Raven; 8.5 trail miles. Hiking, nature study/pleasure walking, camping.

Inks Lake State Park, Burnet County; Hwy. 29 west of Burnet on Inks Lake; 7.5 trail miles. Backpacking, hiking, nature study/pleasure walking.

Jim Hogg State Historical Park, Cherokee County;

Hwy. 84 east of Rusk; 4.0 trail miles. Hiking, nature study/pleasure walking. No camping; day use only.

*Lake Arrowhead State Park, Clay County; FM 1954 southeast of Wichita Falls on Lake Arrowhead; 80 acres trail area. Horseback riding, camping, but horses must be kept in trailers.

Lake Brownwood State Park, Brown County; Hwy. 279 northwest of Brownwood on Lake Brownwood; 4.3 trail miles. Hiking, nature study/pleasure walking, 10 acres trail area; motorbiking, camping.

Lake Livingston State Park, Polk County; FM 3126 southwest of Livingston on Lake Livingston; 6.0 trail miles through East Texas Piney Woods. Bicycling, hiking, jogging, nature study/pleasure walking, camping.

*Lake Mineral Wells State Park, Parker County; Hwy. 180 east of Mineral Wells on Lake Mineral Wells. 13.5 trail miles. Backpacking, hiking, horseback riding, nature study/pleasure walking, camping and designated equestrian camping.

*Lake Somerville State Park, Birch Creek and Nails Creek units, Burleson and Lee counties; Hwy. 36 northwest of Brenham on Somerville Lake; 21.6 trail miles in both units. Backpacking, bicycling, hiking, horseback riding, jogging, nature study/pleasure walking, camping and designated equestrian camping.

Lost Maples State Natural Area, Bandera and Real counties; RR 187 north of Vanderpool, 10.4 trail miles. Backpacking, hiking, nature study/pleasure walking, camping.

McKinney Falls State Park, Travis County; Hwy. 183 south of Austin; 4.5 trail miles. Bicycling, hiking, jogging, nature study/pleasure walking, camping.

Meridian State Park, Bosque County; Hwy. 22 southwest of Meridian on Lake Meridian; 5.0 trail miles. Hiking, nature study/pleasure walking, camping.

*Palo Duro Canyon State Park, Randall County; Hwy. 217 east of Canyon; 9.2 trail miles through spectacular canyon scenery. Hiking, horseback riding, nature study/pleasure walking, camping, but horses must be kept in trailers.

Pedernales Falls State Park, Blanco County; FM 2766 east of Johnson City; 19.4 trail miles. Backpacking, hiking, nature study/pleasure walking, camping.

Seminole Canyon State Historical Park, Val Verde County; Hwy. 90 northwest of Del Rio; 5.0 trail miles with views of Chihuahuan Desert. Hiking, nature study/pleasure walking, camping.

Tyler State Park, Smith County; FM 14 north of Tyler; 3.3 trail miles. Hiking, jogging, nature study/pleasure walking, camping.

Recreational Special Events

Fairs, festivals and other special events provide year-round recreation in Texas. Some are of national interest, and many attract attendance from over the state. Most of them are primarily of local and regional interest.

In addition to those listed here, the recreational paragraphs in the county descriptions refer to numerous events.

The list of fairs and expositions below was compiled from information furnished by the Texas Association of Fairs and Expositions, 411 W. Front, Tyler 75702; the State Department of Highways and Public Transportation, Travel and Information Div., Box 5064, Austin 78763; and local chambers of commerce. Most of the addresses listed below are for local chambers of commerce. Specific dates and more information for listed events, as well as other events taking place in their areas, may be obtained from them.

Fairs, Festivals and Livestock Shows

Abilene—West Texas Fair; Sept.; Box 2281 (79604).

Albany—Fort Griffin Fandangle; June; Box 185 (76430).

Alvarado—Pioneers and Old Settlers Reunion; Aug.; Box 577 (76009).

Amarillo—Tri-State Fair; Sept.; Box 9480 (79105).

Angleton—Brazoria Co. Fair; Oct.; Box 1356 (77515).

Athens—Black-Eyed Pea Jamboree; July; Box 2600 (75751).

Athens—Old Fiddlers' Reunion; May; Box 2600 (75751).

Austin—Aqua Festival; Aug.; Box 1967 (78767).

Austin—Austin-Travis Co. Livestock Show; March or April; Box 1967 (78767).

Austin—Highland Lakes Bluebonnet Trail; April; Box 1967 (78767).

Austin—Laguna Gloria Fiesta; May; 3809 W. 35th (78703).

Bay City—Bay City Rice Festival; Oct.; Box 768 (77404).

Bay City—Matagorda Co. Fair; March; Box 768 (77404).

Beaumont—Neches River Festival; April; Box 3150 (77704).

Beaumont—South Texas State Fair; Oct.; Box 3150 (77704).

Bellville—Austin Co. Fair; Oct.; Box 670 (77418).

Belton—Belton Rodeo and Celebration; July; Box 659 (76513).

Big Spring—Howard Co. Fair; Sept.; Box 1395 (79721).

Boerne—Boerne Berges Fest; June; 1209 S. Main (78006).

Boerne—Kendall Co. Fair; Sept.; 1209 S. Main (78006).

Brackettville—Western Horse Races and Barbecue; Sept.; Box 386 (78832).

Brenham—Washington Co. Fair; Sept.; 314 S. Austin (77833).

Brownsville—Charro Days; Feb.; Box 752 (78520).

Caldwell—Burleson Co. Fair; June; Box 126 (77836).

Canyon—"TEXAS" Historical Musical Drama; June; Box 268 (79015).

Clifton—Central Texas Fair & Rodeo; Aug.; Box 104 (76634).

Columbus—Colorado Co. Fair; Sept.; Box 343 (78934).

Columbus—Magnolia Homes Tour; May; Box 343 (78934).

Conroe—Montgomery Co. Fair; March; Box 2347 (77305).

Corpus Christi—Bayfest; Sept.; Box 640 (78403).

Corpus Christi—Buccaneer Days; April-May; Box 640 (78403).

Dalhart—Inter State Fair; Sept.; Box 967 (79022).

Dalhart—XIT Rodeo & Reunion; Aug.; Box 967 (79022).

Dallas—State Fair of Texas; Oct.; Box 26010 (75226).

DeLeon—DeLeon Peach & Melon Festival; Aug.; Box 44 (76444).

Decatur—Wise Co. Old Settlers Reunion; July; Box 474 (76234).

Denton—North Texas State Fair; Aug.; Box P (76202).

Donna—South Texas Lamb & Sheep Expo.; Jan.; 301 S. 8th (78537).

Edna—Jackson Co. Fair; Sept.-Oct.; Box 788 (77957).

El Paso—Southwestern International Livestock Show & Rodeo; Feb.; Box 10239 (79993).

Ennis—National Polka Festival; May; Box 1177 (75120).

Fairfield—Freestone Co. Fair; Aug.; Box 956 (75840).

Flatonia—Czhilispiel; Oct.; Box 651 (78941).

Fort Stockton—Pecos Co. Fair; Oct.; Box C (79735).

Fort Worth—Pioneer Days; Sept.; 131 E. Exchange Ave. (76106).

Fort Worth—Southwestern Expositioin and Livestock Show; Jan.-Feb.; 777 Taylor, 900 (76102).

Fredericksburg—Easter Fires Pageant; Easter; Box 506 (78624).

Fredericksburg—Gillespie Co. Fair; Aug.; Box 506 (78624).

Fredericksburg—Oktoberfest; Oct.; Box 506 (78624).

Freer—Freer Rattlesnake Roundup; April; Box 717 (78357).

Galveston—Dickens' Evening on the Strand; Dec.; 621 Moody, 300 (77550).

Giddings—Lee County Jr. Livestock Show; March; Box 180 (78942).

Gilmer—East Texas Yamboree; Oct.; Box 854 (75644).

Graham—Young Co. Fair; Sept.; Box 299 (76046).

Grand Prairie—National Championship Pow-Wow; Sept.; Box 531227 (75053).

Greenville—Hunt Co. Fair; Aug.; Box 1055 (75403).

Groesbeck—Limestone Co. Fair; June; Box 326 (76642).

Hallettsville—Lavaca Co. Fair; Oct.-Nov.; Box 313 (77964).

Harker Heights—Heights Oktober Fest; Oct.; Box 2167 (76543).

Hearne—Robertson Co. Fair; March; Box 713 (77859).

Helotes—Helotes Festival; May; Box 376 (78023).

Hempstead—Waller Co. Fair; Sept.; Box 921 (77445).

Hico—Old Settlers Reunion; July; Rt. 1 (76457).

Hidalgo—Border Fest; March; 611 E. Coma (78557).

Hondo—Medina Co. Fair; Sept.; Box 126 (78861).

Houston—Houston-Harris Co. Fair; Oct.; One Abercrombie Dr. (77084).

Houston—Houston Livestock Show & Rodeo; Feb.-March; 1100 Milam Bldg. (77002).

Houston—The Houston Festival; March; 1100 Milam Bldg. (77002).

More on Page 132.

TEXAS STATE PARKS

PARK/†TYPE OF PARK/SPECIAL FEATURES	NEAREST TOWN	CAMPING††	SCREENED SHELTERS	GROUP FACILITY	RESTROOMS	SHOWERS	CABINS	PICNICKING	GROCERIES	FISHING	SWIMMING	WATER SKIING	BOAT RAMP	MUSEUM/EXHIBIT	HISTORIC STRUCTURE	DAY USE ONLY	TRAILER DUMP STATION	NATURE/HIKING TRAILS	MISCELLANEOUS
ABILENE SP	BUFFALO GAP	9	●	DG	●	●		●			●					●	●	●	
ACTON SHP (Grave of Davy Crockett's wife)	GRANBURY			DG	●			●							●	●			
ADMIRAL NIMITZ MUSEUM SHP	FREDERICKSBURG			●				●						●	●	●		●	A
ATLANTA SP	ATLANTA	10		DG	●	●		●		○	○	○	●			●	●		
BALMORHEA SP (San Solomon Springs Courts)	BALMORHEA	9			●	●		●			●					●	●		I
BASTROP SP	BASTROP	6		BG	●	●	●	●	●	●	○						●	●	P G,D
BATTLESHIP TEXAS HS (At San Jacinto Battleground)	HOUSTON													●	●	●			
BENTSEN-RIO GRANDE VALLEY SP	MISSION	11		BG	●	●		●		○			●				●	●	
BIG BEND RANCH SNA	PRESIDIO	1																	
BIG SPRING SP	BIG SPRING				●			●					●			●		●	D
BLANCO SP	BLANCO	10	●	DG	●	●		●		○	○						●		B
BONHAM SP	BONHAM	12		BG	●	●		●		●	○		●				●		B
BRAZOS BEND SP	RICHMOND	6	●	DG	●	●		●		●			●				●	●	P T1,2
BRYAN BEACH SP (Undeveloped Gulf Beach)	FREEPORT	1						○		○	○								
BUESCHER SP	SMITHVILLE	9	●	BG	●	●		●		○	○						●	●	
CADDO LAKE SP	KARNACK	10	●	BG	●	●	●	●		●	○	○	●	●			●	●	B
CADDOAN MOUNDS SHP	ALTO				●			●						●	●	●		●	
CAPROCK CANYONS SP	QUITAQUE	6		DG	●	●		●		●	○		●				●	●	EC S,P
CASSELLS BOYKIN SP	ZAVALLA	2			●			●		○	○	○	●			●			
CEDAR HILL SP	DALLAS	3		DG	●	●		●		●	●	○	●			●			
CHOKE CANYON SP, Calliham Unit	THREE RIVERS	9	●	DG	●	●		●	●	○	○	●	●				●		A,B
CHOKE CANYON SP, South Shore Unit	THREE RIVERS	9		DG	●	●		●		○	○	○	●			●			
CHRISTMAS BAY SP (Undeveloped Gulf Beach)	LA PORTE	1						○		○	○	○							
CLEBURNE SP	CLEBURNE	10	●	BG	●	●		●	●	○	●		●				●	●	B
COLORADO BEND SP (Only 300 Vehicles Allowed)	BEND	1			●					●	○							●	P,T1
CONFEDERATE REUNION GROUNDS SHP	MEXIA			DG				●		○	○				●	●	●		
COPANO BAY SFP*	ROCKPORT				●					●			●						
COPPER BREAKS SP	QUANAH	6			●	●		●		●	○		●				●	●	L,S
DAINGERFIELD SP	DAINGERFIELD	10		BG	●	●	●	●	●	●	●	○					●	●	B
DAVIS MOUNTAINS SP (Indian Lodge)	FORT DAVIS	10		DG	●	●		●							●		●	●	D,I
DINOSAUR VALLEY SP (Dinosaur Footprints)	GLEN ROSE	9		DG	●	●		●		○	○						●	●	L,S
EISENHOWER SP (Marina)	DENISON	10	●	BG	●	●		●		●	○	○	●				●	●	
EISENHOWER BIRTHPLACE SHP	DENISON			●				●						●	●	●			
ENCHANTED ROCK SNA	FREDERICKSBURG	5		DG	●	●		●										●	R,P
FAIRFIELD LAKE SP	FAIRFIELD	6			●	●		●		●	○	○	●				●	●	P
FALCON SP (Airstrip)	ZAPATA	10	●		●	●		●		○	○	○	●			●			
FANNIN BATTLEGROUND SHP	GOLIAD			DG	●			●						●		●			
FANTHORP INN SHP	ANDERSON				●			●						●	●	●			
FORT GRIFFIN SHP	ALBANY	9		DG	●	●		●		○					●	●		●	L
FORT LANCASTER SHP	OZONA				●									●	●	●			
FORT LEATON SHP	PRESIDIO				●			●						●	●	●			
FORT McKAVETT SHP	FORT McKAVETT				●			●						●	●	●		●	
FORT PARKER SP	MEXIA	9	●	BG	●	●		●		●	○	○	●				●	●	B
FORT RICHARDSON SHP	JACKSBORO	6		DG	●	●		●		○				●	●	●	●	●	
FRANKLIN MOUNTAINS SP (Pedestrian Access Only)	EL PASO				●	●		●										●	
FULTON MANSION HSP	FULTON													●	●	●			
GALVESTON ISLAND SP ("The Lone Star" Drama)	GALVESTON	3	●	BG	●	●		●		○	○						●	●	
GARNER SP	CONCAN	9	●	BG	●	●	●	●	●	●	○	○					●	●	M,B T2
GOLIAD SHP	GOLIAD	8	●	BG	●	●		●		○	○			●	●	●	●	●	
GOOSE ISLAND SP	ROCKPORT	9		BG	●	●		●		●	○	○	●				●	●	
GOVERNOR HOGG SHRINE SHP	QUITMAN			DG	●			●						●	●	●		●	
GUADALUPE RIVER SP	BOERNE	9			●	●		●		○	○						●	●	
HILL COUNTRY SNA	BANDERA	1						●										●	S,EC P,T1
HONEY CREEK SNA (Guided Tour Only)	BOERNE														●			●	
HUECO TANKS SHP (Indian Pictographs)	EL PASO	9			●	●		●									●	●	R
HUNTSVILLE SP	HUNTSVILLE	9	●	DG	●	●		●	●	●	●		○	●	●		●	●	B T1,2
INKS LAKE SP	BURNET	6	●	BG	●	●		●	●	●	●	○	●				●	●	P G,B
JIM HOGG SHP	RUSK				●			●						●	●	●		●	
JOSE ANTONIO NAVARRO SHP	SAN ANTONIO				●									●	●	●			
KERRVILLE-SCHREINER SP	KERRVILLE	10	●	BG	●	●		●		●	○		●				●	●	
LAKE ARROWHEAD SP	WICHITA FALLS	9		DG	●	●		●	●	●	○	○	●				●	●	S,B
LAKE BOB SANDLIN SP	MOUNT PLEASANT	6	●	DG	●	●		●		●	○	○	●				●	●	P

TEXAS STATE PARKS

Park	City	CAMPING††	SCREENED SHELTERS	GROUP FACILITY	RESTROOMS	SHOWERS	CABINS	PICNICKING	GROCERIES	FISHING	SWIMMING	WATER SKIING	BOAT RAMP	MUSEUM/EXHIBIT	HISTORIC STRUCTURE	DAY USE ONLY	TRAILER DUMP STATION	NATURE/HIKING TRAILS	MISCELLANEOUS
LAKE BROWNWOOD SP	BROWNWOOD	10	●	BG	●	●	●	●	●	●	●	○	●				●	●	
LAKE COLORADO CITY SP	COLORADO CITY	9	●	DG	●	●		●		●	●	○	●				●		
LAKE CORPUS CHRISTI SP	MATHIS	10	●	DG	●	●		●		●	●	○	●	●			●		B
LAKE LEWISVILLE SP	LEWISVILLE	9	●	BG	●	●		●		○	○	○	●	●			●		
LAKE LIVINGSTON SP	LIVINGSTON	9	●	BG	●	●		●	●	●	●	○	●				●	●	T1,2
LAKE MINERAL WELLS SP	MINERAL WELLS	6	●	DG	●	●		●		●	●	○	●				●	●	EC,R,P,S
LAKE SOMERVILLE SP	SOMERVILLE	6		BG	●	●		●		●	○	○	●	●			●	●	P,T1
LAKE TEXANA SP	EDNA	5		DG	●	●		●		●	○	○	●				●	●	
LAKE WHITNEY SP (Airstrip)	WHITNEY	10	●	BG	●	●		●		○	○	○	●				●	●	
LANDMARK INN SHP (Hotel Rooms)	CASTROVILLE			DG	●			●							●	●		●	I
LIPANTITLAN SHP	ORANGE GROVE	1			●			●											
LOCKHART SP	LOCKHART	9		BG	●	●		●		●							●		G
LONGHORN CAVERN SP (Cavern Tours)*	BURNET				●			●						●	●		●		
LOST MAPLES SNA	VANDERPOOL	7			●	●		●		○	○			●			●	●	P
LUBBOCK LAKE LANDMARK SHP	LUBBOCK				●			●						●	●	●		●	
LYNDON B. JOHNSON SHP	STONEWALL			DG	●			●		○	●			●	●	●		●	L,A
MACKENZIE SP (Prairie Dog Town)*	LUBBOCK				●			●	●					●					G
MAGOFFIN HOME SHP	EL PASO				●									●	●	●			
MARTIN CREEK LAKE SP	TATUM	6	●	DG	●	●		●		●	○	○	●				●	●	P
MARTIN DIES JR. SP	JASPER	10	●	DG	●	●		●		●	○	○	●				●	●	
MATAGORDA ISLAND SP (Boat or Air Access Only)	PORT O'CONNOR	1			●			○		○	○	○			●			●	
MATAGORDA PENINSULA SP (Undeveloped Gulf Beach)	LA PORTE	1						○		○	○	○							
McKINNEY FALLS SP	AUSTIN	5	●	BG	●	●		●		○				●	●		●	●	T2
MERIDIAN SP	MERIDIAN	8	●	BG	●	●		●		○	○	○	●				●	●	
MISSION TEJAS SHP	WECHES	6	●	DG	●	●		●		○	○				●		●	●	
MONAHANS SANDHILLS SP	MONAHANS	9			●	●		●						●			●	●	S
MONUMENT HILL/KREISCHE BREWERY SHP	LA GRANGE				●			●						●	●	●		●	
MOTHER NEFF SP	MOODY	9		DG	●	●		●		●							●	●	
MUSTANG ISLAND SP	PORT ARANSAS	7			●	●		●		○	○						●		
OLD FORT PARKER SHP	GROESBECK				●			●						●	●	●			
PALMETTO SP	LULING	9		DG	●	●		●		●	○						●	●	
PALO DURO CANYON SP (Summer Drama: "Texas")	CANYON	9			●	●		●	●	●				●			●	●	H,S,L,O
PEDERNALES FALLS SP	JOHNSON CITY	7		OG	●	●		●		○	○						●	●	P
PORT ISABEL LIGHTHOUSE SHP	PORT ISABEL														●	●			
PORT LAVACA SFP*	PORT LAVACA				●			●		●			●						
POSSUM KINGDOM SP	CADDO	9			●	●	●	●	●	●	○	○	●				●		L,B
PURTIS CREEK SP	EUSTACE	6			●	●		●		●			●				●	●	P
RUSK/PALESTINE SP (Texas State RR Terminals)	RUSK/PALESTINE	10		DG	●	●		●		○							●	●	
SABINE PASS BATTLEGROUND SHP	PORT ARTHUR				●			●		●			○			●		●	
SAM BELL MAXEY HOUSE SHP	PARIS				●										●	●	●		
SAN JACINTO BATTLEGROUND SHP (Battleship Texas)	HOUSTON			DG	●			●		○				●	●	●			
SAN JOSE MISSION SHP*	SAN ANTONIO				●										●	●	●		
SEA RIM SP	PORT ARTHUR	7			●	●		●		○	○	○	●				●	●	
SEBASTOPOL SHP	SEGUIN				●			●							●	●	●		
SEMINOLE CANYON SHP (Indian Pictographs)	LANGTRY	9			●	●		●						●			●	●	T1
SHELDON SP	HOUSTON							○		●			●						
SOUTH LLANO RIVER SP	JUNCTION	7			●	●		●		●	○						●	●	
STARR MANSION SHP	MARSHALL				●			●						●	●	●			
STEPHEN F. AUSTIN SHP	SAN FELIPE	11	●	DG	●	●		●		○	●			●			●	●	G
TEXAS STATE RAILROAD SHP (Contact Park for Schedule of Runs)	RUSK				●									●		●			
TIPS SP*	THREE RIVERS	9		DG	●	●		●		○							●		
TYLER SP	TYLER	12	●	BG	●	●		●	●	●	●		●				●	●	B
VARNER-HOGG PLANTATION SHP (Guided Tours)	WEST COLUMBIA				●			●						●	●	●		●	
WASHINGTON-ON-THE-BRAZOS SHP (Anson Jones Home)	WASHINGTON			DG	●			●						●	●	●		●	A

†Types of Parks: SP, State Park; SHP, State Historical Park; SNA, State Natural Area; SFP, State Fishing Pier.

††Type(s) of Camping: 1—Primitive; 2—Water Connections; 3—Water & Electricity; 4—Water, Electricity & Sewage; 5—1 & 2; 6—1, 2 & 3; 7—1 & 3; 8—1,3 & 4; 9—2 & 3; 10—2, 3 & 4; 11—2 & 4; 12—3 & 4.

FACILITIES

* FACILITIES NOT OPERATED BY PARKS AND WILDLIFE
** ONLY WALK-IN TENT CAMPING NO VEHICULAR CAMPING PERMITTED
○ PERMITTED BUT FACILITIES NOT PROVIDED
● FACILITIES OR SERVICES PROVIDED FOR ACTIVITY

A AUDITORIUM
B BOATS FOR RENT
BG BOTH DAY AND NIGHT GROUP FACILITIES
CT CHEMICAL TOILETS
D SCENIC DRIVE
DG DAY USE GROUP FACILITIES
EC EQUESTRIAN CAMPING AREA
G GOLF
H HORSES FOR RENT
I HOTEL-TYPE FACILITIES
L TEXAS LONGHORN HERD
M MINIATURE GOLF
OG OVERNIGHT GROUP FACILITIES

P CAMPING — BACKPACKING
R ROCK CLIMBING
S HORSEBACK AREAS/TRAILS
T1 MOUNTAIN BIKE
T2 SURFACED BIKE TRAIL

For information on those park facilities accessible to and usable by the handicapped, ask for park brochure on handicapped facilities.

From Page 129.

Hughes Springs—Wildflower Trails of Texas; April; Box 218 (75656).

Huntsville—Walker Co. Fair; April; Box 538 (77342).

Jefferson—Historical Pilgrimage; May; 116 W. Austin (75657).

Jefferson—Marion Co. Fair; Oct.; 116 W. Austin (75657).

Johnson City—Blanco Co. Fair; Aug.; Box 261 (78636).

Kenedy—Bluebonnet Days; April-May; Box 1929 (78119).

Kerrville—Kerr Co. Fair; June; 1200 Sidney Baker (78028).

Kerrville—Texas Folk Festival; May; 1200 Sidney Baker (78028).

Kerrville—Texas State Arts & Crafts Fair; May; Box 1527 (78028).

Killeen—Central Texas Exposition; March-April; Box 548 (76540).

La Grange—Fayette Co. Fair; Aug.- Sept.; 163 W. La Fayette (78945).

Lamesa—Dawson Co. Fair; Sept.; Drawer J (79331).

Laredo—Laredo Frontier Days & Rattlesnake Roundup; May; Box 790 (78042).

Laredo—Laredo Int'l Fair & Exposition; March; Box 790 (78042).

Laredo—Washington's Birthday Celebration; Feb.; Box 790 (78040).

Longview—Gregg Co. Fair; Sept.; Box 472 (75606).

Lubbock—Panhandle-South Plains Fair; Sept.; Box 561 (79408).

Luling—Watermelon Thump; June; Box 710 (78648).

Marshall—Central East Texas Fair; Sept.; Box 520 (75670).

Mercedes—Rio Grande Valley Livestock Show; March; Box 37 (78570).

Mesquite—Mesquite Championship Rodeo; April-Sept.; 1818 Rodeo Dr. (75149).

Mexia—Limestone Co. Fair; June; Box 352 (76667).

Mission—Texas Citrus Fiesta; Jan.; Box 431 (78572).

Mount Pleasant—Titus Co. Fair; Sept.; Box 1237 (75455).

Nacogdoches—Piney Woods Fair; Oct.; Box 631918 (75963).

Navasota—Grimes Co. Fair; June; Box 530 (77868).

New Braunfels—Comal Co. Fair; Sept.; Box 311417 (78131).

New Braunfels—Wurstfest; Nov.; Box 311417 (78131).

Odessa—Permian Basin Fair & Exposition; Sept.; Box 3626 (79760).

Palestine—Anderson Co. Fair; May; Box 1177 (75802).

Palestine—Dogwood Trails Festival; March; Box 1177 (75802).

Paris—Red River Valley Fair; Aug.-Sept.; Box 1096 (75461).

Pasadena—Pasadena Livestock Show & Rodeo; Sept. 4334 Fairmont Pkwy. (77504).

Plantersville—Texas Renaissance Festival; Oct.-Nov.; Rt. 2, Box 219A-1 (77363).

Port Arthur—CavOILcade; Oct.; 4749 Twin City Hwy, 300N (77642).

Port Lavaca—Calhoun Co. Fair; Oct.; Box 528 (77979).

Refugio—Refugio Co. Fair; Oct.; Box 127 (78377).

Rio Grande City—Starr Co. Fair; March; Box 841 (78582).

Rosenberg—Fort Bend Co. Fair; Sept.-Oct.; 4120 Ave. H (77471).

Salado—Gathering of the Scottish Clans of Texas; Nov.; Box 81 (76571).

San Angelo—San Angelo Stock Show & Rodeo; March; 500 Rio Concho Dr. (76903).

San Antonio—Fiesta San Antonio; April; Box 1628 (78296).

San Antonio—Texas Folklife Festival; Aug.; Box 1628 (78296).

Santa Fe—Galveston Co. Fair & Rodeo; April-May; Box 681 (77510).

Seguin—Guadalupe Co. Fair; Sept.; Box 710 (78156).

Shamrock—St. Patrick's Day Celebration; March; Box 588 (79079).

Snyder—Scurry Co. Fair; Sept.; Drawer CC (79549).

Stamford—Texas Cowboy Reunion; July; Box 1206 (79553).

Sulphur Springs—Hopkins Co. Fall Festival; Sept.; Box 347 (75482).

Sweetwater—Rattlesnake Roundup; March; Box 1148 (79556).

Texarkana—Four States Fair; Sept.-Oct.; Box 1468 (75504).

Tyler—East Texas Fair; Sept.-Oct.; 411 W. Front (75702).

Tyler—Texas Rose Festival; Oct.; Box 390 (75710).

Victoria—Victoria Livestock Show; March; Box 2465 (77904).

Waco—Brazos River Festival & Cotton Palace Pageant; April; Drawer 1220 (76703).

Waco—Heart O'Texas Fair; Oct.; Box 1220 (76703).

Waxahachie—Flea Market Cajunfest; Aug.; Box 187 (75165).

Waxahachie—Scarborough Faire; May; Box 538 (75165).

Weatherford—Parker County Peach Festival; July; Box 310 (76086).

Wharton—Texas Beef Exposition; Nov.-Dec.; Box 868 (77488).

Wharton—Wharton Co. Youth Fair & Exposition; April; Box 868 (77488).

Winnsboro—Autumn Trails Festival; Oct.; 201 W. Broadway (75494).

Woodville—Tyler Co. Dogwood Festival; March; 201 N. Magnolia (75979).

Yorktown—Western Days; Oct.; Box 488 (78164).

National Parks, Historical Sites, Recreation Areas in Texas

Texas has two national parks, a national seashore, a biological preserve, several historic sites, memorials and recreation areas and 10 national wildlife refuges under supervision of the U.S. Department of Interior. In addition, the state has four national forests (see index) under jurisdiction of U.S. Department of Agriculture.

For the number of visitors to national parks in Texas since 1980, see table on following page.

Alibates Flint Quarries National Monument consists of 1,079 acres in Potter County. For more than 10,000 years, pre-Columbian Indians dug agatized limestone from the quarries to make projectile points, knives, scrapers and other tools. The area is presently undeveloped. There were 3,418 daily visits made to the area in 1990. You may visit the flint quarries on guided walking tours with a park ranger. Tours are at 10:00 a.m. and 2:00 p.m., from Memorial Day to Labor Day. Off-season tours can be arranged by writing to Lake Meredith Recreation Area, P.O. Box 1460, Fritch 79036 or by calling (806) 857-3151.

Amistad National Recreation Area contains the U.S. portion of **Amistad Reservoir** on the Rio Grande. Of 65,000 acres in the area, 43,250 acres are in United States. Limited camping space, and camping from boats permitted on shore. Commercial campgrounds, motels, hotels in area. Open year round. In 1990, there were 22,033 overnight stays reported, and 1,307,602 daily visits.

Big Bend National Park, established in 1944, has spectacular mountain and desert scenery, a variety of unusual geological structures. Located in the great bend of the **Rio Grande,** the international boundary between United States and Mexico. Park contains 801,-163 acres. Numerous campsites are located in park, and the Chisos Mountain Lodge has accommodations for approximately 345 guests. Write for reservations to National Park Concessions, Inc., Big Bend National Park, Texas 79834. Park open year round. There were 214,982 overnight stays in 1990, and 258,400 daily visits.

Big Thicket National Preserve, established in 1974, consists of 86,000 acres of diverse flora and fauna, often nicknamed the "biological crossroads of North America." The preserve has been designated a "Man and the Biosphere" by the United Nations Educational, Scientific and Cultural Organization (UNESCO). The Visitor Information Station (409/246-2337), which is handicapped accessible, is located on FM 420, approximately seven miles north of Kountze. It is open daily from 9:00 a.m. to 5:00 p.m. Naturalist activities are available by reservation only. Reservations can be made through the station. The eight hiking trails, ranging in length from one-half mile to 18 miles visit a variety of forest communities that demonstrate the diversity of the Big Thicket. Parking and detailed maps are available at the trailheads. Also, the two shortest trails, the Pitcher Plant Trail and the Sundew Trail, are handicapped accessible. The trails are open year round, but keep in mind that some flooding may occur after heavy rains. For your comfort, bring drinking water, wear comfortable shoes, and don't forget insect repellent during warm weather. Horses are permitted on the Big Sandy Horse Trail only. Pets, off-road vehicles and firearms are not permitted on any trails. Backcountry camping and hunting are allowed in certain areas by permit only. Fishing is allowed in accordance with state law. Boating and canoeing are popular on Preserve corridor units. There were 77,930 daily visits recorded in 1990. Park headquarters is temporarily located at 3785 Milam, Beaumont 77701; telephone: (409) 839-2689.

Chamizal National Memorial, established in 1963 and opened to the public in 1973, consists of 54.9 acres dedicated to the peaceful settlement of a 99-year-old boundary dispute between the United States and Mexico. Located in the south-central part of El Paso, the park is open year-round from 8:00 a.m. to 5:00 p.m., and from 7:00 p.m. to 11:00 p.m. during performances.

It hosts a variety of programs throughout the year, some of which include: the Border Folk Festival (first weekend in October); the Siglo de Oro "Spanish Golden Age Presentation" (February-March); the Border Jazz Festival (May); the Zarzuela Festival (July-August); and the Sixteenth of September "Grito" Celebration. All programs are held in the park's quest to commemorate the signing of the Chamizal Treaty through the promotion of intercultural communication, understanding and harmony. There were 205,073 daily visits in 1990.

Fort Davis National Historic Site in Jeff Davis County was a key post in the West Texas defense system, guarding immigrants and tradesmen on the San Antonio-El Paso Road. Fort Davis was manned by black troops for many of the years it was active. These troops, called "Buffalo Soldiers" because of their curly hair, fought with great distinction in the Indian Wars. Henry O. Flipper, the first black graduate of West Point, served at Fort Davis in the early 1880s. The 460-acre historic site is located in the **Davis Mountains,** the second-highest mountain range in the state. The site includes a museum, an auditorium with daily audio-visual programs, restored and refurnished buildings, picnic area and hiking trails. An annual festival is held on the grounds the Saturday of Labor Day weekend. The site was established in 1961. Lodging is available in the nearby community of Fort Davis. Open year round; 56,619 visits in 1990.

Guadalupe Mountains National Park, established Sept. 15, 1972, consists of 86,416 acres in Hudspeth and Culberson counties. A mountain mass of Permian limestone rises abruptly from the surrounding desert and contains one of the most extensive fossil reefs on record. Deep canyons cut through this exposed fossil reef and provide a rare opportunity for geologic study. Special points of interest are **McKittrick Canyon,** a fragile riparian environment, and **Guadalupe Peak,** the highest in Texas. Campground near Pine Springs Headquarters area has 20 tent sites plus RV parking, and is hub for 80 miles of trails. Dog Canyon area located one mile south of Texas-New Mexico state line, at end of NM State Road 137 and County Road 414, contains 18 tent spaces. A comfort station and parking spaces for five self-contained recreational vehicles are also available. Visit the headquarters Visitor Center for orientation, free information and exhibits. Open year round. Lodging at Van Horn, Texas; White's City or Carlsbad, N.M. There were 18,115 overnight stays in 1990 and 192,890 visits.

Lake Meredith National Recreation Area, about 35 miles northeast of Amarillo, consists of a reservoir behind **Sanford Dam** on the Canadian River, in Moore, Hutchinson and Potter counties. Occupies 44,977 acres;

popular for water-based activities. Marine launching ramps, picnic areas, unimproved campsites. Commercial lodging and trailer hookups available in nearby towns. Open year round. There were 165,907 recorded overnight stays in 1990 and 1,358,871 visits. Headquarters is located at 419 E. Broadway, Fritch 79036; phone (806) 857-3151.

Lyndon B. Johnson National Historical Park includes the boyhood home of the 36th President of United States, and the Johnson Settlement in Johnson City; free bus tour starting at the LBJ State Park includes the **LBJ Birthplace,** old school, cemetery and close-up exterior look at the **Texas White House.** Site in Blanco and Gillespie counties was established Dec. 2, 1969, and contains 554 acres. Open year round. No camping on site; commercial campground, motels in area. There were 193,066 visits in 1990.

Padre Island National Seashore consists of a 67.5-mile stretch of a barrier island along the Gulf Coast; noted for its wide sand beaches, excellent fishing and abundant bird and marine life. Contains 130,355 acres in Kleberg, Willacy and Kenedy counties. Open year round. One paved campground (fee charged) located north of Malaquite Beach, unpaved (primitive) campground area south of beach. Five miles of beach are accessible by regular vehicles (including motor homes) and are open to camping. Fifty-five miles of beach are accessible only by 4x4 vehicles. All 55 miles of beach are also open to camping. Commercial lodging available outside boundaries of National Seashore. There were 78,267 recorded overnight stays in 1990 and 593,270 visits.

Palo Alto Battlefield National Historic Site, Brownsville, contains the site of the first major battle in the Mexican-American War. The battle was fought on May 8, 1846, and represents the first battle of the campaign in northeast Mexico led by General Zachary Taylor. Historical markers are located at the junction of state highways 1847 and 511. There is no site access at this time and there are no public facilities. For additional information contact the Southwest Region, National Park Service, P.O. Box 728, Santa Fe, New Mexico 87504-0728.

Rio Grande Wild and Scenic River, is a 191.2-mile strip on the American shore of the Rio Grande in the Chihuahuan Desert that protects the river. It begins in **Big Bend National Park** and continues downstream to the Terrell-Val Verde County line. There are federal facilities in **Big Bend National Park** only. There were 525 daily visits in 1990, with 4,394 overnight stays.

San Antonio Missions National Historical Park consists of four Spanish Colonial Missions — Concepcion, San Jose, San Juan and Espada — and two of the best preserved remains of the Spanish Colonial irrigation system in the United States represented in the Espada dam and aqueduct. All were crucial elements to Spanish settlement on the Texas frontier. When Franciscan attempts to establish a chain of missions in East Texas in the late 1600s failed, the Spanish Crown ordered the missions transferred to the lush valley of the San Antonio River in 1731, where they flourished until secularization in 1824. One of the principal institutions of settlement on Spain's northern frontier, the missions of San Antonio, today part of the National Park System, are physical reminders of a glorious chapter in **More on Next Page.**

Recreational Visits to National Parks in Texas

This information on National Parks in Texas was furnished by the **National Park Service.** Recreation visits to National Park Service Areas in Texas, by years, numbered 4,747,800 in 1982; 4,664,800 in 1983; 4,800,795 in 1984; 4,539,084 in 1985; 4,573,390 in 1986; 4,817,794 in 1987; 4,517,006 in 1988; 4,488,658 in 1989; and 4,773,653 in 1990. Because of rounding, totals may not add up.

Name of Facility	1987	1988	1989	1990
Alibates Flint Quarries National Monument	2,500	2,142	3,831	3,418
Amistad National Recreation Area	1,219,980	1,284,600	1,321,170	1,527,340
Big Bend National Park	227,940	239,600	281,750	257,390
Big Thicket Preserve	62,460	71,760	102,180	77,950
Chamizal National Memorial	220,970	211,510	200,680	199,000
Fort Davis National Historic Site	52,240	54,540	55,030	56,550
Guadalupe Mountains National Park	156,360	181,730	192,200	192,890
Lake Meredith National Recreation Area	1,280,510	1,321,740	1,274,910	1,358,790
Lyndon B. Johnson National Historical Park	330,850	303,210	200,540	193,080
Padre Island National Seashore	605,990	587,290	586,260	593,270
Rio Grande Wild and Scenic River	734	834	677	525
San Antonio Missions National Historical Park	257,260	258,050	269,430	313,450

Woodland Trails

Below is given brief description of the 11 Texas Forestry Association's Woodland Trails. For further information, write Texas Forestry Assn., P.O. Box 1488, Lufkin, Texas 75902, or phone (409) 632-TREE.

Four-C Trail—Eastern Houston County, 18 miles east of Crockett on Texas 7. Follows old rail tramways along Neches River bottom. Camping. Length, 20 miles.

Bull Creek Trail—Northwestern Polk County, 8.5 miles west of Corrigan on U.S. 287. Winds along banks of Bull Creek. Noted for its large magnolias, oaks, gums and pines. Length, 1½ miles.

Griff Ross Trail—Southern Rusk County, 2.2 miles east of Mount Enterprise on U.S. 84. Follows gentle slope of hill to edge of a forest stream. Donated to TFA by Dr. and Mrs. William F. Ross, Dallas, in memory of his parents, Dr. and Mrs. Griff Ross, Mount Enterprise. No picnicking or camping. Three-quarter mile loop.

Dogwood Trail—Central Tyler County, 3 miles east of Woodville off U.S. 190. Winding along banks of Theuvenin Creek, trail is noted for dogwood blooms in spring. Length, 1½ miles.

Longleaf Pine Trail—Northeastern Polk County, 3 miles east of Camden on Farm Road 62. Noted for large longleaf pines, many 100 years or older. Features nesting holes of rare red-cockaded woodpecker. Length, 2 miles.

Big Creek Trail—East Central San Jacinto County, 6 miles west of Shepherd on Forest Service Road 217. Four loops, partially following Big Creek, clear running stream. Camping, picnicking, swimming and showers at Double Lake Recreation Area. Length, 3½ miles.

Moscow Trail—Northern Polk County, 1 mile south of Moscow on U.S. 59. Meanders along banks of Long King Creek and is noted for tall pines and large variety of other forest plants. Length, 2 miles.

Sawmill Trail—North Jasper County, off Texas 63 seven miles southeast of Zavalla. One trailhead at **Boykin Springs campground** and one at **Bouton Lake campground**, with a spur to abandoned **Aldridge Sawmill** site. Length, 5½ miles.

Sylvan Trail—Central Newton County, opposite roadside park on U.S. 190, 4 miles southeast of Newton. Meanders through area noted for picturesque loblolly pines. Location of two old logging railroads. Length, ½ mile.

Yellow Poplar Trail—Northern Marion County, 8.5 miles north of Jefferson on U.S. 59 opposite roadside park. Winds through only stand of yellow poplar in Texas, and includes state champion tree. Length, 1 mile.

Wild Azalea Canyons Trail—Northern Newton County, 4.4 miles north of Newton on Texas 87, then 6.7 miles east on Farm Road 1414, then 1.8 miles on unpaved roads. Inside pocket wilderness noted for longleaf pines, rock cliffs and wild azaleas that bloom each spring. Several trails of varying lengths; trails open only during bloom season, March-April.

From previous page.

Spanish Colonial history. The 475-acre park is located in the city of San Antonio. The four missions, which are still in use today as active parishes, are open to the public from 8-5 CST and 9-6 DST. For more information, contact San Antonio Missions National Historical Park, 2202 Roosevelt Avenue, San Antonio 78210-4919; (512) 229-5701. There were 313,450 visits in 1990.

Recreation Facilities and Visitation Data Corps of Engineers' Lakes Texas 1990

Facilities available for visitors at U.S. Army Corps of Engineers' lakes in Texas in 1990 are listed below. Since facilities change often, it is best to check at the time of visit.

More than 240 million visitor hours were spent in 1990 by visitors enjoying the recreational facilities at lakes in Texas under the management of the U.S. Army Corps of Engineers. Lake Texoma, with more than 82 million visitor hours spent, led in usage.

Name of Reservoir	Swim Areas	Launch Ramps	Picnic Sites	Camp Sites	Rental Units	Visitation (in visitor hours)
Addicks & Barker	...	...	746	...	...	12,062,400
Aquilla	...	2	...	...	...	312,800
Bardwell	2	7	51	149	...	1,415,500
Belton	5	21	386	279	10	10,551,300
Benbrook	1	15	129	165	...	3,583,400
Canyon	6	25	196	665	45	6,986,900
Georgetown	1	3	118	234	...	4,888,600
Granger	2	5	130	118	...	923,400
Grapevine	3	15	140	168	...	4,003,700
Hords Creek	1	10	5	150	...	1,151,400
Joe Pool	2	4	118	201	...	3,938,900
Lake O' The Pines	7	29	187	556	...	8,689,900
Lavon	4	22	371	178	...	5,983,700
Lewisville	6	25	325	428	...	7,672,800
Navarro Mills	3	6	12	257	...	5,391,900
O. C. Fisher	...	16	133	168	...	2,045,500
Pat Mayse	5	10	14	321	...	1,966,000
Proctor	...	6	59	191	...	2,941,300
Ray Roberts	...	...	3	...	...	203,000
Sam Rayburn	4	31	12	645	17	18,308,300
Somerville	2	12	264	656	0	18,539,300
Stillhouse Hollow	3	5	31	164	...	3,458,700
Texoma	4	30	170	1,212	234	82,487,500
Town Bluff	2	12	126	355	...	4,731,100
Waco	1	9	60	262	...	6,526,900
Whitney	4	26	52	659	6	6,738,600
Wright Patman	5	20	240	645	4	15,153,600
Total	73	366	4,078	8,826	316	240,656,400

Texas Population: Growing and Increasingly Diverse

This article was prepared for this edition of the Texas Almanac by Steve H. Murdock, professor and head of the Department of Rural Sociology in the Texas Agricultural Experiment Station in the Texas A&M University System and Chief Demographer for the Texas State Data Center; David R. Ellis, a Senior Research Associate; and Md. Nazrul Hoque, an Assistant Research Scientist in the Department of Rural Sociology in the Texas Agricultural Experiment Station in the Texas A&M University System.

Population Change in the 1980s

General Patterns and Trends

The results of the 1990 Census show Texas to have had substantial growth during the 1980s, but the rate of population growth was less than in the 1970s and more concentrated in Texas' larger metropolitan areas than in the 1970s. The results also suggest that the state's **population became increasingly diverse,** with the state's ethnic minorities showing large numerical and proportional increases during the decade.

According to the recently released results of the 1990 Census, Texas has maintained its 140-year tradition of **growing more rapidly than the nation as a whole** (see Table 1). The state's population increased from

Population

14,229,191 in 1980 to 16,986,510 in 1990. This was an increase of 2,757,319 persons or 19.4 percent. The nation increased its population from 226,545,805 in 1980 to 248,709,873 in 1990, an increase of 22,164,068 or 9.8 percent.

Texas remained the **third-largest state** behind California, with a population of 29,760,021, and New York, with a population of 17,990,455, and continued to be substantially larger than the fourth-largest state, Florida, which had a population of 12,937,926 in 1990. Texas had the **third-largest numerical increase** of any state in the nation during the 1980s. Only California, which increased its population by 6,092,119 from 1980 to 1990, and Florida, which increased its population by 3,191,602, had larger numerical increases in population than Texas. In fact, these three states accounted for 54 percent of all population growth in the United States. Only one other state, Georgia, with an increase of 1,015,111, increased its population by as much as one million persons. The other three states with populations of more than 10 million persons in 1990 (Pennsylvania with a population of 11.9 million, Illinois with 11.4 million and Ohio with 10.8

million) showed very small population increases during the 1980s (18,538, 4,084 and 49,485 respectively).

In percentage terms, Texas was the **seventh fastest-growing state** behind Nevada with an increase of 50.1 percent, Alaska with 36.9 percent, Arizona with 34.8 percent, Florida with 32.8 percent, California with 25.7 percent, and New Hampshire, which increased its population by 20.5 percent. Whether examined in numerical or percentage terms, Texas' population growth was extensive during the 1980s.

It is clear, however, that Texas' **most rapid population growth** occurred during the first few years of the 1980s, while the mid-1980s showed periods of net outmigration and very slow population growth, followed by a moderate upturn in growth during the last few years of the 1980s. In addition, it is evident that the growth of the 1980s was both less and less pervasive than during the 1970s and was due to quite different patterns of migration and natural increase. A majority of the population

Table 1
Total Population and Percent Population Change in Texas and the United States, 1850-1990

Year	Total Population		Percent Change	
	Texas	U.S.	Texas	U.S.
1850 ..	212,592	23,191,876	—	—
1860 ..	604,215	31,443,321	184.2	35.6
1870 ..	818,579	39,818,449	35.5	26.6
1880 ..	1,591,749	50,155,783	94.5	26.0
1890 ..	2,235,527	62,947,714	40.4	25.5
1900 ..	3,048,710	75,994,575	36.4	20.7
1910 ..	3,896,542	91,972,266	27.8	21.0
1920 ..	4,663,228	105,710,620	19.7	14.9
1930 ..	5,824,715	122,775,046	24.9	16.1
1940 ..	6,414,824	131,669,275	10.1	7.2
1950 ..	7,711,194	150,697,361	20.2	14.5
1960 ..	9,579,677	179,323,175	24.2	19.0
1970 ..	11,196,730	203,302,031	16.9	13.4
1980 ..	14,229,191	226,545,805	27.1	11.4
1990 ..	16,986,510	248,709,873	19.4	9.8

Table 2
Population Counts 1980 and 1990, Population Change, Natural Increase and Net Migration 1980-90 in Metropolitan Statistical Areas in Texas

Metropolitan Statistical Area	1980 Census Count	1990 Census Count	1980-90 Population Change	1980-90 Natural Increase	1980-90 Net Migration
Abilene.	110,932	119,655	8,723	14,243	—5,520
Amarillo.	173,699	187,547	13,848	19,458	—5,610
Austin.	536,688	781,572	244,884	87,002	157,882
Beaumont-Port Arthur	375,497	361,226	—14,271	27,315	—41,586
Brazoria.	169,587	191,707	22,120	22,589	—469
Brownsville-Harlingen	209,727	260,120	50,393	41,038	9,355
Bryan-College Station	93,588	121,862	28,274	13,173	15,101
Corpus Christi.	326,228	349,894	23,666	42,148	—18,482
Dallas.	1,957,378	2,553,362	595,984	291,822	304,162
El Paso.	479,899	591,610	111,711	90,928	20,783
Ft. Worth-Arlington	973,138	1,332,053	358,915	137,643	221,272
Galveston-Texas City	195,940	217,399	21,459	20,181	1,278
Houston.	2,735,766	3,301,937	566,171	430,889	135,282
Killeen-Temple.	214,656	255,301	40,645	42,726	—2,081
Laredo.	99,258	133,239	33,981	23,359	10,622
Longview-Marshall.	151,752	162,431	10,679	11,220	—541
Lubbock.	211,651	222,636	10,985	25,947	—14,962
McAllen-Edinburg-Mission	283,229	383,545	100,316	64,001	36,315
Midland	82,636	106,611	23,975	16,216	7,759
Odessa	115,374	118,934	3,560	19,156	—15,596
San Angelo	84,784	98,458	13,674	9,239	4,435
San Antonio	1,071,954	1,302,099	230,145	144,349	85,796
Sherman-Denison	89,796	95,021	5,225	3,382	1,843
Texarkana	75,301	81,665	6,364	4,100	2,264
Tyler	128,366	151,309	22,943	11,117	11,826
Victoria	68,807	74,361	5,554	9,130	—3,576
Waco	170,755	189,123	18,368	12,854	5,514
Wichita Falls	121,082	122,378	1,296	10,416	—9,120
State of Texas	14,229,191	16,986,510	2,757,319	1,822,385	934,934

Metropolitan Statistical Areas as defined in the 1990 Census.

increase during the 1980s was due to **natural increase** (the difference between the number of births and deaths) rather than net migration. Only about one-third of the state's population increase was due to net inmigration during the 1980s, compared to nearly 60 percent from 1970 to 1980.

Slower patterns of growth and differences in the sources of growth were evident in all types of areas in the state. Thus, although all but one of the state's Metropolitan Statistical Areas (MSAs) increased their populations from 1980 to 1990 (see Tables 2 and 3), all showed increases in the 1970s, 11 MSAs showed net outmigration during the 1980s, while none had outmigration during the 1970s, and 23 of these 28 metropolitan areas had slower rates of population growth in the 1980s than in the 1970s.

Similar patterns were evident for Texas **cities and counties.** From 1980 to 1990, 51 percent of the state's towns and cities showed population increases, compared to 80 percent from 1970-80. The number of Texas' 254 counties declining in population increased to 98 from 1980 to 1990 compared to only 44 during the 1970s. Figure 1 provides two maps, one (in the top panel) showing different rates of population change among Texas counties from 1970-80 and the other (in the bottom panel) showing population change from 1980-90. An examination of these maps clearly reveals that population growth in Texas was less pervasive in the 1980s than the 1970s.

Among the most notable **differences in growth were** those between the small towns and larger cities of the state and between metropolitan and non-metropolitan areas in the state. Although 80 percent of all towns and cities in the state with populations of fewer than 10,000 persons in 1990 increased in population in the 1970s, only 47 percent of such places showed increases during the 1980s. For places of 10,001 to 25,000, nearly 79 percent showed increases in population from 1970-80, but 68 percent showed increases in the 1980s. For places with populations of 25,001 to 100,000, 83 percent showed population increases in the 1970s, while 81 percent continued to show increases in the 1980s. Among the state's largest places, those with populations of more than 100,000, 90 percent showed population increases in the 1970s, and 93 percent showed population increases during the 1980s.

Metropolitan counties of the state (those counties that are part of the state's Metropolitan Statistical Areas), which contained 79.5 of the state's population in 1980 (using 1990 definitions of Metropolitan Statistical Areas), accounted for 81.6 percent of the population and received 92.8 percent of the increase in the state's population from 1980 to 1990. **Non-metropolitan counties** (those counties not in an MSA) had 20.5 percent of the population of the state in 1980 but 18.4 percent in 1990 and received only 7.2 percent of the state's growth during the 1980s.

Growth Among Counties, Places and Metropolitan Statistical Areas

Harris County maintained its position as the state's largest county, with 2,818,199 persons, an increase of 17 percent from 1980 to 1990. **Dallas** (1,842,810), **Bexar** (1,185,394), **Tarrant** (1,170,103), and **Travis** (576,407) were the next-largest counties in the state. Taken together, these five largest counties accounted for 44.9 percent of the state's total population in 1990 compared to 44.2 percent in 1980.

Harris, with an increase of 408,652 residents, Tarrant (309,223), Dallas (296,420), Bexar (196,594), and Travis (156,834) were the five **counties with the largest numerical increases in population.** Denton County showed the **largest percentage increase** during the decade, with a 91.1 percent increase, followed by Collin (82.6), Williamson (82.4), Rockwall (76.2), and Fort Bend (72.7) counties.

Jefferson County, with a decrease of -11,541, **lost the most residents,** followed by Lamb (-3,597), Orange (-3,329), Kleberg (-3,084), and Hale (- 2,921) counties. The five counties with the **largest percentage losses** in population were Hall (-30.2), Hemphill (-29.9), Dickens (-27.4), Cottle (-23.8), and Briscoe (-23.6).

Among Texas cities, San Antonio had the **largest numerical increase,** with an addition of 150,056 residents during the decade, followed by Austin with an increase of 120,129. El Paso ranked fifth in numerical increase with a gain of 90,083 residents. The remaining seven of the state's ten cities with the largest numerical population gains were in the Dallas-Fort Worth Metroplex. Dallas, with a gain of 102,800 residents ranked third in the state, followed by Arlington (with a gain of 101,608 residents), Fort Worth (62,455), Plano (56,384), Irving (45,094), Garland (41,793), and Carrollton (41,575).

Of the **535 communities in Texas that lost population** during the decade, Port Arthur (-4,329), Orange (-4,247) and Beaumont (-3,779) ranked first through third. Kingsville (-3,582) and Galveston (-2,832) completed the list of the five cities with the largest numerical declines.

Among the state's **metropolitan areas** (see Tables 2 and 3) the Houston MSA remained the state's **largest,** with a population of 3,301,937 in 1990, an increase of 566,171, or 20.7 percent over 1980. The Dallas MSA, however, posted the **largst numerical gain** during the decade, with an increase of 591,610 (or 34.3 percent) from a

Table 3

Numerical Change in Population 1970-80 and 1980-90, and Percent Change 1970-80 and 1980-90 for Metropolitan Statistical Areas in Texas

Metropolitan Statistical Areas	Population Change 1970-80	Population Change 1980-90	Percent Change 1970-80	Percent Change 1980-90
Abilene	13,079	8,723	13.4	7.9
Amarillo	29,303	13,848	20.3	8.0
Austin	176,225	244,884	48.9	45.6
Beaumont-Port Arthur-Orange	27,929	—14,271	8.0	—3.8
Brazoria	61,275	22,120	56.6	13.0
Brownsville-Harlingen-San Benito	69,359	50,393	49.4	24.0
Bryan-College Station	35,610	28,274	61.4	30.2
Corpus Christi	41,396	23,666	14.5	7.3
Dallas	401,054	595,984	25.8	30.4
El Paso	120,608	111,711	33.6	23.3
Ft. Worth-Arlington	177,894	358,915	22.4	36.9
Galveston-Texas City	26,128	21,459	15.4	11.0
Houston	844,762	566,171	44.7	20.7
Killeen-Temple	54,862	40,645	34.3	18.9
Laredo	26,399	33,981	36.2	34.2
Longview-Marshall	30,982	10,679	25.7	7.0
Lubbock	32,356	10,985	18.0	5.2
McAllen-Edinburg-Mission	101,694	100,316	56.0	35.4
Midland	17,203	23,975	26.3	29.0
Odessa	22,714	3,560	24.5	3.1
San Angelo	13,737	13,674	19.3	16.1
San Antonio	183,775	230,145	20.7	21.5
Sherman-Denison	6,571	5,225	7.9	5.8
Texarkana	6,392	6,364	9.3	8.5
Tyler	31,270	22,943	32.2	17.9
Victoria	15,041	5,554	28.0	8.1
Waco	23,202	18,368	15.7	10.8
Wichita Falls	519	1,296	0.4	1.1
State of Texas	3,030,536	2,757,319	27.1	19.4

Metropolitan Statistical Area as defined in the 1990 Census.

population of 1,957,378 to 2,553,362 in 1990. In terms of **percentage increase,** the Austin MSA, with an increase of 45.6 percent during the decade, showed the greatest gain. Only one MSA, Beaumont-Port Arthur, experienced a net loss of population during the decade.

Texas Population Patterns by Ethnicity, 1980 to 1990

Statewide Patterns

Perhaps the most dramatic results from the 1990 Census reported to date are those related to the **increase in Texas' minority populations** (see Table 4). The state's **Hispanic** population increased by more than 45 percent from 1980 to 1990, while the **Black** population increased by nearly 17 percent and the **Other** population by more than 88 percent from 1980 to 1990. Because the population base for the Other population is quite small however, it is growth in the Hispanic, and to a lesser extent the Black, population which has markedly changed in the last decade. From 1980 to 1990, the Black population increased by nearly 300,000 persons and the Hispanic population increased by more than 1.3 million. Thus although the Hispanic population was only one-third as large as the **Anglo** population in 1980, its numerical increase from 1980 to 1990 was more than 300,000 greater than that for Anglos.

Hispanics accounted for 49 percent of the net increase in population from 1980 to 1990, Blacks for 10 percent of the increase and persons from Other ethnic groups for 6.5 percent. By 1990, Hispanics accounted for 25.6 percent of the population, Blacks for 11.6 percent and persons from Other ethnic groups for 2.2 percent of the Texas population. Thus Texas' population in 1990 was 40 percent minority compared to 25 percent of the population that is minority in the United States as a whole (see Table 4).

Patterns of Ethnic Change in Counties, Places and Metropolitan Areas

Of the state's 254 counties, only 26 (10.2 percent) did not show an increase in their Hispanic populations and only 74 did not show increases in their Other population category. On the other hand, 132 counties (52 percent) showed a loss in their Anglo populations and 141 (55.5 percent) experienced decline in their Black populations.

Seven counties in the state increased their Hispanic populations by more than 50,000 persons between 1980 and 1990. These were Bexar County with an increase of 128,269, Cameron County (51,341), Dallas County (161,069), El Paso County (114,618), Harris County (275,858), Hidalgo County (96,760), and Tarrant County (72,247). Overall, 47 counties showed increases of more than 100 percent in their Hispanic populations.

By contrast, although the Anglo population base was more than three times as large as the Hispanic population base in 1980, only four counties had increases of 50,000 or more in their Anglo populations from 1980 to 1990 — Collin (97,213), Denton (105,155), Tarrant (177,389) and Travis (80,230) — and not a single county increased its Anglo population by 100 percent.

For Blacks, only Dallas County, with an increase of 76,343, and Harris County, with an increase of 58,674, increased their Black populations by as much as 50,000 persons. Only Denton and Fort Bend had numerical increases of more than 1,000 persons that also involved

Table 4
Population 1980 and 1990, Percent Change in Population 1980 to 1990 and Proportion of Population 1980 and 1990 by Ethnicity for Texas and the United States

Ethnic Category	Number 1980	1990	Percent Change 1980-90	Proportion of Population 1980	1990
	Texas				
Anglo...	9,350,297	10,291,680	10.1	65.7	60.6
Black...	1,692,542	1,976,360	16.8	11.9	11.6
Hispanic	2,985,824	4,339,905	45.4	21.0	25.6
Other...	200,528	378,565	88.8	1.4	2.2
Total...	14,229,191	16,986,510	19.4	100.0	100.0
	United States				
Anglo...	180,602,838	188,128,296	4.2	79.7	75.7
Black...	26,091,857	29,216,293	12.0	11.5	11.7
Hispanic	14,603,683	22,354,059	53.1	6.5	9.0
Other...	5,247,427	9,011,225	71.7	2.3	3.6
Total...	226,545,805	248,709,873	9.8	100.0	100.0

percentage increases of more than 100 percent. In the Other population, increases of more than 10,000 persons occurred in Dallas County (33,567), Fort Bend County (10,097), Harris County (55,437), Tarrant County (21,822), and Travis County (10,627). A total of 54 counties increased their Other populations by more than 100 percent from 1980 to 1990.

As a result of these changes, the proportion of counties' populations that was Hispanic tended to increase while the proportion that was Anglo and Black declined. Of the 254 counties in the state, 218 showed decreases in the proportion of their populations that were Anglo, 174 showed decreases in the proportion of their populations that were Black, but only 11 showed decreases in the proportion of their populations that were composed of Hispanics and 76 experienced decreases in the proportions of persons from Other ethnic groups in their populations.

The **patterns of ethnic change in Texas cities** varied by the size of the place, and within each size-of-place by ethnic group. Hispanic growth accounted for 29 percent of the increase in places of 1,000 or less; for 55 percent of the increase in places of 1,001 to 2,499; for 49 percent of the increase in places of 2,500 to 10,000; for 37 percent of the increase in places of 10,001 to 25,000; and for 34 percent of the increase in places between 25,001 and 100,000 from 1980 to 1990. In places of more than 100,000, Hispanics accounted for 690,593, or 74 percent, of the 931,447-person increase that occurred from 1980 to 1990.

Anglos, by contrast, accounted for a much smaller proportion of the growth than their proportion of the population in each size-of-place category. In places of 1,000 or less, Anglos accounted for 80.2 percent of the population in 1990, but for 72.2 percent of the change from 1980 to 1990. For each of the other size-of-place categories, except that inclusive of the largest-size places, Anglos accounted for 65 to 70 percent of the population in 1990, but accounted for only 41-46 percent of the net change in population from 1980 to 1990. The most startling pattern for Anglos, however, was that in the state's largest cities. Of the 931,447 increase in population from 1980 to 1990 in the population of the 19 places with more than 100,000 residents, only 28,380 was due to growth in the Anglo population. Anglos accounted for 49.4 percent of the population in such cities in 1990 (compared to 56.5 percent in 1980), but accounted for only 3 percent of the net population increase in these largest Texas cities from 1980 to 1990.

Among Blacks, population decline occurred in places of 1,000 or fewer residents, and the proportion of the net change accounted for by Black residents was less than their share of the population in places between 1,001 and 10,000 residents. Blacks accounted for about 2 percent more of the increase in population from 1980 to 1990 than they were of the population in places of 10,001 to 100,000 in 1990. In the largest places, Blacks accounted for more than 16 percent of the population, but were only 13.3 percent of the increase in population from 1980 to 1990.

The Other population showed patterns similar to those for Hispanics, with those in the Other population category contributing more to the overall growth in each size-of-place category than they were of the population in each category. However, the impact of the Other population was clearly the largest in the larger size-of-place categories. In places with fewer than 2,500 persons, the rate of growth in the Other population was only 1 to 2 percent larger than their share of the 1990 populations in these areas and were small overall. In places with populations between 10,001 and 100,000, persons from Other ethnic groups accounted for about 4 to 6 percent of the growth but were only 1 to 2 percent of the population. Finally, in places of more than 100,000, the Other population group made up only 2.8 percent of the population in 1990 (and 1.8 percent in 1980), but accounted for 9.5 percent of the growth.

Overall, only 220 places showed declines in their Hispanic populations, 402 showed declines in their Black populations, and 702 places showed declines in their Anglo populations. As a result of such patterns, declines generally occurred in the proportion of Anglos in places, while increases occurred in the proportions of Hispanics in the populations of places.

The patterns of **ethnic change in Metropolitan Statistical Areas** are similar to those for counties. Every metropolitan area showed an increase in the number and proportion of its population that was Hispanic, with four areas increasing their Hispanic populations by more than 100 percent and eight others showing increases of 50 to 100 percent (see Table 5). Hispanics

Table 5

Populations 1980 and 1990, Numerical Change 1980 and 1990, and Percent Change 1980 and 1990 in Metropolitan Statistical Areas (MSAs) in Texas by Ethnicity

Metropolitan Area	HISPANIC				ANGLO				BLACK				OTHER			
	1980	1990	Change	% Chg.	1980	1990	Change	% Chg.	1980	1990	Change	% Chg.	1980	1990	Change	% Chg.
State of Texas	2,985,824	4,339,905	1,354,081	45.35	9,350,297	10,291,680	941,383	10.07	1,692,542	1,976,360	283,818	16.77	200,528	378,565	178,037	88.78
Abilene	13,203	17,511	4,308	32.63	89,703	92,955	3,252	3.63	6,590	7,336	746	11.32	1,436	1,853	417	29.04
Amarillo	14,897	25,390	10,493	70.44	147,075	148,241	1,166	0.79	8,443	9,542	1,099	13.02	3,284	4,374	1,090	33.19
Austin	94,367	159,942	65,575	69.49	383,947	530,664	146,717	38.21	49,523	69,626	20,103	40.59	8,851	21,340	12,489	141.10
Beaumont-Port Arthur	12,613	15,241	2,628	20.84	277,533	255,481	-22,052	-7.95	81,046	83,972	2,926	3.61	4,305	6,532	2,227	51.73
Brazoria	22,679	33,797	11,118	49.02	132,332	139,683	7,351	5.55	13,013	15,425	2,412	18.54	1,563	2,802	1,239	79.27
Brownsville-Harlingen	161,654	212,995	51,341	31.76	46,488	45,354	-1,134	-2.44	591	567	-24	-4.06	994	1,204	210	21.13
Bryan-College Station	9,455	16,713	7,258	76.76	71,989	87,139	15,150	21.04	10,267	13,409	3,142	30.60	1,877	4,601	2,724	145.13
Corpus Christi	158,119	181,860	23,741	15.01	152,274	151,385	-889	-0.58	12,868	12,809	-59	-0.46	2,967	3,840	873	29.42
Dallas	176,065	368,884	192,819	109.52	1,436,248	1,703,736	267,488	18.62	313,476	402,662	89,186	28.45	31,589	78,080	46,491	147.17
El Paso	297,001	411,619	114,618	38.59	157,842	151,313	-6,529	-4.14	17,590	20,525	2,935	16.69	7,466	8,153	687	9.20
Ft. Worth-Arlington	71,758	150,033	78,275	109.08	785,049	1,004,656	219,607	27.97	102,837	141,321	38,484	37.42	13,494	36,043	22,549	167.10
Galveston-Texas City	23,557	30,962	7,405	31.43	133,898	144,852	10,954	8.18	35,895	37,414	1,519	4.23	2,590	4,171	1,581	61.04
Houston	402,224	707,536	305,312	75.91	1,755,671	1,863,449	107,778	6.14	510,459	596,860	86,401	16.93	67,412	134,092	66,680	98.91
Killeen-Temple	22,070	31,238	9,168	41.54	150,158	167,589	17,431	11.61	33,881	45,377	11,496	33.93	6,386	8,204	1,818	28.47
Laredo	90,842	125,069	34,227	37.68	8,124	7,427	-697	-8.58	75	68	-7	-9.33	1,044	1,318	274	26.25
Longview-Marshall	2,813	5,053	2,240	79.63	114,014	120,265	6,251	5.48	12,228	12,919	691	5.65	217	675	458	211.06
Lubbock	41,428	51,011	9,583	23.13	151,854	151,414	-440	-0.29	15,558	16,646	1,088	6.99	2,811	3,565	754	26.82
McAllen-Edinburg-Mission	230,212	326,972	96,760	42.03	51,719	54,259	2,540	4.91	422	518	96	22.75	876	1,796	920	105.02
Midland	12,323	22,780	10,457	84.86	62,650	74,499	11,849	18.91	7,000	8,016	1,016	14.51	663	1,316	653	98.49
Odessa	24,831	37,315	12,484	50.28	84,362	74,822	-9,540	-11.31	5,027	5,391	364	7.24	1,154	1,406	252	21.84
San Angelo	17,953	25,501	7,548	42.04	62,696	67,642	4,946	7.89	3,329	3,955	626	18.80	806	1,360	554	68.73
San Antonio	481,511	620,290	138,779	28.82	505,007	576,836	71,829	14.22	71,497	85,228	13,731	19.21	13,939	19,745	5,806	41.65
Sherman-Denison	1,349	2,795	1,446	107.19	81,265	84,271	3,006	3.70	6,286	6,511	225	3.58	896	1,444	548	61.16
Texarkana	993	1,334	341	34.34	57,565	61,964	4,399	7.64	16,322	17,697	1,375	8.42	421	670	249	59.14
Tyler	4,037	8,986	4,949	122.59	95,585	109,853	14,268	14.93	28,059	31,289	3,230	11.51	685	1,181	496	72.41
Victoria	20,944	25,372	4,428	21.14	42,815	43,835	1,020	2.38	4,619	4,638	19	0.41	429	516	87	20.28
Waco	14,988	23,643	8,655	57.75	127,585	134,507	6,922	5.43	27,068	29,036	1,968	7.27	1,114	1,937	823	73.88
Wichita Falls	7,793	10,555	2,762	35.44	100,300	98,127	-2,173	-2.17	10,773	10,986	213	1.98	2,216	2,710	494	22.29

accounted for the largest numerical increase of any ethnic group from 1980 to 1990 in 17 of the state's 28 metropolitan areas.

Both Dallas and Fort Worth-Arlington MSAs increased their Hispanic populations by more than 100 percent. Taken together, the Dallas and Fort Worth-Arlington areas increased their Hispanic populations by more than 271,000 from 1980 to 1990. Less dramatic on a percentage basis, but the largest in numerical terms, was the growth in the Hispanic population in Houston, with an increase of 305,312 Hispanics from 1980 to 1990. In fact, nine of every 10 Hispanics added to the Texas population from 1980 to 1990 were added to a metropolitan area's population. By 1990, Texas had five metropolitan areas that were more than 50 percent Hispanic — Brownsville-Harlingen (82 percent), Corpus Christi (52 percent), El Paso (70 percent), Laredo (94 percent) and McAllen-Edinburg-Mission (85 percent) — and one other metropolitan area, San Antonio, had a population that was nearly 48 percent Hispanic.

All of the state's metropolitan areas showed a decline between 1980 and 1990 in the proportion of their populations that were Anglo, and seven areas showed absolute numerical declines in their Anglo population base. The largest percentage declines occurred in Odessa, which lost 11.3 percent of its Anglo population from 1980 to 1990, and in Laredo (8.6 percent) and Beaumont-Port Arthur (8 percent). Dallas showed the largest numerical increase in its Anglo population from 1980 to 1990, 267,488 (18.62 percent), followed by Fort Worth- Arlington (219,607 or 27.97 percent) and Austin (146,717 or 38.21 percent).

Of the state's 28 metropolitan areas, 19 showed slower growth in their Black populations than the total rate of increase for the Black population at the state level (16.8 percent). The growth of the Black population was concentrated in a few areas. Dallas increased its Black population by 89,186, and Houston increased its Black population by 86,401. In fact, these two areas alone accounted for 62 percent of all the persons added to the Black population between 1980 and 1990, while containing 50 percent of the total Black population in the state.

The population in the Other ethnic group showed patterns similar to those for Hispanics. All but two metropolitan areas showed increases in the proportion of their populations in the Other ethnic category. Six areas showed increases of more than 100 percent, and another 10 experienced increases of more than 50 percent. Houston has a substantially larger population in the Other racial category than any other metropolitan area, with a population of 134,092 in 1990 (35 percent of all persons in the Other category in the state in 1990) and an increase of 66,680 (98.91 percent) from 1980 to 1990. The next-largest population is in Dallas, with a population of 78,080 in 1990 and an increase of 46,491 from 1980 to 1990, followed by Fort Worth-Arlington (36,043), Austin (21,340) and San Antonio (19,745). No other metropolitan area in the state had as many as 10,000 persons in the Other population category in 1990.

Conclusion

As the remaining results from the 1990 Census are released during the coming years, it seems likely that the diversity among Texas population groups and regions of the state will become even more apparent. This diversity reflects Texas' rich cultural heritage, its size and its decades of rapid population change. Although the state's present level of growth appears to be quite slow (although more rapid than during the late 1980s), we anticipate that Texas' population will not only continue to increase, so that the state will remain among the faster-growing states in the nation, but that its diversity will also continue to increase, creating an equally diverse range of opportunities for the people of Texas.

Texas' reputation for wide open spaces is belied by crowds like this one at a concert in Dallas' West End Marketplace. Dallas Morning News photo.

Population of Cities and Towns

Population: Population of **incorporated places** and certain **Census Designated Places** is from the **U.S. Census Bureau for 1990.** Places incorporated before 1990 are printed in lightface capital letters, e.g., "ABBOTT." Places incorporated since 1990 are printed in boldface type, e.g., **"Cross Timbers."** Population figures for towns incorporated since August 1990 are local estimates.

Population of **unincorporated places** is not enumerated by the U.S. Census Bureau except for Census Designated Places; the population figure given here for unincorporated towns is an estimate of the number of persons considered locally as living in that community. The names are printed in lightface type, e.g., "Acton." In some cases we could not obtain a reliable population estimate; these places show "NA" (Not Available) in place of population.

Metropolitan Statistical Area population is from the

U.S. Census Bureau for 1990.

County Seats: County seats are marked with a section mark (§). If more than one county is listed, the town is the county seat of the first-named county.

Post Offices: Places with post offices are marked with an asterisk (*) e.g., "*Ace."

Banking Towns: Towns with one or more banks as of May 1, 1990, are marked with a dagger, e.g., "†ALAMO." (This includes national, state and private banking institutions.) Information from **Federal Reserve Bank,** Dallas.

Location: County in which town is located immediately follows name of town, e.g., "Aberfoyle, Hunt," meaning Aberfoyle in Hunt County. If town is in more than one county, the county names are separated with hyphens.

Town and County—	Pop.
A	
A & D Acres, Llano	NA
*ABBOTT, Hill	314
Aberfoyle, Hunt	35
*†ABERNATHY, Hale-Lubbock	2,720
Abex, Navarro	NA
§*†ABILENE, Taylor-Jones	106,654
1990 metro. pop.	119,655
Ables Springs, Kaufman	NA
Abner, Kaufman	NA
Abram-Perezville, Hidalgo	3,999
Acala, Hudspeth	25
*Ace, Polk	40
*ACKERLY, Dawson-Martin	243
Acme, Hardeman	14
Acton, Hood	450
Acuff, Lubbock	30
Acworth, Red River	52
Adams, Lamar	NA
Adams Acres, Montgomery	NA
Adams Gardens, Cameron	200
Adams Hill, Bexar	NA
Adams Oaks, Montgomery	NA
Adams Store, Panola	NA
Adamsville, Lampasas	28
Addielou, Red River	31
*†ADDISON, Dallas	8,783
Addran, Hopkins	NA
Adell, Parker	NA
*Adkins, Bexar	241
Admiral, Callahan	18
*ADRIAN, Oldham	220
Advance, Parker	NA
*Afton, Dickens	100
Afton Park, Montgomery	NA

Town and County—	Pop.
Agnes, Parker	NA
*AGUA DULCE, Nueces	794
Agua Nueva, Jim Hogg	20
Agua Verde, Travis	NA
Aguilares, Webb	10
*Aiken, Floyd	60
Aiken, Shelby	75
Aikin Grove, Red River	26
Air Country Estates, Williamson	NA
Airport City, Bexar	106
Airville, Bell	NA
Alabama-Coushatta Indian Res., Polk	478
Alabama Creek, Trinity	20
*†ALAMO, Hidalgo	8,210
Alamo Alto, El Paso	25
Alamo Beach, Calhoun	NA
*ALAMO HEIGHTS, Bexar	6,502
*Alanreed, Gray	60
Alazan, Nacogdoches	NA
*ALBA, Wood-Rains	489
§*†ALBANY, Shackelford	1,962
*Albert, Gillespie	25
Albion, Red River	50
Alderbranch, Anderson	NA
Aldine, Harris	11,133
*†ALEDO, Parker	1,169
Aleman, Hamilton	60
Alethia, Montgomery	NA
Alexander, Erath	40
Alexanders Store, Shelby	NA
Aley, Henderson	NA
Alfred, Jim Wells	10
Algerita, San Saba	48
Algoa, Galveston	135
§*†ALICE, Jim Wells	19,788
Allamoore, Hudspeth	NA

Town and County—	Pop.
*†ALLEN, Collin	18,309
Allendale, Montgomery	NA
Allenfarm, Brazos	30
Allenhurst, Matagorda	NA
Allen's Chapel, Fannin	41
Allen's Point, Fannin	76
*Alleyton, Colorado	165
*Allison, Wheeler	135
Allison, Wise	NA
Allmon, Floyd	NA
Allred, Yoakum	NA
ALMA, Ellis	205
Almeda, Harris	NA
Almira, Cass	NA
Almont, Bowie	NA
§*†ALPINE, Brewster	5,637
Alpine Village, Travis	NA
Alsa, Van Zandt	30
Alsdorf, Ellis	NA
*Altair, Colorado	30
Altavista, Jim Hogg	NA
*†ALTO, Cherokee	1,027
Alto Bonito, Starr	70
Altoga, Collin	367
*ALTON, Hidalgo	3,069
Alum, Wilson	NA
Alum Creek, Bastrop	NA
*†ALVARADO, Johnson	2,918
*†ALVIN, Brazoria	19,220
*ALVORD, Wise	865
§*†AMARILLO, Potter-Randall	157,615
1990 metro. pop.	187,547
Ambia, Lamar	20
Ambrose, Grayson	41
Ames, Coryell	NA
*AMES, Liberty	989
Amherst, Lamar	NA

Town and County-	Pop.
*†AMHERST, Lamb	742
Amity, Comanche	NA
Ammannsville, Fayette	42
Amphion, Atascosa	NA
Amsterdam, Brazoria	NA
Anadarko, Rusk	NA
§*†ANAHUAC, Chambers	1,993
Anchorage, Atascosa	NA
Ander, Goliad	35
§*†Anderson, Grimes	370
Anderson Mill, Williamson-Travis	9,468
*Andice, Williamson	25
§*†ANDREWS, Andrews	10,678
§*ANGLETON, Brazoria	17,140
ANGUS, Navarro	363
Anhalt, Comal	NA
*†ANNA, Collin	904
Annarose, Live Oak	NA
ANNETTA, Parker	672
ANNETTA NORTH, Parker	265
ANNETTA SOUTH, Parker	413
*ANNONA, Red River	329
§*†ANSON, Jones	2,644
*Antelope, Jack	65
*ANTHONY, El Paso	3,328
Anthony, Fannin	10
Anthony Harbor, San Augustine	NA
Antioch, Cass	29
Antioch, Delta	25
Antioch, Madison	20
Antioch, Panola	121
Antioch, Shelby	NA
Antioch, Smith	NA
*†ANTON, Hockley	1,212
Apache Shores, Travis	NA
*APPLEBY, Nacogdoches	449
*Apple Springs, Trinity	130
April Sound, Montgomery	NA
*AQUILLA, Hill	136
Arah, Scurry	NA
*†ARANSAS PASS, San Patricio-Aransas-Nueces	7,180
Arbala, Hopkins	41
*Arcadia, Shelby	20
§*†ARCHER CITY, Archer	1,748
ARCOLA, Fort Bend	666
Arden, Irion	1
Argo, Titus	26
*ARGYLE, Denton	1,575
Arkadelphia, Bowie	NA
Arkansas Colony, Baylor	NA
Arlie, Childress	NA
*†ARLINGTON, Tarrant	261,721
1990 metro. pop.	1,332,053
Armstrong, Bell	22
*Armstrong, Kenedy	20
Arneckeville, DeWitt	50
Arnett, Coryell	NA
Arnett, Hockley	26
Arney, Castro	NA
*†ARP, Smith	812
Arrowhead Lake, Montgomery	NA
Arrowhead Shores, Hood	NA
Arrowhead Village, Comal	NA
Arroyo City, Cameron	NA
*Art, Mason	18
Artesian Lakes Estates, Montgomery	NA
*Artesia Wells, La Salle	30
*Arthur City, Lamar	200
Arvana, Dawson	25
Asa, McLennan	46
Ash, Houston	NA
Ashby, Matagorda	NA
*ASHERTON, Dimmit	1,608
Ashland, Upshur	20
Ashmore, Gaines	25
Ashtola, Donley	20
Ashwood, Matagorda	NA
Asia, Polk	NA
§*†ASPERMONT, Stonewall	1,214
Astro Hills, Comal	NA
*Atascosa, Bexar	300
Ater, Coryell	NA
§*†ATHENS, Henderson	10,967
*†ATLANTA, Cass	6,118
Atlas, Lamar	20

Town and County-	Pop.
Atoy, Cherokee	NA
Attoyac, Nacogdoches	NA
Attoyac Village, Nacogdoches	NA
Atwell, Callahan	NA
*AUBREY, Denton	1,138
Auburn, Ellis	12
Augusta, Houston	20
AURORA, Wise	623
§*†AUSTIN, Travis-Williamson	465,622
1990 metro. pop.	715,958
Austin Lake Estates, Travis	NA
*Austonio, Houston	37
*AUSTWELL, Refugio	189
Authon, Parker	5
*Avalon, Ellis	130
*AVERY, Red River	430
*†AVINGER, Cass	478
*Avoca, Jones	121
*Axtell, McLennan	105
*†AZLE, Tarrant-Parker	8,868

B

Babyhead, Llano	20
Back, Gray	14
*Bacliff, Galveston	5,549
Bagby, Fannin	NA
*Bagwell, Red River	150
*BAILEY, Fannin	187
Baileyboro, Bailey	NA
BAILEY'S PRAIRIE, Brazoria	634
Baileyville, Milam	45
Bainer, Lamb	NA
Bainville, Karnes	NA
§*†BAIRD, Callahan	1,658
Baker, Floyd	NA
Bakersfield, Pecos	30
Balboa Acres, Hidalgo	NA
*BALCH SPRINGS, Dallas	17,406
BALCONES HEIGHTS, Bexar	3,022
Balcones Village, Travis-Williamson	NA
Bald Hill, Angelina	NA
Bald Prairie, Robertson	31
Baldwin, Harrison	NA
§*†BALLINGER, Runnels	3,975
*BALMORHEA, Reeves	765
Balsora, Wise	50
Bammel, Harris	NA
§*†BANDERA, Bandera	877
Bandera Falls, Bandera	NA
*†BANGS, Brown	1,555
Bankersmith, Kendall	NA
*Banquete, Nueces	449
Barbarosa, Guadalupe	25
Barclay, Falls	72
*BARDWELL, Ellis	387
*Barker, Harris	160
*Barksdale, Edwards	617
Barnes, Polk	NA
Barnes Switch, Trinity	15
*Barnhart, Irion	135
*Barnum, Polk	20
*Barrett, Harris	3,052
*BARRY, Navarro	175
*BARSTOW, Ward	535
*†BARTLETT, Williamson-Bell	1,439
Bartley Woods, Fannin	30
Bartons Chapel, Jack	NA
BARTONVILLE, Denton	849
Barwise, Floyd	30
Bascom, Smith	NA
Bassett, Bowie	373
§*†BASTROP, Bastrop	4,044
Bastrop Bayou Acres, Brazoria	NA
Bastrop Beach, Brazoria	NA
Bateman, Bastrop	NA
Batesville, Red River	14
*Batesville, Zavala	1,313
*Batson, Hardin	140
Battle, McLennan	NA
Bavarian Hills, Bexar	NA
Baxter, Henderson	20
§*†BAY CITY, Matagorda	18,170
Bay Harbor, Galveston	NA
Baylake, Angelina	NA
Baylor Lake, Childress	27
Bayou Village, Angelina	NA

Town and County-	Pop.
BAYOU VISTA, Galveston	1,320
*BAYSIDE, Refugio	400
Bayside Terrace, Harris	NA
*†BAYTOWN, Harris-Chambers	63,850
*BAYVIEW, Cameron	231
Baywood Estates, Henderson	NA
Bazette, Navarro	30
Beach, Montgomery	NA
BEACH CITY, Chambers	852
Beans, Jasper	NA
Bear Creek, Dallas	1,000
Bear Creek Oaks, Hays	NA
Bear Creek Park, Travis	NA
Bear Creek Ranch, Montgomery	NA
*BEASLEY, Fort Bend	485
Beattie, Comanche	50
Beaukiss, Williamson	20
§*†BEAUMONT, Jefferson	114,323
1990 metro. pop.	361,226
Beaumont Place, Harris	NA
Beaux Art Gardens, Jefferson	NA
Beaver Dams, Bowie	NA
*Bebe, Gonzales	52
Beck, Lamb	NA
Becker, Kaufman	NA
*BECKVILLE, Panola	783
Becton, Lubbock	125
*†BEDFORD, Tarrant	43,762
*†Bedias, Grimes	301
BEE CAVE, Travis	241
Beechwood, Sabine	NA
*Bee House, Coryell	40
§*†BEEVILLE, Bee	13,547
Beeville Naval Air Station, Bee	1,250
Behrnville, Williamson	30
Belcherville, Montague	34
Belfalls, Bell	20
Belgrade, Newton	NA
Belk, Lamar	55
*†BELLAIRE, Harris	13,842
Bella Vista, Fort Bend	NA
Bell Branch, Ellis	NA
*BELLEVUE, Clay	333
*BELLMEAD, McLennan	8,336
*†BELLS, Grayson	962
§*†BELLVILLE, Austin	3,378
Belmena, Milam	15
*Belmont, Gonzales	60
Belott, Houston	NA
§*†BELTON, Bell	12,476
Ben-Roy Bay, Smith	NA
*Ben Arnold, Milam	148
*BENAVIDES, Duval	1,788
Ben Bolt, Jim Wells	110
*†BENBROOK, Tarrant	19,564
Benchley, Robertson	110
*Bend, San Saba	115
*Ben Franklin, Delta	75
Ben Hur, Limestone	100
§*BENJAMIN, Knox	225
Bennett, Parker	85
Bennett Estates, Montgomery	NA
Benoit, Runnels	NA
Bentonville, Jim Wells	15
Bentwood Acres, Grayson	NA
*†Ben Wheeler, Van Zandt	400
*Berclair, Goliad	70
Berea, Houston	NA
Berea, Marion	74
*Bergheim, Kendall	22
*Bergstrom Air Force Base, Travis	2,945
Berlin, Washington	NA
Bernard Acres, Brazoria	NA
Bernardo, Colorado	155
Berryhill, Shackelford	NA
Berry's Creek, Williamson	50
BERRYVILLE, Henderson	749
*†BERTRAM, Burnet	849
Bess, Duval	20
*Best, Reagan	25
Bethany, Panola	50
Bethel, Anderson	31
Bethel, Ellis	NA
Bethel, Henderson	NA

Town and County-	Pop.	Town and County-	Pop.	Town and County-	Pop.
Buffalo Mop, Limestone	NA	Camp San Saba, McCulloch	36	Carroll Springs, Anderson	NA
Buffalo Springs, Clay	51	Camp Scenic, Kerr	NA	*†CARROLLTON, Denton-	
BUFFALO SPRINGS, Lubbock	247	Camp Seale, Polk	NA	Dallas-Collin	82,169
Buford, El Paso	NA	Camp Springs, Scurry	10	Carson, Fannin	22
Buford, Mitchell	25	Camp Swift, Bastrop	2,681	*Carswell Air Force Base,	
Bugbee Heights, Hutchinson	75	Camp Switch, Gregg	70	Tarrant	3,162
Bug Tussle, Fannin	15	Campti, Shelby	NA	*Carta Valley, Edwards	20
*Bula, Bailey	105	*Camp Verde, Kerr	41	Carter Lake, Brazos	NA
Bulcher, Cooke	NA	Camp Willow, Guadalupe	NA	Carterville, Cass	25
*†BULLARD, Smith-Cherokee	890	*CAMP WOOD, Real	595	Carterville, Harrison	NA
Bull Run, Newton	NA	Camp Worth, San Augustine	NA	§*†CARTHAGE, Panola	6,496
*Bulverde, Comal	25	Canada Verde, Wilson	123	Cartwright, Kaufman	NA
Bulverde Estates, Comal	NA	§*†CANADIAN, Hemphill	2,417	Cartwright, Wood	61
Bulverde Hills, Comal	NA	Canal City, Galveston	NA	Carver, Leon	NA
*Buna, Jasper	2,127	Canary, Leon	NA	Carver Park, Bexar	NA
Buncombe, Panola	87	Candelaria, Presidio	55	Casa Piedra, Presidio	21
Bunger, Young	26	Caney, Matagorda	296	Casey, El Paso	115
Bunker Hill, Jasper	NA	CANEY CITY, Henderson	170	Cash, Hunt	56
Bunker Hill, Lamar	NA	Caney Creek, Henderson	NA	*Cason, Morris	173
BUNKER HILL VILLAGE,		Caney Creek Estates,		Cass, Cass	50
Harris	3,391	Matagorda	NA	Cassie, Burnet	NA
Bunns Bluff, Orange	NA	Caney Creek Estates,		Cassin, Bexar	NA
Bunyan, Erath	20	Montgomery	NA	*Castell, Llano	72
*†BURKBURNETT, Wichita	10,145	Cannon, Grayson	75	CASTLE HILLS, Bexar	4,198
BURKE, Angelina	314	Canterbury Estates, Smith	NA	Castle Terrace, Burnet	NA
*Burkett, Coleman	30	§*†CANTON, Van Zandt	2,949	Castlewood Forest, Travis	NA
*Burkeville, Newton	515	Cantu, Hidalgo	NA	*†CASTROVILLE, Medina	2,159
Burleigh, Austin	69	*Canutillo, El Paso	4,442	*Catarina, Dimmit	45
*†BURLESON, Johnson-		Canyon, Lubbock	40	*Cat Spring, Austin	76
Tarrant	16,113	§*†CANYON, Randall	11,365	Causeway Beach, Henderson	NA
*Burlington, Milam	140	Canyon City, Comal	100	Cavazos, Cameron	NA
§*†BURNET, Burnet	3,423	Canyon Corners, Comal	NA	Cave Creek, Gillespie	NA
Burns, Bowie	NA	Canyon Creek Estates, Comal	NA	Caviness, Lamar	80
Burns City, Cooke	61	*Canyon Lake, Comal	9,975	Cawthon, Brazos	75
Burrantown, Houston	NA	Canyon Lake Acres, Comal	NA	Cayote, Bosque	75
Burroughsville, Victoria	NA	Canyon Lake Estates, Comal	NA	*Cayuga, Anderson	56
Burrow, Hunt	NA	Canyon Lake Forest, Comal	NA	Cedar Bay, Smith	NA
*†BURTON, Washington	311	Canyon Lake Hills, Comal	NA	Cedar Bayou, Harris-	
Busby, Fisher	12	Canyon Lake Island, Comal	NA	Chambers	1,287
*Bushland, Potter	130	Canyon Lake Mobile Home Est.,		Cedar Branch Park, Henderson	NA
Bushwhacker Peninsula,		Comal	NA	Cedar Creek, Anderson	NA
Henderson	NA	Canyon Lake Shores, Comal	NA	*Cedar Creek, Bastrop	145
Bustamante, Zapata	25	Canyon Lake Village, Comal	NA	Cedar Creek, Waller	NA
Busterville, Hockley	NA	Canyon Lake Village West,		Cedar Creek Park, Hill	NA
Butler, Bastrop	NA	Comal	NA	*†CEDAR HILL, Dallas-Ellis	19,976
Butler, Freestone	67	Canyon Oak Estates, Comal	NA	Cedar Hill, Floyd	NA
*†BYERS, Clay	510	Canyon Park Estates, Comal	NA	Cedar Lake, Matagorda	148
*BYNUM, Hill	192	Canyon Springs, Comal	NA	*Cedar Lane, Matagorda	85
Byrd, Ellis	15	Canyon Valley, Crosby	NA	Cedar Mills, Grayson	NA
Byrds, Brown	NA	Canyon View Acres, Comal	NA	*CEDAR PARK, Williamson-	
Byrdtown, Lamar	NA	Cape Conroe, Montgomery	NA	Travis	5,161
C		Cape Malibu, Montgomery	NA	Cedar Point, Llano	NA
C.H. Rouse Estates,		Cape Tranquility, Henderson	NA	Cedar Shores Estates, Bosque	170
Montgomery	NA	Capitola, Fisher	NA	Cedar Springs, Falls	90
Cabot Kingsmill, Gray	62	Caplen, Galveston	30	Cedar Springs, Upshur	NA
*CACTUS, Moore	1,529	Capps Addition, Montgomery	NA	Cedarvale, Kaufman	NA
Caddell Cove, San Augustine	NA	Capps Corner, Montague	NA	Cedar Valley, Bell	4
*Caddo, Stephens	40	Cap Rock, Crosby	NA	Cedar Valley, Travis	70
Caddo Camp, Hunt	NA	Caps, Taylor	100	*Cee Vee, Cottle	71
Caddo Lake Estates, Marion	NA	Cara Blanca, Baylor	NA	Cego, Falls	98
*†CADDO MILLS, Hunt	1,068	Caradan, Mills	20	Cele, Travis	NA
Cade Chapel, Navarro	NA	Carancahua, Jackson	NA	*†CELESTE, Hunt	733
Cade Lake, Burleson	NA	*CARBON, Eastland	255	*†CELINA, Collin	1,737
Cadiz, Bee	15	Carbondale, Bowie	30	Celotex, Fisher	NA
Cain City, Gillespie	NA	Cardinal Hills, Travis	NA	Centennial, Coleman	NA
Calaveras, Wilson	100	Carey, Childress	60	Center, Fisher	NA
§*†CALDWELL, Burleson	3,181	Carl, Travis	NA	Center, Limestone	76
Caledonia, Rusk	NA	Carlisle, Rusk	161	§*†CENTER, Shelby	4,950
Calf Creek, McCulloch	23	Carlisle, Trinity	95	Center City, Mills	15
Calina, Limestone	NA	Carlos, Grimes	NA	Center Grove, Franklin	NA
*Call, Jasper-Newton	170	*Carlsbad, Tom Green	100	Center Grove, Houston	NA
*Calliham, McMullen	90	CARL'S CORNER, Hill	94	Center Grove, Titus	NA
CALLISBURG, Cooke	344	Carlson, Travis	61	Center Hill, Houston	NA
Call Junction, Jasper	50	*Carlton, Hamilton	70	Center Line, Burleson	NA
*CALVERT, Robertson	1,536	*†CARMINE, Fayette	192	Center Mill, Hood	NA
Cambridge Shores, Grayson	NA	Carmona, Polk	50	Center Plains, Swisher	NA
*Camden, Polk	1,200	Caro, Nacogdoches	113	Center Point, Camp	NA
Camelot, Travis	NA	Carolina, Walker	NA	Center Point, Ellis	NA
§*†CAMERON, Milam	5,580	Carpenter, Wilson	NA	Centerpoint, Hays	NA
Cameron Park, Cameron	3,802	Carpenters Bluff, Grayson	NA	Center Point, Howard	NA
Camilla, San Jacinto	70	Carriage Hills, Montgomery	NA	Center Point, Hunt	NA
Camp Air, Mason	15	Carricitos, Cameron	25	*Center Point, Kerr	623
*CAMPBELL, Hunt	683	Carrizo Creek Estates,		Center Point, Panola	NA
*Campbellton, Atascosa	275	Nacogdoches	NA	Center Point, Upshur	NA
Camp Creek Lake, Robertson	241	§*†CARRIZO SPRINGS,		Centerview, Leon	NA
Campo Alto, Hidalgo	NA	Dimmit	5,745	§*CENTERVILLE, Leon	812
Camp Ruby, Polk	35	Carroll, Smith	60	Centerville, Trinity	40

Town and County-	Pop.
Center Vine, Morris	NA
Central, Angelina	105
Central Gardens, Jefferson	4,026
Central Heights, Nacogdoches	NA
Central High, Cherokee	NA
*Centralia, Trinity	26
Cestohowa, Karnes	110
Chaille, Grimes	20
Chalk, Cottle	45
Chalk Bluff Estates, McLennan	NA
Chalk Hill, Rusk	NA
Chalk Mountain, Erath	25
Chambersville, Collin	40
Chambliss, Collin	25
Champion, Nolan	16
Champions, Harris	17,125
Chances Store, Burleson	NA
*†CHANDLER, Henderson	1,630
Chaney, Eastland	35
*†Channelview, Harris	25,564
§*CHANNING, Hartley	277
Chaparral Estates, Liberty	NA
Chapel Hill, Smith	NA
Chapman, Rusk	20
Chapman Lakeside, San Augustine	NA
*Chapman Ranch, Nueces	100
Chapparal Park, Hays	NA
Chappel, San Saba	25
*†Chappell Hill, Washington	310
Charco, Goliad	68
Charleston, Delta	120
Charlie, Clay	65
*†CHARLOTTE, Atascosa	1,475
Chase Field Naval Air Stn., Bee	1,221
CHATEAU WOODS, Montgomery	641
*Chatfield, Navarro	40
Chatt, Hill	NA
*Cheapside, Gonzales	31
Cheek, Jefferson	62
Cheneyboro, Navarro	NA
*Cherokee, San Saba	175
Cherokee Club Estates, Cherokee	NA
Cherokee Cove, Hunt	NA
Cherokee Hill, Smith	NA
Cherry Spring, Gillespie	75
*†CHESTER, Tyler	285
Chesterville, Colorado	NA
*†CHICO, Wise	800
*Chicota, Lamar	125
Chihuahua, Hidalgo	NA
Chihuahua Farm, Zapata	NA
§*†CHILDRESS, Childress	5,055
*†CHILLICOTHE, Hardeman	816
*Chilton, Falls	310
*CHINA, Jefferson	1,144
CHINA GROVE, Bexar	872
China Grove, Scurry	15
*China Spring, McLennan	181
Chinati, Presidio	NA
Chinquapin, Matagorda	NA
*†CHIRENO, Nacogdoches	415
Chita, Trinity	75
Choate, Karnes	NA
Chocolate Bayou, Brazoria	60
Choice, Shelby	21
*Chriesman, Burleson	30
*CHRISTINE, Atascosa	368
*Christoval, Tom Green	216
Church Hill, Rusk	15
Churchill Bridge, Brazoria	NA
*CIBOLO, Guadalupe-Bexar	1,757
Cibolo Oaks Landing, Kendall	NA
Cipres, Hidalgo	20
Circle, Cherokee	NA
Circle, Lamb	NA
Circleback, Bailey	10
Circle D-KC Estates, Bastrop	1,247
Circleville, Travis	NA
Circleville, Williamson	42
*†CISCO, Eastland	3,813
Cistern, Fayette	75
Citrus City, Hidalgo	NA
Citrus Grove, Matagorda	NA
Clairemont, Kent	15
Clairette, Erath	55

Town and County-	Pop.
Clara, Wichita	100
Clardy, Lamar	NA
§*†CLARENDON, Donley	2,067
Clareville, Bee	23
Clark, Liberty	NA
Clark, Victoria	NA
Clarkson, Milam	10
§*CLARKSVILLE, Red River	4,311
*CLARKSVILLE CITY, Gregg-Upshur	720
§*†CLAUDE, Armstrong	1,199
Clauene, Hockley	24
Clawson, Angelina	195
CLAY, Burleson	61
Clays Corner, Parmer	NA
*Clayton, Panola	79
Claytonville, Fisher	21
Claytonville, Swisher	116
Clear Creek, Burnet	NA
Clear Creek, Henderson	NA
Clear Creek Forest, Montgomery	NA
Clear Lake, Collin	50
CLEAR LAKE SHORES, Galveston	1,096
Clear Springs, Guadalupe	60
Clearview Estates, Henderson	NA
Clearview Point, Henderson	NA
Clearwater, Franklin	NA
Clear Water Bay, Henderson	NA
Clear Water Cove, San Patricio	NA
Clear Water Estates, Comal	NA
§*†CLEBURNE, Johnson	22,205
Clegg, Live Oak	25
Clemons, Waller	NA
*Clemville, Matagorda	54
Cleo, Kimble	3
Cleveland, Austin	78
*†CLEVELAND, Liberty	7,124
Cliffside, Potter	206
*CLIFTON, Bosque	3,195
Clifton, Van Zandt	NA
Climax, Collin	40
Cline, Uvalde	10
*CLINT, El Paso	1,035
Clinton, Hunt	NA
*Clodine, Fort Bend	31
Clopton, Franklin	15
Close City, Garza	107
Cloverleaf, Harris	18,230
Club Lake, Collingsworth	NA
Club Lakeview, Waller	NA
*CLUTE, Brazoria	8,910
*†CLYDE, Callahan	3,002
*†COAHOMA, Howard	1,133
Cobb, Archer	NA
Cobbs, Kaufman	NA
Coble, Hockley	NA
Cochran, Austin	116
*COCKRELL HILL, Dallas	3,746
COFFEE CITY, Henderson	216
Coffeeville, Upshur	50
Cofferville, Lamb	NA
Coit, Limestone	NA
Coke, Wood	105
§*†COLDSPRING, San Jacinto	538
Cold Springs, Coryell	NA
Coldwater, Dallam	NA
§*†COLEMAN, Coleman	5,410
Coleman Cove, San Augustine	NA
Colfax, Van Zandt	35
Colita, Polk	NA
College Hill, Bowie	116
College Mound, Kaufman	350
*Collegeport, Matagorda	91
*†COLLEGE STATION, Brazos	52,456
Bryan-College Station 1990 metro. pop.	121,862
*COLLEYVILLE, Tarrant	12,724
*COLLINSVILLE, Grayson	1,033
*†COLMESNEIL, Tyler	569
Cologne, Goliad	85
Colony, Fayette	NA
Colony, Rains	70
Colonys Estates, Medina	NA
Colorado, Jim Hogg	23
§*†COLORADO CITY,	

Town and County-	Pop.
Mitchell	4,749
Colorado River Ranchettes, Travis	NA
Colquitt, Kaufman	NA
Coltexo, Gray	5
Coltharp, Houston	NA
Colton, Travis	50
Columbia Lakes, Brazoria	NA
§*†COLUMBUS, Colorado	3,367
Comal, Comal	40
Comal Hills, Comal	NA
§*†COMANCHE, Comanche	4,087
Comanche Cove, Hood	560
Comanche Harbor, Hood	250
Comanche Pass, Travis	NA
Comanche Rancheros, Llano	NA
*COMBES, Cameron	2,042
COMBINE, Kaufman-Dallas	1,329
Cometa, Zavala	NA
*†Comfort, Kendall	1,477
*COMMERCE, Hunt	6,825
*COMO, Hopkins	563
Compton, Rusk	NA
*Comstock, Val Verde	375
Comyn, Comanche	27
*Concan, Uvalde	71
*Concepcion, Duval	25
Concho, Concho	NA
Concord, Cherokee	NA
Concord, Hunt	30
Concord, Johnson	NA
*Concord, Leon	28
Concord, Liberty	26
Concord, Madison	50
Concord, Rusk	23
Concordia, Nueces	NA
Concrete, DeWitt	46
*Cone, Crosby	110
Conlen, Dallam	61
Connor, Madison	NA
§*†CONROE, Montgomery	27,610
Conroe Bay, Montgomery	NA
Content, Bell	25
*†CONVERSE, Bexar	8,887
Conway, Carson	50
Cooks Point, Burleson	60
Cooks Store, Anderson	NA
*Cookville, Titus	105
COOL, Parker	214
Cool Crest, Bexar	NA
*†COOLIDGE, Limestone	748
Coon Creek, Bosque	NA
§*†COOPER, Delta	2,153
Cooper, Houston	NA
Copano Village, Aransas	210
Copeland, Montgomery	NA
Copeland, Smith	NA
Copeland Creek, Marion	NA
*Copeville, Collin	NA
*†COPPELL, Dallas-Denton	16,881
*†COPPERAS COVE, Coryell-Lampasas	24,079
COPPER CANYON, Denton	978
Corbet, Navarro	80
Cordele, Jackson	74
CORINTH, Denton	3,944
Corinth, Jones	25
Corinth, Leon	NA
Corinthian Point, Montgomery	NA
Corley, Bowie	35
Cornersville, Hopkins	NA
Cornett, Cass	30
Corn Hill, Williamson	NA
Cornudas, Hudspeth	NA
§*†CORPUS CHRISTI, Nueces-San Patricio-Kleberg	257,453
1990 metro. pop.	349,894
*Corpus Christi Naval Air Stn, Nueces	500
CORRAL CITY, Denton	46
*†CORRIGAN, Polk	1,764
Corry, Lamb	NA
§*†CORSICANA, Navarro	22,911
Coryell City, Coryell	125
*Cost, Gonzales	62
Cotton Center, Fannin	5
*Cotton Center, Hale	205

Town and County—	Pop.
*†Enloe, Delta	113
*†ENNIS, Ellis	13,883
Ennis, Scurry	3
Enoch, Upshur	NA
*Enochs, Bailey	164
Enright, Brazos	NA
Ensign, Ellis	10
Enterprise, Van Zandt	90
*Eola, Concho	218
Eolian, Stephens	9
Equestrian Estates, Brazos	NA
*Era, Cooke	200
Ericksdahl, Jones	75
Erin, Jasper	40
Erlins Green, Comal	NA
Ernies Acres, Brazoria	NA
Erwin, Grimes	NA
Escobares, Starr	1,705
Escobas, Zapata	25
Eskota, Fisher	NA
Esperanza, Hudspeth	75
Espey, Atascosa	NA
Esquire Estates, Henderson	NA
Esseville, Live Oak	NA
Estacado, Lubbock	80
*ESTELLINE, Hall	194
Estes, Aransas	50
Ethel, Grayson	25
*Etoile, Nacogdoches	70
Etter, Moore	160
Eubank Acres, Travis	NA
Eula, Callahan	125
*†EULESS, Tarrant	38,149
Eulogy, Bosque	45
Eunice, Leon	NA
Eureka, Franklin	NA
EUREKA, Navarro	242
Eureka, Stephens	NA
*EUSTACE, Henderson	662
*Evadale, Jasper	1,422
*†EVANT, Coryell-Hamilton	444
Evergreen, Hamilton	NA
Evergreen, San Jacinto	50
Evergreen Park, Orange	NA
*EVERMAN, Tarrant	5,672
Ewell, Upshur	100
Eylau, Bowie	2,962
Ezzell, Lavaca	55
F	
*†Fabens, El Paso	5,599
Fails, Walker	NA
Fairbanks, Harris	1,050
Fairchilds, Fort Bend	150
§*†FAIRFIELD, Freestone	3,234
Fairland, Burnet	NA
Fairlie, Hunt	80
Fairmount, Sabine	NA
Fair Oaks, Freestone	23
Fair Oaks, Limestone	NA
*FAIR OAKS RANCH, Bexar-Comal-Kendall	1,860
Fair Play, Panola	80
Fairview, Angelina	NA
Fairview, Armstrong	NA
Fairview, Brazos	NA
Fairview, Cass	NA
FAIRVIEW, Collin	1,554
Fairview, Comanche	NA
Fairview, Crosby	NA
Fairview, Gaines	NA
Fairview, Hockley	10
Fairview, Hood	NA
Fairview, Howard	85
Fairview, Rusk	NA
Fairview, Wilson	322
FAIRVIEW, Wise	206
Fairy, Hamilton	31
Falcon, Zapata	50
*Falcon Heights, Starr	361
Falcon Village, Starr	NA
§*†FALFURRIAS, Brooks	5,788
Fallon, Limestone	NA
*†FALLS CITY, Karnes	478
Fambrough, Stephens	NA
Famuliner, Cochran	NA
Fannett, Jefferson	105
*Fannin, Goliad	105
Fargo, Wilbarger	161

Town and County—	Pop.
Farmers Academy, Titus	NA
*†FARMERS BRANCH, Dallas	24,250
Farmers Valley, Wilbarger	50
*†FARMERSVILLE, Collin	2,640
Farmington, Grayson	20
*Farnsworth, Ochiltree	149
Farr, Ward	NA
Farrar, Limestone	51
Farrsville, Newton	150
§*†FARWELL, Parmer	1,373
Fashing, Atascosa	50
*FATE, Rockwall	475
Faught, Lamar	25
Faulkner (or Pinhook), Lamar	48
Fawil, Newton	NA
Fayburg, Collin	NA
*†FAYETTEVILLE, Fayette	283
Fays Corner, Hidalgo	NA
Faysville, Hidalgo	300
Fedor, Lee	76
*Fentress, Caldwell	85
*FERRIS, Ellis	2,212
Fetzer, Waller	NA
Field Schoolhouse, Erath	12
Field Senate, Jack	NA
Fields Store, Waller	NA
*Fieldton, Lamb	126
*Fife, McCulloch	32
Files Valley, Hill	50
Fincastle, Henderson	NA
Fink, Grayson	25
Finney, Hale	15
Finney, King	70
First Colony, Fort Bend	18,327
*Fischer, Comal	20
Fisk, Coleman	40
Five Notch, Harrison	NA
Five Points, Ellis	NA
Flaccus, Karnes	NA
Flagg, Castro	50
Flamingo Isles, Galveston	NA
Flamingo Lake, Montgomery	NA
*Flat, Coryell	210
Flat Fork, Shelby	NA
*†FLATONIA, Fayette	1,295
Flat Prairie, Trinity	NA
Flats, Rains	100
Flat Top, Stonewall	NA
Flatwoods, Eastland	56
*Flint, Smith	150
Flint Rock Hills, Travis	NA
Flo, Leon	20
*Flomot, Motley	181
Flora, Hopkins	NA
Flora Bluff, Franklin	NA
*†FLORENCE, Williamson	829
§*†FLORESVILLE, Wilson	5,247
Florey, Andrews	25
Flowella, Brooks	NA
Flower Hill, Colorado	NA
*FLOWER MOUND, Denton	15,527
Floy, Fayette	NA
Floyd, Hunt	220
§*†FLOYDADA, Floyd	3,896
Flugrath, Blanco	NA
*Fluvanna, Scurry	180
Fly Gap, Mason	NA
*Flynn, Leon	81
Foard City, Foard	10
Fodice, Houston	49
*†FOLLETT, Lipscomb	441
Folsom, Shelby	NA
Foncine, Collin	20
Foot, Collin	20
Footes, Gregg	NA
Ford, Deaf Smith	NA
Ford Oaks, Travis	NA
Fords Corner, San Augustine	NA
Fordtran, Victoria	18
*Forest, Cherokee	85
*Forestburg, Montague	200
Forest Chapel, Lamar	NA
Forest Cove, Montgomery	NA
Forest Creek, Bexar	NA
*Forest Glade, Bexar	NA
Forest Glade, Limestone	340

Town and County—	Pop.
Forest Grove, Collin	20
Forest Grove, Milam	60
Forest Heights, Orange	250
Forest Hill, Lamar	NA
FOREST HILL, Tarrant	11,482
Forest Hill, Wood	NA
Forest Hill Estates, Coryell	125
Forest Hills, Montgomery	NA
Forest Lake, Brazos	NA
Forest Lake, Gregg	NA
Forest North Estates, Williamson	NA
Forest Park, Henderson	NA
Forest Springs, Polk	NA
Forest Trail, Montgomery	NA
Forest View North, Comal	NA
*†FORNEY, Kaufman	4,070
*Forreston, Ellis	300
*FORSAN, Howard	256
*Fort Bliss, El Paso	13,915
Fort Clark Springs, Kinney	1,070
§*†Fort Davis, Jeff Davis	1,212
FORT GATES, Coryell	818
Fort Griffin, Shackelford	96
*Fort Hancock, Hudspeth	400
*†Fort Hood, Bell-Coryell	35,580
*Fort McKavett, Menard	45
Fort Parker, Limestone	2
Fort Parker State Park, Limestone	30
*Fort Sam Houston, Bexar	10,000
Fort Spunky, Hood	15
Fort Stanley Creek, Angelina	NA
§*†FORT STOCKTON, Pecos	8,524
§*†FORT WORTH, Tarrant-Denton	447,619
Dallas-Fort Worth 1990 CMSA pop.	3,885,415
Foster, Fort Bend	NA
Foster, Terry	NA
Foster Creek Estates, Fort Bend	NA
Fostoria, Montgomery	NA
Fouke, Wood	NA
Four Corners, Brazoria	NA
Four Corners, Chambers	NA
Four Corners, Fort Bend	NA
Four Corners, Harris	NA
Four Corners, Montgomery	NA
Four Points, Travis	NA
Four Way, Moore	NA
*Fowlerton, La Salle	100
Fox Chase Farms, Kendall	NA
Fox Hill, Comal	NA
Fox Run, Bexar	NA
Foxwood, Montgomery	NA
Frame Switch, Williamson	20
*Francitas, Jackson	30
Frank, Fannin	3
*Frankel City, Andrews	NA
Frankell, Stephens	NA
§*†FRANKLIN, Robertson	1,336
Franklin Center, Scurry	NA
*†FRANKSTON, Anderson	1,122
Fred, Tyler	239
§*†FREDERICKSBURG, Gillespie	6,934
Fredonia, Gregg	NA
*Fredonia, Mason	50
Freedom, Rains	60
Freeneytown, Rusk	NA
*†FREEPORT, Brazoria	11,389
*†FREER, Duval	3,271
*Freestone, Freestone	35
Freeway Forest, Montgomery	NA
Freeway Oaks Estates, Montgomery	NA
Freheit, Comal	NA
Frelsburg, Colorado	75
Frenstat, Burleson	NA
Fresno, Collingsworth	NA
*Fresno, Fort Bend	3,182
Freyburg, Fayette	40
Friday, Trinity	40
Friendly, Van Zandt	NA
Friendship, Dawson	8
Friendship, Lamb	NA
Friendship, Leon	NA

Town and County-	Pop.	Town and County-	Pop.	Town and County-	Pop.
Friendship, Smith	NA	Geronimo Village, Bexar	NA	§*†GRAHAM, Young	8,986
Friendship, Trinity	NA	Gethsemane, Marion	NA	Granada Hills, Travis	NA
Friendship, Upshur	NA	GHOLSON, McLennan	692	§*†GRANBURY, Hood	4,045
Friendship, Williamson	48	Gibtown, Jack	NA	Grand Bluff, Panola	97
Friendship Village, Bowie	200	§*†GIDDINGS, Lee	4,093	*GRANDFALLS, Ward	583
*†FRIENDSWOOD, Galveston-		Gifco, Ellis	NA	*†GRAND PRAIRIE, Dallas-	
Harris	22,814	Gilbert, Angelina	NA	Tarrant-Ellis	99,616
Frio, Castro	60	*Gilchrist, Galveston	750	*GRAND SALINE, Van Zandt	2,630
*†FRIONA, Parmer	3,688	Gill, Harrison	NA	Grandview, Dawson	NA
Frio Town, Frio	38	*Gillett, Karnes	120	Grandview, Gray	13
*FRISCO, Collin-Denton	6,141	Gilliland, Knox	103	*†GRANDVIEW, Johnson	1,245
*†FRITCH, Hutchinson-Moore	2,335	§*†GILMER, Upshur	4,822	Grandview Beach, Burnet	NA
Frog, Kaufman	NA	Gilpin, Childress	NA	Grange Hall, Harrison	NA
Frognot, Collin	NA	Gilpin, Dickens	NA	*†GRANGER, Williamson	1,190
Front, Panola	NA	Ginger, Rains	96	*Grangerland, Montgomery	NA
Frontier Lakes, Montgomery	NA	*Girard, Kent	125	*GRANITE SHOALS, Burnet	1,378
Fronton, Starr	110	Girlstown USA, Cochran	NA	Granite Shoals Lake Estates,	
*†FROST, Navarro	579	*Girvin, Pecos	30	Llano	NA
Fruitland, Montague	20	Gist, Jasper	NA	Granjeno, Hidalgo	NA
*FRUITVALE, Van Zandt	349	Givens, Lamar	135	Gran Sabana, Burnet	NA
Frydek, Austin	150	Glade Branch, Franklin	NA	Gran Sabana, Llano	NA
Fulbright, Red River	150	*†GLADEWATER, Gregg-		Grape Creek, Tom Green	NA
*FULSHEAR, Fort Bend	557	Upshur	6,027	*†GRAPELAND, Houston	1,450
*FULTON, Aransas	763	Gladys, Montague	NA	Grapetown, Gillespie	NA
Funston, Jones	76	Glass, Somervell	NA	*†GRAPEVINE, Tarrant-	
Furrh, Panola	40	Glaze City, Gonzales	10	Dallas-Denton	29,202
		*Glazier, Hemphill	45	Grassland, Lynn	61
G		Glen Cove, Coleman	40	Grassyville, Bastrop	50
Gadston, Lamar	NA	Glendale, Trinity	78	Gray, Marion	NA
Gafford, Hopkins	NA	Glenfawn, Rusk	16	Grayback, Wilbarger	25
§*Gail, Borden	202	*Glen Flora, Wharton	210	GRAYBURG, Hardin	257
§*†GAINESVILLE, Cooke	14,256	Glenmont Estates, Montgomery	NA	Gray Rock, Franklin	NA
Galena, Smith	NA	Glen More, Comal	NA	GRAYS PRAIRIE, Kaufman	286
*GALENA PARK, Harris	10,033	Glenn, Dickens	NA	Graytown, Wilson	64
Galilee, Smith	NA	GLENN HEIGHTS, Dallas-Ellis	4,564	Great N.W. Emerald Valley,	
Galilee, Walker	NA	Glenn Oaks, Henderson	NA	Bexar	NA
*GALLATIN, Cherokee	368	Glen Oaks, Kerr	NA	Great Oaks, Williamson	NA
Galle, Guadalupe	80	Glen Oaks, San Augustine	NA	Green, Karnes	35
Galleon Bay, Nueces	NA	Glenrio, Deaf Smith	NA	Green Acres, Hunt	NA
Galloway, Panola	71	§*†GLEN ROSE, Somervell	1,949	Green Acres, Sabine	NA
§*†GALVESTON, Galveston	59,070	Glenwood, Upshur	NA	Green Brier Cove, Henderson	NA
Galveston-Texas City		*Glidden, Colorado	255	Green Glenn Acres, Medina	NA
1990 metro. pop.	217,399	Globe, Lamar	NA	Green Hill, Titus	NA
*†GANADO, Jackson	1,701	Glory, Lamar	30	Green Lake, Calhoun	51
Gannon, Fisher	NA	*Gober, Fannin	146	Green Pastures, Hays	NA
Garceno, Starr	45	*GODLEY, Johnson	569	Greenpond, Hopkins	NA
Garcia, Deaf Smith	NA	*Golden, Wood	156	Greenridge North, Bexar	NA
Garcias, Starr	NA	Golden Beach, Llano	NA	Greens Creek, Erath	75
§*Garden City, Glasscock	293	Golden Oaks, Williamson	NA	Greenshores, Travis	NA
Gardendale, Bexar	NA	Golden Trails, Montgomery	NA	Green Spring Valley, Bexar	NA
*Gardendale, Ector	1,103	Goldfinch, Frio	35	Greenview, Hopkins	NA
Gardendale, La Salle	59	*Goldsboro, Coleman	30	§*†GREENVILLE, Hunt	23,071
†GARDEN RIDGE, Comal	1,450	*GOLDSMITH, Ector	297	Greenvine, Washington	35
Garden Valley, Childress	NA	§*†GOLDTHWAITE, Mills	1,658	Greenway, Bexar	NA
Garden Valley, Smith	150	§*†GOLIAD, Goliad	1,946	Greenwood, Hopkins	35
Garfield, DeWitt	NA	GOLINDA, Falls-McLennan	347	Greenwood, Midland	32
Garfield, Travis-Bastrop	1,336	Golly, DeWitt	NA	Greenwood, Red River	20
Garland, Bowie	NA	Gomez, Terry	NA	*Greenwood, Wise	76
*†GARLAND, Dallas-Collin-		§*†GONZALES, Gonzales	6,527	Greenwood Acres, Llano	NA
Rockwall	180,650	Goober Hill, Shelby	NA	Greenwood Acres, Orange	NA
Garner, Parker	98	*Goodfellow Air Force Base, Tom		Greenwood Forest, Kerr	NA
Garner State Park, Uvalde	40	Green	345	*GREGORY, San Patricio	2,458
GARRETT, Ellis	340	Good Hope, Franklin	NA	Gresham, Smith	100
Garretts Bluff, Lamar	20	*Goodland, Bailey	25	GREY FOREST, Bexar	425
*†GARRISON, Nacogdoches	883	Goodlett, Hardeman	80	Greystone, Comal	NA
*Garwood, Colorado	975	GOODLOW, Navarro	319	Grice, Upshur	20
*GARY, Panola	271	Good Neighbor, Hopkins	NA	Griffin, Cherokee	21
Gas Plant, Terrell	31	Goodnight, Armstrong	25	Griffith, Cochran	NA
Gastonia, Kaufman	30	Goodnight, Navarro	NA	Griffith Switch, Ellis	10
§*†GATESVILLE, Coryell	11,492	*GOODRICH, Polk	239	Grigsby, Shelby	45
*Gause, Milam	400	Goodsprings, Rusk	21	Grit, Mason	30
Gay Hill, Washington	145	Goodwill, Burleson	NA	§*†GROESBECK, Limestone	3,185
Gayle Estates, Brazoria	NA	Goodwin, San Augustine	NA	*†GROOM, Carson	613
*Geneva, Sabine	100	*GORDON, Palo Pinto	465	Grossville, Mason	NA
Geneva Estates, Travis	NA	*Gordonville, Grayson	220	*GROVES, Jefferson	16,513
Geneview, Stonewall	NA	*GOREE, Knox	412	§*†GROVETON, Trinity	1,071
Gentrys Mill, Hamilton	NA	*†GORMAN, Eastland	1,290	Grow, King	70
Geola Estates, Llano	NA	Goshen, Walker	NA	Gruenau, DeWitt	NA
George's Creek, Somervell	66	Gould, Cherokee	NA	Gruene Oaks, Comal	NA
§*†GEORGETOWN,		*Gouldbusk, Coleman	70	*†GRUVER, Hansford	1,172
Williamson	14,842	Gourdneck, Panola	30	Guadalupe, Victoria	106
§*†GEORGE WEST, Live Oak	2,586	Graball, Washington	NA	Guadalupe Heights, Kerr	NA
Georgia, Lamar	NA	Grace, King	20	Guadalupe Station, Culberson	80
Germania, Midland	27	Graceton, Upshur	40	*Guerra, Jim Hogg	75
Germany, Houston	NA	*†GRAFORD, Palo Pinto	561	Guion, Taylor	18
*Geronimo, Guadalupe	250	Graham, Garza	183	Gulf Dial, Hutchinson	80
Geronimo Forest, Bexar	NA	Graham, Jasper	NA	Gulf Haven, Galveston	NA

Town and County-	Pop.	Town and County-	Pop.	Town and County-	Pop.
Gum Springs, Cass	NA	Harvey, Brazos	310	High Chapparal, Montgomery	NA
Gum Springs, Harrison	NA	Harwell Point, Burnet	NA	High Gabriel East, Williamson	NA
†GUN BARREL CITY,		*Harwood, Gonzales	112	High Gabriel West, Williamson	NA
Henderson	3,526	§*†HASKELL, Haskell	3,362	High Hill, Fayette	116
Gunsight, Stephens	6	Haslam, Shelby	101	*High Island, Galveston	500
*GUNTER, Grayson	898	*HASLET, Tarrant-Denton	795	Highland, Erath	60
Gus, Burleson	NA	*Hasse, Comanche	43	Highland, Smith	NA
*†GUSTINE, Comanche	430	Hatchel, Runnels	16	Highland Acres, Hunt	NA
§*Guthrie, King	160	Hatchetville, Hopkins	NA	Highland Addition, Parker	NA
*Guy, Fort Bend	60	Havana, Hidalgo	NA	Highland Bayou, Galveston	1,209
Guys Store, Leon	NA	*†HAWKINS, Wood	1,309	Highland Haven, Burnet	NA
		*HAWLEY, Jones	606	Highland Hollow, Montgomery	NA
H		Hawthorne, Shelby	NA	HIGHLAND PARK, Dallas	8,739
Haciendito, Presidio	NA	Hawthorne, Walker	NA	Highland Park, Nacogdoches	NA
Hackberry, Cottle	81	Hawthorn Ridge, Montgomery	NA	*†Highlands, Harris	6,632
HACKBERRY, Denton	200	Haynesville, Wichita	60	†HIGHLAND VILLAGE,	
Hackberry, Edwards	NA	Haynie Flat, Travis-Burnet	NA	Denton	7,027
Hackberry, Garza-Lynn	NA	HAYS, Hays	251	High Point, Collin	NA
Hackberry, Lavaca	NA	Hays City, Hays	NA	High Point, Grimes	15
Hagansport, Franklin	40	Hays Country Oaks, Hays	NA	Highsaw, Henderson	NA
Hagerville, Houston	NA	Hazle Dell, Comanche	NA	Hightower, Liberty	30
Hail, Fannin	30	Hazy Hollow, Montgomery	NA	Hightown, Polk	NA
Hainesville, Wood	74	Headsville, Robertson	NA	Highway 90 Ranch, Medina	NA
*†HALE CENTER, Hale	2,067	*†HEARNE, Robertson	5,132	Hilda, Mason	NA
Halfway, Hale	58	*HEATH, Rockwall	2,108	Hilger, Fannin	NA
Hall, Marion	NA	Heatherstone, Harris	NA	Hill and Dale Acres,	
Hall, San Saba	NA	§*†Hebbronville, Jim Hogg	4,465	Montgomery	NA
§*†HALLETTSVILLE, Lavaca	2,718	HEBRON, Denton	1,128	Hill Country Ranches, Hays	NA
Halls Bluff, Houston	NA	Heckville, Lubbock	NA	HILL COUNTRY VILLAGE,	
HALLSBURG, McLennan	450	*HEDLEY, Donley	391	Bexar	1,038
Halls Store, Panola	NA	Hedwigs Hill, Mason	10	Hillcrest, Colorado	25
*†HALLSVILLE, Harrison	2,288	HEDWIG VILLAGE, Harris	2,616	HILLCREST VILLAGE,	
Halsted, Fayette	46	Hefner, Knox	76	Brazoria	695
*†HALTOM CITY, Tarrant	32,856	Hegar, Waller	NA	*Hillister, Tyler	200
Hamby, Taylor	100	Heidelberg, Hidalgo	NA	Hillje, Wharton	51
Hamilton, Franklin	NA	*Heidenheimer, Bell	144	Hills, Lee	20
§*†HAMILTON, Hamilton	2,937	Helena, Karnes	35	§*†HILLSBORO, Hill	7,072
*†HAMLIN, Jones-Fisher	2,791	Helmic, Trinity	NA	Hillside Estates, Henderson	NA
Hammond, Robertson	44	*HELOTES, Bexar	1,535	Hills Prairie, Bastrop	35
Hamon, Gonzales	15	§*†HEMPHILL, Sabine	1,182	Hilltop Acres, Bexar	NA
Hampton, Nacogdoches	NA	§*†HEMPSTEAD, Waller	3,551	Hilltop Acres, Kaufman	NA
*Hamshire, Jefferson	350	§*†HENDERSON, Rusk	11,139	*Hilltop Lakes, Leon	300
Hancock Oak Hills, Comal	NA	Henderson Chapel, Concho	NA	HILSHIRE VILLAGE, Harris	665
*Hankamer, Chambers	189	Hendricks, Hunt	NA	Hinckley, Lamar	40
Hannibal, Erath	NA	Henly, Hays	55	Hindes, Atascosa	14
Hanover, Milam	27	§*†HENRIETTA, Clay	2,896	Hines, Johnson	NA
Hansford, Hansford	NA	Henry's Chapel, Cherokee	75	Hinkles Ferry, Brazoria	35
*†HAPPY, Swisher-Randall	588	§*†HEREFORD, Deaf Smith	14,745	Hippie Ridge, Wise	
Happy Hill, Johnson	NA	Heritage Farm, Bexar	NA	(See Draper Addition)	
Happy Landing, Shelby	NA	Heritage Hills, Hays	NA	Hiram, Kaufman	34
Happy Union, Hale	15	Heritage Oaks, Hays	NA	*†HITCHCOCK, Galveston	5,868
Happy Valley, Taylor	NA	Heritage Oaks, Montgomery	NA	Hitchland, Hansford	27
Haralson Lakes, Tyler	NA	Hermits Cove, Rains	40	Hitson, Fisher	NA
Harbin, Erath	21	*Hermleigh, Scurry	200	Hix, Burleson	35
Harborlight, Sabine	NA	Herty, Angelina	605	Hoard, Wood	NA
Harbor Point, Henderson	NA	Hester, Navarro	35	Hobbs, Fisher	91
Harborview, Brazoria	NA	*†HEWITT, McLennan	8,983	*Hobson, Karnes	135
Hardin, Coleman	NA	*Hext, Menard	64	*Hochheim, DeWitt	70
Hardin, Hardin	NA	HICKORY CREEK, Denton	1,893	*Hockley, Harris	300
*HARDIN, Liberty	563	Hickory Creek, Fort Bend	NA	Hodges, Jones	250
Hardy, Montague	NA	Hickory Creek, Houston	NA	Hogan Acres, Johnson	NA
Hare, Williamson	70	Hickory Creek, Hunt	NA	Hogansville, Rains	200
*Hargill, Hidalgo	1,349	Hickory Forrest, Guadalupe	300	Hogg, Burleson	NA
†HARKER HEIGHTS, Bell	12,841	Hickory Hills, Montgomery	NA	Holcomb Store, Cherokee	NA
Harkeyville, San Saba	12	Hickory Hills, Sabine	NA	Holiday Beach, Aransas	1,000
*Harleton, Harrison	260	Hickory Hollow, Hunt	NA	Holiday Estates, Hunt	NA
*†HARLINGEN, Cameron	48,735	Hickory Hollow, San Augustine	NA	Holiday Forest, Sabine	NA
Brownsville-Harlingen		Hicksbaugh, Tyler	NA	Holiday Harbor, Marion	NA
1990 metro. pop.	260,120	*†HICO, Hamilton	1,342	Holiday Hills, Smith	NA
Harlow, Hunt	NA	*†HIDALGO, Hidalgo	3,292	Holiday Hills Estates, Stephens	NA
Harmon, Lamar	35	Hidden Acres, Henderson	NA	Holiday Lake Estates, Polk	NA
Harmon Creek Ridge, Walker	NA	Hidden Acres, Williamson	NA	HOLIDAY LAKES, Brazoria	1,039
Harmony, Floyd	NA	Hidden Forest Estates,		Holiday Oaks, Montgomery	NA
Harmony, Grimes	12	Montgomery	NA	Holiday Shores, Brazoria	NA
Harmony, Limestone	NA	Hidden Hill Lakes, Smith	NA	Holiday Shores, Collin	NA
Harmony, Nacogdoches	NA	Hidden Hills, Travis	NA	*†HOLLAND, Bell	1,118
Harmony Hall, Austin	NA	Hidden Hills Harbor, Henderson	NA	Holland Quarters, Panola	40
*Harper, Gillespie	383	Hidden Meadows, Williamson	NA	*HOLLIDAY, Archer	1,475
Harpersville, Stephens	NA	Hidden Valley, Travis	NA	Holly, Houston	NA
Harriet, Tom Green	NA	Hide-A-Way Lake, Smith	NA	Holly Acres, Angelina	NA
Harris Chapel, Panola	180	Hide Away, Brazoria	NA	Holly Beach, Cameron	NA
Harrison, McLennan	25	Hideaway, Comal	NA	Holly Grove, Polk	NA
*Harrold, Wilbarger	320	Higginbotham, Gaines	210	Holly Hills, Polk	NA
*HART, Castro	1,221	*HIGGINS, Lipscomb	464	Holly Springs, Jasper	50
Hartburg, Newton	275	High, Lamar	55	Holly Terrace, Montgomery	NA
Hart Camp, Lamb	NA	Highbank, Falls	126	HOLLYWOOD PARK, Bexar	2,841
*Hartley, Hartley	370	High Chaparral, Williamson	NA	Holman, Fayette	116
Harvard Switch, Camp	NA				
Harvest Acres, Montgomery	NA				

Town and County-	Pop.	Town and County-	Pop.	Town and County-	Pop.
Homer, Angelina	360	Hurnville, Clay	15	JAMAICA BEACH, Galveston	624
Homestead Meadows, El Paso	4,978	Huron, Hill	NA	James, Shelby	NA
§*†HONDO, Medina	6,018	*†HURST, Tarrant	33,574	James, Upshur	NA
Honea Forrest Estates, Montgomery	NA	Hurstown, Shelby	NA	Jamestown, Newton	70
Honey Creek, Comal	NA	Hurst Springs, Coryell	NA	Jamestown, Smith	75
*†HONEY GROVE, Fannin	1,681	*HUTCHINS, Dallas	2,719	JA Ranch, Armstrong	20
Honey Island, Hardin	401	*†HUTTO, Williamson	630	Jardin, Hunt	22
Hood, Cooke	75	HUXLEY, Shelby	335	*†Jarrell, Williamson	410
*HOOKS, Bowie	2,684	Huxley Bay, Shelby	NA	§*†JASPER, Jasper	6,959
Hooker Ridge, Rains	250	*Hye, Blanco	105	§*†JAYTON, Kent	608
Hoop and Holler, Liberty	NA	Hylton, Nolan	28	Jean, Young	91
Hoover, Gray	5	Hynds City, Montague	NA	Jeddo, Bastrop	75
Hoover, Lamar	NA			§*†JEFFERSON, Marion	2,199
Hope, Lavaca	45	**I**		Jenkins, Morris	NA
Hopewell, Franklin	35	Iago, Wharton	56	Jennings, Lamar	NA
Hopewell, Houston	NA	Ibex, Shackelford	25	Jericho, Shelby	NA
Hopewell, Leon	NA	Ida, Grayson	50	*Jermyn, Jack	75
Hopewell, Red River	150	*†IDALOU, Lubbock	2,074	Jerrys Quarters, Washington	NA
HORIZON CITY, El Paso	2,308	Idle Hour Acres, Travis	NA	JERSEY VILLAGE, Harris	4,826
Hornsby Bend, Travis	20	Ike, Ellis	10	*†JEWETT, Leon	668
*Horseshoe Bay, Llano-Burnet	1,546	Illinois Bend, Montague	NA	Jiba, Kaufman	NA
Horseshoe Bay South, Burnet	NA	IMPACT, Taylor	25	*†JOAQUIN, Shelby	805
Horseshoe Bay West, Llano	NA	Impala Point, Henderson	NA	Joe Lee, Bell	2
Horseshoe Bend, Liberty	NA	Impala Woods, Polk	NA	Johnson, Anderson	NA
Horseshoe Falls, Comal	NA	*Imperial, Pecos	720	Johnson, Terry	NA
Horseshoe Lake, Smith	NA	Imperial Valley, Travis	NA	§*†JOHNSON CITY, Blanco	932
Hortense, Polk	25	Inadale, Scurry	8	Johnson Creek, Marion	NA
Horton, Delta	25	Independence, Washington	140	Johnston Store, Nacogdoches	NA
Horton, Panola	NA	India, Ellis	12	Johnsville, Erath	25
Hostetter Creek Estates, Montgomery	NA	Indian Creek, Smith	NA	Johntown, Red River	175
Houmont Park, Harris	NA	Indian Gap, Hamilton	36	Joiner, Fayette	NA
§*†HOUSTON, Harris-Fort Bend-Montgomery	1,630,553	Indian Harbor Estates, Hood	691	*Joinerville, Rusk	140
Houston-Galveston-Brazoria 1990 CMSA pop.	3,771,043	Indian Hill, Newton	NA	Joliet, Caldwell	NA
Howard, Ellis	26	Indian Hills, Bexar	NA	Jolly, Clay	201
HOWARDWICK, Donley	211	Indian Hills, Comal	NA	Jolly Oaks, Williamson	NA
*†HOWE, Grayson	2,173	Indian Hills, Llano	NA	Jollyville, Williamson-Travis	15,206
Howellville, Harris	36	INDIAN LAKE, Cameron	390	Jonah, Williamson	60
Howland, Lamar	90	Indian Lake, Newton	NA	Jones, Van Zandt	NA
Howth, Waller	65	Indian Lodge, Bosque	NA	*Jonesboro, Coryell-Hamilton	200
Hoxie, Williamson	50	Indian Mound Estates, Sabine	NA	JONES CREEK, Brazoria	2,160
Hoyte, Milam	20	Indian Oaks, Henderson	NA	Jones Prairie, Milam	35
Hub, Parmer	NA	Indian Oaks, Waller	NA	*JONESTOWN, Travis	1,250
Hubbard, Bowie	269	Indian Oaks, Williamson	NA	*Jonesville, Harrison	28
*†HUBBARD, Hill	1,589	Indianola, Calhoun	NA	Joplin, Jack	NA
Huber, Shelby	NA	Indian Rock, Upshur	NA	Joppa, Burnet	NA
Huckabay, Erath	150	Indian Springs, Polk	NA	Jordans Store, Shelby	NA
Hudd, Scurry	NA	Indian Woods, Montgomery	NA	*JOSEPHINE, Collin-Hunt	503
Huddleston, Montague	NA	Indio, Presidio	NA	*†JOSHUA, Johnson	3,828
HUDSON, Angelina	2,374	*†Industry, Austin	475	Josselet, Haskell	NA
Hudson Bend, Travis	NA	*Inez, Victoria	1,371	Josserand, Trinity	NA
HUDSON OAKS, Parker	711	*†INGLESIDE, San Patricio	5,696	Jot-Em-Down, Hunt-Delta	10
Hudsons Chapel, Cherokee	NA	Ingleside-on-the-Bay, San Patricio	NA	§*†JOURDANTON, Atascosa	3,220
Hudsonville, Fannin	5	*INGRAM, Kerr	1,408	Joy, Clay	150
Huff, Archer	NA	Inks Lake Village, Llano	NA	Joyce, Webb	20
Huffines, Cass	90	Inverness Point, Travis	NA	Jud, Haskell	40
*Huffman, Harris	50	*†Iola, Grimes	331	*Judson, Gregg	650
*Hufsmith, Harris	250	IOWA COLONY, Brazoria	675	Jumbo, Castro	NA
*†HUGHES SPRINGS, Cass-Morris	1,938	*†IOWA PARK, Wichita	6,072	Jumbo, Panola	NA
Hughey, Gregg	NA	*Ira, Scurry	250	Junction, Coleman	NA
*†Hull, Liberty	1,800	*†IRAAN, Pecos	1,322	§*†JUNCTION, Kimble	2,654
Hulon Lakes, Montgomery	NA	Irby, Haskell	NA	Juno, Val Verde	10
*†HUMBLE, Harris	12,060	*IREDELL, Bosque	339	*Justiceburg, Garza	76
Humble Colorado Camp, Jim Hogg	NA	Ireland, Coryell	60	*†JUSTIN, Denton	1,234
Humble Government Wells Camp, Duval	NA	*Irene, Hill	160		
Hume, Cherokee	NA	Irish Meadows, Smith	NA	**K**	
*Hungerford, Wharton	178	Ironton, Cherokee	110	Kalgary, Crosby	140
*Hunt, Kerr	708	*†IRVING, Dallas	155,037	*Kamay, Wichita	642
Hunter, Comal	30	Isla, Sabine	29	Kamey, Calhoun	NA
Hunter Hills, Comal	NA	Island Village, Llano	NA	Kanawha, Red River	149
Hunter Oaks, Comal	NA	Israel, Polk	25	*Karnack, Harrison	775
Hunters Creek, Comal	NA	*†ITALY, Ellis	1,699	§*†KARNES CITY, Karnes	2,916
HUNTERS CREEK VILLAGE, Harris	3,954	*†ITASCA, Hill	1,523	Karon, Live Oak	20
Hunters Glen, Hays	NA	Ivan, Stephens	15	*Katemcy, Mason	90
Hunters Retreat, Montgomery	NA	*Ivanhoe, Fannin	110	*†KATY, Harris-Waller-Fort Bend	8,005
*†HUNTINGTON, Angelina	1,794	Iverson, Hill	NA	§*†KAUFMAN, Kaufman	5,238
Huntoon, Ochiltree	21	*Izoro, Lampasas	31	Kaufman Estates, Kaufman	240
§*†HUNTSVILLE, Walker	27,925			Keechi, Leon	67
Hurley, Wood	NA	**J**		*†KEENE, Johnson	3,944
Hurlwood, Lubbock	115	*†JACINTO CITY, Harris	9,343	Keeter, Wise	NA
		§*†JACKSBORO, Jack	3,350	Keith, Grimes	NA
		Jackson, Marion	NA	Keith Lake, Jefferson	NA
		Jackson, Shelby	NA	*†KELLER, Tarrant	13,683
		Jackson, Van Zandt	NA	Kellers Corner, Cameron	NA
		*†JACKSONVILLE, Cherokee	12,765	*Kellerville, Wheeler	50
		Jacobia, Hunt	60	Kellogg, Hunt	NA
		Jacobs, Rusk	NA	Kelly, Collin	NA
		Jakes Colony, Guadalupe	30	*Kelly Air Force Base, Bexar	2,363

Town and County—	Pop.	Town and County—	Pop.	Town and County—	Pop.
Lamar, Aransas	1,600	*LEFORS, Gray	656	Locker, San Saba	16
Lamar, Shelby	NA	*Leggett, Polk	375	Lockett, Wilbarger	200
*†LA MARQUE, Galveston	14,120	Legion, Kerr	NA	Lockettville, Hockley	20
Lamasco, Fannin	32	Lehman, Cochran	NA	§*†LOCKHART, Caldwell	9,205
§*†LAMESA, Dawson	10,809	Leigh, Harrison	100	*†LOCKNEY, Floyd	2,207
Lamkin, Comanche	88	Leisure Acres, Coryell	25	Loco, Childress	NA
§*†LAMPASAS, Lampasas	6,382	Leisure Land, Henderson	NA	Locust, Grayson	NA
Lanark, Cass	NA	Lela, Wheeler	135	*Lodi, Marion	164
*†LANCASTER, Dallas	22,117	*Lelia Lake, Donley	125	Lodwick, Marion	NA
Landrum Station, Cameron	125	*Leming, Atascosa	250	Loeb, Hardin	NA
*Lane City, Wharton	111	*Lenorah, Martin	70	Loebau, Lee	20
Laneley, Freestone	27	Lenz, Karnes	20	Logan, Panola	40
Laneport, Williamson	60	Leo, Cooke	80	LOG CABIN, Henderson	487
*Laneville, Rusk	200	Leo, Lee	NA	*Lohn, McCulloch	149
Langford Place, Orange	NA	*LEONA, Leon	178	Loire, Wilson	50
*Langtry, Val Verde	145	*†LEONARD, Fannin	1,744	Lois, Cooke	60
Lanham, Hamilton	NA	Leona Schroder, Nueces	40	Lolaville, Collin	NA
Lanier, Cass	40	Leonidas, Montgomery	NA	*Lolita, Jackson	300
Lannius, Fannin	79	*Leon Junction, Coryell	25	Lollipop, Henderson	NA
Lansing, Harrison	NA	Leon Springs, Bexar	137	Loma, Walker	NA
Lantana, Cameron	NA	*LEON VALLEY, Bexar	9,581	Loma Alta, McMullen	25
La Paloma, Cameron	110	*LEROY, McLennan	292	Loma Alta, Val Verde	30
La Parita, Atascosa	NA	Lesley, Hall	45	Lomax, Howard	3,554
*†LA PORTE, Harris	27,910	§*†LEVELLAND, Hockley	13,986	*†LOMETA, Lampasas	625
*La Pryor, Zavala	1,343	Leverett's Chapel, Rusk	450	*London, Kimble	180
§*†LAREDO, Webb	122,899	Levi, McLennan	50	London, Rusk	NA
1990 metro. pop.	133,239	Levita, Coryell	70	Londonderry, Harris	NA
La Reforma, Starr	45	*†LEWISVILLE, Denton-		Lone Camp, Palo Pinto	32
*Lariat, Parmer	200	Dallas	46,521	Lone Cedar, Ellis	18
Lark, Carson	NA	*†LEXINGTON, Lee	953	Lone Elm, Ellis	20
La Rose, Nueces	20	Liberty, Coleman	NA	Lone Elm, Kaufman	NA
*Larue, Henderson	160	Liberty, Freestone	75	*Lone Grove, Llano	50
*LaSalle, Jackson	75	Liberty, Hopkins	NA	Lone Oak, Bexar	NA
LaSalle Estates, Montgomery	NA	§ *†LIBERTY, Liberty	7,733	Lone Oak, Colorado	NA
*Lasara, Willacy	100	Liberty, Lubbock	10	Lone Oak, Erath	NA
Las Escobas, Starr	NA	Liberty, Milam	40	*†LONE OAK, Hunt	521
Las Milpas-Hidalgo Park, Hidalgo-		Liberty, Newton	NA	Lone Oak Estates, Bexar	NA
Annexed by Pharr, 1987	4,178	Liberty, Rusk	NA	Lone Pine, Houston	NA
Las Playas, Brazoria	NA	Liberty Chapel, Johnson	NA	Lone Star, Cherokee	NA
Las Rusias, Cameron	NA	Liberty City, Gregg	1,607	Lone Star, Floyd	NA
Lassater, Marion	48	*Liberty Grove, Collin	NA	Lone Star, Franklin	NA
Las Yescas, Cameron	NA	Liberty Hill, Houston	NA	Lone Star, Kaufman	NA
Latch, Upshur	50	*Liberty Hill, Milam	25	Lone Star, Lamar	NA
Latex, Harrison	NA	*Liberty Hill, Williamson	300	*†LONE STAR, Morris	1,615
*LATEXO, Houston	289	Liberty Oaks, Williamson	NA	*Long Branch, Panola	181
La Tina, Cameron	NA	Lilbert, Nacogdoches	NA	Long Hollow, Leon	NA
Latium, Washington	30	*Lillian, Johnson	105	Long Lake, Anderson	NA
Lauback, Guadalupe	13	*Lincoln, Lee	276	Long Lake Estates,	
*Laughlin Air Force Base,		LINCOLN PARK, Denton	287	Montgomery	NA
Val Verde	2,556	*†LINDALE, Smith	2,428	*Long Mott, Calhoun	76
La Union, Cameron	20	§*†LINDEN, Cass	2,375	Long Mountain, Mason	NA
Laurel, Newton	125	Lindenau, DeWitt	50	Longpoint, Washington	80
Laureles, Cameron	20	Lindendale, Kendall	NA	§*†LONGVIEW, Gregg-Harrison-	
Laurel Estates, Hays	NA	*LINDSAY, Cooke	610	Upshur	70,311
Lavada, Franklin	NA	*Lingleville, Erath	100	Longview-Marshall	
*Lavender, Limestone	NA	*Linn, Hidalgo	450	1990 metro. pop.	162,431
*†LA VERNIA, Wilson	639	Linn Flat, Nacogdoches	NA	Longworth, Fisher	65
*LA VILLA, Hidalgo	1,388	Linwood, Cherokee	40	Lonnie, Childress	NA
*LAVON, Collin	303	*†LIPAN, Hood	354	Loon Bay, Henderson	NA
Lavon Beach Estates, Collin	NA	§*Lipscomb, Lipscomb	45	Looneyville, Nacogdoches	NA
Lavon Shores Estates, Collin	NA	*Lissie, Wharton	70	*Loop, Gaines	315
Law, Brazos	NA	Littig, Travis	37	*Lopeno, Zapata	100
*LA WARD, Jackson	162	Little Cypress, Orange	1,050	Lopezville, Hidalgo	2,827
*LAWN, Taylor	358	*LITTLE ELM, Denton	1,255	*†LORAINE, Mitchell	731
*LAWRENCE, Kaufman	231	§*†LITTLEFIELD, Lamb	6,489	*†LORENA, McLennan	1,158
Lawsonville, Rusk	NA	Little Hope, Wood	NA	*†LORENZO, Crosby	1,208
Lazare, Cottle-Hardeman	26	Little Midland, Burnet	NA	*Los Angeles, La Salle	140
*Lazbuddie, Parmer	248	Little New York, Gonzales	20	Los Barreras, Starr	125
Lazy Acres, Nacogdoches	NA	Little Ridge Estates, Collin	NA	Los Coyotes, Willacy	NA
Lazy Caney Pines, Montgomery	NA	*LITTLE RIVER-ACADEMY,		*Los Ebanos, Hidalgo	100
Lazy Forest, Montgomery	NA	Bell	1,390	Los Escondidos, Burnet	NA
Lazy River Resort, Austin	NA	Littleville, Hamilton	NA	*†LOS FRESNOS, Cameron	2,473
*Leaday, Coleman	55	Lively, Kaufman	NA	*Los Indios, Cameron	206
League, Crosby	NA	*LIVE OAK, Bexar	10,023	Losoya, Bexar	322
*†LEAGUE CITY, Galveston	30,159	Live Oak, Concho	NA	Lost Creek, Coleman	NA
Leagueville, Henderson	NA	Liveoak, Newton	NA	Lost Creek, Travis	4,095
§*†LEAKEY, Real	399	Live Oak Bend, Matagorda	NA	Lost Hollow Creek, Llano	NA
*†LEANDER, Williamson-		Live Oak Ranchettes,		Lost Lakes, Montgomery	NA
Travis	3,398	Williamson	NA	Lost Prairie, Limestone	2
Leander Heights, Williamson	NA	Live Oak Resorts, Hill	NA	Lost River Estates, Williamson	NA
*LEARY, Bowie	395	Liveoak Estates, Montgomery	NA	LOS YBANEZ, Dawson	83
Lebanon, Collin	50	*LIVERPOOL, Brazoria	396	*†LOTT, Falls	775
*Ledbetter, Fayette	76	§*†LIVINGSTON, Polk	5,019	Lotta, Harrison	10
Leedale, Bell	16	§*†LLANO, Llano	2,962	*†Louise, Wharton	310
Lees, Glasscock	NA	Lobo, Culberson	40	Lovelace, Hill	NA
*Leesburg, Camp	115	Loch Ness Cove, Montgomery	NA	*†LOVELADY, Houston	587
Lee Spring, Smith	NA	Lochridge, Brazoria	NA	*Loving, Young	240
*Leesville, Gonzales	150				

Town and County–	Pop.	Town and County–	Pop.	Town and County–	Pop.
*Lowake, Concho	40	*MAGNOLIA, Montgomery	940	*Maxwell, Caldwell	185
Lowman, Lamar	NA	Magnolia, San Jacinto	30	*May, Brown	285
LOWRY CROSSING, Collin	865	Magnolia Beach, Calhoun	NA	*Maydelle, Cherokee	250
Loyal Valley, Mason	50	Magnolia Bend, Montgomery	NA	Mayfield, Hale	NA
Loyola Beach, Kleberg	NA	Magnolia Gardens, Harris	NA	Mayfield, Hill	NA
*Lozano, Cameron	200	Magnolia Hills, Montgomery	NA	Mayflower, Newton	100
§*†LUBBOCK, Lubbock	186,206	Magnolia Lake, Montgomery	NA	Mayhill, Denton	150
1990 metro. pop.	222,636	Magnolia Oaks, Montgomery	NA	Maynard, San Jacinto	25
*LUCAS, Collin	2,205	*Magnolia Springs, Jasper	80	*†MAYPEARL, Ellis	781
Luckenbach, Gillespie	25	Maha, Travis	NA	*Maysfield, Milam	140
*LUEDERS, Jones-Shackelford	365	Mahl, Nacogdoches	NA	*MEADOW, Terry	547
LUELLA, Grayson	559	Mahomet, Burnet	47	Meadowbrook, Montgomery	NA
§*†LUFKIN, Angelina	30,206	Mahoney, Hopkins	NA	Meadowbrook, Smith	NA
*†LULING, Caldwell	4,661	Majors, Franklin	NA	Meadowcreek, Kaufman	240
Lull, Hidalgo	NA	*MALAKOFF, Henderson	2,038	Meadow Grove, Bell	10
*†LUMBERTON, Hardin	6,640	Mallard, Montague	NA	Meadow Lake, Guadalupe	250
Lumkins, Ellis	20	*MALONE, Hill	306	MEADOWLAKES, Burnet	514
Lums Chapel, Lamb	NA	Malta, Bowie	297	Meadowood Acres, Bexar	NA
Lund, Travis	50	Malvern, Leon	NA	MEADOWS, Fort Bend	4,606
Lusk, Throckmorton	NA	Mambrino, Hood	74	Meadowview, Hunt	NA
Luther, Howard	335	*Manchaca, Travis	4,700	Meadow Village, Bexar	NA
Lutie, Collingsworth	35	Manchester, Red River	185	Mecca, Madison	6
Lux Ranch, Kendall	NA	Mangum, Eastland	15	Medicine Mound, Hardeman	50
Lydia, Red River	109	Mangus Corner, Bexar	NA	Medill, Lamar	50
*LYFORD, Willacy	1,674	Manheim, Lee	40	*Medina, Bandera	515
Lynchburg, Harris	100	Mankin, Henderson	NA	Medina Base, Bexar	NA
Lynn Grove, Grimes	NA	Mankins, Archer	45	Medina River West, Medina	NA
Lynnwood Lakes, Waller	NA	*MANOR, Travis	1,041	Meeker, Jefferson	NA
*Lyons, Burleson	360	*†MANSFIELD, Tarrant-		Meek Estates, Henderson	NA
Lytle Ranch Acres, Medina	NA	Johnson-Ellis	15,607	Meeks, Bell	15
*†LYTLE, Atascosa-Medina-		*MANVEL, Brazoria	3,733	*MEGARGEL, Archer	244
Bexar	2,255	*Maple, Bailey	130	Meldrum, Shelby	NA
Lytton Springs, Caldwell	76	Maple, Red River	30	*MELISSA, Collin	557
		Maple Spring, Titus	NA	Mellon, Frio	14
Mc		Mapleton, Houston	NA	Melrose, Nacogdoches	150
*McAdoo, Dickens	169	*Marathon, Brewster	800	*MELVIN, McCulloch	184
*†MCALLEN, Hidalgo	84,021	*†MARBLE FALLS, Burnet	4,007	§*†MEMPHIS, Hall	2,465
McAllen-Edinburg-Mission		§*†MARFA, Presidio	2,424	§*†MENARD, Menard	1,606
1990 metro. pop.	383,545	Margaret, Foard	51	Mendoza, Caldwell	50
*†MCCAMEY, Upton	2,493	Marie, Runnels	NA	Menlow, Hill	10
*McCaulley, Fisher	96	*MARIETTA, Cass	161	§*Mentone, Loving	50
McClanahan, Falls	60	*†MARION, Guadalupe	984	Mentz, Colorado	NA
McClelland, Shelby	NA	Marion Ferry Park, Angelina	NA	*†MERCEDES, Hidalgo	12,694
McCollum, Montague	NA	*Markham, Matagorda	1,206	Mercers Gap, Comanche	NA
McCook, Hidalgo	91	Mark Heights, Smith	NA	Mercury, McCulloch	166
*McCoy, Atascosa	25	Markley, Young	31	*Mereta, Tom Green	75
McCoy, Floyd	NA	Markout, Kaufman	80	§*†MERIDIAN, Bosque	1,390
McCoy, Kaufman	20	Marlboro Country, Hays	NA	*Merit, Hunt	215
McCoy, Panola	NA	§*†MARLIN, Falls	6,386	*†MERKEL, Taylor	2,469
McCoy, Red River	175	Marlow, Milam	45	Merle, Burleson	NA
McCullough, Ellis	NA	*MARQUEZ, Leon	270	Merriam, Eastland	14
*McDade, Bastrop	345	Mars, Van Zandt	NA	*MERTENS, Hill	104
McDade Estates, Montgomery	NA	§*†MARSHALL, Harrison	23,682	§*†MERTZON, Irion	778
McDaniels, Brown	NA	Longview-Marshall		Mesa, El Paso	50
*McFaddin, Victoria	320	1990 metro. pop.	162,431	Mescalero Park, Randall	NA
McGee Landing, Sabine	NA	MARSHALL CREEK, Denton	315	*†MESQUITE, Dallas	101,484
McGirk, Hamilton	NA	Marshall Ford, Travis	NA	Mesquite Acres Island,	
*†MCGREGOR, McLennan	4,683	Marshall Northeast, Harrison	1,500	San Patricio	NA
§*†MCKINNEY, Collin	21,283	Marston, Polk	25	Metcalf Gap, Palo Pinto	NA
McKinney Acres, Andrews	NA	*†MART, McLennan	2,004	*†MEXIA, Limestone	6,933
McKnight, Rusk	NA	*MARTINDALE, Caldwell	904	Mexico, Hunt	NA
*†MCLEAN, Gray	849	Martinez, Bexar	NA	*Meyersville, DeWitt	110
MCLENDON-CHISHOLM,		Martin Prairie, Grimes	75	§*†MIAMI, Roberts	675
Rockwall	646	Martins Mills, Van Zandt	125	*Mico, Medina	98
*McLeod, Cass	50	Martin Springs, Hopkins	115	Midcity, Lamar	NA
McMahan, Caldwell	125	*Martinsville, Nacogdoches	126	Middle Gabriel Estates,	
McMillan, San Saba	NA	Marvin, Lamar	NA	Williamson	NA
McNair, Harris	2,039	Maryetta, Jack	7	Middleton, Leon	26
*McNary, Hudspeth	250	*Maryneal, Nolan	75	Middle Water, Hartley	10
McNeel, Brazoria	NA	Marys Creek, Baylor	NA	Midessa Heights, Midland	NA
McNeil, Caldwell	NA	Marysville, Cooke	NA	*Midfield, Matagorda	70
*McNeil, Travis	70	§*†MASON, Mason	2,041	*Midkiff, Upton	68
*McQueeney, Guadalupe	2,063	Mason Lake Estates, Liberty	NA	Midlake Village, Sabine	NA
		Massey, Hill	NA	§*†MIDLAND, Midland	89,443
M		Massey Lake, Anderson	NA	1990 metro. pop.	106,611
*MABANK, Kaufman-		Masters, Throckmorton	NA	*†MIDLOTHIAN, Ellis	5,141
Henderson	1,739	*Masterson, Moore	15	Midway, Bell	122
Mabelle, Baylor	6	§*†MATADOR, Motley	790	Midway, Bexar	NA
Mabry, Red River	60	*Matagorda, Matagorda	605	Midway, Dawson	20
*Macdona, Bexar	297	*†MATHIS, San Patricio	5,423	Midway, Fannin	7
Macedonia, Harrison	NA	Matthews, Colorado	NA	Midway, Franklin	NA
Macey, Brazos	NA	Matthey Estate, Bexar	NA	Midway, Hill	NA
Macon, Franklin	NA	*MAUD, Bowie	1,049	Midway, Howard	NA
Macune, San Augustine	100	Maudlowe, Refugio	NA	Midway, Jim Wells	NA
Madero, Hidalgo	NA	*†Mauriceville, Orange	2,046	Midway, Lavaca	NA
§*†MADISONVILLE, Madison	3,569	Maverick, Runnels	31	Midway, Limestone	NA
Madras, Red River	61	Maxdale, Bell	4	*MIDWAY, Madison	274
Mae, Jim Wells	NA	Maxey, Lamar	55		
Magnet, Wharton	42				

Town and County–	Pop.
New Hope, Rusk	NA
New Hope, San Augustine	NA
New Hope, Smith	NA
New Hope, Wood	NA
Newlin, Hall	31
*NEW LONDON, Rusk	926
New Lynn, Lynn	18
Newman, El Paso	60
New Mesquite, Collin	NA
New Moore, Lynn	NA
New Mountain, Upshur	NA
*Newport, Clay-Jack	70
New Prospect, Rusk	NA
New River Lake Estates, Liberty	NA
New Salem, Palo Pinto	NA
New Salem, Rusk	31
Newsome, Camp	100
*NEW SUMMERFIELD, Cherokee	521
New Sweden, Travis	60
Newt, Fannin	2
§*†NEWTON, Newton	1,885
*New Ulm, Austin	650
*†NEW WAVERLY, Walker	936
New Wehdem, Austin	100
New Willard, Polk	160
New York, Henderson	NA
NEYLANDVILLE, Hunt	94
Nickel Creek, Culberson	16
Nickleberry, Cass	NA
Nickleville, Wise	NA
NIEDERWALD, Hays-Caldwell	233
Nigton, Trinity	34
Nimrod, Eastland	85
Nineveh, Leon	101
Nix, Lampasas	NA
*†NIXON, Gonzales-Wilson	1,995
Noack, Williamson	60
Nob Hill, Llano	NA
Nobility, Fannin	21
Noble, Lamar	40
Nockenut, Wilson	10
*NOCONA, Montague	2,870
Nogalus Prairie, Trinity	41
*Nolan, Nolan	131
*NOLANVILLE, Bell	1,834
Nolte, Guadalupe	25
*NOME, Jefferson	448
Noodle, Jones	40
NOONDAY, Smith	466
Nopal, DeWitt	25
*NORDHEIM, DeWitt	344
Norman, Williamson	20
Normandy, Maverick	98
*†NORMANGEE, Leon-Madison	689
*Normanna, Bee	75
Norse, Bosque	110
North Alamo, Hidalgo	NA
North Bancroft Estates, Kendall	NA
North Cedar, Trinity	NA
NORTH CLEVELAND, Liberty	176
Northcliff, Guadalupe	1,800
North Country, Montgomery	NA
North Cowden, Ector	80
NORTHCREST, McLennan	1,725
*Northfield, Motley	15
North Groesbeck, Hardeman	NA
North Hopkins, Hopkins	NA
North Houston, Harris	NA
North Jericho, Shelby	NA
NORTHLAKE, Denton	250
North Lake Estates, Comal	NA
Northlake Estates, Williamson	NA
North Line Oaks, Montgomery	NA
North Oaks, Travis	NA
North Orange Heights, Orange	NA
North Park Estates, Travis	NA
*†NORTH RICHLAND HILLS, Tarrant	45,895
Northrup, Lee	71
North San Antonio Hills, Bexar	NA
North San Pedro, Nueces	953
North Shore Colony, Travis	NA
North Star, Archer	NA
Northwest Oaks, Burnet	NA
Northwest Woods, Williamson	NA

Town and County–	Pop.
Northwoods,	NA
North Woods, Montgomery	NA
*North Zulch, Madison	100
*Norton, Runnels	76
Notla, Ochiltree	20
*Notrees, Ector	338
Nottingham Forest, Orange	NA
Nottingham Woods, Houston	NA
*NOVICE, Coleman	183
Novice, Lamar	NA
Noxville, Kimble	3
Nubia, Taylor	NA
Nugent, Jones	41
Nunelee, Fannin	25
*Nursery, Victoria	106

O

Town and County–	Pop.
Oak, Ellis	NA
Oakalla, Burnet	45
Oak Bend, Brazoria	NA
Oak Branch, Ellis	NA
Oak Cliff Acres, Comal	NA
Oak Creek, Bexar	NA
Oak Creek, Comal	NA
Oak Crest Estates, Williamson	NA
Oakdale, Hopkins	NA
Oakdale, Polk	25
Oak Flat, Nacogdoches	NA
Oak Flats, Rusk	NA
Oak Forest, Gonzales	25
Oak Forest, Montgomery	NA
Oak Forest Haven, Hunt	NA
Oak Grove, Bowie	294
Oak Grove, Colorado	NA
Oak Grove, Ellis	10
Oak Grove, Hopkins	NA
OAK GROVE, Kaufman	557
Oak Grove, Wood	74
Oak Harbor, Henderson	NA
Oak Heights, Kerr	NA
Oak Hill, Hood	NA
Oak Hill, Rusk	24
Oakhill Ranches, Bexar	NA
*OAKHURST, San Jacinto	219
Oak Island, Chambers	NA
Oaklake, McLennan	60
Oakland, Brazoria	NA
Oakland, Cherokee	NA
*Oakland, Colorado	80
Oakland, Jack	NA
Oakland, Van Zandt	26
Oak Lane, Montgomery	NA
OAK LEAF, Ellis	984
Oak Manor, Brazoria	NA
Oak Meadows Estates, Montgomery	NA
Oak Moss, Bexar	NA
Oak Park, Travis	NA
OAK POINT, Denton	645
Oak Ridge, Fannin	90
Oak Ridge, Grayson	NA
Oak Ridge, Llano	NA
Oak Ridge, Nacogdoches	NA
Oak Ridge Estates, Marion	NA
OAK RIDGE (Cooke Co.), Cooke	180
OAK RIDGE (Kaufman Co.), Kaufman	268
OAK RIDGE NORTH, Montgomery	2,454
Oak Shade, Polk	NA
Oaks North, Bexar	NA
Oak Springs, Hill	NA
Oak Terrace, Montgomery	NA
Oak Terrace Estates, Polk	NA
Oak Trail Shores, Hood	1,750
OAK VALLEY, Navarro	388
Oak Valley Park, Travis	NA
Oakview, Comal	NA
Oak Village, Bexar	NA
Oak Village North, Comal	NA
*Oakville, Live Oak	260
*†OAKWOOD, Leon	527
Oakwood Acres, Bexar	NA
Oatmeal, Burnet	20
*O'BRIEN, Haskell	152
Oceanshore, Galveston	NA
Ocee, McLennan	35
Ochiltree, Ochiltree	NA

Town and County–	Pop.
Odds, Limestone	NA
*Odell, Wilbarger	131
*†ODEM, San Patricio	2,366
§*†ODESSA, Ector-Midland	89,699
1990 metro. pop.	118,934
*†O'DONNELL, Lynn-Dawson	1,102
Oenaville, Bell	120
O'Farrell, Cass	20
Ogburn, Wood	NA
*†OGLESBY, Coryell	452
*Oilton, Webb	458
Oklahoma, Montgomery	NA
Oklahoma Flat, Hockley	NA
Oklahoma Lane, Parmer	64
*Oklaunion, Wilbarger	138
Okra, Eastland	20
Ola, Kaufman	50
*Old Boston, Bowie	NA
Old Bowling, Leon	20
Old Center, Panola	83
Old Diana, Upshur	NA
Old Dime Box, Lee	200
*Olden, Eastland	110
Oldenburg, Fayette	54
Old Ferry, Travis	NA
*Old Glory, Stonewall	125
Oldham, Tyler	NA
Old Larissa, Cherokee	NA
Old Midway, Leon	NA
*Old Ocean, Brazoria	915
Old River Lake, Liberty	NA
OLD RIVER-WINFREE, Chambers	1,233
Old Sabinetown, Sabine	NA
Old Salem, Bowie	NA
Old Salem, Newton	NA
Old Snake River, Liberty	NA
Old Town Meadows, Williamson	NA
Old Union, Bowie	238
Old Union, Limestone	25
Oletha, Limestone	NA
Olfen, Runnels	NA
Olin, Hamilton	12
Olivia, Calhoun	215
Ollie, Polk	NA
*†Olmito, Cameron	200
Olmos, Guadalupe	30
OLMOS PARK, Bexar	2,161
*†OLNEY, Young	3,519
*†OLTON, Lamb	2,116
*OMAHA, Morris	833
Omega, Gregg	NA
Omen, Smith	150
*ONALASKA, Polk	728
One Seventy-Seven Lake Est., Montgomery	NA
Onion Creek, Travis	1,544
Opdyke, Hockley	20
OPDYKE WEST, Hockley	100
Open Air Estates, Smith	NA
Oplin, Callahan	75
O'Quinn, Fayette	25
Oran, Palo Pinto	NA
§*†ORANGE, Orange	19,381
Beaumont-Port Arthur 1990 metro. pop.	361,226
Orangedale, Bee	35
*Orangefield, Orange	725
*†ORANGE GROVE, Jim Wells	1,175
Orangeville, Fannin	23
*ORCHARD, Fort Bend	373
*†ORE CITY, Upshur	898
Orient, Tom Green	40
*Orla, Reeves	183
Osage, Coryell	30
Oscar, Bell	40
Osceola, Hill	90
Oslo, Hansford	NA
Otey, Brazoria	318
Otis Chalk, Howard	79
*Ottine, Gonzales	90
*Otto, Falls	85
*Ovalo, Taylor	NA
*†OVERTON, Rusk-Smith	2,105
*OVILLA, Ellis-Dallas	2,027
Owens, Brown	NA
Owens, Crosby	75

Town and County-	Pop.	Town and County-	Pop.	Town and County-	Pop.
Owensville, Robertson	NA	Peach Creek Oaks, Montgomery	NA	*†PILOT POINT, Denton	2,538
Owentown, Smith	NA	*Peacock, Stonewall	125	Pinckney, Polk	NA
Owl Creek, Bell	45	Peadenville, Palo Pinto	NA	Pine, Camp	78
OYSTER CREEK, Brazoria	912	Pearl, Coryell	125	Pine Acres, Montgomery	NA
§*†Ozona, Crockett	3,181	*†PEARLAND, Brazoria-		Pine Branch, Red River	NA
		Harris	18,697	Pine Crest, Montgomery	NA
P		Pearl City, DeWitt	NA	Pinedale, Walker	NA
Pacio, Delta	15	§*†PEARSALL, Frio	6,924	Pine Forest, Hopkins	51
Padgett, Young	23	Pearson, Medina	NA	Pine Forest, Montgomery	NA
Padre Island, Nueces	NA	Pearsons Chapel, Houston	NA	PINE FOREST, Orange	709
§*†PADUCAH, Cottle	1,788	*Pear Valley, McCulloch	37	Pine Grove, Cherokee	NA
*Paige, Bastrop	275	*Peaster, Parker	80	Pine Grove, Harris	NA
§*†PAINT ROCK, Concho	227	Pebble Beach, Llano	NA	Pine Grove, Newton	160
*†PALACIOS, Matagorda	4,418	Pebble Beach-Sunset Acres,		Pinehill, Rusk	49
Palava, Fisher	12	Collin	NA	*Pinehurst, Montgomery	3,284
Paleface Lake Country Est.,		Pecan Acres, Wise-Tarrant	1,587	PINEHURST, Orange	2,682
Travis	NA	Pecan Creek, Fort Bend	NA	Pine Island, Jefferson	350
§*†PALESTINE, Anderson	18,042	Pecan Creek, Tom Green	NA	Pine Island, Waller	571
Palito Blanco, Jim Wells	35	*PECAN GAP, Delta-Fannin	245	Pine Lake, Montgomery	NA
*†PALMER, Ellis	1,659	Pecan Grove, Collin	NA	*†PINELAND, Sabine	882
Palm Harbor, Aransas	125	Pecan Grove, Fort Bend	9,502	Pine Mills, Wood	2
PALMHURST, Hidalgo	326	PECAN HILL, Ellis	564	Pine Park, Sabine	NA
Palm Park, Bexar	NA	Pecan Hill, Fort Bend	NA	Pine Prairie, Walker	NA
PALM VALLEY, Cameron	1,199	Pecan Plantation, Hood	990	Pine Springs, Culberson	20
PALMVIEW, Hidalgo	1,818	Pecan Wells, Hamilton	NA	Pine Springs, Smith	NA
Palo Alto, Nueces	15	§*†PECOS, Reeves	12,069	Pine Trail Shores, Smith	NA
Palo Alto Park, Bexar	NA	Peeltown, Kaufman	NA	Pineview, Wood	NA
Paloduro, Armstrong	NA	Peerless, Hopkins	NA	Pinewood Estates, Hardin	1,174
Palomino Park, Travis	NA	*Peggy, Atascosa	20	Pinewood Estates, Montgomery	NA
§*Palo Pinto, Palo Pinto	350	Pelham, Navarro	NA	Piney, Austin	NA
*Paluxy, Hood	76	PELICAN BAY, Tarrant	1,271	Piney Creek, Austin	NA
§*†PAMPA, Gray	19,959	*Pendleton, Bell	60	Piney Point, Montgomery	NA
Pancake, Coryell	NA	Pendleton Harbor, Sabine	NA	Piney Point, Sabine	NA
Pandale, Val Verde	20	*PENELOPE, Hill	210	PINEY POINT VILLAGE,	
*Pandora, Wilson	125	*Penitas, Hidalgo	1,077	Harris	3,197
§*†PANHANDLE, Carson	2,353	*Pennington, Trinity-Houston	100	Pinhook (or Faulkner), Lamar	48
*Panna Maria, Karnes	96	*Penwell, Ector	74	Pinwah Pines, Polk	NA
*Panola, Panola	296	Peoria, Hill	81	Pioneer, Eastland	40
PANORAMA, Montgomery	1,556	*Pep, Hockley	50	Pioneer Town, Hays	NA
Panorama Estates, Hunt	NA	Percilla, Houston	95	Pioneer Trails, Montgomery	NA
Panoramic Hills, Travis	NA	PERNITAS POINT, Live Oaks-		*Pipe Creek, Bandera	66
*PANTEGO, Tarrant	2,371	Jim Wells	174	Pirates Beach, Galveston	NA
Pantex, Carson	115	*Perrin, Jack	300	Pirates Cove, Galveston	NA
Panther Chapel, Franklin	NA	*Perry, Falls	96	Pitner Junction, Rusk	NA
Papalote, Bee	70	§*†PERRYTON, Ochiltree	7,607	§*†PITTSBURG, Camp	4,007
*Paradise, Wise	275	Perryville, Wood	52	Placation Estates, Sabine	NA
Paradise Bay, Montgomery	NA	Personville, Freestone	NA	*Placedo, Victoria	515
Paradise Hills, San Augustine	NA	Personville, Limestone	NA	Placid, McCulloch	32
Paradise Manor, Travis	NA	Pert, Anderson	35	Plain, Houston	NA
Paradise Point, Llano	NA	Peters, Austin	95	Plains, Borden	NA
*†PARIS, Lamar	24,699	*†PETERSBURG, Hale	1,292	§*†PLAINS, Yoakum	1,422
Parita, Bexar	NA	Peter's Prairie, Red River	40	§*†PLAINVIEW, Hale	21,700
Park, Fayette	22	Petersville, DeWitt	NA	Plainview, Sabine	NA
Park Community, Navarro	NA	Petroleum, Jim Hogg	15	Plainview, Scurry	NA
*PARKER, Collin	1,235	*PETROLIA, Clay	762	Plank, Hardin	205
Parker, Johnson	21	PETRONILA, Nueces	155	*†PLANO, Collin-Denton	128,713
Parkers Point, Angelina	NA	Petteway, Robertson	25	*Plantersville, Grimes	212
Parklane, Comal	NA	Pettibone, Milam	25	Plaska, Hall	28
Parks Camp, Stephens	NA	*Pettit, Hockley	26	Plateau, Culberson	5
Park Springs, Wise	NA	*Pettus, Bee	400	PLEAK, Fort Bend	746
Parkview Estates, Guadalupe	500	*Petty, Lamar	100	Pleasant Farms, Ector	NA
Parnell, Hall	43	Petty, Lynn	24	Pleasant Grove, Bastrop	NA
Parsley Hill, Wilbarger	40	Petty's Chapel, Navarro	25	Pleasant Grove, Bowie	2,312
Parvin, Denton	44	*PFLUGERVILLE, Travis	4,444	Pleasant Grove, Falls	35
*†PASADENA, Harris	119,363	Phalba, Van Zandt	58	Pleasant Grove, Hopkins	NA
Paso Real, Willacy	NA	*†PHARR, Hidalgo	32,921	Pleasant Grove, Limestone	NA
Patillo, Erath	10	Phelan, Bastrop	NA	Pleasant Grove, Upshur	NA
Patman Switch, Cass	NA	Phelps, Walker	98	Pleasant Grove, Wood	NA
Patonia, Polk	NA	Phillips, Angelina	NA	Pleasant Hill, Eastland	15
Patricia, Dawson	60	*Phillips, Hutchinson	1,624	Pleasant Hill, Franklin	NA
Patrick, McLennan	NA	Phillipsburg, Washington	40	Pleasant Hill, Nacogdoches	NA
Patrole, Reeves	16	Phillips Camp, Hansford	NA	Pleasant Hill, Yoakum	NA
Patroon, Shelby	55	Pickens, Henderson	NA	Pleasant Oaks, Bexar	NA
*PATTISON, Waller	327	Pickett, Navarro	NA	Pleasant Oaks, Henderson	NA
Pattonfield, Upshur	NA	Pickney, Polk	NA	*†PLEASANTON, Atascosa	7,678
PATTON VILLAGE,		*Pickton, Hopkins	90	Pleasant Ridge, Leon	NA
Montgomery	1,155	Pidcoke, Coryell	30	Pleasant Springs, Leon	NA
*Pattonville, Lamar	180	Piedmont, Grimes	46	Pleasant Valley, Blanco	NA
Pawelekville, Karnes	105	Piedmont, Upshur	NA	Pleasant Valley, Dallas	NA
*Pawnee, Bee	249	*Pierce, Wharton	49	Pleasant Valley, Kendall	NA
Paxton, Shelby	161	Pierces Chapel, Cherokee	NA	Pleasant Valley, Lamb	NA
Paynes Corner, Gaines	NA	Pike, Collin	80	PLEASANT VALLEY, Wichita	378
PAYNE SPRINGS, Henderson	606	Pilgrim, Gonzales	60	Pleasant Valley Acres,	
Payton Colony, Blanco	NA	Pilgrim Point, Grimes	12	Montgomery	NA
Peach Creek, Brazos	NA	Pilgrim Rest, Rains	72	Pleasant Valley Estates, Comal	NA
Peach Creek Estates,		Pilot Grove, Grayson	75	Pleasant View Estates, Stephens	NA
Montgomery	NA	Pilot Knob, Travis	NA	Pleasure Point, Angelina	NA
Peach Creek Forest,					
Montgomery	NA				

Town and County-	Pop.	Town and County-	Pop.	Town and County-	Pop.
Pleasure Point, Marion	NA	*Priddy, Mills	215	Ratibor, Bell	10
*Pledger, Matagorda	159	PRIMERA, Cameron	2,030	Rattan, Delta	10
Pluck, Polk	NA	Primrose, Van Zandt	24	*Ravenna, Fannin	186
*Plum, Fayette	95	*†PRINCETON, Collin	2,321	Ravenwood, Brazos	NA
Plum Creek, Freestone	NA	Pringle, Hutchinson	40	Ray, Grayson	NA
Plum Grove, Ellis	NA	Pritchett, Upshur	125	Rayburn, Liberty	30
PLUM GROVE, Liberty	480	*Proctor, Comanche	220	*Rayburn Country, Jasper	600
Plum Ridge, Angelina	NA	*Progreso, Hidalgo	1,951	Rayburn Hideaway,	
Pluto, Ellis	NA	PROGRESO LAKES, Hidalgo	154	Nacogdoches	NA
Poetry, Kaufman	NA	Progress, Bailey	49	Rayford Forest, Montgomery	NA
*†POINT, Rains	645	Prospect, Rains	40	Raylake, Angelina	NA
Point Aquarius, Montgomery	NA	*†PROSPER, Collin	1,018	Rayland, Foard	30
*POINTBLANK, San Jacinto	443	Providence, Floyd	NA	§*†RAYMONDVILLE, Willacy	8,880
*POINT COMFORT, Calhoun	956	Providence, Polk	NA	Ray Point, Live Oak	75
Point Enterprise, Limestone	200	Pruitt, Cass	NA	*Raywood, Liberty	231
Point Loma, San Patricio	NA	Pruitt, Van Zandt	NA	Razor, Lamar	15
Point Royal, Henderson	NA	Pueblo, Callahan	NA	*Reagan, Falls	200
Point Venture, Travis	NA	Pueblo, Eastland	46	Reagan Wells, Uvalde	20
Polar, Kent	10	Pueblo Nuevo, Webb	130	Reagor Springs, Ellis	45
*Pollok, Angelina	300	Puerto Rico, Hidalgo	91	*Realitos, Duval	250
*PONDER, Denton	432	Pullman, Potter	31	Reata Trails, Williamson	NA
Pond Springs, Williamson	NA	Pumphrey, Runnels	NA	Rebecca Creek Park, Comal	NA
Pone, Rusk	NA	Pumpkin, San Jacinto	20	Red Bank, Bowie	NA
Ponta, Cherokee	50	Pumpville, Val Verde	21	Red Bluff, Jackson	NA
*Pontotoc, Mason	125	Punkin Center, Dawson	NA	Red Bluff, Reeves	40
Poole, Rains	50	Punkin Center, Eastland	12	Red Branch, Grayson	NA
*Poolville, Parker	230	Punkin Center, Hardeman	NA	Red Branch, Leon	NA
Porfirio, Willacy	NA	*Purdon, Navarro	133	Redbud Acres, Williamson	NA
Port-Au-Prince, Brazoria	NA	Purley, Franklin	81	Red Cut Heights, Bowie	563
Port Alto, Calhoun	NA	*Purmela, Coryell	61	Redfield, Nacogdoches	NA
*†PORT ARANSAS, Nueces	2,233	Pursley, Navarro	40	*Redford, Presidio	107
*PORT ARTHUR, Jefferson	58,724	Purves, Erath	50	Red Gate, Hidalgo	NA
Beaumont-Port Arthur		*PUTNAM, Callahan	103	Red Hill, Cass	20
1990 metro. pop.	361,226	*PYOTE, Ward	348	Red Hill, Limestone	NA
*Port Bolivar, Galveston	1,200			Red Lake, Freestone	NA
Port Brownsville, Cameron	NA	**Q**		Redland, Angelina	NA
*Porter, Montgomery	2,146	*Quail, Collingsworth	92	Redland, Leon	35
Porter Heights, Montgomery	1,448	Quail Creek, San Jacinto	NA	Redland, Van Zandt	NA
Porter Springs, Houston	50	Quail Valley, Williamson	NA	Redlawn, Cherokee	NA
Porterville Timbers,		§*†QUANAH, Hardeman	3,413	Red Lick, Bowie	NA
Montgomery	NA	Quarry, Washington	NA	*†RED OAK, Ellis	3,124
*PORT ISABEL, Cameron	4,467	Quarterway, Hale	12	Red Ranger, Bell	12
*†PORTLAND, San Patricio-		*QUEEN CITY, Cass	1,748	*Red Rock, Bastrop	100
Nueces	12,224	*Quemado, Maverick	426	*Red Springs, Baylor	81
§*†PORT LAVACA, Calhoun	10,886	Quicksand, Newton	NA	Red Springs, Smith	NA
*Port Mansfield, Willacy	731	Quihi, Medina	104	Redtown, Angelina	NA
*†PORT NECHES, Jefferson	12,974	*†QUINLAN, Hunt	1,360	*REDWATER, Bowie	824
*Port O'Connor, Calhoun	1,184	QUINTANA, Brazoria	51	Redwood, Guadalupe	400
Port Sullivan, Milam	15	*†QUITAQUE, Briscoe	513	Reeds Settlement, Red River	50
Porvenir, Presidio	NA	§*†QUITMAN, Wood	1,684	Reedville, Caldwell	NA
Posey, Hopkins	NA			Reese, Cherokee	75
Posey, Lubbock	125	**R**		Reese Air Force Base,	
§*†POST, Garza	3,768	R.O. Ranch Estates, Travis	NA	Lubbock	1,263
Post Oak, Blanco	NA	Rabb, Nueces	20	Reese Village, Lubbock	2,600
Postoak, Jack	79	Rabbit Hollow, Williamson	NA	Reeves, Hardin	NA
Postoak, Lamar	NA	Rabbs Prairie, Fayette	31	Refuge, Houston	NA
Post Oak, Lee	NA	Raccoon Bend, Austin	NA	§*†REFUGIO, Refugio	3,158
Post Oak, Robertson	NA	Rachal, Brooks	36	Regency, Mills	25
POST OAK BEND, Kaufman	264	Radium, Jones	26	Rehburg, Washington	NA
Post Oak Point, Austin	NA	Ragtown, Lamar	25	Reilly Springs, Hopkins	44
*POTEET, Atascosa	3,206	*Rainbow, Somervell	76	Rek Hill, Fayette	NA
*†POTH, Wilson	1,642	Rainbow Hills, Bexar	NA	*REKLAW, Cherokee-Rusk	266
Potosi, Taylor	1,441	Raintree Country, Montgomery	NA	Relampago, Hidalgo	NA
*†POTTSBORO, Grayson	1,177	Raisin, Victoria	50	Reliance, Brazos	NA
*Pottsville, Hamilton	312	Raleigh, Navarro	NA	Rendon, Tarrant	90
*Powderly, Lamar	185	*†RALLS, Crosby	2,172	RENO, Lamar	1,784
*†POWELL, Navarro	101	Ralph, Randall	NA	RENO, Parker	2,322
Powell Point, Fort Bend	NA	Ramireno, Zapata	NA	Reservation, Kerr	NA
*POYNOR, Henderson	237	Ramirez, Duval	40	Retreat, Grimes	NA
Praesel, Milam	115	Ranch Branch, Mason	NA	Retreat, Hill	NA
Praha, Fayette	25	Ranch Harbor Estates, Hill	NA	RETREAT, Navarro	334
Prairie Center, Matagorda	NA	Ranchito, Cameron	NA	Retta, Johnson	NA
Prairie Chapel, McLennan	NA	Ranchland Acres, Midland	NA	Reyes, Duval	NA
Prairie Dell, Bell	12	Rancho Alegre, Jim Wells	1,950	Reynard, Houston	NA
Prairie Grove, Franklin	NA	Rancho de la Parita, Jim Wells	NA	Rhea, Parmer	98
*Prairie Hill, Limestone	150	RANCHO VIEJO, Cameron	885	Rhea Mills, Collin	47
Prairie Hill, Washington	NA	Rand, Kaufman	NA	Rhineland, Knox	196
*Prairie Lea, Caldwell	100	Randado, Jim Hogg	15	*RHOME, Wise	605
Prairie Mountain, Llano	NA	*Randolph, Fannin	70	Rhonesboro, Upshur	40
Prairie Point, Cooke	30	*Randolph Air Force Base,		Ricardo, Kleberg	120
Prairieview, Hale	NA	Bexar	3,015	*†RICE, Navarro-Ellis	564
*PRAIRIE VIEW, Waller	4,004	*†RANGER, Eastland	2,803	Rices Crossing, Williamson	100
Prairieville, Kaufman	50	Ranger Country, Williamson	NA	*Richards, Grimes	296
Preiss Heights, Comal	NA	Ranger Estates, Midland	NA	*†RICHARDSON, Dallas-	
*†PREMONT, Jim Wells	2,914	RANGERVILLE, Cameron	280	Collin	74,840
*†PRESIDIO, Presidio	3,072	Rankin, Ellis	12	*RICHLAND, Navarro	244
Preston, Grayson	250	§*†RANKIN, Upton	1,011	Richland, Rains	100
*Price, Rusk	275	*RANSOM CANYON, Lubbock	750		
		*Ratcliff, Houston	106		

Town and County—	Pop.	Town and County—	Pop.	Town and County—	Pop.
Richland, Travis	NA	Rockhouse, Austin	NA	Royal Oaks, Llano	NA
RICHLAND HILLS, Tarrant	7,978	Rock House, Williamson	NA	Royal Oaks, Montgomery	NA
*RICHLAND SPRINGS,		*Rock Island, Colorado	160	Royal Oaks, Orange	NA
San Saba	344	Rock Island, Marion	NA	Royal Oaks, Smith	NA
§*RICHMOND, Fort Bend	9,801	*Rockland, Tyler	105	*Royalty, Ward	196
†RICHWOOD, Brazoria	2,732	Rockne, Bastrop	400	Royal View, Bexar	NA
Rico Ranchos, Travis	NA	§*†ROCKPORT, Aransas	4,753	Royder, Brazos	NA
Riderville, Panola	50	§*†ROCKSPRINGS, Edwards	1,339	*†ROYSE CITY, Rockwall-	
Ridge, Mills	NA	§*†ROCKWALL, Rockwall	10,486	Collin	2,206
Ridge, Robertson	67	*Rockwood, Coleman	80	Royston, Fisher	30
Ridgeheights, Midland	NA	Rocky Branch, Morris	135	Rucker, Comanche	NA
Ridgemar Landing, Williamson	NA	Rocky Creek, Angelina	NA	Rucker's Bridge, Lamar	20
Ridgeway, Hopkins	54	Rocky Creek, Blanco	NA	Rugby, Red River	24
Ridgewood, Midland	NA	Rocky Hill, Angelina	NA	Ruidosa, Presidio	43
Ridings, Fannin	10	ROCKY MOUND, Camp	53	*†RULE, Haskell	783
*†RIESEL, McLennan	839	Rocky Point, Burnet	NA	Rumley, Lampasas	NA
Rimwick Forest, Montgomery	NA	Rocky Point, Rains	80	RUNAWAY BAY, Wise	700
Rincon, Starr	NA	Roddy, Van Zandt	NA	*RUNGE, Karnes	1,139
*Ringgold, Montague	100	Rodney Calm, Navarro	NA	Runn, Hidalgo	NA
Rio Bravo, Webb	4,000	Roeder, Titus	NA	Running Water, Hale	NA
Rio del Sol, Cameron	NA	*Roganville, Jasper	100	Rural Shade, Navarro	30
*Rio Frio, Real	50	*ROGERS, Bell	1,131	Rushing, Navarro	NA
§*†Rio Grande City, Starr	9,891	Rogers, Taylor	NA	Rush Prairie, Navarro	NA
*RIO HONDO, Cameron	1,793	Rogers Hill, McLennan	NA	§*†RUSK, Cherokee	4,366
Rio Llano Ranch, Llano	NA	Rogers Plantation, Brazos	NA	Russell, Leon	27
*Riomedina, Medina	53	Roland, Collin	NA	Russelltown, Cameron	NA
Rios, Duval	75	Rolling Hills, Hunt	NA	Rustic Acres, Angelina	NA
*†RIO VISTA, Johnson	541	Rolling Hills, Potter	1,000	Rutersville, Fayette	72
*RISING STAR, Eastland	859	Rolling Hills, Waller	NA	Ruth Springs, Henderson	NA
Rita, Burleson	50	Rolling Hills Shores, Hood	NA	Ryanville, Refugio	NA
River, Zavala	NA	ROLLING MEADOWS, Gregg	291	*Rye, Liberty	76
River Acres, Tyler	NA	Rolling Oaks, Hays	NA		
River Bend, Newton	NA	ROLLINGWOOD, Travis	1,388	**S**	
River Bend, Sabine	NA	*†ROMA-LOS SAENZ, Starr	8,059	Sabanna, Eastland	12
Riverbend Oaks, Williamson	NA	ROMAN FOREST,		*†SABINAL, Uvalde	1,584
Riverbrook, Montgomery	NA	Montgomery	1,033	Sabine, Gregg	750
Riverby, Fannin	15	Roman Hills, Montgomery	NA	Sabine Farms, Harrison	NA
River Club Estates,		*Romayor, Liberty	96	Sabine Sands, Newton	NA
Montgomery	NA	Romero, Hartley	25	*†SACHSE, Dallas-Collin	5,346
Rivercrest, Travis	NA	Romney, Eastland	12	*Sacul, Nacogdoches	170
River Crest Estates, Angelina	NA	*Roosevelt, Kimble	98	Saddle and Surrey,	
River Hill, Panola	NA	Roosevelt, Lubbock	3,500	Montgomery	NA
River Hills, Travis	NA	*ROPESVILLE, Hockley	494	*SADLER, Grayson	316
River Meadows, Hays	NA	Rosalie, Red River	100	*Sagerton, Haskell	115
River Oaks, Brazos	NA	*Rosanky, Bastrop	210	*SAGINAW, Tarrant	8,551
River Oaks, Burnet	NA	Rosborough Springs, Harrison	NA	Saint Clair Cove, Galveston	NA
River Oaks, Hays	NA	*†ROSCOE, Nolan	1,446	Saint Elmo, Freestone	NA
RIVER OAKS, Tarrant	6,580	*†ROSEBUD, Falls	1,638	St. Francis, Potter	NA
River Oaks, Travis	NA	ROSE CITY, Orange	572	*ST. HEDWIG, Bexar	1,443
River Oaks, Williamson	NA	Rose Hill, Harris	NA	Saint Holland, Grimes	50
River Oaks Estates,		Rose Hill, San Jacinto	10	*†ST. JO, Montague	1,048
Montgomery	NA	ROSE HILL ACRES, Hardin	468	Saint John, Harrison	NA
River Plantation, Montgomery	NA	*†ROSENBERG, Fort Bend	20,183	Saint John Colony, Caldwell	NA
Riverpoint Estates, Comal	NA	Rosevine, Sabine	50	Saint Lawrence, Glasscock	NA
River Ridge, Montgomery	NA	Rosewood, Upshur	100	ST. PAUL, Collin	415
Rivers End, Brazoria	NA	Rosewood Hill, Harris	NA	St. Paul, San Patricio	180
*RIVERSIDE, Walker	451	*Rosharon, Brazoria	435	*†Salado, Bell	1,216
Riverside Estates, Brazoria	NA	Rosita, Duval	NA	Salem, Cherokee	NA
River Terrace, Harris	NA	Rosita, Starr	220	Salem, Grimes	50
River Trail, Nueces	NA	*ROSS, McLennan	188	Salem, Newton	85
Riverwood, Montgomery	NA	Ross City, Howard	81	Salem, Victoria	25
*Riviera, Kleberg	550	*ROSSER, Kaufman	366	Salesville, Palo Pinto	40
Riviera Beach, Kleberg	NA	*Rosston, Cooke	110	Saline, Menard	58
Riviera Estates, Polk	NA	Rossville, Atascosa	47	*Salineno, Starr	155
Roach, Cass	NA	*†ROTAN, Fisher	1,913	Salmon Lake, Anderson	20
Roane, Navarro	120	Rough Creek, San Saba	NA	*Salt Flat, Hudspeth	35
*†ROANOKE, Denton	1,616	Round House, Navarro	NA	Salt Gap, McCulloch	25
Roans Prairie, Grimes	56	*†ROUND MOUNTAIN, Blanco	59	*Saltillo, Hopkins	200
*ROARING SPRINGS, Motley	264	Round Mountain, Travis	59	Samaria, Navarro	NA
Robbins, Leon	20	Round Prairie, Navarro	40	Sam Houston Lake Estates,	
§*†ROBERT LEE, Coke	1,276	Round Prairie, Robertson	NA	Liberty	NA
Robertson, Crosby	35	*†ROUND ROCK, Williamson-		*Samnorwood, Collingsworth	110
†ROBINSON, McLennan	7,111	Travis	30,923	Sample, Gonzales	25
Robinson Arms Landing, Reeves	21	Round Timber, Baylor	8	Sanaloma Estates, Williamson	NA
*†ROBSTOWN, Nueces	12,849	*†ROUND TOP, Fayette	81	§*†SAN ANGELO, Tom Green	84,474
§*†ROBY, Fisher	616	Round Top, Fisher	NA	1990 metro. pop.	98,458
*Rochelle, McCulloch	163	Roundup, Hockley	27	§*†SAN ANTONIO, Bexar	935,933
*†ROCHESTER, Haskell	458	Rowden, Callahan	30	1990 metro. pop.	1,302,099
Rock Bluff, Burnet	NA	*†Rowena, Runnels	466	San Antonio Prairie, Burleson	NA
Rock Creek, McLennan	25	Rowland, Montague	NA	Sanatorium, Tom Green	450
Rock Creek, Somervell	36	*†ROWLETT, Dallas-		§*†SAN AUGUSTINE, San	
*†ROCKDALE, Milam	5,235	Rockwall	23,260	Augustine	2,337
Rockett, Ellis	124	*†ROXTON, Lamar	639	*†SAN BENITO, Cameron	20,125
Rockford, Lamar	NA	Royal Forest, Comal	NA	San Carlos, Hidalgo	100
Rock Harbor, Hood	NA	Royal Forest, Montgomery	NA	San Carlos, Starr	NA
Rockhill, Collin	25	Royal Oaks, Henderson	NA	Sanco, Coke	30
Rock Hill, Franklin	NA	Royal Oaks, Kerr	NA	SANCTUARY, Parker	234
Rock Hill, Wood	21			Sand, Dawson	20

Town and County–	Pop.	Town and County–	Pop.	Town and County–	Pop.
Sandbranch, Dallas	400	Scenic Brook, Travis	NA	Shady Grove, Panola	NA
§*†Sanderson, Terrell	1,128	Scenic Brook West, Travis	NA	Shady Grove, Smith	NA
Sand Flat, Johnson	NA	Scenic Hills, Guadalupe	150	Shady Grove, Upshur	NA
Sand Flat, Rains	100	Scenic Terrace, Comal	NA	Shady Meadow, Montgomery	NA
Sand Flat, Smith	NA	Scharbauer City, Ector	20	Shady Oaks, Brazoria	NA
Sandhill, Floyd	NA	Schattel, Frio	130	SHADY SHORES, Denton	1,045
Sand Hill, Upshur	NA	*†SCHERTZ, Guadalupe-		Shady Shores, Henderson	NA
*Sandia, Jim Wells	215	Comal-Bexar	10,555	Shady Shores, Marion	NA
§*†SAN DIEGO, Duval-		Schicke Point, Calhoun	NA	*Shafter, Presidio	31
Jim Wells	4,983	Schoolerville, Hamilton	NA	*†SHALLOWATER, Lubbock	1,708
Sand Jack, Newton	NA	School Hill, Erath	22	*†SHAMROCK, Wheeler	2,286
Sand Lake, Ellis	NA	Schoolland, Gonzales	NA	Shamrock Estates, Collin	NA
Sandlin, Stonewall	NA	Schroeder, Goliad	350	Shamrock Shores, Sabine	NA
Sandoval, Williamson	50	*SCHULENBURG, Fayette	2,455	Shangri La, Burnet	NA
Sand Ridge, Houston	NA	Schumannsville, Guadalupe	400	Shankleville, Newton	NA
Sand Springs, Howard	903	Schwab City, Polk	NA	Shannon, Clay	23
Sandusky, Grayson	NA	*†Schwertner, Williamson	150	Sharp, Milam	75
*Sandy, Blanco	25	Science Hall, Jasper	NA	SHAVANO PARK, Bexar	1,708
Sandy, Limestone	5	Scissors, Hidalgo	1,513	Shawnee Prairie, Angelina	NA
Sandy Acres, Burnet	NA	*SCOTLAND, Archer-Clay	490	Shawnee Shores, Hunt	NA
Sandy Acres, Midland	NA	*SCOTTSVILLE, Harrison	283	Shawnee Shores, Sabine	NA
Sandy Harbor, Llano	85	Scranton, Eastland	40	Shaws Bend, Colorado	NA
Sandy Hill, Washington	50	Scrappin Valley, Newton	NA	*Sheffield, Pecos	600
Sandy Hills, Montgomery	NA	*Scroggins, Franklin	125	Shelby, Austin	175
Sandy Point, Brazoria	30	*Scurry, Kaufman	315	*Shelbyville, Shelby	215
*San Elizario, El Paso	4,385	*SEABROOK, Harris-		Sheldon, Harris	1,653
*SAN FELIPE, Austin	618	Chambers-Galveston	6,685	Shell Camp, Gregg	225
*SANFORD, Hutchinson	218	*†SEADRIFT, Calhoun	1,277	Shell Shore, Smith	NA
Sanford Estates, Hutchinson	70	*†SEAGOVILLE, Dallas-		Shelter Cove, Polk	NA
San Gabriel, Milam	100	Kaufman	8,969	SHENANDOAH, Montgomery	1,718
San Gabriel Heights, Williamson	NA	*†SEAGRAVES, Gaines	2,398	Shep, Taylor	60
San Gabriel River Ranch,		Seale, Robertson	26	*†SHEPHERD, San Jacinto	1,812
Williamson	NA	*†SEALY, Austin	4,541	*Sheppard Air Force Base,	
*†SANGER, Denton	3,508	Seaton, Bell	60	Wichita	3,825
San Geronimo, Bexar	NA	Seawillow, Caldwell	NA	*Sheridan, Colorado	225
*San Isidro, Starr	130	*Sebastian, Willacy	1,598	§*†SHERMAN, Grayson	31,601
San Jacinto, Walker	NA	Sebastopol, Trinity	31	Sherman-Denison	
San Jose, Duval	15	Seco Mines, Maverick	NA	1990 metro. pop.	95,021
*†SAN JUAN, Hidalgo	10,815	Security, Montgomery	24	Sherry, Red River	15
SAN LEANNA, Travis	325	Sedalia, Collin	25	Sherwood, Irion	73
*San Leon, Galveston	3,328	Sedwick, Shackelford	NA	Sherwood Forest, Bexar	NA
San Manuel, Hidalgo	NA	*Segno, Polk	80	Sherwood Shores, Bell	600
§*†SAN MARCOS, Hays-		Segovia, Kimble	25	Sherwood Shores, Burnet	NA
Caldwell	28,743	§*†SEGUIN, Guadalupe	18,853	Sherwood Shores, Grayson	NA
San Martin Hills, Medina	NA	Sejita, Duval	22	Sherwood Shores 3, Burnet	NA
SAN PATRICIO, San Patricio	369	Selden, Erath	71	Shields, Coleman	13
San Pedro, Cameron	NA	Selfs, Fannin	30	Shiloh, Bastrop	NA
San Pedro, Zapata	25	*SELMA, Bexar-		Shiloh, Lavaca	NA
*SAN PERLITA, Willacy	512	Guadalupe-Comal	520	Shiloh, Leon	NA
San Roman, Starr	NA	*Selman City, Rusk	271	Shiloh, Limestone	110
§*†SAN SABA, San Saba	2,626	§*†SEMINOLE, Gaines	6,342	Shiloh, Williamson	NA
SANSOM PARK, Tarrant	3,928	Sempronius, Austin	NA	*†SHINER, Lavaca	2,074
*†SANTA ANNA, Coleman	1,249	Senior, Bexar	NA	Shinnery Lake, Stonewall	NA
Santa Anna, Starr	30	Sentinel Oaks, Montgomery	NA	Shire, Rusk	200
Santa Catarina, Starr	48	Serbin, Lee	90	Shirley, Hopkins	NA
*Santa Elena, Starr	64	Serenada, Williamson	3,242	Shirley Creek, Nacogdoches	NA
*SANTA FE, Galveston	8,429	Serene Hills, Bexar	NA	*Shiro, Grimes	205
Santa Margarita, Willacy	NA	Seth Ward, Hale	1,402	Shive, Hamilton	61
*Santa Maria, Cameron	210	Settlers Village, Harris	NA	SHOREACRES, Harris-	
*Santa Monica, Willacy	NA	Seven Coves, Montgomery	NA	Chambers	1,316
Santa Rita, Reagan	NA	SEVEN OAKS, Polk	171	Shore Acres, Hunt	NA
*SANTA ROSA, Cameron	2,223	Seven Pines, Gregg-Upshur	NA	Shore Ridge, Kerr	NA
*†Santo, Palo Pinto	312	*†SEVEN POINTS,		Short, Shelby	NA
*San Ygnacio, Zapata	895	Henderson-Kaufman	723	Shovel Mountain, Burnet	NA
San Ysidro, El Paso	400	Seven Sisters, Duval	60	*Sidney, Comanche	196
*Saragosa, Reeves	185	Seward Junction, Williamson	NA	§*†Sierra Blanca, Hudspeth	700
*Saratoga, Hardin	1,000	Sexton, Sabine	27	Siesta Shores, Travis	NA
Sarber, Marion	NA	Sexton City, Rusk	NA	Siesta Verde, Hays	NA
Sarco, Goliad	40	Seymore, Hopkins	NA	Signal Peak, Culberson	NA
Sardis, Cass	NA	§*†SEYMOUR, Baylor	3,185	Silas, Shelby	NA
Sardis, Ellis	NA	Seymour Colony, Baylor	NA	Siloam, Bowie	50
Sardis, Fisher	12	Shadow Bay, Montgomery	NA	*†SILSBEE, Hardin	6,368
*Sargent, Matagorda	76	Shadow Lake Estates,		*Silver, Coke	60
§*Sarita, Kenedy	185	Montgomery	NA	Silver City, Fannin	NA
Saron, Trinity	NA	Shadowland Retreat,		Silver City, Milam	25
Saspamco, Wilson	443	Montgomery	NA	Silver City, Montgomery	NA
*Satin, Falls	138	Shadowood Estates, Smith	NA	Silver City, Navarro	NA
Satsuma, Harris	NA	Shady Acres, Burnet	NA	Silver City, Red River	25
Sattler, Comal	30	Shady Brook Acres,		Silver Creek Village 1, Burnet	NA
Saturn, Gonzales	15	Montgomery	NA	Silver Creek Village 2, Burnet	NA
Sauney Stand, Washington	NA	Shady Creek Ranch, Burnet	NA	Silver Hills, Comal	NA
Savage, Crosby	NA	Shady Dale, Montgomery	NA	Silver Hills, Kendall	NA
*SAVOY, Fannin	877	Shady Grove, Burnet	NA	Silver Lake, Van Zandt	42
Sayers, Bexar	NA	Shady Grove, Cherokee	20	Silver Pines, Smith	NA
Sayersville, Bastrop	NA	Shady Grove, Franklin	NA	§*†SILVERTON, Briscoe	779
Scatter Branch, Hunt	NA	Shady Grove, Houston	NA	Silver Valley, Coleman	20
Scenic Oaks, Bexar	2,352	Shady Grove, Kerr	NA	Simmons, Live Oak	35

Town and County-	Pop.
Simmons Bottom, Liberty	NA
*Simms, Bowie	240
Simms, Deaf Smith	NA
*SIMONTON, Fort Bend	717
Simpsonville, Matagorda	NA
Simpsonville, Upshur	100
Sims, Brazos	NA
Simsboro, Freestone	NA
Sinclair City, Smith	NA
Singing Sands, Galveston	NA
Singletary Sites, Newton	NA
*Singleton, Grimes	44
§*†SINTON, San Patricio	5,549
Sion, Walker	NA
Sipe Springs, Comanche	75
*Sisterdale, Kendall	63
Sivells Bend, Cooke	100
Six Lakes, Liberty-Polk	NA
Sixmile, Calhoun	NA
Skeeterville, San Saba	NA
*SKELLYTOWN, Carson	664
Skellyville, Travis	NA
*Skidmore, Bee	500
Sky Harbor, Hood	NA
Sky Lakes, Waller	NA
Skyline Acres, Comal	NA
Skyline Acres, Hays	NA
Skyview Acres, Kendall	NA
Slabtown, Lamar	NA
Slate Shoals, Lamar	NA
*†SLATON, Lubbock	6,078
Slaughter Creek Acres, Travis	NA
Slay, Ellis	NA
Slayden, Gonzales	15
Sleepy Hollow, Hays	NA
Sleepy Hollow, Montgomery	NA
Slide, Lubbock	44
*Slidell, Wise	175
Sloan, San Saba	NA
*Slocum, Anderson	125
Smetana, Brazos	80
*SMILEY, Gonzales	463
Smithfield, Tarrant	1,000
Smith Grove, Houston	NA
*Smithland, Marion	179
Smith Oaks, Grayson	50
Smith Point, Chambers	150
Smiths Bluff, Jefferson	NA
Smithson Valley, Comal	15
*†SMITHVILLE, Bastrop	3,196
Smithwick, Burnet	NA
*SMYER, Hockley	442
Smyrna, Cass	NA
Smyrna, Harrison	NA
Smyrna, Rains	25
*†SNOOK, Burleson	489
Snow Hill, Collin	20
Snow Hill, Upshur	NA
Snuff Ridge, Liberty	NA
Snug Harbor, Brazoria	NA
Snyder, Hale	NA
§*†SNYDER, Scurry	12,195
*SOCORRO, El Paso	22,995
Soldier Mound, Dickens	NA
Solms, Comal	40
*†SOMERSET, Bexar	1,144
*†SOMERVILLE, Burleson	1,542
Sommers Mill, Bell	6
§*†SONORA, Sutton	2,751
Sorghumville, Houston	NA
*†SOUR LAKE, Hardin	1,547
*South Bend, Young	100
South Bosque, McLennan	80
South Brice, Hall	15
South Camp, King	NA
Southern Oaks, Montgomery	NA
South Franklin, Franklin	30
South Gale, Grayson	NA
South Groveton, Trinity	175
South Haven, Howard	NA
*SOUTH HOUSTON, Harris	14,207
South Jonestown Hills, Travis	NA
*†SOUTHLAKE, Tarrant-Denton	7,065
*Southland, Garza	168
Southland Plantation, Polk	NA
*SOUTHMAYD, Grayson	643
SOUTH MOUNTAIN, Coryell	301

Town and County-	Pop.
*†SOUTH PADRE ISLAND, Cameron	1,677
*South Plains, Floyd	25
South Purmela, Coryell	3
Southridge Estates, Guadalupe	100
South San Gabriel Ranches, Williamson	NA
South San Pedro, Nueces	1,912
South Shore, Bell	40
SOUTHSIDE PLACE, Harris	1,392
South Sulphur, Hunt	60
South Texarkana, Bowie	370
Southton, Bexar	113
Sowells Bluff, Fannin	5
*Spade, Lamb	174
Spanish Fort, Montague	50
Spanish Oak Estates, Williamson	NA
Spanish Oak Terrace, Williamson	NA
Spanish Shores, Henderson	NA
Spanish Trail, Hood	400
Sparenberg, Dawson	20
Sparks, Bell	30
Sparks, El Paso	1,276
*Speaks, Lavaca	60
§*†SPEARMAN, Hansford	3,197
Specht Store, Bexar	NA
Speegleville, McLennan	111
Spencer, Montague	NA
*Spicewood, Burnet	110
Spicewood Beach, Burnet	NA
Spicewood Springs, Travis	NA
Spider Mountain, Burnet	NA
Spillers Store, Leon	NA
Spillview Estates, Henderson	NA
*SPLENDORA, Montgomery	745
Splendora Estates, Montgomery	NA
Splendora Farms, Montgomery	NA
*SPOFFORD, Kinney	68
Spoke Hills, Hays	NA
Sportsman Village, Marion	NA
Spraberry, Midland	46
*†Spring, Harris	33,111
*Spring Branch, Comal	200
Spring Branch, Smith	NA
Spring Creek, Hutchinson	139
Spring Creek, San Saba	NA
Spring Creek, Throckmorton	NA
Spring Creek Estates, Montgomery	NA
Springdale, Cass	30
Springfield, Anderson	20
Springfield, Jim Wells	NA
Spring Forest, Montgomery	NA
Spring Hill, Bowie	209
†Spring Hill, Guadalupe	400
Spring Hill, Navarro	60
Spring Hill, San Jacinto	NA
Spring Hills, Montgomery	NA
Spring Hills, Sabine	NA
Spring Hills North, Montgomery	NA
*SPRINGLAKE, Lamb	132
Spring Lake Estates, Montgomery	NA
Spring Oaks, Montgomery	NA
Spring Place, Franklin	NA
*†SPRINGTOWN, Parker	1,740
†SPRING VALLEY, Harris	3,392
Spring Valley, McLennan	NA
Spring Valley, Travis	NA
Spring Woods, Montgomery	NA
Sprinkle, Travis	NA
*SPUR, Dickens	1,300
*Spurger, Tyler	472
Stacy, McCulloch	20
Staff, Eastland	65
*†STAFFORD, Fort Bend-Harris	8,397
Stag Creek, Comanche	50
STAGECOACH, Montgomery	340
Stage Coach Farms, Montgomery	NA
Stage Coach Hills, Bexar	NA
Stage Coach Hills Estates, Bexar	NA
Stairtown, Caldwell	35
Staley, San Jacinto	30

Town and County-	Pop.
*†STAMFORD, Jones-Haskell	3,817
Stampede, Bell	10
Stamps, Upshur	NA
Stanfield, Clay	25
§*†STANTON, Martin	2,576
*Staples, Guadalupe	75
*Star, Mills	85
STAR HARBOR, Henderson	368
Star Route, Cochran	NA
Starrville, Smith	75
Startzville, Comal	30
State Line, Culberson	18
Steele Hill, Dickens	NA
Steep Creek, San Augustine	NA
Steep Hollow, Brazos	NA
Steiner, Bosque	20
Stephens Creek, San Jacinto	135
§*†STEPHENVILLE, Erath	13,502
Sterley, Floyd	10
§*†STERLING CITY, Sterling	1,096
Sterrett, Ellis	28
Stewards Mill, Freestone	22
Stewart, Rusk	NA
Stiles, Reagan	16
Stillwell Crossing, Brewster	3
§*†STINNETT, Hutchinson	2,166
Stith, Jones	18
*†STOCKDALE, Wilson	1,268
Stockholm, Hidalgo	50
Stockman, Shelby	52
Stoneburg, Montague	51
Stone City, Brazos	NA
Stone Creek, Harris	NA
Stonegate, Kendall	NA
Stoneham, Grimes	12
Stonehurst, Williamson	NA
Stone Point, Van Zandt	32
Stone Ridge, Smith	NA
*Stonewall, Gillespie	245
Stony, Denton	25
Stout, Wood	86
*Stowell, Chambers	1,419
Stranger, Falls	27
§*†STRATFORD, Sherman	1,781
Stratton, DeWitt	25
*STRAWN, Palo Pinto	709
Streeter, Mason	100
*STREETMAN, Freestone-Navarro	260
Strickland Crossing, Sabine	NA
String Prairie, Bastrop	75
Stringtown, Hunt	NA
Stringtown, Newton	NA
Strong, Shelby	NA
Structure, Williamson	60
Stuart Place, Cameron	NA
Stubblefield, Houston	NA
Stubbs, Kaufman	NA
Study Butte, Brewster	120
Styx, Kaufman	NA
*Sublime, Lavaca	75
*†SUDAN, Lamb	983
*SUGAR LAND, Fort Bend	24,529
Sugar Valley, Matagorda	NA
*Sullivan City, Hidalgo	2,371
*Sulphur Bluff, Hopkins	280
Sulphur Springs, Angelina	NA
§*†SULPHUR SPRINGS, Hopkins	14,062
Summerall, Henderson	NA
*Summerfield, Castro	60
Summerfield, Cherokee	25
Summer Hill, Henderson	NA
Summerville, Gonzales	NA
Summit Oaks, Bexar	NA
*Sumner, Lamar	80
*†SUNDOWN, Hockley	1,759
Sunniland, Live Oak	75
Sunnyside, Castro	106
Sunnyside, Waller	120
Sunnyside, Wilson	300
SUNNYVALE, Dallas	2,228
Sun Oil Camp, Starr	100
*†SUNRAY, Moore	1,729
Sunrise, Falls	1,220
*SUNRISE BEACH, Llano	497
*Sunset, Montague	200

Town and County—	Pop.	Town and County—	Pop.	Town and County—	Pop.
*Turnertown, Rusk	76	Vandyke, Comanche	20	Walnut Grove, Collin	200
Turney, Cherokee	100	§*†VAN HORN, Culberson	2,930	Walnut Grove, Kendall	NA
Turtle Bayou, Chambers	42	Van Raub, Bexar	NA	Walnut Grove, Smith	NA
Turtle Cove, Brazoria	NA	Van Sickle, Hunt	NA	Walnut Hills, Montgomery	NA
Turtle Creek, Montgomery	NA	*Van Vleck, Matagorda	1,534	Walnut Hills, Potter	60
*†TUSCOLA, Taylor	620	Vasco, Delta	20	Walnut Place, Travis	NA
Tuxedo, Jones	42	Vashti, Clay	140	Walnut Ridge, Angelina	NA
Twichell, Ochiltree	22	Vattman, Kleberg	NA	*WALNUT SPRINGS, Bosque	716
Twin Cedar Retreat, Sabine	NA	Vaughan, Hill	70	Walnut Springs, Ellis	NA
Twin Creek, Bexar	NA	Veach, San Augustine	NA	Walnut Springs, Montgomery	NA
Twin Isles, Burnet	NA	*Vealmoor, Howard	179	Walton, Van Zandt	35
Twin Lake Estates, Montgomery	NA	§*†VEGA, Oldham	840	Wamba, Bowie	70
Twin Lake Ranch Estates, Medina	NA	*VENUS, Johnson-Ellis	977	Waneta, Houston	NA
Twin Lakes, Smith	NA	*Vera, Knox	276	Waples, Hood	NA
Twin Shores, Montgomery	NA	Verde Mills, Bexar	NA	*Warda, Fayette	67
Twin Sisters, Blanco	78	Verdi, Atascosa	NA	Wards Creek, Bowie	164
Twin Valley Terrace, Bexar	NA	*Verhalen, Reeves	52	*Waring, Kendall	73
*Twitty, Wheeler	60	*Veribest, Tom Green	40	Warlock, Marion	NA
*TYE, Taylor	1,088	§*†VERNON, Wilbarger	12,001	Warner Junction, Grayson	NA
§*†TYLER, Smith	75,450	Verona, Collin	NA	*Warren, Tyler	304
1990 metro. pop.	151,309	Vessey, Red River	14	WARREN CITY, Gregg-Upshur	250
*Tynan, Bee	200	Veterans, Ward	NA	*Warrenton, Fayette	50
Type, Williamson	40	Viboras, Starr	22	Warsaw, Kaufman	58
Tyson, Hill	NA	Vick, Concho	20	Warwick, Smith	NA
		Vicksburg, Montgomery	NA	Washburn, Armstrong	104
U		Victoria, Limestone	25	*Washington, Washington	265
UHLAND, Caldwell-Hays	368	§*†VICTORIA, Victoria	55,076	*†WASKOM, Harrison	1,812
*Umbarger, Randall	327	1990 metro. pop.	74,361	Wastella, Nolan	13
UNCERTAIN, Harrison	194	Victory City, Bowie	NA	†WATAUGA, Tarrant	20,009
Union, Brazos	NA	Vidauri, Refugio	85	Water Front Park, Comal	NA
Union, San Augustine	NA	*†VIDOR, Orange	10,935	Waterloo, Williamson	60
Union, Scurry	20	Vienna, Lavaca	40	Waterman, Shelby	53
Union, Terry	85	View, Taylor	75	Waters Bluff, Smith	NA
Union, Wilson	22	Viewpoint, Lamar	NA	Waters Park, Travis	NA
Union Bluff, Hill	NA	*Vigo Park, Swisher	31	*Water Valley, Tom Green	120
Union Center, Eastland	NA	Villa Cavazos, Cameron	NA	Waterwood, San Jacinto	NA
Union Flat, Childress	NA	*Village Mills, Hardin	300	Watkins, Van Zandt	NA
Union Grove, Bell	4	Village Oaks, Williamson	NA	Watson, Burnet	NA
Union Grove, Erath	12	Village Shores, Comal	NA	Watt, Limestone	NA
UNION GROVE, Upshur	271	Village West, Travis	NA	Watterson, Bastrop	NA
Union High, Navarro	NA	Villa Nueva, Cameron	NA	Watts, Marion	NA
Union Valley, Hunt	25	Villareales, Starr	NA	Waverly, San Jacinto	50
Unity, Lamar	NA	Vincent, Howard	500	§*†WAXAHACHIE, Ellis	18,168
*UNIVERSAL CITY, Bexar	13,057	Vinegarone, Val Verde	NA	Wayland, Stephens	15
University Acres, Brazos	NA	Vineyard, Jack	37	Wayne, Cass	NA
UNIVERSITY PARK, Dallas	22,259	VINTON, El Paso	605	*Wayside, Armstrong	40
Upper Meyersville, DeWitt	NA	Violet, Nueces	160	Wayside, Lynn	NA
Upshaw, Nacogdoches	NA	Virginia Estates, Montgomery	NA	Wealthy, Leon	NA
Upton, Bastrop	25	Vista, Hamilton	NA	§*†WEATHERFORD, Parker	14,804
Urbana, San Jacinto	10	Vistula, Houston	NA	Weatherly, Hall	20
Utley, Bastrop	30	Vivian, Foard	NA	Weaver, Hopkins	35
*Utopia, Uvalde	360	*Voca, McCulloch	56	Webb, Shelby	NA
§*†UVALDE, Uvalde	14,729	Volente, Travis	NA	Webb, Webb	40
Uz, Montague	NA	Volga, Houston	NA	Webberville, Travis	50
		*Von Ormy, Bexar	264	Webbville, Coleman	50
V		Von Ormy Heights, Bexar	NA	*†WEBSTER, Harris	4,678
Valdasta, Collin	40	Vontress, Haskell	NA	Weches, Houston	26
*VALENTINE, Jeff Davis	217	*Voss, Coleman	20	Weedhaven, Jackson	NA
*Valera, Coleman	80	*Votaw, Hardin	160	Weekend Retreats, Montgomery	NA
Valley Creek, Fannin	12	Vsetin, Lavaca	NA	Weeks Settlement, Newton	NA
Valley Grove, Rusk	NA	Vysehrad, Lavaca	NA	Weeping Mary, Cherokee	NA
Valley Hi, Bexar	NA			*Weesatche, Goliad	525
*†VALLEY MILLS, Bosque-McLennan	1,085	**W**		*†WEIMAR, Colorado	2,052
Valley Ridge, Brazos	NA	§*†WACO, McLennan	103,590	Weinert, Guadalupe	10
*Valley Spring, Llano	50	1990 metro. pop.	189,123	*WEINERT, Haskell	235
Valley View, Comal	NA	*Wadsworth, Matagorda	152	Weir, Hopkins	NA
*VALLEY VIEW, Cooke	640	*WAELDER, Gonzales	745	*WEIR, Williamson	220
Valley View, Cottle	20	Wagner, Hunt	NA	Weiss Bluff, Jasper	NA
Valley View, Mitchell	NA	*Waka, Ochiltree	145	*Welch, Dawson	110
Valley View, Runnels	NA	Wakefield, Polk	NA	Welcome, Austin	150
Valley View, Upshur	NA	*WAKE VILLAGE, Bowie	4,757	Weldon, Houston	131
Valley View, Wichita	200	*†Walburg, Williamson	250	Welfare, Kendall	36
Valley View, Williamson	NA	Walco Hills, Montgomery	NA	*Wellborn, Brazos	100
Valleyview Acres, Smith	NA	Waldeck, Fayette	35	Wellborn Oaks, Brazos	NA
Valley Wells, Dimmit	25	Walden, Montgomery	NA	§*†WELLINGTON, Collingsworth	2,456
Valley Wood Acres, Montgomery	NA	Waldrip, McCulloch	NA	*WELLMAN, Terry	239
Val Verde, Hidalgo	NA	Walhalla, Fayette	37	*†WELLS, Cherokee	761
Val Verde, Milam	NA	Walkers Mill, Harrison	NA	Wells, Lynn	NA
*†VAN, Van Zandt	1,854	*Wall, Tom Green	200	Wells Branch, Travis	7,094
*†VAN ALSTYNE, Grayson	2,090	Wallace, Van Zandt	NA	Wells Creek, Anderson	NA
Vance, Real	20	Wallace Prairie, Grimes	75	Wellswood, San Augustine	NA
*Vancourt, Tom Green	125	*WALLER, Waller-Harris	1,493	Wentworth, Van Zandt	32
Vandalia, Red River	35	Walling, Hill	NA	Wesco, Gray	7
*Vanderbilt, Jackson	667	*†WALLIS, Austin	1,001	Weser, Goliad	50
*Vanderpool, Bandera	20	*Wallisville, Chambers	377	*†WESLACO, Hidalgo	21,877
		Walnut Bend, Cooke	100		
		Walnut Creek, Montgomery	NA		
		Walnut Forest, Travis	NA		

County Population History, 1850-1990

The population of each Texas county for each United States census report beginning with 1850, or first census after date of organization for counties organized after 1850, is given in the table below.

County	1850	1860	1870	1880	1890	1900	1910	1920	1930	1940	Change 40-50	1950	Change 50-60	1960	Change 60-70	1970	Change 70-80	1980	Change 80-90	1990
Anderson	2,884	10,398	9,229	17,395	20,923	28,015	29,650	34,318	34,643	37,092	-14.1	31,875	-11.6	28,162	-1.3	27,789	38.1	38,381	25.1	48,024
Andrews	0	0	0	0	24	87	975	350	736	1,277	291.7	5,002	168.9	13,450	-22.9	10,372	28.5	13,323	7.6	14,338
Angelina	1,165	4,271	3,985	5,239	6,306	13,481	17,705	22,287	27,803	32,201	11.9	36,032	10.5	39,814	23.9	49,349	30.0	64,172	8.9	69,884
Aransas	0	0	0	596	1,824	1,716	2,106	2,064	2,219	3,469	22.6	4,252	64.8	7,006	27.1	8,902	60.2	14,260	25.5	17,892
Archer	0	0	0	31	2,101	2,508	6,525	5,254	9,684	7,599	-10.3	6,816	-10.4	6,110	-5.7	5,759	26.2	7,266	9.7	7,973
Armstrong	0	0	0	0	944	1,205	2,682	2,816	3,329	2,495	-11.2	2,215	-11.2	1,966	-3.6	1,895	5.2	1,994	1.4	2,021
Atascosa	0	1,578	2,915	4,217	6,459	7,143	10,004	12,702	15,654	19,275	4.0	20,048	-6.1	18,828	-0.7	18,696	34.0	25,055	21.9	30,533
Austin	3,841	10,139	15,087	14,429	17,859	20,676	17,699	18,874	18,860	17,384	-15.7	14,663	-6.0	13,777	0.4	13,831	28.2	17,726	11.9	19,832
Bailey	0	0	0	0	0	4	312	517	5,186	6,318	20.2	7,592	19.7	9,090	-6.6	8,487	-3.8	8,168	-13.5	7,064
Bandera[1]	0	399	649	2,158	3,795	5,332	4,921	4,001	3,784	4,234	4.2	4,410	-11.7	3,892	22.0	4,747	49.2	7,084	49.1	10,562
Bastrop	3,099	7,006	12,290	17,215	20,736	26,845	25,344	26,649	23,888	21,610	-9.2	19,622	-13.7	16,925	2.2	17,297	42.9	24,726	54.7	38,263
Baylor	0	0	0	715	2,595	3,052	8,411	7,027	7,418	7,755	-11.3	6,875	-14.3	5,893	-11.4	5,221	-5.8	4,919	-10.9	4,385
Bee	0	910	1,082	2,298	3,720	7,720	12,090	12,137	15,721	16,481	10.3	18,174	30.7	23,755	-4.3	22,737	14.5	26,030	-3.4	25,135
Bell	0	4,799	9,771	20,518	33,377	45,535	49,186	46,412	50,030	44,863	64.6	73,824	27.5	94,097	32.3	124,483	26.8	157,889	21.0	191,088
Bexar	6,052	14,454	16,043	30,470	49,432	69,422	119,676	202,096	292,533	338,176	48.0	500,460	37.3	687,151	20.9	830,460	19.1	988,800	19.9	1,185,394
Bexar Dist.[2]																				
Blanco	0	1,281	1,187	3,583	4,649	4,703	4,311	4,063	3,842	4,264	-11.4	3,780	-3.3	3,657	-2.5	3,567	31.2	4,681	27.6	5,972
Borden	0	0	0	35	222	776	1,386	965	1,505	1,396	-20.8	1,106	-2.7	1,076	-17.5	888	-3.3	859	-7.0	799
Bosque	0	2,005	4,981	11,217	14,224	17,390	19,013	18,032	15,750	15,761	-24.9	11,836	-8.7	10,809	1.5	10,966	22.2	13,401	12.9	15,125
Bowie	2,912	5,052	4,684	10,965	20,267	26,676	34,827	39,472	48,563	50,208	23.4	61,966	-3.2	59,971	13.1	67,813	11.0	75,301	8.5	81,665
Brazoria	4,841	7,143	7,527	9,774	11,506	14,861	18,919	20,614	23,054	27,069	72.0	46,549	63.7	76,204	42.1	108,312	56.6	169,587	13.0	191,707
Brazos	614	2,776	9,205	13,576	16,650	18,859	21,975	21,822	21,835	26,977	42.3	38,390	16.9	44,895	29.1	57,978	61.4	93,588	30.2	121,862
Brewster[3]	0	0	0	0	710	2,356	5,220	4,822	6,624	6,478	12.8	7,309	-12.0	6,434	20.9	7,780	-2.7	7,573	14.6	8,681
Briscoe[3]	0	0	0	0	0	1,253	2,162	2,948	5,590	4,056	-13.0	3,528	1.4	3,577	-21.9	2,794	-7.7	2,579	-23.6	1,971
Brooks[4,9]	0	0	0	0	0	0	0	4,560	5,901	6,362	44.5	9,195	-6.4	8,609	-7.0	8,005	5.3	8,428	-2.7	8,204
Brown[6]	0	244	544	8,414	11,421	16,019	22,935	21,682	26,382	25,924	10.3	28,607	-13.6	24,728	4.6	25,877	27.7	33,057	4.0	34,371
Buchanan[8]	0	0	0	0	0	0	0	0	0	0										0
Buchel[7]	0	0	0	0	298	0	0	0	0	0										0
Burleson	1,713	5,683	8,072	9,243	13,001	18,367	18,687	16,855	18,334	18,334	-29.1	13,000	-14.0	11,177	-10.5	9,999	23.1	12,313	10.7	13,625
Burnet	0	2,487	3,688	6,855	10,747	10,755	10,755	9,499	10,355	10,777	-3.9	10,356	-10.5	9,265	23.0	11,420	55.9	17,803	27.4	22,677
Caldwell	1,329	4,481	6,572	11,757	15,769	21,765	24,237	25,160	31,397	24,893	-22.3	19,350	-11.0	17,222	23.0	21,178	11.6	23,637	11.7	26,392
Calhoun	1,110	2,642	3,443	1,739	815	2,395	3,635	4,700	5,385	5,911	56.0	9,222	79.9	16,592	7.5	17,831	9.8	19,574	-2.7	19,053
Callahan	0	0	0	3,453	5,487	8,768	12,973	11,844	12,785	11,568	-21.4	9,087	-12.7	7,929	3.5	8,205	34.0	10,992	7.9	11,859
Cameron[9,50]	8,541	6,028	10,999	14,959	14,424	16,095	27,158	36,662	77,540	83,202	50.4	125,170	20.7	151,098	-7.1	140,368	49.4	209,680	24.1	260,120
Camp	0	0	0	5,931	6,624	9,146	9,551	11,103	7,745	8,740	-15.0	7,429	5.7	7,849	2.0	8,005	15.9	9,275	6.8	9,904
Carson	0	0	0	0	356	469	2,127	3,078	6,624	6,624	3.4	6,852	13.6	7,781	-18.3	6,358	4.9	6,672	-1.4	6,576
Cass[10]	4,991	8,411	8,875	16,724	22,554	22,841	27,587	30,041	30,030	33,496	-20.2	26,732	-12.1	23,496	2.7	24,133	21.9	29,430	1.9	29,982
Castro	0	0	0	0	9	400	1,850	1,948	4,720	4,631	17.0	5,417	64.7	8,923	16.5	10,394	1.6	10,556	-14.1	9,070
Chambers	0	1,508	1,503	2,187	2,241	3,046	4,234	4,162	5,710	7,511	4.8	7,871	31.9	10,379	17.4	12,187	52.1	18,538	8.4	20,088
Cherokee	6,673	12,098	11,079	16,723	22,975	25,154	29,038	37,633	43,180	43,970	-12.0	38,694	-14.4	33,120	-3.4	32,008	19.1	38,127	7.7	41,049
Childress[11]	0	0	0	0	1,175	5,004	9,538	10,933	14,545	12,149	-0.2	12,123	-30.5	8,421	-21.6	6,605	5.2	6,950	-14.3	5,953
Clay[51]	0	109	-52	5,045	7,503	9,231	17,043	16,864	14,461	12,524	-21.0	9,896	-15.6	8,351	-3.3	8,079	18.6	9,582	4.6	10,024
Cochran	0	0	0	0	0	25	65	67	1,963	3,735	58.7	5,928	8.2	6,417	-17.0	5,326	-9.4	4,825	-9.3	4,377
Coke[12]	0	0	0	0	2,059	3,430	6,412	4,557	5,253	4,590	-11.9	4,045	-11.3	3,589	-14.0	3,087	3.5	3,196	7.1	3,424
Coleman	0	0	347	3,603	6,112	10,077	22,618	18,805	23,669	20,571	-24.6	15,503	-19.6	12,458	-17.4	10,288	1.5	10,439	-7.0	9,710
Collin	1,950	9,264	14,013	25,983	36,736	50,087	49,021	49,609	46,180	47,190	-11.7	41,692	-1.1	41,247	62.2	66,920	115.9	144,490	82.7	264,036
Collingsworth[11]	0	0	0	6	357	1,233	5,224	9,154	19,129	10,331	-11.5	9,139	-31.3	6,276	-24.2	4,755	-2.3	4,648	-23.1	3,573
Colorado	2,257	7,885	8,326	16,673	19,512	22,203	18,897	19,013	19,119	17,812	-1.3	17,576	5.0	18,463	-4.5	17,638	6.7	18,823	-2.3	18,383
Comal	1,723	4,030	5,283	5,546	6,398	7,008	8,434	8,824	11,984	12,321	32.8	16,357	21.3	19,844	21.8	24,165	50.8	36,446	42.2	51,832

County Population History, 1850-1990 (Cont'd.)

County	1850	1860	1870	1880	1890	1900	1910	1920	1930	1940	Change 40-50	1950	Change 50-60	1960	Change 60-70	1970	Change 70-80	1980	Change 80-90	1990
Comanche[4]	0	709	1,001	8,608	15,608	23,009	27,186	25,748	18,430	19,245	-19.4	15,516	-23.5	11,865	0.3	11,898	6.0	12,617	6.1	13,381
Concho	0			800	1,065	1,427	6,654	5,847	7,645	6,192	-18.0	5,078	-27.7	3,672	-20.0	2,937	-0.7	2,915	4.4	3,044
Cooke	220	3,760	5,315	20,391	24,696	27,494	26,603	25,667	24,123	24,909	-11.1	22,146	1.9	22,560	4.0	23,471	17.8	27,656	11.3	30,777
Coryell	0	2,666	4,124	10,924	16,873	21,308	21,703	20,601	19,999	20,226	-19.5	16,284	47.1	23,961	47.4	35,311	60.8	56,767	13.1	64,213
Cottle	0			24	240	1,002	4,396	6,901	9,395	7,079	-13.8	6,099	-31.0	4,207	-23.8	3,204	-8.0	2,947	-23.8	2,247
Crane[12]	0				15	51	331	37	2,221	2,841	39.6	3,965	18.5	4,699	-11.2	4,172	10.3	4,600	1.1	4,652
Crockett[13]	0				194	1,591	1,296	1,500	2,590	2,809	41.7	3,981	5.7	4,209	-7.7	3,885	18.6	4,608	-11.5	4,078
Crosby	0			127	346	788	1,765	6,084	11,023	10,046	-4.6	9,582	8.0	10,347	-12.2	9,085	-2.5	8,859	-17.6	7,304
Culberson[15]	0							912	1,228	1,653	10.4	1,825	53.1	2,794	22.7	3,429	-3.3	3,315	2.8	3,407
Dallam	0					146	4,001	4,528	7,830	6,494	17.6	7,640	-17.5	6,302	-4.6	6,012	8.6	6,531	-16.4	5,461
Dallas	2,743	8,665	13,314	33,488	67,042	82,726	135,748	210,551	325,691	398,564	54.3	614,799	54.8	951,527	39.5	1,327,321	17.3	1,556,549	19.0	1,852,810
Dawson[16]	0			24	29	29	2,320	4,309	13,573	15,367	24.4	19,113	0.4	19,185	-13.5	16,604	-2.5	16,184	-11.3	14,349
Davis[10]	0																			
Deaf Smith	0			38	179	843	3,942	3,747	5,979	6,056	50.4	9,111	44.7	13,187	44.1	18,999	11.4	21,165	-9.5	19,153
Delta	641	5,031	7,251	5,597	9,117	15,249	14,566	15,887	13,138	12,858	-30.3	8,964	-34.6	5,860	-15.9	4,927	-1.8	4,839	0.4	4,857
Denton	1,716	5,108	6,443	18,143	21,289	28,318	31,258	35,355	32,822	33,658	22.9	41,365	14.7	47,432	59.5	75,633	89.2	143,126	91.1	273,525
DeWitt	0			10,082	14,307	21,311	23,501	27,971	27,441	24,935	-7.9	22,973	-10.0	20,683	-9.8	18,660	1.3	18,903	-0.3	18,840
Dickens	0			28	295	1,151	3,092	5,876	8,601	7,847	-8.5	7,177	-30.8	4,963	-24.7	3,737	-5.3	3,539	-27.4	2,571
Dimmit	0			665	1,049	1,106	3,460	5,296	8,035	8,542	24.7	10,654	-5.2	10,095	-10.5	9,039	25.8	11,367	-8.2	10,433
Donley	0			160	1,056	2,756	5,284	8,035	10,262	7,487	-17.0	6,216	-28.4	4,449	-18.2	3,641	11.9	4,075	-9.3	3,696
Dunn[17]	0		109																	
Duval[17][18]	0		1,083	5,732	7,598	8,483	8,964	8,251	12,191	20,565	-23.9	15,643	-14.4	13,398	-12.5	11,722	6.8	12,517	3.2	12,918
Eastland	0	99	88	4,855	10,373	17,971	23,421	58,505	34,156	30,345	-21.1	23,942	-18.4	19,526	-7.3	18,092	7.7	19,480	-5.1	18,488
Ector[19]	0				224	381	1,178	760	3,958	15,051	179.7	42,102	116.1	90,995	0.9	91,805	25.7	115,374	3.1	118,934
Edwards[20]	0			266	1,970	3,108	3,768	2,283	2,764	2,934	-0.9	2,908	-20.3	2,317	-9.1	2,107	2.1	2,033	11.5	2,266
Ellis	989	5,246	7,514	21,294	31,774	50,059	53,629	55,700	53,936	47,733	-4.4	45,645	-4.9	43,395	7.5	46,638	28.1	59,743	42.6	85,167
El Paso[21]	0	4,051	3,671	3,845	15,678	24,886	52,599	101,877	131,597	131,067	48.8	194,968	61.1	314,070	14.4	359,291	28.1	479,899	23.3	591,610
Encinal[22]	0	43	427	1,902	2,744															
Erath	0	2,425	1,801	11,796	21,594	29,966	32,095	23,264	20,804	20,760	-11.2	18,434	-11.9	16,236	11.7	18,141	24.4	22,560	24.1	27,991
Falls	0	3,614	9,851	16,240	20,706	33,342	35,649	36,217	38,771	35,984	-25.7	26,724	-20.4	21,263	-18.6	17,300	3.7	17,946	-1.3	17,712
Fannin	3,788	9,217	13,207	25,501	38,709	51,793	44,801	48,186	41,163	41,064	-23.9	31,253	-23.6	23,880	-4.9	22,705	7.0	24,285	2.7	24,804
Fayette	3,756	11,604	16,863	27,996	31,481	36,542	29,796	29,965	29,954	29,238	-17.3	24,176	-15.7	20,384	-13.4	17,650	6.7	18,832	6.7	20,095
Fisher	0			136	2,996	3,708	12,596	12,596	13,563	12,932	-14.8	11,023	-28.6	7,865	-19.3	6,344	-11.0	5,891	-17.8	4,842
Floyd	0			3	529	2,020	4,638	9,758	12,490	10,659	-1.2	10,535	17.4	12,369	-10.7	11,044	-0.0	9,834	-13.6	8,497
Foard[23]	0					1,568	5,726	4,747	6,315	5,237	-19.5	4,216	-25.9	3,125	-29.2	2,211	-2.4	2,158	-16.9	1,794
Foley[24]	0				25															
Fort Bend	2,533	6,143	7,114	9,380	10,586	16,538	18,168	18,168	29,718	32,963	-5.8	31,056	30.5	40,527	29.1	52,314	150.1	130,846	72.3	225,421
Franklin	0			5,280	6,481	8,674	8,910	9,304	8,494	8,389	-25.4	6,257	-18.5	5,101	3.7	5,291	30.3	6,893	13.2	7,802
Freestone	0	6,881	8,139	14,921	15,987	18,910	20,557	23,264	21,589	21,138	-25.7	15,696	-20.2	12,525	-11.2	11,116	33.4	14,830	6.7	15,818
Frio	0	42	309	2,130	3,112	4,200	8,895	9,286	9,411	9,207	12.5	10,357	-2.4	10,112	10.4	11,159	13.5	13,785	-2.3	13,472
Gaines	0				68	55	1,255	1,018	2,800	8,136	9.5	8,909	37.7	12,267	-5.5	11,593	13.4	13,150	7.4	14,123
Galveston	4,529	8,229	15,290	24,121	31,476	44,116	44,479	53,150	64,401	81,173	39.3	113,066	24.1	140,364	21.0	169,812	15.4	195,940	-3.6	217,399
Garza	0				14	185	1,995	555	5,586	5,586	12.4	6,281	5.3	6,611	-20.0	5,289	0.9	5,336	27.1	5,143
Gillespie	1,240	2,736	3,566	5,228	7,056	8,229	9,447	10,015	11,020	10,670	-1.4	10,520	-4.5	10,048	5.0	10,553	28.9	13,532	27.1	17,204
Glasscock[14]	0				208	286	1,143	555	1,263	1,193	-8.7	1,089	2.7	1,118	3.3	1,155	12.9	1,304	15.2	1,447
Goliad	648	3,384	3,628	5,832	5,910	8,310	9,909	9,348	10,093	8,798	-29.3	6,219	-12.7	5,429	-10.3	4,869	6.7	5,193	6.7	5,980
Gonzales	1,492	8,059	8,951	14,840	18,016	28,882	28,055	23,264	28,337	26,075	-18.8	21,164	-15.7	17,845	-8.2	16,375	3.1	16,883	1.5	17,205
Gray	0			56	203	480	3,405	4,663	22,090	23,911	3.4	24,728	27.5	31,535	-14.5	26,949	-2.1	26,386	-9.2	23,967
Grayson	2,008	8,184	14,387	38,108	53,211	63,661	65,996	74,165	65,843	69,499	1.4	70,467	3.7	73,043	13.9	83,225	7.9	89,796	5.8	95,021
Greer[52]	0			5,336																
Gregg	0			8,530	9,402	12,343	14,140	16,767	15,778	58,027	5.6	61,258	13.4	69,436	9.4	75,929	31.0	99,487	5.5	104,948
Grimes	4,008	10,307	13,218	18,603	21,312	26,106	21,005	23,101	23,101	21,960	-31.1	15,135	-16.0	12,709	-6.7	11,855	14.6	13,580	38.6	18,828
Guadalupe	1,511	5,444	7,282	12,202	15,217	21,385	24,913	27,719	28,925	25,596	-0.8	25,392	14.3	29,017	15.6	33,554	39.2	46,708	38.9	64,873
Hale	0			721	721	1,680	7,566	10,104	20,189	18,813	50.0	28,211	30.4	36,798	-7.2	34,137	10.1	37,592	-7.8	34,671

County Population History, 1850-1990 (Cont'd.)

County	1850	1860	1870	1880	1890	1900	1910	1920	1930	1940	Change 40-50	1950	Change 50-60	1960	Change 60-70	1970	Change 70-80	1980	Change 80-90	1990
Hall	0	0	0	0	703	1,660	8,279	11,137	16,966	12,117	-9.8	10,930	-33.0	7,322	-17.9	6,015	-7.0	5,594	-30.2	3,905
Hamilton[6]	0	489	733	6,365	6,313	13,520	15,315	14,676	13,523	13,303	-19.9	10,660	-20.4	8,488	-15.2	7,198	15.3	8,297	-6.8	7,733
Hansford	0	0	0	18	133	167	935	1,354	3,548	2,783	51.0	4,202	47.7	6,208	2.3	6,351	-2.2	6,209	-5.8	5,848
Hardeman[23]	0	0	0	50	3,904	3,634	11,213	12,487	14,532	11,073	-7.8	10,212	-19.0	8,275	-17.9	6,795	-6.3	6,368	-17.0	5,283
Hardin	0	1,353	1,460	1,870	3,956	5,049	12,947	15,983	13,918	15,875	23.1	19,535	26.1	24,629	21.8	29,996	35.8	40,721	1.5	41,320
Harris	4,668	9,070	17,375	27,985	37,249	63,786	115,693	186,667	359,328	528,961	52.5	806,701	54.1	1,243,158	40.1	1,741,912	38.3	2,409,544	17.0	2,818,199
Harrison	*,***	15,001	13,241	25,177	26,721	31,878	37,243	43,565	48,937	50,900	-6.2	47,745	-4.5	45,594	-1.7	44,841	16.6	52,265	10.0	57,483
Hartley	0	0	0	100	252	377	1,298	1,109	2,185	1,873	2.1	1,913	13.5	2,171	28.1	2,782	43.3	3,987	-8.9	3,634
Haskell	0	0	0	48	1,665	2,637	16,249	14,193	16,669	14,905	-7.8	13,736	-18.7	11,174	-23.8	8,512	-9.2	7,725	-11.7	6,820
Hays	387	2,126	4,088	7,555	11,352	14,142	15,518	15,920	14,915	15,349	16.2	17,840	11.7	19,934	38.7	27,642	46.9	40,594	61.6	65,614
Hemphill	0	0	0	149	519	815	3,170	4,170	4,637	4,170	-1.1	4,123	-22.8	3,185	-3.2	3,084	72.0	5,304	-29.9	3,720
Henderson	1,237	4,595	6,786	9,735	12,285	19,970	20,131	28,327	30,583	31,822	-26.5	23,405	-6.9	21,786	21.5	26,466	61.0	42,606	37.4	58,543
Hidalgo[25][49]	0	1,182	2,387	4,347	6,534	6,837	13,728	38,110	77,004	106,059	51.3	160,446	12.8	180,904	0.3	181,535	56.0	283,229	35.4	383,545
Hill	0	3,653	7,453	16,554	27,583	41,355	46,760	43,332	43,036	38,355	-18.4	31,282	-24.4	23,650	-4.5	22,596	10.7	25,024	8.5	27,146
Hockley	0	0	0	0	0	44	137	137	9,298	12,693	60.8	20,407	9.5	22,340	-8.7	20,396	13.9	23,230	4.2	24,199
Hood	0	0	2,585	6,125	7,614	9,146	10,008	8,759	6,779	6,674	-20.8	5,287	3.0	5,443	17.0	6,368	178.2	17,714	63.6	28,981
Hopkins	2,623	7,745	12,651	15,461	20,572	27,950	31,038	34,791	29,410	30,264	-22.4	23,490	-20.8	18,594	11.4	20,710	21.9	25,247	14.2	28,833
Houston	2,721	8,058	8,147	16,702	19,360	25,452	31,038	28,601	31,137	29,417	-22.4	22,822	-15.5	19,276	-7.4	17,855	24.9	22,299	-4.1	21,375
Howard	0	0	0	50	1,210	2,528	8,881	6,962	22,888	20,990	27.3	26,722	50.2	40,139	-5.8	37,796	-12.3	33,142	-2.4	32,343
Hudspeth[26]	0	0	0	0	0	0	0	1,445	3,728	3,149	36.5	4,298	-22.2	3,343	-28.4	2,392	14.0	2,728	6.9	2,915
Hunt	1,520	6,630	10,291	17,911	31,885	47,295	48,116	50,350	49,016	48,793	-12.4	42,731	-7.8	39,399	21.7	47,948	15.2	55,248	16.5	64,343
Hutchinson	0	0	0	50	58	303	692	721	14,848	19,069	65.6	31,580	9.0	34,419	-29.0	24,443	7.6	26,304	-2.3	25,689
Irion[12]	0	0	0	0	870	848	892	1,610	2,049	1,963	-19.0	1,590	-25.6	1,183	-9.6	1,070	29.5	1,386	17.5	1,629
Jack	0	1,000	694	6,626	9,740	10,224	11,817	9,863	9,046	10,206	-24.0	7,755	-4.3	7,418	-9.5	6,711	10.4	7,408	-5.8	6,981
Jackson	996	2,612	2,278	2,723	3,281	6,094	9,442	11,244	12,916	11,720	10.2	12,916	8.7	14,040	-7.6	12,975	2.9	13,352	-2.3	13,039
Jasper	1,767	4,037	4,218	5,779	5,592	7,138	14,000	15,569	13,040	17,491	14.6	20,049	10.2	22,100	11.7	24,692	24.7	30,781	1.0	31,102
Jeff Davis[27]	0	0	0	0	1,394	1,150	1,678	1,914	1,800	2,375	-12.0	2,090	-24.3	1,582	-3.5	1,527	7.9	1,647	18.2	1,946
Jefferson	1,836	1,995	1,906	3,489	5,857	14,239	38,182	73,120	133,391	145,329	34.2	195,083	25.9	245,659	-0.4	244,773	2.5	250,938	-4.6	239,397
Jim Hogg[28][49]	0	0	0	0	0	0	0	4,919	5,449	5,449	-1.1	5,389	-6.8	5,022	-7.3	4,654	11.0	5,168	-1.1	5,109
Jim Wells[29]	0	0	0	0	0	0	0	13,456	17,286	20,239	38.3	27,991	23.4	34,548	-4.4	33,032	10.5	36,498	3.2	37,679
Johnson	0	4,305	4,923	17,911	22,313	33,819	24,460	37,286	33,337	30,384	3.3	31,390	10.6	34,720	31.8	45,769	47.8	67,649	43.6	97,165
Jones	0	0	0	546	3,797	7,053	24,299	22,323	24,233	23,378	-5.3	22,147	-12.9	19,299	-16.5	16,106	7.2	17,268	-4.5	16,490
Karnes	0	2,171	1,705	3,637	8,681	8,866	14,942	19,049	23,316	17,853	-4.0	17,139	-12.5	14,995	-10.2	13,462	1.0	13,593	-8.4	12,455
Kaufman	1,047	3,936	6,895	15,448	21,598	33,376	35,322	41,276	40,905	38,308	-18.6	31,170	-4.0	29,931	8.2	32,392	20.4	39,015	33.8	52,220
Kendall	0	0	1,536	2,763	3,826	4,103	3,826	3,746	4,119	5,080	6.8	5,423	8.6	5,889	18.3	6,964	52.7	10,635	37.2	14,589
Kenedy[30][50]	0	0	0	0	0	0	0	0	700	700	-9.7	632	39.9	884	-23.3	678	-19.9	543	-15.3	460
Kent	0	0	0	92	324	899	2,655	3,335	3,851	3,413	-34.1	2,249	-23.2	1,727	-17.0	1,434	-20.2	1,145	-11.8	1,010
Kerr[31]	0	634	1,042	2,168	4,462	4,980	5,505	5,842	10,151	11,650	20.4	14,022	19.8	16,800	15.8	19,454	47.9	28,780	26.1	36,304
Kimble[31]	0	0	72	40	341	2,503	3,261	3,781	4,919	5,064	-8.8	4,619	-14.6	3,943	-1.0	3,904	4.1	4,063	1.5	4,122
King	0	0	0	40	173	490	810	655	1,193	1,066	-18.4	870	-26.4	640	-27.5	464	-8.4	425	-16.7	354
Kinney[31]	0	61	1,204	4,487	3,781	2,447	3,401	3,746	3,980	2,902	-8.1	2,668	-8.1	2,452	-18.2	2,006	13.6	2,279	36.9	3,119
Kleberg[29]	0	0	0	0	0	0	0	5,779	10,686	13,344	64.8	21,991	36.7	30,052	10.4	33,166	0.6	33,358	-9.2	30,274
Knox[23]	0	0	0	77	1,134	2,322	9,625	9,240	11,368	10,090	-0.1	10,082	-22.1	7,857	-24.0	5,972	-10.8	5,329	-9.2	4,837
Lamar	3,978	10,136	15,790	27,193	37,302	48,627	46,544	55,742	57,606	50,425	-14.7	43,033	-20.4	34,234	5.3	36,062	16.9	42,156	4.3	43,949
Lamb	0	0	0	0	4	31	540	1,175	17,452	17,606	13.7	20,015	8.3	21,896	-18.8	17,770	5.1	18,669	-19.3	15,072
Lampasas[5]	0	1,028	1,344	5,421	7,584	8,625	9,532	8,800	8,677	9,167	8.3	9,929	-5.1	9,418	-1.0	9,323	28.8	12,005	12.6	13,521
La Salle	0	0	69	789	2,139	2,303	4,747	4,821	8,228	8,003	-6.5	7,485	-20.2	5,972	-16.0	5,014	10.0	5,514	-4.7	5,254
Lavaca	1,571	5,945	9,168	13,641	21,887	28,121	26,418	28,964	27,550	25,485	-13.1	22,159	-9.0	20,174	-11.3	17,903	6.1	19,004	-1.7	18,690
Lee	0	0	0	8,937	11,952	14,595	13,132	14,014	13,390	12,751	-5.7	12,024	-25.6	8,949	-10.1	8,048	36.1	10,952	17.4	12,854
Leon	1,946	6,781	6,523	12,817	13,841	18,072	16,583	18,286	19,898	17,733	-32.2	12,024	-17.2	9,951	-12.2	8,738	9.8	9,594	32.0	12,665
Liberty	2,522	3,189	4,414	4,999	4,230	8,102	10,686	14,637	19,886	24,541	8.9	26,729	18.2	31,595	4.5	33,014	42.6	47,088	12.0	52,726
Limestone	2,608	4,537	8,591	16,246	21,678	32,573	34,621	33,283	39,497	33,781	-25.3	25,251	-19.2	20,413	-11.3	18,100	11.7	20,224	3.6	20,946
Lipscomb[11]	0	0	0	69	632	790	2,634	4,102	4,512	3,764	-2.8	3,658	-6.9	3,406	2.3	3,486	8.0	3,766	-16.5	3,143
Live Oak	0	593	852	1,994	2,055	2,268	3,442	4,171	8,956	9,799	-7.6	9,054	-13.3	7,846	-14.6	6,697	43.4	9,606	-0.5	9,556

County Population History, 1850-1990 (Cont'd.)

County	1850	1860	1870	1880	1890	1900	1910	1920	1930	1940	Change 40-50	1950	Change 50-60	1960	Change 60-70	1970	Change 70-80	1980	Change 80-90	1990
Llano	0	1,101	1,379	4,962	6,772	7,301	6,520	5,360	5,538	5,996	-10.3	5,377	-2.5	5,240	33.2	6,979	45.4	10,144	14.7	11,631
Loving[14]	0	0	0	0	3	33	249	82	195	285	-20.4	227	-0.4	226	-27.4	164	-44.5	91	17.6	107
Lubbock	0	0	0	25	33	293	3,624	11,096	39,104	51,782	95.1	101,048	54.7	156,271	14.7	179,295	18.0	211,651	5.2	222,636
Lynn	0	0	0	9	24	17	1,713	4,751	12,372	11,931	-7.6	11,030	-1.1	10,914	-16.6	9,107	-5.5	8,605	-21.5	6,758
Madison	0	2,238	4,061	8,512	10,862	10,754	10,432	11,956	12,227	12,029	-33.5	7,996	-15.6	6,749	14.8	7,693	38.4	10,649	2.6	10,931
Marion	0	3,977	8,562	10,983	10,959	10,754	10,472	10,886	12,277	11,427	-11.2	10,172	-20.9	8,049	-5.8	8,517	21.6	10,360	-3.6	9,984
Martin	0	0	0	12	264	332	1,549	1,146	5,785	5,556	-0.3	5,541	-8.5	5,068	-5.8	4,774	-1.9	4,684	5.8	4,956
Mason	0	630	678	2,655	5,180	5,573	5,683	4,824	5,511	5,378	7.4	4,945	-23.6	3,780	-11.2	3,356	9.7	3,683	-7.1	3,423
Matagorda	2,124	3,454	3,377	3,940	3,985	6,097	13,594	16,589	17,678	20,066	22.1	21,559	19.4	25,744	8.4	27,913	35.5	37,828	-2.4	36,928
Maverick	0	726	1,951	2,967	3,698	4,066	5,151	7,418	6,120	10,071	22.1	12,292	18.0	14,508	24.7	18,093	73.5	31,398	15.9	36,378
McCulloch	0	0	173	1,533	3,217	3,960	13,405	11,020	13,208	13,208	-11.4	11,701	-24.7	8,815	-2.8	8,571	1.9	8,735	0.5	8,778
McLennan	0	6,206	13,500	26,934	39,204	59,772	73,250	82,921	98,682	101,898	27.8	130,194	15.3	150,091	-1.7	147,553	15.7	170,755	10.8	189,123
McMullen	0	0	230	701	1,038	1,024	1,091	952	1,351	1,374	-13.6	1,187	-6.0	1,116	-1.9	1,095	-27.9	789	3.5	817
Medina	909	1,838	2,078	4,492	5,730	7,783	13,415	11,677	13,589	16,106	5.6	17,013	-7.1	18,904	7.1	20,249	14.4	23,164	17.9	27,312
Menard	0	0	667	1,239	1,215	2,011	2,707	3,162	4,447	4,521	-7.7	4,175	-29.0	2,964	-10.7	2,646	-11.3	2,346	-4.0	2,252
Midland[33]	0	0	0	0	1,033	1,741	3,464	2,449	8,005	11,721	120.0	25,785	162.6	67,717	-3.4	65,433	26.3	82,636	29.0	106,611
Milam	2,907	5,175	8,984	18,659	24,773	39,666	36,780	38,104	37,915	33,120	-28.8	23,585	-5.6	22,263	-10.0	20,028	13.5	22,732	0.9	22,946
Mills[34]	0	0	0	0	5,493	7,851	9,694	9,019	8,293	7,951	-24.6	5,999	-25.5	4,467	-5.7	4,212	6.3	4,477	1.2	4,531
Mitchell	0	0	0	117	2,059	2,855	8,956	7,527	14,183	12,477	15.1	14,357	-21.6	11,255	-19.4	9,073	0.2	9,088	-11.8	8,016
Montague	0	849	890	11,257	18,863	24,800	25,123	22,200	19,159	20,442	15.1	17,070	-12.8	14,893	2.9	15,326	13.6	17,410	-0.8	17,274
Montgomery	2,384	5,479	6,483	10,154	11,765	17,067	15,679	17,334	14,588	23,055	6.3	24,504	9.5	26,839	84.4	49,479	159.7	128,487	41.8	182,201
Moore	0	0	0	0	15	209	561	571	1,555	4,461	199.2	13,349	10.7	14,773	-4.8	14,060	17.9	16,575	7.8	17,865
Morris	0	0	0	5,032	6,580	8,220	10,489	11,055	10,028	9,810	-3.8	9,433	33.3	12,576	-2.1	12,310	18.8	14,629	-9.8	13,200
Motley	0	0	0	24	139	1,257	2,396	4,107	6,812	4,994	-20.6	3,963	-27.6	2,870	-24.1	2,178	-10.5	1,950	-21.4	1,532
Nacogdoches	5,193	8,292	9,614	11,590	15,984	24,663	27,406	28,457	30,290	35,392	-14.3	30,326	-7.5	28,046	29.5	36,362	28.1	46,786	17.0	54,753
Navarro	2,190	5,996	8,879	21,702	26,373	43,374	47,070	50,624	60,507	51,308	-22.2	39,916	-13.8	34,423	-9.5	31,150	13.4	35,323	13.0	39,926
Newton	1,689	3,119	2,187	4,350	4,650	7,282	10,850	12,196	12,524	13,700	-20.9	10,832	-4.2	10,372	12.4	11,657	13.7	13,254	2.4	13,569
Nolan	0	0	0	640	1,573	2,611	11,999	10,868	19,323	17,309	14.4	19,808	-4.3	18,963	-14.5	16,220	7.0	17,359	-4.8	16,594
Nueces[35]	698	2,906	3,975	7,673	8,093	10,439	21,955	22,807	51,779	92,661	78.6	165,471	33.9	221,573	7.2	237,544	12.9	268,215	8.5	291,145
Ochiltree	0	0	0	198	270	267	1,602	2,331	5,224	3,764	43.0	6,024	55.7	9,380	3.5	9,704	-1.2	9,588	-4.8	9,128
Oldham	0	0	0	387	270	349	812	709	1,404	1,385	20.7	1,672	15.3	1,928	17.1	2,258	1.1	2,283	-0.2	2,278
Orange	0	1,916	1,255	2,938	4,770	5,905	9,528	15,377	15,149	17,382	133.4	40,567	48.8	60,357	17.9	71,170	17.8	83,838	-4.0	80,509
Palo Pinto	0	1,524	1,524	5,885	8,320	12,291	19,506	23,431	17,576	18,456	-7.1	17,154	19.6	20,516	41.2	28,962	-16.9	24,062	4.1	25,055
Panola	3,871	8,475	10,119	12,219	14,328	21,404	21,755	21,755	24,063	22,513	-14.5	19,250	-12.4	16,870	-6.3	15,894	30.4	20,724	6.3	22,035
Parker	0	4,213	4,186	15,870	21,682	25,823	26,331	23,382	20,541	20,482	19.8	24,528	-6.7	22,880	48.1	33,888	31.6	44,609	45.2	64,785
Parmer	0	0	0	0	7	34	1,555	1,699	5,869	5,890	-1.7	5,787	65.6	9,583	9.7	10,509	5.0	11,038	-10.6	9,863
Pecos[36]	0	0	0	1,807	1,326	2,360	2,071	3,857	7,812	8,185	21.4	9,939	20.3	11,957	15.0	13,748	6.3	14,618	0.4	14,675
Polk	2,348	8,300	8,707	7,189	10,332	14,447	17,459	16,784	17,555	20,635	-21.5	16,194	-14.4	13,861	4.3	14,457	68.8	24,407	25.7	30,687
Potter	0	0	0	28	849	1,820	12,424	16,710	46,080	54,265	35.2	73,366	57.5	115,580	-21.7	90,511	7.1	98,637	-0.8	97,874
Presidio[37]	0	580	1,636	2,873	1,698	3,673	5,218	8,099	10,154	10,925	-32.7	7,354	-25.8	5,460	-11.3	4,842	7.1	5,188	27.9	6,637
Rains	0	0	0	3,035	3,909	6,127	6,787	3,675	7,114	7,185	-41.8	4,266	-29.8	2,993	25.4	3,752	29.0	4,839	38.8	6,715
Randall	0	0	0	3	187	963	3,312	1,461	7,071	7,185	91.7	13,774	146.2	33,913	58.9	53,885	39.3	75,062	19.5	89,673
Reagan[38]	0	0	0	0	0	0	392	377	3,028	1,997	56.6	3,127	20.9	3,782	-14.4	3,239	27.7	4,135	9.2	4,514
Real[39]	0	0	0	0	0	0	0	2,197	2,197	2,420	2.4	2,479	-16.1	2,079	-3.2	2,013	22.7	2,469	-2.3	2,412
Red River	3,906	8,535	10,653	17,194	21,452	29,893	28,564	35,829	30,923	29,769	-26.6	21,851	-28.2	15,682	-8.8	14,298	-4.4	16,101	-11.1	14,317
Reeves[40]	0	0	2,324	1,247	1,239	1,847	4,392	4,457	6,407	8,006	46.7	11,745	50.2	17,644	-6.3	16,526	-8.8	15,801	0.3	15,852
Refugio	288	1,600	0	1,585	1,239	1,641	2,814	4,050	7,691	10,383	-2.6	10,113	8.5	10,975	-13.5	9,494	-2.2	9,289	-14.1	7,976
Roberts	0	0	0	32	326	620	1,469	1,457	1,457	1,289	-20.0	1,031	4.3	1,075	-10.0	967	22.8	1,187	-13.6	1,025
Robertson	934	4,997	9,990	22,383	26,506	31,480	27,454	27,933	27,240	25,710	-22.6	19,908	-18.8	16,157	-10.9	14,389	1.8	14,653	5.9	15,511
Rockwall	0	0	0	2,984	3,193	8,531	8,072	4,072	7,658	7,051	-12.7	6,156	-4.5	5,878	19.9	7,046	106.2	14,528	76.2	25,604
Runnels	0	0	0	980	3,193	5,379	20,858	16,710	21,821	18,903	-11.3	16,771	-10.5	15,016	-19.4	12,108	-1.9	11,872	-4.9	11,294
Rusk	8,148	15,803	16,916	18,986	18,559	26,099	26,946	26,710	32,484	51,023	-17.0	42,348	-14.0	36,421	-6.4	34,102	21.3	41,382	5.7	43,735
Sabine	2,498	2,750	3,256	4,161	4,969	6,394	8,582	12,299	11,998	10,896	-21.4	8,568	-14.8	7,302	-1.6	7,187	21.1	8,702	10.2	9,586
San Augustine	3,648	4,094	4,196	5,084	6,688	8,434	11,264	13,737	12,471	12,471	-29.1	8,837	-12.6	7,722	1.8	7,858	11.8	8,785	-8.9	7,999

County Population History, 1850-1990 (Cont'd.)

County	1850	1860	1870	1880	1890	1900	1910	1920	1930	1940	Change 40-50	1950	Change 50-60	1960	Change 60-70	1970	Change 70-80	1980	Change 80-90	1990
San Jacinto	0	0	0	6,186	7,360	10,277	9,542	9,867	9,711	9,056	-20.8	7,172	-14.2	6,153	8.9	6,702	70.6	11,434	43.2	16,372
San Patricio	0	620	602	1,010	1,312	2,372	7,307	11,386	23,836	28,871	24.1	35,842	25.6	45,021	5.0	47,288	22.7	58,013	1.3	58,749
San Saba	200	913	1,425	5,324	6,641	7,569	11,245	10,045	10,273	11,012	-21.3	8,666	-26.4	6,381	-13.2	5,540	2.8	5,693	-5.1	5,401
Schleicher[41]	0	0	0	0	0	515	1,893	1,851	3,166	3,083	-7.5	2,852	-2.1	2,791	-18.4	2,277	23.8	2,820	6.0	2,990
Scurry	0	0	0	102	1,415	4,158	10,924	9,003	12,188	11,545	97.3	22,779	-10.6	20,369	-22.6	15,760	15.4	18,192	2.4	18,634
Shackelford	0	44	455	2,037	2,012	2,461	4,960	4,960	6,695	5,001	-19.5	3,479	14.7	3,990	-16.7	3,323	17.8	3,915	-15.3	3,316
Shelby	4,239	5,362	5,732	9,532	14,365	20,452	26,423	27,464	28,627	29,235	-19.7	23,479	-12.8	20,479	-3.9	19,672	17.3	23,084	-4.5	22,034
Sherman	0	0	0	34	34	104	1,376	1,473	2,314	2,026	20.6	2,443	6.6	2,605	40.4	3,657	-13.2	3,174	-10.0	2,858
Smith	4,292	13,392	16,532	21,863	28,324	37,370	41,746	46,769	53,123	69,090	8.1	74,701	15.6	86,350	12.4	97,096	32.2	128,366	17.9	151,309
Somervell[8]	0	0	0	2,649	3,419	3,498	3,931	3,563	3,016	3,071	-17.2	2,542	1.4	2,577	8.4	2,793	48.7	4,154	29.0	5,360
Starr[49]	0	2,406	4,154	8,304	10,749	11,469	13,151	11,089	11,409	13,312	4.8	13,948	22.9	17,137	3.3	17,707	54.0	27,266	48.6	40,518
Stephens[8]	0	230	330	4,725	4,926	6,466	7,980	16,560	16,560	12,356	-14.2	10,597	-16.2	8,885	-5.3	8,414	18.0	9,926	-9.2	9,010
Sterling[42]	0	0	0	0	0	1,127	1,493	1,053	1,431	1,404	-8.7	1,282	-8.2	1,177	-10.3	1,056	14.2	1,206	19.2	1,438
Stonewall	0	0	0	104	1,024	2,183	5,320	4,086	5,667	5,589	-34.2	3,679	-18.0	3,017	-20.5	2,397	0.4	2,406	-16.3	2,013
Sutton[41]	0	0	0	0	658	1,727	1,569	1,598	2,807	3,977	-5.8	3,746	-0.2	3,738	-15.1	3,175	61.6	5,130	-19.4	4,135
Swisher	0	0	0	4	100	1,227	4,012	4,388	7,343	6,528	26.4	8,249	28.6	10,607	-2.2	10,373	-6.3	9,723	-16.4	8,133
Tarrant	664	6,020	5,788	24,671	41,142	52,376	108,572	152,800	197,553	225,521	60.2	361,253	49.1	538,495	33.0	716,317	20.2	860,880	35.9	1,170,103
Taylor	0	0	0	1,736	6,957	10,499	26,293	24,081	41,023	44,147	43.5	63,370	59.5	101,078	-3.2	97,853	13.4	110,932	7.9	119,655
Terrell[43]	0	0	0	0	0	48	1,430	2,952	2,660	2,952	8.0	3,189	-18.5	2,600	-25.4	1,940	-17.8	1,595	-11.6	1,410
Terry	0	0	0	21	21	48	1,474	2,236	8,883	11,160	17.4	13,107	24.3	16,286	-13.3	14,118	3.3	14,581	-9.3	13,218
Throckmorton[51]	0	124	0	711	902	1,750	4,563	1,480	5,253	2,906	24.5	3,618	-23.5	2,767	-20.3	2,205	-6.9	2,053	-8.4	1,880
Titus	0	9,648	11,339	5,959	8,190	12,292	16,422	18,128	16,003	17,052	1.5	17,302	-3.0	16,785	-0.5	16,702	28.4	21,442	12.0	24,009
Tom Green[44]	0	0	0	3,615	5,152	6,804	17,882	25,210	37,777	39,302	49.9	58,929	9.7	64,630	9.9	71,047	19.3	84,784	16.1	98,458
Travis	3,138	8,080	13,153	27,028	36,322	47,386	55,620	57,616	77,777	111,053	45.0	160,980	31.8	212,136	39.3	295,516	41.9	419,335	37.5	576,407
Trinity	0	4,392	4,141	4,915	7,648	10,976	12,768	13,623	13,637	13,705	-26.7	10,040	-24.9	7,539	1.2	7,628	23.9	9,450	21.1	11,445
Tyler	1,894	4,525	4,915	5,825	10,877	11,899	10,250	10,415	11,448	11,948	-5.5	11,292	-5.5	10,666	16.4	12,417	30.7	16,223	2.6	16,646
Upshur	3,394	10,645	12,039	10,266	12,695	16,266	19,960	20,472	22,297	26,178	-20.5	20,822	-4.9	19,793	6.0	20,976	36.3	28,595	9.7	31,370
Upton[14]	0	0	0	0	0	48	501	253	5,968	4,297	23.5	5,307	17.6	6,239	-24.7	4,697	-1.7	4,619	-3.7	4,447
Uvalde	0	506	851	2,541	3,804	4,647	11,233	12,706	14,924	13,246	20.9	16,015	5.0	16,814	3.2	17,348	29.4	22,441	4.0	23,340
Val Verde[45]	0	0	0	0	2,874	5,263	8,613	14,123	14,924	15,453	7.6	16,635	47.0	24,461	12.3	27,471	30.7	35,910	7.8	38,721
Van Zandt	1,348	3,777	6,494	12,619	16,225	25,481	25,651	30,784	32,315	23,741	-4.8	22,593	-15.5	19,091	16.0	22,155	41.8	31,426	20.7	37,944
Victoria	2,019	4,171	4,860	6,289	8,737	13,678	14,990	18,556	18,528	19,868	57.2	31,241	48.8	46,475	15.7	53,766	28.0	68,807	8.1	74,361
Walker	3,964	8,191	9,766	12,024	12,874	15,813	16,061	18,328	18,014	18,868	6.9	20,163	6.5	21,475	28.9	27,680	51.0	41,789	21.8	50,917
Waller	0	0	0	9,024	10,888	14,246	12,138	12,138	14,292	10,280	16.4	11,961	0.9	12,071	18.3	14,285	38.6	19,798	18.1	23,390
Ward[14]	0	0	0	0	77	1,451	2,389	2,615	4,599	9,575	39.4	13,346	11.8	14,917	-12.7	13,019	7.4	13,976	-6.2	13,115
Washington	5,983	15,215	23,104	27,565	29,161	32,931	25,561	25,394	25,387	25,387	-19.1	20,542	-6.8	19,145	-1.6	18,842	16.7	21,998	18.9	26,154
Webb[46]	1,397	1,397	2,615	5,273	14,842	21,851	29,152	29,152	42,128	45,916	22.3	56,141	15.4	64,791	12.5	72,859	36.2	99,258	34.2	133,239
Wharton	1,752	3,380	3,426	4,459	7,584	16,942	21,123	27,397	29,681	36,158	-0.2	36,077	5.8	38,152	-3.7	36,729	9.6	40,242	-0.7	39,955
Wheeler[11]	0	0	0	512	778	636	5,258	7,397	19,555	12,411	-16.9	9,484	-23.0	7,947	-19.0	6,434	10.9	7,137	-17.6	5,879
Wichita	0	0	0	433	4,831	5,806	16,094	72,911	74,416	73,604	33.8	98,493	25.4	123,528	-2.4	120,563	0.4	121,082	1.1	122,378
Wilbarger	0	0	0	126	7,092	5,759	12,000	15,112	24,579	17,066	20.4	20,552	-13.6	17,748	-13.5	15,355	3.8	15,931	-5.1	15,121
Willacy[47]	0	0	0	0	0	0	0	0	20,128	13,230	58.1	20,920	-4.0	20,084	-22.5	15,570	12.4	17,495	1.2	17,705
Williamson	1,568	4,529	6,368	15,155	25,909	38,072	42,228	42,934	44,146	41,698	-6.8	38,853	-9.8	35,044	6.5	37,305	105.1	76,521	82.4	139,551
Wilson	0	0	2,556	7,118	10,655	13,961	17,289	17,289	17,606	17,066	-14.0	14,672	-9.6	13,267	-1.7	13,041	28.5	16,756	35.2	22,650
Winkler[14]	0	0	0	0	18	60	442	81	6,784	6,141	63.9	10,064	35.7	13,652	-29.4	9,640	3.2	9,944	-13.3	8,626
Wise	0	3,160	1,450	16,601	24,134	27,116	26,450	23,363	19,178	19,074	-15.4	16,141	5.4	17,012	15.7	19,687	35.0	26,575	30.5	34,679
Wood	0	4,968	6,894	11,212	13,932	21,048	23,363	23,417	20,128	24,360	-12.5	21,308	-17.2	17,653	5.3	18,589	32.9	24,697	19.0	29,380
Yoakum	0	0	0	0	4	26	602	504	1,263	5,354	-19.0	4,339	85.1	8,032	-8.6	7,344	13.0	8,299	5.9	8,786
Young	592	592	135	4,726	5,049	6,540	13,657	11,258	20,128	19,004	-11.5	16,810	2.6	17,254	-10.7	15,400	23.4	19,001	-4.6	18,126
Zapata[48][49]	1,248	1,248	1,488	3,636	3,562	4,760	3,809	2,929	2,867	3,916	12.5	4,405	-0.3	4,393	-0.9	4,352	52.3	6,628	40.0	9,279
Zavala	0	26	26	410	1,097	792	1,889	3,108	10,349	11,603	-3.5	11,201	13.3	12,696	-10.4	11,370	2.6	11,666	4.3	12,162
Others	0	324	138	1,902	8,403	0	3,108	0	0	0	***.*	0	***.*	0	***.*	0	***.*	0	***.*	0

[1]Part of Bandera taken to form Real in 1913.

[2]Comprised the greater part of West Texas until 1876, when it was divided into counties. It was usually referred to as a part of Bexar County, but there was a separate organization, and it was listed separately in the United States Census report of 1870, referred to as Bexar Territory and Bexar District.

County Population History, 1850-1990 (Cont'd.)

3Organized from part of Presidio in 1887; Buchel and Foley annexed in 1897.

4Part of Comanche taken to form part of Mills in 1887.

5No population reported for Briscoe County in 1890.

6Population to form Mills in 1887.

7Created from part of Presidio in 1887; annexed to Brewster in 1897.

8Name changed from Buchanan to Stephens in 1861.

9Cameron, Starr and Webb reported together in 1850; population credited to Cameron.

10Name of Cass County changed to Davis in 1861; changed back to Cass in 1871.

11Relocation of the 100th meridian (United States Supreme Court decision of March 17, 1930) resulted in the following changes in Texas counties: Part of Harmon County, Okla., acquired by Childress County, Texas; parts of Beckham and Harmon, Okla., acquired by Collingsworth, Texas; parts of Ellis and Roger Mills, Okla., acquired by Hemphill, Texas; part of Ellis, Okla., by Lipscomb, Texas; parts of Beckham and Roger Mills, Okla., by Wheeler, Texas.

12Created from, by part of Tom Green in 1889.

13Pest of Crockett taken to form Schleicher and Sutton in 1887, and part of Val Verde in 1885.

14Created from part of Tom Green in 1887.

15Culberson created from El Paso in 1911.

16There was an old Dawson County existing in 1860 a number of years before the creation of the present Dawson County of the South Plains. The older Dawson was west of present Uvalde county.

17Formed from part of Duval County in 1913; later disorganized; no census report.

18Parts of Duval taken to form Jim Hogg in 1913.

19Part of Duval taken to form part of Tom Green in 1887.

20Ector formed from part of Tom Green in 1887.

21Part of Edwards taken to form part of Real in 1913.

22Parts of El Paso taken to form Culberson in 1911 and Hudspeth in 1917.

23Annexed to Webb in 1899.

24Organized from parts of Hardeman and Knox in 1891.

25Oard organized from part of Presidio in 1887; annexed to Brewster in 1897.

26Organized from parts of Willacy and Brooks in 1911, and to form new boundaries of Willacy in 1921.

27Parts of Hidalgo taken to form parts of Willacy and Brooks in 1911, and to form new boundaries of Willacy in 1921.

28Hudspeth created from El Paso in 1917.

29Hudspeth created part of Presidio in 1887.

30Jim Hogg created from part of Duval and Brooks in 1913.

31Jim Wells created from part of Nueces in 1911; Kleberg organized from part of Nueces in 1913.

32Kenedy created from part of Willacy in 1921.

33Part of Kerr taken to form part of Real in 1913.

34Part taken to form part of Val Verde in 1885.

35Created from part of Tom Green in 1885.

36Created from parts of Brown, Comanche, Hamilton and Lampasas in 1887.

37Parts of Nueces taken to form Jim Wells in 1911, Kleberg in 1913.

38Parts of Pecos taken to form Reeves in 1883, part of Val Verde in 1885 and part of Terrell in 1905.

39Parts of Presidio taken to form Buchel, Brewster, Foley and Jeff Davis in 1887.

40Reagan created from part of Tom Green in 1903.

41Real created from parts of Bandera, Edwards and Kerr in 1913.

42Created from part of Pecos in 1883.

43Created from part of Crockett in 1887.

44Sterling formed from part of Tom Green in 1891.

45Terrell created from part of Pecos in 1905.

46Parts taken to form Midland in 1885, Ector, Glasscock, Loving, Upton, Ward and Winkler in 1887; Coke and Irion in 1889, Sterling in 1891, and Reagan in 1903.

47Parts taken to form Midland in 1885.

48Created from parts of Kinney, Crockett and Pecos in 1885.

49Encinal annexed in 1899.

50Old Willacy created from parts of Cameron and Hidalgo in 1911; name changed to Kenedy in 1921; new Willacy organized from parts of Cameron and Hidalgo in 1921.

51Part of Zapata taken to form part of Brooks in 1911.

52Brooks created from parts of Hidalgo, Starr, Zapata in 1911; part taken for part of Jim Hogg in 1913.

53Part of Cameron taken to form Willacy in 1911; part was taken again in 1921 to form part of new area of Willacy when Kenedy was created from Willacy.

54No population for Clay, Palo Pinto or Throckmorton reported in 1870.

55Greer County was organized as Texas civil unit and under Texas administration until 1896, when it was transferred to Oklahoma by decision of the United States Supreme Court.

City Population History, 1850-1990

The table below shows, for a selected list of Texas cities, a complete record of population for each decennial year, insofar as such record exists.

The official census record is presented below with few exceptions. In some instances, however, unofficial figures are given where census figures are unavailable. These are explained in footnotes. In recent years, the official census has included not only incorporated towns, but also unincorporated towns that meet certain federal criteria. These are called "Census Designated Places," and some are included in this list. At least one town from each county is listed.

Where no figure is given, it means that the town was not incorporated (or did not qualify as a Census Designated Place) on that date and that no census was taken for it. It does not necessarily mean that the town did not exist. Some Texas towns were in existence many years before incorporating.

City, County	1850	1860	1870	1880	1890	1900	1910	1920	1930	1940	Change 40-50	1950	Change 50-60	1960	Change 60-70	1970	Change 70-80	1980	Change 80-90	1990
Abernathy, Hale	0	0	0	0	0	0	0	0	0	858	99.8	1,692	47.2	2,491	5.4	2,625	10.6	2,904	-6.3	2,720
Abilene, Taylor	0	0	0	0	3,194	3,411	9,204	10,274	23,175	26,612	71.2	45,570	98.3	90,368	-0.8	89,653	9.7	98,315	8.5	106,654
Addison, Dallas	0	0	0	0	0	0	0	0	0	0	***	0	***	308	92.5	593	836.4	5,553	58.2	8,783
Alamo, Hidalgo	0	0	0	0	0	0	0	0	1,018	1,944	55.2	3,017	36.6	4,121	4.1	4,291	35.9	5,831	40.8	8,210
Alamo Heights, Bexar	0	0	0	0	0	0	0	0	3,874	5,700	40.4	8,000	-5.6	7,552	-8.2	6,933	-9.8	6,252	4.0	6,502
Albany, Shackelford	0	0	0	129	857	999			2,422	2,230	1.1	2,255	-2.4	2,200	-10.1	1,978	23.9	2,450	-19.9	1,962
Alice, Jim Wells	0	0	0	0	0	0		2,136	4,239	7,792	111.1	16,449	26.8	20,861	-3.5	20,121	4.2	20,961	-5.6	19,788
Allen, Collin	0	0	0	0	0	0		931			***		***	659	194.4	1,940	328.6	8,314	120.2	18,309
Alpine, Brewster	0	0	0	0	0	0			3,495	3,866	36.1	5,261	-9.9	4,740	26.0	5,971	-8.5	5,465	3.1	5,637
Alton, Hidalgo	0	0	0	0	0	0	0	0	0	0	***	0	***	0	***	0	***	2,732	12.3	3,069
Alvarado, Johnson	0	0	0	0	1,543	1,342	1,155	1,284	1,210	1,324	25.1	1,656	15.2	1,907	11.6	2,129	26.9	2,701	8.0	2,918
Alvin, Brazoria	0	0	0	0	261	996	1,453	1,519	1,511	3,087	19.9	3,701	52.5	5,643	89.1	10,671	54.8	16,515	16.4	19,220
Amarillo, Potter	0	0	0	0	482	1,442	9,957	15,494	43,132	51,686	43.6	74,246	85.8	137,969	-7.9	127,010	17.5	149,230	5.6	157,615
Anahuac, Chambers	0	0	0	0	0	0	0	0	0	‡1,500	-14.5	1,282	-0.1	1,281	46.8	1,881	-2.2	1,840	8.3	1,993
Andrews, Andrews	0	0	0	0	0	0	0	‡500	‡800	611	439.1	3,294	238.0	11,135	-22.5	8,625	28.2	11,061	-3.5	10,678
Angleton, Brazoria	0	0	0	0	0	0	1,842		2,093	1,763	92.8	3,399	115.1	7,312	33.6	9,770	42.6	13,929	23.1	17,140
Anson, Jones	0	0	0	0			1,425			2,338	15.8	2,708	6.7	2,890	-9.5	2,615	8.3	2,831	-6.6	2,644
Anthony, El Paso	0	0	0	0	0	0	0	0	0	0	***	839	28.9	1,082	99.1	2,154	22.6	2,640	26.1	3,328
Aransas Pass, San Patricio	0	0	0	0	187		1,197		2,482	4,095	31.8	5,396	28.9	6,956	-16.4	5,813	23.4	7,173	0.1	7,180
Archer City, Archer	0	0	0	0			825	689	1,512	1,675	13.1	1,895	4.2	1,974	-12.8	1,722	8.1	1,862	-6.1	1,748
Arlington, Tarrant	0	0	0	0	664	1,079	1,794	3,031	3,661	4,240	81.4	7,692	482.1	44,775	100.4	89,723	78.5	160,123	63.4	261,721
Aspermont, Stonewall	0	0	0	0			205	436	769	1,041	1.8	1,060	20.3	1,275	-6.0	1,198	13.3	1,357	-10.5	1,214
Athens, Henderson	*177	0	†500		1,764		2,261	3,176	4,342	4,765	9.0	5,194	36.4	7,086	35.2	9,582	6.4	10,197	7.6	10,967
Atlanta, Cass	0	0	0	0		1,301	1,604	1,685		2,453	54.2	3,782	7.8	4,076	22.8	5,007	25.3	6,272	-2.5	6,118
Austin, Travis	629	3,494	4,428	11,013	14,575	22,258	29,860	34,876	53,120	87,930	50.6	132,459	40.8	186,545	35.0	251,808	37.2	345,496	34.8	465,622
Azle, Tarrant	0	0	0	0	0	0	0	0	0	0	***	0	***	2,969	51.3	4,493	29.6	5,822	52.3	8,868
Balch Springs, Dallas	0	0	0	0	0	0	0	0	0	0	***	0	***	6,821	53.4	10,464	31.4	13,746	26.6	17,406
Balcones Heights, Bexar	0	0	0	0	0	0	0	0	0	0	***	0	***	950	163.6	2,504	13.9	2,853	5.9	3,022
Ballinger, Runnels	0	0	0	0	1,390	1,128	3,536	2,767	4,187	4,472	18.6	5,302	-4.9	5,043	-16.7	4,203	0.1	4,207	-5.5	3,975
Bandera, Bandera	0	0	0	0		419		‡700	‡580	‡1,250	6.0	‡1,325	-19.6	1,065	-16.3	891	6.3	947	-7.4	877
Barrett, Harris	0	0	0	0	0	0	0	0	0	0	***	0	***	2,364	16.3	2,750	***	3,052	***	2,872
Bastrop, Bastrop	*151	0	0			1,707	1,828			1,976	60.7	3,176	-5.5	3,001	3.7	3,112	21.8	3,789	6.7	4,044
Bay City, Matagorda	0	0	0	0	0	2,145	3,156	3,454	4,070	6,594	43.0	9,427	23.5	11,656	0.7	11,733	52.0	17,837	1.9	18,170
**Baytown, Harris	0	0	0	0	0	0	0	0	0	0	***	22,983	22.5	28,159	56.2	43,980	29.4	56,923	12.2	63,850
Beaumont, Jefferson	0	0	0	0	3,296	9,427	20,640	40,422	57,732	59,061	59.2	94,014	26.8	119,175	-2.7	115,919	1.9	118,102	-3.2	114,323
Bedford, Tarrant	0	0	0	0	0	0	0	0	0	0	***	1,386	95.3	2,706	271.4	10,049	107.2	20,821	110.2	43,762
Beeville, Bee	0	0	0	0	†1,311	‡2,311	3,269		4,806	6,789	37.7	9,348	47.7	13,811	-2.2	13,506	7.9	14,574	-7.0	13,547
Bellaire, Harris	0	0	0	0	0	0	0	0	390	1,124	805.1	10,173	95.3	19,872	-4.3	19,009	-21.4	14,950	-7.4	13,842
Bellmead, McLennan	0	0	0	0	0	0	0	0	0	0	***	0	***	5,127	50.1	7,698	-1.7	7,569	10.1	8,336
Bellville, Austin	0	0	0	0					1,533	1,347	56.8	2,112	5.0	2,218	6.9	2,371	20.6	2,860	18.1	3,378
Belton, Bell	300	305	777	1,797	3,000	3,700	4,164	5,098	3,779	3,572	74.9	6,246	30.7	8,163	6.5	8,696	22.6	10,660	17.0	12,476
Benavides, Duval	0	0	0	0	0	0	0	0		3,081	-2.1	3,016	-18.5	2,459	-14.1	2,112	-6.3	1,978	-9.6	1,788
Benbrook, Tarrant	0	0	0	0	0	0	0	0	0	0	***	617	427.4	3,254	151.0	8,169	66.2	13,579	44.1	19,564
Benjamin, Knox	0	0	0	0	0	0	0	0	832	599	-11.4	531	-42.0	308	0.0	308	-16.6	257	-12.5	225
Big Lake, Reagan	0	0	0	0	0	0	0		485	763	182.0	2,152	24.0	2,668	-6.7	2,489	36.8	3,404	7.9	3,672
Big Spring, Howard	0	0	0	0		‡1,255	4,102	4,273	13,735	12,604	37.1	17,286	80.7	31,230	-8.0	28,735	-13.7	24,804	-6.9	23,093

City Population History, 1850-1990 (Cont'd.)

City, County	1850	1860	1870	1880	1890	1900	1910	1920	1930	1940	Change 40-50	1950	Change 50-60	1960	Change 60-70	1970	Change 70-80	1980	Change 80-90	1990
Bishop, Nueces	0	0	0	0	0	0	0	0	953	1,329	105.5	2,731	36.3	3,722	-6.9	3,466	6.9	3,706	-10.0	3,337
Boerne, Kendall	0	0	0	0	0	0	886	1,153	1,117	1,271	41.8	1,802	20.4	2,169	12.1	2,432	32.8	3,229	32.4	4,274
Bonham, Fannin	*477	0	0	1,880	3,361	5,042	4,844	5,655	6,008	6,349	11.0	7,049	4.4	7,357	4.6	7,698	-4.7	7,338	-8.9	6,686
Borger, Hutchinson	0	0	0	0	0	0	0	0	6,532	10,018	80.3	18,059	15.8	20,911	-32.1	14,195	11.6	15,837	-1.0	15,675
Bowie, Montague	0	0	0	0	0	2,600	2,874	3,131	2,653	3,470	31.0	4,544	0.5	4,566	13.6	5,185	8.2	5,610	-11.1	4,990
Brackettville, Kinney	0	0	0	0	0	690	2,197	2,197	3,131	1,429	30.0	1,858	-10.5	1,662	-7.4	1,539	8.9	1,676	3.8	1,740
Brady, McCulloch	0	0	0	115	560	690	2,669	2,669	3,983	5,002	18.8	5,944	-10.2	5,338	4.1	5,557	7.4	5,969	-0.4	5,946
Brazoria, Brazoria	0	0	0	0	0	0	0	0	704	715	***	776	66.4	1,291	30.2	1,681	80.0	3,025	-10.2	2,717
Breckenridge, Stephens	0	0	0	0	0	0	0	1,846	7,569	5,826	13.5	6,610	-5.1	6,273	-5.2	5,944	16.4	6,921	-18.1	5,665
Brenham, Washington	0	0	2,221	4,101	5,209	5,968	4,718	5,066	5,974	6,435	7.9	6,941	11.5	7,740	15.3	8,922	22.9	10,966	9.0	11,952
Bridge City, Orange	0	0	0	0	0	0	0	0	0	0	***	0	***	4,677	74.6	8,164	-6.1	7,667	4.8	8,034
Bridgeport, Wise	0	0	0	0	498	900	2,000	1,872	1,907	1,735	18.1	2,049	57.1	3,218	12.3	3,613	3.4	3,737	-4.2	3,581
Brownfield, Terry	0	0	0	0	0	0	0	0	2,021	4,009	53.7	6,161	67.0	10,286	-6.2	9,647	7.7	10,387	-8.0	9,560
Brownsville, Cameron	0	2,734	4,905	4,938	6,134	6,305	10,517	11,791	22,021	22,083	63.3	36,066	33.2	48,040	9.3	52,522	61.8	84,997	16.4	98,962
Brownwood, Brown	0	0	0	725	2,176	3,965	6,967	8,223	12,789	13,398	50.6	20,181	-15.9	16,974	2.3	17,368	10.6	19,203	-4.2	18,387
Bryan, Brazos	0	0	0	0	2,979	3,589	4,132	6,307	7,814	11,842	52.9	18,102	52.1	27,542	22.4	33,719	31.5	44,337	24.1	55,002
Buffalo, Leon	0	0	0	190	310	310	310	510	470	737	31.1	966	14.7	1,108	12.1	1,242	21.3	1,507	3.2	1,555
Bunker Hill Village, Harris	0	0	0	0	0	0	0	0	0	0	***	0	***	2,216	79.5	3,977	-5.7	3,750	-9.6	3,391
Burkburnett, Wichita	0	0	0	0	0	0	0	5,300	3,281	2,814	61.9	4,555	67.3	7,621	21.1	9,230	15.6	10,668	-4.9	10,145
Burleson, Johnson	0	0	0	0	0	0	0	241	573	573	38.0	791	196.5	2,345	228.9	7,713	52.1	11,734	37.3	16,113
Burnet, Burnet	0	0	0	0	0	1,003	1,476	1,535	1,724	1,945	23.1	2,394	-7.5	2,214	29.4	2,864	19.1	3,410	0.4	3,423
Caldwell, Burleson	0	0	0	0	1,454	1,689	981	2,099	2,103	2,165	-2.6	2,109	4.5	2,204	4.7	2,308	27.9	2,953	7.7	3,181
Calvert, Robertson	0	0	0	2,280	1,250	3,322	1,476	2,366	2,366	2,366	7.7	2,548	-18.6	2,073	-0.0	2,072	-16.4	1,732	-11.3	1,536
Cameron, Milam	0	0	0	0	1,608	3,341	2,579	4,298	4,565	5,040	0.2	5,052	11.6	5,640	-1.7	5,546	3.2	5,721	-2.5	5,580
Canadian, Hemphill	0	0	0	0	0	0	1,648	2,187	2,068	2,151	25.5	2,700	-17.1	2,239	2.3	2,292	52.3	3,491	-30.8	2,417
Canton, Van Zandt	0	0	0	0	0	0	0	573	704	715	23.2	881	26.4	1,114	104.9	2,283	24.6	2,845	3.7	2,949
Canyon, Randall	0	0	0	0	0	0	1,400	1,618	2,821	2,622	66.4	4,364	34.0	5,864	42.1	8,333	28.7	10,724	6.0	11,365
Carrizo Springs, Dimmit	0	0	0	0	0	0	0	954	2,171	2,494	73.1	4,316	32.0	5,699	-5.7	5,374	28.1	6,886	-16.6	5,745
Carrollton, Dallas	0	0	0	0	0	0	0	573	689	921	74.8	1,610	163.5	4,242	226.6	13,855	193.0	40,591	102.4	82,169
Carthage, Panola	0	0	0	0	0	0	0	1,366	1,651	2,178	118.1	4,750	10.8	5,262	2.5	5,392	19.6	6,447	0.8	6,496
Castle Hills, Bexar	0	0	0	0	0	0	0	0	0	0	***	0	***	2,622	102.6	5,311	-10.1	4,773	-12.0	4,198
Cedar Hill, Dallas	0	0	0	0	0	0	0	0	0	476	53.8	732	152.5	1,848	41.2	2,610	162.4	6,849	191.7	19,976
Cedar Park, Williamson	0	0	0	0	0	0	0	0	0	0	***	0	***	0	***	0	***	3,474	48.6	5,161
Center, Shelby	0	0	0	0	0	318	1,684	1,838	2,510	3,010	43.6	4,323	4.3	4,510	10.6	4,989	16.8	5,827	-15.1	4,950
Centerville, Leon	0	0	0	0	288	204	318	‡475	‡500	900	6.8	961	-13.0	836	-0.6	831	-3.9	799	1.6	812
Channing, Hartley	0	0	0	0	0	0	‡475	‡475	‡500	‡475	-36.8	‡300	30.0	390	-13.8	336	-9.5	304	-8.9	277
Childress, Childress	0	0	0	0	0	1,063	3,818	5,003	7,163	6,434	18.4	7,619	-16.0	6,399	-15.5	5,408	7.6	5,817	-13.1	5,055
Cisco, Eastland	0	0	0	0	0	692	2,410	7,422	6,027	4,934	6.0	5,230	-14.0	4,499	-7.5	4,160	8.6	4,517	-15.6	3,813
Clarendon, Donley	0	0	0	0	0	1,514	1,946	2,456	2,756	2,431	6.0	2,577	-15.7	2,172	-9.1	1,974	12.5	2,220	-6.9	2,067
Clarksville, Red River	‡700	0	0	0	0	2,069	2,065	3,386	2,952	4,095	6.3	4,353	-11.5	3,851	-13.1	3,346	47.0	4,917	-12.3	4,311
Claude, Armstrong	0	0	0	0	0	310	692	770	1,041	761	7.8	820	22.6	1,005	-1.3	992	12.1	1,112	7.8	1,199
Cleburne, Johnson	0	0	0	1,855	3,278	7,493	10,364	12,820	11,539	10,558	22.2	12,905	19.2	15,381	4.1	16,015	20.0	19,218	15.5	22,205
Cleveland, Liberty	0	0	683	285	0	0	0	1,327	1,422	1,217	190.7	3,541	27.1	4,501	25.0	5,627	6.2	5,977	19.2	7,124
Clifton, Bosque	0	0	0	0	0	0	1,137	0	1,422	1,732	6.1	1,837	27.1	2,335	10.4	2,578	18.8	3,063	4.3	3,195
Clute, Brazoria	0	0	0	0	0	0	0	0	0	0	***	0	***	3,104	54.0	4,781	59.0	7,602	17.2	8,910
Clyde, Callahan	0	0	0	0	439	0	495	610	706	800	13.5	908	22.9	1,116	46.5	1,635	56.7	2,562	17.2	3,002
Cockrell Hill, Dallas	0	0	0	0	0	0	0	0	0	1,246	77.1	2,207	65.6	3,655	-3.8	3,515	-7.2	3,262	14.8	3,746
Coldspring, San Jacinto	0	0	0	0	0	0	0	‡500	‡500	‡500	0.0	‡500	31.0	655	3.1	675	-15.7	569	-5.4	538
Coleman, Coleman	0	0	0	‡400	906	1,362	3,046	2,868	6,078	6,054	7.9	6,530	-2.2	6,371	-12.0	5,608	6.3	5,960	-9.2	5,410
College Station, Brazos	‡700	*400	0	0	0	0	0	0	0	2,184	262.9	7,925	43.8	11,396	55.1	17,676	110.9	37,272	40.7	52,456
Colleyville, Tarrant	0	0	0	0	0	0	0	0	0	0	***	0	***	1,491	125.9	3,368	98.9	6,700	89.9	12,724
Colorado City, Mitchell	0	0	0	‡1,200	1,959	1,840	1,840	1,766	4,671	5,213	29.9	6,774	-4.7	6,457	-19.0	5,227	3.4	5,405	-12.1	4,749
Columbus, Colorado	0	0	683	1,959	0	1,766	1,840	2,054	2,054	2,422	18.8	2,878	27.0	3,656	-8.6	3,342	17.4	3,923	-14.2	3,367
Comanche, Comanche	‡400	0	0	704	1,226	2,070	2,756	3,524	2,435	3,209	19.7	3,840	-11.1	3,415	15.2	3,933	3.6	4,075	0.3	4,087

Table: City Population History, 1850-1990 (Cont'd.)

City, County	1850	1860	1870	1880	1890	1900	1910	1920	1930	1940	Change 40-50	1950	Change 50-60	1960	Change 60-70	1970	Change 70-80	1980	Change 80-90	1990
Commerce, Hunt	0	0	0	0	810	1,800	2,818	3,842	4,267	4,699	25.3	5,889	-1.7	5,789	64.7	9,534	-14.7	8,136	-16.1	6,825
Conroe, Montgomery	0	0	0	0	0	0	1,374	1,858	2,457	4,624	57.8	7,298	26.0	9,192	30.2	11,969	50.7	18,034	53.1	27,610
Converse, Bexar	0	0	0	0	0	0	0	0	0	0			***		***	1,383	254.8	4,907	81.1	8,887
Cooper, Delta	0	0	0	0	629	1,518	1,513	2,563	2,023	2,537	-7.4	2,350	-5.8	2,213	2.0	2,258	3.5	2,338	-7.9	2,153
Coppell, Dallas	0	0	0	0	0	0	0	0	0	0			***	666	159.5	1,728	121.4	3,826	341.2	16,881
Copperas Cove, Coryell	0	0	0	0	0	0	0	509	406	356	195.5	1,052	334.1	4,567	136.9	10,818	80.0	19,469	23.7	24,079
Corpus Christi, Nueces	0	175	2,140	3,257	4,387	4,703	8,222	10,522	27,741	57,301	89.0	108,287	54.9	167,690	22.0	204,525	13.4	231,999	11.0	257,453
Corsicana, Navarro	0	0	0	3,373	6,285	9,313	9,749	11,356	15,202	15,232	26.1	19,211	5.9	20,344	-1.8	19,972	8.7	21,712	5.5	22,911
Cotulla, La Salle	0	0	0	0	0	0	1,880	1,058	3,175	3,633	21.6	4,418	-10.4	3,960	-13.8	3,415	14.6	3,912	-5.6	3,694
Crane, Crane	0	0	0	0	0	0	0	0	0	1,420	51.7	2,154	76.2	3,796	-9.7	3,427	5.7	3,622	-2.5	3,533
Crockett, Houston	‡600	‡1,500	0	599	1,445	2,612	3,947	3,061	4,441	4,536	30.8	5,932	-9.7	5,356	23.5	6,616	11.9	7,405	-5.1	7,024
Crosbyton, Crosby	0	0	0	0	0	0	0	809	1,250	1,615	16.3	1,878	41.1	2,650	-15.1	2,251	1.7	2,289	-11.5	2,026
Crowell, Foard	0	0	0	0	0	278	1,341	1,175	1,946	1,817	5.8	1,922	-11.0	1,710	-18.2	1,399	7.9	1,509	-18.5	1,230
Crowley, Tarrant	0	0	0	0	0	0	0	0	0	0			26.4	583	356.6	2,662	119.8	5,852	19.2	6,974
Crystal City, Zavala	0	0	0	0	0	0	0	±800	6,609	6,529	10.2	7,198	26.4	9,101	-11.0	8,104	2.8	8,334	-0.9	8,263
Cuero, DeWitt	0	0	0	0	0	3,422	3,109	3,671	4,672	5,474	37.0	7,498	-2.1	7,338	-5.2	6,956	2.4	7,124	-6.0	6,700
Daingerfield, Morris	0	0	0	0	0	0	0	0	0	1,032	61.6	1,668	87.8	3,133	-16.1	2,630	15.2	3,030	-15.1	2,572
Dalhart, Dallam	*430	0	0	0	0	0	2,580	2,676	4,691	4,682	26.4	5,918	-12.8	5,160	10.6	5,705	20.1	6,854	-8.9	6,246
Dallas, Dallas	*430	‡2,000	‡3,000	10,358	38,067	42,638	92,104	158,976	260,475	294,734	47.4	434,462	56.4	679,684	24.2	844,401	7.1	904,078	11.4	1,006,877
Dayton, Liberty	0	0	0	0	0	0	0	0	1,207	1,279	42.3	1,820	85.0	3,367	13.0	3,804	29.0	4,908	5.0	5,151
Decatur, Wise	0	0	0	579	1,746	1,562	1,651	2,205	2,037	2,578	13.3	2,922	21.9	3,563	-9.1	3,240	26.7	4,104	3.6	4,252
Deer Park, Harris	0	0	0	0	0	0	0	0	0	0	***	736	561.0	4,865	162.5	12,773	77.3	22,648	22.1	27,652
Del Rio, Val Verde	0	0	0	0	0	0	2,551	0	11,693	13,343	6.5	14,211	31.0	18,612	14.6	21,330	40.8	30,034	2.2	30,705
Denison, Grayson	0	0	0	3,975	10,958	11,807	13,632	17,065	13,850	15,581	12.3	17,504	30.0	22,748	9.6	24,923	-4.2	23,884	-10.0	21,505
Denton, Denton	0	0	0	1,194	2,558	4,187	4,732	7,626	9,587	11,192	91.0	21,372	25.6	26,844	48.5	39,874	20.5	48,063	37.9	66,270
Denver City, Yoakum	0	0	0	0	0	0	0	0	0	0	***	298	560.7	1,969	109.9	4,133	13.8	4,704	9.4	5,145
DeSoto, Dallas	0	0	0	0	0	0	0	0	0	1,398	19.6	1,672	50.8	2,522	162.4	6,617	134.8	15,538	96.6	30,544
Devine, Medina	0	0	0	0	0	0	1,042	995	1,093	0	***	2,391	4.8	2,506	31.3	3,311	13.4	3,756	4.6	3,928
Diboll, Angelina	0	0	0	0	0	0	0	±150	0	0				2,506	41.9	3,557	46.6	5,227	-17.0	4,341
Dickens, Dickens	0	0	0	0	0	176	0	±400	1,363	465	-10.5	416	-3.8	400	-26.3	295	38.6	409	-21.3	322
Dickinson, Galveston	0	0	0	0	0	0	0	0	0	0	***	0	***	4,715	11.5	5,257	42.7	7,505	26.5	9,497
Dilley, Frio	0	0	0	0	0	0	0	0	760	1,244	45.4	1,809	17.1	2,118	11.5	2,362	9.2	2,579	2.1	2,632
Dimmitt, Castro	0	0	0	0	0	0	0	0	929	943	54.9	1,461	100.9	2,935	47.4	4,327	16.0	5,019	-12.2	4,408
Donna, Hidalgo	0	0	0	0	0	0	0	1,579	4,103	4,712	52.2	7,171	4.9	7,522	-2.1	7,365	35.1	9,952	27.1	12,652
Dublin, Erath	0	0	0	50	1,980	2,370	2,551	3,229	2,271	2,546	8.4	2,761	-11.5	2,443	15.0	2,810	-3.1	2,723	17.2	3,190
Dumas, Moore	0	0	0	0	0	0	0	0	0	735	189.4	2,127	298.5	8,477	15.3	9,771	24.8	12,194	5.6	12,871
Duncanville, Dallas	0	0	0	0	0	0	0	0	0	0	***	841	348.8	3,774	273.7	14,105	97.0	27,781	28.7	35,748
Eagle Lake, Colorado	0	0	0	0	769	1,107	1,717	2,017	2,343	2,124	31.2	2,787	27.9	3,565	0.6	3,587	9.3	3,921	-9.4	3,551
Eagle Pass, Maverick	0	0	0	0	0	596	3,536	5,765	5,059	6,459	12.6	7,276	66.2	12,094	27.0	15,364	39.3	21,407	-3.5	20,651
Eastland, Eastland	0	0	0	0	0	0	855	9,368	4,648	3,849	-5.8	3,626	-9.2	3,292	-3.5	3,178	17.9	3,747	-1.5	3,690
Edcouch, Hidalgo	0	0	0	0	0	0	0	0	914	1,758	66.4	2,925	-3.8	2,814	-5.6	2,656	16.4	3,092	-6.9	2,878
Eden, Concho	0	0	0	0	0	0	0	593	1,194	1,603	23.4	1,978	-24.2	1,500	-13.9	1,291	0.2	1,294	21.1	1,567
Edgecliff, Tarrant	0	0	0	0	0	0	0	0	0	0			***	339	237.2	1,143	135.8	2,695	0.7	2,715
Edinburg, Hidalgo	0	0	0	0	0	0	0	±150	4,821	8,718	42.0	12,383	51.1	18,706	-8.2	17,163	40.3	24,075	24.1	29,885
Edna, Jackson	0	0	0	0	0	0	0	1,406	1,752	2,724	41.5	3,855	30.7	5,038	5.8	5,332	6.0	5,650	-5.4	5,343
El Campo, Wharton	0	0	0	0	0	0	1,778	1,766	2,034	3,906	59.7	6,237	23.5	7,700	21.2	9,332	12.1	10,462	0.5	10,511
Eldorado, Schleicher	0	0	0	0	0	112	0	0	1,404	1,530	8.0	1,653	11.9	1,850	-21.8	1,446	42.5	2,061	-2.0	2,019
Electra, Wichita	0	0	0	0	0	0	640	4,744	6,712	5,588	-11.1	4,970	-4.2	4,759	-18.2	3,895	-3.6	3,755	-17.1	3,113
Elgin, Bastrop	0	0	0	0	0	0	1,707	1,630	1,823	2,008	57.8	3,168	10.8	3,511	9.1	3,832	18.3	4,535	6.9	4,846
El Lago, Harris	0	0	0	0	0	0	0	0	0	0			***	0	***	2,308	35.6	3,129	4.5	3,269
El Paso, El Paso	0	‡2,000	0	736	10,338	15,906	39,279	77,560	102,421	96,810	34.8	130,485	112.0	276,687	16.5	322,261	32.0	425,259	21.2	515,342
Elsa, Hidalgo	0	0	0	0	0	0	0	0	750	1,006	216.0	3,179	21.0	3,847	14.4	4,400	15.0	5,061	3.6	5,242
Emory, Rains	0	0	0	0	353	426	0	±800	0	750	-7.4	648	-12.0	570	21.6	693	17.3	813	18.5	963
Ennis, Ellis	0	0	1,351	1,351	2,171	4,919	5,669	7,224	7,069	7,087	10.3	7,815	19.6	9,347	18.2	11,046	9.6	12,110	14.6	13,883

City Population History, 1850-1990 (Cont'd.)

City, County	1850	1860	1870	1880	1890	1900	1910	1920	1930	1940	Change 40-50	1950	Change 50-60	1960	Change 60-70	1970	Change 70-80	1980	Change 80-90	1990
Euless, Tarrant	0	0	0	0	0	0	0	0	0	0	***	0	***	4,263	353.1	19,316	24.3	24,002	58.9	38,149
Everman, Tarrant	0	0	0	0	0	0	0	0	0	0	***	451	138.6	1,076	324.7	4,570	17.9	5,387	5.3	5,672
Fabens, El Paso	0	0	0	0	0	0	0	0	1,623	0	***	3,089	1.5	3,134	3.4	3,241	***	0	***	0
Fairfield, Freestone	0	0	0	0	0	0	0	0	0	1,047	66.4	1,742	2.2	1,781	16.5	2,074	69.0	3,505	-7.7	3,234
Falfurrias, Brooks	0	0	0	0	0	895	1,398	1,518	1,581	1,708	***	6,712	-2.9	6,515	-2.5	6,355	-4.0	6,103	-5.2	5,788
Farmers Branch, Dallas	0	0	0	0	913	0	0	1,384	2,637	0	***	915	***	13,441	104.5	27,492	-9.6	24,863	-2.5	24,250
Floresville, Wilson	0	0	0	0	0	0	0	0	0	1,708	14.1	1,949	9.1	2,126	74.4	3,707	18.2	4,381	19.8	5,247
Flower Mound, Denton	0	0	0	0	0	0	0	0	0	0	***	0	***	0	***	1,685	161.2	4,402	252.7	15,527
Floydada, Floyd	0	0	0	0	0	0	664	1,384	2,637	2,726	17.8	3,210	17.4	3,769	9.0	4,109	2.0	4,193	-7.1	3,896
Forest Hill, Lamar	0	0	615	1,162	0	0	0	0	±1,200	±1,000	***	1,519	112.0	3,221	155.7	8,236	41.9	11,684	-1.7	11,482
Fort Davis, Jeff Davis	0	0	0	0	0	1,061	0	±1,061	1,297	±1,000	20.0	±1,200	-29.2	850	5.4	896	0.4	900	***	0
Fort Stockton, Pecos	0	0	500	6,663	23,076	0	0	±1,297	2,695	3,294	34.9	1,444	43.4	6,373	30.0	8,283	4.9	8,688	-1.9	8,524
Fort Worth, Tarrant	4,117	0	13,818	6,663	23,076	26,688	73,312	106,482	163,447	177,662	56.9	278,778	27.8	356,268	10.4	393,476	-2.1	385,141	16.2	447,619
Fredericksburg, Gillespie	0	0	0	0	0	0	0	1,798	2,416	3,544	8.7	3,854	20.1	4,629	15.1	5,326	20.4	6,412	8.1	6,934
Freeport, Brazoria	0	0	0	0	0	0	0	0	3,162	2,579	133.1	6,012	93.3	11,619	3.3	11,997	12.1	13,444	-15.3	11,389
Freer, Duval	0	0	0	0	0	0	0	0	0	2,346	-2.8	2,280	19.5	2,724	2.9	2,804	14.6	3,213	1.8	3,271
Friendswood, Galveston	0	0	0	0	0	0	0	0	0	0	***	0	***	0	***	5,675	88.9	10,719	112.8	22,814
Friona, Parmer	0	0	0	0	0	0	0	0	731	803	49.7	1,202	70.4	2,048	51.9	3,111	22.4	3,809	-3.2	3,688
Frisco, Collin	0	0	0	0	0	126	332	733	618	670	9.9	736	60.9	1,184	55.8	1,845	85.4	3,420	79.6	6,141
Gail, Borden	0	0	0	0	0	0	0	±126	±175	±200	0.0	±200	0.0	200	-11.0	178	6.2	189	***	0
Gainesville, Cooke	0	0	0	2,667	6,594	7,874	7,624	8,643	8,915	9,651	16.5	11,246	16.3	13,083	5.7	13,830	1.8	14,081	1.2	14,256
Galena Park, Harris	0	0	0	0	0	0	0	0	0	1,562	360.1	7,186	51.0	10,852	-3.4	10,479	-5.7	9,879	-1.6	10,033
Galveston, Galveston	4,117	7,307	13,818	22,248	29,084	37,788	36,981	44,255	52,938	60,862	9.4	66,568	0.9	67,175	-8.0	61,809	0.2	61,902	-4.6	59,070
Garden City, Glasscock	0	0	0	0	0	0	0	±100	±250	±200	8.0	±270	0.0	270	5.9	286	2.4	293	***	0
Garland, Dallas	0	0	0	0	0	819	804	1,421	1,584	2,233	373.4	10,571	264.2	38,501	111.5	81,437	70.5	138,857	30.1	180,650
Gatesville, Coryell	0	0	0	434	478	1,865	1,929	2,499	2,601	3,177	21.4	3,856	50.0	4,626	2.7	6,260	48.1	6,260	83.6	11,492
Georgetown, Williamson	0	0	±320	1,354	2,447	2,790	3,096	2,871	3,583	3,682	34.5	4,951	5.4	5,218	7.7	6,395	29.9	9,468	56.8	14,842
George West, Live Oak	0	0	0	0	0	0	0	0	0	0	***	0	22.5	1,878	-1.3	2,022	29.9	2,627	-1.6	2,586
Giddings, Lee	0	0	0	624	0	0	1,484	1,650	1,835	2,166	16.9	2,532	11.4	2,821	-1.3	2,783	41.9	3,950	3.6	4,093
Gilmer, Upshur	0	0	0	0	0	0	0	2,268	1,963	3,138	30.5	4,096	5.3	4,312	-2.7	4,196	29.9	2,627	-6.7	4,822
Gladewater, Gregg	0	0	0	132	400	890	0	±1,000	983	4,454	19.1	5,305	8.2	5,742	-2.9	5,574	23.1	5,167	-8.0	6,027
Glen Rose, Somervell	0	0	0	0	0	1,261	0	±2,500	1,424	1,446	18.9	1,248	19.8	1,495	-2.3	1,554	33.5	2,075	-2.2	1,949
Goliad, Goliad	648	1,212	0	0	0	0	0	±1,000	3,859	4,722	9.3	1,580	10.8	1,750	-2.3	1,709	16.4	1,990	-8.7	1,946
Gonzales, Gonzales	1,072	0	0	1,581	1,641	4,297	3,139	3,128	5,208	6,929	19.8	5,659	3.0	5,829	0.4	5,854	22.2	7,152	***	6,527
**Goose Creek, Harris	0	0	0	0	0	0	0	0	4,981	0	***	0	***	0	***	0	***	0	***	0
Graham, Young	0	0	0	0	667	878	1,569	2,544	4,981	5,175	30.3	6,742	26.1	8,505	-12.1	7,477	21.1	9,055	-0.8	8,986
Granbury, Hood	0	0	0	0	1,164	1,410	1,336	1,364	996	1,166	44.3	1,683	32.3	2,227	11.0	2,473	34.7	3,332	21.4	4,045
Grand Prairie, Dallas	0	0	0	0	0	0	994	1,263	1,529	1,595	815.0	14,594	108.2	30,386	67.5	50,904	40.4	71,462	39.4	99,616
Grand Saline, Van Zandt	0	0	0	0	0	1,065	994	1,528	1,799	1,641	10.3	1,824	10.8	2,006	12.5	2,257	20.0	2,006	-2.9	2,630
Grapevine, Tarrant	0	0	0	0	0	681	1,065	821	936	1,043	74.9	1,824	54.7	2,821	149.0	7,023	68.0	11,801	147.5	29,202
Greenville, Hunt	*246	0	0	4,330	4,330	6,860	8,850	12,384	12,407	13,995	5.2	14,727	29.6	19,087	15.5	22,043	0.5	22,161	4.1	23,071
Gregory, San Patricio	0	0	0	0	0	0	0	0	0	0	***	0	***	1,970	14.0	2,246	22.0	2,739	-10.3	2,458
Groesbeck, Limestone	0	0	0	0	663	1,462	1,454	1,522	2,059	2,272	-4.0	2,182	14.5	2,498	-4.1	2,396	40.8	3,373	-5.6	3,185
Groves, Jefferson	0	0	0	0	0	0	0	0	0	0	***	0	14.5	17,304	4.4	18,067	-5.4	17,090	-3.4	16,513
Guthrie, King	0	0	0	0	0	101	0	±101	0	±101	-4.0	±150	4.4	±210	-40.5	125	12.0	±140	***	0
Halletsville, Lavaca	0	0	0	0	1,011	1,457	1,379	1,444	1,406	1,581	48.5	2,000	40.0	2,808	-3.4	2,712	5.6	2,865	-5.1	2,718
Haltom City, Tarrant	0	0	0	0	0	0	0	0	0	0	26.5	5,760	301.6	23,133	21.6	28,127	3.2	29,014	13.2	32,856
Hamilton, Hamilton	0	0	0	0	1,011	1,457	1,379	1,444	1,406	2,716	13.3	3,077	0.9	3,106	-11.1	3,189	15.5	2,760	-7.9	2,937
Hamlin, Jones	0	0	0	0	0	0	1,548	2,018	2,048	2,406	52.1	3,659	3.6	3,791	-12.3	3,325	-2.3	3,248	-14.1	2,791
Harker Heights, Bell	0	0	0	0	0	0	0	0	0	0	***	0	***	0	***	4,216	74.2	7,345	74.8	12,841
Harlingen, Cameron	0	0	0	0	0	0	1,978	1,784	12,124	13,306	74.6	23,229	77.4	41,207	-18.7	33,503	30.0	43,543	11.9	48,735
Haskell, Haskell	0	0	0	0	0	0	2,346	2,300	3,051	3,836	25.7	4,016	4.7	4,016	-9.0	3,655	3.5	3,782	-11.1	3,362
Hearne, Robertson	0	0	0	1,421	0	±800	2,346	2,300	2,956	3,511	38.8	4,872	6.2	5,172	-3.7	4,982	8.8	5,418	-5.3	5,132
Hebbronville, Jim Hogg	0	0	0	0	0	2,129	2,353	2,741	2,956	3,511	38.8	4,302	-7.3	3,987	2.3	4,079	***	0	***	0

City Population History, 1850-1990 (Cont'd.)

City, County	1850	1860	1870	1880	1890	1900	1910	1920	1930	1940	Change 40-50	1950	Change 50-60	1960	Change 60-70	1970	Change 70-80	1980	Change 80-90	1990
Hedwig Village, Harris	0	0	0	0	0	0	0	0	0	0	***	0	***	1,182	175.4	3,255	-23.0	2,506	4.4	2,616
Hemphill, Sabine	0	0	0	0	0	279	0	0	731	739	31.1	969	-5.8	913	10.1	1,005	34.6	1,353	-12.6	1,182
Hempstead, Waller	*705	0	0	2,100	2,541	0	0	‡3,100		1,674	-16.7	1,395	581.4	9,505	-80.1	1,891	82.8	3,456	2.7	3,551
Henderson, Rusk	0	0	0	0	0	0	0	2,273	2,932	6,437	6.2	6,833	41.5	9,666	5.4	10,187	12.6	11,473	-2.9	11,139
Henrietta, Clay	0	0	0	0	0	0	0	2,563	2,020	2,391	17.6	2,813	8.8	3,062	-5.4	2,897	8.7	3,149	-8.0	2,896
Hereford, Deaf Smith	0	0	0	0	0	1,614	2,104	1,696	2,458	2,584	101.5	5,207	29.7	6,752	98.7	13,414	18.2	15,853	-7.0	14,745
Hewitt, McLennan	0	0	0	0	0	0	0	0	0	0	***	0	***		***	569	822.1	5,247	71.2	8,983
Highland Park, Dallas	0	0	0	0	0	0	1,750	2,321	8,422	10,288	10.9	11,405	-8.7	10,411	-2.7	10,133	-12.1	8,909	-1.9	8,739
Highlands, Harris	0	0	0	0	0	0	0	0	0	0	***	2,723	59.2	4,336	-20.2	3,462			***	
Highland Village, Denton	0	0	0	0	0	0	0	0	0	0					***	516	529.1	3,246	116.5	7,027
Hillsboro, Hill	0	0	†313	0	0	5,346	6,115	6,952	7,823	7,799	7.2	8,363	-11.5	7,402	-2.4	7,224	2.4	7,397	-4.4	7,072
Hitchcock, Galveston	0	0	0	0	0	0	0	0	0	0	***	1,105	372.0	5,216	6.7	5,565	19.6	6,655	-11.8	5,868
Hollywood Park, Bexar	0	0	0	0	0	0	0	0	0	0	***	0	***	783	193.6	2,299	40.5	3,231	-12.1	2,841
Hondo, Medina	0	0	0	0	0	0	0	0	0	0		4,188	19.2	4,992	9.9	5,487	10.4	6,057	-0.6	6,018
Hooks, Bowie	0	0	0	0	0	0	0	0	0	0		2,319	-11.7	2,048	24.3	2,545	-1.5	2,507	7.1	2,684
Houston, Harris	2,396	4,845	9,382	16,513	27,557	44,633	78,800	138,276	292,352	384,514	55.0	596,163	57.4	938,219	31.4	1,232,802	29.3	1,594,086	2.3	1,630,553
Humble, Harris	0	0	0	0	0	0	0	0	0	1,371	1.2	1,388	23.3	1,711	91.6	3,278	105.3	6,729	79.2	12,060
Hunters Creek Village, Harris	0	0	0	0	0	0	0	0	0	0	***	0	***	2,478	59.8	3,959	6.5	4,215	-6.2	3,954
Huntsville, Walker	*892	0	†1,600	‡2,536	1,509	2,485	2,072	4,689	5,028	5,108	92.2	9,820	22.2	11,999	46.8	17,610	35.9	23,936	16.7	27,925
Hurst, Tarrant	0	0	0	0	0	0	0	0	0	0	***	0	***	10,165	167.7	27,215	15.5	31,420	6.9	33,574
Hutchins, Dallas	0	0	0	0	0	0	0	0	0	0		743	48.0	1,100	59.5	1,755	70.7	2,996	-9.2	2,719
Ingleside, San Patricio	0	0	0	0	0	0	603	0	0	0	***	1,424	112.2	3,022	24.5	3,763	44.5	5,436	4.8	5,696
Iowa Park, Wichita	0	0	0	0	0	0	0	2,041	2,009	1,980	6.6	2,110	56.2	3,295	75.9	5,796	6.7	6,184	-1.8	6,072
Irving, Dallas	0	0	0	0	0	0	0	357	731	1,089	140.7	2,621	***	45,985	111.5	97,260	13.0	109,943	41.0	155,037
Jacinto City, Harris	0	0	0	0	0	0	0	0	0	0	***	6,856	39.3	9,547	0.2	9,563	-6.4	8,953	4.4	9,343
Jacksboro, Jack	0	0	0	0	751	1,311	1,480	1,373	1,837	2,368	24.6	2,951	29.3	3,816	-6.9	3,554	12.5	4,000	-16.3	3,350
Jacksonville, Cherokee	0	0	0	0	970	1,568	2,875	3,723	6,748	7,213	19.3	8,607	11.4	9,590	1.5	9,734	26.0	12,264	4.1	12,765
Jasper, Jasper	0	0	‡360	‡500	‡473	0	0	‡750	3,393	3,497	25.9	4,403	11.0	4,889	27.9	6,251	11.3	6,959	0.0	6,959
Jayton, Kent	0	0	0	0	0	0	314	0	623	770	-17.8	633	10.6	700	0.4	703	-9.2	638	-4.7	608
Jefferson, Marion	0	988	4,190	3,260	3,072	2,850	2,515	2,549	2,329	2,797	13.1	3,164	-2.6	3,082	-7.0	2,866	-7.8	2,643	-16.8	2,199
Jersey Village, Harris	0	0	0	0	0	0	0	0	0	0			***	493	55.2	765	433.9	4,084	18.2	4,826
Johnson City, Blanco	0	0	0	0	0	0	0	‡400				645	-7.8	595	28.9	767	13.7	872	6.9	932
Jones Creek, Brazoria	0	0	0	0	0	0	0	0			***	1,481	1.6	1,504	17.2	1,763	49.4	2,634	-18.0	2,160
Jourdanton, Atascosa	0	0	0	0	0	0	344	0			-14.0	2,562	1.6	2,603	-6.3	2,440	12.4	2,743	17.4	3,220
Junction, Kimble	0	0	0	0	0	0	0	0		1,571	55.9	2,471	-1.2	2,441	8.7	2,654	-2.3	2,593	2.4	2,654
Karnes City, Karnes	0	0	0	0	0	0	1,959	0	767	2,086	18.5	2,588	0.6	2,603	12.4	2,926	12.6	3,296	-11.5	2,916
Katy, Harris	0	0	0	0	0	0	0	682	1,415	950	64.7	849	84.8	1,569	86.3	2,923	93.6	5,660	41.4	8,005
Kaufman, Kaufman	0	0	0	0	1,282	1,378	1,147	2,501	3,264	2,654	2.3	2,714	13.7	3,087	30.0	4,012	16.1	4,658	12.5	5,238
Keene, Johnson	0	0	0	156	0	0	0	787	0	0	***	0	***	1,532	59.3	2,440	23.5	3,013	30.9	3,944
Keller, Tarrant	0	0	0	0	0	0	0	0	0	0	***	0	***	827	78.2	1,474	181.1	4,143	230.3	13,683
Kenedy, Karnes	0	0	†226	0	0	0	0	2,015	2,610	2,891	46.5	4,234	1.6	4,301	-3.4	4,156	4.8	4,356	-13.6	3,763
Kennedale, Tarrant	0	0	0	0	0	0	0	0	0	0	***	1,046	45.4	1,521	102.2	3,076	-15.7	2,594	57.9	4,096
Kermit, Winkler	0	0	0	0	0	0	0	0	0	2,584	167.5	6,912	51.4	10,465	-24.7	7,884	1.7	8,015	-14.2	6,875
Kerrville, Kerr	0	0	0	0	1,044	1,423	1,834	2,353	4,546	5,572	38.0	7,691	15.7	8,901	42.4	12,672	20.5	15,276	13.8	17,384
Kilgore, Gregg	0	0	0	0	0	0	0	0		6,708	43.7	9,638	4.7	10,092	-5.9	9,495	15.5	10,968	0.9	11,066
Killeen, Bell	0	0	0	0	285	780	1,265	1,298	1,260	1,263	457.8	7,045	231.8	23,377	51.9	35,507	30.4	46,296	37.2	63,535
Kingsville, Kleberg	0	0	0	0	0	0	0	4,770	6,815	7,782	117.1	16,898	49.7	25,297	14.6	28,995	-0.6	28,808	-12.3	25,276
Kirby, Bexar	0	0	0	0	0	0	0	0	0	0	***	0	***	680	276.2	2,558	149.6	6,385	30.4	8,326
‡Kleberg, Dallas	0	0	0	0	0	0	0	0	0	0	***	0	***	3,572	33.5	4,768	***		***	
Kountze, Hardin	0	0	0	0	0	0	0	0	0	0		1,651	7.1	1,768	22.9	2,173	25.0	2,716	-24.3	2,056
Lacy-Lakeview, McLennan	0	0	0	0	0	0	0	0	0	0	***	0	***	2,272	12.6	2,558	7.6	2,752	31.4	3,617
La Feria, Cameron	0	0	0	0	0	0	0	236	1,594	1,644	79.6	2,952	3.2	3,047	-13.3	2,642	32.3	3,495	24.7	4,360
La Grange, Fayette	0	0	1,165	1,325	1,626	2,392	1,850	1,669	1,594	2,531	8.2	2,738	32.3	3,623	-14.7	3,092	21.9	3,768	4.9	3,951

City Population History, 1850-1990 (Cont'd.)

City, County	1850	1860	1870	1880	1890	1900	1910	1920	1930	1940	Change 40-50	1950	Change 50-60	1960	Change 60-70	1970	Change 70-80	1980	Change 80-90	1990
Lake Dallas, Denton	0	0	0	0	0	0	0	0	0	0	***	2,897	233.1	9,651	***	1,431	122.0	3,177	15.1	3,656
Lake Jackson, Brazoria	0	0	0	0	0	0	0	0	0	0	***	3,091	24.5	3,849	38.6	13,376	42.8	19,102	19.2	22,776
Lakeview, Floyd	0	0	0	0	0	0	0	0	0	852	262.8		***				***		***	202
Lakeway, Travis	0	0	0	0	0	0	0	0	0	0							***	790	411.9	4,044
Lake Worth, Tarrant	0	0	0	0	0	0	0	0	0	0	***	2,351	63.0	3,833	29.4	4,958	-11.4	4,394	4.5	4,591
La Marque, Galveston	0	0	0	0	0	0	0	0	0	6,038	77.3	7,359	89.8	13,969	15.5	16,131	-4.7	15,372	-8.1	14,120
Lamesa, Dawson	0	0	0	0	0	0	0	0	3,528	3,426	42.1	10,704	16.2	12,438	-7.1	11,559	2.0	11,790	-8.3	10,809
Lampasas, Lampasas	0	0	+420	653	2,408	2,107	2,119	2,107	2,709	3,151	41.8	4,869	3.9	5,061	17.0	5,922	4.1	6,165	3.5	6,382
Lancaster, Dallas	0	0	0	0	741	1,045	1,115	1,190	1,133	1,151	44.2	1,632	359.6	7,501	40.3	10,522	40.7	14,807	49.4	22,117
La Porte, Harris	0	0	0	0	0	537	678	889	1,280	3,072	32.2	4,429	1.9	4,512	58.4	7,149	96.7	14,062	98.5	27,910
Laredo, Webb	0	1,256	2,046	3,521	11,319	13,429	14,855	22,710	32,618	39,274	32.2	51,910	16.9	60,678	13.8	69,024	32.5	91,449	34.4	122,899
League City, Galveston	0	0	0	0	0	318	980	‡150	‡700	‡550	0.0	‡550	-18.2	2,622	312.6	10,818	53.2	16,578	81.9	30,159
Leakey, Real	0	0	0	0	0	0	0	0	0	0	***	450	95.5	450	-12.7	393	19.1	468	-14.7	399
Leon Valley, Bexar	0	0	0	0	0	0	0	1,117	0	3,091	167.4	8,264	22.9	536	364.0	2,487	259.9	8,951	7.0	9,581
Levelland, Hockley	0	0	0	0	0	0	0	0	1,661	873	73.7	1,516	160.9	10,153	12.7	11,445	20.7	13,809	1.3	13,986
Lewisville, Denton	0	0	0	497	0	865	980	0	853	3,087	34.9	4,163	47.2	3,956	134.2	9,264	162.0	24,273	91.7	46,521
Liberty, Liberty	0	0	458	0	0	0	0	0	2,187	3,817	71.3	6,540	10.6	6,127	-8.7	5,591	42.1	7,945	-2.7	7,733
Littlefield, Lamb	0	0	0	0	0	0	0	0	3,218	3,817	71.3	6,540	10.6	7,236	-6.9	6,738	10.0	7,409	-12.4	6,489
Live Oak, Bexar	0	0	0	0	0	0	1,687	928	1,165	1,851	54.8	2,865	18.6	3,398	16.7	2,779	194.5	8,183	22.5	10,023
Livingston, Polk	*423	0	0	718	1,233	2,306	2,945	1,645	2,124	2,658	11.1	2,954	-10.1	2,656	-1.8	3,965	24.3	4,928	1.8	5,019
Llano, Llano	0	0	+500	0	2,034	3,591	0	3,731	4,367	5,018	11.1	5,573	9.2	6,084	6.7	2,608	17.8	3,071	-3.5	2,965
Lockhart, Caldwell	0	0	0	1,525	0	0	5,155	5,713	5,036	13,758	78.1	24,502	63.5	439	103.6	894	22.6	7,953	15.7	9,205
Lomax, Howard	0	0	0	0	0	0	1,938	4,051	20,520	31,853	125.8	71,747	79.4	40,050	16.7	46,744	34.3			
Longview, Gregg	0	0	0	0	529	1,527	2,749	4,878	5,970	9,567	58.2	15,135	16.6	128,691	30.7	149,101	34.3	62,762	12.0	70,311
Lubbock, Lubbock	0	0	0	0	1,792	1,349	1,404	1,502	7,311	4,437	-3.2	4,297	17.6	17,641	15.9	28,562	16.7	173,979	7.0	186,206
Lufkin, Angelina	0	0	0	0	0	694	627	1,079	1,294	2,095	24.5	2,393	2.7	4,412	23.0	4,719	23.9	28,562	5.8	30,206
Luling, Caldwell	0	0	0	0	418	0	0	719	635	774	24.5	964	-2.9	2,324	7.0	2,881	6.8	5,039	-7.5	4,661
Madisonville, Madison	0	0	0	0	0	0	1,061	0	0	1,021	100.2	2,044	42.6	1,375	24.0	3,658	27.0	3,660	-2.5	3,569
Mansfield, Tarrant	0	0	0	575	0	1,137	0	1,079	865	3,805	-5.3	3,603	***	2,161	166.0	106	121.2	8,092	92.9	15,607
Manvel, Brazoria	0	0	0	0	2,058	158	3,878	3,553	3,909	6,542	8.5	7,099	-22.3	2,799	2.2	2,209	47.2	3,252	23.2	3,733
Marble Falls, Burnet	0	0	0	5,624	7,207	3,092	11,452	4,310	5,338	18,410	21.3	2,269	-2.5	6,918	-4.2	2,682	-8.1	2,466	-1.7	4,007
Marfa, Presidio	0	0	0	0	0	‡300	2,939	14,271	6,203	‡1,500	-20.6	2,269	6.8	23,846	-3.8	6,351	11.8	7,099	-10.0	2,424
Marlin, Falls	0	0	0	0	0	‡300	0	1,200	2,853	2,856	63.2	2,448	-3.2	2,197	-0.6	1,806	8.6	24,921	-5.0	6,386
Marshall, Harrison	‡1,189	‡4,000	1,920	0	0	1,137	0	‡1,200	‡12,000	‡1,500	-3.7	1,325	-25.9	1,815	-10.4	2,183	19.2	24,921	-13.8	23,682
Mart, McLennan	0	0	0	0	0	158	692	692	0	1,376	107.7	4,050	-8.2	1,217	-11.9	1,091	-3.6	2,153	-13.8	2,041
Mason, Mason	0	0	0	0	774	1,435	1,864	5,331	9,074	1,950	69.0	1,877	50.0	6,075	15.0	5,351	5.9	1,052	-5.2	2,041
Matador, Motley	0	0	0	0	0	0	0	2,081	3,446	11,877	20.3	20,067	63.1	32,728	-21.6	37,636	78.1	5,667	-24.9	790
Mathis, San Patricio	0	0	0	1,479	2,489	4,342	4,714	6,677	2,041	2,595	29.4	3,121	73.9	3,375	-6.0	2,647	-8.0	5,667	-4.3	5,423
McAllen, Hidalgo	0	0	0	0	0	0	0	5,331	9,074	11,877	69.0	20,067	63.1	32,728	14.3	37,636	78.1	67,042	25.3	84,021
McCamey, Upton	0	0	0	0	0	0	0	0	3,446	2,595	20.3	3,121	30.3	4,642	-21.6	2,647	-8.0	2,436	2.3	2,493
McGregor, McLennan	0	0	0	774	774	1,435	1,864	2,081	2,041	2,062	29.4	2,669	30.3	4,642	-6.0	4,365	3.4	4,513	3.8	4,683
McKinney, Collin	*523	0	0	1,479	2,489	4,342	4,714	6,677	7,307	8,555	13.1	10,560	30.3	13,763	10.4	15,193	7.0	16,249	31.0	21,283
Memphis, Hall	0	0	0	0	0	1,435	1,936	2,839	4,257	3,869	-1.5	3,810	-12.5	3,332	-9.1	3,227	3.9	3,352	-26.5	2,465
Menard, Menard	0	0	0	0	0	1,137	1,164	1,164	1,969	2,375	13.1	2,685	-28.7	1,914	-3.1	1,740	-2.5	1,697	-5.4	1,606
Mentone, Loving	0	0	0	0	0	0	1,209	0	0	‡150	-26.7	‡110	0.0	‡110	-60.0	‡44	13.6	‡50	***	
Mercedes, Hidalgo	0	0	0	0	135	406	687	3,414	6,608	7,624	32.2	10,081	8.6	10,943	-14.5	9,355	13.6	11,851	7.1	12,694
Mertzon, Irion	0	0	0	0	0	0	0	‡400	684	869	-12.0	765	-22.4	594	-13.6	513	33.9	687	13.2	778
Mesquite, Dallas	0	0	0	135	1,674	2,393	2,694	674	729	1,045	63.3	1,696	***	27,526	100.3	55,131	21.6	67,053	51.3	101,484
Mexia, Limestone	0	0	0	1,298	0	286	0	3,482	6,579	6,410	3.4	6,627	-7.6	6,121	-2.9	5,943	19.4	7,094	-2.3	6,933
Miami, Roberts	0	0	0	0	0	0	0	937	953	713	-9.5	645	1.7	656	-6.9	611	33.1	813	-17.0	675
Midland, Midland	0	0	0	0	1,674	832	2,192	1,795	5,484	9,352	132.2	21,713	188.4	62,625	-5.0	59,463	18.6	70,525	26.8	89,443
Midlothian, Ellis	0	0	0	0	297	1,725	868	1,298	1,168	1,027	14.6	1,177	29.2	1,521	-5.0	2,322	38.6	3,219	59.7	5,141
Mineola, Wood	0	0	0	1,175	1,323	2,048	1,706	2,299	3,304	3,223	12.5	3,626	5.1	3,810	52.7	3,926	10.7	4,346	-0.6	4,321
Mineral Wells, Palo Pinto	0	0	0	0	577	0	3,950	7,890	5,986	6,303	23.8	7,801	41.7	11,053	66.6	18,411	-21.4	14,468	2.8	14,870

City Population History, 1850-1990 (Cont'd.)

City, County	1850	1860	1870	1880	1890	1900	1910	1920	1930	1940	Change 40-50	1950	Change 50-60	1960	Change 60-70	1970	Change 70-80	1980	Change 80-90	1990
Mission, Hidalgo	0	0	0	0	0	0	0	3,847	5,120	5,982	80.0	10,765	30.8	14,081	-7.4	13,043	73.2	22,589	26.8	28,653
Missouri City, Fort Bend	0	0	0	0	0	0	0	0	0	0	***	***	***	604	584.8	4,136	493.2	24,533	47.5	36,176
Monahans, Ward	0	0	0	0	0	0	0	0	816	3,944	60.0	6,311	35.7	8,567	-2.7	8,333	0.8	8,397	-3.5	8,101
Mont Belvieu, Chambers	0	0	0	0	0	0	0	‡20	‡600	‡600	-16.7	‡500	0.0	‡500	128.8	1,144	51.2	1,730	-23.5	1,323
Morton, Cochran	0	0	0	0	0	0	0	0	0	1,137	100.0	2,274	20.1	2,731	0.3	2,738	-2.3	2,674	-2.9	2,597
Mount Pleasant, Titus	*227	0	0	0	0	0	3,137	4,099	3,541	4,528	40.1	6,342	26.6	8,027	17.8	9,459	16.3	11,003	11.7	12,291
Mount Vernon, Franklin	0	0	0	0	0	972	0	0	779	1,443	-1.4	1,423	-6.0	1,338	35.0	1,806	12.1	2,025	9.6	2,219
Muleshoe, Bailey	0	0	0	0	0	0	0	0	1,318	1,327	86.7	2,477	56.3	3,871	16.9	4,525	7.0	4,842	-5.6	4,571
Munday, Knox	0	0	0	0	0	0	956	998	1,318	1,545	46.9	2,270	-12.9	1,978	-12.7	1,726	0.7	1,738	-7.9	1,600
Nacogdoches, Nacogdoches	‡468	*383	0	1,611	1,138	1,827	3,369	3,546	5,687	7,538	63.5	12,327	2.8	12,674	77.9	22,544	20.4	27,149	13.7	30,872
Nassau Bay, Harris	0	0	0	0	0	0	0	0	0	0	***	***	***	***	***	***	***	4,526	-4.6	4,320
Navasota, Grimes	0	0	0	0	2,997	3,857	3,284	5,060	5,128	6,138	-15.5	5,188	-4.8	4,937	3.5	5,111	16.8	5,971	5.4	6,296
Nederland, Jefferson	0	0	0	0	0	0	0	0	0	1,111	141.9	3,805	216.3	12,036	39.7	16,810	0.3	16,855	-3.9	16,192
New Boston, Bowie	0	0	0	0	0	0	0	0	949	‡1,000	168.8	2,688	3.2	2,773	45.5	4,034	14.7	4,628	9.3	5,057
New Braunfels, Comal	*1,727	‡3,500	2,261	1,938	1,608	2,097	3,165	3,590	6,242	6,976	75.0	12,210	28.0	15,631	14.3	17,859	25.4	22,402	22.0	27,334
Newton, Newton	0	0	0	0	0	0	0	0	‡1,000	‡1,200	-22.2	934	32.0	1,233	24.0	1,529	6.0	1,620	16.4	1,885
Nocona, Montague	0	0	0	0	381	961	1,338	1,422	2,352	2,605	16.0	3,022	3.5	3,127	-8.2	2,871	4.2	2,992	-4.1	2,870
North Richland Hills, Tarrant	0	0	0	0	0	0	0	0	0	0	***	***	***	8,662	90.6	16,514	85.2	30,592	50.0	45,895
Oak Ridge North, Montgomery	0	0	0	0	0	0	0	0	0	0	***	***	***	***	***	2,216	13.0	2,504	-2.0	2,454
Odessa, Ector	0	0	0	0	0	0	0	0	2,407	9,573	208.1	29,495	172.4	80,338	-2.4	78,380	14.9	90,027	-0.4	89,699
Olmos Park, Bexar	0	0	0	0	0	0	0	0	0	1,822	55.9	2,841	-13.5	2,457	-8.4	2,250	-8.0	2,069	4.4	2,161
Olney, Young	0	0	0	0	0	0	1,095	1,164	4,138	3,497	7.7	3,765	2.8	3,872	-6.4	3,624	12.0	4,060	-13.3	3,519
Orange, Orange	0	0	0	0	3,173	3,835	5,527	9,212	7,913	7,472	183.4	21,174	20.9	25,605	-4.5	24,457	-3.4	23,628	-18.0	19,381
Ozona, Crockett	0	0	0	0	0	0	0	0	0	2,677	***	2,885	***	3,361	***	3,642	***	3,766	***	3,181
Paducah, Cottle	0	0	0	0	0	0	1,389	1,335	1,318	2,677	10.3	2,952	-19.0	2,392	-14.2	2,052	8.0	2,216	-19.3	1,788
Paint Rock, Concho	0	0	0	0	0	0	0	‡750	‡1,000	‡800	0.0	‡800	1.3	810	-76.2	193	32.6	256	-11.3	227
Palacios, Matagorda	0	0	0	0	0	323	1,350	1,357	2,802	2,288	22.3	2,799	31.3	3,676	-0.9	3,642	28.1	4,667	-5.3	4,418
Palestine, Anderson	‡2,000	0	0	2,997	5,838	8,297	10,482	11,039	11,445	12,144	3.0	12,503	11.8	13,974	3.9	14,525	9.8	15,948	13.1	18,042
Pampa, Gray	0	0	0	0	0	0	521	987	10,470	12,895	28.6	16,583	48.7	24,664	-11.9	21,726	-1.5	21,396	-6.7	19,959
Panhandle, Carson	0	0	0	0	0	468	0	638	978	978	43.5	1,403	35.9	1,907	12.3	2,141	4.0	2,226	5.7	2,353
Paris, Lamar	*1,003	‡1,500	0	3,980	8,254	9,358	11,269	15,040	15,649	18,678	15.9	21,643	-3.1	20,977	11.7	23,441	8.8	25,498	-3.1	24,699
Pasadena, Harris	0	0	0	0	0	0	0	0	1,647	3,436	554.3	22,483	161.3	58,737	52.0	89,277	26.1	112,560	6.0	119,363
Pearland, Brazoria	0	0	0	0	0	0	0	0	0	1,198	69.4	2,029	-26.2	1,497	330.5	6,444	105.6	13,248	42.9	18,927
Pear Ridge, Jefferson	0	0	0	0	0	0	0	0	0	0	***	***	***	***	***	***	***	1,869	-85.9	263
Pearsall, Frio	0	0	0	0	393	639	1,799	2,161	2,536	3,164	41.6	4,481	10.6	4,957	11.9	5,545	33.1	7,383	-6.2	6,924
Pecos, Reeves	0	0	0	0	0	0	1,856	1,445	3,304	4,855	65.9	8,054	58.0	12,728	-0.4	12,682	1.4	12,855	-6.1	12,069
**Pelly, Harris	0	0	0	0	0	0	0	0	0	0	***	***	***	***	***	***	***	***	***	***
Perryton, Ochiltree	0	0	0	0	0	0	0	‡500	2,824	2,325	90.0	4,417	78.9	7,903	-1.2	7,810	2.3	7,991	-4.8	7,607
Pflugerville, Travis	0	0	0	0	0	0	0	0	‡580	‡500	-24.0	‡380	0.0	‡380	44.5	549	35.7	745	496.5	4,444
Pharr, Hidalgo	0	0	0	0	0	0	0	1,565	3,225	4,784	81.6	8,690	62.3	14,106	12.2	15,829	35.1	21,381	54.0	32,921
Phillips, Hutchinson	0	0	0	0	0	0	0	0	0	0	***	***	***	1,703	29.1	2,198	39.0	3,055	-12.2	2,682
Pinehurst, Montgomery	0	0	0	0	0	0	0	0	0	0	***	***	***	1,790	42.3	2,548	16.1	2,958	8.1	3,197
Piney Point Village, Harris	0	0	0	0	0	0	0	0	0	0	***	***	***	***	***	***	***	2,991	-5.6	3,380
Pittsburg, Camp	0	0	0	0	1,203	1,783	1,916	2,540	2,640	2,916	7.8	3,142	20.8	3,796	1.3	3,844	10.4	4,245	-5.6	4,007
Plainview, Hale	0	0	0	0	0	0	2,829	3,989	8,834	8,263	70.0	14,044	33.4	18,735	1.9	19,096	16.2	22,187	-2.2	21,700
Plano, Collin	0	0	0	0	824	1,304	1,258	1,715	1,554	1,582	34.4	2,126	73.8	3,695	383.7	17,872	304.7	72,331	77.9	128,713
Pleasanton, Atascosa	0	0	0	0	0	0	0	1,036	1,154	2,074	40.5	2,913	19.0	3,467	56.0	5,407	17.4	6,346	21.0	7,678
Port Arthur, Jefferson	0	0	0	0	0	900	7,663	22,251	50,902	46,140	24.7	57,530	15.9	66,676	-14.0	57,371	6.7	61,195	-4.0	58,724
Port Isabel, Cameron	0	0	0	0	0	0	0	0	1,177	1,440	64.7	2,372	50.7	3,575	-14.2	3,067	22.9	3,769	18.5	4,467
Portland, San Patricio	0	0	0	0	0	0	0	0	0	0	***	1,292	96.4	2,538	187.7	7,302	64.7	12,023	1.7	12,224
Port Lavaca, Calhoun	0	0	0	0	0	0	0	1,213	1,367	2,069	170.6	5,599	58.3	8,864	18.4	10,491	4.0	10,911	-0.2	10,886
Port Neches, Jefferson	0	0	0	0	0	0	0	0	2,327	2,487	119.1	5,448	59.6	8,696	25.3	10,894	28.0	13,944	-7.0	12,974
Post, Garza	0	0	0	0	0	0	1,699	1,436	1,668	2,046	53.5	3,141	48.5	4,663	-17.3	3,854	2.8	3,961	-4.9	3,768

City Population History, 1850-1990 (Cont'd.)

City, County	1850	1860	1870	1880	1890	1900	1910	1920	1930	1940	Change 40-50	1950	Change 50-60	1960	Change 60-70	1970	Change 70-80	1980	Change 80-90	1990
Poteet, Atascosa	0	0	0	0	0	0	0	0	1,231	2,315	7.4	2,487	13.0	2,811	7.2	3,013	2.4	3,086	3.9	3,206
Prairie View, Waller	0	0	0	0	0	0	0	0	0	1,080	142.5	2,619	***	2,326	54.3	3,589	11.3	3,993	0.3	4,004
Premont, Jim Wells	0	0	0	0	0	0	0	500	459	564	***	540	16.4	3,049	7.6	3,282	-9.1	2,984	-2.3	2,914
Princeton, Collin	0	0	0	0	0	0	0	3,691	4,464	3,767	-4.3	4,589	10.0	594	86.0	1,105	208.4	3,408	-31.9	2,321
Quanah, Hardeman	0	0	0	0	1,477	1,651	3,127	±500	1,365	1,512	21.8	1,771	10.0	4,564	-13.5	3,948	-1.5	2,422	-12.3	3,413
Ralls, Crosby	0	0	0	0	0	0	0	16,201	6,208	1,771	17.1	3,989	29.9	2,300	-14.7	1,962	23.4	2,142	-10.3	2,172
Ranger, Eastland	0	0	0	0	0	0	0	0	2,050	4,553	-12.4	9,136	-0.5	3,313	-6.6	3,094	1.6	3,142	-10.8	2,803
Raymondville, Willacy	0	0	0	0	0	0	0	933	2,019	4,050	125.6	4,666	-16.9	9,385	-14.9	7,987	18.9	9,493	-6.5	8,880
Refugio, Refugio	0	0	479	0	0	0	773	0	629	4,077	14.4	1,289	2.7	4,944	-12.2	4,340	-10.2	3,898	-19.0	3,158
Richardson, Dallas	0	0	0	0	0	0	0	0	0	720	79.0	0	***	16,810	189.0	48,582	49.2	72,496	3.2	74,840
Richland Hills, Tarrant	0	0	0	0	0	0	0	0	0	0	0.2	2,030	80.7	7,804	13.6	8,865	67.8	7,977	***	7,978
Richmond, Fort Bend	0	0	‡1,000	0	1,477	1,651	1,371	1,273	1,432	2,026	***	3,992	57.5	5,835	57.5	5,777	67.8	9,692	1.1	9,801
Richwood, Brazoria	0	0	0	0	0	0	0	0	0	0	***	7,097	***	649	123.7	1,452	78.4	2,591	5.4	2,732
Rio Grande City, Starr	439	0	0	1,968	0	582	0	±582	2,283	662		1,070	-8.9	8,444	-2.7	8,193	***	0	***	0
River Oaks, Brazos	0	0	0	0	0	0	0	0	0	0	61.6	3,992	46.2	5,835	-3.0	8,193	-15.9	6,890	-4.5	6,580
Robert Lee, Coke	0	0	0	0	0	582	0	0	490	662	***	1,070	19.0	975	14.8	1,119	7.4	1,202	6.2	1,276
Robinson, McLennan	0	0	0	0	0	0	0	948	4,183	6,780	7.3	7,278	41.1	10,266	80.4	3,807	59.5	6,074	17.1	7,111
Robstown, Nueces	0	0	0	0	0	2,515	2,073	2,323	2,204	6,780	8.7	7,278	93.1	10,266	9.3	11,217	7.9	12,100	-6.2	12,849
Rockdale, Milam	0	0	0	0	1,505	1,153	1,382	1,545	2,204	2,136	31.1	2,321	31.9	2,989	3.9	4,655	20.5	5,611	-6.7	5,235
Rockport, Aransas	0	0	0	0	1,069	389	1,136	±600	1,140	1,729	7.0	2,266	-11.0	1,275	29.8	3,879	-5.0	3,686	28.9	4,753
Rocksprings, Edwards	0	0	0	0	0	0	0	1,388	998	1,339	13.9	1,501	-4.2	1,275	-4.2	1,221	1.7	1,317	1.7	1,339
Rockwall, Rockwall	0	0	0	843	0	1,245	0	1,279	1,071	1,414	11.5	1,576	-5.1	1,496	44.1	3,121	90.3	5,939	76.6	10,486
Roma-Los Saenz, Starr	0	0	0	0	0	0	1,198	1,000	1,632	1,941	79.6	6,210	56.2	9,698	24.7	2,154	57.1	3,384	138.2	8,059
Rosenberg, Fort Bend	0	0	0	0	0	0	1,126	900	998	2,029	55.9	3,163	-11.9	2,788	-13.8	12,098	48.7	17,995	12.2	20,183
Rotan, Fisher	0	0	0	0	0	0	0	0	1,941	1,240	16.0	1,438	30.6	1,878	49.7	2,404	-5.0	2,284	-16.2	1,913
Round Rock, Williamson	0	0	0	0	0	0	0	0	0	0	***	6,598	-25.7	1,015	154.1	2,811	320.2	11,812	161.8	30,923
Rowlett, Dallas	0	0	0	0	0	0	0	0	0	0		561	78.4	1,001	0.3	2,579	191.7	7,522	209.2	23,260
Rusk, Cherokee	‡355	*395	1,383	0	0	846	1,558	2,348	3,859	5,699	15.8	6,598	-25.7	4,900	138.0	4,914	-4.7	4,681	-6.7	4,366
Saginaw, Tarrant	0	0	0	0	0	0	0	0	0	0	***	561	78.4	1,001	0.3	2,382	140.8	5,736	49.1	8,551
San Angelo, Tom Green	0	*395	0	0	0	0	10,321	10,050	25,308	25,802	60.9	52,093	12.9	58,815	8.6	63,884	14.6	73,240	15.3	84,474
San Antonio, Bexar	3,488	8,235	12,256	20,550	37,673	53,321	96,614	161,379	231,542	253,854	60.9	408,442	43.9	587,718	11.3	654,153	20.1	785,410	19.2	935,933
San Augustine, San Augustine	0	0	920	503	744	261	1,204	1,268	1,247	1,516	65.6	2,510	2.9	2,584	-1.7	2,539	15.4	2,930	-20.2	2,337
San Benito, Cameron	0	0	0	0	0	0	0	5,070	10,753	9,501	39.7	13,271	23.7	16,422	-7.6	15,176	18.5	17,988	11.9	20,125
Sanderson, Terrell	0	0	0	0	0	112	0	±500	±1,000	±1,875	14.7	±2,150	9.3	±2,350	-47.7	±1,229	22.1	±1,500	***	0
San Diego, Duval	0	0	0	0	0	0	0	0	1,119	2,674	64.4	4,397	-1.0	4,351	4.4	4,490	16.4	5,225	-4.6	4,983
Sanger, Denton	0	0	0	0	0	0	0	1,204	1,203	2,000	17.0	1,170	1.7	1,190	34.7	1,603	60.6	2,574	36.3	3,508
San Juan, Hidalgo	0	0	0	0	0	0	0	1,203	1,615	2,264	50.8	3,413	28.1	4,371	2.0	5,070	50.1	7,608	42.2	10,815
San Marcos, Hays	0	0	741	1,232	2,335	2,292	4,071	4,527	5,134	6,006	66.2	9,980	27.4	12,713	48.4	18,860	24.2	23,420	22.7	28,743
San Pedro, Cameron	0	0	0	0	0	0	0	0	0	0	***	8,127	-6.1	7,634	***	0	***	0	***	0
San Saba, San Saba	0	0	0	0	0	0	0	2,011	2,240	2,927	16.2	1,611	-19.8	4,175	14.3	2,555	-8.6	2,336	12.4	2,626
Sansom Park, Tarrant	0	0	0	0	0	0	0	0	0	0	***	3,400	159.2	4,175	***	4,771	-17.8	3,921	0.2	3,928
Santa Fe, Galveston	0	0	0	0	0	0	0	0	0	0	***	1,611	***	0	***	0	***	5,413	55.7	8,429
Sarita, Kenedy	0	0	0	0	0	0	0	±200	±250	0	0.0	±200	0.0	±200	-2.0	±196	-5.6	±185	***	0
Schertz, Guadalupe	0	0	0	0	0	0	0	0	0	±250	***	0	***	2,281	78.0	3,811	78.8	7,262	45.3	10,555
Seabrook, Harris	0	0	0	0	0	0	0	±200	604	760	153.6	1,927	94.3	3,745	17.2	4,061	22.5	4,670	43.1	6,685
Seagoville, Dallas	0	0	0	0	0	0	0	0	505	3,225	-34.9	2,101	9.8	2,307	5.8	3,811	66.4	7,304	22.8	8,969
Seagraves, Gaines	0	0	0	0	0	0	0	0	0	760	***	1,942	19.9	2,328	2.2	2,440	6.4	2,596	-7.6	2,398
Sealy, Austin	0	0	0	1,363	1,716	2,421	3,116	3,631	5,225	7,006	38.9	1,942	46.9	2,328	11.4	2,685	44.3	3,875	17.2	4,541
Seguin, Guadalupe	0	*792	‡830	1,363	1,716	2,421	3,116	3,631	5,225	7,006	97.6	9,733	64.9	14,299	12.0	15,934	12.0	17,854	5.6	18,853
Seminole, Gaines	0	0	0	0	0	0	0	2,121	1,761	1,761	97.6	3,479	0.3	5,737	-12.7	5,007	21.4	6,080	4.3	6,342
Seymour, Baylor	0	0	0	0	0	0	2,029	2,121	2,626	3,328	13.6	3,779	-6.3	3,789	-8.4	3,469	21.4	3,657	-12.9	3,185
Shamrock, Wheeler	0	0	0	0	0	0	0	1,227	3,780	3,123	6.4	3,322	271.4	3,113	-15.1	2,644	7.2	2,834	-19.3	2,286
Shepherd, San Jacinto	0	0	0	0	0	278	0	±500	±450	±500	-30.0	±350	0	±1,300	-28.6	928	80.4	1,674	8.2	1,812

City Population History, 1850-1990 (Cont'd.)

City, County	1850	1860	1870	1880	1890	1900	1910	1920	1930	1940	Change 40-50	1950	Change 50-60	1960	Change 60-70	1970	Change 70-80	1980	Change 80-90	1990
Sherman, Grayson	0	0	1,439	6,093	7,335	10,243	12,412	15,031	15,713	17,156	17.5	20,150	24.0	24,988	16.3	29,061	4.7	30,413	3.9	31,601
Sierra Blanca, Hudspeth	0	0	0	0	0	0	0	‡600	873	‡723	17.6	‡850	0.0	‡850	-29.4	‡416	16.7	‡700	***	0
Silsbee, Hardin	0	0	0	0	0	241	0	416	1,852	2,525	25.9	3,179	97.5	6,277	15.8	7,271	5.7	7,684	-17.1	6,368
Silverton, Briscoe	0	0	0	0	0	0	0	1,058	873	684	25.0	855	36.6	1,168	-7.4	1,026	-10.5	918	-15.1	779
Sinton, San Patricio	0	0	0	0	0	0	0	1,525	1,852	3,770	12.8	4,254	41.2	6,008	0.2	5,563	8.6	6,044	-8.2	5,549
Slaton, Lubbock	0	0	0	0	0	0	0	3,204	3,896	3,587	40.4	5,036	30.4	6,568	0.9	5,583	3.4	6,804	-10.7	6,078
Smithville, Bastrop	0	0	0	0	909	2,577	0	2,179	3,008	3,100	9.0	3,379	-13.2	2,933	-19.3	2,959	17.3	3,470	-7.9	3,196
Snyder, Hale	0	0	0	616	500	612	2,514	2,179	3,008	3,815	214.8	12,010	15.3	13,850	-14.4	11,171	13.7	12,705	-4.0	12,195
Snyder, Scurry	0	0	0	500	500	612	2,514	1,009	1,942	3,815	214.9	12,012	8.6	13,850	-17.9	11,171	13.7	12,705	-4.0	12,195
Sonora, Sutton	0	0	0	0	0	0	0	0	612	2,528	4.2	2,633	-0.5	2,619	-17.9	2,149	79.4	3,856	-28.7	2,751
South Houston, Harris	0	0	0	0	0	0	0	0	2,708	982	320.2	4,126	82.3	7,523	53.2	11,527	15.3	13,293	6.9	14,207
Southlake, Denton	0	0	0	0	0	0	0	0	0	0	***	0	98.5	1,023	98.5	2,031	38.3	2,808	151.6	7,065
††South San Antonio, Bexar	*441	0	0	0	0	0	0	0	0	0	***	0	***	0	***	0	***	0	***	0
South San Pedro, Nueces	0	0	0	0	0	0	0	0	0	0	***	1,852	92.0	3,555	-3.4	3,065	-0.6	3,413	-6.3	3,197
Spearman, Hansford	0	0	0	0	0	0	0	1,100	1,580	1,105	67.6	1,852	***	3,004	5.5	3,435	5.8	3,353	1.2	3,392
Spring Valley, Harris	0	0	0	0	0	0	0	0	0	0	1.7	2,173	5.8	3,004	-24.0	3,170	-3.3	1,690	-23.1	1,300
Spur, Dickens	0	0	0	0	0	0	0	0	1,899	2,136	***	1,852	***	1,485	95.7	1,747	63.6	4,755	76.6	8,397
Stafford, Fort Bend	0	0	0	0	0	0	3,902	3,704	4,095	4,810	21.0	5,819	-9.6	5,259	-13.3	2,906	-0.4	4,542	-16.0	3,817
Stamford, Jones	0	0	0	0	0	1,902	2,561	‡600	1,384	1,245	28.0	1,594	68.8	2,690	-21.3	4,558	9.3	2,314	11.3	2,576
Stanton, Martin	0	0	0	0	909	532	0	3,891	3,994	4,768	50.1	7,155	2.9	7,359	26.1	2,117	28.1	11,881	13.6	13,502
Stephenville, Erath	0	0	0	0	909	1,902	2,561	472	‡700	‡886	84.3	1,170	34.1	875	-10.9	9,277	17.3	915	19.8	1,096
Sterling City, Sterling	0	0	0	0	0	532	520	472	‡700	635	56.9	1,376	1.9	1,850	-25.3	780	10.3	1,917	-2.5	2,166
Stinnett, Hutchinson	0	0	0	0	0	0	0	0	873	877	***	2,285	22.6	2,802	-25.3	2,014	-10.4	2,222	-7.1	1,781
Stratford, Sherman	0	0	0	0	0	0	0	0	873	877	33.4	1,393	18.4	2,802	18.4	2,139	20.3	1,917	177.9	24,529
Sugar Land, Fort Bend	0	*2,500	0	0	0	0	0	0	5,417	6,742	***	8,991	-1.9	9,160	16.2	3,318	166.0	8,826	9.8	14,062
Sulphur Springs, Hopkins	0	0	0	1,854	3,033	3,635	5,151	5,558	10,848	10,367	33.4	13,619	2.2	13,914	3.4	10,642	20.3	12,804	-6.8	3,297
Sweeny, Brazoria	0	0	0	0	0	0	0	4,307	1,792	2,686	10.9	2,978	16.3	3,087	-13.6	3,191	1.8	3,538	-6.8	11,967
Sweetwater, Nolan	0	0	0	614	614	670	4,176	786	1,620	2,129	33.8	2,848	5.8	13,463	-5.5	12,020	12.6	12,242	-2.2	3,222
Taft, San Patricio	0	0	0	0	0	0	0	5,965	7,463	7,875	15.2	9,071	4.0	3,012	-1.9	3,274	10.4	3,686	-12.6	2,868
Tahoka, Lynn	0	0	0	0	0	0	0	0	3,509	3,157	***	2,925	***	9,434	1.9	2,956	10.4	3,262	-12.1	11,472
Taylor, Williamson	0	0	0	2,584	2,584	4,211	5,314	3,306	15,345	15,344	-7.3	25,467	-6.7	2,728	5.1	990	270.6	10,619	-7.5	3,394
Taylor Lake Village, Harris	0	0	0	0	0	0	0	0	0	0	66.0	11,544	19.4	30,419	9.9	2,867	18.2	3,669	-3.6	3,268
Teague, Freestone	0	0	0	0	0	0	3,288	11,033	8,795	15,344	111.9	11,544	19.6	13,803	2.7	3,431	27.1	3,390	8.5	46,109
Temple, Bell	0	0	0	2,003	4,047	7,065	10,993	8,349	15,345	15,344	45.4	25,467	105.8	30,419	-6.2	33,431	18.2	42,483	8.5	46,109
Terrell, Kaufman	0	0	0	2,003	2,988	6,330	7,050	8,349	8,795	10,481	189.1	11,544	22.1	13,803	0.9	14,182	-6.7	13,225	-5.6	12,490
Terrell Hills, Bexar	0	0	0	0	0	0	0	0	0	1,236	***	2,708	***	5,572	-6.2	5,225	-11.1	4,644	-1.1	4,592
Texarkana, Bowie	0	0	0	1,833	2,852	5,256	9,790	11,480	16,602	17,019	16.4	24,753	22.1	30,218	0.9	30,497	2.5	31,271	-1.1	31,656
Texas City, Galveston	0	0	0	0	0	0	0	2,509	3,534	5,748	189.1	16,620	92.9	32,065	21.3	38,908	6.4	41,403	-1.4	40,822
The Colony, Denton	0	0	0	0	0	0	0	0	0	0	***	0	***	0	***	0	***	11,586	90.9	22,113
Throckmorton, Throckmorton	0	0	0	37	240	240	0	686	1,135	1,133	16.4	1,319	-4.5	1,260	-12.3	1,105	6.2	1,174	-11.8	1,036
Tilden, McMullen	0	0	0	0	506	506	0	‡250	0	‡500	-24.0	‡380	0.0	‡380	9.5	‡416	20.2	‡500	***	0
Tomball, Harris	0	0	0	0	0	0	0	0	0	668	59.4	1,065	60.8	1,713	59.6	2,734	46.2	3,996	59.4	6,370
Trinity, Trinity	0	0	0	0	0	0	1,216	1,363	2,036	2,217	-7.4	2,054	-13.0	1,787	40.6	2,512	-2.4	2,452	8.0	2,648
Tulia, Swisher	0	0	0	0	0	0	0	1,189	2,202	2,055	56.8	3,222	36.9	4,410	20.0	5,294	-4.9	5,033	-6.6	4,699
Tyler, Smith	‡1,024	0	0	2,423	6,908	8,069	10,400	12,085	17,113	28,279	37.8	38,968	31.5	51,230	12.8	57,770	22.0	70,508	7.0	75,450
Universal City, Bexar	0	0	0	0	0	0	0	0	0	0	***	‡380	***	‡380	***	7,613	40.8	10,720	21.8	13,057
University Park, Dallas	0	0	0	0	0	0	0	0	4,200	14,458	67.9	24,275	-4.4	23,202	1.3	23,498	-5.3	22,254	1.9	22,259
Uvalde, Uvalde	0	0	0	0	1,265	1,889	3,998	3,885	5,286	6,679	29.9	8,674	18.7	10,293	4.6	10,764	31.7	14,178	3.9	14,729
Van Horn, Culberson	0	0	0	0	0	0	0	0	0	515	36.4	1,161	68.2	1,953	47.9	2,889	-4.0	2,772	5.7	2,930
Vega, Oldham	0	0	0	0	0	0	0	‡200	519	0	20.2	619	6.3	658	27.5	839	7.3	900	-6.7	840
Vernon, Wilbarger	0	0	0	0	2,857	1,993	3,195	5,142	9,137	9,277	36.4	12,651	-4.0	12,141	-5.7	11,454	10.8	12,695	-5.5	12,001
Victoria, Victoria	*1,440	‡2,500	0	0	3,046	4,010	3,673	5,957	7,421	11,566	39.4	16,126	104.9	33,047	25.1	41,349	22.6	50,695	8.6	55,076
Vidor, Orange	0	0	0	0	0	0	0	0	0	0	***	2,136	131.2	4,938	97.2	9,738	24.4	12,117	-9.8	10,935

City Population History, 1850-1990 (Cont'd.)

City, County	1850	1860	1870	1880	1890	1900	1910	1920	1930	1940	Change 40-50	1950	Change 50-60	1960	Change 60-70	1970	Change 70-80	1980	Change 80-90	1990
Waco, McLennan	*749	0	3,008	7,295	14,445	20,686	26,425	38,500	52,848	55,982	51.3	84,706	15.5	97,808	-2.5	95,326	6.2	101,261	2.3	103,590
Wake Village, Bowie	0	0	0	0	0	0	0	0	0	0	***	1,066	6.9	1,140	111.2	2,408	60.5	3,865	23.1	4,757
Watauga, Tarrant	0	0	0	0	0	0	0	0	0	0	***	0	***	0	***	3,778	172.2	10,284	94.6	20,009
Waxahachie, Ellis	0	0	0	1,354	3,076	4,215	6,205	7,958	8,042	8,655	29.5	11,204	13.8	12,749	5.5	13,452	8.7	14,624	24.2	18,168
Weatherford, Parker	*175	†1,823	0	2,046	3,369	4,786	5,074	6,203	4,912	5,924	36.6	8,093	20.6	9,759	20.4	11,750	2.5	12,049	22.9	14,804
Wellington, Collingsworth	0	0	0	0	0	0	576	1,968	3,570	3,308	11.1	3,676	-14.7	3,137	-8.1	2,884	5.5	3,043	-19.3	2,456
Weslaco, Hidalgo	0	0	0	0	0	0	0	0	4,879	6,883	9.2	7,514	108.3	15,649	-2.1	15,313	26.2	19,331	13.2	21,877
West Columbia, Brazoria	0	0	0	0	0	0	0	0	0	1,573	33.5	2,100	40.3	2,947	13.2	3,335	23.2	4,109	6.4	4,372
West Orange, Orange	0	0	0	0	0	0	0	0	0	0	***	2,539	90.9	4,848	-0.6	4,820	-4.4	4,610	-9.2	4,187
West University Place, Harris	0	0	0	0	0	0	0	0	1,322	9,221	85.2	17,074	-14.3	14,628	-9.0	13,317	-9.8	12,010	7.6	12,920
Westworth Village, Tarrant	0	0	0	0	0	0	0	0	0	0	***	529	527.8	3,321	37.9	4,578	-20.2	3,651	-35.6	2,350
Wharton, Wharton	0	0	0	0	0	0	1,505	2,346	2,691	4,386	1.5	4,450	28.9	5,734	37.4	7,881	14.6	9,033	-0.2	9,011
White Oak, Gregg	0	0	0	0	0	0	0	0	0	0	***	0	***	1,250	84.0	2,300	92.0	4,415	16.3	5,136
Whitesboro, Grayson	0	0	0	773	1,170	1,243	1,219	1,810	1,535	1,560	18.8	1,854	34.0	2,485	17.8	2,927	9.2	3,197	0.4	3,209
White Settlement, Tarrant	0	0	0	0	0	0	0	0	0	0	***	10,827	6.3	11,513	16.8	13,449	0.4	13,508	14.5	15,472
Wichita Falls, Wichita	0	0	0	0	1,978	2,480	8,200	40,079	43,690	45,112	50.8	68,042	49.5	101,724	-5.4	96,265	-2.1	94,201	2.2	96,259
Wills Point, Van Zandt	0	0	0	0	1,025	1,347	1,398	1,811	2,023	1,976	2.7	2,030	12.4	2,281	15.6	2,636	-0.2	2,631	13.5	2,986
Windcrest, Bexar	0	0	0	0	0	0	0	0	0	0	***	0	***	441	664.4	3,371	58.2	5,332	***	5,331
Wink, Winkler	0	0	0	0	0	0	0	0	3,963	1,945	-21.8	1,521	22.5	1,863	-45.1	1,023	15.5	1,182	0.6	1,189
Winnie, Chambers	0	0	0	0	0	0	0	0	‡370	‡200	62.5	‡325	242.8	‡1,114	38.5	‡1,543	***		***	
Winnsboro, Wood	0	0	0	0	388	899	1,741	2,184	1,905	2,092	20.1	2,512	6.5	2,675	14.5	3,064	12.9	3,458	-16.0	2,904
Winters, Runnels	0	0	0	0	0	0	1,347	1,509	2,423	2,335	14.6	2,676	22.0	3,266	-11.0	2,907	5.3	3,061	-5.1	2,905
Woodville, Tyler	0	0	0	0	0	0	0	0	969	1,521	22.5	1,863	3.1	1,920	38.6	2,662	6.0	2,821	-6.6	2,636
Woodway, McLennan	0	0	0	0	0	0	0	0	0	0	***	0	***	1,244	287.4	4,819	47.1	7,091	22.6	8,695
Wylie, Collin	0	0	0	0	239	773	620	945	771	914	41.7	1,295	39.3	1,804	48.3	2,675	17.8	3,152	176.5	8,716
Yoakum, Lavaca	0	0	0	0	1,745	3,499	4,657	6,184	5,656	4,733	10.5	5,231	10.1	5,761	-0.1	5,755	6.8	6,148	-8.7	5,611
Yorktown, DeWitt	0	0	0	430	522	846	1,180	1,723	1,882	2,081	24.7	2,596	-2.7	2,527	-4.6	2,411	3.6	2,498	-11.6	2,207
Zapata, Zapata	0	0	0	0	0	0	0	0	‡450	‡500	70.0	‡850	138.9	‡2,031	3.5	‡2,102	66.5	‡3,500	***	0

*Census of incorporated towns of Texas taken in 1858 by tax assessors and collectors in each county.
†Federal census of western part of Texas for 1870, as given in Texas Almanac for 1871.
‡An estimate of that date.
***Pelly, Goose Creek and Baytown merged in 1947, and the single community took the name of the latter — Baytown. Baytown was unincorporated prior to this merger and did not show any previous census. However, Pelly and Goose Creek were previously incorporated, hence the census figures for them in 1930 and 1940.
§Includes Huntsville prison population.
††South San Antonio was annexed by San Antonio in 1944.
‡‡Kleberg annexed by Dallas in 1979.

Counties

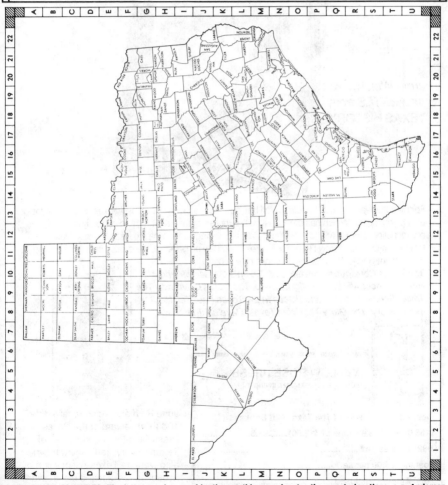

LOCATION OF COUNTIES: The letter-number combination on this map denotes the county locations; e.g. Anderson County (J-19) can be located by using the horizontal and vertical scales at top and bottom of this map.

Demographics of Texas Counties

These pages describe Texas' 254 counties and hundreds of towns. Descriptions are based on reports from chambers of commerce, Texas Agricultural Extension Service, federal and state agencies and many others. Consult the index for other county information.

County maps are based on those of the State Department of Highways and Public Transportation and are copyrighted, 1991, as are the entire contents.

LETTER-NUMBER COMBINATIONS in parentheses with each county denote location on the map on the facing page. For example, Anderson County (J-19) means that Anderson County can be found near the intersection of lines J and 19 on the larger map.

TOPOGRAPHY: Descriptions are from U.S. Geological Survey and local sources.

HISTORY, ORGANIZATION, COUNTY NAMES: From Texas Statutes, Fulmore's History and Geography of Texas as Told in County Names, WPA Historical Records Survey and Texas Centennial Commission Report.

COURTS, CONGRESSIONAL DISTRICTS, ETC.: The following abbreviations are used: Cong. Dist., Congressional District; St. Sen. Dist., State Senatorial District; St. Rep. Dist., State Representative District; St. Dist. Cts., State District Courts; U.S. Jud. Dist., U.S. Judicial District; Ct. Appeals, Court of Appeals; Admin. Jud. Dist., Administrative Judicial District.

The designations used in the following counties were districts as constituted in 1991.

Texas is divided into four U.S. Judicial Districts: Northern, Southern, Eastern and Western. These abbreviations are used to designate the city in which the court sits: N-Ab: Abilene; N-Am: Amarillo; N-Dl: Dallas; N-FW: Fort Worth; N-Lb: Lubbock; N-SAng: San Angelo; N-WF: Wichita Falls; S-Br: Brownsville; S-CC: Corpus Christi;

LEGEND FOR MAPS

Following is explanation of signs and symbols used:

▬▬▬ Paved road of all types.

◣▬◤ Indicates divided roads.

▬□□□□▬ Surfaced roads—all-weather gravel, shell, etc.

= = = =: Roads under construction.

(With few exceptions roads shown on these maps are state and federal highways. Local roads of all types of improvement thread the counties of Texas.)

▬▦▬ Incorporated towns.

▬○▬ Unincorporated towns.

▬◉▬ County seats.

◀20▶ Interstate highway numbers.

◀2▶ U.S. highway numbers.

◀2A▶ Alternate U.S. highway numbers.

◀2▶ State highway numbers.

◀2▶ Farm to market roads.

◀2▶ Park roads, temporary designations.

◀LR▶ County or local roads.

+++++ Railroads.

✈ Airports.

🌲 Notable parks.

S-Gn: Galveston; S-Hn: Houston; S-La: Laredo; S-Va: Victoria; E-Bt: Beaumont; E-Ml: Marshall; E-Ps: Paris; E-Sh: Sherman; E-Tx: Texarkana; E-Ty: Tyler; W-An: Austin; W-DR: Del Rio; W-EP: El Paso; W-Pe: Pec-a: Victoria; E-Bt: Beaumont; E-Ml: Marshall; E-Ps: Paris; E-Sh: Sherman; E-Tx: Texarkana; E-Ty: Tyler; W-An: Austin; W-DR: Del Rio; W-EP: El Paso; W-Pe: Pecos; W-SAnt; San Antonio; W-Wa: Waco; W-M-O: Midland-Odessa.

1. Population	14. Av. Weekly Wage
2. Area (sq. mi.)	15. Density
3. Land Area	16. Water Area
4. Civilian Labor	17. Jobless Rate
5. Altitude (ft.)	18. Retail Sales
6. Rainfall (in.)	19. Gross Sales
7. Jan. min.	20. Reg. Voters
8. July max.	21. Election Turnout
9. Grow. Season (days)	22. Vehicles
10. Total Income (mil.)	23. Lane Miles
11. Per Capita Income	24. Tax Value
12. Total Wages	25. Fed. Spending (000)
13. Housing	26. Defense Spending (000)

Sources of County Demographics

The following are the sources for the demographic information on Texas counties that appears in the following section of the Almanac.

1. **Population:** The official count of the U.S. census bureau as of January 1991. These figures are subject to change after the Almanac goes to press.

2. **Area (sq. mi.):** The total land and surface water area as determined by the census bureau, 1990.

3. **Land Area:** The total land area in square miles as determined by the census bureau, 1990.

4. **Civilian Labor:** The civilian labor force as determined by the Texas Employment Commission for 1990.

5. **Altitude (ft.):** From the U.S. Geological Survey list of highest and lowest points measured in each county.

6. **Rainfall (in.):** Provided by the National Oceanic and Atmospheric Administration state climatologist.

7. **Jan. min.:** Provided by NOAA state climatologist.

8. **July max.:** Provided by NOAA state climatologist.

9. **Grow. Season (days):** Provided by the NOAA state climatologist.

10. **Total Income (mil.):** From the Census of Business, April 1991, by the U.S. census bureau. Figure represents 1989 income in millions of dollars.

11. **Per Capita Income:** From the Census of Business, April 1991, by the U.S. census bureau. Figure represents the 1989 per-capita income.

12. **Total Wages:** Based on the quarterly figures for 1990 provided by the Texas Employment Commission.

13. **Housing:** From the official 1990 U.S. census.

14. **Av. Weekly Wage:** Calculated by the Texas Almanac staff from figures provided by the Texas Employment Commission for 1990.

15. **Density:** Population density of people per square mile determined by dividing the population by the land area of each county as determined by the U.S. census bureau as of Jan. 1991.

16. **Water Area:** The surface water area as determined by the census bureau, 1990.

17. **Jobless Rate:** The unemployment rate for 1990 as calculated by the Texas Employment Commission.

18. **Retail Sales:** Preliminary figures compiled by the Texas Almanac from quarterly reports for 1990 as reported to the state comptroller. The figures are subject to change in the comptroller's final report.

19. **Gross Sales:** Preliminary figures compiled by the Texas Almanac from quarterly reports for 1990 as reported to the state comptroller. The figures are subject to change in the comptroller's final report.

20. **Reg. Voters:** The number of people registered to vote in the 1990 general election as reported to the Texas Secretary of State.

21. **Election Turnout:** The percentage of registered voters who participated in the 1990 gubernatorial election as reported to the Texas Secretary of State.

22. **Vehicles:** The number of vehicles of all types registered in each county in 1990 as reported by the State Department of Highways and Public Transportation.

23. **Lane Miles:** The number of lane miles in 1990 as determined by the highway department. Lane miles are the number of miles of roadway times the width in lanes. For example, one mile of six-lane freeway would be six lane miles.

24. Tax Value: The reported value of real and personal property in each county in 1989 as reported to the State Property Tax Board.

25. Fed. Spending: The total amount of federal spending in millions of dollars as reported in the "Consolidated Federal Funds Report, Fiscal 1989" by the U.S. Department of Commerce, Bureau of the Census.

26. Defense Spending: The total amount of federal defense spending as reported in the "Consolidated Federal Funds Report, Fiscal 1989" by the U.S. Department of Commerce, Bureau of the Census.

27. Vital Statistics: These statistics for calendar year 1989 were compiled by the State Department of Health.

28. Ethnicity: These percentages are as reported by the census bureau in January 1991 based on the 1990 census. They are subject to change. The percentages do not add up to 100 because Hispanics are considered an ethnic group, not racial. A Hispanic person can be white or black, Native American or Asian. (**.*%) indicates an ethnic group constitutes less than one-tenth of one percent of the total population.

Anderson County

LOCATION: East Texas (J-19).

Cong. Dist. 2	U.S. Jud. Dist. .... E-Tyler
St. Sen. Dist. 3	Ct. Appeals..................... 12
St. Rep. Dist. 11	Admin. Jud. Dist. 1
St. Dist. Cts. 3, 87, 349	

History: First settled in 1830s; created from Houston County and organized in 1846; named for K.L. Anderson, last vice-president of the Republic of Texas.

Physical Features: Hilly, slopes to Trinity and Neches rivers; sandy, clay, black soils; pines, hardwoods used commercially.

Population................ 48,024	Av. Weekly Wage $360.82
Area (sq. mi) 1,078.0	Density 45
Land Area 1,070.9	Water Area 7.1
Civilian Labor 21,930	Jobless Rate.................. 6.1
Altitude (ft.) 624-198	Retail Sales $251,967,713
Rainfall (in.) 41.7	Gross Sales $904,949,956
Jan. min. 35	Reg. Voters 20,005
July max. 95	Election Turnout 49.6
Grow. Season(days) 264	Vehicles 36,170
Total Income (mil.) $575	Lane Miles 931
Per Capita Income...$11,975	Tax Value... $1,452,705,957
Total Wages.....$257,649,567	Fed. Spending $122,368
Housing.................. 16,886	Defense Spending $4,701

Vital Statistics, 1989: Births, 626; Deaths, 447; Marriages, 431; Divorces, 33.

Ethnicity, 1990: White, 33,354 (69.5%); Black, 11,143 (23.2%); American Indian, 129 (0.3%); Asian, 125 (0.3%); Hispanic, 3,953 (8.2%); Other, 3,273 (6.8%).

Recreation: Fishing, hunting, manystreams, lakes; Dogwood Trails; historic sites; **Engeling Wildlife Refuge; Texas State Railroad Park; Museum for East Texas Culture;** professional bicycle racing; civic auditorium; county fair; arts, crafts festival; tour of old homes. Tourist information center in restored 1890 depot.

Minerals: Oil and gas.

Agriculture: Principal agricultural income from beef cattle, dairy cattle, hogs also raised; hay is top crop with truck vegetables, melons, peaches, blackberries raised; Christmas trees raised; timber sold.

Business: Manufacturing, distribution, agribusiness, tourism; hunting and fishing leases; three Texas Department of Corrections units.

PALESTINE (18,042) county seat; wholesale meats, auto parts, clothing, metal, wood products manufactured; aluminum smelting plant; transportation center; agribusiness center; shipping center; Scientific Balloon Station; hospital; library; vocational-technical facilities; hospitals; **Trinity Valley Community College.**

Other towns include **Elkhart** (1,076), **Frankston** (1,127), and **Tennessee Colony**(est. 120), site of Coffield and Beto Units I and II, Texas Department of Criminal Justice.

Andrews County

LOCATION: Borders New Mexico (I-7).

Cong. Dist. 19	U.S. Jud. Dist. .... W-M-O
St. Sen. Dist. 28	Ct. Appeals..................... 8
St. Rep. Dist. 77	Admin. Jud. Dist. 7
St. Dist. Cts. 109	

History: Created 1876 from Bexar Territory; organized 1910; named for Texas Revolutionary soldier Richard Andrews.

Physical Features: Plains, drain to playas; grass, mesquite, shin oak; red clay, sandy soils.

Population................ 14,338	Av.Weekly Wage $433.88
Area (sq. mi) 1,501.0	Density 10
Land Area 1,500.7	Water Area 0.3
Civilian Labor 6,998	Jobless Rate.................. 4.0
Altitude (ft.) 2,297-2,915	Retail Sales $67,434,575
Rainfall (in.) 14.1	Gross Sales $219,096,401
Jan. min. 29	Reg. Voters 6,057
July max. 95	Election Turnout 50.5
Grow. Season(days) 213	Vehicles 13,749
Total Income (mil.) $204	Lane Miles 540
Per Capita Income...$13,496	Tax Value...... $2,270,527,504
Total Wages......$117,095,199	Fed. Spending $25,965
Housing...................5,462	Defense Spending $315

Vital Statistics, 1989: Births, 277; Deaths, 103; Marriages, 151; Divorces, 88.

Ethnicity, 1990: White, 10,834 (75.6%); Black, 274 (1.9%); American Indian, 82 (0.6%); Asian, 154 (1.1%); Hispanic, 4,552 (31.7%); Other, 2,994 (20.9%).

Recreation: Prairie dog town; oil museum; local arts, crafts, other local events; camper facilities.

Minerals: A leading producer of oil and gas.

Agriculture: Cattle major revenue producer; cotton, sorghums contribute; grains, corn, hay raised; significant irrigation.

Business: Chiefly oil related; vacuum cleaner manufacturing, fiberglass tank manufacturing; agribusiness.

ANDREWS (10,678) county seat; oil marketing center; amphitheatre; hospital, rest home, mental health center; parks.

See map on next page.

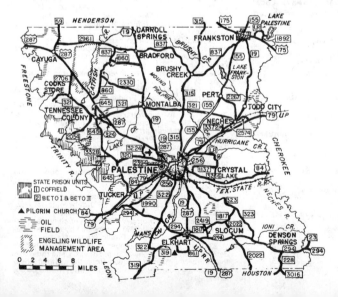

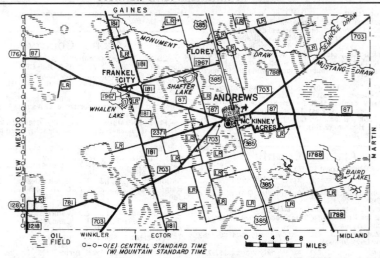

O-O-O(E) CENTRAL STANDARD TIME
(W) MOUNTAIN STANDARD TIME

Angelina County

LOCATION: In east (K-21).

Cong. Dist. 2	U.S. Jud. Dist. .... E-Tyler
St. Sen. Dist. 3	Ct. Appeals...................... 9
St. Rep. Dist. 17	Admin. Jud. Dist. 2
St. Dist. Cts. 159, 217	

History: Created, organized 1846 from Nacogdoches County; river and county named for legendary Indian maiden Angelina.

Physical Features: Rolling, hilly; black, red, gray soils; Angelina National Forest.

Population................ 69,884	Av. Weekly Wage $369.59
Area (sq. mi) 864.4	Density 87
Land Area 801.6	Water Area 62.8
Civilian Labor 32,995	Jobless Rate.................. 6.3
Altitude (ft.) 404-139	Retail Sales $502,813,786
Rainfall (in.) 41.5	Gross Sales.... $1,436,379,160

Jan.min......................38	Reg. Voters 34,685
July max. 94	Election Turnout......... 46.3
Grow. Season(days) 244	Vehicles 63,635
Total Income (mil.) $980	Lane Miles 904
Per Capita Income...$14,261	Tax Value...... $2,089,318,935
Total Wages......$547,960,455	Fed. Spending $177,200
Housing................... 28,751	Defense Spending $5,904

Vital Statistics, 1989: Births, 1,058; Deaths, 603; Marriages, 833; Divorces, 510.

Ethnicity, 1990: White, 54,752 (78.3%); Black, 10,731 (15.4%); American Indian, 153 (0.2%); Asian, 295 (0.4%); Hispanic, 6,072 (8.7%); Other, 3,953 (5.7%).

Recreation: Sam Rayburn Reservoir; national, state forests, parks; historic sites; Texas Forest Festival third weekend in September; **Forestry Association Museum** and historical locomotive exhibit; museum; woodland trails; **Ellen Trout Park and Zoo**; county rodeo.

Minerals: Limited output of natural gas and oil.

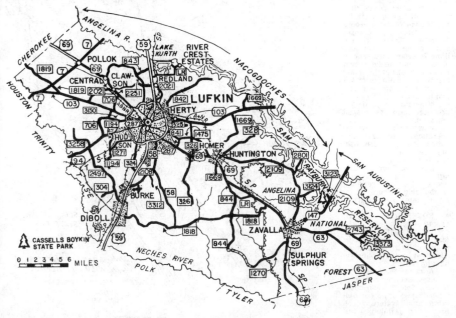

Angelina Co. (Cont.)

Agriculture: Leading timber-producing county with 70% of land in commercial forests; beef cattle, poultry significant revenue sources; some hay, vegetables marketed.

Business: Many plants make oil-field pumping units, newsprint, other paper products; wood products, iron and steel castings, truck trailers; mobile home units, horse stables.

LUFKIN (30,206) county seat; manufacturing center; **Angelina College;** two hospitals; **Texas Forest Service Cudlipp Forestry Center; U.S. Forest Service; Ellen Trout Park Zoo; Museum of East Texas, Lufkin Civic Center, Angelina County Exposition Center.** Other towns are **Diboll** (4,341); **Hudson** (2,374), **Huntington** (1,794), **Homer** (360), **Zavalla** (701).

Aransas County

LOCATION: On Coast (Q-17).

Cong. Dist. 14	U.S. Jud. Dist. ....S-CC
St. Sen. Dist. 18	Ct. Appeals......................13
St. Rep. Dist. 36	Admin. Jud. Dist. 4
St. Dist. Cts........ 36, 156, 343	

History: Created, organized 1871 from Refugio County; named for Rio Nuestra Senora de Aranzazu, derived from a Spanish palace.

Physical Features: Flat; sandy loam, coastal clay soils; many bays, inlets; mesquites, live oaks.

Population................ 17,892	Av. Weekly Wage $292.48
Area (sq. mi) 527.9	Density 64
Land Area 251.9	Water Area 276.0
Civilian Labor 7,776	Jobless Rate..................4.4
Altitude (ft.) 24-6	Retail Sales $166,420,441
Rainfall (in.) 36.9	Gross Sales $193,138,955
Jan. min. 45	Reg. Voters 8,218
July max. 92	Election Turnout 54.6
Grow. Season(days) 312	Vehicles 13,306
Total Income (mil.) $230	Lane Miles 161
Per Capita Income...$13,171	Tax Value......... $889,776,111
Total Wages....... $58,143,905	Fed. Spending $45,694
Housing.................... 10,876	Defense Spending $3,895

Vital Statistics, 1989: Births, 228; Deaths, 169; Marriages, 238; Divorces, 83.

Ethnicity, 1990: White, 15,282 (85.4%); Black, 319 (1.8%); American Indian, 111 (0.6%); Asian, 589 (3.3%); Hispanic, 3,588 (20.1%); Other, 1,591 (8.9%).

Recreation: Many fishing, hunting,tourist facilities; **Fulton Mansion; Goose Island State Park; Aransas National Wildlife Refuge;** state marine lab; **Texas Maritime Museum;** bird sanctuaries (a nationally known birding "hotspot"); many resort homes; **Rockport Art Center;** demonstration garden for birds.

Minerals: Oil and gas produced, also oyster shell and sand.

Agriculture: Cow-calf operations; major crops are cotton, sorghum, corn; fishing becoming important; redfish hatchery.

Business: Tourism, fishing andshrimping; oil production; refining; shipbuilding,offshore equipment fabricated; carbon plant.

ROCKPORT (4,753) county seat; fishing; tourist center; art festival; oyster fest; sea fair in October; Hummer/Bird celebration; Fiesta en La Playa; library; nursing centers.

Aransas Pass (912 in Aransas County, partly in Nueces, San Patricio counties); deepwater port on **Gulf Intracoastal Waterway;** oil production, refining; indus-

trial plants; tourism; hospital, nursing home. Other town, **Fulton** (763).

Archer County

LOCATION: North Central (F-14).

Cong. Dist. 13	U.S. Jud. Dist. .... N-WF
St. Sen. Dist. 30	Ct. Appeals...................... 2
St. Rep. Dist. 80	Admin. Jud. Dist. 8
St. Dist. Cts....................97	

History: Created from Fannin Land District, 1858; organized, 1880. Named for Dr. B.T. Archer, Republic of Texas commissioner to United States.

Physical Features: Rolling, hilly, drained by Wichita River forks; black, red loams, sandy soils; mesquites, post oaks.

Population.................7,973	Av. Weekly Wage $334.06
Area (sq. mi) 925.7	Density 9
Land Area 909.7	Water Area 16.0
Civilian Labor 3,247	Jobless Rate..................3.9
Altitude (ft.) 1,286-934	Retail Sales $29,750,804
Rainfall (in.) 27.7	Gross Sales $57,813,187
Jan. min. 28	Reg. Voters 4,859
July max. 98	Election Turnout 60.3
Grow. Season(days) 220	Vehicles 8,641
Total Income (mil.) $121	Lane Miles 524
Per Capita Income...$15,074	Tax Value......... $445,786,430
Total Wages....... $24,892,879	Fed. Spending $28,373
Housing....................3,664	Defense Spending $6,632

Vital Statistics, 1989: Births, 106; Deaths, 60;Marriages, 48; Divorces, 41.

Ethnicity,1990: White, 7,789 (97.7%); Black, 11 (0.1%); American Indian, 36 (0.5%); Asian, 4 (0.1%); Hispanic, 189 (2.4%); Other, 133 (1.7%).

Recreation:

Minerals: Oil, gas, stone produced.

Agriculture: Beef, stocker cattle big revenue sources; dairy operations; wheat, major crop, other grains also produced; some irrigation.

Business: Cattle; oil-field services.

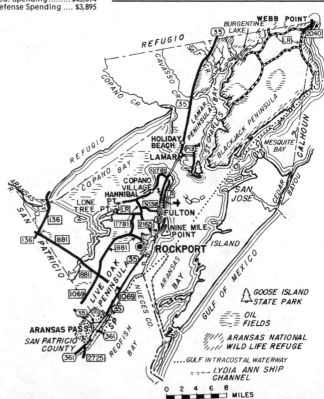

Archer Co. (Cont.)

ARCHER CITY (1,748) county seat; cattle, oil-field service center; hospital, library, museum; some manufacturing; other towns are **Holliday** (1,475), **Lakeside City** (865, partly in Wichita County), **Megargel** (244), **Scotland** (380 in Archer County, partly in Clay County); **Windthorst** (364 in Archer County, partly in Clay County), and part of Wichita Falls.

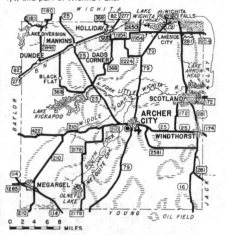

Armstrong County

LOCATION: Northwest, in Panhandle (D-9).

Cong. Dist.	13	U.S. Jud. Dist.	N-Am.
St. Sen. Dist.	31	Ct. Appeals	7
St. Rep. Dist.	84	Admin. Jud. Dist.	9
St. Dist. Cts.	47		

History: Created from Bexar District, 1876; organized 1890; name honors a pioneer family.

Physical Features: Plain, broken by Palo Duro Canyon, Caprock. Chocolate loam, gray soils.

Population	2,021	Av. Weekly Wage	$302.63
Area (sq. mi)	913.7	Density	2
Land Area	913.6	Water Area	0.1
Civilian Labor	976	Jobless Rate	5.3
Altitude (ft.)	3,512-2,829	Retail Sales	$6,788,436
Rainfall (in.)	20.6	Gross Sales	$10,789,092
Jan. min.	19	Reg. Voters	1,306
July max.	92	Election Turnout	53.9
Grow. Season (days)	213	Vehicles	2,635
Total Income (mil.)	$39	Lane Miles	372

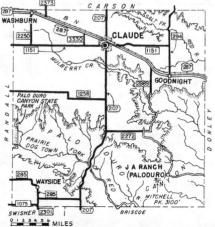

Per Capita Income...$17,983
Total Wages.........$5,885,565
Housing.........916
Tax Value.........$148,030,960
Fed. Spending..........$9,607
Defense Spending.......$108

Vital Statistics, 1989: Births, 23; Deaths, 28; Marriages, 20; Divorces, 13.

Ethnicity, 1990: White, 1,976 (97.8%); Black, 0 (0.0%); American Indian, 10 (0.5%); Asian, 7 (0.3%); Hispanic, 55 (2.7%); Other, 28 (1.4%).

Recreation: Palo Duro Canyon State Park; pioneer **Goodnight Ranch Home**; Caprock Roundup in July; Cowboy Morning.

Minerals: Sand, gravel produced.

Agriculture: Stocker cattle, cow- calf operations important; crops include wheat, sorghums, cotton and hay; 7,500 acres irrigated.

Business: Agribusiness center.

CLAUDE (1,199) county seat; farm, ranch supplies; glass company; medical center; nursing home; spring fair.

Atascosa County

LOCATION: South, near San Antonio (P-14).

Cong. Dist.	15	U.S. Jud. Dist.	W-SAnt.
St. Sen. Dist.	21	Ct. Appeals	4
St. Rep. Dist.	45	Admin. Jud. Dist.	4
St. Dist. Cts.	81, 218		

History: Created, organized from Bexar District, 1856. Atascosa means boggy in Spanish.

Physical Features: Grassy prairie, drained by Atascosa River, tributaries; mesquites, other brush.

Population	30,533	Av. Weekly Wage	$312.74
Area (sq. mi)	1,235.7	Density	25
Land Area	1,232.2	Water Area	3.5
Civilian Labor	11,392	Jobless Rate	7.2
Altitude (ft.)	725-241	Gross Sales	$206,999,392
Rainfall (in.)	27.8	Retail Sales	$118,715,302
Jan. min.	39	Reg. Voters	15,407
July max.	97	Election Turnout	42.9
Grow. Season (days)	282	Vehicles	21,875
Total Income (mil.)	$326	Lane Miles	1,007
Per Capita Income	$10,782	Tax Value	$1,374,581,570
Total Wages	$91,670,548	Fed. Spending	$68,469
Housing	11,589	Defense Spending	$3,160

Vital Statistics, 1989: Births, 471; Deaths, 254; Marriages, 226; Divorces, 95.

Ethnicity, 1990: White, 25,019 (81.9%); Black, 143 (0.5%); American Indian, 109 (0.4%); Asian, 65 (0.2%); Hispanic, 16,064 (52.6%); Other, 5,197 (17.0%).

Recreation: Local events; quail, deer hunting; Longhorn Museum; river park; little theater group; county fair; stock show in January; **Strawberry Festival** at Poteet in April; home of the cowboy homecoming in August.

Minerals: Oil, gas and lignite.

Agriculture: Beef, dairy cattle raised; crops include peanuts, hay, corn, grain sorghums, strawberries; 40,000

Atascosa Co. (Cont.)
acres irrigated, mostly peanuts, corn, hay.
   Business: Agribusinesses, oil-well supplies, services; coal plant; light manufacturing, shipping.
   JOURDANTON (3,220) county seat; hospital, rest home. Other towns, **Charlotte** (1,475), **Christine** (368), **Lytle** (1,911 in Atascosa County, partly in Medina, Bexar counties), **Pleasanton** (7,678), hospital, nursing homes; "home of the cowboy"; **Poteet** (3,206), "strawberry capital."

Austin County

LOCATION: Southwest (N-18).

Cong. Dist. 14	U.S. Jud. Dist. ....S-Hn.
St. Sen. Dist. 5	Ct. Appeals..................1,14
St. Rep. Dist. 30	Admin. Jud. Dist. 3
St. Dist. Cts...................155	

History: Birthplace of Anglo-American colonization; named for Stephen F. Austin, father of Texas. County created, organized 1837.

Physical Features: Level to hilly, drained by San Bernard, Brazos rivers; black prairie to sandy upland soils.

Vital Statistics, 1989: Births, 250; Deaths, 260; Marriages, 138; Divorces, 91.

Ethnicity, 1990: White, 16,244 (81.9%); Black, 2,608 (13.2%); American Indian, 46 (0.2%); Asian, 26 (0.1%); Hispanic, 2,073 (10.5%); Other, 908 (4.6%).

Recreation: Fishing and hunting; local events; **Stephen F. Austin State Park**, other historic sites; Pioneer Trail; county fair in October, Christmas on the Square in Bellville.

Minerals: Oil and natural gas.

Agriculture: Livestock, poultry top cash source; also produced are sorghums, small grains, rice, corn, peanuts, cotton.

Business: Agribusiness; steel, other manufacturing.

BELLVILLE (3,378) county seat; varied manufacturing; hospital; oil production. Other towns are **San Felipe** (618), colonial capital of Texas; **Sealey** (4,541), oil-field manufacturing, picturesque downtown; **Wallis** (1,001).

Population................ 19,832	Av. Weekly Wage $379.93
Area (sq. mi) 656.3	Density 30
Land Area 652.6	Water Area 3.7
Civilian Labor 10,174	Jobless Rate...................3.5
Altitude (ft.) 263-23	Retail Sales $136,662,510
Rainfall (in.) 40.4	Gross Sales....... $386,944,489
Jan. min. 43	Reg. Voters 9,949
July max. 94	Election Turnout......... 55.9
Grow. Season (days)..... 282	Vehicles 20,227
Total Income (mil.) $344	Lane Miles 607
Per Capita Income...$17,346	Tax Value...... $1,264,747,116
Total Wages.....$119,841,894	Fed. Spending.........$50,623
Housing.....................8,871	Defense Spending $362

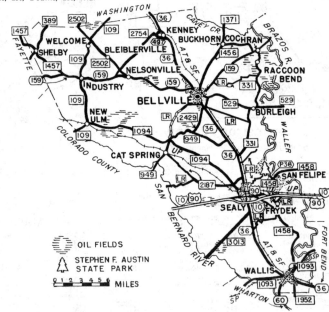

OIL FIELDS

STEPHEN F. AUSTIN STATE PARK

0 1 2 3 4 5 6 MILES

Bailey County

LOCATION: Northwest (E-7).

Cong. Dist. 19	U.S. Jud. Dist. .... N-Lb.
St. Sen. Dist. 31	Ct. Appeals......................7
St. Rep. Dist. 85	Admin. Jud. Dist. 9
St. Dist. Cts..................287	

History: Created from Bexar District, 1876, organized 1917. Named for Alamo hero Peter J. Bailey.

Physical Features: Plain; mostly sandy loam soils; mesquite brush; drains to Brazos River, playas.

Population..................7,064	Av. Weekly Wage $295.84
Area (sq. mi) 827.3	Density 9
Land Area 826.7	Water Area 0.6
Civilian Labor 3,131	Jobless Rate...................3.7
Altitude (ft.) 4,060-3,790	Retail ales $43,949,239
Rainfall (in.) 16.1	Gross Sales....... $97,156,838
Jan. min. 20	Reg. Voters 3,468
July max. 91	Election Turnout......... 48.8
Grow. Season (days).....181	Vehicles 6,830
Total Income (mil.) $130	Lane Miles 473
Per Capita Income...$16,367	Tax Value........ $276,803,375
Total Wages.......$32,321,272	Fed. Spending.........$28,763
Housing.....................3,109	Defense Spending $133

Vital Statistics, 1989: Births, 109; Deaths, 49; Marriages, 74; Divorces, 21.

Ethnicity, 1990: White, 6,537 (92.5%); Black, 124 (1.8%); American Indian, 10 (0.1%); Asian, 12 (0.2%); Hispanic, 2,740 (38.8%); Other, 381 (5.4%).

Recreation: Muleshoe National Wildlife Refuge; "Old Pete," the national Mule memorial; historical building park; museum; local events; hunting.

Minerals: Insignificant.

Agriculture: Stocker cattle, cow-calf operations; crops include cotton, wheat, corn, grain sorghums, vegetables; about 160,000 acres irrigated.

Business: Farm supply manufacturing, food-processing plants; muffler manufacturing; other agribusiness.

MULESHOE (4,571) county seat; agribusiness center; manufacture auto mufflers, flour; nursing home, hospital; **Mule Days** in August, county fair in September, other local events.

See map on next page.

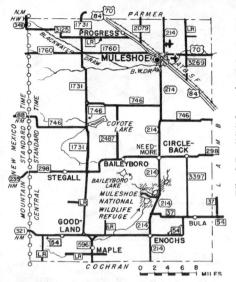

Agriculture: Beef cattle, sheep, goats, are major revenue sources; crops include apple production increasing, pecans.

Business: Tourism, hunting, fishing, purse factory, ranching supplies, marketing, forest products.

BANDERA (877) county seat; cedar mill, shingle factory; purse factory; hunting, guest-ranching center; museums; local events; nursing home; **Medina** (est. 500), "apple capital of Texas."

Bastrop County

LOCATION: Near Austin (M-16).

Cong. Dist. 10	U.S. Jud. Dist. ....W-An.
St. Sen. Dist. 18	Ct. Appeals........................ 3
St. Rep. Dist. 30	Admin. Jud. Dist. 2
St. Dist. Cts. 21, 335	

History: First settled 1829; county created 1836, organized 1837; named for Baron de Bastrop, who aided Moses Austin and Anglo colonists.

Physical Features: Rolling; alluvial, sandy, loam soils; varied timber, "Lost Pines"; bisected by Colorado River.

Population................ 38,263	Av. Weekly Wage $295.72
Area (sq. mi) 895.9	Density 43
Land Area 888.4	Water Area 7.5
Civilian Labor 16,960	Jobless Rate..................4.8
Altitude (ft.) 729-356	Retail Sales $155,102,946
Rainfall (in.) 36.5	Gross Sales...... $218,202,688
Jan. min. 38	Reg. Voters 19,942
July max. 96	Election Turnout........ 51.3
Grow. Season (days)..... 268	Vehicles 32,771
Total Income (mil.) $471	Lane Miles 776
Per Capita Income...$11,872	Tax Value...... $1,556,196,682
Total Wages...... $88,726,765	Fed. Spending $95,603
Housing.................... 16,220	Defense Spending $8,156

Vital Statistics, 1989: Births, 604; Deaths, 336; Marriages, 245; Divorces, 196.

Ethnicity, 1990: White, 29,607 (77.4%); Black, 4,512 (11.8%); American Indian, 181 (0.5%); Asian, 129 (0.3%); Hispanic, 6,933 (18.1%); Other, 3,834 (10.0%).

Recreation: Center of **Lost Pines** region; fishing, hunting; **Bastrop, Buescher State Parks; Lake Bastrop**; historic sites; museum; railroad park and museum; Elgin Western Days in July; Smithville Jamboree in April; Texas State Championship BBQ Cookoff in July.

Minerals: Clay, oil, gas and lignite.

Agriculture: Livestock provide most income; crops include corn, grain sorghums, pecans, peanuts; minor irrigation for alfalfa; some forest products.

Business: Agribusiness, brick, electronic equipment, other manufacturing; tourism attracting residents from Austin.

Bandera County

LOCATION: Southwest (N-13).

Cong. Dist. 21	U.S. Jud. Dist. ....W-SAnt.
St. Sen. Dist. 25	Ct. Appeals...................... 4
St. Rep. Dist. 45	Admin. Jud. Dist. 6
St. Dist. Cts. 216	

History: Created, organized from Bexar, Uvalde counties, 1856; named for Bandera (flag) Mountains.

Physical Features: Hilly, plateau; Medina River, Lake; limestone, sandy soils; dominated by various species of oaks, walnuts, native cherry and Uvalde maple.

Population................ 10,562	Av. Weekly Wage $269.96
Area (sq. mi) 797.5	Density 13
Land Area 791.7	Water Area 5.8
Civilian Labor 4,437	Jobless Rate.................2.7
Altitude (ft.) 2,185-1,175	Retail Sales $42,201,823
Rainfall (in.) 35.1	Gross Sales....... $59,704,463
Jan. min. 31	Reg. Voters 6,220
July max. 94	Election Turnout......... 55.0
Grow. Season (days)..... 235	Vehicles 10,071
Total Income (mil.) $158	Lane Miles 393
Per Capita Income...$15,123	Tax Value........ $889,938,389
Total Wages....... $24,987,145	Fed. Spending $29,908
Housing.........................6,475	Defense Spending $4,350

Vital Statistics, 1989: Births, 149; Deaths, 114; Marriages, 107; Divorces, 73.

Ethnicity, 1990: White, 10,027 (94.9%); Black, 23 (0.2%); American Indian, 66 (0.6%); Asian, 26 (0.2%); Hispanic, 1,172 (11.1%); Other, 420 (4.0%).

Recreation: Dude and resort ranches, RV parks; hunting leases, fishing; **Frontier Times Museum; Lost Maples** and **Hill Country State Natural Areas; Bandera Downs Race Track;** Fun-tier Days celebration, youth rodeo, numerous other local events; Medina Lake.

Minerals: Not significant.

More on next page.

Bastrop Co. (Cont.)

BASTROP (4,044) county seat; oil-well supply, some manufacturing; hospital; University of Texas cancer research center; federal correctional center. Other towns, **Elgin** (4,846), a Main Street City; famous for sausages, brick plants; various other manufacturing; nursing home; Western Days in July; **Garfield** (103 in Bastrop County, mostly in Travis County), **Smithville** (3,196) railroad maintenance, light manufacturing, environmental science park, research; hospital, nursing home; municipal airport; jamboree in April, barbeque cookoff in July.

Baylor County

LOCATION: North central (F-13).

Cong. Dist. 13	U.S. Jud. Dist. ....N-WF
St. Sen. Dist. 30	Ct. Appeals......................11
St. Rep. Dist. 80	Admin. Jud. Dist. 9
St. Dist. Cts....................50	

History: Created from Fannin County 1858, organized 1879. Named for H.W. Baylor, Texas Ranger surgeon.

Physical Features: Level to hilly; drains to Brazos, Wichita rivers; sandy, loam, red soils; grassy, mesquites, cedars.

Population...................4,385	Av. Weekly Wage $269.48
Area (sq. mi) 901.0	Density 5
Land Area 870.8	Water Area 30.2
Civilian Labor 2,305	Jobless Rate...................3.7
Altitude (ft.) 1,394-1,053	Retail Sales $21,886,059
Rainfall (in.) 25.7	Gross Sales $50,142,836
Jan. min.........................26	Reg. Voters 3,090
July max.........................98	Election Turnout.........46.4
Grow. Season (days).....214	Vehicles 5,473
Total Income (mil.) $74	Lane Miles 434
Per Capita Income...$16,797	Tax Value.........$302,741,399
Total Wages.......$16,983,772	Fed. Spending.........$21,362
Housing.......................2,997	Defense Spending $212

Vital Statistics, 1989: Births, 68; Deaths, 71; Marriages, 53; Divorces, 30.

Ethnicity, 1990: White, 3,962 (90.4%); Black, 180 (4.1%); American Indian, 9 (0.2%); Asian, 13 (0.3%); Hispanic, 334 (7.6%); Other, 221 (5.0%).

Recreation: Lake Kemp; Millers Creek Reservoir; park, pavilions for reunions.

Minerals: Oil, gas produced.

Agriculture: Cow-calf operations, stocker cattle produced; wheat, cotton, hay grown; some irrigation for cotton, wheat.

Business: Chiefly agribusiness; oil, gas production; light manufacturing.

SEYMOUR (3,185) county seat; agribusinesses; hospital, nursing home; local events.

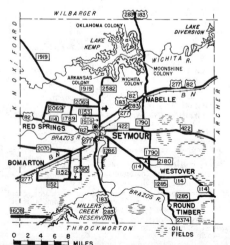

Bee County

LOCATION: Southeast (P-15).

Cong. Dist. 14	U.S. Jud. Dist. ....S-CC
St. Sen. Dist. 21	Ct. Appeals......................13
St. Rep. Dist. 33	Admin. Jud. Dist. 4
St. Dist. Cts........ 36, 156, 343	

History: Created from Karnes, Live Oak, Goliad, Refugio, San Patricio counties, 1857; organized 1858; named for Gen. Barnard Bee.

Physical Features: Level to rolling; black clay, sandy, loam soils; brushy.

Population...............25,135	Av. Weekly Wage....$327.12
Area (sq. mi) 880.3	Density 29
Land Area 880.2	Water Area 0.1
Civilian Labor 10,967	Jobless Rate...................6.5
Altitude (ft.) 422-87	Retail Sales $115,370,582
Rainfall (in.) 31.1	Gross Sales $210,053,866
Jan. min.........................41	Reg. Voters 13,779
July max. 95	Election Turnout.........47.8
Grow. Season (days).....285	Vehicles 18,331
Total Income (mil.) $290	Lane Miles 639
Per Capita Income...$11,086	Tax Value.........$784,291,124
Total Wages......$111,893,049	Fed. Spending ...$103,265
Housing...................10,171	Defense Spending ...$40,058

Vital Statistics, 1989: Births, 509; Deaths, 200; Marriages, 224; Divorces, 160.

Ethnicity, 1990: White, 19,443 (77.4%); Black, 727 (2.9%); American Indian, 103 (0.4%); Asian, 231 (0.9%); Hispanic, 12,909 (51.4%); Other, 4,631 (18.4%).

Recreation: Hunting leases, camping; historical sites; western week in October, junior livestock show, 16th of September celebration.

Minerals: Oil, gas produced, also gravel, sand.

Agriculture: Cow-calf production, feedlot; cotton increasing, other crops grain sorghums, corn, wheat; some irrigation for corn, grass, sod production.

Business: Oil supplies, agribusiness; small feedlots; military installations.

BEEVILLE (13,547) county seat; **Naval Air Station;** oil-field services; agribusiness; **Bee County College;** hospital, nursing homes.

Bell County

LOCATION: Central (K-16).

Cong. Dist. 11	U.S. Jud. Dist. ...... W-Waco
St. Sen. Dist. 24	Ct. Appeals......................3
St. Rep. Dist. 53, 54	Admin. Jud. Dist. 3

History: Created from Milam County and organized 1850; named for Gov. P.H. Bell.

Physical Features: Level to hilly; black to light soils; mixed timber.

Population...............191,088	Av. Weekly Wage $337.28
Area (sq. mi) 1,087.1	Density 181
Land Area 1,058.9	Water Area 28.2
Civilian Labor 79,601	Jobless Rate...................6.7
Altitude (ft.) 1,245-429	Retail Sales ... $1,075,120,482

More on page 190.

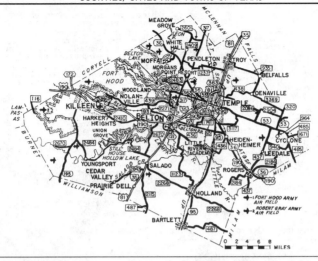

TEMPLE, The "Wildflower Capital of Texas" continues to flourish all year long through continuing beautification projects and real community pride.

Located within three hours drive time of 80% of the state, Temple is easily accessible by train, plane, or automobile. Two of Texas cleanest lakes, Lakes Belton and Stillhouse, provide recreation and relaxation, as well as a bountiful supply of drinking water. Sporting events find Temple the perfect host, with beautiful complexes, and ample hotels.

With the 40,000 sq. ft. Mayborn Convention Center, wonderful museums and exceptional cultural facilities, meeting planners and citizens alike can rest assured that Temple is the superb choice.

Ranked by a university study as among the "most desirable places in Texas to live", Temple's diverse economy is reflected by the wide variety of industry, exceptional educational facilities, and low cost of living.

Temple is proof that cosmopolitan outlook and country values can not only co-exist but actually complement each other. The diverse mixture of talents and interests creates a rich composite that promotes personal professional, and spiritual growth.

While in TEMPLE, visit the Historic Railroad and Pioneer Museum, the SPJST Museum, and the Cultural Activities Center.

For more information on tourism and or industry in Temple please write: Connie Kuehl
Director of Tourism and Promotions,
Municipal Building
Temple, Texas 76501 or Call:
(817)770-5606 —FAX(817)770-5594

Bell Co. (Cont.)

Rainfall in.) 33.8	Gross Sales.... $2,506,517,941
Jan. min. 36	Reg. Voters 63,423
July max. 96	Election Turnout 49.7
Grow. Season (days)..... 260	Vehicles 156,544
Total Income (mil.) .. $2,446	Lane Miles 1,373
Per Capita Income...$13,620	Tax Value...... $4,184,845,083
Total Wages......$992,574,327	Fed. Spending 1,445,585
Housing.................... 75,504	Defense Spending 1,059,871

Vital Statistics, 1989: Births, 4,812; Deaths, 1,299; Marriages, 3,279; Divorces, 2,069.

Ethnicity, 1990: White, 136,066 (71.2%); Black, 36,095 (18.9%); American Indian, 944 (0.5%); Asian, 5,531 (2.9%); Hispanic, 24,995 (13.1%); Other, 12,452 (6.5%).

Recreation: Fishing, hunting; Fort Hood Community Festival; **Belton, Stillhouse Hollow lakes;** historic sites include Stagecoach Inn at Salado; Independence Day celebration, rodeo in Belton; **Bell County Exposition Center;** Salado art fair in August, gathering of Scottish clans in November, antique show in April, country Christmas weekend.

Minerals: Stone, sand and gravel.

Agriculture: Cow-calf, stocker cattle operations provide most revenue; crops include corn, wheat, sorghums, cotton; soybeans introduced; cedar posts produced.

Business: Diversified manufacturing includes computer equipment, plastic goods, furniture, clothing; agribusiness; distribution center; Fort Hood; tourism.

BELTON (12,476) county seat; **University of Mary Hardin-Baylor**, Bell County Exposition Center; manufactures include school, office furniture, roofing felt, athletic equipment; **Central Texas State Fair** in September.

Killeen (63,535); site of **Fort Hood** military installation; **University of Central Texas, Central Texas College;** varied manufacturing; convention facilities; medical center.

Temple (46,109), rail, market, distribution center; diversified industries; convention, exposition center; **Temple Junior College;** one of nation's leading medical centers, **Scott and White Clinic and Hospital; Olin E. Teague VA Center.**

Other towns include **Bartlett** (621 in Bell County, mostly in Williamson County); **Fort Hood** (17,021 in Bell County, partly in Coryell County); **Harker Heights** (12,841), **Holland** (1,118), **Little River-Academy** (1,390), **Morgan's Point Resort** (1,766), **Nolanville** (1,834), **Rogers** (1,131), **Salado** (1,216), **Troy** (1,395).

Bexar County

LOCATION: South (N-14).

Cong. Dist. 20, 21, 23	U.S. Jud. Dist. ....W-SAnt.
St. Sen. Dist. 19, 21, 25, 26	Ct. Appeals..................... 4

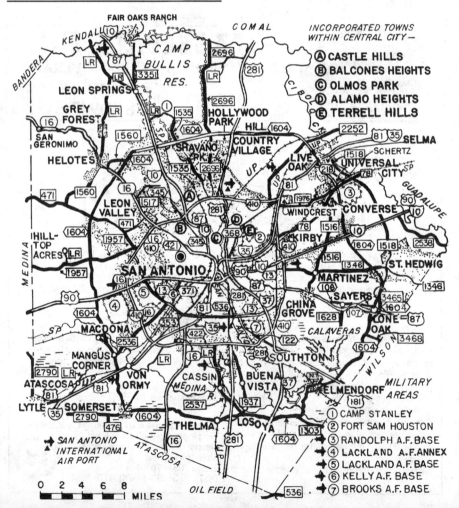

INCORPORATED TOWNS WITHIN CENTRAL CITY —
- (A) CASTLE HILLS
- (B) BALCONES HEIGHTS
- (C) OLMOS PARK
- (D) ALAMO HEIGHTS
- (E) TERRELL HILLS

MILITARY AREAS
- (1) CAMP STANLEY
- (2) FORT SAM HOUSTON
- (3) RANDOLPH A.F. BASE
- (4) LACKLAND A.F.ANNEX
- (5) LACKLAND A.F. BASE
- (6) KELLY A.F. BASE
- (7) BROOKS A.F. BASE

0 2 4 6 8 MILES

St. Rep. Dist. ....115-124 Admin. Jud. Dist. 4

History: Created 1836, organized 1837, from Spanish municipality named for Duke de Bexar; a colonial capital of Texas.

Physical Features: Hilly; heavy black to thin limestone soils; spring-fed streams; underground water; mesquite, other brush.

Population............ 1,185,394	Av. Weekly Wage $374.09
Area (sq. mi) 1,256.7	Density 950
Land Area 1,246.9	Water Area 9.8
Civilian Labor 551,122	Jobless Rate....................7.1
Altitude (ft.) 1,892-486	Retail Sales .. $8,252,044,686
Rainfall (in.) 29.1	Gross Sales.... 21,292,139,952
Jan. min. 39	Reg. Voters 513,132
July max. 95	Election Turnout 42.9
Grow. Season (days)..... 265	Vehicles 867,358
Total Income (mil.) .$17,368	Lane Miles 2,876
Per Capita Income...$14,053	Tax Value..... $35,968,372,498
Total Wages.. $8,501,652,247	Fed. Spending...... 5,660,554
Housing..................453,948	Defense Spending 2,675,153

Vital Statistics, 1989: Births, 21,829; Deaths, 8,368; Marriages, 10,398; Divorces, 7,228.

Ethnicity, 1990: White, 878,736 (74.1%); Black, 84,670 (7.1%); American Indian, 4,265 (0.4%); Asian, 15,429 (1.3%); Hispanic, 589,180 (49.7%); Other, 202,294 (17.1%).

Recreation: Major tourist and retirement area; historic sites include the **Alamo**, other missions, many buildings; **River Walk; Seaworld of Texas;** El Mercado (market), La Villita; Tower of the Americas; Brackenridge Park; zoo; symphony orchestra; HemisFair Plaza; Folk Life Festival; Fiesta San Antonio; **Institute of Texan Cultures;** many military posts; parks, museums; hunting, fishing; many special events; major livestock show (check with chamber of commerce for dates).

Minerals: Cement, stone, oil, gas, sand and gravel, lime, clays.

Agriculture: Income from beef, dairy cattle, other livestock; crops include sorghums, vegetables, hay, corn, nursery plant production; significant irrigation.

Business: Government center with large federal payroll, five military bases; tourism second-largest industry; developing high-tech industrial park, research center; education center with 14 colleges including **Our Lady of the Lake University of San Antonio, San Antonio College, St. Mary's University, Trinity University, University of Texas Health Science Center at San Antonio, University of Texas at San Antonio.**

SAN ANTONIO (935,933) county seat; Texas' third largest city; state's largest military center; varied manufacturing with emphasis on high-tech industries; other products include construction equipment, concrete and dairy products; Alamo and other historic sites attract tourists; many local events; popular retirement area.

Other towns include **Alamo Heights** (6,502); **Balcones Heights** (3,022); **Castle Hills** (4,198); **China Grove** (872); **Converse** (8,887); **Cross Mountain** (1,112); **Dominion** (1,196); **Elmendorf** (568); **Fair Oaks Ranch** (1,640, partly in Comal, Kendall counties); **Grey Forest** (425); **Helotes** (1,535); **Hill Country** (1,038); **Hollywood Park** (2,841); **Kirby** (8,326); **Lackland Air Force Base** (9,352); **Leon Valley** (9,581); **Live Oak** (10,023); **Lytle** (4 in Bexar, partly in Atascosa, Medina counties); **Olmos Park** (2,161); **St. Hedwig** (1,443); **Scenic Oaks** (2,352); **Schertz** (414, partly in Guadalupe, Comal counties); **Selma** (447); **Shavano Park** (1,708); **Somerset** (1,144); **Terrell Hills** (4,592); **Timberwood Park** (2,578); **Universal City** (13,057); **Windcrest** (5,331).

Blanco County

LOCATION: Central (M-14).

Cong. Dist. 10	U.S. Jud. Dist. ....W-An.
St. Sen. Dist. 25	Ct. Appeals..................... 3
St. Rep. Dist. 47	Admin. Jud. Dist. 3
St. Dist. Cts..................33	

History: Created, organized, 1858, from Burnet, Comal, Gillespie, Hays counties; named for Blanco (white) River.

Physical Features: Hilly; Blanco, Pedernales rivers; cedars, pecans, other trees.

Population................5,972	Av. Weekly Wage $347.79
Area (sq. mi)..............713.3	Density 8
Land Area 711.2	Water Area 2.1
Civilian Labor 2,903	Jobless Rate....................2.5
Altitude (ft.)......... 1,801-978	Retail Sales $23,425,553
Rainfall (in.) 34.7	Gross Sales....... $144,926,047
Jan. min. 33	Reg. Voters 3,624
July max. 95	Election Turnout 63.1
Grow. Season (days)..... 234	Vehicles 6,728
Total Income (mil.) $96	Lane Miles 451
Per Capita Income...$15,206	Tax Value........ $774,065,359

Total Wages....... $30,997,585 Fed. Spending......... $23,354
Housing....................3,128 Defense Spending $1,600

Vital Statistics, 1989: Births, 93; Deaths, 80; Marriages, 64; Divorces, 21.

Ethnicity, 1990: White, 5,598 (93.7%); Black, 56 (0.9%); American Indian, 17 (0.3%); Asian, 22 (0.4%); Hispanic, 840 (14.1%); Other, 279 (4.7%).

Recreation: President Lyndon B. Johnson's boyhood home; **Blanco State Park; Pedernales Falls State Park;** hunting, fishing; scenic drives; county fair; jamboree, fiddlefest in June; historic courthouse.

Minerals: Insignificant.

Agriculture: Cow-calf operation, some stocker cattle; nursery plants, wheat, hay, peaches, pecans.

Business: Livestock trailer manufacturing, tourism, ranch supplies, marketing.

JOHNSON CITY (932) county seat; tourist center; nursing home; electric co-op; livestock center; **Blanco** (1,238), ranch supply center; horticultural products; two nursing homes; **Round Mountain** (59).

Borden County

LOCATION: West (H-9).

Cong. Dist. 17	U.S. Jud. Dist. .... N-Lb.
St. Sen. Dist. 28	Ct. Appeals..................... 11
St. Rep. Dist. 69	Admin. Jud. Dist. 7
St. Dist. Cts..................132	

History: Created 1876 from Bexar County, organized 1891; named for Gail Borden, pioneer patriot, inventor, editor.

Physical Features: Rolling, broken by Caprock Escarpment; drains to Colorado River, Lake J.B. Thomas; sandy loam, clay soils.

Population....................799	Av. Weekly Wage $376.94
Area (sq. mi)..............906.0	Density 1
Land Area 898.8	Water Area 7.2
Civilian Labor 396	Jobless Rate..................4.3
Altitude (ft.).......2,964-1,247	Retail Sales $153,282
Rainfall (in.) 18.7	Gross Sales........... $621,636
Jan. min. 30	Reg. Voters 544
July max. 96	Election Turnout 71.7
Grow. Season (days)..... 214	Vehicles 1,066
Total Income (mil.) $15	Lane Miles 344
Per Capita Income...$18,231	Tax Value........ $335,376,430
Total Wages.........$2,842,091	Fed. Spending $3,635
Housing....................... 474	Defense Spending $9

Vital Statistics, 1989: Births, 4; Deaths, 4; Marriages, 7; Divorces, 3.

Ethnicity, 1990: White, 769 (96.2%); Black, 2 (0.3%); American Indian, 10 (1.3%); Asian, 0 (0.0%); Hispanic, 120 (15.0%); Other, 18 (2.3%).

Recreation: Fishing, hunting; **Lake J.B. Thomas**; museum; junior coyote opry in September.

Minerals: Oil, gas, sand and gravel.

Agriculture: Beef cattle, horses provide most income; crops include cotton, wheat for grazing, pecans, alfalfa; some irrigation for cotton.

Business: Oil, agribusiness; service station.

GAIL (est. 202) county seat; county museum; antique shop; horse sale in spring; ambulance service.

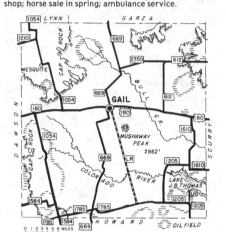

Bosque County

LOCATION: Central (J-15).

Cong. Dist. 11	U.S. Jud. Dist. ...... W-Waco
St. Sen. Dist. 22	Ct. Appeals..................... 10
St. Rep. Dist. 57	Admin. Jud. Dist. 3
St. Dist. Cts. 220	

History: Created, organized, 1854, from Milam District, McLennan County; named for Bosque (woods) River.

Physical Features: Hilly, broken by Bosque, Brazos rivers; limestone to alluvial soils; cedars, oaks, mesquites.

Population................ 15,125	Av. Weekly Wage $303.05
Area (sq. mi) 1,002.6	Density 15
Land Area 989.2	Water Area 13.4
Civilian Labor 6,456	Jobless Rate................. 6.2
Altitude (ft.) 122-503	Retail Sales $50,585,529
Rainfall (in.) 31.6	Gross Sales...... $136,323,176
Jan. min........................ 33	Reg. Voters 8,533
July max. 97	Election Turnout 58.6
Grow. Season (days)..... 243	Vehicles 15,077
Total Income (mil.) $225	Lane Miles 695

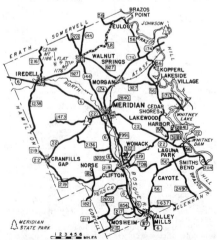

Per Capita Income...$15,402   Tax Value......... $829,750,738
Total Wages....... $49,986,640   Fed. Spending......... $49,821
Housing......................8,073   Defense Spending $2,759

Vital Statistics, 1989: Births, 220; Deaths, 237; Marriages, 95; Divorces, 71.

Ethnicity, 1990: White, 14,173 (93.7%); Black, 319 (2.1%); American Indian, 26 (0.2%); Asian, 41 (0.3%); Hispanic, 1,430 (9.5%); Other, 566 (3.7%).

Recreation: Whitney Lake, **Meridian State Park, Bosque Memorial Museum** at Clifton; fishing, hunting; scenic routes, golf course, Norwegian smorgasbord at Norse community in November, Central Texas Youth Fair in Clifton in August; **Texas Safari Wildlife Park** in Clifton.

Minerals: Lime, stone.

Agriculture: Cattle, Angora goats, sheep, swine are major producers; crops include wheat, grain sorghums, oats, coastal Bermuda hay, corn, peaches; some irrigation.

Business: Agribusiness; tourism, small industries; tree supplier.

MERIDIAN (1,390) county seat; distribution center; varied manufacturing.

Other towns are **Clifton** (3,195), trade center; light manufacturing; hospital, rest home; **Cranfills Gap** (269), **Iredell** (339); **Morgan** (451); **Valley Mills** (1,085, partly in McLennan County); **Walnut Springs** (716).

Bowie County

LOCATION: Northeast (F-21).

Cong. Dist. 1	U.S. Jud. Dist. .... E-Tx.
St. Sen. Dist. 1	Ct. Appeals..................... 6
St. Rep. Dist. 1	Admin. Jud. Dist. 1
St. Dist. Cts. 5, 102, 202	

History: Created 1840 from Red River County, organized 1841; named for Alamo hero, James Bowie.

Physical Features: Hilly, forested; clay, sandy, alluvial soils; drained by Red and Sulphur rivers.

Population................ 81,665	Av. Weekly Wage $347.65
Area (sq. mi) 922.7	Density 92
Land Area 887.9	Water Area 34.8
Civilian Labor 39,344	Jobless Rate................. 6.4
Altitude (ft.) 437-225	Retail Sales $614,626,505
Rainfall (in.) 45.3	Gross Sales .. $1,353,261,606
Jan. min........................ 35	Reg. Voters 41,608
July max. 93	Election Turnout 42.8
Grow. Season (days)..... 235	Vehicles 76,146
Total Income (mil.) .. $1,156	Lane Miles 1,151
Per Capita Income...$14,495	Tax Value...... $2,221,650,786
Total Wages......$489,166,833	Fed. Spending......... $496,861
Housing.................... 34,182	Defense Spending . $242,564

Vital Statistics, 1989: Births, 1,144; Deaths, 802; Marriages, 819; Divorces, 572.

Ethnicity, 1990: White, 62,878 (77.0%); Black, 17,798 (21.8%); American Indian, 412 (0.5%); Asian, 262 (0.3%); Hispanic, 1,334 (1.6%); Other, 315 (0.4%).

Recreation: Wright Patman Lake, Crystal Springs beach, other lakes; hunting, fishing, historic sites; four-states fair in October, pioneer days, other local events.

Minerals: Oil, gas, sand, gravel.

Agriculture: Beef, dairy cattle, poultry, horses are major revenue sources; crops include wheat, soybeans, rice, milo, corn, blueberries, truck crops, cotton, alfalfa; pine timber, hardwoods, pulpwood harvested; some irrigation for peanuts.

Business: Manufacturing; agribusiness; government employment; tourism; U.S. Army Depot, ordnance plant.

BOSTON county seat (but courthouse now located in New Boston).

Texarkana (31,656, in Texas, 22,631 in Arkansas), distribution, manufacturing, medical center; **Red River Army Depot;** state-line tourist attractions; **Texarkana College, East Texas State University at Texarkana;** federal correctional unit; Four States Fair in October and Quadrangle Festival in September, Perot Theatre.

Other towns include **New Boston** (5,057) site of courthouse; Lone Star Army Ammunition Plant, paper mill; **De Kalb** (1,976), **Hooks** (2,684), **Leary** (395), **Maud** (1,049), **Nash** (2,162), **Redwater** (824), **Wake Village** (4,757).

See map on next page.

Brazoria County

LOCATION: On coast (O-20).

Cong. Dist. 14, 22	U.S. Jud. Dist. ....S-Gn.
St. Sen. Dist. 17, 18	Ct. Appeals................. 1, 14
St. Rep. Dist. 27, 28, 29	Admin. Jud. Dist. 2
St. Dist. Cts. ...23, 149, 239, 300	

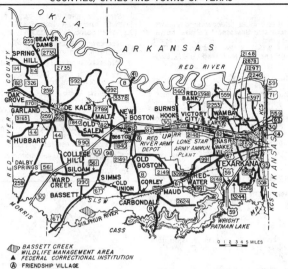

IIIII BASSETT CREEK
WILDLIFE MANAGEMENT AREA
▲ FEDERAL CORRECTIONAL INSTITUTION
Ⓐ FRIENDSHIP VILLAGE

0 1 2 3 4 5 MILES

Brazoria Co (Cont.)

History: Created 1836, organized 1837 from Municipality of Brazoria; name derived from Brazos River; settled by Stephen F. Austin colonists.

Physical Features: Flat, coastal soils, drained by Brazos and San Bernard rivers.

Vital Statistics, 1989: Births, 3,147; Deaths, 1,100; Marriages, 1,641; Divorces, 1,215.

Population	191,707
Area (sq. mi)	1,597.4
Land Area	1,386.8
Civilian Labor	87,156
Altitude (ft.)	146-5
Rainfall (in.)	52.3
Jan. min.	42
July max.	92
Grow. Season (days)	268
Total Income (mil.)	$3,139
Per Capita Income	$17,099
Total Wages	$1,747,029,097
Housing	74,362
Av. Weekly Wage	$504.68
Density	136
Water Area	210.6
Jobless Rate	5.5
Retail Sales	$1,145,065,559
Gross Sales	$3,006,090,237
Reg. Voters	85,378
Election Turnout	50.9
Vehicles	167,686
Lane Miles	1,154
Tax Value	$9,544,345,390
Fed. Spending	$365,918
Defense Spending	$71,532

Ethnicity, 1990: White, 154,875 (80.8%); Black, 15,981 (8.3%); American Indian, 812 (0.4%); Asian, 1,961 (1.0%); Hispanic, 33,797 (17.6%); Other, 18,078 (9.4%).

Recreation: Water sports, 20 miles natural beach; fishing, hunting; many historic sites; **Varner-Hogg State Park; Bryan Beach State Park; Bayou Wildlife Park Exotic Animal Paradise;** replica of first capitol of Republic of Texas at West Columbia; county parks.

Minerals: Oil, gas produced, limestone.

Agriculture: Rice, sorghums major revenue producers, aquaculture introduced; beef cattle, horses significant; over 35,000 acres of rice irrigated.

Business: Extensive petroleum and chemical industry; fishing; tourism; agribusiness.

ANGLETON (17,140) county seat; banking, distribution center for large oil, chemical, agricultural area; fish-processing plant; large county fair; hospital, nursing home.

Brazosport is a community of nine cities; world's

OIL FIELD
VARNER-HOGG STATE PARK
STATE PRISON UNITS
▲ 1 DARRINGTON
▲ 2 RAMSEY
▲ 3 RETRIEVE
▲ 4 CLEMENS
✦ BRYAN BEACH STATE PARK
IIIII PEACH POINT WILDLIFE MGMT. AREA

0 1 2 3 4 5 6 MILES

Brazoria Co. (Cont.)
largest basic-chemical complex; deepwater seaport; commercial fishing; tourism; **Brazosport College**; hospital; Brazosport cities include **Clute** (8,910), **Freeport** (11,389), **Jones Creek** (2,160), **Lake Jackson** (22,776), **Oyster Creek** (912), **Quintana** (51), **Richwood** (2,732), **Surfside Beach** (611).

Other towns include **Alvin** (19,220), rice, chemical processing; **Alvin Community College**, hospital, numerous local events; **Home of Nolan Ryan**, pitcher for Texas Rangers. Also **Bailey's Prairie** (634), **Bonney** (339), **Brookside Village** (1,470), **Danbury** (1,447), **Hillcrest Village** (695), **Holiday Lakes** (1,039), **Iowa Colony** (675), **Liverpool** (396), **Manvel** (3,733), **Pearland** (17,234 in Brazoria County, partly in Harris County), **Sweeny** (3,297), **West Columbia** (4,372), San Jacinto Festival, Varner-Hogg State Park Plantation Days in April; **Wild Peach** (2,440).

Brazos County

LOCATION: Southeast (L-18).

Cong. Dist. 6	U.S. Jud. Dist. .... S-Hn.
St. Sen. Dist. 5	Ct. Appeals............. 1, 10, 14
St. Rep. Dist. 14	Admin. Jud. Dist. 2
St. Dist. Cts........ 85, 272, 361	

History: Created 1841 from Robertson, Washington counties and named Navasota; renamed for Brazos River in 1842, organized 1843.

Physical Features: Between Brazos and Navasota rivers; rich bottom soils, sandy, clays on rolling uplands; mostly oak trees.

Population...............121,862	Av. Weekly Wage $322.04
Area (sq. mi) 590.3	Density 207
Land rea.....................585.8	Water Area 4.5
Civilian Labor 61,806	Jobless Rate.................. 3.5
Altitude (ft.) 312-197	Retail Sales $879,449,884
Rainfall (in.) 39.1	Gross Sales .. $1,619,300,223
Jan. min. 39	Reg. Voters 56,949
July max. 95	Election Turnout........ 55.5
Grow. Season (days).... 274	Vehicles 82,894
Total Income (mil.) .. $1,467	Lane Miles 729
Per Capita Income...$12,760	Tax Value...... $3,285,954,679
Total Wages....$922,718,915	Fed. Spending $285,494
Housing....................48,558	Defense Spending .. $28,640

Vital Statistics, 1989: Births, 1,772; Deaths, 609; Marriages, 1,208; Divorces, 432.

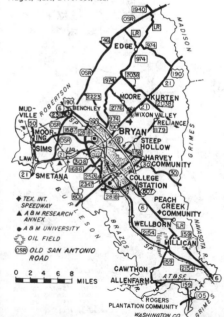

Ethnicity, 1990: White, 94,866 (77.8%); Black, 13,672 (11.2%); American Indian, 274 (0.2%); Asian, 4,313 (3.5%); Hispanic, 16,713 (13.7%); Other, 8,737 (7.2%).

Recreation: Fishing, hunting; Texas World Speedway, many springtime festivals; Texas A&M events.

Minerals: Sand and gravel, lignite, gas, oil.

Agriculture: Most income from cattle, hogs; chief crops are sorghums, corn, cotton, wheat, oats, pecans.

Business: Agribusiness center; computers, research and development; offshore technology; four industrial parks; Texas A&M University enterprises are major economic factor.

BRYAN (55,002) county seat; university enterprises; defense electronics, other varied manufacturing; agribusiness center; hospitals, psychiatric facilities.

College Station (52,456) home of **Texas A&M University**, varied high-tech manufacturing; research; other town, **Wixon Valley** (186).

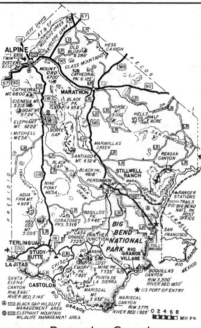

Brewster County

LOCATION: In Rio Grande's Big Bend (N-6).

Cong. Dist. 21	U.S. Jud. Dist. .... W-Pe.
St. Sen. Dist. 25	Ct. Appeals...................... 8
St. Rep. Dist. 68	Admin. Jud. Dist. 6
St. Dist. Cts........................83	

History: Created, organized, 1887, from Presidio County; named for Henry P. Brewster, Republic of Texas secretary of war.

Physical Features: Largest Texas county; area equal to Connecticut plus Rhode Island; mountains and deep canyons, distinctive geology, plant life, animals.

Population...................8,681	Av . Weekly Wage....$283.34
Area (sq. mi) 6,193.1	Density 1
Land Area 6,193.0	Water Area 0.1
Civilian Labor 3,912	Jobless Rate.................. 4.1
Altitude (ft.) 7,825-1,355	Retail Sales $49,024,048
Rainfall (in.) 14.8	Gross Sales $71,468,770
Jan. min. 32	Reg. Voters 5,195
July max. 89	Election Turnout........ 43.5
Grow. Season (days)...... 223	Vehicles 6,608
Total Income (mil.) $94	Lane Miles 588
Per Capita Income...$12,192	Tax Value......... $410,080,439
Total Wages....... $42,889,994	Fed. Spending $25,183
Housing.....................4,491	Defense Spending $913

Vital Statistics, 1989: Births, 101; Deaths, 92; Marriages, 75; Divorces, 20.

Brewster Co. (Cont.)

Ethnicity, 1990: White, 8,300 (95.6%); Black, 85 (1.0%); American Indian, 20 (0.2%); Asian, 52 (0.6%); Hispanic, 3,702 (42.6%); Other, 224 (2.6%).

Recreation: Many tourist attractions; **Big Bend National Park**; ghost mining towns; scenic drives, canyons, mountains; among last unspoiled "frontier" in United States; **Museum of the Big Bend** at Sul Ross State University; **Woodward Ranch and Stillwell Ranch rockhound areas**; annual Chili Cookoff at Terlingua; retirement area; Big Bend summer theater at Alpine; cavalry post at **Lajitas**; hunting leases.

Minerals: Sand and gravel, fluorspar.

Agriculture: Nearly all agricultural income from cattle, sheep, goats; pecans, apples raised; minor irrigation.

Business: Sul Ross State University; ranching; tourism; retirement developments; hunting leases; some curio manufacturing.

ALPINE (5,637) county seat; ranch trade center; tourism; **Sul Ross State University**; hospital; local events; varied manufacturing. Other community, **Marathon**, ranching center, gateway to **Big Bend National Park**.

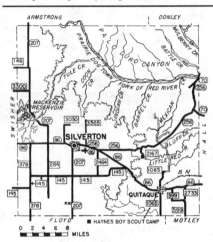

Briscoe County

LOCATION: Northwest (D-9).

Cong. Dist.	13	U.S. Jud. Dist.	N-Am.
St. Sen. Dist.	31	Ct. Appeals	7
St. Rep. Dist.	84	Admin. Jud. Dist.	9
St. Dist. Cts.	110		

History: Created from Bexar District, 1876, organized 1892; named for Andrew Briscoe, Republic of Texas soldier.

Physical Features: Partly on High Plains, broken by Caprock Escarpment, fork of Red River; sandy, loam soils.

Population	1,971	Av. Weekly Wage	$264.64
Area (sq. mi)	901.6	Density	2
Land Area	900.3	Water Area	1.3
Civilian Labor	1,186	Jobless Rate	2.4
Altitude (ft.)	3,316-2,174	Gross Sales	$15,748,027
Rainfall (in.)	20.4	Retail Sales	$4,447,682
Jan. min.	19	Reg. Voters	1,331
July max.	91	Election Turnout	60.3
Grow. Season (days)	214	Vehicles	2,374
Total Income (mil.)	$36	Lane Miles	328
Per Capita Income	$17,855	Tax Value	$111,454,870
Total Wages	$5,146,639	Fed. Spending	$13,863
Housing	1,074	Defense Spending	$79

Vital Statistics, 1989: Births, 26; Deaths, 19; Marriages, 17; Divorces, 6.

Ethnicity, 1990: White, 1,559 (79.1%); Black, 68 (3.5%); American Indian, 5 (0.3%); Asian, 0 (0.0%); Hispanic, 367 (18.6%); Other, 339 (17.2%).

Recreation: Hunting, fishing; scenic drives; local events; **Briscoe County Museum; Caprock Canyons State**

Park, Mackenzie Reservoir.

Minerals: Insignificant.

Agriculture: Wheat, grain sorghums, cotton, corn are main crops; vegetables, melons introduced; beef cattle, stockers; an estimated 40,000 acres of grains irrigated.

Business: Agribusiness.

SILVERTON (779) county seat; agribusiness center; irrigation supplies manufactured; clinics; Briscoe County Celebration in August; **Quitaque** (513), trade center.

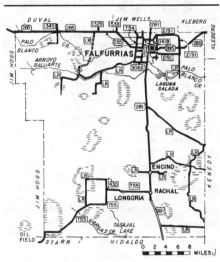

Brooks County

LOCATION: South (S-15).

Cong. Dist.	15	U.S. Jud. Dist.	S-CC
St. Sen. Dist.	20	Ct. Appeals	4
St. Rep. Dist.	37	Admin. Jud. Dist.	5
St. Dist. Cts.	79		

History: Created from Hidalgo, Starr, Zapata counties, 1911; organized same year. Named for J.A. Brooks, Texas Ranger and legislator.

Physical Features: Level to rolling; brushy; light to dark sandy loam soils.

Population	8,204	Av. Weekly Wage	$275.08
Area (sq. mi)	943.6	Density	9
Land Area	943.3	Water Area	0.3
Civilian Labor	3,800	Jobless Rate	7.1
Altitude (ft.)	367-46	Retail Sales	$40,584,736
Rainfall (in.)	25.8	Gross Sales	$53,643,621
Jan. min.	44	Reg. Voters	6,045
July max.	98	Election Turnout	34.8
Grow. Season (days)	303	Vehicles	5,437
Total Income (mil.)	$77	Lane Miles	264
Per Capita Income	$8,217	Tax Value	$649,838,620
Total Wages	$28,035,946	Fed. Spending	$27,741
Housing	3,084	Defense Spending	$284

Vital Statistics, 1989: Births, 159; Deaths, 56; Marriages, 90; Divorces, 25.

Ethnicity, 1990: White, 6,748 (82.3%); Black, 3 (**.*%); American Indian, 13 (0.2%); Asian, 10 (0.1%); Hispanic, 7,338 (89.4%); Other, 1,430 (17.4%).

Recreation: Hunting, fishing; Texas Ranger Museum, Don Pedrito Shrine.

Minerals: Oil, gas production.

Agriculture: Most income from cow-calf operations, stocker cattle, dairy cattle, hunting leases; crops include watermelons, grain sorghums, corn; honeydews introduced; some irrigations for melons, grass

Business: Chiefly oil, gas, cattle raising.

FALFURRIAS (5,788) county seat; retail; agribusiness; some manufacturing; hospital, nursing home; museum, library.

Brown County

LOCATION: Central (J-13).

Cong. Dist. 11	U.S. Jud. Dist. ...... N-SAng.
St. Sen. Dist. 24	Ct. Appeals....................11
St. Rep. Dist. 65	Admin. Jud. Dist. 7
St. Dist. Cts.....................35	

History: Named for Indian fighter Henry S. Brown; created 1856 from Comanche, Travis counties; organized 1857.

Physical Features: Rolling, hilly; drains to Colorado River; varied soils, timber.

Population................ 34,371	Av. Weekly Wage $334.03
Area (sq. mi) 956.9	Density 37
Land Area 943.9	Water Area 13.0
Civilian Labor 16,501	Jobless Rate.................. 6.4
Altitude (ft.) 1,894-1,321	Retail Sales $214,650,000
Rainfall (in.) 26.1	Gross Sales....... $374,388,142
Jan. min. 31	Reg. Voters 16,788
July max. 97	Election Turnout 52.3
Grow. Season (days)..... 242	Vehicles 33,124
Total Income (mil.) $454	Lane Miles 736
Per Capita Income...$13,646	Tax Value...... $1,117,390,966
Total Wages......$203,239,161	Fed. Spending....... $107,955
Housing................... 16,894	Defense Spending $7,241

Vital Statistics, 1989: Births, 508; Deaths, 403; Marriages, 403; Divorces, 150.

Ethnicity, 1990: White, 30,267 (88.1%); Black, 1,552 (4.5%); American Indian, 131 (0.4%); Asian, 88 (0.3%); Hispanic, 3,799 (11.1%); Other, 2,333 (6.8%).

Recreation: Lake Brownwood State Park; **MacArthur Academy of Freedom at Howard Payne University**; fishing, hunting; Brown County youth fair in January, other local events.

Minerals: Oil, gas, paving materials, gravel, clays.

Agriculture: Beef cattle, swine, sheep and goats for mohair, peanuts chief crops, others are hay, wheat oats; 3,800 acres irrigated for peanuts and hay.

Business: Agribusinesses, general manufacturing plants, distribution center.

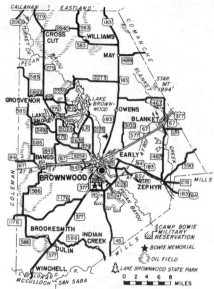

BROWNWOOD (18,387) county seat; retail trade center; varied industries; distribution center; **Howard Payne University, MacArthur Academy of Freedom**; mental health/mental retardation center; state 4-H Club center; hospitals. Other towns include **Bangs** (1,555), **Blanket** (381), **Early** (2,380).

Burleson County

LOCATION: East central (L-17).

Cong. Dist. 14	U.S. Jud. Dist. ....W-An.
St. Sen. Dist. 5	Ct. Appeals.................1, 14
St. Rep. Dist. 13	Admin. Jud. Dist. 2
St. Dist. Cts............. 21, 335	

History: Created, organized, 1846, from Milam, Washington counties; named for Edward Burleson, a hero of the Texas Revolution.

Population............... 13,625	Av. Weekly Wage $312.12
Area (sq. mi) 677.8	Density 20
Land Area 665.6	Water Area 12.2
Civilian Labor 6,002	Jobless Rate.................. 5.6
Altitude (ft.) 417-221	Retail Sales $53,474,436
Rainfall (in.) 39.1	Gross Sales....... $130,292,792
Jan. min. 37	Reg. Voters 7,487
July max. 94	Election Turnout 55.9
Grow. Season (days)..... 275	Vehicles 13,271
Total Income (mil.) $164	Lane Miles 517
Per Capita Income...$11,475	Tax Value......... $834,805,319
Total Wages....... $42,085,110	Fed. Spending......... $47,324
Housing...................7,033	Defense Spending $1,411
	More on next page.

Physical Features: Rolling to hilly; drains to Brazos, Yegua Creek, Somerville Lake; loam and heavy bottom soils; oaks, other trees.

Vital Statistics, 1989: Births, 202; Deaths, 171; Marriages, 82; Divorces, 74.

Ethnicity, 1990: White, 10,173 (74.7%); Black, 2,430 (17.8%); American Indian, 53 (0.4%); Asian, 18 (0.1%); Hispanic, 1,624 (11.9%); Other, 7.0%).

Recreation: Fishing, limited hunting; **Somerville Lake** recreation; **Birch Creek Park; Big Creek Park;** historic sites; **Burleson County Kolache Festival, County Fair** in September.

Minerals: Oil, gas, sand and gravel.

Agriculture: Beef cattle, swine, horses top agricultural products; cotton, corn, wheat major crops, soybeans, grain sorghums, oats also grown; about 70 percent of crops irrigated because of drought.

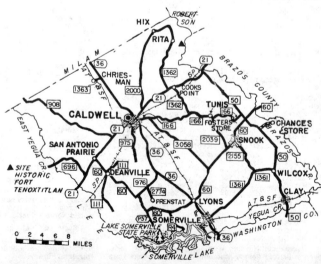

Burleson Co. (Cont.)

Business: Agribusiness, oil and natural gas; varied manufacturing.

CALDWELL (3,181) county seat; light manufacturing; oil-field tool and servicing; tourist center; hospital, nursing home; historical museum; youth rodeo in July; "Kolache capital of Texas"; other towns **Clay** (est. 61), **Snook** (489). **Somerville** (1,542), tourist, railroad center, some manufacturing, local events.

Burnet County

LOCATION: Central (L-15).

Cong. Dist. 10	U.S. Jud. Dist. ....W-An.
St. Sen. Dist. 24	Ct. Appeals......................3
St. Rep. Dist. 52	Admin. Jud. Dist. 3
St. Dist. Cts.....................33	

History: Created from Bell, Travis, Williamson counties, 1852; organized 1854; named for David G. Burnet, provisional president of the Republic of Texas.

Physical Features: Many lakes; hilly; caves; sandy, red, black waxy soils; cedars, other trees.

Population................22,677	Av. Weekly Wage $311.54
Area (sq. mi) 1,020.0	Density 23
Land Area 995.2	Water Area 24.8
Civilian Labor 9,531	Jobless Rate...................4.1
Altitude (ft.).........1,585-779	Retail Sales $144,953,173
Rainfall (in.) 30.4	Gross Sales......$251,865,912
Jan. min. 33	Reg. Voters.............12,793
July max. 98	Election Turnout........59.8
Grow. Season (days).....230	Vehicles 24,235
Total Income (mil.) $353	Lane Miles 793
Per Capita Income...$14,167	Tax Value...$1,337,997,168
Total Wages.......$85,148,015	Fed. Spending.........$75,715
Housing 12,793	Defense Spending ...$7,361

Vital Statistics, 1989: Births, 318; Deaths, 295; Marriages, 221; Divorces, 150.

Ethnicity, 1990: White, 20,793 (91.7%); Black, 269 (1.2%); American Indian, 109 (0.5%); Asian, 59 (0.3%); Hispanic, 2,440 (10.8%); Other, 1,447 (6.4%).

Recreation: Water sports on lakes; sites of historic forts; Granite Mt. furnished stone for Texas Capitol;

deer, other hunting; major tourist center; **Longhorn Cavern** and **Inks Lake State Parks**; Bluebonnet Trail in Spring.

Minerals: Stone, graphite, sand and gravel.

Agriculture: Cattle, sheep, goats top revenue producers; income also from cedar posts, pecans, hay; some grains.

Business: Stone processing, manufacturing, agribusinesses, tourist trade, hunting leases.

BURNET (3,423) county seat; other towns, **Marble Falls** (4,007), ranching; precision instruments, sporting goods manufactured; stone quarry; tourist center; nursing home; **Bertram** (849), **Cottonwood Shores** (548), **Granite Shoals** (1,378), **Meadowlakes** (514).

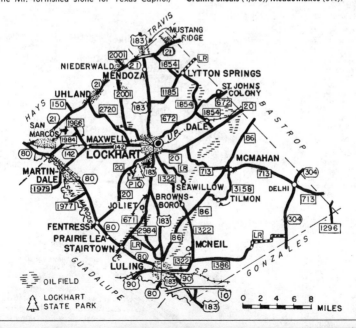

Caldwell County

LOCATION: South Central (N-16).

Cong. Dist. 10
St. Sen. Dist. 18
St. Rep. Dist. 31
St. Dist. Cts. 22, 207, 274

U.S. Jud. Dist. .... W-An.
Ct. Appeals...................... 3
Admin. Jud. Dist. 3

History: Created, organized from Bastrop, Gonzales counties, 1848; named for Indian fighter Mathew Caldwell.

Physical Features: Varied soils ranging from black clay to waxy; level, draining to San Marcos River.

Population............... 26,392	Av. Weekly Wage $292.42
Area (sq. mi) 547.3	Density 48
Land Area 545.7	Water Area 1.6
Civilian Labor 10,009	Jobless Rate..................5.7
Altitude (ft.) 705-388	Retail Sales $95,019,641
Rainfall (in.) 34.7	Gross Sales $143,591,490
Jan. min. 37	Reg. Voters 12,309
July max. 97	Election Turnout 45.2
Grow. Season (days)..... 275	Vehicles 18,922
Total Income (mil.) $316	Lane Miles 602
Per Capita Income...$10,859	Tax Value........ $823,241,749
Total Wages....... $77,686,838	Fed. Spending......... $62,100
Housing................... 10,085	Defense Spending $3,971

Vital Statistics, 1989: Births, 379; Deaths, 247; Marriages, 168; Divorces, 111.

Ethnicity, 1990: White, 18,919 (71.7%); Black, 2,825 (10.7%); American Indian, 65 (0.2%); Asian, 86 (0.3%); Hispanic, 9,988 (37.8%); Other, 4,497 (17.0%).

Recreation: Fishing; **Lockhart State Park**; Luling Watermelon Thump; Chisholm Trail roundup at Lockhart; oldest library in Texas; museums; nature trails; rodeo.

Minerals: Oil, gas, sand and gravel.

Agriculture: Cow-calf operations, turkeys, eggs top revenue sources; hay, grain sorghums, cotton, corn, wheat, hay major crops; some irrigation for grass, vegetables, pasture.

Business: Petroleum, agribusiness, varied manufacturing.

LOCKHART (9,205) county seat, agribusiness center, tourism; hospital, nursing home; 16th of September celebration; light manufacturing. Other towns, **Luling** (4,66½), oil industry center; hospital, nursing home; **Martindale** (904), **Mustang Ridge** (319 in Caldwell County, partly in Travis and Bastrop counties); **Niederwald** (74 in Caldwell County, mostly in Hays County); **San Marcos** (mostly in Hays County), **Uhland** (153 in Caldwell County, partly in Hays County).

Calhoun County

LOCATION: On coast (P-18).

Cong. Dist. 14
St. Sen. Dist. 18
St. Rep. Dist. 32
St. Dist. Cts. 24, 135, 267

U.S. Jud. Dist. .... S-Va.
Ct. Appeals...................... 13
Admin. Jud. Dist. 4

History: Created, organized from Jackson, Matagorda, Victoria counties, 1846. Named for John C. Calhoun, U.S. statesman.

Physical Features: Sandy, broken by bays; partly on Matagorda Island.

Vital Statistics, 1989: Births, 318; Deaths, 139; Marriages, 158; Divorces, 123.

Ethnicity, 1990: White, 14,819 (77.8%); Black, 556 (2.9%); American Indian, 35 (0.2%); Asian, 556 (2.9%); Hispanic, 6,893 (36.2%); Other, 3,087 (16.2%).

Recreation: Beaches, fishing, water sports, duck, goose hunting; historic sites, county park, **Matagorda Island, Green Lake**; Labor Day summerfest and fishing festival, La Salle Days in April, county fair; convention center.

Minerals: Oil, gas.

Agriculture: Top crops are rice, cotton, grain sorghums, corn; some rice irrigated; beef cattle significant, shrimp, crayfish farming increasing.

Business: Aluminum manufacturing, plastics plant, marine construction, agribusinesses; petroleum; tourism, fishing and fish processing.

PORT LAVACA (10,886) county seat; commercial seafood operations; offshore drilling operations; tourist center; some manufacturing; convention center; hospital, nursing home. Other towns, **Point Comfort** (956), aluminum, plastic plants, deepwater port; **Port O'Connor** (est. 1,184), tourist center; seafood processing; some manufacturing; **Seadrift** (1,277).

Population............... 19,053	Av. Weekly Wage $514.33
Area (sq. mi) 1,032.1	Density 35
Land Area 512.3	Water Area 519.8
Civilian Labor 9,601	Jobless Rate..................5.8
Altitude (ft.) 27-4	Retail ales ... $120,286,376
Rainfall (in.) 42.2	Gross Sales $611,123,650
Jan. min. 44	Reg. Voters 10,446
July max. 93	Election Turnout 51.7
Grow. Season (days)..... 300	Vehicles 16,397
Total Income (mil.) $269	Lane Miles 383
Per Capita Income...$13,355	Tax Value...... $1,800,460,520
Total Wages......$264,055,083	Fed. Spending......... $43,819
Housing...................9,544	Defense Spending $4,297

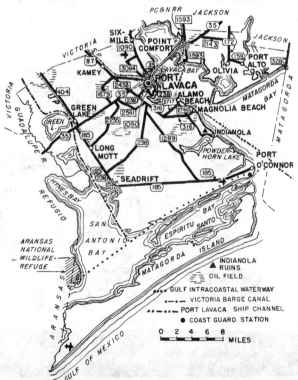

Callahan County

LOCATION: West central (I-13).

Cong. Dist. 17	U.S. Jud. Dist. ....N-Ab.
St. Sen. Dist. 30	Ct. Appeals......................11
St. Rep. Dist. 64	Admin. Jud. Dist. 7
St. Dist. Cts. 42	

History: Created 1858 from Bexar, Bosque, Travis counties; organized 1877; named for Texas Ranger J.H. Callahan.

Physical Features: On divide between Brazos, Colorado rivers' watersheds; level to rolling.

Population................ 11,859	Av. Weekly Wage $288.29
Area (sq. mi) 901.2	Density 13
Land Area 898.6	Water Area 2.6
Civilian Labor 5,396	Jobless Rate.................. 4.6
Altitude (ft.) 2,204-1,604	Retail Sales $31,638,476
Rainfall (in.) 24.5	Gross Sales........ $50,993,624
Jan. min. 32	Reg. Voters 7,011
July max. 96	Election Turnout......... 56.2
Grow. Season (days)..... 228	Vehicles 13,904
Total Income (mil.) $151	Lane Miles 743
Per Capita Income...$11,738	Tax Value....$448,471,631
Total Wages....... $22,351,677	Fed. Spending $36,736
Housing.....................5,433	Defense Spending $1,908

Vital Statistics, 1989: Births, 147; Deaths, 146; Marriages, 80; Divorces, 68.

Ethnicity, 1990: White, 11,482 (96.8%); Black, 2 (**.*%); American Indian, 44 (0.4%); Asian, 40 (0.3%); Hispanic, 489 (4.1%); Other, 291 (2.5%).

Recreation: Hunting, local events; Lake Clyde; county museum; old settlers reunion in July.

Minerals: Oil and gas.

Agriculture: Beef cattle significant; crops include wheat, peanuts, grain sorghums; some irrigation of peanuts and coastal Bermuda.

Business: Oil-field services, agribusiness.

BAIRD (1,658) county seat; ranching, oil-field supply center; some manufacturing, shipping; hospital, clinic, nursing home. Other towns are **Clyde** (3,002), small manufacturing; **Cross Plains** (1,063); **Putnam** (103).

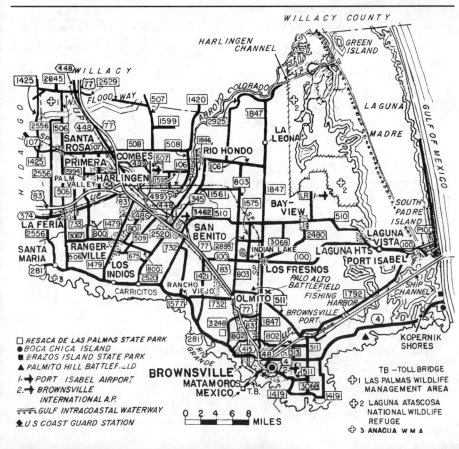

Cameron County

LOCATION: Southern tip (U-16).

Cong. Dist. 15	U.S. Jud. Dist. .... S-Br.
St. Sen. Dist. 27	Ct. Appeals.....................13
St. Rep. Dist. 37, 38, 39	Admin. Jud. Dist. 5
St. Dist. Cts. 103, 107, 138, 197, 357	

History: Created, organized from Nueces County, 1848; named for Capt. Ewen Cameron of Mier Expedition.

Physical Features: Rich Rio Grande Valley soils; flat; semitropical climate.

Population................260,120	Av. Weekly Wage $297.27
Area (sq. mi) 1,276.3	Density 287
Land Area 905.5	Water Area 370.8
Civilian Labor 104,812	Jobless Rate................ 11.7
Altitude (ft.) 67-3	Retail Sales ... $1,550,208,997
Rainfall (in.) 25.4	Gross Sales.... $3,933,943,722
Jan. min. 51	Reg. Voters 94,489
July max. 93	Election Turnout 37.8
Grow. Season (days)..... 341	Vehicles 153,287
Total Income (mil.) .. $2,260	Lane Miles 1,493
Per Capita Income... $8,435	Tax Value...... $4,902,730,236
Total Wages... $1,181,469,519	Fed. Spending....... $630,307
Housing...................87,714	Defense Spending ... $29,392

Vital Statistics, 1989: Births, 6,214; Deaths, 1,586; Marriages, 2,786; Divorces, 396.

Ethnicity, 1990: White, 214,424 (82.4%); Black, 825 (0.3%); American Indian, 413 (0.2%); Asian, 750 (0.3%); Hispanic, 212,995 (81.9%); Other, 43,708 (16.8%).

Recreation: Year-round resort; fishing, hunting, water sports; historical sites; Mexican gateway; South Padre Island; Brazos Island State Park; Laguna Atascosa Wildlife Refuge; numerous local events; recreational vehicle center; air shows at Harlingen; Iwo Jima Monument.

Minerals: Natural gas, oil.

Agriculture: A leading agricultural county; cotton top crop with corn, grain sorghums, citrus and sugar cane raised; small feedlot operations; 200,000 acres irrigated, mostly cotton, corn.

Business: Fruit, vegetables, seafood processing; fishing, shipping, tourism; agribusiness; manufacturing.

BROWNSVILLE (98,962) county seat; varied industries, shipping, **Port of Brownsville**, fishing, tourism, agribusiness; **Texas Southmost College, University of Texas - Pan American** branch; hospitals, nursing homes, crippled children health center; **Gladys Porter Zoo** for endangered species.

Harlingen (48,735), agribusiness, tourist center; varied manufacturing; distribution center; **Texas State Technical Institute**; Valley Baptist Medical Center; mental health/mental retardation center, psychiatric centers, nursing homes; **South Texas Hospital**; Valley International Airport; greyhound racing.

San Benito (20,125), varied manufacturing, bottling; tourism; hospital; recreation facilities. Other towns are **Bayview** (231), **Combes** (2,042), **Encantada-Ranchito El Calaboz** (1,143), **Indian Lake** (390), **La Feria** (4,360), **Laguna Vista** (1,166), **Los Fresnos** (2,473), **Palm Valley** (1,199), **Port Isabel** (4,467), **Primera** (2,030), **Rancho Viejo** (885), **Rio Hondo** (1,793), **Rangerville** (280), **Santa Rosa** (2,223), **South Padre Island** (1,677).

Camp County

LOCATION: Northeast (G-20).

Cong. Dist. 1	U.S. Jud. Dist. .... E-MI.
St. Sen. Dist. 1	Ct. Appeals.....................6
St. Rep. Dist. 8	Admin. Jud. Dist. 1
St. Dist. Cts.............. 76, 276	

History: Third smallest county in Texas; created, organized from Upshur County 1874; named for jurist-legislator J.L. Camp.

Physical Features: Hilly, forested; drains to Cypress Creek on north; Lake O' the Pines, Lake Bob Sandlin.

Population..................9,904	Av. Weekly Wage $262.61
Area (sq. mi) 203.1	Density 49
Land Area 197.5	Water Area 5.6
Civilian Labor 6,158	Jobless Rate.................5.8
Altitude (ft.) 538-277	Retail Sales $61,583,337
Rainfall (in.) 43.3	Gross Sales....... $93,208,140
Jan. min. 32	Reg. Voters 5,745
July max. 94	Election Turnout 50.3
Grow. Season (days)..... 238	Vehicles 10,151
Total Income (mil.) ...$167	Lane Miles 266
Per Capita Income...$16,692	Tax Value......... $338,130,212
Total Wages....... $42,987,920	Fed. Spending......... $32,020
Housing....................4,525	Defense Spending $883

Vital Statistics, 1989: Births, 151; Deaths, 127; Marriages, 92; Divorces, 41.

Ethnicity, 1990: White, 7,130 (72.0%); Black, 2,360 (23.8%); American Indian, 35 (0.4%); Asian, 5 (0.1%); Hispanic, 501 (5.1%); Other, 374 (3.8%).

Recreation: Water sports, fishing on six lakes within 20 miles of Pittsburg; local events.

Minerals: Oil, gas, clays, coal.

Agriculture: Broilers, eggs top agriculture products; beef, dairy cattle produced; top crops are hay, peaches, blueberries, greenhouse plants, vegetables; some irrigation.

Business: Agribusiness; timber industries; light manufacturing, food processing; retirement center; rural heritage center in late 1991; Pilgrim Foundation chapel.

PITTSBURG (4,007) county seat; agribusiness; timber; tourism; food processing; light manufacturing; **Northeast Texas Community College;** Chick Fest in April, Pioneer Days in September, junior livestock show in March; celebrated centennial in 1991; other town, **Rocky Mound** (53).

Carson County

LOCATION: Northwestern (C-9).

Cong. Dist. 13	U.S. Jud. Dist. ....N-Am.
St. Sen. Dist. 31	Ct. Appeals.....................7
St. Rep. Dist. 88	Admin. Jud. Dist. 9
St. Dist. Cts................... 100	

History: Created from Bexar District, 1876; organized 1888; named for Republic of Texas secretary of state S.P. Carson.

Physical Features: Level, some broken land; loam soils.

Population..................6,576	Av. Weekly Wage $550.15
Area (sq. mi)..............924.1	Density 7
Land Area 923.2	Water Area 0.9
Civilian Labor 3,959	Jobless Rate...................3.4
Altitude (ft.).......3,536-3,204	Retail Sales $22,370,646
Rainfall (in.) 19.7	Gross Sales....... $57,743,699
Jan. min. 21	Reg. Voters................4,104
July max. 97	Election Turnout......... 59.3
Grow. Season (days)..... 191	Vehicles 6,892
Total Income (mil.) $106	Lane Miles 776
Per Capita Income...$15,672	Tax Value $633,223,954
Total Wages......$105,448,830	Fed. Spending $57,873
Housing.......................2,855	Defense Spending ... $35,300

Vital Statistics, 1989: Births, 87; Deaths, 63; Marriages, 55; Divorces, 29.

Ethnicity, 1990: White, 6,315 (96.0%); Black, 11 (0.2%); American Indian, 44 (0.7%); Asian, 9 (0.1%); Hispanic, 354 (5.4%); Other, 197 (3.0%).

Recreation: Museum, local events, sausage festivals.

Minerals: Oil, gas production.

Agriculture: Beef cattle significant; crops include hay, wheat, corn; some irrigation.

Business: Agribusinesses, oil-field services.

PANHANDLE (2,353) county seat; agribusiness, petroleum center; nursing homes; airport; varied manufacturing. Other towns, **Groom** (613), **Skellytown** (664), **White Deer** (1,125).

Cass County

LOCATION: Northeast (G-21).

Cong. Dist. 1	U.S. Jud. Dist. .... E-MI.
St. Sen. Dist. 1	Ct. Appeals......................6
St. Rep. Dist. 8	Admin. Jud. Dist. 1
St. Dist. Cts.....................5	

History: Named for U.S. Sen. Lewis Cass; created, organized 1846 from Bowie County.

Physical Features: Rolling, forested; timber produced; drained by Cypress Bayou, Sulphur River.

Population................ 29,982	Av. Weekly Wage $370.74
Area (sq. mi) 960.3	Density 32
Land Area 937.4	Water Area 22.9
Civilian Labor 14,727	Jobless Rate...................6.9
Altitude (ft.)............486-219	Retail ales $138,233,530
Rainfall (in.) 46.3	Gross Sales....... $253,532,804
Jan. min.........................31	Reg. Voters................ 17,023
July max. 93	Election Turnout......... 43.4
Grow. Season (days)..... 237	Vehicles 27,137
Total Income (mil.) $387	Lane Miles 970
Per Capita Income...$12,888	Tax Value...... $1,176,629,193
Total Wages....$136,106,990	Fed. Spending $86,636
Housing..................... 13,161	Defense Spending ... $3,176

Vital Statistics, 1989: Births, 431; Deaths, 341; Marriages, 229; Divorces, 214.

Ethnicity, 1990: White, 23,651 (78.9%); Black, 6,057 (20.2%); American Indian, 105 (0.4%); Asian, 25 (0.1%); Hispanic, 373 (1.2%); Other, 144 (0.5%).

Recreation: Fishing, hunting, water sports, county park; **Wright Patman Lake, Atlanta State Park,** wildflower trails in April, forest festival in September.

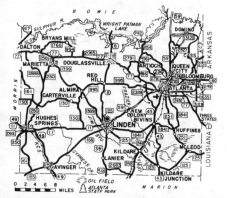

Minerals: Gas, oil, iron ore.

Agriculture: Timber major revenue; beef cattle; forages; broilers; fruit, vegetables; Christmas trees; blueberries introduced.

Business: Paper mill, wood products, varied manufacturing; agribusinesses, sawmill.

LINDEN (2,375) county seat; wood-treating plants; timber; oldest courthouse still in use as courthouse; hospital, nursing home. Other towns are **Atlanta** (6,118), varied manufacturing; timber; cattle; two hospitals; **Avinger** (478); **Bloomburg** (376); **Domino** (101); **Douglassville** (192); **Hughes Springs** (1,927 in Cass County, partly in Morris County), varied manufacturing, warehousing; two nursing homes; **Marietta** (161); **Queen City** (1,748).

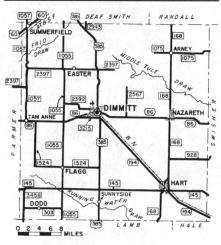

Castro County

LOCATION: Northwest (D-8).

Cong. Dist. 19	U.S. Jud. Dist. .... N-Am.
St. Sen. Dist. 31	Ct. Appeals......................7
St. Rep. Dist. 85	Admin. Jud. Dist. 9
St. Dist. Cts.............. 64, 242	

History: Created 1876 from Bexar District, organized 1891. Named for Henri Castro, Texas colonizer.

Physical Features: Flat, drains to creeks, draws, playas; underground water.

Population..................9,070	Av. Weekly Wage $298.25
Area (sq. mi) 899.3	Density 10
Land Area 898.4	Water Area 0.9
Civilian Labor 4,467	Jobless Rate...................4.3
Altitude (ft.).......3,942-3,731	Retail ales $38,905,751
Rainfall (in.) 16.6	Gross Sales....... $82,520,655
Jan. min.........................19	Reg. Voters................4,515
July max. 91	Election Turnout......... 45.5
Grow. Season (days)..... 193	Vehicles 8,339
Total Income (mil.) $138	Lane Miles 529
Per Capita Income...$13,751	Tax Value........ $414,382,012
Total Wages....... $39,733,876	Fed. Spending $36,733
Housing.......................3,357	Defense Spending $499

Vital Statistics, 1989: Births, 179; Deaths, 67; Marriages, 65; Divorces, 35.

Ethnicity, 1990: White, 5,526 (60.9%); Black, 261 (2.9%); American Indian, 10 (0.1%); Asian, 15 (0.2%); Hispanic, 4,187 (46.2%); Other, 3,258 (35.9%).

Recreation: Local events; pheasant hunting.

Minerals: Not significant.

Agriculture: A leading agricultural county; fed cattle, sheep important, hogs raised; crops include corn and cotton with sorghums, wheat, sunflowers, sugar beets, vegetables raised.

Business: Varied agribusinesses.

DIMMITT (4,408) county seat; agribusiness center; library, hospital, nursing home; harvest festival. Other towns, **Hart** (1,221), **Nazareth** (293).

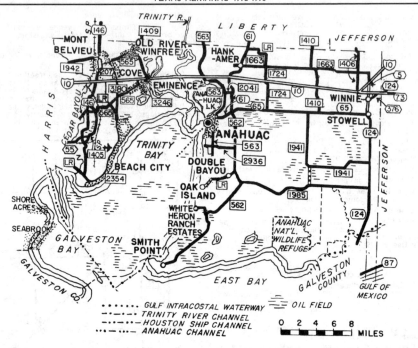

•••••• GULF INTRACOSTAL WATERWAY   **≡≡ OIL FIELD**
—•—•— TRINITY RIVER CHANNEL
—•••— HOUSTON SHIP CHANNEL
—••— ANAHUAC CHANNEL

0 2 4 6 8 MILES

Chambers County

LOCATION: On Galveston, other bays (M-21).

Cong. Dist. 9	U.S. Jud. Dist. ....S-Gn.
St. Sen. Dist. 4	Ct. Appeals..................1, 14
St. Rep. Dist. 21	Admin. Jud. Dist. 2
St. Dist. Cts............. 253, 344	

History: Named for Gen. T. J. Chambers, surveyor; created, organized 1858 from Liberty, Jefferson counties.

Physical Features: Level, coastal soils; some forests.

Population............... 20,088	Av. Weekly Wage $483.48
Area (sq. mi) 868.5	Density 33
Land Area 599.3	Water Area 269.2
Civilian Labor 7,897	Jobless Rate................... 4.6
Altitude (ft.)................. 73-2	Retail Sales $117,670,484
Rainfall (in.) 51.6	Gross Sales....... $263,322,997
Jan. min. 41	Reg. Voters 10,336
July max. 91	Election Turnout......... 46.8
Grow. Season (days)..... 261	Vehicles 20,653
Total Income (mil.) $245	Lane Miles 700
Per Capita Income...$13,824	Tax Value...... $2,882,902,438
Total Wages......$141,342,036	Fed. Spending......... $60,698
Housing....................8,032	Defense Spending $2,861

Vital Statistics, 1989: Births, 267; Deaths, 176; Marriages, 271; Divorces, 116.

Ethnicity, 1990: White, 16,725 (83.3%); Black, 2,550 (12.7%); American Indian, 53 (0.3%); Asian, 116 (0.6%); Hispanic, 1,195 (5.9%); Other, 644 (3.2%).

Recreation: Fishing, hunting; all water sports; camping facilities; 10 county parks; **Anahuac National Wildlife Refuge;** historic sites; Wallisville Heritage Park; Texas Rice Festival in October, Texas Gatorfest in September.

Minerals: Oil, gas, salt, clays, sand and gravel.

Agriculture: Rice, soybeans top crops; beef cattle raised; significant irrigation; 15,000 acres of timber.

Business: Petroleum, chemicals, steel plants; agribusinesses; varied manufacturing; fish processing; tourism.

ANAHUAC (1,993) county seat; canal connects with Houston Ship Channel; agribusiness; nursing home, hospital. Other towns are **Baytown** (2,724 in Chambers County, mostly in Harris County), **Beach City** (852), **Cove**

(402), **Mont Belvieu** (1,323 in Chambers County, partly in Liberty County), **Old River-Winfree** (1,233), **Stowell** (1,419), **Winnie** (2,238) fertilizer manufacturing, wholesale greenhouse, medical center.

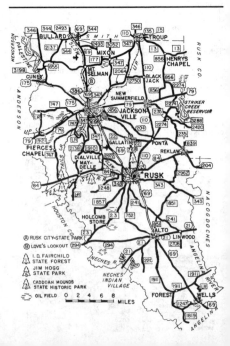

Cherokee County

LOCATION: East (J-20).

Cong. Dist. 1	U.S. Jud. Dist. .... E-Ty.
St. Sen. Dist. 3	Ct. Appeals.................... 12
St. Rep. Dist. 11	Admin. Jud. Dist. 1
St. Dist. Cts. 2	

History: Named for Indians; created, organized in 1846 from Nacogdoches County.

Physical Features: Hilly, partly forested; drains to Angelina, Neches rivers; many streams, lakes; sandy, clay soils.

Population 41,049	Av. Weekly Wage $297.75
Area (sq. mi) 1,062.0	Density 39
Land Area 1,052.3	Water Area 9.7
Civilian Labor 20,415	Jobless Rate 5.7
Altitude (ft.) 708-204	Retail Sales $206,706,552
Rainfall (in.) 44.6	Gross Sales $503,513,479
Jan. min. 35	Reg. Voters 19,831
July max. 94	Election Turnout 45.1
Grow. Season (days)..... 258	Vehicles 34,513
Total Income (mil.) $515	Lane Miles 1,110
Per Capita Income...$12,824	Tax Value.... $1,292,532,261
Total Wages......$212,722,540	Fed. Spending....... $114,614
Housing 17,620	Defense Spending ... $4,185

Vital Statistics, 1989: Births, 574; Deaths, 503; Marriages, 318; Divorces, 201.

Ethnicity, 1990: White, 32,039 (78.1%); Black, 6,931 (16.9%); American Indian, 108 (0.3%); Asian, 196 (0.5%); Hispanic, 2,697 (6.6%); Other, 1,775 (4.3%).

Recreation: Water activities; fishing, hunting on many lakes; numerous historical sites, homes; **Texas State Railroad** excursion train; state parks. Among points of interest are **Love's Lookout Park, Jim Hogg State Park**, birthplace of first native Texan to become governor; **Caddoan Mounds State Park** near Alto; site of ghost town of **New Birmingham; I.D. Fairchild State Forest;** nature trails through forests and several lakes; tomato fest in September, county fair in October, other local events.

Minerals: Oil, gas, iron ore.

Agriculture: Greenhouse plants a major factor; forages, vegetables, peaches, Christmas trees raised; dairy and beef cattle important; timber produced.

Business: Varied manufacturing; agribusinesses; tourism.

RUSK (4,366) county seat; agribusiness; tourism, state hospital; **Jacksonville** (12,765), manufacturing center; agribusiness; tourism; retail center; hospital, clinic; **Lon Morris College, Jacksonville College, Baptist M.A. Theological Seminary.**

Other towns are **Alto** (1,027); **Bullard** (52 in Cherokee County, mostly in Smith County); **Cuney** (170); **Gallatin** (368); **New Summerfield** (521); **Reklaw** (151 in Cherokee County, partly in Rusk County);**Troup** (33 in Cherokee County, mostly in Smith County); **Wells** (761).

Childress County

LOCATION: Northwest (D-11).

Cong. Dist. 13	U.S. Jud. Dist. .... N-Am.
St. Sen. Dist. 30	Ct. Appeals.................... 7
St. Rep. Dist. 84	Admin. Jud. Dist. 9
St. Dist. Cts.................. 100	

History: Created 1876 from Bexar, Young districts; organized 1887; named for author of Texas Declaration of Independence, George C. Childress.

Physical Features: Rolling prairie, draining to Prairie Dog Town Fork of Red River; mixed soils.

Population.................5,953	Av. Weekly Wage $276.88
Area (sq. mi) 713.5	Density 8
Land Area 710.3	Water Area 3.2
Civilian Labor 2,366	Jobless Rate 6.1
Altitude (ft.) 1,934-1,782	Retail Sales $44,619,303
Rainfall (in.) 19.9	Gross Sales....... $62,180,241
Jan. min. 26	Reg. Voters 3,182
July max. 96	Election Turnout 51.3
Grow. Season (days)...... 217	Vehicles 6,108
Total Income (mil.) $83	Lane Miles 470
Per Capita Income...$13,600	Tax Value........ $157,609,153
Total Wages....... $23,496,721	Fed. Spending....... $27,205
Housing 3,042	Defense Spending $373

Vital Statistics, 1989: Births, 70; Deaths, 124; Marriages, 58; Divorces, 33.

Ethnicity, 1990: White, 4,969 (83.5%); Black, 321 (5.4%); American Indian, 26 (0.4%); Asian, 17 (0.3%); Hispanic, 853 (14.3%); Other, 620 (10.4%).

Recreation: Water recreation on **Lakes Childress and Baylor Creek**, fishing, hunting; parks; county museum;

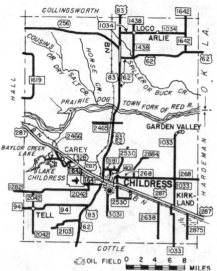

local events.

Minerals: Small production of oil, gas.

Agriculture: Agricultural income from cotton, wheat, hay, grain sorghums, peanuts; cattle, Angora goats introduced; some cotton, peanuts irrigated; some mesquite marketed.

Business: Agribusinesses; food processing, varied manufacturing.

CHILDRESS (5,055) county seat; varied manufacturing, hospital, nursing homes; home of Greenbelt Bowl, high school all-star football game; settlers reunion; youth livestock show; hospital clinic; prison unit under construction.

Clay County

LOCATION: North central (F-14).

Cong. Dist. 13	U.S. Jud. Dist. .... N-WF
St. Sen. Dist. 30	Ct. Appeals.................... 2
St. Rep. Dist. 80	Admin. Jud. Dist. 8
St. Dist. Cts.................... 97	

History: Created, organized from Cooke County, 1857; Indians forced disorganization, 1862; reorganized, 1873; named for Henry Clay, U.S. statesman.

Physical Features: Hilly, rolling; drains to Red, Trinity rivers, Lake Arrowhead; sandy loam, chocolate soils; mesquites, post oaks.

Population 10,024	Av. Weekly Wage $335.45
Area (sq. mi) 1,116.1	Density 9
Land Area 1,097.8	Water Area 18.3
Civilian Labor 4,925	Jobless Rate.................. 3.9
Altitude (ft.) 1,083-862	Retail Sales $35,500,992
Rainfall (in.) 30.1	Gross Sales $58,941,786
Jan. min. 27	Reg. Voters 6,011
July max. 97	Election Turnout 52.7
Grow. Season (days)..... 232	Vehicles 8,885
Total Income (mil.) $143	Lane Miles 789
Per Capita Income...$15,423	Tax Value........ $522,631,376
Total Wages....... $24,507,814	Fed. Spending....... $24,162
Housing 4,693	Defense Spending $911

Vital Statistics, 1989: Births, 97; Deaths, 103; Marriages, 82; Divorces, 44.

Ethnicity, 1990: White, 9,751 (97.3%); Black, 33 (0.3%); American Indian, 88 (0.9%); Asian, 23 (0.2%); Hispanic, 242 (2.4%); Other, 129 (1.3%).

Recreation: Fishing, water sports at **Lake Arrowhead;** local events.

Minerals: Oil and gas, stone.

Agriculture: Beef and dairy cattle top producers; swine raised; top crops are wheat, cotton, pecan, peaches.

Business: Oil; agribusinesses; varied manufacturing.

HENRIETTA (2,896) county seat; varied manufacturing; hospital, rest homes; pioneer reunion in Sep-

Clay Co. (Cont.)

tember, agricultural seminar in January; other towns are **Bellevue** (333), **Byers** (510), **Dean** (277), **Jolly** (201), **Petrolia** (762), **Scotland** (110 in Clay County, mostly in Archer County), **Windthorst** (3 in Clay County, mostly in Archer County).

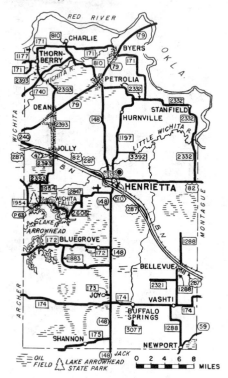

Agriculture: Agricultural income from cotton, grain sorghums, wheat; cattle, extensive cattle feeding; 120,500 acres irrigated for cotton, wheat, grain sorghums; onions introduced.

Business: Agribusinesses; feedlots; meat packing.

MORTON (2,597) county seat; oil, agriculture center, meat packing; hospital, nursing home; rodeo, barbeque cookoff in August; junior livestock show in February. Other town, **Whiteface** (512).

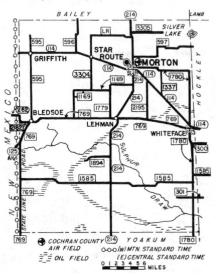

Coke County

LOCATION: West central (J-11).

Cong. Dist. 17	U.S. Jud. Dist. ...... N-SAng.
St. Sen. Dist. 15	Ct. Appeals.......................3
St. Rep. Dist. 66	Admin. Jud. Dist. 7
St. Dist. Cts. 51	

History: Created, organized 1889 from Tom Green County; named for Gov. Richard Coke.

Physical Features: Prairie, hills, Colorado River valley; sandy loam, red soils; E.V. Spence Reservoir.

Population.................3,424	Av. Weekly Wage $338.81
Area (sq. mi) 927.9	Density 4
Land Area 898.8	Water Area 29.1
Civilian Labor 1,718	Jobless Rate..................1.8
Altitude (ft.) 2,608-1,758	Retail ales $21,755,513
Rainfall (in.) 20.7	Gross Sales........$27,367,181

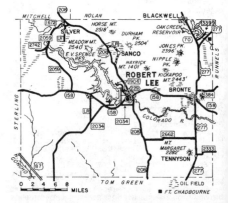

Cochran County

LOCATION: Adjoins New Mexico (F-7).

Cong. Dist. 19	U.S. Jud. Dist. .... N-Lb.
St. Sen. Dist. 28	Ct. Appeals.......................7
St. Rep. Dist. 77	Admin. Jud. Dist. 9
St. Dist. Cts. 286	

History: Created from Bexar, Young districts, 1876; organized 1924; named for Robert Cochran, who died in the Alamo.

Physical Features: Many small lakes (playas); level prairie; underground water; loam, sandy loam soils.

Population.................4,377	Av. Weekly Wage $327.05
Area (sq. mi) 775.2	Density 6
Land Area 775.2	Water Area 0.0
Civilian Labor 1,912	Jobless Rate..................4.0
Altitude (ft.) 3,965-3,687	Retail Sales $18,096,567
Rainfall (in.) 16.6	Gross Sales $24,250,512
Jan. min. 22	Reg. Voters 2,181
July max. 91	Election Turnout.........45.7
Grow. Season (days).....189	Vehicles 4,109
Total Income (mil.) $64	Lane Miles 470
Per Capita Income...$15,146	Tax Value.........$655,684,303
Total Wages.......$22,006,449	Fed. Spending.........$21,419
Housing......................1,761	Defense Spending $48

Vital Statistics, 1989: Births, 73; Deaths, 34; Marriages, 29; Divorces, 18.

Ethnicity, 1990: White, 2,997 (68.5%); Black, 234 (5.3%); American Indian, 13 (0.3%); Asian, 1 (**.*%); Hispanic, 1,857 (42.4%); Other, 1,132 (25.9%).

Recreation: Rodeo; county fair; museum; golf course.

Minerals: Oil, gas.

Coke Co. (Cont.)

Jan. min. 28	Reg. Voters 2,226
July max. 97	Election Turnout 53.9
Grow. Season (days).....226	Vehicles 4,289
Total Income (mil.) $51	Lane Miles 357
Per Capita Income...$15,675	Tax Value.........$306,522,720
Total Wages.......$15,327,899	Fed. Spending........$12,168
Housing 2,787	Defense Spending $328

Vital Statistics, 1989: Births, 31; Deaths, 40; Marriages, 24; Divorces, 15.

Ethnicity, 1990: White, 3,222 (94.1%); Black, 6 (0.2%); American Indian, 17 (0.5%); Asian, 2 (0.1%); Hispanic, 422 (12.3%); Other, 177 (5.2%).

Coleman County

LOCATION: West central (J-12).

Cong. Dist. 17	U.S. Jud. Dist. ......N-SAng.
St. Sen. Dist. 24	Ct. Appeals...................11
St. Rep. Dist. 65	Admin. Jud. Dist. 7
St. Dist. Cts................35, 42	

History: Created 1858 from Brown, Travis counties; organization began 1862, completed 1864; named for Houston's aide, R.M. Coleman.

Physical Features: Hilly, rolling; drains to Colorado River, Pecan Bayou; lakes; some mesquite, oaks.

Population..................9,710	Av. Weekly Wage $274.27
Area (sq. mi) 1,281.5	Density 8
Land Area 1,272.9	Water Area 8.6
Civilian Labor 4,665	Jobless Rate..................7.7
Altitude (ft.) 2,173-1,488	Retail Sales $39,966,613
Rainfall (in.) 26.9	Gross Sales $73,922,396
Jan. min. 32	Reg. Voters 6,301
July max. 96	Election Turnout 47.3
Grow. Season (days).....235	Vehicles 10,716
Total Income (mil.) $147	Lane Miles 740
Per Capita Income...$15,527	Tax Value......$464,021,763
Total Wages.......$32,089,684	Fed. Spending........$38,651
Housing 5,373	Defense Spending $1,165

Vital Statistics, 1989: Births, 137; Deaths, 183; Marriages, 99; Divorces, 45.

Ethnicity, 1990: White, 8,995 (92.6%); Black, 246 (2.5%); American Indian, 29 (0.3%); Asian, 7 (0.1%); Hispanic, 1,139 (11.7%); Other, 433 (4.5%).

Recreation: Fishing, hunting; water sports; local events; historic sites; **Coleman Lake, O. H. Ivie Reservoir, Hord's Creek Lake,** other lakes; Santa Anna Peak.

Minerals: Oil, gas, coal, stone, clays.

Agriculture: Beef cattle, sheep, goats, horses, hogs top producers; crops include wheat, cotton, oats, grain sorghums; mesquite for firewood and furniture.

Business: Agribusinesses, petroleum, tile, brick plants, other manufacturers.

Recreation: Hunting, fishing; **E.V. Spence and Oak Creek Reservoirs;** historic sites, county museum, local events.

Minerals: Oil, gas, sand and gravel.

Agriculture: Majority income from cattle, sheep, goats; cotton, grain sorghums, small grains, hay leading crops; some irrigation for cotton, Bermuda grass.

Business: Oil-well supplies, agribusinesses, tourism.

ROBERT LEE (1,276) county seat; ranching, petroleum center; hospital, nursing home. Other towns, **Blackwell** (7 in Coke County, mostly in Nolan County), **Bronte** (962).

COLEMAN (5,410) county seat; varied manufacturing, aircraft restoration, agribusiness; hospital, nursing homes; city park, museum, bass tournament, rodeos, county fair. Other towns, **Santa Anna** (1,249), **Novice** (183).

Collin County

LOCATION: North central (G-17).

Cong. Dist. 3, 4, 26	U.S. Jud. Dist. ....E-Sh.
St. Sen. Dist. 2, 8	Ct. Appeals...................5
St. Rep. Dist. 60, 61, 62	Admin. Jud. Dist. 1
St. Dist. Cts.......199, 219, 296	

History: Created from Fannin County and organized, 1846. Named for pioneer settler Collin McKinney.

Physical Features: Heavy, black clay soil; level to rolling; drains to Trinity, Lake Lavon.

Population..................264,036	Av . Weekly Wage....$484.68
Area (sq. mi) 885.8	Density 310
Land Area 847.7	Water Area 38.1
Civilian Labor 121,078	Jobless Rate..................4.6
Altitude (ft.) 753-472	Retail Sales ... $2,023,111,192
Rainfall (in.) 36.9	Gross Sales ... $3,980,495,733
Jan. min. 33	Reg. Voters 122,114
July max. 96	Election Turnout 55.6
Grow. Season (days).....230	Vehicles 227,286
Total Income (mil.) ..$5,386	Lane Miles 1,212
Per Capita Income...$22,777	Tax Value.....$18,313,490,109
Total Wages.....$2,021,455,188	Fed. Spending....$333,636
Housing 103,469	Defense Spending .. $49,990

Vital Statistics, 1989: Births, 4,213; Deaths, 994; Marriages, 3,170; Divorces, 1,245.

Ethnicity, 1990: White, 235,290 (89.1%); Black, 10,925 (4.1%); American Indian, 1,112 (0.4%); Asian, 7,480 (2.8%); Hispanic, 18,158 (6.9%); Other, 9,229 (3.5%).

Recreation: Fishing, water sports on **Lake Lavon,** other lakes; historic sites; old homes restoration, tours; **Heard Natural Science Museum,** McKinney Historical District, Old Collin County Post Office, **Bolin Wildlife Ex-**hibit; hot-air balloon festival in September and local events in Plano.

Minerals: Limited stone production.

Agriculture: Agricultural income equally divided between crops, livestock; sorghums, wheat, hay, cotton, chief crops; beef cattle, horses raised.

Business: Varied manufacturing plants, agribusinesses, retail and wholesale center; many residents work in Dallas.

McKINNEY (21,283) county seat; agribusiness, trade center; varied industry; hospital, nursing homes; fashion outlet; museums.

Plano (128,673 in Collin, partly in Denton County); one of the state's fastest-growing cities; varied manufacturing; newspaper printing; research center; growing commercial and financial center; hospital, nursing homes, medical and psychiatric centers.

Other towns are **Allen** (18,309); **Anna** (904); **Blue Ridge** (521); **Celina** (1,737); **Dallas** (26,325 in Collin, mostly in Dallas County); **Fairview** (1,554); **Farmersville** (2,640); **Frisco** (5,873 in Collin, partly in Denton County); **Garland** (15 in Collin, mostly in Dallas County); **Josephine** (492 in Collin, mostly in Hunt County); **Lavon** (303); **Lowry Crossing** (865); **Lucas** (2,205); **Melissa** (557); **Murphy** (1,547); **Nevada** (456); **New Hope** (523); **Parker** (1,235); **Princeton** (2,321); **Prosper** (1,018); **Richardson** (9,979 in Collin, mostly in Dallas County); **Royse City** (167 in Collin, mostly in Rockwall County); **Sachse** (194 in Collin, mostly in Dallas County); **Saint Paul** (415); **Westminister** (388); **Weston** (362); **Wylie** (8,662).

See map on next page.

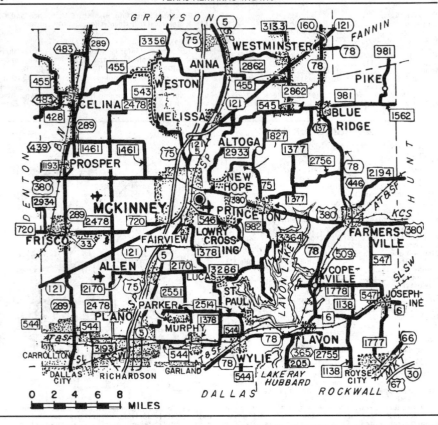

Collingsworth County

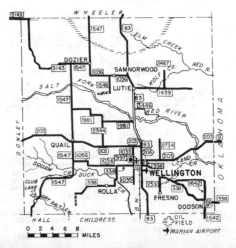

LOCATION: In Panhandle (D-11).

Cong. Dist. 13	U.S. Jud. Dist. ....N-Am.
St. Sen. Dist. 31	Ct. Appeals......................7
St. Rep. Dist. 84	Admin. Jud. Dist. 9
St. Dist. Cts. 100	

History: Created, 1876, from Bexar and Young districts, organized 1890. Named for Republic of Texas' first chief justice, James Collinsworth (name misspelled in law).

Physical Features: Rolling, broken terrain, draining to Red River forks; sandy and loam soils.

Population..................3,573	Av. Weekly Wage $278.67
Area (sq. mi) 919.4	Density 4
Land Area 918.8	Water Area 0.6
Civilian Labor 1,990	Jobless Rate 4.7
Altitude (ft.) 2,389-1,789	Retail Sales $11,933,051
Rainfall (in.) 21.2	Gross Sales........ $35,091,893
Jan. min. 23	Reg. Voters 2,368
July max. 96	Election Turnout......... 47.0
Grow. Season (days)..... 212	Vehicles 3,826
Total Income (mil.) $46	Lane Miles 453
Per Capita Income...$12,801	Tax Value...$130,527,310
Total Wages....... $11,911,382	Fed. Spending.........$18,308
Housing.....................1,951	Defense Spending $414

Vital Statistics, 1989: Births, 50; Deaths, 51; Marriages, 51; Divorces, 11.

Ethnicity, 1990: White, 2,977 (83.3%); Black, 230 (6.4%); American Indian, 32 (0.9%); Asian, 3 (0.1%); Hispanic, 561 (15.7%); Other, 331 (9.3%).

Recreation: Children's camp, county museum, pioneer park.

Minerals: Gas, oil production.

Agriculture: Major income from cotton, grains, peanuts; cow-calf operation, stocker cattle; 25,000 acres cotton, peanuts, alfalfa irrigated.

Business: Chiefly agribusinesses, varied manufacturing.

WELLINGTON (2,456) county seat; railroad spikes, furniture, mattresses manufactured; agribusiness; hospital, nursing home. Other town, **Dodson** (113).

Colorado County

LOCATION: Southeast (N-18).

Cong. Dist. 14	U.S. Jud. Dist. ....S-Hn.
St. Sen. Dist. 5	Ct. Appeals..................1, 14
St. Rep. Dist. 30	Admin. Jud. Dist. 3
St. Dist. Cts...........25, 2D25	

History: Created 1836, an original county, organized 1837. Named for Colorado River.

Physical Features: Three soil areas; level to rolling; bisected by Colorado River; oaks leading timber.

Population................	18,383	Av . Weekly Wage....	$309.36
Area (sq. mi)	973.6	Density	19
Land Area	963.0	Water Area	10.6
Civilian Labor	7,022	Jobless Rate.................	3.6
Altitude (ft.)	450-151	Retail les	$145,458,649
Rainfall (in.)	41.4	Gross Sales.......	$310,685,546
Jan. min.	39	Reg. Voters	11,012
July max.	96	Election Turnout.........	46.8
Grow. Season (days).....	280	Vehicles	18,525
Total Income (mil.)	$284	Lane Miles	761
Per Capita Income...	$15,485	Tax Value......	$1,296,978,789
Total Wages.......	$88,703,080	Fed. Spending	$65,583
Housing......................	8,538	Defense Spending	$2,810

Vital Statistics, 1989: Births, 244; Deaths, 245; Marriages, 123; Divorces, 63.

Ethnicity, 1990: White, 13,352 (72.6%); Black, 3,118 (17.0%); American Indian, 30 (0.2%); Asian, 16 (0.1%); Hispanic, 2,833 (15.4%); Other, 1,867 (10.2%).

Recreation: Hunting, many historic sites, homes; **Attwater Prairie Chicken Refuge**; Wild and Wooly Weekend, first weekend in October.

Minerals: Gas, oil, sand and gravel, stone.

Agriculture: Major crops are rice, corn, grain sorghums; cow-calf operations important; 48,000 acres of rice irrigated.

Business: Agribusinesses; oil-field services and equipment manufacturing; plants process minerals.

COLUMBUS (3,367) county seat; agribusiness center; oil-field servicing; oil-field tanks manufactured; hospital, nursing home; historical sites, homes, walking tour. Other towns are **Eagle Lake** (3,551), wildflower celebration; **Weimar** (2,052), feed mill, light industry, hospital; "Gedenke" on Saturday before Mother's Day.

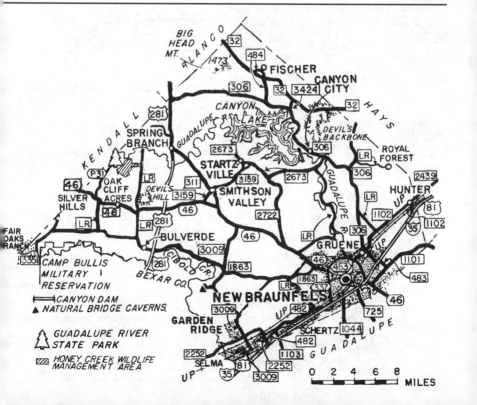

Comal County

LOCATION: South central (N-14).

Cong. Dist. 21   U.S. Jud. Dist. ....W-SAnt.
St. Sen. Dist. 21   Ct. Appeals...................... 3
St. Rep. Dist. 46   Admin. Jud. Dist. 3
St. Dist. Cts........ 22, 207, 274

History: Created and organized from Bexar, Gonzales, Travis counties, 1846; named for Comal River.

Physical Features: Hilly; spring-fed streams; 2.5-mile-long Comal River called "shortest U.S. river," Guadalupe River; Canyon Lake.

Population................ 51,832	Av. Weekly Wage $311.55
Area (sq. mi) 574.5	Density 93
Land Area 561.4	Water Area 13.1
Civilian Labor 25,177	Jobless Rate................. 5.0
Altitude (ft.) 1,473-623	Retail Sales $847,926,913
Rainfall (in.) 33.6	Gross Sales.... $1,190,153,186
Jan. min. 38	Reg. Voters 27,565
July max. 96	Election Turnout 51.3
Grow. Season (days)..... 261	Vehicles 50,568
Total Income (mil.) $873	Lane Miles 598
Per Capita Income...$16,653	Tax Value...... $2,961,005,049
Total Wages......$272,772,761	Fed. Spending $187,336
Housing.................... 22,933	Defense Spending ... $71,972

Vital Statistics, 1989: Births, 767; Deaths, 431; Marriages, 598; Divorces, 286.

Ethnicity, 1990: White, 46,821 (90.3%); Black, 443 (0.9%); American Indian, 148 (0.3%); Asian, 164 (0.3%); Hispanic, 11,864 (22.9%); Other, 4,256 (8.2%).

Recreation: Tourist center; fishing, hunting; historic sites, museum; scenic drives; **Canyon Lake** facilities; **Landa Park** with 76 species of trees, **Prince Solms Park**, other county parks; **Natural Bridge Caverns; New Braunfels Rose Garden;** river resorts, lodges, river sports; Schlitterbohn water park; Wurstfest in November, other local events, old homes.

Minerals: Stone, lime, sand and gravel.

Agriculture: Beef cattle, sheep, Angora goats, swine, exotic animals top revenue; corn, grain sorghums, wheat, oats; some low-volume drip irrigation for Christmas trees.

Business: Varied manufacturing; tourist business; county in San Antonio MSA.

NEW BRAUNFELS (27,091, partly in Guadalupe County) county seat; varied manufacturing; retail, distribution; tourist center, rose garden; hospital, nursing homes; library; center for retarded; local events. Other towns, **Canyon Lake** (9,975), **Fair Oaks Ranch** (51 in Comal County, partly in Bexar, Kendall counties), **Garden Ridge** (1,450), **Schertz** (129 in Comal County, partly in Guadalupe, Bexar counties), **Selma** (15 in Comal County, partly in Bexar, Guadalupe counties).

Comanche County

LOCATION: Central (J-14).

Cong. Dist. 17   U.S. Jud. Dist. .... N-WF
St. Sen. Dist. 22   Ct. Appeals...................... 11
St. Rep. Dist. 65   Admin. Jud. Dist. 3
St. Dist. Cts.................. 220

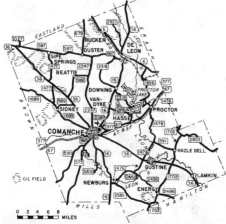

History: Created, organized, 1856, from Bosque, Coryell counties; named for plains Indians.

Physical Features: Rolling, hilly; sandy, loam, waxy soils; drains to Leon River, Proctor Lake; pecans, oaks, mesquites, cedars.

Population............... 13,381	Av . Weekly Wage.... $285.92
Area (sq. mi) 947.6	Density 14
Land Area 937.7	Water Area 9.9
Civilian Labor 5,090	Jobless Rate................. 6.4
Altitude (ft.) 1,847-1,056	Retail Sales $69,752,781
Rainfall (in.) 29.3	Gross Sales....... $151,750,345
Jan. min. 30	Reg. Voters 7,178
July max. 95	Election Turnout 49.0
Grow. Season (days)..... 238	Vehicles 13,416
Total Income (mil.) $176	Lane Miles 726
Per Capita Income...$14,385	Tax Value...... $568,336,877
Total Wages....... $44,053,104	Fed. Spending $48,536
Housing....................6,718	Defense Spending $1,820

Vital Statistics, 1989: Births, 181; Deaths, 202; Marriages, 93; Divorces, 56.

Ethnicity, 1990: White, 12,297 (91.9%); Black, 16 (0.1%); American Indian, 51 (0.4%); Asian, 8 (0.1%); Hispanic, 2,205 (16.5%); Other, 1,009 (7.5%).

Recreation: Hunting, fishing, water sports, **Proctor Lake;** parks, community center, museums; Pow-Wow in September, rodeo in July, other local events.

Minerals: Limited gas, oil, stone, clay.

Agriculture: Beef, dairy cattle, swine, sheep and goats top revenue; peanuts, grains, hay leading crops; pecans, fruit also produced; substantial irrigation, mostly peanuts.

Business: Peanut- and pecan-shelling plants; other agribusinesses; food, other processing; manufacturing.

COMANCHE (4,087) county seat; plants process feed, food; chemical warfare suit factory; varied manufacturing; agribusiness; hospital, nursing home; public library; state's oldest courthouse, "Old Cora," on display on town square. Other towns are **De Leon** (2,190), marketing center for peanuts, pecans; **Gustine** (430).

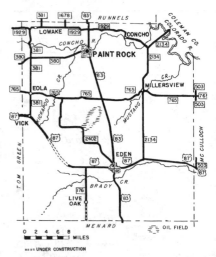

Concho County

LOCATION: Central (K-12).

Cong. Dist. 17   U.S. Jud. Dist. ...... N-SAng
St. Sen. Dist. 24   Ct. Appeals......................
St. Rep. Dist. 67   Admin. Jud. Dist. ....
St. Dist. Cts............. 119, 198

History: Created from Bexar District, 1858, organized 1879; named for Concho River.

Physical Features: Rough, broken area to south; level in north; sandy, loam and dark soils; drains to creeks and Colorado River.

Population.................3,044	Av. Weekly Wage $251.2
Area (sq. mi) 993.7	Density ....
Land Area 991.5	Water Area .... 2.

Civilian Labor 1,786	Jobless Rate................... 3.9
Altitude (ft.) 2,083-1,631	Retail Sales $6,453,483
Rainfall (in.) 23.9	Gross Sales.......... $9,091,801
Jan. min. 33	Reg. Voters 1,730
July max. 97	Election Turnout 56.1
Grow. Season (days)..... 228	Vehicles 3,128
Total Income (mil.) $45	Lane Miles 418
Per Capita Income...$18,002	Tax Value......... $281,282,637
Total Wages........$8,701,424	Fed. Spending $15,502
Housing...................... 1,514	Defense Spending $485

Vital Statistics, 1989: Births, 24; Deaths, 34; Marriages, 14; Divorces, 11.

Ethnicity, 1990: White, 2,718 (89.3%); Black, 16 (0.5%); American Indian, 5 (0.2%); Asian, 5 (0.2%); Hispanic, 1,194 (39.2%); Other, 300 (9.9%).

Recreation: Famed for 1,500 **Indian pictographs**, largest collection known; local events; **O. H. Ivie Reservoir.**

Minerals: Oil, gas, stone produced.

Agriculture: Leading sheep-producing county; cattle, goats also raised; wheat, feed grains, cotton chief crops; 10,000 acres irrigated for cotton.

Business: Chiefly agribusinesses.

PAINT ROCK (227) county seat; named for Indian pictographs; farming, ranching center; **Eden** (1,567) steel fabrication, detention center; hospital, nursing home; fall fest in September.

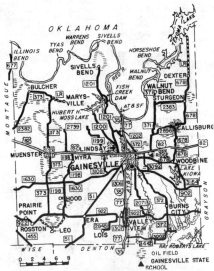

Cooke County

LOCATION: North central, adjoins Oklahoma (F-16).

Cong. Dist. 17, 26	U.S. Jud. Dist. .... E-Sh.
St. Sen. Dist. 30	Ct. Appeals..................... 2
St. Rep. Dist. 63	Admin. Jud. Dist. 8
St. Dist. Cts. 235	

History: Created, organized, 1848, from Fannin County; named for Capt. W.G. Cooke of the Texas Revolution.

Physical Features: Drains to Red, Trinity rivers; Texoma Lake in northeast corner; sandy, red, loam soils.

Population................. 30,777	Av. Weekly Wage $337.62
Area (sq. mi) 898.7	Density 34
Land Area 873.7	Water Area 25.0
Civilian Labor 12,409	Jobless Rate.................... 5.1
Altitude (ft.) 1,007-636	Retail Sales $217,842,300
Rainfall (in.) 33.0	Gross Sales....... $381,551,479
Jan. min. 28	Reg. Voters 15,571
July max. 96	Election Turnout 50.5
Grow. Season (days)..... 226	Vehicles 30,056
Total Income (mil.) $405	Lane Miles 832
Per Capita Income...$13,242	Tax Value..... $1,197,581,455
Total Wages......$167,308,711	Fed. Spending $79,233
Housing.................... 13,311	Defense Spending $6,917

Vital Statistics, 1989: Births, 464; Deaths, 300; Marriages, 628; Divorces, 195.

Ethnicity, 1990: White, 28,375 (92.2%); Black, 1,169

(3.8%); American Indian, 232 (0.8%); Asian, 131 (0.4%); Hispanic, 1,408 (4.6%); Other, 870 (2.8%).

Recreation: Water sports; **Ray Roberts Lake, Moss Lake;** hunting, fishing; **Frank Buck Zoo;** museum; park; local events.

Minerals: Oil, gas, sand and gravel.

Agriculture: Most income from beef, dairy operations, sheep, goats hogs, horses; crops include wheat, oats, grain sorghums, peanuts, hay; some irrigation for hay, peanuts; some firewood sold.

Business: Agribusinesses, oil industries, varied manufacturing.

GAINESVILLE (14,256) county seat; aircraft, steel fabrication, tourism; agribusiness center; zoo, parks, Victorian homes, walking tours; historic homes; **Cooke County College, Gainesville State School; Camp Sweeney** for diabetic children.

Other towns, **Muenster** (1,387), dairy center, food processing, oil production, varied manufacturing; hospital, nursing home; Germanfest in April; **Callisburg** (344); **Lindsay** (610); **Oak Ridge** (180); **Valley View** (640).

Coryell County

LOCATION: Central (K-15).

Cong. Dist. 11	U.S. Jud. Dist. .... W-Wa.
St. Sen. Dist. 24	Ct. Appeals..................... 10
St. Rep. Dist. 57	Admin. Jud. Dist. 3
St. Dist. Cts. 52	

History: Created from Bell County, organized, 1854; named for local pioneer, James Coryell.

Physical Features: Leon Valley in center, remainder rolling, hilly.

Population................ 64,213	Av. Weekly Wage $308.64
Area (sq. mi) 1,056.7	Density 61
Land Area 1,051.8	Water Area 4.9
Civilian Labor 17,269	Jobless Rate.................... 8.6
Altitude (ft.) 1,839-1,365	Retail Sales $135,482,354
Rainfall in.) 32.5	Gross Sales....... $197,801,034
Jan. min. 34	Reg. Voters 17,059
July max. 97	Election Turnout 45.8
Grow. Season (days)..... 241	Vehicles 32,638
Total Income (mil.) $740	Lane Miles 680
Per Capita Income...$11,906	Tax Value..... $914,766,591
Total Wages......$137,895,091	Fed. Spending $112,522
Housing.................... 18,841	Defense Spending ... $36,350

Vital Statistics, 1989: Births, 1,003; Deaths, 288; Marriages, 335; Divorces, 201.

Ethnicity, 1990: White, 45,078 (70.2%); Black, 13,592 (21.2%); American Indian, 461 (0.7%); Asian, 1,670 (2.6%); Hispanic, 6,243 (9.7%); Other, 3,412 (5.3%).

Recreation: **Mother Neff State Park;** hunting; nearby lakes and Leon River. **Fort Hood** brings many visitors; historic homes; log jail; Shivaree in June, Rabbit Fest in May, Oktoberfest in October, other local events.

Minerals: Small stone, sand and gravel production.

Agriculture: Beef cattle, horses, sheep, goats, turkeys, hogs are revenue producers; grains, hay, pecans produced, soybeans introduced; some irrigation; cedar posts.

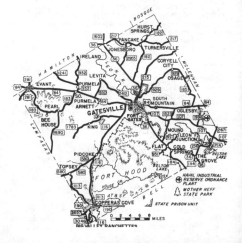

Coryell Co. (Cont.)

Business: Fort Hood military business, agribusinesses, plastics and other manufacturing.

GATESVILLE (11,492) county seat; varied manufacturing; four state prison units; refurbished courthouse; museum; historic buildings; Harvest Fest in October, antique shows, branch **Central Texas College.** Other towns include **Copperas Cove** (24,079 in Coryell County, partly in Lampasas County), business center for Fort Hood; industrial filters, other manufacturing; hospital; **Central Texas College; Evant** (335, partly in Hamilton County); **Fort Gates** (818, partly in Bell County); **Fort Hood** (18,559 in Coryell County, partly in Bell County); **Oglesby** (452); **South Mountain** (301).

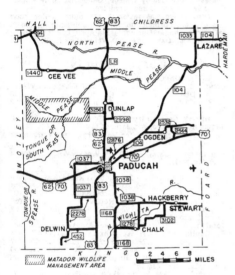

Cottle County

LOCATION: Northwest (E-11).

Cong. Dist. ....13 U.S. Jud. Dist. ....N-WF
St. Sen. Dist. ....30 Ct. Appeals......................7
St. Rep. Dist. ....78 Admin. Jud. Dist. 9
St. Dist. Cts......................50

History: Created 1876 from Fannin County; organized 1892; named for George W. Cottle, Alamo hero.

Physical Features: Rough in west, level in east; gray, black, sandy and loam soils; drains to Pease River.

Population..................2,247	Av. Weekly Wage $328.10
Area (sq. mi) 901.6	Density 3
Land Area 901.2	Water Area 0.4
Civilian Labor 1,101	Jobless Rate..................3.0
Altitude (ft.) 2,149-1,605	Retail Sales $10,628,005
Rainfall (in.) 22.0	Gross Sales.......$13,600,860
Jan. min. 26	Reg. Voters 1,623
July max. 97	Election Turnout.........46.3
Grow. Season (days).....219	Vehicles 2,432
Total Income (mil.) $37	Lane Miles 391
Per Capita Income...$17,620	Tax Value.........$133,146,933
Total Wages.......$25,625,992	Fed. Spending.........$13,308
Housing.....................1,286	Defense Spending $74

Vital Statistics, 1989: Births, 27; Deaths, 36; Marriages, 11; Divorces, 6.

Ethnicity, 1990: White, 1,853 (82.5%); Black, 199 (8.9%); American Indian, 4 (0.2%); Asian, 3 (0.1%); Hispanic, 367 (16.3%); Other, 188 (8.4%).

Recreation: Settlers reunion in April, junior rodeo in August; hunting; **Matador Wildlife Management Area.**

Minerals: Not significant.

Agriculture: Major income from cotton, grains, alfalfa; cow-calf operations, stocker cattle, horses raised; some irrigation.

Business: Chiefly agribusinesses; gasoline manufacturing.

PADUCAH (1,788) county seat; agribusiness, petroleum center; hospital; local events.

Crane County

LOCATION: Southwest (J-7).

Cong. Dist. ....21 U.S. Jud. Dist. ....W-M-O
St. Sen. Dist. ....25 Ct. Appeals......................8
St. Rep. Dist. ....69 Admin. Jud. Dist. 7
St. Dist. Cts..................109

History: Created from Tom Green County, 1887, organized 1927; named for Baylor University President W. C. Crane.

Physical Features: Rolling prairie, Pecos Valley, some hills; sandy, loam soils; Juan Cordona Lake.

Population..................4,652	Av. Weekly Wage $480.26
Area (sq. mi.) 785.6	Density 6
Land Area 785.6	Water Area 0.0
Civilian Labor 1,450	Jobless Rate..................4.3
Altitude (ft.).......2,902-2,475	Retail Sales $22,182,023
Rainfall (in.) 12.0	Gross Sales.......$53,472,833
Jan. min. 29	Reg. Voters 2,680
July max. 96	Election Turnout.........62.4
Grow. Season (days).....225	Vehicles 5,468
Total Income (mil.) $61	Lane Miles 318
Per Capita Income...$14,305	Tax Value......$1,310,705,020
Total Wages.......$41,905,635	Fed. Spending..........$6,576
Housing.....................1,795	Defense Spending $47

Vital Statistics, 1989: Births, 87; Deaths, 33; Marriages, 37; Divorces, 16.

Ethnicity, 1990: White, 3,097 (66.6%); Black, 130 (2.8%); American Indian, 11 (0.2%); Asian, 10 (0.2%); Hispanic, 1,577 (33.9%); Other, 1,404 (30.2%).

Recreation: Local events; sites of pioneer trails and historic Horsehead Crossing on Pecos River; camping park.

Minerals: Among leaders in oil, gas production.

Agriculture: Cattle ranching top revenue producer; very little farming.

Business: Oil-based economy.

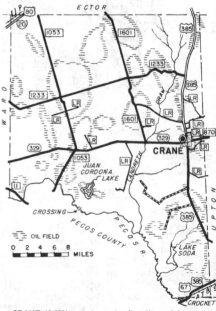

CRANE (3,533) county seat; oil-well servicing, production; foundry; steel, surfboard manufacturing; hospital, nursing home.

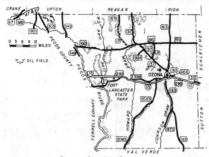

Crockett County

LOCATION: Southwest (L-9).

Cong. Dist.	21	U.S. Jud. Dist. ...... N-SAng.
St. Sen. Dist.	25	Ct. Appeals 8
St. Rep. Dist.	67	Admin. Jud. Dist. 6
St. Dist. Cts.	112	

History: Created 1875 from Bexar, organized 1891; named for Alamo hero, David Crockett.

Physical Features: Level to rough, hilly terrain; drains to Pecos River on south; rocky soils.

Population	4,078	Av. Weekly Wage	$330.32
Area (sq. mi.)	2,807.6	Density	1
Land Area	2,807.6	Water Area	0.0
Civilian Labor	1,756	Jobless Rate	5.8
Altitude (ft.)	3,958-1,824	Retail Sales	$23,946,850
Rainfall (in.)	18.2	Gross Sales	$35,118,250
Jan. min.	31	Reg. Voters	2,568
July max.	97	Election Turnout	39.7
Grow. Season (days)	233	Vehicles	3,919
Total Income (mil.)	$61	Lane Miles	781
Per Capita Income	$14,743	Tax Value	$644,757,172
Total Wages	$23,514,637	Fed. Spending	$14,597
Housing	1,897	Defense Spending	$155

Vital Statistics, 1989: Births, 57; Deaths, 29; Marriages, 23; Divorces, 1.

Ethnicity, 1990: White, 4,018 (98.5%); Black, 39 (1.0%); American Indian, 9 (0.2%); Asian, 4 (0.1%); Hispanic, 2,021 (49.6%); Other, 8 (0.2%).

Recreation: Hunting; historic sites, **Fort Lancaster State Park;** county museum; Davy Crockett statue in park.

Minerals: Oil, gas production.

Agriculture: A major sheep, Angora goat producing county; income also from beef cattle.

Business: Oil, ranching.

OZONA (3,181) county seat; trade center for ranching; hunting leases; tourism; hospital, nursing home.

Crosby County

LOCATION: Northwest (F-9).

Cong. Dist.	17	U.S. Jud. Dist. .... N-Lb.
St. Sen. Dist.	28	Ct. Appeals 7
St. Rep. Dist.	84	Admin. Jud. Dist. 9
St. Dist. Cts.	72	

History: Created from Bexar District 1876, organized 1886; named for Texas Land Commissioner Stephen Crosby.

Physical Features: Flat, rich soil above Caprock, broken below; drains into Brazos River forks and playas.

Population	7,304	Av. Weekly Wage	$291.07
Area (sq. mi.)	901.6	Density	8
Land Area	899.5	Water Area	2.1
Civilian Labor	3,092	Jobless Rate	4.7
Altitude (ft.)	3,167-2,369	Retail Sales	$33,810,051
Rainfall (in.)	20.5	Gross Sales	$65,706,440
Jan. min.	24	Reg. Voters	3,820
July max.	93	Election Turnout	44.8
Grow. Season (days)	206	Vehicles	6,452
Total Income (mil.)	$96	Lane Miles	569
Per Capita Income	$12,529	Tax Value	$264,831,735
Total Wages	$30,241,223	Fed. Spending	$29,675
Housing	3,312	Defense Spending	$106

Vital Statistics, 1989: Births, 123; Deaths, 86; Marriages, 32; Divorces, 27.

Ethnicity, 1990: White, 5,784 (79.2%); Black, 321 (4.4%); American Indian, 13 (0.2%); Asian, 8 (0.1%); Hispanic, 3,111 (42.6%); Other, 1,178 (16.1%).

Recreation: White River Lake; Silver Falls Park; Crosby County Pioneer Museum at Crosbyton and Ralls Historical Museum have many American Indian artifacts; Crosbyton solar power plant; God's Country outdoor theater in August, county fair in September.

Minerals: Sand, gravel, oil and gas.

Agriculture: Cotton, grain sorghums, wheat, hay, vegetables produced; cattle, hogs, sheep raised; about 142,000 acres irrigated.

Business: Agribusinesses, food processing, clothes manufacturing, gasohol plant; tourism; drug and alcohol treatment center.

CROSBYTON (2,026) county seat; agribusiness center; hospital, nursing homes. Other towns are **Lorenzo** (1,208), **Ralls** (2,172), nursing home.

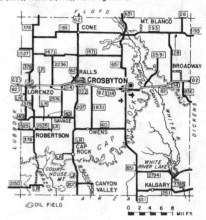

Culberson County

LOCATION: Far west (J-4).

Cong. Dist. 16	U.S. Jud. Dist. ....W-Pe.
St. Sen. Dist. 25	Ct. Appeals.....................8
St. Rep. Dist. 69	Admin. Jud. Dist. 6
St. Dist. Cts........ 34, 205, 210	

History: Created from El Paso County 1911, organized 1912; named for D.B. Culberson, Texas congressman.

Physical Features: Texas' highest mountains, entire county over 3,000 feet in elevation; slopes toward Pecos Valley on east, Diablo Bolson on west; salt lakes; unique vegetation in canyons.

Population.................3,407	Av . Weekly Wage.... $405.29
Area (sq. mi.) 3,812.8	Density 1
Land Area 3,812.6	Water Area 0.2
Civilian Labor 1,648	Jobless Rate..................6.8
Altitude (ft.).......8,749-3,021	Retail Sales $25,360,702
Rainfall (in.) 11.1	Gross Sales $35,754,704
Jan. min. 30	Reg. Voters 1,747
July max. 95	Election Turnout 39.8
Grow. Season (days).....224	Vehicles 2,344
Total Income (mil.) $35	Lane Miles 744
Per Capita Income...$11,240	Tax Value......... $397,172,984
Total Wages....... $28,134,930	Fed. Spending $7,065
Housing.....................1,297	Defense Spending $92

Vital Statistics, 1989: Births, 71; Deaths, 19; Marriages, 29; Divorces, 10.

Ethnicity, 1990: White, 2,400 (70.4%); Black, 2 (0.1%); American Indian, 16 (0.5%); Asian, 27 (0.8%); Hispanic, 2,-419 (71.0%); Other, 962 (28.2%).

Recreation: Guadalupe Mountains National Park; Guadalupe and El Capitan, twin peaks; scenic canyons and mountains; historical museum at Van Horn; historical salt deposits.

Minerals: Sulphur, gas, marble.

Agriculture: Income from beef cattle; crops include cotton, pecans; 2,500 acres in irrigation.

Business: Agribusinesses; tourism; talc mining, processing; oil production; county fair in September, frontier days in June.

VAN HORN (2,930) county seat; convention center; ranching; rock crushing; hospital; airport; tourism.

Dallam County

LOCATION: Northwestern corner (A-7).

Cong. Dist. 13	U.S. Jud. Dist. .... N-Am.
St. Sen. Dist. 31	Ct. Appeals.....................7
St. Rep. Dist. 88	Admin. Jud. Dist. 9
St. Dist. Cts.................69	

History: Created from Bexar District, 1876, organized 1891. Named for lawyer-editor James W. Dallam.

Physical Features: Prairie, over 3,800-foot elevation, broken by creeks; playas; sandy, loam soils; **Rita Blanca National Grasslands.**

Population.................5,461	Av. Weekly Wage $304.58
Area (sq. mi.) 1,505.3	Density 4
Land Area 1,504.8	Water Area 0.5
Civilian Labor 3,231	Jobless Rate..................3.5
Altitude (ft.).......4,693-3,869	Retail Sales $50,619,365
Rainfall (in.) 16.5	Gross Sales $124,682,816
Jan. min. 18	Reg. Voters 2,467
July max. 91	Election Turnout 52.6
Grow. Season (days)..... 178	Vehicles 5,624
Total Income (mil.) $95	Lane Miles 592
Per Capita Income...$17,761	Tax Value......... $261,447,098
Total Wages....... $32,199,003	Fed. Spending $31,786
Housing.....................2,574	Defense Spending $311

Vital Statistics, 1989: Births, 90; Deaths, 67; Marriages, 76; Divorces, 29.

Ethnicity, 1990: White, 4,600 (84.2%); Black, 112 (2.1%); American Indian, 43 (0.8%); Asian, 14 (0.3%); Hispanic, 1,-151 (21.1%); Other, 692 (12.7%).

Recreation: Local events; Interstate Fair in September; XIT Museum; **XIT Rodeo and Reunion** in August; La Rita Theater in June-August; **Lake Rita Blanca** in Hartley County.

Minerals: Not significant.

Agriculture: Income from beef cattle, feedlots; corn, wheat, grain sorghums; pinto beans introduced; substantial irrigation.

Business: Agribusinesses, tourism, small manufacturing.

DALHART (4,001 in Dallam County, partly in Hartley County) county seat; **Frank Phillips College** branch, agribusiness center for parts of Texas, New Mexico, Oklahoma; railroad; feedlots; some manufacturing; hospital, nursing home. Other town, **Texline** (425).

Dallas County

LOCATION: North central (H-17).

Cong. Dist. 3, 5, 6, 24	St. Dist. Cts. 14, 44, 68,
St. Sen. Dist....... 2, 8, 9, 10,	95, 101, 116, 134, 160, 162,
16, 23	191, 192, 193, 194, 195, 203,
Rep. Dist..............98-114	204, 254, 255, 256, 265, 282,
U.S. Jud. Dist. .... N-Dl.	283, 291, 292, 298, 301, 302,
Ct. Appeals 5	303, 304, 305, 330, Cr. 1,
Admin. Jud. Dist. 1	Cr. 2, Cr. 3, Cr. 4, Cr. 5

History: Created, organized, 1846 from Nacogdoches, Robertson counties; named for U.S. Vice President **George Mifflin Dallas.**

Physical Features: Mostly flat, heavy Blackland soils, sandy clays in west; drains to Trinity River tributaries.

Population.............1,852,810	Av. Weekly Wage $516.16
Area (sq. mi.)..............908.7	Density 2,105
Land Area 879.8	Water Area 28.9
Civilian Labor 1,095,660	Jobless Rate..................5.3
Altitude (ft.)............584-382	Retail Sales .. 21,170,622,158
Rainfall (in.) 35.9	Gross Sales .. 79,365,336,060
Jan. min. 36	Reg. Voters 802,952
July max. 95	Election Turnout 50.3
Grow. Season (days).... 235	Vehicles 1,551,252
Total Income (mil.) ..$36,744	Lane Miles 3,008
Per Capita Income...$19,602	Tax Value..... $95,565,296,097
Total Wages.. $30,748,449,011	Fed. Spending 5,766,776
Housing.................793,938	Defense Spending 1,862,128

Vital Statistics, 1989: Births, 36,153; Deaths, 12,295; Marriages, 16,330; Divorces, 12,221.

Ethnicity, 1990: White, 1,241,455 (67.0%); Black, 369,597 (19.9%); American Indian, 9,437 (0.5%); Asian, 52,238 (2.8%); Hispanic, 315,630 (17.0%); Other, 180,083 (9.7%).

Recreation: Dallas County is one of the state's top tourist destinations and one of the nation's most popular convention centers. Its major attractions include cultural, athletic and special events including the **State Fair of Texas** in October, conventions and trade shows. Year-round attractions include the **Hall of State, Museum of Art, the Science Place, Museum of Natural History, SMU Owens Fine Arts Center, Biblical Arts Center; Dallas Zoo; Dallas Theater Center, the West End Historic District, Mobil Cotton Bowl on Jan. 1;** many historical sites, including a museum in the old Texas School Book Depository, from which the shot was fired that killed President John F. Kennedy in 1963. Other attractions include the **Morton H. Meyerson Symphony Center;** performing arts and professional theater; professional and amateur sports; the Texas broadcast museum; special shows; nearby lakes; several theme and amusement parks.

Minerals: Production of sand, gravel, cement, stone, clays.

Agriculture: Horticultural crops top revenue source; grain sorghums, wheat, hay, assorted fruits and vegetables grown; horses, calves, breeder cattle raised.

Business: A national center for insurance, banking, transportation, electronics manufacturing, data processing, conventions and trade shows; more than 3,000 plants make apparel, building material, food, oil-field supplies, electronics and many other products; **Dallas Market Center** is the focal point for many international exhibitions, 500 foreign firms, 18 foreign banks have offices in the city; foreign-trade zone located at D/FW International Airport, U.S. Customs point of entry; more than 130 million feet of office space; more than 100 companies relocated to Dallas in the past decade.

EDUCATION: The following universities and colleges are located in Dallas County: **Southern Methodist University, University of Dallas, Dallas Baptist College, University of Texas at Dallas, Dallas Theological Seminary, University of Texas Southwestern Medical Center, Baylor College of Dentistry, Baylor University School of Nursing, Texas Woman's University Dallas Center** on two campuses, **Dallas County Community College System** with seven campuses, **Northwood Institute, Amber University, East Texas State University Metroplex Commuter Facility, Dallas Bible College** and Dallas Christian College.

DALLAS (966,168 in Dallas County, partly in Collin, Denton, Kaufman counties) county seat; second-largest city in Texas; center for commerce, transportation, banking, insurance, retail and wholesale trade; manufacturing, distribution, data-processing center; a major tourist center; **D/FW International Airport** is world's largest in acreage and one of the world's busiest in emplanements; world headquarters for the **U.S. Army and Air Force Exchange Service;** 11th District, Federal Reserve Bank; Naval Air Station; more than 1,800 corporate headquarters; a leader in fashions and in computer operations; outstanding medical centers, whose researchers have won two Nobel Prizes in the past decade; headquarters for the Boy Scouts of America and many trade associations; second nationally in the number of conventions, trade and marketing shows; **Dallas Convention Center** in downtown Dallas has 1.9 million square feet under one roof with more than 600,000 square feet of exhibit space and 75 meeting rooms; **Dallas Market Hall** has more than 200,000 square feet of exhibit space, 17 meeting rooms and a seating capacity of 27,000; other facilities are located on the State Fair grounds; **World Trade Center** is an international market center; Infomart, a large computer-sales complex; Reunion Arena, home of many professional and amateur sporting events, also has convention space and parking facilities; many hotels in downtown area offer adequate accomodations for most conventions (40,000 rooms in greater Dallas area).

Garland (180,635 in Dallas County, partly in Collin, Rockwall counties); varied manufacturing; community college branch; hospital, nursing homes; performing arts center.

Irving (155,037); location of **Texas Stadium, home of the Dallas Cowboys; Las Colinas** business development; medical facilities; some manufacturing, food process-

The water sculpture, Boy and Girl on the Beach, is a central feature at the Dallas Arboretum. Dallas Morning News Photo by William Snyder.

ing; distribution center; University of Dallas, Northlake College, DeVry Institute.

Other large cities include **Mesquite** (101,484); residential city with varied industries; distribution center; Eastfield College; **Mesquite Championship Rodeo;** retail malls; Devil's Bowl Speedway, Mesquite Opry, other events.

Richardson (64,861 in Dallas County, partly in Collin Couny); electronics, telecommunications manufacturing center; Richland College; hospital, nursing homes; Spring Valley Creek Farm, many local events. **Grand Prairie** (81,527 in Dallas County, partly in Ellis, Tarrant counties); defense industries; distribution center; tourist attractions include new wax museum, Traders' Village; hospital, nursing homes; **Joe Pool Reservoir** nearby. **Carrollton** (40,024 in Dallas County, partly in Denton, Collin counties); residential community; distribution center; Perry Homstead Museum, fall heritage festival. **Duncanville** (35,748); varied manufacturing; residential community; near Joe Pool Reservoir, Iris Garden, local events. **Farmers Branch** (24,250); distribution center; varied manufacturing; Brookhaven College; hospital; Folklore Festival in May, other local events.

Smaller communities include **Lancaster** (22,117); industrial, agricultural center; warehouse, distribution facilities; Cedar Valley College; airport; hospital, nursing homes; **DeSoto** (30,544); residential community, varied light industry; annual CityFest in May; nursing homes; **Addison** (8,783), general aviation airport; **Balch Springs** (17,406); **Buckingham** (102); **Cedar Hill** (19,926 in Dallas County, partly in Ellis County), Northwood Institute; **Cockrell Hill** (3,746); **Combine** (434 in Dallas County, mostly in Kaufman County); **Coppell** (16,878 in Dallas County, partly in Denton County); **Glenn Heights** (3,768); **Grapevine** (3 in Dallas County, mostly in Denton, Tarrant counties), gateway to D-FW International Airport; **Highland Park** (8,739); **Hutchins** (2,719), varied manufacturing; **Lewisville** (555 in Dallas County, mostly in Denton County); **Ovilla** (279 in Dallas County, mostly in Ellis County); **Rowlett** (19,907 in Dallas County, partly in Rockwall County), varied manufacturing; hospital; local events; **Sachse** (5,152 in Dallas County, partly in Collin County); **Seagoville** (8,969 in Dallas County, partly in Kaufman County); federal correctional institution; some manufacturing; corporate headquarters; **Sunnyvale** (2,228); **University Park** (22,259), home of **Southern Methodist University; Wilmer** (2,479).

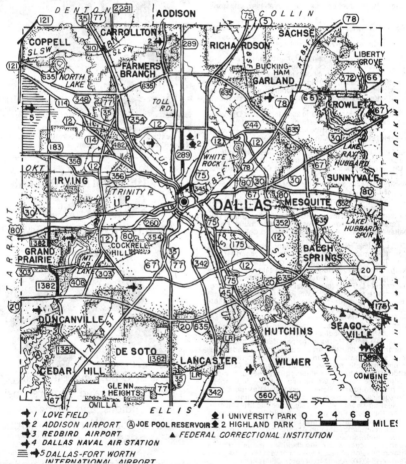

1 *LOVE FIELD*
2 *ADDISON AIRPORT*   Ⓐ*JOE POOL RESERVOIR*
3 *REDBIRD AIRPORT*
4 *DALLAS NAVAL AIR STATION*
5 *DALLAS-FORT WORTH INTERNATIONAL AIRPORT*

♦ 1 *UNIVERSITY PARK*
♦ 2 *HIGHLAND PARK*
▲ *FEDERAL CORRECTIONAL INSTITUTION*

0 2 4 6 8 MILES

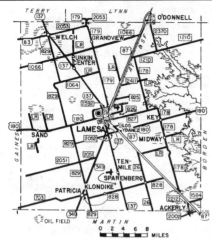

Dawson County

LOCATION: West (H-8).

Cong. Dist. 19	U.S. Jud. Dist. .... N-Lb.
St. Sen. Dist. 28	Ct. Appeals.....................11
St. Rep. Dist. 77	Admin. Jud. Dist. 7
St. Dist. Cts..................106	

History: Created from Bexar District, 1876, organized 1905; named for Nicholas M. Dawson, San Jacinto veteran.

Physical Features: Rolling prairie, broken on the east; loam and sandy soils.

Population................ 14,349	Av. Weekly Wage $304.88
Area (sq. mi.)..............902.1	Density 16
Land Area 902.1	Water Area 0.0
Civilian Labor 7,023	Jobless Rate....................7.4
Altitude (ft.) 3,095-2,860	Retail Sales $96,413,304
Rainfall (in.) 16.2	Gross Sales ... $166,919,264
Jan. min. 25	Reg. Voters 8,316
July max. 95	Election Turnout 44.5
Grow. Season (days)..... 210	Vehicles 12,456
Total Income (mil.) $201	Lane Miles 710
Per Capita Income...$13,819	Tax Value.......... $724,411,551
Total Wages....... $65,381,434	Fed. Spending $51,200
Housing......................5,821	Defense Spending $332

Vital Statistics, 1989: Births, 237; Deaths, 154; Marriages, 139; Divorces, 66.

Ethnicity, 1990: White, 9,789 (68.2%); Black, 622 (4.3%); American Indian, 23 (0.2%); Asian, 19 (0.1%); Hispanic, 6,120 (42.7%); Other, 3,896 (27.2%).

Recreation: Local parks; Dawson County Museum; campground; May Fun Fest; rodeo, county fair, Southwestern Art Show.

Minerals: Oil, natural gas produced.

Agriculture: A major cotton-producing county; also grain sorghums, wheat; cow-calf operation, hogs raised; 38,000 acres irrigated for cotton.

Business: Agribusinesses; oil industries; apparel, farm, gin equipment manufacturing.

LAMESA (10,809) county seat; agribusiness center; food processing, oil-field services; some manufacturing; computerized cotton-classing office; hospital, nursing homes; library, museum; campus of **Howard College**; prison unit under construction.

Other towns are **Ackerly** (153 in Dawson County, partly in Martin County); **Los Ybanez** (83); **O'Donnell** (134 in Dawson County, mostly in Lynn County).

Deaf Smith County

LOCATION: Northwest (C-7).

Cong. Dist. 19	U.S. Jud. Dist. .... N-Am.
St. Sen. Dist. 31	Ct. Appeals..................... 7
St. Rep. Dist. 86	Admin. Jud. Dist. 9
St. Dist. Cts. 222	

History: Created 1876, from Bexar District; organized 1890. Named for famed scout, Erastus (Deaf) Smith.

Physical Features: Level plain, partly broken; chocolate and sandy loam soils; drains to Palo Duro and Tierra Blanca creeks.

Population............... 19,153	Av. Weekly Wage $316.86
Area (sq. mi.).......... 1,498.3	Density 13
Land Area 1,497.4	Water Area 0.9
Civilian Labor 9,028	Jobless Rate....................5.7
Altitude (ft.) 4,362-3,789	Retail Sales $93,139,801
Rainfall (in.) 16.0	Gross Sales ... $299,505,084
Jan. min. 21	Reg. Voters 8,502
July max. 90	Election Turnout 46.2
Grow. Season (days)..... 195	Vehicles 17,424
Total Income (mil.) $293	Lane Miles 601
Per Capita Income...$14,872	Tax Value.......... $670,160,684
Total Wages......$102,385,431	Fed. Spending $62,455
Housing......................7,147	Defense Spending $165

Vital Statistics, 1989: Births, 430; Deaths, 131; Marriages, 167; Divorces, 52.

Ethnicity, 1990: White, 14,522 (75.8%); Black, 307 (1.6%); American Indian, 49 (0.3%); Asian, 39 (0.2%); Hispanic, 9,356 (48.8%); Other, 4,236 (22.1%).

Recreation: Local events, museum, tours; **National Cowgirl Hall of Fame.**

Minerals: Not significant.

Agriculture: One of the state's leading farm-producing counties; large cattle feedlot operations; crops include sorghums, wheat, oats, barley, sugar beets, corn, cotton, onions, other vegetables, sunflowers; 205,000 acres irrigated.

Business: Sugar refinery; meat packers; offset printing; other varied industries, mostly agribusiness.

HEREFORD (14,745) county seat; agribusinesses, food processing; varied manufacturing; hospital, nursing home.

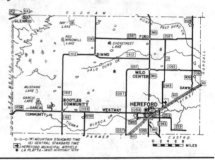

Delta County

LOCATION: Northeast (F-19).

Cong. Dist. 1	U.S. Jud. Dist. ....E-Ps.
St. Sen. Dist. 1	Ct. Appeals..................... 6
St. Rep. Dist. 2	Admin. Jud. Dist. 1
St. Dist. Cts. 8, 62	

History: Created from Lamar, Hopkins counties and organized, 1870. Greek letter delta origin of name, because of shape of the county.

Physical Features: Between two forks of Sulphur River; black, sandy loam soils.

Population...................4,857	Av. Weekly Wage $261.06
Area (sq. mi.).............277.8	Density 17

Delta Co. (Cont.)

Land Area 277.1	Water Area 0.7
Civilian Labor 2,360	Jobless Rate 5.4
Altitude (ft.) 536-396	Retail Sales $10,414,679
Rainfall (in.) 42.7	Gross Sales $16,521,737
Jan. min. 30	Reg. Voters 2,913
July max. 94	Election Turnout 49.8
Grow. Season (days) 233	Vehicles 5,191
Total Income (mil.) $63	Lane Miles 344
Per Capita Income...$13,232	Tax Value......... $136,840,641
Total Wages...... $11,525,107	Fed. Spending $35,689
Housing 2,302	Defense Spending ... $17,660

Vital Statistics, 1989: Births, 58; Deaths, 88; Marriages, 45; Divorces, 19.

Ethnicity, 1990: White, 4,388 (90.3%); Black, 404 (8.3%); American Indian, 41 (0.8%); Asian, 7 (0.1%); Hispanic, 67 (1.4%); Other, 17 (0.4%).

Recreation: Fishing, hunting, local events; **Big Creek Lake** and **Cooper Lake** under construction.

Minerals: Not significant.

Agriculture: Beef, dairy cattle top producers; crops include hay, wheat, soybeans, cotton, grain sorghums.

Business: Agribusinesses; tourism; manufacturing.

COOPER (2,153) county seat; industrial park, some manufacturing; agribusiness; clinic; county museum; county fair in May; other town, **Pecan Gap** (233 in Delta County, partly in Fannin County).

Denton County

LOCATION: North central (G-16).

Cong. Dist. 26	U.S. Jud. Dist. .... E-Sh.
St. Sen. Dist. 10, 22, 30	Ct. Appeals..................... 2
St. Rep. Dist. 59, 61	Admin. Jud. Dist. 8
St. Dist. Cts. 16, 158, 211	

History: Created, organized out of Fannin County, 1846; named for John B. Denton, pioneer minister.

Physical Features: Partly hilly, draining to Trinity River, two lakes; Blackland and Grand Prairie soils.

Population............... 273,525	Av. Weekly Wage.... $372.76
Area (sq. mi.) 957.6	Density 300
Land Area 888.4	Water Area 69.2
Civilian Labor 131,960	Jobless Rate 4.8
Altitude (ft.) 844-515	Retail Sales ... $1,440,590,656
Rainfall (in.) 33.5	Gross Sales.... $3,571,391,966

C O O K E

GRAYSON

PILOT POINT

BOLIVAR

SANGER

AUBREY

KRUGER-VILLE

KRUM

DENTON

CROSS ROADS

LINCOLN PARK

LITTLE ELM

FRISCO

PONDER

CORINTH

SHADY SHORES

NORTH LAKE

ARGYLE

LAKE DALLAS

LEWIS-VILLE LAKE

JUSTIN

COPPER CANYON

HIGHLAND VILLAGE

DOUBLE OAK

LEWISVILLE

PLANO

FLOWER MOUND

HEBRON

DALLAS

ROANOKE

WESTLAKE

CARROLLTON

TARRANT

DALLAS

OIL FIELD

① OAK POINT
② LAKEWOOD VILLAGE
③ THE COLONY
④ MARSHALL CREEK
⑤ HICKORY CREEK
⑥ HACKBERRY
⑦ EASTVALE
⑧ BARTONVILLE
⑨ CORRAL CITY
⑩ COPPELL
⑪ TROPHY CLUB

0 2 4 6 8 MILES

⑫ LAKE LEWISVILLE STATE PARK

Jan. min. 32	Reg. Voters 114,779
July max. 96	Election Turnout 50.1
Grow. Season (days)..... 226	Vehicles 211,892
Total Income (mil.) .. $4,563	Lane Miles 1,217
Per Capita Income...$18,688	Tax Value... $12,824,921,133
Total Wages... $1,280,494,220	Fed. Spending....... $771,263
Housing 111,190	Defense Spending . $503,306

Vital Statistics, 1989: Births, 4,808; Deaths, 1,158; Marriages, 2,354; Divorces, 1,356.

Ethnicity, 1990: White, 241,982 (88.5%); Black, 13,569 (5.0%); American Indian, 1,416 (0.5%); Asian, 6,870 (2.5%); Hispanic, 19,013 (7.0%); Other, 9,688 (3.5%).

Recreation: Water activities at **Lewisville, Grapevine** lakes, seven U.S. Corps of Engineers parks; **Ray Roberts Lake;** universities' cultural, athletic activities, including "Texas Women; A Celebration of History" exhibit at TWU library; State D.A.R. Museum "First Ladies of Texas" collection of gowns and memorabilia, Little Chapel-in-the-Woods, Botanical Gardens and local events; annual Denton Jazzfest in September; **North Texas State Fair** in August.

Minerals: Limited output oil, sand, gravel, gas, clay.

Agriculture: Beef cattle, horses, poultry, hay, wheat top revenue sources; nursery crops, grain sorghums, peanuts, cotton, oats, other principal crops; peanuts, turf irrigated.

Business: Varied industries; colleges; tourism; part of Dallas-Fort Worth CMSA.

DENTON (66,270) county seat; **University of North Texas, Texas Woman's University, Denton State School** (for the retarded); plants make variety of products; hospitals, nursing homes; airport; women's museum.

Lewisville (45,966 in Denton County, partly in Dallas County), retail center, electronics and varied industries; Lewisville Lake, hospital; local events.

Other towns include **Argyle** (1,575); **Aubrey** (1,138); **Bartonville** (849); **Carrollton** (42,145 in Denton County, partly in Dallas, Collin counties); **Coppell** (3 in Denton County, mostly in Dallas County); **Copper Canyon** (978); **Corinth** (3,944); **Corral City** (46); **Cross Roads** (361); **Dallas** (14,338 in Denton County, partly in Collin, Rockwall Kaufman counties, mostly in Dallas County); **Double Oak** (1,664); **Flower Mound** (15,527); **Frisco** (268 in Denton County, mostly in Collin County); **Hebron** (1,128); **Hickory Creek** (1,893); **Highland Village** (7,027); **Hackberry** (200); **Justin** (1,234); **Krugerville** (735); **Krum** (1,542); **Lake Dallas** (3,656), electronics manufacturing; **Lakewood Village** (169); **Little Elm** (1,255); **Lincoln Park** (287); **Marshall Creek** (315); **Northlake** (250); **Oak Point** (645); **Pilot Point** (2,538), light manufacturing, agribusinesses, near Lake Ray Roberts, pioneer days in June; **Ponder** (432); **Roanoke** (1,616); **Sanger** (3,508); **Shady Shores** (1,045); **Southlake** (242 in Denton County, partly in Tarrant County), varied manufacturing, computer training, local events; **The Colony** (22,131), tourist center, IBM, sail fair in September; **Trophy Club** (3,922); and **Westlake** (80 in Denton County, mostly in Tarrant County); and part of Plano.

DeWitt County

LOCATION: South (O-16).

Cong. Dist. 14	U.S. Jud. Dist. ....S-Va.
St. Sen. Dist. 18	Ct. Appeals................... 13
St. Rep. Dist. 31	Admin. Jud. Dist. 4
St. Dist. Cts........ 24, 135, 267	

History: Created from Gonzales, Goliad, Victoria counties and organized, 1846; named for Green DeWitt, colonizer.

Physical Features: Drained by Guadalupe and tributaries; rolling to level; waxy, loam, sandy soils.

Population............... 18,840	Av. Weekly Wage $285.72
Area (sq. mi.) 910.4	Density 21
Land Area 909.2	Water Area 1.2
Civilian Labor 8,099	Jobless Rate.................. 94.7
Altitude (ft.)............462-163	Retail Sales $101,929,781
Rainfall (in.) 36.2	Gross Sales ... $188,365,002
Jan. min. 42	Reg. Voters 9,778
July max. 96	Election Turnout 45.2
Grow. Season (days)..... 270	Vehicles 16,168
Total Income (mil.) $253	Lane Miles 641
Per Capita Income...$14,070	Tax Value........ $845,196,261
Total Wages....... $82,531,825	Fed. Spending......... $55,489
Housing 8,570	Defense Spending $1,902

Vital Statistics, 1989: Births, 265; Deaths, 269; Marriages, 108; Divorces, 37.

Ethnicity, 1990: White, 14,356 (76.2%); Black, 2,114 (11.2%); American Indian, 22 (0.1%); Asian, 17 (0.1%); Hispanic, 4,567 (24.2%); Other, 2,331 (12.4%).

Recreation: Hunting, fishing, local events; historic homes; museum.

Minerals: Oil and natural gas production.

Agriculture: Beef cattle, dairy products, hogs, poultry top revenue producers; crops include grain sorghums, corn, oats, wheat, pecans.

Business: Wood, furniture plants, textile mill; varied manufacturing; agribusinesses.

CUERO (6,700) county seat; agribusiness, turkey center; varied manufacturing; food processing; hospital, nursing homes; annual Turkeyfest. Other towns, **Nordheim** (344); **Yoakum** (2,154 in DeWitt, mostly in Lavaca County); **Yorktown** (2,207), hospital, nursing homes; museum; oil-well servicing.

Dickens County

LOCATION: Northwest (F-10).

Cong. Dist. 13	U.S. Jud. Dist. .... N-Lb.
St. Sen. Dist. 30	Ct. Appeals..................... 7
St. Rep. Dist. 84	Admin. Jud. Dist. 9
St. Dist. Cts.................. 110	

History: Created 1876, from Bexar District; organized 1891; named for Alamo hero who is variously listed as James R. Demkins, James R. Dimpkins and J. Dickens (according to noted authority Dr. Amelia Williams, writing in the Southwestern Historical Quarterly).

Physical Features: Broken land, Caprock in northwest; sandy, chocolate, red soils; drains to Croton, Duck creeks.

Population................2,571	Av. Weekly Wage $274.70
Area (sq. mi.) 905.2	Density 3
Land Area 904.2	Water Area 1.0
Civilian Labor 1,103	Jobless Rate.................. 4.4
Altitude (ft.).......2,991-1,933	Retail Sales $7,663,082
Rainfall (in.) 20.7	Gross Sales ... $33,875,426
Jan. min. 26	Reg. Voters 1,746
July max. 95	Election Turnout 48.7
Grow. Season (days)..... 217	Vehicles 2,682
Total Income (mil.) $38	Lane Miles 460

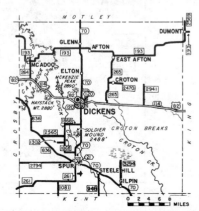

Dickens Co. (Cont.)
Per Capita Income...$14,076   Tax Value......... $109,239,774
Total Wages.........$9,484,881   Fed. Spending......... $16,627
Housing......................1,568   Defense Spending $73
    Vital Statistics, 1989: Births, 31; Deaths, 36; Marriages, 20; Divorces, 4.
    Ethnicity, 1990: White, 2,193 (85.3%); Black, 113 (4.4%); American Indian, 13 (0.5%); Asian, 1 (**.*%); Hispanic, 479 (18.6%); Other, 251 (9.8%).
    Recreation: Hunting, fishing, local events.
    Minerals: Small oil, gas output.
    Agriculture: Most revenue from beef cattle, cotton, wheat; some irrigation.
    Business: Chiefly ranching, farming supplies; some manufacturing.
    DICKENS (322) county seat; **Spur** (1,300), principal agribusiness center.

Dimmit County

    LOCATION: Southwest (Q-12).
Cong. Dist. 23   U.S. Jud. Dist. ....W-SAnt.
St. Sen. Dist. 21   Ct. Appeals......................4
St. Rep. Dist. 44   Admin. Jud. Dist. 4
St. Dist. Cts.................. 293
    History: Named for Philip Dimitt of Texas Revolution; law misspelled name; created 1858 from Bexar, Maverick, Uvalde, Webb counties; organized 1880.
    Physical Features: Level to rolling; much brush; sandy, loam, red soils; drained by Nueces River and tributaries.

Population................ 10,433   Av. Weekly Wage $276.16
Area (sq. mi.).......... 1,334.5   Density 8
Land Area ....1,331.0   Water Area 3.5
Civilian Labor 4,208   Jobless Rate................ 11.9
Altitude (ft.)............591-461   Retail Sales $41,827,698
Rainfall (in.) .... 21.5   Gross Sales....... $63,100,618
Jan. min. 41   Reg. Voters 6,748
July max. 100   Election Turnout 50.4
Grow. Season (days)..... 290   Vehicles 6,606
Total Income (mil.) ......$73   Lane Miles 506
Per Capita Income.. $6,576   Tax Value......... $568,805,905
Total Wages....... $36,259,807   Fed. Spending.........$30,239
Housing....................3,911   Defense Spending $245
    Vital Statistics, 1989: Births, 189; Deaths, 79; Marriages, 75; Divorces, 17.
    Ethnicity, 1990: White, 7,599 (72.8%); Black, 60 (0.6%); American Indian, 16 (0.2%); Asian, 12 (0.1%); Hispanic, 8,688 (83.3%); Other, 2,746 (26.3%).
    Recreation: Hunting, fishing, lake campsites; local events; mild climate makes area **Winter Garden** for tourists.
    Minerals: Oil, gas production.
    Agriculture: Principal crops cotton, hay, pecans,

vegetables; beef cattle raised; among leading irrigated vegetable-growing counties since early in century; 10,000 acres irrigated.
    Business: Agribusinesses; petroleum products; varied manufacturing; tourism.
    CARRIZO SPRINGS (5,745) county seat; agribusiness center, feedlot, food processing; oil and gas processing; hunting center; hospitals, nursing home. Other towns, **Asherton** (1,608), **Big Wells** (756).

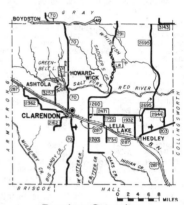

Donley County

    LOCATION: Northwest (D-10).
Cong. Dist. 13   U.S. Jud. Dist. .... N-Am.
St. Sen. Dist. 31   Ct. Appeals...................... 7
St. Rep. Dist. 84   Admin. Jud. Dist. 9
St. Dist. Cts.................. 100
    History: Created 1876, organized 1882, out of Bexar District; named for Texas Supreme Court Justice S.P. Donley.
    Physical Features: Bisected by Red River Salt Fork; rolling to level; clay, loam, sandy soils.

Population..................3,696   Av. Weekly Wage $282.33
Area (sq. mi.)............933.0   Density 4
Land Area ....929.8   Water Area 3.2
Civilian Labor 1,950   Jobless Rate.................3.7
Altitude (ft.).......3,213-2,388   Retail Sales $16,931,753
Rainfall (in.) .... 21.5   Gross Sales........ $26,410,213

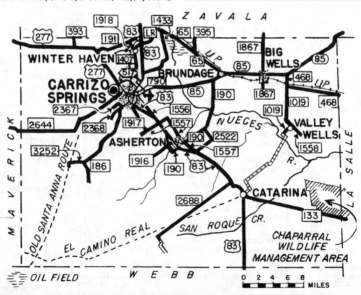

Donley Co. (Cont.)

Jan. min.	22
July max.	95
Grow. Season (days)	206
Total Income (mil.)	$64
Per Capita Income	$16,796
Total Wages	$12,434,993
Housing	2,304
Reg. Voters	2,306
Election Turnout	54.9
Vehicles	3,950
Lane Miles	447
Tax Value	$166,339,026
Fed. Spending	$15,411
Defense Spending	$206

Vital Statistics, 1989: Births, 45; Deaths, 53; Marriages, 33; Divorces, 16.

Ethnicity, 1990: White, 3,522 (95.3%); Black, 127 (3.4%); American Indian, 13 (0.4%); Asian, 2 (0.1%); Hispanic, 139 (3.8%); Other, 32 (0.9%).

Recreation: Greenbelt Lake, hunting, fishing, camping, water sports; Saints Roost celebration, rodeo in July; museum.

Minerals: Small amount of natural gas.

Agriculture: Beef cattle top revenue source; pigs, horses also raised; crops are cotton, hay, wheat, peanuts, grain sorghums; 8,000 acres irrigated for cotton, peanuts.

Business: Agribusinesses; distribution; varied manufacturing; nursing home; junior livestock show in January.

CLARENDON (2,067) county seat; **Clarendon Junior College; Saints Roost museum; Burton Memorial Library;** agribusinesses, varied manufacturing; tourism; medical center, nursing home. Other towns **Hedley** (391), **Howardwick** (211).

Duval County

LOCATION: South (R-15).

Cong. Dist.	15
St. Sen. Dist.	21
St. Rep. Dist.	44
St. Dist. Cts.	229
U.S. Jud. Dist.	S-CC
Ct. Appeals	4
Admin. Jud. Dist.	5

History: Created from Live Oak, Nueces, Starr counties, 1858, organized 1876; named for B.H. Duval, a victim of Goliad massacre.

Physical Features: Level to hilly, brushy in most areas; varied soils.

Population	12,918	Av. Weekly Wage	$319.82
Area (sq. mi.)	1,795.7	Density	7
Land Area	1,792.8	Water Area	2.9
Civilian Labor	5,660	Jobless Rate	7.9
Altitude (ft.)	783-244	Retail Sales	$36,471,984
Rainfall (in.)	24.4	Gross Sales	$72,539,305
Jan. min.	41	Reg. Voters	8,973
July max.	97	Election Turnout	45.2
Grow. Season (days)	298	Vehicles	7,702

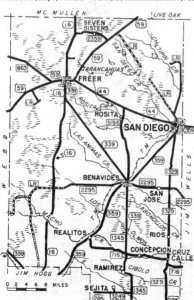

Total Income (mil.)	$139
Per Capita Income	$10,816
Total Wages	$48,329,213
Housing	5,112
Lane Miles	630
Tax Value	$887,961,073
Fed. Spending	$44,548
Defense Spending	$643

Vital Statistics, 1989: Births, 222; Deaths, 111; Marriages, 82; Divorces, 40.

Ethnicity, 1990: White, 10,183 (78.8%); Black, 12 (0.1%); American Indian, 12 (0.1%); Asian, 17 (0.1%); Hispanic, 11,267 (87.2%); Other, 2,694 (20.9%).

Recreation: Hunting, tourist crossroads, rattlesnake roundup, local events.

Minerals: Production of oil, gas, salt, uranium, sand and gravel.

Agriculture: Most income from beef cattle; remainder from grains, cotton, vegetables, hay.

Business: Ranching; petroleum; tourism.

SAN DIEGO (4,109 in Duval County, partly in Jim Wells County) county seat; ranching, oil field, tourist center; hospital. Other towns are **Benavides** (1,788), **Freer** (3,271).

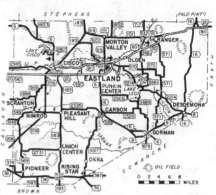

Eastland County

LOCATION: Central (I-13).

Cong. Dist.	17
St. Sen. Dist.	22
St. Rep. Dist.	65
St. Dist. Cts.	91
U.S. Jud. Dist.	N-Ab.
Ct. Appeals	11
Admin. Jud. Dist.	8

History: Created from Bosque, Coryell, Travis counties, 1858, organized 1873; named for W.M. Eastland, Mier Expedition casualty.

Physical Features: Hilly, rolling; sandy, loam soils; drains to Leon River forks.

Population	18,488	Av. Weekly Wage	$284.68
Area (sq. mi.)	931.8	Density	20
Land Area	926.0	Water Area	5.8
Civilian Labor	8,090	Jobless Rate	6.1
Altitude (ft.)	1,882-1,303	Retail Sales	$97,467,004
Rainfall (in.)	27.2	Gross Sales	$294,390,774
Jan. min.	30	Reg. Voters	10,707
July max.	95	Election Turnout	51.4
Grow. Season (days)	299	Vehicles	18,780
Total Income (mil.)	$233	Lane Miles	1,024
Per Capita Income	$12,312	Tax Value	$676,441,489
Total Wages	$73,364,460	Fed. Spending	$66,309
Housing	9,760	Defense Spending	$1,890

Vital Statistics, 1989: Births, 183; Deaths, 274; Marriages, 173; Divorces, 65.

Ethnicity, 1990: White, 17,474 (94.5%); Black, 397 (2.1%); American Indian, 52 (0.3%); Asian, 37 (0.2%); Hispanic, 1,404 (7.6%); Other, 528 (2.9%).

Recreation: Fishing, **Lake Leon, Lake Cisco;** water sports; hunting; festivals; historic sites and displays.

Minerals: Production of oil, gas, stone, clays, sand and gravel.

Agriculture: Fed beef and dairy cattle, turkeys top revenue producers; peanuts, hay, wheat, grain sorghums major crops; 20,000 acres irrigated, mostly peanuts, some coastal Bermuda.

Business: Agribusinesses; education; petroleum industries; varied manufacturing.

EASTLAND (3,690) county seat; plants make various goods; agribusiness; printing; mental health center; hospital, nursing home.

Eastland Co. (Cont.)

Cisco (3,813) agribusiness; plants make clothing, other products; Conrad Hiltons's first hotel renovated, museum; **Cisco Junior College**; hospital, nursing home.

Other towns, **Ranger** (2,803), oil center, varied manufacturing, **Ranger Junior College**, hospital, nursing home; **Carbon** (255); **Gorman** (1,290), peanut processing; agribusiness; hospital, nursing home; peanut festival in September; **Rising Star** (859), cap manufacturing.

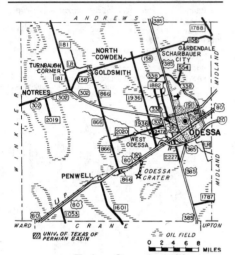

Ector County

LOCATION: West (J-7).

Cong. Dist. 16, 19	U.S. Jud. Dist. .... W: M-O
St. Sen. Dist. 28	Ct. Appeals....................... 8
St. Rep. Dist. 75, 76	Admin. Jud. Dist. 7
St. Dist. Cts.. 70, 161, 244, 358	

History: Created from Tom Green County, 1887; organized, 1891; named for Texas legislator-jurist M.D. Ector.

Physical Features: Level to rolling, some sand dunes; meteor crater; desert vegetation.

Population............... 118,934	Av. Weekly Wage $403.90
Area (sq. mi.) 901.7	Density 132
Land Area 901.1	Water Area 0.6
Civilian Labor 51,268	Jobless Rate.................. 6.0
Altitude (ft.) 3,275-2,817	Retail Sales .. $1,093,793,204
Rainfall (in.) 12.7	Gross Sales.... $2,525,188,538
Jan. min. 28	Reg. Voters 47,754
July max. 95	Election Turnout 51.9
Grow. Season (days)..... 217	Vehicles 109,674
Total Income (mil.) .. $1,685	Lane Miles 889
Per Capita Income... $13,850	Tax Value...... $4,538,856,722
Total Wages...... $922,044,708	Fed. Spending $206,588
Housing 48,613	Defense Spending $4,385

Vital Statistics, 1989: Births, 2,326; Deaths, 825; Marriages, 1,187; Divorces, 909.

Ethnicity, 1990: White, 91,309 (76.8%); Black, 5,557 (4.7%); American Indian, 647 (0.5%); Asian, 662 (0.6%); Hispanic, 37,315 (31.4%); Other, 20,759 (17.5%).

Recreation: Metropolitan cultural centers; second largest U.S. meteor crater; **Globe Theatre** replica; presidential museum; Permian playhouse theatre; art institute for the Permian Basin.

Minerals: Leading oil-producing county with more than 2 billion barrels produced since 1926; gas, cement, stone.

Agriculture: Beef cattle, poultry chief producers; pecans, hay.

Business: Oil-based economy; center for Permian Basin oil field operations.

ODESSA (89,504 in Ector County, partly in Midland County) county seat; oil field services, supplies; petrochemical complex; medical center; cultural center; **Odessa College, University of Texas of Permian Basin.** Other towns, **Goldsmith** (297), **Gardendale** (1,103), **West Odessa** (16,568).

Edwards County

LOCATION: Southwest (M-11).

Cong. Dist. 21	U.S. Jud. Dist. ... W-Del Rio
St. Sen. Dist. 25	Ct. Appeals....................... 4
St. Rep. Dist. 67	Admin. Jud. Dist. 6
St. Dist. Cts. 63	

History: Created from Bexar District, 1858; organized 1883; named for Nacogdoches empresario Hayden Edwards.

Physical Features: Rolling, hilly; caves; spring-fed streams; rocky, thin soils; drained by Llano, Nueces rivers; varied timber.

Population................. 2,266	Av. Weekly Wage $272.38
Area (sq. mi.) 2,120.0	Density 1
Land Area 2,119.9	Water Area 0.1
Civilian Labor 865	Jobless Rate.................. 7.1
Altitude (ft.) 2,410-1,507	Retail Sales $7,026,986
Rainfall (in.) 23.6	Gross Sales........ $10,203,895
Jan. min. 35	Reg. Voters 1,315
July max. 95	Election Turnout 60.8
Grow. Season (days)..... 250	Vehicles 2,016
Total Income (mil.) $29	Lane Miles 500
Per Capita Income... $14,369	Tax Value........ $467,755,346
Total Wages...... $5,382,284	Fed. Spending $12,537
Housing 1,550	Defense Spending $94

Vital Statistics, 1989: Births, 43; Deaths, 13; Marriages, 18; Divorces, 10.

Ethnicity, 1990: White, 2,114 (93.3%); Black, 0 (0.0%); American Indian, 4 (0.2%); Asian, 4 (0.2%); Hispanic, 1,182 (52.2%); Other, 144 (6.4%).

Recreation: Leading deer, turkey hunting area; fishing; scenic drives; local events; state park planned.

Minerals: Oil and gas produced.

Agriculture: Almost all agricultural income from Angora goats, sheep, cattle; center of nation's goat-mohair production.

Business: Ranching economy; revenue also from hunting leases; tourism; oil, gas production.

ROCKSPRINGS (1,339) county seat; ranching, hunting center; tourism, hospital.

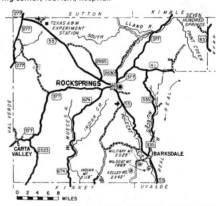

Ellis County

LOCATION: Central (I-17).

Cong. Dist. 6	U.S. Jud. Dist. ...... N-Dallas
St. Sen. Dist. 9	Ct. Appeals..................... 10
St. Rep. Dist. 4	Admin. Jud. Dist. 1
St. Dist. Cts. 40	

History: Created 1849, organized 1850, from Navarro County. Named for Richard Ellis, president of Convention of 1836 that declared Texas' independence from Mexico.

Physical Features: Rich Blackland soils; level to rolling; Chambers Creek, Trinity River.

Population............... 85,167	Av. Weekly Wage $369.08
Area (sq. mi.) 951.6	Density 91
Land Area 939.9	Water Area 11.7
Civilian Labor 41,386	Jobless Rate.................. 5.6
Altitude (ft.) 755-395	Retail Sales $416,218,401
Rainfall (in.) 36.3	Gross Sales.... $1,675,710,304
Jan. min. 33	Reg. Voters 41,504
July max. 97	Election Turnout 50.5

Ellis Co. (Cont.)

Grow. Season (days).....	246	Vehicles	78,373
Total Income (mil.) ..	$1,291	Lane Miles	1,419
Per Capita Income...	$15,055	Tax Value......	$3,537,305,763
Total Wages......	$431,712,005	Fed. Spending.......	$326,630
Housing..................	31,236	Defense Spending	$5,695

Vital Statistics, 1989: Births, 1,478; Deaths, 688; Marriages, 937; Divorces, 287.

Ethnicity, 1990: White, 69,049 (81.1%); Black, 8,525 (10.0%); American Indian, 370 (0.4%); Asian, 214 (0.3%); Hispanic, 11,243 (13.2%); Other, 7,009 (8.2%).

Recreation: Scarborough Faire; National Polka Festival at Ennis; Gingerbread Trail homes tour, Italian Festival in Italy; Bluebonnet Trails in April; hunting.

Minerals: Oil, gas and limestone.

Agriculture: Cow-calf operations, stocker cattle, horses, dairy production, honey; crops include cotton, corn, wheat, milo, hay.

Business: Varied manufacturing; agribusinesses; many residents employed in Dallas; the U.S. Department of Energy is building the Superconducting Super Collider.

WAXAHACHIE (18,168) county seat; varied manufacturing; motion picture production; tourism; hospital, nursing homes; **Southwestern Assemblies of God College,** Navarro College/Ellis County; Scarborough Faire begins in April, Gingerbread Trail in June.

Ennis (13,883), agribusiness; manufacturing; bluebonnet trails in April, National Polka Festival in May; tourism; hospitals; nursing home.

Other towns are **Alma** (205); **Bardwell** (387); **Cedar Hill** (50 in Ellis County, mostly in Dallas County); **Ferris** (2,212); **Garrett** (340); **Glenn Heights** (796 in Ellis County, mostly in Dallas County); **Italy** (1,699); **Mansfield** (142 in Ellis County, mostly in Tarrant County); **Maypearl** (781); **Midlothian** (5,141), trade zone planned, cement plant, factories; local events; **Milford** (711); **Ovilla** (1,748 in Ellis County, partly in Dallas County); **Oak Leaf** (984); **Palmer** (1,659); **Pecan Hill** (564); **Red Oak** (3,124); **Rice** (10 in Ellis County, mostly in Navarro County); and part of Grand Prairie.

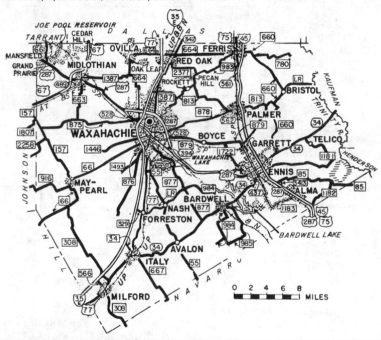

El Paso County

LOCATION: Most western county (J-1).

Cong. Dist.	16	U.S. Jud. Dist. ...	W-El Paso
St. Sen. Dist.	25, 29	Ct. Appeals......................	8
St. Rep. Dist.	70-74	Admin. Jud. Dist.	6
St. Dist. Cts. ... 34, 41, 65, 120, 168, 171, 205, 210, 243, 327, 346			

History: Created from Bexar District, 1849; organized 1850; named for historic northern pass (Paso del Norte).

Physical Features: Fertile Rio Grande Valley; 7,000-foot mountains; desert vegetation except where irrigated.

Population..............	591,610	Av. Weekly Wage	$331.17
Area (sq. mi.).........	1,014.6	Density	583
Land Area	1,013.0	Water Area	1.6
Civilian Labor	250,793	Jobless Rate...............	10.7
Altitude (ft.).......7,192-3,582		Retail Sales ...	$3,706,845,333
Rainfall (in.)	7.8	Gross Sales ...	$8,685,260,666
Jan. min.	30	Reg. Voters	197,735
July max.	95	Election Turnout........	37.6
Grow. Season (days).....	248	Vehicles	361,966
Total Income (mil.) ..	$6,423	Lane Miles	1,358
Per Capita Income...	$10,735	Tax Value.....	$12,911,803,363

Total Wages... $3,386,322,649   Fed. Spending...... 1,933,350
Housing.................. 185,931   Defense Spending . $720,147

Vital Statistics, 1989: Births, 13,831; Deaths, 3,232; Marriages, 7,562; Divorces, 2,968.

Ethnicity, 1990: White, 452,512 (76.5%); Black, 22,110 (3.7%); American Indian, 2,590 (0.4%); Asian, 6,485 (1.1%); Hispanic, 411,619 (69.6%); Other, 107,913 (18.2%).

Recreation: Gateway to Mexico; varied U.S.- Mexican metropolitan events, Chamizal Museum; major tourist center; December Sun Carnival with annual John Hancock Bowl football game; El Paso Festival in July; Border Folk Festival in October; Southwestern International Livestock Show, Rodeo in February; **Franklin Mountains and Hueco Tanks State Parks,** missions and other historic sites; near Carlsbad Caverns, White Sands, bullfighting, horse and dog racing; amusement park.

Minerals: Production of cement, stone, sand and gravel.

El Paso Co. (Cont.)

Agriculture: Dairy and beef cattle, hogs leading revenue producers; cotton, grain, pecans, hay raised; 47,000 acres irrigated, mostly cotton.

Business: Government, military is major economic factor; wholesale, retail distribution center; education; Tigua Indian reservation, tourism; maquiladora plants, varied manufacturers; ore smelting, refining, cotton, food processing.

EL PASO (515,342) county seat; fourth-largest Texas city; lowest all-weather pass through Rocky Mountains; a center for government operations; manufactured products include clothing, electronics, auto equipment, plastics; trade and distribution; refining and processing of ore, oil, food, cotton, and other farm, ranch products;

University of Texas at El Paso; El Paso Community College; UT School of Nursing at El Paso; Texas Tech University Health Science Center; home of **U.S. Army Air Defense Command**; 16 hospitals; museums; numerous tourist attractions; convention, civic center; community theater, symphony orchestra, gateway to Mexico and largest U.S. city on Mexican border.

Federal installations include **Fort Bliss, William Beaumont General Hospital, La Tuna** correctional institution.

Ysleta, the oldest town in Texas, is now part of El Paso; other towns include **Anthony** (3,328), **Canutillo** (4,442), **Clint** (1,035), **Fabens** (5,599), **Fort Bliss** (13,915), **Homestead Meadows** (4,978), **Horizon City** (2,308), **Socorro** (22,995), **Sparks** (1,276), **San Elizario** (4,385), **Vinton** (605), **Westway** (2,381).

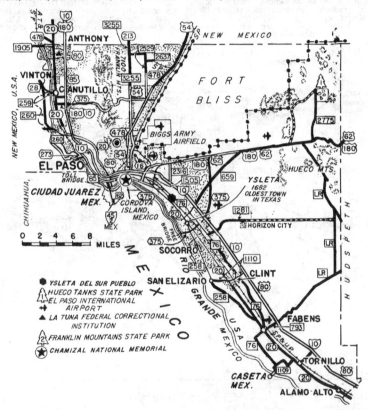

Erath County

LOCATION: North central (I-14).

Cong. Dist.	17	U.S. Jud. Dist.	N-FW
St. Sen. Dist.	22	Ct. Appeals	11
St. Rep. Dist.	58	Admin. Jud. Dist.	8
St. Dist. Cts.	266		

History: Created from Bosque, Coryell counties, 1856, organized same year; named for George B. Erath, Texas Revolution figure.

Physical Features: Hilly, rolling plains; clay loam, sandy soils; drains to Bosque River, Paluxy Creek.

Population	27,991	Av. Weekly Wage	$313.44
Area (sq. mi.)	1,089.8	Density	26
Land Area	1,086.4	Water Area	3.4
Civilian Labor	13,611	Jobless Rate	4.6
Altitude (ft.)	1,558-943	Retail Sales	$192,357,705
Rainfall (in.)	30.1	Gross Sales	$332,717,079
Jan. min.	31	Reg. Voters	12,096
July max.	95	Election Turnout	56.2

Grow. Season (days)	238	Vehicles	25,315
Total Income (mil.)	$396	Lane Miles	784
Per Capita Income	$15,235	Tax Value	$1,194,589,784
Total Wages	$158,686,198	Fed. Spending	$68,973
Housing	12,746	Defense Spending	$3,050

Vital Statistics, 1989: Births, 377; Deaths, 310; Marriages, 295; Divorces, 165.

Ethnicity, 1990: White, 26,413 (94.4%); Black, 195 (0.7%); American Indian, 94 (0.3%); Asian, 115 (0.4%); Hispanic, 2,458 (8.8%); Other, 1,174 (4.2%).

Recreation: Tarleton State University with fine arts center; Historical House museum; old courthouse; log cabins; Thurber, ghost town; museums; nearby lakes, **Bosque River Park;** St. Patrick's celebration in Dublin; junior livestock show.

Minerals: Gas, oil.

Agriculture: A leading county in milk production;

beef cattle important; peanuts, the major cash crop, small grains, sorghums chief crops; horticulture industry, especially tree growing and greenhouses, expanding; some irrigation, mostly peanuts and forage crops.

Business: Agricultural, industrial and educational enterprises.

STEPHENVILLE (13,502) county seat; **Tarleton State University;** various manufacturing plants; hospital, clinics, mental health/mental retardation center; **Texas A&M Research and Extension Center.** Other town, **Dublin** (3,190), agribusiness center; food processing; hospital, nursing home.

Falls County

LOCATION: Central (K-17).

Cong. Dist. 11	U.S. Jud. Dist. ....W-Wa.
St. Sen. Dist. 9	Ct. Appeals......................10
St. Rep. Dist. 55	Admin. Jud. Dist. 3
St. Dist. Cts. 82	

History: Created and organized, 1850, from Limestone, Milam counties; named for Brazos River falls.

Physical Features: Level to rolling; bisected by Brazos; Blackland, red, sandy loam soils; mineral springs.

Population................. 17,712	Av. Weekly Wage $288.35
Area (sq. mi.)..............773.8	Density 23
Land Area 769.1	Water Area 4.7
Civilian Labor 7,545	Jobless Rate................. 4.4
Altitude (ft.)............590-314	Retail Sales $70,489,528
Rainfall (in.) 36.0	Gross Sales....... $115,665,748
Jan. min. 36	Reg. Voters 9,272
July max. 97	Election Turnout......... 47.1
Grow. Season (days)..... 257	Vehicles 13,538

Total Income (mil.) $204

Total Income (mil.) $204	Lane Miles 706
Per Capita Income...$12,242	Tax Value......... $549,993,460
Total Wages....... $49,316,596	Fed. Spending $73,184
Housing.....................7,695	Defense Spending $1,773

Vital Statistics, 1989: Births, 236; Deaths, 279; Marriages, 128; Divorces, 49.

Ethnicity, 1990: White, 11,390 (64.3%); Black, 4,810 (27.2%); American Indian, 41 (0.2%); Asian, 21 (0.1%); Hispanic, 2,072 (11.7%); Other, 1,450 (8.2%).

Recreation: Fishing, camping, mineral baths attract visitors; Falls County Youth Fair at Marlin; Highland Mansion and Falls on the Brazos.

Minerals: Gas, stone, small oil production.

Agriculture: Stocker cattle, cow-calf operations important; crops include corn, grain sorghums, cotton, small grains; 5,000 acres of corn irrigated.

Business: Varied manufacturing; agribusinesses.

MARLIN (6,386) county seat; agribusiness, small industries; mineral water and spas; hospital; printing; veterans hospital; tourism; festival; prison unit. Other towns, **Bruceville-Eddy** (1 in Falls County, mostly in McLennan County); **Golinda** (289 in Falls County, partly in McLennan County); **Lott** (775); **Rosebud** (1,638), feed, fertilizer processing; clothing manufactured; nursing home.

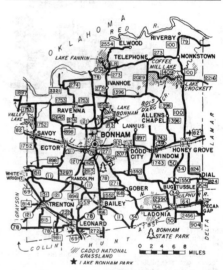

Fannin County

LOCATION: Borders Oklahoma (F-18).

Cong. Dist......................4	U.S. Jud. Dist ....E-Paris
St. Sen. Dist. 2	Ct. Appeals......................6
St. Rep. Dist. 2	Admin. Jud. Dist. 1
St. Dist. Cts. 6, 336	

History: Created from Red River County, 1837, organized, 1838; named for James W. Fannin, a victim of Goliad massacre.

Physical Features: Rolling prairie, drained by Red River, Bois d' Arc Creek; mostly Blackland soils; Caddo National Grassland.

Population............... 24,804	Av. Weekly Wage $317.13
Area (sq. mi.)..............891.5	Density 28
Land Area 891.5	Water Area 7.6
Civilian Labor 12,608	Jobless Rate................. 6.2
Altitude (ft.)............767-478	Retail Sales $125,969,385
Rainfall (in.) 41.6	Gross Sales....... $345,827,011
Jan. min. 31	Reg. Voters 13,066
July max. 95	Election Turnout......... 46.6
Grow. Season (days)..... 228	Vehicles 23,986
Total Income (mil.) $321	Lane Miles 903
Per Capita Income...$13,295	Tax Value......... $821,814,899
Total Wages....... $88,341,023	Fed. Spending $107,501
Housing.....................11,491	Defense Spending $6,255

Vital Statistics, 1989: Births, 313; Deaths, 363; Marriages, 229; Divorces, 162.

Fannin Co. (Cont.)

Ethnicity, 1990: White, 22,722 (91.6%); Black, 1,633 (6.6%); American Indian, 182 (0.7%); Asian, 54 (0.2%); Hispanic, 485 (2.0%); Other, 213 (0.9%).

Recreation: Sam Rayburn home, Sam Rayburn Memorial Library; Bonham State Park; water activities on several area lakes; hunting; Ivanhoe Winery.

Minerals: Not significant; some sand produced.

Agriculture: Beef cattle important; crops include sorghums, soybeans, peanuts, cotton, grapes; 3,500 acres irrigated, mainly peanuts; firewood marketed.

Business: Varied manufacturing; agribusinesses, distribution, meat packing; timber.

BONHAM (6,686) county seat; varied manufacturing; hospitals, Sam Rayburn Veterans Memorial Center; Bois D'Arc Festival in May, county fair in October, rodeo in July. Other towns include **Bailey** (187); **Dodd City** (350); **Ector** (494); **Honey Grove** (1,681); agribusiness center, varied manufacturing, local events; **Ladonia** (658), restored historical downtown, varied manufacturing; **Leonard** (1,744), varied manufacturing; **Pecan Gap** (12 in Fannin County, mostly in Delta County); **Savoy** (877); **Trenton** (655); **Wisdom** (269).

Fayette County

LOCATION: Central (K-17).

Cong. Dist. 11	U.S. Jud. Dist. .... W-Wa.
St. Sen. Dist. 9	Ct. Appeals.................... 10
St. Rep. Dist. 55	Admin. Jud. Dist. 3
St. Dist. Cts. 82	

History: Created from Bastrop, Colorado counties, 1837; organized, 1838; named for French hero of U.S. Revolution, Marquis de Lafayette.

Physical Features: Rolling to level, bisected by Colorado River; sandy loam, black waxy soils.

Population................ 20,095	Av. Weekly Wage $314.15
Area (sq. mi.)............. 959.8	Density 21
Land Area 950.1	Water Area 9.7
Civilian Labor 9,351	Jobless Rate.................. 2.8
Altitude (ft.)..........590-245	Retail Sales $147,054,253
Rainfall (in.) 37.4	Gross Sales .. $324,631,502
Jan. min. 41	Reg. Voters 11,008
July max. 95	Election Turnout 63.9
Grow. Season (days)..... 277	Vehicles 20,293
Total Income (mil.) $324	Lane Miles 955
Per Capita Income..$16,539	Tax Value...... $1,546,160,543
Total Wages......$108,190,823	Fed. Spending......... $67,139
Housing................... 10,748	Defense Spending $3,226

Vital Statistics, 1989: Births, 254; Deaths, 272; Marriages, 131; Divorces, 69.

Ethnicity, 1990: White, 17,323 (86.2%); Black, 1,686 (8.4%); American Indian, 29 (0.1%); Asian, 15 (0.1%); Hispanic, 1,702 (8.5%); Other, 1,042 (5.2%).

Recreation: Many historical restorations at Round Top and Winedale, including **Winedale Inn**; museums; **Monument Hill State Park, Faison Home Museum, Kreische Brewery**, other historic sites; hunting, fishing, Fayette Power Project Lake; piano festival at Round Top; Czech chili cookoff at Flatonia; Fayette County Fair and Heritage Days at LaGrange; spring festival at Ellinger; Bluebonnet Festival in Schulenburg.

Minerals: Oil, gas, clays, sand and gravel.

Agriculture: Cow-calf production; crops include corn, grain sorghums, peanuts, pecans.

Business: Agribusinesses; oil production; manufacturing includes steel fencing; tourism.

LA GRANGE (3,951) county seat; varied manufacturing; food processing; power generation; hospital, rest home.

Schulenburg (2,455) varied manufacturing; food processing; rest home, clinics. Other towns, **Carmine** (192), **Fayetteville** (283), **Flatonia** (1,291), **Round Top**, (81).

Fisher County

LOCATION: West central (H-11).

Cong. Dist. 17	U.S. Jud. Dist. .... N-Ab.
St. Sen. Dist. 30	Ct. Appeals.................... 11
St. Rep. Dist. 78	Admin. Jud. Dist. 7
St. Dist. Cts. 32	

History: Created from Bexar District, 1876; organized, 1886; named for S.R. Fisher, Republic of Texas secretary of navy.

Physical Features: Rolling; red, sandy loam soils; drains to forks of Brazos River.

Population................ 4,842	Av. Weekly Wage $398.91
Area (sq. mi.)............. 901.7	Density 5
Land Area 901.2	Water Area 0.5
Civilian Labor 2,437	Jobless Rate.................. 6.4
Altitude (ft.) 2,235-1,723	Retail Sales $11,876,174
Rainfall (in.) 22.5	Gross Sales........ $26,518,484
Jan. min. 30	Reg. Voters 3,153
July max. 97	Election Turnout 54.1
Grow. Season (days).... 218	Vehicles 4,645
Total Income (mil.) $68	Lane Miles 553
Per Capita Income..$12,924	Tax Value........ $356,226,823
Total Wages....... $21,531,806	Fed. Spending $23,383
Housing...................... 2,431	Defense Spending $277

Vital Statistics, 1989: Births, 51; Deaths, 78; Marriages, 24; Divorces, 23.

Ethnicity, 1990: White, 4,445 (91.8%); Black, 190 (3.9%); American Indian, 19 (0.4%); Asian, 0 (0.0%); Hispanic, 997 (20.6%); Other, 188 (3.9%).

Recreation: Quail, dove, turkey hunting, fishing; county fair, rodeo in August, quail cookoff in November.

Minerals: Production of oil, gas, gypsum.

Agriculture: Beef cattle, swine, Angora goats important; crops include cotton, wheat, grain sorghums, hay; some irrigation.

Business: Oil; gypsum; agribusinesses; electric co-op.

ROBY (616) county seat; agribusiness, cotton gin, electric co-op headquarters. Other towns, **Hamlin** (3 in Fisher County, mostly in Jones County), farming center; **Rotan** (1,913), gypsum plant; oil mill; agribusinesses.

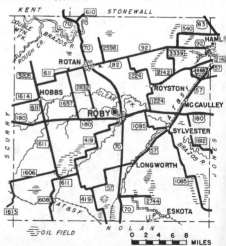

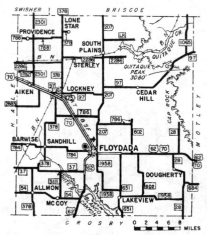

Floyd County

LOCATION: Northwest (E-9).

Cong. Dist. 13	U.S. Jud. Dist. ....N-Lb.
St. Sen. Dist. 30	Ct. Appeals......................7
St. Rep. Dist. 84	Admin. Jud. Dist. 9
St. Dist. Cts. 110	

History: Created from Bexar District, 1876; organized 1890. Named for D.W. Floyd, Alamo martyr.

Physical Features: Flat, broken by Caprock on east, by White River on south; many playas; red, black loam soils.

Population....................8,497	Av. Weekly Wage $278.43
Area (sq. mi.)...............992.5	Density 9
Land Area 992.3	Water Area 0.2
Civilian Labor 4,241	Jobless Rate..................4.5
Altitude (ft.) 3,316-2,574	Retail Sales $35,515,931
Rainfall (in.) 19.0	Gross Sales ... $92,316,707
Jan. min. 23	Reg. Voters 4,875
July max. 93	Election Turnout 48.5
Grow. Season (days)..... 213	Vehicles 8,412
Total Income (mil.) $110	Lane Miles 668
Per Capita Income...$13,071	Tax Value.........$310,168,087
Total Wages....... $31,867,097	Fed. Spending.........$42,138
Housing......................3,535	Defense Spending $145

Vital Statistics, 1989: Births, 169; Deaths, 85; Marriages, 59; Divorces, 26.

Ethnicity, 1990: White, 5,523 (65.0%); Black, 320 (3.8%); American Indian, 16 (0.2%); Asian, 15 (0.2%); Hispanic, 3,381 (39.8%); Other, 2,623 (30.9%).

Recreation: Hunting, fishing; museum; local events; county fair at Lockney.

Minerals: Not significant.

Agriculture: Major income from wheat, cotton; also beef and stocker cattle; corn, grain sorghums also raised; 246,000 acres irrigated.

Business: Livestock feedlots; farm machinery and oil-field manufacturing; agribusinesses; metal products; printing.

FLOYDADA (3,896) county seat; some manufacturing; meat, vegetable processing; distribution center; hospital, nursing home; Punkin Days in October, Old Settlers Reunion in May, county fair; **Texas A&M Engineering Extension Service.** Other town, **Lockney** (2,207), agriculture center; manufacturing; hospital, nursing home.

Foard County

LOCATION: Northwest (E-12).

Cong. Dist. 13	U.S. Jud. Dist. ....N-WF
St. Sen. Dist. 30	Ct. Appeals......................7
St. Rep. Dist. 80	Admin. Jud. Dist. 9
St. Dist. Cts.....................46	

History: Created out of Cottle, Hardeman, King, Knox counties, 1891, and organized same year; named for Maj. Robert L. Foard of Confederate army.

Physical Features: Drains to North Wichita, Pease rivers; sandy, loam soils, rolling surface.

Population....................1,794	Av. Weekly Wage $233.89
Area (sq. mi.)...............707.7	Density 3
Land Area 706.7	Water Area 1.0
Civilian Labor 1,163	Jobless Rate..................2.1
Altitude (ft.) 1,784-1,300	Retail Sales $4,625,924
Rainfall (in.) 23.9	Gross Sales ... $7,690,969
Jan. min. 24	Reg. Voters 1,242
July max. 97	Election Turnout 51.2
Grow. Season (days)..... 219	Vehicles 1,652
Total Income (mil.) $31	Lane Miles 299
Per Capita Income...$18,156	Tax Value.........$107,080,073
Total Wages........$6,336,620	Fed. Spending.........$10,469
Housing.......................... 898	Defense Spending $50

Vital Statistics, 1989: Births, 19; Deaths, 40; Marriages, 13; Divorces, 5.

Ethnicity, 1990: White, 1,552 (86.5%); Black, 88 (4.9%); American Indian, 11 (0.6%); Asian, 4 (0.2%); Hispanic, 233 (13.0%); Other, 139 (7.7%).

Recreation: Copper Breaks State Park across county line, eight miles north of Crowell; local events.

Minerals: Oil, gas.

Agriculture: Wheat, cotton, alfalfa top crops; cow-calf operations, stockers raised; some irrigation for alfalfa.

Business: Agribusiness; clothes manufacturing; oil economy; nursing home.

CROWELL (1,230) county seat; agriculture center; clothing manufactured; hospital, nursing home; local events.

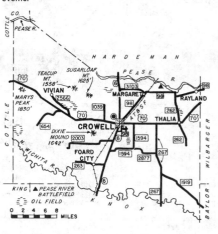

Fort Bend County

LOCATION: Southeast (N-19).

Cong. Dist. 22	U.S. Jud. Dist. ....S-Hn.
St. Sen. Dist. 13, 17,18	Ct. Appeals................1, 14
St. Rep. Dist. 26, 27	Admin. Jud. Dist 2
St. Dist. Cts.......240, 268, 328	

History: Named for river bend where Austin's colonists settled, among state's more historic counties; created 1837 from Austin County, organized 1838; scene of early Jaybird-Woodpecker War.

Physical Features: Drained by Brazos, San Bernard rivers; level to rolling; rich alluvial soils; some loams, clays.

Population....................225,421	Av . Weekly Wage....$461.04
Area (sq. mi.)................886.0	Density 257
Land Area 875.0	Water Area 11.0
Civilian Labor 101,103	Jobless Rate..................3.5
Altitude (ft.) 127-46	Retail Sales ... $2,000,660,122
Rainfall (in.) 43.9	Gross Sales.... $4,059,508,008
Jan. min. 41	Reg. Voters 86,349
July max. 94	Election Turnout 53.7
Grow. Season (days)....296	Vehicles 152,586
Total Income (mil.) .. $3,630	Lane Miles 947
Per Capita Income...$17,164	Tax Value...... $9,969,758,303
Total Wages... $1,116,596,827	Fed. Spending.......$252,978
Housing......................77,087	Defense Spending $20,879

Vital Statistics, 1989: Births, 3,958; Deaths, 880; Marriages, 1,402; Divorces, 900.

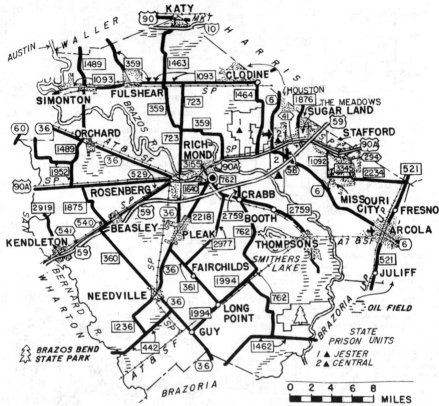

Franklin County

LOCATION: Northeast (C-21).

Cong. Dist. 1	U.S. Jud. Dist. .... E-Tx.
St. Sen. Dist. 1	Ct. Appeals...................... 6
St. Rep. Dist. 8	Admin. Jud. Dist. 1
St. Dist. Cts. 8, 62	

History: Created, organized 1875 from Titus County; named for Judge B.C. Franklin of Texas.

Physical Features: Many wooded hills; drained by numerous streams; alluvial to sandy clay soils; two lakes.

Population......................7,802	Av. Weekly Wage $284.75
Area (sq. mi.)...............294.7	Density 27
Land Area 285.6	Water Area 9.1
Civilian Labor 3,978	Jobless Rate.................4.9
Altitude (ft.)..........493-377	Retail Sales $30,939,016
Rainfall (in.) 46.8	Gross Sales $41,238,161
Jan. min. 33	Reg. Voters 4,299
July max. 93	Election Turnout 50.0
Grow. Season (days).....234	Vehicles 6,701
Total Income (mil.) $104	Lane Miles 328

Per Capita Income...$13,698	Tax Value......... $414,068,460
Total Wages....... $23,024,596	Fed. Spending.........$16,774
Housing....................4,211	Defense Spending $1,258

Vital Statistics, 1989: Births, 85; Deaths, 90; Marriages, 65; Divorces, 43.

Ethnicity, 1990: White, 7,139 (91.5%); Black, 349 (4.5%); American Indian, 47 (0.6%); Asian, 18 (0.2%); Hispanic, 357 (4.6%); Other, 249 (3.2%).

Recreation: Fishing, water sports on Cypress Springs and Bob Sandlin lakes; Aqua-Fest in August; local events, county fair.

Minerals: Oil, gas and lignite produced.

Agriculture: A top dairy county; beef cattle, broilers major economic factors; hay is principal crop; blueberries, peaches also raised; timber marketed.

RED RIVER COUNTY

Business: Agribusinesses; oil.
MOUNT VERNON (2,219) county seat; varied manufacturing; livestock market; supply center; hospital; airport. Other town, **Winnsboro** (671 in Franklin County, mostly in Wood County).

Freestone County

LOCATION: East central (J-18).

Cong. Dist.	6	U.S. Jud. Dist. ...... W-Wa.
St. Sen. Dist.	9	Ct. Appeals 10
St. Rep. Dist.	11	Admin. Jud. Dist. 2
St. Dist. Cts.	77, 87	

History: Named for indigenous stone; created 1850 from Limestone County, organized 1851.

Physical Features: Rolling, drains to Trinity River; Blackland, sandy, loam soils.

Population	15,818	Av. Weekly Wage	$413.80
Area (sq. mi.)	892.1	Density	18
Land Area	885.2	Water Area	6.9
Civilian Labor	5,857	Jobless Rate	6.4
Altitude (ft.)	608-209	Retail Sales	$68,529,374
Rainfall (in.)	38.3	Gross Sales	$154,596,988
Jan. min.	35	Reg. Voters	8,815
July max.	95	Election Turnout	51.2
Grow. Season (days)	263	Vehicles	14,992
Total Income (mil.)	$205	Lane Miles	823
Per Capita Income	$12,530	Tax Value	$1,226,283,800
Total Wages	$77,850,144	Fed. Spending	$48,130
Housing	7,811	Defense Spending	$894

Vital Statistics, 1989: Births, 199; Deaths, 200; Marriages, 117; Divorces, 92.

Ethnicity, 1990: White, 12,382 (78.3%); Black, 3,013 (19.0%); American Indian, 53 (0.3%); Asian, 37 (0.2%); Hispanic, 619 (3.9%); Other, 333 (2.1%).

Recreation: Fishing, hunting; **Fairfield Lake** recreation area; fair, rodeo in August, other local events; historic sites; railroad museum at Teague; coon hunting championship in September; golf course.

Minerals: Stone, gas, coal, oil, iron ore.

Agriculture: Cattle, hogs, horses important; hay; commercial orchards grow peaches, other fruits; vegetables, melons, pecans, corn other crops; little irrigation; some hardwood, firewood marketed.

Business: Mining, stone quarry, brick plant; varied manufacturing; agribusinesses; two electricity generating plants.

FAIRFIELD (3,234) county seat; headquarters Continental Telephone Co.; lignite mining; trade center; hospital, nursing home; county museum.

Other towns are **Kirvin** (107); **Streetman** (260 in Freestone County, partly in Navarro County); **Teague** (3,268); manufacturing, railroad museum; hospital, nursing home; **Wortham** (1,020).

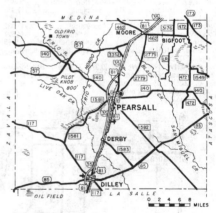

Frio County

LOCATION: South (P-13).

Cong. Dist.	15	U.S. Jud. Dist. ...... W-SAnt.
St. Sen. Dist.	21	Ct. Appeals 4
St. Rep. Dist.	45	Admin. Jud. Dist. 4
St. Dist. Cts.	81, 218	

History: Created, organized, 1871, from Atascosa, Bexar, Uvalde counties; named for Frio (cold) River.

Physical Features: Rolling, much brush; bisected by Frio River; sandy, red sandy loam soils.

Population	13,472	Av. Weekly Wage	$292.74
Area (sq. mi.)	1,134.3	Density	12
Land Area	1,133.1	Water Area	1.2
Civilian Labor	6,409	Jobless Rate	6.9
Altitude (ft.)	763-435	Retail Sales	$88,015,941
Rainfall (in.)	23.9	Gross Sales	$161,211,778
Jan. min.	39	Reg. Voters	7,549
July max.	98	Election Turnout	34.3
Grow. Season (days)	291	Vehicles	8,822

Frio Co. (Cont.)

Total Income (mil.) $116	Lane Miles 759
Per Capita Income.... $8,274	Tax Value......... $600,146,082
Total Wages....... $56,307,964	Fed. Spending $37,217
Housing.......................4,880	Defense Spending $467

Vital Statistics, 1989: Births, 233; Deaths, 118; Marriages, 102; Divorces, 21.

Ethnicity, 1990: White, 9,119 (67.7%); Black, 183 (1.4%); American Indian, 23 (0.2%); Asian, 38 (0.3%); Hispanic, 9,749 (72.4%); Other, 4,109 (30.5%).

Recreation: Hunting: local events; Big Foot Wallace Museum, other museums; in **Winter Garden** area; potato festival in June.

Minerals: Production of oil, natural gas, stone.

Agriculture: A leading peanut-producing county; other crops vegetables, grain sorghums, melons, corn, vegetables; cattle, hogs raised.

Business: Chiefly agribusinesses; oil-field services.

PEARSALL (6,924) county seat; oil, ranching center; food processing; leather working; shipping; old jail museum; hospital, rest homes. Other town is **Dilley** (2,632).

Gaines County

LOCATION: Adjoins New Mexico (H-7).

Cong. Dist. 19	U.S. Jud. Dist. .... N-Lb.
St. Sen. Dist. 28	Ct. Appeals...................... 8
St. Rep. Dist. 77	Admin. Jud. Dist. 7
St. Dist. Cts. 106	

History: Created from Bexar District, 1876, organized 1905; named for James Gaines, a signer of the Texas Declaration of Independence.

Physical Features: Flat, drains to draws; many playas; underground water supply.

Population............... 14,123	Av . Weekly Wage.... $353.80
Area (sq. mi.) 1,502.8	Density 9
Land Area 1,502.4	Water Area 0.4
Civilian Labor 5,598	Jobless Rate.................. 4.8
Altitude (ft.) 3,581-3,039	Retail Sales $76,443,945
Rainfall (in.) 15.8	Gross Sales....... $150,232,991
Jan. min. 25	Reg. Voters 5,536
July max. 95	Election Turnout 49.2
Grow. Season (days)..... 210	Vehicles 11,916
Total Income (mil.) $148	Lane Miles 668
Per Capita Income...$11,041	Tax Value...... $3,889,911,432
Total Wages....... $70,149,992	Fed. Spending $44,527
Housing.....................5,215	Defense Spending $198

Vital Statistics, 1989: Births, 295; Deaths, 83; Marriages, 191; Divorces, 52.

Ethnicity, 1990: White, 10,378 (73.5%); Black, 334 (2.4%); American Indian, 38 (0.3%); Asian, 15 (0.1%); Hispanic, 4,608 (32.6%); Other, 3,358 (23.8%).

Recreation: Local events.

Minerals: Production of oil, gas, sodium sulphate; one of the leading oil-producing counties.

Agriculture: A leading cotton and peanut producing county; other grains, vegetables raised; cattle, sheep, hogs produced; substantial irrigation.

Business: Major oil-producing county, as well as a leader in cotton, peanut production; oil-field activities; agribusinesses; varied manufacturing.

SEMINOLE (6,342) county seat; market center; golf course; hospital. Other town, **Seagraves** (2,398), market for three-county area; manufacturing; state mental health clinic.

Galveston County

LOCATION: On coast, island (N-21).

Cong. Dist. 9	U.S. Jud. Dist. ....S-Gn.
St. Sen. Dist. 4, 11	Ct. Appeals.................1, 14
St. Rep. Dist. 24, 25	Admin. Jud. Dist. 2
St. Dist. Cts....... 10, 56, 122, 212, 306	

History: Among most historic counties; created from Brazoria County 1838; organized 1839; named for Spanish governor of Louisiana and major figure in frontier reorganization, Count Bernardo de Galvez.

Physical Features: Partly island, partly coastal; flat, artificial drainage; sandy, loam, clay soils; broken by bays.

Population...............217,399	Av. Weekly Wage ... $409.96
Area (sq. mi.) 876.3	Density 545
Land Area 398.6	Water Area 477.7
Civilian Labor 109,581	Jobless Rate.................. 7.1
Altitude (ft.) 23-8	Retail Sales ... $1,225,340,718
Rainfall (in.) 40.2	Gross Sales... $4,863,227,457
Jan. min. 48	Reg. Voters 106,430
July max. 87	Election Turnout......... 47.3
Grow. Season (days)..... 335	Vehicles 172,246
Total Income (mil.) .. $3,545	Lane Miles 947
Per Capita Income...$16,995	Tax Value...... $9,454,935,484
Total Wages... $1,588,654,280	Fed. Spending $611,655
Housing.....................99,219	Defense Spending . $112,216

Vital Statistics, 1989: Births, 3,753; Deaths, 1,770; Marriages, 1,754; Divorces, 658.

Ethnicity, 1990: White, 164,210 (75.5%); Black, 38,154 (17.6%); American Indian, 752 (0.3%); Asian, 3,569 (1.6%); Hispanic, 30,962 (14.2%); Other, 10,714 (4.9%).

Recreation: One of Texas' most historic cities; popular tourist and convention center; fishing, surfing, boating, sailing and other water sports on 93-mile Gulf beach (32 miles on Bolivar Peninsula), bay, tributaries; mild climate; **Galveston Island State Park**; Historical District tour in spring includes many homes, sites; Mardi Gras celebration; Rosenberg Library; handicapped fishing tournament; Texas Seaport Museum, other mu-

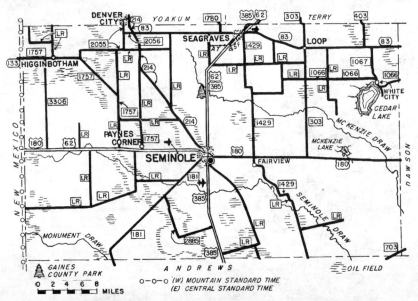

Galveston Co. (Cont.)

seums, Shrimp Festival; strawberry festival at Dickinson; drama "Lone Star" presented in outdoor amphitheater in summer; restored sailing ship, "Elissa," railroad museum; Dickens Winter Festival on the Strand; lighted boat parade, sports fest in Texas City.

Minerals: Production of oil, gas, clays, sand and gravel.

Agriculture: Rice a major crop; substantial irrigation; cattle, horses also raised; other crops soybeans, grain sorghums, corn; aquaculture developing.

Business: Port activities dominate economy; insurance and finance center; petrochemical plants; varied manufacturing; tourism; medical education center; oceanographic research center; ship building; commercial fishing.

GALVESTON (59,070) county seat; tourist center; shipping, shipyard; other industries; port container facility; **University of Texas Medical Branch; National Maritime Research Center; Texas A&M University** at Galveston (only city with both A&M and UT campuses); **Galveston College;** hospitals.

Texas City (40,822), refining, petrochemical plants; **College of the Mainland;** hospitals; varied local events.

Other towns include **Bacliff** (5,549), **Bayou Vista** (1,320), **Clear Lake Shores** (1,096), **Dickinson** (9,497), **Friendswood** (14,979 in Galveston County, partly in Harris County), **Hitchcock** (5,868), **Jamaica Beach** (624), **Kemah** (1,094), **La Marque** (14,120), **League City** (30,026 in Galveston County, partly in Harris County), **San Leon** (3,328), **Santa Fe** (8,429), **Tiki Island Village** (537).

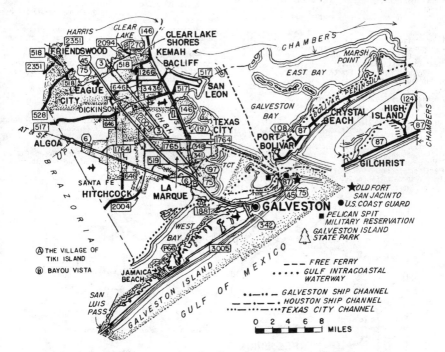

Garza County

LOCATION: Northwest (G-9).

Cong. Dist. 17	U.S. Jud. Dist. ....N-Lb.
St. Sen. Dist. 28	Ct. Appeals.....................7
St. Rep. Dist. 78	Admin. Jud. Dist. 7
St. Dist. Cts..................106	

History: Created from Bexar District, 1876; organized 1907; named for early Texas family.

Physical Features: Rough, broken land, with playas, gullies, canyons, Brazos River forks; sandy, loam, clay soils; Caprock on west.

Population...................5,143	Av. Weekly Wage $313.82
Area (sq. mi.).............896.2	Density 6
Land Area 895.6	Water Area 0.6
Civilian Labor 2,016	Jobless Rate................5.0
Altitude (ft.).......2,986-2,176	Retail Sales $22,741,817
Rainfall (in.) 19.4	Gross Sales $38,868,108
Jan. min. 26	Reg. Voters 2,838
July max. 94	Election Turnout.........45.2
Grow. Season (days).....216	Vehicles 4,850
Total Income (mil.) $56	Lane Miles 453
Per Capita Income...$11,740	Tax Value.........$494,910,191
Total Wages.......$21,263,270	Fed. Spending $16,254
Housing.....................2,183	Defense Spending $87

Vital Statistics, 1989: Births, 78; Deaths, 60; Marriages, 58; Divorces, 21.

Ethnicity, 1990: White, 4,588 (89.2%); Black, 328 (6.4%); American Indian, 9 (0.2%); Asian, 21 (0.4%);

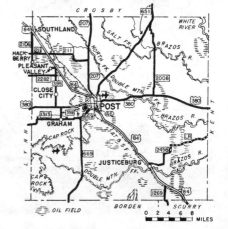

Garza Co. (Cont.)
Hispanic, 1,454 (28.3%); Other, 197 (3.8%).

Recreation: Fourth of July "Family in the Park," founders day in September; historical markers; scenic areas; **Post-Garza Museum; White River Lake**.

Minerals: Production of oil and gas.

Agriculture: Cotton, grains raised; cattle, egg production, hogs sold; some irrigation.

Business: Economy based on oil, farming.

POST (3,768) county seat; founded by **C.W. Post**, cereal manufacturer; oil, agribusiness center; hospital, nursing homes; Texas Main Street city; Algerita Art Center.

Gillespie County

LOCATION: West central (M-13).

Cong. Dist. 21	U.S. Jud. Dist. ....W-An.
St. Sen. Dist. 25	Ct. Appeals.....................4
St. Rep. Dist. 67	Admin. Jud. Dist. 6
St. Dist. Cts....................216	

History: Created and organized, 1848, from Bexar, Travis counties; named for Texas Ranger Capt. R.A. Gillespie; historic German settlement in heart of Comanche country; birthplace of President Lyndon B. Johnson and Fleet Admiral Chester W. Nimitz.

Physical Features: Plateau and hills, broken by spring-fed streams.

Population................17,204	A v. Weekly Wage....$263.99
Area (sq. mi.) 1,061.5	Density 16
Land Area 1,061.1	Water Area 0.4
Civilian Labor 7,770	Jobless Rate.................2.4
Altitude (ft.) 2,244-1,477	Retail Sales $121,516,868
Rainfall (in.) 28.7	Gross Sales.......$248,973,517
Jan. min. 36	Reg. Voters 9,775
July max. 95	Election Turnout 56.4
Grow. Season (days)..... 219	Vehicles 17,516
Total Income (mil.) $291	Lane Miles 703
Per Capita Income...$17,757	Tax Value......$1,548,744,557
Total Wages.......$67,361,265	Fed. Spending.........$58,198

Housing......................8,250 Defense Spending $6,504

Vital Statistics, 1989: Births, 193; Deaths, 230; Marriages, 148; Divorces, 76.

Ethnicity, 1990: White, 16,325 (94.9%); Black, 34 (0.2%); American Indian, 60 (0.3%); Asian, 27 (0.2%); Hispanic, 2,426 (14.1%); Other, 758 (4.4%).

Recreation: Among leading deer-hunting areas; fishing; numerous historic sites and tourist attractions include **Lyndon B. Johnson National Historic Park, LBJ Ranch and Lyndon B. Johnson State Park, Admiral Nimitz State Historical Park; Pioneer Museum Complex, Enchanted Rock State Park**; Easter Fires Pageant in Fredericksburg in March, night in old Fredericksburg in July, county fair in August, Oktoberfest in October, other local events.

Minerals: Sand, gravel, granite, gypsum.

Agriculture: Most income from cattle, other livestock; largest peach-producing county in state; hay, grain sorghums, oats, wheat also raised.

Business: Agribusinesses; tourism; food processing; hunting leases; small manufacturing; granite for markers.

FREDERICKSBURG (6,934) county seat; varied manufacturing; wine production; food processing; museum; tourist attractions; hospital; **Stonewall** (est. 245) agribusiness, tourism, Peach JAMboree in June.

Glasscock County

LOCATION: West (J-9).

Cong. Dist. 17	U.S. Jud. Dist. ...... N-SAng.
St. Sen. Dist. 25	Ct. Appeals.....................8
St. Rep. Dist. 69	Admin. Jud. Dist. 7
St. Dist. Cts..................118	

History: Created 1887, from Tom Green County; organized, 1893; named for Texas pioneer George W. Glasscock.

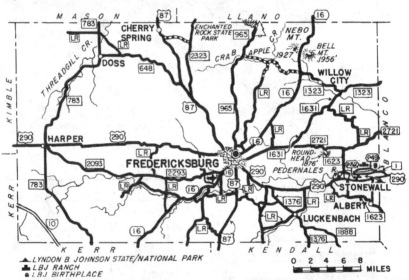

▲ LYNDON B JOHNSON STATE/NATIONAL PARK
▲ LBJ RANCH
● LBJ BIRTHPLACE

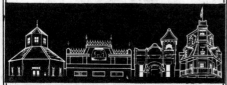

MILES 0 2 4 6 8

Physical Features: Level, broken by several small streams; sandy, loam soils.

Population 1,447	Av. Weekly Wage $338.59
Area (sq. mi.) 900.9	Density 2
Land Area 900.8	Water Area 0.1
Civilian Labor 1,250	Jobless Rate 1.8
Altitude (ft.) 2,727-2,495	Retail Sales $1,574,283
Rainfall (in.) 15.8	Gross Sales $5,678,753
Jan. min. 21	Reg. Voters 703
July max. 93	Election Turnout 74.3
Grow. Season (days) 222	Vehicles 2,151
Total Income (mil.) $22	Lane Miles 274
Per Capita Income ... $18,788	Tax Value $414,528,580
Total Wages $5,792,638	Fed. Spending $6,064
Housing 600	Defense Spending $28

Vital Statistics, 1989: Births, 28; Deaths, 2; Marriages, 14; Divorces, 6.

Ethnicity, 1990: White, 1,156 (79.9%); Black, 0 (0.0%); American Indian, 2 (0.1%); Asian, 0 (0.0%); Hispanic, 424 (29.3%); Other, 289 (20.0%).

Recreation: Local events.

Minerals: Production of oil, gas.

Agriculture: Crops include cotton, grain sorghums, watermelons, wheat, pecans, grapes; cattle, sheep, swine, Angora goats and milk goats raised; 52,000 acres irrigated, mostly cotton.

Business: Economy based on oil, farming and ranching.

GARDEN CITY (est. 300) county seat; serves sparsely settled ranching, oil area.

Goliad County

LOCATION: South (P-16).

Cong. Dist. 14	U.S. Jud. Dist. .... S-Va.
St. Sen. Dist. 18	Ct. Appeals 13
St. Rep. Dist. 31	Admin. Jud. Dist. 4
St. Dist. Cts. 24, 135, 267	

History: Among the state's most historic areas; created 1836 from Spanish municipality, organized 1837; name is anagram of (H)idalgo.

Physical Features: Rolling, brushy; bisected by San Antonio River; sandy, loam, alluvial soils.

Population 5,980	Av. Weekly Wage $315.14
Area (sq. mi.) 859.3	Density 7
Land Area 853.5	Water Area 5.8
Civilian Labor 2,641	Jobless Rate 5.8
Altitude (ft.) 242-63	Retail Sales $20,449,491
Rainfall (in.) 36.8	Gross Sales $25,870,041
Jan. min. 43	Reg. Voters 3,633
July max. 96	Election Turnout 53.7
Grow. Season (days) 285	Vehicles 5,183
Total Income (mil.) $83	Lane Miles 500
Per Capita Income ... $13,892	Tax Value $738,909,774
Total Wages $18,927,128	Fed. Spending $16,671
Housing 2,834	Defense Spending $766

Vital Statistics, 1989: Births, 68; Deaths, 67; Marriages, 47; Divorces, 22.

Ethnicity, 1990: White, 4,953 (82.8%); Black, 407 (6.8%); American Indian, 19 (0.3%); Asian, 5 (0.1%); Hispanic, 2,145 (35.9%); Other, 596 (10.0%).

Goliad Co. (Cont.)

Recreation: Many historic sites including missions, restored **Presidio La Bahia, Fannin Battleground** and **Goliad State Historical Parks**; Gen. Ignacio Zaragoza statue, **Mission Espirtu Santo de Zuniga**; Old Market House museum; fishing, hunting, camping; horse races, golf courses; many local events.

Minerals: Production of oil, gas.

Agriculture: Beef cattle, stocker operations and fed cattle are top revenue producers; corn, grain sorghums, hay raised, fruits introduced; some irrigation.

Business: Primarily based on oil; agribusiness; tourism, electricity-generating plant.

GOLIAD (1,946) county seat; one of state's oldest towns; many historic sites of interest; tourism; oil; agriculture; hospital; library; county fair in March, Longhorn Stampede in June, Christmas in Goliad in December.

Gonzales County

LOCATION: South central (N-16).

Cong. Dist. 14, 15	U.S. Jud. Dist. .... W-SAnt.
St. Sen. Dist. 18	Ct. Appeals.................... 13
St. Rep. Dist. 31	Admin. Jud. Dist. 3
St. Dist. Cts. 25, 2D25	

History: Among most historic areas and first Anglo-American settlements; original county, created 1836, organized 1837; named for Coahuila y Texas Gov. Rafael Gonzales.

Physical Features: Rolling, rich bottom soils along Guadalupe River and its tributaries; some sandy areas; many oaks, pecans.

Population............... 17,205	Av . Weekly Wage.... $274.49
Area (sq. mi.) 1,069.8	Density 16

Land Area 1,067.8	Water Area 2.0
Civilian Labor 6,800	Jobless Rate................. 3.8
Altitude (ft.) 504-201	Retail Sales $100,789,559
Rainfall (in.) 32.6	Gross Sales...... $243,864,817
Jan. min. 41	Reg. Voters 9,884
July max. 97	Election Turnout 40.6
Grow. Season (days)..... 276	Vehicles 15,612
Total Income (mil.) $240	Lane Miles 871
Per Capita Income...$13,209	Tax Value......... $782,264,150
Total Wages....... $73,137,570	Fed. Spending......... $82,767
Housing.....................7,803	Defense Spending ... $31,266

Vital Statistics, 1989: Births, 296; Deaths, 218; Marriages, 109; Divorces, 85.

Ethnicity, 1990: White, 13,025 (75.7%); Black, 1,716 (10.0%); American Indian, 46 (0.3%); Asian, 23 (0.1%); Hispanic, 6,142 (35.7%); Other, 2,395 (13.9%).

Recreation: Historic sites, homes; 86 officially recognized homes or historical markers; **Pioneer Village Living History Center; Palmetto State Park; Gonzales Museum, Gonzales County jail and museum, Independence Park;** other historical attractions; "Come and Take It" festival in Gonzales, Settlers Set-To in Smiley, Feather Fest in Nixon, Guacamole Fest in Waelder.

Minerals: Production of gas, oil, clay, gravel.

Agriculture: Top poultry and egg producing county in state; cow-calf operations important; crops include watermelons, corn, peanuts, pecans, grain sorghums, some wheat; tomatoes introduced; some irrigation, mostly corn, grains.

Business: Agribusinesses, poultry processing; feed plants; tile, clay plants; boots manufactured.

GONZALES (6,527) county seat; first shot in Texas Revolution fired here, called **Lexington of Texas;** shipping, processing center; manufacturing; hospital, nursing home; museum; children's rehabilitation hospitals. Other towns, **Nixon** (1,995 in Gonzales County, partly in Wilson County); **Smiley** (463); **Waelder** (745); **Ottine** (est. 90),**Palmetto State Park, Elks Crippled Children's Hospital; Gonzales Warm Springs Foundation Hospital.**

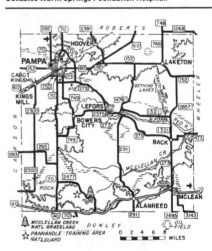

Gray County

LOCATION: In Panhandle (C-10).

Cong. Dist. 13	U.S. Jud. Dist. .... N-Am.
St. Sen. Dist. 31	Ct. Appeals.................... 7
St. Rep. Dist. 84	Admin. Jud. Dist. 9
St. Dist. Cts. 31, 223	

History: Created 1876, from Bexar District; organized, 1902; named for Peter W. Gray, member of first State Legislature.

Physical Features: Level, broken by Red River forks, tributaries; sandy loam, waxy soils.

Population............... 23,967	Av. Weekly Wage $396.44
Area (sq. mi.) 929.2	Density 26
Land Area 928.3	Water Area 0.9
Civilian Labor 11,447	Jobless Rate................. 4.6
Altitude (ft.) 3,296-2,558	Retail Sales $188,773,113
Rainfall (in.) 19.6	Gross Sales...... $365,868,026
Jan. min. 22	Reg. Voters 13,119
July max. 92	Election Turnout 57.4
Grow. Season (days)..... 195	Vehicles 27,076

Gray Co. (Cont.)

Total Income (mil.) $426	Lane Miles 769
Per Capita Income...$18,103	Tax Value...... $1,120,952,604
Total Wages......$179,575,827	Fed. Spending......... $80,503
Housing................... 11,496	Defense Spending ... $10,512

Vital Statistics, 1989: Births, 321; Deaths, 291; Marriages, 268; Divorces, 166.

Ethnicity, 1990: White, 21,566 (90.0%); Black, 899 (3.8%); American Indian, 216 (0.9%); Asian, 115 (0.5%); Hispanic, 1,895 (7.9%); Other, 1,171 (4.9%).

Recreation: Water sports, **Lake McClellan National Grasslands Park; White Deer Land Museum;** barbed-wire museum, golf tournaments; rodeos, other local events.

Minerals: Production of oil, gas.

Agriculture: Fed cattle, stocker operations provide most revenue; wheat, grain sorghums, corn, hay and forage raised; more than 17,000 acres irrigated, mostly grains.

Business: Economy based on petroleum, agriculture, feedlot operations, chemical plant, other manufacturing.

PAMPA (19,959) county seat; petroleum processing; varied manufacturing; other industries; hospital, nursing home; **Clarendon College, Pampa Center.** Other towns, **Lefors** (656), **McLean** (849).

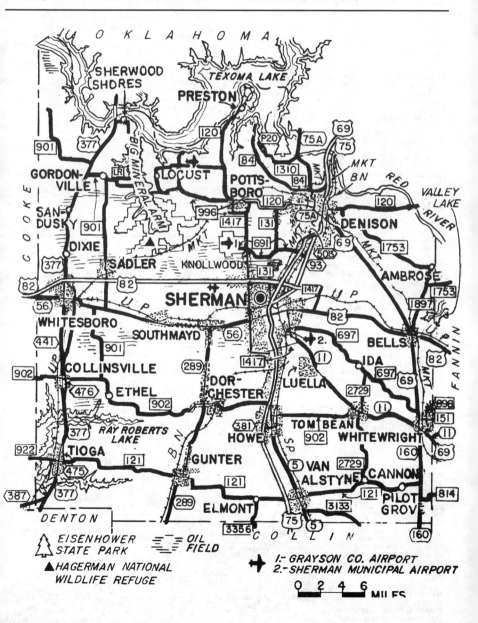

Legend:
- EISENHOWER STATE PARK
- OIL FIELD
- ▲ HAGERMAN NATIONAL WILDLIFE REFUGE
- 1.- GRAYSON CO. AIRPORT
- 2.- SHERMAN MUNICIPAL AIRPORT

0 2 4 6 MILES

Grayson County

LOCATION: North; adjoins Oklahoma (F-17).

Cong. Dist. 4	U.S. Jud. Dist. .... E-Sh.
St. Sen. Dist. 30	Ct. Appeals..................... 5
St. Rep. Dist. 62	Admin. Jud. Dist. 1
St. Dist. Cts. 15, 59, 336	

History: Created, organized, 1846, from Fannin County; named for Republic of Texas Atty. Gen. Peter W. Grayson.

Physical Features: Level, some low hills; sandy loam, Blackland soils; drains to Red River on north and to tributaries of the Trinity River on the south.

Population............... 95,021	Av. Weekly Wage $401.54
Area (sq. mi.)............. 979.1	Density 102
Land Area 933.6	Water Area 45.5
Civilian Labor 47,282	Jobless Rate................. 5.3
Altitude (ft.)............867-535	Retail Sales $677,524,138
Rainfall (in.) 38.2	Gross Sales.... $1,425,643,714
Jan. min. 30	Reg. Voters 46,696
July max. 95	Election Turnout 47.1
Grow. Season (days)..... 227	Vehicles 91,973
Total Income (mil.) .. $1,478	Lane Miles 1,158
Per Capita Income...$15,040	Tax Value...... $3,387,794,137
Total Wages......$773,695,498	Fed. Spending $285,725
Housing................... 44,181	Defense Spending ... $23,072

Vital Statistics, 1989: Births, 1,339; Deaths, 1,162; Marriages, 1,097; Divorces, 733.

Ethnicity, 1990: White, 85,553 (90.0%); Black, 6,565 (6.9%); American Indian, 1,046 (1.1%); Asian, 412 (0.4%); Hispanic, 2,795 (2.9%); Other, 1,445 (1.5%).

Recreation: Texoma Lake is a leading fishing, tourist attraction; annual striper fishing derby on lake and Red River; **Ray Roberts Lake**; Western Week; President Dwight D. Eisenhower birthplace; **Eisenhower State Park**; varied cultural activities; **Hagerman Wildlife Refuge; Grayson County Pioneer Village**; antique boat motor museum; many local events.

Minerals: Production of oil, gas and stone.

Agriculture: Most income from cattle, other livestock, including hogs, horses, poultry; crops include wheat, grain sorghums, peanuts; some peanuts irrigated.

Business: Primarily a manufacturing, distribution and trade center for northern Texas and southern Oklahoma; tourism; minerals; agribusinesses significant.

SHERMAN (31,601) county seat; varied manufacturing; many processors, distributors for major companies; **Austin College**; hospitals.

Denison (21,505), manufacturing; food processing; transportation center; tourism; hospitals.

Grayson County College located between Sherman and Denison.

Other towns, **Bells** (962); **Collinsville** (1,033); **Dorchester** (137); **Gunter** (898); **Howe** (2,173); **Knollwood** (205); **Luella** (559); **Pottsboro** (1,177); **Sadler** (316); **Southmayd** (643); **Tom Bean** (827); **Tioga** (625); **Van Alstyne** (2,090), window screen, electronics, saddles, tack manufacturing; local events; **Whitesboro** (3,209), agribusiness, tourism, Mayfest in May, Peanut Festival in October; clinic; **Whitewright** (1,713 in Grayson County, partly in Fannin County).

Gregg County

LOCATION: Northeast (H-20).

Cong. Dist. 4	U.S. Jud. Dist. .... E-Ty.
St. Sen. Dist. 1	Ct. Appeals.............6, 12
St. Rep. Dist. 7	Admin. Jud. Dist. 1
St. Dist. Cts. 124, 188, 307	

History: Created, organized, 1873, from Rusk, Upshur counties; named for Confederate Gen. John Gregg.

Physical Features: Hilly, timbered; sandy, clay, alluvial soils; bisected by Sabine River.

Population.............104,948	Av. Weekly Wage $372.80
Area (sq. mi.)............. 276.3	Density 384
Land Area 274.0	Water Area 2.3
Civilian Labor 54,585	Jobless Rate................. 7.3
Altitude (ft.)............436-289	Retail Sales $1,129,704,039
Rainfall (in.) 46.5	Gross Sales.... $3,890,827,544
Jan. min. 35	Reg. Voters 54,361
July max. 94	Election Turnout 50.4
Grow. Season (days)..... 247	Vehicles 119,943
Total Income (mil.) .. $1,647	Lane Miles 729
Per Capita Income...$15,238	Tax Value.... $5,169,196,764
Total Wages......$976,009,471	Fed. Spending $278,063
Housing................... 44,446	Defense Spending ... $11,086

Vital Statistics, 1989: Births, 1,840; Deaths, 1,032; Marriages, 1,455; Divorces, 776.

Ethnicity, 1990: White, 81,883 (78.0%); Black, 19,937 (19.0%); American Indian, 478 (0.5%); Asian, 491 (0.5%); Hispanic, 3,775 (3.6%); Other, 2,159 (2.1%).

Recreation: Water activities on area lakes; hunting; varied cultural events; **East Texas Oil Museum**, tourism, Glory Days in Kilgore in April, Depot Fest Art Festival and Loblolly Festival in October.

Minerals: Leading oil-producing county with more than 3 billion barrels produced since 1931, mostly from East Texas Field; also, sand and gravel and natural gas.

Agriculture: Agricultural income from beef cattle, hay production, race-horse breeding, timber, Christmas tree production; crops negligible.

Business: Oil-based economy, but with significant other manufacturing; tourism, conventions; agribusinesses and lignite coal production.

LONGVIEW (68,655, partly in Harrison County) county seat; center for East Texas industry; convention center; hospitals; **LeTourneau College** and **Kilgore College Longview Center.**

Kilgore (8,258 in Gregg County, partly in Rusk County), oil center; manufacturing; hospitals; **Kilgore College,** East Texas Treatment Center.

Other towns include **Clarksville City** (720 in Gregg County, partly in Upshur County), **Easton** (355 in Gregg County, partly in Rusk County), **Gladewater** (3,747 in Gregg County, partly in Upshur County), **Lakeport** (710), **Liberty City** (1,607),**Rolling Meadows** (291), **Warren City** (241 in Gregg County, partly in Upshur County), **White Oak** (5,136).

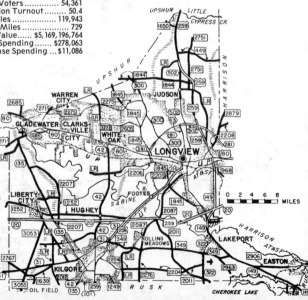

Grimes County

LOCATION: Southeast (L-18).

Cong. Dist. 6	U.S. Jud. Dist. ....S-Hn.
St. Sen. Dist. 5	Ct. Appeals...................1, 14
St. Rep. Dist. 15	Admin. Jud. Dist. 2
St. Dist. Cts. 12, 278	

History: Created from Montgomery County and organized, 1846; named for Jesse Grimes, who signed Texas Declaration of Independence.

Physical Features: Rich bottom soils along Brazos, Navasota rivers; remainder hilly, partly forested.

Population................ 18,828	Av. Weekly Wage $388.70
Area (sq. mi.)..............801.2	Density 24
Land Area 793.8	Water Area 7.4
Civilian Labor 10,634	Jobless Rate 4.0
Altitude (ft.) 415-193	Retail Sales $94,642,601
Rainfall (in.) 40.4	Gross Sales....... $204,133,691
Jan. min. 40	Reg. Voters 8,513
July max. 96	Election Turnout 45.7
Grow. Season (days)..... 278	Vehicles 14,829
Total Income (mil.) $225	Lane Miles 610
Per Capita Income...$12,000	Tax Value......... $957,899,703
Total Wages...... $97,647,173	Fed. Spending........ $47,637
Housing......................7,735	Defense Spending $781

Vital Statistics, 1989: Births, 256; Deaths, 197; Marriages, 140; Divorces, 70.

Ethnicity, 1990: White, 12,879 (68.4%); Black, 4,614 (24.5%); American Indian, 52 (0.3%); Asian, 30 (0.2%); Hispanic, 2,657 (14.1%); Other, 1,253 (6.7%).

Recreation: Hunting, fishing; historic sites; Renaissance Festival in October; county fair; Nostalgic Days in May.

Minerals: Some oil, gas, coal production.

Agriculture: Beef, milk cattle top producers; crops include corn, hay, vegetables, fruit production increasing; honey significant; some forest products sold.

Business: Varied manufacturing; agribusinesses.

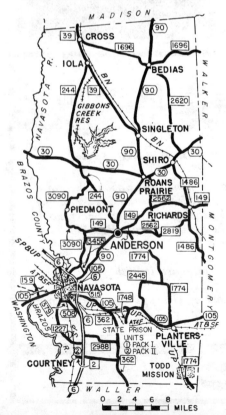

ANDERSON (est. 320) county seat; rural center; **Fanthorp Inn** historical site; Go-Texan weekend in February, Nostalgia Days in May, county fair.

Navasota (6,296), agribusiness center for parts of three counties; varied manufacturing; food, wood processing; hospitals. Other town, **Todd Mission** (54).

Guadalupe County

LOCATION: South central (N-15).

Cong. Dist. 14	U.S. Jud. Dist. ....W-SAnt.
St. Sen. Dist. 21	Ct. Appeals..................... 4
St. Rep. Dist. 46	Admin. Jud. Dist. 3
St. Dist. Cts. 25, 2D25, 274	

History: Created, organized, 1846, from Bexar, Gonzales counties; named for river.

Physical Features: Bisected by Guadalupe River; level to slightly rolling surface; sandy, loam, Blackland soils.

Population................ 64,873	Av. Weekly Wage $337.88
Area (sq. mi.).............714.2	Density 91
Land Area 711.2	Water Area 3.0
Civilian Labor 29,403	Jobless Rate 4.4
Altitude (ft.) 726-372	Retail Sales $245,729,746
Rainfall (in.) 31.4	Gross Sales... $884,407,424
Jan. min. 40	Reg. Voters 29,608
July max. 96	Election Turnout 48.4
Grow. Season (days)..... 267	Vehicles 54,064
Total Income (mil.) $865	Lane Miles 914
Per Capita Income...$13,838	Tax Value..... $2,311,116,782
Total Wages......$260,755,873	Fed. Spending....... $164,439
Housing.................. 25,444	Defense Spending ...$31,981

Vital Statistics, 1989: Births, 971; Deaths, 472; Marriages, 468; Divorces, 272.

Ethnicity, 1990: White, 52,948 (81.6%); Black, 3,665 (5.6%); American Indian, 235 (0.4%); Asian, 465 (0.7%); Hispanic, 19,246 (29.7%); Other, 7,560 (11.7%).

Recreation: Fishing, hunting; historic sites; high school rodeo, Earth Day in April, Cinco de Mayo Celebration, many other local events.

Minerals: Production of oil, gas, sand and gravel, clays.

Agriculture: Beef cattle top producers; horses, hogs, poultry, exotic animals raised; crops include grain sorghums, corn, wheat, oats, cotton, peanuts, pecans, Christmas trees, peaches, nursery plants; little irrigation for vegetables, fruits, pasture, cotton.

Business: Agribusinesses; varied manufacturing; tourism; many residents work in San Antonio; county in San Antonio MSA.

SEGUIN (18,853) county seat; varied manufacturing, hospitals, clinics, nursing home; **Texas Lutheran College**, many local events. Other towns include **Cibolo** (1,757) **Marion** (984), **McQueeney** (2,063), **New Berlin** (188), **New Braunfels** (243 in Guadalupe County, mostly in Comal County), **Shertz** (10,012 in Guadalupe County, partly in Comal, Bexar counties), **Selma** (58 in Guadalupe County partly in Bexar, Comal counties).

Hale County

LOCATION: Northwest (E-8).

Cong. Dist. 19	U.S. Jud. Dist. .... N-Lb
St. Sen. Dist. 31	Ct. Appeals.....................
St. Rep. Dist. 85	Admin. Jud. Dist. ....
St. Dist. Cts. 64, 242	

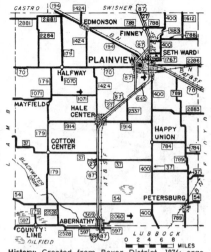

History: Created from Bexar District, 1876; organized, 1888; named for Lt. J.C. Hale, who died at San Jacinto.

Physical Features: Level; fertile sandy, loam soils; many playas; large underground water supply.

Population................. 34,671	Av . Weekly Wage.... $307.18
Area (sq. mi.) 1,004.8	Density 34
Land Area 1,004.7	Water Area 0.1
Civilian Labor 17,342	Jobless Rate................... 5.4
Altitude (ft.).......3,515-3,501	Retail Sales $707,378,451
Rainfall (in.) 19.0	Gross Sales.... $1,128,662,931
Jan. min. 23	Reg. Voters 14,230
July max. 92	Election Turnout......... 44.5
Grow. Season (days).... 211	Vehicles 30,346
Total Income (mil.) $417	Lane Miles 1,052
Per Capita Income...$13,080	Tax Value...... $1,080,001,615
Total Wages......$194,669,041	Fed. Spending....... $116,327
Housing.................... 13,156	Defense Spending $1,333

Vital Statistics, 1989: Births, 637; Deaths, 296; Marriages, 363; Divorces, 194.

Ethnicity, 1990: White, 23,823 (68.7%); Black, 1,852 (5.3%); American Indian, 148 (0.4%); Asian, 136 (0.4%); Hispanic, 14,428 (41.6%); Other, 8,712 (25.1%).

Recreation: Local events; Llano Estacado Museum.

Minerals: Production of oil, gas.

Agriculture: One of leading farm-producing counties; cotton, major crop; others include corn, grain sorghums, wheat, soybeans; fed cattle, stockers raised; 310,000 acres irrigated, primarily cotton.

Business: Many agribusinesses, food processing plants; manufacturing.

PLAINVIEW (21,700) county seat; packing plants, distribution center; other industries; **Wayland Baptist University;** hospitals, mental health/mental retardation center; international occupational center; Queens Classic on Thanksgiving weekend, Pioneer Classic in November; other local events.

Other towns include **Abernathy** (2,132 in Hale County, partly in Lubbock County), **Edmonson** (107), **Hale Center** (2,067), **Petersburg** (1,292), **Seth Ward** (1,402).

Hall County

LOCATION: Northwest (D-10).

Cong. Dist. 13	U.S. Jud. Dist. .... N-Am.
St. Sen. Dist. 31	Ct. Appeals....................... 7
St. Rep. Dist. 84	Admin. Jud. Dist. 9
St. Dist. Cts.................. 100	

History: Created 1876 from Bexar, Young districts; organized 1890; named for Republic of Texas secretary of war W.D.C. Hall.

Physical Features: Rolling to hilly, broken by Red River forks, tributaries; red and black sandy loam.

Population.................3,905	Av. Weekly Wage $265.46
Area (sq. mi.).............904.0	Density 4
Land Area 903.1	Water Area 0.9

Civilian Labor 2,046	Jobless Rate................... 6.9
Altitude (ft.) 2,238-3,315	Retail Sales $19,126,520
Rainfall (in.) 20.3	Gross Sales........ $28,444,198
Jan. min. 25	Reg. Voters 2,752
July max. 97	Election Turnout........ 46.0
Grow. Season (days)..... 213	Vehicles 3,704
Total Income (mil.) $54	Lane Miles 449
Per Capita Income...$13,813	Tax Value......... $146,077,427
Total Wages....... $12,810,181	Fed. Spending......... $22,071
Housing.....................2,189	Defense Spending $112

Vital Statistics, 1989: Births, 37; Deaths, 63; Marriages, 33; Divorces, 23.

Ethnicity, 1990: White, 2,908 (74.5%); Black, 303 (7.8%); American Indian, 15 (0.4%); Asian, 7 (0.2%); Hispanic, 727 (18.6%); Other, 672 (17.2%).

Recreation: Fishing, hunting; museum; Bob Wills Day Celebration in April in Turkey; local events.

Minerals: Not significant.

Agriculture: Most income from crops including cotton, sorghums, peanuts, wheat, vegetables; also beef cattle, hogs; some irrigation.

Business: Grain, cotton processing; farm, ranch supplies, marketing for large rural area.

MEMPHIS (2,465) county seat; foundry; cotton gins; food processing; manufacturing; hospital, nursing home. Other towns include **Estelline** (194), **Lakeview** (202), **Turkey** (507).

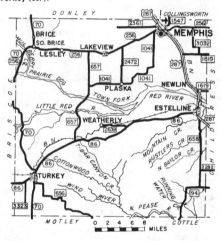

Hamilton County

LOCATION: Northwest (D-10).

Cong. Dist. 13	U.S. Jud. Dist. .... N-Am.
St. Sen. Dist. 31	Ct. Appeals.......................
St. Rep. Dist. 84	Admin. Jud. Dist. 9
St. Dist. Cts.................. 100	

History: Created 1842; then re-created, organized 1858, from Bosque, Comanche, Lampasas counties; named for South Carolinian, Gov. James Hamilton, who aided Texas Revolution and Republic.

Physical Features: Hilly, broken by scenic valleys; loam soils.

Population.................7,733	Av. Weekly Wage $280.64
Area (sq. mi.).............836.3	Density 9
Land Area 835.7	Water Area 0.6
Civilian Labor 3,870	Jobless Rate................... 4.0
Altitude (ft.) 1,590-967	Retail Sales $35,468,925
Rainfall (in.) 29.8	Gross Sales.... $112,094,617
Jan. min. 33	Reg. Voters 4,480
July max. 97	Election Turnout........ 64.7
Grow. Season (days)..... 239	Vehicles 8,011
Total Income (mil.) $115	Lane Miles 575
Per Capita Income...$14,629	Tax Value......... $459,610,542
Total Wages....... $26,107,034	Fed. Spending......... $29,339
Housing.....................4,263	Defense Spending $914

Vital Statistics, 1989: Births, 92; Deaths, 142; Marriages, 49; Divorces, 40.

Ethnicity, 1990: White, 7,389 (95.6%); Black, 2 (**.*%); American Indian, 21 (0.3%); Asian, 24 (0.3%); Hispanic, 403 (5.2%); Other, 297 (3.8%).

Hamilton Co. (Cont.)

Recreation: Deer, quail, dove, duck hunting; dove festival in September; Old Settlers Reunion in July in Hico, other local events.

Minerals: Limited gas, oil, gravel.

Agriculture: Beef cattle, dairies top revenue sources; sheep, goats raised; crops include wheat, sorghums, hay; minor crops are corn, oats, barley.

Business: Agribusinesses include 40 dairies; varied manufacturing; hunting leases; many residents commute to cities to work.

HAMILTON (2,937) county seat; varied manufacturing; hospital, nursing homes; library; other towns, **Evant** (109 in Hamilton County, partly in Coryell County), **Hico** (1,342).

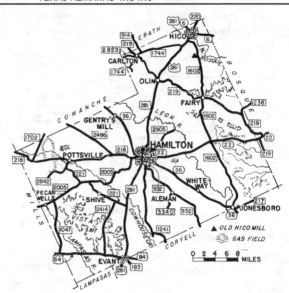

Hansford County

LOCATION: Top of Panhandle (A-9).

Cong. Dist. 13	U.S. Jud. Dist. ....N-Am.
St. Sen. Dist. 31	Ct. Appeals....................7
St. Rep. Dist. 88	Admin. Jud. Dist. 9
St. Dist. Cts....................84	

History: Created 1876, from Bexar, Young districts; organized 1889; named for Judge J.M. Hansford.

Physical Features: Level, many playas, creeks, draws; sandy, loam, black soils; underground water.

Population.................5,848	Av. Weekly Wage $396.94
Area (sq. mi.) 920.4	Density 6
Land Area 919.8	Water Area 0.6
Civilian Labor 3,645	Jobless Rate.................3.0
Altitude (ft.) 3,237-2,986	Retail Sales $41,624,623
Rainfall (in.) 19.2	Gross Sales.......$80,113,056
Jan. min. 20	Reg. Voters 3,290
July max. 95	Election Turnout 59.9
Grow. Season (days).....186	Vehicles 7,584
Total Income (mil.) $142	Lane Miles 509

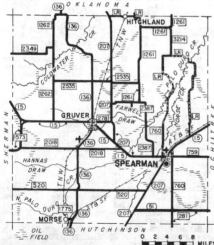

Per Capita Income...$23,690 Tax Value.........$468,038,314
Total Wages.......$41,880,284 Fed. Spending.........$25,529
Housing......................2,525 Defense Spending $69

Vital Statistics, 1989: Births, 89; Deaths, 48; Marriages, 44; Divorces, 7.

Ethnicity, 1990: White, 4,821 (82.4%); Black, 0 (0.0%); American Indian, 23 (0.4%); Asian, 14 (0.2%); Hispanic, 1,174 (20.1%); Other, 990 (16.9%).

Recreation: Stationmasters House Museum; hunting; local events.

Minerals: Production of gas, oil, stone, helium.

Agriculture: Large cattle-feeding operations; crops include sorghums, wheat, corn; substantial irrigation.

Business: Agribusinesses; mineral operations.

SPEARMAN (3,197) county seat; feedlots; grain marketing, storage center; gas processing; hospital; retirement center; airport. Other town, **Gruver** (1,172).

Hardeman County

LOCATION: Borders Oklahoma (E-12).

Cong. Dist. 13	U.S. Jud. Dist. ....N-WF
St. Sen. Dist. 30	Ct. Appeals....................7
St. Rep. Dist. 80	Admin. Jud. Dist. 9
St. Dist. Cts....................46	

History: Created 1858, from Fannin County; re-created, 1876, organized, 1884; named for pioneer Texas brothers, Bailey and T.J. Hardeman.

Physical Features: Rolling, broken area on divide between Pease, Red rivers' forks; sandy, sandy loam soils.

Population.................5,283	Av. Weekly Wage $294.75
Area (sq. mi.) 697.0	Density 8
Land Area 695.4	Water Area 1.6
Civilian Labor 2,596	Jobless Rate.................6.3
Altitude (ft.) 1,749-1,287	Retail Sales $20,675,765
Rainfall (in.) 23.4	Gross Sales.......$59,266,348
Jan. min. 24	Reg. Voters 2,932
July max. 97	Election Turnout.........45.9
Grow. Season (days) ...221	Vehicles 4,906
Total Income (mil.) $84	Lane Miles 466
Per Capita Income...$14,888	Tax Value $268,604,707
Total Wages.......$20,814,120	Fed. Spending.......$24,706
Housing......................2,677	Defense Spending $329

Vital Statistics, 1989: Births, 74; Deaths, 73; Marriages, 39; Divorces, 30.

Ethnicity, 1990: White, 4,427 (83.8%); Black, 321 (6.1%); American Indian, 26 (0.5%); Asian, 16 (0.3%);

Hispanic, 589 (11.1%); Other, 493 (9.3%).

Recreation: Copper Breaks State Park; Lake Pauline activities; museum; Quanah Parker monument, special day; many local events.

Minerals: Production of oil, gas, gypsum.

Agriculture: Wheat, cotton, peanuts, other crops top revenue producers; beef cattle, stockers, sheep, goats, horses; some cotton irrigated.

Business: Agribusinesses; some manufacturing.

QUANAH (3,413) county seat; agribusinesses; cotton oil mill; manufacturing; hospital, rest homes; Copper Breaks Fun Day on Memorial Day, arts, crafts show in fall, other local events. **Chillicothe** (816), other town.

Hardin County

LOCATION: Southeast (L-21).

Cong. Dist.	2	U.S. Jud. Dist.	E-Bt.
St. Sen. Dist.	3	Ct. Appeals	9
St. Rep. Dist.	20	Admin. Jud. Dist.	2
St. Dist. Cts.	88, 356		

History: Created, organized, 1858, from Jefferson, Liberty counties. Named for Texas Revolutionary leader William Hardin.

Physical Features: Heavily timbered; many streams; sandy, loam soils; Big Thicket covers much of area.

Population	41,320	Av. Weekly Wage	$308.62
Area (sq. mi.)	897.3	Density	46
Land Area	894.3	Water Area	3.0
Civilian Labor	17,385	Jobless Rate	6.5
Altitude (ft.)	126-29	Retail Sales	$225,944,717
Rainfall (in.)	55.4	Gross Sales	$357,042,552
Jan. min.	38	Reg. Voters	24,299
July max.	93	Election Turnout	37.4
Grow. Season (days)	246	Vehicles	39,068
Total Income (mil.)	$514	Lane Miles	528
Per Capita Income	$12,691	Tax Value	$1,370,730,616
Total Wages	$111,615,836	Fed. Spending	$98,937
Housing	16,458	Defense Spending	$2,514

Vital Statistics, 1989: Births, 596; Deaths, 385; Marriages, 425; Divorces, 322.

Ethnicity, 1990: White, 37,485 (90.7%); Black, 3,485 (8.4%); American Indian, 123 (0.3%); Asian, 58 (0.1%); Hispanic, 679 (1.6%); Other, 169 (0.4%).

Recreation: Big Thicket with rare plant, animal life; part of Big Thicket National Preserve; **Big Thicket Museum** at Saratoga; Red Cloud Water Park; hunting, fishing; local events.

Minerals: Production of oil, gas and gravel.

Agriculture: Timber provides most income; more than 85 percent of county forested; beef cattle, leading livestock; crops include forage, nursery plants, rice, hay, Christmas trees; some honey sold; some irrigation.

Business: Paper manufacturing; wood processing; minerals; food processing; county in Beaumont-Port Arthur-Orange MSA.

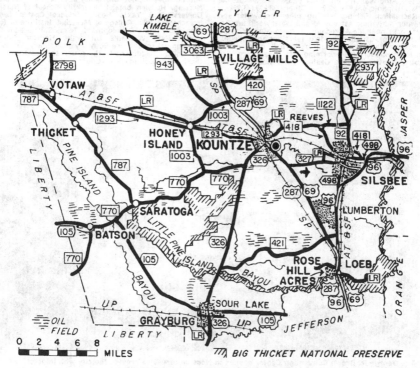

KOUNTZE (2,056) county seat; sawmill; some manufacturing; tourism; nursing home; library; other towns are **Silsbee** (7,391) trade, manufacturing center; oil, gas processing; hospital, nursing home; **Grayburg** (257); **Lumberton** (6,640); **Pinewood Estates** (1,174); Rose Hill Acres (468); **Sour Lake** (1,547).

Harris County

LOCATION: Southeast (M-20).

Cong. Dist. . 7, 8, 9, 18, 22, 25	St. Dist. Cts. 11, 55, 61,
St. Sen.	80, 113, 125, 127, 129, 133,
Dist. 4, 5, 6, 7, 11, 13, 15, 17	151, 152, 157, 164, 165, 174,
St. Rep. Dist. 125-150	176, 177, 178, 179, 180, 182,
U.S. Jud. Dist. .... S-Hn.	183, 184, 185, 189, 190, 208,
Ct. Appeals 1, 14	209, 215, 228, 230, 232, 234,
Admin. Jud. Dist. 2	245, 246, 247, 248, 257, 262,
	263, 269, 270, 280, 281, 295,
	308, 309, 310, 311, 312, 313,
	314, 315, 333, 334, 337, 338,
	339, 351

History: Created 1836, organized 1837; named for John R. Harris, founder of Harrisburg (now part of Houston) in 1824.

Physical Features: Level; typically coastal surface and soils; many bayous, lakes, canals for artificial drainage; partly forested.

Population............ 2,818,199	Av. Weekly Wage $513.85
Area (sq. mi.) 1,777.8	Density 1,625
Land Area 1,728.9	Water Area 48.9
Civilian Labor 1,504,242	Jobless Rate.................. 5.3
Altitude (ft.) 171-6	Retail Sales ... 26,338,167,251
Rainfall (in.) 42.6	Gross Sales... 101,704,393,053
Jan. min. 46	Reg. Voters 1,175,883
July max. 93	Election Turnout 45.9
Grow. Season (days)..... 300	Vehicles 2,218,651
Total Income (mil.) .$50,003	Lane Miles 3,787
Per Capita Income...$17,948	Tax Value..... 113,959,607,497
Total Wages..$38,252,305,937	Fed. Spending 7,414,317
Housing............... 1,170,848	Defense Spending . $815,849

Vital Statistics, 1989: Births, 54,450; Deaths, 17,097; Marriages, 27,466; Divorces, 16,251.

Ethnicity, 1990: White, 1,824,137 (64.7%); Black, 541,180 (19.2%); American Indian, 8,044 (0.3%); Asian, 110,848 (3.9%); Hispanic, 644,935 (22.9%); Other, 333,990 (11.9%).

Recreation: Fishing, boating, other freshwater and saltwater activities; **Astroworld and WaterWorld** amusement parks near the **Astrodome;** numerous athletic and cultural events associated with universities and colleges; professional football, baseball, basketball, other activities; **Jones Hall for the Performing Arts, Nina Vance Alley Theatre, Houston Theatre Center, Music Hall Coliseum,**

Convention Center, the Summit, a 17,000-seat sports and entertainment center; Sam Houston Park, with restored early Houston homes, church, stores; **Museum of Fine Arts, Contemporary Arts Museum,** Rice Museum; Sarah Campbell Blaffer Gallery at the University of Houston; museum of natural science, planetarium, zoological gardens in Hermann Park; **San Jacinto Battleground State Park** with museum, Battleship Texas; Lyndon B. Johnson Space Center; annual livestock show; festival in spring; Azalea Trail, numerous art shows, cultural events, other tourist attractions. (Consult chambers of commerce or Greater Houston Convention and Visitors Council for details and dates.)

Minerals: Among leading oil, gas, petrochemical areas; production of petroleum, cement, natural gas, liquids, salt, lime, sand and gravel, clays, stone; approximately 1 billion barrels of oil produced since 1905; center of multi-county petrochemical processing plants that are among the world's largest.

Agriculture: Beef cattle, cow-calf operations, dairy products major revenue producers; crops include rice, nursery plants, corn, peanuts; about 9,000 acres irrigated for rice; substantial income from forest products.

Business: Highly industrialized county with more than 3,500 manufacturing plants; corporate management center; nation's largest concentration of petrochemical plants; largest U.S wheat-exporting port, among top U.S. ports in the value of foreign trade and total tonnage; petroleum refining, chemicals, food, kindred products, fabricated metal products, non-electrical machinery, primary metals, scientific instruments; paper and allied products, printing and publishing, numerous other products manufactured; center for energy, space and medical research; center of international business.

EDUCATION: Houston is a major center of higher education in Texas, with more than 140,000 students enrolled in 28 colleges and universities in the county. Among these are **Rice University, the University of Houston** (three branches in county), **Texas Southern University, University of St. Thomas, Houston Baptist University, South Texas College of Law, Hispanic International University;** Junior colleges include the Houston Community College system, Lee College, San Jacinto College, North Harris County Junior College. Medical schools and colleges include **University of St. Thomas School of Nursing, Houston Baptist University School of Nursing, University of Texas Health Science Center (seven branches), Baylor College of Medicine,** Institute of Religion and Human Development, Texas Chiropractic College, Texas Woman's University—Houston Center. Theological schools are St. Mary's Seminary, Texas Bible College; additionally there are several trade and technical schools in Harris County.

The George R. Brown Convention Center opened in Houston in 1987 to provide the city with impressive facilities for attracting major meetings and trade shows. Associated Press Photo.

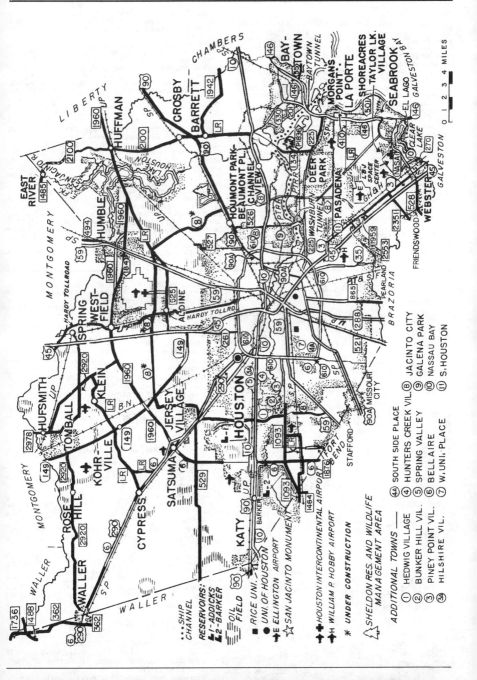

Harris Co. (Cont.)

HOUSTON (1,603,524 in Harris County, partly in Fort Bend, Montgomery counties) county seat; largest Texas city; ranks first in manufacture of petroleum equipment, agricultural chemicals, fertilizers, pesticides, oil and gas pipeline transmission; ranks high in commercial bank demand deposits, wholesale sales, retail sales, value added by manufacture and manufacturing payrolls; many foreign bank branches; several foreign consulates; foreign-trade investment and tourism offices; a leading scientific center; ranks high in manufacture of machinery, fabricated metals; a major distribution, shipping center; engineering and research center; food processing and textile mills; plants make apparel, lumber and wood products; furniture, paper, chemical, petroleum and coal products; publishing center; many other products manufactured; major medical and education center; one of the nation's largest public school systems; prominent corporate center, with more than 200 firms relocating corporate headquarters, divisions or subsidaries to county since 1970.

Pasadena (119,363), residential city with large industrial area manufacturing petrochemicals and other petroleum-related products; civic center; retail mall; San Jacinto College, Texas Chiropractic College; four hospitals; historical museum; Strawberry Festival and other local events.

Bellaire (13,842), residential city with several major office buildings. The **Clear Lake Area** includes **Seabrook** (6,685 in Harris County, partly in Chambers, Galveston counties), **Nassau Bay** (4,320); **El Lago** (3,269); **Webster**

(4,678); **Taylor Lake Village** (3,394), **Lyndon B. Johnson Space Center, University of Houston-Clear Lake**; **Bayport Industrial Complex** includes Port of Bayport; 12 major marinas; two hospitals; **Baytown** (61,126), refining, petrochemical center; Lee College; major shopping mall; hospital center; historical homes; **Tomball**, petrochemicals; retail center; regional hospital; airport; **Humble** (12,060), oil-field equipment manufactured; retail center; hospital; various local events.

Other cities include **Aldine** (11,133); **Bunker Hill Village** (3,391); **Barrett** (3,052); **Channelview** (25,564); **Cloverleaf** (18,230); **Crosby** (1,811); **Deer Park** (27,652), ship-channel industries; fall festival; hospital; **Friendswood** (7,835 in Harris County, mostly in Galveston County); **Galena Park** (10,033); **Hedwig Village** (2,616); **Hilshire Village** (665); **Hunters Creek Village** (3,954); **Highlands** (6,632); **Jacinto City** (9,343); **Jersey Village** (4,826); **Katy** (6,453 in Harris County, partly in Fort Bend, Waller counties), varied manufacturing, hospital, nursing home; **Kingwood** (37,350); **La Porte** (27,910), varied manufacturing; Sylvan Beach Festival in April; **League City** (133 in Harris County, mostly in Galveston County; **Mission Bend** (10,750 in Harris County, partly in Fort Bend County); **Missouri City** (3,957 in Harris County, mostly in Fort Bend County); **Morgan's Point** (341); **Pearland** (1,463 in Harris County, mostly in Brazoria County); **Piney Point Village** (3,197); **Shoreacres** (1,316 in Harris County, partly in Chambers County); **South Houston** (14,207); **Southside Place** (1,392); **Spring** (33,111); **Spring Valley** (3,392); **Stafford** (307 in Harris County, mostly in Fort Bend County); **Sheldon** (1,653; **Waller** (170 in Harris County, partly in Waller County); and **West University Place** (12,920).

Harrison County

LOCATION: Northeast (H-21).

Cong. Dist. 1	U.S. Jud. Dist. .... E-MI.
St. Sen. Dist. 1	Ct. Appeals..................... 6
St. Rep. Dist. 9	Admin. Jud. Dist. 1
St. Dist. Cts.................71	

History: Created 1839, from Shelby County; organized, 1842; named for eloquent advocate of Texas Revolution, Jonas Harrison.

Physical Features: Hilly, rolling; over half forested; Sabine River; Caddo Lake.

Population................ 57,483	Av. Weekly Wage $454.00
Area (sq. mi.).............915.1	Density 63
Land Area 898.8	Water Area 16.3
Civilian Labor 25,049	Jobless Rate................. 6.0
Altitude (ft.) 417-168	Retail Sales ... $294,397,728
Rainfall (in.) 46.4	Gross Sales $944,858,369
Jan. min. 33	Reg. Voters 30,664
July max. 94	Election Turnout 46.6
Grow. Season (days)..... 245	Vehicles 49,485
Total Income (mil.) $738	Lane Miles 1,153
Per Capita Income...$12,839	Tax Value...... $2,850,818,284
Total Wages....$434,339,826	Fed. Spending $195,340
Housing.................. 23,440	Defense Spending ... $64,351

Vital Statistics, 1989: Births, 787; Deaths, 589; Marriages, 770; Divorces, 373.

Ethnicity, 1990: White, 40,387 (70.3%); Black, 16,038 (27.9%); American Indian, 192 (0.3%); Asian, 144 (0.3%); Hispanic, 1,278 (2.2%); Other, 722 (1.3%).

Recreation: Fishing, other water activities; hunting; many plantation homes, many historic sites; Stagecoach Days in May; Old Courthouse Museum; Old World Store; **Caddo Lake and State Park, Lake O' The Pines, Pirkey Lake.**

Minerals: Production of oil, gas, coal, clays, sand and gravel.

Agriculture: Cattle, hogs provide most revenue; crops include nursery plants, hay, timber.

Business: Oil, gas processing; lumbering; pottery, other varied manufacturing.

MARSHALL (23,682) county seat; petroleum, lumber processing; varied manufacturing; civic center; historic sites; hospital, nursing home; **Wiley College; East Texas Baptist University.** Other towns, **Hallsville** (2,288); **Longview** (1,656 in Harrison County, partly in Gregg, Upshur counties); **Nesbitt** (327); **Scottsville** (283); **Uncertain** (194); **Waskom** (1,812).

Hartley County

LOCATION: Borders New Mexico (B-8).

Cong. Dist. 13	U.S. Jud. Dist. .... N-Am.
St. Sen. Dist. 31	Ct. Appeals..................... 7
St. Rep. Dist. 88	Admin. Jud. Dist. 9
St. Dist. Cts..................69	

History: Created 1876 from Bexar, Young districts; organized 1891; named for Texas pioneers O.C. and R.K. Hartley.

Physical Features: Level; drains to Canadian River, tributaries; playas; sandy, loam, chocolate soils; Rita Blanca Lake.

Population..................3,634	Av. Weekly Wage $317.85
Area (sq. mi.) 1,463.2	Density 2
Land Area 1,462.3	Water Area 0.9
Civilian Labor 1,997	Jobless Rate................. 2.5
Altitude (ft.) 4,397-3,439	Retail Sales $20,052,429
Rainfall (in.) 16.1	Gross Sales $27,145,094
Jan. min. 21	Reg. Voters 2,266
July max. 92	Election Turnout 64.4
Grow. Season(days) 180	Vehicles 4,714
Total Income (mil.) $78	Lane Miles 505
Per Capita Income...$22,066	Tax Value......... $199,042,380
Total Wages....$8,082,323	Fed. Spending $12,305
Housing..................... 1,541	Defense Spending $0

Vital Statistics, 1989: Births, 39; Deaths, 37; Marriages, 3; Divorces, 15.

Ethnicity, 1990: White, 3,510 (96.6%); Black, 9 (0.2%); American Indian, 30 (0.8%); Asian, 7 (0.2%); Hispanic, 201 (5.5%); Other, 78 (2.1%).

Recreation: Rita Blanca Lake activities; ranch museum; local events; **XIT Rodeo and Reunion** at Dalhart.

Minerals: Natural gas.

Agriculture: Major income from sorghums, wheat,

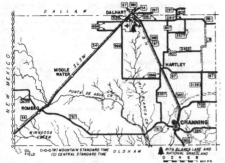

corn; cattle; about 100,000 acres irrigated.

Business: Economy based on agriculture, gas production; varied manufacturing.

CHANNING (277) county seat; **Dalhart** (2,245 in Hartley County, mostly in Dallam County), feedlots; feed, meat processing; other industries.

Haskell County

LOCATION: West central (G-12).

Cong. Dist. 17	U.S. Jud. Dist. .... N-Ab.
St. Sen. Dist. 30	Ct. Appeals.....................11
St. Rep. Dist. 64	Admin. Jud. Dist. 7
St. Dist. Cts. 39	

History: Created 1858, from Milam, Fannin counties; re-created 1876; organized 1885; named for Goliad victim C.R. Haskell.

Physical Features: Rolling; broken areas; drained by Brazos tributaries; Lake Stamford; sandy loam, gray, black soils.

Population....................6,820	Av. Weekly Wage $267.80
Area (sq. mi.)..............910.2	Density 8
Land Area 903.0	Water Area 7.2
Civilian Labor 3,350	Jobless Rate...................3.5
Altitude (ft.).......1,681-1,416	Retail Sales $36,280,626
Rainfall (in.) 24.1	Gross Sales........ $50,428,117
Jan. min. 28	Reg. Voters 4,202
July max. 97	Election Turnout........ 54.5
Grow. Season(days) 232	Vehicles 7,682
Total Income (mil.) $107	Lane Miles 641
Per Capita Income.......$16,289	Tax Value........ $382,042,863
Total Wages....... $22,336,640	Fed. Spending.........$31,896
Housing....................3,828	Defense Spending $1,544

Vital Statistics, 1989: Births, 80; Deaths, 114; Marriages, 60; Divorces, 26.

Ethnicity, 1990: White, 5,481 (80.4%); Black, 244 (3.6%); American Indian, 17 (0.2%); Asian, 16 (0.2%); Hispanic, 1,312 (19.2%); Other, 1,062 (15.6%).

Recreation: Lake Stamford activities; local events; hunting.

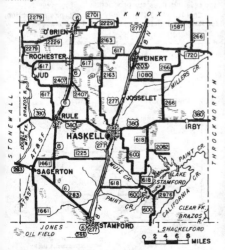

Minerals: Production of oil and gas.

Agriculture: Most income from cotton, grains; remainder from beef cattle, hogs; substantial irrigation.

Business: Agribusinesses, oil-field operations.

HASKELL (3,362) county seat; farming trade center. Other towns **O'Brien** (152), **Rochester** (458), **Rule** (783), **Stamford** (36 in Haskell County, mostly in Jones County), **Weinert** (235).

Hays County

LOCATION: South central (M-15).

Cong. Dist. 10	U.S. Jud. Dist. ....W-An.
St. Sen. Dist. 14	Ct. Appeals.....................3
St. Rep. Dist. 47	Admin. Jud. Dist. 3
St. Dist. Cts........ 22, 207, 274	

History: Created 1843 from Travis County; organized same year; named for Capt. Jack Hays, famous Texas Ranger.

Physical Features: Partly hilly, partly Blackland.

Population 65,614	Weekly Wage $309.23
Area (sq. mi.)..............679.8	Density 97
Land Area 677.9	Water Area 1.9
Civilian Labor 32,116	Jobless Rate...................4.6
Altitude (ft.) 1,501-582	Retail Sales $320,394,294
Rainfall (in.) 34.3	Gross Sales..... $659,647,889
Jan. min. 36	Reg. Voters 31,917
July max. 95	Election Turnout........ 53.9
Grow. Season(days) 254	Vehicles 47,411
Total Income (mil.) $810	Lane Miles 622
Per Capita Income...$12,174	Tax Value...... $2,563,257,196
Total Wages......$288,269,060	Fed. Spending....... $139,924
Housing.................... 25,160	Defense Spending .. $13,581

Vital Statistics, 1989: Births, 921; Deaths, 323; Marriages, 498; Divorces, 235.

Ethnicity, 1990: White, 55,360 (84.4%); Black, 2,220 (3.4%); American Indian, 230(0.4%); Asian, 427 (0.7%); Hispanic, 18,249 (27.8%); Other, 7,377 (11.2%).

Recreation: Major tourist center; retirement area; fine fishing, hunting; **Aquarena; Pioneer Town; Wonder World**; university cultural, athletic events; Cypress

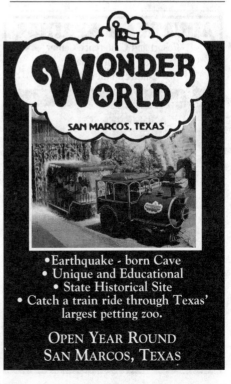

Creek and Blanco River resorts and recreation, guest ranches; antique shops at Wimberley; numerous local events.

Minerals: Sand and gravel, cement produced.

Agriculture: Most agricultural income from beef cattle, some sheep, goats; crops include hay, cotton, grain sorghums, wheat, corn, peaches; a little irrigation; cedar posts.

Business: Tourism, education, retirement village, some manufacturing; part of Austin MSA.

SAN MARCOS (28,743 in Hays County, partly in Caldwell County), county seat; recreation, education center; varied manufacturing including aircraft assemblies, metal stamping; distribution center; hospital, sports medicine, physical therapy center; **Southwest Texas State University, San Marcos Baptist Academy, Gary Job Corps Training Center; Scheib Center** for mentally handicapped; Mardi Gras, Cinco de Mayo in April, Texas Chilympiad in September, many other events. Other towns include **Buda** (1,795), **Dripping Springs** (1,033), **Hays** (251), **Kyle** (2,225), **Mountain City** (377), **Niederwald** (159 in Hays County, partly in Caldwell County), **Uhland** (215 in Hays County, partly in Caldwell County); **Wimberley** (2,403) retirement community, some light manufacturing, artists; Wimberley Fest in July, Gospel Music Festival in October, bike tour; nursing home; **Woodcreek** (889).

Hemphill County

LOCATION: Eastern Panhandle (B-11).

Cong. Dist.	13	U.S. Jud. Dist.	N-Am.
St. Sen. Dist.	31	Ct. Appeals	7
St. Rep. Dist.	88	Admin. Jud. Dist.	9
St. Dist. Cts.	31		

History: Created from Bexar, Young districts, 1876; organized 1887; named for Republic of Texas Justice John Hemphill.

Physical Features: Sloping surface, broken by Canadian, Washita rivers, Lake Marvin; sandy, red, dark soils.

Population	3,720	Av. Weekly Wage	$361.56
Area (sq. mi.)	912.0	Density	4
Land Area	909.7	Water Area	2.3
Civilian Labor	1,797	Jobless Rate	4.0
Altitude (ft.)	2,843-2,185	Retail Sales	$17,080,785
Rainfall (in.)	20.1	Gross Sales	$31,900,341
Jan. min.	22	Reg. Voters	2,168
July max.	95	Election Turnout	67.2
Grow. Season(days)	204	Vehicles	4,580
Total Income (mil.)	$69	Lane Miles	384
Per Capita Income	$18,212	Tax Value	$834,696,275
Total Wages	$22,880,886	Fed. Spending	$10,383
Housing	1,708	Defense Spending	$1,249

Vital Statistics, 1989: Births, 49; Deaths, 32; Marriages, 38; Divorces, 7.

Ethnicity, 1990: White, 3,503 (94.2%); Black, 7 (0.2%); American Indian, 22 (0.6%); Asian, 5 (0.1%); Hispanic, 412 (11.1%); Other, 183 (4.9%).

Recreation: Lake Marvin activities; fall foliage tours; hunting, fishing; **Buffalo Wallow Indian Battleground, Gene Howe Wildlife Management Area**, golf course; fall foliage tour, junior rodeo, county fair, other events.

Minerals: Production of oil, natural gas.

Agriculture: Fed beef cattle, swine top revenue sources; crops include wheat, hay, grain sorghums, improved pastures; some irrigation.

Business: Economy based on petroleum production and refining, livestock production.

CANADIAN (2,417) county seat; oil, gas production; feedlot; hospital, nursing home; golf course.

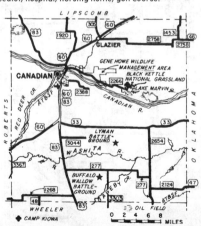

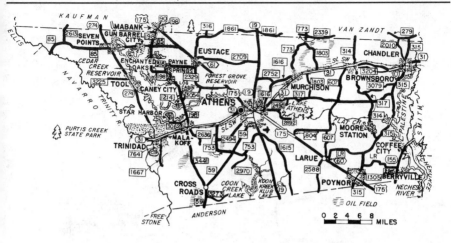

Henderson County

LOCATION: East (I-19).

Cong. Dist. 1
St. Sen. Dist. 9
St. Rep. Dist. 12
St. Dist. Cts. 3, 173

U.S. Jud. Dist. .... E-Ty.
Ct. Appeals...................... 12
Admin. Jud. Dist. 1

History: Created and organized 1846 from Houston, Nacogdoches counties; named for Gov. J. Pinckney Henderson.

Physical Features: Hilly, rolling; one-third forested; bounded by Neches, Trinity rivers; sandy, loam, clay soils; commercial timber; Cedar Creek, other lakes.

Population................ 58,543	Av.Weekly Wage $308.08
Area (sq. mi.)..............949.0	Density 66
Land Area 874.3	Water Area 74.7
Civilian Labor 26,461	Jobless Rate................... 8.9
Altitude (ft.)............763-256	Retail Sales $305,012,418
Rainfall (in.) 39.4	Gross Sales....... $560,286,841
Jan. min. 36	Reg. Voters 30,718
July max. 96	Election Turnout......... 53.7
Grow. Season(days) 260	Vehicles 54,957
Total Income (mil.) $708	Lane Miles 905
Per Capita Income...$12,519	Tax Value...... $2,450,186,835
Total Wages......$173,628,153	Fed. Spending $122,246
Housing................... 31,763	Defense Spending $5,296

Vital Statistics, 1989: Births, 718; Deaths, 651; Marriages, 583; Divorces, 144.

Ethnicity, 1990: White, 52,216 (89.2%); Black, 4,755 (8.1%); American Indian, 181(0.3%); Asian, 141 (0.2%); Hispanic, 2,368 (4.0%);Other, 1,250 (2.1%).

Recreation: Cedar Creek Reservoir, Lake Palestine, Lake Athens, other public, private lakes; **Purtis Creek State Park**; hunting, fishing; annual Black-eyed Pea Jamboree in July, fiddlers' reunion in May, Lakefest in October.

Minerals: Production of oil, gas, clays, lignite, sulphur, sand and gravel.

Agriculture: Most income from cattle, horses, swine, poultry; crops include grain, hay, fruits, vegetables, melons, nursery crops; hardwood timber marketed.

Business: Varied manufacturing; agribusinesses; minerals; recreation.

ATHENS (10,967) county seat; agribusiness center; some industry; tourism; hospital, mental health/mental retardation center; **Trinity Valley Community College**. Other towns, **Berryville** (749); **Brownsboro** (545); **Caney City** (170); **Chandler** (1,630); **Coffee City** (216); **Enchanted Oaks** (290); **Eustace** (662); **Gun Barrel City** (3,526); **Log Cabin** (487); **Mabank** (281 in Henderson County, partly in Kaufman County); **Malakoff** (2,038), brick factory, varied industry, Lakefest in October; **Moore Station** (256); **Murchison** (510); **Payne Springs** (606); **Poynor** (237); **Seven Points** (723 in Henderson County, partly in Kaufman County); **Star Harbor** (368); **Tool** (1,712); **Trinidad** (1,056).

Hidalgo County

LOCATION: Extreme south (U-15).

Cong. Dist. 15
St. Sen. Dist. 20, 27
St. Rep. Dist 40-42,
St. Dist. Cts. 92, 93, 139,
206, 275, 332

U.S. Jud. Dist. .... S-Br.
Ct. Appeals...................... 13
Admin. Jud. Dist. 5

History: Settled early by Spaniards; created, organized, 1852, from Cameron, Starr counties; named for leader of Mexico's independence movement, Miguel Hidalgo y Costillo.

Physical Features: Rich alluvial soils along Rio Grande; sandy, loam soils in north; semitropical vegetation.

Population...............383,545	Av. Weekly Wage $277.79
Area (sq. mi.).......... 1,582.7	Density 244
Land Area 1,569.0	Water Area 13.7
Civilian Labor 164,362	Jobless Rate............... 19.1
Altitude (ft.) 325-28	Retail Sales .. $2,551,491,730
Rainfall (in.) 23.0	Gross Sales .. $4,687,345,956
Jan.min. 48	Reg. Voters 143,524
July max. 95	Election Turnout......... 36.3
Grow. Season(days) 327	Vehicles 228,339
Total Income (mil.) .. $3,118	Lane Miles 1,890
Per Capita Income....$7,814	Tax Value.. $7,418,233,304
Total Wages.. $1,550,767,256	Fed. Spending $917,356
Housing................... 126,434	Defense Spending ... $85,027

Vital Statistics, 1989: Births, 9,834; Deaths, 2,116; Marriages, 4,135; Divorces, 84.

Ethnicity, 1990: White, 286,858 (74.8%); Black, 806 (0.2%); American Indian, 668 (0.2%); Asian, 1,088 (0.3%); Hispanic, 326,972 (85.2%); Other, 94,125 (24.5%).

Recreation: Winter resort, retirement area; fishing, hunting; gateway to Mexico; historical sites; **Bentsen-Rio Grande Valley State Park**; live steam museum at Alamo, Weslaco Bicultural Museum, other museums; many attractions; Rio Grande Valley livestock show at Mercedes; South Texas Lamb and Sheep show at Donna; **Citrus Fiesta** at Mission; Fiesta Hidalgo in March and annual Spring Arts and Plant Sale in April at Edinburg; All-Valley Winter Vegetable Show at Pharr; consult chambers of commerce for special events.

BENTSEN-RIO GRANDE VALLEY STATE PARK

SANTA ANA NATIONAL WILD LIFE REFUGE

★ U.S. BORDER PORT OF ENTRY

0 2 4 6 8 MILES

Minerals: Production of oil, gas, stone, sand and gravel.

Agriculture: Ninety percent of farm cash receipts from crops, principally from cotton, grain, vegetables, citrus, sugar cane; livestock includes cattle; 270,000 acres irrigated.

Business: Food processing, shipping; other agribusinesses; tourism; mineral operations; diversified metro area.

EDINBURG (29,855) county seat; vegetable processing, packing; petroleum operations; clothing; tourist center, planetarium; hospitals; South Texas High School for special education; **Tropical Texas Center for Mental Health/Mental Retardation;** museum; Fiesta Hidalgo in February.

McAllen (84,021) tourist center; varied manufacturing; food processing, packing, shipping; near port of entry to Mexico; foreign trade zone;

Pharr (32,921), agriculture, trading center; trucking; tourism; local events.

Mercedes (12,694), "boot capital," citrus, vegetable center; tourism; clinic; many local events.

Other towns are **Abram-Perezville** (3,999); **Alamo** (8,210); **Alton** (3,069); **Donna** (12,652), citrus center, varied manufacturing, lamb, sheep show in January; **Edcouch** (2,878); **Elsa** (5,242); **Hidalgo** (3,292); **La Homa** (1,403); **La Joya** (2,604); **La Villa** (1,388); **Lopezville** (2,827); **Mila Doce** (2,089); **Mission** (28,653); **Palmhurst** (326); **Palmview** (1,818); **Penitas** (1,077); **Progreso** (1,951); **Progreso Lakes** (154); **San Juan** (10,815); **Scissors** (1,513); **Sullivan City** (2,371); **Weslaco** (21,877).

Hill County

LOCATION: Central (I-16).

Cong. Dist. 6	U.S. Jud. Dist. .... W-Wa.
St. Sen. Dist. 9	Ct. Appeals.....................10
St. Rep. Dist. 57	Admin. Jud. Dist. 3
St. Dist. Cts. 66	

History: Created from Navarro County, organized, 1853; named for G.W. Hill, Republic of Texas official.

Physical Features: Level to rolling; Blackland soils, some sandy loams; drains to Brazos; Whitney Lake, Navarro Mills Reservoir.

Population................ 27,146	Av. Weekly Wage $299.98
Area (sq. mi.)..............985.6	Density 28
Land Area 962.4	Water Area 23.2
Civilian Labor 10,832	Jobless Rate..................6.2
Altitude (ft.) 864-481	Retail Sales $188,880,093
Rainfall (in.) 34.2	Gross Sales...... $303,064,470
Jan. min. 33	Reg. Voters 13,309
July max. 96	Election Turnout 55.1
Grow. Season(days) 250	Vehicles 26,697
Total Income (mil.) $358	Lane Miles 1,086
Per Capita Income...$13,130	Tax Value......... $892,097,286
Total Wages....... $88,928,247	Fed. Spending $95,767
Housing................... 12,851	Defense Spending $3,935

Vital Statistics, 1989: Births, 362; Deaths, 368; Marriages, 262; Divorces, 151.

Ethnicity, 1990: White, 23,669 (87.2%); Black, 2,520 (9.3%); American Indian, 80 (0.3%); Asian, 38 (0.1%); Hispanic, 2,230 (8.2%); Other, 839 (3.1%).

Recreation: Whitney Lake, Aquilla Lake, Navarro Mills Lake activities; excursion boat on Whitney; Hill College, **Confederate Museum, Audie Murphy Gun Museum,** historic structures; art festival in June; motorcycle track, varied activities.

Hill Co. (Cont.)

Minerals: Limestone, gas, oil.

Agriculture: Farm income almost evenly split between crops, livestock; crops include grain sorghums, wheat, corn, cotton, hay; beef, dairy cattle, horses, swine raised.

Business: Agribusinesses, varied manufacturing, tourism.

HILLSBORO (7,072) county seat; varied manufacturing; **Hill College;** regional hospital; retail center; courthouse, antique shops, depot restoration; hospital, nursing homes; arts and crafts fair in June, county fair, other local events. Other towns are **Abbott** (314); **Aquilla** (136); **Blum** (358); **Bynum** (192); **Covington** (238); **Carl's Corner** (94); **Hubbard** (1,589); **Itasca** (1,523); **Malone** (306); **Mertens** (104); **Mount Calm** (303); **Penelope** (210); **Whitney** (1,626), tourist center; nursing homes, hospital, varied manufacturing.

Hockley County

LOCATION: Northwest (F-7).

Cong. Dist.	19	U.S. Jud. Dist. ..... N-Lb.
St. Sen. Dist.	31	Ct. Appeals 7
St. Rep. Dist.	77	Admin. Jud. Dist. 9
St. Dist. Cts.	286	

History: Created 1876, from Bexar, Young districts; organized 1921; named for Republic of Texas secretary of war Gen. G.W. Hockley.

Physical Features: Flat, numerous playas, drains to **Yellow House River, Lake;** loam, sandy loam soils.

Population	24,199	Av. Weekly Wage $363.86
Area (sq. mi.)	908.5	Density 27
Land Area	908.3	Water Area 0.2
Civilian Labor	10,477	Jobless Rate 4.8
Altitude (ft.)	3,633-3,388	Retail Sales $112,075,717
Rainfall (in.)	18.1	Gross Sales $241,190,362
Jan. min.	23	Reg. Voters 11,424
July max.	92	Election Turnout 41.6
Grow. Season(days)	196	Vehicles 21,669
Total Income (mil.)	$293	Lane Miles 750
Per Capita Income	$12,385	Tax Value $2,299,310,955
Total Wages	$147,659,084	Fed. Spending $61,939
Housing	9,273	Defense Spending $796

Vital Statistics, 1989: Births, 379; Deaths, 168; Marriages, 225; Divorces, 134.

Ethnicity, 1990: White, 18,937 (78.3%); Black, 1,023 (4.2%); American Indian, 86 (0.4%); Asian, 33 (0.1%); Hispanic, 7,654 (31.6%);Other, 4,120 (17.0%).

Recreation: Early Settlers' Day in July, Marigolds Arts, Crafts Festival in November.

Minerals: Production of oil, gas, stone; one of leading oil-producing counties with more than 1 billion barrels produced.

Agriculture: Cotton, grain sorghums are top crops; cattle, hogs raised; substantial irrigation.

Business: Economy based on extensive oil, gas production and services; manufacturing; varied agribusiness.

LEVELLAND (13,986) county seat; oil, cotton, cattle center; hospital, nursing home; **South Plains College.**

Other towns are **Anton** (1,212), **Opdyke West** (100), **Ropesville** (494), **Smyer** (442), **Sundown** (1,759).

Hood County

LOCATION: Central (I-15).

Cong. Dist.	6	U.S. Jud. Dist. ..... N-FW
St. Sen. Dist.	22	Ct. Appeals 2
St. Rep. Dist.	64	Admin. Jud. Dist. 8
St. Dist. Cts.	355	

History: Created, organized 1866 from Johnson County; named for Confederate Gen. John B. Hood.

Physical Features: Hilly; broken by Paluxy, Brazos rivers; sandy, sandy loam soils.

Population	28,981	Av.Weekly Wage $325.76
Area (sq. mi.)	436.7	Density 68
Land Area	421.6	Water Area 15.1
Civilian Labor	15,593	Jobless Rate 8.2
Altitude (ft.)	1,230-722	Retail Sales $182,751,843
Rainfall (in.)	30.9	Gross Sales $244,793,375
Jan. min.	33	Reg. Voters 15,933
July max.	97	Election Turnout 58.4
Grow. Season(days)	232	Vehicles 31,677
Total Income (mil.)	$523	Lane Miles 375
Per Capita Income	$15,894	Tax Value $1,256,582,831
Total Wages	$94,591,064	Fed. Spending $69,944
Housing	14,930	Defense Spending $6,277

Vital Statistics, 1989: Births, 380; Deaths, 252; Marriages, 302; Divorces, 213.

Ethnicity, 1990: White, 28,054 (96.8%); Black, 52 (0.2%); American Indian, 154 (0.5%); Asian, 177 (0.6%); Hispanic, 1,353 (4.7%); Other, 544 (1.9%).

Recreation: Fishing, scenic areas; summer theater; **Granbury Lake; Acton State Park;** livestock show in

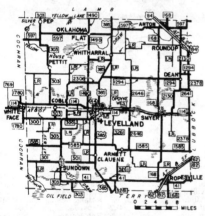

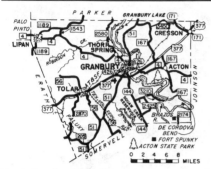

March, Gen. Granbury's Birthday in March; 4th of July celebration.

Minerals: Oil, gas, stone.

Agriculture: Fed beef, cow-calf operations, horses are top revenue sources; crops include pecans, hay, peanuts; some irrigation.

Business: Agribusinesses; tourism; gas production.

GRANBURY (4,045) county seat; agribusiness; tourism; historic downtown area; hospital, nursing home; nuclear-power plant nearby. Other towns are **Lipan** (354), **Oak Trail Shores** (1,750), **Tolar** (523).

Hopkins County

LOCATION: Northeast (G-19).

Cong. Dist. 1	U.S. Jud. Dist. ....E-Ps.
St. Sen. Dist. 1	Ct. Appeals..................6, 12
St. Rep. Dist. 2	Admin. Jud. Dist. 1
St. Dist. Cts.................. 8, 62	

History: Created, organized 1846 from Lamar, Nacogdoches counties; named for the pioneer Hopkins family.

Physical Features: Drains northward to South Sulphur River; light, sandy to heavier black soils; varied timber, including pines.

Population............... 28,833	Av.Weekly Wage $337.02
Area (sq. mi.) 792.7	Density 37
Land Area 784.7	Water Area 8.0
Civilian Labor 13,955	Jobless Rate.................. 5.9
Altitude (ft.).........649-420	Retail Sales ... $268,417,648
Rainfall (in.) 44.2	Gross Sales....... $758,853,392
Jan. min........................31	Reg. Voters 14,095
July max. 94	Election Turnout......... 56.3
Grow. Season(days) 238	Vehicles 29,662
Total Income (mil.) $413	Lane Miles 953
Per Capita Income...$14,094	Tax Value...... $1,232,536,816
Total Wages......$156,851,320	Fed. Spending......... $72,016
Housing................... 12,666	Defense Spending $2,151

Vital Statistics, 1989: Births, 382; Deaths, 317; Marriages, 303; Divorces, 201.

Ethnicity, 1990: White, 25,381 (88.0%); Black, 2,476 (8.6%); American Indian, 126(0.4%); Asian, 70 (0.2%); Hispanic, 1,407 (4.9%); Other, 780 (2.7%).

Recreation: Fishing, hunting; Sulphur Springs Lake activities; museum; dairy festival, state homemade ice cream contest in June; world champion stew contest in September.

Minerals: Production of oil, gas and lignite.

Agriculture: Leading dairy county in Texas and Southwest; also leader in beef cattle production; crops include hay, wheat, silage, corn, rice, soybeans.

Business: Dairies, large milk-processing plants; agribusinesses; varied manufacturing.

SULPHUR SPRINGS (14,062) county seat; dairy center; food processing, distribution; varied manufacturing; hospital. Other towns, **Como** (563), **Cumby** (571), **Tira**(237).

Houston County

LOCATION: East (K-19).

Cong. Dist. 2	U.S. Jud. Dist. .... E-Ty.
St. Sen. Dist. 5	Ct. Appeals..................... 12
St. Rep. Dist. 15	Admin. Jud. Dist. 1
St. Dist. Cts...............3, 349	

History: Created, organized 1837 from Nacogdoches County by Republic of Texas; named for Sam Houston.

Physical Features: Rolling, draining to Neches, Trinity rivers; over half forested; commercial timber production.

Population............... 21,375	Av. Weekly Wage $357.60
Area (sq. mi.) 1,236.8	Density 24
Land Area 1,230.9	Water Area 5.9
Civilian Labor 7,979	Jobless Rate................... 5.2
Altitude (ft.).........552-167	Retail Sales ... $102,344,319
Rainfall (in.) 42.2	Gross Sales....... $261,449,988
Jan. min........................35	Reg. Voters 11,667
July max. 95	Election Turnout......... 49.4
Grow. Season(days) 265	Vehicles 18,585
Total Income (mil.) $314	Lane Miles 838
Per Capita Income...$13,699	Tax Value...... $1,054,783,682
Total Wages......$112,555,345	Fed. Spending......... $70,452
Housing................... 10,263	Defense Spending $2,324

Vital Statistics, 1989: Births, 294; Deaths, 290; Marriages, 198; Divorces, 86.

Ethnicity, 1990: White, 14,373 (67.2%); Black, 6,326 (29.6%); American Indian, 32(0.1%); Asian, 49 (0.2%); Hispanic, 965 (4.5%); Other, 595 (2.8%).

Recreation: Fishing, hunting; **Davy Crockett National Forest; Mission Tejas State Park;** 75 historical markers; historic buildings; Houston County Lake; many local events.

Minerals: Production of oil, gas and sand and gravel.

Agriculture: Cattle principal income source; horses, hogs also raised; crops include hay, corn, cotton, peanuts, watermelons; blueberries introduced; timber harvested; 3,000 acres of peanuts irrigated.

Business: Economy based on livestock, timber, manufacturing, tourism.

CROCKETT (7,024) county seat; varied manufacturing; hospital, nursing homes; local events; **Crockett State School;** fifth oldest town in Texas, many historic sites; fiddlers festival in June, coon hunters finals in September, other local events. Other towns are **Grapeland** (1,450), **Kennard** (341), **Latexo** (289), **Lovelady** (587).

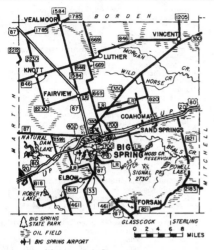

+| BIG SPRING AIRPORT

Howard County

LOCATION: West (I-9).

Cong. Dist. 17	U.S. Jud. Dist. ....N-Ab.
St. Sen. Dist. 28	Ct. Appeals....................11
St. Rep. Dist. 69	Admin. Jud. Dist. 7
St. Dist. Cts..................118	

History: Named for V.E. Howard, Texas legislator; created 1876 from Bexar, Young districts; organized, 1882.

Physical Features: On southern edge Llano Estacado; sandy, sandy loam soils.

Population................. 32,343	Av. Weekly Wage $366.06
Area (sq. mi.).............904.2	Density 36
Land Area 902.9	Water Area 1.3
Civilian Labor 14,396	Jobless Rate...................5.0
Altitude (ft.) 2,776-2,271	Retail Sales $216,518,476
Rainfall (in.) 17.7	Gross Sales.......$498,647,339
Jan. min. 30	Reg. Voters 15,188
July max. 95	Election Turnout......... 51.2
Grow. Season(days) 217	Vehicles 29,848
Total Income (mil.) $474	Lane Miles 834
Per Capita Income...$14,213	Tax Value...... $1,449,826,719
Total Wages......$202,781,577	Fed. Spending $122,077
Housing 13,626	Defense Spending ... $3,374

Vital Statistics, 1989: Births, 535; Deaths, 326; Marriages, 298; Divorces, 63.

Ethnicity, 1990: White, 25,282 (78.2%); Black, 1,225 (3.8%); American Indian, 179(0.6%); Asian, 162 (0.5%); Hispanic, 8,607 (26.6%); Other, 5,495 (17.0%).

Recreation: Big Spring State Park; campground in Comanche Trail Park; Native Plant Trail; several small parks; Moss Creek Reservoir; various other area lakes; museum; historical sites; county fair.

Minerals: Production of oil, gas, sand, gravel and stone.

Agriculture: Crops, principally dry-land cotton, wheat and sorghum, provide most income; beef cattle raised, sheep increasing; some irrigation.

Business: Oil, gas operations; agribusinesses; varied manufacturing, including clothing.

BIG SPRING (23,093) county seat; petrochemicals produced; other varied manufacturing; Howard College; six hospitals, including a state institution and a veterans administration hospital; federal prison unit; numerous local events. Other towns, Coahoma (1,133), Forsan (256).

Hudspeth County

LOCATION: Far west (K-2).

Cong. Dist. 16	U.S. Jud. Dist. ....W-Pe.
St. Sen. Dist. 25	Ct. Appeals.....................8
St. Rep. Dist. 69	Admin. Jud. Dist. 6
St. Dist. Cts..........34,205,210	

History: Named for Texas political leader Claude B. Hudspeth; created, organized 1917 from El Paso County.

Physical Features: Plateau, basin terrain, draining to salt lakes; Rio Grande; mostly rocky, alkaline, clay soils, except alluvial along Rio Grande; desert, mountain vegetation.

Population..................2,915	Av. Weekly Wage $264.70
Area (sq. mi.)........... 4,572.2	Density 1
Land Area 4,571.3	Water Area 0.9
Civilian Labor 1,237	Jobless Rate...................3.5
Altitude (ft.).......7,484-3,492	Retail Sales $5,462,844
Rainfall (in.) 8.0	Gross Sales $7,318,145
Jan. min. 27	Reg. Voters 1,266
July max. 94	Election Turnout 44.9
Grow. Season (days)..... 231	Vehicles 2,000
Total Income (mil.) $33	Lane Miles 818
Per Capita Income...$13,029	Tax Value......... $364,532,402
Total Wages........$7,955,799	Fed. Spending.......... $7,368
Housing.....................1,250	Defense Spending $133

Vital Statistics, 1989: Births, 45; Deaths, 19; Marriages, 21; Divorces, 1.

Ethnicity, 1990: White, 2,345 (80.4%); Black, 15 (0.5%); American Indian, 9 (0.3%); Asian, 2 (0.1%); Hispanic, 1,935 (66.4%); Other, 544 (18.7%).

Recreation: Part of Guadalupe Mountains National Park, containing unique plant life, canyons; scenic drives; fort ruins; hot springs; salt basin; white sands; hunting; many local events.

Minerals: Talc, stone, gypsum.

Agriculture: Most income from cotton, alfalfa, vegetables; fed cattle, hogs raised; 40,000 acres irrigated.

Business: Agribusiness, mining, tourism, hunting leases.

SIERRA BLANCA (est. 700) county seat; ranching center; tourist stop on interstate highway; 4th of July fair; livestock show in January. Other city, Dell City (569) feedlots; clinic; trade center; home of tumbleweed creations.

Hunt County

LOCATION: North (G-18).

Cong. Dist. 1, 4	U.S. Jud. Dist. ....N-Dl.
St. Sen. Dist. 2	Ct. Appeals..................5, 6
St. Rep. Dist. 3	Admin. Jud. Dist. 1
St. Dist. Cts............. 196, 354	

History: Named for Memucan Hunt, Republic of Texas secretary of navy; created, organized 1846 from Fannin, Nacogdoches counties.

Physical Features: Mostly heavy Blackland soil, some loam, sandy loams; level to rolling; Sabine, Sulphur rivers; Lake Tawakoni.

Population............... 64,343	Av. Weekly Wage $397.87
Area (sq. mi.).............882.0	Density 77
Land Area 841.2	Water Area 40.8

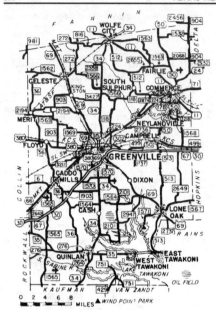

Land Area 887.4
Civilian Labor 12,356
Altitude (ft.) 3,313-2,736
Rainfall (in.) 19.3
Jan. min. 24
July max. 93
Grow. Season(days) 187
Total Income (mil.) $421
Per Capita Income...$17,400
Total Wages......$243,306,841
Housing 11,410

Water Area 7.5
Jobless Rate.....................4.3
Retail Sales $130,361,017
Gross Sales...... $322,772,953
Reg. Voters 14,377
Election Turnout......... 54.0
Vehicles 29,340
Lane Miles 478
Tax Value... $1,472,129,197
Fed. Spending $63,055
Defense Spending $1,099

Vital Statistics, 1989: Births, 365; Deaths, 258; Marriages, 242; Divorces, 131.

Ethnicity, 1990: White, 22,661 (88.2%); Black, 677 (2.6%); American Indian, 362 (1.4%); Asian, 105 (0.4%); Hispanic, 2,509 (9.8%); Other, 1,884 (7.3%).

Recreation: Lake Meredith activities; fishing, camping, boating; **Alibates Flint Quarries National Monument** (in nearby Potter County); **Adobe Walls**, historic Indian battle site; "world's largest" fish fry in June; other local events.

Minerals: Production of gas, oil, sand and gravel.

Agriculture: Feedlot cattle, cow-calf and stocker operations; crops include wheat, grain sorghums, corn, forage; about 45,000 acres irrigated for wheat, grain sorghums, corn.

Business: Oil, gas, petrochemicals; agribusiness; varied manufacturing; tourism.

STINNETT (2,166) county seat; petroleum refining; farm center. Other cities, **Borger** (15,675), carbon-black production, oil-field servicing; varied manufacturing; **Frank Phillips College**; hospital, nursing homes; **Fritch** (2,325 in Hutchinson County, partly in Moore County), **Sanford** (218).

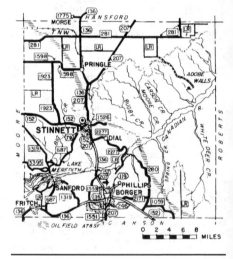

Civilian Labor 35,795
Altitude (ft.) 1,553-688
Rainfall (in.) 40.4
Jan.min..........................30
July max. 95
Grow. Season(days) 237
Total Income (mil.) $953
Per Capita Income...$14,150
Total Wages......$490,049,380
Housing 28,931

Jobless Rate................... 6.1
Retail Sales $392,019,528
Gross Sales... $1,438,223,608
Reg. Voters 30,046
Election Turnout......... 50.0
Vehicles 58,126
Lane Miles 1,282
Tax Value... $1,971,272,355
Fed. Spending $355,557
Defense Spending . $170,325

Vital Statistics, 1989: Births, 996; Deaths, 645; Marriages, 631; Divorces, 379.

Ethnicity, 1990: White, 55,705 (86.6%); Black, 6,802 (10.6%); American Indian, 266 (0.4%); Asian, 351 (0.5%); Hispanic, 2,876 (4.5%); Other, 1,219 (1.9%).

Recreation: Lake Tawakoni; East Texas State University events; local events; county fair; cotton jubilee in October; July 4th celebration.

Minerals: Gas, oil, sand and gravel.

Agriculture: Beef cattle, race horse activity, dairy products top revenue sources; hay, cotton, wheat; some Christmas, fruit trees.

Business: Agribusinesses, education, varied manufacturing; many residents employed in Dallas CMSA.

GREENVILLE (23,071) county seat; varied manufacturing; hospital, nursing homes, local events; **Commerce** (6,825), **East Texas State University**; some manufacturing; hospital, nursing homes. Other towns, **Caddo Mills** (1,068); **Campbell** (683); **Celeste** (733); **Josephine** (11 in Hunt County, mostly in Collin County); **Lone Oak** (521); **Neylandville** (94); **Quinlan** (1,360); **West Tawakoni** (932), tourist center, light industry; catfish tournament in May, lakefest; **Wolfe City** (1,505).

Hutchinson County

LOCATION: North Panhandle (B-9).
Cong. Dist. 13
St. Sen. Dist. 31
St. Rep. Dist. 88
St. Dist. Cts. 84, 316

U.S. Jud. Dist. .... N-Am.
Ct. Appeals.......................7
Admin. Jud. Dist. 9

History: Created 1876 from Bexar Territory; organized 1901; named for pioneer jurist Anderson Hutchinson.

Physical Features: Plain, broken by Canadian River and tributaries, Lake Meredith; many fertile valleys along streams.

Population............... 25,689
Area (sq. mi.) 894.9

Av. Weekly Wage $481.28
Density 29

Irion County

LOCATION: Southwest (K-10).
Cong. Dist. 21
St. Sen. Dist. 25
St. Rep. Dist. 67
St. Dist. Cts. 51

U.S. Jud. Dist. .... N-SAng.
Ct. Appeals......................3
Admin. Jud. Dist. 7

History: Named for Republic of Texas leader R.A. Irion; created, organized 1889 from Tom Green County.

Physical Features: Hilly, broken by Middle Concho, tributaries; clay, sandy soils.

Population............... 1,629
Area (sq. mi.) 1,051.6
Land Area 1,051.5
Civilian Labor 818
Altitude (ft.) 2,725-2,084
Rainfall (in.) 18.0
Jan. min. 30
July max. 95
Grow. Season (days)..... 232
Total Income (mil.) $31
Per Capita Income...$16,935

Av. Weekly Wage $398.94
Density 2
Water Area 0.1
Jobless Rate....................3.1
Retail Sales $2,726,901
GrossSales $10,058,138
Reg. Voters 1,122
Election Turnout......... 53.2
Vehicles 2,009
Lane Miles 247
Tax Value........ $287,490,100

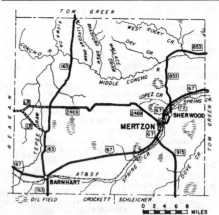

Total Wages.........$9,355,991 Fed. Spending.......... $5,235
Housing........................ 842 Defense Spending $133

Vital Statistics, 1989: Births, 24; Deaths, 14; Marriages, 12; Divorces, 8.

Ethnicity, 1990: White, 1,609 (98.8%); Black, 2 (0.1%); American Indian, 1 (0.1%); Asian, 0 (0.0%); Hispanic, 385 (23.6%); Other, 17 (1.0%).

Recreation: Hunting; historic sites; old Sherwood courthouse built 1900; county fair.

Minerals: Oil, natural gas.

Agriculture: Angora goats, sheep, cattle provide most income; crops include some cotton, grain sorghums; some hay irrigated.

Business: Ranching; oil, gas production.

MERTZON (778) county seat; farm center; wool warehousing.

Jack County

LOCATION: North (G-14).

Cong. Dist. 17	U.S. Jud. Dist. .... N-FW
St. Sen. Dist. 30	Ct. Appeals...................... 2
St. Rep. Dist. 80	Admin. Jud. Dist. 8
St. Dist. Cts...................271	

History: Named for brothers, P.C. and W.H. Jack, leaders in Texas' independence effort; created 1856 from Cooke County; organized 1857.

Physical Features: Rolling, broken by West Fork of the Trinity, other streams; sandy, dark brown, loam

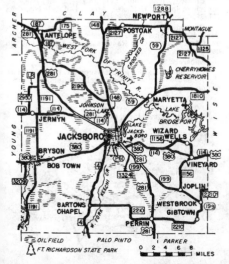

soils; Lakes Bridgeport and Jacksboro.

Population..................6,981	Av. Weekly Wage $348.91
Area (sq. mi.)..............920.1	Density 8
Land Area 917.4	Water Area 2.7
Civilian Labor 3,064	Jobless Rate..................4.5
Altitude (ft.) 1,297-976	Retail Sales $23,218,126
Rainfall (in.) 28.0	Gross Sales....... $42,078,468
Jan. min. 32	Reg. Voters 4,233
July max. 97	Election Turnout......... 48.5
Grow. Season(days) 218	Vehicles 7,793
Total Income (mil.) $93	Lane Miles 564
Per Capita Income...$13,510	Tax Value........ $560,041,557
Total Wages....... $26,743,043	Fed. Spending.........$19,363
Housing......................3,431	Defense Spending $571

Vital Statistics, 1989: Births, 85; Deaths, 66; Marriages, 62; Divorces, 38.

Ethnicity,1990: White, 6,748 (96.7%); Black, 51 (0.7%); American Indian, 18 (0.3%); Asian, 10 (0.1%); Hispanic, 232 (3.3%); Other, 154 (2.2%).

Recreation: Lakes Bridgeport, Jacksboro activities; **Fort Richardson State Historical Park**, museum, other historic sites; rattlesnake hunt, rodeo, golf tournaments; Weekend in Old Mesquiteville Festival in June.

Minerals: Oil, gas produced.

Agriculture: Cow-calf operations provide most income; crops include wheat; firewood significant.

Business: Economy based on petroleum production, oil-field services, livestock, manufacturing, tourism and recreation.

JACKSBORO (3,350) county seat; oil-well servicing, supplies; agribusinesses; hospital; nursing home; library; airport; Mesquiteville Festival in June; lake under construction. **Bryson** (520), other town.

Jackson County

LOCATION: On coast (O-18).

Cong. Dist. 14	U.S. Jud. Dist. .... S-Va.
St. Sen. Dist. 18	Ct. Appeals.................... 13
St. Rep. Dist. 31	Admin. Jud. Dist. 4
St. Dist. Cts.... 24, 135, 267	

History: Mexican municipality, created 1835, became original county the following year; named for U.S. President Andrew Jackson.

Physical Features: Loam, clay, black soils; drains to creek, rivers, bays; prairie and motts of trees.

Population............... 13,039	Av.Weekly Wage $344.96
Area (sq. mi.)..............857.0	Density 15
Land Area 829.5	Water Area 27.5
Civilian Labor 5,482	Jobless Rate..................3.6
Altitude (ft.) 109-11	Retail Sales $83,504,617
Rainfall (in.) 40.9	Gross Sales....... $143,669,822
Jan. min. 42	Reg. Voters 6,939
July max. 94	Election Turnout......... 52.9
Grow. Season(days) 290	Vehicles 13,058
Total Income (mil.) $193	Lane Miles 636
Per Capita Income...$15,569	Tax Value........ $932,728,490
Total Wages....... $54,207,859	Fed. Spending......... $43,113
Housing......................5,831	Defense Spending $489

Jackson Co. (Cont.)

Vital Statistics, 1989: Births, 168; Deaths, 125; Marriages, 87; Divorces, 47.

Ethnicity, 1990: White, 10,857 (83.3%); Black, 1,218 (9.3%); American Indian, 41 (0.3%); Asian, 12 (0.1%); Hispanic, 2,772 (21.3%); Other, 911 (7.0%).

Recreation: Hunting, fishing; historic sites; **Texana Museum; Lake Texana, Brackenridge Plantation campground, Lake Texana State Park;** county fair, rodeo.

Minerals: Production of oil and natural gas.

Agriculture: Rice top revenue source; corn, grain sorghums, cotton also raised; beef cattle; 30,000 acres of rice, limited pasture irrigated; miscellaneous firewood sold.

Business: Petroleum production and operation; metal fabrication and tooling, sheet-metal works, other manufacturing; agribusinesses; lake recreation.

EDNA (5,343) county seat; oil, gas; tourism; agriculture; varied manufacturing; hospitals, nursing homes; county fair in October. Other towns, **Ganado** (1,701), **La Ward** (162).

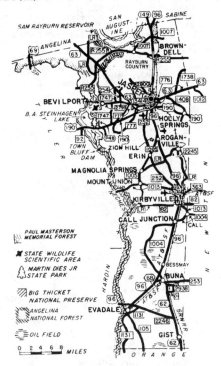

Jasper County

LOCATION: Southeast (L-22).

Cong. Dist. 2	U.S. Jud. Dist. .... E-Bt.
St. Sen. Dist. 3	Ct. Appeals..................... 9
St. Rep. Dist. 20	Admin. Jud. Dist. 2
St. Dist. Cts................ 1, 1A	

History: Created 1836, organized 1837, from Mexican municipality; named for Sgt. William Jasper of U.S. Revolution.

Physical Features: Angelina and Sabine National Forests; **Sam Rayburn Reservoir; B.A. Steinhagen Lake;** Neches River.

Population................. 31,102	Av. Weekly Wage $360.52
Area (sq. mi.).............969.6	Density 34
Land Area 937.4	Water Area 32.2
Civilian Labor 14,284	Jobless Rate..................8.0
Altitude (ft.) 438-68	Retail Sales $242,134,937
Rainfall (in.) 55.4	Gross Sales....... $761,841,870
Jan. min. 38	Reg. Voters 18,410
July max. 93	Election Turnout 38.3
Grow. Season(days) 229	Vehicles 30,859
Total Income (mil.) $397	Lane Miles 682
Per Capita Income...$12,772	Tax Value...... $1,349,736,080
Total Wages....$159,668,268	Fed. Spending....... $100,289
Housing................... 13,807	Defense Spending $3,256

Vital Statistics, 1989: Births, 455; Deaths, 366; Marriages, 335; Divorces, 201.

Ethnicity, 1990: White, 24,750 (79.6%); Black, 5,868 (18.9%); American Indian, 76(0.2%); Asian, 38 (0.1%); Hispanic, 594 (1.9%); Other, 370 (1.2%).

Recreation: Lake activities; hunting; **Martin Dies Jr. State Park;** azalea trail in spring; rodeo.

Minerals: Oil, gas produced.

Agriculture: Cattle, hogs, poultry, horses major revenue source; crops include vegetables, fruit, pecans; 87 percent of area forested, timber is major income producer.

Business: Economy based on timber industries; oil; tourism; fishing; agriculture.

JASPER (6,959) county seat; wood industries; plywood mill, sawmills. Other towns, **Browndell** (192), **Buna** (2,127), **Evadale** (1,422), **Kirbyville** (1,871).

Jeff Davis County

LOCATION: Southwest (I-5).

Cong. Dist. 16	U.S. Jud. Dist. .... W-Pe.
St. Sen. Dist. 25	Ct. Appeals..................... 8
St. Rep. Dist. 69	Admin. Jud. Dist. 6
St. Dist. Cts...................83	

History: Named for Jefferson Davis, U.S. war secretary, Confederate president; created, organized 1887 from Presidio County.

Physical Features: Highest average elevation in Texas, one mile or higher; peaks, canyons, plateaus; intermountain wash, clay, loam soils; cedars, oaks in highlands.

Population................. 1,946	Av. Weekly Wage $316.78
Area (sq. mi.) 2,264.6	Density 1
Land Area 2,264.5	Water Area 0.1
Civilian Labor 894	Jobless Rate.................. 3.5
Altitude (ft.) 8,378-3,871	Retail Sales $4,041,792
Rainfall (in.) 18.9	GrossSales $5,380,342
Jan. min. 32	Reg. Voters 1,189
July max. 83	Election Turnout 56.6
Grow. Season (days)........0	Vehicles 1,925
Total Income (mil.) $24	Lane Miles 469
Per Capita Income...$12,932	Tax Value......... $177,518,762
Total Wages........$9,274,128	Fed. Spending $6,365
Housing................... 1,358	Defense Spending $255

Vital Statistics, 1989: Births, 24; Deaths, 20; Marriages, 10; Divorces, 9.

Ethnicity, 1990: White, 1,671 (85.9%); Black, 7 (0.4%); American Indian, 12 (0.6%); Asian, 4 (0.2%); Hispanic, 770 (39.6%); Other, 252 (12.9%).

Recreation: Scenic drives; hunting; **Fort Davis National Historic Site; Davis Mountains State Park; McDonald Observatory; Prude Ranch** summer camp; July 4th celebration.

Minerals: Not significant.

Agriculture: Cattle top cash supplier; hunting leases significant; wine grapes, feed grains raised; minor irrigation.

Business: Ranching; tourism; hunting.

FORT DAVIS (1,212 est.) county seat; trade, scenic tourist center. Other town, **Valentine** (217).

Jefferson County

LOCATION: Southeast (M-22).

Cong. Dist. 9
St. Sen. Dist. 4
St. Rep. Dist. 20-23
St. Dist. Cts. 58, 60, 136,
172, 252, 279, 317, Cr. 1
U.S. Jud. Dist................. E-Bt.
Ct. Appeals..........................9
Admin. Jud. Dist. 2

History: Created 1836 from Mexican municipality; organized 1837; named for U.S. President Thomas Jefferson.

Physical Features: Grassy plain, with timber in northwest; beach sands, sandy loams, black clay soils; drains to Neches River, Gulf of Mexico.

Vital Statistics, 1989: Births, 3,747; Deaths, 2,345; Marriages, 2,690; Divorces, 1,529.

Ethnicity, 1990: White, 154,-273 (64.4%); Black, 74,412 (31.1%); American Indian, 578 (0.2%); Asian, 5,145 (2.1%); Hispanic,12,629 (5.3%); Other, 4,989 (2.1%).

Recreation: Beaches, fresh- and salt-water fishing; duck, goose hunting; water activities; **Dick Dowling Monument and Park; Spindletop site, Texas Energy Museum,** and boomtown restoration; museum; saltwater lake; **Murphree wildlife refuge; Lamar University,** other events; historic sites; South Texas Fair, many festivals; Tex Ritter memorial and park at Nederland, also heritage festival in March, arts and crafts fair in November.

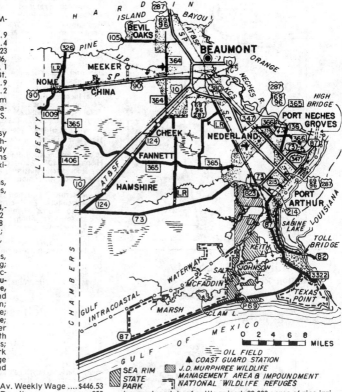

Population..............239,397	Av. Weekly Wage $446.53
Area (sq. mi.).......... 1,111.2	Density 255
Land Area 903.5	Water Area 207.7
Civilian Labor 110,326	Jobless Rate...................7.0
Altitude (ft.)................42-3	Retail Sales ... $1,884,992,177
Rainfall (in.) 52.8	Gross Sales... $6,371,557,787
Jan.min............................42	Reg. Voters 131,173
July max. 93	Election Turnout 47.3
Grow. Season(days) 250	Vehicles 201,415
Total Income (mil.) .. $3,854	Lane Miles 982
Per Capita Income...$16,375	Tax Value... $10,322,365,825
Total Wages.. $2,453,506,585	Fed. Spending....... $874,803
Housing..................101,153	Defense Spending . $189,764

Minerals: Large producer of oil, gas, sulphur, salt, sand and gravel; Spindletop, first major Texas oil field; large petrochemical industry, some wood products; state and federal prison facilities.

Agriculture: Rice top agricultural product, soybeans also produced; beef cattle raised; 32,000 acres of rice irrigated.

Business: Petrochemicals, other chemical plants; shipbuilding; steel mill; port activity; oil-field supplies dominate economy.

BEAUMONT (114,323) county seat; varied petrochemical production; refining; shipbuilding; port activities; rice milling; **Lamar University;** many hospitals, nursing homes; South Texas Fair. Ethnic Heritage Festival in November, Main Street on the Neches.

Port Arthur (58,724), center for oil, chemical activities; shipping; drydock; food processing; tourism. Other towns, **Nederland** (16,192) tourism, Windmill and French museums; hospital; **Bevil Oaks** (1,350); **Central Gardens** (4,026); **China** (1,144); **Groves** (16,513); **Nome** (448); **Port Neches** (12,974) oil, chemical plants; varied manufacturing; riverfront festival.

Jim Hogg County

LOCATION: South (S-14).

Cong. Dist. 15	U.S. Jud. Dist. .... S-La.
St. Sen. Dist. 21	Ct. Appeals...................... 4
St. Rep. Dist. 44	Admin. Jud. Dist. 5
St. Dist. Cts.................. 229	

History: Named for Texas Gov. James Stephen Hogg; created, organized 1913 from Brooks, Duval counties.

Physical Features: Rolling plain, with heavy brush cover; white blow sand and sandy loam; parts hilly, broken.

Population..................5,109	Av.Weekly Wage $249.30
Area (sq. mi.).......... 1,136.1	Density 4
Land Area 1,136.1	Water Area 0.0
Civilian Labor 2,528	Jobless Rate...................8.7
Altitude (ft.)............742-249	Retail Sales $29,213,149
Rainfall (in.) 22.4	Gross Sales $46,319,309
Jan. min. 42	Reg. Voters 3,711
July max. 97	Election Turnout 45.8
Grow. Season(days) 303	Vehicles 3,651

Total Income (mil.) $60	Lane Miles 288
Per Capita Income...$11,682	Tax Value........ $448,815,638
Total Wages....... $15,620,860	Fed. Spending.........$16,055
Housing.....................2,094	Defense Spending $179

Vital Statistics, 1989: Births, 90; Deaths, 41; Marriages, 45; Divorces, 0.

Ethnicity, 1990: White, 4,375 (85.6%); Black, 4 (0.1%); American Indian, 12 (0.2%); Asian, 4 (0.1%); Hispanic, 4,-659 (91.2%); Other, 714 (14.0%).

Recreation: Center of white-tailed deer and bobwhite quail hunting; local events.

Minerals: Oil and gas.

Agriculture: Most income from cattle, ranching; grain sorghums principal crop; some irrigation.

Business: Oil, cattle operations.

HEBBRONVILLE (4,465) county seat; ranching, oilfield center.

See map on next page.

nized 1912; named for developer J.B. Wells Jr.

Physical Features: Level to rolling; sandy to dark soils; grassy, mesquite brush.

Population	37,679	Av.Weekly Wage	$321.07
Area (sq. mi.)	868.2	Density	43
Land Area	864.6	Water Area	3.6
Civilian Labor	16,406	Jobless Rate	6.7
Altitude (ft.)	314-62	Retail Sales	$215,385,247
Rainfall (in.)	28.5	Gross Sales	$456,787,615
Jan. min.	43	Reg. Voters	21,203
July max.	97	Election Turnout	38.1
Grow. Season(days)	289	Vehicles	27,914
Total Income (mil.)	$397	Lane Miles	634
Per Capita Income	$10,496	Tax Value	$1,001,207,233
Total Wages	$184,204,915	Fed. Spending	$98,737
Housing	13,925	Defense Spending	$2,956

Vital Statistics, 1989: Births, 679; Deaths, 320; Marriages, 261; Divorces, 144.

Ethnicity, 1990: White, 28,504 (75.6%); Black, 218 (0.6%); American Indian, 82 (0.2%); Asian, 103 (0.3%); Hispanic, 27,201 (72.2%); Other, 8,772 (23.3%).

Recreation: Hunting; fiestas, other local events; wildflower tour at Premont in March; county fair, youth rodeo.

Minerals: Production of oil, gas, caliche.

Agriculture: Beef cattle primary income source; cotton, sorghums, wheat, corn, vegetables, watermelons raised; some irrigation.

Business: Oil, gas production, cotton and cattle dominate economy.

ALICE (19,788) county seat; oil-field service center; agribusinesses; hospital, nursing home; Fiesta Bandana; Bee County College extension. Other towns, **Orange Grove** (1,175), **Premont** (2,914), **Pernitas Point** (49 in Jim Wells County, partly in Live Oak County); **San Diego** (874 in Jim Wells County, mostly in Duval County).

Jim Wells County

LOCATION: South (R-5).

Cong. Dist.	15
St. Sen. Dist.	20
St. Rep. Dist.	44
St. Dist. Cts.	79
U.S. Jud. Dist.	S-CC
Ct. Appeals	4
Admin. Jud. Dist.	5

History: Created 1911 from Nueces County; orga-

Johnson County

LOCATION: North (I-16).

Cong. Dist.	6
St. Sen. Dist.	22
St. Rep. Dist.	58
St. Dist. Cts.	18, 249
U.S. Jud. Dist.	N-Dl.
Ct. Appeals	10
Admin. Jud. Dist.	3

History: Named for Col. M.T. Johnson of Mexican War, Confederacy; created, organized 1854 out of Ellis, Hill, Navarro counties.

Physical Features: Hilly, rolling, many soil types; Brazos, Trinity rivers; Lake Pat Cleburne.

Population	97,165	Av. Weekly Wage	$325.99
Area (sq. mi.)	734.3	Density	133
Land Area	729.3	Water Area	5.0
Civilian Labor	51,264	Jobless Rate	5.1
Altitude (ft.)	1,065-651	Retail Sales	$472,273,231
Rainfall (in.)	32.4	Gross Sales	$1,079,060,977
Jan.min.	33	Reg. Voters	45,399
July max.	98	Election Turnout	49.4
Grow. Season (days)	233	Vehicles	89,976
Total Income (mil.)	$1,437	Lane Miles	876
Per Capita Income	$14,215	Tax Value	$2,811,618,775
Total Wages	$345,371,434	Fed. Spending	$187,448
Housing	37,001	Defense Spending	$11,983

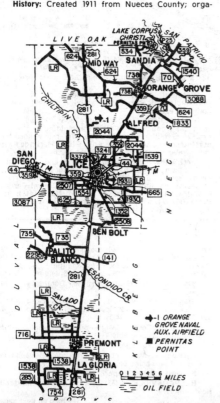

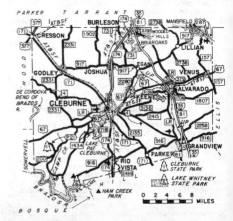

Johnson Co. (Cont.)
Vital Statistics, 1989: Births, 1,434; Deaths, 740; Marriages, 890; Divorces, 601.

Ethnicity, 1990: White, 90,328 (93.0%); Black, 2,521 (2.6%); American Indian, 419(0.4%); Asian, 447 (0.5%); Hispanic, 7,457 (7.7%);Other, 3,450 (3.6%).

Recreation: Excellent bird, deer hunting; water activities on **Lake Pat Cleburne, Whitney Lake** and at **Cleburne State Park;** museum; local events.

Minerals: Limestone, sand, gravel.

Agriculture: A leading dairy county; 85 percent of annual income from cattle, horses, hogs, and dairy products; crops include wheat, grain sorghums, wheat, corn.

Business: Agribusinesses; railroad shops; manufacturing; distribution; lake activities; residents employed in Fort Worth; county is part of Fort Worth-Arlington PMSA.

CLEBURNE (22,205) county seat; dairy center; railshipping terminal; varied manufacturing; hospital; Layland Museum; Hill College, Cleburne campus. Other towns are **Alvarado** (2,918), Johnson County Pioneer Days; **Briaroaks** (535), **Burleson** (14,153 in Johnson County, part in Tarrant County); **Godley** (569); **Grandview** (1,245), **Joshua** (3,828); **Keene** (3,944), **Southwestern Adventist College;** **Mansfield** (617 in Johnson County, mostly in Tarrant County); **Rio Vista** (541); **Venus** (960).

Jones County

LOCATION: West Central (H-12).

Cong. Dist. 17	U.S. Jud. Dist. ....N-Ab.
St. Sen. Dist. 30	Ct. Appeals..............11
St. Rep. Dist. 78	Admin. Jud. Dist. 7
St. Dist. Cts.................259	

History: Named for the last president of the Republic of Texas, Anson Jones; created 1858 from Bexar, Bosque counties; re-created 1876; organized 1881.

Physical Features: Level to rolling prairie; drained by Brazos River fork, tributaries; Lake Stamford.

Population...............16,490	Av. Weekly Wage $307.25
Area (sq. mi.).............937.1	Density 18
Land Area 931.0	Water Area 6.1
Civilian Labor 5,727	Jobless Rate.................5.9
Altitude (ft.)......1,855-1,560	Retail Sales $85,162,088
Rainfall (in.) 25.3	Gross Sales $142,610,520
Jan. min. 31	Reg. Voters...............8,475
July max. 97	Election Turnout 48.8
Grow. Season(days) 223	Vehicles 14,999
Total Income (mil.) $225	Lane Miles 973
Per Capita Income...$13,593	Tax Value......... $562,727,131
Total Wages....... $54,225,272	Fed. Spending $60,727
Housing....................7,610	Defense Spending $2,977

Vital Statistics, 1989: Births, 248; Deaths, 232; Marriages, 111; Divorces, 77.

Ethnicity, 1990: White, 13,786 (83.6%); Black, 666 (4.0%); American Indian, 47 (0.3%); Asian, 31 (0.2%); Hispanic, 2,786 (16.9%);Other, 1,960 (11.9%).

Recreation: Lake activities; **Fort Phantom Hill** site; Cowboys Christmas Ball; Cowboy Reunion on July 4 weekend; old courthouse, restored opera house, museum, art show.

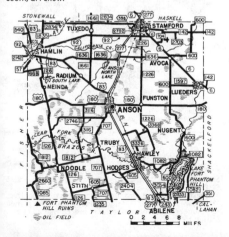

Minerals: Oil, gas, sand and gravel, stone.

Agriculture: Cotton, wheat, milo, hay, watermelons, peanuts major crops; beef cattle, hogs, horses, sheep raised; some irrigation for cotton, peanuts and hay.

Business: Agribusiness center; varied manufacturing.

ANSON (2,644) county seat; farming center; boat, trailer factory, Western clothing manufacturing; hospital, nursing home; historic buildings. Other towns, **Stamford** (3,781 in Jones County, partly in Haskell County), **Hamlin** (2,788 in Jones County, partly in Fisher County), **Hawley** (606), **Lueders** (365 in Jones County, partly in Shackelford County), **Abilene** (797 in Jones County, mostly in Taylor County).

Karnes County

LOCATION: South (O-15).

Cong. Dist. 15	U.S. Jud. Dist. ....W-SAnt.
St. Sen. Dist. 18	Ct. Appeals...............4
St. Rep. Dist. 33	Admin. Jud. Dist. 4
St. Dist. Cts.............. 81, 218	

History: Created, organized 1854 from Bexar, Goliad, San Patricio counties; named for Texas Revolutionary figure Henry W. Karnes.

Physical Features: Sandy loam, dark clay, alluvial soils in rolling terrain; traversed by San Antonio River; mesquite, oak trees.

Population............12,455	Av. Weekly Wage $305.39
Area (sq. mi.).............753.5	Density 17
Land Area 750.3	Water Area 3.2
Civilian Labor 4,329	Jobless Rate.................4.7
Altitude (ft.).............525-225	Retail Sales $50,818,171
Rainfall (in.) 33.2	Gross Sales $112,611,969
Jan. min. 41	Reg. Voters...............7,077
July max. 97	Election Turnout 44.8
Grow. Season(days) 281	Vehicles 10,237
Total Income (mil.) $147	Lane Miles 691
Per Capita Income...$11,796	Tax Value......... $561,799,839
Total Wages... $49,118,360	Fed. Spending $47,243
Housing....................5,112	Defense Spending $936

Vital Statistics, 1989: Births, 223; Deaths, 154; Marriages, 30; Divorces, 22.

Ethnicity, 1990: White, 9,548 (76.7%); Black, 362 (2.9%); American Indian, 35 (0.3%); Asian, 14 (0.1%); Hispanic, 5,916 (47.5%);Other, 2,496 (20.0%).

Recreation: Historic sites include Old Helena; **Panna Maria,** Texas' oldest Polish settlement, founded Dec. 24, 1854; bird hunting; local events, golf course and tennis courts; restored courthouse and museum at Helena; local events.

Minerals: Oil, gas, stone; uranium-producing plant at Falls City.

Agriculture: Most income from beef, dairy cattle, hogs; crops include grain sorghums, wheat, corn; some irrigation for grain, grass.

Business: Agribusiness, mineral production, tourism; varied manufacturing.

More on next page.

Karnes Co. (Cont.)

KARNES CITY (2,916) county seat; farm trade, processing center; oil-field servicing; varied manufacturing; hospitals, nursing home; library. Other towns **Falls City** (478) uranium processing; **Kenedy** (3,763); **Runge** (1,139).

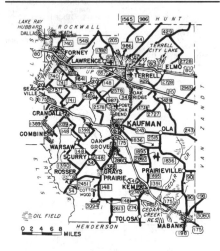

Kaufman County

LOCATION: North (H-18).

Cong. Dist. 4	U.S. Jud. Dist. .... N-DI.
St. Sen. Dist. 2	Ct. Appeals 5, 12
St. Rep. Dist. 4	Admin. Jud. Dist. 1
St. Dist. Cts. 86	

History: Created from Henderson County and organized, 1848; named for member of Texas and U.S. Congresses D.S. Kaufman.

Physical Features: Largely Blackland prairie, draining to Trinity River, Cedar Creek and Lake.

Population 52,220	Av. Weekly Wage $324.09
Area (sq. mi.) 806.8	Density 66
Land Area 786.1	Water Area 20.7
Civilian Labor 27,616	Jobless Rate 4.9
Altitude (ft.) 539-359	Retail Sales $296,335,584
Rainfall (in.) 38.2	Gross Sales $589,044,425
Jan. min. 32	Reg. Voters 24,326
July max. 96	Election Turnout 48.8
Grow. Season(days) 248	Vehicles 48,880
Total Income (mil.) $801	Lane Miles 1,156
Per Capita Income ... $13,779	Tax Value $1,761,811,843
Total Wages $218,696,172	Fed. Spending $148,777
Housing 20,029	Defense Spending $5,556

Vital Statistics, 1989: Births, 765; Deaths, 515; Marriages, 606; Divorces, 295.

Ethnicity, 1990: White, 42,810 (82.0%); Black, 7,295 (14.0%); American Indian, 198 (0.4%); Asian, 229 (0.4%); Hispanic, 3,340 (6.4%); Other, 1,688 (3.2%).

Recreation: Activities at Cedar Creek and Ray Hubbard lakes; **Porter Farm** near Terrell is historic site of origin of U.S.-Texas Agricultural Extension program; historic homes at Terrell; Jackrabbit Stampede in September in Forney, chili cookoff in September; Scarecrow festival in October in Kaufman; other local events.

Minerals: Oil, gas, stone.

Agriculture: Most income from cattle, hogs, poultry, horses; crops include cotton, hay, oats, corn, sorghums, wheat; timber; nursery products marketed.

Business: Antique center; varied manufacturing; trade center; part of Dallas PMSA.

KAUFMAN (5,238) county seat; varied manufacturing; **Terrell** (12,490) agribusiness, varied manufacturing; **Terrell State Hospital, Trinity Valley Community College Health-Science Center**; other towns are **Forney** (4,070) wholesale, retail antiques, light manufacturing, historical homes; **Mabank** (1,458 in Kaufman County, partly in Henderson County); **Kemp** (1,184); **Combine** (895 in Kaufman County, partly in Dallas County); **Cottonwood** (156); **Crandall** (1,652); **Oak Grove** (557); **Oak Ridge** (268); **Post**

Oak Bend (264); **Grays Prairie** (286); **Rosser** (366); **Dallas** (7 in Kaufman County, mostly in Dallas County, partly in Collin, Denton counties).

Kendall County

LOCATION: South central (M-14).

Cong. Dist. 21	U.S. Jud. Dist. ......W.-SAnt.
St. Sen. Dist. 25	Ct. Appeals 4
St. Rep. Dist. 46	Admin. Jud. Dist. 6
St. Dist. Cts. 216	

History: Created, organized from Blanco, Kerr counties 1862; named for pioneer journalist-sheepman and early contributor to Texas Almanac, George W. Kendall.

Physical Features: Hilly, plateau, with springfed streams; caves; scenic drives.

Population 14,589	Av. Weekly Wage $276.27
Area (sq. mi.) 662.9	Density 22
Land Area 662.4	Water Area 0.5
Civilian Labor 7,248	Jobless Rate 2.7
Altitude (ft.) 2,011-1,159	Retail Sales $148,089,242
Rainfall (in.) 32.2	Gross Sales $193,079,682
Jan. min. 35	Reg. Voters 7,734
July max. 93	Election Turnout 58.7
Grow. Season(days) 236	Vehicles 17,856
Total Income (mil.) $297	Lane Miles 436
Per Capita Income ... $18,504	Tax Value $1,080,549,110
Total Wages $48,226,260	Fed. Spending $46,421
Housing 6,138	Defense Spending $6,735

Vital Statistics, 1989: Births, 215; Deaths, 129; Marriages, 182; Divorces, 64.

Ethnicity, 1990: White, 13,682 (93.8%); Black, 58 (0.4%); American Indian, 71 (0.5%); Asian, 38 (0.3%); Hispanic, 2,392 (16.4%); Other, 740 (5.1%).

Recreation: Hunting, fishing, **Guadalupe River State Park**; tourist center; **Cascade Caverns**; historic sites; festival, other local celebrations.

Minerals: Natural gas.

Agriculture: Most income from cattle, sheep, Angora goats, swine, poultry; some wheat, oats, hay, other grains.

Business: Agribusinesses; some manufacturing.

BOERNE (4,274) county seat; livestock center; tourism; some manufacturing; nursing homes. Other towns, **Comfort** (1,477) has state's only Civil War monument honoring Union soldiers; tourism; many local events; **Fair Oaks Ranch**(169 in Kendall County, partly in Bexar, Comal counties).

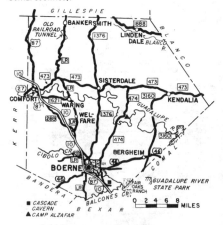

Kenedy County

LOCATION: Southern, coastal (S-16).

Cong. Dist. 27	U.S. Jud. Dist. .... S-CC
St. Sen. Dist. 20	Ct. Appeals 13
St. Rep. Dist. 37	Admin. Jud. Dist. 5
St. Dist. Cts. 105	

History: Among last counties created, organized, 1921, from Cameron, Hidalgo, Willacy counties; named for pioneer steamboat operator and cattleman, Capt. Mifflin Kenedy.

Kenedy Co. (Cont.)

Physical Features: Typical coastal flat, sandy terrain, some loam soils; motts of live oaks.

Population.................... 460	Av. Weekly Wage $341.69
Area (sq. mi.).......... 1,945.5	Density 0
Land Area 1,456.8	Water Area 488.7
Civilian Labor 357	Jobless Rate.................. 1.7
Altitude (ft.)............... 79-9	Retail Sales $401,166
Rainfall (in.) 29.7	Gross Sales............ $432,969
Jan. min....................... 45	Reg. Voters 324
July max. 95	Election Turnout......... 45.4
Grow. Season(days) 319	Vehicles 405
Total Income (mil.) $10	Lane Miles 187
Per Capita Income...$20,548	Tax Value......... $716,720,770
Total Wages.........$4,282,110	Fed. Spending............. $828
Housing........................ 212	Defense Spending $9

Vital Statistics, 1989: Births, 4; Deaths, 3; Marriages, 3; Divorces, 0.

Ethnicity, 1990: White, 378 (82.2%); Black, 0 (0.0%); American Indian, 0 (0.0%); Asian, 0 (0.0%); Hispanic, 362 (78.7%); Other, 82 (17.8%).

Recreation: Hunting a major enterprise; livestock show, fair in January; fishing.

Minerals: Oil, gas.

Agriculture: Cattle, horse production major factors; some watermelons, pasture principal crops.

Business: Oil, ranching economy; hunting leases a factor.

SARITA (est. 185) county seat; cattle-shipping point; ranch headquarters; gas processing; one of state's least populous counties.

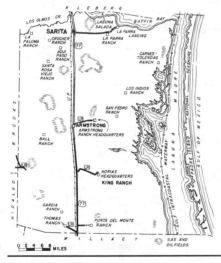

Kent County

LOCATION: West (G-10).

Cong. Dist. 13	U.S. Jud. Dist. .... N-Lb.
St. Sen. Dist. 30	Ct. Appeals...................... 7
St. Rep. Dist. 78	Admin. Jud. Dist. 7
St. Dist. Cts.................... 39	

History: Created 1876, from Bexar, Young territories; organized 1892. Name honors Andrew Kent, one of 32 volunteers from Gonzales who died at the Alamo.

Physical Features: Rolling, broken terrain; drains to Salt and Double Mountain forks of Brazos River; sandy, loam soils.

Population.................... 1,010	Av. Weekly Wage $332.90
Area (sq. mi.) 902.8	Density 1
Land Area 902.3	Water Area 0.5
Civilian Labor 540	Jobless Rate.................. 1.9
Altitude (ft.).......2,830-1,823	Retail Sales $3,097,143
Rainfall (in.) 20.6	GrossSales $6,761,716
Jan. min........................ 24	Reg. Voters 868
July max. 97	Election Turnout......... 22.7
Grow. Season (days)..... 216	Vehicles 1,572

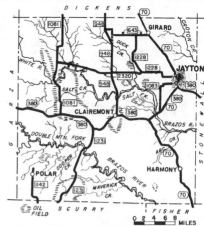

Total Income (mil.) $15	Lane Miles 326
Per Capita Income...$13,723	Tax Value......... $926,186,396
Total Wages.........$4,189,179	Fed. Spending $5,344
Housing........................ 610	Defense Spending $275

Vital Statistics, 1989: Births, 7; Deaths, 15; Marriages, 10; Divorces, 5.

Ethnicity, 1990: White, 902 (89.3%); Black, 6 (0.6%); American Indian, 1 (0.1%); Asian, 0 (0.0%); Hispanic, 120 (11.9%); Other, 101 (10.0%).

Recreation: Hunting, local events; scenic croton breaks and salt flat.

Minerals: Oil, gas, sand and gravel.

Agriculture: Income from cow-calf, stocker operations; crops include cotton, wheat, peanuts; some irrigation.

Business: Agribusinesses, oil-field operations.

JAYTON (608) county seat; oil-field services; farming center.

Kerr County

LOCATION: Southwest central (M-13).

Cong. Dist. 21	U.S. Jud. Dist. ....W-SAnt.
St. Sen. Dist. 25	Ct. Appeals...................... 4
St. Rep. Dist. 67	Admin. Jud. Dist. 6
St. Dist. Cts............. 198, 216	

History: Created, organized 1856 from Bexar County; named for member of Austin's Colony, James Kerr.

Physical Features: Hills, spring-fed streams are scenic attractions; dams, lakes on Guadalupe River.

Population................ 36,304	Av. Weekly Wage $306.98
Area (sq. mi.).......... 1,107.6	Density 33
Land Area 1,106.2	Water Area 1.4
Civilian Labor 16,891	Jobless Rate.................. 3.1
Altitude (ft.).......2,303-1,524	Retail Sales $245,278,115
Rainfall (in.) 29.8	Gross Sales $428,463,385
Jan. min........................ 32	Reg. Voters 20,049
July max. 94	Election Turnout......... 50.2
Grow. Season(days) 216	Vehicles 32,625
Total Income (mil.) $628	Lane Miles 703
Per Capita Income...$17,550	Tax Value...... $1,851,345,431
Total Wages......$176,819,141	Fed. Spending........ $147,998
Housing................... 17,132	Defense Spending .. $11,024

Vital Statistics, 1989: Births, 428; Deaths, 466; Marriages, 335; Divorces, 215.

Ethnicity, 1990: White, 32,842 (90.5%); Black, 805 (2.2%); American Indian, 128 (0.4%); Asian, 141 (0.4%); Hispanic, 5,994 (16.5%); Other, 2,388 (6.6%).

Recreation: Very popular area for tourists, hunters, fishermen; many private and youth camps; dude ranches; **Kerrville State Park;** wildlife management area; hatchery; **Texas Arts and Crafts Fair, Folk Festival, Folk Music Festival** in Kerrville; experimental aircraft fly-in; **Cowboy Artists Museum.**

Minerals: Limited sand, gravel.

Agriculture: Cattle, sheep and goats for wool, mohair primary economic factors; crops include hay, pe-

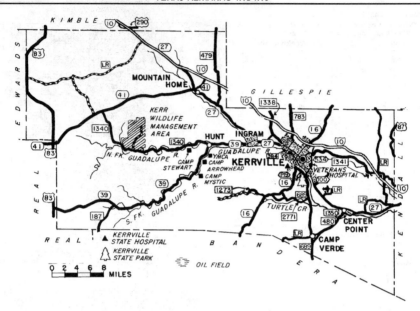

Kerr Co. (Cont.)
cans, oats, wheat; apples introduced; some irrigation for apples, pecans; cedar posts sold.

Business: Tourism; agribusinesses; manufacturing; medical services.

KERRVILLE (17,384) county seat; major tourist center; agribusiness; medical facilities; aircraft and parts and other varied manufacturing; **Schreiner College;** hospital; **Kerrville State Hospital; VA Medical Center;** retirement center; retail trade; numerous local events (check with chamber of commerce). Other town, **Ingram** (1,408).

Kimble County

LOCATION: Central southwest (L-12).

Cong. Dist. 21	U.S. Jud. Dist. ....W-An.
St. Sen. Dist. 25	Ct. Appeals......................4
St. Rep. Dist. 67	Admin. Jud. Dist. 6
St. Dist. Cts. 198	

History: Created from Bexar County 1858; organized 1876; named for George C. Kimble, a Gonzales volunteer who died at the Alamo.

Physical Features: Broken, rolling plain; drains to Llano River; sandy, gray, chocolate loam soils.

Population...................4,122	Av. Weekly Wage $266.76
Area (sq. mi.) 1,250.9	Density 3
Land Area 1,250.7	Water Area 0.2
Civilian Labor 2,210	Jobless Rate 2.4
Altitude (ft.) 2,372-1,783	Retail Sales $36,835,441
Rainfall (in.) 22.5	Gross Sales........ $52,820,951
Jan. min. 32	Reg. Voters 2,307
July max. 97	Election Turnout........ 65.2
Grow. Season(days) 213	Vehicles 4,906
Total Income (mil.) $65	Lane Miles 684
Per Capita Income...$15,704	Tax Value...........................*
Total Wages....... $17,284,231	Fed. Spending $15,641
Housing....................2,604	Defense Spending $577

*Not reported by county.

Vital Statistics, 1989: Births, 56; Deaths, 53; Marriages, 39; Divorces, 25.

Ethnicity,1990: White, 3,654 (88.6%); Black, 2 (**.*%); American Indian, 5 (0.1%); Asian, 10 (0.2%); Hispanic, 772 (18.7%); Other, 451 (10.9%).

Recreation: Hunting, fishing in spring-fed streams; among leading deer counties; **South Llano River State Park, Lake Junction;** Kimble Kounty Kow Kick, flea markets, other local events.

Minerals: Limited sand, gravel, gas, oil.

Agriculture: Cattle, sheep, Angora and Spanish goats are primary products; pecans raised; some irrigation for forage sorghum, coastal Bermuda.

Business: Livestock production, state's largest goat market, wool, mohair, tourism, hunting, fishing dominate economy; cedar oil and wood products sold; metal building materials manufactured.

JUNCTION (2,654) county seat; livestock center; cedar oil, wood products produced; **Texas Tech University Center;** hospital, nursing home; library.

King County

LOCATION: Northwest (F-11).

Cong. Dist. 13	U.S. Jud. Dist. ....N-WF
St. Sen. Dist. 30	Ct. Appeals......................7
St. Rep. Dist. 78	Admin. Jud. Dist. 9
St. Dist. Cts. 50	

History: Created 1876 from Bexar District; organized 1891; named for William P. King, a volunteer from Gonzales who died at the Alamo.

Physical Features: Hilly, broken by Wichita, Brazos tributaries; extensive grassland; dark loam to red soils.

Population....................354	Av. Weekly Wage $390.63
Area (sq. mi.)..............913.3	Density 0
Land Area 912.3	Water Area 1.0
Civilian Labor 339	Jobless Rate 1.5
Altitude (ft.) 2,081-1,739	Retail Sales $1,144,193
Rainfall (in.) 21.5	Gross Sales..........$1,198,285

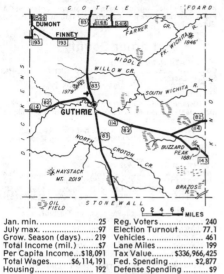

Jan. min. 25	Reg. Voters 240
July max. 97	Election Turnout......... 77.1
Grow. Season (days)..... 219	Vehicles 461
Total Income (mil.) $7	Lane Miles 199
Per Capita Income...$18,091	Tax Value......... $336,966,425
Total Wages......$6,114,191	Fed. Spending $2,877
Housing 192	Defense Spending $9

Vital Statistics, 1989: Births, 4; Deaths, 1; Marriages, 2; Divorces, 0.

Ethnicity, 1990: White, 317 (89.5%); Black, 0 (0.0%);American Indian, 0 (0.0%); Asian, 0 (0.0%); Hispanic, 53 (15.0%); Other, 37 (10.5%).

Recreation: Local events; 6666 Ranch; county fair in October.

Minerals: Oil, gas.

Agriculture: Cow-calf, stocker cattle operations, horses principal sources of income; cotton, wheat, hay, grain sorghums raised.

Business: Minerals, ranching provide most income.

GUTHRIE (est. 160) county seat; ranch-supply center; museum, library.

Kinney County

LOCATION: Southwest (O-11).

Cong. Dist. 23	U.S. Jud. Dist. ....W-DR
St. Sen. Dist. 21	Ct. Appeals...................... 4
St. Rep. Dist. 68	Admin. Jud. Dist. 6
St. Dist. Cts.....................63	

History: Created from Bexar County 1850; organized 1874; named for H.L. Kinney, founder of Corpus Christi.

Physical Features: Hilly, broken by many Rio Gran-

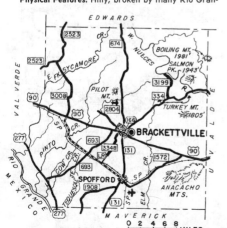

de tributaries; Anacacho Mountains; Nueces Canyon.

Population.................3,119	Av.Weekly Wage $261.12
Area (sq. mi.) 1,365.3	Density 2
Land Area 1,363.5	Water Area 1.8
Civilian Labor 1,039	Jobless Rate................... 5.6
Altitude (ft.) 1,981-909	Retail Sales $6,171,608
Rainfall (in.) 21.1	GrossSales $21,261,076
Jan. min. 36	Reg. Voters 1,744
July max. 96	Election Turnout......... 61.8
Grow. Season (days)..... 270	Vehicles 2,352
Total Income (mil.) $34	Lane Miles 407
Per Capita Income...$12,849	Tax Value....... $333,135,395
Total Wages........$7,250,842	Fed. Spending.........$14,546
Housing......................1,812	Defense Spending $1,090

Vital Statistics, 1989: Births, 39; Deaths, 40; Marriages, 16; Divorces, 8.

Ethnicity, 1990: White, 2,746 (88.0%); Black, 57 (1.8%); American Indian, 26 (0.8%); Asian, 9 (0.3%); Hispanic, 1,570 (50.3%); Other, 281 (9.0%).

Recreation: Hunting; **Alamo Village Guest Ranch;** Seminole Cemetery; **Fort Clark Springs;** 4-H livestock show in January; frontier fair in June.

Minerals: Not significant.

Agriculture: Most income from cattle, sheep, goats; cotton, corn, vegetables produced; some irrigation.

Business: Agribusinesses, tourist trade.

BRACKETTVILLE (1,740) county seat; tourist, local market center; clinic. Other town, **Spofford** (68).

Kleberg County

LOCATION: Southern coast (R-16).

Cong. Dist. 27	U.S. Jud. Dist. ....S-CC
St. Sen. Dist. 20	Ct. Appeals.................... 13
St. Rep. Dist. 37	Admin. Jud. Dist. 5
St. Dist. Cts. 105	

History: Created, organized 1913 from Nueces County; named for San Jacinto veteran and rancher, Robert Kleberg.

Physical Features: Coastal plain, broken by bays; sandy, loam, clay soils; tree motts.

Population................. 30,274	Av.Weekly Wage $311.79
Area (sq. mi.).......... 1,090.4	Density 35
Land Area 871.0	Water Area 219.4
Civilian Labor 15,061	Jobless Rate................... 6.2
Altitude (ft.) 151-3	Retail Sales $170,052,093
Rainfall (in.) 27.5	Gross Sales $250,885,510
Jan. min. 46	Reg. Voters 14,055
July max. 95	Election Turnout......... 44.4
Grow. Season(days) 314	Vehicles 21,127
Total Income (mil.) $400	Lane Miles 364
Per Capita Income...$12,969	Tax Value...... $1,493,095,949
Total Wages......$150,070,512	Fed. Spending $274,293
Housing................... 12,141	Defense Spending $196,066

Vital Statistics, 1989: Births, 609; Deaths, 235; Marriages, 326; Divorces, 186.

Ethnicity, 1990: White, 20,650 (68.2%); Black, 998 (3.3%); American Indian, 81 (0.3%); Asian, 414 (1.4%); Hispanic, 18,529 (61.2%); Other, 8,131 (26.9%).

Recreation: Fishing, water activities, park on **Baffin Bay;** wildlife sanctuary; winter bird watching; Texas A&I events, museum; King Ranch headquarters, tours; livestock show, fair in March and other local events.

Minerals: Production of oil, gas, stone.

Agriculture: Cattle, horses, swine, poultry, top products; crops are cotton, grain sorghums, vegetables; minor irrigation.

More on next page.

Kleberg Co. (Cont.)

Business: Economy based on petroleum, cattle ranching; some manufacturing; military installation; FCC monitoring station.

KINGSVILLE (25,276) county seat; oil, gas center; agribusiness; tourism; chemical and plastic plant; **Texas A&I University;** headquarters of **King Ranch;** hospital; winter home for migratory birds; golf course; **Naval Air Station;** part of Corpus Christi.

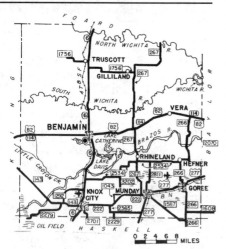

Knox County

LOCATION: Northwest (F-12).

Cong. Dist.	13	U.S. Jud. Dist.	N-WF
St. Sen. Dist.	30	Ct. Appeals	11
St. Rep. Dist.	78	Admin. Jud. Dist.	9
St. Dist. Cts.	50		

History: Created from Bexar, Young territories 1858; re-created 1876; organized 1886; named for U.S. Secretary of War Gen. Henry Knox.

Physical Features: Eroded breaks on rolling plains; Brazos, Wichita rivers; sandy, loam soils.

Population	4,837	Av. Weekly Wage $306.41
Area (sq. mi.)	855.4	Density ... 6
Land Area	854.1	Water Area ... 1.3
Civilian Labor	2,374	Jobless Rate ... 3.2
Altitude (ft.)	1,646-1,401	Retail Sales ... $19,938,721
Rainfall (in.)	24.3	Gross Sales ... $54,131,217
Jan. min.	29	Reg. Voters ... 2,708
July max.	98	Election Turnout ... 51.5
Grow. Season(days)	217	Vehicles ... 4,762
Total Income (mil.)	$64	Lane Miles ... 428
Per Capita Income	$12,995	Tax Value ... $207,313,127
Total Wages	$19,957,386	Fed. Spending ... $23,932
Housing	2,485	Defense Spending ... $234

Vital Statistics, 1989: Births, 82; Deaths, 72; Marriages, 36; Divorces, 26.

Ethnicity, 1990: White, 3,765 (77.8%); Black, 338 (7.0%); American Indian, 7 (0.1%); Asian, 5 (0.1%); Hispanic, 1,088 (22.5%); Other, 722 (14.9%).

Recreation: Lake activities, fishing; hunting; vegetable fair in June, local events.

Minerals: Oil, gas.

Agriculture: Crops include cotton, wheat, hay, vegetables, melons, black-eyed peas top agricultural revenue; stocker, dairy cattle, hogs raised; more than 69,000 acres irrigated.

Business: Agribusinesses, petroleum operations.

BENJAMIN (225) county seat; farm center; **Munday** (1,600) portable buildings, other manufacturing; **Texas A&M Vegetable Research Station; vegetable festival;**

Knox City (1,440) agribusiness, petroleum center; **USDA Plant Materials Research Center;** hospital, nursing home; **Goree** (412).

Lamar County

LOCATION: Northeast (F-19).

Cong. Dist.	1	U.S. Jud. Dist.	E-Ps.
St. Sen. Dist.	1	Ct. Appeals	6
St. Rep. Dist.	2	Admin. Jud. Dist.	1
St. Dist. Cts.	6, 62		

History: Created 1840 from Red River County; organized 1841; named for second president of Republic of Texas, Mirabeau B. Lamar.

Physical Features: On divide between Red, Sulphur rivers; soils chiefly Blackland, except along Red; pines, hardwoods.

Population	43,949	Av. Weekly Wage $358.65
Area (sq. mi.)	932.4	Density ... 48
Land Area	917.0	Water Area ... 15.4
Civilian Labor	21,650	Jobless Rate ... 6.6
Altitude (ft.)	602-390	Retail Sales ... $330,279,547
Rainfall (in.)	45.0	Gross Sales ... $534,285,524
Jan. min.	30	Reg. Voters ... 22,831
July max.	94	Election Turnout ... 45.3
Grow. Season(days)	235	Vehicles ... 43,427
Total Income (mil.)	$624	Lane Miles ... 996
Per Capita Income	$13,858	Tax Value ... $1,338,730,174
Total Wages	$312,418,633	Fed. Spending ... $138,209
Housing	18,955	Defense Spending $5,659

Vital Statistics, 1989: Births, 692; Deaths, 514; Marriages, 548; Divorces, 329.

Ethnicity, 1990: White, 36,814 (83.8%); Black, 6,397 (14.6%); American Indian, 406 (0.9%); Asian, 153 (0.3%); Hispanic, 475 (1.1%); Other, 179 (0.4%).

Recreation: Pat Mayse Lake activities; Gambill goose refuge; hunting, fishing; Sam Bell Maxey Home; State Sen. A.M. Aikin Archives; other museums; fishing tournament in April, heritage festival in July, crafts fair, fiddlers contest in October, many other local events.

Minerals: Negligible.

Agriculture: Beef, dairy cattle top agricultural products; hay, wheat, soybeans, cotton raised; some peanuts irrigated.

Business: Varied manufacturing; agribusinesses; tourism.

PARIS (24,699) county seat; varied manufacturing; medical center, hospitals; five Fortune 500 companies in city; **Paris Junior College.** Other towns include **Blossom** (1,440), **Deport** (712 in Lamar County, partly in Red River County); **Reno** (1,784), **Roxton** (639), **Sun Valley** (60), **Toco** (127).

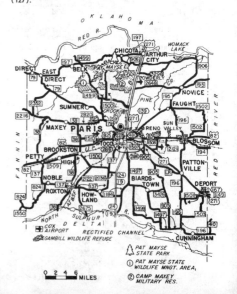

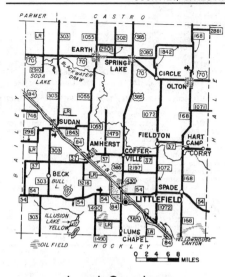

Population................ 13,521	Av. Weekly Wage $261.74
Area (sq. mi.)............ 713.9	Density 19
Land Area 712.0	Water Area 1.9
Civilian Labor 6,221	Jobless Rate.................. 6.0
Altitude (ft.)...... 1,190-339	Retail Sales $49,620,715
Rainfall (in.) 29.5	Gross Sales $93,302,720
Jan. min. 31	Reg. Voters 6,815
July max. 96	Election Turnout........ 53.5
Grow. Season(days) 223	Vehicles 12,531
Total Income (mil.) $182	Lane Miles 468
Per Capita Income...$12,710	Tax Value........ $547,126,939
Total Wages....... $36,013,029	Fed. Spending $47,155
Housing..................... 6,159	Defense Spending $7,919

Vital Statistics, 1989: Births, 212; Deaths, 146; Marriages, 193; Divorces, 70.

Ethnicity, 1990: White, 12,164 (90.0%); Black, 268 (2.0%); American Indian, 79 (0.6%); Asian, 136 (1.0%); Hispanic, 1,753 (13.0%); Other, 874 (6.5%).

Recreation: Hunting, fishing in streams; Spring Ho Festival in July; other local events.

Minerals: Sand and gravel, building stone.

Agriculture: Beef cattle the major economic factor; dairy products, goats, sheep, hogs also sold; crops include hay, wheat, oats, grain sorghums, peanuts, pecans, peaches.

Business: Many employed at Fort Hood; several industrial plants; tourism; agribusinesses.

LAMPASAS (6,382) county seat; ranching, hunting center; varied manufacturing; historic downtown; hospital, nursing home; golf course. Other town, **Lometa** (625) and part of Copperas Cove.

Lamb County

LOCATION: Northwest (E-8).

Cong. Dist. 19	U.S. Jud. Dist. .... N-Lb.
St. Sen. Dist. 31	Ct. Appeals................. 7
St. Rep. Dist. 85	Admin. Jud. Dist. 9
St. Dist. Cts.	154

History: Created 1876 from Bexar District; organized 1908; named for Lt. G.A. Lamb, who died in battle of San Jacinto.

Physical Features: Rich, red, brown soils on plain; some hills; drains to Brazos Double Mountain Fork; numerous playas.

Population................ 15,072	Av. Weekly Wage $318.82
Area (sq. mi.).......... 1,017.7	Density 15
Land Area 1,016.2	Water Area 1.5
Civilian Labor 6,277	Jobless Rate.................. 5.0
Altitude (ft.)......3,849-3,486	Retail Sales $55,266,985
Rainfall (in.) 18.6	Gross Sales....... $218,378,306
Jan. min. 23	Reg. Voters 8,371
July max. 92	Election Turnout........ 40.4
Grow. Season(days) 194	Vehicles 14,285
Total Income (mil.) $253	Lane Miles 809
Per Capita Income...$16,625	Tax Value...... $1,109,554,975
Total Wages....... $68,303,528	Fed. Spending $63,938
Housing..................... 6,465	Defense Spending $554

Vital Statistics, 1989: Births, 229; Deaths, 193; Marriages, 124; Divorces, 61.

Ethnicity, 1990: White, 13,036 (86.5%); Black, 822 (5.5%); American Indian, 88 (0.6%); Asian, 25 (0.2%); Hispanic, 5,509 (36.6%); Other, 1,101 (7.3%).

Recreation: Local events; pioneer independence day celebration in June.

Minerals: Production of oil, stone, gas.

Agriculture: Fed cattle, crops, inlcuding cotton, hay, grains top revenue producers.

Business: Agribusinesses.

Littlefield (6,489) county seat; agribusiness center; varied manufacturing; hospital, nursing home; airport. Other towns, **Earth** (1,228) farming center; farm goods manufacturing; feed lot; **Amherst** (724); **Olton** (2,116); Springlake (132); **Sudan** (983).

Lampasas County

LOCATION: Central (K-14).

Cong. Dist. 11	U.S. Jud. Dist. ....W-An.
St. Sen. Dist. 24	Ct. Appeals..................... 3
St. Rep. Dist. 54	Admin. Jud. Dist. 3
St. Dist. Cts.....................27	

History: Name is Spanish for lilies found nearby streams; county created, organized 1856 from Bell, Travis counties.

Physical Features: Rolling, hilly; Colorado, Lampasas rivers; cedars, oaks, pecans.

La Salle County

LOCATION: South (Q-13).

Cong. Dist. 15	U.S. Jud. Dist. .... S-La.
St. Sen. Dist. 21	Ct. Appeals..................... 4
St. Rep. Dist. 44	Admin. Jud. Dist. 4
St. Dist. Cts............. 81, 218	

History: Created from Bexar Land Dist, organized 1880; named for Robert Cavalier Sieur de la Salle, French explorer who died in Texas.

Physical Features: Brushy plain, broken by Nueces, Frio rivers and their tributaries; chocolate, dark gray, sandy loam soils.

Population.................. 5,254	Av. Weekly Wage $247.20
Area (sq. mi.)........... 1,494.2	Density 3
Land Area 1,488.9	Water Area 5.3
Civilian Labor 1,950	Jobless Rate.................. 7.5
Altitude (ft.)........... 558-326	Retail Sales $16,792,745
Rainfall (in.) 21.6	Gross Sales $23,938,523
Jan. min. 42	Reg. Voters 3,548
July max. 99	Election Turnout........ 43.4
Grow. Season(days) 288	Vehicles 3,169
Total Income (mil.) $46	Lane Miles 648
Per Capita Income...... $9,427	Tax Value....... $378,389,630
TotalWages....... $11,864,404	Fed. Spending $22,578
Housing..................... 2,241	Defense Spending $260

Vital Statistics, 1989: Births, 78; Deaths, 63; Marriages, 40; Divorces, 6.

Ethnicity, 1990: White, 3,567 (67.9%); Black, 53 (1.0%); American Indian, 9 (0.2%); Asian, 10 (0.2%); Hispanic, 4,068 (77.4%); Other, 1,615 (30.7%).

Recreation: Nature trails; **Chaparral Wildlife Management Area**; deer, bird, javelina hunting; wild hog cookoff; county fair; Cotulla school where the late President Lyndon B. Johnson taught attracts tourists.

More on next page.

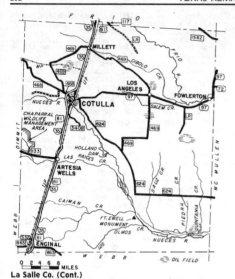

MILES

La Salle Co. (Cont.)

Minerals: Production of oil, gas.

Agriculture: Feedlot, stocker and cow-calf operations top revenue producers; crops include grain sorghums, corn, peanuts, watermelons; some irrigation for peanuts.

Business: Agribusinesses, hunting leases.

COTULLA (3,694) county seat; livestock, hunting center; **Encinal** (620) other town.

Lavaca County

LOCATION: South (N-17).

Cong. Dist. 14	U.S. Jud. Dist. ....S-Va.
St. Sen. Dist. 18	Ct. Appeals.....................13
St. Rep. Dist. 31	Admin. Jud. Dist. 3
St. Dist. Cts............25, 2D25	

History: Name is Spanish word for cow, la vaca, from name of river; created, organized 1846 from Colorado, Jackson, Gonzales, Victoria counties.

Physical Features: North rolling, south plains; sandy loam, black waxy soils; drains to Lavaca, Navidad rivers.

Population................ 18,690	Av. Weekly Wage $259.08
Area (sq. mi.).............970.3	Density 19
Land Area 969.9	Water Area 0.4
Civilian Labor 8,080	Jobless Rate..................2.0
Altitude (ft.)............503-133	Retail Sales $102,855,113

MILES

Rainfall (in.) 38.4		Gross Sales....... $242,269,328
Jan. min. 41		Reg. Voters.............. 10,629
July max. 96		Election Turnout......... 48.8
Grow. Season(days) 280		Vehicles 18,709
Total Income (mil.) $284		Lane Miles 636
Per Capita Income...$15,470		Tax Value...... $1,019,533,600
Total Wages....... $63,630,118		Fed. Spending.........$64,747
Housing.....................9,542		Defense Spending $995

Vital Statistics, 1989: Births, 226; Deaths, 254; Marriages, 87; Divorces, 66.

Ethnicity, 1990: White, 16,541 (88.5%); Black, 1,342 (7.2%); American Indian, 20 (0.1%); Asian, 14 (0.1%); Hispanic, 1,596 (8.5%); Other, 773 (4.1%).

Recreation: Deer, other hunting, fishing; spring wildflower trails, fiddlers frolic, gaslight dinner theater, museum, brewery; local events.

Minerals: Some oil, gas.

Agriculture: Livestock, especially cattle, are largest revenue sources; crops include hay, milo, corn.

Business: Varied manufacturing; leather goods center; agribusinesses; oil and gas production.

HALLETTSVILLE (2,718) county seat; varied manufacturing, medical center, nursing home; **Yoakum** (3,457 in Lavaca County, partly in DeWitt County); local events; hospital, nursing home; **Shiner** (2,074) brewery, other industry; museum; clinic, nursing home; trade fairs in October, April, other local events; **Moulton** (923) agribusiness; clinic, nursing home; local events.

MILES

Lee County

LOCATION: Southeast (M-17).

Cong. Dist. 14	U.S. Jud. Dist. ....W-An.
St. Sen. Dist. 18	Ct. Appeals.....................3
St. Rep. Dist. 30	Admin. Jud. Dist. 2
St. Dist. Cts.............. 21, 335	

History: Created from Bastrop, Burleson, Fayette, Washington counties and organized in 1874; named for Confederate Gen. Robert E. Lee.

Physical Features: Rolling, broken by Yegua and its tributaries; red to black soils, sandy to heavy loams.

Population................ 12,854		Av.Weekly Wage $330.55
Area (sq. mi.).............634.0		Density 20
Land Area 628.5		Water Area 5.5
Civilian Labor 4,832		Jobless Rate..................4.7
Altitude (ft.)............513-238		Retail Sales $76,391,215
Rainfall (in.) 35.1		Gross Sales....... $208,264,641
Jan. min. 34		Reg. Voters.............. 6,735
July max. 94		Election Turnout......... 62.0
Grow. Season(days) 273		Vehicles 12,918
Total Income (mil.) $179		Lane Miles 514
Per Capita Income...$13,475		Tax Value........$804,844,795
Total Wages....... $68,856,831		Fed. Spending.........$26,117
Housing.....................5,765		Defense Spending $494

Vital Statistics, 1989: Births, 186; Deaths, 111; Marriages, 94; Divorces, 52.

Ethnicity, 1990: White, 10,057 (78.2%); Black, 1,780 (13.8%); American Indian, 14 (0.1%); Asian, 15 (0.1%); Hispanic, 1,410 (11.0%); Other, 988 (7.7%).

Recreation: Fishing, hunting; **Lake Somerville State Park;** pioneer village, Wendish museum and structures; Geburtstag celebration in September; sheriff's posse rodeo in May; other local events, historic sites.

Minerals: Oil, natural gas, lignite.

Agriculture: Cattle are principal agricultural in-

Lee Co. (Cont.)

come; hogs raised; crops include peanuts, corn, grain sorghums, wheat, oats; soybeans introduced; some irrigation of peanuts, hay.

Business: Varied manufacturing; agribusinesses; oil, gas operations.

GIDDINGS (4,093) county seat; varied manufacturing, food processing; hospital, nursing home. Other towns, **Lexington** (953), livestock-marketing center; **Serbin** (est. 90), Wendish museum.

Leon County

LOCATION: East central (K-18).

Cong. Dist. ....13 U.S. Jud. Dist. .... N-WF
St. Sen. Dist. ....30 Ct. Appeals...................... 2
St. Rep. Dist. ....80 Admin. Jud. Dist. 8
St. Dist. Cts.................97

History: Created, organized 1846 from Robertson County; named for Mexican founder of Victoria, Martin de Leon.

Physical Features: Hilly, rolling, almost half covered by timber; drains to Navasota, Trinity rivers and tributaries; sandy, dark, alluvial soils.

Population................	12,665	Av.Weekly Wage	$400.86
Area (sq. mi.)..........	1,080.4	Density	12
Land Area	1,072.1	Water Area	8.3
Civilian Labor	5,817	Jobless Rate..................	5.4
Altitude (ft.)............	496-190	Retail Sales	$63,918,060
Rainfall (in.)	39.3	Gross Sales.......	$321,881,108
Jan. min.	35	Reg. Voters	8,100
July max.	96	Election Turnout.........	47.7
Grow. Season(days)	270	Vehicles	12,171
Total Income (mil.)	$179	Lane Miles	834
Per Capita Income...	$14,876	Tax Value......	$1,345,217,773
Total Wages.......	$54,654,315	Fed. Spending.........	$47,357
Housing....................	7,019	Defense Spending	$1,031

Vital Statistics, 1989: Births, 188; Deaths, 193; Marriages, 77; Divorces, 44.

Ethnicity, 1990: White, 10,730 (84.7%); Black, 1,615 (12.8%); American Indian, 39(0.3%); Asian, 8 (0.1%); Hispanic, 509 (4.0%); Other, 273 (2.2%).

Recreation: Hilltop Lakes resort area; sites of **Camino Real, Fort Boggy**; deer hunting.

Minerals: Oil, gas, iron ore, lignite.

Agriculture: Top cow-calf production in state; hogs raised; crops include hay, watermelons, vegetables, small grains; minor irrigation; Christmas trees introduced; some forest products.

Business: Agribusinesses, oil production.

CENTERVILLE (812) county seat; varied manufacturing; farm center; clinic, nursing home; July 4th celebration, local events. Other towns, **Buffalo** (1,555); farm center; electricity-generating plant; clinic, nursing home; golf tournament in August, stampede in September; **Normangee** (639 in Leon County, partly in Madison County); **Oakwood** (527); **Jewett** (668); **Leona** (178); **Marquez** (270).

Liberty County

LOCATION: Southeast (M-20).

Cong. Dist. .... 2 U.S. Jud. Dist. .... E-Bt.
St. Sen. Dist. .... 4 Ct. Appeals...................... 9
St. Rep. Dist. ....21 Admin. Jud. Dist. 2
St. Dist. Cts. 75, 253

History: Named for Spanish municipality, Libertad; created 1836, organized 1837.

Physical Features: Rolling; 60 percent in pine, hardwood timber; bisected by Trinity River; sandy, loam, black soils; Wallisville Lake; Big Thicket.

Population................	52,726	Av. Weekly Wage	$319.81
Area (sq. mi.)..........	1,176.3	Density	45
Land Area	1,159.8	Water Area	16.5
Civilian Labor	22,311	Jobless Rate..................	6.9
Altitude (ft.)	261-23	Retail Sales	$319,591,876
Rainfall (in.)	50.7	Gross Sales.......	$632,551,875
Jan. min.	40	Reg. Voters	25,917
July max.	94	Election Turnout.........	43.8
Grow. Season(days)	261	Vehicles	46,912
Total Income (mil.)	$689	Lane Miles	806
Per Capita Income...	$13,124	Tax Value......	$2,031,863,366
Total Wages......	$219,813,639	Fed. Spending......	$141,513
Housing....................	22,080	Defense Spending	$3,907

Vital Statistics, 1989: Births, 779; Deaths, 527; Marriages, 617; Divorces, 320.

Ethnicity, 1990: White, 44,014 (83.5%); Black, 6,911 (13.1%); American Indian, 181 (0.3%); Asian, 124 (0.2%); Hispanic, 2,880 (5.5%); Other, 1,496 (2.8%).

Recreation: Big Thicket; Wallisville Lake; hunting, fishing; historic sites; Trinity Valley exposition in October.

Minerals: Oil, gas, sulphur, sand and gravel.

Agriculture: Rice top crop with soybeans second; sorghums, corn grown; cow-calf operations important; more than 35,000 acres irrigated for rice; some lumbering.

Business: Agribusinesses; chemical plants; varied manufacturing; tourism; forest industries; many residents work in Houston; part of Houston PMSA.

LIBERTY (7,733) county seat; government center; petroleum-related industry; agribusiness; library; museum; regional historical resource depository; liberty bell tower, plaza; hospital, nursing homes. Other towns, **Cleveland** (7,124) forest products processed, shipped; tourism; library; museum; hospital, nursing home; **Ames** (989), **Daisetta** (969), **Dayton** (5,151), **Dayton Lakes** (191), **Devers** (318), **Hardin** (563), **Kenefick** (435), **North Cleveland** (176), **Plum Grove** (480).

Limestone County

LOCATION: East central (J-17).

Cong. Dist. .... 6 U.S. Jud. Dist. .... W-Wa.
St. Sen. Dist. .... 9 Ct. Appeals................... 10
St. Rep. Dist. ....12 Admin. Jud. Dist. 2
St. Dist. Cts. 77, 87

History: Created from Robertson County and organized 1846; named for indigenous rock.

Physical Features: Borders Blacklands, level to rolling; drained by Navasota and tributaries; on divide be-

Total Income (mil.) $53	Lane Miles 447
Per Capita Income...$17,227	Tax Value........ $415,483,598
Total Wages....... $12,485,923	Fed. Spending $12,921
Housing 1,683	Defense Spending $53

Vital Statistics, 1989: Births, 27; Deaths, 30; Marriages, 27; Divorces, 17.

Ethnicity, 1990: White, 3,092 (98.4%); Black, 1 (**.*%); American Indian, 34 (1.1%); Asian, 13 (0.4%); Hispanic, 379 (12.1%); Other, 3 (0.1%).

Recreation: Darrouzett festival, Will Rogers Day and other local events.

Minerals: Production of oil, natural gas.

Agriculture: Cow-calf, stocker operations top revenue producers; crops include wheat, milo, forage sorghums; more than 20,000 acres of wheat, milo, grass irrigated.

Business: Agribusinesses; oil, gas operations.

LIPSCOMB (est. 45) county seat; livestock center; junior livestock show in March. Other towns, **Booker** (1,231 in Lipscomb County, partly in Ochiltree County); **Darrouzett** (343), local events; **Follett** (441); **Higgins** (464), local events.

tween Brazos and Trinity rivers; Lake Mexia, Lake Springfield, Lake Limestone.

Population................ 20,946	Av. Weekly Wage $336.41
Area (sq. mi.) 933.1	Density 22
Land Area 908.8	Water Area 24.3
Civilian Labor 9,350	Jobless Rate.................4.6
Altitude (ft.) 665-375	Retail Sales $116,688,605
Rainfall (in.) 38.3	Gross Sales....... $293,306,448
Jan. min.......................34	Reg. Voters 10,140
July max. 95	Election Turnout......... 48.6
Grow. Season(days) 255	Vehicles 18,884
Total Income (mil.) $263	Lane Miles 757
Per Capita Income...$11,792	Tax Value...... $1,805,231,806
Total Wages.....$120,282,639	Fed. Spending.........$64,802
Housing.....................9,923	Defense Spending $1,554

Vital Statistics, 1989: Births, 330; Deaths, 296; Marriages, 192; Divorces, 133.

Ethnicity, 1990: White, 15,695 (74.9%); Black, 4,156 (19.8%); American Indian, 41(0.2%); Asian, 50 (0.2%); Hispanic, 1,459 (7.0%); Other, 1,004 (4.8%).

Recreation: Fishing, activities at three lakes; restored Fort Parker, Fort Parker State Park; Confederate Reunion Grounds; other historic sites; museum; hunting; fiddle festival in May, coon-dog show, hunt in January; junior livestock show; other events.

Minerals: Oil, gas, sand and gravel, clay, stone, lignite.

Agriculture: Cow-calf, stocker cattle operations important; sheep, goats, horses, swine, dairy cattle raised; crops include hay, wheat, corn, cotton, peaches, pecans, vegetables; some commercial nursery activity.

Business: Varied manufacturing; agribusinesses; tourism; mineral operations.

GROESBECK (3,185) county seat; varied manufacturing; mining; private prison; agribusiness; power generating; mining; hospital; nursing homes. Other towns, **Mexia** (6,933), agribusiness center; grocery distribution; **Mexia State School;** hospital; **Coolidge** (748); **Kosse** (505); **Tehuacana** (322); **Thornton** (540).

Lipscomb County

LOCATION: Northeast corner of Panhandle (A-11).

Cong. Dist. 13	U.S. Jud. Dist. .... N-Am.
St. Sen. Dist. 31	Ct. Appeals...................... 7
St. Rep. Dist. 88	Admin. Jud. Dist. 9
St. Dist. Cts. 31	

History: Created 1876 from Bexar District; organized 1887; named for A.S. Lipscomb, Republic of Texas leader.

Physical Features: Plain, broken in east; drains to tributaries of Canadian, Wolf Creek; sandy loam, black soils.

Population..................3,143	Av. Weekly Wage $322.30
Area (sq. mi.) 932.2	Density 3
Land Area 932.1	Water Area 0.1
Civilian Labor 1,541	Jobless Rate.................3.1
Altitude (ft.) 2,834-2,506	Retail Sales $8,751,177
Rainfall (in.) 21.3	GrossSales $117,952,887
Jan. min.......................20	Reg. Voters 1,911
July max. 93	Election Turnout......... 57.8
Grow. Season (days)..... 202	Vehicles 4,037

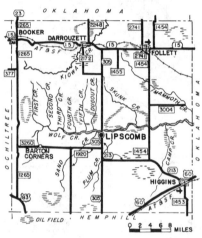

Live Oak County

LOCATION: South (Q-15).

Cong. Dist. 15	U.S. Jud. Dist. ....S-CC
St. Sen. Dist. 21	Ct. Appeals.................... 13
St. Rep. Dist. 45	Admin. Jud. Dist. 4
St. Dist. Cts. 36, 156, 343	

History: Named for predominant tree; created, organized 1856 from Nueces, San Patricio counties.

Physical Features: Brushy plains, partly broken by Nueces and tributaries; black waxy, gray sandy, other soils.

Population..................9,556	Av. Weekly Wage $321.99
Area (sq. mi.) 1,078.8	Density 9
Land Area 1,036.3	Water Area 42.5
Civilian Labor 4,326	Jobless Rate.................4.3
Altitude (ft.) 479-96	Retail Sales $42,223,396
Rainfall (in.) 27.6	Gross Sales $61,639,579
Jan. min.......................41	Reg. Voters 6,033
July max. 95	Election Turnout......... 41.9
Total Income (mil.) $127	Vehicles 9,271
Per Capita Income...$14,244	Lane Miles 946
Total Wages.....$39,715,514	Tax Value........ $888,862,460
Housing...................5,517	Fed. Spending.........$67,719
	Defense Spending $42,673

Vital Statistics, 1989: Births, 120; Deaths, 84; Marriages, 59; Divorces, 44.

Ethnicity, 1990: White, 8,316 (87.0%); Black, 10 (0.1%); American Indian, 36 (0.4%); Asian, 31 (0.3%); Hispanic, 3,324 (34.8%); Other, 1,163 (12.2%).

Recreation: Lake Corpus Christi activities; Mathis Lake, Choke Canyon Reservoir and State Park, Tips State Park; hunting; county fair.

Minerals: Production of oil, gas, sand and gravel.

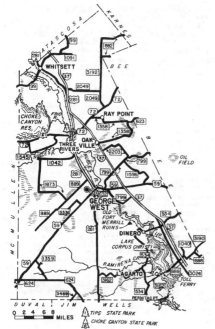

Area (sq. mi.)	966.1	Density	12
Land Area	934.8	Water Area	31.3
Civilian Labor	4,745	Jobless Rate	3.0
Altitude (ft.)	1,867-1,038	Retail Sales	$55,944,497
Rainfall (in.)	26.6	Gross Sales	$117,195,725
Jan. min.	32	Reg. Voters	7,993
July max.	97	Election Turnout	67.9
Grow. Season(days)	229	Vehicles	13,593
Total Income (mil.)	$212	Lane Miles	498
Per Capita Income	$16,911	Tax Value	$1,300,544,502
Total Wages	$40,508,367	Fed. Spending	$51,608
Housing	9,773	Defense Spending	$3,824

Vital Statistics, 1989: Births, 110; Deaths, 227; Marriages, 87; Divorces, 76.

Ethnicity, 1990: White, 11,386 (97.9%); Black, 22 (0.2%); American Indian, 39 (0.3%); Asian, 20 (0.2%); Hispanic, 453 (3.9%); Other, 164 (1.4%).

Recreation: Top deer-hunting county; fishing; **Highland Lakes** activities; major tourist area; **Enchanted Rock State Park;** spring bluebonnet festival; hang gliding; many local events.

Minerals: Stone, granite, vermiculite, llanite.

Agriculture: Beef cattle top agricultural product; swine raised; crops include peanuts, hay; some irrigation of peanuts, grass.

Business: Tourism; ranch trading center; granite mined.

LLANO (2,962) county seat; tourist, hunting center; livestock trading; some manufacturing; hospital; museum; national downtown historic district; golf course. Other towns, **Kingsland** (2,725), tourism, retirement community; metal fabrication; wood work; library; nursing home; local events; **Buchanan Dam** (1,099); **Horseshoe Bay** (1,222 in Llano County, partly in Burnet County); **Sunrise Beach** (497).

Loving County

LOCATION: New Mexico line (J-6).

Cong. Dist.	16	U.S. Jud. Dist.	N-Pe.
St. Sen. Dist.	25	Ct. Appeals	8
St. Rep. Dist.	69	Admin. Jud. Dist.	7
St. Dist. Cts.	143		

History: Last county organized; created 1887 from Tom Green; organized 1931; named for Oliver Loving, trail driver. Loving is Texas' least populous county.

Physical Features: Rolling prairies drain to Pecos River; Red Bluff Reservoir; sandy, loam, clay soils.

Population	107	Av. Weekly Wage	$264.89
Area (sq. mi.)	676.8	Density	0
Land Area	673.1	Water Area	3.7
Civilian Labor	67	Jobless Rate	0.0
Altitude (ft.)	3,311-2,685	Retail Sales	$490,026
Rainfall (in.)	9.1	Gross Sales	$1,328,825
Jan. min.	28	Reg. Voters	112
July max.	96	Election Turnout	85.7
Grow. Season (days)	222	Vehicles	308
Total Income (mil.)	$3	Lane Miles	67
Per Capita Income	$37,122	Tax Value	$222,950,029
Total Wages	$316,804	Fed. Spending	$315
Housing	59	Defense Spending	$0

Vital Statistics, 1989: Births, 1; Deaths, 1; Marriages, 9; Divorces, 1.

Ethnicity, 1990: White, 93 (86.9%); Black, 0 (0.0%);

Agriculture: Cow-calf operations dropping, but significant; swine produced; crops include corn, grain sorghums, cotton; some irrigation for hay, coastal Bermuda pastures.

Business: Oil activities, agribusinesses dominate economy.

GEORGE WEST (2,568) county seat; agribusiness, petroleum refineries. Other towns, **Three Rivers** (1,889), refineries; **Pernitas Point** (125 in Live Oak County, mostly in Jim Wells County).

Llano County

LOCATION: West Central (L-14).

Cong. Dist.	21	U.S. Jud. Dist.	W-An.
St. Sen. Dist.	24	Ct. Appeals	3
St. Rep. Dist.	47	Admin. Jud. Dist.	3
St. Dist. Cts.	33		

History: Name is Spanish for plains; created, organized 1856 from Bexar District, Gillespie County.

Physical Features: Drains to Colorado, Llano rivers; rolling to hilly; Buchanan, Inks, Lyndon B. Johnson lakes.

Population 11,631   Av. Weekly Wage $301.36

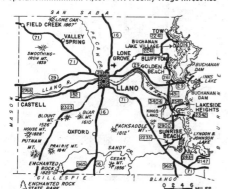

Loving Co. (Cont.)
American Indian, 0 (0.0%); Asian, 0 (0.0%); Hispanic, 14 (13.1%); Other, 14 (13.1%).
  Recreation: N.A.
  Minerals: Production of oil, gas.
  Agriculture: Some cattle; no crops.
  Business: Petroleum operations; some cattle.
  MENTONE (50 est.) county seat; oil-field supply center; only town.

Lubbock County

  LOCATION: Northwest (F-8).

Cong. Dist. 13	U.S. Jud. Dist. .... N-WF
St. Sen. Dist. 30	Ct. Appeals......................2
St. Rep. Dist. 80	Admin. Jud. Dist. 8
St. Dist. Cts.................72,99,	
137, 140, 237	

  History: Named for Col. Tom S. Lubbock, an organizer of Confederate Terry's Rangers; county created 1876 from Bexar District; organized 1891.
  Physical Features: Level plains, broken by 1,500 playas, Yellow House River; rich soils with underground water.

Population...............222,636	Av. Weekly Wage $357.06
Area (sq. mi.).............900.6	Density 247
Land Area 899.5	Water Area 1.1
Civilian Labor 115,267	Jobless Rate...................4.8
Altitude (ft.).......3,402-3,015	Retail Sales ... $1,975,089,457
Rainfall (in.) 17.8	Gross Sales.... $4,888,537,495
Jan.min....................24	Reg. Voters 100,347
July max....................92	Election Turnout.........49.6
Grow. Season(days) 208	Vehicles 189,169
Total Income (mil.) .. $3,240	Lane Miles 1,579
Per Capita Income...$14,208	Tax Value...... $5,882,450,426
Total Wages... $1,747,842,952	Fed. Spending $638,183
Housing...................91,375	Defense Spending . $125,055

  Vital Statistics, 1989: Births, 3,959; Deaths, 1,544; Marriages, 2,214; Divorces, 1,404.
  Ethnicity, 1990: White, 176,037 (79.1%); Black, 17,154 (7.7%); American Indian, 686 (0.3%); Asian, 2,722 (1.2%); Hispanic,51,011 (22.9%); Other, 26,037 (11.7%).
  Recreation: Lubbock Lake Landmark State Historical **Park** and archaeological site; lake activities; Texas Tech events; Lubbock Civic Center, **The Museum of Texas Tech, and Moody Planetarium; Mackenzie State Park; Ranching Heritage Center;** Panhandle-South Plains Fair; Lubbock Arts Festival in April; Buffalo Springs Lake.
  Minerals: Oil, gas, stone, sand and gravel.
  Agriculture: A top agricultural county; fed beef, cow-calf operations, major producers, swine, sheep, poultry raised; cotton major crop, others are grain sorghums, wheat, hay, vegetables; more than 230,000 acres irrigated, mostly cotton.
  Business: World's largest cottonseed processing center; Texas' leading agribusiness center; headquarters for large cotton cooperative; cattle feedlots; manufacturing; higher education center.
  LUBBOCK (186,206) county seat; center for large agricultural area; manufacturing includes electronics, earth-moving equipment, food containers, fire-protection equipment, clothing, other products; distribution center for South Plains; feedlots; medical center; psychiatric hospital; museum; **Texas Tech University** with law and medical schools; **Lubbock Christian University, South Plains College; Wayland Baptist University** off-campus center; **Reese Air Force Base;** numerous hospitals, nursing homes, state school for mentally retarded.
  Other towns include **Abernathy** (558 in Lubbock County, partly in Hale County); **Idalou** (2,074); **New Deal** (521); **Ransom Canyon** (750); **Reese Air Force Base** (1,263); **Shallowater** (1,708); **Slaton** (6,078); **Wolfforth** (1,941).

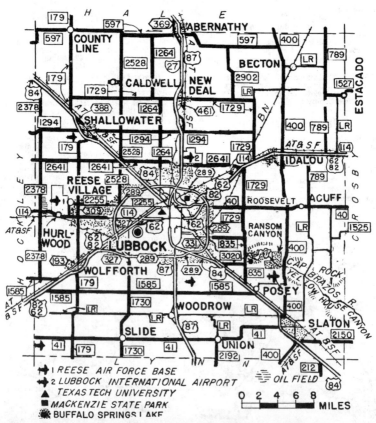

REESE AIR FORCE BASE
LUBBOCK INTERNATIONAL AIRPORT
TEXAS TECH UNIVERSITY
MACKENZIE STATE PARK
BUFFALO SPRINGS LAKE

0 2 4 6 8   MILES

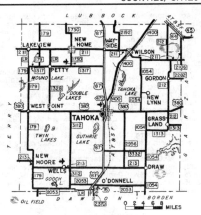

Lynn County

LOCATION: Northwest (G-8).

Cong. Dist. 17	U.S. Jud. Dist. .... N-Lb.
St. Sen. Dist. 28	Ct. Appeals............. 7
St. Rep. Dist. 78	Admin. Jud. Dist. 7
St. Dist. Cts. 106	

History: Created 1876 from Bexar District; organized 1903; named for Alamo victim, W. Lynn (or Linn).

Physical Features: Plain, broken by Caprock Escarpment, playas and draws; sandy loam, black, gray soils.

Population..................6,758	Av. Weekly Wage $322.85
Area (sq. mi.).............893.4	Density 8
Land Area 891.9	Water Area 1.5
Civilian Labor 2,550	Jobless Rate.................4.4
Altitude (ft.).......3,274-2,881	Retail Sales $12,969,559
Rainfall (in.) 18.3	Gross Sales....... $62,853,214
Jan. min. 24	Reg. Voters 3,911
July max. 92	Election Turnout 42.5
Grow. Season(days) 217	Vehicles 6,705
Total Income (mil.) $93	Lane Miles 708
Per Capita Income...$13,849	Tax Value.........$318,316,240
Total Wages $21,623,146	Fed. Spending.........$29,350
Housing......................2,978	Defense Spending $137

Vital Statistics, 1989: Births, 128; Deaths, 77; Marriages, 69; Divorces, 21.

Ethnicity,1990: White, 5,214 (77.2%); Black, 223 (3.3%); American Indian, 22 (0.3%); Asian, 11 (0.2%); Hispanic, 2,819 (41.7%); Other, 1,288 (19.1%).

Recreation: Local events; pioneer museum in Tahoka; Dan Blocker museum in O'Donnell.

Minerals: Oil, natural gas, stone.

Agriculture: Crops, including cotton, grain sorghums, wheat, produce largest income; cattle, sheep, hogs raised; 60,000 acres of cotton irrigated.

Business: Cotton, grain sorghums industries.

TAHOKA (2,868) county seat; agribusiness center; cotton compress; some manufacturing; hospital, nursing home. Other towns, **New Home** (175), **O'Donnell** (968 in Lynn County, partly in Dawson County); **Wilson** (568).

McCulloch County

LOCATION: Texas' geographical center in county (K-13).

Cong. Dist. 21	U.S. Jud. Dist. ....W-An.
St. Sen. Dist. 24	Ct. Appeals..................... 3
St. Rep. Dist. 65	Admin. Jud. Dist. 7
St. Dist. Cts. 198	

History: Created from Bexar District 1856; organized 1876; named for Texas pioneer Gen. Ben McCulloch.

Physical Features: Hilly and rolling; drains to Colorado, Brady Creek and Lake, San Saba River; black loams to sandy soils.

Population..................8,778	Av. Weekly Wage $286.98
Area (sq. mi.)..........1,073.3	Density 8
Land Area 1,069.3	Water Area 4.0
Civilian Labor 3,706	Jobless Rate................. 10.2
Altitude (ft.).......2,021-1,442	Retail Sales $47,741,131
Rainfall (in.) 24.7	Gross Sales...... $108,263,193

Jan. min. 30	Reg. Voters 4,538
July max. 96	Election Turnout 55.7
Grow. Season (days).....226	Vehicles 9,003
Total Income (mil.) $120	Lane Miles 608
Per Capita Income...$13,107	Tax Value.........$450,389,717
Total Wages...... $33,501,788	Fed. Spending.........$31,874
Housing......................4,420	Defense Spending $916

Vital Statistics, 1989: Births, 139; Deaths, 132; Marriages, 86; Divorces, 50.

Ethnicity, 1990: White, 7,855 (89.5%); Black, 166 (1.9%); American Indian, 14 (0.2%); Asian, 8 (0.1%); Hispanic, 2,317 (26.4%); Other, 735 (8.4%).

Recreation: Hunting; **Brady Creek Reservoir** activities; muzzle-loading rifle association state championship; rodeos; golf, tennis tournaments; many local events.

Minerals: Production of oil, sand, gravel, stone, gas.

Agriculture: Beef cattle provide most income; crops include wheat, hay, cotton, oats, peanuts; some irrigation for peanuts.

Business: Agribusiness; manufacturing; tourism; hunting leases.

BRADY (5,946) county seat; ranching, tourist center; mohair, wool processed; oil-field equipment, other manufacturing; hospital, nursing homes; **Central Texas College**; goat cookoff in September, other events. Other town, **Melvin** (184).

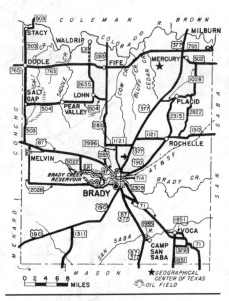

McLennan County

LOCATION: Central (J-16).

Cong. Dist. 11	U.S. Jud. Dist. ....W-Wa.
St. Sen. Dist. 22	Ct. Appeals................. 10
St. Rep. Dist. 55, 56	Admin. Jud. Dist. 3
St. Dist. Cts. 19, 54, 74, 170	

History: Created from Milam County and organized in 1850; named for an original settler, Neil McLennan Sr.

Physical Features: Mostly Blackland prairie, but rolling hills in west; drains to Bosque, Brazos rivers and Lake Waco; heavy, loam, sandy soils.

Population..............189,123	Av. Weekly Wage $353.40
Area (sq. mi.)..........1,060.2	Density 183
Land Area 1,041.9	Water Area 18.3
Civilian Labor 92,420	Jobless Rate.................5.8
Altitude (ft.)............734-381	Retail Sales ... $1,392,600,900
Rainfall (in.) 31.0	Gross Sales.... $4,109,270,214
Jan. min. 36	Reg. Voters 92,481
July max. 97	Election Turnout ....
Grow. Season (days).....253	Vehicles 164,124
Total Income (mil.) .. $2,697	Lane Miles 1,582

McLennan Co. (Cont.)

Per Capita Income...$14,276	Tax Value...... $4,770,636,120
Total Wages... $1,353,355,550	Fed. Spending....... $707,918
Housing.................. 78,736	Defense Spending . $183,017

Vital Statistics, 1989: Births, 2,994; Deaths, 1,780; Marriages, 1,971; Divorces, 1,017.

Ethnicity, 1990: White, 146,100 (77.3%); Black, 29,520 (15.6%); American Indian, 563 (0.3%); Asian, 1,384 (0.7%); Hispanic, 23,643 (12.5%); Other, 11,556 (6.1%).

Recreation: Varied metropolitan activies (contact chambers of commerce for dates); **Fort Fisher Park** with camping facilities; **Homer Garrison Jr. Texas Ranger Museum; Texas Ranger Hall of Fame, Dr Pepper Museum; Cameron Park; Lake Waco; Brazos River** festival and local events; zoo; historic sites and homes; museums; libraries, art center; symphony orchestra; civic theater; private telephone museum in McGregor; Baylor University events; Heart o' Texas Fair, Rodeo, Brazos festival; **Westfest** in West in September; farm show.

Minerals: Sand and gravel, stone, clays, oil, gas.

Agriculture: Feeder calves, breeder cattle, slaughter and stocker cattle, hogs and milk important; crops include corn, grain sorghums, wheat, oats, cotton and hay; some irrigation; cedar posts sold.

Business: A leading distribution, government center for Central Texas; diversified manufacturing; agribusiness; education.

WACO (103,590) county seat; varied manufacturing; tourism center, conventions; agribusiness; hospitals, nursing homes; **Baylor University; McLennan Community College; Texas State Technical Institute; Veterans Administration** regional office, hospital; **Bellmead** (8,336); **Beverly Hills** (2,048); **Bruceville-Eddy** (1,074 in McLennan County, partly in Falls County); **Crawford** (631); **Gholson** (692); **Golinda** (58 in McLennan County, mostly in Falls County); **Hallsburg** (450); **Hewitt** (8,983), iron works, other manufacturing; **Lacy-Lakeview** (3,617); **Leroy** (292); **Lorena** (1,158); **Mart** (2,004); **McGregor** (4,683), farming center, some manufacturing; local events; **Moody** (1,329); **Northcrest** (1,725); **Riesel** (839); **Robinson** (7,111); **Ross** (188); **West** (2,515), famous for Czech foods; varied manufacturing; **Woodway** (8,695).

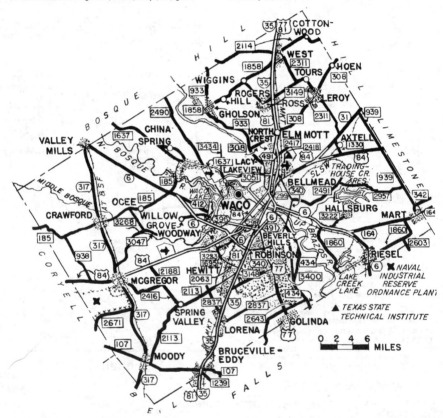

McMullen County

LOCATION: South (Q-14).

Cong. Dist. 15	U.S. Jud. Dist. ....S-La.
St. Sen. Dist. 21	Ct. Appeals......................4
St. Rep. Dist. 44	Admin. Jud. Dist. 4
St. Dist. Cts........ 36, 156, 343	

History: Created from Atascosa, Bexar, Live Oak counties 1858; organized 1862; reorganized 1877; named for Irish empresario John McMullen.

Physical Features: Brushy plain, sloping to Frio, Nueces rivers and tributaries; saline clay soils.

Population.................... 817		Av. Weekly Wage $439.89	
Area (sq. mi.).......... 1,142.6		Density 1	
Land Area 1,113.0		Water Area 29.6	
Civilian Labor 530		Jobless Rate..................0.6	
Altitude (ft.) 642-230		Retail Sales $1,969,029	
Rainfall (in.) 24.4		Gross Sales..........$3,416,223	
Jan. min. 39		Reg. Voters 576	
July max. 97		Election Turnout......... 53.1	
Grow. Season (days)..... 291		Vehicles 1,295	
Total Income (mil.) $20		Lane Miles 317	

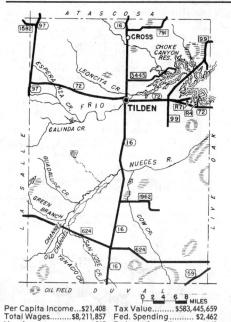

Land Area	469.6
Civilian Labor	4,813
Altitude (ft.)	364-213
Rainfall (in.)	41.1
Jan. min.	39
July max.	96
Grow. Season (days)	272
Total Income (mil.)	$147
Per Capita Income	$12,870
Total Wages	$52,518,241
Housing	4,323

Water Area	2.7
Jobless Rate	3.7
Retail Sales	$54,849,545
Gross Sales	$76,742,348
Reg. Voters	5,350
Election Turnout	52.5
Vehicles	9,026
Lane Miles	569
Tax Value	$551,527,950
Fed. Spending	$25,616
Defense Spending	$609

Vital Statistics, 1989: Births, 138; Deaths, 114; Marriages, 96; Divorces, 49.

Ethnicity, 1990: White, 7,984 (73.0%); Black, 2,575 (23.6%); American Indian, 67 (0.6%); Asian, 13 (0.1%); Hispanic, 1,178 (10.8%); Other, 292 (2.7%).

Recreation: Fishing, hunting; water activities at **Lake Madison**; historic sites; local events.

Minerals: Production of gas, oil, gravel.

Agriculture: Cattle, horses, swine raised; principal crop is forage for livestock.

Business: Agribusinesses; oil production; manufacturing.

MADISONVILLE (3,569) county seat; farm-trade center; varied manufacturing; hospital, nursing home; library. Other towns, **Midway** (274); **Normangee** (50 in Madison County, mostly in Leon County).

Marion County

LOCATION: Northeast (G-21).

Cong. Dist.	1	U.S. Jud. Dist.	E-MI.
St. Sen. Dist.	1	Ct. Appeals.	6
St. Rep. Dist.	8	Admin. Jud. Dist.	1
St. Dist. Cts.	115, 276		

History: Created, organized 1860 from Cass County; named for U.S. Gen. Francis Marion.

Physical Features: Hilly, three-quarters forested with pines, hardwoods; drains to Caddo Lake, Lake O' the Pines, Cypress Bayou.

Population	9,984
Area (sq. mi.)	420.3
Land Area	381.2
Civilian Labor	4,914
Altitude (ft.)	379-168
Rainfall (in.)	44.7
Jan. min.	32
July max.	94

Av. Weekly Wage	$285.99
Density	26
Water Area	39.1
Jobless Rate	5.9
Retail Sales	$29,089,087
Gross Sales	$58,831,832
Reg. Voters	6,630
Election Turnout	51.3

Grow. Season (days)	236
Total Income (mil.)	$109
Per Capita Income	$11,662
Total Wages	$28,642,617
Housing	5,710

Vehicles	7,922
Lane Miles	309
Tax Value	$406,968,487
Fed. Spending	$33,066
Defense Spending	$3,867

Vital Statistics, 1989: Births, 131; Deaths, 116; Marriages, 112; Divorces, 56.

Ethnicity, 1990: White, 6,792 (68.0%); Black, 3,100 (31.0%); American Indian, 44 (0.4%); Asian, 7 (0.1%); Hispanic, 147 (1.5%); Other, 41 (0.4%).

Recreation: Lake O' the Pines, Caddo Lake activities; hunting; **Excelsior Hotel;** 84 medallions on historic sites including Jay Gould railroad car, House of Four Seasons; Freeman Plantation; historical museum; historical pilgrimage in May, founder's day in October, other local events.

Minerals: Oil, gas, clays, lignite.

Agriculture: Beef cattle, horses top producers; hogs raised; coastal Bermuda major crop; also truck crops grown; blueberries introduced; some forest products produced.

Business: Oil; timber; recreation; jams, jellies processed.

JEFFERSON (2,199) county seat; tourism; livestock; timber; minerals; library; many historical sites.

Per Capita Income	$21,408
Total Wages	$8,211,857
Housing	565

Tax Value	$583,445,659
Fed. Spending	$2,462
Defense Spending	$49

Vital Statistics, 1989: Births, 12; Deaths, 6; Marriages, 7; Divorces, 4.

Ethnicity, 1990: White, 713 (87.3%); Black, 0 (0.0%); American Indian, 3 (0.4%); Asian, 0 (0.0%); Hispanic, 320 (39.2%); Other, 101 (12.4%).

Recreation: Deer hunting; many local events; **Choke Canyon Reservoir** and wildlife management area.

Minerals: Production of gas, oil, coal and uranium.

Agriculture: Cattle raising major factor; crops are corn, milo.

Business: Oil, gas production; cattle raising.

TILDEN (est. 500) county seat; kitty-litter production; natural gas processing; ranch center; tourism.

Madison County

LOCATION: East Central (K-18).

Cong. Dist.	6	U.S. Jud. Dist.	S-Hn.
St. Sen. Dist.	5	Ct. Appeals.	10
St. Rep. Dist.	15	Admin. Jud. Dist.	2
St. Dist. Cts.	12, 278		

History: Named for U.S. President James Madison; created from Grimes, Leon, Walker counties 1853; organized 1854.

Physical Features: Hilly, draining to Trinity, Navasota rivers, Bedias Creek on boundaries; one-fifth of area timbered; alluvial, loam, sandy soils.

Population	10,931
Area (sq. mi.)	472.3

Av. Weekly Wage	$323.50
Density	23

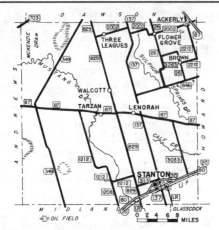

Altitude (ft.) 1,981-1,258	Retail Sales $16,453,468
Rainfall (in.) 24.8	Gross Sales........ $25,846,408
Jan. min. 32	Reg. Voters 2,284
July max. 96	Election Turnout 55.7
Grow. Season (days)..... 217	Vehicles 3,765
Total Income (mil.) $51	Lane Miles 416
Per Capita Income...$15,933	Tax Value......... $543,412,828
Total Wages...$8,889,315	Fed. Spending $13,737
Housing.....................2,356	Defense Spending $293

Vital Statistics, 1989: Births, 42; Deaths, 56; Marriages, 26; Divorces, 15.

Ethnicity, 1990: White, 3,084 (90.1%); Black, 6 (0.2%); American Indian, 13 (0.4%); Asian, 4 (0.1%); Hispanic, 671 (19.6%); Other, 316 (9.2%).

Recreation: Major tourist area; outstanding deer, turkey hunting, river fishing; camping; pinto bean cookoff in June; historic homes; restored town; **Fort Mason Museum;** many local events; golf course.

Minerals: Topaz.

Agriculture: Cattle, goats, sheep top producers; crops include peanuts, hay, watermelons; some 6,000 acres of peanuts, hay irrigated.

Business: Ranching; hunting; tourism; soft-drink bottling.

MASON (2,041) county seat; ranching center; tourism; museum; nursing home; large historical district.

Martin County

LOCATION: West (I-8).

Cong. Dist. 17	U.S. Jud. Dist. .... W:M-O
St. Sen. Dist. 28	Ct. Appeals...................... 8
St. Rep. Dist. 77	Admin. Jud. Dist. 7
St. Dist. Cts. 118	

History: Created from Bexar District 1876; organized 1884; named for Wylie Martin, senator of Republic of Texas.

Physical Features: Sandy, loam soils on plain, broken by playas, creeks.

Population...................4,956	Av. Weekly Wage $488.05
Area (sq. mi.) 915.6	Density 5
Land Area 914.8	Water Area 0.8
Civilian Labor 2,392	Jobless Rate................... 1.5
Altitude (ft.) 2,888-2,518	Retail Sales $22,233,406
Rainfall (in.) 17.2	Gross Sales $330,476,390
Jan. min. 30	Reg. Voters 2,484
July max. 94	Election Turnout 48.6
Grow. Season (days)..... 215	Vehicles 5,466
Total Income (mil.) $75	Lane Miles 572
Per Capita Income...$15,173	Tax Value......... $471,952,609
Total Wages....... $29,159,873	Fed. Spending $23,177
Housing.....................2,038	Defense Spending $91

Vital Statistics, 1989: Births, 92; Deaths, 34; Marriages, 50; Divorces, 26.

Ethnicity, 1990: White, 3,159 (63.7%); Black, 89 (1.8%); American Indian, 11 (0.2%); Asian, 8 (0.2%); Hispanic, 1,960 (39.5%); Other, 1,689 (34.1%).

Recreation: Museum, settlers reunion, local events.

Minerals: Oil, gas.

Agriculture: Cotton, small grains top revenue sources; cattle, sheep, goats, hogs also raised; about 5,000 acres irrigated.

Business: Petroleum production, agribusinesses dominate economy.

STANTON (2,576) county seat; oil, farming, ranching center; some manufacturing; electric co-op; hospital, nursing home; restored convent, other historic buildings; settlers reunion in July, soup cookoff in January, local events. Other town, **Ackerly** (90 in Martin County, partly in Dawson County).

Mason County

LOCATION: Central (L-13).

Cong. Dist. 21	U.S. Jud. Dist. ....W-An.
St. Sen. Dist. 25	Ct. Appeals...................... 4
St. Rep. Dist. 67	Admin. Jud. Dist. 3
St. Dist. Cts....................33	

History: Created from Bexar, Gillespie counties; organized 1858; named for Mexican War victim Lt. G.T. Mason.

Physical Features: Hilly, draining to Llano, San Saba rivers and tributaries; limestone, red soils; varied timber.

Population...................3,423	Av. Weekly Wage $218.60
Area (sq. mi.) 932.2	Density 4
Land Area 932.1	Water Area 0.1
Civilian Labor 1,681	Jobless Rate................... 2.7

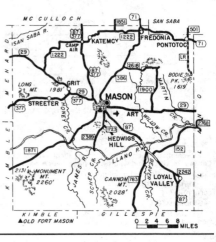

Matagorda County

LOCATION: On coast (O-19).

Cong. Dist. 14	U.S. Jud. Dist. ....S-Gn.
St. Sen. Dist. 18	Ct. Appeals................... 13
St. Rep. Dist. 29	Admin. Jud. Dist. 2
St. Dist. Cts. 23,130	

History: An original county, created 1836 from Spanish municipality, named for canebrake; organized 1837; settled by Stephen F. Austin colonists.

Physical Features: Flat, broken by bays; contains part of Matagorda Island; many different soils; drains to Colorado River, creeks, coast.

Population................ 36,928	Av. Weekly Wage $485.80
Area (sq. mi.) 1,612.2	Density 33
Land Area 1,114.5	Water Area 497.7
Civilian Labor 16,062	Jobless Rate................. 10.4
Altitude (ft.) 56-2	Retail Sales ... $194,788,875
Rainfall (in.) 43.2	Gross Sales $421,550,440
Jan. min. 46	Reg. Voters 17,244
July max. 91	Election Turnout 50.6
Grow. Season (days)..... 296	Vehicles 31,091
Total Income (mil.) $591	Lane Miles 682
Per Capita Income...$15,320	Tax Value...... $4,132,257,590
Total Wages......$303,744,631	Fed. Spending........ $95,735
Housing................... 18,511	Defense Spending $8,278

Vital Statistics, 1989: Births, 679; Deaths, 318; Marriages, 384; Divorces, 241.

Ethnicity, 1990: White, 26,622 (72.1%); Black, 5,106 (13.8%); American Indian, 88 (0.2%); Asian, 842 (2.3%); Hispanic, 9,088 (24.6%); Other, 4,270 (11.6%).

Recreation: Coastal activities, including fishing, water sports, hunting; historic sites, museums; rice fes-

Matagorda Co. (Cont.)
tival, county fair, rodeo in March; boat show in November; antique show in January.

Minerals: Production of gas, oil, salt.

Agriculture: Rice, cotton, grains provide most revenue; beef cattle produced; 44,000 acres irrigated for rice, turf.

Business: Petroleum operations, petrochemicals, agribusinesses dominate the economy; varied manufacturing; tourism significant.

BAY CITY (18,170) county seat; petrochemicals produced; oil, gas processing; nuclear power plant; commercial fishing; hospital, nursing home. Other towns, **Markham** (1,206); **Palacios** (4,418), seafood industry; hospital, library, airport; fishing tournament in August; bayfest in October; public fishing piers; **Van Vleck** (1,534).

crops include oats, sorghums, wheat, pecans, vegetables; some irrigation from Rio Grande.

Business: Oil production, operations; agribusinesses; feedlots; tourist trade with Mexico.

EAGLE PASS (20,651) county seat; varied manufacturing; tourism center; rail, highway entry point to Mexico; hospital.

Maverick County

LOCATION: On Rio Grande (P-11).

Cong. Dist. 23	U.S. Jud. Dist. ....W-DR
St. Sen. Dist. 21	Ct. Appeals......................4
St. Rep. Dist. 68	Admin. Jud. Dist. 4
St. Dist. Cts. 293	

History: Named for pioneer Sam A. Maverick, whose name is a synonym for unbranded cattle; created 1856 from Kinney County; organized 1871.

Physical Features: Broken, rolling surface, with dense brush; clay, sandy, alluvial soils.

Population................ 36,378	Av. Weekly Wage $258.02
Area (sq. mi.) 1,291.7	Density 28
Land Area 1,280.1	Water Area 11.6
Civilian Labor 13,952	Jobless Rate............... 26.8
Altitude (ft.) 918-703	Retail Sales $220,206,488
Rainfall (in.) 21.0	Gross Sales $282,563,094
Jan. min. 38	Reg. Voters 12,038
July max. 99	Election Turnout 41.5
Grow. Season (days)..... 285	Vehicles 20,065
Total Income (mil.) $250	Lane Miles 451
Per Capita Income......$6,155	Tax Value......... $791,266,809
Total Wages......$103,470,278	Fed. Spending $86,419
Housing.................... 11,053	Defense Spending $868

Vital Statistics, 1989: Births, 843; Deaths, 172; Marriages, 579; Divorces, 83.

Ethnicity, 1990: White, 23,748 (65.3%); Black, 32 (0.1%); American Indian, 714 (2.0%); Asian, 71 (0.2%); Hispanic, 34,024 (93.5%); Other, 11,813 (32.5%).

Recreation: Tourist gateway to Mexico; white-tailed deer, bird hunting; fishing; many local events at Eagle Pass.

Minerals: Production of oil, gas, sand and gravel.

Agriculture: Cattle feedlots provide most income;

Medina County

LOCATION: Southwest (O-13).

Cong. Dist. 23	U.S. Jud. Dist. ....W-SAnt.
St. Sen. Dist. 25	Ct. Appeals......................4
St. Rep. Dist. 45	Admin. Jud. Dist. 6
St. Dist. Cts.....................38	

History: Created, organized 1848 from Bexar; settled by Alsatians led by Henri Castro; named for river, probably for Spanish engineer Pedro Medina.

Physical Features: Scenic hills in north; south has fertile valleys, rolling surface; Medina River, Lake.

Population............... 27,312	Av. Weekly Wage $279.41
Area (sq. mi.) 1,334.5	Density 21
Land Area 1,327.8	Water Area 6.7
Civilian Labor 10,762	Jobless Rate................. 5.8
Altitude (ft.)........ 1,995-635	Retail Sales $159,738,851
Rainfall (in.) 28.5	Gross Sales $241,905,744
Jan. min. 39	Reg. Voters 14,176
July max. 98	Election Turnout 47.1
Grow. Season (days)..... 263	Vehicles 25,070
Total Income (mil.) $335	Lane Miles 724
Per Capita Income...$12,121	Tax Value...... $1,277,638,008
Total Wages....... $76,161,973	Fed. Spending $76,745
Housing.................... 10,835	Defense Spending ... $10,834

Vital Statistics, 1989: Births, 418; Deaths, 245; Marriages, 226; Divorces, 103.

Ethnicity, 1990: White, 23,608 (86.4%); Black, 92 (0.3%); American Indian, 119 (0.4%); Asian, 68 (0.2%); Hispanic, 12,134 (44.4%); Other, 3,425 (12.5%).

Recreation: A leading deer area; scenic drives; camping, fishing; 97 historic buildings; museum; **Landmark Inn** at Castroville; market trail days each month; antique shows; St. Louis Day celebration in August.

Minerals: Oil, gas, clay, sand, gravel.

Agriculture: Most income from livestock; crops include grains, peanuts, hay, cotton, vegetables; some irrigation.

0 2 4 6 8
MILES

≡ OIL FIELD
HILL COUNTRY STATE NATURAL AREA

Business: Agribusinesses; tourism; varied manufacturing.

HONDO (6,018) county seat; varied manufacturing; Air Force screening center; hospital, nursing homes. Other towns, **Castroville** (2,159), farm center; food processing; light manufacturing; **Devine** (3,928); **La Coste** (1,021); **Lytle** (340 in Medina County, partly in Atascosa, Bexar counties); **Natalia** (1,216).

Menard County

LOCATION: Southwest (O-13).

Cong. Dist. 23	U.S. Jud. Dist. ....W-SAnt.
St. Sen. Dist. 25	Ct. Appeals.......................4
St. Rep. Dist. 45	Admin. Jud. Dist. 6
St. Dist. Cts....................38	

History: Created from Bexar County in 1858, organized, 1871; named for Galveston's founder, Michel B. Menard.

Physical Features: Rolling, draining to San Saba River and tributaries; limestone soils.

Population....................2,252	Av. Weekly Wage $262.53
Area (sq. mi.)..............902.2	Density 2
Land Area 901.9	Water Area 0.3
Civilian Labor 921	Jobless Rate 4.8
Altitude (ft.)........2,346-1,690	Retail Sales $7,589,186
Rainfall (in.) 22.2	Gross Sales $21,823,070
Jan. min. 29	Reg. Voters...............1,565
July max. 95	Election Turnout 59.0
Grow. Season (days).....220	Vehicles 6,500
Total Income (mil.) $35	Lane Miles 346
Per Capita Income...$14,749	Tax Value.........$259,648,610
Total Wages.........$6,238,751	Fed. Spending $10,283
Housing....................1,562	Defense Spending $191

Vital Statistics, 1989: Births, 21; Deaths, 42; Marriages, 16; Divorces, 13.

Ethnicity, 1990: White, 2,076 (92.2%); Black, 7 (0.3%); American Indian, 5 (0.2%); Asian, 0 (0.0%); Hispanic, 726 (32.2%); Other, 164 (7.3%).

Recreation: Hunting, fishing; historic sites include

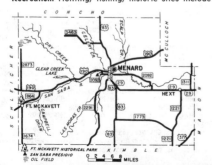

0 2 4 6 8
MILES
▲ FT. MCKAVETT HISTORICAL PARK
▲ SAN SABA PRESIDIO
≡ OIL FIELD

Real Presidio de San Saba, Fort McKavett State Park; museum; country store; **San Saba River;** Jim Bowie days in September, lamb show.

Minerals: Oil, gas.

Agriculture: Income mostly from beef cattle, sheep, goats; crops include grains, pecans; some irrigation; peach orchard introduced with mist system to protect against frost.

Business: Agribusiness; tourism; oil, gas production.

MENARD (1,606) county seat; hunting, ranching center, hospital.

Midland County

LOCATION: West (J-8).

Cong. Dist. 21	U.S. Jud. Dist. .... W:M-O
St. Sen. Dist. 25	Ct. Appeals.......................8
St. Rep. Dist. 25	Admin. Jud. Dist. 7
St. Dist. Cts....................76	

History: Created from Tom Green County and organized, 1885; name came from midway location on railroad between El Paso and Fort Worth.

Physical Features: Flat, broken by draws; sandy, loam soils.

Population...............106,611	Av . Weekly Wage....$471.86
Area (sq. mi.).............902.0	Density 118
Land Area 900.3	Water Area 1.7
Civilian Labor 47,885	Jobless Rate 5.5
Altitude (ft.)......2,936-2,613	Retail Sales $908,687,949
Rainfall (in.) 13.7	Gross Sales... $1,870,847,728
Jan. min. 30	Reg. Voters 48,936
July max. 94	Election Turnout 61.0
Grow. Season (days)..... 218	Vehicles 97,053
Total Income (mil.) .. $1,898	Lane Miles 890
Per Capita Income...$17,765	Tax Value...... $3,888,709,805
Total Wages... $1,069,633,168	Fed. Spending $196,862
Housing....................44,877	Defense Spending $6,143

Vital Statistics, 1989: Births, 2,009; Deaths, 648; Marriages, 994; Divorces, 570.

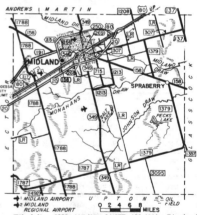

0 2 4 6 8
MILES
✈ 1 MIDLAND AIRPORT
✈ 2 MIDLAND REGIONAL AIRPORT
≡ OIL FIELD

Ethnicity, 1990: White, 86,977 (81.6%); Black, 8,281 (7.8%); American Indian, 414 (0.4%); Asian, 888 (0.8%); Hispanic, 22,780 (21.4%); Other, 10,051 (9.4%).

Recreation: Permian Basin Petroleum Museum, Library and Hall of Fame; Museum of the Southwest; Pliska Aviation Museum; Confederate Air Force and Museum; polo, golf, tennis, professional baseball; community theater; metropolitan events (ask chamber of commerce for dates).

Minerals: Major producer of oil, natural gas; some stone produced.

Agriculture: Annual income from beef, horses; cotton top crop, others are alfalfa, pecans; some irrigation.

Business: Among leading petroleum-producing counties; distribution, administrative center for oil industry; varied manufacturing.

MIDLAND (89,443) county seat; petroleum, petrochemical center; varied manufacturing; livestock sale center; hospital, nursing homes; cultural activities. Other town, **Odessa** (195 in Midland County, mostly in Ector County).

Milam County

LOCATION: East central (L-16).

Cong. Dist. 11	U.S. Jud. Dist. ....W-Wa.
St. Sen. Dist. 5	Ct. Appeals.......................3
St. Rep. Dist. 13	Admin. Jud. Dist. 3
St. Dist. Cts.....................20	

History: Created 1836 from municipality named for Ben Milam, a leader who died at the battle for San Antonio in December 1835; organized 1837.

Physical Features: Partly level Blackland; southeast rolling; Brazos, Little rivers.

Population.................22,946	Av . Weekly Wage....$437.85
Area (sq. mi.)...........1,021.6	Density 23
Land Area 1,016.7	Water Area 4.9
Civilian Labor 8,829	Jobless Rate...................6.1
Altitude (ft.)............648-306	Retail Sales $108,446,479
Rainfall (in.) 34.3	Gross Sales $204,146,815
Jan. min. 38	Reg. Voters 12,051
July max. 96	Election Turnout 56.7
Grow. Season (days).....256	Vehicles 20,865
Total Income (mil.) $306	Lane Miles 682
Per Capita Income...$13,882	Tax Value......$1,337,225,057
Total Wages......$137,336,685	Fed. Spending.........$67,986
Housing....................10,460	Defense Spending $2,016

Vital Statistics, 1989: Births, 281; Deaths, 264; Marriages, 150; Divorces, 99.

Ethnicity, 1990: White, 18,603 (81.1%); Black, 2,940 (12.8%); American Indian, 69 (0.3%); Asian, 37 (0.2%); Hispanic, 3,456 (15.1%); Other, 1,297 (5.7%).

Recreation: Fishing, hunting; historic sites include **Fort Sullivan,** Indian battlegrounds, mission sites; Milam County Museum in old jail at Cameron; festivals, other local events; **Alcoa Lake.**

Minerals: Large lignite deposits; limited oil, natural gas production.

Agriculture: Cattle, hogs, poultry, some sheep provide most income; crops are sorghums, cotton, wheat, hay, corn; soybeans introduced; little irrigation.

Business: Many employed at aluminum plant; varied manufacturing; lignite mining; agribusiness.

CAMERON (5,580) county seat; varied manufacturing; power plant; hospital, nursing homes; library; arts fair in October. Other towns, **Buckholts** (335); **Milano** (408); **Rockdale** (5,235) aluminum plant, golf tournament, fair in October; hospital; **Thorndale** (1,092 in Milam County, partly in Williamson County).

Mills County

LOCATION: Central (J-14).

Cong. Dist. 11	U.S. Jud. Dist. ......N-SAng.
St. Sen. Dist. 24	Ct. Appeals.......................3
St. Rep. Dist. 54	Admin. Jud. Dist. 7
St. Dist. Cts.....................35	

History: Created, organized, 1887 from Brown, Comanche, Hamilton, Lampasas counties; named for pioneer jurist John T. Mills.

Physical Features: Hills, plateau draining to Colorado River on southwest; sandy, loam soils.

Population...................4,531	Av. Weekly Wage $260.49
Area (sq. mi.)...............749.8	Density 6
Land Area 748.1	Water Area 1.7
Civilian Labor 2,041	Jobless Rate...................3.2
Altitude (ft.).......1,762-1,250	Retail Sales $16,318,566
Rainfall (in.) 28.5	Gross Sales $31,290,132
Jan. min. 34	Reg. Voters 2,502
July max. 96	Election Turnout 61.6
Grow. Season (days).....230	Vehicles 5,124
Total Income (mil.) $72	Lane Miles 419
Per Capita Income...$16,398	Tax Value.........$331,913,180
Total Wages.......$15,726,154	Fed. Spending.........$18,697
Housing......................2,578	Defense Spending $292

Vital Statistics, 1989: Births, 42; Deaths, 66; Marriages, 30; Divorces, 15.

Ethnicity, 1990: White, 4,238 (93.5%); Black, 10 (0.2%); American Indian, 4 (0.1%); Asian, 1 (**.*%); Hispanic, 484 (10.7%); Other, 278 (6.1%).

Recreation: Fishing, deer, dove and turkey hunting; historic suspension bridge; fiddlers' contest, fair in May, other local events.

Minerals: Not significant.

Agriculture: Beef cattle strong; dairy cattle, sheep, goats also raised; some irrigation for pecans, pasture.

Business: Chiefly agribusiness, hunting leases.

GOLDTHWAITE (1,658) county seat; agribusiness, livestock center; light manufacturing; hospital, clinics, nursing homes; bike rally in April, old timers rodeo in May. Other town, **Mullin** (194).

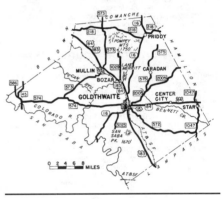

Mitchell County

LOCATION: West (I-10).

Cong. Dist. 17	U.S. Jud. Dist. ....N-Ab.
St. Sen. Dist. 30	Ct. Appeals.....................11
St. Rep. Dist. 66	Admin. Jud. Dist. 7
St. Dist. Cts.....................32	

History: Created 1876 from Bexar District; organized 1881; named for pioneer brothers Asa and Eli Mitchell.

Physical Features: Rolling, draining to Colorado and tributaries; sandy, red, dark soils; Lake Colorado City and Champion Creek Reservoir.

Population...................8,016	Av. Weekly Wage $299.00
Area (sq. mi.)...............915.9	Density 9
Land Area 910.1	Water Area 5.8
Civilian Labor 3,618	Jobless Rate...................6.7
Altitude (ft.).......2,616-2,004	Retail Sales $37,854,484
Rainfall (in.) 19.8	Gross Sales $63,878,775
Jan. min. 30	Reg. Voters 4,773
July max. 97	Election Turnout 51.9
Grow. Season (days).....217	Vehicles 7,478
Total Income (mil.) $109	Lane Miles 657
Per Capita Income...$12,795	Tax Value.........$591,931,439
Total Wages.......$31,158,004	Fed. Spending.........$30,219
Housing......................4,569	Defense Spending $292

Vital Statistics, 1989: Births, 114; Deaths, 115; Marriages, 64; Divorces, 13.

Ethnicity, 1990: White, 6,317 (78.8%); Black, 363 (4.5%); American Indian, 14 (0.2%); Asian, 5 (0.1%); Hispanic, 2,389 (29.8%); Other, 1,317 (16.4%).

Recreation: Lake activities; **Lake Colorado City State Park;** museum, hunting; railhead arts, crafts show in October, other local events.

Minerals: Production of oil and natural gas.

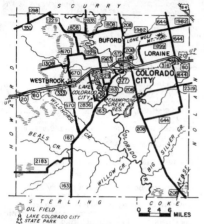

Agriculture: Beef cattle top revenue source, sheep raised; cotton principal crop, grains also produced; some irrigation for cotton, alfalfa.

Business: Oil, agribusiness; some manufacturing.

COLORADO CITY (4,749) county seat; varied manufacturing; electric service center; hospital, nursing home. Other towns, **Loraine** (731), **Westbrook** (237).

Montague County

LOCATION: North (F-15).

Cong. Dist. 17	U.S. Jud. Dist. ....N-WF
St. Sen. Dist. 30	Ct. Appeals.....................2
St. Rep. Dist. 80	Admin. Jud. Dist. 8
St. Dist. Cts. 97	

History: Created from Cooke County 1857, organized 1858; named for pioneer Daniel Montague.

Physical Features: Rolling, draining to tributaries of Trinity, Red rivers; sandy loams, red, black soils; Farmers Creek Reservoir, Lake Amon G. Carter; Lyndon B. Johnson National Grasslands.

Population................17,274	Av. Weekly Wage $278.83
Area (sq. mi.).............938.4	Density 19
Land Area 930.7	Water Area 7.7
Civilian Labor 6,591	Jobless Rate.................5.1

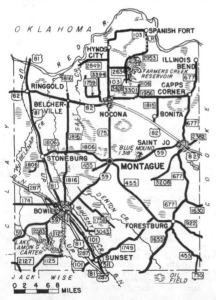

Altitude (ft.) 1,318-766		Retail Sales $86,008,899	
Rainfall (in.) 32.3		Gross Sales...... $172,445,888	
Jan. min. 31		Reg. Voters.............. 10,121	
July max. 97		Election Turnout......... 47.3	
Grow. Season (days)..... 229		Vehicles 18,808	
Total Income (mil.) $228		Lane Miles 808	
Per Capita Income...$13,063		Tax Value........ $606,128,823	
Total Wages...... $59,780,567		Fed. Spending $56,274	
Housing......................9,124		Defense Spending $2,009	

Vital Statistics, 1989: Births, 230; Deaths, 302; Marriages, 177; Divorces, 72.

Ethnicity, 1990: White, 16,834 (97.5%); Black, 5 (**.*%); American Indian, 72 (0.4%); Asian, 13 (0.1%); Hispanic, 548 (3.2%); Other, 350 (2.0%).

Recreation: Lake activities; quail, turkey, deer hunting; scenic drives; museums; historical sites; Chisholm Trail Days, Jim Bowie Days; cattleman's roundup in February; other local events.

Minerals: Production of oil, gas, stone.

Agriculture: Beef, dairy cattle are chief products; crops include wheat, peanuts, watermelons, cantaloupe; some irrigation for peanuts, fruits.

Business: Agribusinesses; oil production; varied manufacturing.

MONTAGUE (est. 400) county seat; agribusiness center. Other towns, **Bowie** (4,990), varied manufacturing, livestock sales, hospital, nursing home, library; fall bash, other local events; **Nocona** (2,870), boot manufacturing; hospital; **Saint Jo** (1,048), farm center.

Montgomery County

LOCATION: Southeast (M-19).

Cong. Dist. 2, 6, 8	U.S. Jud. Dist. ....S-Hn.
St. Sen. Dist. 3, 4, 5	Ct. Appeals.....................9
St. Rep. Dist. 15, 16	Admin. Jud. Dist. 2
St. Dist. Cts........9, 2D9, 221, 284,359	

History: Created, organized 1837 from Washington County; named for U.S. Revolutionary Gen. Richard Montgomery.

Physical Features: Rolling, over three-fourths timbered; Sam Houston National Forest over large area; loam, sandy, alluvial soils.

Population................182,201	Av. Weekly Wage....$390.18
Area (sq. mi.)........... 1,076.8	Density 174
Land Area 1,044.3	Water Area 32.5
Civilian Labor 85,775	Jobless Rate.................5.1
Altitude (ft.) 380-86	Retail Sales ... $1,058,260,383
Rainfall (in.) 46.6	Gross Sales... $2,777,185,648
Jan. min. 38	Reg. Voters............. 84,722
July max. 95	Election Turnout......... 51.9
Grow. Season (days)..... 270	Vehicles 156,394
Total Income (mil.) .. $2,751	Lane Miles 1,012
Per Capita Income...$14,705	Tax Value...... $6,977,155,988
Total Wages......$802,178,104	Fed. Spending $299,600
Housing................... 73,454	Defense Spending .. $25,259

Vital Statistics, 1989: Births, 2,889; Deaths, 1,123; Marriages, 1,898; Divorces, 993.

Ethnicity, 1990: White, 166,107 (91.2%); Black, 7,763 (4.3%); American Indian, 687 (0.4%); Asian, 1,232 (0.7%); Hispanic, 13,237 (7.3%); Other, 6,412 (3.5%).

Recreation: Hunting, fishing; **Lake Conroe** activities; **Sam Houston National Forest; W.G. Jones State Forest;** county fair, safari world and animal park, Heritage Museum, **Lake Woodlands;** hiking, boating, horseback riding; main street festival.

Minerals: Production of oil, gas, sand and gravel.

Agriculture: Agricultural income from horses, cattle; nursery and greenhouse products, forage raised; substantial income from timber products; ostrich, emu introduced.

Business: Many residents work in Houston; center for lumber, oil production; part of Houston PMSA.

CONROE (27,610) county seat; residential community with many people working in Houston; some manufacturing; food processing; hospital, nursing home. Other towns, **Chateau Woods** (641), **Cut and Shoot** (903), **Kingwood** (47 in Montgomery County, mostly in Harris County), **Magnolia** (940), **Montgomery** (356), **Oak Ridge North** (2,454), **Panorama** (1,556), **Patton Village** (1,155), **Pinehurst** (3,284), **Porter Heights** (1,448), **Roman Forest** (1,033), **Shenandoah** (1,718), **Splendora** (745), **Stagecoach** (340), **The Woodlands** (29,205), **Willis** (2,764), **Woodbranch** (1,312), **Woodloch** (291).

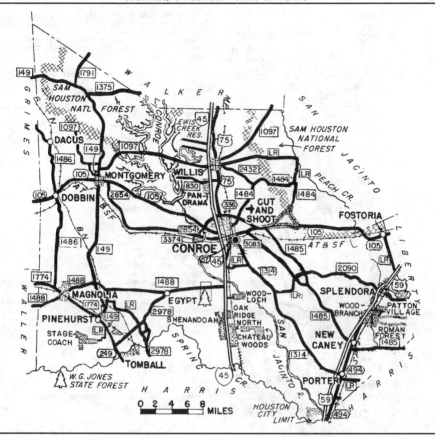

Moore County

LOCATION: Northwest (B-8).

Cong. Dist. 13	U.S. Jud. Dist. ....N-Am.
St. Sen. Dist. 31	Ct. Appeals......................7
St. Rep. Dist. 88	Admin. Jud. Dist. 9
St. Dist. Cts.....................69	

History: Created 1876 from Bexar District; organized 1892; named for Republic of Texas navy commander E.W. Moore.

Physical Features: Flat to rolling, broken by creeks; sandy loams; Lake Meredith.

Population................ 17,865	Av. Weekly Wage $368.09
Area (sq. mi.) 909.6	Density 20
Land Area 899.7	Water Area 9.9
Civilian Labor 9,061	Jobless Rate...................3.5
Altitude (ft.) 3,770-3,221	Retail Sales $104,803,201
Rainfall (in.) 18.5	Gross Sales.... $1,168,026,081
Jan. min. 19	Reg. Voters 7,429
July max. 92	Election Turnout......... 54.6
Grow. Season (days)..... 185	Vehicles 17,682
Total Income (mil.) $281	Lane Miles 469
Per Capita Income...$16,797	Tax Value...... $1,218,481,310
Total Wages......$136,798,272	Fed. Spending $44,946
Housing 6,849	Defense Spending $3,650

Vital Statistics, 1989: Births, 371; Deaths, 112; Marriages, 205; Divorces, 121.

Ethnicity, 1990: White, 12,789 (71.6%); Black, 95 (0.5%); American Indian, 123 (0.7%); Asian, 282 (1.6%); Hispanic, 5,693 (31.9%); Other, 4,576 (25.6%).

Recreation: Lake Meredith activities; historical museum; local events.

Minerals: Production of natural gas, helium, oil.

Agriculture: Most income from feedlot cattle; crops include sorghums, wheat, corn; significant irrigation.

Business: Extensive petroleum operations; major natural gas producing county; varied agribusiness.

DUMAS (12,871) county seat; tourist, retail trade center; varied agribusiness; hospital; nursing home. Other towns, **Cactus** (1,529), **Fritch** (10 in Moore County, mostly in Hutchinson County), **Sunray** (1,729).

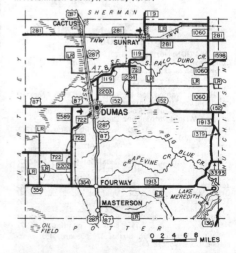

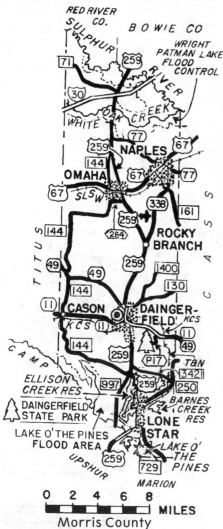

Morris County

LOCATION: Northeast (G-20).

Cong. Dist. 1	U.S. Jud. Dist. .... E-MI.
St. Sen. Dist. 1	Ct. Appeals..................... 6
St. Rep. Dist. 8	Admin. Jud. Dist. 1
St. Dist. Cts............. 76, 276	

History: Named for legislator-jurist W.W. Morris; created from Titus County and organized in 1875.

Physical Features: Rolling, forested hills; drains to streams, Wright Patman and Daingerfield lakes.

Population............... 13,200	Av. Weekly Wage $412.08
Area (sq. mi.).............258.6	Density 52
Land Area 254.5	Water Area 4.1
Civilian Labor 3,912	Jobless Rate................ 13.6
Altitude (ft.)..........537-268	Retail Sales $46,442,636
Rainfall (in.) 44.2	Gross Sales.......$386,358,828
Jan. min. 35	Reg. Voters 8,162
July max. 95	Election Turnout........ 47.5
Grow. Season (days)..... 236	Vehicles 14,447
Total Income (mil.) $169	Lane Miles 355
Per Capita Income...$12,155	Tax Value........$730,405,023
Total Wages....... $98,569,804	Fed. Spending $42,696
Housing......................5,795	Defense Spending $1,177

Vital Statistics, 1989: Births, 170; Deaths, 153; Marriages, 125; Divorces, 66.

Ethnicity, 1990: White, 9,770 (74.0%); Black, 3,227 (24.4%); American Indian, 70 (0.5%); Asian, 18 (0.1%); Hispanic, 239 (1.8%); Other, 115 (0.9%).

Recreation: Activities on **Lake O' the Pines**, many small lakes; fishing, hunting; **Daingerfield State Park;** museum in Daingerfield; local events.

Minerals: Iron ore.

Agriculture: Beef cattle principal income source; poultry increasing; crops include peanuts, hay, watermelons, peaches; minor irrigation; timber products important.

Business: Steel products; manufacturing; tourism; livestock, timber production.

DAINGERFIELD (2,572) county seat; varied manufacturing; hospital, clinics, nursing home; library; Captain Daingerfield Day in October. Other towns, **Hughes Springs** (11 in Morris County, mostly in Cass County); **Lone Star** (1,615), oil-field equipment manufactured; hospital; Starfest in September; **Naples** (1,508), hospital; **Omaha** (833).

Motley County

LOCATION: Northwest (E-10).

Cong. Dist. 13	U.S. Jud. Dist. .... N-Lb.
St. Sen. Dist. 30	Ct. Appeals..................... 7
St. Rep. Dist. 84	Admin. Jud. Dist. 9
St. Dist. Cts............. 110	

History: Created out of Bexar District 1876; organized 1891; named for Dr. J.W. Mottley, a signer of Texas Declaration of Independence, but name was misspelled in the law.

Physical Features: Rough terrain, broken by Pease tributaries; sandy to red clay soils.

Population...................1,532	Av. Weekly Wage $308.87
Area (sq. mi.)..............989.8	Density 2
Land Area 989.4	Water Area 0.4
Civilian Labor 1,035	Jobless Rate................ 2.5
Altitude (ft.)........3,034-1,928	Retail Sales $5,676,621
Rainfall (in.) 20.4	Gross Sales........$22,962,912
Jan. min. 27	Reg. Voters 1,127
July max. 96	Election Turnout........ 51.9
Grow. Season (days)..... 218	Vehicles 1,815
Total Income (mil.) $25	Lane Miles 331
Per Capita Income...$13,566	Tax Value........$126,835,833
Total Wages........$5,091,492	Fed. Spending $8,638
Housing......................1,026	Defense Spending $59

Vital Statistics, 1989: Births, 10; Deaths, 29; Marriages, 10; Divorces, 5.

Ethnicity, 1990: White, 1,362 (88.9%); Black, 68 (4.4%); American Indian, 5 (0.3%); Asian, 4 (0.3%); Hispanic, 136 (8.9%); Other, 93 (6.1%).

Recreation: Local events; quail, dove, deer hunting; Matador Ranch headquarters; spring-fed pool at Roaring Springs; livestock show in March.

Minerals: Oil, gas, sand and gravel.

Agriculture: Beef cattle, cow-calf operations, horses most profitable; crops include cotton, wheat, peanuts; some irrigation for peanuts.

Business: Economy based on livestock, oil production.

MATADOR (790) county seat; farm trade center; **Roaring Springs** (264).

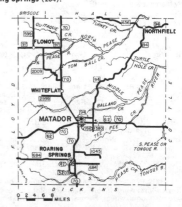

Nacog-doches County

LOCATION: East (J-21).

Cong. Dist. 2
U.S. Jud. Dist.... E-Ty.
St. Sen. Dist. 3
Ct. Appeals 12
St. Rep. Dist. 10
Admin. Jud. Dist. 1
St. Dist. Cts. 145

History: Original county; created 1836, organized 1837; named for Indians; one of state's most historic areas.

Physical Features: On divide between streams; hilly; two-thirds forested; red, gray, sandy soils; Sam Rayburn Reservoir.

Vital Statistics, 1989: Births, 764; Deaths, 480; Marriages, 553; Divorces, 174.

Ethnicity, 1990: White, 43,772 (79.9%); Black, 9,020 (16.5%); American Indian, 144 (0.3%); Asian, 311 (0.6%); Hispanic, 2,788 (5.1%); Other, 1,506 (2.8%).

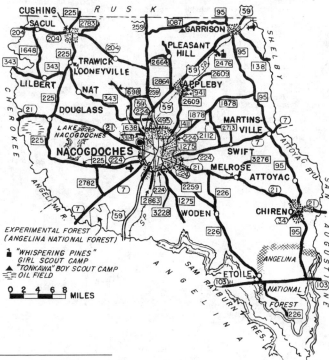

EXPERIMENTAL FOREST (ANGELINA NATIONAL FOREST)

"WHISPERING PINES" GIRL SCOUT CAMP
"TONKAWA" BOY SCOUT CAMP
OIL FIELD

0 2 4 6 8 MILES

Recreation: Lake, river activities; **Stephen F. Austin University** events; **Angelina National Forest**; historic sites major tourist attractions, including Old Stone Fort, pioneer homes, museums, Piney Woods Fair in October, Heritage Days Festival in June.

Population................ 54,753	Av. Weekly Wage $300.74
Area (sq. mi.) 981.3	Density 58
Land Area 946.8	Water Area 34.5
Civilian Labor 27,890	Jobless Rate.................5.1
Altitude (ft.) 655-182	Retail Sales $354,129,017
Rainfall (in.) 47.5	Gross Sales....... $835,651,595
Jan. min. 36	Reg. Voters 26,222
July max. 94	Election Turnout......... 46.7
Grow. Season (days)..... 243	Vehicles 41,508
Total Income (mil.) $686	Lane Miles 903
Per Capita Income...$13,208	Tax Value..... $1,679,628,188
Total Wages......$306,409,582	Fed. Spending....... $130,123
Housing.................... 22,749	Defense Spending $5,292

Minerals: First Texas oil found here, 1866; production of gas, oil, clay, stone.

Agriculture: A leading poultry county; 33 dairies; beef cattle raised; commercial vegetables produced; timber sold.

Business: Agribusinesses; manufacturing; education; tourism.

NACOGDOCHES (30,872) county seat; varied manufacturing; trade center; hospitals, nursing home; **Stephen F. Austin University**; local events. Other towns, **Appleby** (449), **Chireno** (415), **Cushing** (587), **Garrison** (883).

Navarro County

LOCATION: North central (I-17).

Cong. Dist. 6   U.S. Jud. Dist. ....N-DI.
St. Sen. Dist. 9   Ct. Appeals.................... 10
St. Rep. Dist. 12   Admin. Jud. Dist. 3
St. Dist. Cts. 13

History: Created from Robertson County, organized in 1846; named for Republic of Texas leader Jose Antonio Navarro.

Navarro Co. (Cont.)

Physical Features: Level Blackland, some rolling; Chambers, Richland creeks, Trinity River; Navarro Mills Lake, Richland/Chambers Reservoir.

Population................ 39,926	Av. Weekly Wage $325.12
Area (sq. mi.) 1,086.2	Density 37
Land Area 1,071.2	Water Area 15.0
Civilian Labor 18,248	Jobless Rate................. 6.9
Altitude (ft.)........536-293	Retail Sales $235,125,884
Rainfall (in.) 36.6	Gross Sales...... $712,256,877
Jan. min. 34	Reg. Voters 19,887
July max. 96	Election Turnout 50.8
Grow. Season (days)..... 253	Vehicles 34,941
Total Income (mil.) $530	Lane Miles 1,137
Per Capita Income...$13,428	Tax Value...... $1,514,125,075
Total Wages......$206,710,467	Fed. Spending $114,487
Housing.................... 17,209	Defense Spending $4,186

Vital Statistics, 1989: Births, 644; Deaths, 534; Marriages, 406; Divorces, 305.

Ethnicity, 1990: White, 30,322 (75.9%); Black, 7,574 (19.0%); American Indian, 127 (0.3%); Asian, 271 (0.7%); Hispanic, 2,891 (7.2%); Other, 1,632 (4.1%).

Recreation: Navarro Mills Lake activities; Pioneer Village; historic sites, homes; **Richland/Chambers Reservoir;** Fall TPRA Rodeo Finals.

Minerals: Longest continuous Texas oil flow; more than 200 million barrels produced since 1895; production of oil; natural gas, sand and gravel also produced.

Agriculture: Income split between livestock, crops; beef, stocker, dairy cattle, horses raised; crops include cotton, grain sorghums, wheat, oats, hay, corn.

Business: Diversified manufacturing; agribusinesses; oil-field operations, distribution.

CORSICANA (22,911) county seat; growing industrial center; varied manufacturing; distribution center; hospital; **Navarro College;** Amtrak passenger service. Other towns, **Angus** (363); **Barry** (175); **Blooming Grove** (847); **Dawson** (766); **Emhouse** (195); **Eureka** (242); **Frost** (579); **Goodlow** (319); **Kerens** (1,702), some manufacturing; local events; **Mustang** (35); **Mildred** (173); **Navarro** (193); **Oak Valley** (388); **Powell** (101); **Retreat** (334); **Rice** (554 in Navarro County, partly in Ellis County); **Richland** (244).

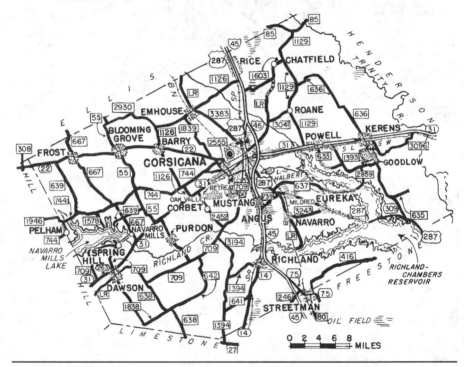

Newton County

LOCATION: Easternmost county (L-22).

Cong. Dist. 2	U.S. Jud. Dist. .... E-Bt.
St. Sen. Dist. 3	Ct. Appeals..................... 9
St. Rep. Dist. 19	Admin. Jud. Dist. 2
St. Dist. Cts.................1, 1-A	

History: Created, organized 1846 from Jasper County; named for U.S. Revolutionary soldier John Newton.

Physical Features: Densely forested hills, valleys; Sabine National Forest; spring-fed streams; highest Texas rainfall; Toledo Bend Reservoir; Sabine River; mostly sandy soils.

Population................ 13,569	Av. Weekly Wage $330.01
Area (sq. mi.).............939.5	Density 15
Land Area 932.7	Water Area 6.8
Civilian Labor 4,906	Jobless Rate................. 9.3
Altitude (ft.).........510-23	Retail Sales $75,802,049
Rainfall (in.) 56.0	Gross Sales..... $95,910,990
Jan. min. 40	Reg. Voters 8,648
July max. 93	Election Turnout 36.8
Grow. Season (days).....228	Vehicles 8,414
Total Income (mil.) $129	Lane Miles 547

Per Capita Income.... $9,699	Tax Value......... $709,367,120
Total Wages....... $30,923,204	Fed. Spending $32,005
Housing.....................6,377	Defense Spending $816

Vital Statistics, 1989: Births, 188; Deaths, 150; Marriages, 151; Divorces, 112.

Ethnicity, 1990: White, 10,402 (76.7%); Black, 3,039 (22.4%); American Indian, 44 (0.3%); Asian, 11 (0.1%); Hispanic, 153 (1.1%); Other, 73 (0.5%).

Recreation: Toledo Bend Reservoir; water sports; fishing, hunting; tourism; **E.O. Siecke State Forest;** Azalea Canyons.

Minerals: Oil, gas.

Agriculture: Forestry is main agricultural activity; peaches, vegetables raised.

Business: Forestry, tourism are main economic factors.

NEWTON (1,885) county seat; lumber manufacturing; plywood mill; hospital; tourist center; airport; **Deweyville** (1,218).

See map on next page.

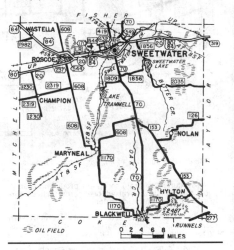

Total Wages....... $95,692,923   Fed. Spending......... $49,957
Housing......................7,395   Defense Spending $1,128

Vital Statistics, 1989: Births, 241; Deaths, 206; Marriages, 178; Divorces, 74.

Ethnicity, 1990: White, 12,942 (78.0%); Black, 775 (4.7%); American Indian, 46 (0.3%); Asian, 18 (0.1%); Hispanic, 4,246 (25.6%); Other, 2,813 (17.0%).

Recreation: Sweetwater and Oak Creek lakes; hunting; rattlesnake roundup in March; pioneer museum; rodeo, other local events booked at Nolan County Coliseum.

Minerals: Production of oil, gas, cement, gypsum, stone, sand and gravel, clays.

Agriculture: Most income from beef cattle, sheep, Angora goats, hogs; crops include cotton, wheat, sorghums; some irrigation.

Business: Varied manufacturing; ranching; oil and gas production.

SWEETWATER (11,967) county seat; All-American city in 1988; varied manufacturing; hospital; **Texas State Technical Institute.** Other towns, **Blackwell** (332 in Nolan County, partly in Coke County), **Roscoe** (1,446).

Nueces County

LOCATION: Southern coast (R-16).

Cong. Dist. 15, 27	U.S. Jud. Dist. ....S-CC
St. Sen. Dist. 20	Ct. Appeals......................13
St. Rep. Dist. 34-36	Admin. Jud. Dist. 5
St. Dist. Cts.............. 28, 94,		
105, 117, 148, 214, 319, 347		

History: Name is Spanish for nuts; county named for river; created, organized 1846 out of San Patricio County.

Physical Features: Flat, rich soils, broken by bays, Nueces River, Petronila Creek; includes Mustang Island, north tip of Padre Island.

Population...............291,145	Av. Weekly Wage $387.46
Area (sq. mi.) 1,166.4	Density 344
Land Area 835.8	Water Area 330.6
Civilian Labor 138,999	Jobless Rate 4.6
Altitude (ft.) 129-6	Retail Sales ... $2,298,662,436
Rainfall (in.) 30.2	Gross Sales .. $6,496,086,751
Jan. min.......................46	Reg. Voters 138,455
July max. 94	Election Turnout 44.3
Grow. Season (days)..... 309	Vehicles 220,856
Total Income (mil.) .. $4,035	Lane Miles 1,295
Per Capita Income...$13,561	Tax Value....$10,744,850,335
Total Wages.. $2,257,211,258	Fed. Spending...... 1,033,013
Housing..................114,225	Defense Spending . $363,433

Vital Statistics, 1989: Births, 5,108; Deaths, 2,075; Marriages, 2,787; Divorces, 1,610.

Ethnicity, 1990: White, 220,168 (75.6%); Black, 12,691 (4.4%); American Indian, 1,175 (0.4%); Asian, 2,483 (0.9%); Hispanic, 152,051 (52.2%); Other, 54,608 (18.8%).

Recreation: Major resort area; fishing, water sports; **Padre Island National Seashore; Mustang Island State Park; Lipantitlan State Historical Park; Art Museum of South Texas, Corpus Christi Museum of Science and History; Texas State Aquarium;** various metropolitan events (check with chamber of commerce); greyhound race track.

Nolan County

LOCATION: West central (I-11).

Cong. Dist. 17	U.S. Jud. Dist. .... N-Ab.
St. Sen. Dist. 24	Ct. Appeals......................11
St. Rep. Dist. 78	Admin. Jud. Dist. 7
St. Dist. Cts.....................32		

History: Created from Bexar, Young districts 1876; organized 1881; named for adventurer Philip Nolan.

Physical Features: On divide between Brazos, Colorado watersheds; mostly red sandy loams, some waxy, sandy soils; Sweetwater, Trammell, Oak Creek lakes.

Population................ 16,594	Av. Weekly Wage $321.50
Area (sq. mi.) 913.9	Density 18
Land Area 912.0	Water Area 1.9
Civilian Labor 7,827	Jobless Rate 7.2
Altitude (ft.) 2,603-1,990	Retail Sales $87,838,961
Rainfall (in.) 23.4	Gross Sales....... $229,301,669
Jan. min. 30	Reg. Voters 8,231
July max. 95	Election Turnout 50.3
Grow. Season (days)..... 221	Vehicles 15,189
Total Income (mil.) $246	Lane Miles 684
Per Capita Income...$14,598	Tax Value......... $619,496,874

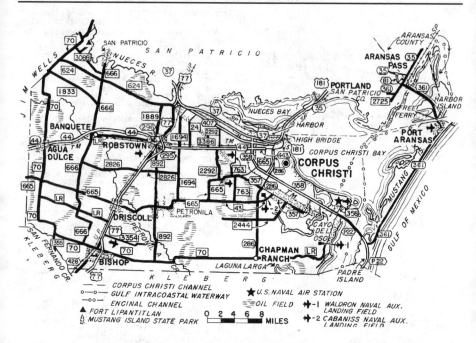

CORPUS CHRISTI CHANNEL
GULF INTRACOASTAL WATERWAY
ENCINAL CHANNEL
▲ FORT LIPANTITLAN
Å MUSTANG ISLAND STATE PARK
★ U.S. NAVAL AIR STATION
OIL FIELD
✛-1 WALDRON NAVAL AUX. LANDING FIELD
✛-2 CABANISS NAVAL AUX. LANDING FIELD
0 2 4 6 8 MILES

Minerals: Production of oil, gas, cement, lime, sand and gravel.

Agriculture: Top grain sorghums producing county; cotton, corn, wheat also raised; beef cattle declined during drought; substantial irrigation.

Business: Diversified economy includes petroleum processing and production; agriculture; tourism; coastal shipping; manufacturing; military complex.

CORPUS CHRISTI (257,453 in Nueces County, partly in San Patricio, Kelberg counties) county seat; varied manufacturing; petroleum processing; seaport; hospitals; museums; recreation centers; tourist destination; **Naval Air Station; Army depot; Corpus Christi State University; Del Mar College.** Other towns, **Agua Dulce** (794); **Aransas Pass** (22 in Nueces County, partly in San Patricio, Aransas counties); **Bishop** (3,337), chemical, pharmaceutical manufacturing; fall carnival in October; **Driscoll** (688); **North San Pedro** (953); **Port Aransas** (2,233), sea research institute; fishing accomodations; fisheries management; **Petronila** (155); **Robstown** (12,849).

Ochiltree County

LOCATION: Extreme northwest (A-10).

Cong. Dist. 13	U.S. Jud. Dist. .... N-Am.
St. Sen. Dist. 31	Ct. Appeals.......................7
St. Rep. Dist. 88	Admin. Jud. Dist. 9
St. Dist. Cts......................84	

History: Created from Bexar District 1876, organized 1889; named for Republic of Texas leader W.B. Ochiltree.

Physical Features: Level, broken by creeks; deep loam, clay soils.

Population...................9,128	Av. Weekly Wage $381.52
Area (sq. mi.).............918.1	Density 10
Land Area 917.6	Water Area 0.5
Civilian Labor 4,422	Jobless Rate..................3.8
Altitude (ft.)......3,007-2,642	Retail Sales $62,973,342
Rainfall (in.) 19.6	Gross Sales.......$164,080,312
Jan. min. 16	Reg. Voters................4,725
July max. 94	Election Turnout 56.7
Grow. Season (days).....191	Vehicles 10,977
Total Income (mil.) $148	Lane Miles 428
Per Capita Income...$16,060	Tax Value.........$553,543,331
Total Wages.......$68,544,300	Fed. Spending $27,761
Housing 3,995	Defense Spending $135

Vital Statistics, 1989: Births, 153; Deaths, 61; Marriages, 109; Divorces, 50.

Ethnicity, 1990: White, 8,023 (87.9%); Black, 2 (**.*%); American Indian, 105 (1.2%); Asian, 8 (0.1%); Hispanic, 1,641 (18.0%); Other, 990 (10.8%).

Recreation: Local events; Springfest in June, Wheatheart of the Nation celebration in August; **Museum of** the Plains; **Wolf Creek Park;** Indian "Buried City" site.

Minerals: Oil, natural gas.

Agriculture: Annual income from beef cattle, swine,

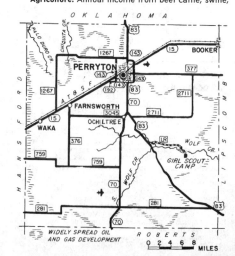

Ochiltree Co. (Cont.)
sheep, horses; crops include wheat, grain sorghums, corn, alfalfa; 70,000 acres irrigated for most crops.

Business: Oil; agribusiness, center of large feedlot operations.

PERRYTON (7,607) county seat; oil-field services, equipment manufacturing; cattle feeding; grain center; hospital, nursing home; convention center, local events. Other town, **Booker** (5 in Ochiltree County, mostly in Lipscomb County).

Oldham County

LOCATION: Northwest (C-7).

Cong. Dist. 13	U.S. Jud. Dist. .... N-Am.
St. Sen. Dist. 31	Ct. Appeals...................... 7
St. Rep. Dist. 88	Admin. Jud. Dist. 9
St. Dist. Cts................... 222	

History: Created 1876 from Bexar District; organized 1880; named for editor-Confederate senator W.S. Oldham.

Physical Features: Level, broken by Canadian River and tributaries.

Population...................2,278	Av. Weekly Wage $316.63
Area (sq. mi.) 1,501.4	Density 2
Land Area 1,500.7	Water Area 0.7
Civilian Labor 1,284	Jobless Rate 4.3
Altitude (ft.)......4,171-3,238	Retail Sales $15,739,463
Rainfall (in.) 17.4	Gross Sales........ $24,316,573
Jan. min........................19	Reg. Voters 1,274
July max. 91	Election Turnout......... 54.6
Grow. Season (days).....186	Vehicles 2,417
Total Income (mil.) $54	Lane Miles 456
Per Capita Income...$18,441	Tax Value......... $119,970,567
Total Wages....... $11,986,326	Fed. Spending $10,491
Housing 861	Defense Spending $105

Vital Statistics, 1989: Births, 29; Deaths, 22; Marriages, 33; Divorces, 1.

Ethnicity, 1990: White, 2,112 (92.7%); Black, 9 (0.4%); American Indian, 29 (1.3%); Asian, 18 (0.8%); Hispanic, 200 (8.8%); Other, 110 (4.8%).

Recreation: Old Tascosa, with Boot Hill Cemetery, pioneer cowboy towns; Oldham County Roundup in August.

Minerals: Sand and gravel, oil, natural gas, stone.

Agriculture: Beef cattle major revenue source; crops include grain sorghums, wheat; some irrigation.

Business: Ranching center.

VEGA (840) county seat; ranch trade center; Cal Farley's Boys Ranch. Other town, **Adrian** (220).

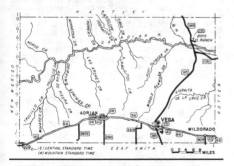

Orange County

LOCATION: Extreme southeast (M-22).

Cong. Dist. 2	U.S. Jud. Dist. .... E-Bt.
St. Sen. Dist. 4	Ct. Appeals...................... 9
St. Rep. Dist. 19	Admin. Jud. Dist. 2
St. Dist. Cts.......128, 163, 260	

History: Created from Jefferson County, organized in 1852; named for early orange grove.

Physical Features: Bounded by Sabine, Neches rivers, Sabine Lake; coastal soils; two-thirds timbered.

Population...............80,509	Av. Weekly Wage $442.12
Area (sq. mi.) 379.5	Density 222
Land Area 356.4	Water Area 23.1
Civilian Labor 37,355	Jobless Rate..................8.8
Altitude (ft.)................25-16	Retail Sales $415,405,622
Rainfall (in.) 59.2	Gross Sales...... $818,648,695
Jan. min.........................40	Reg. Voters 41,810
July max. 91	Election Turnout......... 45.7
Grow. Season (days).... 240	Vehicles 70,878
Total Income (mil.) .. $1,132	Lane Miles 563
Per Capita Income...$13,687	Tax Value...... $3,202,898,903
Total Wages...... $527,285,221	Fed. Spending $188,801
Housing 31,940	Defense Spending ... $12,274

Vital Statistics, 1989: Births, 1,120; Deaths, 700; Marriages, 895; Divorces, 566.

Ethnicity, 1990: White, 72,607 (90.2%); Black, 6,768 (8.4%); American Indian, 189 (0.2%); Asian, 484 (0.6%); Hispanic, 1,933 (2.4%); Other, 461 (0.6%).

Recreation: Fishing, hunting; other water sports; county park; museums; historical homes; crawfish promotion day; metropolitan area events.

Minerals: Production of oil, gas, clays, sand and gravel.

Agriculture: Horticultural plants, forestry products are top revenue sources; some cow-calf operations, horses; citrus grown; crawfish farming, red-fish farming introduced; some irrigation.

Business: Petrochemicals; shipbuilding; shipping; agribusinesses; tourism; lumber processing; county part of Beaumont-Port Arthur MSA.

ORANGE (19,381) county seat; seaport; petrochemical plants; varied manufacturing; food, timber processing; shipping; hospital, theater, museums; Lamar University branch. Other towns **Bridge City** (8,034) varied manufacturing; nursing home; library; local events; new suspension bridge; Mayhaw Mania Festival in April; a rest stop for Monarch butterfly in fall during its migration to Mexico; **Mauriceville** (2,046); **Pine Forest** (709); **Pinehurst** (2,682); **Rose City** (709); **Vidor** (10,935), steel processing; nursing home; **West Orange** (4,187).

See map on next page.

Palo Pinto County

LOCATION: North central (H-14).

Cong. Dist. 17	U.S. Jud. Dist. .... N-FW
St. Sen. Dist. 22	Ct. Appeals......................11
St. Rep. Dist. 64	Admin. Jud. Dist. 8
St. Dist. Cts....................29	

History: Created 1856 from Bosque, Navarro counties; organized 1857; named for creek (in Spanish name means painted stick).

Physical Features: Broken, hilly, wooded in parts; Possum Kingdom Lake, Lake Palo Pinto; sandy, gray, black soils.

Population................. 25,055	Av. Weekly Wage $310.01
Area (sq. mi.) 985.4	Density 26
Land Area 952.9	Water Area 32.5
Civilian Labor 11,477	Jobless Rate..................6.4
Altitude (ft.).........1,470-782	Retail Sales $159,305,133
Rainfall (in.) 29.3	Gross Sales....... $311,011,499
Jan. min.........................32	Reg. Voters 11,943
July max. 97	Election Turnout......... 53.0
Grow. Season (days).... 221	Vehicles 24,618
Total Income (mil.) $335	Lane Miles 829
Per Capita Income...$13,428	Tax Value...... $1,014,869,655
Total Wages...... $114,826,335	Fed. Spending $71,407
Housing 13,117	Defense Spending ... $7,206

Vital Statistics, 1989: Births, 369; Deaths, 297; Marriages, 243; Divorces, 189.

Ethnicity, 1990: White, 22,810 (91.0%); Black, 792 (3.2%); American Indian, 87 (0.3%); Asian, 171 (0.7%); Hispanic, 2,301 (9.2%); Other, 1,195 (4.8%).

Recreation: Tourist center; lake activities; hunting, fishing, water sports; Possum Kingdom Lake, State Park; Mineral Wells State Park; Lake Palo Pinto; Crazy Water Festival in May.

Minerals: Oil, gas, clays, sand and gravel.

Agriculture: Livestock, mostly beef cattle, is prime revenue producer; crops include wheat, oats, grain sorghums, peanuts, cotton; some irrigation.

Business: Varied manufacturing; tourism; petroleum; agribusiness.

PALO PINTO (est. 350) county seat; old settlers reunion; government center. **Mineral Wells** (14,388 in Palo Pinto County, part in Parker County), varied manufacturing; county hospital; tourist center; Weatherford College extension. Other towns, **Gordon** (465), **Graford** (561), **Mingus** (215), **Strawn** (709).

See map on next page.

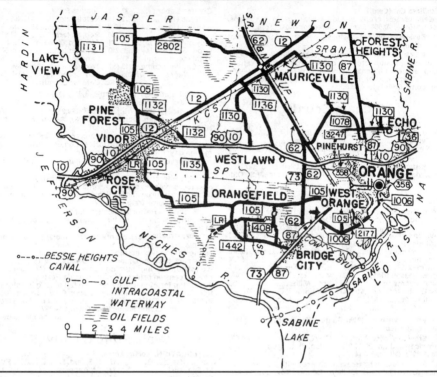

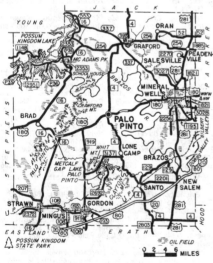

Panola County

LOCATION: On Louisiana line (I-21).

Cong. Dist.	....	1
St. Sen. Dist.	....	1
St. Rep. Dist.	....	10
St. Dist. Cts.	....	123

U.S. Jud. Dist.	.... E-Ty.
Ct. Appeals	..................6, 12
Admin. Jud. Dist.	 1

History: Name is Indian word for cotton; created from Harrison, Shelby counties and organized 1846.

Physical Features: Sixty percent forested, rolling plain; broken by Sabine, Murvaul Creek and Lake, Tole-

do Bend Reservoir.

Population	22,035	Av. Weekly Wage	$373.65
Area (sq. mi.)	821.3	Density	27
Land Area	800.9	Water Area	20.4
Civilian Labor	14,076	Jobless Rate	4.4
Altitude (ft.)	481-192	Retail Sales	$102,627,766
Rainfall (in.)	46.2	Gross Sales	$179,727,120
Jan. min.	37	Reg. Voters	12,627
July max.	95	Election Turnout	48.1
Grow. Season (days)	240	Vehicles	22,379
Total Income (mil.)	$326	Lane Miles	742
Per Capita Income	$14,791	Tax Value	$1,621,860,869
Total Wages	$144,383,117	Fed. Spending	$52,984
Housing	9,692	Defense Spending	$1,622

Vital Statistics, 1989: Births, 258; Deaths, 227; Marriages, 213; Divorces, 153.

Ethnicity, 1990: White, 17,702 (80.3%); Black, 4,057

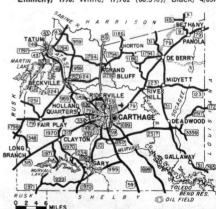

Panola Co. (Cont.)
(18.4%); American Indian, 57 (0.3%); Asian, 23 (0.1%); Hispanic, 477 (2.2%); Other, 196 (0.9%).

Recreation: Lake Murvaul fishing, other water activities; hunting; scenic drives; Jim Reeves memorial; historic sites, homes; museum; **Pirtle Boy Scout Reservation.**

Minerals: Natural gas, oil, coal.

Agriculture: A leading broiler-producing county; cattle, hogs also raised; timber sales significant.

Business: Agribusinesses; varied manufacturing; forest industries; gas processing; oil-field operation.

CARTHAGE (6,496) county seat; petroleum processing; poultry; sawmills; county hospital, clinics, nursing home; **Panola Junior College.** Other towns, **Beckville** (783), **Gary** (271), **Tatum** (255 in Panola County, mostly in Rusk County).

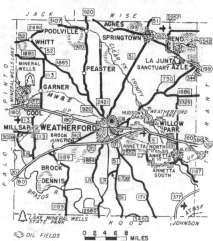

Parker County

LOCATION: North central (H-15).

Cong. Dist.	17	U.S. Jud. Dist.	N-FW
St. Sen. Dist.	22	Ct. Appeals	2
St. Rep. Dist.	63	Admin. Jud. Dist.	8
St. Dist. Cts.	43		

History: Named for pioneer legislator Isaac Parker; created, organized 1855 from Bosque, Navarro counties.

Physical Features: Hilly, broken by Brazos, Trinity tributaries; varied soils; Weatherford Lake and Granbury Lake.

Population	64,785	Av. Weekly Wage $325.50
Area (sq. mi.)	910.0	Density	72
Land Area	903.5	Water Area	6.5
Civilian Labor	32,449	Jobless Rate	4.4
Altitude (ft.)	966-718	Retail Sales	$344,425,603
Rainfall (in.)	31.1	Gross Sales	$753,178,066
Jan. min.	30	Reg. Voters	30,699
July max.	97	Election Turnout	54.5
Grow. Season (days)	225	Vehicles	63,072
Total Income (mil.)	$987	Lane Miles	847
Per Capita Income	$14,553	Tax Value	$2,324,312,869
Total Wages	$202,012,295	Fed. Spending	$114,949
Housing	26,150	Defense Spending	$16,320

Vital Statistics, 1989: Births, 945; Deaths, 498; Marriages, 611; Divorces, 394.

Ethnicity, 1990: White, 62,267 (96.1%); Black, 589 (0.9%); American Indian, 367 (0.6%); Asian, 231 (0.4%); Hispanic, 2,697 (4.2%); Other, 1,331 (2.1%).

Recreation: Railroad museum; park; water sports; **Mineral Wells State Park;** nature trails; hunting; rattlesnake hunt in March; peach festival and frontier days in July; first Monday trade days monthly.

Minerals: Production of natural gas, oil, stone, sand and gravel, clays.

Agriculture: Beef and dairy cattle, horses chief income source; horticultural plants, hay, peaches, peanuts, pecans raised; firewood sales significant.

Business: Primarily agribusiness; varied manufacturing; many residents work in Fort Worth; county part of Fort Worth-Arlington PMSA.

WEATHERFORD (14,804) county seat; agribusiness center; varied manufacturing; hospital, nursing homes; **Weatherford College;** local events. Other towns include **Aledo** (1,169); **Annetta** (672); **Anetta North** (265); **Anetta South** (413); **Azle** (1,203 in Parker County, mostly in Tarrant County); **Briar** (588); **Cool** (214); **Hudson Oaks** (711); **Millsap** (485); **Mineral Wells** (482 in Parker County, mostly in Palo Pinto County); **Reno** (2,322); **Sanctuary** (234); **Springtown** (1,740); **Willow Park** (2,328).

Parmer County

LOCATION: Northwest (D-7).

Cong. Dist.	19	U.S. Jud. Dist.	N-Am.
St. Sen. Dist.	31	Ct. Appeals	7
St. Rep. Dist.	85	Admin. Jud. Dist.	9
St. Dist. Cts.	287		

History: Named for Republic of Texas figure Martin Parmer; created from Bexar District 1876, organized 1907.

Physical Features: Level, broken by draws, playas; sandy, clay, loam soils.

Population	9,863	Av. Weekly Wage $304.48
Area (sq. mi.)	885.2	Density	11
Land Area	881.7	Water Area	3.5
Civilian Labor	5,908	Jobless Rate	3.6
Altitude (ft.)	4,163-3,926	Retail Sales	$33,726,468
Rainfall (in.)	15.3	Gross Sales	$269,049,101
Jan. min.	21	Reg. Voters	3,846
July max.	91	Election Turnout	51.3
Grow. Season (days)	183	Vehicles	9,912
Total Income (mil.)	$215	Lane Miles	539
Per Capita Income	$21,362	Tax Value	$416,899,279
Total Wages	$65,721,557	Fed. Spending	$48,279
Housing	3,686	Defense Spending	$265

Vital Statistics, 1989: Births, 165; Deaths, 99; Marriages, 221; Divorces, 32.

Ethnicity, 1990: White, 8,980 (91.0%); Black, 123 (1.2%); American Indian, 29 (0.3%); Asian, 24 (0.2%); Hispanic, 4,096 (41.5%); Other, 707 (7.2%).

Recreation: Border Town Days in July; other local events.

Minerals: Not significant.

Agriculture: Agricultural income from cattle, hogs, sheep, crops; among leading counties in total farm income; large cattle-feeding operations. Crops include corn, wheat, cotton, grain sorghums, sugar beets, soybeans, barley, sunflowers and vegetables; more than 190,000 acres irrigated for corn, wheat, cotton, sorghums.

Business: Cattle feeding; grain elevators; meat-packing plant; varied other agribusinesses.

FARWELL (1,373) county seat; agribusiness and trade center on New Mexico line; grain storage; plants make farm equipment. Other towns, **Bovina** (1,549), farm trade center; **Friona** (3,688), grain elevators; meat packing; feedlots; hospital, nursing home.

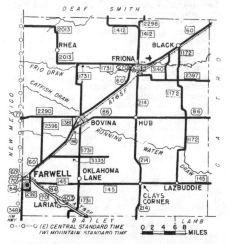

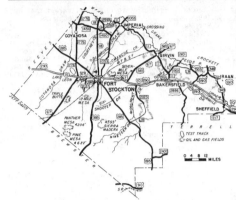

Pecos County

LOCATION: West (L-7).

Cong. Dist. 21	U.S. Jud. Dist. ....W-Pe.
St. Sen. Dist. 25	Ct. Appeals......................8
St. Rep. Dist. 68	Admin. Jud. Dist. 6
St. Dist. Cts.............. 83, 112	

History: Second-largest county in land area; created from Presidio 1871; organized 1872; named for Pecos River, name origin uncertain.

Physical Features: High, broken plateau; draining to Pecos and tributaries; sandy, clay, loam soils.

Population................ 14,675	Av. Weekly Wage $355.76
Area (sq. mi.) 4,765.0	Density 3
Land Area 4,764.0	Water Area 1.0
Civilian Labor 5,874	Jobless Rate..................6.1
Altitude (ft.).......4,797-2,168	Retail Sales $93,103,328
Rainfall (in.) 12.2	Gross Sales....... $161,243,630
Jan. min. 30	Reg. Voters................7,662
July max. 95	Election Turnout 61.3
Grow. Season (days)..... 224	Vehicles 12,998
Total Income (mil.) $153	Lane Miles 1,656
Per Capita Income.... $9,964	Tax Value.... $4,234,938,952
Total Wages....... $82,971,190	Fed. Spending $27,101
Housing....................5,842	Defense Spending $320

Vital Statistics, 1989: Births, 300; Deaths, 96; Marriages, 111; Divorces, 23.

Ethnicity, 1990: White, 9,449 (64.4%); Black, 62 (0.4%); American Indian, 45 (0.3%); Asian, 31 (0.2%); Hispanic, 8,331 (56.8%); Other, 5,088 (34.7%).

Recreation: A major tourist area for recreational, scenic, historical attractions; **Old Fort Stockton, Annie Riggs Museum,** stagecoach stop; scenic drives; **Dinosaur Track Roadside Park;** cattle-trail sites; Alley Oop Park, celebration at Iraan; archaeological museum with oil, ranch-heritage collections.

Minerals: A leading petroleum-producing county; natural gas, oil.

Agriculture: Most annual income from cattle, sheep, goats; crops include cotton, grains, vegetables, alfalfa, pecans, grapes; more than 29,000 acres irrigated.

Business: Oil, gas chief factors in economy; agribusiness center; some manufacturing; tourism.

FORT STOCKTON (8,524) county seat; distribution center for petroleum industry; oil, gas processing; tire-testing center; varied manufacturing; winery; hospital; nursing home; historical tours, local events, new tourist-information center. Other town, **Iraan** (1,322), oil, gas center; tourism; ranching; hospital; local events; birthplace of Alley Oop comic strip.

Polk County

LOCATION: Southeast (K-20).

Cong. Dist. 2	U.S. Jud. Dist. ....S-Hn.
St. Sen. Dist. 3	Ct. Appeals......................9
St. Rep. Dist. 18	Admin. Jud. Dist. 2
St. Dist. Cts........9, 2D9, 258	

History: Named for U.S. President James K. Polk; created from Liberty County, organized 1846.

Physical Features: Rolling; densely forested, with Big Thicket, unique plant, animal life; Neches, Trinity rivers, tributaries.

Population................ 30,687	Av. Weekly Wage $322.01
Area (sq. mi.) 1,109.8	Density 29
Land Area 1,057.3	Water Area 52.5
Civilian Labor 11,013	Jobless Rate..................6.8
Altitude (ft.) 404-68	Retail Sales $195,301,164
Rainfall (in.) 48.0	Gross Sales....... $336,504,636
Jan. min. 37	Reg. Voters............. 19,172
July max. 94	Election Turnout 44.8
Grow. Season (days)..... 250	Vehicles 28,311
Total Income (mil.) $370	Lane Miles 833
Per Capita Income...$11,833	Tax Value...... $1,398,178,033
Total Wages......$115,137,045	Fed. Spending $101,966
Housing.................... 18,324	Defense Spending $4,836

Vital Statistics, 1989: Births, 417; Deaths, 384; Marriages, 283; Divorces, 116.

Ethnicity, 1990: White, 25,100 (81.8%); Black, 3,896 (12.7%); American Indian, 662 (2.2%); Asian, 78 (0.3%); Hispanic, 1,610 (5.2%); Other, 951 (3.1%).

Recreation: Tourist center; **Livingston Lake and State Park;** fishing, other water activities; hunting; **Alabama-Coushatta Indian Reservation, Museum; Big Thicket;** woodlands trails, champion trees; historic homes; local events.

Minerals: Oil, natural gas, sand and gravel.

Agriculture: Leading Texas county in lumber products delivered to mill and rail sidings, Christmas trees; income also from livestock, poultry; crops include peaches, blueberries, vegetables.

Business: Timber; lumber production; tourism; oil.

LIVINGSTON (5,019) county seat; lumber, tourist, oil center. Other towns, **Corrigan** (1,764), plywood plant; **Goodrich** (239); **Onalaska** (728); **Seven Oaks** (171).

Potter County

LOCATION: Northwest (C-8).

Cong. Dist. 13	U.S. Jud. Dist. .... N-Am.
St. Sen. Dist. 31	Ct. Appeals......................7
St. Rep. Dist. 87	Admin. Jud. Dist. 9
St. Dist. Cts....... 47, 108, 181, 251, 320	

History: Named for Robert Potter, Republic of Texas leader; created 1876 from Bexar District; organized 1887.

Physical Features: Mostly level, part rolling; broken by Canadian River and tributaries; sandy, sandy loam, chocolate loam, clay soils; Lake Meredith.

Population................ 97,874	Av. Weekly Wage $376.23
Area (sq. mi.) 922.0	Density 109
Land Area 909.4	Water Area 12.6
Civilian Labor 48,569	Jobless Rate..................6.2

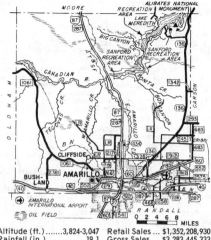

Altitude (ft.) 3,824-3,047
Rainfall (in.) 19.1
Jan. min. 22
July max. 91
Grow. Season (days)..... 190
Total Income (mil.) .. $1,506
Per Capita Income...$14,863
Total Wages... $1,117,860,384
Housing....................42,759

Retail Sales ... $1,352,208,930
Gross Sales.... $3,283,445,333
Reg. Voters 33,884
Election Turnout......... 56.3
Vehicles 96,462
Lane Miles 857
Tax Value...... $3,548,860,461
Fed. Spending....... $597,941
Defense Spending ... $15,653

Vital Statistics, 1989: Births, 2,043; Deaths, 1,023; Marriages, 1,865; Divorces, 639.

Ethnicity, 1990: White, 73,884 (75.5%); Black, 8,673 (8.9%); American Indian, 901 (0.9%); Asian, 2,570 (2.6%); Hispanic, 19,246 (19.7%); Other, 11,846 (12.1%).

Recreation: Metropolitan events (ask chamber of commerce); **Lake Meredith** activities; **Alibates Flint Quarries National Monument;** hunting, fishing; Tri-State Fair.

Minerals: Natural gas, oil, cement, stone, clays, sand and gravel.

Agriculture: Income mostly from beef cattle; wheat, sorghums, chief crops; more than 6,000 acres of wheat, sorghums irrigated.

Business: Transportation, distribution hub for large area; feedlot operations; petrochemicals; gas processing; agribusinesses.

AMARILLO (91,502 in Potter County, part in Randall County) county seat; urban hub for northern Panhandle oil, ranching; distribution, marketing center; varied manufacturing; food processing; five hospitals, 12 clinics; nursing homes; airport; museum; varied cultural, athletic and recreational events; **Amarillo College, Northwest Hospital School of Nursing; Texas State Technical Institute** branch.

Presidio County

LOCATION: Extreme southwest (M-5).
Cong. Dist. 21
St. Sen. Dist. 25
St. Rep. Dist. 68
St. Dist. Cts.....................83

U.S. Jud. Dist. ....W-Pe.
Ct. Appeals.................... 8
Admin. Jud. Dist. 6

History: Created 1850 from Bexar District; organized 1875; now fourth-largest county; named for Spanish Presidio del Norte (fort of the north).

Physical Features: Rugged, mountainous; some of Texas' tallest mountains; many scenic drives; clays, loams, sandy loams on uplands; intermountain wash; timber sparse; **Capote Falls,** state's highest.

Population.................6,637
Area (sq. mi.) 3,856.4
Land Area 3,855.7
Civilian Labor 2,236
Altitude (ft.) 7,728-2,518
Rainfall (in.) 14.8
Jan. min. 25
July max. 90
Grow. Season (days)..... 238
Per Capita Income...$8,486
Total Wages....... $15,960,295

Av. Weekly Wage $196.88
Density 2
Water Area 0.7
Jobless Rate.................16.6
Retail Sales $26,735,228
Gross Sales........ $36,235,298
Reg. Voters 3,098
Election Turnout......... 54.8
Vehicles 4,494
Lane Miles 542
Tax Value........ $267,875,833
Fed. Spending..........$26,280

Housing.....................2,921   Defense Spending $240

Vital Statistics, 1989: Births, 125; Deaths, 64; Marriages, 58; Divorces, 18.

Ethnicity, 1990: White, 5,624 (84.7%); Black, 6 (0.1%); American Indian, 16 (0.2%); Asian, 16 (0.2%); Hispanic, 5,417 (81.6%); Other, 975 (14.7%).

Recreation: Tourist center; near **Big Bend National Park;** mild climate and scenic surroundings; extensive hunting; scenic drives along Rio Grande, in mountains; ghost towns, **mysterious Marfa Lights; Fort D.A. Russell; Fort Leaton State Park;** gateway to Mexico's West Coast by rail; Kingston hot springs.

Minerals: Sand and gravel.

Agriculture: Most income from cattle, goat ranching; cantaloupes, lettuce, watermelons, onions, alfalfa chief crops; some irrigation.

Business: Ranching; income from hunting leases; tourism are major factors in economy.

MARFA (2,424) county seat; ranching supply, tourist center; gateway to mountainous area on Rio Grande in Texas and Mexico; Border Patrol sector headquarters. Other town, **Presidio** (3,072), international bridge.

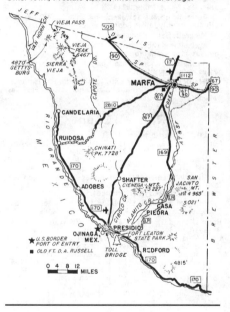

Rains County

LOCATION: Northeast (G-18).
Cong. Dist. 4
St. Sen. Dist. 2
St. Rep. Dist. 3
St. Dist. Cts.............. 8, 354

U.S. Jud. Dist. .... E-Ty.
Ct. Appeals.................... 12
Admin. Jud. Dist. 1

History: County, county seat named for Emory Rains, Republic of Texas leader; county created, organized 1870 from Hopkins, Hunt and Wood counties.

Physical Features: Rolling; partly Blackland, sandy loams, sandy soils; Sabine River, Lake Tawakoni.

Population.................6,715
Area (sq. mi.) 258.8
Land Area 232.0
Civilian Labor 2,433
Altitude (ft.) 491-406
Rainfall (in.) 42.2
Jan. min. 31
July max. 95
Grow. Season (days)..... 242
Total Income (mil.) $79
Per Capita Income...$11,811
Total Wages....... $14,464,006
Housing.....................3,532

Av. Weekly Wage $303.66
Density 28
Water Area 26.8
Jobless Rate.................. 5.8
Retail Sales $17,899,945
Gross Sales........ $34,085,880
Reg. Voters 3,877
Election Turnout......... 53.1
Vehicles 7,054
Lane Miles 270
Tax Value........ $374,209,650
Fed. Spending........ $14,459
Defense Spending $330

Vital Statistics, 1989: Births, 67; Deaths, 85; Marriages, 67; Divorces, 46.

Ethnicity, 1990: White, 6,310 (94.0%); Black, 286

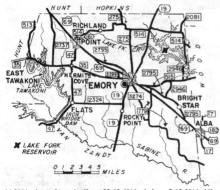

(4.3%); American Indian, 29 (0.4%); Asian, 8 (0.1%); Hispanic, 158 (2.4%); Other, 82 (1.2%).

Recreation: Lake Tawakoni and Lake Fork Reservoir activities; county fair in September; other local events.

Minerals: Natural gas, oil and coal.

Agriculture: Most income from beef, dairy cattle; chief crops are vegetables, watermelons, wheat, hay.

Business: Economy based on oil, tourism, agribusinesses, some manufacturing.

EMORY (963) county seat; local trade, tourism center; some manufacturing; clinic. Other towns, **East Tawakoni** (642), **Point** (645).

Randall County

LOCATION: Northwest (C-8).

Cong. Dist. 13	U.S. Jud. Dist. .... N-Am.
St. Sen. Dist. 31	Ct. Appeals 7
St. Rep. Dist. 86	Admin. Jud. Dist. 9
St. Dist. Cts. 47, 181, 251	

History: Created 1876 from Bexar District; organized 1889; named for Confederate Gen. Horace Randal (county name misspelled when created).

Physical Features: Level, but broken by scenic Palo Duro Canyon, Buffalo Lake; silty clay, loam soils.

Population 89,673	Av. Weekly Wage $332.33
Area (sq. mi.) 922.4	Density 98
Land Area 914.4	Water Area 8.0
Civilian Labor 47,649	Jobless Rate 3.9
Altitude (ft.) 3,748-3,158	Retail Sales $417,195,397
Rainfall (in.) 18.4	Gross Sales $1,016,143,143
Jan. min. 23	Reg. Voters 47,312
July max. 92	Election Turnout 60.8
Grow. Season (days) 195	Vehicles 82,880
Total Income (mil.) .. $1,530	Lane Miles 849
Per Capita Income ... $15,960	Tax Value $2,742,193,804

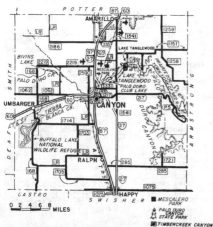

Total Wages ...... $283,736,459 **Fed. Spending** $70,927
Housing .... 37,773 **Defense Spending** $4,822

Vital Statistics, 1989: Births, 1,265; Deaths, 522; Marriages, 278; Divorces, 512.

Ethnicity, 1990: White, 84,633 (94.4%); Black, 1,115 (1.2%); American Indian, 454 (0.5%); Asian, 646 (0.7%); Hispanic, 6,144 (6.9%); Other, 2,825 (3.2%).

Recreation: Palo Duro Canyon State Park, with "Texas" drama a major tourist attraction each summer (ask chamber of commerce for dates); **Panhandle-Plains Historical Museum; West Texas State University** events; Aoudad sheep, migratory waterfowl hunting in season; **Buffalo Lake National Wildlife Refuge.**

Minerals: Not significant.

Agriculture: Most income from beef, dairy cattle, horses; wheat, milo, sugar beets, hay principal crops; 61,000 acres irrigated.

Business: Agribusinesses; education; some manufacturing; tourism; part of Amarillo MSA.

CANYON (11,365) county seat; **West Texas University**, a major economic factor; ranching, feedlot, farm center; gateway to **Palo Duro Canyon State Park**; hospital. Other towns, **Amarillo** (66,113 in Randall County, mostly in Potter County), **Happy** (37 in Randall County, part in Swisher County), Lake Tanglewood (637), **Timbercreek Canyon** (277).

Reagan County

LOCATION: Southwest (K-9).

Cong. Dist. 21	U.S. Jud. Dist. ...... N-SAng.
St. Sen. Dist. 25	Ct. Appeals 8
St. Rep. Dist. 69	Admin. Jud. Dist. 6
St. Dist. Cts. 83, 112	

History: Named for Sen. John H. Reagan, first chairman, Texas Railroad Commission; county created, organized 1903 from Tom Green County.

Physical Features: Level to hilly, broken by draws, Big Lake; sandy, loam, clay soils.

Population 4,514	Av. Weekly Wage $405.66
Area (sq. mi.) 1,176.0	Density 4
Land Area 1,175.4	Water Area 0.6
Civilian Labor 1,862	Jobless Rate 4.0
Altitude (ft.) 2,953-2,406	Retail Sales $23,382,145
Rainfall (in.) 19.5	Gross Sales $51,559,759
Jan. min. 28	Reg. Voters 1,907
July max. 94	Election Turnout 55.0
Grow. Season (days) 229	Vehicles 3,898
Total Income (mil.) $56	Lane Miles 320
Per Capita Income ... $12,225	Tax Value $439,066,710
Total Wages $24,869,997	Fed. Spending $7,418
Housing 1,684	Defense Spending $109

Vital Statistics, 1989: Births, 81; Deaths, 21; Marriages, 30; Divorces, 12.

Ethnicity, 1990: White, 3,550 (78.6%); Black, 127

Reagan Co. (Cont.)
(2.8%); American Indian, 7 (0.2%); Asian, 1 (**.*%); Hispanic, 1,941 (43.0%); Other, 829 (18.4%).

Recreation: Texon reunion; rodeo; other local events.

Minerals: Gas, oil.

Agriculture: Income from beef cattle, goats, sheep; cotton, grains principal crops; grapes introduced; 20,000 acres irrigated.

Business: Oil production; natural gas; ranching.

BIG LAKE (3,672) county seat; center for oil activities, ranching trade; hospital, clinic, nursing home; airport.

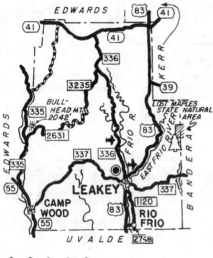

```
0   2   4   6   8
|___|___|___|___|  MILES
```

Real County

LOCATION: Southwest central (N-12).

Cong. Dist. ....21 U.S. Jud. Dist. ....W-SAnt.
St. Sen. Dist. ....25 Ct. Appeals......................4
St. Rep. Dist. ....67 Admin. Jud. Dist. 6
St. Dist. Cts.....................38

History: Created, organized 1913 from Bandera, Edwards, Kerr counties; named for legislator-ranchman Julius Real.

Physical Features: Hilly, spring-fed streams, scenic canyons; Frio, Nueces rivers; cedars, pecans, walnuts, many live oaks, including second-largest oak in state; other vegetation.

Population...................2,412	Av. Weekly Wage $225.40
Area (sq. mi.) 700.0	Density 3
Land Area 699.9	Water Area 0.1
Civilian Labor 1,426	Jobless Rate...................5.7
Altitude (ft.) 2,381-1,494	Retail Sales $7,443,767
Rainfall (in.) 25.7	Gross Sales..........$8,443,623
Jan. min. 31	Reg. Voters 1,929
July max. 92	Election Turnout........56.5
Grow. Season (days)..... 236	Vehicles 2,706
Total Income (mil.) $33	Lane Miles 297
Per Capita Income...$11,840	Tax Value........$302,027,896
Total Wages........$5,297,872	Fed. Spending..........$9,370
Housing.......................2,050	Defense Spending $539

Vital Statistics, 1989: Births, 35; Deaths, 28; Marriages, 25; Divorces, 12.

Ethnicity, 1990: White, 2,064 (85.6%); Black, 0 (0.0%); American Indian, 23 (1.0%); Asian, 0 (0.0%); Hispanic, 574 (23.8%); Other, 325 (13.5%).

Recreation: Major tourist, hunting center; many deer killed each season; fishing; **Frio, Nueces** rivers; camping; artists' haven; Spanish mission site, **Camp Wood**; scenic drives.

Minerals: Not significant.

Agriculture: A leading mohair-producing county;

cattle, sheep, goats produce practically all of farm income; hunting leases; cedar oil processed.

Business: Tourism, hunting leases major sources of income; ranch supplies; cedar sales; popular area for artists, recreational "second homes."

LEAKEY (399) county seat; center for ranching, tourism; cedar-oil mill; medical facilities; July Jubilee in July; **Camp Wood** (595), a tourist, ranching hub for parts of three counties.

Red River County

LOCATION: Northeast (F-20).

Cong. Dist. ....1 U.S. Jud. Dist. ....E-Ps.
St. Sen. Dist. ....1 Ct. Appeals......................6
St. Rep. Dist. ....1 Admin. Jud. Dist. 1
St. Dist. Cts.................6, 102

History: Created 1836 as original county; organized 1837; named for Red River, its northern boundary.

Physical Features: On Red-Sulphur rivers' divide; 39 different soil types; half timbered.

Population...............14,317	Av. Weekly Wage $267.58
Area (sq. mi.)..........1,057.6	Density 14
Land Area 1,050.2	Water Area 7.4
Civilian Labor 6,322	Jobless Rate...................7.0
Altitude (ft.) 525-287	Retail Sales $55,879,699
Rainfall (in.) 44.1	Gross Sales......$130,618,256
Jan. min. 30	Reg. Voters 8,782
July max. 93	Election Turnout........44.3
Grow. Season (days)..... 234	Vehicles 13,233
Total Income (mil.) $173	Lane Miles 742
Per Capita Income...$11,632	Tax Value........$460,332,581
Total Wages.......$44,511,137	Fed. Spending........$59,724
Housing.......................6,642	Defense Spending $1,141

Vital Statistics, 1989: Births, 180; Deaths, 226; Marriages, 154; Divorces, 88.

Ethnicity, 1990: White, 11,203 (78.2%); Black, 2,872 (20.1%); American Indian, 75 (0.5%); Asian, 14 (0.1%); Hispanic, 273 (1.9%); Other, 153 (1.1%).

Recreation: Historical sites; water activities; hunting; county fair, stew cookoff in September.

Minerals: Small oil flow, gas.

Agriculture: Stocker, cow-calf operations, dairy cattle, hogs, poultry account for most income; crops include soybeans, corn, cotton, alfalfa, wheat; some alfalfa irrigated; timber sales substantial.

Business: Agribusinesses; lumbering; manufacturing.

CLARKSVILLE (4,311) county seat; varied manufacturing; hospital, nursing home; library; century-old courthouse. Other towns, **Annona** (329), **Avery** (430), **Bogata** (1,421), **Deport** (34 in Red River County, mostly in Lamar County), **Detroit** (706).

```
0   2   4   6
|___|___|___|  MILES
```

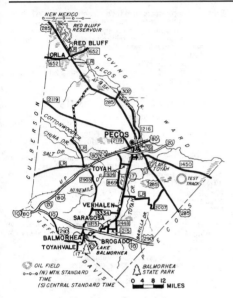

Reeves County

LOCATION: Southwest (K-6).

Cong. Dist. 16	U.S. Jud. Dist. ....W-Pe.
St. Sen. Dist. 25	Ct. Appeals.....................8
St. Rep. Dist. 69	Admin. Jud. Dist. 7
St. Dist. Cts...................143	

History: Created 1883 from Pecos County; organized 1884; named for Confederate Col. George R. Reeves.

Physical Features: Rolling plains, broken by many draws, Pecos River tributaries, Balmorhea, Toyah lakes, Red Bluff Reservoir; Davis Mountains on the south; chocolate loam, clay, sandy, mountain wash soils.

Population...............15,852	Av. Weekly Wage $278.58
Area (sq. mi.)..........2,642.0	Density 6
Land Area 2,636.0	Water Area 6.0
Civilian Labor 6,561	Jobless Rate..................8.7
Altitude (ft.).......4,210-2,538	Retail Sales $75,088,573
Rainfall (in.) 12.7	Gross Sales ...$123,913,198
Jan. min.........................31	Reg. Voters 7,531
July max........................96	Election Turnout 43.6
Grow. Season (days).....226	Vehicles 10,370
Total Income (mil.) $154	Lane Miles 1,167
Per Capita Income...$10,593	Tax Value........$513,227,668
Total Wages.......$62,507,764	Fed. Spending $32,769
Housing.......................6,054	Defense Spending $279

Vital Statistics, 1989: Births, 284; Deaths, 111; Marriages, 116; Divorces, 62.

Ethnicity, 1990: White, 15,293 (96.5%); Black, 347 (2.2%); American Indian, 36 (0.2%); Asian, 36 (0.2%); Hispanic, 11,545 (72.8%); Other, 140 (0.9%).

Recreation: A major "western" tourist area; replica of **Judge Roy Bean** Store, **"Law West of Pecos";** western museum; park with javelina, prairie dogs, other animals; scenic drives; annual rodeo, night in old Pecos in July, cantaloupe festival in August, fair in October; water activities; **Balmorhea State Park and Lake.**

Minerals: Production of oil, natural gas, sand, gravel.

Agriculture: Most income from fed beef, stocker, dairy cattle; crops include cotton, cantaloupes, bell peppers, alfalfa; substantial irrigation.

Business: Petroleum production; agribusinesses; tourism; feedlots; some manufacturing.

PECOS (12,069) county seat; ranching, oil industry center; food processing; produce marketing, shipping; hospital, nursing home; tourism. Other towns, **Balmorhea** (765), **Toyah** (115).

Refugio County

LOCATION: Southern coast (Q-17).

Cong. Dist. 14	U.S. Jud. Dist. ....S-Va.
St. Sen. Dist. 18	Ct. Appeals.....................13
St. Rep. Dist. 32	Admin. Jud. Dist. 4
St. Dist. Cts....... 24, 135, 267	

History: Original county, created 1836, organized 1837; named for Mission of Our Lady of Refuge.

Physical Features: Coastal plain, broken by streams, bays; sandy, loam, black soils; mesquite, oak, huisache motts.

Population...............7,976	Av. Weekly Wage $354.33
Area (sq. mi.)...........818.6	Density 10
Land Area 770.3	Water Area 48.3
Civilian Labor 3,543	Jobless Rate..................3.4
Altitude (ft.)...............78-7	Retail Sales $38,079,091
Rainfall (in.) 38.8	Gross Sales ...$66,301,396
Jan. min.........................43	Reg. Voters 5,164
July max........................94	Election Turnout 54.2
Grow. Season (days)....304	Vehicles 7,274
Total Income (mil.) $143	Lane Miles 464
Per Capita Income...$16,592	Tax Value........$954,283,254
Total Wages.......$42,101,314	Fed. Spending $25,171
Housing.......................3,736	Defense Spending $417

Vital Statistics, 1989: Births, 107; Deaths, 75; Marriages, 62; Divorces, 38.

Ethnicity, 1990: White, 6,201 (77.7%); Black, 645 (8.1%); American Indian, 25 (0.3%); Asian, 5 (0.1%); Hispanic, 3,164 (39.7%); Other, 1,100 (13.8%).

Recreation: Water activities; hunting, fishing; historic sites; **Aransas National Wildlife Refuge, "home of the whooping crane."**

Minerals: Production of oil, natural gas.

Agriculture: Income from grain sorghums, corn, cotton; beef cattle raising, hunting leases also important.

Business: Petroleum, petrochemical production, agribusinesses, tourism main economic factors.

REFUGIO (3,158) county seat; petroleum, agribusiness center; hospital, nursing home; museum, historic buildings, homes; many local events. Other towns, **Austwell** (189), **Bayside** (400), **Woodsboro** (1,731).

Roberts County

LOCATION: Northwestern Panhandle (B-10).

Cong. Dist. 13	U.S. Jud. Dist. ....N-Am.
St. Sen. Dist. 31	Ct. Appeals.....................7
St. Rep. Dist. 88	Admin. Jud. Dist. 9
St. Dist. Cts...................31	

History: Created 1876 from Bexar District; organized 1889; named for Texas leaders John S. Roberts and Gov. O.M. Roberts.

Physical Features: Rolling, broken by Canadian and many tributaries; Red Deer Creek; black, sandy loam, alluvial soils.

Population...................1,025	Av. Weekly Wage $403.64
Area (sq. mi.)..............924.1	Density 1
Land Area 924.1	Water Area 0.0
Civilian Labor 615	Jobless Rate..................6.0
Altitude (ft.).......3,219-2,467	Retail Sales $2,370,174
Rainfall (in.) 20.7	Gross Sales $6,552,162
Jan. min.........................19	Reg. Voters 739

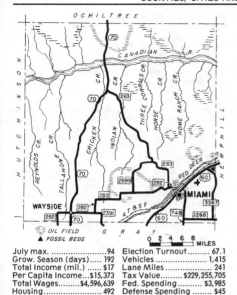

July max. 94
Grow. Season (days)..... 192
Total Income (mil.) $17
Per Capita Income...$15,373
Total Wages.........$4,596,639
Housing........................ 492

Election Turnout 67.1
Vehicles 1,415
Lane Miles 241
Tax Value......... $229,255,705
Fed. Spending $3,985
Defense Spending $45

Vital Statistics, 1989: Births, 13; Deaths, 11; Marriages, 10; Divorces, 2.

Ethnicity, 1990: White, 1,002 (97.8%); Black, 0 (0.0%); American Indian, 1 (0.1%); Asian, 2 (0.2%); Hispanic, 34 (3.3%); Other, 20 (2.0%).

Recreation: National cow-calling contest; scenic drives; county museum.

Minerals: Production of gas, oil.

Agriculture: Beef cattle top producer; hogs raised; crops include wheat, milo, corn; substantial irrigation.

Business: Agribusinesses; oil-field operations.

MIAMI (675) county seat; ranching, oil center; some manufacturing.

Robertson County

LOCATION: East central (K-17).

Cong. Dist. 6	U.S. Jud. Dist. .... W-Wa.
St. Sen. Dist. 5	Ct. Appeals.................... 10
St. Rep. Dist. 13	Admin. Jud. Dist. 2
St. Dist. Cts.....................82	

History: Among first counties, created 1837, organized 1838, subdivided into many others later; named for pioneer Sterling Clack Robertson.

Physical Features: Drains to Brazos, Navasota rivers; sandy soils, heavy in bottoms.

Population................ 15,511
Area (sq. mi.).............865.7
Land Area 854.6
Civilian Labor 5,982
Altitude (ft.) 491-277
Rainfall (in.) 39.3
Jan. min. 37
July max. 96
Grow. Season (days).... 268
Total Income (mil.) $199
Per Capita Income...$13,239
Total Wages....... $62,059,500
Housing......................7,318

Av. Weekly Wage $328.68
Density 18
Water Area 11.1
Jobless Rate.................6.3
Retail Sales $54,632,057
Gross Sales....... $171,974,714
Reg. Voters 9,428
Election Turnout......... 48.4
Vehicles 12,931
Lane Miles 625
Tax Value...... $1,046,620,239
Fed. Spending.........$51,054
Defense Spending $827

Vital Statistics, 1989: Births, 289; Deaths, 195; Marriages, 94; Divorces, 33.

Ethnicity, 1990: White, 10,047 (64.8%); Black, 4,259 (27.5%); American Indian, 36 (0.2%); Asian, 15 (0.1%); Hispanic, 1,904 (12.3%); Other, 1,154 (7.4%).

Recreation: Hunting, fishing; historic sites; historic-homes tour; Country Music Jamboree; county fair at Hearne in March; dogwood trails, wildlife preserves.

Minerals: Gas, oil, lignite.

Agriculture: Most revenue from beef cattle, dairy

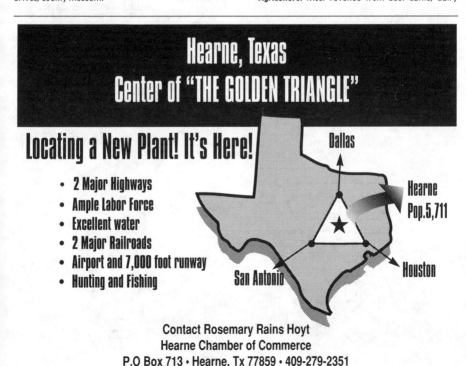

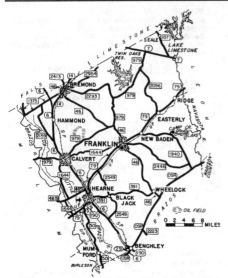

Total Wages....... $92,684,873   Fed. Spending......... $33,556
Housing....................9,788   Defense Spending $2,770

Vital Statistics, 1989: Births, 373; Deaths, 153; Marriages, 2,474; Divorces, 143.

Ethnicity, 1990: White, 23,991 (93.7%); Black, 855 (3.3%); American Indian, 102 (0.4%); Asian, 164 (0.6%); Hispanic, 1,500 (5.9%); Other, 492 (1.9%).

Recreation: Lake Ray Hubbard activities; proximity to Dallas; unusual rock outcrop.

Minerals: Not significant.

Agriculture: Most income from cow-calf operations; crops include wheat, grain sorghums, hay.

Business: Industrial employment in local plants and in Dallas; in Dallas PMSA; tourist and residential development around Lake Ray Hubbard.

ROCKWALL (10,486) county seat; varied manufacturing; hospital, clinics, nursing home; youth fair in April. Other towns, **Fate** (475); **Heath** (2,108); **McLendon-Chisholm** (646); **Rowlett** (3,353 in Rockwall County, mostly in Dallas County); **Royse City** (2,039 in Rockwall County, part in Collin County), some manufacturing; **Wylie** (54 in Rockwall County, mostly in Collin County).

Runnels County

LOCATION: Central (J-11).
Cong. Dist. 17   U.S. Jud. Dist. ...... N-SAng.
St. Sen. Dist. 24   Ct. Appeals......................3
St. Rep. Dist. 65   Admin. Jud. Dist. 7
St. Dist. Cts. 119

History: Named for planter-legislator H.G. Runnels; created 1858 from Bexar, Travis counties; organized 1880.

Physical Features: Level to rolling; bisected by Colorado and tributaries; sandy loam, black waxy soils.

Population....................11,294   Av. Weekly Wage $284.11
Area (sq. mi.)..........1,057.2   Density 11
Land Area ....1,054.5   Water Area 2.7
Civilian Labor 5,646   Jobless Rate.................4.1
Altitude (ft.) 2,301-1,628   Retail Sales $44,546,170
Rainfall (in.) ....22.1   Gross Sales....... $119,105,400
Jan. min. 30   Reg. Voters 6,249
July max. 96   Election Turnout 49.5
Grow. Season (days).....228   Vehicles 12,138
Total Income (mil.) .....$181   Lane Miles 730
Per Capita Income....$15,930   Tax Value........ $460,779,943
Total Wages....... $51,058,722   Fed. Spending $43,239
Housing........................5,345   Defense Spending $54.5

Vital Statistics, 1989: Births, 159; Deaths, 155; Marriages, 91; Divorces, 38.

Ethnicity, 1990: White, 10,438 (92.4%); Black, 183 (1.6%); American Indian, 16 (0.1%); Asian, 16 (0.1%);

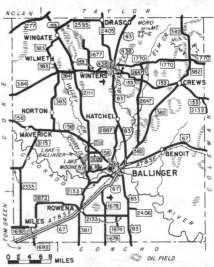

products, hogs, horses, poultry; crops include cotton, sorghums, small grains, watermelons, corn; significant irrigation, mostly cotton.

Business: Agribusinesses; brick manufacturing; power-generating plant.

FRANKLIN (1,336) county seat; farm-trade center, power plants. Other towns, **Bremond** (1,110); **Calvert** (1,536), antique shops; **Hearne** (5,132), some manufacturing; hospital, nursing home.

Rockwall County

LOCATION: North central (G-17).
Cong. Dist. 4   U.S. Jud. Dist. ....N-DI.
St. Sen. Dist. 2   Ct. Appeals......................5
St. Rep. Dist. 3   Admin. Jud. Dist. 1
St. Dist. Cts. 86

History: Texas' smallest county; created, organized 1873 from Kaufman; named for wall-like rock formation.

Physical Features: Rolling prairie, mostly Blackland soil; Trinity River; Lake Ray Hubbard.

Population....................25,604   Av. Weekly Wage $325.55
Area (sq. mi.)..............148.6   Density 200
Land Area ....128.7   Water Area 19.9
Civilian Labor 15,175   Jobless Rate.................3.3
Altitude (ft.) 588-489   Retail Sales $174,215,104
Rainfall (in.) ....36.9   Gross Sales $255,833,359
Jan. min. 33   Reg. Voters 13,651
July max. 96   Election Turnout 54.0
Grow. Season (days).....236   Vehicles 24,615
Total Income (mil.) .....$493   Lane Miles 317
Per Capita Income...$16,409   Tax Value...... $1,336,957,642

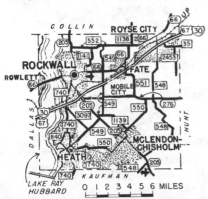

Runnels Co. (Cont.)
Hispanic, 2,740 (24.3%); Other, 641 (5.7%).

Recreation: Deer and turkey hunting, fishing; many local events; 47 historical markers in county.

Minerals: Production of oil, natural gas, sand and gravel.

Agriculture: Most annual income from beef and stocker cattle, sheep; crops include cotton, sorghums, wheat.

Business: Agribusiness; oil activity; manufacturing.

BALLINGER (3,975) county seat; Carnegie Library; varied manufacturing; oil-field services; food processing; hospital; Western Texas College extension. Other towns, **Miles** (793); **Winters** (2,905), varied manufacturing, museum; nursing home, hospital.

Rusk County

LOCATION: East (I-20).

Cong. Dist. 1	U.S. Jud. Dist. .... E-Ty.
St. Sen. Dist. 3	Ct. Appeals 6, 12
St. Rep. Dist. 9	Admin. Jud. Dist. 1
St. Dist. Cts. 4	

History: Named for Republic of Texas, state leader Thomas J. Rusk; created from Nacogdoches County and organized 1843.

Physical Features: On Sabine-Angelina divide; varied deep, sandy soils; over half in pines, hardwoods; Striker Creek Reservoir; Cherokee Lake; Martin Creek Lake.

Population	43,735	Av. Weekly Wage	$381.12
Area (sq. mi.)	938.6	Density	47
Land Area	923.6	Water Area	15.0
Civilian Labor	17,174	Jobless Rate	7.4
Altitude (ft.)	662-280	Retail Sales	$176,657,100
Rainfall (in.)	44.7	Gross Sales	$371,838,849
Jan. min.	35	Reg. Voters	24,786
July max.	93	Election Turnout	44.0
Grow. Season (days)	250	Vehicles	35,241
Total Income (mil.)	$596	Lane Miles	1,132
Per Capita Income...	$14,222	Tax Value......	$2,337,063,810
Total Wages......	$219,429,211	Fed. Spending	$104,782
Housing	19,079	Defense Spending	$2,361

Vital Statistics, 1989: Births, 579; Deaths, 523; Marriages, 344; Divorces, 256.

Ethnicity, 1990: White, 33,730 (77.1%); Black, 8,984 (20.5%); American Indian, 150 (0.3%); Asian, 51 (0.1%); Hispanic, 1,736 (4.0%); Other, 820 (1.9%).

Recreation: Water sports, **Martin Creek Lake State Park;** historic homes, sites; scenic drives; marked site of East Texas Field discovery oil well; golf tournaments.

Minerals: A leading oil county; over 1.5 billion barrels produced since 1930; part of East Texas Field; natural gas, lignite, clays also produced.

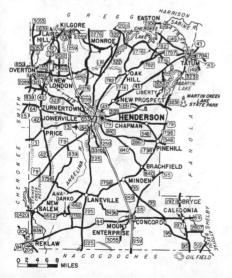

Agriculture: Beef cattle top producer; dairy products, hogs, poultry, horses raised; crops include watermelons, vegetables, hay, grains, corn; timber income substantial.

Business: Economy based on oil, lumbering, agribusinesses, tourism.

HENDERSON (11,139) county seat; center for agribusiness, oil activities; varied manufacturing; hospital. Other towns, **Overton** (1,982 in Rusk County, part in Smith County), oil, lumbering center; petroleum processing; **Texas A&M Research and Extension Center; Easton** (46 in Rusk County, mostly in Gregg County); **Kilgore** (2,808 in Rusk County, mostly in Gregg County); **Mount Enterprise** (501); **New London** (926), site of March 18, 1937, **school explosion** that killed 293 students and faculty; **Reklaw** (115 in Rusk County, mostly in Cherokee County); **Tatum** (1,034 in Rusk County, partly in Panola County).

SAM RAYBURN RESERVOIR
▲ MC MAHAN CHAPEI

Sabine County

LOCATION: Borders Louisiana (J-22).

Cong. Dist. 2	U.S. Jud. Dist. .... E-Bt.
St. Sen. Dist. 3	Ct. Appeals 12
St. Rep. Dist. 17	Admin. Jud. Dist. 2
St. Dist. Cts. 1, 273	

History: An original county, created 1836; organized 1837; name is cypress in Spanish.

Physical Features: Eighty percent forested; 114,498 acres in Sabine National Forest; Sabine River, Toledo Bend Reservoir on east; Sam Rayburn Reservoir on southwest.

Population	9,586	Av. Weekly Wage	$317.96
Area (sq. mi.)	576.5	Density	20
Land Area	490.2	Water Area	86.3
Civilian Labor	3,494	Jobless Rate	7.3
Altitude (ft.)	590-174	Retail Sales	$36,114,071
Rainfall (in.)	52.5	Gross Sales	$94,585,563
Jan. min.	36	Reg. Voters	6,166
July max.	93	Election Turnout	49.7
Grow. Season (days)	236	Vehicles	8,636
Total Income (mil.)	$112	Lane Miles	454
Per Capita Income...	$11,324	Tax Value.........	$375,863,422
Total Wages.......	$29,793,921	Fed. Spending	$39,417
Housing	6,996	Defense Spending	$1,429

Vital Statistics, 1989: Births, 113; Deaths, 142; Marriages, 107; Divorces, 30.

Ethnicity, 1990: White, 8,394 (87.6%); Black, 1,117 (11.7%); American Indian, 10 (0.1%); Asian, 12 (0.1%); Hispanic, 111 (1.2%); Other, 53 (0.6%).

Recreation: Toledo Bend, Sam Rayburn reservoirs activities; many campsites; marinas; McMahan's Chapel, pioneer Protestant church; Sabine National Forest; hunting; May fest in May, county fair in October, other local events.

Minerals: Not significant.

Agriculture: Beef cattle, poultry; vegetables, fruit

Sabine Co. (Cont.)
raised; some irrigation; significant timber marketing.

Business: Economy based on tourism, broilers, timber industries.

HEMPHILL (1,182) county seat; timber, livestock center; tourism. Other towns, **Bronson** (259); **Pineland** (882), timber processing.

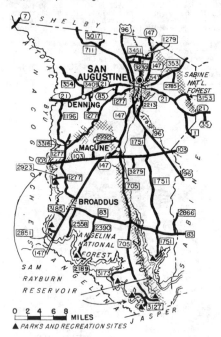

▲ PARKS AND RECREATION SITES

San Augustine County

LOCATION: East (J-21).

Cong. Dist. 1	U.S. Jud. Dist. .... E-Bt.
St. Sen. Dist. 3	Ct. Appeals..................... 12
St. Rep. Dist. 17	Admin. Jud. Dist. 2
St. Dist. Cts............... 1, 273	

History: Among most historic counties; created and named for Mexican municipality in 1836; an original county; organized 1837.

Physical Features: Hilly, 80 percent forested with 66,-799 acres in Angelina National Forest, 4,317 in Sabine National Forest; Sam Rayburn Reservoir; varied soils, sandy to black alluvial.

Population..................7,999	Av. Weekly Wage $277.58
Area (sq. mi.).............592.2	Density 15
Land Area 527.9	Water Area 64.3
Civilian Labor 3,821	Jobless Rate.................. 4.9
Altitude (ft.) 502-156	Retail Sales $35,995,617
Rainfall (in.) 46.3	Gross Sales $79,641,588
Jan. min. 35	Reg. Voters 6,400
July max.........................93	Election Turnout 47.5
Grow. Season (days)..... 238	Vehicles 7,700
Total Income (mil.) $93	Lane Miles 516
Per Capita Income...$10,729	Tax Value........ $306,647,097
Total Wages....... $21,925,765	Fed. Spending $38,665
Housing......................4,162	Defense Spending ... $10,044

Vital Statistics, 1989: Births, 108; Deaths, 129; Marriages, 92; Divorces, 14.

Ethnicity, 1990: White, 5,663 (70.8%); Black, 2,244 (28.1%); American Indian, 15 (0.2%); Asian, 6 (0.1%); Hispanic, 148 (1.7%); Other, 71 (0.9%).

Recreation: Lake activities; pine fest, annual tour of homes in April, sassafras festival in October, other local events; many historic homes; McMahan's Chapel, pioneer Protestant church in nearby Sabine County; tourist facilities in national forests.

Minerals: Small amount of oil.

Agriculture: Income mostly from broilers, cow-calf

operation, horses; crops include watermelons, peas, corn, truck crops; timber sales significant.

Business: Lumbering; shipping; varied manufacturing.

SAN AUGUSTINE (2,337) county seat; tourism; livestock center; varied manufacturing; Deep East Texas Electric Cooperative; lumbering; hospital; claims to be **"Oldest Anglo-Saxon Town in Texas."** Other town, **Broaddus** (212).

San Jacinto County

LOCATION: Southeast (L-20).

Cong. Dist. 2	U.S. Jud. Dist. ....S-Hn.
St. Sen. Dist. 3	Ct. Appeals..................... 9
St. Rep. Dist. 18	Admin. Jud. Dist. 2
St. Dist. Cts........9, 2D9, 258	

History: Created from Liberty, Montgomery, Polk, Walker counties 1869; re-created, organized 1870; named for Battle of San Jacinto.

Physical Features: Rolling hills; 80 percent forested; 58,625 acres in Sam Houston National Forest; Trinity, San Jacinto rivers.

Population............... 16,372	Av. Weekly Wage $319.87
Area (sq. mi.) 627.9	Density 29
Land Area 570.7	Water Area 57.2
Civilian Labor 5,897	Jobless Rate.................. 4.9
Altitude (ft.) 386-74	Retail Sales $35,238,291
Rainfall (in.) 48.0	Gross Sales $43,949,915
Jan. min. 36	Reg. Voters 9,208
July max.........................94	Election Turnout 43.8
Grow. Season (days)..... 261	Vehicles 12,290
Total Income (mil.) $151	Lane Miles 504
Per Capita Income.... $9,854	Tax Value........ $803,233,858
Total Wages....... $21,107,417	Fed. Spending $38,444
Housing......................9,734	Defense Spending $1,351

Vital Statistics, 1989: Births, 184; Deaths, 169; Marriages, 137; Divorces, 109.

Ethnicity, 1990: White, 13,525 (82.6%); Black, 2,544 (15.5%); American Indian, 74 (0.5%); Asian, 14 (0.1%); Hispanic, 431 (2.6%); Other, 215 (1.3%).

Recreation: Livingston Lake water activities; **Double Lake; Wolf Creek Park;** hunting; county fair; **Sam Houston National Forest;** old courthouse and jail are tourist attractions. Approximately 60 percent of county in national forest.

Minerals: Oil, gas and iron ore.

Agriculture: Income from beef cattle, horses, swine; hay grown; timber revenue significant.

Business: Economy based on timber and oil.

COLDSPRING (538) county seat; lumbering; farming center; county fair in September; historic sites. Other towns, **Oakhurst** (219), **Pointblank** (443), **Shepherd** (1,812).

▲ DOUBLE LAKE RECREATION AREA

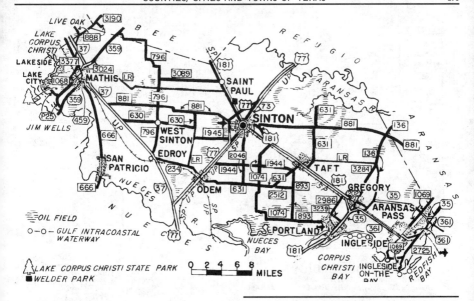

San Patricio County

LOCATION: Southern coast (Q-16).

Cong. Dist. 15	U.S. Jud. Dist. ....S-CC
St. Sen. Dist. 20	Ct. Appeals...................... 13
St. Rep. Dist. 33	Admin. Jud. Dist. 4
St. Dist. Cts........ 36, 156, 343	

History: Created from and named for earlier municipality in 1836; organized 1837, reorganized 1847. San Patricio means Saint Patrick in Spanish.

Physical Features: Between Aransas, Nueces rivers, draining to them and bays; sandy loam, clay, black loam soils; Lake Corpus Christi.

Population............... 58,749	Av. Weekly Wage $385.21
Area (sq. mi.) 707.0	Density 85
Land Area 691.7	Water Area 15.3
Civilian Labor 25,149	Jobless Rate...................7.1
Altitude (ft.) 137-11	Retail Sales $234,432,109
Rainfall (in.) 34.4	Gross Sales...... $703,733,437
Jan. min. 44	Reg. Voters 29,067
July max. 94	Election Turnout 38.8
Grow. Season (days)..... 303	Vehicles 42,972
Total Income (mil.) $707	Lane Miles 874
Per Capita Income...$11,834	Tax Value...... $1,961,436,360
Total Wages......$253,849,551	Fed. Spending $150,892
Housing................... 22,100	Defense Spending $6,380

Vital Statistics, 1989: Births, 965; Deaths, 470; Marriages, 327; Divorces, 287.

Ethnicity, 1990: White, 44,834 (76.3%); Black, 968 (1.6%); American Indian, 219 (0.4%); Asian, 163 (0.3%); Hispanic, 29,809 (50.7%); Other, 12,565 (21.4%).

Recreation: Water activities; hunting; Corpus Christi Bay; **Lake Corpus Christi State Park; Welder Wildlife Foundation;** Rob and Bessie Welder Park; fiddlers festival in Sinton in October, shimporee, other local activities; birdwatching.

Minerals: Production of oil, gas, stone, clays, caliche.

Agriculture: Beef, fed cattle major revenue source; crops include cotton, grain sorghums, corn; fisheries income significant; some irrigation for corn, cotton.

Business: Oil center; petrochemicals; agribusinesses; manufacturing; tourism; in Corpus Christi MSA.

SINTON (5,549) county seat; oil, agribusiness center; fiddlers' festival, other local events; golf course.

Aransas Pass (6,246 in San Patricio County, part in Nueces, Aransas counties); shrimping and tourist center; offshore oil-well drilling servicing; aluminum, chemical plants; hospitals.

Other towns include **Gregory** (2,458), **Ingleside** (5,696), **Lake City** (465), **Lakeside** (292), **Mathis** (5,423), **Odem** (2,366), **Portland** (12,224 in San Patricio County, partly in Nueces County), **San Patricio** (369), **Taft** (3,222), some manufacturing, processing; local events; drug rehabilitation center, hospital; **Taft Southwest** (2,012); and part of **Corpus Christi.**

San Saba County

LOCATION: Central (K-14).

Cong. Dist. 11	U.S. Jud. Dist. .... N-An.
St. Sen. Dist. 24	Ct. Appeals...................... 3
St. Rep. Dist. 54	Admin. Jud. Dist. 3
St. Dist. Cts....................33	

History: Created from Bexar and organized 1856; named for river.

Physical Features: Hilly, rolling; bisected by San Saba River; Colorado River on east; black, gray sandy loam, alluvial soils.

Population..................5,401	Av. Weekly Wage $248.63
Area (sq. mi.) 1,138.2	Density 5
Land Area 1,134.5	Water Area 3.7
Civilian Labor 2,925	Jobless Rate...................5.2
Altitude (ft.) 1,971-1,110	Retail Sales $20,344,481
Rainfall (in.) 25.9	Gross Sales........ $40,644,170
Jan. min. 32	Reg. Voters 3,046
July max. 96	Election Turnout 50.5
Grow. Season (days)..... 227	Vehicles 5,928
Total Income (mil.) $82	Lane Miles 427
Per Capita Income...$14,993	Tax Value... $435,930,228
Total Wages....... $18,617,146	Fed. Spending $23,561
Housing......................3,079	Defense Spending $480

Vital Statistics, 1989: Births, 76; Deaths, 101; Marriages, 40; Divorces, 21.

Ethnicity, 1990: White, 4,944 (91.5%); Black, 14 (0.3%); American Indian, 8 (0.1%); Asian, 1 (**.*%); Hispanic, 998 (18.5%); Other, 434 (8.0%).

Recreation: A leading deer hunting area; many local events; historic sites; log cabin museum; fishing; scenic drives; Gorman Falls.

Minerals: Limited stone production.

Agriculture: Most income from cattle, sheep, goats; crops include pecans, wheat, peanuts, hay; about 7,900 acres irrigated for pecans, peanuts, hay.

Business: Agribusinesses; pecans; stone processing; tourist and hunting-lease income.

SAN SABA (2,626) county seat; claims title "Pecan Capital of the World"; stone processing; range of manufacturing; prison unit; hospital, nursing homes; livestock show in January. Other town, **Richland Springs** (344).

See map on next page.

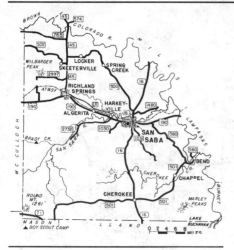

Scurry County

LOCATION: West (H-10).

Cong. Dist.	17	U.S. Jud. Dist.	N-Lb.
St. Sen. Dist.	30	Ct. Appeals.	11
St. Rep. Dist.	78	Admin. Jud. Dist.	7
St. Dist. Cts.	132		

History: Created from Bexar 1876; organized 1884; named for Confederate Gen. W.R. Scurry.

Physical Features: Drained by Colorado, Brazos tributaries; Lake J.B. Thomas; prairie, some hills; sandy, loam soils.

Population	18,634	Av. Weekly Wage	$373.81
Area (sq. mi.)	907.5	Density	21
Land Area	902.5	Water Area	5.0
Civilian Labor	10,677	Jobless Rate	4.6
Altitude (ft.)	2,822-2,129	Retail Sales	$108,409,367

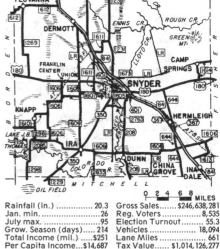

Rainfall (in.)	20.3	Gross Sales	$246,638,281
Jan. min.	26	Reg. Voters	8,535
July max.	95	Election Turnout	55.3
Grow. Season (days)	214	Vehicles	18,094
Total Income (mil.)	$251	Lane Miles	661
Per Capita Income	$14,687	Tax Value	$1,014,126,277
Total Wages	$122,557,663	Fed. Spending	$49,534
Housing	7,698	Defense Spending	$538

Vital Statistics, 1989: Births, 271; Deaths, 147; Marriages, 139; Divorces, 80.

Ethnicity, 1990: White, 14,113 (75.7%); Black, 879 (4.7%); American Indian, 62 (0.3%); Asian, 35 (0.2%); Hispanic, 4,454 (23.9%); Other, 3,545 (19.0%).

Recreation: Lake J.B. Thomas water recreation; **Sandstone Canyon Indian pictographs; Towle Memorial Park**; museums, national finals American Junior Rodeo Association in August; white buffalo days in October, other local events.

Minerals: Nation's leading oil-producing county; also gas, stone.

Agriculture: Livestock include beef cattle, hogs, dairy cows and sheep; croms are cotton, hay, grain sorghums, ensilage, wheat, pecans.

Business: Oil production major economic factor; agribusinesses; manufacturing.

SNYDER (12,195) county seat; oil center; varied manufacturing; **Western Texas College**; hospital, nursing homes.

Schleicher County

LOCATION: Southwest (L-11).

Cong. Dist.	21	U.S. Jud. Dist.	N-SAng.
St. Sen. Dist.	25	Ct. Appeals.	3
St. Rep. Dist.	67	Admin. Jud. Dist.	7
St. Dist. Cts.	51		

History: Named for Gustav Schleicher, founder of German colony; county created from Crockett 1887, organized 1901.

Physical Features: Plateau, broken by Devils River, Concho, San Saba tributaries; part hilly; black soils.

Population	2,990	Av. Weekly Wage	$369.98
Area (sq. mi.)	1,310.6	Density	2
Land Area	1,310.6	Water Area	0.0
Civilian Labor	1,443	Jobless Rate	5.3
Altitude (ft.)	2,467-2,125	Retail Sales	$6,183,136
Rainfall (in.)	19.0	Gross Sales	$27,553,916
Jan. min.	28	Reg. Voters	1,645
July max.	93	Election Turnout	52.0
Grow. Season (days)	229	Vehicles	3,074
Per Capita Income	$38	Lane Miles	362
Total Income (mil.)	$38	Tax Value	$329,103,988
Total Wages	$14,217,415	Fed. Spending	$12,464
Housing	1,288	Defense Spending	$3,039

Vital Statistics, 1989: Births, 38; Deaths, 23; Marriages, 10; Divorces, 9.

Ethnicity, 1990: White, 2,078 (69.5%); Black, 27 (0.9%); American Indian, 3 (0.1%); Asian, 1 (**.*%); Hispanic, 1,062 (35.5%); Other, 881 (29.5%).

Recreation: Hunting; livestock show in January, youth and open rodeos; other local events.

Minerals: Production of oil, natural gas.

Agriculture: Sheep, cattle and goats top producers; crops include cotton, milo, small grain, hay; little irrigation.

Business: Oil and ranching economy.

ELDORADO (2,019) county seat; center for livestock, woolen mill, mohair marketing; oil activities; medical center.

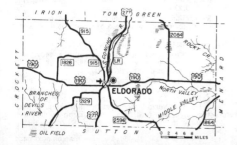

Shackelford County

LOCATION: Central (H-13).

Cong. Dist.	17	U.S. Jud. Dist.	N-Ab.
St. Sen. Dist.	30	Ct. Appeals.	11
St. Rep. Dist.	64	Admin. Jud. Dist.	7
St. Dist. Cts.	259		

History: Created from Bosque County 1858; organized 1874; named for Dr. Jack Shackelford (sometimes referred to as John), Texas Revolutionary hero.

Physical Features: Rolling, hilly, numerous tribu-

Shackelford Co. (Cont.)

taries of Brazos; sandy and chocolate loam soils; McCarthy Lake.

Population..................3,316	Av. Weekly Wage $319.97
Area (sq. mi.)..............915.5	Density 4
Land Area....................914.0	Water Area 1.5
Civilian Labor 1,729	Jobless Rate...................2.9
Altitude (ft.)........1,788-1,217	Retail Sales $10,809,497
Rainfall (in.) 27.1	Gross Sales........$19,479,799
Jan. min. 29	Reg. Voters 2,167
July max. 98	Election Turnout 51.9
Grow. Season (days).....224	Vehicles 3,754
Total Income (mil.) $57	Lane Miles 353
Per Capita Income...$17,342	Tax Value.........$287,215,780
Total Wages.......$16,239,186	Fed. Spending $10,359
Housing....................1,717	Defense Spending $443

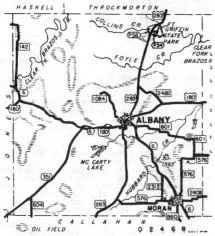

Vital Statistics, 1989: Births, 43; Deaths, 33; Marriages, 30; Divorces, 11.

Ethnicity, 1990: White, 3,125 (94.2%); Black, 12 (0.4%); American Indian, 9 (0.3%); Asian, 2 (0.1%); Hispanic, 272 (8.2%); Other, 168 (5.1%).

Recreation: Fort Griffin State Park (in National Register of Historic Places), June **Fandangle** musical production major tourist attractions, many local activities; courthouse historical district; lake activities, hunting.

Minerals: Production of oil, natural gas.

Agriculture: Most income from cattle, sheep, horses, hogs; crops include cotton, wheat.

Business: Oil and ranching economy; some manufacturing; June Fandangle is tourist attraction.

ALBANY (1,962) county seat; tourism; oil and agriculture center; quarter-horse breeding, training; historical district. Other town, **Moran** (285).

Shelby County

LOCATION: Borders Louisiana (I-21).

Cong. Dist. 1	U.S. Jud. Dist. ....E-Ty.
St. Sen. Dist. 3	Ct. Appeals.....................12
St. Rep. Dist. 10	Admin. Jud. Dist. 1
St. Dist. Cts.............123, 273	

History: Original county, created 1836; organized 1837; named for Isaac Shelby of American Revolution.

Physical Features: Partly hills, much bottomland; well timbered, 67,762 acres in Sabine National Forest; Toledo Bend and Pinkston reservoirs; Sabine, Attoyac rivers, other streams; sandy, clay, alluvial soils.

Population.................22,034	Av. Weekly Wage $280.76
Area (sq. mi.)..............834.5	Density 28
Land Area....................794.1	Water Area 40.4
Civilian Labor 10,617	Jobless Rate...................5.7
Altitude (ft.) 630-213	Retail Sales $125,135,406
Rainfall (in.) 49.7	Gross Sales........$354,570,631
Jan. min. 34	Reg. Voters 13,282
July max. 94	Election Turnout 41.5
Grow. Season (days) 240	Vehicles 22,827
Total Income (mil.) $284	Lane Miles 857
Per Capita Income...$11,883	Tax Value.........$669,717,834
Total Wages.......$86,633,613	Fed. Spending $78,449

Housing...................10,610	Defense Spending $1,804

Vital Statistics, 1989: Births, 346; Deaths, 306; Marriages, 233; Divorces, 132.

Ethnicity, 1990: White, 17,047 (77.4%); Black, 4,727 (21.5%); American Indian, 36 (0.2%); Asian, 31 (0.1%); Hispanic, 539 (2.4%); Other, 193 (0.9%).

Recreation: Toledo Bend Reservoir activities; **Sabine National Forest**; hunting, fishing; camping; historic sites; poultry festival, antique-gun show, wolf hunt in October.

Minerals: Natural gas, oil.

Agriculture: A leader in broiler and egg production; most income from poultry, beef cattle; hay, vegetables; timber sales significant.

Business: Broiler, egg production, cattle, timber leading economic factors; tourism contributes.

CENTER (4,950) county seat; poultry, lumber processing; hospitals, nursing homes; **Shelby College Center.** Other towns, **Huxley** (335), **Joaquin** (805), **Tenaha** (1,072), **Timpson** (1,029).

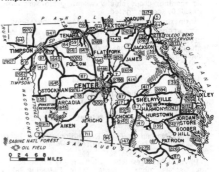

Sherman County

LOCATION: Top of Panhandle (A-8).

Cong. Dist. 13	U.S. Jud. Dist. ....N-Am.
St. Sen. Dist. 31	Ct. Appeals.....................7
St. Rep. Dist. 88	Admin. Jud. Dist. 9
St. Dist. Cts...................69	

History: Named for Texas Gen. Sidney Sherman; county created from Bexar District 1876; organized 1889.

Physical Features: Level, broken by creeks, playas; sandy to dark loam soils; underground water.

Population..................2,858	Av. Weekly Wage $334.68
Area (sq. mi.)..............923.2	Density 3
Land Area....................923.1	Water Area 0.1
Civilian Labor 1,572	Jobless Rate...................2.4

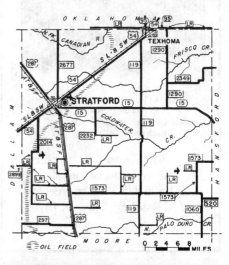

Altitude (ft.) 3,743-3,485	Retail Sales $13,091,850	Area (sq. mi.) 949.4	Density 162
Rainfall (in.) 16.9	Gross Sales........ $25,827,974	Land Area 928.4	Water Area 21.0
Jan. min. 18	Reg. Voters 1,713	Civilian Labor 74,118	Jobless Rate....................6.2
July max. 93	Election Turnout 54.8	Altitude (ft.) 631-52	Retail Sales ... $1,281,229,886
Grow. Season (days)..... 182	Vehicles 3,639	Rainfall (in.) 43.1	Gross Sales.... $3,405,745,167
Total Income (mil.) $78	Lane Miles 429	Jan. min. 33	Reg. Voters 75,235
Per Capita Income...$26,900	Tax Value......... $389,295,153	July max. 94	Election Turnout 52.3
Total Wages....... $14,827,532	Fed. Spending $22,980	Grow. Season (days)..... 259	Vehicles 136,752
Housing......................1,293	Defense Spending $116	Total Income (mil.) .. $2,472	Lane Miles 1,495
		Per Capita Income...$16,139	Tax Value...... $5,624,576,080
		Total Wages... $1,301,761,623	Fed. Spending $397,076
		Housing.................. 64,285	Defense Spending ... $40,574

Vital Statistics, 1989: Births, 40; Deaths, 32; Marriages, 16; Divorces, 7.

Ethnicity, 1990: White, 2,816 (98.5%); Black, 4 (0.1%); American Indian, 12 (0.4%); Asian, 7 (0.2%); Hispanic, 538 (18.8%); Other, 19 (0.7%).

Recreation: County fair, jamboree in September, livestock show in February, other local events; pheasant hunting.

Minerals: Production of natural gas, oil.

Agriculture: Beef and stocker cattle important, much cattle feeding; crops chiefly wheat, grain sorghums, corn; 130,300 acres irrigated.

Business: Agribusinesses, large feedlot operations.

STRATFORD (1,781) county seat; agribusiness center; feedlot operations; industrial authority; some manufacturing; nursing home. **Texhoma** (291 in Texas, 746 in Oklahoma), other principal town.

Smith County

LOCATION: Northeast (H-19).

Cong. Dist. 4	U.S. Jud. Dist. .... E-Ty.
St. Sen. Dist. 2	Ct. Appeals..................... 12
St. Rep. Dist. 5, 6	Admin. Jud. Dist. 1
St. Dist. Cts... 7, 114, 241, 321	

History: Named for Texas Revolutionary Gen. James Smith; county created, organized 1846 from Nacogdoches.

Physical Features: Rolling hills, many timbered; Sabine, Neches, other streams; Tyler, Palestine lakes; alluvial, gray, sandy loam, clay soils.

Population...............151,309 Av. Weekly Wage $398.69

Vital Statistics, 1989: Births, 2,266; Deaths, 1,353; Marriages, 1,637; Divorces, 909.

Ethnicity, 1990: White, 113,676 (75.1%); Black, 31,572 (20.9%); American Indian, 520 (0.3%); Asian, 638 (0.4%); Hispanic, 8,986 (5.9%); Other, 4,903 (3.2%).

Recreation: Activities on Palestine, Tyler lakes and others; famed **Tyler Rose Garden; Texas Rose Festival** in October; **Azalea Trail** in spring; **Tyler State Park;** Goodman Museum; East Texas Fair in fall, onion festival at Noonday; collegiate events.

Minerals: Production of oil, gas, clays, sand and gravel, stone.

Agriculture: A major producer of rose bushes and horticultural crops; livestock include beef, dairy cattle, horses, hogs; other crops include hay, watermelons, fruits, pecans; timber sales substantial; irrigation minor.

Business: Agribusiness; petroleum production; distribution center; education.

TYLER (75,450) county seat; claims title "Rose Capital of the World"; administrative for oil production; varied manufacturing; **Texas College, University of Texas at Tyler, Tyler Junior College; University of Texas Health Center;** medical center, nursing school.

Other towns are **Arp** (812); **Bullard** (838 in Smith County, part in Cherokee County); **Dogwood City** (est. 500); **Lindale** (2,428), food processing; county fest, rodeo; **New Chapel Hill** (439); **Noonday** (466); **Overton** (123 in Smith County, mostly in Rusk County); **Troup** (1,626 in Smith County, partly in Cherokee County); **Whitehouse** (4,032); **Winona** (457).

See map on next page.

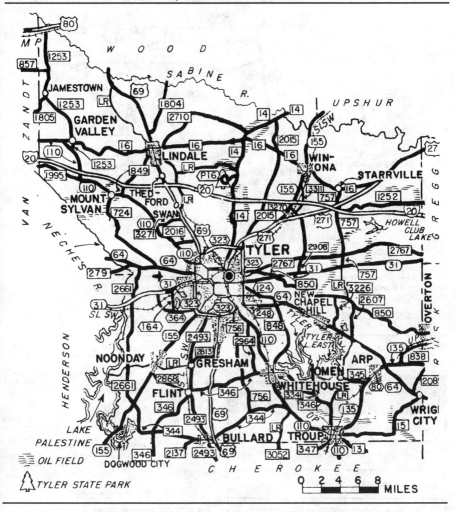

Somervell County

LOCATION: North central (I-15).

Cong. Dist. 17	U.S. Jud. Dist. ....W-Wa.
St. Sen. Dist. 22	Ct. Appeals.....................10
St. Rep. Dist. 58	Admin. Jud. Dist. 3
St. Dist. Cts..............18, 249	

History: Second-smallest county in land area in Texas; created, organized as Somerville County 1875 from Hood, Bosque; name changed to proper spelling 1876; named for Republic of Texas General Alexander Somervell.

Physical Features: Hilly; Brazos, Paluxy rivers; gray, dark, alluvial soils.

Population..................5,360	Av. Weekly Wage $790.21
Area (sq. mi.).............191.8	Density 29
Land Area 187.1	Water Area 4.7
Civilian Labor 1,879	Jobless Rate................18.7
Altitude (ft.) 1,013-627	Retail Sales $19,979,899
Rainfall (in.) 32.2	Gross Sales........ $37,150,996
Jan. min. 32	Reg. Voters 3,279
July max. 98	Election Turnout.........54.0
Grow. Season (days).....236	Vehicles 5,472
Total Income (mil.) $78	Lane Miles 184
Per Capita Income...$14,020	Tax Value.... $4,554,205,584
Total Wages......$158,898,415	Fed. Spending........ $10,080
Housing.....................2,429	Defense Spending $394

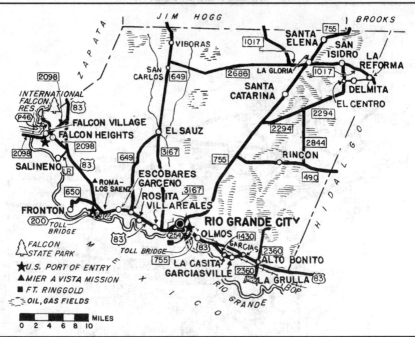

Somervell Co. (Cont.)

Vital Statistics, 1989: Births, 79; Deaths, 43; Marriages, 87; Divorces, 44.

Ethnicity, 1990: White, 4,849 (90.5%); Black, 10 (0.2%); American Indian, 34 (0.6%); Asian, 22 (0.4%); Hispanic, 749 (14.0%); Other, 445 (8.3%).

Recreation: Fishing, hunting; unique geological formations; **Dinosaur Valley State Park; Glen Rose Big Rock Park; Fossil Rim Wildlife Center**; nature trails, museum; local events.

Minerals: Limited sand, gravel.

Agriculture: Most income from beef cattle, dairy products; crops include hay, peanuts, small grains; minor irrigation.

Business: Tourism, agribusinesses.

GLEN ROSE (1,949) county seat; tourism, farm trade center; hospital, nursing home; nuclear power plant; wildlife center.

Starr County

LOCATION: Far south (U-14).

Cong. Dist.	15	U.S. Jud. Dist.	S-Br.
St. Sen. Dist.	21	Ct. Appeals	4
St. Rep. Dist.	37	Admin. Jud. Dist.	5
St. Dist. Cts.	229		

History: Named for Dr. J.H. Starr, a secretary of treasury of Republic of Texas; county created from Nueces, organized 1848.

Physical Features: Rolling, some hills; dense brush; clay, loam, sandy soils, alluvial on Rio Grande; Falcon Reservoir.

Population	40,518	Av. Weekly Wage	$240.13
Area (sq. mi.)	1,229.3	Density	33
Land Area	1,223.1	Water Area	6.2
Civilian Labor	17,944	Jobless Rate	36.1
Altitude (ft.)	531-143	Retail Sales	$140,048,833
Rainfall (in.)	20.6	Gross Sales	$174,729,583
Jan. min.	44	Reg. Voters	16,233
July max.	99	Election Turnout	26.1
Grow. Season (days)	314	Vehicles	22,544
Total Income (mil.)	$186	Lane Miles	464
Per Capita Income	$4,549	Tax Value	$966,523,044
Total Wages	$77,516,953	Fed. Spending	$87,957
Housing	12,164	Defense Spending	$500

Vital Statistics, 1989: Births, 1,008; Deaths, 199; Marriages, 492; Divorces, 76.

See map at top of page.

Starr Co. (Cont.)

Ethnicity, 1990: White, 25,067 (61.9%); Black, 25 (0.1%); American Indian, 31 (0.1%); Asian, 25 (0.1%); Hispanic, 39,390 (97.2%); Other, 15,370 (37.9%).

Recreation: Falcon Reservoir activities; deer, white-wing dove hunting; access to Mexico; historic houses; grotto at Rio Grande City.

Minerals: Production of oil, natural gas, sand and gravel.

Agriculture: Most income from crops, including sorghums, cotton, vegetables; beef cattle, hogs, sheep, horses; substantial irrigation for vegetables.

Business: Vegetable packing, shipping, other agri-businesses; oil processing; tourism.

RIO GRANDE CITY (9,891) county seat; agriculture center; food processing; exports to Mexico; hospital. Other towns, **Escobares** (1,705), **La Casita-Garciasville** (1,186), **La Grulla** (1,335), **Roma** (8,059).

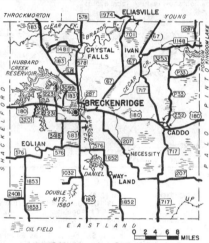

Stephens County

LOCATION: North central (H-13).

Cong. Dist. 17	U.S. Jud. Dist. ....N-Ab.
St. Sen. Dist. 22	Ct. Appeals....................11
St. Rep. Dist. 64	Admin. Jud. Dist. 8
St. Dist. Cts...................90	

History: Created as Buchanan 1858 from Bosque; renamed 1861 for Confederate Vice President Alexander H. Stephens; organized 1876.

Physical Features: Broken, hilly; Hubbard Creek Reservoir, Possum Kingdom, Daniel lakes; Brazos River; loam, sandy soils.

Population...................9,010	Av. Weekly Wage $318.37
Area (sq. mi.)..............921.5	Density 10
Land Area 894.7	Water Area 26.8
Civilian Labor 4,112	Jobless Rate..................4.4
Altitude (ft.).......1,578-1,127	Retail Sales $53,611,936
Rainfall (in.) 26.4	Gross Sales........$96,874,741
Jan. min. 31	Reg. Voters 5,397
July max. 97	Election Turnout.........50.8
Grow. Season (days).....222	Vehicles 9,364
Total Income (mil.) $120	Lane Miles 546
Per Capita Income...$12,564	Tax Value....$668,951,457
Total Wages.......$45,195,648	Fed. Spending.........$26,259
Housing......................4,689	Defense Spending $1,001

Vital Statistics, 1989: Births, 140; Deaths, 135; Marriages, 83; Divorces, 56.

Ethnicity, 1990: White, 8,187 (90.9%); Black, 252 (2.8%); American Indian, 30 (0.3%); Asian, 28 (0.3%); Hispanic, 767 (8.5%); Other, 513 (5.7%).

Recreation: Lake activities; hunting; campsites; historical points; **Swenson Museum; Sandefer Oil Museum;** aviation museum and annual air show; rattlesnake hunt; local events.

Minerals: Oil, natural gas, stone.

Agriculture: Most income from beef cattle, horses,

hogs, goats, sheep; crops include wheat, oats, hay, peanuts, grain sorghums, cotton, pecans; some firewood, fence posts sold.

Business: Oil, agribusinesses, recreation, some manufacturing.

BRECKENRIDGE (5,665) county seat; oil and agriculture center; some manufacturing; petrochemical production; hospital, nursing homes; airport; arts center and library; many local events.

Sterling County

LOCATION: Southwest (J-10).

Cong. Dist. 17	U.S. Jud. Dist. ......N-SAng.
St. Sen. Dist. 25	Ct. Appeals....................3
St. Rep. Dist. 66	Admin. Jud. Dist. 7
St. Dist. Cts...................51	

History: Named for buffalo hunter W.S. Sterling; created, organized 1891 from Tom Green County.

Physical Features: Central prairie, surrounded by hills, broken by Concho River and tributaries; sandy to black soils.

Population..................1,438	Av. Weekly Wage $334.03
Area (sq. mi.)..............923.5	Density 2
Land Area 923.4	Water Area 0.1
Civilian Labor 802	Jobless Rate..................2.2
Altitude (ft.).......2,623-2,167	Retail Sales $6,680,143
Rainfall (in.) 18.6	Gross Sales....$13,517,113
Jan. min. 27	Reg. Voters 839
July max. 96	Election Turnout........60.0
Grow. Season (days).....224	Vehicles 1,684
Total Income (mil.) $19	Lane Miles 240
Per Capita Income...$13,112	Tax Value........$396,660,949
Total Wages.........$8,441,485	Fed. Spending..........$3,454
Housing.........................623	Defense Spending $96

Vital Statistics, 1989: Births, 22; Deaths, 17; Marriages, 16; Divorces, 3.

Ethnicity, 1990: White, 1,244 (86.5%); Black, 0 (0.0%); American Indian, 9 (0.6%); Asian, 0 (0.0%); Hispanic, 366 (25.5%); Other, 185 (12.9%).

Recreation: Hunting, local events.

Minerals: Oil, natural gas.

Agriculture: Most income from beef cattle and sheep; some wheat raised; about 1,000 acres irrigated.

Business: Oil and ranching economy; hunting leases.

STERLING CITY (1,096) county seat; farm, ranch trade center; oil-field services; hospital, nursing home.

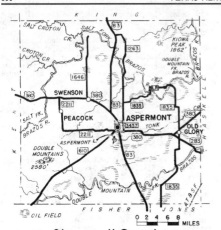

Stonewall County

LOCATION: Northwest, below Caprock (G-11).

Cong. Dist. 17	U.S. Jud. Dist. ....N-Ab.
St. Sen. Dist. 30	Ct. Appeals......................11
St. Rep. Dist. 78	Admin. Jud. Dist. 7
St. Dist. Cts. 39	

History: Named for Confederate Gen. T.J. (Stonewall) Jackson; created from Bexar 1876, organized 1888.

Physical Features: Level, bisected by Brazos forks; sandy loam, sandy, other soils; some hills.

Population..................2,013	Av. Weekly Wage $333.65
Area (sq. mi.)..............920.2	Density 2
Land Area 918.7	Water Area 1.5
Civilian Labor 1,255	Jobless Rate..................3.8
Altitude (ft.)....1,964-1,659	Retail Sales $8,135,037
Rainfall (in.) 22.2	Gross Sales........$15,519,801
Jan. min. 27	Reg. Voters 1,513
July max. 98	Election Turnout 54.7
Grow. Season (days).....220	Vehicles 2,451
Total Income (mil.) $35	Lane Miles 319
Per Capita Income...$16,703	Tax Value........$251,460,089
Total Wages......$10,930,487	Fed. Spending..........$9,483
Housing......................1,080	Defense Spending $88

Vital Statistics, 1989: Births, 38; Deaths, 36; Marriages, 16; Divorces, 10.

Ethnicity, 1990: White, 1,898 (94.3%); Black, 89 (4.4%); American Indian, 2 (0.1%); Asian, 7 (0.3%); Hispanic, 237 (11.8%); Other, 17 (0.8%).

Recreation: Rodeo in June, other local events.

Minerals: Production of oil, natural gas, gypsum.

Agriculture: Most income from beef cattle; crops include wheat, cotton, peanuts, grain sorghums; about 2,-000 acres of peanuts irrigated.

Business: Oil, agribusinesses leading economic factors.

ASPERMONT (1,214) county seat; oil field, ranching center.

Sutton County

LOCATION: Southwest (L-11).

Cong. Dist. 21	U.S. Jud. Dist. ......N-SAng.
St. Sen. Dist. 25	Ct. Appeals......................4
St. Rep. Dist. 67	Admin. Jud. Dist. 6
St. Dist. Cts. 112	

History: Created from Crockett 1887; organized 1890; named for Confederate officer Col. John S. Sutton.

Physical Features: Level, broken by tributaries of Devils, Llano rivers; black, red loam soils.

Population..................4,135	Av. Weekly Wage $338.64
Area (sq. mi.) 1,454.4	Density 3
Land Area 1,453.8	Water Area 0.6
Civilian Labor 2,038	Jobless Rate..................4.8
Altitude (ft.)......2,461-1,942	Retail Sales $23,579,064
Rainfall (in.) 20.7	Gross Sales........$54,217,385
Jan. min. 32	Reg. Voters 2,259
July max. 95	Election Turnout 45.2
Grow. Season (days).....235	Vehicles 4,931
Total Income (mil.) $59	Lane Miles 592
Per Capita Income...$14,835	Tax Value........$593,842,730

Total Wages.......$28,668,045	Fed. Spending.........$11,945
Housing......................1,924	Defense Spending $153

Vital Statistics, 1989: Births, 69; Deaths, 48; Marriages, 38; Divorces, 22.

Ethnicity, 1990: White, 3,125 (75.6%); Black, 2 (**.*%); American Indian, 16 (0.4%); Asian, 6 (0.1%); Hispanic, 1,-866 (45.1%); Other, 986 (23.8%).

Recreation: Among leading hunting counties; **Meirs Museum; Caverns of Sonora**; local events; county park, rodeo, goat cookoff, national 4-H wool-judging competition.

Minerals: Production of oil, natural gas, stone.

Agriculture: Livestock provide most income, beef cattle, Angora goats, meat goats, fine-wool sheep; wheat raised for grazing; minor irrigation.

Business: Agribusinesses, oil, tourism; hunting leases.

SONORA (2,751) county seat; oil field, mohair, wool center; **Texas A&M Agricultural Research Substation**; hospital, nursing home; dinner theater in summer; wool, mohair show in June, local events.

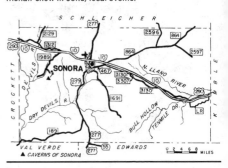

Swisher County

LOCATION: Northwest (D-8).

Cong. Dist. 13	U.S. Jud. Dist. ....N-Am.
St. Sen. Dist. 31	Ct. Appeals......................7
St. Rep. Dist. 85	Admin. Jud. Dist. 9
St. Dist. Cts. 64, 242	

History: Named for J.G. Swisher of Texas Revolution; county created from Bexar, Young territories 1876; organized 1890; among last Indian strongholds.

Physical Features: Level, broken by Tule Canyon and Creek; playas; large underground water supply; rich soils.

Population..................8,133	Av. Weekly Wage $290.14
Area (sq. mi.)..............900.6	Density 9
Land Area 900.4	Water Area 0.2
Civilian Labor 3,636	Jobless Rate..................4.3
Altitude (ft.)......3,604-3,354	Retail Sales $36,522,605
Rainfall (in.) 17.5	Gross Sales........$82,953,692
Jan. min. 22	Reg. Voters 4,437
July max. 92	Election Turnout 50.5
Grow. Season (days).....205	Vehicles 7,989
Total Income (mil.) $153	Lane Miles 808
Per Capita Income...$17,863	Tax Value........$306,037,447
Total Wages.......$33,583,820	Fed. Spending.......$40,973
Housing......................3,494	Defense Spending $165

Vital Statistics, 1989: Births, 150; Deaths, 85; Marriages, 59; Divorces, 40.

Ethnicity, 1990: White, 5,702 (70.1%); Black, 340 (4.2%); American Indian, 26 (0.3%); Asian, 17 (0.2%); Hispanic, 2,496 (30.7%); Other, 2,048 (25.2%).

Recreation: Mackenzie Reservoir, Tule Lake activities; museum; local events.

Minerals: Not significant.

Agriculture: A major agricultural county; fed cattle lead income, stocker cattle raised; crops include wheat, cotton, corn, grain sorghums; about 150,000 acres irrigated.

Business: Large feedlots, grain storage, other agribusinesses; varied manufacturing; tourism; new prison unit open.

TULIA (4,699) county seat; farming center; varied manufacturing; grain storage; food processing; hospital, nursing home; library, museum; new prison unit; county celebration in July. Other towns, **Happy** (551 in Swisher County, part in Randall County), **Kress** (739).

See map on next page.

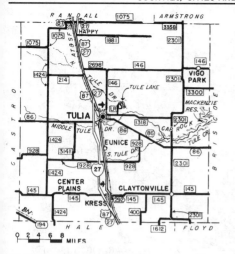

Tarrant County

LOCATION: North (H-16).

Cong. Dist. 12, 24, 26	Ct. Appeals...................... 2
St. Sen. Dist. 10, 12, 22, 23	St. Dist. Cts. 17, 48, 67,
St. Rep. Dist. 89-97	96, 141, 153, 213, 231, 233,
Admin. Jud. Dist. 8	236, 297, 322, 323, 324, 325,
U.S. Jud. Dist............N-FW	342, 348, 352, 360, 371, 372,
	Cr. 1, Cr. 2, Cr. 3, Cr.4,
	Imp. 1, Imp. 2

History: Named for Gen. Edward H. Tarrant, who helped drive Indians from area; county created 1849 from Navarro County; organized 1850.

Physical Features: Part Blackland, level to rolling; drains to Trinity; Worth, Grapevine, Eagle Mountain, Benbrook lakes.

Population............ 1,170,103	Av. Weekly Wage $454.82
Area (sq. mi.)............897.5	Density 1,348
Land Area 863.5	Water Area 34.0
Civilian Labor 650,164	Jobless Rate.................5.3
Altitude (ft.)............864-484	Retail Sales ... 10,814,093,852
Rainfall (in.) 31.3	Gross Sales.... 29,703,739,514
Jan. min. 35	Reg. Voters 529,598
July max. 96	Election Turnout........ 51.2
Grow. Season (days)..... 230	Vehicles 1,028,001
Total Income (mil.) .$20,371	Lane Miles 2,598
Per Capita Income...$17,686	Tax Value..... $47,140,518,214
Total Wages..$12,398,511,164	Fed. Spending 5,972,757
Housing..................489,807	Defense Spending 3,814,422

Vital Statistics, 1989: Births, 22,055; Deaths, 7,735; Marriages, 12,130; Divorces, 7,742.

Ethnicity, 1990: White, 917,501 (78.4%); Black, 140,740 (12.0%); American Indian, 5,551 (0.5%); Asian, 29,705 (2.5%); Hispanic, 139,879 (12.0%); Other, 76,606 (6.5%).

Recreation: Numerous metropolitan events (ask chambers of commerce); **Scott Theatre; Amon G. Carter Museum; Kimbell Art Museum; Fort Worth Art Museum; Museum of Science and History; Casa Manana;** famed **Botanic Gardens; Forest Park Zoo; Log Cabin Village; Six Flags Over Texas** at Arlington; **Southwestern Esposition, Stock Show; Convention Center; Stockyards Historical District;** Colonial National Golf Tournament; Texas Rangers major league baseball at Arlington, other athletic events.

Minerals: Production of cement, sand, gravel, stone, gas.

Agriculture: $21.2 million average farm income; dairy and beef cattle, hogs and poultry; headquarters for large dairy producers' organization at Arlington; large production eggs, milk; horses; major nursery-stock production; crops include grain sorghums, small grains, cotton, pecans, vegetables.

Business: Diversified urban economy; planes, helicopters, foods, mobile homes, electronic equipment, chemicals, plastics among products of more than 1,000 factories; large federal expenditure due to defense industries; D/FW International Airport nation's largest; fourth most populous Texas county; economy closely associated with Dallas urban area.

Education: Texas Christian University, Texas Wesleyan University, Southwestern Baptist Theological Seminary, Tarrant County Junior College System (three campuses), **Texas College of Osteopathic Medicine** (merged with University of North Texas in 1975) all in Fort Worth; **University of Texas at Arlington, Arlington Baptist College, Bauder Fashion College** in Arlington.

FORT WORTH (447,619) county seat; a major mercantile, commercial and financial center; wholesale trade center for much of West Texas; a leader in aerospace activities with large airplane, helicopter and other plants; an outstanding cultural center with renowned art museums; many conventions held in large downtown center; **Carswell Air Force Base;** agribusiness center for wide area with large grain-storage and feed-mill operations; adjacent to **D/FW International Airport;** hospitals, nursing homes, many local events (check with chamber of commerce for dates).

Among leading educational centers in state (see list of schools above).

Arlington (261,721); an industrial and distribution center; industries make and distribute automobiles, food products, electronic components, aircraft and parts, rubber and plastic products; medical center, hospitals, nursing homes; a major tourist center with **Six Flags Over Texas,** the **Texas Rangers** baseball team, numerous restaurants; educational facilities are listed above.

Other towns include, **Azle** (7,665 in Tarrant, partly in Parker County), varied industries, hospital, local events; **Bedford** (43,762); **Benbrook** (19,564); **Blue Mound** (2,133); **Briar** (2,409 in Tarrant, partly in Wise County);

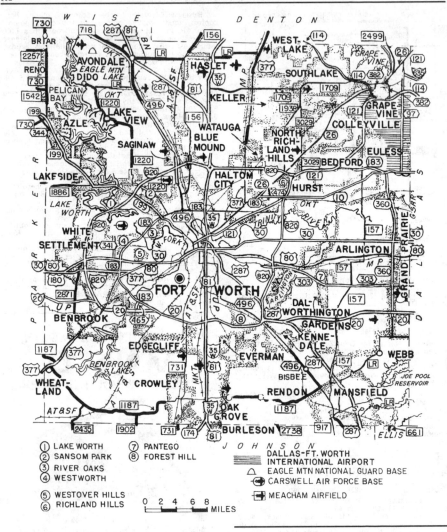

① LAKE WORTH ⑦ PANTEGO
② SANSOM PARK ⑧ FOREST HILL
③ RIVER OAKS
④ WESTWORTH
⑤ WESTOVER HILLS
⑥ RICHLAND HILLS

0 2 4 6 8 MILES

DALLAS-FT. WORTH
INTERNATIONAL AIRPORT
△ EAGLE MTN NATIONAL GUARD BASE
⊙ CARSWELL AIR FORCE BASE
⊞ MEACHAM AIRFIELD

Tarrant Co. (Cont.)

Burleson (1,960 in Tarrant, mostly in Johnson County); **Colleyville** (12,724); **Crowley** (6,974 in Tarrant, partly in Johnson County), varied manufacturing, hospital; **Dalworthington Gardens** (1,758); **Eagle Mountain** (5,847); **Edgecliff Village** (2,715); **Euless** (38,149); **Everman** (5,672); **Forest Hill** (11,482); **Grand Prairie** (18,086 in Tarrant County, partly in Dallas and Ellis counties); **Grapevine** (29,199 in Tarrant, partly in Denton County), varied manufacturing; near D/FW International Airport; tourist center; **Haltom City** (32,856); **Haslet** (795 in Tarrant, partly in Denton County); **Hurst** (33,574); **Keller** (13,683); **Kennedale** (4,096); **Lakeside** (816); **Lake Worth** (4,591); **Mansfield** (14,848 in Tarrant, partly in Johnson County), varied manufacturing; hospital; Frontier Days, hometown celebration in fall; **North Richland Hills** (45,895); **Pantego** (2,371); **Pecan Acres** (310 in Tarrant, mostly in Wise County); **Pelican Bay** (1,271); **Rendon** (7,658); **Richland Hills** (7,978); **River Oaks** (6,580); **Saginaw** (8,551); **Sansom Park** (3,928); **Southlake** (6,823); **Watauga** (20,009); **Westlake** (105 in Tarrant, partly in Denton County); **Westover Hills** (672); **Westworth Village** (2,350); **White Settlement** (15,472), near aircraft manufacturing, air force base; hospital, nursing homes; industrial park.

Taylor County

LOCATION: Central (I-12).

Cong. Dist. 17	U.S. Jud. Dist. ....N-Ab.
St. Sen. Dist. 24	Ct. Appeals...............11
St. Rep. Dist. 78, 79	Admin. Jud. Dist. 7
St. Dist. Cts. 42, 104, 326, 350	

History: Named for Alamo heroes Edward, James, George Taylor, brothers; county created from Bexar, Travis 1858; organized 1878.

Physical Features: Prairies, with Callahan Divide, draining to Colorado tributaries, Brazos forks; Lakes Abilene, Kirby; mostly loam soils.

Population.............119,655	Av. Weekly Wage $352.91
Area (sq. mi.)..........919.3	Density 130
Land Area 915.7	Water Area 3.6
Civilian Labor 50,932	Jobless Rate................6.1
Altitude (ft.) 2,410-1,672	Retail Sales $884,060,290
Rainfall (in.) 23.3	Gross Sales .. $2,350,144,507
Jan. min. 31	Reg. Voters 54,003
July max. 95	Election Turnout 53.1
Grow. Season (days).....225	Vehicles 107,792
Total Income (mil.) .. $1,820	Lane Miles 1,153

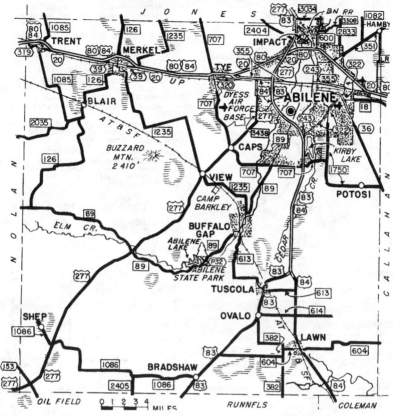

Taylor Co. (Cont.)

Per Capita Income...$15,001	Tax Value...... $3,168,646,281
Total Wages......$826,112,110	Fed. Spending....... $529,751
Housing.................... 49,810	Defense Spending . $272,358

Vital Statistics, 1989: Births, 2,260; Deaths, 912; Marriages, 1,409; Divorces, 823.

Ethnicity, 1990: White, 100,237 (83.8%); Black, 7,547 (6.3%); American Indian, 450 (0.4%); Asian, 1,449 (1.2%); Hispanic, 17,511 (14.6%); Other, 9,972 (8.3%).

Recreation: Metropolitan, school events (ask chamber of commerce): Abilene State Park; lake activities; Nelson Park Zoo; Texas Cowboy Reunion, West Texas Fair; Fort Phantom Hill; Buffalo Gap historical tour and art festival; rodeo, other events.

Minerals: Production of oil, natural gas, stone, caliche, clays, sand and gravel.

Agriculture: Fed cattle most productive, cow-calf operation; crops include wheat, cotton, grain sorghums, hay; less than 5,000 acres irrigated, mostly improved pasture.

Business: Major economic factors include Dyess Air Force Base, feedlots, agribusinesses, diversified manufacturing; education.

ABILENE (105,857 in Taylor County, part in Jones County) county seat; distribution center; plants make a variety of products; meat, dairy processing; oil-field service center; **Abilene Christian University, Hardin-Simmons University, McMurry University, Cisco Junior College** branch; medical center; **Abilene State School; West Texas Rehabilitation Center.**

Other communities are **Buffalo Gap** (499); **Impact** (25); **Lawn** (358); **Merkel** (2,469), manufacturing; oil-field services; nursing home; **Potosi** (1,441); **Trent** (319); **Tuscola** (620); **Tye** (1,088).

Terrell County

LOCATION: Borders Mexico (M-8).

Cong. Dist. 21	U.S. Jud. Dist. ....W-DR
St. Sen. Dist. 25	Ct. Appeals...................... 8
St. Rep. Dist. 68	Admin. Jud. Dist. 6
St. Dist. Cts. 63	

History: Named for Confederate Gen. A.W. Terrell; county created, organized 1905 from Pecos County.

Physical Features: Semi-mountainous, many canyons; rocky, limestone soils.

Population.................1,410		Av. Weekly Wage $340.83	
Area (sq. mi.) 2,357.9		Density 1	
Land Area 2,357.9		Water Area 0.0	
Civilian Labor 935		Jobless Rate.................. 1.9	
Altitude (ft.) 2,792-1,668		Retail Sales $3,721,031	
Rainfall (in.) 12.8		Gross Sales $6,180,282	
Jan. min. 29		Reg. Voters 920	
July max. 93		Election Turnout......... 53.5	
Grow. Season (days)..... 237		Vehicles 1,388	
Total Income (mil.) $28		Lane Miles 330	
Per Capita Income...$19,381		Tax Value......... $261,053,259	
Total Wages.........$6,291,714		Fed. Spending......... $7,620	
Housing........................ 810		Defense Spending $50	

Vital Statistics, 1989: Births, 21; Deaths, 7; Marriages, 15; Divorces, 6.

Ethnicity, 1990: White, 1,189 (84.3%); Black, 1 (0.1%); American Indian, 5 (0.4%); Asian, 2 (0.1%); Hispanic, 751 (53.3%); Other, 213 (15.1%).

Recreation: Hunting, especially white-tailed, mule deer; lower canyons of Rio Grande accessible by boat; county fair in June, local events.

Minerals: Production of natural gas, oil.

Agriculture: Most income from sheep, goats, wool, mohair, some beef cattle; no crops; only 19 acres irrigated from flowing springs.

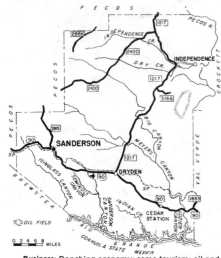

≡□ OIL FIELD

0 2 4 6 8 MILES

Business: Ranching economy; some tourism; oil and natural gas exploration increasing.

SANDERSON (1,128) county seat; ranching, petroleum operations center; rail terminal; called "gateway to Big Bend"; county fair in January.

Terry County

LOCATION: West (G-7).
Cong. Dist. 19   U.S. Jud. Dist. .... N-Lb.
St. Sen. Dist. 28   Ct. Appeals........................ 7
St. Rep. Dist. 77   Admin. Jud. Dist. 9
St. Dist. Cts. 121

History: Named for head of famed Texas Ranger troop, Col. B.F. Terry; county created from Bexar District 1876; organized 1904.

Physical Features: Level, broken by draws, playas; sandy, sandy loam, loam soils.

Population................. 13,218	Av. Weekly Wage $362.21
Area (sq. mi.) 890.8	Density 15
Land Area 889.8	Water Area 1.0
Civilian Labor 5,258	Jobless Rate................... 6.1
Altitude (ft.) 3,447-3,183	Retail Sales $77,613,695
Rainfall (in.) 17.5	Gross Sales .. $167,439,443
Jan. min. 24	Reg. Voters 7,083
July max. 93	Election Turnout 45.9
Grow. Season (days)..... 206	Vehicles 14,135
Total Income (mil.) $164	Lane Miles 631

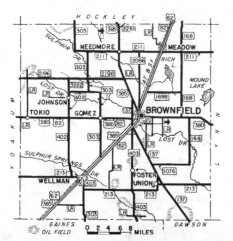

0 2 4 6 8 MILES

Per Capita Income...$11,424   Tax Value......... $958,446,810
Total Wages....... $67,278,436   Fed. Spending......... $50,332
Housing.......................5,296   Defense Spending $1,449

Vital Statistics, 1989: Births, 277; Deaths, 134; Marriages, 104; Divorces, 70.

Ethnicity, 1990: White, 10,202 (77.2%); Black, 449 (3.4%); American Indian, 38 (0.3%); Asian, 28 (0.2%); Hispanic, 5,194 (39.3%); Other, 2,501 (18.9%).

Recreation: Local events; Terry County Heritage Museum, fair, harvest festival in October, junior livestock show in February.

Minerals: Production of oil, natural gas, sodium sulphate.

Agriculture: Stocker cattle important; crops include cotton, wheat, peanuts, vegetables; 125,000 acres irrigated, mostly cotton.

Business: Petroleum, agribusinesses.

BROWNFIELD (9,560) county seat; oil-field services; agribusiness; minerals processed; prison unit; hospital, medical center, nursing homes. Other towns, **Meadow** (547), **Wellman** (239).

Throckmorton County

LOCATION: North central (G-13).
Cong. Dist. 17   U.S. Jud. Dist. .... N-Ab.
St. Sen. Dist. 30   Ct. Appeals..................... 11

St. Rep. Dist. 64   Admin. Jud. Dist. 7
St. Dist. Cts. 39

History: Named for Dr. W.E. Throckmorton, father of Gov. J.W. Throckmorton; county created from Fannin 1858; organized 1879.

Physical Features: Rolling, between Brazos forks; red to black soils.

Population................. 1,880	Av. Weekly Wage $273.21
Area (sq. mi.) 915.5	Density 2
Land Area 912.4	Water Area 3.1
Civilian Labor 943	Jobless Rate................... 1.6
Altitude (ft.) 1,583-1,153	Retail Sales $5,820,049
Rainfall (in.) 25.0	Gross Sales .. $8,762,128
Jan. min. 28	Reg. Voters 1,308
July max. 97	Election Turnout 56.7
Grow. Season (days)..... 220	Vehicles 2,088
Total Income (mil.) $33	Lane Miles 340
Per Capita Income...$16,799	Tax Value......... $206,058,396
Total Wages........$7,131,819	Fed. Spending......... $8,410
Housing.......................1,099	Defense Spending $91

Vital Statistics, 1989: Births, 22; Deaths, 31; Marriages, 11; Divorces, 7.

Ethnicity, 1990: White, 1,778 (94.6%); Black, 0 (0.0%); American Indian, 4 (0.2%); Asian, 8 (0.4%); Hispanic, 136 (7.2%); Other, 90 (4.8%).

Recreation: Hunting, fishing; historic sites include **Camp Cooper, Camp Wilson**, site of former Comanche reservation; restored ranch home, **Miller's Creek Lake**.

Minerals: Production of natural gas, oil.

Agriculture: Cattle, sheep, horses provide most income; crops include wheat, oats, cotton, sorghums, hay.

Business: Oil and agribusiness economy.

THROCKMORTON (1,036) county seat; varied manufacturing; oil-field services; hospital, nursing home. Other town, **Woodson** (262).

Titus County

LOCATION: Northeast (G-20).

Cong. Dist. 1	U.S. Jud. Dist. .... E-Tx.
St. Sen. Dist. 1	Ct. Appeals...................... 6
St. Rep. Dist. 8	Admin. Jud. Dist. 1
St. Dist. Cts............. 76, 276	

History: Named for pioneer settler A.J. Titus; county created from Bowie, Red River counties; organized 1846.

Physical Features: Small and hilly; drains to Big Cypress Creek, Sulphur River; timbered.

Population................ 24,009	Av. Weekly Wage $373.86
Area (sq. mi.).............425.6	Density 58
Land Area 410.5	Water Area 15.1
Civilian Labor 14,285	Jobless Rate................... 5.6
Altitude (ft.).............462-301	Retail Sales $188,881,274
Rainfall (in.) 45.5	Gross Sales....... $657,765,177
Jan. min. 30	Reg. Voters 12,130
July max. 95	Election Turnout 46.5
Grow. Season (days).... 233	Vehicles 22,546
Total Income (mil.) $338	Lane Miles 531
Per Capita Income...$14,809	Tax Value.. $1,607,864,740
Total Wages......$235,697,570	Fed. Spending $65,946
Housing......................9,355	Defense Spending ... $1,966

Vital Statistics, 1989: Births, 446; Deaths, 231; Marriages, 273; Divorces, 69.

Ethnicity, 1990: White, 18,664 (77.7%); Black, 3,229 (13.4%); American Indian, 107 (0.4%); Asian, 27 (0.1%); Hispanic, 2,556 (10.6%); Other, 1,982 (8.3%).

Recreation: Fishing, hunting; activities on **Monticello Reservoir, Lake Bob Sandlin, Welsh Reservoir, Wright Patman Lake**, other area lakes; railroad museum; river-

boat; many varied local events (check with chamber of commerce).

Minerals: Production of oil, gas, lignite.

Agriculture: Most income from cattle, dairy products, poultry; among leading counties in broilers; crops include corn, watermelons, grain sorghums, hay, peanuts.

Business: Economy based largely on oil, agribusinesses, tourism; lignite mining and power generation.

MOUNT PLEASANT (12,291) county seat; tourism; varied manufacturing; food-processing plants; hospital, nursing homes; **Northeast Texas Community College**. Other towns, **Miller's Cove** (75), **Talco** (592), **Winfield** (345).

Tom Green County

LOCATION: West central (K-11).

Cong. Dist. 21	U.S. Jud. Dist. ...... N-SAng.
St. Sen. Dist. 25	Ct. Appeals...................... 3
St. Rep. Dist. 66	Admin. Jud. Dist. 7
St. Dist. Cts........ 51, 119, 340	

History: Created from Bexar District 1874, named for Gen. Tom Green of Texas Revolution; organized 1875; 12 other counties created from this original area.

Physical Features: Plains, rolling hills, broken by Concho forks; loams in basin, stony hillsides; Nasworthy, O.C. Fisher lakes; Twin Buttes Reservoir.

Population............... 98,458	Av. Weekly Wage $339.87
Area (sq. mi.).......... 1,540.5	Density 65
Land Area 1,522.1	Water Area 18.4
Civilian Labor 43,827	Jobless Rate................... 5.6
Altitude (ft.).......2,480-1,717	Retail Sales $642,152,307
Rainfall (in.) 18.2	Gross Sales.... $1,940,393,316

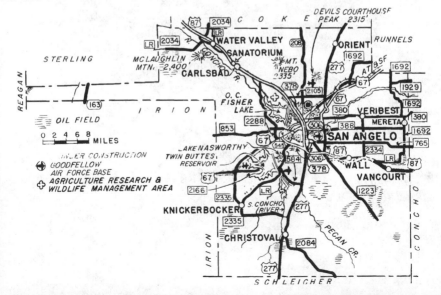

Tom Green Co. (Cont.)

Jan. min. 32	Reg. Voters 44,449
July max. 97	Election Turnout 51.0
Grow. Season (days)..... 235	Vehicles 86,686
Total Income (mil.) .. $1,462	Lane Miles 911
Per Capita Income...$14,658	Tax Value...... $2,963,208,182
Total Wages......$628,344,862	Fed. Spending $351,746
Housing................... 40,076	Defense Spending . $122,546

Vital Statistics, 1989: Births, 1,672; Deaths, 813; Marriages, 1,249; Divorces, 605.

Ethnicity, 1990: White, 79,533 (80.8%); Black, 4,136 (4.2%); American Indian, 373 (0.4%); Asian, 998 (1.0%); Hispanic, 25,501 (25.9%); Other, 13,418 (13.6%).

Recreation: Water sports; hunting; Fort Concho Museum; metropolitan, collegiate activities (ask chamber of commerce for dates); roping fiesta, **Fiesta del Concho**; stock show and rodeo.

Minerals: Production of oil, natural gas, stone.

Agriculture: Income mostly from beef, dairy cattle, sheep, goats; a leading producer of wool, mohair; crops raised are cotton, wheat, oats, sorghums; about 35,000 acres irrigated, mostly cotton, some grain sorghums.

Business: "Sheep and Wool Capital"; economy based on varied agribusinesses, manufacturing; trade center for large area, educational center, medical center.

SAN ANGELO (84,474) county seat; varied agribusiness; plants make a variety of products, distribution center; hospital, nursing homes; **Angelo State University, Texas A&M Research and Extension Center.**

Travis County

LOCATION: Central (M-15).

Cong. Dist. 10	U.S. Jud. Dist. ....W-An.
St. Sen. Dist. 14	Ct. Appeals...................... 3
St. Rep. Dist. 47-51	Admin. Jud. Dist. 3

St. Dist. Cts.. 53, 98, 126, 147, 167, 200, 201, 250, 261, 299, 331, 345, 353

History: Created 1840, when Austin became Texas Capital, from Bastrop County; organized 1843; named for Alamo commander Col. William B. Travis; many other counties created from original area.

Physical Features: Scenic hills, broken by Colorado River and lakes; cedars, pecans, other trees; diverse soils, mineral deposits.

Population...............576,407	Av. Weekly Wage $436.94
Area (sq. mi.).......... 1,022.1	Density 583
Land Area 989.4	Water Area 32.7

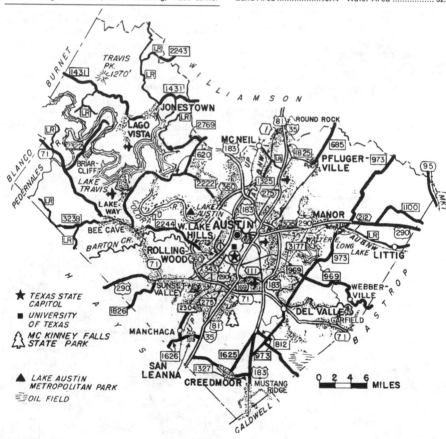

Civilian Labor 333,969	Jobless Rate..................4.6
Altitude (ft.) 1,330-444	Retail Sales ... $5,112,157,962
Rainfall (in.) 31.5	Gross Sales... 11,512,096,064
Jan. min. 39	Reg. Voters 305,582
July max. 95	Election Turnout 62.7
Grow. Season (days).....270	Vehicles 460,366
Total Income (mil.) .. $9,639	Lane Miles 1,431
Per Capita Income...$17,097	Tax Value.....$25,900,211,822
Total Wages... $7,270,919,336	Fed. Spending 3,144,527
Housing....................263,589	Defense Spending . $544,001

Vital Statistics, 1989: Births, 10,106; Deaths, 3,004; Marriages, 6,571; Divorces, 3,338.

Ethnicity, 1990: White, 422,749 (73.3%); Black, 63,173 (11.0%); American Indian, 2,089 (0.4%); Asian, 16,497 (2.9%); Hispanic, 121,689 (21.1%); Other, 71,899 (12.5%).

Recreation: Major tourist center; 95 miles of Colorado River lakes from Austin northwestward; hunting, fishing; **McKinney Falls State Park; Austin Aqua Festival;** livestock exposition; many collegiate, metropolitan, governmental events (ask chamber of commerce or State Department of Highways and Public Transportation).

Minerals: Production of lime, stone, sand, gravel, oil and gas.

Agriculture: Annual income from beef, dairy cattle, horses, hogs; crops include sorghums, cotton, small grains, pecans.

Business: Urbanized area with economy based on education, state government, tourism, research and industry; many conventions.

EDUCATION: University of Texas main campus; **St. Edwards's University, Maryhill College, Concordia Lutheran College, Huston-Tillotson College, Austin Community College,** Episcopal and Presbyterian seminaries; many state eleemosynary schools, institutions.

AUSTIN (463,178 in Travis County, part in Williamson County, county seat and state capital; large state and federal payrolls; a leading convention, tourist city; **Lyndon B. Johnson Library;** many research, high-tech industries; hospitals, including state institutions; popular retirement area; **Bergstrom Air Force Base.**

Other towns are **Anderson Mill** (169 in Travis County, part in Williamson County, **Bee Cave** (241), **Briarcliff** (335), **Creedmoor** (194), **Garfield** (1,233 in Travis County, part in Bastrop County), **Jonestown** (1,250), **Lakeway** (4,044), **Lago Vista** (2,199), **Lost Creek** (4,095), **Manor** (1,041), **Mustang Ridge** (257 in Travis County, part in Caldwell County), **Onion Creek** (1,544), **Pflugerville** (4,444), **Rollingwood** (1,388), **San Leanna** (325), **Sunset Valley** (327), **Tanglewood Forest** (2,941), **Wells Branch** (7,094), **West Lake Hills** (2,542), **Windemere** (3,207).

Trinity County

LOCATION: Southeast (K-20).

Cong. Dist. 2	U.S. Jud. Dist. ....S-Hn.
St. Sen. Dist. 5	Ct. Appeals.................1, 14
St. Rep. Dist. 17	Admin. Jud. Dist. 2
St. Dist. Cts...........2D9, 258	

History: Named for river; county created, organized 1850 out of Houston County.

Physical Features: Heavily forested hills, between Neches and Trinity rivers; rich alluvial soils, sandy upland; 67,910 acres in Davy Crockett National Forest.

Population................11,445	Av. Weekly Wage $271.43
Area (sq. mi.).............713.9	Density 17
Land Area 692.8	Water Area 21.1
Civilian Labor 4,495	Jobless Rate...................5.4
Altitude (ft.)...........362-169	Retail Sales $44,956,894
Rainfall (in.) 46.9	Gross Sales........$97,908,337
Jan. min. 38	Reg. Voters 8,363
July max. 94	Election Turnout 43.4
Grow. Season (days).....260	Vehicles 10,879
Total Income (mil.) $133	Lane Miles 416
Per Capita Income...$10,770	Tax Value.........$575,243,983
Total Wages.......$27,353,460	Fed. Spending $39,702
Housing....................7,195	Defense Spending $1,097

Vital Statistics, 1989: Births, 146; Deaths, 142; Marriages, 103; Divorces, 55.

Ethnicity, 1990: White, 9,619 (84.0%); Black, 1,645 (14.4%); American Indian, 24 (0.2%); Asian, 21 (0.2%); Hispanic, 272 (2.4%); Other, 136 (1.2%).

Recreation: Livingston Lake activities; fishing, hiking, hunting; Davy Crockett National Forest; local events; historic sites.

Minerals: Limited oil, gas, lignite, sand and gravel.

Agriculture: Timber sales produce substantial

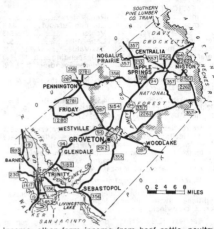

income; other farm income from beef cattle, poultry, hogs; crops include hay, vegetables, peaches, pecans.

Business: Forestry, tourism, cattle chief sources of income.

GROVETON (1,071) county seat; gateway to **Davy Crockett National Forest** recreation areas; lumber center; petroleum processing; nursing home; airport. Other town, **Trinity** (2,648), steel fabrication; hospital, nursing home; forest-industries center; near **Livingston Lake.**

Tyler County

LOCATION: Southeast (K-21).

Cong. Dist. 2	U.S. Jud. Dist. ....E-Bt.
St. Sen. Dist. 3	Ct. Appeals......................9
St. Rep. Dist. 18	Admin. Jud. Dist. 2
St. Dist. Cts.............88, 1-A	

History: Named for U.S. President John Tyler; county created, organized 1846 from Liberty.

Physical Features: Hilly, densely timbered; drains to Neches, Angelina rivers, other streams; B.A. Steinhagen Lake; Big Thicket is unique plant and animal area.

Population................16,646	Av. Weekly Wage $295.55
Area (sq. mi.).............935.7	Density 18
Land Area 922.9	Water Area 12.8
Civilian Labor 7,426	Jobless Rate...................6.0
Altitude (ft.)...........443-109	Retail Sales $70,914,652
Rainfall (in.) 52.0	Gross Sales.......$111,540,930

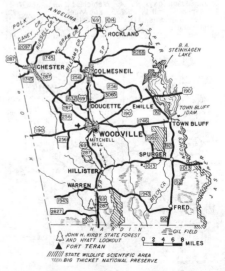

Tyler Co. (Cont.)

Jan. min.	38	Reg. Voters	10,585
July max.	94	Election Turnout	43.5
Grow. Season (days)	241	Vehicles	15,545
Total Income (mil.)	$234	Lane Miles	509
Per Capita Income	$13,074	Tax Value	$789,854,326
Total Wages	$52,728,780	Fed. Spending	$54,540
Housing	9,041	Defense Spending	$1,675

Vital Statistics, 1989: Births, 188; Deaths, 241; Marriages, 174; Divorces, 92.

Ethnicity, 1990: White, 14,550 (87.4%); Black, 1,994 (12.0%); American Indian, 46 (0.3%); Asian, 12 (0.1%); Hispanic, 177 (1.1%); Other, 44 (0.3%).

Recreation: Big Thicket National Preserve; guest ranch; Heritage Village; lake activities; Allan Shivers Museum; **John Henry Kirby State Forest;** historic sites, buildings; near **Alabama-Coushatta Indian Reservation;** dogwood festival in April; county fair, rodeo, western weekend in March, other local events.

Minerals: Production of oil, natural gas.

Agriculture: Timber sales major income source; additional farming income from cattle, hogs, poultry, horses; crops include fruit.

Business: Lumbering, poultry processing, some manufacturing; tourism; catfish production.

WOODVILLE (2,636) county seat; lumber, cattle-marketing center; varied manufacturing; tourist center; hospital, nursing homes. Other towns, **Chester** (285), **Colmesneil** (569).

Upshur County

LOCATION: Northeast (H-20).

Cong. Dist.	1	U.S. Jud. Dist.	E-MI.
St. Sen. Dist.	1	Ct. Appeals	6, 12
St. Rep. Dist.	5	Admin. Jud. Dist.	1
St. Dist. Cts.	115		

History: Created from Harrison, Nacogdoches counties 1846; organized same year; named for U.S. Secretary of State A.P. Upshur.

Physical Features: Rolling to hilly, over half forested; drains to Sabine, Cypress Creek, Lake O' the Pines, Lake Gladewater.

Population	31,370	Av. Weekly Wage	$273.60
Area (sq. mi.)	592.6	Density	53
Land Area	587.7	Water Area	4.9
Civilian Labor	18,964	Jobless Rate	4.9
Altitude (ft.)	685-228	Retail Sales	$120,264,105
Rainfall (in.)	45.1	Gross Sales	$231,954,125
Jan. min.	32	Reg. Voters	16,799
July max.	94	Election Turnout	47.7
Grow. Season (days)	245	Vehicles	27,362
Total Income (mil.)	$385	Lane Miles	738
Per Capita Income	$12,112	Tax Value	$1,013,247,337
Total Wages	$72,643,042	Fed. Spending	$77,082
Housing	12,873	Defense Spending	$2,511

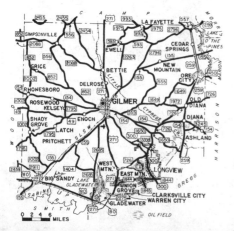

Vital Statistics, 1989: Births, 473; Deaths, 261; Marriages, 290; Divorces, 236.

Ethnicity, 1990: White, 27,076 (86.3%); Black, 3,881 (12.4%); American Indian, 121 (0.4%); Asian, 29 (0.1%); Hispanic, 641 (2.0%); Other, 263 (0.8%).

Recreation: Scenic trails; hunting, fishing; East Texas October "Yamboree," other local events.

Minerals: Production of oil, natural gas, sand and gravel.

Agriculture: Most from beef, dairy cattle, poultry; among leading broiler and dairy producing counties; vegetable crops, hay, peaches raised; timber a major product.

Business: Manufacturing, agribusinesses, petroleum products and lumber mill are leading economic factors; many residents work at nearby area plants.

GILMER (4,822) county seat; varied manufacturing; meat, timber, vegetable processing; **Ambassador College;** hospital, nursing homes. Other towns are **Big Sandy** (1,185), **Ambassador College; East Mountain** (762); **Gladewater** (2,280 in Upshur County, mostly in Gregg County); **Ore City** (898); **Union Grove** (271); **Warren City** (9 in Upshur County, partly in Gregg County).

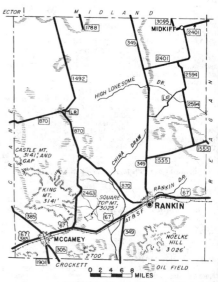

Upton County

LOCATION: West (K-8).

Cong. Dist.	21	U.S. Jud. Dist.	W:M-O
St. Sen. Dist.	25	Ct. Appeals	8
St. Rep. Dist.	69	Admin. Jud. Dist.	6
St. Dist. Cts.	83, 112		

History: Created in 1887 from Tom Green County; organized 1910; name honors brothers John and William Upton, Confederate colonels.

Physical Features: North flat, south rolling, hilly; limestone, sandy loam soils, drains to creeks.

Population	4,447	Av. Weekly Wage	$438.48
Area (sq. mi.)	1,241.8	Density	4
Land Area	1,241.7	Water Area	0.1
Civilian Labor	1,903	Jobless Rate	3.4
Altitude (ft.)	3,141-2,441	Retail Sales	$13,854,494
Rainfall (in.)	12.7	Gross Sales	$33,615,976
Jan. min.	31	Reg. Voters	2,380
July max.	96	Election Turnout	55.4
Grow. Season (days)	232	Vehicles	4,346
Total Income (mil.)	$60	Lane Miles	386
Per Capita Income	$11,956	Tax Value	$654,689,614
Total Wages	$31,078,053	Fed. Spending	$9,314
Housing	1,868	Defense Spending	$128

Vital Statistics, 1989: Births, 84; Deaths, 36; Marriages, 36; Divorces, 20.

Ethnicity, 1990: White, 3,487 (78.4%); Black, 94 (2.1%); American Indian, 20 (0.4%); Asian, 2 (**.*%); Hispanic, 1,666 (37.5%); Other, 844 (19.0%).

Recreation: Historic sites, **Mendoza Trail Museum;** scenic areas; chili cookoff, pecan show, other local events.

Minerals: Production of oil, natural gas.

Agriculture: Annual income divided among sheep, goats, cattle and cotton; also wheat, pecan prduction; some cotton, pecans irrigated.

Business: Petroleum production, ranching, tourism.

RANKIN (1,011) county seat, and **McCamey** (2,493) are both centers for oil and ranching; hospitals; nursing homes; annual pecan show.

Uvalde County

LOCATION: Southwest (Q-12).

Cong. Dist. 23	U.S. Jud. Dist. ....W-DR
St. Sen. Dist. 21	Ct. Appeals......................4
St. Rep. Dist. 67	Admin. Jud. Dist. 6
St. Dist. Cts.....................38	

History: Created from Bexar 1850; organized 1853; re-created, organized 1856; named for noted Indian fighter and governor of Coahuila, Juan de Ugalde, with name Anglicized.

Physical Features: Part on Edwards Plateau, most is rolling hills below escarpment; spring-fed Sabinal, Frio, Leona, Nueces rivers; cypress, cedar, other trees; unique maple groves.

Population................ 23,340	Av. Weekly Wage $252.94
Area (sq. mi.) 1,558.6	Density 15
Land Area 1,556.6	Water Area 2.0
Civilian Labor 13,774	Jobless Rate................ 10.1
Altitude (ft.).......... 1,957-699	Retail Sales $130,534,230
Rainfall (in.) 24.1	Gross Sales $272,957,510
Jan. min. 37	Reg. Voters 12,195
July max. 97	Election Turnout 44.0
Grow. Season (days)..... 255	Vehicles 18,037
Total Income (mil.) $279	Lane Miles 720
Per Capita Income...$11,486	Tax Value......... $882,343,168
Total Wages......$105,485,348	Fed. Spending $66,767
Housing....................9,685	Defense Spending $3,116

Vital Statistics, 1989: Births, 451; Deaths, 180; Marriages, 233; Divorces, 83.

Ethnicity, 1990: White, 15,078 (64.6%); Black, 47 (0.2%); American Indian, 49 (0.2%); Asian, 70 (0.3%); Hispanic, 14,104 (60.4%); Other, 8,096 (34.7%).

Recreation: Major deer, turkey hunting area; **Garner State Park;** water activities on scenic rivers; **John Nance Garner Museum;** Uvalde Memorial Park; scenic trails; historic sites; local events; recreational homes.

Minerals: Production asphalt, stone, sand and gravel.

Agriculture: Annual income from beef cattle, hogs, sheep, goats; crops include wheat, corn, oats, grain sorghums, cotton, vegetables; substantial number of acres irrigated.

Business: Agribusinesses; light manufacturing; tourism; hunting leases.

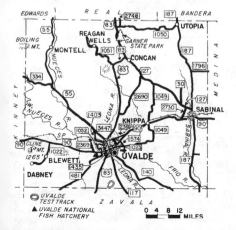

UVALDE (14,729) county seat; plants make variety of products; vegetable, wool, mohair processing; **Southwest Texas Junior College; Texas A&M Research and Extension Center;** hospital. Other town, **Sabinal** (1,584), farm, ranch center; gateway to Frio and Sabinal canyons; tourist, retirement area.

Val Verde County

LOCATION: Southwest (N-10).

Cong. Dist. 21	U.S. Jud. Dist. ....W-DR
St. Sen. Dist. 25	Ct. Appeals......................4
St. Rep. Dist. 68	Admin. Jud. Dist. 6
St. Dist. Cts.....................63	

History: Only county named for a Civil War battle; Val Verde means green valley; county created, organized 1885 from Crockett, Kinney, Pecos counties.

Physical Features: Rolling, hilly; brushy; Devils, Pecos rivers, Amistad Reservoir; limestone, alluvial soils.

Population................ 38,721	Av. Weekly Wage $281.96
Area (sq. mi.) 3,232.6	Density 12
Land Area 3,170.6	Water Area 62.0
Civilian Labor 13,435	Jobless Rate................ 12.6
Altitude (ft.)......... 2,248-925	Retail Sales $205,398,845
Rainfall (in.) 17.2	Gross Sales $277,451,494
Jan. min. 38	Reg. Voters 13,874
July max. 98	Election Turnout 47.1
Grow. Season (days)..... 300	Vehicles 28,550
Total Income (mil.) $391	Lane Miles 665
Per Capita Income.... $9,678	Tax Value......... $874,871,134
Total Wages......$117,853,667	Fed. Spending $185,507
Housing................... 13,776	Defense Spending ... $83,143

Vital Statistics, 1989: Births, 891; Deaths, 210; Mar-

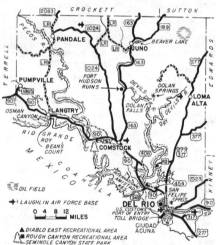

riages, 543; Divorces, 146.

Ethnicity, 1990: White, 26,694 (68.9%); Black, 757 (2.0%); American Indian, 126 (0.3%); Asian, 244 (0.6%); Hispanic, 27,299 (70.5%); Other, 10,900 (28.2%).

Recreation: Gateway to Mexico; deer hunting, fishing; **Amistad Reservoir** activities; **Seminole Canyon State Park;** Langtry restoration of **Judge Roy Bean's** saloon; San Felipe Springs.

Minerals: Production sand and gravel, gas, oil.

Agriculture: Most income from sheep, Angora goats, cattle.

Business: Agribusiness; tourism; area trade center; large military, other federal expenditures.

DEL RIO (30,705) county seat; center for tourism and trade with Mexico; varied manufacturing; hospital; nursing homes; **Laughlin Air Force Base** (2,556).

Van Zandt County

LOCATION: Northeast (H-18).

Cong. Dist. 4	U.S. Jud. Dist. .... E-Ty.
St. Sen. Dist. 2	Ct. Appeals................5, 12
St. Rep. Dist. 5	Admin. Jud. Dist. 1
St. Dist. Cts.................. 294	

History: Named for Republic of Texas leader Isaac Van Zandt; county created, organized from Henderson 1848.

Physical Features: In three soil belts; level to rolling; Sabine, Neches rivers; Lake Tawakoni; partly forested.

Population................37,944	Av. Weekly Wage $306.07
Area (sq. mi.).............859.5	Density 44
Land Area 848.8	Water Area 10.7
Civilian Labor 17,035	Jobless Rate..................5.5
Altitude (ft.)............573-421	Retail Sales $149,771,515
Rainfall (in.) 42.4	Gross Sales...... $202,082,128
Jan. min. 32	Reg. Voters 21,067
July max. 97	Election Turnout......... 48.2
Grow. Season (days)..... 250	Vehicles 39,884
Total Income (mil.) $521	Lane Miles 1,153
Per Capita Income...$12,942	Tax Value.... $1,474,199,919
Total Wages....... $96,463,375	Fed. Spending......... $93,949
Housing....................16,999	Defense Spending $3,054

Vital Statistics, 1989: Births, 455; Deaths, 504; Marriages, 299; Divorces, 233.

Ethnicity, 1990: White, 35,351 (93.2%); Black, 1,451 (3.8%); American Indian, 155 (0.4%); Asian, 47 (0.1%); Hispanic, 1,515 (4.0%); Other, 940 (2.5%).

Recreation: Lake activities; **Purtis Creek State Park;** historic sites; Canton "First Monday" trades day, county fair in July, Van oil festival in July, other local events.

Minerals: Production of oil, gas, salt, iron ore, clays.

Agriculture: Most annual income from cattle, hogs, dairy products; a leading county in beef cows and calves; a major hay and sweet potato producer, also nursery stock, vegetables, grains, cotton; limited irrigation.

Business: Economy based on oil, tourism, agribusinesses, light manufacturing; many commute to jobs in Dallas.

CANTON (2,949) county seat; popular "Trades Day" first Monday of each month plus weekend before; agribusiness center; health-care center, nursing homes.

Other towns are **Edgewood** (1,284), heritage square; **Edom** (300), fall art fair; **Fruitvale** (349); **Grand Saline** (2,630), salt plant, manufacturing, clinic, nursing home; salt palace; **Van** (1,854) oil center, clinic, nursing home; **Wills Point** (2,986), some manufacturing, livestock marketing, clinic, nursing home.

Victoria County

LOCATION: South (P-17).

Cong. Dist. 14	U.S. Jud. Dist. ....S-Va.
St. Sen. Dist. 18	Ct. Appeals..................... 13
St. Rep. Dist. 32	Admin. Jud. Dist. 4
St. Dist. Cts ... 24, 135, 267	

History: An original county, created 1836 from Mexican municipality named for President Guadalupe Victoria of Mexico.

Physical Features: Rolling, intersected by many streams; sandy loams, clays, alluvial soils.

Population................ 74,361   Av. Weekly Wage $374.46

Area (sq. mi.)..............888.7	Density 84
Land Area 882.5	Water Area 6.2
Civilian Labor 35,896	Jobless Rate..................5.0
Altitude (ft.)............205-38	Retail Sales $607,620,632
Rainfall (in.) 36.9	Gross Sales.... $1,431,186,615
Jan. min. 43	Reg. Voters 35,801
July max. 94	Election Turnout......... 50.2
Grow. Season (days)..... 290	Vehicles 67,610
Total Income (mil.) .. $1,164	Lane Miles 693
Per Capita Income...$15,749	Tax Value...... $3,046,915,154
Total Wages...... $546,382,569	Fed. Spending....... $165,680
Housing...................29,155	Defense Spending $5,427

Vital Statistics, 1989: Births, 1,332; Deaths, 586; Marriages, 706; Divorces, 402.

Ethnicity, 1990: White, 59,251 (79.7%); Black, 4,906 (6.6%); American Indian, 208 (0.3%); Asian, 257 (0.3%); Hispanic, 25,372 (34.1%); Other, 9,739 (13.1%).

Recreation: Fishing, hunting; saltwater activities; many historic homes, sites; recreational park; zoo; many local events.

Minerals: Production of oil, natural gas, sand and gravel.

Agriculture: Beef cattle provide most income, dairies important; crops include grain sorghums, cotton, corn, rice, soybeans; cotton acreage increasing; about 2,500 acres irrigated for corn and pasture.

Business: Income from oil, manufacturing, petrochemical plants, agribusinesses, tourism.

VICTORIA (55,076) county seat; tourism, agribusiness center; on barge canal; petrochemicals; foundry equipment; **Victoria College, University of Houston at Victoria;** community theater, symphony; hospitals. Other towns, **Bloomington** (1,888), **Inez** (1,371).

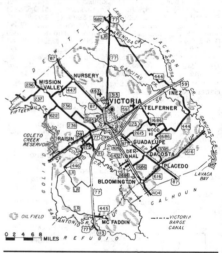

Walker County

LOCATION: Southeast (L-19).

Cong. Dist. 2	U.S. Jud. Dist. ....S-Hn.
St. Sen. Dist. 5	Ct. Appeals.................1, 14
St. Rep. Dist. 18	Admin. Jud. Dist. 2
St. Dist. Cts............. 12, 278	

History: Created, organized 1846 from Montgomery County; first named for U.S. Secretary of Treasury R.J. Walker; renamed 1863 for Texas Ranger Capt. S.H. Walker.

Physical Features: Rolling hills; more than 70 percent forested; Sam Houston National Forest; San Jacinto, Trinity rivers.

Population................50,917	Av. Weekly Wage $365.88
Area (sq. mi.)..............801.4	Density 65
Land Area 787.5	Water Area 13.9
Civilian Labor 21,480	Jobless Rate..................3.5
Altitude (ft.)............404-140	Retail Sales $265,143,063
Rainfall (in.) 44.2	Gross Sales....... $435,174,970
Jan. min. 38	Reg. Voters 18,492
July max. 95	Election Turnout......... 54.5

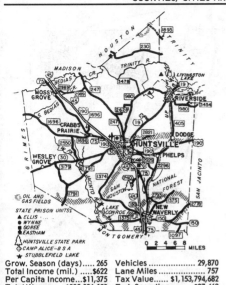

Grow. Season (days)..... 265
Total Income (mil.) $622
Per Capita Income...$11,375
Total Wages......$335,086,129
Housing.................... 18,311

Vehicles 29,870
Lane Miles 757
Tax Value...... $1,153,794,682
Fed. Spending......... $97,463
Defense Spending $6,869

Vital Statistics, 1989: Births, 570; Deaths, 322; Marriages, 473; Divorces, 262.

Ethnicity, 1990: White, 34,946 (68.6%); Black, 12,334 (24.2%); American Indian, 187 (0.4%); Asian, 323 (0.6%); Hispanic, 5,493 (10.8%); Other, 3,127 (6.1%).

Recreation: Fishing, hunting; **Lake Conroe and Livingston Lake** activities; **Sam Houston Museum,** homes, grave; prison museum, other historic sites; **Huntsville State Park; Sam Houston National Forest;** county fair in April.

Minerals: Clays, natural gas, oil, sand and gravel, stone.

Agriculture: Most income from cattle, horses; crops include hay, cotton, grain sorghums; minor irrigation; timber sales substantial.

Business: Economy based on state employment in prison system, education, agribusiness, lumbering, tourism.

HUNTSVILLE (27,925) county seat; Texas Department of Criminal Justice headquarters; **Sam Houston State University,** museum; varied manufacturing; oil, gas, lignite exploration; hospital. Other towns, **New Waverly** (936), **Riverside** (451).

Waller County

LOCATION: Southeast (M-18).

Cong. Dist. 14
St. Sen. Dist. 5
St. Rep. Dist. 13
St. Dist. Cts. 19, 155

U.S. Jud. Dist. ....S-Hn.
Ct. Appeals...................1, 14
Admin. Jud. Dist. 2

History: Named for Edwin Waller, Republic of Texas leader; county created, organized 1873 from Austin, Grimes counties.

Physical Features: Rolling prairie; drains to Brazos and San Jacinto rivers; alluvial soils; almost 20 percent forested.

Population................ 23,390
Area (sq. mi.) 518.4
Land Area 513.6
Civilian Labor 9,985
Altitude (ft.)............249-110
Rainfall (in.)............... 38.2
Jan. min. 38
July max.........................95
Grow. Season (days)..... 283
Total Income (mil.) $306
Per Capita Income...$13,051
Total Wages......$125,112,148
Housing....................8,764

Av. Weekly Wage $340.36
Density 46
Water Area 4.8
Jobless Rate...................5.0
Retail Sales $260,080,298
Gross Sales...... $368,087,886
Reg. Voters 12,976
Election Turnout........ 48.8
Vehicles 26,248
Lane Miles 535
Tax Value...... $1,406,163,017
Fed. Spending......... $62,069
Defense Spending $1,511

Vital Statistics, 1989: Births, 327; Deaths, 163; Marriages, 199; Divorces, 96.

Ethnicity, 1990: White, 12,987 (55.5%); Black, 8,796 (37.6%); American Indian, 28 (0.1%); Asian, 69 (0.3%); Hispanic, 2,592 (11.1%); Other, 1,510 (6.5%).

Recreation: Fishing, hunting; historic sites; historical museum, county fair in July, FFA shows in April and May.

Minerals: Oil, natural gas, sand and gravel.

Agriculture: Major income from beef cattle, hogs, goats; crops include rice, hay, corn; 10,000 acres irrigated for rice; some timber marketed.

Business: Economy based on oil, agribusiness, proximity to Houston, manufacturing; county part of Houston PMSA.

HEMPSTEAD (3,551) county seat; agribusiness center; varied manufacturing; hospital, clinic, nursing home; watermelon fest in July. Other towns, **Brookshire** (2,922), **Katy** (843 in Waller County, part in Harris, Fort Bend counties), **Pattison** (327), **Prairie View** (4,004), home of **Prairie View A&M University; Pine Island** (571), **Waller** (1,323 in Waller County, partly in Harris County).

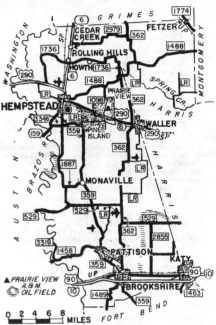

Ward County

LOCATION: Far west (J-6).

Cong. Dist. 16
St. Sen. Dist. 25
St. Rep. Dist. 69
St. Dist. Cts. 143

U.S. Jud. Dist. ....W-Pe.
Ct. Appeals....................... 8
Admin. Jud. Dist. 7

History: Named for Republic of Texas leader Thomas W. Ward; county created from Tom Green 1887; organized 1892.

Physical Features: Plain, sloping to Pecos River; sandy, loam soils.

Population................ 13,115
Area (sq. mi.) 835.7
Land Area 835.5
Civilian Labor 5,776
Altitude (ft.).......2,799-2,467
Rainfall (in.) 12.3
Jan. min. 29
July max.........................96
Grow. Season (days)..... 223
Total Income (mil.) $181
Per Capita Income...$13,684
Total Wages....... $88,917,593
Housing....................5,361

Av. Weekly Wage $414.13
Density 16
Water Area 0.2
Jobless Rate...................5.3
Retail Sales $63,320,740
Gross Sales...... $135,621,382
Reg. Voters 6,507
Election Turnout........ 57.7
Vehicles 12,387
Lane Miles 670
Tax Value...... $1,033,576,320
Fed. Spending......... $26,147
Defense Spending $338

Vital Statistics, 1989: Births, 227; Deaths, 116; Mar-

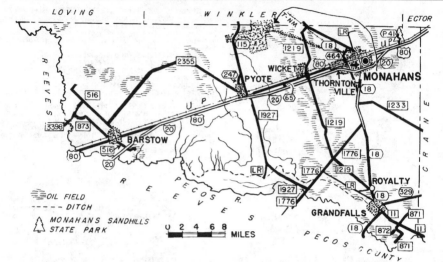

OIL FIELD

---- DITCH

MONAHANS SANDHILLS
STATE PARK

0 2 4 6 8
MILES

riages, 97; Divorces, 72.

Ethnicity, 1990: White, 9,905 (75.5%); Black, 457 (3.5%); American Indian, 75 (0.6%); Asian, 25 (0.2%); Hispanic, 4,830 (36.8%); Other, 2,653 (20.2%).

Recreation: Monahans Sandhills State Park, Museum; Pyote Rattlesnake Museum; Million Barrel Museum; county park; local events.

Minerals: Production of oil, gas, sand and gravel.

Agriculture: Income mostly from beef cattle; cotton, hay grown; some irrigation for cotton.

Business: Oil, gas, other minerals dominate economy.

MONAHANS (8,101) county seat; center for oil, agribusiness; gasoline plant; pecan shelling; county hospital, nursing home. Other towns, **Barstow** (535); **Grandfalls** (583); **Pyote** (348), **West Texas Children's Home; Thorntonville** (693); **Wickett** (560).

Washington County

LOCATION: Southeast (M-18).
Cong. Dist. .... 10　U.S. Jud. Dist. ....W-An.

St. Sen. Dist. .... 5　Ct. Appeals 1, 14
St. Rep. Dist. .... 13　Admin. Jud. Dist. 2
St. Dist. Cts. 21, 335

History: Named for George Washington; an original county; created 1836; organized 1837.

Physical Features: Rolling prairie of sandy loam, alluvial soils; Brazos River and tributaries.

Population 26,154	Av. Weekly Wage $334.46
Area (sq. mi.) 621.3	Density 43
Land Area 609.2	Water Area 12.1
Civilian Labor 12,909	Jobless Rate 3.0
Altitude (ft.) 460-343	Retail Sales $173,770,059
Rainfall (in.) 39.7	Gross Sales $602,662,360
Jan. min. 39	Reg. Voters 13,868
July max. 96	Election Turnout 60.9
Grow. Season (days) 277	Vehicles 24,529
Total Income (mil.) $457	Lane Miles 624
Per Capita Income ...$17,529	Tax Value $1,409,218,145
Total Wages $180,389,495	Fed. Spending $70,324
Housing 11,664	Defense Spending $2,623

Vital Statistics, 1989: Births, 361; Deaths, 290; Marriages, 197; Divorces, 102.

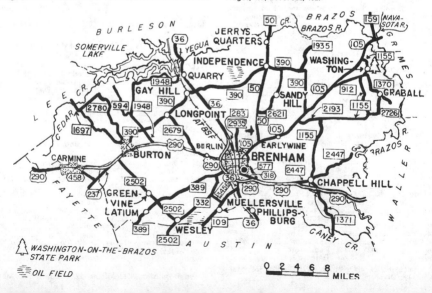

WASHINGTON-ON-THE-BRAZOS
STATE PARK

OIL FIELD

0 2 4 6 8
MILES

Washington Co. (Cont.)
Ethnicity, 1990: White, 19,782 (75.6%); Black, 5,463 (20.9%); American Indian, 46 (0.2%); Asian, 186 (0.7%); Hispanic, 1,158 (4.4%); Other, 677 (2.6%).
Recreation: Many historic sites; **Washington-on-the-Brazos State Park;** Texas Baptist Historical Museum; **Star of Republic Museum; Somerville Lake;** fishing, hunting; old homes; bluebonnet trails in spring, cotton-gin festival in April.
Minerals: Oil, natural gas and stone.
Agriculture: Most income from cattle, hogs, horses, dairy products, poultry; crops chiefly hay, cotton, horticultural plants.
Business: Agribusinesses, oil, tourism, manufacturing.
BRENHAM (11,952) county seat; cotton processing; varied manufacturing; **Blinn College, Brenham State School.** Other town, **Burton** (311), national landmark cotton gin, local activities.

Webb County

LOCATION: Southwest (R-13).
Cong. Dist. 23	U.S. Jud. Dist. ....S-La.
St. Sen. Dist. 21	Ct. Appeals..................... 4
St. Rep. Dist. 43	Admin. Jud. Dist. 4
St. Dist. Cts........ 49, 111, 341	

History: Named for Republic of Texas leader James Webb; created, organized 1848 from Nueces and Bexar counties.
Physical Features: Rolling, some hills; much brush; sandy, gray soils; alluvial along Rio Grande.

Population.............133,239	Av. Weekly Wage $293.94
Area (sq. mi.).........3,375.6	Density 40
Land Area 3,356.9	Water Area 18.7
Civilian Labor 53,159	Jobless Rate................ 10.8
Altitude (ft.)...........899-372	Retail Sales ... $1,494,265,174
Rainfall (in.) 20.1	Gross Sales... $2,629,969,590
Jan. min.........................45	Reg. Voters............. 47,221
July max. 99	Election Turnout 30.6
Grow. Season (days).....322	Vehicles 79,809
Total Income (mil.) ..$1,066	Lane Miles 885
Per Capita Income.... $8,043	Tax Value...... $3,956,555,217
Total Wages......$662,179,952	Fed. Spending $307,889
Housing...................37,053	Defense Spending ... $11,476

Vital Statistics, 1989: Births, 3,614; Deaths, 711; Marriages, 1,262; Divorces, 270.

Ethnicity, 1990: White, 93,657 (70.3%); Black, 156 (0.1%); American Indian, 201 (0.2%); Asian, 484 (0.4%); Hispanic, 125,069 (93.9%); Other, 38,741 (29.1%).

Recreation: Major tourist gateway to Mexico; hunting, fishing; **Casa Blanca Lake,** water recreation, golf; Border Olympics in March; Rio Grande art festival in April; **Washington's Birthday** celebration; historic sites; museum; **Fort McIntosh.**

Minerals: Production of natural gas, oil, stone, sand and gravel.

Agriculture: Among leading beef-cattle counties; stocker production growing; crops include vegetables, grain sorghums, cotton; about 4,500 acres irrigated.

Business: International trade, tourism, oil and gas operations; government center; manufacturing; agribusinesses; a major gateway for trade and tourism with Mexico.

LAREDO (122,899) county seat; founded in 1755 by Tomas Sanchez; varied manufacturing; meat packing; major rail, highway gateway to Mexico; **Laredo Junior College, Laredo State University;** mental health center; hospitals, nursing homes; many tourist facilities. Other town, **El Cenizo** (1,399).

Wharton County

LOCATION: Southeast (Q-18).
Cong. Dist. 14	U.S. Jud. Dist. ....S-Hn.
St. Sen. Dist. 5	Ct. Appeals..................... 13
St. Rep. Dist. 29	Admin. Jud. Dist. 2
St. Dist. Cts............. 23, 329	

History: Named for John A. and William H. Wharton, brothers active in the Texas Revolution; county created, organized 1846 from Jackson, Matagorda counties.
Physical Features: Prairie; bisected by Colorado River; alluvial, black, sandy loam soils.

Population...............39,955	Av. Weekly Wage $321.98
Area (sq. mi.).........1,094.5	Density 37
Land Area 1,090.2	Water Area 4.3
Civilian Labor 21,969	Jobless Rate...................4.3
Altitude (ft.).............148-71	Retail Sales $260,119,694
Rainfall (in.) 41.3	Gross Sales...... $551,757,013
Jan. min.........................44	Reg. Voters............. 18,816
July max. 93	Election Turnout......... 46.4
Grow. Season (days).....266	Vehicles 36,009
Total Income (mil.) $574	Lane Miles 919
Per Capita Income...$14,670	Tax Value...... $2,116,357,161
Total Wages......$225,072,437	Fed. Spending $115,491
Housing...................16,262	Defense Spending $2,721

Vital Statistics, 1989: Births, 666; Deaths, 393; Marriages, 308; Divorces, 165.
Ethnicity, 1990: White, 29,127 (72.9%); Black, 6,308 (15.8%); American Indian, 38 (0.1%); Asian, 131 (0.3%); Hispanic, 10,103 (25.3%); Other, 4,351 (10.9%).
Recreation: Hunting, fishing; big-game trophy, art and historical museums; historic sites; festivals.
Minerals: Production of oil, gas, sulphur.
Agriculture: Most income from crops; leading rice-producing county; other crops are sorghums, cotton, corn; cow-calf operations, poultry important; about 115,-000 acres irrigated, mostly rice and corn.
Business: Economy based on oil, sulphur, other minerals; agribusinesses, varied manufacturing.
WHARTON (9,011) county seat; mineral, produce processing; hospitals, clinics, nursing homes; **Wharton County Junior College.** Other towns, **El Campo** (10,511), aluminum processing, manufacturing, rice processing, storage; plastic, styrofoam processing; wholesale nursery; hospital, nursing home; local events; **East Bernard** (1,544), agribusiness, varied manufacturing; **Boling-Iago** (1,119).

Wheeler County

LOCATION: Eastern Panhandle (C-11).
Cong. Dist. 13	U.S. Jud. Dist. ....N-Am.
St. Sen. Dist. 31	Ct. Appeals..................... 7
St. Rep. Dist. 88	Admin. Jud. Dist. 9
St. Dist. Cts....................31	

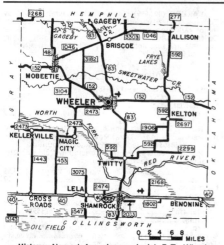

History: Named for pioneer jurist R.T. Wheeler; county created from Bexar, Young districts 1876; organized 1879.

Physical Features: Plain, on edge of Caprock; Red River, Sweetwater Creek; some canyons; red sandy loam, black clay soils.

Population...................5,879	Av. Weekly Wage $290.54
Area (sq. mi.).............915.3	Density 6
Land Area 914.2	Water Area 1.1
Civilian Labor 2,978	Jobless Rate.................3.9
Altitude (ft.).......2,869-2,127	Retail Sales $33,324,407
Rainfall (in.) 22.6	Gross Sales....... $62,267,395

Jan. min. 22	Reg. Voters...............3,962
July max. 96	Election Turnout.........52.4
Grow. Season (days).....208	Vehicles 6,368
Total Income (mil.) $101	Lane Miles 670
Per Capita Income...$16,605	Tax Value...$568,096,181
Total Wages.......$24,913,584	Fed. Spending........$25,966
Housing......................3,082	Defense Spending $233

Vital Statistics, 1989: Births, 65; Deaths, 100; Marriages, 98; Divorces, 29.

Ethnicity, 1990: White, 5,424 (92.3%); Black, 154 (2.6%); American Indian, 42 (0.7%); Asian, 23 (0.4%); Hispanic, 378 (6.4%); Other, 236 (4.0%).

Recreation: Shamrock St. Patrick's Day event, Octoberfest; Pioneer West museum at Shamrock; historic sites; Old Mobeetie, Fort Elliott.

Minerals: Production of oil, natural gas.

Agriculture: Most annual income from fed beef, cowcalf and stocker cattle; crops include wheat, grain sorghums, cotton.

Business: Oil, agribusiness, tourism important.

WHEELER (1,393) county seat; large feedlots; agribusiness; petroleum center; tourism; slaughter plant; hospital, nursing home. Other towns, Mobeetie (154), Shamrock (2,286).

Wichita County

LOCATION: North (E-14).

Cong. Dist. 13	U.S. Jud. Dist. ....N-WF
St. Sen. Dist. 30	Ct. Appeals.....................2
St. Rep. Dist. 80, 81	Admin. Jud. Dist. 8
St. Dist. Cts. 30, 78, 89	

History: Named for Indian tribe; county created from Young Territory 1858; organized 1882.

Physical Features: Prairie; Red, Wichita rivers; North Fork Buffalo Creek Reservoir, Lake Wichita; sandy, loam soils.

Population...............122,378	Av. Weekly Wage $355.50
Area (sq. mi.).............632.9	Density 202
Land Area 627.6	Water Area 5.3
Civilian Labor 55,057	Jobless Rate.................6.1

Wichita Co. (Cont.)

Altitude (ft.) 1,225-954	Retail Sales $875,634,499
Rainfall (in.) 26.7	Gross Sales.... $1,687,594,849
Jan. min. 28	Reg. Voters 57,662
July max. 99	Election Turnout 50.9
Grow. Season (days)..... 229	Vehicles 112,172
Total Income (mil.) .. $1,985	Lane Miles 1,067
Per Capita Income...$16,014	Tax Value...... $3,592,684,924
Total Wages......$883,021,619	Fed. Spending $548,726
Housing.................... 51,351	Defense Spending . $251,334

Vital Statistics, 1989: Births, 2,054; Deaths, 1,194; Marriages, 2,078; Divorces, 909.

Ethnicity, 1990: White, 102,427 (83.7%); Black, 11,221 (9.2%); American Indian, 903 (0.7%); Asian, 1,851 (1.5%); Hispanic, 10,555 (8.6%); Other, 5,976 (4.9%).

Recreation: Metropolitan events (ask chamber of commerce): museums; historic **Kell House,** historic tour; Oil Bowl football game in August; collegiate activities; water sports on several lakes; **Lake Arrowhead State Park.**

Minerals: Production of oil, natural gas, sand, gravel, stone.

Agriculture: Cow-calf production, stocker cattle important; cotton, wheat, top crops; 2,000 acres irrigated for cotton and coastal Bermuda pastures.

Business: Economy based on retail trade for large area, government, manufacturing, oil and agribusiness; vocational training center.

WICHITA FALLS (96,259 in Wichita County, partly in Archer, Clay counties) county seat; distribution center for large area in Texas, Oklahoma; varied manufacturing; oil-field services; hospitals; **Midwestern State University,** vocational-technical training center; **Sheppard Air Force Base; Wichita Falls State Hospital;** major bicycle race, local events.

Other cities, **Burkburnett** (10,145), some manufacturing, nursing home; **Electra** (3,113), agribusiness, oil center; library, hospital, nursing home; **Iowa Park** (6,072), some manufacturing, clinic, nursing home; **Pleasant Valley** (378).

Wilbarger County

LOCATION: North (E-13).

Cong. Dist. 13	U.S. Jud. Dist. .... N-WF
St. Sen. Dist. 30	Ct. Appeals.....................7
St. Rep. Dist. 80	Admin. Jud. Dist. 9
St. Dist. Cts...................46	

History: Named for pioneers Josiah and Mathias Wilbarger; created from Bexar District 1858; organized 1881.

Physical Features: Rolling, Red, Pease rivers, tributaries; sandy, loam, waxy soils; Santa Rosa Lake.

Population................ 15,121	Av. Weekly Wage $325.02
Area (sq. mi.) 978.1	Density 16
Land Area 971.1	Water Area 7.0
Civilian Labor 8,358	Jobless Rate.................. 4.3
Altitude (ft.) 1,361-1,099	Retail Sales $82,909,878
Rainfall (in.) 25.3	Gross Sales...... $258,401,786
Jan. min. 28	Reg. Voters 7,344
July max. 99	Election Turnout 45.7
Grow. Season (days)..... 221	Vehicles 14,308
Total Income (mil.) $219	Lane Miles 725
Per Capita Income...$14,357	Tax Value...... $962,534,097
Total Wages....... $94,898,554	Fed. Spending $51,157
Housing.....................6,815	Defense Spending $1,115

Vital Statistics, 1989: Births, 192; Deaths, 202; Marriages, 338; Divorces, 91.

Ethnicity, 1990: White, 12,010 (79.4%); Black, 1,349 (8.9%); American Indian, 80 (0.5%); Asian, 82 (0.5%); Hispanic, 2,185 (14.5%); Other, 1,600 (10.6%).

Recreation: Doan's Crossing, site of cattle drive; other historic sites; Red River Valley Museum; hunting, fishing; local events.

Minerals: Production of oil, natural gas.

Agriculture: Crops include cotton, wheat, alfalfa; cattle, hogs, horses raised; substantial irrigation.

Business: Agribusinesses and oil.

VERNON (12,001) county seat; agribusiness, oil center; varied manufacturing; electricity-generating plant; **Vernon Regional Junior College;** mental health center, hospital. **Lockett** (est. 200) is home of **Texas A&M Research and Extension Center.**

Willacy County

LOCATION: South (T-16).

Cong. Dist. 27	U.S. Jud. Dist. .... S-Br.
St. Sen. Dist. 20	Ct. Appeals.................... 13
St. Rep. Dist. 37	Admin. Jud. Dist. 5
St. Dist. Cts......103, 107, 138,	.... 197, 357

History: Named for Texas legislator John G. Willacy; county created, organized 1911 from Cameron, Hidalgo counties; reorganized 1921.

Physical Features: Flat, sloping to Laguna Madre; alluvial, sandy, marshy soils; Padre Island; La Sal Vieja, salt lake; Laguna Atascosa Wildlife Refuge.

Population................ 17,705	Av. Weekly Wage $246.22
Area (sq. mi.) 784.2	Density 30
Land Area 596.7	Water Area 187.5
Civilian Labor 7,133	Jobless Rate................. 15.2
Altitude (ft.) 55-7	Retail Sales $55,044,372
Rainfall (in.) 27.5	Gross Sales...... $94,439,085
Jan. min. 47	Reg. Voters 8,600
July max. 96	Election Turnout 44.1
Grow. Season (days)..... 331	Vehicles 11,521
Total Income (mil.) $136	Lane Miles 480
Per Capita Income... $7,199	Tax Value........ $586,709,149
Total Wages....... $46,642,127	Fed. Spending $53,897
Housing.....................6,057	Defense Spending $555

Vital Statistics, 1989: Births, 364; Deaths, 126; Marriages, 133; Divorces, 47.

Ethnicity, 1990: White, 13,820 (78.1%); Black, 79 (0.4%); American Indian, 29 (0.2%); Asian, 13 (0.1%); Hispanic, 14,937 (84.4%); Other, 3,764 (21.3%).

Recreation: Fresh and saltwater fishing, hunting; local events; mild climate attracts many winter tourists; Port Mansfield fishing tournament in July; stock show, rodeo in January.

Minerals: Production of oil, natural gas.

Agriculture: Most income from crops, chiefly cotton, sorghums, sugar cane, corn, vegetables; cattle, hogs, horses, Spanish goats raised; about 16,000 acres irrigated, mostly cotton, sugar cane, corn.

Business: Primarily oil, agribusinesses; tourism; shipping from Port Mansfield.

RAYMONDVILLE (8,880) county seat; agribusiness, oil center; some manufacturing; food processing, shipping; tourist center; hospital. Other towns, **Lyford** (1,674); **San Perlita** (512); **Port Mansfield** (est. 731) is popular fishing port; shrimp processing; **Sebastian** (1,598).

See map on next page.

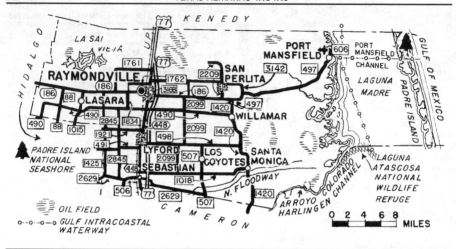

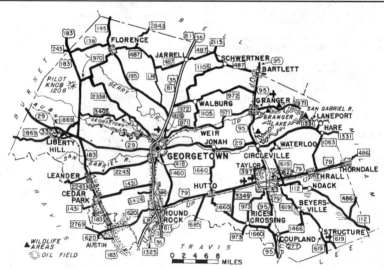

Williamson County

LOCATION: Central (L-16).

Cong. Dist. 11, 14	U.S. Jud. Dist. ....W-An.
St. Sen. Dist. 5, 18	Ct. Appeals...................... 3
St. Rep. Dist. 52	Admin. Jud. Dist. 3
St. Dist. Cts............. 26, 277	

History: Named for Robert M. Williamson, pioneer leader; county created from Milam, organized 1848.

Physical Features: Level to rolling; mostly Blackland soil, some loam, sand; drained by San Gabriel, tributaries.

Population...............139,551	Av. Weekly Wage $333.12
Area (sq. mi.).......... 1,136.4	Density 123
Land Area 1,124.3	Water Area 12.1
Civilian Labor 69,197	Jobless Rate 4.1
Altitude (ft.)......... 1,265-454	Retail Sales $697,879,688
Rainfall (in.) 34.2	Gross Sales.... $1,404,976,045
Jan. min. 35	Reg. Voters 61,001
July max. 97	Election Turnout 62.1
Grow. Season (days)..... 258	Vehicles 114,288
Total Income (mil.) .. $1,899	Lane Miles 1,372
Per Capita Income...$13,961	Tax Value...... $5,920,753,018
Total Wages......$490,283,624	Fed. Spending ... $235,381
Housing.................... 54,398	Defense Spending ... $21,448

Vital Statistics, 1989: Births, 2,388; Deaths, 749; Marriages, 1,085; Divorces, 682.

Ethnicity, 1990: White, 121,914 (87.4%); Black, 6,861 (4.9%); American Indian, 508 (0.4%); Asian, 1,846 (1.3%); Hispanic, 20,004 (14.3%); Other, 8,422 (6.0%).

Recreation: San Gabriel Park; water recreation on lakes; **Inner Space Cavern;** historic sites; hunting; **Dan Moody Museum** at Taylor; rattlesnake sacking in March, barbecue cookoff in August, frontier days in July.

Minerals: Building stone, oil, sand and gravel.

Agriculture: Grain sorghum, cotton, wheat, corn, oats raised; cow-calf operations, stocker cattle important.

Business: Agribusinesses, varied manufacturing, education are main economic factors; part of Austin MSA.

GEORGETOWN (14,842) county seat; agribusiness center; manufacturing; hospital, nursing homes; **Southwestern University; Inner Space Cavern.**

Taylor (11,472), agribusiness, publishing center; varied manufacturing; cottonseed, meat processing; hospital, nursing homes; Temple Junior College extension.

Round Rock (30,923 in Williamson County, partly in Travis County), varied manufacturing; hospital, nursing homes; **Texas Baptist Children's Home.** Other towns are

Anderson Mill (9,299 in Williamson County, partly in Travis County); Austin (2,444 in Williamson County, mostly in Travis County); Bartlett (818 in Williamson County, partly in Bell County), first rural electrification in nation in 1933; clinic, rest home; library; Brushy Creek (5,833); Cedar Park (5,161); Florence (829); Granger (1,190); Hutto (630); Jollyville (14,094 in Williamson County, partly in Travis County); Leander (3,398); Weir (220); Serenada (3,242); Thrall (550).

Wilson County

LOCATION: South (O-15).

Cong. Dist. 15	U.S. Jud. Dist. ....W-SAnt.
St. Sen. Dist. 21	Ct. Appeals......................4
St. Rep. Dist. 45	Admin. Jud. Dist. 4
St. Dist. Cts.............. 81, 218	

History: Created from Bexar, Karnes counties and organized 1860; named for James C. Wilson, member of the Mier Expedition.

Physical Features: Rolling plains; mostly sandy soils, some heavier; San Antonio River, Cibolo Creek.

Population................ 22,650	Av. Weekly Wage $280.22
Area (sq. mi.).............808.5	Density 28
Land Area 807.1	Water Area 1.4
Civilian Labor 9,330	Jobless Rate...................4.2
Altitude (ft.)............781-362	Retail Sales $67,274,147
Rainfall (in.) 29.4	Gross Sales....... $120,735,749
Jan. min. 38	Reg. Voters 13,345
July max. 97	Election Turnout......... 50.5
Grow. Season (days)..... 280	Vehicles 19,174
Total Income (mil.) $259	Lane Miles 703
Per Capita Income...$12,317	Tax Value......... $854,249,083
Total Wages.. $43,583,910	Fed. Spending.........$49,346
Housing.......................8,501	Defense Spending $2,945

Vital Statistics, 1989: Births, 333; Deaths, 151; Marriages, 183; Divorces, 79.

Ethnicity, 1990: White, 19,652 (86.8%); Black, 242

(1.1%); American Indian, 45 (0.2%); Asian, 22 (0.1%); Hispanic, 8,054 (35.6%); Other, 2,689 (11.9%).

Recreation: Stockdale watermelon festival in June; Floresville peanut festival in October; Wilson County Junior Livestock Show in January; arts, crafts in May.

Minerals: Production of oil, gas, clays.

Agriculture: Majority income from beef, dairy cat-

---

tle, hogs, poultry; crops include peanuts, sorghums, corn, small grains, vegetables, melons, sunflowers, fruit; some irrigation.

Business: Chiefly agribusinesses; some residents employed in San Antonio.

FLORESVILLE (5,247) county seat; agribusiness center; nursing home, hospital; shopping mall. Other towns, **La Vernia** (639), **Poth** (1,642); **Stockdale** (1,268), food processing; medical center, nursing home; recreation facilities.

Winkler County

LOCATION: West (J-7).

Cong. Dist. 16   U.S. Jud. Dist. .... W-Pe.
St. Sen. Dist. 25   Ct. Appeals................... 8
St. Rep. Dist. 69   Admin. Jud. Dist. 7
St. Dist. Cts. 109

History: Named for Confederate Col. C.M. Winkler; county created from Tom Green 1887; organized 1910.

Physical Features: Plains, partly sandy hills.

Population.................. 8,626	Av. Weekly Wage $374.05
Area (sq. mi.) 841.2	Density 10
Land Area 841.1	Water Area 0.1
Civilian Labor 3,765	Jobless Rate................. 5.2
Altitude (ft.) 3,193-2,671	Retail Sales $33,550,953
Rainfall (in.) 11.0	Gross Sales...... $106,328,261
Jan. min. 28	Reg. Voters 4,018
July max. 96	Election Turnout 51.3
Grow. Season (days) 219	Vehicles 8,278
Total Income (mil.) $102	Lane Miles 295
Per Capita Income... $12,621	Tax Value............ $739,816,960
Total Wages....... $46,953,951	Fed. Spending........ $17,705
Housing..................... 3,702	Defense Spending $268

Vital Statistics, 1989: Births, 140; Deaths, 79; Marriages, 68; Divorces, 33.

Ethnicity, 1990: White, 6,184 (71.7%); Black, 167 (1.9%); American Indian, 48 (0.6%); Asian, 9 (0.1%); Hispanic, 3,172 (36.8%); Other, 2,218 (25.7%).

Recreation: Monahans Sandhills State Park in nearby Ward County; museum; zoo; wooden oil derrick; local events.

Minerals: A leading petroleum-producing county; gas, salt also produced.

Agriculture: Income from cow-calf production, horses.

Business: Oil and natural gas economy, among leading petroleum-producing counties.

KERMIT (6,875) county seat, and **Wink** (1,189) are oil-activity centers; hospital, nursing home; part of **Monahans** in county.

Wise County

LOCATION: North (G-15).

Cong. Dist. 17   U.S. Jud. Dist. .... N-FW
St. Sen. Dist. 22   Ct. Appeals................... 2
St. Rep. Dist. 63   Admin. Jud. Dist. 8
St. Dist. Cts. 271

History: Created, organized 1856 from Cooke County;

named for Virginian, U.S. Sen. Henry A. Wise, who favored annexation of Texas.

Physical Features: Rolling, hilly; clay, loam, sandy soils; Lake Bridgeport; Eagle Mountain Lake.

Population................ 34,679	Av. Weekly Wage ... $373.56
Area (sq. mi.) 922.7	Density 38
Land Area 904.6	Water Area 18.1
Civilian Labor 14,179	Jobless Rate................. 4.7
Altitude (ft.) 1,180-693	Retail Sales $160,362,434
Rainfall (in.) 28.9	Gross Sales....... $330,379,626
Jan. min. 29	Reg. Voters 16,406
July max. 100	Election Turnout 53.1
Grow. Season (days)..... 220	Vehicles 37,913
Total Income (mil.) $447	Lane Miles 836
Per Capita Income...$12,491	Tax Value..... $1,767,832,089
Total Wages......$136,616,996	Fed. Spending......... $64,504
Housing................... 14,172	Defense Spending $3,478

Vital Statistics, 1989: Births, 484; Deaths, 284; Marriages, 302; Divorces, 220.

Ethnicity, 1990: White, 32,550 (93.9%); Black, 390 (1.1%); American Indian, 210 (0.6%); Asian, 83 (0.2%); Hispanic, 2,663 (7.7%); Other, 1,446 (4.2%).

Recreation: Lake Bridgeport activities; hunting; exotic deer preserve; historical sites; **Lyndon B. Johnson National Grasslands;** museum, little theater; Chisholm Trail Days in June; old courthouse; many local events.

Minerals: Production of natural gas, oil, stone, clays, sand, gravel.

Agriculture: Most revenue from dairy operations, beef cattle, horses, sheep, poultry; a leading dairy county; crops include sorghums, small grains, peanuts, vegetables, cantaloupes, watermelons, pecans; limited irrigation.

Business: Agribusinesses, petroleum, recreation leading economic factors; many residents work in Fort Worth.

DECATUR (4,252) county seat; petroleum center; dairying; cattle marketing; some manufacturing; hospital, nursing homes; youth fair in April, dairy festival in May, other local events.

Bridgeport (3,581), trade center for lake resort; oil, gas production; manufacturing; hospital, nursing homes. Other towns include **Alvord** (865), **Aurora** (623), **Boyd** (1,041), **Briar** (902 in Wise County, partly in Tarrant, Parker counties), **Chico** (800), **Fairview** (206), **Lake Bridgeport** (322), **Newark** (651), **Pecan Acres** (1,277 in Wise County, partly in Tarrant County), **Rhome** (605), **Runaway Bay** (700).

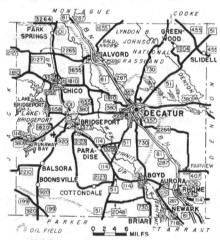

Wood County

LOCATION: Northeast (G-19).

Cong. Dist. 4   U.S. Jud. Dist. .... E-Ty.
St. Sen. Dist. 2   Ct. Appeals................ 6, 12
St. Rep. Dist. 3   Admin. Jud. Dist. 1
St. Dist. Cts. 114, 294

History: Created from Van Zandt County and organized 1850; named for Gov. George T. Wood.

Physical Features: Hilly, almost half forested; sandy to alluvial soils; drained by Sabine and tributaries; four county lakes; many private lakes.

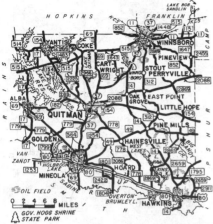

GOV. HOGG SHRINE STATE PARK

Population	29,380	Av. Weekly Wage	$297.60
Area (sq. mi.)	695.7	Density	43
Land Area	650.2	Water Area	45.5
Civilian Labor	12,751	Jobless Rate	5.7
Altitude (ft.)	630-299	Retail Sales	$153,093,693
Rainfall (in.)	45.0	Gross Sales	$283,167,795
Jan. min.	31	Reg. Voters	15,219
July max.	94	Election Turnout	53.6
Grow. Season (days)	246	Vehicles	31,365
Total Income (mil.)	$397	Lane Miles	890
Per Capita Income	$13,819	Tax Value	$1,652,520,527
Total Wages	$99,893,014	Fed. Spending	$93,584
Housing	14,519	Defense Spending	$5,082

Vital Statistics, 1989: Births, 349; Deaths, 389; Marriages, 292; Divorces, 175.

Ethnicity, 1990: White, 26,363 (89.7%); Black, 2,402 (8.2%); American Indian, 109 (0.4%); Asian, 40 (0.1%); Hispanic, 788 (2.7%); Other, 466 (1.6%).

Recreation: Activities at **Lake Fork Reservoir, Lake Bob Sandlin;** hunting; **Gov. Hogg Shrine State Park** and museum; historic sites; scenic drives; Mineola May Days in May, moonlight madness in October, dogwood fiesta in April, settlers reunion in August, other local events.

Minerals: A leading petroleum-producing county; natural gas, sand, gravel, clays also produced.

Agriculture: Most income from dairy, beef cattle, hogs, horses, broilers; truck crops, hay, corn, small grains; some Christmas trees, timber sold.

Business: Minerals, agribusinesses, tourism.

QUITMAN (1,684) county seat; tourism; food processing; some manufacturing; hospital; nursing homes.

Mineola (4,321), farm, railroad center; some manufacturing; nursing home; museum. Other towns include **Alba** (489 in Wood County, partly in Rains County); **Hawkins** (1,309); **Winnsboro** (2,233 in Wood County, partly in Franklin County); **Yantis** (210).

Yoakum County

LOCATION: Borders New Mexico (G-7).

Cong. Dist.	19	U.S. Jud. Dist.	N-Lb.
St. Sen. Dist.	28	Ct. Appeals.	8
St. Rep. Dist.	77	Admin. Jud. Dist.	9
St. Dist. Cts.	121		

History: Named for Henderson Yoakum, pioneer historian; created from Bexar District 1876; organized 1907.

Physical Features: Level to rolling; playas, draws; sandy, loam, chocolate soils.

Population	8,786	Av. Weekly Wage	$454.72
Area (sq. mi.)	799.7	Density	11
Land Area	799.7	Water Area	0.0
Civilian Labor	4,546	Jobless Rate	3.5
Altitude (ft.)	3,891-3,490	Retail Sales	$47,922,031
Rainfall (in.)	16.2	Gross Sales	$140,389,506
Jan. min.	23	Reg. Voters	3,650
July max.	92	Election Turnout	51.5
Grow. Season (days)	199	Vehicles	9,586
Total Income (mil.)	$129	Lane Miles	403
Per Capita Income	$13,982	Tax Value	$2,951,784,451
Total Wages	$82,025,150	Fed. Spending	$23,039
Housing	3,371	Defense Spending	$101

Vital Statistics, 1989: Births, 145; Deaths, 53; Marriages, 95; Divorces, 37.

Ethnicity, 1990: White, 6,300 (71.7%); Black, 86 (1.0%); American Indian, 31 (0.4%); Asian, 11 (0.1%); Hispanic, 3,217 (36.6%); Other, 2,358 (26.8%).

Recreation: Local events; **Tsa Mo Ga Museum** at Plains; settlers reunion in August.

Minerals: Production of oil, natural gas, salt makes this a leading minerals-producing county.

Agriculture: Most income from grains, cotton, sorghums, wheat, peanuts; beef cattle raised; substantial irrigation.

Business: Oil, agriculture dominate economy.

PLAINS (1,422) county seat; oil, agribusiness center; hospital planned. Other town, **Denver City** (5,145), center for oil, agriculture activities in two counties; hospital, library.

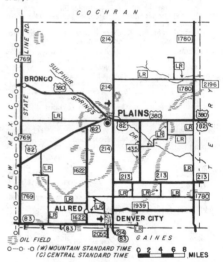

Young County

LOCATION: North (G-14).

Cong. Dist.	17	U.S. Jud. Dist.	N-WF
St. Sen. Dist.	30	Ct. Appeals.	2
St. Rep. Dist.	64	Admin. Jud. Dist.	8
St. Dist. Cts.	90		

History: Named for early Texan, Col. W.C. Young; county created, organized from Bosque, Fannin 1856; reorganized 1874.

Physical Features: Hilly, broken; drained by Brazos and tributaries; Possum Kingdom, Lake Graham.

Population	18,126	Av. Weekly Wage	$360.93
Area (sq. mi.)	930.8	Density	20
Land Area	922.3	Water Area	8.5
Civilian Labor	8,139	Jobless Rate	4.2
Altitude (ft.)	1,389-1,038	Retail Sales	$98,588,476
Rainfall (in.)	28.0	Gross Sales	$275,513,477
Jan. min.	28	Reg. Voters	9,939
July max.	97	Election Turnout	55.9
Grow. Season (days)	216	Vehicles	21,158
Total Income (mil.)	$309	Lane Miles	715
Per Capita Income	$17,324	Tax Value	$674,911,570
Total Wages	$115,689,726	Fed. Spending	$54,667
Housing	8,039	Defense Spending	$1,913

Vital Statistics, 1989: Births, 268; Deaths, 270; Marriages, 193; Divorces, 110.

Ethnicity, 1990: White, 17,023 (93.9%); Black, 268 (1.5%); American Indian, 62 (0.3%); Asian, 49 (0.3%); Hispanic, 1,164 (6.4%); Other, 724 (4.0%).

Recreation: Fishing, boating and water sports at **Possum Kingdom and Lake Graham; Fort Belknap** restoration; site of former large Indian reservation; marker at oak tree in Graham where ranchers formed forerunner of Texas and Southwestern Cattle Raisers Association; one-arm dove hunt at Olney.

Minerals: Production of oil, natural gas, sand and gravel.

Agriculture: Majority income from beef cattle, hogs, sheep, goats; wheat chief crop, also cotton, grain sorghums; hunting leases.

Business: Oil, agribusinesses, tourism.

GRAHAM (8,986) county seat; manufacturing; oil-well servicing; hospital, nursing homes, mental health clinic; Ranger Junior College extension. Other towns, **Olney** (3,519), agribusiness center; some manufacturing; hospital, nursing homes; art in the park in June; **Newcastle** (505).

Zapata County

LOCATION: South (S-13).

Cong. Dist. 15	U.S. Jud. Dist. .... S-La.
St. Sen. Dist. 21	Ct. Appeals...................... 4
St. Rep. Dist. 44	Admin. Jud. Dist. 4
St. Dist. Cts...................... 49	

History: Named for Col. Antonio Zapata, pioneer Mexican rancher; county created, organized 1858 from Starr, Webb counties.

Physical Features: Rolling; brushy; broken by tributaries of Rio Grande; Falcon Reservoir.

Population.................. 9,279	Av. Weekly Wage $263.35
Area (sq. mi.) 1,058.1	Density 9
Land Area 996.8	Water Area 61.3
Civilian Labor 3,213	Jobless Rate................ 10.5
Altitude (ft.) 562-327	Retail Sales $26,182,925
Rainfall (in.) 19.8	Gross Sales....... $34,237,762
Jan. min. 45	Reg. Voters 5,094
July max. 99	Election Turnout 33.3
Grow. Season (days)...... 304	Vehicles 6,339
Total Income (mil.) $65	Lane Miles 244
Per Capita Income.... $7,334	Tax Value... $1,145,788,400
Total Wages....... $19,774,684	Fed. Spending $23,702
Housing.................. $4,217	Defense Spending $618

Vital Statistics, 1989: Births, 198; Deaths, 84; Marriages, 87; Divorces, 3.

Ethnicity, 1990: White, 6,680 (72.0%); Black, 1 (**.*%); American Indian, 9 (0.1%); Asian, 8 (0.1%); Hispanic, 7,519 (81.0%); Other, 2,-581 (27.8%).

Recreation: Falcon Reservoir and State Park are tourist attractions; historic sites; winter tourist center.

Minerals: Production of natural gas, oil.

Agriculture: Most revenue from beef cattle; crops not significant.

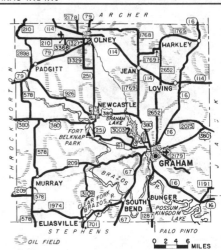

Business: Economy based on oil, ranching, **Falcon Reservoir** activities.

ZAPATA (7,119) county seat; tourist, agribusiness, oil center; retirement center; tourism, clinic.

Zavala County

LOCATION: Southwest (P-12).

Cong. Dist. 23	U.S. Jud. Dist. .... W-DR
St. Sen. Dist. 21	Ct. Appeals...................... 4
St. Rep. Dist. 44	Admin. Jud. Dist. 4
St. Dist. Cts................... 293	

History: Created from Maverick, Uvalde counties 1858; organized 1884; named for Texas Revolutionary leader Lorenzo de Zavala.

Physical Features: Level to rolling; much brush; Nueces, Leona, other streams.

Population............... 12,162	Av. Weekly Wage $248.31
Area (sq. mi.) 1,301.7	Density 9
Land Area 1,298.5	Water Area 3.2
Civilian Labor 5,425	Jobless Rate................ 17.1
Altitude (ft.) 956-540	Retail Sales $22,510,537
Rainfall (in.) 21.3	Gross Sales....... $143,053,100
Jan. min. 41	Reg. Voters 6,910
July max. 98	Election Turnout 35.8
Grow. Season (days)..... 280	Vehicles 5,760
Total Income (mil.) $81	Lane Miles 541
Per Capita Income.... $6,739	Tax Value......... $519,698,650
Total Wages.... $33,881,046	Fed. Spending $32,522
Housing.................. 4,178	Defense Spending $242

Vital Statistics, 1989: Births, 242; Deaths, 95; Marriages, 98; Divorces, 30.

Ethnicity, 1990: White, 6,443 (53.0%); Black, 296 (2.4%); American Indian, 16 (0.1%); Asian, 3 (**.*%); Hispanic, 10,875 (89.4%); Other, 5,404 (44.4%).

Recreation: Hunting, fishing; annual spinach festival; local events.

Minerals: Production of oil, natural gas.

Agriculture: Fed cattle top agricultural production; beef, goats, sheep important; top crops are cotton, vegetables, corn, pecans, wheat, grain sorghums; about 45,-000 acres irrigated for variety of crops; some firewood sold; hunting leases significant.

Business: Chiefly agribusinesses, leading county in **Winter Garden** truck area; oil, gas, hunting income.

CRYSTAL CITY (8,263) county seat; varied agribusinesses; headquarters for Crystal City railroad; food processing; oil-field services; cotton gin; hospital; spinach capital, **Home of Popeye**. Other towns, **Batesville** (1,313), **La Pryor** (1,343).

Courageous Texans

"Troops from other states have their reputations to gain, but sons of the Alamo have theirs to maintain."
— Jefferson Davis, U.S. Secretary of War

By Mike Kingston, editor of the Texas Almanac

Texans, in a land born in revolution and forced by circumstances to defend their land against foreign invasion and depredations by native people, have long honored their military leaders and soldiers.

Since the so-called Indian Wars of the 19th century, 65 Texans have earned the highest honor for valor bestowed by a appreciative nation: the Congressional Medal of Honor. Thirty-seven of the medals were awarded posthumously, after recipients sacrificed their own lives for their comrades and for the nation.

The Congressional Medal of Honor was instituted in 1862 to recognize the courage and valor of the men of the Union Army In the Civil War. (See the brief history of the medal on a succeeding page.)

To be nominated for the medal of honor, a study presented by the U.S. Senate Committee on Veterans' Affairs notes that the deed must be proved by uncontestable evidence of at least two eyewitnesses. ". . .(the deed) must be so outstanding that it clearly distinguishes his gallantry beyond the call of duty from lesser acts of bravery; it must involve the risk of life; and it must be the type of deed which, if he had not done it, would not subject him to any justified criticism." A recipient is eligible for a $200 a month stipend.

The Texans who received the highest military honor offered by an appreciative nation came from all walks of life. Many were humbled by the honor and others relished the well-deserved attention. Some like **Finnis McCleery of San Angelo**, who at 41 was the oldest Texan to receive the Congressional Medal of Honor, has never been comfortable around crowds and likes his anonymity. Others, like **Audie Murphy of Farmersville**, enjoyed the attention, and indeed, Murphy built an acting career around the notice he received as World War II's most decorated soldier.

The first Congressional Medals of Honor were awarded in 1863. The **first Texan to receive the honor was Sgt. John Ward** of the 24th U.S. Infantry Indian Scouts. While on patrol by the Pecos River on April 25, 1875, Sgt. Ward and three companions charged 25 hostiles. He received the medal a month later on May 25, 1875.

Private Adam Paine, also of the Indian Scouts, actually acted before Sgt. Ward, but received his medal later. Pvt. Paine "rendered invaluable service to Col. R. S. Mackenzie" during a battle in Canyon Blanco on a tributary of the Red River on Sept. 26, 1874. The medal was awarded on Oct. 13, 1875.

Present-day citations for the medal of honor give a fairly detailed account of the incidents in which the honoree performed heroically. In the 19th century, the citation were briefer. **Second Lt. Robert L. Howze's** citation noted only that the recipient was honored for "Bravery in Action" in an engagement at White River, South Dakota, on Jan. 1, 1891. And **John McLennon,** a musician with Company A, 7th U.S. Infantry, was cited for "Gallantry in Action" in an battle at Big Hole, Mont., on Aug. 9, 1877.

Between the Indian Wars and World War I, three other Texans received the nation's highest military honor. **Lt. George M. Shelton of Bellington** received the

award for heroism in the Philippine insurrection in 1900; **U.S. Navy Comdr. William Kelly Harrison of Waco** received a medal for action in the Mexican campaign of 1914; and **Navy Shipfitter First Class George H. Wheeler of San Antonio** received a medal for courageous action in Chile in 1909.

(Space limitations prohibit us from running descriptions of all the courageous actions that brought honor to fighting men from Texas. Following are condensed descriptions of the valorous exploits of a representative number of Congressional Medal of Honor recipients from Texas. A full list of recipients appears at the end of this article.)

World War I

Army Pvt. David B. Barkeley of Laredo: Swam the Meuse River near Pouilly, France, on Nov. 9, 1918, under heavy enemy fire on a reconnaissance mission. After gaining vital information, Barkeley re-entered the river to return to friendly lines, but he drowned after experiencing cramps.

Hospital Apprentice 1st Class, U.S. Navy, David E. Hayden of Florence: Under heavy enemy fire near Thiaucourt, France, on Sept. 15, 1918, Hayden rescued a wounded soldier, first giving medical treatment while under hostile fire and then helping the man back to friendly lines.

Army Pfc. Daniel R. Edwards of Moorville: Returning to duty after recuperation from serious wounds, Edwards crawled into a trench to engage the enemy. After killing four of the enemy, he took four prisoners and was seriously wounded again while returning them to American territory. His courageous actions became a tradition in the 3rd Machine Gun Battalion, and his comrades morale soare.

World War II

Army Air Corps Maj. Horace S. Carswell Jr. of Fort Worth: Maj. Carswell, for whom Carswell Air Force Base in Fort Worth was named, piloted a one-plane strike against a Japanese naval convoy in the South China Sea on Oct. 26, 1944. After making one surprise run on the convoy, he turned the plane around and made another, facing withering fire from the alerted Japanese war ships. Maj. Carswell's plane was badly damaged, losing two engines. Turning inland, the courageous pilot kept the craft in the air until a third engine failed. Maj. Carswell ordered his crew to evacuate the plane. He stayed aboard with a crewman whose parachute was damaged, and both were killed when the plane crashed into a mountain.

Army Lt. Col. Robert G. Cole of San Antonio: Lt. Col. Cole led a courageous bayonet charge on an entrenched German position, initially with only a pistol. Later he retrieved a rifle from a fallen comrade to continue to lead the assault.

Navy Comndr. Samuel David Dealey, Dallas: Commander Dealey distinguished himself as commander of the U.S.S. Harder on patrol of Japanese-controlled Pacific waters. During one two-day period, the Harder sank five vital Japanese destroyers. Two of the torpedo shots were of the "down-the-throat" variety, with the submarine directly facing the bow of the enemy ship. This remarkable record, the citation asserts, "attests to valiant fighting spirit of Comdr. Dealey and his indomitable command."

The Congressional Medal of Honor Shown: Army
Artist: Ben McConnell, The Dallas Morning News

Audie Murphy

Roy Benavidez

Army 1st Lt. James H. Fields, a native of Caddo: Led a charge on an entrenched enemy position, despite several wounds. When he was wounded in the face and lost the ability to speak, Lt. Fields continued to lead the attack using hand signals. When a light machine gun crew was immobilized, he took up the weapon, shooting from the hip and inspired his depleted platoon to continue fighting until the enemy position was taken.

Army 2nd Lt. Thomas Fowler of Wichita Falls: This tank commander took command of two disorganized infantry platoons and led an attack against a superior German force. He personally cleared paths through mine fields and led tanks and soldiers through the deadly ground.

Army Staff Sgt. Marcario Garcia of Sugar Land: Near Grosshau, Germany, on Nov. 27, 1944, (then Pvt.) Garcia's squad was pinned down by enemy machine gun fire and mortars in a country with meager cover. Throwing grenades as he went, Garcia made his way to the enemy emplacement, sustaining wounds in the process. He destroyed the gun and killed several enemy. When Garcia returned to his men, a second machine gun opened up, and the intrepid soldier attacked again, knocking out the weapon. Only after his squad had taken its objective did Garcia submit to medical attention.

Army 2nd Lt. James L. Harris of Hillsboro: Although mortally wounded, Lt. Harris directed a counterattack against a surprise thrust by Germans near Vagney, France, in October, 1944. The tank commander, armed only with a pistol, scouted ahead of his vehicle until he was hit by machine-gun fire. He crawled back to his tank, but could not enter it. So he directed fire from outside the vehicle. Caught in a battle between his own tank and an attacking German tank, Harris continued his leadership. Harris' leg was blown off, but he directed medics to attend to another soldier. When they returned, the valiant Harris was dead.

Army Sgt. Jose M. Lopez of Mission: Sgt. Lopez almost single-handedly repelled a German attack on Company K near Krinkelt, Belgium, on Dec. 17, 1944. He first carried a heavy machine gun to a position on the flank to hold Germans at bay. When the enemy charged another part of the American line, Lopez toted the weapon to a new position, firing until ammunition was exhausted. He is credited with killing 100 Germans, while gaining time for new forces to arrive to repel the attack.

Army 2nd Lt. Audie L. Murphy of Farmersville: The legendary Murphy was the most decorated American soldier in World War II. His citation for the medal of honor relates his single-handed repulsion of an attack by six German tanks and waves of infantry near Kaysersberg, France, on Dec. 16, 1944. He directed fire until the enemy almost overran him. Then Murphy jumped aboard a burning American tank, which could have exploded at any time, and used its .50 caliber machine gun against

the advancing infantry, killing dozens. With infantry support lagging, the German tanks retreated. After obtaining grenades and a rifle to launch them, he returned to a point position and directed artillery fire with the grenades. Using automatic weapons, he continued his assault on the German infantry. A grenade explosion inflicted eight wounds on this courageous soldier, who provided an inspiring example for the men of his command.

Army Tech Sgt. Cleto Rodriguez of San Marcos: On Feb. 9, 1945, (then Pvt.) Rodriguez and a comrade led an attack on a railroad station near Manila. They moved ahead of a stalled attack and fired at targets of opportunity for several hours. Then moving closer to the station, they caught numerous Japanese soldiers making their way to pill boxes and stopped the advance. Rodriguez made his way to the railroad building, attacking with five grenades that killed seven Japanese and destroyed a 20-mm. machine gun. Rodriquez' comrade was killed, but two days later, the Texan destroyed another 20-mm. gun, killing six more Japanese soldiers. These exploits materially aided the American advance in Manila.

Marine Staff Sgt. William James Bordelon of San Antonio: On Nov. 20, 1943, Sgt. Bordelon was part of the force that invaded Tarawa in the Gilbert Islands. Under withering enemy fire, Bordelon set demolition that knocked out two pill boxes and was wounded while attacking a third. Out of demolition, he returned to the beach, where he rescued several wounded men from the surf. Getting more demolition, he attacked a fourth pill box and was killed by enemy fire. His deeds helped secure a beachhead on the small atoll.

Marine Reserve 1st Lt. Jack Lummus of Ennis: After two days of continuous fighting on Iwo Jima, Lt. Lummus led his men on an assault on entrenched Japanese positions. Under withering hostile fire, Lummus personally knocked out two pill boxes, despite wounds from two nearby grenade explosions. He returned to his troops, inspired their advance and then attacked and destroyed a third pill box. Leading a mop-up action against fox holes and trenches, Lummus was fatally wounded when he stepped on a land mine.

Marine Pfc. Charles Howard Roan of Claude: During the attack on Peleliu, Palau Islands, on Sept. 18, 1944, Roan and his comrades were cut off from the main U.S. force and pinned down by a Japanese grenade attack from higher ground. Roan was wounded by one grenade blast near the depression in which he and four comrades had taken cover. When another grenade rolled into the depression, Roan unhesitatingly threw his body on the explosive, absorbing the full force of the blast with his body and saving his companions lives.

Korea

Air Force Maj. George Andrew Davis Jr. of Dublin: While on air patrol near the Sinuiju-Yulu River in Korea on Feb. 10, 1952, Maj. Davis without hesitation attacked a 12-plane formation of North Korean MIG-15s. He knocked out two of the enemy planes and was fighting a third when his plane was destroyed in a blast, killing the valiant pilot. Maj. Davis' heroic actions protected a low-level bomber attack.

Army Pfc. Jack G. Hanson of Galveston: On June 7, 1951, on a hillside near Pachi-dong, Korea, machine-gunner Hanson voluntarily stuck to his weapon when the position was attacked by an overwhelming enemy force. Several comrades were wounded and crawled to safety while Hanson continued his one-man defense of the hillside. When platoon reorganized and retook the position two a one-half hours later, Pfc. Hanson was found dead. But he had taken his toll. His machine gun ammunition was exhausted, and he was found with an empty pistol in one hand and a bloody machete in the other. Twenty-two dead enemy were strewn around his position.

Army Cpl. Benito Martinez of Fort Hancock: Cpl. Martinez fought a determined defense against an overwhelming hostile force near Satae-ri, Korea, on Sept. 6, 1952. Manning a machine gun, Martinez stayed at his forward listening post when his comrades withdrew. Several times he refused rescue attempts because it would have increased the danger to his companions. Finally, under relentless pressure from the enemy, Martinez retreated a short distance with only an automatic rifle and a pistol. For six hours before his death, Martinez fought a delaying action that allowed his unit to reorganize and regain the lost ground.

Marine 1st Lt. Frank N. Mitchell of Indian Springs: Near Hansan-ni, Korea, on Nov. 26, 1950, Lt. Mitchell led a rifle platoon that was attacked by the enemy. In the face of withering fire, Lt. Mitchell led an assault with a machine gun and was wounded. Injured, the officer reorganized his unit, and directed a brutal hand-to-hand battle against an enemy counterattack. After the battle, Lt. Mitchell sought volunters to retrieve the wounded. He covered the rescuers until the removal of the wounded was complete. Lt. Mitchell was killed by a burst of small arms fire.

Marine Pfc. Whitt L. Moreland of Austin: This young Marine volunteered to accompany a rifle company in its assault on a fortified hill position near Kwagch'i-Dong on May 29, 1951. When the initial objective was taken, Pfc. Moreland and others started for a fortified bunker 400 meters away. Near the bunker, the enemy began a grenade attack. Moreland kicked several of the grenades off the ridge, but he slipped and fell while attempting to kick another off. To protect his comrades, Moreland rolled over on the grenade and absorbed the full blast with his body, saving his companions.

Vietnam

Army Master Sgt. Roy P. Benavidez of El Campo: On May 2, 1968, near Loc Ninh, Vietnam, Benavidez volunteered to aid in the rescue of a 12-man Special Forces Reconnaissance Team that had come under heavy fire. Arriving by helicopter, Benavidez learned that all team members were dead or wounded and could not reach the pickup area. He ran 75 meters under heavy fire to reach the soldiers, suffering several wounds during his advance. After directing team fire to facilitate the landing of a chopper, he dragged half the dead and wounded to the craft. He provided protective fire to cover the others as they made their way to the helicopter, and then ran with the craft as it moved to a cache of secret papers that had to be retrieved. When a second 'copter arrived he helped other wounded to the craft. At one point while severely wounded, he fought hand-to-hand with an enemy soldier before killing him. Benavidez was credited with saving eight comrades, despite his numerous and painful wounds. He is the last Texan to have been honored with a Congressional Medal of Honor.

Army Ranger Spec. 4 Robert D. Law of Fort Worth: On Feb. 22, 1969, while on a long-range reconnaissance patro, Law helped defend against an enemy attack by covering his team's flank. When a grenade was thrown into the team's parameter, Law unhesitatingly threw himself on the explosive, absorbing the full impact of the blast and saving his comrades' lives at the cost of his own.

Army Spec. 5 Clarence E. Sasser of Chenango: During an air assault in Ding Tuong Province on Jan. 10, 1968, this medical corpsman repeatedly exposed himself to hostile fire from three sides of the landing area to treat wounded soldiers. After suffering two wounds, which incapacitated his legs, he crawled 100 meters to treat another wounded man. Then he led a group of wounded soldiers 200 meters to relative safety. Though seriously wounded himself, Sasser continued to provide medical care for injured comrades before evacuation five hours later.

Army Staff Sgt. Marvin R. Young of Alpine: While on a reconnaissance mission near Ben Cui on Aug. 21, 1968, Young's squad came under heavy fire by a superior enemy force. When the platoon leader was killed, Young assumed command and exposed himself to deadly fire while maneuvering and encouraging his soldiers. When withdrawal was ordered, he provide covering fire, despite suffering a serious head wound. The courageous soldier refused to accept assistance that would have slowed the withdrawal. Young elected to stay behind to cover the maneuver until an enemy force engulfed his position, and he was killed.

These and other accounts of the courage and selfless sacrifice of valiant Texans are sources of pride and appreciation for those of us who benefit from the freedoms many of the honorees died to defend.

FOR FURTHER READING: *The Congressional Medal of Honor: The Names, The Deeds;* Sharp & Dunnigan Publications, Forest Ranch, CA., 1984.

Medal of Honor Recipients, 1863-1978; U.S. Senate Committee on Veterans' Affairs, Washington, D.C., 1979.

The Medal of Honor

Nations have long honored military prowess and service to the state. The Jewish historian Josephus in the 1st century A.D. recorded the Greek practice of awarding a gold button for gallantry on the field. Romans crowned outstanding soldiers with oak or laurel wreaths.

The United States instituted its highest memorial, the Congressional Medal of Honor, at the beginning of the Civil War. Congress approved a medal of honor for enlisted men of the Navy and Marine Corps in December 1861; two months later, a similar award for members of the Army was approved.

After the turn of the century, Congress considered the problems of honoring persons whose acts of heroism were courageous and noteworthy, but not of the caliber to receive the medal of honor. A pyramid of awards was designed with the medal of honor at its pinnacle. Awards now are available to civilians, as well as military personnel. (See the order of precedence of military decorations at the end of this article.)

The first medals of honor were awarded to 19 Union soldiers who infiltrated the South in April 1862 to sabotage an important railroad link between Atlanta and Chattanooga. Disguised as civilians, the soldiers captured a locomotive 200 miles deep in the Confederacy and led Confederate officials on a 90-mile chase before being captured. In a few days, eight of the group were tried and executed. On March 25, 1863, six members of the party arrived in Washington after being paroled by the Confederacy. They were presented with the first medals of honor by Secretary of War Stanton. Medals subsequently given to the rest of the raiding party, in some cases posthumously, of course.

Through the early years, standards for giving the medal were loose. Some 1,537 medals of honor were awarded in the Civil War alone, many more than have been given in subsequent conflicts.

A total of 3,412 Congressional Medals of Honor have been awarded since the honor was instituted. Some 726 were given to foreign-born soldiers fighting for the United States. (Irish- born fighters received about one-third of these.) Eighteen recipients have received two medals of honor, and one man, John Henry Pruitt of Arizona, received medals of honor from both the Army and the Navy for the same act of bravery. He captured 40 Germans and knocked out two machine guns in France in 1918 to merit the recognition.

In 1917, 910 names were stricken from the rolls of recipients by a special Army Medal of Honor Board because it was deemed the individuals had not performed acts of sufficient merit to earn the award.

Angelo (Charles) Liteky renounced the Medal of Honor he received for service in Vietnam to protest U.S. policies in Nicaragua. It was the only time a recipient had renounced the medal.

Medal of Honor Recipients from Texas

*Posthumous
Name, Rank, Unit, Place of Entry, Conflict

Army-Air Force

ADAMS, Lucian, S/Sgt., 3d Inf. Div. (Port Arthur), WWII.
BARKELEY, David B., Pvt., 89th Div. (San Antonio), WWI.
BENAVIDEZ, Roy P., M/Sgt., Det. B-56, 5th Sp. Fr. Gp. (DeWitt County, Cuero), Viet.
*CARSWELL, Horace S., Jr., Maj., AC, 308th Bomb. Gp. (San Angelo), WWII.
*COLE, Robert G., Lt. Col., 101st Airborne Div. (San Antonio), WWII.
*DAVIS, George Andrew, Jr., Maj., USAF (Lubbock), WWI.
EDWARDS, Daniel R., Pfc., Co. C, 1st Div. (Bruceville), WWI.
EVERHART, Forrest E., T/Sgt., 90th Inf. Div. (Texas City) (b. Ohio), WWII.
FIELDS, James H., 1st Lt., 4th Armd. Div. (Houston), WWII.
*FOWLER, Thomas W., 2d Lt., 1st Armd. Div. (Wichita Falls), WWII.
GARCIA, Marcario, S/Sgt., 4th Inf. Div. (Sugar Land) (b. Mexico), WWII.
*HANSON, Jack G., Pfc., 7th Inf. Div. (Galveston) (b. Miss.), Kor.
*HARRIS, James L., 2d Lt., 756th Tank Bn. (Hillsboro), WWII.
HOWZE, Robert L., 2d Lt., 6th U.S. Cav. (Overton), Ind.
*HUGHES, Lloyd H., 2d Lt., A.C. (San Antonio) (b. La.), WWII.
KEARBY, Neel E., Col., A.C. (Dallas), WWII.
*KEATHLEY, George D., S/Sgt., 85th Inf. Div. (Lamesa), WWII.
*KIMBRO, Truman, T4g., 2d Inf. Div. (Houston), WWII.
*KNIGHT, Jack L., 1st Lt., 124th Cav. Reg. (Weatherford), WWII.
*KNIGHT, Raymond L., 1st Lt., A.C. (Houston), WWII.
*LAW, Robert .D, Spec. 4, 1st Inf. Div. (Fort Worth), Viet.
*LEE, Milton A., Pfc., 101st Airborne Div. (San Antonio) (b. La.), Viet.
*LEONARD, T. W., 1st Lt., 893d T.D. Bn. (Dallas), WWII.
LOGAN, James M., Sgt., 36th Inf. Div. (Luling), WWII.
LOPEZ, Jose M., Sgt., 2d Inf. Div. (Brownsville), WWII.
*MARTINEZ, Benito, Cpl., 25th Inf. Div. (Fort Hancock), Kor.
*MATHIS, Jack W., 1st Lt., A.C. (San Angelo), WWII.
McCLEERY, Finnis D., P/Sgt., 6th U.S. Inf. (San Angelo), Viet.
McLENNON, John, Musician, 7th U.S. Inf., Ind.
McNERNEY, David H., 1st Sgt., 4th Inf. Div. (Fort Bliss) (b. Mass.), Viet.
MORGAN, John C., 2d Lt., A.C. (Entered service: London, England), WWII.
MURPHY, Audie L., 1st Lt., 3d Inf. Div. (Hunt County, near Kingston), WWII.
PAINE, Adam, Indian Scouts, U.S. Army (Fort Duncan) (b. Fla.), Ind.
*PENDLETON, Charles F., Cpl., 3d Inf. Div. (Fort Worth) (b. Tenn.), Kor.
*ROBINSON, James E., Jr., 1st Lt., 63d Inf. Div. (Waco) (b. Ohio), WWII.
RODRIGUEZ, Cleto, T/Sgt., 37th Inf. Div. (San Antonio), WWII.
SASSER, Clarence Eugene, Spec. 5, 9th Inf. Div. (Rosharon), WWII, Viet.
SHELTON, George M., Pvt., 23d U.S. Inf. (Bellington), Phi. Ins.
*STEINDAM, Russell A., 1st Lt., 25th Inf. Div. (Austin), Viet.
STONE, James L., 1st Lt., 1st Cav. Div. (Houston) (b. Ark.), Kor.
*WALLACE, Herman C., Pfc., 76th Inf. Div. (Lubbock) (b. Okla.), WWII.
WARD, John, Sgt., 24th U.S. Inf., Indian Scouts (Fort Duncan) (b. Ark.), Ind.
*WATKINS, Travis E., M/Sgt., 2d Inf. Div. (Overton) (b. Ark.), Kor.
WHITELEY, Eli, 1st Lt., 3d Inf. Div. (Georgetown), WWII.
*YOUNG, Marvin R., S/Sgt., 25th Inf. Div. (Odessa), Viet.

Navy-Marine Corps

*ANDERSON, Richard Allen, L/Cpl., 1st Mar. Div. (Edinburg) (b. D.C.), Viet.
*BORDELON, William James, S/Sgt., USMC (San Antonio), WWII.
BULKELEY, John Duncan, Lt. Comdr., USN (b. N.Y.), WWII.
*CREEK, THomas E., L/Cpl., 3rd Mar. Div. USMC (Amarillo) (b. Mo.), Viet.
*DEALEY, Samuel David, Comdr., USN, (Dallas) WWII.
*GONZALEZ, Alfredo, Sgt., 1st Mar. Div., USMC (Edinburg), Viet.
*GUILLEN, Ambrosio, S/Sgt., 1st Mar. Div. USMC (b. Colo.), Kor.
HARRELL, William George, Sgt., USMC (Rio Grande City), WWII.
HARRISON, William Kelly, Comdr., USN (Waco), Mex.
*HAWKINS, William Dean, 1st Lt., USMC (El Paso) (b. Kans.), WWII.
HAYDEN, David E., HA1c., USN (Florence), WWI.
*HUTCHINS, Johnnie David, Sfc., USNR (Weimer), WWII.
*KILMER, John E., Hospital Corpsman, USN (b. Ill.), Kor.
*LUMMUS, Jack, 1st Lt., USMCR (Ennis), WWII.
*MITCHELL, Frank N., 1st Lt., 1st Marine Div., USMC (Roaring Springs), Kor.
*MORELAND, Whitt L., Pfc., 1st Marine Div., USMCR (Austin), Kor.
O'BRIEN, George H., Jr., 2d Lt., 1st Marine Div., USMCR (Big Spring), Kor.
*ROAN, Charles Howard, Pfc., USMCR (Claude), WWII.
WHEELER, George H., SF1c., USN (San Antonio), Int. 1900-10.
*WILSON, Alfred M., Pfc., 3rd Mar. Div., USMC (Abilene) (b. Ill.), Viet.

Recipient born in Texas unless noted otherwise.

Conflicts: Indian Wars, Ind.; Interim 1900-10, Int. 1900-10; Mexican Campaign, 1914, Mex.; Philippine Insurrection, 1899, Phi. Ins.; World War I, WWI; World War II, WWII; Korea, Kor.; Vietnam, Viet.

Summary of Congressional Medals for Texans

Conflict	Medals
Indian Wars	4
Interim, 1901-1910	1
Mexican Campaign, 1914	1
Philippines Campaign, 1990	1
World War I	3
World War II	32
Korea	11
Vietnam	12
Total	65

The following information is based on 28 recipients for whom dates of birth are available.

Oldest Recipient: Finnis McCleery, Vietnam, 41 years, 2 months, 19 days.
Youngest Recipient: Thomas E. Creek, Vietnam, 18 years, 10 months, 14 days
Average Age of Recipient, 25 years, 1 month, 16 days.

Precedence of Military Honors

Cross: Given to all ranks for exceptional heroism in combat.
Shown: Navy

Distinguished Service Medal: Given to high-ranking officers for exceptional meritorious service.
Shown: Air Force

Silver Star: Given to all ranks for gallantry in action.

Purple Heart: Given to all ranks for wounds or death in combat.

Source: World Book Encyclopedia, 1988. Artist: Carol Zuber-Mallison, The Dallas Morning News.

The order of precedence of military decorations and the year in which it was instituted is as follows:

U.S. Army and Air Force
1. Medal of Honor (1862)
2. Distinguished Service Cross (1918)/Air Force Cross (1960)
3. Defense Distinguished Service Medal (1970)
4. Distinguished Service Medal (1918)
5. Silver Star (1918)
6. Defense Superior Service Medal (1976)
7. Legion of Merit (1942)
8. Distinguished Flying Cross (1926)
9. Soldier's Medal (1926)/Airman's Medal (1960)
10. Bronze Star (1942)
11. Meritorious Service Medal (1969)
12. Air Medal (1942)
13. Joint Service Commendation Medal (1963)
14. Army Commendation Medal (formerly Commendation Ribbon)(1945)/Air Force Commendation Medal (1958)
15. Purple Heart (1782)

U.S. Navy and Marine Corps
1. Medal of Honor (1862)
2. Navy Cross (1919)
3. Defense Distinguished Service Medal (1970
4. Distinguished Service Medal (1918)
5. Silver Star (1918)
6. Defense Superior Service Medal (1976)
7. Legion of Merit (1942)
8. Navy and Marine Corps Medal (1942)
9. Bronze Star (1942)
10. Meritorious Service Medal (1969)
11. Air Medal (1942)
12. Joint Service Commendation Medal (1967)
13. Navy Commendation Medal (formerly Navy Commendation Ribbon)(1944)
14. Purple Heart (1782)

Medals for Civilians
1. Medal for Merit (1942)
2. Presidential Medal of Freedom (1963) (Supersedes Medal of Freedom)
3. Certain military medals may also be awarded to civilians under specificized conditions.

The Bombing of North Texas

This article was prepared by Mike Kingston, editor of the Texas Almanac.

In the spring of 1945, the war in Europe was nearing an end, and attention was turning to finishing the job against the Japanese in the Pacific. In either case, however, both conflicts were thousands of miles away from the rural Texas communities of Woodson in Throckmorton County and Desdemona in Eastland County.

History Highlights

While both communities sent people to the armed forces, the daily dangers of wartime were hardly a consideration. No bombs fell near them nor were shots fired by enemy soldiers. Both communities were in farming and ranching country, and only a quarter century earlier, Desdemona had been one of Texas' first oil boom towns.

On March 23 and 24 of 1945, Woodson and Desdemona were "bombed" by the Japanese, though no damage was done in either community. On March 23, C.M. "Pug" Guthery, just shy of his 15th birthday, was getting off the afternoon school bus that had taken him home. In the southeastern sky, he saw what looked like a basketball drifting quickly to earth.

With youthful enthusiasm, Guthery began chasing the object on foot, running almost two miles before the balloon finally fluttered to the ground. By the time he reached the object, the school bus also had arrived and several children already were off the bus and examining the contraption.

Guthery, now a grandfather, didn't follow the lead of the other children. "The thing smelled bad," he recalls, "something like creosote. So I didn't fool with it."

The other youngsters, however, busily gathered souvenirs. Some cut lengths of the quarter-inch grass rope that encircled the balloon, and others took pieces of the balloon itself.

"It looked like leather," Guthery recalls. "Whatever it was, it was a tough material."

Most of the 6,000 balloons the Japanese released were made of paper gathered by school students, probably no older than Guthery. The odor undoubtedly was from a weatherproofing treatment of some type.

The balloon was gray, and the only marking on it was a large fading rising sun on its top.

Government officials arrived the next day to pick up the balloon, and they came to the school to ask all the students to return the souvenirs they had taken from the balloon. "The pieces were needed to reconstruct it," Guthery said.

After that no more was heard of the balloon, and it didn't last as a topic of conversation for more than a couple of days.

Sixty miles to the northwest, a similar scenario was acted out the following day. Ivan Miller, a cowboy on the Barney Davis ranch eight miles north of Woodson in southeast Throckmorton County, was checking cattle near his home about 8:30 on the morning of March 24 when he came upon a collapsed balloon.

His widow, Florence Miller, recalls that Ivan described the balloon "as big around as a house." The balloon also had a large rising sun painted on its top, and several smaller versions of the sun were located around the bottom.

Mrs. Miller said her husband started to raise the balloon to see if any people or calves were trapped under it, but he decided to leave it alone.

The postmaster was notified soon after the discovery, and in the early afternoon, government officials arrived to take charge of the situation. As at Desdemona, school children showed great interest. Several visited the site and took souvenirs from the balloon. Government officials asked them to return the pieces of rope and balloon.

Just when the balloon landed is unknown. But Mrs. Miller says it could not have been in the pasture for more than a day or two because her husband regularly checked cattle in the area.

The Japanese launched the first of the balloons in November of 1944. It is thought the bombardment was made in retaliation of Jimmy Doolittle's raid on Tokyo in 1942. Manufacture of the balloons was a national project. School children donated the paper used in construction of the balloons themselves.

Each balloon was equipped with an incendiary bomb that was to be released by an automatic mechanism operated through barometric pressure. No reports were made of any of the bombs causing fires, and the five deaths in southern Oregon resulting from one bomb explosion were caused by children playing with the device after it landed.

American officials blacked out news of the balloon bombardment in the belief that if the Japanese thought the effort unsuccessful they would stop releasing the balloons. The strategy apparently worked because the Japanese stopped releasing the balloons in April 1945, although some balloons were found in Canada as late as July.

Nevertheless, the balloon bombs brought some West Texans closer to the war in the Pacific than was comfortable during this brief period before the end of the conflict.

Prisoner-of-War Camps

During World War II, Texas played host to some reluctant guests. Twenty-one prisoner base camps and more than 20 branch camps were located in the Lone Star State, housing approximately 45,000 German, Italian and Japanese prisoners from 1942 to 1945. Several of these were in Central Texas. Some were established at existing army camps, while others were built especially to house prisoners.

Camp Hearne was one of those built as a prison camp. When the business leaders of Hearne learned that a camp was to be located somewhere in the Brazos bottomlands, they actively campaigned for the camp to be built nearby.

When the first prisoners arrived at Camp Hearne, curious citizens crowded the roadways to get a glimpse of the Germans. Many of Hearne's POWs were members of the elite Afrika Korps. Later in the war, Camp Hearne also housed 323 Japanese soldiers. Camp Hearne was responsible for distribution of mail to all prisoners across the United States.

Camp Swift, already an army camp seven miles north of Bastrop, was a temporary home to 3,865 Germans before the war ended.

The Germans were model prisoners: Accustomed to strict discipline, they obeyed orders instantly, and they were hard workers. They were also inventive. When officials cut off sales of beer to POWs because of public complaints, the Germans hoarded their sugar rations and made their own home brew with fermented fruit and vegetable peelings.

Amusements were mostly homemade. Some Central Texans were introduced to the game of soccer by watching the prisoners at Camp Hearne play on an improvised soccer field. Other Camp Hearne prisoners constructed detailed concrete replicas — waist-high — of old German castles. Those incarcerated at Camp Swift had their own band and chorus.

Some of the prisoners attended classes arranged through nearby universities: Those at Camp Brady could take courses at the University of Texas; Fort Sam Houston's prisoners could do college work at St. Mary's University.

Some prisoners were assigned to help Texas farmers, who were short-handed because so many able-bodied Texans were in military service. Farmers applied for prisoners, in groups of not less than 15, through their county agents. They agreed to pay the minimum wage, about $1.50 a day, and to supply food, transportation and tools. German prisoners picked Central Texas peaches, baled hay, gathered pecans and chopped cotton. Many had grown up on farms and the work was familiar. As one said philosophically, "Hitler said we would be in America in 1945; and here we are — chopping cotton."

Because of their discipline, the Germans rarely tried to escape, but there were at least two attempts made at Camp Hearne. One prisoner was found in civilian clothes marching along the highway between Hearne and Franklin loudly singing German army marching songs. On another occasion, six prisoners fashioned a boat out of waterproof ponchos using umbrellas for sails. They intended to find the coast, then proceed to the Guadalupe River and work their way upstream to what they thought would be the sanctuary of the German communities in Central Texas.

The industrious prisoners published camp newspapers in German — nine separate weeklies statewide. In the Central Texas region, *Spiegel* was published at Camp Hearne, and *Neuland* was produced at Camp Hood.

The prisoner-of-war camps were deactivated beginning in November 1945, and the prisoners were sent home. Some alumni of the camps have held reunions, and some former prisoners and their families on U.S. vacations stop by their old camps for a look.

Transportation

Texans Move by Land, Sea, Air

Texas is a leader among the states in a number of transportation indicators, including total road and street mileage, total railroad mileage and total number of airports. **Texas ranks second** behind California in motor vehicle registrations and in number of general aviation aircraft.

The Texas transportation system includes **223,450 miles of municipal and rural highways, 13,707 miles of railroad line,** approximately **1,600 landing facilities** and **13 major Gulf Coast ports.** Texans own and operate almost **15 million motor vehicles** and about **21,000 aircraft.**

The transportation industry is a major employer in Texas. Statistics compiled by the Texas Employment Commission indicate that over 300,000 Texans are **employed** in the transportation industry. The largest group — 108,637 — is employed in trucking and warehousing. Railroads employ 11,400, air transportation 77,492 and water transportation 16,030.

The largest state government agency involved in transportation is the **Texas State Department of Highways and Public Transportation.** The **Railroad Commission of Texas** has intrastate authority over railroad safety, truck lines, buses and pipelines. Another state agency with a major role in transportation is the **Texas Department of Aviation.**

Texas Highways

Texas has the largest road network in the nation. There are more than 300,000 miles of roadways in the state, of which 76,564, including access roads on interstate highways as separate routes for the first time, are maintained by the Texas Department of Highways and Public Transportation. The state-maintained system, however, includes practically all the freeways and other high traffic-carrying highways. With less than three-tenths of the total center-line miles, the state-maintained system carries almost three-fourths of all the miles driven in Texas. (The total lane-miles in the state system is 181,665 in which one lane of highway one mile long is considered one lane mile.)

Highway Statistics, Fiscal 1990

Source: Texas Department of Highways and Public Transportation

County	Vehicles Registered	Miles Driven Per Day	Lane Miles of Highway	Maintenance Expenditure	Construction Expenditure	Vehicles Reg. Fees	County Net Receipts	State Net Receipts
Anderson	36,170	909,397	931	$3,723,535	$2,244,227	$1,951,954	$596,212	$1,355,742
Andrews	13,749	358,824	540	1,108,236	945,025	782,727	320,444	462,283
Angelina	63,635	1,490,943	904	3,676,579	8,507,687	3,723,618	785,838	2,937,780
Aransas	13,306	311,600	161	625,083	174,411	686,024	347,371	338,653
Archer	8,641	326,379	524	1,248,452	1,199,199	431,458	326,978	104,480
Armstrong	2,635	228,844	372	783,052	9,428	139,177	137,712	1,465
Atascosa	21,875	854,000	1,007	3,060,866	1,605,504	1,157,039	498,308	658,731
Austin	20,227	793,705	607	1,955,695	227,031	1,188,064	488,607	699,457
Bailey	6,830	169,272	473	1,341,068	98,056	383,713	329,244	54,469
Bandera	10,071	193,130	393	775,558	436,622	531,218	425,482	105,736
Bastrop	32,771	970,774	776	2,186,764	1,668,208	1,762,533	667,130	1,095,403
Baylor	5,473	169,750	434	1,943,802	155,109	278,287	236,316	41,971
Bee	18,331	499,011	639	1,892,514	430,661	1,064,863	533,624	531,239
Bell	156,544	3,221,435	1,373	4,078,665	8,201,467	8,403,227	1,433,901	6,969,326
Bexar	867,358	14,368,551	2,876	15,229,084	121,561,555	50,927,411	8,777,965	42,149,446
Blanco	6,728	279,548	451	1,093,388	87,195	369,268	272,383	96,885
Borden	1,066	51,423	344	773,276	26,439	47,384	46,958	426
Bosque	15,077	373,629	695	2,361,153	1,202,807	797,660	456,296	341,364
Bowie	76,146	1,957,517	1,151	3,996,064	4,172,903	4,009,428	862,608	3,146,820
Brazoria	167,686	3,096,254	1,154	6,852,263	28,543,547	9,110,544	1,459,298	7,651,246
Brazos	82,894	1,490,488	729	2,677,140	11,392,251	4,537,761	907,620	3,630,141
Brewster	6,608	169,226	588	1,567,955	753,498	333,577	300,908	32,669
Briscoe	2,374	52,601	328	682,989	36,970	123,922	122,211	1,711
Brooks	5,437	306,017	264	735,211	702,555	295,917	218,874	77,043
Brown	33,124	578,623	736	1,661,018	4,469,317	1,738,824	580,764	1,158,060
Burleson	13,271	465,443	517	1,657,534	2,657,147	706,057	426,491	279,566
Burnet	24,235	620,075	793	1,529,109	116,223	1,235,798	489,548	746,250
Caldwell	18,922	519,907	602	1,973,957	2,070,424	1,076,807	519,843	556,964
Calhoun	16,397	361,667	383	990,295	805,718	850,708	380,161	470,547
Callahan	13,904	636,667	743	1,790,553	3,270,446	677,458	416,643	260,815
Cameron	153,287	3,047,942	1,493	6,536,719	19,172,078	8,443,316	1,424,339	7,018,977
Camp	10,151	193,312	266	689,448	806,637	676,974	336,644	340,330
Carson	6,892	550,799	776	2,044,426	90,839	371,260	322,953	48,307
Cass	27,137	800,460	970	3,711,048	11,949,172	1,417,279	535,852	881,427
Castro	8,339	225,797	529	1,023,097	217,052	524,564	416,674	107,890
Chambers	20,653	1,413,243	700	1,741,982	16,746,232	1,159,583	463,364	696,219
Cherokee	34,513	925,566	1,110	4,066,799	1,080,117	1,887,672	584,976	1,302,696
Childress	6,108	238,909	470	1,000,278	3,590,733	300,226	280,005	20,221
Clay	8,885	586,997	789	1,392,472	115,178	468,502	376,576	91,926

County	Vehicles Registered	Miles Driven Per Day	Lane Miles of Highway	Maintenance Expenditure	Construction Expenditure	Vehicles Reg. Fees	County Net Receipts	State Net Receipts
Cochran	4,109	96,658	470	875,548	19,028	223,518	220,935	2,583
Coke	4,289	163,168	357	1,042,433	1,336,867	216,292	213,268	3,024
Coleman	10,716	289,204	740	1,562,254	1,268,700	543,521	424,980	118,541
Collin	227,286	2,938,975	1,212	5,552,508	45,616,175	13,113,759	2,584,903	10,528,856
Collingsworth	3,826	87,608	453	803,251	125,336	181,929	179,518	2,411
Colorado	18,525	1,070,835	761	3,024,740	726,284	1,122,321	476,767	645,554
Comal	50,568	1,447,806	598	2,083,376	2,947,569	2,943,525	767,580	2,175,945
Comanche	13,416	377,873	726	1,884,345	939,437	710,114	448,505	261,609
Concho	3,128	196,711	418	969,719	3,945,750	142,698	140,637	2,061
Cooke	30,056	859,642	832	2,513,116	8,835,113	1,734,697	649,906	1,084,791
Coryell	32,638	645,942	680	1,775,789	1,402,515	1,630,796	575,148	1,055,648
Cottle	2,432	74,442	391	2,879,307	0	121,402	119,779	1,623
Crane	5,468	159,199	318	671,430	0	380,045	254,073	125,972
Crockett	3,919	310,033	781	1,549,786	2,147,328	205,632	203,415	2,217
Crosby	6,452	187,316	569	1,889,733	105	331,685	300,532	31,153
Culberson	2,344	421,036	744	1,407,424	934,050	119,601	118,230	1,371
Dallam	5,624	282,450	592	2,346,303	1,172,300	322,485	283,988	38,497
Dallas	1,551,252	25,034,496	3,008	19,129,062	96,813,485	95,002,130	15,868,592	79,133,538
Dawson	12,456	329,002	710	1,323,124	101,958	705,075	435,978	269,097
DeWitt	16,168	349,878	641	2,019,883	1,241,172	889,564	508,726	380,838
Deaf Smith	17,424	300,333	601	1,182,708	2,740,021	1,211,055	531,372	679,683
Delta	5,191	148,561	344	1,476,971	1,938,006	257,342	227,669	29,673
Denton	211,892	4,127,471	1,217	4,855,926	41,322,604	12,089,745	2,490,007	9,599,738
Dickens	2,682	94,343	460	660,293	937,655	129,007	127,221	1,786
Dimmit	6,606	204,182	506	934,940	894,231	387,048	287,534	99,514
Donley	3,950	331,640	447	996,117	1,824,923	176,428	174,226	2,202
Duval	7,702	343,124	630	1,276,459	2,815,823	452,129	365,091	87,038
Eastland	18,780	889,013	1,024	2,333,873	2,316,896	1,028,462	480,355	548,107
Ector	109,674	1,280,752	889	2,048,277	3,246,995	6,575,798	1,115,887	5,459,911
Edwards	2,016	67,522	500	963,195	1,259,991	106,057	104,618	1,439
El Paso	361,966	5,382,888	1,358	5,588,737	21,791,366	21,028,109	4,024,059	17,004,050
Ellis	78,373	2,354,315	1,419	6,069,990	9,009,041	4,602,234	1,117,928	3,484,306
Erath	25,315	721,737	784	3,894,921	341,899	1,362,895	521,511	841,384
Falls	13,538	475,999	706	1,557,181	3,120,645	706,290	443,612	262,678
Fannin	23,986	489,636	903	2,650,631	6,935,879	1,236,694	512,008	724,686
Fayette	20,293	886,235	955	2,730,856	13,228,574	1,176,557	542,720	633,837
Fisher	4,645	136,215	553	1,006,166	348,724	230,942	223,404	7,538
Floyd	8,412	174,224	668	978,818	115,996	474,691	390,586	84,105
Foard	1,652	59,088	299	2,234,585	27,655	83,844	82,788	1,056
Fort Bend	152,586	2,997,116	947	6,798,585	25,457,169	8,412,198	1,369,068	7,043,130
Franklin	6,701	287,865	328	1,137,688	985,801	335,693	268,903	66,790
Freestone	14,992	962,051	823	1,995,873	1,484,982	740,525	449,078	291,447
Frio	8,822	475,895	759	2,055,829	597,827	541,593	414,466	127,127
Gaines	11,916	369,481	668	1,602,022	1,220,013	699,080	411,224	287,856
Galveston	172,246	3,218,788	947	7,966,249	20,630,330	9,642,170	2,001,060	7,641,110
Garza	4,850	290,182	453	913,285	1,900,187	338,685	273,278	65,407
Gillespie	17,516	409,627	703	2,126,337	382,236	965,065	523,857	441,208
Glasscock	2,151	143,026	274	547,714	188,510	139,734	138,111	1,623
Goliad	5,183	250,311	500	1,015,045	1,158,370	239,964	225,825	14,139
Gonzales	15,612	717,620	871	2,879,327	470,176	868,902	458,913	409,989
Gray	27,076	494,684	769	1,722,051	204,225	1,596,067	578,335	1,017,732
Grayson	91,973	1,892,657	1,158	5,701,930	8,521,249	5,179,525	1,260,424	3,919,101
Gregg	119,943	1,944,632	729	2,574,404	8,640,260	6,603,757	505,797	6,097,960
Grimes	14,829	494,923	610	2,095,110	2,320,133	803,468	499,885	303,583
Guadalupe	54,064	1,530,982	914	2,158,353	6,131,268	2,960,852	714,598	2,246,254
Hale	30,346	626,485	1,052	2,203,278	1,898,190	1,651,340	556,208	1,095,132
Hall	3,704	158,466	449	1,083,377	108,289	198,084	195,216	2,868
Hamilton	8,011	235,276	575	1,991,681	15,615	452,800	377,649	75,151
Hansford	7,584	119,210	509	917,853	178,496	431,966	354,308	77,658
Hardeman	4,906	249,899	466	983,749	1,266,365	278,298	269,879	8,419
Hardin	39,068	929,857	528	1,692,968	2,980,383	2,216,685	741,393	1,475,292
Harris	2,218,651	34,380,925	3,787	25,327,173	476,345,195	128,854,237	15,974,610	112,879,627
Harrison	49,485	1,530,806	1,153	3,230,690	4,924,124	2,383,052	451,619	1,931,433
Hartley	4,714	213,499	505	773,518	225,469	269,528	238,471	31,057
Haskell	7,682	200,558	641	1,702,184	1,250,327	386,192	338,532	47,660
Hays	47,411	1,690,362	622	2,334,923	10,063,573	2,474,149	670,433	1,803,716
Hemphill	4,580	125,074	384	1,110,354	1,412,296	224,414	202,445	21,969
Henderson	54,957	1,155,311	905	2,746,773	11,082,265	2,790,855	709,718	2,081,137
Hidalgo	228,339	4,495,736	1,890	6,354,125	11,446,318	13,265,864	2,025,880	11,239,984
Hill	26,697	1,247,538	1,086	2,367,079	1,440,921	1,439,137	612,744	826,393
Hockley	21,669	477,766	750	1,392,624	22,809	1,296,869	498,963	797,906
Hood	31,677	713,685	375	1,632,376	680,023	1,644,459	536,604	1,107,855
Hopkins	29,662	1,041,160	953	2,238,026	1,948,638	1,722,130	555,422	1,166,708
Houston	18,585	483,892	838	1,890,461	562,179	978,504	478,703	499,801
Howard	29,848	735,894	834	1,616,847	4,824,412	1,764,666	652,579	1,112,087
Hudspeth	2,000	714,492	818	1,773,509	2,497,912	101,595	99,924	1,671
Hunt	58,126	1,691,062	1,282	4,214,670	4,914,542	2,955,202	748,731	2,206,471
Hutchinson	29,340	335,204	478	902,418	520,903	1,562,982	410,291	1,152,691
Irion	2,009	91,951	247	982,460	2,242,348	112,883	111,511	1,372
Jack	7,793	256,556	564	1,934,329	1,048,951	468,038	368,609	99,429
Jackson	13,058	567,506	636	3,282,948	2,196,625	719,818	436,612	283,206
Jasper	30,859	880,245	682	1,897,379	3,259,495	1,636,580	556,106	1,080,474
Jeff Davis	1,925	131,174	469	970,874	787,209	117,448	105,109	12,339

County	Vehicles Registered	Miles Driven Per Day	Lane Miles of Highway	Maintenance Expenditure	Construction Expenditure	Vehicles Reg. Fees	County Net Receipts	State Net Receipts
Jefferson	201,415	3,555,987	982	4,867,716	40,453,270	10,973,593	1,710,643	9,262,950
Jim Hogg	3,651	95,489	288	695,539	1,768	203,064	160,109	42,955
Jim Wells	27,914	734,452	634	2,296,453	1,727,015	1,785,624	538,861	1,246,763
Johnson	89,976	1,715,370	876	3,161,289	7,689,348	5,009,652	1,245,466	3,764,186
Jones	14,999	412,077	973	1,460,670	487,789	901,070	498,771	402,299
Karnes	10,237	318,972	691	1,578,192	3,053,932	543,331	416,889	126,442
Kaufman	48,880	2,101,344	1,156	3,446,151	8,221,612	2,447,588	667,300	1,780,288
Kendall	17,856	441,050	436	892,443	1,666,767	935,885	429,087	506,798
Kenedy	405	293,598	187	1,986,975	1,027	18,026	17,819	207
Kent	1,572	51,206	326	600,656	56,958	67,540	66,772	768
Kerr	32,625	688,253	703	1,856,025	2,580,809	1,751,355	575,156	1,176,199
Kimble	4,906	319,161	684	1,422,375	804,930	245,472	214,501	30,971
King	461	64,132	199	406,252	1,218,203	23,089	22,907	182
Kinney	2,352	128,387	407	1,422,370	15,462	117,121	102,988	14,133
Kleberg	21,127	469,242	364	1,042,414	841,369	1,201,132	410,798	790,334
Knox	4,762	132,190	428	694,541	952,147	283,096	260,396	22,700
Laalle	3,169	296,780	648	1,375,787	1,473,343	155,611	153,524	2,087
Lamar	43,427	915,908	996	3,315,915	1,917,451	2,358,407	646,342	1,712,065
Lamb	14,285	364,878	809	1,726,019	631,652	759,457	446,311	313,146
Lampasas	12,531	293,353	468	1,121,657	864,634	639,496	435,965	203,531
Lavaca	18,709	390,563	636	1,787,336	1,204,766	1,089,312	530,658	558,654
Lee	12,918	444,928	514	1,026,177	33,412	712,670	431,924	280,746
Leon	12,171	900,193	834	1,910,209	1,554,198	606,426	434,786	171,640
Liberty	46,912	1,310,854	806	3,860,771	2,032,146	2,854,920	801,158	2,053,762
Limestone	18,884	523,528	757	1,944,120	5,273,999	951,464	394,790	556,674
Lipscomb	4,037	69,406	447	722,791	1,355,655	217,421	214,986	2,435
Live Oak	9,271	761,656	946	2,490,363	3,382,497	554,429	385,240	169,189
Llano	13,593	287,449	498	923,836	1,033,946	680,880	442,455	238,425
Loving	308	10,844	67	118,902	0	20,415	20,284	131
Lubbock	189,169	2,599,596	1,579	4,823,238	52,939,103	11,041,740	1,881,368	9,160,372
Lynn	6,705	251,473	708	1,149,077	820,039	326,269	290,417	35,852
Madison	9,026	567,040	569	1,742,952	702,056	463,756	333,107	130,649
Marion	7,922	252,529	309	1,507,126	619,342	427,743	334,418	93,325
Martin	5,466	304,671	572	875,890	1,896,328	298,268	269,972	28,296
Mason	3,765	126,539	416	937,426	14,377	184,159	179,678	4,481
Matagorda	31,091	697,888	682	2,516,415	1,326,343	1,544,597	417,511	1,127,086
Maverick	20,065	327,716	451	1,532,080	212,846	1,173,318	432,337	740,981
McCulloch	9,003	240,087	608	1,732,758	776,184	441,521	342,756	98,765
McLennan	164,124	3,553,245	1,582	4,027,298	8,845,637	10,802,002	1,802,237	8,999,765
McMullen	1,295	84,042	317	824,544	196,628	68,460	67,855	605
Medina	25,070	649,589	724	2,421,622	3,912,228	1,335,296	523,044	812,252
Menard	6,500	103,294	346	674,135	0	808,466	239,736	568,730
Midland	97,053	1,358,412	890	2,748,187	5,619,098	5,603,177	1,003,093	4,600,084
Milam	20,865	655,037	682	2,274,979	874,923	1,074,341	491,513	582,828
Mills	5,124	164,487	419	895,614	940,856	239,497	236,256	3,241
Mitchell	7,478	407,957	657	1,534,523	1,913,255	392,820	333,373	59,447
Montague	18,808	539,092	808	1,682,358	2,598,267	1,071,045	538,687	532,358
Montgomery	156,394	3,721,396	1,012	6,790,219	45,347,943	8,534,532	1,437,068	7,097,464
Moore	17,682	353,300	469	998,180	1,618,940	1,032,264	420,133	612,131
Morris	14,447	360,159	355	1,357,212	911,971	876,540	390,501	486,039
Motley	1,815	59,351	331	741,614	555,113	84,892	83,602	1,290
Nacogdoches	41,508	1,213,106	903	2,568,242	5,716,747	2,279,775	631,191	1,648,584
Navarro	34,941	1,295,656	1,137	4,510,023	5,848,046	1,964,542	613,623	1,350,919
Newton	8,414	347,623	547	2,129,538	302,809	465,719	374,866	90,853
Nolan	15,189	669,905	684	1,863,648	970,926	858,680	506,908	351,772
Nueces	220,856	3,484,415	1,295	4,714,238	46,032,605	13,456,455	2,538,571	10,917,884
Ochiltree	10,977	177,428	428	896,583	23,675	717,728	461,525	256,203
Oldham	2,417	546,938	456	771,446	741,119	140,759	139,188	1,571
Orange	70,878	1,827,155	563	2,111,094	10,206,287	3,656,504	821,674	2,834,830
Palo Pinto	24,618	697,321	829	4,044,614	1,743,716	1,327,044	525,704	801,340
Panola	22,379	709,243	742	2,058,894	5,313,431	1,081,445	400,857	680,588
Parker	63,072	1,682,376	847	4,440,271	2,711,521	3,309,750	768,541	2,541,209
Parmer	9,912	291,079	539	1,101,922	1,432,910	619,199	451,436	167,763
Pecos	12,998	640,355	1,656	2,807,218	1,687,815	661,078	380,670	280,408
Polk	28,311	1,082,795	833	3,299,984	4,606,068	1,550,324	546,121	1,004,203
Potter	96,462	1,772,365	857	3,658,549	3,615,132	5,563,125	1,005,136	4,557,989
Presidio	4,494	131,428	542	1,605,139	841,808	240,368	236,450	3,918
Rains	7,054	189,973	270	961,119	526,468	336,259	281,809	54,450
Randall	82,880	831,909	849	2,068,767	3,218,386	4,823,939	1,167,878	3,656,061
Reagan	3,898	117,633	320	1,205,767	47,611	256,635	224,666	31,969
Real	2,706	63,147	297	535,075	10,451	138,982	137,085	1,897
Red River	13,233	344,992	742	2,166,213	1,078,359	636,877	441,177	195,700
Reeves	10,370	535,651	1,167	2,373,639	1,486,466	571,030	411,672	159,358
Refugio	7,274	475,941	464	1,308,030	109,311	402,378	284,886	117,492
Roberts	1,415	63,146	241	326,979	8,734	66,556	65,816	740
Robertson	12,931	465,453	625	1,849,278	2,157,668	630,391	434,687	195,704
Rockwall	24,615	764,172	317	964,904	758,311	1,420,885	394,245	1,026,640
Runnels	12,138	298,785	730	1,307,404	548,810	675,559	427,427	248,132
Rusk	35,241	979,510	1,132	4,131,626	3,250,361	1,957,704	591,243	1,366,461
Sabine	8,636	223,468	454	1,068,421	148,217	447,813	342,144	105,669
San Augustine	7,700	223,666	516	1,432,409	1,961,212	436,766	365,169	71,597

County	Vehicles Registered	Miles Driven Per Day	Lane Miles of Highway	Maintenance Expenditure	Construction Expenditure	Vehicles Reg. Fees	County Net Receipts	State Net Receipts
San Jacinto	12,290	468,439	504	1,445,421	1,305,040	642,270	430,100	212,170
San Patricio	42,972	1,266,578	874	3,855,278	11,644,473	2,339,815	642,490	1,697,325
San Saba	5,928	123,893	427	1,036,382	1,158,185	322,291	301,795	20,496
Schleicher	3,074	107,632	362	365,200	3,040	142,078	140,490	1,588
Scurry	18,094	479,081	661	1,345,448	4,670,868	1,075,369	473,418	601,951
Shackelford	3,754	131,113	353	866,226	43,364	194,855	177,563	17,292
Shelby	22,827	580,192	857	2,418,675	2,714,153	1,350,496	506,934	843,562
Sherman	3,639	217,214	429	819,396	566,851	190,509	188,808	1,701
Smith	136,752	3,347,935	1,495	5,888,869	10,162,246	7,509,394	1,304,459	6,204,935
Somervell	5,472	202,662	184	815,378	0	264,648	191,619	73,029
Starr	22,544	519,332	464	1,172,747	643,130	1,349,336	587,513	761,823
Stephens	9,364	206,499	546	1,360,023	784,610	535,908	380,037	155,871
Sterling	1,684	146,045	240	603,733	0	75,708	67,065	8,643
Stonewall	2,451	85,563	319	614,579	307,336	135,427	133,998	1,429
Sutton	4,931	339,373	592	1,537,533	6,142	300,903	236,165	64,738
Swisher	7,989	315,983	808	1,152,731	5,077,123	421,981	351,419	70,562
Tarrant	1,028,001	17,757,082	2,598	11,118,923	118,734,060	58,426,579	8,212,539	50,214,040
Taylor	107,792	1,586,691	1,153	3,516,862	4,531,824	6,410,864	1,419,406	4,991,458
Terrell	1,388	68,015	330	495,910	922,677	66,279	65,422	857
Terry	14,135	355,091	631	1,555,256	37,780	845,244	449,143	396,101
Throckmorton	2,088	77,036	340	813,873	127,385	108,291	107,010	1,281
Titus	22,546	682,648	531	1,712,991	2,725,183	1,233,675	499,507	734,168
Tom Green	86,686	1,089,060	911	2,352,535	9,371,680	4,679,792	926,587	3,753,205
Travis	460,366	8,088,999	1,431	10,285,361	95,942,511	26,341,184	4,808,551	21,532,633
Trinity	10,879	275,979	416	1,255,919	1,956,898	579,262	376,136	203,126
Tyler	15,545	424,850	509	1,926,510	364,017	830,068	457,634	372,434
Upshur	27,362	658,960	738	1,791,484	3,561,117	1,378,947	538,031	840,916
Upton	4,346	141,427	386	403,468	900,207	291,540	265,333	26,207
Uvalde	18,037	491,442	720	1,574,728	676,333	1,151,431	494,746	656,685
Val Verde	28,550	337,789	665	1,288,631	835,413	1,489,205	491,456	997,749
Van Zandt	39,884	1,402,688	1,153	4,030,557	2,606,134	2,053,918	719,810	1,334,108
Victoria	67,610	1,249,551	693	2,695,996	9,374,656	3,745,011	799,081	2,945,930
Walker	29,870	1,326,944	757	2,642,611	5,589,563	1,709,923	642,490	1,067,433
Waller	26,248	873,080	535	1,985,650	7,662,176	1,403,488	527,438	876,050
Ward	12,387	417,366	670	1,346,503	213,727	671,844	373,017	298,827
Washington	24,529	679,429	624	2,008,035	3,200,074	1,521,115	585,141	935,974
Webb	79,809	982,208	885	2,979,508	3,290,635	5,188,478	878,130	4,310,348
Wharton	36,009	1,123,181	919	2,606,149	6,099,334	2,152,297	597,667	1,554,630
Wheeler	6,368	411,150	670	1,345,936	284,656	298,888	264,628	34,260
Wichita	112,172	1,653,454	1,067	3,407,677	8,536,619	6,115,351	1,080,333	5,035,018
Wilbarger	14,308	524,217	725	1,405,368	1,374,015	758,253	454,337	303,916
Willacy	11,521	311,608	480	2,642,904	259,155	679,836	441,263	238,573
Williamson	114,288	2,681,335	1,372	5,453,256	30,331,479	6,033,262	1,128,348	4,904,914
Wilson	19,174	484,260	703	2,253,894	1,485,129	964,093	479,055	485,038
Winkler	8,278	138,178	295	541,956	24,931	456,314	273,859	182,455
Wise	37,913	1,250,536	836	3,396,396	7,019,201	2,257,293	614,353	1,642,940
Wood	31,365	592,145	890	2,434,110	1,118,710	1,502,898	460,882	1,042,016
Yoakum	9,586	179,417	403	1,056,701	1,371,261	604,467	430,074	174,393
Young	21,158	355,709	715	1,977,110	1,127,228	1,242,183	496,390	745,793
Zapata	6,339	237,710	244	556,659	200,215	311,760	200,980	110,780
Zavala	5,760	189,467	541	1,741,443	2,717,797	317,395	244,685	72,710
Unknown Co	28,625	0	0	7,279,471	0	0	0	0
State Collect	0	0	0	0	0	21,828,542	0	21,828,542
Exempt	512,307	0	0	0	0	0	0	0
State Totals	14,496,096	284,807,726	181,665	$597,159,733	$1,879,703,475	$820,119,447	$183,631,516	$636,487,931

Note: The final three entries under county are for categories of expense or enumeration not assigned to a particular county.

Motor Vehicle Accidents, Losses

The following statistics for motor vehicle accidents, deaths and injuries, miles traveled and economic losses are from the Texas Department of Public Safety, Austin.

Year	No. Killed	+No. Injured	No. Fatal	+No. Involving Injury	+No. Non-Injury	+Total	*Number	Deaths per 100 million Miles	✓Economic Loss
				Accidents by Kinds			Vehicle Miles Traveled		
1970	3,560	223,000	2,965	124,000	886,000	1,012,965	‡68,031,000,000	5.2	$1,042,200,000
1978	**3,980	178,228	3,468	117,998	††304,830	††426,296	102,624,000,000	3.9	2,430,000,000
1979	4,229	184,550	3,685	122,793	322,336	448,814	101,909,000,000	4.1	2,580,000,000
1980	4,424	185,964	3,863	123,577	305,500	432,940	103,255,000,000	4.3	3,010,000,000
1981	4,701	206,196	4,137	136,396	317,484	458,017	111,036,000,000	4.2	3,430,000,000
1982	4,271	204,666	3,752	135,859	312,159	451,770	‡‡124,910,000,000	3.4	3,375,000,000
1983	3,823	208,157	§§3,328	137,695	302,876	443,899	129,309,000,000	3.0	3,440,000,000
1984	3,913	220,720	3,466	145,543	293,285	442,294	137,280,000,000	2.9	3,795,000,000
1985	3,682	231,009	3,270	151,657	300,531	452,188	143,500,000,000	2.6	3,755,000,000
1986	3,568	234,120	3,121	154,514	298,079	452,593	150,474,000,000	2.4	3,782,000,000

			Accidents by Kinds				Vehicle Miles Traveled			
Year	No. Killed	+No. Injured	No. Fatal	+No. Involving Injury	+No. Non-Injury	+Total	*Number	Deaths per 100 million Miles	✔Economic Loss
1987.............	3,261	226,895	2,881	146,913	246,175	395,969	151,221,000,000	2.2	3,913,000,000
1988.............	3,395	238,845	3,004	152,004	237,703	392,711	152,819,000,000	2.2	4,515,000,000
1989.............	3,361	243,030	2,926	153,356	233,967	390,249	159,679,000,000	2.1	4,873,000,000
1990.............	3,243	262,576	2,882	162,424	216,140	381,446	163,103,000,000	2.0	4,994,000,000

*Vehicle miles traveled since 1964 were estimated on the basis of new data furnished by U.S. Bureau of Public Roads through National Safety Council. Vehicle miles and deaths per 100 million vehicle miles after 1964 cannot, therefore, be compared with previous years.

+In August 1967, amended estimating formula received from National Safety Council. Starting with 1972, actual reported injuries are listed rather than estimates.

‡Vehicle miles traveled estimated by Texas Highway Department starting with 1970. Method of calculation varies from that used for prior years. Vehicle miles and deaths per 100,000,000 vehicle miles for 1969 and before cannot be compared to subsequent years.

✔Economic loss formula last changed 1984.

**Change in counting fatalities. Counted when injury results in death within 90 days of vehicle accident in which the injury occurred.

††Total accidents and non-injury accidents for 1978-84 cannot be compared with years prior to 1978 due to changes in reporting laws.

‡‡Method of calculating vehicle miles traveled revised for 1982 by the Texas State Department of Highways and Public Transportation. Vehicle miles and deaths per 100,000,000 miles cannot be compared to prior years.

§§Change in counting fatalities. Counted when injury results in death within 30 days of vehicle accident in which the injury occurred.

Aviation in Texas

The following was prepared for the Texas Almanac by George B. Dresser, Program Manager, and his staff, Texas Transportation Institute, Texas A&M University, College Station.

Air transportation is a vital and vigorous part of the Texas economy. Texans are major users of air transportation and the state's airport system ranks as one of the busiest and largest in the nation. In 1989, 17 domestic airlines served 22 Texas airports with scheduled passenger service and enplaned over 45 million passengers. The more than 21,000 active general aviation aircraft are being flown by a resident pilot population of nearly 51,000 utilizing over 1,600 landing facilities.

The State of Texas has long been committed to providing air transportation to the public. In 1945, the **Texas Aeronautics Commission (TAC)** was created and directed by the Legislature to encourage, foster and assist in the development of aeronautics within the state, and to encourage the establishment of airports and air navigational facilities. The commission's first annual report of Dec. 31, 1946, stated that Texas had 592 designated airports and 7,756 civilian aircraft.

Drivers' Licenses

The following report from Texas Department of Public Safety shows the number of drivers' licenses issued during the fiscal year and number of valid licenses at the end of each fiscal year.

Fiscal Year Ending	*Licenses Issued During Year	Valid Licenses at Year's End
Aug. 31, 1990	4,205,385	11,738,602
Aug. 31, 1989	4,397,140	11,672,696
Aug. 31, 1988	4,130,447	11,641,984
Aug. 31, 1987	3,886,622	11,550,219
Aug. 31, 1986	4,325,742	11,436,780
Aug. 31, 1985	4,677,788	11,241,367
Aug. 31, 1984	4,498,902	11,009,567
Aug. 31, 1983	4,090,602	10,805,539
Aug. 31, 1982	4,281,652	10,463,962
Aug. 31, 1981	3,818,303	9,909,721
Aug. 31, 1980	3,699,543	9,551,683
Aug. 31, 1979	3,616,754	9,189,198
Aug. 31, 1978	3,529,926	8,805,604
Aug. 31, 1977	3,418,606	8,420,678
Aug. 31, 1976	3,233,610	8,127,188
Aug. 31, 1975	2,980,024	7,806,703
Aug. 31, 1974	2,887,456	7,588,372
Aug. 31, 1973	2,807,828	7,334,913
Aug. 31, 1972	2,573,010	7,098,425
Aug. 31, 1971	2,418,170	6,768,319
Aug. 31, 1970	2,321,416	6,420,602
Aug. 31, 1969	3,403,122	6,035,944
Aug. 31, 1968	3,603,082	5,849,126

*Includes renewals during year.

The commitment to providing air transportation was strengthened in Oct. 18, 1989, when the TAC became the **Texas Department of Aviation (TDA).** One of the goals of the TDA is to develop a statewide system of airports that will meet the goal of providing adequate access to the population and economic centers.

Texas leads the nation in the number of landing facilities: 1,697 as of December 1989, followed by Illinois with 938. These include 1,287 airports, 402 heliports and eight stolports.

In its **Texas Aeronautical Facilities Plan,** the TDA identified 307 of those airports as being critical to the state's development. These facilities are needed to serve the population, the business community and the agricultural and mineral-production industries. Of these 307 sites, 27 are commercial-service airports, 24 are reliever airports, 82 are business-service airports, 116 are community-service airports, and 57 are basic-service airports. Commercial-service airports provide scheduled passenger service. The reliever airports provide alternative landing facilities in metropolitan areas separate from the commercial-service airports and, together with the business-service airports, provide access for business and executive turbine-powered aircraft. The community and basic-service airports provide access for single- and multi-engine piston-powered aircraft to smaller communities throughout the state.

The TDA is charged by the Legislature with planning, programming and implementing improvement projects at approximately 255 general-aviation airports. In carrying out these responsibilities, TDA channels the Airport Improvement Program (AIP) funds provided by the **Federal Aviation Administration** for all general aviation airports in Texas. The TDA's **Aviation Facilities Development and Financial Assistance Program** oversees planning and research; assists with engineering and technical services; and provides financial assistance through state grants and loans to public bodies operating airports for the purpose of establishing, constructing, reconstructing, enlarging or repairing airports, airstrips or navigational facilities. To implement and administer the Aviation Facilities Development Program, the 71st Legislature appropriated $4 million for the 1990-91 biennium.

TDA's **Aeronautical Services and Information Section** provides specialized training programs, aeronautical publications and safety information to Texans who are involved with or interested in aviation.

In Texas, scheduled passenger traffic (commercial air carriers and commuters) experienced strong growth during 1989, and this trend is expected to continue based on preliminary 1990 figures. Nationwide total scheduled passenger enplanements showed a slight decrease of 0.4 percent from 1988 to 1989, while scheduled passenger enplanements in Texas increased 6.3 percent during the same period. Texas, with 6.8 percent of the nation's population, accounted for 11 percent of the nation's enplanements.

Texas ranks second in the United States, after California, in aircraft departures and in passengers enplaned by commercial air carriers. Over 91 percent of the state's population lives within 50 miles of an airport with scheduled air-passenger service. As of January 1989, 17 U.S. carriers were serving 22 Texas airports in 20 cities. These carriers enplaned more than 45 million passengers in 1989. Dallas/Fort Worth International, Dallas Love Field, Houston Intercontinental and Houston's William P. Hobby together accounted for 82 percent of these enplanements.

Texas was served by seven commuter airlines as of January 1989. Commuter airlines operate aircraft of 60 seats or less and perform at least five scheduled round trips per week between two or more cities. Commuters provided service from 25 cities and provided the only scheduled service from 14 of these cities. In 1989, commuter airlines enplaned over 1.8 million passengers at Texas airports. Since passage of the federal Airline Deregulation Act of 1978, route expansion by commuter airlines has been vigorous in Texas and throughout the nation, although developing successful new commuter markets in Texas has proven to be difficult. Numerous routes have been initiated only to be subsequently abandoned. The most recent trend has been for commuter airlines to associate themselves with major airlines as "code-sharing" partners. The code-sharing commuters provide connecting flights with major carriers, principally at Dallas/Fort Worth International and Houston Intercontinental airports and, to a lesser extent, at other hub airports. Commuter carriers have upgraded their equipment, and the quality of commuter service continues to improve.

The Texas general-aviation fleet (all aircraft except military and commercial airlines) consisted of 21,680 registered aircraft as of Dec. 31, 1989. The size of the general-aviation fleet has remained relatively stable during the 1980s and is expected to remain stable during the 1990s. While the proportion of the general-aviation fleet consisting of single-engine airplanes — planes associated with personal or pleasure flying — is decreasing, the proportion of multi-engine airplanes — planes associated with business and executive transportation — is increasing. Business continues to increase its use of general-aviation aircraft. In 1989, 24 percent of aircraft hours flown were for executive and business transportation, 29 percent were for personal transportation, 19 percent were for instructional flying, 14 percent were for commuter and air taxi, six percent were aerial application, and eight percent were for other purposes. Texas has eight percent of the nation's registered aircraft, including 9.4 percent of the turbine-powered aircraft. The state's 51,809 active pilots represent eight percent of the nation's pilots.

Texas Enplaned Passengers—1989
Source: Air Carrier Activity Information System, FAA

This table shows passenger enplanements at Texas cities having scheduled air carrier or commuter service during calendar year 1989.

City	Enplanements	City	Enplanements
Abilene	65,911	Laredo	56,515
Amarillo	458,538	Longview	37,817
Austin	2,032,862	Lubbock	628,996
Beaumont-Port Arthur	102,998	McAllen	217,585
Brownwood	1,620	Midland	597,115
College Station	68,686	San Angelo	58,145
Corpus Christi	417,569	San Antonio	2,593,261
Dallas-Fort Worth	23,823,229	Temple	3,429
El Paso	1,677,290	Texarkana	44,730
Fort Worth	1,754	Tyler	77,650
Harlingen	538,332	Victoria	20,663
Houston	11,441,186	Waco	34,890
Killeen	44,096	Wichita Falls	58,222

Texas Enplaned Traffic—1989
FAA Certificated Carriers
Source: FAA

This table shows domestic airline traffic at Texas cities during calendar year 1989, as reported by the Federal Aviation Administration. In addition, U.S. carriers' traffic to foreign destinations is shown.

City	Aircraft Departures	Enplaned Passengers	Air Mail Tons	Cargo Tons
DOMESTIC				
Amarillo	6,544	441,677	608.83	212.18
Austin	30,878	2,022,269	3,630.64	9,733.12
Brownsville-Harlingen-San Benito	7,158	534,945	5.54	2,745.02
Corpus Christi	6,507	408,374	477.90	218.05
Dallas-Fort Worth	284,167	24,578,425	75,425	123,607
El Paso	26,283	1,672,402	1,233.77	4,283.66
Houston	153,138	10,345,846	22,632.13	52,083.33
Lubbock	11,249	627,500	509.81	6,502.06
Midland-Odessa	9,040	596,702	165.72	613.55
Mission-McAllen-Edinburg	1,776	157,495	578.43	339.13
San Antonio	36,047	2,463,014	7,057.39	8,315.55
Other	1,136	13	-0-	819.64
Total Domestic	573,923	43,848,662	112,325.87	209,472.99
INTERNATIONAL				
Dallas-Fort Worth	7,721	818,476	1,504.65	16,469.70
Houston	6,028	611,484	406.33	7,939.76
Mission-McAllen-Edinburg	589	39,325	.63	573.51
San Antonio	386	30,379	.02	477.34
Other	206	-0-	-0-	150.60
Total Intl.	14,930	1,499,664	1,911.63	25,610.91
TOTAL	588,853	45,348,326	114,237.50	235,083.90

Top Ten Texas Cities—1989
Source: FAA

City	Aircraft Departures Performed	Percent of Total	Enplaned Passengers	Percent of Total
Dallas-Fort Worth	291,888	50	25,396,901	56
Houston	159,166	27	10,957,330	24
San Antonio	36,415	6	2,493,393	6

City	Aircraft Departures Performed	Percent of Total	Enplaned Passengers	Percent of Total
Austin	30,879	5	2,022,269	4
El Paso	26,283	4	1,672,402	4
Lubbock	11,249	2	627,500	1
Midland/Odessa	9,040	2	596,702	1
Brownsville-Harlingen-San Benito	7,259	1	534,945	1
Amarillo	6,544	1	441,677	1
Corpus Christi	6,507	1	408,374	1

Total Texas Aircraft Departures Performed 585,230
Total Texas Enplaned Passengers 45,151,493

Texas Air Traffic

Source: FAA

Airline passenger traffic enplaned in Texas by scheduled certificated carriers.

Source: CAB-FAA

Year	Domestic	International	Total
1957	2,699,393	109,165	2,808,558
1958	2,658,897	83,870	2,742,767
1959*	2,750,391	78,150	2,828,541
1960	3,045,391	68,191	3,113,582

Year	Domestic	International	Total
1961	3,431,788	72,680	3,505,275
1962*	3,599,658	83,325	3,682,983
1963*	3,914,309	105,150	4,019,459
1964*	4,514,200	108,257	4,622,457
1965	5,635,179	122,510	5,757,689
1966	6,991,148	178,464	7,169,612
1967	7,983,634	189,251	8,172,885
1968	9,286,973	220,026	9,506,999
1969	9,924,696	218,352	10,142,048
1970*	10,039,886	216,805	10,256,691
1971	9,936,887	225,024	10,161,911
1972	11,022,538	232,875	11,255,413
1973	11,954,536	276,325	12,230,861
1974	12,934,999	274,569	13,209,568
1975	12,918,790	264,248	13,182,957
1976	14,218,189	267,151	14,485,340
1977	15,595,237	275,910	15,871,147
1978	17,805,693	435,336	18,241,029
1979	20,966,571	580,223	21,546,794
1980	24,693,080	610,134	25,303,214
1981	26,853,393	596,087	27,449,480
1982	29,031,114	510,674	29,541,788
1983	30,291,548	561,749	30,853,297
1984	34,524,502	606,259	35,130,762
1985	38,152,612	760,415	38,913,027
1986	39,127,357	830,035	39,957,392
1987	40,391,079	1,102,146	41,493,225
1988	41,328,616	1,327,355	42,655,971
1989	43,848,662	1,499,295	45,348,326

*Fiscal year July 1 through June 30; all others are calendar years.

Tonnage Handled by Texas Ports, 1980-1989

Source: Corps of Engineers, U.S. Army

Table below gives consolidated tonnage handled by ports and moving through Gulf Intracoastal Waterway. All figures are in short tons.

Ports	1989	1988	1987	1986	1985	1984	1983	1982	1981	1980
Brwnsvle	1,360,964	1,237,027	1,234,039	1,212,743	1,442,790	1,481,422	1,338,550	2,200,132	2,810,018	2,569,697
Port Isabel	263,335	318,466	298,789	291,713	279,578	257,781	284,758	307,856	313,036	304,964
Corpus Christi	58,440,714	56,310,445	51,239,602	48,053,926	41,057,313	44,081,109	39,131,318	37,974,192	41,980,354	45,001,096
Freeport	15,176,018	15,137,891	13,980,280	13,370,117	12,918,289	15,122,761	15,671,990	14,989,683	23,357,106	20,131,067
Galveston	11,837,611	12,354,709	8,684,216	7,987,857	7,791,729	11,752,974	10,177,718	9,349,856	11,268,337	9,631,091
Houston	125,583,156	124,886,883	112,546,187	101,659,064	90,669,169	96,777,619	88,706,519	94,649,549	100,966,741	108,937,268
Texas City	41,272,401	42,746,698	37,233,420	35,479,909	33,440,917	30,656,673	35,496,241	33,370,791	27,852,242	25,948,936
Sabine	726,141	1,248,308	722,151	385,202	547,160	605,050	605,108	1,164,632	1,063,238	949,404
Port Arthur	31,127,913	23,801,409	20,615,945	18,879,546	15,754,931	16,430,368	18,338,237	19,945,958	26,037,529	29,796,633
Beaumont	31,668,257	31,947,319	29,758,759	27,453,660	26,842,008	33,004,372	36,001,675	33,286,791	40,358,920	52,260,728
Orange	727,454	657,627	771,673	661,570	648,350	452,488	399,092	279,728	484,942	567,157
Port Lavaca	4,715,349	5,061,695	4,995,099	4,858,515	4,365,748	3,636,922	3,422,854	4,308,436	4,148,664	3,991,089
Anahuac	21,399	3,033	2,850	48,662	52,859	6,242	0	31,122	25,276	41,665
Moss Bluff	294,125	0	0	0	0	0	0	128,747	196,402	207,471
Channel to Liberty	4,791	4,433	0	0	0	58,726	0	0	0	20,700
Double Bayou	0	2,850	14,445	14,145	20,845	2,412	12,915	11,843	26,136	48,554
Cedar Bayou	308,807	275,458	247,093	275,900	218,608	391,946	454,993	404,816	231,485	328,513
Colo. Riv.	618,147	682,328	693,885	571,818	480,181	324,075	380,744	392,933	403,016	436,585
Sweeny	529,648	480,519	360,272	324,528	519,417	619,837	629,816	726,684	660,291	673,740
Palacios	0	0	0	0	10,116	0	86	54,545	100,293	85,862
Dickinson	475,275	722,645	420,062	330,172	194,932	176,905	16,055	17,921	23,275	19,275
Aransas Pass	1,893	84,325	14,445	821	9,649	3,314	959	12,243	9,953	9,113
Port Mansfld	88	3,909	11,949	3,883	204,007	57,894	62,871	1,431	115,874	13,432
Harlingen	728,954	753,937	718,645	668,733	692,170	801,003	702,242	862,969	655,127	623,292
Channel to Victoria	3,142,614	3,562,336	3,655,454	3,078,476	3,414,087	3,674,375	3,342,181	2,744,633	2,930,820	3,303,122
Choc. Byu	3,278,422	3,526,758	2,750,380	2,874,357	4,076,999	3,401,910	2,608,300	3,043,107	4,301,199	2,934,850
Johnsons Bayou	765,454	839,594	0	0	0	0	0	0	0	0
Rockport	0	2,336	0	0	0	0	0	0	0	0
Clear Crk.	0	0	0	0	0	0	0	0	0	0
*Other Ports	0	0	614,273	388,265	307,445	143,381	149,118	437,953	848,517	772,349

Total . . . . . 1989, 330,068,930; 1988, 326,652,938; 1987, 291,583,913; 1986, 268,873,582; 1985, 245,959,297; 1984, 263,921,559; 1983, 257,934,340; 1982, 260,698,551; 1981, 291,168,791; 1980, 309,607,653.

Transportation in Texas has advanced far from the spring day in 1871 when this mule-car service brought Dallas its first transit facility. The city's original system consisted of two of these mule-drawn streetcars.

Ports	1989	1988	1987	1986	1985	1984	1983	1982	1981	1980
				Gulf Intracoastal Waterway (Through Traffic)						
Sabine R. to Galv.	53,586,769	53,365,999	46,942,071	47,401,050	42,443,030	43,810,015	40,165,385	38,796,688	43,092,704	41,976,730
Galv. to Corpus Christi . . .	26,000,866	26,249,081	23,055,688	23,809,550	22,937,710	20,991,540	19,340,594	18,975,500	22,692,629	21,142,516
Corpus Christi to Mexico . . .	1,900,609	2,005,427	1,862,828	1,723,040	2,128,564	1,877,348	1,782,427	2,066,270	2,231,646	2,388,221
Total.	81,488,244	81,620,507	71,860,587	72,933,640	67,509,304	66,678,903	61,288,406	59,838,458	68,016,979	65,507,467

*Other ports include Rockport, Johnsons Bayou and Channel to Liberty prior to 1988.

Foreign and Domestic Commerce Through Major Texas Ports

Data in table below represent receipts and shipments for only the 13 major Texas ports in 1989. Total receipts and shipments for these 13 ports amounted to 320,247,691 tons. Total receipts and shipments for all Texas ports amounted to 330,068,930.

Source: U.S. Army Corps of Engineers
(All figures in short tons)

Port	Total	Foreign		Domestic				
				Coastwise		Internal		
		Imports	Exports	Receipts	Shipments	Receipts	Shipments	Local
Sabine Pass	726,141	961	. . .	. . .	. . .	306,944	418,236	. . .
Orange	727,454	100	42,678	. . .	. . .	542,497	142,179	. . .
Beaumont	31,668,257	7,163,459	3,454,752	5,210,047	3,567,446	5,521,028	6,082,209	669,316
Port Arthur	31,127,913	16,626,216	3,012,713	898,189	2,480,953	1,996,147	5,933,384	180,311
Houston	125,583,156	39,760,085	23,763,308	4,041,459	9,557,842	22,538,025	16,073,629	9,848,808
Texas City	41,272,401	20,170,819	1,932,922	2,958,100	3,966,389	4,901,675	7,085,313	257,183
Galveston.	11,837,611	2,131,671	5,541,054	278,337	2,445,196	975,178	422,088	44,087
Freeport	15,176,018	5,376,422	1,327,776	3,175,626	497,360	2,375,053	2,326,872	96,909
Corpus Christi	58,440,714	30,663,160	5,046,923	226,033	9,356,134	2,335,505	8,975,189	1,837,770
Port Isabel	263,335	. . .	. . .	. . .	. . .	112,246	151,089	. . .
Brownsville	1,360,964	271,507	137,755	3,500	50,424	835,218	60,254	2,306
Port Aransas (Harbor Island) . . .	2,063,640	1,996,159	. . .	. . .	. . .	25,465	42,016	. . .
Port Mansfield	88	. . .	. . .	. . .	. . .	88	. . .	. . .
Total	320,247,691	124,160,559	44,259,881	16,791,291	31,921,744	42,465,069	47,712,458	12,936,690

Constitution of Texas

Following is the complete text of the Constitution of Texas. It includes the original document which was adopted on Feb. 15, 1876, plus the 326 amendments approved through the election of Nov. 6, 1990.

Each amendment is accompanied by a footnote explaining when it was adopted. This text, with footnotes, of the constitution is copyrighted by the A. H. Belo Corporation and may not be reprinted without written permission from the publisher.

Amendment of the Texas Constitution requires a two-thirds favorable vote by both the Texas House of Representatives and the Senate, followed by a majority vote of approval by voters in a statewide election.

Prior to 1973, amendments to the constitution could not be submitted by a special session of the Legislature. But the constitution was amended in 1972 to allow submission of amendments if the special session were opened to the subject by the governor.

Constitutional amendments are not subject to a gubernatorial veto. Once submitted, voters have the final decision on whether to change the constitution as proposed.

The following table lists the total number of amendments submitted to voters by the Texas Legislature and shows the year in which the Legislature approved them for submission to voters; e.g., the Seventieth Legislature in 1987 approved 28 amendments to be submitted to voters — 25 in 1987 and three in 1988.

Year	No.	Year	No.	Year	No.
1879	1	1921	5	1961	14
1881	2	1923	2	1963	7
1883	5	1925	4	1965	27
1887	6	1927	8	1967	20
1889	2	1929	7	1969	16
1891	5	1931	9	1971	18
1893	2	1933	12	1973	9
1895	2	1935	13	1975	12
1897	5	1937	7	1977	15
1899	1	1939	4	1978	1
1901	1	1941	5	1979	12
1903	3	1943	3	1981	10
1905	3	1945	8	1982	3
1907	9	1947	9	1983	19
1909	4	1949	10	1985	17
1911	5	1951	7	1986	1
1913	7	1953	11	1987	28
1915	7	1955	9	1989	21
1917	2	1957	12	1990	1
1919	13	1959	4	1991	11

Amendments, 1989

Twenty-one amendments were voted on Nov. 7, 1989:

HJR 4 — Authorizing the members of a hospital district board to serve four-year terms. Approved 710,018 to 411,778.

HJR 13 — Authorizing the Legislature to exempt from ad valorem taxation certain property of nonprofit veterans organizations. Approved 603,333 to 539,012.

HJR 19 — Providing a bill of rights for crime victims. Approved 819,399 to 317,111.

HJR 32 — Authorizing the Legislature to permit and regulate raffles conducted by certain nonprofit organizations for charitable purposes. Approved 704,694 to 423,699.

HJR 33 — Authorizing the state to provide scholarships, grants, loans and other financial assistance to local fire departments and other public fire-fighting organizations. Approved 665,913 to 462,686.

HJR 40 — Relating to the oath of office prescribed for members of the Legislature, the secretary of state, and other elected and appointed officials. Approved 796,323 to 353,661.

HJR 51 — Authorizing the Legislature to provide for the issuance of bonds and state financing of development and production of Texas products and businesses. Approved 597,178 to 543,631.

HJR 101 — Authorizing the Legislature to organize and combine various state agencies that perform criminal justice functions. Approved 794,006 to 328,831.

HJR 102 (1) — Relating to the salaries of the lieutenant governor, the speaker and members of the Legislature. Defeated 732,417 to 424,704.

HJR 102 (2) — Relating to the per diem allowed members of the Legislature. Defeated 592,412 to 531,550.

SJR 4 — Authorizing jury instructions on good time and eligibility for parole and mandatory supervision. Approved 901,297 to 239,714.

SJR 5 — Authorizing the issuance of an additional $500 million of Texas water development bonds for water supply, water quality, and flood control purposes. Approved 686,735 to 460,742.

SJR 11 — Authorizing the exemption from ad valorem taxation certain personal property temporarily in the state for certain purposes. Approved 742,405 to 408,573.

SJR 16 — Abolishing the office of county surveyor in Bexar, Cass, Ector, Garza, Harris, Smith and Webb counties. Approved 736,963 to 302,617.

SJR 24 — Providing for the issuance of general obligation bonds for acquiring, constructing or equipping corrections institutions, youth corrections institutions, statewide law enforcement facilities and mental health and mental retardation institutions. Approved 779,641 to 357,154.

SJR 34 — Relating to the authority of the Legislature to provide for the creation, establishment, maintenance and operation of a hospital district. Approved 776,806 to 332,298.

SJR 44 — Eliminating certain time limitations relating to the issuance of Texas agricultural water conservation bonds. Approved 537,990 to 535,724.

SJR 53 — Relating to the guarantee by the permanent school fund of bonds issued by the state to fund local schools. Approved 628,812 to 495,090.

SJR 59 — Authorizing local governments to invest their funds as authorized by law. Approved 658,826 to 431,794.

SJR 71 — Relating to the election of a district attorney in Fort Bend County. Approved 704,699 to 338,529.

SJR 74 — Providing for the issuance of general obligation bonds as college savings bonds by the Texas Higher Education Coordinating Board to provide educational loans to students and to encourage the public to save for a college education. Approved 682,251 to 435,182.

Amendment, 1990

One amendment was voted on Nov. 6, 1990:

SJR 2 (Sixth Called Session) — Clarifying the authority of the Senate to consider certain nominees to state and district offices and to provide for filling vacancies in those offices. Approved 1,740,374 to 916,162.

Amendments, 1991

The first two amendments in the list below were to be voted on Aug. 10, 1991, and the 9 others were to be voted on Nov. 5, 1991:

SJR 5 — Providing for the issuance of general obligation bonds by the Higher Education Coordinating Board to provide educational loans to students.

SJR 42 — Relating to partial exemption of residence homesteads from ad valorem taxation by county education districts.

HJR 114 — Relating to the amending of a home rule charter by a city under 5,000 population.

SJR 6 — Relating to investments by statewide public retirement systems.

SJR 8 — Relating to establishing the Election and Ethics Commission.

SJR 11 — Authorizing the commissioner of the General Land Office to issue patents for certain public free school fund land held in good faith under color of title for at least 50 years.

SJR 15 — Authorizing the exemption from ad valorem taxation of property owned by a non-profit water supply or waste-water service corporation.

SJR 21 — Authorizing the Legislature to submit debt questions to the voters in proposition form.

SJR 26 — Relating to investments made by the Veteran's Land Board of funds in the Veterans' Land Fund or the Veterans' Housing Assistance Fund.

SJR 34 — Increasing from 20 percent to 50 percent the percentage of water development bonds previously authorized that may be issued to economically distressed areas.

SJR 39 — Relating to exemptions from property taxes for certain property in an enterprise zone.

Index to State Constitution

The following index to the Texas State Constitution includes all amendments voted on through the election of Nov. 6, 1990. In some instances, reference may be to a section that has been deleted from the text of the Constitution as carried here. However, these references are included when it is clear in the note telling that a section has been deleted that the reference was once a part of the text.

In some instances, an article number is given after the main heading and then there may be references to other articles under the heading (See **Courts, Art. V**: and then under **Impeachment of judges: XV, Secs. 2, 6**).

We trust that this index will be helpful to readers in finding particular sections they are looking for. The Texas Almanac welcomes any suggestions for improving this index, or any criticisms that might help us make this index more useful to our readers.

Contracts:
Not to be impaired: I, Sec. 16.
Public, how let: XVI, Sec. 21.
Convict labor on roads: XVI, Sec. 24.
Convicts denied vote: VI, Sec. 1.

Corporations, Art. XII:
Created by general laws: Secs. 1, 2.
Franchises under legislative control: Sec. 3.
Charges for freights, etc., prohibited except by law: Secs. 4, 5.
Issuance of stocks and bonds prohibited certain instances: Sec. 6.
Vested rights protected: Sec. 7.
Corruption of blood: I, Sec. 21.

Counties:
Cities, can't become stockholders, exceptions: III, Sec. 52.
Consolidation of govt. offices, functions: III, Secs. 63, 64.
County-wide hospital districts: IX, Secs. 4, 5, 6, 7, 8, 9, 11.
Creation and organization of: IX, Sec. 1.
Legal subdivisions of state: XI, Sec. 1.
Home rule: IX, Sec. 3.
How county seats created, changed: IX, Sec. 2.
Can't invest in stock of private corporations: XI, Sec. 3.
Provide workhouses, poorhouses: XVI, Sec. 8.
Tax limitations on: VIII, Sec. 1.
Taxation in unorganized: VIII, Sec. 12.

County:
Commissioners: V, Sec. 18.

Courts, Art. V:
County judges, terms: Sec. 30.
Election, term of office, etc.: Sec. 15.
Jurisdiction of, appeals, etc.: Sec. 16.
Jurisdiction of may be changed: Sec. 22.
Probate business, prosecutions: Sec. 29.
Terms for criminal business: Sec. 17.
And District Attorneys, duties, etc.: V, Sec. 21.
Employees, workmen's compensation for: III, Sec. 60.
Hospital districts: IX, Secs. 4, 5, 6, 7, 8, 9, 11.
Lines, changing of: IX, Sec. 1.
Offices, elective: XVI, Sec. 64.

Officials:
Medical expenses: III, Sec. 52-e.
Removal from office: V, Sec. 24.
Terms, compensation, etc.: XVI, Secs. 61, 62, 65.

School:
Districts: VII, Secs. 3-a, 3-b.
Lands: VII, Secs. 6, 6-a.
Seats, how created, changed: IX, Sec. 2.
Tax Assessor and Collector: VIII, Secs. 14, 16, 16-a.
Treasurer and Surveyor: XVI, Sec. 44.

Courts, Art. V:
Appeal in criminal cases, none allowed: Sec. 26.
Civil Appeals, term, etc.: Secs. 1, 6.
Commissioners, terms of justices of peace, commissioners: Sec. 18.
County, election, term of judges, etc.: Secs. 15, 16, 17, 29.
Criminal Appeals, jurisdiction, etc.: Secs. 4, 5.
Criminal jurisdiction of justices of peace: Sec. 19.
Disqualification of judges: Sec. 11.
District, clerk of, term, etc.: Sec. 9.
Districts fixed by ordinance: Sec. 14.
District, jurisdiction and powers of: Sec. 8.
Impeachment of judges: XV, Secs. 2, 6.
Judges conservators of peace: Sec. 12.
Judicial districts, term of office, etc.: Sec. 7.
Jurisdiction, terms of: Secs. 3, 6, 22.
Jurors, grand and petit: Sec. 13.
Jury trial, who pays fee: Sec. 10.
Kinds of: Sec. 1.
Removal of judges for misconduct: XV, Sec. 8.
Remove county officials for misconduct, etc.: Sec. 24.
Retirement and compensation of judges: Sec. 1-a; XVI, Sec. 67 (d).
Salaries: Secs. 2, 4, 6, 7, 15.

Supreme:
Direct appeal: Sec. 3-b.
Qualifications, election, etc.: Sec. 2.
To regulate practice: Sec. 25.
Time of sitting: Sec. 3-a.
Transfer of cases by Legislature: Sec. 27.
Vacancies in office of judges, how filled: Sec. 28.
Creation of counties: IX, Sec. 1.

Credit of State:
For toll roads prohibited: III, Sec. 52-b.
Not to be pledged: III, Sec. 50.

Criminal Appeals Court, Art. V:
How set up: Sec. 4.
Jurisdiction, term, etc.: Secs. 1, 5.
Retirement and compensation of judges: Sec. 1-a.

Criminal:
District Attorneys: V, Sec. 30.
Prosecutions, rights of accused persons: I, Sec. 10.
Criminals disfranchised: XVI, Sec. 2.
Dallas County road bonds: III, Sec. 52-e.
Deaf and Dumb asylum, taxes for support: III, Sec. 48.
Death compensation funds for state employees: XVI, Secs. 62, 63, 67.
Debate, freedom in: III, Sec. 21.

Debt:
Imprisonment for: I, Sec. 18.
Power of Legislature to release: III, Sec. 55.
Debts, purpose for which may be created: III, Sec. 49.
Deductions from salaries to be provided for: XVI, Sec. 10.
Delinquent taxes: III, Sec. 55.
Defeated bill or resolution not considered again: III, Sec. 34.
Departments of Government: II, Sec. 1.
Deportations: I, Sec. 20.
Disabled, assistance to: III, Sec. 51-a.

Disability:
Aid, municipal: III, Secs. 51-e, 51-f, 51-g.
Funds for state employees: XVI, Secs. 62, 63, 67.
Disorderly conduct in Legislature: III, Sec. 15.

District:
Attorneys, Criminal: V, Sec. 30.
And County Attorneys, duties, etc.: V, Sec. 21.

Courts, Art. V:
Clerk of, term of office, etc.: Sec. 9.
Districts fixed by ordinance: Sec. 14.
Judges, qualifications, residence, etc.: Sec. 7.
Jurisdiction and powers: Sec. 8.
Jurors, grand and petit: Sec. 13.
Jury trial, who pays fee: Sec. 10.
Judges, removal by impeachment: XV, Secs. 2, 6, 8.
Offices, elective: XVI, Sec. 64.
Officials, compensation, etc.: XVI, Secs. 61, 65.

Districts:
Representative, how apportioned: III, Secs. 26, 26-a, 28.
Senatorial, how apportioned: III, Secs. 25, 28.
Divorce, how granted: III, Sec. 56.
Doctors, qualifications to be prescribed: XVI, Sec. 31.
Double jeopardy: I, Sec. 14.
Due course of law: I, Sec. 19
Dueling prohibited: XVI, Sec. 4.
Duration of special sessions: III, Sec. 40.

Education, Art. VII:
Agricultural & Mechanical College: Sec. 13.
Board of, terms and duties: Sec. 8.
Building bonds authorized for UT and A&M: Secs. 17, 18.
College building fund tax: Sec. 17.
County-line districts, validation, bonds, etc.: Sec. 3-a.
County school lands: Sec. 6.
Land appropriated for university: Sec. 15.
Lands to be sold: Secs. 12, 15.
Medical board: III, Sec. 50-a.
Patents for school lands: 4A.
Permanent school fund; sectarian schools: Sec. 5.
Permanent university fund: Secs. 11, 11-a, 17, 18.
Public schools established: Sec. 1.
Sale of school lands: Sec. 4.
School taxes, how derived: Sec. 3.
Segregation in schools: Sec. 7.
Taxation of county school lands: Sec. 6-a.
Taxation of university lands: Sec. 16-a.
Taxes for support of public schools: Secs. 2, 3; III, Sec. 48.
Terms of office in school system: Sec. 16.
University for colored: Sec. 14.
University funds, how invested: Sec. 11.
University lands and funds: Sec. 10.

Election:
Executive officers: IV, Secs. 1, 2.
Legislature: III, Secs. 3, 4, 27.
Results, ties, contests: IV, Sec. 3.

Elections:
By ballot, registration in cities of 10,000 or more: VI, Sec. 4
Bribery in, disqualification: XVI, Sec. 5.
Poll tax required: VI, Sec. 2.
Votes, how taken: III, Sec. 41.
Voters privileged from arrest: VI, Sec. 5.
Who can vote: VI, Secs. 1, 3, 3-a.

Text of Texas Constitution

The following is a complete text of the Constitution of Texas, containing all amendments adopted through Nov. 6, 1990, with explanatory footnotes:

Preamble

Humbly invoking the blessings of Almighty God, the people of the State of Texas do ordain and establish this Constitution.

ARTICLE I — BILL OF RIGHTS

That the general, great and essential principles of liberty and free government may be recognized and established, we declare:

Sec. 1. Texas Free and Independent — Texas is a free and independent State, subject only to the Constitution of the United States, and the maintenance of our free institutions and the perpetuity of the Union depend upon the preservation of the right of local self-government, unimpaired to all the states.

Sec. 2. All Political Power Is Inherent in the People — All political power is inherent in the people, and all free governments are founded on their authority, and instituted for their benefit. The faith of the people of Texas stands pledged to the preservation of a republican form of government, and subject to this limitation only, they have at all times the inalienable right to alter, reform or abolish their government in such manner as they may think expedient.

Sec. 3. All Free Men Have Equal Rights — All free men, when they form a social compact, have equal rights, and no man, or set of men, is entitled to exclusive separate public emoluments or privileges but in consideration of public services.

Sec. 3-a. Equality under the law shall not be denied or abridged because of sex, race, color, creed or national origin. This amendment is self-operative.

[Note — Sec. 3-a of Art. I is an added amendment setting forth civil rights for all. Submitted by the Sixty-second Legislature (1971) and adopted in an election Nov. 7, 1972.]

Sec. 4. There Shall Be No Religious Test for Office — No religious test shall ever be required as a qualification to any office or public trust in this State; nor shall anyone be excluded from holding office on account of his religious sentiments, provided he acknowledge the existence of a Supreme Being.

Sec. 5. How Oaths Shall Be Administered — No person shall be disqualified to give evidence in any of the courts of this State on account of his religious opinions, or for want of any religious belief, but all oaths or affirmations shall be administered in the mode most binding upon the conscience, and shall be taken subject to the pains and penalties of perjury.

Sec. 6. Freedom in Religious Worship Guaranteed — All men have a natural and indefeasible right to worship Almighty God according to the dictates of their own consciences. No man shall be compelled to attend, erect or support any place of worship, or to maintain any ministry against his consent. No human authority ought, in any case whatever, to control or interfere with the rights of conscience in matters of religion, and no preference shall ever be given by law to any religious society or mode of worship. But it shall be the duty of the Legislature to pass such laws as may be necessary to protect equally every religious denomination in the peaceable enjoyment of its own mode of public worship.

Sec. 7. No Appropriation for Sectarian Purposes — No money shall be appropriated or drawn from the Treasury for the benefit of any sect, or religious society, theological or religious seminary, nor shall property belonging to the State be appropriated for any such purposes.

Sec. 8. Liberty of Speech and Press Guaranteed; Libel. Every person shall be at liberty to speak, write or publish his opinions, on any subject, being responsible for the abuse of that privilege; and no law shall ever be passed curtailing the liberty of speech or of the press. In prosecutions for the publication of papers, investigating the conduct of officers or men in public capacity, or when the matter published is proper for public information, the truth thereof may be given in evidence. And in all indictments for libels, the jury shall have the right to determine the law and the facts, under the direction of the court, as in other cases.

Sec. 9. No Unreasonable Seizures and Searches Allowed — The people shall be secure in their persons, houses, papers and possessions from all unreasonable seizures or searches, and no warrant to search any place, or to seize any person or thing, shall issue without describing them as near as may be, or without probable cause, supported by oath or affirmation.

Sec. 10. Rights of Accused Persons in Criminal Prosecutions — In all criminal prosecutions the accused shall have a speedy public trial by an impartial jury. He shall have the right to demand the nature and cause of the accusation against him, and to have a copy thereof. He shall not be compelled to give evidence against himself and shall have the right of being heard by himself or counsel, or both; shall be confronted with the witnesses against him and shall have compulsory process for obtaining witnesses in his favor, except that when the witness resides out of the State and the offense charged is a violation of any of the antitrust laws of this State, the defendant and the State shall have the right to produce and have the evidence admitted by deposition, under such rules and laws as the Legislature may hereafter provide; and no person shall be held to answer for a criminal offense, unless on an indictment of a grand jury, except in cases in which the punishment is by fine or imprisonment, otherwise than in the penitentiary; in cases of impeachment and in cases arising in the army or navy, or in the militia, when in actual service in time of war or public danger.

[Note — The foregoing is an amended section, the amendment consisting of the addition of that clause relating to depositions of witnesses resident outside of the State in antitrust suits. Submitted by the Thirty-fifth Legislature (1917) and adopted at election on Nov. 5, 1918.]

Sec. 11. Bail — All prisoners shall be bailable by sufficient sureties, unless for capital offenses, when the proof is evident; but this provision shall not be so construed as to prevent bail after indictment found upon examination of the evidence, in such manner as may be prescribed by law.

Sec. 11-a. Multiple Convictions; Denial of Bail — Any person (1) accused of a felony less than capital in this State, who has been theretofore twice convicted of a felony, the second conviction being subsequent to the first, both in point of time of commission of the offense and conviction therefor, (2) accused of a felony less than capital in this State, committed while on bail for a prior felony for which he has been indicted, or (3) accused of a felony less than capital in this State involving the use of a deadly weapon after being convicted of a prior felony, after a hearing, and upon evidence substantially showing the guilt of the accused of the offense in (1) or (3) above or of the offense committed while on bail In (2) above, may be denied bail pending trial, by a district judge in this State, if said order denying bail pending trial is issued within seven calendar days subsequent to the time of incarceration of the accused; provided, however, that if the accused is not accorded a trial upon the accusation under (1) or (3) above or the accusation and indictment used under (2) above within sixty (60) days from the time of his incarceration upon the accusation, the order denying bail shall be automatically set aside, unless a continuance is obtained upon the motion or request of the accused; provided, further, that the right of appeal to the Court of Criminal Appeals of this State is expressly accorded the accused for a review of any judgment or order made hereunder, and said appeal shall be given preference by the Court of Criminal Appeals.

[Note — Sec. 11-a of Art. I is an added amendment permitting denial of bail to a person charged with a felony less than capital who has been theretofore twice convicted of a felony. Submitted by the Fifty-fourth Legislature (1955) and adopted in election Nov. 6, 1956. This section was amended to provide for further denial of bail under circumstances (2) and (3) above, and providing for 60-day limit to that person's incarceration without trial; and providing for that person's right of appeal. Submitted by the Sixty-fifth Legislature (1977) and adopted in election Nov. 8, 1977.]

Sec. 12. The Writ of Habeas Corpus — The writ of habeas corpus is a writ of right, and shall never be suspended. The Legislature shall enact laws to render the remedy speedy and effectual.

Sec. 13. Excessive Bail and Fine and Unusual Punishment Prohibited; Courts Open — Excessive bail shall not be required, nor excessive fines imposed, nor cruel or unusual punishment inflicted. All courts shall be open, and every person for an injury done him in his lands, goods, person or reputation, shall have due course of law.

Sec. 14. No Person Shall Be Put Twice in Jeopardy — No person, for the same offense, shall be twice put in jeopardy of life or liberty, nor shall a person be again put upon trial for the same offense after a verdict of not guilty in a court of competent jurisdiction.

Sec. 15. Right of Trial by Jury — The right of trial by jury shall remain inviolate. The Legislature shall pass such laws as may be needed to regulate the same, and to maintain its purity and efficiency. Provided, that the Legislature may provide for the temporary commitment, for observation and/or treatment, of mentally ill persons not charged with a criminal offense, for a period of time not to exceed ninety (90) days, by order of the County Court without the necessity of a trial by jury.

[Note — The original Sec. 15 of Art. I was amended to add the last sentence. Submitted by the Forty-fourth Legislature (1935) and adopted in an election Aug. 24, 1935.]

Section 15-a. No person shall be committed as a person of unsound mind except on competent medical or psychiatric testimony. The Legislature may enact all laws necessary to provide for the trial, adjudication of insanity and commitment of persons of unsound mind and to provide for a method of appeal from judgments rendered in such cases. Such laws may provide for a waiver of trial by jury. In cases where the person under inquiry has not been charged with the commission of a criminal offense, by the concurrence of the person under inquiry, or his next of kin, and an attorney

Article I — (Cont'd.); Article II and III

ad litem appointed by a judge of either the County or Probate Court of the county where the trial is being held, and shall provide for a method of service of notice of such trial upon the person under inquiry and of his right to demand a trial by jury.

[Note — Sec. 15-a of Art. I is an added amendment relating to requiring medical or psychiatric testimony for commitment of persons of unsound mind and authorizing Legislature to provide for trial and commitment of such persons and for waiver of trial by jury where the person under inquiry has not been charged with commission of a criminal offense. Submitted by the Fifty-fourth Legislature (1955) and adopted in election Nov. 5, 1956.]

Sec. 16. There Shall Be No Bill of Attainder or Ex-Post Facto Laws — No bill of attainder or ex post facto law, retroactive law, or any other law impairing the obligation of contracts shall be made.

Sec. 17. Privileges and Franchises: Eminent Domain — No person's property shall be taken, damaged or destroyed for or applied to public use without adequate compensation being made, unless by the consent of such person; and when taken, except for the use of the State, such compensation shall be first made or secured by a deposit of money; and no irrevocable or uncontrollable grant of special privileges or immunities shall be made; but all priviliedges and franchises granted by the Legislature, or created under its authority, shall be subject to the control thereof.

Sec. 18. No imprisonment for Debt — No person shall ever be imprisoned for debt.

Sec. 19. Due Course of Law — No citizen of this State shall be deprived of life, liberty, property, privileges or immunities, or in any manner disfrancised, except by the due course of the law of the land.

Sec. 20. No Outlawrry or Deportations — No citizen shall be outlawed. No person shall be transported out of the State for any offense committed within the same. This section does not prohibit an agreement with another state providing for the confinement of inmates of this State in the penal or correctional facilities of that state.

[Note — The foregoing Sec. 20 of Art. I was amended to permit state prisoners to be placed in penal facilities of another state pursuant to an interstate agreement. Submitted by the Sixty-ninth Legislature (1985) and adopted in an election Nov. 5, 1985.]

Sec. 21. Corruption of Blood, Forfeiture; Suicide —No conviction shall work corruption of blood or forfeiture of estate, and the estates of those who destroy their own lives shall descend or vest as in the case of natural death.

Sec. 22. Treason —Treason against the State shall consist only in levying war against it, or adhering to its enemies, giving ;them aid and comfort; and no person shall be convicted of treason except on the testimony of two witnesses to the same overt act or on confession in open court.

Sec. 23. Right to Bear Arms —Every citizen shall have the right to keep and bear arms in the lawful defense of himself or the State; but the Legislature shall have power, by law, to regulate the wearing of arms, with a view to prevent crime.

Sec. 24. Military Subordinate to Civil Authority — The military shall at all times be subordinate to the civil authority.

Sec. 25. Quartering Soldiers — No soldier shall in time of peace be quartered in the house of any citizen without the consent of the owner, nor in time of war but in a manner prescribed by law.

Sec. 26 Prepetuities; Monopolies; Primeogeniture; Entailments — Prepetuities and monopolies are contrary to the genius of a free government, and shall never be allowed, nor shall the law of primogeniture or entailments ever be in force in ths State.

Sec. 27. Right of Petition Guaranteed — The citizens shall have the right, in a peaceable manner, to assemble together for their common good and apply to those invested with the powers of geovernment for redress of grievances or other purposes, by petition, address or remonstrance.

Sec. 28. Power to Suspend Laws — No power of suspending laws in this State shall be exercised except by the Legislature.

Sec. 29. "Bill of Rights" Inviolate — To guard against transgressions of the high powers being delegated, we declare that everything in this "Bill of Rights" is excepted out of the general powers of government, and shall forever remain inviolate, and all laws contrary thereto, or the following provisions, shall be void.

Sec. 30. Rights of Crime Victims — (a) A crime victim has the following rights:

(1) the right to be treated with fairness and with respect for the victim's dignity and privacy throughout the criminal justice process; and

(2) the right to be reasonably protected from the accused throughout the criminal justice process.

(b) On the request of a crime victim, the crime victim has the following rights:

(1) the right to notification of court proceedings;

(2) the right to be present at all public court proceedings related to the offense, unless the victim is to testify and the court determines that the victim's testimony would be materially affected if the victim hears other testimony at the trial;

(3) the right to confer with a representative of the prosecutor's office;

(4) the right to restitution; and

(5) the right to information about the conviction, sentence, imprisonment, and release of the accused.

(c) The legislature may enact laws to define the term "victim" and to enforce these and other rights of crime victims.

(d) The state, through its prosecuting attorney, has the right to enforce the rights of crime victims.

(e) The legislature may enact laws to provide that a judge, attorney for the state, peace officer, or law enforcement agency is not liable for a failure or inability to provide a right enumerated in this section. The failure or inability of any person to provide a right or service enumerated in this section may not be used by a defendant in a criminal case as a ground for appeal or post-conviction writ of habeas corpus. A victim or guardian or legal representative of a victim has standing to enforce the rights enumerated in this section but does not have standing to participate as a party in a criminal proceeding or to contest the disposition of any charge.

[Note — Sec. 30 of Art. I is an amendment relating to the rights of crime victims. Submitted by the Seventy-first Legislature (1989) and adopted in an election Nov. 7, 1989.]

ARTICLE II — THE POWERS OF GOVERNMENT

Sec. 1. Departments of Governments to Be Kept Distinct — The powers of the government of the State of Texas shall be divided into three distinct departments, each of which shall be confined to a separate body of magistracy, to wit: Those which are legislative to one, those which are executive to another, and those which are judicial to another; and no person, or collection of persons, being of one of these departments shall exercise any power properly attached to either of the others, except in the instances herein expressly L permitted.

ARTICLE III — LEGISLATIVE DEPARTMENT

Sec. 1 The Legislature: House and Senate — The legislature power of this State shall be vested in a Senate and House of Representatives, which together shall be styled "The Legislature of the State of Texas."

Sec. 2 Number of Members Limited — The Senate shall consist of thirty-one members, and shall never be increased above this number. The House of Representatives shall consist of ninety-three members until the first apportionment after the adoption of this Constitution, when or at any apportionment thereafter the number of Representatives may be increased by the Legislature, upon the ration of not more than one Representative for every 15,000 inhabitants; provided, the number of Representative shall never exceed 150.

Sec. 3 Election of Senators; New Apportionment —The Senators shall be chosen by the qualified electors for the term of four years; but a new Senate shall be chosen after every apportionment, and the Senators elected after each apportionment shall be divided by lot into two classes. The seats of the Senators of the first class shall be vacated at the expiration of the first two years, and those of the second class at the expiration of four years, so that one half of the Senators shall be chosen biennially thereafter. Senators shall take office following their election, on the day set by law for the convening of the regular session of the Legislature, and shall serve thereafter for the full term of years to which elected and until their successors have been elected and qualified.

[Note — The foregoing Sec. 3 of Art. III was amended to establish the date on which newly elected members of the Senate shall qualify and take office. Submitted by the Fifty-ninth Legislature (1965) and adopted in election Nov. 8, 1966.]

Sec. 4 Election of Representatives; Term of Office — The members of the House of Representatives shall be chosen by the qualified electors for the terms of two years. Representatives shall take office following their election, on the day set by law for the convening of the regular session of the Legislature, and shall serve thereafter for the full term of years to which elected and until their successors shall have been elected and qualifed.

[Note — The foregoing Sec. 4 of Art. III was ameneded to provide for the date on which newly elected members of the House of Representatives shall qualify and take office. Submitted by the Fifty-ninth Legislature (1965) and adopted in an election Nov. 8, 1966.]

Sec. 5 Time of Meeting; Method of Procedure — The Legislature shall meet every two years at such time as may be provided by law and at other times when convened by the

Article III — (Cont'd.)

Governor. When convened in regular session, the first thirty days thereof shall be devoted to the introduction of bills and resolutions, acting upon emergency appropriations, passing upon the confirmation of the recess appointees of the Governor and such emergency matters as may be submitted by the Governor in special messages to the Legislature; provided, that during the succeeding thirty days of the regular session of the Legislature the various committees of each house shall hold hearings to consider all bills and resolutions and other matters then pending; and such emergency matters as may be submitted by the Governor; provided, further that during the following sixty days the Legislature shall act upon such bills and resolutions as may be then pending and upon such emergency matters as may be submitted by the Governor in special messages to the Legislature; provided, however, either house may other wise determine its order of business by an affirmative vote of four fifths of its membership.

[Note — The foregoing Sec. 5 of Art. III has been amended once, to provide for a 120-day session. It was submitted together with the amendement of Sec. 24 of Art. III. Submitted by the Forty-first Legislature (1929); ratified Nov. 4, 1930.]

Sec. 6 **Qualifications of Senators** —No person shall be a Senator unless he be a citizen of the United States, and, at the time of his election, a qualified elector of this State, and shall have been a residen of this State five years next preceding his election and the last year thereof a resident of the district for which he shall be chosen, and shall have attained the age of twenty-six years.

Sec. 7 **Qualifications of Representatives** — No person shall be a Representative unless he be a citizen of the United States, and, at the time of his election, a qualified elector of this State, and shall have been a resident of this State two years preceding his election, the last year thereof a resident of the district for which he shall be chosen, and shall have attained the age of twenty-one years.

Sec. 8 **Each House to Judge Qualifications of Its Own Members** — Each house shall be the judge of the qualifications and election of its own members; but contested elections shall be determined in such manner as shall be provided by law.

Sec. 9. **President Pro Tem of the Senate; Speaker of the House; Officers** — (a) The Senate shall, at the beginning and close of each session, and at such other times as may be necessary, elect one of its members President pro tempore, who shall perform the duties of the Lieutenant Governor in any case of absence or disability of that officer. If the said office of Lieutenant Governor becomes vacant, the President pro tempore of the Senate shall convene the Committee of the Whole Senate within 30 days after the vacancy occurs. The Committee of the Whole shall elect one of its members to perform the duties of the Lieutenant Governor in addition to his duties as Senator until the next general election. If the Senator so elected ceases to be a Senator before the election of a new Lieutenant Governor, another Senator shall be elected in the same manner to perform the duties of the Lieutenant Governor until the next general election. Until the Committee of the Whole elects one of its members for this purpose, the President pro tempore shall perform the duties of the Lieutenant Governor as provided by this subsection.

(b) The House of Representatives shall, when it first assembles, organize temporarily, and thereupon proceed to the election of a Speaker from its own members.

(c) Each House shall choose its other officers.

[Note — Sec. 9 of Art. III was amended to provide for method of filling a vacancy in the office of Lieutenant Governor. Submitted by the Sixty-eighth Legislature (1983) and approved in election Nov. 6, 1984.]

Sec. 10. **Quorum** — Two thirds of each house shall constitute a quorum to do business, but a smaller number may adjourn from day to day and compel the attendance of absent members, in such manner and under such penalties as each house may provide.

Sec. 11. **Rules: Power to Punish and Expel** — Each house may determine the rules of its own proceedings, punish members for disorderly conduct, and, with the consent of two thirds, expel a member, but not a second time for the same offense.

Sec. 12. **Journal: Yeas and Nays** — Each house shall keep a journal of its proceedings, and publish the same; and the yeas and nays of the members of either house on any question shall, at the desire of any three members present, be entered on the journals.

Sec. 13. **Vacancies, How Filled** — When vacancies occur in either house, the Governor, or the person exercising the power of the Governor, shall issue writs of election to fill such vacancies; and should the Governor fail to issue a writ of election to fill any such vacancy within twenty days after the returning officer of the district in which such vacancy may have happened shall be authorized to order an election for that purpose.

Sec. 14. **Members of Legislature Privileged From Arrest** — Senators and Representatives shall, except in cases of treason, felony or breach of the peace, be privileged from arrest during the session of the Legislature, and in going to or returning from the same, allowing one day for every twenty miles such member may reside from the place at which the Legislature is convened.

Sec. 15. **Each House May Punish Disorderly Conduct** — Each house may punish, by imprisonment, during its sessions, any person not a member for disrespectful or disorderly conduct in its presence, or for obstructing any of its proceedings; provided, such imprisonment shall not, at any one time, exceed forty-eight hours.

Sec. 16. **Sessions to Be Open** — The sessions of each house shall be open, except the Senate when in executive session.

Sec. 17. **Adjournments** — Neither house shall, without the consent of the other, adjourn for more than three days, nor to any other place than that where the Legislature may be sitting.

Sec. 18. **Ineligibility of Members to Certain Offices; Not to Be Interested in Contracts** — No Senator or Representative shall, during the term for which he was elected, be eligible to (1) any civil office of profit under this State which shall have been created, or the emoluments of which may have been increased, during such term, or (2) any office or place, the appointment to which may be made, in whole or in part, by either branch of the Legislature; provided, however, the fact that the term of office of Senators and Representatives does not end precisely on the last day of December but extends a few days into January of the succeeding year shall be considered as de minimis, and the ineligibility herein created shall terminate on the last day in December of the last full calendar year of the term for which he was elected. No member of either House shall vote for any other member for any office whatever, which may be filled by a vote of the Legislature, except in such cases as are in this Constitution provided, nor shall any member of the Legislature be interested, either directly or indirectly, in any contract with the State, or any county thereof, authorized by any law passed during the term for which he was elected.

[Note — Sec. 18 of Art. III was amended to fix the time during which members of Legislature shall be ineligible to hold other office. Submitted by the Sixtieth Legislature (1967) and adopted in election Nov. 5, 1968.]

Sec. 19. **What Officers Ineligible to Membership in Legislature** — No judge of any court, Secretary of State, Attorney General, clerk of any court of record, or any person holding a lucrative office under the United States, or this State, or any foreign government, shall, during the term for which he is elected or appointed, be eligible to the Legislature.

Sec. 20. **Receivers or Disbursers of Public Funds Not Eligible to Membership in the Legislature Until Discharge Received** — No person who at any time may have been a collector of taxes or who may have been otherwise entrusted with public money, shall be eligible to the Legislature, or to any office of profit or trust under the State Government, until he shall have obtained a discharge for the amount of such collections, or for all public moneys with which he may have been entrusted.

Sec. 21. **Freedom in Debate** — No member shall be questioned in any other place for words spoken in debate in either house.

Sec. 22. **Personal Interest in Measure or Bill** — A member who has a personal or private interest in any measure or bill, proposed or pending before the Legislature, shall disclose the fact to the house of which he is a member, and shall not vote thereon.

Sec. 23. **Removal Vacates Office** — If any Senator or Representative remove his residence from the district or county for which he was elected, his office shall thereby become vacant, and the vacancy shall be filled as provided in Sec. 13 of this article.

Sec. 23-a. **John Tarleton Contract Validated** — The Legislature is authorized to appropriate so much money as may be necessary, not to exceed seventy-five thousand ($75,000) dollars, to pay claims incurred by John Tarleton Agricultural College for the construction of a building on the campus of such college pursuant to deficiency authorization by the Governor of Texas on Aug. 31, 1937.

[Note — Sec. 23-a. of Art. III is an added amendment to provide for payment of a contractor whose contract had been annulled. Submitted by the Forty-ninth Legislature (1945) and ratified in election Nov. 5, 1946.]

Sec. 24. **Mileage and Per Diem** — Members of the Legislature shall receive from the Public Treasury a salary of Six Hundred Dollars ($600) per month. Each member shall also receive a per diem of Thirty Dollars ($30) for each day during each Regular and Special Session of the Legislature. No Regular Session shall be of longer duration than one hundred and forty (140) days.

Article III — (Cont'd.)

In addition to the per diem the Members of each House shall be entitled to mileage at the same rate as prescribed by law for employees of the State of Texas. This amendment takes effect on April 22, 1975.

[Note — Sec. 24 of Art. III has been amended four times, first raising the per diem and decreasing the mileage. It was submitted with the amendment of Sec. 5 of Art. III. Submitted by Forty-first Legislature (1929); ratified Nov. 4, 1930. Further amended to raise per diem to $25 for first 120 days only. Submitted by Fifty-third Legislature (1953) and adopted in election Nov. 2, 1954. Further amended to fix the salary at $4,800 per year and setting the per diem at $12 per day for first 120 days of regular session and 30 days of each special session. Submitted by Fifty-sixth Legislature (1959) and adopted in election Nov. 8, 1960. It was amended to set salaries of members of Legislature at $600 per month and set per diem of $30 per day during legislative sessions and a mileage allowance at the same rate provided by law for state employees. Submitted by Sixty-fourth Legislature (1975) and adopted in election April 22, 1975.]

Sec. 25. **Senatorial Districts, How Apportioned** — The State shall be divided into senatorial districts of contiguous territory according to the number of qualified electors, as nearly as may be, and each district shall be entitled to elect one Senator; and no single county shall be entitled to more than one Senator.

Sec. 26. **Representative Districts, How Apportioned** — The members of the House of Representatives shall be apportioned among the several counties, according to the number of population in each, as nearly as may be, on a ratio obtained by dividing the population of the State, as ascertained by the most recent United States census, by the number of members of which the House is composed; provided that whenever a single county has sufficient population to be entitled to a Representative, such county shall be formed into a separate representative district, and when two or more counties are required to make up the ratio of representation, such counties shall be contiguous to each other; and when any one county has more than sufficient population to be entitled to one or more Representatives, such Representative or Representatives shall be apportioned to such county, and for any surplus of population it may be joined in a representative district with any other contiguous county or counties.

Sec. 26-a. **Redistricting According to Population** — Provided, however, that no county shall be entitled to or have under any apportionment more than seven (7) Representatives unless the population of such county shall exceed seven hundred thousand (700,000) people as ascertained by the most recent United States census, in which event such county shall be entitled to one additional Representative for each one hundred thousand (100,000) population in excess of seven hundred thousand (700,000) population as shown by the latest United States census; nor shall any district be created which would permit any county to have more than seven (7) Representatives except under the conditions set forth above.

[Note — Sec. 26-a of Art. III is an added amendment, to place limitation on representation of counties with large population. Adopted in election Nov. 3, 1936.]

Sec. 27. **Election of Members** — Elections for Senators and Representatives shall be general throughout the State, and shall be regulated by law.

Sec. 28. **Reapportionment After Each Census** — The Legislature shall, at its first regular session after the publication of each United States decennial census, apportion the State into senatorial and representative districts, agreeable to the provisions of Sections 25, 26 and 26-a of this Article. In the event the Legislature shall at any such first regular session following the publication of a United States decennial census, fail to make such apportionment, same shall be done by the Legislative Redistricting Board of Texas, which is hereby created, and shall be composed of five (5) members, as follows: The Lieutenant Governor, the Speaker of the House of Representatives, the Attorney General, the Comptroller of Public Accounts and the Commissioner of the General Land Office, a majority of whom shall constitute a quorum. Said board shall assemble in the City of Austin within ninety (90) days after the final adjournment of such regular session. The board shall, within sixty (60) days after assembling, apportion the State into senatorial and representative districts, or into senatorial or representative districts, as the failure of action of such Legislature may make necessary. Such apportionment shall be in writing and signed by three (3) or more of the members of such board duly acknowledged as the act and deed of such board, and when so executed and filed with the Secretary of State, shall have force and effect of law. Such apportionment shall become effective at the next succeeding statewide general election. The Supreme Court of Texas shall have jurisdiction to compel such commission to perform its duties in accordance with the provisions of this section by writ of mandamus or other extraordinary writs conformable to the usages of law. The Legislature shall provide necessary funds for clerical and technical aid and for other expenses incidental to the work of the board, and the Lieutenant Governor and the Speaker of the House of Representatives shall be entitled to receive per diem and

travel expense during the board's session in the same manner and amount as they would receive while attending a special session of the Legislature. This amendment shall become effective Jan. 1, 1951.

[Note — The foregoing Section 28 of Art. III was amended to provide for the Legislative Redistricting Board of Texas, this action being taken because of failure of past Legislatures to obey the mandate in the original Sec. 28 to redistrict the state after each decennial census. Submitted by the Fiftieth Legislature (1947) and adopted Nov. 2, 1948.]

Proceedings

Sec. 29. **Enacting Clause** — The enacting clause of all laws shall be: ''Be it enacted by the Legislature of the State of Texas.''

Sec. 30. **Laws to Be Passed by Bill; Amendments** — No law shall be passed, except by bill, and no bill shall be so amended in its passage through either house as to change its original purpose.

Sec. 31. **Bills May Originate in Either House and May Be Amended or Rejected by the Other House** — Bills may originate in either house, and when passed by such house may be amended, altered or rejected by the other.

Sec. 32. **Bills to Be Read on Three Several Days; Suspension of Rule** — No bill shall have the force of a law until it has been read on three several days in each house, and free discussion allowed thereon; but in cases of imperative public necessity (which necessity shall be stated in a preamble or in the body of the bill) four fifths of the house in which the bill may be pending may suspend this rule, the yeas and nays being taken on the question of suspension and entered upon the journals.

Sec. 33. **Bills for Raising Revenue** — All bills for raising revenue shall originate in the House of Representatives, but the Senate may amend or reject them as other bills.

Sec. 34. **Bill or Resolution Defeated, Not to Be Considered Again** — After a bill has been considered and defeated by either house of the Legislature, no bill containing the same substance shall be passed into a law during the same session. After a resolution has been acted on and defeated, no resolution containing the same substance shall be considered at the same session.

Sec. 35. **Bills to Contain but One Subject, Which Must Be Expressed in Title** — (a) No bill (except general appropriation bills, which may embrace the various subjects and accounts for and on account of which moneys are appropriated) shall contain more than one subject.

(b) The rules of procedure of each house shall require that the subject of each bill be expressed in its title in a manner that gives the Legislature and the public reasonable notice of that subject. The Legislature is solely responsible for determining compliance with the rule.

(c) A law, including a law enacted before the effective date of this subsection, may not be held void on the basis of an insufficient title.

[Note — The foregoing Sec. 35 of Art. III was amended to require each house to include in its rules of procedure a rule that each bill contain title expressing bill's subject. Submitted by Sixty-ninth Legislature (1985) and adopted in an election Nov. 4, 1986.]

Sec. 36. **Reviving or Amending Laws** — No law shall be revived or amended by reference to its title; but in such case the act revived, or the section or sections amended, shall be re-enacted and published at length.

Sec. 37. **Reference to Committees** — No bill shall be considered unless it has been first referred to a committee and reported thereon, and no bill shall be passed which has not been presented and referred to and reported from a committee at least three days before the final adjournment of the Legislature.

Sec. 38. **Signing Bills** — The presiding officer of each house shall, in the presence of the house over which he presides, sign all bills and joint resolutions passed by the Legislature, after their titles have been publicly read before signing, and the fact of signing shall be entered on the journals.

Sec. 39. **When Laws Take Effect** — No law passed by the Legislature, except the general appropriation act, shall take effect or go into force until ninety days after the adjournment of the session at which it was enacted, unless in case of an emergency, which emergency must be expressed in a preamble or in the body of the act, the Legislature shall, by a vote of two thirds of all the members elected to each house, otherwise direct; said vote to be taken by yeas and nays, and entered upon the journals.

Sec. 40. **Business and Duration of Special Sessions** — When the Legislature shall be convened in special session, there shall be no legislation upon subjects other than those designated in the proclamation of the Governor calling such session, or presented to them by the Governor; and no such session shall be of longer duration than thirty days.

Sec. 41. **Elections: Votes, How Taken** — In all elections by the Senate and House of Representatives, jointly or sepa-

Article III – (Cont'd.)

rately, the vote shall be given viva voce, except in the election of their officers.

[Note — Sec. 42 of Art. III, relating to passage of laws, was deleted by constitutional amendment in election Aug. 5, 1969.]

Requirements and Limitations

Sec. 43. **Revision and Publication of Laws** — (a) The Legislature shall provide for revising, digesting and publishing the laws, civil and criminal; provided, that in the adoption of and giving effect to any such digest or revision the Legislature shall not be limited by Secs. 35 and 36 of this article.

(b) In this section, "revision" includes a revision of the statutes on a particular subject and any enactment having the purpose, declared in the enactment, of codifying without substantive change statutes that individually relate to different subjects.

[Note — The foregoing Sec. 43 of Art. III was amended to provide for the continuing revision of state laws. Submitted by the Sixty-ninth Legislature (1985) and adopted in an election Nov. 4, 1986.]

Sec. 44. **Compensation of Officers: Payment of Claims** — The Legislature shall provide by law for the compensation of all officers, servants, agents and public contractors, not provided for in this Constitution, but shall not grant extra compensation to any officer, agent, servant or public contractors, after such public service shall have been performed or contract entered into for the performance of the same; nor grant, by appropriation or otherwise, any amount of money out of the Treasury of the State, to any individual, on a claim, real or pretended, when the same shall not have been provided for by pre-existing law; nor employ anyone in the name of the State, unless authorized by pre-existing law.

Sec. 45. **Change of Venue** — The power to change the venue in civil and criminal cases shall be vested in the courts, to be exercised in such manner as shall be provided by law; and the Legislature shall pass laws for that purpose.

[Note — Sec. 46 of Art. III, relating to vagrant laws, was deleted by constitutional amendment in election Aug. 5, 1969.]

Sec. 47. **Lotteries Shall Be Prohibited** — (a) The Legislature shall pass laws prohibiting lotteries and gift enterprises in this State other than those authorized by Subsections (b) and (d) of this section.

(b) The Legislature by law may authorize and regulate bingo games conducted by a church, synagogue, religious society, volunteer fire department, nonprofit veterans organization, fraternal organization, or nonprofit organization supporting medical research or treatment programs. A law enacted under this subsection must permit the qualified voters of any county, justice precinct, or incorporated city or town to determine from time to time by a majority vote of the qualified voters voting on the question at an election whether bingo games may be held in the county, justice precinct, city or town. The law must also require that:

(1) all proceeds from the games are spent in Texas for charitable purposes of the organizations;

(2) the games are limited to one location as defined by law on property owned or leased by the church, synagogue, religious society, volunteer fire department, nonprofit veterans organization, fraternal organization, or nonprofit organization supporting medical research or treatment programs; and

(3) the games are conducted, promoted, and administered by members of the church, synagogue, religious society, volunteer fire department, nonprofit veterans organization, fraternal organization, or nonprofit organization supporting medical research or treatment programs.

(c) The law enacted by the Legislature authorizing bingo games must include:

(1) a requirement that the entities conducting the games report quarterly to the Comptroller of Public Accounts about the amount of proceeds that the entities collect from the games and the purposes for which the proceeds are spent; and

(2) criminal or civil penalties to enforce the reporting requirement.

(d) The Legislature by general law may permit charitable raffles conducted by a qualified religious society, qualified volunteer fire department, qualified volunteer emergency medical service, or qualified nonprofit organizations under the terms and conditions imposed by general law.

The law must also require that:

(1) all proceeds from the sale of tickets for the raffle must be spent for the charitable purposes of the organizations; and

(2) the charitable raffle is conducted, promoted, and administered exclusively by members of the qualified religious

society, qualified volunteer fire department, qualified volunteer emergency medical service, or qualified nonprofit organization.

[Note — The foregoing Sec. 47 of Art. III was amended to authorize bingo games on local option basis if games are conducted by religious society or other charitable society and proceeds are to be spent in Texas for charitable purposes of the organization. Submitted by the Sixty-sixth Legislature (1979) and adopted in election Nov. 4, 1980. It was further amended by the addition of subsection (d) authorizing the Legislature to permit and regulate raffles conducted for charitable purposes by certain non-profit organizations. Submitted by the Seventy-first Legislature (1989) and adopted in an election Nov. 7, 1989.]

[Note — Sec. 48 of Art. III, relating to power to levy taxes, was deleted by constitutional amendment in election Aug. 5, 1969.]

[Note — Sec. 48a and Sec. 48b, relating to the Teachers' Retirement Fund and Teachers' Retirement System, respectively, were deleted by constitutional amendment in an election April 22, 1975. See also note under Art. III, Sec. 51e and Sec. 51f; Art. XVI, Sec. 62 and Sec. 63. See also Art. XVI, Sec. 67, which replaces the foregoing Sections.]

Sec. 48-d. **Rural Fire Prevention Districts** — The Legislature shall have the power to provide for the establishment and creation of rural fire-prevention districts and to authorize a tax on the ad valorem property situated in said districts not to exceed three (3c) cents on the one hundred ($100) dollars valuation for the support thereof; provided that no tax shall be levied in support of said districts until approved by vote of the people residing therein.

[Note — The foregoing Sec. 48-d of Art. III was submitted as an amendment by the Fifty-first Legislature (1949) and ratified in an election Nov. 8, 1949. The absence of Section 48-c is explained by the fact that such section was proposed as an amendment but failed to carry.]

Sec. 48-e. **Jail Districts** — The legislature, by law, may provide for the creation, operation, and financing of jail districts and may authorize each district to issue bonds and other obligations and to levy an ad valorem tax on property located in the district to pay principal of and interest on the bonds and to pay for operation of the district. An ad valorem tax may not be levied and bonds secured by a property tax may not be issued until approved by the qualified electors of the district voting at an election called and held for that purpose.

[Note — The foregoing Sec. 48-e of Art. III, an amendment, was added to provide for the creation, operation and financing of jail districts. Submitted by the Seventieth Legislature (1987) and adopted in an election Nov. 3, 1987.]

Sec. 48-e. **Emergency Services Districts** — Laws may be enacted to provide for the establishment and creation of special districts to provide emergency services and to authorize the commissioners courts of participating counties to levy a tax on the ad valorem property situated in said districts not to exceed Ten Cents (10c) on the One Hundred Dollars ($100.00) valuation for the support thereof; provided that no tax shall be levied in support of said districts until approved by a vote of the qualified electors residing therein. Such a district may provide emergency medical services, emergency ambulance services, rural fire prevention and control services, or other emergency services authorized by the Legislature.

[Note — The foregoing Sec. 48-e of Art. III, an amendment, was added to provide for the creation of emergency medical services districts. Submitted by the Seventieth Legislature (1987) and adopted in an election Nov. 3, 1987.]

[Note — The foregoing two sections of Art. III were both numbered 48-e by the Seventieth Legislature (1987), and they shall remain so designated unless changed by a future Legislature.]

Sec. 49. **Purpose for Which Debts May Be Created** — No debt shall be created by or on behalf of the State, except to supply casual deficiencies of revenue, repel invasion, suppress insurrection, defend the State in war or pay existing debt; and the debt created to supply deficiencies in the revenue shall never exceed in the aggregate at any one time $200,000.

Sec. 49-a. **Limiting Appropriations to Anticipated Revenue; Comptroller's Certification Required; Issuance of Certain General Revenue Bonds Authorized** — It shall be the duty of the Comptroller of Public Accounts in advance of each regular session of the Legislature to prepare and submit to the Governor and to the Legislature upon its convening a statement under oath showing fully the financial condition of the State Treasury at the close of the last fiscal period and an estimate of the probable receipts and disbursements for the then current fiscal year. There shall also be

Article III — (Cont'd.)

contained in said statement an itemized estimate of the anticipated revenue based on the laws then in effect that will be received by and for the State from all sources showing the fund accounts to be credited during the succeeding biennium and said statement shall contain such other information as may be required by law. Supplemental statements shall be submitted at any special session of the Legislature and at such other times as may be necessary to show probable changes.

From and after Jan. 1, 1945, save in the case of emergency and imperative public necessity and with a four-fifths vote of the total membership of each house, no appropriation in excess of the cash and anticipated revenue of the funds from which such appropriation is to be made shall be valid. From and after Jan. 1, 1945, no bill containing an appropriation shall be considered as passed or be sent to the Governor for consideration until and less the Comptroller of Public Accounts endorses his certificate thereon showing that the amount appropriated is within the amount estimated to be available in the affected funds. When the Comptroller finds an appropriation bill exceeds the estimated revenue he shall endorse such finding thereon and return to the house in which same originated. Such information shall be immediately made known to both the House of Representatives and the Senate, and the necessary steps shall be taken to bring such appropriation to within the revenue, either by providing additional revenue or reducing the appropriation.

For the purpose of financing the outstanding obligations of the general revenue fund of the State and placing its current accounts on a cash basis the Legislature of the State of Texas is hereby authorized to provide for the issuance, sale and retirement of serial bonds equal in principal to the total outstanding, valid and approved obligations owing by said fund on Sept. 1, 1943, provided such bonds shall not draw interest in excess of 2 per cent per annum and shall mature within twenty years from date.

[Note — The foregoing Sec. 49-a of Art. III is an amendment added to provide for Comptroller's estimates of receipts and disbursements and limit legislative appropriations, as stated. Adopted in an election Nov. 3, 1942.]

Sec. 49-b. **Veterans' Land Board: Bonds Authorized for Creation of Veterans' Land Fund; Purchase of Land by State and Sales to Veterans** — By virtue of prior amendments to this Constitution, there has been created a governmental agency of the State of Texas performing governmental duties which has been designated the Veterans' Land Board. Said Board shall continue to function for the purposes specified in all of the prior Constitutional Amendments except as modified herein. Said Board shall be composed of the Commissioner of the General Land Office and two (2) citizens of the State of Texas, one (1) of whom shall be well versed in veterans' affairs and one (1) of whom shall be well versed in finances. One (1) such citizen member shall, with the advice and consent of the Senate, be appointed biennially by the Governor to serve for a term of four (4) years; but the members serving on said Board on the date of adoption hereof shall complete the terms to which they were appointed. In the event of the resignation or death of any such citizen member, the Governor shall appoint a replacement to serve for the unexpired portion of the term to which the deceased or resigning member had been appointed. The compensation for said citizen members shall be as is now or may hereafter be fixed by the Legislature; and each shall make bond in such amount as is now or may hereafter be prescribed by the Legislature.

The Commissioner of the General Land Office shall act as Chairman of said Board and shall be the administrator of the Veterans' Land Program under such terms and restrictions as are now or may hereafter be provided by law. In the absence or illness of said Commissioner, the Chief Clerk of the General Land Office shall be the Acting Chairman of said Board with the same duties and powers that said Commissioner would have if present.

The Veterans' Land Board may provide for, issue and sell not to exceed Nine Hundred and Fifty Million Dollars ($950,000,000) in bonds or obligations of the State of Texas for the purpose of creating a fund to be known as the Veterans' Land Fund, Seven Hundred Million Dollars ($700,000,000) of which have heretofore been authorized. Such bonds or obligations shall be sold for not less than par value and accrued interest; shall be issued in such forms, denominations, and upon such terms as are now or may hereafter be provided by law; shall be issued and sold at such times, at such places, and in such installments as may be determined by said Board; and shall bear a rate or rates of interest as may be fixed by said Board but the weighted average annual interest rate, as that phrase is commonly and ordinarily used and understood in the municipal-bond market, of all the bonds issued and sold in any installment of any bonds may not exceed the rate specified in Sec. 65 of this article. All bonds or obligations issued and sold hereunder shall, after execution

by the Board, approval by the Attorney General of Texas, registration by the Comptroller of Public Accounts of the State of Texas, and delivery to the purchaser or purchasers, be incontestable and shall constitute general obligations of the State of Texas under the Constitution of Texas; and all bonds heretofore issued and sold by said Board are hereby in all respects validated and declared to be general obligations of the State of Texas. In order to prevent default in the payment of principal or interest on any such bonds, the Legislature shall appropriate a sufficient amount to pay the same.

In the sale of any such bonds or obligations, a preferential right of purchase shall be given to the administrators of the various Teacher Retirement Funds, the Permanent University Funds, and the Permanent School Funds.

Said Veterans' Land Fund shall consist of any lands heretofore or hereafter purchased by said Board, until the sale price therefor, together with any interest and penalties due, have been received by said Board (although nothing herein shall be construed to prevent said Board from accepting full payment for a portion of any tract), and of the moneys attributable to any bonds heretofore or hereafter issued and sold by said Board which moneys so attributable shall include but shall not be limited to the proceeds from the issuance and sale of such bonds; the moneys received from the sale or resale of any lands, or rights therein, purchased with such proceeds; the moneys received from the sale or resale of any lands, or rights therein, purchased with other moneys attributable to such bonds; the interest and penalties received from the sale or resale of such lands, or rights therein; the bonuses, income, rents, royalties, and any other pecuniary benefit received by said Board from any such lands; sums received by way of indemnity or forfeiture for the failure of any bidder for the purchase of any such bonds to comply with his bid and accept and pay for such bonds or for the failure of any bidder for the purchase of any lands comprising a part of said Fund to comply with his bid and accept and pay for any such lands; and interest received from investments of any such moneys. The principal and interest on the bonds heretofore and hereafter issued by said Board shall be paid out of the moneys of said Fund in conformance with the Constitutional provisions authorizing such bonds; but the moneys of said Fund which are not immediately committed to the payment of principal and interest on such bonds, the purchase of lands as herein provided, or the payment of expenses as herein provided may be invested in bonds or obligations of the United States until such funds are needed for such purposes.

All moneys comprising a part of said Fund and not expended for the purposes herein provided shall be a part of said Fund until there are sufficient moneys therein to retire fully all of the bonds heretofore or hereafter issued and sold by said Board, at which time all such moneys remaining in said Fund, except such portion thereof as may be necessary to retire all such bonds which portion shall be set aside and retained in said Fund for the purpose of retiring all such bonds, shall be deposited to the credit of the General Revenue Fund to be appropriated to such purposes as may be prescribed by law. All moneys becoming a part of said Fund thereafter shall likewise be deposited to the credit of the General Revenue Fund.

When a Division of said Fund (each Division consisting of the moneys attributable to the bonds issue and sold pursuant to a single Constitutional authorization, and the lands purchased therewith) contains sufficient moneys to retire all of the bonds secured by such Division, the moneys thereof, except such portion as may be needed to retire all of the bonds secured by such Division which portion shall be set aside and remain a part of such Division for the purpose of retiring all such bonds, may be used for the purpose of paying the principal and the interest thereon, together with the expenses herein authorized, or any other bonds heretofore or hereafter issued and sold by said Board. Such use shall be a matter for the discretion and direction of said Board; but there may be no such use of any such moneys contrary to the rights of any holder of any of the bonds issued and sold by said Board or violative of any contract to which said Board is a party.

The Veterans' Land Fund shall be used by said Board for the purpose of purchasing lands situated in the State of Texas as owned by the United States or any governmental agency thereof, owned by the Texas Prison System or any other governmental agency of the State of Texas, or owned by any person, firm, or corporation. All lands thus purchased shall be acquired at the lowest price obtainable, to be paid for in cash, and shall be a part of such Fund. Such lands heretofore or hereafter purchased and comprising a part of said Fund are hereby declared to be held for a governmental purpose, although the individual purchasers thereof shall be subject to taxation to the same extent and in the same manner as are purchasers of lands dedicated to the Permanent Free Public School Fund.

The lands of the Veterans' Land Fund shall be sold by said Board in such quantities, on such terms, at such prices, at such rates of interest and under such rules and regulations as are now or may hereafter be provided by law to veterans as they are now or may hereafter be defined by the

Article III – (Cont'd.)

laws of the State of Texas. The foregoing notwithstanding, any lands in the Veterans' Land Fund which have been first offered for sale to veterans and which have not been sold may be sold or resold to such purchasers, in such quantities, and on such terms, and at such prices and rates of interest, and under such rules and regulations as are now or may hereafter be provided by law.

Said Veterans' Land Fund, to the extent of the moneys attributable to any bonds hereafter issued and sold by said Board may be used by said Board, as is now or may hereafter be provided by law, for the purpose of paying the expenses of surveying, monumenting, road construction, legal fees, recordation fees, advertising and other like costs necessary or incidental to the purchase and sale, or resale, of any lands purchased with any of the moneys attributable to such additional bonds, such expenses to be added to the price of such lands when sold, or resold, by said Board; for the purpose of paying the expenses of issuing, selling, and delivering any such additional bonds; and for the purpose of meeting the expenses of paying the interest or principal due or to become due on any such additional bonds.

All of the moneys attributable to any series of bonds hereafter issued and sold by said Board (a 'series of bonds' being all of the bonds issued and sold in a single transaction as a single installment of bonds) may be used for the purchase of lands as herein provided, to be sold as herein provided, for a period ending eight (8) years after the date of sale of such series of bonds; provided, however, that so much of such moneys as may be necessary to pay interest on bonds hereafter issued and sold shall be set aside for that purpose in accordance with the resolution adopted by said Board authorizing the issuance and sale of such series of bonds. After such eight (8) year period, all of such moneys shall be set aside for the retirement of any bonds hereafter issued and sold and to pay interest thereon, together with any expenses as provided herein, in accordance with the resolution or resolutions authorizing the issuance and sale of such additional bonds, until there are sufficient moneys to retire all of the bonds hereafter issued and sold, at which time all such moneys then remaining a part of said Veterans' Land Fund and thereafter becoming a part of said Fund shall be governed as elsewhere provided herein.

This amendment being intended only to establish a basic framework and not to be a comprehensive treatment of the Veterans' Land Program, there is hereby reposed in the Legislature full power to implement and effectuate the design and objects of this amendment, including the power to delegate such duties, responsibilities, functions, and authority to the Veterans' Land Board as it believes necessary.

Should the Legislature enact any enabling laws in anticipation of this amendment, no such law shall be void by reason of its anticipatory nature.

[Note — The foregoing Sec. 49-b of Art. III has been amended ten times: First, for the purpose of aiding war veterans in land purchases. Submitted by Forty-ninth Legislature (1945), and ratified in a special election Nov. 7, 1946. (It was by error that the date was set as Nov. 7 instead of Nov. 5, which was the general election date.) Second, it was amended to increase the authorized bond issue from $25,000,-000 to $100,000,000 and to make minor changes. Submitted by Fifty-second Legislature (1951), and ratified in an election Nov. 13, 1951. Third, it was amended to change membership of the Veterans' Land Board and to raise the total of bonds authorized to $200,000,000. Submitted by Fifty-fourth Legislature (1955) and adopted in election Nov. 6, 1956. Fourth, it was amended to fix the rate of interest not to exceed 3½ per cent per annum. Submitted by Fifty-sixth Legislature (1959) and adopted in election Nov. 8, 1960. Fifth, it was amended to provide for offering land in the Veterans' Land Fund to non-veteran purchasers after land has first been offered to veterans. Submitted by Fifty-seventh Legislature (1961) and adopted in election Nov. 6, 1962. Sixth, to extend Veterans' Land Program by authorizing sale of bonds to increase Veterans' Land Fund for purchasing land to be sold to Texas veterans who served between Sept. 16, 1940, and date of formal withdrawal of U.S. troops from Viet Nam; and providing for additional $200,000,000 in bonds for this program. Submitted by Sixtieth Legislature (1967) and adopted in election Nov. 11, 1967. Seventh, to provide for additional $100 million in bonds for the Veterans' Land Fund and to make all veterans eligible to participate who served in armed forces after Sept. 16, 1940. Submitted by Sixty-third Legislature (1973) and adopted in election Nov. 6, 1973. Eighth, to provide for additional $200 million in bonds for the Veterans' Land Fund and to extend the right to apply to purchase land to unmarried surviving spouses of veterans who meet requirements set out herein. Submitted by Sixty-fifth Legislature (1977) and adopted in election Nov. 8, 1977. Ninth, to raise to $950 million the amount of bonds authorized for the Veterans' Land Fund. Submitted by Sixty-seventh Legislature (1981) and adopted in election Nov. 3, 1981. Tenth, to define an eligible veteran for purposes of this program. Submitted

by Sixty-ninth Legislature (1985) and adopted in an election Nov. 5, 1985.]

Sec. 49-b-1. Bonds Authorized to Finance Veterans' Land Program and Veterans' Housing Assistance Program — (a) In addition to the general obligation bonds authorized to be issued and to be sold by the Veterans' Land Board by Sec. 49-b of this article, the Veterans' Land Board may provide for, issue, and sell not to exceed $1.3 billion in bonds of the State of Texas, $800 million of which have heretofore been authorized to provide financing to veterans of the state in recognition of their service to their state and country.

(b) For purposes of this section, "veteran" means a person who satisfies the definition of "veteran" as is now or may hereafter be set forth by the laws of the State of Texas.

(c) The bonds shall be sold for not less than par value and accrued interest; shall be issued in such forms and denominations, upon such terms, at such times and places, and in such installments as may be determined by the board; and, notwithstanding the rate of interest specified by any other provision of this Constitution, shall bear a rate or rates of interest fixed by the board. All bonds issued and sold pursuant to Subsections (a) through (f) of this section shall, after execution by the board, approval by the Attorney General of Texas, registration by the Comptroller of Public Accounts of the State of Texas, and delivery to the purchaser or purchasers, be incontestable and shall constitute general obligations of the state under the Constitution of Texas.

(d) Three hundred million dollars of the state bonds authorized by this section shall be used to augment the Veterans' Land Fund. The Veterans' Land Fund shall be used by the board for the purpose of purchasing lands situated in the State of Texas owned by the United States government or any agency thereof, the State of Texas or any subdivision or agency thereof, or any person, firm, or corporation. The lands shall be sold to veterans in such quantities, on such terms, at such prices, at such rates of interest, and under such rules and regulations as may be authorized by law. The expenses of the board in connection with the issuance of the bonds and the purchase and sale of the lands may be paid from money in the fund. The Veterans' Land Fund shall continue to consist of any lands purchased by the board until the sale price therefor, together with any interest and penalties due, have been received by the board (although nothing herein shall prevent the board from accepting full payment for a portion of any tract) and of the money attributable to any bonds issued and sold by the board for the Veterans' Land Fund, which money so attributable shall include but shall not be limited to the proceeds from the issuance and sale of such bonds; the money received from the sale or resale of any lands, or rights therein, purchased from such proceeds; the money received from the sale or resale of any lands, or rights therein, purchased with other money attributable to such bonds; the interest and penalties received from the sale or resale of such lands, or rights therein; the bonuses, income, rents, royalties, and any other pecuniary benefit received by the board from any such lands; sums received by way of indemnity or forfeiture for the failure of any bidder for the purchase of any such bonds to comply with his bid and accept and pay for such bonds or for the failure of any bidder for the purchase of any lands comprising a part of the fund to comply with his bid and accept and pay for any such lands; and interest received from investments of any such money. The principal of and interest on the general obligation bonds previously authorized by Sec. 49-b of this Constitution shall be paid out of the money of the fund in conformance with the constitutional provisions authorizing such bonds. The principal of and interest on the general obligation bonds authorized by this section for the benefit of the Veterans' Land Fund shall be paid out of the money of the fund, but the money of the fund which is not immediately committed to the payment of principal and interest on such bonds, the purchase of lands as herein provided, or the payment of expenses as herein provided may be invested in bonds or obligations of the United States until the money is needed for such purposes.

(e) The Veterans' Housing Assistance Fund is created, and $1 billion of the state bonds authorized by this section shall be used for the Veterans' Housing Assistance Fund, $500 million of which have heretofore been authorized. Money in the Veterans' Housing Assistance Fund shall be administered by the Veterans' Land Board and shall be used for the purpose of making home mortgage loans to veterans for housing within the State of Texas in such quantities, on such terms, at such rates of interest, and under such rules and regulations as may be authorized by law. The expenses of the board in connection with the issuance of the bonds and the making of the loans may be paid from money in the fund. The Veterans' Housing Assistance Fund shall consist of any interest of the board in all home mortgage loans made to veterans by the board pursuant to a Veterans' Housing Assistance Program which the Legislature may establish by appropriate legislation until, with respect to any such home mortgage loan, the principal amount, together with any interest and penalties due, have been received by the board; the money attributable to any bonds issued and sold by the

Article III — (Cont'd.)

board to provide money for the fund, which money so attributable shall include but shall not be limited to the proceeds from the issuance and sale of such bonds; income, rents, and any other pecuniary benefit received by the board as a result of making such loans; sums received by way of indemnity or forfeiture for the failure of any bidder for the purchase of any such bonds to comply with his bid and accept and pay for such bonds; and interest received from investments of any such bonds. The principal of and interest on the general obligation bonds authorized by this section for the benefit of the Veterans' Housing Assistance Fund shall be paid out of the money of the fund, but the money of the fund which is not immediately committed to the payment of principal and interest on such bonds, the making of home mortgage loans as herein provided, or the payment of expenses as herein provided may be invested in bonds or obligations of the United States until the money is needed for such purposes.

(f) To the extent there is not money in either the Veterans' Land Fund or the Veterans' Housing Assistance Fund, as the case may be, available for payment of principal of and interest on the general obligation bonds authorized by this section to provide money for either of the funds, there is hereby appropriated out of the first money coming into the treasury in each fiscal year, not otherwise appropriated by this Constitution, an amount which is sufficient to pay the principal of and interest on such general obligation bonds that mature or become due during that fiscal year.

(g) Receipt of all kinds of the funds determined by the board not to be required for the payment of principal of and interest on the general obligation bonds herein authorized, heretofore authorized, or hereafter authorized by this Constitution to be issued by the board to provide money for either of the funds may be used by the board, to the extent not inconsistent with the proceedings authorizing such bonds, to pay the principal of and interest on general obligation bonds issued to provide money for the other fund, or to pay the principal of and interest on revenue bonds of the board issued for the purposes of providing funds for the purchasing of lands and making the sale thereof to veterans or making home mortgage loans to veterans as provided by this section. The revenue bonds shall be special obligations and payable only from the receipt of the funds and shall not constitute indebtedness of the state or the Veterans' Land Board. The board is authorized to issue such revenue bonds from time to time which shall not exceed an aggregate principal amount that can be fully retired from the receipts of the funds and other revenues pledged to the retirement of the revenue bonds. The revenue bonds shall be issued in such forms and denominations, upon such terms, at such times and places, and in such installments as may be determined by the board; and, notwithstanding the rate of interest specified by any other provision of the Constitution, shall bear a rate or rates of interest fixed by the board.

[Note — The foregoing Sec. 49-b-1 of Art. III was added to provide financial assistance to veterans and to authorize issuance of bonds to finance the Veterans' Land Program and the Veterans' Housing Assistance Program. Submitted by Sixty-eighth Legislature (1983) and adopted in election Nov. 8, 1983. It was further amended to provide $500 million additional bonding authority for the veterans' housing assistance program and changing definition of veterans eligible to participate in veterans' land program and veterans' housing program. Submitted by Sixty-ninth Legislature (1985) and adopted in an election Nov. 5, 1985.]

Sec. 49-c. **Texas Water Development Board, Fund; Purpose** — There is hereby created as an agency of the State of Texas the Water Development Board to exercise such powers as necessary under this provision together with such other duties and restrictions as may be prescribed by law. The qualifications, compensation and number of members of said Board shall be determined by law. They shall be appointed by the Governor with the advice and consent of the Senate in the manner and for such terms as may be prescribed by law.

The Texas Water Development Board shall have the authority to provide for, issue and sell general obligation bonds of the State of Texas in an amount not to exceed One Hundred Million Dollars ($100,000,000). The Legislature of Texas, upon two-thirds (⅔) vote of the elected Members of each House, may authorize the Board to issue additional bonds in an amount not exceeding One Hundred Million Dollars ($100,000,000). The bonds authorized herein or permitted to be authorized by the Legislature shall be called "Texas Water Development Bonds," shall be executed in such form, denominations and upon such terms as may be prescribed by law, provided, however, that the bonds shall not bear more than four percent (4%) interest per annum; they may be issued in such installments as the Board finds feasible and practical in accomplishing the purpose set forth herein.

All moneys received from the sale of State bonds shall be deposited in a fund hereby created in the State Treasury to be known as the Texas Water Development Fund to be administered (without further appropriation) by the Texas Wa-

ter Development Board in such manner as prescribed by law.

Such fund shall be used only for the purpose of aiding or making funds available upon such terms and conditions as the Legislature may prescribe, to the various political subdivisions or bodies politic and corporate of the State of Texas including river authorities, conservation and reclamation districts and districts created or organized or authorized to be created or organized under Article XVI, Section 59 or Article III, Section 52, of this Constitution, interstate compact commissions to which the State of Texas is a party and municipal corporations, in the conservation and development of the water resources of this State, including the control, storing and preservation of its storm and flood waters and the waters of its rivers and streams, for all useful and lawful purposes by the acquisition, improvement, extension, or construction of dams, reservoirs and other water storage projects, including any system necessary for the transportation of water from storage to points of treatment and/or distribution, including facilities for transporting water therefrom to wholesale purchasers, or for any one or more of such purposes or methods.

Any or all financial assistance as provided herein shall be repaid with interest upon such terms, conditions and manner of repayment as may be provided by law.

While any of the bonds authorized by this provision or while any of the bonds that may be authorized by the Legislature under this provision, or any interest on any of such bonds, is outstanding and unpaid, there is hereby appropriated out of the first moneys coming into the Treasury in each fiscal year, not otherwise appropriated by this Constitution, an amount which is sufficient to pay the principal and interest on such bonds that mature or become due during such fiscal year, less the amount in the sinking fund at the close of the prior fiscal year.

The Legislature may provide for the investment of moneys available in the Texas Water Development Fund, and the interest and sinking funds established for the payment of bonds issued by the Texas Water Development Board. Income from such investment shall be used for the purposes prescribed by the Legislature. The Legislature may also make appropriations from the General Revenue Fund for paying administrative expenses of the Board.

From the moneys received by the Texas Water Development Board as repayment of principal for financial assistance or as interest thereon, there shall be deposited in the interest and sinking fund for the bonds authorized by this Section sufficient moneys to pay the interest and principal to become due during the ensuing year and sufficient to establish and maintain a reserve in said fund equal to the average annual principal and interest requirements on all outstanding bonds issued under this Section. If any year prior to December 31, 1982 moneys are received in excess of the foregoing requirements then such excess shall be deposited to the Texas Water Development Fund, and may be used for administrative expenses of the Board and for the same purposes and upon the same terms and conditions prescribed for the proceeds derived from the sale of such State bonds. No grant of financial assistance shall be made under the provisions of this Section after December 31, 1982, and all moneys thereafter received as repayment of principal for financial assistance or as interest thereon shall be deposited in the interest and sinking fund for the State bonds; except that such amount as may be required to meet the administrative expenses of the Board may be annually set aside; and provided, that after all State bonds have been fully paid with interest, or after there are on deposit in the interest and sinking fund sufficient moneys to pay all future maturities of principal and interest, additional moneys so received shall be deposited to the General Revenue Fund.

All bonds issued hereunder shall after approval by the Attorney General, registration by the Comptroller of Public Accounts of the State of Texas, and delivery to the purchasers, be incontestable and shall constitute general obligations of the State of Texas under the Constitution of Texas.

[Note — The foregoing Sec. 49-c of Art. III, an amendment, was added, setting up the Texas Water Development Board and Fund and providing for supervision thereof. Submitted by the Fifty-fifth Legislature (1957) and adopted in election Nov. 5, 1957.]

Sec. 49-d. **Development and Conservation of Public Waters** — It is hereby declared to be the policy of the State of Texas to encourage the optimum development of the limited number of feasible sites available for the construction or enlargement of dams and reservoirs for the conservation of the public waters of the state, which waters are held in trust for the use and benefit of the public, and to encourage the optimum regional development of systems built for the filtration, treatment, and transmission of water and wastewater. The proceeds from the sale of the additional bonds authorized hereunder deposited in the Texas Water Development Fund and the proceeds of bonds previously authorized by Art. III, Sec. 49-c of this Constitution, may be

Article III - (Cont'd.)

used by the Texas Water Development Board, under such provisions as the Legislature may prescribe by general law, including the requirement of a permit for storage or beneficial use, for the additional purposes of acquiring and developing storage facilities, and any system or works necessary for the filtration, treatment and transportation of water or wastewater, or for any one or more of such purposes or methods, whether or not such a system or works is connected with a reservoir in which the state has a financial interest; provided however, the Texas Water Development Fund or any other state fund provided for water development, transmission, transfer or filtration shall not be used to finance any project which contemplates or results in the removal from the basin of origin of any surface water necessary to supply the reasonably foreseeable future water requirements for the next ensuing fifty-year period within the river basin of origin, except on a temporary, interim basis.

Under such provisions as the Legislature may prescribe by general law the Texas Water Development Fund may be used for the conservation and development of water for useful purposes by construction or reconstruction or enlargement of reservoirs constructed or to be constructed or enlarged within the State of Texas or on any stream constituting a boundary of the State of Texas, together with any system or works necessary for the filtration, treatment and/or transportation of water, by any one or more of the following governmental agencies; by the United States of America or any agency, department or instrumentality thereof; by the State of Texas or any agency, department or instrumentality thereof; by political subdivisions or bodies politic and corporate of the state; by interstate compact commissions to which the State of Texas is a party; and by municipal corporations. The Legislature shall provide terms and conditions under which the Texas Water Development Board may sell, transfer or lease, in whole or in part, any reservoir and associated system or works which the Texas Water Development Board has financed in whole or in part.

Under such provisions as the Legislature may prescribe by general law, the Texas Water Development Board may also execute long-term contracts with the United States or any of its agencies for the acquisition and development of storage facilities in reservoirs constructed or to be constructed by the Federal Government. Such contracts when executed shall constitute general obligations of the State of Texas in the same manner and with the same effect as state bonds issued under the authority of the preceding Sec. 49-c of this Constitution, and the provisions in said Sec. 49-c with respect to payment of principal and interest on state bonds issued shall likewise apply with respect to payment of principal and interest required to be paid by such contracts. If storage facilities are acquired for a term of years, such contracts shall contain provisions for renewal that will protect the state's investment.

The aggregate of the bonds authorized hereunder shall not exceed $200,000,000 and shall be in addition to the aggregate of the bonds previously authorized by said Sec. 49-c of Art. III of this Constitution. The Legislature upon two-thirds (2/3) vote of the elected members of each House, may authorize the board to issue all or any portion of such $200,000,000 in additional bonds herein authorized.

The Legislature shall provide terms and conditions for the Texas Water Development Board to sell, transfer or lease, in whole or in part, any acquired facilities or the right to use such facilities at a price not less than the direct cost of the board in acquiring same; and the Legislature may provide terms and conditions for the board to sell any unappropriated public waters of the state that might be stored in such facilities. As a prerequisite to the purchase of such storage or water, the applicant therefor shall have secured a valid permit from the Texas Water Commission or its successor authorizing the acquisition of such storage facilities or the water impounded therein. The money received from any sale, transfer or lease of facilities shall be used to pay principal and interest on state bonds issued or contractual obligations incurred by the Texas Water Development Board, provided that when moneys are sufficient to pay the full amount of indebtedness then outstanding and the full amount of interest to accrue thereon, any further sums received from the sale, transfer or lease of such facilities shall be deposited and used as provided by law. Money received from the sale of water, which shall include standby service, may be used for the operation and maintenance of acquired facilities, and for the payment of principal and interest on debt incurred.

Should the Legislature enact enabling laws in anticipation of the adoption of this amendment, such acts shall not be void by reason of their anticipatory character.

[Note — The foregoing Sec. 49-d of Art. III, an amendment, was added to authorize the Texas Water Development Board to acquire and develop storage facilities in reservoirs and to dispose of such storage facilities and water upon such terms as Legislature shall prescribe. Submitted by the Fifty-seventh Legislature (1961) and adopted in election Nov. 6, 1962. It was further amended to provide for optimum development of water reservoirs and investment of the Texas Wa-

ter Development Fund. Submitted by the Fifty-ninth Legislature (1965) and adopted in an election Nov. 8, 1966. It was again amended to encourage optimum regional development of systems built for filtration, treatment and transmission of water and wastewater. Submitted by the Sixty-ninth Legislature (1985) and adopted in an election Nov. 5, 1985.]

Sec. 49-d-1. **Water Development Bonds** — (a) The Texas Water Development Board shall upon direction of the Texas Water Quality Board, or any successor agency designated by the Legislature, issue additional Texas Water Development Bonds up to an additional aggregate principal amount of Two Hundred Million Dollars ($200,000,000) to provide grants, loans, or any combination of grants and loans for water quality enhancement purposes as established by the Legislature. The Texas Water Quality Board or any successor agency designated by the Legislature may make such grants and loans to political subdivisions or bodies politic and corporate of the State of Texas, including municipal corporations, river authorities, conservation and reclamation districts, and districts created or organized or authorized to be created or organized under Art. XVI, Sec. 59, or Art. III, Sec. 52, of this Constitution, State agencies, and interstate agencies and compact commissions to which the State of Texas is a party, and upon such terms and conditions as the Legislature may authorize by general law. The bonds shall be issued for such terms, in such denominations, form and installments, and upon such conditions as the Legislature may authorize.

(b) The proceeds from the sale of such bonds shall be deposited in the Texas Water Development Fund to be invested and administered as prescribed by law.

(c) The bonds authorized in this Sec. 49-d-1 and all bonds authorized by Sections 49-c and 49-d of Art. III shall bear interest at not more than 6 percent per annum and mature as the Texas Water Development Board shall prescribe, subject to the limitations as may be imposed by the Legislature.

(d) The Texas Water Development Fund shall be used for the purposes heretofore permitted by, and subject to the limitations in Sections 49-c, 49-d and 49-d-1; provided, however, that the financial assistance may be made pursuant to the provisions of Sections 49-c, 49-d and 49-d-1 subject only to the availability of funds and without regard to the provisions in Sec. 49-c that such financial assistance shall terminate after Dec. 31, 1982.

(e) Texas Water Development Bonds are secured by the general credit of the State and shall after approval by the Attorney General, registration by the Comptroller of Public Accounts of the State of Texas, and delivery to the purchasers, be incontestable and shall constitute general obligations of the State of Texas under the Constitution of Texas.

(f) Should the Legislature enact enabling laws in anticipation of the adoption of this amendment, such acts shall not be void by reason of their anticipatory character.

[Note — The foregoing Sec. 49-d-1, an amendment, was added to provide for an additional $100 million for grants and loans for water improvement; also to raise the interest rate on water bonds to 6 percent. Submitted by the Sixty-second Legislature (1971) and adopted in an election May 18, 1971. It was amended to increase to $200 million the amount available for water quality enhancement. Submitted by the Sixty-fourth Legislature (1975) and adopted in an election Nov. 2, 1976.]

Sec. 49-d-2. (a) The Texas Water Development Board may issue additional Texas Water Development Bonds up to an additional aggregate principal amount of $980 million. Of the additional bonds authorized to be issued, $590 million of those bonds are dedicated for use for the purposes provided by Sec. 49-c and Sec. 49-d of this article with $400 million of those bonds to be used for state participation in the acquisition and development of facilities for the storage, transmission, transportation, and treatment of water and wastewater as authorized by Sec. 49-d of this article. The Legislature may set limits on the extent of state participation in projects in each fiscal year through the General Appropriations Act or other law, and state participation is limited to 50 percent of the funding for any single project. Of the additional bonds authorized, $190 million are dedicated for use for the purposes provided by Sec. 49-d-1 of this article and $200 million are dedicated exclusively for flood control projects and may be made available for any acquisition or construction necessary to achieve structural and nonstructural flood control purposes.

(b) The Texas Water Development Board shall issue the additional bonds authorized by this section for the terms, in the denominations, form, and installments, on the conditions, and subject to the limitations provided by Sec. 49-c, Sec. 49-d, and Sec. 49-d-1 of this article and by laws adopted by the Legislature implementing those sections.

Article III — (Cont'd.)

(c) Proceeds from the sale of the bonds authorized by this section shall be deposited in the Texas water development fund to be administered and invested as provided by law.

(d) Financial assistance made available for the purposes provided by this section is subject only to availability of funds. The requirement of Sec. 49-c of this article that financial assistance terminate on Dec. 31, 1982, does not apply to financial assistance made available under this section.

(e) Bonds issued under this section shall bear interest as provided by Sec. 65 of this article.

[Note — The foregoing Sec. 49-d-2 Art. III, an amendment, was added to authorize issuance of an additional $980 million of Texas Water Development Bonds. Submitted by the Sixty-ninth Legislature (1985) and adopted in an election Nov. 5, 1985.]

Sec. 49-d-3. (a) The Legislature by law may create one or more special funds in the state treasury for use for or in aid of water conservation, water development, water quality enhancement, flood control, drainage, subsidence control, recharge, chloride control, agricultural soil and water conservation, desalinization or any combination of those purposes, may make money in a special fund available to cities, counties, special governmental districts and authorities, and other political subdivisions of the state for use for the purposes for which the fund was created by grants, loans, or any other means, and may appropriate money to any of the special funds to carry out the purposes of this section.

(b) Money deposited in a special fund created under this section may not be used to finance or aid any project that contemplates or results in the removal from the basin of origin of any surface water necessary to supply the reasonably foreseeable water requirements for the next ensuing 50-year period within the river basin of origin, except on a temporary, interim basis.

[Note — The foregoing Sec. 49-d-3, of Art. III, an amendment, was added to create special water funds for water conservation, development, quality enhancement, flood control, drainage, subsidence control, recharge, chloride control, agricultural soil and water conservation and desalinization of water. Submitted by Sixty-ninth Legislature (1985) and adopted in an election Nov. 5, 1985.]

Sec. 49-d-4. (a) In addition to other programs authorized by this constitution, the Legislature by law may provide for the creation, administration, and implementation of a bond insurance program to which the state pledges its general credit in an amount not to exceed $250 million to insure the payment in whole or in part of the principal of and interest on bonds or other obligations that are issued by cities, counties, special governmental districts and authorities, and other political subdivisions of the state as defined by law for use for or in aid of water conservation, water development, water quality enhancement, flood control, drainage, recharge, chloride control, desalinization, or any combination of those purposes.

(b) The Legislature by law shall designate the state agency to administer the bond insurance program and may authorize that agency to execute insurance contracts that bind the state to pay the principal of and interest on the bonds if the bonds are in default or the bonds are subject to impending default, subject to the limits provided by this section and by law.

(c) The payment by the state of any insurance commitment made under this section must be made from the first money coming into the state treasury that is not otherwise dedicated by this constitution.

(d) Notwithstanding the total amount of bonds insured under this section, the total amount paid and not recovered by the state under this section, excluding the costs of administration, may not exceed $250 million.

(e) Except on a two-thirds vote of the members elected to each house of the Legislature, the ratio of bonds insured to the total liability of the state must be two to one.

(f) Except on a two-thirds vote of the members elected to each house of the Legislature, the state agency administering the bond insurance program may not authorize bond insurance coverage under the program in any state fiscal year that exceeds a total of $100 million.

(g) Unless authorized to continue by a two-thirds vote of the members elected to each house, this section and the bond insurance program authorized by this section expire on the sixth anniversary of the date on which this section becomes a part of the constitution. However, bond insurance issued before the expiration of this section and the program is not affected by the expiration of this section and the program and remains in effect according to its terms, and the state is required to fulfill all of the terms of that previously issued insurance.

[Note — The foregoing Sec. 49-d-4 of Art. III, an amendment, was added to authorize a bond insurance program. Submitted by the Sixty-ninth Legislature (1985) and adopted in an election Nov. 5, 1985.]

Sec. 49-d-5. For the purpose of any program established or authorized by Sec. 49-c, Sec. 49-d, Sec. 49-d-1, Sec. 49-d-2, or Sec. 49-d-4 of this article, the Legislature by law may extend any benefits to nonprofit water supply corporations that it may extend to a district created or organized under Art. XVI, Sec. 59, of this constitution.

[Note — The foregoing Sec. 49-d-5 of Art. III, an amendment, was added to clarify the purpose for which Texas Water Development Bonds may be issued. Submitted by Sixty-ninth Legislature (1985) and adopted in an election Nov. 5, 1985.]

Sec. 49-d-6. (a) The Texas Water Development Board may issue additional Texas Water Development Bonds up to an additional aggregate principal amount of $400 million. Of the additional bonds authorized to be issued, $200 million of those bonds shall be used for purposes provided by Section 49-c of this article, $150 million of those bonds shall be used for purposes provided by Section 49-d-1 of this article, and $50 million of those bonds shall be used for flood control as provided by law.

(b) The legislature may require review and approval of the issuance of the bonds, of the use of the bond proceeds, or of the rules adopted by an agency to govern use of the bond proceeds. Notwithstanding any other provision of this constitution, any entity created or directed to conduct this review and approval may include members or appointees of members of the executive, legislative, and judicial departments of state government.

(c) The Texas Water Development Board shall issue the additional bonds authorized by this section for the terms, in the denominations, form, and installments, on the conditions, and subject to the limitations provided by Sections 49-c and 49-d-1 of this article and by laws adopted by the legislature implementing this section.

(d) Subsections (c) through (e) of Section 49-d-2 of this article apply to the bonds authorized by this section.

[Note — The foregoing Sec. 49-d-6 of Art. III, an amendment, was added to authorize the issuance of an additional $400 million of Texas Water Development Bonds for water supply, water quality, and flood control purposes. Submitted by the Seventieth Legislature (1987) and adopted in an election Nov. 3, 1987.]

Sec. 49-d-7. (a) The Texas Water Development Board may issue additional Texas water development bonds up to an additional aggregate principal amount of $500 million. Of the additional bonds authorized to be issued, $250 million of those bonds shall be used for purposes provided by Section 49-c of this article, $200 million of those bonds shall be used for purposes provided by Section 49-d-1 of this article, and $50 million of those bonds shall be used for flood control as provided by law.

(b) The Texas Water Development Board may use the proceeds of Texas water development bonds issued for the purposes provided by Section 49-c of this article for the additional purpose of providing financial assistance, on terms and conditions provided by law, to various political subdivisions and bodies politic and corporate of the state and to nonprofit water supply corporations to provide for acquisition, improvement, extension, or construction of water supply projects that involve the distribution of water to points of delivery to wholesale or retail customers.

(c) The legislature may require review and approval of the issuance of the bond, the use of the bond proceeds, or the rules adopted by an agency to govern use of the bond proceeds. Notwithstanding any other provision of this constitution, any entity created or directed to conduct this review and approval may include members or appointees of members of the executive, legislative, and judicial departments of state government.

(d) Except as specifically provided by Subsection (e) of this section, the Texas Water Development Board shall issue the additional bonds authorized by this section for the terms, in the denominations, form, and installments, on the conditions, and subject to the limitations provided by Sections 49-c and 49-d-1 of this article and by laws adopted by the legislature implementing this section.

(e) The legislature may provide by law for subsidized loans and grants from the proceeds of bonds authorized by this section to provide wholesale and retail water and wastewater facilities to economically distressed areas of the state as defined by law, provided, the principal amount of bonds that may be issued for the purposes under this subsection may not exceed 20 percent of the total amount of bonds authorized by this section. Separate accounts shall be established in the water development fund for administering the proceeds of bonds issued for purposes under this subsection,

Article III – (Cont'd.)

and an interest and sinking fund separate from and not subject to the limitations of the interest and sinking fund created pursuant to Section 49-c for other Texas water development bonds is established in the State Treasury to be used for paying the principal of and interest on bonds for the purposes of this subsection. While any of the bonds authorized for the purposes of this subsection or any of the interest on those bonds is outstanding and unpaid, there is appropriated out of the first money coming into the State Treasury in each fiscal year, not otherwise appropriated by this constitution, an amount that is sufficient to pay the principal of and interest on those bonds issued for the purposes under this subsection that mature or become due during that fiscal year.

(f) Subsections (c) through (e) of Section 49-d-2 of this article apply to the bonds authorized by this section.

[Note — The foregoing Sec. 49-d-7 of Art. III, an amendment, was added to authorize the issuance of an additional $500 million of Texas water development bonds for water supply, water quality and flood control purposes. Proposed by the Seventy-first Legislature (1989) and adopted in an election Nov. 7, 1989.]

Sec. 49-e. **Texas Park Development Bonds** — The Parks and Wildlife Department, or its successor vested with the powers, duties, and authority which deals with the operation, maintenance, and improvement of State Parks, shall have the authority to provide for, issue and sell general obligation bonds of the State of Texas in an amount not to exceed Seventy-Five Million Dollars ($75,000,000). The bonds authorized herein shall be called "Texas Park Development Bond," shall be executed in such form, denominations, and upon such terms as may be prescribed by law, provided, however, that the bonds shall bear a rate or rates of interest as may be fixed by the Parks and Wildlife Department or its successor, but the weighted average annual interest rate, as that phrase is commonly and ordinarily used and understood in the municipal bond market, of all the bonds issued and sold in any installment of any bonds, shall not exceed four and one-half percent (4½%) interest per annum; they may be issued in such installments as said Parks and Wildlife Department, or its said successor, finds feasible and practical in accomplishing the purpose set forth herein.

All moneys received from the sale of said bonds shall be deposited in a fund hereby created with the State Treasurer to be known as the Texas Park Development Fund to be administered (without further appropriation) by the said Parks and Wildlife Department, or its said successor, in such manner as prescribed by law.

Such fund shall be used by said Parks and Wildlife Department, or its said successor, under such provisions as the Legislature may prescribe by general law, for the purposes of acquiring lands from the United States, or any governmental agency thereof, from any governmental agency of the State of Texas, or from any person, firm, or corporation, for State Park Sites and for developing said sites as State Parks.

While any of the bonds authorized by this provision, or any interest on any such bonds, is outstanding and unpaid, there is hereby appropriated out of the first moneys coming into the Treasury in each fiscal year, not otherwise appropriated by this Constitution, an amount which is sufficient to pay the principal and interest on such bonds that mature or become due during such fiscal year, less the amount in the interest and sinking fund at the close of the prior fiscal year, which includes any receipts derived during the prior fiscal year by said Parks and Wildlife Department, or its said successor, from admission charges to State Parks, as the Legislature may prescribe by general law.

The Legislature may provide for the investment of moneys available in the Texas Park Development Fund and the interest and sinking fund established for the payment of bonds issued by said Parks and Wildlife Department, or its said successor. Income from such investment shall be used for the purposes prescribed by the Legislature.

From the moneys received by said Parks and Wildlife Department, or its said successor, from the sale of the bonds issued hereunder, there shall be deposited in the interest and sinking fund for the bonds authorized by this section sufficient moneys to pay the interest to become due during the State fiscal year in which the bonds were issued. After all bonds have been fully paid with interest, or after there are on deposit in the interest and sinking fund sufficient moneys to pay all future maturities of principal and interest, additional moneys received from admission charges to State Parks shall be deposited to the State Parks Fund, or any successor fund which may be established by the Legislature as a depository for Park revenue earned by said Parks and Wildlife Department, or its said successor.

All bonds issued hereunder shall after approval by the Attorney General, registration by the Comptroller of Public Accounts of the State of Texas, and delivery to the purchasers, be incontestable and shall constitute general obligations of the State of Texas under the Constitution of Texas.

Should the Legislature enact enabling laws in anticipation of the adoption of this amendment, such acts shall not be void by reason of their anticipatory nature.

[Note — The foregoing Sec. 49-e of Art. III, an amendment, was added to authorize issuance and sale of $75,000,000 in bonds to create the Texas Park Development Fund to acquire lands for State Park sites and to develop State Parks. Submitted by the Sixtieth Legislature (1967) and adopted in election Nov. 11, 1967.]

Sec. 49-f. (a) The Legislature by general law may provide for the issuance of general obligation bonds of the state, the proceeds of which shall be used to make loans and provide other financing assistance for the purchase of farm and ranch land.

(b) All money received from the sale of the bonds shall be deposited in a fund created with the state treasurer to be known as the farm and ranch finance program fund. This fund shall be administered by the Veterans' Land Board in the manner prescribed by law.

(c) Sec. 65(b) of this article applies to the payment of interest on the bonds.

(d) The principal amount of bonds outstanding at one time may not exceed $500 million.

(e) While any of the bonds authorized by this section or any interest on those bonds is outstanding and unpaid, there is appropriated out of the first money coming into the treasury in each fiscal year not otherwise appropriated by this constitution an amount that is sufficient to pay the principal and interest on the bonds that mature or become due during the fiscal year less the amount in the interest and sinking fund at the close of the prior fiscal year.

(f) The bonds shall be approved by the attorney general and registered with the comptroller of public accounts. The bonds, when approved and registered, are general obligations of the state and are incontestable.

[Note — The foregoing Sec. 49-f of Art. III, an amendment, was added to authorize the issuance of general obligation bonds to provide financing for purchase of farm and ranch land. Submitted by Sixty-ninth Legislature (1985) and adopted in an election Nov. 5, 1985.]

Sec. 49-g. **Superconducting Super Collider: Bonds Authorized for Facilities** —(See also second Sec. 49-g below, regarding the economic stabilization fund, and the explanatory note which follows it.) (a) The legislature may authorize (1) the appropriate agency to issue up to $500 million in general obligation bonds and to use the proceeds of the bonds (without further appropriation) to establish a superconducting super collider fund to be used in any manner appropriate to fund undertakings related to a superconducting super collider research facility sponsored or authorized by the United States government, and (2) the appropriate agency to grant land or property, whether or not acquired from proceeds of the bonds, to the United States government for undertakings related to a superconducting super collider research facility. The superconducting super collider fund shall contain a project account, an interest and sinking account and such other accounts as may be authorized by the legislature. The fund shall be composed of the proceeds of the bonds authorized by this section, together with any income from investment of money in the fund, amounts received pursuant to Subsection (b) hereof, and any other amounts authorized to be deposited in the fund by the legislature.

(b) Bonds issued under this section constitute a general obligation of the state. While any of the bonds or interest on the bonds is outstanding and unpaid, there is appropriated out of the first money coming into the treasury in each fiscal year, not otherwise appropriated by this constitution, the amount sufficient to pay the principal of and interest on the bonds that mature or become due during the fiscal year, less any amount in the interest and sinking account at the end of the preceding fiscal year that is pledged to payment of the bonds or interest.

(c) The legislature may require review and approval of the issuance of the bonds, of the use of the bond proceeds, or of the rules adopted by an agency to govern use of the bond proceeds. Notwithstanding any other provision of this constitution, any entity created or directed to conduct this review and approval may include members, or appointees of members, of the executive, legislative, and judicial departments of state government.

(d) Should the legislature enact enabling laws in anticipation of the adoption of this section, such acts shall not be void by reason of their anticipatory character.

[Note — The foregoing Sec. 49-g of Art. III, an amendment, was added to provide for issuance of bonds relating to a superconducting super collider research facility. Submitted by the Seventieth Legislature (1987) and adopted in an election Nov. 3, 1987.]

Article III — (Cont'd.)

Sec. 49-g. **Economic Stabilization Fund** — (See also first Sec. 49-g above, regarding the superconducting super collider, and the explanatory note which follows the second Sec. 49-g below.) (a) The economic stabilization fund is established as a special fund in the state treasury.

(b) The comptroller shall, not later than the 90th day of each biennium, transfer to the economic stabilization fund one-half of any unencumbered positive balance of general revenues on the last day of the preceding biennium. If necessary, the comptroller shall reduce the amount transferred in proportion to the other amounts prescribed by this section to prevent the amount in the fund from exceeding the limit in effect for that biennium under Subsection (g) of this section.

(c) Not later than the 90th day of each fiscal year, the comptroller of public accounts shall transfer from general revenue to the economic stabilization fund the amounts prescribed by Subsections (d) and (e) of this section. However, if necessary, the comptroller shall reduce proportionately the amounts transferred to prevent the amount in the fund from exceeding the limit in effect for that biennium under Subsection (g) of this section.

(d) If in the preceding year the state received from oil production taxes a net amount greater than the net amount of oil production taxes received by the state in the fiscal year ending August 31, 1987, the comptroller shall transfer to the economic stabilization fund an amount equal to 75 percent of the difference between those amounts. The comptroller shall retain the remaining 25 percent of the difference as general revenue. In computing the net amount of oil production taxes received, the comptroller may not consider refunds paid as a result of oil overcharge litigation.

(e) If in the preceding year the state received from gas production taxes a net amount greater than the net amount of gas production taxes received by the state in the fiscal year ending August 31, 1987, the comptroller shall transfer to the economic stabilization fund an amount equal to 75 percent of the difference between those amounts. The comptroller shall retain the remaining 25 percent of the difference as general revenue. For the purposes of this subsection, the comptroller shall adjust his computation of revenues to reflect only 12 months of collection.

(f) The legislature may appropriate additional amounts to the economic stabilization fund.

(g) During each fiscal biennium, the amount in the economic stabilization fund may not exceed an amount equal to 10 percent of the total amount, excluding investment income, interest income, and amounts borrowed from special funds, deposited in general revenue during the preceding biennium.

(h) In preparing an estimate of anticipated revenues for a succeeding biennium as required by Article III, Section 49a, of this constitution, the comptroller shall estimate the amount of the transfers that will be made under Subsections (b), (d), and (e) of this section. The comptroller shall deduct that amount from the estimate of anticipated revenues as if the transfers were made on August 31 of that fiscal year.

(i) The state treasurer shall credit to general revenue interest due to the economic stabilization fund that would result in an amount in the economic stabilization fund that exceeds the limit in effect under Subsection (g) of this section.

(j) The comptroller, with the consent of the state treasurer, may transfer money from the economic stabilization fund to general revenue to prevent or eliminate a temporary cash deficiency in general revenue. The comptroller shall return the amount transferred to the economic stabilization fund as soon as practicable, but not later than August 31 of each odd-numbered year. The state treasurer shall allocate the depository interest as if the transfers had not been made. If the comptroller submits a statement to the governor and the legislature under Article III, Section 49a, of this constitution when money from the economic stabilization fund is in general revenue, the comptroller shall state that the transferred money is not available for appropriation from general revenue.

(k) Amounts from the economic stabilization fund may be appropriated during a regular legislative session only for a purpose for which an appropriation from general revenue was made by the preceding legislature and may be appropriated in a special session only for a purpose for which an appropriation from general revenue was made in a preceding legislative session of the same legislature. An appropriation from the economic stabilization fund may be made only if the comptroller certifies that appropriations from general revenue made by the preceding legislature for the current biennium exceed available general revenues and cash balances for the remainder of that biennium. The amount of an appropriation from the economic stabilization fund may not exceed the difference between the comptroller's estimate of general revenue for the current biennium at the time the comptroller receives for certification the bill making the appropriation and the amount of general revenue appropriations for that biennium previously certified by the comptroller. Appropriations from the economic stabilization

fund under this subsection may not extend beyond the last day of the current biennium. An appropriation from the economic stabilization fund must be approved by a three-fifths vote of the members present in each house of the legislature.

(l) If an estimate of anticipated revenues for a succeeding biennium prepared by the comptroller pursuant to Article III, Section 49a, of this constitution, is less than the revenues that are estimated at the same time by the comptroller to be available for the current biennium, the legislature may, by a three-fifths vote of the members present in each house, appropriate for the succeeding biennium from the economic stabilization fund an amount not to exceed this difference. Following each fiscal year, the actual amount of revenue shall be computed, and if the estimated difference exceeds the actual difference, the comptroller shall transfer the amount necessary from general revenue to the economic stabilization fund so that the actual difference shall not be exceeded. If all or a portion of the difference in revenue from one biennium to the next results, at least in part, from a change in a tax rate or base adopted by the legislature, the computation of revenue difference shall be adjusted to the amount that would have been available had the rate or base not been changed.

(m) In addition to the appropriation authority provided by Subsections (k) and (l) of this section, the legislature may, by a two-thirds vote of the members present in each house, appropriate amounts from the economic stabilization fund at any time and for any purpose.

(n) Money appropriated from the economic stabilization fund is subject to being withheld or transferred, within any limits provided by statute, by any person or entity authorized to exercise the power granted by Article XVI, Section 69, of this constitution.

(o) In this section, "net" means the amount of money that is equal to the difference between gross collections and refunds before the comptroller allocates the receipts as provided by law.

[Note — The foregoing Sec. 49-g of Art. III, an amendment, was added to establish the economic stabilization fund. Submitted by the Seventieth Legislature and adopted in an election Nov. 8, 1988. Please also note that the Seventieth Legislature submitted two different Section 49-g's for Article III: the first, having to do with the superconducting super collider, approved in an election Nov. 3, 1987, and the second, having to do with the economic stabilization fund, approved in an election Nov. 8, 1988. They are printed here in the order in which they were adopted.]

Sec. 49-h. (a) The legislature may authorize the issuance of up to $500 million in general obligation bonds and the use of the bond proceeds for acquiring, constructing, or equipping new facilities or for major repair or renovation of existing facilities of corrections institutions, including youth corrections institutions, and mental health and mental retardation institutions. The legislature may require the review and approval of the issuance of the bonds and the projects to be financed by the bond proceeds. Notwithstanding any other provision of this constitution, the issuer of the bonds or any entity created or directed to review and approve projects may include members or appointees of members of the executive, legislative, and judicial departments of state government.

(b) Bonds issued under this section constitute a general obligation of the state. While any of the bonds or interest on the bonds is outstanding and unpaid, there is appropriated out of the first money coming into the treasury in each fiscal year, not otherwise appropriated by this constitution, the amount sufficient to pay the principal of and interest on the bonds that mature or become due during the fiscal year, less any amount in any sinking fund at the end of the preceding fiscal year that is pledged to payment of the bonds or interest.

(c) (1) The legislature may authorize the issuance of up to $400 million in general obligation bonds, in addition to the amount authorized by Subsection (a) of this section, and use the proceeds of the bonds for acquiring, constructing, or equipping new corrections institutions, mental health and mental retardation institutions, youth corrections institutions, and statewide law enforcement facilities and for major repair or renovation of existing facilities of those institutions.

(2) The provisions of Subsection (a) of this section relating to the review and approval of bonds and the provisions of Subsection (b) of this section relating to the status of the bonds as a general obligation of the state and to the manner in which the principal and interest on the bonds are paid apply to bonds authorized under this subsection.

[Note — The foregoing Sec. 49-h of Art. III, an amendment, was added to provide for issuance of general obligation bonds for construction projects for corrections institutions and mental health and mental retardation institutions. Submitted by the Seventieth Legislature and adopted in an election Nov. 3 1987. It was further amended by

Article III – (Cont'd.)

the addition of subsection (c) providing for the issuance of general obligation bonds for acquiring, constructing or equipping corrections institutions, youth corrections institutions, statewide law enforcement facilities and mental health and mental retardation institutions. Proposed by the Seventy-first Legislature (1989) and adopted in a election Nov. 7, 1989.]

Sec. 49-i. (a) The legislature by law may provide for the issuance of general obligation bonds of the state for the purpose of providing money to establish a Texas agricultural fund in the state treasury to be used without further appropriation in the manner provided by law and for the purpose of providing money to establish a rural microenterprise development fund in the state treasury to be used without further appropriation in the manner provided by law. The Texas agricultural fund shall be used only to provide financial assistance to develop, increase, improve, or expand the production, processing, marketing, or export of crops or products grown or produced primarily in this state by agricultural businesses domiciled in the state. The rural microenterprise development fund shall be used only in furtherance of a program established by the legislature to foster and stimulate the creation and expansion of small businesses in rural areas. The financial assistance offered by both funds may include loan guarantees, insurance, coinsurance, loans, and indirect loans or purchases or acceptances of assignments of loans or other obligations.

(b) The principal amount of bonds outstanding at one time may not exceed $25 million for the Texas agricultural fund and $5 million for the rural microenterprise development fund.

(c) The legislature may establish an interest and sinking account and other accounts within the Texas agricultural fund and within the rural microenterprise development fund. The legislature may provide for the investment of bond proceeds and of the interest and sinking accounts. Income from the investment of money in the funds that is not immediately committed to the payment of the principal of and interest on the bonds or the provision of financial assistance shall be used to create new employment and business opportunities in the state through the diversification and expansion of agricultural or rural small businesses, as provided by the legislature.

(d) Bonds authorized under this section constitute a general obligation of the state. While any of the bonds or interest on the bonds is outstanding and unpaid, there is appropriated out of the first money coming into the treasury in each fiscal year, not otherwise appropriated by this constitution, the amount sufficient to pay the principal of and interest on the bonds that mature or become due during the fiscal year, less any amounts in the interest and sinking accounts at the close of the preceding fiscal year that are pledged to payment of the bonds or interest.

[Note – The foregoing Sec. 49-i of Art. III, an amendment, authorizes the Legislature to provide for issuance of bonds and state financing of development and producton of Texas products and businesses. Proposed by the Seventy-first Legislature (1989) and adopted in an election Nov. 7, 1989.]

Sec. 50. **Credit of State Not to Be Pledged** – The Legislature shall have no power to give or to lend or to authorize the giving or lending of the credit of the State in aid of, or to any person, association or corporation, whether municipal or other, or to pledge the credit of the State in any manner whatsoever, for the payment of the liabilities, present or prospective, of any individual, association of individuals, municipal or other corporation whatsoever.

Sec. 50-a. **State Medical Education Board, Fund; Purpose** – The Legislature shall create a State Medical Education Board to be composed of not more than six (6) members whose qualifications, duties and terms of office shall be prescribed by law. The Legislature shall also establish a State Medical Education Fund and make adequate appropriations therefor to be used by the State Medical Education Board to provide grants, loans or scholarships to students desiring to study medicine and agreeing to practice in the rural areas of this State, upon such terms and conditions as shall be prescribed by law. The term "rural areas" as used in this section shall be defined by law.

[Note – The foregoing Sec. 50-a of Art. III, an amendment, was added for the stated purpose of providing scholarships and to set up a State Medical Education Board. Submitted by the Fifty-second Legislature and adopted in an election Nov. 4, 1952.]

Sec. 50-b. **Student Loans** – (a) The Legislature may provide that the Coordinating Board, Texas College and University System, or its successor or successors, shall have the authority to provide for, issue and sell general obligation bonds of the State of Texas in an amount not to exceed Eighty-five Million Dollars ($85,000,000). The bonds authorized herein, shall be called "Texas College Student Loan

Bonds," shall be executed in such form, denominations and upon such terms as may be prescribed by law, provided, however, that the bonds shall not bear more than four per cent (4%) interest per annum; they may be issued in such installments as the Board finds feasible and practical in accomplishing the purposes of this section.

(b) All moneys received from the sale of such bonds shall be deposited in a fund hereby created in the State Treasury to be known as the Texas Opportunity Plan Fund to be administered by the Coordinating Board, Texas College and University System, or its successor or successors to make loans to students who have been admitted to attend any institution of higher education within the State of Texas, public or private, including Junior Colleges, which are recognized or accredited under terms and conditions prescribed by the Legislature, and to pay interest and principal on such bonds and provide a sinking fund therefor under such conditions as the Legislature may prescribe.

(c) While any of the bonds, or interest on said bonds authorized by this section is outstanding and unpaid, there is hereby appropriated out of the first moneys coming into the Treasury in each fiscal year, not otherwise appropriated by this Constitution, an amount sufficient to pay the principal and interest on such bonds that mature or become due during such fiscal year, less the amount in the sinking fund at the close of the prior fiscal year.

(d) The Legislature may provide for the investment of moneys available in the Texas Opportunity Plan Fund, and the interest and sinking funds established for the payment of bonds issued by the Coordinating Board, Texas College and University System, or its successor or successors. Income from such investment shall be used for the purposes prescribed by the Legislature.

(e) All bonds issued hereunder shall, after approval by the Attorney General, registration by the Comptroller of Public Accounts of the State of Texas, and delivery to the purchasers, be incontestable and shall constitute general obligations of the State of Texas under this Constitution.

(f) Should the Legislature enact enabling laws in anticipation of the adoption of this amendment, such acts shall not be void because of their anticipatory nature.

[Note — The foregoing Sec. 50-b of Art. III, an amendment, was added to provide a system of student loans at institutions of higher education and to provide for creation of the Texas Opportunity Plan Fund. Submitted by the Fifty-ninth Legislature (1965) and adopted in an election Nov. 2, 1965.]

Sec. 50-b-1. (a) The Legislature may provide that the Coordinating Board, Texas College and University System, or its successor or successors, shall have authority to provide for, issue and sell general obligation bonds of the State of Texas in an amount not to exceed Two Hundred Million Dollars ($200,000,000) in addition to those heretofore authorized to be issued pursuant to Sec. 50-b of the Constitution. The bonds authorized herein shall be executed in such form, upon such terms and be in such denomination as may be prescribed by such law and shall bear interest, and be issued in such installments as shall be prescribed by the Board provided that the maximum net effective interest rate to be borne by such bonds may be fixed by law.

(b) The moneys received from the sale of such bonds shall be deposited to the credit of the Texas Opportunity Plan Fund created by Sec. 50-b of the Constitution and shall otherwise be handled as provided in Sec. 50-b of the Constitution and the laws enacted pursuant thereto.

(c) The said bonds shall be general obligations of the state and shall be payable in the same manner and from the same sources as bonds heretofore authorized pursuant to Sec. 50-b.

(d) All bonds issued hereunder shall, after approval by the Attorney General, registration by the Comptroller of Public Accounts of the State of Texas, and delivery to the purchasers, be incontestable and shall constitute general obligations of the State of Texas under this Constitution.

(e) Should the Legislature enact enabling laws in anticipation of the adoption of this amendment such acts shall not be void because of their anticipatory nature.

[Note—The foregoing Sec. 50-b-1 of Art. III, an amendment, was added to provide for additional loans to students at higher educational institutions under the Texas Opportunity Plan. Submitted by the Sixty-first Legislature (1969) and adopted in election Aug. 5, 1969.]

Sec. 50-b-2. **Additional Student Loans** – (a) The legislature by general law may authorize the Texas Higher Education Coordinating Board or its successor or successors to provide for, issue, and sell general obligation bonds of the State of Texas in an amount not to exceed $75 million in addition to those bonds issued under Sections 50-b and 50-b-1 of this constitution. Bonds issued under this section shall be issued as college savings bonds as provided by law.

Article III — (Cont'd.)

(b) The bonds shall:

(1) be executed in the form, on the terms, and in the denominations as prescribed by law; and

(2) bear interest and be issued in installments as prescribed by the Texas Higher Education Coordinating Board or its successor or successors.

(c) The maximum net effective interest rate to be borne by bonds issued under this section must be set by law.

(d) The proceeds from the sale of bonds issued under this section shall be credited to the Texas opportunity plan fund created by Section 50-b of this constitution and shall be administered as provided by Section 50-b of this constitution and the law enacted under that constitutional provision.

(e) Bonds issued under this section are payable in the same manner and from the same sources as bonds authorized under Section 50-b of this constitution.

(f) Bonds issued under this section, after approval by the attorney general, registration by the comptroller of public accounts, and delivery to the purchasers, are incontestable and are general obligations of the State of Texas under this constitution.

[Note — The foregoing Sec. 50-b-2 of Art. III, an amendment, was added to provide for the issuance of general obligation bonds as college savings bonds to provide educational loans to students and to encourage the public to save for a college education. Proposed by the Seventy-first Legislature (1989) and adopted in an election Nov. 7, 1989.]

Sec. 50-c. **Farm and Ranch Loan Security Fund** — (a) The Legislature may provide that the commissioner of agriculture shall have the authority to provide for, issue, and sell general obligation bonds of the State of Texas in an amount not to exceed $10 million. The bonds shall be called "Farm and Ranch Loan Security Bonds" and shall be executed in such form, denominations, and on such terms as may be prescribed by law. The bonds shall bear interest rates fixed by the Legislature of the State of Texas.

(b) All money received from the sale of Farm and Ranch Loan Security Bonds shall be deposited in a fund hereby created with the State Treasurer to be known as the "Farm and Ranch Loan Security Fund." This fund shall be administered without further appropriation by the commissioner of agriculture in the manner prescribed by law.

(c) The Farm and Ranch Loan Security Fund shall be used by the commissioner of agriculture under provisions prescribed by the Legislature for the purpose of guaranteeing loans used for the purchase of farm and ranch real estate, for acquiring real estate mortgages or deeds of trust on lands purchased with guaranteed loans, and to advance to the borrower a percentage of the principal and interest due on those loans; provided that the commissioner shall require at least six percent interest be paid by the borrower on any advance of principal and interest. The Legislature may authorize the commissioner to sell at foreclosure any land acquired in this manner, and proceeds from that sale shall be deposited in the Farm and Ranch Loan Security Fund.

(d) The Legislature may provide for the investment of money available in the Farm and Ranch Loan Security Fund and the interest and sinking fund established for the payment of bonds issued by the commissioner of agriculture. Income from the investment shall be used for purposes prescribed by the Legislature.

(e) While any of the bonds authorized by this section or any interest on those bonds is outstanding and unpaid, there is hereby appropriated out of the first money coming into the treasury in each fiscal year not otherwise appropriated by this constitution an amount that is sufficient to pay the principal and interest on the bonds that mature or become due during the fiscal year less the amount in the interest and sinking fund at the close of the prior fiscal year.

[Note — Sec. 50-c of Art. III, an amendment, was added to provide for the guarantee of loans for purchase of farm and ranch real estate for qualified borrowers by the sale of general obligation bonds of the State of Texas. Submitted by the Sixty-sixth Legislature (1979) and adopted in election Nov. 6, 1979.]

Sec. 50-d. (a) On a two-thirds vote of the members elected to each house of the Legislature, the Texas Water Development Board may issue and sell Texas agricultural water conservation bonds in an amount not to exceed $200 million.

(b) The proceeds from the sale of Texas agricultural water conservation bonds shall be deposited in a fund created in the state treasury to be known as the agricultural water conservation fund.

(c) Texas agricultural water conservation bonds are general obligations of the State of Texas. During the time that Texas agricultural water conservation bonds or any interest on those bonds is outstanding and unpaid, there is appropri-

ated out of the first money coming into the state treasury in each fiscal year, not otherwise appropriated by this constitution, an amount that is sufficient to pay the principal of and interest on those bonds that mature or become due during that fiscal year, less the amount in the sinking fund at the close of the prior fiscal year.

(d) The terms, conditions, provisions, and procedures for issuance and sale and management of proceeds of Texas agricultural water conservation bonds shall be provided by law.

[Note — The foregoing Sec. 50-d of Art. III, an amendment, was added to authorize issuance and sale of $200 million of Texas agricultural water conservation bonds. Submitted by the Sixty-ninth Legislature (1985) and adoped in an election Nov. 5, 1985. Subsection (e) of Sec. 50-d was repealed in order to eliminate certain time limitations relating to the issuance of Texas agricultural water conservation bonds. Repeal proposed by the Seventy-first Legislature (1989) and adopted in an election Nov. 7, 1989.]

Sec. 50-e. (a) For the purposes of providing surety for the Texas grain warehouse self-insurance fund, the legislature by general law may establish or provide for a guarantee of the fund not to exceed $50 million.

(b) At the beginning of the fiscal year after the fund reaches $5 million, as certified by the comptroller of public accounts, the guarantee of the fund shall cease and this provision shall expire.

(c) Should the legislature enact any enabling laws in anticipation of this amendment, no such law shall be void by reason of its anticipating nature.

(d) If the provisions of this section conflict with any other provisions of this constitution, the provisions of this section shall prevail.

[Note — The foregoing section 50-e, an amendment, was added to establish a self-insurance pool for grain storage facilities. Submitted by the Seventieth Legislature (1987) and adopted in an election Nov. 3, 1987.]

Sec. 51. **Tax Levy Authorized for Confederate Soldiers and Sailors and Their Widows** — The Legislature shall have no power to make any grant or authorize the making of any grant of public moneys to any individual, association of individuals, municipal or other corporations whatsoever; provided, however, the Legislature may grant aid to indigent and disabled Confederate soldiers and sailors under such regulations and limitations as may be deemed by the Legislature as expedient, and to their widows in indigent circumstances under such regulations and limitations as may be deemed by the Legislature as expedient; provided that the provisions of this Section shall not be construed so as to prevent the grant of aid in cases of public calamity.

[Note—The foregoing Sec. 51 of Art. III, in its present form, is the result of much amendment. The original Sec. 51, which prohibited all grants of public money to individuals, associations, etc., with the single exception of cases of "public calamity," has been amended nine times, as follows: (1) Establishing Confederate Home. Submitted by Twenty-third Legislature (1893) and ratified at election, Nov. 6, 1894, and proclaimed adopted Dec. 21, 1894. (2) Providing for pensions for Confederate veterans from appropriations not to exceed $250,000 annually. Submitted by Twenty-fifth Legislature (1897), adopted at election, Nov. 1, 1898, and proclaimed Dec. 22, 1898. (3) Raising amount that might be appropriated for Confederate pensions from $250,000 to $500,000 annually. Submitted by Twenty-eighth Legislature (1903), adopted in election, Nov. 8, 1904, and proclaimed Dec. 29, 1904. (4) Increasing authorized maximum appropriations for Confederate Home from $100,000 to $150,000 annually. Submitted by Thirty-first Legislature (1909), adopted in election, Nov. 8, 1910, and declared adopted Dec. 31, 1910. (5) Authorizing 5c ad valorem tax for Confederate pension fund— also omitting "public calamity" clause. Submitted by Thirty-second Legislature (1911), adopted Nov. 3, 1912, and proclaimed Dec. 30, 1912. (6) Authorizing 7c ad valorem tax for Confederate pension fund — also reinstating "public calamity" clause. Submitted by Thirty-eighth Legislature (1923) and adopted Nov. 4, 1924. (7) Eliminating specific restrictions upon grants of aid to Confederate soldiers, sailors and others with respect to date of removal to Texas, etc.; and conferring such authority upon the Legislature. Submitted by Fortieth Legislature (1927); ratified Nov. 6, 1928; proclaimed Feb. 6, 1929. (8) Cutting tax from 7c to 2c by addition of Sec. 17 of Art. VII, which was deleted by Constitutional amendment in 1982. (9) Further amended to provide for abolition of the two cents ad valorem tax for this purpose by Dec. 31, 1976, but making provision for aiding these veterans and their widows. (See also Art. VIII, Sec. 1-e.) Submitted by Sixtieth Legislature (1967) and adopted in election Nov. 5, 1968.]

Sec. 51-a—**Assistance and Medical Care to Needy Aged, Needy Blind, Needy Children and Totally Disabled; Limitation on Expenditures for Same** — The Legislature shall

Article III - (Cont'd.)

have the power, by General Laws, to provide; subject to limitations herein contained, and such other limitations, restrictions and regulations as may by the Legislature be deemed expedient, for assistance grants to dependent children and the caretakers of such children, needy persons who are totally and permanently disabled because of a mental or physical handicap, needy aged persons and needy blind persons.

The Legislature may provide by General Law for medical care, rehabilitation and other similar services for needy persons. The Legislature may prescribe such other eligibility requirements for participation in these programs as it deems appropriate and may make appropriations out of state funds for such purposes. The maximum amount paid out of state funds for assistance grants to or on behalf of needy dependent children and their caretakers shall not exceed the amount of Eighty Million Dollars ($80,000,000) during any fiscal year, except that the limit shall be One Hundred Sixty Million Dollars ($160,000,000) for the two years of the 1982-1983 biennium. For the two years of each subsequent biennium, the maximum amount shall not exceed one percent of the state budget. The Legislature by general statute shall provide for the means for determining the state budget amounts, including state and other funds appropriated by the Legislature, to be used in establishing the biennial limit.

Provided further, that if the limitations and restrictions herein contained are found to be in conflict with the provisions of appropriate federal statutes, as they now are or as they may be amended to the extent that federal matching money is not available to the state for these purposes, then and in that event the Legislature is specifically authorized and empowered to prescribe such limitations and restrictions and enact such laws as may be necessary in order that such federal matching money will be available for assistance and/or medical care for or on behalf of needy persons.

Nothing in this section shall be construed to amend, modify or repeal Sec. 31 of Art. XVI of this Constitution; provided further, however, that such medical care, services or assistance shall also include the employment of objective or subjective means, without the use of drugs, for the purpose of ascertaining and measuring the powers of vision of the human eye, and fitting lenses or prisms to correct or remedy any defect or abnormal condition of vision. Nothing herein shall be construed to permit optometrists to treat the eyes for any defect whatsoever in any manner nor to administer nor to prescribe any drug or physical treatment whatsoever, unless such optometrist is a regularly licensed physician or surgeon under the laws of this State.

[Note—The foregoing Sec. 51-a of Art. III, an amendment, was first submitted by Forty-ninth Legislature and adopted in an election Aug. 25, 1945. It supplanted four earlier amendments, as follows: An original Sec. 51-a which provided for issuance of $20,000,000 in state bonds for relief (the so-called "Bread bonds") this amendment having been submitted by Forty-third Legislature and adopted Aug. 26, 1933; and also Secs. 51-b, 51-c and 51-d, which originally provided for old-age pensions and other welfare measures, adopted in elections Aug. 24, 1935 and Aug. 23, 1937. Because of this consolidation, the Constitution skip from Sec. 51-a to Sec. 51-e until a Sec. 51-b was added in election Nov. 2, 1954, and a Subsection 51-a was added in election Nov. 5, 1957. It was further amended to raise the limit from $35,000,000 to $42,000,000. Submitted by Fifty-third Legislature (1953) and adopted in election Nov. 2, 1954. It was again amended to raise the limit from $42,000,000 to $47,000,000 and authorizing legislative appropriations to raise the needed money. Submitted by Fifty-fifth Legislature (1957) and adopted in election Nov. 5, 1957. It was further amended to raise the total amount of assistance to $52,000,000 per year. Submitted by Fifty-seventh Legislature (1961) and adopted in election Nov. 6, 1962. It was further amended to combine the former Sections 51-a and 51-b-1 of Art. III into one section to be known as Sec. 51-a; further raising the total amount of assistance to $60,000,000 per year and providing that Legislature shall prescribe the residence requirements. Submitted by Fifty-eighth Legislature (1963) and adopted in election Nov. 9, 1963. It was further amended in 1965 to create a new Sec. 51-a which consolidates the old Sec. 51-a and Subsections 51-a-1 and 51-a-2. The new Sec. 51-a enables the State of Texas to cooperate with the U.S. government in providing assistance and medical care for the needy aged, needy blind, needy children and needy totally disabled; expands age categories of those eligible for blind assistance and of needy children; and extends eligibility for the aged to citizens of the U.S. or noncitizens who have resided in the U.S. for 25 years. Submitted by Fifty-ninth Legislature (1965) and adopted in election Nov. 2, 1965. It was again amended to raise the limit on amount to be expended from $60,000,000 to $80,000,000 a year. It further provided that certain amounts be allocated out of the Omnibus Tax Clearance Fund for aid to permanently and totally disabled, families with dependent children and for old-age assistance. Submitted by Sixty-first Legislature (1969) and adopted in an election Aug. 5, 1969. The regular session of the Sixty-seventh Legislature (1981) submitted an amendment to raise the amount to be expended on Aid for Dependent Children in the 1982-1983 biennium to a maximum of $160 million and, for each subsequent biennium, the maximum amount would not exceed one percent of the state budget. This proposed amendment inadvertently cut out other needy recipients and SJR 10 of the Called Session of the Sixty-seventh Legis-

lature (1982) amended the proposed amendment to include other needy recipients in this fund. Adopted in election Nov. 2, 1982.]

Sec. 51-a-1. (a) The legislature by general law may authorize the use of public money to provide to local fire departments and other public fire-fighting organizations:

(1) loans or other financial assistance to purchase fire-fighting equipment and to aid in providing necessary equipment and facilities to comply with federal and state law; and

(2) scholarships and grants to educate and train the members of local fire departments and other public fire-fighting organizations.

(b) A portion of the money used under this section may be used for the administrative costs of the program. The legislature shall provide for the terms and conditions of scholarships, grants, loans, and other financial assistance to be provided under this section.

[Note — The foregoing Sec. 51-a-1 of Art. III, an amendment, was added to authorize the state to provide scholarships, grants, loans and other financial assistance to local fire departments and other public fire-fighting organizations. Proposed by the Seventy-first Legislature (1989) and adopted in an election Nov. 7, 1989.]

[Note — Sec. 51-b of Art. III, creating the State Building Commission and the State Building Fund, was eliminated by a constitutional amendment in an election Nov. 7, 1978.]

Sec. 51-c. **False Imprisonment** — The Legislature may grant aid and compensation to any person who has heretofore paid a fine or served a sentence in prison, or who may hereafter pay a fine or serve a sentence in prison, under the laws of this State for an offense for which he or she is not guilty, under such regulations and limitations as the Legislature may deem expedient.

[Note — Sec. 51-c of Art. III was added to provide that Legislature may grant aid and compensation to persons who have been fined or imprisoned under laws of this state for offenses of which they are not guilty. Submitted by the Fifty-fourth Legislature (1955) and adopted in election Nov. 6, 1956.]

Sec. 51-d. **Assistance to Survivors of Law Enforcement Officers Killed on Duty** — The Legislature shall have the power, by general law, to provide for the payment of assistance by the State of Texas to the surviving spouse, minor children, and surviving dependent parents, brothers, and sisters of officers, employees and agents, including members of organized volunteer fire departments and members of organized police reserve or auxiliary units with authority to make an arrest, of the state or of any city, county, district, or other political subdivision who, because of the hazardous nature of their duties, suffer death in the course of the performance of those official duties. Should the Legislature enact any enabling laws in anticipation of this amendment, no such law shall be void by reason of its anticipatory nature.

[Note — The foregoing Sec. 51-d, an amendment, was added to provide assistance for survivors of law enforcement officers killed in performance of their duty. Submitted by the Fifty-ninth Legislature (1965), and adopted in election Nov. 8, 1966. It was further amended to provide for assistance to survivors of members of volunteer fire departments and organized police reserve, or auxiliary units with authority to make arrests, of political subdivisions of the state. Submitted by the Sixty-first Legislature (1969) and adopted in election Aug. 5, 1969. It was again amended to provide compensation for dependent parents, brothers and sisters of officers killed in performing their duties. Submitted by the Sixty-eighth Legislature (1983) and adopted in election Nov. 6, 1984.]

[Note — Sec. 51e and Sec. 51f, relating to City and Town Pension System and Local Pension Plans, respectively, were deleted by a constitutional amendment election April 22, 1975. See also note under Art. III, Sec. 48a and Sec. 48b; Art. XVI, Sec. 62 and Sec. 63. See also Art. XVI, Sec. 67, which replaces the foregoing Sections.]

Sec. 51-g. **Social Security Coverage for Municipal Employees** — The Legislature shall have the power to pass such laws as may be necessary to enable the State to enter into agreements with the Federal Government to obtain for proprietary employees of its political subdivisions coverage under the old-age and survivors insurance provisions of Title II of the Federal Social Security Act as amended. The Legislature shall have the power to make appropriations and authorize all obligations necessary to the establishment of such Social Security coverage program.

Article III — (Cont'd.)

[Note — The foregoing Sec. 51-g of Art.III, an amendment, was added for the stated purpose of extending Social Security coverage to municipal employees. Submitted by the Fifty-third Legislature (1953) and adopted in an election Nov. 2, 1954.]

Sec. 52. Counties, Cities, Etc., Not Authorized to Grant Money or Become Stockholders; Exceptions —

(a) Except as otherwise provided by this section, the Legislature shall have no power to authorize any county, city, town or other political corporation or subdivision of the State to lend its credit or to grant public money or thing of value in aid of, or to any individual, association or corporation whatsoever, or to become a stockholder in such corporation, association or company. However, this section does not prohibit the use of public funds or credit for the payment of premiums on non-assessable life, health, or accident insurance policies and annuity contracts issued by a mutual insurance company authorized to do business in this State.

[Note — Sec. 52(a) was amended to allow political subdivisions the opportunity to engage in and transact business with authorized mutual insurance companies in same manner as with other insurance companies. Submitted by Sixty-ninth Legislature (1985) and adopted in an election Nov. 4, 1986.]

(b) Under legislative provision any county, any political subdivision of a county, any number of adjoining counties or any political subdivision of the State or any defined district now or hereafter to be described and defined within the State of Texas, and which may or may not include towns, villages or municipal corporations, upon a vote of a two-thirds majority of the resident property taxpayers voting thereon who are qualified electors of such district or territory, to be affected thereby, in addition to all other debts, may issue bonds or otherwise lend its credit in any amount not to exceed one fourth of the assessed valuation of the real property of such district or territory, except that the total bonded indebtedness of any city or town shall never exceed the limits imposed by other provisions of this Constitution, and levy and collect taxes to pay the interest thereon and provide a sinking fund for the redemption thereof, as the Legislature may authorize, and in such manner as it may authorize the same, for the following purposes, to wit:

(1) The improvement of rivers, creeks and streams to prevent overflows and to permit of navigation thereof or irrigation thereof, or in aid of such purposes.

(2) The construction and maintenance of pools, lakes, reservoirs, dams, canals and waterways for the purposes of irrigation, drainage or navigation, or in aid thereof.

(3) The construction, maintenance and operation of macadamized, graveled or paved roads and turnpikes or in aid thereof.

(c) Notwithstanding the provisions of Subsection (b) of this section, bonds may be issued by any county in an amount not to exceed one fourth of the assessed valuation of the real property in the county, for the construction, maintenance, and operation of macadamized, graveled, or paved roads and turnpikes, or in aid thereof, upon a vote of a majority of the resident property taxpayers voting thereon who are qualified electors of the county, and without the necessity of further or amendatory legislation. The county may levy and collect taxes to pay the interest on the bonds as it becomes due and to provide a sinking fund for redemption of the bonds.

(d) Any defined district created under this section that is authorized to issue bonds or otherwise lend its credit for the purposes stated in Subdivisions (1) and (2) of Subsection (b) of this section may engage in fire-fighting activities and may issue bonds or otherwise lend its credit for fire-fighting purposes as provided by law and this constitution.

(e) A county, city, town, or other political corporation or subdivision of the state may invest its funds as authorized by law.

[Note — The foregoing Sec. 52 of Art. III, is an amended section, the amendment authorizing formation of districts for issuance of bonds for leveeing, drainage, irrigation, highway construction and other public improvements. Submitted by the Twenty-eighth Legislature (1903), adopted in election, Nov. 8, 1904, and proclaimed Dec. 29, 1904. It was further amended to permit any county, on vote of a majority of qualified property taxpaying electors, to issue road bonds in an amount not exceeding one fourth of assessed valuation of the real property in the county. Submitted by the Sixty-first Legislature (1969) and adopted in election Nov. 3, 1970. It was further amended by adding Subsection (d) to authorize certain districts to engage in fire-fighting activities and to issue bonds or otherwise lend their credit for fire-fighting purposes. (See also Subsection (f) of Sec. 59, Art. XVI.) Submitted by the Sixty-fifth Legislature (1977) and adopted in

election Nov. 7, 1978. Subsection (e) was added to authorize local governments to invest their funds as authorized by law. (See related amendment at Art. XI, Sec. 3.) Proposed by Seventy-first Legislature (1989) and adopted in an election Nov. 7, 1989.]

Sec. 52-a.

Notwithstanding any other provision of this constitution, the legislature may provide for the creation of programs and the making of loans and grants of public money, other than money otherwise dedicated by this constitution to use for a different purpose, for the public purposes of development and diversification of the economy of the state, the elimination of unemployment or underemployment in the state, the stimulation of agricultural innovation, the fostering of the growth of enterprises based on agriculture, or the development or expansion of transportation or commerce in the state. Any bonds or other obligations of a county, municipality, or other political subdivision of the state that are issued for the purpose of making loans or grants in connection with a program authorized by the legislature under this section and that are payable from ad valorem taxes must be approved by a vote of the majority of the registered voters of the county, municipality, or political subdivision voting on the issue. An enabling law enacted by the legislature in anticipation of the adoption of this amendment is not void because of its anticipatory character.

[Note — The foregoing Sec. 52-a of Art. III, an amendment, was added to authorize the Legislature to provide assistance to encourage economic development in the state. Submitted by the Seventieth Legislature (1987) and adopted in an election Nov. 3, 1987.]

Sec. 52-b. Legislature Prohibited to Lend Credit of State in Building or Maintaining Toll Roads and Turnpikes —

The Legislature shall have no power or authority to in any manner lend the credit of the State or grant any public money to, or assume any indebtedness, present or future, bonded or otherwise, of any individual, person, firm, partnership, association, corporation, public corporation, public agency, or political subdivision of the State, or anyone else, which is now or hereafter authorized to construct, maintain or operate toll roads and turnpikes within this State.

[Note — The foregoing Sec. 52-b of Art. III, an amendment, was added for the stated purpose of prohibiting Legislature from lending credit of State in building or maintaining toll roads and turnpikes. Submitted by the Fifty-third Legislature (1953) and adopted in an election Nov. 2, 1954.]

Sec. 52-d. Harris County Road Districts —

Upon the vote of a majority of the resident qualified electors owning rendered taxable property therein so authorizing, a county or road district may collect an annual tax for a period not exceeding five (5) years to create a fund for constructing lasting and permanent roads and bridges or both. No contract involving the expenditure of any of such fund shall be valid unless, when it is made, money shall be on hand in such fund.

At such election, the Commissioners Court shall submit for adoption a road plan and designate the amount of special tax to be levied; the number of years said tax is to be levied; the location, description and character of the roads and bridges; and the estimated cost thereof. The funds raised by such taxes shall not be used for purposes other than those specified in the plan submitted to the voters. Elections may be held from time to time to extend or discontinue said plan or to increase or diminish said tax. The Legislature shall enact laws prescribing the procedure hereunder.

The provisions of this section shall apply only to Harris County and road districts therein.

[Note — The foregoing Sec. 52-d of Art. III, an amendment, was added for the stated purpose of giving special local tax powers to Harris County. Adopted in an election Aug. 23, 1937.]

Note that Secs. 52-a and 52-c are omitted. Such sections never existed. The Fifty-third Legislature (1953) submitted an amendment to be numbered 52-b, and same was adopted in an election Nov. 2, 1954. Obviously, the designation, "Sec. 52-d," in Senate Joint Resolution No. 16 of the Forty-fifth Legislature resulted from confusion of a new section number with the sequence of paragraphs "a, b and c" under section 52 immediately above. Some published texts of the State Constitution give this as "Paragraph d," under Sec. 52, as it might properly have been designated, but SJR No. 16 of the Fifty-third Legislature definitely gave it as a separate "Sec. 52-d." Since Sec. 52-b was added in 1954, Secs. 52-a and 52-c are still missing.

Sec. 52-e. Dallas County Road Bonds —

Bonds to be issued by Dallas County under Sec. 52 of Art. III of this Constitution for the construction, maintenance and operation of

Article III — (Cont'd.)

macadamized, graveled or paved roads and turnpikes, or in aid thereof, may, without the necessity of further or amendatory legislation, be issued upon a vote of a majority of the resident property taxpayers voting thereon who are qualified electors of said county, and bonds heretofore or hereafter issued under Subsections (a) and (b) of said Sec. 52 shall not be included in determining the debt limit prescribed in said Section.

[Note — The foregoing Sec. 52-e of Art. III, an amendment, was added to allow Dallas County to issue bonds for construction of roads upon majority vote of resident property taxpayers. Submitted by the Sixtieth Legislature (1967) and adopted in election Nov. 5, 1968.]

Note: As in the case of Sec. 52-d above, this section might more properly have been designated as paragraph "e" under Sec. 52, but the Sixtieth Legislature designated it as Sec. 52-e, which resulted in there being two Sections 52-e, as they also designated the section below, relating to payment of medical expenses for county and precinct officials, as Sec. 52-e.

Sec. 52-e. Payment of Medical Expenses for County and Precinct Officials

— Each county in the State of Texas is hereby authorized to pay all medical expenses, all doctor bills and all hospital bills for Sheriffs, Deputy Sheriffs, Constables, Deputy Constables and other county and precinct law enforcement officials who are injured in the course of their official duties; providing that while said Sheriff, Deputy Sheriff, Constable, Deputy Constable or other county or precinct law enforcement official is hospitalized or incapacitated that the county shall continue to pay his maximum salary; providing, however, that said payment of salary shall cease on the expiration of the term of office to which such official was elected or appointed. Provided, however, that no provision contained herein shall be construed to amend, modify, repeal or nullify Art. XVI, Sec. 31, of the Constitution of the State of Texas.

[Note — The foregoing Sec. 52-e of Art. III, an amendment, was added to authorize counties to pay medical bills for county and precinct law enforcement officials who are injured in line of duty; and the county shall continue to pay maximum salary for duration of term to which they were elected or appointed. Submitted by the Sixtieth Legislature (1967) and adopted in election Nov. 11, 1967.]

Sec. 52-f. Private Roads in County

— A county with a population of 5,000 or less, according to the most recent federal census, may construct and maintain private roads if it imposes a reasonable charge for the work. The Legislature by general law may limit this authority. Revenue received from private road work may be used only for the construction, including right-of-way acquisition, or maintenance of public roads.

[Note — Sec. 52-f of Art. III, an amendment, was added to authorize counties with population of 5,000 or less to perform private road work. Submitted by the Sixty-sixth Legislature (1979) and adopted in election Nov. 4, 1980.]

Sec. 53. Extra Compensation by Municipal Corporations

— The Legislature shall have no power to grant or to authorize any county or municipal authority to grant any extra compensation, fee or allowance to a public officer, agent, servant or contractor, after service has been rendered or a contract has been entered into and performed in whole or in part; nor pay, nor authorize the payment of any claim created against any county or municipality of the State under any agreement or contract made without authority of law.

Sec. 54. Liens on Railroads

— The Legislature shall have no power to release or alienate any lien held by the State upon any railroad, or in anywise change the tenor or meaning or pass any act explanatory thereof; but the same shall be enforced in accordance with the original terms upon which it was acquired.

Sec. 55. Power of Legislature to Release Debt

— The Legislature shall have no power to release or extinguish, or to authorize the releasing or extinguishing, in whole or in part, the indebtedness, liability or obligation of any corporation or individual, to this State or to any county or defined subdivision thereof, or other municipal corporation therein, except delinquent taxes which have been due for a period of at least ten years.

[Note—The foregoing Sec. 55 of Art. III is an amendment of an original section, the amendment having been adopted to include the clause "except delinquent taxes which have been due for a period of at least ten years." Submitted by the Forty-second Legislature (1931) and adopted in an election Nov. 8, 1932. Proclaimed Jan. 9, 1933.]

Sec. 56. Special Laws; Limitations

— The Legislature shall not, except as otherwise provided in this Constitution, pass any local or special law authorizing:

The creation, extension or impairing of liens;
Regulating the affairs of counties, cities, towns, wards or school districts;
Changing the names of persons or places;
Changing the venue in civil or criminal cases;
Authorizing the laying out, opening, altering or maintaining of roads, highways, streets or alleys;
Relating to ferries or bridges, or incorporating ferry or bridge companies, except for the erection of bridges crossing streams which form boundaries between this and any other State;
Vacating roads, town plats, streets or alleys;
Relating to cemeteries, graveyards or public grounds not of the states;
Authorizing the adoption or legitimation of children;
Locating or changing county seats;
Incorporating cities, towns or villages, or changing their charter;
For the opening and conducting of election or fixing or changing the places of voting;
Granting divorces;
Creating offices, or prescribing the powers and duties of officers in counties, cities, towns, election or school districts;
Changing the law of descent or succession;
Regulating the practice or jurisdiction of, or changing the rules of evidence in any judicial proceeding or inquiry before courts, justices of the peace, sheriffs, commissioners, arbitrators or other tribunals, or providing or changing methods for the collection of debts or the enforcing of judgments or prescribing the effect of judicial sales of real estate;
Regulating the fees or extending the powers and duties of aldermen, justices of the peace, magistrates or constables;
Regulating the management of public schools, the building or repairing of schoolhouses, and the raising of money for such purposes;
Fixing the rate of interest;
Affecting the estates of minors or persons under disability;
Remitting fines, penalties and forfeitures and refunding moneys legally paid into the Treasury;
Exempting property from taxation;
Regulating labor, trade, mining and manufacturing;
Declaring any named person of age;
Extending the time for the assessment or collection of taxes, or otherwise relieving any assessor or collector of taxes from the due performance of his official duties or his securities from liability;
Giving effect to informal or invalid wills or deeds;
Summoning or impaneling grand or petit juries;
For limitation of civil or criminal actions;
For incorporating railroads or other works of internal improvements;
And in all other cases where a general law can be made applicable no local or special law shall be enacted; provided, that nothing herein contained shall be construed to prohibit the Legislature from passing special laws for the preservation of the game and fish of this State in certain localities.

Sec. 57. Notice of Local or Special Laws

— No local or special law shall be passed unless notice of the intention to apply therefor shall have been published in the locality where the matter or thing to be affected may be situated, which notice shall state the substance of the contemplated law, and shall be published at least thirty days prior to the introduction into the Legislature of such bill and in the manner to be provided by law. The evidence of such notice having been published shall be exhibited in the Legislature before such act shall be passed.

Sec. 58. Sessions to Be Held at Austin, Seat of Government

— The Legislature shall hold its sessions at the City of Austin, which is hereby declared to be the seat of government.

Sec. 59. Workmen's Compensation for State Employees

— The Legislature shall have power to pass such laws as may be necessary to provide for workmen's compensation insurance for such State employees, as in its judgment is necessary or required; and to provide for the payment of all costs, charges and premiums on such policies of insurance; providing, the state shall never be required to purchase insurance for any employee.

[Note — The foregoing Sec. 59 of Art. III, an amendment, was added for the stated purpose of providing for workmen's compensation for state employees. Adopted in an election, Nov. 3, 1936.]

Sec. 60. Workmen's Compensation Insurance for County Employees

— The Legislature shall have the power to pass such laws as may be necessary to enable all counties and other political subdivisions of this State to provide Workmen's Compensation insurance, including the right to provide its own insurance risk, for all employees of the county or political subdivision as in its judgment is necessary or

Article III — (Cont'd.)

required; and the Legislature shall provide suitable laws for the administration of such insurance in the counties or political subdivisions of this State and for the payment of the costs, charges and premiums on such policies of insurance and the benefits to be paid thereunder.

[Note — The foregoing Sec. 60 of Art. III was first added for the stated purpose of providing workmen's compensation insurance for county employees. Adopted in election Nov. 2, 1948. Further amended to include all political subdivisions. Submitted by the Fifty-seventh Legislature (1961) and adopted in election Nov. 6, 1962.]

Sec. 61. The Legislature shall have the power to enact laws to enable cities, towns and villages of this state to provide Workmen's Compensation Insurance, including the right to provide their own insurance risk for all employees; and the Legislature shall provide suitable laws for the administration of such insurance in the said municipalities and for payment of the costs, charges, and premiums on policies of insurance and the benefits to be paid thereunder.

[Note — The foregoing Sec. 61 of Art. III, an amendment, was added for the stated purpose of providing workmen's compensation insurance for municipal employees. Submitted by the Fifty-second Legislature and adopted in an election Nov. 4, 1952.]

Sec. 61-a. **Salary of Governor, Attorney General, Comptroller of Public Accounts, Treasurer, Commissioner of General Land Office and Secretary of State** — The Legislature shall not fix the salary of the Governor, Attorney General, Comptroller of Public Accounts, the Treasurer, Commissioner of the General Land Office or Secretary of State at a sum less than that fixed for such officials in the Constitution on Jan. 1, 1953.

[Note — The foregoing Sec. 61-a of Art. III, an amendment, was added to fix the salaries of the aforementioned officials. Submitted by the Fifty-third Legislature (1953) and adopted in an election Nov. 2, 1954; as submitted in SJR 5, this amendment was designated merely as "Section 61" duplicating the number of an existing section. To distinguish between the two, it is here designated as "Section 61-a."]

Sec. 62. **Continuity of State and Local Governmental Operations** — (a) The Legislature, in order to insure continuity of state and local governmental operations in periods of emergency resulting from disasters caused by enemy attack, shall have the power and the immediate duty to provide for prompt and temporary succession to the powers and duties of public offices, of whatever nature and whether filled by election or appointment, the incumbents of which may become unavailable for carrying on the powers and duties of such offices. Provided, however, that Article I of the Constitution of Texas, known as the "Bill of Rights" shall not be in any manner affected, amended, impaired, suspended, repealed or suspended hereby.

(b) When such a period of emergency or the immediate threat of enemy attack exists, the Legislature may suspend procedural rules imposed by this Constitution that relate to:

(1) the order of business of the Legislature;

(2) the percentage of each house of the Legislature necessary to constitute a quorum;

(3) the requirement that a bill must be read on three days in each house before it has the force of law;

(4) the requirement that a bill must be referred to and reported from committee before its consideration; and

(5) the date on which laws passed by the Legislature take effect.

(c) When such a period of emergency or the immediate threat of enemy attack exists, the Governor, after consulting with the Lieutenant Governor and the Speaker of the House of Representatives, may suspend the constitutional requirement that the Legislature hold its sessions in Austin, the seat of government. When this requirement has been suspended, the Governor shall determine a place other than Austin at which the Legislature will hold its sessions during such period of emergency or immediate threat of enemy attack. The Governor shall notify the Lieutenant Governor and the Speaker of the House of Representatives of the place and time at which the Legislature will meet. The Governor may take security precautions, consistent with the state of emergency, in determining the extent to which that information may be released.

(d) To suspend the constitutional rules specified by Subsection (b) of this section, the Governor must issue a proclamation and the House of Representatives and the Senate must concur in the proclamation as provided by this section.

(e) The Governor's proclamation must declare that a period of emergency resulting from disasters caused by enemy attack exists, or that the immediate threat of enemy attack exists, and that suspension of constitutional rules relating to legislative procedure is necessary to assure continuity of state government. The proclamation must specify the period, not to exceed two years, during which the constitutional rules specified by Subsection (b) of this section are suspended.

(f) The House of Representatives and the Senate, by concurrent resolution approved by the majority of the members present, must concur in the Governor's proclamation. A resolution of the House of Representatives and the Senate concurring in the Governor's proclamation suspends the constitutional rules specified by Subsection (b) of this section for the period of time specified by the Governor's proclamation.

(g) The constitutional rules specified by Subsection (b) of this section may not be suspended for more than two years under a single proclamation. A suspension may be renewed, however, if the Governor issues another proclamation as provided by Subsection (e) of this section and the House of Representatives and the Senate, by concurrent resolution, concur in that proclamation.

[Note — The foregoing Sec. 62 of Art. III, an amendment, was added to provide for temporary succession to powers and duties of public offices in periods of emergency resulting from disaster caused by enemy attack. Submitted by the Fifty-seventh Legislature (1961) and adopted in election Nov. 6, 1962. It was further amended to authorize suspension of certain constitutional rules relating to legislative procedure during disasters or during immediate threat of enemy attack. Submitted by Sixty-eighth Legislature (1983) and adopted in election Nov. 8, 1983.]

Sec. 63. **Consolidation of Governmental Functions in Counties of 1,200,000 or More Inhabitants** — (1) The Legislature may by statute provide for the consolidation of some functions of government of any one or more political subdivisions comprising or located within any county in this state having one million, two hundred thousand (1,200,000) or more inhabitants. Any such statute shall require an election to be held within the political subdivisions affected thereby with approval by a majority of the voters in each of these political subdivisions, under such terms and conditions as the Legislature may require.

(2) The county government, or any political subdivision(s) comprising or located therein, may contract one with another for the performance of governmental functions required or authorized by this Constitution or the laws of this state, under such terms and conditions as the Legislature may prescribe. The term "governmental functions," as it relates to counties, includes all duties, activities and operations of statewide importance in which the county acts for the state, as well as of local importance, whether required or authorized by this Constitution or the laws of this state.

[Note — The foregoing Sec. 63 of Art. III, an amendment, was added to provide for consolidation of governmental functions between political subdivisions within counties of 1,-200,000 or more inhabitants. Submitted by the Fifty-ninth Legislature (1965) and adopted in election Nov. 8, 1966.]

Sec. 64. **Consolidation of Governmental Offices and Functions in Counties** — (a) The Legislature may by special statute provide for consolidation of governmental offices and functions of government of any one or more political subdivisions comprising or located within any county. Any such statute shall require an election to be held within the political subdivisions affected thereby with approval by a majority of the voters in each of these subdivisions, under such terms and conditions as the Legislature may require.

(b) The county government, or any political subdivision(s) comprising or located therein, may contract one with another for the performance of governmental functions required or authorized by this Constitution or the Laws of this State, under such terms and conditions as the Legislature may prescribe. No person acting under a contract made pursuant to this Subsection (b) shall be deemed to hold more than one office of honor, trust or profit or more than one civil office of emolument. The term "governmental functions," as it relates to counties, includes all duties, activities and operations of statewide importance in which the county acts for the State, as well as of local importance, whether required or authorized by this Constitution or the Laws of this State.

[Note — The foregoing Sec. 64 of Art. III, an amendment, was first added to provide for consolidation of governmental functions in El Paso and Tarrant Counties. Submitted by the Sixtieth Legislature (1967) and adopted in election Nov. 5, 1968. It was further amended to provide for consolidation of governmental functions in any county. Submitted by the Six-

Article III — (Cont'd.); Article IV

ty-first Legislature (1969) and adopted in election Nov. 3, 1970.]

Sec. 65. **Interest Rate on State Bonds** — (a) Wherever the Constitution authorizes an agency, instrumentality, or subdivision of the State to issue bonds and specifies the maximum rate of interest which may be paid on such bonds issued pursuant to such constitutional authority, such bonds may bear interest at rates not to exceed a weighted average annual interest rate of 12 percent unless otherwise provided by Subsection (b) of this section. All Constitutional provisions specifically setting rates in conflict with this provision are hereby repealed.

(b) Bonds issued by the Veterans' Land Board after the effective date of this subsection bear interest at a rate or rates determined by the board, but the rate or rates may not exceed a net effective interest rate of 10 percent per year unless otherwise provided by law. A statute that is in effect on the effective date of this subsection and that sets as a maximum interest rate payable on bonds issued by the Veterans' Land Board a rate different from the maximum rate provided by this subsection is ineffective unless reenacted by the Legislature after that date.

[Note — Sec. 65 of Art. III is an added amendment to set the interest rate on state bonds not to exceed a weighted average annual interest of 6 per cent. Submitted by the Sixty-second Legislature (1971) and adopted in an election Nov. 7, 1972. The interest rate was raised to 12 percent in an amendment submitted by a special session of the Sixty-seventh Legislature (1982) and adopted in election Nov. 2, 1982.]

ARTICLE IV — EXECUTIVE DEPARTMENT

Sec. 1. **Officers of Executive Department** — The executive department of the State shall consist of a Governor, who shall be the chief executive officer of the State; a Lieutenant Governor, Secretary of State, Comptroller of Public Accounts, Treasurer, Commissioner of the General Land Office and Attorney General.

Sec. 2. **Election of Executive Officers** — All the above officers of the executive department (except Secretary of State) shall be elected by the qualified voters of the State at the time and places of election for members of the Legislature.

Sec. 3. **Election Results; Ties; Contests** — The returns of every election for said executive officers, until otherwise provided by law, shall be made out, sealed up and transmitted by the returning officers prescribed by law, to the seat of government, directed to the Secretary of State, who shall deliver the same to the Speaker of the House of Representatives as soon as the Speaker shall be chosen, and the said Speaker shall, during the first week of the session of the Legislature, open and publish them in the presence of both houses of the Legislature. The person voted for at said election having the highest number of votes for each of said offices, respectively, and being constitutionally eligible, shall be declared by the Speaker, under sanction of the Legislature, to be elected to said office. But if two or more persons shall have the highest and an equal number of votes for either of said offices, one of them shall be immediately chosen to such office by a joint vote of both houses of the Legislature. Contested elections for either of said offices shall be determined by both houses of the Legislature in joint session.

Sec. 3-a. **Gubernatorial Succession** — If, at the time the Legislature shall canvass the election returns for the offices of Governor and Lieutenant Governor, the person receiving the highest number of votes for the office of Governor, as declared by the Speaker, has died, then the person having the highest number of votes for the office of Lieutenant Governor shall act as Governor until after the next general election. It is further provided that in the event the person with the highest number of votes for the Office of Governor as declared by the Speaker, shall become disabled, or fail to qualify, then the Lieutenant Governor shall act as Governor until a person has qualified for the office of Governor or until after the next general election. Any succession to the governorship not otherwise provided for in this Constitution may be provided for by law; provided, however, that any person succeeding to the office of Governor shall be qualified as otherwise provided in this Constitution, and shall, during the entire term to which he may succeed, be under all the restrictions and inhibitions imposed in this Constitution on the Governor.

[Note — An added amendment, for the purpose stated herein. Submitted by the Fiftieth Legislature (1947) and adopted in election, Nov. 2, 1948.]

Sec. 4. **Governor, When Installed; Term; Qualifications** — The Governor elected at the general election in 1974, and hereafter, shall be installed on the first Tuesday after the organization of the Legislature, or as soon thereafter as practicable, and shall hold his office for the term of four years, or until his successor shall be duly installed. He shall be at least thirty years of age, a citizen of the United States, and shall have resided in this State at least five years immediately preceding his election.

[Note — Sec. 4 of Art. IV was amended to raise to four

years the term of office of Governor. Submitted by the Sixty-second Legislature (1971) and adopted in an election Nov. 7, 1972.]

Sec. 5. **Governor's Salary and Mansion** — The Governor shall, at stated times, receive as compensation for his service an annual salary in an amount to be fixed by the Legislature, and shall have the use and occupation of the Governor's Mansion, fixtures and furniture.

[Note — The foregoing Sec. 5 of Art. IV was first amended to raise Governor's salary from $4,000 to $12,000. Adopted in an election Nov. 3, 1936. Further amended to give Legislature authority to fix salary. Submitted by the Fifty-third Legislature (1953) and adopted in election Nov. 2, 1954.]

Sec. 6. **Governor to Hold No Other Office, Etc.** — During the time he holds the office of Governor he shall not hold any other office, civil, military or corporate; nor shall he practice any profession or receive compensation, reward, fee or the promise thereof for the same; nor receive any salary, reward or compensation or the promise thereof from any person or corporation for any service rendered or performed during the time he is Governor or to be thereafter rendered or performed.

Sec. 7. **Commander in Chief; May Call Out Militia** — He shall be commander in chief of the military forces of the State, except when they are called into actual service of the United States. He shall have power to call forth the militia to execute the laws of the State, to suppress insurrections, repel invasions and protect the frontier from hostile incursions by Indians or other predatory bands.

Sec. 8. **Governor May Convene Legislature** — The Governor may, on extraordinary occasions, convene the Legislature at the seat of government or at a different place in case that should be in possession of the public enemy, or in case of the prevalence of disease threat. His proclamation therefor shall state specifically the purpose for which the Legislature is convened.

Sec. 9. **Governor's Message; to Account for Moneys; Present Estimates, Etc.** — The Governor shall, at the commencement of each session of the Legislature, and at the close of his term of office, give to the Legislature information, by message, of the condition of the State; and he shall recommend to the Legislature such measures as he may deem expedient. He shall account to the Legislature for all public moneys received and paid out by him from any funds subject to his order, with vouchers; and shall accompany his message with a statement of the same. And at the commencement of each regular session he shall present estimates of the amount of money required to be raised by taxation for all purposes.

Sec. 10. **Governor Shall Cause the Laws to Be Executed; Intercourse With Other States** — He shall cause the laws to be faithfully executed and shall conduct, in person, or in such manner as shall be prescribed by law, all intercourse and business of the State with other States and with the United States.

Sec. 11. **Board of Pardons and Paroles: Advisory Authority to Governor in Granting Reprieves, Paroles, Pardons, Etc.** — (a) The Legislature shall by law establish a Board of Pardons and Paroles and shall require it to keep record of its actions and the reasons for its actions. The Legislature shall have authority to enact parole laws and laws that require or permit courts to inform juries about the effect of good conduct time and eligibility for parole or mandatory supervision on the period of incarceration served by a defendant convicted of a criminal offense.

(b) In all criminal cases, except treason and impeachment, the Governor shall have power, after conviction, on the written signed recommendation and advice of the Board of Pardons and Paroles, or a majority thereof, to grant reprieves and commutations of punishment and pardons; and under such rules as the Legislature may prescribe; and upon the written recommendation and advice of a majority of the Board of Pardons and Paroles, he shall have the power to remit fines and forfeitures. The Governor shall have the power to grant one reprieve in any capital case for a period not to exceed thirty (30) days; and he shall have the power to revoke conditional pardons. With the advice and consent of the Legislature, he may grant reprieves, commutations of punishment and pardons in cases of treason.

[Note—The foregoing Sec. 11 of Art. IV was amended from the original to establish the stated procedure for granting pardons and paroles, which was originally vested exclusively in the Governor's office. Submitted by the Forty-fourth Legislature (1935) and adopted in an election Nov. 3, 1936. It was again amended to make the Board of Pardons and Paroles a statutory agency and to give the board power to revoke paroles. Submitted by the Sixty-eighth Legislature (1983) and adopted in election Nov. 8, 1983. It was once again amended to authorize jury instructions on good time and eligibility for parole and mandataory supervision. Proposed by the Seventy-first Legislature (1989) and adopted in an election Nov. 7, 1989.]

Sec. 11A. **Suspension of Sentences; Probation** — The courts of the State of Texas shall have original jurisdiction of criminal actions shall have the power, after conviction, to suspend the imposition or execution of sentence and to place the defendant upon probation and to reimpose such sen-

Article IV — (Cont'd.)

tence, under such conditions as the Legislature may prescribe.

[Note — The foregoing Sec. 11A of Art. IV, an amendment, was added for the stated purpose of providing suspended sentences. Submitted by the Forty-fourth Legislature (1935) and adopted in an election Aug. 24, 1935.]

Sec. 11B. (a) The legislature by law may organize and combine into one or more agencies all agencies of the state that:

(1) have authority over the confinement or supervision of persons convicted of criminal offenses;

(2) set standards or distribute state funds to political subdivisions that have authority over the confinement or supervision of persons convicted of criminal offenses; or

(3) gather information about the administration of criminal justice.

(b) The legislature by law may authorize the appointment of members of more than one department of government to serve on the governing body.

[Note — The foregoing Sec. 11B of Art. IV, an amendment, was added to authorize the legislature to organize and combine various state agencies that perform criminal justice functions. Proposed by the Seventy-first Legislature (1989) and adopted in an election Nov. 7, 1989.]

Sec. 12. **Governor to Fill Vacancies in State and District Offices** — (a) All vacancies in State or district offices, except members of the Legislature, shall be filled, unless otherwise provided by law, by appointment of the Governor.

(b) An appointment of the Governor made during a session of the Senate shall be with the advice and consent of two thirds of the Senate present.

(c) In accordance with this section, the Senate may give its advice and consent on an appointment of the Governor made during a recess of the Senate. To be confirmed, the appointment must be with the advice and consent of two-thirds of the Senate present. If an appointment of the Governor is made during the recess of the Senate, the Governor shall nominate the appointee, or some other person to fill the vacancy, to the Senate during the first ten days of its next session following the appointment. If the Senate does not confirm a person under this subsection, the Governor shall nominate in accordance with this section the recess appointee or another person to fill the vacancy during the first ten days of each subsequent session of the Senate until a confirmation occurs. If the Governor does not nominate a person to the Senate during the first ten days of a session of the Senate as required by this subsection, the Senate at that session may consider the recess appointee as if the Governor had nominated the appointee.

(d) If the Senate, at any special session, does not take final action to confirm or reject a previously unconfirmed recess appointee or another person nominated to fill the vacancy for which the appointment was made:

(1) the Governor after the session may appoint another person to fill the vacancy; and

(2) the appointee, if otherwise qualified and if not removed as provided by law, is entitled to continue in office until the earlier of the following occurs:

(A) the Senate rejects the appointee at a subsequent session; or

(B) the Governor appoints another person to fill the vacancy under Subdivision (1) of this subsection.

(e) If the Senate, at a regular session, does not take final action to confirm or reject a previously unconfirmed recess appointee or another person nominated to fill the vacancy for which the appointment was made, the appointee or other person, as appropriate, is considered to be rejected by the Senate when the Senate session ends.

(f) If an appointee is rejected, the office shall immediately become vacant, and the Governor shall, without delay, make further nominations, until a confirmation takes place. If a person has been rejected by the Senate to fill a vacancy, the Governor may not appoint the person to fill the vacancy or, during the term of the vacancy for which the person was rejected, to fill another vacancy in the same office or on the same board, commission, or other body.

(g) Appointments to vacancies in offices elective by the people shall only continue until the next general election.

(h) The Legislature by general law may limit the term to be served by a person appointed by the Governor to fill a vacancy in a state or district office to a period that ends before the vacant term otherwise expires or, for an elective office, before the next election at which the vacancy is to be filled, if the appointment is made on or after November 1 preceding the general election for the succeeding term of the office of Governor and the Governor is not elected at that election to the succeeding term.

(i) For purposes of this section, the expiration of a term of office or the creation of a new office constitutes a vacancy.

[Note — The foregoing Sec. 12(a) was changed and Sec. 12(b) was added to Art. IV to limit the authority of a governor to fill vacancies in state and district offices if the governor is not re-elected. Submitted by the Seventieth Legislature (1987) and adopted in an election Nov. 3, 1987. It was further amended to clarify the authority of the Senate to consider certain nominees to state and district offices and to

provide for filling vacancies in those offices. Submitted by the Seventy-first Legislature (1990) and adopted in an election Nov. 6, 1990.]

Sec. 13. **Where Governor Shall Reside** — During the session of the Legislature the Governor shall reside where its sessions are held and at all other times at the seat of government, except when, by act of the Legislature, he may be required or authorized to reside elsewhere.

Sec. 14. **Approval of Bills; Veto Bill Not Returned to Become a Law** — Every bill which shall have passed both houses of the Legislature shall be presented to the Governor for his approval. If he approve, he shall sign it, but if he disapprove it, he shall return it with his objections to the house in which it originated, which house shall enter the objections at large upon its journal, and proceed to reconsider it. If, after such reconsideration, two thirds of the members present agree to pass the bill, it shall be sent, with the objections, to the other house, by which likewise it shall be reconsidered, and if approved by two thirds of the members of that house, it shall become a law; but in such cases the votes of both houses shall be determined by yeas and nays; and the names of the members voting for and against the bill shall be entered on the journal of each house, respectively. If any bill shall not be returned by the Governor with his objections within ten days (Sundays excepted) after it shall have been presented to him, the same shall be a law in like manner as if he had signed it, unless the Legislature, by its adjournment, prevent its return, in which case it shall be a law, unless he shall file the same, with his objections, in the office of the Secretary of State and give notice thereof by public proclamation within twenty days after such adjournment. If any bill presented to the Governor contains several items of appropriation he may object to one or more of such items, and approve the other portion of the bill. In such case he shall append to the bill, at the time of signing it, a statement of the items to which he objects, and no item so objected to shall take effect. If the Legislature be in session he shall transmit to the house in which the bill originated a copy of such statement, and the items objected to shall be separately considered. If, on reconsideration, one or more of such items be approved by two thirds of the members present, of each house, the same shall be part of the law, notwithstanding the objections of the Governor. If any such bill containing several items of appropriation not having been presented to the Governor ten days (Sundays excepted) prior to adjournment, be in the hands of the Governor at the time of adjournment, he shall have twenty days from such adjournment within which to file objections to any items thereof and make proclamation of the same, and such item or items shall not take effect.

Sec. 15. **What to Be Presented for Approval** — Every order, resolution or vote to which the concurrence of both houses of the Legislature may be necessary except on questions of adjournment shall be presented to the Governor, and before it shall take effect shall be approved by him; or, being disapproved, shall be repassed by both houses, and all the rules, provisions and limitations shall apply thereto as prescribed in the last preceding section in the case of a bill.

Sec. 16. **Lieutenant Governor; Election; Term; Powers and Duties** — There shall also be a Lieutenant Governor who shall be chosen at every election for Governor by the same electors, in the same manner, continue in office for the same time and possess the same qualifications. The electors shall distinguish for whom they vote as Governor and for whom as Lieutenant Governor. The Lieutenant Governor shall, by virtue of his office, be President of the Senate and shall have, when in committee of the whole, a right to debate, and vote on all questions; and when the Senate is equally divided, to give the casting vote. In case of the death, resignation, removal from office, inability or refusal of the Governor to serve, or of his impeachment or absence from the State, the Lieutenant Governor shall exercise the power and authority appertaining to the office of Governor until another be chosen at the periodical election, and be duly qualified; or until the Governor, impeached, absent or disabled, shall be acquitted, return or his disability be removed.

Sec. 17. **Vacancy in Office; Compensation** — If, during the vacancy in the office of Governor, the Lieutenant Governor should die, resign, refuse to serve or be removed from office or be unable to serve; or if he shall be impeached or absent from the State, the President of the Senate, for the time being, shall, in like manner, administer the government until he shall be superseded by a Governor or Lieutenant Governor. The Lieutenant Governor shall, while he act as President of the Senate, receive for his services the same compensation and mileage which shall be allowed to the members of the Senate, and no more; and during the time he administers the government as Governor, he shall receive in like manner the same compensation which the Governor would have received had he been employed in the duties of his office, and no more. The President, for the time being, of the Senate, shall, during the time he administers the government, receive in like manner the same compensation which the Governor would have received had he been employed in the duties of his office.

Sec. 18. **Succession to Governorship** — The Lieutenant Governor, or President of the Senate, succeeding to the office of Governor shall, during the entire terms to which he may succeed, be under all the restrictions and inhibitions imposed in this Constitution on the Governor.

Sec. 19. **Seal of State; Secretary of State to Keep, Etc.** - There shall be a seal of the State which shall be kept by the Secretary of State and used by him officially under the d

Article IV — (Cont'd.); Article V

rection of the Governor. The seal of the State shall be a star of five points, encircled by olive and live oak branches, and the words "The State of Texas."

Sec. 20. **Commissions to Be Signed and Sealed** — All commissions shall be in the name and by the authority of the State of Texas, sealed with the State seal, signed by the Governor, and attested by the Secretary of State.

Sec. 21. **Secretary of State; Term; Duties; Compensation** — There shall be a Secretary of State, who shall be appointed by the Governor, by and with the advice and consent of the Senate, and who shall continue in office during the term of service of the Governor. He shall authenticate the publication of the laws and keep a fair register of all official acts and proceedings of the Governor, and shall, when required, lay the same and all papers, minutes and vouchers relative thereto, before the Legislature or either house thereof, and shall perform such other duties as may be required of him by law. He shall receive for his services an annual salary in an amount to be fixed by the Legislature.

[Note — The foregoing Sec. 21 of Art. IV was first amended from the original to raise the salary of the Secretary of State from $2,000 to $6,000 a year. Amendment adopted in an election Nov. 3, 1936. Further amended to give Legislature authority to fix salary. Submitted by the Fifty-third Legislature (1953) and adopted in election Nov. 2, 1954.]

Sec. 22. **Attorney General; Term; Duties; Residence; Salary** — The Attorney General elected at the general election in 1974, and thereafter, shall hold his office for four years and until his successor is duly qualified. He shall represent the State in all suits and pleas in the Supreme Court of the State in which the state may be a party, and shall especially inquire into the charter rights of all private corporations, and from time to time in the name of the State, take such action in the courts as may be proper and necessary to prevent any private corporation from exercising any power or demanding or collecting any species of taxes, tolls, freight or wharfage not authorized by law. He shall whenever sufficient cause exists, seek a judicial forfeiture of such charters, unless otherwise expressly directed by law, and give legal advice in writing to the Governor and other executive officers, when requested by them, and perform such other duties as may be required by law. He shall reside at the seat of government during his continuance in office. He shall receive for his services an annual salary in an amount to be fixed by the Legislature.

[Note — The foregoing Sec. 22 of Art. IV was amended from the original to raise the Attorney General's fixed salary from $2,000 to $10,000 a year and to eliminate provisions for fees not to exceed $2,000 a year. Amendment adopted in an election Nov. 3, 1936. Further amended to give Legislature authority to fix salary. Submitted by the Fifty-third Legislature (1953) and adopted in election Nov. 2, 1954. It was further amended to lengthen the term of office from two to four years. Submitted by the Sixty-second Legislature (1971) and adopted in an election Nov. 7, 1972.]

Sec. 23. **Comptroller; Treasurer, and Commissioner of the General Land Office; Terms; Salaries; Residence; Fees** — The Comptroller of Public Accounts, the Treasurer and the Commissioner of the General Land Office and any statutory state officer who is elected by the electorate of Texas at large, unless a term of office is otherwise specifically provided in this Constitution, shall each hold office for the term of four years and until his successor is qualified. The four-year term applies to these officers who are elected at the general election in 1974 or thereafter. Each shall receive an annual salary in an amount to be fixed by Legislature; reside at the capital of the State during his continuance in office, and perform such duties as are or may be required by law. They and the Secretary of State shall not receive to their own use any fees, costs or perquisites of office. All fees that may be payable by law for any service performed by any officer specified in this section, or in his office, shall be paid, when received into the State Treasury.

[Note — The foregoing Sec. 23 of Art. IV was first amended from the original to raise salaries of three state officials mentioned from $2,500 each to $6,000 each annually. Amendment adopted in an election Nov. 3, 1936. Further amended to give Legislature authority to fix salary. Submitted by the Fifty-third Legislature (1953) and adopted in election Nov. 2, 1954. It was further amended to raise to four years the term of office of the above-named officials. Submitted by the Sixty-second Legislature (1971) and adopted in an election Nov. 7, 1972.]

Sec. 24. **Officers to Account to the Governor; Duty of Governor; False Reports** — An account shall be kept by the officers of the executive department and by all officers and managers of State institutions of all moneys and choses in action received and disbursed or otherwise disposed of by them, severally, from all sources, and for every service performed; and a semi-annual report thereof shall be made to the Governor, under oath. The Governor may, at any time, require information in writing from any and all of said officers or managers upon any subject relating to the duties,

conditions, management and expenses of their respective offices and institutions, which information shall be required by the Governor under oath, and the Governor may also inspect their books, accounts, vouchers and public funds; and any officer or manager who, at any time shall willfully make a false report or give false information, shall be guilty of perjury and so adjudged and punished accordingly and removed from office.

Sec. 25. **Laws for Investigation of Breaches of Trust** — The Legislature shall pass efficient laws facilitating the investigation of breaches of trust and duty by all custodians of public funds and providing for their suspensions from office on reasonable cause shown, and for the appointment of temporary incumbents of their offices during such suspensions.

Sec. 26. **Notaries Public** — (a) The Secretary of State shall appoint a convenient number of notaries public for the state who shall perform such duties as now are or may be prescribed by law. The qualifications of notaries public shall be prescribed by law.

(b) The terms of office of notaries public shall not be less than two years nor more than four years as provided by law.

[Note — The foregoing Sec. 26 of Art. IV was amended from the original to give the Secretary of State the authority, formerly held by the Governor, to appoint notaries public, and to include the stated contents of paragraphs (b) and (c). Submitted by the Forty-sixth Legislature (1939), and adopted in an election Nov. 5, 1940. It was further amended to establish terms of notaries public for not less than two years nor more than four years; did away with old sections (b) and (c) and provided for terms of office for notaries. Submitted by the Sixty-sixth Legislature (1979) and adopted in election Nov. 6, 1979.]

ARTICLE V — JUDICIAL DEPARTMENT

Temporary Provision. (a) This temporary provision applies to the constitutional amendment proposed by S.J.R. No. 14, 69th Legislature, Regular Session, 1985, and expires Jan. 1, 1992.

(b) Courts of Appeals Districts and Judges. The supreme judicial districts of the state become courts of appeals districts. Associate justices of the courts of appeals become justices of the courts of appeals.

(c) County Courts and County Judges. Unless otherwise provided by law, all county courts in existence under the Constitution continue in effect with jurisdiction as provided by law. The judges of those courts remain as county court judges and as presiding officers of the county commissioners courts.

(d) Municipal Courts, County Courts at Law, and Justice of the Peace Courts. Unless otherwise provided by law, order, charter, or ordinance, these courts and judges of them remain as they exist at the time of adoption of the amendments, including any new courts authorized by law but not taking effect until after the date of adoption of these amendments.

(e) Judicial Districts and Judges. Unless otherwise provided by law, judicial districts in existence at the time of adoption of these amendments remain in effect, including any districts authorized by law but not taking effect until after the date of adoption of these amendments.

(f) Laws and Rules Continued. Except to the extent inconsistent with the provisions of these amendments, all laws and rules of court in force on the effective date of these amendments continue in effect until otherwise provided by law.

(g) Other Provisions. In the event a transfer or transition has not been provided for in by these amendments or other law, the Supreme Court shall provide by rule for the orderly transfer or transition.

(h) The initial term of the member of the Judicial Districts Board appointed by the governor expires Dec. 31, 1990.

[Note — The foregoing Temporary Provision to Art. V was added to provide for reapportionment of judicial districts by the Judicial Districts Board or by the Legislative Redistricting Board, and to provide for administration and jurisdiction of constitutional courts. It will expire Jan. 1, 1992. Submitted by Sixty-ninth Legislature (1985) and adopted in election Nov. 5, 1985.]

Sec. 1. **The Several Courts; Criminal Courts** — The judicial power of this State shall be vested in one Supreme Court, in one Court of Criminal Appeals, in Courts of Appeals, in District Courts, in County Courts, in Commissioners' Courts, in courts of Justices of the Peace and in such other courts as may be provided by law.

The Legislature may establish such other courts as it may deem necessary and prescribe the jurisdiction and organization thereof and may conform the jurisdiction of the district and other inferior courts thereto.

[Note — The foregoing Sec. 1 of Art. V is an amended section, being a general revision of the original, to provide for "Courts of Civil Appeals" and a "Court of Criminal

Article V — (Cont'd.)

Appeals" in place of the old "Court of Appeals," making minor changes. Submitted by the Twenty-second Legislature (1891), ratified at an election Aug. 11, 1891, and declared adopted Sept. 22, 1891. It was amended to provide for a Court of Criminal Appeals with nine judges and to permit the court to sit in panels of three judges. (See also note under Sec. 4 below.) Submitted by the Sixty-fifth Legislature (1977) and adopted in election Nov. 8, 1977. It was further amended to change Courts of Civil Appeals to Courts of Appeal. Submitted by the Sixty-sixth Legislature (1979) and adopted in election Nov. 4, 1980.]

Sec. 1-a. **Retirement and Compensation of Judges** — (1) Subject to the further provisions of this section, the Legislature shall provide for the retirement and compensation of justices and judges of the Appellate Courts and District and Criminal District Courts on account of length of service, age and disability, and for their reassignment to active duty where and when needed. The office of every such justice and judge shall become vacant when the incumbent reaches the age of seventy-five (75) years or such earlier age, not less than seventy (70) years, as the Legislature may prescribe; but, in the case of an incumbent whose term of office includes the effective date of this Amendment, this provision shall not prevent him from serving the remainder of said term nor be applicable to him before his period or periods of judicial service shall have reached a total of ten (10) years.

(2) The name of the State Judicial Qualifications Commission is changed to the State Commission on Judicial Conduct. The Commission consists of eleven (11) members, to wit: (i) one (1) Justice of a Court of Appeals; (ii) one (1) District Judge; (iii) two (2) members of the State Bar, who have respectively practiced as such for over ten (10) consecutive years next preceding their selection; (iiii) four (4) citizens, at least thirty (30) years of age, not licensed to practice law nor holding any salaried public office or employment; (v) one (1) Justice of the Peace; (vi) one (1) Judge of a Municipal Court; and, (vii) one (1) Judge of a County Court at Law; provided that no person shall be or remain a member of the Commission, who does not maintain physical residence within this state, or who resides in, or holds a judgeship within or for, the same Supreme Judicial District as another member of the Commission, or who shall have ceased to retain the qualifications above specified for his respective class of membership, except that the Justice of the Peace and the Judges of a Municipal Court and/or a County Court at Law shall be selected at large without regard to whether they reside or hold a judgeship in the same Supreme Judicial District as another member of the Commission. Commissioners of classes (i), (ii) and (vii) above shall be chosen by the Supreme Court with advice and consent of the Senate, those of class (iii) by the Board of Directors of the State Bar under regulations to be prescribed by the Supreme Court with advice and consent of the Senate, those of class (iiii) by appointment of the Governor with advice and consent of the Senate, and the commissioners of classes (v) and (vi) by appointment of the Supreme Court as provided by law, with the advice and consent of the Senate.

(3) The regular term of office of Commissioners shall be six (6) years; but the initial members of each of classes (i), (ii) and (iii) shall respectively be chosen for terms of four (4) and six (6) years, and the initial members of class (iiii) for respective terms of two (2), four (4) and six (6) years. Interim vacancies shall be filled in the same manner as vacancies due to expiration of a full term, but only for the unexpired portion of the term in question. Commissioners may succeed themselves in office only if having served less than three (3) consecutive years.

(4) Commissioners shall receive no compensation for their services as such. The Legislature shall provide for the payment of the necessary expense for the operation of the Commission.

(5) The Commission may hold its meetings, hearings and other proceedings at such times and places as it shall determine but shall meet at Austin at least once each year. It shall annually select one of its members as chairman. A quorum shall consist of six (6) members. Proceedings shall be by majority vote of those present, except that recommendations for retirement, censure, suspension, or removal of any person holding an office named in paragraph A of Subsection (6) of this section shall be by affirmative vote of at least six (6) members.

(6) A. Any justice or judge of the courts established by this Constitution or created by the Legislature as provided in Sec. 1, Art. V, of this Constitution, may, subject to the other provisions hereof, be removed from office for willful or persistent violation of rules promulgated by the Supreme Court of Texas, incompetence in performing the duties of the office, willful violation of the Code of Judicial Conduct, or willful or persistent conduct that is clearly inconsistent with the proper performance of his duties or casts public discredit upon the judiciary or administration of justice. Any person holding such office may be disciplined or censured, in lieu of removal from office, as provided by this section. Any person

holding an office specified in this subsection may be suspended from office with or without pay by the Commission immediately on being indicted by a State or Federal grand jury for a felony offense or charged with a misdemeanor involving official misconduct. On the filing of a sworn complaint charging a person holding such office with willful or persistent violation of rules promulgated by the Supreme Court of Texas, incompetence in performing the duties of the office, willful violation of the Code of Judicial Conduct, or willful and persistent conduct that is clearly inconsistent with the proper performance of his duties or casts public discredit on the judiciary or on the administration of justice, the Commission, after giving the person notice and an opportunity to appear and be heard before the Commission, may recommend to the Supreme Court the suspension of such person from office. The Supreme Court, after considering the record of such appearance and the recommendation of the Commission, may suspend the person from office with or without pay, pending final disposition of the charge.

B. Any person holding an office named in paragraph A of this subsection who is eligible for retirement benefits under the laws of this state providing for judicial retirement may be involuntarily retired, and any person holding an office named in that paragraph who is not eligible for retirement benefits under such laws may be removed from office, for disability seriously interfering with the performance of his duties, which is, or is likely to become, permanent in nature.

C. The law relating to the removal, discipline, suspension, or censure of a Justice or Judge of the courts established by this Constitution or created by the Legislature as provided in this Constitution applies to a master or magistrate appointed as provided by law to serve a trial court of this State and to a retired or former Judge who continues as a judicial officer subject to an assignment to sit on a court of this State. Under the law relating to the removal of an active Justice or Judge, the Commission and the review tribunal may prohibit a retired or former Judge from holding judicial office in the future or from sitting on a court of this State by assignment.

(7) The Commission shall keep itself informed as fully as may be of circumstances relating to the misconduct or disability of particular persons holding an office named in paragraph A of Subsection (6) of this section, receive complaints or reports, formal or informal, from any source in this behalf and make such preliminary investigations as it may determine. Its orders for the attendance or testimony of witnesses or for the production of documents at any hearing or investigation shall be enforceable by contempt proceedings in the District Court or by a Master.

(8) After such investigation as it deems necessary, the Commission may in its discretion issue a private or public admonition, warning, reprimand, or requirement that the person obtain additional training or education, or if the Commission determines that the situation merits such action, it may institute formal proceedings and order a formal hearing to be held before it concerning the public censure, removal, or retirement of a person holding an office or position specified in Subsection (6) of this section, or it may in its discretion request the Supreme Court to appoint an active or retired District Judge or Justice of a Court of Appeals, or retired Judge or Justice of the Court of Criminal Appeals or the Supreme Court, as a Master to hear and take evidence in any such matter, and to report thereon to the Commission. The Master shall have all the power of a District Judge in the enforcement of orders pertaining to witnesses, evidence, and procedure. If, after formal hearing, or after considering the record and report of a Master, the Commission finds good cause therefor, it shall issue an order of public censure or it shall recommend to a review tribunal the removal or retirement, as the case may be, of the person in question holding an office or position specified in Subsection (6) of this section and shall thereupon file with the tribunal the entire record before the Commission.

(9) A tribunal to review the Commission's recommendation for the removal or retirement of a person holding an office or position specified in Subsection (6) of this section is composed of seven (7) Justices or Judges of the Courts of Appeals who are selected by lot by the Chief Justice of the Supreme Court. Each Court of Appeals shall designate one of its members for inclusion in the list from which the selection is made. Service on the tribunal shall be considered part of the official duties of a judge, and no additional compensation may be paid for such service. The review tribunal shall review the record of the proceedings on the law and facts and in its discretion may, for good cause shown, permit the introduction of additional evidence. Within 90 days after the date on which the record is filed with the review tribunal, it shall order public censure, retirement or removal, as it finds just and proper, or wholly reject the recommendation. A Justice, Judge, Master, or Magistrate may appeal a decision of the review tribunal to the Supreme Court under the substantial evidence rule. Upon an order for involuntary retirement for disability or an order for removal, the office in question shall become vacant. The review tribunal, in an order for involuntary retirement for disability or an order for removal, may

Article V — (Cont'd.)

prohibit such person from holding judicial office in the future. The rights of an incumbent so retired to retirement benefits shall be the same as if his retirement had been voluntary.

(10) All papers filed with and proceedings before the Commission or a Master shall be confidential, unless otherwise provided by law, and the filing of papers with, and the giving of testimony before the Commission or a Master shall be privileged, unless otherwise provided by law. However, the Commission may issue a public statement through its executive director or its Chairman at any time during any of its proceedings under this Section when sources other than the Commission cause notoriety concerning a Judge or the Commission itself and the Commission determines that the best interests of a Judge or of the public will be served by issuing the statement.

(11) The Supreme Court shall by rule provide for the procedure before the Commission, Masters, review tribunal, and the Supreme Court. Such rule shall provide the right of discovery of evidence to a Justice, Judge, Master, or Magistrate after formal proceedings are instituted and shall afford to any person holding an office or position specified in Subsection (6) of this section, against whom a proceeding is instituted to cause his retirement or removal, due process of law for the procedure before the Commission, Masters, review tribunal, and the Supreme Court in the same manner that any person whose property rights are in jeopardy in an adjudicatory proceeding is entitled to due process of law, regardless of whether or not the interest of the person holding an office or position specified in Subsection (6) of this section in remaining in active status is considered to be a right or a privilege. Due process shall include the right to notice, counsel, hearing, confrontation of his accusers, and all such other incidents of due process as are ordinarily available in proceedings whether or not misfeasance is charged, upon proof of which a penalty may be imposed.

(12) No person holding an office specified in Subsection (6) of this section shall sit as a member of the Commission in any proceeding involving his own suspension, discipline, censure, retirement or removal.

(13) This Sec. 1-a is alternative to and cumulative of, the methods of removal of persons holding an office named in paragraph A of Subsection (6) of this section provided elsewhere in this Constitution.

(14) The Legislature may promulgate laws in furtherance of this Section that are not inconsistent with its provisions.

TEMPORARY PROVISION. (a) This temporary provision applies to the constitutional amendment proposed by H.J.R. No. 4, Sixty-eighth Legislature, Regular Session, 1983, and expires Jan. 1, 1988.

(b) The consitutional amendment takes effect Jan. 1, 1985.

(c) The initial term of the commissioner of class (v) added by amendment in 1977 expired on Nov. 19, 1979. The initial term of the commissioner of class (vi) and (vii) expires on Nov. 19, 1985.

(d) Each person holding office as a member of the Commission on Judicial Conduct on Jan. 1, 1985, continues to hold the office for the term for which he was appointed.

(e) The offices of the first commissioner of class (i) and the first commissioner of class (ii) whose terms expire after Jan. 1, 1985, are abolished on the expiration of the terms.

(f) Changes made in the constitution by this amendment do not apply to investigations and formal proceedings where the investigation of judicial conduct by the commission began before Jan. 1, 1985.

[Note — The foregoing Sec. 1-a was added to provide for retirement and compensation of judges. Submitted by Fiftieth Legislature (1947) and adopted in election, Nov. 2, 1948. It was amended to provide for automatic retirement of district and appellate judges for old age; to create the State Judicial Qualifications Commission and defining its functions; and empowering the Supreme Court to remove district and appellate judges for misconduct and to retire such judges in cases of disability. Submitted by Fifty-ninth Legislature (1965) and adopted in election Nov. 2, 1965. It was further amended to specifically name those offices under the jurisdiction of the Commission and to broaden the Commission's duties and powers. Submitted by Sixty-first Legislature (1969) and adopted in election Nov. 3, 1970. It was further amended to change the name of the State Judicial Qualifications Commission to the State Commission on Judicial Conduct; raise the number of members of the Commission to eleven; set out specific qualifications for membership; and provide for the suspension, censure, removal or involuntary retirement of a justice under certain circumstances. Submitted by Sixty-fifth Legislature (1977) and adopted in election Nov. 8, 1977. It was again amended to specify ways to discipline active judges, certain retired and former judges,

and certain masters and magistrates of courts. Submitted by Sixty-eighth Legislature (1983) and adopted in election Nov. 6, 1984.]

Sec. 2. **Supreme Court; Quorum; Qualifications; Election; Salary; Vacancy** — The Supreme Court shall consist of the Chief Justice and eight Justices, any five of whom shall constitute a quorum, and the concurrence of five shall be necessary to a decision of a case; provided, that when the business of the court may require, the court may sit in sections as designated by the court to hear argument of causes and to consider applications for writs of error or other preliminary matters. No person shall be eligible to serve in the office of Chief Justice or Justice of the Supreme Court unless the person is licensed to practice law in this state and is, at the time of election, a citizen of the United States and of this State and has attained the age of thirty-five years and has been a practicing lawyer or a lawyer and judge of a court of record together at least ten years. Said Justices shall be elected (three of them each two years) by the qualified voters of the State at a general election; shall hold their offices six years or until their successors are elected and qualified; and shall each receive such compensation as shall be provided by law. In case of a vacancy in the office of the Chief Justice or any Justice of the Supreme Court, the Governor shall fill the vacancy until the next general election for State officers, and at such general election the vacancy for the unexpired term shall be filled by election by the qualified voters of the State. The Justices of the Supreme Court who may be in office at the time this amendment takes effect shall continue in office until the expiration of their terms of office under the present Constitution and until their successors are elected and qualified.

[Note — The foregoing Sec. 2 of Art. V has been thrice amended: (1) To raise salaries and make minor adjustments, by amendment submitted by the Twenty-second Legislature, ratified in an election Aug. 11, 1891, and declared adopted Sept. 22, 1891; (2) to raise the number of justices on the Supreme Court from three to nine and make other adjustments, by amendment submitted by the Forty-ninth Legislature and adopted in an election Aug. 25, 1945; and (3) to change name of Commission of Appeals and qualifications of Supreme Court Justices. Submitted by the Sixty-sixth Legislature (1979) and adopted in election Nov. 4, 1980.]

Sec. 3. **Jurisdiction; Terms of Court** — The Supreme Court shall exercise the judicial power of the state except as otherwise provided in this Constitution. Its jurisdiction shall be co-extensive with the limits of the State and its determinations shall be final except in criminal law matters. Its appellate jurisdiction shall be final and shall extend to all cases except in criminal law matters and as otherwise provided in this Constitution or by law. The Supreme Court and the Justices thereof shall have power to issue writs of habeas corpus, as may be prescribed by law; and under such regulations as may be prescribed by law, the said courts and the Justices thereof may issue the writs of mandamus, procedendo, certiorari and such other writs as may be necessary to enforce its jurisdiction. The Legislature may confer original jurisdiction on the Supreme Court to issue writs of quo warranto and mandamus in such cases as may be specified, except as against the Governor of the State.

The Supreme Court shall also have power, upon affidavit or otherwise as by the court may be determined to ascertain such matters of fact as may be necessary to the proper exercise of its jurisdiction.

The Supreme Court shall appoint a clerk, who shall give bond in such manner as is now or may hereafter be required by law, and he may hold his office for four years and shall be subject to removal by said court for good cause entered of record on the minutes of said court, who shall receive such compensation as the Legislature may provide.

[Note—The foregoing Sec. 3 of Art. V has been thrice amended, as follows: (1) To readjust jurisdiction of the Supreme Court to that of the Courts of Civil Appeals which were established by amendment of the same date, and also to consolidate the original Sec. 4, providing for a clerk of the court, with Sec. 3, by amendment submitted by the Twenty-second Legislature (1891), ratified Aug. 11, 1891, and proclaimed Sept. 22, 1891; (2) to eliminate provisions that the Supreme Court "sit from first Monday in October of each year until the last Saturday in June of the next year," by amendment submitted as part of the amendment, which added Sec. 3-a. See note of that section; and (3) redefining the jurisdiction of the Supreme Court. Submitted by the Sixty-sixth Legislature (1979) and adopted in election Nov. 4, 1980.]

Sec. 3-a. **Time of Sitting** — The Supreme Court may sit at any time during the year at the seat of government for the transaction of business and each term thereof shall begin and end with each calendar year.

[Note—The foregoing Sec. 3-a of Art. V was added to make the time of sitting of the Supreme Court discretionary with that court. It was substituted for a provision formerly

Article V — (Cont'd.)

incorporated in Sec. 3. (See note on Sec. 3.) Submitted by the Forty-first Legislature (1929), ratified in an election Nov. 4, 1930, and proclaimed Dec. 17, 1930.]

Sec. 3-b. **Direct Appeal** — The Legislature shall have the power to provide by law, for an appeal direct to the Supreme Court of this State from an order of any trial court granting or denying an interlocutory or permanent injunction on the grounds of the constitutionality or unconstitutionality of any statute of this State, or on the validity or invalidity of any administrative order issued by any state agency under any statute of this State.

[Note—The foregoing Sec. 3-b of Art. V was added for the stated purpose of providing for direct appeals. Submitted by the Forty-sixth Legislature and adopted in an election Nov. 5, 1940.]

Sec. 3-c. (a) The supreme court and the court of criminal appeals have jurisdiction to answer questions of state law certified from a federal appellate court.

(b) The supreme court and the court of criminal appeals shall promulgate rules of procedure relating to the review of those questions.

[Note — The foregoing Sec. 3-c of Art. V, an amendment, was added to grant the Supreme Court and the Court of Criminals Appeals jurisdiction to answer questions of state law certified from a federal appellate court. Submitted by the Sixty-ninth Legislature (1985) and adopted in an election Nov. 5, 1985.]

Sec. 4. **Court of Criminal Appeals** — The Court of Criminal Appeals shall consist of eight Judges and one Presiding Judge. The Judges shall have the same qualifications and receive the same salaries as the Associate Justices of the Supreme Court, and the Presiding Judge shall have the same qualifications and receive the same salary as the Chief Justice of the Supreme Court. The Presiding Judge and the Judges shall be elected by the qualified voters of the state at a general election and shall hold their offices for a term of six years. In case of a vacancy in the office of a Judge of the Court of Criminal Appeals, the Governor shall, with the advice and consent of the Senate, fill said vacancy by appointment until the next succeeding general election.

For the purpose of hearing cases, the Court of Criminal Appeals may sit in panels of three Judges, the designation thereof to be under rules established by the court. In a panel of three Judges, two Judges shall constitute a quorum and the concurrence of two Judges shall be necessary for a decision. The Presiding Judge, under rules established by the court, shall convene the court en banc for the transaction of all other business and may convene the court en banc for the purpose of hearing cases. The court must sit en banc during proceedings involving capital punishment and other cases as required by law. When convened en banc, five Judges shall constitute a quorum and the concurrence of five Judges shall be necessary for a decision. The Court of Criminal Appeals may appoint Commissioners in aid of the Court of Criminal Appeals as provided by law.

[Note—The foregoing Sec. 4 of Art. V is an amendment, superseding, in part, the original Sec. 5 which provided for the former "Court of Appeals." The original Sec. 4 provided for the appointment of Supreme Court clerks, and was absorbed in the amended Sec. 3. Submitted by the Twenty-second Legislature (1891); ratified Aug. 11, 1891, and adopted Sept. 22, 1891. It was further amended to raise number of judges from three to five and define their terms of office. Submitted by the Fifty-ninth Legislature (1965) and adopted in election Nov. 8, 1966. It was again amended to raise the number of judges from five to nine and to provide that the Court of Criminal Appeals may sit in panels of three judges. Submitted by the Sixty-fifth Legislature (1977) and adopted in election Nov. 8, 1977.]

Sec. 5. **Jurisdiction; Power; Terms; Clerk, Etc.** — The Court of Criminal Appeals shall have final appellate jurisdiction coextensive with the limits of the State and its determinations shall be final in all criminal cases of whatever grade, with such exceptions and under such regulations as may be provided in this Constitution or as prescribed by law.

The appeal of all cases in which the death penalty has been assessed shall be to the Court of Criminal Appeals. The appeal of all other criminal cases shall be to the Courts of Appeal as prescribed by law. In addition, the Court of Criminal Appeals may, on its own motion, review a decision of a Court of Appeals in a criminal case as provided by law. Discretionary review by the Court of Criminal Appeals is not a matter of right, but of sound judicial discretion.

Subject to such regulations as may be prescribed by law, the Court of Criminal Appeals and the Judges thereof shall have the power to issue the writ of habeas corpus, and in criminal law matters, the writs of mandamus, procedendo, prohibition, and certiorari. The court and the judges thereof shall have the power to issue such other writs as may be necessary to protect its jurisdiction or enforce its judgments. The court shall have the power upon affidavit or otherwise to ascertain such matters of fact as may be necessary to the exercise of its jurisdiction.

The Court of Criminal Appeals may sit for the transaction of business at any time during the year and each term shall begin and end with each calendar year. The Court of Criminal Appeals shall appoint a clerk of the court who shall give bond in such manner as is now or may hereafter be required by law, and who shall hold his office for a term of four years unless sooner removed by the court for good cause entered of record on the minutes of said court.

The clerk of the Court of Criminal Appeals who may be in office at the time when this amendment takes effect shall continue in office for the term of his appointment.

[Note—The foregoing Sec. 5 of Art. V is an amendment, superseding primarily the original Sec. 6, which defined jurisdiction, powers, etc. of the old "Court of Appeals." (See also note on Sec. 6 below.) Submitted by Twenty-second Legislature (1891); ratified at an election Aug. 11, 1891, and declared adopted Sept. 22, 1891. It was further amended to redefine jurisdiction, powers and terms of office. Submitted by Fifty-ninth Legislature (1965) and adopted in election Nov. 8, 1966. (See note under Sec. 4 above.) It was again amended to enlarge the court's jurisdiction and to redefine its term of office. Submitted by Sixty-fifth Legislature (1977) and adopted in election Nov. 8, 1977. It was again amended to redefine jurisdiction of Courts of Criminal Appeals. Submitted by Sixty-sixth Legislature (1979) and adopted in election Nov. 4, 1980.]

Sec. 6. **Supreme Judicial Districts; Courts of Civil Appeals; Jurisdiction; Term; Justices; Election; Salary; Clerk** — The state shall be divided into courts of appeals districts, with each district having a Chief Justice, two or more other Justices, and such other officials as may be provided by law. The Justices shall have the qualifications prescribed for Justices of the Supreme Court. The Court of Appeals may sit in sections as authorized by law. The concurrence of a majority of the judges sitting in a section is necessary to decide a case. Said Court of Appeals shall have appellate jurisdiction coextensive with the limits of their respective districts, which shall extend to all cases of which the District Courts or County Courts have original or appellate jurisdiction under such restrictions and regulations as may be prescribed by law. Provided, that the decisions of said courts shall be conclusive on all questions of fact brought before them on appeal or error. Said courts shall have such other jurisdiction, original and appellate, as may be prescribed by law.

Each of said Courts of Appeals shall hold its sessions at a place in its district to be designated by the Legislature and at such time as may be prescribed by law. Said justices shall be elected by the qualified voters of their respective districts at a general election for a term of six years and shall receive for their services the sum provided by law. Each Court of Appeals shall appoint a clerk in the same manner as the clerk of the Supreme Court, which clerk shall receive such compensation as may be fixed by law.

All constitutional and statutory references to the Courts of Civil Appeals shall be construed to mean the Courts of Appeals.

[Note—The foregoing Sec. 6 of Art. V, establishing the Courts of Civil Appeals, is an amendment, superseding parts of the original Secs. 5 and 6, which provided for the old "Court of Appeals," and defined its jurisdiction, powers, etc. Submitted by the Twenty-second Legislature (1891), ratified at an election Aug. 11, 1891, and declared adopted Sept. 22, 1891. It was further amended to increase the number of justices on a Court of Civil Appeals, permitting a Court of Civil Appeals to sit in sections and requiring a concurrence of a majority of justices to decide a case. Submitted by the Sixty-fifth Legislature (1977) and adopted in election Nov. 7, 1978. It was again amended to change the name of the Courts of Civil Appeals to the Courts of Appeal and to redefine the jurisdiction of said courts. Submitted by the Sixty-sixth Legislature (1979) and adopted in election Nov. 4, 1980. It was again amended to redefine the membership and duties of the Courts of Appeals. Submitted by the Sixty-ninth Legislature (1985) and adopted in an election Nov. 5, 1985.]

Sec. 7. **Judicial Districts; Judges; Their Qualifications; Residence; Term of Office; Salary; Terms of Court** — The State shall be divided into judicial districts, with each district having one or more Judges as may be provided by law or by this Constitution. Each district judge shall be elected by the qualified voters at a General Election and shall be a citizen of the United States and of this State, who is licensed to practice law in this State and has been a practicing lawyer or a

Article V — (Cont'd.)

Judge of a Court in this State, or both combined, for four (4) years next preceding his election, who has resided in the district in which he was elected for two (2) years next preceding his election, and who shall reside in his district during his term of office and hold his office for the period of four (4) years, and who shall receive for his services an annual salary to be fixed by the Legislature. The Court shall conduct its proceedings at the county seat of the county in which the case is pending, except as otherwise provided by law. He shall hold the regular terms of his Court at the County Seat of each County in his district in such manner as may be prescribed by law. The Legislature shall have power by General or Special Laws to make such provisions concerning the terms or sessions of each Court as it may deem necessary.

The Legislature shall also provide for the holding of District Court when the Judge thereof is absent, or is from any cause disabled or disqualified from presiding.

———

[Note—The foregoing Sec. 7 of Art. V has been amended three times: (1) Effecting a general revision of the original Sec. 7 to eliminate specification that judge must be "twenty-five years of age" and making minor changes. Submitted by the Twenty-second Legislature (1891) and ratified in election Aug. 11, 1891. (2) Providing that the District Court shall conduct its proceedings in the county seat of the county in which the case is pending "except as otherwise provided by law." Submitted by the Fifty-first Legislature (1949) and adopted in election Nov. 8, 1949. (3) It was again amended to redefine the membership and terms of office of the district courts. Submitted by the Sixty-ninth Legislature (1985) and adopted in an election Nov. 5, 1985.]

———

Sec. 7a. (a) The Judicial Districts Board is created to reapportion the judicial districts authorized by Art. V, Sec. 7, of this constitution.

(b) The membership of the board consists of the Chief Justice of the Texas Supreme Court who serves as chairman, the presiding judge of the Texas Court of Criminal Appeals, the presiding judge of each of the administrative judicial districts of the state, the president of the Texas Judicial Council, and one person who is licensed to practice law in this state appointed by the governor with the advice and consent of the senate for a term of four years. In the event of a vacancy in the appointed membership, the vacancy is filled for the unexpired term in the same manner as the original appointment.

(c) A majority of the total membership of the board constitutes a quorum for the transaction of business. The if0;nt
adoption of a reapportionment order requires a majority vote of the total membership of the board.

(d) The reapportionment powers of the board shall be exercised in the interims between regular sessions of the Legislature, except that a reapportionment may not be ordered by the board during an interim immediately following a regular session of the Legislature in which a valid and subsisting statewide apportionment of judicial districts is enacted by the Legislature. The board has other powers and duties as provided by the Legislature and shall exercise its powers under the policies, rules, standards, and conditions, not inconsistent with this section, that the Legislature provides.

(e) Unless the Legislature enacts a statewide reapportionment of the judicial districts following each federal decennial census, the board shall convene not later than the first Monday of June of the third year following the year in which the federal decennial census is taken to make a statewide reapportionment of the districts. The board shall complete its work on the reapportionment and file its order with the secretary of state not later than Aug. 31 of the same year. If the Judicial Districts Board fails to make a statewide apportionment by that date, the Legislative Redistricting Board established by Art. III, Sec. 28, of this constitution shall make a statewide reapportionment of the judicial districts not later than the 150th day after the final day for the Judicial Districts Board to make the reapportionment.

(f) In addition to the statewide reapportionment, the board may reapportion the judicial districts of the state as the necessity for reapportionment appears by redesignating, in one or more reapportionment orders, the county or counties that comprise the specific judicial districts affected by those reapportionment orders. In modifying any judicial district, no county having a population as large or larger than the population of the judicial district being reapportioned shall be added to the judicial district.

(g) Except as provided by Subsection (i) of this section, this section does not limit the power of the Legislature to reapportion the judicial districts of the state, to increase the number of judicial districts, or to provide for consequent matters on reapportionment. The Legislature may provide for the effect of a reapportionment made by the board on pending cases or the transfer of pending cases, for jurisdiction of a county court where county court jurisdiction has

been vested by law in a district court affected by the reapportionment, for terms of the courts upon existing officers and their duties, and for all other matters affected by the reapportionment. The Legislature may delegate any of these powers to the board. The Legislature shall provide the necessary expenses of the board.

(h) Any judicial reapportionment order adopted by the board must be approved by a record vote of the majority of the membership of both the senate and house of representatives before such order can become effective and binding.

(i) The Legislature, the Judicial Districts Board, or the Legislative Redistricting Board may not redistrict the judicial districts to provide for any judicial district smaller in size than an entire county except as provided by this section. Judicial districts smaller in size than the entire county may be created subsequent to a general election where a majority of the persons voting on the proposition adopt the proposition "to allow the division of _____County into judicial districts composed of parts of _____Coun-ty." No redistricting plan may be proposed or adopted by the Legislature, the Judicial Districts Board, or the Legislative Redistricting Board in anticipation of a future action by the voters of any county.

———

[Note — The foregoing Sec. 7a of Art. V, an amendment, was added to create the Judicial Districts Board and to define its membership and duties. Submitted by the Sixty-ninth Legislature (1985) and adopted in an election Nov. 5, 1985.]

———

Sec. 8. Jurisdiction and Powers of the District Courts — District Court jurisdiction consists of exclusive, appellate, and original jurisdiction of all actions, proceedings, and remedies, except in cases where exclusive, appellate, or original jurisdiction may be conferred by this Constitution or other law on some other court, tribunal, or administrative body. District Court judges shall have the power to issue writs necessary to enforce their jurisdiction. The District Court shall have appellate jurisdiction and general supervisory control over the County Commissioners' Court with such exceptions and under such regulations as may be prescribed by law.

———

[Note—The foregoing Sec. 8 of Art. V is an amendment of the original Sec. 8, including the words "of contested elections" in the first paragraph and adding the last sentence in the second paragraph. Submitted by the Twenty-second Legislature (1891), ratified at an election Aug. 11, 1891, and declared adopted Sept. 22, 1891. It was further amended to give District and County Courts general jurisdiction over probate matters; and further provided that Legislature may increase, diminish or eliminate jurisdiction of District Court or County Court in probate matters; and further provided that Legislature may provide that all appeals in such matters be to Courts of Civil Appeals. Submitted by the Sixty-third Legislature (1973) and adopted in election Nov. 6, 1973. It was again amended to define the exact duties of the judges of the district courts. Submitted by the Sixty-ninth Legislature (1985) and adopted in an election Nov. 5, 1985.]

———

Sec. 9. Clerk of the District Court; Term of Office; How Removed; How Vacancy Is Filled — There shall be a Clerk for the District Court of each county, who shall be elected by the qualified voters for state and county officers, and who shall hold his office for four years, subject to removal by information, or by indictment of a grand jury and conviction by a petit jury. In case of vacancy the judge of a District Court shall have the power to appoint a Clerk, who shall hold until the office can be filled by election.

———

[Note—The foregoing Sec. 9 of Art. V has been amended to change the term of office from two to four years. Submitted by the Fifty-third Legislature (1953) and adopted in election Nov. 2, 1954.]

———

Sec. 10. Jury Trial; by Whom Fee Is to Be Paid — In the trial of all cases in the District Courts, the plaintiff or defendant shall, upon application made in open court, have the right of trial by jury; but no jury shall be impaneled in any civil case unless demanded by a party to the case, and a jury fee be paid by the party demanding a jury, for such sum and with such exceptions as may be prescribed by the Legislature.

Sec. 11. Disqualification of Judges; Special Judges; Exchange of Districts; Vacancies — No judge shall sit in any case wherein he may be interested, or where either of the parties may be connected with him either by affinity or consanguinity, within such a degree as may be prescribed by law, or when he shall have been counsel in the case. When the Supreme Court, the Court of Criminal Appeals, the Court of Civil Appeals, or any member of either, shall be thus disqualified to hear and determine any case or cases in said court, the same shall be certified to the Governor of the State, who shall immediately commission the requisite num-

Article V — (Cont'd.)

ber of persons, learned in the law, for the trial and determination of such cause or causes. When a Judge of the District Court is disqualified by any of the causes above stated, the parties may, by consent, appoint a proper person to try said case; or, upon their failing to do so, a competent person may be appointed to try the same in the county where it is pending in such manner as may be prescribed by law.

And the District Judges may exchange districts or hold courts for each other when they may deem it expedient, and shall do so when required by law. This disqualification of Judges of inferior tribunals shall be remedied, and vacancies in their offices filled, as may be prescribed by law.

[Note — The foregoing Sec. II of Art. V is an amended section, having been amended to use correct references to courts as established in amended Secs. 1, 3, 4, 5 and 6. Submitted by the Twenty-second Legislature (1891), ratified at an election Aug. 11, 1891, and declared adopted Sept. 22, 1891.]

Sec. 12. **Judges Conservators of Peace; Style of Writs; Prosecution by State** — (a) All judges of courts of this State, by virtue of their office, are conservators of the peace throughout the State.

(b) An indictment is a written instrument presented to a court by a grand jury charging a person with the commission of an offense. An information is a written instrument presented to a court by an attorney for the State charging a person with the commission of an offense. The practice and procedures relating to the use of indictments and informations, including their contents, amendment, sufficiency, and requisites, are as provided by law. The presentment of an indictment or information to a court invests the court with jurisdiction of the cause.

[Note — The foregoing Sec. 12 of Art. V has been amended from the original to substitute "Courts of the State" for enumeration of kinds of courts contained in original sections and applying to courts before general revision of judiciary in 1891. Submitted by the Twenty-second Legislature (1891), ratified at an election Aug. 11, 1891, and declared adopted Sept. 22, 1891. It was further amended to explain the manner in which a person is charged with a criminal offense and certain requirements applicable to state writs and processes. Submitted by the Sixty-ninth Legislature (1985) and adopted in an election Nov. 5, 1985.]

Sec. 13. **Jurors, Grand and Petit; Number Required to Return Verdict** — Grand and petit juries in the District Courts shall be composed of twelve men; but nine members of a grand jury shall be a quorum to transact business and present bills. In trials of civil cases and in trials of criminal cases below the grade of felony in the District Courts, nine members of the jury concurring may render a verdict, but when the verdict shall be rendered by less than the whole number, it shall be signed by every member of the jury concurring in it. When, pending the trial of any case, one or more jurors, not exceeding three, may die, or be disabled from sitting, the remainder of the jury shall have the power to render the verdict; provided, that the Legislature may change or modify the rule authorizing less than the whole number of the jury to render a verdict.

[Note — Sec. 14 of Art. V, defining judicial districts and time of holding courts therein was deleted by constitutional amendment in an election Nov. 5, 1985.]

Sec. 15. **County Court; Election; Term of Office of County Judges; Fees** — There shall be established in each county in this State, a County Court, which shall be a court of record; and there shall be elected in each county by the qualified voters a County Judge, who shall be well informed in the law of the state, shall be a conservator of the peace, and shall hold his office for four years and until his successor shall be elected and qualified. He shall receive as compensation for his services such fees and perquisites as may be prescribed by law.

[Note — The foregoing Sec. 15 of Art. V has been amended to change the term of office from two to four years. Submitted by the Fifty-third Legislature (1953) and adopted in election Nov. 2, 1954.]

Sec. 16. **Jurisdiction of County Court; Appeals; Probate Jurisdiction; May Issue Writs; Judge Disqualified, When** — The County Court has jurisdiction as provided by law. The County Judge is the presiding officer of the County Court and has judicial functions as provided by law. County court

judges shall have the power to issue writs necessary to enforce their jurisdiction.

County Courts in existence on the effective date of this amendment are continued unless otherwise provided by law. When the Judge of the County Court is disqualified in any case pending in the County Court the parties interested may, by consent, appoint a proper person to try said case, or upon their failing to do so a competent person may be appointed to try the same in the county where it is pending in such manner as may be prescribed by law.

[Note — The foregoing Sec. 16 of Art. V is an amendment from the original to make changes relating to appeals to the county court, relating to disqualification of the judge, and minor changes. Submitted by the Twenty-second Legislature (1891), ratified at an election Aug. 11, 1891, and declared adopted Sept. 22, 1891. It was further amended to extend jurisdiction of Justices of Peace in civil cases. (See also Sec. 19 of Art. V.) Submitted by the Sixty-fifth Legislature (1977) and adopted in election Nov. 7, 1978. It was amended again to redefine jurisdiction of appellate courts. Submitted by the Sixty-sixth Legislature (1979) and adopted in election Nov. 4, 1980. It was again amended to define the jurisdiction of the County Judge and his duties. Submitted by the Sixty-ninth Legislature (1985) and adopted in an election Nov. 5, 1985.]

[Note — Sec. 16-a of Art. V, providing for probate courts, was deleted by constitutional amendment in an election Nov. 5, 1985.]

Sec. 17. **Terms of County Court for Criminal Business; Prosecution Commenced by Information; Grand Jury to Inquire Into Misdemeanors; Quashing of Grand Jury Indictments; Jury** — The County Court shall hold terms as provided by law. Prosecutions may be commenced in said court by information filed by the County Attorney, or by affidavit, as may be provided by law. Grand juries empaneled in the District Courts shall inquire into misdemeanors, and all indictments therefor returned into the District Courts shall forthwith be certified to the County Courts, or other inferior courts having jurisdiction to try them, for trial; and if such indictment be quashed in the county, or other inferior court, the person charged shall not be discharged if there is probable cause of guilt, but may be held by such court or magistrate to answer an information or affidavit. A jury in the County Court shall consist of six men; but no jury shall be empaneled to try a civil case, unless demanded by one of the parties, who shall pay such jury fee therefor in advance as may be prescribed by law, unless he makes affidavit that he is unable to pay the same.

[Note — The foregoing Sec. 17 of Art. V was amended to redefine the terms of office of county judges. Submitted by the Sixty-ninth Legislature (1985) and adopted in an election Nov. 5, 1985.]

Sec. 18. **Terms of Justices of the Peace; County Commissioners and Commissioners' Court** — (a) Each county in the state, with a population of 30,000 or more, according to the most recent federal census, from time to time, for the convenience of the people, shall be divided into not less than four and not more than eight precincts. Each county in the State with a population of 18,000 or more but less than 30,000 according to the most recent federal census, from time to time, for the convenience of the people, shall be divided into not less than two and not more than five precincts. Each county in the State with a population of less than 18,000, according to the most recent federal census, from time to time, for the convenience of the people, shall be designated as a single precinct or, if the Commissioners Court determines that the county needs more than one precinct, shall be divided into not more than four precincts. Notwithstanding the population requirements of this subsection, Chambers County, from time to time, for the convenience of the people, shall be divided into not less than two and not more than six precincts. A division or designation under this subsection shall be made by the Commissioners Court provided for by this Constitution. In each such precinct there shall be elected one Justice of the Peace and one Constable, each of whom shall hold his office for four years and until his successor shall be elected and qualified; provided that in a county with a population of less than 150,000, according to the most recent federal census, in any precinct in which there may be a city of 18,000 or more inhabitants, there shall be elected two Justices of the Peace, and in a county with a population of 150,000 or more, according to the most recent federal census, each precinct may contain more than one Justice of the Peace Court.

(b) Each county shall, in the manner provided for justice of the peace and constable precincts, be divided into four Commissioners' precincts in each of which there shall be

Article V — (Cont'd.)

elected by the qualified voters thereof one County Commissioner, who shall hold his office for four years and until his successor shall be elected and qualified. The County Commissioners so chosen, with the County Judge as presiding officer, shall compose the County Commissioners Court, which shall exercise such powers and jurisdiction over all county business as is conferred by this Constitution and the laws of the state, or as may be hereafter prescribed.

(c) When the boundaries of justice of the peace and constable precincts are changed, each Justice and Constable in office on the effective date of the change, or elected to a term of office beginning on or after the effective date of the change, shall serve in the precinct in which the person resides for the term to which each was elected or appointed, even though the change in boundaries places the person's residence outside the precinct for which he was elected or appointed, abolishes the precinct for which he was elected or appointed, or temporarily results in extra Justices or Constables serving in a precinct. When, as a result of a change of precinct boundaries, a vacancy occurs in the office of Justice of the Peace or Constable, the Commissioners Court shall fill the vacancy by appointment until the next general election.

(d) When the boundaries of commissioners precincts are changed, each commissioner in office on the effective date of the change, or elected to a term of office beginning on or after the effective date of the change, shall serve in the precinct to which each was elected or appointed for the entire term to which each was elected or appointed, even though the change in boundaries places the person's residence outside the precinct for which he was elected or appointed.

[Note — The foregoing Sec. 18 of Art. V was first amended to change the term of office for Justices of the Peace and Constables from two to four years. Submitted by the Fifty-third Legislature (1953) and adopted in election Nov. 2, 1954. It was again amended to authorize fewer justice of the peace and constable precincts in counties with populations of less than 30,000 and to provide for continuous service by Justices of Peace, Constables and County Commissioners when precinct boundaries are changed. Submitted by Sixty-eighth Legislature (1983) and adopted in election Nov. 8, 1983. It was again amended to allow Chambers County to be divided into two to six precincts. Submitted by Sixty-ninth Legislature (1985) and adopted in an election Nov. 5, 1985. It was further amended to provide that certain justice precincts may contain more than one justice of the peace court. Submitted by the Seventieth Legislature (1987) and adopted in an election Nov. 3, 1987.]

Sec. 19. Criminal Jurisdiction of Justices of the Peace; Appeals; Justices of the Peace ex-Officio Notaries — Justice of the peace courts shall have original jurisdiction in criminal matters of misdemeanor cases punishable by fine only, exclusive jurisdiction in civil matters where the amount in controversy is two hundred dollars or less, and such other jurisdiction as may be provided by law. Justices of the peace shall be ex officio notaries public.

[Note — The foregoing Sec. 19 of Art. V was amended to extend jurisdiction of Justices of Peace and to give them jurisdiction in civil matters involving $200 or less. (See also Sec. 16 of Art. V.) Submitted by the Sixty-fifth Legislature (1977) and adopted in election Nov. 7, 1978. It was again amended to redefine the duties of Justices of the Peace and to make them ex officio notaries public. Submitted by the Sixty-ninth Legislature (1985) and adopted in an election Nov. 5, 1985.]

Sec. 20. County Clerk; Election; Terms; Duties; Vacancies — There shall be elected for each county, by the qualified voters, a County Clerk, who shall hold his office for four years, who shall be clerk of the County and Commissioners' Courts and recorder of the county, whose duties, perquisites and fees of office shall be prescribed by the Legislature, and a vacancy in whose office shall be filled by the Commissioners' Court until the next general election; provided, that in counties having a population of less than 8,000 persons there may be an election of a single clerk, who shall perform the duties of District and County Clerks.

[Note — The foregoing Sec. 20 of Art. V has been amended to change the term of office from two to four years. Submitted by the Fifty-third Legislature (1953) and adopted in election Nov. 2, 1954.]

Sec. 21. County and District Attorneys; Duties; Vacancies; Fees — A County Attorney, for counties in which there is not a resident Criminal District Attorney, shall be elected by the qualified voters of each county, who shall be commissioned by the Governor and hold his office for the term of four years. In case of vacancy the Commissioners' Court of the county shall have power to appoint a County Attorney until the next general election. The County Attorneys shall represent the State in all cases in the District and inferior courts in their respective counties; but if any county shall be included in a district in which there shall be a District Attor-

ney, the respective duties of District Attorneys and County Attorneys shall, in such counties, be regulated by the Legislature. The Legislature may provide for the election of District Attorneys in such districts as may be deemed necessary, and make provisions for the compensation of District Attorneys and County Attorneys. District Attorneys shall hold office for a term of four years, and until their successors have qualified.

[Note — The foregoing Sec. 21 of Art. V has been amended to change the term of office from two to four years; also leaves solely to Legislature provision for annual salary to be paid by State to District and County Attorneys. Submitted by the Fifty-third Legislature (1953) and adopted in election Nov. 2, 1954.]

[Note — Sec. 22 of Art. V, giving Legislature power to change jurisdiction of county courts, was deleted by constitutional amendment in an election Nov. 5, 1985.]

Sec. 23. Sheriff; Term of Office; Vacancy — There shall be elected by the qualified voters of each county a Sheriff, who shall hold his office for the term of four years, whose duties and perquisites and fees of office shall be prescribed by the Legislature, and vacancies in whose office shall be filled by the Commissioners' Court until the next general election.

[Note — The foregoing Sec. 23 of Art. V has been amended to change the term of office from two to four years. Submitted by the Fifty-third Legislature (1953) and adopted in election Nov. 2, 1954.]

Sec. 24. Certain Officers Removed by District Courts for Drunkenness, Incompetency, Official Misconduct, Etc. — County Judges, County Attorneys, Clerks of the District and County Courts, Justices of the Peace, Constables and other county officers may be removed by the Judges of the District Courts for incompetency, official misconduct, habitual drunkenness or other causes defined by law, upon the cause therefor being set forth in writing, and the finding of its truth by a jury.

[Note — Sec. 25 of Art. V, giving the Supreme Court power to make rules of procedure was deleted by constitutional amendment in an election Nov. 5, 1985.]

Sec. 26. No Appeal in Criminal Cases by the State — The State is entitled to appeal in criminal cases, as authorized by general law.

[Note — The foregoing Sec. 26 of Art. V has been amended to give the state a limited right to appeal in criminal cases. Submitted by the Seventieth Legislature and adopted in an election Nov. 3, 1987.]

Sec. 27. Transfer of Cases by the Legislature — The Legislature shall, at its first session provide for the transfer of all business, civil and criminal, pending in District Courts, over which jurisdiction is given by this Constitution to the County Courts or other inferior courts, to such county or inferior courts, and for the trial or disposition of all such causes by such county or other inferior courts.

Sec. 28. Vacancies in Offices of Judges of Superior Courts to Be Filled by the Governor — Vacancies in the office of the Judges of the Supreme Court, the Court of Criminal Appeals, the Court of Civil Appeals and District Courts shall be filled by the Governor until the next succeeding general election, and vacancies in the office of County Judge and Justices of the Peace shall be filled by the Commissioners' Court until the next succeeding general election.

[Note — The foregoing Sec. 28 of Art. V has been amended from the original to make names of courts harmonize with names in amended Secs. 1, 3, 4, 5 and 6. Submitted by the Twenty-second Legislature (1891), ratified in an election Aug. 11, 1891, and declared adopted Sept. 22, 1891. This section was again amended to provide that appointments to the offices of County Judge and Justice of the Peace should be filled only to the next succeeding general election instead of for the full elected term. Submitted by the Fifty-fifth Legislature (1957) and adopted in election Nov. 4, 1958.]

Sec. 29. Terms of County Courts; Probate Business; Prosecutions — The County Court shall hold at least four terms for both civil and criminal business annually, as may be provided by the Legislature, or by the Commissioners' Court of the county under authority of law, and such other terms each year as may be fixed by the Commissioners' Court; provided, the Commissioners' Court of any county having fixed the times and number of terms of the County Court shall not change the same again until the expiration of one year. Said court shall dispose of probate business either in term time or vacation, under such regulations as may be

Article V — (Cont'd.); Article VI

prescribed by law. Prosecutions may be commenced in said courts in such manner as is or may be provided by law, and a jury therein shall consist of six men. Until otherwise provided, the terms of the County Court shall be held on the first Mondays in February, May, August and November, and may remain in session three weeks.

[Note — Sec. 29 of Art. V, an amendment, was added for stated purpose of prescribing county court terms. Submitted by the Eighteenth Legislature (1883), ratified in an election Aug. 14, 1883, and proclaimed adopted Sept. 25, 1883.]

Sec. 30. **County Judges and Criminal District Attorneys; Terms** — The Judges of all courts of county-wide jurisdiction heretofore or hereafter created by the Legislature of this State, and all Criminal District Attorneys now or hereafter authorized by the laws of this State, shall be elected for a term of four years, and shall serve until their successors have qualified.

[Note — Sec. 30 of Art. V, an amendment, was added for purpose of prescribing term of office of County Judges and Criminal District Attorneys. Submitted by the Fifty-third Legislature (1953) and adopted in election Nov. 2, 1954.]

Sec. 31. **Court Administration and Rule-making Authority** — (a) The Supreme Court is responsible for the efficient administration of the judicial branch and shall promulgate rules of administration not inconsistent with the laws of the state as may be necessary for the efficient and uniform administration of justice in the various courts.

(b) The Supreme Court shall promulgate rules of civil procedure for all courts not inconsistent with the laws of the state as may be necessary for the efficient and uniform administration of justice in the various courts.

(c) The Legislature may delegate to the Supreme Court or Court of Criminal Appeals the power to promulgate such other rules as may be prescribed by law or this Constitution, subject to such limitations and procedures as may be provided by law.

[Note — The foregoing Sec. 31 of Art. V, an amendment, was added to provide for the administration and jurisdiction of constitutional courts. Submitted by the Sixty-ninth Legislature (1985) and adopted in an election Nov. 5, 1985.]

[Note — For further clarification of rules of procedure for the different courts, see Temporary Provision at the beginning of Article V.]

ARTICLE VI. — SUFFRAGE

Sec. 1. **Persons Who Cannot Vote** — The following classes of persons shall not be allowed to vote in this State, to wit:

*First: Persons under eighteen (18) years of age.

Second: Idiots and lunatics.

Third: All paupers supported by any county.

Fourth: All persons convicted of any felony, subject to such exceptions as the Legislature may make.

[Note — The foregoing Sec. 1 of Art. VI has been twice amended from the original to give privilege of ballot to officers and enlisted men of National Guard, National Guard Reserves, Officers Reserve Corps, Organized Reserves and retired officers and enlisted men of Army, Navy and Marine Corps. Submitted by the Forty-second Legislature (1931) and adopted in an election Nov. 8, 1932. Proclaimed Jan. 9, 1933. It was further amended by HJR 10 submitted by the Fifty-third Legislature (1953) and adopted in an election Nov. 2, 1954, to remove restrictions against members of the Armed Forces. This amendment also repealed the original Sec. 2-a of Art. VI which provided for paid poll tax exemption for war veterans. See also note under Sec. 2 and new Sec. 2-a.* Texas on April 27, 1971, became the twenty-first state to ratify an amendment to the U.S. Constitution lowering the voting age to 18 from 21. When Ohio ratified the amendment in July, 1971, it was the 38th state to do so, the number required to change the voting age.]

Sec. 2. **Annual Registration; Absentee Voting** — Every person subject to none of the foregoing disqualifications, who shall have attained the age of *21 years and who shall be a citizen of the United States and who shall have resided in this State one year next preceding an election and the last six months within the district or county in which such person offers to vote, shall be deemed a qualified elector; provided, however, that before offering to vote at an election a voter shall have registered annually, but such requirement for registration shall not be considered a qualification of an elector within the meaning of the term "qualified elector" as used in any other Article of this Constitution in respect to any matter except qualification and eligibility to

vote at an election. Any legislation enacted in anticipation of the adoption of this Amendment shall not be invalid because of its anticipatory nature. The Legislature may authorize absentee voting. And this provision of the Constitution shall be self-enacting without the necessity of further legislation.

[Note — The foregoing Sec. 2 of Art. VI has been amended six times, as follows: (1) To include provision that declaration of foreigner must be filed at least six months before election to enable him to vote in such election. Submitted by Twenty-fourth Legislature (1895), ratified in an election Nov. 3, 1896, and declared adopted Dec. 18, 1896. (2) To make poll tax receipt certificate of registration for voting. Submitted by Twenty-seventh Legislature (1901), ratified in an election Nov. 4, 1902, and declared adopted Dec. 26, 1902. (3) To limit suffrage to citizens; allowing husband or wife to pay poll tax for other; authorizing absentee voting. Submitted by Thirty-seventh Legislature (1921) and ratified in election July 23, 1921. (4) To extend suffrage to members of the Armed Forces of the United States. Submitted by Fifty-third Legislature (1953) and adopted in an election Nov. 2, 1954. (5) To omit the requirement that members of armed services may vote only in county in which they resided at time of entering the service. Submitted by Fifty-ninth Legislature (1965) and adopted in election Nov. 8, 1966. (6) To repeal the poll tax as a voting requirement and substituting therefor annual registration. Submitted by Fifty-ninth Legislature (1965), adopted in election Nov. 8, 1966. *See also note under Sec. 1 above.]

Sec. 2-a. **Vote for Electors for President and Vice President and Statewide Offices** — (a) Notwithstanding any other provision of this Constitution, the Legislature may enact laws and provide a method of registration, including the time of such registration, permitting any person who is qualified to vote in this state except for the residence requirements within a county or district, as set forth in Sec. 2 of this article, to vote for (1) electors for president and vice president of the United States and (2) all offices, questions or propositions to be voted on by all electors throughout this state.

(b) Notwithstanding any other provision of this Constitution, the Legislature may enact laws and provide for a method of registration, including the time for such registration, permitting any person (1) who is qualified to vote in this state except for the residence requirements of Sec. 2 of this article, and (2) who shall have resided anywhere within this state at least thirty (30) days next preceding a general election in a presidential election year, and (3) who shall have been a qualified elector in another state immediately prior to his removal to this state or would have been eligible to vote in such other state had he remained there until such election, to vote for electors for president and vice president of the United States in that election.

(c) Notwithstanding any other provision of this Constitution, the Legislature may enact laws and provide for a method of registration, including the time for such registration, permitting absentee voting for electors for president and vice president of the United States in this state by former residents of this state (1) who have removed to another state, and (2) who meet all qualifications, except residence requirements, for voting for electors for president and vice president in this state at the time of the election, but the privileges of suffrage so granted shall be only for such period of time as would permit a former resident of this state to meet the residence requirements for voting in his new state of residence, and in no case for more than twenty-four (24) months.

[Note — The foregoing Sec. 2-a, an amendment, was added to provide for voting on electors for president and vice president and on all statewide offices. Submitted by the Fifty-ninth Legislature (1965) and adopted in election Nov. 8, 1966.]

Sec. 3. **Electors in Towns and Cities; Only Property Taxpayers to Vote in Certain Instances** — All qualified electors of the State, as herein described, who shall have resided for six months immediately preceding an election within the limits of any city or corporate town, shall have the right to vote for Mayor and all other elective officers; but in all elections to determine expenditure of money or assumption of debt, only those shall be qualified to vote who pay taxes on property in said city or incorporated town; provided, that no poll tax for the payment of debts thus incurred shall be levied upon the persons debarred from voting in relation thereto.

Sec. 3-a. **Only Those Who Have Rendered Property for Taxation May Vote in Bond Elections** — When an election is held by any county, or any number of counties, or any political subdivision of the State, or any political subdivision of a county, or any defined district now or hereafter to be described and defined within the State and which may or may not include towns, villages or municipal corporations, or any city, town or village, for the purpose of issuing bonds or

Article VI — (Cont'd.); Article VII

otherwise lending credit, or expending money or assuming any debt, only qualified electors who own taxable property in the State, county, political subdivision, district, city, town or village where such election is held, and who have duly rendered the same for taxation, shall be qualified to vote and all electors shall vote in the election precinct of their residence.

[Note — The foregoing Sec. 3-a of Art. VI, an amendment, was added for the purpose of limiting voters participating in bond elections to those who have rendered property for taxation. Submitted by the Forty-second Legislature (1931) and adopted in an election Nov. 8, 1932; proclaimed Jan. 9, 1933.]

Sec. 4. **Voter Registration** — In all elections by the people the vote shall be by ballot, and the Legislature shall provide for the numbering of tickets and make such other regulations as may be necessary to detect and punish fraud and preserve the purity of the ballot box; and the Legislature shall provide by law for the registration of all voters.

[Note — The foregoing Sec. 4 of Art. VI has been amended twice as follows: A provision for the registration of voters in cities of 10,000 or more population was added by amendment submitted by the Twenty-second Legislature (1891), ratified in election Aug. 11, 1891, and declared adopted Sept. 22, 1891. It was further amended to delete this provision for registration of voters in cities of 10,000 or more population. (See also note under Sec. 2, Art. VI.) Submitted by the Fifty-ninth Legislature (1965) and adopted in election Nov. 8, 1966.]

Sec. 5. **Voters Privileged From Arrest** — Voters shall, in all cases except treason, felony or breach of the peace, be privileged from arrest during their attendance at elections and in going to and returning therefrom.

ARTICLE VII.—EDUCATION— THE PUBLIC FREE SCHOOLS

Sec. 1. **Public Schools to Be Established** — A general diffusion of knowledge being essential to the preservation of the liberties and rights of the people, it shall be the duty of the Legislature of the State to establish and make suitable provision for the support and maintenance of an efficient system of public free schools.

Sec. 2. **Provisions Governing the Levy and Collection of Taxes for the Support of the Public Free Schools** — All funds, lands and other property heretofore set apart and appropriated for the support of public schools, all the alternate sections of land reserved by the State out of grants heretofore made or that may hereafter be made to railroads or other corporations, of any nature whatsoever, one half of the public domain of the State, and all sums of money that may come to the State from the sale of any portion of the same shall constitute a perpetual public school fund.

Sec. 3. **School Taxes** — One fourth of the revenue derived from the State occupation taxes and a poll tax of one ($1.00) dollar on every inhabitant of this State, between the ages of 21 and 60 years, shall be set apart annually for the benefit of the public free schools; and in addition thereto, there shall be levied and collected an annual ad valorem State tax of such an amount not to exceed 35c on the one hundred ($100.00) dollars valuation, as, with the available school fund arising from all other sources, will be sufficient to maintain and support the public schools of this State for a period of not less than six months in each year, and it shall be the duty of the State Board of Education to set aside a sufficient amount out of the said tax to provide free textbooks for the use of children attending the public free schools of this State; provided, however, that should the limit of taxation herein named be insufficient the deficit may be met by appropriation from the general funds of the State, and the Legislature may also provide for the formation of school districts by general laws, and all such school districts may embrace parts of two or more counties. And the Legislature shall be authorized to pass laws for the assessment and collection of taxes in all said districts and for the management and control of the public school or schools of such districts, whether such districts are composed of territory wholly within a county or in parts of two or more counties. And the Legislature may authorize an additional ad valorem tax to be levied and collected within all school districts heretofore formed or hereafter formed, for the further maintenance of public free schools, and for the erection and equipment of school buildings therein; provided, that a majority of the qualified property taxpaying voters of the district voting at an election to be held for that purpose shall vote such tax not to exceed in any one year $1 on the $100 valuation of the property subject to taxation in such district, but the limitation upon the amount of school district tax herein authorized shall not apply to incorporated cities or towns constituting separate and independent school districts, nor to independent or common school districts created by general or special law.

[Note — The foregoing Sec. 3 of Art. VII is an amended section, having been altered six times: (1) To authorize a State ad valorem school tax of not more than 20c, and further to authorize creation by Legislature of school districts for local taxation not to exceed 20c. Submitted by Eighteenth Legislature (1883), ratified in election Aug. 14, 1883, and declared adopted Sept. 25, 1883. (2) To authorize maximum tax in school districts of 50c. Submitted by Thirtieth Legislature (1907), ratified in an election Nov. 3, 1908, and declared adopted Feb. 2, 1909. (3) To authorize intercounty school districts and authorizing Legislature to pass laws for management and control of districts. Submitted by Thirty-first Legislature (1909), ratified in an election Aug. 3, 1909. See note on 3-a below. (4) To increase maximum tax for State school purposes from 20c to 35c and provide for free textbooks. Submitted by Thirty-fifth Legislature (1917) and adopted at election of Nov. 5, 1918. (5) To remove 50c limit on school district tax submitted by Thirty-sixth Legislature (1919) and adopted at election of Nov. 2, 1920. (6) To eliminate the provision authorizing the Legislature to create districts by special law. Submitted by Thirty-ninth Legislature (1925) and ratified in an election Nov. 2, 1926, and proclaimed Jan. 20, 1927.]

See Sec. 1-e of Art. VIII for provisions to gradually abolish the ad valorem tax as a source for state school support.

[Note — Sec. 3-a of Art. VII, relating to county line districts, validation, bonds and taxation, was deleted by constitutional amendment in election Aug. 5, 1969.]

Sec. 3-b. **County School Districts** — No tax for the maintenance of public free schools voted in any independent school district and no tax for the maintenance of a junior college voted by a junior college district, nor any bonds voted in any such district, but unissued, shall be abrogated, canceled or invalidated by change of any kind in the boundaries thereof. After any change in boundaries, the governing body of any such district, without the necessity of an additional election, shall have the power to assess, levy and collect ad valorem taxes on all taxable property within the boundaries of the district as changed, for the purposes of the maintenance of public free schools or the maintenance of a junior college, as the case may be, and the payment of principal of and interest on all bonded indebtedness outstanding against, or attributable, adjusted or allocated to, such district or any territory therein, in the amount, at the rate, or not to exceed the rate, and in the manner authorized in the district prior to the change in its boundaries, and further in accordance with the laws under which all such bonds, respectively, were voted; and such governing body also shall have the power, without the necessity of an additional election, to sell and deliver any unissued bonds voted in the district prior to any such change in boundaries, and to assess, levy and collect ad valorem taxes on all taxable property in the district as changed, for the payment of principal of and interest on such bonds in the manner permitted by the laws under which such bonds were voted. In those instances where the boundaries of any such independent school district are changed by the annexation of, or consolidation with, one or more whole school districts, the taxes to be levied for the purposes herein-above authorized may be in the amount or at not to exceed the rate theretofore voted in the district having at the time of such change the greatest scholastic population according to the latest scholastic census and only the unissued bonds of such district voted prior to such change, may be subsequently sold and delivered and any voted, but unissued, bonds of other school districts involved in such annexation or consolidation shall not thereafter be issued.

[Note. The foregoing Sec. 3-b of Art. VII, an amendment, was added originally for the purpose of allowing independent school districts in Dallas County to work out adjustment of boundaries without abrogating, canceling or invalidating existing tax rates and bonds. Submitted by the Fifty-seventh Legislature (1961) and adopted in election Nov. 6, 1962. Further amended to include school districts in any county of Texas. Submitted by the Fifty-ninth Legislature (1965) and adopted in election Nov. 8, 1966.]

Sec. 4. **Sale of School Lands; No Release to Purchasers; the Investment of Proceeds** — The lands herein set apart to the public free school fund shall be sold under such regulations, at such times and on such terms as may be prescribed by law; and the Legislature shall not have power to grant any relief to purchasers thereof. The proceeds of such sales must be used to acquire other land for the Public Free School fund as provided by law or the proceeds shall be invested by the comptroller, as may be directed by the Board of Education herein provided for, in the bonds of the United States, the State of Texas, or counties in said State, or in such other securities and under such restrictions as may be prescribed by law; and the State shall be responsible for all investments.

[Note — The foregoing Sec. 4 of Art. VII is an amended section, the amendment authorizing investment of money from sale of State public school lands in securities other than

Article VII — (Cont'd.)

State and United States bonds, as was required by the original section. The amendment also added the clause making the State responsible for such investments. Submitted by the Eighteenth Legislature (1883), ratified in an election Aug. 14, 1883, and declared adopted Sept. 25, 1883. It was again amended to authorize proceeds from sale of land dedicated to permanent school fund to be used to acquire other land for that fund. Submitted by Sixty-ninth Legislature (1985) and adopted in an election Nov. 5, 1985.]

Sec. 4A. **Patents Issued for Free Public School Lands** — (a) On application to the School Land Board, a natural person is entitled to receive a patent to land from the commissioner of the General Land Office if:

(1) the land is surveyed public free school land, either surveyed or platted according to records of the General Land Office;

(2) the land was not patentable under the law in effect immediately before adoption of this section;

(3) the person acquired the land without knowledge of the title defect out of the State of Texas or Republic of Texas and held the land under color of title, the chain of which dates from at least as early as January 1, 1932; and

(4) the person, in conjunction with his predecessors in interest:

(A) has a recorded deed on file in the respective county courthouse and has claimed the land for a continuous period of at least 50 years as of November 15, 1981; and

(B) for at least 50 years has paid taxes on the land together with all interest and penalties associated with any period of delinquency of said taxes; provided, however, that in the event that public records concerning the tax payments on the land are unavailable for any period within the past 50 years, the tax assessors-collectors of the taxing jurisdictions in which the land is located shall provide the School Land Board with a sworn certificate stating that, to the best of their knowledge, all taxes have been paid for the past 50 years and there are no outstanding taxes nor interest or penalties currently due against the property.

(b) The applicant for the patent must submit to the School Land Board certified copies of his chain of title and a survey of the land for which a patent is sought, if requested to do so by the board. The board shall determine the qualifications of the applicant to receive a patent under this section. Upon a finding by the board that the applicant meets the requirements of Subsection (a) of this section, the commissioner of the General Land Office shall award the applicant a patent. If the applicant is denied a patent, he may file suit against the board in a district court of the county in which the land is situated within 60 days from the date of the denial of the patent under this section. The trial shall be de novo and not subject to the Administrative Procedure and Texas Register Act, and the burden of proof is on the applicant.

(c) This section does not apply to beach land, submerged land, or islands, and may not be used by an applicant to resolve a boundary dispute. This section does not apply to land that, previous to the effective date of this section, was found by a court of competent jurisdiction to be state owned or to land on which the state has given a mineral lease that on the effective date of this section was productive.

(d) Application for a patent under this section must be filed with the School Land Board within five years from the effective date of this section.

(e) This section is self-executing.

(f) This section expires on January 1, 1990.

[Note — The foregoing Sec. 4A of Art. VII, an amendment, was added to authorize the Commissioner of the General Land Office to issue patents for certain public free school fund land held in good faith under color of title for at least 50 years as of Nov. 15, 1981. Submitted by the Sixty-seventh Legislature (1981) and adopted in election Nov. 3, 1981.]

Sec. 5. **Permanent School Fund; Interest; Alienation; Sectarian Schools** — (a) The principal of all bonds and other funds, and the principal arising from the sale of the lands hereinbefore set apart to said school fund, shall be the permanent school fund, and all the interest derivable therefrom and the taxes herein authorized and levied shall be the available school fund. The available school fund shall be applied annually to the support of the public free schools. Except as provided by this section, no law shall ever be enacted appropriating any part of the permanent or available school fund to any other purpose whatever; nor shall the same or any part thereof ever be appropriated to or used for the support of any sectarian school; and the available school fund herein provided shall be distributed to the several counties according to their scholastic population and applied in such manner as may be provided by law.

(b) The Legislature by law may provide for using the permanent school fund and the income from the permanent school fund to guarantee bonds issued by school districts or by the state for the purpose of making loans to or purchasing the bonds of school districts for the purpose of acquisition, construction, or improvement of instructional facilities including all furnishings thereto. If any payment is required to be made by the permanent school fund as a result of its guarantee of bonds issued by the state, an amount equal to this payment shall be immediately paid by the state from the treasury to the permanent school fund. An amount owed by the state to the permanent school fund under this section shall be a general obligation of the state until paid. The amount of bonds authorized hereunder shall not exceed $750 million or a higher amount authorized by a two-thirds record vote of both houses of the legislature. If the proceeds of bonds issued by the state are used to provide a loan to a school district and the district becomes delinquent on the loan payments, the amount of the delinquent payments shall be offset against state aid to which the district is otherwise entitled.

[Note — The foregoing Sec. 5 (b) of Art. VII was amended to provide for using the permanent school fund and its income to guarantee bonds issued by the state for the purpose of aiding school districts. Proposed by the Seventy-first Legislature (1989) and adopted in an election Nov. 7 1989.]

(c) The Legislature may appropriate part of the available school fund for administration of the permanent school fund or of a bond guarantee program established under this section.

(d) Notwithstanding any other provision of this constitution, in managing the assets of the permanent school fund, the State Board of Education may acquire, exchange, sell, supervise, manage, or retain, through procedures and subject to restrictions it establishes and in amounts it considers appropriate, any kind of investment, including investments in the Texas growth fund created by Article XVI, Section 70, of this constitution, that persons of ordinary prudence, discretion, and intelligence, exercising the judgment and care under the circumstances then prevailing, acquire or retain for their own account in the management of their affairs, not in regard to speculation but in regard to the permanent disposition of their funds, considering the probable income as well as the probable safety of their capital.

[Note — The foregoing Sec. 5 of Art. VII is an amended section. It was first amended to allow Legislature to add not exceeding 1 per cent annually of the total value of the permanent school fund to the available school fund. Submitted by the Twenty-second Legislature (1891), ratified in an election Aug. 11, 1891, and declared adopted Sept. 22, 1891. It was further amended to delete this provision. Submitted by the Fifty-eighth Legislature (1963), and adopted in election Nov. 3, 1964. It was again amended to authorize use of the permanent school fund to guarantee bonds issued by school districts. Submitted by Sixty-eighth Legislature (1983) and adopted in election Nov. 8, 1983. It was further amended to authorize the investment of Permanent School Fund monies in the Texas Growth Fund. Submitted by the Seventieth Legislature (1987) and adopted in an election Nov. 8, 1988.]

Sec. 6. **County School Lands; Limitations; Settlers; Proceeds** — All lands heretofore or hereafter granted to the several counties of this State for educational purposes are of right the property of said counties respectively to which they were granted, and title thereto is vested in said counties, and no adverse possession or limitation shall ever be available against the title of any county. Each county may sell or dispose of its lands in whole or in part in manner to be here provided by the Commissioners' Court of the county. Actual settlers residing on said land shall be protected in the prior right of purchasing the same to the extent of their settlement, not to exceed 160 acres, at the price fixed by said court, which price shall not include the value of existing improvements made thereon by such settlers. Said lands, and the proceeds thereof, when sold, shall be held by said counties alone as a trust for the benefit of public schools therein; said proceeds to be invested in bonds of the United States, the State of Texas, or counties in said State, or in such other securities and under such restrictions as may be prescribed by law; and the counties shall be responsible for all investments; the interest thereon and other revenue, except principal, shall be available fund.

[Note — The foregoing Sec. 6 of Art. VII is an amended section, the amendment authorizing the investment of money from sale of county public school lands in securities other than State and United States bonds (as was required in the original section), and making counties responsible for such investments. Submitted by the Eighteenth Legislature (1883), ratified in an election August 14, 1883, and declared adopted Sept. 25, 1883.]

Sec. 6-a. **Taxation of County School Lands** — All agriculture or grazing school land mentioned in Sec. 6 of this article owned by any county shall be subject to taxation except for State purposes to the same extent as lands privately owned.

Article VII — (Cont'd.)

[Note — The foregoing Sec. 6-a of Art. VII, an amendment, was added for the stated purpose of providing taxation of lands mentioned in Sec. 6. Submitted by the Thirty-ninth Legislature (1925), ratified in an election Nov. 2, 1926, and proclaimed Jan. 20, 1927.]

Sec. 6-b. Notwithstanding the provisions of Sec. 6, Art. VII, Constitution of the State of Texas, any county, acting through the commissioners court, may reduce the county permanent school fund of that county and may distribute the amount of the reduction to the independent and common school districts of the county on a per scholastic basis to be used solely for the purpose of reducing bonded indebtedness of those districts or for making permanent improvements. The commissioners court shall, however, retain a sufficient amount of the corpus of the county permanent school fund to pay ad valorem taxes on school lands or royalty interests owned at the time of the distribution. Nothing in this Section affects financial aid to any school district by the State.

[Note — Sec. 6-b of Art VII is an added amendment to allow a county to reduce its county permanent school fund and distribute the money to independent and common school districts on a per capita basis. Submitted by the Sixty-second Legislature (1971) and adopted in an election Nov. 7, 1972.]

[Note — Sec. 7 of Art. VII, relating to separate schools for white and colored, was deleted by constitutional amendment in election Aug. 5, 1969.]

Sec. 8. **Board of Education; Terms and Duties** — The Legislature shall provide by law for a State Board of Education, whose members shall be appointed or elected in such manner and by such authority and shall serve for such terms as the Legislature shall prescribe not to exceed six years. The said board shall perform such duties as may be prescribed by law.

[Note — The foregoing Sec. 8 of Art. VII is an amended section, reconstituting the State Board of Education. The original text provided for a Board of Education consisting of Governor, Comptroller and Secretary of State, serving ex officio. Submitted by the Fortieth Legislature (1927); ratified Nov. 6, 1928; proclaimed Feb. 6, 1929.]

Asylums

Sec. 9. **Lands of Asylums; Sale.** All lands heretofore granted for the benefit of the lunatic, blind, deaf and dumb, and orphan asylums, together with such donations as may have been or may hereafter be made to either of them, respectively, as indicated in the several grants, are hereby set apart to provide a permanent fund for the support, maintenance and improvement of said asylums. And the Legislature may provide for the sale of the lands and the investment of the proceeds in the manner as provided for the sale and investment of school lands in Sec. 4 of this article.

University

Sec. 10. **University Lands and Funds** — The Legislature shall, as soon as practicable, establish, organize and provide for the maintenance, support and direction of a University of the first class, to be located by a vote of the people of this State and styled "The University of Texas," for the promotion of literature and the arts and sciences, including an agricultural, and mechanical department.

Sec. 11. **University Funds; How Invested** — In order to enable the Legislature to perform the duties set forth in the foregoing section, it is hereby declared all lands and other property heretofore set apart and appropriated for the establishment and maintenance of the University of Texas, together with all the proceeds of sales of the same, heretofore made or hereafter to be made, and all grants, donations and appropriations that may hereafter be made by the State of Texas, or from any other source, except donations limited to specific purposes, shall constitute and become a permanent university fund. And the same as realized and received into the treasury of the State (together with such sums belonging to the fund, as may now be in the treasury) shall be invested in bonds of the United States, the State of Texas, or counties of said State, or in school bonds of municipalities or in bonds of any city of this State or in bonds issued under and by virtue of the Federal Farm Loan Act approved by the President of the United States July 17, 1916, and amendments thereto; and the interest accruing thereon shall be subject to appropriation by the Legislature to accomplish the purpose declared in the foregoing section; provided, that the one tenth of the alternate sections of the lands granted to railroads reserved by the State, which were set apart and appropriated to the establishment of the University of Texas by an act of the Legislature of Feb. 11, 1858, entitled "An act to establish the University of Texas" shall not be included in or constitute a part of, the permanent university fund.

[Note — The foregoing Sec. 11 of Art. VII has been twice amended as follows: (1) Adding a clause giving the Board of Regents of the University of Texas latitude in expending part of the permanent fund for buildings. Submitted by the Forty-first Legislature (1929); ratified Nov. 4, 1930. (2) Eliminating this latitude allowed the Board of Regents and restoring the original provisions of the Constitution which limited investments to bonds of the United States, State or civil subdivisions. This last amendment added also the clause "except donations limited to specific purposes." Submitted by the Forty-second Legislature (1931); adopted Nov. 8, 1932. Proclaimed Jan. 9, 1933.]

Sec. 11-a. In addition to the bonds enumerated in Section 11 of Article VII of the Constitution of the State of Texas, the Board of Regents of The University of Texas may invest the Permanent University Fund in securities, bonds or other obligations issued, insured, or guaranteed in any manner by the United States Government, or any of its agencies, and in such bonds, debentures, or obligations, and preferred and common stocks issued by corporations, associations, and other institutions as the Board of Regents of The University of Texas System may deem to be proper investments for said funds; provided, however, that not more than one per cent (1%) of said fund shall be invested in the securities of any one (1) corporation, nor shall more than five per cent (5%) of the voting stock of any one corporation be owned; provided, further, that stocks eligible for purchase shall be restricted to stocks of companies incorporated within the United States which have paid dividends for five (5) consecutive years or longer immediately prior to the date of purchase and which, except for bank stocks and insurance stocks, are listed upon an exchange registered with the Securities and Exchange Commission or its successors.

In making each and all of such investments said Board of Regents shall exercise the judgment and care under the circumstances then prevailing which men of ordinary prudence, discretion, and intelligence exercise in the management of their own affairs, not in regard to speculation but in regard to the permanent disposition of their funds, considering the probable income therefrom as well as the probable safety of their capital.

The interest, dividends and other income accruing from the investments of the Permanent University Fund, except the portion thereof which is appropriated by the operation of Sec. 18 of Art. VII for the payment of principal and interest on bonds or notes issued thereunder, shall be subject to appropriation by the Legislature to accomplish the purposes declared in Sec. 10 of Article VII of this Constitution.

This amendment shall be self-enacting, and shall become effective upon its adoption, provided, however, that the Legislature shall provide by law for full disclosure of all details concerning the investments in corporate stocks and bonds and other investments authorized herein.

[Note — Sec.11-a of Art. VII was added to provide for broader investment of the Permanent University Fund in corporate bonds and stocks under certain conditions and limitations. Submitted by the Fifty-fourth Legislature (1955) and adopted in election Nov. 6, 1956. It was further amended to increase the types of securities available for investment to the Permanent University Fund by allowing securities, bonds or other obligations issued, insured or guaranteed in any manner by the federal government. Submitted by the Sixtieth Legislature (1967) and adopted in election Nov.5, 1968.]

Sec. 11-b. Notwithstanding any other provision of this constitution, in managing the assets of the permanent university fund, the Board of Regents of The University of Texas System may acquire, exchange, sell, supervise, manage, or retain, through procedures and subject to restrictions it establishes and in amounts it considers appropriate, any kind of investment, including investments in the Texas growth fund created by Article XVI, Section 70, of this constitution, that persons of ordinary prudence, discretion, and intelligence, exercising the judgment and care under the circumstances then prevailing, acquire or retain for their own account in the management of their affairs, not in regard to speculation but in regard to the permanent disposition of their funds, considering the probable income as well as the probable safety of their capital. This section does not affect the state treasurer's custodial responsibilities for public funds, securities, and other evidences of investment.

[Note — The foregoing section 11-b, an amendment, was added to allow the Permanent University Fund to be invested in the Texas Growth Fund. Submitted by the Seventieth Legislature (1987) and adopted in an election Nov. 8, 1988.]

Sec. 12. **Lands to Be Sold; No Relief of Purchasers** — The land herein set apart to the university fund shall be sold under such regulations at such times and on such terms as

Article VII — (Cont'd.)

may be provided by law, and the Legislature shall provide for the prompt collection, at maturity, of all debts due on account of university lands heretofore sold, or that may hereafter be sold, and shall in neither event have the power to grant relief to the purchasers.

Sec. 13. **Agricultural and Mechanical College; Appropriations** — The Agricultural and Mechanical College of Texas, established by an act of the Legislature passed April 17, 1871, located in the County of Brazos, is hereby made and constituted a branch of the University of Texas, for instruction in agriculture, the mechanic arts and the natural sciences connected therewith. And the Legislature shall at its next session make an appropriation not to exceed $40,000 for the construction and completion of the buildings and improvements, and for providing the furniture necessary to put said college in immediate and successful operation.

Sec. 14. **Prairie View A&M** — Prairie View A&M University in Waller County is an institution of the first class under the direction of the same governing board as Texas A&M University referred to in Article VII, Section 13, of this constitution as the Agricultural and Mechanical College of Texas.

[Note — The foregoing Sec. 14 of Art. VII was substituted for an earlier Sec. 14. It sets out that Prairie View A&M University is an institution of the first class under direction of Texas A&M University governing board. (See also Sections 17 and 18 of Art. VII.) Submitted by the Sixty-eighth Legislature (1983) and adopted in election Nov. 6, 1984.]

Sec. 15. **Land Appropriated for University; How Sold** — In addition to the lands heretofore granted to the University of Texas, there is hereby set apart and appropriated, for the endowment, maintenance and support of said university and its branches, 1,000,000 acres of the unappropriated public domain of the State, to be designated and surveyed as may be provided by law; and said lands shall be sold under the same regulations and the proceeds invested in the same manner as is provided for the sale and investment of the permanent university fund; and the Legislature shall not have the power to grant any relief to the purchasers of said lands.

Sec. 16. **Terms of Office in School Systems** — The Legislature shall fix by law the terms of all offices of the public school system and of the State institutions of higher education, inclusive, and the terms of members of the respective boards, not to exceed six years.

[Note — The foregoing Sec. 16 of Art. VII is the first of two amendments numbered 16. (See following section and note thereon.) This amendment was added for the stated purpose of providing for fixing of terms of office in public school system. Submitted by the Fortieth Legislature (1927); ratified Nov. 6, 1928; proclaimed Feb. 6, 1929.]

Sec. 16 [a.] **Taxation of University Lands** — All land mentioned in Secs. 11, 12 and 15 of Article VII of the Constitution of the State of Texas, now belonging to the University of Texas, shall be subject to the taxation for county purpose to the same extent as lands privately owned; provided, they shall be rendered for taxation upon values fixed by the State Tax Board; and providing, that the State shall remit annually to each of the counties in which said lands are located an amount equal to the tax imposed upon said land for county purposes.

[Note — The foregoing section, which obviously should have been numbered either 16-a or 17, was designated as No. 16 in H.J.R. No. 11 of the Forty-first Legislature (1929) in which the amendment was submitted. It is customarily printed in legal references as Sec. 16 [a.] This amendment was added for the stated purpose of providing for taxation of University of Texas lands. It was ratified Nov. 4, 1930. Declared adopted Dec. 17, 1930.]

Sec. 17. **Support for Higher Education** — (a) In the fiscal year beginning September 1, 1985, and each fiscal year thereafter, there is hereby appropriated out of the first money coming into the state treasury not otherwise appropriated by the constitution $100 million to be used by eligible agencies and institutions of higher education for the purpose of acquiring land either with or without permanent improvements, constructing and equipping buildings or other permanent improvements, major repair or rehabilitation of buildings or other permanent improvements, and acquisition of capital equipment, library books and library materials. During the regular session of the legislature that is nearest to, preceding, the beginning of each fifth fiscal year dating from September 1, 1985, the legislature may by two-thirds vote of the membership of each house adjust the amount of the constitutional appropriation for the ensuing five years but may not adjust the appropriation in such a way as to impair any obligation created by the issuance of bonds or notes in accordance with this section.

(b) The funds appropriated under Subsection (a) of this section shall be for the use of the following eligible agencies and institutions of higher education (even though their names may be changed):

(1) East Texas State University including East Texas State University at Texarkana; (2) Lamar University including Lamar University at Orange and Lamar University at Port Arthur; (3) Midwestern State University; (4) North Texas State University; (5) Pan American University including Pan American University at Brownsville; (6) Stephen F. Austin State University; (7) Texas College of Osteopathic Medicine; (8) Texas State University System Administration and the following component institutions: (9) Angelo State University; (10) Sam Houston State University; (11) Southwest Texas State University; (12) Sul Ross State University including Uvalde Study Center; (13) Texas Southern University; (14) Texas Tech University; (15) Texas Tech University Health Sciences Center; (16) Texas Woman's University; (17) University of Houston System Administration and the following component institutions: (18) University of Houston — University Park; (19) University of Houston — Victoria; (20) University of Houston — Clear Lake; (21) University of Houston — Downtown; (22) University System of South Texas System Administration and the following component institutions: (23) Corpus Christi State University; (24) Laredo State University; (25) Texas A&I University; and (26) West Texas State University.

(c) Pursuant to a two-thirds vote of the membership of each house of the legislature, institutions of higher education may be created at a later date by general law, and, when created, such an institution shall be entitled to participate in the funding provided by this section if it is not created as a part of The University of Texas System or The Texas A&M University System. An institution that is entitled to participate in dedicated funding provided by Article VII, Section 18, of this constitution may not be entitled to participate in the funding provided by this section.

(d) In the year 1985 and every 10 years thereafter, the legislature or an agency designated by the legislature no later than August 31 of such year shall allocate by equitable formula the annual appropriations made under Subsection (a) of this section to the governing boards of eligible agencies and institutions of higher education. The legislature shall review, or provide for a review, of the allocation formula at the end of the fifth year of each 10-year allocation period. At that time adjustments may be made in the allocation formula, but no adjustment that will prevent the payment of outstanding bonds and notes, both principal and interest, may be made.

(e) Each governing board authorized to participate in the distribution of money under this section is authorized to expend all money distributed to it for any of the purposes enumerated in Subsection (a). In addition, unless a single bonding agency is designated as hereinafter provided, such governing board may issue bonds and notes for the purposes of refunding bonds or notes issued under this section or prior law, acquiring land either with or without permanent improvements, constructing and equipping buildings or other permanent improvements, and for major repair and rehabilitation of buildings or other permanent improvements, and may pledge up to 50 percent of the money allocated to such governing board pursuant to this section to secure the payment of the principal and interest of such bonds or notes. Proceeds from the issuance of bonds or notes under this subsection shall be maintained in a local depository selected by the governing board issuing the bonds or notes. The bonds and notes issued under this subsection shall be payable solely out of the money appropriated by this section and shall mature serially or otherwise in not more than 10 years from their respective dates. All bonds issued under this section shall be sold only through competitive bidding and are subject to approval by the attorney general. Bonds approved by the attorney general shall be incontestable. The permanent university fund may be invested in the bonds and notes issued under this section. In lieu of the authority granted to each governing board herein, the legislature by general law may designate a single agency to issue bonds and notes authorized under this section and transfer to that agency the authority to collect and pledge money to the payment of such bonds and notes for the purposes, to the extent, and subject to the restrictions of this section. Provided, that such agency shall be authorized to issue such bonds and notes for the benefit of an eligible institution and pledge money collected hereunder only as directed by the governing board of each eligible institution.

(f) The funds appropriated by this section may not be used for the purpose of constructing, equipping, repairing, or rehabilitating buildings or other permanent improvements that are to be used for student housing, intercollegiate athletics, or auxiliary enterprises.

(g) Except for that portion of the allocated funds that may be required to be transferred to a single bonding agency, if one is created, the comptroller of public accounts shall make annual transfers of the funds allocated pursuant to Subsection (d) directly to the governing boards of the eligible institutions.

Article VII — (Cont'd.)

(h) To assure efficient use of construction funds and the orderly development of physical plants to accommodate the state's real need, the legislature may provide for the approval or disapproval of all new construction projects at the eligible agencies and institutions entitled to participate in the funding provided by this section.

(i) The legislature by general law may dedicate portions of the state's revenues to the creation of a dedicated fund ("the higher education fund") for the purposes expressed in Subsection (a) of this section. The legislature shall provide for administration of the fund, which shall be invested in the manner provided for investment of the permanent university fund. The income from the investment of the higher education fund shall be credited to the higher education fund until such time as the fund totals $2 billion. The principal of the higher education fund shall never be expended. At the beginning of the fiscal year after the fund reaches $2 billion, as certified by the comptroller of public accounts, the dedication of general revenue funds provided for in Subsection (a) of this section shall cease. At the beginning of the fiscal year after the fund reaches $2 billion, and each year thereafter, 10 percent of the interest, dividends, and other income accruing from the investments of the higher education fund during the previous fiscal year shall be deposited and become part of the principal of the fund, and out of the remainder of the annual income from the investment of the principal of the fund there shall be appropriated an annual sum sufficient to pay the principal and interest due on the bonds and notes issued under this section and the balance of the income shall be allocated, distributed, and expended as provided for the appropriations made under Subsection (a).

(j) The state systems and institutions of higher education designated in this section may not receive any additional funds from the general revenue of the state for acquiring land with or without permanent improvements, for constructing or equipping buildings or other permanent improvements, or for major repair and rehabilitation of buildings or other permanent improvements except that:

(1) In the case of fire or natural disaster the legislature may appropriate from the general revenue an amount sufficient to replace the uninsured loss of any building or other permanent improvement; and

(2) the legislature, by two-thirds vote of each house, may, in cases of demonstrated need, which need must be clearly expressed in the body of the act, appropriate additional general revenue funds for acquiring land with or without permanent improvements, for constructing or equipping buildings or other permanent improvements, or for major repair and rehabilitation of buildings or other permanent improvements.

This subsection does not apply to legislative appropriations made prior to the adoption of this amendment.

(k) Without the prior approval of the legislature, appropriations under this section may not be expended for acquiring land with or without permanent improvements, or for constructing and equipping buildings or other permanent improvements, for a branch campus or educational center that is not a separate degree-granting institution created by general law.

(l) This section is self-enacting upon the issuance of the governor's proclamation declaring the adoption of the amendment, and the state comptroller of public accounts and the state treasurer shall do all things necessary to effectuate this section. This section does not impair any obligation created by the issuance of any bonds and notes in accordance with prior law, and all outstanding bonds and notes shall be paid in full, both principal and interest, in accordance with their terms. If the provisions of this section conflict with any other provisions of this constitution, then the provisions of this section shall prevail, notwithstanding all such conflicting provisions.

[Note — The foregoing Sec. 17 of Art. VII is an added amendment that supersedes the old Sec. 17 which provided for a confederate pension fund tax, college building fund tax and reduced the ad valorem ceiling for general purposes. That section was deleted in an election Nov. 2, 1982. This added Sec. 17 was proposed to create from general revenue a special higher education assistance fund for construction and related activities, to restructure the permanent university fund and to increase the number of institutions eligible to benefit from the permanent university fund. (See also Sections 14 and 18 of Art. VII.) Submitted by the Sixty-eighth Legislature (1983) and adopted in election Nov. 6, 1984.]

Sec. 18. Building Bonds Authorized for the University of Texas and Texas A&M University; Retired From Income From the Permanent University Fund; Etc.

— (a) The Board of Regents of The Texas A&M University System may issue bonds and notes not to exceed a total amount of 10 percent of the cost value of the investments and other assets of the permanent university fund (exclusive of real estate) at the time of the issuance thereof, and may pledge all or any part of its one-third interest in the available university fund to secure the payment of the principal and interest of those bonds and notes, for the purpose of acquiring land either with or without permanent improvements, constructing and equipping buildings or other permanent improvements, major repair and rehabilitation of buildings and other permanent improvements, acquiring capital equipment and library books and library materials, and refunding bonds or notes issued under this Section or prior law, at or for The Texas A&M University System administration and the following component institutions of the system:

(1) Texas A&M University, including its medical college which the legislature may authorize as a separate medical institution; (2) Prairie View A&M University, including its nursing school in Houston; (3) Tarleton State University; (4) Texas A&M University at Galveston; (5) Texas Forest Service; (6) Texas Agricultural Experiment Stations; (7) Texas Agricultural Extension Service; (8) Texas Engineering Experiment Stations; (9) Texas Transportation Institute; and (10) Texas Engineering Extension Service.

(b) The Board of Regents of The University of Texas System may issue bonds and notes not to exceed a total amount of 20 percent of the cost value of investments and other assets of the permanent university fund (exclusive of real estate) at the time of issuance thereof, and may pledge all or any part of its two-thirds interest in the available university fund to secure the payment of the principal and interest of those bonds and notes, for the purpose of acquiring land either with or without permanent improvements, constructing and equipping buildings or other permanent improvements, major repair and rehabilitation of buildings and other permanent improvements, acquiring capital equipment and library books and library materials, and refunding bonds or notes issued under this section or prior law, at or for The University of Texas System administration and the following component institutions of the system:

(1) The University of Texas at Arlington; (2) The University of Texas at Austin; (3) The University of Texas at Dallas; (4) The University of Texas at El Paso; (5) The University of Texas of the Permian Basin; (6) The University of Texas at San Antonio; (7) The University of Texas at Tyler; (8) The University of Texas Health Science Center at Dallas; (9) The University of Texas Medical Branch at Galveston; (10) The University of Texas Health Science Center at Houston; (11) The University of Texas Health Science Center at San Antonio; (12) The University of Texas System Cancer Center; (13) The University of Texas Health Center at Tyler; and (14) The University of Texas Institute of Texan Cultures at San Antonio.

(c) Pursuant to a two-thirds vote of the membership of each house of the legislature, institutions of higher education may be created at a later date as a part of The University of Texas System or The Texas A&M University System by general law, and, when created, such an institution shall be entitled to participate in the funding provided by this section for the system in which it is created. An institution that is entitled to participate in dedicated funding provided by Article VII, Section 17, of this constitution may not be entitled to participate in the funding provided by this section.

(d) The proceeds of the bonds or notes issued under Subsection (a) or (b) of this section may not be used for the purpose of constructing, equipping, repairing, or rehabilitating buildings or other permanent improvements that are to be used for student housing, intercollegiate athletics, or auxiliary enterprises.

(e) The available university fund consists of the dividends, interest and other income from the permanent university fund (less administrative expenses) including the net income attributable to the surface of permanent university fund land. Out of one-third of the available university fund, there shall be appropriated an annual sum sufficient to pay the principal and interest due on the bonds and notes issued by the Board of Regents of The Texas A&M University System under this section and prior law, and the remainder of that one-third of the available university fund shall be appropriated to the Board of Regents of The Texas A&M University System which shall have the authority and duty in turn to appropriate an equitable portion of the same for the support and maintenance of The Texas A&M University System administration, Texas A&M University, and Prairie View A&M University. The Board of Regents of The Texas A&M University System, in making just and equitable appropriations to Texas A&M University and Prairie View A&M University, shall exercise its discretion with due regard to such criteria as the board may deem appropriate from year to year, taking into account all amounts appropriated from Subsection (f) of this section. Out of the other two-thirds of the available university fund there shall be appropriated an annual sum sufficient to pay the principal and interest due on the bonds and notes issued by the Board of Regents of The University of Texas System under this section and prior law, and the remainder of such two-thirds of the available university fund, shall be appropriated for the support and maintenance of The University of Texas at Austin and The University of Texas as System administration.

(f) It is provided, however, that, for 10 years beginning upon the adoption of this amendment, before any other allo-

Article VII — (Cont'd.); Article VIII

cation is made of The University of Texas System's two-thirds share of the available university fund, remaining after payment of principal and interest on its bonds and notes issued under this section and prior law, $6 million per year shall be appropriated out of that share to the Board of Regents of The Texas A&M University System for said board's use in making appropriations to Prairie View A&M University. This subsection expires and is deleted from this constitution 10 years from the adoption of this amendment.

(g) The bonds and notes issued under this section shall be payable solely out of the available university fund, mature serially or otherwise in not more than 30 years from their respective dates, and, except for refunding bonds, be sold only through competitive bidding. All of these bonds and notes are subject to approval by the attorney general and when so approved are incontestable. The permanent university fund may be invested in these bonds and notes.

(h) To assure efficient use of construction funds and the orderly development of physical plants to accommodate the state's real need, the legislature may provide for the approval or disapproval of all new construction projects at the eligible agencies and institutions entitled to participate in the funding provided by this section except The University of Texas at Austin, Texas A&M University in College Station, and Prairie View A&M University.

(i) The state systems and institutions of higher education designated in this section may not receive any funds from the general revenue of the state for acquiring land with or without permanent improvements, for constructing or equipping buildings or other permanent improvements, or for major repair and rehabilitation of buildings or other permanent improvements except that:

(1) In the case of fire or natural disaster the legislature may appropriate from the general revenue an amount sufficient to replace the uninsured loss of any building or other permanent improvement; and

(2) The legislature, by two-thirds vote of each house, may, in cases of demonstrated need, which need must be clearly expressed in the body of the act, appropriate general revenue funds for acquiring land with or without permanent improvements, for constructing or equipping buildings or other permanent improvements, or for major repair and rehabilitation of buildings or other permanent improvements.

This subsection does not apply to legislative appropriations made prior to the adoption of this amendment.

(j) This section is self-enacting on the issuance of the governor's proclamation declaring the adoption of this amendment, and the state comptroller of public accounts and the state treasurer shall do all things necessary to effectuate this section. This section does not impair any obligation created by the issuance of bonds or notes in accordance with prior law, and all outstanding bonds and notes shall be paid in full, both principal and interest, in accordance with their terms, and the changes herein made in the allocation of the available university fund shall not affect the pledges thereof made in connection with such bonds or notes heretofore issued. If the provisions of this section conflict with any other provision of this constitution, then the provisions of this section shall prevail, notwithstanding any such conflicting provisions.

[Note — Sec. 18 and Sec. 17 of Art. VII were originally added to the Constitution as a single amendment to provide for funding of construction at Texas universities and colleges. Submitted by the Fiftieth Legislature (1947) and adopted in election Aug. 23, 1947. It was further amended in election Nov. 6, 1956 and again in an election Nov. 8, 1968. Sec. 17 was repealed in election Nov. 2, 1982. A new Sec. 17 and Sec. 18 were submitted by the Sixth-eighth Legislature (1983) and adopted in election Nov. 6, 1984. (See also notes under Sec. 14 and Sec. 17.)]

ARTICLE VIII — TAXATION AND REVENUE

Sec. 1. **Taxation to Be Equal and Uniform; Occupation and Income Taxes; Exemptions; Limitations Upon Counties, Cities, Etc.** — (a) Taxation shall be equal and uniform.

(b) All real property and tangible personal property in this State, unless exempt as required or permitted by this Constitution, whether owned by natural persons or corporations, other than municipal, shall be taxed in proportion to its value, which shall be ascertained as may be provided by law.

(c) The Legislature may provide for the taxation of intangible property and may also impose occupation taxes, both upon natural persons and upon corporations, other than municipal, doing any business in this State. It may also tax incomes of both natural persons and corporations, other than municipal, except that persons engaged in mechanical and agricultural pursuits shall never be required to pay an occupation tax.

(d) The Legislature by general law shall exempt from ad valorem taxation household goods not held or used for production of income and personal effects not held or used for

the production of income. The Legislature by general law may exempt from ad valorem taxation: (1) all or part of the personal property homestead of a family or single adult, "personal property homestead" meaning that personal property exempt by law from forced sale for debt; and (2) subject to Subsection (e) of this section, all other tangible personal property, except structures which are personal property and are used or occupied as residential dwellings and except property held or used for the production of income.

(e) The governing body of a political subdivision may provide for the taxation of all property exempt under a law adopted under Subdivision (2) of Subsection (d) of this section and not exempt from ad valorem taxation by any other law.

(f) The occupation tax levied by any county, city or town for any year, on persons or corporations pursuing any profession or business, shall not exceed one half of the tax levied by the State for the same period on such profession or business.

[Note — Sec. 1 of Art. VIII was amended to provide tax relief for residential homesteads and to provide personal property exemptions. (See also Sec. 1-b, and Sec. 23 of Art. VIII.) Submitted by the Sixty-fifth Legislature, (1977) and adopted in election Nov. 7, 1978. Sec. 1 was further amended to provide exemption from ad valorem taxation for certain tangible personal property located in the state. Submitted by the Seventieth Legislature (1987) and adopted in an election Nov. 3, 1987. Sec. 1 (b) was amended to authorize the exemption from ad valorem taxation certain personal property temporarily in the state for certain purposes. (See related amendment at Sec. 1-j, Art. VIII.) Submitted by Seventy-first Legislature (1989) and adopted in an election Nov. 7, 1989.]

Sec. 1-a. **Abolishing Ad Valorem Tax for State's General Fund Purposes; Providing Local Tax Rate, Etc.** — From and after Jan 1, 1951, no State ad valorem tax shall be levied upon any property within this State for general revenue purposes. From and after January 1, 1951, the several counties of the State are authorized to levy ad valorem taxes upon all property within their respective boundaries for county purposes, except the first three thousand dollars ($3,000) value of residential homesteads of married or unmarried adults, male or female, including those living alone, not to exceed thirty cents (30c) on each one hundred dollars ($100) valuation, in addition to all other ad valorem taxes authorized by the Constitution of this State, provided the revenue derived therefrom shall be used for construction and maintenance of farm-to-market roads or for flood control, except as herein otherwise provided.

Provided that in those counties or political subdivisions or areas of the State from which tax donations have heretofore been granted, the State Automatic Tax Board shall continue to levy the full amount of the State ad valorem tax for the duration of such donation, or until all legal obligations heretofore authorized by the law granting such donation or donations shall have been fully discharged, whichever shall first occur; provided that if such donation to any such county or political subdivision is for less than the full amount of State ad valorem taxes so levied, the portion of such taxes remaining over and above such donation shall be retained by said county or subdivision.

[Note — Sec. 1-a of Art. VIII was first added and then amended, as follows: (1) Giving homesteads $3,000 exemption from State taxes. Submitted by the Forty-second Legislature (1931), and adopted in an election Nov. 8, 1932. (2) Making more definite the provision for extending the exemption to counties and subdivisions having tax remission as soon as tax remission ceased, whether by expiration of the period designated in the act granting remission or voluntarily by action of local authorities. The original amendment failed to make provision for the latter contingency. Submitted by the Forty-third Legislature (1933), and adopted in an election Aug. 26, 1933. (3) Reducing maximum ad valorem tax for general revenue from 35c to 30c. (4) Abolishing ad valorem tax for state general fund purposes and providing for local taxation as indicated in text of section. (See also Sec. 1-b immediately below and note thereon.) Submitted by the Fiftieth Legislature (1947) and adopted in election Nov. 2, 1948. (5) Extending the $3,000 ad valorem tax exemption to homesteads of unmarried adults. Submitted by the Sixty-third Legislature (1973) and adopted in election Nov. 6, 1973.]

Sec. 1-b. **Homestead Exemption Under State Tax** — (a) Three thousand dollars ($3,000) of the assessed taxable value of all residence homesteads of married or unmarried adults, male or female, including those living alone, shall be exempt from all taxation for all State purposes.

(b) From and after January 1, 1973, the governing body of any county, city, town, school district, or other political subdivision of the State may exempt by its own action not less than three thousand dollars ($3,000) of the market value of residence homesteads of persons, married or unmarried, including those living alone, who are under a disability for purposes of payment of disability insurance benefits under Federal Old-Age, Survivors, and Disability Insurance or its

Article VIII — (Cont'd.)

successor or of married or unmarried persons sixty-five (65) years of age or older, including those living alone, from all ad valorem taxes thereafter levied by the political subdivision. As an alternative, upon receipt of a petition signed by twenty per cent (20%) of the voters who voted in the last preceding election held by the political subdivision, the governing body of the subdivision shall call an election to determine by majority vote whether an amount not less than three thousand dollars ($3,000) as provided in the petition, of the market value of residence homesteads of disabled persons or of persons sixty-five (65) years of age or over shall be exempt from ad valorem taxes thereafter levied by the political subdivision. An eligible disabled person who is sixty-five (65) years of age or older may not receive both exemptions from the same political subdivision in the same year but may choose either if the subdivision has adopted both. Where any ad valorem tax has theretofore been pledged for the payment of any debt, the taxing officers of the political subdivision shall have authority to continue to levy and collect the tax against the homestead property at the same rate as the tax so pledged until the debt is discharged, if the cessation of the levy would impair the obligation of the contract by which the debt was created.

An exemption adopted under this subsection based on assessed value is increased, effective January 1, 1979, to an amount that, when converted to market value, provides the same reduction in taxes, except that the market value exemption shall be rounded to the nearest $100.

(c) Five Thousand Dollars ($5,000) of the market value of the residence homestead of a married or unmarried adult, including one living alone, is exempt from ad valorem taxation for general elementary and secondary public school purposes. In addition to this exemption, the Legislature by general law may exempt an amount not to exceed Ten Thousand Dollars ($10,000) of the market value of the residence homestead of a person who is disabled as defined in Subsection (b) of this section and of a person sixty-five (65) years of age or older from ad valorem taxation for general elementary and secondary public school purposes. The Legislature by general law may base the amount of and condition eligibility for the additional exemption authorized by this subsection for disabled persons and for persons sixty-five (65) years of age or older on economic need. An eligible disabled person who is sixty-five (65) years of age or older may not receive both exemptions from a school district but may choose either. An eligible person is entitled to receive both the exemption required by this subsection for all residence homesteads and any exemption adopted pursuant to Subsection (b) of this section, but the Legislature shall provide by general law whether an eligible disabled or elderly person may receive both the additional exemption for the elderly and disabled authorized by this subsection and any exemption for the elderly or disabled adopted pursuant to Subsection (b) of this section. Where ad valorem tax has previously been pledged for the payment of debt, the taxing officers of a school district may continue to levy and collect the tax against the value of homesteads exempted under this subsection until the debt is discharged if the cessation of the levy would impair the obligation of the contract by which the debt was created. The Legislature shall provide for formulas to protect school districts against all or part of the revenue loss incurred by the implementation of Article VIII, Sections 1-b(c), 1-b(d), and 1-d-1, of this constitution. The Legislature by general law may define residence homestead for purposes of this section.

(d) Except as otherwise provided by this subsection, if a person receives the residence homestead exemption prescribed by Subsection (c) of this section for homesteads of persons sixty-five (65) years of age or older, the total amount of ad valorem taxes imposed on that homestead for general elementary and secondary public school purposes may not be increased while it remains the residence homestead of that person or that person's spouse who receives the exemption. If a person sixty-five (65) years of age or older dies in a year in which the person received the exemption, the total amount of ad valorem taxes imposed on the homestead for general elementary and secondary public school purposes may not be increased while it remains the residence homestead of that person's surviving spouse if the spouse is fifty-five (55) years of age or older at the time of the person's death, subject to any exceptions provided by general law. However, taxes otherwise limited by this subsection may be increased to the extent the value of the homestead is increased by improvements other than repairs or improvements made to comply with governmental requirements.

[Note — The foregoing Subsection (d) of Sec. 1-b of Art. VIII was amended to limit school tax increases on the residence homestead of the surviving spouse of an elderly person. Submitted by the Seventieth Legislature (1987) and adopted in an election Nov. 3, 1987.]

(e) The governing body of a political subdivision may exempt from ad valorem taxation a percentage of the market value of the residence homestead of a married or unmar-

ried adult, including one living alone. The percentage may not exceed forty percent (40%) for the years 1982 through 1984, thirty percent (30%) for the years 1985 through 1987, and twenty percent (20%) in 1988 and each subsequent year. However, the amount of an exemption authorized pursuant to this subsection may not be less than Five Thousand Dollars ($5,000) unless the Legislature by general law prescribes other monetary restrictions on the amount of the exemption. An eligible adult is entitled to receive other applicable exemptions provided by law. Where ad valorem tax has previously been pledged for the payment of debt, the governing body of a political subdivision may continue to levy and collect the tax against the value of the homesteads exempted under this subsection until the debt is discharged if the cessation of the levy would impair the obligation of the contract by which the debt was created. The Legislature by general law may prescribe procedures for the administration of residence homestead exemptions.

[Note — Sec. 1-b of Art. VIII was amended to allow county, city, school district or other political subdivision to exempt not less than Three Thousand Dollars of the assessed value of residence homesteads of persons 65 years and older from all ad valorem taxes levied by the subdivision. Submitted by Sixty-second Legislature (1971) and adopted in election Nov. 7, 1972. See also note under 1-c below. It was further amended to extend to unmarried persons the $3,000 ad valorem exemption on homesteads. Submitted by Sixty-third Legislature (1973) and adopted in election Nov. 6, 1973. See also Art. XVI, Secs. 50, 51 and 52. It was further amended to give added tax relief to disabled persons and persons over sixty-five and to provide for administration of property tax. It also added Subsections (c) and (d). (See also Sec. 1, Sec. 21, and Sec. 23 of Art. VIII.) Submitted by Sixty-fifth Legislature (1977) and adopted in election Nov. 7, 1978. It was again amended to add subsection (e) to authorize political subdivisions to provide property tax relief for owners of residence homesteads and changing certain property tax administrative procedures. (See also Sec. 21, Subsection (c) of Art. VIII.) Submitted by Sixty-seventh Legislature (1981) and adopted in election Nov. 3, 1981.]

Sec. 1-c. **Optional Provisions Relating to Sec. 1-a and Sec. 1-b** — Provided, however, the terms of this resolution shall not be effective unless House Joint Resolution No. 24 is adopted by the people and in no event shall this resolution go into effect until January 1, 1951.

[Note — Sec. 1-b and Sec. 1-c were added because of an oversight in writing the text of Sec. 1-a (adopted by joint resolution at an earlier date) which would have abolished the $3,000 homestead exemption under the state school tax on adoption of Sec. 1-a by the people. Submitted by the Fiftieth Legislature (1947) and adopted in election Nov. 2, 1948.]

Sec. 1-d. **Taxation of Agricultural Land** — (a) All land owned by natural persons which is designated for agricultural use in accordance with the provisions of this section shall be assessed for all tax purposes on the consideration of only those factors relative to such agricultural use. "Agricultural use" means the raising of livestock or growing of crops, fruit, flowers, and other products of the soil under natural conditions as a business venture for profit, which business is the primary occupation and source of income of the owner.

(b) For each assessment year the owner wishes to qualify his land under provisions of this section as designated for agricultural use he shall file with the local tax assessor a sworn statement in writing describing the use to which the land is devoted.

(c) Upon receipt of the sworn statement in writing the local tax assessor shall determine whether or not such land qualifies for the designation as to agricultural use as defined herein and in the event it so qualifies he shall designate such land as being for agricultural use and assess the land accordingly.

(d) Such local tax assessor may inspect the land and require such evidence of use and source of income as may be necessary or useful in determining whether or not the agricultural use provision of this article applies.

(e) No land may qualify for the designation provided for in this act unless for at least three (3) successive years immediately preceding the assessment date the land has been devoted exclusively for agricultural use, or unless the land has been continuously developed for agriculture during such time.

(f) Each year during which the land is designated for agricultural use, the local tax assessor shall note on his records the valuation which would have been made had the land not qualified for such designation under this section. If designated land is subsequently diverted to a purpose other than that of agricultural use, or is sold, the land shall be subject to an additional tax. The additional tax shall equal the

Article VIII — (Cont'd.)

difference between taxes paid or payable, hereunder, and the amount of tax payable for the preceding three years had the land been otherwise assessed. Until paid, there shall be a lien for additional taxes and interest on land assessed under the provisions of this section.

(g) The valuation and assessment of any minerals or sub-surface rights to minerals shall not come within the provisions of this section.

[Note — The foregoing Sec. 1-d of Art. VIII, an amendment, was added for the stated purpose of providing that all land designated for agricultural use be assessed only as such. Submitted by the Fifty-ninth Legislature (1965) and adopted in an election Nov. 8, 1966.]

Sec. 1-d-1. **Open-Space Land Taxation** — (a) To promote the preservation of open-space land, the legislature shall provide by general law for taxation of open-space land devoted to farm or ranch purposes on the basis of its productive capacity and may provide by general law for taxation of open-space land devoted to timber production on the basis of its productive capacity. The legislature by general law may provide eligibility limitations under this section and may impose sanctions in furtherance of the taxation policy of this section.

(b) If a property owner qualifies his land for designation for agricultural use under Section 1-d of this article, the land is subject to the provisions of Section 1-d for the year in which the designation is effective and is not subject to a law enacted under this Section 1-d-1 in that year.

[Note — The foregoing Sec. 1-d-1 of Art. VIII is an amendment to promote preservation of open-space land and to provide for taxation of production of timber thereon; also redefines use of open land for agricultural purposes and taxation thereon. Submitted by the Sixty-fifth Legislature (1977) and adopted in election Nov. 7, 1978.]

Sec. 1-e. **Gradual Abolition of Ad Valorem Tax** — (1) No State ad valorem taxes shall be levied upon any property within this State.

(2) All receipts from previously authorized State ad valorem taxes that are collected on or after the effective date of the 1982 amendment to this section shall be deposited to the credit of the general fund of the county collecting the taxes and may be expended for county purposes. Receipts from taxes collected before that date shall be distributed by the Legislature among institutions eligible to receive distributions under prior law. Those receipts and receipts distributed under prior law may be expended for the purposes provided under prior law or for repair and renovation of existing permanent improvements.

[Note — Sec. 1-e of Art. VIII was added to provide for the gradual abolition of the ad valorem tax for all state purposes except those that were listed under Art. VII, Sec. 17 (which was repealed by constitutional amendment in an election Nov. 2, 1982) for certain institutions of higher education and for pension funds for Confederate veterans and their widows, and for Texas Rangers and their widows. Submitted by the Sixtieth Legislature (1967) and adopted in an election Nov. 5, 1968. Sec. 1-e was amended to abolish the state property tax and to add Subsection (2), which is self-explanatory. Submitted by Called Session of the Sixty-seventh Legislature (1982) and adopted in election Nov. 2, 1982. (See also Art. III, Sec. 51 and Art. XVI, Sec. 66.)]

Sec. 1-f. **Ad Valorem Tax Relief** — The legislature by law may provide for the preservation of cultural, historical, or natural history resources by:

(1) granting exemptions or other relief from state ad valorem taxes on appropriate property so designated in the manner prescribed by law; and

(2) authorizing political subdivisions to grant exemptions or other relief from ad valorem taxes on appropriate property so designated by the political subdivision in the manner prescribed by general law.

[Note — Sec. 1-f of Art. VIII was added to authorize tax relief to preserve certain cultural, historical or natural history resources. Submitted by the Sixty-fifth Legislature (1977) and adopted in election Nov. 8, 1977.]

Sec. 1-g. **Tax Relief to Encourage Development and Improvement of Property** — (a) The legislature by general law may authorize cities, towns, and other taxing units to grant exemptions or other relief from ad valorem taxes on property located in a reinvestment zone for the purpose of encouraging development or redevelopment and improvement of the property.

(b) The Legislature by general law may authorize an incorporated city or town to issue bonds or notes to finance the development or redevelopment of an unproductive, undeveloped, or blighted area within the city or town and to

pledge for repayment of those bonds or notes increases in ad valorem tax revenues imposed on property in the area by the city or town and other political subdivisions.

[Note — Sec. 1-g of Art. VIII was added to encourage development and improvement of certain areas through tax relief. Submitted by the Sixty-seventh Legislature (1981) and adopted in election Nov. 3, 1981.]

Sec. 1-h — **Validation of Assessment Ratio** — Sec. 26.03, Tax Code, is validated as of January 1, 1980.

[Note — Sec. 1-h of Art. VIII, an amendment, was added to give validation date of Sec. 26.03 of the Tax Code. Submitted by Called Session of the Sixty-seventh Legislature (1982) and adopted in election Nov. 2, 1982.]

Sec. 1-i. — The legislature by general law may provide ad valorem tax relief for mobile marine drilling equipment designed for offshore drilling of oil or gas wells that is being stored while not in use in a county bordering on the Gulf of Mexico or on a bay or other body of water immediately adjacent to the Gulf of Mexico.

[Note — The foregoing Sec. 1-i of Art. VIII, an amendment, was added to provide ad valorem tax relief for certain offshore drilling equipment that is not in use. Submitted by the Seventieth Legislature (1987) and adopted in an election Nov. 3, 1987.]

Sec. 1-j. (a) To promote economic development in the State, goods, wares, merchandise, other tangible personal property, and ores, other than oil, natural gas, and other petroleum products, are exempt from ad valorem taxation if:

(1) the property is acquired in or imported into this State to be forwarded outside this State, whether or not the intention to forward the property outside this State is formed or the destination to which the property is forwarded is specified when the property is acquired in or imported into this State:

(2) the property is detained in this State for assembling, storing, manufacturing, processing, or fabricating purposes by the person who acquired or imported the property; and

(3) the property is transported outside of this State not later than 175 days after the date the person acquired or imported the property in this State.

(b) Tangible personal property exempted from taxation in Subsection (a) of this section is subject to the following:

(1) A county, common, or independent school district, junior college district, or municipality, including a home-rule city, may tax such property otherwise exempt, if the governing body of the county, common, or independent school district, junior college district, or municipality takes official action as provided in this section and in the manner provided by law to provide for the taxation of such property.

(2) Any official action to tax such exempt property must be taken before April 1, 1990. If official action is taken to tax such exempt property before January 1, 1990, such property is taxable effective for the tax year 1990. However, if such official action to tax such exempt property is taken prior to April 1, 1990, but after January 1, 1990, the official action shall not become effective to tax such property until the 1991 tax year.

(3) Any of the above-named political subdivisions shall have the authority to exempt from payment of taxation such property located in such above-named political subdivisions for the taxing year 1989. If a governing body exempts the property from 1989 taxes, the governing body shall waive 1989 taxes already imposed and refund 1989 taxes already paid on such property for that year.

(4) The governing body of a county, common, or independent school district, junior college district, or municipality that acts under Subdivision (2) of Subsection (b) of this section to tax the property otherwise exempt by Subsection (a) of this section may subsequently exempt the property from taxation by rescinding its action to tax the property. The exemption applies to each tax year that begins after the date the action is taken and applies to the tax year in which the action is taken if the governing body so provides. A governing body that rescinds its action to tax the property may not take action to tax such property after the rescission.

(c) For purposes of this section:

(1) tangible personal property shall include aircraft and aircraft parts:

(2) property imported into this State shall include property brought into this State;

(3) property forwarded outside this State shall include property transported outside this State or to be affixed to an aircraft to be transported outside this State; and

(4) property detained in this State for assembling, storing, manufacturing, processing, or fabricating purposes shall include property, aircraft, or aircraft parts brought into this State or acquired in this State and used by the per-

Article VIII — (Cont'd.)

son who acquired the property, aircraft, or aircraft parts in or who brought the property, aircraft, or aircraft parts into this State for the purpose of repair or maintenance of aircraft operated by a certificated air carrier.

[Note — The foregoing Sec. 1-j of Art. VIII, an amendment, was added to authorize the exemption from ad valorem taxation of certain personal property temporarily in the state for certain purposes. (See related amendment in Sec. 1 (a) of Art. VIII.) Proposed by Seventy-first Legislature (1989) and adopted in an election Nov. 7, 1989.]

Sec. 2. **Occupation Taxes Equal and Uniform; Exemptions Therefrom** — (a) All occupation taxes shall be equal and uniform upon the same class of subjects within the limits of the authority levying the tax; but the Legislature may, by general laws, exempt from taxation public property used for public purposes; actual places of religious worship, also any property owned by a church or by a strictly religious society for the exclusive use as a dwelling place for the ministry of such church or religious society, and which yields no revenue whatever to such church or religious society; provided that such exemption shall not extend to more property than is reasonably necessary for a dwelling place and in no event more than one acre of land; places of burial not held for private or corporate profit; solar or wind-powered energy devices; all buildings used exclusively and owned by persons or associations of persons for school purposes and the necessary furniture of all schools and property used exclusively and reasonably necessary in conducting any association engaged in promoting the religious, educational and physical development of boys, girls, young men or young women operating under a State or National organization of like character; also, the endowment funds of such institutions of learning and religion not used with a view to profit; and when the same are invested in bonds or mortgages, or in land or other property which has been and shall hereafter be bought in by such institutions under foreclosure sales made to satisfy or protect such bonds or mortgages, that such exemption of such land and property shall continue only for two years after the purchase of the same at such sale by such institutions and no longer, and institutions of purely public charity; and all laws exempting property from taxation other than the property mentioned in this Section shall be null and void.

(b) The Legislature may, by general law, exempt property owned by a disabled veteran or by the surviving spouse and surviving minor children of a disabled veteran. A disabled veteran is a veteran of the armed services of the United States who is classified as disabled by the Veterans Administration or by a successor to that agency; or the military service in which he served. A veteran who is certified as having a disability of less than 10 per cent is not entitled to an exemption. A veteran having a disability rating of not less than 10 per cent nor more than 30 per cent may be granted an exemption from taxation for property valued at up to $1,500. A veteran having a disability rating of more than 30 per cent but not more than 50 per cent may be granted an exemption from taxation for property valued at up to $2,000. A veteran having a disability rating of more than 50 per cent but not more than 70 per cent may be granted an exemption from taxation for property valued at up to $2,500. A veteran who has a disability rating of more than 70 per cent, or a veteran who has a disability rating of not less than 10 per cent and has attained the age of 65, or a disabled veteran whose disability consists of the loss or loss of use of one or more limbs, total blindness in one or both eyes, or paraplegia, may be granted an exemption from taxation for property valued at up to $3,000. The spouse and children of any member of the United States Armed Forces who loses his life while on active duty will be granted an exemption from taxation for property valued at up to $2,500. A deceased disabled veteran's surviving spouse and children may be granted an exemption which in the aggregate is equal to the exemption to which the decedent was entitled at the time he died.

(c) The Legislature by general law may exempt from ad valorem taxation property that is owned by a nonprofit organization composed primarily of members or former members of the armed forces of the United States or its allies and chartered or incorporated by the United States Congress.

[Note — Sec. 2 or Art. VIII has been amended five times as follows: (1) Adding clause with reference to endowment fund. Submitted by the Twenty-ninth Legislature (1905); ratified Nov. 6, 1906, and proclaimed adopted Jan. 7, 1907. (2) Permitting exemption of ministers' dwellings and certain other property of religious organizations, the original amendment having provided only for exemption for "actual places of worship." Submitted by the Fortieth Legislature (1927); ratified Nov. 6, 1928; proclaimed Feb. 6, 1929. (3) To allow certain tax exemptions to disabled veterans, their surviving spouses and surviving minor children and to survivors of members of the armed forces who lose their life while on active duty. Submitted by the Sixty-second Legislature (1971) and adopted in an election Nov. 7, 1972. (4) Authorizing Legislature to exempt from taxation solar and wind-powered energy devices. Submitted by the Sixty-fifth

Legislature (1977) and adopted in election Nov. 7, 1978. (5) Authorizing the legislature to exempt from ad valorem taxation certain property of non-profit veterans organizations. Submitted by Seventy-first Legislature (1989) and adopted in an election Nov. 7, 1989.]

Sec. 3. **Taxes to Be Collected for Public Purposes Only** — Taxes shall be levied and collected by general laws and for public purposes only.

Sec. 4. **Power to Tax Corporations Not to Be Surrendered** — The power to tax corporations and corporate property shall not be surrendered or suspended by act of the Legislature, by any contract or grant to which the State shall be a party.

Sec. 5. **Railroad Taxes Due Cities and Towns** — All property of railroad companies, of whatever description lying or being within the limits of any city or incorporated town within this State, shall bear its proportionate share of municipal taxation, and if any such property shall not have been heretofore rendered, the authorities of the city or town within which it lies shall have power to require its rendition and collect the usual municipal tax thereon, as on other property lying within said municipality.

Sec. 6. **Appropriations; How Made and for What Period** — No money shall be drawn from the Treasury but in pursuance of specific appropriations made by law; nor shall any appropriation of money be made for a longer term than two years, except by the First Legislature to assemble under this Constitution, which may make the necessary appropriations to carry on the government until the assembling of the Sixteenth Legislature.

Sec. 7. **Special Funds Not to Be Borrowed or Diverted** — The Legislature shall not have power to borrow, or in any manner divert from its purpose any special fund that may, or ought to, come into the Treasury; and shall make it penal for any person or persons to borrow, withhold or in any manner to divert from its purpose, any special fund or any part thereof.

Sec. 7-a. **Net Motor License Fees and Motor Fuel Tax Revenues Restricted, Except One Fourth of Fuel Taxes to Schools, to Highway Improvement Policing and Administration** — Subject to legislative appropriation, allocation and direction, all net revenues remaining after payment of all refunds allowed by law and expenses of collection derived from motor vehicle registration fees, and all taxes, except gross production and ad valorem taxes, on motor fuels and lubricants used to propel motor vehicles over public roadways, shall be used for the sole purpose of acquiring rights of way, constructing, maintaining, and policing such public roadways and for the administration of such laws as may be prescribed by the Legislature pertaining to the supervision of traffic and safety on such roads; and for the payment of the principal and interest on county and road district bonds or warrants voted or issued prior to January 2, 1939, and declared eligible prior to January 2, 1945, for payment out of the County and Road District Highway Fund under existing law, provided, however, that one fourth (¼) of such net revenue from the motor fuel tax shall be allocated to the Available School Fund; and, provided, however, that the net revenue derived by counties from motor vehicle registration fees shall never be less than the maximum amounts allowed to be retained by each county and the percentage allowed to be retained by each county under the laws in effect on January 1, 1945. Nothing contained herein shall be construed as authorizing the pledging of the State's credit for any purpose.

[Note — Sec. 7-a of Art. VIII is an amendment, restricting revenues from motor vehicle registration and motor fuel taxes to the stated purposes of highway improvement, policing and administration. Submitted by the Forty-ninth Legislature (1945), ratified in an election Nov. 5, 1946.]

Sec. 7-b. All revenues received from the federal government as reimbursement for state expenditures of funds that are themselves dedicated for acquiring rights-of-way and constructing, maintaining, and policing public roadways are also constitutionally dedicated and shall be used only for those purposes.

[Note — Sec. 7-b of Art. VIII, an amendment, provides for the dedication of certain funds for highway purposes. Submitted by the Seventieth Legislature (1987) and adopted in an election Nov. 8, 1988.]

Sec. 8. **Railroad Property; How Assessed** — All property of railroad companies shall be assessed, and the taxes collected in the several counties in which said property is situated, including so much of the roadbed and fixtures as shall be in each county. The rolling stock may be assessed in gross in the county where the principal office of the company is located, and the county tax paid upon it shall be apportioned

Article VIII — (Cont'd.)

as provided by general law in proportion to the distance such road may run through any such county, among the several counties through which the road passes, as part of their tax assets.

[Note — The foregoing Sec. 8 of Art. VIII, an amendment, was added to allow Legislature to provide by general law for apportionment of value of railroad rolling stock among counties for purposes of property taxation. Submitted by Sixty-ninth Legislature (1985) and adopted in an election Nov. 4, 1986.]

Sec. 9. **Rate of State and Municipal Taxation** — The State tax on property, exclusive of the tax necessary to pay the public debt, and of the taxes provided for the benefit of the public free school, shall never exceed thirty-five cents (35c) on the One Hundred Dollars ($100) valuation; and no county, city or town shall levy a tax rate in excess of Eighty Cents (80c) on the One Hundred Dollars ($100) valuation in any one (1) year for general fund, permanent improvement fund, road and bridge fund and jury fund purposes; provided further that at the time the Commissioners Court meets to levy the annual tax rate for each county it shall levy whatever tax rate may be needed for the four (4) constitutional purposes; namely, general fund, permanent improvement fund, road and bridge fund and jury fund so long as the Court does not impair any outstanding bonds or other obligations and so long as the total of the foregoing tax levies does not exceed Eighty Cents (80c) on the One Hundred Dollars ($100) valuation in any one (1) year. Once the Court has levied the annual tax rate, the same shall remain in force and effect during that taxable year; and the Legislature may also authorize an additional annual ad valorem tax to be levied and collected for the further maintenance of the public roads; provided that a majority of the qualified property tax-paying voters of the county voting at an election to be held for that purpose shall vote such tax, not to exceed fifteen cents (15c) on the One Hundred Dollars ($100) valuation of the property subject to taxation in such county. Any county may put all tax money collected by the county into one general fund, without regard to the purpose or source of each tax. And the Legislature may pass local laws for the maintenance of the public roads and highways, without the local notice required for special or local laws. This section shall not be construed as a limitation of powers delegated to counties, cities or towns by any other section or sections of this Constitution.

[Note — The foregoing Sec. 9 of Art. VIII has been amended seven times as follows: (1) To lower State tax rate from 50c to 35c, a separate State school tax having been provided by companion amendment, Sec. 3 of Art. VII. Submitted by Eighteenth Legislature (1883), ratified in an election Aug. 14, 1883, and declared adopted Sept. 25, 1883. (2) To authorize Legislature to provide for a 15c local road tax. Submitted by Twenty-first Legislature (1889), ratified in an election Nov. 3, 1890, and declared adopted Dec. 19, 1890. (3) To authorize 15c tax for jurors. Submitted by Twenty-ninth Legislature (1905), ratified in an election Nov. 6, 1906, and declared adopted Jan. 7, 1907. (4) Providing that County Commissioners "may re-allocate the foregoing county taxes by changing the rates provided for any of the foregoing purposes" if approved by "a majority of the qualified property taxpaying voters," but restricting the period to six years, and restricting total to 80c on the $100 valuation. Submitted by Forty-eighth Legislature and adopted in an election Nov. 7, 1944. (5) Abolishing ad valorem tax for State general revenue fund purposes, and making other provisions. (See Sec. 1-a of Art. VIII and note thereon.) Submitted by Fiftieth Legislature (1947) and adopted in election Nov. 2, 1948. (6) Giving Commissioners Court authority to levy whatever sums may be necessary for general fund purposes, permanent improvement fund purposes, road and bridge purposes and jury purposes, so long as total of these tax rates does not exceed 80c on the $100 valuation in any one year. Submitted by Fifty-fourth Legislature (1955) and adopted in election Nov. 6, 1956. (7) To allow counties to put all county taxes into one general fund. Submitted by Sixtieth Legislature (1967) and adopted in election Nov. 11, 1967.]

Sec. 10. **Taxes Not to Be Released Except by Two-Thirds Vote of Each House** — The Legislature shall have no power to release the inhabitants of, or property in, any county, city or town, from the payment of taxes levied for State or county purposes, unless in case of great public calamity in any such county, city or town, when such release may be made by a vote of two-thirds of each house of the Legislature.

Sec. 11. **Where Property Is to Be Assessed** — All property, whether owned by persons or corporations, shall be assessed for taxation and the taxes paid in the county where situated, but the Legislature may by a two-thirds vote authorize the payment of taxes of non-residents of counties to be made at the office of the Comptroller of Public Accounts. And all lands and other property not rendered for taxation by the owner thereof shall be assessed at its fair value by the proper officer.

[Note — Sec. 12 of Art. VIII, relating to unorganized

counties, was deleted by constitutional amendment in election Aug. 5, 1969.]

Sec. 13. **Tax Sales; Tax Deeds; Redemptions** — Provision shall be made by the first Legislature for the speedy sale, without the necessity of a suit in court, of a sufficient portion of all lands and other property for the taxes due thereon, and every year thereafter for the sale, in like manner, of all lands and other property upon which the taxes have not been paid; and the deed of conveyance to the purchaser for all lands and other property thus sold shall be held to vest a good and perfect title in the purchaser thereof, subject to be impeached only for actual fraud; provided, that the former owner shall within two years from date of filing for record of purchaser's deed have the right to redeem the land upon the following basis:

(1) Within the first year of the redemption period upon the payment of the amount of money paid for the land, including one ($1) dollar tax deed recording fee and all taxes, penalties, interest and costs paid plus not exceeding twenty-five (25%) percent of the aggregate total;

(2) Within the last year of the redemption period upon the payment of the amount of money paid for the land, including one ($1) dollar tax deed recording fee and all taxes, penalties, interest and costs paid plus not exceeding fifty (50%) percent of the aggregate total.

[Note — The foregoing Sec. 13 of Art. VIII was amended to insert the provisions for redemption given above for the original clause, which provided for "double the amount of money paid for the land" to be paid by the original owner for redemption. Submitted by the Forty-second Legislature (1931), and adopted in an election Nov. 8, 1932. Proclaimed July 26, 1933.]

Sec. 14. **County Tax Assessor and Collector** — Except as provided in Sec. 16 of this Article, there shall be elected by the qualified electors of each county an Assessor and Collector of Taxes, who shall hold his office for four years and until his successor is elected and qualified; and such Assessor and Collector of Taxes shall perform all the duties with respect to assessing property for the purpose of taxation and of collecting taxes as may be prescribed by the Legislature.

[Note — Sec. 14 of Art. VIII was first amended to consolidate offices of Tax Assessor and Tax Collector. (See also Sec. 16.) Submitted by the Forty-second Legislature (1931), and adopted in an election Nov. 8, 1932. Proclaimed Jan. 9, 1933. It was again amended to change term of office from two to four years. Submitted by the Forty-third Legislature (1953) and adopted in election Nov. 2, 1954.]

Sec. 15. **Tax Liens and Sales** — The annual assessment made upon landed property shall be a special lien thereon; and all property, both real and personal, belonging to any delinquent taxpayer shall be liable to seizure and sale for the payment of all the taxes and penalties due by such delinquent, and such property may be sold for the payment of the taxes and penalties due by such delinquent, under such regulations as the Legislature may provide.

Sec. 16. **Sheriff to Be County Tax Assessor-Collector in Some Counties** — The Sheriff of each county, in addition to his other duties, shall be the Assessor and Collector of Taxes therefor. But in counties having ten thousand (10,000) or more inhabitants, to be determined by the last preceding census of the United States, an Assessor and Collector of Taxes shall be elected, as provided in Sec. 14 of this Article and shall hold office for four years and until his successor shall be elected and qualified.

[Note — Sec. 16 of Art. VIII was first amended to harmonize with section consolidating offices of Assessor and Collector of Taxes. (See also Sec. 14.) Submitted by the Forty-second Legislature (1931) and adopted in an election Nov. 8, 1932. Proclaimed Jan. 9, 1933. It was again amended to change term of office from two to four years. Submitted by the Fifty-third Legislature (1953) and adopted in election Nov. 2, 1954.]

Sec. 16-a. **Assessor-Collector of Taxes in Counties of Less Than Ten Thousand** — In any county having a population of less than ten thousand (10,000) inhabitants, as determined by last preceding census of the United States, the Commissioners' Court may submit to the qualified property taxpaying voters of such county at an election the question of adding an Assessor-Collector of Taxes to the list of authorized county officials. If a majority of such voters voting in such election shall approve of adding an Assessor-Collector of Taxes to such list, then such official shall be elected at the next General Election for such Constitutional term of office as is provided for other Tax Assessor-Collectors in this State.

Article VIII — (Cont'd.); Article IX

[Note — The foregoing Sec. 16-a of Art. VIII, an amendment, was added for the stated purpose of providing for a Tax Assessor-Collector in counties of less than 10,000 population. Submitted by the Fifty-third Legislature (1953) and adopted in an election Nov. 2, 1954.]

Sec. 17. **Power of Legislature as to Taxes** — The specification of the objects and subjects of taxation shall not deprive the Legislature of the power to require other subjects or objects to be taxed, in such manner as may be consistent with the principles of taxation fixed in this Constitution.

Sec. 18. **Equalization of Taxes** — (a) The Legislature shall provide for equalizing, as near as may be, the valuation of all property subject to or rendered for taxation and may also provide for the classification of all lands with reference to their value in the several counties.

(b) A single appraisal within each county of all property subject to ad valorem taxation by the county and all other taxing units located therein shall be provided by general law. The Legislature, by general law, may authorize appraisals outside a county when political subdivisions are situated in more than one county or when two or more counties elect to consolidate appraisal services.

(c) The Legislature, by general law, shall provide for a single board of equalization for each appraisal entity consisting of qualified persons residing within the territory appraised by that entity. Members of the board of equalization may not be elected officials of the county or of the governing body of a taxing unit.

(d) The Legislature shall prescribe by general law the methods, timing and administrative process for implementing the requirements of this section.

[Note — Sec. 18 of Art. VIII was amended to provide for a single appraisal and a single board of equalization within each county for ad valorem tax purposes. Submitted by the Sixty-sixth Legislature (1979) and adopted in election Nov. 4, 1980.]

Sec. 19. **Farm Products in the Hands of the Producer Exempt From All Taxation** — Farm products, livestock, and poultry in the hands of the producer, and family supplies for home and farm use, are exempt from all taxation until otherwise directed by a two-thirds vote of all the members *elect to both houses of the Legislature.

*Explanatory Note — Expressed thus in official draft of Constitution.

[Note — The foregoing Sec. 19 of Art. VIII, an amendment, was added for the stated purpose of exempting farm products from taxation. Submitted by the Sixteenth Legislature (1879); ratified in an election Sept. 2, 1879, and declared adopted Oct. 14, 1879. It was amended to change the wording to include livestock and poultry with farm products as exempt from taxation. Submitted by the Sixty-seventh Legislature (1981) and adopted in election Nov. 3, 1981.]

Sec. 19-a. **Farm Implements Exempt From Taxation** — Implements of husbandry that are used in the production of farm or ranch products are exempt from ad valorem taxation.

[Note — The foregoing Sec. 19-a of Art. VIII, an amendment, was added to exempt implements of farm husbandry from ad valorem taxation. Submitted by Called Session of the Sixty-seventh Legislature (1982) and adopted in election Nov. 2, 1982.]

Sec. 20. **Limiting Ad Valorem Tax Assessment; Discount for Prompt Payment of Taxes** — No property of any kind in this State shall ever be assessed for ad valorem taxes at a greater value than its fair cash market value nor shall any Board of Equalization of any governmental or political subdivision or taxing district within this State fix the value of any property for tax purposes at more than its fair cash market value; provided, that in order to encourage the prompt payment of taxes, the Legislature shall have the power to provide that the taxpayer shall be allowed by the State and all governmental and political subdivisions and taxing districts of the State a three per cent discount on ad valorem taxes due the State or due any governmental or political subdivision or taxing district of the State if such taxes are paid ninety days before the date when they would otherwise become delinquent; and the taxpayer shall be allowed a two per cent discount on said taxes if paid sixty days before said taxes would become delinquent; and the taxpayer shall be allowed a one per cent discount if said taxes are paid thirty days before they would otherwise become delinquent. This amendment shall be effective Jan. 1, 1939. The Legislature shall pass necessary laws for the proper administration of this Section.

[Note — The foregoing Sec. 20 of Art. VIII, an amendment, was added (1) to restrict assessed value to true market value, and (2) to provide for stated discounts for prepayment of taxes. Adopted in an election Aug. 23, 1937.]

Sec. 21. **Limitation on Property Taxes** — (a) Subject to any exceptions prescribed by general law, the total amount of property taxes imposed by a political subdivision in any year may not exceed the total amount of property taxes imposed by that subdivision in the preceding year unless the governing body of the subdivision gives notice of its intent to consider an increase in taxes and holds a public hearing on the proposed increase before it increases those total taxes. The legislature shall prescribe by law the form, content, timing, and methods of giving the notice and the rules for the conduct of the hearing.

(b) In calculating the total amount of taxes imposed in the current year for the purposes of Subsection (a) of this section, the taxes on property in territory added to the political subdivision since the preceding year and on new improvements that were not taxable in the preceding year are excluded. In calculating the total amount of taxes imposed in the preceding year for the purposes of Subsection (a) of this section, the taxes imposed on real property that is not taxable by the subdivision in the current year are excluded.

(c) The Legislature by general law shall require that, subject to reasonable exceptions, a property owner be given notice of a revaluation of his property and a reasonable estimate of the amount of taxes that would be imposed on his property if the total amount of property taxes for the subdivision were not increased according to any law enacted pursuant to Subsection (a) of this section. The notice must be given before the procedures required in Subsection (a) are instituted.

[Note—The foregoing Sec. 21 of Art. VIII, an amendment, was added to limit increases in property revaluation and to prescribe method of giving notice before property revaluated. (See also Sec. 1, Sec. 1-b and Sec. 23 of Art. VIII.) Submitted by the Sixty-fifth Legislature (1977) and adopted in election Nov. 7, 1978. It was further amended to change wording of administrative procedures in notifying property owners. (See also Subsection (e) of Section 1-b of Art. VIII.) Submitted by the Sixty-seventh Legislature (1981) and adopted in election Nov. 3, 1981.]

Sec. 22. **State Tax Revenues** — (a) In no biennium shall the rate of growth of appropriations from state tax revenues not dedicated by this constitution exceed the estimated rate of growth of the state's economy. The Legislature shall provide by general law procedures to implement this subsection.

(b) If the Legislature by adoption of a resolution approved by a record vote of a majority of the members of each house finds that an emergency exists and identifies the nature of the emergency, the Legislature may provide for appropriations in excess of the amount authorized by Subsection (a) of this section. The excess authorized under this subsection may not exceed the amount specified in the resolution.

(c) In no case shall appropriations exceed revenues as provided in Article III, Sec. 49-a, of this constitution. Nothing in this section shall be construed to alter, amend, or repeal Article III, Sec. 49-a, of this constitution.

[Note—The foregoing Sec. 22 of Art. VIII, an amendment, was added to limit the rate of growth of appropriations from state tax revenues; and to provide for emergency spending by state. (See also Sec. 49-a of Art. III. Submitted by the Sixty-fifth Legislature (1977) and adopted in election Nov. 7, 1978.]

Sec. 23. **No Statewide Real Property Appraisal** — (a) There shall be no statewide appraisal of real property for ad valorem tax purposes; however, this shall not preclude formula distribution of tax revenues to political subdivisions of the state.

(b) Administrative and judicial enforcement of uniform standards and procedures for appraisal of property for ad valorem tax purposes, as prescribed by general law, shall originate in the county where the tax is imposed, except that the Legislature may provide by general law for political subdivisions with boundaries extending outside the county.

[Note — The foregoing Sec. 23 of Art. VIII, an amendment, was added to prohibit a statewide appraisal of real property for ad valorem tax purposes; but allows local subdivisions to administer tax rate. (See also Sec. 1, Sec. 1-b, Sec. 21 of Art. VIII.) Submitted by the Sixty-fifth Legislature (1977) and adopted in election Nov. 7, 1978.]

ARTICLE IX — COUNTIES

Sec. 1. **Creation and Organization of Counties; Changing of County Lines** — The Legislature shall have power to create counties for the convenience of the people, subject to the following provisions:

Article IX — (Cont'd.)

First. In the territory of the State exterior to all counties now existing, no new counties shall be created with a less area than 900 square miles in a square form, unless prevented by pre-existing boundary lines. Should the State lines render this impracticable in border counties, the area may be less. The territory referred to may, at any time, in whole or in part, be divided into counties in advance of population and attached for judicial and land surveying purposes to the most convenient organized county or counties.

Second. Within the territory of any county or counties now existing, no new county shall be created with a less area than 700 square miles, nor shall any such county now existing be reduced to a less area than 700 square miles. No new counties shall be created so as to approach nearer than twelve miles of the county seat of any county from which it may, in whole or in part, be taken. Counties of a less area than 900, but of 700 or more square miles, within counties now existing, may be created by a two-thirds vote of each house of the Legislature, taken by yeas and nays, and entered on the journals. Any county now existing may be reduced to an area of not less than 700 square miles by a like two-thirds vote. When any part of a county is stricken off and attached to or created into another county, the part stricken off shall be holden for and obliged to pay its proportion of all the liabilities then existing of the county from which it was taken, in such manner as may be prescribed by law.

Third. No part of any existing county shall be detached from it and attached to another existing county until the proposition for such change shall have been submitted, in such manner as may be provided by law, to a vote of the electors of both counties, and shall have received a majority of those voting on the question in each.

Sec. 1-a. **Regulation of Travel on Gulf Coast Beaches** — The Legislature may authorize the governing body of any county bordering on the Gulf of Mexico or the tidewater limits thereof to regulate and restrict the speed, parking and travel of motor vehicles on beaches available to the public by virtue of public right and the littering of such beaches.

Nothing in this amendment shall increase the rights of any riparian or littoral landowner with regard to beaches available to the public by virtue of public right or submerged lands.

The Legislature may enact any laws not inconsistent with this Section which it may deem necessary to permit said counties to implement, enforce and administer the provisions contained herein.

[Note — The foregoing Sec. 1-a of Art. IX, an amendment, was added to authorize regulation of travel on Gulf Coast beaches open to the public. Submitted by the Fifty-seventh Legislature (1961) and adopted in election Nov. 6, 1962.]

County Seats

Sec. 2. **How County Seats Are Created and Changed** — The Legislature shall pass laws regulating the manner of removing county seats, but no county seat situated within five miles of the geographical center of the county shall be removed except by a vote of two-thirds of all electors voting on the subject. A majority of such electors, however, voting at such election, may remove a county seat from a point more than five miles from a geographical center of the county to a point within five miles of such center, in either case the center to be determined by a certificate from the Commissioner of the General Land Office.

[Note — Sec. 3 of Art. IX, relating to home rule, was deleted by constitutional amendment in election Aug. 5, 1969.]

Sec. 4. **County-Wide Hospital Districts** — The Legislature may by law authorize the creation of county-wide Hospital Districts in counties having a population in excess of 190,000 and in Galveston County, with power to issue bonds for the purchase, acquisition, construction, maintenance and operation of any county-owned hospital, or where the hospital system is jointly operated by a county and city within the county, and to provide for the transfer to the county-wide hospital district of the title to any land, buildings or equipment, jointly or separately owned, and for the assumption by the district of any outstanding bonded indebtedness theretofore issued by any county or city for the establishment of hospitals or hospital facilities; to levy a tax not to exceed seventy-five (75c) cents on the One Hundred ($100.00) Dollars valuation of all taxable property within such district, provided, however, that such district shall be approved at an election held for that purpose, and that only qualified, property taxpaying voters in such county shall vote therein; provided further, that such hospital district shall assume full responsibility for providing medical and hospital care to needy inhabitants of the county, and thereafter such county and cities therein shall not levy any other tax for hospital purposes; and provided further that should such hospital district construct, maintain and support a hospital or hospital system, that the same shall never become a charge against the State of Texas, nor shall any direct appropriation ever be made by the Legislature for the construction, maintenance or improvement of the said hospital or hospitals. Should the Legislature enact enabling laws in anticipation of the adoption of this amendment, such acts shall not be invalid because of their anticipatory character.

[Note — The foregoing Sec. 4 of Art. IX, an amendment, was added to the Constitution for the purpose of providing for county-wide hospital districts. Submitted by the Fifty-third Legislature (1953) and adopted in election Nov. 2, 1954.]

Sec. 5 (a). The Legislature may by law authorize the creation of two hospital districts, one to be coextensive with and have the same boundaries as the incorporated City of Amarillo, as such boundaries now exist or as they may hereafter be lawfully extended, and the other to be coextensive with Wichita County.

If such district or districts are created, they may be authorized to levy a tax not to exceed Seventy-five Cents (75c) on the One Hundred Dollars ($100.00) valuation of taxable property within the district; provided, however no tax may be levied until approved by a majority vote of the participating resident qualified property taxpaying voters who have duly rendered their property for taxation. The maximum rate of tax may be changed at subsequent elections so long as obligations are not impaired, and not to exceed the maximum limit of Seventy-five Cents (75c) per One Hundred Dollars ($100.00) valuation, and no election shall be required by subsequent changes in the boundaries of the City of Amarillo.

If such tax is authorized, no political subdivision or municipality within or having the same boundaries as the district may levy a tax for medical or hospital care for needy individuals, nor shall they maintain or erect hospital facilities, but the district shall by resolution assume all such responsibilities and shall assume all of the liabilities and obligations (including bonds and warrants) of such subdivisions or municipalities or both. The maximum tax rate submitted shall be sufficient to discharge such obligations, liabilities, and responsibilities, and to maintain and operate the hospital system, and the Legislature may authorize the district to issue tax bonds for the purpose of the purchase, construction, acquisition, repair or renovation of improvements and initially equipping the same, and such bonds shall be payable from said Seventy-five Cents (75c) tax. The Legislature shall provide for transfer of title to properties to the district.

(b). The Legislature may by law permit the County of Potter (in which the City of Amarillo is partially located) to render financial aid to that district by paying a part of the expenses of operating and maintaining the system and paying a part of the debts of the district (whether assumed or created by the district) and may authorize the levy of a tax not to exceed Ten Cents (10c) per One Hundred Dollars ($100.00) valuation (in addition to other taxes permitted by this Constitution) upon all property within the county but without the City of Amarillo at the time such levy is made for such purposes. If such tax is authorized, the district shall by resolution assume the responsibilities, obligations, and liabilities of the county in the manner and to the extent hereinabove provided for political subdivisions having boundaries coextensive with the district, and the county shall not thereafter levy taxes (other than herein provided) for hospital purposes nor for providing hospital care for needy individuals of the county.

(c). The Legislature may by law authorize the creation of a hospital district within Jefferson County, the boundaries of which shall include only the area comprising the Jefferson County Drainage District No. 7 and the Port Arthur Independent School District, as such boundaries existed on the first day of January, 1957, with the power to issue bonds for the sole purpose of purchasing a site for, and the construction and initial equipping of, a hospital system, and with the power to levy a tax of not to exceed Seventy-five Cents (75c) on the One Hundred Dollars ($100) valuation of property therein for the purpose of paying the principal and interest on such bonds.

The creation of such hospital district shall not be final until approved at an election by a majority of the resident property taxpaying voters voting at said election who have duly rendered their property for taxation upon the tax rolls of either said Drainage or said School District, nor shall such bonds be issued or such tax be levied until so approved by such voters.

The district shall not have the power to levy any tax for maintenance or operation of the hospital or facilities, but shall contract with other political subdivisions of the state or private individuals, associations, or corporations for such purposes.

If the district hereinabove authorized is finally created, no other hospital district may be created embracing any part of the territory within its boundaries, but the Legislature by law may authorize the creation of a hospital district incorporating herein the remainder of Jefferson County, having the powers and duties and with the limitations presently provided by Art. IX, Section 4, of the Constitution of

Article IX — (Cont'd.)

Texas, except that such district shall be confirmed at an election wherein the resident qualified property taxpaying voters who have duly rendered their property within such proposed district for taxation on the county rolls, shall be authorized to vote. A majority of those participating in the election voting in favor of the district shall be necessary for its confirmation and for bonds to be issued.

(d). Should the Legislature enact enabling laws in anticipation of adoption of this amendment, such acts shall not be invalid because of their anticipatory character.

[Note — The foregoing Sec. 5 of Art. IX, an amendment, was added to provide for the creation of special hospital districts and authorizing the levying of taxes for their support. Submitted by the Fifty-fifth Legislature (1957) and adopted in an election Nov. 4, 1958.]

(e). The legislature by law may authorize Randall County to render financial assistance to the Amarillo Hospital District by paying part of the district's operating and maintenance expenses and the debts assumed or created by the district and to levy a tax for that purpose in an amount not to exceed seventy-five cents (75¢) on the One Hundred Dollars ($100.00) valuation on all property in Randall County that is not within the boundaries of the City of Amarillo or the South Randall County Hospital District. This tax is in addition to any other tax authorized by this constitution. If the tax is authorized by the legislature and approved by the voters of the area to be taxed, the Amarillo Hospital District shall, by resolution, assume the responsibilities, obligations, and liabilities of Randall County in accordance with Subsection (a) of this section and, except as provided by this subsection, Randall County may not levy taxes or issue bonds for hospital purposes or for providing hospital care for needy inhabitants of the county. Not later than the end of the first tax year during which taxes are levied under this subsection, Randall County shall deposit in the State Treasury to the credit of the state General Revenue Fund $45,000 to reimburse the state for the cost of publishing the resolution required by this subsection.

(f). Notwithstanding the provisions of Article IX of this constitution, if a hospital district was created or authorized under a constitutional provision that includes a description of the district's boundaries or jurisdiction, the legislature by law may authorize the district to change its boundaries or jurisdiction. The change must be approved by a majority of the qualified voters of the district voting at an election called and held for that purpose.

[Note — The foregoing Subsection (e) of Sec. 5 of Art. IX, an amendment, was added to expand services provided by the Amarillo Hospital District. Submitted by the Seventieth Legislature (1987) and adopted in an election Nov. 3, 1987.]

Sec. 6. Lamar County Hospital District Abolished

On the effective date of this Amendment, the Lamar County Hospital District is abolished. The Commissioners Court of Lamar County may provide for the transfer or for the disposition of the assets of the Lamar County Hospital District.

[Note — the foregoing Sec. 6 of Art. IX, an amendment, was added to authorize creation of a hospital district in Lamar County and authorizing the levying of taxes for its support. Submitted by the Fifty-sixth Legislature (1959) and adopted in an election Nov. 8, 1960. It was amended to abolish the hospital district. Submitted by the Sixty-second Legislature (1971) and adopted in an election Nov. 7, 1972.]

Sec. 7. Hidalgo County Hospital District; Creation, Tax Rate

The Legislature may by law authorize the creation of a Hospital District coextensive with Hidalgo County, having the powers and duties and with the limitations presently provided in Art. IX, Sec. 5 (a), of the Constitution of Texas, as it applies to Hidalgo County, except that the maximum rate of tax that the said Hidalgo County Hospital District may be authorized to levy shall be ten cents (10¢) per One Hundred Dollars ($100) valuation of taxable property within the District subject to district taxation.

[Note — The foregoing Sec. 7 of Art. IX, an amendment, was added to authorize creation of a hospital district in Hidalgo County and authorizing the levying of taxes for its support. Submitted by the Fifty-sixth Legislature (1959) and adopted in an election Nov. 8, 1960.]

Sec. 8. Comanche County Hospital District; Creation, Tax Rate

The Legislature may by law authorize the creation of a Hospital District to be coextensive with the limits of County Commissioners Precinct No. 4 of Comanche County, Texas.

If such District is created, it may be authorized to levy a tax not to exceed seventy-five cents (75¢) on the One Hundred Dollar ($100) valuation of taxable property within the District; provided, however, no tax may be levied until approved by a majority vote of the participating resident qualified property taxpaying voters who have duly rendered their property for taxation. The maximum rate of tax may be changed at subsequent elections so long as obligations are not impaired, and not to exceed the maximum limit of seventy-five cents (75¢) per One Hundred Dollar ($100) valuation, and no election shall be required by subsequent changes in the boundaries of the Commissioners Precinct No. 4 of Comanche County.

If such tax is authorized, no political subdivision or municipality within or having the same boundaries as the District may levy a tax for medical or hospital care for needy individuals, nor shall they maintain or erect hospital facilities, but the District shall by resolution assume all such responsibilities and shall assume all of the liabilities and obligations (including bonds and warrants) of such subdivisions or municipalities or both. The maximum tax rate submitted shall be sufficient to discharge such obligations, liabilities, and responsibilities and to maintain and operate the hospital system, and the Legislature may authorize the District to issue tax bonds for the purpose of the purchase, construction, acquisition, repair or renovation of improvements and initially equipping the same, and such bonds shall be payable from said seventy-five cents (75¢) tax. The Legislature shall provide for transfer of title to properties to the District.

(b) The Legislature may by law permit the County of Comanche to render financial aid to that District by paying a part of the expenses of operating and maintaining the system and paying a part of the debts of the District (whether assumed or created by the District) and may authorize the levy of a tax not to exceed ten cents (10¢) per One Hundred Dollar ($100) valuation (in addition to other taxes permitted by this Constitution) upon all property within the County but without the County Commissioners Precinct No. 4 of Comanche County at the time such levy is made for such purposes. If such tax is authorized, the District shall by resolution assume the responsibilities, obligations and liabilities of the County in the manner and to the extent hereinabove provided for political subdivisions having boundaries coextensive with the District, and the County shall not hereafter levy taxes (other than herein provided) for hospital purposes nor for providing hospital care for needy individuals of the county.

(c) Should the Legislature enact enabling laws in anticipation of the adoption of this amendment, such Acts shall not be invalid because of their anticipatory character.

[Note — The foregoing Sec. 8 of Art. IX, an amendment, was added to authorize creation of a hospital district in Comanche County and authorizing the levying of taxes for its support. Submitted by the Fifty-sixth Legislature (1959) and adopted in an election Nov. 8, 1960.]

Sec. 9.

The Legislature may by general or special law provide for the creation, establishment, maintenance and operation of hospital districts composed of one or more counties or all or any part of one or more counties with power to issue bonds for the purchase, construction, acquisition, repair or renovation of buildings and improvements and equipping same, for hospital purposes; providing for the transfer to the hospital district of the title to any land, buildings, improvements and equipment located wholly within the district which may be jointly or separately owned by any city, town or county, providing that any district so created shall assume full responsibility for providing medical and hospital care for its needy inhabitants and assume the outstanding indebtedness incurred by cities, towns and counties for hospital purposes prior to the creation of the district, if same are located wholly within its boundaries, and a pro rata portion of such indebtedness based upon the then last approved tax assessment rolls of the included cities, towns and counties if less than all the territory thereof is included within the district boundaries; providing that after its creation no other municipality or political subdivision shall have the power to levy taxes or issue bonds or other obligations for hospital purposes or for providing medical care within the boundaries of the district; providing for the levy of annual taxes at a rate not to exceed seventy-five cents (75¢) on the one hundred dollar valuation of all taxable property within such district for the purpose of meeting the re-

Article IX— (Cont'd.)

quirements of the district's bonds, the indebtedness assumed by it and its maintenance and operating expenses, providing that such district shall not be created or such tax authorized unless approved by a majority of the qualified voters thereof voting at an election called for the purpose; and providing further that the support and maintenance of the district's hospital system shall never become a charge against or obligation of the State of Texas nor shall any direct appropriation be made by the Legislature for the construction, maintenance or improvement of any of the facilities of such district.

Provided, however, that no district shall be created by special law except after thirty (30) days' public notice to the district affected, and in no event may the Legislature provide for a district to be created without the affirmative vote of a majority of the qualified voters in the district concerned.

The Legislature may also provide for the dissolution of hospital districts provided that a process is afforded by statute for:

(1) Determining the desire of a majority of the qualified voters within the district to dissolve it;

(2) Disposing of or transferring the assets, if any, of the district; and

(3) Satisfying the debts and bond obligations, if any, of the district, in such manner as to protect the interest of the citizens within the district, including their collective property rights in the assets and property of the district, provided, however, that any grant from federal funds, however dispensed, shall be considered an obligation to be repaid in satisfaction and provided that no election to dissolve shall be held more often than once each year. In such connection, the statute shall provide against disposal or transfer of the assets of the district except for due compensation unless such assets are transferred to another governmental agency, such as a county, embracing such district and using such transferred assets in such a way as to benefit citizens formerly within the district.

[Note — The foregoing Sec. 9 of Art. IX, an amendment, was added to provide for the creation of special hospital districts and authorizing the levying of taxes for their support. Submitted by the Fifty-seventh Legislature (1961) and adopted in an election Nov. 6, 1962. It was further amended to provide method of dissolution of hospital districts. Submitted by the Fifty-ninth Legislature (1965) and adopted in election Nov. 8 1966. It was again amended to authorize the legislature to provide by general or special law for the creation, establishment, maintenance and operation of a hospital district. Submitted by the Seventy-first Legislature (1989) and adopted in an election Nov. 7, 1989.]

Sec. 9A. The Legislature by law may determine the health care services a hospital district is required to provide, the requirements a resident must meet to qualify for services, and any other relevant provisions necessary to regulate the provision of health care to residents.

[Note — Sec. 9a of Art. IX, an amendment, was added to authorize Legislature to regulate the provision of health care by hospital districts. Submitted by Sixty-ninth Legislature (1985) and adopted in an election Nov. 5, 1985.]

Sec. 9B. The legislature by general or special law may provide for the creation, establishment, maintenance, and operation of hospital districts located wholly in a county with a population of 75,000 or less, according to the most recent federal decennial census, and may authorize the commissioners court to levy a tax on the ad valorem property located in the district for the support and maintenance of the district. A district may not be created or a tax levied unless the creation and tax are approved by a majority of the registered voters who reside in the district. The legislature shall set the maximum tax rate a district may levy. The legislature may provide that the county in which the district is located may issue general obligation bonds for the district and provide other services to the district. The district may provide hospital care, medical care, and other services authorized by the legislature.

[Note — The foregoing Sec. 9B of Art. XI, an amendment, was added to authorize the legislature to provide by general or special law for the creation, establishment, maintenance and operation of a hospital district. Submitted by the Seventy-first Legislature (1989) and adopted in an election Nov. 7, 1989.]

[Note — Sec. 10 of Art. IX is blank.]

Sec. 11. The Legislature may by law authorize the creation of hospital districts in Ochiltree, Castro, Hansford and Hopkins Counties, each district to be coextensive with the limits of such county.

If any such district is created, it may be authorized to levy a tax not to exceed Seventy-five Cents (75c) on the One Hundred Dollar ($100) valuation of taxable property within the district; provided, however, no tax may be levied until approved by a majority vote of the participating resident qualified property taxpaying voters who have duly rendered their property for taxation. The maximum rate of tax may be changed at subsequent elections so long as obligations are not impaired, and not to exceed the maximum limit of Seventy-five Cents (75c) per One Hundred Dollar ($100) valuation.

If such tax is authorized, no political subdivision or municipality within or having the same boundaries as the district may levy a tax for medical or hospital care for needy individuals, nor shall they maintain or erect hospital facilities, but the district shall by resolution assume all such responsibilities and shall assume all of the liabilities and obligations (including bonds and warrants) of such subdivisions or municipalities or both. The maximum tax rate submitted shall be sufficient to discharge obligations, liabilities, and responsibilities, and to maintain and operate the hospital system, and the Legislature may authorize the district to issue tax bonds for the purpose of the purchase, construction, acquisition, repair or renovation of improvements and initially equipping the same, and such bonds shall be payable from said Seventy-five Cent (75c) tax. The Legislature shall provide for transfer of title to properties to the district.

[Note—The foregoing Sec. 11 of Art. IX, an amendment, was added to provide for the creation of special hospital districts and to authorize the levying of taxes for their support. It is obviously misnumbered, as there is no Sec. 10 of Art. IX. Submitted by the Fifty-seventh Legislature (1961) and adopted in an election Nov. 6, 1962.]

Sec. 12. **Establishment of Airport Authorities** — The Legislature may by law provide for the creation, establishment, maintenance and operation of Airport Authorities composed of one or more counties, with power to issue general obligation bonds, revenue bonds, either or both of them, for the purchase, acquisition by the exercise of the power of eminent domain or otherwise, construction, reconstruction, repair or renovation of any airport or airports, landing fields and runways, airport buildings, hangars, facilities, equipment, fixtures, and any and all property, real or personal, necessary to operate, equip and maintain an airport; shall provide for the option by the governing body of the city or cities whose airport facilities are served by certificated airlines and whose facility or some interest therein, is proposed to be or has been acquired by the authority, to either appoint or elect a board of directors of said authority; if the directors are appointed such appointment shall be made by the County Commissioners Court after consultation with and consent of the governing body or bodies of such city or cities, and if the board of directors is elected they shall be elected by the qualified taxpaying voters of the county which chooses to elect the directors to represent that county, such directors shall serve without compensation for a term fixed by the Legislature not to exceed six (6) years, and shall be selected on the basis of the proportionate population of each county based upon the last preceding federal census, and shall be a resident or residents of such county; provide that no county shall have less than one (1) member on the board of directors; provide for the holding of an election in each county proposing the creation of an authority to be called by the Commissioners Court or Commissioners Courts, as the case may be, upon petition of five percent (5%) of the qualified taxpaying voters within the county or counties, said elections to be held on the same day if more than one county is included, provided that no more than one (1) such election may be called in a county until after the expiration of one (1) year; in the event such an election has failed, and thereafter only upon a petition of ten percent (10%) of the qualified taxpaying voters being presented to the Commissioners Court or Commissioners Courts of the county or counties in which such an election has failed, and in the event that two or more counties vote on the proposition of the creation of an authority therein, the proposition shall not be deemed to carry unless the majority of the qualified taxpaying voters in each county voting thereon vote in favor thereof; provided, however, that an Airport Authority may be created and be composed of the county or counties that vote in favor of its creation if separate propositions are submitted to the voters of each county so that they may vote for a two or more county authority or a single county authority; provide for the appointment by the board of directors of an assessor and collector of taxes in the authority, whether constituted of one or more counties, whose duty it shall be to assess all taxable property, both real and personal, and collect the taxes thereon, based upon the tax rolls approved by the board of directors, the tax to be levied not to exceed seventy-five cents (75c) per one hundred dollars ($100) assessed valuation of the property, provided, however, that the property of state regulated common carriers required by law to pay a tax upon intangible assets shall not be subject to taxation by the authority, said taxable property shall be assessed on a valuation not to exceed the market value and shall be equal and

Article IX — (Cont'd.); Article X and XI

uniform throughout the authority as is otherwise provided by the Constitution; the Legislature shall authorize the purchase or acquisition by the authority of any existing airport facility publicly owned and financed and served by certificated airlines, in fee or of any interest therein, or to enter into any lease agreement therefor, upon such terms and conditions as may be mutually agreeable to the authority and the owner of such facilities, or authorize the acquisition of same through the exercise of the power of eminent domain, and in the event of such acquisition, if there are any general obligation bonds that the owner of the publicly owned airport facility has outstanding, the same shall be fully assumed by the authority and sufficient taxes levied by the authority to discharge said outstanding indebtedness; and likewise any city or owner that has outstanding revenue bonds where the revenues of the airport have been pledged or said bonds constitute a lien against the airport facilities, the authority shall assume and discharge all the obligations of the city under the ordinances and bond indentures under which said revenue bonds have been issued and sold. Any city which owns airport facilities not serving certificated airlines which are not purchased or acquired or taken over as herein provided by such authority, shall have the power to operate the same under the existing laws or as the same may hereafter be amended. Any such authority when created may be granted the power and authority to promulgate, adopt and enforce appropriate zoning regulations to protect the airport from hazards and obstructions which would interfere with the use of the airport and its facilities for landing and take-off; an additional county or counties may be added to an existing authority if a petition of five percent (5%) of the qualified taxpaying voters is filed with and an election is called by the Commissioners Court of the county or counties seeking admission to an authority and the vote is favorable, then admission may be granted to such county or counties by the board of directors of the then existing authority upon such terms and conditions as they may agree upon and evidenced by a resolution approved by two-thirds (⅔) of the then existing board of directors, provided, however, the county or counties that may be so added to the then existing authority shall be given representation on the board of directors by adding additional directors in proportion to their population according to the last preceding federal census.

[Note—The foregoing Sec. 12 was added to provide by law for the establishment of airport authorities. Submitted by the Fifty-ninth Legislature (1965) and adopted in election Nov. 8, 1966.]

Sec. 13. **Mental Health Services** — Notwithstanding any other section of this article, the Legislature in providing for the creation, establishment, maintenance, and operation of a hospital district, shall not be required to provide that such district shall assume full responsibility for the establishment, maintenance, support, or operation of mental health services or mental retardation services including the operation of any community mental health centers, community mental retardation centers or community health and mental retardation centers which may exist or be thereafter established within the boundaries of such district, nor shall the Legislature be required to provide that such district shall assume full responsibility of public health department units and clinics and related public health activities or services, and the Legislature shall not be required to restrict the power of any municipality or political subdivision to levy taxes or issue bonds or other obligations or to expend public moneys for the establishment, maintenance, support, or operation of mental health services, mental retardation services, public health units or clinics or related public health activities or services or the operation of such community mental health or mental retardation centers within the boundaries of the hospital districts; and unless a statute creating a hospital district shall expressly prohibit participation by any entity other than the hospital district in the establishment, maintenance, or support of mental health services, mental retardation services, public health units or clinics or related public health activities within or partly within the boundaries of any hospital district, any municipality or any other political subdivision or state-supported entity within the hospital district may participate in the establishment, maintenance, and support of mental health services, mental retardation services, public health units and clinics and related public health activities and may levy taxes, issue bonds or other obligations, and expend public moneys for such purposes as provided by law.

[Note—The foregoing Sec. 13 of Art. IX, an amendment, was added to permit municipalities and other political subdivisions within hospital districts to participate in establishment, maintenance, support or operation of mental health, mental retardation or public health services. Submitted by the Sixtieth Legislature (1967) and adopted in election Nov. 11, 1967.]

ARTICLE X — RAILROADS

[Note—All of Art. X relating to railroads, except Sec. 2,

was deleted by constitutional amendment in election Aug. 5, 1969.]

*Article [Sec.] 2. **Public Highways; Common Carriers; Duty of the Legislature; Fixing Rates** — Railroads heretofore constructed or which may hereafter be constructed in this State are hereby declared public highways and railroad companies common carriers. The Legislature shall pass laws to regulate railroad freight and passenger tariffs to correct abuses, and prevent unjust discrimination and extortion in the rates of freight and passenger tariffs on the different railroads in this State, and enforce the same by adequate penalties; and to the further accomplishments of these objects and purposes may provide and establish all requisite means and agencies invested with such powers as may be deemed adequate and advisable.

[Note—The foregoing *'Article Sec. 2" of Art. X is an amended section, the amendment being in the last clause which permitted establishment of the Railroad Commission of Texas. Submitted by the Twenty-first Legislature (1889), ratified in an election Nov. 4, 1890, and declared adopted Dec. 19, 1890.]

*Explanatory Note—The legislative resolution submitting this amendment erroneously used the word, "Article," instead of the usual abbreviation, "Sec." Order used above is according to official draft of the Constitution.

ARTICLE XI — MUNICIPAL CORPORATIONS

Sec. 1. **Counties Are Legal Subdivisions of the State** — The several counties of this State are hereby recognized as legal subdivisions of the State.

Sec. 2. **Public Buildings and Roads** — The construction of jails, courthouses and bridges and the establishment of county poorhouses and farms and the laying out, construction and repairing of county roads shall be provided for by general laws.

Sec. 3. **No County or Municipal Corporation Shall Become a Subscriber to the Capital Stock of Any Private Corporation or Make Any Donation to the Same** — No county, city or other municipal corporation shall hereafter become a subscriber to the capital of any private corporation or association, or make any appropriation or donation to the same, or in anywise loan its credit; but this shall not be construed to in any way affect any obligation heretofore undertaken pursuant to law or to prevent a county, city, or other municipal corporation from investing its funds as authorized by law.

[Note — The foregoing Sec. 3 of Art. XI was amended to authorize local governments to invest their funds as authorized by law. (See related amendment at Art. III, Sec. 52(e).) Proposed by Seventy-first Legislature (1989) and adopted in an election Nov. 7, 1989.]

Sec. 4. **Cities and Towns Having a Population of 5,000 or Less Inhabitants to Be Chartered by General Laws; Dues to Be Collected in Current Money** — Cities and towns having a population of 5,000 or less may be chartered alone by general laws. They may levy, assess and collect such taxes as may be authorized by law, but no tax for any purpose shall ever be lawful for any one year which shall exceed 1½ percent of the taxable property of such city; and all taxes shall be collectible only in current money, and all licenses and occupation taxes levied, and all fines, forfeitures and penalties accruing to said cities and towns shall be collectible only in current money.

[Note—The foregoing Sec. 4 of Art. XI has been twice amended, as follows: (1) To provide that towns of 5,000 or less (instead of 10,000 or less, as provided by the original section) may be chartered alone by general law. Submitted by the Thirty-first Legislature (1909), ratified in an election Aug. 3, 1909, and declared adopted Sept. 24, 1909. (2) To authorize a maximum tax rate, in towns of 5,000 or less, of 1½ percent of taxable values in lieu of the originally specified maximum of one fourth of 1 percent. Submitted by the Thirty-sixth Legislature (1919) and adopted at election of Nov. 2, 1920.]

Sec. 5. **Cities of More Than 5,000 Inhabitants May by a Majority Vote of the Qualified Voters Adopt Their Own Charter; Limitation as to Taxation and Debt** — Cities having more than five thousand (5,000) inhabitants may, by a majority vote of the qualified voters of said city, at an election held for that purpose, adopt or amend their charters, subject to such limitations as may be prescribed by the Legislature, and providing that no charter or any ordinance passed under said charter shall contain any provision inconsistent with the Constitution of the State or of the general laws enacted by the Legislature of this State; said cities may

Article XI — (Cont'd.); Article XII

levy, assess and collect such taxes as may be authorized by law or by their charters; but no tax for any purpose shall ever be lawful for any one year which shall exceed 2½ percent of the taxable property of such city, and no debt shall ever be created by any city unless at the same time provision be made to assess and collect annually a sufficient sum to pay the interest thereon and creating a sinking fund of at least 2 percent thereon; and provided, further, that no city charter shall be altered, amended or repealed oftener than every two years.

[Note—The foregoing Sec. 5 of Art. XI has been twice amended, as follows: (1) To authorize towns of more than 5,000 population (instead of more than 10,000, as provided in the original section) to be chartered by special act, and allowing in such cities a maximum tax rate of 2½ percent. Submitted by the Thirty-first Legislature (1909), ratified in an election Aug. 3, 1909, and proclaimed Sept. 24, 1909. (2) To grant home rule to cities of more than 5,000 population. Submitted by the Thirty-second Legislature (1911), adopted at election of Nov. 5, 1912, and proclaimed Dec. 30, 1912.]

Sec. 6. **Municipal Taxation** — Counties, cities, and towns are authorized, in such mode as may now or may hereafter be provided by law, to levy, assess and collect the taxes necessary to pay the interest and provide a sinking fund to satisfy any indebtedness heretofore legally made and undertaken; but all such taxes shall be assessed and collected separately from that levied, assessed and collected for current expenses of municipal government and shall, when levied, specify in the act of levying the purpose therefor; and such taxes may be paid in the coupons, bonds or other indebtedness for the payment of which such tax may have been levied.

Sec. 7. **Taxation of Seawalls, Etc.; Restrictions and Limitations; Eminent Domain** — All counties and cities bordering on the coast of the Gulf of Mexico are hereby authorized upon a vote of the majority of the resident property taxpayers voting thereon at an election called for such purpose, to levy and collect such tax for construction of seawalls, breakwaters or sanitary purposes, as may now or may hereafter be authorized by law, and may create a debt for such works and issue bonds in evidence thereof. But no debt for any purpose shall ever be incurred in any manner by any city or county unless provision is made at the time of creating the same, for levying and collecting a sufficient tax to pay the interest thereon and provide at least 2 percent as a sinking fund; and the condemnation of the right of way for the erection of such work shall be fully provided for.

[Note—The foregoing Sec. 7 of Art. XI was amended to simplify language describing electors' qualifications. Submitted by the Forty-second Legislature (1931), adopted in election Nov. 8, 1932. Proclaimed Jan. 9, 1933. Further amended to provide that a majority of resident property taxpayers may vote to issue bonds for construction of seawalls and breakwaters. Submitted by the Sixty-third Legislature (1973) and adopted in election Nov. 6, 1973.]

Sec. 8. **State Aid for Seawalls, Etc.** — The counties and cities on the Gulf Coast being subject to calamitous overflows, and a very large proportion of the general revenue being derived from those otherwise prosperous localities.* The Legislature is specially authorized to aid, by donation of such portion of the public domain as may be deemed proper, and in such mode as may be provided by law, the construction of seawalls or breakwaters, such aid to be proportioned to the extent and value of the works constructed, or to be constructed, in any locality.

*Explanatory Note—The starting of a new sentence at this point follows the official draft of the Constitution, but it is evident that the foregoing phrase ending with "localities" was meant to modify the following sentence.

Sec. 9. **Public Buildings, Etc.** — The property of counties, cities and towns owned and held only for public purposes, such as public buildings and the sites therefor, fire engines and the furniture thereof, and all property used or intended for extinguishing fires, public grounds and all other property devoted exclusively to the use and benefit of the public, shall be exempt from forced sale and from taxation; provided, nothing herein shall prevent the enforcement of the vendor's lien, the mechanic's or builder's lien, or other liens now existing.

[Note—Sec. 10 of Art. XI, relating to special taxes and school districts, was deleted by constitutional amendment in

election Aug. 5, 1969.]

Sec. 11. **Term of Office for City Officials** — A home rule city may provide by charter or charter amendment, and a city, town or village operating under the general laws may provide by majority vote of the qualified voters voting at an election called for that purpose, for a longer term of office than two (2) years for its officers, either elective or appointive, or both, but not to exceed four (4) years; provided, however, that tenure under Civil Service shall not be affected hereby.

Provided, however, if any of such officers, elective or appointive, shall announce their candidacy, or shall in fact become a candidate, in any general, special or primary election, for any office of profit or trust under the laws of this State or the United States other than the office then held, at any time when the unexpired term of the office then held shall exceed one (1) year, such announcement or such candidacy shall constitute an automatic resignation of the office then held, and the vacancy thereby created shall be filled pursuant to law in the same manner as other vacancies for such office are filled.

A municipality so providing a term exceeding two (2) years but not exceeding four (4) years for any of its non-civil service officers must elect all of the members of its governing body by majority vote of the qualified voters in such municipality, and any vacancy or vacancies occurring on such governing body shall not be filled by appointment but must be filled by majority vote of the qualified voters at a special election called for such purpose within one hundred and twenty (120) days after such vacancy or vacancies occur.

[Note—The foregoing Sec. 11 of Art. XI, an amendment, was added to provide four-year terms for city officials. Submitted by the Fifty-fifth Legislature (1957), adopted in election Nov. 4, 1958.]

Sec. 12. **Sanitation Sewer Lines** — The Legislature by general law may authorize a city or town to expend public funds for the relocation or replacement of sanitation sewer laterals or water laterals on private property if the relocation or replacement is done in conjunction with or immediately following the replacement or relocation of sanitation sewer mains or water mains serving the property. The law must authorize the city or town to affix, with the consent of the owner of the private property, a lien on the property for the cost of relocating or replacing the sewer laterals on the property and must provide that the cost shall be assessed against the property with repayment by the property owner to be amortized over a period not to exceed five years at a rate of interest to be set as provided by the law. The lien may not be enforced until after five years have expired since the date the lien was affixed.

[Note — The foregoing Sec. 12 of Art. XI, an amendment, was added to permit a city or town to expend public funds and levy assessments for relocation or replacement of sanitation sewer laterals on private property. Submitted by Sixty-eighth Legislature (1983) and adopted in election Nov. 8, 1983. It was again amended to allow Legislature to enact laws permitting a city or town to spend public funds for the relocation or replacement of water laterals on private property. Submitted by the Sixty-ninth Legislature (1985) and adopted in an election Nov. 5, 1985.]

Sec. 13. **Classification of Municipal Functions** — (a) Notwithstanding any other provision of this constitution, the legislature may by law define for all purposes those functions of a municipality that are to be considered governmental and those that are proprietary, including reclassifying a function's classification assigned under prior statute or common law.

(b) This section applies to laws enacted by the 70th Legislature, Regular Session, 1987, and to all subsequent regular or special sessions of the legislature.

[Note — The foregoing Sec. 13, Art. XI, an amendment, was added to define the governmental and proprietary functions of a municipality. Submitted by the Seventieth Legislature (1987) and adopted in an election Nov. 3, 1987.]

ARTICLE XII — PRIVATE CORPORATIONS

Sec. 1. **Corporations Created by General Laws** — No private corporation shall be created except by general laws.

Sec. 2. **General Laws to be Enacted** — General laws shall be enacted providing for the creation of private corporations, and shall therein provide fully for the adequate protection of the public and of the individual stockholders.

Article XII — (Cont'd.); Article XIII, XIV, XV and XVI

[Note—Sections 3, 4, 5 and 7 of Art. XII—relating to franchises, and wharfage and freight tolls—were deleted by constitutional amendment in election Aug. 5, 1969.]

Sec. 6. The Issuance of Stocks and Bonds by Corporations Prohibited Except for Money Paid and Labor Done, Etc. — No corporation shall issue stock or bonds except for money paid, labor done, or property actually received, and all fictitious increase of stock or indebtedness shall be void.

ARTICLE XIII — SPANISH AND MEXICAN LAND TITLES

[Note—The entire Art. XIII, relating to Spanish and Mexican Land Titles, was deleted by constitutional amendment in election Aug. 5, 1969.]

ARTICLE XIV — PUBLIC LANDS AND LAND OFFICE

Sec. 1. General Land Office; Grants to Be Registered in; Land Office to Be Self-Sustaining — There shall be one General Land Office in the State, which shall be at the seat of government, where all land titles which have emanated or may hereafter emanate from the State shall be registered, except those titles the registration of which may be prohibited by this Constitution. It shall be the duty of the Legislature at the earliest practicable time to make the Land Office self-sustaining, and from time to time the Legislature may establish such subordinate offices as may be deemed necessary.

[Note—All of Art. XIV relating to public lands and the Land Office, except Sec. 1, was deleted by constitutional amendment in election Aug. 5, 1969.]

ARTICLE XV — IMPEACHMENT

Sec. 1. Power of Impeachment Vested in the House of Representatives — The power of impeachment shall be vested in the House of Representatives.

Sec. 2. Trial by Senate — Impeachment of the Governor, Lieutenant Governor, Attorney General, Treasurer, Commissioner of the General Land Office, Comptroller, and the Judges of the Supreme Court, Courts of Appeal and District Courts shall be tried by the Senate.

Sec. 3. Oath of Senators — When the Senate is sitting as a court of impeachment, the Senators shall be on oath, or affirmation, impartially to try the party impeached, and no person shall be convicted without the concurrence of two thirds of the Senators present.

Sec. 4. Judgment; Party Convicted Subject to Indictment Under the Criminal Laws — Judgment in cases of impeachment shall extend only to removal from office and disqualification from holding any office of honor, trust or profit under this State. A party convicted on impeachment shall also be subject to indictment, trial and punishment, according to law.

Sec. 5. Officers Suspended During Pending Proceedings — All officers against whom articles of impeachment may be preferred shall be suspended from the exercise of the duties of their office during the pendency of such impeachment. The Governor may make a provisional appointment to fill the vacancy occasioned by the suspension of an officer until the decision on the impeachment.

Sec. 6. Removal of District Judges — Any Judge of the District Courts of the State who is incompetent to discharge the duties of his office, or who shall be guilty of partiality, or oppression, or other official misconduct, or whose habits and conduct are such as to render him unfit to hold such office or who shall negligently fail to perform his duties as Judge, or who shall fail to execute in a reasonable measure the business in his courts, may be removed by the Supreme Court. The Supreme Court shall have original jurisdiction to hear and determine the causes aforesaid when presented in writing, upon the oaths, taken before some Judge of a court of record, of not less than ten lawyers, practicing in the courts held by such Judge, and licensed to practice in the Supreme Court; said presentment to be founded either upon the knowledge of the persons making it or upon the written oaths as to facts of creditable witnesses. The Supreme Court may issue all needful process and prescribe all needful rules to give effect to this section. Causes of this kind shall have precedence and be tried as soon as practicable.

Sec. 7. Trial and Removal of Other Officers — The Legislature shall provide by law for the trial and removal from office of all officers of this State, the modes for which have not been provided in this Constitution.

Address

Sec. 8. Removal of Judges of Supreme Court and Courts of Appeals and of District Courts — The Judges of the Supreme Court, Courts of Appeals and District Courts shall be removed by the Governor on the address of two thirds of each house of the Legislature, for willful neglect of duty, incompetency, habitual drunkenness, oppression in office, or other reasonable cause which shall not be sufficient ground for impeachment; provided, however that the cause or causes for which such removal shall be required shall be stated at length in such address and entered on the journals of each house; and provided, further, that the cause or causes shall be notified to the Judge so intended to be removed, and he shall be admitted to a hearing in his own defense before any vote for such address shall pass; and in all such cases the vote shall be taken by yeas and nays and entered on the journals of each house, respectively.

Sec. 9. Removal of Appointed Officials by Governor; Special Session of Senate for This Purpose — (a) In addition to the other procedures provided by law for removal of public officers, the governor who appoints an officer may remove the officer with the advice and consent of two-thirds of the members of the senate present.

(b) If the Legislature is not in session when the governor desires to remove an officer, the governor shall call a special session of the senate for consideration of the proposed removal. The session may not exceed two days in duration.

[Note — The foregoing Sec. 9 of Art. XV, an amendment, was added to authorize the governor to remove appointed officers with the advice and consent of the senate. Submitted by the Sixty-sixth Legislature (1979) and adopted in election Nov. 4, 1980.]

ARTICLE XVI — GENERAL PROVISIONS

Sec. 1. Official Oaths — (a) Members of the Legislature, and all other elected officers, before they enter upon the duties of their offices, shall take the following Oath or Affirmation:

"I,   , do solemnly swear (or affirm), that I will faithfully execute the duties of the office of   of the State of Texas, and will to the best of my ability preserve, protect, and defend the Constitution and laws of the United States and of this State so help me God."

(b) Each member of the Legislature and all other elected officers, before taking the Oath or Affirmation of office prescribed by this section and entering upon the duties of office, shall subscribe to the following statement:

"I,   , do solemnly swear (or affirm) that I have not directly or indirectly paid, offered, promised to pay, contributed, or promised to contribute any money or thing of value, or promised any public office or employment for the giving or witholding of a vote at the election at which I was elected so help me God."

The Secretary of State, and all other appointed officers before they enter upon the duties of their offices, shall take the following Oath or Affirmation:

"I,   , do solemnly swear (or affirm), that I will faithfully execute the duties of the office of   of the State of Texas, and will to the best of my ability preserve, protect, and defend the Constitution and laws of the United States and of this State so help me God."

(d) The Secretary of State, and all other appointed officers, before taking the Oath or Affirmation of office prescribed by this section and entering upon the duties of office, shall subscribe to the following statement:

"I,   , do solemnly swear (or affirm) that I have not directly or indirectly paid, offered, or promised to pay, contributed, or promised to contribute any money, or valuable thing, or promised any public office or employment, as a reward to secure my appointment or confirmation thereof, so help me God."

(e) Members of the Legislature and all other elected officers shall file the signed statement required by Subsection (b) of this section with the Secretary of State before taking the Oath or Affirmation of office prescribed by Subsection (a) of this section.

(f) The Secretary of State and all other appointed officers shall file the signed statement required by Subsection (d) of this section with the Secretary of State before taking the Oath or Affirmation of office prescribed by Subsection (c) of this section.

[Note — The foregoing Sec. 1 of Art. XVI was amended from the original text to eliminate that part of the oath stating that the incoming official had not fought a duel or sent or accepted a challenge to a duel or acted as a second in a duel. Submitted by the Forty-fifth Legislature (1937) and adopted in an election Nov. 8, 1938. It was further amended to change the form of the oath of office to include appointive officers of the State. Submitted by the Fifty-fourth Legislature (1955) and adopted in an election Nov. 6, 1956. It was again amended to change the oath of office prescribed for members of the legislature, the secretary of state and other elected and appointed officers. Proposed by the Seventy-first Legislature (1989) and adopted in an election Nov. 7, 1989.]

Sec. 2. Right of Suffrage to Be Protected; Criminals Disfranchised — Laws shall be made to exclude from office, serving on juries, and from the right of suffrage, those who may have been or shall hereafter be convicted of bribery, perjury, forgery or other high crimes. The privilege of free suffrage shall be protected by laws, regulating elections

Article XVI — (Cont'd.)

and prohibiting, under adequate penalties, all undue influence therein from power, bribery, tumult, or other improper practice.

[Note—Sections 3 and 4 of Art. XVI—relating to fines, and dueling—were deleted by constitutional amendment in election Aug. 5, 1969.]

Sec. 5. Bribery in Elections Disqualification for Holding Office — Every person shall be disqualified from holding any office of profit or trust in this State who shall have been convicted of having given or offered a bribe to procure his election or appointment.

Sec. 6. Appropriations for Private Purposes Prohibited; Expenditures to Be Published — (a) No appropriation for private or individual purposes shall be made, unless authorized by this Constitution. A regular statement, under oath, and an account of the receipts and expenditures of all public money shall be published annually, in such manner as shall be prescribed by law.

(b) State agencies charged with the responsibility of providing services to those who are blind, crippled, or otherwise physically or mentally handicapped may accept money from private or federal sources, designated by the private or federal source as money to be used in and establishing and equipping facilities for assisting those who are blind, crippled, or otherwise physically or mentally handicapped in becoming gainfully employed, in rehabilitating and restoring the handicapped, and in providing other services determined by the state agency to be essential for the better care and treatment of the handicapped. Money accepted under this subsection is state money. State agencies may spend money accepted under this subsection, and no other money, for specific programs and projects to be conducted by local level or other private, nonsectarian associations, groups, and nonprofit organizations, in establishing and equipping facilities for assisting those who are blind, crippled, or otherwise physically or mentally handicapped in becoming gainfully employed, in rehabilitating and restoring the handicapped, and in providing other services determined by the state agency to be essential for the better care or treatment of the handicapped.

The state agencies may deposit money accepted under this subsection either in the state treasury or in other secure depositories. The money may not be expended for any purpose other than the purpose for which it was given. Notwithstanding any other provision of this Constitution, the state agencies may expend money accepted under this subsection without the necessity of an appropriation, unless the Legislature, by law, requires that the money be expended only on appropriation. The Legislature may prohibit state agencies from accepting money under this subsection or may regulate the amount of money accepted, the way the acceptance and expenditure of the money is administered, and the purposes for which the state agencies may expend the money. Money accepted under this subsection for a purpose prohibited by the Legislature shall be returned to the entity that gave the money.

This subsection does not prohibit state agencies authorized to render services to the handicapped from contracting with privately-owned or local facilities for necessary and essential services, subject to such conditions, standards, and procedures as may be prescribed by law.

[Note—The foregoing Sec. 6 of Art. XVI was amended to authorize public grants to private groups for assistance to the blind, crippled or otherwise physically and mentally handicapped. Submitted by the Fifty-ninth Legislature (1965) and adopted in election Nov. 8, 1966.]

[Note—Sec. 7 of Art. XVI, relating to paper money, was deleted by constitutional amendment in election Aug. 5, 1969.]

Sec. 8. Counties May Provide Workhouses, Poorhouses and Farms — Each county in the State may provide, in such manner as may be prescribed by law, a manual labor poorhouse and farm, for taking care of, managing, employing and supplying the wants of its indigent and poor inhabitants.

Sec. 9. Absence on Business of the State or United States Shall Not Forfeit a Residence Once Obtained — Absence on business of the State or of the United States shall not forfeit a residence once obtained, so as to deprive anyone of the right of suffrage, or of being elected or appointed to any office, under the exceptions contained in this Constitution.

Sec. 10. Deductions From Salaries to be Provided for — The Legislature shall provide for deductions from the salaries of public officers who may neglect the performance of any duty that may be assigned them by law.

Sec. 11. Usurious Interest Prohibited — The Legislature shall have authority to classify loans and lenders, license and regulate lenders, define interest and fix maximum rates of interest; provided, however, that in the absence of legislation fixing maximum rates of interest all contracts for a greater rate of interest than ten per centum (10%) per annum shall be deemed usurious; provided, further, that in contracts where no rate of interest is agreed upon, the rate shall not exceed six per centum (6%) per annum. Should any regulatory agency, acting under the provisions of this Section, cancel or refuse to grant any permit under any law passed by the Legislature; then such applicant or holder shall have the right of appeal to the courts and granted a trial de novo as that term is used in appealing from the justice of peace court to the county court.

[Note—The foregoing Sec. 11 of Art. XVI has been twice amended—first setting 10 percent and 6 percent as interest rates, in place of original provision for 12 percent and 8 percent. Submitted by the Twenty-second Legislature (1891), ratified in election Aug. 11, 1891, and declared adopted Sept. 22, 1891. Further amended to grant right of appeal from justice of peace court to county court. Submitted by the Fifty-sixth Legislature (1959) and adopted in election Nov. 8, 1960.]

Sec. 12. Officers Not Eligible — No member of Congress, nor person holding or exercising any office of profit or trust under the United States, or either of them, or under any foreign power, shall be eligible as a member of the Legislature or hold or exercise any office of profit or trust under this State.

[Note—Sec. 13 of Art. XVI, relating to arbitration laws, was deleted by constitutional amendment in election Aug. 5, 1969.]

Sec. 14. Residence of Officers — All civil officers shall reside within the State, and all district or county officers within their districts or counties, and shall keep their offices at such places as may be required by law; and failure to comply with this condition shall vacate the office so held.

Sec. 15. Community Property of Husband and Wife; Partition Thereof — All Property, both real and personal, of a spouse owned or claimed before marriage, and that acquired afterward by gift, devise or descent, shall be the separate property of that spouse; and laws shall be passed more clearly defining the rights of the spouses, in relation to separate and community property; provided that persons about to marry and spouses, without the intention to defraud pre-existing creditors, may by written instrument from time to time partition between themselves all or part of their property, then existing or to be acquired, or exchange between themselves the community interest of one spouse or future spouse in any property for the community interest of the other spouse or future spouse in other community property then existing or to be acquired, whereupon the portion or interest set aside to each spouse shall be and constitute a part of the separate property and estate of such spouse or future spouse; spouses may also from time to time, by written instrument, agree between themselves that the income or property from all or part of the separate property then owned or which thereafter might be acquired by only one of them, shall be the separate property of that spouse; if one spouse makes a gift of property to the other that gift is presumed to include all the income or property which might arise from that gift of property; and spouses may agree in writing that all or part of their community property becomes the property of the surviving spouse on the death of a spouse.

[Note—Sec. 15 of Art. XVI originally had no provision for partition of community property of husband and wife. Provision for partition was the purpose of the amended section. Submitted by the Fiftieth Legislature (1947) and adopted in election Nov. 2, 1948. It was further amended to allow spouses to agree that income or property arising from separate property is to be separate property. Submitted by the Sixty-sixth Legislature (1979) and adopted in election Nov. 4, 1980. It was again amended to permit spouses to hold community property with right of survivorship. Submitted by the Seventieth Legislature (1987) and adopted in an election Nov. 3, 1987.]

Sec. 16. Banking Corporations — (a) The Legislature shall, by general laws, authorize the incorporation of state banks and savings and loan associations and shall provide for a system of state supervision, regulation and control of such bodies which will adequately protect and secure the depositors and creditors thereof.

No state bank shall be chartered until all of the authorized capital stock has been subscribed and paid in full in cash. Except as may be permitted by the Legislature pursuant to subsections (b), (d), and (e) of this Section 16, state bank shall not be authorized to engage in business at more than one place, which shall be designated in its charter; however, this restriction shall not apply to any other type of financial institution chartered under the laws of this state.

No foreign corporation, other than the national banks of the United States domiciled in this State, shall be permitted to exercise banking or discounting privileges in this State.

Article XVI — (Cont'd.)

(b) If it finds that the convenience of the public will be served thereby, the Legislature may authorize state and national banks to establish and operate unmanned teller machines within the county or city of their domicile. Such machines may perform all banking functions. Banks which are domiciled within a city lying in two or more counties may be permitted to establish and operate unmanned teller machines within both the city and the county of their domicile. The Legislature shall provide that a bank shall have the right to share in the use of these teller machines, not situated at a banking house, which are located within the county or the city of the bank's domicile, on a reasonable, nondiscriminatory basis, consistent with anti-trust laws. Banks may share the use of such machines within the county or city of their domicile with savings and loan associations and credit unions which are domiciled in the same county or city.

(c) A state bank created by virtue of the power granted by this section, notwithstanding any other provision of this section, has the same rights and privileges that are or may be granted to national banks of the United States domiciled in this State.

Should the Legislature enact legislation in anticipation of the adoption of this amendment, such law shall not be invalid because of its anticipatory character.

(d) The Legislature may authorize a state bank or national bank of the United States domiciled in this State to engage in business at more than one place if it does so through the purchase and assumption of certain assets and liabilities of a failed state bank or a failed national bank of the United States domiciled in this State.

(e) The Legislature shall authorize a state bank or national bank of the United States domiciled in this State to establish and operate banking facilities at locations within the county or city of its domicile, subject to limitations the Legislature imposes. The Legislature may permit a bank domiciled within a city located in two or more counties to establish and operate branches within both the city and the county of its domicile, subject to limitations the Legislature imposes.

(f) A bank may not be considered a branch or facility of another bank solely because it is owned or controlled by the same stockholders as the other bank, has common accounting and administrative systems with the other bank, or has a name similar to the other bank's or because of a combination of those factors.

[Note—The foregoing Sec. 16 of Art. XVI has been amended from the original, as follows: (1) To eliminate the original provision that "No corporate body shall hereafter be created, renewed or extended with banking or discounting privileges," and making possible the establishment of the present state banking system. Submitted by the Twenty-eighth Legislature (1903), ratified in an election Nov. 8, 1904, and declared adopted Dec. 29, 1904. (2) Eliminating a provision, contained in the amendment of 1904, making shareholders of banks liable to the extent of twice the par value of the shares owned. Submitted by the Forty-fifth Legislature (1937), and adopted in an election Aug. 23, 1937. (3) Authorizing banks to use unmanned teller machines within the county or city of their domicile on a shared basis. Submitted by the Sixty-sixth Legislature (1979) and adopted in election Nov. 4, 1980. (4) Adding Subsection (c), providing state banks same rights and privileges as national banks. Submitted by the Sixty-eighth Legislature (1983) and adopted in election Nov. 6, 1984. (5) Amending sections (a) and (c) and adding sections (d), (e) and (f) to provide that a bank may offer full service banking at more than one location within the city or county where its principal facility is located, subject to limitations and restrictions provided by law. Submitted by the Sixty-ninth Legislature (1986) and adopted in an election Nov. 4, 1986.]

Sec. 17. **Officers to Perform Duties Until Successor Qualified** — All officers within this State shall continue to perform the duties of their offices until their successors shall be duly qualified.

Sec. 18. **Vested Rights** — The rights of property and of action, which have been acquired under the Constitution and the laws of the Republic and State, shall not be divested; nor shall any rights or actions, which have been divested, barred or declared null and void by the Constitution of the Republic and State be reinvested, renewed or reinstated by this Constitution; but the same shall remain precisely in the situation which they were before the adoption of this Constitution, unless otherwise herein provided; and provided, further, that no cause of action heretofore barred shall be revived.

Sec. 19. **Qualifications of Jurors** — The Legislature shall prescribe by law the qualifications of grand and petit jurors; provided that neither the right nor the duty to serve on grand and petit juries shall be denied or abridged by reason of sex. Whenever in the Constitution the term "men" is used in reference to grand or petit juries, such term shall include persons of the female as well as the male sex.

[Note—The foregoing Sec. 19 of Art. XVI was amended to include women jurors. Submitted by the Fifty-third Legislature (1953) and adopted in an election Nov. 2, 1954.]

Sec. 20. **Manufacture and Sale of Intoxicants** — (a) The Legislature shall have the power to enact a Mixed Beverage Law regulating the sale of mixed alcoholic beverages on a local option election basis. The Legislature shall also have the power to regulate the manufacture, sale, possession and transportation of intoxicating liquors, including the power to establish a state monopoly on the sale of distilled liquors.

Should the Legislature enact any enabling laws in anticipation of this amendment, no such law shall be void by reason of its anticipatory nature.

(b) The Legislature shall enact a law or laws whereby the qualified voters of any county, justices precinct or incorporated town or city may, by a majority vote of those voting, determine from time to time whether the sale of intoxicating liquors for beverage purposes shall be prohibited or legalized within the prescribed limits; and such laws shall contain provisions for voting on the sale of intoxicating liquors of various types and various alcoholic content.

(c) In all counties, justices precincts or incorporated towns or cities wherein the sale of intoxicating liquors had been prohibited by local option elections held under the laws of the State of Texas and in force at the time of the taking effect of Section 20, Article XVI of the Constitution of Texas, it shall continue to be unlawful to manufacture, sell, barter or exchange in any such county, justices precinct or incorporated town or city, any spiritous, vinous or malt liquors or medicated bitters capable of producing intoxication or any other intoxicants whatsoever, for beverage purposes, unless and until a majority of the qualified voters in such county or political subdivision thereof voting in an election held for such purposes shall determine such to be lawful; provided that this subsection shall not prohibit the sale of alcoholic beverages containing not more than 3.2 percent alcohol by weight in cities, counties or political subdivisions thereof in which the qualified voters have voted to legalize such sale under the provisions of Chapter 116, Acts of the Regular Session of the Forty-third Legislature.

[Note—The foregoing Sec. 20 of Art. XVI has been amended from the original (which merely provided for local option elections in "any county, justices precinct, town or city") five times, as follows: (1) To insert a clause in original section "or such subdivision of a county as may be designated by Commissioners' Court of said county," with reference to local option elections. Submitted by Twenty-second Legislature (1891), ratified in an election Aug. 11, 1891, and declared adopted Sept. 22, 1891. (2) To declare state-wide prohibition. Submitted by Thirty-sixth Legislature (1919), and declared adopted May 24, 1919. (3) To legalize sale of vinous and malt liquors of not more than 3.2 percent alcohol. Submitted by Forty-third Legislature (1933), and adopted in an election Aug. 26, 1933. (4) To legalize sale of all liquors, as stated in the section printed above. Submitted by Forty-fourth Legislature (1935), and adopted in an election Aug. 24, 1935. (5) To give Legislature power to enact a Mixed Beverage Law regulating sale of mixed drinks on local option election basis. Submitted by Sixty-first Legislature (1969) and adopted in election Nov. 3, 1970.]

Sec. 21. **Stationery; Public Printing** — All stationery, printing, fuel used in the Legislature and departments of the government other than the judicial department, printing and binding of the laws, journals, and department reports, and all other printing and binding and the repairing and furnishing of the halls and rooms used during meetings of the Legislature and in committees, except proclamations and such products and services as may be done by handicapped individuals employed in nonprofit rehabilitation facilities providing sheltered employment to the handicapped in Texas, shall be performed under contract, to be given to the lowest responsible bidder, below such maximum price and under such regulations as shall be prescribed by law. No member or officer of any department of the government shall in any way have a financial interest in such contracts, and all such contracts or programs involving the state use of the products and services of handicapped individuals shall be subject to such requirements as might be established by the Legislature.

[Note—The foregoing Sec. 21 of Art. XVI was amended to eliminate reference to the Deaf and Dumb Asylum; to allow certain products and services of handicapped persons to be used by agencies of state government; to require other products and services required for operation of state government be acquired under bids by lowest responsible bidder; and to eliminate requirement that Governor, Secretary of State and Comptroller of Public Accounts be personally involved with such transactions. Submitted by the Sixty-fifth Legislature (1977) and adopted in election Nov. 7, 1978.]

Article XVI — (Cont'd.)

Sec. 22. **Fence Laws** — The Legislature shall have the power to pass such fence laws, applicable to any subdivision of the State or county, as may be needed to meet the wants of the people.

Sec. 23. **Stock Laws** — The Legislature may pass laws for the regulation of livestock and the protection of stock raisers in the stock raising portion of the State, and exempt from the operation of such laws other portions, sections or counties; and shall have power to pass general and special laws for the inspection of cattle, stock and hides, and for the regulation of brands; provided, that any local law thus passed shall be submitted to the freeholders of the section to be affected thereby, and approved by them before it shall go into effect.

Sec. 24. **Roads; Convict Labor** — The Legislature shall make provision for laying out and working public roads, for the building of bridges, and for utilizing fines, forfeitures, and convict labor to all these purposes.

Sec. 25. **Drawbacks and Rebates in Freight Insurance, Transportation, Storage, Etc., Prohibited** — That all drawbacks and rebatement of insurance, freight, transportation, carriage, wharfage, storage, compressing, bailing, repairing, or for any other kind of labor or service of, or to any cotton, grain or any other produce or article of commerce in this State, paid or allowed or contracted for to any common carrier, shipper, merchant, commission merchant, factor, agent or middleman of any kind not the true and absolute owner thereof, are forever prohibited; and it shall be the duty of the Legislature to pass effective laws punishing all persons in this State who pay, receive or contract for or respecting the same.

Sec. 26. **Homicide: Civil Action For** — Every person, corporation or company that may commit a homicide, through willful act or omission or gross neglect, shall be responsible in exemplary damages to the surviving husband, widow, heirs of his or her body, or such of them as there may be, without regard to any criminal proceeding that may or may not be had in relation to the homicide.

Sec. 27. **Vacancies in Offices Filled for Unexpired Term Only** — In all elections to fill vacancies of office in this State, it shall be to fill the unexpired term only.

Sec. 28. **Wages Exempt From Garnishment** — No current wages for personal service shall ever be subject to garnishment, except for the enforcement of court-ordered child support payments.

[Note — The foregoing Sec. 28 of Art. XVI was amended to allow Legislature to provide for additional remedies to enforce court-ordered child support payments. Submitted by Sixty-eighth Legislature (1983) and adopted in election Nov. 8, 1983.]

[Note—Sec. 29 of Art. XVI, relating to barratry, was deleted by constitutional amendment in election Aug. 5, 1969.]

Sec. 30. **Duration of Offices; Term of Railroad Commissioner** — (a) The duration of all offices not fixed by this Constitution shall never exceed two years.

(b) When a Railroad Commission is created by law it shall be composed of three Commissioners, who shall be elected by the people at a general election for state officers, and their term of office shall be six years. Railroad Commissioners first elected after this amendment goes into effect shall hold office as follows: One shall serve two years, and one four years, and one six years; their terms to be decided by lot immediately after they shall have qualified. And one Railroad Commissioner shall be elected every two years thereafter. In case of vacancy in said office the Governor of the State shall fill said vacancy by appointment until the next general election.

(c) The Legislature may provide that members of the governing board of a district or authority created by authority of Art. III, Sec. 52(b) (1) or (2), or Art. XVI, Sec. 59, of this Constitution serve terms not to exceed four years.

(d) The Legislature by general or special law may provide that members of the governing board of a hospital district serve terms not to exceed four years.

[Note — The foregoing Sec. 30 of Art. XVI was amended from the original to permit six-year terms for the newly created offices of the three-place Railroad Commission of Texas. The original section consisted only of the first clause of the amendment as printed above. Submitted by the Twenty-third Legislature (1893), ratified in an election Nov. 6, 1894, and declared adopted Dec. 21, 1894. It was further amended to provide four-year terms for members of governing boards of certain water districts and conservation and reclamation districts. Submitted by the Sixty-seventh Legislature (1981) and adopted in an election Nov. 2, 1982. It was again amended by adding Subsection (d) to authorize the members of a hospital district board to serve four-year terms. Proposed by the Seventy-first Legislature (1989) and adopted in an election Nov. 7, 1989.]

Sec. 30-A. **Board of Regents, Trustees, Managers, Etc.; Term of Office** — The Legislature may provide by law that the members of the Board of Regents of the State University and boards of trustees or managers of the educational, eleemosynary and penal institutions of this State, and such boards as have been or may hereafter be established by law, may hold their respective offices for the term of six (6) years, one third of the members of such boards to be elected or appointed every two years in such manner as the Legislature may determine; vacancies in such offices to be filled as may be provided by law, and the Legislature shall enact suitable laws to give effect to this section.

[Note—The foregoing Sec. 30-A of Art. XVI , an amendment, was added to give the Legislature authority to provide official terms of more than two years. (See Sec. 30 above and note thereunder.) Submitted by the Thirty-second Legislature (1911), ratified at an election Nov. 5, 1912, and declared adopted Dec. 30, 1912.]

Sec. 30-B. **Tenure Under Municipal Civil Service** — Wherever by virtue of stature or charter provisions appointive officers of any municipality are placed under the terms and provisions of Civil Service and rules are set up governing appointment to and removal from such offices. The provisions of Article 16, Section 30, of the Texas Constitution limiting the duration of all offices not fixed by the Constitution to two (2) years shall not apply, but the duration of such offices shall be governed by the provisions of the Civil Service law or charter provisions applicable thereto.

[Note—The foregoing Sec. 30-B of Art. XVI, an amendment, was added to extend to local officials terms under the Civil Service exemption from the two-year restriction in the first clause of Sec. 30. (See Secs. 30 and 30-a and notes thereunder.) Submitted by the Forty-sixth Legislature; ratified in an election Nov. 5, 1940.]

Sec. 31. **Qualifications of Physicians to Be Prescribed** — The Legislature may pass laws prescribing the qualifications of practitioners of medicine in this State, and to punish persons for malpractice, but no preference shall ever be given by law to any schools of medicine.

[Note—Sec. 32 of Art. XVI, relating to Board of Health and Vital Statistics, was deleted by constitutional amendment in election Aug. 5, 1969.]

Sec. 33. **Condition Under Which a Person Can Not Receive Compensation From the State** — The accounting officers in this State shall neither draw nor pay a warrant or check on funds of the State of Texas, whether in the treasury or otherwise, to any person for salary or compensation who holds at the same time more than one civil office of emolument, in violation of Sec. 40.

[Note—The foregoing Sec. 33 of Art. XVI has been amended four times, as follows: (1) To release National Guard of Texas, National Guard Reserve and Officers' Reserve Corps and United States Organized Reserves from the prohibition against holding remunerative office. Submitted by Thirty-ninth Legislature (1925), and adopted in an election Nov. 2, 1926. Proclaimed Jan. 20, 1927. (2) To add to those released from the prohibition against holding remunerative office all retired officers and enlisted men of the United States Army, Navy and Marine Corps. Submitted by Forty-second Legislature (1931), and adopted in an election Nov. 8, 1932. Proclaimed Jan. 9, 1933. (3) To allow nonelective state officers and employees to serve in other nonelective offices under this state or the U.S. until Sept. 1, 1969, and thereafter only if authorized by Legislature, if the offices are of benefit to Texas or are required by state or federal law and there is no conflict of interest; prohibiting elected officers from holding any other office under this state; and adding members of Air National Guard, Air National Guard Reserve, Air Force Reserve and retired members of Air Force to list of persons exempted. Submitted by Sixtieth Legislature (1967) and adopted in election Nov. 11, 1967. (4) It was amended to delete the old Sec. 33 of Art. XVI and substitute the foregoing therefor. (See also note under Sec. 40 of Art. XVI.) Submitted by the Sixty-second Legislature (1971) and adopted in election Nov. 7, 1972.]

[Note—Sections 34, 35, 36 and 38 of Art. XVI—relating to military forts, laborers on public works, payments to school-teachers, and a Commissioner of Insurance, Statistics and History—were deleted by constitutional amendment in election Aug. 5, 1969.]

Sec. 37. **Mechanic's Liens to Be Enforced** — Mechanics, artisans and material men of every class shall have a lien upon the buildings and articles made or repaired by them, for the value of their labor done thereon, or material furnished therefor; and the Legislature shall provide by law for the speedy and efficient enforcement of said liens.

Sec. 39. **Memorials of Texas History** — The Legislature may, from time to time, make appropriations for preserving

Article XVI — (Cont'd.)

and perpetuating memorials of the history of Texas, by means of monuments, statues, paintings and documents of historical value.

Sec. 40. **Provision Against Holding More Than One Office; Exceptions** — No person shall hold or exercise at the same time, more than one civil office of emolument, except that of Justice of the Peace, County Commissioner, Notary Public and Postmaster, Officer of the National Guard, the National Guard Reserve, and the Officers Reserve Corps of the United States and enlisted men of the National Guard, the National Guard Reserve, and the Organized Reserves of the United States, and retired officers of the United States Army, Air Force, Navy, Marine Corps, and Coast Guard, and retired warrant officers, and retired enlisted men of the United States Army, Air Force, Navy, Marine Corps, and Coast Guard, and the officers and directors of soil and water conservation districts, unless otherwise specially provided herein. Provided, that nothing in this Constitution shall be construed to prohibit an officer or enlisted man of the National Guard, and the National Guard Reserve, or an officer in the Officers Reserve Corps of the United States, or an enlisted man in the Organized Reserves of the United States, or retired officers of the United States Army, Air Force, Navy, Marine Corps, and Coast Guard, and retired warrant officers, and retired enlisted men of the United States Army, Air Force, Navy, Marine Corps, and Coast Guard, and officers of the State and water conservation districts, from holding at the same time any other office or position of honor, trust or profit, under this State or the United States, or from voting at any election, general, special or primary in this State when otherwise qualified. State employees or other individuals who receive all or part of their compensation either directly or indirectly from funds of the State of Texas and who are not State officers, shall not be barred from serving as members of the governing bodies of school districts, cities, towns, or other local governmental districts; provided, however, that such State employees or other individuals shall receive no salary for serving as members of such governing bodies. It is further provided that a non-elective State officer may hold other non-elective offices under the State or the United States, if the other office is of benefit to the State of Texas or is required by the State or Federal law, and there is no conflict with the original office for which he receives salary or compensation. No member of the Legislature of this State may hold any other office or position of profit under this State, or the United States, except as a notary public if qualified by law.

[Note—The foregoing Sec. 40 of Art. XVI has been amended three times as follows: (1) To release National Guard, National Guard Reserve and Officers' Reserve Corps and United States Organized Reserves from the prohibition against holding remunerative office. Submitted by Thirty-ninth Legislature (1925), and adopted in an election Nov. 2, 1926. Proclaimed Jan. 20, 1927. (2) To add to those released from the prohibition against holding remunerative office all retired officers and enlisted men of the United States Army, Navy and Marine Corps. Submitted by Forty-second Legislature (1931) and adopted in an election Nov. 8, 1932. Proclaimed Jan. 9, 1933. (3) To add to those released from the prohibition against holding remunerative office retired officers or enlisted men of the Air Force and Coast Guard; and officers and directors of soil and water conservation districts, unless otherwise specially prohibited; also certain other state employees who are not officers of the state. Submitted by Sixty-second Legislature (1971) and adopted in an election Nov. 7, 1972.]

Sec. 41. **Bribery of Certain Officials to Be Prohibited** — Any person who shall, directly or indirectly, offer, give or promise any money or thing of value, testimonial, privilege or personal advantage to any executive or judicial officer or member of the Legislature, to influence him in the performance of any of his public or official duties, shall be guilty of bribery and be punished in such manner as shall be provided by law. And any member of the Legislature, or executive or judicial officer, who shall solicit, demand or receive, or consent to receive, directly or indirectly, for himself or for another, from any company, corporation or person any money, appointment, employment testimonial, reward, thing of value or employment, or of personal advantage or promise thereof, for his vote or official influence, or for withholding the same, or with any understanding, expressed or implied, that his vote or official action shall be in any way influenced thereby, or who shall solicit, demand and receive any such money or other advantage, matter or thing aforesaid, for another, as the consideration of his vote or official influence, in consideration of the payment or promise of such money, advantage, matter or thing to another, shall be held guilty of bribery within the meaning of the Constitution, and shall incur the disabilities provided for said offenses, with a forfeiture of the office they may hold, and such other additional punishment as is or shall be provided by law.

[Note—Sec. 42 of Art. XVI, relating to an asylum for ine-

briates, was deleted by constitutional amendment in election Aug. 5, 1969.]

Sec. 43. **Exemption From Public Service** — No man or set of men shall ever be exempted, relieved or discharged from the performance of any public duty or service imposed by general law, by any special law. Exemptions from the performance of such public duty or service shall only be made by general law.

Sec. 44. **County Treasurer and Surveyor** — (a) Except as otherwise provided by this section, the Legislature shall prescribe the duties and provide for the election by the qualified voters of each county in this State, of a County Treasurer and a County Surveyor, who shall have an office at the county seat, and hold their office for four years, and until their successors are qualified; and shall have such compensation as may be provided by law.

(b) The office of County Treasurer in the counties of Tarrant and Bee is abolished and all the powers, duties, and functions of the office in each of these counties are transferred to the County Auditor or to the officer who succeeds to the auditor's functions. The office of County Treasurer in the counties of Bexar and Collin are abolished and all the powers, duties, and functions of the office in each of these counties are transferred to the County Clerk. However, the office of County Treasurer shall be abolished in the counties covered by this subsection only after a local election has been held in each county and the proposition ''to abolish the elective office of county treasurer'' has passed by a majority of those persons voting in said election.

(c) The office of County Treasurer in the counties of Andrews and Gregg is abolished. In Andrews County, the powers, duties, and functions of the office are transferred to the County Auditor of the county or to the officer who succeeds to the auditor's functions. In Gregg County, the functions of the office are transferred to an elected official or the County Auditor as designated by the Commissioners Court, and the Commissioners Court may from time to time change its designation as it considers appropriate.

(d) The office of County Treasurer in the counties of El Paso and Fayette is abolished. In El Paso County, the Commissioners Court may employ or contract with a qualified person or may designate another county officer to perform any of the functions that would have been performed by the County Treasurer if the office had not been abolished. In Fayette County, the functions of the abolished office are transferred to the County Auditor or to the officer who succeeds to the auditor's functions. However, the office of County Treasurer in El Paso or Fayette County is abolished under this subsection only if, at the statewide election at which the constitutional amendment providing for the abolition of the office in that county is submitted to the voters, a majority of the voters of that county voting on the question at that election favor the amendment.

(e) The office of County Surveyor in the counties of Denton, Randall, Collin, Dallas, El Paso, and Henderson is abolished upon the approval of the abolition by a majority of the qualified voters of the respective county voting on the question at an election that the Commissioners Court of the county may call. If the election is called, the Commissioners Court shall order the ballot at the election to be printed to provide for voting for or against the proposition: ''Abolishing the office of county surveyor.'' Each qualified voter of the county is entitled to vote in the election. If the office of County Surveyor is abolished under this subsection, the maps, field notes, and other records in the custody of the County Surveyor are transferred to the County Clerk of the county. After abolition, the Commissioners Court may employ or contract with a qualified person to perform any of the functions that would have been performed by the County Surveyor if the office had not been abolished.

(f) This subsection applies only to the counties of Cass, Ector, Garza, Smith, Bexar, Harris, and Webb. The office of County Surveyor in the county is abolished on January 1, 1990, if at the statewide election at which the addition to the Constitution of this subsection is submitted to the voters, a majority of the voters of that county voting on the question at that election favor the addition of this subsection. If the office of County Surveyor is abolished in a county under this subsection, the powers, duties, and functions of the office are transferred to the county officer or employee designated by the Commissioners Court of the county in which the office is abolished, and the Commissioners Court may from time to time change its designation as it considers appropriate.

[Note — Subsection (f) of Art. XVI, Sec. 44, an amendment, was added to abolish the office of county surveyor in designated counties. Proposed by the Seventy-first Legislature (1989) and adopted in an election Nov. 7, 1989. A previous Subsection (f) relating to the abolishing the office of county treasurer in Gregg and Fayette counties had expired on Jan. 2, 1988. It had replaced the previous Subsection (f), which expired Jan. 2, 1986.]

Article XVI — (Cont'd.)

(g) The office of County Treasurer in Nueces County is abolished and all powers, duties, and functions of this office are transferred to the County Clerk. However, the office of County Treasurer in Nueces County is abolished under this subsection only if, at the statewide election at which this amendment is submitted to the voters, a majority of the voters of Nueces County voting on the question at that election favor the amendment. The office of County Treasurer of Nueces County is abolished on January 1, 1988, if the conditions of this subsection are met. If that office in Nueces County is not abolished, this subsection expires on January 1, 1988.

[Note — The foregoing Sec. 44 of Art. XVI was amended to raise term of office from two to four years. Submitted by the Fifty-third Legislature (1953) and adopted in election Nov. 2, 1954. It was further amended to abolish the office of County Treasurer in Tarrant and Bee counties. Submitted by the Sixty-seventh Legislature (1981) and adopted in election Nov. 2, 1982. It was amended again to abolish the office of County Treasurer in Bexar and Collin counties. Submitted by Sixty-eighth Legislature (1983) and adopted in election Nov. 6, 1984. It was again amended to abolish the office of county treasurer in Andrews and El Paso counties; to abolish the office of county surveyor in Collin, Dallas, Denton, El Paso, Henderson and Randall counties. Submitted by the Sixty-ninth Legislature (1985) and adopted in an election Nov. 5, 1985. It was further amended to abolish the office of county treasurer in Gregg, Fayette and Nueces counties. Submitted by the Seventieth Legislature (1987) and adopted in an election Nov. 3, 1987. It was again amended to abolish the office of county surveyor in Cass, Ector, Garza, Smith, Bexar, Harris and Webb counties. Proposed by the Seventy-first Legislature (1989) and adopted in an election Nov. 7, 1989.]

[Note—Sections 45 and 46 of Art. XVI—relating to records of the history of Texas and organization of a militia — were deleted by constitutional amendment in election Aug. 5, 1969.]

Sec. 47. **Scruples Against Bearing Arms** — Any person who conscientiously scruples to bear arms shall not be compelled to do so, but shall pay an equivalent for personal service.

Sec. 48. **Laws to Remain in Force** — All laws and parts of laws now in force in the State of Texas which are not repugnant to the Constitution of the United States or to this Constitution shall continue and remain in force as the laws of this State until they expire by their own limitation or shall be amended or repealed by the Legislature.

Sec. 49. **Exemptions From Forced Sales** — The Legislature shall have power, and it shall be its duty, to protect by law from forced sale a certain portion of the personal property of all heads of families, and also of unmarried adults, male and female.

Sec. 50. **Homestead Exemptions; Encumbrances, Pretended Sales** — The homestead of a family, or of a single adult person, shall be, and is hereby protected from forced sale, for the payment of all debts except for the purchase money thereof, or a part of such purchase money, the taxes due thereon, or for work and material used in constructing improvements thereon, and in this last case only when the work and material are contracted for in writing, with the consent of both spouses, in the case of a family homestead, given in the same manner as is required in making a sale and conveyance of the homestead; nor may the owner or claimant of the property claimed as homestead, if married, sell or abandon the homestead without the consent of the other spouse, given in such manner as may be prescribed by law. No mortgage, trust deed, or other lien on the homestead shall ever be valid, except for the purchase money therefor, or improvements made thereon, as hereinbefore provided, whether such mortgage, or trust deed, or other lien, shall have been created by the owner alone, or together with his or her spouse, in case the owner is married. All pretended sales of the homestead involving any condition of defeasance shall be void.

[Note—The foregoing Sec. 50 of Art. XVI was amended to include single persons under the homestead exemption provision; and it further made the wife an equal partner under the homestead provision. Submitted by the Sixty-third Legislature (1973) and adopted in election Nov. 6, 1973.]

Sec. 51. **Homestead Defined** — The homestead, not in a town or city, shall consist of not more than two hundred acres of land, which may be in one or more parcels, with the improvements thereon; the homestead in a city, town or village, shall consist of lot or lots amounting to not more than one acre of land, together with any improvements on the land; provided, that the same shall be used for the purposes of a home, or as a place to exercise the calling or business of the homestead claimant, whether a single adult person, or the head of a family; provided also, that any temporary renting of the homestead shall not change the character of the same, when no other homestead has been acquired.

[Note—The foregoing Sec. 51 was amended to raise the value of lots, exclusive of improvements, from $5,000 to $10,000 when designated as homesteads. Submitted by the Sixty-first Legislature (1969) and adopted in election Nov. 3, 1970. It was further amended to provide that family homesteads may not be abandoned except with consent of both spouses. Submitted by the Sixty-third Legislature (1973) and adopted in election Nov. 6, 1973. It was again amended to replace the limitation on the value of an urban homestead with a limitation based on size. Submitted by Sixty-eighth Legislature (1983) and adopted in election Nov. 8, 1983.]

Sec. 52. **Descent of Homestead** — On the death of the husband or wife, or both, the homestead shall descend and vest in like manner as other real property of the deceased, and shall be governed by the same laws of descent and distribution, but it shall not be partitioned among the heirs of the deceased during the lifetime of the surviving husband or wife, or so long as the survivor may elect to use or occupy the same as a homestead, or so long as the guardian of the minor children of the deceased may be permitted, under the order of the proper court having jurisdiction, to use and occupy the same.

Sec. 53. **Declaration Validating Process and Writs** — That no inconvenience may arise from the adoption of this Constitution, it is declared that all process and writs of all kinds which have been or may be issued and not returned or executed when this Constitution is adopted shall remain valid, and shall not be in any way affected by the adoption of this Constitution.

[Note—Sections 54 and 55 of Art. XVI—relating to pensions, and the indigent lunatics—were deleted by constitutional amendment in election Aug. 5, 1969.]

Sec. 56. **Advertising Texas' Resources** — The Legislature of the State of Texas shall have the power to appropriate money and establish the procedure necessary to expend such money for the purpose of developing information about the historical, natural, agricultural, industrial, educational, marketing, recreational and living resources of Texas, and for the purpose of informing persons and corporations of other states through advertising in periodicals having national circulation, and the dissemination of factual information about the advantages and economic resources offered by the State of Texas; providing, however, that neither the name nor the picture of any living state official shall ever be used in any of said advertising, and providing that the Legislature may require that any sum of money appropriated hereunder shall be matched by an equal sum paid into the State Treasury from private sources before any of said money may be expended.

[Note—The foregoing Sec. 56 of Art. XVI is substituted for the original Section 56 which prohibited the expenditure of state funds for attracting immigrants. Submitted by the Fifty-fifth Legislature (1957) and adopted in an election Nov. 4, 1958.]

[Note—Sections 57, 58 and 60 of Art. XVI—relating to land for state capitol, management of the prison system and the Texas Centennial—were deleted by constitutional amendment in election Aug. 5, 1969.]

*Sec. 59-a. **Conservation and Development of Natural Resources** — The conservation and development of all the natural resources of this State, including the control, storing, preservation and distribution of its storm and flood waters, the waters of its rivers and streams, for irrigation, power and all other useful purposes, the reclamation and irrigation of its arid, semi-arid and other lands needing irrigation, the reclamation and drainage of its overflowed lands, and other lands needing drainage, the conservation and development of its forests, water and hydro-electric power, the navigation of its inland and coastal waters, and the preservation and conservation of all such natural re-

Article XVI — (Cont'd.)

sources of the State are each and all hereby declared public rights and duties; and the Legislature shall pass all such laws as may be appropriate thereto.

*The resolution submitting this amendment was headed "Sec. 59-a," followed by paragraphs "(b)" and "(c)." Obviously, the first heading should have been "Sec. 59 (a)," the parenthetical (a) referring only to the first paragraph.

(b) There may be created within the State of Texas or the State may be divided into, such number of conservation and reclamation districts as may be determined to be essential to the accomplishment of the purposes of this amendment to the Constitution, which districts shall be governmental agencies and bodies politic and corporate with such powers of government and with the authority to exercise such rights, privileges and functions concerning the subject matter of this amendment as may be conferred by law.

(c) The Legislature shall authorize all such indebtedness as may be necessary to provide all improvements and the maintenance thereof requisite to the achievement of the purposes of this amendment, and all such indebtedness may be evidenced by bonds of such conservation and reclamation districts, to be issued under such regulations as may be prescribed by law and shall, also, authorize the levy and collection within such districts of all such taxes, equitably distributed, as may be necessary for the payment of the interest and the creation of a sinking fund for payment of such bonds; and also for the maintenance of such districts and improvements, and such indebtedness shall be a lien upon the property assessed for the payment thereof; provided, the Legislature shall not authorize the issuance of any bonds or provide for any indebtedness against any reclamation district unless such proposition shall first be submitted to the qualified property taxpaying voters of such district and the proposition adopted.

(d) No law creating a conservation and reclamation district shall be passed unless notice of the intention to introduce such a bill setting forth the general substance of the contemplated law shall have been published at least thirty (30) days and not more than ninety (90) days prior to the introduction thereof in a newspaper or newspapers having general circulation in the county or counties in which said district or any part thereof is or will be located and by delivering a copy of such notice and such bill to the Governor who shall submit such notice and bill to the Texas Water Commission, or its successor, which shall file its recommendation as to such bill with the Governor, Lieutenant Governor and Speaker of the House of Representatives within thirty (30) days from date notice was received by the Texas Water Commission. Such notice and copy of bill shall also be given of the introduction of any bill amending a law creating or governing a particular conservation and reclamation district if such bill (1) adds additional land to the district, (2) alters the taxing authority of the district, (3) alters the authority of the district with respect to the issuance of bonds, or (4) alters the qualifications or terms of office of the members of the governing body of the district.

(e) No law creating a conservation and reclamation district shall be passed unless, at the time notice of the intention to introduce a bill is published as provided in Subsection (d) of this section, a copy of the proposed bill is delivered to the commissioners court of each county in which said district or any part thereof is or will be located and to the governing body of each incorporated city or town in whose jurisdiction said district or any part thereof is or will be located. Each such commissioners court and governing body may file its written consent or opposition to the creation of the proposed district with the governor, lieutenant governor, and speaker of the house of representatives. Each special law creating a conservation and reclamation district shall comply with the provisions of the general laws then in effect relating to consent by political subdivisions to the creation of conservation and reclamation districts and to the inclusion of land within the district.

(f) A conservation and reclamation district created under this section to perform any or all of the purposes of this section may engage in fire-fighting activities and may issue bonds or other indebtedness for fire-fighting purposes as provided by law and this constitution.

[Note—The foregoing Sec. 59-a, obviously meant to be Sec. 59 (see footnote), was added to establish a conservation policy. Submitted by Thirty-fifth Legislature (1917), and adopted in an election of Aug. 21, 1917, and proclaimed Oct. 2, 1917. It was amended by adding paragraph (d) to require notice at both the local level and state level through publication in a newspaper having general circulation in county in which district is to be set up at least 30 days prior to introduction of bill in Legislature. Submitted by Fifty-eighth Legislature (1963) and adopted in election Nov. 3, 1964. It was

further amended to establish certain requirements relative to enactment of laws creating certain conservation and reclamation districts. Submitted by Sixty-third Legislature (1973) and adopted in election Nov. 6, 1973. It was further amended by adding Subsection (f), authorizing certain districts to engage in fire-fighting activities and to issue bonds or otherwise lend their credit for fire-fighting purposes. (See also Subsection (d), Sec. 52, Art. III.) Submitted by Sixty-fifth Legislature (1977) and adopted in election Nov. 7, 1978.]

[Note—See note after Sec. 56 for Sec. 60.]

Sec. 61. **Compensation of District and County Officials** — All district officers in the State of Texas and all county officers in counties having a population of twenty thousand (20,000) or more, according to the then last preceding Federal Census, shall be compensated on a salary basis. In all counties in this State, the Commissioners Courts shall be authorized to determine whether precinct officers shall be compensated on a fee basis or on a salary basis, with the exception that it shall be mandatory upon the Commissioners Courts to compensate all justices of the peace, constables, deputy constables and precinct law enforcement officers on a salary basis beginning January 1, 1973; and in counties having a population of less than twenty thousand (20,000), according to the then last preceding Federal Census, the Commissioners Court shall also have the authority to determine whether county officers shall be compensated on a fee basis or on a salary basis, with the exception that it shall be mandatory upon the Commissioners Courts to compensate all sheriffs, deputy sheriffs, county law enforcement officers, including sheriffs who also perform the duties of assessor and collector of taxes, and their deputies, on a salary basis beginning January 1, 1949.

All fees earned by district, county and precinct officers shall be paid into the county treasury where earned for the account of the proper fund, provided that fees incurred by the State, county and any municipality, or in case where a pauper's oath is filed, shall be paid into the county treasury when collected and provided that where any officer is compensated wholly on a fee basis such fees may be retained by such officer or paid into the treasury of the county as the Commissioners Court may direct. All notaries public, county surveyors and public weighers shall continue to be compensated on a fee basis.

[Note—The foregoing Sec. 61 of Art. XVI has been amended three times, as follows: (1) To put all district and county officials in counties of more than 20,000 population on a salary basis, substituting for fee basis, and making it optional with the Commissioners Courts whether precinct officers in counties of less than 20,000 should be on salary or fee basis and optional with reference to county officers in counties of less than 20,000. Submitted by the Forty-fourth Legislature (1935), and adopted in an election Aug. 24, 1935. (2) To make mandatory a salary basis for constables and precinct enforcement officers in counties of more than 20,000 and making it mandatory, in counties of less than 20,000 population, that all sheriffs, deputy sheriffs and other county enforcement officers, be on salary basis. Submitted by the Fiftieth Legislature (1947) and adopted in election Nov. 2, 1948. (3) To include justices of the peace with those to be compensated on salary basis beginning Jan. 1, 1973. Submitted by the Sixty-second Legislature (1971) and adopted in an election Nov. 7, 1972.]

[Note—Sec. 62 and Sec. 63 of Art. XVI, pertaining to **Retirement, Disability and Death Compensation Funds** and **Teacher and State Employee Retirement System,** respectively, were repealed in a constitutional amendment election April 22, 1975. See also note under Art. III, Sec. 48-a, 48-b, 51-e and 51-f; also see Sec. 67 of Art. XVI, which replaces the foregoing Sections.]

Sec. 64. **Inspector of Hides and Animals; Elective District, County and Precinct Offices; Terms of Office** — The office of Inspector of Hides and Animals, the elective district, county and precinct offices which have heretofore had terms of two years, shall hereafter have terms of four years; and the holders of such terms shall serve until their successors are qualified.

[Note — The foregoing Sec. 64 of Art. XVI, an amendment, was added for the purpose of setting term of office for these officials. Submitted by the Fifty-third Legislature (1953) and adopted in election Nov. 2, 1954.]

Sec. 65. **District and County Officials; Terms of Office** — The following officers elected at the general election in November, 1954, and thereafter, shall serve for the full terms provided in this Constitution.

Article XVI — (Cont'd.)

(a) District Clerks; (b) County Clerks; (c) County Judges; (d) Judges of County Courts-at-Law, County Criminal Courts, County Probate Courts, and County Domestic Relations Courts; (e) County Treasurers; (f) Criminal District Attorneys; (g) County Surveyors; (h) Inspectors of Hides and Animals; (i) County Commissioners for Precincts Two and Four; (j) Justices of the Peace.

Notwithstanding other provisions of this Constitution, the following officers elected at the general election in November, 1954, shall serve only for terms of two years: (a) Sheriffs; (b) Assessors and Collectors of Taxes; (c) District Attorneys; (d) County Attorneys; (e) Public Weighers; (f) County Commissioners for Precincts One and Three; (g) Constables. At subsequent elections, such officers shall be elected for the full terms provided in this Constitution.

In any district, county or precinct where any of the aforementioned officers is of such nature that two or more persons hold such office, with the result that candidates file for "Place No. 1," "Place No. 2," etc., the officers elected at the general election in November, 1954, shall serve for a term of two years if the designation of their office is an uneven number, and for a term of four years, if the designation of their office is an even number. Thereafter, all such officers shall be elected for the term provided in this Constitution.

Provided, however, if any of the officers named herein shall announce their candidacy, or shall in fact become a candidate, in any General, Special or Primary Election, for any office of profit or trust under the laws of this state or the United States other than the office then held, at any time when the unexpired term of the office then held shall exceed one (1) year, such announcement or such candidacy shall constitute an automatic resignation of the office then held, and the vacancy thereby created shall be filled pursuant to law in the same manner as other vacancies for such office are filled.

[Note — The foregoing Sec. 65 of Art. XVI, an amendment, was added for the purpose of setting the terms of office of the aforementioned officers. Submitted by the Fifty-third Legislature (1953) and adopted in an election Nov. 2, 1954. This section was further amended by adding the provision that a person must resign his present term of office if same has more than a year to run when he becomes a candidate for another office. Submitted by the Fifty-fifth Legislature (1957) and adopted in an election Nov. 4, 1958.]

Sec. 65A. Notwithstanding Section 65 of this article, the election and term of office of a district attorney serving a judicial district composed entirely of Fort Bend County are governed by the law relating to criminal district attorneys.

[Note — The foregoing Sec. 65A of Art. XVI, an amendment, was added relating to the election of a district attorney in Fort Bend County. Proposed by the Seventy-first Legislature (1989) and adopted in an election Nov. 7, 1989. Subsections (a), (b) and (c), proposed and adopted at the same time, constituted a temporary provision requiring a district attorney serving in a judicial district composed entirely of Fort Bend County to be elected and serve a term in the manner provided by general law for criminal district attorneys. The temporary provision took effect upon adoption and expired Jan. 2, 1990.]

Sec. 66. **Pensions for Texas Rangers** — The Legislature shall have authority to provide for a system of retirement and disability pensions for retiring Texas Rangers who have not been eligible at any time for membership in the Employees Retirement System of Texas as that retirement system was established by Chapter 352, Acts of the Fiftieth Legislature, Regular Session, 1947, and who have had as much as two (2) years service as a Texas Ranger, and to their widows; providing that no pension shall exceed Eighty Dollars ($80) per month to any such Texas Ranger or his widow, provided that such widow was legally married prior to January 1, 1957, to a Texas Ranger qualifying for such pension.

These pensions may be paid only from the special fund created by *Sec. 17, Art. VII for a payment of pensions for services in the Confederate army and navy, frontier organizations, and the militia of the State of Texas, and for widows of such soldiers serving in said armies, navies, organizations or militia.

---

*Sec. 17, Art. VII was repealed by amendment adopted in election Nov. 2, 1982. No provision has been made for deletion of this reference in Art. XVI to Sec. 17, Art. VII. (See Art. VIII, Sec. 1-e.)

[Note — The foregoing Sec. 66 of Art. XVI, an amendment, was added to provide for retirement pensions for Texas Rangers and their widows. Submitted by the Fifty-fifth Legislature (1957), adopted in an election Nov. 4, 1958. (See also Art. VIII, Sec. 1-e.)]

Sec. 67. **State Retirement Systems** — (a) General Provisions. (1) The Legislature may enact general laws establishing systems and programs of retirement and related disability and death benefits for public employees and officers. Financing of benefits must be based on sound actuarial principles. The assets of a system are held in trust for the benefit of members and may not be diverted.

(2) A person may not receive benefits from more than one system for the same service, but the Legislature may provide by law that a person with service covered by more than one system or program is entitled to a fractional benefit from each system or program based on service rendered under each system or program calculated as to amount upon the benefit formula used in that system or program. Transfer of service credit between the Employees Retirement System of Texas and the Teacher Retirement System of Texas also may be authorized by law.

(3) Each statewide benefit system must have a board of trustees to administer the system and to invest the funds of the system in such securities as the board may consider prudent investments. In making investments, a board shall exercise the judgment and care under the circumstances then prevailing that persons of ordinary prudence, discretion, and intelligence exercise in the management of their own affairs, not in regard to speculation, but in regard to the permanent disposition of their funds, considering the probable income therefrom as well as the probable safety of their capital. The Legislature by law may further restrict the investment discretion of a board.

(4) General laws establishing retirement systems and optional retirement programs for public employees and officers in effect at the time of the adoption of this section remain in effect, subject to the general powers of the Legislature established in this subsection.

(b) **State Retirement Systems.** (1) The Legislature shall establish by law a Teacher Retirement System of Texas to provide benefits for persons employed in the public schools, colleges, and universities supported wholly or partly by the state. Other employees may be included under the system by law.

(2) The Legislature shall establish by law an Employees Retirement System of Texas to provide benefits for officers and employees of the state and such state-compensated officers and employees of appellate courts and judicial districts as may be included under the system by law.

(3) The amount contributed by a person participating in the Employees Retirement System of Texas or the Teacher Retirement System of Texas shall be established by the Legislature but may not be less than six percent of current compensation. The amount contributed by the state may not be less than six percent nor more than 10 percent of the aggregate compensation paid to individuals participating in the system. In an emergency, as determined by the governor, the Legislature may appropriate such additional sums as are actuarially determined to be required to fund benefits authorized by law.

(c) **Local Retirement Systems.** (1) The Legislature shall provide by law for:

(A) The creation by any city or county of a system of benefits for its officers and employees;

(B) A statewide system of benefits for the officers and employees of counties or other political subdivisions of the state in which counties or other political subdivisions may voluntarily participate; and

(C) A statewide system of benefits for officers and employees of cities in which cities may voluntarily participate.

(2) Benefits under these systems must be reasonably related to participant tenure and contributions.

(d) **Judicial Retirement System.** (1) Notwithstanding any other provision of this section, the system of retirement, disability, and survivors' benefits heretofore established in the constitution or by law for justices, judges, and commissioners of the appellate courts and judges of the district and criminal district courts is continued in effect. Contributions required and benefits payable are to be as provided by law.

(2) General administration of the Judicial Retirement System of Texas is by the Board of Trustees of the Employees Retirement System of Texas under such regulations as may be provided by law.

(e) **Anticipatory Legislation.** Legislation enacted in anticipation of this amendment is not void because it is anticipatory.

[Note — The foregoing Sec. 67 of Art. XVI, an amendment, was added to revise and consolidate provisions relating to state and local retirement systems and programs, and providing for a maximum state contribution to state systems of 10 percent of aggregate compensation paid to individuals. Submitted by the Sixty-fourth Legislature (1975) and adopted in an election April 22, 1975. See also notes under Art. III, Sections 48-a, 48-b, 51-e and 51-f; and Art. XVI, Sections 62 and 63.]

Article XVI — (Cont'd.)

Sec. 68. **Promoting, Marketing Agricultural Products —** The Legislature may provide for the advancement of food and fiber in this state by providing representative associations of agricultural producers with authority to collect such refundable assessments on their product sales as may be approved by referenda of producers. All revenue collected shall be used solely to finance programs of marketing, promotion, research, and education relating to that commodity.

[Note — The foregoing Sec. 68 of Art. XVI, an amendment, was added to provide for the advancement of food and fiber production and marketing through research, education and promotion, financed by producers of agricultural products. Submitted by Sixty-eighth Legislature (1983) and adopted in election Nov. 8, 1983.]

Sec. 69. The Legislature may require, by rider in the General Appropriations Act or by separate statute, the prior approval of the expenditure or the emergency transfer of any funds appropriated by the agencies of state government.

[Note — The foregoing Sec. 69 of Art. XVI, an amendment, was added to protect public funds by authorizing prior approval of expenditure or emergency transfer of state appropriations. Submitted by Sixty-ninth Legislature (1985) and adopted in an election Nov. 5, 1985.]

Sec. 70. **Texas Growth Fund —** (a) In this section:

(1) "Board of trustees" means the board of trustees of the Texas growth fund.

(2) "Fund" means the Texas growth fund.

(3) "Venture capital investment" means an investment in debt, equity, or a combination of debt and equity that possesses the potential for substantial investment returns, and includes investments in new or small businesses, investments in businesses with rapid growth potential, or investments in applied research and organizational activities leading to business formation and opportunities involving new or improved processes or products.

(b) The Texas growth fund is created as a trust fund. Except as otherwise provided by this section, the fund is subject to the general laws of this state governing private sector trusts. The governing boards of the permanent university fund, the permanent school fund, the Teacher Retirement System of Texas, the Employees Retirement System of Texas, and any other pension system created under this constitution or by statute of this state in their sole discretion may make investments in the fund.

(c) The fund is managed by a board of trustees consisting of four public members appointed by the governor and one member from and elected by the membership of each of the following:

(1) the Board of Regents of The University of Texas System;

(2) the Board of Regents of The Texas A&M University System;

(3) the Board of Trustees of the Teacher Retirement System of Texas;

(4) the Board of Trustees of the Employees Retirement System of Texas; and

(5) the State Board of Education.

(d) Each public member of the board must have demonstrated substantial investment expertise. A public member serves for a six-year term expiring February 1 of an odd-numbered year.

(e) A person filling an elected position on the board of trustees ceases to be a member of the board of trustees when the person ceases to be a member of the board the person represents or as otherwise provided by procedures adopted by the board the person represents. The governor shall designate a chairman from among the members of the board of trustees who serves a term of two years expiring February 1 of each odd-numbered year. A member may serve more than one term as chairman.

(f) The board of trustees shall manage the investment of the fund, and may:

(1) employ and retain staff, including a chief executive officer;

(2) analyze and structure investments;

(3) set investment policy of the fund;

(4) take any action necessary for the creation, administration, and protection of the fund;

(5) enter into investment contracts with the participating funds or systems;

(6) adopt rules regarding the operation of the fund;

(7) pay expenses of the fund based on an assessment on investor contributions; and

(8) alternatively, or in combination with its own staff, contract for the management of investments under this section with a private investment management firm or with an investing fund or system electing a member of the board of trustees.

(g) In making investments, including venture capital investments, the board of trustees shall exercise the judgment and care under the circumstances then prevailing that persons of ordinary prudence, discretion, and intelligence exercise in the management of their own affairs, not in regard to speculation but in regard to the permanent disposition of their funds, considering the probable income as well as the probable safety of the capital of the fund. All investments of the fund shall be directly related to the creation, retention, or expansion of employment opportunity and economic growth in Texas. In making venture capital investments, all other material matters being equal, the board of trustees shall invest in technological advances that could be expected to result in the greatest increase in employment opportunity and economic growth in Texas.

(h) The board of trustees shall establish and operate the fund to the extent practical under the generally accepted business procedures relating to a mutual fund and shall value the investments for determining the purchase or sales price of participating shares of investing funds or systems participating in the fund consistent with investment contracts. Evidences of participation in the fund shall be held by the state treasurer in keeping with the custodial responsibilities of that office.

(i) An investing fund or system, without liability at law or in equity to members of the governing board of the fund or system in their personal or official capacities, may cumulatively invest in the Texas growth fund not more than one percent of the book or cost value of the investing fund or system, as determined at the end of each fiscal year.

(j) The board of trustees shall establish criteria for the investment of not more than 10 percent of the fund in venture capital investments. Not more than 25 percent of the funds available for venture capital investments may be used for unilateral investment. Investments of the remainder of the funds available for venture capital investments must be matched at least equally by funds from sources other than the fund, with matching amounts established by the board of trustees. The board of trustees shall also establish criteria for the investment of not less than 50 percent of the fund in equity or debt security, or a combination of equity and debt security, for the initial construction, expansion, or modernization of business or industrial facilities in Texas. The board of trustees may invest in money funds whose underlying investments are consistent and acceptable under the investment policy of the fund.

(k) On a quarterly basis, the amount of income realized on investments under this section shall be distributed to each of the systems and funds investing in the Texas growth fund in proportion to the number of participating shares of each investing system and fund. Capital appreciation becomes a part of the corpus of the Texas growth fund and shall be distributed in accordance with the investment contracts.

(l) The board of trustees shall make arrangements to begin liquidation, phase out investments, and return the principal and capital gains on investments to the investors in the fund not later than the 10th anniversary of the date of the adoption of this section. Except under unusual circumstances where it may be necessary to protect investments previously made, further investments may not be made in or by the fund after the 10th anniversary of the date of the adoption of this section.

(m) At the regular legislative session next preceding the 10th anniversary of the date of the adoption of this section, the legislature, by two-thirds vote of each house, may authorize the creation of Texas growth fund II, which shall operate under this section and under the board of trustees created by this section in the same manner as the Texas growth fund. Funds in Texas growth fund II may not be commingled with funds in the Texas growth fund.

(n) The board of trustees may purchase liability insurance for the coverage of the trustees, employees, and agents of the board.

(o) The legislature shall provide by law for the periodic review of the board of trustees in the same manner and at the same intervals as it provides for review of other state agencies, except that the legislature shall provide that the board of trustees is not subject to abolishment as part of the review process.

(p) This section expires September 1, 1998, except that if the legislature authorizes the creation of Texas growth fund II as provided by Subsection (m) of this section, this section expires September 1, 2008.

(q) This section is self-executing and takes effect on its adoption by the voters. All state officials named in this section, the state treasurer, and the comptroller of public accounts shall take all necessary actions for the implementation of this section. The legislature shall provide by law for full disclosure of all details concerning investments authorized by this section.

Article XVI — (Cont'd.); Article XVII

(r) The board of trustees may not invest money from the Texas growth fund in a business unless the business has submitted to the board of trustees an affidavit disclosing whether the business has any direct financial investment in or with South Africa or Namibia.

[Note — The foregoing Sec. 70 of Article XVI, an amendment, was added to establish the Texas growth fund. Submitted by the Seventieth Legislature (1987) and adopted in an election Nov. 8, 1988.]

Sec. 71. (a) The legislature by law may establish a Texas product development fund to be used without further appropriation solely in furtherance of a program established by the legislature to aid in the development and production of new or improved products in this state. The fund shall contain a program account, an interest and sinking account, and other accounts authorized by the legislature. To carry out the program authorized by this subsection, the legislature may authorize loans, loan guarantees, and equity investments using money in the Texas product development fund and the issuance of up to $25 million of general obligation bonds to provide initial funding of the Texas product development fund. The Texas product development fund is composed of the proceeds of the bonds authorized by this subsection, loan repayments, guarantee fees, royalty receipts, dividend income, and other amounts received by the state from loans, loan guarantees, and equity investments made under this subsection and any other amounts required to be deposited in the Texas product development fund by the legislature.

(b) The legislature by law may establish a Texas small business incubator fund to be used without further appropriation solely in furtherance of a program established by the legislature to foster and stimulate the development of small businesses in the state. The fund shall contain a project account, an interest and sinking account, and other accounts authorized by the legislature. A small business incubator operating under the program is exempt from ad valorem taxation in the same manner as an institution of purely public charity under Article VIII, Section 2, of this constitution. To carry out the program authorized by this subsection, the legislature may authorize loans and grants of money in the Texas small business incubator fund and the issuance of up to $20 million of general obligation bonds to provide initial funding of the Texas small business incubator fund. The Texas small business incubator fund is composed of the proceeds of the bonds authorized by this subsection, loan repayments, and other amounts received by the state for loans or grants made under this subsection and any other amounts required to be deposited in the Texas small business incubator fund by the legislature.

(c) The legislature may require review and approval of the issuance of bonds under this section, of the use of the bond proceeds, or of the rules adopted by an agency to govern use of the bond proceeds. Notwithstanding any other provision of this constitution, any entity created or directed to conduct this review and approval may include members, or appointees of members, of the executive, legislative, and judicial departments of state goverment.

(d) Bonds authorized under this seciton constitute a general obligation of the state. While any of the bonds or interest on the bonds is outstanding and unpaid, there is appropriated out of the first money coming into the treasury in each fiscal year, not otherwise appropriated by this constitution, the amount sufficient to pay the principal of and interest on the bonds that mature or become due during the fiscal year, less any amount in any interest and sinking account at the end of the preceding fiscal year that is pledged to payment of the bonds or interest.

[Note — The foregoing Sec. 71 of Art. XVI, an amendment, was added to establish a Texas product development fund to aid in the development and production of new or improved products in this state. Proposed by the Seventy-first Legislature (1989) and adopted in an election Nov. 7, 1989.]

ARTICLE XVII — MODE OF AMENDING THE CONSTITUTION OF THIS STATE

Sec. 1. **How the Constitution Is to Be Amended** — The Legislature, at any regular session, or at any special session when the matter is included within the purposes for which the session is convened, may propose amendments revising the Constitution, to be voted upon by the qualified electors for statewide offices and propositions, as defined in the Constitution and statutes of this State. The date of the elections shall be specified by the Legislature. The proposal for submission must be approved by a vote of two-thirds of all the members elected to each House, entered by yeas and nays on the journals.

A brief explanatory statement of the nature of a proposed amendment, together with the date of the election and the wording of the proposition as it is to appear on the ballot, shall be published twice in each newspaper in the State which meets requirements set by the Legislature for the publication of official notices of officers and departments of the state government. The explanatory statement shall be prepared by the Secretary of State and shall be approved by the Attorney General. The Secretary of State shall send a full and complete copy of the proposed amendment or amendments to each county clerk who shall post the same in a public place in the courthouse at least 30 days prior to the election on said amendment. The first notice shall be published not more than 60 days nor less than 50 days before the date of the election, and second notice shall be published on the same day in the succeeding week. The Legislature shall fix the standards for the rate of charge for the publication, which may not be higher than the newspaper's published national rate for advertising per column inch.

The election shall be held in accordance with procedures prescribed by the Legislature, and the returning officer in each county shall make returns to the Secretary of State of the number of legal votes cast at the election for and against each amendment. If it appears from the returns that a majority of the votes cast have been cast in favor of an amendment, it shall become a part of this Constitution, and proclamation thereof shall be made by the Governor.

[Note—Sec. 1 of Art. XVII was amended to revise provisions on time and method of proposing amendments to State Constitution and publishing notice of proposed amendments. Submitted by the Sixty-second Legislature (1971) and adopted in an election Nov. 7, 1972.]

Sec. 2. **Rewriting State Constitution** — (a) When the Legislature convenes in regular session in January, 1973, it shall provide by concurrent resolution for the establishment of a constitutional revision commission. The Legislature shall appropriate money to provide an adequate staff, office space, equipment, and supplies for the commission.

(b) The commission shall study the need for constitutional change and shall report its recommendations to the members of the Legislature not later than November 1, 1973.

(c) The members of the Sixty-third Legislature shall be convened as a constitutional convention at noon on the second Tuesday in January, 1974. The Lieutenant Governor shall preside until a chairman of the convention is elected. The convention shall elect other officers it deems necessary, adopt temporary and permanent rules, and publish a journal of its proceedings. A person elected to fill a vacancy in the Sixty-third Legislature before dissolution of the convention becomes a member of the convention on taking office as a member of the Legislature.

(d) Members of the convention shall receive compensation, mileage, per diem as determined by a five-member committee, to be composed of the Governor, Lieutenant Governor, Speaker of the House, Chief Justice of the Supreme Court, and Chief Justice of the Court of Criminal Appeals. This shall not be held in conflict with Art. XVI, Sec. 33 of the Texas Constitution. The convention may provide for the expenses of its members and for the employment of a staff for the convention, and for these purposes may by resolution appropriate money from the general revenue fund of the State Treasury. Warrants shall be drawn pursuant to vouchers signed by the chairman or by a person authorized by him in writing to sign them.

(e) The convention, by resolution adopted on the vote of at least two-thirds of its members, may submit for a vote of the qualified electors of this State a new Constitution which may contain alternative articles or sections, or may submit revisions of the existing Constitution which may contain alternative articles or sections. Each resolution shall specify the date of the election, the form of the ballots, and the method of publicizing the proposals to be voted on. To be adopted, each proposal must receive the favorable vote of the majority of those voting on the proposal. The conduct of the election, the canvassing of the votes, and the reporting of the returns shall be as provided for elections under Sec. 1 of this article.

(f) The convention may be dissolved by resolution adopted on the vote of at least two-thirds of its members; but it is automatically dissolved at 11:59 p.m. on May 31, 1974, unless its duration is extended for a period not to exceed 60 days by resolution adopted on the vote of at least two thirds of its members.

(g) The Bill of Rights of the present Texas Constitution shall be retained in full.

[Note—The foregoing Sec. 2 of Art. XVII is an added amendment, providing for a constitutional convention for the purpose of submitting to the voters a new constitution or revisions of the existing state constitution. Submitted by the Sixty-second Legislature (1971) and adopted in an election Nov. 7, 1972.]

A technician adjusts the small transmitter that powered the first radio station owned by the Belo Corporation in 1922. The 50-watt station broadcast from the roof of The Dallas Morning News' building in downtown Dallas.

Newspapers, Radio and Television Stations

The radio and television stations in the list below are those with valid current operating licenses. Not included are those with only construction permits or with applications pending. The names of daily newspapers are followed by (D); all others are weeklies.

Abernathy—Newspaper: Weekly Review.

Abilene—Newspaper: Reporter-News (D). **Radio-AM:** KEAN,1280 Khz; KORQ, 1340; KNTS, 1470; KEYJ, 1560. **Radio-FM:** KGNZ, 88.1 MHz; KACU, 89.7; KAGN, 91.3; KORQ, 100.7; KEAN, 105.1; KHXS, 106.3; KEYJ, 107.9. **TV:** KRBC-Ch. 9; KTAB-Ch. 32.

Alamo—Radio-FM: KJAV, 104.9 MHz.

Alamo Heights—Radio-AM: KDRY, 1100 Khz.

Albany—Newspaper: News.

Aledo—Newspaper: Clear Fork News.

Alice—Newspaper: Echo-News (D). **Radio-AM:** KDSI, 1070 Khz. **Radio-FM:** KOPY, 92.1 MHz; KBIC, 102.3.

Allen—Newspaper: American.

Alpine—Newspaper: Avalanche. **Radio-AM:** KVLF, 1240 Khz. **Radio-FM:** KALP, 92.7 MHz.

Alvarado—Newspaper: Post.

Alvin—Newspaper: Sun. **Radio-AM:** KTEK, 1110 Khz. **Radio-FM:** KACC, 91.3 MHz.

Amarillo—Newspaper: News & Globe-Times (D). **Radio-AM:** KGNC, 710 Khz; KIXZ, 940; KDJW, 1010; KZIP, 1310; KFNS, 1360; KPUR, 1440. **Radio-FM:** KLMN, 89.1 MHz; KQIZ, 93.1; KBUY, 94.1; KLSF, 96.9; KMLT, 97.9; KMML, 98.7; KRGN, 103.1. **TV:** KACV-Ch. 2; KAMR-Ch. 4; KVII-Ch. 7; KFDA-Ch. 10; KCIT-Ch. 14.

Amherst—Newspaper: Press.

Anahuac—Newspaper: Progress.

Andrews—Newspaper: Andrews County News. **Radio-AM:** KACT, 1360 Khz. **Radio-FM:** KACT, 105.5 MHz.

Angleton—Newspaper: Times (D).

Anson—Newspaper: Western Observer. **Radio-FM:** KKHR, 98.1 MHz.

Aransas Pass—Newspaper: Progress.

Archer City—Newspaper: Archer County News.

Arlington—Newspaper: News. **Radio-FM:** KHYI, 94.9 MHz.

Aspermont—Newspaper: Stonewall County Courier.

Athens—Newspaper: Daily Review (D). **Radio-AM:** KLVQ, 1410 Khz.

Atlanta—Newspaper: Citizens Journal. **Radio-AM:** KALT, 900 Khz. **Radio-FM:** KPYN, 99.3 MHz.

Austin—Newspapers: American-Statesman (D); Austin Area Legal Record (D); Jollyville Record; Lake Travis View; Westlake Picayune. **Radio-AM:** KLBJ, 590 Khz; KVET, 1300; KMOW, 1490. **Radio-FM:** KAZI, 88.7 MHz; KMFA, 89.5; KUT, 90.5; KLBJ, 93.7; KKMJ, 95.5; KVET, 98.1; KLTD, 99.1; KASE, 100.7; KPEZ, 102.3. **TV:** KTBC-Ch. 7; KLRU-Ch. 18; KVUE-Ch. 24; KXAN-Ch. 36; KBVO-Ch. 42.

Azle—Newspaper: News-Advertiser.

Baird—Newspaper: Callahan County Star.

Balch Springs—Radio-AM: KSKY, 660 Khz.

Ballinger—Newspaper: Ledger. **Radio-AM:** KRUN, 1400 Khz. **Radio-FM:** KRUN, 103.1 MHz.

Bandera—Newspaper: Bulletin. **Radio-FM:** KHLC, 98.3 MHz.

Bangs—Newspaper: Brown County Gazette.

Bartlett—Newspaper: Tribune Progress.

Bastrop—Newspaper: Advertiser. **Radio-FM:** KGSR, 107.1 MHz.

Bay City—Newspaper: Daily Tribune (D). **Radio-AM:** KIOX, 1270 Khz. **Radio-FM:** KMKS, 92.1 MHz.

Baytown—Newspaper: Sun (D). **Radio-AM:** KWWJ, 1360 Khz. **TV:** KRTW-Ch. 57.

Beaumont—Newspaper: Enterprise (D). **Radio-AM:** KLVI, 560 Khz; KZZB, 990; KWIC, 1380; KAYC, 1450. **Radio-FM:** KVLU, 91.3 MHz; KQXY, 94.1; KZZB, 95.1; KAYD, 97.5; KWIC, 107.9. **TV:** KFDM-Ch. 6; KBMT-Ch. 12; KITU-Ch. 34.

Beeville—Newspaper: Bee-Picayune. **Radio-AM:** KIBL, 1490 Khz. **Radio-FM:** KYTX, 97.9 MHz; KIBL, 104.9.

Bellville—Newspaper: Times. **Radio-AM:** KACO, 1090 Khz.

Belton—Newspaper: Journal. **Radio-AM:** KTON, 940 Khz. **Radio-FM:** KYZZ, 106.3 MHz. **TV:** KNCT-Ch. 46.

Big Lake—Newspaper: Wildcat. **Radio-AM:** KWGH, 1290 Khz.

Big Sandy—Newspaper: Big Sandy & Hawkins Journal.

Big Spring—Newspaper: Herald (D). **Radio-AM:** KWKI, 1270 Khz; KBYG, 1400; KBST, 1490. **Radio-FM:** KBST, 95.3 MHz. **TV:** KWAB-Ch. 4.

Bishop—Radio-FM: KFLZ, 107.1 MHz.
Blanco—Newspaper: Blanco County News.
Blossom—Newspaper: Times.
Boerne—Newspapers: Hill Country Recorder; Star. **Radio-AM:** KBRN, 1500 Khz.
Bogata—Newspaper: News.
Bonham—Newspaper: Daily Favorite (D). **Radio-AM:** KFYN, 1420 Khz. **Radio-FM:** KFYZ, 98.3 MHz.
Booker—Newspaper: News.
Borger—Newspaper: News-Herald (D). **Radio-AM:** KQTY, 1490 Khz; KBBB, 1600. **Radio-FM:** KDXR, 104.3 MHz.
Bovina—Newspaper: Blade.
Bowie—Newspaper: News. **Radio-AM:** KRJT, 1410 Khz. **Radio-FM:** KRJT, 100.7 Mhz.
Brackettville—Newspaper: Kinney Cavalryman; Brackett News.
Brady—Newspapers: Herald; Standard. **Radio-AM:** KNEL, 1490 Khz. **Radio-FM:** KNEL, 95.3 MHz.
Breckenridge—Newspaper: American. **Radio-AM:** KSTB, 1430 Khz. **Radio-FM:** KROO, 93.5 MHz.
Bremond—Newspaper: Press.
Brenham—Newspaper: Banner-Press (D). **Radio-AM:** KTTX, 1280 Khz. **Radio-FM:** KULF, 94.1 Mhz; KWHI, 106.3.
Bridgeport—Newspaper: Index. **Radio-FM:** KWCS, 96.7 MHz.
Brookshire—Newspaper: Bluebonnet Banner.
Brownfield—Newspaper: News. **Radio-AM:** KKUB, 1300 Khz. **Radio-FM:** KLCU, 103.9 MHz.
Brownsboro—Newspaper: Statesman.
Brownsville—Newspaper: Herald (D). **Radio-AM:** KBOR, 1600 Khz. **Radio-FM:** KBNR, 88.3 MHz; KRIX, 99.5; KTEX, 100.3. **TV:** KVEO-Ch. 23.
Brownwood—Newspaper: Bulletin (D). **Radio-AM:** KXYL, 1240 Khz; KBWD, 1380. **Radio-FM:** KBUB, 90.3 MHz; KPSM, 99.3; KOXE, 101.5; KISJ, 104.1.
Bryan—Newspaper: Eagle (D). **Radio-AM:** KTAM, 1240 Khz; KAGC, 1510. **Radio-FM:** KORA, 98.3 MHz; KKYS, 104.7. **TV:** KBTX-Ch. 3.
Buda—Newspaper: Onion Creek Free Press.
Buffalo—Newspaper: Press.
Burkburnett—Newspaper: Informer Star. **Radio-FM:** KYYI, 104.7 MHz.
Burleson—Newspaper: Star.
Burnet—Newspaper: Bulletin. **Radio-AM:** KHLB, 1340 Khz. **Radio-FM:** KHLB, 106.9 MHz.
Caldwell—Newspaper: Burleson County Citizen-Tribune.
Cameron—Newspaper: Herald. **Radio-AM:** KMIL, 1330 Khz. **Radio-FM:** KCRM, 103.1 MHz.
Canadian—Newspaper: Record. **Radio-FM:** KEZP, 103.1 MHz.
Canton—Newspaper: Herald.
Canyon—Newspaper: News. **Radio-AM:** KAKS, 1550 Khz. **Radio-FM:** KWTS, 91.1 MHz; KPUR, 107.1; KAKS, 107.9.
Canyon Lake—Newspaper: Times Guardian/ Chronicle.
Carrizo Springs—Newspaper: Javelin. **Radio-AM:** KBEN, 1450 Khz.
Carthage—Newspapers: Panola County Post; Watchman. **Radio-AM:** KGAS, 1590 Khz. **Radio-FM:** KTUX, 98.9 MHz.
Castroville—Newspaper: News Bulletin.
Cedar Hill—Newspaper: Chronicle.
Celina—Newspaper: Record.
Center—Newspaper: Light & Champion. **Radio-AM:** KDET, 930 Khz. **Radio-FM:** KLCR, 102.3 MHz.
Centerville—Newspaper: News.
Chico—Newspaper: Texan.
Childress—Newspaper: Index. **Radio-AM:** KCTX, 1510 Khz. **Radio-FM:** KSRW, 96.1 MHz.
Chillicothe—Newspaper: Valley News.
Cibolo—Radio-AM: KBUC, 830 Khz.
Cisco—Newspaper: Press.
Clarendon—Newspaper: News.
Clarksville—Newspaper: Times. **Radio-AM:** KCAR, 1350 Khz.
Claude—Newspaper: News.
Clear Lake City—Newspaper: Citizen (D).
Cleburne—Newspaper: Times-Review (D). **Radio-AM:** KCLE, 1120 Khz.
Cleveland—Newspaper: Advocate. **Radio-AM:** KLEV, 1410 Khz.
Clifton—Newspaper: Record. **Radio-FM:** KWOW, 103.3 MHz.
Clute—Newspaper: Brazosport Facts (D).

Clyde—Newspaper: Journal.
Coleman—Newspaper: Chronicle & Democrat-Voice. **Radio-AM:** KSTA, 1000 Khz. **Radio-FM:** KSTA, 107.1 MHz.
College Station—Newspaper: Battalion (D). **Radio-AM:** WTAW, 1150 Khz. **Radio-FM:** KAMU, 90.9 MHz; KTSR, 92.1. **TV:** KAMU-Ch. 15.
Colleyville—Newspaper: News & Times.
Colorado City—Newspaper: Record. **Radio-AM:** KVMC, 1320 Khz. **Radio-FM:** KAUM, 106.3 MHz.
Columbus—Newspapers: Banner Press; Colorado County Citizen. **Radio-FM:** KULM, 98.3 MHz.
Comanche—Newspaper: Chief. **Radio-AM:** KCOM, 1550 Khz.
Comfort—Newspaper: News.
Commerce—Newspaper: Journal. **Radio-FM:** KETR, 88.9 MHz; KEMM, 92.1.
Conroe—Newspaper: Courier (D). **Radio-AM:** KIKR, 880 Khz; KSSQ, 1140. **Radio-FM:** KJOJ, 106.9 MHz. **TV:** KTFH-Ch. 49.
Cooper—Newspaper: Review.
Coppell—Newspaper: Citizens' Advocate.
Copperas Cove—Newspaper: Leader Press. **Radio-FM:** KOOV, 103.1 MHz.
Corpus Christi—Newspapers: Caller-Times (D); Legal & Business News (D). **Radio-AM:** KCTA, 1030 Khz; KCCT, 1150; KSIX, 1230; KRYS, 1360; KUNO, 1400; KEYS, 1440. **Radio-FM:** KEDT, 90.3 MHz; KBNJ, 91.9; KMXR, 93.9; KZFM, 95.5; KLTG, 96.5; KRYS, 99.1. **TV:** KIII-Ch. 3; KRIS-Ch. 6; KZTV-Ch. 10; KEDT-Ch. 16; KORO-Ch. 28.
Corrigan—Newspaper: Times.
Corsicana—Newspaper: Daily Sun (D). **Radio-AM:** KAND, 1340 Khz. **Radio-FM:** KAND, 107.9 MHz.
Cotulla—Newspaper: Record. **Radio-FM:** KDCY, 97.7 MHz.
Crane—Newspaper: News. **Radio-AM:** KXOI, 810 Khz.
Crockett—Newspaper: Houston County Courier. **Radio-AM:** KIVY, 1290 Khz. **Radio-FM:** KIVY, 92.7 MHz; KBHT, 93.5.
Crosbyton—Newspaper: Crosby County News & Chronicle.
Cross Plains—Newspaper: Review.
Crowell—Newspaper: Foard County News.
Crowley—Newspaper: Review.
Crystal City—Newspaper: Zavala County Sentinel. **Radio-FM:** KHER, 94.3 MHz.
Cuero—Newspaper: Record. **Radio-AM:** KQRO, 1600 Khz. **Radio-FM:** KQRO, 97.7 MHz.
Cypress—Radio-AM: KYND, 1520 Khz.
Daingerfield—Newspaper: Bee. **Radio-AM:** KEGG, 1560 Khz.
Dalhart—Newspaper: Texan (D). **Radio-AM:** KXIT, 1240 Khz. **Radio-FM:** KXIT, 95.9 MHz.
Dallas—Newspapers: The Dallas Morning News (D); Dallas Times Herald (D); Business Journal; Commercial Record (D); Oak Cliff Tribune; Park Cities News; Park Cities People; Suburban Tribune; Texas Jewish Post; White Rocker.**Radio-AM:** KLIF, 570 Khz; KGGR, 1040; KRLD, 1080; KYII, 1190; KAAM, 1310; KDBN, 1480. **Radio-FM:** KRSM, 88.5 MHz; KNON, 89.3; KERA, 90.1; KCBI, 90.9; KVTT, 91.7; KZPS, 92.5; KKWM, 97.9; KLUV, 98.7; KJMZ, 100.3; WRR, 101.1; KMGC, 102.9; KKDA, 104.5; KRSR, 105.3.**TV:** KDFW-Ch. 4; WFAA-Ch. 8; KERA-Ch. 13; KDFI-Ch. 27; KDAF-Ch. 33; KXTX-Ch. 39; KDTX-Ch. 58.
Decatur—Newspapers: Wise County Messenger; Wise Times.
Deer Park—Newspaper: Progress.
De Kalb—Newspaper: News.
DeLeon—Newspaper: Free Press.
Dell City—Newspaper: Hudspeth County Herald.
Del Rio—Newspaper: News-Herald (D). **Radio-AM:** KLKE, 1230 Khz; KWMC, 1490. **Radio-FM:** KDLK, 94.3 MHz; KTDR, 96.3.
Del Valle—Radio-AM: KIXL, 970 Khz.
Denison—Newspaper: Herald (D). **Radio-AM:** KDSX, 950 Khz. **Radio-FM:** KTCY, 104.9 MHz; KDSQ, 101.7.
Denton—Newspapers: Denton County Enterprise; Record-Chronicle (D). **Radio-AM:** KDNT, 1440 Khz. **Radio-FM:** KNTU, 88.1 MHz; KWDC, 99.1; KOAI, 106.1. **TV:** KDTN-Ch. 2.
Denver City—Newspaper: Press.
Deport—Newspaper: Times.
DeSoto—Newspaper: News-Advertiser.
Devine—Newspaper: Medina Valley Times; News. **Radio-FM:** KTXX, 92.1 MHz.
Diboll—Newspaper: Free Press. **Radio-AM:** KDFX, 1260 Khz. **Radio-FM:** KAFX, 95.5 MHz.
Dilley—Newspaper: Herald.
Dimmitt—Newspaper: Castro County News. **Radio-AM:** KDHN, 1470 Khz.

Donna—Newspaper: Events.
Dublin—Newspaper: Progress.
Dumas—Newspaper: Moore County News-Press. **Radio-AM:** KDDD, 800 Khz. **Radio-FM:** KMRE, 95.3 MHz.
Duncanville—Newspaper: Suburban.
Eagle Lake—Newspaper: Headlight.
Eagle Pass—Newspaper: News-Guide. **Radio-AM:** KEPS, 1270 Khz. **Radio-FM:** KINL, 92.7 MHz.
East Bernard—Newspaper: Tribune.
Eastland—Newspaper: Telegram. **Radio-AM:** KEAS, 1590 Khz. **Radio-FM:** KVMX, 96.7 MHz.
Eden—Newspaper: Echo.
Edgewood—Newspaper: Enterprise.
Edinburg—Newspaper: Review (D). **Radio-AM:** KURV, 710 Khz. **Radio-FM:** KOIR, 88.5 MHz; KBFM, 104.1; KVLY, 107.9.
Edna—Newspaper: Herald. **Radio-AM:** KTMR, 1130 Khz.
El Campo—Newspaper: Leader-News. **Radio-AM:** KULP, 1390 Khz. **Radio-FM:** KXGC, 96.9 MHz.
Eldorado—Newspaper: Success.
Electra—Newspaper: Star News.
Elgin—Newspaper: Courier. **Radio-AM:** KELG, 1440 Khz.
El Paso—Newspapers: Herald-Post (D); Times (D). **Radio-AM:** KROD, 600 Khz; KHEY, 690; KAMA, 750; KBNA, 920; KFNA, 1060; KEZB, 1150; KVIV, 1340; KTSM, 1380; KELP, 1590. **Radio-FM:** KTEP, 88.5 MHz; KXCR; 89.5; KOFX, 92.3; KAMZ, 93.1; KEZB, 93.9; KLTO, 94.7; KLAQ, 95.5; KHEY, 96.3; KBNA, 97.5; KTSM, 99.9; KPRR, 102.1. **TV:** KDBC-Ch. 4; KVIA-Ch. 7; KTSM-Ch. 9; KCOS-Ch. 13; KCIK-Ch. 14; KINT-Ch. 26; KSCE-Ch. 38.
Emory—Newspaper: Rains County Leader.
Ennis—Newspapers: Daily News (D); Ellis County News; The Press.
Everman—Newspaper: Times.
Fabens—Radio-FM: KPAS, 103.1 MHz.
Fairfield—Newspaper: Recorder. **Radio-FM:** KNES, 92.1 MHz.
Falfurrias—Newspaper: Facts. **Radio-AM:** KPSO, 1260 Khz. **Radio-FM:** KPSO, 106.3 MHz.
Farmersville—Newspaper: Times.
Farwell—Newspaper: State Line Tribune. **Radio-AM:** KIJN, 1060 Khz.**Radio-FM:** KIJN, 92.3 MHz; KLZK, 98.3.
Ferris—Radio-AM: KDFT, 540 Khz.
Flatonia—Newspaper: Argus.
Floresville—Newspaper: Chronicle-Journal. **Radio-FM:** KWCB, 94.3 MHz.
Floydada—Newspaper: Floyd County Hesperian. **Radio-AM:** KKAP, 900 Khz. **Radio-FM:** KKAP, 95.3 MHz.
Follett—Newspaper: The Golden Spread.
Forney—Newspaper: Messenger.
Fort Davis—Newspaper: Jeff Davis County Mountain Dispatch.
Fort Stockton—Newspaper: Pioneer. **Radio-AM:** KFST, 860 Khz. **Radio-FM:** KFST, 94.3 MHz.
Fort Worth—Newspapers: Business Press; Commercial Recorder (D); Lake Worth Times-Record; Star Telegram (D); Weekly Livestock Reporter. **Radio-AM:** WBAP, 820 Khz; KFJZ, 870; KHVN, 970; KESS, 1270; KNRB, 1360; KSGB, 1540; KSSA, 1600. **Radio-FM:** KTCU, 88.7 MHz; KLTY, 94.1; KSCS, 96.3; KPLX, 99.5; KMEX, 107.5; KEGL, 97.1; KTXQ, 102.1. **TV:** KXAS-Ch. 5; KTVT-Ch. 11; KTXA-Ch. 21; KFWD-Ch. 52.
Franklin—Newspaper: News Weekly.
Frankston—Newspaper: Citizen.
Fredericksburg—Newspaper: Standard/Radio Post. **Radio-AM:** KNAF, 910 Khz. **Radio-FM:** KFAN, 101.1 MHz.
Freeport—Radio-AM: KBRZ, 1460 Khz. **Radio-FM:** KGLF, 103.3 MHz.
Freer—Newspaper: Press. **Radio-FM:** KBRA, 95.9 MHz.
Friendswood—Newspaper: Journal.
Friona—Newspaper: Star.
Frisco—Newspaper: Enterprise.
Fritch—Newspaper: Eagle Press.
Gail—Newspaper: Borden Star.
Gainesville—Newspaper: Register(D). **Radio-AM:** KGAF, 1580 Khz. **Radio-FM:** KDGE, 94.5 MHz.
Galveston—Newspaper: Daily News (D). **Radio-AM:** KTUS, 1400 Khz; KGBC, 1540. **Radio-FM:** KRTX, 104.9 MHz; KQQK, 106.5. **TV:** KLTJ-Ch. 22; KTMD-Ch. 48.
Ganado—Newspaper: Tribune.
Garland—Newspaper: News. **Radio-AM:** KPBC, 770 Khz. **TV:** KUVN-Ch. 23.
Gatesville—Newspaper: Messenger. **Radio-FM:** KRYL, 98.3 MHz.
Georgetown—Newspapers: Sunday Sun; Williamson County Sun. **Radio-AM:** KGTN, 1530 Khz. **Radio-FM:** KHFI, 96.5 MHz.

Giddings—Newspaper: Times & News. **Radio-FM:** KOKE, 101.7 MHz.
Gilmer—Newspaper: Mirror. **Radio-AM:** KHYM, 1060 Khz. **Radio-FM:** KLSQ, 95.3 MHz.
Gladewater—Newspaper: Mirror. **Radio-AM:** KEES, 1430 Khz.
Glen Rose—Newspaper: Reporter.
Goldthwaite—Newspaper: Eagle.
Goliad—Newspapers: Advance Guard; Texan Express.
Gonzales—Newspapers: Daily Inquirer (D); Weekly Inquirer. **Radio-AM:** KCTI, 1450 Khz. **Radio-FM:** KPJN, 106.3 MHz.
Gorman—Newspaper: Progress.
Graham—Newspaper: Leader. **Radio-AM:** KSWA, 1330 Khz. **Radio-FM:** KWKQ, 107.1 MHz.
Granbury—Newspaper: Hood County News. **Radio-AM:** KPAR, 1420 Khz.
Grand Prairie—Newspaper: News. **Radio-AM:** KKDA, 730 Khz.
Grand Saline—Newspaper: Sun.
Grandview—Newspaper: Tribune.
Granger—Newspaper: News.
Grapeland—Newspaper: Messenger.
Greenville—Newspaper: Herald-Banner (D). **Radio-AM:** KGVL,1400 Khz. **Radio-FM:** KIKT, 93.5 MHz.
Groesbeck—Newspaper: Journal.
Groom—Newspaper: Groom/McLean News.
Groves—Radio-FM: KTFA, 92.1 MHz.
Groveton—Newspaper: News.
Gun Barrel City—Newspaper: Cedar Creek Pilot.
Hale Center—Newspaper: American.
Hallettsville—Newspaper: Tribune-Herald. **Radio-AM:** KRJH, 1520 Khz.
Hallsville—Newspaper: Herald.
Hamilton—Newspaper: Herald-News. **Radio-AM:** KOES, 900 Khz.
Hamlin—Newspaper: Herald. **Radio-AM:** KWZD, 103.7 MHz.
Harker Heights—Radio-FM: KLFX, 105.5 MHz.
Harlingen—Newspaper: Valley Star (D). **Radio-AM:** KGBT, 1530 Khz. **Radio-FM:** KELT, 94.5 MHz; KIWW, 96.1. **TV:** KGBT-Ch. 4; KLUJ-Ch. 44; KMBH-Ch. 60.
Harper—Newspaper: Herald.
Hart—Newspaper: Beat.
Haskell—Newspaper: Free Press. **Radio-FM:** KVRP, 95.5 MHz.
Hawley—Newspaper: Jones County Journal.
Hearne—Newspaper: Democrat. **Radio-FM:** KHRN, 94.3 MHz.
Hebbronville—Newspapers: Enterprise; View.
Hemphill—Newspaper: Sabine County Reporter & Rambler. **Radio-AM:** KAWS, 1240 Khz.
Hempstead—Newspaper: Waller County News-Citizen.
Henderson—Newspaper: Daily News (D). **Radio-AM:** KWRD, 1470 Khz. **Radio-FM:** KGRI, 100.1 MHz.
Henrietta—Newspaper: Clay County Leader.
Hereford—Newspaper: Brand (D). **Radio-AM:** KPAN, 860 Khz. **Radio-FM:** KPAN, 106.3 MHz.
Hico—Newspaper: News-Review.
Highland Park—Radio-AM: KVIL, 1150 Khz. **Radio-FM:** KVIL, 103.7 MHz.
Highlands—Newspaper: Star.
Hillsboro—Newspaper: Reporter. **Radio-AM:** KHBR, 1560 Khz. **Radio-FM:** KJNE, 102.5 MHz.
Hondo—Newspaper: Anvil Herald. **Radio-AM:** KRME, 1460 Khz.
Honey Grove—Newspaper: Signal-Citizen.
Hooks—Radio- FM: KLLI, 95.9 MHz.
Houston—Newspapers: Business Journal; Chronicle (D); Daily Court Review (D); Forward Times; Informer; Jewish Herald Voice; Post (D). **Radio-AM:** KILT, 610 Khz; KTRH, 740; KKBQ, 790; KEYH, 850; KPRC, 950; KLAT, 1010; KRBE, 1070; KNUZ, 1230; KXYZ, 1320; KCOH, 1430; KYOK, 1590. **Radio-FM:** KHMF, 88.7 MHz; KPFT, 90.1; KTSU 90.9; KTRU, 91.7; KLTR, 93.7; KLDE, 94.5; KIKK, 95.7; KHMX, 96.5; KHMF, 97.9; KODA, 99.1; KILT, 100.3; KLOL, 101.1; KMJQ, 102.1; KQUE, 102.9; KRBE, 104.1; KHCB, 105.7. **TV:** KPRC-Ch. 2; KUHT-Ch. 8; KHOU-Ch. 11; KTRK-Ch. 13; KETH-Ch. 14; KTXH-Ch. 20; KRIV-Ch. 26; KHTV-Ch. 39.
Howe—Newspaper: Enterprise.
Hubbard—Newspaper: City News.
Humble—Radio-AM: KGOL, 1180 Khz. **Radio-FM:** KSBJ, 89.3 MHz.
Huntington—Radio-FM: KAQU, 101.9 MHz.
Huntsville—Newspaper: Item (D).**Radio-AM:** KKNX, 1400 Khz; KSAM, 1490. **Radio-FM:** KSHU, 90.5 MHz; KHUN, 101.7.

Hurst—Newspaper: Mid-Cities News.
Hutto—Radio-FM: KRGT, 92.1 MHz.
Idalou—Newspaper: Beacon.
Ingleside—Newspaper: Index.
Iowa Park—Newspaper: Leader.
Iraan—Newspaper: News.
Irving—Newspaper: News. **TV:** KHSX-Ch. 49.
Jacksboro—Newspapers: Gazette-News; Jack County Herald.
Jacksonville—Newspaper: Progress (D). **Radio-AM:** KEBE, 1400 Khz. **Radio-FM:** KBJS, 90.3 MHz; KOOI, 106.5. **TV:** KETK-Ch. 56.
Jasper—Newspaper: News-Boy. **Radio-AM:** KTXJ, 1350 Khz. **Radio-FM:** KJAS, 100.9 MHz; KWYX, 102.3.
Jefferson—Newspaper: Jimplecute.
Jewett—Newspaper: Messenger.
Johnson City—Newspaper: Record-Courier.
Joshua—Newspaper: Tribune.
Junction—Newspaper: Eagle. **Radio-AM:** KMBL, 1450 Khz.
Karnes City—Newspaper: Karnes Citation. **Radio-AM:** KAML, 990 Khz.
Katy—Newspaper: Times.
Kaufman—Newspaper: Herald.
Keene—Radio-FM: KJCR; 88.3 MHz.
Kenedy—Newspaper: Advance Times. **Radio-AM:** KAML, 990 Khz. **Radio-FM:** KTNR, 92.1 MHz.
Kennedale—Newspaper: News.
Kerens—Newspaper: Tribune.
Kermit—Newspaper: Winkler County News. **Radio-AM:** KERB, 600 Khz. **Radio-FM:** KERB, 106.3 MHz.
Kerrville—Newspapers: Daily Times (D); Mountain Sun. **Radio-AM:** KERV, 1230 Khz. **Radio-FM:** KRVL, 94.3 MHz. **TV:** KRRT-Ch. 35.
Kilgore—Newspaper: News Herald (D). **Radio-AM:** KKTX, 1240 Khz. **Radio-FM:** KKTX, 96.1 MHz.
Killeen—Newspaper: Daily Herald (D). **Radio-AM:** KIIZ, 1050 Khz. **Radio-FM:** KNCT, 91.3 MHz; KBTS, 93.3.
Kingsville—Newspaper: Record. **Radio-AM:** KINE, 1330 Khz. **Radio-FM:** KTAI, 91.1 MHz; KNGV, 92.7; KWVS, 97.5.
Kirbyville—Newspaper: East Texas Banner.
Knox City—Newspaper: Knox County News.
Kress—Newspaper: Chronicle.
Ladonia—Newspaper: News.
La Feria—Newspaper: News.
La Grange—Newspaper: Fayette County Record. **Radio-AM:** KVLG, 1570 Khz. **Radio-FM:** KBUK, 104.9 MHz.
Lake Dallas—Newspaper: Lake Cities Sun.
Lake Jackson—Newspaper: Brazorian News. **Radio-FM:** KZFX, 107.5 MHz.
La Marque—Newspaper: Times.
Lamesa—Newspaper: Press Reporter. **Radio-AM:** KPET, 690 Khz. **Radio-FM:** KLSC, 100.3 MHz; KIOL, 104.7.
Lampasas—Newspaper: Dispatch Record. **Radio-AM:** KCYL, 1450 Khz. **Radio-FM:** KLTD, 99.1 MHz.
Lancaster—Newspaper: News.
La Porte—Newspaper: Bayshore Sun.
Laredo—Newspaper: Morning Times (D). **Radio-AM:** KVOZ, 890 Khz; KLAR, 1300. **Radio-FM:** KHOY, 88.1 MHz; KBNL, 89.9; KJBZ, 92.7; KOYE, 94.9; KRRG, 98.1. **TV:** KGNS-Ch. 8; KVTV-Ch. 13; KLDO-Ch. 27.
La Vernia—Newspaper: News.
Leakey—Newspaper: Real County American.
Leonard—Newspaper: Graphic.
Levelland—Newspaper: Hockley County News-Press. **Radio-AM:** KLVT, 1230 Khz. **Radio-FM:** KHOC, 105.5 MHz.
Liberty—Newspaper: Vindicator. **Radio-AM:** KPXE, 1050 Khz.
Lindale—Newspaper: News.
Linden—Newspaper: Cass County Sun.
Littlefield—Newspaper: Lamb County Leader-News. **Radio-AM:** KZZN, 1490 Khz.
Livingston—Newspaper: Polk County Enterprise. **Radio-AM:** KETX, 1140 Khz. **Radio-FM:** KETX, 92.1 MHz.
Llano—Newspaper: News. **Radio-FM:** KLKM, 104.9 MHz.
Lockhart—Newspaper: Post-Register. **Radio-AM:** KFIT, 1060 Khz.
Lockney—Newspaper: Beacon.
Longview—Newspaper: News-Journal (D). **Radio-AM:** KLGV, 1280 Khz; KFRO, 1370. **Radio-FM:** KYKX, 105.7 MHz. **TV:** KLMG-Ch. 51.
Lorenzo—Newspaper: Examiner. **Radio-FM:** KKCL, 98.1 MHz.
Lubbock—Newspaper: Avalanche-Journal (D). **Radio-AM:** KJBX, 580 Khz; KFYO, 790; KXTQ, 950; KFMX,1340; KLFB, 1420,; KTLK, 1460; KLLL, 1590. **Radio-FM:** KTXT, 88.1 MHz; KOHM, 89.1; KKIK, 93.7; KFMX, 94.5; KLLL, 96.3; KJBX, 99.5; KTEZ, 101.1; KZII, 102.5. **TV:** KTXT-Ch. 5; KCBD-Ch. 11; KLBK-Ch. 13; KAMC-Ch. 28; KJTV- Ch. 34.

Lufkin—Newspaper: Daily News (D). **Radio-AM:** KRBA, 1340 Khz; KBLZ, 1420. **Radio-FM:** KSWP, 91.1 MHz; KUEZ, 99.3; KYKS, 105.1. **TV:** KTRE-Ch. 9.
Luling—Newspaper: Newsboy & Signal. **Radio-FM:** KATG, 94.7 MHz.
Mabank—Newspaper: Monitor.
Madisonville—Newspaper: Meteor. **Radio-AM:** KMVL, 1220 Khz. **Radio-FM:** KAGG, 96.1 MHz.
Malakoff—Newspaper: News. **Radio-FM:** KCKL, 95.9 MHz.
Mansfield—Newspaper: News-Mirror.
Marble Falls—Newspaper: Highlander.
Marfa—Newspaper: Independent Sentinel.
Marion—Radio-AM: KBIB, 1000 Khz.
Marlin—Newspaper: Democrat. **Radio-FM:** KEYR, 92.9 MHz.
Marshall—Newspaper: News-Messenger (D). **Radio-AM:** KCUL, 1410 Khz; KMHT, 1450. **Radio-FM:** KBWC, 91.1 MHz; KEEP, 92.3; KMHT, 103.9.
Mart—Newspaper: Herald.
Mason—Newspaper: Mason County News.
Matador—Newspaper: Motley County Tribune.
Mathis—Newspaper: News.
McAllen—Newspaper: Monitor (D). **Radio-AM:** KRIO, 910 Khz. **Radio-FM:** KVMV, 96.9 MHz; KQXX, 98.5.
McCamey—Newspaper: News.
McGregor—Newspaper: Mirror.
McKinney—Newspaper: Courier-Gazette (D). **Radio-FM:** KSSA, 95.3 MHz.
Memphis—Newspaper: Democrat. **Radio-AM:** KLSR, 1130 Khz. **Radio-FM:** KLSR, 105.3 MHz.
Menard—Newspaper: News.
Mercedes—Newspaper: Enterprise. **Radio-FM:** KBOR, 106.3 MHz.
Merkel—Newspaper: Mail. **Radio-AM:** KMXO, 1500 Khz. **Radio-FM:** KFQX, 102.3 MHz.
Mesquite—Radio-FM: KEOM, 88.3 MHz.
Mexia—Newspaper: Daily News (D). **Radio-AM:** KRQX, 1590 Khz. **Radio-FM:** KYCX, 104.9 MHz.
Miami—Newspaper: Chief.
Midland—Newspaper: Reporter-Telegram (D). **Radio-AM:** KCRS, 550 Khz; KWEL, 1070; KJBC, 1150; KMND, 1510. **Radio-FM:** KNFM, 92.3 MHz; KBAT, 93.3; KCRS, 103.3; KCHX, 106.7. **TV:** KMID-Ch. 2.
Midlothian—Newspaper: Mirror; Reporter.
Miles—Newspaper: Messenger.
Mineola—Newspaper: Monitor. **Radio-AM:** KMOO, 1510 Khz. **Radio-FM:** KMOO, 96.7 MHz.
Mineral Wells—Newspaper: Index (D). **Radio-AM:** KJSA, 1140 Khz. **Radio-FM:** KYXS, 95.9 MHz.
Mission—Newspaper: Progress-Times. **Radio-AM:** KIRT, 1580 Khz. **Radio-FM:** KITM, 105.5 MHz.
Monahans—Newspaper: News. **Radio-AM:** KLBO, 1330 Khz. **Radio-FM:** KGEE, 99.9 MHz; KMGP, 102.1.
Moody—Newspaper: Courier.
Morton—Newspaper: Tribune. **Radio-AM:** KRAN, 1280 Khz.
Moulton—Newspaper: Eagle.
Mount Pleasant—Newspaper: Tribune (D). **Radio-AM:** KIMP, 960 Khz. **Radio-FM:** KPXI, 100.7 MHz.
Mount Vernon—Newspaper: Optic-Herald.
Muenster—Newspaper: Enterprise.
Muleshoe—Newspapers: Bailey County Journal; Journal. **Radio-AM:** KMUL, 1380 Khz. **Radio-FM:** KMUL, 103.1 MHz.
Munday—Newspaper: Courier.
Nacogdoches—Newspaper: Daily Sentinel (D). **Radio-AM:** KSFA, 860 Khz; KEEE, 1230. **Radio-FM:** KSAU, 90.1 MHz; KTBQ, 92.1; KJCS, 103.3.
Naples—Newspaper: Monitor.
Navasota—Newspaper: Examiner-Review. **Radio-AM:** KWBC, 1550 Khz. **Radio-FM:** KNAV, 92.5 MHz.
Nederland—Radio-AM: KDVE, 1510 Khz.
Needville—Newspaper: Gulf Coast Tribune.
New Boston—Newspaper: Bowie County Citizens Tribune. **Radio-AM:** KNBO, 1530 Khz.
New Braunfels—Newspaper: Herald-Zeitung (D). **Radio-AM:** KGNB, 1420 Khz. **Radio-FM:** KNBT, 92.1 MHz.
Newton—Newspaper: Newton County News.
New Ulm—Newspaper: Enterprise.
Nixon—Newspaper: News-Star.
Nocona—Newspaper: News.
Normangee—Newspaper: Star.
Odem—Newspaper: Odem-Edroy Times. **Radio-FM:** KKHQ, 98.3 MHz.

The 1991 Pulitzer Prize for Feature Photography was awarded to Dallas Morning News photographer William Snyder (right) for his pictures of orphaned, ill and abandoned children in Romania. This was Snyder's second Pulitzer: He was part of a News team, along with David Hanners and Karen Blessen, that won the 1989 Pulitzer for Explanatory Journalism for its report on the investigation of a plane crash. Dallas Morning News staff photo.

Odessa—Newspaper: American (D).**Radio-AM:** KENT, 920 Khz; KNDA, 1000; KOZA, 1230; KOYL, 1310; KRIL, 1410. **Radio-FM:** KOCV, 91.3 MHz; KQIP, 96.9; KODM, 97.9; KKKK, 99.1. **TV:** KOSA-Ch. 7; KTPX-Ch. 9; KPEJ-Ch. 24; KOCV-CH. 36; KMLM-Ch. 42.

O'Donnell—Newspaper: Index-Press.

Olney—Newspaper: Enterprise.

Olton—Newspaper: Enterprise.

Orange—Newspaper: Leader (D). **Radio-AM:** KOGT, 1600 Khz. **Radio-FM:** KKMY, 104.5 MHz; KIOC, 106.1.

Overton—Newspaper: Press.

Ozona—Newspaper: Stockman. **Radio-FM:** KYXX, 94.3 MHz.

Paducah—Newspaper: Post.

Paint Rock—Newspaper: Concho Herald.

Palacios—Newspaper: Beacon.

Palestine—Newspaper: Herald Press (D). **Radio-AM:** KNET, 1450 Khz. **Radio-FM:** KTDN, 91.5 MHz; KLIS, 96.7; KYYK, 98.3.

Pampa—Newspaper: News (D). **Radio-AM:** KGRO, 1230 Khz; KPDN, 1340. **Radio-FM:** KOMX, 100.3 MHz.

Panhandle—Newspaper: Herald.

Paris—Newspaper: News (D). **Radio-AM:** KGDD, 1250 Khz; KPLT, 1490. **Radio-FM:** KOYN, 93.9 MHz; KBUS, 101.9; KPLT, 107.7.

Pasadena—Newspaper: Citizen (D). **Radio-AM:** KIKK, 650 Khz; KLVL, 1480. **Radio-FM:** KJIC, 88.1 MHz; KKBQ, 92.9.

Pearland—Newspaper: Journal.

Pearsall—Newspaper: Leader. **Radio-AM:** KVWG, 1280 Khz. **Radio-FM:** KVWG, 95.3 MHz.

Pecos—Newspaper: Enterprise (D). **Radio-AM:** KIUN, 1400 Khz. **Radio-FM:** KPTX, 98.3 MHz.

Perryton—Newspaper: Herald. **Radio-AM:** KEYE, 1400 Khz. **Radio-FM:** KEYE, 95.9 MHz.

Petersburg—Newspaper: Post.

Pflugerville—Newspaper: Pflag.

Pharr—Newspaper: Pharr/San Juan/Alamo Advance News. **Radio-AM:** KVJY, 840 Khz.

Pilot Point—Newspaper: Post-Signal.

Pittsburg—Newspaper: Gazette. **Radio-FM:** KXAL, 103.1 MHz.

Plains—Newspaper: Pride. **Radio-FM:** KPLN, 90.3 MHz.

Plainview—Newspaper: Herald (D). **Radio-AM:** KKYN, 1090 Khz; KVOP, 1400. **Radio-FM:** KWLD, 91.5 MHz; KATX, 97.3; KKYN, 103.9.

Plano—Newspaper: Star-Courier (D). **Radio-AM:** KSSA, 1600 Khz.

Pleasanton—Newspaper: Express. **Radio-AM:** KBOP, 1380 Khz. **Radio-FM:** KBOP, 98.3 MHz.

Port Aransas—Newspaper: South Jetty.

Port Arthur—Newspaper: News (D). **Radio-AM:** KALO, 1250 Khz; KOLE, 1340;. **Radio-FM:** KYKR, 93.3 MHz; KHYS, 98.5. **TV:** KJAC-Ch. 4.

Port Isabel—Newspaper: Port Isabel/South Padre Press.

Portland—Newspaper: News. **Radio-FM:** KCGR, 105.5 MHz.

Port Lavaca—Newspaper: Wave (D). **Radio-AM:** KGUL, 1560 Khz. **Radio-FM:** KPLV, 93.3 MHz.

Port Neches—**Radio-AM:** KDLF, 1150 Khz.

Post—Newspaper: Dispatch. **Radio-AM:** KPOS, 1370 Khz.

Pottsboro—Newspaper: Press.

Prairie View—**Radio-FM:** KPVU, 91.3 MHz.

Premont—**Radio-FM:** KMFM, 104.9 MHz.

Presidio—Newspaper: The International.

Princeton—Newspaper: Herald.

Quanah—Newspaper: Tribune-Chief. **Radio-AM:** KIXC, 1150 Khz. **Radio-FM:** KIXC, 100.9 MHz.

Quinlan—Newspaper: Tawakoni News.

Quitaque—Newspaper: Valley Tribune.

Quitman—Newspaper: Wood County Democrat.

Ralls—**Radio-AM:** KCLR, 1530 Khz.

Ranger—Newspaper: Times.

Rankin—Newspaper: News.

Raymondville—Newspaper: Chronicle/News. **Radio-AM:** KSOX, 1240 Khz. **Radio-FM:** KSOX, 101.7 MHz.

Red Oak—Newspapers: North Ellis County Review; Rambler.

Refugio—Newspaper: County Advantage Press. **Radio-FM:** KZTX, 106.3 MHz.

Richardson—Newspaper: News.

Riesel—Newspaper: Rustler.

Rio Grande City—Newspaper: Rio Grande Herald. **Radio-FM:** KCTM, 103.1 MHz.

Rising Star—Newspaper: Rising Star.

Robert Lee—Newspaper: Observer/Enterprise.

Robstown—Newspaper: Nueces County Record-Star. **Radio-AM:** KROB, 1510 Khz. **Radio-FM:** KLUX, 89.5 MHz; KROB, 99.9; KMIQ, 105.1.

Rochester—Newspaper: Twin Cities News.

Rockdale—Newspaper: Reporter. **Radio-FM:** KRXT, 98.5 MHz.

Rockport—Newspapers: Herald; Pilot. **Radio-FM:** KPCB, 102.3 Mhz.

Rocksprings—Newspaper: Texas Mohair Weekly.

Rockwall—Newspaper: Rockwall Journal-Success.

Rollingwood—**Radio-AM:** KFON, 1370 Khz.

Roma—Newspaper: South Texas Reporter. **Radio-FM:** KBMI, 97.7 MHz.

Rosebud—Newspaper: News.

Rosenberg—Newspaper: Herald-Coaster (D). **Radio-AM:** KMPQ, 980 Khz. **Radio-FM:** KMIA, 104.9 Mhz. **TV:** KXLN-Ch. 45.

Rotan—Newspaper: Advance-Star-Record.

Round Rock—Newspaper: Leader. **Radio-FM:** KNLE, 88.1 MHz.

Rowena—Newspaper: Press.

Rowlett—Newspaper: Lakeshore Times.

Royse City—Newspaper: News.

Rusk—Newspapers: Cherokeean/Herald; Cherokee

County Banner. **Radio-AM:** KTLU, 1580 Khz. **Radio-FM:** KWRW, 97.7 Mhz.
Sachse—Newspaper: Sentinel.
Saint Jo—Newspaper: Tribune.
San Angelo—Newspaper: Standard-Times (D). **Radio-AM:** KGKL, 960 Khz; KAYJ, 1260; KTEO, 1340; KBIL, 1420. **Radio-FM:** KBIL, 92.9 Mhz; KTEO, 93.9; KIXY, 94.7; KGKL, 97.5; KELI, 98.7; KSJT, 107.5. **TV:** KACB-Ch. 3; KIDY-Ch. 6; KLST-Ch. 8.
San Antonio—Newspapers: Commercial Recorder (D); Express-News (D); Light (D); North San Antonio Times; Texas Farm & Ranch News. **Radio-AM:** KTSA, 550 Khz; KSLR, 630; KKYX, 680; KSJL, 760; KONO, 860; KFHM, 1160; WOAI, 1200; KZEP, 1250; KXTN, 1310; KCOR, 1350; KCHL, 1480; KEDA, 1540. **Radio-FM:** KSTX, 89.1 Mhz; KSYM, 90.1; KPAC, 90.9; KRTU, 91.7; KSRR, 92.9; KSAQ, 96.1; KAJA, 97.3; KISS, 99.5; KCYY, 100.3; KQXT, 101.9; KTFM, 102.7; KZEP, 104.5; KZVE, 107.5. **TV:** KMOL-Ch. 4; KENS-Ch. 5; KLRN-Ch. 9; KSAT-Ch. 12; KHCE-Ch. 23; KABB-Ch. 29; KWEX-Ch. 41; KVDA-Ch. 60.
San Augustine—Newspaper: Tribune.
San Benito—Newspaper: News.
Sanderson—Newspaper: Times.
San Diego—Newspaper: Duval County Picture.
Sanger—Newspaper: Courier.
San Juan—Radio-AM: KUBR, 1210 Khz.
San Marcos—Newspapers: News; Record (D). **Radio-AM:** KSPL, 1470 Khz. **Radio-FM:** KEYI, 103.5 MHz.
San Saba—Newspaper: News & Star. **Radio-AM:** KBAL, 1410 Khz.
Santa Anna—Newspaper: News.
Schulenburg—Newspaper: Sticker.
Seabrook—Radio-FM: KRTS, 92.1 MHz.
Seagoville—Newspaper: Suburbia News.
Seagraves—Newspaper: Gaines County News.
Sealy—Newspaper: News.
Seguin—Newspaper: Gazette-Enterprise (D). **Radio-AM:** KWED, 1580 Khz. **Radio-FM:** KSMG, 105.3 MHz.
Seminole—Newspaper: Sentinel. **Radio-AM:** KIKZ, 1250 Khz. **Radio-FM:** KSEM, 106.3 MHz.
Seymour—Newspaper: Baylor County Banner. **Radio-AM:** KSEY, 1230 Khz. **Radio-FM:** KSEY, 94.3 MHz.
Shamrock—Newspaper: Texan.
Shepherd—Newspaper: San Jacinto News-Times.
Sherman—Newspaper: Democrat (D). **Radio-AM:** KXEB, 910 Khz; KTXO, 1500. **Radio-FM:** KIKM, 96.7; KDSQ, 101.7 MHz; KWSM, 104.1.
Shiner—Newspaper: Gazette.
Silsbee—Newspaper: Bee. **Radio-AM:** KKAS, 1300 Khz. **Radio-FM:** KWDX, 101.7 MHz.
Silverton—Newspaper: Briscoe County News.
Sinton—Newspaper: San Patricio County News. **Radio-AM:** KDAE, 1590 Khz. **Radio-FM:** KNCN, 101.3 MHz; KOUL, 103.7.
Slaton—Newspaper: Slatonite. **Radio-AM:** KCAS, 1050 Khz. **Radio-FM:** KJAK, 92.7 MHz.
Smithville—Newspaper: Bastrop County Times.
Snyder—Newspaper: Daily News (D). **Radio-AM:** KSNY, 1450 Khz. **Radio-FM:** KSNY, 101.7 MHz.
Somerset—Radio-AM: KCHG, 810 Khz.
Somerville—Newspaper: Tribune.
Sonora—Newspaper: Devil's River News. **Radio-AM:** KHOS, 980 Khz. **Radio-FM:** KHOS, 92.1 MHz.
Spearman—Newspaper: Hansford Reporter Statesman. **Radio-FM:** KRDF, 98.3 MHz.
Springtown—Newspaper: Epigraph. **Radio-FM:** KMQX, 89.1 MHz.
Spur—Newspaper: Texas Spur.
Stamford—Newspaper: American. **Radio-AM:** KVRP, 1400 Khz.
Stephenville—Newspaper: Empire-Tribune (D). **Radio-AM:** KSTV, 1510 Khz. **Radio-FM:** KSTV, 105.7 MHz.
Sterling City—Newspaper: News-Record.
Stinnett—Newspaper: Adobe Press.
Stratford—Newspaper: Star.
Sudan—Newspaper: Beacon-News.
Sugar Land—Newspaper: Fort Bend Mirror.
Sulphur Springs—Newspaper: News-Telegram (D). **Radio-AM:** KSST, 1230 Khz. **Radio-FM:** KDXE, 95.9 MHz.
Sweetwater—Newspaper: Reporter (D). **Radio-AM:** KXOX, 1240 Khz. **Radio-FM:** KXOX, 96.7 MHz. **TV:** KTXS-Ch. 12.
Taft—Newspaper: Tribune.
Tahoka—Newspaper: Lynn County News.
Talco—Newspaper: Times.
Tatum—Newspaper: Trammel Trace Tribune.
Taylor—Newspaper: Daily Press (D). **Radio-AM:** KTAE, 1260 Khz.
Teague—Newspaper: Chronicle.
Temple—Newspaper: Telegram (D). **Radio-AM:**

KTEM, 1400 Khz. **Radio-FM:** KPLE, 104.9 MHz. **TV:** KCEN-Ch. 6.
Terrell—Newspaper: Tribune (D). **Radio-AM:** KTER, 1570 Khz. **Radio-FM:** KTLR, 107.1 MHz.
Terrell Hills—Radio-AM: KISS, 930 Khz. **Radio-FM:** KMMX, 106.7 MHz.
Texarkana—Newspaper: Gazette (D). **Radio-AM:** KCMC, 740 Khz; KTWN, 940; KTFS, 1400. **Radio-FM:** KTXK, 91.5 MHz; KTAL, 98.1; KKYR, 102.5. **TV:** KTAL-Ch. 6.
Texas City—Newspaper: Sun (D). **Radio-AM:** KYST, 920 Khz.
Thorndale—Newspaper: Champion.
Three Rivers—Newspaper: Progress.
Throckmorton—Newspaper: Tribune.
Timpson—Newspaper: News.
Tomball—Radio-AM: KSEV, 700 Khz.
Trenton—Newspaper: Tribune.
Trinity—Newspaper: Standard.
Tulia—Newspaper: Herald. **Radio-AM:** KTUE, 1260 Khz.
Tuscola—Newspaper: Journal.
Tye—Radio-FM: KTLC, 99.7 MHz.
Tyler—Newspaper: Courier-Times-Telegraph (D). **Radio-AM:** KTBB, 600 Khz; KZEY, 690; KDOK, 1330; KYZS, 1490. **Radio-FM:** KVNE, 89.5 MHz; KGLY, 91.3; KROZ, 92.1; KTYL, 93.1; KNUE, 101.5. **TV:** KLTV-Ch. 7.
Universal City—Radio-AM: KSAH, 720 Khz.
Uvalde—Newspaper: Leader-News. **Radio-AM:** KVOU, 1400 Khz. **Radio-FM:** KLXQ, 102.3 MHz; KYUF, 104.9.
Van Alstyne—Newspaper: Leader.
Van Horn—Newspaper: Advocate.
Vega—Newspaper: Enterprise.
Vernon—Newspaper: Daily Record (D). **Radio-AM:** KVWC, 1490 Khz. **Radio-FM:** KVWC, 102.3 MHz.
Victoria—Newspaper: Advocate (D). **Radio-AM:** KAMG, 1340 Khz; KNAL, 1410. **Radio-FM:** KVIC, 95.1 MHz; KTXN, 98.7; KEPG, 100.9; KZEU, 107.9. **TV:** KVCT-Ch. 19; KAVU-Ch. 25.
Vidor—Newspaper: Vidorian.
Waco—Newspaper: Citizen; Tribune-Herald (D). **Radio-AM:** KWTX, 1230 Khz; WACO, 1460; KRZI, 1580; KBBW, 1010. **Radio-FM:** KNFO, 95.5 MHz; KWTX, 97.5; WACO, 99.9; KWBU, 107.1. **TV:** KWTX-Ch. 10; KXXV-Ch. 25; KCTF-Ch. 34; KWKT-Ch. 44.
Wallis—Newspaper: News Review.
Waskom—Newspaper: Review.
Waxahachie—Newspaper: Daily Light (D). **Radio-AM:** KBEC, 1390 Khz.
Weatherford—Newspaper: Democrat(D); Leader/Times. **Radio-AM:** KZEE, 1220 Khz. **Radio-FM:** KYQX, 89.5 MHz.
Weimar—Newspaper: Mercury.
Wellington—Newspaper: Leader.
Weslaco—Radio-AM: KRGE, 1290 Khz. **TV:** KRGV-Ch. 5.
West—Newspaper: News.
West Lake Hills—Radio-AM: KTXZ, 1560 Khz.
Wharton—Newspaper: Journal-Spectator. **Radio-AM:** KANI, 1500 Khz.
Wheeler—Newspaper: Times. **Radio-FM:** KPDR, 90.5 MHz.
White Deer—Newspaper: News.
Whitehouse—Newspaper: Tri County Leader. **Radio-FM:** KISX, 107.3 MHz.
White Oak—Newspaper: Independent.
Whitesboro—Newspaper: News-Record.
Whitewright—Newspaper: Sun.
Whitney—Newspaper: Messenger.
Wichita Falls—Newspaper: Times-Record-News (D). **Radio-AM:** KWFT, 620 Khz; KKCR, 990; KLLF, 1290. **Radio-FM:** KMOC, 89.5 MHz; KNIN, 92.9; KLUR, 99.9; KWFS, 103.3; KTLT, 106.3. **TV:** KFDX-Ch. 3; KAUZ-Ch. 6; KJTL-Ch. 18.
Wills Point—Newspapers: Chronicle; Van Zandt News.
Wimberley—Newspaper: View.
Winfield—Radio-FM: KYKM, 97.7 MHz.
Wink—Newspaper: Bulletin.
Winnsboro—Newspaper: News. **Radio-FM:** KWNS, 104.9 MHz.
Winters—Newspaper: Enterprise.
Wolfe City—Newspaper: Mirror.
Woodville—Newspapers: Tyler County Booster; Woodsman. **Radio-AM:** KVLL, 1490 Khz.
Wylie—Newspapers: News; Sentinel.
Yoakum—Newspaper: Herald-Times. **Radio-FM:** KYOC, 102.3 MHz.
Yorktown—Newspapers: DeWitt County View; News.
Zapata—Newspaper: Zapata County News.

Crime and Punishment

Violent Crime Lurches Ahead

While the overall crime rate in Texas dropped for the past two years, violent crime made a comeback in 1990 that concerns law-enforcement officials and citizens alike.

In 1990, the crime rate dropped 1.4 percent, which coming on the heels of a 1.2 percent decline in 1989, gave the state the first back-to-back declines in the crime rate in the past 17 years. The crime rate is calculated on the basis of the incidence of seven so-called index crimes as set out by the Federal Bureau of Investigation. Index crimes include murder, rape, robbery, aggravated assault, burglary, theft and motor vehicle theft. The crime rate is a reflection of the number of index crimes committed per 100,000 population.

But the 18 percent increase in murder, 10 percent rise in rape, 17 percent hike in robbery and the 15 percent jump in aggravated assaults raised concerns that the state may be in for another spiral in the crime rate. The 2,388 persons murdered in 1990 was just below the number killed in the record years of 1982 when 2,463 died and 1981 in which 2,438 were killed.

Rapes, robberies and aggravated assaults all reached all-time highs in Texas in 1990, in part because of the growing population.

Violence against law-enforcement officers also increased during 1990. A total of 5,059 officers were assaulted during the year, an increase of almost 13 percent. Another 16 officers died in the line of duty, two killed feloniously and 14 accidentally.

Texas has 847 state and local law-enforcement agencies, including 254 sheriff's departments and 593 local police departments. A total of 35,164 sworn officers were certified to enforce the law in 1990.

Statewide, one in every five (20 percent) of the index crimes reported to law-enforcement agencies was cleared by the arrest of a suspect. Clearance rates typically are highest for the more serious crimes. Clearance rates in 1990 ranged from 69 percent for murder to 14 percent for burglary. For other crimes, clearance rates were 59 percent for rape and for aggravated assault, 30 percent for robbery, 19 percent for theft and 15

High Crime Rates Hit Cities of All Sizes

Crime in Texas is not confined in the big cities, but it has also moved to the suburbs and medium-sized communities. The following is a list of cities of more than 10,000 population and their crime rates based on incidents per 100,000 inhabitants.

Rank, City, County	Crime Rate
1. Greenville, Hunt	16,176
2. Dallas, Dallas	15,520
3. Fort Worth, Tarrant	14,977
4. Humble, Harris	14,204
5. Odessa, Ector	13,532
6. Orange, Orange	13,441
7. Balch Springs, Dallas	12,680
8. San Antonio, Bexar	12,477
9. Paris, Lamar	12,000

percent for auto theft. A total of 204,135 arrests were made for these seven categories of crime.

Texas is hardly soft on criminals either. A total of 521,923 persons were under some form of supervision by the criminal justice system. That is almost 4.3 percent of the adult population (18 years of age and over) that is either on felony or misdemeanor probation (361,720), on parole from prison (72,793), in prison (49,589) or in the local jail (37,821). This figure is 36 percent higher than in 1986, the first year it was calculated by the Texas Almanac.

In the following tables, the crime rates and other information about crime are presented for each of the jurisdictions in Texas. In addition, a second table presents the number of people under some form of criminal justice supervision by county in 1990-91.

Despite the good intentions of many Texans, the crime problem is not being solved in the state. These statistics reflect the failure.

—MIKE KINGSTON.

*Texas Crime History 1974-1990**

Year—	Murder	Rape	Robbery	Aggravated Assault	Burglary	Theft	Car Theft	Rate Per 100,000 Population
1974	1,646	3,521	19,420	21,931	184,562	289,900	44,787	4,695.2
1975	1,639	3,430	20,076	22,658	203,821	362,665	47,386	5,407.2
1976	1,519	3,666	17,352	21,885	193,208	400,767	43,871	5,464.4
1977	1,705	4,338	19,552	26,714	205,672	383,451	51,018	5,397.1
1978	1,853	4,927	21,395	28,475	209,770	398,923	57,821	5,556.8
1979	2,226	6,028	25,636	33,909	239,263	411,555	72,687	5,911.7
1980	2,389	6,694	29,532	39,251	262,332	450,209	79,032	6,135.7
1981	2,438	6,816	28,516	40,673	275,652	454,210	83,244	6,042.4
1982	2,463	6,814	33,603	45,221	285,757	501,312	87,090	6,297.5
1983	2,238	6,334	29,769	42,195	262,214	503,555	82,522	5,907.1
1984	2,091	7,340	28,537	42,764	266,032	529,469	87,781	6,029.2
1985	2,124	8,367	31,693	47,868	289,913	596,130	99,561	6,570.9
1986	2,255	8,605	40,018	59,002	341,560	664,832	119,095	7,408.2
1987	1,960	8,068	38,049	57,903	355,732	711,739	123,378	7,724.3
1988	2,021	8,122	39,307	60,084	362,099	739,784	134,271	8,019.6
1989	2,029	7,953	37,910	63,978	342,360	741,642	150,974	7,926.8
1990	2,388	8,746	44,316	73,860	314,346	730,926	154,387	7,823.7

*Crime figures provided by Texas Department of Public Safety, Austin, and the Federal Bureau of Investigation, Washington. Population figures used to determine crime rate per 100,000 population based on U.S. Bureau of Census. The population figure used in determining the crime rate for 1990 in Texas was 16,986,510.

Crime Rates, 1990

County/Agency	Total Crime	Crime Rate	Sworn Staff	Civilian Staff	Murder	Rape	Robbery	Assault	Burglary	Theft	Car Theft	Crimes Cleared	Clearance Rate	Arrested
Anderson — 3	2,301	4,791	59	40	5	19	38	248	653	1,226	112	622	27.0	517
Anderson SO	598	2,072	18	26	3	4	6	102	188	264	31	177	29.6	232
Palestine PD	1,640	9,090	36	11	2	15	31	145	437	931	79	414	25.2	277
Frankston PD	63	5,590	5	3	0	0	1	1	28	31	2	31	49.2	8
Andrews — 2	521	3,634	24	11	3	1	2	39	129	316	31	96	18.4	134
Andrews SO	194	5,301	10	9	2	1	0	12	48	110	21	43	22.2	77
Andrews PD	327	3,062	14	2	1	0	2	27	81	206	10	53	16.2	57
Angelina — 4	3,718	5,320	93	52	9	26	49	143	1,125	2,186	180	1,560	42.0	808
Angelina SO	780	2,325	21	29	4	11	8	11	248	454	44	420	53.8	230
Diboll PD	198	4,561	9	5	0	1	2	16	49	114	16	76	38.4	47
Huntington PD	19	1,059	3	0	0	0	0	2	10	7	0	10	52.6	10
Lufkin PD	2,721	9,008	60	18	5	14	39	114	818	1,611	120	1,054	38.7	521
Aransas — 2	1,204	6,729	30	19	1	12	4	72	361	686	68	287	23.8	137
Aransas SO	611	4,991	13	12	1	10	2	22	247	282	47	192	31.4	65
Rockport PD	593	12,476	17	7	0	2	2	50	114	404	21	95	16.0	72
Archer — 1	65	815	7	4	2	0	0	4	24	33	2	13	20.0	15
Archer SO	65	815	7	4	2	0	0	4	24	33	2	13	20.0	15
Armstrong — 1	26	1,286	2	3	0	0	0	1	21	1	3	4	15.4	1
Armstrong SO	26	1,286	2	3	0	0	0	1	21	1	3	4	15.4	1
Atascosa — 4	626	2,050	34	42	1	6	4	46	189	359	21	204	32.6	211
Atascosa SO	315	1,917	16	38	0	3	4	12	112	175	9	68	21.6	79
Pleasanton PD	177	2,305	9	4	0	2	0	10	49	108	8	92	52.0	85
Poteet PD	67	2,090	4	0	1	0	0	18	16	31	1	24	35.8	26
Jourdanton PD	67	2,081	5	0	0	1	0	6	12	45	3	20	29.9	21
Austin — 4	443	2,234	32	11	2	4	4	73	101	244	15	140	31.6	131
Austin SO	118	1,081	16	9	2	2	2	18	51	39	4	28	23.7	69
Bellville PD	122	3,612	7	2	0	0	1	19	20	75	7	35	28.7	27
Sealy PD	198	4,360	8	0	0	2	1	34	27	130	4	75	37.9	35
Wallis PD	5	500	1	0	0	0	0	2	3	0	0	2	40.0	0
Bailey — 2	235	3,327	9	11	0	3	0	22	34	166	10	95	40.4	73
Bailey SO	53	2,126	3	5	0	0	0	3	14	32	4	16	30.2	17
Muleshoe PD	182	3,982	6	6	0	3	0	19	20	134	6	79	43.4	56
Bandera — 1	407	3,853	12	6	1	4	2	43	199	138	20	99	24.3	95
Bandera SO	407	3,853	12	6	1	4	2	43	199	138	20	99	24.3	95
Bastrop — 4	1,263	3,301	41	62	2	19	4	123	475	589	51	217	17.2	313
Bastrop SO	740	2,827	20	49	1	16	2	68	341	282	30	54	7.3	261
Bastrop PD	162	4,006	8	2	0	0	0	2	33	121	6	40	24.7	34
Elgin PD	248	5,118	7	7	0	0	1	29	80	124	14	84	33.9	1
Smithville PD	113	3,536	6	4	1	3	1	24	21	62	1	39	34.5	17
Baylor — 1	57	1,300	2	6	0	0	0	14	22	21	0	14	24.6	17
Baylor SO	57	1,300	2	6	0	0	0	14	22	21	0	14	24.6	17
Bee — 2	1,135	4,516	30	23	0	0	7	174	311	606	37	523	46.1	544
Bee SO	155	1,338	12	17	0	0	0	17	75	56	7	30	19.4	59
Beeville PD	980	7,234	18	6	0	0	7	157	236	550	30	493	50.3	485
Bell — 8	9,657	5,054	323	215	22	146	172	578	2,327	5,985	427	3,270	33.9	2,378
Bell SO	862	1,677	64	134	4	25	6	72	278	424	53	352	40.8	245
Belton PD	492	3,944	17	9	2	0	7	33	110	330	10	171	34.8	103
Harker Heights PD	482	3,754	26	8	0	10	4	56	108	275	29	160	33.2	64
Killeen PD	4,401	6,927	109	36	11	47	94	129	1,151	2,774	195	1,059	24.1	919
Nolanville PD	25	1,363	1	1	0	0	0	1	11	13	0	2	8.0	2
Temple PD	3,357	7,281	100	27	5	63	61	287	661	2,142	138	1,518	45.2	1,041
Morgans Point R PD	34	1,925	5	0	0	0	0	0	5	27	2	5	14.7	0
Holland PD	4	358	1	0	0	1	0	0	3	0	0	3	75.0	4
Bexar — 20	131,294	11,076	2,320	1,012	226	513	3,025	2,928	30,031	78,106	16,465	19,289	14.7	16,913
Bexar SO	8,352	5,015	509	621	13	53	87	422	2,740	4,072	965	1,180	14.1	2,891
San Antonio PD	116,774	12,477	1,565	290	208	430	2,864	2,228	26,015	70,150	14,879	16,993	14.6	13,170
Alamo Heights PD	469	7,213	19	7	0	1	4	7	122	284	51	192	40.9	53
Balcones Height PD	888	29,385	16	6	0	3	16	34	138	549	148	84	9.5	158
Castle Hills PD	425	10,124	18	5	1	2	9	6	128	225	54	100	23.5	63
Converse PD	433	4,872	17	1	0	2	4	65	177	161	24	105	24.2	47
Hill Country PD	54	5,202	5	0	0	0	0	0	20	30	4	7	13.0	2
Hollywood Park PD	72	2,534	8	0	0	0	3	0	11	51	7	13	18.1	0
Kirby PD	609	7,314	9	5	0	8	8	19	96	423	55	93	15.3	62
Leon Valley PD	839	8,757	26	8	0	7	8	26	146	569	83	226	26.9	199
Olmos Park PD	86	3,980	10	0	0	0	2	1	16	54	13	8	9.3	11
Shavano Park PD	25	1,464	4	0	0	0	0	3	8	13	1	3	12.0	1
Terrell Hills PD	338	7,361	16	0	0	1	0	1	6	118	197	15	16	4.7	18
Universal City PD	698	5,346	24	8	2	4	7	58	116	468	43	78	11.2	109
Windcrest PD	494	9,267	16	6	1	1	9	19	87	316	61	94	19.0	67
Live Oak PD	388	3,871	18	3	0	1	2	28	59	262	36	56	14.4	32
UT-Hea Sci Cen PD	87	*****	17	32	0	0	0	0	2	78	7	6	6.9	5
UT-San Antonio PD	133	*****	14	19	0	0	0	1	0	127	5	17	12.8	8
Selma PD	53	10,192	7	1	0	0	1	2	17	21	12	7	13.2	2
Somerset PD	77	6,731	2	0	0	0	0	3	15	56	2	11	14.3	15
Blanco — 1	48	804	6	4	0	0	0	0	32	13	3	4	8.3	11
Blanco SO	48	804	6	4	0	0	0	0	32	13	3	4	8.3	11
Borden — 1	17	2,128	1	0	0	0	0	0	14	3	0	11	64.7	0
Borden SO	17	2,128	1	0	0	0	0	0	14	3	0	11	64.7	0

County/Agency	Total Crime	Crime Rate	Sworn Staff	Civilian Staff	Murder	Rape	Robbery	Assault	Burglary	Theft	Car Theft	Crimes Cleared	Clearance Rate	Arrested
Bosque — 3	301	1,990	11	11	0	1	0	11	118	163	8	71	23.6	68
Bosque SO	153	1,451	5	10	0	1	0	6	74	65	7	10	6.5	46
Clifton PD	133	4,163	5	1	0	0	0	4	35	94	0	52	39.1	20
Meridian PD	15	1,079	1	0	0	0	0	1	9	4	1	9	60.0	2
Bowie — 6	4,159	5,093	132	17	8	34	77	284	1,049	2,460	247	1,525	36.7	1,437
Bowie SO	685	1,928	35	5	5	9	9	42	250	307	63	212	30.9	204
De Kalb PD	121	6,123	4	1	0	2	1	10	29	75	4	79	65.3	34
New Boston PD	211	4,172	7	4	0	0	0	13	54	136	8	49	23.2	36
Texarkana PD	2,940	9,287	78	7	3	20	67	211	689	1,791	159	1,116	38.0	1,084
Wake Village PD	116	2,439	4	0	0	0	0	5	14	91	6	37	31.9	46
Hooks PD	86	3,204	4	0	0	3	0	3	13	60	7	32	37.2	33
Brazoria — 16	7,744	4,039	291	174	13	59	72	608	1,670	4,742	580	1,776	22.9	1,748
Brazoria SO	1,669	2,285	84	100	5	10	19	288	554	682	111	300	18.0	377
Alvin PD	1,274	6,629	33	7	1	5	13	76	186	927	66	363	28.5	294
Angleton PD	770	4,492	26	9	0	13	5	36	139	526	51	139	18.1	107
Clute PD	581	6,521	16	8	1	7	6	24	113	394	36	191	32.9	167
Freeport PD	847	7,437	26	8	1	7	11	38	179	541	70	261	30.8	249
Lake Jackson PD	739	3,245	31	11	1	2	2	9	73	588	64	141	19.1	242
Manvel PD	117	3,134	5	0	2	3	0	7	41	56	8	14	12.0	2
Pearland PD	1,032	5,520	28	11	1	3	8	73	215	590	142	167	16.2	150
Richwood PD	130	4,758	6	1	0	0	1	14	19	88	8	32	24.6	11
Sweeny PD	111	3,367	5	1	0	2	0	6	31	69	3	41	36.9	30
West Columbia PD	193	4,414	7	4	0	1	6	12	42	128	4	48	24.9	59
Alvin Comm Col PD	27	*****	6	3	0	0	0	0	1	26	0	3	11.1	0
Brazoria PD	76	2,797	7	5	0	0	0	8	23	42	3	25	32.9	20
Jones Creek PD	25	1,157	2	0	0	0	0	0	10	15	0	2	8.0	3
Surfside Beach PD	76	12,439	4	2	0	3	0	11	23	31	8	27	35.5	22
Oyster Creek PD	77	8,443	5	4	1	3	1	6	21	39	6	22	28.6	15
Brazos — 4	7,834	6,429	229	124	2	58	152	437	1,828	4,997	360	1,849	23.6	1,232
Brazos SO	290	2,013	42	39	0	0	1	3	138	139	9	87	30.0	38
Bryan PD	4,360	7,927	78	19	2	46	125	345	1,135	2,519	188	1,270	29.1	780
College Station PD	2,402	4,579	67	26	0	8	25	87	491	1,648	143	394	16.4	344
TX A&M Col Sta PD	782	*****	42	40	0	4	1	2	64	691	20	98	12.5	70
Brewster — 3	266	3,064	16	13	0	1	0	26	66	164	9	57	21.4	37
Brewster SO	2	66	4	7	0	0	0	1	0	1	0	2	100.0	6
Alpine PD	209	3,708	6	5	0	1	0	25	55	120	8	55	26.3	31
Sul Ross U. PD	55	*****	6	1	0	0	0	0	11	43	1	0	0.0	0
Briscoe — 1	34	1,725	2	1	0	0	0	2	13	19	0	5	14.7	6
Briscoe SO	34	1,725	2	1	0	0	0	2	13	19	0	5	14.7	6
Brooks — 2	220	2,682	14	12	0	0	2	35	125	54	4	18	8.2	48
Brooks SO	39	1,614	6	11	0	0	0	0	22	16	1	0	0.0	42
Falfurrias PD	181	3,127	8	1	0	0	2	35	103	38	3	18	9.9	6
Brown — 4	1,944	5,656	47	18	1	18	15	125	624	1,106	55	394	20.3	417
Brown SO	306	2,540	14	10	1	3	1	20	137	138	6	42	13.7	97
Bangs PD	69	4,437	2	0	0	1	0	5	30	33	0	22	31.9	6
Brownwood PD	1,473	8,011	27	7	0	14	12	98	454	854	41	301	20.4	267
Early PD	96	4,034	4	1	0	0	2	2	3	81	8	29	30.2	47
Burleson — 3	447	3,281	19	10	1	14	2	82	129	203	16	182	40.7	169
Burleson SO	270	3,033	7	8	0	12	0	50	95	102	11	93	34.4	92
Caldwell PD	90	2,829	7	1	0	1	1	24	14	47	3	52	57.8	48
Somerville PD	87	5,642	5	1	1	1	1	8	20	54	2	37	42.5	29
Burnet — 5	774	3,413	45	24	0	8	3	37	234	474	18	237	30.6	199
Burnet SO	308	2,399	20	15	0	5	1	15	119	158	10	66	21.4	83
Burnet PD	112	3,272	7	1	0	3	1	6	49	48	5	42	37.5	36
Marble Falls PD	281	7,013	11	7	0	0	1	10	54	213	3	100	35.6	70
Bertram PD	29	3,416	1	0	0	0	0	1	3	25	0	22	75.9	8
Horseshoe Bay PD	44	2,824	6	1	0	0	0	5	9	30	0	7	15.9	2
Caldwell — 4	1,084	4,107	29	42	3	8	5	176	304	558	30	288	26.6	296
Caldwell SO	184	1,615	10	36	2	6	0	43	63	68	2	19	10.3	90
Lockhart PD	631	6,855	12	0	0	1	5	73	182	353	17	150	23.8	105
Luling PD	217	4,656	6	6	1	1	0	55	40	111	9	101	46.5	94
Martindale PD	52	5,752	1	0	0	0	0	5	19	26	2	18	34.6	7
Calhoun — 3	686	3,600	39	13	1	2	6	45	208	413	11	172	25.1	177
Calhoun SO	177	2,569	21	8	0	0	0	2	75	100	0	26	14.7	45
Port Lavaca PD	455	4,180	16	5	1	2	6	39	123	275	9	128	28.1	113
Seadrift PD	54	4,229	2	0	0	0	0	4	10	38	2	18	33.3	19
Callahan — 1	100	843	7	5	0	0	1	13	37	48	1	20	20.0	52
Callahan SO	100	843	7	5	0	0	1	13	37	48	1	20	20.0	52
Cameron — 10	17,250	6,632	353	234	37	53	237	1,095	5,142	9,181	1,505	3,816	22.1	3,453
Cameron SO	1,806	2,400	48	132	16	2	15	155	1,095	477	46	86	4.8	299
Brownsville PD	9,163	9,259	143	50	13	36	172	552	2,414	4,908	1,068	2,260	24.7	1,891
Combes PD	82	4,016	4	0	0	0	0	10	36	36	0	1	1.2	4
Harlingen PD	3,842	7,883	81	23	4	6	36	241	935	2,355	265	968	25.2	823
La Feria PD	189	4,335	7	4	0	3	0	19	76	88	3	31	16.4	56
Los Fresnos PD	87	3,518	6	4	0	2	0	2	25	55	3	11	12.6	9
Port Isabel PD	274	6,134	16	5	0	0	0	35	42	183	14	123	44.9	90
San Benito PD	1,014	5,039	29	9	4	0	9	64	283	593	61	239	23.6	126
S. Padre Island PD	752	44,842	16	7	0	4	5	17	215	468	43	92	12.2	151
Primera PD	41	2,020	3	0	0	0	0	0	21	18	2	5	12.2	4
Camp — 2	370	3,736	12	6	0	3	1	56	95	197	18	132	35.7	109
Camp SO	161	2,730	4	5	0	1	0	31	63	60	6	40	24.8	38
Pittsburg PD	209	5,216	8	1	0	2	1	25	32	137	12	92	44.0	71

County/Agency	Total Crime	Crime Rate	Sworn Staff	Civilian Staff	Murder	Rape	Robbery	Assault	Burglary	Theft	Car Theft	Crimes Cleared	Clearance Rate	Arrested
Carson — 2	61	928	9	1	1	0	0	3	17	33	7	24	39.3	33
Carson SO	41	971	5	1	1	0	0	1	15	19	5	6	14.6	30
Panhandle PD	20	850	4	0	0	0	0	2	2	14	2	18	90.0	3
Cass — 2	548	1,828	24	18	4	7	3	71	176	266	21	195	35.6	319
Cass SO	325	1,362	12	13	2	5	2	35	130	139	12	71	21.8	211
Atlanta PD	223	3,645	12	5	2	2	1	36	46	127	9	124	55.6	108
Castro — 2	244	2,690	13	9	1	0	0	21	52	158	12	57	23.4	60
Castro SO	66	1,416	6	8	0	0	0	1	21	38	6	14	21.2	19
Dimmitt PD	178	4,038	7	1	1	0	0	20	31	120	6	43	24.2	41
Chambers —	641	3,191	31	31	2	8	7	34	176	345	69	142	22.2	116
Chambers SO	467	2,489	25	30	2	8	7	25	144	229	52	98	21.0	91
Mont Belvieu PD	174	13,152	6	1	0	0	0	9	32	116	17	44	25.3	25
Cherokee — 4	1,724	4,200	50	31	1	10	45	173	519	895	81	565	32.8	378
Cherokee SO	675	2,956	18	24	0	5	16	102	265	243	44	127	18.8	126
Jacksonville PD	914	7,160	23	6	1	2	28	51	210	593	29	398	43.5	237
Rusk PD	108	2,474	8	1	0	3	1	16	36	44	8	33	30.6	13
Alto PD	27	2,629	1	0	0	0	0	4	8	15	0	7	25.9	2
Childress — 2	180	3,024	11	10	0	2	2	37	63	76	0	51	28.3	58
Childress SO	38	4,232	4	5	0	0	0	8	15	15	0	23	60.5	24
Childress PD	142	2,809	7	5	0	2	2	29	48	61	0	28	19.7	34
Clay — 1	241	2,404	10	4	0	0	1	4	99	129	8	5	2.1	41
Clay SO	241	2,404	10	4	0	0	1	4	99	129	8	5	2.1	41
Cochran — 1	143	3,267	7	4	0	0	0	20	39	77	7	32	22.4	34
Cochran SO	143	3,267	7	4	0	0	0	20	39	77	7	32	22.4	34
Coke — 1	31	905	4	1	0	0	0	0	25	6	0	1	3.2	0
Coke SO	31	905	4	1	0	0	0	0	25	6	0	1	3.2	0
Coleman — 3	199	2,049	15	7	0	4	6	9	100	76	4	46	23.1	74
Coleman SO	77	2,524	5	4	0	3	0	2	47	24	1	2	2.6	33
Coleman PD	85	1,571	9	3	0	1	6	6	36	35	1	32	37.6	21
Santa Anna PD	37	2,962	1	0	0	0	0	1	17	17	2	12	32.4	20
Collin — 9	11,000	4,166	341	232	9	81	106	771	2,814	6,481	738	3,429	31.2	2,541
Collin SO	839	2,334	79	119	2	7	6	56	340	383	45	202	24.1	1,430
Allen PD	673	3,676	25	11	0	1	6	30	175	432	29	114	16.9	78
Farmersville PD	87	3,295	4	0	1	0	0	6	37	36	7	25	28.7	17
Frisco PD	201	3,273	13	4	0	0	1	13	71	99	17	34	16.9	18
McKinney PD	1,715	8,058	32	8	0	29	27	294	320	940	105	853	49.7	333
Plano PD	6,954	5,403	167	82	4	36	64	339	1,720	4,282	509	2,084	30.0	617
Wylie PD	324	3,717	15	5	2	4	1	10	85	208	14	70	21.6	22
Princeton PD	190	8,186	5	3	0	4	0	17	65	94	10	45	23.7	24
Parker PD	17	1,377	1	0	0	0	1	6	1	7	2	2	11.8	2
Collingsworth — 1	84	2,351	9	3	0	1	0	7	19	54	3	32	38.1	37
Collingsworth SO	84	2,351	9	3	0	1	0	7	19	54	3	32	38.1	37
Colorado — 3	715	3,889	23	7	2	3	4	60	219	401	26	171	23.9	196
Colorado SO	258	2,250	12	5	2	2	2	13	114	115	10	43	16.7	82
Columbus PD	214	6,356	6	1	0	1	1	16	48	139	9	82	38.3	72
Eagle Lake PD	243	6,843	5	1	0	0	1	31	57	147	7	46	18.9	42
Comal — 2	2,197	4,239	78	76	3	3	30	190	705	1,110	156	674	30.7	614
Comal SO	785	3,204	36	61	1	2	5	23	315	389	50	162	20.6	212
New Braunfels PD	1,412	5,166	42	15	2	1	25	167	390	721	106	512	36.3	402
Comanche — 2	173	1,293	12	19	0	0	1	7	74	83	8	23	13.3	186
Comanche SO	86	925	6	15	0	0	0	0	47	36	3	1	1.2	151
Comanche PD	87	2,129	6	4	0	0	1	7	27	47	5	22	25.3	35
Concho — 2	95	3,121	5	6	0	0	0	11	34	48	2	15	15.8	24
Concho SO	41	2,776	3	5	0	0	0	1	23	16	1	3	7.3	5
Eden PD	54	3,446	2	1	0	0	0	10	11	32	1	12	22.2	19
Cooke — 2	1,234	4,009	44	26	0	8	5	90	384	675	72	253	20.5	129
Cooke SO	375	2,270	13	16	0	4	2	38	129	173	29	93	24.8	51
Gainesville PD	859	6,026	31	10	0	4	3	52	255	502	43	160	18.6	78
Coryell — 3	1,691	2,633	56	32	1	29	4	196	399	981	81	647	38.3	710
Coryell SO	187	653	10	12	0	2	0	12	72	86	15	38	20.3	325
Copperas Cove PD	1,215	5,046	37	14	1	25	4	166	257	718	44	505	41.6	322
Gatesville PD	289	2,515	9	6	0	2	0	18	70	177	22	104	36.0	63
Cottle — 1	37	1,647	2	3	0	1	2	4	13	16	1	19	51.4	24
Cottle SO	37	1,647	2	3	0	1	2	4	13	16	1	19	51.4	24
Crane — 2	147	3,160	12	9	0	0	0	16	29	98	4	34	23.1	25
Crane SO	52	4,647	6	4	0	0	0	2	14	35	1	8	15.4	4
Crane PD	95	2,689	6	5	0	0	0	14	15	63	3	26	27.4	21
Crockett — 1	96	2,354	7	4	2	1	0	13	24	51	5	28	29.2	39
Crockett SO	96	2,354	7	4	2	1	0	13	24	51	5	28	29.2	39
Crosby — 1	24	329	6	6	0	1	1	0	11	8	3	7	29.2	30
Crosby SO	24	329	6	6	0	1	1	0	11	8	3	7	29.2	30
Culberson — 1	32	939	5	6	3	1	0	6	5	15	2	30	93.8	50
Culberson SO	32	939	5	6	3	1	0	6	5	15	2	30	93.8	50
Dallam — 2	120	2,197	13	12	4	1	2	3	17	85	8	60	50.0	81
Dallam SO	6	484	3	6	3	0	0	1	1	1	0	6	100.0	21
Dalhart PD	114	1,825	10	6	1	1	2	2	16	84	8	6	5.3	60
Dallas — 32	229,864	12,406	4,747	2,479	498	1,738	11,879	15,154	48,277	120,155	32,163	55,029	23.9	28,411
Dallas SO	700	5,181	428	928	4	0	17	193	179	269	38	267	38.1	17
Dallas PD	156,267	15,520	2,877	845	447	1,344	10,565	12,194	32,975	74,229	24,513	37,829	24.2	16,806
Addison PD	1,155	13,150	48	16	1	5	39	46	161	803	100	216	18.7	104
Balch Springs PD	2,207	12,680	23	10	1	14	26	325	319	1,362	160	460	20.8	188
Carrollton PD	5,190	6,316	123	49	1	13	71	108	1,180	3,313	504	1,129	21.8	591
Cedar Hill PD	1,013	5,071	27	8	1	4	15	31	396	501	65	657	64.9	90
Cockrell Hill PD	168	4,485	9	5	0	0	1	14	54	64	35	21	12.5	6

County/Agency	Total Crime	Crime Rate	Sworn Staff	Civilian Staff	Murder	Rape	Robbery	Assault	Burglary	Theft	Car Theft	Crimes Cleared	Clearance Rate	Arrested
Dallas Cont'd.)														
Coppell PD	668	3,957	23	7	0	2	6	20	272	337	31	193	28.9	70
DeSoto PD	1,823	5,968	37	19	1	5	31	33	457	1,114	182	444	24.4	304
Duncanville PD	2,258	6,316	50	26	1	8	60	101	608	1,271	209	478	21.2	322
Farmers Branch PD	2,242	9,245	66	13	2	4	37	87	410	1,393	309	578	25.8	256
Garland PD	11,627	6,436	215	85	11	132	204	370	2,903	6,889	1,118	4,062	34.9	2,549
Grand Prairie PD	8,870	8,904	146	73	5	52	194	614	1,879	4,702	1,424	2,184	24.6	1,492
Highland Park PD	593	6,786	51	9	0	2	17	3	128	395	48	144	24.3	162
Hutchins PD	113	4,156	9	4	0	0	2	25	32	37	17	40	35.4	34
Irving PD	13,832	8,922	246	86	13	90	231	352	2,430	9,280	1,436	2,854	20.6	2,216
Lancaster PD	1,247	5,638	30	11	1	0	32	9	284	763	158	148	11.9	106
Mesquite PD	10,647	10,491	160	46	4	21	178	377	1,666	7,274	1,127	2,151	20.2	1,809
Richardson PD	4,829	6,452	136	70	2	22	107	126	1,124	3,035	413	692	14.3	936
Sachse PD	123	2,301	9	6	0	2	0	6	51	62	2	35	28.5	20
Seagoville PD	587	6,545	12	4	0	6	5	30	151	334	61	57	9.7	37
University Park PD	983	4,416	34	8	1	3	20	7	185	668	99	85	8.6	81
Wilmer PD	119	4,800	7	5	0	1	1	9	49	53	6	19	16.0	25
UT Med Sch PD	153	*****	16	30	0	0	0	1	5	138	9	4	2.6	2
UT Dallas PD	55	*****	8	21	0	0	0	0	1	52	2	7	12.7	6
Eastfield Col PD	87	*****	8	1	0	0	0	0	0	84	3	1	1.1	0
Rowlett PD	875	3,762	31	12	2	6	6	40	279	511	31	158	18.1	107
Richland Col PD	103	*****	9	1	0	0	0	1	0	95	7	7	6.8	3
North Lake Col PD	58	*****	8	1	0	0	0	1	0	56	1	3	5.2	0
Glenn Heights PD	101	2,213	7	5	0	0	2	4	30	53	12	20	19.8	9
Dallas Co Hosp PD	902	*****	7	59	0	1	8	27	36	817	13	55	6.1	45
SMU PD	269	*****	17	16	0	1	4	0	33	201	30	31	11.5	9
Dawson — 2.	612	4,265	23	10	1	1	5	59	167	368	11	237	38.7	95
Dawson SO	77	2,175	7	4	0	0	0	8	26	38	5	12	15.6	38
Lamesa PD	535	4,950	16	6	1	1	5	51	141	330	6	225	42.1	57
Deaf Smith — 2	955	4,986	37	25	1	0	3	92	159	655	45	287	30.1	239
Deaf Smith SO	95	2,155	14	19	1	0	0	17	22	52	3	23	24.2	125
Hereford PD	860	5,832	23	6	0	0	3	75	137	603	42	264	30.7	114
Delta — 1.	74	1,524	6	9	0	1	2	3	41	20	7	15	20.3	38
Delta SO	74	1,524	6	9	0	1	2	3	41	20	7	15	20.3	38
Denton — 12	13,273	4,853	371	227	8	86	138	617	3,238	8,289	897	2,711	20.4	1,883
Denton SO	955	2,908	74	110	1	11	2	76	374	417	74	198	20.7	495
Denton PD	5,436	8,203	104	27	1	34	73	305	1,432	3,363	228	1,166	21.4	758
Lake Dallas PD	155	4,240	8	7	2	0	0	17	44	80	12	29	18.7	13
Lewisville PD	4,381	9,417	74	29	4	28	48	90	847	2,889	475	1,026	23.4	446
Pilot Point PD	80	3,152	3	0	0	1	1	8	22	45	3	9	11.3	4
TWU PD	49	*****	15	12	0	2	0	0	12	32	3	4	8.2	5
UNT PD	416	*****	22	16	0	2	4	6	50	333	21	66	15.9	20
Flower Mound PD	497	3,201	29	8	0	7	4	79	133	248	26	113	22.7	52
The Colony PD	1,077	4,870	23	11	0	0	5	30	269	731	42	58	5.4	60
Highland Village PD	135	1,921	10	6	0	1	0	4	28	96	6	26	19.3	27
Corinth PD	84	2,130	9	1	0	0	1	2	25	49	7	13	15.5	3
Trophy Club PD	8	186	0	0	0	0	0	0	2	6	0	3	37.5	0
DeWitt — 3	140	743	17	10	3	1	2	8	59	63	4	27	19.3	44
DeWitt SO	46	602	7	10	1	0	0	0	28	15	2	5	10.9	16
Cuero PD	88	1,313	7	0	1	1	2	8	27	47	2	16	18.2	19
Yorktown PD	6	272	3	0	1	0	0	0	4	1	0	6	100.0	9
Dickens — 2.	68	2,645	4	4	0	1	1	7	25	29	5	36	52.9	28
Dickens SO	25	1,967	2	4	0	0	0	3	11	8	3	11	44.0	4
Spur PD	43	3,308	2	0	0	1	1	4	14	21	2	25	58.1	24
Dimmit — 2.	50	479	10	8	1	0	0	0	27	22	0	1	2.0	15
Dimmit SO	50	479	10	8	1	0	0	0	27	22	0	1	2.0	15
Carrizo Springs PD	0	*****	0	0	0	0	0	0	0	0	0	0	***.*	0
Donley — 1	66	1,786	5	3	0	4	0	5	22	33	2	36	54.5	33
Donley SO	66	1,786	5	3	0	4	0	5	22	33	2	36	54.5	33
Duval — 2	425	3,290	18	13	2	4	2	48	157	205	7	97	22.8	147
Duval SO	266	2,548	15	9	2	2	1	30	107	120	4	58	21.8	97
Freer PD	159	4,861	3	4	0	2	1	18	50	85	3	39	24.5	50
Eastland — 5	621	3,359	23	10	4	3	4	32	158	373	47	136	21.9	303
Eastland SO	81	1,175	4	8	2	1	0	0	3	38	28	9	11	13.6	173
Cisco PD	208	5,455	7	0	0	0	1	7	41	142	17	73	35.1	75
Eastland PD	169	4,580	8	2	0	1	1	15	34	99	19	34	20.1	42
Gorman PD	0	0	1	0	0	0	0	0	0	0	0	0	***.*	0
Ranger PD	163	5,815	3	0	2	1	2	7	45	104	2	18	11.0	13
Ector — 3	14,242	11,975	249	108	20	79	133	481	2,945	10,110	474	2,632	18.5	1,852
Ector SO	2,093	7,159	81	28	9	19	19	15	530	1,395	106	302	14.4	230
Odessa PD	12,138	13,532	167	70	11	60	114	466	2,415	8,704	368	2,330	19.2	1,622
UT-Per. Basin PD	11	*****	1	10	0	0	0	0	0	11	0	0	0.0	0
Edwards — 1	41	1,809	4	5	0	0	0	3	25	12	1	16	39.0	22
Edwards SO	41	1,809	4	5	0	0	0	3	25	12	1	16	39.0	22
Ellis — 7	4,550	5,342	129	101	5	16	37	474	1,207	2,540	271	1,197	26.3	1,024
Ellis SO	919	2,248	34	73	1	5	0	196	409	296	12	169	18.4	244
Ennis PD	934	6,728	27	7	1	5	14	49	263	539	63	181	19.4	291
Ferris PD	169	7,640	10	1	0	3	0	16	59	72	19	36	21.3	43
Midlothian PD	221	4,299	16	6	0	0	3	19	44	148	7	69	31.2	50
Palmer PD	50	3,014	2	0	0	0	0	9	13	27	1	11	22.0	12
Red Oak PD	262	8,387	7	5	0	0	3	36	41	161	21	48	18.3	36
Waxahachie PD	1,995	10,981	33	9	3	3	17	149	378	1,297	148	683	34.2	348

County/Agency	Total Crime	Crime Rate	Sworn Staff	Civilian Staff	Murder	Rape	Robbery	Assault	Burglary	Theft	Car Theft	Crimes Cleared	Clearance Rate	Arrested
El Paso — 4	60,858	10,287	995	645	45	290	1,430	3,718	10,558	39,004	5,813	8,731	14.3	9,168
El Paso SO	2,463	3,377	175	363	11	33	49	243	912	1,053	162	378	15.3	395
Anthony PD	300	9,014	6	0	0	1	0	33	60	200	6	95	31.7	97
El Paso PD	57,921	11,239	799	251	34	256	1,381	3,440	9,565	37,609	5,636	8,236	14.2	8,658
UT-El Paso PD	174	*****	15	31	0	0	0	2	21	142	9	22	12.6	18
Erath — 4	929	3,319	58	30	0	3	3	38	214	639	32	279	30.0	334
Erath SO	172	1,522	15	21	0	1	1	13	85	69	3	34	19.8	170
Dublin PD	44	1,379	5	1	0	0	0	0	4	40	0	0	0.0	0
Stephenville PD	593	4,392	28	7	0	1	2	23	91	450	26	223	37.6	159
Tarleton St U PD	120	*****	10	1	0	1	0	2	34	80	3	22	18.3	5
Falls — 3	535	3,021	13	4	0	0	7	67	221	232	8	108	20.2	118
Falls SO	0	0	0	0	0	0	0	0	0	0	0	0	***.*	0
Marlin PD	481	7,532	9	4	0	0	6	52	210	205	8	90	18.7	106
Rosebud PD	54	3,297	4	0	0	0	1	15	11	27	0	18	33.3	12
Fannin — 2	622	2,508	25	13	4	0	4	33	232	322	27	174	28.0	221
Fannin SO	274	1,512	11	8	3	0	0	17	133	106	15	50	18.2	119
Bonham PD	348	5,205	14	5	1	0	4	16	99	216	12	124	35.6	102
Fayette — 3	229	1,140	17	15	1	0	2	15	108	90	13	62	27.1	93
Fayette SO	109	683	12	14	1	0	2	4	61	30	11	22	20.2	65
Carmine PD	0	0	0	0	0	0	0	0	0	0	0	0	***.*	0
La Grange PD	120	3,037	5	1	0	0	0	11	47	60	2	40	33.3	28
Fisher — 1	63	1,301	5	4	0	0	0	0	36	25	2	3	4.8	8
Fisher SO	63	1,301	5	4	0	0	0	0	36	25	2	3	4.8	8
Floyd — 3	193	2,271	13	5	1	0	1	21	62	101	7	35	18.1	27
Floyd SO	44	1,838	7	5	1	0	0	2	11	28	2	5	11.4	12
Floydada PD	116	2,977	4	0	0	0	1	16	40	57	2	26	22.4	14
Lockney PD	33	1,495	2	0	0	0	0	3	11	16	3	4	12.1	1
Foard — 1	18	1,003	3	2	0	0	0	2	12	3	1	12	66.7	10
Foard SO	18	1,003	3	2	0	0	0	2	12	3	1	12	66.7	10
Fort Bend — 8	9,439	4,187	309	95	15	51	228	553	2,859	4,854	879	1,667	17.7	1,366
Fort Bend SO	3,264	2,626	146	43	4	14	50	101	1,304	1,462	329	359	11.0	570
Missouri City PD	1,701	4,702	36	13	1	6	47	53	527	860	207	263	15.5	190
Richmond PD	908	9,264	14	6	4	14	48	132	253	427	30	168	18.5	87
Rosenberg PD	1,825	9,042	39	13	2	11	49	179	374	1,109	101	562	30.8	325
Stafford PD	684	8,146	20	9	2	3	22	29	157	375	96	118	17.3	101
Sugar Land PD	857	3,494	40	9	2	1	12	33	194	527	88	155	18.1	72
Needville PD	71	3,229	5	1	0	1	0	21	22	27	0	32	45.1	8
Meadows PD	129	2,801	9	1	0	1	0	5	28	67	28	10	7.8	13
Franklin — 1	122	1,564	5	7	1	0	1	3	50	60	7	35	28.7	58
Franklin SO	122	1,705	5	7	1	0	1	3	50	60	7	35	28.7	58
Freestone —	451	2,851	22	14	2	0	2	46	183	192	26	153	33.9	110
Freestone SO	251	2,694	10	9	1	0	2	28	111	96	13	48	19.1	81
Fairfield PD	78	2,412	6	4	1	0	0	13	26	32	6	37	47.4	19
Teague PD	122	3,733	6	1	0	0	0	5	46	64	7	68	55.7	10
Frio — 2	531	3,942	19	43	1	5	0	75	170	248	32	100	18.8	100
Frio SO	162	2,474	11	42	0	0	0	28	42	77	15	10	6.2	20
Pearsall PD	369	5,329	8	1	1	5	0	47	128	171	17	90	24.4	80
Dilley PD	0	*****	4	0	0	0	0	0	0	0	0	0	***.*	0
Gaines — 3	522	3,696	22	6	0	2	2	31	214	250	23	95	18.2	85
Gaines SO	139	2,582	9	6	0	0	0	0	36	97	6	18	12.9	60
Seagraves PD	45	1,877	3	0	0	2	2	16	7	16	2	29	64.4	11
Seminole PD	338	5,330	10	0	0	0	0	15	171	137	15	48	14.2	14
Galveston — 16	16,590	7,631	503	292	29	111	585	731	4,046	9,771	1,317	3,211	19.4	3,010
Galveston SO	1,074	4,554	90	142	4	10	20	65	474	424	77	157	14.6	115
Dickinson PD	832	8,761	16	4	0	5	16	134	167	446	64	164	19.7	176
Friendswood PD	618	2,709	29	11	3	0	8	34	165	374	34	91	14.7	86
Galveston PD	6,994	11,840	164	35	16	49	386	293	1,552	4,075	623	1,545	22.1	1,414
Hitchcock PD	278	4,738	13	4	0	4	1	4	103	153	13	74	26.6	34
Kemah PD	85	7,770	4	4	0	0	0	2	15	64	4	7	8.2	5
La Marque PD	954	6,756	21	8	2	9	17	14	296	557	59	148	15.5	170
League City PD	1,079	3,578	37	11	0	9	12	14	267	670	107	268	24.8	143
Texas City PD	4,084	10,004	71	11	4	24	122	126	911	2,583	314	633	15.5	766
UT-Galveston PD	108	*****	23	49	0	0	0	0	0	105	3	5	4.6	4
A&M-Galveston PD	3	*****	6	7	0	0	0	0	0	3	0	1	33.3	0
Jamaica Beach PD	28	4,487	5	1	0	0	0	1	4	19	4	15	53.6	19
Crystal Beach PD	0	*****	0	0	0	0	0	0	0	0	0	0	***.*	0
Santa Fe PD	397	4,710	12	5	0	1	2	44	91	248	11	97	24.4	75
Bayou Vista PD	0	*****	4	0	0	0	0	0	0	0	0	0	***.*	0
Col of Mainland PD	56	*****	8	0	0	0	1	0	1	50	4	6	10.7	3
Garza — 1	173	3,364	7	4	0	4	2	13	61	91	2	43	24.9	29
Garza SO	173	3,364	7	4	0	4	2	13	61	91	2	43	24.9	29
Gillespie — 2	314	1,825	25	14	1	0	2	8	83	207	13	69	22.0	87
Gillespie SO	145	1,412	9	12	1	0	0	4	57	80	3	14	9.7	32
Fredericksburg PD	169	2,437	16	2	0	0	2	4	26	127	10	55	32.5	55
Glasscock — 1	12	829	2	2	1	0	0	1	3	7	0	5	41.7	4
Glasscock SO	12	829	2	2	1	0	0	1	3	7	0	5	41.7	4
Goliad — 1	24	401	7	8	0	0	0	0	9	12	3	14	58.3	50
Goliad SO	24	401	7	8	0	0	0	0	9	12	3	14	58.3	50
Gonzales — 2	458	2,662	20	14	6	0	3	65	106	257	21	152	33.2	245
Gonzales SO	219	2,051	11	9	3	0	0	36	52	115	13	59	26.9	133
Gonzales PD	239	3,662	9	5	3	0	3	29	54	142	8	93	38.9	112
Gray — 2	1,496	6,242	41	11	3	13	14	244	333	851	38	540	36.1	245
Gray SO	148	3,693	13	3	0	3	0	7	52	78	8	23	15.5	78
Pampa PD	1,348	6,754	28	8	3	10	14	237	281	773	30	517	38.4	167

County/Agency	Total Crime	Crime Rate	Sworn Staff	Civilian Staff	Murder	Rape	Robbery	Assault	Burglary	Theft	Car Theft	Crimes Cleared	Clearance Rate	Arrested
Grayson — 5	6,465	6,804	159	51	14	38	127	304	1,890	3,738	354	1,232	19.1	1,003
Grayson SO	1,053	2,721	48	18	3	11	4	25	506	457	47	290	27.5	394
Denison PD	2,165	10,067	41	8	3	6	40	159	565	1,271	121	352	16.3	299
Sherman PD	3,134	9,917	56	20	8	20	82	112	801	1,931	180	550	17.5	298
Whitesboro PD	95	2,960	6	4	0	0	1	8	17	65	4	34	35.8	12
Austin Col Pol PD	18	*****	8	1	0	1	0	0	1	14	2	6	33.3	0
Gregg — 5	8,712	8,301	231	104	10	79	159	1,042	1,993	4,865	564	2,467	28.3	1,802
Gregg SO	681	3,987	54	39	2	10	12	82	227	308	40	262	38.5	288
Gladewater PD	429	7,118	13	5	2	0	3	21	110	272	21	66	15.4	50
Kilgore PD	739	6,678	26	6	1	3	3	48	190	440	54	97	13.1	178
Longview PD	6,735	9,579	127	50	5	66	141	887	1,435	3,760	441	2,018	30.0	1,261
White Oak PD	128	2,492	11	4	0	0	0	4	31	85	8	24	18.8	25
Grimes — 2	661	3,511	20	15	2	6	10	72	184	334	53	221	33.4	196
Grimes SO	205	1,636	9	8	2	0	1	6	93	79	24	35	17.1	46
Navasota PD	456	7,243	11	7	0	6	9	66	91	255	29	186	40.8	150
Guadalupe — 3	2,966	4,572	71	96	4	18	39	186	1,012	1,626	81	712	24.0	874
Guadalupe SO	613	1,728	22	71	0	0	3	9	307	276	18	38	6.2	206
Shertz PD	512	4,851	17	6	0	0	2	40	89	363	18	59	11.5	54
Seguin PD	1,841	9,765	32	19	4	18	34	137	616	987	45	615	33.4	614
Hale — 3	1,702	4,909	56	21	1	10	17	140	422	1,070	42	707	41.5	343
Hale SO	139	1,259	23	14	0	0	0	20	51	68	0	75	54.0	80
Abernathy PD	60	2,206	3	0	0	0	2	7	17	33	1	22	36.7	7
Plainview PD	1,503	6,926	30	7	1	10	15	113	354	969	41	610	40.6	256
Hall — 2	38	973	5	4	0	0	0	4	13	17	4	12	31.6	29
Hall SO	16	1,111	3	4	0	0	0	0	6	7	3	3	18.8	15
Memphis PD	22	892	2	0	0	0	0	4	7	10	1	9	40.9	14
Hamilton — 2	208	2,690	10	9	0	0	1	20	57	127	3	75	36.1	36
Hamilton SO	151	2,363	7	9	0	0	1	19	53	76	2	39	25.8	28
Hico PD	57	4,247	3	0	0	0	0	1	4	51	1	36	63.2	8
Hansford — 3	116	1,984	11	7	0	1	0	3	19	89	4	48	41.4	33
Hansford SO	43	2,907	3	4	0	0	0	2	6	34	1	11	25.6	12
Gruver PD	17	1,451	2	0	0	1	0	0	1	14	1	7	41.2	0
Spearman PD	56	1,752	6	3	0	0	0	1	12	41	2	30	53.6	21
Hardeman — 2	138	2,612	8	4	0	2	1	11	42	72	10	23	16.7	35
Hardeman SO	65	3,476	4	4	0	2	1	4	14	38	6	23	35.4	29
Quanah PD	73	2,139	4	0	0	0	0	7	28	34	4	0	0.0	6
Hardin — 5	943	2,282	44	23	1	7	4	111	248	529	43	339	35.9	330
Hardin SO	393	1,591	14	16	0	6	2	50	130	193	12	112	28.5	127
Kountze PD	98	4,767	4	1	0	0	0	7	40	51	0	25	25.5	23
Silsbee PD	243	3,816	14	5	0	0	1	38	29	156	19	124	51.0	140
Lumberton PD	130	1,958	7	1	0	1	1	8	32	85	3	47	36.2	28
Sour Lake PD	79	5,107	5	0	1	0	0	8	17	44	9	31	39.2	12
Harris — 34	257,820	9,148	6,768	2,387	657	1,716	15,148	11,385	60,886	113,999	54,029	36,836	14.3	25,919
Harris SO	42,621	5,249	1,718	382	74	210	1,469	2,004	12,185	17,568	9,111	4,622	10.8	2,714
Houston PD	184,869	11,338	4,104	1,549	568	1,335	12,921	7,813	42,946	78,393	40,853	26,987	14.6	18,169
Baytown PD	6,053	9,480	101	35	1	51	175	225	1,377	3,385	839	1,269	21.0	1,004
Bellaire PD	736	5,317	34	12	1	1	22	53	155	420	84	182	24.7	132
Deer Park PD	850	3,074	41	10	1	4	9	73	254	449	60	184	21.6	194
Galena Park PD	285	2,841	16	5	0	0	8	5	86	146	40	14	4.9	75
Humble PD	1,713	14,204	42	11	0	1	34	33	207	1,059	379	452	26.4	509
Jacinto City PD	386	4,131	15	5	0	2	15	8	53	231	77	67	17.4	86
Jersey Village PD	386	7,998	14	7	0	0	10	7	36	300	33	24	6.2	1
La Porte PD	972	3,483	47	20	2	12	22	51	239	558	88	105	10.8	189
Pasadena PD	10,688	8,937	195	53	4	76	237	886	2,150	5,907	1,408	1,607	15.1	1,586
Seabrook PD	344	5,146	20	4	0	2	1	11	73	223	34	54	15.7	72
South Houston PD	1,233	8,679	28	8	2	4	39	46	255	666	221	302	24.5	189
Southside Place PD	86	6,178	6	3	0	1	7	1	13	54	10	29	33.7	32
Spring Valley PD	126	3,715	14	5	1	0	2	2	28	70	23	15	11.9	19
Tomball PD	445	6,986	18	3	0	0	1	6	26	76	285	51	123	27.6	99
Village PD	281	2,448	26	5	1	0	6	3	83	165	23	24	8.5	20
Webster PD	1,260	26,935	26	10	2	5	12	13	104	863	261	163	12.9	282
W. University P PD	439	3,398	21	7	0	3	10	3	132	242	49	15	3.4	33
Katy PD	279	3,485	18	5	0	0	8	17	73	156	25	69	24.7	53
Nassau Bay PD	293	6,782	13	6	0	1	8	7	38	199	40	30	10.2	46
UT Houston PD	412	*****	46	120	0	0	0	7	5	385	17	20	4.9	15
U of Houston PD	602	*****	34	21	0	0	5	2	15	516	64	60	10.0	52
Texas Southern PD	248	*****	15	17	0	0	10	11	37	175	15	3	1.2	11
Hou-Clear Lake PD	35	*****	11	7	0	0	0	1	1	32	1	4	11.4	1
Hedwig Village PD	453	17,317	16	6	0	2	11	11	64	264	101	155	34.2	123
Hou-Downtown PD	145	*****	13	10	0	0	3	1	8	119	14	33	22.8	23
Hou Metro Trans PD	432	*****	53	39	0	3	91	20	6	268	44	74	17.1	37
N. Harris Co Co PD	40	*****	3	1	0	0	0	0	12	24	4	1	2.5	0
Klein ISD PD	283	*****	18	7	0	0	1	3	24	241	14	40	14.1	69
Lakeview PD	186	2,709	10	4	0	0	0	10	43	123	9	37	19.9	26
Katy ISD PD	189	*****	6	4	0	0	0	23	6	159	1	32	16.9	34
Spring Brch ISD PD	228	*****	11	1	0	1	5	11	32	179	0	33	14.5	18
Rice University PD	242	*****	15	5	0	0	1	0	30	175	36	7	2.9	6
Harrison — 2	2,303	4,006	76	25	5	50	46	225	505	1,376	95	689	29.9	447
Harrison SO	553	1,636	36	15	1	25	4	42	189	289	3	38	6.9	93
Marshall PD	1,749	7,385	40	10	4	25	42	183	316	1,087	92	651	37.2	354
Hartley — 1	8	220	2	2	0	0	0	0	3	5	0	0	0.0	2
Hartley SO	8	497	2	2	0	0	0	0	3	5	0	0	0.0	2
Haskell — 1	79	1,158	3	5	0	0	1	2	32	43	1	12	15.2	32
Haskell SO	79	1,165	3	5	0	0	1	2	32	43	1	12	15.2	32

County/Agency	Total Crime	Crime Rate	Sworn Staff	Civilian Staff	Murder	Rape	Robbery	Assault	Burglary	Theft	Car Theft	Crimes Cleared	Clearance Rate	Arrested
Hays — 4	3,382	5,154	131	129	5	24	27	240	790	2,125	171	715	21.1	648
Hays SO	783	2,260	62	107	4	4	3	67	292	381	32	242	30.9	273
San Marcos PD	1,978	6,882	46	13	1	17	21	146	383	1,286	124	361	18.3	285
SWTU PD	537	*****	19	9	0	3	1	21	85	414	13	99	18.4	81
Kyle PD	84	3,775	4	0	0	0	2	6	30	44	2	13	15.5	9
Hemphill — 2	44	1,183	8	6	0	1	0	3	11	28	1	15	34.1	11
Hemphill SO	35	2,686	8	6	0	1	0	2	8	23	1	10	28.6	8
Canadian PD	9	372	0	0	0	0	0	1	3	5	0	5	55.6	3
Henderson — 6	2,445	4,176	68	51	4	8	21	241	927	1,155	89	694	28.4	599
Henderson SO	981	2,386	26	36	3	5	3	118	499	313	40	101	10.3	274
Athens PD	850	7,751	20	6	1	1	10	75	284	446	33	401	47.2	230
Malakoff PD	164	8,047	5	0	0	0	4	17	60	77	6	53	32.3	36
Seven Points PD	157	21,715	5	5	0	1	3	4	9	135	5	22	14.0	6
Gun Barrel City PD	272	7,714	10	4	0	0	0	20	67	184	1	104	38.2	45
Caney City PD	21	12,353	2	0	0	1	1	7	8	0	4	13	61.9	8
Hidalgo — 16	25,276	6,590	577	350	35	97	282	1,476	7,063	13,900	2,423	5,534	21.9	4,691
Hidalgo SO	4,422	3,498	122	167	17	29	62	201	2,641	1,247	225	274	6.2	805
Alamo PD	340	4,141	10	5	0	1	2	13	124	179	21	41	12.1	62
Donna PD	879	6,948	16	8	1	0	1	99	176	547	55	136	15.5	98
Edcouch PD	207	7,192	5	1	0	0	1	46	57	94	9	43	20.8	17
Edinberg PD	1,716	5,742	39	18	1	17	26	217	464	833	158	243	14.2	425
Elsa PD	215	4,101	6	5	3	0	1	28	38	139	6	94	43.7	30
Hidalgo PD	226	6,865	18	4	0	1	9	1	51	149	15	19	8.4	89
La Villa PD	19	1,369	2	1	0	0	0	7	9	3	0	5	26.3	11
McAllen PD	8,709	10,365	165	74	3	16	104	340	1,624	5,562	1,060	1,558	17.9	1,531
Mercedes PD	595	4,687	17	8	0	10	12	97	187	253	36	173	29.1	73
Mission PD	1,763	6,153	45	10	1	8	12	67	382	1,117	176	398	22.6	474
Pharr PD	3,240	9,842	57	23	1	11	35	149	695	2,018	331	1,761	54.4	514
San Juan PD	940	8,692	19	5	4	3	7	83	237	520	86	168	17.9	63
Weslaco PD	1,791	8,187	40	13	4	1	8	112	344	1,086	236	611	34.1	484
La Joya PD	69	2,650	5	4	0	0	2	5	24	34	4	3	4.3	10
UT-Pan Am U PD	145	*****	11	4	0	0	0	11	10	119	5	7	4.8	5
Hill — 3	915	3,371	37	21	6	4	4	43	329	483	44	196	21.4	171
Hill SO	329	1,783	14	14	4	5	1	16	171	106	26	58	17.6	108
Hillsboro PD	501	7,084	17	6	2	1	3	22	143	315	15	113	22.6	52
Whitney PD	85	5,228	6	1	0	0	0	5	15	62	3	25	29.4	11
Hockley — 4	771	3,186	34	17	2	0	4	33	174	538	20	162	21.0	189
Hockley SO	193	1,986	9	11	1	0	1	3	67	115	6	28	14.5	71
Levelland PD	551	3,940	20	6	1	0	3	30	100	403	14	131	23.8	116
Ropesville PD	7	1,417	1	0	0	0	0	0	2	5	0	0	0.0	1
S Plains Col PD	20	*****	4	0	0	0	0	0	5	15	0	3	15.0	1
Hood — 2	838	2,892	31	28	1	1	3	53	274	464	42	119	14.2	308
Hood SO	570	2,286	16	25	1	0	1	49	245	245	29	63	11.1	277
Granbury PD	268	6,625	15	3	0	1	2	4	29	219	13	56	20.9	31
Hopkins — 2	1,391	4,824	46	26	1	8	6	118	303	884	71	337	24.2	293
Hopkins SO	296	2,004	18	19	1	0	3	35	80	163	14	46	15.5	89
Sulphur Springs PD	1,095	7,787	28	7	0	8	3	83	223	721	57	291	26.6	204
Houston — 2	572	2,676	19	10	6	3	6	77	162	300	18	182	31.8	196
Houston SO	169	1,178	8	5	1	0	1	20	62	79	6	27	16.0	89
Crockett PD	403	5,737	11	5	5	3	5	57	100	221	12	155	38.5	107
Howard — 2	1,893	5,853	56	30	7	15	8	177	312	1,305	69	312	16.5	411
Howard SO	228	2,465	12	10	2	2	1	24	39	152	8	66	28.9	50
Big Spring PD	1,665	7,210	44	20	5	13	7	153	273	1,153	61	246	14.8	361
Hudspeth — 1	28	961	6	20	1	1	0	8	1	17	0	22	78.6	32
Hudspeth SO	28	961	6	20	1	1	0	8	1	17	0	22	78.6	32
Hunt — 7	5,510	8,563	101	52	5	29	79	986	1,376	2,791	244	1,672	30.3	1,040
Hunt SO	715	2,300	20	22	2	0	6	52	305	303	47	155	21.7	347
Commerce PD	706	10,344	16	6	1	2	3	111	176	389	24	179	25.4	68
Greenville PD	3,732	16,176	45	17	2	26	66	811	806	1,861	160	1,275	34.2	588
ETSU PD	124	*****	14	5	0	0	2	2	25	91	4	18	14.5	7
Caddo Mills PD	52	4,869	2	0	0	1	1	2	17	30	1	14	26.9	8
West Tawakoni PD	21	2,253	1	1	0	0	0	0	7	14	0	0	0.0	0
Quinlan PD	160	11,765	3	1	0	0	1	8	40	103	8	31	19.4	22
Hutchinson — 3	914	3,558	37	26	0	1	7	23	242	610	31	185	20.2	302
Hutchinson SO	211	2,689	13	17	0	1	0	9	61	135	5	36	17.1	153
Borger PD	689	4,396	21	8	0	0	7	13	174	469	26	147	21.3	145
Stinnett PD	14	646	3	1	0	0	0	1	7	6	0	2	14.3	4
Irion — 1	29	1,780	3	3	0	0	0	4	8	17	0	7	24.1	4
Irion SO	29	1,780	3	3	0	0	0	4	8	17	0	7	24.1	4
Jack — 2	139	1,991	11	10	1	2	0	9	55	68	4	24	17.3	37
Jack SO	69	1,900	5	9	0	0	0	1	35	33	0	2	2.9	25
Jacksboro PD	70	2,090	6	1	1	2	0	8	20	35	4	22	31.4	12
Jackson — 2	273	2,094	14	11	2	3	2	22	122	112	10	43	15.8	64
Jackson SO	86	1,117	7	10	2	1	2	5	41	36	1	7	8.1	14
Edna PD	187	3,500	7	1	0	2	0	17	81	76	9	36	19.3	50
Jasper — 3	771	2,479	33	15	2	2	9	40	210	490	18	367	47.6	325
Jasper SO	324	1,455	15	9	1	1	1	5	148	153	15	52	16.0	106
Jasper PD	381	5,475	15	6	1	1	8	34	41	294	2	263	69.0	166
Kirbyville PD	66	3,528	3	0	0	0	0	1	21	43	1	52	78.8	53
Jeff Davis — 1	16	822	2	2	0	0	3	5	7	0	1	15	93.8	19
Jeff Davis SO	16	822	2	2	0	0	3	5	7	0	1	15	93.8	19
Jefferson — 7	21,687	9,059	454	251	32	197	837	1,931	6,304	10,574	1,812	5,472	25.2	2,967
Jefferson SO	612	5,331	70	156	1	8	4	27	219	300	53	96	15.7	31

County/Agency	Total Crime	Crime Rate	Sworn Staff	Civilian Staff	Murder	Rape	Robbery	Assault	Burglary	Theft	Car Theft	Crimes Cleared	Clearance Rate	Arrested
Jefferson (Cont'd.)														
Beaumont PD	13,099	11,458	219	47	19	126	562	1,136	3,842	6,151	1,263	3,233	24.7	1,860
Groves PD	684	4,142	12	1	2	0	5	11	164	465	37	163	23.8	71
Nederland PD	873	5,392	18	5	0	0	7	14	164	659	29	200	22.9	148
Port Arthur PD	5,565	8,194	107	28	9	59	253	713	1,777	2,359	395	1,504	27.0	778
Port Neches PD	522	4,023	17	3	1	4	2	27	118	348	22	218	41.8	55
Lamar U. Beaum PD	332	*****	11	11	0	0	4	3	20	292	13	58	17.5	24
Jim Hogg — 1	40	783	14	15	0	0	0	4	28	8	0	42	105.0	38
Jim Hogg SO	40	783	14	15	0	0	0	4	28	8	0	42	105.0	38
Jim Wells — 4	2,292	6,083	53	22	4	7	8	95	759	1,355	64	416	18.2	408
Jim Wells SO	376	2,890	16	13	2	1	2	24	180	157	10	97	25.8	69
Alice PD	1,864	9,420	30	9	2	5	6	67	566	1,165	53	307	16.5	322
Premont PD	12	412	4	0	0	0	0	0	7	5	0	2	16.7	11
Orange Grove PD	40	3,404	3	0	0	1	0	4	6	28	1	10	25.0	6
Johnson — 6	3,691	3,799	112	115	3	15	32	101	957	2,354	229	948	25.7	619
Johnson SO	972	1,963	26	86	2	2	3	43	432	408	82	101	10.4	134
Alvarado PD	209	7,162	5	5	0	2	4	15	66	109	13	45	21.5	23
Burleson PD	953	5,914	30	7	1	7	11	12	233	629	60	363	38.1	97
Cleburne PD	1,343	6,048	37	11	0	1	13	7	158	1,099	65	401	29.9	339
Joshua PD	148	3,866	7	1	0	3	0	19	40	81	5	26	17.6	18
Keene PD	66	1,673	7	5	0	0	1	5	28	28	4	12	18.2	8
Jones — 4	399	2,420	19	18	1	3	2	62	125	185	21	103	25.8	71
Jones SO	146	2,273	4	10	1	0	0	10	52	76	7	24	16.4	33
Anson PD	80	3,026	4	1	0	0	0	12	22	41	5	16	20.0	6
Hamlin PD	24	860	4	4	0	0	0	6	11	5	2	4	16.7	4
Stamford PD	149	3,904	7	3	0	3	2	34	40	63	7	59	39.6	28
Karnes — 1	79	634	8	11	1	0	0	14	43	17	4	33	41.8	90
Karnes SO	79	634	8	11	1	0	0	14	43	17	4	33	41.8	90
Kaufman — 5	2,690	5,151	72	41	9	8	58	233	812	1,411	159	579	21.5	492
Kaufman SO	954	3,263	20	25	3	4	3	48	365	461	70	309	32.4	194
Forney PD	135	3,317	8	4	0	0	3	12	39	73	8	17	12.6	20
Kaufman PD	412	7,866	13	4	1	0	4	55	121	209	22	91	22.1	102
Kemp PD	42	3,547	4	0	0	0	2	2	18	18	2	7	16.7	4
Terrell PD	1,147	9,183	27	8	5	4	46	116	269	650	57	155	13.5	172
Kendall — 2	610	4,181	27	13	0	1	0	51	248	280	30	86	14.1	61
Kendall SO	452	4,382	16	12	0	1	0	49	209	174	19	48	10.6	33
Boerne PD	158	3,697	11	1	0	0	0	2	39	106	11	38	24.1	28
Kenedy — 1	25	5,435	5	1	0	0	1	2	14	3	5	5	20.0	4
Kenedy SO	25	5,435	5	1	0	0	1	2	14	3	5	5	20.0	4
Kent — 1	7	693	2	2	0	0	0	4	2	0	1	6	85.7	2
Kent SO	7	693	2	2	0	0	0	4	2	0	1	6	85.7	2
Kerr — 2	1,386	3,818	62	29	2	8	11	91	407	813	54	508	36.7	430
Kerr SO	307	1,623	21	19	1	2	1	61	123	113	6	51	16.6	265
Kerrville PD	1,079	6,207	41	10	1	6	10	30	284	700	48	457	42.4	165
Kimble — 1	37	898	2	5	0	0	0	4	10	21	2	11	29.7	46
Kimble SO	37	898	2	5	0	0	0	4	10	21	2	11	29.7	46
King — 1	9	2,542	1	0	0	0	0	0	0	9	0	2	22.2	4
King SO	9	2,542	1	0	0	0	0	0	0	9	0	2	22.2	4
Kinney — 1	14	449	3	8	0	0	0	1	5	6	2	10	71.4	12
Kinney SO	14	449	3	8	0	0	0	1	5	6	2	10	71.4	12
Kleberg — 3	2,151	7,105	88	16	3	14	32	171	572	1,310	49	355	16.5	365
Kleberg SO	155	3,101	36	1	2	2	2	12	50	79	8	39	25.2	72
Kingsville PD	1,857	7,347	41	10	1	11	30	158	475	1,141	41	313	16.9	289
Texas A&I U. PD	139	*****	11	5	0	1	0	1	47	90	0	3	2.2	4
Knox — 2	15	310	8	1	0	0	0	2	9	4	0	11	73.3	11
Knox SO	6	185	6	1	0	0	0	2	2	2	0	5	83.3	5
Munday PD	9	563	2	0	0	0	0	0	7	2	0	6	66.7	6
Lamar — 2	3,472	7,900	54	46	2	23	40	449	688	2,102	168	961	27.7	742
Lamar SO	508	2,639	14	28	1	3	3	50	163	250	38	90	17.7	234
Paris PD	2,964	12,000	40	18	1	20	37	399	525	1,852	130	871	29.4	508
Lamb — 3	397	2,634	21	12	2	1	0	33	93	258	10	144	36.3	82
Lamb SO	55	850	7	5	1	1	0	4	14	33	2	12	21.8	50
Littlefield PD	305	4,700	11	7	1	0	0	26	58	213	7	131	43.0	30
Olton PD	37	1,749	3	0	0	0	0	3	21	12	1	1	2.7	2
Lampasas — 2	473	3,498	17	14	1	3	3	10	114	321	21	151	31.9	168
Lampasas SO	67	939	8	8	0	0	0	1	42	20	4	7	10.4	65
Lampasas PD	406	6,362	9	6	1	3	3	9	72	301	17	144	35.5	103
La Salle — 3	67	1,275	6	14	2	0	1	10	26	15	13	30	44.8	52
La Salle SO	67	1,275	6	14	2	0	1	10	26	15	13	30	44.8	52
Lavaca — 3	366	1,958	24	15	5	0	1	19	87	236	18	103	28.1	116
Lavaca SO	74	585	11	8	1	0	0	10	23	36	4	20	27.0	39
Hallettsville PD	82	3,017	4	1	1	0	0	5	13	59	4	22	26.8	13
Yoakum PD	210	3,743	9	6	3	0	1	4	51	141	10	61	29.0	64
Lee — 3	293	2,279	17	11	1	4	2	31	72	170	13	91	31.1	143
Lee SO	101	1,294	8	5	0	2	0	10	45	39	2	31	30.7	117
Giddings PD	185	4,520	8	6	1	1	2	0	21	26	9	57	30.8	26
Lexington PD	7	735	1	0	0	0	0	0	1	4	2	3	42.9	0
Leon — 1	184	1,453	7	3	0	0	7	10	88	57	22	16	8.7	60
Leon SO	184	1,453	7	3	0	0	7	10	88	57	22	16	8.7	60
Liberty — 4	1,993	3,780	72	47	3	10	28	209	621	987	135	563	28.2	509
Liberty SO	683	2,088	35	29	1	3	4	99	296	234	46	136	19.9	215
Cleveland PD	694	9,742	18	7	1	1	16	66	114	443	53	275	39.6	199
Dayton PD	194	3,766	9	5	0	6	3	24	44	107	10	80	41.2	22
Liberty PD	422	5,457	10	6	1	0	5	20	167	203	26	72	17.1	73

County/Agency	Total Crime	Crime Rate	Sworn Staff	Civilian Staff	Murder	Rape	Robbery	Assault	Burglary	Theft	Car Theft	Crimes Cleared	Clearance Rate	Arrested
Limestone — 3	817	3,901	30	29	2	13	10	72	187	497	36	358	43.8	302
Limestone SO	263	2,429	15	23	0	4	0	15	100	126	18	82	31.2	129
Groesbeck PD	42	1,319	5	1	1	0	0	2	9	28	2	13	31.0	8
Mexia PD	512	7,385	10	5	1	9	10	55	78	343	16	263	51.4	165
Lipscomb — 1	71	2,259	5	4	0	0	0	11	14	43	3	20	28.2	14
Lipscomb SO	71	2,259	5	4	0	0	0	11	14	43	3	20	28.2	14
Live Oak — 1	123	1,287	8	9	0	0	2	8	32	73	8	29	23.6	78
Live Oak SO	123	1,287	8	9	0	0	2	8	32	73	8	29	23.6	78
Llano — 2	300	2,579	16	9	1	1	1	2	120	167	8	76	25.3	80
Llano SO	199	2,296	11	9	1	1	0	2	78	114	3	56	28.1	59
Llano PD	101	3,410	5	0	0	0	1	0	42	53	5	20	19.8	21
Loving — 1	2	1,869	2	0	0	0	0	0	1	1	0	0	0.0	0
Loving SO	2	1,869	2	0	0	0	0	0	1	1	0	0	0.0	0
Lubbock — 10	14,246	6,399	467	253	16	186	314	764	3,343	8,779	844	3,897	27.4	2,216
Lubbock SO	796	3,526	92	163	0	24	8	91	236	396	41	193	24.2	69
Idalou PD	8	386	3	0	0	0	0	0	1	1	6	0	4	50.0	6
Lubbock PD	12,302	6,607	317	44	16	160	304	636	2,893	7,516	777	3,527	28.7	2,055
Shallowater PD	23	1,347	3	2	0	0	0	3	8	10	2	2	8.7	0
Slaton PD	266	4,376	8	6	0	1	1	20	65	164	15	41	15.4	55
Texas Tech PD	658	*****	29	22	0	0	1	6	123	521	7	105	16.0	22
Wolfforth PD	58	2,988	3	0	0	1	0	5	13	38	1	10	17.2	4
Ransom Canyon PD	5	667	1	0	0	0	0	0	1	4	0	0	0.0	0
TT Hea Sci Cen PD	121	*****	10	16	0	0	0	1	0	120	0	12	9.9	5
New Deal PD	9	1,727	1	0	0	0	0	1	3	4	1	3	33.3	0
Lynn — 2	165	2,442	9	6	0	0	0	9	62	88	6	50	30.3	62
Lynn SO	109	2,802	5	6	0	0	0	1	52	50	6	33	30.3	50
Tahoka PD	56	1,953	4	0	0	0	0	8	10	38	0	17	30.4	12
Madison — 2	492	4,501	13	9	0	4	2	73	131	265	17	125	25.4	111
Madison SO	169	2,296	8	8	0	4	0	51	57	47	10	73	43.2	53
Madisonville PD	323	9,050	5	1	0	0	2	22	74	218	7	52	16.1	58
Marion — 2	391	3,916	15	4	2	1	2	37	141	180	28	136	34.8	134
Marion SO	262	3,365	10	4	2	1	2	8	108	122	19	75	28.6	97
Jefferson PD	129	5,866	5	0	0	0	0	29	33	58	9	61	47.3	37
Martin — 2	59	1,190	7	4	0	0	0	3	16	36	4	7	11.9	16
Martin SO	28	1,176	3	4	0	0	0	1	3	22	2	1	3.6	9
Stanton PD	31	1,203	4	0	0	0	0	2	13	14	2	6	19.4	7
Mason — 1	22	643	3	2	3	0	0	1	14	4	0	12	54.5	8
Mason SO	22	643	3	2	3	0	0	1	14	4	0	12	54.5	8
Matagorda — 3	2,582	6,992	67	34	4	21	35	136	655	1,628	103	1,084	42.0	381
Matagorda SO	561	3,912	35	22	2	13	2	28	195	272	49	217	38.7	84
Bay City PD	1,773	9,758	26	9	1	6	31	82	377	1,237	39	795	44.8	254
Palacios PD	248	5,613	6	3	1	2	2	26	83	119	15	72	29.0	43
Maverick — 2	1,452	3,991	49	33	3	4	4	83	325	972	61	264	18.2	416
Maverick SO	150	954	17	23	1	0	1	35	83	29	1	3	2.0	113
Eagle Pass PD	1,302	6,305	32	10	2	4	3	48	242	943	60	261	20.0	303
McCulloch — 2	250	2,848	15	10	0	0	0	21	62	160	7	89	35.6	64
McCulloch SO	57	2,013	8	4	0	0	0	7	18	31	1	19	33.3	21
Brady PD	193	3,246	7	6	0	0	0	14	44	129	6	70	36.3	43
McLennan — 16	14,591	7,715	363	215	28	126	384	1,030	4,202	8,039	782	2,914	20.0	2,911
McLennan SO	928	2,678	44	111	3	8	8	51	407	420	31	119	12.8	345
Bellmead PD	563	6,754	12	4	3	2	9	10	140	357	42	171	30.4	146
Beverly Hills PD	138	6,738	6	0	0	1	3	2	26	97	9	19	13.8	6
Hewitt PD	236	2,627	15	7	0	0	0	11	64	153	8	46	19.5	41
Lacy-Lakeview PD	270	7,465	7	5	0	2	2	5	38	217	6	87	32.2	96
Lorena PD	42	3,627	3	0	0	0	0	0	11	27	4	9	21.4	10
McGregor PD	125	2,669	6	6	0	1	1	10	46	60	7	34	27.2	37
Mart PD	112	5,589	4	0	0	0	0	1	23	36	3	1	0.9	9
Northcrest PD	23	1,333	4	0	0	0	0	0	9	13	1	1	4.3	2
Robinson PD	229	3,220	11	6	0	3	1	17	63	141	4	17	7.4	49
Waco PD	11,204	10,816	199	52	22	108	354	882	3,171	6,030	637	2,282	20.4	2,097
West PD	84	3,340	4	0	0	0	1	4	24	42	13	12	14.3	9
Woodway PD	160	1,840	16	9	0	1	1	11	50	92	5	43	26.9	40
McLennan Col. PD	8	*****	3	3	0	0	0	0	3	5	0	0	0.0	0
Baylor U. PD	269	*****	18	11	0	0	3	0	66	194	6	38	14.1	14
TSTI Waco PD	200	*****	11	1	0	0	0	4	48	142	6	35	17.5	10
McMullen — 1	26	3,182	2	1	1	0	0	0	11	12	2	1	3.8	0
McMullen SO	26	3,182	2	1	1	0	0	0	11	12	2	1	3.8	0
Medina — 3	952	3,486	33	19	3	8	3	86	375	430	47	240	25.2	177
Medina SO	329	1,895	14	12	0	3	1	23	168	116	18	60	18.2	54
Devine PD	233	5,932	6	5	0	0	2	14	62	140	15	90	38.6	81
Hondo PD	390	6,481	13	2	3	5	0	49	145	174	14	90	23.1	42
Menard — 1	38	1,687	4	5	0	0	0	3	25	8	2	12	31.6	10
Menard SO	38	1,687	4	5	0	0	0	3	25	8	2	12	31.6	10
Midland — 2	6,413	6,015	232	113	7	78	121	346	1,850	3,609	402	1,801	28.1	858
Midland SO	849	4,945	76	82	0	13	0	44	296	465	31	209	24.6	50
Midland PD	5,564	6,221	156	31	7	65	121	302	1,554	3,144	371	1,592	28.6	808
Milam — 3	581	2,532	20	22	2	3	5	34	168	350	19	261	44.9	337
Milam SO	171	1,410	7	12	0	1	1	0	83	74	12	16	9.4	130
Cameron PD	141	2,527	6	5	2	0	2	11	32	91	3	63	44.7	77
Rockdale PD	269	5,138	7	5	0	2	2	23	53	185	4	182	67.7	130
Mills — 1	11	243	4	5	0	0	0	2	0	8	2	1	18.2	5
Mills SO	11	243	4	5	0	0	0	2	0	8	2	1	18.2	5

County/Agency	Total Crime	Crime Rate	Sworn Staff	Civilian Staff	Murder	Rape	Robbery	Assault	Burglary	Theft	Car Theft	Crimes Cleared	Clearance Rate	Arrested
Mitchell — 2	263	3,281	11	12	1	2	1	35	83	135	6	78	29.7	58
Mitchell SO	73	2,234	4	6	1	2	0	14	36	19	1	26	35.6	29
Colorado City PD	190	4,001	7	6	0	0	1	21	47	116	5	52	27.4	29
Montague — 3	591	3,421	21	23	0	3	2	34	185	306	61	125	21.2	110
Montague SO	277	2,942	8	12	0	2	2	13	116	106	38	33	11.9	56
Bowie PD	183	3,667	8	6	0	0	0	7	36	125	15	51	27.9	31
Nocona PD	131	4,564	5	5	0	1	0	14	33	75	8	41	31.3	23
Montgomery — 6	9,854	5,408	314	102	18	58	124	693	2,588	5,562	811	1,792	18.2	1,211
Montgomery SO	6,561	4,392	228	82	15	35	50	382	1,938	3,607	534	1,209	18.4	772
Conroe PD	2,943	10,659	54	14	3	23	67	292	577	1,735	246	490	16.6	382
Roman Forest PD	26	2,517	2	1	0	0	0	0	15	10	1	2	7.7	0
Shenandoah PD	64	3,725	6	0	0	0	1	1	4	47	11	12	18.8	2
Oak Ridge North PD	152	6,194	6	1	0	0	3	5	46	85	13	47	30.9	15
Conroe ISD PD	108	*****	18	4	0	0	3	13	8	78	6	32	29.6	40
Moore — 2	599	3,353	32	18	1	6	3	13	209	352	15	94	15.7	262
Moore SO	146	2,924	11	13	0	3	2	13	63	61	4	9	6.2	144
Dumas PD	453	3,520	21	5	1	3	1	0	146	291	11	85	18.8	118
Morris — 4	413	3,129	19	7	2	5	7	54	108	226	11	284	68.8	85
Morris SO	140	1,865	8	6	1	3	1	25	37	68	5	52	37.1	50
Daingerfield PD	196	7,621	5	1	0	2	6	14	43	125	6	199	102.0	20
Lone Star PD	76	4,706	3	0	0	0	0	15	28	33	0	32	42.1	15
Naples PD	1	66	3	0	1	0	0	0	0	0	0	1	100.0	0
Motley — 1	16	1,044	1	0	1	0	0	1	7	7	0	3	18.8	2
Motley SO	16	1,044	1	0	1	0	0	1	7	7	0	3	18.8	2
Nacogdoches — 3	2,681	4,897	82	46	5	9	42	247	637	1,645	96	671	25.0	657
Nacogdoches SO	501	2,098	16	20	3	0	8	58	183	211	38	270	53.9	120
Nacogdoches PD	1,815	5,879	49	14	2	8	34	186	401	1,130	54	344	19.0	494
S.F. Austin U. PD	365	*****	17	12	0	1	0	3	53	304	4	57	15.6	43
Navarro — 2	2,455	6,149	56	47	2	37	34	91	566	1,633	92	726	29.6	450
Navarro SO	492	2,892	20	37	2	3	4	32	201	230	20	107	21.7	91
Corsicana PD	1,963	8,568	36	10	0	34	30	59	365	1,403	72	619	31.5	359
Newton — 1	186	1,371	11	1	1	0	2	8	98	62	15	54	29.0	67
Newton SO	186	1,371	11	1	1	0	2	8	98	62	15	54	29.0	67
Nolan — 3	790	4,761	32	12	1	1	8	49	203	501	27	182	23.0	104
Nolan SO	40	1,257	10	8	0	0	1	6	19	14	0	9	22.5	22
Roscoe PD	10	692	1	0	0	0	0	2	5	3	0	4	40.0	3
Sweetwater PD	740	6,184	21	4	1	1	7	41	179	484	27	169	22.8	79
Nueces — 6	27,840	9,562	498	328	29	247	468	962	6,643	18,190	1,301	5,712	20.5	6,637
Nueces SO	294	1,925	89	166	0	7	3	13	99	158	14	61	20.7	648
Bishop PD	122	3,656	5	4	0	0	1	15	39	64	3	17	13.9	23
Corpus Christi PD	26,535	10,307	370	146	29	240	446	892	6,131	17,548	1,249	5,512	20.8	5,756
Robstown PD	689	5,362	17	6	0	0	17	35	330	282	25	83	12.0	159
Port Aransas PD	177	7,927	9	5	0	0	1	7	40	119	10	39	22.0	51
Corpus C. Univ PD	23	*****	8	1	0	0	0	0	4	19	0	0	0.0	0
Ochiltree — 2	317	3,473	19	16	0	3	1	20	61	225	7	92	29.0	133
Ochiltree SO	93	6,114	9	10	0	2	0	9	24	55	3	17	18.3	51
Perryton PD	224	2,945	10	6	0	1	1	11	37	170	4	75	33.5	82
Oldham — 1	49	2,151	5	5	0	0	0	0	12	34	3	7	14.3	11
Oldham SO	49	2,151	5	5	0	0	0	0	12	34	3	7	14.3	11
Orange — 7	4,594	5,706	134	68	6	46	181	247	1,411	2,485	218	902	19.6	512
Orange SO	770	2,218	46	37	1	4	13	27	311	368	46	219	28.4	122
Bridge City PD	310	3,859	12	5	1	3	4	17	64	207	14	81	26.1	21
Orange PD	2,605	13,441	42	12	4	36	154	152	785	1,375	99	314	12.1	211
Pinehurst PD	212	7,905	6	4	0	3	3	19	55	125	7	42	19.8	49
Vidor PD	439	4,015	21	8	0	0	3	24	96	286	30	173	39.4	69
West Orange PD	231	5,517	6	2	0	0	4	2	95	111	19	63	27.3	38
Rose City PD	27	4,720	1	0	0	0	0	6	5	13	3	10	37.0	2
Palo Pinto — 2	1,223	4,881	35	27	1	6	10	132	380	624	70	416	34.0	217
Palo Pinto SO	268	2,590	12	20	0	2	4	18	109	123	12	45	16.8	70
Mineral Wells PD	955	6,422	23	7	1	4	6	114	271	501	58	371	38.8	147
Panola — 2	412	1,870	25	20	3	3	8	22	119	234	23	103	25.0	101
Panola SO	219	1,436	12	14	3	1	0	9	78	111	17	55	25.1	53
Carthage PD	193	2,971	13	6	0	2	8	13	41	123	6	48	24.9	48
Parker — 3	2,163	3,339	64	46	3	23	12	123	764	1,157	81	334	15.4	332
Parker SO	1,053	2,252	26	30	3	14	4	49	492	466	25	90	8.5	202
Weatherford PD	1,021	6,897	33	12	0	9	8	64	256	631	53	240	23.5	119
Springtown PD	89	5,115	5	4	0	0	0	10	16	60	3	4	4.5	11
Parmer — 2	215	2,180	13	10	3	1	0	42	65	92	12	50	23.3	34
Parmer SO	76	1,231	6	6	3	0	0	0	26	42	5	10	13.2	13
Friona PD	139	3,769	7	4	0	1	0	42	39	50	7	40	28.8	21
Pecos — 2	501	3,414	28	16	2	0	0	61	109	309	20	174	34.7	203
Pecos SO	137	2,227	13	8	1	0	0	31	60	36	9	47	34.3	122
Fort Stockton PD	364	4,270	15	8	1	0	0	30	49	273	11	127	34.9	81
Polk — 4	1,181	3,849	37	26	4	9	16	87	443	572	50	372	31.5	530
Polk SO	544	2,347	19	17	2	4	7	25	257	229	20	120	22.1	412
Livingston PD	462	9,205	10	6	1	5	6	51	129	251	19	186	40.3	104
Corrigan PD	128	7,256	5	3	1	0	3	8	36	70	10	35	27.3	9
Onalaska PD	47	6,456	3	0	0	0	0	3	21	22	1	31	66.0	5
Potter — 5	13,963	14,266	359	131	23	81	248	616	3,331	9,072	592	2,810	20.1	2,805
Potter SO	219	3,758	99	53	1	6	0	29	51	120	12	40	18.3	43
Amarillo PD	13,643	8,656	241	76	22	75	248	581	3,262	8,876	579	2,744	20.1	2,745
Amarillo Col PD	54	*****	6	2	0	0	0	4	6	44	0	13	24.1	6
TSTI Campus PD	35	*****	9	0	0	0	0	0	0	12	0	11	31.4	9
Airport PD	12	*****	4	0	0	0	0	2	0	9	1	2	16.7	2

County/Agency	Total Crime	Crime Rate	Sworn Staff	Civilian Staff	Murder	Rape	Robbery	Assault	Burglary	Theft	Car Theft	Crimes Cleared	Clearance Rate	Arrested
Presidio — 1	51	768	4	7	0	2	0	10	17	11	11	37	72.5	47
Presidio SO	51	768	4	7	0	2	0	10	17	11	11	37	72.5	47
Rains — 1	146	2,174	7	10	0	1	2	7	52	70	14	28	19.2	40
Rains SO	146	2,174	7	10	0	1	2	7	52	70	14	28	19.2	40
Randall — 3	636	709	69	18	1	7	1	39	155	409	24	160	25.2	297
Randall SO	276	2,166	48	14	1	4	1	18	85	153	14	74	26.8	237
Canyon PD	226	1,989	14	2	0	1	0	15	40	160	10	64	28.3	57
WTSU PD	134	*****	7	2	0	2	0	6	30	96	0	22	16.4	3
Reagan — 1	70	1,551	4	5	0	1	0	4	15	49	1	16	22.9	40
Reagan SO	70	1,551	4	5	0	1	0	4	15	49	1	16	22.9	40
Real — 1	20	829	2	3	0	0	0	2	11	6	1	1	5.0	4
Real SO	20	829	2	3	0	0	0	2	11	6	1	1	5.0	4
Red River — 2	574	4,009	15	8	1	3	1	66	243	232	28	119	20.7	173
Red River SO	259	2,588	8	7	1	3	0	36	112	89	18	8	3.1	90
Clarksville PD	315	7,307	7	1	0	0	1	30	131	143	10	111	35.2	83
Reeves — 2	577	3,640	28	39	2	1	3	48	165	347	11	122	21.1	215
Reeves SO	132	3,489	12	32	1	0	0	5	55	64	7	47	35.6	108
Pecos PD	445	3,687	16	7	1	1	3	43	110	283	4	75	16.9	107
Refugio — 2	167	2,094	15	10	1	3	2	34	63	61	3	53	31.7	56
Refugio SO	66	1,370	10	9	1	0	1	8	36	18	2	6	9.1	36
Refugio PD	101	3,198	5	1	0	3	1	26	27	43	1	47	46.5	20
Roberts — 1	12	1,171	4	1	0	0	0	1	2	9	0	3	25.0	2
Roberts SO	12	1,171	4	1	0	0	0	1	2	9	0	3	25.0	2
Robertson — 2	803	5,177	15	20	1	13	23	144	212	372	38	294	36.6	389
Robertson SO	148	1,426	6	12	1	3	5	19	59	55	6	35	23.6	210
Hearne PD	655	12,763	9	8	0	10	18	125	153	317	32	259	39.5	179
Rockwall — 4	854	3,335	50	29	2	3	6	29	210	529	75	197	23.1	192
Rockwall SO	153	2,489	13	17	1	1	0	10	67	55	19	12	7.8	43
Rockwall PD	518	4,940	24	11	1	0	4	11	112	342	48	121	23.4	124
Royce City PD	149	6,754	7	1	0	2	2	5	25	110	5	44	29.5	16
Heath PD	34	1,613	6	0	0	0	0	3	6	22	3	20	58.8	9
Runnels — 3	189	1,673	14	8	0	2	0	25	52	107	3	49	25.9	33
Runnels SO	48	1,087	6	5	0	1	0	2	22	22	1	9	18.8	10
Ballinger PD	84	2,113	5	3	0	1	0	8	19	56	0	16	19.0	12
Winters PD	57	1,962	3	0	0	0	0	15	11	29	2	24	42.1	11
Rusk — 4	2,126	4,861	254	30	6	12	18	184	639	1,146	121	438	20.6	243
Rusk SO	798	2,934	223	21	5	6	3	35	348	348	53	233	29.2	99
Henderson PD	1,145	10,279	25	6	1	5	14	111	211	740	63	174	15.2	134
Overton PD	167	7,933	4	1	0	1	1	38	74	49	4	30	18.0	8
Tatum PD	16	1,241	2	2	0	0	0	0	6	9	1	1	6.3	2
Sabine — 2	174	1,815	8	6	1	2	2	16	68	77	8	61	35.1	60
Sabine SO	148	1,761	5	6	1	0	1	12	55	72	7	41	27.7	42
Hemphill PD	26	2,200	3	0	0	2	1	4	13	5	1	20	76.9	18
San Augustine — 2	197	2,463	10	5	0	1	1	43	42	107	3	81	41.1	67
San Augustine SO	93	1,643	5	5	0	1	0	13	31	47	1	21	22.6	36
San Augustine PD	104	4,450	5	0	0	0	1	30	11	60	2	60	57.7	31
San Jacinto — 1	484	2,956	9	10	0	1	4	61	207	193	18	68	14.0	215
San Jacinto SO	484	2,956	9	10	0	1	4	61	207	193	18	68	14.0	215
San Patricio — 8	2,634	4,483	96	47	4	12	8	164	922	1,415	109	781	29.7	568
San Patricio SO	576	3,219	29	24	0	0	0	20	234	297	25	96	16.7	170
Ingleside PD	301	5,284	9	5	0	0	3	13	119	154	12	281	93.4	39
Aransas Pass PD	518	7,213	17	5	2	2	4	19	206	257	28	182	35.1	162
Mathis PD	398	7,339	5	2	1	0	0	64	120	201	12	6	1.5	26
Portland PD	502	4,107	21	10	0	5	1	1	154	324	17	91	18.1	74
Sinton PD	233	4,199	7	1	1	3	0	29	48	141	11	95	40.8	57
Taft PD	64	1,986	5	0	0	2	0	2	31	27	2	20	31.3	27
Gregory PD	42	1,709	3	0	0	0	0	16	10	14	2	10	23.8	13
San Saba — 1	115	2,129	2	5	0	0	0	27	56	28	4	15	13.0	24
San Saba SO	115	2,129	2	5	0	0	0	27	56	28	4	15	13.0	24
Schleicher — 1	85	2,843	5	4	0	1	0	10	40	33	1	41	48.2	27
Schleicher SO	85	2,843	5	4	0	1	0	10	40	33	1	41	48.2	27
Scurry — 2	520	2,791	24	10	1	11	1	43	97	350	17	229	44.0	128
Scurry SO	166	2,578	8	6	0	1	0	7	48	106	4	69	41.6	28
Snyder PD	354	2,903	16	4	1	10	1	36	49	244	13	160	45.2	100
Shackelford — 1	28	844	3	9	0	0	0	0	8	17	3	5	17.9	27
Shackelford SO	28	844	3	9	0	0	0	0	8	17	3	5	17.9	27
Shelby — 2	831	3,771	18	19	3	11	13	74	232	467	31	296	35.6	226
Shelby SO	199	1,165	5	15	3	2	2	29	79	65	19	40	20.1	80
Center PD	632	12,768	13	4	0	9	11	45	153	402	12	256	40.5	146
Sherman — 2	20	700	7	5	0	0	0	2	7	9	2	1	5.0	6
Sherman SO	12	1,114	4	5	0	0	0	1	3	8	0	1	8.3	6
Stratford PD	8	449	3	0	0	0	0	1	4	1	2	0	0.0	0
Smith — 9	11,264	7,444	247	142	17	106	185	575	2,646	7,142	593	3,477	30.9	1,905
Smith SO	2,255	3,373	85	73	5	35	20	135	676	1,257	127	664	29.4	470
Arp PD	17	2,094	1	0	0	0	0	0	0	10	6	3	17.6	3
Lindale PD	151	6,219	6	4	0	0	0	2	41	105	3	35	23.2	34
Troup PD	74	4,461	4	1	0	0	0	8	23	39	4	16	21.6	8
Tyler PD	8,469	11,225	132	46	12	70	164	403	1,851	5,516	453	2,693	31.8	1,362
Whitehouse PD	146	3,621	7	3	0	1	1	23	29	92	0	54	37.0	23
Tyler Jr. Col. PD	99	*****	7	1	0	0	0	2	16	78	3	10	10.1	5
UT-Tyler PD	25	*****	2	7	0	0	0	0	0	25	0	0	0.0	0
UTHea Cen PD	28	*****	3	7	0	0	0	2	0	24	2	2	7.1	0
Somervell — 1	180	3,358	13	12	0	0	0	9	64	94	13	28	15.6	45
Somervell SO	180	3,358	13	12	0	0	0	9	64	94	13	28	15.6	45

County/Agency	Total Crime	Crime Rate	Sworn Staff	Civilian Staff	Murder	Rape	Robbery	Assault	Burglary	Theft	Car Theft	Crimes Cleared	Clearance Rate	Arrested
Starr — 2	920	2,271	38	35	4	2	8	116	370	340	80	71	7.7	171
Starr SO	661	2,036	30	29	3	2	5	93	260	239	59	46	7.0	148
Roma PD	259	3,214	8	6	1	0	3	23	110	101	21	25	9.7	23
Stephens — 2	242	2,686	14	10	0	3	1	9	69	150	10	73	30.2	57
Stephens SO	98	2,930	5	4	0	2	1	7	35	47	6	12	12.2	12
Breckenridge PD	144	2,542	9	6	0	1	0	2	34	103	4	61	42.4	45
Sterling — 1	24	1,669	3	1	0	0	0	1	8	15	0	6	25.0	4
Sterling SO	24	1,669	3	1	0	0	0	1	8	15	0	6	25.0	4
Stonewall — 1	29	1,441	2	4	0	0	0	2	8	18	1	14	48.3	12
Stonewall SO	29	1,441	2	4	0	0	0	2	8	18	1	14	48.3	12
Sutton — 2	142	3,434	9	8	0	0	1	6	26	105	4	31	21.8	21
Sutton SO	29	2,095	5	8	0	0	1	0	6	18	4	5	17.2	5
Sonora PD	113	4,108	4	0	0	0	0	6	20	87	0	26	23.0	16
Swisher — 2	209	2,570	10	10	2	2	0	27	46	123	9	72	34.4	74
Swisher SO	83	2,417	4	5	2	2	0	6	27	42	4	17	20.5	26
Tulia PD	126	2,681	6	5	0	0	0	21	19	81	5	55	43.7	48
Tarrant — 36	118,889	10,161	2,437	1,558	156	743	3,783	6,741	26,104	66,890	14,472	22,664	19.1	15,318
Tarrant SO	1,843	3,888	117	785	2	7	20	181	634	886	113	374	20.3	125
Arlington PD	22,309	8,524	350	107	8	139	586	1,143	4,498	13,192	2,743	5,554	24.9	2,549
Azle PD	575	6,484	19	7	0	6	3	30	95	418	23	166	28.9	116
Bedford PD	2,433	5,560	60	24	1	23	31	25	476	1,682	195	474	19.5	292
Benbrook PD	699	3,573	33	8	1	8	13	29	158	427	63	243	34.8	121
Blue Mound PD	53	2,485	4	4	0	0	2	4	9	30	8	14	26.4	13
Crowley PD	254	3,642	13	6	0	0	0	29	60	150	15	50	19.7	17
Dalworth. Gard. PD	105	5,973	6	1	0	0	1	0	29	69	6	12	11.4	51
Euless PD	2,351	6,163	52	30	3	13	31	88	490	1,520	206	496	21.1	282
Everman PD	257	4,531	15	6	0	2	7	42	70	110	26	34	13.2	36
Forest Hill PD	959	8,352	20	8	1	8	52	43	228	499	128	199	20.8	116
Fort Worth PD	67,040	14,977	953	307	130	432	2,801	4,463	15,298	34,710	9,206	10,160	15.2	8,848
Grapevine PD	1,444	4,945	52	25	0	6	15	48	297	986	92	520	36.0	208
Haltom City PD	3,472	10,567	48	11	0	25	65	70	1,007	1,877	428	137	3.9	159
Hurst PD	2,695	8,027	55	29	4	35	38	112	514	1,702	290	1,023	38.0	623
Kennedale PD	169	4,126	13	5	1	0	5	8	83	60	12	35	20.7	60
Lakeside PD	32	3,699	2	1	0	0	0	1	12	17	2	17	53.1	6
Lake Worth PD	948	20,649	19	7	1	1	6	58	81	769	32	236	24.9	141
Mansfield PD	943	6,042	26	2	0	2	8	49	208	623	53	211	22.4	136
N.Richland Hill PD	3,248	7,077	64	28	2	26	46	107	663	2,064	340	941	29.0	522
Richland Hills PD	553	6,932	14	6	0	1	7	3	182	332	28	118	21.3	49
River Oaks PD	403	6,125	14	6	0	0	8	25	113	225	32	125	31.0	42
Saginaw PD	376	4,397	18	7	0	0	3	9	78	256	30	74	19.7	65
Sansom Pk Vill PD	259	6,594	5	8	0	0	2	15	76	142	24	10	3.9	24
Watauga PD	520	2,599	30	10	0	0	6	10	124	352	28	49	9.4	106
Westover Hills PD	36	5,357	12	1	0	0	0	0	14	17	5	7	19.4	7
Westworth PD	50	2,128	4	4	0	0	0	3	11	30	6	15	30.0	10
W. Settlement PD	1,405	9,081	23	10	1	1	15	21	158	1,064	145	416	29.6	235
Keller PD	426	3,113	22	8	0	2	1	66	115	223	19	72	16.9	47
Pantego PD	204	8,604	11	5	0	0	2	5	59	118	20	48	23.5	27
Southlake PD	271	3,836	19	7	0	5	3	22	77	154	10	44	16.2	52
UT-Arlington PD	457	*****	22	32	0	1	1	7	28	398	22	97	21.2	80
DFW It'l PD	1,583	*****	276	26	0	0	3	13	33	1,422	112	613	38.7	106
TCU PD	104	*****	17	12	0	0	1	1	22	80	0	1	1.0	0
Colleyville PD	369	2,900	18	7	1	0	1	11	101	246	9	77	20.9	44
Col. Osteo Med PD	44	*****	11	8	0	0	0	0	3	40	1	2	4.5	3
Taylor — 5	6,083	5,084	235	87	8	100	189	655	1,773	3,086	272	1,818	29.9	1,295
Taylor SO	180	1,748	67	33	0	4	2	13	69	90	2	66	36.7	337
Abilene PD	5,739	5,381	160	49	7	92	187	628	1,647	2,912	266	1,704	29.7	927
Merkel PD	64	2,592	3	0	1	1	0	6	23	30	3	22	34.4	11
Tye PD	81	7,445	2	1	0	3	0	5	28	44	1	23	28.4	20
H-SU PD	19	*****	3	4	0	0	0	3	6	10	0	3	15.8	0
Terrell — 1	23	1,631	3	2	0	0	0	2	15	6	0	4	17.4	8
Terrell SO	23	1,631	3	2	0	0	0	2	15	6	0	4	17.4	8
Terry — 2	695	5,258	20	11	1	15	5	38	247	369	20	133	19.1	132
Terry SO	151	4,128	6	8	0	5	0	4	38	97	7	21	13.9	78
Brownsfield PD	544	5,690	14	3	1	10	5	34	209	272	13	112	20.6	54
Throckmorton — 1	19	1,011	2	5	0	0	0	2	7	9	1	2	10.5	6
Throckmorton SO	19	1,011	2	5	0	0	0	2	7	9	1	2	10.5	6
Titus — 2	1,107	4,611	27	18	6	1	6	60	310	681	43	238	21.5	371
Titus SO	283	2,415	10	12	3	0	1	13	81	168	17	140	49.5	184
Mount Pleasant PD	824	6,704	17	6	3	1	5	47	229	513	26	98	11.9	187
Tom Green — 4	6,421	6,522	209	69	5	60	45	505	1,662	3,922	222	1,707	26.6	1,888
Tom Green SO	378	2,703	39	27	0	3	4	92	111	157	11	135	35.7	709
San Angelo PD	5,970	7,067	159	40	5	57	41	413	1,539	3,704	211	1,569	26.3	1,176
Angelo St. U. PD	64	*****	9	2	0	0	0	0	7	57	0	1	1.6	0
SanAngelo Park 0P	9	*****	2	0	0	0	0	0	5	4	0	2	22.2	3
Travis — 13	61,185	10,615	3,900	3,649	49	346	1,520	1,716	13,209	40,113	4,232	12,872	21.0	11,777
Travis SO	4,799	5,081	138	660	3	61	48	139	1,559	2,692	297	1,305	27.2	763
DPSAustin	0	*****	2,870	2,554	0	0	0	0	0	0	0	0	***.*	0
Austin PD	54,543	11,714	768	293	46	280	1,461	1,539	11,371	35,955	3,891	11,211	20.6	10,691
Manor PD	12	1,153	4	0	0	0	0	1	3	5	0	0	0.0	1
Rollingwood PD	54	3,890	4	0	0	0	0	0	21	28	4	6	11.1	5
West Lake Hills PD	173	6,806	11	5	0	0	0	2	39	132	0	80	46.2	67
UT-Austin PD	929	*****	58	109	0	3	5	5	33	857	26	147	15.8	110
Pflugerville PD	117	2,633	7	5	0	0	0	7	6	100	4	39	33.3	56
Lakeway Village PD	72	1,780	12	5	0	0	0	0	15	56	1	7	9.7	6

County/Agency	Total Crime	Crime Rate	Sworn Staff	Civilian Staff	Murder	Rape	Robbery	Assault	Burglary	Theft	Car Theft	Crimes Cleared	Clearance Rate	Arrested
Sunset Valley PD	12	3,670	2	0	0	0	0	2	4	6	0	4	33.3	3
Lago Vista PD	67	3,047	7	5	0	0	0	1	22	41	3	7	10.4	2
Mustang Ridge PD	9	1,563	1	0	0	0	0	2	2	4	1	3	33.3	6
Austin ISD PD	398	*****	18	13	0	2	6	15	133	237	5	63	15.8	67
Trinity — 2	322	2,813	11	10	0	3	0	31	141	130	17	56	17.4	102
Trinity SO	261	2,967	7	5	0	3	0	22	126	99	11	36	13.8	75
Trinity PD	61	2,304	4	5	0	0	0	9	15	31	6	20	32.8	27
Tyler — 2	392	2,355	16	17	2	4	1	58	162	157	8	71	18.1	119
Tyler SO	294	2,099	10	16	2	4	1	25	142	112	8	26	8.8	84
Woodville PD	98	3,718	6	1	0	0	0	33	20	45	0	45	45.9	35
Upshur — 4	730	2,327	29	18	0	4	3	83	233	369	38	109	14.9	145
Upshur SO	368	1,657	16	17	0	3	0	19	151	174	21	61	16.6	93
Big Sandy PD	66	5,570	3	0	0	0	3	0	17	38	8	26	39.4	26
Gilmer PD	276	5,724	7	1	0	1	0	61	56	152	6	16	5.8	19
Ore City PD	20	2,227	3	0	0	0	0	3	9	5	3	6	30.0	7
Upton — 1	80	1,799	8	6	1	0	1	19	17	37	5	33	41.3	19
Upton SO	80	1,799	8	6	1	0	1	19	17	37	5	33	41.3	19
Uvalde — 3	635	2,721	31	20	2	2	5	85	217	291	33	336	52.9	187
Uvalde SO	150	2,135	9	15	0	0	0	19	75	48	8	29	19.3	28
Uvalde PD	442	3,001	20	5	2	2	5	60	137	213	23	282	63.8	149
Sabinal PD	43	2,715	2	0	0	0	0	6	5	30	2	25	58.1	10
Val Verde — 2	1,847	4,770	58	65	0	1	5	125	501	1,142	73	356	19.3	585
Val Verde SO	153	1,909	9	54	0	1	1	8	88	49	6	8	5.2	59
Del Rio PD	1,694	5,517	49	11	0	0	4	117	413	1,093	67	348	20.5	526
Van Zandt — 6	940	2,477	44	20	2	3	14	63	304	499	55	303	32.2	250
Van Zandt SO	509	1,940	19	15	2	2	10	32	190	243	30	190	37.3	153
Canton PD	151	5,120	7	4	0	0	2	21	27	90	11	36	23.8	22
Edgewood PD	11	857	3	0	0	0	0	0	5	6	0	1	9.1	0
Grand Saline PD	67	2,548	5	0	0	1	1	7	17	35	6	21	31.3	18
Van PD	47	2,535	4	0	0	0	0	1	13	30	3	14	29.8	17
Wills Point PD	155	5,191	6	1	0	0	1	2	52	95	5	41	26.5	40
Victoria — 2	4,891	6,577	139	53	7	32	67	469	1,285	2,858	173	1,301	26.6	810
Victoria SO	520	2,696	49	19	1	9	4	24	180	293	9	126	24.2	44
Victoria PD	4,371	7,936	90	34	6	23	63	445	1,105	2,565	164	1,175	26.9	766
Wheeler SO	35	974	6	4	2	0	0	3	13	16	1	12	34.3	8
Walker — 2	2,545	4,998	59	39	3	20	33	202	646	1,491	150	713	28.0	343
Walker SO	970	4,219	26	27	2	11	8	80	293	514	62	195	20.1	51
Huntsville PD	1,575	5,640	33	12	1	9	25	122	353	977	88	518	32.9	292
Waller — 5	1,410	6,028	41	35	4	13	19	144	355	790	85	420	29.8	248
Waller SO	198	1,392	9	25	2	6	1	15	100	59	15	114	57.6	53
Brookshire PD	367	12,560	6	4	1	4	2	57	60	229	14	151	41.1	115
Waller PD	125	6,846	7	0	0	1	1	0	38	78	7	50	40.0	26
Hempstead PD	472	13,292	6	1	1	0	15	54	75	287	40	90	19.1	39
Prairie View A& PD	248	*****	13	5	0	2	0	18	82	137	9	15	6.0	15
Ward — 2	498	3,797	29	22	1	1	5	22	91	355	23	182	36.5	187
Ward SO	158	3,151	15	15	1	1	4	5	41	94	12	37	23.4	83
Monahans PD	340	4,197	14	7	0	0	1	17	50	261	11	145	42.6	104
Washington — 2	707	2,703	38	21	1	6	11	96	173	400	20	207	29.3	241
Washington SO	164	1,155	13	9	0	3	2	7	81	65	6	16	9.8	87
Brenham PD	543	4,543	25	12	1	3	9	89	92	335	14	191	35.2	154
Webb — 3	11,289	8,473	332	176	18	20	159	606	2,355	7,029	1,102	1,306	11.6	1,934
Webb SO	291	2,814	145	149	4	3	1	45	113	96	29	53	18.2	306
Laredo PD	10,927	8,891	178	26	14	17	158	561	2,231	6,876	1,070	1,231	11.3	1,627
Laredo Jr Col PD	71	*****	9	1	0	0	0	0	11	57	3	22	31.0	1
Wharton — 3	1,997	4,998	56	25	2	17	32	135	599	1,165	47	531	26.6	429
Wharton SO	507	2,481	24	19	0	7	4	25	204	247	20	136	26.8	104
El Campo PD	833	7,925	18	5	2	3	16	48	258	496	10	172	20.6	185
Wharton PD	657	7,291	14	1	0	7	12	62	137	422	17	223	33.9	140
Wheeler — 2	120	2,041	8	7	2	0	0	13	24	77	4	50	42.0	27
Wheeler SO	35	974	6	4	2	0	0	3	13	16	1	12	34.0	8
Shamrock PD	85	3,718	2	3	0	0	0	10	11	61	3	38	44.7	19
Wichita — 6	11,599	9,478	232	156	11	80	334	521	3,011	7,120	522	2,705	23.3	2,096
Wichita SO	255	3,756	31	72	0	5	6	25	106	99	14	26	10.2	255
Burkburnett PD	332	3,273	12	5	0	0	2	22	90	205	13	54	16.3	50
Electra PD	38	1,221	5	3	0	1	0	4	16	16	1	7	18.4	10
Iowa Park PD	131	2,157	11	4	0	0	0	8	46	71	6	36	27.5	35
Wichita Falls PD	10,785	11,204	166	71	11	74	326	455	2,744	6,687	488	2,579	23.9	1,744
Midwestern Uni PD	58	*****	7	1	0	0	0	7	9	42	0	3	5.2	2
Wilbarger — 2	574	3,796	25	12	2	3	8	95	218	236	12	163	28.4	124
Wilbarger SO	72	2,308	6	6	0	0	0	1	32	38	1	11	15.3	52
Vernon PD	502	4,183	19	6	2	3	8	94	186	198	11	152	30.3	72
Willacy — 2	836	4,722	19	20	1	5	6	133	288	388	15	223	26.7	172
Willacy SO	198	2,244	10	13	1	0	2	18	97	75	5	54	27.3	52
Raymondville PD	638	7,185	9	7	0	5	4	115	191	313	10	169	26.5	120
Williamson — 8	5,148	3,689	162	108	3	64	45	374	1,146	3,275	241	1,625	31.6	1,382
Williamson SO	1,951	2,668	52	69	1	30	12	165	481	1,164	98	588	30.1	629
Georgetown PD	743	5,006	26	11	2	2	8	62	155	472	42	204	27.5	109
Hutto PD	28	4,444	4	0	0	1	0	3	6	17	1	6	21.4	2
Round Rock PD	1,230	3,978	42	10	0	27	11	80	208	846	58	458	37.2	363
Taylor PD	814	7,096	15	7	0	4	12	46	235	489	28	254	31.2	188
Southwestern U PD	13	*****	5	0	0	0	0	1	4	8	0	5	38.5	4
Cedar Park PD	253	4,902	12	6	0	0	1	6	34	202	10	67	26.5	42
Leander PD	116	3,414	6	5	0	0	1	11	23	77	4	43	37.1	45

County/Agency	Total Crime	Crime Rate	Sworn Staff	Civilian Staff	Murder	Rape	Robbery	Assault	Burglary	Theft	Car Theft	Crimes Cleared	Clearance Rate	Arrested
Wilson — 3	516	2,278	15	14	2	3	2	52	164	271	22	70	13.6	99
Wilson SO	292	1,742	8	14	2	3	1	15	113	137	21	29	9.9	63
Floresville PD	224	4,269	6	0	0	0	1	37	51	134	1	41	18.3	36
La Vernia PD	0	0	1	0	0	0	0	0	0	0	0	0	***.*	0
Winkler — 2	187	2,168	15	12	0	0	1	19	48	112	7	75	40.1	77
Winkler SO	23	1,314	6	6	0	0	0	5	4	14	0	8	34.8	33
Kermit PD	164	2,385	9	6	0	0	1	14	44	98	7	67	40.9	44
Wise — 3	866	2,497	37	29	0	5	1	36	292	451	81	78	9.0	243
Wise SO	533	1,985	20	19	0	4	0	20	210	262	37	55	10.3	205
Bridgeport PD	199	5,557	7	6	0	1	1	13	43	129	12	10	5.0	22
Decatur PD	134	3,151	10	4	0	0	0	3	39	60	32	13	9.7	16
Wood — 5	861	2,931	46	33	1	1	6	100	348	372	33	212	24.6	223
Wood SO	632	3,190	20	23	0	0	2	92	227	284	27	168	26.6	181
Hawkins PD	49	3,743	3	0	0	0	0	3	9	37	0	11	22.4	17
Mineola PD	82	1,898	9	7	0	1	2	0	64	14	1	1	1.2	1
Quitman PD	39	2,316	6	0	1	0	1	0	19	17	1	16	41.0	8
Winnsboro PD	59	2,032	8	3	0	0	1	5	29	20	4	16	27.1	16
Yoakum — 2	212	2,413	16	14	0	1	0	23	41	134	13	54	25.5	53
Yoakum SO	94	2,582	9	9	0	1	0	4	22	62	5	23	24.5	26
Denver City PD	118	2,293	7	5	0	0	0	19	19	72	8	31	26.3	27
Young — 3	603	3,327	29	20	0	0	5	32	201	349	16	66	10.9	80
Young SO	218	3,878	12	15	0	0	2	18	73	124	1	23	10.6	52
Graham PD	269	2,994	12	1	0	0	3	10	81	164	11	36	13.4	21
Olney PD	116	3,296	5	4	0	0	0	4	47	61	4	7	6.0	7
Zapata — 1	114	1,229	21	10	0	0	0	6	43	62	3	24	21.1	31
Zapata SO	114	1,229	21	10	0	0	0	6	43	62	3	24	21.1	31
Zavala — 2	226	1,858	14	20	5	0	3	32	74	106	6	71	31.4	105
Zavala SO	90	2,308	8	17	2	0	2	12	32	38	4	35	38.9	65
Crystal City PD	136	1,646	6	3	3	0	1	20	42	68	2	36	26.5	40

Criminal Supervision, 1990-91

County (Adult Pop.)	Jail (1)	Prison (2)	Probation (3)	Parole (4)	Total
Anderson (36,744)	74	86	3,802	110	4,101
Andrews (9,375)	20	35	446	29	535
Angelina (49,869)	98	215	3,026	207	3,576
Aransas (13,386)	27	62	0	59	155
Archer (5,741)	4	7	0	13	24
Armstrong (1,459)	3	3	0	2	8
Atascosa (20,441)	92	93	0	66	258
Austin (14,519)	35	26	0	50	115
Bailey (4,814)	9	9	336	15	371
Bandera (8,054)	8	10	0	14	35
Bastrop (27,242)	138	55	2,610	97	2,909
Baylor (3,406)	7	5	325	11	350
Bee (17,210)	121	83	0	60	283
Bell (136,055)	390	722	5,847	444	7,462
Bexar (839,453)	2,155	2,798	28,504	3,278	37,213
Blanco (4,482)	5	9	0	2	18
Borden (575)	0	0	0	2	3
Bosque (11,563)	20	22	0	25	69
Bowie (59,471)	193	190	2,188	293	2,897
Brazoria (135,462)	420	328	3,485	394	4,699
Brazos (95,689)	231	366	2,819	369	3,836
Brewster (6,629)	12	5	0	13	33
Briscoe (1,420)	0	1	0	2	3
Brooks (5,490)	8	12	0	33	56
Brown (25,134)	58	74	982	132	1,269
Burleson (9,912)	12	33	0	46	100
Burnet (17,101)	23	36	1,025	35	1,124
Caldwell (18,562)	54	102	3,445	92	3,704
Calhoun (13,435)	33	22	0	38	100
Callahan (8,601)	6	21	0	18	47
Cameron (168,280)	591	488	6,858	494	8,506
Camp (7,297)	13	53	0	35	109
Carson (4,609)	7	20	0	12	40
Cass (21,785)	25	68	675	96	873
Castro (5,774)	16	21	0	30	68
Chambers (14,113)	60	81	0	58	206
Cherokee (30,290)	69	79	1,137	117	1,414
Childress (4,400)	8	14	0	17	42
Clay (7,383)	9	10	0	8	27
Cochran (2,918)	8	6	0	4	18
Coke (2,632)	1	9	0	4	14
Coleman (7,382)	9	15	0	21	47
Collin (187,534)	303	365	4,894	399	6,009
Collingsworth (2,622)	4	5	0	4	13
Colorado (13,490)	16	37	0	44	102
Comal (38,576)	106	83	0	74	276
Comanche (10,242)	40	19	794	30	888
Concho (2,344)	0	5	0	8	13
Cooke (22,068)	40	61	508	37	663
Coryell (47,273)	18	66	832	55	978
Cottle (1,669)	4	2	0	4	12
Crane (3,038)	11	9	108	10	138
Crockett (2,822)	14	8	0	1	23
Crosby (5,022)	11	6	0	25	47
Culberson (2,219)	7	7	0	2	16
Dallam (3,801)	13	18	0	14	53
Dallas (1,357,162)	4,754	9,312	40,402	10,390	66,444
Dawson (9,807)	15	42	988	58	1,111
Deaf Smith (12,387)	57	58	770	78	984
Delta (3,680)	0	16	0	8	27
Denton (199,880)	265	334	3,631	435	4,713
DeWitt (13,783)	37	57	0	34	133
Dickens (1,960)	5	8	0	6	22
Dimmit (6,642)	5	12	0	12	30
Donley (2,895)	5	5	0	10	21
Duval (8,690)	8	20	973	27	1,032
Eastland (14,185)	18	39	466	42	574
Ector (81,223)	180	402	2,105	602	3,371
Edwards (1,520)	18	1	0	1	20
Ellis (58,765)	119	143	1,634	239	2,159
El Paso (398,798)	1,095	912	11,561	1,065	14,959
Erath (21,294)	30	77	906	52	1,069
Falls (13,188)	15	38	1,109	48	1,215
Fannin (18,832)	20	56	0	49	131
Fayette (15,271)	30	22	1,677	42	1,775
Fisher (3,590)	7	8	0	5	20
Floyd (5,811)	14	15	403	30	465
Foard (1,365)	1	1	0	2	4
Fort Bend (150,599)	284	213	3,113	441	4,119
Franklin (5,815)	8	26	0	19	54
Freestone (11,531)	30	84	0	44	165
Frio (8,787)	158	32	0	55	253

County (Adult Pop.)	Jail (1)	Prison (2)	Probation (3)	Parole (4)	Total
Gaines (8,982)	17	21	0	27	67
Galveston (157,498)	479	575	3,978	741	5,876
Garza (3,515)	3	11	0	19	39
Gillespie (13,196)	12	22	0	13	48
Glasscock (936)	1	0	0	0	1
Goliad (4,343)	15	19	0	6	44
Gonzales (12,250)	12	39	0	33	89
Gray (17,630)	19	45	666	61	797
Grayson (70,913)	92	185	2,019	229	2,566
Gregg (76,227)	170	437	3,116	387	4,155
Grimes (13,889)	20	37	0	52	115
Guadalupe (46,382)	109	157	1,961	129	2,376
Hale (23,507)	109	90	1,213	183	1,608
Hall (2,978)	5	9	614	18	648
Hamilton (6,007)	7	22	0	12	44
Hansford (4,028)	9	0	0	7	17
Hardeman (3,904)	3	16	0	9	31
Hardin (29,206)	62	62	840	107	1,093
Harris (2,013,190)	7,638	12,322	46,080	17,070	86,016
Harrison (40,928)	62	163	1,100	190	1,529
Hartley (2,581)	2	1	0	5	8
Haskell (5,117)	6	21	183	17	229
Hays (49,624)	266	119	0	107	504
Hemphill (2,570)	4	4	0	2	11
Henderson (44,481)	60	113	0	170	378
Hidalgo (243,124)	475	430	8,122	461	9,571
Hill (20,292)	40	51	1,105	65	1,269
Hockley (16,386)	36	32	693	51	818
Hood (21,579)	48	76	775	80	988
Hopkins (21,172)	45	78	1,267	99	1,499
Houston (15,991)	30	44	0	38	123
Howard (23,626)	19	94	1,011	92	1,227
Hudspeth (1,987)	142	10	0	2	155
Hunt (47,338)	84	128	1,445	246	1,938
Hutchinson (18,216)	43	22	699	66	850
Irion (1,167)	0	0	0	1	2
Jack (5,110)	12	11	1,210	24	1,257
Jackson (9,363)	38	35	0	27	109
Jasper (22,293)	30	46	1,429	71	1,586
Jeff Davis (1,433)	0	4	0	0	4
Jefferson (174,707)	719	813	3,863	1,242	6,836
Jim Hogg (3,441)	7	6	0	3	18
Jim Wells (25,425)	35	86	1,950	99	2,182
Johnson (68,829)	171	159	2,618	210	3,183
Jones (11,939)	17	45	516	45	634
Karnes (8,657)	15	61	1,891	31	1,999
Kaufman (36,858)	80	93	1,121	217	1,554
Kendall (10,759)	12	20	0	15	51
Kenedy (322)	1	1	0	0	2
Kent (749)	0	1	0	0	1
Kerr (27,873)	45	70	2,362	153	2,642
Kimble (3,070)	4	14	0	8	26
King (245)	0	0	0	1	1
Kinney (2,334)	25	3	0	3	31
Kleberg (21,429)	31	40	1,359	50	1,487
Knox (3,507)	8	4	0	10	23
Lamar (32,510)	85	196	1,815	197	2,325
Lamb (10,558)	18	21	279	36	360
Lampasas (9,774)	15	50	0	47	115
La Salle (3,509)	54	13	0	13	82
Lavaca (14,087)	15	25	1,215	17	1,276
Lee (9,040)	12	17	0	25	59
Leon (9,390)	9	17	0	23	55
Liberty (37,323)	120	159	2,376	262	2,956
Limestone (15,438)	51	59	2,253	94	2,470
Lipscomb (2,228)	3	2	0	3	8
Live Oak (6,941)	14	15	0	14	45
Llano (9,729)	13	9	0	15	39
Loving (79)	0	0	0	0	0
Lubbock (163,771)	476	670	4,723	807	6,831
Lynn (4,706)	14	8	0	12	36
Madison (8,579)	15	24	0	26	70
Marion (7,513)	7	13	0	35	58
Martin (3,262)	4	3	0	10	19
Mason (2,618)	2	1	0	3	6
Matagorda (25,325)	51	98	1,988	144	2,304
Maverick (22,544)	115	27	442	20	611
McCulloch (6,410)	17	15	496	18	551
McLennan (139,885)	449	541	3,664	919	5,693
McMullen (615)	0	1	0	2	4
Medina (19,209)	12	46	0	32	99
Menard (1,703)	2	5	0	2	10
Midland (73,168)	281	314	2,520	420	3,577
Milam (16,471)	25	51	524	80	690
Mills (3,448)	5	2	0	4	12
Mitchell (5,813)	13	16	0	10	42
Montague (13,028)	20	24	748	45	841
Montgomery (128,109)	495	379	3,941	474	5,357
Moore (11,963)	15	25	437	35	521
Morris (9,577)	20	37	919	47	1,034
Motley (1,175)	0	3	0	2	5
Nacogdoches (42,069)	105	127	1,391	165	1,811
Navarro (29,168)	136	187	1,162	180	1,685
Newton (9,560)	9	22	0	28	63
Nolan (11,976)	26	57	843	54	985
Nueces (202,321)	651	746	6,193	874	8,581
Ochiltree (6,306)	14	16	1,696	17	1,746
Oldham (1,338)	4	5	0	3	12
Orange (57,508)	105	209	0	256	602
Palo Pinto (18,445)	60	89	486	128	778
Panola (15,896)	28	43	1,029	41	1,149
Parker (46,641)	92	71	1,558	174	1,915
Parmer (6,601)	8	9	0	16	33
Pecos (9,609)	30	25	836	14	908
Polk (23,083)	52	58	1,500	101	1,725
Potter (69,734)	362	420	4,318	472	5,648
Presidio (4,494)	28	11	0	6	45
Rains (5,031)	13	19	0	25	60
Randall (65,169)	59	115	0	57	242
Reagan (2,798)	5	6	0	2	13
Real (1,847)	1	4	0	4	11
Red River (10,874)	9	44	428	42	527
Reeves (10,537)	80	55	761	57	961
Refugio (5,782)	15	16	0	6	40
Roberts (718)	1	4	0	1	6
Robertson (11,075)	27	94	0	114	350
Rockwall (18,082)	40	34	589	38	709
Runnels (8,206)	13	31	0	33	87
Rusk (31,567)	56	82	541	90	777
Sabine (7,572)	5	17	0	20	44
San Augustine (6,046)	6	23	0	22	53
San Jacinto (12,074)	36	38	0	41	120
San Patricio (39,757)	65	147	2,963	164	3,365
San Saba (4,001)	5	5	0	5	16
Schleicher (2,017)	8	4	0	1	15
Scurry (13,319)	46	59	437	61	614
Shackelford (2,428)	3	5	0	9	17
Shelby (16,269)	52	50	0	58	171
Sherman (2,022)	2	1	0	4	8
Smith (111,026)	463	432	4,417	554	5,952
Somervell (3,643)	4	10	0	14	29
Starr (24,553)	175	16	0	41	240
Stephens (6,550)	7	22	0	20	53
Sterling (955)	0	1	0	3	5
Stonewall (1,501)	5	7	0	2	16
Sutton (2,866)	18	9	0	4	31
Swisher (5,675)	25	20	0	49	101
Tarrant (852,582)	3,148	2,889	19,277	4,686	30,806
Taylor (87,053)	347	354	3,005	327	4,087
Terrell (993)	3	1	0	1	5
Terry (8,844)	9	49	807	31	905
Throckmorton (1,435)	0	3	0	5	9
Titus (17,157)	42	60	0	79	197
Tom Green (71,840)	145	294	2,615	302	3,412
Travis (438,196)	1,570	1,650	17,433	2,738	23,795
Trinity (8,765)	6	29	0	32	73
Tyler (12,493)	24	30	449	64	574
Upshur (22,704)	52	44	806	64	976
Upton (2,859)	7	4	0	4	18
Uvalde (15,848)	34	40	1,574	32	1,685
Val Verde (25,965)	167	38	1,103	77	1,404
Van Zandt (28,223)	34	31	566	74	723
Victoria (51,824)	164	185	4,366	204	4,956
Walker (41,231)	79	126	2,038	161	2,452
Waller (17,460)	43	44	0	67	163
Ward (8,769)	63	49	0	47	171
Washington (19,501)	18	60	0	63	149
Webb (84,362)	478	159	2,052	191	2,923
Wharton (28,013)	35	85	0	151	294
Wheeler (4,312)	7	13	333	4	360
Wichita (90,399)	210	184	1,604	341	2,418
Wilbarger (11,130)	14	34	0	23	74
Willacy (11,231)	23	22	0	34	86
Williamson (96,362)	250	311	3,413	238	4,256

Several Views of Texas Crime

Here are ratings of Texas sheriff's departments and police departments in several categories dealing with crimes.

The statistics are broken down into two categories because sheriff's offices have a different jurisdiction than do police departments. In general, the sheriff's responsibilities for law enforcement are confined to unincorporated areas in the counties they serve, although the department does have countywide jurisdiction.

In rural areas, sheriff's departments usually have a much larger physical area, but lightly populated, to patrol. Police departments have more densely populated areas in which to enforce the law, which brings about a different set of challenges.

For the purpose of these rankings, the crime rate is the number of offenses committed per 100,000 population. The clearance rate is the number of offenses cleared by the arrest of suspect. And the murder rate, like the overall crime rate, is the number of offenses committed per 100,000 population.

Clearance Rate, Low
Sheriffs

Rank, County, Agency	Rate
1. Brooks, so	0.0
2. Hartley, so	0.0
3. Loving, so	0.0
4. Comanche, so	1.2
5. Maverick, so	2.0
6. Dimmit, so	2.0

Clearance Rate, Low
Police

Rank, City, Agency, County	Rate
1. Dublin, pd, Erath	0.0
2. Ropesville, pd, Hockley	0.0
3. Ransom Canyon, pd, Lubbock	0.0
4. West Tawakoni, pd, Hunt	0.0
5. Quanah, pd, Hardeman	0.0
6. Manor, pd, Travis	0.0

Clearance Rate, High
Sheriffs

Rank, County, Agency	Rate
1. Jim Hogg, so	105.0
2. Brewster, so	100.0
3. Dallam, so	100.0
4. Jeff Davis, so	93.8
5. Culberson, so	93.8
6. Kent, so	85.7

From Previous Page

County (Adult Pop.)	Jail (1)	Prison (2)	Probation (3)	Parole (4)	Total
Wilson (15,637)	11	27	0	37	80
Winkler (5,757)	7	16	230	18	272
Wise (24,869)	51	37	1	79	180
Wood (22,317)	40	55	912	69	1,078
Yoakum (5,725)	11	17	0	14	44
Young (13,302)	23	29	58	46	159
Zapata (6,051)	3	4	0	8	18
Zavala (7,815)	18	10	0	12	45
Other (0)	1,053	370	0	0	1,423
Statewide (12,150,671)	37,821	49,589	361,720	72,793	521,923

(1) Jail figures represent the average daily population in Texas jails as of March 1, 1991, as reported by the Texas Commission on Jail Standards.

(2) Prison figures reflect the inmate population of the Texas Department of Criminal Justice, Institutional Division by county of origin as of March 1991.

(3) Probation figures are for Feb. 1991, as reported by the Texas Department of Criminal Justice, Community Justice Assistance Division. Statistics for rural areas are given for the home county of the district court; these figures, therefore, represent the total number of probationers for the counties in the judicial district, not just a single county.

(4) Parole figures are from the annual report of the Board of Pardons and Paroles as of Aug. 31, 1990.

Clearance Rate, High
Police

Rank, City, Agency, County	Rate
1. Daingerfield, pd, Morris	102.0
2. Naples, pd, Morris	100.0
3. Yorktown, pd, DeWitt	100.0
4. Ingleside, pd, San Patricio	93.4
5. Panhandle, pd, Carson	90.0
6. Kirbyville, pd, Jasper	78.8
7. Hemphill, pd, Sabine	76.9

Crime Rate, Low
Sheriffs

Rank, County, Agency	Rate
1. Falls, so	0
2. Brewster, so	66
3. Knox, so	185
4. Mills, so	243
5. Crosby, so	329
6. Goliad, so	401
7. Kinney, so	449

Crime Rate, Low
Police

Rank, City, Agency, County	Rate
1. Gorman, pd, Eastland	0
2. Carmine, pd, Fayette	0
3. Bayou Vista, pd, Galveston	0
4. La Vernia, pd, Wilson	0
5. Naples, pd, Morris	66
6. Trophy Club, pd, Denton	186
7. Yorktown, pd, DeWitt	272

Crime Rate, High
Sheriffs

Rank, County, Agency	Rate
1. Ector, so	7,159
2. Ochiltree, so	6,114
3. Kenedy, so	5,435
4. Jefferson, so	5,331
5. Andrews, so	5,301
6. Harris, so	5,249
7. Dallas, so	5,181
8. Travis, so	5,081

Crime Rate, High
Police

Rank, City, Agency, County	Rate
1. South Padre Island, pd, Cameron	44,842
2. Balcones Heights, pd, Bexar	29,385
3. Webster, pd, Harris	26,935
4. Seven Points, pd, Henderson	21,715
5. Lake Worth, pd, Tarrant	20,649
6. Hedwig Village, pd, Harris	17,317
7. Greenville, pd, Hunt	16,176
8. Dallas, pd, Dallas	15,520
9. Fort Worth, pd, Tarrant	14,977

Murder Rate, High
Sheriffs

Rank, County, Agency	Rate
1. Dallam, so	242
2. McMullen, so	122
3. Mason, so	88
4. Culberson, so	88
5. Glasscock, so	69
6. Motley, so	65
7. Swisher, so	58

Murder Rate, High
Police

Rank, City, Agency, County	Rate
1. Oyster Creek, pd, Brazoria	110
2. Ranger, pd, Eastland	71
3. Crockett, pd, Houston	71
4. Naples, pd, Morris	66
5. Somerville, pd, Burleson	65
6. Sour Lake, pd, Hardin	65
7. Quitman, pd, Wood	59

UNITED STATES

SPAIN

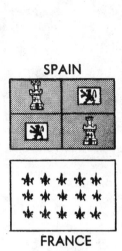

FRANCE

CONFEDERACY

MEXICO

TEXAS

State Flags and Other Symbols

Texas often is called the **Lone Star State** because of its state flag with a single star; this also was the **flag of the Republic of Texas.** The following information about the flag and other Texas symbols may be supplemented by information available from the Texas State Library, Austin.

At the Convention of 1836, at Washington-on-the-Brazos, **Lorenzo de Zavala** is reported to have designed a flag for the Republic — a blue field with a white star of five points central, with the letters T E X A S, one letter between each star point. Probably because of the hasty dispersion of the Convention and loss of part of the Convention notes, nothing further was done with the De Zavala recommendation.

The **first official flag of the Republic,** known as **David G. Burnet's flag,** was adopted on Dec. 10, 1836, as the national standard, "the conformation of which shall be an azure ground with a large golden star central." A new national standard was worked out and approved by Mirabeau B. Lamar on Jan. 25, 1839. This flag consisted of a blue perpendicular stripe of the width of one-third of the whole length of the flag with a white star of five points in the center thereof, and two horizontal stripes of equal breadth, the upper stripe white, the lower red, of the length of two-thirds of the whole flag. This is the **Lone Star Flag.**

Six Flags of Texas

Six different flags have flown over Texas during eight changes of sovereignty. The accepted sequence of these flags follows:

Spanish—1519-1685.
French—1685-1690.
Spanish—1690-1821.
Mexican—1821-1836.
Republic of Texas—1836-1845.
United States—1845-1861.
Confederate States—1861-1865.
United States—1865 to the present.

State Flag

The Lone Star Flag consists of a blue field with a single white star and white and red horizontal stripes, with white uppermost. This flag was adopted by the Third Congress of the Republic, Jan. 25, 1839, at Houston. Although generally used, the state flag was not officially described and usage rules adopted until 1933. These rules are from Acts of 43rd Legislature (p. 186, ch. 87).

Flown out-of-doors, the Texas flag must be on flagpole or staff at least 2½ times as long as the flag. It should not be unfurled earlier than sunrise and should not be left out in rain, snow or other inclement weather. It should be flown with the white stripe uppermost except in case of distress. When the flag is displayed against a wall, the blue field should be at the flag's own right (observer's left). The Texas flag should be displayed on all state memorial days; it should fly at every school on every regular school day.

The Texas flag should be on the marching left in a procession in which the flag of the United States is carried; its staff should be behind the staff of the flag of the United States when the two are displayed with crossed staffs. The Texas flag should be underneath the national flag when the two are flown from the same halyard. When flown from separate, adjacent flagpoles, the United States flag and the Texas flag should be of approximately the same size and on flagpoles of equal length, and the United States flag should be on "the flag's own right," i.e., to the observer's left. The Texas flag should never be used for any utilitarian or strictly decorative purpose. No advertising should be placed upon the flag or flagstaff, and no picture of the flag should be used in an advertisement. When the Texas flag is in such condition that it is no longer a suitable emblem for display, it should be destroyed, preferably by burning, "with the spirit of respect and reverence which all Texans owe the emblem."

Salute to the Texas Flag

A pledge to the Texas flag also was adopted by the 43rd Legislature and from 1933 until 1965 that pledge was used. It contained a phrase, "Flag of 1836," which was historically incorrect, as Texas did not have a flag in 1836. On April 3, 1965, Gov. John Connally signed an act of the 59th Legislature officially designating the salute to the Texas flag as follows:

"Honor the Texas Flag.
I pledge allegiance to thee,
Texas, one and indivisible."

An act of the 71st Legislature in 1989 further stipulated that a person reciting the salute to the Texas flag shall: (1) face the flag and place the right hand over the heart; (2) remove any hat worn by the person; and (3) recite the salute with pride and patriotism. The salute to the Texas flag may be recited at all public and private meetings at which the pledge of allegiance to the United States flag is recited and at historical Texas events and celebrations. The salute to the Texas flag shall be recited after the pledge of allegiance to the United States flag if both are recited.

Other Symbols

State Seal — The seal of the State of Texas consists of "a star of five points, encircled by olive and live oak branches, and the words, 'The State of Texas'." (State Constitution, Art. IV, Sec. 19.) The state seal is a slight modification of the Great Seal of the Republic of Texas, adopted by the Congress of the Republic, Dec. 10, 1836, and readopted with modifications in 1839.

State Citizenship Designation — The people of Texas usually call themselves **Texans**. However, **Texian** was generally used in the early period of history.

State Motto — The state motto of Texas is **"Friendship."** The word, Texas, or Tejas, was the Spanish pronunciation of a Caddo Indian word meaning "friends" or "allies." (Acts of 1930, fourth called session of the 41st Legislature, p. 105.)

State Tree — The **pecan** is the state tree of Texas. The sentiment that led to its official adoption probably grew out of the request of Gov. James Stephen Hogg that a pecan tree be planted at his grave. (Acts of 1919, 36th Legislature, regular session, p. 155; also Acts of 1927, 40th Legislature, p. 234.)

State Stone — **Petrified palmwood** was adopted as the official state stone by the 61st Legislature in 1969.

State Flower — The state flower of Texas is the **bluebonnet,** also called **buffalo clover, wolf flower, "el conejo"** (the rabbit). The bluebonnet was adopted as the State Flower, on request of the Society of Colonial Dames in Texas, by the 27th Legislature, 1901. (See acts of regular session, p. 232.) The original resolution designated Lupinus subcarnosus as the **state flower,** but a resolution (HCR 44) signed March 8, 1971, by Gov. Preston Smith provided legal status as the state flower of Texas for "Lupinus Texensis and any other variety of bluebonnet."

State Bird — The **mockingbird** (Mimus polyglottos) is the state bird of Texas, adopted by the Legislature at the request of the Texas Federation of Women's Clubs. (Acts of 1927, 40th Legislature, regular session, p. 486.)

State Air Force — The Confederate Air Force, based in Midland at the Midland International Airport, was proclaimed the official air force of the State of Texas by the 71st Legislature in 1989.

State Dish — **Chili** was proclaimed the Texas state dish by the Texas Legislature in 1977.

State Fish — The Guadalupe bass, a member of the sunfish family, was named the official state fish of Texas by the 71st Legislature in 1989.

State Folk Dance — The **square dance** was designated the official state folk dance by the 72nd Legislature in 1991.

State Gem — **Texas blue topaz** is the official Texas gem, found in Llano uplift area, especially west to northwest of Mason. It was designated by the 61st Legislature in 1969.

State Grass — **Sideoats grama,** (Bouteloua curtipendula), a native grass found on many different soils, was designated by the Legislature as the **state grass of Texas** in 1971.

State Seashell — The lightning whelk (Busycon perversum pulleyi) was adopted as the official state seashell by the 70th Legislature on April 2, 1987. One of the few shells that opens on the left side, the lightning whelk is named for its colored stripes. It is found only on the Gulf Coast.

State Holidays — Texas has four state holidays and several special observance days. The four holidays are **Texas Independence Day,** March 2, **San Jacinto Day,**

Square dancing has been a popular form of entertainment and recreation for thousands of Texans over the years. The 72nd Legislature gave official recognition to the dance as the state's official folk dance. Dallas Morning News Photo.

April 21, **Emancipation Day,** June 19, and **Lyndon B. Johnson's Birthday,** August 27. (See index for list of Texas holidays and special observances.)

State Song — The state song of Texas is **"Texas, Our Texas."** The music was written by the late William J. Marsh (who died Feb. 1, 1971, in Fort Worth at age 90), and the words by Marsh and Gladys Yoakum Wright, both of Fort Worth. It was adopted as the result of an award offered by the Legislature. (Acts of 1929, first called session, 41st Legislature, p. 286.) Its text follows:

TEXAS, OUR TEXAS

Texas, our Texas! All hail the mighty State!
Texas, our Texas! So wonderful, so great!
Boldest and grandest, withstanding every test;
O empire wide and glorious, you stand supremely blest.

Chorus

God bless you, Texas! And keep you brave and strong.

That you may grow in power and worth, throughout the ages long.

Refrain

Texas, O Texas! Your freeborn single star,
Sends out its radiance to nations near and far.
Emblem of freedom! It sets our hearts aglow.
With thoughts of San Jacinto and glorious Alamo.
Texas, dear Texas! From tyrant grip now free,
Shines forth in splendor your star of destiny!
Mother of Heroes! We come your children true.
Proclaiming our allegiance, our faith, our love for you.
— Words by Gladys Yoakum Wright and William J. Marsh. Music by William J. Marsh.

The adopted song of the University of Texas, **"The Eyes of Texas,"** is also frequently sung at public gatherings. It is usually sung by a standing audience and has a measure of recognition as a state song. Origin of this song is as follows: William Lamdin Prather, president of the University of Texas, 1899-1906, frequently said to the students, "The eyes of Texas are upon you." A university minstrel, as a prank when President Prather was present, sang a song, using this phrase, which had been written by a student, John Lang Sinclair, to the tune of "I've Been Working on the Railroad (Levee)." Gradually it became the adopted song of the University and is popular throughout Texas.

THE EYES OF TEXAS

The eyes of Texas are upon you

All the livelong day.

The eyes of Texas are upon you

You cannot get away.

Do not think you can escape them,

At night or early in the morn,

The eyes of Texas are upon you

Till Gabriel blows his horn.

Politics & Government

Ann Richards celebrates on election night after pulling off one of the biggest upsets in Texas political history to gain the governor's office. Dallas Morning News photo by Gary Kanadjian.

Texas Politics, 1990

This interpretive article on state politics was written by Mike Kingston, editor of the Texas Almanac.

Several firsts cropped up in Texas politics in 1990, a year known more for the nastiness of campaigns and the expense of seeking high office in the state. For the first time, more than $50 million was spent in the governor's race. The total expenditure was easily a state record and maybe a national standard, too.

Amid this shower of money, Texas voters effected the following political magic:

(1) For only the third time in the state's history Texans elected a woman governor. State Treasurer Ann W. Richards, an Austin Democrat, took her place beside Miriam A. Ferguson, who, with the help of her popular husband, James E., a former Democratic governor, sandwiched victories in 1924 and 1932 around a loss in 1926.

(2) Republican Kay Bailey Hutchison of Dallas defeated Nikki Van Hightower, a Houston Democrat, and Libertarian Suzanne Love of Austin for state treasurer in the first all-woman statewide race for a top executive office in state government. (Mrs. Hutchison also defeated a lone woman opponent in the Republican primary, leaving her path to office strewn with female political hopefuls.)

(3) Democrat Dan Morales of San Antonio became the first Hispanic ever to win a non-judicial office in a statewide election in Texas, beating Republican Buster Brown of Lake Jackson for attorney general.

(4) Democrat Morris L. Overstreet of Amarillo defeated Republican Louis Sturns of Fort Worth for Place 5 on the State Court of Criminal Appeals in the first statewide race between black candidates in the state's history.

The governor's race opened quietly enough with Republican Gov. William P. Clements announcing early that he would not seek a third term in 1990. Atty. Gen. Jim Mattox, a Democrat, announced early that he would seek the nomination, and he became the front runner almost immediately. Mattox, a tough campaigner, had victories in 1982 and 1986 statewide elections under his belt.

Ms. Richards also had statewide experience, but in less demanding races for state treasurer in 1982 and 1986. Former Gov. Mark White was a late entry into the race, and four other lesser-known hopefuls vied with the top three in the Democratic primary.

Clayton Williams was a political unknown in the Republican primary. Railroad Commissioner Kent Hance probably was the early favorite, and he could expect tough opposition from Jack Rains of Houston, secretary of state under Clements, and Dallas attorney Tom Luce.

Williams grabbed attention early on with an extensive television campaign featuring slick commercials laying out his views on handling drug offenders and other simplistic solutions to state problems. With $9 million, he easily out spent his six opponents combined and soaked the airwaves with a good-old-boy image that appealed to the conservative Republican electorate. "Texan from central casting," one supporter said of the stereotypical Texas image Williams projected.

The West Texan waltzed to victory over his six primary opponents without a runoff. Williams' victory caught national attention, and he rode a wave of euphoria though the cat fight taking place in the Democratic primary.

In the Democratic party, voters had problems embracing either Mattox or White, the early front runners. Mattox is abrasive, and he had held statewide office long enough to make some enemies. White, too, carried battle scars from bruising fights with the Legislature and teachers' groups over education in his previous term as governor. Ms. Richards was in the enviable position of having performed competently in a statewide office that generates little political heat. Mattox and White could batter each other and open old political wounds, and she could stand outside the bitter give-and-take.

By primary election day, Ms. Richards had convinced many Democratic voters that she deserved the nomination. She led Mattox into a runoff by a little more than 34,000 votes, and increased the margin to almost 160,000 votes in a bitterly contested second primary. At the time, it did not seem a notable accomplishment, since the Democratic nominee was expected only to be a whipping boy for the Republican political "phenom," Clayton Williams. Polls showed the bitter Democratic runoff had turned most voters off, and Williams had a lead of better than 20 points as the general election campaign began.

One of Williams' perceived strengths was his lack of political experience. Backers said Texans were tired of "professional politicians." But this strength quickly turned into a weakness, for the Republican nominee stumbled into a series of gaffes led by a smutty joke about rape victims that even his big bank roll could not ameliorate. Near the end of the general election campaign, Williams capped his goofs by admitting ignorance about a constitutional amendment on the ballot dealing with the governor's appointive procedures and by revealing that he paid no federal income tax in 1986.

Consensus among veteran political observers holds that Williams' severe case of foot-in-mouth disease cost him the election. Ms. Richards' strategy of giving him the rope to hang himself probably is underrated. Exit polls showed that 44 percent of the voters made their decisions in the final month of the race when Williams blew a 15-point lead in the polls and flayed his own credibility almost daily. Even visits by President George Bush and other nationally prominent Republicans in Williams' behalf failed to sway the electorate. Republicans were stunned when Ms. Richards not only won, but carried many usual Republican strongholds such as Dallas and Harris counties.

And while a great deal of attention was given to Williams' goof-ups, his reliance on television to get his message across while ignoring grassroots political organization also played a part. Republican Tom James of Dallas noted that Williams' organization did not even set up phone banks, a basic cog for contacting voters and getting them to the polls in any campaign machine.

Republican Disappointments

Entering 1990, Texas Republicans envisioned the possibility of sweeping top state offices, gaining control of the Legislature and generally strengthening their popularity with Texans. The goals were not unreasonable. The party had many things going for it.

President George Bush was popular with his fellow Texans, and he had many Texas ties in his administration. Democrats were unable to field a popular, well-financed candidate against arch-conservative Republican Sen. Phil Gramm, and usually conservative Texas appeared to be moving even further to the political right than usual.

When the 1990 elections were complete, the Republicans had a few gains. Kay Bailey Hutchison of Dallas had been elected state treasurer, and Rick Perry of Haskell had defeated Democratic incumbent Jim Hightower for agriculture commissioner. Republicans held two lower-echelon statewide offices for the first time. And the party moved to within a seat of a majority on the Texas Supreme Court, where Tom Phillips was re-elected presiding judge.

Sen. Gramm had won his projected 60 percent of the statewide vote against challenger state Sen. Hugh Parmer of Fort Worth, but the incumbent's coattails proved to be short. In the important battle for control of the Texas Legislature, where redistricting battles determine the makeup of both the lawmaking body and Texas' congressional delegation for the next decade, Republicans lost three seats in the House and stood even in the Senate where it holds one-third of the seats. The results broke a string of almost uninterrupted gains in the Legislature for the past decade.

Also in some local elections, Republican incumbents faced tougher battles than anticipated, although many won anyway. For example, in Dallas County, the popular Republican County Judge Lee Jackson polled just over 52 percent of the vote in a race that was thought to have been a runaway victory in the beginning.

Democrats fielded some formidable candidates themselves. Former state comptroller Bob Bullock easily defeated Rob Mosbacher of Houston for lieutenant governor, and Dan Morales, a three-term legislator from San Antonio, became the first Hispanic when he claimed a statewide executive office when he claimed the attorney general's office.

In another historic race, Morris Overstreet of Amarillo defeated Louis E. Sturns of Fort Worth for Place 5 on the Texas Court of Criminal Appeals in the first statewide election of a black to the court. Both candidates were black.

Voter Registration, Participation

A total of 7,701,499 Texans were registered to vote in the 1990 general election, which is a record registration for a non-presidential election year. And 63.4 percent of these registered voters went to the polls on election day. But the figure is misleading, for only 32 percent of the Texans old enough to vote actually took part in the election. According to the 1990 U.S. Census, 12,150,671 people were of voting age in the state. (The largest voter registration in Texas came in 1988 when 8.2 million persons made themselves eligible to participate in the political process.)

The primaries attracted a 2.3 million turnout, a record for a gubernatorial election year dating back to the first primary 1906. A turnout of 2.8 million in the presidential primary of 1988 is still the record high.

1990 Primaries
Republican Primary, 1990

Below are the official returns for contests in the Republican Primary held March 13, 1990, and the Republican Primary Runoff, held April 10, 1990. Included are statewide races and district races for Congress, State Senate, Courts of Appeals and State Board of Education in contested races only. Following these are the results of the Democratic Primary and the Democratic Primary Runoff, held on the same dates.

Governor

Ed Cude	1,077
Kent Hance	132,142
Tom Luce	115,835
W.N. Otwell	2,310
Royce X. Owens	1,392
Jack Rains	82,461
Clayton Williams	520,014
Total Vote	855,231

Attorney General

J.E. "Buster" Brown	359,721
Pat Hill	200,255
H. Tex Lezar	109,549
Bobby Steelhammer	48,643
Total Vote	718,168

Comptroller of Public Accounts

Irby Max Ford	70,782
Jon Hall	173,673
Warren G. Harding Jr.	377,172
Total Vote	621,627

State Treasurer

Kay Bailey Hutchison	509,701
Charlotte Boylan Self	144,374
Total Vote	654,075

Commissioner of the General Land Office

Wes Gilbreath	283,638
William James John	113,987
Grady Yarbrough	205,275
Total Vote	602,900

Republican Primary (Cont'd.)

Commissioner of Agriculture

Gene L. Duke	132,497
Richard McIver	176,976
Rick Perry	276,558
Total Vote	586,031

Railroad Commissioner

Beau Boulter	397,574
Ted Lawson	265,693
Total Vote	663,267

Chief Justice, Supreme Court

Tom Phillips	469,956
Daniel R. Rutherford	170,134
Total Vote	640,090

Justice, Supreme Court, Place 1

George Barbary	272,796
John Cornyn	323,703
Total Vote	596,499

Justice, Supreme Court, Place 2

Charles Ben Howell	312,665
Lamar McCorkle	264,057
Total Vote	576,722

Judge Court of Criminal Appeals, Place 1

Joseph A. (Joe) Devany	309,023
Allen C. Isbell	242,107
Total Vote	551,130

U.S. HOUSE OF REPRESENTATIVES

Below are listed results of contested races only in the election for U.S. House of Representatives in the Republican Primary held March 13, 1990:

District 9

Steve Clifford	2,435
Maury Meyers	7,383
Steve Stockman	6,755
Total Vote	16,573

District 10

David Beilharz	15,870
Matt Harnest	14,130
Total Vote	30,000

District 11

Jim Mathis	8,239
Hugh D. Shine	11,852
David Sibley	8,017
Total Vote	28,108

District 13

Bob Price	9,324
Dick Waterfield	21,117
Total Vote	30,441

STATE SENATE

Below are listed the results of contested races only in the election for State Senate in the Republican Primary held March 13, 1990:

District 9

Chris Harris	27,808
Bill Meier	18,597
Total Vote	46,405

District 12

Dick Andersen	9,913
John Lively	13,094
Total Vote	23,007

COURTS OF APPEALS

Following are the results of the only contested race for Courts of Appeals in the Republican Primary held March 13, 1990:

Chief Justice, Twelfth District

Alvin G. Khoury	10,041
Tom B. Ramey Jr.	21,756
Total Vote	31,797

STATE BOARD OF EDUCATION

Below are given the results of the only contested race for State Board of Education in the Republican Primary held March 13, 1990:

District 6

John H. Alexander	17,013
Jack Christie	30,214
Elsie Huang	13,102
Total Vote	60,329

REPUBLICAN PRIMARY RUNOFF

Below are listed the results of the Republican Primary Runoff election held April 10, 1990:

Commissioner of the General Land Office

Wes Gilbreath	94,487
Grady Yarbrough	47,351
Total Vote	141,838

Commissioner of Agriculture

Richard McIver	43,921
Rick Perry	96,649
Total Vote	140,570

U.S. Representative, Dist. 9

Maury Meyers	5,907
Steve Stockman	3,777
Total Vote	9,684

U.S. Representative, Dist. 11

Jim Mathis	6,504
Hugh D. Shine	10,018
Total Vote	16,522

Democratic Primary, 1990

Below are the official returns for contested races only in the Democratic Primary held March 13, 1990, and the Democratic Primary Runoff held April 10, 1990:

U.S. Senator

Hugh Parmer	766,284
Harley Schlanger	249,445
Total Vote	1,015,729

Governor

Stanley Adams	16,118
Theresa Hearn-Haynes	31,395
Earl Holmes	17,904
Jim Mattox	546,103
Ray Rachal	9,388
Ann W. Richards	580,191
Mark White	286,161
Total Vote	1,487,260

Attorney General

Dan Morales	674,975
John Odam	577,451
Total Vote	1,252,426

State Treasurer

Tom Bowden	331,886
Karen Friend	232,973
Armando Gutierrez	263,132
Nikki Van Hightower	424,027
Total Vote	1,252,018

Commissioner of Agriculture

Neal Burnett	79,397
Clyde W. Chandler	80,111
Jim Hightower	821,192
Dan A. Krenek	63,107
Paul McDaniel	75,426
Dan Pustejovsky	73,228
John Earl Smith	92,728
Total Vote	1,285,189

Railroad Commissioner

Clint Hackney	358,031
Robert (Bob) Krueger	883,804
Total Vote	1,241,835

Justice, Supreme Court, Place 1

Fred Biery	371,373
Gene Kelly	673,911
Total Vote	1,045,284

Justice, Supreme Court, Place 2

Bob Gammage	356,022
Scrappy Holmes	280,939
Ross Sears	421,509
Total Vote	1,058,470

Judge, Court of Criminal Appeals, Place 1

Frank Maloney	380,097
Morris L. Overstreet	355,320
Jeff Van Horn	317,757
Total Vote	1,053,174

Judge, Court of Criminal Appeals, Place 3

Pat Barber	445,023
Bill White	589,527
Total Vote	1,034,550

Democratic Primary (Cont'd.)

Judge, Court of Criminal Appeals, Place 4
(unexpired term)

Charles F. (Charlie) Baird	560,074
Herb Hancock	435,446
Total Vote	995,520

U.S. HOUSE OF REPRESENTATIVES

Below are listed results of contested races only in the election for U.S. House of Representatives in the Democratic Primary held March 13, 1990:

District 9

Jack Brooks	44,781
Jack Brookshire	17,268
Total Vote	62,049

District 10

John Longsworth	4,589
Robin Mills	6,116
J.J. "Jake" Pickle	83,989
Total Vote	94,694

District 26

John Wayne Caton	17,051
Craig Holtzclaw	9,208
Total Vote	26,259

STATE SENATE

Below are listed results of contested races only in the election for State Senate in the Democratic Primary held March 13, 1990:

District 5

Ron DeLord	18,683
Jim Turner	39,970
Total Vote	58,653

District 11

Chet Brooks	20,249
Lloyd Criss	17,964
Total Vote	38,213

District 12

Art Brender	11,611
Nelda Harris	3,539
Glenn Lewis	3,055
Mike Moncrief	19,901
Total Vote	38,106

District 19

Gerard D. Martinez	1,546
Steve Price	5,520
Frank Tejeda	28,987
Virginia Tejeda	1,696
Total Vote	37,749

District 27

Eddie Lucio Jr.	15,752
Alex Moreno	13,273
Hector Uribe	16,545
Total Vote	45,570

District 29

Peggy Rosson	28,882
Tati Santiesteban	18,556
Total Vote	47,438

COURTS OF APPEALS

Following are the results of contested races only for Courts of Appeals in the Democratic Primary held March 13, 1990:

Chief Justice, Third Distrct

Jimmy Carroll	62,555
Charles Chapman	41,920
Total Vote	104,475

Justice, Thirteenth District

J. Bonner Dorsey	58,683
Larry Warner	41,727
Total Vote	100,410

DEMOCRATIC RUNOFF

Below are listed the results of the Democratic Primary Runoff election held April 10, 1990:

Governor

Jim Mattox	481,739
Ann W. Richards	640,995
Total Vote	1,122,734

State Treasurer

Tom Bowden	333,355
Nikki Van Hightower	666,407
Total Vote	999,762

Justice, Supreme Court, Place 2

Bob Gammage	539,412
Ross Sears	383,844
Total Vote	923,256

Judge, Court of Criminal Appeals, Place 1

Frank Maloney	449,695
Morris L. Overstreet	447,583
Total Vote	897,278

State Senator, District 27

Eddie Lucio Jr.	25,584
Hector Uribe	22,667
Total Vote	48,251

General Election, 1990

Below are given results of the general election held Nov. 6, 1990, for all statewide races and for contested congressional, state senate and court of appeals races. These are official returns as canvassed by the **State Canvassing Board**. Abbreviations used are: (Dem.) Democrat, (Rep.) Republican, (Lib.) Libertarian, (Ind.) Independent and (Wri.) Write-In.

U.S. Senator

Phil Gramm (Rep.)	2,302,357
Hugh Parmer (Dem.)	1,429,986
Gary Johnson (Lib.)	89,089
Other	725
Total Vote	3,822,157

Governor

Clayton Williams (Rep.)	1,826,431
Ann W. Richards (Dem.)	1,925,670
Jeff Daiell (Lib.)	*129,128
James Bridges (Wri.)	1,027
Bubbles Cash (Wri.)	3,275
Tyler Pierson (Wri.)	1,395
James "Jim" Wright (Wri.)	1,566

(There were 15 additional official write-in candidates, each of which received fewer than 1,000 votes: Ira Calkins, William Christopher, Evelynn deHart Fain, Robert Louis Garrett Jr., Theresa Hearn-Haynes, Carl Hickerson-Bull, William M. Landry, Arthur A. (Art) Larson, Marc Mabrito, Gene Mitchell, Lloyd "Alamo" Scott, David Winthrop Southmayd, Randy Summers, Denise M. Wolfe and Dennis E. Yancy. Total vote count for these 15 candidates was 4,254*.)

Total Vote	*3,892,746

*This is the total statewide vote as calculated by the Secretary of State's office using the official canvassed couny-by-county election returns as reported by the Legislature, which canvasses the governor's and lieutenant governor's races. However, the Legislature itself, using the same county returns, reported Jeff

Daiell's statewide total as 129,157. In addition, their official statewide total for one of the write-in candidates was 188 instead of the calculated total of 186. Therefore the official total of votes for write-in candidates is 4,256 and the official total of votes cast in the gubernatorial race is 3,892,777.

Lieutenant Governor

Rob Mosbacher (Rep.)	1,741,89
Bob Bullock (Dem.)	2,002,36
Tom Owens (Lib.)	128,71
Other	84
Total Vote	3,873,81

Attorney General

J.E. "Buster" Brown (Rep.)	1,708,11
Dan Morales (Dem.)	1,963,71
Ray E. Dittmar (Lib.)	110,51
Other	97
Total Vote	3,783,30

Comptroller of Public Accounts

Warren G. Harding Jr. (Rep.)	1,150,22
John Sharp (Dem.)	2,314,68
William E. "Bill" Grisham (Lib.)	211,99
Other	72
Total Vote	3,677,62

State Treasurer

Kay Bailey Hutchison (Rep.)	1,895,65
Nikki Van Hightower (Dem.)	1,772,20
Suzanne Love (Lib.)	130,54
Other	53
Total Vote	3,798,93

Commissioner of the General Land Office

Wes Gilbreath (Rep.)	1,336,402
Garry Mauro (Dem.)	2,200,931
Richard C. Donaldson (Lib.)	143,900
Other	489
Total Vote	3,681,722

Commissioner of Agriculture

Rick Perry (Rep.)	1,864,463
Jim Hightower (Dem.)	1,820,145
Karen A. Tegtmeyer (Lib.)	112,017
Other	490
Total Vote	3,797,115

Railroad Commissioner

Beau Boulter (Rep.)	1,495,082
Robert (Bob) Krueger (Dem.)	2,094,082
C.W. Steinbrecher (Lib.)	128,120
Other	583
Total Vote	3,717,867

Chief Justice, Supreme Court

Tom Phillips (Rep.)	2,201,687
Oscar H. Mauzy (Dem.)	1,519,998
Total Vote	3,721,685

Justice, Supreme Court, Place 1

John Cornyn (Rep.)	1,992,447
Gene Kelly (Dem.)	1,586,437
Total Vote	3,578,884

Justice, Supreme Court, Place 2

Charles Ben Howell (Rep.)	1,532,207
Bob Gammage (Dem.)	1,985,215
Total Vote	3,517,422

Judge, Court of Criminal Appeals, Place 1

Joseph A. (Joe) Devany (Rep.)	1,582,817
Frank Maloney (Dem.)	1,882,742
Total Vote	3,465,559

Judge, Court of Criminal Appeals, Place 2

Oliver S. Kitzman (Rep.)	1,696,708
Sam Houston Clinton (Dem.)	1,746,615
Total Vote	3,443,323

Judge, Court of Criminal Appeals, Place 3

Bill White (Dem.)	2,498,471
Carol Caul (Lib.)	444,434
Total Vote	2,942,905

Judge, Court of Criminal Appeals, Place 4 (unexpired term)

David Berchelmann (Rep.)	1,658,728
Charles F. (Charlie) Baird (Dem.)	1,755,075
Total Vote	3,413,803

Judge, Court of Criminal Appeals, Place 5 (unexpired term)

Louis E. Sturns (Rep.)	1,666,778
Morris L. Overstreet (Dem.)	1,757,025
Total Vote	3,423,803

U.S. HOUSE OF REPRESENTATIVES

Below are results in contested races only for the U.S. House of Representatives in the general election held Nov. 6, 1990:

District 1

Hamp Hodges (Rep.)	56,954
Jim Chapman (Dem.)	89,241
Total Vote	146,195

District 2

Donna Peterson (Rep.)	61,555
Charles Wilson (Dem.)	76,974
Total Vote	138,529

District 3

Steve Bartlett (Rep.)	153,857
Joel Kopala (Wri.)	617
Total Vote	154,474

District 4

Ralph M. Hall (Dem.)	108,300
Jim J. McCord (Wri.)	394
Total Vote	108,694

District 5

Jerry Rucker (Rep.)	41,307
John Bryant (Dem.)	65,228
Kenneth Ashby (Lib.)	2,939
Total Vote	109,474

District 6

Joe Barton (Rep.)	125,049
John E. Welch (Dem.)	62,344
Other	737
Total Vote	188,130

District 9

Maury Meyers (Rep.)	58,399
Jack Brooks (Dem.)	79,786
Total Vote	138,185

District 10

David Beilharz (Rep.)	73,766
J.J. "Jake" Pickle (Dem.)	152,784
Jeff Davis (Lib.)	8,905
Other	41
Total Vote	235,496

District 11

Hugh D. Shine (Rep.)	64,269
Chet Edwards (Dem.)	73,810
Total Vote	138,079

District 12

Mike McGinn (Rep.)	39,438
Pete Geren (Dem.)	98,026
Total Vote	137,464

District 13

Dick Waterfield (Rep.)	63,045
Bill Sarpalius (Dem.)	81,815
Total Vote	144,860

District 14

Joe Dial (Rep.)	75,098
Greg Laughlin (Dem.)	89,251
Total Vote	164,349

District 16

Ronald Coleman (Dem.)	62,455
William Burgett (Wri.)	2,854
Total Vote	65,309

District 18

Craig Washington (Dem.)	54,477
Other	243
Total Vote	54,720

District 21

Lamar Smith (Rep.)	144,570
Kirby J. Roberts (Dem.)	48,585
Total Vote	193,155

District 22

Tom DeLay (Rep.)	93,425
Bruce Director (Dem.)	37,721
Total Vote	131,146

District 23

Jerome L. "Jerry" Gonzales (Rep.)	40,856
Albert Bustamante (Dem.)	71,052
Total Vote	111,908

District 26

Dick Armey (Rep.)	147,856
John Wayne Caton (Dem.)	62,158
Total Vote	210,014

STATE SENATE

Below are given the results of contested races only for State Senate in the general election held Nov. 6, 1990:

District 5

Richard A. Smith (Rep.)	64,542
Jim Turner (Dem.)	73,231
Lou "English" Zaeske (Ind.)	8,703
Total Vote	146,476

District 6

Linda L. Rowland (Rep.)	22,285
Gene Green (Dem.)	50,092
Total Vote	72,377

District 11

Jerry Patterson (Rep.)	45,721
Chet Brooks (Dem.)	56,399
Total Vote	102,120

District 12

John Lively (Rep.)	39,259
Mike Moncrief (Dem.)	73,759
J.R. Grover (Lib.)	3,297
Total Vote	116,315

District 13

Bill Batts (Rep.)	22,418
Rodney Ellis (Dem.)	68,398
Other	21
Total Vote	90,837

District 16

John N. Leedom (Rep.)	74,356
Jack F. Borden (Dem.)	49,968
Total Vote	124,324

District 21

Larry Vick (Rep.)	37,781
Judith Zaffirini (Dem.)	81,363
Total Vote	119,144

District 29

Frank Lozito (Rep.)	23,920
Peggy Rosson (Dem.)	51,487
Total Vote	75,407

COURTS OF APPEALS

Below are results in contested races only for Courts of Appeals in the general election held Nov. 6, 1990:

Chief Justice, Twelfth District

Tom B. Ramey Jr. (Rep.)	97,206
Melvin D. Whitaker (Dem.)	88,764
Total Vote	185,970

Chief Justice, Fourteenth District

Curtiss Brown (Dem.)	462,348
Jim Scott (Ind.)	116,788
Total Vote	579,136

Justice, First District, Place 1

D. Camille Dunn (Rep.)	353,584
Elaine Brady (Dem.)	332,229
Total Vote	685,813

Justice, First District, Place 2

Albert Pruett (Rep.)	298,162
Margaret G. Mirabal (Dem.)	386,786
Total Vote	684,948

Justice, First District, Place 3
(unexpired term)

Davie L. Wilson (Rep.)	361,255
Jamie J. Elick (Dem.)	311,889
Total Vote	673,144

Justice, Second District, Place 7

John Narsutis (Rep.)	179,816
John Hill (Dem.)	218,748
Total Vote	398,564

Justice, Third District
(unexpired term)

Jim Keahey (Rep.)	137,384
Mack Kidd (Dem.)	205,320
Total Vote	342,704

Justice, Fourth District
(unexpired term)

Karen Burkhart Angelini (Rep.)	165,755
Orlando L. Garcia (Dem.)	167,733
Total Vote	333,488

Justice, Tenth District

Terry R. Means (Rep.)	87,221
Bill Vance (Dem.)	92,458
Total Vote	179,679

Justice, Tenth District
(unexpired term)

Wes Peylon (Rep.)	71,423
Bob Cummings (Dem.)	101,731
Total Vote	173,154

Justice, Thirteenth District
(unexpired term)

Bill Keys (Rep.)	92,444
Gilberto Hinojosa (Dem.)	139,786
Total Vote	232,230

Justice, Fourteenth District

Paul Murphy (Rep.)	363,357
Ben G. Levy (Dem.)	314,401
Total Vote	677,752

STATE BOARD OF EDUCATION

Below are results in the only contested race for State Board of Education in the general election held Nov. 6, 1990:

District 10

Charles B. Jones (Rep.)	123,661
Will Davis (Dem.)	207,882
Other	57
Total Vote	331,601

†Morris L. Overstreet lost a primary bid for Place 1 on Court of Criminal Appeals and was put on the general election ballot for Place 5, which opened up after the primary, by the State Democratic Executive Committee.

Gubernatorial Primaries, 1990

Below are given the results of the gubernatorial races in the Republican and Democratic primaries, held March 13, 1990, and the Democratic runoff, held April 10, 1990. Information was furnished by the Texas Secretary of State's office.

County	Republican Primary							Democratic Primary								Democratic Runoff	
	Ed Cude	Kent Hance	Tom Luce	W. N. Otwell	Royce X. Owens	Jack Rains	Clayton Williams	Stanley Adams	Theresa Hearn-Haynes	Earl Holmes	Jim Mattox	Ray Rachal	Ann W. Richards	Mark White	Jim Mattox	Ann W. Richards
Anderson	1	175	85	2	3	822	822	87	89	281	2,962	145	2,271	1,502	2,940	2,96
Andrews	1	149	2	3	1	5	363	56	45	56	1,070	35	452	311	795	49
Angelina	4	213	78	0	1	63	554	204	136	237	4,960	121	4,473	1,721	4,342	5,63
Aransas	3	128	216	9	4	59	1,220	20	17	24	736	5	613	268	374	53
Archer	0	18	14	0	0	14	192	18	18	21	1,277	5	464	166	874	55
Armstrong	0	28	3	0	1	9	73	10	3	16	266	2	98	59	125	9
Atascosa	4	85	24	0	0	20	559	157	120	72	1,827	52	1,574	869	1,398	1,54
Austin	3	99	86	0	0	115	721	37	26	43	1,329	6	746	714	1,210	68
Bailey	0	71	0	1	0	5	68	21	18	17	872	13	213	235	541	22
Bandera	0	118	93	7	3	63	1,096	16	15	11	354	5	328	93	213	28
Bastrop	1	149	79	4	1	54	783	82	95	90	2,756	34	2,852	1,052	2,720	3,07
Baylor	0	10	5	0	0	0	36	29	13	13	804	4	314	146	450	35
Bee	3	119	75	0	1	36	617	59	55	60	1,676	20	1,060	836	1,378	1,04
Bell	16	867	621	47	35	407	6,808	81	165	66	3,078	132	3,865	2,145	2,571	4,55
Bexar	257	6,833	6,819	666	89	2,710	34,504	1,403	2,271	624	21,957	308	38,880	10,237	15,968	35,49
Blanco	0	37	29	2	0	20	368	4	5	6	146	2	229	90	126	22
Borden	0	11	2	0	0	1	20	5	2	10	170	1	70	39	78	5
Bosque	0	50	28	0	2	52	471	75	40	80	1,451	37	1,210	572	1,295	1,38
Bowie	9	213	143	3	7	48	843	95	64	108	4,611	75	2,479	1,417	4,120	2,84
Brazoria	7	1,313	844	20	18	1,403	7,931	100	201	131	4,687	63	4,858	3,518	5,405	5,9
Brazos	5	1,264	383	23	22	1,014	4,720	94	44	36	1,281	24	3,174	1,630	1,295	3,6
Brewster	1	38	20	0	2	6	484	18	31	9	439	6	364	337	189	26
Briscoe	0	12	0	0	0	4	13	5	5	11	448	4	134	100	382	22
Brooks	0	0	0	0	0	0	0	40	52	35	1,814	58	1,142	599	1,565	1,39
Brown	1	229	70	5	1	68	1,150	50	51	71	1,769	19	1,302	732	1,110	1,27
Burleson	0	14	2	0	0	7	92	48	76	37	1,499	28	1,064	745	1,779	1,4
Burnet	0	118	89	2	1	83	1,017	70	80	116	2,086	23	1,955	803	2,349	2,2
Caldwell	0	67	23	2	0	25	365	53	82	81	1,679	45	1,833	824	1,715	2,3

County	Republican Primary							Democratic Primary							Democratic Runoff	
	Ed Cude	Kent Hance	Tom Luce	W. N. Otwell	Royce X. Owens	Jack Rains	Clayton Williams	Stanley Adams	Theresa Hearn-Haynes	Earl Holmes	Jim Mattox	Ray Rachal	Ann W. Richards	Mark White	Jim Mattox	Ann W. Richards
Calhoun	2	81	15	0	3	32	283	77	71	76	1,334	20	1,490	893	1,779	1,787
Callahan	0	36	8	0	1	8	192	43	73	84	1,468	17	618	339	1,165	851
Cameron	5	693	135	26	21	108	3,189	250	323	171	9,286	289	5,133	5,050	10,320	9,167
Camp	0	17	9	0	1	7	77	26	14	90	935	14	776	444	1,054	990
Carson	1	110	8	2	0	23	249	26	21	26	899	10	356	171	655	421
Cass	0	63	26	0	4	3	209	49	25	67	2,640	27	1,437	742	2,841	1,940
Castro	0	263	2	0	0	8	109	23	33	29	866	8	244	308	333	242
Chambers	0	61	21	0	0	31	223	100	38	59	1,463	31	805	875	850	649
Cherokee	0	128	61	0	0	37	709	120	68	160	2,370	27	1,898	979	2,029	2,095
Childress	0	59	0	1	0	12	138	17	3	12	356	3	210	120	197	229
Clay	0	18	6	0	0	4	75	34	33	29	1,533	4	713	298	1,272	1,112
Cochran	0	40	1	0	0	1	38	18	10	12	583	8	137	186	574	223
Coke	0	0	0	0	0	0	0	74	16	32	371	13	272	188	417	478
Coleman	0	16	9	0	0	13	155	54	42	67	1,364	23	668	368	1,076	803
Collin	78	3,755	5,576	66	28	2,874	12,369	52	61	36	1,940	38	5,458	2,142	1,922	5,723
Collingsworth	0	50	3	0	0	3	35	12	9	15	466	5	169	81	275	146
Colorado	0	30	25	0	1	24	275	60	64	76	2,170	77	1,051	1,146	1,962	1,027
Comal	13	1,033	658	19	23	352	5,088	37	20	23	573	5	1,129	348	385	1,105
Comanche	0	17	23	3	0	11	181	52	44	71	1,012	18	1,045	406	608	747
Concho	0	12	0	0	0	2	49	7	26	22	290	11	218	169	372	384
Cooke	0	187	170	4	0	88	977	42	48	122	1,415	42	1,286	593	965	1,096
Coryell	1	133	89	4	3	107	1,180	82	36	56	1,848	13	1,274	695	1,595	1,495
Cottle	0	0	0	0	0	0	0	11	15	18	524	3	226	142	313	213
Crane	0	12	0	0	0	1	47	20	34	40	702	10	270	204	983	508
Crockett	0	0	0	0	0	0	0	37	22	18	433	17	312	265	671	520
Crosby	1	87	8	0	0	5	102	11	13	8	605	5	220	204	378	266
Culberson	0	2	2	0	0	1	15	10	14	7	309	7	88	251	309	164
Dallam	0	44	4	1	1	12	122	13	8	21	471	9	162	145	199	141
Dallas	62	20,097	36,728	243	116	14,297	60,831	275	1,071	301	30,731	212	53,995	18,659	30,538	59,677
Dawson	0	133	6	0	0	14	258	38	34	75	1,510	19	378	520	585	252
Deaf Smith	2	378	20	2	3	35	376	54	51	67	1,237	22	494	457	491	300
Delta	0	2	3	0	0	0	21	21	14	37	573	25	492	344	646	590
Denton	18	3,040	3,067	39	32	2,060	10,744	55	76	40	2,019	30	5,693	1,839	1,818	6,320
DeWitt	0	110	35	4	3	23	706	19	18	45	866	7	579	378	798	696
Dickens	0	0	0	0	0	0	0	6	4	6	396	3	112	105	252	128
Dimmit	0	4	2	0	0	1	31	37	74	31	930	31	893	872	954	965
Donley	0	38	10	0	0	26	105	10	7	6	429	11	183	84	182	132
Duval	0	0	0	0	0	0	0	207	37	39	1,464	64	1,922	854	1,424	1,907
Eastland	2	84	23	1	0	24	382	88	70	194	2,055	63	1,110	475	1,201	1,196
Ector	3	2,104	234	19	11	291	8,114	51	105	63	2,220	52	1,908	1,294	1,559	2,107
Edwards	0	34	5	0	0	8	166	5	6	7	113	1	44	41	33	32
Ellis	6	849	826	7	9	537	4,291	51	56	54	2,089	31	2,559	1,125	1,580	2,293
El Paso	129	1,022	167	30	56	260	7,038	273	678	426	20,544	260	14,488	9,467	13,177	13,951
Erath	1	87	44	1	1	54	587	85	63	79	1,288	31	1,952	620	1,189	1,789
Falls	1	35	20	0	0	16	291	81	27	47	1,158	14	857	588	572	686
Fannin	1	51	52	1	0	29	304	25	33	54	1,014	14	1,267	702	928	1,359
Fayette	0	108	44	2	0	60	818	56	53	95	2,087	27	1,070	796	1,864	1,019
Fisher	0	3	0	0	0	0	7	20	28	19	813	4	430	194	734	656
Floyd	0	84	2	0	0	2	128	16	21	29	965	7	321	325	357	283
Foard	0	6	0	0	0	0	10	7	5	4	371	1	136	70	285	225
Fort Bend	8	1,851	1,359	13	20	1,999	8,782	59	177	48	2,811	35	3,925	2,614	3,738	5,160
Franklin	0	10	17	0	0	4	169	10	15	26	632	15	403	276	613	494
Freestone	0	67	38	1	0	57	483	40	32	77	1,178	23	1,087	457	529	757
Frio	0	2	2	0	0	2	33	56	105	52	1,277	32	1,105	645	844	1,086
Gaines	0	116	2	2	0	3	207	24	43	39	963	22	316	281	915	432
Galveston	4	947	542	12	5	826	4,482	219	235	154	8,941	81	10,176	6,090	8,692	9,827
Garza	0	14	0	0	0	0	25	32	13	28	906	10	143	169	724	280
Gillespie	9	419	376	1	8	168	2,676	0	3	8	137	4	308	86	117	330
Glasscock	0	5	3	0	0	7	63	9	5	11	139	5	55	44	77	36
Goliad	0	11	3	0	0	7	100	15	24	25	593	16	348	253	644	450
Gonzales	0	19	26	0	1	13	286	62	73	67	1,496	21	1,115	488	980	979
Gray	2	454	114	10	2	153	1,834	23	23	35	990	7	421	245	466	439
Grayson	0	422	452	7	5	190	2,133	149	100	121	3,074	53	4,354	1,986	3,460	5,255
Gregg	16	1,021	1,358	30	38	407	5,386	51	104	129	2,895	173	3,276	1,629	2,882	3,938
Grimes	1	75	41	2	1	37	424	25	17	42	1,034	4	649	587	1,362	830
Guadalupe	2	442	339	10	6	205	3,184	21	52	42	1,140	20	1,544	410	615	1,265
Hale	0	817	14	2	0	30	711	42	28	89	1,159	37	493	483	541	532
Hall	0	0	0	0	0	0	0	19	18	11	738	8	344	152	491	351
Hamilton	0	23	16	1	1	11	201	33	28	54	693	8	742	293	785	917
Hansford	0	137	17	5	1	9	380	18	13	23	616	9	191	121	592	264
Hardeman	0	9	4	0	0	4	49	26	11	24	869	4	303	153	608	410
Hardin	1	97	25	2	0	19	239	84	79	106	4,869	42	2,164	1,334	4,092	2,570
Harris	111	16,488	16,882	149	191	22,910	73,178	523	13,003	605	30,318	446	60,184	35,413	37,434	66,199
Harrison	0	468	89	13	6	35	728	224	97	116	3,450	99	2,053	1,905	3,725	2,721
Hartley	0	82	5	1	0	12	217	24	12	20	457	4	159	136	395	206
Haskell	0	35	15	0	1	7	206	16	11	31	514	6	477	174	313	570
Hays	3	323	302	4	28	223	1,865	72	106	117	2,605	33	4,003	1,460	2,377	4,207

County	Republican Primary							Democratic Primary							Democratic Runoff	
	Ed Cude	Kent Hance	Tom Luce	W. N. Otwell	Royce X. Owens	Jack Rains	Clayton Williams	Stanley Adams	Theresa Hearn-Haynes	Earl Holmes	Jim Mattox	Ray Rachal	Ann W. Richards	Mark White	Jim Mattox	Ann W. Richards
Hemphill	0	111	13	1	1	30	368	3	4	9	178	1	152	49	60	131
Henderson	0	305	386	3	5	226	2,444	75	72	128	3,226	68	3,384	1,270	2,812	3,438
Hidalgo	5	575	114	16	9	331	2,886	198	389	188	14,390	344	8,161	7,855	14,427	15,308
Hill	2	147	88	3	0	81	860	64	38	85	1,670	16	1,465	719	1,237	1,408
Hockley	0	106	0	0	1	3	180	63	40	58	1,996	28	572	776	1,190	627
Hood	1	316	286	4	1	246	1,805	21	34	37	1,046	8	1,639	462	851	1,765
Hopkins	0	150	68	0	0	66	680	50	36	99	1,431	15	1,565	931	1,719	1,904
Houston	0	52	24	0	0	7	172	103	36	51	1,850	18	1,428	866	1,447	1,185
Howard	0	146	41	0	1	56	1,196	91	27	69	1,457	16	1,149	791	1,244	1,227
Hudspeth	1	4	0	0	0	1	20	4	8	3	208	7	124	122	83	89
Hunt	1	418	396	6	0	293	2,038	73	69	77	1,881	38	2,297	1,445	2,096	2,626
Hutchinson	4	612	118	7	10	223	2,018	45	41	56	1,506	5	561	350	731	606
Irion	0	3	4	0	0	1	24	15	22	18	223	8	180	124	138	158
Jack	0	15	4	0	0	12	90	30	25	50	780	13	653	234	369	421
Jackson	0	31	7	1	0	13	86	87	37	38	1,304	23	752	662	1,085	662
Jasper	0	49	22	3	1	14	216	59	62	123	3,503	27	1,630	1,075	3,672	2,270
Jeff Davis	0	4	1	0	0	1	64	9	17	7	186	2	123	91	283	208
Jefferson	26	1,488	812	26	42	821	3,860	163	268	150	14,762	245	11,185	5,412	12,993	12,136
Jim Hogg	0	1	1	0	0	0	22	17	25	27	968	21	503	767	576	445
Jim Wells	1	49	31	3	0	7	380	66	77	64	2,489	78	2,103	1,171	2,988	3,201
Johnson	7	800	460	15	2	339	3,461	106	74	98	2,855	63	3,974	1,462	2,605	4,290
Jones	0	62	19	0	1	4	269	46	28	48	1,421	12	790	258	1,080	1,050
Karnes	0	8	5	0	0	11	97	62	77	134	1,494	44	744	596	1,453	1,104
Kaufman	1	299	241	6	12	169	1,426	78	79	81	2,031	42	2,137	1,296	2,441	2,438
Kendall	0	241	174	7	3	133	1,728	30	3	2	96	1	294	96	97	298
Kent	0	1	2	0	0	0	3	1	4	1	83	1	42	51	52	4
Kenedy	0	3	0	0	0	0	8	7	5	8	347	2	102	79	309	15
Kerr	9	1,019	701	14	33	285	5,307	5	32	17	321	2	540	152	211	56
Kimble	0	20	15	0	0	14	172	13	12	21	213	5	161	153	169	152
King	0	0	0	0	0	0	0	4	3	2	101	1	48	24	77	6
Kinney	0	13	3	1	0	4	38	30	20	16	442	16	274	212	261	216
Kleberg	1	45	21	4	5	15	357	65	66	44	2,503	118	1,071	638	1,435	980
Knox	0	25	3	0	0	0	72	7	8	18	405	1	231	107	290	353
Lamar	0	92	112	0	2	65	420	142	111	152	2,216	51	2,663	1,630	2,027	2,590
Lamb	0	174	1	1	0	2	175	23	32	35	1,227	16	413	287	1,126	705
Lampasas	0	50	40	2	1	43	549	39	39	32	758	11	699	301	501	614
La Salle	0	1	2	0	0	0	2	21	29	10	618	20	318	638	971	702
Lavaca	0	86	33	0	0	26	487	51	27	57	1,243	14	695	415	1,009	737
Lee	0	47	25	3	0	18	413	34	42	82	1,120	15	705	411	1,239	796
Leon	0	58	37	1	0	36	405	34	21	58	1,215	14	750	471	558	567
Liberty	0	298	49	1	6	52	732	79	114	122	3,458	73	2,452	2,452	2,604	1,801
Limestone	2	64	45	0	0	29	377	51	48	48	1,469	33	1,421	607	939	1,332
Lipscomb	0	114	7	1	0	9	121	11	11	18	378	5	185	110	325	253
Live Oak	0	57	13	0	1	12	288	36	35	33	801	12	455	227	390	334
Llano	0	165	203	2	4	150	1,470	22	6	38	819	8	887	302	764	98
Loving	0	1	0	0	0	1	18	2	0	3	16	1	11	7	4	1
Lubbock	29	9,793	263	12	10	441	9,347	107	100	84	4,919	59	3,492	1,870	2,961	4,531
Lynn	0	30	0	0	0	2	49	19	19	22	858	5	173	242	279	171
McCulloch	0	12	11	0	0	20	239	27	35	50	547	23	643	348	359	581
McLennan	10	1,537	1,197	22	11	764	8,359	177	205	163	6,772	107	9,060	3,898	6,314	11,311
McMullen	0	0	0	0	0	0	0	6	10	12	110	2	68	77	85	7
Madison	0	57	8	2	1	8	200	34	8	23	763	9	538	320	514	409
Marion	0	6	8	0	0	2	30	49	23	60	1,684	23	1,069	497	2,048	1,311
Martin	0	36	0	0	0	8	154	14	8	14	259	7	161	114	266	187
Mason	0	34	14	0	0	20	306	12	4	12	231	7	185	99	153	181
Matagorda	0	96	30	0	0	72	446	106	102	73	2,442	35	1,815	1,473	1,823	1,630
Maverick	0	13	1	0	0	1	40	67	150	52	1,149	46	1,569	923	448	911
Medina	0	87	48	1	1	32	874	77	90	58	1,895	36	1,495	697	1,166	1,091
Menard	0	11	4	0	0	8	38	9	17	29	256	6	211	166	106	161
Midland	5	2,228	715	19	9	710	13,880	30	40	17	925	9	1,115	603	469	1,151
Milam	1	80	31	4	1	44	519	53	66	59	2,131	31	1,515	932	2,140	1,837
Mills	0	9	8	0	0	5	122	21	14	16	293	4	245	142	229	251
Mitchell	0	21	4	0	0	1	63	57	35	38	1,318	19	570	365	1,175	888
Montague	0	23	14	1	0	4	125	54	53	87	2,424	19	1,275	562	2,041	1,531
Montgomery	18	2,376	1,484	27	35	1,875	10,795	58	66	86	2,821	52	3,450	1,955	3,024	3,691
Moore	0	113	19	1	0	31	371	54	57	72	1,570	22	527	338	476	371
Morris	0	28	13	0	0	14	95	51	28	50	1,603	16	993	553	1,321	951
Motley	0	16	0	0	0	1	42	7	7	11	348	6	81	63	226	9
Nacogdoches	5	245	125	34	1	115	648	82	46	131	2,649	139	2,633	1,481	2,395	3,131
Navarro	1	189	135	3	3	91	1,014	100	86	114	2,274	51	2,301	1,627	2,543	2,931
Newton	0	14	8	2	2	0	71	43	58	23	1,971	21	909	633	1,852	1,261
Nolan	0	60	33	1	0	10	294	67	26	45	1,076	13	693	357	782	831
Nueces	8	1,171	787	14	13	571	6,396	277	726	1,011	12,195	396	8,964	4,520	10,114	10,611
Ochiltree	1	219	15	3	1	32	633	39	15	150	811	12	281	172	918	531
Oldham	0	9	1	0	0	1	20	24	23	19	396	0	121	84	223	131
Orange	1	171	45	14	6	38	472	161	140	121	7,746	51	3,871	2,097	7,134	5,081
Palo Pinto	1	102	51	3	0	89	524	88	65	69	1,311	27	1,833	666	988	1,621

| | Republican Primary | | | | | | | Democratic Primary | | | | | | | Democratic Runoff | |
County	Ed Cude	Kent Hance	Tom Luce	W. N. Otwell	Royce X. Owens	Jack Rains	Clayton Williams	Stanley Adams	Theresa Hearn-Haynes	Earl Holmes	Jim Mattox	Ray Rachal	Ann W. Richards	Mark White	Jim Mattox	Ann W. Richards
Panola	0	11	6	0	1	6	67	118	40	79	2,831	17	1,417	718	2,780	1,844
Parker	1	617	327	10	4	290	3,027	54	67	108	1,812	29	2,730	945	1,439	2,579
Parmer	1	78	1	2	0	7	95	46	18	29	797	18	241	267	847	456
Pecos	1	108	14	1	0	13	788	62	75	54	999	31	671	733	999	671
Polk	3	154	35	0	1	42	369	116	129	88	3,076	69	1,958	1,421	3,458	2,683
Potter	8	1,439	249	20	14	465	3,367	70	117	62	2,986	37	1,817	1,001	1,771	2,257
Presidio	0	4	1	0	0	5	44	32	42	45	612	17	262	310	864	485
Rains	0	15	13	0	0	12	65	25	29	49	932	9	557	414	1,159	700
Randall	7	3,085	561	49	30	1,173	6,988	26	30	33	1,856	27	1,674	684	918	1,676
Reagan	0	37	5	0	0	1	252	13	6	11	194	2	63	78	111	50
Real	0	4	4	0	0	2	68	28	19	17	388	8	244	110	107	127
Red River	1	17	3	0	1	1	59	66	43	96	2,238	41	841	746	917	537
Reeves	0	0	0	0	0	0	0	52	126	59	1,593	38	709	868	744	454
Refugio	0	10	2	0	0	1	45	41	54	39	1,169	22	632	367	797	687
Roberts	0	24	4	0	1	15	99	5	2	8	120	6	56	24	61	29
Robertson	0	34	8	2	1	17	263	52	40	47	1,751	26	1,305	951	1,533	1,474
Rockwall	1	549	450	8	3	361	1,919	18	14	47	476	27	720	373	595	822
Runnels	0	26	18	0	0	9	256	39	26	79	951	23	508	279	885	822
Rusk	0	246	82	3	2	55	963	93	73	267	3,148	43	1,906	1,385	3,082	2,538
Sabine	0	15	4	0	1	14	98	25	27	68	1,541	19	842	499	1,418	1,035
San Augustine	1	8	7	1	0	0	25	54	25	36	1,485	16	712	638	1,754	1,438
San Jacinto	0	33	15	1	2	16	213	40	49	48	1,490	92	916	734	1,197	825
San Patricio	3	144	73	15	1	78	895	262	98	159	3,658	58	1,972	1,299	1,924	1,689
San Saba	0	7	7	0	0	5	233	6	8	27	281	6	273	189	343	371
Schleicher	0	12	6	0	1	3	74	30	24	17	237	10	207	183	269	294
Scurry	0	108	17	0	1	39	405	96	57	61	1,423	23	643	412	896	591
Shackelford	0	19	7	1	0	8	82	19	20	19	334	4	225	97	216	172
Shelby	0	0	0	0	0	0	0	91	23	56	2,825	36	1,648	1,083	1,801	1,649
Sherman	0	31	2	0	0	4	99	12	9	23	327	13	98	87	232	139
Smith	14	1,646	1,281	25	25	1,376	9,438	61	55	125	3,034	43	4,470	1,643	2,331	4,508
Somervell	0	27	2	0	0	10	54	38	39	36	699	15	651	323	829	871
Starr	0	14	0	0	1	1	29	22	57	36	1,763	21	594	1,593	651	408
Stephens	0	24	18	1	0	2	95	47	54	86	1,194	16	575	311	741	589
Sterling	1	16	3	0	0	1	94	2	4	5	114	6	69	40	36	49
Stonewall	0	0	0	0	0	1	11	6	14	14	525	9	225	83	281	228
Sutton	0	7	11	0	0	3	140	12	16	11	237	13	157	105	61	64
Swisher	0	33	4	0	0	3	49	15	10	25	849	7	475	477	400	513
Tarrant	36	13,649	12,098	179	90	7,822	45,662	266	574	324	17,578	167	39,370	12,682	16,159	40,912
Taylor	6	1,466	923	12	45	288	5,224	72	47	52	2,774	36	2,900	1,017	1,694	3,247
Terrell	0	0	0	0	0	0	0	18	12	12	143	5	149	189	65	60
Terry	0	128	6	0	0	5	168	46	49	43	1,725	27	462	537	1,569	848
Throckmorton	0	0	0	0	0	0	0	10	8	16	386	4	168	80	115	152
Titus	1	58	34	1	1	17	322	98	45	91	1,943	43	1,395	913	1,791	1,449
Tom Green	15	751	498	16	14	310	5,056	69	60	64	1,297	42	2,266	1,274	1,003	2,667
Travis	14	4,076	6,813	64	37	3,069	21,613	313	714	252	14,945	132	47,578	10,569	16,708	53,722
Trinity	0	21	11	0	0	9	140	54	31	66	1,853	26	950	695	1,058	793
Tyler	0	12	10	0	1	3	80	71	37	38	2,581	23	1,218	727	1,625	1,091
Upshur	0	84	43	8	1	15	435	111	42	262	3,203	27	2,177	798	3,170	2,564
Upton	0	11	1	1	0	0	104	13	27	17	525	17	166	163	604	324
Uvalde	0	55	13	1	1	14	263	99	71	108	1,781	85	1,681	851	1,446	1,367
Val Verde	2	69	43	3	3	20	567	42	103	58	1,437	43	1,714	698	1,660	2,090
Van Zandt	0	143	130	1	1	125	1,213	66	79	147	2,237	69	2,085	1,007	1,915	2,059
Victoria	0	495	121	20	8	244	2,063	133	121	95	2,013	105	2,238	1,402	1,313	1,519
Walker	2	193	144	1	0	134	959	64	66	96	2,096	34	1,771	1,559	1,217	1,255
Waller	1	49	34	1	1	54	396	68	88	55	1,536	29	1,527	1,007	1,730	1,936
Ward	1	59	3	1	0	6	193	97	64	64	1,349	56	623	428	1,400	1,003
Washington	2	125	103	0	0	170	1,166	26	18	41	1,079	15	794	960	752	583
Webb	4	67	14	1	7	13	238	72	248	83	5,138	92	4,799	4,027	8,159	8,173
Wharton	1	171	68	0	1	142	1,004	56	64	58	2,089	32	1,461	1,518	1,860	1,310
Wheeler	0	90	5	0	0	15	147	43	22	24	925	12	221	171	621	305
Wichita	0	636	426	7	10	135	2,771	79	130	80	4,508	46	3,456	1,114	2,793	4,070
Wilbarger	0	38	10	0	0	10	128	33	29	25	1,373	3	444	281	433	369
Willacy	0	17	8	0	1	11	122	39	102	40	1,644	39	541	664	1,992	1,224
Williamson	7	1,358	997	14	13	753	6,441	49	74	87	3,169	34	5,765	1,910	3,140	6,250
Wilson	1	84	31	2	2	31	983	81	69	64	2,025	71	1,593	776	1,258	1,233
Winkler	0	43	4	0	2	2	156	28	42	50	698	26	320	218	223	173
Wise	0	141	91	1	2	100	850	85	103	124	1,905	49	2,415	858	2,144	2,766
Wood	0	174	148	3	0	78	1,012	34	39	237	1,675	28	1,580	804	1,084	1,306
Yoakum	0	75	0	1	0	17	137	31	12	22	715	12	228	200	535	307
Young	0	74	44	1	0	17	303	52	36	80	1,978	39	999	475	1,536	1,244
Zapata	0	16	1	2	3	5	102	10	41	25	961	12	598	440	224	217
Zavala	0	3	0	0	0	0	33	41	53	21	827	24	1,029	446	802	1,228

State Totals: Republicans: Ed Cude, 1,077; Kent Hance, 132,142; Tom Luce, 115,835; W. N. Otwell, 2,310; Royce X. Owens, 1,392; Jack Rains, 82,461; Clayton Williams, 520,014; **Democrats:** Stanley Adams, 16,118; Theresa Hearn-Haynes, 31,395; Earl Holmes, 17,904; Jim Mattox, 546,103; Ray Rachal, 9,388; Ann W. Richards, 580,191; Mark White, 286,161; **Democratic Runoff:** Jim Mattox, 481,739; Ann W. Richards, 640,995.

Statewide Offices, 1990

County	Registered Voters	Total Vote	Turnout (%)	Governor Clayton Williams (R.)	Ann W. Richards (D.)	Jeff Daiell (L.)	Lt. Governor Rob Mosbacher (R.)	Bob Bullock (D.)	Tom Owens (L.)	U.S. Senate Phil Gramm (R.)	Hugh Parmer (D.)	Gary Johnson (L.)
Anderson....	20,005	10,081	50.4	5,133	4,796	111	4,414	5,670	290	6,263	3,826	167
Andrews	6,057	3,123	51.6	2,272	787	62	1,796	1,234	83	2,152	530	48
Angelina	34,685	16,568	47.8	7,385	8,665	505	7,053	9,218	417	9,522	6,828	259
Aransas	8,218	4,765	58.0	2,405	2,079	206	1,842	2,755	166	3,229	1,416	112
Archer......	4,859	3,052	62.8	1,419	1,509	121	1,013	1,958	64	1,813	1,194	42
Armstrong...	1,306	759	58.1	433	271	30	382	339	31	523	209	25
Atascosa....	15,407	6,877	44.6	3,420	3,185	246	2,853	3,669	312	3,920	2,622	210
Austin	9,949	5,717	57.5	3,465	2,093	138	2,698	2,902	128	3,890	1,706	78
Bailey	3,468	1,750	50.5	996	696	46	761	892	44	1,163	530	24
Bandera.....	6,220	3,624	58.3	2,266	1,152	200	1,993	1,458	207	2,474	985	176
Bastrop	19,942	10,489	52.6	4,135	6,101	235	3,566	6,497	423	4,842	5,206	335
Baylor	3,090	1,460	47.2	538	895	23	382	1,020	19	669	733	15
Bee	13,779	6,777	49.2	3,026	3,556	181	2,268	4,354	142	3,814	2,838	103
Bell	63,423	32,374	51.0	15,903	15,621	841	14,729	16,432	723	18,596	12,590	631
Bexar.......	513,132	229,288	44.7	99,478	120,468	8,914	103,783	112,228	8,795	124,138	87,040	7,174
Blanco......	3,624	2,377	65.6	1,392	895	84	1,088	1,161	98	1,441	790	87
Borden.....	544	397	73.0	250	140	5	164	200	6	258	109	6
Bosque.....	8,533	5,154	60.4	2,592	2,409	132	2,133	2,873	89	2,891	2,167	59
Bowie......	41,608	18,514	44.5	8,180	9,640	680	7,519	10,210	627	10,211	6,935	474
Brazoria.....	85,378	45,685	53.5	23,579	19,850	2,158	21,159	22,563	1,914	27,430	14,763	1,141
Brazos.....	56,949	32,936	57.8	17,225	14,357	1,304	18,154	13,640	1,026	22,233	9,120	663
Brewster	5,195	2,311	44.5	1,321	940	48	931	1,207	109	1,328	819	77
Briscoe	1,331	833	62.6	319	484	25	255	551	19	403	401	8
Brooks.....	6,045	2,134	35.3	420	1,685	23	209	1,834	26	592	1,463	34
Brown.....	16,788	9,045	53.9	4,762	4,017	231	4,120	4,756	258	5,651	3,333	115
Burleson ...	7,487	4,251	56.8	2,012	2,174	63	1,690	2,350	107	2,219	1,956	42
Burnet.....	12,793	7,840	61.3	4,088	3,561	170	3,427	4,163	221	4,254	3,359	146
Caldwell....	12,309	5,697	46.3	1,906	3,659	121	2,202	3,849	222	2,903	3,140	173
Calhoun.....	10,446	5,618	53.8	2,634	2,771	201	2,092	3,386	175	3,392	2,118	89
Callahan	7,011	4,043	57.7	2,333	1,607	91	2,052	1,871	106	2,636	1,319	51
Cameron	94,489	36,533	38.7	14,989	20,704	820	15,172	17,734	1,111	18,211	14,367	914
Camp......	5,745	2,968	51.7	1,245	1,646	61	1,038	1,763	58	1,496	1,345	24
Carson......	4,104	2,577	62.8	1,296	1,136	117	1,228	1,312	100	1,661	921	53
Cass........	17,023	7,509	44.1	3,141	4,244	107	2,776	4,437	105	3,885	3,355	63
Castro.....	4,515	2,147	47.6	1,046	1,008	59	876	1,185	68	1,362	742	27
Chambers ...	10,336	5,049	48.8	2,554	2,284	201	2,140	2,706	190	2,986	1,809	107
Cherokee....	19,831	9,220	46.5	4,808	4,141	270	4,183	4,716	247	5,774	3,262	124
Childress	3,182	1,647	51.8	751	881	12	704	919	31	965	668	12
Clay........	6,011	3,300	54.9	1,331	1,836	102	891	2,295	66	1,709	1,506	30
Cochran.....	2,181	1,042	47.8	529	468	44	374	620	51	643	361	30
Coke	2,226	1,229	55.2	678	522	26	587	599	31	787	395	20
Coleman	6,301	3,033	48.1	1,676	1,307	50	1,400	1,497	64	1,921	1,018	24
Collin.......	122,114	71,844	58.8	40,427	27,435	3,711	44,425	24,559	3,233	54,151	15,516	2,125
Collingsworth	2,368	1,167	49.3	476	638	41	479	637	18	630	495	9
Colorado	11,012	5,280	47.9	2,934	2,222	111	2,325	2,923	112	3,380	1,850	74
Comal......	27,565	14,923	54.1	8,763	5,369	720	8,281	6,012	757	10,193	4,093	626
Comanche ...	7,178	3,620	50.4	1,542	1,978	100	1,296	2,198	108	1,773	1,773	50
Concho......	1,730	990	57.2	521	450	14	409	516	19	577	357	15
Cooke......	15,571	8,305	53.3	4,770	3,097	409	4,157	3,722	281	5,359	2,651	170
Coryell.....	17,059	8,123	47.6	4,055	3,753	300	3,579	4,360	54	4,666	3,340	176
Cottle......	1,623	774	47.7	224	528	22	165	577	15	260	474	14
Crane.......	2,680	1,729	64.5	1,208	464	53	829	754	64	1,218	419	20
Crockett.....	2,568	1,034	40.3	679	340	15	463	531	13	752	245	18
Crosby......	3,820	1,761	46.1	844	869	40	593	1,139	35	1,008	725	24
Culberson ...	1,747	712	40.8	373	322	14	156	486	13	369	225	15
Dallam.....	2,467	1,405	57.0	762	535	79	671	680	54	910	453	34
Dallas......	802,952	421,984	52.6	192,105	211,728	17,125	208,076	196,643	15,866	254,951	153,363	11,660
Dawson.....	8,316	3,800	45.7	2,534	1,168	83	1,686	1,909	94	2,611	994	4
DeWitt......	9,778	4,521	46.2	2,728	1,689	94	2,111	2,269	87	3,056	1,327	60
Deaf Smith...	8,502	4,116	48.4	2,491	1,435	148	2,013	1,998	135	2,896	1,158	9
Delta.......	2,913	1,470	50.5	550	901	19	466	949	24	753	678	1
Denton......	114,779	61,088	53.2	30,971	26,560	3,355	33,435	25,022	3,009	41,751	17,132	2,01
Dickens.....	1,746	875	50.1	402	448	20	293	559	19	406	474	
Dimmit.....	6,748	3,425	50.8	1,194	2,205	25	739	2,352	41	1,266	2,012	4
Donley.....	2,306	1,339	58.1	692	574	42	622	657	36	814	484	1
Duval.......	8,973	4,203	46.8	881	3,174	146	419	3,386	42	797	2,895	3
Eastland	10,707	5,668	52.9	3,008	2,493	153	2,776	2,848	177	3,429	2,096	9
Ector.......	47,754	25,513	53.4	16,458	8,347	678	14,056	10,471	915	17,238	5,521	46
Edwards	1,315	811	61.7	527	272	12	360	373	24	581	184	1
El Paso......	197,735	76,863	38.9	32,740	41,624	2,389	21,803	51,980	2,655	45,185	29,033	2,04
Ellis.......	41,504	21,949	52.9	11,210	9,746	924	10,710	10,857	913	14,227	7,751	53
Erath.......	12,096	7,005	57.9	3,515	3,286	198	3,125	3,796	217	4,279	2,645	14
Falls	9,272	4,436	47.8	1,792	2,576	62	1,467	2,798	52	1,963	2,399	3
Fannin......	13,066	6,312	48.3	2,272	3,822	204	1,961	4,117	180	2,859	3,239	11

Statewide Offices,1990

| Attorney General | | | State Treasurer | | | Agriculture Comm. | | | Crim. Ct., Pl. 5 | | |
Buster Brown (R.)	Dan Morales (D.)	Ray E. Dittmar (L.)	Kay B. Hutchison (R.)	Nikki Van Hightower (D.)	Suzanne Love (L.)	Rick Perry (R.)	Jim Hightower (D.)	Karen A. Tegtmeyer (L.)	Louis E. Sturns (R.)	Morris L. Overstreet (D.)	County
4,188	5,799	178	4,911	5,126	219	5,117	4,960	186	3,773	5,670	... Anderson
1,861	1,101	92	1,981	1,017	71	1,730	1,261	63	1,755	1,109	.... Andrews
6,828	9,109	307	8,177	7,984	347	7,931	8,198	354	6,239	9,050	.... Angelina
2,591	1,887	200	2,362	2,142	181	2,392	2,123	155	2,262	2,018	.... Aransas
1,205	1,646	51	1,274	1,610	75	1,162	1,781	63	857	1,773	..... Archer
363	319	27	436	260	34	493	242	15	250	462	.. Armstrong
2,524	3,988	271	2,699	3,683	339	3,196	3,303	248	2,652	3,466	.... Atascosa
3,123	2,273	160	3,295	2,215	135	3,672	1,903	90	2,829	2,244	...... Austin
806	815	29	992	591	45	1,086	569	29	600	806	...... Bailey
1,836	1,512	217	1,943	1,358	243	2,164	1,228	191	1,981	1,181	.... Bandera
3,436	6,479	388	3,420	6,472	429	3,287	6,805	315	3,325	6,262	.... Bastrop
446	938	15	502	874	24	609	801	15	360	874	...... Baylor
2,601	4,011	129	2,644	3,899	155	3,059	3,604	88	2,550	3,763	.... Bee
15,189	14,959	590	15,219	14,685	767	15,364	14,812	621	12,800	14,083	.... Bell
72,725	144,887	7,476	102,721	106,253	10,215	98,063	111,056	9,118	98,297	98,113	...... Bexar
1,104	1,066	106	1,102	1,042	105	1,189	1,035	65	1,034	966	...... Blanco
169	172	9	195	138	12	294	90	4	127	166	..... Borden
2,248	2,609	81	2,549	2,304	121	2,840	2,132	72	1,844	2,535	..... Bosque
7,022	10,363	484	7,513	9,608	692	5,970	11,292	569	6,496	9,947	...... Bowie
27,918	16,307	1,199	23,917	19,656	1,635	24,418	18,646	1,493	20,100	19,402	.... Brazoria
15,855	14,381	957	16,863	13,574	1,073	18,882	12,460	815	15,561	11,238	..... Brazos
994	1,047	111	1,000	1,051	94	917	1,190	85	869	1,049	... Brewster
281	494	11	304	468	17	397	429	5	184	516	...... Briscoe
481	1,791	27	312	1,752	33	463	1,627	31	304	1,737	...... Brooks
4,010	4,835	169	5,135	3,685	241	5,243	3,662	172	3,767	4,661	...... Brown
1,409	2,501	78	1,457	2,535	75	2,175	1,924	54	1,243	2,348	.... Burleson
3,258	4,133	180	3,427	4,024	197	3,361	4,168	161	3,953	3,884	...... Burnet
2,135	3,853	163	2,064	3,889	201	2,171	3,871	149	1,860	3,779	.... Caldwell
2,517	2,904	148	2,076	3,292	166	2,241	3,143	147	1,844	3,222	.... Calhoun
1,709	2,136	69	2,158	1,671	110	2,869	1,129	52	1,541	1,943	.... Callahan
12,921	20,252	936	13,547	18,638	1,227	15,563	17,585	788	12,099	17,707	... Cameron
948	1,760	40	1,039	1,682	46	1,160	1,646	33	814	1,728	...... Camp
1,115	1,359	80	1,326	1,142	101	1,480	1,082	69	897	1,528	...... Carson
2,323	4,399	69	2,432	4,450	116	2,162	4,924	77	2,099	4,406	...... Cass
978	1,066	42	1,134	914	51	1,333	806	24	647	1,239	...... Castro
2,183	2,511	158	2,358	2,401	184	2,410	2,308	163	1,843	2,540	... Chambers
4,147	4,662	163	4,773	4,021	203	5,300	3,700	132	3,456	4,651	... Cherokee
663	917	26	702	875	32	785	838	20	557	970	... Childress
1,001	2,098	53	1,312	1,806	70	1,190	1,964	39	828	2,003	...... Clay
503	472	34	532	432	33	675	363	15	336	552	...... Cochran
481	646	26	549	588	34	749	425	18	373	632	...... Coke
1,240	1,575	41	1,472	1,383	50	1,950	989	26	1,054	1,524	..... Coleman
41,273	25,609	2,936	48,106	19,123	3,411	45,154	21,848	2,989	43,242	19,142	...... Collin
421	657	17	471	596	19	616	518	9	367	646	Collingsworth
2,575	2,574	98	2,814	2,387	101	3,257	1,987	63	2,157	2,512	.... Colorado
7,556	6,433	862	8,467	5,470	837	8,774	5,462	653	8,455	4,860	...... Comal
1,295	2,116	68	1,626	1,797	76	2,096	1,456	57	970	2,168	.... Comanche
363	527	20	381	512	19	524	405	11	262	504	..... Concho
3,763	3,889	210	4,681	3,000	236	5,251	2,606	171	3,754	3,248	...... Cooke
3,743	4,047	210	3,845	3,948	321	3,985	3,870	241	3,303	4,152	...... Coryell
161	539	20	188	522	20	272	496	9	113	548	...... Cottle
871	631	56	739	781	58	538	987	39	560	809	...... Crane
498	446	14	532	402	23	552	428	12	428	373	.... Crockett
651	1,029	35	869	764	43	1,076	672	19	495	1,010	..... Crosby
233	384	16	218	357	20	228	360	11	183	319	.... Culberson
687	645	27	739	594	43	753	610	34	523	759	..... Dallam
189,927	203,502	14,550	229,898	165,141	16,651	210,589	184,589	15,599	197,512	171,307	..... Dallas
1,917	1,640	47	2,114	1,303	91	2,858	874	24	1,525	1,573	..... Dawson
2,082	1,884	96	2,436	1,470	153	2,583	1,505	67	1,830	2,069	.. Deaf Smith
454	919	17	512	847	24	581	822	18	297	954	...... Delta
31,713	24,983	2,801	36,350	20,212	3,365	34,115	22,907	2,862	32,671	21,097	..... Denton
2,315	1,985	67	2,147	2,079	99	2,735	1,605	57	2,045	1,854	..... DeWitt
318	523	13	385	442	17	471	398	10	179	574	.... Dickens
696	2,426	39	738	2,181	56	786	2,262	45	691	2,104	.... Dimmit
558	694	17	645	607	31	746	566	11	458	751	...... Donley
378	3,536	26	419	3,407	52	509	3,385	28	346	3,400	...... Duval
2,406	2,968	121	2,979	2,443	133	3,582	2,021	70	2,207	2,920	.... Eastland
15,877	8,431	673	14,893	9,415	782	11,931	12,162	669	14,060	9,011	...... Ector
403	322	17	387	308	20	406	321	14	364	275	..... Edwards
10,792	10,389	731	11,888	9,201	890	12,578	9,000	644	10,015	10,055	...... Ellis
29,662	42,497	3,059	25,526	44,222	4,503	21,852	50,121	3,412	29,161	40,932	..... El Paso
3,175	3,562	178	3,819	2,972	193	4,406	2,548	121	2,773	3,558	...... Erath
1,579	2,673	41	1,640	2,493	0	1,975	2,341	33	1,213	2,710	...... Falls
1,859	4,151	127	2,267	3,677	180	2,342	3,721	141	1,659	4,051	..... Fannin

County	Registered Voters	Total Vote	Turnout (%)	Governor Clayton Williams (R.)	Ann W. Richards (D.)	Jeff Dalell (L.)	Lt. Governor Rob Mosbacher (R.)	Bob Bullock (D.)	Tom Owens (L.)	U.S. Senate Phil Gramm (R.)	Hugh Parmer (D.)	Gary Johnson (L.)
Fayette	11,008	7,206	65.5	4,224	2,811	166	2,953	4,155	176	4,630	2,456	119
Fisher	3,153	1,750	55.5	582	1,123	44	486	1,209	33	742	965	16
Floyd	4,875	2,412	49.5	1,405	958	44	1,066	1,262	31	1,608	745	11
Foard	1,242	643	51.8	182	454	7	109	497	7	232	379	2
Fort Bend	86,349	47,930	55.5	25,040	21,333	1,279	24,431	22,826	1,186	32,115	15,310	797
Franklin	4,299	2,211	51.4	1,088	1,061	58	917	1,196	68	1,255	896	29
Freestone	8,815	4,628	52.5	2,364	2,153	104	2,090	2,458	109	2,729	1,838	53
Frio	7,549	2,622	34.7	1,130	1,458	34	858	1,670	77	1,252	1,279	43
Gaines	5,536	2,825	51.0	1,820	905	92	1,261	1,476	89	1,666	647	41
Galveston	106,430	52,013	48.9	21,006	29,303	1,545	20,374	30,167	1,745	26,576	24,138	1,241
Garza	2,838	1,323	46.6	788	494	35	560	692	32	829	429	17
Gillespie	9,775	5,772	59.0	3,895	1,619	233	3,423	2,092	272	4,284	1,297	207
Glasscock	703	535	76.1	421	101	11	282	215	17	407	95	6
Goliad	3,633	2,000	55.1	1,079	872	44	795	1,081	52	1,306	601	24
Gonzales	9,884	4,100	41.5	2,234	1,783	75	1,709	2,212	81	2,546	1,379	48
Gray	13,119	8,128	62.0	4,845	2,679	490	4,692	3,088	422	6,043	1,942	203
Grayson	46,696	23,048	49.4	10,410	11,597	1,013	9,514	12,827	881	13,551	8,910	543
Gregg	54,361	28,329	52.1	15,344	12,053	909	13,236	13,377	748	18,485	1,850	530
Grimes	8,513	4,008	47.1	2,020	1,873	105	1,818	2,042	102	2,361	1,565	61
Guadalupe	29,608	15,179	51.3	8,586	5,756	754	7,878	6,679	766	10,111	4,587	586
Hale	14,230	6,492	45.6	3,971	2,363	149	3,279	3,218	134	4,632	1,905	71
Hall	2,752	1,294	47.0	514	753	15	415	835	20	596	636	12
Hamilton	4,480	2,966	66.2	1,535	1,363	67	1,256	1,561	87	1,636	1,211	52
Hansford	3,290	2,079	63.2	1,495	476	76	1,303	653	58	1,677	347	32
Hardeman	2,932	1,390	47.4	518	827	28	392	968	28	641	714	12
Hardin	24,299	9,491	39.1	3,931	5,151	368	3,793	5,542	297	5,497	3,868	176
Harris	1,175,883	556,735	47.3	259,821	280,159	15,545	262,937	274,929	15,279	327,411	203,551	11,277
Harrison	30,664	14,697	47.9	7,104	7,186	331	6,423	7,817	411	8,688	5,611	254
Hartley	2,266	1,560	68.8	891	569	54	810	714	42	1,115	430	18
Haskell	4,202	2,330	55.4	922	1,366	42	820	1,472	36	1,216	1,123	22
Hays	31,917	17,736	55.6	7,157	10,044	515	6,606	10,423	695	9,081	7,823	588
Hemphill	2,168	1,548	71.4	862	595	66	817	670	43	1,120	376	27
Henderson	30,718	17,257	56.2	8,032	8,472	562	7,694	8,958	674	9,711	7,163	312
Hidalgo	143,524	53,063	37.0	18,942	33,167	946	18,685	29,162	1,409	23,882	23,369	1,374
Hill	13,309	7,601	57.1	3,519	3,816	253	2,646	4,831	221	4,158	3,330	152
Hockley	11,424	4,957	43.4	2,761	1,994	193	2,281	2,560	183	3,412	1,389	114
Hood	15,933	9,827	61.7	5,053	4,257	449	4,836	4,707	418	6,169	3,558	238
Hopkins	14,095	8,184	58.1	3,714	4,219	239	3,277	4,583	182	4,515	3,381	80
Houston	11,667	5,923	50.8	2,728	3,037	125	2,461	3,326	110	3,536	2,305	43
Howard	15,188	8,027	52.9	4,512	3,270	224	3,587	4,137	297	4,332	2,583	143
Hudspeth	1,266	585	46.2	335	234	9	138	385	19	350	183	6
Hunt	30,046	15,672	52.2	7,978	7,030	565	7,763	7,499	580	9,814	5,584	344
Hutchinson	14,377	8,390	58.4	4,645	3,118	568	4,581	3,628	406	6,014	2,377	197
Irion	1,122	616	54.9	352	245	15	295	283	21	436	152	13
Jack	4,233	2,128	50.3	1,053	999	68	863	1,158	69	1,188	847	38
Jackson	6,939	3,785	54.5	2,080	1,591	88	1,656	2,001	69	2,496	1,203	36
Jasper	18,410	7,411	40.3	2,881	4,176	333	2,764	4,459	249	3,915	3,362	117
Jeff Davis	1,189	693	58.3	416	257	16	289	337	19	449	179	15
Jefferson	131,173	63,978	48.8	21,718	40,288	1,901	21,105	41,258	1,420	32,018	30,431	895
Jim Hogg	3,711	1,704	45.9	381	1,318	5	225	1,447	19	567	1,081	16
Jim Wells	21,203	8,211	38.7	2,624	5,464	120	1,735	6,134	82	3,455	4,372	64
Johnson	45,399	23,663	52.1	11,491	10,945	1,102	10,785	11,969	1,231	14,388	8,909	662
Jones	8,475	4,231	49.9	2,080	2,057	91	1,883	2,223	90	2,546	1,583	45
Karnes	7,077	3,252	46.0	1,902	1,267	65	1,420	1,691	91	1,958	1,136	63
Kaufman	24,326	12,366	50.8	5,885	5,987	467	5,413	6,464	556	6,992	4,861	361
Kendall	7,734	4,793	62.0	3,177	1,359	238	2,867	1,722	235	3,617	1,043	183
Kenedy	324	151	46.6	65	82	4	55	98	1	84	59	5
Kent	868	214	24.7	99	98	5	192	370	18	319	243	13
Kerr	20,049	10,617	53.0	6,761	3,301	520	6,452	3,764	521	7,477	2,791	447
Kimble	2,307	1,559	67.6	976	529	53	652	813	46	1,115	370	33
King	240	190	79.2	109	76	2	70	106	11	121	59	2
Kinney	1,744	1,110	63.6	590	487	33	430	572	42	631	392	25
Kleberg	14,055	6,399	45.5	2,500	3,743	153	1,750	4,251	137	3,257	2,800	93
Knox	2,708	1,427	52.7	519	876	32	418	980	21	680	733	14
La Salle	3,548	1,558	43.9	481	1,059	10	340	1,143	22	513	969	16
Lamar	22,831	10,623	46.5	4,517	5,826	276	3,557	6,891	220	6,110	4,490	72
Lamb	8,371	3,481	41.6	2,017	1,364	82	1,686	1,774	81	2,313	1,136	45
Lampasas	6,815	3,734	54.8	2,023	1,622	73	1,655	1,972	84	2,129	1,535	52
Lavaca	10,629	5,348	50.3	2,675	2,510	135	1,954	3,181	114	3,128	2,017	76
Lee	6,735	4,255	63.2	2,537	1,642	65	1,734	2,319	74	2,446	1,648	44
Leon	8,100	3,967	49.0	2,040	1,821	93	1,778	2,001	96	2,411	1,503	40
Liberty	25,917	11,690	45.1	5,961	5,389	329	5,024	6,403	356	6,873	4,613	193
Limestone	10,140	5,050	49.8	2,141	2,788	111	1,888	3,079	117	2,505	2,502	55
Lipscomb	1,911	1,225	64.1	676	428	58	645	541	34	885	307	26
Live Oak	6,033	2,627	43.5	1,465	1,060	100	1,100	1,428	91	1,724	830	59
Llano	7,993	5,535	69.2	3,205	2,223	102	2,707	2,710	146	3,271	2,215	89
Loving	112	96	85.7	65	31	0	44	45	1	62	19	1
Lubbock	100,347	51,445	51.3	29,100	20,643	1,480	25,085	25,808	1,316	38,147	12,526	877

| Attorney General | | | State Treasurer | | | Agriculture Comm. | | | Crim. Ct., Pl. 5 | | |
Buster Brown (R.)	Dan Morales (D.)	Ray E. Diftmar (L.)	Kay B. Hutchison (R.)	Nikki Van Hightower (D.)	Suzanne Love (L.)	Rick Perry (R.)	Jim Hightower (D.)	Karen A. Tegtmeyer (L.)	Louis E. Sturns (R.)	Morris L. Overstreet (D.)	County
3,309	3,693	147	3,490	3,556	145	3,842	3,299	111	2,754	3,728	..... Fayette
393	1,276	26	567	1,084	32	896	826	16	315	1,146	..... Fisher
1,261	996	16	1,498	662	26	1,805	584	6	889	1,068	...... Floyd
122	458	2	125	454	11	168	448	4	75	440	...... Foard
26,605	19,949	980	26,396	20,600	993	26,517	19,633	1,103	24,836	17,930	... Fort Bend
780	1,273	52	901	1,066	56	1,060	1,048	41	662	1,230	.... Franklin
2,066	2,426	77	2,250	2,241	110	2,492	2,020	84	1,829	2,429	... Freestone
756	1,763	70	852	1,643	61	1,047	1,484	50	815	1,528	...... Frio
1,532	1,123	63	1,600	1,066	77	1,862	902	34	1,180	1,240	..... Gaines
22,121	28,098	1,348	23,134	27,354	1,378	21,669	27,897	1,609	18,935	27,790	... Galveston
526	710	29	709	479	37	815	459	16	400	673	...... Garza
3,638	1,760	302	3,893	1,587	223	3,852	1,715	188	3,691	1,422	.... Gillespie
335	121	10	316	151	9	430	97	3	247	151	... Glasscock
848	992	43	779	1,010	61	969	891	23	695	874	...... Goliad
1,674	2,167	77	1,823	1,980	78	2,194	1,676	53	1,498	1,897	.... Gonzales
4,645	3,110	286	5,011	2,760	334	5,055	2,853	225	3,982	3,779	...... Gray
9,338	12,667	757	11,022	10,818	937	10,714	11,524	747	9,427	11,563	..... Grayson
11,831	13,655	543	14,834	10,658	729	13,662	12,282	505	11,599	9,920	...... Gregg
1,617	2,081	90	1,743	2,034	100	2,228	1,653	59	1,366	1,941	..... Grimes
7,343	7,058	753	7,998	6,233	839	8,472	5,965	698	8,091	5,717	.. Guadalupe
3,780	2,628	112	4,526	1,909	115	4,755	1,790	88	3,114	2,944	...... Hale
427	782	7	460	768	11	580	685	7	327	839	.... Hall
1,247	1,438	58	1,469	1,218	79	1,858	976	47	887	1,428	... Hamilton
1,218	650	43	1,325	564	47	1,425	548	40	958	838	... Hansford
435	879	13	452	863	27	531	811	14	319	908	.. Hardeman
3,264	5,958	195	3,525	5,615	268	2,847	6,230	298	3,293	5,466	..... Hardin
271,623	254,673	13,527	281,851	258,197	12,609	270,837	251,348	14,943	255,499	226,911	..... Harris
5,235	8,727	296	6,551	7,395	369	6,278	7,868	302	5,936	7,416	... Harrison
812	673	35	871	626	28	963	578	17	667	761	.... Hartley
673	1,575	23	984	1,051	29	1,536	859	23	586	1,400	.... Haskell
6,704	10,002	683	7,015	9,501	749	6,030	10,859	569	6,682	8,981	...... Hays
770	622	34	838	563	45	939	544	26	632	693	... Hemphill
7,488	9,139	439	8,065	8,505	552	8,913	7,793	446	6,819	9,115	.. Henderson
16,068	32,323	1,035	17,031	30,161	1,686	20,774	27,899	1,068	15,351	28,873	..... Hidalgo
3,123	4,133	189	3,624	3,654	235	4,370	3,053	162	2,680	4,109	.... Hill
2,431	2,284	161	3,041	1,679	175	3,212	1,637	121	2,087	2,357	.... Hockley
4,881	4,466	327	5,254	4,071	402	6,265	3,328	287	4,571	4,420	..... Hood
2,865	4,549	124	3,321	4,176	213	4,087	3,671	106	2,314	4,287	.... Hopkins
2,300	3,202	68	2,508	3,133	82	3,017	2,774	51	1,741	3,361	.... Houston
3,919	3,717	216	3,999	3,683	226	4,079	3,689	159	3,324	3,904	.... Howard
262	248	9	201	275	24	220	290	12	172	260	... Hudspeth
7,325	7,631	467	8,242	6,711	567	8,365	6,732	456	6,818	7,215	...... Hunt
4,500	3,678	281	4,984	3,192	337	4,978	3,299	254	3,997	4,225	.. Hutchinson
245	301	10	282	262	17	352	222	11	212	258	...... Irion
852	1,079	57	981	977	62	1,085	935	44	625	1,100	...... Jack
1,769	1,776	51	1,813	1,742	67	2,187	1,450	42	1,306	1,725	.... Jackson
2,315	4,830	161	2,653	4,450	209	2,197	4,882	215	2,107	4,617	..... Jasper
340	249	20	324	256	22	310	302	22	277	249	... Jeff Davis
18,081	43,296	966	21,234	39,171	1,633	16,163	43,756	1,672	18,216	38,988	... Jefferson
201	1,468	15	236	1,396	24	264	1,390	11	257	1,362	... Jim Hogg
2,133	5,686	72	2,030	5,682	126	2,631	5,216	62	1,832	5,556	... Jim Wells
11,014	11,550	958	12,156	10,496	1,025	12,492	10,257	937	10,390	11,429	.... Johnson
1,581	2,467	67	2,074	1,955	87	2,858	1,340	48	1,471	2,168	...... Jones
1,317	1,749	69	1,323	1,712	87	1,873	1,254	49	1,163	1,548	..... Karnes
5,431	6,138	470	6,078	5,539	567	5,988	5,760	470	4,890	6,095	... Kaufman
2,553	1,919	234	2,882	1,478	247	3,201	1,336	187	2,971	1,178	.... Kendall
62	85	1	41	105	2	72	71	3	46	91	..... Kenedy
210	316	10	228	286	21	283	289	10	117	348	...... Kent
6,208	3,818	543	6,781	3,207	567	6,988	3,100	486	6,549	2,907	...... Kerr
732	639	46	760	627	35	816	630	21	627	607	..... Kimble
65	104	2	74	88	7	112	72	1	47	93	...... King
407	563	36	419	530	45	452	502	37	346	497	..... Kinney
2,248	3,671	122	2,153	3,741	142	2,563	3,494	93	1,889	3,477	.... Kleberg
368	993	18	527	822	18	829	604	8	332	891	...... Knox
3,856	6,305	136	4,653	5,561	192	4,342	6,001	143	3,418	6,039	..... Lamar
1,649	1,659	51	2,138	1,182	80	2,463	995	41	1,230	1,632	...... Lamb
1,744	1,794	75	1,742	1,802	82	1,895	1,717	60	1,442	1,797	... Lampasas
323	1,163	12	342	1,097	20	394	1,070	19	292	1,070	... La Salle
2,147	2,836	105	2,182	2,784	111	2,462	2,599	71	1,743	2,650	...... Lavaca
1,662	2,230	71	1,669	2,284	81	2,030	2,028	38	1,471	2,128	.... Lee
1,659	1,987	51	1,836	1,979	75	1,988	1,816	44	1,311	1,930	...... Leon
5,245	6,008	271	5,373	5,973	292	5,700	5,662	236	4,648	6,193	.... Liberty
1,919	2,982	106	2,191	2,727	108	2,238	2,714	80	1,780	2,926	.. Limestone
625	502	18	669	465	32	754	422	24	496	561	... Lipscomb
1,229	1,233	97	1,178	1,278	102	1,574	975	45	1,037	1,256	.... Live Oak
2,658	2,582	130	2,806	2,518	133	2,818	2,541	99	2,482	2,482	...... Llano
47	33	3	46	35	2	42	43	2	35	37	..... Loving
28,402	21,856	1,063	35,309	14,561	1,323	34,786	16,016	950	27,853	18,956	.... Lubbock

County	Registered Voters	Total Vote	Turnout (%)	Governor Clayton Williams (R.)	Ann W. Richards (D.)	Jeff Daiell (L.)	Lt. Governor Rob Mosbacher (R.)	Bob Bullock (D.)	Tom Owens (L.)	U.S. Senate Phil Gramm (R.)	Hugh Parmer (D.)	Gary Johnson (L.)
Lynn	3,911	1,700	43.5	998	663	33	703	958	32	1,049	612	20
Madison	5,350	2,825	52.8	1,392	1,417	10	1,292	1,505	8	293	290	4
Marion	6,630	3,528	53.2	1,385	2,015	104	1,211	1,916	101	1,730	1,348	54
Martin	2,484	1,226	49.4	876	330	18	646	514	27	838	333	11
Mason	2,284	1,303	57.0	787	485	28	592	635	33	840	422	22
Matagorda . . .	17,244	9,018	52.3	4,574	4,146	286	3,703	5,089	270	5,310	3,547	151
Maverick	12,038	5,061	42.0	1,439	3,553	67	1,025	3,552	164	2,147	2,486	112
McCulloch . . .	4,538	2,573	56.7	1,323	1,204	43	1,031	1,456	42	1,610	912	21
McLennan . . .	92,481	50,377	54.5	21,671	27,414	1,112	20,791	29,165	970	28,094	22,121	631
McMullen . . .	576	324	56.3	217	89	17	187	131	6	249	74	3
Medina	14,176	6,952	49.0	3,953	2,727	266	3,268	3,384	306	4,358	2,317	205
Menard	1,565	954	61.0	465	458	26	375	517	22	593	319	10
Midland	48,936	30,641	62.6	23,184	6,672	707	20,302	9,179	1,235	24,496	5,379	776
Milam	12,051	6,945	57.6	2,758	4,069	105	2,080	4,670	102	2,907	3,787	83
Mills	2,502	1,572	62.8	832	709	28	675	858	20	858	686	35
Mitchell	4,773	2,515	52.7	1,216	1,259	33	944	1,462	40	1,490	896	19
Montague . . .	10,121	5,083	50.2	2,280	2,510	281	1,822	2,930	116	2,799	2,032	88
Montgomery .	84,722	45,575	53.8	27,499	16,454	1,425	25,304	18,404	1,454	31,806	12,266	942
Moore	7,429	4,415	59.4	2,513	1,542	240	2,266	2,011	182	3,167	1,191	84
Morris	8,162	3,956	48.5	1,353	2,528	67	1,118	2,676	75	1,704	2,107	38
Motley	1,127	618	54.8	362	223	32	270	323	17	403	192	8
Nacogdoches .	26,222	12,634	48.2	6,298	5,958	324	6,096	6,280	309	8,365	4,056	268
Navarro	19,887	10,478	52.7	4,763	5,343	344	4,318	5,929	324	5,826	4,508	196
Newton	8,648	3,269	37.8	909	2,274	77	822	2,284	78	1,246	1,862	37
Nolan	8,231	4,283	52.0	2,058	2,080	131	1,751	2,352	182	2,561	1,583	87
Nueces	138,455	63,299	45.7	24,317	37,019	1,963	19,510	40,408	1,535	36,102	23,711	1,199
Ochiltree	4,725	2,824	59.8	2,042	636	94	1,794	935	92	2,386	399	53
Oldham	1,274	764	60.0	422	274	64	350	364	40	512	224	15
Orange	41,810	19,860	47.5	6,727	12,366	651	6,899	12,546	673	9,954	9,628	379
Palo Pinto . . .	11,943	6,618	55.4	3,128	3,197	233	2,877	3,521	186	3,705	2,715	142
Panola	12,627	6,194	49.1	2,908	3,166	99	2,293	3,703	97	3,417	2,566	79
Parker	30,699	17,803	58.0	9,380	7,344	869	8,612	8,457	942	11,245	6,224	553
Parmer	3,846	2,061	53.6	1,288	685	58	1,116	971	54	1,417	678	38
Pecos	7,662	4,761	62.1	3,256	1,441	64	1,974	2,432	117	2,471	1,416	82
Polk	19,172	8,938	46.6	4,265	4,321	331	3,885	4,805	254	4,869	3,839	182
Potter	33,884	20,102	59.3	9,855	9,233	873	10,116	9,011	986	12,991	6,493	549
Presidio	3,098	1,720	55.5	635	1,062	19	351	1,219	37	649	933	20
Rains	3,877	2,120	54.7	1,016	1,041	53	855	1,141	65	1,097	926	31
Randall	47,312	30,239	63.9	17,924	10,842	1,273	18,371	11,125	925	22,460	6,156	518
Reagan	1,907	1,065	55.8	807	242	13	582	424	26	864	173	3
Real	1,929	1,132	58.7	671	418	43	572	495	41	785	299	27
Red River . . .	8,782	4,014	45.7	1,711	2,179	119	1,307	2,539	84	1,948	1,888	44
Reeves	7,531	3,336	44.3	1,686	1,600	43	1,073	2,109	100	1,536	1,360	45
Refugio	5,164	2,865	55.5	1,246	1,553	65	840	1,915	46	1,670	1,073	40
Roberts	739	528	71.4	331	165	22	285	219	19	393	123	8
Robertson . . .	9,428	4,638	49.2	1,676	2,883	75	1,428	3,082	69	2,001	2,601	43
Rockwall	13,651	7,828	57.3	4,625	2,752	440	4,699	2,854	348	5,660	1,851	226
Runnels	6,249	3,192	51.1	1,894	1,200	80	1,571	1,487	82	2,132	946	44
Rusk	24,786	11,286	45.5	6,197	4,699	378	5,494	5,331	369	7,413	3,361	182
Sabine	6,166	3,147	51.0	1,336	1,728	72	1,152	1,845	70	1,555	1,414	44
San Augustine	6,400	3,136	49.0	1,290	1,753	83	990	1,870	70	1,500	1,291	54
San Jacinto . .	9,208	4,154	45.1	2,023	2,009	109	1,748	2,195	98	2,239	1,708	74
San Patricio . .	29,067	11,769	40.5	5,088	6,202	473	3,762	7,250	328	6,492	4,525	229
San Saba	3,046	1,560	51.2	847	692	20	578	925	25	801	729	15
Schleicher . . .	1,645	882	53.6	535	321	19	413	441	10	620	240	7
Scurry	8,535	4,896	57.4	3,107	1,614	165	2,384	2,397	125	3,000	1,059	63
Shackelford . .	2,167	1,152	53.2	719	406	25	621	475	34	776	334	15
Shelby	13,282	5,640	42.5	2,264	3,247	113	2,165	3,358	130	3,090	2,334	153
Sherman	1,713	1,039	60.7	627	311	56	578	433	47	749	281	57
Smith	75,235	40,855	54.3	23,493	15,874	1,454	22,548	17,279	1,413	27,984	12,025	786
Somervell . . .	3,279	1,883	57.4	951	819	98	810	914	109	1,107	666	59
Starr	16,233	4,260	26.2	653	3,582	24	592	3,568	54	988	3,144	54
Stephens	5,397	2,865	53.1	1,707	1,033	94	1,347	1,409	90	1,967	826	35
Sterling	839	510	60.8	357	146	6	258	217	6	396	80	5
Stonewall	1,513	840	55.5	308	519	13	239	590	16	386	437	11
Sutton	2,259	1,042	46.1	639	383	20	521	483	18	764	259	6
Swisher	4,437	2,318	52.2	799	1,440	48	721	1,555	42	1,027	1,244	27
Tarrant	529,598	285,772	54.0	131,234	139,788	12,849	135,874	139,251	12,753	175,629	104,985	8,147
Taylor	54,003	29,469	54.6	16,705	11,976	754	16,501	12,314	813	21,220	7,603	485
Terrell	920	499	54.2	242	250	6	139	314	8	242	213	5
Terry	7,083	3,369	47.6	1,897	1,354	91	1,416	1,904	82	2,268	1,087	53
Throckmorton	1,308	775	59.3	367	374	34	265	448	8	424	327	13
Titus	12,130	5,776	47.6	2,503	3,138	118	1,889	3,783	82	3,215	2,460	58
Tom Green . . .	44,449	23,542	53.0	13,040	9,607	779	12,486	10,326	750	16,730	6,321	434
Travis	305,582	195,829	64.1	63,376	128,120	4,135	61,585	125,593	6,938	87,145	98,983	5,833
Trinity	8,363	3,740	44.7	1,712	1,919	109	1,478	2,075	88	2,008	1,567	41
Tyler	10,585	4,775	45.1	1,840	2,763	164	1,703	2,934	116	2,480	2,139	59

Attorney General			State Treasurer			Agriculture Comm.			Crim. Ct., Pl. 5		
Buster Brown (R.)	Dan Morales (D.)	Ray E. Dittmar (L.)	Kay B. Hutchison (R.)	Nikki Van Hightower (D.)	Suzanne Love (L.)	Rick Perry (R.)	Jim Hightower (D.)	Karen A. Tegmeyer (L.)	Louis E. Sturns (R.)	Morris L. Overstreet (D.)	County
809	808	23	970	627	28	1,284	435	8	544	917	...... Lynn
1,039	1,365	37	1,097	1,272	49	1,303	1,164	26	771	1,443	.. McCulloch
21,760	27,507	850	23,462	23,738	1,131	24,842	24,711	912	21,373	25,822	.. McLennan
168	137	8	190	112	5	230	84	4	156	107	... McMullen
198	354	7	206	360	3	203	362	8	150	378	.... Madison
964	2,023	64	1,036	1,941	85	945	2,076	73	823	1,904	..... Marion
664	448	14	606	494	22	823	364	7	475	480	..... Martin
601	578	41	664	518	36	714	517	22	543	543	..... Mason
4,437	4,293	190	4,214	4,539	255	5,304	3,585	162	3,392	4,642	.. Matagorda
812	3,862	92	977	3,417	253	1,129	3,359	131	1,101	3,307	... Maverick
2,832	3,781	286	3,131	3,353	306	4,143	2,587	174	3,180	2,980	..... Medina
350	523	23	382	463	19	425	453	14	280	461	..... Menard
21,128	7,970	1,081	21,379	7,954	905	19,090	10,089	847	20,224	7,455	.... Midland
2,267	4,264	98	2,158	4,369	125	2,720	3,983	90	1,759	4,331	..... Milam
654	813	17	824	665	30	978	546	8	508	785	...... Mills
892	1,397	25	1,021	1,272	42	1,362	1,057	20	691	1,306	... Mitchell
1,829	2,763	110	2,077	2,549	145	2,293	2,480	94	1,442	2,697	... Montague
26,530	16,107	1,298	27,135	16,192	1,358	26,826	15,946	1,273	24,780	15,522	Montgomery
2,278	1,948	126	2,451	1,744	172	2,584	1,736	111	1,807	2,369	..... Moore
895	2,806	45	1,155	2,531	76	1,102	2,650	45	788	2,674	..... Morris
315	247	19	368	196	18	415	188	8	218	279	..... Motley
6,032	6,141	229	7,431	4,834	271	6,809	5,458	256	5,337	5,673	Nacogdoches
4,280	5,805	220	4,314	5,701	308	4,582	5,280	256	3,807	5,767	... Navarro
642	2,382	54	810	2,246	61	666	2,393	52	556	2,286	..... Newton
1,562	2,460	139	1,867	2,157	170	2,431	1,740	94	1,443	2,406	...... Nolan
24,385	34,242	1,682	24,376	34,343	1,959	25,519	33,597	1,583	21,311	32,966	..... Nueces
1,757	858	63	1,861	737	93	1,978	743	55	1,210	1,300	... Ochiltree
345	329	25	386	305	25	447	277	16	242	446	..... Oldham
5,603	13,716	462	6,135	12,992	623	5,061	13,992	646	5,662	12,947	..... Orange
2,836	3,332	182	3,305	2,923	218	4,005	2,423	176	2,468	3,390	.... Palo Pinto
2,052	3,739	80	2,305	3,444	117	1,938	3,959	84	1,936	3,532	.... Panola
8,820	8,098	756	9,446	7,292	913	10,615	6,571	661	8,217	8,249	..... Parker
1,199	812	48	1,245	770	49	1,469	627	28	850	1,008	..... Parmer
2,067	2,276	91	1,896	2,350	122	1,704	2,589	63	1,669	2,338	...... Pecos
3,774	4,736	218	4,142	4,498	229	4,336	4,279	229	3,129	4,857	...... Polk
9,757	9,366	661	12,587	8,383	864	11,018	8,358	628	8,834	10,771	...... Potter
399	1,152	18	432	1,050	45	369	1,140	34	331	1,087	..... Presidio
749	1,155	53	845	1,074	66	960	1,000	48	592	1,139	...... Rains
18,417	10,811	714	20,333	8,841	877	20,227	9,459	590	16,516	13,088	.... Randall
606	374	10	618	363	15	611	386	11	480	389	..... Reagan
583	442	38	535	468	47	610	435	27	467	418	.... Real
1,156	2,545	45	1,415	2,227	87	1,516	2,279	46	960	2,408	... Red River
1,146	2,039	61	1,092	2,020	97	1,063	2,053	68	933	1,941	..... Reeves
1,091	1,558	51	929	1,699	51	1,119	1,572	37	772	1,544	..... Refugio
266	222	14	334	166	11	352	153	11	229	233	... Roberts
1,288	3,093	55	1,359	3,076	68	1,640	2,854	45	1,158	2,996	... Robertson
4,354	2,876	332	5,037	2,221	413	4,799	2,517	318	4,357	2,379	... Rockwall
1,278	1,632	61	1,613	1,302	80	2,145	949	29	1,146	1,438	.... Runnels
5,037	5,381	242	5,590	4,718	334	5,571	5,067	252	4,805	4,633	...... Rusk
1,048	1,750	57	1,227	1,636	58	1,180	1,685	63	857	1,772	..... Sabine
968	1,758	58	1,160	1,583	79	1,350	1,487	52	752	1,726	San Augustine
1,694	1,932	113	1,871	2,024	114	2,220	1,734	65	1,303	2,156	.. San Jacinto
4,794	5,914	330	4,554	6,194	304	5,457	5,555	198	4,127	5,765	. San Patricio
619	824	20	748	746	21	817	704	14	469	852	.... San Saba
407	395	13	427	386	22	469	373	10	314	393	.. Schleicher
2,638	2,080	93	2,826	1,825	128	3,455	1,390	58	2,214	2,129	..... Scurry
483	586	15	632	438	28	826	299	11	441	485	. Shackelford
1,935	3,488	92	2,266	3,156	120	2,636	2,882	76	1,739	3,372	..... Shelby
555	415	26	612	372	35	689	330	24	413	519	.... Sherman
22,857	16,561	963	25,004	14,312	1,324	24,219	15,367	1,004	21,522	15,625	..... Smith
725	864	72	788	833	101	942	759	59	522	884	... Somervell
387	3,790	30	532	3,556	78	762	3,402	42	529	3,544	...... Starr
1,257	1,399	61	1,667	1,023	77	2,129	689	43	1,170	1,259	.... Stephens
254	197	4	281	167	13	332	150	3	240	161	.... Sterling
227	555	17	272	522	13	420	415	7	159	547	... Stonewall
507	484	12	544	413	27	558	427	11	429	440	..... Sutton
754	1,487	40	944	1,300	40	1,098	1,185	24	507	1,651	.... Swisher
134,154	134,675	11,104	153,519	115,139	12,602	144,822	125,255	11,902	144,221	114,681	.... Tarrant
13,023	15,423	664	18,637	9,767	817	21,214	7,933	509	15,742	10,944	..... Taylor
191	258	4	173	246	17	161	280	6	152	232	..... Terrell
1,491	1,822	57	1,870	1,318	77	2,382	1,008	29	1,162	1,683	...... Terry
292	438	18	305	395	20	459	309	13	193	413	Throckmorton
1,811	3,721	63	2,178	3,354	73	2,645	3,005	57	1,697	3,539	.... Titus
11,403	11,143	618	12,623	9,748	764	13,626	9,623	502	11,724	9,593	.. Tom Green
63,470	119,433	6,570	68,954	112,362	7,965	55,686	129,928	5,370	64,811	104,378	..... Travis
1,415	2,008	57	1,595	1,907	64	1,808	1,786	53	1,059	2,073	..... Trinity
1,229	3,336	80	1,647	2,778	118	1,362	3,113	101	1,103	2,881	...... Tyler

John Tower: The GOP's Godfather

A Texas political legend ended when former U.S. Senator John Goodwin Tower died in a tragic plane crash in Brunswick, Ga., on April 5, 1991. For practical purposes, Texas' political history can be dated before and after the diminutive Texan's election to the U.S. Senate in a special election in the spring of 1961.

Former President Lyndon B. Johnson set the stage for Tower's election by running for two offices — the vice-presidency and senator — in the same election. A political unknown, Tower was considered nothing more than a Republican irritant to the Democratic Senate majority leader. But he polled a surprising 41 percent of the general election vote, as many Texans expressed their displeasure at Johnson's dual appearance on the ballot.

The following spring, more than 70 candidates crowded the ballot for the special election to fill Johnson's seat. The favorite was William A. Blakley, a millionaire businessman and Gov. Price Daniel's interim appointee to the senate seat. (Blakley previously had served an interim appointment to the senate seat vacated by Daniel in 1957 before losing a special election to Ralph W. Yarborough. However, Blakley is the only Texan to serve in both the Sam Houston and Thomas J. Rusk, the state's first two senators, successions in the Senate.)

Tower's race the previous fall gave him name recognition in the special election and put in place a political organization. He led the field in the special election with 30.9 percent of the vote and defeated Blakley in the runoff with 50.6 percent of the vote. The election gave Republicans their first U.S. Senate seat from Texas since 1875, and sent after shocks through the ranks of the firmly entrenched Democratic party. Most observers at the time thought Tower's election was an aberration and that he would never be re-elected.

The election invigorated Texas Republicans. For most of the 20th century, Republicans were more a party of patronage than a legitimate political force in Texas. The action was within the ranks of Democratic party where conservatives battled liberals, and the Democratic nomination was tantamount to election.

Dissatisfaction with Democratic President John F. Kennedy allowed the state Republican to score victories in special elections for legislative seats in 1963, and the party appeared to be on a roll. After President Kennedy's assassination in Dallas, however, the party's fortunes tumbled. Usually conservative Texas gave Lyndon Johnson a resounding landslide in the 1964 presidential election over conservative Republican Barry Goldwater of Arizona and in the process wiped out the GOP's hard-earned gains across the state.

Only John Tower remained as the highly visible patron saint of the party, a lone rallying point. He spoke at fund-raisers across the state and in Washington developed a reputation as a solid, articulate conservative voice in the liberal atmosphere of that day in Washington. At five feet five inches tall, Tower was hardly a stereotypical rangy Texan, but he used his size to his advantage. "I'm John Tower, but I don't," he opened many after-dinner talks to the laughter of diners — and contributors. Tower, a powerful speaker whose voice would have done justice to any pulpit, was a popular orator.

Waggoner Carr, a popular conservative Democrat and former speaker of the Texas House of Representatives, challenged Tower in the 1966 general election and lost when internal strife racked the Democratic party. Barefoot Sanders, a moderate and now a federal judge in Dallas, did little better in 1970, and current Railroad Commissioner and former U.S. representative Robert Krueger ran a close campaign in 1976, only to be nipped at the wire by the now-seasoned Sen. Tower.

Though a political unknown in 1960, Tower was well prepared for office. The son and grandson of Methodist ministers, he was born in Houston on Sept. 29, 1925 and graduated from high school in Beaumont in 1942. After serving on a U.S. Navy gunboat in the Pacific in World War II, Tower took a B.A. in political science at Southwestern University in Georgetown in 1948. He worked as a radio announcer in Taylor and Beaumont and as an insurance agent in Dallas before joining the faculty as an associate professor of political science at Midwestern University in Wichita Falls in 1951.

One irony of Tower's career was his attendance at the prestigious London School of Economic and Political Science, an anathema to conservatives at the time. Tower later earned a master's degree in political

County	Registered Voters	Total Vote	Turnout (%)	Governor			Lt. Governor				U.S. Senate		
				Clayton Williams (R.)	Ann W. Richards (D.)	Jeff Daiell (L.)	Rob Mosbacher (R.)	Bob Bullock (D.)	Tom Owens (L.)	Phil Gramm (R.)	Hugh Parmer (D.)	Gary Johnson (L.)
Upshur......	16,799	8,300	49.4	3,851	4,159	269	3,392	4,694	265	4,755	3,391	152
Upton.......	2,380	1,356	57.0	1,005	313	33	680	540	66	1,010	261	25
Uvalde......	12,195	5,519	45.3	2,891	2,472	132	2,335	2,918	153	3,384	1,923	99
Val Verde....	13,874	6,675	48.1	2,682	3,856	126	2,196	4,293	175	3,394	3,125	125
Van Zandt ...	21,067	10,579	50.2	5,406	4,750	363	4,936	5,136	339	6,221	4,014	165
Victoria.....	35,801	18,567	51.9	10,373	7,600	537	8,130	9,460	470	12,750	5,001	256
Walker......	18,492	10,346	55.9	4,924	5,160	237	5,162	5,072	269	6,810	3,452	177
Waller......	12,976	6,475	49.9	2,790	3,541	119	2,426	3,917	130	3,271	3,012	73
Ward	6,507	3,860	59.3	2,527	1,229	101	1,735	1,904	132	2,185	996	65
Washington ..	13,868	8,660	62.4	5,324	3,128	188	4,039	4,547	162	6,069	2,490	108
Webb.......	47,221	14,643	31.0	3,521	10,947	170	3,015	11,086	274	6,982	7,026	285
Wharton.....	18,816	8,962	47.6	4,794	3,939	221	3,808	5,062	205	5,629	3,250	114
Wheeler.....	3,962	2,212	55.8	1,191	884	87	1,079	1,035	69	1,458	689	29
Wichita	57,662	30,699	53.2	12,926	16,397	1,360	11,088	18,688	950	18,038	12,002	588
Wilbarger ...	7,344	3,477	47.3	1,586	1,769	102	1,103	2,294	67	1,974	1,441	29
Willacy	8,600	3,867	45.0	1,385	2,410	72	1,270	2,324	89	1,719	1,814	56
Williamson..	61,001	38,930	63.8	18,148	19,737	1,034	16,969	20,724	1,511	23,068	15,033	1,033
Wilson	13,345	6,928	51.9	3,624	3,109	191	2,862	3,549	224	3,746	2,664	162
Winkler	4,018	2,091	52.0	1,419	644	28	1,100	918	65	1,247	494	28
Wise.......	16,406	9,139	55.7	4,255	4,458	403	3,951	4,935	412	4,957	3,993	276
Wood.......	15,219	8,488	55.8	4,678	3,479	296	4,193	4,023	327	5,425	2,869	183
Yoakum.....	3,650	1,976	54.1	1,204	676	85	935	971	74	1,172	436	34
Young	9,939	5,845	58.8	3,142	2,414	251	2,284	3,387	155	3,862	1,918	76
Zapata	5,094	1,711	33.6	587	1,111	13	452	1,167	32	767	889	12
Zavala	6,910	2,499	36.2	483	1,989	27	333	2,002	20	531	1,777	20
StateTotals...	7,701,499	3,892,746	50.5	1,826,431	1,925,670	129,128	1,741,893	2,002,360	128,714	2,302,357	1,429,986	89,089

science at Southern Methodist University in Dallas before returning to teach at Midwestern.

In 1956, Tower attended his first national political convention, traveling to San Francisco for the renomination of President Dwight D. Eisenhower. At home, he was a member of the 23rd Senatorial District executive committee and served as chairman of the state education and research committee.

Tower did his homework in the Senate, becoming an authority in national defense and the military. Under his guidance, defense spending rose to $211 billion a year. He was credited with bringing many lucrative defense contracts to Texas. When Republicans gained the majority in the Senate in 1981, Tower became chairman of the powerful Armed Services Committee. As important, he put together a highly competent staff to deal with his constituents' relations with the federal government, which earned him many friends among the grassroots of the state's voters.

He also was an active fund-raiser for the party and chaired the Republican Senate Campaign Committee to elect more GOP faithful to the upper house.

As surprising as his election 23 years earlier was Tower's decision not to seek re-election in 1984, after holding some fund-raisers for his anticipated campaign. In his retirement, the former senator became a high-paid defense consultant.

The following year, President Ronald Reagan named Tower to the post of strategic arms negotiator with the Soviet Union. In 1986, Reagan appointed Tower to chair a three-member bipartisan committee to investigate the infamous Iran-contra scandal.

Ironically, it was his experience in defense that opponents used against him when President George Bush tried to appoint Tower Secretary of Defense in 1989. Critics claimed the former senator was too close to defense contractors to perform the duties of the office properly. In one of the few personal setbacks of his political career, Tower's appointment was rejected by the same Senate in which he served for more than two decades. It was the first rejection of a cabinet nominee in more than 30 years.

In a book published just before his death, *Consequences: A Personal and Political Memoir*, Tower lashed out at many who contributed to defeat of his nomination.

Tower's personal life was turbulent, including two

Sen. John Tower

publicized divorces. He had three daughters by his first wife, Lou, including Marian, who died with her father in the plane crash that ended his life.

At the time of Tower's death, Republicans held 10 of 27 Texas seats in the U.S. House and more than 60 seats in the Texas Legislature. Republicans also hold many local government positions, an unheard-of circumstance before Tower opened the door and led the way for development of the two-party system in the state. Despite his quips about his height, in Texas political history, John Tower indeed did — tower.

—Mike Kingston

Attorney General			State Treasurer			Agriculture Comm.			Crim. Ct., Pl. 5		
Buster Brown (R.)	Dan Morales (D.)	Ray E. Dittmar (L.)	Kay B. Hutchison (R.)	Nikki Van Hightower (D.)	Suzanne Love (L.)	Rick Perry (R.)	Jim Hightower (D.)	Karen A. Tegtmeyer (L.)	Louis E. Sturns (R.)	Morris L. Overstreet (D.)	County
3,102	4,924	174	3,655	4,308	263	3,786	4,243	211	2,954	4,677	..... Upshur
675	485	41	662	510	48	569	624	37	465	552	...... Upton
2,275	2,951	123	2,480	2,623	148	3,209	2,140	71	2,155	2,425	..... Uvalde
2,300	4,142	153	2,270	4,060	227	2,261	4,120	181	2,342	3,947	... Val Verde
4,606	5,202	219	5,143	4,705	302	5,783	4,286	212	3,760	5,306	... Van Zandt
8,722	8,665	390	8,385	8,593	455	8,588	8,688	334	7,996	7,293	.... Victoria
4,751	5,234	205	5,172	4,963	225	5,623	4,569	167	4,459	4,828	..... Walker
2,453	3,719	116	2,602	3,643	154	2,857	3,408	117	2,197	3,700	..... Waller
2,011	1,540	106	1,748	1,970	118	1,324	1,989	91	1,504	1,838	...... Ward
4,745	3,554	190	4,992	3,467	149	5,626	2,964	84	4,164	3,432	. Washington
1,672	12,634	176	2,490	11,245	515	2,185	11,684	331	2,933	10,709	...... Webb
4,534	4,219	171	4,556	4,239	190	5,608	3,309	114	3,804	4,354	..... Wharton
1,019	1,011	35	1,102	930	52	1,337	808	23	753	1,160	..... Wheeler
12,613	16,920	755	14,155	15,372	998	10,754	18,745	903	12,094	15,968	..... Wichita
1,277	1,993	56	1,459	1,824	72	1,515	1,857	52	1,121	1,971	... Wilbarger
1,314	2,322	62	1,134	2,364	102	1,650	1,997	47	990	2,321	..... Willacy
17,513	19,615	1,273	17,794	19,097	1,486	16,542	20,981	1,165	17,661	17,262	.. Williamson
2,554	3,786	223	2,662	3,520	235	3,342	3,033	155	2,325	3,230	..... Wilson
1,248	741	46	1,119	896	45	867	1,124	38	983	960	.... Winkler
3,801	4,915	343	4,265	4,426	392	5,006	3,888	298	3,405	4,973	...... Wise
4,049	4,064	215	4,479	3,613	290	4,679	3,523	208	3,810	3,814	...... Wood
1,102	781	61	1,231	624	89	1,382	554	30	985	782	.... Yoakum
2,644	2,808	105	2,899	2,568	127	3,644	2,082	100	2,183	2,781	..... Young
416	1,223	18	457	1,113	38	490	1,119	19	413	1,103	..... Zapata
300	2,101	17	339	1,944	29	394	1,910	19	283	1,901	..... Zavala
1,708,110	1,963,714	110,511	1,895,651	1,772,200	130,543	1,864,463	1,820,145	112,017	1,666,778	1,757,025	.. State Totals

ELECTIONS OF TEXAS GOVERNORS, 1845-1990

Following are the results of all elections of Texas governors since Texas became a state in 1845. Party primaries, as well as general elections, are included whenever possible, although Republican totals are not available for some elections. Prior to 1857, many candidates ran independently; whenever candidates were party nominees, the party is given in parentheses.

1ST ELECTION, 1845
J. P. Henderson	7,853
J. B. Miller	1,673
Scattering	52
Total vote	9,578

2ND ELECTION, 1847
George T. Wood	7,154
J. B. Miller	5,106
N. H. Darnell	1,276
J. J. Robinson	379
Scattering	852
Total vote	14,767

3RD ELECTION, 1849
P. H. Bell	10,319
George T. Wood	8,764
John T. Mills	2,632
Total vote	21,715

4TH ELECTION, 1851
P. H. Bell	13,595
M. T. Johnson	5,262
John A. Greer	4,061
B. H. Epperson	2,971
T. J. Chambers	2,320
Scattering	100
Total vote	28,309

5TH ELECTION, 1853
E. M. Pease	13,091
W. B. Ochiltree	9,178
George T. Wood	5,983
L. D. Evans	4,677
T. J. Chambers	2,449
John Dancy	315
Total vote	35,693

6TH ELECTION, 1855
E. M. Pease	26,336
D. C. Dickson	18,968
M. T. Johnson	809
George T. Wood	226
Total vote	46,339

7TH ELECTION, 1857
H. R. Runnels (Dem.)	32,552
Sam Houston	28,628
Total vote	61,180

8TH ELECTION, 1859
*Sam Houston	36,227
H. R. Runnels (Dem.)	27,500
Scattering	61
Total vote	63,788

*Ran as independent but received the support of the Know-Nothing Party.

Note.—Edward Clark succeeded Sam Houston on March 16, 1861, shortly after Texas seceded from the Union.

9TH ELECTION, 1861
F. R. Lubbock	21,854
Edward Clark	21,730
T. J. Chambers	13,759
Total vote	57,343

10TH ELECTION, 1863
Pendleton Murrah	17,511
T. J. Chambers	12,455
Scattering	1,070
Total vote	31,036

Note.—A. J. Hamilton was named Governor under Reconstruction administration June 17, 1865.

11TH ELECTION, 1866
J. W. Throckmorton	49,277
E. M. Pease	12,168
Total vote	61,445

Note. — E. M. Pease was ap-pointed Governor July 30, 1867.

12TH ELECTION, 1869
E. J. Davis	39,901
A. J. Hamilton	39,092
Hamilton Stuart	380
Total vote	79,373

13TH ELECTION, 1873
Richard Coke (Dem.)	85,549
E. J. Davis (Rep.)	42,633
Total vote	128,182

14TH ELECTION, 1876
Richard Coke (Dem.)	150,581
William Chambers (Rep.)	47,719
Total vote	198,300

Note. — R. B. Hubbard, Lieutenant Governor, succeeded Coke Dec. 1, 1876, when Coke became United States Senator.

15TH ELECTION, 1878
O. M. Roberts (Dem.)	158,933
W. H. Hamman (Greenback)	55,002
A. B. Norton (Rep.)	23,402
Scattering	99
Total vote	237,436

16TH ELECTION, 1880
O. M. Roberts (Dem.)	166,101
E. J. Davis (Rep.)	64,382
W. H. Hamman (Greenback)	33,721
Total vote	264,204

17TH ELECTION, 1882
John Ireland (Dem.)	150,809
G. W. Jones (Greenback)	102,501
J. B. Robertson (I.Dem.)	334
Total vote	253,644

18TH ELECTION, 1884
John Ireland (Dem.)	212,234
Geo. W. Jones (Greenback)	88,450
A. B. Norton (Rep.)	25,557
Total vote	326,241

19TH ELECTION, 1886
L. S. Ross (Dem.)	228,776
A. M. Cochran (Rep.)	65,236
E. L. Dohoney (Prohi.)	19,186
Scattering	102
Total vote	313,300

20TH ELECTION, 1888
L. S. Ross (Dem.)	250,338
Marion Martin (Ind.Fus.)	98,447
Total vote	348,785

21ST ELECTION, 1890
J. S. Hogg (Dem.)	262,432
W. Flanagan (Rep.)	77,742
E. C. Heath (Prohi.)	2,235
Total vote	342,409

22ND ELECTION, 1892
J. S. Hogg (Dem.)	190,486
George Clark (Dem.)	133,395
T. L. Nugent (Peo.)	108,483
A. J. Houston (Ref.Rep.)	1,322
D. M. Prendergast (Prohi.)	1,605
Scattering	176
Total vote	435,467

23RD ELECTION, 1894
C. A. Culberson (Dem.)	207,167
T. L. Nugent (Peo)	152,731
W. K. Makemson (Rep.)	54,520
J. B. Schmidt (L. W. Rep.)	5,036

J. M. Dunn (Prohi.)	2,196
Scattering	1,076
Total vote	422,726

24TH ELECTION, 1896
C. A. Culberson (Dem.)	298,528
J. C. Kearby (Peo.)	238,692
Randolph Clark (Prohi.)	1,876
Scattering	682
Total vote	539,778

25TH ELECTION, 1898
J. D. Sayers (Dem.)	291,548
Barnett Gibbs (Peo.)	114,955
R. P. Bailey (Prohi.)	2,437
G. H. Royall (Soc. Lab.)	552
Scattering	62
Total vote	409,554

26TH ELECTION, 1900
J. D. Sayers (Dem.)	303,586
R. E. Hanney (Rep.)	112,864
T. J. McMinn (Peo.)	26,864
G. H. Royall (Soc. Lab.)	155
Scattering	6,155
Total vote	449,624

27TH ELECTION, 1902
S. W. T. Lanham (Dem.)	219,076
George W. Burkett (Rep.)	65,706
J. M. Mallett (Peo.)	12,387
G. W. Carroll (Prohi.)	8,708
Scattering	3,273
Total vote	309,150

28TH ELECTION, 1904
S. W. T. Lanham (Dem.)	206,160
J. G. Lowden (Rep.)	56,865
Pat B. Clark (Peo.)	9,301
W. D. Jackson (Prohi.)	4,509
Frank Leitner (Soc. Lab.)	552
W. H. Mills (Soc. Dem.)	2,487
Total vote	279,874

DEMOCRATIC PRIMARY ELECTION, 1906

Previous to the election of 1906 all nominations of the Democratic party for state offices had been made in convention. This campaign was the first held under the **Terrell election law**, which required the Democratic Party (as the law was first passed) to provide for a twofold system for nomination of state and district officers. The primary election was held, but the convention vote of each county was to be prorated among the several candidates for each office on the basis of the primary election vote for such candidates in each of such counties.

The popular vote for Governor in the primary of 1906 was as follows:

Thomas M. Campbell	90,345
M. M. Brooks	70,064
O. B. Colquitt	68,529
Charles K. Bell	65,168
Total vote	294,106

The law required the convention to drop the low man at the end of each ballot and authorized each county delegation to prorate the released vote among the other candidates according to its choice. On the first convention ballot the prorated vote was Campbell 213,345, Colquitt 169,934, Bell 163,367 and Brooks 56,318. Brooks was dropped and Colquitt withdrew. Bell also withdrew after finishing but before announcement of the results of the second ballot which was Campbell 418,656. Bell 257,234.

29TH ELECTION, 1906

T. M. Campbell (Dem.) .	148,264
C. A. Gray (Rep.)	23,711
J. W. Pearson (Prohi.) . .	5,252
G. C. Edwards (Soc.) . . .	2,958
A. S. Dowler (Soc. Lab.) .	260
A. W. Atcheson (Reor. Rep.)	5,395
Total vote	185,840

DEMOCRATIC PRIMARY, 1908

In 1907 the primary election law was amended, providing for plurality nomination of state and district officers, i.e., leading candidates won, even though they received less than a majority of all votes cast. The primary of 1908 resulted as follows:

T. M. Campbell	202,608
R. R. Williams	117,459
Total vote	320,067

30TH ELECTION, 1908

T. M. Campbell (Dem.) .	218,956
J. N. Simpson (Rep.) . .	73,305
J. C. Rhodes (Soc.)	8,100
W. B. Cook (Soc. Lab.) . .	234
E. C. Heath (Prohi.)	148
Total vote	300,743

DEMOCRATIC PRIMARY, 1910

O. B. Colquitt	146,526
William Poindexter	79,711
R. V. Davidson	53,187
Cone Johnson	76,050
J. Marion Jones	1,906
Total vote	357,380

31ST ELECTION, 1910

O. B. Colquitt (Dem.) . . .	174,596
J. O. Terrell (Rep.)	26,191
Redding Andrews (Soc.)	11,538
A. J. Houston (Prohi.) . .	6,052
Carl Schmitz (Soc. Lab.)	426
Total vote	218,803

DEMOCRATIC PRIMARY, 1912

O. B. Colquitt	218,812
William F. Ramsey.	177,183
Total vote	395,995

32ND ELECTION, 1912

O. B. Colquitt (Dem.) . . .	234,352
Ed Lasater (Prog.)	15,794
C. W. Johnson (Rep.) . . .	23,089
A. J. Houston (Prohi.) . .	2,356
Redding Andrews (Soc.)	25,258
K. E. Choate (Soc. Lab.)	308
Total vote	301,157

DEMOCRATIC PRIMARY, 1914

James E. Ferguson	237,062
Thomas H. Ball	191,558
Total vote	428,620

33RD ELECTION, 1914

J. E. Ferguson (Dem.) . .	176,599
F. M. Etheridge (Prog.)	1,794
John W. Philp (Rep.) . . .	11,411
E. O. Meitzen (Soc.)	24,977
Total vote	214,781

DEMOCRATIC PRIMARY, 1916

James E. Ferguson	240,561
Charles H. Morris.	174,611
H. C. Marshall	6,731
Total vote	421,903

34TH ELECTION, 1916

J. E. Ferguson (Dem.) . .	296,667
R. B. Creager (Rep.) . . .	49,118
E. O. Meitzen (Soc.)	14,580
H. W. Lewis (Prohi.)	3,200
Total vote	363,565

Note. — In 1917 Governor Ferguson was removed from office and succeeded by Lt. Gov. William P. Hobby.

DEMOCRATIC PRIMARY, 1918

W. P. Hobby.	461,479
James E. Ferguson	217,012
Total vote	678,491

35TH ELECTION, 1918

W. P. Hobby (Dem.)	148,982
Chas. A. Boynton (Rep.)	26,713
Wm. D. Simpson (Soc.). .	1,660
Total vote	177,355

DEMOCRATIC PRIMARIES, 1920

Note. — In 1918 the primary election law had been amended, requiring a majority for nomination for all state and district offices through a double primary election system. In that year, however, only one primary election was necessary in the Governor's race, as there were but two candidates. The first double primary in the Governor's race was in 1920.

First Primary.

Pat M. Neff	149,818
Robert E. Thomason . . .	99,002
Joseph W. Bailey	152,340
Ben F. Looney	48,640
Total vote	449,800

Second Primary.

Pat M. Neff	264,075
Joseph W. Bailey	184,702
Total vote	448,777

36TH ELECTION, 1920

Pat M. Neff (Dem.)	289,188
J. G. Culberson (Rep.) . .	90,217
H. Capers (B. T. Rep.) . .	26,091
T. H. McGregor (Amer.)	69,380
L. L. Rhodes (Soc.).	6,796
Scattering	59
Total vote	481,731

DEMOCRATIC PRIMARY, 1922

Pat M. Neff	318,000
W. W. King.	18,368
Fred S. Rogers.	195,941
Harry T. Warner	57,671
Total vote	589,926

37TH ELECTION, 1922

Pat M. Neff (Dem.)	334,199
W. H. Atwell (Rep.)	73,329
Total vote	407,528

DEMOCRATIC PRIMARIES, 1924

First Primary.

Felix D. Robertson.	193,508
George W. Dixon	4,035
W. E. Pope.	17,136
Joe Burkett	21,720
Mrs. Miriam A. Ferguson	146,424
Lynch Davidson	141,208
V. A. Collins	24,864
T. W. Davidson.	125,011
Thomas D. Barton	29,217
Total vote	703,123

Second Primary.

Mrs. Miriam A. Ferguson	413,751
Felix D. Robertson.	316,019
Total vote	729,770

38TH ELECTION, 1924

Mrs. Miriam A. Ferguson (Dem.).	422,558
George C. Butte (Rep.) .	294,970
Total vote	717,528

DEMOCRATIC PRIMARIES, 1926

First Primary.

Lynch Davidson.	122,449
Mrs. Miriam A. Ferguson	283,482
Mrs. Kate M. Johnston . .	1,029
Dan Moody	409,732
Mrs. Edith E. Wilmans . .	1,580
O. F. Zimmerman	2,962
Total vote	821,234

Second Primary.

Mrs. Miriam A. Ferguson	270,595
Dan Moody	495,723
Total vote	766,318

REPUBLICAN PRIMARY, 1926

Note—First state-wide primary held by Republican party.

H. H. Haines.	11,215
E. P. Scott	4,074
Total vote	15,289

39TH ELECTION, 1926

Dan Moody (Dem.)	233,068
H. H. Haines (Rep.)	31,531
M. A. Smith (Soc.)	908
Total vote	265,507

DEMOCRATIC PRIMARY, 1928

Wm. E. Hawkins.	32,076
Dan Moody	442,080
Louis J. Wardlaw	245,508
Edith E. Wilmans.	18,237
Total vote	737,901

40TH ELECTION, 1928

Dan Moody (Dem.)	582,972
W. H. Holmes (Rep.). . . .	120,504
T. Stedman (Com.)	109
L. L. Rhodes (Soc.).	738
Scattering	2,683
Total vote	707,006

DEMOCRATIC PRIMARIES, 1930

First Primary.

Mrs. Miriam A. Ferguson	242,959
Thomas B. Love	87,068
Paul Loven	2,724
Earle B. Mayfield.	54,459
Barry Miller	54,652
C. C. Moody.	4,382
Frank Putnam	2,365
Clint C. Small	138,934
Ross S. Sterling	170,754
James Young.	73,385
C. E. Walker.	1,760
Total vote	833,442

Second Primary.

Ross S. Sterling	473,371
Mrs. Miriam A. Ferguson	384,402
Total vote	857,773

REPUBLICAN PRIMARY, 1930

George C. Butte	5,001
H. E. Exum	2,773
John F. Grant	1,800
John P. Gaines.	203
Total vote	9,777

41ST ELECTION, 1930

Ross S. Sterling (Dem.) .	252,738
Wm. E. Talbot (Rep.) . . .	62,224
Total vote	314,962

DEMOCRATIC PRIMARIES, 1932

First Primary.

Roger Q. Evans	3,974
Mrs. Miriam A. Ferguson	402,238
C. A. Frakes.	2,338
J. Ed Glenn	2,089
Tom F. Hunter	220,391
Frank Putnam	2,962
Ross S. Sterling	296,383
M. H. Wolfe	32,241
George W. Armstrong . .	5,312
Total vote	967,928

Second Primary.

Ross S. Sterling	473,846
Mrs. Miriam A. Ferguson	477,644
Total Vote.	951,490

42ND ELECTION, 1932

Mrs. Miriam A. Ferguson (Dem.).	528,986
Orville Bullington (Rep.)	317,807
George C. Edwards (Soc.)	1,866
George W. Armstrong (*J. Dem.)	706
Otho L. Heitt (Liberty) . .	101
Philip L. Howe (Com.) . .	72
Total vote	849,538

*Jackson Democratic party.

DEMOCRATIC PRIMARIES, 1934

First Primary.

C. C. McDonald	206,007
James V. Allred	297,656

Clint C. Small. 124,206
Tom F. Hunter. 241,339
Edgar Witt. 62,208
Edward K. Russell 4,408
Maury Hughes. 58,187
Total vote 994,011

Second Primary
James V. Allred 497,808
Tom F. Hunter 457,785
Total vote 995,593

REPUBLICAN PRIMARY, 1934
Note.—This was the third Republican primary.
D. E. Waggoner 13,043

43RD ELECTION, 1934
James V. Allred 421,422
D. E. Wagonner (Rep.). . 13,534
George C. Edwards (Soc.) 1,877
Enoch Hardaway (Com.) 244
Total vote 437,077

DEMOCRATIC PRIMARY, 1936
James V. Allred 553,219
P. Pierce Brooks 33,391
F. W. Fischer 145,877
Tom F. Hunter 239,460
Roy Sanderford 81,170
Total vote 1,053,117

44TH ELECTION, 1936
James V. Allred (Dem.) . 782,083
C. O. Harris (Rep) 58,842
Carl Brannin (Soc.) . . . 962
Homer Brooks (Com.) . . 283
Total vote 482,170

DEMOCRATIC PRIMARY,1938
W. Lee O'Daniel 573,166
Ernest O. Thompson . . . 231,630
William McCraw 152,278
Tom F. Hunter 117,634
S. T. Brogdon 892
Joseph King 773
Clarence E. Farmer 3,869
P. D. Renfro. 8,127
Karl A. Crowley 19,153
Clarence R. Miller 667
James A. Ferguson 3,800
Thomas Self. 1,405
Marvin P. McCoy. 1,491
Total vote 1,114,885

45TH ELECTION, 1938
W. Lee O'Daniel (Dem.) 473,526
Alexander Boynton (Rep.) 10,940
Earl E. Miller (Soc.). . . . 398
Homer Brooks (Com.) . . 424
Total vote 485,288

DEMOCRATIC PRIMARY, 1940
W. Lee O'Daniel 645,646
Ernest O. Thompson . . . 256,923
Harry Hines. 119,121
Mrs. Miriam A. Ferguson 100,578
Jerry Sadler 61,396
Arlon B. Cyclone Davis Jr. 3,625
R. P. Condron 2,001
Total vote 1,189,290

46TH ELECTION, 1940
W. Lee O'Daniel (Dem.) 1,019,338
George C. Hopkins
(Rep.) 59,885
Ben H. Lauderdale
(Com.) 202
Scattering 113
Total vote 1,079,538

DEMORATIC PRIMARY, 1942
Hal H. Collins. 272,469
Alex M. Ferguson. 8,370
Gene S. Porter 4,933
Charles L. Somerville. . . 4,853
Coke R. Stevenson. . . . 651,218
Hope Wheeler 9,373
Total vote 951,216

47TH ELECTION, 1942
Coke R. Stevenson (Dem.) 280,735
C. K. McDowell (Rep.) . . 9,204
Total vote 289,939

DEMOCRATIC PRIMARY, 1944
Coke R. Stevenson 696,586
Martin Jones 21,379
W. J. Minton 8,537
Alex M. Ferguson. 12,649
Minnie F. Cunningham . 48,039
Gene S. Porter 15,243
Edward L. Carey 4,633
William F. Grimes 9,443
Herbert E. Mills. 6,640
Write-in votes 311
Total vote 823,460

48TH ELECTION, 1944
Coke R. Stevenson (Dem.) 1,007,826
B. J. Peasley (Rep.) 100,287
Total vote 1,108,113

DEMOCRATIC PRIMARIES, 1946
First Primary.
Floyd Brinkley. 4,249
William V. Brown. 3,902
A. J. Burks. 4,881
Chas. B. Hutchison 4,616
Beauford Jester. 443,804
Walter Scott McNutt. . . . 4,353
Caso March 20,529
W. J. Minton 2,398
Homer P. Rainey 291,282
Jerry Sadler 103,120
Grover Sellers 162,431
C. R. Shaw 9,764
John Lee Smith 102,941
Reese Turner. 4,914
Total vote 1,163,184
Second Primary.
Beauford H. Jester 701,018
Homer P. Rainey 335,654
Total vote 1,056,672

49TH ELECTION, 1946
Beauford H. Jester
(Dem.). 345,513
Eugene Nolte Jr. (Rep.) 33,231
Total vote 378,744

DEMOCRATIC PRIMARY, 1948
Beauford H. Jester. 642,025
Sumpter W. Stockton . . . 21,243
Roger Q. Evans 279,602
Charles B. Hutchison . . . 24,441
Holmes A. May. 20,538
Caso March 187,658
W. J. Minton 13,659
Denver S. Whiteley. 16,090
Write-in votes 1
Total vote 1,205,257

50TH ELECTION, 1948
Beauford H. Jester
(Dem.). 1,024,160
Alvin H. Lane (Rep.) . . . 177,399
Gerald Overholt (Prohi.) 3,554
Herman Wright (Prog.) . 3,747
Total vote 1,208,860

DEMOCRATIC PRIMARY, 1950
Allan Shivers 829,730
Caso March 195,997
Charles B. Hutchison . . 16,048
Gene S. Porter 14,728
J. M. Wren. 14,138
Mrs. Benita Louise
Marek Lawrence 9,542
Wellington Abbey 6,381
Total vote 1,086,564

51ST ELECTION, 1950
Allan Shivers (Dem.) . . . 833,861
Ralph W. Currie (Rep.) . . 39,737
Total vote 374,747

DEMOCRATIC PRIMARY, 1952
Allan Shivers 883,861
Ralph W. Yarborough . . 488,345
Mrs. Allene M. Trayler. . 34,186
Total vote 1,356,392

52ND ELECTION, 1952
*Allan Shivers (Dem.) . . 1,375,547
*Allan Shivers (Rep.) . . . 468,319
Total vote 1,843,866

*Ran on both Democratic and
Republican tickets.

DEMOCRATIC PRIMARIES, 1954
First Primary.
Allan Shivers 668,913
Ralph W. Yarborough . . 645,994
J. J. Holmes. 19,591
Arlon B. Cyclone Davis. . 16,254
Total vote 1,350,752
Second Primary.
Allan Shivers 775,088
Ralph W. Yarborough . . 683,132
Total vote 1,458,220

53RD ELECTION, 1954
Allan Shivers (Dem.) . . 569,533
Tod R. Adams (Rep.) . . . 66,154
Other. 1,205
Total vote 636,892

DEMOCRATIC PRIMARIES, 1956
First Primary.
Price Daniel 628,914
J. Evetts Haley. 88,772
J. J. Holmes. 10,165
W. Lee O'Daniel. 347,757
Reuben Senterfitt 37,774
Ralph Yarborough. 463,416
Write-in. 72
Total Vote. 1,576,870
Second Primary.
Price Daniel 698,001
Ralph Yarborough 694,830
Total vote 1,392,831

54TH ELECTION, 1956
Price Daniel (Dem.) . . . 1,350,736
William M. Bryant (Rep.) 261,283
W. Lee O'Daniel
(Write-in). 110,234
Other. 1,838
Total vote 1,724,091

DEMOCRATIC PRIMARY, 1958
Price Daniel 799,107
Henry B. Gonzalez 246,969
Joe A. Irwin. 33,643
W. Lee O'Daniel. 238,767
Write-in. 6
Total vote 1,317,492

55TH ELECTION, 1958
Price Daniel (Dem.) . . . 695,779
Edward S. Mayer (Rep.) 94,086
Total vote 789,865

DEMOCRATIC PRIMARY, 1960
Jack Cox 619,834
Price Daniel 908,992
Write-in. 8
Total vote 1,528,834

56TH ELECTION, 1960
Price Daniel (Dem.) . . . 1,627,698
Wm. M. Steger (Rep.) . . 609,808
Total vote 2,237,506

DEMOCRATIC PRIMARIES, 1962
First Primary.
John Connally 431,498
Price Daniel 248,524
Marshall Formby. 139,094
Edwin A. Walker 138,387
Will Wilson. 171,617
Don Yarborough 317,986
Write-in. 9
Total vote 1,447,115
Second Primary.
John Connally 565,174
Don Yarborough 538,924
Total vote 1,104,098

REPUBLICAN PRIMARY, 1962
Jack Cox 99,170
Roy Whittenburg 16,136
Total vote 115,306

57TH ELECTION, 1962
John Connally (Dem.) . . 847,038
Jack Cox (Rep.). 715,025
Jack Carswell (Con.) . . . 7,135
Total vote 1,569,198

DEMOCRATIC PRIMARY, 1964
John Connally	1,125,884
Don Yarborough	471,411
M. T. Banks	22,047
Johnnie Mae Hackworthe	10,955
Total vote	1,630,297

REPUBLICAN PRIMARY, 1964
Jack Crichton	128,146

58TH ELECTION, 1964
John Connally (Dem.)	1,877,793
Jack Crichton (Rep.)	661,675
John C. Williams (Con.)	5,257
Write-in	28
Total vote	2,544,753

DEMOCRATIC PRIMARY, 1966
John Connally	932,641
Stanley C. Woods	291,651
Johnnie Mae Hackworthe	31,105
Write-in votes	3
Total vote	1,255,400

REPUBLICAN PRIMARY, 1966
T. E. Kennerly	49,568

59TH ELECTION, 1966
John Connally (Dem.)	1,037,517
T. E. Kennerly (Rep.)	368,025
Tommye Gillespie (Con.)	10,454
Bard Logan (Conserv.)	9,810
Write-ins	55
Total vote	1,425,861

DEMOCRATIC PRIMARIES, 1968
First Primary.
Preston Smith	386,875
Pat O'Daniel	47,912
John Hill	154,908
Waggoner Carr	257,543
Eugene Locke	218,118
Dolph Briscoe	225,686
Edward L. Whittenburg	22,957
Don Yarborough	421,607
Alfonso Veloz	9,562
Johnnie Mae Hackworthe	5,484
Total vote	1,750,652

Second Primary.
Preston Smith	767,490
Don Yarborough	621,226
Total vote	1,388,716

REPUBLICAN PRIMARY, 1968
Paul Eggers	65,501
John Trice	28,849
Wallace Sisk	10,415
Total vote	104,765

60TH ELECTION, 1968
Preston Smith (Dem.)	1,662,019
Paul Eggers (Rep.)	1,254,333
Total vote	2,916,352

DEMOCRATIC PRIMARY, 1970
Preston Smith	1,011,300

REPUBLICAN PRIMARY, 1970
Paul Eggers	101,875
Roger Martin	7,146
Total vote	109,021

61ST ELECTION, 1970
Preston Smith (Dem.)	1,232,506
Paul Eggers (Rep.)	1,073,831
Other	428
Total vote	2,306,765

DEMOCRATIC PRIMARIES, 1972
First Primary.
Ben Barnes	392,356
Dolph Briscoe	963,397
Frances Farenthold	612,051
Robert E. Looney	10,225
William H. Posey	13,727
Preston Smith	190,709
Gordon F. Wills	10,438
Total vote	2,192,903

Second Primary.
Dolph Briscoe	1,095,168
Frances Farenthold	884,594
Total vote	1,979,762

REPUBLICAN PRIMARIES, 1972
First Primary.
Albert Fay	24,329
Henry C. Grover	37,118
John A. Hall Sr.	8,018
J. A. Jenkins	4,864
Tom McElroy	19,559
David Reagan	20,119
Total vote	114,007

Second Primary.
Albert Fay	19,166
Henry C. Grover	37,842
Total vote	57,008

62ND ELECTION, 1972
Dolph Briscoe (Dem.)	1,633,493
Henry C. Grover (Rep.)	1,533,986
Ramsey Muniz (Raza)	214,118
Deborah Leonard (Soc.)	24,103
Other	3,891
Total vote	3,409,501

DEMOCRATIC PRIMARY, 1974
Dolph Briscoe	1,025,632
Frances Farenthold	437,287
W. H. Posey	31,498
Steve S. Alexander	26,889
Total vote	1,521,306

REPUBLICAN PRIMARY, 1974
Jim Granberry	53,617
Odell McBrayer	15,484
Total vote	69,101

63RD ELECTION, 1974
Dolph Briscoe (Dem.)	1,016,334
Jim Granberry (Rep.)	514,725
Ramsey Muniz (Raza)	93,295
Sherry Smith (Soc.)	8,171
S. W. McDonnell (Am.)	22,208
Other	251
Total vote	1,654,984

DEMOCRATIC PRIMARY, 1978
Donald R. Beagle	14,791
Dolph Briscoe	753,309
John Hill	932,345
Ray Allen Mayo	20,249
Preston Smith	92,202
Total vote	1,812,896

REPUBLICAN PRIMARY, 1978
William P. Clements Jr.	115,345
Ray Hutchison	38,268
Clarence Thompson	4,790
Total vote	158,403

64TH ELECTION, 1978
John Hill (Dem.)	1,166,919
Bill Clements (Rep.)	1,183,828
Mario C. Compean (Raza)	14,213
Sara Jean Johnston (Soc.)	4,624
Other	115
Total vote	2,369,699

DEMOCRATIC PRIMARY, 1982
First Primary.
David L. Young	25,386
Bob Armstrong	262,189
Mark White	592,658
Donald R. Beagle	15,649
Ray Allen Mayo	20,088
*Buddy Temple	402,693
Total vote	1,318,663

*Temple declined to participate in runoff; White declared winner this race.

REPUBLICAN PRIMARY, 1982
William P. Clements Jr.	246,120
Duke Embs	19,731
Total vote	265,851

65TH ELECTION, 1982
Mark White (Dem.)	1,697,870
William P. Clements Jr. (Rep.)	1,465,937
David Hutzelman (Ind.)	19,143
Bob Poteet (Con.)	8,065
Other	76
Total vote	3,191,091

DEMOCRATIC PRIMARY, 1986
Sheila Bilyeu	39,370
Andrew C. Briscoe III	248,850
A. Don Crowder	120,999
Bobby Locke	58,936
Ron Slover	38,861
Mark White	589,536
Total vote	1,096,552

REPUBLICAN PRIMARY, 1986
William P. Clements Jr.	318,808
Kent Hance	108,238
Tom Loeffler	117,673
Total vote	544,719

Following are the vote totals as canvassed by the Republican Party:
William P. Clements Jr.	318,938
Kent Hance	108,583
Tom Loeffler	118,224
Total vote	545,745

66TH ELECTION, 1986
Mark White (Dem.)	1,584,515
William P. Clements Jr. (Rep.)	1,813,779
Theresa Doyle (Lib.)	42,496
Other	670
Total vote	3,441,460

DEMOCRATIC PRIMARY, 1990
First Primary
Stanley Adams	16,118
Theresa Hearn-Haynes	31,395
Earl Holmes	17,904
Jim Mattox	546,103
Ray Rachal	9,388
Ann W. Richards	580,191
Mark White	288,161
Total vote	1,487,280

Second Primary
Jim Mattox	481,739
Ann W. Richards	640,995
Total vote	1,122,734

REPUBLICAN PRIMARY, 1990
Ed Cude	1,077
Kent Hance	132,142
Tom Luce	115,835
W. N. Otwell	2,310
Royce X. Owens	1,392
Jack Rains	82,461
Clayton Williams	520,014
Total vote	855,231

67TH ELECTION, 1990
Governor
Clayton Williams (Rep.)	1,826,431
Ann W. Richards (Dem.)	1,925,670
Jeff Daiell (Lib.)	129,128
Write-Ins (19)	11,517
Total vote	3,892,746

Gubernatorial Candidates

From 1845-1990

Compiled by the staff of the Texas Almanac

In 66 gubernatorial elections since Texas joined the Union in 1845, 322 people—310 men and 12 women—have sought the top office in state government. Miriam A. Ferguson was on the ballot six times, being elected twice, and Preston Smith was successful three times in five tries. Here is the list of people who have run for governor of Texas.

Candidate; Years; Party

Abbey, Wellington; 1950; dem.
Adams, Stanley; 1990; dem.
Adams, Tod R.; 1954; rep.
Alexander, Steve S.; 1974; dem.
*Allred, James V.; 1934, 1936; dem.
Andrews, Redding; 1910, 1912; soc.
Armstrong, Bob; 1982; dem.
Armstrong, George W.; 1932; dem.
Atcheson, A.W.; 1906; reorep.
Atwell, W.H.; 1922; rep.
Bailey, Joseph W.; 1920; dem.
Bailey, R.P.; 1898; proh.
Ball, Thomas H.; 1914; dem.
Banks, M.T.; 1964; dem.
Barnes, Ben; 1972; dem.
Barton, Thomas D.; 1924; dem.
Beagle, Donald R.; 1978, 1982; dem.
Bell, Charles K.; 1906; dem.
*Bell, P.H.; 1849, 1851; none.
†Bilyeu, Sheila; 1986; dem.
Boynton, Alexander; 1938; rep.
Boynton, Charles A.; 1918; rep.
Brannin, Carl; 1936; soc.
Brinkley, Floyd; 1946; dem.
*Briscoe, Dolph; 1968, 1972, 1974, 1978; dem.
Briscoe III, Andrew C.; 1986; dem.
Brogdon, S.T.; 1938; dem.
Brooks, Homer; 1936, 1938; comm.
Brooks, M.M.; 1906; dem.
Brooks, P.Pierce; 1936; dem.
Brown, William V.; 1946; dem.
Bryant, William R.; 1956; rep.
Bullington, Orville; 1932; rep.
Burkett, George W.; 1902; rep.
Burkett, Joe; 1924; dem.
Burks, A.J.; 1946; dem.
Butte, George C.; 1924, 1930; rep.
*Campbell, T.M.; 1906, 1908; dem.
Capers, H.; 1920; btrep.
Carey, Edward L.; 1944; dem.
Carr, Waggoner; 1968; dem.
Carroll, G.W.; 1902; proh.
Carswell, Jack; 1962; conser.
Chambers, T.J.; 1851, 1853, 1861, 1863; none.
Chambers, William; 1876; rep.
Choate, K.E.; 1912; soclab.
Clark, Edward; 1861; none.
Clark, George; 1892; rep.
Clark, Pat B.; 1904; peo.
Clark, Randolph; 1896; proh.
*Clements, Bill; 1978, 1982, 1986; rep.
Cochran, A.M.; 1886; rep.
*Coke, Richard; 1873, 1876; dem.
Collins, Hall H.; 1942; dem.
Collins, V.A.; 1924; dem.
*Colquitt, O.B.; 1906, 1910, 1912; dem.
Compeah, Mario C.; 1978; laraza.
Condron, R.P.; 1940; dem.
*Connally, John; 1962, 1964, 1966; dem.
Cook, W.B.; 1908; soclab.
Cox, Jack; 1960, 1962; dem., rep.
Creager, R.B.; 1916; rep.
Crichton, Jack; 1964; rep.
Crowder, A. Don; 1986; dem.
Crowley, Karl A.; 1938; dem.
Cude, Ed; 1990; rep.
*Culberson, C.A.; 1894, 1896; dem.
Culberson, J.G.; 1920; dem.
†Cunningham, Minnie F.; 1944; dem.
Currie, Ralph W.; 1950; rep.
Dancy, John; 1853; none.
*Daniel, Price; 1956, 1958, 1960, 1962; dem.
Darnell, N.H.; 1847; none.
Davidson, Lynch; 1924, 1926; dem.
Davidson, R.V.; 1910; dem.
Davidson, T.W.; 1924; dem.
Davis, A.B.Cyclon; 1954; dem.

*Davis, E.J.; 1869, 1873, 1880; nonc.
Davis Jr., Cyclone; 1940; dem.
Dickson, D.C.; 1855; none.
Dixon, George W.; 1924; dem.
Dohoney, E.L.; 1886; proh.
Dowler, A.S.; 1906; soclab.
†Doyle, Theresa; 1986; libetar.
Dunn, J.M.; 1894; proh.
Edwards, G.C.; 1906; soc.
Edwards, George C.; 1932, 1934; soc.
Eggers, Paul; 1968, 1970; rep.
Embs, Duke; 1982; rep.
Epperson, B.H.; 1851; none.
Etheridge, F.M.; 1914; prog.
Evans, L.D.; 1853; none.
Evans, Roger Q.; 1932, 1940; dem.
Exum, H.E.; 1930; rep.
†Farenthold, Frances; 1972, 1974; dem.
Farmer, Clarence E; 1938; dem.
Fay, Albert; 1972; rep.
Ferguson, Alex M.; 1942, 1944; dem.
Ferguson, James A.; 1938; dem.
*Ferguson, James E.; 1914, 1916, 1918; dem.
*†Ferguson, Miriam A.; 1924, 1926, 1930, 1932, 1938, 1940; dem.
Fischer, F.W.; 1936; dem.
Flanagan, W.; 1890; rep.
Formby, Marshall; 1962; dem.
Frakes, C.A.; 1932; dem.
Gaines, John P.; 1930; rep.
Gibbs, Barnett; 1898; peo.
†Gillespie, Tommye; 1966; con.
Glenn, J. Ed; 1932; dem.
Gonzalez, Henry B.; 1958; dem.
Granberry, Jim; 1974; rep.
Grant, John F.; 1930; rep.
Gray, C.A.; 1906; rep.
Greer, John A.; 1851; none.
Grimes, William F.; 1944; dem.
Grover, Henry C.; 1972; rep.
†Hackworthe, Johnnie M.; 1964, 1966, 1968; dem.
Haines, H.H.; 1926; rep.
Haley, J.Evetts; 1956; dem.
Hall Sr., John A.; 1972; rep.
Hamilton, A.J.; 1869; none.
Hamman, W.H.; 1878; grbk.
Hance, Kent; 1986, 1990; rep.
Hanney, R.E.; 1900; rep.
Hardaway, Enoch; 1934; comm.
Harris, C.O.; 1936; rep.
Hawkins, William E.; 1928; dem.
†Hearn-Haynes, Theresa; 1990; dem.
Heath, E.C.; 1890, 1908; proh.
Heitt, Otho L.; 1932; liberty.
*Henderson, J.P.; 1845; none.
Hill, John; 1968, 1978; dem.
Hines, Harry; 1940; dem.
*Hobby, William P.; 1918; dem.
*Hogg, Jim S.; 1890, 1892; dem.
Holmes, Earl; 1990; dem.
Holmes, J.J.; 1954, 1956; dem.
Holmes, W.H.; 1928; rep.
Hopkins, George C.; 1940; rep.
Houston, A.J.; 1892, 1910, 1912; refrep, proh.
*Houston, Sam; 1857, 1859; none.
Howe, Philip L.; 1932; comm.
Hughes, Maury; 1934; dem.
Hunter, Tom F.; 1932, 1934, 1936, 1938; dem.
Hutchison, Charles B.; 1946, 1948, 1950; dem.
Hutchison, Ray; 1978; rep.
Hutzelman, David; 1982; ind.
*Ireland, John; 1882, 1884; dem.
Irwin, Joe A.; 1958; dem.
Jackson, W.D.; 1904; proh.
Jenkins, J.A.; 1972; rep.
*Jester, Beauford; 1946, 1948; dem.
Johnson, C.W.; 1912; rep.
Johnson, Cone; 1910; dem.
Johnson, M.T; 1851, 1855; none.

Candidate; Years; Party

†Johnston, Kate M.; 1926; dem.
†Johnston, Sara Jean; 1978; soc.
Jones, G.W.; 1882, 1884; grbk.
Jones, J. Marion; 1910; dem.
Jones, Martin; 1944; dem.
Kearby, J.C.; 1896; peo.
Kennerly, T.E.; 1966; rep.
King, Joseph; 1938; dem.
King, W.W.; 1922; dem.
Lane, Alvin H.; 1948; rep.
*Lanham, S.W.T; 1902, 1904; dem.
Lasater, Ed; 1912; prog.
Lauderdale, Ben H.; 1940; comm.
†Lawrence, Benita L.M; 1950; dem.
Leitner, Frank; 1904; soclab.
†Leonard, Deborah; 1972; soc.
Lewis, H.W.; 1916; proh.
Locke, Bobby; 1986; dem.
Locke, Eugene; 1968; dem.
Loeffler, Tom; 1986; rep.
Logan, Bard; 1966; conser.
Looney, Ben F.; 1920; dem.
Looney, Robert E.; 1972; dem.
Love, Thomas B.; 1930; dem.
Loven, Paul; 1930; dem.
Lowden, J.G.; 1904; rep.
*Lubbock, F.R.; 1861; none.
Luce, Tom; 1990; rep.
Makemson, W.K.; 1894; rep.
Mallett, J.M.; 1902; peo.
March, Caso; 1946, 1948, 1950; dem.
Marshall, H.C.; 1916; dem.
Martin, Marion; 1888; indfus.
Martin, Roger; 1970; rep.
Mattox, Jim; 1990; dem.
May, Holmes A.; 1948; dem.
Mayer, Edward S.; 1958; rep.
Mayfield, Earle B.; 1930; dem.
Mayo, Ray Allen; 1978, 1982; dem.
McBrayer, Odell; 1974; rep.
McCoy, Marvin P.; 1938; dem.
McCraw, William; 1938; dem.
McDonald, C.C.; 1934; dem.
McDonnell, S.W.; 1974; amer.
McDowell, C.K.; 1942; rep.
McElroy, Tom; 1972; rep.
McGregor, T.H.; 1920; amer.
McMinn, T.J.; 1900; peo.
McNutt, Walter S.; 1946; dem.
Meltzen, E.O.; 1914, 1916; soc.
Miller, Barry; 1930; dem.
Miller, Clarence R; 1938; dem.
Miller, Earl E.; 1938; soc.
Miller, J.B.; 1845, 1847; none.
Mills, Herbert E.; 1944; dem.
Mills, John T.; 1849; none.
Mills, W.H.; 1904; socdem.
Minton, W.J.; 1944, 1946, 1948; dem.
Moody, C.C.; 1930; dem.
*Moody, Dan; 1926, 1928; dem.
Morris, Charles H.; 1916; dem.
Muniz, Ramsey; 1972, 1974; laraza.
*Murrah, Pendleton; 1863; none.
*Neff, Pat M.; 1920, 1922; dem.
Nolte Jr., Eugene; 1946; dem.
Norton, A.B.; 1878, 1880, 1884; rep.
Nugent, T.L.; 1892, 1894; peo.
O'Daniel, Pat; 1968; dem.
*O'Daniel, W.Lee; 1938, 1940, 1956, 1958; dem.
Ochiltree, W.B.; 1853; none.
Otwell, W.N.; 1990; rep.
Overholt, Gerald; 1948; proh.
Owens, Royce X.; 1990; rep.
Pearson, J.V.; 1906; proh.
*Pease, E.M.; 1853, 1855, 1866; none.
Peasley, B.J.; 1944; rep.
Philp, John W.; 1914; rep.
Poindester, William; 1910; dem.
Pope, W.E.; 1924; dem.
Porter, Gene S.; 1942, 1944, 1950; dem.
Posey, William H.; 1972, 1974; dem.
Poteet, Bob; 1982; con.
Prendergast, D.M.; 1892; proh.
Putnam, Frank; 1930, 1932; dem.
Rachal, Ray; 1990; dem.
Rainey, Homer P.; 1946; dem.
Rains, Jack; 1990; rep.
Ramsey, William F.; 1912; dem.
Reagan, David; 1972; rep.
Renfro, P.D.; 1938; dem.

Candidate; Years; Party

Rhodes, J.C.; 1908; soc.
Rhodes, L.L.; 1920, 1928; soc.
*†Richards, Ann W.; 1990; dem.
*Roberts, O.M.; 1878, 1880; dem.
Robertson, Felix D.; 1924; dem.
Robertson, J.B.; 1882; inddem.
Robinson, J.J.; 1847; none.
Rogers, Fred S.; 1922; dem.
*Ross, L.S.; 1886, 1888; dem.
Royall, G.H.; 1898, 1900; soclab.
*Runnels, Hardin; 1857, 1859; none.
Russell, Edward K.; 1934; dem.
Sadler, Jerry; 1940, 1946; dem.
Sanderford, Roy; 1936; dem.
*Sayers, J.D.; 1898, 1900; dem.
Schmidt, J.B.; 1894; lwrep.
Schmitz, Carl; 1910; soc lab.
Scott, E.P.; 1926; rep.
Self, Thomas; 1938; dem.
Sellers, Grover; 1946; dem.
Senterfitt, Reuben; 1956; dem.
Shaw, C.R.; 1946; dem.
*Shivers, Allan; 1950, 1952, 1954; dem, rep.
Simpson, J.N.; 1908; rep.
Simpson, William D.; 1918; soc.
Sisk, Wallace; 1968; rep.
Slover, Ron; 1986; dem.
Small, Clint C.; 1930, 1934; dem.
Smith, John Lee; 1946; dem.
Smith, M.A.; 1926; soc.
*Smith, Preston; 1968, 1970, 1972, 1974, 1978; dem.
†Smith, Sherry; 1974; soc.
Sommerville, Charles L.; 1942; dem.
Stedman, T.; 1928; commun.
Steger, William M.; 1960; rep.
*Sterling, Ross S.; 1930, 1932; dem.
*Stevenson, Coke R.; 1942, 1944; dem.
Stockton, Sumpter W.; 1948; dem.
Stuart, Hamilton; 1869; none.
Talbot, William E.; 1930; rep.
Temple, Buddy; 1982; dem.
Terrell, J.O.; 1910; rep.
Thomason, Robert E.; 1920; dem.
Thompson, Clarence; 1978; rep.
Thompson, Ernest O.; 1938, 1940; dem.
*Throckmorton, J.W.; 1866; none.
†Trayler, Allene M.; 1952; dem.
Trice, John; 1968; rep.
Turner, Reese; 1946; dem.
Veloz, Alfonso; 1968; dem.
Waggoner, D.E.; 1934; rep.
Walker, C.E.; 1930; dem.
Walker, Edwin A.; 1962; dem.
Wardlaw, Louis J.; 1928; dem.
Warner, Harry T.; 1922; dem.
†Wheeler, Hope; 1942; dem.
White, Mark; 1982, 1986, 1990; dem.
Whiteley, Denver S.; 1948; dem.
Whittenburg, Edward L.; 1968; dem.
Whittenburg, Roy; 1962; rep.
Williams, Clayton; 1990; rep.
Williams, John C.; 1964; conser.
Williams, R.R.; 1908; dem.
Wills, Gordon R.; 1972; dem.
†Wilmans, Edith E.; 1926, 1928; dem.
Wilson, Will; 1962; dem.
Witt, Edgar; 1934; dem.
Wolfe, M.H.; 1932; dem.
*Wood, George T.; 1847, 1849, 1853, 1855; none.
Woods, Stanley C.; 1966; dem.
Wren, J.M.; 1946; dem.
Wright, Herman; 1948; prog.
Yarborough, Don; 1962, 1964, 1968; dem.
Yarborough, Ralph W.; 1952, 1954, 1956; dem.
Young, David L.; 1982; dem.
Young, James; 1930; dem.
Zimmerman, O.F.; 1926; dem.

* — Indicates candidate was elected to the office of Governor of Texas.

† — Indicates a woman.

Party designations: dem., Democrat; rep., Republican; btrep., Black-and-Tan Republican; amer., American; comm., Communist; con., Constitution; conser., Conservative; grbk., Greenback; inddem., Independent Democrat; indfus., Independent-Fusion; laraza, La Raza; liberty, Liberty; libetar., Libertarian; peo., Populist; prog., Progressive; proh., Prohibition; refrep., Reform Republican; reorep., Reorganized Republican; soc., Socialist; socdem., Social Democrat; soclab., Socialist-Labor

Counties' Political Batting Averages

This article was written by Mike Kingston, Editor of the Texas Almanac.

By the slimmest of margins Texas remains a state where Democratic candidates running statewide can expect to win. Qualifications to the rule are needed. Democratic gubernatorial candidates have a better than even chance at elections. U.S. Senatorial candidates need to pick the right seat. But presidential candidates are another matter, since only Jimmy Carter in 1976 carried Texas for the Democrats in the past six races for the White House. He was subsequently trounced by Republican Ronald Reagan in 1980.

The Texas Almanac reviewed the results of 22 statewide elections for governor, U.S. Senate and president beginning in 1968. This year was selected because it was a watershed year between Democrat Lyndon Johnson's landslide victory in 1964 in the wake of the assassination of John F. Kennedy and Republican Richard Nixon's romp over George McGovern in 1972, when many Texas counties voted Republican for the first time since Reconstruction. Indeed, in 1968, American party George Wallace carried 21 counties, the only third-party presidential candidate to carry counties in Texas. (For rating purposes, Wallace's victories in Angelina, Bowie, Cass, Chambers, Cherokee, Crane, Glasscock, Hardin, Harrison, Jasper, Loving, Martin, Montgomery, Newton, Orange, Panola, Rusk, San Augustine, Shelby, Tyler and Upshur counties are discounted, and the county is given to the Democrats or Republicans, depending on their vote.)

Senatorial candidates fall into two distinct camps: the Houston succession and the Rusk succession (named for Sam Houston and Thomas J. Rusk, the first holders of the U.S. Senate seats from Texas). Republicans have held the Houston succession since 1961 when John Tower emerged from a field of 71 candidates to win the special election to fill the seat vacated by Lyndon B. Johnson's election as vice president in 1960. Tower was re-elected in 1966, 1972 and 1978, and Republican Phil Gramm won election to the seat in 1984, upon Towers' retirement, so Republicans have won all four races for the seat since 1968. Democrats have held the Rusk succession seat since 1875, when the radical Republican James Flanigan left office. Incumbent Lloyd Bentsen Jr. won the office in 1970 and has been re-elected in 1976, 1982 and 1988, giving the Democats a split in the eight senatorial elections since 1968.

Of eight gubernatorial elections begining in 1968, Democrats have won six, including the 1990 match between Ann Richards and Republican Clayton Williams, who entered the general election campaign with a huge lead at the polls. Only William P. Clements Jr., in 1978 and 1986, has been able to break the Democrats' strangle hold on the governor's mansion in Texas. And both his victories — over John Hill in 1978 and incumbent Mark White in 1986 — were considered major upsets. (Clements himself was an upset victim at the hands of White in 1982.)

Breaking each of these 22 selected statewide elections since 1968 down by county, Democrats hold a statistical lead in victories, mostly run up in the 1960s and 1970s in gubernatorial races. In 5,588 chances to win counties (22 elections times 254 counties), Democrats have won 3,265 counties for a "batting average" of .584; Republicans have hit .416 in the same period.

There are 34 counties ranked "Heavy Democratic" by virtue of supporting the Democratic candidate 19 or more times in the 22 elections. Another 130 counties are "Leaning Democratic" with Democratic victories in 13 to 18 elections. Republicans have 11 counties considered "Heavily Republican" and 55 counties "Leaning Republican." Twenty-four small counties are considered "Swing" by virtue of giving each party 10 to 12 victories.

Seven counties — Brooks, Cottle, Duval, Maverick, Starr, Zapata and Webb — voted straight Democratic in all 22 of the statewide elections surveyed. Five counties, Hutchinson, Randall, Smith, Ochiltree and Midland, voted for Republican candidates in 21 of the 22 races.

The coin is still in the air for future projections. In 1990, voter registration in the 164 counties rated either "Heavy" or "Leaning" Democratic totaled 3,720,-735, while in the 66 counties with high Republican preferences registration stood at 3,863,497. In the 24 small "Swing" counties, 117,267 persons were qualified to vote.

The face of Texas politics has changed in the past 22 statewide elections for governor, U.S. Senate and president, but it is uncertain whether the patterns of swings to Republicans are permanent or are an aberration.

(The following is a breakdown of the by-county votes in each of the selected statewide elections since 1968.)

Votes by County
Presidential, Senatorial, Gubernatorial Elections
Statewide 1968-1990

D=Democrat; R=Republican; T=Tie; NR=No Returns

'Heavy' means 19 or more victories; 'Lean' means 13-18 victories; 'Swing' indicates 10-12 wins.

County	P68	G68	S70	G70	P72	S72	G72	G74	P76	S76	S78	G78	P80	S82	G82	P84	S84	G86	P88	S88	S90	G90	DW/RW	Rating
Anderson	D	D	D	D	R	R	D	D	D	D	D	D	R	D	D	R	R	R	R	D	R	R	13/9	Lean Dem
Andrews	R	D	D	D	R	R	D	D	R	R	R	R	R	R	R	R	R	R	R	R	R	R	5/17	Lean GOP
Angelina	D	D	D	D	R	R	D	D	R	R	R	D	R	R	R	R	R	R	R	D	R	R	16/6	Lean Dem
Aransas	D	D	D	D	R	R	D	D	D	D	R	R	R	D	R	R	R	R	R	D	R	R	10/12	Swing
Archer	D	D	D	D	R	R	D	D	D	D	D	R	R	D	R	R	R	R	R	D	R	R	15/7	Lean Dem
Armstrong	R	R	D	D	R	R	D	D	D	D	R	R	R	R	R	R	R	R	R	R	R	R	7/15	Lean GOP
Atascosa	D	D	D	D	R	R	D	D	R	D	R	D	R	R	R	R	R	R	R	R	R	R	12/10	Swing
Austin	R	D	R	D	R	R	D	D	R	R	R	R	R	R	R	R	R	R	R	R	R	R	8/14	Lean GOP
Bailey	R	D	D	D	R	R	D	D	D	D	R	R	R	R	R	R	R	R	R	R	R	R	9/13	Lean GOP
Bandera	R	R	D	D	R	R	D	D	R	R	R	R	R	R	R	R	R	R	R	R	R	R	6/16	Lean GOP
Bastrop	D	D	D	D	R	R	D	D	D	D	D	D	D	D	R	R	D	D	D	D	D	D	18/4	Lean Dem
Baylor	D	D	D	D	R	R	D	D	D	D	D	D	R	R	D	D	R	D	R	D	R	D	18/4	Lean Dem
Bee	D	D	D	D	R	R	D	D	R	R	R	D	R	D	R	R	R	D	R	D	R	D	13/9	Lean Dem
Bell	D	D	D	D	R	R	D	D	R	R	R	D	R	R	R	R	R	R	R	D	R	D	13/9	Lean Dem
Bexar	D	D	D	D	R	D	D	D	D	D	D	D	R	D	R	R	R	D	R	D	R	D	15/7	Lean Dem
Blanco	D	D	D	D	R	R	D	D	R	R	R	D	R	R	R	R	R	R	R	R	R	D	9/13	Lean GOP
Borden	D	D	D	D	R	R	D	D	R	R	R	R	R	R	R	R	R	R	R	R	R	R	10/12	Swing
Bosque	D	D	D	D	R	R	D	D	D	D	R	D	R	R	R	R	R	R	R	D	R	D	13/9	Lean Dem
Bowie	D	D	D	D	R	R	D	D	R	D	R	D	R	R	R	D	R	R	R	D	R	D	15/7	Lean Dem
Brazoria	D	D	D	D	R	R	D	R	R	R	R	R	R	D	R	R	R	R	R	R	R	D	14/8	Lean Dem
Brazos	R	D	R	R	R	R	D	D	R	R	R	R	R	R	R	R	R	R	R	R	R	R	7/15	Lean GOP

County	P68	G68	S70	G70	P72	S72	G72	G74	P76	S76	S78	G78	P80	S82	G82	P84	S84	G86	P88	S88	S90	G90	DW/RW	Rating
Brewster	D	D	D	D	R	R	D	D	R	D	D	R	D	D	R	R	R	R	D	R	R	R	11/11	Swing
Briscoe	D	D	D	D	R	D	D	D	D	D	D	D	R	D	D	R	D	D	R	D	R	D	17/5	Lean Dem
Brooks	D	D	D	D	D	D	D	D	D	D	D	D	D	D	D	D	D	D	D	D	D	D	22/0	Heavy Dem
Brown	D	D	D	D	R	R	D	D	D	D	D	D	R	D	D	R	R	R	D	R	R	D	13/9	Lean Dem
Burleson	D	D	D	D	R	D	D	D	D	D	D	D	D	D	D	R	D	D	D	D	R	D	19/3	Heavy Dem
Burnet	D	D	D	D	R	D	D	D	D	D	D	D	R	D	D	R	R	R	D	R	R	D	13/9	Lean Dem
Caldwell	D	D	D	D	R	D	D	D	D	D	D	D	D	D	D	R	D	D	D	D	D	D	20/2	Heavy Dem
Calhoun	D	D	D	D	D	R	D	D	D	D	D	D	D	D	R	R	R	D	D	R	R	D	16/6	Lean Dem
Callahan	D	D	D	D	R	D	D	D	D	D	D	D	R	D	D	R	R	R	D	R	R	D	13/9	Lean Dem
Cameron	D	D	D	D	R	R	D	D	D	D	D	D	D	D	D	R	D	D	D	D	R	D	18/4	Lean Dem
Camp	D	D	D	D	R	D	D	D	D	D	D	D	D	D	D	R	D	D	D	R	D	D	19/3	Heavy Dem
Carson	R	R	D	D	R	R	D	D	D	D	D	D	R	D	D	R	R	R	R	D	R	R	11/11	Swing
Cass	D	D	D	D	D	D	D	D	D	D	D	D	D	D	D	R	D	D	D	R	D	D	17/5	Lean Dem
Castro	D	D	D	D	R	D	D	D	D	D	D	D	R	D	D	R	R	R	D	R	R	R	14/8	Lean Dem
Chambers	D	D	D	D	R	R	D	D	D	D	D	D	R	D	D	R	D	R	D	R	R	R	15/7	Lean Dem
Cherokee	D	D	D	D	R	R	D	D	D	D	D	D	D	D	D	R	R	R	R	D	R	R	14/8	Lean Dem
Childress	D	D	D	D	R	R	D	D	D	D	D	R	D	D	R	R	R	R	D	R	D	D	14/8	Lean Dem
Clay	D	D	D	D	R	R	D	D	D	D	D	D	D	D	D	R	R	R	D	D	R	D	17/5	Lean Dem
Cochran	D	D	D	D	R	R	D	D	D	D	D	D	R	D	D	R	R	R	R	D	R	R	13/9	Lean Dem
Coke	D	D	D	D	R	R	D	D	D	D	D	D	D	D	D	R	R	R	R	D	R	R	14/8	Lean Dem
Coleman	R	D	D	D	R	R	D	D	D	D	D	R	D	D	R	R	R	R	D	R	R	R	11/11	Swing
Collin	R	D	D	D	R	R	D	R	D	R	R	R	R	R	R	R	R	R	R	R	D	R	4/18	Lean GOP
Collingsworth	D	D	D	D	R	R	D	D	D	D	D	D	D	D	D	R	R	R	R	R	D	R	14/8	Lean Dem
Colorado	R	D	D	D	R	R	D	D	D	D	D	R	D	D	R	R	R	R	D	R	R	R	12/10	Swing
Comal	R	D	R	R	R	R	R	D	R	D	R	R	R	R	R	R	R	R	R	R	R	R	3/19	Heavy GOP
Comanche	D	D	D	D	R	R	D	D	D	D	D	D	D	D	D	R	R	R	D	D	T	D	16/5	Lean Dem
Concho	D	D	D	D	R	R	D	D	D	D	D	D	D	D	R	R	R	R	D	D	R	R	15/7	Lean Dem
Cooke	R	D	D	D	R	R	D	D	D	R	R	D	R	R	R	R	R	R	D	R	R	R	7/15	Lean GOP
Corvell	D	D	D	D	R	R	D	D	D	D	R	D	R	D	R	R	R	D	R	D	R	R	12/10	Swing
Cottle	D	D	D	D	D	D	D	D	D	D	D	D	D	D	D	D	D	D	D	D	D	D	22/0	Heavy Dem
Crane	D	D	D	D	R	R	D	D	R	D	T	R	R	R	D	R	R	R	D	R	R	R	9/12	Swing
Crockett	D	D	D	D	R	R	D	D	D	D	D	D	R	D	R	R	R	R	D	R	R	R	11/11	Swing
Crosby	D	D	D	D	R	D	D	D	D	D	D	D	R	D	D	D	D	D	D	D	R	D	19/3	Heavy Dem
Culberson	D	D	D	D	R	R	D	D	D	D	D	R	R	R	R	D	R	R	D	D	R	D	13/9	Lean Dem
Dallam	R	R	D	D	R	R	D	D	D	D	D	R	R	D	R	R	R	R	R	R	R	R	7/15	Lean GOP
Dallas	R	R	R	R	R	R	R	D	R	R	R	R	R	D	R	R	R	R	R	D	R	D	4/18	Lean GOP
Dawson	R	D	D	D	R	R	D	D	R	D	R	D	R	R	R	D	R	R	R	R	R	R	9/13	Lean Dem
DeWitt	R	D	D	D	R	R	D	D	R	D	R	R	R	R	R	R	R	R	R	R	R	R	8/14	Lean GOP
Deaf Smith	R	D	R	D	R	R	D	D	R	R	R	R	R	R	R	R	R	R	R	R	R	R	5/17	Lean GOP
Delta	D	D	D	D	R	D	D	D	D	D	D	D	D	D	D	R	D	D	D	D	R	D	19/3	Heavy Dem
Denton	R	D	D	R	R	D	D	R	D	R	R	R	R	R	R	R	R	R	R	R	R	D	3/19	Heavy GOP
Dickens	D	D	D	D	R	D	D	D	D	D	D	D	D	D	D	D	D	D	D	D	D	D	21/1	Heavy Dem
Dimmit	D	D	D	D	R	D	D	D	D	D	D	D	D	D	D	D	D	D	D	D	D	D	21/1	Heavy Dem
Donley	R	D	D	D	R	R	D	D	D	D	D	D	R	D	D	R	R	R	R	R	R	R	12/10	Swing
Duval	D	D	D	D	D	D	D	D	D	D	D	D	D	D	D	D	D	D	D	D	D	D	22/0	Heavy Dem
Eastland	D	D	D	D	R	R	D	D	D	D	D	D	D	D	R	R	R	R	D	D	R	D	13/9	Heavy Dem
Ector	R	R	R	D	R	R	R	D	R	R	R	R	R	R	R	R	R	R	R	R	R	R	2/20	Heavy GOP
Edwards	R	D	D	D	R	R	D	D	D	D	R	R	R	R	R	R	D	D	R	R	R	R	7/15	Lean GOP
El Paso	D	D	D	D	R	R	D	D	D	D	R	D	D	D	D	R	R	R	D	D	R	D	16/6	Lean Dem
Ellis	D	D	D	D	R	R	D	D	D	D	D	D	R	D	D	R	R	R	D	R	R	D	13/9	Lean Dem
Erath	D	D	D	D	R	R	D	D	D	D	D	D	D	D	D	R	R	R	D	R	R	D	14/8	Lean Dem
Falls	D	D	D	D	R	R	D	D	D	D	D	D	D	D	R	D	D	D	D	D	R	D	19/3	Heavy Dem
Fannin	D	D	D	D	R	D	D	D	D	D	D	D	R	D	D	R	D	D	D	D	R	D	19/3	Heavy Dem
Fayette	R	D	D	D	R	R	D	D	D	D	D	D	D	D	D	R	R	R	D	R	R	R	12/10	Swing
Fisher	D	D	D	D	R	D	D	D	D	D	D	D	D	D	D	D	D	D	D	D	D	D	21/1	Heavy Dem
Floyd	R	D	D	D	R	R	D	D	D	D	D	D	D	D	D	R	R	R	D	R	R	R	12/10	Swing
Foard	D	D	D	D	R	D	D	D	D	D	D	D	D	D	D	R	D	D	D	D	D	D	20/2	Heavy Dem
Fort Bend	R	D	D	D	R	R	D	R	D	R	D	R	R	R	R	R	R	R	D	R	R	R	7/15	Lean GOP
Franklin	D	D	D	D	R	R	D	D	D	D	D	D	D	D	R	R	R	R	D	R	R	D	16/6	Lean Dem
Freestone	D	D	D	D	R	R	D	D	D	D	D	D	D	D	D	R	R	R	D	R	R	D	14/8	Lean Dem
Frio	D	D	D	D	R	D	D	D	D	D	D	D	D	D	D	D	D	D	D	D	D	D	21/1	Heavy Dem
Gaines	R	D	D	D	R	R	D	D	D	D	D	D	R	D	D	R	R	R	D	R	R	D	11/11	Swing
Galveston	D	D	D	D	R	R	D	D	D	D	D	D	R	D	D	R	D	D	D	D	R	D	19/3	Heavy Dem
Garza	D	D	D	D	R	R	D	D	D	D	D	D	R	D	D	R	R	R	D	R	R	D	13/9	Lean Dem
Gillespie	R	R	R	R	R	D	D	D	R	R	R	R	R	R	R	R	R	R	R	R	R	R	2/20	Heavy GOP
Glasscock	R	D	D	D	R	R	D	D	D	R	R	R	R	R	R	R	R	R	D	R	R	R	7/15	Lean GOP
Goliad	R	D	D	D	R	D	D	D	D	R	D	D	D	R	R	R	R	R	D	R	R	R	10/12	Swing
Gonzales	D	D	D	D	R	R	D	D	D	D	D	D	R	D	D	R	R	R	D	R	R	D	13/9	Lean Dem
Gray	R	R	D	D	R	R	R	D	R	R	R	R	R	R	R	R	R	R	R	R	R	R	2/20	Heavy GOP
Grayson	D	D	D	D	R	D	D	D	D	D	D	D	R	D	D	R	R	R	D	R	R	R	15/7	Lean Dem
Gregg	R	D	R	R	R	R	R	D	R	R	R	R	R	R	R	R	R	R	R	R	R	R	4/18	Lean GOP
Grimes	D	D	D	D	R	R	D	D	D	D	D	D	R	D	D	R	R	R	D	R	R	R	15/7	Lean Dem
Guadalupe	R	D	D	D	R	R	D	D	R	D	R	R	R	R	R	R	R	R	D	R	R	D	8/14	Lean GOP
Hale	R	D	D	D	R	R	D	D	R	D	R	D	R	R	R	D	R	R	R	R	R	R	9/13	Lean Dem
Hall	D	D	D	D	R	D	D	D	D	D	D	D	D	D	D	R	D	D	D	D	R	D	18/4	Lean Dem
Hamilton	R	D	D	D	R	R	D	D	D	D	D	D	D	D	D	R	R	R	D	R	R	R	12/10	Swing
Hansford	R	R	R	R	R	R	D	D	R	R	R	R	R	R	R	R	R	R	R	R	R	R	2/20	Heavy GOP
Hardeman	D	D	D	R	R	D	D	D	D	D	D	D	D	D	D	R	R	R	D	R	R	D	16/6	Lean Dem
Hardin	D	D	D	D	R	D	D	D	D	D	D	D	D	D	D	R	D	D	D	D	R	D	18/4	Lean Dem
Harris	R	D	D	D	R	R	D	D	R	D	R	R	R	R	R	R	R	R	D	R	R	R	7/15	Lean GOP
Harrison	D	D	D	D	R	R	D	D	D	D	D	D	R	D	D	R	R	R	D	R	R	D	14/8	Lean Dem
Hartley	R	R	R	D	R	R	D	D	R	R	R	R	R	R	R	R	R	R	R	R	R	R	4/18	Lean GOP
Haskell	D	D	D	D	R	D	D	D	D	D	D	D	R	D	D	R	D	D	R	D	R	D	17/5	Lean Dem
Hays	D	D	D	D	R	R	D	D	D	D	D	D	R	D	D	R	R	R	D	R	R	R	15/7	Lean Dem
Hemphill	R	R	D	R	R	R	D	D	D	D	D	D	R	R	R	R	R	R	R	R	R	D	4/18	Lean GOP
Henderson	D	D	D	D	R	R	D	D	D	D	D	D	R	D	D	R	R	R	D	R	R	D	15/7	Lean Dem

County	P68	G68	S70	G70	P72	S72	G72	G74	P76	S76	S78	G78	P80	S82	G82	P84	S84	G86	P88	S88	S90	G90	DW/RW	Rating
Hidalgo	D	D	D	D	R	R	D	D	D	D	D	D	D	D	D	D	D	D	D	D	R	D	19/3	Heavy Dem
Hill	D	D	D	D	R	R	D	D	D	D	D	D	D	D	D	R	R	R	D	R	D	D	15/7	Lean Dem
Hockley	D	D	D	D	R	R	D	D	D	D	D	D	R	D	D	R	R	R	R	D	R	R	13/9	Lean Dem
Hood	D	D	D	D	R	D	D	D	D	D	D	D	D	D	D	R	R	R	R	D	R	D	14/8	Lean Dem
Hopkins	D	D	D	D	R	D	D	D	D	D	D	D	D	D	D	R	R	R	R	D	R	D	16/6	Lean Dem
Houston	D	D	D	D	R	D	D	D	D	D	D	D	D	D	D	R	R	R	R	D	R	D	16/6	Lean Dem
Howard	D	D	D	D	R	R	D	D	D	D	R	R	R	D	D	R	R	R	R	D	R	R	11/11	Swing
Hudspeth	D	D	D	D	R	R	D	D	D	D	R	R	R	D	D	R	R	R	D	D	R	R	12/10	Swing
Hunt	D	D	D	D	R	R	D	D	D	D	D	D	R	D	D	R	R	R	R	D	R	R	13/9	Lean Dem
Hutchinson	R	R	R	R	R	R	R	D	R	R	R	R	R	R	R	R	R	R	R	R	R	R	1/21	Heavy GOP
Irion	R	D	D	D	R	R	D	D	R	D	D	R	D	R	R	R	R	R	R	D	R	R	9/13	Lean GOP
Jack	D	D	D	D	R	R	D	D	D	D	D	D	R	D	D	R	R	R	R	D	R	R	13/9	Lean Dem
Jackson	D	D	D	D	R	R	D	D	D	D	D	D	R	D	D	R	R	R	R	D	R	R	13/9	Lean Dem
Jasper	D	D	D	D	R	D	D	D	D	D	D	D	D	D	D	R	D	R	D	D	R	D	18/4	Lean Dem
Jeff Davis	D	D	D	D	R	D	D	D	D	D	R	R	D	R	R	R	R	R	R	D	R	R	10/12	Swing
Jefferson	D	R	D	D	R	R	D	D	D	D	D	D	D	D	D	D	D	D	D	D	R	D	18/4	Lean Dem
Jim Hogg	D	D	D	D	D	R	D	D	D	D	D	D	D	D	D	D	D	D	D	D	D	D	21/1	Heavy Dem
Jim Wells	D	D	D	D	D	R	D	D	D	D	D	D	D	D	D	D	D	D	D	D	D	D	21/1	Heavy Dem
Johnson	D	D	D	D	R	R	D	D	D	D	D	D	R	D	D	R	R	R	R	D	R	R	13/9	Lean Dem
Jones	D	D	D	D	R	R	D	D	D	D	D	D	D	D	D	R	R	R	R	D	R	R	14/8	Lean Dem
Karnes	D	D	D	D	R	D	D	D	D	D	R	D	R	D	D	R	R	R	R	D	R	R	14/8	Lean Dem
Kaufman	D	D	D	D	R	R	D	D	D	D	D	D	D	D	D	R	R	R	R	D	R	R	16/6	Lean Dem
Kendall	R	R	R	R	R	R	D	D	R	R	R	R	R	R	R	R	R	R	R	R	R	R	2/20	Heavy GOP
Kenedy	D	D	D	D	R	D	D	D	D	D	D	D	R	D	D	D	D	D	D	D	R	D	19/3	Heavy Dem
Kent	D	D	D	D	R	D	D	D	D	D	D	D	D	D	D	R	R	D	D	R	R	R	16/6	Lean Dem
Kerr	R	D	R	R	R	R	D	D	R	R	R	R	R	R	R	R	R	R	R	R	R	R	3/19	Heavy GOP
Kimble	R	D	D	D	R	R	D	D	D	R	D	R	R	D	R	R	R	R	D	R	R	R	8/14	Lean GOP
King	D	D	D	D	R	R	D	D	D	D	D	D	R	R	R	R	R	R	D	R	R	R	11/11	Swing
Kinney	D	D	D	D	R	D	NR	D	D	D	D	R	R	R	D	D	D	R	D	R	R	R	11/10	Swing
Kleberg	D	D	D	D	R	D	D	D	D	D	D	D	D	R	D	R	R	D	D	D	R	D	18/4	Lean Dem
Knox	D	D	D	D	D	R	D	D	D	D	D	D	D	D	D	R	D	R	D	D	D	D	19/3	Heavy Dem
LaSalle	D	D	D	D	D	R	D	D	D	D	D	D	D	R	D	D	D	D	D	D	D	D	20/2	Heavy Dem
Lamar	D	D	D	D	R	R	D	D	D	D	R	D	D	D	D	D	D	R	D	R	R	D	15/7	Lean Dem
Lamb	R	D	D	D	R	R	D	D	D	D	D	D	R	D	D	R	R	R	R	D	R	R	11/11	Swing
Lampasas	D	D	D	D	R	R	D	D	D	D	D	D	R	R	R	D	R	R	R	D	R	R	10/12	Swing
Lavaca	D	D	D	D	R	R	D	D	D	D	D	D	R	D	D	R	R	R	R	D	R	R	14/8	Lean Dem
Lee	D	D	D	D	R	R	D	D	D	D	D	D	R	D	D	R	R	R	R	D	R	R	14/8	Lean Dem
Leon	D	D	D	D	R	R	D	D	D	D	D	D	R	D	D	R	R	R	R	D	R	R	14/8	Lean Dem
Leon	D	D	D	D	R	R	D	D	D	D	D	D	D	D	D	R	R	R	R	D	R	R	15/7	Lean Dem
Liberty	D	D	D	D	R	D	D	D	D	D	D	D	D	D	D	R	R	R	R	D	R	R	15/7	Lean Dem
Limestone	D	D	D	D	R	D	D	D	D	D	D	D	D	D	D	R	R	R	R	D	R	D	17/5	Lean Dem
Lipscomb	R	R	R	R	R	R	D	R	D	R	R	R	R	R	R	R	R	R	R	R	R	R	2/20	Heavy GOP
Live Oak	R	D	D	D	R	R	D	D	D	D	R	R	D	R	R	R	R	R	R	D	R	R	9/13	Lean GOP
Llano	D	D	D	D	R	R	D	D	D	D	D	D	R	D	R	D	R	R	R	D	R	R	12/10	Swing
Loving	R	D	D	D	R	R	D	D	D	D	R	R	D	R	R	R	R	R	R	D	R	R	7/15	Lean GOP
Lubbock	R	D	R	D	R	R	D	R	D	R	R	R	R	R	R	R	R	R	R	D	R	R	3/19	Heavy GOP
Lynn	D	D	D	D	R	R	D	D	D	D	D	D	D	D	D	R	R	R	R	D	R	R	13/9	Lean Dem
Madison	D	D	D	D	R	R	D	D	D	D	D	D	D	D	D	R	R	R	R	D	R	D	15/7	Lean Dem
Marion	D	D	D	D	R	R	D	D	D	D	D	D	D	D	D	D	D	D	D	D	R	D	18/4	Lean Dem
Martin	R	D	D	D	R	R	D	D	D	D	R	D	D	D	D	R	R	R	R	D	R	R	11/11	Swing
Mason	R	D	D	D	R	R	D	D	D	D	R	R	R	D	R	R	R	R	R	D	R	R	8/14	Lean GOP
Matagorda	D	D	D	D	R	D	D	D	D	D	D	D	D	D	D	D	D	D	D	D	D	D	22/0	Heavy Dem
McCulloch	D	D	D	D	R	R	D	D	D	D	D	D	R	D	D	D	R	R	R	D	R	R	14/8	Lean Dem
McLennan	D	D	D	D	R	R	D	D	D	D	D	D	D	D	D	R	R	R	R	D	R	D	14/8	Lean Dem
McMullen	R	D	D	D	R	R	D	D	D	R	D	R	R	R	R	R	R	R	R	R	R	R	6/16	Lean GOP
Medina	D	D	D	D	R	R	D	D	D	D	R	R	R	D	D	R	R	R	R	D	R	R	11/11	Swing
Menard	R	D	D	D	R	R	D	D	D	D	D	D	R	D	D	R	R	R	D	R	R	R	12/10	Swing
Midland	R	R	R	R	R	R	R	D	R	R	R	R	R	R	R	R	R	R	R	R	R	R	1/21	Heavy GOP
Milam	D	D	D	D	R	R	D	D	D	D	D	D	D	D	D	D	D	D	D	D	D	D	20/2	Heavy Dem
Mills	D	D	D	D	R	R	D	D	D	D	D	D	D	D	D	R	R	R	D	D	R	D	14/8	Lean Dem
Mitchell	D	D	D	D	R	R	D	D	D	D	D	D	D	D	D	R	R	R	D	D	R	D	15/7	Lean Dem
Montague	D	D	D	D	R	R	D	D	D	D	D	D	D	D	D	R	R	R	R	D	R	D	16/6	Lean Dem
Montgomery	D	R	D	R	D	R	R	D	D	D	D	R	R	R	D	R	R	R	R	D	R	R	5/17	Lean GOP
Moore	R	R	D	D	R	R	D	R	D	R	D	R	R	R	R	R	R	R	R	R	R	R	5/17	Lean GOP
Morris	D	D	D	D	R	R	D	D	D	D	D	D	D	D	D	D	D	R	D	D	R	D	20/2	Heavy Dem
Motley	R	D	D	D	R	R	D	D	D	R	D	R	R	D	R	R	R	R	D	R	R	R	9/13	Lean GOP
Nacogdoches	D	D	D	D	D	R	D	D	D	R	D	D	D	D	D	D	D	D	D	R	D	R	12/10	Swing
Navarro	D	D	D	D	R	R	D	D	D	D	D	D	D	D	D	D	D	R	D	D	R	D	18/4	Lean Dem
Newton	D	D	D	D	R	R	D	D	D	D	D	D	D	D	D	D	D	R	D	D	R	R	21/1	Heavy Dem
Nolan	D	D	D	D	R	R	D	D	D	D	D	D	D	D	D	R	R	R	D	D	R	D	15/7	Lean Dem
Nueces	D	D	D	D	R	R	D	D	D	D	D	D	D	D	D	D	R	D	D	D	R	R	17/5	Lean Dem
Ochiltree	R	R	R	R	R	R	R	D	R	R	D	R	R	R	R	R	R	R	R	R	R	R	1/21	Heavy GOP
Oldham	R	R	D	D	R	R	D	D	D	D	D	R	D	R	R	R	R	R	R	D	R	R	11/11	Swing
Orange	D	D	D	D	R	R	D	D	D	D	D	D	D	D	D	D	D	D	D	D	R	D	20/2	Heavy Dem
Palo Pinto	D	D	D	D	R	R	D	D	D	D	D	D	D	D	D	R	R	R	R	D	R	D	15/7	Lean Dem
Panola	D	D	D	D	R	R	D	D	D	D	D	D	D	D	D	R	R	R	R	D	R	R	14/8	Lean Dem
Parker	D	D	D	D	R	R	D	D	D	D	D	D	D	D	R	R	R	R	R	D	R	R	13/9	Lean Dem
Parmer	R	D	D	D	R	R	D	D	D	D	R	D	R	D	R	R	R	R	D	R	R	R	7/15	Lean GOP
Pecos	D	D	D	D	R	R	D	D	D	D	D	D	R	D	D	R	R	R	R	D	R	R	11/11	Swing
Polk	D	D	D	D	R	D	D	D	D	D	D	D	D	D	D	R	R	R	R	D	R	D	17/5	Lean Dem
Potter	R	R	R	R	R	R	D	R	D	R	R	R	R	R	R	R	R	R	R	R	R	R	3/19	Heavy GOP
Presidio	D	D	D	D	D	R	D	D	D	D	D	D	D	D	D	D	D	R	D	D	D	D	21/1	Heavy Dem
Rains	D	D	D	D	R	R	D	D	D	D	D	D	D	D	D	D	R	R	D	D	R	R	17/5	Lean Dem
Randall	R	R	R	R	R	R	D	D	R	D	R	R	D	R	R	R	R	R	D	R	R	R	1/21	Heavy GOP
Reagan	R	D	D	D	R	R	D	D	R	D	D	R	D	R	R	R	R	R	D	R	R	R	10/12	Swing

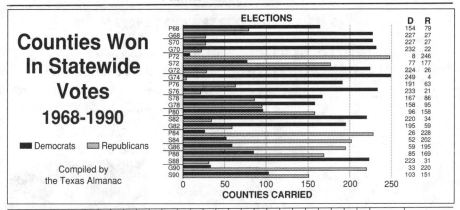

Counties Won In Statewide Votes 1968-1990

■ Democrats ▨ Republicans

Compiled by the Texas Almanac

County	P68	G68	S70	G70	P72	S72	G72	G74	P76	S76	S78	G78	P80	S82	G82	P84	S84	G86	P88	S88	S90	G90	DW/RW	Rating
Real..........	R	D	D	D	R	R	R	D	D	D	D	D	R	R	D	R	R	R	R	D	R	R	11/11	Swing
Red River......	D	D	D	D	R	D	D	D	D	D	D	D	D	D	D	R	D	D	D	D	R	D	19/3	Heavy Dem
Reeves........	R	D	D	D	R	R	R	D	D	D	D	D	R	R	D	R	D	D	D	R	D	R	15/7	Lean Dem
Refugio.......	D	D	D	D	R	R	D	D	D	D	D	D	D	D	D	R	R	R	R	D	R	R	16/6	Lean Dem
Roberts.......	R	R	R	R	R	R	R	D	D	R	D	R	R	R	R	R	R	R	R	R	R	R	3/19	Heavy GOP
Robertson.....	D	D	D	D	R	R	D	D	D	R	D	R	R	R	D	D	D	D	D	D	D	D	21/1	Heavy Dem
Rockwall......	D	D	D	D	R	R	R	D	D	D	R	R	R	R	R	R	R	R	R	R	R	R	6/16	Lean GOP
Runnels	R	D	D	D	R	R	R	D	D	D	R	R	R	R	R	R	R	R	R	R	R	R	10/12	Swing
Rusk..........	D	D	D	D	R	R	R	D	D	R	D	R	R	R	D	R	R	R	R	D	R	R	9/13	Lean GOP
Sabine........	D	D	D	D	D	R	R	D	D	D	D	D	D	D	D	R	D	R	D	D	D	D	18/4	Lean Dem
San Augustine....	D	D	D	D	D	R	R	D	D	D	D	D	D	D	D	D	R	D	D	D	R	D	18/4	Lean Dem
San Jacinto	D	D	D	D	D	R	R	D	D	D	D	D	D	D	D	R	R	R	D	D	R	D	16/6	Lean Dem
San Patricio	D	D	D	D	R	R	D	D	D	D	D	D	D	R	D	D	R	R	R	D	R	D	16/6	Lean Dem
San Saba......	D	D	D	D	R	R	D	D	D	R	D	R	R	R	D	D	R	R	R	D	R	R	15/7	Lean Dem
Schleicher.......	R	D	D	D	R	R	R	D	D	R	D	R	R	R	D	R	R	R	R	D	R	R	9/13	Swing
Scurry........	D	D	D	D	R	R	R	D	D	R	D	R	R	R	D	R	R	R	R	D	R	R	13/9	Lean Dem
Shackelford......	D	D	D	D	R	R	R	D	D	D	D	D	D	R	D	R	R	D	D	D	R	D	13/9	Lean Dem
Shelby........	D	D	D	D	R	R	R	D	D	D	D	D	D	D	D	R	D	D	D	D	R	D	17/5	Lean Dem
Sherman.......	R	R	R	D	R	R	R	D	D	D	R	R	R	R	R	R	R	R	R	R	R	R	4/18	Lean GOP
Smith	R	R	R	R	R	R	R	R	R	R	R	R	R	R	R	R	R	R	R	D	R	R	1/21	Heavy GOP
Somervell	D	D	D	D	R	D	D	D	D	D	D	D	D	D	R	R	R	R	R	D	R	R	15/7	Lean Dem
Starr.........	D	D	D	D	R	R	D	D	D	D	D	D	D	D	D	D	D	D	D	D	D	D	22/0	Heavy Dem
Stephens........	R	D	D	D	R	R	R	D	D	D	R	R	R	R	R	R	R	R	R	R	R	R	10/12	Swing
Sterling......	R	D	D	D	R	R	R	D	D	D	R	R	R	D	R	R	R	R	R	D	R	R	9/13	Lean GOP
Stonewall.....	D	D	D	D	R	D	D	D	D	D	D	D	D	D	D	R	D	D	D	D	D	D	20/2	Heavy Dem
Sutton........	R	D	D	D	R	R	R	D	D	R	D	R	R	R	R	R	R	R	R	D	R	R	8/14	Lean GOP
Swisher.......	D	D	D	D	R	D	D	D	D	D	D	D	D	D	D	R	D	D	D	D	D	D	21/1	Heavy Dem
Tarrant........	R	D	D	R	R	R	R	R	D	R	D	R	R	R	R	R	R	R	R	D	R	R	8/14	Lean GOP
Taylor........	R	D	D	D	R	R	R	R	D	R	D	R	R	R	D	R	R	R	R	D	R	R	7/15	Lean GOP
Terrell	R	D	R	D	R	R	R	D	D	D	R	D	R	R	D	R	R	D	D	R	D	D	12/10	Swing
Terry.........	R	D	D	D	R	R	R	D	D	D	R	D	R	R	D	R	R	D	R	R	D	D	12/10	Swing
Throckmorton....	D	D	D	D	D	R	D	D	D	D	D	D	D	D	D	R	R	D	D	R	D	D	17/5	Lean Dem
Titus.........	D	D	D	D	R	R	D	D	D	D	D	D	R	R	D	R	R	D	D	D	R	D	18/4	Lean Dem
Tom Green	R	D	D	D	R	R	R	D	D	R	D	R	R	R	D	R	R	R	R	D	R	R	9/13	Lean GOP
Travis........	D	D	D	D	R	R	D	D	D	D	D	D	D	D	D	D	D	D	D	D	D	D	18/4	Lean Dem
Trinity	D	D	D	D	R	R	D	D	D	D	D	D	D	D	D	R	D	D	D	D	R	D	18/4	Lean Dem
Tyler..........	D	D	D	D	R	R	D	D	D	D	D	D	D	D	D	R	R	D	D	D	R	D	15/7	Lean Dem
Upshur........	D	D	D	D	R	R	R	D	D	D	D	D	D	R	D	R	R	R	R	D	R	D	15/7	Lean Dem
Upton	R	D	D	D	R	R	R	R	D	R	D	R	R	R	D	R	R	R	R	D	R	R	8/14	Lean GOP
Uvalde........	R	D	D	D	R	R	R	D	D	R	D	R	R	R	D	R	R	R	R	D	R	R	9/13	Lean GOP
Val Verde	D	D	D	D	R	R	R	D	D	D	D	D	R	D	D	R	R	R	D	D	R	D	15/7	Lean Dem
Van Zandt.....	D	D	D	D	R	R	D	D	D	D	R	R	R	R	D	R	R	R	R	D	R	R	14/8	Lean Dem
Victoria......	R	D	D	D	R	R	R	D	D	R	R	R	R	R	D	R	R	R	R	D	R	R	6/16	Lean GOP
Walker........	D	D	D	D	R	R	D	D	D	D	R	D	R	R	D	R	R	R	R	D	R	D	15/7	Lean Dem
Waller........	D	D	D	D	R	R	D	D	D	D	R	D	R	R	D	R	R	D	D	R	D	D	18/4	Lean Dem
Ward..........	R	D	D	D	R	R	R	D	D	R	D	R	R	R	D	R	R	R	R	D	R	R	9/13	Lean GOP
Washington......	R	D	R	D	R	R	R	R	D	R	D	R	R	R	D	R	R	D	D	R	D	D	7/15	Lean GOP
Webb..........	D	D	D	D	D	D	D	D	D	D	D	D	D	D	D	D	D	D	D	D	D	D	22/0	Heavy Dem
Whaton........	D	D	D	D	R	R	D	D	D	D	D	D	R	R	D	R	R	R	R	D	R	D	14/8	Lean Dem
Wheeler.......	R	R	D	D	R	R	R	D	D	D	R	R	R	R	D	R	R	R	R	D	R	D	12/10	Swing
Wichita........	D	D	D	D	R	R	D	D	D	D	R	R	R	R	D	R	R	R	R	D	R	D	14/8	Swing
Wilbarger.....	D	D	D	D	R	R	D	D	D	D	R	R	R	R	D	R	R	R	R	D	R	D	14/8	Lean Dem
Willacy.......	D	D	D	D	R	R	D	D	D	D	D	D	D	D	D	R	D	D	D	D	R	D	20/2	Heavy Dem
Williamson	D	D	D	D	R	R	D	D	D	D	R	R	R	R	D	R	R	R	R	D	R	D	13/9	Lean Dem
Wilson	D	D	D	D	R	R	D	D	D	D	R	D	R	R	D	R	R	R	R	D	R	D	14/8	Lean Dem
Winkler.......	R	D	D	D	R	R	R	D	D	R	D	R	R	R	D	R	R	R	R	D	R	R	9/13	Lean GOP
Wise	D	D	D	D	R	R	R	D	D	D	D	D	R	R	D	R	R	R	R	D	R	D	15/7	Lean Dem
Wood	D	D	D	D	R	R	R	D	D	D	D	D	R	R	D	R	R	R	R	D	R	D	13/9	Lean Dem
Yoakum........	R	D	D	D	R	R	R	D	D	R	D	R	R	R	D	R	R	R	R	D	R	R	7/15	Lean GOP
Young.........	D	D	D	D	R	R	R	D	D	D	R	R	R	R	D	R	R	R	R	D	R	D	13/9	Lean Dem
Zapata........	D	D	D	D	R	D	D	D	D	D	D	D	D	D	D	D	D	D	D	D	D	D	22/0	Heavy Dem
Zavala........	D	D	D	D	R	D	D	D	D	D	D	D	D	D	D	D	D	D	D	D	D	D	21/1	Heavy Dem

Summary: Heavy Dem: 34; Lean Dem: 130; Swing: 24; Heavy GOP: 11; Lean GOP: 55

Party Organizations

Democratic State Executive Committee

Chairman, Bob Slagle, Box 1244, Sherman 75090; **Vice Chairman,** Hazel Obey, Box 6095, Austin 78762; **Vice Chairman For Financial Affairs,** Hugo Berlanga, Box 2910, Austin 78768; **Secretary,** Steve Corley, 314 Birchwood, Garland 75043; **Treasurer,** Sandra Martinez, Box 543, Kyle 78640. **Office Address:** 815 Brazos, Ste. 200, Austin 78701.

National Committee Members: Millie Bruner, Grand Prairie; Billie Carr, Houston; Paul G. Gray, Austin; Al Edwards, Houston; Ed Miller, Texarkana; Domingo Garcia, Dallas; Elizabeth Lara, Houston; K. T. McLeaish, Odessa; Wm. "Billy" Leo, La Joya; Martha Singleton, Fort Worth; Ruth Ann Skaff, Washington, D.C.

District—Member and Address.

1.—Lynda Phillips, Box 591, Gilmer; Lowell Cable, 858 Gilmer, Sulphur Springs 75482.
2.—Mary Elizabeth Jackson, Box 7678, Tyler 75711; Charles P. Elliott, 1407 Cowan, Commerce 75428.
3.—Erma Lewis, 114 Belvedere, Conroe 77301; J. A. McMahon, Rt. 8, Box 511, Livingston 77351.
4.—Irmalyn Thomas, 2235 Lela, Beaumont 77705; Dewey Updegraff, 4463 Memorial Dr., Orange 77630.
5.—Jennifer Yezak, Box 488, Bremond 76629; Jim Carter, 1724 18th, Huntsville 77340.
6.—Sheryl Roppolo, 602 Lakeside, Channelview 77530; R. C. Jones, 6019 Mohawk, Houston 77016.
7.—Mary C. Burke, 9933 Neunes, Houston 77080; Stephen I. Marak III, 11922 Pebble Rock, Houston 77077.
8.—Cynthia Morton, 3710 Corona, Garland 75044; Robert Mayer Jr., 4423 Woodfin, Dallas 75220.
9.—Martha McGregor, 1206 E. Franklin, Hillsboro 76645; John Cullar, 125 Karem, Waco 76710.
10.—Brenda Brimer, 5600 Oak Hills Dr., Colleyville 76034; T. C. Gillespie, 909 Jerry Ln., Bedford 76022.
11.—F.G. (Jean) Wortham, 3707 Longwood, Pasadena 77503; James Edwards, 5817 Woodrow, Texas City 77591.
12.—Barbara McMahon, 1805 Barron Lane, Fort Worth 76112; Grover Swift, 749 N. Main, Fort Worth 76106.
13.—Willie Belle Boone, 9211 Dulcimer, Houston 77051; Raphus Foley Jr., 511 Idaho, Houston 77021.
14.—Thressa Ali, 1706 Gatlinburg, Pflugerville 78660; Paz Pena, 1104 Austin Highland, Austin 78745.
15.—Esther Campos, 1126 Weaver, Houston 77023; Ray Paige, 3806 Keeland, Houston 77093.
16.—Bobbie Holbrook, 6554 Kingsbury, Dallas 75231; Ken Molberg, 5640 Swiss, Dallas 75214.
17.—Kay Bell, 8532 Maplecrest, Houston 77099; Harrison Gregg Jr., 3442 El Dorado Blvd., Missouri City 77459.
18.—Diana Rhodes, Box 37, Nursery 77976; Clint Winters, 418 Wichita, Lockhart 78644.
19.—Ruth McClendon, 3811 Willowwood, San Antonio 78219; Nicki Roberson, 5111 Idaho, San Antonio 78218.
20.—Lana Peterson, 2208 Post Oak Dr., Portland 78374; Martin Garcia, Box 578, Kingsville 78363.
21.—Rebecca Trevino, Box 219, Leming 78050; John Taylor, 5 Spyglass, McQueeney 78123.
22.—Nancy Brannon, 4222 Springmeadow, Flower Mound 75028; Harris Worcester, 107 Vineyard, Weatherford 76087.
23.—Yvonne Davis, 4036 Shadyhollow, Dallas 75233; Tim Thetford, 1411 Ferndale, Dallas 75224.
24.—Kim Lanham, Box 697, Little River 76554; Eddie Shell, Box 719, Burnet 78611.
25.—Janet Massey, Box 138, Midland 79702; Raul Garcia, 3209 Rock Brook, San Angelo 76904.
26.—Bonnie Terry, 2552 W. Woodlawn, San Antonio 78228; John J. Murnin, 319 Montfort, San Antonio 78216.
27.—Frances Domanski, Rt. 1, Box 120, San Benito 78586; Mike Sinder, 821 Nolana, McAllen 78504.
28.—V. E. Hollingsworth, 4613 Dakota, Odessa 79762; Sam Ellis, Rt. 2, Box 120, Southland 79364.
29.—Jesse Carrasco, 3300 Pershing, El Paso 79903; Jose Raul Kennard, 72 Waltham, El Paso 79922.
30.—Dorthy Wise, 1308 Sunnyside Ln., Wichita Falls 76303; Calvin Gambill, 711 W. California, Box 526, Seymour 76380.
31.—Brenda Barrett, 4 Havenwood Circle, Canyon 79015; Mack Sansing, Box 126, Canadian 79014.

YOUNG DEMOCRATS

Pres., Marissa Marmalejo, 1024 W. Schunior, Edinburg 78539; Vice Pres., Patrick Barkman, 8014 Woodway, 1086, Waco 76712.

COUNTY CHAIRMAN'S ASSOCIATION

Robert Mica, Box 394, Flatonia 78941; Maxine Molberg, 143 E. Main, Fredericksburg 78624.

Republican State Executive Committee

Chairman, Fred Meyer, 2121 San Jacinto, 895, LB-5, Dallas 75201; **Vice Chairman,** Gayle D. West, 4030 Fox Meadow, Pasadena 77504; **Secretary,** Diane Rath, 138 Sharon Dr., San Antonio 78216; **Treasurer,** Martha Weisend, 8238 San Benito Way, Dallas 75218; **Office Address:** 211 E. 7th, 620, Austin 78701; **General Counsel,** Kenneth W. Anderson Jr., 1601 Elm, 3000, Dallas 75201.

Fred Meyer of Dallas is state chairman of the Republican party.

National Committeeman, Ernest Angelo Jr., 410 N. Main, Midland 79701; **National Committeewoman,** Mrs. Penny Butler, 819 Briar Ridge, Houston 77057.

1.—Joyce Hugman, Rt. 3, Box 310, Gladewater 75647; Jay Wommack, 6500 Summerhill Rd., Texarkana 75503.
2.—Don W. Kent, 909 ESE Loop 323, 777, Tyler 75701; Jane Oswalt, Rt. 8, Box 905, Tyler 75703.
3.—John J. Naugle, 58 Savannah Park, Conroe 77302; Mary Pluff, 386 Olive, Jasper 75951.
4.—Thurl E. Wood, 228 Ridgewood, Bridge City 77611; Barbara Jackson, 1412 N. 18th, Nederland 77627.
5.—Richard W. Stadelmann, Rt. 5, Box 57, Brenham 77833; Florace Kling, 309 Pershing, College Station 77840.
6.—Tom Cottar, 1204 Mesquite Ln., Baytown 77521; Wilda Lindstrom, 12843 Eastbrook, Houston 77013.
7.—Jim Vaughn, 3803 Black Cricket Ct., Humble 77396; Judy Smith, 9547 Enstone Cr., Spring 77379.
8.—Bob Driegert, 3 Shadywood Pl., Richardson 75080; Harriett J. Armstrong, 4843 Stony Ford Dr., Dallas 75287.
9.—Scott Kurth, 1666 N. Hampton, 200, DeSoto 75115; Sarilee Ferguson, 2317 North 50th, Waco 76710.
10.—James Cribbs, Box 13060, Arlington 76094; Karen K. Cameron, 1210 Timber Ridge Dr., Euless 76039.
11.—Paul J. Cunningham, P.O. Box 1984, Galveston 77550; Patricia Musgrave, 426 Biscayne Blvd., Seabrook 77586.
12.—Nick Acuff, 3880 Hulen, 310, Fort Worth 76107; Marjorie Nunn, 4004 Briarhaven Ct., Fort Worth 76109.
13.—Al Clements, 5627 Bankside Dr., Houston 77096; Mamie Proctor, 4311 Wuthering Heights, Houston 77045.
14.—Clarke Stranghan, 3304 Western Dr., Austin 78745; Cynthia Hall, 8504 Soho Dr., Austin 78748.
15.—Doug Johnson, 2006 Counter Point, Houston 77055; Nelda Eppes, 5426 Poinciana, Houston 77092.
16.—Jay Patterson, 8080 N. Central Expy., 400, Dallas 75206; Lynne Tweedell, 9911 Coldwater Circle, Dallas 75228.
17.—Bill Borden Jr., 4617 Oakdale, Bellaire 77401; Audrey J. Cannon, 2815 Broadmoore Cir., Missouri City 77459.
18.—Darryl Pool, 1809 Wind Spirit, Round Rock 78681; Charla A. Borchers, 2203 N. DeLeon, Victoria 77901.
19.—Wilson M. Petefish, 102 Madrid Dr., Universal City 78148; Theo Wickersham, 201 Scott Ave., Universal City 78148.
20.—Eugene J. Seaman, 5656 S. Staples, 240, Corpus Christi 78411; Karen Bonner, 326 Haroldson, Corpus Christi 78412.
21.—Jay T. Kimbrough, P.O. Drawer 520, Beeville 78104; Barbara Schoolcraft, Rt. 3, Box 720, Seguin 78155.
22.—David H. Arno, 2004 Georgetown, Denton 76201; Naomi Godfrey, 28 Legend Rd., Fort Worth 76132.
23.—Jimmy Morgan, Box 610204, Dallas 75261; Barbara Martin, 3229 Kiesthill Dr., Dallas 75233.

24.—Randy Leifeste, Box 7876, Horseshoe Bay 78654; Gloria Ribbeck, 3509 Meadow Oak Dr., Temple 76502.
25.—John R. Groseclose, 114 E. Twohig, San Angelo 76903; Willie Lawley, 308 S. Someday Dr., Boerne 78006.
26.—Jess Young, Box 15948, San Antonio 78212; Diane Rath, 138 Sharon Dr., San Antonio 78216.
27.—Sam G. Reed, Box 51, Mercedes 78570;; Loddell Batsell, 1515 Whitewing, Brownsville 78521.
28.—Leon Kelley, 2137 71st, Lubbock 79412; Janelle Evans, Box 3, Brownfield 79316.
29.—Kenneth R. Carr, Drawer 1977, El Paso 79950; Marica Waugh, 1435 Rim Rd., El Paso 79902.
30.—Harry Robards, Box 950, Sherman 75091; Jacque Allen, 2206 Clarinda, Wichita Falls 76308.
31.—Mac Thornberry, 3441 Irving, Amarillo 79121; Bonnie Maynard, 5814 Radiant, Amarillo 79109.

Republican State Party Auxiliaries: Texas Asian Republican Caucus: Chmn., Helen Chang, 10723 Braes Bayou, Houston 77071. **Republican National Hispanic Assembly of Texas:** Chmn., Isaac Oliveras, 819 Briarcliff, San Antonio 78213. **Texas Young Republican Federation:** Chmn., Ed Hodges, Box 792082, Dallas 75379. **Black Republican Council of Texas:** Chmn., Reby Cary, 1804 Bunche Dr., Fort Worth 76112. **College Republicans of Texas:** Chmn., Amanda Innis, 2308 Wickersham, 1809, Austin 78741. **Texas Federation of Republican Women:** Pres., Jan Patterson, 9854 Estate Ln., Dallas 75238. **Texas Republican County Chairman's Assn.:** Dan Ouellette, 16 Windsor Dr., Beeville 78102.

Members of Texas Legislature

The Texas Legislature has 181 members—31 in the Senate and 150 in the House of Representatives. Regular sessions convene on the second Tuesday of January in odd-numbered years, but the governor may call special sessions. Article III of the Texas Constitution deals with the legislative branch.

The following lists are members of the 72nd Legislature, which convened on Jan. 8, 1991, following the Nov. 6, 1990, election.

STATE SENATE

Thirty-one members of the State Senate are elected for four-year, overlapping terms. Date in parentheses after each name below indicates expiration of term of office. Chet Brooks of Pasadena is dean of the Senate. Salary: The salary of all members of the Legislature, including both Senators and Representatives, was set by a constitutional amendment, adopted April 22, 1975, as follows: $600 per month and $30 per diem during legislative sessions; mileage allowance at same rate provided by law for state employees. The rate of $30 per diem applies during each regular and special session of the Legislature. The address of senators is Texas Senate, P.O. Box 12068, Capitol Station, Austin, Texas 78711.

Senatorial Districts include one or more whole counties and some counties have more than one Senator.

President of the Senate is Lt. Gov. Robert D. Bullock. Other officers are: President Pro Tempore, Bob Glasgow, Stephenville. Secretary of the Senate, Betty King, Austin. Sergeant-at-Arms, Carleton Turner, Austin.

Dist., Name, Address, Term of Office, Occupation.
18—Armbrister, Ken, Victoria (1-1-95); businessman.
14—Barrientos, Gonzalo, Austin (1-1-93); advertising-public relations.
*31—Bivins, Teel, Amarillo (1-1-93); businessman/cattleman.
11—Brooks, Chet, Pasadena (1-1-95); Appraiser/marketing specialist.
*17—Brown, James E. "Buster," Lake Jackson (1-1-93); attorney.
30—Carriker, Steve, Roby (1-1-93); farmer.
24—Dickson, Temple, Sweetwater (1-1-93); lawyer/rancher.
13—Ellis, Rodney, Houston (1-1-95); attorney.
22—Glasgow, Bob, Stephenville (1-1-95); attorney.
6—Green, Gene, Houston (1-1-95); attorney.
3—Haley, Bill, Center (1-1-93); teacher/businessman.
*10—Harris, Chris, Arlington (1-1-95); attorney.
*8—Harris, Ike, Dallas (1-1-93); attorney.
*7—Henderson, Don, Houston (1-1-95); attorney-businessman.
23—Johnson, Eddie Bernice, Dallas (1-1-95); agency vice president.
*26—Krier, Cyndi T., San Antonio (1-1-93); attorney.
*16—Leedom, John, Dallas (1-1-95); businessman.
27—Lucio, Eddie Jr., Brownsville (1-1-95); advertising executive.
2—Lyon, Ted, Rockwall (1-1-93); attorney.
12—Moncrief, Mike, Fort Worth (1-1-95); businessman.
28—Montford, John, Lubbock (1-1-93); attorney.
4—Parker, Carl, Port Arthur (1-1-93); attorney.
*1—Ratliff, Bill, Mount Pleasant (1-1-93); engineer.
29—Rosson, Peggy, El Paso (1-1-95); homemaker.
*9—Sibley, David, Waco (1-1-95); attorney.
25—Sims, Bill, San Angelo (1-1-95); businessman-rancher.
19—Tejeda, Frank, San Antonio (1-1-95); attorney.
20—Truan, Carlos, Corpus Christi (1-1-93); insurance.
5—Turner, Jim, Crockett (1-1-95); attorney.
15—Whitmire, John, Houston (1-1-95); attorney.
21—Zaffirini, Judith, Laredo (1-1-95); communications.

HOUSE OF REPRESENTATIVES

This list shows the 150 members of the House of Representatives in the 72nd Legislature. They were elected on Nov. 6, 1990, from districts shown in the list below. Doyle Willis, Fort Worth, is the senior House member. Members are elected for 2-year terms. Representatives and senators receive the same salary; see State Senate. Numbers before names denote district. The address of representatives is House of Representatives, P.O. Box 2910, Austin, Texas 78768-2910. FAX: (512) 463-0695.

Speaker, Gib Lewis. Chief Clerk, Betty Murray. Sergeant-at-Arms, Ron Hinkle.

Dist., Name, Home Town, Occupation.
12—Alexander, Clyde, Athens; rancher, businessman.
106—Arnold, Bill, Grand Prairie; school administrator.
140—Bailey, Kevin, Houston; college teacher.
144—Barton, Erwin W., Pasadena; businessman.
34—Berlanga, Hugo, Corpus Christi; businessman.
54—Black, Layton, Goldthwaite; rancher, banker.
*105—Blackwood, Bill, Mesquite; engineer.
110—Blair, Fred, Dallas; real estate broker.
11—Bomer, Elton, Montalba; banker.
128—Bosse, Fred M., Houston; attorney.
*15—Brady, Kevin, The Woodlands; pres., chamber of commerce.
*96—Brimer, Kenneth, Arlington; insurance agent.
107—Cain, David, Dallas; attorney.
*61—Campbell, Ben, Lewisville; consultant.
*109—Carona, John, Dallas; pres., Trans-Cities.
*91—Carter, Bill, Fort Worth; insurance.
45—Cate, Tom, Lytle; lawyer.
35—Cavazos, Eddie, Corpus Christi; real estate broker.
84—Chisum, Warren, Pampa; oil & gas exploration.
17—Clemons, Billy, Lufkin; transit director.
132—Colbert, Paul, Houston; consultant.
23—Collazo, Frank, Port Arthur; public relations consultant.
120—Conley, Karyne, San Antonio; college professor.
64—Cook, John, Breckenridge; rancher, attorney, oil prodn.
78—Counts, David, Knox City; insurance, real estate.
*76—Craddick, Tom, Midland; sales representative.
*87—Crawford, Richard, Amarillo; real estate broker/developer.
43—Cuellar, Henry, Laredo; attorney, customs broker.
42—Cuellar, Renato, Weslaco; retired businessman.
*125—Culberson, John, Houston; attorney.
137—Danburg, Debra, Houston; attorney.
40—De la Garza, Eddie, Edinburg; attorney.
50—Delco, Wilhelmina, Austin; housewife.
*53—Delisi, Dianne W., Temple; self-employed.
56—Denton, Betty, Waco; attorney.
142—Dutton, Harold, Houston; business consultant.
33—Earley, Robert, Beeville; international commodities.
*133—Eckels, Robert, Houston; insurance.
146—Edwards, Al, Houston; real estate.
147—Evans, Larry, Houston; attorney.
80—Finnell, Charles, Holliday; businessman/attorney.
*38—Fleuriet, Kenneth, Harlingen; consultant.
*69—Fraser, Troy, Big Spring; pres., Fraser Industries.
68—Gallego, Pete, Alpine; attorney, restaurant owner.
143—Gallegos, Mario Jr., Houston; sr. capt., Houston Fire Dept.
58—Gibson, Bruce, Cleburne; dairy farmer/attorney.
5—Glaze, Bob, Gilmer; chiropractor.
44—Glossbrenner, Ernestine, Alice; state rep.
*93—Goodman, Toby, Arlington; attorney.
*114—Goolsby, Tony, Dallas; insurance, investments.
108—Granoff, Al, Dallas; attorney.
48—Greenberg, Sherri, Austin; public finance specialist.

*94—Grusendorf, Kent, Arlington; pres., Cyco Mfg.
41—Gutierrez, Roberto, Pharr; businessman.
*71—Haggerty, Pat, El Paso; real estate.
*126—Hamric, Peggy, Houston; community activist.
*27—Harris, Jack, Pearland; dentist.
*102—Hartnett, Will, Dallas; attorney.
*149—Heflin, Talmadge, Houston; businessman.
124—Hernandez, Christine, San Antonio; education consultant.
18—Hightower, Allen, Huntsville; businessman.
*150—Hilbert, Paul, Spring; attorney.
*67—Hilderbran, Harvey, Uvalde; real estate.
*101—Hill, Anita, Garland; state rep.
*112—Hill, Fred, Richardson; businessman.
81—Hirschi, John, Wichita Falls; real estate.
*32—Holzheauser, Steve, Victoria; rancher.
*59—Horn, Jim, Denton; businessman.
100—Hudson, Sam, Dallas; attorney.
*79—Hunter, Robert, Abilene; university administrator.
36—Hunter, Todd, Corpus Christi; attorney.
24—Hury, James, Galveston; attorney.
*129—Jackson, Mike, La Porte; general contractor.
10—Johnson, Jerry, Nacogdoches; financial svcs./cattleman.
*83—Jones, Delwin, Lubbock; investor.
66—Junell, Robert, San Angelo; attorney.
*6—Kamel, Ted, Tyler; restaurant management.
13—Kubiak, Dan, Rockdale; rancher/real estate.
*46—Kuempel, Edmund, Seguin; salesman.
85—Laney, Pete, Hale Center; farmer.
111—Larry, Jerald, Dallas; tax consultant.
89—Lewis, Gib, Fort Worth; pres., Lewis Label Prod.
19—Lewis, Ron, Mauriceville; real estate developer.
47—Linebarger, Libby, Manchaca; homemaker.
116—Luna, Gregory, San Antonio; attorney.
117—Madla, Frank, San Antonio; insurance agent/teacher.
*99—Marchant, Ken, Carrollton; home builder/investor.
25—Martin, Mike, Galveston; attorney.
148—Martinez, Roman, Houston; investments.
51—Maxey, Glen, Austin; lobbyist.
*60—McCall, Brian, Plano; insurance executive.
52—McCollough, Parker, Georgetown; attorney.
73—McDonald, Nancy, El Paso; registered nurse.
72—Moreno, Paul, El Paso; attorney/state rep.
*97—Mowery, Anna, Fort Worth; state rep.
49—Naishtat, Elliott, Austin; attorney.
4—Oakley, Keith, Terrell; rancher/businessman.
*14—Ogden, Steve, Bryan; oil & gas producer.
39—Oliveira, Rene O., Brownsville; attorney.
*113—Ovard, A.R., Dallas; real estate broker.
*92—Park, Carolyn, Bedford; state rep.
2—Patterson, Pete, Brookston; farmer/rancher/real estate.
*130—Pennington, Randy, Houston; chmn. of board, Control Spec.

74—Perez, Nicholas J., El Paso; attorney.
*122—Pierce, George, San Antonio; vice-pres., Transcicso Rwy.
57—Place, Allen, Gatesville; attorney.
22—Price, Al, Beaumont; pilot.
119—Puente, Robert, San Antonio; attorney.
*16—Rabuck, Bob, Conroe; orthodontist.
37—Rangel, Irma, Kingsville; attorney.
*104—Repp, Glenn, Duncanville; aerospace consultant.
*82—Robnett, Nolan J., Lubbock; stockbroker.
118—Rodriguez, Ciro, San Antonio; college professor.
77—Rudd, Jim, Brownfield; attorney.
8—Russell, Sam, Mt. Pleasant; attorney.
9—Sadler, Paul, Henderson; attorney.
30—Saunders, Robert, La Grange; pres., M&S Distrib.
134—Schechter, Sue, Houston; attorney.
*121—Schoolcraft, Alan, San Antonio; attorney.
62—Seidlits Jr., Curtis, Sherman; attorney.
*98—Shea, Gwyn C., Irving; businesswoman.
*127—Shelley, Dan, Crosby; attorney.
*136—Smith, Ashley, Houston; attorney/businessman.
*135—Smith, Dalton, Houston; builder/developer.
*86—Smithee, John, Amarillo; attorney.
20—Soileau, Curtis, Lumberton; attorney.
21—Stiles, Mark, Beaumont; businessman.
*88—Swinford, David, Dumas; grain elevator owner.
*26—Tallas, Jim, Sugar Land; insurance agency.
*55—Taylor, M.A., Waco; retired businessman.
1—Telford, Barry, DeKalb; businessman.
*3—Thomas, Bill, Greenville; life insurance/securities.
95—Thompson, Garfield, Fort Worth; retired.
141—Thompson, Senfronia, Houston; attorney.
65—Turner, Bob, Voss; rancher.
139—Turner, Sylvester, Houston; attorney.
29—Uher, Tom, Bay City; attorney.
115—Van de Putte, Leticia, San Antonio; pharmacist.
31—Von Dohlen, Tim, Goliad; attorney/pharmacist.
*70—Vowell, Jack, El Paso; investor.
145—Wallace, Ralph, Houston; vice-pres., engineering co.
75—Watkins, Gary, Odessa; attorney.
*123—Wentworth, Jeff, San Antonio; attorney.
63—Williamson, Ric, Weatherford; enterpreneur.
90—Willis, Doyle, Fort Worth; attorney/farmer.
*28—Willy, John, Angleton; real estate investments.
131—Wilson, Ron, Houston; attorney.
103—Wolens, Steve, Dallas; attorney.
138—Yarbrough, Ken, Houston; business rep.
*7—Yost, Gerald, Longview; advertising/marketing consult.

*Republicans; all others are Democrats.

Texans in Congress

Texas is allocated 30 members in the U.S. House of Representatives beginning in 1992, and two in the U.S. Senate. The salary of members of both houses is $89,500 with limitations on outside income.

The term of office for members of the House is two years, and the terms of all members will expire on Jan. 1, 1993. Senators serve six-year terms. Lloyd Bentsen will serve until Jan. 1995, and Phil Gramm's term will end in 1997.

Addresses and phone numbers of the lawmakers' Washington and district offices are given below. Washington zip codes are 20515 for members of the House and 20510 for senators.

Senate

Lloyd Bentsen (Dem.)—Washington Office: 703 Hart Senate Office Bldg., (202) 224-5922; District Offices: 961 Federal Bldg., Austin, 78701, (512) 482-5834; 7C14 Earle Cabell Bldg., Dallas, 75242, (214) 767-0577; Suite 800, 1919 Smith St., Houston, 77002, (713) 653-3456.

Phil Gramm (Rep.)—Washington Office: 370 Russell Senate Office Bldg., (202) 224-2934; District Offices: Federal Bldg., 2323 Bryan, #1500, Dallas, 75201, (214) 767-3000; 102 N. College St., Rm. 201, Tyler, 75710, (903) 593-0902; 115 E. Travis, #1631, San Antonio, 78205, (512) 229-4600; 222 E. Van Buren, #404, Harlingen, 78550, (512) 423-6118; 712 Main, #2400, Houston 77002, (713) 229-2766; 112 Federal Bldg., 1205 Texas Ave., Lubbock, 79401, (806) 743-7533; 123 Pioneer Plaza, #665, El Paso, 79901, (915) 534-6896.

House

District

1. Jim Chapman (Dem.), Washington Office: 236 Cannon House Office Bldg., (202) 225-3035; District Offices: U. S. Federal Bldg. G-15, 100 E. Houston, Marshall, 75671, (903) 938-8386; 210 Post Office Bldg., Paris, 75460, (903) 785-0783; 410 Post Office Bldg., Texarkana, 75504, (903) 793-6728; P.O. Box 248, New Boston, 75570, (903) 628-5594.

2. Charles Wilson (Dem.), Washington Office: 2256 Rayburn House Office Bldg., (202) 225-2401; FAX (202) 225-1764; District Office: 701 North First, Rm. 201, Lufkin, 75901, (409) 637-1770.

3. Sam Johnson (Rep.), Washington Office: 1223 Longworth House Office Bldg., (202) 225-1485; District Office: 2825 Regal Road, Ste. 110, Plano, 75075, (214) 985-8868; FAX (214) 985-0798.

4. Ralph Hall (Dem.), Washington Office: 2236 Rayburn House Office Bldg., (202) 225-6673, FAX (202) 225-3332; District Offices: 104 N. San Jacinto, Rockwall, 75087, (214) 771-9118; 119 Federal Bldg., Sherman, 75090, (903) 892-1112; 211 Federal Bldg., Tyler, 75702; (903) 597-3729.

5. John Bryant (Dem.), Washington Office: 208 Cannon House Office Bldg., (202) 225-2231; District Office: 8035 East R. L. Thornton, #518, Dallas, 75228, (214) 767-6554.

Texans chair three important committees in the U.S. Congress. Rep. Kida de la Garza (left) heads the Agricultural Committee in the House; Rep. Jack Brooks (center) chairs the House Judiciary Committee; and Sen. Lloyd Bentsen (right) guides the important Finance Committee in the Senate. Associated Press Photos.

6. Joe Barton (Rep.), Washington Office; 1225 Longworth House Office Bldg., (202) 225-2002, FAX (202) 225-3052; District Offices: 3509 Hulen, Suite 110, Fort Worth, 76107, (817) 737-7737; 303 W. Knox, Suite 101, Ennis, 75119, (214) 875-8488; 809 E. University, 222, College Station, 77805, (409) 846-1985; 300 W. Davis, 507, Conroe, 77301, (409) 760-2291.

7. Bill Archer (Rep.), Washington Office: 1236 Longworth House Office Bldg., (202) 225-2571; FAX (202) 225-4381; District Office: 1003 Wirt Rd., 311, Houston, 77055, (713) 467-7493.

8. Jack Fields (Rep.), Washington Office: 108 Cannon House Office Bldg., (202) 225-4901; District Office: 12605 East Freeway, Suite 320, Houston, 77015, (713) 451-6334.

9. Jack Brooks (Dem.), Washington Office: 2449 Rayburn House Office Bldg., (202) 225-6565; FAX (202) 225-1584; District Offices: 201 Federal Bldg., Beaumont, 77701, (409) 839-2508; U.S. Post Office Bldg., Rm. 216, 601 25th St., Galveston, 77550, (409) 766-3608.

10. J. J. Pickle (Dem.), Washington Office: 242 Cannon House Office Bldg., (202) 225-4865; District Office: 763 Federal Bldg., Austin, 78701, (512) 482-5921.

11. Chet Edwards (Dem.); Washington: 425 Cannon House Office Bldg., (202) 225-6105; District Office: 700 S. University Parks Dr., Waco, 76706, (817) 752-9600.

12. Pete Geren (Dem.); Washington: 1730 Longworth House Office Bldg., (202) 225-5071; FAX (202) 225-2786; District Office: 100 E. 15th St., Fort Worth, 76102, (817) 338-0909, (817) 338-5852.

13. Bill Sarpalius (Dem.), Washington Office: 126 Cannon House Office Bldg., (202) 225-3706; District Offices: 817 S. Polk, Amarillo, 79101, (806) 371-8844; 1000 Lamar, Suite 208, Wichita Falls, 76301, (817) 767-0541.

14. Greg Laughlin (Dem.), Washington Office: 218 Cannon House Office Bldg., (202) 225-2831; FAX (202) 225-1108; District Offices: 312 S. Main, Victoria, 77901, (512) 576-1231; 221 E. Main, Suite 203, Round Rock, 78664, (512) 244-3765.

15. Kika de la Garza (Dem.), Washington Office: 1401 Longworth House Office Bldg., (202) 225-2531; FAX (202) 225-2534; District Offices: 1418 Beech, Rm. 135, McAllen, 78501, (512) 682-5545; 401 E. 2nd, Rm. 201, Alice, 78332, (512) 664-2215.

16. Ron Coleman (Dem.), Washington Office: 440 Cannon House Office Bldg., (202) 225-4831; District Offices: Federal Building, Room C-723, El Paso, 79901, (915) 534-6200; U.S. Post Office Bldg., 304, Pecos, 79772, (915) 445-9213.

17. Charles Stenholm (Dem.), Washington Office: 1226 Longworth House Office Bldg., (202) 225-6605; District Offices: P.O. Box 1237, Stamford, 79553, (915) 773-3623; P.O. Box 1101, Abilene, 79604, (915) 673-7221.

18. Craig Washington (Dem.), Washington Office: 1631 Longworth House Office Bldg., (202) 225-3816; FAX (202) 225-6186; District Office: 1919 Smith, Suite 820, Houston, 77004, (713) 739-7339.

19. Larry Combest (Rep.), Washington Office: 1527 Longworth House Office Bldg., (202) 225-4005; District Offices: Federal Bldg., Suite 613, 1205 Texas Ave., Lubbock, 79401, (806) 763-1611; 419 W. 4th St., Odessa, 79761, (915) 337-1669.

20. Henry Gonzalez (Dem.), Washington Office: 2413 Rayburn House Office Bldg., (202) 225-3236; District Office: Federal Bldg., Rm. B-124, 727 E. Durango, San Antonio, 78206, (512) 229-6195.

21. Lamar Smith (Rep.), Washington Office: 422 Cannon House Office Bldg., (202) 225-4236; District Offices: 10010 San Pedro, Suite 530, San Antonio, 78216, (512) 229-5880; 201 W. Wall St., Suite 104, Midland, 79701, (915) 687-5234; 33 E. Twohig, Suite 302, San Angelo, 76903, (915) 653-3971; 1006 Junction Highway, Kerrville, 78028, (512) 895-1414.

22. Tom DeLay (Rep.), Washington Office, (202) 225-5951; District Offices: 9000 S.W. Freeway, Suite 205, Houston, 77074, (713) 270-4000; 500 N. Chenango, Suite 312, Angleton, 77515, (409) 849-4446.

23. Albert Bustamante (Dem.), 1116 Longworth House Office Bldg., (202) 225-4511; District Offices: 727 E. Durango, B-146, San Antonio, 78206, (512) 229-6191; 1300 Matamoros, 115, Laredo, 78040, (512) 724-7774; 100 E. Broadway, 103, Del Rio, 78841, (512) 774-6545; Uvalde County Courthouse, Uvalde, 78801, (512) 278-5021; 101 E. Dimmit, West Annex, Crystal City, 78839, (512) 374-5200; Dimmit County Courthouse, Carrizo Springs, 78834, (512) 876-2323; Maverick County Courthouse, Eagle Pass, 78852, (512) 773-4110.

24. Martin Frost (Dem.), Washington Office: 2459 Rayburn House Office Bldg., (202) 225-3605; District Offices: 1319 NCNB-Oak Cliff Tower, 400 S. Zang Blvd., Dallas, 75208, (214) 767-2816; 720 NCNB Tower, 801 W. Freeway, Grand Prairie, 75051, (214) 262-1503.

25. Mike Andrews (Dem.), Washington Office: 322 Cannon House Office Bldg., (202) 225-7508; FAX (202) 225-4210; District Offices: Federal Bldg., 515 Rusk, 12102, Houston, 77002, (713) 229-2244; 1001 E. Southmore, 810, Pasadena, 77502, (713) 473-4334.

26. Dick Armey (Rep.), Washington Office: 130 Cannon House Office Bldg., (202) 225-7772; District Offices: 250 S. Stemmons Freeway, Suite 210, Lewisville, 75067, (214) 221-4527; 1301 S. Bowen Rd., Suite 422, Arlington, 76013, (817) 461-2555.

27. Solomon Ortiz (Dem.), Washington Office: 1524 Longworth House Office Bldg., (202) 225-7742; District Offices: 3649 Leopard, Suite 510, Corpus Christi, 78408, (512) 883-5868; 3505 Boca Chica Blvd., 438, Brownsville, 78521, (512) 541-1242; 635 E. King, Kingsville, 78363, (512) 592-5906.

Local Governments

Texas has 254 counties, a number which has not changed since 1931 when Loving County was organized. Loving had 107 population in the 1990 U.S. Census Bureau counts, compared with 164 in 1970 and its peak of 285 in 1940. It is the least-populous county in Texas. In contrast, Harris County is the most-populous in Texas, with a population in 1990 of 2,818,199.

Counties range in area from Rockwall's 148.6 square miles to the 6,193.1 square miles in Brewster, which is equal to the combined area of the states of Connecticut and Rhode Island.

The Texas Constitution makes a county a legal subdivision of the state. Each county has a commissioners court. It consists of four commissioners, each elected from a commissioner's precinct, and a county judge elected from the entire county. In smaller counties, the county judge retains judicial responsibilities in probate and insanity cases.

Eleven hundred and seventy-five incorporated Texas municipalities range in size from 25 residents to Houston's 1,630,553 in the 1990 Census. More than 80 percent of the state's population lives in cities and towns meeting the U.S. Census Bureau definition of urban areas.

Texas had 298 municipalities with more than 5,000 population in the 1990 Census. Under law, these cities may adopt their own charters by a majority vote. Cities of less than 5,000 population may be chartered only under the general law.

There were 286 home-rule cities on June 1, 1991, most of them cities with over 5,000 residents. Some of these cities now show fewer than 5,000 residents, because population has declined since they adopted their home-rule charters. A list of home-rule cities follows this list of mayors and city managers.

Councils of Government

The concept of regional planning and cooperation, fostered by enabling legislation in 1965, has spread across Texas since organization of the **North Central Texas Council of Governments** in 1966.

Legal responsibilities of regional councils include making studies and plans to guide the unified development of their areas, elimination of duplication and promotion of economy and efficiency in coordinated area development. They make recommendations to their member governments and may, upon request, assist in implementation of those plans.

Financing is provided by the local governments, the state and the federal government.

A list of the 24 regional councils, the counties served and the executive director as of February 1991, follows:

Alamo Area Council of Governments: Counties — Atascosa, Bandera, Bexar, Comal, Frio, Gillespie, Guadalupe, Karnes, Kendall, Kerr, Medina and Wilson. Executive director, Al Notzon, 118 Broadway, Ste. 400, San Antonio 78205.

Ark-Tex Council of Governments: Counties — Bowie, Cass, Delta, Franklin, Hopkins, Lamar, Morris, Red River and Titus. Executive director, James D. Goerke, Box 5307, Texarkana, Texas 75505.

Brazos Valley Development Council: Counties — Brazos, Burleson, Grimes, Leon, Madison, Robertson and Washington. Executive director, Glenn J. Cook, Box 4128, Bryan 77805-4128.

Capital Area Planning Council: Counties — Bastrop, Blanco, Burnet, Caldwell, Fayette, Hays, Lee, Llano, Travis and Williamson. Executive director, Richard G. Bean, 2520 IH 35 South, Suite 100, Austin 78704.

Central Texas Council of Governments: Counties — Bell, Coryell, Hamilton, Lampasas, Milam, Mills and San Saba. Executive director, A. C. Johnson, Box 729, Belton 76513-0729.

Coastal Bend Council of Governments: Counties — Aransas, Bee, Brooks, Duval, Jim Wells, Kenedy, Kleberg, Live Oak, McMullen, Nueces, Refugio and San Patricio. Executive director, John Buckner, Box 9909, Corpus Christi 78469.

Concho Valley Council of Governments: Counties — Coke, Concho, Crockett, Irion, Kimble, McCulloch, Mason, Menard, Reagan, Schleicher, Sterling, Sutton and Tom Green. Executive director, Robert R. Weaver, Box 60050, San Angelo 76906.

Deep East Texas Council of Governments: Counties — Angelina, Houston, Jasper, Nacogdoches, Newton, Polk, Sabine, San Augustine, San Jacinto, Shelby, Trinity and Tyler. Executive director, Lewis Johnson, 274 E. Lamar, Jasper 75951.

East Texas Council of Governments: Counties — Anderson, Camp, Cherokee, Gregg, Harrison, Henderson, Marion, Panola, Rains, Rusk, Smith, Upshur, Van Zandt and Wood. Executive director, Glynn Knight, 3800 Stone Rd., Kilgore 75662.

Golden Crescent Regional Planning Commission: Counties — Calhoun, De Witt, Goliad, Gonzales, Jackson, Lavaca and Victoria. Executive director, Patrick J. Kennedy, Box 2028, Victoria 77902.

Heart of Texas Council of Governments: Counties — Bosque, Falls, Freestone, Hill, Limestone and McLen-nan. Executive director, Hugh Davis, 320 Franklin Ave., Waco 76701-2297.

Houston-Galveston Area Council: Counties — Austin, Brazoria, Chambers, Colorado, Fort Bend, Galveston, Harris, Liberty, Matagorda, Montgomery, Walker, Waller and Wharton. Executive director, Jack Steele, Box 22777, Houston 77227.

Lower Rio Grande Valley Development Council: Counties — Cameron, Hidalgo and Willacy. Executive director, Robert A. Chandler, 4900 N. 23rd, McAllen 78504.

Middle Rio Grande Development Council: Counties — Dimmit, Edwards, Kinney, La Salle, Maverick, Real, Uvalde, Val Verde and Zavala. Executive director, Michael M. Patterson, Box 1199, Carrizo Springs 78834-7199.

Nortex Regional Planning Commission: Counties — Archer, Baylor, Childress, Clay, Cottle, Foard, Hardeman, Jack, Montague, Wichita, Wilbarger and Young. Executive director, Vacant, Box 5144, Wichita Falls 76307.

North Central Texas Council of Governments: Counties — Collin, Dallas, Denton, Ellis, Erath, Hood, Hunt, Johnson, Kaufman, Navarro, Palo Pinto, Parker, Rockwall, Somervell, Tarrant and Wise. Executive director, William J. Pitstick, P.O. Drawer COG, Arlington 76005-5888.

Panhandle Regional Planning Commission: Counties — Armstrong, Briscoe, Carson, Castro, Collingsworth, Dallam, Deaf Smith, Donley, Gray, Hall, Hansford, Hartley, Hemphill, Hutchinson, Lipscomb, Moore, Ochiltree, Oldham, Parmer, Potter, Randall, Roberts, Sherman, Swisher and Wheeler. Executive director, Gary Pitner, Box 9257, Amarillo 79105-9257.

Permian Basin Regional Planning Commission: Counties — Andrews, Borden, Crane, Dawson, Ector, Gaines, Glasscock, Howard, Loving, Martin, Midland, Pecos, Reeves, Terrell, Upton, Ward and Winkler. Executive director, Ernest W. Crawford, Box 60669, Midland 79711-0660.

Rio Grande Council of Governments: Counties — Brewster, Culberson, El Paso, Hudspeth, Jeff Davis and Presidio. Executive director, Justin R. Ormsby, 123 Pioneer Plaza, Ste. 210, El Paso 79901.

South East Texas Regional Planning Commission: Counties — Hardin, Jefferson and Orange. Executive director, Don Kelly, P.O. Drawer 1387, Nederland 77627.

South Plains Association of Governments: Counties — Bailey, Cochran, Crosby, Dickens, Floyd, Garza, Hale, Hockley, King, Lamb, Lubbock, Lynn, Motley, Terry and Yoakum. Executive director, Jerry D. Casstevens, Box 3730, Freedom Sta., Lubbock 79452.

South Texas Development Council: Counties — Jim Hogg, Starr, Webb and Zapata. Executive director, Amando Garza Jr., Box 2187, Laredo 78044-2187.

Texoma Regional Planning Commission: Counties — Cooke, Fannin and Grayson. Executive director, Frances Pelley, 10000 Grayson Dr., Denison 75020.

West Central Texas Council of Governments: Counties — Brown, Callahan, Coleman, Comanche, Eastland, Fisher, Haskell, Jones, Kent, Knox, Mitchell, Nolan, Runnels, Scurry, Shackelford, Stephens, Stonewall, Taylor and Throckmorton. Executive director, Brad Helbert, Box 3195, Abilene 79604.

COUNTY APPRAISERS

The following list of Chief Appraisers for Texas counties was furnished by the State Property Tax Board. It includes t he mailing address for each appraiser and is current to July 1, 1991.

Anderson— R. Cliff Wooten, Box 279, Palestine 75802
Andrews—Mickey Green, 405 N.W. 3rd, Andrews 79714
Angelina—Marvin Hahn Jr., Box 2357, Lufkin 75901
Aransas—Jad Smith, 601 S. Church, Rockport 78382
Archer—Edward H. Trigg III, Box 1141, Archer City 76351
Armstrong—Ron Patterson, Drawer D, Claude 79019
Atascosa—Vernon A. Warren, Box 139, Poteet 78065
Austin—Glen Whitehead, 5 E. Main, Bellville 77418
Bailey—Margaret L. Johnson, 104 E. Ave. C, Muleshoe 79347
Bandera—Larry Reagan, Box 1119, Bandera 78003
Bastrop—Dana Ripley, Drawer 578, Bastrop 78602
Baylor—Marilyn Thurmond, 101 S. Washington, Seymour 76380
Bee—Blaine Luthringer, Box 1262, Beeville 78104
Bell—Mike Watson, Box 390, Belton 76513
Bexar—Walter Stoneham, Box 830248, San Antonio 78283
Blanco—Mrs. Hollis Petri, Box 338, Johnson City 78636
Borden—R. D. Lewis, Box 298, Courthouse, Gail 79738
Bosque—Don Whitney, Box 393, Meridian 76665
Bowie—Wayne Hawkins, Box 6527, Texarkana 75505
Brazoria—J. R. Gayle Jr., 500 N. Chenango, Angleton 77515
Brazos—Buddy Winn, 1673 Briarcrest Dr., A-101, Bryan 77802
Brewster—Jerry Ratcliff, Box 1231, Alpine 79831
Briscoe—Carlye Fleming, Box 728, Silverton 79257
Brooks—Humberto Rivera, Drawer A, Falfurrias 78355
Brown—Robert L. Young Jr., 403 Fisk, Brownwood 76801
Burleson—Elizabeth Plagens, Box 1000, Caldwell 77836
Burnet—Stan Hemphill, Drawer E, Burnet 78611
Caldwell—Russell K. Sanders, Box 59, Lockhart 78644
Calhoun—Ken Monroe, Box 48, Port Lavaca 77979
Callahan—Rodney Lewallen, Box 806, Baird 79504
Cameron—Ken Wright, Box 1010, San Benito 78586
Camp—Vaudene Bennett, Box 739, Pittsburg 75686
Carson—Dianne B. Lavake, Box 970, Panhandle 79068
Cass—Janelle Clements, Box 1150, Linden 75563
Castro—Jerry Ratcliff, 204 S.E. 3rd (Rear), Dimmitt 79027
Chambers—Sherwood Blair, Box 1520, Anahuac 77514
Cherokee—S. R. Danner, Box 494, Rusk 75785
Childress—Nadine Parr, Courthouse Box 13, Childress 79201
Clay—A. G. Reis, 101 E. Omega, Henrietta 76365
Cochran—Glen McDaniel, 109 S.E. 1st, Morton 79346
Coke—Patsy Dunn, Box 2, Robert Lee 76945
Coleman—Bill W. Jones, Box 914, Coleman 76834
Collin—Jimmie Honea, 1024 S. Greenville, 120, Allen 75002
Collingsworth—Ann Wauer, Courthouse 1st Floor, Rm. 6, Wellington 79095
Colorado—William Youens Jr., Box 10, Columbus 78934
Comal—Lynn Rodgers (Acting), Box 311222, New Braunfels 78131
Comanche—Clay Fowler, Box 6, Comanche 76442
Concho—Eugene Dillard, Box 68, Paint Rock 76866
Cooke—Ross Fry, 200 W. California, Gainesville 76240
Coryell—Darrell Lisenbe, Box 142, Gatesville 76528
Cottle—Rue Young, Box 459, Paducah 79248
Crane—Peggy Dickson, 511 West 8th, Crane 79731
Crockett—Tom Stokes, Drawer H, Ozona 76943
Crosby—Darla Doss, Box 479, Crosbyton 79322
Culberson—Sally Carrasco, Box 550, Van Horn 79855
Dallam—H. V. Stanley, Box 592, Dalhart 79022
Dallas—Foy Mitchell Jr., 2949 N. Stemmons Frwy., Dallas 75247
Dawson—Tom Anderson, Box 797, Lamesa 79331
Deaf Smith—Fred E. Fox, Box 2298, Hereford 79045
Delta—Toyce Phillips, Box 47, Cooper 75432
Denton—Joe Rogers, Box 2816, Denton 76202
DeWitt—John Haliburton, Box 4, Cuero 77954
Dickens—Jerrie Ballard, Box 119, Dickens 79229
Dimmit—Rolando Cruz, 402 N, 7th, Carrizo Springs 78834
Donley—Charles SoRelle, Box 1220, Clarendon 79226
Duval—Ernesto Molina Jr., Box 809, San Diego 78384
Eastland—Steve Thomas, Box 914, Eastland 76448
Ector—James A. Goodwin, 817 Central, Odessa 79761
Edwards—Natalie Goggans, Box 378, Rocksprings 78880
Ellis—Richard Rhodes, Box 878, Waxahachie 75165
El Paso—Cora Viescas, 1720 Murchison, El Paso 79902
Erath—Jerry Lee, Box 94, Stephenville 76401
Falls—Joyce Collier, Drawer 430, Marlin 76661
Fannin—Carrol Garrison, 920 N. Center, Bonham 75418
Fayette—James Parker, Box 836, La Grange 78945

Fisher—Teddy Kral, Box 516, Roby 79543
Floyd—Sheila Faulkenberry, County Courthouse Rm. 107, Floydada 79235
Foard—Jo Ann Vecera, Box 419, Crowell 79227
Fort Bend—Gene Brewer, 12946 Dairy Ashford Rd., 100, Sugar Land 77487
Franklin—Edward Morrow, Box 720, Mount Vernon 75457
Freestone—Sherrill Minze, Box 675, Fairfield 75840
Frio—Irma Gonzalez, Box 1129, Pearsall 78061
Gaines—Betty Caudle, Box 490, Seminole 79360
Galveston—Guy Emanis, Box 3647, Texas City 77592
Garza—Billie Windham, Drawer F, Post 79356
Gillespie—Olan Tisdale, Box 429, Fredericksburg 78624
Glasscock—Royce Pruit, Box 89, Garden City 79739
Goliad—E. J. Bammert, Box 34, Goliad 77963
Gonzales—Glenda Strackbein, Box 867, Gonzales 78629
Gray—W. Pat Bagley, Box 836, Pampa 79066
Grayson—Robert H. Tollison, 205 N. Travis, Sherman 75090
Gregg—Bill Carroll, Box 6700, Longview 75608
Grimes—Bill Sullivan, Box 489, Anderson 77830
Guadalupe—Pat Fox, Box 1226, Seguin 78155
Hale—Linda Jaynes, Box 29, Plainview 79072
Hall—Jack Scott, 721 Robertson, Memphis 79245
Hamilton—Doyle Roberts, 119 E. Henry, Hamilton 76531
Hansford—Alice Peddy, Box 567, Spearman 79081
Hardeman—Twila Butler, Box 388, Quanah 79252
Hardin—Edwin Barry, Box 670, Kountze 77625
Harris—Jim Robinson, Box 920975, Houston 77292
Harrison—David E. Whitmire, Box 818, Marshall 75670
Hartley—Donna Bryant, Box 405, Hartley 79044
Haskell—Jamie Weaver, Box 467, Haskell 79521
Hays—Bill Backus, 632-A E. Hopkins, San Marcos 78666
Hemphill—James McCarley, Box 65, Canadian 79014
Henderson—Burt Lively, Box 430, Athens 75751
Hidalgo—Daniel Boone, Box 632, Pharr 78577
Hill—Shirley Holub, Box 416, Hillsboro 76645
Hockley—Nick Williams, Box 1090, Levelland 79336
Hood—Harold Chestnut, Box 819, Granbury 76048
Hopkins—Charles Stone, Box 753, Sulphur Springs 75482
Houston—Katherine Keith, Box 1125, Crockett 75835
Howard—Keith Toomire, Box 1151, Big Spring 79721
Hudspeth—John L. Ferrell, Box 186, Sierra Blanca 79851
Hunt—Melda Hart, Box 1339, Greenville 75401
Hutchinson—William Hodge, Box 5065, Borger 79007
Irion—Frances Grice, Box 980, Mertzon 76941
Jack—J.D. Garcia, Box 958, Jacksboro 76056
Jackson—James Surratt, 112 E. Main, Edna 77957
Jasper—David Luther, Box 1300, Jasper 75951
Jeff Davis—John L. Ferrell, Box 373, Fort Davis 79734
Jefferson—Roland Bieber, Box 1470, Groves 77619
Jim Hogg—Carmen J. Dugi (Acting), Box 459, Hebbronville 78361
Jim Wells—Sidney Vela, Box 607, Alice 78333
Johnson—Don Gilmore, 109 N. Main, Cleburne 76031
Jones—John Steele, Box 348, Anson 79501
Karnes—Doris Ahrens, 120 W. Calvert, Karnes City 78118
Kaufman—Jackie Self, Box 819, Kaufman 75142
Kendall—Charles M. Mikulenka (Int.), Box 788, Boerne 78006
Kenedy—D. Clyde Hamilton, Box 1520, Sarita 78385
Kent—Jarri Parker, Box 167, Jayton 79528
Kerr—Travis E. Chalmers, Box 1885, Kerrville 78029
Kimble—Paul Bierschwale, Box 307, Junction 76849
King—Bama Nell Oliver, Box 117, Guthrie 79236
Kinney—Marcus Tidwell, Box 1377, Brackettville 78832
Kleberg—Judy Prince, Box 1027, Kingsville 78363
Knox—Stanton Brown, Box 2, Benjamin 79505
Lamar—Joe Welch, Box 400, Paris 75460
Lamb—Vaughn McKee, Box 552, Littlefield 79339
Lampasas—F. Janice Henry, Box 175, Lampasas 76550
La Salle—Juanita Lozano, Drawer O, Cotulla 78014
Lavaca—Diane Munson, Box 386, Hallettsville 77964
Lee—Roy Holcomb, 218 E. Richmond, Giddings 78942
Leon—Robert Winn, Box 536, Centerville 75833
Liberty—Alan Conner, Box 10016, Liberty 77575
Limestone—Clydene Hyden, Drawer 831, Groesbeck 76642
Lipscomb—Jerry Reynolds, Box 128, Darrouzett 79024
Live Oak—Robert Dirks, Box MM, George West 78022
Llano—Bill Stewart, Box 608, Llano 78643
Loving—Mary Belle Jones, Box 188, Mentone 79754
Lubbock—Dave Kimbrough, Box 10542, Lubbock 79408
Lynn—Dovie Miller, Box 789, Tahoka 79373

McCulloch—Marjorie D. Neal, 104 N. College, Brady 76825
McLennan—Charles Gauer, Box 2297, Waco 76703
McMullen—Mary K. Edwards, Box 38, Tilden 78072
Madison—Dan Singletary, Box 1328, Madisonville 77864
Marion—Jim Muckleroy, Box 690, Jefferson 75657
Martin—Delbert Dickenson, Box 1349, Stanton 79782
Mason—Deborah Geistweidt, Drawer 1119, Mason 76856
Matagorda—Vince Maloney, Box 179, Bay City 77404
Maverick—Victor Perry, Box 2628, Eagle Pass 78852
Medina—James Garcia, 1410 Ave. K, Hondo 78861
Menard—Peggy Decker, Box 1058, Menard 76859
Midland—Ron Stegall, Box 908002, Midland 79708
Milam—Patricia Moraw, Box 769, Cameron 76520
Mills—Doran Lemke, Box 565, Goldthwaite 76844
Mitchell—Clarence Burt, Box 358, Colorado City 79512
Montague—Wanda Russell, Box 121, Montague 76251
Montgomery—Jimmy Foreman, Box 2233, Conroe 77305
Moore—Joyce Jones Cearley, Box 717, Dumas 79029
Morris—Rhonda Hall, Box 563, Daingerfield 75638
Motley—Betty L. Luckett, Box 779, Matador 79244
Nacogdoches—Gary Woods, 216 W. Hospital, Nacog-
doches 75961
Navarro—Harry Hudson, Box 3118, Corsicana 75110
Newton—Margie Herrin, Drawer X, Newton 75966
Nolan—Patricia Davis, Box 1256, Sweetwater 79556
Nueces—George Moff, 1305 N. Shoreline Blvd., Corpus
Christi 78401
Ochiltree—Terry Symons, 825 S. Main, 100, Perryton 79070
Oldham—Jen Carter, Drawer 449, Vega 79092
Orange—Faye Gillet, Box 457, Orange 77630
Palo Pinto—Jackie Samford, Box 250, Palo Pinto 76072
Panola—Charles D. Holmes (Acting), 2 Ball Park Rd.,
Carthage 75633
Parker—Larry Hammonds, 118 W. Columbia, Weather-
ford 76086
Parmer—Ron Procter, Box 56, Bovina 79009
Pecos—Mary Sedlacek, Box 237, Fort Stockton 79735
Polk—Clyde Arrendell, Box 305, Livingston 77351
Potter—Dale Brauchi, Box 7190, Amarillo 79114
Presidio—Steve Zilliox, Box 879, Marfa 79843
Rains—Loudele Dowdy, Box 70, Emory 75440
Randall—Dale Brauchi, Box 7190, Amarillo 79114
Reagan—Byron Bitner, Reagan Co. Courthouse, Big
Lake 76932
Real—Ruth Sanderlin, Box 158, Leakey 78873
Red River—Melvin Carlton, Box R, Clarksville 75426
Reeves—Carol K. Markham, Box 1229, Pecos 79772
Refugio—Bettye Kret, Box 156, Refugio 78377
Roberts—Debbie Stribling, Box 476, Miami 79059
Robertson—Dan Brewer, Box 998, Franklin 77856
Rockwall—Ray Helm, 106 N. San Jacinto, Rockwall 75087
Runnels—Sandee Giles, Box 524, Ballinger 76821
Rusk—Melvin Cooper, Box 7, Henderson 75653-0007
Sabine—Jim Nethery, Box 137, Hemphill 75948
San Augustine—Jamie Doherty, 122 N. Harrison, San Au-
gustine 75972
San Jacinto—Mac Ridley, Box 1170, Coldspring 77331
San Patricio—Kathryn Vermillion, Box 938, Sinton 78387
San Saba—Billy C. Bush, Courthouse, San Saba 76877
Schleicher—Ray Ballew, Box 936, El Dorado 76936
Scurry—L. R. Peveler, 2612 College Ave., Snyder 79549
Shackelford—Betty Viertel, Box 565, Albany 76430
Shelby—Harold Robertson, 5907 Loop 500, Center 75935
Sherman—Marillyn Albert, Box 239, Stratford 79084
Smith—Michael D. Barnett, 245 South S.E. Loop 323, Tyl-
er 75702
Somervell—Sandra Montgomery, Box 747, Glen Rose
76043
Starr—Jose Jaime Trevino, Box 137, Rio Grande City
78582
Stephens—Troy Sloan, Box 351, Breckenridge 76024
Sterling—Linda Low, Box 28, Sterling City 76951
Stonewall—Melissa Burkham, Box 308, Aspermont 79502
Sutton—Rex Ann Friess, 300 E. Oak, Sonora 76950
Swisher—Rose Lee Powell, Box 8, Tulia 79088
Tarrant—Bill Roberts, 2315 Gravel Rd., Fort Worth 76118
Taylor—Richard Petree, Box 1800, Abilene 79604
Terrell—Blain Chriesman, Box 747, Sanderson 79848
Terry—Ronny Burran, Box 426, Brownfield 79316
Throckmorton—Ruby Dunlap, Box 788, Throckmorton
76083
Titus—Lois McKibben, Box 528, Mount Pleasant 75455
Tom Green—Elvin W. Field, Box 3307, San Angelo 76902
Travis—Art Cory, Box 149012, Austin 78714
Trinity—Allen McKinley, Box 950, Groveton 75845
Tyler—Linda Lewis, Drawer X, Woodville 75979
Upshur—Louise Stracener, Box 280, Gilmer 75644

Upton—W. J. Campbell Jr., Box 1110, McCamey 79752
Uvalde—Brownie J. Jones, 209 N. High, Uvalde 78801
Val Verde—Lillie Sue Stout, Box 1059, Del Rio 78841
Van Zandt—Ron Groom, Box 926, Canton 75103
Victoria—Jim Williams, 1611-A E. North, Victoria 77901
Walker—Grover Cook, Box 1798, Huntsville 77340
Waller—Preston Kelly, Box 159, Katy 77492
Ward—Arlice Wittie, Box 905, Monahans 79756
Washington—Charles Gaskamp, Box 681, Brenham 77833
Webb—Ezequiel P. Laurel, Box 719, Laredo 78040
Wharton—Larry Holub, Box 1068, Wharton 77488
Wheeler—Larry Schoenhals, Box 1200, Wheeler 79096
Wichita—Lanier Wilson, Box 5172, Wichita Falls 76307
Wilbarger—Doyle Graham Sr., Box 1519, Vernon 76384
Willacy—Agustin Colchado, Rt. 2, Box 256, Raymondville
78580
Williamson—Donna Moff, Box 1085, Georgetown 78626-
1085
Wilson—Leon Stoeltje, Box 849, Floresville 78114
Winkler—John R. Oglesby, Box 1219, Kermit 79745
Wise—Mickey Hand (Interim), 206 S. State, Decatur 76234
Wood—Carson Wages, Box 951, Quitman 75783
Yoakum—J. D. Brown, Box 748, Plains 79355
Young—Pat Butler, Box 337, Graham 76046
Zapata—Rosalva Villarreal, Box 2315, Zapata 78076
Zavala—Neal Little, 323 W. Zavala, Crystal City 78839

Wet and Dry Counties

When approved in local option elections in "wet"
precincts of counties, sale of **liquor by the drink** is permitted in Texas. This resulted from adoption of an
amendment to the Texas Constitution in 1970 and subsequent legislation, followed by local option elections.
For the first time in more than 50 years liquor by the
drink was made legal in Texas.

Below are compilations showing the status of wet
and dry counties in Texas as of Dec. 31, 1990. A dagger
(†) indicates counties in which the sale of mixed beverages is legal in all or part of the county (94). An asterisk (*) indicates counties wholly wet (37). All others are
dry in part (77).

Counties in Which Distilled Spirits Are Legal (181):
Anderson, †*Aransas, Archer, Atascosa, †*Austin,
†Bandera, *Bastrop, †*Bee, †Bell, †*Bexar, †Blanco,
Bosque, †Brazoria, †*Brazos, †*Brewster, Brooks,
Brown, Burleson, †Burnet, †Calhoun, Callahan, †*Cam-
eron, †Camp, Carson, Cass, Castro, Chambers, Chil-
dress, Clay, Coleman, Collin, †*Colorado, †*Comal, Co-
manche, Cooke, Coryell, *Crockett, Crane, *Culberson,
Dallam, †Dallas, †Dawson, Deaf Smith, †Denton, †De-
Witt, Dickens, †Dimmit, †Donley, †*Duval, Eastland,
†Ector, Edwards, Ellis, †*El Paso, †Falls, Fannin,
Fayette, †*Fort Bend, †Frio, †Galveston, Garza, †Gil-
lespie, †Goliad, Gonzales, Gray, Grayson, Gregg,
†Grimes, †Guadalupe, Hall, Hamilton, Hardin, †Harris,
Harrison, Haskell, †Hays, †Henderson, †*Hidalgo,
†Hill, †Hockley, Hood, †Howard, †*Hudspeth, Hunt,
Hutchinson, †Jackson, †Jasper, Jeff Davis, †Jefferson,
†*Jim Hogg, †Jim Wells, *Karnes, Kaufman, †*Ken-
dall, Kenedy, †Kerr, Kimble, King, †*Kinney, †Kle-
berg, †Lamar, Lampasas, †La Salle, †Lavaca, †Lee,
Leon, Liberty, Lipscomb, Live Oak, †Llano, †*Loving,
†Lubbock, Marion, †Matagorda, †Maverick, †McCul-
loch, †McLennan, †Medina, Menard, †Midland,
Milam, †Mills, Mitchell, Montague, †Montgomery,
†*Moore, Nacogdoches, †Navarro, Newton, Nolan,
†Nueces, †Orange, Palo Pinto, Pecos, †Polk, †Potter,
†*Presidio, Rains, †Randall, *Reagan, Red River,
†Reeves, Refugio, Robertson, Runnels, San Augustine,
San Jacinto, †San Patricio, San Saba, †Schleicher,
Shackelford, Shelby, †Starr, Stonewall, †*Sutton,
†Tarrant, †Taylor, *Terrell, †Titus, †Tom Green,
†*Travis, *Trinity, Upshur, †Upton, Uvalde, †Val
Verde, †Victoria, †Walker, †Waller, Ward, †*Washing-
ton, †*Webb, †Wharton, †Wichita, Wilbarger, †Wilson,
†Williamson, †*Wilson, *Winkler, †*Zapata, †Zavala.

Counties in Which Only 4 Percent Beer Is Legal (12):
Baylor, Caldwell, Cherokee, Concho, Hartley, Irion,
Mason, McMullen, Oldham, Rockwall, Sabine, Stephens.

**Counties in Which 14 Percent Beverages Are Legal
(4):** Glasscock, Limestone, Somervell, Wise.

Counties Wholly Dry (57): Andrews, Angelina, Arm-
strong, Bailey, Borden, Bowie, Briscoe, Cochran,
Coke, Collingsworth, Cottle, Crosby, Delta, Erath,
Fisher, Floyd, Foard, Franklin, Freestone, Gaines,
Hale, Hansford, Hardeman, Hemphill, Hopkins, Hous-
ton, Jack, Johnson, Jones, Kent, Knox, Lamb, Lynn,
Madison, Martin, Morris, Motley, Ochiltree, Panola,
Parker, Parmer, Real, Roberts, Rusk, Scurry, Sher-
man, Smith, Sterling, Swisher, Terry, Throckmorton,
Tyler, Van Zandt, Wheeler, Wood, Yoakum, Young.

TEXAS COUNTY AND DISTRICT OFFICIALS—TABLE NO. 1

County Seats, County Judges, County Clerks, County Attorneys, County Treasurers, Tax Assessors-Collectors and Sheriffs.

See following page for another table of county and district officials. The officials listed in this table are elected by popular vote.

County	County Seat	County Judge	County Clerk	County Attorney	County Treasurer	Assessor-Collector	Sheriff
Anderson	Palestine	*John B. McDonald	Jo Huddleston	James L. Rex	Virginia Salmon	Betty Broyles	Gary Thomas
Andrews	Andrews	Gary W. Gaston	F. Wm. Hoermann	Ed Jones	Office abolished 11-5-85.	Evelyn Hancock	Wayne Farmer
Angelina	Lufkin	†Joe Berry	Pauline Grisham	James Anderson Jr.	Joan Denby	Bill Shanklin	Mike Lawrence
Aransas	Rockport	Agnes A. Harden	Val Jean Eaton	Gary Southard	Marvine Wix	Allena Jones	Robert O. Hewes
Archer	Archer City	Paul O. Wylie	Jane Adams		Betty Tarno	Teresa Martin	P.L. Pippin Jr.
Armstrong	Claude	Hugh Reed	Kathy Byrd		Bernice Stephenson	Ronald Patterson	Charles D. Strange
Atascosa	Jourdanton	‡J.B. Gates	Laquita Hayden	R. T. Franklin	Gloria Smith	Barbara Schorsch	Tommy Williams
Austin	Bellville	‡J. Lee Dittert	Dorothy Himly		Betty Krueger	Joe Spacek	Vernon Brozozowski
Bailey	Muleshoe	Marilyn Cox	Barbara McCamish	Linda Elder	Dorothy Turner	Kathleen Hayes	Jerry Hicks
Bandera	Bandera	Ray F. Mauer	Bernice Bates	Sam L. Darden	Elizabeth James	Marguerite Stevens	R. Stevens Forest Sr.
Bastrop	Bastrop	§Randy Fritz	Shirley Wilhelm		Doris Oldfield	Barbara Brinkmeyer	Con Keirsey
Baylor	Seymour	Joe Dickson	Doris Rushing	Lee Fernon	Pat Coker	Grady Hicks	Wayne Brown
Bee	Beeville	Robert E. Walk	Julia V. Torres	Jose Luis Aliseda	Office abolished 11-2-82.	Lulan Fraser	Robert L. Horn
Bell	Belton	¶John Garth	Vada Sutton	Patrick Ridley	Charles Jones	Betty Willingham	Dan Smith
Bexar	San Antonio	**John A. Longoria	Robert D. Green		Office abolished 11-6-84.	Rudy A. Garza	Harlon Copeland
Blanco	Johnson City	Charles Scott	Dorothy Uecker	Dean Myane	Doris Cage	Joyce Koch	Holton Burleson
Borden	Gail	Van L. York	Dorothy Browne		Melissa Ludecke	Royale Lewis	Royale Lewis
Bosque	Meridian	Ernest M. Reinke Jr.	Patsy Owen Mize	B. J. Shepherd	Randy Outlaw Pullin	Denise Wallace	Dewell Harper
Bowie	Boston	James M. Carlow	Marylene Megason		Pansy Baird	Aleatha Lyle Hanna	Mary Choate
Brazoria	Angleton	††James W. Phillips	Dolly Bailey		Sharon L. Reynolds	Ray Cornett	E.J. Joe King
Brazos	Bryan	‡‡R. J. Holmgreen	Mary Ann Ward	Jim Kuboviak	Sandra Walker	Gerald L. Winn	Ronnie Miller
Brewster	Alpine	Tom Connor	Betty Peters	Val Clark Bead	Hortencia Ramos	Jerry Ratcliff	Jack McDaniel
Briscoe	Silverton	Jimmy Burson	Bess McWilliams	Sharon Sutton Pigg	Janice S. Hill	Betty Ann Stephens	Richard C. Roehr
Brooks	Falfurrias	Homer Mora	Ruben Castellano	David T. Garcia	Gilbert Vela	Ramiro Castellano	Ramiro Castellano
Brown	Brownwood	G. Lee Haney	Margaret Woods		Connie Cline	Colline Nabers	William B. Donahoo
Burleson	Caldwell	Woods A. Caperton	Evelyn M. Henry	J.J. Skrivanek III	Beth Andrews Bills	Floy Stephens	Alfred G. Wilhelm
Burnet	Burnet	Martin McLean	Janet Parker	Jim Cross	Katy Gilmore	Doris Lewis	Weldon Buck
Caldwell	Lockhart	§§Rebecca Hawener	Nina S. Sells		Amelia G. Rizzuto	Mary Smith	Mike Bading
Calhoun	Port Lavaca	¶¶Howard G. Hartzog	Marlene Paul		Sharron Marek	Annette Baker	Kenneth D. Bowden
Callahan	Baird	Bill Johnson	Darlene Walker	Brad Harris	Dora Hounshell	Wauneta Esres	Bill Skinner
Cameron	Brownsville	***Antonio Garza Jr.	Joe G. Rivera	Luis V. Saenz	Michael Puckett	Tony Yzaguirre Jr.	Alex Perez
Camp	Pittsburg	Larry McCasland	Elaine Young	Michael Lantrip	LaJuana Law	Brenda Irby	Charles Elwonger
Carson	Panhandle	Jay Robert Reselius	Sue Persons	Ed Hinshaw	Peggy Butler	Roslyn Watson	Terry Timmons
Cass	Linden	Tommy E. Kessler	Wilma O'Rand		Jo Ellen Whatley	Bobbie Derrick	Paul W. Boone
Castro	Dimmitt	Mrs. M. L. Simpson Jr.	Joy Jones	Jimmy F. Davis	Oleta Raper	Billy W. Hackleman	Lonny N. Rhynes
Chambers	Anahuac	Oscar Nelson	Norma M. Rowland	Charles Brack	Maggie Cryer	Irene Clore	C.E. (Chuck) Morris
Cherokee	Rusk	†††Craig D. Caldwell	Fairy Upshaw	Robert McNatt	Diann Norton	Linda Beard	William Dickson
Childress	Childress	Dean Decker	Nancy Garrison	Derrill Nippert Jr.	Liz Kitchens	E.R. Howard	Claude B. Lane
Clay	Henrietta	Bill Nobles	Kay Hutchison	Eddy Atkins	Sue Brock	Tom Whitley	Jake Bogard
Cochran	Morton	Robert Yeary	Rita Tyson	J.C. Adams Jr.	Betty Hudson	Betty Akins	Royce Fred
Coke	Robert Lee	Royce Lee	Effie Hubbard	Bill J. Helwig	Phelan Wrinkle	D. Kristeen Roe	Marshall Millican
Coleman	Coleman	W.W. Skelton	Glenn Thomas	Joe D. LeMay	Barbara Freeman	Billie Baker	Wade Turner
Collin	McKinney	‡‡‡Ron Harris	Helen Starnes		Office abolished 11-5-85.	Kenneth L. Maun	Terry G. Box
Collingsworth	Wellington	Zook Thomas	Karen Coleman	Charles W. Darter	Yvonne Brewer	Rose Mary Throne	Dale Tarver
Colorado	Columbus	H.O. Strunk	Darlene Hayek	Stephen Sebesta	Joyce M. Stancik	Evelyn Thomas	Bill Esterling

*Anderson County Court at Law: J. Christopher Kolstad. †Angelina County Court at Law: Joe Martin. ‡Atascosa County Courts at Law: No. 1, Edward Johnson; No. 2, John Barina. **Bexar County Courts at Law: No. 1, Anthony J. Ferro; No. 2, H. Paul Canales; No. 3, Shay Gebhardt; No. 4, Sarah E. Garrahan; No. 5, Timothy F. Johnson; No. 6, R. Robert Lozano; No. 7, Tony Jimenez III; No. 8, Miguel Rodriguez; No. 9, Bonnie Reed. County Probate Courts: No. 1, Polly J. Spencer; No. 2, Keith Burris. ††Brazoria County Courts at Law: No. 1, Anthony Willy; No. 2, Garvin Germany Jr.; No. 3, James Blackstock. ‡‡Brazos County Courts at Law: No. 1, Claude Davis; No. 2, Sarah Ryan. §§Caldwell County Court at Law: Edward L. Jarrett. ¶¶Calhoun County Court at Law: Michael M. Fricke. ***Cameron County Courts at Law: No. 1, Everardo Garcia; No. 2, Adolph Betancourt. †††Cherokee County Court at Law: LeRue Dixon. ‡‡‡Collin County Courts at Law: No. 1, Weldon Copeland Jr.; No. 2, Jerry Lewis; No. 3, John O'Keefe Barry.

County Officials — Table No. 1: Judges, Clerks, Attorneys, Treasurers, Tax Assessor-Collectors, Sheriffs (Cont'd.)

County	County Seat	County Judge	County Clerk	County Attorney	County Treasurer	Assessor-Collector	Sheriff
Comal	New Braunfels	*Carter Casteel	Rosie Bosenbury	Nathan Rheinlander	R. A. Bartholomew	Gloria K. Clennan	Jack Bremer
Comanche	Comanche	John M. Weaver	Betty Conway	James L. Edwards	Billy Ruth Rust	Gay Horton	W. G. Garmon
Concho	Paint Rock	Charles J. Dankworth	Margaret T. Taylor	William Campbell	Dorothy Kirkpatrick	William J. Fiveash	William J. Fiveash
Cooke	Gainesville	Jim A. Robertson	Frank Scoggin	D. August Boto	Janet Johnson	Joyce Zwinggi	John S. Aston
Coryell	Gatesville	John Hull	Greta Dysinger	E. E. Powell Jr.	Vesta Leonard	Joan Blanchard	Gerald Kitchens
Cottle	Paducah	Billy J. Gilbert	Geneva Bragg	John H. Richards	Atha Prater	Rue Young	Frank Taylor
Crane	Crane	Charles Blue	Mary Grimes	Gene Clack	Gayla Phillips	Diana Earp	Raymond Weatherby
Crockett	Ozona	Kathryn Mayfield	Debbi Puckett	Orlando DeHoyos	Jim Dudley	Tom Stokes	Jim Wilson
Crosby	Crosbyton	Jerry Robertson	Floyd McGinnes	Tom J. Brian	Joyce M. Whitehead	Buran House	Lavoice "Red" Riley
Culberson	Van Horn	John Conoly	Linda Urias	Stephen Mitchell	Norma Hernandez	Amalia Y. Hernandez	Richard E. Upchurch
Dallam	Dalhart	David D. Field	LuAnn Taylor	Barry Blackwell	Francis "Jiggs" Payne	Patricia Radford	E. H. Little
Dallas	Dallas	†Lee Jackson	Earl Bullock		Bill Melton	David Childs	Jim Bowles
Dawson	Lamesa	Charles Arthur	Gloria Vera	Steven B. Payson	Gene DeFee	Diane Hogg	J. Terry Brown
DeWitt	Cuero	Ben E. Prause	Ann Drehr	Robert W. Post	Peggy Ledbetter	Margaret L. Mueller	Bobby J. McMahan
Deaf Smith	Hereford	Tom Simons	David Ruland	Roland Saul	Vesta Mae Nunley	Margaret Perez	Joe C. Brown Jr.
Delta	Cooper	John I. Hickman	Patsy P. Barton	Frank D. Moore	Glynana Stockton	Kim Helms	Billy Louis Allen
Denton	Denton	‡Jeff Moseley	Tim Hodges		Claudia Mulkey	Herb Barnhart	Kirby Robinson
Dickens	Dickens	Woodie McArthur Jr.	Helen Arrington	D. Vaughan (pro tem)	Druline Rape	Jerrie Ballard	Doyle King
Dimmit	Carrizo Springs	Rodrigo L. Guerra	Mario Z. Garcia	Charles Johnson	Arturo Juarez	Esther Z. Perez	Raul N. Medina Jr.
Donley	Clarendon	W. R. Christal	Fay Vargas	James T. Shelton	Wanda Smith	Wilma Lindley	William J. Thompson
Duval	San Diego	Gilberto Uresti	Oscar Garcia Jr.	Abelardo Garza	Daniel S. Lopez Jr.	Fernando Caballero	Santiago Barrera Jr.
Eastland	Eastland	Scott Bailey	Joann Johnson		Ruth Pugliese Hart	Nancy Trout	Ronnie White
Ector	Odessa	§Jim T. Jordan	Barbara Bedford	Tracey Bright	Carolyn Bowen	Lea Taylor	O. A. Brookshire
Edwards	Rocksprings	Neville G. Smart Jr.	Dorothy R. Hatley	Allen Ray Moody	Jewell V. Merritt	Teresa Sweeten	Donald G. Letsinger
Ellis	Waxahachie	¶Penny Redington	Cindy Polley	Mary Lou Shipley	Theata White	Betty Meador	John Gage
El Paso	El Paso	**Alicia Chacon	Hector Enriquez Jr.	Joseph Lucas	Office abolished 1-1-86.	James Hicks	Leo Samaniego
Erath	Stephenville	Bill M. Hailey	Nelda Crockett	Phil Nichols	Doris LaBaume	Jennifer Schlicke	David O. Coffee
Falls	Marlin	Robert Cunningham	Ruth H. Wood	Thomas B. Sehon	Marilyn Eierm	Gwen Atkins	Larry Pamplin
Fannin	Bonham	Jimmy Doyle	Margaret Gilbert	Dan Meehan	Florence Keahey	C. W. Bond Jr.	Talmage Moore
Fayette	La Grange	Edward F. Janecka	Irene Praka	John W. Wied	Office abolished 11-3-87	Carol Johnson	Vastine Koopmann
Fisher	Roby	Marshal Bennett	Bettie River	Rudy V. Hamric	Ilene Hale	Teddy Kral	Mickey Counts
Floyd	Floydada	William D. Hardin	Margaret Collier		Glenna M. Orman	Penny Golightly	Fred A. Cardinal
Foard	Crowell	Charlie Bell	Jana Payne	Daryl Halencak	Jan Bond	Bobby Bond	Bobby Bond
Fort Bend	Richmond	††Roy Cordes	Dianne Wilson		Kathy Hynson	Marsha Gaines	Perry Hillegeist
Franklin	Mount Vernon	Wayne Foster	Wanda Johnson	Walt Sears Jr.	Sue Ann Harper	Shirley Johnson	Wesley Wayne Foster
Freestone	Fairfield	Joe Roger Alderman	Doris T. Welch	Robert W. Gage	Patricia Robinson	Patsy Stroud	J. R. Sessions Jr.
Frio	Pearsall	Sid Williams III	Mona Hoyle	J. W. Smith Jr.	Mattie B. Saunders	Ysabela Pena	Gabriel Del Toro Jr.
Gaines	Seminole	Max Townsend	Pat Lacy	Bonnie Ericson	Linda Clark	Edith Renfroe	Jon Key
Galveston	Galveston	‡‡Ray Holbrook	Jessie G. Kirkendall	Harvey Bazaman	Richard Kirkpatrick	Charles E. Wilson	Joe Max Taylor
Garza	Post	Giles W. Dalby	Sonny Gossett	Preston Poole	Ruth Ann Young	Laura Hataway	Freddy Cockrell
Gillespie	Fredericksburg	Jay Weinheimer	Doris Lange	Gerald W. Schmidt	Jeanie Bel Crenwelge	Leola Brodbeck	Milton E. Jung
Glasscock	Garden City	Welburn Bednar	Betty Pate	Rick Hamby	Judy Kingston	Royce Pruit	Royce Pruit
Goliad	Goliad	John R. Barnhill	Gail M. Turley	S. G. Paulsgrove	La Nell Oehlke	Neva Thigpen	J. K. McMahan
Gonzales	Gonzales	Henry H. Vollentine	Sonny Sievers	R. B. Scheske	Marie Scoggins	Norma Jean DuBose	D. J. Brzozowski
Gray	Pampa	Carl Kennedy	Wanda Carter	R. D. McPherson	Scott B. Hahn	Margie Gray	Jimmy Free

*Comal County Court at Law: Fred Clark. †Dallas County Courts at Law: No. 1, Charles Lundy; No. 2, Martin Richter; No. 3, Victoria Welcome; No. 4, Bob Day; No. 5, Charles Stokes. County Criminal Courts: Ben Ellis; No. 2, Cas Dunlap; No. 3, Mike Schwille; No. 4, Ralph Taite; No. 5, Tom Fuller; No. 6, Phil Barker; No. 7, John P. McCall; No. 8, John C. Hendrik; No. 9, Molly Lenoir; No. 10, Marshall W. Gandy. County Probate Courts: Nikki DeShazo; No. 2, Robert E. Price; No. 3, Bill Bedard. County Criminal Courts of Appeal: Kenneth Vaughan; No. 2, Lynn Burson. ‡Denton County Courts at Law: No. 1, Darlene Whitten; No. 2, Virgil Vahlenkamp; No. 3, Hollis Godfrey. §Ector County Courts at Law: No. 1, J. A. Bobo; No. 2, Robert Hollman. ¶Ellis County Court at Law: Al Scoggins. **El Paso County Courts at Law: No. 1, Phillip Martinez; No. 2, Virgil Vahlenkamp; No. 3, Jack Ferguson; No. 4, Kitty Schield; No. 5, Herbert Cooper. ††Fort Bend County Courts at Law: No. 1, Larry Wagenbach; No. 2, Walter McMeans. ‡‡Galveston County Courts at Law: No. 1, John Thoma; No. 2, Ronald L. Wilson. Galveston County Probate Court: Jerome Jones.

County Officials — Table No. 1: Judges, Clerks, Attorneys, Treasurers, Tax Assessor-Collectors, Sheriffs (Cont'd.)

County	County Seat	County Judge	County Clerk	County Attorney	County Treasurer	Assessor-Collector	Sheriff
Grayson	Sherman	*Horace Groff	Pat Norman	R.T. Jarvis	Virginia Hughes	John W. Ramsey	L.E. "Jack" Driscoll
Gregg	Longview	†Kenneth Walker	Mollie Barber	David Brabham	Office abolished 1-1-88	Bobby Crawford	Bobby Weaver
Grimes	Anderson	Larry Snook	David Pasket	Joe Falco Jr.	Alvina B. Schroeder	Claude Jolly Jr.	Bill Foster
Guadalupe	Seguin	‡James E. Sagebiel	Lizzie M. Lorenz	Elizabeth C. Jandt	Larry Jones	Betty Boyd	Melvin L. Harborth
Hale	Plainview	Bill Hollars	Mildred Tucker		Evelyn Carroll	Christine Vinson	Charles Tue
Hall	Memphis	Kenneth E. Dale	Dean Cochran	John E. Chamberlain	Sandra Braddock	Sherri Smith	Kenneth W. Schull
Hamilton	Hamilton	Charles Garrett	Virginia Lovell	Thomas E. White	Karen S. Tyson	Ray Horner	Randy Murphree
Hansford	Spearman	Jim Brown	Amelia C. Johnson	John L. Hutchison	Norma Jean Mackie	Helen Dry	R.L. McFarlin Jr.
Hardeman	Quanah	K.D. McNabb	Judy Cokendolpher	Stanley K. Watson	Van R. White Jr.	Betty Lay	Chester Ingram
Hardin	Kountze	T.D. Mayfield Jr.	Dee Hatton	Bevil B. Wright	Eddie Doggett	Jeanette McWright	H.R. Holzapfel
Harris	Houston	§Jon Lindsay	Anita Rodeheaver	Mike Driscoll	Katy Caldwell	Carl S. Smith	Johnny Klevenhagen
Harrison	Marshall	¶Rodney Gilstrap	Glenn Link	Wm. A. Cunningham	Betty C. Anderson	Marie Noland	Bill Oldham
Hartley	Channing	Shane Rieken	Diane Thompson	Art Williams	Betty Edwards	Johnny Williams	Johnny Williams
Haskell	Haskell	B.O. Roberson	Rhonda Moeller	Marcos Hernandez	Willie Faye Tidrow	Bobbye Collins	Johnny Mills
Hays	San Marcos	**Eddy A. Etheredge	Ronnie Dannelley		Dorothy P. Sims	Ruth G. Clayton	Paul Hastings
Hemphill	Canadian	Bob Gober	Davene Hendershot	Charles Kessie	Claudette Hand	Gladene Woodside	Billy Bowen
Henderson	Athens	††Tommy Smith	Gwen Moffett	John Owens	Carolyn Sorrell	Milburn Chaney	H.B. Alfred
Hidalgo	Edinburg	‡‡J. Edgar Ruiz	William Leo		Arturo Solis	Ciro Trevino	Brig Marmolejo
Hill	Hillsboro	Charles R. Herd	Ruth Pelham	Pat Dohoney	Jewel Burton	Tommy Joe Davis	Brent Button
Hockley	Levelland	Don Avery	Mary K. Walker	Kirk Palmer	Jo Beth Hittson	Christy Clevenger	Leroy Schulle
Hood	Granbury	Don Cleveland	Anjanette Ables	John Hughes	Reva Hendrix	Ann Smith	Edwin Tomlinson
Hopkins	Sulphur Springs	Joe R. Pogue	Mary Attlesey	John F. Perry	Betty Moore	Jo Ruth Hodge	Billy G. Dirks
Houston	Crockett	§§John E. Musgrove	Nancy Huff	John Bobbitt	Dianne Rhone	Joan Lucas	Claudie Kendrick
Howard	Big Spring	Ben Lockhart	Margaret Ray	Hardy L. Wilkerson	Bonnie Franklin	Kathy Sayles	A.N. Standard
Hudspeth	Sierra Blanca	Billy R. Love	Patricia Bramblett		Pilar West	Stella C. Kelcy	Richard Love
Hunt	Greenville	¶¶Mike Farris	Jim Hamilton	Toby Wilkinson	Louise Walker	Joyce Barrow	Bobby Young
Hutchinson	Stinnett	David M. Willard	Carol Ann Herbst	Bill Smith	Kathy Sargent	Mary Henderson	Lon Blackmon
Irion	Mertzon	James D. Westfall	Jane Ethridge	Coleta Stewart	Betty Dennis	Joyce Gray	Jimmy Martin
Jack	Jacksboro	Mitchell G. Davenport	Patsy Ramzy	Michael G. Mask	Floyd Easter	Betty Cleveland	W.B. Mathis
Jackson	Edna	Harrison Stafford II	Martha Knapp		Marcell Maresh Jr.	LaVerne Ellison	Kelly Janica
Jasper	Jasper	Corbit Whitehead	Evelyn Stott	Guy James Gray	Brenda Call	Robert C. Pace Jr.	Aubrey E. Cole
Jeff Davis	Fort Davis	Bob Dillard	Peggy Robertson	Ann Barker	Geen Parrott	Harvey Adams	Harvey Adams
Jefferson	Beaumont	***R.P. LeBlanc Jr.	Lolita Ramos	Richard R. Gonzales	Linda Robinson	Nick Lampson	Carl Griffith Jr.
Jim Hogg	Hebbronville	Horacio S. Ramirez	Lilia Pena	J. Sanchez-Vera	Rosa Elia G. Gomez	Margarita R. Vera	Gilberto Ybanez
Jim Wells	Alice	T.L. Harville	Arnoldo Gonzalez		Adan Valadez Jr.	A. Lozano Jr.	Oscar Lopez Jr.
Johnson	Cleburne	†††Joe B. Durham	Robby G. Goodnight	Dale Hannah	Callier Mahanay	W.E. Carroll	Eddy G. Boggs
Jones	Anson	Brad Rowland	Buryl Rye	Dwade R. King	Irene Hudson	Tom Isbell	Mike Middleton
Karnes	Karnes City	Kenneth Pearce	Elizabeth Swize	John W. Berry	Charlene Blaschke	Ruth Lindsey	Robert R. Mutz
Kaufman	Kaufman	Maxine Darst	Crissy Gann		Linda Spencer	Donna Sprague	Robert Harris
Kendall	Boerne	Garland A. Perry	Darlene Herrin	Pamela K. McKay	Barbara J. Schwope	Betty J. Asher	H.A. Stevens
Kenedy	Sarita	J.A. Garcia Jr.	Barbara B. Turcotte	Roy C. Turcotte	John W. Turcotte	Lynwood G. Weiss	James M. Chandler Jr.
Kent	Jayton	Mark A. Geeslin	Cornelia Cheyne	Howard Freemyer	Laverna Harrison	Olen Roy Cheyne	Olen Roy Cheyne
Kerr	Kerrville	‡‡‡W.G. Stacy	Patricia Dye	David Motley	Dorothy Hilburn	Paula Rector	Frances Kaiser
Kimble	Junction	Wilbur R. Dunk	Elaine Carpenter	Callan Graham	Sheila D'Spain	Hal A. Bynum	Hal A. Bynum
King	Guthrie	Kerry Havins	Tavia Vinson		Mary Lee Hurt	Bama Nell Oliver	Jim Waller

*Grayson County Courts at Law: No. 1, Richard Pennell; No. 2, Kellis Sampson. †Gregg County Court at Law: John Sharp. ‡Guadalupe County Court at Law: Fred J. Moore. §Harris County Courts at Law: No. 1, Ed Landry; No. 2, Tom Sullivan; No. 3, Carolyn D. Hobson; No. 4, Charles Coussons. County Criminal Courts at Law: No. 1, Bill Ragan; No. 2, Michael Peters; No. 3, Jimmie Duncan; No. 4, James E. Anderson; No. 5, Hannah Chow; No. 6, J.R. Musslewhite; No. 7, Shelly P. Hancock; No. 8, Neel Richardson; No. 9, Alfred G. Leal; No. 10, Sherman P. Ross; No. 11, David Mendoza; No. 12, Joe Terracina; No. 13, Mark Atkinson; No. 14, Jim Barkley. County Probate Courts: No. 1, John Hutchison; No. 2, Pat Gregory; No. 3, Jim Scanlan; No. 4, William McCulloch. ¶Harrison County Court at Law: Max A. Sandlin. **Hays County Court at Law: No. 1, Howard S. Warner II; No. 2, Linda A. Rodriguez. ††Henderson County Court at Law: D. Matt Livingston. ‡‡Hidalgo County Courts at Law: No. 1, Rodolfo Delgado; No. 2, G. Jaime Garza; No. 3, Richard H. Garcia; No. 4, Leticia Hinojosa. §§Houston County Court at Law: Lynn Markham. ¶¶Hunt County Court at Law: Joe Leonard. ***Jefferson County Courts at Law: No. 1, Alfred Gerson; No. 2, Harold Plessala; No. 3, John Paul Davis. †††Johnson County Court at Law: Tommy Altaras. ‡‡‡Kerr County Court at Law: Spencer W. Brown.

County Officials — Table No. 1: Judges, Clerks, Attorneys, Treasurers, Tax Assessor-Collectors, Sheriffs (Cont'd.)

County	County Seat	County Judge	County Clerk	County Attorney	County Treasurer	Assessor-Collector	Sheriff
Kinney	Brackettville	Tim Ward	Dolores Raney	Tully Shahan	Carlotta de la Rosa	Martha P. Smallwood	Norman H. Hooten
Kleberg	Kingsville	*W.C. McDaniel	Sam D. Deanda	Pete de la Garza	Elaine Maca	Juanita R. Lara	Adan Munoz Jr.
Knox	Benjamin	David Neil Perdue	Gloria L. West		Evelyn B. Balis	Stanton Brown	Henry L. Dancer
La Salle	Cotulla	Leodoro Martinez Jr.	Nora Mae Tyler	Edward Hargrove	Jimmy P. Patterson	Elsa G. Sanchez	Darwin D. Avant
Lamar	Paris	Deane A. Loughmiller	Kathy Poole	Tom Wells	Latricia Miller	Kathy Bolton	Gene Burns
Lamb	Littlefield	Wayne Whiteaker	Bill Johnson	Martha M. Rose	Janice B. Wells	Linda Charlton	E.D. McNeese
Lampasas	Lampasas	Norris Monroe	Connie Hartmann	Larry Allison	Leona Hurst	Glenda Henderson	Gordon Morris
Lavaca	Hallettsville	W.A. Hobbs	Henry J. Sifka	James W. Carr	Thomas M. Grahmann	Mary Lee Supak	Larry J. Meinkowsky
Lee	Giddings	E.W. Kraus	Carol Dismukes	Steven Keng	Rose Fritsche	Virginia Jackson	Joe G. Goodson
Leon	Centerville	Robert L. Gresham	Margaret Wells	Gary Joe Taylor	William D. Lemons	Louise Wilson	Royce G. Wilson
Liberty	Liberty	†Dempsie Henley	Wanda Barker	A.J. Hartel	Winn Skidmore	Mark McClelland	O.J. Stewart
Limestone	Groesbeck	Ray Sealy	Sue Lown	Don Cantrell	Imogene Archibald	Barbara Rader	Dennis Walker
Lipscomb	Lipscomb	Willis V. Smith	Coeta Sperry	Randy M. Phillips	Pat Wyatt	Mary Gunn	Calvin Babitzke
Live Oak	George West	Jim Huff	Mildred James	W.L. Hardwick	LaVona Staithorpe	Larry R. Busby	Larry R. Busby
Llano	Llano	H. Howard Coleman	Bette Sue Hoy	L.T. DesChamps	LaVerne Miller	Margie Jung	Gale Ligon
Loving	Mentone	Donald C. Creager	Juanita Busby		Faye Busby	Elgin R. Jones	Elgin R. Jones
Lubbock	Lubbock	‡Don McBeath	Ann Davidson	Jimmy B. Wright	Connie H. Nicholson	Frank A. Stuart	D.L. "Sonny" Keesee
Lynn	Tahoka	J.F. Brandon	C.W. Roberts	John L. Oxley	Janet Porterfield	George D. McCracken	Jack Miller
Madison	Madisonville	James R. Fite	Joyce M. Coleman	Tony Hileman	Judy Weathers	Guslyn Hairston	Travis Neeley
Marion	Jefferson	Jerry M. Taylor	Clairece Ford		Dorothy T. Whatley	Mary Biggs	Walter Thomas
Martin	Stanton	Bob Deavenport	Virginia James	James L. McGivray	H.D. Howard	Leona Louder	Dan Saunders
Mason	Mason	Fritz E. Landers	Beatrice Langehennig	Harold R. Schmidt	Jane Hoerster	Don K. Grote	Don K. Grote
Matagorda	Bay City	Burt O'Connell	Sarah Vaughn	John C. Dickerson III	Suzanne Kucera	Bill Wiginton	Sammy Hurta
Maverick	Eagle Pass	Enriqueta D. Lane	E. Linda Sumpter	Alberto Ramon	Manuel Reyes Jr.	E.A. Luna	Tom Bowles
McCulloch	Brady	Randy Young	Rose Marie Luttrell	Robert Bond	Norma Gene Holloway	Deena G. Moore	Bill Strickland
McLennan	Waco	§Jim Lewis	Frank Denny		Bill Helton	A.F. "Buddy" Skeen	Jack Harwell
McMullen	Tilden	Elaine Franklin	Neil Hodgin	Maida Modgling	Donald Haynes	Mary K. Edwards	Eddie Reeves
Medina	Hondo	¶Donald E. Campsey	Anna T. Van De Walle	Ben Neel	Rita L. Moos	Loraine Newman	Wesley Scott
Menard	Menard	Otis H. Lyckman	Kay Kennemer		Linda Andrews	Madelon Highsmith	Floyd Rendon
Midland	Midland	**Charles W. Seltzer	Rosenelle Cherry	Mark Dettman	Dee Thompson	Frances Shuffield	Gary Painter
Milam	Cameron	Roger Hashem	La Verne Soefje	Hollis C. Lewis Jr.	Charlie J. Maddox	Porter E. Young Jr.	Leroy Broadus
Mills	Goldthwaite	T.W. Johnson	Walter A. Bryant	Clyde Cockrum	Gloria Marler	Glenn Carr	Glenn Carr
Mitchell	Colorado City	Ray Mayo	Joan Beach	Clay Strange	Ann Hallmark	Clarence C. Burt	Wendell Bryant
Montague	Montague	Jack Winn	Christine Cook	Jeb McNew	James M. Johnson	Christine P. Brock	C.R. (Glen) Whatley
Montgomery	Conroe	††Barb Sadler	Roy Harris	Jim Dozier	Martha Gustavsen	J.R. Moore	Joe Corley
Moore	Dumas	‡‡Jack D. Powell	Rhonnie C. Mayer	Rayford A. Ratliff	Phyllis Holmes	Jane Hendrix	H.T. Montgomery
Morris	Daingerfield	Vanoy Boozer	Doris McNatt	Richard Townsend	Peggy Campbell	Jerry L. Chambliss	Joe E. Skipper
Motley	Matador	Boyce Hart	Lucretia Campbell		Joe E. Campbell	Alton Marshall	Alton Marshall
Nacogdoches	Nacogdoches	§§O.L. Westmoreland	Carol Roberts	Bryan Holt Davis	Kay Watkins	Patsy Cates	Joe Evans
Navarro	Corsicana	Robert Jackson	James F. Doolen		Clyde Johnson	Peggy Jean Blackwell	Jim Hodge
Newton	Newton	Lon Sharver	Melba Canty	Edward J. Tracy	Ruth Dickerson	Beatrice Westbrook	Wayne Powell
Nolan	Sweetwater	‡‡Jack Aycock	Judy Brazelton	Lisa Peterson	Gayle Biggerstaff	Betty Bryant	Jim Blackley
Nueces	Corpus Christi	***Robert N. Barnes	Ernest M. Briones	Carlos Valdez	Office abolished 11-3-87.	Ramiro R. Canales	James T. Hickey
Ochiltree	Perryton	J. Kenny Norris	Jane Hammerbeck	Bruce Roberson	Ginger Hays	Ruby Lee Malaney	Joe Hataway
Oldham	Vega	Donnie Allred	Martha Thompson	Richard Brainerd	Shirley Galbraith	Carolyn Slutz	David Medlin
Orange	Orange	†††John McDonald Jr.	Molly Theriot	Stephen C. Howard	Vergie Moreland	Louvenia Hryhorchuk	Huel R. Fontenot
Palo Pinto	Palo Pinto	Harold M. Couch	Bobbie Smith	Phil Garrett	Tanya Fallin	Max Wheeler	Larry Watson
Panola	Carthage	‡‡‡John Cordray	Joyce Burgess	Morris Samford Jr.	Sue Parker	Lurlene Wilson	Jack Ellett

*Kleberg County Court at Law: †Liberty County Court at Law: Chap Cain. ‡Lubbock County Courts at Law: No. 1, Will Dodson; No. 2, Tom Cannon; No. 3, Mackey Hancock. §McLennan County Courts at Law: No. 1, David Hodges; No. 2, Mike Gassaway. ¶Medina County Court at Law: Hugh Meyer. **Midland County Courts at Law: No. 1, Al Walvoord; No. 2, James FitzGerald. ††Montgomery County Courts at Law: No. 1, Suzanne Stovall; No. 2, Jerry Winfree; No. 3, Mason Martin. ‡‡Moore County Court at Law: No. 1, Robert J. Vargas; No. 2, Delwin McGee. §§Nacogdoches County Court at Law: J. Jack Yarbrough. Nolan County Court at Law: Jack Aycock. ***Nueces County Courts at Law: No. 1, Robert J. Vargas; No. 2, Hector de Pena Jr.; No. 3, Hilda Tagle; No. 4, James E. Klager. Orange County Court at Law: Michael W. Shuff. Panola County Court at Law: Crawford Parker Jr.

County Officials — Table No. 1: Judges, Clerks, Attorneys, Treasurers, Tax Assessor-Collectors, Sheriffs (Cont'd.)

County	County Seat	County Judge	County Clerk	County Attorney	County Treasurer	Assessor-Collector	Sheriff
Parker	Weatherford	*Harris Worcester	Carrie Reed	Patrick J. Fleming	Kenneth Woody	Marjorie King	Ben Whiteman
Parmer	Farwell	Bonnie J. Clayton	Bonnie Warren	Charles F. Aycock	Anne G. Norton	Doris Herington	Rex Williams
Pecos	Fort Stockton	Fredie Capers	Billy Hodges	W.C. McDonald Jr.	Barry McCallister	E.F. Triplett	Bruce Wilson
Polk	Livingston	†John Thompson	Martha Johnson		Cheryl Henry	Robert Willis	Leamon Cain
Potter	Amarillo	‡Arthur Ware	Sue Daniel	Dale W. Elliott	Lawrence Youngblood	Rebecca F. McGee	Jimmy Don Boydston
Presidio	Presidio	Monroe Elms	Ramona Lara		Mario S. Rivera	Richard D. Thompson	Richard D. Thompson
Rains	Emory	Marshall C. Smith	Mary Sheppard	L.M. Braziel	Teresa Northcutt	Richard Wilson	Richard Wilson
Randall	Canyon	§C.W. McMenamy	LeRoy Hutton		Geneva Bagwell	Carol Autry	Harold Hooks
Reagan	Big Lake	Frank Sandel	Hazel S. Carr	Mark Edwards	Nancy L. Ratliff	Venitta Terral	Paul Weatherby
Real	Leakey	G.W. Twilligear Jr.	Rosemary Brice	John A. Daniel	Kathy Brooks	Donna Brice	James E. Brice
Red River	Clarksville	L.D. Williamson	Mary Hausler	Clayton Hall	Belinda Pryor	Juanita Benningfield	Bob Storey
Reeves	Pecos	‖Michael A. Harrison	Catherine Ashley	Scott W. Johnson	Nina V. Abila	Alicia Navarette	Raul Florez
Refugio	Refugio	Charles S. Stone	Janelle Morgan	Robert P. McGuill	Betty Greebon	Veronica Rocha	Jim Hodges
Roberts	Miami	Vernon H. Cook	Jackie M. Jackson	Richard J. Roach	Sarah E. Gill	Carol Billingsley	Lando Brown
Robertson	Franklin	Billy Lee Stellbauer	Mary B. Reagan	Jimmie McCullough	Jacqueline Vann	Charlene Bush	Lee Scott Hurley
Rockwall	Rockwall	William B. Lofland	Paulette Burks	Kendai Granzin	Scott Self	Gail Haire	Jacques I. Kiere
Runnels	Ballinger	Michael B. Murchison	Linda Bruchmiller	Wm. L. Ferguson	Nora Halfmann	VaRue McWilliams	William A. Baird
Rusk	Henderson	**Sandra Hodges	Helen Sillick	Dwight P. McDaniel	Nora Rousseau	Tommy Haskins	Cecil West
Sabine	Hemphill	Richard L. Smith	Nadine Gary	John W. Mitchell	Ollie Faye Sparks	Diane Husband	Blan Greer
San Augustine	San Augustine	Jack B. Nichols	Geraldine Smith		Carol W. Vaughn	Deborah Kay Woods	Charles Bryan
San Jacinto	Coldspring	Joe L. McMurrey	Joyce Hogue	David Aken	Charlene Everett	Vernon Lilley	Lacy Rogers
San Patricio	Sinton	Josephine Miller	Dottie Maley	David Williams	Judy Burr	Polly Nelson	Leroy Moody
San Saba	San Saba	Harlen Barker	Nila Ruth Barker	Thomas Giovaninni	Gerald D. Reavis	John Benner	John Benner
Schleicher	Eldorado	Johnny F. Griffin	Helen Blakeway	Lealand Greene	Karen Henderson	Dorothy M. Evans	Ronnie Norris
Scurry	Snyder	James R. Doolittle	Frances Billingsley		Rita Staton	Rona Sikes	Keith Collier
Shackelford	Albany	Marie Smith	Frances Wheeler	Joe Thigpen	Joy Grun	Ben J. Riley	Ben J. Riley
Shelby	Center	Floyd A. Watson	Peaches Conway	Gary W. Rholes	Lamerie Davis	Harlon Eakin	Paul Ross
Sherman	Stratford	††W.C. Fesler	M.L. Albert	Jack Q. Barton	Linda R. Keener	Zelda Pickens	Jack Haile
Smith	Tyler	‡‡Larry Craig	Mary Morris		Joyce W. Smith	Harris Oswalt	J.B. Smith
Somervell	Glen Rose	Dale McPherson	Lovella Williams	Timothy L. Rudolph	Vicki Crisp	Sandra Montgomery	Bill Hall
Starr	Rio Grande City	§§J.M. Martinez Jr.	Juan J. Mills	Romero Molina	Aurelio Sanchez	Maria Ofelia Saenz	Eugenio Falcon Jr.
Stephens	Breckenridge	Miller Tuttle	Helen Haddock	Jimmy L. Browning	Nancy Clary	Allena Dover	James Cain
Sterling	Sterling City	Robert L. Browne	Diane A. Haar	Drew T. Durham	Beth Kilpatrick	Don Howard	Don Howard
Stonewall	Aspermont	Bobby F. McGough	Betty L. Smith	Dwight Gibson	Linda Messick	Joyce McNutt	Bill Mullen
Sutton	Sonora	Carla Fields	Bobbie Smith	David W. Wallace	Joyce Chalk	Ann Hill	W.W. Webster
Swisher	Tulia	Jay Johnson	Pat Wesley	Donald L. Bookout	Lanelle Dovel	Shirley Whitehead	Paul Scarborough
Tarrant	Fort Worth	¶¶Tom Vandergriff	Suzanne Henderson		Office abolished 4-2-83	June Garrison	Don Carpenter
Taylor	Abilene	***Jesse A. Holloway	Janice Lyons		Anna Moore	Lavena Cheek	John Middleton
Terrell	Sanderson	Charles Stavley	Martha Allen	Marsha Monroe	Ginette Litton	Y.E. Duarte	Y.E. Duarte
Terry	Brownfield	Douglas Ryburn	Ann Willis	G. Dwayne Pruitt	Bobbie Jo McClure	Redelle Davis	Jerry Johnson
Throckmorton	Throckmorton	Joe Ed Thompson	Cathey Mitchell	Dwain Gibson	Brenda Rankin	Greg Dunlap	Greg Dunlap
Titus	Mt. Pleasant	Alford L. Flanagan	Eugenia Roach	Timothy Taylor	Cynthia Agan	June Roach	John A. Moss
Tom Green	San Angelo	†††Robert P. Post	Marie Russell	Paula Davidson	Billie J. McDaniel	Evelyn Vordick	Ernest Haynes
Travis	Austin	‡‡‡Bill Aleshire	Dana DeBeauvoir	Ken Oden	Dolores Ortega-Carter	Cecelia Burke	Doyne Bailey
Trinity	Groveton	Jimmie Thornton	Elaine I. Lockhart	Joe Warner Bell	Frances Worsham	Charlene Carr	Kenneth Moore
Tyler	Woodville	Jerome P. Owens Jr.	Donece Gregory		Jean Phillips	Barbara Tolbert	Gary Hennigan
Upshur	Gilmer	Everett Dean	Rex A. Shaw		Vernon Vick	Michael L. Smith	R.D. "Buck" Cross

*Parker County Court at Law: Fred M. Barker. †Polk County Court at Law: Stephen Phillips. ‡Potter County Courts at Law: No. 1, W.F. Roberts; No. 2, Richard P. Dambold. §Randall County Court at Law: Darrell R. Carey. ‖Reeves County Court at Law: Lee S. Green. **Rusk County Court at Law: Darrell Hyatt. ††Sherman County Court at Law: Dewin McQuee. ‡‡Smith County Courts at Law: No. 1, Joe D. Clayton; No. 2, Randall L. Rogers. §§Starr County Courts at Law: Alex W. Gabert. ¶¶Tarrant County Courts at Law: No. 1, R. Brent Keis; No. 2, Steve Wallace; No. 3, Vincent G. Sprinkle. County Criminal Courts at Law: No. 1, Sherry Hill; No. 2, Michael Mitchell; No. 3, Billy Mills; No. 4, Wallace Bowman; No. 5, Jake Cook; No. 6, R.J. Adcock; No. 7, Howard M. Fender. Probate Courts: No. 1, Robert M. Burnett; No. 2, Pat Ferchill. ***Taylor County Courts at Law: No. 1, Jack Grant; No. 2, Barbara Rollins. †††Tom Green County Court at Law: Ronald L. Blann. ‡‡‡Travis County Courts at Law: No. 1, David Phillips; No. 2, Steve Russell; No. 3, Michael Schless; No. 4 (Probate), Guy Herman; No. 5, Wilfred Aguilar; No. 6, David Puryear; No. 7, Brenda P. Kennedy.

County Officials — Table No. 1: Judges, Clerks, Attorneys, Treasurers, Tax Assessor-Collectors, Sheriffs (Cont'd.)

County	County Seat	County Judge	County Clerk	County Attorney	County Treasurer	Assessor-Collector	Sheriff
Upton	Rankin	Peggy Garner	Phyllis Stephens	Roy L. Scott	Nancy Poage	Dan W. Brown	Dan W. Brown
Uvalde	Uvalde	William R. Mitchell	Lucille C. Hutcherson	David R. White Jr.	Joni Deorsam	Helen Angermiller	Aubrey Smith
Val Verde	Del Rio	*Val Cadena	Maria Elena Cardenas	Carmen R. Worley	Morris L. Taylor	Wayne H. Hyde	James R. Koog
Van Zandt	Canton	Truett Mayo	Elizabeth Everitt		Shirley Morgan	Joyce Fugate	Pat Jorden
Victoria	Victoria	†Helen R. Walker	Val D. Huvar		Cathy Bailey	Bessie Lassmann	Dalton G. Meyer
Walker	Huntsville	‡Frank J. Robinson	James D. Patton	David P. Weeks	Barbara T. McGilberry	Oscar Thorne	Dale Myers
Waller	Hempstead	§Freddie R. Zach	Elva D. Mathis	Valda Combs-Jordan	Susan Winfree	Ellen C. Shelburne	Randy Smith
Ward	Monahans	Sam G. Massey	Pat V. Finley	John Stickels	Nell Berry	Dolores Hannah Fine	Ben Keele
Washington	Brenham	¶Dorothy Morgan	Gertrude Lehrmann	James R. Jones	Norman Draehn	Vennie Herzog	Billy W. Rosenbaum
Webb	Laredo	**Mercurio Martinez	Henry Flores	Anna L.C. Ramirez	Mike Urdiales	Ezequiel Laurel	Juan Garza
Wharton	Wharton	I.J. Irvin Jr.	Delfin Marek	Scott Cline	Gus Wessels Jr.	Frank H. Konvicka	R.R. Machala
Wheeler	Wheeler	Wendell Morgan	Margaret Dorman	Steven R. Emmert	Jerrie Moore	Jerry Dan Hefley	Jimmy Adams
Wichita	Wichita Falls	††Nick Gipson	Vernon Cannon		Marsha Watson	Miles Graham	Thomas J. Callahan
Wilbarger	Vernon	Bob Arnold	Frances McGee	Paul Scott	Janice King	JoAnn Bourland	David Quisenberry
Willacy	Raymondville	Eustolio Gonzales	Terry Flores	Diana Cisneros	Dolores Duron	La Quita Garza	Larry G. Spence
Williamson	Georgetown	‡‡John Doerfler	James N. Boydston	Billy Ray Stubblefield	Irvin Leschber	Dorothy E. Jones	Jim Boutwell
Wilson	Floresville	Martha Schnabel	Eva S. Martinez	Jerry Heltzel	Carolyn Orth	Anna D. Gonzales	Martin H. Baumann
Winkler	Kermit	Frances Clark	Ruth Godwin	Tom Cameron	John W. Stout	Patti Franks	W.H. Sage
Wise	Decatur	§§L.B. McDonald	Sherry Parker	Jean Bishop	Emma Ray	J.C. Stockton	Leroy E. Burch
Wood	Quitman	Lee E. Williams	Martha Bridges		June Robinson	Fred Morrow	Frank White
Yoakum	Plains	Dallas Brewer	Ruby Bruton	Imajean Gray	Toni Jones	Wanda Smith	Jimmie Rice
Young	Graham	Fred Thigpen	Shirley Choate	Arturo A. Figueroa Jr.	Barbara Shoemate	Jean Hester	Carey W. Pettus
Zapata	Zapata	Jose Luis Guevara	Arnoldo Flores		Alejandro R. Ramirez	Rosalva Villarreal	Romeo R. Ramirez
Zavala	Crystal City	Pablo Avila	Teresa P. Flores	Joe Taylor	Susie Perez	Martha P. Cruz	Jose Serna

*Val Verde County Court at Law: James M. Simmonds. †Victoria County Courts at Law: No. 1, Laura A. Weiser; No. 2, Juan Velasquez III. ‡Walker County Court at Law: Ann P. Baker. §Waller County Court at Law: June Jackson. ¶Washington County Court at Law: Robert S. Pieratt. **Webb County Court at Law: Raul Vasquez. ††Wichita County Courts at Law: No. 1, Jim Hogan; No. 2, Tom Bacus. ‡‡Williamson County Courts at Law: No. 1, Timothy G. Maresh; No. 2, Robert F. B. Morse. §§Wise County Court at Law: Melton D. Cude.

TEXAS COUNTY AND DISTRICT OFFICIALS—TABLE NO. 2

District Judges, District Clerks, District Attorneys and County Commissioners. See also Table 1.

County	Dist.	District Judge	District Clerk	District Attorney	Comm. Precinct 1	Comm. Precinct 2	Comm. Precinct 3	Comm. Precinct 4
Anderson	3; 87; 349; 369	R.W. Lawrence; Sam B. Bournias; Melvin W. Whitaker; Bascom W. Bentley III	Maxine Barnette	Jeff Herrington	Truman Starr	Rodney A. Howard	T.L. Beard	J.T. (Tommy) Davis
Andrews	109; 159	James Clack; Gerald A. Goodwin	Imogene Tate	James L. Rex	Bill Chesney	John Hogue	Jerry McPherson	Willard Snow
Angelina	217	David V. Wilson	Jimmie Robinson	Clyde Herrington	Delbert Aldredge	I.D. Henderson	Jim Nerren	James A. Stanley
Aransas	36; 156; 343	Ronald M. Yeager; Rachel Littlejohn; Alonzo T. Rodriguez	Bobbie Rogers	Tom Bridges	Oscar Pina	Ray Longino	W.B. Sanders	Larry Barnebey
Archer	97	Roger E. Towery	Jane Adams	Jack McGaughey	Evon Carter	James R. Wolf	Ben Buerger	D.W. Stone
Armstrong	47	David L. Gleason	Kathy Byrd	Danny Hill	Rex A. Bagwell	Wes Stockett	Stanley Gillham	C.M. Bryant
Atascosa	81; 218	Olin B. Strauss; Stella Saxon	Sally Starr	Alger Kendall	Victor Holguin	Emmett Mikolajczyk	Freddie Ogden	Weldon Cude
Austin	155	Dan Beck	Lorri Coody	Travis Koehn	Curtis Hempel	Mark C. Wittner	James Duke	J. Royce Burger
Bailey	287	Jack D. Young	Nelda Merriott	Johnny Actkinson	R.L. Scott	C.E. Grant Jr.	Joey R. Kindle	Bennie Claunch
Bandera	216	Stephen B. Ables	Bernice Bates	E. Bruce Curry	Bennie Barker	Dan C. Alanis III	Roger Raser	N.P. Thompson
Bastrop	21; 335	John L. Placke; Harold R. Towslee	Peggy Walicek	Charles Penick	Johnny Sanders	Elaine Seidel	Pat Meuth	Lee Dildy
Baylor	50	David Wayne Hajek	Doris Rushing	Bobby D. Burnett	Don Matus	Jimmy Smalstria	Jim Richardson	Felton Mayers
Bee	36; 156; 343	Ronald W. Yeager; Rachel Littlejohn; Alonzo T. Rodriguez	Margie P. Carter	Clarence F. Moore	Victor Salazar	Grady C. Hogue	Santiago Martinez	Walter E. Smith
Bell	146; 169; 264	Joe Carroll; Rick Morris; Stanton Pemberton; Jack Prescott	Daffy Carpenter	Arthur C. Eads	Cliff Jones	Robert Shoemaker	Roy Goad	Royce Matkin
Bexar	37; 45; 57; 73; 131; 144; 150	Vacancy; Carol R. Haberman; Charles A. Gonzalez; Andy Mireles; Rose Spector; Susan D. Reed; Carleton Spears	David J. Garcia	Steven C. Hilbig	Robert Tejeda	Paul Elizondo	Walter Bielstein	Bob Lee
Bexar (Dist. Judges Cont'd.)			166 Peter Michael Curry; 175 Phil G. Chavarria Jr.; 186 Terry Mcdonald; 187 Patrick Priest	224 Carolyn H. Spears; 225 John J. Specia Jr.; 226 Sid L. Harle; 227 Mike Machado	235 Michael P. Peden; 288 Raul Rivera; 289 Tom Rickoff; 290 Sharon S. MacRea			
Blanco	33	Clayton E. Evans	Dorothy Uecker	Sam Oatman	Charles Jones	Robert Riddell	George Byars	Paul Granberg
Borden	132	Gene L. Dulaney	Dorothy Browne	Ernie B. Armstrong	Frank Currey	Larry D. Smith	Vernon Wolf	Hurston Lemons Jr.
Bosque	220	James Morgan	Diane Wellborn	Andy McMullin	J.E. McDowell	Steve McCoy	Calvin Rueter	Carl Smith
Bowie	5; 102; 202	Jack E. Carter; Leon F. Pesek; Guy Jones	Billy Fox	John F. Miller Jr.	Jack Stone	L.B. Grimes	Dale Barrett	Paul Fannin
Brazoria	23; 149; 239; 300	Neil Caldwell; Robert May; James Ray Gayle Jr.; Ogden Bass	Frances Bennett	Jim Mapel	Ronnie Broaddus	James D. Clawson	Billy Joe Plaster	M.A. Mickey Brooks
Brazos	85; 272; 361	William McDonald Jr.; John Martin Delaney; Carolyn L. Ruffino	Travis E. Nelson	William Turner	Gary Norton	Walter Wilcox	Randy Sims	Milton Turner
Brewster	83	Alex R. Gonzalez	Betty Peters	Richard Barajas	Mickey Clouse	J.W. "Red" Pattillo	Emilio Salmon	Abelardo Leyva
Briscoe	110	John R. Hollums	Bess McWilliams	Becky McPherson	Aaron Younger	J.L. Chandler	L.B. Garvin Jr.	Fred A. Strange
Brooks	79	Terry A. Canales	Pete Martinez	Richard Terrell	J.M. Alaniz	Lonnie Cavazos	Roel Villarreal	Salvador Gonzales
Brown	35	Ernest Cadenhead	Jan Brown	Fred Franklin	Kenneth Boyd	J.D. Chastain	Chester Damron	Byron Levisay
Burleson	21; 335	John L. Placke; Harold Towslee	Doris H. Brewer	Charles Sebesta Jr.	Franklin J. Beran	Don L. Groce	W.J. Stracener	Bobby E. Schoppe
Burnet	33	Clayton E. Evans	Modena Curington	Sam Oatman	Mac Hammond	Carroll McCoy	Kenny Baker	Allan Cunningham
Caldwell	22; 207; 274	Charles R. Ramsey; Robert T. Pfeuffer; Fred A. Moore	Emma Jean Schulle	Charles Kimbrough	Morris Alexander	Charles C. Bullock	Ronnie Duesterheft	Joe Ivan Roland

District Judges, District Clerks, District Attorneys and County Commissioners. (Cont'd.) See also Table 1.

County	Dist.	District Judge	District Clerk	District Attorney	Comm. Precinct 1	Comm. Precinct 2	Comm. Precinct 3	Comm. Precinct 4
Calhoun	24	Clarence Stevenson	Ollie Harris Cuellar	Jack Whitlow	Leroy Belk	Stanley L. Mikula	Roy Smith	Oscar Hahn
	135	Marion M. Lewis						
	267	Whayland Kilgore						
Callahan	42	Don Lane	Cubelle Harris	Roy LaFoy		Lowell Johnson	Tommy Holland	Joe Ingram
Cameron	103	Menton Murray	Aurora de la Garza	Luis V. Saenz	Lucindo Rosenbaum	Carlos Cascos	Adolph Thomae Jr.	Tivie Valencia
	107	Benjamin Uresti						
	138	Robert Garza						
	197	Darrell B. Hester						
	357	Rogelio Valdez						
Camp	76	Bill D. Moye	Doloria Bradshaw	Charles C. Bailey	Jack Efurd	Larry Shelton	O.C. Taylor	Curtis Wall
	276	William R. Porter						
Carson	100	John T. Forbis	Sue Persons	David M. McCoy	Mike Britten	Choc Smith	Jerry Strawn	Tracy Kotara
Cass	5	Jack Carter	Becky Wilbanks	Neal Birmingham	Taylor Duncan	B. George Parker	Robert J. Buzbee	J.H. (Hap) Clements
Castro	64	Jack R. Miller	Joy Jones	Jimmy F. Davis	Harold Smith	Dale Winders	Jeff Robertson	Vincent Guggemos
Chambers	242	Marvin F. Marshall	R.B. Scherer		Kenneth Bettis	S. Desormeaux Jr.	Earl Porter	Paul Lott
	253	W.G. Woods Jr.						
Cherokee	2	Morris W. Hassell	Marlys Sue Mason	Charles Holcomb	E.R. (Bob) Gregg	Alton J. Hicks	F.E. Hassell	Billy McCutcheon
	344	Carroll Wilborn Jr.						
	369	Bascom W. Bentley III						
Childress	100	John T. Forbis	Nancy Garrison	David M. McCoy	Stanley Terry	Dan Imhof	Glenn Channell	Mike Wilson
Clay	97	Roger Towery	Dan Slagle	Jack McGaughey	G.E. Liggett	Charles Green	J.I. Johnson	Brice Jackson
Cochran	286	Andy Kupper	Rita Tyson	Gary A. Goff	Billy D. Carter	Frank Davidson	A.W. Coffman	Kenneth Burke
Coke	51	Royal Hart	Ettie Hubbard	Gerald A. Fohn	Paul Burns	Billy Joe Luckett	Tim Millican	James Tidwell
Coleman	42	Donald H. Lane	Louise Thompson	Ross L. Jones	Jack Strickland	Billy McCrary	Vernon Slate	Max Horne
Collin	199	John R. Roach	Hannah Kunkle	Tom O'Connell	Phyllis Cole	Jerry Hoagland	John D. Witherspoon	Jack Hatchell
	219	Curt Henderson						
	296	Verla Sue Holland						
	366	Nathan White Jr.						
Collingsworth	100	John T. Forbis						
Colorado	25	B.B. Schraub	Karen Coleman	David McCoy	Dan Langford	Zeb Roberson	Elvis Pitts	Dudley Coleman
	2D25	Gus J. Strauss	Harvey G. Vornsand		Otto Loessin	Johnnie Eistner	Jerome C. Wicke	Leon Spanihel
Comal	22	Charles R. Ramsay	Margaret Herbrich	Bill M. Reimer	J.L. Evans	Neil V. Craigmile	Patricio Hernandez	Morris Schwab
	207	Robert T. Pfeuffer						
	274	Fred A. Moore						
Comanche	220	James E. Morgan	LaNell S. Williams	Andy J. McMullen	Wade Davis	Murlin Elliott	Brent Daniel	Clyde Brinson
Concho	119	John E. Sutton	Margaret T. Taylor	Stephen Smith	Jerry Conley	John Hruska	Bobby Medders	John B. Williams
	198	Emil Karl Prohl		Ronald L. Sutton				
Cooke	235	Jerry W. Woodlock	Bobbie Calhoun	Phil L. Adams	Danny Knight	Kenneth Alexander	Jerry Lewis	Virgil J. Hess
Coryell	52	Phillip H. Zeigler	Carolyn Pollard	Sandy Gately	John Carlton	Don Thompson	Hiram Davidson	Kyle Pruitt
Cottle	50	David W. Hajek	Geneva Bragg	Bobby D. Burnett	Paul Whitener	A.R. Defoor	Lester Moss	Jimmy Branson
Crane	109	James H. Clack	Mary Grimes	Michael Fostel	Fred Harrelson	John Dee Daniell	Dick Hall	W. McCutchen Jr.
Crockett	112	M. Brock Jones Jr.	Debbi Puckett	J.W. Johnson Jr.	Sostenes DeHoyos	Fred Deaton	Jim House	Rudy Martinez
Crosby	72	Blair Cherry Jr.	Billie Jo Freeman	Tom J. Brian	Nelton Shote	R.W. Self	Herschel Bird	James A. Boydstun
Culberson	34	William E. Moody	Linda Urias	Steve Simmons	Cornelio Garibay	Manuel Molinar	James Stone	Lupe Escajeda
	205	Sam W. Callan						
	210	Sam M. Paxson						
Dallam	69	Ron Enns	LuAnn Taylor	Barry Blackwell	Bob Sheets	Oscar Przilas	Don Bowers	Eulan Sheets
Dallas	14	John M. Marshall	Bill Long	John Vance	Jim Jackson	Nancy Judy	John W. Price	Chris Semos
	44	Candace G. Tyson						

Dallas County Dist. Judges (Cont'd.)

68 Gary Hall	191 David Brooks	254 Dee Miller	330 Theo Bedard	292 Mike Keasler
95 Joe B. Brown	193 Merrill Hartman	255 Don Koons	363 Faith Johnson	298 Adolph Canales
101 Joseph B. Morris	193 Michael O'Neill	256 Carolyn Wright	Cr. 1 Ron Chapman	301 Bob O'Donnell
116 Frank Andrews	194 Harold Entz	265 Keith T. Dean	Cr. 2 Larry W. Baraka	302 Frances Harris
134 Anne Packer	195 Joe Kendall	282 Tom Price	Cr. 3 Mark Tolle	303 Sue Lykes
160 Mark Whittington	203 Thomas B. Thorpe	283 Jack Hampton	Cr. 4 Frances Maloney	304 Harold C. Gaither Jr.
162 Bill Rhea	204 Richard Mays	291 Gerry Meier	Cr. 5 Pat McDowell	305 Catherine S. Evans

District Judges, District Clerks, District Attorneys and County Commissioners. (Cont'd.) See also Table I.

County	Dist.	District Judge	District Clerk	District Attorney	Comm. Precinct 1	Comm. Precinct 2	Comm. Precinct 3	Comm. Precinct 4
Dawson	106	George H. Hansard	Terrye Brown	Ricky Smith	Delmar Moore	Bill Meares	Gene Hendon	Guy Kinnison
DeWitt	24	Clarence N. Stevenson	Gerry Smith	Wiley L. Cheatham	Wallace W. Beck	Billy Moore	Gilbert Pargmann	Odell White
	135	Marion M. Lewis						
	267	Whayland W. Kilgore						
Deaf Smith	222	David Wesley Gulley	Lola Faye Veazey	Roland Saul	John Stribling Jr.	Lupe Chavez	Troy Don Moore	Johnny Latham
Delta	8	Lanny R. Ramsay	Patsy P. Barton	Frank J. Long	C.D. Goforth	Gaston Dodd	Ardell Allison	Ted Carrington
	62	Jim N. Thompson						
Denton	16	John Narsutis	Tracy Kunkel	Bruce Isaacks	Buddy Cole	Sandy Jacobs	Lee Walker	Don Hill
	158	Phillip Vick						
	211	Sam Houston						
	362	David C. White						
	367	E. Lee Gabriel						
Dickens	110	John R. Hollums	Helen Arrington	Becky McPherson	Eldon Williams	R.J. Bell	Vernon Wright	Darrell Thomason
Dimmit	293	Rey Perez	A.G. Martinez Jr.	Roberto Serna	Donald F. Urban	Joaquin Salgado	Oscar Alvarado	Rodrigo Jaime
	365	Amado Abascal III						
Donley	100	John T. Forbis	Fay Vargas	David M. McCoy	Steve Reynolds	C.W. Cornell	T. Mullins	W. Chamberlain
Duval	229	Ricardo H. Garcia	Antonio Salinas	Heriberto Silva	Alejo C. Garcia	Jose Noe Martinez	Richard M. Barton	Robert S. Lee
Eastland	91	Jim R. Wright	Bill Miears	Leslie B. Vance	Richard A. Robinson	Calvin Ainsworth	L.T. Owen	Reggie Pittman
Ector	70	Gene Ater	Jackie Sue Barnes	Gary Garrison	Jack Crider	Bryan Henderson	Ricky Jorgenson	Bob Bryant
	161	Tryon Lewis						
	244	Joe Connally						
	358	Bill McCoy						
Edwards	63	George M. Thurmond	Dorothy R. Hatley	Thomas F. Lee	Mario R. Ruiz	Robert Cottle	Ivan H. Smart	Rex Johnson
El Paso	34	William E. Moody	Edie Rubalcaba	Steve W. Simmons	Charles C. Hooten	Orlando Fonseca	Rogelio Sanchez	Jim Goldman
	41	Mary Anne Bramblett						
	65	Edward S. Marquez						
	120	Robert Dinsmoor						
	168	Jose E. Troche						
	171	Peter S. Peca						

El Paso County Dist. Judges (Cont'd.)
205 Sam W. Callan
210 Sam M. Paxson

El Paso County Dist. Judges (Cont'd.)
243 Herbert E. Marsh
327 Enrique H. Pena

El Paso County Dist. Judges (Cont'd.)
346 Jose J. Baca

County	Dist.	District Judge	District Clerk	District Attorney	Comm. Precinct 1	Comm. Precinct 2	Comm. Precinct 3	Comm. Precinct 4
Ellis	40	Gene Knize	Billie Fuller	Mary Lou Shipley	James Harper	Jerry Holland	Del McLane	Ron Brown
Erath	266	Donald R. Jones	Thomas Pack	John E. Terrill	Kenneth Robertson	Don Stone	Duane Oakes	Hurrsell Whitefield
Falls	82	Robert M. Stem	Larry Hoelscher	Thomas B. Sehon	Roy Jund	Bishop Williams	Tony Hoelscher	Clinton Jacques
Fannin	6	Henry G. Braswell	Eva Lindsey	Derrell Hall	Lloyd Flanagan	Kurt Fogelberg	Choice Wilson	
	336	Ray F. Grisham						
Fayette	155	Dan Beck	Virginia Wied	John W. Wied	Lawrence Adamcik	Ronnie Stork	Wilbert L. Gross	Tom Muras
Fisher	32	Weldon Kirk	Bettie Hargrove	Frank W. Conard III	Charles Meek	Billy Henderson	Jay Hendon	Gene Terry
Floyd	110	John R. Hollums	Barbara Edwards	Becky McPherson	Connie D. Bearden	Floyd W. Jackson	George Taylor	Howard G. Bishop
Foard	46	Thomas A. Neely	Jana Payne	Dan Mike Bird	T.R. Cates	Johnny Urquizo	Wilson Myers	Dayton Everson
Fort Bend	240	Thomas Culver III	Glory Ketelers	Jack Stern	R.L. O'Shieles	Grady Prestage	Alton Pressley	Bob Lutts
Franklin	8	Lanny R. Ramsay	Wanda Johnson	Frank Long	Jearl Cooper	Bobby R. Elbert	B.F. Ingram	Leon Keith
	62	Jim Thompson						
Freestone	77	H.D. Black Jr.	Sue Gregory	Danny Tate Willard	W.R. McSwane	Stanley Gregory	Johnny B. Massey	
	87	Sam B. Bournias						
Frio	81	Olin D. Strauss	Brenda Fudge	Alger Kendall	Antonio Moreno Jr.	J.M. Lindsey III	Adolfo Alvarez	Humberto Berrones
	218	Stella Saxton						
Gaines	106	George H. Hansard	Wilma McNew	Ricky Smith	Jean Bagley	Joe Rowlett	Ray Garrett	J.W. Allen
Galveston	10	Ed. J. Harris	V.J. Beninati Jr.	Michael J. Guarino	Eddie Barr	Eddie Janek	Wayne Johnson III	Billy J. Pegues
	56	I. Allan Lerner						
	122	Henry G. Dalehite						
	212	Roy C. Engelke Jr.						
	306	Susan Baker Olsen						
Garza	106	George H. Hansard	Sonny Gossett	Ricky Smith	Sam E. Ellis	Albert Stone	John Valdez	Herbert Walls
Gillespie	216	Stephen B. Ables	Alberta Gaddy	Bruce Curry	Dayton F. Herber	William A. Roeder	Levy Kusenberger	Eldon Ray Feller
Glasscock	118	Robert H. Moore III	Betty Pate	Rick Hamby	Jimmy Strube	Ervin Wooten	Randell Sherrod	Donald Cypert

District Judges, District Clerks, District Attorneys and County Commissioners. (Cont'd.) See also Table 1.

County	Dist.	District Judge	District Clerk	District Attorney	Comm. Precinct 1	Comm. Precinct 2	Comm. Precinct 3	Comm. Precinct 4
Goliad	24 / 135 / 267	Clarence N. Stevenson / Marion M. Lewis / Whayland W. Kilgore	Gail M. Turley	Wiley L. Cheatham	Ralph Medrano	Jerry Rodriguez	Louis Fromme Jr.	F.F. Post Jr.
Gonzales	25 / 2D25	B.B. Schraub / Gus J. Strauss	Patricia Heinemeyer	W.C. Kirkendall	E.R. Breitschopf	J.V. Ochs	David Kuntschik	Welly Gibson
Gray	31 / 223	M. Kent Sims / Lee Waters	Vickie Walls	Harold L. Comer	Joe Wheeley	Jim Greene	Gerald L. Wright	Ted Simmons
Grayson	15 / 59 / 336	James R. Fry / Lloyd W. Perkins / Ray F. Grisham	Cyndi Mathis		Doug Walker	Johnnie McCraw Jr.	C.E. Kretsinger	C.E. "Gene" Short
Gregg	124 / 188 / 307	Alvin G. Khoury / Larry W. Starr / Robin Sage	Ruby Cooper	David Brabham	G.A. McLaughlin	James Gray	Nelson Tyl	James E. Johnson
Grimes	12 / 278	William L. McAdams / Jerry A. Sandel	Wayne Rucker	David Barron	Jack Carrell	Jerald Dyer	Albin Finke	Marcus Mallard
Guadalupe	25 / 2D25	B.B. Schraub / Gus J. Strauss	James Behrendt	W.C. Kirkendall	Charles J. Willmann	Monroe Schubert	James M. Brannon	Charles Davis
Hale	64 / 242	Jack R. Miller / Marvin F. Marshall	Anna Evans	Terry McEachern	Nina Jo Morris	Homes Roberson	Henry Rieff	James Belk
Hall	100	John T. Forbis	Dean Cochran	David McCoy	Jerry D. Smith	Bobby H. Barbee	Troy E. Phillips	U.F. Coker Jr.
Hamilton	220	James E. Morgan	LaJuan Mizell	Andy J. McMullen	W.O. McCollum	Ora Dell Tyson	George Kilgo	Garland Short
Hansford	84	Juan E. Blackburn	Amelia C. Johnson	Stephen F. Cross	Garland Head	Joe T. Venneman	B.J. Renner	Val Winger
Hardeman	46	Thomas A. Neely	Judy Cokendolpher	Dan Mike Bird	Charles McSpadden	James Rine	Charles Taylor	Van D. Foster
Hardin	88 / 356	Earl B. Stover / Britton E. Plunk	Aline Harper	R.F. Horka	Bob Burgess	John Golden	Bill Fregia	J.D. Brown
Harris	11 / 55 / 61 / 80 / 113 / 125 / 127 / 129 / 133 / 151 / 152 / 157 / 164 / 165	Mark Davidson / Kathy Stone / R. Shearn Smith / William R. Powell / Geraldine Tennant / Don E. Wittig / Sharolyn Wood / Hugo A. Touchy / Lamar McCorkle / Vacant / Jack O'Neill / Mike Schneider / Peter S. Solito / Kenneth D. Harrison	Katherine Tyra	John B. Holmes Jr.	El Franco Lee	Jim Fonteno	Steve Radack	Jerry Eversole

Harris County Dist. Judges (Cont'd.)

Dist.	Judge	Dist.	Judge	Dist.	Judge	Dist.	Judge
174	George Godwin	190	Eileen Frances O'Neill	248	Woody R. Densen	310	Allen J. Daggett
176	James Brian Rains	208	John H. Kyles	257	Norman R. Lee	311	Bill Elliott
177	Miron A. Love	209	Michael T. McSpadden	262	Doug Shaver	312	Robert S. Webb III
178	William T. Harmon	215	Eugene Chambers	263	Charles J. Hearn	313	Robert Lowry
179	Mike Wilkinson	228	Ted Poe	269	W. David West	314	Robert B. Baum
180	Patricia R. Lykos	230	Joe Kegans	270	Ann Cochran	315	Eric G. Andell
182	Donald K. Shipley	232	A.D. Azios	280	Tony Lindsay	333	Richard Bianchi
183	Jay W. Burnett	234	Scott Brister	281	Louis M. Moore	334	Russell Lloyd
184	Bob Burdette	245	Henry G. Schuble III	295	Daniel M. Downey	337	Jim Barr
185	Carl Walker Jr.	246	Wm. W. Peavy Jr.	308	Bob Robertson	338	Mary Bacon
189	Richard W. Millard	247	Charles D. Huckabee	309	John D. Montgomery	339	Norman Lanford
						351	Lupe Salinas

County	Dist.	District Judge	District Clerk	District Attorney	Comm. Precinct 1	Comm. Precinct 2	Comm. Precinct 3	Comm. Precinct 4
Harrison	71	Bonnie Leggat	Betty Cawood	Richard Berry	James D. Mooney	Wm. D. Power	Michael Adkisson	H.W. McCoy
Hartley	69	Ron Enns	Diane Thompson	John Fouts	John Ray Frantz II	Bob Hunnicutt	Jim Yoder	Joe Billups
Haskell	39	Charles L. Chapman	Carolyn Reynolds		J.L. Grand	Ronnie Chapman	J.R. Perry	C.A. Turnbow
Hays	22 / 207 / 274	Charles R. Ramsay / Robert T. Pfeuffer / Fred A. Moore	W.H. Moore	Marcos Hernandez	Rafael Gonzales	Wayne R. Ford	Craig D. Payne	Oran Hill Rippy
Hemphill	31	M. Kent Sims	Davene Hendershot	Harold Comer	Kenneth Osborne	Don Thomason	Leonard Powledge	Robert Forrest
Henderson	3 / 173	R.W. Lawrence / Jack H. Holland	Lelia May Garner	Billy Bandy	Jim Blakeney	Harold Hammer	Cleburn Shavor	Norman Tumlinson
Hidalgo	92 / 93 / 139 / 206 / 275 / 332	Homer Salinas / Fernando Mancias / Raul L. Longoria / Joe B. Evins / Juan R. Partida / Mario E. Ramirez Jr.	Pauline Gonzalez	Rene Guerra	Ramiro Cavazos	Lalo Arcaute	Norberto Salinas	Leonard Camarrillo

District Judges, District Clerks, District Attorneys and County Commissioners. (Cont'd.) See also Table 1.

County	Dist.	District Judge	District Clerk	District Attorney	Comm. Precinct 1	Comm. Precinct 2	Comm. Precinct 3	Comm. Precinct 4
Hill	66	Robert G. Dohoney	Virginia Clements	Dan V. Dent	Bud Raulston	Kenneth Reid	Jim Carmichall	John W. Erwin
Hockley	286	Andy Kupper	Wynelle Donnell	Gary Goff	Sam Langford	El Lea Hensley	J.R. Stanley	Billy W. Thefford
Hood	355	Tom Crum	Tonna Trumble	Richard Hattox	Joe Brown	Melvin Gifford	David Cleveland	Kennith Umphress
Hopkins	8	Lanny R. Ramsay	Patricia Dorner	Frank Long	Elton Stewart	H.W. Halcomb	Delbert Tully	Calvin Prince
	62	Jim N. Thompson						
Houston	3	R.W. Lawrence	Linda Hunt	Don Gordon	George (Buzzy) Bush	Gene Musick	Otis Wooten	Charles Bobbitt
	349	Melvin D. Whitaker						
Howard	118	Robert H. Moore III	Glenda Brasel	Rick Hamby	O.L. Brown	John R. Stanley	W.B. Crooker	Bobby C. Cathey
Hudspeth	34	William E. Moody	Patricia Bramblett	Steve Simmons	Leon Snyder	Lester Ray Talley	Larry Karr	Frank Archuleta
	205	Sam W. Callan						
	210	Sam M. Paxson						
Hunt	196	E. Paul Banner	Ann Prince	Duncan Thomas	Johnnie Lyon	Henry Hensley	W.D. Gooch	Allen Martin
	354	Richard Bosworth						
Hutchinson	84	Juan E. Blackburn	Rena Gay Dorsett	Stephen F. Cross	Clay Ballman	J.C. Berry	Litch Sparks Jr.	John Bayless
Irion	316	John La Grone	Jane Ethridge	Gerald Fohn	Mike Dolan	O.K. Wolfenbarger	Steve Elkins	Stan Keen
Jack	51	Royal Hart						
	271	John R. Lindsey	Lela Vene Cozart	Patrick Morris	Clide Ogle	Linda C. Jones	Raymond Matlock	J.T. Rumage
Jackson	24	Clarence N. Stevenson	Dolores Gabrysch	Robert E. Bell	Miller Rutledge	Erwin Skalicky	Edwin Hurta Jr.	W.O. Walker
	135	Marion M. Lewis						
	267	Whayland W. Kilgore						
Jasper	1-A	Joe Bob Golden	Nell Powers	Guy James Gray	Edgar W. Lewis	Cecil "Buddy" Ellis	James E. Smith	Mack Rose
		Monte D. Lawlis						
Jeff Davis	83	Alex R. Gonzalez	Peggy Robertson	Richard Barajas	John Robert Prude	Chris Lacy	Billie Weston	Ben Gearhart
Jefferson	58	J. Michael Bradford	John Appleman	Tom Maness	Norman J. Troy	Mark Domingue	Dave Smith Jr.	Edward C. Moore
	60	Gary Sanderson						
	136	Jack R. King						
	172	Donald J. Floyd						
	252	Leonard J. Giblin Jr.						
	279	Robert P. Walker						
	317	James Farris						
	Cr.	Lawrence J. Gist						
Jim Hogg	229	Ricardo H. Garcia	Lilia Pena	Heriberto Silva	Jose Zuniga III	Agapito Molina Jr.	Arnoldo Garza	Ruben Rodriguez
Jim Wells	79	Terry A. Canales	Olga Villarreal	Richard Terrell	Lucila de Leon	Hubert Adami	J.B. Freiley	Javier N. Garcia
Johnson	18	C.C. "Kit" Cooke	Jeaniv Johnson	Dan Boulware	Jack Hewlett	Ron Harmon	Bobby Estes	Benny Briscoe
	249	Wayne Bridewell						
Jones	259	Quay Parker	Nona Carter	John Willingham	James Clawson	Jerry Manske	Virgil Ashworth	Steve Lollar
Karnes	81	Olin Strauss	Patricia Brysch	Alger Kendall	L.B. Hailey Jr.	Tom Dworaczyk Sr.	Albert Banduch	Gus Osburn
	218	Stella Saxon						
Kaufman	86	Glen M. Ashworth	Sandra Featherston	Louis W. Conradt Jr.	George Mayfield	John Darden	Ivan Johnson	James Nixon
Kendall	216	Stephen B. Ables	Shirley R. Stehling	E. Bruce Curry	Charles Goodman	James W. Gooden	Victor Phillip	Victor King
Kenedy	105	J. Manuel Banales	Barbara B. Turcotte	Grant Jones	Leonard May	L.E. Turcotte Jr.	Tobin Armstrong	Gus A. Puente
Kent	39	Charles Chapman	Cornelia Cheyne	John Fouts	W.H. Parks	Don Long	Roy H. Parker	Don Trammel
Kerr	198	Emil Karl Prohl	Linda Uecker	Ron Sutton	Gordon Morgan	T.H. "Butch" Lackey	Glenn K. Holekamp	Bruce Oehler
	216	Stephen B. Ables		E. Bruce Curry				
Kimble	198	Emil Karl Prohl	Elaine Carpenter	Ronald A. Sutton	Ray Jacoby	A. Ilee Simon	Russell Fleming	Archie K. Lennon
King	50	David W. Hajek	Tavia Vinson	Bobby Burnett	Jordan Rogers	Sammy Fulton	Bobby Tidmore	Darwood Marshall
Kinney	63	George M. Thurmond	Dolores Raney	Thomas F. Lee	Jose Garza	Plunker Sheedy	Ruben Fuentes	Alvin McClure
Kleberg	105	J. Manuel Banales	Martha I. Soliz	Grant Jones	Doyle Dreyer	Mike Ybarra	Allen May	Romeo L. Lomas
Knox	50	David W. Hajek	Gloria L. West	Bobby D. Burnett	Billy Gene Johnston	Bobby J. Roberson	Johnny Birkenfeld	Philip F. Homer
La Salle	81	Olin D. Strauss	Nora Mae Tyler	Alger Kendall	James R. Black	Roberto F. Aldaco	Arcenio A. Garcia	G. Rodriguez
	218	Stella Saxon						
Lamar	6	Henry G. Braswell	Marvin Ann Patterson	Tom Wells	Troy L. Owens	Carl L. Steffey	Glynn D. Stephens	Alan R. Weatherford
	62	Jim N. Thompson						
Lamb	154	Pat H. Boone Jr.	Ray Lynn Britt	Arthur C. Eads	A.J. Spain	Thurman Lewis	Emil Macha	Leonard Pierce
Lampasas	27	Joe Carroll	Margy Jones		Robert L. Vincent Jr.	Wayne Faught	Willard Potts	Tommy Harkey

District Judges, District Clerks, District Attorneys and County Commissioners. (Cont'd.) See also Table 1.

County	Dist.	District Judge	District Clerk	District Attorney	Comm. Precinct 1	Comm. Precinct 2	Comm. Precinct 3	Comm. Precinct 4
Lavaca	25; 2D25	B.B. Schraub; Gus J. Strauss	Calvin J. Albrecht	W.C. Kirkendall	Jimmie J. Steffek	Eddie Vrana	Daniel Peters	Edward Hermes
Lee	21; 335	John L. Placke; Harold R. Towslee	Adeline Melcher		Verneal Leitko	Otto Becker Jr.	Wilson Boyd	Larry Wachsmann
Leon	12; 87; 278	William L. McAdams; Sam Bill Bournias; Jerry A. Sandel	Gloria McCarty	David Barron	Julian Wakefield	F.G. Lipsey	Craig Graham	Curtis Neyland
Liberty	75; 253	J.C. Zbranek; W.G. Woods	Joy McManus	Michael Little	Bobby D. Blake	Lee Groce	Melvin Hunt	Bobby Payne
Limestone	77; 87	Horace D. Black Jr.; Sam Bill Bournias	Mary D. Budde	Don Cantrell	John Rasco	Billy Waldrop	G.Z. Stone	Jeff Stuver
Lipscomb	31	M. Kent Sims	Coeta Sperry	Harold Comer	John W. Floyd	Verle Woods	Marvin V. Born	Ross G. Zenor
Live Oak	36; 156; 343	Ronald M. Yeager; W. Rachel Littlejohn; Alonzo T. Rodriguez	Ellen Jane McCarley	C.F. "Spike" Moore	Clem McKinney	Hilbert Kopplin	W.L. O'Brien	Emilio Garza
Llano	33; 143	Clayton E. Evans; Bob Parks	Wanda Osbourn	Sam Oatman	Randy Leifeste	Jesse James	J.T. Dotson	Leonard Grenwelge
Loving	72	Blair Cherry	Juanita Busby	David Zavado	Ernest T. Hopper	Joe R. Renteria	John E. Wilkinson	Royce Creager
Lubbock	99; 137; 140; 237; 364	Thomas L. Clinton; Cecil G. Puryear; William R. Shaver; John R. McFall; Bradley S. Underwood	Wayne LeCroy	Travis Ware	Randall Carpenter	James Kitten	Eliseo Solis	Alton Brazell
Lynn	106	George H. Hansard	Joy Laws	Ricky Smith	Gerald Gerner	T.A. Stone	Bobby Cox	J.T. Miller
Madison	12; 278	William L. McAdams; Jerri A. Sandel	Joyce Batson	David Barron	Billy Wilson	Walton Reynolds	Ford Hooper	Milton Wager Jr.
Marion	115; 276	F.L. Garrison; William R. Porter	Syble Blackburn	Tony Hileman	R.M. Blevins Jr.	T.W. (Sam) Smith	Eugene Robinson	C.W. Treadwell
Martin	118	Robert H. Moore III	Virginia James	Rick Hamby	James Biggs	Don Tollison	Ronnie Deatherage	Charles J. McKaskle
Mason	33	Clayton E. Evans	Beatrice Langehennig	Sam Oatman	Carl Marfin	T.J. Webster	Drew Tallent	Mike Jordan
Matagorda	23; 130	Neil Caldwell; Jack Salyer	Paul Hatchett	Danny Shindler	Michael J. Pruett	George W. Deshotels	F.P. "Sonny" Brhlik	E.R. Vacek
Maverick	293	Rey Perez	Diamantina Trevino	Roberto Serna	A. Guajardo Jr.	Guillermo Mancha	Eduardo Trevino	Roberto Ruiz
McCulloch	198	Emil Karl Prohl	Mackye Johnson	Ronald Sutton	Paul Willis	Jackie Behrens	Zane Carroll	Preston Cowan
McLennan	19; 54; 74; 170	Bill Logue; George H. Allen; Derwood Johnson; Joe N. Johnson	Joe Johnson	John Segrest	Wayne Davis	Lester Gibson	Fred Binner	Ray Meadows
McMullen	36; 156; 343	Ronald M. Yeager; W. Rachel Littlejohn; Alonzo T. Rodriguez	Nell Hodgin	C.F. "Spike" Moore	Allen Goff	Rodney Swaim Jr.	Herman Smith	M. Quintanilla Jr.
Medina	38	Mickey R. Pennington	Jean Marty	Rojelio Munoz	Marvin C. Bendele	Stanley Keller Jr.	Enrique G. Santos	Louis Ehlinger
Menard	198	Emil Karl Prohl	Kay Kennemer	Ronald L. Sutton	Harvey Carriger	Richard Cordes	Ray McGuffin	Tim Childers
Midland	142; 238; 318	Pat M. Baskin; John W. Hyde; Dean Rucker	Vivian Wood	Al Schorre	Durward Wright	Guy McCrary	Louisa Valencia	Winfree L. Brown
Milam	20	Charles E. Lance	Leola L. Komar	Fred Franklin	V.W. Hauk	Jesse Weathers	Dale Jaecks	Dalton Caffey
Mills	35	Ernest Cadenhead Jr.	Walter A. Bryant		Marvin Lindsay	Bill Parker	Lee Roy Schwartz	Charles H. Griffin
Mitchell	32	Weldon Kirk	Sharon Hammond	Frank Conard II	Edward B. Roach	Carl Guelker	Buddy Hertenberger	Billy H. Preston
Montague	97; 9	Roger E. Towery; Lynn J. Coker	Condell Lowrie	Jack McGaughey	Jon Kernek	Sherwood McKinley	Glenn Seay	Tommie Sappington
Montgomery	2nd9; 221; 284; 359	John C. Martin; Lee G. Allworth; Olen Underwood; James H. Keeshan	Peggy Stevens	Peter Spears	John Martin	Malcolm Purvis	Ed Chance	Charles Hayden
Moore	69; 76	Ron Enns; Bill D. Moye	June Mills	Barry Blackwell	Jess Starkey	Ernest O. Hanna	Keith Christie	M.O. (Jack) Bain
Morris	276	William R. Porter	Welton D. Walker	Richard Townsend	Robert L. McCain	Weldon Lilley	Forrest A. Clair	Willie G. Smith

District Judges, District Clerks, District Attorneys and County Commissioners. (Cont'd.) See also Table 1.

County	Dist.	District Judge	District Clerk	District Attorney	Comm. Precinct 1	Comm. Precinct 2	Comm. Precinct 3	Comm. Precinct 4
Motley	110	Randy Hollums	Lucretia Campbell	Becky McPherson	John M. Russell	Donald Hughes	Franklin Jameson	J.N. Fletcher
Nacogdoches	145	Jack Pierce	Shelby Solomon	Mike Graham	Billy Reneau	Norman Henderson	Charles Simmons	George Self
Navarro	13	Kenneth A. Douglas	Marilyn Greer	Patrick C. Batchelor	Betty Armstrong	Olin Nickelberry	Thomas Dyer	Paul Slaughter
Newton	1 1-A	Joe Bob Golden Monte D. Lawlis	Abbie Nell Stark	Charles Mitchell	Joe Bill Powell	Anderson White	Melton G. Jarrell	Ricky Jarrell
Nolan	32	Weldon Kirk	Vera Holloman	Frank Conard II	Edsel Bankhead	Harold Ware	Tommy White	Dalton Owens
Nueces	28 94 105 117 148 214 319 347	Eric Brown Jack E. Hunter J. Manuel Banales Robert M. Blackmon Margarito Garza Mike Westergren Max Leon Bennett Joaquin Villarreal III	Oscar Soliz	Grant Jones	George D. Shaffer	David Berlanga Sr.	R. Borchard Jr.	Carol Karter
Ochiltree	84	Juan E. Blackburn	Wilma Srof	Bruce Roberson	Jack Kile	Tom O'Dell	Cliff McGarraugh	Larry Hardy
Oldham	222 128	David Wesley Gulley Patrick A. Clark	Martha Thompson		Kirk Montgomery	Donnie Knox	Tom Baynham	Grady Skaggs
Orange	163 260	David A. Dunn Buddie J. Hahn	Billye Minter		Joe Ware	Marcelle Adams	James R. Burns	Kell M. Bradford Sr.
Palo Pinto	29	David Cleveland	Helen Slemmons	Nick Irsfeld	David Lee	Jimmy McKee	George Nowak	James Youngblood
Panola	123	Bennie C. Boles	Sandra King	Karren Price	Herbert Koonce	Forrest Harris	Dick Haynes	Lovil Hudson
Parker	43 287	James O. Mullin Jack D. Young	Lana O. Tibbitts Marjorie Watkins	Amy Adams Johnny Actkinson	Waymon Wright Ernest Anthony	Mack Dobbs Thomas Ware	Harold Anderson Robert White	Mark Riley Raymond McGehee
Pecos	83 112	Alex R. Gonzalez M. Brock Jones Jr.	Peggy Young	J.W. Johnson	Gregg McKenzie	Tony Villarreal	Neal Sconiers	Paul Valenzuela Jr.
Polk	9 2nd 9 258	Lynn J. Coker John C. Martin Joe Ned Dean	Nell Lowe	Terry Brown	Clarence Ellis	Bobby Smith	James Purvis	R.R. Hubert
Potter	47 108 181 251 320	David L. Gleason Abe Lopez Samuel C. Kiser Patrick A. Pirtle Don R. Emerson	Cindy Groomer	Danny E. Hill	Richard O. Harris	Manny P. Villasenor	Ray Berry	Will C. Thirkill
Presidio	83	Alex R. Gonzalez	Ramona Lara	Richard Barajas	Felipe A. Cordero	Juan Jose Muniz	Ben Benavidez	Jack W. Brunson
Rains	8 354	Lanny R. Ramsay Richard A. Bosworth	Mary Sheppard	J. Frank Long	Jimmy Roberts	William Potts	Ralph Middleton	Rayford Briggs
Randall	47 181 251	David L. Gleason Samuel Kiser Patrick A. Pirtle	LaQuitta Polvadore	Randall L. Sherrod	John J. Currie	William S. Thomas	George Huskey	John M. Dodson
Reagan	83 112	Alex R. Gonzalez H. Brock Jones Jr.	Hazel S. Carr	J.W. Johnson Jr.	Jim O'Bryan	Mike Elkins	Bill Schneemann	Jimmy Matthews
Real	38	Mickey R. Pennington	Rosemary Brice	Richard Barajas Rogelio Munoz	W. B. Sansom Jr.	Kenneth Shackelford	Castelo San Miguel	Milburn Wooldridge
Red River	6 102	Henry G. Braswell Leon F. Pesek	Clara Gaddis		H. Drue Pirtle	James Carson	Ben Storey	Lane Duncan
Reeves	143 24	Bob Parks Clarence N. Stevenson	Juana Jaquez	David P. Zavoda	Marcos Martinez	W. J. Bang	Ismael Dutchover	Bernardo Martinez
Refugio	135 267	Marion M. Lewis Whayland W. Kilgore	Rudy Garcia	Wiley L. Cheatham	James Henry	Ronald Hicks	James Pfeil	Frank Rocha
Roberts	31	M. Kent Sims	Jackie M. Jackson	Harold Comer	William H. Clark	Ronnie Gill	Don Morrison	James F. Duvall Jr.
Robertson	82 354	Robert M. Stem Richard Bosworth	Cornelia Starkey Marty Beaty	Jimmie McCullough Galen Ray Sumrow	Tommy C. Singleton Jerry Wimpee	Bobby Ray Madden Dale E. Troutt	Joe Smith Buford D. Waldrop	Sam Abraham Don Wooldridge
Rockwall	119	John E. Sutton	Loretta Michalewicz		Skipper Wheeless	J.D. Wilson	James Thurman Self	Richard W. Strube
Runnels	4	Donald R. Ross	Pat Endsley	Wm. L. Ferguson	Talmadge Mercer	Harold Kuykendall	Dan Cates	Kenneth Ashby
Rusk	1	Joe Bob Golden	Tanya Walker	Charles R. Mitchell	C. Carlin McDaniel	Lynn Smith	James H. Conn	Chester D. Cox Sr.
Sabine	273	J.L. Smith						
San Augustine	273	J.L. Smith	Jo Anna Johnson	Charles R. Mitchell	Charles Henry Smith	Edward Wilson	Kenneth Stanley	Harlon A. Hall

District Judges, District Clerks, District Attorneys and County Commissioners. (Cont'd.) See also Table 1.

County	Dist.	District Judge	District Clerk	District Attorney	Comm. Precinct 1	Comm. Precinct 2	Comm. Precinct 3	Comm. Precinct 4
San Jacinto	9; 2nd; 258	Lynn J. Coker; John C. Martin; Joe Ned Dean	Edna M. Cox	Robert Hill Trapp	Norman Street	Roy Lewis	Donald Cox	Wayne Conley
San Patricio	36; 156; 343	Ronald M. Yeager; W. Rachel Littlejohn; Alonzo T. Rodriguez	Patricia Norton	Tom Bridges	Nina Trevino	Carl Duncan	Pedro G. Rodriguez	Gordon Porter
San Saba	33	Clayton E. Evans	Nila Ruth Barker	Sam Oatman	Ronald G. McBride	Hollis Lord	Wilson Kuykendall	Bennie L. Lively
Schleicher	51	Royal Hart	Helen Blakeway	Gerald A. Fohn	Johnny Mayo	Kerry Idom	Prissy Paxton	Ross Whitten
Scurry	132	Gene L. Dulaney	Elios Pruitt	Ernie Armstrong	Duaine Davis	Roy Idom	C.D. Gray Jr.	Jerry Gannaway
Shackelford	259	Quay F. Parker	Frances Wheeler	Jack Willingham	Fred Coulter	James H. Balliew	Jimmy Brooks	W.O. McKeever
Shelby	123; 273	Bennie C. Boles; J.L. Smith	Marsha Singletary	Karen Kirkley	Charles Williams	O.K. (Buddy) Hagler	Spencer Hamilton	Virgil Wedgeworth
Sherman	69	Ron Enns	M.L. Albert	Barry Blackwell	Wayne Cummings	Wayland Brown	Dale Hamilton	Tommy Asher
Smith	7; 114; 241; 321	William E. Coats; Cynthia Stevens Kent; Joe Tunnell; Ruth J. Blake	R. Brad Burger	Jack Skeen	Bill Wallis	G.T. Shamburger	Roy Stanley	Andrew Melontree
Somervell	18; 249	C.C. Cooke; Wayne Bridewell	Lovella Williams	Dan Boulware	Elizabeth Hammond	Joe G. Whitworth	Billy C. Miller	Jim Gartrell
Starr	229	Ricardo H. Garcia	Juan Erasmo Saenz	Heriberto Silva	Jose Maria Alvarez	Amando Pena	Eloy Garza	Reynaldo Alaniz
Stephens	90	C.J. Eden	Juanita Speake	John Neal	Jerry Toland	D.C. "Button" Sikes	Ozell Devenport	Carter Fore
Sterling	51	Royal Hart	Diane A. Haar	Gerald A. Fohn	Billy Joe Blair	Russell Noletubby	Billy R. Bynum	Melvin Foster
Stonewall	39	Charles L. Chapman	Betty L. Smith	John Fouts	Johnnie Smith	Pat Cumbie	J.D. Parker	Dickey Parker
Sutton	112; 64	M. Brock Jones Jr.; Jack R. Miller	Bobbie Smith	J.W. Johnson Jr.	Miguel Villanueva	Bill Wade	Bill Keel	Ernest Barrera
Swisher	242	Marvin Marshall	Pat Wesley	Terry McEachern	F.L. McGavock	A.G. House	Harvey Foster	W.C. Weatherred
Tarrant	17; 48; 67; 96; 141; 153; 213; 231	Fred W. Davis; Wm. L. Hughes Jr.; George Allen Crowley; Jeff Walker; Catherine Gant; Sidney C. Farrar Jr.; George S. Kredell; Maryellen Hicks. **Tarrant County Dist. Judges (Cont'd.):** 233 William H. Brigham; 236 Albert L. White Jr.; 297 Everett Young; 322 Frank Sullivan; 323 Scott D. Moore; 324 Brian A. Carper; 325 Mary Sean O'Reilly; 342 Joe Bruce Cunningham; 348 Michael D. Schattman; 352 Bruce Auld; 360 V. Sue Koenig; 371 William Burdock; 372 Pete Perez; Cr.1 Sharen Wilson; Cr.2 Lee Ann Dauphinot; Cr.3 Don Leonard; Cr.4 Joe Drago III; Imp.1 R. E. Thornton; Imp.2 Harry Hopkins	Thomas Hughes	Tim Curry	Dionne Bagsby	M. VanRavenswaay	Bob Hampton	J.D. Johnson
Taylor	42; 104; 326; 350	Donald H. Lane; Billy John Edwards; Aleta Hacker; Jorge A. Solis	Rilla Mahoney	James Eidson	Jack Turner	Don Dudley	John G. Thompson	Neil Fry
Terrell	63	George M. Thurmond	Martha Allen	Tom Lee	Shirly Spence	S.V. Flores	Henry M. Petty	Marshall N. Cooke
Terry	121	Ray D. Anderson	Frances Hyman	John Fouts	Harvey Smith	Bill Keesee	Jasper Jowers	Jimmie Berryhill
Throckmorton	39	Charles L. Chapman	Cathey Mitchell	Charles Bailey	Doyle Wells	John Jones	Carlton Sullivan	George Seedig
Titus	76; 276	Bill D. Moye; William R. Porter	Bobby LaPrade		Mike Price	Mike Fields	J.W. Terrell Jr.	Thomas E. Hockaday
Tom Green	51; 119; 340	Royal Hart; John E. Sutton; Dick Alcala	Sue Bramhall	Gerald Fohn; Stephen H. Smith	B.C. Dominguez	Leon Abbott	Delbert Caffey	Tim Weatherby
Travis	53; 98; 126; 147	Mary P. Williams; Jeanne Meurer; Joe Hart; Wil Flowers. **Travis County Dist. Judges (Cont'd.):** 167 Bob Jones; 200 Paul R. Davis Jr.; 201 Jerry Dellana; 250 John Dietz; 261 Peter Lowry; 299 Jon Wisser; 331 Bob Perkins; 345 Scott McCown; 353 Joe Dibrell	A. Rodriguez-Mendoza	Ronald Earle	Sam Biscoe	Bruce Todd	Pam Reed	Marcos DeLeon

District Judges, District Clerks, District Attorneys and County Commissioners. (Cont'd.) See also Table 1.

County	Dist.	District Judge	District Clerk	District Attorney	Comm. Precinct 1	Comm. Precinct 2	Comm. Precinct 3	Comm. Precinct 4
Trinity	2nd9	John C. Martin	Cheryl Cartwright	Joe L. Price	Lynn Reynolds	Dean Price	Cecil Webb	Wayne Odom
	258	Joe Ned Dean						
Tyler	1-A	Monte D. Lawis	Patricia Brown	James A. Clark	Maxie Riley	Arthur M. Barnes	Jerry Mahan	Henry E. Sawyer Sr.
	88	Earl B. Stover						
Upshur	115	F. L. Garrison	Horace A. Ray	Tim Cone	Gaddis Lindsey	Tommy L. Stanley	David Loyd	Tommy Eatherton
Upton	83	Alex R. Gonzalez	Phyllis Stephens	Richard Barajas	Morris E. McKenzie	T.D. Workman	Dale Kluthe	Eugene Kelton
	112	M. Brock Jones Jr.		J.W. Johnson Jr.				
Uvalde	38	Mickey R. Pennington	Lydia Steele	Rogelio R. Munoz	Randy Scheide	Robert B. Tafolla	Ed Jones	Jesse Moreno
Val Verde	63	George M. Thurmond	Martha Germany	Tom Lee	Ricardo G. Padilla	Robert V. Rodriguez	John M. Cody	John Francis Qualia
Van Zandt	294	Tommy W. Wallace	Nancy Young	John Sickel	A.L. (Bud) Herron	W.A. Warran Jr.	Charles Holland	John Veazey
Victoria	24	Clarence N. Stevenson	Alice Lee	George J. Filley III	Frank Targac	Jerry Nobles	John J. Hammack	Rex L. Easley
	135	Marion L. Lewis						
	267	Whayland W. Kilgore						
	277	Robert C. Cheshire						
Walker	12	William L. McAdams	Betty Tackett	David P. Weeks	B.J. Gaines Jr.	Cecil Williams	James Reynolds	Joe Malak Jr.
	278	Jerry A. Sandel						
Waller	9	Lynn J. Coker	Beverly A. Kluna	James B. Hicks	Delmar Barry	Frank Pokluda	Richard Frey	Eddie Neuman
	155	Dan Beck						
Ward	143	Bob Parks	Jo Ann Roark	David P. Zavoda	Ben Villalobos	Bill Middlebrooks	Larry Hunt	Bob J. Meek
Washington	21	John L. Placke	Blondean Kuecker	Charles Sebesta Jr.	Joe E. Renn	Rudolph Schroeder	Gilbert Janner	Paul Pipes
	335	Harold R. Towslee						
Webb	49	Manuel Flores	Manuel Gutierrez	Joe Rubio	R. Centeno-Hinojosa	Judith Gutierrez	Jose L. Rodriguez	Arnulfo Santos
	111	Antonio Zardanetta						
	341	Elma S. Ender						
Wharton	23	Neil Caldwell	Evelyn Kramr	Daniel Shindler	Carl Nichols	D.C. King	Arvid Schoeneberg	Catherine Drapela
	329	Daniel R. Sklar						
Wheeler	31	M. Kent Sims	Paul Topper	Harold Comer	Elmer Ray Harrison	Billie V. Atherton	Bryan Close	Boyd Hiltbrunner
Wichita	30	Robert P. Brotherton	Dorsey Trapp	Barry L. Macha	Woodrow Gossom Jr.	Weldon Nix	Gordon Griffith	Harold White
	78	Keith Nelson						
	89	R. Temple Driver						
Wilbarger	46	Thomas A. Neely	Wilda Byers	Dan Mike Bird	O.J. Walker	Charles Colbert	Glen Turner	Lenville Morris
Willacy	103	Menton Murray Jr.	Iris O. McGlothin		Israel Tamez	Gene McGee	Alfredo Serrato	Jose I. Jimenez
	107	Benjamin Uresti						
	138	Robert Garza						
	197	Darrell B. Hester						
	357	Ray Valdez						
Williamson	26	William S. Lott	Bonnie Wolbrueck	Ken Anderson	Mike Heiligenstein	Greg Boatright	Raymond Rister	Jerry Mehevec
	277	John R. Carter						
	368	Burt Carnes						
Wilson	81	Olin B. Strauss	Jody Gregory	Alger Kendall	Benito Talamantez	Albert Pruski	Mark A. Johnson	John F. Wiatrek
	218	Stella Saxon						
Winkler	109	James H. Clack	Virginia Healy	Michael L. Fostel	Tommy Smith	James A. Winn	Joe Ethridge	W.T. White
Wise	271	John R. Lindsey	Doris Claborn	Patrick M. Morris	Tom Rattan	Vernon L. Clower	Allen P. Dickey	Bryan A. Farris Jr.
Wood	114	Cynthia S. Kent	Jo Anna Nelson	Marcus D. Taylor	Glenn Bevill	Kenneth Wilson	Roger Pace	Roger Tinney
	294	Tommy W. Wallace						
Yoakum	121	Ray D. Anderson	Mae Barnett	Linda Lowrey	John Avara	R.W. Thurston	Jim Barron	Macky McWhirter
Young	90	C.J. Eden	George C. Birdwell	John Neal	Sam Whittenburg	John Charles Bullock	R.L. Spivey	F.H. Green Sr.
Zapata	49	Manuel R. Flores	Arnoldo Flores	Jose Rubio	Jose Luis Flores	Angel Garza	David Morales	Felix Garcia
Zavala	293	Rey Perez	Rosa Elva Mata	Roberto Serna	Hector Gomez	Mike Acosta	Henry Flores	Esteban Najera
	365	Amado Abascal						

Mayors and City Managers of Texas Cities

The list below was compiled from questionnaires sent out immediately after the municipal elections in May 1991. Name of the city manager is included for municipalities having that form of government.

The authority by which managers hold their positions is explained by footnotes to which the symbols *, †, ‡ and § refer. For explanation of symbols, see end of list. If no symbol precedes name of City Manager, it denotes that the information was not made available to the Almanac.

Abbott . . . . Ronald E. Kaska
Abernathy . . . Shane Cunningham
†City Mgr., Frank D. Russell
Abilene . . . . . . Gary D. McCaleb
*City Mgr., Jim C. Blagg
Ackerly . . . . . Jimmie L. Schuelke
Addison . . . . D. Lynn Spruill
*City Mgr., Ron Whitehead
Adrian . . . . Robt. A. Gruhlkey
City Mgr., Ralph Guest
Agua Dulce . . . . Carl Vajdos
¶Alamo . . . . Rodolfo Villarreal
Alamo Heights (6616 Broadway, San Antonio 78209) . . Wm. D. Balthrope
¶Alba . . . . Orvin Carroll
Albany . . . . Wayne Hogan
City Mgr., Bobby Russell
Aledo . . . . Knox Ross
Alice . . . . Octavio Figueroa Jr.
*City Mgr., Roel Valadez
Allen . . . . Joe Farmer
*City Mgr., Jon McCarty
Alma (Rt. 1, Box 109, Ennis 75119). . . . . . . Lloyd D. Keilers
Alpine . . . . Ernesto S. Gallego
‡City Mgr., Jerry Caravajal
Alto . . . . Garwin A. Baugh
¶Alton (P.O. Drawer 9004, Mission 78572). . . . . Mike Lopez
Alvarado . . . . . . Amon T. Adcock
Alvin . . . . Allen Gray
*City Mgr., Greg Harrison
Alvord . . . . Paul Wright
Amarillo. . . . . Keith Adams
*City Mgr., John Q. Ward
Ames . . . . Roy E. Rollins
Amherst . . . . . George Thompson
Anahuac . . . Monroe Kreuzer Jr.
City Mgr., (Vacancy)
Andrews . . . . . Z. W. Hutcheson Jr.
*City Mgr., Len L. Wilson
Angleton. . . . . B. G. Peck
*City Mgr., Ruth Hertel
Angus (Rt. 3, Box 3060, Corsicana 75110). . . . . Eben D. Stover
Anna . . . . A.L. Geer
Annetta (Box 191, Aledo 76008). . . . . Olan Usher
Annetta North (P.O. Box 262, Aledo 76008). . . . . Edward K. Hensley
Annetta South (P.O. Box 61, Aledo 76008). . . . . Doub Koldin
¶Annona . . . . Carol McNally
Anson . . . . . . Thurman Simmons
City Mgr., David Fenwick
Anthony . . . Jerry M. Montgomery
Anton . . . . Louis E. Boothe
City Mgr., Larry Conkin
Appleby (Rt. 10, Box 5186, Nacogdoches 75961) . . . . . . N. F. Burt
¶Aquilla . . . . . . Larry Maddox
Aransas Pass . . Robert B. Watson
*City Mgr., Rick Ewaniszyk
Archer City . . . . . . Max Wood Sr.
City Mgr., L. B. Boren Jr.
Arcola . . . . Mike R. Saenz
Argyle . . . . . . Yvonne A. Jenkins
Arlington . . . Richard E. Greene
*City Mgr., George C. Campbell
Arp. . . . . Vernon L. Bedair
¶Asherton . Ramon de la Fuente Jr.
¶Aspermont . . . . P. C. Carr
Athens . . . . Bill Underhill
*City Mgr., Kevin P. Evans
Atlanta . . . . . Lawson McKelvey
*City Mgr., Jim Long
Aubrey . . . . . Margarete Redding
Aurora (P.O. Box 558, Rhome 76078). . . . . Owen Landers
Austin. . . . . Bruce Todd

*City Mgr., Camille C. Barnett
Austwell . . . . P. J. Martinez
Avery . . . . Dick W. Handley
Avinger . . . . L. Dee Tallent
Azle . . . . C. Y. Rone
City Mgr., Harry H. Dulin Jr.
Bailey . . . . . . Jewel A. Mims (Mr.)
¶Bailey's Prairie (Box 71, Angleton 77515). . . . . Jo Mapel
Baird . . . . Steve Bowen
City Mgr., Bill Denman
¶Balch Springs . . . . Rick Burridge
City Mgr., (Vacancy)
¶Balcones Heights (123 Altgelt, San Antonio 78201) . . . Emil E. Deike
Ballinger . . . . Larry Lange
*City Mgr., Judy Miller
Balmorhea . . . . Sharon Lippe
Bandera . . . Raymond J. Adamietz
Bangs . . . . M. E. Petross
Bardwell . . . . Larry Gilbert
Barry . . . . John W. Braly Sr.
¶Barstow . . . . Angel Abila
Bartlett. . . . . Wilson Franz
Bartonville (1941 E. Jeter Road, Argyle 76226) . . . . Tom Ott
¶Bastrop. . . . . David Lock
‡City Mgr., Hank Cunningham
Bay City . . . . . . Tommy Z. LeTulle
¶Bayou Vista (2929 Hwy. 6, ‡100, Hitchcock 77563). . Roy C. Corley
Bayside . . . . Kay Phillips
Baytown . . . . Emmett Hutto
*City Mgr., Bobby Lee Rountree
Bayview (P.O. Box 4043, Los Fresnos 78566). Philip M. Loveless Jr.
Beach City . . . . A. R. Senac
Beasley. . . . . Ben W. Hoefke
Beaumont. . . . . . Evelyn M. Lord
*City Mgr., Ray A. Riley
Beckville . . . . . Thomas R. Adams
Bedford . . . . L. Don Dodson
*City Mgr., Jim W. Walker
Bee Cave (3932 RR 620 So., Austin 78734). . . . . Gene Butler
†City Mgr., John Figer
Beeville . . . . Carlos Salazar
*City Mgr., Joe B. Montez
Bellaire . . . . Tim Carter
*City Mgr., Lea Dunn
Bellevue . . . . J.W. Horton
§City Mgr., Jay Anderson
Bellmead (3015 Bellmead Dr., Waco 76705). . . . . . Joe M. Rodriguez
*City Mgr., S. G. Radcliffe
Bells. . . . . A. L. Isom
Bellville . . . . . Abner E. Jackson
City Mgr., John Mumme
Belton. . . . . Clark Potter
*City Mgr., Jeff Holberg
¶Benavides . . . . . Archer Barton
Benbrook (P.O. Box 26569, Fort Worth 76126). . . . Jerry J. Dunn
‡City Mgr., Ken Neystel
Benjamin . . . . Bud Clower
§City Mgr., Jack Waldron
Berryville (Rt. 1, Box 142, Frankston 75763) . . John T. McElvaney
Bertram . . . Johnnie Mae Wheeler
Beverly Hills (3418 Memorial Dr., Waco 76711) . . . . . Betty Gibbs
¶Bevil Oaks (Rt. 1, Box 293, Beaumont 77713) . . . Jerry W. Pickett
Big Lake. . . . . H. F. Ritchie
Big Sandy . . . . . Johnnie L. Baird
Big Spring . . . . Maxwell D. Green
*City Mgr., Hal Boyd
Big Wells. . . . . . Alicia M. Oregel
Bishop . . . . Keith Bellamy
Blackwell . . . . . William E. Tucker
¶Blanco . . . . Phyllis Owen

Blanket. . . . . C.T. Ham
Bloomburg . . . Shannon B. Duncan
Blooming Grove . . . Keith Tunnell
Blossom . . . . Rickey Thomas
Blue Mound (1600 Bell, Fort Worth 76131). . . . . A.R. Perkins
¶Blue Ridge . . . . A. L. Sagely
Blum . . . . Bernilla F. Gunn
Boerne . . . . Patrick Heath
§City Mgr., Ronald C. Bowman
Bogata . . . . Mildred F. Eudy
¶Bonham . . . . William E. Munger
*City Mgr., Thomas L. Mattis
Bonney (19007 Mottesheard Rd., Rosharon 77583)
. . . . Mary M. Coleman
Booker . . . . Kay Smith
§City Mgr., A. Keith Burdett
Borger . . . . Judy Flanders
*City Mgr., James G. Layton
Bovina . . . . Keith Knight
Bowie . . . . Bert Cunningham
§City Mgr., Gerald Hartley Jr.
Boyd . . . . Ray Jordan
Brackettville. . . . . . Larry Moore
Brady . . . . H. L. Gober Jr.
City Mgr., Jack Caffall
Brazoria . . . . Joe Ann Miller
§City Mgr., K. C. Timmermann
¶Breckenridge . . Weldon Leonard
*City Mgr., Dwain Tolle
Bremond . . . . Ricky Swick
Brenham . . . . Robert Appel Jr.
*City Mgr., Leonard Addicks
Briarcliff (HCO 1, Box 24, Spicewood 78669) . . . . Max Hoyt
Briaroaks (Rt. 5, Box 963, Burleson 76028). . . . . . . Alan W. Myers
Bridge City . . . . John W. Banken
‡City Mgr., Robert K. Coffelt
Bridgeport . . . Robert W. Hawkins
Broaddus . . . . W. E. Sheffield
Bronson . . . . Ralph McBride
Bronte . . . . J. T. Henry
Brookshire . . . . . Harry K. Searle
Brookside Village (Rt. 3, Box 3440, Pearland 77581)
. . . . Natividad Martinez
¶Browndell (P.O. Box 430, Brookeland 75931) . . . Erma L. Garrett
Brownfield . . . . Jack Cargill
*City Mgr., R. C. Fletcher
Brownsboro . . . . Thomas A. Crow
City Mgr., Jack E. Beall
¶Brownsville. . . Ygnacio D. Garza
*City Mgr., Steve Fitzgibbons
Brownwood. . . . . Bert V. Massey II
*City Mgr., Virgil C. Gray
Bruceville-Eddy (Box 1418, Bruceville 76630) . . . . . Gene McBride
Bryan . . . . Marvin Tate
*City Mgr., Ernest R. Clark
Bryson . . . . Willard Schlittler
Buckholts . . . . Gwen Hauk
Buckingham (P.O. Box 831452, Richardson 75083) Frank Malone
Buda. . . . . James W. Hollis
Buffalo . . . . Byron Ryder
Buffalo Gap . . . . . Charlie Young
Buffalo Springs (Rt. 10, Box 500, Lubbock 79404). . Jeffrey Driver
Bullard. . . . . S. Ray McCugh
Bunker Hill Village (Box 19429, Houston 77224)
. . . . . . George G. Stubblefield III
§City Mgr., David F. Eby
Burkburnett . . Pat Norriss (Mrs.)
*City Mgr., Gary B. Bean
¶Burke (Rt. 2, Box 122, Diboll 75541). . . . . Zusle Rush Jr.
Burleson. . . . . Vera Calvin
*City Mgr., Jack Eades

Burnet . . . . Bill B. Wilcox
†City Mgr., Johnny Sartain
Burton . . . . Virginia McCune
Byers . . . . W. A. Landrum
¶Bynum . . . . Roscoe E. Waller
Cactus . . . . Leon W. Graham
City Mgr., J.J. Almendinger
Caddo Mills. . . . . Ron Olson
§City Mgr., James Green
¶Caldwell . . . . Jonnie Vic Barnett
City Mgr., William L. Broaddus
Callisburg (Rt. 2, Gainesville
76240). . . . . Bobby McDaniel
¶Calvert . . . . Cooper Wiese
Cameron . . . . . Milton J. Schiller
§City Mgr., Lanny C. French
Campbell . . . . Jack White
Camp Wood . . . Richard A. Tucker
Canadian . . . . Micah Lewis
†City Mgr., Dean Looper
¶Caney City (Rt. 2, Box 2250, Mala-
koff 75148) . . . . Joe Barron
Canton . . . . Richard W. Lawrence
City Mgr., Johnny M. Mallory
¶Canyon . . . . David C. West
*City Mgr., Glen R. Metcalf
Carbon. . . . . . . Kenneth Halford
¶Carl's Corner (Rt. 3, Box 500, Hills-
boro 76645). . . . . Carl Cornelius
Carmine. . . . . . . Stuart Bruchey
Carrizo Springs. . Rufus Lozano Jr.
*City Mgr., Ricardo Cantu
Carrollton. . . . Milburn R. Gravley
*City Mgr., Mike Eastland
Carthage . . . . . . Carson C. Joines
*City Mgr., Charles Thomas
Castle Hills (6915 West Ave., San
Antonio 78213) . Perry Burnham
‡City Mgr., David R. Seyfarth
Castroville . . . . Madelyn Koepp
§City Mgr., Stevan R. Gallegos
¶Cedar Hill . . . . . W. S. Permenter
‡City Mgr., Gregory T. Vick
Cedar Park. . . . . Dorthey Duckett
‡City Mgr., Daron K. Butler
Celeste . . . . Michael D. Stout
¶Celina. . . . . Lloyd Rucker
City Mgr., Stephen K. Shutt
Center . . . . George W. Ihlo
‡City Mgr., Jeff K. Ellington
Centerville . . . . George G. Barnes
Chandler . . . . . . Winston Reagan
Channing . . . . . . Ethel Hunnicutt
Charlotte . . . . Mark Weatherston
Chateau Woods (10224 Fairview,
Conroe 77385). . . John W. Brown
Chester. . . . . Bryan Davis
Chico . . . . Nobie Tucker
Childress . . . . Pat Y. Steed
‡City Mgr., David Galligan
Chillicothe . . . . Wallace Clay
China . . . . Russell Gallier
China Grove (Box 367, Adkins
78101). . . . . . . Harry L. Boyd Sr.
Chireno . . . . . . Orland Strickland
City Mgr., Alton Holt
Christine . . . Patti B. Bedingfield
Cibolo. . . . . Sam Bauder
§City Mgr., David D. Walker
Cisco . . . . Joe Wheatley
§City Mgr., Michael D. Moore
Clarendon. . . . . . . James Sharrar
Clarksville . . . Gavin Watson Jr.
†City Mgr., Wilt Brown
Clarksville City (Box 1209,
Gladewater 75647)
. . . . Harvey E. Griffin
City Mgr., Billy F. Silvertooth Jr.
Claude . . . . Alton L. Goodin
¶Clay (Rt. 2, Box 70-2, Somerville
77879). . . . . Mary F. Mack
Clear Lake Shores (931 Cedar Road,
Kemah 77565). . . . . Sandy Drake
Cleburne . . . Katherine P. Raines
*City Mgr., Joel Victory
Cleveland . . . . Rayburn L. Hanson
‡City Mgr., W. N. Petropolis
Clifton . . . . . . Paul Hollingsworth
Clint. . . . . . . G. Michael Goodwin

Clute . . . . Jerry Adkins
*City Mgr., Barbara Hester
Clyde . . . . Don R. Haley
Coahoma . . . . . . Eleanor Garrett
Cockrell Hill (4125 W. Clarendon,
Dallas 75211) . . . Sam Rodriguez
Coffee City (Box 716, Frankston
75763). . . . . Wayne Phillips
§City Mgr., Jan McGully
Coldspring . . . . John Benestante
Coleman. . . . . . . Woody Maddox
*City Mgr., Roy McCorkle
College Station . . . Larry J. Ringer
*City Mgr., Ron Ragland
Colleyville . . . . . Chris Hawkins
City Mgr., C. Robert Stripling
Collinsville . . . O. M. Quattlebaum
Colmesneil . . . . C.J. Riley
Colorado City . . . . Jim Baum
*City Mgr., Buddy Foster
Columbus . . . . . Dwain K. Dungen
†City Mgr., (Vacancy)
Comanche . . . . . John Beaty Jr.
Combes . . . . . . J. Frank Saldana
Combine (P.O. Box 231, Seagoville
75159). . . . . Charles Stringer
City Mgr., (Vacancy)
¶Commerce . . . . . David M. Ayers
*City Mgr., Truitt Gilbreath
Como . . . . Bobby Clark
Conroe . . . . Carter Moore
§City Mgr., Bill Storey
Converse . . . . Bruce Friesenhahn
‡City Mgr., John L. Klaiber
¶Cool (R. Rte, Box 150, Weatherford
76086). . . . . . Charlie O'Bannon
¶Coolidge . . . . . Glenn McGuire
§City Mgr., Jean H. Davis
Cooper . . . . Richard C. Huie
Coppell. . . . . Mark Wolfe
‡City Mgr., Alan D. Ratliff
Copperas Cove . . . Jim Schmitz
§City Mgr., Johnny P. Smith
Copper Canyon . . Hugh Meilinger
Corinth (2003 S. Corinth, Denton
76205). . . . . . Shirley Spellerberg
§City Mgr., Ken McDonald
Corpus Christi. . . . . Mary Rhodes
*City Mgr., Juan Garza
¶Corral City (P.O. Box 54, Argyle
76226). . . . . Gary Hulstein
Corrigan. . . . . . Robert R. Smiley
‡City Mgr., B.K. Johnson
Corsicana . . . . . Gus Gappelberg
*City Mgr., Craig Lonon

Cottonwood (P.O. Box 348, Kemp
75143). . . . . Tom Anderson
Cottonwood Shores (P.O. Box 191,
Marble Falls 78654)
. . . . Joseph F. Beyer
¶Cotulla . . . . W. L. Cotulla
Cove . . . . Carl Crowder
Covington. . . . James Clinkscales
¶Crandall . . . . Perry Marshak
Crane . . . . Terry L. Schul
§City Mgr., Bill Sanders
Cranfills Gap . . . . . Marc Johnson
Crawford . . . . Russell L. Blenden
Creedmoor (Creedmoor Station,
Austin 78747) . . . . Joe Click
Crockett . . . . W.F. Adler
*City Mgr., Roger G. Johnson
Crosbyton. . . . . Lance Morris
City Mgr., Gary Mitchell
Cross Plains . . . . . Ross Gerking
City Mgr., Debbie Gosnell
¶Cross Roads (P.O. Box 412, Aubrey
76227). . . . . Mark A. Coats
Cross Timbers (Rt. 5, Box 371, Bur-
leson 76028) . . (Election 8/27/91)
¶Crowell . . . . Robert Kincaid
Crowley . . . . . . Nancy Behrens
Crystal City Maria Sanchez-Rivera
*City Mgr., Ramon de la Fuente
Cuero . . . . John Post
*City Mgr., James C. Morgan
Cumby . . . . H. C. Battle
¶Cuney . . . . Billy C. Roberts

Cushing . . . . . . James W. Dawson
City Mgr., Jerry L. Bowers
Cut and Shoot (Box 7364, Conroe
77303). . . . . Mark Patterson
Daingerfield. . . William L. Thorne
§City Mgr., Margie Hargrove
Daisetta . . . . Pat Abshier
Dalhart. . . . . Gene Rahll
*City Mgr., Gregg Duggan
Dallas. . . . . **Annette Strauss
*City Mgr., Jan Hart

Dalworthington Gardens (2600
Roosevelt Dr., Arlington
76016). . . . . Albert A. Taub
Danbury . . Kenneth W. Walters Jr.
Darrouzett . . . . J.P. Rogers
Dawson . . . . Wayne S. Smith
Dayton . . . . Guy L. Harris
§City Mgr., C.P. Coward
Dayton Lakes (P.O. Box 1476, Day-
ton 77535). . . . . . Paul Chalifoux
¶Dean (Hwy. 79, Wichita Falls
76031). . . . . Randall L. Paden
Decatur . . . . Bobby Wilson
Deer Park. . . . . Jimmy Burke
*City Mgr., Ronald V. Crabtree
De Kalb (110 S.E. Front St., DeKalb
75559). . . . . Orval C. Miller
De Leon . . . . Kent Boswell
Dell City . . . . . Leroy Wayne Perry
¶Del Rio . . . Alfredo Gutierrez Jr.
*City Mgr., Jeffrey A. Pomeranz
Denison . . . . Ben Munson
*City Mgr., Larry Cruise
Denton . . . . Bob Castleberry
*City Mgr., Lloyd V. Harrell
Denver City . . Royce Hemmeline
City Mgr., Ray A. Hohstadt
Deport . . . . Charles Foster
DeSoto . . . . David Doyle
*City Mgr., Mark Sowa
Detroit . . . . Charles T. Boyer
Devers . . . . R.B. Evans
Devine . . . . Jerry Beck
Diboll . . . . James P. Simms
‡City Mgr., Vernon Cupit
Dickens . . . . Bill Scott
Dickinson . . . . Veta Winick
City Mgr., Luther Morgan
Dilley . . . . Frank Moffett
Dimmitt . . . . Wayne Collins
City Mgr., Reeford Burrous
Dodd City . . . . . Johnnie Mills Sr.
Dodson. . . . . Rayburn Hightower
¶Dogwood City (Rt. 2, Box 111A,
Flint 75762). . . Elise Mae Perkins
¶Domino (Box 298, Queen City
75572). . . . . Frank Propps
¶Donna. . . . . Hector Casiano
City Mgr., Ricardo T. Cortes
Dorchester (Box 838, Howe
75059). . . . . Stanley Stewart
§City Mgr., W.F. Fritcher Jr.
Double Oak. . . . James R. Handzel
City Mgr., Mary Ann Hauser
¶Douglassville . . . . . W. A. McCoy
Dripping Springs . . Galen Dodson
¶Driscoll . . . . Dan Capehart
Dublin . . . . Jim Leatherwood
‡City Mgr., David Johnson
Dumas . . . . Brent Futrell
*City Mgr., Larry A. Smith
Duncanville . . . . . James L. Tow
*City Mgr., Dan Savage

Eagle Lake . . . . . Roy D. Van Nort
‡City Mgr., Lucille Perry (Acting)
Eagle Pass . . . Roberto Barrientos
City Mgr., Oscar Rodriguez
Early (Box 3100, Brownwood
76803). . . . . Bill Ingley
§City Mgr., Ken Thomas
Earth . . . . R. R. Daniel Jr.
Eastland. . . . . C.W. Hoffmann Jr.
*City Mgr., Paul Catoe
East Mountain (Rt. 1, Box 500,
Gilmer 75644) . . Ralph B. Collins
¶Easton . . . . E. T. Bell
East Tawakoni . . . . Duane Travis

Ector . . . . Lynwood Hogue
Edcouch . . . . Tom Rocchio
  City Mgr., Mario A. Espinosa
Eden . . . . James C. Schumann
Edgecliff . . . . Bob Wershay
  §City Mgr., Rebecca Stark
Edgewood . . . . . Finis Skinner Jr.
Edinburg . . . P.R. Rudy de la Vina
  *City Mgr., Hector Solis
Edmonson . . . . . . Don Ketchum
Edna . . . . Joe D. Hermes
  *City Mgr., James R. Elium III
Edom (Rt. 1, Box 512, Brownsboro
  75756) . . . . Loy Hutchins
El Campo . . . . . . Paul Soechting
  *City Mgr., Terry K. Roberts
¶El Cenizo (P.O. Box 6180, Laredo
  78042) . . . .
Eldorado . . . . John Nikolauk
Electra . . . . Ted Miller
Elgin . . . . Jan Schroeder
  §City Mgr., Jack Harzke
Elkhart . . . . Garth Moran
El Lago (98 Lakeshore Dr., Sea-
  brook 77586) . . . . . Bill McElwain
Elmendorf . . . . . . Simon R. Tarin
¶El Paso . . . . Jonathan W. Rogers
  §City Mgr., K. E. Beasley
¶Elsa . . . . Armando Garza
  City Mgr., Ramiro Rosa
Emhouse . . . . . . Joe E. Johnson
Emory . . . . Rubye McKeown
Enchanted Oaks (Box 517, Mabank
  75147) . . . . Blair Whitelaw
Encinal . . . . Alberto Ochoa
  §City Mgr., Susanna Zarate
¶Ennis . . . . C. T. Abram
  *City Mgr., Steve Howarton
Estelline . . . . T.H. Seay
Euless . . . . . . Harold D. Samuels
  *City Mgr., Tom Hart
Eureka . . . . Bea Murphree
Eustace . . . . . . Harold R. Griffith
¶Evant . . . . C. L. Yarbrough
Everman . . . . Joe Sample
  City Mgr., Jack Chaney
Fairfield . . . . Monte Cole
  ‡City Mgr., Ted Mayo
Fair Oaks Ranch . . . E.L. Gaubatz
Fairview (Collin Co.) (Box 551,
  McKinney 75069) Leahray Wroten
Fairview (Wise Co.) (Rt. 1, Box 16A,
  Rhome 76078)
  . . . . D. Paulette Layfield
Falfurrias . . . . Jimmie Dunn
  §City Mgr., Aurora C. Rodriguez
Falls City . . . . Ray Pollok
Farmers Branch David D. Blair Jr.
  *City Mgr., Richard L. Escalante
Farmersville . . . George C. Crump
  City Mgr., Randall E. Holly
Farwell . . . . Wendol Christian
Fate . . . . Mary Rolfe
Fayetteville . . . . William Graeter
¶Ferris . . . . Jimmie Birdwell
¶Flatonia . . . . Marvin Finger
  City Mgr., James Davis
Florence . . . . . . Lee Roy Knauth
Floresville . . . . . . Roy G. Sanchez
  §City Mgr., H. G. Lumbreras
Flower Mound . . . . . Gary Acker
  ‡City Mgr., Van James
Floydada . . . . . . Wayne A. Russell
  City Mgr., Gary Brown
Follett . . . . . Betty Redelsperger
  City Mgr., Robert Williamson
Forest Hill (6800 Forest Hill Dr.,
  Fort Worth 76140)
  . . . . Donald R. Walker
  City Mgr., Edward Badgett
Forney . . . . Don T. Cates
  §City Mgr., James McConnell
Forsan . . . . Roger Hudgins
Fort Gates (Box 428, Gatesville
  76528) . . . . Lee Bartlett Jr.
Fort Stockton . . . . . . Joe Shuster
  †City Mgr., Jesse Garcia
Fort Worth . . . . . . Kay Granger
  *City Mgr., David Ivory

¶Franklin . . . . . . Charles Ellison
Frankston . . . . . . James Gouger
Fredericksburg . . Boyd K. Harper
  City Mgr., Gary Neffendorf
¶Freeport . . . . . Allen R. Faulk Sr.
  *City Mgr., Earl W. Heath Jr.
Freer . . . . Malloy A. Hamilton
Friendswood. . . . Paul W. Schrader
  *City Mgr., Ron E. Cox
Friona . . . . . . Clarence Monroe
  †City Mgr., Beelee Goodwin
Frisco. . . . . Robert Warren
  City Mgr., George Purefoy
Fritch . . . . H. C. Heard
  ‡City Mgr., Dan Graves
Frost . . . . J. O. Williams
Fruitvale . . . . . . Bea Whisenhunt
Fulshear . . . . Frances Smart
Fulton . . . . Leslie Cole Sr.
Gainesville . . . Charles L. Woolfolk
  *City Mgr., Lyle Dresher
Galena Park . . . . Alvin D. Baggett
Gallatin . . . . . . Richard K. Snow
Galveston . . . . Barbara K. Crews
  *City Mgr., Douglas Matthews
Ganado . . . . Phillip A. Allen
Garden Ridge (Rt. 20, Box 508, San
  Antonio 78218) . Linda M. Klekar
  §City Mgr., Kandi M. Waterstreet
Garland . . . . . . Bill E. Tomlinson
  *City Mgr., James K. Spore
Garrett . . . . . . David W. Clemons
Garrison . . . . . . M. H. Stoddard
  §City Mgr., Melvis Bell
Gary . . . . Robert E. Young
Gatesville . . . . John R. Ward
  *City Mgr., Bob R. Stevens
Georgetown . . . . . . Bill Connor
  *City Mgr., Bob Hart
George West . . . . August Caron Jr.
  City Mgr., Jack Fendley
Gholson (Rt. 5, Box 495, Waco
  76705). . . . . . Howard T. Sexton
Giddings
  . . . . Lavonne Droemer-Morrow
  §City Mgr., James E. Dover
Gilmer . . . . Roy G. Owens
  City Mgr., James D. Mullins
Gladewater . . . . . Jackie D. Wood
  *City Mgr., Douglas R. Driggers
Glenn Heights (1938 S. Hampton
  Rd., DeSoto 75115) N. L. Craddock
  City Mgr., Sam Phelps
Glen Rose . . . . Carroll Gann
¶Godley . . . . Larry Richeson
Goldsmith. . . . . . Ben K. Bilbrey
Goldthwaite . . . . Richard H. Poss
  †City Mgr., Dale Allen
Goliad . . . . . . Linda Swickheimer
Golinda (Rt. 2, Box 629, Lorena
  76655). . . . . . Ennis Degrate Jr.
Gonzales. . . . . . Carroll E. Wiley
  *City Mgr., E.T. Gibson
¶Goodlow (Box 248, Kerens
  75144). . . . . . Willie Marie Isles
Goodrich. . . . . . . Miller Moffett
Gordon. . . . . Jack Coleman
Goree. . . . . . . George K. Cotton
  City Mgr., Terry Hamilton
Gorman . . . . C.M. Avery
Graford . . . . . . Randy Burleson
Graham . . . . . . Ed M. Hinson
  *City Mgr., Larry M. Fields
Granbury . . . . . . Charles E. Baker
  †City Mgr., Robt. D. Brockman
Grandfalls . . . . John Mark Kuhn
Grand Prairie
  . . . . . . Kenneth D. McGuffey
  *City Mgr., Gary Gwyn
Grand Saline . . . . . Larry Martin
  §City Mgr., Sam Beeler
Grandview . . . . Larry Moore
Granger . . . . Dollie Hajda
Granite Shoals . . Maxine Thurman
Grapeland . . . . . Calvin Skidmore
Grapevine . . . . . William D. Tate
  *City Mgr., Mark S. Watson
¶Grayburg (P.O. Box 23, Sour Lake
  77659). . . . . Johnie Floyd

¶Grays Prairie (Rt. 2, Box 627,
  Scurry 75158) . . . . Kenneth York
Greenville . . Everett B. Gladding
  *City Mgr., Edward D. Thatcher
Gregory . . . . Jerry A. Rivers
Grey Forest (18502 Scenic Loop Rd.,
  Helotes 78023). . . . Don Reddout
Groesbeck . . . . Jim Longbotham
Groom . . . . Jimmy Britten
Groves . . . . . . Sylvester Moore
  *City Mgr., A. R. Kilmer
Groveton . . . . Don E. LaRoe
¶Gruver . . . . Roy Byrd
  ‡City Mgr., A. J. Ratliff
Gun Barrel City. . . . . . Ben Flach
  §City Mgr., W. H. Adams Jr.
Gunter . . . . Mark Millar
¶Gustine. . . . . . Roger L. Oliver
¶Hackberry (P.O. Box 945, Little
  Elm 75068) . . . . . Brenda Polley
Hale Center. . . . . . Bob W. Brown
Hallettsville . . . . . . Sam B. Devall
  §City Mgr., Maxine Mikulenka
Hallsburg (Rt. 7, Box 428, Waco
  76705). . . . Margie N. Wilbanks
Hallsville . . . . . . T. Bynum Hatley
Haltom City . . Charles E. Womack
  City Mgr., Linda Tidwell
Hamilton . . . . . . Joe M. Crane
¶Hamlin . . . . Melvin Scott
Happy. . . . . R.N. McDonald
¶Hardin . . . . C. H. Riley
Harker Heights . . Robert E. Green
  City Mgr., Harold Weiler
Harlingen . . . . . H. Wm. Card Jr.
  *City Mgr., Mike R. Perez
Hart . . . . Joe D. Bailey
  §City Mgr., Virginia Reed
Haskell . . . . Greg Melton
  City Mgr., Robert Baker
Haslet. . . . . Odie M. Cowart
Hawkins . . . . . . W. C. Maynard
Hawley . . . . Don Tatum
Hays (P.O. Box 1285, Buda
  78610). . . . . . . Lamont Ramage
Hearne. . . . . . . Billy R. McDaniel
  *City Mgr., Floyd T. Hafley
Heath . . . . Charles Pratt
¶Hebron (Rt. 2, Box 184, Carrollton
  75010). . . . . Stanley Dozier
  City Mgr., C. W. Morris
¶Hedley . . . . Jon L. Leggitt
Hedwig Village (955 Piney Point
  Rd., Houston 77024)
  . . . . . . Victor H. Thompson Jr.
Helotes . . . . Vivian Hultz
Hemphill . . . . Richard Bass
  City Mgr., Tommy Neal
Hempstead . . . Herbert L. Johnson
  §City Mgr., James Vines
Henderson . . . . . . Tony Wooster
  ‡City Mgr., Randall Freeman
  (Interim)
Henrietta . . . . . . Charles S. Catlin
  §City Mgr., Joe Pence
Hereford. . . . . Tom LeGate
  *City Mgr., Chester Nolen

Hewitt . . . . Louis Mexia
  City Mgr., Dennis H. Woodard
Hickory Creek (Box 453, Lake Dal-
  las 75065) . . . . . Mike Flowers
¶Hico . . . . . . W. W. Rutledge Jr.
Hidalgo. . . . . . John David Franz
  City Mgr., Benito Lopez
Higgins. . . . . . . Billy B. Cornett
Highland Park (4700 Drexel Dr.,
  Dallas 75205) . Robert O. Mullins
  ‡City Mgr., George Patterson
Highland Village (948 Highland Vil-
  lage, Lewisville 75067)
  . . . . Kay Stephens
  City Mgr., Robert McDaniel
Hill Country Village (116 Aspen
  Ln., San Antonio 78232)
  . . . . . . Edward R. McNabb Jr.
Hillcrest Village (Box 1172, Alvin
  77512). . . . . Jimmy Hatley
Hillsboro. . . . . Henry Moore
  *City Mgr., Mack Wofford

Hilshire Village (P.O. Box 55233, Houston 77055) . . Jane M. Fisher
Hitchcock . . . . C. E. Clifford
§City Mgr., Bruce Clawson
Holiday Lakes (Rt. 4, Box 747, Angleton 77515) . . Claude M. Hunter
Holland . . . . Arthur Bielss
¶Holliday . . . . Grady Graves
City Mgr., Gary W. Jones
Hollywood Park (2 Mecca Dr., San Antonio 78232) . Bala K. Srinivas
¶Homer (Rt. 2, Box 319N, Lufkin 75901) . . . . R. A. Noel
Hondo . . . . Anthony L. Hardt
City Mgr., Mike Rhea
Honey Grove . . . . . Evelyn F. Wise
City Mgr., Pauline Rodgers
Hooks . . . . James B. Earnest
Horizon City (3614 Buxton Drive, El Paso 79927) Desmond P. Corcoran
Houston . . . . Kathryn J. Whitmire
Howardwick (Box 1143, Clarendon 79226) . . . . Neal Lee
Howe . . . . Ray Bledsoe
City Mgr., Ray Houston
¶Hubbard . . . . Don Anderson
§City Mgr., Harvey H. Schronk
Hudson (Rt. 5, Box 3270, Lufkin 75901) . . . . J.W. Reeves
¶Hudson Oaks . . . . . J. Y. McClure
Hughes Springs . . . . Reba Simpson
Humble . . . . Haden E. McKay
‡City Mgr., James P. Baker
Hunters Creek Village (8333 Katy Fwy., Houston 77024)
. . . . Cebe Sue Barnett
Huntington . . . . Dean McMullen
Huntsville . . . . W.H. Hodges
*City Mgr., Gene Pipes
Hurst . . . . Bill Souder
*City Mgr., Jim D. Starr
Hutchins . . . Joe Edd Wallace Sr.
City Mgr., Steven A. Reed
Hutto . . . . Jeffrey Phillips
Huxley (Rt. 1, Box 1410, Shelbyville 75973) . . . . Larry Vaughn
Idalou . . . . Mike Mauldin
City Mgr., Russell Hamilton
Impact (Box 3116, Abilene 79604) . . . . Dallas Perkins
¶Indian Lake (62 So. Aztec Cove Dr., Los Fresnos 78566)
. . . . Robert J. Wilson
Ingleside . . . . Mark Crawford
City Mgr., Steve Fitzgibbons
¶Ingram . . . . Donald Oehler
¶Iowa Colony (12003 County Road 65, Rosharon 77583)
. . . . Maurice Bright
Iowa Park . . . . Wayne House
‡City Mgr., Gary Jones
¶Iraan . . . . S. E. Turpin
¶Iredell . . . . A. D. Woody Jr.
Irving . . . . Roy F. Brown
*City Mgr., Jack D. Huffman
Italy . . . . Darrell Cockerham
Itasca . . . . Carroll C. Curry
§City Mgr., Mel Coker
Jacinto City (10301 Market St. Rd., Houston 77029) . David A. Gongre
§City Mgr., Joann Griggs
Jacksboro . . . . Jerry Craft
‡City Mgr., LeRoy Lane
Jacksonville . . . Gene Brumbelow
*City Mgr., Jim Dunaway
Jamaica Beach (P.O. Box 5264, Galveston 77554) Kenneth R. Dennis
Jasper . . . . . . Frank Lindsey Jr.
*City Mgr., Wayne DuBose
Jayton . . . . Travis R. Smith
Jefferson . . . . Victor A. Perot
Jersey Village (16501 Jersey Dr., Houston 77040) . Richard Ambrus
City Mgr., Debra Andrews
Jewett . . . . . . Herman Hammond
Joaquin . . . . . . Paul Jackson Jr.
Johnson City . . . . Ralph Moss
Jones Creek (Rt. 1, 7207 SFA Rd., Freeport 77541) Willie Cervenka

Jonestown . . . . . . Weldon Horton
Josephine . William D. McCroan Jr.
Joshua . . . . . . Johnnie Parrish
Jourdanton . . . . . Ed McClure Jr.
§City Mgr., Roy D. Underwood
Junction . . . . . Gordon A. Robbins
Justin . . . . Virgil Eaves
Karnes City . . . . Don Tymrak
Katy . . . . J.W. Conner
§City Mgr., Charles H. Ehlert
Kaufman . . . . Jess M. Murrell
City Mgr., John M. Trayhan
Keene . . . . Gary Heinrich
Keller . . . . Wallace D. Perry
‡City Mgr., Allen Bogard
Kemah . . . . Ben Blackledge
Kemp . . . . . . James Stroman Jr.
Kendleton . . . . Ernest Zomalt
Kenedy . . . . . . Ruhman c. Franklin
Kenefick (Rt. 5, Box 525-A, Dayton 77535) . . . . . . Verlon I. Moore Sr.
Kennard . . . . Bill Thomas
Kennedale . . . . Steve Radakovich
‡City Mgr., Ted Rowe
Kerens . . . . O. R. Spurlock
Kermit . . . . Fred W. Pearson
‡City Mgr., Wayne Reynolds
Kerrville . . . . . Leonard Holloway
*City Mgr., Glenn D. Brown
Kilgore . . . . . . E. Robert Barbee
*City Mgr., Ronald H. Stephens
Killeen . . . . Major E. Blair
*City Mgr., Daniel G. Hobbs
Kingsville . . . . Ron Sadler
*City Mgr., Carlos Lerma
Kirby (112 Baumann, San Antonio 78219) . . . . . . Lloyd Oppermann
City Mgr., Rick T. Cortes
Kirbyville . . . . Jerry E. Nobles
¶Kirvin . . . . Billie Walthall
¶Knollwood (100 Collins Dr., Sherman 75090) . Richard Ross Roelke
Knox City . . . . . . Lynward Wilcox
City Mgr., Kenneth Neal
Kosse . . . . W. C. Graeber
Kountze . . . . . Carl A. Richardson
City Mgr., Clyde T. Townson
Kress . . . . Joe Frausto
Krugerville (‡8 Carrington Center, Aubrey 76227) . . . Harry Richards
City Mgr., Marilyn Carrigan
Krum . . . . Jan Farris
Kyle . . . . Merle D. Wilkins
La Coste . . . . . George T. Lagleder
Lacy-Lakeview (501 E. Craven, Waco 76705) . Charles W. Doherty
Ladonia . . . . Lester Loftice
La Feria . . . . Jesse F. Byars
City Mgr., Thos. V. Kolterman
Lago Vista . . . . Russell Allen
City Mgr., Dennis Jones
La Grange . . . . . Don Chovanec
‡City Mgr., Ronald Holland
¶La Grulla (City Hall, Grulla 78548) . . . . Ruben L. Solis
Laguna Vista . . Rafael Hinojosa Jr.
La Joya . . . . Rodolfo Farias
City Mgr., Oscar Cuellar Jr.
Lake Bridgeport (Rt. 2, Box 244F, Bridgeport 76026) Jeanita Carney
Lake City (Box 177, Mathis 78368) . . . . Orville Downs
Lake Dallas . . . . Ronald E. Honse
Lake Jackson . . . . Doris Williams
*City Mgr., William P. Yenne
Lakeport (P.O. Box 7728, Longview 75607) . . . . . . Norman Pepper
Lakeside (San Patricio Co. (P.O. Box 1191, Mathis 78368)
. . . . Douglass Thompson
Lakeside (Tarrant Co.) (9830 Confederate Park, Fort Worth 76108) . . . . Raymond Beck
Lakeside City (Box 4287, Wichita Falls 76308) . . Charles Ortega
Lake Tanglewood (Rt. 8, Box 35-15, Amarillo 79118). John C. Ricketts
Lakeview . . . . . Russell J. Payne
Lakeway (104 Cross Creek, Austin

78734) . . . . Cole Rowland
§City Mgr., Sam Huser
Lakewood Village (100 Highridge Dr., Little Elm 75068)
. . . . Mary F. Revland
Lake Worth (6720 Telephone Rd., Fort Worth 76135) . . . J.T. Hinkle
§City Mgr., Linda A. Ingram
¶La Marque . . . . Carlton A. Getty
*City Mgr., Gary Jackson
Lamesa . . . . Ronnie Payton
*City Mgr., Paul Feazelle
Lampasas . . . . Jack Calvert
City Mgr., J. O. Tanner
Lancaster . . . . . Margie Waldrop
*City Mgr., William A. Gaither
La Porte . . . . . Norman L. Malone
*City Mgr., Robert T. Herrera
Laredo . . . . . . Saul N. Ramirez Jr.
*City Mgr., Peter Vargas
¶Latexo . . . . Billie Jo Bennett
La Vernia . . . . . . Theo F. Gerlich
La Villa . . . . Carlos Perez
City Mgr., Guadalupe Gonzalez
Lavon . . . . John K. Smith
La Ward . . . . . Tillman M. Hunt Sr.
Lawn . . . . Johnny B. Hudson
§City Mgr., Sue Raper
League City . . . . Joe L. Lamb
¶Leakey . . . . J. H. Chisum
Leander . . . . Mike Lowe
§City Mgr., Joe Ventura
¶Leary (Rt. 5, Box 435, Texarkana 75501) . . . . Elmer E. Line
Lefors . . . . Gene Gee
¶Leona . . . . F. L. Thompson
Leonard . . . . Billy H. Martin
§City Mgr., Lanna Jackson
Leon Valley (6400 El Verde Rd., San Antonio 78238) . Irene Baldridge
§City Mgr., James J. Malone
Leroy . . . . Tim Harrington
Levelland . . . . . Raymond Dennis
*City Mgr., Gregory M. Ingham
Lewisville . . . . . . B.C. Groves
*City Mgr., Charles R. Owens
Lexington . . . . Louis H. Knipstein
Liberty . . . . . C. Scott Parker
*City Mgr., Roy Bennett
¶Lincoln Park (Rt. 1, Box 701, Aubrey 76227) . . . . Roger Pock
Lindale . . . . Bobby McClenny
§City Mgr., Owen Scott
Linden . . . . . . E.W. Roundtree Jr.
City Mgr., Sammy C. Wells
Lindsay . . . . . Robert D. Cogburn
¶Lipan . . . . Gaston Grogan
Little Elm . . . . Jim Pelley
Littlefield . . . . . . Paul D. Bennett
*City Mgr., Marty Mangum
Little River-Academy (Box 521, Little River 76554) Charles R. Rogers
Live Oak (800 Shin Oak Dr., San Antonio 78233) . Norm Tremblay
*City Mgr., Douglas G. Faseler
¶Liverpool . . . . . . Allan F. Moore
Livingston . . . Ben R. Ogletree Jr.
†City Mgr., Sam Gordon
Llano . . . . Jeff Hopf
City Mgr., George Rogers
Lockhart . . . . . M. Louis Cisneros
§City Mgr., Joe A. Michie
Lockney . . . . Kenneth R. Wofford
Log Cabin (P.O. Box 127, Malakoff 75148) . . . . Leta Hunter
Lometa . . . . . . Mary E. McAnelly
Lone Oak . . . . Roy O'Hara
Lone Star . . . . James W. Smith
Longview . . . . Martha Whitehead
*City Mgr., James B. Baugh
Loraine . Catarino G. Martinez Jr.
¶Lorena . . . . . Jerry D. Fountain
Lorenzo . . . . . Tommy D. Fondren
§City Mgr., Leon Moore
Los Fresnos . . . . James Keillor
City Mgr., Tommy M. Brooks
¶Los Ybanez (HCR 7, Box 52, Lamesa 79331) . Mary A. Ybanez

Lott . . . . Walter D. Ford
Lovelady . . . . . . Troy R. Driskell
Lowry Crossing (360 Bridgefarmer Rd., McKinney 75069)
. . . . Jim Champlin
Lubbock . . . . B. C. McMinn
*City Mgr., Larry Cunningham
Lucas . . . . Gerry Ann Guzman
Lueders . . . . Floyd R. Jones
¶Luella . . . . Jerry MacNeill
Lufkin . . . . . . Louis A. Bronaugh
*City Mgr., C.G. Maclin
Luling . . . . Martin E. Weiner
*City Mgr., Harold L. Watts
Lumberton . . . . . Wilton Dunaway
Lyford . . . . Morris W. Dodd
Lytle . . . . John McGinnis
Mabank . . . . Jack Salter
§City Mgr., L.R. Stryker
Madisonville . . . . . . E.B. Andrews
‡City Mgr., J.T. Closs
Magnolia Dorothy "Dickey" Dyer
Malakoff . . . . . Martin Walling Jr.
§City Mgr., Howard Julian
Malone . . . . James Lucko
¶Manor . . . . . . Sidney E. Donnell Sr.
§City Mgr., Michael Bamer
Mansfield . . . . Gary Dalton
‡City Mgr., Clayton W. Chandler
Manvel . . . . Doyle Fenn
¶Marble Falls . . . . . . Tony Hogue
‡City Mgr., Jack Chaney
Marfa . . . . Genevieve P. Bassham
§City Mgr., Bobby R. Martinez
¶Marietta . . . . . . Delton W. Miller
Marion . . . . Glenn A. Hild
Marlin . . . . Clark Morris
‡City Mgr., Sue Philley
Marquez . . . . Terry K. Watson
Marshall . . . . Carl Swendson
*City Mgr., Tony Williams
Marshall Creek . . . Charles R. Cox
Mart . . . . M.C. Tony Wayland
Martindale . . . . . . Walter Bagley
Mason . . . . . . R. Clinton Schulze
Matador . . . . . Gary L. Lancaster
Mathis . . . . . . Eva F. Medrano
Maud . . . . Billy D. Foster
Maypearl . . . . Kyle E. Neal
McAllen . . . . . . Othal E. Brand Sr.
‡City Mgr., Jose Escamilla
McCamey . . . . . John Max Tucker
McGregor . . . . . . Kathleen Anglin
*City Mgr., Bill Dake
McKinney . . . . John E. Gay
*City Mgr., D. E. Paschal Jr.
McLean . . . . Sam A. Haynes
McLendon-Chisholm (P.O. Box 157, Rockwall 75087) . . Chuck Hodges
Meadow . . . . Dale Wylie
¶Meadowlakes (209 Meadowlakes, Marble Falls 78654) Randy Savage
Meadows (12002 Southwest Frwy., Stafford 77477) . . . Jim McDonald
Megargel . . . Charlie J. Kulhanek
Melissa . . . . Buck Weatherby
Melvin . . . . . . Charlie Flores Jr.
§City Mgr., Ken Normand
Memphis . . . . . . Homer Tucker
Menard . . . . Max E. Hooten
§City Mgr., James F. Cannon

¶Mercedes . . . . Norma G. Garcia
*City Mgr., Alan Kamasaki
Meridian . . . . Joe Rickard
Merkel . . . . J.T. Naron
§City Mgr., Kent Satterwhite
Mertens . . . . . . Ledlow Joe Crass
Mertzon . . . . Virginia Wales
Mesquite . . . . Cathye Ray
*City Mgr., James A. Prugel Jr.
Mexia . . . . Richard Duncan
*City Mgr., Gerald Yarbrough
Miami . . . . Newton M. Cox
Midland . . . . . Carroll M. Thomas
‡City Mgr., Fred W. Poe
Midlothian . . . . Maurice Osborn
*City Mgr., Robert G. Powers
¶Midway . . . . Patrick H. Wakefield
¶Milano . . . . Roger Hashem

Mildred (Rt. 6, Corsicana 75110)
. . . . E. L. Manire Jr.
Miles . . . . Werner Harsch
Milford . . . . Bobby D. Cooper
Miller's Cove (Rt. 3, Box 3, Mt. Pleasant 75455)
. . . . . Raymond Wayne Miller
Millsap . . . . Mary French
Mineola . . . . Glenn Smith
§City Mgr., Thomas R. Taylor
Mineral Wells . . . . . Willie Casper
*City Mgr., Natalie Flores-Kelly
Mingus . . . . Milo Moffit
Mission . . . . . . Pat Townsend Jr.
*City Mgr., Michael H. Talbot
Missouri City . . . . . John B. Knox
‡City Mgr., John R. Milford
Mobeetie . . . . Dale Corcoran
Mobile City (813 Lilac Lane, Rockwall 75087) . . . . Billie M. Easley
Monahans . . . . . Walter W. Roeber
*City Mgr., Jack Forga
Mont Belvieu . . . . . Fred R. Miller
§City Mgr., Ruthie P. Sager
Montgomery . . . . . John A. Butler
¶Moody . . . . Marvin Evans
§City Mgr., Charleen Dowell
Moore Station (Rt. 1, Box 133, Larue 75770) . . . . Arthur T. Earl
Moran . . . . Marvin Kays
Morgan . . Harold E. Vandiver Jr.
Morgan's Point (P.O. Box 839, La Porte 77571) . . . . John A. Grimes
City Mgr., David A. Paulissen
Morgan's Point Resort (8 Morgan's Point Blvd, Belton 76513)
. . . . Carl P. Brown
†City Mgr., Gerry G. Giles
Morton . . . . Ray Lewis
City Mgr., Mitch Grant
Moulton . . . . Minnie Lee Fisbeck
¶Mountain City (116 Cedar, Buda 78610) . . . . Beth H. Smith
Mount Calm . . . . James Johansen
Mount Enterprise . . Carl D. Allen
Mount Pleasant . . . Jim Blanchard
*City Mgr., T. Clay Collins
Mount Vernon . . . . Mike Edwards
§City Mgr., Eddie G. Turner
Muenster . . . . Ted Henscheid
§City Mgr., Joseph M. Fenton
Muleshoe . . . . . Darrell E. Turner
*City Mgr., Dave Marr Jr.
¶Mullin . . . . A. C. Spinks
¶Munday . . . . . Doris Dickerson
§City Mgr., Walter M. Hertle
Murchison . . . . . . A.D. McCurley
¶Murphy (205 N. Murphy Rd., Plano 75094) Reginald W. George
Mustang (P.O. Box 325, Corsicana 75151) . . . . Glenn Albritton
Mustang Ridge (1699 Laws Rd., Buda 78610) . . . . Robert A. Lee
Nacogdoches . . . . Judy McDonald
*City Mgr., Gordon C. Pierce
Naples . . . . Howard Belville
Nash . . . . Jay Smith
Nassau Bay (1800 NASA Rd. One, Houston 77058) . . . Johnny Jones
*City Mgr., Jim McFellin
¶Natalia . . Martin B. Hardison Jr.
Navarro (P.O. Box 7501, Corsicana 75110) . . . . . Yvonne Capehart
Navasota . . . . B.J. Gruner
*City Mgr., Alva McDonald
Nazareth . . . . . . Ralph Brockman
Nederland . . . . . Carl N. LeBlanc
*City Mgr., D. E. Sosa

Needville . . . . . Kermit Blezinger
¶Nesbitt (Rt. 5, Box 88, Marshall 75670) . . . . Roy A. Nesbitt
Nevada . . . . Giles Caldwell
Newark . . . . . . Bobby Williams
New Berlin (Rt. 1, Box 215-A, La Vernia 78121) Freddie Friederick
New Boston . . . . . John H. McCoy
New Braunfels
. . . . James E. Goodbread
*City Mgr., Paul Grohman

Newcastle . . . . Earline Swarts
¶New Chapel Hill (Rt. 25, Box 834, Tyler 75707) . . . . J. T. Pinkerton
New Deal . . . . Terry Martin
New Home . . . . Roy Blevins
New Hope (Box 562, McKinney 75069) . . . . . . Tamara J. Blazier
New London . . Charlie McConnico
New Summerfield . . . Bill Poteet
Newton . . . . . . Charles M. Glover
New Waverly . . . Grady Chandler
¶Neylandville (General Delivery, Greenville 75401) . Robert L. Lee
Niederwald (Rt. 1, Box 175 N, Kyle 78640) . . . . Jack Clay Hodges
¶Nixon . . . . W. G. Millington
City Mgr., James E. Talley
Nocona . . . . Robert R. Smith
‡City Mgr., Melvin D. Adams
Nolanville . . . . . Noah Van Kirk Sr.
Nome . . . . Hugh R. Ferguson
Noonday (P.O. Box 6425, Tyler 75711) . . . . Bennie H. Smith
¶Nordheim . . . . Elo Pfeifer
¶Normangee . . . . J. C. Traylor III
North Cleveland (Box 1266, Cleveland 77327) . . . . Woodrow Squier
Northcrest (613 N. Lacy Dr., Waco 76705) . . . . Dahon E. Tynes
¶Northlake (Rt. 1, Box 89, Justin 76247) . . . . W. T. Yarbrough
North Richland Hills (P.O. Box 18609, Fort Worth 76180)
. . . . Tommy Brown
*City Mgr., Rodger Line
Novice . . . . Jim White
Oak Grove (P.O. Box 309, Kaufman 75142) . . . . Jim D. Terry
Oakhurst . . . . . . Jackie R. Elliott
Oak Leaf . . . . James Ezell
Oak Point (P.O. Box 818, Little Elm 75068) . . . . Carl F. Busch
Oak Ridge (Cooke Co.) (Rt. 3, Box 325, ‡27, Gainesville 76240) . . . . Donna Skaggs
Oak Ridge (Kaufman Co.) (Rt. 1, Box 228, Terrell 75160)
. . . . Marge Betts
Oak Ridge North (27326 Robinson Rd., Conroe 77385) Gary A. Louie
*City Mgr., Richard Derr
¶Oak Valley (P.O. Box 2193, Corsicana 75151) . . . . Jim Venable
Oakwood . . . . Ruby R. Johnson
O'Brien . . . . Charlene Brothers
Odem . . . . . Jessie Rodriguez Sr.
Odessa . . . . Lorraine Bonner
*City Mgr., Ray Kendall (Acting)
O'Donnell . . . . . . David M. Smith
Oglesby . . . . . Kenneth Goodwin
¶Old River-Winfree (Box 1169, Mont Belvieu 77580) . . Arthur LaFour
City Mgr., Patti McCall
Olmos Park (119 W. El Prado Dr., San Antonio 78212)
. . . . Gerald Z. Dubinski
†City Mgr., A. T. Brainerd
Olney . . . . Jeff McClatchy
Olton . . . . Leon Noack
Omaha . . . . . . Tommy G. Knight
Onalaska . . . . R.E. Maddox
Opdyke West (P.O. Box 1179, Levelland 79336) . . . . Wayne Riggins
Orange . . . . Dan Mohon
*City Mgr., Michael J. Van Wickler
Orange Grove . . Truett L. Thomas
§City Mgr., Perry R. Young
Orchard . . . . . . Eugene L. Demny
Ore City . . . . Albert J. Hiles
Overton . . . . Robert Raney
City Mgr., Ray Litton
Ovilla . . . . . . Charles B. Morton
Oyster Creek Richard D. Merriman
Paducah . . . . Lee Currey
City Mgr., Bill Cartwright
Paint Rock . . . . . Patricia Sue Sims
Palacios . . . . . Leonard L. Lamar
Palestine . . . . . . Jackson Hanks
*City Mgr.,
Richard R. Rockenbaugh

Palmer . . . . Wallace Hughey
¶Palmhurst (Rt. 2, Box 80, Mission 78572). . . . . . Sandford E. Orme
City Mgr., Gary Toothaker
Palm Valley (Rt. 4, Harlingen 78552). . . . . John Puhl

Palmview (Rt. 10, Box 598-B, Mission 78572) . . . . Jose R. Pena
City Mgr., Sergio Munoz
Pampa . . . . Richard D. Peet
*City Mgr., Glen E. Hackler
Panhandle . . . . Jack Miller
‡City Mgr., Thomas Blazek
Panorama (98 Hiwon Dr., Conroe 77304). . . . Donald R. Branham
Pantego . . . . R.D. Surratt
‡City Mgr., Larry W. Smith
Paris . . . . George Fisher Jr.
*City Mgr., Michael E. Malone
Parker . . . . Jack Albritton
§City Mgr., Betty McMenamy
Pasadena . . . . . . John R. Harrison
Pattison . . . . . Linda A. Mladenka
Patton Village (P.O. Box 437, Splendora 77372). . Kenneth E. Jenkins
¶Payne Springs. . . . . . Gary Walsh
Pearland . . . . . . C.V. Coppinger
*City Mgr., James O. DeShazer
¶Pearsall . . . . Ruben Leal
§City Mgr., Andres Garza Jr.
¶Pecan Gap . . . . John Reid
Pecan Hill (P.O. Box 443, Red Oak 75154). . . . . Linda White
Pecos . . . . Marilea Parsons
‡City Mgr., H.W. Nagel
Pelican Bay (1300 Pelican Circle, Azle 76020) . . . . . . Vickie Lynch
¶Penelope. . . . . Robert E. Tobola
Pernitas Point (HCR-1, Box 621, Sandia 78383) . . Dorothy Keetch
Perryton . . . . Doug Hale
†City Mgr., David Landis
Petersburg . . . . Jim Fox
§City Mgr., Jesse J. Nave
Petrolia . . . . James L. Elledge Jr.
Petronila (Rt. 3, Box 51, Robstown 78380). . . . . . William J. Ordner
Pflugerville . . . . . . Scott Winton
§City Mgr., Clarence Bohls
Pharr . . . . Rubio Salinas Jr.
‡City Mgr., Joel Zarate
Pilot Point . . . . T. Ray Dane
§City Mgr., Eric Kuykendall
Pine Forest (Box 1004, Vidor 77662). . . . . . William G. Elliott
City Mgr., G.T. Sharp
Pinehurst (3640 Mockingbird, Orange 77630) . . . . . . A.R. Morgan
§City Mgr., Walter E. Cobb
Pineland. . . . John O. Booker Jr.
Piney Point Village (7745 San Felipe, Houston 77063)
. . . . A. Lee Smith
Pittsburg . . . . . . D. H. Abernathy
†City Mgr., Ned C. Muse
Plains. . . . . T. J. Miller
Plainview . . . . . E. V. Ridlehuber
*City Mgr., James P. Jeffers
Plano . . . . Florence Shapiro
*City Mgr., Thomas Muehlenbeck
Pleak (5809 Pleak Rd., Richmond 77469). . . . . . William J. Poncik
Pleasanton . . . . . . Michael J. Olle
‡City Mgr., Larry Pippin
Pleasant Valley. . . . . Leon T. Little
¶Plum Grove (Rt. 5, Box 322-G, Cleveland 77327). . . Noble Enloe
Point . . . . Joe Ben Cason
Pointblank . . . . Tom Tyson
Point Comfort. . . Theresa R. Tanner
Ponder . . . . Ema Lu Long
Port Aransas. . . . . . J. C. Barr
‡City Mgr., Gordon N. Beck
Port Arthur Mary Ellen Summerlin
*City Mgr., Cornelius Boganey
Port Isabel . . . . Calvin Byrd
City Mgr., Leo F. Sanders

Portland. . . . . Billy G. Webb
*City Mgr., (Vacancy)
Port Lavaca . . . . Tiney Browning
*City Mgr., C. J. Webster
Port Neches . . Gary C. Graham Sr.
*City Mgr., James Harrington
Post . . . . Jim Jackson
City Mgr., Robert J. Turner
Post Oak Bend (Rt. 4, Box 32, Kaufman 75142). . . . . Al Ray
Poteet. . . . . . Robert Z. Enriquez
Poth . . . . Gene Maeckel
¶Pottsboro . . . . George E. Cassell
¶Powell. . . . . Paul J. Sloan
Poynor. . . . . Allen Bragg
¶Prairie View . . . Ronald Leverett
City Mgr., U. R. Bell
Premont. . . . . Luis S. Saenz
Presidio . . . . John Ferguson
¶Primera . . . . . Ronald D. Harwell
Princeton . . . . Bill Caldwell
¶Progreso Lakes (Box 511, Progreso 78579) . . . Bill Swinnea
Prosper . . . . Grady Smothermon
Putnam . . . . Winford Fry
¶Pyote . . . . Darral M. Shirey
Quanah. . . . . . Weldon Dickerson
City Mgr., Ronnie Ingram
Queen City . . . James McCormack
Quinlan . . . . Lois Cagle
City Mgr., Richard Torres
Quintana (P.O. Box 2379, Freeport 77541). . . . . . Mary J. Cornett
Quitaque . . . . Elgin Conner
§City Mgr., David Brunson
Quitman . . . . Erwin Jordan
Ralls. . . . . David A. Prewitt
Rancho Viejo (3461 Carmen, Brownsville 78520)
. . . . Walter F. Halleman Jr.
¶Ranger . . . . David Rogers
Rangerville (Rt. 4, Box 77, San Benito 78586) . Wayne M. Halbert
Rankin . . . . Elveen Phillips West
Ransom Canyon . . . Lee Kitchens
City Mgr., E. Wayne Gentry
Raymondville. . . . . C. M. Crowell
Red Oak . . . . . . Debra Griswold
Redwater . . . . . . John J. Rooney
Refugio . . . . Bart Wales
Reklaw. . . . . . Harlan Crawford
Reno (Lamar Co.) (165 Bybee St., Paris 75460) . . . . Pat Bailey
§City Mgr., Debbie Spencer
Reno (Parker Co.) (Rt. 4, Box 270, Azle 76020) . . . . . F. E. Pugh
¶Retreat (Rt. 3, Box 2050, Corsicana 75110). . . . . . Frances Robinson
Rhome . . . . Karl Little
Rice . . . . Sid Schutte
Richardson. . . . . Gary Slagel
*City Mgr., Bob Hughey
Richland. . . . . Guy Lansford
Richland Hills (3200 Diana Dr., Fort Worth 76118). . . . James R. Truitt
City Mgr., Stephen Hughes
Richland Springs
. . . . John E. McPherson
¶Richmond . . . . Hilmar G. Moore
§City Mgr., Jack L. Tyler
Richwood . . . . David Head
Riesel. . . . . . Burney B. Mullens
¶Rio Bravo (P.O. Box 420585, Laredo 78042). . . . .
Rio Hondo . . Alejandro Chavez Jr.
Rio Vista. . . . . Sam Bigham
Rising Star . . . . . . Jerrell Bible
City Mgr., Gene Moore
River Oaks (4900 River Oaks Blvd, Fort Worth 76114)
. . . . Thomas M. Holland
City Mgr., W. C. Ray
Riverside. . . . . Randell L. Vincent
Roanoke. . . . . . . Max L. Watson
Roaring Springs . . . Joey Thacker
§City Mgr., Frances Walters
Robert Lee . . . . . . Jackie Walker

Robinson (111 W. Lyndale, Waco 76706). . . . . Billy Simons
§City Mgr., Curtis McLemore
Robstown . . . . . . Julio Garcia Jr.
Roby . . . . Cecil J. King
City Mgr., Jimmy C. Price
Rochester. . . . . . Rod Townsend
Rockdale . . . . Bill T. Avrett
‡City Mgr., Marshall Martin
¶Rockport. . . . . Danny Adams
City Mgr., Frederick W. Robison
Rocksprings Heriberto M. Gallegos
Rockwall . . . . . . Frank R. Miller
‡City Mgr., William R. Eisen
Rocky Mound (Box 795, Pittsburg 75686). . . . . Noble T. Smith
City Mgr., Frederick Kimble
Rogers . . . . Billy Ray Crow

¶Rolling Meadows (105 McKinnon Dr., Kilgore 75662) E. N. Roberson
Rollingwood (403 Nixon Dr., Austin 78746). . . Courtland L. Logue Jr.
¶Roma . . . . Jose C. Saenz
§City Mgr., Andy Canales
Roman Forest (Box 397, New Caney 77357). . . . . . . Marie H. Coose
Ropesville. . . . . . . James Pierce
Roscoe . . . . Ron Stovall
City Mgr., Don Allen

Rosebud. . . . . . Evelyn Longwell
†City Mgr., Wanda Fischer
Rose City (370 Rose City Dr., Vidor 77662). . . . . . O. Hector Cantu
Rose Hill Acres (Box 8285, Lumberton 77711). . Rayedene S. Graves
Rosenberg . . . . Larry Wilkinson
City Mgr., Robert Eskridge
Ross . . . . James L. Jaska
¶Rosser . . . . . . Fred F. Alford Jr.
Rotan . . . . Jerry A. Marshall
§City Mgr., Joe Dickson
Round Mountain. . . . . E.B. Seals
Round Rock . . . . Mike Robinson
‡City Mgr., Robert L. Bennett Jr.
Round Top . . . . . . Dave Nagel
Rowlett. . . . . John Schroy
*City Mgr., Mike Gibson

Roxton . . . . Luther Smith
¶Royse City. . . . . . Don Becknell
City Mgr., Michael G. Duehring
Rule . . . . Jerry Cannon
City Mgr., Danny Hisey
Runaway Bay . . . . . Clay N. Dent
§City Mgr., Mike Evans
Runge . . . . Daulton Bassett
Rusk. . . . . Mike Crysup
‡City Mgr., Bill Collum
Sabinal . . . . . . James D. Reavis
Sachse . . . . Larry Holden
City Mgr., Lloyd Henderson
¶Sadler. . . . . O. L. Woods
Saginaw . . . . . . John Ed Keeter
City Mgr., Roy L. Moffatt
¶St. Hedwig (Box 40, Saint Hedwig 78152). . . . Albert Strzelczyk
St. Jo (P.O. Box 186, Saint Jo 76265). . . . . J. C. Donnell
St. Paul (745 Parker Rd. Loop, Saint Paul 75098). . . . . . Carl Sherrin
San Angelo . . . . . . Don Butts
*City Mgr., Stephen Brown
¶San Antonio. . . . . . Nelson Wolff
*City Mgr., Alex Briseno
San Augustine. . . . . Curt Goetz
‡City Mgr., Alton B. Shaw
¶San Benito . . . . Gilbert Galvan
City Mgr., Manuel Hinojosa
¶Sanctuary (316 Ash Creek Dr., Azle 76020) . . . .
¶San Diego . . . . Amando S. Garcia
San Felipe. . . . . . . Diana Boring
Sanford . . . . . Douglas Whipkey
Sanger . . . . Nel Armstrong
City Mgr., John Hamilton
San Juan. . . . . . Arturo Guajardo
*City Mgr., Raul L. Rubio

¶San Leanna (Box 86, Manchaca 78652)......... Damon O'Neal
San Marcos..... Kathy M. Morris
*City Mgr., Larry D. Gilley
¶San Patricio (Rt. 2, Box 40, Mathis 78368).... Lonnie Glasscock III
¶San Perlita ..... David J. Dawe
San Saba......... Joe Ragsdale
§City Mgr., James Reavis
Sansom Park (5500 Buchanan, Fort Worth 76114).. Merle Easterling
Santa Anna.... Gale Allen-Brock
Santa Fe......... Jack L. Long
City Mgr., Vince Di Piazza
Santa Rosa..... Ruben Ochoa Jr.
Savoy......... James Teems
Schertz......... Earl W. Sawyer
‡City Mgr., Kerry R. Sweatt
Schulenburg....... Leo Kopecky
†City Mgr., Robert A. Hoot
Scotland....... Robert W. Krahl
Scottsville..... John P. Verhalen
¶Seabrook....... Harold L. Graham
*City Mgr., Mark Neff
Seadrift.......... Mark Daniel
Seagoville......... Neal Wooley
§City Mgr., Al Lemond
Seagraves.... Patrick L. McAdoo
Sealy.......... Betty Reinbeck
†City Mgr., Roger Carlisle
Seguin.......... Ed Gotthardt
City Mgr., Jake Krauskopf
Selma........ Kenneth Fleenor
§City Mgr., Margie Lubianski
Seminole...... Robert M. Cosby
City Mgr., Thomas L. Adams
Seven Oaks (Rt. 1, Box 833, Livingston 77351)........ Viola Jones
Seven Points. Paul E. Mooneyham
Seymour............ Dick Wirz
§City Mgr., Mary Alice Smith
Shady Shores (Box 362, Lake Dallas 75065)......... Olive Stephens
Shallowater........ Moe Dozier
Shamrock.... Douglas O. V. Rives
†City Mgr., Johnny Rhodes
Shavano Park (99 Saddletree Rd., San Antonio 78231). Linda Zuflacht
Shenandoah (801 Maplewood, Spring 77381).... Charles Bradt
City Mgr., Jose Cantu
Shepherd....... Frances Shank
Sherman..... Harry R. Reynolds
*City Mgr., Talmadge N. Buie
Shiner.......... Arthur T. Ward
Shoreacres (619 Shoreacres Blvd., La Porte 77571)... James L. Neal
Silsbee....... Wesley C. Latham
*City Mgr., Ronald M. Hickerson
Silverton......... Wayne Nance
Simonton...... Maurice Berkman
Sinton............ Tom Harrison
*City Mgr., Warren Driver
Skellytown .... Tommy J. Owens
Slaton............ Don Kendrick
§City Mgr., Jim Estes
Smiley.......... Paul D. Elder
Smithville..... Vernon Richards
§City Mgr., Gerald Decker
¶Smyer....... Foy E. Thompson Jr.
Snook......... Richard Kovar
Snyder...... Troy D. Williamson
*City Mgr., John Gayle
Socorro....... Reuben R. Chavez
Somerset...... Paul G. Cuellar
§City Mgr., Luke W. Parchman
Somerville....... Tanya Roush
§City Mgr., David Lozano
Sonora......... Billy G. Gosney
†City Mgr., M. H. Gildon
Sour Lake..... Charlie Lyons Jr.
City Mgr., Robert Ewart
South Houston (Box 238, Houston 77587)......... Dennis Cordray
Southlake.......... Gary Fickes
City Mgr., Curtis E. Hawk
Southmayd......... Billy Kerr
City Mgr., Diane Moore
¶South Mountain (Rt. 2, Box 298 A, Gatesville 76528)...........

South Padre Island (Box 3410, Port Isabel 78597)
...... Robert N. Pinkerton Jr.
‡City Mgr., Eduardo A. Campirano
Southside Place (6309 Edloe, Houston 77005).. David Bellamy
City Mgr., Seth M. Young
Spearman....... Burl Buchanan
†City Mgr., James R. Murray
Splendora........ Grace Myers
¶Spofford........ J. B. Herndon
Springlake...... Harlon Watson
Springtown....... Doug Hughes
§City Mgr., Lance Howerton
Spring Valley (1025 Campbell Rd., Houston 77055)
.... William R. Denison
City Mgr., George R. Parker
Spur........... Glen T. Williams
Stafford....... Leonard Scarcella
Stagecoach (Box 364, Tomball 77377)......... T. H. Wilson
Stamford....... Louis E. Johnson
*City Mgr., Ken Roberson
Stanton......... Lester Baker
§City Mgr., Danny Fryar
Star Harbor (P.O. Drawer 949, Malakoff 75148)...... John A. Lott
†City Mgr., Wyatt E. Parkins
Stephenville
.... George Swearingen
§City Mgr., Donald B. Davis
Sterling City... Clyde Ross Foster
¶Stinnett....... Ronnie E. Griffin
City Mgr., Bruce Titus
Stockdale...... Willard Jordan
§City Mgr., Carl R. Lambeck
Stratford..... Dwight D. Reese
City Mgr., Wayland Brown
¶Strawn..... Gordon S. Thomason
Streetman....... Arnold Lewis
Sudan.......... H. Carl Burnett
¶Sugar Land...... Lee Duggan
City Mgr., David E. Neeley
Sulphur Springs. Ronald Lummus
*City Mgr., Olen Petty
Sundown....... Joe Craddock
‡City Mgr., Tommy Phillips
Sunnyvale......... Paul E. Cash
§City Mgr., Robert J. Ewalt
Sunray.......... Dow Brewer
City Mgr., Greg Smith
Sunrise Beach.... Edward W. Houy
Sunset Valley (2 Lone Oak Trail, Austin 78745).... Helen C. Besse
¶Sun Valley (Rt. 2, Paris 75460)
.... Maria Wagnon
Surfside Beach (Rt. 2, Box 909, Freeport 77541). Charles Schulte
Sweeny............ Vivian Brooks
§City Mgr., Exa Mae Keller
Sweetwater........ Rick Rhodes
*City Mgr., David Maddox
Taft......... Herbert O. Grebe Jr.
‡City Mgr., Al Veselka
Tahoka....... James A. Solomon
‡City Mgr., Barry Pittman
Talco......... K.M. (Mike) Sloan
Tatum......... Murry E. Adams
Taylor......... Donald Hill
*City Mgr., Ken Taylor
Taylor Lake Village (1202 Kirby, Seabrook 77586)
.... James E. Cumming
Teague......... Bobby Wilkinson
City Mgr., Stan Smith
Tehuacana.. Charles D. Yelverton
Temple......... Dennis Hobbs
*City Mgr., Jack Parker
Tenaha....... George N. Bowers
Terrell......... Don L. Lindsey
*City Mgr., Lanny S. Lambert
Terrell Hills (5100 N. New Braunfels, San Antonio 78209)
.... Barbara B. Christian
*City Mgr., Henry U.B. Brummett
Texarkana...... John M. Jarvis
*City Mgr., George Shackleford
Texas City...... Charles T. Doyle
Texhoma..... Mark H. Freeman

Texline......... Doug Antwiler
City Mgr., Bernard Eads
The Colony.... Wm. W. Manning
*City Mgr., William M. Hall
Thompsons..... G. W. Longserre
Thorndale........... Don Culp
Thornton...... Charles M. Peery
Thorntonville (2414 W. 2nd, Monahans 79756).... Harold Callaway
Thrall......... James Dvorak
Three Rivers.... Louise Shumate
Throckmorton.... D. K. Weaver
Tiki Island, Village of (802 Tiki Drive, Rt.2, Tiki Island 77554)......... Richard Hensley
Timbercreek Canyon (Rt. 7, Box 4-5, Amarillo 79118)
.... Weldon Hill
Timpson........... Ross Graves
¶Tioga......... Billy J. McKnight
¶Tira (Rt. 7, Box 240, Sulphur Springs 75482)... Coy O. Vicars
Toco (2103 Chestnut, Brookston 75421)...... Hugh D. Thompson
Todd Mission (Rt. 2, Box 650, Plantersville 77363).. George Coulam
¶Tolar............ A. D. Haddock
City Mgr., Howard Nance
Tomball......... Bill T. Webb
City Mgr., Don R. Taylor
Tom Bean........ Bill W. Garner
¶Tool (Rt. 6, Box 843, Kemp 75143)........ James R. Green
Toyah........ Charlotte Waight
Trent......... James Wallis
Trenton...... William E. Dodson
¶Trinidad..... Ernest L. Jenkins
Trinity......... Sam R. Barnes
§City Mgr., Buddy Drake
Trophy Club..... James P. Carter
§City Mgr., Donna Welsh
Troup............. Gene Cottle
†City Mgr., Kenneth N. Berry
Troy........... David Walston
Tulia........... David Edwardst
*City Mgr., Mike McDonough
Turkey........ Steve Farley
Tuscola........ Mark Young
Tye........... Gayland Childers
Tyler..... Smith P. Reynolds Jr.
City Mgr. (Interim), Pinkney Butler
Uhland.......... Dan T. Sorrels
Uncertain......... Bill Mauthe
¶Union Grove (Box 1326, Gladewater 75647).. Randy Lee Simcox
Universal City. Carmeline Squires
*City Mgr., Gene Thorpe
University Park (P.O. Box 8005, Dallas 75205).... John G. Roach
‡City Mgr., Bob Livingston
Uvalde......... Bill McWhorter
*City Mgr., James Thurmond
¶Valentine...... Jesus Calderon
*City Mgr., Albert Miller
Valley Mills....... Howard Hillin
Valley View...... Owen D. Roane
Van........... V. M. Camper
Van Alstyne...... David Schatz
Van Horn....... Okey D. Lucas
Vega......... Mark J. Groneman
Venus........... James Flatt
§City Mgr., John Daniel
Vernon.... George E. Maxon Jr.
*City Mgr., Paul Hawkins
Victoria.......... Ted B. Reed
*City Mgr., James J. Miller
Vidor............ Ruth Woods
City Mgr., Curtis F. Jeanis
Vinton (436 Vinton Rd., Canutillo 79835)...... Samuel Monrreal
Waco............ Charles Reed
*City Mgr., John D. Harrison
Waelder......... Zora Schultz
Wake Village.... Mike Huddleston
§City Mgr., Mike Burke
Waller..... Danny L. Marburger
Wallis........ John C. Lockwood
Walnut Springs. John T. McDowell
Warren City (Rt. 2, Box 72-C,

Gladewater 75647)
.... John W. Shearer
Waskom .... Jimmy Moore
Watauga...... Virgil R. Anthony
  City Mgr., W. E. Keating
Waxahachie .... Joe Grubbs
  *City Mgr., Robert W. Sokoll
Weatherford..... Sherry Watson
  *City Mgr., Kenneth Reneau
Webster ...... Dennis J. Waggett
  §City Mgr., Albert A. Holquin
Weimar .... Julius E. Bartek
  †City Mgr., F. E. Parks
¶Weinert........... J. E. Jetton
  City Mgr., R. M. Walker
Weir........... Mervin Walker
Wellington .. Milburn Derryberry
  City Mgr., Glen Taylor
¶Wellman .... Lynn Hudson
Wells .... Robert F. English
Weslaco ..... Eugene A. Braught
  *City Mgr., Wai- Lin Lam
West .... William F. Pareya
  Westbrook ...... J. L. Rees
West Columbia .. Robert R. Dixon
  City Mgr., Vicki S. Knight
¶Westlake (Box 501, Dove Rd., Roa-
  noke 76262)...... Dale L. White
West Lake Hills (911 Westlake Dr.,
  Austin 78746) .... Tom H. Taylor
  §City Mgr., Dick Hargarten
¶Westminster ... Richard J. Davis
¶West Mountain (Rt. 8, Box 664,
  Gilmer 75644).............
Weston ...... Kenneth R. Cowan
West Orange (2700 Austin Ave.,
  Orange 77630) Carl K. Thibodeaux

Westover Hills (1200 Summit Ave.,
  Fort Worth 76107) . Sam H. Berry
West Tawakoni (Rt. 1, Box 354,
  Quinlan 75474) .. Ken L. Stinogel
West University Place (3800 Univer-
  sity Blvd., Houston 77005)
.... Whitt F. Johnson
  ‡City Mgr., Mike Tanner
Westworth Village (311 Burton
  Hill Rd., Fort Worth 76114)
.... W.O. Henker
Wharton ..... Garland Novosad
  *City Mgr., Robert A. Miller
Wheeler .... Wanda Herd
White Deer ... R. W. Standefer Jr.
Whiteface...... Mack Ashmore
  City Mgr., Mary Lou Martin
Whitehouse....... Acker Hanks
  City Mgr., C. C. Pledger
¶White Oak ..... George F. Kutch
Whitesboro...... Alfred C. Miller
  ‡City Mgr., Joe N. West
White Settlement James M. Herring
  *City Mgr., J. E. Keaton
Whitewright .. Clarence Tillett Jr.
Whitney .... Bill Sawyer
Wichita Falls.... Michael A. Lam
  *City Mgr., James B. Berzina
Wickett........ W.W. Randolph
Willis ..... Edgar Straughter Sr.
Willow Park ..... Sharon Suarez
Wills Point ..... Bobby Springer
  City Mgr., Wilson Read
Wilmer .... Preston Parks
  City Mgr., James Douglas
Wilson .... Jackie Bishop

Windcrest (8601 Midcrown, San
  Antonio 78239) Watson Burnfield
Windom ...... Billy Joe Roberts
Windthorst .... Donald F. Frerich
¶Winfield .... Margarett Gandy
Wink.......... Linda McDonald
Winnsboro .... Jerry Hopper
  City Mgr., Jerry Poe
Winona ...... Carl W. Granberry
Winters.......... Sandy Griffin
  §City Mgr., Charles C. Ludwick
Wixon Valley (P.O. Box 105, Kurten
  77862)........... Joe Krolczyk
Wolfe City..... Ronald H. Wensel
Wolfforth .... Donald Preston
Woodbranch (P.O. Box 804, New
  Caney 77357) .. Stephan L. Early
Woodcreek (P.O. Box 1570, Wim-
  berley 78676) .. Jeannine C. Pool
Woodloch (2626 Woodloch Dr., Con-
  roe 77385).... David B. Houston
Woodsboro ... Ronald S. Williams
Woodson....... Bobby Mathiews
Woodville ..... Thomas C. Knapp
Woodway (P.O. Box 20937, Waco
  76702)............. Don Moes
  *City Mgr., Marvin Norwood
Wortham .. Mary Mathison Price
Wylie .... John W. Akin
  ‡City Mgr., Bill Dashner
Yantis........ Brian E. Harris
Yoakum ..... M. W. Harbus Jr.
  *City Mgr., William H. Lewis
Yorktown .... Eugene Czaja
  City Mgr., Milton Ledwig
Zavalla .... Opal C. Gant

*Cities having charter provision for city manager.
†General law cities adopting plan by election.
‡Cities adopting manager plan by ordinance.
§Cities having officer performing duties of manager. These are city secretaries, city administrators and other paid officials who are city managers in fact, though not by strict definition of the term. All are places operating under general law.
¶No answer to 1991 questionnaire; data here are the latest available.
**Holdover in office. Municipal election in Dallas was postponed pending Justice Department clearance of new City Council districts.

Home-Rule Cities

The home-rule cities of Texas are listed below, as reported by the cities themselves May 1991.

City	Present Form of Government	Present Form Adopted	*First Charter	City	Present Form of Government	Present Form Adopted	*First Charter
Abilene	Council-Mgr.	1981	1911	Breckenridge	Commission-Mgr.	1954	1954
Addison	Council-Mgr.	1988	1978	Brenham	Council-Mgr.	1920	1920
Alamo	Mayor-Council	1978	1978	Bridge City	Council-Mgr.	1974	1974
Alamo Heights	Mayor-Council	1954	1954	Brownfield	Council-Mgr.	1954	1954
Alice	Council-Mgr.	1981	1949	Brownsville	Commission-Mgr.	1915	1915
Allen	Council-Mgr.	1979	1979	Brownwood	Council-Mgr.	1955	1914
Alvin	Council-Mgr.	1990	1963	Bryan	Council-Mgr.	1941	1917
Amarillo	Council-Mgr.	1913	1913	Burleson	Council-Mgr.	1969	1969
Andrews	Council-Mgr.	1959	1959	Caddo Mills	Council-Mgr.	1985	1985
Angleton	Council-Mgr.	1991	1967	Cameron	Mayor-Council	1956	1956
Anson	Council-Mgr.	1920	1913	Canyon	Commission-Mgr.	1959	1959
Aransas Pass	Council-Mgr.	1986	1951	Carrizo Springs	Council-Mgr.	1971	1959
Arlington	Council-Mgr.	1990	1920	Carrollton	Council-Mgr.	1987	1961
Athens	Council-Mgr.	1966	1966	Carthage	Commission-Mgr.	1948	1948
Atlanta	Council-Mgr.	1968	1968	Cedar Hill	Council-Mgr.	1975	1975
Austin	Council-Mgr.	1991	1919	Cedar Park	Council-Mgr.	1987	1987
Azle	Council-Mgr.	1971	1971	Center	Council-Mgr.	1984	1984
Ballinger	Mayor-Council	1963	1963	Centerville	Mayor-Council	1945	1945
Bay City	Mayor-Council	1989	1989	Childress	Council-Mgr.	1917	1917
Baytown	Council-Mgr.	1948	1948	Cisco	Council-Mgr.	1974	1919
Beaumont	Council-Mgr.	1986	1913	Cleburne	Council-Mgr.	1950	1914
Bedford	Council-Mgr.	1967	1952	Cleveland	Council-Mgr.	1981	1981
Beeville	Council-Mgr.	1951	1951	Clute	Council-Mgr.	1976	1957
Bellaire	Council-Mgr.	1987	1947	Coleman	Council-Mgr.	1949	1949
Bellmead	Council-Mgr.	1961	1955	College Station	Council-Mgr.	1983	1952
Belton	Council-Mgr.	1990	1914	Colleyville	Council-Mgr.	1984	1976
Benbrook	Council-Mgr.	1990	1983	Colorado City	Council-Mgr.	1989	1948
Big Spring	Council-Mgr.	1972	1926	Commerce	Commission-Mgr.	1954	1954
Bonham	Commission-Mgr.	1947	1914	Conroe	Mayor-Council	1965	1965
Borger	Council-Mgr.	1988	1926	Converse	Council-Mgr.	1984	1981
Bowie	Mayor-Council	1984	1984	Coppell	Council-Mgr.	1988	1986
Brady	Council-Mgr.	1989	1982	Copperas Cove	Council-Mgr.	1979	1979

City	Present Form of Government	Present Form Adopted	*First Charter	City	Present Form of Government	Present Form Adopted	*First Charter
Corpus Christi	Council-Mgr.	1987	1926	Kerrville	Council-Mgr.	1942	1942
Corsicana	Commission-Mgr.	1956	1917	Kilgore	Commission-Mgr.	1960	1960
Crockett	Council-Mgr.	1964	1964	Killeen	Council-Mgr.	1991	1948
Crystal City	Council-Mgr.	1986	1946	Kingsville	Commission-Mgr.	1951	1916
Cuero	Council-Mgr.	1969	1944	Kirby	Council-Mgr.	1988	1988
Daingerfield	Council-Mgr.	1980	1980	La Feria	Commission-Mgr.	1990	1990
Dalhart	Council-Mgr.	1979	1960	La Grange	Council-Mgr.	1983	1983
Dallas	Council-Mgr.	1931	1889	Lake Jackson	Council-Mgr.	1989	1954
Dayton	Council-Mgr.	1983	1976	Lakeway	Mayor-Council	1990	1990
Deer Park	Council-Mgr.	1960	1960	Lake Worth	Mayor-Council	1965	1965
De Leon	Mayor-Council	1919	1919	La Marque	Council-Mgr.	1975	1957
Del Rio	Council-Mgr.	1967	1918	Lamesa	Council-Mgr.	1945	1945
Denison	Council-Mgr.	1984	1925	Lampasas	Council-Mgr.	1986	1986
Denton	Council-Mgr.	1959	1914	Lancaster	Council-Mgr.	1974	1956
Denver City	Council-Mgr.	1985	1985	La Porte	Council-Mgr.	1985	1949
De Soto	Council-Mgr.	1991	1969	Laredo	Council-Mgr.	1982	1921
Dickinson	Mayor-Council	1987	1987	League City	Mayor-Council	1962	1962
Dimmitt	Council-Mgr.	1990	1990	Levelland	Council-Mgr.	1949	1949
Donna	Council-Mgr.	1957	1957	Lewisville	Council-Mgr.	1989	1962
Dumas	Commission-Mgr.	1969	1955	Liberty	Council-Mgr.	1958	1958
Duncanville	Council-Mgr.	1962	1962	Littlefield	Council-Mgr.	1958	1958
Eagle Pass	Council-Mgr.	1964	1964	Live Oak	Council-Mgr.	1976	1976
Eastland	Commission-Mgr.	1926	1919	Lockhart	Council-Mgr.	1990	1973
Edinburg	Council-Mgr.	1949	1949	Longview	Council-Mgr.	1979	1943
Edna	Council-Mgr.	1984	1966	Lubbock	Council-Mgr.	1988	1917
El Campo	Council-Mgr.	1991	1954	Lufkin	Commission-Mgr.	1966	1919
Electra	Mayor-Council	1917	1917	Luling	Council-Mgr.	1977	1977
Elgin	Council-Mgr.	1989	1985	McAllen	Commission-Mgr.	1927	1927
El Paso	Council	1907	1873	McGregor	Council-Mgr.	1989	1979
‡§Elsa	...	...	...	McKinney	Council-Mgr.	1988	1959
Ennis	Commission-Mgr.	1956	1913	Mansfield	Council-Mgr.	1975	1924
Euless	Council-Mgr.	1975	1962	Marble Falls	Council-Mgr.	1986	1986
Everman	Council-Mgr.	1989	1945	Marlin	Council-Mgr.	1977	1915
Farmers Branch	Council-Mgr.	1989	1956	Marshall	Commission-Mgr.	1958	1913
Flower Mound	Council-Mgr.	1989	1981	Mercedes	Commission-Mgr.	1973	1931
Forest Hill	Council-Mgr.	1976	1976	Mesquite	Council-Mgr.	1953	1953
Fort Worth	Council-Mgr.	1925	1919	Mexia	Council-Mgr.	1924	1924
Fredericksburg	Council-Mgr.	1991	1991	Midland	Council-Mgr.	1985	1940
Freeport	Council-Mgr.	1960	1949	Midlothian	Council-Mgr.	1980	1980
Friendswood	Council-Mgr.	1961	1961	Mineral Wells	Council-Mgr.	1966	1966
Frisco	Council-Mgr.	1987	1987	Mission	Council-Mgr.	1987	1961
Gainesville	Council-Mgr.	1990	1920	Missouri City	Council-Mgr.	1986	1974
Galena Park	Mayor-Council	1975	1946	Monahans	Council-Mgr.	1954	1954
Galveston	Council-Mgr.	1960	1913	Mount Pleasant	Council-Mgr.	1948	1948
Garland	Council-Mgr.	1990	1951	Muleshoe	Council-Mgr.	1960	1960
Gatesville	Council-Mgr.	1966	1966	Nacogdoches	Commission-Mgr.	1988	1929
Georgetown	Council-Mgr.	1968	1968	Nassau Bay	Council-Mgr.	1988	1973
George West	Mayor-Council	1979	1979	Navasota	Council-Mgr.	1947	1927
Giddings	Council-Mgr.	1984	1982	Nederland	Council-Mgr.	1972	1955
Gladewater	Council-Mgr.	1985	1955	New Braunfels	Council-Mgr.	1967	1964
Glenn Heights	Council-Mgr.	1987	1987	North Richland Hills	Council-Mgr.	1989	1963
Gonzales	Council-Mgr.	1957	1957	Odessa	Council-Mgr.	1985	1945
Gorman	Mayor-Council	1925	1925	Olney	Mayor-Aldermen	1985	1979
Graham	Council-Mgr.	1930	1920	Orange	Council-Mgr.	1986	1960
Granbury	Mayor-Council	1989	1989	Palestine	Council-Mgr.	1983	1917
Grand Prairie	Council-Mgr.	1987	1948	Palm Valley	Mayor-Aldermen	1984	1981
Grapevine	Council-Mgr.	1965	1965	Pampa	Council-Mgr.	1927	1927
Greenville	Council-Mgr.	1953	1921	Paris	Council-Mgr.	1948	1919
Groves	Council-Mgr.	1959	1953	Pasadena	Mayor-Council	1964	1943
Haltom City	Council-Mgr.	1989	1955	Pearland	Council-Mgr.	1971	1971
Harker Heights	Council-Mgr.	1991	1971	Pecos	Council-Mgr.	1983	1983
Harlingen	Commission-Mgr.	1955	1927	Pharr	Commission-Mgr.	1989	1949
Hearne	Council-Mgr.	1971	1964	Plainview	Council-Mgr.	1985	1949
Henderson	Council-Mgr.	1985	1947	Plano	Council-Mgr.	1988	1988
Hereford	Commission-Mgr.	1952	1952	Pleasanton	Council-Mgr.	1989	1982
Hewitt	Council-Mgr.	1983	1983	Port Aransas	Council-Mgr.	1978	1978
Highland Park	Council-Mgr.	1975	1975	Port Arthur	Council-Mgr.	1932	1915
Highland Village	Council-Mgr.	1986	1986	Port Isabel	Commission-Mgr.	1984	1978
Hillsboro	Council-Mgr.	1981	1915	Portland	Council-Mgr.	1967	1967
Hitchcock	Mayor-Commission	1960	1960	Port Lavaca	Mayor-Council	1972	1956
Houston	Council	1946	1913	Port Neches	Council-Mgr.	1967	1955
Humble	Council-Mgr.	1987	1973	Quanah	Mayor-Council	1911	1911
Huntsville	Council-Mgr.	1986	1968	Ranger	Commission-Mgr.	1919	1919
Hurst	Council-Mgr.	1985	1956	Raymondville	Commission-Mgr.	1955	1955
Ingleside	Council-Mgr.	1979	1979	Richardson	Council-Mgr.	1989	1956
Irving	Council-Mgr.	1989	1952	Richland Hills	Council-Mgr.	1986	1986
Jacinto City	Council-Mgr.	1980	1980	River Oaks	Mayor-Council	1949	1949
Jacksonville	Council-Mgr.	1978	1921	Robstown	Mayor-Council	1948	1948
Jasper	Council-Mgr.	1967	1964	Rockdale	Council-Mgr.	1978	1978
Jersey Village	Council-Mgr.	1986	1986	Rockport	Council-Mgr.	1983	1983
Katy	Aldermen-Admin.	1989	1981	Rockwall	Council-Mgr.	1985	1985
Kaufman	Council-Mgr.	1987	1987	Rosenberg	Council-Mgr.	1985	1956
Keller	Council-Mgr.	1982	1982				
Kermit	Council-Mgr.	1989	1989				

City	Present Form of Government	Present Form Adopted	*First Charter
Round Rock	Council-Mgr.	1978	1978
Rowlett	Council-Mgr.	1979	1979
Rusk	Council-Mgr.	1986	1986
Sachse	Council-Mgr.	1988	1986
Saginaw	Council-Mgr.	1988	1988
San Angelo	Council-Mgr.	1915	1915
San Antonio	Council-Mgr.	1951	1914
San Benito	Commission-Mgr.	1920	1920
San Juan	Mayor-Council	1975	1975
San Marcos	Council-Mgr.	1967	1967
Santa Fe	Council-Mgr.	1981	1981
Schertz	Council-Mgr.	1989	1974
Seabrook	Council-Mgr.	1979	1979
Seagoville	Council-Mgr.	1991	1969
Seguin	Council-Mgr.	1986	1971
Seminole	Mayor-Council	1991	1991
Sherman	Council-Mgr.	1975	1915
Silsbee	Council-Mgr.	1956	1956
Sinton	Council-Mgr.	1966	1966
Slaton	Mayor-Council	1929	1929
Snyder	Council-Mgr.	1989	1952
Southlake	Council-Mgr.	1991	1987
Stamford	Council-Mgr.	1918	1918
Stephenville	Council-Mgr.	1961	1961
Sugar Land	Council-Mgr.	1981	1981
Sulphur Springs	Council-Mgr.	1983	1947
Sweetwater	Commission-Mgr.	1984	1947
Taylor	Commission-Mgr.	1988	1914
Temple	Council-Mgr.	1990	1922
Terrell	Council-Mgr.	1973	1913
Terrell Hills	Council-Mgr.	1957	1957
Texarkana	Council-Mgr.	1960	1917
Texas City	Mayor-Commission	1946	1946
The Colony	Council-Mgr.	1986	1979
Tomball	Council-Mgr.	1987	1987
Tulia	Council-Mgr.	1972	1972
Tyler	Council-Mgr.	1915	1915
Universal City	Council-Mgr.	1988	1972

Kay Granger of Fort Worth became in 1991 the latest woman to be elected mayor of a major Texas city.

City	Present Form of Government	Present Form Adopted	*First Charter
University Park	Council-Mgr.	1989	1924
Uvalde	Council-Mgr.	1951	1934
Vernon	Commission-Mgr.	1962	1916
Victoria	Council-Mgr.	1957	1915
Vidor	Mayor-Council	1969	1969
Waco	Council-Mgr.	1958	1913
Watauga	Mayor-Council	1990	1980
Waxahachie	Council-Mgr.	1971	1916
Weatherford	Council-Mgr.	1983	1918
Weslaco	Council-Mgr.	1927	1927
West Orange	Mayor-Aldermen	1988	1955
West University sity Place	Council-Mgr.	1989	1940
Wharton	Council-Mgr.	1978	1970
White Settlement	Council-Mgr.	1968	1954
Wichita Falls	Council-Mgr.	1920	1913
Woodway	Council-Mgr.	1955	1955
Wylie	Council-Mgr.	1985	1985
Yoakum	Council-Mgr.	1915	1915

*Present (1985) home-rule amendment (Art. XI, Sec. 5) ratified Nov. 5, 1912.
‡Date present form of charter adopted and date of first charter adoption not available.
§Data on form of government not available.

State Government

State government is divided into **executive, legislative** and **judicial branches** under the Texas Constitution, adopted in 1876. The chief executive is the **Governor** whose term, effective in 1975, is for 4 years, according to a constitutional amendment approved by Texas voters in 1972. Other elected state officials with executive responsibilities include the **Lieutenant Governor, Attorney General, Comptroller of Public Accounts, Treasurer, Commissioner of the General Land Office** and **Commissioner of Agriculture.** The terms of these officials also were increased from 2 to 4 years by the constitutional

amendment. Three members of the **Railroad Commission** are elected for 6-year terms.

Except for making numerous appointments, the governor's powers are limited in comparison with those in most states.

The legislative branch comprises 31 members of the Senate and 150 members of the House of Representatives.

The judiciary consists of the **Supreme Court** and its co-ordinate **State Court of Criminal Appeals, 14 Courts of Appeals** and more than 370 district courts. Members are elected.

State and Federal Courts

The following lists include U.S. district courts in Texas, Texas district courts, Texas higher courts and administrative judicial districts. The lists were compiled from reports of the Texas Judicial Council and other sources.

The section — Counties, Cities and Towns of Texas — shows, alphabetically by counties, judicial districts to which each county is assigned.

Table No. 2 of District and County Officials also shows the district judges by counties.

U.S. District Courts In Texas

Texas is divided into four federal judicial districts, and each district is composed of several divisions. Appeal from all Texas federal district courts is to the **Fifth Circuit Court of Appeals,** New Orleans. Judges are appointed for life and receive a salary of $125,100 annually.

NORTHERN TEXAS DISTRICT

District Judges. — Chief Judge, Barefoot Sanders, Dallas. **Senior Judges,** Robert W. Porter, Dallas; David O. Beloew Jr. and Eldon B. Mahon, Fort Worth; and Halbert O. Woodard, Lubbock. **Judges:** Jerry Buchmeyer, Dallas; Sam R. Cummings, Lubbock; A. Joe Fish, Sidney A. Fitzwater, and Robert B. Maloney, Dallas; and Mary Lou Robinson, Amarillo. **Clerk of District Court:** Nancy Doherty, Dallas. **U.S. Attorney:** Marvin Collins, Dallas. **U.S. Marshal:** Bruce Beaty, Dallas. Court is in continuous session in each division of the Northern Texas District. Following are the different divisions of the Northern District and the counties in each division:

Dallas Division
Dallas, Ellis, Hunt, Johnson, Kaufman, Navarro and Rockwall. **Magistrates:** William F. Sanderson Jr., John B. Tolle and Jane Jackson, Dallas. **Chief Deputy Clerk:** Michael E. Ruhnow.

Fort Worth Division
Comanche, Erath, Hood, Jack, Palo Pinto, Parker, Tarrant and Wise. **Magistrate:** Alex H. McGlinchey, Fort Worth. **Deputy in charge:** Pam Murphy.

Amarillo Division
Armstrong, Briscoe, Carson, Castro, Childress, Collingsworth, Dallam, Deaf Smith, Donley, Gray, Hall, Hansford, Hartley, Hemphill, Hutchinson, Lipscomb, Moore, Ochiltree, Oldham, Parmer, Potter, Randall, Roberts, Sherman, Swisher and Wheeler. **Magistrate:** Clinton E. Averitte, Amarillo. **Deputy in charge:** May Harris.

Abilene Division
Callahan, Eastland, Fisher, Haskell, Howard, Jones, Mitchell, Nolan, Shackelford, Stephens, Stonewall, Taylor and Throckmorton. **Magistrate:** Billy W. Boone, Abilene. **Deputy in charge:** Georgia Sanders.

San Angelo Division
Brown, Coke, Coleman, Concho, Crockett, Glasscock, Irion, Menard, Mills, Reagan, Runnels, Schleicher, Sterling, Sutton and Tom Green. **Magistrate:** Philip R. Lane, San Angelo. **Deputy in charge:** Ann Loyd.

Wichita Falls Division
Archer, Baylor, Clay, Cottle, Foard, Hardeman, King, Knox, Montague, Wichita, Wilbarger and Young. **Magistrate:** Robert K. Roach, Wichita Falls. **Deputy in charge:** Connie Faulkner.

Lubbock Division
Bailey, Borden, Cochran, Crosby, Dawson, Dickens, Floyd, Gaines, Garza, Hale, Hockley, Kent, Lamb, Lubbock, Lynn, Motley, Scurry, Terry and Yoakum. **U.S. District Judge:** Sam R. Cummings, Lubbock. **Magistrate:** J. Q. Warnick Jr., Lubbock. **Deputy in charge:** Kristy Weinheimer.

WESTERN TEXAS DISTRICT

District Judges. Chief Judge, Lucius D. Bunton III, Midland. **Judges:** Edward C. Prado, San Antonio; H. F. Garcia, San Antonio; Harry Lee Hudspeth, El

Paso; James R. Nowlin, Austin; Walter S. Smith Jr., Waco; and one vacancy. **Senior Judge:** D. W. Suttle, San Antonio. **Clerk of District Court:** Charles W. Vagner, San Antonio. **Chief Deputy Clerk** is C. M. Saunders. **U.S. Attorney:** Ronald F. Ederer, San Antonio. **U.S. Marshal:** William J. Jonas Jr., San Antonio. Following are the different divisions of the Western District, and the counties in each division.

San Antonio Division
Atascosa, Bandera, Bexar, Comal, Dimmit, Frio, Gonzales, Guadalupe, Karnes, Kendall, Kerr, Medina, Real and Wilson. Court is in continuous session at San Antonio. **Magistrates:** Robert B. O'Connor, John W. Primomo and Nancy Stein Nowak, San Antonio. **Bankruptcy Judges:** Leif M. Clark and Ronald B. King, San Antonio. **Deputy in charge:** Larry Bick.

Austin Division
Bastrop, Blanco, Burleson, Burnet, Caldwell, Gillespie, Hays, Kimble, Lampasas, Lee, Llano, Mason, McCulloch, San Saba, Travis, Washington and Williamson. Court for the Austin division shall be held at Austin. **Magistrate:** Stephen H. Copelle, Austin. **Bankruptcy Judges:** Chief, Larry E. Kelly, and Frank P. Monroe. **Deputy in charge:** Robert J. Williams.

El Paso Division
El Paso County only. Court is in continuous session in El Paso. **Magistrates:** Janet Ruesch and Philip T. Cole, El Paso. **Bankruptcy Judge:** Leif M. Clark, San Antonio. **Deputy in charge:** Richard Delgado.

Waco Division
Bell, Bosque, Coryell, Falls, Freestone, Hamilton, Hill, Leon, Limestone, McLennan, Milam, Robertson and Somervell. Court for the Waco division shall be held at Waco. **Magistrate:** Dennis Green, Waco. **Bankruptcy Judge:** Larry E. Kelly, Austin. **Deputy in charge:** Mark Borchardt.

Del Rio Division
Edwards, Kinney, Maverick, Terrell, Uvalde, Val Verde and Zavala. Court for the Del Rio division shall be held at Del Rio. **Magistrate:** Durwood Edwards, Del Rio. **Bankruptcy Judge:** Ronald B. King, San Antonio. **Deputy in charge:** Katherine K. West.

Pecos Division
Brewster, Culberson, Hudspeth, Jeff Davis, Loving, Reeves, Pecos, Presidio, Ward and Winkler. Court for the Pecos division shall be held at Pecos. **Magistrates:** Katherine H. Baker (part-time) and Walter Holcombe (part-time), Pecos. **Bankruptcy Judge:** Ronald B. King, San Antonio. **Deputy in charge:** Karen W. White.

Midland-Odessa Division
Andrews, Crane, Ector, Martin, Midland and Upton. Court for the Midland-Odessa Division shall be held at Midland. Court may be held, in the discretion of the court, in Odessa, when courtroom facilities are made available at no expense to the government. **Magistrate:** Robert R. Sykes (part-time), Midland. **Bankruptcy Judge:** Ronald B. King, San Antonio. **Deputy in charge:** John D. Neil, Midland.

EASTERN TEXAS DISTRICT
District Judges.—Chief Judge, Robert M. Parker, Tyler. **Judges:** Joe J. Fisher, Beaumont; Richard A. Schell, Beaumont; William M. Steger, Tyler; William Wayne Justice, Tyler; Howell Cobb, Beaumont; Sam Hall, Marshall; Paul N. Brown, Sherman. **Clerk of District Court:** Murray L. Harris, Tyler. **U.S. Attorney:** Rob-

ert J. Wortham, Beaumont. **U.S. Marshal:** Keith Gary, Tyler. **Chief U.S. Probation Officer:** Wade E. French, Tyler. **Judges in Bankruptcy:** C. Houston Abel, Tyler, and Donald R. Sharp, Beaumont. Following are the different divisions of the Eastern District, and the counties in each division:

Tyler Division
Anderson, Cherokee, Gregg, Henderson, Panola, Rains, Rusk, Smith, Van Zandt and Wood. Court in continuous session. **Magistrates:** Henry W. McKee, Tyler, and Judith Guthrie, Tyler. **Chief Deputy:** Frank Monge.

Beaumont Division
Hardin, Jasper, Jefferson, Liberty, Newton, Orange. Court in continuous session. **Magistrates:** Earl Hines and J. Michael Bradford, Beaumont. **Deputy in charge:** Kelly Gavagan.

Marshall Division
Camp, Cass, Harrison, Marion, Morris, Upshur. Court in continuous session. **Deputy in charge:** Peggy Anderson.

Sherman Division
Collin, Cooke, Denton and Grayson. Court in continuous session. **Magistrate:** Roger Sanders. **Deputy in charge:** Sandra Southerland.

Texarkana Division
Bowie, Franklin and Titus. Sessions held as business dictates and as announced by the court. **Magistrate:** Charles Attaway. **Deputy in charge:** Doris Stanley.

Paris Division
Delta, Fannin, Lamar, Red River and Hopkins. Sessions held as business dictates and as announced by the court.

Lufkin Division
Angelina, Houston, Nacogdoches, Polk, Sabine, San Augustine, Shelby, Trinity, Tyler. Sessions held as business dictates and as announced by the court.

SOUTHERN TEXAS DISTRICT
District Judges.—Chief Judge, James DeAnda, Houston. **Judges:** Kenneth M. Hoyt, Sim Lake, Norman W. Black, Lynn N. Hughes, John D. Rainey, Melinda Harmon and David Hittner, Houston; Hayden W. Head

Jr., Corpus Christi; Hugh Gibson, Sr. Judge, and Samuel B. Kent, Galveston; Filemon B. Vela, Brownsville; George P. Kazen, Laredo; Ricardo H. Hinojosa, McAllen. **Senior Judge:** John V. Singleton Jr, Houston. **Clerk of District Court:** Jesse E. Clark, Houston. **U. S. Attorney:** Ronald G. Woods, Houston. **U.S. Marshal:** Basil S. Baker, Houston. **Bankruptcy Judges:** Chief, R. F. Wheless Jr., Manuel Leal, Letitia Z. Clark, William Greendyke and Karen K. Brown, Houston; Richard Schmidt, Corpus Christi. Following are the different divisions of the Southern District and the counties in each division:

Houston Division
Austin, Brazos, Colorado, Fayette, Fort Bend, Grimes, Harris, Madison, Montgomery, San Jacinto, Walker, Waller and Wharton. **Magistrates:** Calvin Botley, Frances Stacy, Nancy Pecht and George A. Kelt Jr., Houston. **Clerk:** Jesse E. Clark.

Brownsville Division
Cameron and Willacy. **Magistrates:** Fidencio Garza Jr. and Robert Guerra (part-time), Brownsville. **Deputy in charge:** Juan M. Barbosa.

Corpus Christi Division
Aransas, Bee, Brooks, Duval, Jim Wells, Kenedy, Kleberg, Live Oak, Nueces and San Patricio. **Magistrate:** Eduardo E. de Ases, Corpus Christi. **Deputy in charge:** Monica Seaman.

Galveston Division
Brazoria, Chambers, Galveston and Matagorda. **Magistrate:** John R. Froeschner. **Deputy in charge:** Leo Garza.

Laredo Division
Jim Hogg, LaSalle, McMullen, Webb and Zapata. **Magistrate:** Marcel C. Notzon, Laredo. **Deputy in charge:** Beatriz Garcia.

Victoria Division
Calhoun, DeWitt, Goliad, Jackson, Lavaca, Refugio and Victoria. **Deputy in charge:** Maxine Gammon.

McAllen Division
Hidalgo and Starr, **Magistrate:** William M. Mallett, McAllen. **Deputy in charge:** Sofia Anderson.

State Higher Courts

The state's higher courts are listed below with corrections to July 1, 1991. Notations in parentheses indicate dates of expiration of **terms of office.** Judges of the Supreme Court, Court of Criminal Appeals and Courts of Appeals are elected to 6-year, overlapping terms. District Court judges are elected to 4-year terms. As of Fiscal Year 1991, the Chief Justice of the Supreme Court and the Presiding Judge of the Court of Criminal Appeals each received $91,875; Justices each received $89,250; Chief Justices of the Courts of Appeals received $80,850; justices received $76,309 from the state. In addition a supplemental amount may be paid by counties but total salary must be at least $1,000 less than that received by Supreme Court justices. District Court judges received $57,257 from the state, plus supplemental pay from various subdivisions. Their total salary must be $2,000 less than that received by Supreme Court justices.

The judiciary of the state consists of nine members of the **State Supreme Court;** nine of the **Court of Criminal Appeals;** 80 of the **Courts of Appeals;** 376 of the **State District Courts;** 10 of the **Criminal District Courts;** 174 of the **County Courts at Law;** 254 of the **County Courts;** 917 **Justice of the Peace Courts;** and 1,181 **Municipal Courts.**

Below is given information on only the Supreme Court, Court of Criminal Appeals, Courts of Appeals and state District Courts. Names of county court judges, as well as names of the various district court judges, are given by counties in two tables beginning on page 457.

Supreme Court
Chief Justice, Thomas R. Phillips (12-31-96). **Justices,** Raul A. Gonzalez (12-31-94); Oscar Mauzy (12-31-92); Eugene A. Cook (12-31-92); Jack Hightower (12-31-92); Nathan L. Hecht (12-31-94); Lloyd Doggett (12-31-94); John Cornyn (12-31-96); Bob Gammage (12-31-96). **Clerk of Court,** John T. Adams. **Location of court,** Austin.

Court of Criminal Appeals
Presiding Judge, Michael J. McCormick (12-31-94). **Judges:** Sam Houston Clinton (12-31-96); Chuck Miller (12-31-94); Charles F. Campbell (12-31-94); Bill White (12-31-90); Charles Baird (12-31-92); Morris Overstreet (12-31-92); Frank Maloney (12-31-96); Fortunato P. Benavides (12-31-92). **State's Attorney,** Robert Huttash. **Clerk of Court,** Thomas Lowe. **Location of court,** Austin.

Courts of Appeals
These courts have jurisdiction within their respective supreme judicial districts. A constitutional amendment approved in 1978 raised the number of associate justices for Courts of Appeals where needed. Judges are elected from the district for 6-year terms. Another amendment adopted in 1980 changed the name of the old **Courts of Civil Appeals** to the **Courts of Appeals** and changed the jurisdiction of the courts. See Art. V, Sec. 6 of the State Constitution.

First District—*Houston. Chief Justice, Alice Oliver Trevathan (12-31-92). Justices: Sam H. Bass Jr. (12-31-94); Lee Duggan Jr. (12-31-94); Murry B. Cohen (12-31-94); D. Camille Dunn (12-31-96); Margaret G. Mirabal (12-31-96); Jon N. Hughes (12-31-94); Michol O'Connor (12-31-94); Davie L. Wilson (12-31-92). Clerk of court, Kathryn Cox. Counties in the First District are as follows: Austin, Brazoria, Brazos, Burleson, Chambers, Colorado, Fort Bend, Galveston, Grimes, Harris, Trinity, Walker, Waller, Washington.

Second District—Fort Worth: Chief Justice, H. Tod Weaver (12-31-94). Justices: Joe Spurlock II (12-31-92); John Hill (12-31-96); David Farris (12-31-94); Hal Lattimore (12-31-96); Lawrence Meyers (12-31-94); and Sam Day (12-31-94). Clerk of court, Yvonne Palmer. Counties in Second District are as follows: Archer, Clay, Cooke, Denton, Hood, Jack, Montague, Parker, Tarrant, Wichita, Wise, Young.

Third District—Austin: Chief Justice, James L. Carroll (12-31-96). Justices: John Powers (12-31-92); Marilyn Aboussie (12-31-94); J. Woodfin Jones (12-31-94); Mack Kidd (12-31-94); and Bea Ann Smith (12-31-92). Clerk of court, Susan K. Bage. Counties in the Third District are as follows: Bastrop, Bell, Blanco, Burnet, Caldwell, Coke, Comal, Concho, Fayette, Hays, Irion, Lampasas, Lee, Llano, McCulloch, Milam, Mills, Runnels, San Saba, Schleicher, Sterling, Tom Green, Travis, Williamson.

Fourth District—San Antonio: Chief Justice, Blair Reeves (12-31-96). Justices: Shirley W. Butts (12-31-94); Alfonso Chapa (12-31-94); David Peeples (12-31-94); Fred Biery (12-31-94); Ron Carr (12-31-92); and Orlando Garcia (12-31-94). Clerk of court, Herb Schaefer. Counties in the Fourth District are as follows: Atascosa, Bandera, Bexar, Brooks, Dimmit, Duval, Edwards, Frio, Gillespie, Guadalupe, Jim Hogg, Jim Wells, Karnes, Kendall, Kerr, Kimble, Kinney, La Salle, McMullen, Mason, Maverick, Medina, Menard, Real, Starr, Sutton, Uvalde, Val Verde, Webb, Wilson, Zapata, Zavala.

Fifth District—Dallas: Chief Justice, Craig T. Enoch (12-31-94); Justices: Warren Whitham (12-31-94); Annette Stewart (12-31-92); Gordon Rowe (12-31-96); James A. Baker (12-31-94); Sue Lagarde (12-31-94); Linda Thomas (12-31-92); Ed Kinkeade (12-31-94); John Ovard (12-31-94); Joe Burnett (12-31-94); John Whittington (12-31-94); Frances Maloney (12-31-96); and Ron Chapman (12-31-92). Clerk of Court, Kenneth P. Stripling. Counties in the Fifth District are as follows: Collin, Dallas, Grayson, Hunt, Kaufman, Rockwall, Van Zandt.

Sixth District—Texarkana: Chief Justice, William J. Cornelius (12-31-92); Justices: Charles M. Bleil (12-31-94) and Ben Z. Grant (12-31-96). Clerk of court, Tibby Thomas. Counties in the Sixth District are as follows: Bowie, Camp, Cass, Delta, Fannin, Franklin, Gregg, Harrison, Hopkins, Hunt, Lamar, Marion, Morris, Panola, Red River, Rusk, Titus, Upshur, Wood.

Seventh District—Amarillo: Chief Justice, Charles L. Reynolds (12-31-96). Justices: Carlton B. Dodson (12-31-92); H. Bryan Poff Jr. (12-31-94) and John T. Boyd (12-31-94). Clerk of court, Peggy Culp. Counties in the Seventh District are as follows: Armstrong, Bailey, Briscoe, Carson, Castro, Childress, Cochran, Collingsworth, Cottle, Crosby, Dallam, Deaf Smith, Dickens, Donley, Floyd, Foard, Garza, Gray, Hale, Hall, Hansford, Hardeman, Hartley, Hemphill, Hockley, Hutchinson, Kent, King, Lamb, Lipscomb, Lubbock, Lynn, Moore, Motley, Ochiltree, Oldham, Parmer, Potter, Randall, Roberts, Sherman, Swisher, Terry, Wheeler, Wilbarger, Yoakum.

Eighth District—El Paso: Chief Justice, Max Osborn (12-31-90). Justices: Jerry Woodard (12-31-92); Larry Fuller (12-31-94) and Ward L. Koehler (12-31-94). Clerk of court, Barbara B. Dorris. Counties in the Eighth District are as follows: Andrews, Brewster, Crane, Crockett, Culberson, Ector, El Paso, Gaines, Glasscock, Hudspeth, Jeff Davis, Loving, Martin, Midland, Pecos, Presidio, Reagan, Reeves, Terrell, Upton, Ward, Winkler.

Ninth District—Beaumont: Chief Justice, Ronald L. Walker (12-31-96). Justices: Jack Brookshire (12-31-94) and Don Burgess (12-31-92). Clerk of court, Shirley Forrest. Counties in the Ninth District are as follows: Angelina, Hardin, Jasper, Jefferson, Liberty, Montgomery, Newton, Orange, Polk, San Jacinto, Tyler.

Tenth District—Waco: Chief Justice, Bob L. Thomas (12-31-94). Justices: Bobby L. Cummings (12-31-92) and

Bill Vance (12-31-96). Clerk of court, Robert G. Watts. Counties in the Tenth District are as follows: Bosque, Brazos, Coryell, Ellis, Falls, Freestone, Hamilton, Hill, Johnson, Leon, Limestone, McLennan, Madison, Navarro, Robertson, Somervell.

Eleventh District—Eastland: Chief Justice, Austin O. McCloud (12-31-94). Justices: William G. Arnot (12-31-90) and Charles R. Dickenson (12-31-92). Clerk of court, Oleta Moseley. Counties in the Eleventh District are as follows: Baylor, Borden, Brown, Callahan, Coleman, Comanche, Dawson, Eastland, Erath, Fisher, Haskell, Howard, Jones, Knox, Mitchell, Nolan, Palo Pinto, Scurry, Shackelford, Stephens, Stonewall, Taylor, Throckmorton.

Twelfth District—Tyler: Chief Justice, Tom B. Ramey Jr. (12-31-96). Justices: Bill Bass (12-31-94) and Paul S. Colley (12-31-92). Clerk of court, Carolyn Allen. Counties in the Twelfth District are as follows: Anderson, Cherokee, Gregg, Henderson, Hopkins, Houston, Kaufman, Nacogdoches, Panola, Rains, Rusk, Sabine, Smith, San Augustine, Shelby, Upshur, Van Zandt.

Thirteenth District—Corpus Christi: Chief Justice, Paul W. Nye (12-31-94). Justices: Noah O. Kennedy (12-31-94); Robert J. Seerden (12-31-92); and J. Bonner Dorsey (12-31-96); Gilberto Hinojosa (12-31-94), and one vacancy. Clerk of court, Cathy Wilborn. Counties in the Thirteenth District are as follows: Aransas, Bee, Calhoun, Cameron, DeWitt, Goliad, Gonzales, Hidalgo, Jackson, Kenedy, Kleberg, Lavaca, Live Oak, Matagorda, Nueces, Refugio, San Patricio, Victoria, Wharton, Willacy.

Fourteenth District—†Houston: Chief Justice, J. Curtiss Brown (12-31-96). Justices: Paul Pressler (12-31-92); William E. Junell (12-31-92); Paul C. Murphy (12-31-96); Ross A. Sears (12-31-94); George T. Ellis (12-31-94); Joe L. Draughn (12-31-94); Bill Cannon (12-31-94); and Samuel H. Robertson Jr. (12-31-94). Clerk of court, Mary Jane Smart. Counties in the Fourteenth District are as follows: Austin, Brazoria, Brazos, Burleson, Chambers, Colorado, Fort Bend, Galveston, Grimes, Harris, Trinity, Walker, Waller, Washington.

*The location of the First Court of Appeals was changed from Galveston to Houston by the Fifty-fifth Legislature, with the provision that all cases originated in Galveston County be tried in that city and with the further provision that any case may, at the discretion of the court, be tried in either city.

†Because of the heavy workload of the Houston area Court of Appeals, the Sixtieth Legislature, in 1967, provided for the establishment of a Fourteenth Appeals Court at Houston.

Administrative Judicial Districts of Texas

There are nine administrative judicial districts in the state for administrative purposes. An active or retired district judge or an active or retired appellate judge with judicial experience in a district court serves as the Presiding Judge upon appointment by the Governor. They receive extra compensation of $5,000 paid by counties in the respective administrative districts.

The Presiding Judge convenes an annual conference of the judges in the administrative district to consult on the state of business in the courts. This conference is empowered to adopt rules for the administration of cases in the district. The Presiding Judge may assign active or retired district judges residing within the administrative district to any of the district courts within the administrative district. The Presiding Judge of one administrative district may request the Presiding Judge of another administrative district to assign a judge from that district to sit in a district court located in the administrative district of the Presiding Judge making the request.

The Chief Justice of the Supreme Court of Texas convenes an annual conference of the nine Presiding Judges to determine the need for assignment of judges and to promote the uniform administration of the assignment of judges. The Chief Justice is empowered to assign judges of one administrative district for service in another whenever such assignments are necessary for the prompt and efficient administration of justice.

First District—Presiding Judge, Pat McDowell, Dallas: Anderson, Bowie, Camp, Cass, Cherokee, Collin, Dallas, Delta, Ellis, Fannin, Franklin, Grayson, Gregg, Harrison, Henderson, Hopkins, Houston, Hunt, Kaufman, Lamar, Marion, Morris, Nacogdoches, Panola, Rains, Red River, Rockwall, Rusk, Shelby, Smith, Titus, Upshur, Van Zandt and Wood.

Second District—Thomas J. Stovall Jr., Seabrook:

Angelina, Bastrop, Brazoria, Brazos, Burleson, Chambers, Fort Bend, Freestone, Galveston, Grimes, Hardin, Harris, Jasper, Jefferson, Lee, Leon, Liberty, Limestone, Madison, Matagorda, Montgomery, Newton, Orange, Polk, Robertson, Sabine, San Augustine, San Jacinto, Trinity, Tyler, Walker, Waller, Washington and Wharton.

Third District—B. B. Schraub, Seguin: Austin, Bell, Blanco, Bosque, Burnet, Caldwell, Colorado, Comal, Comanche, Coryell, Falls, Fayette, Gonzales, Guadalupe, Hamilton, Hays, Hill, Johnson, Lampasas, Lavaca, Llano, McLennan, Mason, Milam, Navarro, San Saba, Somervell, Travis and Williamson.

Fourth District—John Cornyn, San Antonio: Aransas, Atascosa, Bee, Bexar, Calhoun, DeWitt, Dimmit, Frio, Goliad, Jackson, Karnes, LaSalle, Live Oak, Maverick, McMullen, Refugio, San Patricio, Victoria, Webb, Wilson, Zapata and Zavala.

Fifth District—Darrell Hester, Brownsville: Brooks, Cameron, Duval, Hidalgo, Jim Hogg, Jim Wells, Kenedy, Kleberg, Nueces, Starr and Willacy.

Sixth District—Sam M. Paxson, El Paso: Bandera, Brewster, Crockett, Culberson, Edwards, El Paso, Gillespie, Hudspeth, Jeff Davis, Kendall, Kerr, Kimble, Kinney, Medina, Pecos, Presidio, Reagan, Real, Sutton, Terrell, Upton, Uvalde and Val Verde.

Seventh District—Weldon Kirk, Sweetwater: Andrews, Borden, Brown, Callahan, Coke, Coleman, Concho, Crane, Dawson, Ector, Fisher, Gaines, Garza, Glasscock, Haskell, Howard, Irion, Jones, Kent, Loving, Lynn, McCulloch, Martin, Menard, Midland, Mills, Mitchell, Nolan, Reeves, Runnels, Schleicher, Scurry, Shackelford, Sterling, Stonewall, Taylor, Throckmorton, Tom Green, Ward and Winkler.

Eighth District—Jeff Walker, Fort Worth: Archer, Clay, Cooke, Denton, Eastland, Erath, Hood, Jack,

Montague, Palo Pinto, Parker, Stephens, Tarrant, Wichita, Wise and Young.

Ninth District—Ray D. Anderson, Brownfield: Armstrong, Bailey, Baylor, Briscoe, Carson, Castro, Childress, Cochran, Collingsworth, Cottle, Crosby, Dallam, Deaf Smith, Dickens, Donley, Floyd, Foard, Gray, Hale, Hall, Hansford, Hardeman, Hartley, Hemphill, Hockley, Hutchinson, King, Knox, Lamb, Lipscomb, Lubbock, Moore, Motley, Ochiltree, Oldham, Parmer, Potter, Randall, Roberts, Sherman, Swisher, Terry, Wheeler, Wilbarger and Yoakum.

Texas Main Street Project

To encourage Texas cities to rehabilitate and reuse existing historic buildings, the Texas Historical Commission began the Texas Main Street Project in 1981. The project is primarily a technical assistance program. Each year, several cities or neighborhoods of large cities are selected to be officially designated Main Street cities. Sponsorship of the project can be by the municipal government, community development corporation, chamber of commerce or downtown organization.

The Texas Main Street Project office provides architectural design assistance and supervision for the Main Street managers, and each city receives a three-day visit by a professional team of consultants who provide immediate and long-term suggestions for the community's revitalization. Other state agencies, including the Texas Department of Commerce, the Texas Department of Community Affairs, the Texas Department of Agriculture and the Governor's Office, provide additional assistance.

Following is a list of Texas Main Street cities/neighborhoods as of January 1991, grouped by year of designation. An asterisk before the name denotes a city no longer active in the program. Self-initiated cities are listed last.

1981: *Eagle Pass, Hillsboro, *Navasota, *Plainview, Sequin. 1982: *Gainesville, Georgetown, *Kingsville, *Marshall, McKinney. 1983: Brenham, *Harlingen, Lufkin, *Stamford, Waxahachie. 1984: *Belton, *Brownwood, Ennis, Goliad, Paris. 1985: Corsicana, Cuero, Lampasas, Mineral Wells, Sweetwater. 1986: Greenville, Palestine, *Pampa, Pittsburg, San Marcos. 1987: Kilgore, Post, Terrell, Weatherford; Wharton. 1988: Center, Daingerfield, Gonzales, Henderson, Temple. 1989: Denison, Fort Stockton, Mineola, Sulphur Springs, Yoakum. 1990: Athens, Denton, El Campo, Elgin, Jasper, Tyler. 1991: Abilene, Angleton, Glen Rose, Jefferson Avenue/Dallas, Market Square/Houston, New Braunfels, and Odessa.

Self-initiated cities include: Fort Worth-Polytechnic, Grapevine, Houston Heights, *Longview and Mount Vernon.

Department of Human Services

The **Texas Department of Human Services (DHS),** administers programs that provide financial and medical assistance and social services to those who are eligible. It also is responsible for licensing child-care facilities and child-placing agencies. The department's headquarters is in Austin, but its services are available in all 254 Texas counties.

The **Texas Board of Human Services** is responsible for adoption of all policies, rules and regulations of the department. (See **State Boards and Commissions** for membership.)

Department services are provided through 10 administrative regions, each supervised by a regional administrator. The department's Austin headquarters staff develops program policy and provides support functions, such as legal, personnel, data-processing and fiscal services, that serve all programs.

DHS has three major program divisions: Client Self-support Services, Protective Services and Health Care Services.

CLIENT SELF-SUPPORT SERVICES — The emphasis in Client Self-support Services (CSS) is on helping build the capacity of families to become and remain self-sufficient. CSS programs include those that provide assistance to meet basic needs, along with support services to promote economic independence.

The **Aid to Families with Dependent Children (AFDC)** program provides financial assistance to needy dependent children and the parents or relatives with whom they live. Financial need must be the result of the absence or disability of a parent, or the unemployment of the principal wage-earner parent. The average monthly payment per recipient is $57.

The AFDC-related **Medicaid** program provides medical coverage to all recipients of AFDC and to other groups of low-income families, women and children to ensure that they have access to adequate medical care, including prenatal care for pregnant women. Medical benefits are also available for 12 months after a family is denied AFDC cash assistance due to earned income. This helps support the family in its transition to economic independence.

The **Food Stamp** program provides coupons to low-income families to supplement their food-purchasing power and help them to obtain a nutritionally adequate diet. Households composed of individuals receiving AFDC or Supplemental Security Income (SSI) grants also receive food stamps. Other households eligible for food stamps include those with incomes below 130 percent of the poverty level.

Employment services help promote the long-term self-sufficiency of AFDC and food-stamp recipients. The **Job Opportunities and Basic Skills (JOBS)** program provides case management, education, vocational training, life-skills training, job preparation and job-search assistance to AFDC-eligible adults and teens. The **Food Stamp Employment and Training** program provides limited case management, job preparation and job-search assistance to food-stamp clients. Support services for clients participating in employment services include child care and allowances for transportation and certain other work- or training-related expenses.

The **Child Care** program uses a mix of funding sources to provide care for children of low-income parents so the parents can work, seek work or receive training that will lead to employment. Child care is also available to children in danger of abuse or neglect, and to children in foster care when the foster parents work or when care is needed to stimulate the child's development.

Other CSS programs include a 100 percent federally funded **Refugee Resettlement** program that provides financial, medical and social services to eligible refugees to assist them in becoming self-sufficient as quickly as possible after arrival in the United States. The **Energy Assistance** program assists low-income households in meeting the cost of residential energy. The **Food Services** program distributes food donated by the U.S. Department of Agriculture to local organizations. Reimbursement is also provided for meals served to low-income children and adults in institutional settings, such as schools, non-profit day-care centers and summer programs. The **Disaster Assistance** program provides grants to families who are victims of a presidentially declared disaster.

PROTECTIVE SERVICES — The DHS provides protective services for abused and neglected children, families, spouses, and elderly or disabled adults and administers the licensing program.

Child Protective Services include investigation of reports of child abuse or neglect; follow-up services to children in their own homes; foster-care services for children who are temporarily unable to remain in their homes; adoption and post-adoption services for children who cannot be safely returned to their homes; and services for delinquent, emotionally disturbed, truant and runaway children.

The **Family Violence Services** program works to reduce and prevent family violence by supporting services for battered women and their families.

The **Adult Protective Services** program investigates reports of abuse, neglect or exploitation of elderly or disabled adults and, when a report is validated, provides or arranges for services to remedy the situation in the least restrictive manner possible.

The **Licensing** program regulates day-care and residential (24-hour) child-care facilities to protect the health, safety and well-being of children in care outside of their own homes.

HEALTH-CARE SERVICES — The DHS purchases health-care services for eligible clients under Title XIX of the Social Security Act (Medicaid). In addition to the AFDC-related clients described previously, Medicaid coverage is provided for certain elderly clients and people with disabilities.

The **Texas Medicaid** program offers a wide array of health-care services, including inpatient and outpatient hospital, physician, prescription drugs, laboratory and X-ray, certified nurse midwife, maternity clinic, rural health clinic, ambulance, optometry and eyeglasses, certain dental services, hearing aids, emergency hospital, ambulatory surgical center, birthing center, chiropractic, home health care, hospice care, respiratory therapy, family planning, health and dental screenings for children, nursing facility, intermediate-care facility for mentally retarded people; medical transportation services, and others.

The **Community Care Services** program helps prevent or delay the long-term institutionalization of eligible individuals through community-based services. This program provides in-home services, such as family care, primary home care, electronic monitoring, and home-delivered meals. Out-of-home services include day activity and health services, adult foster-care services and respite services. Residential care is available for those persons who need 24-hour supervision but not daily nursing intervention.

Federal waivers allow DHS to provide supportive, community-based services that are not normally available under the Medicaid program. These waivers allow special-needs populations, such as people with related conditions or medically fragile children, an alternative to institutionalization.

DHS provides services to more than 2 million Texans each year. Most department services are provided to people with incomes considerably lower than the federal poverty guidelines. Protective services and licensing services are provided without regard to income. Costs of most programs are shared by the state and federal governments.

COSTS/SERVICES

Costs of most programs are shared by the state and fedeal governments. Expenditures by method of finance for fiscal year 1990 are as follows:

Income Assistance and Self-support Services: $801,235,183 (61 percent federally funded).

Health Care Services: $1,946,286,056 (61 percent federally funded).

Services for Families and Children: $211,462,242 (56 percent federally funded).

Services to Aged and Disabled: $1,211,940,813 (69 percent federally funded).

Agency Administration: $80,075,880 (60 percent federally funded).

Grand Total: $4,251,000,174 (64 percent federally funded).

Health Care

The following information has been supplied chiefly by the **Texas Hospital Association** and the **Texas Department of Health.**

As our population increases and technological advances continue, this field of essential services has greatly expanded in Texas. Houston, Dallas and other Texas cities are internationally known for their medical centers. However, many small communities of the state have no hospital or access to professional medical care. As our population ages, access to health care becomes a greater concern for many Texans, as evidenced by the coverage of health care issues in the Texas media.

Hospitals

In 1989, Texas hospitals employed 235,278 full-time equivalent people (FTEs) with a payroll, including benefits of more than $6.6 billion. These employees were reported by the 538 hospitals, with approximately 79,000 beds, registered with the American Hospital Association. One of every 12 U.S. hospitals is located in Texas.

The average length of stay in the 433 community hospitals was 6.3 days in 1989, compared to 6.8 days in 1975. The average length of stay in Texas community hospitals was one day less than the U.S. average and the average cost per admission in Texas was $6,240, which was 4 percent less than the U.S. average of $6,525. Admissions to Texas community hospitals totaled 1,975,235, or 89 percent of the total admissions to all Texas hospitals. There were 18,181,214 out-patient visits in 1989, of which 12,555,506 or 69 percent were provided by community hospitals. Psychiatric admissions of 63,575 represented 3 percent of total admissions in 1989. Of the total 3,920,384 births in U.S. hospitals in 1989, 296,883 were in Texas hospitals. There were 49,565 Registered Nurse FTEs, 18,934 Licensed Vocational Nurse FTEs, and 4,259 FTE health care professions trainees working in Texas hospitals in 1989.

Allied Health Training

Hospitals are the leading source of allied health education in Texas. All allied health personnel are either completely or partially educated in a hospital, clinical, internship or residency program.

Texas continues to experience a shortage of workers in health-care fields. Student enrollments and the number of graduates have increased steadily over the past five years. However, there is still a great demand for physical therapists, occupational therapists, respiratory therapists, medical technologists, radiologic technologists, pharmacists and registered nurses. In the forseeable future, these demands will continue, due largely to the population growth and the expanding requirements for health services.

The Texas Health Careers Program, sponsored by the THA Health Education and Research Foundation, P.O. Box 15587, Austin, Texas 78761, collects information on nursing, allied health and other medical and dental education programs, and provides free information to anyone interested in a career in the health field.

Nursing

For nursing professionals, the Texas Organization of Nurse Executives and the Texas Society of Infection

LIVE BIRTHS AND DEATHS

(Rates per 1,000 Estimated Population)

Year	Live Births No.	Rate	Deaths No.	Rate
1967	203,790	19.2	86,193	8.1
1968	207,191	19.2	92,098	8.5
1969	220,647	20.0	93,336	8.5
1970	230,624	20.6	94,287	8.4
1971	228,983	20.0	94,724	8.3
1972	214,613	18.4	99,275	8.5
1973	209,651	17.8	101,487	8.6
1974	210,787	17.5	99,426	8.3
1975	215,426	17.6	98,354	8.0
1976	218,447	17.5	100,620	8.1
1977	228,871	17.8	100,077	7.8
1978	236,612	18.2	103,670	8.0
1979	254,263	19.0	104,745	7.8
1980	273,433	19.2	108,018	7.6
1981	281,558	19.1	110,498	7.5
1982	297,683	19.5	111,263	7.3
1983	295,178	18.8	114,714	7.3
1984	298,756	18.7	116,755	7.3
1985	308,027	18.8	118,183	7.2
1986	307,003	18.4	118,637	7.1
1987	301,827	17.8	119,734	7.1
1988	303,314	17.6	122,731	7.1
1989	307,540	17.6	124,563	7.1

CAUSES OF DEATH

The 10 leading causes of death in Texas in 1989 were:

Cause	Deaths	*Rate	% of Total Deaths
All Causes	124,563	713.0	100.0
Heart Disease	40,162	229.9	32.2
Malignant Neoplasms...	27,318	156.4	21.9
Cerebrovascular Diseases	8,343	47.8	6.7
Accidents and Adverse Effects	6,540	37.4	5.3
Chronic Obstructive Pulmonary Disease and Allied Conditions	4,337	24.8	3.5
Pneumonia, Influenza	3,869	22.1	3.1
Diabetes Mellitus	2,872	16.4	2.3
Homicide	2,086	11.9	1.7
Suicide	2,073	11.9	1.7
Chronic Liver Disease and Cirrhosis	1,606	9.2	1.3
All Other Causes	25,357	145.1	20.4

*Rates per 100,000 estimated population

Control Practitioners offer opportunities for continuing education and networking with others in the profession. They also serve as advocates for nursing and provide representatives to regulatory agency committees, legislative study groups and other related nursing organizations. These societies are affiliated with the Texas Hospital Association, the principal advocate and leadership organization for hospitals and health-care providers. The association helps the industry better serve Texans through representation, education and services.

Schools of Nursing

There are currently 71 schools of nursing in Texas accredited by the **Board of Nurse Examiners** for the State of Texas. Forty-six offer associate degree programs, 26 offer baccalaureate degree programs and 2 have hospital diploma programs.

The **associate degree** programs include: **Abilene Intercollegiate** School of Nursing, Abilene; **Alvin Community College** Department of Nursing, Alvin; **Amarillo College** Associate Degree Nursing Program, Amarillo; **Austin Community College,** Austin; **Lee College** Associate Degree Nursing Program, Baytown; **Lamar University** Associate Degree Nursing Program, Beaumont; **Howard County Junior College** Associate Degree Nursing Program, Big Spring; **Texas Southmost College** School of Nursing, Brownsville; **Blinn College,** Bryan; **Del Mar College** Department of Registered Nurse Education, Corpus Christi; **Navarro College** School of Nursing, Corsicana; **El Centro College** Division of Associate Degree Nursing, Dallas; **Grayson County College** Associate Degree Nursing Program, Denison; **University of Texas-Pan American** Department of Nursing, Edinburg; **El Paso Community College** Department of Nursing, El Paso; **Tarrant County Junior College** Department of Nursing, Fort Worth; **Cooke County College** Department of Nursing, Gainesville; **Galveston College,** Galveston; **Houston Baptist University** Associate Degree Nursing Program, Houston; **Houston Community College** Department of Nursing, Houston; **North Harris County College** Associate Degree Nursing Program, Houston; **Trinity Valley Community College,** Kaufman; **Southwestern Adventist College** Department of Nursing, Keene; **Kilgore College** Department of Nursing, Kilgore; **Central Texas College** School of Nursing, Killeen; **Brazosport College** Associate Degree Nusing Program, Lake Jackson; **Laredo Junior College** Department of Nursing, Laredo; **South Plains College,** Levelland; **Angelina College** Division of Nursing, Lufkin; **Collin County Community College,** McKinney; **Midland College** School of Nursing, Midland; **Northeast Texas Community College,** Mt. Pleasant; **Odessa College** Associate Degree Nursing Program, Odessa; **Lamar University,** Orange; **Paris Junior College** Department of Nursing, Paris; **San Jacinto College** Department of Nursing Education, Pasadena; **Angelo State University** Department of Nursing, San Angelo; **San Antonio College** Department of Nursing, San Antonio; **Western Texas College** Associate Degree Nursing Program, Snyder; **Tarleton State University** School of Nursing, Stephenville; **Texarkana College** William Buchanan Department of Nursing, Texarkana; **College of the Mainland** Nursing Department, Texas City; **Tyler Junior College,** Tyler; **Victoria College** Associate Degree Nursing Program, Victoria; **McLennan Community College** Department of Nursing, Waco; **Wharton County Junior College** School of Nursing, Wharton.

Baccalaureate degree programs include: **Abilene Intercollegiate** School of Nursing, Abilene; **University of Texas** School of Nursing at Arlington, Arlington; **The University of Texas** School of Nursing at Austin, Austin; **Lamar University** School of Nursing, Beaumont; **Mary Hardin-Baylor University** Department of Nursing, Belton; **West Texas State University** School of Nursing, Canyon; **Baylor University** School of Nursing, Dallas; **Dallas Baptist University** Division of Nursing, Dallas; **Texas Woman's University** College of Nursing (which also offers the master's and doctoral degrees in nursing), Denton; **The University of Texas** School of Nursing at El Paso, El Paso; **Texas Christian University** Harris College of Nursing, Fort Worth; **The University of Texas Medical Branch** School of Nursing, Galveston; **Houston Baptist University** School of Nursing, Houston; **Texas Woman's University,** Houston; **The University of Texas Health Science Center at Houston** School of Nursing, Houston; **Prairie View A&M University** College of Nursing, Houston; **Incarnate Word College** Department of Nursing, San Antonio; **The University of Texas Health Science Center at San Antonio** School of Nursing, San Antonio; **Texas Tech University Health Science Center** School of Nursing, Lubbock; **Stephen F. Austin University** School of Nursing, Nacogdoches; **University of Texas at Tyler** School of Nursing, Tyler; **Midwestern University** Department of Nursing, Whichita Falls.

The **hospital diploma** programs are: **Methodist Hospital School of Nursing,** Lubbock; **Baptist Memorial Hospital School of Nursing,** San Antonio.

Texas Department of Commerce

The Texas Department of Commerce was created in September 1987 in response to major changes that had taken place in the state's economy in the preceding decade. At the time, emphasis was shifting from heavy manufacturing and natural resources to services and trade. The focus on development and expansion of local businesses was changing to national and international business development. The Texas Department of Commerce was formed by the consolidation of eight state boards or agencies (Texas Economic Development Commission, Texas Tourist Development Agency, Texas World Trade Council, Texas World Trade Development Authority, Enterprise Zone Board, Technology Training Board, Texas Music Commission and Texas Film Commission) into one department with various programs and divisions.

During a major reorganization in 1991, the Texas Department of Commerce implemented a new organizational structure that enacted changes designed to make the agency more efficient, credible and accountable to the citizens of Texas.

This improvement plan is based on the concept of providing legendary customer service with the emphasis on customer satisfaction, not the marketing of the agency as a whole.

The purpose of the department is to build and maintain a diverse and dynamic state economy and create jobs for Texans. Its programs focus on attracting national and international industries to Texas, promoting tourism in the state, retaining and expanding businesses in Texas, assisting small businesses, and training a capable work force. Divisions within the department include:

• **The Work Force Development Division** administers job-training programs statewide to ensure a highly trained labor force for businesses through a network of 34 serve providers. The Job Training Partnership Act (JTPA) that offers programs on skills assessment, training and job assistance for program participants including the economic disadvantaged, handicapped and "hard-to-serve" individuals. JTPA also provides financial incentives for participating businesses and funds the Dislocated Worker Program. Also under the Work Force Development Division are the Texas Literacy Council, the Summer Youth Employment and Training Programs and the Work Force Incentive Program.

• **The Community Development Block Grant Division** (CDBG) administers the program that provides small cities and counties with financial assistance for public works, housing, economic development and planning through a variety of funds. The program benefits primarily persons of low to moderate incomes. Two of these programs are the Texas Capital Fund and the Texas Rental Rehabilitation Program.

• **The Business Development Division** concentrates on retaining and expanding the state's existing business and industrial base and marketing Texas nationally and internationally as an ideal state for business location and expansion. It also promotes the film and music industries through the Texas Music and Film offices, aids businesses in exporting Texas products, helps communities create and execute economic development plans, encourages the transfer of high technology to business applications, assists small businesses in Texas and operates the state's foreign offices.

• **The Tourism Division** promotes travel to Texas by working with travel industry planners, executing national and international advertising and public relations campaigns and assists local communities in maximizing their tourism business.

Under Commerce's new position of the Chief Administrative Officer are Data Services, Human Resources, Intergovernmental Relations, Research & Planning, Administration and Communication Divisions. Ms. Cathy Bonner is interim director of the department.

Institutional Division TDCJ

The Institutional Division of the Texas Department of Criminal Justice operates the state prison system for adult felony offenders. The headquarters is in Huntsville, with James A. Collins as director. The system maintains more than 100,000 acres of land on 35 units, and houses in excess of 46,000 inmates.

Since 1982, the Institutional Division has been under federal court order to relieve overcrowding and to upgrade various services. In March 1990, active monitoring of the prison system by the Special Master appointed by the court was terminated.

The following summary of current operations deals only with the Institutional Division. Juvenile offenders are under the jurisdiction of a separate state agency, the **Texas Youth Commission.**

The **Texas Board of Criminal Justice** guides the administration and operation of the department in the areas of policy, planning and budgetary matters; the nine board members are nonsalaried and appointed for 6-year overlapping terms by the governor. James A. Collins has served as director since January 1990.

The average number of inmates during fiscal year 1988 was 39,221. Prison population has grown from 18,151 on Aug. 31, 1975, to 20,976 on Aug. 31, 1976, to 20,862 on Aug. 31, 1977, to 24,615 on Aug. 31, 1978, to 25,164 on Aug. 31, 1979, to 28,543 on Aug. 31, 1980, to 30,315 on Aug. 31, 1981, to 34,393 on Aug. 31, 1982, to 36,769 on Aug. 31, 1983, to 35,772 on Aug. 31, 1984, to 37,320 on Aug. 31, 1985, to 38,246 on Aug. 31, 1986, to 39,652 on Aug. 31, 1987, and to 39,664 on Aug. 31, 1988. Currently, the recidivism rate is approximately 43 percent.

On Aug. 31, 1990, total assets of the division were $982,934,497.52, including land, buildings and equipment. Total monies appropriated to the division by the Texas Legislature for the 1990-91 biennium amounted to $1.45 billion (this includes $210.1 million for building programs).

Agriculture and livestock operations are under efficient management and provide a savings to taxpayers. Combined with prison industries and construction projects utilizing inmate labor, this financial effort gives Texas one of the lowest per capita inmate costs to taxpayers in the nation. Costs **daily** per inmate were: 1990 - $37.03; 1989 - $34.07; 1988 - $32.66; 1987 - $26.94; 1986 - $25.07; 1985 - $21.00; 1984 - $17.70; 1983 - $14.57; 1982 - $12.11; 1981 - $9.80; - 1980 - $8.61; 1979 - $7.34; 1978 - $7.15; 1977 - $7.32; 1976 - $5.97; 1975 - $5.20; 1974 - $4.59; 1973 - $3.89 and 1972 - $3.31.

Most treatment programs in the areas of education, recreation, medicine and worship are funded by legislative appropriations or other state funds. Supplemental monies to extend these programs are derived from prison commissary operations.

Cooperative programs in **higher education** are being carried out on all units. Junior college programs leading to associate degrees are in effect with **Lee College, Brazosport College, Alvin College, Central Texas College, Blinn College** and **Trinity Valley Community College.** Bachelors degrees can be earned through **Sam Houston State University, the University of Houston—Clear Lake, Tarleton State University** or **Stephen F. Austin State University.** A Master of Arts degree can be earned at the **University of Houston—Clear Lake.** During the 1989-1990 school year, 11,306 inmates participated in college programs. In addition, 1,287 inmates participated in Apprenticeships, Related Training and **Texas A&M University Extension Programs** to qualify for craft certificates.

In 1969, an independent school **(Windham School System)** was created within the division to offer education in grades 1-12 and special education leading to a G.E.D., or high school diploma. One-third of those who function at or above the sixth grade level when enrolled will attain the GED before leaving prison.

More than 40 different programs are offered in various vocational skills through the Windham School System. Participants in the college and secondary level vocational courses numbered more than 9,100 students during fiscal year 1990.

Rehabilitative programs are also available in the fields of physiological and psychiatric health care, varied recreational programs, legal services, religious activities, inmate self-help groups, work-release programs, job placement services, pre-release programs and support programs in conjunction with other state agencies.

Units

Beto Units, Tennessee Colony, Anderson County: Agricultural operations include livestock, field crops and edible crops, horse breeding and swine farrowing. Industrial operations include a highway sign factory and a concrete block plant. Beto is divided into Beto I and Beto II.

Central Unit, Sugar Land, Fort Bend County: Agricultural operations include field and edible crops, livestock, central agricultural commissary, agriculture administrative offices, veterinary clinic and harvesting equipment repair. Industrial operations include a soap and detergent factory, a transportation warehouse, and the central industrial distribution warehouse.

Clemens Unit, Brazoria, Brazoria County: Agricultural operations include field and edible crops, livestock and grain dryer.

Coffield Unit, Tennessee Colony, Anderson County: Agricultural operations include livestock, field and edible crops, feedlot, feed mill and a poultry house. Industrial operations include records conversion and metal fabrication.

Darrington Unit, Rosharon, Brazoria County: Agricultural operations include field and edible crops, livestock, poultry layers, grain dryer and cold storage facility. Other operations include tire recapping and a concrete batch plant.

Diagnostic Unit, Huntsville, Walker County: Special operations include testing and classifying of all newly received male inmates in order to assign them to a permanent unit.

Eastham Unit, Lovelady, Houston County: Agricultural operations include field crops, livestock, dairy, gin, feed mill, poultry house and swine farrowing. Other operations include a garment factory.

Ellis Units, Huntsville, Walker County: Agricultural operations include field crops, livestock, gin, farrowing barn, forestry program and sawmill. Industrial operations include a dental lab, garment factory, woodworking shop, textile mill and bus repair facility. Other operations include the headquarters for central area maintenance, medical treatment center (acute and intermediate) and the central area region fire and safety office. Ellis is divided into Ellis I and Ellis II.

Ferguson Unit, Midway, Madison County: Agricultural operations include field crops, livestock and swine farrowing. Other operations include a mop and broom factory, a shoe factory and the headquarters for the central area construction program.

Gatesville Unit, Gatesville, Coryell County **(Women's Unit):** Special operations include a garment factory, regional medical facilities, and the testing and classifying of all newly received female inmates in order to assign them to a permanent unit.

Goree Unit, Huntsville, Walker County: Agricultural operations include a horse breeding program and a dairy calf operation.

Hilltop Unit, Gatesville, Coryell County: Agricultural operations include edible crops and livestock. Industrial operations include a garment factory. Other operations include a satellite headquarters for northern area maintenance.

Huntsville Unit, Walker County: Industrial operations include textile mill, mechanical department and print shop. Other operations include regional infirmary, Windham Media Center; headquarters for construction department, maintenance warehouse operations.

Jester Units, Richmond, Fort Bend County: Agricultural operations include field and edible crops and livestock. Industrial operations include a garment factory. Pre-release program for males is located on Jester II; mobility impaired inmates are housed at Jester III. Jester is divided into Jester I, Jester II and Jester III.

Michael Unit, Tennessee Colony, Anderson County: Agricultural operations include a meatpacking plant.

Mountain View Unit, Gatesville, Coryell County **(Women's Unit):** Special operations include a Braille facility, psychiatric facility and pre-release for female inmates.

Pack Units, Navasota, Grimes County: Agricultural operations include field and edible crops and livestock.

Other operations include a stainless steel products factory. Pack is divided into Pack I and Pack II.

Ramsey Units, Rosharon, Brazoria County: Agricultural operations include field and edible crops, livestock, grain dryer, storage, dehydrator and gin. Other operations include furniture refinishing and the headquarters for southern area maintenance. Ramsey is divided into Ramsey I, Ramsey II and Ramsey III.

Retrieve Unit, Angleton, Brazoria County: Agricultural operations include field and edible crops and livestock.

Skyview Unit, at Rusk State Hospital, Cherokee County: Houses in-patient, mentally ill male inmates.

Wynne Unit, Huntsville, Walker County: Agricultural operations include field and edible crops, livestock, dairy, heifer breeding and dog kennel program. Industrial operations include a license plate plant, validation sticker plant, mattress factory, corrugated box factory, plastic sign shop, records conversion, transportation department, prison store and laundries. Other operations include administrative offices for the **Windham School District,** laundries and in-house construction.

Clements Unit, Amarillo, Potter County: Industrial operations consist of a shoe factory. Agricultural operations include edible and field crops. A 450-bed psychiatric treatment facility is also part of the unit.

Daniel Unit, Snyder, Scurry County: Industrial operations include modular furniture factory/upholstery.

Hightower Unit, Dayton, Liberty County: Industrial operations consist of a garment factory.

Hobby Unit, Marlin, Falls County: Industrial operations consist of a print shop. Agricultural operations include edible crops.

Hughes Unit, Gatesville, Coryell County: Industrial operations consist of a garment factory.

Lewis Unit, Woodville, Tyler County: Industrial operations consist of a woodworking factory.

Division Hospital, Galveston, Galveston County: Special operations include facilities for major surgery, acute care and specialized treatment.

As of February 1991, the Institutional Division had plans to build 10 more units in the communities of Teague, Dilley, Childress, Lamesa, Hondo, Pampa, Abilene, Beeville, Beaumont and Livingston. Construction of the units was expected to continue through March 1993.

Youth Institutions

The following institutions are under the direction of the **Texas Youth Commission.**

RESIDENTIAL TREATMENT CENTER

Corsicana State Home—Corsicana; 1897; Sandra L. Burnam, superintendent; 88 students.

INSTITUTIONS

Brownwood State School—Brownwood; 1970; Linda Steen, superintendent; 228 students.

Crockett State School—Crockett; 1947 as **Brady State School for Colored Girls;** changed to **Crockett State School for Girls;** and in 1975 name changed to present form; David Cocoros, superintendent; 118 students.

Gainesville State School—Gainesville; 1916; Jerry Day, superintendent; 295 students.

Giddings State School—Giddings; 1972; Calvin Crenshaw, superintendent; 269 students.

West Texas State School—Pyote; 1966; Johnny B. Williams, superintendent; 182 students.

In addition, all youth committed to the Texas Youth Commission are processed through either the Statewide Reception Center (Brownwood, 1970, Bill Doggett, acting superintendent) or the Mobile Diagnostic Unit operating from the Evins Regional Juvenile Center in Edinburg (Joseph Martinez, regional director), which exclusively serves youth from South Texas.

State Institutions For MHMR Services

Texas Department of Mental Health and Mental Retardation is responsible for conserving the mental health of Texas citizens and helping citizens of the state who have mental retardation to achieve their potential. It administers state hospitals and state centers for persons with mental illness, schools and state centers for persons with mental retardation and genetic screening and counseling units, and participates in administering community mental health and mental retardation centers. The department's address is Box 12668, Austin 78711-2668.

MENTAL HEALTH HOSPITALS

Austin State Hospital—Austin; 1857; Harold K. Dudley Jr., superintendent; 450 patients.

Big Spring State Hospital—Big Spring; 1937; Robert von Rosenberg, superintendent; 310 patients.

Kerrville State Hospital—Kerrville; 1950; Dr. Luther W. Ross, superintendent; 349 patients.

Rusk State Hospital—Rusk; 1919; Dr. Allen C. Chittenden, superintendent; 374 patients.

San Antonio State Hospital—San Antonio; 1892; Steven B. Schnee, Ph. D., superintendent; 518 patients.

Terrell State Hospital—Terrell; 1885; Benny Britton, interim superintendent; 470 patients.

Vernon State Hospital—Vernon; 1969; James E. Smith, superintendent; 430 patients: 110 in Drug Dependent Youth Program, South Campus; 320 in maximum-security hospital, North Campus.

Waco Center for Youth—Waco; 1979; Charles Locklin, director; 96 clients.

Wichita Falls State Hospital—Wichita Falls; 1922; Richard M. Bruner, superintendent; 480 patients.

SCHOOLS FOR PERSONS WITH MENTAL RETARDATION

Abilene State School—Abilene; 1901; Bill Waddill, superintendent; 771 individuals.

Austin State School—Austin; 1917; James G. Armstrong, Ph. D., superintendent; 500 individuals.

Brenham State School—Brenham; 1974; Jimmy R. Haskins, Ed. D., superintendent; 500 individuals.

Corpus Christi State School—Corpus Christi; 1970; Aurelio Valdez Jr., superintendent; 410 individuals.

Denton State School—Denton; 1960; Patricia Jessee, superintendent; 670 individuals.

Fort Worth State School—Fort Worth; 1976; Gileen Reynolds, interim superintendent; 375 individuals.

Lubbock State School—Lubbock; 1969; Lonnie H. Willis, superintendent; 440 individuals.

Lufkin State School—Lufkin; 1962; Harry G. Heyman, superintendent; 492 individuals.

Mexia State School—Mexia; 1946; W. H. Lowry, Ph. D., superintendent; 783 individuals.

Richmond State School—Richmond; 1968; Gerald N. Brunette, M.S., superintendent; 749 individuals.

San Angelo State School—Carlsbad; 1969; R. Allen Williams, superintendent; 435 individuals.

San Antonio State School—San Antonio; 1978; Tom Deliganis, Ph. D., superintendent; 327 individuals.

Travis State School—Austin; 1934; Richard L. Smith, Ed. D., superintendent; 640 individuals.

STATE CENTERS

Amarillo State Center—Amarillo; 1967; Richard D. Browder, director; 600 individuals.

Beaumont State Center—Beaumont; 1968; Gary Hidalgo, director; 440 individuals.

El Paso State Center—El Paso; 1974; Beatrice Butler, director; 189 individuals.

Laredo State Center—Laredo; 1969; Delores V. Rodriguez, director; 1,503 individuals.

Rio Grande State Center—Harlingen; 1962; Rigoberto T. F. Gonzalez, R.N., M.A., director; 1,375 individuals. Includes outreach centers in Alice, Falfurrias, Kingsville and San Diego.

COMMUNITY MENTAL HEALTH AND MENTAL RETARDATION CENTERS

Abilene — Abilene Regional MHMR Center; 1971; Russell B. Evans, executive director; 2,000 individuals.

Amarillo — Texas Panhandle Mental Health Authority; 1968; Claire Rigler, executive director; 2,795 individuals.

Austin — Austin-Travis County MHMR Center; 1967; John E. Brubaker, executive director; 9,000 individuals.

Beaumont — MHMR of Southeast Texas (Life Resource); 1967; Roger Pricer, Ph. D., executive director; 7,506 individuals.

Brownwood — Central Texas MHMR Center; 1969; Roy A. Cronenberg, executive director; 636 individuals.

Bryan-College Station — MHMR Authority of Brazos Valley; 1972; Jack Leon Bawcom, executive director; 2,300 individuals.

Cleburne — Johnson County MHMR Center; 1985; Joseph P. Mirisciotti, executive director; 832 individuals.

Conroe — Tri-County MHMR Services; 1983; Leon Evans, executive director; 7,500 individuals.

Corpus Christi — Nueces County MHMR Community

Center; 1970; Wallace E. Whitworth Jr., executive director; 5,000 individuals.

Corsicana — Navarro County MHMR Center; 1979; Julia W. Lang, executive director; 1,000 individuals.

Dallas — Dallas County MHMR Center; 1967; Marcia B. Bryan, Ed. D., executive director; 14,351 individuals.

Denison — MHMR Services of Texoma; 1974; Carl Kelly, executive director; 2,234 individuals.

Denton — Denton County MHMR Center; 1987; Cynthia Sill, excutive executive director; 2,630 individuals.

Edinburg — Tropical Texas Center for MHMR; 1967; Marion G. Shirah, executive director; 7,186 individuals.

El Paso — Life Management Center; 1968; Michael Nash, Ph. D., executive director; 6,365 individuals.

Fort Worth — Tarrant County MHMR Services; 1969; Jim McDermott, Ph.D., executive director; 15,051 individuals.

Galveston — Gulf Coast Center; 1969; G. Michael Winburn, executive director; 2,818 individuals.

Greenville — Hunt County Family Services Center Inc.; 1971; Jim Putnam, executive director; 1,062 individuals.

Houston — MHMR Authority of Harris County; 1965; Jan Duker, Ph. D., executive director; 20,000 individuals.

Longview — Sabine Valley Center; 1970; Mack O. Blackwell, executive director; 6,218 individuals.

Lubbock — Lubbock Regional MHMR Center; 1969; Gene Menefee, executive director; 4,000 individuals.

Lufkin — Deep East Texas Regional MHMR Services; 1975; Susan Rushing, executive director; 3,829 individuals.

McKinney — Collin County MHMR Center; 1986; Randy Routon, executive director; 2,217 individuals.

Midland/Odessa — Permian Basin Community Center for MHMR; 1969; Clyde McLean, executive director; 3,336 individuals.

Plainview — Central Plains Comprehensive Commu- nity MHMR Center; 1969; Rick Van Hersh, executive director; 2,200 individuals.

San Angelo — MHMR Services for the Concho Valley; 1969; James M. Young, executive director; 1,118 individuals.

San Antonio — The Center for Health Care Services; 1966; Ruben R. Cardenas, executive director; 15,000 individuals.

Stephenville — Pecan Valley MHMR Center; 1977; Theresa Mulloy, Ed. D., executive director; 2,540 individuals.

Temple — Central Counties Center for MHMR Services; 1967; Michael K. Muegge, executive director; 2,056 individuals.

Texarkana — Northeast Texas MHMR Center; 1974; Joe Bob Hall, executive director; 1,105 individuals.

Tyler — MHMR Regional Center of East Texas; 1970; Richard J. DeSanto, executive director; 4,715 individuals.

Victoria — Gulf Bend MHMR Center; 1970; Bill Dillard, executive director; 2,605 individuals.

Waco — Heart of Texas MHMR Center; 1969; Dean Maberry, executive director; 2,312 individuals.

Wharton — Riceland Regional Mental Health Authority; 1988; Bascom Hodges, executive director; 1,166 individuals.

Wichita Falls — Wichita Falls Community MHMR Center; 1969; Henrilu Smith, M.S., executive director; 1,800 individuals.

SPECIAL UNITS

Genetic Screening and Counseling Service — Denton; 1975; Dr. Donald W. Day, director; makes medical genetic services available to all Texans regardless of ability to pay.

Leander Rehabilitation Center — Cedar Park; 1969; Roy Jones, director; recreational center serving residents of other department and community MHMR facilities.

History of Texas Public Lands

The History of Texas Public Lands was revised for the Texas Almanac by **Commissioner Garry Mauro** and the staff of the General Land Office of Texas. It is a summary of a longer history of the Texas **public domain** in the General Land Office.

The **Texas General Land Office** is one of the oldest governmental entities in the state, dating back to the Republic. The practice of having a commissioner to administer public lands reaches even farther back into Texas history when proprietors of Spanish and Mexican land grants "commissioned" representatives to handle land transactions.

Before the American Revolution, proprietors of the colonies along the eastern seaboard established land offices under the supervision of the commissioned representative to sell land and control squatting or trespassing. Later in Texas, when the Mexican government began issuing land grants for colonization, each empresario colony had a land commissioner to issue individual land titles and settle disputes.

The first General Land Office was established in the constitution of the Republic of Texas in 1836, and the first Texas Congress enacted the provision into law in 1837. However, President Sam Houston vetoed the act on the grounds that the office would not be able to function properly until the records of the various empresario colonies, Spanish and Mexican land grants, and the appropriate archives could be properly gathered together. But the new Congress was so anxious to settle land questions that it overrode his veto.

The sale of public lands had been temporarily suspended during the War for Texas Independence from Mexico, and there was a great clamor to open up the public lands again. New settlers were arriving every day and the demand for free or cheap land was tremendous.

Because the new Texas government needed to become stable and productive, it sought to attract and keep these settlers. The Texas Congress enacted generous laws offering large tracts of land to just about anyone who wanted them. For example, all heads of households in Texas as of March 2, 1836, were entitled to a league and a labor of land (about 4,605 acres). Single men could claim a third of a league. In the 10 years Texas existed as a Republic, it alloted 41,570,733 acres to encourage settlement, to reward veterans of the War for Independence, to pay the Republic's debts and to finance its operations.

In 1844, as negotiations proceeded for Texas to join the Union, the resulting treaty stipulated that the U.S. would pay $10 million of the Republic's debts and acquire 175 million acres of the public domain. Opponents to statehood in the U.S. Congress felt that Texas' land were not worth the assumption of the $10 million debt and refused to make the trade. In the final resolution for annexation, Texas was to keep its public domain and the U.S. was to disclaim any responsibility fo Texas' debt. Texas officially came into the Union Dec 29, 1845, keeping both its debt and its public lands.

When the first **state constitution** was drawn up i July, 1845, it provided no major change in the administration of the Texas public domain. All land titles issue under the laws of Spain, Mexico and the Republic o Texas were recognized. The Commissioner of the General Land Office became one of the elected constitutional officials of the state government.

In the early years of statehood, Texas establishe the precedent of using its vast public domain for publi benefit. The first use was to sell or trade off land t eliminate the huge debt remaining from the War fo Independence and early years of the Republic. A wes ern area of 67 million acres, now part of New Mexicc Colorado, Oklahoma, Kansas and Wyoming, was tran ferred to the United States by the Texas Legislature o Nov. 25, 1850. Texas received $10 million in governmen bonds. The state had shed all its debts by 1855 and sti had over 98 million acres of open domain. Texas gav away land for **internal improvements, homesteads, vete ans grants, capitol construction,** and for **settlement** + **boundary disputes.** More than 32 million acres were gi en away to promote **railroad construction.** And 50 millic acres were set aside as an **endowment to public schoo and colleges.**

By 1898, there was very little remaining unappr priated public land in Texas. The **homestead polic** which had seen 4.8 million acres of land given away f settlers, was finally abandoned in 1899. The Legislatur in 1900 determined that the public schools and the **Pe manent School Fund** would receive all unsurveyed lan and the few remaining unappropriated public land Finally in 1939, all lakes, bays, islands and the su merged areas off the Texas coast accrued to the Scho Fund.

Public Lands of Texas

Taken from the records of the General Land Office of Texas, the following summary shows the disposition of the public domain. The total area given here differs from the U.S. Census Bureau figure of 171,096,320 given elsewhere in this volume.

	Acres.	Subtotals
Total area to tidewater		172,193,269
Total area to 3-league (10.36-mile) limit		3,997,000
		176,190,269
Grants to promote citizenship and to induce immigration—		
By governments of Spain and Mexico	26,280,000	
Headrights and bounties	36,876,492	
Colonies—(Peter's, Mercer's et al.)	4,494,806	
Homestead donations (pre-emptions)	4,847,136—	72,498,434
Donations to veterans—		
San Jacinto veterans—Act of 1879 and 1881	1,169,382	
Confederate veterans—Act of 1881	1,979,852—	3,149,234
Sold to pay public debts by Republic	1,329,200	
50c Sales scrip act of 1879 and $2 sales scrip act of 1887	1,660,936—	2,990,136
Internal improvements—		
State Capitol Building	3,025,000	
Irrigation, drainage, iron works, Kiamasha Road and sundry	4,088,640—	7,113,640
To acquire transportation facilities—		
Grants to railroads	32,153,878—	32,153,878
For education—		
State University and A&M	2,329,168	
County school purposes	4,229,166	
Eleemosynary institutions	410,600	
Public free school	44,443,744	
Unsold public school land	863,540—	52,276,218
Total surveyed land		170,181,540
Less conflicts (estimated at one half of 1 percent)		850,908
Net as per original surveys		169,330,632
Excess (estimated at approximately 1.1 percent)		1,862,637
River beds and vacancies (estimated)		1,000,000
Submerged coastal areas to three-league limit		3,997,000
Total		176,190,269

The end of the vast unappropriated public domain might have signaled the end of the use of public land for the benefit of all Texans. But when oil was discovered in 1921 on state lands under lease, this remaining public land became a most valuable economic asset to the state. After selling off 91.4 percent of its surface land without reserving mineral rights, Texas finally had established the right to its subsurface minerals in 1895. And the Relinquishment Act of 1919 gave the surface owners of the land rights to participate in the mineral wealth as "agents" of the state. The economic value of the public lands of Texas in the 20th Century thus resulted from the belated development of its mineral ownership.

Today 20.6 million acres are considered to be in the public domain. This includes almost 4 million acres of submerged coastal lands, which are bays, inlets and the area from the Texas shoreline to the three marine league line (10.36 miles) in the Gulf of Mexico. In addition, more than one million acres are estimated to make up the state's riverbeds and vacant areas. The University of Texas System holds title to 2,109,000 fee acres and other state agencies or special schools hold title to approximately 1.9 million acres. Texas owns mineral rights alone in approximately 7.4 million covered under the Relinquishment Act, Free Royalty Act and the various sales acts and has outright ownership to approximately 860,000 upland acres, mostly west of the Pecos. Texas has liens on 1.5 million acres of land in the active accounts of the Veterans Land Board and another 1.7 million acres of excess land that are not calculated into any category.

Perhaps the most valuable segment of the Texas public domain is its coastal submerged land. And for some time, there was serious question about the state's ownership. The Republic of Texas had proclaimed its Gulf boundaries as three marine leagues, recognized by international law as traditional national boundaries. These boundaries were never seriously questioned when Texas joined the Union in 1845, and Texas continued to claim jurisdiction. A congressional resolution in 1930 authorized the U.S. Attorney General to file suit to establish the offshore lands as properties of the federal government.

The legal question was more important to Texas in the 20th century than it would have been upon entering the Union, since offshore oil and gas production had become a source of tremendous income to the state. Gulf of Mexico leases between the three-mile and the three-marine league limit (the area claimed by the federal government) have brought the state approximately $1.5 billion in revenue since the first oil lease there in 1922. Congress returned the disputed lands to Texas in 1953, and the Supreme Court finally confirmed Texas' ownership to the 1,878,394 acres in 1960. (See Tidelands History in 1972-73 Texas Almanac.)

In 1978, the federal government also granted states a "fair and equitable" share of the revenues from offshore federal leases within three miles of the states' outermost boundary. The states did not receive any such revenue until April 1986 when Congress clarified the meaning of "fair and equitable" through additional legislation. Under the 1986 law, coastal states are entitled to 27 percent of all revenues in perpetuity from federal leases within three miles of the state-federal boundary. In addition, Texas received a one-time settlement to cover the 1978 to 1985 period amounting to $426 million in Fiscal Year 1986 and a deferred payment of $134 million over 15 years.

The General Land Office handles leases and revenue accounting on all lands dedicated to the **Permanent School Fund** and on land owned by various state agencies. The Land Commissioner, two members of the University of Texas Board of Regents and one A&M University Board of Regents member make up the Board for Lease of lands dedicated to the **Permanent University Fund**. Revenue accounting for income from Permanent University Lands is processed by the University of Texas; investment income from the fund is divided approximately two-thirds to one-third between the University of Texas and Texas A&M University, respectively. As of May 31, 1991, the **Permanent University Fund** has a book value of more than $3.2 billion; the **Permanent School Fund** has a book value of more than $6.7 billion.

All activities on state lands are reviewed for their environmental impact, and restrictions are placed in offshore drilling lessons where needed to protect resources.

Veterans Land Program

In 1946, the Legislature created a bond program to aid veterans in purchasing farm land. Up to $1.25 billion in bonding authority has been authorized over the years in a series of constitutional amendments; as of

Jan. 1, 1991, more than $1.1 billion of the bonds had been sold to fund loans.

Loans cannot exceed $20,000, and tracts purchased through the program must be at least five acres. To date, 104,000 veterans have participated in the land program, purchasing more than 4.5 million acres of land.

Veterans Housing Assistance Program

The 68th Legislature created the Veterans Housing Assistance Program, which also is funded through bond proceeds. With the passage of two constitutional amendments, the people of Texas have authorized the selling of $1 billion in bonds to finance the veterans housing program. To date, $750 million in bonds have been sold to fund housing loans.

Eligible veterans may borrow up to $45,000 toward the purchase of a home; the balance of the purchase price is financed through private sector lending institutions. When the low interest veterans loan is combined with private sector interest rates, monthly payments are significantly reduced. Since the program began op-

eration in January 1984, more than 23,000 veterans have received housing loans.

Veterans Home Improvement Program

In 1986, the Veterans Land Board implemented the Veterans Home Improvement Program, which is funded through the Housing Assistance Program. The Home Improvement Program allows Texas Veterans to borrow between $4,000 and $17,500 to make substantial home repairs and improvements.

To date, 2,000 or more veterans have received Veterans Home Improvement loans. In excess of $27 million has been loaned since the program's inception.

All three programs are administered by the Veterans Land Board, which is chaired by the Texas Land Commissioner. The bonded debt for the programs and all administrative costs are completely financed by the veterans who use the programs; there is no cost to Texas taxpayers. Eligible veterans may participate in each of the three veterans programs.

Details about the programs may be obtained from the Veterans Land Board by calling toll free 1-800-252-VETS.

Texas State Officials, Boards, Commissions

A list of Texas State officialdom is given on this and following pages, revised to July 1, 1991. Information includes (1) Date of creation of office or agency; (2) whether elective or appointive; (3) length of term; (4) number of members, if a board or commission; (5) name of officials (or officials). Dates in parentheses indicate termination of appointment. Names of towns in parentheses indicate home of official whose residence is officially in Austin. In some instances the dates of expiration are prior to issuance of this volume; in such instances a holdover term is indicated, no new appointment having been made at time of publication of the Texas Almanac. Most positions marked "apptv." are appointive by the Governor. Where otherwise, appointing authority is designated. Most Advisory Boards are not listed. Salaries were furnished by the Legislative Budget Board and are those effective for the 1991 year.

A&M University System, Board of Regents of — (See **Texas A&M University System Board of Regents.**)

Accident Board, Industrial — (See **Industrial Accident Board.**)

Accountancy, Texas State Board of Public — (1945 with 2-year terms; reorganized 1959 as 9-member board with 6-yr. overlapping terms; number of members increased to 12 in 1979; increased to 15 in 1989); per diem and expenses; 15 members: Cynthia Barnes, Houston (01/31/97); Stanley L. Blend, San Antonio (01/31/95); Leopoldo P. Botello Jr., San Antonio (01/31/95); Roger B. Clark, Stamford (01/31/95); William R. Cox, Houston (01/31/95); Vernon D. Evans, Fort Worth (01/31/97); Carmen C. Garcia, San Antonio (01/31/97); Paul W. Hillier Jr., Dallas (01/31/93); Ladelle M. Hyman, Houston (01/31/93); Earl C. Lairson, Houston (01/31/93); John F. Lanier Jr., Austin (01/31/93); Judy J. Lee, Houston (01/31/97); William H. Quimby, Dallas (01/31/93); Ronnie Rudd, Houston (01/31/95); I. Lee Wilson, Rockwall (01/31/97). Exec. Dir., Bob E. Bradley, 1033 La Posada Dr., Ste. 340, Austin 78752-3894 (non-member) ($50,744).

Ad Valorem Tax Rate, Board to Calculate the — (1907); ex officio; term in other office; 3 members: Governor, State Comptroller of Public Accounts and State Treasurer.

Adjutant General — (1836 by Republic of Texas; present office established 1905); apptv.: William C. Wilson, Commerce (02/01/91). Box 5218, Austin 78763 ($59,790, plus house and utilities).

Adjutant General, Assistant for Air — Lester L. McIntyre, Box 5218, Austin 78763 ($56,039, plus house and utilities).

Adjutant General, Assistant for Army — Walter Jack Dingler, Box 5218, Austin 78763 ($56,039, plus house and utilities).

Administrative Judicial Districts of Texas, Presiding Judge — (Apptv. by Governor; serve terms concurrent with term as District Judge, subject to reappointment if re-elected to bench. No extra compensation: No. 1, Pat McDowell, Dallas; No. 2, Thomas J. Stovall Jr., Huntsville; No. 3, B.B. Schraub, Seguin; No. 4, John N. Cornyn, San Antonio; No. 5, Darrell Hester, Brownsville; No. 6, Sam M. Paxson, El Paso; No. 7, Weldon Kirk, Sweetwater; No. 8, Roger Jeffrey Walker, Fort Worth; No. 9, Ray D. Anderson, Brownfield.

Adult Probation Commission, Texas — (1977 as 9-member board; duties assumed by Texas Board of Criminal Justice in 1990.)

Aging, Texas Board on — (1965 as **Governor's Committee on Aging**; name changed in 1981 to present form); apptv.; 6-yr.; expenses; 9 apptv. members: Penny Butler, Houston (02/01/93); Gary R. Cook, Dallas (02/01/95); Nadine W. Francis, Austin (02/01/93); J. Kenneth Huff

Sr., Whitesboro (02/01/97); Margaret C. Luckie, Wharton (02/01/95); Jan Patterson, Dallas (02/01/95); Evelyn Porter, San Antonio (02/01/91); Dan Roberts, Fort Worth (02/01/97); James W. Roberts, Andrews (02/01/93). Exec. Dir., Polly Sowell, Box 12786, Austin 78711 (non-member) ($52,500).

Agricultural Diversification Board — (1987); 2-yr., expenses; 8 members: 2 ex officio non-voting (one each apptd. by Speaker and Lt. Gov.); 2 ex officio voting (Commissioner of Agriculture and director of Institute for International Agribusiness Studies at Prairie View A&M Univ.; 4 apptd. by Gov.: Polly Cummings, Izoro (01/01/93); Luis Mata, El Paso (01/01/93); Maurice Owens, Hempstead (01/01/93); Joe Bailey Pate Jr., Lubbock (01/01/93).

Agricultural Finance Authority, Texas — (1987); expenses; 2-yr.; 6 members: 2 ex officio: Commissioner of Agriculture and director of Institute for International Agribusiness Studies at Prairie View A&M Univ.; 4 apptd. by Governor: R. David Guerrero, Alice (01/01/93); Leodoro Martinez Jr., Cotulla (01/01/93); F. Gary Valdez, Austin (01/01/93); Mary Esther Webb, Cisco (01/01/91).

Agricultural Resources Protection Authority — (1989); 2-yr., expenses; 9 members: 7 from govt. agencies: Director, Texas Agricultural Experiment Station; Dean, College of Agricultural Sciences of Texas Tech University; Dean, University of Texas School of Public Health, Houston; Director of Environmental Epidemiology at Texas Department of Health; Chief of Groundwater Conservation section, Texas Water Commission; Dir. of Institute for International Agriculture at Prairie View A&M; Commissioner of Agriculture; 2 apptd. by gov.: W. Thomas Beard III, Alpine (02/01/91); Jane N. Saginaw, Dallas (02/01/93).

Agriculture, Commissioner of — (1907); elective; 2-yr. by original constitutional provision, term raised to 4-yr. in 1972, effective in 1975): Rick Perry, (01/01/95). Box 12847, Capitol Sta., Austin 78711-2847 ($74,698).

Air Control Board, Texas — (1965 as 6-member board; membership increased to 9 in 1967); apptv.; 6-yr.; per diem and expenses; 9 members: Bob G. Bailey, Abilene (09/01/93); John L. Blair, Kountze (09/01/91); Marcus M. Key, Houston (09/01/91); Calvin B. Parnell Jr., College Station (09/01/95); William H. Quortrup, Dallas (09/01/95); Charles H. Rivers, Pasadena (09/01/93); Warren H. Roberts, Arlington (09/01/95); Dick Whittington, Lockhart (09/01/91); Mary Ann Wyatt, Victoria (09/01/93). Exec. Dir., Steven N. Spaw, 6330 Highway 290 E., Austin 78723 (non-member) ($63,000).

Aircraft Pooling Board, State — (1979); apptv.; 6-yr.; 5 members — 2 ex officio: representative of State Auditor's Office and representative of State Purchasing and

General Services Commission; 3 apptv. — one by Gov., one by Speaker and one by Lt. Gov. Gov.'s appointee: Richard Arthur Box, Austin (01/31/95). Exec. Dir., Bob DuLaney, 4900 Old Manor Rd., Austin 78723 (non-member) ($55,157).

Alcohol and Drug Abuse, Texas Commission on — (1953 as Texas Commission on Alcoholism; name changed and membership increased to 9 in 1986); apptv.; 6-yr.; per diem and expenses; 9 members: J. Coley Cowden, Midland (06/08/93); Jerry P. Cunningham, Dallas (06/08/95); Jerry Deere, Freeport (06/08/93); Cervando Martinez Jr., San Antonio (06/08/91); Mary Lou Parsons, Odessa (06/08/95); Joe Samuel Ratliff, Houston (06/08/95); C.C. Reed, Kress (06/08/91); Randall L. Schmidt, Fort Worth (06/08/93); Robb Southerland, Austin (06/08/91). Exec. Dir., Bob Dickson, 720 Brazos, Ste. 403, Austin 78701 (non-member) ($63,000).

Alcoholic Beverage Commission, Texas — (1935 as Liquor Control Board; name changed 1970); apptv.; 6-yr.; per diem and expenses; administrator apptd. by commission; 3 members: Renee Higginbotham-Brooks, Fort Worth (11/15/95); Louis M. Pearce Jr., Houston (11/15/91); R. Allan Shivers Jr., Austin (11/15/93). Admin., Sherman McBeath, Box 13127, Austin 78711 (non-member) ($68,250).

Alzheimer's Disease and Related Disorders, Council on — (1987); 2- yr.; expenses; 17 members: 5 agency heads or their designees: Depts. of Aging, Health, Human Services, Mental Health and Mental Retardation and the Long-Term Care Coordinating Council for the Elderly. Lt. Gov. appts. 2 public and 2 professional members; Speaker appts. 1 public and 3 professional members; Gov. appts. 2 public and 2 professional: J. Howard Frederick, San Antonio (09/01/92); Betty Haisten, Beaumont (09/01/92); S.T. Harris, Dallas (09/01/91); Donald E. Moss, El Paso (09/01/91).

Angelina and Neches River Authority, Board of Directors — (1935 as Sabine-Neches Conservation Dist.; reorganized 1950 and name changed to Neches River Conservation Dist.; changed to present name in 1977); apptv.; expenses; 6-yr.; 9 members: William S. Lilly, Nacogdoches (09/05/91); Harold C. Maxwell, Diboll (09/05/95); Wendel Carl Messec, Henderson (09/05/93); George F. Middlebrook III, Nacogdoches (09/05/95); C. Wayland Quisenberry, Lufkin (09/05/95); Joe E. Rich Sr., Lufkin (09/05/93); Paul Richard Riehle, Lufkin (09/05/91); Joyce Swearingen, Nacogdoches (09/05/93); Walter R. Volz, Jacksonville (09/05/95). Gen. Mgr., Gary L. Neighbors, Box 387, Lufkin 75902-0387 (non-member).

Animal Health Commission, Texas — (1893 as Texas Livestock Sanitary Commission; name changed in 1959, membership increased to 9 in 1973; raised to 12 in 1983); apptv.; per diem and expenses; 6-yr.; 12 members: Delvin R. Barrett, Bryan (09/06/91); Donald Lee Berend, Wichita Falls (09/06/95); John S. Cargile, San Antonio (09/06/91); Joe B. Hathoot, Canadian (09/06/91); Claude J. Kelley Jr., Fredericksburg (09/06/95); Allan C. Oltjen, Canyon (09/06/93); James B. Owen, Tyler (09/06/91); Florence Rieck, Roosevelt (09/06/95); Bruce Benjamin Rigler, Plainview (09/06/93); Sparks Rust Jr., Del Rio (09/06/95); James D. Sartwelle, Houston (09/06/91); Gaye Lynn Seawright, DeSoto (09/06/93). Exec. Dir., Dr. John W. Holcombe, Box 12966, Austin 78711 (non-member) ($65,100).

Antiquities Committee — (1969 as 7-member board; membership increased to 9 in 1983); apptv.; per diem and expenses; 2-yr.; 9 members — 6 ex officio, term in other office: Chmn., Texas Historical Commission; Dir., State Parks and Wildlife Dept.; Commissioner of General Land Office; State Archeologist; State Engineer-Dir., State Department of Highways and Public Transportation; and Exec. Dir., Texas Dept. of Water Resources; 3 apptv. members: Randolph P. "Mike" Campbell, Denton (01/31/91); Anne E. Fox, San Antonio (01/31/91); D. Ryan Smith, Canyon (01/31/91). Staff Dir., J. Barto Arnold III, P.O. Box 12276, Austin 78711.

Architectural Examiners, Texas Board of — (1937 as 3-member board; raised to 6 members in 1951; membership increased to 9 in 1977); apptv.; 6-yr.; per diem and expenses; 9 members: Dee Lynn Aguilar, Fort Worth (01/31/93); Earl P. Broussard Jr., Austin (01/31/93); Morris Allen Graves, Houston (01/31/91); James M. Langford, El Paso (01/31/91); Thomas W. Parker, Bryan (01/31/93); George Ray Rodgers, Marshall (01/31/95); Cleveland Turner III, Amarillo (01/31/95); Bobbie Joe Wise Jr., San Antonio (01/31/95); Jerry E. Yancey, Plano (01/31/95). Exec. Dir., Robert H. Norris, 8213 Shoal Creek Blvd., Ste. 107, Austin 78758 (non-member) ($50,744).

Arts and Industries (A&I), Texas College of — (See University System of South Texas.)

Arts, Texas Commission on the — (1965 as Texas Fine Arts Commission; name changed to **Texas Commission on the Arts and Humanities** and membership increased to 18 in 1971; name changed to present form in 1979); apptv.; 6-yr.; expenses; 18 members: Richard Alvarado, El Paso (08/31/95); Kenneth E. Bentsen, Houston (08/31/91); Margaret B. Brown, Waco (08/31/87); Kenneth Q. Carlile, Marshall (08/31/91); Alice Carrington, San Antonio (08/31/93); George Ann Carter, Fort Worth (08/31/95); Ruth Fox, Austin (08/31/95); Robert L. Gerry, Houston (08/31/93); Lisa Hembry, Dallas (08/31/95); William J. Hill, Houston (08/31/95); Mary Ellen Jericho, Dallas (08/31/93); Adair W. Margo, El Paso (08/31/93); Henry S. Miller Jr., Dallas (08/31/91); Martha W. Morriss, Texarkana (08/31/93); Aaronetta H. Pierce, San Antonio (08/31/91); Frances Annette Strake, Houston (08/31/93); James D. Tittle, Abilene (08/31/95); Jeffrey Weiss, Dallas (08/31/91). Exec. Dir., John Paul Batiste, Box 13406, Austin 78711 (non-member) ($50,400).

Athletic Trainers, Advisory Board of — (1971 as Texas Board of Athletic Trainers; name changed and membership increased to 6 in 1973); expenses; 6-yr.; 6 members: Sanford E. Miller, Nacogdoches (01/31/93); James Glenn Murray, Lubbock (01/31/93); Wilford F. Pickard Jr., Bryan (01/31/91); Cynthia Louise Raines, El Paso (01/31/89); Michael Kay Stephens, Austin (01/31/91); Thomas D. Wilson Jr., Houston (01/31/95). Exec. Secy., Allen Eggert, Texas Department of Health, 1100 W. 49th, Austin 78756.

Attorney General, State — (1836 by original Constitution of Republic of Texas, 1876 by present Constitution); elective; (2-yr. by original Constitution; term raised to 4-yr. in 1972, effective 1975): Dan Morales, (01/01/95). Box 12548, Austin 78711 ($74,698).

Attorney, State's — Apptv.: Robert Huttash, Box 12405, Austin 78711 ($77,490).

Auditor, State — (1929); apptv. by Legislative Audit Committee, a joint Senate-House committee; 2-yr.: Lawrence F. Alwin, Houston. Office Address: Box 12067, Austin 78711 ($66,950).

Automated Information and Telecommunications Council — (1981); apptv.; 2-yr; expenses; 7 members: 3 apptd. by Gov., 2 apptd. by Lt. Gov., and 2 apptd by Speaker. Gov.'s apptees.: Gary L. Hammon, San Antonio (02/01/91); Donald A. Maxwell, College Station (02/01/93); Nancy Norris, Austin (02/01/89). Exec. Dir., Jo King McCrorey, Box 13564, Austin 78711 (non-member) ($31,518).

Aviation, Texas Board of — (1989); replaced **Aeronautics Commission;** apptv.; per diem and expenses; 6 members: Oliver Kendall Kelley, Amarillo (02/01/93); Dennis A. Blackburn, Kingwood (02/01/97); Charles D. Nash Sr., Austin (02/01/95); Stephanie R. Roberts, Tyler (02/01/93); Zena Rucker, Grapevine (02/01/97); Elton Rust, Waring (02/01/95). Exec. Dir., C.A. (Clay) Wilkins, Dept. of Aviation, Box 12607, Austin 78711.

Bandera County River Authority — (1971); apptv.; 6-yr.; expenses; 9 members: Phillip F. Becker, Bandera (01/31/93); Jose Manuel Cantu, Pipe Creek (01/31/93); Morgan Keith Cox, Bandera (01/31/91); Tom Denyer, Bandera (01/31/91); J.B. Edwards, Pipe Creek (01/31/95); Paul Garrison Jr., Medina (01/31/93); Don E. Karr, Bandera (01/31/89); Joel K. Leighton, Vanderpool (01/31/95); Craig A. Tips, Bandera (01/31/93). Exec. Dir., Ray Buck, P.O. Box 771, Bandera 78003.

Banking Board, State — (1909); 2 ex officio members, term in other office: Commissioner of Banking and State Treasurer; one apptd. by Gov. for 2 years: George Willeford III, Austin (01/31/93). Office Address: 2601 N. Lamar, Austin 78705.

Banking Commissioner, State — (1923); apptv. by State Finance Commission; 2-yr.: Kenneth W. Littlefield, 2601 N. Lamar, Austin 78705 ($84,941). (See also **Finance Commission of Texas.**)

Bar of Texas, State — (1939 as administrative arm of Supreme Court); 30 members elected by membership; 3-yr. terms; expenses paid from dues collected from membership. President, president-elect, vice president and immediate past president serve as ex officio members. Exec. Dir., Karen H. Johnson, Box 12487, Austin 78711 (non-member).

Barber Examiners, State Board of — (1929 as 3- member board; membership increased in 1975); apptv.; 6-yr.; per diem and expenses; 6 members: Sharon Jeschke Carper, Lubbock (01/31/95); David B. McCall, Austin (01/31/93); Santa Robles Morales, Brownsville (01/31/93); Helen Spears, Dallas (01/31/95); Joe Wiley Turner, Midland (01/31/91); Thelma R. Walker, Fort Worth (01/31/91). Exec. Dir., Jo King McCrorey, 9101

Burnet Rd., Ste. 103, Austin 78758 ($36,750).

Battleship Texas Advisory Board — (1983; superseded Battleship Texas Commission); apptv.; 6-yr.; 9 members: Charles A. Alcorn, Houston (02/01/95); Richard Burton Ballanfant, Houston (02/01/95); Mike P. Cokinos, Beaumont (02/01/91); Caroline K. Gregory, Houston (02/01/91); David A. Jones, Houston (02/01/91); Robert O. Miller, Houston (02/01/93); Aileen D. Rains, Houston (02/01/93); George W. Strake III, Houston (02/01/95); Robert L. Waldrop, Houston (02/01/93). Office Address: 3527 Battleground Rd., LaPorte 77571.

Blind and Severely Disabled Persons, Commission on Purchases of Products of — (1979); apptv.; 2-yr.; 9 members: Marilyn P. Abercrombie, Conroe (01/31/91); Ronald Wayne Arnett, Georgetown (01/31/91); Carl Cagle, Corpus Christi (01/31/91); Gibson M. DuTerroil, Houston (01/31/91); John Albert Fenoglio, Austin (01/31/91); Mearl Zeek Harris, Austin (01/31/91); Barbara Pace, Jasper (01/31/91); Michael T. Phillips, Austin (01/31/91); Marion Truitt, Abilene (01/31/91); Roger G. Welsch, Austin (01/31/91).

Blind, Governing Board of the Texas School for the — (1979); apptv.; 6-yr.; expenses; 9 members: Mary G. Behnke, Orange (01/31/91); Dr. Michael Connolly, Nacogdoches (01/31/93); Marcia M. Grimsley, Austin (01/31/95); Chris D. Prentice, Lubbock (01/31/95); Crispin E. Sanchez, Laredo (01/31/95); Olivia C. Schonberger, El Paso (01/31/93); Virginia Sowell, Lubbock (01/31/91); Dr. Nalin H. Tolia, Odessa (01/31/93); Don Welch, Dallas (01/31/91). Exec. Dir., Dr. Philip H. Haden, 1110 W. 45th, Austin 78756 (non-member) ($56,700).

Blind, Texas Commission for the — (1931 as 6-member State Commission for the Blind; raised to 9 members in 1979; name changed in 1985); apptv.; 6-yr.; expenses; 9 members: Dr. James L. Caldwell, Austin (02/01/95); Kyle Lance Fulton, Lubbock (02/01/93); C. Robert Keeney Jr., Houston (02/01/93); Ann Masterson, Houston (02/01/95); Robert Peters, Tyler (02/01/91); Carol Santry, San Angelo (02/01/95); Lewis Timberlake, Austin (02/01/91); John M. Turner, Dallas (02/01/91); Leahray S. Wroten, McKinney (02/01/93). Exec. Dir., Pat D. Westbrook, Box 12866, Austin 78711 (non-member) ($61,425).

Board of — (Note: In most instances, state boards are alphabetized under specific reference word, as Accountancy, Texas State Board of Public.)

Brazos River Authority, Board of Directors — (1929 as Brazos River Conservation and Reclamation Dist.; name changed to present form in 1953); apptv.; 6-yr; expenses; 21 members: James C. Atkins Jr., Lake Jackson (02/01/93); Deborah H. Bell, Abilene (02/01/93); Chauncey L. Bogan, Seabrook (02/01/93); Robert G. Boone, Burleson (02/01/91); Brad Crawford, Lubbock (02/01/93); Perry V. Dalby, Salado (02/01/93); Charles J. Farrar, Dublin (02/01/95); Ramiro A. Galindo, Bryan (02/01/95); James J. Gibson, Guthrie (02/01/97); Robert E. Hebert, Sugar Land (02/01/95); Jesse Lee Hibbetts Jr., Lake Jackson (02/01/95); Don T. Kearby, Mineral Wells (02/01/91); Art King, Bryan (02/01/95); John H. Mills, Round Rock (02/01/91); Charles Moser, Brenham (02/01/91); Lyndon Olson Sr., Waco (02/01/97); Robert K. Pace, Wichita Falls (02/01/95); Ruth Schiermeyer, Lubbock (02/01/95); Chester R. Upham III, Mineral Wells (02/01/93); John M. Wehby, Taylor (02/01/91); James F. Wood, Woodway (02/01/93). Gen. Mgr., Carson H. Hoge, Box 7555, Waco 76714 (non-member).

Canadian River Compact Commissioner — (1951); apptv.; salary and expenses; (his function is to negotiate with other states respecting waters of the Canadian). See also Interstate Compact Commission and Caddo Lake Compact Commission: John C. Sims, Lubbock (12/31/91). ($10,149).

Canvassers, State Board of — (1897); 2 ex officio members, term in other office: Governor and Secretary of State; one apptd. by Gov. for 2-yr. term: Billie Jean Carr, Houston (02/01/93). Office Address: Secretary of State's Office, Capitol Bldg., Austin 78701.

Central Colorado River Authority — (See Colorado River Authority, Central.)

Chemist, Texas State — (1911); ex officio, indefinite term: W.Y. Cobb. Texas Agricultural Experiment Station, Box 3160, College Station 77841.

Child Abuse and Neglect Prevention, Council on — (1985); apptv.; 2-yr.; expenses; 9 members: W. B. Howard, Houston (09/01/91); Don T. O'Bannon Jr., Dallas (09/01/91); Ben G. Raimer, Texas City (09/01/95); Michael Atlee Reilly, Arlington (09/01/91); Celia M. Salomons, San Antonio (09/01/95); Mary B. Scruggs, Plano (09/01/91); Emily B. Shelton, Lufkin (09/01/93); Peggy

B. Smith, Houston (09/01/95); Roy Edward Turner Jr., Amarillo (09/01/93).

Childhood Intervention Services, Interagency Council on Early — (1981); apptv.; 2-yr.; 5 members — one apptd. by Gov., one each by Dept. of Health, Dept. of MHMR, Dept. of Human Services and Texas Education Agency. Gov's. apptee: Janet D. Holliday, San Antonio (02/01/91). Acting Administrator, Louise Iscoe, Dept. of Health, 1100 W. 49th, Austin 78756 (non-member).

Chiropractic Examiners, Texas State Board of — (1949); apptv.; 6-yr.; expenses; 9 members: David E. Albracht, Amarillo (04/26/93); George Aubert, Tomball (08/03/95); James E. Franklin, San Antonio (04/26/93); Nancy Z. Jones, Dallas (08/03/95); Ben H. Proctor, Fort Worth (08/03/91); V.C. Salyer Jr., Dublin (08/03/91); Dennis Wayne Teal, Canton (08/03/91); Raymond G. Wheless, Plano (04/26/93); John H. Wright, Houston (08/03/95). Exec. Dir., Jennie Smetana, 8716 MoPac Expy. North, Ste. 301, Austin 78759 (non-member) ($29,400).

Coastal Water Authority, Board of Directors — (1967 as Coastal Industrial Water Authority, Board of Directors of; name changed in 1985); 7 members — 4 to be appointed by mayor of Houston with advice and consent of governing body of Houston; 3 apptd. by Gov.; per diem and expenses; 2-yr.; Gov's. appointees: Buster E. French, Dayton (03/31/92); R. Wayne Smith, Houston (04/01/91); Terry D. Williamson, Baytown (04/01/91). Exec. Dir., Ralph T. Rundle, Citicorp Center, 1200 Smith, Ste. 2260, Houston 77002 (non-member).

College Opportunity Act Committee — (1989); 6-yr.; 9 members: 6 ex officio: Commissioner, General Land Office; Exec. Admin., Texas Water Development Board; Comptroller; State Treasurer; Exec. Dir., Bond Review Board; Commissioner of Higher Education. 3 apptd.: Barbara J. Dugas-Patterson, Houston (02/01/97); Linda Perryman, Dallas (02/01/93); W. Ted Shaw, Dallas (02/01/95).

Colorado River Authority, Central, Board of Directors — (1935); apptv.; 6-yr.; per diem on duty; 9 members: Robert J. Cheaney II, Santa Ana (02/01/93); Zeno Hemphill, Coleman (02/01/95); Clifford L. Horn, Talpa (02/01/93); Cloyce M. Huckabee, Coleman (02/01/95); Ross L. Jones, Coleman (02/01/95); Nicholas J. Knox, Burkett (02/01/93); O.R. Lawlis, Coleman (02/01/91); Louis Pittard, Gouldbusk (02/01/91); Jim Bob Thweatt, Coleman (02/01/91). Operations Mgr., Laneal Maedgen, Box 964, Coleman 76834 (non-member).

Colorado River Authority, Lower, Board of Directors — (1934 as 9-member board; membership increased in 1951 and 1975); apptv.; 6-yr.; per diem on duty; 15 members: Lawrence Roy Bandy, Luling (02/01/93); Raymond F. Barker, Kerrville (02/01/97); J. Randall Grimes, Georgetown (02/01/93); John H. Hill, Cypress Mill (02/01/95); J.M. Johnson Jr., Eagle Lake (02/01/93); Ray S. Knox, Blanco (02/01/95); Burton B. Letulle, Bay City (02/01/97); Cecil B. Long, Bastrop (02/01/95); Michael J. Lucksinger, Burnet (02/01/93); Alexander Hamilton Massad, Austin (02/01/95); Betty Jo Miller, San Saba (02/01/97); Neal L. Norris Jr., Kingsland (02/01/93); Charles Patrick Oles Jr., Austin (02/01/95); Rita Myatt Radley, El Campo (02/01/93). Gen. Mgr., Mark Rose, Box 220, Austin 78767 (non-member).

Colorado River Authority, Upper, Board of Directors — (1935 as 9-member board; reorganized in 1965); apptv.; 6-yr.; per diem and expenses; indefinite number of members: George Ray Alderman, Winters (02/01/95); William J. Cervenka, Ballinger (02/01/91); Victor Wayne Choate, San Angelo (02/01/97); James David Clendennen, Silver (02/01/95); Harry B. Elam, San Angelo (02/01/95); Frances G. Pierce, Bronte (02/01/93); Brian C. Richards, Ballinger (02/01/93); Carl S. Strain, San Angelo (02/01/93); Patricia Ivey, Robert Lee (02/01/97). Office Address: P.O. Box 680, Ballinger 76821.

Commerce, Texas Department of — (1987); apptv.; 6-yr.; 6 members: Ernesto Ancira Jr., San Antonio (02/01/95); Vanessa Diane Gilmore, Houston (02/01/93); Alan R. Kahn, Dallas (02/01/97); James R. Lesch, Houston (02/01/95); J. Jorge Verduzco, Laredo (02/01/97); Edward O. Vetter, Dallas (02/01/95). Interim Exec. Dir., Cathy Bonner, Box 12728, Austin 78711 (non-member) ($74,970).

Commissioner of — (See keyword, as Agriculture, Commissioner of.)

Comptroller of Public Accounts — (1835 by Provisional Government of Texas, 1876 by present Constitution); elective; (2-yr. by original Constitution; term raised to 4-yr. in 1972, effective 1975): John Sharp, (02/01/95). LBJ State Office Bldg., Austin 78774 ($74,698).

Concho River Water and Soil Conservation Authority, Lower — (1939); 6-yr.; 9 members: Leroy Paul Beach, Millersview (02/01/93); Emmett H. Brosig Jr., Paint Rock (02/01/91); Howard E. Loveless, Eden (02/01/93); Billy J. Mikeska, Eola (02/01/93); Benjamin O. Sims, Paint Rock (02/01/97); Alton R. Taylor, Eden (02/01/95); Edwin T. Tickle, Paint Rock (02/01/95); T.E. Wells, Paint Rock (02/01/91); Harvey P. Williams, Eola (02/01/95). Office Address: Paint Rock 76866.

Conservation Foundation, Texas — (1969 as 12-member board; membership reduced to 6 in 1979); apptv.; expenses; 6-yr.; 6 members — 3 ex officio, term in other office: Exec. Dir., Parks and Wildlife Dept.; Commissioner of General Land Office; Exec. Dir., Texas Historical Commission; one each apptd. by Gov., Lt. Gov. and Speaker — Gov's. apptee.: R.C. Allen, Corpus Christi (06/13/93). Office Address: Box 12845, Austin 78711.

Conservatorship Board, State — (1979); apptv.; expenses; 6-yr.; 3 members: Georgina F. Gonzalez, Houston (01/31/93); William Wayne Kilgarlin, Austin (01/31/95); Joseph F. Phillips, Mission (01/31/93).

Corrections, Texas Board of — (1885 as **Texas Prison Board**; superseded **Superintendent of Penitentiaries**, est. in 1849; name changed to Texas Board of Corrections, 1957; duties assumed by Texas Board of Criminal Justice in 1990.

Cosmetology Commission, Texas — (1935 as 3-member **State Board of Hairdressers and Cosmetologists**; name changed and membership increased to 6 apptv. and one ex officio in 1971); apptv.; per diem and expenses; 6-yr.: Lois Miriam Cohen, Graford (12/31/93); Lucille C. Garcia, San Antonio (12/31/91); Evelyn Aileen Hunter, Dallas (12/31/93); Ronald McGehee, Bedford (12/31/91); Nedum C. Muns III, Huntsville (12/31/95); Sergio Shearer, Edinburg (12/31/95). Exec. Dir., Ron Resech, 1111 Rio Grande, Austin 78701 (non-member) ($42,000).

Counselors, Texas State Board of Examiners of Professional — (1981); apptv.; 6-yr.; expenses; 9 members: Daniel W. Adams, Corpus Christi (02/01/91); Rodolfo Arredondo Jr., Lubbock (02/01/91); Julian L. Biggers Jr., Lubbock (02/01/95); Carol E. Champion, Brownsville (02/01/91); Jane Bock Guzman, Dallas (02/01/95); Yvonne Kohutek, San Antonio (02/01/93); Nancy Avery Pressler, Houston (02/01/93); Norma Lee Walston, Austin (02/01/95); Robert Dean Wyrick, Cedar Hill (02/01/93). Exec. Sec., Don Rettberg, 1100 W. 49th, Austin 78756-3183 (non-member).

Court Reporters Certification Board — (1977 as 9-member **Texas Reporters Committee**; name changed to present form and membership increased to 12 in 1983); apptv. by State Supreme Court; 6-yr.; expenses; 12 members: Ronald C. Bird, San Antonio (12/31/86); Charles Griggs, Sweetwater (12/31/90); Joseph H. Hart, Austin (12/31/88); Linda Hyde, Austin (12/31/86); David B. Jackson, Dallas (12/31/90); John M. Keel, Austin (12/31/88); Judy Kulhanek, Houston (12/31/90); Jack B. Moorhead, Houston (12/31/86); Louise Morse, Austin (12/31/88); Jean Nipper, Austin (12/31/90); Tom Prentice, Austin (12/31/86); Jerry Spence, Big Spring (12/31/88). Exec. Secy., Peg Liedtke, Box 13131, Austin 78711 (non-member).

Credit Union Commission — (1949 as 3- member **Credit Union Advisory Commission**; name changed and membership increased to 6 in 1969; increased to 9 in 1981); apptv.; 6-yr.; expenses; 9 members: Gilbert E. Andrews, El Paso (02/15/93); Barbara Fry Arnold, Odessa (02/15/91); Gerald W. Gurney, Plano (02/15/95); Terry R. Stapleton, Houston (02/15/97); Wilfred Navarro, Houston (02/15/95); Jimmy F. Sasser, Edinburg (02/15/93); Gerald R. Sheets, Robstown (02/15/91); Donald Greg Storch, Houston (02/15/93); Joe G. Thornton, Texarkana (02/15/95). Commissioner, John R. Hale, 914 E. Anderson Lane, Austin 78752-1699 (non-member) ($82,735).

Crime Stoppers Advisory Council — (1981); apptv.; 2-yr.; 5 members: Robert B. Aguirre, San Antonio (09/01/91); Sam J. Chase, Abilene (09/01/93); Donald Ray Geen, Lumberton (09/01/91); John Keith McKissick, Forney (09/01/91); H. Dean Wilkerson, Coppell (09/01/91).

Criminal Justice, Texas Board of — (1989: assumed duties of former Texas Board of Corrections and Adult Probation Commission; also oversees Board of Pardons and Paroles Division); apptd; 6-yr.; expenses; 9 members: Joshua W. Allen Sr., Beaumont (02/01/97); James Eller, Bryan (02/01/93); Clarence M. Stevenson, Victoria (02/01/95); Ellen J. Halbert, Austin (02/01/97); Selden B. Hale III, Amarillo (02/01/97); Jerry H. Hodge,

Amarillo (02/01/95); Alan Polunsky, San Antonio (02/01/95); Mamie Moore Proctor, Houston (02/01/93); F.L. Stephens, San Angelo (02/01/93). Exec. Dir., James A. Lynaugh, P.O. Box 13084, Austin 78711.

Deaf, Governing Board of the Texas School for the — Trena L. Baxley, Livingston (01/31/91); Allan F. Bubeck Jr., Garland (01/31/95); Beatrice M. Burke, Big Spring (01/31/95); Nancy Ellen Munger, Kyle (01/31/95); Robert B. Neely, Dallas (01/31/93); Gary Adrian Utley, Baytown (01/31/93); Polly Piercy Walton, Beaumont (01/31/91); Ralph H. White, Austin (01/31/97).

Deaf, Texas Commission for the — (1971 as 6-member board; membership raised to 9 in 1979); apptv.; 6-yr.; expenses; 9 members — 3 deaf persons, 2 parents of deaf, 2 professionals serving deaf and 2 from general public: Clyde S. Black, Temple (01/31/93); Sidney J. Braquet, Houston (01/31/91); Gwendel D. Butler, Austin (01/31/95); Donald Howard England, Austin (01/31/95); Mary Helen Haltom, Fort Worth (01/31/91); Melinda Fry McKee, Waco (01/31/93); Thalia H. Munoz, Rio Grande City (01/31/93); Ann M. Phillips, Dallas (01/31/91); Ruth T. Seeger, Austin (01/31/97). Exec. Dir., Larry D. Evans, Box 12904, Austin 78711 (non-member) ($47,250).

Dental Examiners, Texas State Board of — (1919 as 6-member dental board; increased to 9 members in 1971; increased to 12 in 1981); appt.; 6-yr.; per diem while on duty; 12 members: James L. Bolton, Borger (05/10/95); Roger Byrne, Corpus Christi (05/10/93); Terry Daniel Dickinson, Houston (05/10/91); Clara Hoffman, Dallas (05/10/91); E. Penn Jackson, San Antonio (05/10/95); William J. Kemp, Haskell (05/10/91); Charles T. Ku, Flower Mound (05/10/93); James W. Orr, Austin (05/10/95); I.J. Patterson Jr., Longview (05/10/95); Sam H. Rabon, Kingsville (05/10/91); Ronald Hughes Shamblin, Jasper (05/10/93); Mary Christine Spinks, Houston (05/10/93). Exec. Dir., Crockett Camp, 327 Congress, Ste. 500, Austin 78701 (non-member) ($51,626).

Depository Board, State — (1905); 3 ex officio, term in other office: State Treasurer, Banking Commissioner, Comptroller, one apptd. by Gov. for 2- yr. term: Dorothy Jean Alcorn, Victoria (08/31/93); Debbie Hanna, Austin (08/31/89); Clarence F. Kendall II, Houston (08/31/91); Xavier C. Lemond, Katy (08/31/91); Jose Molina, Houston (08/31/89); Robert Lee Monaghan, Midland (08/22/91); Ralph E. Reamer, Houston (08/31/91); Don A. Sanders, Houston (08/31/89). Office Address: P.O. Box 12608, Austin 78711.

Developmental Disabilities, Texas Planning Council for — (1971); apptv.; 6-yr.; 27 members — 8 ex offico: Representatives from Dept. of Mental Health and Mental Retardation, Rehabilitation Commission, Dept. of Health, Dept. of Human Services, Texas Dept. on Aging, Texas Education Agency, Texas Commission for the Blind, Texas Commission for the Deaf; 19 apptv. members: Ronnie N. Alexander, San Antonio (02/01/91); Oscar P. Bobbitt, Austin (02/01/93); Mary Jane Clark, Pharr (02/01/91); Tom Deliganis, San Antonio (02/01/95); Debbie B. Francis, Dallas (02/01/95); Jerry Glenn Hassell, Austin (02/01/91); J. Robert Hester Jr., Arlington (02/01/95); Aaron Wells Howard, Houston (02/01/92); Theda N. Hoyt, Cypress (02/01/95); Angela K. Lamb, Amarillo (02/01/91); Federico Marquez, El Paso (02/01/97); James McBryde, Abilene (02/01/95); Guy McCrary, Midland (02/01/93); Shirley Ann Menard, Schertz (02/01/91); Hector Saenz, San Antonio (02/01/91); E. Darlene Topp, Harlingen (02/01/93); James E. Vaughn, Humble (02/01/95); Leota G. Veenker, Coppell (02/01/93); Jerijean W. Work, Rusk (02/01/95). Exec. Dir., Roger A. Webb, 4900 N. Lamar, Austin 78751 (non-member).

Diabetes Council, Texas — (1983; with 5 ex officio and 8 public members; changed to present configuration in 1987); 2-yr.; 11 members — 3 ex officio; 8 public members as follows: Michelle C. Cross, Austin (02/01/91); H. Clay Dahlberg, Hunt (02/01/92); Jaime A. Davidson, Dallas (02/01/92); Robert S. Davidson, Midland (02/01/91); Ernest Deal, Dallas (02/01/92); Charles R. Gregg, Houston (02/01/91); Maurilia F. Rodriguez, Brownsville (02/01/92); Michael P. Stern, San Antonio (02/01/91). Office Address: Texas Dept. of Health, 1100 W. 49th, Austin 78756.

Dietitians, Texas State Board of Examiners of — (1983); apptv.; 6-yr.; per diem and expenses; 9 members: 3 from general public and 6 licensed dieticians: Lydia Damrel, Vidor (09/01/93); Pattye Greer, Nacogdoches (09/01/91); James T. Moore, Austin (09/01/91); Helen P. O'Reilly, Richardson (09/01/93); Cheryl Porter, Midland (09/01/95); Gracie Specks, Temple (09/01/91); Johnnie Ruth Stripling, Tyler (09/01/91);

Jeanne Marie Vier, Austin (09/01/95); Alana Davis Webb, Austin (09/01/93). Office Address: Texas Dept. of Health, 1100 W. 49th, Austin 78756.

Disabilities, Council on — (1983); apptv. as indicated; 2-yr.; 21 members: 4 apptd. by Lt. Gov., 4 by Speaker; one member each from Dept. of Human Services, Dept. of Mental Health and Mental Retardation, Dept. of Health, Texas Education Agency, Texas Rehabilitation Commission, Texas Commission for the Deaf, State Commission for the Blind, Texas Dept. on Aging, Texas Commission on Alcoholism; 4 apptd. by Gov. as follows: Mary Carolyn Knott, El Paso (01/31/91); Marvin Richard Marek Jr., San Antonio (01/31/91); Linda Parker, Harper (01/31/91); Martha Wynne, Dallas (01/31/91).

East Texas State University, Board of Regents — (1969); apptv.; 6-yr.; 9 members: John R. Armstrong, Bonham (02/15/95); Raymond B. Cameron, Rockwall (02/15/97); Kerry Noble Cammack, Longview (02/15/95); Robert Kyle Campbell, Dallas (02/15/93); Sally R. Lancaster, Dallas (02/15/91); William Davis Norton, Tyler (02/15/93); Karl C. Rove, Austin (02/15/95); Demetris A. Sampson, Dallas (02/15/97); William T. Taylor III, Houston (02/15/97). Pres., Dr. Jerry Morris, ETSU, Commerce 75429 (non-member).

Economic Development Commission, Texas — (Merged into **Texas Department of Commerce**, 1987.

Economy & Efficiency in State Government, Texas Comm. on — George Beto, Huntsville (09/01/89); Joe Christie, Austin (09/01/89).

Education, Board of Control for Southern Regional — (1969); apptv.; 4-yr.; 5 members: Gov. ex officio, 4 apptd.: Kent Grusendorf, Arlington, Dallas (06/30/93); Carl A. Parker, Austin (06/30/92); Dr. William J. Teague, Abilene (06/30/91); Mike Toomey, Austin (06/30/94). Pres., Southern Regional Education Board, 592 10th St. N.W., Atlanta, GA 30318-5790.

Education, Commissioner of — (1866 as Superintendent of Public Instruction; 1949 changed to present name by Gilmer-Aiken Law); apptv. by **State Board of Education**; 4-yr.: Lionel R. Meno. ($114,474) (See also **Education, State Board of**.)

Education, State Board of — (1866; re-created 1928 and re-formed by **Gilmer-Aikin Act** in 1949 to consist of 21 elective members from districts co-extensive with 21 congressional districts at that time; membership increased to 24 with congressional redistricting in 1971, effective 1973; membership increased to 27 with congressional redistricting in 1981, effective 1983; reorganized by special legislative session as 15-member apptv. board in 1984 to become elective board again in 1988); expenses; 4-yr.; all terms expire 1-1-93; 15 members (numerals before names indicate district numbers): (1) Rene Nunez, El Paso; (2) Mary Helen Berlanga, Corpus Christi; (3) Esteban Sosa, San Antonio; (4) Ray Alexander, Houston; (5) John H. Shields, San Antonio; (6) Jack Christie, Houston; (7) Carolyn H. Crawford, Beaumont; (8) Mary Perkins, Lufkin; (9) A. M. Aikin, Commerce; (10) Will Davis, Austin; (11) Jane Nelson, Lewisville; (12) Geraldine "Tincy" Miller, Dallas; (13) Dr. Emmett Conrad, Dallas; (14) William Hudson, Wichita Falls; (15) Monte Hasie, Lubbock. Office Address: Texas Education Agency, 1701 N. Congress Ave., Austin 78701-1494. (See also **Commissioner of Education**.)

Educational Excellence Committee — (1989); apptv.; 6-yrs.; 15 members: Edward B. Adams, Austin (02/01/93); Brenda F. Arnett, Houston (02/01/93); Patti Clapp, Dallas (02/01/95); Yvonne A. Ewell, Dallas (02/01/97); Irene M. Garcia, Mission (02/01/91); Jacqueline R. Goettsche, Fredericksburg (02/01/97); Nancy Ann Loeffler, San Antonio (02/01/95); Dan Frank Long, Georgetown (02/01/93); Roger C. Minard, Austin (02/01/93); Maxine J. Nance, Atlanta (02/01/97); Bette A. Noble, Victoria (02/01/95); Winston C. Power Jr., Dallas (02/01/95); Donald Reynolds, Goodrich (02/01/91); Glenda Smith, Austin (02/01/91); Larry J. Ward, Richardson (02/01/95).

Egg Marketing Advisory Board — (1957); apptv.; 6-yr.; 11 members — 2 ex officio: Commissioner of Agriculture is chairman, one apptd. by head of Poultry Science Dept., Texas A&M University; 9 apptv.: Roderick L. Benner, San Antonio (09/27/93); Jack Wilson Evans Jr., Dallas (09/27/93); Kervin E. Jacob, Houston (09/27/91); David M. Jenkins, La Grange (09/27/95); Hobert H. Joe, Houston (09/27/95); Terry A. Legan, Dallas (09/27/95); Ernest A. Mahard, Prosper (09/27/93); Emil W. Plasek, Waco (09/27/91); Kenneth R. Vaughan, San Antonio (09/27/91).

Election Commission, State — (1973); 9 members, ex officio and apptv. as indicated: Chmn. of Democratic State Executive Committee; Chmn. of Republican State Executive Committee; Chief Justice of Supreme Court; Presiding Judge, Court of Criminal Appeals; 2 persons to be named, one a justice of the Court of Appeals appointed by Chief Justice of Supreme Court, one a District Judge apptd. by presiding judge of Court of Criminal Appeals; 2 county chairmen, one each from Democratic and Republican parties, named by the parties; Secretary of State.

Emergency Communications, Advisory Commission on State — (1985); expenses; 17 members — 5 ex offico: exec. dir's. of Texas Advisory Commission on Intergovernmental Relations, Depts. of Health, Public Safety, Criminal Justice Policy Council and the major association representing regional planning commissions; 12 public members: 8 apptd. by Gov., 2 by Lt. Gov., 2 by Speaker. Gov's. apptees: Vaughn R. Aldredge, Austin (09/01/93); George E. Cook, Dallas (09/01/91); Patrick A. Craven, Buda (09/01/93); William Charles Deere, Dallas (09/01/91); Ron Harris, Plano (09/01/91); John William Munn, Fort Worth (09/01/93); John P. Schneider Jr., Austin (09/01/95); Mrs. Lee Walker, Denton (09/01/93). Exec. Dir., Mary A. Boyd, 1101 Capital of Texas Hwy., S., Ste. B-100, Austin 78746.

Employee Incentive Commission — (Merged with the Productivity and Bonus Commission into new **Texas Incentive and Productivity Commission** in 1989.)

Employment Commission, Texas — (1936); apptv.; $79,800; 6-yr.; 3 members: Charles E. Haddock, Seagoville (02/01/93); James J. Kaster, Austin (02/01/95); Mary Scott Nabers, Austin (02/01/91). Admin., William Grossenbacher, 638 TEC Bldg., 101 E. 15th, Austin 78778 (non-member) ($77,700).

Engineers, State Board of Registration for Professional — (1937 as 6-member board; membership increased to 9 in 1981); apptv.; per diem and expenses; 6-yr.; 9 members: James G. Abbee, Bedford (09/26/95); Joseph J. Beal, Austin (09/26/91); James Chien-I Chang, Houston (09/26/93); Ernest David Dorchester, Midland (09/26/91); Earnest F. Gloyna, Austin (09/26/95); Carl Ruchell Hubert, Houston (09/26/93); James Ken Newman, Denton (09/26/91); Jose I. Novoa, Dallas (09/26/93); James K. Wilhelm, Houston (09/26/95). Exec. Dir., Charles E. Nemir, Drawer 18329, Austin 78760 (non-member) ($57,042).

Entomologist, State — (1900); ex officio: Entomologist at Texas Agricultural Experiment Station, College Station: Paul W. Jackson.

Ethics Advisory Commission, State — (1983); 11 members: 2 ex officio (non-voting): Secretary of State and Attorney General; 5 apptd. by Gov. — 3 from general public and 2 legal counsels of different major political parties; 2 apptd. by Lt. Gov.; 2 apptd. by Speaker — one state representative and one from general public; expenses; 2-yr.; Gov's. apptees.: Leonard E. Davis, Tyler (02/01/84); Harold Hammett, Fort Worth (02/01/84); Robert C. McKay, Victoria (02/01/85); William Edward Moody, El Paso (02/01/85); John F. Sutton Jr., Austin (02/01/87).

Evergreen Underground Water Conservation District — (1965); 2-yr.; 5 members — 4 elected: 2 each from Wilson and Atascosa counties; one apptd. by Gov.: Carl Hoefelmeyer, Poth (02/01/91).

Family Practice Residency Advisory Committee — (1977); 3-yr.; expenses; 12 members apptv. as follows: one practicing physician apptd. by Texas Osteopathic Medical Assn.; 2 apptd. by Assn. of Directors of Family Practice Training Programs; one apptd. by Texas Medical Assn.; 2 administrators of hospitals apptd. by Texas Hospital Assn.; the president of the Texas Academy of Family Physicians; and 3 public members apptd. by the Gov. Gov's. apptees.: Charlie Allen Britsch, Castroville (08/29/91); Dr. Jack L. Eidson, Weatherford (08/29/93); Georgia Hawks Swift, Amarillo (08/29/92).

Film Commission, Texas — (Merged with **Texas Department of Commerce** in 1987.) Dir., Tom Copeland, P.O. Box 12728, Austin 78711.

Finance Commission, State — (1923 as **Banking Commission**; reorganized as **Finance Commission** in 1943 with 9 members; membership increased to 12 in 1983 — 6 from banking section, 3 from savings and loan section and 3 from general public); apptv.; 6-yr.; per diem and traveling expenses; 12 members: Lewis E. Bracy Jr., Uvalde (02/01/92); Dana H. Cook, Missouri City (02/01/94); John C. Dawson Jr., Houston (02/01/92); James S. DuBose, Fort Worth (02/01/96); David M Laney, Dallas (12/01/96); Leonard B. Rosenberg, Houston (02/01/92); Scott B. Smith, Denison (02/01/94); R Dary Stone, Dallas (02/01/96); Milton H. Thomas Jr. Dallas (02/01/94). **Banking Commissioner**, Kenneth Litt lefield, 2601 N. Lamar, Austin 78705, appointee of Fi nance Commission. (See also **Banking Commissioner, State**.)

Fire Department Emergency Board — (1990); 2-yr., apptv.; per diem and transportation expenses; 7 members: Howard Baughman, Del Rio (02/01/91); Melody B. Chatelle, Austin (02/01/93); Charles C. Harris, Midland (02/01/91); Barney J. Oldham, Bertram (02/01/91); Ernest Reesing, Alpine (02/01/91); Dan W. Stamper, Austin (02/01/91); Ray L. Williamson, Wharton (02/01/91). State Fire Marshal, Ernest A. Emerson, 1110 San Jacinto Blvd., Austin 78701.

Fire Fighters' Relief and Retirement Fund — (1977); apptv.; expenses; 6-yr.; 6 members: Donald Eernisse, Alvin (09/01/91); Benny Paul Kennedy, Andrews (09/01/93); Glenn D. Neutzler, Brenham (09/01/91); Wayne E. Popp, Louise (09/01/93); Robert J. Rice, Canyon (09/01/95); Charles H. Romans, Uvalde (09/01/93). Fire Fighter's Pension Commissioner, Helen L. Campbell, 3910 S. I-35, Ste. 235, Austin 78704.

Fire Protection Personnel Standards and Education, Commission on — (1969); apptv.; expenses; 6-yr.; 2 ex officio members: Commissioner of Higher Education of the Coordinating Board, Texas College and University System, and the Commissioner of the Texas Education Agency; 9 apptv. members: Thomas P. Foster, College Station (06/11/93); Patrick K. Hughes, Keller (06/11/91); Mike B. Perez Jr., Laredo (06/11/91); James L. Roberts, Midland (06/11/95); Otto C. Schattel, Hallsville (06/11/95); Chester A. Shelton, Beaumont (06/11/93); Wayne C. Sibley, Midlothian (06/11/95); Billie Monroe Strickland, Arlington (06/11/93); Lester W. Tyra Jr., ouston (06/11/91). Exec. Dir., Ray L. Goad, 9800 N. Lamar, Ste. 160, Austin 78753 (non-member) ($36,750).

Firemen's Pension Commissioner — (1937); apptv.; 2-yr.: Helen Campbell, Austin (07/01/91). 3910 S. I-35, #235, Austin 78704 ($36,750).

Forester, State — (1959); apptv. by Board of Regents of Texas A&M University: Bruce R. Miles, College Station.

Funeral Service Commission, Texas — (1903 as State Board of Embalming; 1935 as **State Board of Funeral Directors and Embalmers**; 1953 as 6-member board; membership increased to 9 in 1979; name changed to present form in 1987); apptv.; per diem and expenses; 6-yr.; 9 members: Russell Wayne Allen, Benbrook (01/31/95); Robert R. Dixon, West Columbia (01/31/97); C.L. Jackson, Houston (01/31/93); Scott Kurth, Cedar Hill (01/31/95); Percy Parsons, Dimmitt (01/31/93); Ted Karpf, Dallas (01/31/97); Paul Gifford Pond, Port Arthur (01/31/93); Donald H. Taft, Beaumont (05/31/91); Lois Villasenor, Austin (01/31/95). Exec. Dir., Larry A. Farrow, 8100 Cameron Rd., Bldg. B., Ste. 550, Austin 78753.

General Land Office, Commissioner of the — (1836 by Constitution of Republic of Texas; 1876 by present Constitution); elective; (2-yr. by original Constitutional provision; term raised to 4-yr. in 1972, effective 1975): Garry Mauro, (01/01/95). Stephen F. Austin Bldg., Room 835, Austin 78701 ($74,698).

Governor — (1845 by original Constitution, 1876 by present Constitution); elective (2-yr. by original constitutional provision, term raised to 4-yr. in 1972, effective 1975): Ann Richards, (01/01/95). Room 200, State Capitol, Austin 78701 ($93,432).

Growth Fund Board of Trustees, Texas — (1988); apptd.; 6-yr.; 9 members — one member from and elected by membership of each of the following: Board of Regents, University of Texas System; Board of Regents, Texas A&M University System; Board of Trustees, Teacher Retirement System; Board of Trustees, Employees Retirement System; State Board of Education; 4 public members apptd. by Gov.: H. Scott Caven, Houston (02/01/93); John H. Dalton, San Antonio (02/01/97); Richard J. Hanschen, Dallas (02/01/93); Marice Ellis-Kirk, Dallas (02/01/97).

Guadalupe River Authority, Upper — (1939); apptv.; 6-yr.; 9 members: A.J. Brough, Kerrville (02/01/93); Richard G. Eastland, Hunt (02/01/91); Robert Lynn Finch, Kerrville (02/01/95); John R. Furman III, Kerrville (02/01/95); T. Beck Gipson, Kerrville (02/01/93); Mary Virginia Holekamp, Kerrville (02/01/95); R.H. Hoekamp, Kerrville (02/01/91); H. Ritman Jons, Kerrville (02/01/91); Lorita Ann Tipton, Kerrville (02/01/93). Gen. Mgr., B. W. Bruns, Box 1278, Kerrville 78029-1278.

Guadalupe-Blanco River Authority — (1935); apptv.; per diem and expenses on duty; 6-yr.; 9 members: William A. Blackwell, Cuero (02/01/95); Harry A. Fish, Boerne (02/01/93); Joseph Pat Kelly, Victoria (02/01/91); Warren P. Kirksey, Lockhart (02/01/91); Jerry Lloyd Moore Jr., San Marcos (02/01/95); Jen F. Ripley, Waelder (02/01/95); Herbert R. Schneider, New

Braunfels (02/01/93); Preston A. Stofer, Long Mott (02/01/93); John C. Taylor, McQueeney (02/01/97). Gen. Mgr., John H. Specht, Box 271, Seguin 78156 (non-member).

Gulf Coast Waste Disposal Authority — (1969); apptv.; 2-yr.; per diem and expenses on duty; 9 members: 3 apptv. by Gov., 3 by County Commissioners Courts of counties in district, 3 by Municipalities Waste Disposal Councils of counties in district. Gov's. apptees: Jerome J. Pennington, Houston (08/31/91); Oscar G. Weir, Baytown (08/31/92); Philip A. Werner, Galveston (08/31/92). Gen. Mgr., Richard L. Brown, P.O. Box 53150, Houston 77258 (non-member).

Gulf States Marine Fisheries Commission — (1949); apptv.; 3-yr.; 3 members — 2 ex officio: exec. dir., Texas Parks & Wildlife Dept.; one member of House; one apptd. by Gov.: Charles E. Belaire, Fulton (03/17/93). Exec. Dir., Larry B. Simpson, Box 726, Ocean Springs, MS 30564.

Health Care Reimbursement Alternatives, Texas Commission on — (1987); term at pleasure of Gov.; apptd., expenses; 18 member — 4 representatives and 3 public members apptd. by Speaker; 4 senators and 3 public members apptd. by Lt. Gov.; 3 public members and chairman apptd. by Gov.; Gov's apptees: Joel T. Allison, Corpus Christi; Lynda Calcote, Abilene; William P. Daves Jr., Dallas; Carol Carlson Dean, Lakeside City.

Health Coordinating Council, Statewide — (1975); apptv.; 2-yr.; one ex officio, 21 apptv., as follows: Dr. Letha F. Barber, Galveston (09?01/92); John R. Bush, Dallas (02/01/92); Kim A. Caldwell, Athens (09/01/92); Lawrence J. Canfield, Temple (09/01/91); Helen T. Chang, Houston (09/01/92); Evelyn H. Close, Perryton (09/01/91); Larry Thomas Craig, Tyler (09/01/91); Scott Moore Duncan, Houston (09/01/91); Ernest J. Gerlach, San Antonio (09/01/91); Geraldine T. Hester, Bryan (09/01/92); Delmar S. Hilliard, Newton (09/01/91); Betty H. Himmelblau, Austin (09/01/91); Bob Max Hollander, Odessa (09/01/92); Henry Lopez Jr., San Antonio (09/01/92); Mary M. Newsome, Houston (09/01/91); Dr. Damaso A. Oliva, San Antonio (09/01/91); Margaret Purvis, Midland (09/01/92); Edith Schuler, Richardson (09/01/91); Dr. C. William Spencer, Arlington (09/01/92); Dr. A. Bryan Spires Jr., Austin (09/01/92); Kay H. Williamson, Houston (09/01/92). Office Address: Texas Dept. of Health, 1100 W. 49th, Austin 78756.

Health and Human Services Coordinating Council — (1975 as 9-member board; membership increased to 19 in 1983); 6-yr.; 19 members: 7 ex officio: Gov., Lt. Gov., Speaker, Chairmen of Texas Board of Human Services, Texas Board of Health, Texas Board of Mental Health and Mental Retardation, State Board of Education; 2 senators and 2 general public members apptd. by Lt. Gov., 2 representatives and 2 general public members apptd. by Speaker; 2 board members of state agencies and 2 general public members apptd. by Gov., as follows: Jerry P. Cunningham, Dallas (09/01/91); Jerry Kane, Corpus Christi (09/01/91); Gary Michael Polland, Houston (09/01/91); Anne Ashy Shepard, Harlingen (09/01/91). Exec. Dir., James P. Smothermon, 9101 Burnet Rd. Ste. 216, Austin 78758 (non-member) ($52,907).

Health, Commissioner of — (1879 as State Health Officer; 1955 changed to **Commissioner of Health**; 1975 changed to **Director, Texas Department of Health Resources**; 1977 changed to **Commissioner, Texas Department of Health**; apptv.; 2-yr.: Dr. Robert Bernstein, Austin (01/01/91). 1100 W. 49th, Austin 78756 ($84,000).

Health, Texas Board of — (1903 as State Board of Health; superseded similar department created in 1891; name changed in 1975 to **Texas Board of Health Resources** and membership increased to 18; name changed in 1977 to present form); apptv.; per diem and expenses on duty; 6-yr.; 18 members: Ron J. Anderson, Duncanville (02/01/97); Joan W. Biggerstaff, Plano (02/01/95); Dr. Robert E. Bonham, Dallas (02/01/95); Don L. Brewer, Dallas (02/01/93); Dr. Frank Bryant Jr., San Antonio (02/01/93); Ramiro R. Casso, McAllen (02/01/97); David L. Collins, Missouri City (02/01/97); Dr. Bennett L.G. Harber, Boerne (02/01/95); Larry D. Krupala, Cuero (02/01/93); Dr. Donald M. Peterson, Dallas (02/01/95); Dr. Susan B. Place, Plano (02/01/97); William D. Poteet III, Lubbock (02/01/95); Dr. Milton Lee Risinger, Terrell (02/01/97); William A. Scott, Houston (02/01/97); Barbara T. Slover, Fort Worth (02/01/93); Oliver Roy Smith, El Paso (02/01/93); Ruth F. Stewart, San Antonio (02/01/97); Dr. Raleigh R. White IV, Temple (02/01/93). **Commissioner of Health**, Robert Bernstein, 1100 W. 49th, Austin 78756 (non-member) ($84,000).

Hearing Aids, Texas Board of Examiners in the Fitting and Dispensing of — (1969); apptv.; 6-yr.; expenses; 9 members: Florence Pringle Anderson, San Antonio (12/31/93); Suzanne Elizabeth Brennan, Houston (12/31/91); Andrew Louis Burns Jr., Texarkana (12/31/93); Dr. Henry M. Carder, Dallas (12/31/95); Wallace Hamill, Dallas (12/31/93); George Holland Jr., Lubbock (12/31/91); Tom C. Lucenay, Waco (12/31/91); Betty Jeanne Marsh, El Paso (12/31/95); Richard L. Riess, College Station (12/31/95). Exec. Dir., Wanda F. Stewart, 4800 N. Lamar, Ste. 150, Austin 78756 (non-member) ($26,775).

High-Speed Rail Authority, Texas — (1989); 6-yr.; expenses; 9 members — Chmn., State Highway and Public Transportation Comm.; Chmn., Texas Turnpike Authority; Chmn., Railroad Commission; Chmn., board of directors of a metropolitan transit authority; 2 Chmn., boards of directors of regional transportation authorities; 3 apptd. by governor: D. Kent Anderson, Houston (06/01/95); Henry Ruben Munoz III, San Antonio (06/01/97); Charles J. Wyly Jr., Dallas (06/01/95). Exec. Dir., Bob Neely, 823 Congress, Ste. 1502, Austin 78701.

Higher Education Coordinating Board, Texas — (1953 as temporary board; 1955 as permanent 15-member **Texas Commission on Higher Education**; changed to 18-member board in 1965; name changed to present form in 1987); apptv.; 6-yr.; expenses; 18 members: Carolyn R. Bacon, Dallas (08/31/93); W. Mike Baggett, Dallas (08/31/95); Herbert L. Butrum, Houston (08/31/95); Frank K. Cahoon, Midland (08/31/93); Hal Daugherty, El Paso (08/31/93); Dr. Lauro G. Guerra, McAllen (08/31/91); Cipriano F. Guerra Jr., San Antonio (08/31/93); Lawrence E. Jenkins, Austin (08/31/95); Jess Ben Latham III, Amarillo (08/31/91); Gregory E. Mitchell, Amarillo (08/31/93); Patricia S. Prather, Houston (08/31/95); Kathryn A. Priddy, Dallas (08/31/93); Harry M. Reasoner, Houston (08/31/91); Regina J. Rogers, Houston (08/31/91); Ray E. Santos, Lubbock (08/31/91); Charles C. Sprague, Dallas (08/31/95); Philip G. Warner, Houston (08/31/91); Mary Beth Williamson, San Antonio (08/31/95). Commissioner of Higher Education, Dr. Kenneth H. Ashworth, Box 12788, Austin 78711 (non-member) ($117,923).

Highway and Public Transportation Commission, Texas — (1917 as **State Highway Commission**; merged with **Mass Transportation Commission** and name changed to present form in 1975); apptv.; 6-yr.; ($35,123); 3 members: Robert H. Dedman, Dallas (02/15/93); Wayne B. Duddlesten, Houston (02/15/95); Ray C. Stoker Jr., Odessa (02/15/91). Office Address: Dewitt C. Greer State Highway Bldg., 11th and Brazos, Austin 78701.

Highways and Public Transportation, State Engineer-Dir. for — (1917 as **State Highway Engineer**; name changed to present form in 1975); apptd. by Texas Highway and Public Transportation Commission, indefinite term: Arnold Oliver, 11th and Brazos, Austin 78701-2483 ($84,000).

Historical Commission, Texas — (1953); apptv.; expenses; 6-yr.; 18 members: Brian Babin, Woodville (02/01/95); John M. Bennett, San Antonio (02/01/95); Carrielu B. Christensen, Austin (02/01/93); George Christian, Austin (02/01/91); Harold D. Courson, Perryton (02/01/93); Martha K. Crowley, Richardson (02/01/93); Al Davis, Houston (02/01/95); T.R. Fehrenbach, San Antonio (02/01/95); Willie Lee Gay, Houston (02/01/97); Sheldon Hall, El Paso (02/01/95); Betty E. Hanna, Breckenridge (02/01/93); Clotilde P. Garcia, Corpus Christi (02/01/97); Jean W. Kaspar, Shiner (02/01/95); Karl A. Komatsu, Fort Worth (02/01/93); Thomas E. Kroutter Jr., Port Arthur (02/01/97); Archie P. McDonald, Nacogdoches (02/01/97); James S. Nabors, Lake Jackson (02/01/91); Dr. Dan Alvin Willis, Fort Worth (02/01/97). Exec. Dir., Curtis Tunnell, Box 12276, Austin 78711 (non-member) ($50,299).

Historical Records Advisory Board, Texas — (1976); apptv.; 3-yr.; 9 members: David R. Farmer, Southlake (01/23/93); Diana B. Gonzalez, San Antonio (01/23/94); Chris A. LaPlante, Austin (01/23/91); David J. Murrah, Lubbock (01/23/92); Audray B. Randle, Austin (01/23/91); Iris T. Schumann, New Braunfels (01/23/93); Lydia Torrez, McAllen (01/23/92); Ron C. Tyler, Austin (01/23/92); Trisha Wilson, Dallas (01/23/93). State Historical Records Coordinator, Chris LaPlante, State Library and Archives, P.O. Box 12927, Austin 78711.

Hospital Equipment Financing Council, Texas — John A. Adkins, Houston (09/01/91); Jose A. Botello, Dallas (09/01/91); Kippy Caraway, Houston (07/17/89); David R. Garcia, San Antonio (09/01/89); O. Ray Hurst, Austin (07/17/89); Richard F. Kiepfer, Boerne (09/01/93); Elizabeth L. Kimmel, Houston (07/17/89); Dan E. Patterson,

Dallas (09/01/93); Calvin E. Person, Dallas (09/01/93); Miguel San Juan, Houston (09/01/93); Alicia Z. Vera, Brownsville (09/01/91); Mrs. Charles Wilson, Marshall (09/01/91).

Hospital Licensing Advisory Council — 6-yr., 9 members: Susanna E. Bedell, Palestine (12/07/95); David G. Borman, Iowa Park (12/07/93); David C. Bush, Houston (12/07/95); Bob L. Bybee, Canyon (12/07/95); Larry M. Graham, Round Rock (12/07/91); Jake Henry Jr., Lubbock (12/087/91); Mayola E. Lasater, Aledo (12/07/91); Donald B. Lewis, Athens (12/07/93); Bruce D. Purdy, Muleshoe (12/07/93). Texas Department of Health, 1100 W. 49th, Austin 78756.

Housing Agency, Texas — (1979); apptv.; expenses; 6-yr.; Exec. Dir., Texas Dept. of Community Affairs is ex officio member and chmn;.; 9 apptv. members: Margie Lee Bingham, Missouri City (01/31/95); Edmund R. Carrera, El Paso (01/31/93); George R. Farish, Houston (01/31/93); Gary Allen Hammond, Plano (01/31/95); John W. Hazard, Houston (01/31/95); Richard Jordan, Austin (01/31/91); Arthur Navarro, Austin (01/31/97); Paul R. Rodriguez, Mission (01/31/97); Donald W. Sowell, Prairie View (01/31/93). Exec. Admin., (Vacancy), 811 Barton Springs Rd., Ste., 300, Austin 78704 (non-member) ($64,500).

Human Rights, State Commission on — (1983); apptv.; 6-yr.; expenses; 6 members: Jose E. De Santiago, Houston (09/24/95); Maxine Lee, Austin (09/24/91); Mallory Robinson, Houston (09/24/91); Rae Schollmaier, Fort Worth (09/24/93); Frank Thompson Jr., Houston (09/24/95); Laura Zuniga, El Paso (09/24/93). Exec. Dir., Bill Hale, Box 13493, Austin 78711 (non-member) ($52,133).

Human Services, Texas Board of — (1941 as **State Board of Public Welfare**; name changed to present form in 1985); apptv.; 6-yr.; per diem and expenses; 6 members: Maurice Lee Barksdale, Arlington (01/20/93); Cassandra C. Carr, Austin (02/01/93); Robert Geyer, El Paso (01/20/97); David Herndon, Austin (01/20/95); Ida Kern Papert, Dallas (01/20/95); Yava D. Scott, Missouri City (01/20/97). **Commissioner** (interim), Burt Raiford, Box 149030, Austin 78714 ($84,000).

Humanities, Texas Committee for the — (1972); apptv. and elective by committee; 2-yr. for apptv. members, 4-yr. for elective; 22 members — 6 apptd. as follows: Bridget Barry, Fort Worth (12/31/91); Mary Denny, Aubrey (12/31/91); Paul A. Leche, Austin (12/31/91); Homer B. Reynolds III, McKinney (12/31/91); William R. Tucker, Beaumont (12/31/91); Ann J. Willeford, Austin (12/31/90). Exec. Dir., James F. Veninga, Banister Place A, 3809 So. Second, Austin 78704 (non-member).

Incentive and Productivity Commission, Texas — (1987 as **Productivity and Bonus Commission** and **Employee Incentive Commission**; commissions merged and name changed to present form in 1989); 9 members — 6 state officials (term on commission is term in other office): Gov., Lt. Gov., Comptroller, State Treasurer, Administrator of Texas Employment Comm., Chmn. of Texas Higher Education Coordinating Board; 3 apptd. by Gov.: Ralph Cowen, Brownsville (02/01/93); Beryl P. Crowley, Austin (02/01/93); Aurora Sanchez, Austin. Exec. Dir., M. Elaine Powell, P.O. Box 12482, Austin 78711.

Indian Affairs Commission, Texas — (1965 as **Texas Indian Commission**; name changed to present form 1988; abolished by Sunset Commission, 1989.)

Industrial Accident Board — (1913; merged into Worker's Compensation Commission 1989.)

Industrialized Building Code Council, Texas — (1985); apptv.; 2-yr.; 12 members: Charles W. Alexander, Irving (02/01/91); Karen A. Barrett, Spring (02/01/92); Charles L. Clawson, Arlington (02/01/91); Joseph A.C. Cote, San Antonio (02/01/91); Bobby J. Fowler, Abilene (02/01/92); James R. Hickman, Lubbock (02/01/92); Jeffrey B. Lewis, Houston (02/01/92); Raymond D. Powell, Lubbock (02/01/92); Jimmy Furman Rogers, Fort Worth (02/01/91); Michael T. Slataper, Arlington (02/01/91); Douglas Steadman, San Antonio (02/01/91); George E. Walker Sr., Waco (02/01/92). Office Address: P.O. Box 12157, Austin 78711.

Information Resources, Texas Department of — (1990); 6-yr.; expenses; 3 members recommended by Speaker of House, 3 by Lt. Gov.; 3 by Gov.: 9 members: Jon M. Bradley, Dallas (02/01/95); R. Dan Burck, Austin (02/01/91); Temple Dickson, Austin (02/01/97); John Keel, Austin (02/01/97); Donald A. Maxwell, Bryan (02/01/95); Lynn M. Moak, Austin (02/01/93); Harry H. Richardson, San Antonio (02/01/95); William D. Stotesbery, Austin (02/01/93); Richard F. Williamson, Austin (02/01/93). Exec. Dir., Ann S. Fuelberg, P.O. Box 13564, Austin 78711.

Insurance, State Board of — (1927 as **State Board of Insurance Commissioners**; superseded similar commission of 1913; re-created 1957 to form **State Board of Insurance**; apptv.; 6-yr.; 3 members at $71,400 each and **State Insurance Commissioner** at $69,300, who serves 2-yr. term and is apptd. by board members: Jo Ann Howard, Austin (01/31/91); Richard F. Reynolds, Flower Mound (01/31/93); Allene D. Evans, Austin (01/31/95).**Commissioner**, Philip Barnes, 1110 San Jacinto, Austin 78701-1998.

Intergovernmental Relations, Texas Advisory Commission on — (1971); apptv.; 6-yr.; 2 ex officio: Lt. Gov. and Speaker of House; 24 apptd.: 3 senators apptd. by Lt. Gov.; 3 representatives apptd. by Speaker; 18 apptd. by Gov.: Leo Berman, Arlington (09/01/93); Ernest E. Chance, The Woodlands (09/01/93); Patti Clapp, Dallas (09/01/93); Sam Collins, Orange (09/01/89); James D. Dannenbaum, Houston (09/01/89); June Garrison, Fort Worth (09/01/91); Kathlyn J. Gilliam, Dallas (09/01/91); Emmett L. Gloyna, Edna (09/01/93); E.C. Green, Denison (09/01/91); Anthony Hall, Houston (09/01/89); Emmett Hutto, Baytown (09/01/91); Joseph Pena, Carrollton (09/01/91); Mrs. Pic Rivers, Houston (09/01/89); Hollis V. Rutledge Jr., San Antonio (09/01/93); Carroll M. Thomas, Midland (09/01/93); Norman Troy, Beaumont (09/01/87); Tom Vickers, San Antonio (09/01/91); Don R. Windle, Denton (09/01/91). Exec. Dir., Jay G. Stanford, Box 13206, Austin 78711 (non-member) ($42,848).

Interstate Compact for Supervision of Parolees and Probation — (1951); ex officio: Attorney General. Administrator: Tom Vickers, Austin.

Interstate Oil Compact Commission, Texas Representative — (1935); ex officio or apptv., according to Gov's. choice; per diem and expenses. Ex officio member: Land Commissioner. Apptv. members: Bob Armstrong, Lena Guerrero. (Approximately 150 other appointees serve on various committees.) Exec. Dir., W. Timothy Dowd, P.O. Box 53127, Oklahoma City, OK 73152.

Interstate Parole Compact Administrator — (1951); apptv.: Knox Fitzpatrick, Dallas.

Irrigators, Texas Board of — (1979); apptv.; 6-yr.; expenses; 6 members: J. Carl Causey, Weatherford (01/31/95); John Alan Heidman, Dallas (01/31/91); Joe H. Key, Austin (01/31/95); William E. Petty Sr., Tyler (01/31/93); Daniel J. Romo, Laredo (01/31/93); James K. Rourke Jr., Austin (01/31/91). Exec. Sec., Joyce Watson, Box 12337, Austin 78711 (non-member) ($31,500).

Jail Standards, Commission on — (1975); apptv.; 6-yr.; expenses; 9 members: Kenneth W. Anderson Jr., Dallas (01/31/95); Charles E. Chatman, Sherman (01/31/97); Rolando V. Del Carmen, Huntsville (01/31/93); Joe Evans, Nacogdoches (01/31/97); Dr. Charles R. Hurst, Tyler (01/31/93); Ruth J. McClendon, San Antonio (01/31/93); Josephine W. Miller, Sinton (01/31/95); J. David Nelson, Lubbock (01/31/95); Alex F. Perez, Brownsville (01/31/97). Exec. Dir., Jack E. Crump, Box 12985, Austin 78711 (non-member) ($43,243).

Judicial Conduct, State Commission on — (1965 as 9-member **Judicial Qualifications Commission**; name changed in 1977 to present form and membership raised to 11); expenses; 6-yr.; 11 members apptd. as follows: 5 apptd. by Supreme Court; 2 apptd. by State Bar; 4 apptd. by Gov. as follows: Lowell Cable, Sulphur Springs (11/19/91); Gary E. Griffith, Dallas (11/19/91); A.H. "Al" Lock, Fort Worth (11/19/95); Roderick M. Nugent Jr., Amarillo (11/19/93). Exec. Dir., Robert C. Flowers, Box 12265, Austin 78711 (non-member) ($77,490).

Judicial Council, Texas — (1929 as **Texas Civil Judicial Council**; name changed in 1975); ex officio terms vary; apptv.; 6-yr. terms; expenses; 19 members — 6 ex officio: past Chmn. of House Judiciary Committee, Chief Justice of Texas Supreme Court, Judge of Court of Criminal Appeals, Chmn. of House Judiciary Committee, past Chmn. of Senate Jurisprudence Committee, Chmn. of Senate Jurisprudence Committee; 4 apptd. with ex officio qualifications and 9 apptd. from general public: Frank B. Davis, Houston (06/30/91); Robert A. Gammage, Austin (06/30/91); Rae Jackson, Longview (06/30/95); Ward L. Koehler, El Paso (06/30/93); John L. McCraw, McKinney (06/30/91); Alan M. Sager, Austin (06/30/93); Thomas J. Stovall Jr., Seabrook (02/01/91); Blake Tartt, Houston (06/30/93); Nick Taylor, Midland (06/30/95); Ken Towery, Austin (06/30/95). Exec. Dir., C. Raymond Judice, Box 12066, Austin 78711 (non-member).

Judicial Districts Board — (1985); 12 ex officio members (term in other office); one apptv. (4 yrs.); ex officio: Chief Justice of Texas Supreme Court; Presiding Judge, Court of Criminal Appeals; Presiding Judge of

each of 9 Administrative Judicial Districts; pres. of Texas Judicial Council. Apptee: David A. Talbot Jr., Austin (12/21/94).

Judicial Districts of Texas, Admin., Presiding Judges of — (See **Administrative Judicial Districts**).

Juvenile Probation Commission, Texas — Victoria H. Baldwin, Austin (08/31/91); Mary A. Burk, San Angelo (08/31/93); Elvin Lee Caraway, Fort Worth (08/31/93); Catherine Stayman Evans, Dallas (08/31/95); Kimball T. Hillencamp, Jacksonville (08/31/93); W. Clyde Lemon, Houston (08/31/95); Scott D. Moore, Fort Worth (08/31/91); Roy E. Turner, Canyon (08/31/91); Jane A. Wetzel, Dallas (08/31/93). Exec. Dir., Bernard Licorione, P.O. Box 13547, Austin 78711.

Lamar University System, Board of Regents — (1949); apptv.; 6-yr.; expenses; 9 members: Amelia Cobb, Beaumont (10/04/93); Carroll W. Conn Jr., Beaumont (10/04/95); E. Linn Draper Jr., Beaumont (10/04/95); Thomas Maes II, Beaumont (10/04/95); Douglas W. Matthews, Galveston (10/04/91); Ted E. Moor Jr., Beaumont (10/04/93); Wayne A. Reaud, Beaumont (10/04/91); Ronald G. Steinhart, Dallas (10/04/93); H. Wayne Willis, Kountze (10/04/91). Chancellor, Dr. George McLaughlin, Box 11900, Beaumont 77710 (non-member).

Land Board, School — (1939); one ex officio (term in other office); 2 apptd. — one by Atty. Gen. and one by Gov. for 2-yr. term; per diem and expenses; ex officio member: Comm. of General Land Office; Gov's. apptee: Gaylord T. Hughey Jr., Tyler (08/29/91).

Land Office, Commissioner of — (See **General Land Office, Commissioner of.**)

Land Surveying, Texas Board of Professional — (1979); formed from consolidation of membership of **Board of Examiners of Licensed Land Surveyors**, est. 1977, and **State Board of Registration for Public Surveyors**, est. 1955); apptv.; 6-yr.; 10 members — Commissioner of General Land Office serving by statute; 3 members of general public, 2 licensed land surveyors, 4 registered public surveyors, as follows: George H. Clements III, Dallas (01/31/93); Herman Hays Forbes, Round Rock (01/31/95); Walter Fortney, Fort Worth (01/31/91); Fern Maddera, Levelland (01/31/91); Arthur W. Osborn, Tyler (01/31/93); Robert J. Prejean, New Ulm (01/31/95); Andrew L. Sikes, Houston (01/31/93); David A. Vilbig, Dallas (01/31/95); William C. Wilson Jr., San Angelo (01/31/91). Exec. Sec., Betty J. Pope, 7701 N. Lamar, Ste. 400, Austin 78752 (non-member) ($33,425).

Lands, Board for Lease of University — (1929 as 3-member board; membership increased to 4 in 1985); ex officio; term in other office; 4 members: Commissioner of General Land Office, 2 members of Board of Regents of University of Texas, 1 member Board of Regents of Texas A&M University.

Lands, State Board for Lease of State Park — (1965); 2-yr.; 3 members — 2 ex officio: Commissioner of General Land Office and Chmn. of Parks and Wildlife Commission; one apptd.: Charles D. Nash Jr., San Marcos (09/01/89).

Lavaca-Navidad River Authority, Board of Directors — (1954 as 7-member **Jackson County Flood Control District**; reorganized as 9-member board in 1959; name changed to present form in 1969); apptv.; 6-yr.; per diem and expenses; 9 members: M.H. Brock, Ganado (05/01/93); Edwin H. Duenow, Lolita (05/01/91); Harry Lee Hafernick, Edna (05/01/91); J.B. Housson, Ganado (05/01/91); Joyce H. Jarrett, Edna (05/01/95); Gene A. Ratliff, Edna (05/01/93); R. Don Sachtleben, Edna (05/01/93); Dennis S. Simons, Edna (05/01/95); August E. Westhoff II, Edna (05/01/95). Gen. Mgr., Emmett Gloyna, Box 429, Edna 77957 (non-member).

Law Enforcement Officer Standards & Education, Commission on — (1965); expenses; 14 members — 5 ex officio: Atty. Gen., Directory of Public Safety, Commissioner of Education, Exec. Dir. Criminal Justice Division-Governor's Office and Commissioner of Higher Education; 9 apptv. members: John E. Clark, San Antonio (08/30/93); Roger P. Dickey, Abilene (08/30/91); Louis T. Getterman III, Austin (08/30/93); Maxine E. Hannifin, Midland (08/30/93); J.C. Mosier, Houston (08/30/95); Charles W. Phelps, Bryan (08/30/91); J.R. Sonny Sessions, Fairfield (08/30/91); David L. Walker, Terrell (08/30/95); William P. Whitworth, Seguin (08/30/95). Exec. Dir., Fred Toler, 1033 La Posada, Ste. 175, Austin 78752 (non-member) ($50,744).

Law Library Board, State — (1971); ex officio; expenses; 3 members: Chief Justice State Supreme Court, Presiding Judge Court of Criminal Appeals and Atty. General. Dir., Kay Schlueter (non-member), Box 12367, Austin 78711 ($37,728).

Legislative Budget Board — (1949); 10 members: 6 ex officio: Lt. Gov., Speaker of House; Chmn., Senate Finance Comm.; Chmn., Senate State Affairs Comm.; Chmn., House Appropriations Comm.; Chmn., House Ways and Means Comm.; plus 4 other members of Legislature. Director, James P. Oliver, Box 12666, Austin 78711-2666 (non-member).

Legislative Council, Texas — (1949); 17 ex officio members — 4 senators named by Lt. Gov.; 9 representatives named by Speaker; Chmn., House Administration Committee; Chmn., Senate Administration Committee, Lt. Gov. and Speaker. Exec. Dir., Robert I. Kelly, P.O. Box 12128, Austin 78711.

Legislative Redistricting Board — (1948); 5 ex officio members; term in other office: Lt. Gov., Speaker of House, Atty. Gen., Comptroller and Commissioner of General Land Office.

Librarian, State — (Originally est. in 1839; present office est. 1909); apptv., indefinite term: William D. Gooch, Box 12927, Austin 78711 ($48,410).

Library and Archives Commission, Texas State — (1909 as 5-member **Library and State Historical Commission;** number of members increased to 6 in 1953; name changed to present form in 1979); apptv.; per diem and expenses on duty; 6 members: Carolyn Armstrong, Kingsville (09/28/95); James H. Banks, Austin (09/28/95); Jean Daniel, Liberty (09/28/91); Byron L. LeFlore, San Antonio (09/28/93); Auralia Nelson McCreless, San Antonio (09/28/91); Harriette Williford-Whatley, Fairfield (09/28/93). Dir., William D. Gooch, State Librarian, Box 12927, Capitol Sta., Austin 78711 ($54,600).

Library, State Legislative Reference — (1909); indefinite term; Director: Sally Reynolds, Box 12488, Austin 78711.

Licensing and Regulation, Texas Commission on — (1989); apptv.; 6-yr.; expenses; 6 members: Marjorie M. Arsht, Bellaire (02/01/93); Arlen D. Bynum, Dallas (02/01/97); Paul J. Corkery, Fort Worth (02/01/93); Johnnye Davis, Odessa (02/01/95); Carmen Mitchell, Dallas (02/01/97); Earl L. Yeakel III, Austin (02/01/95). Exec. Dir., Larry E. Kosta, P.O. Box 12157, Austin 78711.

Lieutenant Governor, State — (1836 by original constitution of the Republic of Texas; 1876 by present Constitution); elective, salary same as Senators' when acting as Pres. of Senate, Governor's salary when acting as Gov.; (2-yr. by original Constitution, term raised to 4-yr. in 1972, effective 1975): Bob Bullock (01/01/95). Box 12068, Austin 78711.

Liquor Control Board — (See **Alcoholic Beverage Commission.**)

Long-Term Care for the Elderly, Coord. Council on — (1983); apptv. as indicated; 2-yr.; indefinite number of members: 4 apptd. by Gov.; 4 by Lt. Gov.; 4 by Speaker; one each by Texas Dept. on Aging, Texas Dept. of Human Services, Texas Dept. of Health, Texas Dept. of Mental Health and Mental Retardation; Gov's. apptees: Ernestine H. Bridges, Mesquite (01/31/91); Rosemary Castillo, El Paso (01/31/93); Jacqueline S. Martin, Houston (01/31/93); Charlcie White Thompson, Buffalo (01/31/91).

Lower Colorado River Authority — (See **Colorado River Authority, Lower.**)

Marine Fisheries Commission — (See **Gulf States Marine Fisheries Commission.**)

Medical District Review Committee, Dist. 1 — (1977); apptv.; 6-hr.; expenses; 20 members — five from each of 4 districts: Jerome L. Armbruster, Pearland (01/15/94); Richard H. Eppright, Amarillo (01/15/94); Robert W. Feldtman, Houston (01/15/92); William H. Fleming III, Sugar Land (01/15/96); Clara H. Haney, Houston (01/15/94).

Medical District Review Committee, Dist. 2 — Robert K. Bass, Dallas (01/15/94); Linda Kagy, Mesquite (01/15/94); John L. Sawtelle, Trinidad (01/15/94); Phillip E. Williams Jr., Dallas (01/15/96); Richard C. Wootan, Dallas (01/15/92).

Medical District Review Committee, Dist. 3 — Carlos A. Fernandez, El Paso (01/15/92); Carolyn Moorhouse, Seymour (01/15/94); William L. Rector, Wichita Falls (01/15/96); F. Warren Tingley, Arlington (01/15/92); Irvin E. Zeitler Jr., Stamford (01/15/94).

Medical District Review Committee, Dist. 4 — Clyde R. Danks, Austin (01/15/96); Royce K. Keilers, La Grange (01/15/94); Janet McGlasson, Rockport (01/15/94); Harold Skaggs, Austin (01/15/92); Vicente Tavarez, McAllen (01/15/94).

Medical Examiners, Texas State Board of — (1907 as 12-member board, membership raised to 15 in 1981); apptv.; 6-yr.; per diem on duty; 15 members: Gilberto Aguirre, San Antonio (04/13/95); Penny Angelo, Midland (04/13/95); John C. Bagwell, Dallas (04/13/91);

George S. Bayoud, Garland (04/13/93); John H. Boyd, Eden (04/13/93); Barbara J. Coe, Dallas (04/13/93); William H. Fleming III, Sugar Land (04/13/95); Arthur M. Jansa Sr., Houston (04/13/91); Cindy Jenkins, Stowell (04/13/91); Alfred R. Johnson, Dallas (04/13/93); James W. Lively, Corpus Christi (04/13/91); R.A.D. Morton Jr., El Paso (04/13/91); Milam B. Pharo, Dallas (04/13/95); Luis M. Rios, Edinburg (04/13/95); C. Richard Stasney, Houston (04/13/93). Exec. Dir., Homer R. Goehrs, M.D., Box 13562, Austin 78711 ($64,260).

Mental Health and Mental Retardation, Texas Board of — (1965, superseded **Board of Texas State Hospitals and Special Schools**); apptv.; 6-yr.; per diem and expenses; 9 members: Charles M. Cooper, Dallas (01/31/93); Pattilou Dawkins, Amarillo (01/31/93); Louis E. Deere, Dallas (01/31/97); Virginia Eernisse, Alvin (01/31/97); J.L. Huffines, Lewisville (01/31/95); Anne R. Race, Dallas (01/31/95); Fermin Sarabia, San Antonio (01/31/95); Ann K. Utley, Dallas (01/31/97); Edward B. Weyman, Midland (01/31/93). **Commissioner of Mental Health,** Dennis R. Jones, Box 12668, Austin 78711-2668 (non-member) ($88,480).

Midwestern State University, Board of Regents — (1959); apptv.; 6-yr.; 9 members: David H. Allen, Wichita Falls (02/25/94); Jerry K. Estes, Wichita Falls (02/25/92); Martha W. Hendrickson, Wichita Falls (02/25/92); Milburn E. Nutt, Wichita Falls (02/25/96); Dunman Perry Jr., Mineral Wells (02/25/94); Gary H. Shores, Wichita Falls (02/25/96); Joe H. Staley Jr., Dallas (02/25/96); E.L. Watson, Dallas (02/25/92); Kathryn Anne Yeager, Wichita Falls (02/25/94). Pres., Dr. Louis J. Rodriguez, 3400 Taft, Wichita Falls 76308 (non-member).

Motor Vehicle Commission, Texas — (1971 as 6-member board; membership increased to 9 in 1979; reduced to 6 in 1987); apptv.; 6-yr.; per diem and expenses; 6 members: Delma Abalos, Odessa (01/31/97); Leonard E. Burton, Irving (01/31/93); William W. Collins Jr., Fort Worth (01/31/95); T.J. Connolly, San Antonio (01/31/97); John C. Horton III, Austin (01/31/95); Norman Scott Jones, Dallas (01/31/93). Exec. Dir., Russell Harding, Box 2293, Austin 78768 (non-member) ($52,500).

Municipal Retirement System, Texas — (See **Retirement System, Municipal, Board of Trustees.**)

Music Commission, Texas — (Merged with **Texas Department of Commerce,** 1987.)

National Guard Armory Board, Texas — (1935 as 3-member board; reorganized as 6-member board in 1981; 6-yr.; 6 members — 3 members of National Guard, 3 from general public: Hal Boyd, Big Spring (04/30/91); Don O. Daniel, Portland (04/30/93); Charles Driggers, Campbell (04/30/97); Lillian Dunlap, San Antonio (04/30/93); V.C. Eissler, Fredericksburg (04/30/95); Reynaldo Sanchez, El Paso (04/30/95). Exec. Dir., William E. Beaty, P.O. Box 5218, Austin 78763 ($50,400).

National Guard Commander, Texas — (1947); apptv.; Maj. Gen. Willie L. Scott, Austin.

National Research Laboratory Commission, Texas — (1986); apptv.; expenses; 6-yr.; 9 members: J. Fred Bucy, Dallas (02/01/93); Charles W. Duncan Jr., Houston (02/01/93); Martin Goland, San Antonio (02/01/91); Gerald Griffin, Houston (02/01/91); Jerome Johnson, Amarillo (02/01/91); Kenneth A. McCrady, Ennis (02/01/93); Peter O'Donnell Jr., Dallas (02/01/95); Charles R. Perry, Odessa (02/01/95); Warren G. Woodward, Dallas (02/01/95). Exec. Dir., Edward C. Bingler, 1801 N. Hampton, Ste. 400, DeSoto 75115.

Natural Fibers and Food Protein Commission — (1941 as **Cotton Research Committee;** name changed in 1971 and again in 1975); 4 ex officio members and 7 members apptd. to executive advisory committee by chairman with approval of commission members, to serve 2-yr. terms. Ex officio members serve indefinite terms: Pres., Texas Womans's University, Denton; Pres., Texas Tech University, Lubbock; Chancellor, Texas A&M University System; Pres., University of Texas at Austin. Exec. Dir., Carl Cox, 17360 Coit Rd., Dallas 75252 (non-member).

Neches River Municipal Water Authority, Upper — (Est. 1953 as 9-member board; membership changed to 3 in 1959); apptv.; 6-yr.; 3 members: Gordon B. Broyles, Palestine (02/01/93); Marley P. Styner, Palestine (02/01/91); Ben L. Swinney, Palestine (02/01/95). Gen. Mgr., Roy Douglas, Drawer 1965, Palestine 75801 (non-member).

Neches Valley Authority, Lower — (1933); apptv.; per diem and expenses on duty; 9 members: R.C. Aldrich, Nome (07/28/95); F.M. Archer, Woodville (07/28/91); Clyde L. Cole, Silsbee (07/28/93); William Doornbos, Nederland (07/28/93); Paul Georgas Jr., Silsbee (07/28/91); Dan Hallmark, Beaumont (07/28/93);

Thad Heartfield, Beaumont (07/28/95); W.S. Nichols Jr., Woodville (07/28/89); Jack Scott, Port Arthur (07/28/91). Gen. Mgr. A. T. Hebert Jr., P.O. Box 3464, Beaumont 77704 (non-member).

Nonresident Violator Compact Administrator — (1981); apptv.; 2-yr.: Calvin M. Anderson, Austin (02/01/91).

North Texas State University — (See **University of North Texas Board of Regents**.)

Nueces River Authority, Board of Directors — (1953 as **Nueces River Conservation and Reclamation District**; name changed in 1971); apptv.; 6-yr.; per diem and expenses; 21 members: Eugene L. Ames Jr., San Antonio (02/01/93); Mary B. Autry, Pipe Creek (02/01/97); Wayne J. Baldwin, Sandia (02/01/93); Dudley Q. Braly, Beeville (02/01/95); Dolph Briscoe III, Cotulla (02/01/93); Dan O. Dennis, Corpus Christi (02/01/95); George A. Finley III, Corpus Christi (02/01/93); Santiago N. Flores, Mathis (02/01/91); Bruce T. Foster, Hondo (02/01/95); Stevan R. Gallegos, Castroville (02/01/93); Joseph E. Gardner Jr., Corpus Christi (02/01/95); James W. Gorman, San Antonio (02/01/93); Albert A. Ivy, Carrizo Springs (02/01/91); Edward M. Jones, Ingleside (02/01/97); Jay T. Kimbrough, Beeville (02/01/95); Roy Martin, Cotulla (02/01/91); Daniel Martinez, Corpus Christi (02/01/95); Bob Mullen, Alice (02/01/97); Alvaro D. Saenz, Corpus Christi (02/01/95); Kenneth B. Shackelford, Leakey (02/01/93); Robert L. Wagner, Crystal City (02/01/95). Exec. Dir., Con Mims III, Box 349, Uvalde 78802-0349.

Nurse Examiners, State Board of — (1909 as 6-member board; reorganized and membership increased to 9 in 1981); apptv.; per diem and expenses; 6-yr.; 9 members: Pauline Barnes, Texarkana (01/31/91); Lynn C. Besselman, Amarillo (01/31/93); Sara J. Keele, Houston (01/31/95); Teddy L. Langford, Lubbock (01/31/91); Morris H. Parrish, Irving (01/31/95); Eileen Marie Piwetz, Midland (01/31/93); Nelwyn P. Ross, El Paso (01/31/95); Aimee J. Seamans, San Antonio (01/31/93); Patsy Sharpe, Fort Worth (01/31/91). Exec. Dir., Louise Waddill, 9101 Burnet Rd., Ste. 104, Austin 78758 (non-member) ($50,400).

Nurse Examiners, State Board of Vocational — (1951 as 9-member board; membership increased to 12 in 1981); apptv.; 6-yr.; 12 members — one doctor, one registered nurse, one hospital administrator, 7 licensed vocational nurses and 2 from general public: Virginia M. Bauman, South Padre Island (09/06/93); Norma Jean Clark, Corinth (09/06/93); Connie M. Davis, Fort Worth (09/06/95); Lee C. Detenbeck, Horseshoe Bay (09/06/91); Sharon Johnson, Taylor (09/06/91); Sandra U. Knight, Palestine (09/06/93); Ruth Leopard, San Antonio (09/06/95); Betty F. McLemore, Longview (09/06/95); Wayne L. Ogburn, Abilene (09/06/91); Annie Mae Parker, Belton (09/06/95); Doris A. Parker, Frankston (09/06/95); Charlotte J. Sifford, Adrian (09/06/93). Exec. Dir., Joyce A. Hammer, 9101 Burnet Rd., Ste. 105, Austin 78758 (non-member) ($44,100).

Nursing Home Administrators, Texas Board of Licensure for — (1969 as 6-member board; membership raised to 11 in 1979); apptv.; per diem and expenses; 6-yr.; 11 members — 2 ex officio: Commissioner of Human Services and Commissioner of Health; 9 apptv. members: Johnnie Lou Avery, Big Spring (01/31/97); Cindy R. Brockwell, Boerne (01/31/95); Margaret L. Gose, Wichita Falls (01/31/93); Barbara W. Hinson, Gilmer (01/31/93); Rumaldo Z. Juarez, Edinburg (01/31/97); W. Edward McLendon, Richardson (01/31/95); Jarmese Morris, Pearland (01/31/97); Herman D. Sabrsula, Houston (01/31/95); Dr. Jack S. Weinblatt, Temple (01/31/93). Exec. Dir., Dr. Karl E. Bishop, 4800 N. Lamar, Ste. 310, Austin 78756 (non-member) ($36,750).

Occupational Therapy, Texas Advisory Board of — (1983); apptv.; 6 members — 3 occupational therapists, one asst. occupational therapist and 2 from general public; 6-yr.; per diem and expenses: Frances Derrick, Mesquite (02/01/95); Graciela Garcia, Houston (02/01/99); Peggy L. Pickens, Houston (02/01/91); Marianne L. Punchard, Mart (02/01/91); Sally Wise Schultz, Plano (02/01/93); Lewis R. Strickland, Galveston (02/01/95). Exec. Dir., Linda Vaclavik, 4900 N. Lamar, Austin 78751.

Offenders with Mental Impairments, Texas Council on — (1987); apptv.; expenses; 6-yr.; 27 members: 18 heads of agencie or their designees: Texas Dept. of Corrections, Texas Dept. of MHMR, Board of Pardons and Paroles, Texas Adult Probation Commission, Texas Juvenile Probation Commission, Texas Youth Commission, Texas Rehabilitation Commission, Central Education Agency, Criminal Justice Policy Council, Mental

Health Assn. in Texas, Texas Commission on Alcohol and Drug Abuse, Commission on Law Enforcement Officer Standards and Education, Texas Council of Community MHMR Centers, Commission on Jail Standards, Texas Planning Council for Developmental Disabilities, Texas Assn. for Retarded Citizens, Texas Alliance for the Mentally Ill, and Parent Assn. for the Retarded of Texas; 9 apptd. by Gov. as follows: C. Anne Bishop, Austin (02/01/95); Lisa Ann Blue, Dallas (02/01/93); Kevin Chapman, Dallas (02/01/95); Marshall D. Herklotz, Tennessee Colony (02/01/91); Karl B. McLeod, Boling (02/01/89); John D. Nottingham Jr., Houston (02/01/93); Mario E. Ramirez, Edinburg (02/01/97); William B. Schnapp, Houston (02/01/93); Jeffrey C. Siegel, Dallas (02/01/95).

Old San Antonio Road Preservation Commission — (1989); term at pleasure of governor; 9 members: 4 representatives of state agencies: State Dept. of Highways and Public Transportation, Texas Historical Commission, Parks and Wildlife, Texas Dept. of Commerce (Tourism Div.); 5 at large recommended by Texas Historical Commission and apptd. by gov.: Dr. Archie P. McDonald, Nacogdoches; Gen. John R. McGiffert, San Antonio; Ingrid B. Morris, Hemphill; Nan Olsen, Bastrop; Rose T. Trevino, Laredo.

Ombudsman (Citizens' Advocate) — Annette M. Lo-Voi, P.O. Box 12428, Austin 78711.

Optometry Board, Texas — (1921 as 6-member **State Board of Examiners in Optometry**; name changed to present form in 1981 and membership increased to 9); apptv.; per diem; 6-yr.; 9 members: Jimmy Bitner, Fredericksburg (01/31/95); Terry Brown, Dallas (01/31/91); Barry J. Davis, Groves (01/31/95); Clinton M. DeWolfe, Houston (01/31/93); Stanley C. Pearle, Dallas (01/31/93); William D. Pittman, Mexia (01/31/91); Floyd L. Thornton, Wichita Falls (01/31/93); Marilyn Kay Walls, Cleburne (01/31/93); Elzie Mac Wright, Seminole (01/31/95). Exec. Dir., Lois Ewald, 9101 Burnet Rd., Ste. 214, Austin 78758 (non-member) ($37,275).

Pardons and Paroles Division, Board of — (1893 as **Board of Pardon Advisers**; changed in 1936 to Board of Pardons and Paroles with 3 members; membership increased to 6 in 1983; made a division of the Texas Department of Criminal Justice and membership increased to 18 in 1990); apptv.; 6-yr.; 18 members at $71,400: Hubert E. Bechtol, Austin (02/01/95); Irma Cauley, Bryan (02/01/97); Kenneth N. Coleman, Huntsville (02/01/97); Daniel L. Downs, Houston (02/01/95); Frank C. Eikenburg, Dallas (02/01/93); Bennie L. Elmore, Huntsville (02/01/93); John Escobedo, Huntsville (02/01/93); Troy G. Fox, Round Rock (02/01/95); Gloria Gibney, Corpus Christi (02/01/93); Ron D. Givens, Lubbock (02/01/93); James H. Granberry, Lubbock (02/01/95); Mae Johnson Jackson, Waco (02/01/97); Henry B. Keene, Austin (02/01/95); Peggy McAdams, Huntsville (02/01/97); Winona W. Miles, Austin (02/01/97); Stennett D. Posey, Georgetown (02/01/93); Albert G. Sanchez, Crystal City (02/01/97); Donn D. Woolery, Huntsville (02/01/95). Exec. Dir., James A. Lynaugh, Box 13401, Austin 78711 (non-member) ($69,300).

Parks and Wildlife Commission, Texas — (1963 as 3-member board; membership increased to 6 in 1971 and increased to 9 in 1983); apptv.; expenses; 6-yr.; 9 members: Lee M. Bass, Fort Worth (02/01/95); Henry C. Beck III, Dallas (02/01/95); Ygnacio D. Garza, Brownsville (02/01/97); Terese T. Hershey, Houston (02/01/97); George C. Hixon, San Antonio (02/01/95); John W. Kelsey, Houston (02/01/95); Charles D. Nash Jr., San Marcos (02/01/93); Beatrice C. Pickens, Amarillo (02/01/93); Thomas W. Umphrey, Beaumont (02/01/97). Exec. Dir., Andrew Sansom, 4200 Smith School Rd., Austin 78744 (non-member) ($75,600).

Pecos River Compact Commissioner — (1942); apptv.; 2-yr.; expenses: Billy L. Moody, Fort Stockton (01/23/93). Address: 401 N. Main, Fort Stockton 79735 ($19,084.

Pension Boards — For old age, blind and dependent children's assistance, see **Human Services, State Board of**. For unemployment compensation, see **Employment Commission, Texas**. For retirement pay to state and municipal employees and teachers, see proper category under **Retirement**.

Pension Review Board, State — (1979); apptv.; 6-yr.; 9 members — one senator apptd. by Lt. Gov., one representative apptd. by Speaker, 7 apptd. by Gov. as follows: Hugh L. Stephens, Dallas (01/31/97); Gary D. Hughes, Lubbock (01/31/91); Bob Hughey, Richardson (01/31/95); Joe M. Nuessle, Midland (01/31/93); Norman W. Parrish, Houston (01/31/95); Gilbert F. Vasquez, San Antonio (01/31/97); Paul H. Weyrauch, Marble Falls

(03/01/95). Exec. Dir., Rita Horwitz, Box 13498, Austin 78711 (non-member) ($44,100).

Pest Control Board, Texas Structural — (1971 as 7-member board, membership raised to 9 in 1979); apptv.; 6-yr.; expenses; 9 members — 3 ex officio: Commissioner of Agriculture; Commissioner of Health; and head of Entomology Dept., Texas A&M University; 6 apptv. members: Virgil C. Adams Sr., Denton (08/30/90); Merle M. Carlson, Houston (02/01/95); Robert W. Jenkins Sr., Marble Falls (02/01/95); Rayford G. Kay, Houston (02/01/93); David Melass, Lake Jackson (02/01/93); Richard M. Rogers, Dallas (08/30/89); Ray Patrick Thompson, Pasadena (02/01/97). Exec. Dir., Benny M. Mathis, 9101 Burnet Rd., Ste. 201, Austin 78758 ($48,537).

Pharmacy, Texas State Board of — (1907 as 6-member board; membership increased to 9 in 1981); apptv.; 6-yr.; 9 members: Thomas A. Aday, Plainview (08/31/95); Harold D. Eakman, San Angelo (08/31/91); Georgette Erskine-Hankins, Bedford (08/31/91); David Lee Franklin, Dallas (08/31/95); Albert E. Hopkins, Houston (08/31/91); Michael K. Lester, Dallas (08/31/93); Ann Peden, Hondo (08/31/95); Jerry D. Pyle, Arlington (08/31/93); Charles L. Rittenberry, Amarillo (08/31/93). Exec. Dir.-Sec., Fred S. Brinkley Jr., 8505 Cross Park Dr., Ste. 110, Austin 78754 (non-member) ($60,231).

Physical Fitness, Commission on — (1971); apptv., 6-yr., 15 members: Amanda Bullard, Austin (06/13/87); Dr. Kenneth H. Cooper, Dallas (06/13/89); William P. Daves, Dallas (06/13/91); George F. Dillman, Dallas (06/13/91); Dr. Ted L. Edwards, Austin (06/13/87); A.D. Gearner Jr., Dallas (06/13/89); Patrice McKinney, Colorado City (06/13/89); R. Lisa Rico Popp, Austin (06/13/91); Dr. Richard L. Shorkey, Beaumont (06/13/87); Rollin A. Sininger, Denton (06/13/87); Elvin Smith, College Station (06/13/91); Neal Spelce, Austin (06/13/91); Dr. William G. Squires Jr., Seguin (06/13/89); J. Terry Townsend, Austin (06/13/89); Cissy Woomer, Austin (06/13/87).

Physical Therapy Examiners, Texas State Board of — (1971); apptv.; 6-yr.; expenses; 9 members: Cecilia G. Akers, San Antonio (01/31/91); Russell J. Baird, Wharton (01/31/93); Travis B. Cox, San Antonio (01/31/95); Lila C. Cross, Boerne (01/31/95); Dorene P. Goodson, Arlington (01/31/95); Julia Hartman, Odessa (01/31/95); Lynn Laird, Amarillo (01/31/93); Richard Tinsley, Houston (01/31/91); Patricia E. Winchester, Midlothian (01/31/91). Exec. Dir., Sherry L. Lee, 313 Rundberg, Ste. 113, Austin 78753 (non-member) ($37,699).

Plumbing Examiners, State Board of — (1947 as 6-member board; membership increased to 9 in 1981: one each master plumber, journeyman plumber, plumbing inspector; 2 building contractors and 2 from general public); apptv.; expenses; 6-yr.; 9 members: Stanley J. Briers, Seabrook (09/05/91); Joe W. Campbell, Pasadena (09/05/91); Gerald L. Harris, Sugar Land (09/05/93); Phillip A. Lord, Houston (09/05/91); Jerry D. Moore, Pollok (09/05/95); Allison R. Smith, Comfort (09/05/93); Alonzo L. Starkey III, Kerrville (09/05/95); Michael J. Warren, North Richland Hills (09/05/95); William G. Wheeler, Victoria (09/05/93). Admin., Lynn Brown, 929 E. 41st, Austin 78751 (non-member) ($58,355).

Podiatry Examiners, State Board of — (1923 as 6-member State Board of Chiropody Examiners; name changed in 1967; made 9-member board in 1981); apptv.; 6-yr.; expenses; 9 members: Harry V. Burns, San Antonio (07/10/91); Ben Clark Jr., Dallas (07/10/95); Thomas F. Eckert, Tyler (07/10/91); Preston Goforth, Temple (07/10/93); John G. Knecht, Galveston (07/10/91); Eugene R. Scioli, Lubbock (07/10/93); Rick D. Sorrells, Dallas (07/10/95); Betty Frances Walker, Odessa (07/10/93); Peter J. Williams, San Antonio (07/10/95). Exec. Dir., D. Elliott Branson, D.P.M., 8420 Executive Center Dr., Ste. 305, Austin 78731 (non-member) (part-time $16,988).

Polygraph Examiners Board — (1965); apptv.; 6-yr.; 6 members: J. Glen Diviney, Hurst (06/18/93); Ed Hodges, Dallas (06/18/95); Ernie Hulsey, Houston (06/18/91); Horacio Ortiz, Corpus Christi (06/18/95); Eddie Senigaur, Gonzales (06/18/91); William J. Taylor, Round Rock (06/18/93). Exec. Officer, Bryan M. Perot, Box 4087, Austin 78773 (non-member) ($30,005).

Preservation Board, State — (1983); 2-yr.; 7 members — 4 ex officio: Gov., Lt. Gov., Speaker and Architect of Capitol; 3 apptv.: one apptd. by Gov., one senator apptd. by Lt. Gov. and one representative apptd. by Speaker. Gov's. apptee: Joseph F. Pinnelli, Austin (02/01/93). Office Address: Box 13286, Austin 78711.

Prison Board, Texas — (See **Criminal Justice, Texas Board of**.)

Private Investigators and Private Security Agencies, Board of — (1969); apptv.; expenses; 6-yr.; 8 members —

2 ex officio: Dir., Dept. of Public Safety and Atty. Gen.; 6 apptd. members: James Smith Bowie, Houston (01/31/95); Joel K. Glenn, Fort Worth (01/31/93); Patti Ivey, Robert Lee (01/31/91); Jack Montague, Austin (01/31/93); Robert D. Sanders, Sunnyvale (01/31/97); Jess Ann Thomason, Midland (01/31/95). Exec. Dir., Clema D. Sanders, Box 13509, Austin 78711 (non-member) ($41,919).

Produce Recovery Fund Board — (1977 as 3-member board; membership increased to 6 in 1981); apptv.; expenses; 6-yr.; 6 members — 2 each from commission merchants, general public and producer representatives. R.C. Allen, Corpus Christi (01/31/93); Douglas C. Brown, Waco (01/31/93); Humberto M. Garcia, Rio Grande City (01/31/92); Marian Sue Hawkins, Hart (01/31/95); Martin H. Rutchik, Dallas (01/31/91); Steven L. Weltman, Sugar Land (01/31/95). Admin., Margaret Alvarez, P.O. Box 12847, Austin 78711.

Productivity Bonus Commission — (See **Incentive and Productivity Commission, Texas.**)

Property Tax Board, State — (1977 as **School Tax Assessment Practices Board**; name changed in 1980); apptv.; 6-yr.; expenses; 6 members: George F. Bobbitt, Houston (03/01/93); Marvin L. Jones, Spearman (03/01/93); Jim N. Nugent, Amarillo (03/01/95); Roy Orr, DeSoto (03/01/97); Arthur C. White, Dallas (03/01/95); Gerald Winn, Bryan (03/01/91). Exec. Dir., Leon Wilhite, 4301 Westbank Dr., Bldg. B., Ste. 100, Austin 78746 (non-member) ($63,319).

Psychologists, Texas Board of Examiners of — (1969 as 6-member board; membership increased to 9 in 1981); apptv.; 6-yr.; per diem and expenses; 9 members: Barbara A. Bailey, Austin (10/31/91); Ronald A. Brandon, Temple (10/31/93); Kenneth K. Brimer, Livingston (10/31/95); Kenneth F. Kopel, Houston (01/31/95); Harold H. LeCrone Jr., Waco (10/31/91); Lisa Saemann, Dallas (10/31/91); Larry S. Schoenfeld, San Antonio (10/31/93); John Sell, Dallas (10/31/93); Jerome N. Sherman, Houston (10/31/95). Exec. Dir., Patricia S. Bizzell, 9101 Burnet Rd., Ste. 212, Austin 78758 ($40,263).

Public Accountancy, State Board of — (See **Accountancy, State Board of Public.**)

Public Finance Authority, Texas — (1984, assumed duties of **Texas Public Building Authority**); apptv.; per diem and expenses; 6-yr.; 3 members: E. Peter Pincoffs, Austin (02/01/95); Marc R. Stanley, Dallas (02/01/97); Harry M. Whittington, Austin (02/01/93). Exec. Dir., Glen Hartman, P.O. Box 12906, Austin 78711.

Public Safety Commission — (1935); apptv.; expenses; 6-yr.; 3 members: Albert Alkek, Houston (12/31/93); Calvin R. Guest, Bryan (12/31/91); Robert B. Holt, Midland (12/31/95). Dir., Joe E. Milner, Box 4087, Austin 78773 (non-member) ($79,800).

Public Utility Commission — (1975); apptv.; 6-yr., 3 members at $71,400: Jo Campbell, Austin (09/01/91); Marta R. Greytok, Seabrook (09/01/93); Paul D. Meek, Dallas (09/01/95). Exec. Dir., James Crouch, 7800 Shoal Creek Blvd., Ste. 400 N, Austin 78757 ($61,425).

Purchasing and General Services Commission, State — (1915 as **Board of Control**; name changed 1979); apptv.; 6-yr.; expenses; 3 members: Phillip A. Aronoff, Houston (01/31/93); Robert E. Davis, Irving (01/31/95); Anne Shelmire Wynne, Austin (01/31/97). Exec. Dir., Lias B. Steen, Box 13047, Austin 78711-3047 (non-member) ($69,300).

Racing Commission, Texas — (1986); 6-yr.; per diem and expenses; 8 members — 2 ex officio: Chmn. of Public Safety Commission and Comptroller; 6 apptv.: Glenn Blodgett, Guthrie (02/01/95); Anne Dunigan-Wilson, Abilene (02/01/97); Hugh A. Fitzsimons Jr., Carrizo Springs (02/01/95); Demarious L. Frey, Corpus Christi (02/01/93); A.L. Mangham Jr., Nacogdoches (02/01/95); Patricia H. Pangburn, Southlake (02/01/97). Exec. Secy., David J. Freeman, Box 12080, Austin 78711 (non-member) ($64,260).

Radiation Advisory Board — (1961 as 9-member board, membership increased to 18 in 1981); apptv.; 6-yr.; expenses; 18 members: Fred J. Bonte, Dallas (04/16/91); Ralph Buell, Lake Jackson (04/16/91); Thomas M. Burnette, Plano (04/16/95); William G. Hendrick, Austin (04/16/97); Joseph M. Kenworthy, Gatesville (04/16/91); Glen Keith King, Sugar Land (04/16/91); Jack S. Krohmer, Georgetown (04/16/93); Jesse W. Locke, Dallas (04/16/95); James C. Martin, Duncanville (04/16/95); Benjamin M. McKibbens, Harlingen (04/16/95); Anne W. Orr, Austin (04/16/91); Dr. Jack D. Ramsey, Abilene (04/16/91); Jeannette Rogers, Houston (04/16/95); Robert Daniel Smith, Austin (04/16/91); Michael D. Spence, Richardson (04/16/95); Vernie A. Stembridge, Dallas (04/16/93); William R. Underdown Jr., Bruni (04/16/93); Dr. Rodolfo L. Villarreal, Houston

(04/16/95).

Radioactive Waste Disposal Authority, Texas Low-Level — (1981); apptv.; 6-yr.; expenses; 6 members — one medical doctor, one health physicist, one attorney, one geologist and 2 from general public: James P. Allison, Austin (02/01/91); William L. Fisher, Austin (02/01/93); Milton J. Guiberteau, Houston (02/01/95); Tom Ingram, Midland (02/01/93); David Ojeda Jr., Carrizo Springs (02/01/97); John E. Simek, Bryan (02/01/95). Gen. Mgr., Lawrence R. Jacobi Jr., 7701 N. Lamar Blvd., Ste. 300, Austin 78752 (non-member) ($62,658).

Railroad Commission of Texas — Lena Guerrero, Austin (Austin) (12/31/92); Kent R. Hance Sr., Austin (Lubbock) (12/31/90); James E. Nugent, Austin (Kerrville) (12/31/88). Office Address: P.O. Box 12967, Austin 78711.

Real Estate Commission, Texas — Deborah Ann Aikin, Commerce (01/31/97); Weldon E. Traylor Sr., Houston (01/31/97); Robert T. Martin, Fort Worth (01/31/93); John L. Minor Jr., Houston (01/31/95); Henry Santamaria, El Paso (01/31/95); Marsha Shanklin, Victoria (01/31/91); Marsha Spencer, Houston (01/31/95); Michael N. Wieland, El Paso (01/31/91); Florence Willess, Dallas (01/31/93). Admin., Wallace Collins, P.O. Box 12188, Austin 78711.

Real Estate Research Advisory Committee — (1971); apptv.; 6-yr.; 10 members — one ex officio: representative of **Texas Real Estate Commission**; 9 apptv. members: Patsy Bohannan, Midland (01/31/95); Don R. Ellis, Del Rio (01/31/95); Alberto R. Gonzales, Houston (01/31/93); Bill Jennings, Fort Worth (01/31/91); Frederick D. McClure, San Augustine (01/31/91); Richard S. Seline, Houston (01/31/95); David L. Stirton, Houston (01/31/91); Jack W. Tumlinson, Cameron (01/31/93); Thomas Andrew Wilder, Euless (01/31/93). Dir., Richard F. Floyd, Texas Real Estate Research Center, Texas A&M, College Station 77843.

Red River Authority, Board of Directors — (1959); apptv.; 6-yr.; per diem and expenses; 9 members: George W. Arrington, Canadian (08/11/95); Ben D. Blackburn, Bells (08/11/91); Eric S. Clifford, Paris (08/11/95); Richard O. Harris Jr., Amarillo (08/11/93); Joe L. Johnson Jr., Wichita Falls (08/11/95); Stephen Ledwell, Texarkana (08/11/93); William L. Lindemann, Windthorst (08/11/91); Rex H. McAnelly, Pampa (08/11/91); Albert B. Wharton III, Vernon (08/11/91). Gen. Mgr., Ronald J. Glenn, 520 Hamilton Bldg., Wichita Falls 76301 (non-member).

Red River Compact Commissioner — (1949); apptv.; 4-yr.; (Function of commissioner is to negotiate with other states respecting waters of the Red. See also Canadian River Compact Commission): Nathan I. Reiter Jr., Texarkana (02/01/93). ($22,835).

Retirement System, Municipal, Board of Trustees — Andres Vega Jr., Brownsville (02/01/97).

Redistricting Board, Legislative — (See **Legislative Redistricting Board**.)

Rehabilitation Commission, Texas — (1969); apptv.; expenses; 6-yr.; 6 members: Emanuel Bodner, Houston (08/31/91); Jim Gray, Longview (08/31/93); Jerry Kane, Corpus Christi (08/31/93); Diane Doehne Rath, San Antonio (08/31/91); A. Kent Waldrep Jr., Plano (08/31/95); Ray A. Wilkerson, Austin (08/31/95). Commissioner, Vernon M. Arrell, 4900 N. Lamar Blvd., Austin 78751 (non-member) ($75,600).

Retirement System of Texas, Employees — (1949); apptv.; 6-yr.; 7 members — one apptd. by Gov., one by Chief Justice of State Supreme Court and one by Speaker; 3 are employee members of the system serving 6-yr. overlapping terms. Pamela A. Carley, Austin (08/31/91); Jack D. Kyle, Huntsville (08/31/92); B.L. Parker, Austin (08/31/94); J. Michael Weiss, Lubbock (08/31/94); Marcus Yancey, Austin (08/31/93); Janice R. Zitleman, Austin (08/31/95). Exec. Dir., Clayton T. Garrison, Box 13207, Capitol Sta., Austin 78711 (non-member).

Retirement System, Municipal, Board of Trustees — (1947); apptv.; 6-yr.; expenses; 6 members: Ronald Everett Cox, Kilgore (02/01/93); Rita Harmon, Lubbock (02/01/95); Stephen W. McCullough, Irving (02/01/93); Jim D. Starr, Hurst (02/01/95); Charles E. Wilson, Waco (01/31/97). Dir. and Exec. Sec., Jimmie L. Mormon, 1200 N. I-35, Austin 78701.

Retirement System of Texas, Teacher — (1937 as 6-member board; membership increased to 9 in 1973); expenses; 6-yr.; 9 members — 2 apptd. by State Board of Education, 3 apptd. by Gov. and 4 TRS members apptd. by Gov. after being nominated by popular ballot of members of the retirement system, one of these 4 to be a retired member and another to be a member from

higher education: George M. Crowson, Houston (08/31/95); Stephen C. Mahood, Dallas (08/31/93); Sue McGarvey, Hallsville (08/31/95); Frank Monroe, Dallas (08/31/93); Sheila Jackson Payne, Arlington (08/31/91); A.W. "Dub" Riter, Tyler (08/31/95); Clarence A. Roberson, Fort Worth (08/31/93); Edward H. Wicker, Beeville (08/31/91); Dana Williams, Corpus Christi (08/31/91). Exec. Sec., Bruce Hineman, 1000 Red River, Austin 78701 (non-member) ($65,000).

Retirement System, Texas County and District — (1967); apptv.; 6-yr.; 9 members: Fred R. Clark, New Braunfels (12/31/93); Giles W. Dalby, Post (12/31/91); Bill D. Hicks, Odessa (12/31/93); Kathy Hynson, Rosenberg (12/31/95); Steve Radack, Houston (12/31/95); Sam D. Seale, Port Lavaca (12/31/91); Carl S. Smith, Houston (12/31/91); Bill W. Wallis, Tyler (12/31/95); Durward O. Wright, Midland (12/31/93). Exec. Dir., J. Robert Brown, 400 W. 14th, Austin 78701 (non-member).

Rio Grande Compact Commissioner of Texas — (1929); apptv.; 6-yr.: Jack Hammond, El Paso (06/09/95). Box 12785, El Paso 79913 ($38,830).

Rio Grande Valley Municipal Water Authority — (1969); apptv.; 2-yr.; 10 members: Charles C. Cardenas, McAllen (04/30/92); Dr. Joseph B. Coulter, Brownsville (04/30/91); Sylvia H. Flores, Mercedes (04/30/92); John Halm Jr., Raymondville (04/30/91); Roel R. Ramirez, Roma (04/30/92); J.L. Taylor, McAllen (04/30/92); John W. Topp, Harlingen (04/30/92); Connie de la Garza, Harlingen (04/30/91). Mgr., Ersel Lantz, 3505 Boca Chica, Ste. 333, Brownsville 78521.

Runnels County Water Authority, Board of Directors — (1955); apptv.; 6-yr.; 9 members: James D. Condra, Talpa (02/01/95); Leon Frerich, Norton (02/01/93); Marvin W. Gerhart, Winters (02/01/95); Werner Harsch, Miles (02/01/93); E. Jerry Holden, Ballinger (02/01/91); Elliott J. Kemp, Ballinger (02/01/93); Wilson A. McCown, Miles (02/01/91); Oswald D. Reed, Winters (02/01/91); Kenneth H. Slimp, Winters (02/01/95).

Rural Health Initiatives, Exec. Comm. of the Center for — (1989); 6-yr.; expenses; 9 members: Jim Bob Brame, Eldorado (08/31/95); Lynda Calcote, Abilene (08/31/93); Michael P. Ellis, Daingerfield (08/31/91).

Rural Medical Education Board, State — (1973); apptv.; 6-yr.; per diem and expenses; 6 members: James W. Caldwell, Rockwall (02/27/92); James W. Farris, Paris (02/27/94); Richard M. Hall, Eden (02/27/90); Sam A. Nixon, Houston (02/27/94); Billie Marie Veach, Austin (02/27/90); Leo L. Westerholm, Port Lavaca (02/27/92). Dir., J. C. Randolph, Box 12663, Austin 78711 (non-member).

Sabine River Authority, Board of Directors — (1949); apptv.; per diem and expenses; 6-yr.; 9 members: Nolton L. Brown, Bridge City (07/06/91); John H. Butts, San Augustine (07/06/91); James E. Campbell, Center (07/06/95); John W. Cooke, Carthage (07/06/91); Luther Earl Davis, Hemphill (07/06/93); Jerry G. Forbes, Quinlan (07/06/95); Horace F. McQueen, Tyler (07/06/93); Thomas C. Merritt, Longview (07/06/95); William Y. Rice, Longview (07/06/93). Exec. Vice Pres. & Gen. Mgr., Sam F. Collins, Box 579, Orange 77630 (non-member).

Sabine River Compact Commission — (1953); apptv.; 6-yr.; 5 members — one member and chmn. apptd. by President of United States without a vote; 2 from Texas and 2 from Louisiana. Texas members: David V. Cardner, Orange (07/12/95); Danny Choate, Orange (07/12/92). ($4,070). Office Address: Box 579, Orange 77630.

San Jacinto Historical Advisory Board — (1907 as San Jacinto State Park Commission; changed to San Jacinto Battleground Commission and changed again in 1965 to present name); apptv.; 6-yr.; 5 members — 2 ex officio: Dir., Parks Div., Parks and Wildlife Dept. and pres. of San Jacinto Museum of History Assn. 3 apptd. by Gov.: Helen Alexander, Houston (09/01/91); Cecil D. Ghormely, Houston (09/01/93); Joel Moore Nash, Bellaire (09/01/95). Parks Section, Parks and Wildlife Dept., 4200 Smith School Rd., Austin 78744.

San Jacinto River Authority, Board of Directors — (1937); apptv.; expenses while on duty; 6-yr.; 6 members: Varreece Berry, Pasadena (10/16/91); Henry T. Brooks, Conroe (10/16/93); James T. Edmonds, Houston (10/16/93); R. Gary Montgomery, The Woodlands (10/16/95); Ralph Shirley, Houston (10/16/91); Walter D. Wilkerson Jr., Conroe (10/16/95). Gen. Mgr., James R. Adams, Box 329, Conroe 77305 (non-member).

Savings and Loan Commissioner — Apptv. by State Finance Commission: James L. Pledger, 2601 N. Lamar, Ste. 201, Austin 78705. ($82,735).

School Land Board — (See **Land Board, School**.)

Secretary of State — (1836 by Constitution of Republic of Texas, 1876 by present Constitution); apptv.: John Hannah, Box 12887, Austin 78711-2887 ($72,549).

Securities Board, State — (Est. 1957, the outgrowth of several amendments to the Texas Securities Act, originally passed 1913); act is administered by the **Securities Commissioner,** who is appointed by the board members; expenses; 6-yr.; 3 members: Duncan E. Boeckman, Dallas (01/20/95); Thomas B. McDade, Houston (01/20/93); Thomas D. Warner, Houston (01/20/97). **Securities Commissioner,** Richard D. Latham, Box 13167, Capitol Sta., Austin 78711 ($69,325).

Seed and Plant Board, State — (1959); apptv.; 2-yr.; 6 members: George B. Babcock, Lubbock (10/06/91); William F. Bennett Sr., Lubbock (10/06/91); Gary T. Ivey, Ralls (10/06/92); Charles Leamons, Weimar (10/06/92); Edward C.A. Runge, College Station (10/06/91); Romeo M. Villarreal, Edinburg (10/06/92). Office Address: Texas Dept. of Agriculture, Box 12847, Austin 78711.

Sex Offender Treatment, Interagency Council on — (1983); 12 members — 9 ex officio: one each from Texas Dept. of Corrections, Board of Pardons and Paroles, Texas Adult Probation Commission, Texas Juvenile Probation Commission, Texas Dept. of Mental Health and Mental Retardation, Texas Youth Commission, Sam Houston State University, Texas Dept. of Human Services and one member of Gov's. office administering criminal justice planning; 3 apptv. from general public; 6-yr.; expenses; apptv. members: Collier M. Cole, Dickinson (02/01/91); Walter J. Meyer III, Galveston (02/01/95); Norma W. Reed, El Paso (02/01/93).

Soil and Water Conservation Board, Texas State: 5 members: Joe Antilley, Abilene (05/05/92); Harvey Davis, Temple (05/07/91); Albert H. Evans Jr., Henderson (05/05/92); C.F. "Dick" Schendel, Goliad (05/07/91); Fred Squyres, Dumas (05/07/91). Exec. Dir., Robert G. Buckley, P.O. Box 650, Temple 76503.

Space Commission, Texas — (1988); apptv.; 6-yr.; expenses; 9 members: Joseph P. Allen IV, Houston (02/01/95); Jerry C. Bostick, Seabrook (02/01/91); Lenox Carruth Jr., Dallas (02/01/91); David A. Heuer, Houston (02/01/95); Frank Maresh, Houston (02/91/95); Oran Nicks, College Station (02/01/93); Sarah A. Peterson, Houston (02/01/93); Emyre B. Robinson, Dickinson (02/01/91); Jack M. Webb, Houston (02/01/93).

Speech Pathology & Audiology, State Committee of Examiners for — (1983); apptv.; 6-yr.; per diem and expenses; 9 members — 3 audiologists, 3 speech-language pathologists and 3 from general public: Harold S. Beaver, Holland (08/31/91); Susan Gay Dorsett, Stephenville (08/31/93); Marilyn S. Duncan, Dallas (08/31/93); Carol N. Gore, El Paso (08/31/95); Carol M. Hering, Austin (08/31/91); Gene R. Powers, Austin (08/31/95); Marjorie R. Sanger, Waco (08/31/91); Drew G. Sawyer, Austin (08/31/95); Saundra C. Waters, Houston (08/31/91). Exec. Secy., Dorothy Cawthon, Texas Dept. of Health, 1100 W. 49th, Austin 78756.

Student Loan Corporation, Texas Guaranteed — (1979); 6-yr.; 11 members — one ex officio; Comptroller of Public Accounts; one apptd. by Commissioner of Higher Education and one apptd. by Chmn. of Coordinating Board; 8 apptd. by Gov. as follows: Lee Elliott Brown, Houston (01/31/97); Gary W. Bruner, Arlington (01/31/95); Paul H. Ellis, Austin (01/31/97); Elizabeth G. Flores, Laredo (01/31/97); Mark Griffin, Lubbock (01/31/93); Wright L. Lassiter Jr., Dallas (01/31/95); Alan V. Rash, El Paso (01/31/95); J. Malon Southerland, College Station (01/31/93). Exec. Dir., Joe L. McCormick, Box 15996, Austin 78711 (non-member).

Sulphur River Basin Authority, Board of Directors — (1985); apptd.; 6-yr.; per diem and expenses; 6 members: David Baucom, Sulphur Springs (02/01/95); Curtis R. Fendley, Paris (02/01/91); William O. Morriss, Texarkana (02/01/93); Katherine C. Ramsay, Mount Vernon (02/01/93); Vatra Solomon, Mount Pleasant (02/01/91); Carroll Wheeler, Texarkana (02/01/91).

Sunset Advisory Commission — (1977); 10 members: 4 members of House of Representatives, 4 members of Senate, one public member apptd. by Speaker, one public member apptd. by Lt. Gov.; 4-yr.; expenses; 2 public members: Lynn Eggers, Grapevine (08/31/91); Nancy C. Speck, Nacogdoches (08/31/91). Dir., Bill Wells, P.O. Box 13066, Austin 78711.

Surplus Property Agency, Texas — (1945 as **Texas State Educational Agency for Surplus Property;** name changed to present form 1949); apptv.; 6-yr.; expenses; 9 members: Franklin P. Adams, Richardson (03/19/91); Emmett H. Allen, Fort Worth (03/19/93); Robert Caskey, Johnson City (03/19/91); M.F. Connor, Weslaco (03/19/93); Robert A. Lansford, Austin (03/19/95); Pat Legan, San Antonio (03/19/93); Molly Ann Pryor, Houston (03/19/91); Trevor D. Rees-Jones, Dallas (03/19/95);

Herman H. Wommack Jr., Texarkana (03/19/95). Exec. Dir., Marvin J. Titzman, Box 8120, San Antonio 78208-0120 (non-member) ($51,450).

Tax Board, State — (1905); ex officio; term in other office; no compensation; 3 members: Comptroller, Secretary of State and State Treasurer.

Tax Professional Examiners, Board of — (1977 as **Board of Tax Assessor Examiners;** name changed to present form 1983); apptv.; expenses; 6-yr.; 6 members: Herb Barnhart, Denton (03/01/93); Ruth g. Clayton, San Marcos (03/01/97); Phyllis J. Colon, Corpus Christi (03/01/95); Harris Oswalt, Tyler (03/01/95); Ciro Trevino, Edinburg (03/01/97); Cora B. Viescas, El Paso (03/01/93). Exec. Dir., Sam H. Smith, 4301 Westbank Dr., Bldg. B, Ste. 140, Austin 78761 (non-member) ($40,926).

Teacher Retirement System — (See **Retirement System, Teacher.**)

Teachers' Professional Practices Commission — (1969); apptv.; expenses; 3-yr.; 15 members: Marilyn Adams, Austin (08/31/91); Audean Allman, Houston (08/31/91); Charles W. Blanton, Dallas (08/31/91); Robert W. Caster, Palestine (08/31/92); Jimmye R. Hancock, Paris (08/31/91); Drusilla M. Knight, Corpus Christi (08/31/91); Rosa D. Lavender, Kerrville (08/31/91); Marsha W. Lilly, Stafford (08/31/91); Carroll B. Lockett, Lubbock (08/31/91); Evelyn C. Reed, San Antonio (08/31/91); Irene Rieck, Brownfield (08/31/92); Glenda J. Scarbrough, Andrews (08/31/91); Thomasine Sparks, Kingsville (08/31/91); Susan Tuminello, Houston (08/31/91); John E. Wilson, Amarillo (08/31/91). Dir., Edward Vodicka, 1701 N. Congress, Austin 78701.

Texas A&M University System-Board of Regents — (1875); apptv.; 6-yr.; expenses; 9 members: Billy W. Clayton, Springlake (02/01/95); Douglas R. DeCluitt, Waco (02/01/93); Raul B. Fernandez, San Antonio (02/01/95); Alison W. Leland, Houston (02/01/97); Ross D. Margraves Jr., Houston (02/01/95); William A. McKenzie, Dallas (02/01/93); Wayne Showers, McAllen (02/01/93); Mary Nan West, Batesville (02/01/97); Royce W. Wisenbaker, Tyler (02/01/97). Chancellor, Perry L. Adkisson, College Station 77843-1123 (non-member).

Texas Development Board — (1959); 3 ex officio members; Governor; Chmn., Texas Industrial Commission; and Chmn. of Texas Highway and Public Transportation Commission.

Texas Southern University, Board of Regents — (1947); expenses; 6-yr.; 9 members: Joe M. Bailey, Houston (02/01/97); Rufus Cormier Jr., Houston (02/01/93); Percy P. Creuzot, Houston (02/01/93); Walter H. Criner, Houston (02/01/95); Carole A. Fleming, Sugar Land (02/01/93); David S. Gamble, Houston (02/01/93); Jenard M. Gross, Houston (02/01/97); Odysseus M. Lanier, Houston (02/01/95); Carroll W. Phillips, Houston (02/01/95). Pres., Dr. William H. Harris, 3100 Cleburne, Houston 77004 (non-member).

Texas State Technical Institute, Board of Regents — (1960); apptv.; expenses; 6-yr.; 9 members: E.A. Aguilar Jr., El Paso (08/31/91); George W. Baur, Houston (08/31/93); John E. Davis, Waco (08/31/93); Ricardo Gutierrez, Rio Grande City (08/31/95); Jesse S. Harris, Dallas (08/31/93); George Fred Rhodes, Port Lavaca (08/31/91); Jere J. Ruff, Longview (08/31/95); Mollie Anna Solomon, Groves (08/31/91); David W. Taylor, Houston (08/31/95). Chancellor, Dr. Cecil L. Groves, TSTI System, Waco 76705 (non-member).

Texas State University System, Board of Regents — (1911 as **Board of Regents of State Teachers Colleges;** name changed in 1965 to **Board of Regents of State Senior Colleges;** changed to present form in 1975); apptv.; per diem and expenses; 6-yr.; 9 members: William L. (Bill) Cunningham, San Marcos (02/01/97); Norman D. Elder, Del Rio (02/01/93); Becky R. Espino, Fort Stockton (02/01/97); Thomas R. Kowalski, Austin (02/01/95); Daniel N. Matheson III, Austin (02/01/95); Jane Monday, Huntsville (02/01/97); Daniel S. Ouellette, Beeville (02/01/95); W.C. Perry, Waco (02/01/93); Clyde Waddell Jr., Lubbock (02/01/93). Exec. Dir., Lamar G. Urbanovsky, 505 Sam Houston Bldg., Austin 78701 (non-member).

Texas Tech University, Board of Regents — (1923); apptv.; expenses; 6-yr.; 9 members: Richard E. Cavazos, Leander (01/31/95); Rex P. Fuller, Lubbock (01/31/93); James L. Gulley Jr., Tyler (01/31/95); Claude C. Hobbs, Waco (01/31/93); James L. Johnson, Irving (01/31/95); Patsy W. Martin, Austin (01/31/97); John C. Sims, Lubbock (01/31/97); Elizabeth (Cissy) Ward, Houston (01/31/97); Alan B. White, Lubbock (01/31/95). Secy., Freda Pierce, Box 4039, Lubbock 79409 (non-member).

Texas Woman's University Board of Regents — (1901); apptv.; expenses; 6-yr.; 9 members: Jeanne L.

Johnson, Dallas (02/01/95); Ms. J. Willis Johnson, San Angelo (02/01/93); Jayne Lipe, Fort Worth (02/01/97); Diana E. Marshall, Houston (02/01/97); Darlene T. Medrano, Harlingen (02/01/97); Don C. Reynolds, Fort Worth (02/01/95); Elizabeth B. Sellers, Houston (02/01/93); Glen E. Sparks, Irving (02/01/93); Kris Anne Vogelpohl, Galveston (02/01/95). Pres., Dr. Shirley S. Chater, Box 23025, TWU Sta., Denton 76204 (non-member).

Textbook Committee, State — (1929 as **Textbook Advisory Committee;** under Gilmer-Aikin Act of 1949 name changed to present form); apptd. by **Board of Education** and is recommended by Commissioner of Education; 1-yr., 15 members.

Treasurer, State — (1835 by Provisional Government of Texas, 1876 by present Constitution); elective; (2-yr. by original constitutional provision; raised to 4-yr. in 1972, effective 1975): Kay Bailey Hutchison, (01/01/95). Box 12608, Austin 78711 ($74,698).

Trinity River Authority, Board of Directors — (1955); apptv.; per diem and expenses; 6-yr.; 24 directors — 3 from Tarrant County, 4 from Dallas County, 2 from area-at-large and one each from 15 other districts: Albert C. Barger, Centerville (03/15/93); Jake Caprielian, Crockett (03/15/97); Jack A. Coleman Jr., Palestine (03/15/95); Berlin M. Cummings, Fort Worth (03/15/91); Donald F. Dean, Madisonville (03/15/93); William D. Elliott, Dallas (03/15/95); T. Walter Erwin III, Ennis (03/15/93); Robert A. Estrada, Dallas (03/15/91); Joseph C. Gerard, Malakoff (03/15/95); Blake Gillen, Corsicana (03/15/91); Robert D. Hardy Jr., Huntsville (03/15/95); Roger C. Hunsaker, Fort Worth (03/15/93); William L. Hutchison, Dallas (03/15/95); Melvin W. Jackson Jr., Dallas (03/15/91); David B. Jenkins, Stowell (03/15/91); Erma C. Johnson, Fort Worth (03/15/95); B.C. Lively, Livingston (03/15/91); Maurice Lee Locke, Liberty (03/15/95); C. L. McCuistion Jr., Forney (03/15/93); Stephen L. Tatum, Fort Worth (03/15/97); H. Gene Reynolds Jr., Fairfield (03/15/95); John W. Rhea Jr., Dallas (03/15/93); James H. Sewell, Coldspring (03/15/93); Lee Wayne Vanecek, Trinity (03/15/93). Gen. Mgr., Danny F. Vance, Box 60, Arlington 76004 (non-member).

Turnpike Authority, Texas - Board of Directors — (1953 as 9-member board; increased to 12 members in 1971); 6-yr.; 12 members — 3 ex officio; 3 members of State Highway and Public Transportation Commission; 9 apptv. as follows: Richard L. Bischoff, Houston (02/15/91); Robert L. Collins, Houston (02/15/91); William P. Manomes Jr., Dallas (02/15/95); Charles R. Matthews, Garland (02/15/93); Philip Montgomery, Dallas (02/15/95); James N. Muns, Dallas (02/15/93); Ed Palm, Fort Worth (02/15/91); Clive Runnells, Houston (02/15/93); Jere W. Thompson Jr., Dallas (02/15/95). Exec. Dir., John B. Ramming, 190369, Dallas 75219 (non-member).

Uniform State Laws, Commission on — (1941 as 5-member **Commissioners to the National Conference on Uniform State Laws;** name changed to present form, membership increased to 6 and term of office raised to 6 years in 1977); apptv.; 6-yr.; 6 members: Patrick C. Guillot, Dallas (09/30/94); David Peeples, San Antonio (09/30/92); Rodney W. Satterwhite, Midland (09/30/96); George L. Thompson III, Lubbock (09/30/96); Bradley J.B. Toben, Waco (09/30/94); Edmund R. Wood, Dallas (09/30/92).

University of Houston, Board of Regents — (1963); apptv.; expenses; 6-yr.; 9 members: Dorothy J. Alcorn, Victoria (08/31/93); John T. Cater, Houston (08/31/95); Elizabeth L. Ghrist, Houston (08/31/95); C. F. Kendall III, Houston (08/31/91); James L. Ketelsen, Houston (08/31/93); Kenneth L. Lay, Houston (08/31/93); Xavier C. Lemond, Katy (08/31/91); Vidal G. Martinez, Houston (08/31/95); R. E. Reamer, Houston (08/31/91). Chancellor Dr. Alexander F. Schilt, 1600 Smith, Houston 77002 (non-member).

University of North Texas Board of Regents — (1949); apptv.; 6-yr.; expenses; 9 members: J.S. Farrington, Dallas (05/22/93); Becky Ann Garth, Temple (05/22/89); Nancy S. Halbreich, Dallas (05/22/91); Joe Kirven, Dallas (05/22/95); E. L. Langley, Irving (05/22/95); Lucille G. Murchison, Addison (05/22/93); Billie L. Parker, Fort Worth (05/22/93); Edwin Bruce Street Jr., Graham (05/22/91); Topsy R. Wright, Grand Prairie (05/22/91). Chancellor, Alfred Hurley, Box 13737, NT Sta., Denton 76203-3737 (non-member).

University of Texas System, Board of Regents — (1881); apptv.; expenses; 6-yr.; 9 members: Sam E. Barshop, San Antonio (02/01/93); Louis A. Beecherl Jr., Dallas (02/01/93); Robert J. Cruikshank, Houston (02/01/95); Zan Wesley Holmes Jr., Dallas (02/01/97); Thomas G. Loeffler, Mason (02/01/95); W.A. "Tex"

Moncrief Jr., Fort Worth (02/01/93); Mario E. Ramirez, Roma (02/01/95); Bernard Rapoport, Waco (02/01/97); Ellen C. Temple, Lufkin (02/01/97). Chancellor, Hans Mark, 601 Colorado, Austin 78701 (non-member).

Vehicle Equipment Safety Commissioner — (1965); apptv.; George W. Busby, Dept. of Public Safety, Austin.

Veterans Commission, Texas — (1927 as **Veterans State Service Office;** reorganized as **Veterans Affairs Commission** in 1947 with 5 members; membership increased to 6 in 1981; name changed to present form in 1985); apptv.; 6-yr.; per diem while on duty and expenses; 6 members: Samuel Bier, Austin (12/31/91); Manuel A. Cano, Mercedes (12/31/95); William R. Crawford, Plano (12/31/95); Barnie O. Henderson Jr., Cameron (12/31/93); Billy R. Kirby, Clinton (12/31/91); James S. Novy, San Antonio (12/31/95). Exec. Dir., Douglas K. Brown, Box 12277, Austin 78711 (non-member) ($46,041).

Veterans Land Board — (Est. 1949 as 3-member ex officio board; reorganized 1956); 4-yr.; per diem and expenses; 3 members: one ex officio: Comm. of General Land Office; 2 apptd.: Jonathan Rogers, El Paso (12/19/92); Jim Sale, Dallas (12/29/90). Exec. Sec., Jack Guiberson; Stephen F. Austin Bldg., Austin 78701 (non-member) ($57,474).

Veterinary Medical Examiners, State Board of — (1911; revised 1953; made 9-member board in 1981); apptv.; expenses on duty; 6-yr.; 9 members: Larry M. Dubuisson, Weslaco (08/26/93); Olivia Ruth Eudaly, Fort Worth (08/26/93); Alton F. Hopkins, Dallas (08/26/95); Mike Levi, Spicewood (08/26/91); Robert D. Lewis, Elgin (08/26/93); Mary E. Mainster, San Antonio (08/26/91); Guy Alvin Sheppard, SAn Angelo (08/26/95); Fred K. Soifer, Houston (08/26/91); Clark S. Willingham, Dallas (08/26/95). Exec. Dir., Donald B. Wilson, 1946 S. I-35, Ste. 306, Austin 78704 (non-member) ($45,449).

Water Commission, Texas — (1913 as **State Board of Water Engineers;** name changed in 1962 to **Texas Water Commission;** reorganized and name again changed in 1965 to **Water Rights Commission;** reorganized and name changed to present form in 1977 to perform the judicial function for the **Texas Dept. of Water Resources**); apptv.; 6-yr.; 3 members full-time at $71,400: J.E. Birdwell Jr., Lubbock (08/31/95); John L. Hall, Austin (08/31/91); Buck Jim Wynne III, Dallas (08/31/93). Exec. Dir., Alan P. Beinke Jr., Box 13087, Austin 78711 (non-member) ($70,711).

Water Development Board, Texas — (1957; legislative function for the **Texas Dept. of Water Resources,** 1977); apptv.; per diem and expenses; 6-yr.; 6 members: Thomas M. Dunning, Dallas (12/31/91); Noe Fernandez, McAllen (12/31/95); Charles M. Jenness, Houston (12/31/91); William B. Madden, Dallas (12/31/95); Wesley Edwin Pittman, Midland (12/31/93); one vacancy. Exec. Admin., M. G.E. Gretschmar, Box 13231, Austin 78711 (non-member) ($63,000).

Water Resources Planning Commission, Multi-State — (1985); apptv.; 6-yr.; 6 members: A.L. Black, Friona (02/01/87); T.D. Howell, Marshall (02/01/89); Tom Masterson, Houston (02/01/91); Idris Traylor Jr., Lubbock (02/01/89); Judson William, El Paso (02/01/91).

Water Well Drillers Board, Texas — (1961 as 8-member board; reorganized 1981 and membership increased to 9); apptv.; per diem and expenses; 6-yr.; 9 members — 6 water-well drillers, 3 from general public: Frank Del Rio, Austin (09/15/91); Jerry F. Fontaine, Palestine (09/15/93); Gary Dean Grant, Abernathy (09/15/95); James Frank Grimes, Dallas (09/15/95); Cynthia E. Hall, Austin (09/15/95); Barry Henderson, Longview (09/15/91); Walter O'Neil Loftis, Midland (09/15/93); Frank Rosenkranz Jr., San Antonio (09/15/95); John N. Walker, Alvin (09/15/91). Steve Wiley, TDWR, Box 13087, Capitol Sta., Austin 78711 (non-member).

Workers Compensation Commission, Texas — (1991); 6-yr.; apptv.; expenses; 6 members: Ramon Class, Canyon (02/01/91); Jack Garey, Austin (02/01/95); Joe L. Hanson, Richardson (02/01/97); Edward K. Hayse Jr., North Richland Hills (02/01/95); O.D. Kenemore, Lake Jackson (02/01/95); Dewey Mark, San Antonio (02/01/91). Exec. Dir., Geroge Chapman, 4000 S. I-35, Austin 78704.

Youth Commission, Texas — (1949 as 9-member board; reorganized 1957 and again in 1975); 6-yr.; per diem on duty; 6 apptv. members: Gary D. Compton, Amarillo (08/31/91); Comer J. Cottrell, Dallas (08/31/93); Edna L. Tamayo, Harlingen (08/31/93); Rev. Floyd Williams, Houston (08/31/95); Marilla B. Wood, Houston (08/31/91); Larry F. York, Austin (08/31/91). Exec. Dir., Ron Jackson, Box 4260, Austin 78765 (non-member) ($75,600).

CHIEF TEXAS ADMINISTRATIVE OFFICIALS

On this and following pages are lists of the principal administrative officials who have served the Republic and State of Texas with dates of their tenures of office. In a few instances there are disputes as to the exact beginning and ending of these tenures. Dates given in these lists are those that appear to be most authentic.

*Spanish Royal Governors

Domingo Teran de los Rios	1691-1692
Gregorio de Salinas	1692-1697
Francisco Cuerbo y Valdez	1698-1702
Mathias de Aguirre	1703-1705
Martin de Alarcon	1705-1708
Simon Padilla y Cordova	1708-1712
Pedro Fermin de Echevers y Subisa	1712-1714
Juan Valdez	1714-1716
Martin de Alarcon	1716-1719
Marquis de San Miguel de Aguayo	1719-1722
Fernando Perez de Almazan	1722-1727
Melchor de Media Villa y Ascona	1727-1730
Juan Bustillo Zevallos	1730-1734
Manuel de Sandoval	1734-1736
Carlos Benites Franquis de Lugo	1736-1737
Prudencio de Orobio y Bazterra	1737-1741
Tomas Felipe Wintuisen	1741-1743
Justo Boneo y Morales	1743-1744
Francisco Garcia Larios	1744-1748
Pedro del Barrio Junco y Espriella	1748-1751
Jacinto de Barrios y Jauregui	1751-1759
Angel Martos y Navarrete	1759-1766
Hugo Oconor	1767-1770
Baron de Ripperda	1770-1778
Domingo Cabello	1778-1786
Bernardo Bonavia	1786-1786
Rafael Martinez Pacheco	1787-1788
The office of Governor was ordered suppressed and the province put under a presidial captain for a period in	1788-1789
Manuel Munoz	1790-1798
Josef Irigoyen	1798-1800
Juan Bautista de Elguezabal	1800-1805
Antonio Cordero y Bustamante	1805-1810
Juan Bautista Casas	1811-1811
Manuel de Salcedo	1811-1813
Cristobal Dominguez	1814-1817
Ignacio Perez	1817-1817
Manuel Pardo	1817-1817
Antonio Martinez	1817-1822

Governors Under Mexican Rule

The first two Governors under Mexican rule, Trespalacios and Garcia, were of Texas only as Texas was then constituted. Beginning with Gonzales, 1824, the Governors were for the joint State of Coahuila-Texas.

Jose Felix Trespalacios	1822-1823
Luciano Garcia	1823-1824
Rafael Gonzales	1824-1826
Victor Blanco	1826-1827
Jose Maria Viesca	1827-1830
Jose Maria Letona	1831-1832
Ramon Eca y Musquiz	1830-1831
Ramon Eca y Musquiz	1832-1832
Juan Martin de Beramendi	1832-1833
Juan Jose de Vidauri y Villasenor	1833-1834
Juan Jose Elguezabal	1834-1835
Jose Maria Cantu	1835-1835
Agustin M. Viesca	1835-1835
Marciel Borrego	1835-1835
Ramon Eca y Musquiz	1835-1835

Provisional Colonial Governor, Before Independence

†Henry Smith (Impeached)	1835
†James W. Robinson	

Presidents of the Republic of Texas

David G. Burnet	Mar. 16, 1836-Oct. 22, 1836
Sam Houston	Oct. 22, 1836-Dec. 10, 1838
Mirabeau B. Lamar	Dec. 10, 1838-Dec. 13, 1841
Sam Houston	Dec. 13, 1841-Dec. 9, 1844
Anson Jones	Dec. 9, 1844-Feb. 19, 1846

Governors Since Annexation

J. Pinckney Henderson	Feb. 19, 1846-Dec. 21, 1847
‡Albert C. Horton	
George T. Wood	Dec. 21, 1847-Dec. 21, 1849
P. Hansbrough Bell	Dec. 21, 1849-Nov. 23, 1853
J. W. Henderson	Nov. 23, 1853-Dec. 21, 1853
Elisha M. Pease	Dec. 21, 1853-Dec. 21, 1857
Hardin R. Runnels	Dec. 21, 1857-Dec. 21, 1859
Sam Houston (resigned because of state's secession)	Dec. 21, 1859-Mar. 16, 1861
Edward Clark	Mar. 16, 1861-Nov. 7, 1861
Francis R. Lubbock (resigned to enter Confederate	

Army)	Nov. 7, 1861-Nov. 5, 1863
Pendleton Murrah (administration terminated by fall of Confederacy)	Nov. 5, 1863-June 17, 1865
Fletcher S. Stockdale (Lt. Gov. performed some duties of office on Murrah's departure, but is sometimes included in list of Governors. Hamilton's appointment was for immediate succession as shown by dates.)	
Andrew J. Hamilton (Provisional, appointed by President Johnson)	June 17, 1865-Aug. 9, 1866
Jas. W. Throckmorton	Aug. 9, 1866-Aug. 8, 1867
Elisha M. Pease (appointed July 30, 1867, under martial law)	Aug. 8, 1867-Sept. 30, 1869

Interregnum

Pease resigned and vacated office Sept. 30, 1869; no successor was named until Jan. 8, 1870. Some historians extend Pease's term until Jan. 8, 1870, but in reality Texas was without a head of its civil government from Sept. 30, 1869 until Jan. 8, 1870. Republican Edmund J. Davis (appointed provisional Governor after being elected)

	Jan. 8, 1870-Jan. 15, 1874
Richard Coke (resigned to enter United States Senate)	Jan. 15, 1874-Dec. 1, 1876
Richard B. Hubbard	Dec. 1, 1876-Jan. 21, 1879
Oran M. Roberts	Jan. 21, 1879-Jan. 16, 1883
John Ireland	Jan. 16, 1883-Jan. 18, 1887
Lawrence Sullivan Ross	Jan. 18, 1887-Jan. 20, 1891
James Stephen Hogg	Jan. 20, 1891-Jan. 15, 1895
Charles A. Culberson	Jan. 15, 1895-Jan. 17, 1899
Joseph D. Sayers	Jan. 17, 1899-Jan. 20, 1903
S. W. T. Lanham	Jan. 20, 1903-Jan. 15, 1907
Thos. Mitchell Campbell	Jan. 15, 1907-Jan. 17, 1911
Oscar Branch Colquitt	Jan. 17, 1911-Jan. 19, 1915
James E. Ferguson (impeached)	Jan. 19, 1915-Aug. 25, 1917
William Pettus Hobby	Aug. 25, 1917-Jan. 18, 1921
Pat Morris Neff	Jan. 18, 1921-Jan. 20, 1925
Miriam A. Ferguson	Jan. 20, 1925-Jan. 17, 1927
Dan Moody	Jan. 17, 1927-Jan. 20, 1931
Ross S. Sterling	Jan. 20, 1931-Jan. 17, 1933
Miriam A. Ferguson	Jan. 17, 1933-Jan. 15, 1935
James V. Allred	Jan. 15, 1935-Jan. 17, 1939
W. Lee O'Daniel (resigned to enter United States Senate)	Jan. 17, 1939-Aug. 4, 1941
Coke R. Stevenson	Aug. 4, 1941-Jan. 21, 1947
Beauford H. Jester	Jan. 21, 1947-July 11, 1949
Allan Shivers (Lt. Governor succeeded on death of Governor Jester. Elected in 1950 and re-elected in 1952 and 1954)	July 11, 1949-Jan. 15, 1957
Price Daniel	Jan. 15, 1957-Jan. 15, 1963
John Connally	Jan. 15, 1963-Jan. 21, 1969
Preston Smith	Jan. 21, 1969 to Jan. 16, 1973
**Dolph Briscoe	Jan. 16, 1973 to Jan. 16, 1979
William P. Clements	Jan. 16, 1979 to Jan. 18, 1983
Mark White	Jan. 18, 1983 to Jan. 20, 1987
William P. Clements	Jan. 20, 1987 to Jan. 15, 1991
Ann W. Richards	Jan. 15, 1991 to Present

---

*Some authorities would include Texas under administrations of several earlier Spanish Royal Governors. The late Dr. C. E. Castaneda, Latin-American librarian of University of Texas and authority on history of Texas and Southwestern region, would include the following four: Francisco de Garay, 1523-26; Panfilo de Narvaez, 1526-28; Nuno de Guzman, 1528-30; Hernando de Soto, 1538-43.

†Served as acting Governor just prior to March 2, 1836, after Smith was impeached.

‡Acting Governor while Henderson away in Mexican War.

**Effective in 1975, term of office was raised to 4 years, according to a constitutional amendment approved by Texas voters in 1972. See lead to State Government chapter in this edition for other state officials whose terms were raised to 4 years.

TEXAS VICE PRESIDENTS AND LIEUTENANT GOVERNORS
Vice Presidents of Republic

	Date Elected.
Lorenzo de Zavala (provisional Vice President.) M. B. Lamar	Sept. 5, 1836
David G. Burnet	Sept. 3, 1838
Edward Burleson	Sept. 6, 1841
Kenneth L. Anderson	Sept. 2, 1844

Lieutenant Governors

Albert C. Horton	1846-1847
John A. Greer	1847-1851
J. W. Henderson, Aug. 4, 1851 (Served as Governor of Texas from Nov. 23, 1853, to Dec. 21, 1853.)	
D. C. Dickson	1853-1855
H. R. Runnels	Aug. 6, 1855
(Runnels became Governor of Texas in 1857.)	
F. R. Lubbock	Aug. 4, 1857
(Became Governor of Texas during Confederacy.)	
Edward Clark	Aug. 1, 1859
(Became Governor of Texas during Confederacy.)	
John M. Crockett	1861-1863
Fletcher S. Stockdale	1863-1866
George W. Jones	1866
(Jones was removed by General Sheridan.)	
J. W. Flanagan	1869
(Flanagan was elected a U.S. Senator and was never inaugurated as Lt. Gov.)	
R. B. Hubbard	1873-1876
(Became Governor of Texas in 1876.)	
J. D. Sayers	1878-1880
L. J. Storey	1880-1882
Marion Martin	1882-1884
Barnett Gibbs	1884-1886
T. B. Wheeler	1886-1888
T. B. Wheeler	1888-1890
George C. Pendleton	1890-1892
M. M. Crane	Jan. 17, 1893-Jan. 25, 1895
George T. Jester	1895-1896
George T. Jester	1896-1898
J. N. Browning	1898-1902
George D. Neal	1902-1906
A. B. Davidson	1906-1912
Will H. Mayes	1912-1914
W. P. Hobby	1914-1917
(Became Governor of Texas in September, 1917.)	
W. A. Johnson (succeeded Hobby as Lieutenant Governor, serving his unexpired term and until January, 1920).	
Lynch Davidson	1920-1922
T. W. Davidson	1922-1924
Barry Miller	1924-1931
Edgar E. Witt	1931-1935
Walter Woodul	1935-1939
Coke R. Stevenson	1939-1941
(Became Governor of Texas Aug. 4, 1941.)	
John Lee Smith	1943-Jan. 21, 1947
Allan Shivers	Jan. 21, 1947-July 11, 1949
(Shivers succeeded to the governorship on death of Governor Beauford H. Jester, July 11, 1949.)	
Ben Ramsey	1951-Sept. 18, 1961
(Ben Ramsey resigned to become a member of the State Railroad Commission, Sept. 18, 1961.)	
Preston Smith	1963-1969
Ben Barnes	1969-1973
William P. Hobby	1973 to 1991
Robert D. Bullock	1991 to Present

SECRETARIES OF STATE
Republic of Texas

Raines Yearbook for Texas, 1901, gives the following record of Secretaries of State during the era of the Republic of Texas:

Under President ad interim David G. Burnet—Samuel P. Carson, James Collingsworth and W. H. Jack.

Under Sam Houston (first term)—Stephen F. Austin, 1836. J. Pinckney Henderson and Dr. Robert A. Irion, 1837-38.

Under Mirabeau B. Lamar—Bernard Bee appointed Dec. 16, 1838; James Webb appointed Feb. 6, 1839; D. G. Burnet appointed Acting Secretary of State, May 31, 1839; N. Amory appointed Acting Secretary of State, July 23, 1839; D. G. Burnet appointed Acting Secretary of State, Aug. 5, 1839; Abner S. Lipscomb appointed Secretary of State, Jan. 31, 1840, and resigned Jan. 22, 1841; Joseph Waples appointed Acting Secretary of State, Jan. 23, 1841, and served until Feb. 8, 1841; James S. Mayfield appointed Feb. 8, 1841; Joseph Waples appointed April 30, 1841, and served until May 25, 1841; Samuel A. Roberts appointed May 25, 1841, and reappointed Sept. 7, 1841.

Under President Sam Houston (second term)—E. Lawrence Stickney, Acting Secretary of State until Anson Jones appointed Dec. 13, 1841. Jones served as Secretary of State throughout this term except during the summer and part of this term of 1842, when Joseph Waples filled the position as Acting Secretary of State.

Under President Anson Jones—Ebenezer Allen served from Dec. 10, 1844, until Feb. 5, 1845, when Ashbel Smith became Secretary of State. Allen was again named Acting Secretary of State, March 31, 1845, and later named Secretary of State.

State Secretaries of State

Charles Mariner	Feb. 20, 1846-May 4, 1846
David G. Burnet	May 4, 1846-Jan. 1, 1848
Washington D. Miller	Jan. 1, 1848-Jan. 2, 1850
James Webb	Jan. 2, 1850-Nov. 14, 1851
Thomas H. Duval	Nov. 14, 1851-Dec. 22, 1853
Edward Clark	Dec. 22, 1853-Dec., 1857
T. S. Anderson	Dec. 1857-Dec. 27, 1859
E. W. Cave	Dec. 27, 1859-Mar. 16, 1861
Bird Holland	Mar. 16, 1861-Nov., 1861
Charles West	Nov., 1861-Sept., 1862
Robert J. Townes	Sept., 1862-May 2, 1865
Charles R. Pryor	May 2, 1865-Aug., 1865
James H. Bell	Aug., 1865-Aug., 1866
John A. Green	Aug., 1866-Aug., 1867
D. W. C. Phillips	Aug., 1867-Jan., 1870
J. P. Newcomb	Jan. 1, 1870-Jan. 17, 1874
George Clark	Jan. 17, 1874-Jan. 27, 1874
A. W. DeBerry	Jan. 27, 1874-Dec. 1, 1876
Isham G. Searcy	Dec. 1, 1876-Jan. 23, 1879
J. D. Templeton	Jan. 23, 1879-Jan. 22, 1881
T. H. Bowman	Jan. 22, 1881-Jan. 18, 1883
J. W. Baines	Jan. 18, 1883-Jan. 21, 1887
John M. Moore	Jan. 21, 1887-Jan. 22, 1891
George W. Smith	Jan. 22, 1891-Jan. 17, 1895
Allison Mayfield	Jan. 17, 1895-Jan. 5, 1897
J. W. Madden	Jan. 5, 1897-Jan. 18, 1899
D. H. Hardy	Jan. 18, 1899-Jan. 19, 1901
John G. Tod	Jan. 19, 1901-Jan., 1903
J. R. Curl	Jan., 1903-April, 1905
O. K. Shannon	April, 1905-Jan., 1907
L. T. Dashiel	Jan., 1907-Feb., 1908
W. R. Davie	Feb., 1908-Jan., 1909
W. B. Townsend	Jan., 1909-Jan., 1911
C. C. McDonald	Jan., 1911-Dec., 1912
J. T. Bowman	Dec., 1912-Jan., 1913
John L. Wortham	Jan., 1913-June, 1913
F. C. Weinert	June, 1913-Nov., 1914
D. A. Gregg	Nov., 1914-Jan., 1915
John G. McKay	Jan., 1915-Dec., 1916
C. J. Bartlett	Dec., 1916-Nov., 1917
George F. Howard	Nov., 1917-Nov., 1920
C. D. Mims	Nov., 1920-Jan., 1921
S. L. Staples	Jan., 1921-Aug., 1924
J. D. Strickland	Sept., 1924-Jan. 1, 1925
Henry Hutchings	Jan. 1, 1925-Jan. 20, 1925
Mrs. Emma G. Meharg	Jan. 20, 1925-Jan., 1927
Mrs. Jane Y. McCallum	Jan., 1927-Jan., 1933
W. W. Heath	Jan., 1933-Jan., 1935
Gerald C. Mann	Jan., 1935-Aug. 31, 1935
R. B. Stanford	Aug. 31, 1935-Aug. 25, 1936
B. P. Matocha	Aug. 25, 1936-Jan. 18, 1937
Edward Clark	Jan. 18, 1937-Jan., 1939
Tom L. Beauchamp	Jan., 1939-Oct., 1939
M. O. Flowers	Oct. 26, 1939-Feb. 25, 1941
William J. Lawson	Feb. 25, 1941-Jan., 1943
Sidney Latham	Jan., 1943-Feb., 1945
Claude Isbell	Feb., 1945-Jan., 1947
Paul H. Brown	Jan., 1947-Jan. 19, 1949
Ben Ramsey	Jan. 19, 1949-Feb. 9, 1950
John Ben Shepperd	Feb. 9, 1950-April 30, 1952
Jack Ross	April 30, 1952-Jan. 9, 1953
Howard A. Carney	Jan. 9, 1953-Apr. 30, 1954
C. E. Fulgham	May 1, 1954-Feb. 15, 1955
Al Muldrow	Feb. 16, 1955-Nov. 1, 1955
Tom Reavley	Nov. 1, 1955-Jan. 16, 1957
Zollie Steakley	Jan. 16, 1957-Jan. 2, 1962
P. Frank Lake	Jan. 2, 1962-Jan. 15, 1963
Crawford C. Martin	Jan. 15, 1963-March 12, 1966
John L. Hill	March 12, 1966-Jan. 22, 1968
Roy Barrera	March 7, 1968-Jan. 23, 1969
Martin Dies Jr.	Jan. 23, 1969-Sept. 1, 1971
Robert D. Bullock	Sept. 1, 1971-Jan. 2, 1973
V. Larry Teaver Jr.	Jan. 2, 1973-Jan. 19, 1973
Mark W. White Jr.	Jan. 19, 1973-Oct. 27, 1977
Steven C. Oaks	Oct. 27, 1977-Jan. 16, 1979
George W. Strake Jr.	Jan. 16, 1979-Oct. 6, 1981
David A. Dean	Oct. 22, 1981-Jan. 18, 1983
John Fainter	Jan. 18, 1983-July 31, 1984
Myra A. McDaniel	Sept. 6, 1984-Jan. 26, 1987
Jack Rains	Jan. 26, 1987-June 15, 1989
George Bayoud Jr.	June 19, 1989-Jan. 15, 1991
John Hannah Jr.	Jan. 17, 1991 to Present

ATTORNEYS GENERAL
Attorneys General Under Republic
David Thomas and
  Peter W. Grayson........... Mar. 2-Oct. 22, 1836
J. Pinckney Henderson, Peter W. Grayson,
  John Birdsall, A. S. Thurston............. 1836-1838
J. C. Watrous .... Dec., 1838-June 1, 1840
Joseph Webb and F. A. Morris............ 1840-1841
George W. Terrell, Ebenezer Allen........ 1841-1844
Ebenezer Allen..................... 1844-1846

*Attorneys General, State
Volney E. Howard......... Feb. 21, 1846-May 7, 1846
John W. Harris............ May 7, 1846-Oct. 31, 1849
Henry P. Brewster........ Oct. 31, 1849-Jan. 15, 1850
A. J. Hamilton............ Jan. 15, 1850-Aug. 5, 1850
Ebenezer Allen............ Aug. 5, 1850-Aug. 2, 1852
Thomas J. Jennings........ Aug. 2, 1852-Aug. 4, 1856
James Willie.............. Aug. 4, 1856-Aug. 2, 1858
Malcolm D. Graham........ Aug. 2, 1858-Aug. 6, 1860
George M. Flournoy....... Aug. 6, 1860-Jan. 15, 1862
N. G. Shelley.............. Feb. 3, 1862-Aug. 1, 1864
B. E. Tarver.............. Aug. 1, 1864-Dec. 11, 1865
Wm. Alexander.......... Dec. 11, 1865-June 25, 1866
W. M. Walton .... June 25, 1866-Aug. 27, 1867
Wm. Alexander.......... Aug. 27, 1867-Nov. 5, 1867
Ezekiel B. Turner .... Nov. 5, 1867-July 11, 1870
Wm. Alexander.......... July 11, 1870-Jan. 27, 1874
George Clark .... Jan. 27, 1874-Apr. 25, 1876
H. H. Boone.............. Apr. 25, 1876-Nov. 5, 1878
George McCormick........ Nov. 5, 1878-Nov. 2, 1880
J. H. McLeary............. Nov. 2, 1880-Nov. 7, 1882
John D. Templeton .... Nov. 7, 1882-Nov. 2, 1886
James S. Hogg .... Nov. 2, 1886-Nov. 4, 1890
C. A. Culberson .... Nov. 4, 1890-Nov. 6, 1894
M. M. Crane .... Nov. 6, 1894-Nov. 8, 1898
Thomas S. Smith......... Nov. 8, 1898-Mar. 15,1901
C. K. Bell................ Mar. 20, 1901-Jan., 1904
R. V. Davidson .... Jan., 1904-Dec. 31, 1909
Jewel P. Lightfoot......... Jan. 1, 1910-Aug. 31, 1912
James D. Walthall......... Sept. 1, 1912-Jan. 1, 1913
B. F. Looney.............. Jan. 1, 1913-Jan., 1919
C. M. Cureton .... Jan., 1919-Dec., 1921
W. A. Keeling .... Dec., 1921-Jan., 1925
Dan Moody............... Jan., 1925-Jan., 1927
Claude Pollard .... Jan., 1927-Sept., 1929
R. L. Bobbitt (Apptd.) .... Sept., 1929-Jan., 1931
James V. Allred........... Jan., 1931-Jan., 1935
William McCraw........... Jan., 1935-Jan., 1939
Gerald C. Mann (resigned) ...... Jan., 1939-Jan., 1944
Grover Sellers............ Jan., 1944-Jan., 1947
Price Daniel .... Jan., 1947-Jan., 1953
John Ben Shepperd.......... Jan., 1953-Jan. 1, 1957
Will Wilson .... Jan. 1, 1957-Jan. 15, 1963
Waggoner Carr............ Jan. 15, 1963-Jan. 1, 1967
Crawford C. Martin........ Jan. 1, 1967-Dec. 29, 1972
John Hill................ Jan. 1, 1973-Jan. 16, 1979
Mark White............ Jan. 16, 1979 to Jan. 18, 1983
Jim Mattox............ Jan. 18, 1983 to Jan. 15, 1991
Dan Morales............ Jan. 15, 1991 to Present

*The first few Attorneys General held office by ap-
pointment of the Governor. The office was made elective in 1850 by constitutional amendment and Ebenezer
Allen was first elected Attorney General.

TREASURERS
Treasurers Under Republic
Asa Brigham....................... 1838-1840
James W. Simmons.................... 1840-1841
Asa Brigham....................... 1841-1844
Moses Johnson 1844-1846

State Treasurers
James H. Raymond........ Feb. 24, 1846-Aug. 2, 1858
†C. H. Randolph .... Aug. 2, 1858-June, 1865
†Samuel Harris .... Oct. 2, 1865-June 25, 1866
W. M. Royston........... June 25, 1866-Sept. 1, 1867
John Y. Allen .... Sept. 1, 1867-Jan., 1869
George W. Honey .... Jan., 1869-Jan., 1874
B. Graham .... (short term) beginning May 27, 1872
A. J. Dorn .... Jan., 1874-Jan., 1879
F. R. Lubbock .... Jan., 1879-Jan., 1891
W. B. Wortham .... Jan., 1891-Jan., 1899
John W. Robbins.......... Jan., 1899-Jan., 1907
Sam Sparks............... Jan., 1907-Jan., 1912
J. M. Edwards............ Jan., 1912-Jan., 1919
John W. Baker............ Jan., 1919-Jan., 1921
G. N. Holton .... July, 1921-Nov. 21, 1921
C. V. Terrell .... Nov. 21, 1921-Aug. 15, 1924
S. L. Staples .... Aug. 16, 1924-Jan. 15, 1925

W. Gregory Hatcher .... Jan. 16, 1925-Jan. 1, 1931
Charley Lockhart .... Jan. 1, 1931-Oct. 25, 1941
Jesse James .... Oct. 25, 1941-Sept. 29, 1977
Warren G. Harding .... Oct. 7, 1977-Jan. 3, 1983
Ann Richards .... Jan. 3, 1983 to Jan. 2, 1991
Kay Bailey Hutchison .... Jan. 2, 1991 to Present

*Honey was removed from office for a short period
in 1872 and B. Graham served in his place.
†Randolph fled to Mexico upon collapse of Confederacy. No exact date available for his departure
from office or for Harris' succession to the post. It is
believed Harris took office Oct. 2, 1865.

RAILROAD COMMISSION OF TEXAS
John H. Reagan, June 10, 1891-Jan. 20, 1903.
L. L. Foster, June 10, 1891-April 30, 1895.
W. P. McLean, June 10, 1891-Nov. 20, 1894.
L. J. Storey (succeeding W. P. McLean), Nov. 21,
1894-Mar. 28, 1909.
N. A. Stedman (succeeding L. L. Foster), May 1,
1895-Jan. 4, 1897.
Allison Mayfield (succeeding N. A. Stedman), Jan.
5, 1897-Jan. 23, 1923.
O. B. Colquitt (succeeding John H. Reagan), Jan.
21, 1903-Jan. 17, 1911.
William D. Williams (succeeding L. J. Storey),
April 28, 1909-Oct. 1, 1916.
John L. Wortham (succeeding O. B. Colquitt), Jan.
21, 1911-Jan. 1, 1913.
Earle B. Mayfield (succeeding John L. Wortham),
Jan. 2, 1913-March 1, 1923.
Charles H. Hurdleston (succeeding William D. Wil-
liams), Oct. 10, 1916-Dec. 31, 1918.
Clarence E. Gilmore (succeeding Charles H. Hur-
dleston), Jan. 1, 1919-Jan. 1, 1929.
W. A. Nabors (succeeding Allison Mayfield), March
1, 1923-Jan. 18, 1925.
W. M. W. Splawn (succeeding Earle B. Mayfield),
March 1, 1923-Aug. 1, 1924.
C. V. Terrell (succeeding W. M. W. Splawn), Aug.
15, 1924-Jan. 1, 1939.
Lon A. Smith (succeeding W. A. Nabors), Jan. 19,
1925-Jan. 1, 1941.
Pat M. Neff (succeeding Clarence E. Gilmore),
Jan. 1, 1929-Jan. 1, 1933.
Ernest O. Thompson (succeeding Pat M. Neff),
Jan. 1, 1933-Jan. 8, 1965.
G. A. Sadler (succeeding C. V. Terrell), Jan. 1,
1939-Jan. 1, 1943.
Olin Culberson (succeeding Lon A. Smith), Jan. 1,
1941-June 22, 1961.
Beauford Jester (succeeding G. A. Sadler), Jan. 1,
1943-Jan. 21, 1947.
William J. Murray Jr. (succeeding Beauford Jes-
ter), Jan. 21, 1947-Apr. 10, 1963.
Jim C. Langdon (succeeding William J. Murray
Jr.), May 28, 1963-Jan. 3, 1978.
Ben Ramsey (succeeding Olin Culberson), Sept. 18,
1961-Jan. 1, 1977.
Jon Newton (succeeding Ben Ramsey), Jan. 1,
1977-Jan. 1, 1979.
Byron Tunnell (succeeding Ernest O. Thompson),
Jan. 8, 1965-Sept. 15, 1973.
Mack Wallace (succeeding Byron Tunnell), Sept.
15, 1973 to Present.
John H. Poerner (succeeding Jim C. Langdon),
Jan. 3, 1978 to Jan. 1, 1981.
James E. Nugent (succeeding Jon Newton), Jan. 1,
1979 to Present.
Buddy Temple (succeeding John H. Poerner),
Jan.1,1981 to Jan. 1, 1987.
John Sharp (succeeding Buddy Temple), Jan. 1,
1987 to Present.
Robert Krueger (succeeding Kent Hance, Jan. 3,
1991 to Present.
Lena Guerrero (succeeding John Sharp, Jan. 23,
1991 to Present.

COMPTROLLER OF PUBLIC ACCOUNTS
Comptrollers Under Republic
John H. Money .... Dec. 30, 1835-Jan. 17, 1836
H. C. Hudson .... Jan. 17, 1836-Oct. 22, 1836
E. M. Pease.............. June, 1837-Dec., 1837
F. R. Lubbock .... Dec., 1837-Jan., 1839
Jas. W. Simmons .... Jan. 15, 1839-Sept. 30, 1840
Jas. B. Shaw .... Sept. 30, 1840-Dec. 24, 1841
F. R. Lubbock .... Dec. 24, 1841-Jan. 1, 1842
Jas. B. Shaw .... Jan. 1, 1842-Jan. 1, 1846

State Comptrollers
Jas. B. Shaw .... Feb. 24, 1846-Aug. 2, 1858
Clement R. Johns .... Aug. 2, 1858-Aug. 1, 1864

Willis L. Robards. . . . . Aug. 1, 1864-Oct. 12, 1865	
Albert H. Latimer . . . . Oct. 12, 1865-Mar. 27, 1866	
Robert H. Taylor . . . . Mar. 27, 1866-June 25, 1866	
Willis L. Robards. . . . . June 25, 1866-Aug. 27, 1867	
Morgan C. Hamilton . . . . . . Aug. 27, 1867-Jan. 8, 1870	
A. Bledsoe. . . . . Jan. 8, 1870-Jan. 20, 1874	
Stephen H. Darden . . . . Jan. 20, 1974-Nov. 2, 1880	
W. M. Brown . . . . Nov. 2, 1880-Jan. 16, 1883	
W. J. Swain . . . . Jan. 16, 1883-Jan. 18, 1887	
John D. McCall . . . . Jan. 18, 1887-Jan. 15, 1895	
R. W. Finley . . . . Jan. 15, 1895-Jan. 15, 1901	
R. M. Love . . . . Jan. 15, 1901-Jan., 1903	
J. W. Stephen . . . . Jan., 1903-Jan., 1911	
W. P. Lane . . . . Jan., 1911-Jan., 1915	
H. B. Terrell . . . . Jan., 1915-Jan., 1920	
M. L. Wiginton . . . . Jan., 1920-Jan., 1921	
Lon A. Smith . . . . Jan., 1921-Jan., 1925	
S. H. Terrell . . . . Jan., 1925-Jan., 1931	
Geo. H. Sheppard . . . . Jan., 1931-Jan. 17, 1949	
Robert S. Calvert . . . . Jan. 17, 1949-Jan., 1975	
Robert D. Bullock . . . . Jan., 1975-Jan. 3, 1991	
John Sharp . . . . Jan. 3, 1991 to Present	

TEXAS SENATORIAL SUCCESSION

Following is the succession of Texas representatives in the United States Senate since the annexation of Texas to the Union in 1845:

Houston Succession

Sam Houston. . . . . Feb. 21, 1846-Mar. 4, 1859	
John Hemphill . . . . Mar. 4, 1859-July 11, 1861	

Louis T. Wigfall and W. S. Oldham took their seats in the Confederate Senate, Nov. 16, 1861, and served in that body until fall of Confederacy. After collapse of the Confederacy the State Legislature on Aug. 21, 1866, elected David G. Burnet and Oran M. Roberts to the United States Senate, anticipating immediate readmission to the Union, but they were not allowed to take their seats.

*Morgan C. Hamilton . . . . . . Feb. 22, 1870-Mar. 3, 1877	
Richard Coke . . . . Mar. 4, 1877-Mar. 3, 1895	
Horace Chilton . . . . Mar. 3, 1895-Mar. 3, 1901	
Joseph W. Bailey. . . . . Mar. 3, 1901-Jan. 8, 1913	
R. M. Johnson. . . . . Jan. 8, 1913-Feb. 3, 1913	
Morris Sheppard (died). . . . . . Feb. 13, 1913-Apr. 9, 1941	
Andrew J. Houston . . . . June 2-26, 1941	
W. Lee O'Daniel . . . . Aug. 4, 1941-Jan. 3, 1949	
Lyndon B. Johnson . . . . Jan. 3, 1949-Jan. 20, 1961	
William A. Blakley. . . . . Jan. 20, 1961-June 15, 1961	
*John G. Tower . . . . June 15, 1961-Jan. 21, 1985	
Phil Gramm . . . . Jan. 21, 1985 to Present	

Rusk Succession

Thomas J. Rusk (died) . . . . . Feb 21, 1846-July 29, 1857	
J. Pinckney Henderson (died) . . Nov. 9, 1857-June 4, 1858	
Matthias Ward (appointed interim). . . . . Sept. 29, 1858-Dec. 5, 1859	

Note.—Succession broken by expulsion of Texas Senators following annexation of Texas from Union. See note above under "Houston Succession" on Louis T. Wigfall and W. S. Oldham and Burnet and Roberts.

*James W. Flanagan . . . . Feb. 22, 1870-Mar. 3, 1875	
Samuel B. Maxey . . . . Mar. 3, 1875-Mar. 3, 1887	
John H. Reagan (resigned). . . Mar. 3, 1887-June 10, 1891	
Horace Chilton (filled vacancy on appointment) . . Dec. 7, 1891-Mar. 30, 1892	
Roger Q. Mills. . . . . Mar. 30, 1892-Mar. 3, 1899	
†Charles A. Culberson . . . . Mar. 3, 1899-Mar. 4, 1923	
Earle B. Mayfield . . . . Mar. 4, 1923-Mar. 4, 1929	
Tom Connally . . . . Mar. 4, 1929-Jan. 3, 1953	
Price Daniel . . . . Jan. 3, 1953-Jan. 15, 1957	
William A. Blakley. . . . . Jan. 15, 1957-Apr. 27, 1957	
Ralph W. Yarborough . . . . . . Apr. 27, 1957-Jan. 12, 1971	
Lloyd Bentsen . . . . Jan. 12, 1971 to Present	

*Republican members.
†First election to U.S. Senate held in 1916. Prior to that time, senators were appointed by the Legislature.

COMMISSIONERS OF THE GENERAL LAND OFFICE

Commissioners Under Republic

John P. Borden . . . . Aug. 23, 1837-Dec. 12, 1840	
H. W. Raglin . . . . Dec. 12, 1840-Jan. 4, 1841	
*Thomas William Ward . . . . . Jan. 4, 1841-Mar. 20, 1848	

Commissioners Under State

George W. Smyth . . . . Mar. 20, 1848-Aug. 4, 1851	
Stephen Crosby . . . . Aug. 4, 1851-Mar. 1, 1858	
Francis M. White. . . . . Mar. 1, 1858-Mar. 1, 1862	
Stephen Crosby . . . . Mar. 1, 1862-Sept. 1, 1865	
Francis M. White. . . . . Sept. 1, 1865-Aug. 7, 1866	
Stephen Crosby . . . . Aug. 7, 1866-Aug. 27, 1867	
Joseph Spence . . . . Aug. 27, 1867-Jan. 19, 1870	

Jacob Kuechler. . . . . Jan. 19, 1870-Jan. 20, 1874	
J. J. Groos. . . . . Jan. 20, 1874-June 15, 1878	
W. C. Walsh. . . . . July 30, 1878, Jan. 10, 1887	
R. M. Hall . . . . Jan. 10, 1887-Jan. 16, 1891	
W. L. McGaughey . . . . Jan. 16, 1891-Jan. 26, 1895	
A. J. Baker . . . . Jan. 26, 1895-Jan. 16, 1899	
George W. Finger . . . . Jan. 16, 1899-May 4, 1899	
Charles Rogan . . . . May 11, 1899-Jan. 10, 1903	
John J. Terrell . . . . Jan. 10, 1903-Jan. 11, 1909	
J. T. Robison. . . . . Jan., 1909-Sept. 11, 1929	
J. H. Walker . . . . Sept. 11, 1929-Jan., 1937	
William H. McDonald . . . . Jan, 1937-Jan., 1939	
Bascom Giles . . . . Jan., 1939-Jan. 5, 1955	
J. Earl Rudder . . . . Jan. 5, 1955-Feb. 1, 1958	
Bill Allcorn . . . . Feb. 1, 1958-Jan. 1, 1961	
Jerry Sadler . . . . Jan. 1, 1961-Jan. 1, 1971	
Bob Armstrong. . . . . Jan. 1, 1971-Jan. 1, 1983	
Garry Mauro . . . . Jan. 1, 1983 to Present	

*Part of term after annexation.

FIRST LADIES OF TEXAS

Martha Evans Gindratt Wood 1847-49	
*Bell Administration 1849-53	
Lucadia Christiana Niles Pease 1853-57; 1867-69	
†Runnels Administration. 1857-59	
Margaret Moffette Lea Houston 1859-61	
Martha Evans Clark 1861	
Adele Barron Lubbock 1861-63	
Susie Ellen Taylor Murrah. 1863-65	
Mary Jane Bowen Hamilton. 1865-66	
Annie Rattan Throckmorton. 1866-67	
Ann Elizabeth Britton Davis 1870-74	
Mary Home Coke 1874-76	
Janie Roberts Hubbard 1876-79	
Frances Wickliff Edwards Roberts 1879-83	
Anne Maria Penn Ireland 1883-87	
Elizabeth Dorothy Tinsley Ross 1887-91	
Sarah Stinson Hogg. 1891-95	
Sally Harrison Culberson. 1895-99	
Orlene Walton Sayers 1899-1903	
Sarah Beona Meng Lanham. 1903-07	
Fannie Brunner Campbell 1907-11	
Alice Fuller Murrell Colquitt 1911-15	
‡Miriam A. Wallace Ferguson, 1915-17; 1925-27; 1933-35	
Willie Cooper Hobby 1917-21	
Myrtle Mainer Neff. 1921-25	
Mildred Paxton Moody 1927-31	
Maud Gage Sterling 1931-33	
Jo Betsy Miller Allred 1935-39	
Merle Estella Butcher O'Daniel 1939-41	
**Fay Wright Stevenson 1941-42	
**Stevenson Administration 1942-46	
Mabel Buchanan Jester. 1946-49	
Marialice Shary Shivers 1949-57	
Jean Houston Baldwin Daniel 1957-63	
Idanell Brill Connally. 1963-69	
Ima Mae Smith 1969-73	
Betty Jane Slaughter Briscoe. 1973-79	
Rita Crocker Bass Clements 1979-83	
Linda Gale Thompson White 1983-87	
Rita Crocker Bass Clements 1987-91	

*Gov. Peter Hansbrough Bell was married at expiration of his term of office, March 3, 1857, to Mrs. Ella Reeves Eaton Dickens.

†Gov. Hardin R. Runnels never married.

‡Mistress of the Mansion while her husband, James E. Ferguson, was Governor, 1915-17; both Mansion Mistress and Governor of Texas, 1925-27 and 1933-35.

**Mrs. Coke R. (Fay Wright) Stevenson died in the Governor's Mansion Jan. 3, 1942. Governor Stevenson's mother and daughter-in-law served as Mistresses of the Mansion during the remainder of his term. He was married to Mrs. Marguerite King Heap Jan. 16, 1954.

SUPERINTENDENTS OF PUBLIC INSTRUCTION

Pryor Lea . . . . Nov. 10, 1866-Sept. 12, 1867	
Edwin M. Wheelock. . . . . Sept. 12, 1867-May 6, 1871	
Jacob C. DeGress . . . . May 6, 1871-Jan. 20, 1874	
O. H. Hollingsworth . . . . Jan. 20, 1874-May 6, 1884	
B. M. Baker. . . . . May 6, 1884-Jan. 18, 1887	
O. H. Cooper . . . . Jan 18, 1887-Sept. 1, 1890	
H. C. Pritchett. . . . . Sept. 1, 1890-Sept. 15, 1893	
J. M. Carlisle. . . . . Sept. 15, 1891-Jan. 10, 1899	
J. S. Kendall . . . . Jan. 10, 1899-July 2, 1901	
Arthur Lefevre . . . . July 2, 1901-Jan. 12, 1905	
R. B. Cousins. . . . . Jan. 12, 1905-Jan. 1, 1910	
F. M. Bralley. . . . . Jan. 1, 1910-Sept. 1, 1913	
W. F. Doughty. . . . . Sept. 1, 1913-Jan. 1, 1919	

Annie Webb Blanton . . . . Jan. 1, 1919-Jan. 16, 1923
S. M. N. Marrs. . . . . Jan. 16, 1923-April 28, 1932
C. N. Shaver . . . . April 28, 1932-Oct. 1, 1932
L. W. Rogers . . . . Oct. 1, 1932-Jan. 16, 1933
L. A. Woods. . . . . Jan. 16, 1933-*1951

State Commissioner of Education
J. W. Edgar . . . . May 31, 1951-June 30, 1974
Marlin L. Brockette. . . . . July 1, 1974-Sept. 1, 1979
Alton O. Bowen . . . . Sept. 1, 1979-June 1, 1981
Raymon Bynum . . . . June 1, 1981-Oct. 31, 1984
W. N. Kirby. . . . . April 13, 1985-July 1, 1991
Lionel R. Meno . . . . July 1, 1991 to Present

*The office of State Superintendent of Public Instruction was abolished by the Gilmer-Aikin act of 1949 and the office of Commissioner of Education created, appointed by a new State Board of Education elected by the people.

Speaker of the Texas House

The Speaker of the Texas House of Representatives is the presiding officer of the lower chamber of the State Legislature. The official is elected at the beginning of each regular session by a vote of the members of the House.

Speaker, Residence	Elected	Legislature
William E. Crump, Bellville.	1846	1st
William H. Bourland, Paris	1846	1st
James W. Henderson, Houston	1847	2nd
Charles G. Keenan, Huntsville	1849	3rd
David C. Dickson, Anderson	1851	4th
Hardin R. Runnels, Boston	1853	5th
Hamilton P. Bee, Laredo.	1855	6th
William S. Taylor, Larissa.	1857	7th
Matt F. Locke, Lafayette	1858	7th
Marion DeKalb Taylor, Jefferson	1859	8th
Constantine W. Buckley, Richmond . . .	1861	9th
Nicholas H. Darnell, Dallas	1861	9th
Constantine W. Buckley, Richmond . . .	1863	9th
Marion DeKalb Taylor, Jefferson	1863	10th
Nathaniel M. Burford, Dallas	1866	11th
Ira H. Evans, Corpus Christi	1870	12th
William H. Sinclair, Galveston	1871	12th
Marion DeKalb Taylor, Jefferson	1873	13th
Guy M. Bryan, Galveston	1874	14th
Thomas R. Bonner, Tyler	1876	15th
John H. Cochran, Dallas	1879	16th
George R. Reeves, Pottsboro	1881	17th
Charles R. Gibson, Waxahachie.	1883	18th
Lafayette L. Foster, Groesbeck.	1885	19th
George C. Pendleton, Belton.	1887	20th
Frank P. Alexander, Greenville	1889	21st
Robert T. Milner, Henderson	1891	22nd
John H. Cochran, Dallas	1893	23rd
Thomas Slater Smith, Hillsboro.	1895	24th
L. Travis Dashiell, Jewett	1897	25th
J. S. Sherrill, Greenville	1899	26th
Robert E. Prince, Corsicana	1901	27th
Pat M. Neff, Waco	1903	28th
Francis W. Seabury, Rio Grande City . .	1905	29th
Thomas B. Love, Lancaster	1907	30th
Austin M. Kennedy, Waco.	1909	31st
John W. Marshall, Whitesboro	1909	31st
Sam Rayburn, Bonham.	1911	32nd
Chester H. Terrell, San Antonio.	1913	33rd
John W. Woods, Rotan	1915	34th
Franklin O. Fuller, Coldspring	1917	35th
R. Ewing Thomason, El Paso	1919	36th
Charles G. Thomas, Lewisville	1921	37th
Richard E. Seagler, Palestine	1923	38th
Lee Satterwhite, Amarillo.	1925	39th
Robert L. Bobbitt, Laredo.	1927	40th
W. S. Barron, Bryan	1929	41st
Fred H. Minor, Denton	1931	42nd
Coke R. Stevenson, Junction.	1933	43rd
"	1935	44th
Robert W. Calvert, Hillsboro.	1937	45th
R. Emmett Morse, Houston.	1939	46th
Homer L. Leonard, McAllen	1941	47th
Price Daniel, Liberty	1943	48th
Claud H. Gilmer, Rocksprings.	1945	49th

William O. Reed, Dallas	1947	50th
Durwood Manford, Smiley	1949	51st
Reuben Senterfitt, San Saba	1951	52nd
"	1953	53rd
Jim T. Lindsey, Texarkana.	1955	54th
Waggoner Carr, Lubbock	1957	55th
"	1959	56th
James A. Turman, Gober	1961	57th
Byron M. Tunnell, Tyler	1963	58th
Ben Barnes, DeLeon.	1965	59th
"	1967	60th
Gus F. Mutscher, Brenham.	1969	61st
"	1971	62nd
Rayford Price, Palestine	1972	62nd
Price Daniel Jr., Liberty.	1973	63rd
Bill Clayton, Springlake	1975	64th
"	1977	65th
"	1979	66th
"	1981	67th
Gibson D. Lewis, Fort Worth	1983	68th
"	1985	69th
"	1987	70th
"	1989	71st
"	1991	72nd

CHIEF JUSTICE OF SUPREME COURT
Republic of Texas
James Collinsworth. . . . . . . Dec. 16, 1836-July 23, 1838
John Birdsall . . . . Nov. 19-Dec. 12, 1838
Thomas J. Rusk . . . . Dec. 12, 1838-Dec. 5, 1840
John Hemphill . . . . Dec. 5, 1840-Dec. 29, 1845

Constitutions of 1845 and 1861
John Hemphill . . . . Mar. 2, 1846-Oct. 10, 1858
Royall T. Wheeler . . . . Oct. 11, 1858-April 1864
Oran M. Roberts . . . . Nov. 1, 1864-June 30, 1866

Constitution of 1866 (Presidential Reconstruction)
*George F. Moore . . . . Aug. 16, 1866-Sept. 10, 1867
*Removed under Congressional Reconstruction by military authorities who appointed members of the next court.

Constitution of 1866 (Congressional Reconstruction)
†Amos Morrill. . . . . Sept. 10, 1867-July 5, 1870
†Court on which he sat is generally referred to as the "Military Court" and its decisions have little or no precedential value.

Constitution of 1869
Lemuel D. Evans. . . . . July 5, 1870-Aug. 31, 1873
Wesley Ogden . . . . Aug. 31, 1873-Jan. 29, 1874
Oran M. Roberts . . . . Jan. 29, 1874-Apr. 18, 1876

Constitution of 1876
Oran M. Roberts . . . . Apr. 18, 1876-Oct. 1, 1878
George F. Moore . . . . Nov. 5, 1878-Nov. 1, 1881
Robert S. Gould. . . . . Nov. 1, 1881-Dec. 23, 1882
Asa H. Willie . . . . Dec. 23, 1882-Mar. 3, 1888
John W. Stayton . . . . Mar. 3, 1888-July 5, 1894
Reuben R. Gaines . . . . July 10, 1894-Jan. 5, 1911
Thomas J. Brown . . . . Jan. 7, 1911-May 26, 1915
Nelson Phillips . . . . June 1, 1915-Nov. 16, 1921
C. M. Cureton . . . . Dec. 2, 1921-Apr. 8, 1940
W. F. Moore . . . . Apr. 17, 1940-Jan. 1, 1941
James P. Alexander . . . . Jan. 1, 1941-Jan. 1, 1948
J. E. Hickman . . . . Jan. 5, 1948-Jan. 3, 1961
Robert W. Calvert . . . . Jan. 3, 1961-Oct. 4, 1972
Joe R. Greenhill . . . . Oct. 4, 1972-Oct. 25, 1982
Jack Pope. . . . . Nov. 23, 1982-Jan. 5, 1985
John L. Hill Jr. . . . . Jan. 5, 1985-Jan. 4, 1988
Thomas R. Phillips . . . . Jan. 4, 1988-Present

PRESIDING JUDGES, COURT OF APPEALS (1876-1891) and COURT OF CRIMINAL APPEALS (1891-Present)
Mat D. Ector. . . . . May 6, 1876-Oct. 29, 1879
John P. White. . . . . Nov. 9, 1879-Apr. 26, 1892
James M. Hurt . . . . May 4, 1892-Dec. 31, 1898
W. L. Davidson . . . . Jan. 2, 1899-June 27, 1913
A. C. Prendergast . . . . June 27, 1913-Dec. 31, 1916
W. L. Davidson . . . . Jan. 1, 1917-Jan. 25, 1921
Wright C. Morrow . . . . Feb. 8, 1921-Oct. 16, 1939
Frank Lee Hawkins . . . . Oct. 16, 1939-Jan. 2, 1951
Harry N. Graves . . . . Jan. 2, 1951-Dec. 31, 1954
W. A. Morrison . . . . Jan. 1, 1955-Jan. 2, 1961
Kenneth K. Woodley . . . . . . Jan. 3, 1961-Jan. 4, 1965
W. T. McDonald . . . . Jan. 4, 1965-June 25, 1966
W. A. Morrison . . . . June 25, 1966-Jan. 1, 1967
Kenneth K. Woodley . . . . . . Jan. 1, 1967-Jan. 1, 1971
John F. Onion Jr. . . . . Jan. 1, 1971-Jan. 1, 1989
Michael J. McCormick . . . . Jan. 1, 1989-Present

Military Activities

Since 1845 Texas has been one of the leading states in military activities, with its strategic location on the Gulf of Mexico midway between the East and West Coasts, its generally mild climate and its varied terrain. Back in 1845, however, it was the **Mexican War,** precipitated by the annexation of Texas by the United States, that made Texas the center of operations. Between then and the outbreak of the **Civil War** in 1861, U.S. Army forts were established to protect settlers from Indians and to maintain peace in areas still claimed by Mexico.

Fifth U.S. Army

Fifth U.S. Army headquarters, has been located in the historic **Quadrangle** at **Fort Sam Houston, San Antonio,** since July 1, 1971. One of five continental Armies, Fifth Army is responsible to **U.S. Forces Command, Fort McPherson, Ga.,** for land defense, domestic emergency plans and operations and for specified civil-military programs within the Army area. The headquarters has command responsibility over some 670 assigned military personnel, more than 1,700 civilian employees (220 in the headquarters and more than 1,500 in subordinate field commands) and more than 1,400 full-time unit support personnel.

With "Readiness" its watchword and mission, Fifth Army commands **U.S. Army Reserve (USAR)** units and oversees training and readiness of **Army National Guard (ARNG)** units in its 8-state area of responsibility — Arkansas, Kansas, Louisiana, Missouri, Nebraska, New Mexico, Oklahoma and Texas. The Guard and Reserve comprise more than half of the deployable combat forces of the Army.

The ARNG is the only Army resource with dual status as federal and state military force (a unit is never on both duties at the same time). When the ARNG is in non-federalized status, the governor is commander-in-chief of the Texas National and State Guards, while the command function is exercised through an **adjutant general** appointed by the governor and approved by both federal and state legislative authorities. Office of the Adjutant General of Texas is at Camp Mabry, Austin. There under his jurisdiction is the **Command and Control Headquarters,** also headquarters of the **49th Armored "Lone Star" Division,** one of nine major ARNG commands in the Fifth Army area. There are 22,000 Texas Guard soldiers training at 119 armories. See also **Texas Guard** listing.

U.S. Army Reserve

The **U.S. Army Reserve (USAR),** a vital link in the total Army's national defense role, is well represented throughout Texas. Army reservists from all walks of civilian life devote, usually, one weekend a month and two weeks for annual training a year to make themselves and their units ready for mobilization should the need arise.

These citizen-soldiers of Texas are members of more than 250 separate units that are authorized over 18,200 people. Most of them are subordinate to one of four major Army Reserve commands in Texas. These commands are the **90th U.S. Army Reserve Command (ARCOM),** Fort Sam Houston, San Antonio; **75th Maneuver Area Command (MAC),** Houston; **420th Engineer Brigade,** Bryan; and the **807th Medical Brigade,** Seagoville.

There are 34 units in San Antonio and others in Amarillo, Austin, Beaumont-Port Arthur, Corpus Christi, El Paso, Houston, Laredo, Lubbock, Pasadena, Texarkana and Wichita Falls. Also, smaller communities such as Abilene, Alice, Bay City, Brownsville, Bryan, Conroe, Harlingen, Huntsville, McAllen, Marshall, Midland, Paris, Rio Grande City, San Marcos, Sinton, Tyler, Victoria, Waco and Yoakum have units.

Texas USAR units vary in size and missions, ranging from a 3-soldier military history detachment to combat engineer and medical brigades, to a 1,000-bed hospital unit.

Other USAR units, ranging from small detachments to brigades, belong to major U.S. Army Reserve commands headquartered in other states.

Some elements of the 95th Division (Training), headquartered in Midwest City, OK, and the 122d ARCOM, headquartered in N. Little Rock, AR, are included in the unit and personnel totals above. Similarly, the Texas-headquartered USAR commands have units and soldiers in other states. For instance, the 90th ARCOM, largest of Fifth Army's major USAR commands, has more than 10,000 soldiers in units located in Texas, Arkansas, Louisiana, Missouri and New Mexico.

Desert Shield/Desert Storm

During the first six months of the Mid-East conflict, 45 ARNG and USAR units within Texas were mobilized, with 5,700 citizen soldiers involved.

A Readiness Group at Fort Sam Houston, one of four in the Army area, provides on the spot assistance to ARNG/USAR commanders, and reports directly to the Fifth Army commander. Groups provide combat, combat support, combat service support, and maintenance and administrative teams to assist units.

Texas Guard

Tracing its history to early frontier days, the Texas Guard is organized into three separate entities: The **Texas Army National Guard,** the **Texas Air National Guard** and the **Texas State Guard.**

The Texas State Guard, an all-volunteer backup force, was originally created by the Texas Legislature in 1941. It became an active element of the state military forces in 1965 with a mission of reinforcing the National Guard in state emergencies, and of replacing National Guard units called into federal service. The Texas State Guard, which has a membership of approximately 1,300 personnel, also participates in local emergencies.

When the Guard was reorganized following World War II, the Texas Air National Guard was added. Texas Air National Guard units serve as augmentation units to major Air Force commands, including the Air Defense Command, the Tactical Air Command and the Strategic Air Command. Approximately 3,800 men and women make up the Air Guard in nine Texas cities.

The Army National Guard is available for either national or state emergencies and has been used extensively during hurricanes, tornadoes and floods. There are more than 200 units located in 128 cities in Texas, with a total Army Guard membership of 22,000.

The governor of Texas is commander-in-chief of the Texas National and State Guards. This command function is exercised through an **adjutant general** appointed by the governor and approved by both federal and state legislative authority.

The adjutant general is the active administrative head of the Texas Guard, and head of the Adjutant General's Department, a state agency, working in conjunction with the National Guard Bureau, a federal agency.

When called into active federal service, National Guard units come within the chain of command of the Army and Air Force units. When not in federal service, **Camp Mabry,** in Austin, is the main storage, maintenance and administrative headquarters for the Texas Guard.

Fort Bliss

Located at El Paso in the vast expanse of West Texas, **Fort Bliss** is the home of the **U.S. Army Air Defense Artillery Center,** largest air defense center in the Free World. Its primary mission is to train individual air defense soldiers and units, which also include foreign military students from as many as 25 countries at one time. Here at Fort Bliss are the key training, development and support activities for the Army's vital guided missile and air defense artillery programs.

Fort Bliss is home of the **U.S. Army Air Defense Artillery School,** the **11th Air Defense Artillery Brigade, 6th Air Defense Artillery Brigade, Air Defense Artillery Test Directorate, Range Command, 3d Armored Cavalry Regiment** and the **70th Ordnance Battalion's 2d Platoon, 507th Medical Company (Air Ambulance).** As part of the **Military Assistance to Safety and Traffic (MAST),** the 507th provides emergency air transportation for residents of West Texas and New Mexico to medical facilities in El Paso.

Other activities include the **U.S. Army Sergeants Major Academy** and **William Beaumont Army Medical Center,** as well as a graduate-level Teaching institution of the Army's Dental Activity. In addition, the **German Air Force Command U.S.** and the **German Air Force Air Defense School** are on post through an agreement between the U.S. Government and the Federal Republic of Germany.

Fort Bliss and its ranges cover over 1.2 million acres extending from Texas' Upper Rio Grande Valley into New Mexico — an area greater than that of Rhode Island. The post's almost 20,000 military personnel and some 8,000 civilian employees receive an annual payroll of about $987 million.

Fort Hood

Fort Hood, home of the III Armored Mobile Corps, covers 339 square miles in Central Texas just west of Killeen, midway between Waco and Austin.

Named for **Confederate General John Bell Hood,** the "Great Place," as the post is now known throughout the United States Army, is the largest armored installation in the free world. Originally home of the **Army Tank Destroyer Center** during World War II, Fort Hood today is the only post in the United States that accommodates two armored divisions and the **Apache Training Brigade.**

In addition to the **1st Cavalry Division** and the **2nd Armored Division,** the **6th Cavalry Brigade (Air Combat),** the **13th Support Command (Corps),** the **3rd Signal Brigade, 31st Air Defense Artillery Brigade, 89th Military Police Brigade, 504th Military Intelligence Brigade, 3rd Finance Group, 3rd Personnel Group,** the **U.S. Army Training and Doctrine Command Test and Experimentation Command (TEXCOM)** the **Medical Activity (MEDDAC),** the **Dental Activity (DENTAC),** and various other tenant organizations are an integral part of Fort Hood. The post supports more than 190,000 active and retired military, their dependents and Department of the Army civilians. It maintains more than 4,356 buildings, housing facilities for some 24,356 bachelor enlisted service members and 5,537 family units.

Visitors are welcome at this open post, which boasts two museums sponsored by the two divisions and open daily. Fort Hood also hosts several events during the year, including an annual Fourth of July celebration, to which the public is cordially invited.

Fort Sam Houston

Headquarters Fort Sam Houston is the hub of support to many commands and tenant activities on the post, including a school that trains thousands of medical personnel for Army and other military services. Within its boundaries, Fort Sam Houston has one of the largest collections of historic buildings (more than 900), providing a century and a half of visual history at the post

Fort Sam Houston hosts **Fifth U.S. Army, Health Services Command,** the **Academy of Health Sciences, Brooke Army Medical Center, Institute of Surgical Research, U.S. Army Dental Activity** and the **U.S. Army Area Dental Laboratory, 902d Military Intelligence Group, 546 Ordnance Detachment and the Joint Medical Readiness Training Center.**

Other tenants include Fort Sam Houston National Cemetery; the real estate projects office of the Fort Worth District Corps of Engineers, a West Point Admissions Office, U.S. Army Medical Department Museum and the Fort Sam Houston Museum.

National Guard and Reserve units and high school and college ROTC elements throughout South Texas are also among the functions supported by the posts.

As part of its support, the command manages **Camp Bullis,** a 27,880-acre area. Besides the continuous training at the camp, 20,400 acres are under agricultural grazing leases, and approximately 6,000 acres are home to the threatened Golden-cheeked Warbler. The entire area is managed for both game and non-game wildlife. Numerous governmental agencies, including FBI and Air Force personnel, train there on a year-round basis.

Fort Sam Houston is the birthplace of military aviation, and that legacy is carried on today by the post's 507th Medical Company, a helicopter ambulance unit which transports patients in need of immediate medical care. The 507th spearheaded the Defense Department's part in establishing **Military Assistance to Safety and Traffic (MAST)** in 1970. Working with civil authorities, the pilots and medical aid personnel respond to medical emergencies to evacuate patients, using skills for "MEDEVACing" soldiers in combat environments.

Fort Sam Houston is located in the center of San Antonio, the nation's ninth-largest city. The relationship between the civilian and military communities is strong, and a year-round calendar of civic activities involves the post.

Corpus Christi Army Depot

Corpus Christi Army Depot (CCAD), activted in 1961, on the **Corpus Christi Naval Air Station,** covers 180 acres, mostly under roof. The Army's only complete overhaul and repair facility for helicopters, the depot repairs UH-1 Huey, AH-Cobra, UH-60 Black Hawk, CH-47D Chinook and other helicopters and components. CCAD also overhauls other U.S. armed forces helicopters for use worldwide.

About 130 job skills in the wage grade area and 80 in the general classification series are used by the approximately 4,321 civilians and 20 assigned military. It is the largest industrial employer in South Texas, with an annual budget of about $325 million and an annual payroll of about $163 million.

Red River Army Depot

Red River Army Depot at Texarkana was activated in August 1941 following a government purchase of 116 farms and ranches, plus wooded acreage. Occupying 50 square miles, it has approximately 1,400 buildings and structures.

Red River's primary mission is to receive, store, recondition and issue all types Army ordnance general supplies and ammunition. It is a major Army maintenance point for rebuilding combat and general purpose vehicles and other types Army ordnance. It has a limited number of military personnel and about 4,300 Civil Service employees.

Health Services Command

The **U.S. Army Health Services Command (HSC),** headquartered at Fort Sam Houston, San Antonio, operates the largest military medical care system in the free world.

As one of the Army's largest major commands, HSC supports the day to day activity of eight Army medical centers, 30 Army community hospitals, 41 dental activities and laboratories, along with the Academy of Health Sciences, the Army Environmental Hygiene Agency, and three Army installations.

HSC is also responsible for training of Army medical personnel, both officer and enlisted, through the Academy of Health Sciences. The Academy also develops medical technology and techniques for the battlefield of the future.

The command employs approximately 50,000 military and civilian personnel. Almost half of the work force is civilian.

U.S. Army Medical Museum

The **U.S. Army Medical Museum** is housed in a "Spanish Revival" style building on the northeast corner of the post. On exhibit is an extensive collection of military medical artifacts, including early horse-drawn and motorized ambulances, as well as medical items captured during World Wars, Korea and Vietnam. The facility is open to public and admission is free.

Academy of Health Sciences

The **Academy of Health Sciences,** U.S. Army (AHS) is a major part of the U.S. Army Health Services Command, and is the largest allied health care training center in the world.

Approximately 34,000 resident students per year attend its facilities at Fort Sam Houston; the Medical Equipment and Optical School, Aurora, Colorado; and the School of Aviation Medicine, Fort Rucker, Alabama. In addition, the academy administers the Army Medical Department Student Detachment consisting of about 400 officers at more than 100 colleges and universities across the United States, who are studying to earn their masters or doctorate degrees. These physicians and dentists are serving in internship, residency or fellowship programs with civilian medical facilities. Approximately 33,000 additional students take correspondence courses through the academy each year.

Medical students from 34 foreign countries currently are trained at the academy. The International Military Student Office at the academy also helps administer security assistance training for foreign military personnel at U.S. Army medical facilities throughout the United States.

Qualified students who successfully complete selected programs of study are eligible for award of college credit. Among the programs that are affiliated with civilian colleges and universities is one program that results in a bachelor of science degree for warrant officers, and three result in a master's degree for officer students. The academy maintains graduate-level affiliations with **Baylor** and **Tulane Universities, Texas Wesleyan College,** and undergraduate-level affiliation with the **University of Oklahoma.**

Historically, the academy dates back to 1920, when it was founded as the **Medical Department Field School** at Carlisle Barracks, Pa. In 1946 it was moved to Fort Sam Houston, where it was known first as **Army Medical Service School** and then as **Medical Field Service School.** In 1972, the academy moved to its present location at Fort

Sam Houston and was redesignated Academy of Health Sciences, U.S. Army.

Brooke Army Medical Center

Brooke Army Medical Center (BAMC) at Fort Sam Houston, is the successor to Brooke General Hospital, which was established as a post hospital in April 1881. The second largest of the Army's eight medical centers, BAMC has a worldwide mission of responsibility in every phase of medical education, patient care and medical research.

BAMC operates 645 hospital beds for definitive inpatient treatment, including all phases of surgical and medical primary, secondary and tertiary care. It provides one of three Level I Trauma Centers in San Antonio to assist the city in treatment of trauma patients.

Besides an annual inpatient load of more than 20,000 and outpatient visits of 1.1 million, the Center conducts an intensive education program in 23 medical specialties. Graduate resident training is conducted in health care administration, pharmacy, dietetics, specialized nursing and clinical pastoral education.

The U.S. Army Institute of Surgical Research, attached to BAMC for administrative and logistical support, has an international reputation for its outstanding work in research and treatment of burns. Burn teams flown to scenes of cases in the continental U.S. and sometimes overseas return patients to the Institute for care in a matter of hours.

U.S. Army Area Dental Laboratory

The U.S. Army Area Dental Laboratory at Fort Sam Houston is one of four throughout HSC providing fixed and removable dental prosthetic appliances for eligible beneficiaries in an 8-state area and Panama. It also provides consultation service to directors of dental services at designated Army installations.

The Fort Sam Houston Dental Activity (DENTAC) was organized in May 1978. The DENTAC operates three dental clinics with 56 dental treatment rooms to support over 12,000 active military personnel in the Fort Sam Houston area. In addition to dental care, the DENTAC at Fort Sam Houston offers three residency programs.

William Beaumont Army Medical Center

Standing at the base of the Franklin Mountains in El Paso, **William Beaumont Army Medical Center** uniquely symbolizes the latest developments in military medicine.

William Beaumont is an acute care and teaching institution, with 11 general inpatient wards and many specialty wards, totaling 423 beds. It serves a population of some 80,000 beneficiaries in the El Paso area and also takes medical referrals from other military hospitals in Arizona, New Mexico and West Texas.

In addition to the main hospital building, health care is provided at a number of sites throughout Fort Bliss and White Sands Missile Range. The consolidated troop medical clinic is one of the largest TMCs in the Army, and houses a primary care clinic, aviation medicine clinic, dental clinic, physical examination area, occupational health clinic and community mental health clinic.

A typical day at William Beaumont includes more than 2,500 outpatient clinic visits, filling of 4,600 prescriptions, completion of nearly 25,000 laboratory procedures, more than 2,000 radiology procedures and an average of 4.8 births.

The medical center houses the Army's first Residential Treatment Facility for alcoholism and drug abuse.

Darnall Army Community Hospital

Opened in 1965, **Darnall Army Hospital** (as it was originally named) at **Fort Hood** was the Army's first permanent 200-300 bed hospital and was known as one of the most modern in the military. However, the $12-million, fully equipped hospital was designed only to provide primary care to 40,000 people, and as Fort Hood grew and the retiree population increased, the need for expansion became evident. In 1979, a massive wraparound reconstruction and addition project began, and five years later the hospital had doubled its size.

Darnall is the only Army Medical Department Activity under the U.S. Army Health Services Command with a newborn intensive care unit and nuclear medicine service.

Although not a medical center, Darnall does have an emergency medicine residency program. Additionally, there are training programs in nursing anesthesiology, nursing education training and occupational specialty training.

Darnall presently supports 38,000 active duty, 50,000 family members, and 30,000 retired personnel and their families.

Military Aviation

The birth of military aviation took place at San Antonio in 1910, although some earlier flights were made elsewhere. On Feb. 5, 1910, **Benjamin D. Foulois** arrived at Fort Sam Houston and was instructed to teach himself to fly. His first flight was made March 2, 1910. (See Page 164, 1986-87 Texas Almanac, for more details.)

In 1917, during World War I, San Antonio's **Kelly Field** was activated and became one of the world's largest air training fields. It remained open after the war and **Randolph Field** was activated in 1930. During World War II, thousands of pilots, navigators and bombardiers trained at Texas fields.

Air Force bases in Texas as of July 1, 1991, include: Bergstrom near Austin; Brooks near San Antonio; Carswell in Fort Worth; Dyess in Abilene; Goodfellow at San Angelo; Kelly near San Antonio; Lackland near San Antonio; Laughlin near Del Rio; Randolph at San Antonio; Reese at Lubbock; and Sheppard at Wichita Falls.

Civil Air Patrol

The Civil Air Patrol (CAP) is a volunteer civilian auxiliary of the Air Force. Southwest Regional headquarters, located at Dallas Naval Air Station, Building 1239, directs CAP activities in Texas, Arizona, Arkansas, Louisiana, Oklahoma and New Mexico. There are 3,490 members of the Texas Wing of the CAP, with headquarters at Bergstrom AFB. Its membership includes 1,456 cadet members (ages 13 to 18) and 2,034 senior members, over 18, from many Texas communities. Mailing address of the Texas Wing is Bldg. 207, Bergstrom AFB, Texas 78743.

U.S. Navy and Naval Reserve

The most recent figures available show that the U.S. Navy accounted for over $15 million flowing into the Texas economy in fiscal year 1987. There are 7,222 active-duty military and 2,213 civilian employees stationed throughout the state, but concentrated in four principal locations: Corpus Christi, Kingsville, Beeville and Dallas.

The Chief of Naval Air Training Staff and a major portion of the pilot training pipeline are located at Naval Air Station Corpus Christi, where 1,452 pilots and 411 jet pilots were trained in fiscal year 1988. Additional pilot training facilities are found at Naval Air Stations Kingsville and Chase Field (Beeville).

An important facet of the "Navy presence" in Texas are the approximately 8,162 drilling reservists who serve throughout the state. The largest reserve training site is Naval Air Station Dallas, which is responsible for three reserve aircraft squadrons. VF-201 and VF-202, the two fighter squadrons based in Dallas, operate the F-14 Tomcat fighter aircraft. VR-59, the reserve logistics squadron, transports troops and supplies as part of its mission.

The Navy is constructing a new naval station in the community of Ingleside near Corpus Christi.

Marine Corps Reserve

Marine Corps Reserve units are located at Abilene, Amarillo, Austin, Corpus Christi, Dallas (including a Marine Aircraft Group headquarters at NAS, Dallas), El Paso, Fort Worth, Galveston, Harlingen, Houston, Lubbock, San Antonio, Texarkana and Waco.

Army and Air Force Exchange Service

Dallas is headquarters for the worldwide **Army and Air Force Exchange Service,** which provides quality merchandise to active-duty qualified reserve and retired military people and their families around the world. The Exchange Service is a self-sustaining organization, which employs more than 82,000 people, including almost 8,500 associates in Texas.

Business & Industry

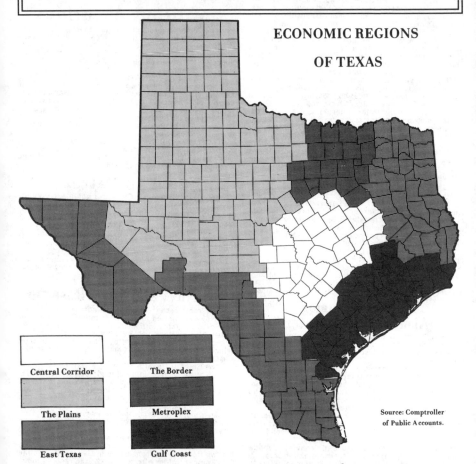

ECONOMIC REGIONS

OF TEXAS

Central Corridor

The Plains

East Texas

The Border

Metroplex

Gulf Coast

Source: Comptroller
of Public Accounts.

The Economic Regions of Texas

The following article was prepared for this edition of the Texas Almanac by John Sharp, Comptroller of Public Accounts of Texas.

INTRODUCTION

Texas' enormous size and diverse geography, climate and natural resources create a special challenge for those analyzing its economy. Changes in the economic conditions of the nation and world affect various regions in Texas in widely different ways.

The swings of the world's oil prices will not influence Amarillo in the same manner as Austin, and declines in defense spending will have a far greater impact on Dallas than Beaumont.

To accurately assess the state's economy, the Comptroller of Public Accounts divides the state into six individual regions — the Plains, the Metroplex, East Texas, the Gulf Coast, the Central Corridor and the Border.

The Plains region is the largest and most sparsely populated area of the state, with an economy based on oil and gas and agriculture. The Metroplex is largely urban, with defense-related and high-tech manufacturing and service industries. East Texas is for the most

part rural and heavily dependent on producing and processing agricultural commodities, timber, oil and gas and coal.

The economy of the most populous region of Texas — the Gulf Coast — is centered on petroleum and petrochemicals. Government, the military and education provide a solid economic base for the Central Corridor. The Border region is closely tied to Mexico through the trade, tourism, manufacturing and transportation sectors, which provide support for the Mexican maquiladora industry.

The Plains

The economic health of the 98-county Plains region, which includes Abilene, Amarillo, Lubbock, Midland, Odessa, San Angelo and Wichita Falls, relies heavily on oil and gas and agriculture.

Cotton, grain sorghum, wheat, corn and other feed grains are the area's main crops, but the region also leads the nation in feedlot cattle production. Oil and gas production dominate the west central and southwest-

ern part of the region, centered around Midland and Odessa.

After a solid recovery in 1988, the growth of the Plains stalled in 1989 as large oil companies consolidated operations and transferred employees out of the region. But Plains oil and gas employment has stabilized, and the region has begun to see some modest job growth again.

The region's agriculture had a good year in 1990. Cotton yields were up, with some counties setting records. Wheat production also provided a good harvest, and strong prices continued to help beef producers.

In 1992, with renewed national growth, the region should begin to post gains in nearly all economic sectors.

In the 1990s, the Plains will continue to lag behind the state's overall growth, due to consolidation in the oil and gas industry. Employment growth will average 1.3 percent annually, compared to 1.8 percent statewide.

Manufacturing and services will be key growth sectors. And the Plains' construction, banking and real-estate industries will get solidly back on track. Transportation and trade also will see steady progress.

The Metroplex

The Metroplex, which includes Dallas, Fort Worth and Sherman-Denison, is a major manufacturing, trade, air transportation, distribution and finance center. It is the most urbanized of the state's regions and has a strong manufacturing base built on high-tech electronics, aerospace and military equipment.

In 1990, the 20-county region continued its three-year rebound from the real-estate recession of 1987, but growth has been dampened by the sluggish performance of the area's high-tech and defense-related manufacturing industries.

The Metroplex will continue to add jobs slowly, and by 1992, economic growth in the area will again parallel the state's growth rate. Nearly all sectors should gain employment in 1992 led by transportation and manufacturing. And coupled with solid gains in services and increased wholesale- and retail-trade activity, total employment will rise to 2.114 million in 1992.

During the nineties, reduced defense spending will cap growth in area defense industries, but jobs in the production of electronics and computers will more than offset job losses in defense and aerospace.

With surplus space being slowly absorbed, the Metroplex construction industry will contribute strongly to regional growth throughout the decade. The Metroplex's strong service sector and transportation and trade industries will move ahead throughout the nineties.

Over the decade, the Metroplex economy will generate 396,700 new jobs, bringing total employment to 2.479 million.

East Texas

The 35-county East Texas region benefits from a wealth of natural resources, primarily timber, oil and gas, coal and water. The area's agricultural operations also are becoming increasingly important as rice, grain sorghum, peanuts, cotton and soybeans find new markets. And the region is experiencing a rise in tourism and health services as the number of retirees living there increases.

In 1990, East Texas' trade and services saw increased economic activity, and a healthy forest products industry contributed to renewed growth. In 1991, jobs in the area, which includes Longview, Marshall, Tyler and Texarkana, should grow to nearly 396,000.

While the forest-products industry will remain a staple of the region's employment in the 1990s, service-producing industries will be responsible for the bulk of East Texas' new jobs. The area's excellent highway network and proximity to major markets will spur growth in warehousing and motor-freight transportation. With real estate markets firming up, the region's construction, banking and real-estate industries will also be back on track.

The region will grow somewhat more slowly than the state during the 1990s because of continuing consolidations in oil and gas, but steady growth in other parts of the economy will help East Texas to register job gains of 1.5 percent annually.

Gulf Coast

The Gulf Coast economy led the state in economic growth in 1990. Total non-farm employment in the 32-county Gulf Coast region — including Houston, Galveston, Brazoria, Beaumont, Corpus Christi and Victoria — increased by 2.9 percent in 1989 to 1990. During this period, the region accounted for more than half of all new jobs added statewide.

Houston, the fourth-largest city in the nation, serves as a natural economic hub of the region. With its enormous energy and petrochemical industries, the giant Port of Houston, the Texas Medical Center, and Johnson Space Center, the city offers an amazing variety of opportunities for both national and international business of all kinds.

In 1991, Gulf Coast growth will slow along with the U.S. economy, but the region should still outpace the rest of Texas except the Border for a job gain of 1.2 percent to 2.146 million.

In 1992, Gulf Coast manufacturers of plastics, chemicals, steel and other fabricated metals, aerospace and other transportation equipment, and instruments will do better as the U.S. economy expands. The region's rejuvenated construction sector will continue to improve, and activity in real estate and finance will mount. Job growth in business and health services will continue at a solid rate, and trade activity will accelerate.

During the 1990s, the Gulf Coast will add about 398,800 new jobs, and by the year 2000, employment will hit 2.545 million.

Manufacturing job growth will be led by high-tech computers and electronics, aerospace, plastics and a revitalized steel industry. Strong construction and real-estate markets will fuel area job gains, while opportunities in the burgeoning health and business service industries will swell employment ranks.

Central Corridor

Historically, the Central Corridor has served as a center for federal and state government and higher education. In recent years, high-tech manufacturing and services have also played increasingly larger roles in the region's economy.

Although weaknesses in the construction industry continued to slow the Central Corridor economy in 1990, the region set new job records for the fourth consecutive year following a severe real-estate slump in 1987. But the pace of growth will ebb due to a national recession and sluggish performance in area high-tech manufacturing industries.

Employment in the 39-county Central Corridor region — including Austin, San Antonio, Waco, Killeen-Temple and Bryan-College Station — will climb to 1.223 million in 1991. The bulk of that growth will be registered by a rebounding trade sector.

In 1992, with an improving U.S. economy, Central Corridor employment will reach 1.242 million. A strong upswing in high-tech manufacturing is expected. Planned federal-defense cutbacks may reduce military and related civilian personnel at some Central Corridor bases. But with new troops being stationed at other bases, the region as a whole will experience a slight net gain in military employment in the coming years.

During the 1990s, with the shakeout in construction, banking and real estate largely complete, employment gains in the Central Corridor will average 2 percent annually.

The area's service industries will remain the biggest source of employment growth, adding almost 80,000 employees during the decade. Over the decade, the Central Corriuor economy will create 255,900 new jobs to bring total area employment to 1.479 million.

The Border

The 30-county Border region — including Brownsville, McAllen, Laredo and El Paso — is unique because of its close cultural and economic relationship to Mexico.

Helped by business from maquiladora plants in Mexico and the transportation companies that support them, and a resurgence in retail trade, the number of jobs in the region grew to 505,100 in 1990.

In 1991, the Border will once again become the fastest-growing area of the state as its economy proves more resistant than others to the national recession. By 1992, total employment will top 522,400.

As Mexican maquiladora plants increase, diversify and become more capital-intensive, they will continue to stimulate the service companies that support them, such as trucking and warehousing, on the Texas side of the national border.

A more open Mexican trade policy, which eliminated sanctions against the import of U.S. electronic goods and reduced tariffs on a broad range of products, should also boost Border retail trade.

Border agriculture has not fared as well as other sectors. A persistent drought has weakened the region's agricultural economy. Pastures are in poor to fair shape, and dryland cotton yields have been below average. Irrigated crops, however, should continue to do well.

The late-December 1989 freeze took a heavy toll on farm income, and citrus crops were damaged severely. Citrus production is not expected to recover before 1993.

Tourism continues to bolster the Border economy, particularly the growth in the number of "winter Texans," Midwesterners and retirees who make South Texas home in the winter.

Relaxed trade restrictions, a growing population and continued growth in maquiladoras will contribute to a 2.1 percent job growth rate in the 1990s to bring total employment up to 621,200.

Texas' Economy: The Envy of Others

"The Texas economy is now back on track. The state has added new jobs at a rate of 2 to 3 percent a year since 1988," Comptroller of Public Accounts John Sharp thinks. In early 1991, while the national economy was slowing down, Texas ranked first among the states in the number of new jobs added over the previous year with an all-time record of about 7.1 million Texans working in non-farm jobs.

More Balanced Growth

The outlook for the Texas economy through 1993 is for steady growth. The state's more diversified economy is less likely than in the 1970s and 1980s to suffer shocks brought about by volatile energy prices. The economy is driven today by manufacturing, trade, and services — a more stable foundation for growth than the state's earlier reliance on oil and gas, real estate, and construction.

A return of consumer confidence and a healthier national economy will help keep Texas growing through 1993. Total non-farm employment will continue to reach new highs, rising by about 250,000 to reach 7.4 million in 1993. State personal income also is expected to grow 7 percent each year in 1992 and 1993.

In addition, low business costs, favorable real-estate prices, a Sunbelt climate and growing markets will continue to lure new business to Texas. From migration alone, Texas will gain about 40,000 new residents a year in 1992 and 1993. Adding these newcomers to the natural increase, Texas' population will grow by about two million people, to more than 19 million, by 2000.

Oil and Gas: A Roller Coaster

The state's oil and gas industry began to recover in 1989 and the success of horizontal-drilling techniques spawned increases in both drilling activity and oil and gas employment in 1990. Growing from a lean base, the oil and gas industry was the fastest growing industry in Texas in early 1991.

Still, oil and gas probably will never regain the prominent role they had in the early 1980s. Oil and gas account for about 15 percent of the state economy, down from a peak of 27 percent in 1981. With declining oil and gas production, employment through 1993 will remain fairly flat, at around 185,000 jobs.

Construction To Improve

It will still be a number of years before the Texas construction industry, battered by overbuilding, returns to normal. But the Texas market for existing home sales is improving. Apartment occupancy rates are above 90 percent in all major Texas cities, and permits for new housing are gradually rising. Consequently, construction employment increased at an annual rate of 4 percent in early 1991. Construction employment should grow by 4 percent in 1992 and nearly 5 percent in 1993, as ongoing business improvement and rising migration to Texas create greater demand for commercial and residential space.

Although hiring again, the construction industry remains far behind its boom in the early 1980s. Housing starts peaked at 334,000 in 1983, before bottoming out at 46,000 starts in 1990. New housing starts are expected to number 75,000 in 1992 and 88,000 in 1993.

Manufacturing

The state's manufacturing industry suffered from defense cutbacks and an ailing national economy in 1990 and 1991, prompting some major layoffs in electronics and defense manufacturing. Since manufactured goods are sold worldwide, manufacturing is more sensitive to the swings of the national and world economies than other Texas economic sectors.

But despite uncertainties nationwide, Texas manufacturing is expected to grow. Texas' low business costs, expansions and relocations will help statewide manufacturing employment to rise by 1.8 percent in 1992 and nearly 3 percent in 1993.

The manufacturing industries that will improve the most in 1992 and 1993 are computers, electronics, food processing, and printing and publishing. The building-

materials industry also will add jobs as the construction industry strengthens.

Finance and Real Estate

The finance, insurance and real estate sector has been slow to respond to four straight years of economic growth in the overall Texas economy. Overbuilding, relatively high interest rates and the lack of available financing have suppressed the industry.

The silver lining to these difficulties is that overbuilding has left Texas with abundant bargain-priced real estate, compared to the rest of the nation. The median price of a house in all major Texas cities is below the nation's. At the end of 1990, the median price for a house was $68,700 in Houston, $85,500 in Dallas, and $63,000 in San Antonio, compared to a national average of $95,500.

In early 1991, the most profitable banks in large national bank-holding companies were in Texas. Contributing to the revival of the state's banking industry is a reduction in bankruptcies, in contrast to the national trend. Finance, insurance and real estate employment should grow by 1.3 percent in 1992 and 2.2 percent in 1993.

Trend Toward Services

In step with the national trend toward a service-based economy, health and business services in Texas grew at about 5 percent a year through the mid-to-late 1980s. An increase in the average age of the population and the success of the Texas Medical Center in Houston have stimulated the demand for health care services. Business services also have grown as manufacturers and government increasingly use independent consultants and business experts.

Texas employment growth in health and business services will slow somewhat, but will still grow at a sustainable 2 percent a year in 1992 and 1993.

The Road Ahead

The outlook for the Texas economy remains bright. Forecasts by three independent organizations place Houston and Dallas-Fort Worth among the top ten U.S. areas for positive real-estate prospects in the short term. Although non-metropolitan recreation areas have some of the fastest employment growth rates in Texas, metropolitan counties will continue to generate most of the new jobs. According to NPA Data Services, Harris County will add 452,000 jobs over the next ten years, Dallas County will add 371,000, Tarrant will add 159,000, Bexar will add 153,000, and Travis will add 129,000.

Diversification has changed the face of the Texas economy. Although Texas is more susceptible today to downturns in the national economy, it will be jolted less in the future by dramatic changes in energy prices. For the next few years, Texas' economic growth is expected to outpace the overall national rate. Through the 1990s, Texas should be a Sunbelt star, with an increasingly resilient economy.

Employment Growth Rates, Texas and the U.S.
Year-over-Year Percent Change

Year	Texas Empl. Growth	U.S. Empl. Growth	Difference from U.S.
1980	4.5	0.7	3.8
1981	5.6	0.8	4.8
1982	1.4	-1.7	3.1
1983	-1.1	0.7	-1.8
1984	4.8	4.8	0.0
1985	2.6	3.2	-0.6
1986	-1.5	2.1	-3.6
1987	-0.7	2.7	-3.4
1988	2.5	3.3	-0.8
1989	2.4	2.7	-0.3
1990	2.8	1.8	1.0

Source: Texas Employment Commission and U.S. Bureau of Labor Statistics.

Texas Bank Resources and Deposits—1905-1990

On Dec. 31, 1990, Texas had a total of 1,183 national and state banks with total deposits of $143,690,107,000 and total resources of $170,829,567,000.

SOURCE: Federal Reserve Bank of Dallas.

(In thousands of dollars)

Date	National Banks No. Banks	National Banks Total Resources	National Banks Deposits	State Banks No. Banks	State Banks Total Resources	State Banks Deposits	Combined Total No. Banks	Combined Total Total Resources	Combined Total Deposits
Sept. 30, 1905	440	$189,484	$101,285	29	$4,341	$2,213	469	$193,825	$103,498
Nov. 10, 1910	516	293,245	145,249	621	88,103	59,766	1,137	381,348	205,015
Dec. 29, 1920	556	780,246	564,135	1,031	391,127	280,429	1,587	1,171,373	844,564
Dec. 31, 1930	560	1,028,420	826,723	655	299,012	231,909	1,215	1,327,432	1,058,632
Dec. 31, 1940	446	1,695,662	1,534,702	393	227,866	179,027	839	1,923,528	1,713,729
Dec. 31, 1950	442	6,467,275	6,076,006	449	1,427,680	1,338,540	891	7,894,955	7,414,546
Dec. 31, 1955	446	8,640,239	7,983,681	472	2,087,066	1,941,706	918	10,727,305	9,925,387
Dec. 31, 1956	452	8,986,456	8,241,159	480	2,231,497	2,067,927	932	11,217,953	10,309,086
Dec. 31, 1957	457	8,975,321	8,170,271	486	2,349,935	2,169,898	943	11,325,256	10,340,169
Dec. 31, 1958	458	9,887,737	9,049,580	499	2,662,270	2,449,474	957	12,550,007	11,499,054
Dec. 31, 1959	466	10,011,949	9,033,495	511	2,813,006	2,581,404	977	12,824,955	11,614,899
Dec. 31, 1960	468	10,520,690	9,560,668	532	2,997,609	2,735,726	1,000	13,518,299	12,296,394
Dec. 30, 1961	473	11,466,767	10,426,812	538	3,297,588	3,009,499	1,011	14,764,355	13,436,311
Dec. 28, 1962	486	12,070,803	10,712,253	551	3,646,404	3,307,714	1,037	15,717,207	14,019,967
Dec. 30, 1963	519	12,682,674	11,193,194	570	4,021,033	3,637,559	1,089	16,703,707	14,830,753
Dec. 31, 1964	539	14,015,957	12,539,142	581	4,495,074	4,099,543	1,120	18,511,031	16,638,685
Dec. 31, 1965	545	14,944,319	13,315,367	585	4,966,947	4,530,675	1,130	19,911,266	17,846,042
Dec. 31, 1966	546	15,647,346	13,864,727	591	5,332,385	4,859,906	1,137	20,979,731	18,724,633
Dec. 31, 1967	542	17,201,752	15,253,496	597	6,112,900	5,574,735	1,139	23,314,652	20,828,231
Dec. 31, 1968	535	19,395,045	16,963,003	609	7,107,310	6,489,357	1,144	26,502,355	23,452,360
Dec. 31, 1969	529	19,937,396	16,687,720	637	7,931,966	7,069,822	1,166	27,869,362	23,757,542
Dec. 31, 1970	530	22,087,890	18,384,922	653	8,907,039	7,958,133	1,183	30,994,929	26,343,055
Dec. 31, 1971	530	25,137,269	20,820,519	677	10,273,200	9,179,451	1,207	35,410,469	29,999,970
Dec. 31, 1972	538	29,106,654	23,892,660	700	12,101,749	10,804,827	1,238	41,208,403	34,697,487
Dec. 31, 1973	550	32,791,219	26,156,659	716	14,092,134	12,417,693	1,266	46,883,353	38,574,352
Dec. 31, 1974	569	35,079,218	28,772,284	744	15,654,983	13,758,147	1,313	50,734,201	42,530,431
Dec. 31, 1975	584	39,138,322	31,631,199	752	17,740,669	15,650,933	1,336	56,878,991	47,282,132
Dec. 31, 1976	596	43,534,570	35,534,285	761	19,846,695	17,835,078	1,357	63,381,265	52,999,363
Dec. 31, 1977	604	49,091,503	39,828,475	773	22,668,498	20,447,012	1,377	71,760,001	60,275,487
Dec. 31, 1978	609	56,489,274	44,749,491	786	25,987,616	23,190,869	1,395	82,476,890	67,940,360
Dec. 31, 1979	615	65,190,891	50,754,782	807	30,408,232	26,975,854	1,422	95,599,123	77,730,636
Dec. 31, 1980	641	75,540,334	58,378,669	825	35,186,113	31,055,648	1,466	110,726,447	89,434,317
Dec. 31, 1981	694	91,811,510	68,750,678	829	42,071,043	36,611,555	1,523	133,882,553	105,362,233
Dec. 31, 1982	758	104,580,333	78,424,478	841	48,336,463	41,940,277	1,599	152,916,796	120,364,755
Dec. 31, 1983	880	126,914,841	98,104,893	848	55,008,329	47,653,797	1,728	181,923,170	145,758,690
Dec. 31, 1984	999	137,565,365	105,862,656	855	60,361,504	52,855,584	1,854	197,926,869	158,718,240
Dec. 31, 1985	1,058	144,674,908	111,903,178	878	64,349,869	56,392,634	1,936	209,024,777	168,295,812
Dec. 31, 1986	1,077	141,397,037	106,973,189	895	65,989,944	57,739,091	1,972	207,386,981	164,712,280
Dec. 31, 1987	953	135,690,678	103,930,262	812	54,361,514	47,283,855	1,765	190,052,192	151,214,117
Dec. 31, 1988	802	130,310,243	106,740,461	690	40,791,310	36,655,253	1,492	171,101,553	143,395,714
Dec. 31, 1989	687	133,163,016	104,091,836	626	40,893,848	36,652,675	1,313	174,056,864	140,744,511
Dec. 31, 1990	605	125,808,263	103,573,445	578	45,021,304	40,116,662	1,183	170,829,567	143,690,107

Total Deposits and Total Assets of All Insured Commercial Banks in Texas by Counties

Source: Federal Reserve Bank of Dallas as of Dec. 31, 1990
(in thousands of dollars)

County	No. of Banks	Total Deposits	Total Assets	County	No. of Banks	Total Deposits	Total Assets
Anderson	5	$311,543	$227,643	Burleson	4	172,290	158,492
Andrews	3	117,424	109,114	Burnett	3	115,232	103,488
Angelina	5	402,686	364,110	Caldwell	4	172,405	158,709
Aransas	2	145,295	136,362	Calhoun	3	293,258	268,438
Archer	2	52,183	48,129	Callahan	3	119,675	106,640
Armstrong	1	20,789	19,096	Cameron	13	1,282,725	1,181,624
Atascosa	4	154,586	137,994	Camp	2	120,805	109,246
Austin	5	259,712	234,151	Carson	3	66,251	60,001
Bailey	2	96,504	87,813	Cass	6	229,801	212,455
Bandera	2	53,255	48,893	Castro	2	78,335	70,480
Bastrop	4	203,616	183,724	Chambers	4	141,104	121,164
Baylor	2	63,257	57,552	Cherokee	7	376,598	336,764
Bee	3	182,827	163,124	Childress	1	32,314	29,809
Bell	13	798,758	728,722	Clay	2	75,626	66,975
Bexar	26	5,234,426	4,722,169	Cochran	1	51,788	47,530
Blanco	3	86,090	74,898	Coke	2	46,664	41,711
Bosque	3	101,267	92,901	Coleman	3	119,204	108,303
Bowie	5	708,562	622,379	Collin	14	743,998	690,281
Brazoria	13	840,408	754,098	Collingsworth	2	55,394	50,545
Brazos	5	820,283	737,710	Colorado	5	269,395	229,104
Brewster	1	57,084	52,463	Comal	4	269,686	253,644
Briscoe	2	52,236	46,622	Comanche	3	166,518	154,310
Brooks	2	60,722	50,609	Concho	2	31,675	28,406
Brown	3	166,976	154,822	Cooke	4	278,958	250,922

County	No. of Banks	Total Deposits	Total Assets	County	No. of Banks	Total Deposits	Total Assets
Coryell	5	252,728	232,104	Lamb	5	109,240	99,117
Cottle	1	38,650	31,780	Lampasas	2	128,255	119,426
Crane	1	28,238	25,693	Lavaca	3	171,683	153,626
Crockett	2	109,598	97,926	Lee	4	261,857	243,178
Crosby	3	72,027	65,108	Leon	4	79,590	69,404
Culberson	1	15,329	13,468	Liberty	7	321,369	299,256
Dallam	3	142,238	128,863	Limestone	6	182,524	168,858
Dallas	77	57,809,424	48,117,190	Lipscomb	1	28,559	25,280
Dawson	2	218,123	196,929	Live Oak	2	109,511	94,797
DeWitt	5	244,295	226,175	Llano	4	191,154	173,784
Deaf Smith	2	168,517	150,241	Lubbock	14	2,409,144	2,055,726
Delta	3	53,306	47,744	Lynn	3	105,127	92,614
Denton	11	733,725	677,542	Madison	2	167,942	152,531
Dickens	1	21,997	19,962	Marion	2	46,874	43,359
Dimmit	2	42,714	40,072	Martin	2	52,207	44,200
Donley	2	66,214	59,114	Mason	2	54,943	51,173
Duval	2	59,670	53,588	Matagorda	2	195,254	158,548
Eastland	4	123,525	109,179	Maverick	2	205,936	197,596
Ector	5	480,231	429,816	McCulloch	2	89,163	78,198
Edwards	1	25,830	22,291	McLennan	17	1,113,725	1,022,384
El Paso	12	3,382,201	2,958,481	McMullen	1	30,680	27,408
Ellis	10	455,065	410,815	Medina	7	172,324	157,491
Erath	4	165,178	153,027	Menard	2	31,740	26,420
Falls	3	87,480	83,935	Midland	5	934,581	792,860
Fannin	7	227,815	212,541	Milam	5	286,760	253,973
Fayette	7	258,553	237,075	Mills	2	100,919	92,539
Fisher	2	75,626	69,254	Mitchell	3	102,643	91,634
Floyd	2	98,356	88,153	Montague	4	408,216	373,889
Foard	1	22,007	19,913	Montgomery	4	181,929	171,827
Fort Bend	5	388,883	351,055	Moore	2	114,172	103,139
Franklin	2	82,219	74,366	Morris	3	102,975	97,517
Freestone	4	95,865	81,975	Motley	1	7,939	7,025
Frio	3	162,837	146,036	Nacogdoches	8	510,419	475,784
Gaines	3	122,521	111,811	Navarro	8	204,391	189,583
Galveston	16	1,150,775	989,082	Newton	1	35,920	33,229
Garza	1	49,553	43,685	Nolan	2	132,149	119,211
Gillespie	3	180,499	166,554	Nueces	14	2,158,826	1,816,848
Goliad	1	30,256	27,487	Ochiltree	2	186,900	165,741
Gonzales	3	102,656	96,480	Oldham	1	23,049	19,769
Gray	4	297,159	263,134	Orange	5	304,317	280,726
Grayson	12	544,108	508,114	Palo Pinto	4	140,093	128,584
Gregg	11	1,038,312	968,004	Panola	3	216,575	191,757
Grimes	5	132,557	122,068	Parker	5	418,735	386,037
Guadalupe	4	282,505	250,921	Parmer	2	131,091	112,668
Hale	5	306,676	283,826	Pecos	3	134,745	120,958
Hall	2	59,767	55,019	Polk	4	279,830	255,124
Hamilton	3	150,702	141,401	Potter	7	1,836,911	1,593,792
Hansford	3	142,141	123,586	Presidio	2	53,289	44,636
Hardeman	3	70,886	65,762	Rains	2	53,499	50,291
Hardin	5	253,309	231,096	Randall	1	81,893	74,738
Harris	95	29,940,173	23,015,693	Reagan	2	43,216	39,597
Harrison	6	268,869	240,591	Real	1	14,951	13,249
Haskell	4	99,834	91,625	Red River	2	49,418	45,588
Hays	3	137,665	127,326	Reeves	2	128,880	113,514
Hemphill	2	110,858	99,467	Refugio	2	101,163	80,388
Henderson	7	439,725	399,660	Roberts	1	14,099	13,092
Hidalgo	17	2,111,582	1,934,076	Robertson	3	149,330	135,413
Hill	5	180,765	159,043	Rockwall	3	88,510	82,295
Hockley	3	55,816	51,094	Runnels	6	124,992	116,836
Hood	4	253,875	234,370	Rusk	5	371,347	328,090
Hopkins	4	301,433	275,410	Sabine	2	90,654	81,476
Houston	7	197,542	183,177	San Augustine	1	45,283	40,024
Howard	4	397,619	348,137	San Jacinto	2	29,776	28,004
Hudspeth	1	8,411	7,525	San Patricio	8	301,714	272,616
Hunt	6	266,184	247,929	San Saba	2	52,492	47,420
Hutchison	3	114,955	106,453	Schleicher	1	35,946	29,959
Irion	1	66,539	59,357	Scurry	2	174,860	155,484
Jack	3	113,505	102,955	Shackelford	2	148,900	137,640
Jackson	2	156,303	145,763	Shelby	4	163,450	150,477
Jasper	3	282,670	257,011	Sherman	1	62,570	55,616
Jeff Davis	1	14,594	13,342	Smith	8	922,890	813,286
Jefferson	6	1,569,384	1,361,434	Somervell	1	29,922	27,822
Jim Hogg	2	78,563	66,186	Starr	2	205,703	187,448
Jim Wells	6	381,494	333,322	Stephens	1	62,291	57,678
Johnson	10	529,935	486,086	Sterling	1	30,155	25,218
Jones	3	119,294	105,772	Stonewall	1	27,995	21,997
Karnes	3	120,765	110,214	Sutton	2	57,310	50,420
Kaufman	6	397,796	368,464	Swisher	4	128,544	117,670
Kendall	1	39,113	35,584	Tarrant	48	8,916,582	7,873,297
Kent	1	8,463	7,815	Taylor	6	658,184	590,494
Kerr	2	242,854	227,750	Terrell	1	17,783	16,181
Kimble	2	40,828	35,671	Terry	2	156,511	140,493
Kinney	1	11,838	10,748	Throckmorton	2	31,721	28,093
Kleberg	2	212,275	189,134	Titus	3	173,607	160,251
Knox	2	57,680	52,064	Tom Green	6	736,319	667,681
La Salle	1	22,925	20,605	Travis	11	2,222,807	1,939,550
Lamar	5	327,690	291,032	Trinity	3	62,543	57,978

County	No. of Banks	Total Deposits	Total Assets	County	No. of Banks	Total Deposits	Total Assets
Tyler	3	54,292	49,289	Wichita	6	381,151	341,210
Upshur	4	269,274	234,906	Wilbarger	3	252,910	224,381
Upton	2	54,531	48,112	Willacy	2	140,743	127,822
Uvalde	3	269,159	247,466	Williamson	14	662,683	609,885
Val Verde	2	200,546	183,783	Wilson	4	155,213	140,819
Van Zandt	7	167,966	157,247	Winkler	2	69,599	60,155
Victoria	5	1,925,821	1,557,397	Wise	4	232,504	210,849
Walker	3	166,873	160,276	Wood	7	320,560	294,239
Waller	2	56,311	51,515	Yoakum	3	89,762	81,296
Ward	2	123,876	106,027	Young	4	265,781	243,208
Washington	4	167,595	155,674	Zapata	2	111,111	103,701
Webb	7	3,092,806	2,828,060	Zavala	1	30,451	28,393
Wharton	6	432,707	390,807	**TOTAL**	**1,183**	**$168,922,390**	**$143,690,107**
Wheeler	4	96,332	83,75?				

Leading Texas Commercial Banks, Ranked by Total Domestic Deposits As of December 31, 1990

Source: Federal Reserve Bank of Dallas
Abbreviations used in this table:
Bk-Bank; St-State; NB-National Bank;
B&TC-Bank and Trust Company.

Rank	Name and Location of Bank	Total Deposits (000 dollars)
1	NCNB Texas NB, Dallas	$25,422,973
2	Bank One Texas NA, Dallas	12,119,623
3	Texas Commerce Bk NA, Houston	6,507,711
4	First Interstate Bk Tx NA, Houston	4,688,297
5	Team Bk, Fort Worth	4,195,035
6	First Cy Tx-Houston NA, Houston	3,818,350
7	Frost NB of San Antonio, San Antonio	2,190,766
8	Texas Commerce Bk-Dallas NA, Dallas	2,030,361
9	First Cy Texas-Dallas, Dallas	1,953,321
10	International Bk of CMRC, Laredo	1,202,396
11	Victoria B&TC, Victoria	1,127,336
12	Texas Commerce Bk-El Ps NA, El Paso	1,113,986
13	Laredo NB, Laredo	1,110,465
14	Comerica Bk-Texas, Dallas	1,025,165
15	Hibernia NB in Texas, Dallas	923,022
16	Texas Commerce Bk, Austin NA, Austin	818,527
17	MBank El Paso NA, El Paso	814,976
18	Texas Cmrc Bk-Rio Grd Vly NA, McAllen	803,213
19	First NB at Lubbock, Lubbock	679,995
20	First NB of Amarillo, Amarillo	647,264
21	First Cy Tx-Beaumont NA, Beaumont	631,765
22	NorthPark NB of Dallas, Dallas	615,906
23	Amarillo NB, Amarillo	592,707
24	First Cy Tx-Austin NA, Austin	570,568
25	First City Tx-Corpus Christi, Corpus Christi	505,321
26	Corpus Christi NB, Corpus Christi	464,103
27	Broadway NB, San Antonio	460,135
28	First NB of Abilene, Abilene	429,562
29	Texas Cmrc Bk Ft Worth, Ft Worth	426,069
30	First Cy Tx-El Paso NA, El Paso	393,300
31	Mercantile Bk NA, Brownsville	389,896
32	American St Bk, Lubbock	371,592
33	River Oaks Bk, Houston	358,293
34	Channelview Bk, Channelview	346,298
35	Texas Commerce Bk-San Antonio NA, San Antonio	342,354
36	Texas Commerce Bk, Beaumont NA, Beaumont	340,503
37	First Victoria NB, Victoria	338,561
38	First Cy Tx-Midland NA, Midland	337,122
39	Central B&TC, Fort Worth	334,269
40	First Cy Texas SA NA, San Antonio	332,261
41	Cullen Center B&TC, Houston	328,006
42	Charter NB - Houston, Houston	327,940
43	First Cy Tx-Bryn/Cllg Stn NA, Bryan	327,340
44	Texas Cmrc Bk-Arlington NA, Arlington	323,471
45	Plains NB of Lubbock, Lubbock	319,043
46	North Dallas B&TC, Dallas	300,242
47	First St Bk, Denton	300,123
48	First Cy Tx-Tyler NA, Tyler	298,382
49	Southside St Bk, Tyler	296,944
50	MBank Waco NA, Waco	278,655
51	Union NB Texas, Laredo	261,326
52	First St B&TC, Mission	257,582
53	Texas Commerce Bk-Midland NA, Midland	256,272
54	Texas Commerce Bk - CRPS NA, Corpus Christi	253,971
55	Groos Bk NA, San Antonio	252,895
56	Overton Park NB, Fort Worth	239,990
57	Bank of the Hills, Austin	237,750
58	Texarkana NB, Texarkana	236,369
59	University St Bk, Houston	234,360
60	Post Oak Bk, Houston	226,416
61	First Bk, Katy	226,152
62	Longview B&TC, Longview	225,234
63	Texas Commerce Bk - Sn An NA, San Angelo	223,440
64	American NB of Terrell, Terrell	220,527
65	Compass Bk-Houston, Houston	220,504
66	First American Bk, Bryan	215,699
67	Texas Commerce Bk - Lngvw NA, Longview	215,550
68	First St Bk, Austin	215,103
69	Cornerstone Bk NA, Dallas	213,190
70	Parker Square Bk NA, Wichita Falls	208,700
71	First B&TC, Groves	206,579
72	Citizens B&TC, Baytown	205,535
73	Merchants Bk, Houston	205,232
74	First St Bk of Uvalde, Uvalde	203,782
75	Cullen/Frost Bk of Dallas NA, Dallas	201,181
76	Provident Bk, Dallas	198,455
77	Lockwood NB, Houston	198,097
78	Sunwest Bk of El Paso, El Paso	197,129
79	Citizens NB of Henderson, Henderson	196,919
80	North Ft Worth Bk, Fort Worth	195,414
81	First NB in Big Spring, Big Spring	191,057
82	First St B&TC, Port Lavaca	186,480
83	First NB of Temple, Temple	183,962
84	Texas Bk, Weatherford	183,210
85	Charter NB Colonial, Houston	182,596
86	Texas Commerce Bk NA, Lubbock	181,502
87	Sterling Bk, Houston	181,218
88	Texas Commerce Bk-Odessa NA, Odessa	175,527
89	First Cy Tx-Alice, Alice	173,039
90	Plano B&TC, Plano	167,702
91	Sugar Creek NB, Fort Bend Cty	166,703
92	Texas Commerce Bk - Amarillo, Amarillo	166,567
93	Kelly Field NB, San Antonio	164,397

Rank	Name and Location of Bank	Total Deposits (000 dollars)
94	First NB of Kerrville, Kerrville	163,528
95	First NB in Pampa, Pampa	163,388
96	Texas St Bk, McAllen	160,255
97	First Cy Tx-Lufkin NA, Lufkin	158,451
98	Promenade NB, Richardson	158,315
99	Kleberg First NB, Kingsville	156,750
100	United States NB of Glvstn, Galveston	156,173
101	Texas Commerce Bk-Bfls NA, New Braunfels	154,849
102	First Cy Tx-San Angelo NA, San Angelo	153,884
103	Southwest Bk Tx NA, Houston	151,084
104	American NB, Corpus Christi	150,185
105	Harlingen NB, Harlingen	149,887
106	Firstbank, Texarkana	147,611
107	Jefferson St Bk, San Antonio	146,014
108	First NB, Marshall	145,218
109	Sulphur Springs St Bk, Sulphur Springs	144,429
110	Texas Gulf Bk NA, Freeport	144,369
111	First NB, Killeen	144,346
112	First Cy Tx-Orange NA, Orange	143,480
113	Citizens Bk, Kilgore	143,031
114	Compass Bk, Plano	142,351
115	Stone Fort NB, Nacogdoches	142,055
116	First St Bk, Rio Vista	141,728
117	First NB of Bowie, Bowie	138,128
118	First NB of Albany, Albany	137,640
119	BancTexas Houston NA, Houston	137,477
120	Texas NB of Waco, Waco	137,376
121	First NB Rio Grande City, Rio Grande City	136,551
122	Bank of North Texas, North Richland Hills	135,808
123	Park NB of Houston, Houston	135,474
124	Citizen St Bk Corpus Christi, Corpus Christi	135,239
125	First NB of Athens, Athens	134,233
126	American Bk, Houston	133,904
127	Fredonia St Bk, Nacogdoches	133,284
128	Bank of Houston, Houston	132,986
129	Liberty NB in Paris, Paris	132,919
130	First NB Texas, Webster	132,572
131	Central NB, Waco	132,470
132	First St Bk, Athens	131,614
133	First Cy Tx-Madisonville NA, Madisonville	131,477
134	First NB of Park Cities, Dallas	130,662
135	Metrobank NA, Houston	130,636
136	Southwest Bk, Fort Worth	130,614
137	First NB, Plainview	129,555
138	Guaranty Bk, Mt Pleasant	129,476
139	NBC Bk - Eagle Pass NA, Eagle Pass	129,363
140	South Main Bk, Houston	129,164
141	First Western NB, Carrollton	129,041
142	American Bk Halton Cy, Haltom City	128,851
143	Citizens St Bk, Giddings	128,522
144	First NB of Bay City, Bay City	128,515
145	Tanglewood Bk NA, Houston	128,480
146	Klein Bk, Harris County	126,307
147	Meadowbrook NB, Fort Worth	125,650
148	Western NB, Odessa	125,611
149	First St B&TC, Carthage	125,239
150	First NB of Grapevine, Grapevine	123,795

Total Domestic Deposits and Total Domestic Assets of All Insured Commercial Banks in Seven Largest Counties

As of December 31, 1990
(In Thousands of Dollars)

County	No. of Banks	Total Assets	Total Deposits
Bexar	26	$5,234,426	$4,722,169
Cameron	13	1,282,725	1,181,624
Dallas	77	57,809,424	48,117,190
Harris	95	29,940,173	23,015,693
Tarrant	48	8,916,582	7,873,297
Travis	11	2,222,807	1,939,550
Webb	7	3,092,806	2,828,060
Total All Counties	277	$108,498,943	$89,677,583

Texas National Banks

Consolidated Statement, Foreign and Domestic Offices, as of Dec. 31, 1990
Source: Federal Reserve Bank of Dallas

Number of Banks 605
(All figures in thousand dollars)

Assets

Cash and due from banks:
Noninterest-bearing balances and currency and coin $10,941,242
Interest-bearing balances 2,023,002
Securities 30,915,593
Fed. funds sold 13,178,105
Securities purchased under agreement to resell 826,722
Loans and lease financing receivables:
Loans and leases, net of unearned income 58,531,524
Less: allowance for loan and lease losses 1,667,069
Less: allocated transfer risk reserve 0
Loans and leases, net 56,864,454
Assets held in trading accounts 281,403
Premises and fixed assets 2,357,616
Other real estate owned 1,265,394
Investments in unconsolidated subsidiaries and associated companies 9,491
Customers liability on acceptances outstanding.................... 288,584
Intangible assets.................. 597,986
Other assets 6,258,660
Total Assets $125,808,263

Liabilities

Deposits:
In domestic offices................ $103,573,445
Noninterest-bearing 23,474,690
Interest-bearing 80,098,753
In foreign offices, edge & agreement subsidiaries, & IBF's............. 1,903,929
Noninterest-bearing 2,353
Interest-bearing 1,901,576
Federal funds purchased 5,446,507
Securities sold under agreement to repurchase 2,130,456
Demand notes issued to the U.S. Treasury 2,350,526
Other borrowed money............. 682,054
Mortgage indebtedness and obligations under capitalized leases........... 87,586
Banks' liability on acceptances executed and outstanding................. 288,584
Notes and debentures subordinated to deposits..................... 359,872
Other liabilities.................. 1,761,216
Total Liabilities $118,584,175

Equity Capital

Perpetual preferred stock............ $67,782
Common stock 1,650,089
Surplus........................ 0
Undivided profits and capital reserves ... 827,233
Cumulative foreign currency translation adjustments 13
Total Equity Capital $7,224,088
Total liabilities, limited preferred stock and equity capital $125,808,263

Texas State Banks

Consolidated Statement, Foreign and Domestic Offices, as of Dec. 31, 1990
Source: Federal Reserve Bank of Dallas

Number of Banks 578
(All figures in thousand dollars)

Assets

Cash and due from banks:
Noninterest-bearing balances and currency and coin $2,921,047
Interest-bearing balances 848,056
Securities....................... 15,448,942
Fed. funds sold and securities purchased under agreement to resell in domestic offices of the bank and of its edge and agreement subsidiaries and in IBFs:
Federal funds sold 3,744,187

Securities Purchased under
agreements to rerell 69,359
Loans and lease financing receivables:
Loans and leases, net of unearned
income 19,352,924
Less: allowance for loan and lease
losses 448,618
Less: Allocated Transfer Risk
Reserve 0
Loans and leases, net of unearned income
Allowance, and reserve 18,904,309
Assets held in trading accounts 22,007
Premises and fixed assets 882,077
Other real estate owned 703,880
Investments in unconsolidated
subsidiaries and associated companies. . 2,276
Customers liability on acceptances
outstanding. 4,835
Intangible assets. 48,289
Other assets 1,422,040
Total Assets $45,021,304

Liabilities

Deposits:
In domestic offices. $40,116,662
Noninterest-bearing 7,729,290
Interest-bearing 32,387,372
In foreign offices, edge & agreement
subsidiaries, & IBF's 48,707
Noninterest-bearing 0
Interest-beearing 48,707

Federal funds purchased and securities
sold under agreements to repurchase in
Domestic offices of the bank and of its
edge and agreement subsidiaries and
in IBFS:
Federal funds purchase 721,744
Securities sold under agreements to
repurchase 269,208
Demand notes issued to the U.S. Treasury 231,705
Other borrowed money 66,443
Mortgage indebtedness and obligations
under capitalized leases. 40,418
Banks' liability on acceptances executed
and outstanding. 4,835
Notes and debentures subordinated to
deposits. 10,283
Other liabilities. 404,869
Total Liabilities $41,914,873
Limited-life preferred stock 0

Equity Capital

Perpetual preferred stock. $5,704
Common stock 613,746
Surplus. 0
Undivided profits and capital reserves . . . 894,669
Cumulative foreign currency
translation adjustments 0
Total Equity Capital $3,106,431
Total liabilities, limited-life preferred
stock and equity capital.. . . . . $45,021,304

Savings and Loan Associations

Texas on Dec. 31, 1990, had 131 insured savings and loan associations and savings banks, with total assets of $72,041,456. This total included federal- and state-chartered associations, which are members of the Federal Home Loan Bank of Dallas and insured by the Federal Savings and Loan Insurance Corporation.
Details in the following table were supplied by the Dallas District of the Office of Thrift Supervision of the U.S. Department of the Treasury.

Texas Savings and Loan Associations
(Thousands of Dollars)

Year	No. Assns.	Total Assets	+Mortgage Loans	✓Cash	✓Investment Securities	Savings Capital	FHLB Advances and other Borrowed Money	*Net Worth
Dec. 31, 1990†	131	$72,041,456	$27,475,664	$20,569,770	. . .	$56,994,387	$17,738,041	−$4,566,656
Conservatorship	51	14,952,402	6,397,466	2,188,820	. . .	16,581,525	4,304,033	−6,637,882
Privately Owned	80	57,089,054	21,078,198	18,380,950	. . .	40,412,862	13,434,008	2,071,226
Dec. 31, 1989†	196	90,606,100	37,793,043	21,218,130	. . .	70,823,464	27,158,238	−9,356,209
Conservatorship	81	22,159,752	11,793,445	2,605,080	. . .	25,381,494	7,103,657	−10,866,213
Privately Owned	115	68,446,348	25,999,598	18,613,050	. . .	45,441,970	20,054,581	1,510,004
Dec. 31, 1988	204	110,499,276	50,920,006	26,181,917	. . .	83,950,314	28,381,573	−4,088,355
Dec. 31, 1987	279	99,613,666	56,884,564	12,559,154	. . .	85,324,796	19,235,506	−6,677,338
Dec. 31, 1986	281	96,919,775	61,489,463	9,989,918	. . .	80,429,758	14,528,311	109,807
Dec. 31, 1985	273	91,798,890	60,866,666	10,426,464	. . .	72,806,067	13,194,147	3,903,611
Dec. 31, 1984	273	77,544,202	45,859,408	10,424,113	. . .	61,943,815	10,984,467	2,938,044
Dec. 31, 1983	273	56,684,508	36,243,290	6,678,808	. . .	46,224,429	6,317,947	2,386,551
Dec. 31, 1982	288	42,505,924	28,533,974	4,713,742	. . .	34,526,483	5,168,343	1,631,139
Dec. 31, 1981	311	38,343,703	30,013,805	3,294,327	. . .	30,075,258	4,846,153	1,493,795
Dec. 31, 1980	318	34,954,129	27,717,383	3,066,791	. . .	28,439,210	3,187,638	1,711,201
Dec. 31, 1979	310	31,280,006	25,238,483	2,512,797	. . .	25,197,598	2,969,838	1,640,049
Dec. 31, 1978	318	27,933,526	22,830,872	142,721	$1,876,882	22,848,519	2,251,631	1,444,607
Dec. 31, 1977	328	24,186,338	19,765,901	154,027	1,579,440	19,994,347	1,515,045	1,235,096
Dec. 31, 1976	316	19,921,694	16,096,166	196,790	1,344,827	16,908,949	949,231	1,044,611
Dec. 31, 1975	303	16,540,181	13,367,569	167,385	1,000,095	13,876,780	919,404	914,502
Dec. 31, 1974	295	13,944,524	11,452,013	117,097	806,302	11,510,259	1,038,386	834,892
Dec. 31, 1973	288	12,629,928	10,361,847	126,106	795,989	10,483,113	740,725	763,618
Dec. 31, 1972	278	10,914,627	8,919,007	155,901	841,904	9,249,305	459,019	678,086
Dec. 31, 1971	272	9,112,590	7,481,751	140,552	670,622	7,647,906	458,152	589,077
Dec. 31, 1970	271	7,706,639	6,450,730	122,420	509,482	6,335,582	559,953	531,733
Dec. 31, 1969	270	7,055,949	5,998,172	105,604	391,175	5,894,398	473,066	487,308

*Net worth includes permanent stock and paid-in surplus general reserves, surplus and undivided profits.
✓Beginning in 1979, cash and investment securities data combined.
+Beginning in 1982, net of loans in process.
†Beginning in 1989, the Office of Thrift Supervision, U.S. Department of the Treasury, separated data on savings and loans (thrifts) into two categories: those under the supervision of the Office of Thrift Supervision (Conservatorship Thrifts) and those still under private management (Privately Owned).

Construction Industry

Contract awards for construction in 1990 totaled $3,922,781,630. While not near the all-time record of $4,806,998,065 set in 1985, and even below the 1989 total of $4,176,355,929, the 1990 amount was dubbed "respectable" by industry observers.

A table below shows the approved Texas construction for 1991. These data were compiled by editors of **Texas Contractor** from official sources.

Comparison of Construction Awards by Years

Source: Texas Contractor

Year	Total Awards	Year	Total Awards	Year	Total Awards
1990	$3,922,781,630	1977	2,270,788,842	1965	1,254,638,051
1989	4,176,355,929	1976	1,966,553,804	1964	1,351,656,302
1988	3,562,336,666	1975	1,737,036,682	1963	1,154,624,634
1987	4,607,051,270	1974	2,396,488,520	1962	1,132,607,006
1986	4,636,310,266	1973	1,926,778,365	1961	988,848,239
1985	4,806,998,065	1972	1,650,897,233	1960	1,047,943,630
1984	3,424,721,025	1971	1,751,331,262	1959	1,122,290,957
1983	4,074,910,947	1970	1,458,708,492	1958	1,142,138,674
1982	3,453,784,388	1969	1,477,125,397	1957	1,164,240,546
1981	3,700,112,809	1968	1,363,629,304	1956	1,220,831,984
1980	3,543,117,615	1967	1,316,872,998	1955	949,213,349
1979	3,353,243,234	1966	1,421,312,029	1954	861,623,224
1978	2,684,743,190				

Approved Texas Construction, 1991

The following is a recapitulation of all approved Texas construction for 1991. The data were compiled by the editors of **Texas Contractor** from official sources.

FEDERAL

General Services Administration	$ 23,000,000
Federal Aviation Administration	95,000,000
Veterans Administration	21,000,000
Soil Conservation Service	5,800,000
Rural Electrification Administration	160,000,000
Department of Defense	289,617,000
Federal Highway Aid	850,000,000
National Aeronautics & Space Administration	27,000,000
U.S. Department of Agriculture	180,000,000
Total	**$1,650,617,000**

STATE

Highway Construction Funds	$1,008,486,005
State Building Programs	302,468,944
State Colleges and Universities	318,706,575
Total	**$1,626,661,524**

WATER PROJECTS

Bureau of Reclamation	$ 214,000
Corps of Engineers	124,000,000
River Authorities	300,000,000
State-Assisted Work	90,000,000
Total	**$ 514,214,000**

CITIES

Schools, Colleges	$ 232,189,628
Streets, Bridges	296,065,512
Waterworks, Sewers	741,085,000
Apartments, Duplexes and Residences	1,273,856,482
Commercial	2,050,676,415
City Buildings	289,752,000
Total	**$4,883,625,037**

COUNTIES

Roads-County Funds	$ 10,542,000
Road Maintenance	116,090,634
Machinery Purchases	36,913,978
County Buildings	40,435,000
Miscellaneous	7,230,604
Total	**$211,212,216**
GRAND TOTAL 1991 APPROVED CONSTRUCTION	**$8,886,327,777**

Analysis of Awards

The following table analyzes and classifies awards in Texas for the year 1990, as compared with the corresponding year of 1989, as reported by **Texas Contractor**.

	1990		1989	
	No.	Amount	No.	Amount
Engineering Awards	1,803	$2,246,723,256	1,767	$2,313,973,182
Non-Residential Awards	1,064	1,676,058,374	1,168	1,862,382,747
Total	2,867	$3,922,781,630	2,935	$4,176,355,929

ENGINEERING AWARDS

	1990		1989	
	No.	Amount	No.	Amount
Highways, Streets, Airports	1,192	$1,685,933,354	1,237	$1,822,073,034
Waterworks, Sewers, etc.	480	430,422,831	447	441,815,230
Irrigation, Drainage, etc.	73	121,774,984	44	41,257,074
Miscellaneous	58	8,592,087	39	8,827,844
Total	1,803	$2,246,723,256	1,767	$2,313,973,182

NON-RESIDENTIAL CONSTRUCTION AWARDS

	1990		1989	
	No.	Amount	No.	Amount
Educational Bldgs.	315	$486,777,644	331	$689,320,767
Churches, Theaters, etc.	39	27,068,285	30	20,184,520
Hospitals, Hotels, Motels Public Bldgs.	66	77,522,232	58	118,515,984
Public Bldgs.	296	520,587,061	390	819,641,539
Commercial-Industrial	337	562,386,840	348	212,383,302
Miscellaneous	11	1,716,312	11	2,336,635
Total	1,064	$1,676,058,374	1,168	$1,862,382,747

Texas Credit Unions

Membership in Texas' 950 credit unions has grown by approximately 120,000 each year during the past decade as credit unions continue to be the fastest-growing segment of the financial industry.

Nationally, there are 15,945 credit unions representing more than $195 billion in assets. Texas remains a leader in the credit union movement: Based on figures compiled by the Texas Credit Union League, Texas credit unions account for more than $146 billion and rank second in the nation according to asset size. Texas also has the fourth highest number of credit union members in the country: more than 4 million. Currently, one Texan of every four belongs to a credit union.

In 1990, share (savings) accounts stood at $136 billion, and loans amounted to $8.5 billion.

Credit unions are chartered at federal or state levels. The National Credit Union Administration (NCUA) is the regulatory agency for the federally chartered credit unions in Texas. The Texas Credit Union Department, Austin, is the regulatory agency for the state-chartered credit unions.

The Texas Credit Union League and Affiliates at 4455 LBJ Freeway, Farmers Branch, Tx. 75244-5998, has been the state association for federal and state-chartered credit unions since October 1934.

Insurance in Texas

The State Board of Insurance reported that, on Aug. 31, 1990, there were 2,451 firms licensed to handle insurance business in Texas, including 816 Texas firms and 1,635 out-of-state companies. Annual premium income of firms operating in Texas caused Dallas and some other cities to rank among the nation's major insurance centers.

Additional details are provided in subsequent tables covering the calendar year 1989.

The former **Robertson Law,** enacted in 1907 and repealed in 1963, encouraged the establishment of many Texas insurance firms. It required life insurance companies operating in the state to invest in Texas three-fourths of all reserves held for payment of policies written in the state. Many out-of-state firms withdrew from

Texas. Later many companies re-entered Texas and the law was liberalized and then repealed.

The State Board of Insurance administers legislation relating to the insurance business. This agency was established in 1957, following discovery of irregularities in some firms and succeeded two previous regulatory groups, established in 1913 and changed in 1927. The governor appoints the three-member board, which, in turn, appoints the State Commissioner of Insurance. The commissioner serves as chief administrator of the agency and has other powers with which to regulate the insurance industry.

In 1991, the legislature moved to revise the operation of the commission.

Insurance Companies in Texas

The following table shows the number and kinds of insurance companies licensed in Texas on Aug. 31, 1990:

	Texas	Out-of-State	Total		Texas	Out-of-State	Total
Stock Life	272	647	919	Risk Retention Groups	2	...	2
Mutual Life	3	83	86	Third Party Administrators	79	118	197
Stipulated Premium Life	67	...	67	Continuing Care Retirement			
Non-profit Life	...	1	1	Communities	15	2	17
Stock Fire	1	8	9	Total Legal Reserve	713	1,635	2,348
Stock Fire and Casualty	111	588	699	Statewide Mutual Assessment			
Mutual Fire and Casualty	8	65	73	Life, Health and Accident	2	...	2
Stock Casualty	5	54	59	Local Mutual Aid Associations	27	...	27
Mexican Casualty	...	9	9	Burial Associations	11	...	11
Lloyds	86	1	87	Exempt Associations	14	...	14
Reciprocal Exchanges	12	14	26	Non-profit Hospital Service	1	...	1
Fraternal Benefit Societies	12	28	40	County Mutual Fire	24	...	24
Titles	6	16	22	Farm Mutual Fire	24	...	24
Non-profit Legal Services	1	...	1	Total Mutual Assessment	103	...	103
Health Maintenance	33	1	34	Grand Total	816	1,635	2,451

LEGAL RESERVE LIFE INSURANCE COMPANIES
Texas Business Only, for Calendar Year 1989:

	Texas	Out-of-State	Total
Premium income during 1989	$1,810,209,728	$3,347,325,119	$5,157,534,847
Claims and benefits paid during 1989	$1,578,223,026	$2,499,603,112	$4,077,826,138

MUTUAL FIRE AND CASUALTY INSURANCE COMPANIES
Texas Business Only, for Calendar Year 1989:

	Premiums	Losses
Texas companies	$455,443,264	$467,105,435
Companies of other states	2,264,659,043	1,728,884,848
Total	$2,720,102,307	$2,195,990,283

LLOYDS INSURANCE
Texas Business Only, for Calendar Year 1989:

	Premiums	Losses
Texas companies	$955,808,868	$613,262,879
Companies of other states	1,975,446	1,831,522
Total	$957,784,314	$615,094,401

RECIPROCAL INSURANCE COMPANIES
Texas Business Only, for Calendar Year 1989:

	Premiums	Losses
Texas companies	$377,097,687	$269,978,527
Companies of other states	208,978,527	183,506,343
Total	$586,076,214	$453,484,870

STOCK FIRE COMPANIES
Texas Business Only, for Calendar Year 1989:

	Premiums	Losses
Texas companies	$9,966,789	$29,632,761
Companies of other states and foreign companies	1,561,649	3,062,939
Total	$11,528,438	$32,695,700

FRATERNAL BENEFIT SOCIETIES
Texas Business Only, for Calendar Year 1989:

	Texas	Out-of-State	Total
No. policies issued during 1989.	12,375	29,391	41,766
Amount of insurance issued during 1989.	$277,421,591	$1,457,491,301	1,734,912,892
Amount of Premiums received during 1989 (Life and H&A)	22,206,966	112,668,878	134,875,844
Losses and claims paid during 1989 (Life and H&A)	6,347,919	30,783,453	37,081,372
No. policies in force Dec. 31, 1989	NA	NA	NA
Amount of insurance in force Dec. 31, 1989	$1,488,177,824	$7,592,683,626	$9,081,861,450

STOCK CASUALTY INSURANCE COMPANIES
Texas Business Only, for Calendar Year 1989:

	Premiums	Losses
Texas companies	$13,822,678	$5,459,726
Companies of other states and foreign companies	213,763,103	303,921,041
Total	$227,585,781	$308,380,767

TITLE GUARANTY COMPANIES
Texas Business Only, for Calendar Year 1989:

	Texas	Out-of-State	Total
Premium income	$321,046,021	$2,673,295,646	$2,994,341,667
Losses paid.	15,727,905	212,157,931	227,885,836

STOCK FIRE AND CASUALTY INSURANCE COMPANIES
Texas Business Only, for Calendar Year 1989:

	Premiums	Losses
Texas companies	$2,031,800,700	$1,601,260,746
Companies of other states.	6,677,806,247	5,432,536,585
Total	$8.709,606.947	$7,033,797,331

Per Capita Personal Income
Source: U.S. Department of Commerce

This table shows the per capita personal income in Texas Metropolitan Statistical Areas as reported in the April 1990 Survey of Current Business. All figures are in dollars. These data are based on MSAs as constituted in 1990.

Per capita personal income for the entire state rose from $1,349 in 1950 to $14,590 in 1988. This compared with the U.S. per capita income which rose from $1,496 in 1950 to $16,490 in 1988, according to U.S. Department of Commerce figures.

Metropolitan Statistical Area*	1980	1981	1982	1983	1984	1985	1986	1987	1988
TEXAS.	$9,439	$10,807	$11,378	$11,686	$12,575	$13,494	$13,489	$13,843	$14,590
Abilene	9,398	11,076	11,465	11,777	12,175	13,369	13,055	13,433	14,243
Amarillo.	9,545	10,769	11,464	11,924	12,666	13,616	13,577	14,166	14,634
Austin	9,065	10,383	11,174	11,937	13,483	14,530	14,548	14,656	15,342
Beaumont-Port Arthur	9,950	11,184	11,784	12,013	12,210	12,811	12,899	13,323	14,203
Brazoria (PMSA)	10,188	11,421	12,065	11,860	13,079	13,770	14,287	14,577	15,642
Brownsville-Harlingen	5,506	6,172	6,365	6,654	6,796	7,138	7,166	7,452	7,868
Bryan-College Station.	6,740	8,032	8,524	9,085	9,561	9,813	10,156	10,743	11,613
Corpus Christi	8,518	9,850	10,345	10,503	10,923	12,110	11,561	11,674	12,408
Dallas (PMSA)	11,179	12,574	13,415	14,222	15,861	17,221	17,400	17,775	18,580
El Paso	6,603	7,413	7,753	8,290	8,745	8,931	9,192	9,541	10,008
Fort Worth-Arlington (PMSA).	10,418	11,755	12,384	13,103	14,138	15,084	15,617	15,876	16,551
Galveston-Texas City (PMSA).	10,370	11,807	12,575	12,323	13,392	13,857	14,126	14,644	15,572
Houston (PMSA)	...	...	...	...	14,517	15,301	14,793	15,169	16,192
Killeen-Temple	7,359	8,224	9,187	9,930	10,320	11,122	11,662	11,987	12,538
Laredo.	5,321	6,028	6,174	6,017	6,030	6,712	6,729	6,963	7,452
Longview-Marshall	9,028	10,374	10,886	11,008	11,710	12,208	12,424	12,738	13,421
Lubbock.	8,674	9,690	10,289	11,123	11,584	12,218	12,152	12,717	13,432
McAllen-Edinburg-Mission.	4,939	5,755	5,979	6,012	6,458	6,740	6,720	6,933	7,302
Midland	13,525	16,149	16,805	15,507	15,094	17,719	15,785	15,860	16,947
Odessa	10,203	12,264	12,478	11,512	11,325	13,582	11,658	12,132	12,663
San Angelo	8,899	10,324	11,181	11,580	12,115	12,803	13,063	13,492	13,969
San Antonio	8,346	9,337	9,991	10,569	11,540	12,514	12,669	12,750	13,436
Sherman-Denison.	8,768	9,841	10,521	11,148	12,158	12,835	13,083	13,623	14,347
Texarkana, Texas-Ark.	7,633	8,617	9,139	9,557	10,375	11,541	11,889	12,288	12,957
Tyler	9,404	10,854	11,749	12,188	13,296	13,728	13,987	14,586	15,154
Victoria	9,498	11,660	12,342	11,928	13,077	13,811	13,476	13,925	14,653
Waco	8,396	9,504	10,252	10,958	11,718	12,209	12,467	12,754	13,411
Wichita Falls	9,857	11,302	12,115	11,835	11,970	12,985	13,734	13,646	14,055	14,930

*Each Metropolitan Statistical Area comprises one county except the following: Amarillo: Potter and Randall; Austin: Hays, Travis and Williamson; Beaumont-Port Arthur: Hardin, Jefferson and Orange; Corpus Christi: Nueces and San Patricio; Dallas PMSA: Collin, Dallas, Denton, Ellis, Kaufman and Rockwall; Fort Worth-Arlington PMSA: Johnson, Parker and Tarrant; Houston PMSA: Fort Bend, Harris, Liberty, Montgomery and Waller; Killeen-Temple: Bell and Coryell; Longview-Marshall: Gregg and Harrison; San Antonio: Bexar, Comal and Guadalupe; Texarkana: Bowie County, TX, and Miller County, AR.

Employment, by Industries and Counties†

This table shows monthly average employment in the fourth quarter of 1990. This survey is limited to employers who are subject to the Texas Unemployment Compensation Act. Figures provided by Texas Employment Commission.

County	Total Employment	Agriculture	Mining	Construction	Manufacturing	Transp., Comm. and Pub. Util.	Trade	Finance, Ins. and Real Estate	Service & Other	State Govt.	Local Govt.
Anderson	13,938	92	604	232	1,318	384	3,422	373	2,237	3,406	1,870
Andrews	5,391	13	1,794	189	*	252	935	156	1,059	39	954
Angelina	28,954	252	27	1,697	7,801	1,686	6,229	973	5,388	1,473	3,428
Aransas	3,789	69	155	210	424	252	1,286	176	495	115	607
Archer	1,522	149	201	71	*	48	328	63	277	33	352
Armstrong	417	32	0	*	*	*	88	28	156	20	93
Atascosa	5,837	349	584	125	92	445	1,692	195	878	114	1,363
Austin	6,341	107	80	617	614	280	2,021	433	1,190	89	910
Bailey	2,126	479	*	47	56	168	591	78	179	29	499
Bandera	1,993	104	*	67	77	*	430	70	842	42	361
Bastrop	6,012	158	49	161	925	133	1,509	245	876	179	1,777
Baylor	1,169	32	43	33	59	92	284	53	300	49	224
Bee	6,646	149	372	166	547	298	1,611	261	1,438	117	1,687
Bell	56,841	252	*	2,060	8,196	1,905	14,777	2,463	15,590	643	10,955
Bexar	445,076	2,919	1,616	19,403	37,933	20,962	124,241	36,618	128,989	12,073	60,322
Blanco	1,787	109	*	90	67	*	439	143	665	48	226
Borden	167	20	*	*	0	0	*	*	60	14	73
Bosque	3,112	*	*	58	785	136	707	127	667	51	581
Bowie	27,124	207	16	1,035	4,484	1,436	7,923	1,219	6,665	431	3,708
Brazoria	68,464	478	1,998	11,016	17,255	2,903	12,440	1,619	9,263	3,085	8,407
Brazos	57,129	554	845	1,892	3,418	1,364	11,926	1,795	9,741	20,897	4,697
Brewster	3,137	101	*	208	68	197	722	104	666	678	393
Briscoe	400	61	*	*	*	*	18	93	*	122	17	89
Brooks	1,963	119	132	26	*	45	488	70	529	49	505
Brown	11,802	67	70	297	2,799	520	2,941	264	2,725	584	1,535
Burleson	2,645	78	253	83	*	71	717	197	581	55	610
Burnet	5,119	55	74	217	1,004	291	1,325	231	762	108	1,052
Caldwell	5,235	87	364	66	673	226	1,083	185	1,353	111	1,087
Calhoun	10,810	85	152	1,810	3,362	251	1,917	323	1,591	64	1,255
Callahan	1,518	18	61	35	67	85	343	109	247	48	505
Cameron	77,538	1,756	12	2,420	12,299	3,247	20,668	3,409	17,421	2,156	14,150
Camp	3,142	726	*	153	541	135	633	105	468	16	365
Carson	3,631	77	88	92	*	101	267	61	2,553	44	348
Cass	7,170	19	86	380	1,909	285	1,463	245	1,193	266	1,324
Castro	2,632	832	0	70	138	106	562	70	239	33	582
Chambers	5,745	151	424	484	*	331	1,078	174	1,912	60	1,131
Cherokee	13,790	867	69	284	3,198	585	2,666	322	2,609	1,875	1,315
Childress	1,645	96	*	23	*	109	534	41	345	133	364
Clay	1,414	50	32	89	94	65	331	51	208	38	456
Cochran	1,402	212	*	*	*	16	231	*	565	21	357
Coke	862	51	189	13	*	*	110	53	107	21	318
Coleman	2,080	57	106	24	*	99	495	111	693	38	457
Collin	81,082	919	*	2,619	14,440	1,770	21,526	4,335	23,138	1,953	10,382
Collingsworth	909	152	0	8	*	41	211	*	210	36	251
Colorado	5,495	301	338	253	792	227	1,623	152	947	93	769
Comal	17,058	104	*	831	3,449	463	5,615	614	3,605	171	2,206
Comanche	3,070	478	*	67	233	147	768	109	572	45	651
Concho	718	69	0	*	*	*	146	*	290	21	192
Cooke	9,757	178	301	152	2,567	568	2,549	279	1,213	360	1,590
Coryell	8,629	55	*	354	568	152	1,530	313	1,349	2,454	1,854
Cottle	2,191	78	39	185	93	126	668	114	729	34	125
Crane	1,788	*	848	63	58	107	197	29	83	22	381
Crockett	1,493	114	249	15	10	77	380	*	292	40	316
Crosby	2,079	551	*	27	89	39	411	55	414	37	456
Culberson	1,328	66	*	*	*	*	330	*	675	33	224
Dallam	2,070	205	*	48	53	112	774	129	308	50	391
Dallas	1,164,758	5,412	16,939	39,982	185,415	77,288	312,534	117,323	315,889	8,237	85,739
Dawson	4,433	792	453	48	302	214	994	195	514	49	872
Deaf Smith	6,318	838	0	220	1,394	322	1,572	191	686	62	1,033
Delta	936	*	*	*	86	*	130	49	407	34	230
Denton	68,430	617	35	2,317	11,711	2,041	18,922	1,894	13,086	9,999	7,808
DeWitt	5,619	56	83	144	1,207	163	1,279	357	893	206	1,231
Dickens	699	134	0	*	*	79	112	26	177	22	149
Dimmit	2,678	362	384	62	*	79	555	86	353	61	736
Donley	862	56	0	*	50	30	226	53	110	23	314
Duval	2,848	60	607	*	*	53	338	41	680	59	1,010
Eastland	5,111	34	296	234	824	261	1,349	159	810	89	1,055
Ector	45,191	146	6,056	2,531	4,387	2,086	13,079	1,397	8,015	765	6,729
Edwards	366	26	*	*	*	*	88	*	99	19	134
Ellis	22,955	239	10	1,155	7,355	1,313	5,157	715	3,567	248	3,196
El Paso	199,000	2,157	47	8,339	41,031	9,911	53,513	7,710	41,510	4,157	30,634
Erath	10,088	961	*	250	1,449	314	2,798	274	1,681	1,441	920
Falls	3,342	153	*	111	408	106	697	204	599	373	69
Fannin	5,428	83	*	159	1,386	213	1,128	483	1,021	96	855
Fayette	6,722	276	264	197	799	210	2,085	250	1,258	114	1,265
Fisher	1,094	142	*	*	*	158	139	65	286	25	271

County	Total Employment	Agriculture	Mining	Construction	Manufacturing	Transp., Comm. and Pub. Util.	Trade	Finance, Ins. and Real Estate	Service & Other	State Govt.	Local Govt.
Floyd	2,415	668	0	30	204	104	501	72	206	31	599
Foard	580	47	0	20	*	20	103	*	277	12	101
Fort Bend	47,849	1,071	1,587	2,151	7,762	2,676	10,357	1,365	9,707	2,950	8,223
Franklin	1,603	39	*	*	*	84	269	88	854	31	238
Freestone	3,645	27	*	91	299	543	693	149	1,096	61	686
Frio	4,098	528	545	117	108	145	916	86	781	82	790
Gaines	4,121	893	473	162	125	234	773	179	347	38	897
Galveston	75,082	325	598	4,478	8,756	4,572	15,105	4,912	13,077	11,918	11,341
Garza	1,358	175	283	9	29	41	272	23	188	41	297
Gillespie	5,061	73	*	273	725	196	1,606	251	1,274	98	565
Glasscock	399	205	*	*	*	*	*	*	74	9	111
Goliad	1,132	58	*	46	*	*	214	44	346	53	371
Gonzales	5,228	645	201	64	889	315	1,238	191	732	89	864
Gray	8,865	116	1,139	669	1,330	365	2,034	311	1,761	99	1,041
Grayson	37,230	220	118	1,615	11,209	1,448	7,993	1,975	8,586	224	3,842
Gregg	51,188	390	2,733	3,172	9,518	2,436	13,991	1,953	10,848	362	5,785
Grimes	5,029	202	*	207	1,182	138	797	186	483	755	1,079
Guadalupe	15,100	285	104	678	4,192	316	3,432	533	2,428	208	2,924
Hale	12,442	1,149	*	329	*	445	3,506	447	4,437	120	2,009
Hall	1,128	155	0	*	*	194	241	44	208	19	267
Hamilton	1,797	144	*	34	*	78	533	76	595	29	308
Hansford	2,065	425	195	167	32	166	416	93	123	19	429
Hardeman	1,334	46	*	7	*	90	274	63	479	53	322
Hardin	7,128	54	417	366	789	288	2,015	202	1,269	113	1,615
Harris	1,466,494	8,268	67,008	107,038	160,133	103,330	364,058	95,483	401,910	33,508	125,758
Harrison	18,577	44	712	500	7,370	869	3,379	604	2,659	234	2,206
Hartley	496	72	*	*	*	17	135	0	57	16	199
Haskell	1,697	207	43	28	36	135	505	85	253	52	353
Hays	18,938	160	*	671	2,167	825	4,101	544	3,733	4,006	2,731
Hemphill	1,230	73	224	*	13	99	210	85	218	27	281
Henderson	10,841	177	266	495	1,537	579	2,843	475	2,253	141	2,075
Hidalgo	109,342	8,154	868	4,263	14,299	3,005	31,210	3,831	17,686	3,064	22,962
Hill	5,719	299	*	284	1,006	207	1,281	210	1,076	91	1,265
Hockley	8,154	519	1,689	315	130	410	1,479	198	1,588	54	1,772
Hood	5,770	97	*	339	152	223	1,939	275	1,565	40	1,140
Hopkins	9,092	324	*	474	1,146	502	3,396	425	1,287	137	1,401
Houston	6,200	101	*	137	1,085	219	1,351	254	1,140	990	923
Howard	11,104	210	928	577	1,112	533	2,587	459	1,917	1,015	1,766
Hudspeth	590	162	*	*	*	42	60	*	83	38	205
Hunt	23,715	118	*	490	8,841	1,235	4,485	583	3,059	1,886	3,018
Hutchinson	9,631	58	1,100	1,421	2,315	334	1,898	183	858	81	1,383
Irion	483	26	122	18	*	*	80	*	111	10	116
Jack	1,495	*	259	37	26	144	292	79	227	45	386
Jackson	3,051	151	416	144	35	199	771	143	380	48	764
Jasper	8,592	214	*	296	2,359	311	1,857	354	1,541	147	1,513
Jeff Davis	613	57	*	26	0	23	89	25	181	134	78
Jefferson	107,897	490	1,277	10,625	17,569	7,625	25,482	4,093	27,040	3,101	10,595
Jim Hogg	1,216	115	113	23	*	26	365	*	143	46	385
Jim Wells	11,414	336	2,606	427	280	443	2,636	423	2,389	148	1,726
Johnson	20,537	324	*	946	4,266	753	5,828	737	4,101	157	3,425
Jones	3,577	255	221	162	358	284	677	146	489	76	909
Karnes	3,120	76	135	87	386	191	778	162	580	68	657
Kaufman	12,977	107	*	478	2,423	391	3,194	409	2,184	1,358	2,433
Kendall	3,530	34	36	214	303	47	1,246	166	761	39	684
Kenedy	229	108	*	0	0	0	*	0	68	2	51
Kent	242	28	*	0	0	*	16	*	75	13	110
Kerr	10,985	264	19	355	1,259	351	2,743	552	2,984	1,170	1,288
Kimble	1,237	38	0	28	171	31	370	50	271	57	221
King	328	*	*	*	*	*	21	0	236	7	64
Kinney	563	58	0	*	*	*	64	20	234	18	169
Kleberg	9,139	464	449	229	582	355	2,154	268	1,870	1,310	1,458
Knox	1,264	157	119	48	9	43	258	41	223	45	321
Lamar	17,051	132	*	654	5,585	677	3,575	439	3,553	399	2,037
Lamb	4,364	1,022	*	66	*	341	1,001	120	877	63	874
Lampasas	2,645	49	*	125	458	72	790	111	473	64	503
La Salle	943	114	64	*	0	15	172	54	152	38	334
Lavaca	4,717	42	67	152	1,672	128	1,179	174	621	84	598
Lee	4,173	202	499	178	408	341	1,015	186	379	389	576
Leon	2,556	99	69	213	*	26	692	164	744	59	490
Liberty	13,487	232	703	468	2,005	481	3,165	457	3,116	435	2,425
Limestone	6,920	81	*	173	699	621	1,325	170	1,007	1,834	1,010
Lipscomb	731	*	65	11	*	7	188	34	140	13	273
Live Oak	2,421	29	427	113	*	68	653	101	463	67	500
Llano	2,611	25	*	89	77	112	756	224	726	59	543
Loving	22	*	*	0	0	0	*	0	11	1	10
Lubbock	95,657	1,419	244	3,008	7,243	5,142	28,431	4,902	23,995	11,574	9,699
Lynn	1,541	535	0	3	75	161	175	59	99	30	404
Madison	3,169	*	74	53	37	83	672	105	806	737	602
Marion	1,946	19	*	35	475	58	519	61	388	52	339
Martin	1,265	238	130	38	*	*	181	39	280	29	330
Mason	811	39	0	19	38	25	278	59	138	24	191
Matagorda	12,112	350	423	1,797	901	*	2,674	280	3,467	151	2,069

County	Total Employment	Agriculture	Mining	Construction	Manufacturing	Transp., Comm. and Pub. Util.	Trade	Finance, Ins. and Real Estate	Service & Other	State Govt.	Local Govt.
Maverick	7,727	496	*	85	1,170	348	2,268	242	797	120	2,201
McCulloch	2,221	55	*	44	224	154	612	80	517	40	495
McLennan	74,773	711	102	2,931	14,666	3,753	19,016	4,771	18,716	2,190	7,917
McMullen	333	19	90	*	0	*	53	*	60	32	79
Medina	5,335	223	99	197	482	160	1,470	187	980	123	1,414
Menard	462	*	*	*	*	10	128	*	143	18	163
Midland	45,172	386	10,088	1,297	2,272	2,541	11,000	2,358	8,754	409	6,067
Milam	6,187	168	77	332	*	285	1,148	249	2,857	69	1,002
Mills	1,216	173	*	9	*	*	227	62	514	24	207
Mitchell	2,065	163	119	65	*	164	419	97	399	53	586
Montague	4,116	21	231	77	963	141	953	181	651	71	827
Montgomery	40,629	521	1,250	2,267	4,897	1,310	10,943	1,842	9,226	291	8,082
Moore	7,053	381	285	170	*	440	1,422	162	3,187	50	956
Morris	4,571	65	*	81	2,078	359	689	130	535	61	573
Motley	337	47	*	*	65	*	90	*	44	14	77
Nacogdoches	20,293	389	*	673	4,547	501	4,944	618	3,256	3,018	2,347
Navarro	12,620	141	331	481	3,009	457	2,808	437	2,819	318	1,819
Newton	1,856	*	*	48	701	37	252	*	201	53	564
Nolan	5,777	131	173	185	1,086	564	1,200	166	839	405	1,028
Nueces	114,599	634	3,428	8,985	10,337	5,947	29,742	5,559	30,592	3,071	16,304
Ochiltree	3,597	78	791	*	150	219	881	172	737	33	536
Oldham	720	83	*	*	*	*	110	*	278	20	229
Orange	23,357	105	186	1,479	6,696	1,098	5,057	611	4,269	363	3,493
Palo Pinto	7,175	44	242	143	1,239	492	2,068	220	1,214	131	1,382
Panola	7,266	155	1,891	351	*	342	1,167	173	1,847	56	1,284
Parker	11,915	318	177	551	2,415	462	3,327	513	1,498	126	2,528
Parmer	4,199	500	0	70	*	179	558	78	2,123	28	663
Pecos	4,484	240	699	88	144	312	1,048	135	612	115	1,091
Polk	6,957	22	200	112	1,469	315	1,794	286	1,228	140	1,391
Potter	58,291	645	1,086	2,430	6,996	4,161	16,257	3,123	13,836	1,955	7,802
Presidio	1,292	315	0	49	*	52	284	48	148	65	331
Rains	915	*	0	82	*	39	164	*	353	26	251
Randall	16,647	376	89	738	1,622	339	6,458	668	2,565	1,626	2,166
Reagan	1,191	33	411	12	34	89	192	*	103	14	303
Real	458	63	0	*	*	*	80	*	121	12	182
Red River	3,198	71	*	142	952	96	514	74	552	67	730
Reeves	4,274	589	187	137	113	346	991	125	772	115	899
Refugio	2,295	146	484	38	31	125	545	120	213	39	554
Roberts	223	9	11	*	*	*	48	20	52	4	79
Robertson	3,520	225	*	*	359	303	652	135	1,026	73	742
Rockwall	5,579	142	*	239	691	543	1,415	255	1,413	45	836
Runnels	3,581	231	265	50	1,202	135	634	111	298	47	608
Rusk	11,800	153	775	1,790	1,592	1,188	2,093	367	2,097	175	1,570
Sabine	1,809	*	*	*	*	100	317	63	945	32	352
San Augustine	1,526	18	0	*	122	*	364	64	493	51	414
San Jacinto	1,318	12	*	80	148	45	227	81	162	37	526
San Patricio	12,887	411	409	1,604	*	453	2,558	392	4,046	185	2,825
San Saba	1,465	72	*	52	*	17	531	59	442	29	263
Schleicher	745	47	216	*	*	74	74	*	86	8	240
Scurry	6,579	105	1,923	206	290	355	1,343	184	660	348	1,165
Shackelford	984	28	325	*	*	28	137	*	241	23	207
Shelby	5,984	*	*	81	2,215	173	1,191	258	1,097	74	891
Sherman	867	197	112	28	*	18	241	*	58	18	193
Smith	63,713	1,048	1,880	1,931	11,510	3,038	16,242	3,249	14,937	2,952	6,920
Somervell	4,006	*	0	*	81	*	230	31	3,248	38	378
Starr	6,472	*	163	53	43	134	1,319	196	1,472	128	2,964
Stephens	2,743	53	466	55	193	174	795	229	313	51	41
Sterling	487	72	81	*	*	*	94	*	100	16	12
Stonewall	629	*	149	79	*	30	73	*	138	12	14
Sutton	1,639	90	440	90	18	74	305	75	180	58	30
Swisher	2,356	614	*	47	164	147	463	99	254	39	52
Tarrant	530,697	2,815	4,100	20,410	111,270	54,919	143,830	24,891	114,355	8,255	45,85
Taylor	45,348	385	1,607	1,417	4,493	2,586	12,509	1,879	12,749	2,370	5,35
Terrell	383	21	*	0	*	*	52	0	180	20	11
Terry	3,736	466	727	98	124	191	807	134	333	62	79
Throckmorton	513	60	99	*	*	38	67	24	72	19	13
Titus	12,181	93	*	453	3,883	1,026	2,134	277	2,522	149	1,64
Tom Green	36,265	520	525	1,140	5,471	2,674	9,306	1,532	8,895	2,287	3,9
Travis	329,604	1,644	563	10,054	42,293	11,070	71,788	21,543	84,622	55,451	30,57
Trinity	1,954	*	*	61	294	51	491	116	362	30	54
Tyler	3,456	39	5	145	717	122	734	95	348	353	89
Upshur	5,780	64	*	164	617	250	1,268	157	2,128	106	1,02
Upton	1,383	50	343	72	*	179	214	48	47	24	40
Uvalde	8,124	1,160	216	251	796	296	1,959	266	1,079	270	1,83
Val Verde	8,186	108	*	226	415	451	2,918	336	1,267	240	2,22
Van Zandt	6,147	278	422	258	385	309	1,530	208	1,314	75	1,36
Victoria	28,564	190	1,686	1,722	3,107	1,187	7,743	1,594	6,456	302	4,57
Walker	18,127	133	*	362	1,406	258	3,613	426	2,462	7,675	1,79
Waller	7,148	208	*	150	1,242	54	1,624	128	816	1,976	95
Ward	4,018	9	880	209	120	381	819	87	408	279	82
Washington	10,435	207	133	435	2,285	169	2,597	655	1,541	1,094	1,31
Webb	44,907	443	1,736	1,430	1,755	6,431	14,815	1,981	7,327	877	8,11
Wharton	13,462	1,278	794	374	1,683	457	3,207	440	2,763	182	2,28

County	Total Employment	Agriculture	Mining	Construction	Manufacturing	Transp., Comm. and Pub. Util.	Trade	Finance, Ins. and Real Estate	Service & Other	State Govt.	Local Govt.
Wheeler	1,637	96	58	0	15	108	449	66	353	32	460
Wichita	47,672	171	1,409	1,656	8,133	2,570	11,347	2,065	13,060	2,614	4,647
Wilbarger	5,753	265	76	136	*	298	1,047	208	1,590	1,236	897
Willacy	3,463	680	*	85	*	145	651	138	607	75	1,082
Williamson	29,062	257	*	1,624	5,775	629	7,038	973	6,044	493	6,229
Wilson	3,094	188	46	88	199	45	874	158	473	106	917
Winkler	2,437	*	636	*	49	180	498	62	392	33	587
Wise	7,105	85	932	164	1,213	496	1,668	223	959	98	1,267
Wood	6,648	127	263	277	847	308	1,442	357	1,634	102	1,291
Yoakum	3,612	198	1,292	178	62	263	544	61	275	22	717
Young	6,280	82	773	136	1,353	332	1,356	326	908	82	932
Zapata	1,420	64	198	15	*	35	236	67	148	23	634
Zavala	2,598	493	89	37	*	29	273	43	798	70	766

†When there was no employment reported in a county in one of the industry groups, a "0" is shown. When one or two employers comprise 80% or more of the employment for an industry group in a county, a "*" is shown. The employment for that industry is included in "Service & Other" so as not to reveal information about individual establishments.

Employment by Industries, 1990

This table shows the number of employing establishments, employment and wages paid as reported by the Texas Employment Commission for the fourth quarter of 1990. Wages are estimates based on four times the wages for the fourth quarter of 1990.

Industry/Group	Reporting Units	Employ-ment	Total Wages 1990
Agriculture, Forestry, Fisheries	11,731	90,311	$1,268,751,340
Agricultural Production—Crops	3,252	22,981	276,407,616
Agricultural Prod. —Livestock	2,596	19,391	318,502,524
Agricultural Services	5,726	46,797	649,712,916
Forestry	50	697	16,738,352
Fishing, Hunting and Trapping	107	444	7,389,936
Mining	6,789	187,485	8,373,980,852
Metal Mining	25	504	21,766,384
Coal Mining	19	3,752	171,408,052
Oil and Gas Ext.	6,548	177,922	8,028,188,236
Nonmetallic Min., Except Fuels	197	5,307	152,618,180
Contract Construction	27,674	338,057	8,636,687,720
General Building Contractors	6,958	63,228	1,745,224,496
Heavy Const. Ex. Building	2.566	104,841	3,110,018,980
Special Trade Contractors	18,150	169,988	3,781,444,244
Manufacturing	19,248	998,967	29,755,554,872
Food and Kindred Products	1,120	101,615	2,302,284,468
Textile Mill Products	79	4,034	73,403,044
Apparel and Other Textile Prods.	987	55,481	829,047,992
Lumber and Wood Products	1,437	31,175	616,465,360
Furniture and Fixtures	490	16,805	322,814,736
Paper and Allied Products	251	25,680	771,552,884
Printing and Publishing	3,813	75,825	1,855,132,596
Chemicals and Allied Products	746	83,145	3,700,418,376
Petroleum and Coal Products	144	29,802	1,444,349,272
Rubber and Misc. Plastics Prods.	842	42,132	1,060,468,232
Leather and Leather Products	148	7,600	139,391,908
Stone, Clay and Glass Products	844	35,868	924,535,400
Primary Metal Inds.	307	30,069	919,097,528
Fabricated Metal Products	2,140	82,668	2,218,607,216
Industrial Mach. and Equipment	3,115	117,985	3,931,581,388
Electronic and Other Electric Equip.	825	107,803	3,712,243,128
Transportation Equipment	618	94,651	3,326,552,780
Instruments and Related Prods.	519	40,018	1,257,541,932
Miscellaneous Mfg. Industries	823	16,612	350,066,636
Transportation, Communication	12,057	411,511	12,793,893,700
Railroad Transp.	3	41	1,138,328
Local & Interurban Pass. Transp.	439	11,197	174,730,700
Trucking and Ware-housing	5,398	107,123	2,447,960,232
Water Transportation	574	15,335	485,430,060
Transportation by Air	663	77,179	2,635,310,900
Pipelines, Exc. Natural Gas.	42	4,398	209,289,768
Transportation Serv.	2,524	26,316	644,631,376
Communication	1,207	90,292	3,066,453,396
Electric, Gas and Sanitary Serv.	1,207	79,629	3,128,948,944
Wholesale and Retail Trade	89,525	1,758,848	31,211,762,940
Wholesale Trade —Durable Goods.	21,554	267,121	9,184,354,576
Wholesale Trade —Nondurable	10,638	169,307	4,997,363,080
Building Materials and Garden Supply	2,995	40,100	712,541,196
Gen. Mdse. Stores	426	190,894	2,497,012,312
Food Stores	7,162	239,080	3,076,032,840
Automotive Dealers and Serv. Sta.	9,146	137,232	2,972,208,116
Apparel and Access. Stores.	4,343	86,282	964,120,280
Furniture and Home Furns. Store	4,153	50,682	959,529,784
Eating and Drinking Places	15,565	432,397	3,769,112,296
Miscellaneous Retail	13,543	145,753	2,079,488,460
Finance, Insurance and Real Estate	27,460	416,905	11,829,679,300
Depository Institutions	2,448	125,197	3,119,788,128
Nondepository Institutions	1,362	27,801	868,542,572
Security and Commodity Brokers	1,022	15,633	1,032,262,604
Insurance Carriers	928	82,468	2,459,103,000
Ins. Agents, Brokers and Service	7,449	45,203	1,321,210,856

Industry/Group	Reporting Units	Employ-ment	Total Wages 1990
Real Estate	12,204	107,654	2,360,827,796
Holding and Other Investment Offices	2,047	12,948	667,944,336
Service Industries	121,000	1,637,658	39,071,431,072
Hotels and Other Lodging Places	2,076	87,247	1,023,237,816
Personal Services	8,965	79,826	1,012,299,532
Business Services	17,224	398,917	7,853,350,072
Auto. Repair, Services & Parking	9,068	61,609	1,080,843,140
Miscellaneous Repair Services	4,573	25,957	600,049,000
Motion Pictures	1,484	21,290	245,077,232
Amusement and Recreation Services	3,429	57,530	841,034,508
Health Services	25,922	485,847	13,400,747,484
Legal Services	9,138	62,858	3,855,064,432

Industry/Group	Reporting Units	Employ-ment	Total Wages 1990
Educational Services	1,212	52,755	1,099,389,064
Social Services	4,060	82,484	949,659,556
Museums, Botanical, Zoological Gardens	108	3,081	47,579,356
Membership Orgs	4,325	36,853	576,681,976
Engineering and Mgmt. Services	14,480	157,951	6,214,879,624
Private Households	14,578	21,916	206,643,972
Services, Nec.	358	1,536	64,894,324
Federal Government	1,976	197,808	6,204,454,660
State and Local Government	6,215	1,074,072	22,500,248,852
All Industries and Federal Agencies	323,675	7,111,623	171,646,445,304
Industries with Texas UI Coverage	321,699	6,913,815	165,441,990,644

Non-Agricultural Employment, 1990

(In Thousands)

Employment in Texas increased to 7,125,500 in December 1990, up from 6,982,400 in December 1989. Average employment for 1990 was 7,031,700.

The following table shows Texas Employment Commission estimates of the non-agricultural labor force in Texas for December 1989 and December 1990 together with the change in the number employed.

Industry	Dec. 1989 (000)	Dec. 1990 (000)	Change For Year (000)
Total Non-agricultural W & S Employment	6,982.4	7,125.5	143.1
Manufacturing	988.0	986.4	−1.6
Durable Goods	566.0	561.1	−4.9
Lumber, Wood Prod	31.5	31.8	0.3
Logging Camps, Sawmills, Planing Mills	7.2	7.7	0.5
Furniture and Fixtures	16.5	15.6	−0.9
Stone, Clay and Glass Products	36.8	34.3	−2.5
Concrete, Gypsum & Plaster Products	16.6	14.7	−1.9
Primary Metals Ind.	28.9	30.0	1.1
Fabricated Metal Industries	79.6	82.2	2.6
Fabricated Struct. Metal Products	39.0	40.3	1.3
Industrial Machinery and Equipment	110.8	115.6	4.8
Oil & Gas Field Machinery	23.7	27.4	3.7
Electronic & Other Electrical Eqpmt.	106.7	102.9	−3.8
Transportation Equipment	100.2	94.1	−6.1
Aircraft & Parts	72.6	68.7	−3.9
Inst. & Related Prods.	38.8	39.0	0.2
Misc. Mfg. Ind.	16.2	15.6	−0.6
Nondurable Goods	422.0	425.3	3.3
Food & Kindred Prod.	100.9	102.8	1.9
Meat Products	30.4	31.6	1.2
Dairy Products	4.6	4.2	−0.4
Bakery Products	10.7	9.8	−0.9
Malt Beverages	2.9	3.0	0.1
Textile Mill Products	4.1	4.2	0.1
Apparel, Other Finished Textile Products	58.9	54.2	−4.7
Paper, Allied Prod.	24.6	24.7	0.1
Printing, Publishing	73.8	74.7	0.9
Newsprs., Periodicals, Books & Misc.	35.8	36.0	0.2
Chemicals & Allied Products	81.6	85.3	3.7
Petroleum & Coal Products	28.9	28.8	0.9
Petroleum Refining	25.7	26.5	0.8
Rubber & Misc. Plastics Prod.	41.4	42.2	0.8
Leather & Leather Products	7.7	7.3	−0.4
Total Nonmanufacturing	5,994.4	6,139.1	144.7

Industry	Dec. 1989 (000)	Dec. 1990 (000)	Change For Year (000)
Mining	177.1	183.8	6.7
Metal & Coal & Nonmet. Mnrls., exc. Fuel	9.7	9.3	−0.4
Oil and Gas Extraction	167.4	174.5	7.1
Construction	323.9	338.4	14.5
Transportation and Public Utilities	417.6	428.6	11.0
Railroad Transportation	19.8	18.6	−1.2
Transportation, Except Railroads	232.6	242.1	9.5
Transportation by Air	71.9	77.2	5.3
Communications	86.8	88.9	2.1
Electric, Gas and Sanitary Services	78.4	79.0	0.6
Electric Services	40.5	40.5	0.0
Gas Production & Distribution	27.7	27.1	−0.6
Wholesale & Retail Trade	1,737.5	1,733.1	−4.4
Wholesale Trade	426.0	423.5	−2.5
Retail Trade	1,311.5	1,309.6	−1.9
Building Materials & Garden Supplies	39.8	40.3	0.5
General Merchandise Stores	199.2	195.0	−4.2
Food Stores	233.6	239.7	6.1
Automotive Dealers & Service Stations	136.1	137.7	1.6
Apparel & Accessory Stores	91.8	83.0	−8.8
Eating & Drinking Places	416.5	424.9	8.4
Other Retail Trade	194.5	189.0	−5.5
Finance, Insurance and Real Estate	435.8	428.6	−7.2
Depository Insts., Incl. Banks	132.7	127.7	−5.0
Ins. Carriers, Agents, and Brokers	141.5	143.5	2.0
Other Finance, Ins. & Real Estate	161.6	157.4	−4.2
Services	1,670.0	1,724.6	54.6
Hotels & Other Lodging Places	85.1	86.2	1.1
Personal Services	76.6	79.2	2.6
Business & Repair Services	435.3	449.5	14.2
Amusement, Incl. Motion Pictures	75.0	75.7	0.7

More on page 608.

Average Hours and Earnings, 1990

The following table shows average weekly hours and earnings for 1990. Figures are provided by the **Texas Employment Commission in cooperation with the U.S. Bureau of Labor Statistics.**

	Average Pay	Average Hours	Average Wage		Average Pay	Average Hours	Average Wage
MANUFACTURING....	$437.65	41.8	$10.47	Leather and Leather Products...........	261.49	39.5	6.62
Durable Goods	433.02	42.0	10.31	NONMANU-FACTURING			
Lumber and Wood Products......	311.96	42.1	7.41	Mining	605.25	44.9	13.48
Furniture and Fixtures............	282.03	39.5	7.14	Oil and Gas Extraction.........	606.58	44.7	13.57
Stone, Clay and Glass Products......	420.11	43.0	9.77	Metal & Bit. Coal and Nonmet. Min. ..	587.66	47.7	12.32
Primary Metal Industries.........	491.89	43.3	11.36	Comm., exc. U.S.P.O....	532.76	40.7	13.09
Fabricated Metal Products...........	405.83	42.9	9.46	Elec., Gas and San. Services	546.04	42.1	12.97
Machinery, except Electrical.........	435.20	42.5	10.24	Whlse. and Retail Trade........	243.29	32.7	7.44
Oilfield Machinery........	549.19	47.1	11.66	Wholesale Trade	425.58	39.7	10.72
Electric and Electronic Equip.....	471.74	41.2	11.45	Wholesale Trade, Durable Goods......	445.20	40.0	11.13
Transportation Equipment.........	548.22	41.5	13.21	Motor Vehicles and Automotive	379.61	38.5	9.86
Instruments and Related Prod........	405.96	40.8	9.95	Lumber and Other Construction........	380.94	42.0	9.07
Miscellaneous Mfg. Industries......	292.92	38.9	7.53	Professional & Commercial	540.80	40.0	13.52
Nondurable Goods.	442.81	41.5	10.67	Electrical Goods	421.34	39.9	10.56
Food and Kindred Products...........	359.96	42.1	8.55	Machinery, Equipment.......	479.40	40.8	11.75
Meat Products	277.38	41.9	6.62	Whlse. Trade — Nondurable	396.14	39.3	10.08
Malt Beverages	872.81	46.9	18.61	Groceries and Related Products.........	385.44	38.2	10.09
Textile Mill Products...........	332.21	42.7	7.78	Petroleum and Petroleum Products	419.24	43.4	9.66
Apparel and Other Textile Products.....	208.50	37.5	5.56	Retail Trade	188.80	30.6	6.17
Paper and Allied Products...........	495.00	44.0	11.25	Bldg. Materials & Garden	278.78	38.4	7.26
Printing and Publishing	419.49	39.8	10.54	Banking	306.23	37.3	8.21
Chemicals and Allied Products......	720.61	43.7	16.49	Nat'l Commercial Banks.............	313.94	38.1	8.24
Petroleum and Coal Products.......	761.17	45.2	16.84	Gen Mdse. Stores......	188.47	30.3	6.22
Petroleum Refining...........	793.66	45.3	17.52	Food Stores	206.70	31.8	6.50
Rubber & Misc. Plastics	382.44	41.3	9.26	Apparel and Accessory Stores...........	185.74	30.4	6.11
				Furniture, Home Furnishings	288.29	31.2	9.24
				Eating & Drinking Places	118.26	27.0	4.38

*Figures cover production workers in manufacturing and mining industries only and non-supervisory employees in other industry divisions. Earnings' averages include premium pay for overtime, holidays and for lateshift work.

Texas Unemployment Compensation Fund

This table summarizes the status of the **Texas Unemployment Compensation Fund** on Aug. 31, 1990, and activities during the fiscal year 1989-90, as reported by the Texas Employment Commission.

Fund Balance Sept. 1, 1989	$959,082,444
Receipts	
Gross Payroll Remittances Allocated....	$1,021,081,906
Less Refunds and Returned Checks ...	−9,854,639
Less Penalties and Interest..........	−10,354,947
Less Surtax	−535,673
Net Payroll Taxes	1,000,336,647
Interest Earned....................	87,785,723
FUTA Tax Credits..................	19,291
Transfers from Advance Interest Fund ..	0
Transfers from Special Adm. Fund	0
Rent to Amortize State Office Buildings ..	107,899
Benefits Reimbursed by Other States....	18,036,445
From Federal Funds (UCFE, UCX, USPS, PSE, TRA and DUA).....................	41,983,901
Federal Share of Extended Benefits.....	0
Federal Supplemental Compensation ...	−71,720
Refunds from Reimbursing Employers ..	28,137,811
Total Receipts..................	$1,176,385,997

Disbursements	
Net Benefits Paid Claimants Under State Law (Includes State Share Extended Benefits)	$726,781,862
Expenditure of Sec. 903 Allotment for Buildings	0
UCFE, USPS, UCX, PSE, TRA and DUA Paid....................	41,909,113
Compensation.....................	−32,716
Federal Supplemental Compensation ...	−32,716
Extended Benefits Paid Federal Share	479
Benefits Paid Reimbursed by Other States.........	20,684,818
Reimbursable Benefits Paid	27,543,628
Total Disbursements...............	$816,887,184
Net Operating Income...............	359,498,813
Sub-Total	000,000,000
FEDERAL ADVANCES	
Title XII Advances	$000,000,000
Less Title XII Repayments	−000,000,000
Net Change in Title XII Advances	−000,000,000
Fund Balance Aug. 31, 1990...........	$1,318,581,257

Agriculture

There's Room for Growth

Information for this article was provided by Agricultural Extension Service specialists, Texas Agricultural Statistics Service, and U.S. Departments of Agriculture and Commerce and was coordinated by Carl G. Anderson, Extension Marketing Economist, Texas A&M University. All references are to Texas unless otherwise specified.

Agriculture is one of the most important industries in Texas. Many businesses, financial institutions, and individuals are involved in providing supplies, credit and services to farmers and ranchers and in processing and marketing agricultural commodities.

Agribusiness, the combined phases of food and fiber production, processing, transporting, and marketing, is a leading Texas industry. Most of the following discussion is devoted to the phase of production on farms and ranches.

Including all its agribusiness phases, agriculture added about $40 billion in 1990 to the economic activity of the state. The **estimated value of farm assets** in Texas — the land, buildings, livestock, machinery, crops, inventory on farms, household goods and farm financial assets — totaled approximately $90 billion at the beginning of 1990.

Texas agriculture is a strong industry. **Receipts from farm and ranch marketings** in 1990 were estimated at $11.5 billion. Ten years earlier this figure stood at $9.1 billion.

The potential for further growth is great. With the increasing demand for food and fiber throughout the world, and because of the importance of agricultural exports to this nation's trade balance, agriculture in Texas is destined to play an even greater role in the future.

Major efforts of research and educational programs by the Texas A&M University System are directed toward developing the state's agricultural industry to its fullest potential. The goal is to capitalize on natural advantages that agriculture has in Texas because of the relatively warm climate, productive soils, and availability of excellent export and transportation facilities.

The number and nature of farms have changed over time. The **number of farms in Texas** has decreased from 418,000 in 1940 to 186,000 in 1990 with an average size of 710 acres. Average value per farm of all farm assets, including land and buildings, has increased from $6,196 in 1940 to $483,870 in 1990.

Balance Sheet, Texas Farms and Ranches Jan. 1, 1981-89

Source: "Economic Indicators of the Farm Sector: State Financial Summary"
Table below shows the financial status of Texas farms and ranches as of Jan. 1 of the years 1981-89.

Item	1981	1982	1983	1984	†1985	1986	1987	1988	§1989
				Million dollars					
Physical Assets:									
Real estate	73,951	74,528	81,122	89,194	80,439	73,101	72,461	68,218	66,792
Nonreal estate:									
Livestock and poultry	4,646	5,121	4,958	4,897	4,729	4,761	6,621	8,439	8,589
Machinery and motor vehicles	6,250	6,256	6,216	6,245	5,461	5,384	5,330	5,412	5,608
*Crops stored on and off farms	1,499	1,805	1,334	378	652	721	786	774	837
Purchased inputs	—	—	—	—	85	136	401	343	252
Household equipment and furnishings	1,430	1,661	1,938	2,601	1,804	1,861	2,133	2,398	2,681
Financial assets:									
Deposits and currency	1,724	1,804	1,924	2,155	—	—	—	—	—
U.S. savings bonds	407	396	414	435	—	—	—	—	—
Investments in co-ops	1,481	1,596	1,712	1,559	1,356	1,538	1,573	1,500	1,609
Other financial	—	—	—	—	2,777	3,286	3,531	3,708	3,689
TOTAL ASSETS	91,388	93,167	99,618	107,463	97,303	90,789	92,835	90,792	90,058
Liabilities:									
**Real estate debt	5,795	6,051	6,357	6,443	6,486	6,071	5,678	5,143	4,833
***Nonreal estate debt:									
****Excluding CCC loans	6,354	6,383	6,536	6,892	6,545	5,878	5,763	5,576	5,406
‡Commodity Credit Corporation loans	428	1,147	799	526	—	—	—	—	—
TOTAL LIABILITIES	12,577	13,581	13,692	13,861	13,031	11,949	11,441	10,718	10,238
Owners' equities	78,811	79,586	85,926	94,428	84,271	78,840	81,394	80,073	79,820
TOTAL CLAIMS	91,388	93,167	99,618	108,288	97,303	90,789	92,835	90,792	90,059

*All crops held on farms including value above loan rates for crops held under CCC.
**Includes CCC storage and drying facilities loans.
***Includes debt owed to institutional lender and to noninstitutional or miscellaneous lenders.
****Nonrecourse CCC loans secured by crops owned by farmers. These crops are included as assets in this balance sheet.
†As of 1985, Purchased Inputs figure added; Commodity Credit Corporation Loans figure excluded.
§Preliminary.
Source: "Economic indicators of the Farm Sector: State Financial Summary 1985, USDA, ERS, January 1987, p.229.; 1988, 1989 (including operator households).

Mechanization of farming continues as new and larger machines replace manpower. Even though machinery price tags are high relative to times past, machine power is much cheaper than manpower. Tractors, mechanical harvesters and numerous cropping machines have virtually eliminated menial tasks that for many years were traditional to farming.

Revolutionary agricultural chemicals have appeared, along with improved plants and animals and methods of handling them. Hazards of farming and ranching were reduced by better use of weather information, machinery and other improvements; but rising costs, labor problems, and escalating energy costs have added to concerns of farmers and ranchers.

Among the major changes in Texas agriculture since World War II are these:

• Farms have become fewer, larger, specialized and much more expensive to own and operate, but far more productive.

• Irrigation has become an important factor in crop production.

• Crops and livestock have made major changes in production areas, as in the concentration of cotton on the High Plains and livestock increases in Central and Eastern Texas.

• Pest and disease control methods have greatly improved. Herbicides are relied upon for weed control.

• Ranchers and farmers are better educated and informed, more science- and business-oriented.

• Feedlot finishing, commercial broiler production, artificial insemination, improved pastures and brush control, reduced feed requirements and other changes have greatly increased livestock and poultry efficiency. Biotechnology and genetic engineering promise new breakthroughs in reaching even higher levels of productivity.

• Cooperation among farmers in marketing, promotion and other fields has increased.

• Agricultural producers have become increasingly dependent on off-the-farm services to supply production inputs such as feeds, chemicals, credit and other essentials.

Agribusiness

Texas farmers and ranchers have developed considerable dependence upon agribusiness. With many producers specializing in the production of certain crops and livestock, they look beyond the farm and ranch for supplies and services. On the input side, they rely on suppliers of production needs and services and, on the output side, they need assemblers, processors and distributors.

Since 1940, the **proportion of Texans whose livelihood is linked to agriculture** has changed greatly. In 1940, about 23 percent were producers on farms and ranches, and about 17 percent were suppliers or were engaged in assembly, processing and distribution of agricultural products. The agribusiness alignment in 1990 was less than 2 percent on farms and ranches with about 20 percent of the labor force providing production or marketing supplies and services and retailing food and fiber products. The **impact of production agriculture on the economy of Texas** is about $40 billion annually.

Cash Receipts

Farm and ranch cash receipts in 1989 totaled $10.760 billion. With estimates of $1.249 billion for **government payments,** $472.1 million of noncash income, and $969.5 million of other farm income are included, realized **gross farm income** totaled $12.905 billion. With farm production expenses of $9.898 billion and a $546.1 million decrease in farm inventories from the year before, net income totaled $3.001 billion or $16,134 per farm.

Farm and Ranch Assets

Farm and ranch assets totaled $90.1 billion on Jan. 1, 1990. This was essentially the same as a year earlier. **Value of real estate** declined 2.1 percent to $66.8 billion. **Liabilities** totaled $10.2 billion, a 4.5 percent decline from the previous year.

Percent of Income From Products

Livestock and livestock products accounted for 63.8 percent of the cash receipts from farm marketings in 1989 with the remaining 36.2 percent from **crops.** This is a somewhat larger proportion of receipts from livestock than in the past because of reduced acreage associated with farm programs. However, these relationships change because of variations in commodity prices and volume of marketings.

From livestock marketings, **meat animals** accounted for 48.52 percent of total receipts received by farmers and ranchers in 1989. Most of these receipts were from cattle and calf sales. **Dairy products** made up 6.87 percent of receipts, **poultry and eggs** 7.2 percent, and **miscellaneous livestock** 1.19 percent.

From crop receipts, **cotton** accounted for 13.85 percent of total receipts; **feed crops,** 7.68 percent; **food grains,** 3.32 percent; **vegetables,** 3.25 percent; **greenhouse/nursery products,** 4.43 percent; **oil crops,** 1.86 percent; **fruits and nuts,** .63 percent; and **other crops,** .86 percent.

Texas' Rank Among States

Measured by **cash receipts for farm and ranch marketings, Texas ranked second in 1989.** California ranked first and Iowa third.

Texas normally leads all other states in numbers of farms and ranches and farm and ranch land, cattle slaughtered, cattle on feed, calf births, sheep and lambs slaughtered, goats, cash receipts from livestock marketings, cattle and calves, beef cows, sheep and lambs, wool production, mohair production, and exports of lard and tallow. The state also usually leads in production of cotton, watermelons and spinach.

Texas' Agricultural Exports

The value of Texas' share of **agricultural exports** in fiscal year 1990 was $2.5254 billion. Cotton accounted for $668.9 million of the exports; feed grains, $408.9 million; wheat and flour, $163.4 million; rice, $120.3 million; tallow and lard, $76.0 million; cottonseed oil, $24.0 million; hides and skins, $289.5 million; meats and meat products, $366.1 million; fruits, $28.8 million; peanuts, $29.3 million; soybeans, $34.1 million; vegetables, $29.0 million; poultry products, $44.0 million; dairy products, $8.8 million; and miscellaneous and other products, $228.0 million.

Texas' 1990 exports of $2.5254 billion of farm and ranch products compares with $2.6367 billion in 1989; $2.2475 billion in 1988; and $1.5295 billion in 1987.

Hunting

The management of wildlife as an economic enterprise through **leasing for hunting** makes a significant contribution to the economy of many counties. Leasing the right of ingress on a farm or ranch for the purpose of hunting is the service marketed. After the leasing, the consumer — the hunter — goes onto the land to seek the harvest of the wildlife commodity. Hunting lease income to farmers and ranchers in 1990 was estimated at $164 million.

The demand for hunting opportunities is growing while the land capable of producing huntable wildlife is decreasing. As a result, farmers and ranchers are placing more emphasis on wildlife management practices to help meet requests for hunting leases.

Irrigation

Texas farmers irrigated approximately 6 million acres of land in 1990. Although some irrigation is practiced in nearly every county of the state, about 68 percent of the total irrigated acreage is on the Southern High Plains of Texas. Other concentrated areas of irrigation are the Gulf Coast rice-producing area, the Lower Rio Grande Valley, the Winter Garden district of South Texas, the Trans-Pecos area of West Texas and the peanut-producing area in North Central Texas centered around Erath, Eastland and Comanche counties. **Sprinkler irrigation** was used on about 45 percent of the total irrigated acreage, with surface irrigation methods — primarily furrow, border and contour-check methods — being used on the remaining 55 percent.

Drip, or trickle, irrigation has attracted much attention in recent years for use on tree crops such as citrus, pecans, avocados, peaches and apples. The use of drip irrigation is increasing, with present acreage estimated to be 35,000 acres.

The use of sprinkler irrigation is also in an upward trend, increasing from about 14 percent of the total irrigated acreage in 1964, to 19 percent in 1969, 32 percent in 1984, and 45 percent in 1990.

Approximately 70 percent of the state's irrigated acreage is supplied with water pumped from wells. Surface water sources supply the remaining area. **Declining groundwater levels in several of the major aquifers** is a serious problem. As the water level declines, well yields decrease and pumping costs increase. Decreasing groundwater supplies and higher fuel prices have contributed to the decrease in irrigated acreage. Further decreases can be expected unless additional sources of water are developed, irrigation efficiencies are significantly improved, and/or crops and cultural techniques are developed to reduce water requirements and irrigation costs. However, recent studies of the availability of water in the Ogallala formation, which supplies water for most of the High Plains irrigation, indicate that a viable irrigated agriculture can be expected to continue in the High Plains area much longer than most predictions in the past have indicated.

Rapidly rising fuel costs pose another serious problem for Texas irrigation farmers. More than half of the irrigation pumps in the state are driven with power units that use natural gas as a fuel. Natural gas prices paid by farmers have increased dramatically in recent years. The cost of other fuels used for pumping irrigation water, primarily electricity and diesel, has also increased significantly. Since fuel costs are a major part of the cost of irrigation water, farmers are facing keen management decisions in the use of irrigation for crop production.

Irrigation is an important factor in the productivity of Texas agriculture. The **value of crop production from irrigated acreage** is 50 to 60 percent of the total value of all crop production, although only about 30 percent of the state's total harvested cropland acreage is irrigated.

The **percentage of total crop production that comes from irrigated lands** varies from year to year, depending primarily upon the amount of rainfall received. In good rainfall years, the proportion of irrigated crop production to total crop production is somewhat less. However, in years of below-average rainfall, the percentage of the total crop production that comes from irrigated lands increases. Thus, irrigation provides a stabilizing influence upon Texas agriculture, enabling Texas farmers to produce a more dependable supply of food and fiber products without total dependence upon natural rainfall.

*Realized Gross Income and Net Income From Farming, Texas, 1958-1989

Year	**Realized Gross Farm Income	Farm Production Expenses	Net Change in Farm Inventories	***Total Net Farm Income	***Total Net Income Per Farm
	Million Dollars				Dollars
1958	$2,666.1	$1,637.5	$17.7	$1,046.3	$3,948.0
1974	6,178.0	5,057.0	—80.3	1,040.7	4,980.0
1975	6,497.4	5,180.3	—106.2	1,210.9	6,407.0
1976	7,029.8	5,926.0	124.8	1,103.8	5,902.7
§1977	7,343.3	6,257.5	—38.4	1,085.8	5,837.6
1978	8,716.4	7,510.7	149.3	1,205.7	6,517.3
1979	11,057.5	9,245.7	—95.6	1,811.7	9,688.2
1980	9,611.4	9,081.1	—542.5	530.4	2,806.3
1981	11,545.7	9,564.7	699.9	1,981.0	10,481.5
1982	11,372.7	9,581.5	—124.3	1,791.2	9,527.7
1983	11,129.2	9,387.9	—590.7	1,741.4	9,312.3
1984	12,058.8	9,762.8	168.8	2,296.0	12,278.1
1985	11,272.7	9,226.3	—9.0	2,046.4	10,658.3
1986	10,282.0	8,722.0	—384.3	1,559.9	8,210.0
1987	12,255.4	9,259.2	—466.7	2,996.2	15,937.2
1988	12,574.7	9,380.9	—9.4	3,193.8	17,079.1
1989	12,904.6	9,897.8	—546.1	3,006.8	16,165.6

*Details for items may not add to totals because of rounding. Series revised, September, 1981.

**Cash receipts from farm marketings, government payments, value of home consumption and gross rental value of farm dwellings.

***Farm income of farm operators.

§Starting in 1977, farms with production of $1,000 or more used to figure income.

Source: "Economic Indicators of the Farm Sector, State Financial Summary, 1985" USDA, ERS, January 1987. pp. 95-97.

"Economic Indicators of the Farm Sector, State Financial Summary, 1987," USDA, ERS, January 1989.

"Economic Indicators of the Farm Sector, State Financial Summary, 1989," USDA, ERS, February 1991, page 54.

Texas' Export Shares of Agricultural Commodities, 1986-90

Commodity*	1986	1987	1988	1989	1990	1990 Texas Share of U.S. Exports %
	Million Dollars					
Rice.	101.7	88.0	104.7	155.5	120.3	18.8
Cotton	203.2	378.5	679.1	705.8	668.9	26.0
Tallow & Lard. .	77.2	67.0	90.6	85.9	76.0	18.7
Hides & Skins . .	212.4	239.0	285.3	268.2	289.5	14.9
Meats other than Poultry .	169.0	206.4	286.5	362.6	366.1	12.9
Feed Grains . . .	185.8	181.3	254.6	415.5	408.9	4.6
Poultry Products. . . .	21.0	30.5	31.5	35.5	44.0	4.0
Fruits	8.7	18.5	31.6	34.7	28.8	1.6
Vegetables. . . .	12.0	14.7	14.9	20.8	29.0	1.0
Wheat & Flour .	236.7	157.0	264.3	284.9	163.4	6.4
Soybeans	19.3	13.0	15.1	23.7	34.1	0.4
Cottonseed Oil	35.1	15.5	38.0	37.6	24.0	48.2
Peanuts	24.0	22.9	19.1	22.3	29.3	9.5
Nuts.	1.5	0.9	1.2	2.2	6.3	0.3
†Dairy Products	8.7	10.7	12.5	11.8	8.8	3.4
All Other	83.1	85.6	118.5	169.7	228.0	2.7
TOTAL.	1,399.4	1,529.5	2,247.5	2,636.7	2,525.4	6.6

*Commodity and related preparations.

†For 1981 and 1982 the USDA changed the variable used to determine export share of dairy products to state fluid milk production.

Source: FATUS, Foreign Agricultural Trade of the United States, various issues, March/April, May/June, January/February, 1980-1991.

Cash Receipts From Farm Marketings 1936-1987

Source: Texas Crop & Livestock Reporting Service

Year	Crop	Livestock and Livestock Production	Total Crops and Livestock	*Government Payments	Total Crops, Livestock and Payments
	1,000 dollars				
1936 . .	$298,361	$186,829	$485,190	$27,121	$512,311
1969 . .	1,202,150	1,851,386	3,053,536	505,248	3,558,784
1970 . .	1,264,766	1,956,991	3,221,757	543,156	3,764,913
1971 . .	1,177,911	2,284,873	3,462,784	468,552	3,931,336
1972 . .	1,463,122	2,614,518	4,077,641	528,567	4,606,208
1973 . .	2,811,135	3,686,236	6,497,371	386,554	6,883,925
1974 . .	2,695,007	2,971,115	5,666,122	80,552	5,746,674
1975 . .	2,759,514	3,076,782	5,836,296	146,562	5,982,858
1976 . .	3,091,434	3,201,974	6,293,408	111,735	6,405,143
1977 . .	3,147,190	3,523,073	6,670,263	157,993	6,828,256
1978 . .	3,015,882	4,628,470	7,644,352	318,843	7,963,195
1979 . .	3,991,103	6,059,942	10,051,045	307,099	10,358,144
1980 . .	3,925,092	5,185,067	9,110,159	231,840	9,341,999
1981 . .	4,371,497	5,448,215	9,819,712	321,365	10,141,077
1982 . .	4,206,582	5,421,060	9,627,642	643,598	10,271,240
1983 . .	3,645,911	5,521,428	9,176,339	1,129,855†	10,306,194
1984 . .	3,754,843	5,900,842	9,655,685	782,441	10,438,126
1985 . .	3,814,575	5,447,863	9,262,438	848,079	10,110,517
1986 . .	3,100,048	5,512,607	8,612,655	978,393	9,591,048
1987 . .	3,034,922	6,089,748	9,124,670	1,441,175	10,565,845
1988 . .	3,689,300	6,562,030	10,251,330	1,155,332	11,406,662
1989 . .	3,897,000	6,863,400	10,760,400	1,248,713	12,009,113

*Includes Payment-in-kind (PiK) of $661 million.

Source: "1985 Texas Agricultural Cash Receipts, Prices Received and Paid by Farmers", Texas Agricultural Statistical Service, USDA, Bulletin 239, August 1986, page 3.

"Economic Indicators of the Farm Sector, State Financial Summary, 1989", USDA, ERS, February 1991, page 54.

Principal Crops

In most recent years, the **value of crop production** in Texas has been less than half of the total value of the state's agricultural output. Cash receipts from farm sales of crops are reduced somewhat because some grain and roughage is fed to livestock on farms where produced and also because of the farm program for crops.

Receipts from all Texas crops totaled $3.9 billion in 1989; $3.7 billion in 1988; and $3 billion in 1987.

Cotton and wheat account for a large part of the total crop receipts. In 1989, cotton contributed about 38.2 percent of the crop total, sorghum grain 8.8 percent, corn 9 percent, and wheat 6.1 percent. Hay, vegetables, rice, cottonseed, peanuts and soybeans are other important cash crops.

Cotton

Cotton has been a major crop in Texas for more than a century. Since 1880, Texas has led all states in cotton production in most years, and today the annual Texas cotton harvest amounts to approximately a third of total production in the United States. The **annual cotton crop** has averaged 3.85 million bales since 1980.

Total value of **upland and pima lint cotton** produced in Texas in 1990 was $1.56 billion. **Cottonseed** value in 1990 was $239,686,000, making the total value of the Texas crop $1.80 billion. In 1989, the cottonseed value was $141,491,000 and total crop was $0.95 billion.

Upland cotton was harvested from 5 million acres in 1990 and American-Pima from 58,000 acres, for a total of 5.06 million acres. Cotton acreage harvested in 1989 totaled 3.83 million. Production amounted to 5.09 million bales in 1990 and 3 million in 1989. Counties leading in production of upland cotton include **Gaines, Lubbock, Lynn, Hockley, Terry and Crosby.**

Cotton is the raw material for processing operations at **gins, oil mills, compresses and a small number of textile mills** in Texas.

Cotton in Texas is machine harvested. Growers in 1988 used **stripper harvesters** to gather 77 percent of the crop and **spindle pickers** to harvest the remaining 23 percent. Field storage of harvested seed cotton is gaining in popularity as gins decline in number. In 1988, 76 percent of the cotton was ginned from modules and 24 percent from trailers. Much of the Texas cotton crop is exported; Japan and South Korea are major buyers. With the development of open-end spinning, more utilization of cotton by mills within the state may develop in the future. Unlike the conventional ring-spinning method, open-end spinning techniques can efficiently produce high-quality yarn from relatively strong, short-staple cotton with fine mature fiber.

The state's major cotton-producing areas are tied together by an **electronic marketing system.** This system is a computer network that links producers through terminals that are usually located at gins to a relatively large number of buyers. The network provides farmers with a centralized market that allows many sellers and buyers to trade with each other on a regular basis.

The **first high-volume instrument cotton-classing office** in the nation was opened at Lamesa, Tex., in 1980.

Grain Sorghum

Grain sorghum usually ranks second in dollar value. Much of the grain is exported as well as being used in livestock and poultry feed throughout the state.

In 1990, 2.60 million acres of grain sorghum were harvested, yielding an average of 2,912 pounds per acre for a total production of 75,712,000 hundredweight. It was valued at $4.14 per hundredweight (cwt.), a total value of $313,664,000. In 1989, 3.10 million acres were harvested, with an average of 2,968 pounds per acre, or 92,008,000 cwt. The season's price was $3.89 cwt. for a total value of $358,174,000. The 1988 crop was valued at $345,398,000. In 1987, 2.65 million acres were harvested, yielding 3,528 pounds per acre. The crop was valued at $278,807,000.

Although also grown to some extent in all counties where crops are important, the largest concentrations are in the High Plains, Rolling Plains, Blackland Prairie, Grand Prairie, Coastal Prairie, Coastal Bend, Rio Grande Plain, and Lower Rio Grande Valley areas. Counties leading in production are **Nueces, Hidalgo, Wharton, Hansford, Moore and Deaf Smith.**

Research to develop high-yielding hybrids resistant to diseases and insect damage continues. A leader in this development, J. Roy Quinby, is principle author of **More on page 537.**

Cash Receipts By Commodities 1987-89

Commodity	Value		
	1987	1988	1989
	— 1,000 dollars —		
All Commodities	$9,124,670	$10,251,368	$10,760,414
Livestock and products	6,089,748	6,562,030	6,863,404
Crops, Fruits and others	3,034,922	3,689,338	3,897,010
Livestock and products			
Cattle and calves	4,616,602	4,969,762	5,049,760
Milk, wholesale	574,304	634,260	724,009
Broilers	337,218	391,461	482,744
Eggs	191,744	181,882	223,295
Hogs	102,331	99,144	94,258
Sheep and lambs	93,207	67,784	77,232
Wool	19,844	35,854	27,180
Mohair	42,606	28,876	24,794
Milk, retail	8,223	4,884	15,321
*Other	103,669	148,123	144,811
Crops			
Cotton lint	846,189	1,150,971	1,347,847
Corn	204,249	348,669	349,276
Sorghum, grain	280,147	341,033	342,456
Wheat	224,808	287,033	237,698
Hay	130,429	128,711	162,927
Cottonseed	129,422	199,336	142,663
Peanuts	119,070	111,890	136,123
Rice	100,362	145,681	123,097
Soybeans	24,745	38,221	57,640
Onions	77,885	48,455	53,540
Sugar beets	14,904	27,185	27,937
Sugar cane	32,659	26,765	26,765
Potatoes	24,848	27,968	25,682
Carrots	18,520	17,269	19,476
Cucumbers	22,933	14,413	17,988
Broccoli	12,524	10,590	14,706
Sweet potatoes	13,247	9,186	12,124
Honeydew melons	19,706	20,640	10,547

Commodity	Value		
	1987	1988	1989
	— 1,000 dollars —		
Seed, sorghum-sudan crosses	6,000	8,000	8,000
Lettuce	5,655	8,752	7,582
Oats	9,579	10,005	6,459
Sunflowers	1,979	2,232	5,959
Tomatoes	6,682	6,739	4,763
Corn, sweet	2,400	2,100	1,738
Cauliflower	792	1,980	1,482
Barley	2,027	1,201	1,099
Cantaloupes	23,205	NA	NA
Cabbage	36,630	NA	NA
Watermelons	43,010	NA	NA
Peppers	33,759	NA	NA
Spinach	11,932	NA	NA
Rye	197	293	NA
†Other crops	54,890	193,905	207,131
Fruits and nuts			
Pecans	24,780	31,500	33,500
Grapefruit	19,333	21,456	19,115
Oranges	9,601	11,411	9,687
Peaches	1,824	5,748	5,000
Other Farm Income			
Greenhouse and nursery	444,000	430,000	477,003

Commodities are listed in order of importance for 1989 by crop items and by livestock items.

*Includes milkfat, turkey eggs, turkeys, honey bees, equine, goats, goat milk and other poultry and livestock.

†Miscellaneous vegetables, field crops, fruits and nuts.

Includes only sales from farms but excluded in cash receipts for all farm commodities.

NA = Not available.

Source: "Economic Indicators of the Farm Sector, State Financial Summary, 1989," USDA, ERS, February 1991, pp. 118-119.

Cotton Gins By Counties

Source: Texas Cotton Ginners' Assn. and U.S. Department of Commerce

Counties	Active Gins Operating During 1989-1990 Crop Year	Running Bales Ginned 1989	1988	1987
Bailey	8	34,164	186,978	86,626
Baylor	2	*	*	*
Bell	1	*	*	*
Borden	1	*	*	*
Brazoria	3	10,528	15,781	6,923
Brazos	5	31,450	35,594	28,654
Briscoe	4	19,658	45,710	28,919
Burleson	2	*	*	*
Caldwell	1	*	*	*
Cameron	12	60,890	149,740	118,003
Castro	9	29,045	35,748	33,690
Childress	3	14,536	9,343	29,341
Clay	1	*	*	*
Cochran	5	18,446	93,703	82,494
Coleman	1	*	*	*
Collin	3	7,147	12,336	6,322
Collingsworth	2	22,625	30,601	40,984
Concho	2	*	*	*
Cottle	4	11,834	8,064	17,424
Crosby	9	115,962	155,570	155,183
Culberson	1	*	*	*
Dawson	17	85,588	204,242	112,469
Deaf Smith	1	*	*	*
Delta	2	*	*	*
Denton	1	*	*	*
Dickens	3	5,663	8,349	14,464
Donley	3	5,485	17,036	19,853
Ellis	6	21,898	24,914	14,664
El Paso	7	94,872	83,290	76,392
Falls	3	8,991	12,002	6,710
Fisher	5	21,366	28,636	55,295
Floyd	13	60,207	170,307	108,251
Foard	2	*	*	8,247
Fort Bend	10	40,507	52,392	23,515
Frio	1	*	*	*
Gaines	17	255,151	318,792	235,588
Garza	3	8,690	20,678	22,719
Glasscock	2	*	*	*
Hale	17	63,521	228,088	213,394
Hall	6	31,072	50,137	64,206
Hardeman	2	*	*	*
Haskell	9	47,643	53,130	70,013
Hidalgo	15	74,569	157,872	145,889
Hill	6	16,237	15,779	11,212
Hockley	15	128,439	258,486	213,478
Houston	2	*	*	*
Howard	7	25,940	114,058	102,937
Hudspeth	2	*	*	*
Hunt	3	3,884	7,245	4,261
Jones	12	29,734	40,728	77,913
Kaufman	2	*	*	*
Kent	1	*	*	*
King	1	*	*	*
Kleberg	1	*	*	*
Knox	4	26,329	25,612	23,911
Lamar	2	*	*	*
Lamb	15	121,162	204,744	201,089
Lubbock	19	168,730	266,357	222,376
Lynn	16	144,779	285,232	210,491
McCulloch	1	*	*	*
McLennan	1	*	*	*
Martin	10	40,907	158,720	122,838
Matagorda	1	*	*	*
Medina	2	*	*	*
Midland	1	*	*	*
Milam	3	13,942	15,680	11,566
Mitchell	5	21,108	32,569	49,822
Motley	4	12,324	15,657	17,251
Navarro	4	17,295	18,884	11,588
Nolan	2	*	*	*
Nueces	12	62,288	114,387	106,672
Parmer	8	34,877	45,449	52,363
Pecos	2	*	*	*
Reagan	2	*	*	*
Reeves	3	21,188	20,286	17,890
Refugio	1	*	*	*
Robertson	4	46,775	48,460	33,031
Runnels	7	27,318	28,317	46,658
San Patricio	10	55,813	123,650	104,678
Schleicher	1	*	*	*
Scurry	7	24,113	44,794	69,784
Starr	1	*	*	*
Stonewall	1	*	*	*
Swisher	7	9,423	42,030	48,151
Taylor	2	*	*	*
Terry	12	110,354	229,843	182,180
Throckmorton	2	*	*	*
Tom Green	8	50,453	48,607	54,187
Travis	1	*	*	*
Upton	1	*	*	*
Uvalde	1	*	*	*
Walker	1	*	*	*
Wharton	6	55,867	65,859	32,194
Wheeler	3	1,590	6,325	6,432
Wichita	1	*	*	*
Wilbarger	5	27,071	19,287	49,362
Willacy	6	25,552	150,247	125,625
Williamson	12	56,291	66,917	51,637
Yoakum	7	65,074	132,669	104,479
Young	2	*	*	*
Zavala	3	27,840	33,786	28,071
All Others	—	271,654	335,242	336,518
Total	507	2,945,859	5,124,948	4,556,877

*—None Reported.
Source: "Texas Cotton Ginner's Association" 1990. U.S. Department of Ariculture.

Value of Texas Cotton and Cottonseed

The following table was compiled by Texas Cottonseed Crushers from their historical records and reports of the U.S. Department of Commerce and Department of Agriculture.

(All Figures in Thousands)

Crop Year	Cotton Production (Bales)	Cotton Value	Cottonseed Production Tons	Cottonseed Value	Crop Year	Cotton Production (Bales)	Cotton Value	Cottonseed Production Tons	Cottonseed Value
1970	3,191	$314,913	1,242	$68,310	1981	5,645	1,259,964	2,438	207,230
*1971	2,579	328,915	1,050	59,325	1982	2,700	664,848	1,122	90,882
1972	4,246	468,758	1,643	79,850	1983	2,380	677,443	1,002	162,324
1973	4,673	1,031,798	1,788	167,178	1984	3,680	927,360	1,563	157,863
1974	2,462	412,434	981	116,739	1985	3,910	968,429	1,634	102,156
1975	2,382	523,659	909	81,628	1986	2,535	560,945	1,053	82,118
1976	3,307	977,814	1,271	124,558	1987	4,635	1,325,981	1,915	157,971
1977	5,465	1,303,730	2,089	133,696	1988	5,215	1,291,651	2,131	238,672
1978	3,792	977,426	1,483	166,096	1989	2,870	812,784	1,189	141,491
1979	5,515	1,474,490	2,264	262,624	1990	5,085	1,565,256	2,049	239,686
1980	3,320	1,091,616	1,361	161,959					

*Beginning in 1971, basis for cotton prices was changed from 500 pound gross weight to 480 pound net weight bale; to compute comparable prices for previous years multiply price times 1.04167.

"Principal Crops" Cont. from Page 535.
a history of grain sorghums that appeared in the 1972-73 edition of the Texas Almanac.

Rice

Rice, which is grown in 20 counties on the Coastal Prairie of Texas, ranked third in value among Texas crops for a number of years. However, in recent years, cotton, grain sorghum, wheat and corn have outranked rice.

Farms are highly mechanized, producing rice through irrigation and using airplanes for much of the planting, fertilizing and application of insecticides and herbicides.

Texas farmers grow **long- and medium-grain rice** only. The Texas rice industry, which has grown from 110 acres in 1850 to a high of 642,000 acres in 1954, has been marked by significant yield increases and improved varieties. Record production was in 1981, with 27,239,000 hundredweights harvested. Highest yield was 6,250 pounds per acre in 1986.

Several different types of **rice-milling procedures** are in use today. The simplest and oldest method produces a product known as regular milled white rice, the most prevalent on the market today.

During this process, rice grains are subjected to additional cleaning to remove chaff, dust, foreign seeds and other debris, and then the husks are removed from the grains. This results in a product that is the whole, unpolished grain of rice with only the outer hull and a small amount of bran removed. This product is called brown rice and is sometimes sold without further treatment other than grading. It has a delightful nutlike flavor and a slightly chewy texture.

When additional layers of the bran are removed, the rice becomes white in color and begins to appear as it is normally recognized at retail level. The removal of the bran layer from the grain is performed in a number of steps using two or three types of machines. After the bran is removed, the product is ready for classification as to size. Rice is more valuable if the grains are not broken. In many cases, additional vitamins are added to the grains to produce what is called "enriched rice."

Another process may be used in rice milling to produce a product called parboiled rice. In this process, the rice is subjected to a combination of steam and pressure prior to the time it is milled in the manner described above. This process gelatinizes the starch in the grain, the treatment aiding in the retention of much of the natural vitamin and mineral content. After cooking, parboiled rice tends to be fluffy, more separate and plump.

Still another type of rice is precooked rice, which is actually milled rice that, after milling, has been cooked. Then the moisture is removed through a dehydration process. Precooked rice requires a minimum of preparation time since it needs merely to have the moisture restored to it.

The United States produces only a small part of the world's total rice, but it is one of the leading exporters. American rice is popular abroad and is exported to more than 100 foreign countries.

Rice production was 21,180,000 cwt. in 1990 on 353,000 harvested acres. In 1989, the crop totaled 19,266,000 cwt. on 338,000 acres, valued at $154,513,000 or an average of $8.02 per cwt. The value of production in 1988 was $168,547,000, $7.24 per cwt., on total production of 23,280,000 cwt. from 388,000 harvested acres.

Wheat

Wheat for grain is one of the state's most valuable cash crops, usually exceeded in value only by cotton and sometimes by grain sorghum. Wheat pastures also provide considerable winter forage for cattle, which is reflected in value of livestock produced.

Texas wheat growers planted 6.7 million acres in 1990 and harvested grain from 4.2 million acres. The yield was 31 bushels per acre for a total production of 130.2 million bushels valued at $358,050,000. In 1989, farmers planted 6.7 million acres of wheat and harvested 3 million acres with a yield of 20 bushels per acre, or 60 million bushels produced, valued at $227,400,000. Comparable figures for 1988 were 6.3 million acres planted, 3.2 million acres harvested, 28 bushels per acre, for a total yield of 89.6 million bushels valued at $303,744,000.

Leading wheat-producing counties, based on acreage planted, are **Ochiltree, Wilbarger, Swisher, Hansford, Deaf Smith, Dallam, Randall and Castro.** The leading counties, based on total bushels harvested, are **Dallam, Wilbarger, Collin, Fannin and Throckmorton.**

Wheat was first grown commercially in Texas near Sherman about 1833. The acreage expanded greatly in North Central Texas after 1850 because of rapid settlement of the state and introduction of the well-adapted Mediterranean strain of wheat. A major family flour industry developed in the Fort Worth/Dallas/Sherman area between 1875 and 1900. Now, around half of the state acreage is planted on the High Plains and about a third of this is irrigated. Most of the Texas wheat acreage is of the hard red winter class. Because of the recent development of varieties with improved disease resistance and the use of wheat for winter pasture, there has been a sizable expansion of acreage in Central and South Texas.

Most all wheat harvested for grain is used in some phase of the milling industry. The better-quality **hard red winter wheat** is used in the production of commercial bakery flour. Lower grades and varieties of **soft red winter wheat** are used in family flours. By-products of milled wheat are used for feed.

Texas Fruit-Vegetable Shipments

(Amounts are shown in units of 1,000 hundredweight for rail (RL), truck (TR) and export (Expt.).)

	1988		1989		1990	
Commodity	RL	TR	RL	TR	RL	TR
Avocados	0	1	0	0	0	0
Beans	0	3	0	0	0	1
Beets	0	102	0	87	0	48
Broccoli	0	258	5	226	1	98
Cabbage.	0	3,918	0	3,366	0	2,273
Cantaloupes . . .	0	2,627	0	2,583	0	1,230
Carrots	10	602	10	536	8	221
Cauliflower. . . .	0	35	0	25	0	2
Celery	0	869	0	922	0	257
Cucumbers. . . .	0	714	0	514	0	365
Eggplant	0	5	0	4	0	0
Grapefruit	5	2,554	2	2,673	0	14
Grapefruit, Expt.	0	94	2	162	0	14
Greens	0	312	0	224	0	140
Honeydews. . . .	16	1,170	15	828	0	477
Lettuce, Iceberg	0	442	0	233	0	74
Misc. Herbs . . .	0	0	0	0	0	4
Mixed Citrus. . .	2	0	0	0	0	0
Mixed Misc. Melons	0	36	0	1	0	0
Okra.	0	43	0	36	0	24
Onions, dry	*102	3,894	‡126	3,915	**29	2,834
Onions, green . .	0	28	0	18	0	8
Oranges	7	1,027	4	1,156	0	3

	1988		1989		1990	
Commodity	RL	TR	RL	TR	RL	TR
Parsley.	0	58	0	53	0	33
Peaches	0	7	0	0	0	4
Peas, other than green.	0	2	0	3	0	2
Peppers, bell. . .	0	562	0	598	1	618
Peppers, other	0	24	0	20	0	24
Potatoes, table	56	1,945	40	2,375	2	1,996
Potatoes, chipper	1	532	0	525	0	652
Spinach	0	298	0	298	0	220
Squash	0	43	0	41	0	12
Tomatoes	0	189	0	81	0	42
Tomatoes, cherry	0	2	0	4	0	1
Turnips- Rutabagas . . .	0	11	0	10	0	4
Watermelons . .	†9	3,211	§1	2,688	††6	3,715
TOTALS	*†208	25,618	‡§203	24,205	**††44	15,410

NOTE: Export data are not complete and should not be interpreted as representing total exports.
*Includes 59 piggyback loads of dry onions.
†Includes 9 piggyback loads of watermelons.
‡Includes 53 piggyback loads of dry onions.
§Includes 1 piggyback load of watermelons.
**Includes 3 piggyback loads of dry onions.
††Includes 3 piggyback loads of watermelons.

Corn

Interest in corn production throughout the state increased during the 1970s. Once the principal grain crop, corn acreage declined as plantings of grain sorghum increased. Only 500,000 acres were harvested annually until the mid-1970s when development of new hybrids occurred.

Harvested acreage was 1,250,000 in 1987; 1,350,000 in 1988; 1,400,000 in 1989; and 1,450,000 in 1990. Yields for the corresponding years (1987-1990) were 107, 96, 106 and 90 bushels per acre, respectively.

Most of the acreage and yield increases have occurred in the irrigated High Plains. In recent years, corn has ranked fourth in value among the state's crops. It was valued at $332,775,000 in 1990 and $390,292,000 in 1989. Earlier values were $351,216,000 in 1988 and $290,238,000 in 1987. The grain is largely used for livestock feed, but other important uses are in food products.

The leading counties in production for 1989 were **Parmer, Castro, Hale, Dallam, Moore and Lamb.**

Rye

Rye is grown mainly on the Northern and Southern High Plains, the Northern Low Plains, Cross Timbers, Blacklands, and East Texas areas. Minor acreages are seeded in South Central Texas, the Edwards Plateau, and the Upper Coast. Rye is grown primarily as a cover crop and for grazing during the fall, winter, and early spring.

In 1990, 100,000 acres were planted to rye with 10,000 acres harvested, averaging 14 bushels per acre. The crop value was estimated at $308,000, or $2.20 per bushel. Comparable figures for 1989 were 90,000 acres planted and 126,000 bushels harvested from 7,000 acres, averaging 18 bushels per acre for a total value of $258,000, or $2.05 per bushel.

In 1988, 150,000 acres were planted and 150,000 bushels were harvested from 10,000 acres, averaging 15 bushels per acre. The harvest was valued at $405,000, or $2.70 per bushel.

Some of the leading rye-producing counties based on 1989 acreages were **Eastland, Houston, Henderson, Comanche, Hall and Navarro.**

Oats

Oats are grown extensively in Texas for winter pasture, hay, silage and greenchop feeding, and some acreage is harvested for grain.

Texas farmers planted 1.1 million acres of oats in 1990. They harvested 225,000 acres, averaging 41 bushels per acre, for a total production of 9,225,000 bushels at an average price of $1.50 per bushel with an estimated value of $13,838,000. Most of the 1986 acreage was used for pasture.

Comparable figures are: in 1989, 1.1 million acres were planted with 200,000 harvested. Yield was 33 bushels per acre for a value of $13,596,000 from 6.6 million bushels. In 1988, 1.1 million acres were planted, 200,000 acres harvested, yielding 9 million bushels, or 45 bushels per acre, for a total value of $21,780,000.

Almost all oat grain produced in Texas is utilized as feed for livestock within the state. A small acreage is grown exclusively for planting seed.

Leading oat grain-producing counties in 1989 were **Hamilton, Collin, Uvalde, Coryell and McLennan.**

Barley

Texas barley acreage and production fall far below that of wheat and oats. In 1990, farmers planted 30,000 acres and harvested 16,000 acres, averaging 38 bushels per acre, for a total production of 608,000 bushels. With the price averaging $2.15 per bushel, the estimated value totaled $1,307,000. This compared with 25,000 acres planted, 15,000 acres harvested, yielding 32 bushels per acre for a total production of 480,000 bushels valued at $1,008,000 in 1989; 35,000 acres planted, 18,000 harvested, yielding 30 bushels per acre for a total production of 540,000 bushels valued at $1,080,000 in 1988.

Leading barley-producing counties in 1989 were **Moore, Parmer, Deaf Smith, Swisher and Sherman.**

Sugar Beets

Sugar beets have been grown on a commercial scale in Texas since 1964 when the first beet-sugar factory was built by Holly Sugar Company at Hereford. The leading counties in production in 1989 were **Deaf Smith, Castro, Parmer and Swisher.**

In 1990, 41,900 acres were planted with 41,000 harvested. The yield averaged 24.7 tons per acre for total production of 1,013,000 tons. In 1989, 36,600 acres were planted and 35,300 acres harvested with an average

yield of 21 tons per acre. Total production amounted to 743,000 tons that averaged $41.30 per ton for a value of $30,686,000.

Comparable figures for 1988 are 34,000 acres planted with 33,000 acres harvested yielding 21.9 tons per acre. Production totaled 723,000 tons with an average price of $37.60 per ton valued at $27,185,000.

Sugar Cane

Sugar cane is grown from seed cane planted in late summer or fall. It is harvested 12 months later and milled to produce raw sugar and molasses. The raw sugar then requires additional refining before it is in final form to be offered to consumers.

The **sugar-cane grinding mill** operated at Santa Rosa, Cameron County, is considered as one of the most modern mills in the United States. Texas sugar cane-producing counties are **Hidalgo, Cameron and Willacy.**

In 1990, 36,200 acres were harvested from which 948,000 tons of sugar cane were milled. The yield averaged 26.2 tons per acre. In 1989, 35,500 acres were harvested yielding 24.7 tons per acre or 878,000 tons valued at $21 per ton, or $18,438,000. Sugar cane was not a commercial crop in Texas for about 50 years following its abandonment in 1923 because of adverse markets.

Hay, Silage, and Other Forage Crops

A large proportion of Texas' agricultural land is devoted to forage-crop production. This acreage produces essentially the total feed requirements for most of the state's large domestic-livestock population as well as game animals.

Approximately 80 million acres of native rangeland, which are primarily in the western half of Texas, provide grazing for beef cattle, sheep, goats, horses and game animals. An additional 20 million acres are devoted to introducing forage species. Of this total, approximately 16 million acres are established to introduce improved perennial grasses and legumes and are harvested by grazing animals. The average annual acreage of crops grown for hay, silage and other forms of machine-harvested forage is close to 4 million acres with an estimated value in excess of $600 million.

Hay accounts for a large amount of this production, with some corn and sorghum silage being produced. The most important hay crops are annual and perennial grasses and alfalfa. In 1990, the production of hay was 8 million tons with a value of $620 million.

In 1989, hay was harvested from 3,910,000 acres producing an average of 2.45 tons per acre or 9,582,000 tons valued at $75 per ton or $718,650,000. Production in 1988 was 5,350,000 tons from 3,200,000 acres valued at $74 per ton or $395,900,000.

Grass hay production is widely distributed with some leading counties being **Hopkins, Lamar, Henderson, Van Zandt, Erath, Lamb, McLennan, Ellis and Anderson.**

Alfalfa hay was harvested from 100,000 acres in 1990, producing an average of 4 tons per acre for total production of 400,000 tons. Value was included with "all hay." In 1989, 462,000 tons were produced on 110,000 acres, averaging 4.2 tons per acre.

An additional sizable acreage of annual forage crops such as **sudan and millet** is grazed, as well as much of the small grain acreage. Alfalfa, sweet corn, vetch, arrowleaf clover, grasses and other forage plants also provide income as seed crops.

Peanuts

Peanuts are grown on approximately 275,000 acres in Texas, with some 40 percent of the acreage irrigated. Yet, well over half of the crop annually produced is on acreage that is irrigated. **Texas ranked second** nationally in production of peanuts in 1990. Among Texas crops, peanuts ranks about seventh in value.

Until 1973, essentially all of the Texas acreage was planted to the Spanish types, which were favored because of their earlier maturity and better drought tolerance than other types. The Spanish varieties are also preferred for some uses due to their distinctive flavor. The Florunner variety, a runner market type, is now planted on a sizable proportion of the acreage where soil moisture is favorable. The variety is later maturing but better yielding than Spanish varieties under good growing conditions. Florunner peanuts have acceptable quality to compete with the Spanish variety in most products.

Production in 1990 amounted to 537,225,000 pounds of peanuts from 290,000 acres planted and 285,000 acres harvested or an average of 1,885 pounds per harvested acre valued at 41.5 cents per pound or $222,948,000. In

1989, the crop amounted to 484,700,000 pounds harvested from 262,000 acres. It was valued at $134,262,000 or 27.7 cents per pound. Leading counties in peanut production are **Comanche, Gaines, Frio, Atascosa and Eastland.**

Soybeans

Production is largely in the areas of the Upper Coast, irrigated High Plains, and Red River Valley of Northeast Texas. Soybeans are adapted to the same general soil and climatic conditions as corn, cotton or grain sorghum, if moisture, disease and insects are not limiting factors. The major counties in soybean production in 1989 were **Hale, Floyd, Liberty, Lamar and Brazoria.**

In low-rainfall areas, yields have been too low or inconsistent for profitable production under dryland conditions. Soybeans' need for moisture in late summer minimizes economic crop possibilities in the Blacklands and Rolling Plains. In the Blacklands, cotton root rot seriously hinders soybean production. Limited moisture at critical growth stages may occasionally prevent economical yields, even in high-rainfall areas of Northeast Texas and the Coastal Prairie.

Because of day-length sensitivity, soybeans should be planted in Texas during the long days of May and June to obtain sufficient vegetative growth for optimum yields. Varieties planted during this period usually cease vegetative development and initiate reproductive processes during the hot, usually dry months of July and August. When moisture is insufficient during the blooming and fruiting period, yields are drastically reduced. In most areas of the state, July and August rainfall is insufficient to permit economical dryland production. The risk of dryland soybean production in the Coastal Prairie and Northeast Texas is considerably less when compared to other dryland areas because moisture is available more often during the critical fruiting period.

In 1990, the Texas soybean crop averaged 25 bushels per acre from 200,000 acres harvested. Total production of 5 million bushels was valued at $28 million or $5.60 per bushel. The figures for 1989 were 12,450,000 bushels harvested from 415,000 acres. Yield was 30 bushels per acre for a total value of $63,122,000 or $5.07 per bushel. In 1988, 6,300,000 bushels were harvested from 225,000 acres. Yield was 28 bushels per acre for a total of $44,415,000 value or $7.05 per bushel.

Sunflowers

Sunflowers constitute **one of the most important annual oilseed crops** in the world. The cultivated types, which are thought to be descendants of the common wild sunflower native to Texas, have been successfully grown in several countries including Russia, Argentina, Romania, Bulgaria, Uruguay, Western Canada and portions of the northern United States. Extensive trial plantings conducted in the Cotton Belt states since 1968 showed sunflowers have considerable potential as an oilseed crop in much of this area, including Texas. This crop exhibits good cold and drought tolerance, is adapted to a wide range of soil and climatic conditions, and tolerates higher levels of hail, wind, and sand abrasion than other crops normally grown in the state.

In 1990, about 20,000 acres were planted to sunflowers of which 20,000 were harvested, yielding 1,275 pounds per acre for a total yield of 25,500,000 pounds valued at $3,105,000. In 1989, 60,000 acres were planted and 56,000 were harvested for total production of 67,120,000 pounds valued at $8,441,000. The leading counties in production in 1989 were **Floyd, Crosby, Hale and Hidalgo.**

Reasons for growing sunflowers include the need for an additional cash crop with low water and plant-nutrient requirements, the development of sunflower hybrids, and interest by food processors in Texas sunflower oil, which has a high oleic-acid content. Commercial users have found many advantages in this high-oleic oil, including excellent cooking stability, particularly for use as a deep-frying medium for potato chips, corn chips and similar products.

Sunflower meal is a high-quality protein source free of nutritional toxins that can be included in rations for swine, poultry and ruminants. The hulls constitute a source of roughage, which can also be included in livestock rations.

Flaxseed

Earliest flax planting was at Victoria in 1900. Since the first planting, Texas flax acreage has fluctuated depending on market, winterkill and drought. Flax acreage has dropped in recent years, and estimates were discontinued in 1980.

Forest Products

The non-industrial, private forest landowners of East Texas, who own 60 percent of the 11.5 million acres of timberlands, sold **timber stumpage** with an estimated value of $234 million in 1988. Forest industry landowners had timber stumpage sales of $76 million. An estimated $17 million in timber stumpage was sold from the National Forests in Texas. The delivered value of this timber to the processing plants (such as sawmills, paper-mills and plywood plants) was over $511 million. In 1990, the volume of pine cut in Texas was estimated to have exceeded the growth by 12 percent. The hardwood harvest was 71 percent of growth.

Pulpwood, sawlogs and veneer bolts for plywood are the leading timber products, with utility poles, piling, fence posts and railroad crossties also providing income to timber growers. Over 750,000 **Christmas trees,** grown primarily in East Texas but found throughout the state, were sold in the Texas market. In Central Texas some timber is harvested for fuelwood, lumber, veneer, crossties, posts and cedar oil.

In addition to timber production, the forests of Texas provide a multitude of additional benefits, such as wildlife habitat, watershed protection, livestock grazing and opportunities for outdoor recreation. Minor products include pine straw, edible berries and nuts, wild honey and decorative plants such as mistletoe.

Texas forests are affected by many problems ranging from urban growth to insect and disease damage. New regulations regarding even-aged management of timber stands in National Forests threaten to decrease cutting and income to East Texas counties.

Horticultural Specialty Crops

The trend to increased production of horticulture specialty crops continues to rise as transportation costs on long-distance hauling makes the importance of plants from other growing areas increasingly costly. This has resulted in a marked increase in the production of **container-grown plants** within the state. This increase is noted especially in the production of **bedding plants, foliage plants, sod and woody landscape plants.**

Plant-rental services have become a multimillion-dollar business. This comparative newcomer in the plant industry provides plants and maintains them in office buildings, shopping malls, public buildings, and even in some homes for a fee. The response has been terrific as evidenced by the growth of companies providing these services.

The interest in plants for interior landscapes is confined to no specific age group. Retail nurseries and florist shops report that people of all ages are buying plants — from the elderly in retirement homes to high school and college students in dormitory rooms and apartments.

Extension specialists estimated cash receipts from horticultural specialty crops in Texas to be around $550 million in 1990.

Truck Crops

Some market vegetables are produced in almost all Texas counties, but most of the commercial crop comes from about 200 counties. **Hidalgo County** is the leading Texas county in vegetable acres harvested, followed by **Starr and Cameron counties.** Other leading producing counties are **Frio, Uvalde, Duval, Webb, Hale and Zavala.**

Most Texas vegetables are marketed fresh rather than processed. Nationally, Texas ranks fifth in harvested acreage and value of fresh-market vegetables, being exceeded by California, Florida and Arizona. Texas had 3.6 percent of the harvested acreage, 2.5 percent of the production, and 2.6 percent of the value of fresh-market vegetables produced in the United States in 1990. The severe freeze in December 1989 had an adverse impact on both acreage and production in 1990.

Vegetables leading in value of production usually are carrots, onions, watermelons, cantaloupes, cabbage and Irish potatoes.

Texas growers harvested principle commercial vegetable crops valued at $111,754,000 from 59,400 acres in 1990. This compared with $148,221,000 from 80,700 acres in 1989 and $425,000,000 from 200,000 acres in 1988.

Onions

Onions were harvested from 17,700 acres and valued at $57,299,000 in 1990. That compared with 19,000 acres harvested valued at $53,540,000 in 1989; 18,100 acres valued at $48,455,000 in 1988; and, 17,200 acres valued at $77,885,000 in 1987.

Carrots

Carrot production was valued at $7,322,000 in 1990

from 5,300 acres harvested. This compared with $19,476,000 from 9,900 acres in 1989; $17,269,000 from 10,000 acres in 1988; and $18,520,000 from 11,500 acres in 1987.

The winter carrot production from South Texas accounts for about three-fourths of total production during the winter season.

Irish Potatoes

Irish potatoes were harvested from 16,800 acres with production of 3,072,000 cwt. valued at $48,145,000 in 1990. This compared with 16,300 acres valued at $41,918,000 in 1989; 15,200 acres valued at $28,672,000 in 1988; and 17,200 acres valued $25,544,000 in 1987.

Cantaloupes and Honeydews

Cantaloupes were harvested from 13,000 acres in 1990 and were valued at $43,524,000. This compared with 17,000 acres valued at $23,205,000 in 1989; 17,000 acres valued at $23,205,000 in 1988; and 22,000 acres valued at $50,336,000 in 1987.

Honeydew melons valued at $17,145,000 were harvested at 5,000 acres in 1990. This compared with $10,547,000 from 6,500 acres in 1989; $20,640,000 from 7,500 acres in 1988; and $19,706,000 from 4,600 acres in 1987.

Cabbage

The 10,000 acres of cabbage harvested in Texas in 1990 brought a value of $35,880,000. This compared with 15,000 acres valued at $36,630,000 in 1989; 15,000 acres valued at $36,630,000 in 1987.

Cauliflower

Cauliflower was harvested from 1,000 acres and valued at $678,000 in 1990. Comparable figures were 1,500 acres valued at $1,482,000 in 1989; 1,500 acres valued at $1,980,000 in 1988; and 700 acres valued at $792,000 in 1987.

Broccoli

Broccoli in 1990 was produced on 5,100 acres with a value of $6,255,000. That compared with 6,700 acres valued at $14,706,000 in 1989; 6,200 acres valued at $10,590,000 in 1988; and 5,400 acres valued at $11,822,000 in 1987. Broccoli is primarily a South-Texas crop.

Watermelons

Watermelons were harvested from 50,000 acres in 1990 with a value of $47,588,000. Comparable figures were 40,000 acres valued at $43,010,000 in 1989; 40,000 acres valued at $43,010,000 in 1988; and 40,000 acres valued at $43,010,000 in 1987.

Tomatoes

Commercial tomatoes are marketed throughout the year from Texas partly as a result of recent increases in greenhouse production during the winter.

The tomato crop in 1990 was valued at $3,042,000 from 2,600 harvested acres. This compared with $4,763,000 from 2,800 acres in 1989; $6,739,000 from 3,200 acres in 1988; and $6,682,000 from 2,600 acres in 1987.

Green Peppers

Green peppers in 1990 were harvested from 5,000 acres valued at $28,050,000. This compared with 6,000 acres valued at $33,759,000 in 1989; 6,000 acres valued at $33,759,000 in 1988; and 6,000 acres valued at $33,759,000 in 1987.

Lettuce

Lettuce was harvested from 500 acres and valued at $311,000 in 1990. Comparable figures were 2,400 acres valued at $7,582,000 in 1989; 1,800 acres valued at $8,752,000 in 1988; and 2,000 acres valued at $5,655,000 in 1987.

Sweet Potatoes

Sweet potatoes in 1990 were harvested from 6,200 acres with a value of $6,696,000. This compared with 7,000 acres valued at $12,474,000 in 1989 and 7,400 acres valued at $8,495,000 in 1988.

Spinach

Spinach production is primarily concentrated in the Winter Garden area of South Texas. The 5,000 acres harvested in 1990 were valued at $7,205,000. This compared with 4,000 acres valued at $10,944,000 in 1989; 4,000 acres valued at $10,944,000 in 1988; and 4,000 acres valued at $10,944,000 in 1987.

Cucumbers

The cucumber crop in Texas during 1990 was harvested from 4,100 acres valued at $7,118,000. This compared with 5,800 acres valued at $11,832,000 in 1989; 5,800 acres valued at $11,832,000 in 1988; and 5,800 acres valued at $11,832,000 in 1987.

Sweet Corn

Sweet corn was harvested in Texas from 2,400 acres valued at $2,232,000 in 1990. This compared with 2,500

acres valued at $1,738,000 in 1989; 3,000 acres valued at $2,100,000 in 1988; and 4,000 acres valued at $2,400,000 in 1987.

Vegetables for Processing

Cucumbers, snap beans and tomatoes for processing in 1990 were harvested from 18,800 acres valued at $14,894,000. Comparable figures were 27,500 acres valued at $22,770,000 in 1989.

Fruits and Nuts

Texas is noted for producing a wide variety of fruit. The **pecan** is the only commercial nut crop in the state. The pecan is native to most of the state's river valleys and is the Texas state tree. **Citrus**, which is produced in the three southernmost counties in the Lower Rio Grande Valley, has been severly damaged by freeze. Some new orchards are being replanted. **Peaches** represent the next most important Texas fruit crop, yet there is a considerable amount of interest in growing **apples.**

Citrus

Prior to the 1989 freeze, Texas ranked with Florida, California and Arizona as leading states in the production of citrus. Most of the Texas production was in **Cameron, Hidalgo and Willacy counties** of the Lower Rio Grande Valley. The 1989 freeze had a devastating effect on the Texas citrus industry.

Peaches

Primary production areas are East Texas, the Hill Country and the West Cross Timbers. Recently, peach production has spread to South and West Texas. Low-chilling varieties for early marketings are being grown in **Atascosa, Frio, Webb, Karnes and Duval** counties.

The Texas peach crop totaled 20,500,000 pounds in 1990 for a value of $7,175,000 or 35 cents per pound. In 1989, 12,500,000 pounds were produced, valued at $5 million, or 40 cents per pound.

The demand for high-quality Texas peaches greatly exceeds the supply. **Texas ranked 11th nationally** in peach production in 1989. Leading Texas counties in production are **Gillespie, Parker, Montague, Comanche, Limestone and Eastland.**

Apples

Small acreages of apples, usually marketed in the state, are grown in a number of counties. The leading counties in production are **Montague and Gillespie.** Other counties growing apples include Callahan, Collingsworth, Clay, Cass, Donley, Eastland, Hudspeth, Jeff Davis, Lampasas, Parker, San Saba and Young. The crop is harvested and marketed from July to October.

A considerable number of apple trees have been planted in the Hill Country. Most of the trees are new varieties of Red and Golden Delicious types on semi-dwarfing rootstocks. Trees are established in high-density plantings of 100 to 200 trees per acre. Most of the apples are sold as roadside stands or go to nearby markets.

Pears

Well adapted for home and small-orchard production, pears are not commercially significant in Texas. **Comanche, Parker, Lampasas, Cooke, McCulloch and Eastland counties** lead in trees. Usually the fruit goes for home consumption or to nearby markets.

Apricots

Not a commercial crop, apricots are grown chiefly in **Comanche, Denton, Wilbarger, Parker and Collingsworth counties.** Others reporting apricots include Martin, Clay, Young, Lampasas, Gillespie, Anderson, Erath, Wichita and Eastland counties.

Plums

Plum production is scattered over a wide area of the state with the heaviest production in East and Central Texas. The leading counties in production are **Smith, Gillespie and Knox.** Most of the production goes to nearby markets or to processors.

Blackberries

Smith County is a blackberry center with the Tyler-Lindale area having processed the crop since 1890. There are about 1,500 acres with blackberries in **Smith, Wood, Van Zandt and Henderson counties.** The Brazos blackberry is grown as a local market or "pick-your-own" fruit in many sections of the state. **Dewberries** grow wild in Central and East Texas and are gathered for home use and local sale in May and June.

Strawberries

Atascosa County is the leading commercial area, although strawberries are grown for local markets in Wood, Van Zandt, and Smith counties in East Texas.

The most concentrated production occurs in the Poteet area below San Antonio.

Avocados

Avocados grow on a small acreage in the Lower Rio Grande Valley. Interest in this crop is increasing and production is expected to expand. Lulu is the principal variety.

Pecans

The pecan, **the state tree**, is one of the most widely distributed trees in Texas. It is native to over 150 counties and is grown commercially in some 30 additional counties. The pecan is also widely used as a dual-purpose yard tree. The commercial plantings of pecans have greatly accelerated in Central and West Texas, with many of the new orchards being irrigated. Many new pecan plantings are being established under trickle-irrigation systems. Two factors that have greatly helped to increase quality and yields have been the development and use of the new UDSA pecan varieties and some 40 county and regional pecan-grading demonstrations.

The 1990 crop totaled 65 million pounds valued at $73,500,000 or $1.13 per pound. In 1989, the crop totaled 55 million pounds valued at $44,250,000 or 80.5 cents per pound. The 1988 crop totaled 60 million pounds valued at $31,500,000 or 52.5 cents per pound.

Nationally, **Texas ranked second in pecan production** in 1989. Leading Texas counties in pecan production are **Hood, El Paso, Pecos, San Saba, Mills, Comanche, Wharton and Gonzales.**

Livestock and Their Products

Livestock and their products usually account for more than half of the agricultural cash receipts in Texas. The **state ranks first nationally** in all cattle, beef cattle, cattle on feed, sheep and lambs, wool, goats and mohair. In 1989 it ranked 10th in dairy cows, 6th in broilers, 8th in eggs and 17th in hogs.

Meat animals normally account for around 80 percent of total cash receipts from marketings of livestock and their products. Sales of livestock and products in 1989 totaled $6.86 billion, up from $6.56 billion in 1988.

Cattle dominate livestock production in Texas, contributing more than 70 percent of cash receipts from livestock and products each year. The Jan. 1, 1991, inventory of all cattle and calves in Texas totaled 13.4 million head, valued at $8,442,000.

Texas sheep raisers have gradually reduced their herds in light of increasing production costs. On Jan. 1, 1991, the **sheep and lamb** inventory stood at 2 million head, compared with 2,090,000 head in 1990. Sheep and lambs numbered 3,214,000 on Jan. 1, 1973, down from a high of 10,829,000 in 1943. Sheep and lamb production fell from 148,295,000 pounds in 1973 to 94,593,000 pounds in 1988. **Wool production** decreased from 26,352,000 pounds valued at $23,190,000 in 1973 to 18,000,000 pounds valued at $27,180,000 in 1989. The price of wool per pound was 88 cents in 1973, $1.21 in 1987, $1.97 in 1988, and $1.51 in 1989. Lamb prices averaged $71.10 per cwt. in 1989, $75.10 per cwt. in 1988, $84.80 per cwt. in 1987. The average value per head of sheep stock on Jan. 1, 1991, was estimated at $54, $64.50 in 1990, and $73.50 in 1989.

Mohair production in Texas dropped from a 1965 high of 31,584,000 pounds to 9.3 million pounds in 1979; 15.4 million in 1989; 15.4 million pounds in 1988; and 16.2 million pounds in 1987. In 1965, mohair was valued at $20,845,000, averaging 66 cents per pound. The value of 1979 production was $47,430,000, an average of $5.10 per pound; in 1986, $40,160,000 or $2.51 per pound; in 1987, $42,606,000 or $2.63 per pound; in 1988, $29,876,000 or $1.94 per pound; and in 1989, $24,794,000 or $1.61 per pound.

Beef Cattle

Raising beef cattle is the most extensive agricultural operation in Texas. In 1989, 46.9 percent of total cash receipts from farm and ranch marketings — $5,049,760,000 of $10,760,414,000 — came from cattle and calves. This compared with $4,969,762,000 of $10,251,368,000 in 1988, and $4,616,602,000 of $9,124,670,000 in 1987. The next leading commodity is cotton.

Nearly all of the 254 counties in Texas derive more revenue from cattle than from any other agricultural commodity, and those that don't usually rank cattle second in importance.

Within the boundaries of Texas are 14 percent of all the cattle in the U.S., as are 16 percent of the beef breeding cows, and 13 percent of the calf crop.

The **number of all cattle** in Texas on Jan. 1, 1991, totaled 13,400,000. This compared with 13,200,000 on Jan. 1, 1990; 13,400,000 in 1989; 13,600,000 in 1988; 13,400,000 in 1987; and 13,600,000 in 1986.

Calves born on Texas farms and ranches in 1991 totaled 5,000,000, compared with 5,000,000 in 1990; 5,100,000 in 1989; 5,250,000 in 1988; and 5,050,000 in 1987.

Receipts of cattle and calves at approximately 153 **livestock auctions** inspected by Texas Animal Health Commission totaled 5,933,000 head in 1990, compared with 6,182,000 head in 1989, and 6,590,000 head in 1988. The number of cattle and calves shipped into Texas totaled 3,296,403 head in 1990; 2,598,158 head in 1989; and 3,097,893 in 1988.

Livestock Industries

A large portion of Texas livestock is sold through local auction markets. In 1988, 153 livestock auctions reported by the Texas Animal Health Commission listed receipts of 6,590,000 cattle and calves; 455,000 hogs; and 1,308,000 sheep and goats. This compared with 6,394,000 cattle and calves, 372,000 hogs, 1,168,000 sheep and goats in 1987. Figures for 1986 were 6,368,000 cattle and calves; 362,000 hogs; 1,151,000 sheep and goats.

During 1988, the commission reported 2,276,133 cattle and calves shipped from Texas to other states and 2,719,958 shipped in, compared with 2,208,827 shipped out and 3,001,742 shipped in during 1987; 1,763,373 shipped out and 3,097,893 shipped in during 1986. (Figures exclude cattle shipped direct to slaughter where no health certificates are required.)

Texas, during 1988, shipped out 85,064 sheep and lambs and shipped in 137,387, compared with 109,152 shipped out and 135,889 shipped in during 1987; 150,963 shipped out in 1986 and 240,038 shipped in.

Feedlot fattening of livestock, mainly cattle, is a ma-

Texas Livestock Numbers And Values

Source: U.S. Department of Agriculture

Class of Livestock	Numbers				Farm Value					
	1989	1990	1991 Preliminary	Percent Change	Value Per Head			Total Value		
					1989	1990	1991	1989	1990	1991
	Thousands			Pct.	Dollars			1,000 Dollars		
All Cattle	13,400	13,200	13,400	102	$540.00	$585.00	$630.00	$7,303,000	$7,222,000	$8,442,000
*Milk Cows.	5,290	5,210	5,360	103	NA	NA	NA	NA	NA	NA
*Beef Cows.	380	390	390	100	NA	NA	NA	NA	NA	NA
†Hogs	500	500	550	110	81.00	81.00	82.00	40,500	40,500	45,100
All Sheep	1,870	2,090	2,000	96	73.50	64.00	54.00	137,445	133,760	108,000
Goats.	1,850	1,900	1,830	96	54.20	49.00	34.00	100,270	93,100	62,200
†Chickens	17,750	17,750	17,200	97	1.85	1.85	2.20	32,838	32,838	37,840
†Turkey Hens.	‡	NA	NA	NA	NA	NA	NA	NA	NA	NA
Total Value	. . .	. . .	. . .	. . .	. . .	. . .	. . .	$7,614,053	$8,022,198	$8,695,140

*Included in "All Cattle."
†Figures are as of Juanary 1.
‡Estimates discontinued in 1985. Turkey figures not released for 1987 to avoid disclosing individual operations.
NA = Not Available.

jor industry in Texas. Texas lots marketed 4,745,000 head of grain-fed cattle in 1989, compared with 5,035,000 in 1988; 5,255,000 in 1987; and 5,260,000 in 1986. In recent years, more cattle have been fed in Texas than any other state in the United States.

During 1989, there were 161 feedlots in Texas with capacity of 1,000 animals or more. This compared with 163 in 1988; 151 in 1987; and 150 in 1986.

Feedlots with capacities of 1,000 head or more accounted for more than 98 percent of the cattle fed in Texas. Total feedlot marketings in 1989 represented about 21 percent of total U.S. fed cattle marketings.

Large amounts of capital are required for feedlot operations. This has forced many lots to become custom feeding facilities.

Feedlots are concentrated on the High Plains largely because of extensive supplies of sorghum and other feed. But beef breeding herds have increased most in East Texas, where grazing is abundant.

Increased feeding of cattle in commercial feedlots has been a major economic development during recent years and has stimulated the establishment and expansion of beef-slaughtering plants. Most of this development has been in the Panhandle-Plains area of Northwest Texas. This area alone accounts for over 70 percent of the cattle fed in the state.

Federally-inspected slaughter plants in Texas numbered 60 in 1990. This compared with 61 in 1989 and 61 in 1988. In 1990, the number of head slaughtered in Texas totaled 5,586,400 cattle; 177,000 hogs; 612,100 sheep and lambs; and 70,100 calves. This compared with 5,786,900 cattle; 719,300 hogs; and 91,600 calves in 1989; and 5,957,100 cattle; 70,100 calves; 924,100 hogs; 542,400 sheep and lambs in 1988.

Dairying

Ninety percent of the state's dairy industry is located east of the line from Wichita Falls to Brownwood, to San Antonio to Corpus Christi. Leading counties in **milk production** are Hopkins, Erath and Johnson, which combined, produce almost 35 percent of the milk in the state, with Hopkins producing almost 17 percent of the total.

All the milk sold by Texas dairy farmers is market-ed under the terms of Federal Marketing Orders. Most Texas dairymen are members of one of four marketing cooperatives. Associated Milk Producers, Inc., is the largest, representing the majority of the state's producers.

Texas dairy farmers received an average price for milk of $14.43 per hundred pounds in 1989, compared with $13.24 per hundred pounds in 1988, and $13.78 per hundred pounds of milk in 1987. A total of 5.124 billion pounds of milk was sold to plants and dealers in 1989, bringing in cash receipts from milk to dairy farmers of $734,679,000 in 1989. This compares with 4.826 billion pounds sold in 1988 that brought in $639,144,000 in cash receipts. In 1987 Texas dairymen sold 4.23 billion pounds of milk, which brought in cash receipts of $582,527,000.

The number of milk cows that have calved on Texas farms on Jan. 1, 1990, was 390,000 head. This compares with 380,000 head on Jan. 1, 1989, and 370,000 head on Jan. 1, 1988. Average production per cow in the state has increased steadily over the past several decades. The average production per cow in 1989 was 13,394 pounds; in 1988, it was 12,997 pounds; in 1987, it was 12,506 pounds. Total **milk production** in Texas in 1989 was 5.170 billion pounds. This compares with 4.874 billion pounds produced in 1988, and 4.277 billion pounds produced in 1987.

There were 6,000 operations reporting milk cows in Texas in 1989. There was an average of 2,162 commercial milk producing units in Texas in 1989. This compares with 6,200 operations reporting milk cows in 1988 and approximately 2,150 commercial milk producing units.

Dairy Manufacturing

The major dairy products manufactured in Texas include condensed, evaporated and dry milk, creamery butter and cheese. However, production and value data are not available because of the small number of manufacturing plants producing these products.

Frozen Desserts

Production of frozen desserts in Texas totaled 118,627,000 gallons in 1990. In 1989, 110,915,000 gallons were produced, and in 1988, the amount was 115,456,000 gallons. **Ice-cream production** in Texas in 1990 amounted to 50,801,000 gallons; in 1989, it was 46,368,000 gallons; in

Texas Cattle Marketed, By Size Of Feedlots

Texas Crop and Livestock Reporting Service

	Feedlot Capacity (head)					
Year	Under 1,000	1,000-1,999	2,000-3,999	4,000-7,999	8,000-15,999	16,000 & Over	Total
	— Cattle Marketed — 1,000 head —						
1962 ..	105	87	109	194	*261	—	756
1963 ..	120	111	144	205	185	131	896
1964 ..	118	100	174	223	177	179	971
1965 ..	104	108	205	324	107	246	1,094
1966 ..	163	127	268	359	205	290	1,412
1967 ..	138	126	194	372	343	481	1,654
1968 ..	112	91	138	321	439	869	1,970
1969 ..	111	78	133	303	514	1,567	2,706
1970 ..	98	53	112	281	727	1,867	3,138
1971 ..	99	49	117	304	697	2,397	3,663
1972 ..	98	57	112	308	558	3,175	4,308
1973 ..	99	47	74	210	625	3,357	4,412
1974 ..	85	31	48	189	544	3,002	3,899
1975 ..	50	22	51	134	485	2,325	3,067
1976 ..	60	33	62	170	583	3,039	3,947
1977 ..	146	22	38	206	604	3,211	4,227
1978 ..	80	20	50	242	697	3,826	4,915
1979 ..	54	19	46	227	556	3,543	4,445
1980 ..	51	18	47	226	533	3,285	4,160
1981 ..	50	20	50	220	510	3,110	3,960
1982 ..	55	20	60	210	540	3,190	4,075
1983 ..	100	20	80	130	490	3,580	4,400
1984 ..	60	20	180	150	540	4,140	5,090
1985 ..	70	10	20	170	620	4,140	5,030
1986 ..	90	10	40	180	550	4,390	5,260
1987 ..	90	20	35	170	625	4,315	5,255
1988 ..	30	15	35	185	650	4,100	5,015
1989 ..	40	15	40	165	675	3,810	4,745

Number of feedlots with 1,000 head or more capacity is number of lots operating any time during the year. Number under 1,000 head capacity and total number of all feedlots is number at end of year.

Source: "1985 Agricultural Facts", Texas Agricultural Statistics Service, April 20, 1989. Numbers for 1986, '87, '88, '89, '90, '91.

Hog Production in Texas

Source: Texas A&M—USDA

Year	Production	Avg. Market Wt.	Avg. Price Per Cwt.	Gross Income
	1,000 Pounds	Pounds	Dollars	1,000 Dollars
1958	262,134	233	$19.50	$44,997
1959	338,343	228	14.40	47,948
1960	288,844	228	14.70	44,634
1961	289,700	229	16.40	49,174
1962	288,815	230	16.30	47,483
1963	282,807	234	15.10	43,685
1964	259,549	240	14.80	43,351
1965	212,404	240	19.80	41,432
1966	234,742	239	22.60	49,992
1967	289,773	240	18.70	51,767
1968	313,515	240	18.10	55,788
1969	325,896	240	21.60	73,027
1970	385,502	241	22.50	75,288
1971	529,986	236	16.60	90,257
1972	449,357	244	24.00	114,730
1973	375,372	242	37.90	148,488
1974	350,811	253	33.30	123,277
1975	271,027	244	43.70	127,323
1976	286,053	247	41.50	117,587
1977	292,290	247	38.00	109,634
1978	303,135	258	43.80	135,006
1979	320,790	261	39.70	125,183
1980	315,827	259	35.90	111,700
1981	264,693	256	41.70	121,054
1982	205,656	256	49.60	112,726
1983	209,621	256	45.20	95,343
1984	189,620	262	45.50	95,657
1985	168,950	266	43.40	75,512
1986	176,660	269	45.90	81,028
1987	216,834	NA	50.60	103,983
1988	236,658	NA	41.30	100,029
1989	228,459	NA	39.90	95,153

Source: "1985 Texas Livestock, Dairy and Poultry Statistics", USDA, Bulletin 235, June 1986, pp. 32, 46. "Texas Agricultural Facts," Texas Agricultural Statistics Service, 4/18/89, 4/91.

1988, it was 49,767,000 gallons. Ice-cream mix produced in Texas in 1990 amounted to 27,830,000 gallons; in 1989, it was 25,467,000 gallons; in 1988, it was 27,058,000 gallons. Ice-milk production in Texas amounted to 21,380,000 gallons in 1990; in 1989, it was 21,639,000 gallons; and in 1988, production totaled 20,034,000 gallons. Mellorine in 1987 totaled 4,690,000 gallons; in 1986, it was 4,622,000 gallons; in 1985, mellorine production totaled 4,184,000 gallons.

Swine

Texas ranked 17th among the states in number of swine on hand, Dec. 1, 1988. Swine producers in the state usually produce about 25 to 30 percent of the pork consumed by the state's population, or about 800,000 head marketed annually.

Production units vary in size from one to over 1,100 sows. Although the number of farms producing hogs has steadily decreased, the size of production units has increased.

With the trend to larger units, there has been increasing swine production in the Panhandle, South Plains and West-Central areas of Texas. In alphabetical order, the 10 leading counties in hog numbers in 1988 were **Archer, Colorado, Fayette, Lee, Llano, Lubbock, Milam, Moore, Uvalde and Wilson.**

Specialization in the swine industry has resulted in a demand for top-quality feeder pigs by those farmers who have grain available. To meet this demand, feeder-pig marketing associations have been established in the feeder-pig producing areas of East and Central Texas. These associations hold feeder-pig sales monthly and auction pigs in uniform lots according to grades and weights.

With the establishment of marketing associations capable of shipping slaughter hogs to any point in the United States, and because of the volume of sorghum grain produced in the state, the potential for increased production is tremendous, for both feeder pigs and slaughter hogs.

In 1989, 860,000 head of hogs were marketed in Texas, producing 235,895,000 pounds of pork valued at $94,258,000 or $39.90 per 100 pounds. Comparable figures for 1988 were 873,000 head marketed, 239,776,000 pounds of pork valued at $100,029,000, or $41.30 per 100 pounds; in 1987, 731,000 head marketed, 202,120,000 pounds of pork valued at $103,983,000, with cash receipts of $102,331,000, or $50.60 per 100 pounds.

Texas Sheep and Wool Production

Year	Sheep *Number	Value	Wool Production (lbs.)	Value
1850	100,530	N. A.	131,917	N. A.
1860	753,363	N. A.	1,493,363	N. A.
1870	1,223,000	$2,079,000	N. A.	N. A.
1880	6,024,000	12,048,000	N. A.	N. A.
1890	4,752,000	7,128,000	N. A.	N. A.
1900	2,416,000	4,590,000	9,630,000	N. A.
1910	1,909,000	5,536,000	8,943,000	$1,699,170
1920	3,360,000	33,600,000	22,813,000	5,019,000
1930	6,304,000	44,758,000	48,262,000	10,135,000
1940	10,069,000	49,413,000	79,900,000	23,171,000
1950	6,756,000	103,877,000	51,480,000	32,947,000
1951	7,119,000	154,962,000	48,712,000	48,225,000
1952	6,188,000	114,910,000	46,277,000	26,841,000
1953	5,574,000	56,833,000	42,511,000	26,782,000
1954	5,331,000	53,829,000	44,220,000	26,090,000
1955	5,659,000	57,125,000	45,137,000	19,409,000
1956	5,376,000	58,337,000	42,653,000	18,767,000
1957	4,749,000	46,769,000	39,409,000	22,069,000
1958	4,891,000	85,306,000	38,716,000	15,099,000
1959	5,458,000	95,154,000	46,726,000	20,559,000
1960	5,938,000	85,801,000	51,980,000	21,832,000
1961	6,140,000	72,859,000	52,225,000	23,501,000
1962	5,854,000	58,300,000	49,752,000	23,881,000
1963	5,538,000	55,175,000	46,602,000	23,767,000
1964	5,185,000	47,668,000	38,836,000	20,195,000
1965	4,539,000	50,811,000	41,109,000	18,499,000
1966	4,795,000	69,587,000	38,777,000	19,001,000
1967	4,802,000	67,686,000	36,998,000	15,169,000
1968	4,419,000	56,800,000	33,363,000	15,347,000
1969	4,029,000	67,284,000	29,717,000	14,561,000
1970	3,708,000	73,602,000	30,784,000	11,082,000
1971	3,789,000	66,308,000	30,397,000	4,864,000
1972	3,524,000	65,194,000	29,430,000	14,126,000
1973	3,214,000	64,280,000	26,352,000	23,190,000
1974	3,090,000	80,340,000	23,900,000	15,535,000
1975	2,715,000	63,803,000	23,600,000	14,868,000
1976	2,600,000	81,900,000	22,000,000	17,380,000
1977	2,520,000	93,240,000	21,000,000	17,220,000
1978	2,460,000	111,930,000	18,500,000	15,355,000
1979	2,415,000	152,145,000	19,075,000	18,503,000
1980	2,400,000	138,000,000	18,300,000	17,751,000
1981	2,360,000	116,820,000	20,500,000	24,600,000
1982	2,400,000	100,800,000	19,300,000	16,212,000
1983	2,225,000	86,775,000	18,600,000	15,438,000
1984	1,970,000	76,830,000	17,500,000	16,100,000
1985	1,930,000	110,975,000	16,200,000	13,284,000
1986	1,850,000	107,300,000	16,400,000	13,284,000
1987	2,050,000	133,250,000	16,400,000	19,844,000
1988	2,040,000	155,040,000	18,200,000	35,854,000
1989	1,870,000	133,445,000	18,000,000	27,180,000
†1990	2,090,000	134,805,000	17,400,000	19,662,000

*Number given here represents all sheep on farms as of Jan. 1; number clipped will vary because of spring and fall clipping.

†Preliminary.

Source: "1985 Texas Livestock, Dairy and Poultry Statistics", USDA Bulletin 235, June 1986, pp. 24-25. "Texas Agricultural Facts", Crop and Livestock Reporting Service, 2/19/88, 4/18/88, 2/23/89, 4/20/89, 2/91, 4/91.

Angora Goats and Mohair

Year	Goats *Number	Farm Value	Mohair Production (lbs.)	Value
1900	627,333	$923,777	961,328	$267,864
1910	1,135,000	2,514,000	1,998,000	468,000
1920	1,753,000	9,967,000	6,786,000	1,816,000
1930	2,965,000	14,528,000	14,800,000	4,995,000
1940	3,300,000	10,560,000	18,250,000	9,308,000
1950	2,295,000	13,082,000	12,643,000	9,735,000
1951	2,433,000	23,114,000	12,280,000	14,613,000
1952	2,054,000	17,664,000	11,561,000	11,330,000
1953	1,910,000	12,224,000	11,972,000	10,775,000
1954	2,082,000	13,741,000	13,097,000	9,561,000
1955	2,546,000	14,003,000	16,401,000	13,613,000
1956	2,700,000	18,900,000	17,616,000	14,974,000
1957	2,808,000	17,400,000	18,432,000	15,483,000
1958	2,864,000	25,800,000	20,207,000	14,751,000
1959	3,150,000	26,145,000	23,512,000	22,807,000
1960	3,339,000	29,383,000	23,750,000	21,375,000
1961	3,473,000	29,520,000	25,690,000	22,093,000
1962	3,647,000	30,270,000	26,418,000	19,021,000
1963	3,683,000	25,781,000	28,153,000	25,056,000
1964	3,904,000	29,280,000	28,872,000	27,428,000
1965	4,060,000	28,420,000	31,584,000	20,845,000
1966	4,222,000	28,710,000	28,770,000	15,536,000
1967	3,969,000	20,639,000	26,335,000	10,797,000
1968	3,572,000	17,503,000	25,272,000	11,448,000
1969	3,215,000	22,184,000	20,100,000	13,246,000
1970	2,572,000	19,033,000	17,985,000	7,032,000
1971	2,133,000	12,158,000	14,855,000	4,480,000
1972	1,650,000	10,230,000	10,190,000	8,458,000
1973	1,775,000	15,798,000	9,930,000	18,569,000
1974	1,560,000	22,620,000	8,400,000	11,508,000
1975	1,350,000	17,820,000	8,600,000	15,910,000
1976	1,270,000	25,273,000	8,100,000	24,057,000
1977	1,400,000	35,000,000	8,000,000	22,960,000
1978	1,355,000	44,038,000	8,100,000	37,179,000
1979	1,360,000	61,200,000	9,300,000	47,430,000
1980	1,400,000	64,400,000	8,800,000	30,800,000
1981	1,380,000	53,130,000	10,100,000	35,350,000
1982	1,410,000	57,810,000	10,000,000	25,500,000
1983	1,420,000	53,250,000	10,600,000	42,930,000
1984	1,450,000	82,215,000	10,600,000	48,160,000
1985	1,590,000	76,797,000	13,300,000	45,885,000
1986	1,770,000	70,977,000	16,000,000	40,160,000
1987	1,780,000	82,592,000	16,200,000	42,606,000
1988	1,800,000	108,180,000	15,400,000	29,876,000
1989	1,850,000	100,270,000	15,400,000	24,794,000
†1990	1,900,000	93,100,000	14,500,000	13,775,000

*Number here represents all goats on farms as of Jan. 1; the number of goats clipped will vary each year, but is usually larger because of spring and fall clipping.

†Preliminary.

Source: "1985 Texas Livestock, Dairy and Poultry Statistics", USDA Bulletin 235, June 1986, page 25. "Texas Agricultural Facts", Crop and Livestock Reporting Service, 2/19/88, 2/23/89, 4/20/89, 2/91, 4/91.

Hay bailing season is a busy time on Texas farms. Hay is raised for home use and for sale on many of the state's farms. Dallas Morning News Photo.

Goats and Mohair

Goats in Texas numbered 1,830,000 on Jan. 1, 1991, compared with 1,900,000 at the beginning of 1990; 1,850,000 in 1989; 1,800,000 in 1988; and 1,780,000 in 1987. They had a value of $62,200,000 or $34 per head in 1991, compared with $93,100,000 or $49 per head in 1990; $100,270,000 or $54.20 per head in 1989; $108,180,000 or $60.10 per head in 1988; and $82,592,000 or $46.40 per head in 1987.

The goat herd largely consists of **Angora goats** for mohair production. Angora goats totaled 1.5 million in 1991, 1.62 million in 1990; 1.6 million in 1989; 1.46 million in 1988; and 1.48 million in 1987. **Spanish goats** and others numbered 330,000 in 1991, compared with 280,000 in 1990; 250,000 in 1989; 340,000 in 1988; and 300,000 in 1987.

Mohair production during 1989 totaled 15.4 million pounds, compared with 15.4 million in 1988; 16.2 million in 1987; and 16 million in 1986. Average price per pound in 1989 was $1.61 from 2,140,000 goats clipped for a total value of $24,794,000. This compared with $1.94 per pound in 1988 from 2 million goats clipped and total value of $29,876,000; $2.63 per pound from 2 million goats and total value of $42,606,000 in 1987; and $2.51 per pound from 2 million goats and total value of $40,160,000 in 1986.

Nearly half of the world's mohair and 97 percent of the U.S. clip are produced in Texas. The leading Texas counties in Angora goats are **Edwards, Val Verde, Sutton, Crockett, Uvalde, Terrell, Kimble, Mason, Mills and Kinney.**

Sheep and Wool

Sheep and lambs in Texas numbered 2 million head on Jan. 1, 1991, down from 2,090,000 in 1990; 1,870,000 in 1989; 2,040,000 in 1988; and 2,050,000 in 1987.

All sheep were valued at $108,000,000 or $54 per head on Jan. 1, 1991, compared with $134,805,000 or $64.50 per head in 1990; $137,445,000 or $73.50 per head in 1989; $155,040,000 or $76 per head in 1988; and $133,250,000 or $65 per head in 1987.

Breeding ewes one year old and over numbered 1,420,000 in 1991; 1,490,000 in 1990; 1,250,000 in 1989; 1,370,000 in 1988; and 1,400,000 in 1987.

Ewe lambs totaled 240,000 head in 1991; 250,000 in 1990; 270,000 in 1989; 310,000 in 1988; and 290,000 in 1987. Lambs saved numbered 1,150,000 in 1991; 1,150,000 in 1990; 1,150,-000 in 1989; and 950,000 in 1988. Early lamb crop estimates were discontinued in January 1983.

Sheep operations in Texas were estimated to be 8,200 in 1990, 8,200 in 1989, and 8,400 in 1988.

Texas **wool production** in 1989 was 18 million pounds from 2,550,000 sheep. Value totaled $27,180,000 or $1.51 per pound. This compared with 18.2 million pounds of wool valued at $35,854,000 or $1.97 per pound in 1988; 16.4 million pounds from 2,250,000 sheep valued at $19,844,000 or $1.21 per pound in 1987; and 16.4 million pounds valued at $13,284,000 or 81 cents per pound in 1986.

Most sheep in Texas are concentrated in the **Edwards Plateau** area of West Central Texas and nearby counties. The 10 leading counties are **Val Verde, Crock-** ett, Castro, Bailey, Kinney, Coryell, Schleicher, McCulloch, Pecos and Waller. Sheep production is largely dual purpose, for both wool and lamb production.

San Angelo long has been the **largest sheep and wool market in the nation** and the center for wool and mohair warehouses, scouring plants and slaughterhouses.

Horses

Nationally, Texas ranks as one of the leading states in horse numbers and is the headquarters for many **national horse organizations.** The largest single horse-breed registry in America, the American Quarter Horse Association, has its headquarters in Amarillo. The National Cutting Horse Association and the American Paint Horse Association are both located in Fort Worth. In addition to these national associations, Texas also has active state associations that include Palominos, Arabians, Thoroughbreds, Appaloosa and Ponies.

Horses are still used to support the state's giant beef cattle and sheep industries. Horses are most abundant in the heavily populated areas of the state. Participation activities consist of horse shows, trail rides, play days, rodeos, polo and horse racing. Residential subdivisions have been developed within the state with facilities for urban and suburban horse owners.

The number of horses in Texas is expected to increase because of legislative approval of parimutuel betting in November 1987.

Poultry and Eggs

Poultry and eggs annually contribute about 6 percent to the average yearly cash receipts of Texas farmers. In 1988, Texas ranked 7th among the states in broilers produced, 7th in eggs produced, and 10th in hens.

In 1989, cash receipts to Texas producers from the production of **broilers and eggs** totaled $706,039,000, compared with $573,343,000 in 1988; $528,962,000 in 1987; and $565,620,000 in 1986.

Gross income from **eggs** was $223,295,000 in 1989, compared with $181,882,000 in 1988; $191,744,000 in 1987; and $196,267,000 in 1986. Eggs produced in 1989 totaled 3.3 billion eggs, compared with 3.36 billion in 1988; 3.42 billion in 1987; and 3.36 billion in 1986. Average price received per dozen in 1989 was 81.1 cents, compared with 64.9 cents in 1988; 67.2 cents in 1987, and 70.2 cents in 1986. Leading egg-producing counties are **Angelina, Camp, Brazos, Fayette, Lavaca, Gonzales, Lubbock, Collin, Shelby and Garza.**

Broiler production in 1989 totaled 291,600,000 birds, compared with 266,300,000 in 1988; 259,000,000 in 1987; and 238,600,000 in 1986. Value of production from broilers in 1989 totaled $482,744,000, compared with $391,461,000 in 1988; $337,218,000 in 1987; and $369,353,000 in 1986. Price per pound averaged 38.5 cents in 1989; 35 cents in 1988; 31 cents in 1987; and 36 cents in 1986. Leading broiler-producing counties are **Camp, Caldwell, Gonzales, Nacogdoches, Panola, San Augustine, Shelby, Titus, Upshur and Wood.**

Education

Public Schools

Public school enrollment in Texas reached a peak of 3,151,659 in 1989-90, according to the **Texas Education Agency.**

The seven largest districts (listed alphabetically), which usually have more than one-fourth of the total pupil population, are: Austin, Dallas, El Paso, Fort Worth, Houston, San Antonio and Ysleta.

History of Public Education

Public education was one of the primary goals of the early settlers of Texas, who listed the failure to provide education as one of their grievances in the Texas Declaration of Independence from Mexico.

As early as 1838, President Mirabeau B. Lamar's message to the Republic of Texas Congress advocated setting aside public domain for public schools. His interest caused him to be called the "Father of Education in Texas." In 1839 Congress designated three leagues of land to support public schools for each Texas county and 50 leagues for a state university. In 1840 each county was allocated one more league of land.

The Republic, however, did not establish a public school system or university. The **1845 State Constitution** advocated public education, instructing the Legislature to designate at least 10 per cent of the tax revenue for schools. Further delay occurred until **Gov. Elisha M.**

School Districts

The following Texas Education Agency table shows the change in the types of school districts in Texas, especially the decline in common school districts.

Year	Common School Districts*	Independent School Districts	Total
1990-91	7	1,058	1,065
1989-90	7	1,061	1,068
1988-89	7	1,064	1,071
1987-88	10	1,076	1,086
1986-87	10	1,058	1,068
1985-86	10	1,053	1,063
1984-85	10	1,052	1,062
1983-84	10	1,059	1,069
1982-83	10	1,061	1,071
1981-82	12	1,087	1,099
1980-81	12	1,087	1,099
1975-76	118	1,009	1,127
1970-71	188	999	1,187
1965-66	322	1,010	1,332
1960-61	530	1,009	1,539
1955-56	849	1,008	1,857
1950-51	1,558	947	2,505
1945-46	4,461	998	5,459
1940-41	5,319	1,090	6,409
1935-36	5,984	1,015	6,999
1930-31	6,425	1,034	7,459
1910-11 (Largest Count)	8,053	546	8,599

*Districts in these columns include Rural High School Districts and Independent School Districts with less than 150 scholastics which are under the county superintendent.

Pease, on Jan. 31, 1854, signed the bill **setting up the Texas public school system.**

The public school system was made possible by setting aside $2 million out of $10 million Texas received for relinquishing its claim to land to the north and west of its present boundaries. (See **Compromise of 1850** in historical section.)

During 1854, legislation provided for state apportionment of funds based upon an annual census and required railroads which were granted land to survey alternate sections that were set aside for public school financing. The first **school census** that year showed **65,463 scholastics; state fund apportionment** was 62c per student.

When adopted in 1876, the present **Texas Constitution** provided: "All funds, lands and other property heretofore set apart and appropriated for the support of public schools; all the alternate sections of land reserved by the state of grants heretofore made or that may hereafter be made to railroads, or other corporations, of any nature whatsoever; one half of the public domain of the state, and all sums of money that may come to the state from the sale of any portion of the same shall constitute a perpetual public school fund."

Over 52,000,000 acres of the Texas public domain were allotted for school purposes. (See table, Public Lands of Texas, in chapter on State Government.)

The Constitution also provided for one fourth of occupation taxes and a poll tax of one dollar for school support, and made provisions for local taxation. No provision was made for direct ad valorem taxation for maintenance of an available school fund, but a maximum 20c state ad valorem school tax was adopted in 1883, and raised to 35c in connection with provision of free textbooks in the amendment of 1918.

In 1949, the **Gilmer-Aikin Laws** reorganized the state system of public schools by making sweeping changes in administration and financing. All schools below college level were, prior to 1984, headed by the **State Board of Education,** whose members were elected from congressional districts as set in 1981. Under the new educational reforms of 1984, a new 15-member board was appointed by the governor to replace the existing 27-member elected panel. This board appoints a **State Commissioner of Education** who is executive head of the **Texas Education Agency,** which administers the public school system. Under the law, TEA consists of (1) the State Board of Education, (2) the State Commissioner of Education, (3) the State Department of Education and (4) the State Board of Vocational Education. The personnel of the State Board of Education and the State

Board of Vocational Education is the same, the members of the State Board of Education serving ex officio as members of the State Board of Vocational Education when considering matters relating to vocational education.

The funding of Texas public school education continues to be a major issue before the Texas Legislature in the 1980s. The Sixty-fourth (1975) Legislature made major changes in the state's guaranteed **Foundation School Program** with enactment of HB 1126, which provided increased funding for salaries, operating allowance and transportation. This bill also provided state funds for compensatory education and equalization aid and revised the method for determining state aid received by school districts under the Foundation Program.

Major changes continued with the passage of SB 1 during a called special session of the Sixty-fifth (1977) Texas Legislature. The **School Tax Assessment Practices Board** was created to determine, on a statewide basis, the property wealth of school districts. The board was also charged with upgrading professional standards for appraising and assessing school district property taxes.

The Sixty-sixth (1979) Legislature passed SB 350, which increased most categorical programs, including salaries, and lowered the rate used in calculating the districts' share of the Foundation School Program cost. In addition, SB 621 required the establishment of countywide appraisal districts.

House Bill 1060, which was enacted by the 66th Texas Legislature, implements provisions of the Constitutional Amendment (HJR-1) approved by voters in November, 1978. This bill provides for state payments to school districts to replace taxes lost because of state-mandated reduction of ad valorem tax base due to residential timber and agricultural land.

The Sixty-seventh (1981) Legislature passed HB 656, which increased most categorical programs, including salaries, and lowered the rate used in calculating the district's share of the Foundation School Program cost.

Members of the 68th Texas Legislature, in special session, forged a historic education reform bill in the summer of 1984. Known as House Bill 72, the reform action, with a $2.8 billion price tag, came in response to a growing national and statewide concern over declining test scores and deteriorating general literacy in America's schoolchildren over two decades, a deterioration generally reflected in Texas test scores.

The nationally recognized Texas school reform act was formulated by a Select Committee headed by Dallas computer magnate Ross Perot and appointed by

Permanent School Fund

The following table, from the Texas Education Agency, Austin, shows the total value of the **Texas permanent school fund** and the income earned by years since the fund was established.

Year	*Total Investment Fund	Total Income Earned by P.S.F.
1854	$2,000,000.00	...
1880	3,542,126.00	...
1898	7,588,712.00	...
1899	8,420,588.85	$691,594.85
1900	9,102,872.75	783,142.08
1970	842,217,721.05	34,762,955.32
1971	884,680,139.49	38,107,272.60
1972	927,690,294.64	40,765,514.29
1973	977,970,414.00	44,462,028.00
1974	1,081,492,087.81	50,898,130.46
1975	1,176,441,741.70	61,050,083.01
1976	1,318,313,917.99	67,573,179.43
1977	1,546,151,708.00	84,817,986.33
1978	1,815,364,050.00	104,618,901.41
1979	2,062,710,780.00	130,629,766.02
1980	2,464,579,397.00	163,000,000.00
1981	2,986,784,696.12	217,695,444.70
1982	3,532,013,181.39	270,648,812.76
1983	3,959,923,160.00	698,567,452.76
1984	4,496,345,276.00	359,080,872.00
1985	5,095,802,979.00	417,080,383.00
1986	5,792,619,707.00	†652,030,987.00
1987	6,143,198,029.00	551,417,861.00
1988	6,493,070,622.00	572,665,253.00
1989	6,873,610,771.00	614,786,823.00
1990	7,328,172,096.00	674,634,994.00

*Includes cash—bonds at par and stocks at book value.
†Includes non-recurring extraordinary income of $140,246,302.

Gov. Mark White at the behest of Lt. Gov. Bill Hobby and Speaker of the House Gib Lewis, following failures by the Legislature — and resistance from the voters — to support teacher pay raises or additional public school funding without education reform.

The result was the reform bill of 1984 that provided equalization formulas for state financial aid for public education, raised teacher salaries and tied those raises to teacher performance, and introduced more stringent teacher certification and initiated competency testing for both entering and existing teachers.

Academic achievement was set as a priority in public education with stricter attendance rules, adoption of a no-pass, no-play rule prohibiting students scoring below 70 in each class from participating in sports and other extracurricular activities, and national norm

Scholastic Population, Apportionment, 1854-1990

The Texas public school system was established and the permanent school fund set up by the Fifth Legislature, Jan. 31, 1854. The first apportionment by the state to public schools was for the school year 1854-55.

Years	Scholastic Age	Scholastic Population	Apportionment Per Capita	Amount
1854-55	...	65,463	$0.62	...
1872-73	...	229,568	1.81	$405,518
1880-81	...	266,439	3.00	679,317
1890-91	8-16	545,616	4.00	2,182,464
1900-01	8-17	706,546	4.25	3,002,820
1910-11	7-17	949,006	6.25	5,931,287
1920-21	7-18	1,271,157	14.50	18,431,716
1930-31	6-17	1,562,427	17.50	27,342,473
1940-41	6-17	1,536,910	22.50	34,580,475
1950-51	6-17	1,566,610	60.00	93,996,600
1960-61	6-17	2,249,157	73.00	164,188,461
1970-71	6-17	2,800,500	119.45	287,159,758
1979-80	6-17	3,012,210	309.00	797,805,346
1980-81	...	...	397.00	3,042,476
1981-82	...	...	457.00	3,089,788
1982-83	...	...	525.00	1,401,767,656
1983-84	...	...	480.00	1,304,921,553
1984-85	...	...	225.00	627,870,430
1985-86	...	...	280.00	807,680,617
1986-87	...	...	280.00	821,854,348
1987-88	...	...	274.00	817,876,984
1988-89	...	...	295.00	882,999,623
1989-90	...	...	303.00	917,608,395

Scholastic age (6-17 until 1979-80) was determined as follows: A child having attained the age of 6 before Sept. 1 was enumerated for the school year beginning on that date. One having attained the age of 18 prior to Sept. 1 was excluded from the school census. There is no longer a school census. Age requirements are generally from 5 to 21, although for special education, ages range from birth through age 22.

Texas School Salaries

Year	Average Annual Salary, Common School Districts	Average Annual Salary, Independent School Districts	Average Annual Salary, State
1872-73	...	...	$210.00
1886-87	$218.27	$502.09	244.76
1899-1900	219.05	474.84	260.26
1910-11	320.57	514.22	391.21
1920-21	699.48	1,021.76	895.20
1930-31	781.30	1,274.00	1,079.07
*1940-41	893.00	1,269.00	1,150.00
1950-51	2,967.19	3,250.78	3,215.93
1960-61	...	...	4,734.00
1970-71	...	...	8,486.00
1980-81	...	...	16,724
1981-82	...	...	18,682
1982-83	...	...	20,745
1983-84	...	...	21,418
1984-85	...	...	24,504
1985-86	...	...	25,581
1986-87	...	...	24,890
1987-88	...	...	24,179
1988-89	...	...	24,876
1989-90	...	...	25,896

*Salaries of both white and black teachers included beginning with the school year, 1940-41. Only white teachers' salaries included prior to that year.

testing through the grades to assure parents of individual schools' performance through a common frame of reference.

A new 10-member oversight panel, the **Legislative Education Board,** would review all aspects of state education policy and school finance.

Higher academic standards had been enacted by the 67th Legislature under H.B. 246 in 1981, which established a statewide curriculum standard for all grades. The reforms of 1984, however, carried a broader price tag and were supported by legislative vote to increase a host of goods, services, gasoline and business franchise taxes — an action that would not have been possible without the education reforms.

Texas has two types of **school districts,** independent and common, each administering local affairs through a board of trustees. Independent school districts deal directly with Texas Education Agency; common districts are supervised by elected county school superintendents and county trustees.

Ad valorem taxes provided most of the financial support for schools by school districts until Jan. 1, 1975, when the 5 cents ad valorem tax for the **available school fund** was abolished. This tax also was a significant source of state support, at a rate not to exceed 35c on each $100 in real and personal property but a constitutional amendment adopted in 1968 provided for gradual phasing out of state ad valorem taxes for all purposes except the tax levied by Sec. 17, Art. VII, for certain institutions of higher learning. Sec. 17, Art. VII, was deleted by a Constitutional amendment adopted in an election Nov. 2, 1982. Other state support comes from designated percentages of several taxes and from the **Permanent School Fund.**

Enrollment By Grades

(Average Daily Attendance)

1989-90	3,151,659	1982-83	2,725,009
1988-89	3,098,092	1981-82	2,675,168
1987-88	3,057,147	1980-81	2,639,794
1986-87	3,039,416	1979-80	2,605,174
1985-86	2,933,081	1978-79	2,589,980

1984-85	2,924,000	1977-78	2,576,552
1983-84	2,745,338	1976-77	2,555,294

The following table shows refined average daily attendance by grades for the school years of 1987-88, 1988-89 and 1989-90.

	1987-88	1988-89	1989-90
Pre-Kindergarten	63,696.77	69,221.32	72,218.22
Kindergarten	189,186.56	190,681.62	190,583.77
Grade 1	283,768.19	287,884.58	290,849.81
Grade 2	261,478.36	265,391.71	268,928.90
Grade 3	249,620.03	260,508.16	265,583.68
Grade 4	241,867.00	250,474.68	262,698.75
Grade 5	237,375.81	241,307.57	251,243.65
Grade 6	232,254.12	239,405.21	244,782.30
Grade 7	235,348.42	234,256.20	242,683.13
Grade 8	224,959.41	227,672.92	228,839.26
Grade 9	247,813.82	246,888.78	254,221.44
Grade 10	213,404.18	208,955.03	210,826.84
Grade 11	186,580.76	189,265.84	187,296.13
Grade 12	178,259.28	186,178.58	180,922.94
TOTAL	3,057,147.48	3,098,092.21	3,151,658.78

High School Graduates

Source: Texas Education Agency

1989-90	172,480	1971-72	153,633
1988-89	176,951	1970-71	148,105
1987-88	171,436	1969-70	139,046
1986-87	168,430	1968-69	135,344
1985-86	161,150	1967-68	127,492
1984-85	159,343	1966-67	125,742
1983-84	161,580	1965-66	121,084
1982-83	168,897	1964-65	121,759
1981-82	172,099	1963-64	97,158
1980-81	171,665	1962-63	87,640
1979-80	171,449	1961-62	86,518
1978-79	168,518	1960-61	85,102
1977-78	167,983	1959-60	76,500
1976-77	163,574	1958-59	71,855
1975-76	159,855	1957-58	67,778
1974-75	159,487	1956-57	65,132
1973-74	156,984	1955-56	64,291
1972-73	152,172	1954-55	60,141
		1953-54	56,363

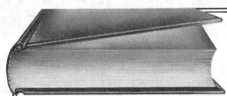

School Spending by County, 1989-90

School finance reform has been an emotional and political issue in Texas for a decade. Legislators, judges, citizen groups and state agencies have searched for equitable and politically acceptable methods of distributing school aid between rich and poor school districts.

The following breakdown of school information, ranging from student population and ethnicity to revenues and spending for the state's 1,058 school districts, gives a statistical view of the state aid picture as it existed in 1989-90, the last full year for which the information was available when the Almanac went to press.

Financial and student information was provided by school district by the Texas Education Agency, and the Texas Almanac staff compiled the totals for each county that are printed in bold-face type.

Compiled by the staff of the Texas Almanac from information provided by the Texas Education Agency.

County/ISD	Districts	Students	% White**	% Hispanic**	% Black**	% Asian**	% American Indian**	Total Revenue	% Local***	% Other***	% State***	% Federal***	Revenue Per Pupil	Total Spending	Spending Per Pupil
Anderson	7	**8,456**	73.9	6.3	19.5	0.3	†	**32,448,428**	34.9	6.3	53.3	5.5	**3,837**	**38,134,173**	**4,510**
Cayuga		553	86.6	3.4	9.0	0.9	0.0	2,541,643	50.1	4.3	43.1	2.5	4,596	2,442,669	4,417
Elkhart		880	93.8	0.7	5.6	0.0	0.0	3,077,690	27.1	6.6	62.0	4.3	3,497	3,961,349	4,502
Frankston		730	83.7	1.5	14.8	0.0	0.0	3,564,326	40.5	9.2	46.5	3.7	4,883	3,926,312	5,379
Neches		210	81.9	0.5	17.6	0.0	0.0	1,052,248	59.0	5.7	28.4	6.9	5,011	1,266,483	6,031
Palestine		4,091	59.0	11.1	29.6	0.3	†	15,269,440	34.6	5.1	53.2	7.1	3,732	19,101,492	4,669
Slocum		313	97.4	0.3	2.2	0.0	0.0	1,252,172	30.1	10.1	54.5	5.3	4,001	1,313,125	4,195
Westwood		1,679	85.9	2.4	11.0	0.5	0.2	5,690,909	26.2	7.8	61.9	4.1	3,389	6,122,743	3,647
Andrews	1	**3,683**	56.2	40.2	2.0	1.2	0.4	**17,260,801**	84.3	6.5	5.2	4.0	**4,687**	**18,536,154**	**5,033**
Andrews		3,683	56.2	40.2	2.0	1.2	0.4	17,260,801	84.3	6.5	5.2	4.0	4,687	18,536,154	5,033
Angelina	6	**14,630**	66.3	12.5	20.6	0.4	0.1	**52,966,692**	29.6	8.2	53.9	8.3	**3,620**	**60,238,133**	**4,117**
Central		1,203	92.9	3.3	3.7	0.2	0.0	3,996,903	15.9	5.0	74.8	4.3	3,322	4,000,985	3,326
Diboll		2,020	42.1	37.0	20.8	0.0	†	9,186,651	20.1	21.6	47.1	11.2	4,548	14,671,012	7,263
Hudson		1,657	87.4	8.7	3.7	0.1	0.1	5,346,281	22.1	5.5	67.6	4.7	3,226	5,408,401	3,264
Huntington		1,313	94.1	1.2	4.6	0.1	0.0	4,002,933	18.3	4.7	72.9	4.0	3,049	4,917,753	3,745
Lufkin		8,066	58.0	11.0	30.2	0.7	0.1	28,821,889	37.7	5.3	47.8	9.2	3,573	29,593,302	3,669
Zavalla		371	99.7	0.3	0.0	0.0	0.0	1,612,035	26.2	8.9	57.6	7.3	4,345	1,646,680	4,438
Aransas	1	**2,832**	58.8	29.7	1.8	9.7	0.0	**11,292,041**	68.2	5.4	20.4	6.0	**3,987**	**11,596,151**	**4,095**
Aransas County		2,832	58.8	29.7	1.8	9.7	0.0	11,292,041	68.2	5.4	20.4	6.0	3,987	11,596,151	4,095
Archer	4	**1,743**	98.9	0.7	0.4	0.0	0.0	**6,704,936**	41.4	6.0	50.2	2.4	**3,847**	**6,938,926**	**3,981**
Archer City		554	99.5	0.4	0.2	0.0	0.0	2,258,683	45.5	4.0	48.2	2.4	4,077	2,324,277	4,195
Holliday		796	99.5	0.3	0.3	0.0	0.0	2,809,100	37.2	7.4	53.0	2.4	3,529	2,885,839	3,625
Megargel		85	95.3	0.0	4.7	0.0	0.0	521,482	72.8	1.7	22.4	3.1	6,135	605,275	7,121
Windthorst		308	97.4	2.6	0.0	0.0	0.0	1,115,671	29.2	8.5	60.1	2.2	3,622	1,123,535	3,648
Armstrong	1	**386**	95.9	3.9	0.0	0.3	0.0	**1,568,763**	37.0	4.0	56.8	2.2	**4,064**	**1,604,971**	**4,158**
Claude		386	95.9	3.9	0.0	0.3	0.0	1,568,763	37.0	4.0	56.8	2.2	4,064	1,604,971	4,158
Atascosa	5	**7,036**	39.5	59.8	0.4	0.2	†	**24,829,042**	25.2	4.3	60.3	10.2	**3,529**	**26,059,457**	**3,704**
Charlotte		504	20.4	79.6	0.0	0.0	0.0	2,177,867	26.6	3.1	60.7	9.7	4,321	2,169,040	4,304
Jourdanton		1,131	48.4	50.8	0.6	0.2	0.0	4,477,220	61.6	5.3	25.3	7.9	3,959	4,979,189	4,402
Lytle		975	38.6	60.9	0.1	0.4	0.0	3,199,867	13.1	3.9	75.7	7.3	3,282	3,363,422	3,450
Pleasanton		2,945	47.7	51.3	0.7	0.3	0.0	9,826,091	19.8	4.3	65.5	10.4	3,337	10,097,176	3,429
Poteet		1,481	23.4	76.4	0.1	0.1	0.1	5,147,997	10.9	4.0	71.3	13.8	3,476	5,450,630	3,680
Austin	3	**4,335**	68.6	13.8	17.2	0.3	0.0	**16,538,312**	48.8	6.8	40.3	4.1	**3,815**	**17,342,458**	**4,001**
Bellville		1,646	74.5	5.7	19.7	0.1	0.0	6,533,506	49.6	7.9	38.7	3.9	3,969	6,882,322	4,181
Sealy		1,920	64.7	18.2	16.6	0.5	0.0	6,254,541	45.3	6.2	43.9	4.5	3,258	6,564,560	3,419
Wallis-Orchard		769	65.7	20.5	13.4	0.4	0.0	3,750,265	53.3	6.1	37.1	3.6	4,877	3,895,576	5,066
Bailey	2	**1,814**	44.6	53.2	2.0	0.1	0.1	**7,321,861**	31.5	6.1	50.4	12.0	**4,036**	**7,859,772**	**4,333**
Muleshoe		1,663	45.7	51.9	2.2	0.1	0.1	6,344,249	28.7	6.3	52.9	12.1	3,815	6,704,274	4,031
Three Way		151	32.5	67.5	0.0	0.0	0.0	977,612	49.7	4.7	34.0	11.5	6,474	1,155,498	7,652
Bandera	2	**1,737**	83.9	15.1	0.7	0.2	0.1	**6,427,934**	54.2	8.5	32.9	4.4	**3,701**	**7,263,346**	**4,182**
Bandera		1,458	82.1	17.1	0.6	0.2	0.0	5,100,047	58.8	8.7	29.1	3.4	3,498	5,942,590	4,076
Medina		279	93.2	4.7	1.4	0.4	0.4	1,327,887	36.4	7.7	47.7	8.2	4,759	1,320,756	4,734
Bastrop	4	**7,742**	62.4	23.3	13.8	0.3	0.3	**28,455,419**	35.3	5.0	52.7	7.0	**3,675**	**29,725,445**	**3,840**
Bastrop		4,249	66.1	21.3	11.9	0.4	0.4	14,947,808	33.7	5.8	53.1	7.4	3,518	15,796,293	3,718
Elgin		2,138	50.3	31.8	17.6	0.1	0.2	7,996,374	35.9	4.8	52.4	7.0	3,740	8,122,969	3,799
McDade		80	90.0	6.3	3.8	0.0	0.0	406,405	58.4	1.6	32.7	7.3	5,080	499,615	6,245
Smithville		1,275	68.5	17.1	14.1	0.2	0.1	5,104,832	37.3	3.3	53.5	5.9	4,004	5,306,568	4,162
Baylor	1	**711**	77.6	15.0	6.8	0.4	0.1	**3,396,918**	34.9	13.5	47.9	3.7	**4,778**	**6,568,555**	**9,238**
Seymour		711	77.6	15.0	6.8	0.4	0.1	3,396,918	34.9	13.5	47.9	3.7	4,778	6,568,555	9,238
Bee	4	**5,437**	34.2	61.9	3.3	0.7	0.0	**20,495,101**	22.8	3.6	60.0	13.6	**3,770**	**21,303,745**	**3,918**
Beeville		4,283	31.1	64.1	4.0	0.8	0.0	15,649,398	19.1	3.5	62.3	15.1	3,654	16,256,763	3,796
Pawnee		111	27.9	72.1	0.0	0.0	0.0	703,730	53.7	5.7	27.8	12.9	6,340	703,730	6,340
Pettus		432	53.7	46.1	0.2	0.0	0.0	1,924,701	39.4	3.3	49.0	8.2	4,455	2,081,409	4,818
Skidmore-Tynan		611	43.7	55.5	0.8	0.0	0.0	2,217,272	24.9	4.3	63.2	7.6	3,629	2,261,843	3,702
Bell	9	**39,804**	56.7	15.6	24.2	3.1	0.3	**139,384,158**	22.4	4.5	57.4	15.7	**3,502**	**147,160,209**	**3,697**
Academy		774	87.2	12.4	0.3	0.1	0.0	2,950,019	21.4	9.3	66.2	3.0	3,811	2,951,198	3,813
Bartlett		398	48.0	32.4	19.3	0.3	0.0	1,733,043	23.8	4.3	63.6	8.3	4,354	1,694,228	4,257
Belton		4,980	75.0	18.5	5.1	0.9	0.5	15,953,137	30.1	5.0	57.0	7.9	3,203	16,214,767	3,256
Holland		463	73.4	15.3	10.6	0.6	0.0	1,966,708	18.8	2.8	71.9	6.5	4,248	1,952,076	4,216
Killeen		22,854	48.6	14.3	31.9	4.7	0.5	78,903,216	12.3	4.1	61.5	22.1	3,452	85,054,562	3,722
Rogers		715	82.0	15.8	2.0	0.0	0.3	2,640,444	19.7	5.8	70.8	3.7	3,693	2,671,433	3,736
Salado		533	89.5	9.8	0.6	0.2	0.0	2,162,668	54.4	4.7	38.3	2.6	4,058	2,237,585	4,198
Temple		8,052	57.3	17.6	24.0	1.0	†	29,414,246	43.5	4.7	43.3	8.5	3,653	30,592,468	3,799
Troy		1,035	83.2	15.1	1.4	0.2	0.1	3,660,677	23.8	7.1	66.1	2.9	3,537	3,791,892	3,664

County/ISD	Districts	Students	% White**	% Hispanic**	% Black**	% Asian**	% American Indian**	Total Revenue	% Local***	% Other***	% State***	% Federal**	Revenue Per Pupil	Total Spending	Spending Per Pupil
Bexar	15	229,385	31.3	60.1	7.5	1.0	†	848,442,403	37.3	4.5	48.4	9.8	3,699	929,180,653	4,051
Alamo Heights		3,470	71.2	25.4	2.7	0.6	0.1	16,799,859	83.2	8.5	5.3	3.0	4,841	17,180,412	4,951
East Central		5,771	55.2	33.1	11.3	0.4	†	20,369,067	28.7	6.4	57.8	7.0	3,530	20,880,010	3,618
Edgewood		15,485	1.4	96.0	2.4	0.2	†	56,927,045	6.8	2.0	75.3	15.9	3,676	62,511,452	4,037
Fort Sam Houston		1,557	53.3	17.3	26.7	2.4	0.2	6,538,148	0.0	6.8	46.6	46.5	4,199	8,653,249	5,558
Harlandale		15,039	10.0	89.1	0.4	0.4	0.1	56,613,736	13.0	4.2	70.3	12.5	3,764	57,195,820	3,803
Judson		12,883	56.6	25.3	15.2	2.7	0.2	43,556,544	48.3	4.9	41.7	5.1	3,381	48,118,341	3,735
Lackland		952	63.6	15.1	17.9	3.4	0.1	3,588,534	0.0	6.1	52.2	41.7	3,769	4,712,102	4,950
North East		39,622	62.5	28.8	6.7	1.9	†	143,384,560	63.4	7.6	26.2	2.8	3,619	161,663,269	4,080
Northside		49,447	45.3	47.1	6.1	1.5	0.1	172,359,530	51.5	5.4	37.2	5.8	3,486	210,320,424	4,253
Randolph Field		1,160	73.2	9.9	13.9	3.0	0.0	4,721,925	0.0	6.2	48.7	45.1	4,071	5,947,988	5,128
San Antonio		61,156	6.7	81.1	11.8	0.4	†	244,630,805	30.4	2.3	53.8	13.5	4,000	245,932,477	4,021
So. San Antonio		10,692	6.9	91.2	1.6	0.2	†	38,027,422	12.1	1.8	72.0	14.1	3,557	38,939,476	3,642
Somerset		1,902	33.0	66.5	0.4	0.1	0.0	6,872,650	15.0	4.1	70.9	10.0	3,613	7,510,612	3,949
Southside		2,819	24.9	74.4	0.4	0.2	†	10,082,603	16.7	2.4	68.5	12.3	3,577	10,283,536	3,648
Southwest		7,430	20.0	74.7	4.7	0.6	0.0	23,969,975	13.9	6.2	72.7	7.2	3,226	29,331,485	3,948
Blanco	2	1,151	78.2	20.8	0.7	0.3	0.0	4,511,989	48.0	4.3	44.5	3.2	3,920	4,816,175	4,184
Blanco		633	73.3	24.8	1.3	0.6	0.0	2,357,867	41.4	4.5	50.1	4.0	3,725	2,317,430	3,661
Johnson City		518	84.2	15.8	0.0	0.0	0.0	2,154,122	55.2	4.1	38.4	2.3	4,159	2,498,745	4,824
Borden	1	197	80.2	19.3	0.0	0.0	0.5	1,618,793	81.6	12.8	3.5	2.1	8,217	1,860,352	9,443
Borden County		197	80.2	19.3	0.0	0.0	0.5	1,618,793	81.6	12.8	3.5	2.1	8,217	1,860,352	9,443
Bosque	8	2,648	81.6	14.5	3.7	0.2	†	10,525,945	34.9	6.2	52.5	6.5	3,975	10,722,090	4,049
Clifton		916	81.0	12.3	6.1	0.4	0.1	3,133,562	42.3	5.2	47.3	5.3	3,421	3,189,141	3,482
Cranfills Gap		125	90.4	9.6	0.0	0.0	0.0	644,714	43.3	5.4	47.0	4.3	5,158	652,845	5,223
Iredell		115	91.3	7.8	0.0	0.9	0.0	576,389	35.9	6.3	53.8	4.0	5,012	571,329	4,968
Kopperl		186	93.5	6.5	0.0	0.0	0.0	836,609	47.2	6.6	42.1	4.0	4,498	922,332	4,959
Meridian		454	76.9	20.9	2.2	0.0	0.0	1,572,074	27.7	5.4	61.3	5.6	3,463	1,629,447	3,589
Morgan		154	61.0	39.0	0.0	0.0	0.0	757,279	27.1	14.9	45.3	12.8	4,917	714,092	4,637
Valley Mills		488	87.3	6.1	6.6	0.0	0.0	2,293,907	29.7	4.8	57.0	8.6	4,701	2,314,519	4,743
Walnut Springs		210	74.8	25.2	0.0	0.0	0.0	711,411	20.9	7.4	65.0	6.7	3,388	728,385	3,469
Bowie	13	16,267	68.3	0.9	30.2	0.4	0.2	55,366,481	28.0	5.5	58.6	7.8	3,404	60,483,124	3,718
DeKalb		1,027	63.0	1.7	35.2	0.0	0.2	3,576,383	15.3	6.9	70.2	7.6	3,482	4,250,074	4,138
Hooks		1,050	77.0	0.8	21.3	0.8	0.2	3,349,022	13.4	7.6	71.9	7.2	3,190	4,012,397	3,821
Hubbard		62	100	0.0	0.0	0.0	0.0	242,668	22.8	3.7	71.5	1.9	3,914	241,972	3,903
Leary		157	87.3	0.0	12.7	0.0	0.0	493,678	15.1	4.5	76.5	3.9	3,144	518,019	3,299
Liberty-Eylau		2,822	56.9	0.4	42.3	0.2	0.3	8,798,929	19.7	6.5	63.5	10.3	3,118	10,443,120	3,701
Malta		61	100	0.0	0.0	0.0	0.0	240,392	21.5	4.4	72.5	1.6	3,941	257,412	4,220
Maud		405	83.5	0.2	15.8	0.0	0.5	1,540,402	11.4	5.6	73.8	9.2	3,803	1,708,025	4,217
New Boston		1,702	72.7	1.5	24.9	0.2	0.7	5,876,881	18.3	5.0	65.5	11.3	3,453	6,599,420	3,877
Pleasant Grove		1,926	92.0	2.3	4.5	1.0	0.3	6,096,772	40.4	7.5	50.1	2.0	3,166	6,388,371	3,317
Red Lick		254	100	0.0	0.0	0.0	0.0	856,056	27.1	8.0	62.2	2.8	3,370	874,081	3,441
Redwater		831	89.4	1.4	8.8	0.1	0.2	2,571,124	15.1	7.1	74.2	3.6	3,094	2,677,243	3,222
Simms		491	100	0.0	0.0	0.0	0.0	1,716,132	16.4	5.8	71.2	6.6	3,495	1,765,482	3,596
Texarkana		5,479	53.9	0.6	44.9	0.5	0.1	20,008,042	40.0	3.7	47.6	8.7	3,652	20,747,508	3,787
Brazoria	8	40,445	68.7	22.0	8.1	1.1	0.1	150,437,984	56.4	6.3	33.4	3.9	3,720	164,187,971	4,060
Alvin		9,495	71.6	24.9	2.5	0.9	0.1	30,523,026	35.6	5.7	54.8	3.9	3,215	28,690,249	3,022
Angleton		6,079	64.0	20.8	14.2	0.9	0.1	23,274,702	58.5	12.1	25.0	4.4	3,829	23,304,706	3,834
Brazosport		11,747	63.2	27.5	8.1	1.2	0.1	45,247,818	71.1	4.6	19.5	4.7	3,852	47,450,886	4,039
Columbia Brazoria		3,705	73.1	11.7	15.0	0.1	†	13,313,384	48.6	4.6	42.2	4.6	3,593	14,986,327	4,045
Damon		147	69.4	27.9	2.7	0.0	0.0	560,076	52.8	5.2	35.7	6.2	3,810	589,651	4,011
Danbury		597	84.6	12.2	2.8	0.3	0.0	2,249,041	45.8	3.5	49.2	1.5	3,767	2,643,605	4,428
Pearland		6,468	75.2	19.4	2.8	2.5	0.0	24,626,628	47.9	5.9	43.3	2.8	3,807	35,311,172	5,459
Sweeny		2,207	67.9	11.4	20.3	0.2	0.2	10,643,309	81.5	5.6	12.0	1.0	4,823	11,211,375	5,080
Brazos	2	16,468	59.0	18.8	20.1	2.1	0.1	63,760,960	49.9	7.7	36.1	6.4	3,872	88,871,843	5,397
Bryan		11,200	51.8	24.1	23.6	0.5	0.1	40,381,847	40.0	7.8	44.8	7.5	3,606	51,711,978	4,617
College Station		5,268	74.2	7.5	12.8	5.4	0.1	23,379,113	67.0	7.6	21.0	4.4	4,438	37,159,865	7,054
Brewster	4	1,464	40.9	58.3	0.6	0.1	0.1	5,915,198	34.2	2.0	52.9	10.8	4,040	6,056,962	4,137
Alpine		1,185	44.9	54.3	0.6	0.1	0.2	4,443,542	33.6	2.0	53.9	10.4	3,750	4,536,883	3,829
Marathon		162	22.2	77.8	0.0	0.0	0.0	705,038	45.5	2.5	48.2	3.8	4,352	761,234	4,699
San Vicente		31	41.9	54.8	3.2	0.0	0.0	339,649	11.9	3.4	67.3	17.4	10,956	339,449	10,950
Terlingua*		86	20.9	77.9	1.2	0.0	0.0	426,969	40.0	0.0	38.6	21.4	4,965	419,396	4,877
Briscoe	1	248	68.5	29.8	1.6	0.0	0.0	1,159,622	34.5	4.0	57.6	3.9	4,676	1,205,511	4,861
Silverton		248	68.5	29.8	1.6	0.0	0.0	1,159,622	34.5	4.0	57.6	3.9	4,676	1,205,511	4,861
Brooks	1	2,051	8.1	91.7	0.0	0.1	0.0	8,248,096	50.7	4.7	34.4	10.2	4,021	9,030,199	4,403
Brooks		2,051	8.1	91.7	0.0	0.1	0.0	8,248,096	50.7	4.7	34.4	10.2	4,021	9,030,199	4,403
Brown	7	6,705	78.6	14.9	6.0	0.3	0.3	25,159,333	35.2	5.7	52.0	7.1	3,752	26,474,400	3,949
Bangs		892	77.6	11.0	11.0	0.0	0.4	3,606,282	33.9	5.4	53.1	7.6	4,043	3,884,205	4,354
Blanket		165	86.1	13.9	0.0	0.0	0.0	821,731	24.9	8.6	58.8	7.6	4,980	897,787	5,441
Brookesmith		150	84.7	13.3	0.0	0.0	2.0	577,291	28.0	6.3	63.5	2.2	3,849	675,904	4,506
Brownwood		4,042	73.5	18.5	7.4	0.3	0.2	14,777,697	38.1	5.1	47.9	8.9	3,656	15,155,444	3,749
Early		1,053	91.1	8.0	0.6	0.3	0.1	3,816,896	27.7	6.6	60.4	5.4	3,625	4,172,431	3,962
May		249	95.2	4.8	0.0	0.0	0.0	995,838	44.3	6.9	46.2	2.6	3,999	1,084,538	4,356
Zephyr		154	90.3	9.7	0.0	0.0	0.0	563,598	17.3	7.7	72.3	2.7	3,660	606,091	3,936
Burleson	3	2,777	57.4	16.7	25.8	0.1	†	11,127,785	42.6	4.4	45.4	7.6	4,007	12,091,594	4,354
Caldwell		1,621	65.9	18.1	15.8	0.1	0.0	6,591,798	41.4	4.9	43.8	9.9	4,067	7,291,003	4,498
Snook		503	42.9	15.5	41.6	0.0	0.0	2,246,436	40.5	2.3	51.0	6.3	4,466	2,293,424	4,559
Somerville		653	47.3	14.1	38.4	0.0	0.2	2,289,551	47.9	4.9	39.4	7.7	3,506	2,507,167	3,839
Burnet	2	4,236	80.8	16.9	1.9	0.2	0.2	18,340,004	62.3	5.1	26.0	6.7	4,330	19,671,806	4,644
Burnet Cons		1,997	82.7	15.7	1.4	0.2	0.1	8,346,319	55.8	4.4	31.4	8.4	4,179	8,602,510	4,308
Marble Falls		2,239	79.1	18.0	2.4	0.2	0.2	9,993,685	67.8	5.6	21.4	5.2	4,463	11,069,296	4,944

County/ISD	Districts	Students	% White**	% Hispanic**	% Black**	% Asian**	% American Indian**	Total Revenue	% Local***	% Other***	% State***	% Federal***	Revenue Per Pupil	Total Spending	Spending Per Pupil
Caldwell	3	4,927	45.6	44.0	10.3	0.1	†	17,991,403	25.1	5.7	59.8	9.3	3,652	18,235,611	3,701
Lockhart		3,333	44.7	45.9	9.2	0.1	†	12,020,534	24.9	5.4	59.8	9.9	3,607	12,116,128	3,635
Luling		1,385	46.3	41.6	12.1	0.0	0.1	5,021,591	23.4	7.0	61.4	8.2	3,626	5,168,819	3,732
Prairie Lea		209	55.0	29.2	15.8	0.0	0.0	949,278	37.3	3.5	51.6	7.5	4,542	950,664	4,549
Calhoun	1	4,202	47.4	45.4	3.3	4.0	0.0	20,061,355	73.8	5.9	11.7	8.6	4,774	21,285,261	5,066
Calhoun County		4,202	47.4	45.4	3.3	4.0	0.0	20,061,355	73.8	5.9	11.7	8.6	4,774	21,285,261	5,066
Callahan	4	2,774	94.7	5.0	0.0	0.1	0.0	10,735,784	33.1	5.2	58.5	3.2	3,870	11,104,546	4,003
Baird		472	90.0	9.1	0.0	0.6	0.2	1,886,727	36.7	4.1	55.7	3.5	3,997	1,916,489	4,060
Clyde Cons		1,385	95.7	3.9	0.0	0.0	0.4	5,023,032	31.8	6.1	59.6	2.5	3,627	5,255,841	3,795
Cross Plains		447	98.2	1.8	0.0	0.0	0.0	1,911,660	23.2	3.9	68.2	4.7	4,277	1,911,861	4,277
Eula		470	92.8	7.0	0.0	0.2	0.0	1,914,365	43.1	5.2	48.6	3.0	4,073	2,020,355	4,299
Cameron	10	71,543	7.6	92.0	0.2	0.1	†	260,710,474	15.6	3.1	67.2	14.2	3,644	283,714,938	3,966
Brownsville		36,538	3.6	96.2	0.1	0.1	†	129,961,180	10.1	2.6	72.9	14.4	3,557	143,815,782	3,936
Harlingen		14,498	15.9	83.2	0.7	0.2	†	50,063,181	19.4	4.5	63.1	13.0	3,453	55,592,755	3,835
La Feria		2,216	12.3	87.5	0.1	0.1	0.0	7,867,010	11.6	3.9	69.3	15.2	3,550	8,163,449	3,684
Los Fresnos Cons		4,403	12.4	87.3	0.2	0.1	0.0	15,135,839	13.5	1.4	68.2	16.9	3,438	16,273,275	3,696
Point Isabel		2,107	19.2	80.7	0.1	0.0	0.0	9,125,217	77.3	3.1	9.2	10.4	4,331	9,312,720	4,420
Rio Hondo		1,769	6.6	93.3	0.1	0.0	0.0	5,942,764	12.6	3.0	69.4	14.9	3,359	5,979,519	3,380
San Benito Cons		7,623	4.6	95.0	0.2	0.1	0.1	27,569,498	8.9	3.0	70.8	17.2	3,617	28,600,213	3,752
Santa Maria		371	0.8	99.2	0.0	0.0	0.0	1,752,918	8.7	1.1	75.7	14.5	4,725	1,719,358	4,634
Santa Rosa		1,046	1.5	98.5	0.0	0.0	0.0	4,308,574	5.8	1.7	74.6	18.0	4,119	4,628,574	4,425
South Texas		972	11.6	87.2	0.8	0.3	0.0	8,984,293	46.3	4.9	43.9	5.0	9,243	9,629,293	9,907
Camp	1	1,991	65.3	4.8	29.8	0.0	0.0	6,480,333	29.8	5.0	57.7	7.5	3,255	6,543,283	3,286
Pittsburg		1,991	65.3	4.8	29.8	0.0	0.0	6,480,333	29.8	5.0	57.7	7.5	3,255	6,543,283	3,286
Carson	3	1,390	93.0	6.5	0.3	0.1	0.0	7,675,579	69.4	5.0	23.7	2.0	5,522	7,809,619	5,618
Groom		214	97.7	2.3	0.0	0.0	0.0	1,134,562	59.7	7.0	29.5	3.9	5,302	1,146,113	5,356
Panhandle		693	89.8	9.5	0.4	0.3	0.0	3,979,108	69.9	4.1	24.7	1.3	5,742	4,023,493	5,806
White Deer		483	95.7	4.1	0.2	0.0	0.0	2,561,909	72.8	5.5	19.5	2.2	5,304	2,640,013	5,466
Cass	8	6,223	72.3	0.8	26.6	0.1	0.2	24,386,879	30.1	8.0	52.5	9.4	3,919	28,131,942	4,521
Atlanta		2,083	65.2	0.5	33.8	0.2	0.2	7,925,833	26.5	2.8	55.5	15.2	3,805	10,780,678	5,176
Avinger		233	72.5	1.3	24.9	0.4	0.9	933,322	20.2	2.9	69.7	7.1	4,006	1,006,175	4,318
Bloomburg		232	90.1	0.0	9.9	0.0	0.0	916,319	18.5	11.8	67.8	1.9	3,950	837,719	3,611
Hughes Springs		913	79.4	1.8	18.6	0.0	0.2	3,771,219	42.6	4.6	45.6	7.2	4,131	3,811,441	4,175
Linden-Kildare		1,252	67.9	1.0	31.2	0.0	0.0	5,266,379	13.8	23.5	57.4	5.3	4,206	5,732,124	4,578
Marietta		78	66.7	0.0	33.3	0.0	0.0	398,852	18.9	2.0	72.1	7.0	5,113	419,305	5,376
McLeod		233	94.0	0.0	6.0	0.0	0.0	836,399	27.3	1.7	65.8	5.2	3,590	762,398	3,272
Queen City		1,199	76.6	0.7	22.6	0.0	0.1	4,338,556	51.6	3.6	35.8	9.0	3,618	4,782,102	3,988
Castro	3	2,523	33.9	62.5	3.5	0.1	0.0	9,925,338	24.0	4.9	56.1	15.0	3,934	10,556,572	4,184
Dimmitt		1,716	30.4	65.2	4.4	0.1	0.0	6,330,249	28.1	5.0	51.8	15.1	3,689	6,405,374	3,733
Hart		566	18.7	79.0	2.3	0.0	0.0	2,524,830	14.6	4.0	64.7	16.7	4,461	3,069,429	5,423
Nazareth		241	95.0	5.0	0.0	0.0	0.0	1,070,259	22.1	6.8	61.0	10.1	4,441	1,081,769	4,489
Chambers	3	3,996	77.2	8.1	14.1	0.6	†	23,946,822	70.5	8.0	18.0	3.4	5,993	23,450,913	5,869
Anahuac		1,361	59.3	13.3	25.9	1.5	0.0	6,639,474	56.0	8.9	28.7	6.4	4,878	6,858,031	5,039
Barbers Hill		1,692	91.4	5.3	3.3	0.1	0.0	12,675,685	88.0	3.7	1.5		7,492	12,084,912	7,142
East Chambers		943	77.5	5.5	16.6	0.2	0.1	4,631,663	43.5	10.2	42.0	4.3	4,912	4,507,970	4,780
Cherokee	5	6,905	68.7	7.1	23.6	0.3	0.2	25,996,680	30.5	4.0	53.3	12.2	3,765	26,359,927	3,818
Alto		654	58.9	2.0	38.8	0.0	0.3	2,665,465	29.6	6.6	65.8	4.0	4,076	2,867,632	4,385
Jacksonville		3,956	67.0	8.4	24.0	0.5	0.1	13,551,869	36.8	4.6	50.4	8.2	3,426	13,398,162	3,387
New Summerfield		270	52.6	23.7	23.7	0.0	0.0	1,122,398	17.8	4.5	69.9	7.8	4,157	1,164,445	4,313
Rusk		1,719	77.0	4.5	17.9	0.2	0.4	7,411,617	23.2	3.7	49.4	23.7	4,312	7,667,401	4,460
Wells		306	81.0	0.0	19.0	0.0	0.0	1,245,331	19.7	5.9	66.6	7.8	4,070	1,262,287	4,125
Childress	1	1,258	67.2	24.2	7.8	0.8	0.0	4,347,700	18.0	6.2	67.5	8.4	3,456	4,438,806	3,528
Childress		1,258	67.2	24.2	7.8	0.8	0.0	4,347,700	18.0	6.2	67.5	8.4	3,456	4,438,806	3,528
Clay	5	1,885	95.7	3.3	0.4	0.2	0.5	7,751,212	34.0	6.0	56.1	3.8	4,110	8,456,169	4,484
Bellevue		183	98.4	1.6	0.0	0.0	0.0	859,314	37.2	7.6	49.8	5.4	4,696	928,831	5,076
Byers		136	93.4	6.6	0.0	0.0	0.0	570,512	25.1	5.5	64.7	4.8	4,195	604,336	4,444
Henrietta		965	95.4	2.7	0.7	0.3	0.8	3,726,101	34.4	5.2	57.0	3.3	3,861	4,149,271	4,300
Midway		168	93.5	6.0	0.0	0.0	0.6	834,571	61.9	7.3	26.6	4.2	4,968	1,007,731	5,998
Petrolia		434	96.8	3.2	0.0	0.0	0.0	1,760,714	21.4	6.6	68.6	3.4	4,057	1,766,000	4,069
Cochran	3	1,179	42.1	52.7	5.3	0.0	0.0	7,078,563	52.3	10.8	28.7	8.2	6,004	8,224,769	6,976
Bledsoe		30	43.3	56.7	0.0	0.0	0.0	498,325	86.4	6.6	3.0	4.0	16,611	446,921	14,897
Morton		810	33.0	60.1	6.9	0.0	0.0	3,561,005	16.6	15.3	54.3	13.7	4,396	4,320,663	5,334
Whiteface Cons		339	63.7	34.5	1.8	0.0	0.0	3,019,233	88.7	6.1	2.7	2.5	8,906	3,457,185	10,198
Coke	2	641	81.9	17.5	0.3	0.0	0.3	3,057,599	46.3	4.2	46.0	3.5	4,770	3,314,969	5,172
Bronte		309	82.8	17.2	0.0	0.0	0.0	1,528,595	32.3	4.2	58.9	4.5	4,947	1,605,433	5,196
Robert Lee		332	81.0	17.8	0.6	0.0	0.6	1,529,004	60.2	4.2	33.1	2.5	4,605	1,709,536	5,149
Coleman	4	1,713	75.9	19.6	4.5	0.0	0.0	8,479,803	30.1	4.7	55.8	9.4	4,950	9,266,937	5,410
Coleman		1,016	73.2	20.7	6.1	0.0	0.0	4,621,906	25.8	5.0	55.9	13.3	4,549	5,068,889	4,989
Novice		94	94.7	5.3	0.0	0.0	0.0	689,782	52.4	4.5	40.1	3.0	7,338	917,931	9,765
Panther Creek		250	90.0	10.0	0.0	0.0	0.0	1,534,711	39.6	2.8	51.8	5.6	6,139	1,512,852	6,051
Santa Anna		353	68.8	26.9	4.2	0.0	0.0	1,633,404	24.1	5.7	65.7	4.6	4,627	1,767,265	5,006
Collin	14	49,545	84.2	7.2	5.3	3.1	0.3	218,136,598	68.1	9.7	19.7	2.5	4,403	247,630,491	4,998
Allen		4,915	91.0	3.7	3.7	0.9	0.8	20,018,274	56.1	12.4	29.8	1.7	4,073	23,322,255	4,745
Anna		608	91.8	8.2	0.0	0.0	0.0	2,276,111	29.8	6.2	62.6	1.4	3,744	2,265,362	3,726
Blue Ridge		425	96.7	2.6	0.2	0.0	0.5	1,360,986	28.0	4.9	64.7	2.3	3,202	1,450,969	3,414
Celina		710	80.1	10.3	8.5	0.1	1.0	2,658,920	37.6	6.4	53.1	2.9	3,745	2,721,340	3,833
Community		843	88.4	7.7	3.3	0.1	0.5	3,160,073	28.6	5.6	63.1	2.6	3,749	3,380,961	4,011
Farmersville		963	76.8	11.2	11.7	0.0	0.2	3,178,004	30.4	6.2	59.6	3.8	3,300	3,218,999	3,343
Frisco		1,298	68.1	28.7	2.5	0.2	0.5	6,457,071	74.1	7.0	15.3	3.6	4,975	7,574,671	5,836
Lovejoy		440	96.1	2.3	0.0	1.4	0.2	2,581,699	86.0	3.6	10.1	0.3	5,867	2,985,941	6,786

County/ISD	Districts	Students	% White**	% Hispanic**	% Black**	% Asian**	% American Indian**	Total Revenue	% Local***	% Other***	% State***	% Federal***	Revenue Per Pupil	Total Spending	Spending Per Pupil
Collin Co. (Con't.)															
McKinney		4,953	64.2	20.9	14.4	0.5	0.1	19,796,894	64.2	5.4	25.3	5.2	3,997	21,496,463	4,340
Melissa		273	87.2	10.3	0.7	0.0	1.8	1,214,559	55.5	7.7	36.2	0.6	4,449	1,282,146	4,697
Plano		29,554	85.7	4.4	4.9	4.8	0.1	136,136,352	76.3	10.1	11.8	1.8	4,606	158,270,629	5,355
Princeton		1,534	92.4	5.3	1.6	0.2	0.4	5,600,992	31.2	9.1	56.1	3.6	3,651	5,795,469	3,778
Prosper		505	82.4	17.2	0.2	0.2	0.0	2,335,019	62.2	5.6	30.0	2.2	4,624	2,449,377	4,850
Wylie		2,524	92.7	5.3	0.7	0.4	0.9	11,361,644	51.9	15.4	25.4	7.3	4,501	11,415,909	4,523
Collingsworth	2	738	65.7	25.7	7.5	0.3	0.8	3,201,074	25.0	3.2	60.5	11.3	4,337	3,719,657	5,040
Samnorwood		105	83.8	16.2	0.0	0.0	0.0	628,575	45.3	2.5	47.4	4.7	5,986	659,214	6,278
Wellington		633	62.7	27.3	8.7	0.3	0.9	2,572,499	20.0	3.4	63.7	12.9	4,064	3,060,443	4,835
Colorado	3	3,592	55.1	22.3	22.6	0.0	0.0	14,458,880	41.3	4.9	44.7	9.1	4,025	15,209,464	4,234
Columbus		1,516	69.2	14.0	16.8	0.0	0.0	5,429,544	39.5	5.7	48.6	6.3	3,581	5,507,645	3,633
Rice Cons		1,540	40.1	34.0	26.0	0.0	0.0	6,523,323	37.6	4.9	44.3	13.1	4,236	6,965,700	4,523
Weimar		536	58.2	12.5	29.3	0.0	0.0	2,506,013	55.0	3.0	37.4	4.6	4,675	2,736,119	5,105
Comal	2	10,687	67.8	31.1	1.0	0.1	†	42,516,440	57.2	5.4	33.1	4.3	3,978	46,120,480	4,316
Comal		5,684	80.2	18.9	0.8	0.1	†	23,869,032	68.9	4.2	23.0	3.9	4,199	27,473,072	4,833
New Braunfels		5,003	53.8	44.8	1.2	0.1	0.1	18,647,408	42.2	7.0	46.1	4.7	3,727	18,647,408	3,727
Comanche	4	2,172	73.2	26.6	0.2	0.0	†	8,164,931	24.0	5.0	63.0	7.9	3,759	8,222,643	3,786
Comanche		1,137	71.3	28.3	0.4	0.0	0.0	3,981,843	24.7	6.6	61.8	6.9	3,502	4,076,128	3,585
De Leon		705	72.3	27.7	0.0	0.0	0.0	2,886,928	24.9	3.3	61.3	10.5	4,095	2,803,936	3,977
Gustine		190	79.5	20.5	0.0	0.0	0.0	704,942	25.3	4.7	62.8	7.2	3,710	744,931	3,921
Sidney		140	84.3	15.0	0.0	0.0	0.7	591,218	13.5	3.2	80.0	3.3	4,223	597,648	4,269
Concho	2	555	52.8	46.7	0.0	0.0	0.5	2,591,031	26.2	4.5	58.7	10.6	4,669	2,665,614	4,803
Eden Cons		399	52.1	47.9	0.0	0.0	0.0	1,855,292	24.1	4.5	60.0	11.4	4,650	1,886,142	4,727
Paint Rock		156	54.5	43.6	0.0	0.0	1.9	735,739	31.5	4.6	55.3	8.6	4,716	779,472	4,997
Cooke	8	5,188	87.8	5.9	5.6	0.5	0.2	18,774,882	39.7	5.9	48.5	5.9	3,619	19,972,555	3,850
Callisburg		765	98.0	1.0	0.1	0.3	0.5	3,237,984	42.9	6.7	46.3	4.1	4,233	3,168,900	4,142
Era		324	94.4	5.6	0.0	0.0	0.0	1,130,332	35.2	8.9	51.9	4.0	3,489	1,380,363	4,260
Gainesville		2,669	79.8	8.7	10.8	0.6	0.1	9,558,104	42.2	4.4	45.2	8.2	3,581	10,070,049	3,773
Lindsay		421	95.2	2.4	0.0	2.4	0.0	1,305,758	29.0	11.6	57.2	2.3	3,102	1,224,091	2,908
Muenster		375	99.2	0.3	0.0	0.3	0.3	1,165,487	41.2	6.5	49.1	3.1	3,108	1,364,002	3,637
Sivells Bend		52	96.2	3.8	0.0	0.0	0.0	271,425	68.0	4.4	25.8	1.8	5,220	275,925	5,306
Valley View		540	93.7	6.3	0.0	0.0	0.0	1,896,898	24.3	6.7	65.8	3.1	3,513	2,280,448	4,223
Walnut Bend		42	95.2	4.8	0.0	0.0	0.0	208,894	61.8	0.0	31.1	7.1	4,974	208,777	4,971
Coryell	5	8,992	75.3	8.4	13.4	2.4	0.4	26,639,205	20.0	6.0	69.0	5.0	2,963	32,173,622	3,578
Copperas Cove		6,238	69.5	8.4	18.1	3.4	0.5	17,600,887	18.6	5.5	71.0	4.9	2,822	22,596,829	3,622
Evant		262	83.2	16.8	0.0	0.0	0.0	981,506	20.3	5.6	63.6	10.5	3,746	1,050,122	4,008
Gatesville		2,070	88.6	7.2	3.9	0.1	0.1	6,553,834	24.3	7.2	63.8	4.7	3,166	6,982,538	3,373
Jonesboro		243	98.4	1.6	0.0	0.0	0.0	863,153	18.0	6.9	70.5	4.5	3,552	904,308	3,721
Oglesby		179	82.7	17.3	0.0	0.0	0.0	639,825	16.4	5.6	73.8	4.2	3,574	639,825	3,574
Cottle	1	459	57.7	28.5	13.5	0.2	0.0	2,287,440	30.7	2.7	58.9	7.6	4,984	2,266,360	4,938
Paducah		459	57.7	28.5	13.5	0.2	0.0	2,287,440	30.7	2.7	58.9	7.6	4,984	2,266,360	4,938
Crane	1	1,310	54.2	41.8	4.0	0.1	0.0	6,552,478	87.4	6.5	4.9	1.1	5,002	7,456,520	5,692
Crane		1,310	54.2	41.8	4.0	0.1	0.0	6,552,478	87.4	6.5	4.9	1.1	5,002	7,456,520	5,692
Crockett	1	922	38.1	61.0	0.7	0.3	0.0	5,170,846	82.7	5.4	9.9	2.0	5,608	5,377,641	5,833
Crockett County		922	38.1	61.0	0.7	0.3	0.0	5,170,846	82.7	5.4	9.9	2.0	5,608	5,377,641	5,833
Crosby	3	1,862	33.9	61.5	4.4	0.2	0.0	8,490,203	21.9	6.7	57.2	14.2	4,560	9,071,449	4,872
Crosbyton		632	36.9	56.8	6.2	0.2	0.0	2,895,087	24.1	2.6	64.6	8.7	4,581	2,903,037	4,593
Lorenzo		467	30.2	64.0	5.1	0.6	0.0	2,422,136	25.1	2.6	49.1	23.3	5,187	2,871,082	6,148
Ralls		763	33.7	63.8	2.5	0.0	0.0	3,172,980	17.4	13.7	56.7	12.2	4,159	3,297,330	4,322
Culberson	1	836	19.4	80.0	0.0	0.6	0.0	3,521,262	61.7	2.7	29.2	6.4	4,212	3,489,196	4,174
Culberson County		836	19.4	80.0	0.0	0.6	0.0	3,521,262	61.7	2.7	29.2	6.4	4,212	3,489,196	4,174
Dallam	2	1,636	76.7	20.2	2.5	0.6	0.1	6,601,279	39.6	6.1	46.1	8.2	4,035	6,842,297	4,182
Dalhart		1,467	76.1	20.4	2.8	0.6	0.1	5,616,543	37.9	6.4	46.6	9.1	3,829	5,794,809	3,950
Texline		169	82.2	17.8	0.0	0.0	0.0	984,736	49.1	4.4	43.1	3.4	5,827	1,047,488	6,198
Dallas	15	316,282	48.2	20.9	27.1	3.4	0.4	1,316,792,809	65.8	8.3	21.5	4.4	4,163	1,608,683,624	5,086
Carrollton-FB		16,484	68.3	16.1	6.1	8.9	0.5	80,059,730	86.0	6.3	5.3	2.3	4,857	82,574,974	5,009
Cedar Hill		4,282	70.0	9.7	17.9	1.8	0.5	17,512,978	66.1	7.5	24.9	1.5	4,090	18,375,358	4,291
Coppell		2,930	82.8	6.6	3.0	7.1	0.6	16,166,325	88.8	6.5	4.4	0.4	5,518	20,635,469	7,043
Dallas		132,366	18.1	32.8	46.9	1.8	0.4	591,721,595	67.6	9.0	17.2	6.1	4,474	798,963,949	6,041
DeSoto		5,889	71.9	5.1	21.8	0.9	0.3	22,075,522	60.6	8.7	29.9	0.9	3,749	23,164,419	3,934
Duncanville		10,008	70.7	7.5	19.4	2.2	0.2	36,555,681	61.2	7.9	28.5	2.4	3,653	41,142,505	4,111
Garland		36,158	71.3	12.2	11.6	4.2	0.7	128,239,084	54.1	8.2	34.0	3.7	3,547	130,937,187	3,621
Grand Prairie		16,464	58.0	28.1	10.3	3.0	0.6	58,776,097	42.3	7.2	44.2	6.2	3,570	68,187,493	4,142
Highland Park		4,066	97.5	0.8	0.3	1.4	†	21,274,708	89.8	5.2	5.0	0.0	5,232	23,596,268	5,803
Irving		22,639	64.3	20.1	9.4	5.5	0.8	85,774,500	70.0	6.0	21.0	3.0	3,789	104,702,066	4,625
Lancaster		4,216	56.4	7.6	35.1	0.4	0.5	18,280,082	61.1	6.9	29.0	3.0	4,336	20,784,210	4,930
Mesquite		24,649	82.0	8.8	5.9	2.9	0.4	80,715,936	39.1	13.3	44.9	2.8	3,275	96,375,639	3,910
Richardson		32,229	72.5	5.8	14.2	7.2	0.3	143,929,260	78.8	7.3	11.9	2.0	4,466	161,720,361	5,018
Sunnyvale		304	94.7	2.6	2.0	0.3	0.3	1,369,655	90.7	2.5	5.8	1.1	4,505	1,375,343	4,524
Wilmer-Hutchins		3,708	8.0	11.6	80.2	0.2	0.1	14,341,656	34.8	3.6	51.2	10.4	3,868	16,148,387	4,355
Dawson	4	3,591	38.2	56.9	4.6	0.2	0.0	15,457,008	34.2	7.7	47.3	10.8	4,304	16,345,804	4,552
Dawson		154	32.5	67.5	0.0	0.0	0.0	1,621,146	82.9	7.7	2.6	6.9	10,527	1,713,992	11,130
Klondike		235	71.1	28.9	0.0	0.0	0.0	1,600,023	69.2	6.6	17.0	7.1	6,809	1,752,073	7,456
Lamesa		2,962	34.0	60.2	5.6	0.3	0.0	10,844,358	19.1	7.8	60.7	12.4	3,661	11,319,401	3,822
Sands		240	62.5	37.5	0.0	0.0	0.0	1,391,481	54.9	7.9	29.8	7.4	5,798	1,560,338	6,501
DeWitt	6	4,552	54.5	32.2	13.3	†	0.0	18,054,630	31.1	6.0	53.8	9.1	3,966	20,777,073	4,564
Cuero		1,848	46.5	35.7	17.7	0.1	0.0	7,344,717	24.7	6.0	56.9	12.5	3,974	7,565,650	4,094
Meyersville		145	93.1	6.9	0.0	0.0	0.0	707,375	65.5	7.6	25.4	1.5	4,878	730,590	5,039
Nordheim		113	53.1	46.9	0.0	0.0	0.0	756,390	60.4	6.3	28.4	4.9	6,694	809,794	7,166
Westhoff		68	57.4	32.4	10.3	0.0	0.0	325,234	38.3	1.7	54.8	5.2	4,783	337,204	4,959

County/ISD	Districts	Students	% White**	% Hispanic**	% Black**	% Asian**	% American Indian**	Total Revenue	% Local***	% Other***	% State***	% Federal**	Revenue Per Pupil	Total Spending	Spending Per Pupil
DeWitt Co. (Con't.)															
Yoakum		1,638	55.6	29.0	15.4	0.0	0.0	5,585,935	30.3	6.6	55.6	7.5	3,410	7,778,256	4,749
Yorktown		740	64.5	33.2	2.3	0.0	0.0	3,334,979	32.0	4.9	55.9	7.1	4,507	3,555,579	4,805
Deaf Smith	2	4,663	34.0	63.9	1.7	0.3	0.1	16,136,446	21.3	3.9	58.2	16.6	3,461	16,807,366	3,604
Hereford		4,593	33.4	64.4	1.8	0.3	0.1	15,681,053	20.7	3.9	58.5	16.9	3,414	16,349,375	3,560
Walcott		70	72.9	27.1	0.0	0.0	0.0	455,393	42.7	2.9	49.1	5.4	6,506	457,991	6,543
Delta	2	1,039	77.9	2.0	19.8	0.1	0.2	4,250,606	25.5	4.8	62.1	7.6	4,091	5,029,964	4,841
Cooper		765	84.6	1.4	13.6	0.1	0.3	2,831,984	21.0	6.1	66.6	6.3	3,702	2,965,352	3,876
Fannindel		274	59.1	3.6	37.2	0.0	0.0	1,418,622	34.6	2.1	53.1	10.2	5,177	2,064,612	7,535
Denton	11	40,125	85.8	7.1	5.2	1.6	0.4	156,667,055	59.8	7.6	29.3	3.3	3,904	197,893,941	4,932
Argyle		515	98.6	0.8	0.2	0.4	0.0	2,493,478	74.6	3.3	21.1	1.0	4,842	4,764,800	9,252
Aubrey		773	96.1	3.9	0.0	0.0	0.0	2,574,931	33.7	7.1	56.4	2.9	3,331	2,942,105	3,806
Denton		10,231	76.7	10.0	11.5	1.5	0.3	42,696,115	61.0	7.8	27.1	4.1	4,173	58,623,577	5,730
Krum		774	92.5	6.1	0.9	0.5	0.0	2,833,620	30.1	7.3	60.9	1.8	3,661	2,951,566	3,813
Lake Dallas		1,620	91.5	4.4	1.1	1.7	1.4	5,590,031	56.0	6.1	33.3	4.5	3,451	5,792,841	3,576
Lewisville		19,554	87.5	6.1	4.0	2.0	0.3	74,053,931	64.5	8.1	25.0	2.4	3,787	95,323,804	4,875
Little Elm		943	84.7	13.8	0.7	0.4	0.3	3,600,293	36.3	6.9	53.8	3.0	3,818	3,667,124	3,889
Northwest		2,998	92.3	6.0	0.4	1.2	0.2	12,864,333	60.8	5.0	28.7	5.6	4,291	13,007,211	4,339
Pilot Point		864	89.2	4.6	6.1	0.0	0.0	3,483,500	41.6	7.4	45.7	5.3	4,032	3,724,350	4,311
Ponder		385	91.9	5.7	0.0	1.3	1.0	1,668,325	36.5	15.7	45.6	2.1	4,333	1,656,339	4,302
Sanger		1,468	90.7	6.4	2.0	0.2	0.7	4,808,498	40.1	7.1	47.5	5.4	3,276	5,440,224	3,706
Dickens	2	550	60.5	32.5	6.7	0.0	0.2	2,763,740	23.0	3.9	63.2	9.9	5,025	2,797,129	5,086
Patton Springs		96	60.4	38.5	0.0	0.0	1.0	725,456	26.7	4.4	60.4	8.5	7,557	724,095	7,543
Spur		454	60.6	31.3	8.1	0.0	0.0	2,038,284	21.7	3.7	64.2	10.4	4,490	2,073,034	4,566
Dimmit	2	2,849	13.3	85.8	0.8	0.2	0.0	13,308,877	25.9	2.6	54.7	16.8	4,671	13,923,858	4,887
Asherton		414	0.7	99.3	0.0	0.0	0.0	2,101,251	15.9	1.2	63.5	19.4	5,075	2,229,581	5,385
Carrizo Springs		2,435	15.4	83.5	0.9	0.2	0.0	11,207,626	27.8	2.9	53.1	16.3	4,603	11,694,277	4,803
Donley	2	656	83.8	8.2	7.9	0.0	0.0	2,809,784	24.5	5.9	63.5	6.1	4,283	3,547,745	5,408
Clarendon		544	82.9	7.5	9.6	0.0	0.0	2,224,742	25.1	3.7	65.4	5.8	4,090	2,933,730	5,393
Hedley		112	88.4	11.6	0.0	0.0	0.0	585,042	22.2	14.2	56.4	7.2	5,224	614,015	5,482
Duval	4	3,401	8.1	91.8	0.1	0.1	0.0	16,769,291	43.9	2.7	42.4	11.0	4,931	16,799,323	4,940
Benavides		712	2.0	98.0	0.0	0.0	0.0	4,461,672	44.6	2.0	40.8	12.5	6,266	4,449,232	6,249
Freer		1,061	23.4	76.2	0.2	0.2	0.0	4,917,182	59.1	3.7	32.4	4.8	4,634	5,158,062	4,862
Ramirez*		31	0.0	†	0.0	0.0	0.0	365,756	56.9	3.3	20.0	19.8	11,799	433,323	13,978
San Diego		1,597	0.8	99.2	0.1	0.0	0.0	7,024,681	32.1	2.4	51.7	13.9	4,399	6,758,706	4,232
Eastland	6	3,290	86.2	11.3	1.9	0.4	0.2	12,587,058	30.1	4.7	57.8	7.4	3,826	13,271,656	4,034
Carbon		114	98.2	1.8	0.0	0.0	0.0	636,440	51.5	4.4	40.0	4.0	5,583	644,765	5,656
Cisco		872	86.8	9.7	3.4	0.0	0.0	3,249,666	26.4	3.9	64.3	5.5	3,727	3,268,602	3,748
Eastland		1,096	89.3	9.1	0.9	0.4	0.3	3,817,314	35.1	5.0	55.3	4.5	3,483	4,067,334	3,711
Gorman		342	76.0	21.3	0.0	2.0	0.6	1,532,211	23.7	4.4	49.5	22.1	4,480	1,892,142	5,533
Ranger		639	80.4	16.0	3.1	0.2	0.3	2,318,496	26.3	5.6	62.2	5.9	3,628	2,349,792	3,677
Rising Star		227	94.7	4.4	0.9	0.0	0.0	1,032,931	28.4	4.2	59.7	7.7	4,550	1,049,021	4,621
Ector	1	26,366	52.1	41.7	5.3	0.6	0.2	93,964,768	44.2	4.5	42.3	9.0	3,564	99,209,139	3,763
Ector County		26,366	52.1	41.7	5.3	0.6	0.2	93,964,768	44.2	4.5	42.3	9.0	3,564	99,209,139	3,763
Edwards	2	830	46.4	53.4	0.0	0.2	0.0	3,750,211	37.4	2.8	48.6	11.2	4,518	3,708,379	4,468
Nueces Canyon		355	74.1	25.6	0.0	0.3	0.0	1,733,130	43.6	3.8	41.7	11.0	4,882	1,728,170	4,868
Rocksprings		475	25.7	74.1	0.0	0.2	0.0	2,017,081	32.1	1.9	54.6	11.4	4,246	1,980,209	4,169
El Paso	9	139,112	17.9	78.1	3.1	0.7	0.1	491,763,017	25.7	2.9	60.2	11.2	3,535	558,633,911	4,016
Anthony		646	7.4	92.1	0.5	0.0	0.0	2,417,393	24.4	2.6	62.1	10.8	3,742	2,654,452	4,109
Canutillo		3,338	9.3	90.4	0.3	†	0.0	12,195,948	16.5	2.1	68.0	13.4	3,654	15,034,123	4,504
Clint		3,253	17.1	82.5	0.5	0.0	0.0	11,573,793	30.4	3.3	59.9	6.4	3,558	17,197,007	5,287
El Paso		64,047	21.9	72.4	4.6	1.0	0.1	228,463,298	31.1	2.7	54.0	12.2	3,567	247,203,298	3,860
Fabens		2,195	4.6	94.9	0.4	0.0	†	7,556,256	11.5	1.9	70.6	16.0	3,442	7,526,684	3,429
San Elizario		1,554	1.0	98.8	0.1	0.0	0.1	5,415,542	7.8	1.3	79.4	11.4	3,485	5,538,378	3,564
Socorro		12,998	9.6	89.2	0.9	0.2	†	44,761,776	22.3	2.6	66.1	9.0	3,444	70,916,349	5,456
Tornillo		372	4.8	95.2	0.0	0.0	0.0	1,697,382	12.7	0.3	73.4	13.6	4,563	1,844,182	4,957
Ysleta		50,709	17.1	79.8	2.3	0.6	0.3	177,681,629	21.1	3.4	65.0	10.4	3,504	190,719,438	3,761
Ellis	10	18,264	69.7	16.9	13.0	0.3	0.1	66,799,815	45.6	5.1	44.4	4.9	3,657	68,879,764	3,771
Avalon		179	62.6	35.2	2.2	0.0	0.0	684,062	13.3	9.5	65.3	11.9	3,822	704,016	3,933
Ennis		4,007	57.1	24.0	18.6	0.3	0.0	13,882,013	39.4	5.1	50.0	5.6	3,464	14,203,014	3,545
Ferris		1,395	50.0	29.9	19.7	0.2	0.1	4,990,445	30.4	4.2	61.4	4.0	3,577	5,797,038	4,156
Italy		574	59.8	10.6	29.3	0.2	0.2	2,270,414	18.3	4.5	68.1	9.1	3,955	2,355,820	4,104
Maypearl		489	80.4	13.9	5.1	0.6	0.0	1,907,266	25.7	4.4	62.1	7.8	3,900	1,900,923	3,887
Midlothian		2,661	89.0	7.9	2.6	0.6	†	11,374,499	66.5	6.9	21.3	5.0	4,275	11,359,341	4,269
Milford		193	64.2	5.2	30.6	0.0	0.0	1,001,276	31.1	2.9	58.3	7.7	5,188	999,216	5,177
Palmer		743	80.1	18.7	0.7	0.0	0.5	2,241,661	25.3	4.7	67.5	2.5	3,017	2,372,231	3,193
Red Oak		3,089	86.7	8.5	4.3	0.3	0.2	10,252,212	49.1	5.0	44.9	1.0	3,319	10,315,595	3,339
Waxahachie		4,934	63.5	18.0	18.1	0.3	0.1	18,195,967	49.4	4.4	40.4	5.8	3,688	18,872,570	3,825
Erath	7	4,545	86.8	12.1	0.5	0.5	0.1	14,888,428	44.1	5.0	43.0	7.9	3,276	15,704,936	3,455
Bluff Dale		60	91.7	5.0	3.3	0.0	0.0	276,075	55.7	3.8	36.2	4.3	4,601	287,413	4,790
Dublin		1,056	80.3	19.4	0.1	0.1	0.1	3,307,995	30.3	6.5	54.1	9.1	3,133	3,687,438	3,492
Huckabay		129	79.1	20.9	0.0	0.0	0.0	711,067	58.9	3.7	31.7	5.8	5,512	790,421	6,127
Lingleville		185	73.0	26.5	0.0	0.0	0.5	837,247	43.8	7.5	43.3	5.5	4,526	847,710	4,582
Morgan Mill		81	95.1	3.7	1.2	0.0	0.0	293,568	61.3	4.1	25.5	9.1	3,624	323,139	3,989
Stephenville		3,005	90.0	8.6	0.7	0.7	0.1	9,287,579	46.3	4.4	41.2	8.1	3,091	9,577,744	3,187
Three Way		29	82.8	17.2	0.0	0.0	0.0	174,897	81.9	3.9	11.9	2.3	6,031	191,071	6,589
Falls	4	3,153	49.2	15.7	35.1	0.0	0.0	12,346,213	17.0	4.4	68.0	10.6	3,916	13,022,422	4,130
Chilton		353	44.5	26.3	29.2	0.0	0.0	1,520,994	15.1	2.3	68.7	13.8	4,309	1,515,400	4,293
Marlin		1,809	40.5	12.9	46.6	0.0	0.0	6,923,132	17.7	4.5	65.7	12.1	3,827	6,947,084	3,840
Rosebud-Lott		892	63.2	18.7	18.0	0.0	0.0	3,613,686	16.3	5.3	71.2	7.2	4,055	4,283,737	4,802
Westphalia		99	97.0	3.0	0.0	0.0	0.0	288,401	19.9	1.0	77.6	1.5	2,913	276,201	2,790

County/ISD	Districts	Students	% White**	% Hispanic**	% Black**	% Asian**	% American Indian**	Total Revenue	% Local***	% Other***	% State***	% Federal***	Revenue Per Pupil	Total Spending	Spending Per Pupil
Fannin...........	8	4,332	90.4	2.1	7.2	0.3	0.1	15,429,426	25.9	6.3	60.8	7.0	3,562	16,270,628	3,756
Bonham........		1,893	89.0	1.7	8.6	0.5	0.2	5,993,712	28.8	7.4	54.2	9.5	3,166	6,219,418	3,285
Dodd City......		188	100	0.0	0.0	0.0	0.0	790,556	17.1	4.6	68.2	10.0	4,205	836,351	4,449
Ector.........		124	89.5	8.9	0.0	0.8	0.8	606,488	20.7	5.5	69.5	4.4	4,891	622,324	5,019
Honey Grove Con..		592	84.6	2.4	12.8	0.2	0.0	2,419,554	22.4	6.1	64.6	6.8	4,087	2,478,320	4,186
Leonard........		599	90.0	0.8	9.2	0.0	0.0	1,947,868	18.3	5.6	72.5	3.7	3,252	2,267,223	3,785
Sam Rayburn		340	96.5	1.8	1.5	0.0	0.3	1,342,803	18.2	4.7	69.4	7.7	3,949	1,379,979	4,059
Savoy.........		248	99.6	0.4	0.0	0.0	0.0	930,307	56.3	6.0	35.3	2.5	3,751	1,034,624	4,172
Trenton........		348	90.8	5.7	3.4	0.0	0.0	1,398,138	24.6	5.8	66.5	3.1	4,018	1,432,389	4,116
Fayette.........	5	3,371	75.7	11.4	12.6	0.2	0.1	13,120,604	54.7	5.5	35.6	4.2	3,892	13,680,271	4,058
Fayetteville		196	92.9	0.0	6.1	1.0	0.0	793,646	44.6	5.9	43.3	6.2	4,049	998,277	5,093
Flatonia		477	57.4	30.6	11.9	0.0	0.0	1,980,157	46.9	3.4	45.4	4.3	4,151	1,991,988	4,176
La Grange.......		1,755	77.8	10.1	11.6	0.2	0.3	6,719,523	60.9	6.4	29.0	3.7	3,829	6,823,210	3,888
Round Tp-Carmine		227	90.7	2.6	6.6	0.0	0.0	1,087,269	80.2	7.8	10.4	1.6	4,790	1,093,551	4,817
Schulenburg		716	73.3	7.5	19.1	0.0	0.0	2,540,009	36.6	3.9	53.7	5.8	3,547	2,773,245	3,873
Fisher...........	4	885	57.2	36.4	6.4	0.0	0.0	4,019,700	36.5	6.4	50.9	6.2	4,542	4,806,723	5,431
Hobbs.........		13	53.8	46.2	0.0	0.0	0.0	235,728	86.6	5.3	3.1	5.0	18,133	332,041	25,542
McCaulley.......		35	65.7	20.0	14.3	0.0	0.0	490,946	72.7	2.1	19.6	5.6	14,027	488,961	13,970
Roby..........		320	64.4	34.4	1.3	0.0	0.0	1,326,352	18.3	8.9	64.6	8.3	4,145	1,824,090	5,700
Rotan..........		517	52.2	38.5	9.3	0.0	0.0	1,966,674	33.7	6.0	55.2	5.1	3,804	2,161,631	4,181
Floyd............	2	2,028	36.6	57.9	5.1	0.2	0.1	8,579,558	18.5	3.0	63.9	14.6	4,231	9,048,198	4,462
Floydada		1,270	37.3	57.1	5.4	0.1	0.2	5,593,663	18.0	3.0	63.7	15.3	4,404	5,746,587	4,525
Lockney........		758	35.5	59.4	4.7	0.4	0.0	2,985,895	19.3	2.9	64.4	13.4	3,939	3,301,611	4,356
Foard	1	349	72.2	18.9	8.9	0.0	0.0	1,523,279	28.8	7.1	57.5	6.5	4,365	1,613,107	4,622
Crowell........		349	72.2	18.9	8.9	0.0	0.0	1,523,279	28.8	7.1	57.5	6.5	4,365	1,613,107	4,622
Fort Bend	5	48,997	46.2	22.6	24.2	6.9	0.1	188,797,806	51.5	6.5	38.2	3.8	3,853	218,013,628	4,450
Fort Bend		33,647	47.5	14.2	28.9	9.4	0.1	116,881,608	47.3	6.4	43.6	2.7	3,474	134,574,760	4,000
Kendleton......		148	1.4	32.4	66.2	0.0	0.0	921,198	37.4	0.8	47.6	14.2	6,224	891,893	6,026
Lamar Consolida..		11,741	39.0	45.7	14.9	0.5	†	56,321,433	57.2	7.4	29.4	6.0	4,797	66,339,192	5,650
Needville		1,920	71.1	19.2	9.3	0.3	0.1	6,496,660	33.6	6.0	56.4	4.0	3,384	7,357,409	3,832
Stafford		1,541	45.1	35.7	9.5	9.2	0.5	8,176,907	87.2	3.7	6.4	2.7	5,306	8,850,374	5,743
Franklin	1	1,186	86.1	5.1	8.5	0.2	0.1	4,482,021	57.4	6.7	32.2	3.8	3,779	4,676,319	3,943
Mount Vernon....		1,186	86.1	5.1	8.5	0.2	0.1	4,482,021	57.4	6.7	32.2	3.8	3,779	4,676,319	3,943
Freestone	4	3,111	75.1	3.9	20.5	0.5	0.1	12,600,652	59.8	6.9	27.3	6.0	4,050	13,747,198	4,419
Dew		51	94.1	2.0	3.9	0.0	0.0	270,001	75.9	4.2	16.0	3.9	5,294	346,660	6,797
Fairfield........		1,573	74.3	3.6	21.2	0.8	0.1	6,940,320	67.3	7.5	17.9	7.4	4,412	7,978,758	5,072
Teague		1,091	73.9	5.4	20.3	0.3	0.1	3,881,449	57.6	6.8	31.5	4.0	3,558	3,881,451	3,558
Wortham........		396	79.0	0.8	20.2	0.0	0.0	1,508,882	28.4	5.2	61.4	5.0	3,810	1,540,329	3,890
Frio	2	3,313	15.5	83.8	0.3	0.3	0.1	13,567,331	20.3	4.5	57.7	17.5	4,095	14,026,291	4,234
Dilley		932	17.8	81.3	0.0	0.6	0.2	4,218,150	21.1	4.8	60.9	13.1	4,526	4,564,157	4,897
Pearsall		2,381	14.6	84.8	0.4	0.2	0.0	9,349,181	20.0	4.3	56.2	19.5	3,927	9,462,134	3,974
Gaines	3	3,243	49.5	46.8	3.4	0.2	0.1	18,541,646	61.4	20.1	12.0	6.4	5,717	19,348,181	5,966
Loop		149	47.0	53.0	0.0	0.0	0.0	1,436,126	77.5	14.4	2.9	5.2	9,638	1,494,692	10,031
Seagraves.......		737	33.5	58.6	7.6	0.3	0.0	3,801,414	30.3	17.5	41.8	10.4	5,158	4,367,559	5,926
Seminole........		2,357	54.6	42.8	2.3	0.2	0.1	13,304,106	68.6	21.5	4.5	5.4	5,645	13,485,930	5,722
Galveston	9	56,312	64.5	13.5	18.5	3.4	0.1	231,005,898	63.0	5.5	28.0	3.5	4,102	238,155,250	4,229
Clear Creek......		21,334	78.6	8.8	6.0	6.4	0.2	83,513,936	65.5	6.0	26.3	2.2	3,915	85,519,262	4,009
Dickinson.......		5,269	68.9	15.4	13.0	2.7	†	23,140,416	58.0	5.6	30.9	5.5	4,392	23,094,344	4,383
Friendswood.....		3,198	94.6	3.0	1.0	1.3	0.1	12,564,022	58.9	5.7	33.8	1.6	3,929	13,013,867	4,069
Galveston		9,871	31.5	24.5	41.7	2.1	0.1	41,838,670	65.6	1.5	29.6	3.2	4,239	44,122,593	4,470
High Island		236	92.4	6.4	0.0	0.8	0.4	1,328,990	65.4	5.1	26.3	3.2	5,631	1,640,726	6,952
Hitchcock		1,250	40.4	17.4	41.9	0.2	0.1	7,081,022	35.5	6.9	45.2	12.4	5,665	6,716,366	5,373
La Marque		1,527	36.2	9.2	53.8	0.7	0.1	22,832,947	61.1	10.4	24.1	4.4	4,453	24,518,562	4,782
Santa Fe		3,917	89.1	10.4	0.2	0.3	0.1	12,855,572	35.7	4.9	55.6	3.8	3,282	13,304,614	3,397
Texas City......		6,110	60.5	20.9	16.8	1.5	0.1	25,850,323	80.0	5.6	10.2	4.3	4,231	26,224,916	4,292
Garza	2	1,187	52.2	39.6	8.1	0.1	0.0	6,064,275	63.5	8.9	22.3	5.3	5,109	6,889,526	5,804
Post		1,034	52.5	38.5	8.9	0.1	0.0	5,084,381	66.9	10.3	18.1	4.7	4,917	5,943,571	5,748
Southland		153	50.3	47.1	2.6	0.0	0.0	979,888	45.8	1.9	44.1	8.3	6,404	945,955	6,183
Gillespie	3	2,539	76.1	23.1	0.3	0.5	†	10,091,389	54.6	8.2	30.2	7.0	3,975	10,432,658	4,109
Doss Cons*		27	96.3	3.7	0.0	0.0	0.0	113,316	66.1	5.2	28.8	0.0	4,197	116,423	4,312
Fredericksburg...		2,258	74.2	24.9	0.4	0.5	†	8,861,996	55.2	8.8	28.5	7.3	3,925	9,018,178	3,994
Harper		254	90.6	9.4	0.0	0.0	0.0	1,116,077	48.5	5.1	43.7	2.6	4,394	1,297,557	5,108
Glasscock	1	382	66.2	33.8	0.0	0.0	0.0	2,338,046	88.8	5.2	4.1	1.7	6,121	2,658,799	6,960
Glasscock		382	66.2	33.8	0.0	0.0	0.0	2,338,046	88.8	5.2	4.1	1.7	6,121	2,658,799	6,960
Goliad	1	1,248	50.1	41.7	8.1	0.0	0.1	5,515,635	55.2	4.5	27.7	12.6	4,420	5,998,294	4,806
Goliad		1,248	50.1	41.7	8.1	0.0	0.1	5,515,635	55.2	4.5	27.7	12.6	4,420	5,998,294	4,806
Gonzales	3	3,720	41.4	46.9	11.6	†	0.0	13,682,067	25.8	3.6	58.9	11.8	3,678	14,975,334	4,026
Gonzales		2,581	45.2	41.1	13.6	†	0.0	8,547,155	28.5	3.6	56.4	11.5	3,312	9,718,504	3,765
Nixon-Smiley		911	38.7	58.8	2.4	0.0	0.0	3,954,694	17.8	3.2	67.5	11.5	4,341	3,990,204	4,380
Waelder		228	9.2	64.9	25.9	0.0	0.0	1,180,218	32.5	5.4	56.4	5.7	5,176	1,266,626	5,555
Gray	5	4,725	79.5	12.9	6.1	0.7	0.8	18,703,306	51.3	4.4	39.1	5.2	3,958	18,578,241	3,932
Alanreed........		18	94.4	5.6	0.0	0.0	0.0	205,450	84.2	10.6	3.1	1.6	11,414	328,221	18,235
Grandvw-Hopkins		26	100	0.0	0.0	0.0	0.0	402,000	92.8	5.0	0.2	1.9	15,462	402,000	15,462
Lefors.........		162	94.4	5.6	0.0	0.0	0.0	1,173,669	84.3	5.7	1.7	7.5	7,245	1,162,395	7,175
McLean........		235	94.5	3.4	1.3	0.0	0.9	1,131,508	56.1	6.6	33.7	3.6	4,815	1,219,493	5,189
Pampa		4,284	77.9	13.8	6.7	0.8	0.9	15,790,679	47.0	4.1	43.2	5.8	3,686	15,466,132	3,610
Grayson.........	13	17,591	86.3	2.9	9.7	0.5	0.6	63,681,303	39.6	7.2	47.3	5.9	3,620	67,127,819	3,816
Bells..........		535	99.8	0.2	0.0	0.0	0.0	1,955,779	19.7	7.0	71.3	1.5	3,656	1,960,606	3,665
Collinsville		372	95.4	4.3	0.0	0.0	0.3	1,266,087	22.1	6.6	69.4	1.9	3,403	1,268,587	3,410
Denison		4,616	84.5	2.0	12.2	0.5	0.8	16,118,638	38.5	6.5	48.4	6.5	3,492	16,651,547	3,607

County/ISD	Districts	Students	% White**	% Hispanic**	% Black**	% Asian**	% American Indian**	Total Revenue	% Local***	% Other***	% State***	% Federal***	Revenue Per Pupil	Total Spending	Spending Per Pupil
Grayson Co. (Con't.)															
Gunter		334	82.6	16.8	0.3	0.3	0.0	1,319,700	20.0	7.8	69.7	2.5	3,951	1,568,959	4,697
Howe		838	96.1	3.1	0.0	0.2	0.6	3,036,684	22.1	8.9	67.4	1.6	3,624	3,120,571	3,724
Pottsboro		996	99.7	0.2	0.0	0.0	0.1	4,415,960	49.0	14.3	33.8	3.0	4,434	4,612,854	4,631
S and S Cons		767	97.1	1.6	0.0	0.4	0.9	2,997,313	48.7	3.3	46.1	1.9	3,908	2,954,563	3,852
Sherman		5,857	76.8	3.6	18.2	0.7	0.8	21,169,209	49.4	6.9	33.9	9.8	3,614	23,359,578	3,988
Tioga		107	95.3	4.7	0.0	0.0	0.0	476,694	31.8	4.8	57.1	6.3	4,455	514,310	4,807
Tom Bean		676	96.4	0.7	0.6	1.9	0.3	2,493,446	18.4	11.0	68.3	2.3	3,689	2,493,446	3,689
Van Alstyne		790	93.8	2.2	3.2	0.3	0.6	2,595,927	32.4	4.8	61.3	1.5	3,286	2,596,139	3,286
Whitesboro		1,149	96.3	3.5	0.0	0.2	0.0	3,964,330	36.0	6.0	54.6	3.4	3,450	4,024,547	3,503
Whitewright		554	83.8	6.3	9.9	0.0	0.0	1,871,536	23.7	5.0	69.3	2.0	3,378	2,002,112	3,614
Gregg	7	22,343	70.6	2.9	25.7	0.5	0.3	90,228,401	55.6	8.7	31.2	4.5	4,038	95,080,557	4,255
Gladewater		2,106	77.0	1.7	20.8	0.3	0.2	9,422,059	60.6	8.4	26.3	4.7	4,474	9,940,237	4,720
Kilgore		3,636	75.4	1.6	22.6	0.1	0.2	12,805,729	42.9	7.6	45.1	4.5	3,522	13,029,898	3,584
Longview		8,138	47.0	3.5	48.9	0.5	0.1	31,316,562	48.7	5.3	38.8	7.1	3,848	32,080,906	3,942
Pine Tree		4,642	88.6	4.2	5.4	1.2	0.6	19,375,901	62.3	16.7	19.7	1.3	4,174	19,465,231	4,193
Sabine		1,201	83.0	1.6	14.4	0.3	0.7	6,151,408	51.8	4.8	37.0	6.4	5,122	6,991,398	5,821
Spring Hill		1,326	93.8	3.9	2.2	0.1	0.0	5,314,563	66.7	7.3	24.5	1.6	4,008	5,980,340	4,510
White Oak		1,294	95.1	0.2	4.1	0.4	0.2	5,842,179	84.5	8.1	5.6	1.6	4,515	7,592,547	5,868
Grimes	4	3,789	55.6	16.2	28.1	†	0.0	14,139,379	30.9	7.1	52.6	9.4	3,732	14,636,531	3,863
Anderson-Shiro		413	71.4	5.3	23.2	0.0	0.0	1,943,038	55.5	11.2	28.9	4.3	4,705	2,072,359	5,018
Iola		378	84.7	9.0	6.3	0.0	0.0	1,657,497	30.9	14.4	48.5	6.2	4,385	1,702,192	4,503
Navasota		2,874	49.2	19.0	31.7	†	0.0	9,718,633	24.7	4.7	59.5	11.1	3,382	10,071,258	3,504
Richards		124	63.7	8.9	27.4	0.0	0.0	820,211	45.9	10.6	35.3	8.2	6,615	790,722	6,377
Guadalupe	4	12,910	55.5	36.9	6.6	0.8	0.2	46,823,643	35.7	5.0	47.9	11.4	3,627	51,021,111	3,952
Marion		917	70.9	25.6	2.8	0.4	0.2	3,214,660	29.2	3.9	63.1	3.7	3,506	3,138,485	3,423
Navarro		520	64.2	33.8	1.9	0.0	0.0	2,221,251	43.0	5.6	46.8	4.6	4,272	2,615,882	5,031
Schertz-Cibolo-U		4,648	70.1	23.5	4.7	1.4	0.3	14,374,902	36.8	6.3	48.3	8.6	3,093	17,673,210	3,802
Seguin		6,825	42.8	47.9	8.8	0.5	†	27,012,830	35.3	4.4	45.9	14.4	3,958	27,593,534	4,043
Hale	5	8,292	37.0	56.3	6.7	0.1	†	29,614,185	28.1	3.8	54.4	13.7	3,571	33,954,514	4,095
Abernathy		869	41.4	54.8	3.7	0.1	0.0	3,985,059	54.5	4.3	26.0	15.1	4,586	4,864,599	5,598
Cotton Center		172	34.9	65.1	0.0	0.0	0.0	859,368	31.8	2.7	48.7	16.8	4,996	990,070	5,756
Hale Center		723	34.6	60.4	5.0	0.0	0.0	2,831,745	17.3	4.7	63.3	14.7	3,917	2,959,578	4,091
Petersburg		414	37.0	62.1	1.0	0.0	0.0	1,975,849	25.5	2.8	60.0	11.7	4,773	2,185,714	5,280
Plainview		6,114	36.7	55.3	7.9	0.1	†	19,962,164	25.0	3.7	57.9	13.4	3,265	22,954,553	3,754
Hall	3	869	54.1	33.4	12.3	0.2	0.0	4,130,972	23.4	6.9	61.2	8.5	4,754	4,566,247	5,255
Lakeview		64	34.4	65.6	0.0	0.0	0.0	493,960	26.1	8.7	48.3	16.8	7,718	707,706	11,058
Memphis		514	53.9	29.8	16.0	0.4	0.0	2,207,701	23.7	6.1	60.8	9.4	4,295	2,373,984	4,619
Turkey-Quitaque		291	58.8	32.6	8.6	0.0	0.0	1,429,311	21.6	7.2	68.0	3.1	4,912	1,484,557	5,102
Hamilton	2	1,247	91.3	8.2	0.1	0.4	0.0	4,983,717	27.6	4.8	59.2	8.4	3,997	5,040,670	4,042
Hamilton		779	92.0	7.3	0.0	0.5	0.1	3,208,190	30.3	5.1	55.8	8.8	4,118	3,209,489	4,120
Hico		468	90.0	9.6	0.2	0.2	0.0	1,775,527	22.8	4.3	65.2	7.7	3,794	1,831,181	3,913
Hansford	3	1,472	73.4	25.9	0.1	0.4	0.1	7,831,329	68.9	5.6	23.0	2.4	5,320	7,709,935	5,238
Gruver		536	70.0	28.9	0.2	0.9	0.0	2,970,000	67.4	5.7	24.2	2.7	5,541	2,970,000	5,54
Pringle-Morse Co		84	67.9	31.0	1.2	0.0	0.0	681,512	87.4	8.2	1.7	2.7	8,113	863,287	10,277
Spearman		852	76.2	23.5	0.0	0.1	0.2	4,179,817	66.0	4.8	26.7	2.5	4,906	3,876,648	4,550
Hardeman	2	1,112	73.4	18.1	8.1	0.2	0.1	5,213,227	39.0	6.2	46.6	8.2	4,688	5,731,042	5,154
Chillicothe		265	75.5	12.8	10.9	0.0	0.8	1,412,256	61.3	5.7	24.9	8.1	5,329	1,468,266	5,54
Quanah		847	72.7	19.7	7.2	0.2	0.1	3,800,971	31.3	6.4	54.1	8.2	4,488	4,262,776	5,03
Hardin	5	9,925	85.5	1.1	13.3	0.1	†	36,635,504	35.3	5.6	52.4	6.7	3,691	38,963,579	3,924
Hardin-Jefferson		1,857	83.3	1.7	15.0	0.1	0.0	8,221,309	53.4	4.4	33.7	8.5	4,427	9,216,614	4,96
Kountze		1,258	80.3	1.1	18.4	0.2	0.0	4,678,356	28.2	4.3	62.9	4.6	3,719	4,856,596	3,86
Lumberton		2,397	98.5	1.2	0.0	0.3	0.0	7,714,704	29.0	6.8	58.7	5.5	3,218	8,009,418	3,34
Silsbee		3,741	77.4	0.8	21.7	0.1	0.1	13,006,375	26.5	6.3	59.8	7.4	3,477	13,699,981	3,66
W. Hardin Co Con		672	99.7	0.3	0.0	0.0	0.0	3,014,760	47.9	5.2	42.9	4.1	4,486	3,180,970	4,73
Harris	20	521,527	42.8	28.3	24.4	4.3	0.1	2,015,471,103	55.0	6.2	32.6	6.1	3,865	2,378,755,244	4,56
Aldine		39,133	36.3	28.8	30.4	4.4	0.1	124,402,480	40.3	5.5	44.9	9.3	3,179	124,802,480	3,18
Alief		28,408	41.9	17.1	22.4	18.5	†	119,493,314	59.9	7.0	31.2	1.9	4,206	138,317,110	4,86
Channelview		5,111	66.3	22.6	8.2	2.9	0.1	20,464,391	56.7	5.3	34.4	3.6	4,004	21,561,570	4,21
Crosby		3,466	66.2	6.9	26.3	0.5	0.1	14,988,793	39.3	17.7	37.2	5.8	4,325	23,563,589	6,79
Cypress-Fairbanks		38,920	73.7	11.4	8.0	6.6	0.3	158,863,735	62.9	7.7	24.5	1.0	4,082	196,695,836	5,05
Deer Park		9,729	82.3	15.4	0.8	1.3	0.1	40,332,024	85.3	8.1	5.3	0.3	4,148	51,952,240	5,34
Galena Park		15,278	43.2	37.3	17.1	2.4	†	46,600,274	36.1	7.2	51.8	4.9	3,050	55,330,899	3,62
Goose Creek		17,150	56.8	26.4	16.3	0.5	†	77,421,932	66.4	5.2	25.5	2.9	4,514	78,026,049	4,55
Houston		191,282	15.2	42.6	39.6	2.6	0.1	705,692,131	52.7	5.3	31.8	10.1	3,689	906,251,005	4,73
Huffman		2,017	95.6	3.5	0.2	0.5	0.2	7,694,640	42.7	5.8	49.2	2.3	3,815	7,972,266	3,95
Humble		18,835	85.5	6.4	5.7	2.3	0.1	74,348,598	54.2	6.4	37.3	2.1	3,947	96,578,973	5,12
Katy		18,385	81.7	9.5	4.7	3.9	0.2	79,673,638	65.7	7.9	24.1	2.3	4,334	87,133,661	4,73
Klein		25,088	75.2	8.9	9.8	5.9	0.2	98,988,987	50.2	6.4	42.1	1.3	3,946	103,474,263	4,12
La Porte		7,596	72.6	16.7	9.1	1.3	0.3	38,002,225	76.8	4.2	14.0	5.0	5,003	38,020,293	5,00
North Forest		11,854	2.7	9.1	88.2	†	†	45,153,437	25.4	6.5	10.8	3,809	4,049	45,153,437	3,80
Pasadena		36,637	52.8	38.0	4.5	4.3	0.4	124,327,649	41.1	6.3	47.6	5.1	3,393	133,623,259	3,64
Sheldon		4,010	66.6	11.9	19.6	1.7	0.2	20,299,385	72.9	6.6	16.5	4.0	5,061	21,016,273	5,24
Spring		17,917	68.5	12.3	14.6	4.3	0.2	73,196,920	38.1	8.1	31.7	1.8	4,085	97,870,637	5,46
Spring Branch		26,044	50.6	31.6	9.0	8.2	0.1	115,542,468	70.6	5.4	22.9	1.0	4,436	125,544,732	4,82
Tomball		4,667	91.0	4.6	3.8	0.5	0.1	23,033,118	69.5	8.8	19.8	1.8	4,935	24,100,049	5,16
Harrison	6	12,456	63.7	1.6	34.4	0.2	0.1	50,166,239	49.4	4.7	38.8	7.0	4,027	50,052,546	4,01
Elysian Fields		913	74.5	1.2	24.0	0.0	0.3	7,649,072	53.7	4.9	37.4	4.0	4,964	4,964,532	5,43
Hallsville		3,061	90.4	1.0	8.0	0.2	0.4	12,247,518	68.2	4.4	21.9	5.5	4,001	12,558,352	4,10
Harleton		496	91.7	0.0	8.2	0.0	0.0	2,073,656	49.2	5.9	41.1	3.8	4,181	2,174,254	4,38
Karnack		484	34.9	0.0	65.1	0.0	0.0	1,932,620	31.7	1.7	57.3	9.3	3,993	1,969,377	4,06

County/ISD	Districts	Students	% White**	% Hispanic**	% Black**	% Asian**	% American Indian**	Total Revenue	% Local***	% Other***	% State***	% Federal***	Revenue Per Pupil	Total Spending	Spending Per Pupil
Harrison Co. (Con't.)															
Marshall		6,669	49.2	2.2	48.3	0.3	0.1	22,817,693	40.8	5.3	45.3	8.6	3,421	24,813,474	3,721
Waskom		833	69.3	1.7	28.7	0.4	0.0	3,445,680	47.0	2.9	44.2	5.8	4,136	3,572,557	4,289
Hartley	2	281	94.0	5.7	0.4	0.0	0.0	**1,895,204**	63.2	8.0	25.0	3.6	6,744	**1,935,100**	6,886
Channing		142	93.7	6.3	0.0	0.0	0.0	1,022,921	67.2	10.2	18.7	3.6	7,204	1,059,817	7,464
Hartley		139	94.2	5.0	0.7	0.0	0.0	872,283	58.4	5.4	32.7	3.5	6,275	875,283	6,297
Haskell	5	1,245	62.6	32.2	4.8	0.2	0.2	**5,517,157**	37.1	5.3	49.7	7.9	4,431	**6,040,500**	4,852
Haskell		749	61.3	32.3	5.7	0.4	0.3	2,669,791	23.3	5.2	63.0	8.4	3,564	3,034,495	4,051
Paint Creek		101	70.3	29.7	0.0	0.0	0.0	699,993	57.7	4.9	32.6	4.9	6,931	729,993	7,228
Rochester		180	58.9	36.1	5.0	0.0	0.0	878,480	53.1	2.7	41.4	2.8	4,880	912,222	5,068
Rule		186	67.2	28.5	4.3	0.0	0.0	978,785	32.6	8.2	47.1	12.1	5,262	975,709	5,246
Weinert		29	62.1	37.9	0.0	0.0	0.0	290,108	79.3	5.7	3.2	11.8	10,004	388,081	13,382
Hays	4	12,485	54.8	41.9	2.9	0.3	0.1	**50,529,814**	50.8	4.0	39.2	6.0	4,047	**52,574,850**	4,211
Dripping Springs		1,488	90.1	8.3	0.7	0.5	0.5	6,676,922	63.0	7.3	27.8	1.9	4,487	7,110,204	4,778
Hays Con		4,056	61.0	36.0	2.5	0.5	0.1	16,899,545	45.3	4.3	43.8	6.6	4,167	17,245,501	4,252
San Marcos		6,014	35.8	59.8	4.1	0.2	†	22,314,196	45.1	3.0	43.8	8.1	3,710	22,700,802	3,775
Wimberley		927	94.3	5.3	0.0	0.3	0.1	4,639,151	75.6	3.4	20.3	0.7	5,004	5,518,343	5,953
Hemphill	1	820	83.3	16.1	0.2	0.1	0.2	**4,819,415**	90.8	3.6	4.3	1.3	5,877	**4,880,039**	5,951
Canadian		820	83.3	16.1	0.2	0.1	0.2	4,819,415	90.8	3.6	4.3	1.3	5,877	4,880,039	5,951
Henderson	8	8,600	81.8	3.9	14.1	0.2	†	**33,030,681**	47.2	7.2	40.5	5.1	3,841	**35,852,001**	4,169
Athens		3,293	75.7	6.3	17.8	0.2	0.0	11,587,798	45.5	5.4	43.0	6.2	3,519	12,495,897	3,795
Brownsboro		1,940	82.2	2.1	15.4	0.2	0.1	8,196,627	40.6	12.6	41.1	5.7	4,225	9,163,376	4,723
Cross Roads		517	95.9	1.9	2.1	0.0	0.0	2,315,124	54.5	7.2	36.2	2.1	4,478	2,324,140	4,495
Eustace		1,003	94.9	4.0	1.0	0.0	0.1	4,024,128	45.1	4.8	46.2	3.9	4,012	4,068,507	4,056
LaPoynor		401	79.3	0.5	20.0	0.2	0.0	1,801,191	72.4	4.0	20.8	2.8	4,492	2,076,238	5,178
Malakoff		1,057	80.7	1.5	17.3	0.5	0.0	3,617,043	55.1	4.9	34.7	5.4	3,422	3,951,919	3,739
Murchison		132	97.0	3.0	0.0	0.0	0.0	539,740	32.1	10.1	55.0	2.7	4,089	652,943	4,947
Trinidad		257	79.0	4.3	16.7	0.0	0.0	949,030	45.8	5.0	44.5	4.7	3,693	1,118,981	4,354
Hidalgo	15	108,251	5.6	94.1	0.1	0.1	0	**411,159,304**	12.5	5.3	67.5	14.7	3,798	**491,712,301**	4,542
Donna		7,023	3.1	96.8	†	†	0.0	25,733,255	7.5	2.4	72.5	17.7	3,664	27,862,666	3,967
Edcouch-Elsa		3,980	1.0	98.9	0.1	†	0.0	15,603,420	3.9	2.8	71.9	21.3	3,920	15,735,274	3,954
Edinburg		15,089	5.7	94.1	0.2	0.1	†	55,823,469	17.4	3.7	65.0	14.0	3,700	66,941,070	4,436
Hidalgo		2,196	0.7	99.2	0.0	0.1	0.0	9,326,851	9.3	0.7	65.4	24.6	4,247	9,703,522	4,419
La Joya		8,981	0.9	98.9	0.1	0.1	0.0	34,463,330	17.9	4.0	63.0	15.0	3,837	42,445,217	4,726
La Villa		660	0.0	100	0.0	0.0	0.0	3,746,947	12.2	3.0	61.1	23.7	5,677	3,731,482	5,654
McAllen		21,169	12.8	86.6	0.2	0.3	†	75,687,558	19.3	5.3	63.3	12.2	3,575	93,079,655	4,397
Mercedes		4,708	2.4	97.4	0.1	0.1	0.0	17,774,387	5.7	3.1	70.7	20.5	3,775	18,214,885	3,869
Mission Con		9,306	4.5	95.2	0.1	0.2	0.1	36,472,578	8.1	4.4	72.0	15.6	3,919	42,687,669	4,587
Monte Alto		465	4.3	95.7	0.0	0.0	0.0	1,998,099	12.4	1.4	69.4	16.8	4,297	2,093,695	4,503
Pharr-SJ-Alamo		18,062	2.3	97.6	0.1	†	0.0	72,157,473	9.3	11.0	68.5	11.3	3,995	102,628,410	5,682
Progreso		1,535	0.0	100	0.0	0.0	0.0	5,761,509	5.4	1.2	74.9	18.4	3,753	6,791,696	4,425
Sharyland		2,856	25.6	74.1	0.3	†	0.0	9,116,247	19.7	5.0	63.0	12.3	3,192	9,866,709	3,455
Valley View		1,276	0.1	99.9	0.0	0.0	0.0	5,367,660	4.7	1.9	73.5	19.9	4,207	5,525,002	4,330
Weslaco		10,945	4.5	95.3	†	0.1	†	42,126,521	9.2	2.2	71.0	17.6	3,849	44,405,349	4,057
Hill	12	5,008	74.1	11.3	14.4	0.1	0.1	**18,425,545**	24.1	4.6	63.3	8.0	3,679	**19,703,037**	3,934
Abbott		189	96.8	2.6	0.5	0.0	0.0	708,749	21.9	6.2	69.2	2.7	3,750	704,055	3,725
Aquilla		136	86.0	3.7	8.8	0.0	1.5	601,902	30.6	2.7	64.3	2.4	4,426	659,013	4,846
Blum		246	93.1	6.9	0.0	0.0	0.0	998,867	31.5	5.9	60.1	2.4	4,060	998,867	4,060
Bynum		113	77.0	2.7	20.4	0.0	0.0	578,822	35.2	4.8	57.4	2.6	5,122	566,424	5,013
Covington		215	95.3	4.7	0.0	0.0	0.0	866,287	16.4	6.5	75.1	2.0	4,029	866,337	4,029
Hillsboro		1,660	57.9	20.4	21.5	0.0	0.2	5,810,588	25.1	3.8	58.2	13.0	3,500	6,076,113	3,660
Hubbard		462	66.2	2.6	31.2	0.0	0.0	1,806,546	20.0	5.8	62.6	5.2	3,910	1,915,947	4,147
Itasca		545	61.1	18.7	19.3	0.6	0.4	2,095,582	27.6	2.9	63.4	6.1	3,845	2,183,253	4,006
Malone		76	75.0	5.3	19.7	0.0	0.0	341,600	24.0	7.1	64.3	4.6	4,495	366,200	4,818
Mount Calm		114	76.3	5.3	18.4	0.0	0.0	648,429	18.3	3.0	50.2	28.4	5,688	1,258,756	11,042
Penelope		130	82.3	12.3	5.4	0.0	0.0	531,973	17.1	3.3	75.2	4.4	4,092	583,671	4,490
Whitney		1,122	92.5	4.2	3.2	0.0	0.1	3,436,200	22.1	5.6	66.8	5.5	3,063	3,524,401	3,141
Hockley	6	5,881	51.9	42.6	5.3	0.2	0.1	**29,222,507**	60.7	7.2	24.3	7.9	4,969	**30,259,894**	5,145
Anton		361	48.2	44.9	6.4	0.0	0.6	1,584,841	34.8	6.5	46.3	12.4	4,390	1,861,037	5,155
Levelland		4,134	51.2	41.9	6.6	0.3	†	18,083,266	57.6	8.7	24.2	9.5	4,374	18,555,102	4,488
Ropes		281	38.8	60.1	1.1	0.0	0.0	1,409,649	26.2	5.8	57.8	10.1	5,017	1,574,213	5,602
Smyer		353	68.0	30.9	1.1	0.0	0.0	1,775,427	62.7	3.0	31.9	2.4	5,030	1,824,832	5,169
Sundown		579	54.1	44.9	1.0	0.0	0.0	5,397,543	90.6	4.3	2.7	2.5	9,322	5,397,543	9,322
Whitharral		173	58.4	41.6	0.0	0.0	0.0	971,781	39.5	5.0	46.7	8.8	5,617	1,047,167	6,053
Hood	3	5,588	93.1	5.5	0.3	0.6	0.5	**17,559,329**	45.9	6.3	42.9	5.0	3,142	**18,323,893**	3,279
Granbury		5,032	92.7	5.6	0.4	0.7	0.5	15,534,696	47.6	6.3	41.1	5.0	3,087	15,893,388	3,158
Lipan		220	96.8	3.2	0.0	0.0	0.0	906,457	45.6	5.1	45.5	3.8	4,120	973,427	4,425
Tolar		336	95.2	4.8	0.0	0.0	0.0	1,118,176	22.3	7.0	65.4	5.4	3,328	1,457,078	4,337
Hopkins	7	5,527	83.5	4.5	11.5	0.3	0.3	**21,008,739**	38.2	7.2	46.7	7.9	3,801	**22,630,826**	4,095
Como-Pickton		526	83.7	9.9	5.7	0.0	0.8	2,075,984	34.4	4.1	57.3	4.2	3,947	1,976,443	3,757
Cumby		210	94.8	2.4	0.5	0.0	2.4	831,467	37.6	4.3	55.3	2.5	3,959	884,456	4,212
Miller Grove		196	88.3	10.7	0.5	0.0	0.5	800,106	35.1	4.3	56.7	3.8	4,082	828,516	4,227
North Hopkins		330	93.9	1.5	3.9	0.6	0.0	1,409,843	38.7	3.7	53.0	4.6	4,272	1,389,015	4,209
Saltillo		200	94.0	4.0	1.5	0.0	0.5	748,918	23.1	5.1	66.4	5.3	3,745	772,919	3,865
Sulphur Bluff		207	85.0	14.0	1.0	0.0	0.0	1,045,656	35.1	12.6	47.2	5.1	5,051	2,058,192	9,943
Sulphur Springs		3,858	81.1	3.3	15.1	0.4	0.1	14,096,765	40.0	8.7	41.7	9.7	3,654	14,721,285	3,816
Houston	5	3,957	60.2	2.9	36.6	0.2	0.1	**15,824,609**	27.9	5.3	55.7	11.1	3,999	**17,135,171**	4,330
Crockett		1,796	40.4	3.7	55.7	0.1	0.1	6,495,574	25.1	5.0	56.5	13.4	3,617	6,744,561	3,755
Grapeland		820	70.5	0.0	29.4	0.1	0.0	2,731,205	30.0	8.4	58.5	6.7	3,331	3,725,743	4,544
Kennard		417	69.8	0.5	29.0	0.5	0.2	1,984,759	18.7	4.9	63.0	13.4	4,760	1,967,295	4,718
Latexo		402	91.0	4.2	3.5	0.7	0.5	2,159,244	27.8	7.1	52.8	12.1	5,371	2,201,944	5,477

County/ISD	Districts	Students	% White**	% Hispanic**	% Black**	% Asian**	% American Indian**	Total Revenue	% Local***	% Other***	% State***	% Federal***	Revenue Per Pupil	Total Spending	Spending Per Pupil
Houston Co. (Cont.)															
Lovelady		522	80.5	5.9	13.6	0.0	0.0	2,453,827	40.3	5.4	47.0	7.4	4,701	2,495,628	4,781
Howard	3	6,099	60.3	34.6	4.5	0.4	0.2	24,557,858	51.5	5.5	36.1	6.9	4,027	26,327,575	4,317
Big Spring		4,601	52.8	40.6	5.9	0.5	0.3	16,358,364	43.3	5.1	42.6	9.0	3,555	17,417,186	3,786
Coahoma		959	80.5	19.3	0.0	0.2	0.0	4,915,753	56.8	6.2	33.8	3.2	5,126	5,203,545	5,426
Forsan		539	88.3	11.5	0.2	0.0	0.0	3,283,741	84.5	6.3	7.3	1.9	6,092	3,706,844	6,877
Hudspeth	4	754	25.3	74.0	0.7	0.0	0.0	3,732,818	35.2	5.2	49.8	9.9	4,951	3,854,508	5,112
Allamoore*		3	100	0.0	0.0	0.0	0.0	38,988	98.0	0.0	2.0	0.0	12,996	35,087	11,696
Dell City		248	37.5	60.5	2.0	0.0	0.0	1,181,673	23.7	9.3	57.3	9.7	4,765	1,175,690	4,741
Fort Hancock		365	11.2	88.8	0.0	0.0	0.0	1,702,972	34.8	3.2	49.4	12.6	4,666	1,779,752	4,876
Sierra Blanca		138	39.1	60.9	0.0	0.0	0.0	809,185	49.7	3.5	42.0	4.8	5,864	863,979	6,261
Hunt	10	12,071	79.1	4.5	15.6	0.5	0.4	42,686,810	41.9	6.5	44.5	7.0	3,536	45,430,121	3,764
Bland		349	97.1	0.3	1.7	0.0	0.9	1,382,885	23.1	4.0	70.0	2.9	3,962	1,272,636	3,647
Boles Home		203	87.2	3.9	8.9	0.0	0.0	801,266	5.0	1.0	90.2	3.8	3,947	801,266	3,947
Caddo Mills		692	91.2	1.7	7.1	0.0	0.0	2,417,276	29.9	4.8	61.2	4.2	3,493	2,423,324	3,502
Campbell		330	97.0	1.8	0.9	0.0	0.3	1,137,191	18.4	3.1	76.2	2.2	3,446	1,324,425	4,013
Celeste		397	93.2	3.8	3.0	0.0	0.0	1,446,923	23.7	10.0	64.0	2.3	3,645	1,643,054	4,139
Commerce		1,588	74.8	1.8	21.9	1.0	0.5	6,090,240	29.0	9.5	48.7	12.7	3,835	6,369,908	4,011
Greenville		5,008	66.4	6.1	26.6	0.7	0.1	18,207,327	44.1	6.3	42.3	7.2	36,383	19,871,673	3,968
Lone Oak		498	88.4	4.0	6.4	0.2	1.0	2,090,102	22.3	16.6	59.0	2.1	4,197	2,063,315	4,143
Quinlan		2,448	93.2	5.4	0.5	0.1	0.8	7,280,799	27.5	7.3	61.0	4.3	2,974	7,835,155	3,201
Wolfe City		558	85.5	2.2	11.8	0.2	0.4	1,832,801	19.3	4.7	73.2	2.8	3,285	1,825,365	3,271
Hutchinson	4	5,579	83.7	12.0	3.6	0.3	0.4	22,475,600	50.3	4.2	42.0	3.5	4,029	26,224,065	4,700
Borger		3,311	77.3	16.6	5.7	0.3	0.1	11,351,076	38.5	4.3	51.5	5.7	3,428	11,705,724	3,535
Plemons-Sti-Phi		846	89.6	8.7	0.2	0.2	1.2	6,176,340	81.2	3.8	14.0	1.0	7,301	9,280,236	10,970
Sanford		1,390	95.0	3.5	0.7	0.4	0.5	4,682,734	35.6	4.6	58.2	1.5	3,369	4,914,210	3,535
Spring Creek		32	96.9	3.1	0.0	0.0	0.0	265,450	94.7	1.4	3.3	0.5	8,295	323,895	10,122
Irion	1	342	73.1	26.9	0.0	0.0	0.0	1,969,516	79.9	6.9	11.9	1.3	5,759	2,101,831	6,146
Irion County		342	73.1	26.9	0.0	0.0	0.0	1,969,516	79.9	6.9	11.9	1.3	5,759	2,101,831	6,146
Jack	3	1,537	94.0	4.0	1.2	0.2	0.7	6,426,407	59.1	5.1	33.2	2.6	4,181	7,350,500	4,782
Bryson		261	94.6	1.9	0.8	0.0	2.7	1,235,434	58.8	5.4	32.1	3.7	4,733	1,439,084	5,514
Jacksboro		955	92.9	4.8	1.7	0.3	0.3	3,948,237	61.1	5.2	31.7	2.1	4,134	4,543,027	4,757
Perrin-Whitt Con.		321	96.9	3.1	0.0	0.0	0.0	1,242,736	52.9	4.7	39.2	3.1	3,871	1,368,389	4,263
Jackson	3	3,098	63.6	26.8	9.5	0.1	0.0	13,364,425	50.6	5.1	38.6	5.6	4,314	16,624,012	5,366
Edna		1,625	55.5	29.4	14.9	0.2	0.0	6,551,649	47.0	5.3	40.4	7.2	4,032	9,945,291	6,120
Ganado		619	62.5	32.5	5.0	0.0	0.0	2,439,170	37.7	3.7	51.7	7.0	3,941	2,515,385	4,064
Industrial		854	79.9	17.8	2.3	0.0	0.0	4,373,606	63.3	5.6	28.6	2.5	5,121	4,163,336	4,875
Jasper	5	7,263	69.8	1.9	28.0	0.1	0.1	26,061,702	34.0	4.1	54.4	7.5	3,588	27,319,221	3,761
Brookeland		248	78.2	0.0	21.8	0.0	0.0	1,185,707	64.9	2.3	22.8	10.0	4,781	1,305,791	5,265
Buna		1,518	91.0	0.6	7.8	0.2	0.4	4,845,952	27.7	3.4	64.9	4.0	3,192	4,889,484	3,221
Evadale		420	100	0.0	0.0	0.0	0.0	2,720,328	85.6	7.8	4.0	2.6	6,477	2,781,212	6,621
Jasper		3,524	52.6	3.3	43.9	0.1	†	12,297,919	27.3	3.5	59.0	10.3	3,490	12,784,379	3,628
Kirbyville		1,553	78.7	1.0	20.3	0.0	0.1	5,011,796	21.2	4.9	67.9	6.0	3,227	5,558,355	3,579
Jeff Davis	2	368	56.3	41.3	2.2	0.3	0.0	2,307,526	35.3	3.5	60.0	1.3	6,270	2,539,864	6,903
Fort Davis		295	61.4	35.6	2.7	0.3	0.0	1,662,537	30.0	4.8	65.2	0.0	5,636	1,894,875	6,423
Valentine		73	35.6	64.4	0.0	0.0	0.0	644,989	48.9	0.0	46.5	4.5	8,835	644,989	8,83
Jefferson	6	44,646	48.5	4.9	42.9	3.6	†	175,243,137	55.0	5.0	31.8	8.3	3,925	194,716,242	4,364
Beaumont		20,690	35.5	3.5	59.0	1.9	0.1	80,453,321	51.5	4.6	33.5	10.4	3,889	92,862,674	4,489
Hamshire-Fannett		1,608	89.9	2.1	7.4	0.6	0.0	6,454,214	58.0	4.3	34.2	3.5	4,014	7,567,606	4,705
Nederland		5,056	94.3	3.1	1.0	1.5	0.1	18,183,832	50.8	5.8	38.7	4.9	3,596	20,190,027	3,995
Port Arthur		12,043	26.4	8.6	56.1	8.9	0.0	49,330,423	57.6	5.0	28.7	8.8	4,096	53,734,761	4,461
Port Neches		5,055	93.8	4.8	0.1	1.3	0.0	18,739,410	61.4	6.9	27.9	3.8	3,707	18,223,774	3,606
Sabine Pass		194	88.1	0.0	11.3	0.5	0.0	2,081,937	94.4	2.1	3.5	0.0	10,732	2,137,400	11,011
Jim Hogg	1	1,274	6.0	93.6	0.1	0.1	0.2	5,821,180	51.1	3.3	39.5	6.2	4,569	6,298,853	4,943
Jim Hogg County		1,274	6.0	93.6	0.1	0.1	0.2	5,821,180	51.1	3.3	39.5	6.2	4,569	6,298,853	4,943
Jim Wells	5	8,741	22.1	77.2	0.6	0.1	0.0	32,759,403	26.3	3.8	60.6	9.3	3,748	33,773,405	3,863
Alice		6,115	20.0	79.1	0.8	0.1	0.0	22,112,085	23.3	3.9	62.3	10.5	3,616	22,235,535	3,637
B.Bolt-Pal Blanc		420	9.8	90.2	0.0	0.0	0.0	2,135,161	34.1	3.2	53.9	8.8	5,084	2,186,544	5,209
La Gloria		48	29.2	70.8	0.0	0.0	0.0	458,084	87.0	0.0	6.9	6.1	9,543	508,658	10,597
Orange Grove		1,211	42.8	57.0	0.1	0.2	0.0	4,026,029	44.4	4.1	51.5	0.0	3,325	4,154,821	3,431
Premont		947	13.9	85.6	0.2	0.1	0.0	4,028,044	43.8	3.6	44.9	7.8	4,253	4,687,847	4,953
Johnson	9	19,923	87.4	8.6	3.0	0.5	0.2	67,167,901	35.4	7.8	51.9	4.8	3,371	76,284,114	3,829
Alvarado		2,333	87.1	7.5	4.9	0.0	0.5	7,666,492	27.9	7.9	56.5	4.9	3,204	7,442,143	3,191
Burleson		5,326	95.2	3.3	0.4	0.9	0.2	16,846,561	45.3	6.9	44.3	3.4	3,163	17,290,689	3,248
Cleburne		5,668	79.9	12.5	6.9	0.6	0.1	19,533,636	38.7	10.0	43.7	7.6	3,446	27,639,191	4,877
Godley		641	93.8	5.9	0.3	0.0	0.0	2,426,096	29.4	5.8	62.4	2.3	3,785	2,437,690	3,802
Grandview		733	82.7	11.6	5.7	0.0	0.0	3,293,191	23.8	6.5	67.4	2.3	4,493	3,351,283	4,572
Joshua		3,016	93.8	5.4	0.6	0.1	0.1	8,644,129	31.2	7.8	58.9	2.2	2,866	9,392,283	3,113
Keene		602	60.8	26.9	9.0	2.3	1.0	2,650,047	25.1	2.3	68.3	4.3	4,402	2,850,056	4,735
Rio Vista		694	92.9	6.6	0.4	0.0	0.0	2,745,700	18.9	10.2	68.4	2.5	3,956	2,769,778	3,991
Venus		910	80.4	17.7	0.9	1.0	0.0	3,554,743	26.4	5.2	65.9	2.5	3,906	3,111,001	3,419
Jones	5	3,256	68.1	25.8	5.8	0.3	0.0	13,347,622	24.5	5.6	62.9	7.0	4,098	13,900,694	4,269
Anson		816	57.8	38.5	3.6	0.1	0.0	3,124,516	21.2	3.3	69.0	6.5	3,829	3,121,813	3,825
Hamlin		741	65.2	25.4	8.8	0.7	0.0	3,125,182	30.3	5.5	57.7	6.5	4,218	3,158,045	4,261
Hawley		614	93.8	6.0	0.2	0.0	0.0	2,264,365	20.2	5.1	69.9	4.8	3,688	2,357,272	3,839
Lueders-Avoca		208	86.1	13.5	0.0	0.0	0.0	1,044,990	44.6	4.7	47.3	3.6	5,024	1,044,991	5,024
Stamford		877	57.7	31.2	10.6	0.5	0.0	3,788,569	19.6	8.2	65.4	6.8	4,320	4,218,573	4,811
Karnes	4	2,831	35.0	61.6	3.2	0.1	0.0	11,201,150	26.2	4.1	59.5	10.1	3,957	11,707,171	4,135
Falls City		308	79.9	20.1	0.0	0.0	0.0	1,308,637	33.9	5.1	55.8	5.1	4,249	1,384,587	4,495
Karnes City		1,032	33.5	61.6	4.8	0.0	0.0	4,018,809	27.2	3.6	59.6	9.6	3,894	4,009,119	3,885

County/ISD	Districts	Students	% White**	% Hispanic**	% Black**	% Asian**	% American Indian**	Total Revenue	% Local***	% Other***	% State***	% Federal***	Revenue Per Pupil	Total Spending	Spending Per Pupil
Karnes Co. (Con't.)															
Kenedy		1,123	24.9	72.0	2.7	0.4	0.0	4,470,971	24.5	4.4	59.5	11.6	3,981	4,671,607	4,160
Runge		368	32.6	64.1	3.3	0.0	0.0	1,402,733	21.5	4.0	63.0	11.5	3,812	1,641,858	4,462
Kaufman	7	13,271	77.0	7.2	15.1	0.6	0.2	46,109,481	33.8	5.7	54.4	6.1	3,474	47,950,512	3,613
Crandall		1,017	91.2	2.8	5.7	0.3	0.0	3,577,197	25.9	8.7	62.4	3.1	3,517	4,012,075	3,945
Forney		1,462	90.1	3.6	5.8	0.1	0.4	6,379,354	46.9	6.8	35.3	11.0	4,363	6,847,705	4,684
Kaufman		2,625	71.3	16.8	11.3	0.5	0.1	8,666,026	24.5	7.4	65.4	2.7	3,301	9,012,117	3,433
Kemp		1,378	91.6	3.3	4.5	0.1	0.5	4,879,989	32.7	5.6	58.3	3.4	3,541	5,159,544	3,744
Mabank		2,408	94.6	2.3	2.7	0.3	0.1	7,583,002	48.9	4.5	43.5	3.1	3,149	7,632,674	3,170
Scurry-Rosser		678	88.6	2.2	8.8	0.1	0.1	2,305,269	21.6	5.3	70.3	2.9	3,400	2,491,472	3,675
Terrell		3,703	53.0	8.5	37.1	1.3	0.1	12,718,644	29.5	4.1	56.2	10.2	3,435	12,794,925	3,455
Kendall	2	3,443	77.4	21.8	0.6	0.1	0.1	12,987,452	58.5	6.0	32.2	3.3	3,772	13,192,973	3,832
Boerne		2,615	81.8	17.3	0.6	0.2	0.2	10,007,243	66.7	5.4	25.5	2.4	3,827	10,136,983	3,876
Comfort		828	63.6	35.9	0.5	0.0	0.0	2,980,209	30.8	7.9	54.9	6.3	3,599	3,055,990	3,691
Kenedy	1	58	0.0	100	0.0	0.0	0.0	475,000	94.5	0.0	5.5	0.0	8,190	659,795	11,376
Kenedy Co Wide*		58	0.0	100	0.0	0.0	0.0	475,000	94.5	0.0	5.5	0.0	8,190	659,795	11,376
Kent	1	187	82.9	15.5	1.6	0.0	0.0	2,583,979	85.4	11.2	2.1	1.3	13,818	2,583,979	13,818
Jayton-Girard		187	82.9	15.5	1.6	0.0	0.0	2,583,979	85.4	11.2	2.1	1.3	13,818	2,583,979	13,818
Kerr	5	5,436	72.0	24.0	3.3	0.6	0.1	22,544,680	54.0	8.1	32.3	5.6	4,147	22,848,706	4,203
Center Point		434	80.4	18.7	0.7	0.2	0.0	1,878,120	34.7	3.8	54.9	6.7	4,327	1,920,377	4,425
Divide		9	88.9	11.1	0.0	0.0	0.0	106,406	94.4	2.8	2.8	0.0	11,823	106,406	11,823
Hunt		113	88.5	11.5	0.0	0.0	0.0	986,537	94.0	2.2	2.8	1.0	8,730	949,954	8,407
Ingram		1,061	89.8	8.9	1.0	0.3	0.0	4,207,571	33.0	12.4	49.5	5.1	3,966	4,264,906	4,020
Kerrville		3,819	65.5	29.2	4.4	0.7	0.1	15,366,046	59.3	7.8	26.9	6.0	4,024	15,607,063	4,087
Kimble	1	756	70.0	30.0	0.0	0.0	0.0	3,160,283	30.7	5.0	59.5	4.9	4,180	3,176,093	4,201
Junction		756	70.0	30.0	0.0	0.0	0.0	3,160,283	30.7	5.0	59.5	4.9	4,180	3,176,093	4,201
King	1	94	87.2	12.8	0.0	0.0	0.0	1,309,734	91.4	5.5	2.1	1.0	13,933	1,309,734	13,933
Guthrie*		94	87.2	12.8	0.0	0.0	0.0	1,309,734	91.4	5.5	2.1	1.0	13,933	1,309,734	13,933
Kinney	1	570	32.5	62.8	4.2	0.4	0.2	2,693,666	26.1	4.5	59.6	9.9	4,726	2,682,154	4,706
Brackett		570	32.5	62.8	4.2	0.4	0.2	2,693,666	26.1	4.5	59.6	9.9	4,726	2,682,154	4,706
Kleberg	5	6,535	25.5	70.3	3.5	0.6	0.1	27,361,135	34.0	6.7	49.8	9.5	4,187	28,156,493	4,309
Kingsville		5,420	23.4	71.6	4.2	0.7	0.1	21,206,347	29.3	7.1	52.6	11.0	3,913	21,388,759	3,946
Laureles		14	0.0	100	0.0	0.0	0.0	438,495	92.0	6.9	1.1	0.0	31,321	414,939	29,639
Ricardo		523	33.8	65.8	0.4	0.0	0.0	2,272,758	31.9	2.6	60.0	5.5	4,346	2,253,175	4,308
Riviera		491	43.4	56.6	0.0	0.0	0.0	2,801,780	49.1	7.6	38.6	4.7	5,706	3,393,969	6,912
Santa Gertrudis		87	8.0	92.0	0.0	0.0	0.0	641,755	91.3	5.6	3.1	0.0	7,376	705,651	8,111
Knox	4	1,089	53.8	35.2	11.0	0.0	0.0	5,439,244	28.4	5.9	56.3	9.3	4,995	5,992,963	5,503
Benjamin		66	87.9	12.1	0.0	0.0	0.0	540,429	76.1	9.1	10.0	4.9	8,188	666,452	10,098
Goree		109	30.3	56.0	13.8	0.0	0.0	746,957	23.3	5.3	61.0	10.4	6,853	768,027	7,046
Knox City-O'Brien		471	54.6	32.9	12.5	0.0	0.0	2,352,034	25.8	4.2	60.5	9.4	4,994	2,644,437	5,615
Munday		443	53.7	35.9	10.4	0.0	0.0	1,799,824	19.5	7.5	62.9	10.1	4,063	1,914,047	4,321
La Salle	1	1,228	14.0	85.8	0.2	0.0	0.0	5,120,656	23.8	0.2	57.7	18.3	4,170	4,946,521	4,028
Cotulla		1,228	14.0	85.8	0.2	0.0	0.0	5,120,656	23.8	0.2	57.7	18.3	4,170	4,946,521	4,028
Lamar	5	8,473	76.4	0.9	21.5	0.4	0.7	30,409,495	28.1	6.4	56.0	9.5	3,589	31,725,049	3,744
Chisum		669	84.8	0.6	14.2	0.0	0.4	2,374,431	37.5	7.4	44.9	10.2	3,549	2,419,518	3,617
North Lamar		2,515	92.8	0.4	5.9	†	0.8	8,525,533	31.2	7.9	54.6	6.3	3,390	9,297,463	3,697
Paris		4,078	60.5	1.5	36.5	0.7	0.8	15,157,809	27.7	5.9	54.5	11.8	3,717	15,525,201	3,807
Prairiland		1,035	96.0	0.4	2.4	0.4	0.8	3,527,155	16.8	4.7	72.7	5.9	3,408	3,589,489	3,468
Roxton		176	63.1	0.0	36.9	0.0	0.0	824,567	24.8	4.4	58.9	11.9	4,685	893,378	5,076
Lamb	6	3,665	39.1	52.6	8.2	0.1	0.1	16,619,432	40.1	3.0	45.6	11.4	4,535	20,205,577	5,513
Amherst		219	47.9	38.4	13.7	0.0	0.0	986,846	24.5	3.6	59.9	12.0	4,506	1,013,638	4,628
Littlefield		1,593	38.7	50.1	11.2	0.0	0.0	6,073,598	32.3	2.7	52.2	12.9	3,813	8,205,640	5,151
Olton		799	29.3	68.2	2.3	0.3	0.0	3,224,023	24.0	3.9	60.1	12.0	4,035	3,607,876	4,515
Spade		100	58.0	42.0	0.0	0.0	0.0	648,037	26.8	4.2	55.7	13.1	6,480	656,073	6,560
Springlake-Earth		557	38.8	56.4	4.8	0.0	0.0	2,449,128	22.0	4.2	57.6	16.1	4,397	2,493,884	4,477
Sudan		397	51.4	36.0	12.1	0.0	0.5	3,237,800	91.9	1.2	3.1	3.8	8,156	4,228,502	10,651
Lampasas	2	2,615	79.7	17.9	1.6	0.4	0.3	8,933,200	26.7	5.1	60.2	7.9	3,416	10,106,998	3,865
Lampasas		2,374	80.1	17.4	1.8	0.4	0.3	8,096,105	27.9	5.1	59.3	7.7	3,410	9,160,748	3,859
Lometa		241	75.9	23.7	0.0	0.0	0.4	837,095	15.5	5.0	69.3	10.2	3,473	946,250	3,926
Lavaca	6	2,030	81.5	6.9	11.5	0.1	0.0	7,847,465	41.7	6.3	47.0	5.0	3,866	8,409,246	4,142
Ezzell		72	97.2	2.8	0.0	0.0	0.0	346,100	84.9	6.4	6.9	1.7	4,807	577,558	8,022
Hallettsville		999	79.7	7.0	13.0	0.3	0.0	3,567,077	45.3	7.8	41.3	5.6	3,571	3,728,351	3,732
Moulton		296	84.1	13.5	2.4	0.0	0.0	1,157,072	27.1	5.2	62.8	4.8	3,909	1,239,256	4,187
Shiner		521	76.2	5.4	18.4	0.0	0.0	2,106,579	31.1	4.7	58.8	5.5	4,043	2,196,895	4,217
Sweet Home		90	100	0.0	0.0	0.0	0.0	358,825	34.8	6.1	57.1	1.9	3,987	359,422	3,994
Vysehrad		52	100	0.0	0.0	0.0	0.0	311,812	86.2	4.5	7.7	1.6	5,996	307,764	5,919
Lee	3	2,495	68.5	15.2	16.2	†	0.1	10,207,038	47.4	8.1	39.5	4.9	4,091	10,535,623	4,223
Dime Box		199	65.3	5.0	29.6	0.0	0.1	1,164,280	41.9	23.0	28.3	6.8	5,851	1,423,392	7,153
Giddings		1,487	60.6	22.3	17.0	0.1	0.0	6,061,062	58.5	5.7	31.2	4.6	4,076	6,121,614	4,117
Lexington		809	83.8	4.6	11.2	0.0	0.4	2,981,696	27.0	7.3	60.9	4.8	3,686	2,990,617	3,697
Leon	5	2,628	80.2	4.7	14.8	0.2	0.1	11,586,715	56.2	5.5	31.9	6.4	4,409	13,527,816	5,148
Buffalo		731	80.7	7.4	11.8	0.1	0.0	2,635,737	30.0	5.6	59.0	5.5	3,606	2,635,737	3,606
Centerville		507	84.2	2.2	13.6	0.0	0.0	2,924,345	68.4	8.8	13.7	9.1	5,768	4,885,497	9,636
Leon		626	86.9	6.4	6.1	0.3	0.3	2,750,168	74.0	4.3	17.6	4.1	4,393	2,754,573	4,400
Normangee		422	83.6	3.6	12.8	0.0	0.0	1,624,416	55.3	3.5	35.0	6.2	3,849	1,558,825	3,694
Oakwood		342	56.7	1.2	41.8	0.3	0.0	1,652,049	47.6	3.6	41.9	6.8	4,831	1,693,184	4,951
Liberty	7	11,889	78.7	5.4	15.7	0.2	0.1	43,506,546	39.2	6.3	49.0	5.4	3,659	45,085,271	3,792
Cleveland		2,881	70.6	9.0	20.2	0.2	†	8,967,776	37.7	4.8	51.0	6.5	3,113	9,843,675	3,417
Dayton		3,288	85.0	4.4	10.3	0.2	0.1	10,470,031	39.7	6.3	51.9	2.0	3,184	10,482,976	3,188
Devers		87	49.4	14.9	35.6	0.0	0.0	625,377	85.4	4.0	4.1	6.4	7,188	709,369	8,154
Hardin		1,069	89.8	5.5	4.6	0.0	0.1	4,359,339	35.6	4.3	54.5	5.7	4,078	4,772,021	4,464

County/ISD	Districts	Students	% White**	% Hispanic**	% Black**	% Asian**	% American Indian**	Total Revenue	% Local***	% Other***	% State***	% Federal***	Revenue Per Pupil	Total Spending	Spending Per Pupil
Liberty Co. (Con't.)															
Hull-Daisetta.....	781	71.1	0.8	27.5	0.6	0.0	3,531,853	40.6	11.1	43.9	4.4	4,522	3,531,853	4,522
Liberty.........	2,380	68.0	5.4	26.2	0.4	†	10,823,624	39.6	7.2	44.2	8.9	4,548	11,040,318	4,639
Tarkington......	1,403	96.4	1.9	1.5	0.0	0.1	4,728,546	36.5	5.9	54.6	3.1	3,370	4,705,059	3,354
Limestone.......	3	3,988	63.0	8.6	28.1	0.3	†	18,862,439	53.3	7.4	33.1	6.2	4,730	20,968,086	5,258
Coolidge........	218	44.5	17.4	38.1	0.0	0.0	954,772	15.1	4.0	70.7	10.2	4,380	1,309,328	6,006
Groesbeck.......	1,491	73.2	7.8	19.0	0.0	0.1	9,829,995	82.5	9.9	4.1	3.5	6,593	11,302,618	7,581
Mexia..........	2,279	58.1	8.3	33.0	0.6	0.0	8,077,672	22.2	4.8	64.0	9.0	3,544	8,356,140	3,667
Lipscomb.........	4	732	81.0	18.2	0.0	0.3	0.5	4,386,400	79.3	4.4	13.4	2.8	5,992	4,696,343	6,416
Booker.........	382	70.2	28.5	0.0	0.3	1.0	1,769,653	72.5	5.0	17.8	4.7	4,633	1,782,258	4,666
Darrouzett......	78	94.9	5.1	0.0	0.0	0.0	737,495	89.0	8.1	2.5	0.4	9,455	917,958	11,769
Follett.........	140	97.1	2.9	0.0	0.0	0.0	1,005,526	82.9	4.6	8.7	3.7	7,182	1,129,041	8,065
Higgins.........	132	87.1	12.1	0.0	0.8	0.0	873,726	80.8	0.0	19.2	0.0	6,619	867,086	6,569
Live Oak	2	2,040	54.1	45.6	†	0.2	0.0	8,419,097	58.6	5.9	29.9	5.6	4,127	8,774,711	4,301
George West	1,262	54.6	45.0	0.0	0.4	0.0	4,946,107	58.5	5.2	30.2	6.1	3,919	5,284,940	4,188
Three Rivers.....	778	53.3	46.5	0.1	0.0	0.0	3,472,990	58.8	6.8	29.4	5.0	4,464	3,489,771	4,486
Llano...........	1	1,227	93.2	6.6	0.2	0.0	0.0	5,464,024	80.1	10.2	6.4	3.3	4,453	5,510,662	4,491
Llano..........	1,227	93.2	6.6	0.2	0.0	0.0	5,464,024	80.1	10.2	6.4	3.3	4,453	5,510,662	4,491
Loving...........	No School	Districts	in County.	See Winkler Co.											
Lubbock..........	8	41,849	53.0	34.4	11.6	0.8	0.1	160,305,791	37.8	4.4	49.6	8.2	3,831	182,003,322	4,349
Frenship........	3,978	71.1	20.8	7.0	1.0	0.1	13,074,141	25.7	5.8	60.6	7.9	3,287	14,831,478	3,728
Idalou.........	826	53.5	45.4	0.8	0.2	0.0	3,250,542	27.4	4.2	59.1	9.2	3,935	3,407,475	4,125
Lubbock........	30,908	48.9	36.1	13.9	1.0	0.1	120,719,505	41.7	4.0	45.8	8.4	3,906	134,211,365	4,342
Lubbock-Cooper ..	1,542	71.5	27.7	0.6	0.1	0.1	5,883,642	28.2	9.7	58.3	3.8	3,816	10,418,800	6,757
New Deal.......	619	62.7	36.7	0.6	0.0	0.0	2,362,249	29.4	4.6	59.0	7.0	3,816	2,499,087	4,037
Roosevelt	1,242	66.7	25.9	7.0	0.1	0.3	4,629,117	22.9	2.9	69.5	4.7	3,727	4,403,102	3,545
Shallowater......	937	72.0	26.8	1.2	0.0	0.0	3,360,391	19.7	5.2	70.7	4.4	3,586	4,275,615	4,563
Slaton..........	1,797	45.3	45.0	9.5	0.2	0.1	7,026,204	26.5	3.8	56.4	13.2	3,910	7,956,400	4,428
Lynn............	4	1,568	41.3	55.2	3.5	0.0	0.0	7,571,640	28.0	4.7	56.4	10.9	4,829	7,905,521	5,042
New Home.......	204	46.6	52.0	1.5	0.0	0.0	978,202	37.3	4.4	46.2	12.1	4,795	1,082,290	5,305
O'Donnell	436	30.3	69.7	0.0	0.0	0.0	2,226,524	29.7	3.5	54.8	12.0	5,107	2,290,007	5,252
Tahoka.........	695	44.9	47.8	7.3	0.0	0.0	3,115,948	20.2	5.4	63.9	10.5	4,483	3,277,358	4,716
Wilson..........	233	46.8	52.8	0.4	0.0	0.0	1,250,966	37.4	5.1	48.6	8.9	5,369	1,255,866	5,390
Madison.........	2	1,851	65.6	8.1	26.1	0.1	0.0	7,122,125	39.2	3.4	48.9	8.5	3,848	7,903,238	4,270
Madisonville Con..	1,653	61.8	8.9	29.2	0.1	0.0	6,034,107	36.7	3.1	50.8	9.4	3,650	6,815,218	4,123
North Zulch......	198	98.0	1.5	0.5	0.0	0.0	1,088,018	53.3	5.0	38.6	3.2	5,495	1,088,020	5,495
Marion..........	1	1,514	52.2	1.0	46.7	0.1	0.0	6,585,939	44.2	3.0	40.5	12.3	4,350	7,752,139	5,120
Jefferson........	1,514	52.2	1.0	46.7	0.1	0.0	6,585,939	44.2	3.0	40.5	12.3	4,350	7,752,139	5,120
Martin..........	2	1,094	49.5	48.6	1.3	0.0	0.6	5,494,430	52.6	6.3	33.7	7.4	5,022	5,512,672	5,044
Grady..........	212	55.7	44.3	0.0	0.0	0.0	1,365,414	87.8	5.6	4.7	1.9	6,441	1,603,312	7,563
Stanton........	882	48.0	49.7	1.6	0.0	0.8	4,129,016	41.0	6.5	43.3	9.2	4,681	5,555,360	6,299
Mason...........	1	608	69.1	30.3	0.5	0.2	0.0	2,753,290	32.7	5.9	53.3	8.1	4,528	2,987,450	4,914
Mason..........	608	69.1	30.3	0.5	0.2	0.0	2,753,290	32.7	5.9	53.3	8.1	4,528	2,987,450	4,914
Matagorda.......	5	8,319	50.9	30.2	15.0	3.8	0.1	37,095,917	60.0	6.7	28.1	5.2	4,459	38,484,870	4,626
Bay City........	4,635	51.0	29.7	17.7	1.5	0.1	16,312,566	46.6	8.4	38.5	6.5	3,519	17,515,533	3,779
Matagorda	108	85.2	13.0	1.9	0.0	0.0	854,714	91.0	2.9	4.0	2.0	7,914	855,864	7,925
Palacios	1,581	37.3	43.5	4.0	15.3	0.0	11,584,915	88.0	4.9	3.7	3.4	7,328	11,525,565	7,290
Tidehaven.......	895	63.5	29.4	7.0	0.1	0.0	3,686,257	43.1	8.6	42.7	5.5	4,119	3,756,263	4,197
Van Vleck	1,100	56.6	15.6	27.7	0.0	0.0	4,657,465	45.3	4.4	44.9	5.4	4,234	4,831,645	4,392
Maverick.........	1	9,567	3.6	96.0	†	0.1	0.4	32,242,701	9.0	2.8	68.8	19.4	3,370	36,603,065	3,826
Eagle Pass	9,567	3.6	96.0	†	0.1	0.4	32,242,701	9.0	2.8	68.8	19.4	3,370	36,603,065	3,826
McCulloch........	3	1,773	61.0	36.2	2.7	0.2	0.0	7,139,734	26.2	4.6	59.1	10.1	4,027	7,372,177	4,158
Brady..........	1,429	57.2	39.3	3.3	0.2	0.0	5,420,455	27.9	4.5	57.1	10.5	3,793	5,654,903	3,957
Lohn...........	100	65.0	34.0	1.0	0.0	0.0	642,117	24.6	5.0	61.7	8.7	6,421	642,117	6,421
Rochelle........	244	81.1	18.9	0.0	0.0	0.0	1,077,162	18.4	5.1	67.9	8.6	4,415	1,075,157	4,406
McLennan........	18	33,701	59.6	16.9	22.8	0.6	0.1	121,601,546	35.0	5.5	51.7	7.7	3,608	144,917,549	4,300
Axtell	666	83.5	6.2	10.1	0.2	0.2	3,604,426	6.4	3.6	68.0	22.0	5,412	5,419,130	8,137
Bosqueville......	289	85.5	6.9	6.9	0.0	0.7	1,092,302	35.0	6.5	55.3	3.2	3,780	1,176,793	4,072
Bruceville-Eddy...	556	86.0	10.8	3.1	0.0	0.0	2,044,898	26.7	4.3	66.3	2.7	3,678	2,154,516	3,875
China Spring.....	912	94.6	4.3	0.1	1.0	0.0	2,690,981	23.9	6.4	68.5	1.1	2,951	2,850,316	3,121
Connally	2,296	75.3	11.4	11.9	1.1	0.2	7,129,143	19.6	5.7	65.4	9.3	3,105	7,654,582	3,334
Crawford	377	87.8	8.5	3.7	0.0	0.0	1,361,523	26.1	7.8	64.1	2.1	3,611	1,453,840	3,856
Gholson........	155	81.3	4.5	14.2	0.0	0.0	569,331	16.9	5.8	73.0	4.3	3,673	573,856	3,702
Hallsburg.......	118	81.4	6.8	11.9	0.0	0.0	611,059	90.7	2.6	5.0	1.6	5,178	544,605	4,615
La Vega	2,229	63.0	16.6	20.0	0.2	0.2	7,953,166	30.6	3.6	59.4	6.4	4,568	8,140,314	3,652
Lorena	1,085	95.3	3.8	0.9	0.0	0.0	3,615,947	23.6	8.0	67.1	1.3	3,333	3,804,921	3,507
Mart...........	680	66.2	4.0	29.9	0.0	0.0	2,331,362	19.3	9.1	67.1	4.5	3,428	2,471,614	3,635
McGregor.......	1,119	56.9	26.3	16.7	0.1	0.0	4,378,262	19.5	12.7	58.6	9.2	3,913	4,569,335	4,083
Midway.........	4,855	89.6	5.3	3.6	1.4	0.1	16,557,754	62.1	6.3	30.5	1.0	3,410	22,376,869	4,609
Moody.........	638	71.8	17.2	10.3	0.2	0.5	2,399,373	18.5	4.0	69.8	7.6	3,761	2,945,613	4,617
Riesel	424	82.8	9.9	6.8	0.2	0.2	1,412,894	23.5	7.1	67.7	1.8	3,332	1,779,923	4,197
Robinson	1,742	85.4	9.4	4.9	0.2	0.1	4,938,241	29.3	7.0	62.5	1.2	2,835	7,677,697	4,407
Waco..........	14,325	30.4	27.1	41.8	0.6	†	55,271,801	36.7	4.4	47.7	11.1	3,858	65,322,533	4,564
West	1,235	91.3	3.9	4.6	0.2	0.0	3,639,083	27.2	7.8	62.5	2.6	2,947	4,001,092	3,240
McMullen	1	173	53.8	46.2	0.0	0.0	0.0	1,758,024	82.6	13.6	2.9	1.0	10,162	3,106,264	17,955
McMullen County .	173	53.8	46.2	0.0	0.0	0.0	1,758,024	82.6	13.6	2.9	1.0	10,162	3,106,264	17,955
Medina	5	6,404	47.3	52.2	0.3	0.1	0.0	21,729,315	25.0	5.3	60.7	8.9	3,393	22,447,80	3,50
D'Hanis........	247	44.1	55.9	0.0	0.0	0.0	1,068,172	26.5	8.5	58.5	6.5	4,325	1,167,480	4,72
Devine.........	1,619	50.4	49.3	0.1	0.2	0.0	5,611,455	26.1	5.2	60.9	7.8	3,466	5,636,200	3,48
Hondo.........	1,808	37.6	62.1	0.3	0.1	0.0	6,202,885	24.2	4.1	59.9	11.8	3,431	6,748,748	3,73

County/ISD	Districts	Students	% White**	% Hispanic**	% Black**	% Asian**	% American Indian**	Total Revenue	% Local***	% Other***	% State***	% Federal***	Revenue Per Pupil	Total Spending	Spending Per Pupil
Medina Co. (Con't.)															
Medina Valley....		1,926	58.7	40.9	0.2	0.2	0.0	6,052,053	30.6	7.0	55.8	6.6	3,142	6,072,395	3,153
Natalia.........		804	36.6	62.1	1.2	0.1	0.0	2,794,750	12.1	3.5	73.8	10.6	3,476	2,823,067	3,511
Menard..........	1	403	55.8	44.2	0.0	0.0	0.0	2,067,356	34.7	4.2	43.9	17.3	5,130	2,228,547	5,530
Menard........		403	55.8	44.2	0.0	0.0	0.0	2,067,356	34.7	4.2	43.9	17.3	5,130	2,228,547	5,530
Midland..........	2	21,558	60.6	28.8	9.6	0.9	0.1	74,886,815	50.0	5.9	39.0	5.3	3,474	78,413,298	3,637
Greenwood......		1,282	85.1	14.3	0.1	0.4	0.2	5,449,460	50.6	4.3	43.7	1.3	4,251	5,667,128	4,421
Midland........		20,276	59.1	29.7	10.2	0.9	0.1	69,437,355	49.9	6.0	38.6	5.6	3,425	72,746,170	3,588
Milam...........	6	4,555	61.3	21.3	17.3	†	†	16,153,609	44.6	5.0	43.4	7.1	3,546	17,096,534	3,753
Buckholts.......		134	53.7	46.3	0.0	0.0	0.0	719,369	23.5	6.1	64.9	5.5	5,368	737,254	5,502
Cameron........		1,688	51.4	24.7	23.8	0.1	0.0	5,536,044	20.9	5.4	65.2	8.5	3,280	5,611,986	3,325
Gause..........		70	68.6	8.6	22.9	0.0	0.0	318,057	33.0	2.8	50.7	13.4	4,544	515,906	7,370
Milano.........		314	86.9	5.7	7.3	0.0	0.0	1,208,022	27.1	4.3	61.7	6.9	3,848	1,468,750	4,678
Rockdale.......		1,961	64.1	19.8	16.1	0.0	0.0	6,725,398	71.2	4.8	17.9	6.1	3,430	7,032,731	3,586
Thorndale......		388	71.4	19.8	8.5	0.0	0.3	1,646,519	39.5	5.3	49.6	5.7	4,244	1,729,907	4,459
Mills...........	4	862	81.6	18.0	0.2	0.1	0.1	3,908,509	22.0	7.1	64.9	6.1	4,534	4,367,547	5,067
Goldthwaite.....		585	80.2	19.5	0.3	0.0	0.0	2,318,012	21.1	7.1	66.4	5.5	3,962	2,787,622	4,765
Mullin.........		113	93.8	6.2	0.0	0.0	0.0	622,952	27.9	3.0	62.9	6.1	5,513	611,951	5,415
Priddy.........		97	80.4	18.6	0.0	0.0	1.0	537,786	13.8	5.6	74.8	5.9	5,544	540,710	5,574
Star...........		67	74.6	23.9	0.0	1.5	0.0	429,759	28.6	14.9	47.2	9.3	6,414	427,264	6,377
Mitchell.........	3	1,734	53.1	40.0	6.9	0.0	0.1	8,543,876	51.4	5.9	34.4	8.4	4,927	8,891,200	5,128
Colorado.......		1,327	53.1	38.7	8.1	0.0	0.1	6,212,449	46.4	7.2	36.7	9.8	4,682	6,516,624	4,911
Loraine........		229	38.0	57.2	4.8	0.0	0.0	1,086,022	34.9	3.1	55.9	6.1	4,742	1,142,071	4,987
Westbrook......		178	71.9	28.1	0.0	0.0	0.0	1,245,405	91.0	1.9	4.0	3.1	6,997	1,232,505	6,924
Montague........	7	3,212	95.0	4.6	†	0.2	0.2	11,927,742	33.5	5.2	56.9	4.3	3,713	12,939,259	4,028
Bowie..........		1,717	97.1	2.6	0.0	0.1	0.2	5,613,486	32.8	6.0	57.0	4.2	3,269	6,002,585	3,496
Forestburg.....		134	92.5	7.5	0.0	0.0	0.0	579,881	29.7	4.0	63.6	2.7	4,327	636,802	4,752
Gold Burg.......		136	99.3	0.7	0.0	0.0	0.0	696,887	41.5	5.8	47.8	4.9	5,124	694,331	5,105
Montague.......		71	80.3	19.7	0.0	0.0	0.0	297,360	19.5	8.0	64.0	8.5	4,188	310,797	4,377
Nocona........		720	91.0	8.2	0.1	0.4	0.3	3,004,817	32.8	4.6	58.5	4.0	4,173	3,379,619	4,694
Prairie Valley....		122	95.9	2.5	0.0	0.0	1.6	589,615	43.0	2.7	51.1	3.2	4,833	773,340	6,339
Saint Jo........		312	94.9	5.1	0.0	0.0	0.0	1,145,696	34.4	4.0	56.0	5.6	3,672	1,141,785	3,660
Montgomery......	6	37,060	85.6	7.5	6.0	0.8	0.1	142,267,872	50.6	5.7	39.9	3.8	3,839	144,908,617	3,910
Conroe.........		22,234	83.0	9.0	6.8	1.1	0.1	83,386,278	52.0	5.9	38.6	3.5	3,750	84,687,076	3,809
Magnolia.......		3,313	90.7	6.6	2.4	0.2	†	11,765,316	43.6	5.5	49.1	1.8	3,551	11,572,781	3,493
Montgomery.....		1,804	82.6	3.2	14.1	0.1	0.1	8,817,769	77.8	3.7	15.7	2.8	4,888	8,887,552	4,927
New Caney......		5,102	93.1	5.3	1.1	0.5	0.1	20,267,811	42.7	6.7	47.6	3.0	3,973	21,490,194	4,212
Splendora......		1,879	95.3	4.3	0.3	0.1	0.0	6,229,815	21.2	6.2	66.4	6.2	3,315	6,226,424	3,314
Willis.........		2,728	82.0	6.2	11.7	†	†	11,800,883	56.5	3.7	31.1	8.7	4,326	12,044,590	4,415
Moore...........	2	4,121	57.9	39.1	0.5	2.3	0.3	15,408,779	64.4	6.2	24.6	4.8	3,739	19,057,788	4,625
Dumas.........		3,595	56.4	40.3	0.5	2.6	0.2	13,169,496	63.9	6.3	24.9	4.8	3,663	16,632,889	4,627
Sunray.........		526	68.4	30.6	0.4	0.0	0.6	2,239,283	67.2	5.4	23.0	4.5	4,257	2,424,899	4,610
Morris...........	2	3,019	66.6	2.0	31.0	0.1	0.2	12,673,861	55.3	4.8	32.0	8.0	4,198	13,600,345	4,505
Daingerfield-LS ..		2,051	65.7	2.2	31.6	0.1	0.2	8,827,091	69.0	5.7	18.7	7.0	4,304	9,480,586	4,622
Pewitt.........		968	68.6	1.4	29.6	0.1	0.2	3,846,770	23.7	2.6	63.5	10.2	3,974	4,119,759	4,256
Motley..........	1	257	79.8	14.8	4.7	0.8	0.0	1,597,599	27.7	3.8	55.3	13.3	6,216	1,706,967	6,642
Motley County...		257	79.8	14.8	4.7	0.8	0.0	1,597,599	27.7	3.8	55.3	13.3	6,216	1,706,967	6,642
Nacogdoches......	9	8,799	69.4	5.3	24.7	0.5	0.1	32,237,751	33.7	5.6	53.1	7.6	3,664	36,362,773	4,133
Central Heights...		454	87.0	1.5	10.8	0.0	0.7	1,810,629	15.6	3.0	77.6	3.7	3,988	1,792,845	3,949
Chireno........		238	81.9	2.1	16.0	0.0	0.0	1,085,730	20.7	5.8	66.6	6.9	4,562	1,112,943	4,676
Cushing........		428	90.9	0.9	8.2	0.0	0.0	1,750,556	53.3	3.7	39.1	1.8	4,090	2,112,200	4,935
Douglass.......		245	88.2	2.0	9.8	0.0	0.0	895,224	40.6	3.4	49.9	6.1	3,654	909,873	3,714
Etoile.........		98	100	0.0	0.0	0.0	0.0	507,613	21.7	8.2	62.6	7.5	5,180	479,275	4,891
Garrison.......		669	69.1	1.0	29.9	0.0	0.0	2,970,318	16.3	6.8	66.0	10.9	4,440	3,075,806	4,598
Martinsville.....		191	95.3	2.6	2.1	0.0	0.0	728,584	21.7	6.7	68.1	3.6	3,815	749,443	3,924
Nacogdoches.....		5,854	61.1	7.2	31.0	0.7	†	20,208,824	39.6	5.6	46.2	8.6	3,452	23,792,009	4,064
Woden.........		622	95.5	1.8	2.3	0.3	0.2	2,280,273	11.8	7.3	76.7	4.2	3,666	2,338,379	3,759
Navarro..........	7	7,454	67.3	7.4	24.7	0.4	0.1	28,052,682	37.9	4.8	50.1	7.3	3,763	28,962,897	3,886
Blooming Grove ..		652	87.1	4.8	7.7	0.0	0.5	2,658,345	27.2	4.7	63.9	4.2	4,077	2,754,987	4,225
Corsicana......		4,837	60.9	8.5	30.0	0.6	0.1	17,591,548	43.0	4.7	43.7	8.6	3,637	17,944,829	3,710
Dawson........		396	82.1	4.0	13.6	0.0	0.3	1,492,600	21.3	9.7	63.4	5.6	3,769	1,515,592	3,827
Frost..........		339	79.9	10.0	10.0	0.0	0.2	1,294,548	19.8	3.3	73.0	3.9	3,819	1,364,930	4,026
Kerens.........		685	60.1	5.4	34.5	0.0	0.0	2,609,923	23.7	4.1	64.2	8.0	3,810	2,877,798	4,201
Mildred........		308	96.1	1.9	1.6	0.3	0.0	1,526,869	59.8	4.3	33.3	2.5	4,957	1,526,869	4,957
Rice...........		237	84.4	8.9	5.9	0.0	0.8	989,834	25.9	3.8	66.5	3.8	3,708	977,892	4,126
Newton..........	3	2,734	69.3	0.6	30.0	†	0.1	12,353,184	32.4	2.7	54.4	10.5	4,518	12,793,263	4,679
Burkeville......		405	47.7	1.2	51.1	0.0	0.0	2,430,686	45.5	3.6	44.6	6.3	6,002	2,470,945	6,101
Deweyville......		673	99.1	0.6	0.0	0.0	0.3	3,050,454	35.6	3.5	55.9	5.1	4,533	3,164,464	4,702
Newton........		1,656	62.6	0.4	37.0	0.1	0.1	6,872,044	26.4	2.0	57.3	14.3	4,150	7,157,854	4,322
Nolan...........	4	3,760	58.2	36.4	5.3	†	0.1	14,270,923	34.4	4.6	51.6	9.3	3,795	15,132,103	4,024
Blackwell Cons ..		154	83.8	16.2	0.0	0.0	0.0	1,192,941	81.4	2.2	14.6	1.8	7,746	1,159,939	7,532
Highland.......		126	94.4	5.6	0.0	0.0	0.0	898,331	66.0	6.5	23.3	4.2	7,130	1,093,409	8,678
Roscoe.........		481	48.4	50.1	1.2	0.0	0.2	1,902,266	26.3	3.3	64.0	6.4	3,955	1,899,384	3,949
Sweetwater.....		2,999	56.9	36.5	6.5	†	†	10,277,385	27.7	5.0	56.1	11.2	3,427	10,979,371	3,661
Nueces..........	13	62,769	31.5	62.8	4.8	0.7	0.2	240,285,564	38.7	4.4	47.3	9.6	3,828	261,525,360	4,166
Agua Dulce.....		405	37.0	62.2	0.0	0.0	0.7	1,832,126	43.6	4.7	47.5	5.4	4,524	2,005,170	4,951
Banquete......		825	28.4	71.5	0.1	0.0	0.0	4,063,984	44.0	3.5	47.9	4.6	4,926	3,988,681	4,835
Bishop Cons		1,381	30.8	67.6	1.6	0.0	0.0	5,369,925	59.8	8.5	24.3	7.5	3,888	5,613,017	4,064
Calallen.......		4,246	71.8	26.7	1.1	0.3	0.1	16,927,171	57.2	6.5	33.2	3.2	3,987	18,263,306	4,301
Corpus Christi....		41,277	25.3	68.2	5.7	0.6	0.2	151,317,003	33.6	4.0	52.0	10.4	3,666	167,368,542	4,055
Driscoll........		228	15.4	84.2	0.4	0.0	0.0	1,211,320	64.0	2.9	25.1	8.1	5,313	1,236,170	5,422

County/ISD	Districts	Students	% White**	% Hispanic**	% Black**	% Asian**	% American Indian**	Total Revenue	% Local***	% Other***	% State***	% Federal***	Revenue Per Pupil	Total Spending	Spending Per Pupil
Nueces Co. (Con't.)															
Flour Bluff		4,798	74.2	18.5	3.5	3.3	0.5	16,691,291	44.8	5.2	42.4	7.6	3,479	18,971,739	3,954
London		142	79.6	20.4	0.0	0.0	0.0	706,189	48.8	14.8	32.6	3.8	4,973	793,736	5,590
Port Aransas		375	90.7	8.3	0.0	1.1	0.0	2,812,722	90.9	4.2	3.3	1.6	7,501	3,180,093	8,480
Robstown		4,360	1.4	97.5	1.1	0.0	0.0	16,946,739	10.3	3.0	68.3	18.5	3,887	17,571,976	4,030
Santa Cruz		29	0.0	100	0.0	0.0	0.0	325,535	75.3	4.7	5.9	14.1	11,225	378,000	13,034
Tuloso-Midway		2,754	47.5	51.2	1.1	0.1	†	14,364,248	75.1	6.6	13.9	4.4	5,216	14,356,594	5,213
West Oso		1,949	2.8	80.2	16.6	0.4	0.0	7,717,311	35.4	1.7	51.2	11.6	3,960	7,798,336	4,001
Ochiltree	2	2,021	77.4	21.8	0.0	0.2	0.5	7,177,422	60.7	6.3	28.7	4.2	3,551	7,572,604	3,747
Perryton		1,983	78.2	21.0	0.0	0.3	0.6	6,889,521	59.8	6.5	29.3	4.3	3,474	7,259,259	3,661
Waka		38	36.8	63.2	0.0	0.0	0.0	287,901	82.6	2.6	13.7	1.2	7,576	313,345	8,246
Oldham	4	946	84.0	13.5	1.1	0.6	0.7	5,415,268	21.3	24.7	47.9	6.2	5,724	5,651,771	5,974
Adrian		112	70.5	29.5	0.0	0.0	0.0	741,814	39.9	5.6	49.1	5.4	6,623	750,686	6,703
Boys Ranch		434	85.9	10.1	2.3	1.2	0.5	2,555,242	0.0	44.8	47.3	8.0	5,888	2,555,242	5,888
Vega		337	86.6	13.4	0.0	0.0	0.0	1,712,702	37.8	7.4	50.9	3.9	5,082	1,929,473	5,725
Wildorado		63	81.0	9.5	0.0	1.6	7.9	405,510	51.2	6.4	36.3	6.2	6,437	416,370	6,609
Orange	5	17,030	86.2	1.9	11.1	0.8	0.1	69,331,648	48.6	5.6	40.0	5.8	4,071	73,782,665	4,333
Bridge City		2,631	96.4	1.4	0.0	2.1	0.0	10,654,071	55.9	4.9	33.9	5.3	4,049	10,894,365	4,141
Lt Cypress-Mrvll		3,364	93.2	1.8	4.2	0.6	0.2	12,390,613	40.1	5.5	50.2	4.2	3,683	13,164,476	3,913
Orangefield		1,337	97.2	1.2	0.1	1.5	0.0	5,231,373	38.0	5.6	52.6	3.9	3,913	5,584,882	4,177
Vidor		5,589	97.3	2.6	0.0	0.1	†	19,386,974	29.4	5.4	60.3	4.9	3,469	20,093,846	3,595
W. Orange-Cove		4,109	55.2	1.4	42.6	0.9	0.0	21,668,653	69.7	6.1	16.0	8.2	5,273	24,045,096	5,852
Palo Pinto	6	4,721	81.8	12.2	4.8	1.1	0.2	17,200,003	37.8	5.1	50.7	6.3	3,643	17,678,985	3,745
Gordon		191	96.3	3.7	0.0	0.0	0.0	861,916	50.2	6.0	40.1	3.6	4,513	912,416	4,777
Graford		379	94.7	4.7	0.0	0.5	0.0	1,850,084	64.5	5.2	28.0	2.3	4,881	1,806,126	4,766
Mineral Wells		3,612	78.0	14.2	6.3	1.3	0.2	11,987,404	27.9	4.8	59.4	7.9	3,319	12,298,664	3,405
Palo Pinto		46	89.1	8.7	0.0	0.0	2.2	374,326	89.7	4.3	3.5	2.5	8,138	364,825	7,931
Santo		353	97.5	2.5	0.0	0.0	0.0	1,519,783	56.3	6.7	35.0	2.1	4,305	1,618,696	4,586
Strawn		140	82.9	17.1	0.0	0.0	0.0	606,490	56.9	6.5	32.9	3.7	4,332	678,258	4,845
Panola	3	4,143	74.7	1.4	23.7	0.1	0.2	16,846,523	62.5	5.4	27.2	5.0	4,066	18,716,568	4,518
Beckville		553	82.3	1.4	15.9	0.0	0.4	2,679,163	76.8	6.6	13.6	3.0	4,845	2,986,038	5,400
Carthage		3,354	71.8	1.3	26.6	0.1	0.2	13,130,861	61.1	5.3	28.5	5.2	3,915	14,599,622	4,353
Gary		236	97.5	2.5	0.0	0.0	0.0	1,036,499	43.8	3.2	45.3	7.7	4,392	1,130,908	4,792
Parker	8	11,507	93.7	4.4	1.3	0.4	0.2	38,218,057	36.6	6.5	51.8	5.2	3,321	43,535,669	3,783
Aledo		1,816	96.1	2.8	0.2	0.7	0.2	5,844,385	48.5	5.5	44.8	1.2	3,218	5,774,491	3,180
Brock		372	97.3	2.2	0.5	0.0	0.0	1,433,622	34.8	8.9	53.8	2.4	3,854	1,677,585	4,510
Garner		154	95.5	4.5	0.0	0.0	0.0	698,581	50.3	4.8	36.0	8.9	4,536	716,541	4,653
Millsap		577	94.5	4.3	1.2	0.0	0.0	2,113,936	25.6	6.9	63.9	3.6	3,664	2,115,937	3,667
Peaster		455	98.5	1.5	0.0	0.0	0.0	1,614,173	28.1	6.4	62.1	3.3	3,548	1,693,186	3,721
Poolville		240	98.8	1.3	0.0	0.0	0.0	951,893	45.2	6.2	46.6	2.0	3,966	949,674	3,957
Springtown		2,426	96.5	2.5	0.3	0.4	0.3	8,217,195	33.7	5.9	56.4	4.0	3,387	9,475,937	3,906
Weatherford		5,467	90.6	6.3	2.3	0.5	0.3	17,344,272	35.2	7.0	50.2	7.7	3,173	21,132,318	3,865
Parmer	4	2,565	43.6	54.9	1.3	0.2	†	10,820,841	27.4	6.0	56.4	10.3	4,219	11,549,437	4,503
Bovina		516	28.3	70.7	1.0	0.0	0.0	2,116,825	22.3	3.1	63.7	11.0	4,102	2,339,137	4,533
Farwell		496	62.3	36.9	0.8	0.0	0.0	2,225,564	36.6	3.8	52.0	7.7	4,487	2,309,750	4,657
Friona		1,286	40.6	57.0	1.9	0.5	0.1	5,123,476	23.9	8.5	57.0	10.6	3,984	5,407,144	4,205
Lazbuddie		267	52.8	47.2	0.0	0.0	0.0	1,354,976	33.3	4.3	50.3	12.1	5,075	1,493,406	5,593
Pecos	3	3,927	34.8	64.6	0.4	0.2	0.0	22,758,575	79.6	3.8	9.6	7.0	5,795	24,224,143	6,169
Buena Vista		176	50.6	49.4	0.0	0.0	0.0	1,558,927	86.0	4.5	4.9	4.6	8,858	1,792,722	10,186
Fort Stockton		3,156	28.4	71.0	0.4	0.2	0.0	14,983,562	73.6	3.8	12.9	9.7	4,748	16,166,845	5,123
Iraan-Sheffield		595	64.5	35.3	0.0	0.2	0.0	6,216,086	92.5	3.8	2.7	1.0	10,447	6,264,576	10,529
Polk	6	5,410	71.4	6.6	19.9	0.3	1.9	22,151,504	39.4	6.8	42.4	11.5	4,095	22,169,351	4,098
Big Sandy		337	75.1	1.2	0.0	0.0	23.7	1,440,974	39.4	5.1	49.0	6.5	4,276	1,481,491	4,396
Corrigan-Camden		1,183	46.6	17.6	35.5	0.3	0.0	5,085,937	35.4	8.2	49.4	7.0	4,299	5,181,631	4,380
Goodrich		302	60.6	8.9	29.8	0.7	0.0	1,197,393	37.8	5.0	53.5	3.7	3,965	1,347,393	4,462
Leggett		171	56.7	9.4	33.9	0.0	0.0	919,154	47.2	3.8	39.7	9.4	5,375	1,017,840	5,952
Livingston		3,052	80.3	3.1	15.6	0.3	0.7	11,762,492	35.4	7.1	41.3	16.2	3,854	11,444,811	3,750
Onalaska		365	89.6	1.6	8.8	0.0	0.0	1,745,554	74.6	4.9	17.4	3.2	4,782	1,696,185	4,647
Potter	4	29,161	68.8	20.0	8.2	2.8	0.2	107,528,935	45.2	6.0	42.6	6.3	3,687	120,699,070	4,139
Amarillo		26,983	67.1	20.9	8.8	3.0	0.2	97,141,823	43.3	6.0	44.1	6.5	3,600	109,678,165	4,065
Bushland		332	89.8	10.2	0.0	0.0	0.0	1,706,364	84.9	6.9	5.9	2.3	5,140	2,328,889	7,015
Highland Park		654	85.0	11.0	1.8	1.7	0.5	4,438,308	87.6	4.5	4.4	3.4	6,786	4,433,562	6,779
River Road		1,192	93.4	5.5	0.0	0.3	0.9	4,242,440	27.8	6.2	59.0	7.0	3,559	4,258,454	3,573
Presidio	2	1,545	9.3	90.4	0.0	0.2	0.1	5,941,920	13.3	2.9	68.2	15.7	3,846	5,728,770	3,708
Marfa		576	23.1	76.6	0.0	0.3	0.0	2,048,182	26.1	1.5	64.1	8.3	3,556	2,058,182	3,573
Presidio		969	1.1	98.7	0.0	0.1	0.1	3,893,738	6.5	3.7	70.3	19.6	4,018	3,670,588	3,788
Rains	1	1,206	90.5	3.2	5.9	0.0	0.3	5,765,039	43.8	16.0	31.2	9.1	4,780	6,264,068	5,194
Rains		1,206	90.5	3.2	5.9	0.0	0.3	5,765,039	43.8	16.0	31.2	9.1	4,780	6,264,068	5,194
Randall	1	5,857	89.9	7.8	1.4	0.6	0.2	19,450,403	48.0	5.7	42.3	3.9	3,321	20,460,193	3,493
Canyon		5,857	89.9	7.8	1.4	0.6	0.2	19,450,403	48.0	5.7	42.3	3.9	3,321	20,460,193	3,493
Reagan	1	1,253	44.8	52.8	2.4	0.0	0.0	4,818,707	55.3	7.6	31.1	6.0	3,846	5,324,446	4,249
Reagan County		1,253	44.8	52.8	2.4	0.0	0.0	4,818,707	55.3	7.6	31.1	6.0	3,846	5,324,446	4,249
Real	1	239	78.2	21.8	0.0	0.0	0.0	958,134	56.2	3.9	29.9	10.0	4,009	1,037,585	4,341
Leakey		239	78.2	21.8	0.0	0.0	0.0	958,134	56.2	3.9	29.9	10.0	4,009	1,037,585	4,341
Red River	4	2,959	69.0	2.5	27.9	0.2	0.3	11,421,373	20.4	4.3	64.5	10.8	3,860	12,138,474	4,102
Avery		328	87.2	3.7	7.6	0.3	1.2	1,252,932	13.7	5.1	73.1	8.1	3,820	1,314,789	4,009
Clarksville		1,524	53.4	2.5	43.8	0.1	0.1	5,880,528	18.9	4.0	63.8	13.3	3,859	6,238,205	4,093
Detroit		410	83.7	1.2	14.6	0.2	0.2	1,505,814	14.1	3.2	73.1	9.5	3,673	1,592,119	3,883
Talco-Bogata Con		697	85.9	2.9	10.6	0.1	0.4	2,782,099	30.0	5.0	57.6	7.4	3,992	2,993,361	4,293

County/ISD	Districts	Students	% White**	% Hispanic**	% Black**	% Asian**	% American Indian**	Total Revenue	% Local***	% Other***	% State***	% Federal***	Revenue Per Pupil	Total Spending	Spending Per Pupil
Reeves	2	3,837	15.2	82.2	2.4	0.2	0.1	14,641,677	43.2	3.3	43.8	9.7	3,816	15,285,872	3,984
Balmorhea		257	9.3	90.7	0.0	0.0	0.0	1,318,735	20.2	2.8	68.0	9.1	5,131	1,533,311	5,966
Pecos Barstow Toy		3,580	15.6	81.6	2.5	0.2	0.1	13,322,942	45.5	3.3	41.4	9.8	3,721	13,752,561	3,841
Refugio	3	1,793	42.8	46.7	10.3	0.1	0.1	8,918,761	70.7	5.2	19.0	5.1	4,974	9,694,844	5,407
Austwell-Tivoli . . .		208	24.5	70.7	4.8	0.0	0.0	1,481,081	86.4	7.3	4.1	2.2	7,121	1,889,808	9,086
Refugio		883	40.0	44.1	15.6	0.2	0.1	4,647,309	82.2	5.7	5.6	6.5	5,263	4,647,312	5,263
Woodsboro		702	51.9	43.0	5.1	0.0	0.0	2,790,371	43.2	3.2	49.2	4.4	3,975	3,157,724	4,498
Roberts	1	222	94.6	4.5	0.0	0.9	0.0	1,394,377	89.1	5.0	3.8	2.0	6,281	1,394,377	6,281
Miami		222	94.6	4.5	0.0	0.9	0.0	1,394,377	89.1	5.0	3.8	2.0	6,281	1,394,377	6,281
Robertson	5	3,210	45.1	17.5	37.4	†	0.0	13,580,737	38.4	5.9	46.9	8.7	4,231	14,360,647	4,474
Bremond		358	69.6	5.9	24.6	0.0	0.0	2,137,086	66.7	2.8	26.0	4.5	5,970	2,119,685	5,921
Calvert		377	15.6	16.2	68.2	0.0	0.0	1,653,938	29.0	1.5	54.3	15.2	4,387	1,575,707	4,180
Franklin		687	80.6	8.7	10.5	0.1	0.0	3,320,683	64.5	2.9	29.3	3.3	4,834	3,726,278	5,424
Hearne		1,746	33.3	22.7	44.0	0.0	0.0	6,133,892	17.9	9.9	61.3	10.8	3,513	6,576,785	3,767
Mumford		42	9.5	54.8	35.7	0.0	0.0	335,138	22.1	5.3	53.7	18.9	7,979	362,192	8,624
Rockwall	2	5,530	87.9	6.9	4.5	0.7	†	16,734,163	55.8	6.8	34.3	3.0	3,026	18,029,542	3,260
Rockwall		4,401	90.8	5.0	3.6	0.6	†	12,924,924	62.8	7.1	27.4	2.6	2,937	13,844,924	3,146
Royse City		1,129	76.5	14.7	8.0	0.8	0.0	3,809,239	32.0	5.9	57.8	4.4	3,374	4,184,618	3,706
Runnels	5	2,478	65.7	32.4	1.7	0.2	0.0	10,230,295	27.9	5.5	57.9	8.8	4,128	10,874,327	4,388
Ballinger		1,081	67.4	31.1	1.4	0.1	0.0	4,523,672	25.2	5.5	58.5	10.9	4,185	4,741,930	4,387
Miles		393	74.3	25.7	0.0	0.0	0.0	1,629,762	26.2	6.2	60.7	6.8	4,147	1,743,753	4,437
Olfen		64	45.3	40.6	14.1	0.0	0.0	296,120	14.4	2.0	79.2	4.4	4,627	296,120	4,627
Wingate		35	57.1	42.9	0.0	0.0	0.0	304,826	40.1	1.4	52.0	6.5	8,709	349,746	9,993
Winters		905	61.5	36.0	2.0	0.4	0.0	3,475,915	32.3	5.8	54.4	7.5	3,841	3,742,778	4,136
Rusk	8	7,767	67.5	5.0	27.2	0.1	0.1	35,587,817	53.2	6.8	34.4	5.7	4,582	36,271,250	4,670
Carlisle		360	79.7	4.4	13.9	0.3	1.7	1,445,515	27.9	4.4	62.6	5.2	4,015	1,452,283	4,034
Henderson		3,805	68.1	3.8	27.9	0.1	0.1	14,772,066	44.1	6.8	42.7	6.4	3,882	14,936,343	3,925
Laneville		366	37.7	7.7	54.6	0.0	0.0	1,850,486	20.3	4.0	66.6	9.2	5,056	1,967,611	5,376
Leveretts Chapel . .		107	56.1	3.7	40.2	0.0	0.0	765,847	61.4	3.7	29.3	5.3	7,157	769,089	7,188
Mount Enterprise		369	67.8	0.3	32.0	0.0	0.0	1,981,150	15.5	21.3	47.4	15.8	5,369	2,118,733	5,742
Overton		442	80.8	1.4	17.4	0.2	0.2	1,794,585	28.1	6.4	60.8	4.8	4,060	1,970,161	4,457
Tatum		1,174	64.2	11.4	24.4	0.0	0.0	7,153,402	89.1	3.9	4.2	2.8	6,093	7,153,403	6,093
West Rusk		1,144	70.4	4.9	24.5	0.1	0.2	5,824,766	68.1	7.4	21.2	3.3	5,092	5,903,627	5,161
Sabine	2	1,400	80.1	0.9	18.9	0.1	0.0	6,272,624	27.9	13.9	49.0	9.1	4,480	6,267,121	4,477
Hemphill		825	78.9	1.2	19.8	0.1	0.0	3,801,129	35.7	7.8	45.3	11.2	4,607	3,818,298	4,628
West Sabine		575	81.7	0.5	17.7	0.0	0.0	2,471,495	15.9	23.4	54.7	5.9	4,298	2,448,823	4,259
San Augustine	2	1,564	52.9	1.3	45.7	0.0	0.1	6,483,988	17.2	4.3	65.3	13.2	4,146	6,453,740	4,126
Broaddus		352	90.1	0.9	9.1	0.0	0.0	1,537,260	22.4	8.9	56.3	12.3	4,367	1,602,019	4,551
San Augustine		1,212	42.1	1.5	56.4	0.0	0.1	4,946,728	15.6	2.9	68.1	13.5	4,081	4,851,721	4,003
San Jacinto	2	2,900	73.7	1.8	24.4	0.0	†	12,203,045	45.6	3.6	42.3	8.5	4,208	12,737,273	4,392
Coldspring Okhurs		1,580	62.3	0.9	36.7	0.0	0.1	6,942,266	59.8	3.4	29.9	6.9	4,394	7,241,616	4,583
Shepherd		1,320	87.4	2.8	9.8	0.0	0.0	5,260,779	26.9	3.9	58.6	10.6	3,985	5,495,657	4,163
San Patricio	7	14,817	39.6	58.2	1.9	0.3	0.1	52,761,113	34.8	4.0	51.5	9.6	3,561	57,669,154	3,892
Aransas Pass		2,088	54.6	40.0	4.7	0.5	0.1	7,060,022	32.0	4.0	54.3	9.7	3,381	7,891,310	3,779
Gregory-Portland		3,831	59.4	38.8	1.0	0.8	0.1	13,099,481	46.4	5.0	43.9	4.6	3,419	13,098,359	3,419
Ingleside		1,588	64.1	34.4	1.2	0.1	0.1	5,662,192	65.7	3.5	26.6	4.2	3,566	7,719,441	4,861
Mathis		2,233	16.3	82.7	1.1	0.0	0.0	8,336,853	12.8	2.6	63.5	21.2	3,733	8,345,289	3,737
Odem-Edroy		1,272	25.3	74.4	0.1	0.0	0.2	4,782,842	23.7	4.4	67.0	4.9	3,760	5,856,050	4,604
Sinton		2,229	23.5	73.8	2.6	0.1	0.0	7,928,729	29.7	4.6	53.4	12.2	3,557	8,536,462	3,830
Taft		1,576	14.1	83.2	2.4	0.3	0.0	5,890,994	29.9	3.4	56.7	10.1	3,738	6,222,243	3,948
San Saba	3	1,094	76.1	23.5	0.4	0.0	0.0	4,684,033	21.9	5.5	63.0	9.6	4,282	4,738,486	4,331
Cherokee		143	76.9	21.0	2.1	0.0	0.0	598,226	27.1	4.2	57.5	11.2	4,183	624,667	4,368
Richland Springs . .		153	91.5	8.5	0.0	0.0	0.0	744,850	27.7	3.6	58.8	9.9	4,868	761,986	4,980
San Saba		798	72.9	26.8	0.1	0.0	0.1	3,340,957	19.7	6.2	64.9	9.2	4,187	3,351,833	4,200
Schleicher	1	710	53.7	45.6	0.4	0.3	0.0	3,502,407	56.5	7.0	32.9	3.6	4,933	3,642,357	5,130
Schleicher		710	53.7	45.6	0.4	0.3	0.0	3,502,407	56.5	7.0	32.9	3.6	4,933	3,642,357	5,130
Scurry	3	3,967	63.6	32.2	4.0	0.1	0.1	13,827,093	64.3	3.9	29.1	2.7	3,486	14,963,311	3,772
Hermleigh		166	62.0	38.0	0.0	0.0	0.0	754,179	50.0	3.6	37.5	9.0	4,543	785,699	4,733
Ira		244	88.9	11.1	0.0	0.0	0.0	1,355,040	72.7	9.3	16.1	1.9	5,553	1,287,352	5,276
Snyder		3,557	61.9	33.4	4.5	0.1	0.1	11,717,874	64.3	3.3	30.2	2.1	3,294	12,890,260	3,624
Shackelford	2	660	86.2	12.7	0.5	0.0	0.6	2,974,476	36.0	7.3	53.1	3.7	4,507	3,200,704	4,850
Albany		547	85.0	14.3	0.5	0.0	0.2	2,245,258	31.4	7.9	57.0	3.8	4,105	2,375,933	4,344
Moran		113	92.0	5.3	0.0	0.0	2.7	729,218	50.0	5.3	41.1	3.5	6,453	824,771	7,299
Shelby	6	4,426	66.9	2.0	30.8	0.2	0.1	16,473,525	20.0	5.2	65.5	9.2	3,722	17,367,030	3,924
Center		2,116	63.2	3.1	33.3	0.3	0.1	7,204,180	22.0	4.5	64.3	9.2	3,405	7,881,917	3,725
Excelsior		82	97.6	2.4	0.0	0.0	0.0	408,896	13.4	6.6	73.9	6.1	4,987	397,303	4,845
Joaquin		619	91.9	0.6	7.4	0.0	0.0	2,250,210	22.2	12.4	58.7	6.7	3,635	2,244,603	3,626
Shelbyville		622	59.3	1.4	39.2	0.0	0.0	2,405,133	13.7	3.7	72.0	10.6	3,867	2,449,182	3,938
Tenaha		390	54.1	0.5	44.9	0.0	0.5	1,535,813	13.0	4.9	71.8	10.4	3,938	1,604,354	4,114
Timpson		597	66.2	1.0	32.7	0.2	0.0	2,669,293	23.7	2.5	64.4	9.4	4,471	2,789,671	4,673
Sherman	2	601	74.4	18.1	7.2	0.3	0.0	3,423,068	59.7	14.2	23.4	2.6	5,696	3,318,592	5,522
Stratford		508	73.4	17.7	8.5	0.4	0.0	2,583,922	62.5	5.7	28.3	3.5	5,086	2,623,871	5,165
Texhoma		93	79.6	20.4	0.0	0.0	0.0	839,146	51.1	40.4	8.5	0.0	9,023	694,721	7,470
Smith	8	27,805	64.6	7.8	27.1	0.4	0.1	96,122,365	44.6	5.9	44.5	5.0	3,457	104,710,735	3,766
Arp		811	69.1	2.5	28.5	0.0	0.0	3,172,588	28.0	4.5	59.3	8.2	3,912	3,595,404	4,433
Bullard		896	92.0	1.6	6.4	0.1	0.0	3,307,301	50.8	5.2	40.7	3.3	3,691	3,595,068	4,012
Chapel Hill		3,003	65.5	5.1	29.0	0.1	0.0	10,217,961	32.4	4.7	55.7	7.2	3,403	10,891,315	3,627
Lindale		2,191	86.8	2.8	10.1	0.1	0.2	7,195,220	34.0	9.1	53.0	3.9	3,284	7,420,954	3,387
Troup		820	75.0	4.6	20.1	0.1	0.1	3,432,984	34.8	5.6	48.4	11.2	4,187	3,702,824	4,515
Tyler		16,091	54.2	11.2	34.1	0.5	0.1	54,723,928	50.2	5.5	38.8	5.5	3,401	58,308,782	3,624
Whitehouse		3,132	88.3	1.3	9.6	0.7	0.2	9,930,181	40.7	6.7	48.9	3.8	3,171	11,643,939	3,718

County/ISD	Districts	Students	% White**	% Hispanic**	% Black**	% Asian**	% American Indian**	Total Revenue	% Local***	% Other***	% State***	% Federal***	Revenue Per Pupil	Total Spending	Spending Per Pupil
Smith Co. (Con't.)															
Winona.........		861	71.5	4.8	23.6	0.0	0.1	4,142,202	45.5	8.1	44.8	1.6	4,811	5,553,192	6,450
Somervell	1	1,345	76.4	22.2	0.3	0.4	0.8	11,687,272	93.5	3.0	2.6	0.9	8,689	10,945,708	8,138
Glen Rose		1,345	76.4	22.2	0.3	0.4	0.8	11,687,272	93.5	3.0	2.6	0.9	8,689	10,945,708	8,138
Starr	3	11,819	1.0	99.0	†	0.0	0.0	47,939,155	13.4	3.7	64.6	18.4	4,056	55,293,701	4,678
Rio Grande City...		6,609	1.1	98.8	†	0.0	0.0	26,934,877	14.4	2.2	66.0	17.4	4,075	30,970,967	4,686
Roma		4,842	0.5	99.4	0.1	0.0	0.0	18,650,209	5.8	5.7	67.4	21.1	3,852	21,592,722	4,459
San Isidro		368	4.1	95.9	0.0	0.0	0.0	2,354,069	61.9	4.7	25.7	7.7	6,397	2,730,012	7,419
Stephens	1	1,910	82.1	13.6	3.1	0.5	0.6	7,042,343	67.2	4.9	23.7	4.2	3,687	7,479,521	3,916
Breckenridge		1,910	82.1	13.6	3.1	0.5	0.6	7,042,343	67.2	4.9	23.7	4.2	3,687	7,479,521	3,916
Sterling	1	328	75.0	25.0	0.0	0.0	0.0	2,190,728	87.5	4.7	4.9	2.9	6,679	2,348,196	7,159
Sterling City		328	75.0	25.0	0.0	0.0	0.0	2,190,728	87.5	4.7	4.9	2.9	6,679	2,348,196	7,159
Stonewall.........	1	369	72.9	19.8	6.5	0.8	0.0	2,015,081	56.8	5.0	33.4	4.8	5,461	2,274,876	6,165
Aspermont		369	72.9	19.8	6.5	0.8	0.0	2,015,081	56.8	5.0	33.4	4.8	5,461	2,274,876	6,165
Sutton	1	1,029	47.9	52.1	0.0	0.0	0.0	4,913,241	73.2	5.0	18.0	3.8	4,775	6,123,718	5,951
Sonora		1,029	47.9	52.1	0.0	0.0	0.0	4,913,241	73.2	5.0	18.0	3.8	4,775	6,123,718	5,951
Swisher	3	1,926	50.9	42.3	6.5	0.2	0.2	8,535,806	27.3	5.1	55.6	12.1	4,432	9,487,760	4,926
Happy		243	85.2	14.0	0.8	0.0	0.0	1,191,506	42.2	4.4	44.6	8.8	4,903	1,335,914	5,498
Kress		366	38.8	56.6	4.6	0.0	0.0	1,625,811	33.2	4.3	53.1	9.4	4,442	1,679,811	4,590
Tulia...........		1,317	48.0	43.5	8.0	0.2	0.2	5,718,489	22.5	5.4	58.6	13.6	4,342	6,472,035	4,914
Tarrant..........	17	201,737	65.9	14.3	16.4	3.2	0.3	758,423,677	56.1	7.1	30.1	6.7	3,759	860,356,748	4,265
Arlington		43,328	75.6	8.6	11.0	4.6	0.3	174,899,666	63.8	8.3	21.3	6.6	4,037	209,042,924	4,825
Azle		4,973	96.1	2.6	0.5	0.5	0.3	15,594,936	33.6	5.9	54.3	6.2	3,136	16,205,359	3,259
Birdville........		18,019	87.1	7.2	1.7	3.8	0.1	65,680,838	57.0	7.5	31.0	4.5	3,645	66,667,368	3,700
Carroll		1,797	97.2	2.3	0.2	0.2	0.1	7,099,098	79.8	5.2	14.4	0.7	3,951	7,240,671	4,029
Castleberry......		2,851	81.1	16.3	0.7	1.6	0.2	8,530,759	26.4	9.1	58.3	6.2	2,992	8,851,644	3,105
Crowley		5,337	79.8	7.5	8.8	3.3	0.6	20,332,418	66.7	6.1	25.1	2.1	3,810	22,570,336	4,229
Eagle Mt-Saginaw		4,616	84.0	9.1	1.2	5.5	0.2	15,997,887	66.5	6.0	24.4	3.2	3,466	16,812,955	3,642
Everman........		3,306	43.8	10.0	44.1	1.8	0.3	12,557,158	50.9	7.6	36.2	5.3	3,798	16,553,438	5,007
Fort Worth		69,435	35.2	27.4	34.9	2.4	0.1	264,854,281	47.1	6.4	35.9	10.6	3,814	308,769,199	4,447
Grapevine Collyvl		7,873	92.3	4.3	2.0	1.3	0.2	28,851,506	75.6	6.8	15.0	2.6	3,665	28,719,271	3,648
H-E-B		18,168	85.1	5.8	3.9	4.6	0.7	69,092,173	65.5	6.3	25.5	2.7	3,803	75,074,556	4,132
Keller		7,564	89.3	4.2	2.4	3.8	0.3	24,481,130	59.3	6.9	31.9	2.0	3,237	28,670,051	3,790
Kennedale		1,686	84.9	7.7	7.0	0.4	0.0	5,738,081	50.0	6.2	40.7	3.1	3,403	5,877,813	3,486
Lake Worth		1,475	75.7	20.2	2.9	0.7	0.5	5,499,759	44.0	10.8	40.1	5.1	3,729	5,505,964	3,733
Mansfield		7,147	85.6	7.7	4.9	1.3	0.5	25,177,527	57.9	6.4	32.6	3.0	3,523	29,561,432	4,136
Masonic Home ...		131	96.2	2.3	0.0	0.0	1.5	730,800	0.0	95.9	4.1	0.0	5,579	730,800	5,579
White Settlement..		4,031	82.1	7.5	7.0	2.9	0.5	13,305,660	50.5	5.3	39.5	4.6	3,301	13,502,967	3,350
Taylor...........	5	22,715	68.7	21.2	8.7	1.1	0.3	80,801,001	36.8	5.0	52.8	5.4	3,557	83,274,715	3,666
Abilene		18,690	64.1	24.0	10.3	1.3	0.3	66,111,487	35.7	4.7	53.8	5.8	3,537	67,367,770	3,604
Jim Ned Cons		723	91.6	7.7	0.7	0.0	0.0	3,049,287	39.6	4.3	52.9	3.2	4,218	3,054,027	4,224
Merkel		1,389	82.7	15.6	1.3	0.3	0.1	4,634,602	24.3	3.8	66.9	4.9	3,337	5,129,930	3,693
Trent		196	87.2	12.8	0.0	0.0	0.0	939,115	48.2	7.8	38.6	5.3	4,791	1,078,677	5,503
Wylie		1,717	95.0	2.6	1.3	1.1	0.0	6,066,510	55.4	8.9	33.8	1.9	3,533	6,644,311	3,870
Terrell...........	1	336	35.7	63.4	0.0	0.6	0.3	2,311,896	52.9	27.1	17.5	2.5	6,881	2,296,366	6,834
Terrell County....		336	35.7	63.4	0.0	0.6	0.3	2,311,896	52.9	27.1	17.5	2.5	6,881	2,296,366	6,834
Terry............	4	3,273	41.5	53.3	5.0	0.2	†	14,685,595	53.5	6.6	27.9	12.0	4,487	15,187,946	4,640
Brownfield		2,746	39.9	53.9	5.9	0.2	†	10,830,564	49.5	6.8	29.8	13.9	3,944	11,067,387	4,030
Meadow		243	43.2	56.4	0.4	0.0	0.0	1,409,728	42.9	5.5	40.8	10.8	5,801	1,481,058	6,095
Union		106	36.8	62.3	0.9	0.0	0.0	980,293	62.9	7.6	25.5	4.0	9,248	1,090,364	10,286
Wellman		178	65.7	33.7	0.0	0.6	0.0	1,465,010	87.4	5.4	3.3	4.0	8,230	1,549,137	8,703
Throckmorton	2	365	89.3	9.3	0.0	0.5	0.8	1,822,378	51.5	7.3	36.1	5.1	4,993	2,124,311	5,820
Throckmorton....		260	86.5	11.5	0.0	0.8	1.2	1,202,881	52.0	8.7	33.4	5.9	4,626	1,386,298	5,332
Woodson		105	96.2	3.8	0.0	0.0	0.0	619,497	50.4	4.6	41.4	3.6	5,900	738,013	7,029
Titus	4	4,473	70.6	11.9	17.2	0.1	0.2	15,107,076	46.8	5.5	41.1	6.6	3,377	16,931,233	3,785
Chapel Hill		216	91.2	1.4	5.1	0.0	2.3	708,979	20.2	5.5	70.0	4.3	3,282	843,814	3,907
Harts Bluff		369	99.2	0.3	0.3	0.0	0.3	1,135,494	17.0	5.0	74.9	3.1	3,077	1,136,582	3,080
Mount Pleasant...		3,787	66.0	13.8	20.0	0.1	0.1	12,715,427	49.7	5.5	38.0	6.8	3,358	14,414,262	3,806
Winfield		101	94.1	5.9	0.0	0.0	0.0	547,176	76.8	6.8	4.4	11.9	5,418	536,575	5,313
Tom Green.......	6	18,527	58.6	35.5	4.8	0.9	0.1	59,767,457	32.2	5.7	56.7	5.3	3,226	62,480,230	3,372
Christoval		293	75.8	24.2	0.0	0.0	0.0	1,477,568	57.1	6.0	35.4	1.5	5,043	1,688,548	5,763
Grape Ck-Pulliam		704	83.8	16.1	0.0	0.1	0.0	2,211,388	30.4	4.0	62.9	2.7	3,141	3,203,270	4,550
San Angelo		16,346	55.3	38.1	5.5	1.0	0.1	49,901,177	31.7	5.7	57.3	5.3	3,053	50,645,337	3,098
Veribest		135	85.9	13.3	0.0	0.7	0.0	549,004	53.0	3.7	40.0	3.3	4,067	770,755	5,709
Wall		694	83.6	16.4	0.0	0.0	0.0	3,814,538	20.7	6.3	62.5	10.1	5,496	4,358,568	6,280
Water Valley		355	87.3	12.4	0.3	0.0	0.0	1,813,752	45.2	6.9	1.7	5,109	1,813,752	5,109
Travis	7	83,375	49.8	30.7	17.2	2.1	0.3	398,170,686	67.1	6.5	21.2	5.0	4,776	417,706,797	5,010
Austin		63,886	44.1	33.9	19.8	1.9	0.3	300,445,381	65.6	6.8	22.0	5.5	4,703	315,826,211	4,944
Del Valle		5,155	40.9	42.6	14.6	1.6	0.2	20,109,978	43.0	5.5	42.0	9.5	3,901	20,825,978	4,040
Eanes		4,916	93.8	2.9	0.5	2.7	†	31,628,997	87.5	6.0	4.5	2.1	6,434	34,163,888	6,950
Lago Vista		410	92.0	7.3	0.5	0.0	0.2	3,179,290	93.4	2.4	3.5	0.7	7,754	3,377,654	8,238
Lake Travis......		1,704	90.4	8.9	0.2	0.2	0.2	12,354,991	90.6	5.3	3.5	0.6	7,251	12,704,313	7,456
Manor..........		1,226	44.0	31.2	23.7	1.0	0.2	6,513,196	66.1	3.8	24.0	6.2	5,313	6,147,900	5,015
Pflugerville......		6,078	69.3	16.3	10.0	4.2	0.1	23,938,853	64.3	6.5	27.0	2.1	3,939	24,660,783	4,057
Trinity	4	2,287	76.1	2.1	21.6	0.2	†	8,924,484	34.4	4.5	53.6	7.5	3,902	10,072,490	4,404
Apple Springs		186	76.9	0.0	23.1	0.0	0.0	700,338	23.1	2.9	63.3	10.7	3,765	913,004	4,909
Centerville		176	97.7	0.6	1.7	0.0	0.0	698,231	19.8	3.9	66.2	10.1	3,967	723,470	4,111
Groveton		742	84.0	1.1	14.8	0.0	0.0	2,960,945	28.2	4.8	60.7	6.3	3,990	3,520,712	4,745
Trinity		1,183	67.8	3.2	28.7	0.3	0.0	4,564,970	42.3	4.7	45.6	7.4	3,859	4,915,304	4,155

County/ISD	Districts	Students	% White**	% Hispanic**	% Black**	% Asian**	% American Indian**	Total Revenue	% Local***	% Other***	% State***	% Federal***	Revenue Per Pupil	Total Spending	Spending Per Pupil
Tyler............	5	3,564	78.1	0.4	19.6	0.1	1.8	14,533,464	36.8	4.9	49.7	8.6	4,078	15,235,202	4,275
Chester......		270	72.6	0.0	27.0	0.0	0.4	1,208,411	42.5	4.2	49.0	4.4	4,476	1,345,367	4,983
Colmesneil		338	88.5	0.0	11.5	0.0	0.0	1,732,344	31.8	4.6	41.1	22.5	5,125	1,996,410	5,907
Spurger		340	94.1	0.0	5.6	0.0	0.3	1,593,530	33.6	3.0	59.0	4.3	4,687	1,585,514	4,663
Warren........		892	95.2	0.8	3.6	0.1	0.3	3,414,568	47.3	4.1	44.8	3.8	3,828	3,696,272	4,144
Woodville		1,724	64.8	0.5	31.0	0.2	3.4	6,584,611	32.5	5.9	52.3	9.3	3,819	6,611,639	3,835
Upshur	7	5,971	82.8	1.9	15.1	0.1	0.1	23,207,939	31.4	8.0	54.7	5.8	3,887	24,637,276	4,126
Big Sandy		655	77.6	5.2	16.9	0.3	0.0	2,773,265	31.9	12.2	49.9	5.9	4,234	2,773,265	4,234
Gilmer		2,178	77.3	1.6	21.0	†	†	8,467,103	32.5	7.6	52.7	7.2	3,888	8,214,558	3,772
Harmony		694	98.3	1.4	0.3	0.0	0.0	2,799,716	45.9	6.5	44.0	3.6	4,034	2,940,026	4,236
New Diana		708	82.2	1.4	16.2	0.0	0.1	2,413,607	18.3	6.2	71.4	4.1	3,409	2,798,579	3,953
Ore City		811	84.1	1.1	14.3	0.5	0.0	2,706,786	18.7	5.1	67.3	8.9	3,338	3,369,121	4,154
Union Grove		615	97.2	2.6	0.0	0.0	0.2	2,689,195	37.3	13.5	46.4	2.7	4,373	2,997,585	4,874
Union Hill		310	67.1	0.0	32.9	0.0	0.0	1,358,267	30.2	3.9	61.0	5.0	4,382	1,544,142	4,981
Upton	2	1,227	52.4	45.5	2.0	0.1	0.0	8,238,415	82.3	5.1	9.0	3.6	6,714	9,020,799	7,352
McCamey		781	48.4	49.6	1.9	0.1	0.0	5,199,215	77.8	5.7	11.5	4.9	6,657	5,664,662	7,253
Rankin		446	59.4	38.3	2.2	0.0	0.0	3,039,200	89.9	4.0	4.6	1.5	6,814	3,356,137	7,525
Uvalde..........	4	5,648	26.7	72.9	0.1	0.2	†	20,808,998	20.3	3.6	60.8	15.2	3,684	22,044,826	3,903
Knippa		163	50.3	49.7	0.0	0.0	0.0	768,278	29.5	5.6	56.5	8.4	4,713	839,408	5,150
Sabinal		495	38.2	61.8	0.0	0.0	0.0	2,314,590	24.8	4.7	58.1	12.4	4,676	2,506,224	5,063
Utopia........		167	98.8	1.2	0.0	0.0	0.0	776,213	56.5	6.4	33.7	3.3	4,648	797,941	4,778
Uvalde Cons		4,823	22.3	77.3	0.2	0.2	†	16,949,917	17.8	3.3	62.5	16.3	3,514	17,901,253	3,712
Val Verde.......	3	9,402	16.3	82.3	1.2	0.2	†	32,812,809	13.3	3.3	66.4	17.0	3,490	35,794,611	3,807
Comstock		120	56.7	42.5	0.0	0.0	0.8	684,967	51.2	4.5	40.0	4.3	5,708	710,983	5,925
Juno*		9	22.2	77.8	0.0	0.0	0.0	87,417	97.3	0.0	2.7	0.0	9,713	87,117	9,680
San Felipe Del Rio		9,273	15.7	82.8	1.2	0.2	†	32,040,425	12.3	3.3	67.1	17.3	3,455	34,996,511	3,774
Van Zandt	7	7,651	89.8	4.3	5.5	0.2	0.1	25,184,003	37.7	5.9	52.5	3.9	3,292	27,661,487	3,615
Canton		1,508	93.7	2.0	3.8	0.4	0.1	4,916,801	36.6	5.2	55.2	3.0	3,260	6,392,609	4,239
Edgewood.......		727	88.6	3.2	8.0	0.0	0.3	2,587,503	33.9	7.4	55.0	3.7	3,559	2,676,370	3,681
Fruitvale		296	95.6	4.4	0.0	0.0	0.0	1,171,717	39.7	2.1	57.3	0.9	3,959	1,442,830	4,874
Grand Saline.....		942	92.9	6.7	0.0	0.4	0.0	2,984,560	30.0	7.0	58.9	4.1	3,168	2,990,525	3,175
Martins Mill		288	87.2	7.6	5.2	0.0	0.0	1,047,726	30.6	4.4	62.2	2.9	3,638	1,012,382	3,515
Van..........		1,711	90.1	4.1	5.5	0.1	0.2	5,910,775	58.0	5.8	32.2	4.0	3,455	6,112,761	3,573
Wills Point......		2,179	85.7	5.0	9.1	†	0.1	6,564,921	26.0	6.2	62.5	5.3	3,013	7,034,010	3,228
Victoria..........	4	15,268	46.8	45.4	7.4	0.4	0.1	60,048,853	49.6	5.0	38.7	6.8	3,933	70,568,501	4,622
Bloomington		871	31.3	63.3	5.4	0.0	0.0	3,155,558	29.9	3.2	60.0	6.9	3,623	3,218,378	3,695
McFaddin.......		13	0.0	100	0.0	0.0	0.0	127,202	91.3	4.7	2.8	1.2	9,785	144,623	11,125
Nursery		106	66.0	33.0	0.9	0.0	0.0	388,447	73.8	1.8	24.2	0.2	3,665	390,803	3,687
Victoria		14,278	47.6	44.3	7.6	0.4	0.1	56,377,646	50.4	5.1	37.7	6.8	3,949	66,814,697	4,680
Walker..........	2	7,146	59.2	10.1	30.1	0.5	0.1	26,589,074	39.6	4.9	49.2	6.3	3,721	30,968,625	4,334
Huntsville		6,353	59.8	9.9	29.5	0.6	0.1	23,641,044	41.5	4.9	47.6	6.0	3,721	27,630,506	4,349
New Waverly.....		793	54.1	11.1	34.4	0.1	0.3	2,948,030	24.0	5.2	62.2	8.6	3,718	3,338,119	4,209
Waller	3	5,112	51.3	15.6	32.4	0.6	†	20,032,395	52.6	4.2	37.7	5.4	3,919	20,775,478	4,064
Hempstead		1,102	40.3	16.5	42.7	0.5	0.0	4,170,389	45.2	3.7	44.6	6.4	3,784	4,352,063	3,949
Royal		1,304	31.2	25.3	42.9	0.5	0.0	5,530,260	59.1	3.3	30.1	7.4	4,241	5,556,169	4,261
Waller.........		2,706	65.5	10.6	23.1	0.7	†	10,331,746	52.1	4.9	39.0	3.9	3,818	10,867,246	4,016
Ward............	2	3,090	52.7	42.4	4.5	0.1	0.3	13,103,706	65.1	5.1	24.5	5.4	4,241	14,267,037	4,617
Grand Falls Royalt		228	48.2	51.3	0.4	0.0	0.0	1,570,146	72.8	2.0	21.5	3.7	6,887	1,607,579	7,051
MonahnsWickPyot		2,862	53.1	41.7	4.8	0.1	0.3	11,533,560	64.0	5.5	24.9	5.6	4,030	12,659,458	4,423
Washington	2	4,797	62.9	5.5	30.4	1.2	†	16,976,460	34.8	6.5	51.6	7.1	3,539	17,278,766	3,602
Brenham........		4,408	62.5	5.5	30.7	1.3	†	15,344,931	33.1	6.6	53.1	7.3	3,481	15,439,254	3,503
Burton		389	67.1	6.4	26.5	0.0	0.0	1,631,529	51.2	5.8	37.9	5.2	4,194	1,839,512	4,729
Webb............	4	35,012	4.5	95.2	†	0.3	†	123,964,119	17.0	2.4	67.8	12.8	3,541	118,669,373	3,389
Laredo		23,161	2.5	97.4	†	0.1	†	85,094,158	9.0	1.7	74.2	15.0	3,674	76,659,935	3,310
Mirando City.....		123	10.6	89.4	0.0	0.0	0.0	1,105,226	59.8	2.1	24.4	13.6	8,986	1,263,141	10,269
United.........		11,478	8.3	91.0	†	0.7	†	35,663,673	30.6	3.8	57.7	7.9	3,107	36,939,360	3,218
Webb Cons		250	11.2	88.8	0.0	0.0	0.0	2,101,062	86.6	7.5	2.3	3.6	8,404	3,806,937	15,228
Wharton	5	8,563	47.6	32.3	19.9	0.1	0.0	32,700,902	44.9	6.1	42.1	6.8	3,819	35,090,741	4,098
Boling		842	49.4	34.0	16.6	0.0	0.0	3,870,376	59.0	6.9	29.8	4.4	4,597	4,089,958	4,857
East Bernard.....		827	70.3	18.4	11.4	0.0	0.0	3,414,149	43.1	6.0	47.0	4.0	4,128	3,580,486	4,329
El Campo		3,596	46.4	37.5	15.9	0.2	0.0	13,199,336	42.8	6.3	42.5	8.3	3,671	14,087,159	3,917
Louise.........		437	64.5	30.0	5.5	0.0	0.0	1,809,347	41.8	5.4	49.5	3.4	4,140	2,085,362	4,772
Wharton		2,861	39.6	29.7	30.4	0.2	0.0	10,407,694	43.4	5.8	43.4	7.3	3,638	11,247,776	3,931
Wheeler..........	7	1,227	82.2	11.4	5.5	0.5	0.3	7,764,759	61.6	7.1	25.8	5.3	6,328	7,900,447	6,439
Allison		81	†	0.0	0.0	0.0	0.0	905,429	94.9	3.1	1.5	0.5	11,178	874,905	10,801
Briscoe........		69	98.6	0.0	1.4	0.0	0.0	806,761	92.7	3.5	2.2	1.5	11,692	857,595	12,429
Kelton.........		72	88.9	8.3	2.8	0.0	0.0	725,729	90.0	6.0	2.7	1.3	10,080	726,729	10,093
Lela		40	75.0	17.5	0.0	7.5	0.0	202,159	65.4	3.3	25.7	5.5	5,054	237,694	5,942
Mobeetie.......		65	98.5	1.5	0.0	0.0	0.0	775,572	65.6	3.5	29.1	1.7	11,932	682,358	10,498
Shamrock		477	70.0	15.7	13.6	0.4	0.4	2,520,024	29.3	13.4	44.9	12.3	5,283	2,532,280	5,309
Wheeler		423	87.0	12.1	0.0	0.2	0.7	1,829,085	62.5	4.5	29.7	2.9	4,324	1,988,886	4,702
Wichita	5	21,422	73.7	11.3	12.8	1.9	0.3	73,747,470	40.1	6.8	46.7	6.5	3,443	79,832,503	3,727
Burkburnett		3,348	85.8	4.3	7.4	1.9	0.6	11,510,903	39.7	5.4	44.0	10.9	3,438	11,971,194	3,576
City View		703	75.2	9.7	9.8	5.1	0.1	2,483,353	30.5	6.0	59.3	4.2	3,533	2,572,541	3,659
Electra		624	85.4	6.6	8.0	0.0	0.0	2,770,985	44.3	4.8	38.1	12.8	4,441	3,211,246	5,146
Iowa Park Cons ...		1,858	96.6	2.5	0.2	0.3	0.4	5,761,697	36.4	9.9	50.3	3.4	3,101	6,126,168	3,297
Wichita Falls		14,889	67.6	14.2	15.9	2.1	0.3	51,220,532	40.8	6.9	46.7	5.6	3,440	55,951,354	3,758
Wilbarger	3	2,822	66.0	21.8	11.2	0.6	0.4	11,524,387	55.7	5.2	30.0	9.3	4,089	12,388,933	4,390
Harrold........		122	78.7	17.2	2.5	0.0	1.6	588,007	53.4	5.1	39.1	2.4	4,820	624,742	5,121
Northside		103	68.0	21.4	6.8	3.9	0.0	486,939	21.9	8.6	65.7	3.7	4,728	626,150	6,079
Vernon........		2,597	65.3	22.0	11.8	0.5	0.4	10,449,371	57.4	5.0	27.8	9.9	4,024	11,138,041	4,289

Texas Higher Education

This article was prepared by the staff of the Texas Higher Education Coordinating Board.

With work on the state budget postponed until July, the 72nd Legislature adjourned May 27, 1991, having passed a number of bills affecting higher education, including bills to provide funding for student loans, expand some institutions, and consolidate university insurance programs under the Employees Retirement System.

The **student loan bond legislation** authorizes the Coordinating Board to immediately sell $75 millon in revenue bonds to fund fall semester student loans under the Hinson-Hazlewood College Student Loan Program. The remainder of this four-bill package authorizes the Coordinating Board, subject to voter approval on Aug. 10, 1991, to issue up to $300 million in general obligation bonds to fund student loans and raises the annual cap on bond sales by the Board from $50 million to $100 million.

Until July 1989, the **Hinson-Hazlewood Loan Program** functioned as a revolving fund, with loan repayments being sufficient to cover new loans. However, annual loan volume ballooned from $12 million in 1986 to almost $80 million in 1990 as a result of changes in federal financial aid programs, the creation of the College Access Loan program to help middle-income families who had been cut off from federal aid, and publicity about the state's low interest rate.

Looking ahead to their budget-writing challenge in July, legislators attempted to "put some teeth" into efforts to **consolidate and eliminate waste in state government** by passing a bill that sunsets every state agency on Dec. 31, 1991, unless the agency is reauthorized by the Legislature. Separate legislation requires all state agencies to complete a comprehensive strategic plan by March 1 of every even-numbered year.

Legislation to address the **nursing shortage** did not move, primarily because of its fiscal implications. Emergency funding of $2.5 million for the remainder of this fiscal year was trusteed to the governor's office for

County/ISD	Districts	Students	% White**	% Hispanic**	% Black**	% Asian**	% American Indian*	Total Revenue	% Local***	% Other***	% State***	% Federal***	Revenue Per Pupil	Total Spending	Spending Per Pupil
Willacy	4	4,985	8.3	91.3	0.5	0.0	0.0	20,544,232	16.4	3.3	62.5	17.7	4,121	21,332,639	4,279
Lasara		229	1.3	98.7	0.0	0.0	0.0	1,266,879	14.4	3.4	67.7	14.5	5,532	1,308,211	5,713
Lyford		1,432	7.0	92.8	0.2	0.0	0.0	6,719,162	26.5	1.6	54.4	17.5	4,692	6,719,162	4,692
Raymondville		3,048	7.8	91.5	0.7	0.0	0.0	11,387,638	8.7	3.9	68.5	18.9	3,736	11,970,462	3,927
San Perlita		276	25.7	74.3	0.0	0.0	0.0	1,170,553	35.5	7.9	45.3	11.3	4,241	1,334,804	4,836
Williamson	11	34,515	77.9	14.9	5.2	1.7	0.2	141,979,636	58.2	6.1	32.8	2.9	4,114	152,952,202	4,431
Coupland		88	87.5	8.0	4.5	0.0	0.0	510,294	44.5	7.5	45.2	2.8	5,799	613,886	6,976
Florence		591	85.6	13.9	0.5	0.0	0.0	2,375,072	27.8	6.2	62.2	3.8	4,019	2,358,034	3,990
Georgetown		4,889	75.9	20.0	3.6	0.4	0.2	18,234,671	53.8	5.6	36.4	4.1	3,730	18,394,685	3,762
Granger		306	64.1	22.9	13.1	0.0	0.0	1,330,522	30.4	4.4	58.0	7.2	4,348	1,418,652	4,636
Hutto		545	75.2	22.2	2.6	0.0	0.0	2,193,115	44.4	4.7	46.7	4.2	4,024	2,331,190	4,277
Jarrell		364	78.6	18.7	2.2	0.3	0.3	1,285,101	36.2	4.6	56.4	2.9	3,530	1,381,871	3,796
Leander		5,044	88.7	9.0	1.2	0.8	0.3	23,407,948	68.3	7.2	21.6	2.8	4,641	28,111,879	5,573
Liberty Hill		972	87.3	11.7	0.6	0.3	0.0	4,215,951	26.1	7.7	61.5	4.8	4,337	4,644,828	4,779
Round Rock		18,735	79.7	12.2	5.1	2.8	0.2	76,920,830	64.0	5.8	28.4	1.8	4,106	81,268,837	4,338
Taylor		2,516	44.5	34.6	20.2	0.3	0.3	9,709,967	34.6	5.9	51.9	7.6	3,859	10,496,835	4,172
Thrall		465	73.1	20.2	6.7	0.0	0.0	1,796,165	21.6	6.9	65.5	6.0	3,863	1,931,505	4,154
Wilson	4	5,051	58.4	40.4	1.2	†	0.0	15,825,858	23.8	3.9	65.4	6.9	3,133	16,938,213	3,353
Floresville		2,486	46.0	52.8	1.2	0.0	0.0	7,377,115	21.5	3.4	66.5	8.6	2,967	7,644,450	3,075
La Vernia		1,210	84.2	14.1	1.6	0.1	0.0	4,011,125	30.0	4.5	61.9	3.6	3,315	4,786,125	3,955
Poth		694	57.6	42.2	0.1	0.0	0.0	2,300,201	22.9	4.7	66.0	6.5	3,314	2,330,366	3,358
Stockdale		661	58.2	40.1	1.7	0.0	0.0	2,137,417	21.1	3.9	67.6	7.4	3,234	2,177,272	3,294
Winkler	2	2,171	49.8	48.3	1.8	0.1	0.1	11,505,543	69.0	5.1	21.4	4.4	5,300	12,880,688	5,933
Kermit		1,767	45.1	52.9	1.8	0.1	0.1	7,439,265	55.7	6.1	31.8	6.3	4,210	8,814,375	4,988
Wink-Loving		404	70.3	28.2	1.5	0.0	0.0	4,066,278	93.3	3.4	2.5	0.8	10,065	4,066,313	10,065
Wise	7	6,028	86.5	12.1	1.1	0.1	0.2	24,642,355	51.7	6.3	37.5	4.4	4,088	25,389,781	4,212
Alvord		424	87.7	10.8	0.7	0.7	0.0	1,947,088	44.2	3.9	49.0	2.9	4,592	2,049,248	4,833
Boyd		1,080	94.4	4.6	0.6	0.0	0.5	4,198,400	34.9	5.3	57.3	2.5	3,887	4,206,494	3,895
Bridgeport		1,586	81.8	18.0	0.0	0.1	0.2	6,295,553	61.5	5.8	28.2	4.5	3,969	6,424,553	4,051
Chico		506	95.5	4.3	0.0	0.0	0.2	1,869,726	63.8	3.3	29.4	3.4	3,695	2,046,948	4,045
Decatur		1,639	78.6	17.9	3.2	0.2	0.1	7,118,583	52.7	10.9	29.6	6.9	4,343	7,372,282	4,498
Paradise		561	97.0	3.0	0.0	0.0	0.0	2,163,000	57.7	0.0	41.2	1.2	3,856	2,159,575	3,850
Slidell		232	91.4	7.8	0.9	0.0	0.0	1,050,005	34.3	6.0	53.7	6.0	4,526	1,130,681	4,874
Wood	6	5,567	87.5	2.9	9.2	0.3	0.1	22,236,111	50.1	9.4	36.9	3.6	3,994	24,205,046	4,348
Alba-Golden		559	96.6	3.4	0.0	0.0	0.0	2,235,096	30.5	6.5	58.4	4.5	3,998	2,450,134	4,383
Hawkins		782	80.4	0.6	18.9	0.0	0.0	4,151,051	81.7	11.7	4.9	1.7	5,308	5,054,463	6,464
Mineola		1,618	80.8	4.6	14.3	0.1	0.2	5,609,750	41.5	6.4	46.8	5.2	3,467	6,178,108	3,818
Quitman		1,050	89.0	2.2	8.3	0.5	0.1	4,424,454	52.0	14.6	31.0	2.4	4,214	3,988,773	3,799
Winnsboro		1,271	93.2	2.2	3.6	0.9	0.0	4,647,898	35.9	8.3	51.4	4.4	3,657	5,413,784	4,259
Yantis		287	95.5	4.5	0.0	0.0	0.0	1,167,862	66.3	5.1	26.3	2.4	4,069	1,119,784	3,902
Yoakum	2	2,521	52.4	45.9	1.5	0.1	0.1	16,033,689	85.4	7.8	4.3	2.6	6,360	21,704,666	8,610
Denver City		2,007	52.3	45.7	1.8	0.1	†	12,610,130	85.5	8.2	4.4	2.0	6,283	17,705,508	8,822
Plains		514	52.9	46.9	0.0	0.0	0.2	3,423,559	84.8	6.3	4.1	4.9	6,661	3,999,158	7,780
Young	3	3,588	88.6	9.1	1.8	0.3	0.2	12,527,426	42.2	6.4	45.3	6.1	3,491	13,170,834	3,671
Graham		2,584	90.5	7.0	1.8	0.5	0.2	8,111,762	46.4	7.0	43.6	3.0	3,139	8,235,715	3,187
Newcastle		182	99.5	0.0	0.0	0.0	0.0	994,627	63.1	3.7	28.7	4.4	5,465	1,061,638	5,833
Olney		822	80.3	17.4	2.1	0.0	0.2	3,421,037	26.3	5.6	54.2	13.9	4,162	3,873,481	4,712
Zapata	1	2,479	7.8	92.2	0.0	0.0	0.0	11,393,597	73.2	3.1	13.1	10.5	4,596	11,300,392	4,558
Zapata		2,479	7.8	92.2	0.0	0.0	0.0	11,393,597	73.2	3.1	13.1	10.5	4,596	11,300,392	4,558
Zavala	2	2,519	3.1	96.5	0.3	0.0	0.1	11,697,033	17.0	1.8	62.8	18.5	4,644	11,655,812	4,627
Crystal City		2,037	0.5	99.0	0.4	0.0	0.1	9,232,212	17.2	1.5	60.9	20.4	4,532	9,348,356	4,589
La Pryor		482	13.9	86.1	0.0	0.0	0.0	2,464,821	16.4	2.7	69.7	11.2	5,114	2,307,456	4,787

*Common school districts; all others are independent school districts. See text for explanation of difference.
†Fewer than one-tenth of one percent.
**May not total 100% because of rounding.
***May not total 100% because of rounding.

distribution to public nursing schools that can increase their enrollments by at least 10 students. The Legislative Budget Board will review the governor's recommendations, and the funds will be distributed by late July. The schools must send reports certifying the enrollment increases to the Coordinating Board by October 1992.

Efforts to dismantle or significantly alter the **Texas Academic Skills Program** failed. TASP was created by the 70th Legislature to assess and improve the basic skills of entering college students. The only TASP-related bill to pass in the regular session exempts students from the TASP Test if they are enrolled in a course offered outside the state by a Texas institution of higher education.

Changes in **teacher education** were enacted through the public-school reform bill. It authorizes the State Board of Education and the Coordinating Board to develop the process for establishing centers for professional development through the colleges of education. The centers would provide pre-service and staff development training of teachers and administrators. The State Board of Education, in consultation with the Coordinating Board, will devise a system for awarding competitive grants to support the centers — with funding to come from future appropriations, gifts and grants.

The reorganization and consolidation of **university insurance programs** under the Employees Retirement System was added as an amendment to the insurance reform bill. As a result, all higher-education health insurance programs will be consolidated into three possible systems — the University of Texas System, Texas A&M University System and another group under the Employees Retirement System for other institutions. Texas Tech and the University of Houston have the option of joining the ERS group or setting up their own insurance program. The Coordinating Board will continue to administer the Optional Retirement Program. Separate legislation passed requiring institutions to include graduate students in their health insurance programs.

Two new **competitive grants programs** were established under the **Texas-Mexico Educational Development Fund** and the **Texas-International Education Development Fund** to be administered by the Coordinating Board. No funds were appropriated for these programs. The Board must also develop rules to govern the international student exchange programs.

A new **financial-aid program** was created for fifth-year Certified Public Accountant students. At the same time, curriculum requirements for this course of study were increased.

Another financial-aid program created by the 71st Legislature, the **Outstanding Rural Scholars Program,** was transferred from the Coordinating Board to the Center for Rural Health Initiatives.

Interest in **faculty issues** continued this session. Institutions must report to the Coordinating Board by July 1, 1992, on the steps they have taken to implement the recommendations of the Coordinating Board's Student Committee on the Use of Part-Time Faculty. The Board will analyze the reports and summarize its findings for legislators.

An advisory committee will be appointed by the Coordinating Board to assess the representation of women on boards, among tenured faculty and in the administration of Texas universities. The Board must report back to the Legislature by the end of this calendar year on ways to improve representation of women.

In an effort to improve the transfer of community college students to universities, legislation was enacted requiring all public universities and their feeder community colleges to establish permanent advisory committees to recommend policies to facilitate transfers.

Institutional changes authorized during the 72nd Session included bills:

• Expanding **The University of Texas of the Permian Basin** into a four-year institution effective Sept. 1, 1991.

• Changing the name of the Texas State Technical Institute to the **Texas State Technical College System** effective Sept. 1, 1991, and establishing a TSTI extension center in the city of Marshall. The Marshall center may not offer general academic or technical courses or programs that duplicate the offerings of Panola College, Northeast Texas Community College, and Kilgore College. The bills also specify that TSTI must obtain prior Coordinating Board approval before it can offer a new course or program.

• Giving the **Texas A&M University System** board of

regents immediate authorization to change the name of the system and component institutions, with the exception of Tarleton State University.

• Designating **Lamar University at Port Arthur and at Orange** as "lower division institutions" and allowing them to issue degrees in their own name.

• Creating the **Texas Academy of Leadership in the Humanities at Lamar University at Beaumont.** The Academy will enroll gifted and talented secondary school students in college courses for college credit.

• Designating The University of Texas-Pan American-Brownsville as a "general academic institution," as opposed to an upper-level center, and renaming it **"The University of Texas at Brownsville"** effective Sept. 1, 1991. The bill also allows the university, with Coordinating Board approval, to enter into a partnership agreement whereby the university will contract with **Texas Southmost College** to teach lower-division, occupational, or technical courses that are not offered at the university.

• Allowing **Laredo State University** to teach only junior, senior and master's level "courses" rather than accept only junior, senior and master's level "students."

• Changing the name of the **University of Houston-University Park** to the University of Houston effective immediately.

• Extending the deadline for Coordinating Board approval of a four-year center **Central Texas University** from Sept. 1, 1994 to Sept. 1, 1999.

Statewide Enrollment

A total of 884,160 students were enrolled in the public and private institutions of higher education in Texas in fall 1990, an increase of 23,579 students from the previous year. Twenty-four four-year public institutions reported combined increases of 9,789 students, while 11 reported a combined loss of 2,276 students. Total enrollment at these 35 institutions was 407,461, up 1.88 percent from 1989. Enrollment increases at 38 of the 49 public junior college districts brought total fall enrollment at these institutions to 369,520 for a net increase of 3.95 percent.

The four campuses of the Texas State Technical Institute experienced a 2.3 percent drop in enrollment, with 193 fewer students enrolled in fall 1990 than in fall 1989. Independent senior institutions saw a slight increase in enrollment from 83,113 students in fall 1989 to 84,857 students in fall 1990. Independent junior colleges lost 53 students in fall 1990 bringing their total enrollment to 808.

Enrollments in all public health-related schools showed a net increase of 4.7 percent in fall 1990 to 11,873. Enrollment rose in medical schools by .22 percent. However, enrollment in dental schools dropped by 2.4 percent and enrollment dropped in the veterinary medicine program by 3.8 percent. In contrast, enrollment rose 9.3 percent in health-related academic programs. where 563 more students enrolled than in 1989. Enrollment at independent medical and dental schools dropped by 10 students to 1,426 in fall 1990 compared to 1,436 in fall 1989.

In summer 1991, Texas' system of public higher education included 26 public four-year institutions, nine upper-level universities or centers, three lower-division centers, 49 public community college districts, one technical institute with four campuses, eight medical schools and health science centers, a school for marine resources and a special institute for the deaf. On September 1, 1991, The University of Texas of the Permian Basin expanded from an upper-level university to a four-year university. In the private sector, Texas has 37 independent senior colleges and universities, three junior colleges, one medical school and one dental school.

Tuition and Fees

Resident tuition at Texas public universities will continue to follow the schedule of increases established by the 69th Legislature in 1985 unless action is taken during a special session of the 72nd Legislature to raise tuition rates. For 1991-92 and 1992-93, **Texas residents** will pay $20 per undergraduate semester credit hour. For the 1993-94 and 1994-95 academic years, Texas residents will pay $22 per undergraduate semester credit hour. Despite these increases, tuition costs for state residents remain among the lowest in the nation. Tuition for a **non-resident student** is $128 per semester credit hour beginning in fall 1991.

Bills permitting regents to raise **building use fees** from $6 to $12 per semester credit hour and raising the ceiling on **non-academic activities** from $90 to $150 per semester hour became law. A number of institutions were also successful in enacting increases in student fees.

History

While there were earlier efforts toward higher education, the first permanent institutions established were these church-supported schools: **Rutersville University,** established in 1840 by Methodist minister Martin Ruter in Fayette County, predecessor of **Southwestern University,** Georgetown, established in 1843; **Baylor University,** now at Waco, but established in 1845 at Independence, Washington County; and **Austin College,** now at Sherman, but founded in 1849 at Huntsville.

Other historic Texas schools of collegiate rank included: **Larissa College,** 1848, at Larissa, Cherokee County; **McKenzie College,** 1841, Clarksville; **Chappell Hill Male and Female Institute,** 1850, Chappell Hill; **Soule University,** 1855, Chappell Hill; **Johnson Institute,** 1852, Driftwood, Hays County; **Nacogdoches University,** 1845, Nacogdoches; **Salado College,** 1859, Salado, Bell County. **Add-Ran College,** established at Thorp Spring in 1873, was the predecessor of present **Texas Christian University,** Fort Worth.

Texas A&M, authorized by the Legislature in 1871, opened its doors in 1876 to become the first publicly supported institution of higher education. In 1881, Texans voted to establish the **University of Texas** in Austin, with a medical branch in Galveston; the Austin institution opened Sept. 15, 1883, the Galveston school in 1891.

In 1901, the 27th Legislature established the **Girls Industrial College** (forerunner of **Texas Woman's University**), which began classes at its campus in Denton in

1903. A campaign to establish a state industrial college for women was led by the State Grange and Patrons of Husbandry. A bill was signed into law on April 6, 1901, creating the college. It was charged with a dual mission, which continues to guide the university today — to provide a liberal education and to prepare young women with a specialized education "for the practical industries of the age." In 1905 the name of the college was changed to the **College of Industrial Arts;** in 1934, it was changed to **Texas State College for Women.** Since 1957 the name of the institution, which is now the largest university for women in the United States, has been the **Texas Woman's University.**

A number of Texas schools were established primarily for **blacks,** although collegiate racial integration is now complete in the state. The black-oriented institutions include state-supported **Prairie View State University,** Prairie View; **Texas Southern University,** Houston; and privately supported **Huston-Tillotson College,** Austin; **Jarvis Christian College,** Hawkins; **Wiley College,** Marshall; **Paul Quinn College,** Waco; **Mary Allen College,** Crockett; and **Butler** and **Texas Colleges,** Tyler.

Wadley Research Institute, Dallas, and M. D. Anderson **Hospital and Tumor Institute,** Houston, grant graduate degrees although they are not primarily educational institutions.

The preceding table gives dates of establishment for leading Texas institutions and enrollments, as reported by the schools. In some cases, dates of establishment differ from those given in the preceding discussion because schools use the date when authorization was given, rather than actual date of first classwork.

Universities and Colleges of Texas

Table below is from data assembled from these institutions during 1991. Enrollment figures are for the 1990-1991 regular term and the 1990 summer term.

Name of Institution; Location; Ownership; 2-yr., 4-yr., Upper Level; Date of Founding; President	Number in Faculty	Regular Term 1990-01	Summer Session 1990	Extension or Continuing Ed.
Abilene Christian University—Abilene; private, 4-yr.; 1906 (as **Childers Classical Institute;** became **Abilene Christian College** by 1914; became university in 1976); Dr. William J. Teague.	251	4,053	1,227	...
ALAMO COMMUNITY COLLEGE DISTRICT—Ivory V. Nelson, Chancellor				
Palo Alto College—San Antonio; state, 2-yr.; 1985; Dr. Byron Skinner	215	4,763	...	...
St. Philip's College—San Antonio; state, 2-yr.; 1898; Dr. Stephen R. Mitchell	200	5,700	2,000	3,000
San Antonio College—San Antonio; municipal, 2-yr.; 1925; Dr. Max Castillo.	419	20,937	16,149	3,200
Alvin Community College—Alvin; private, 2-yr.; 1949; Dr. A. Rodney Allbright	101	3,900	3,516	2,823
Amarillo College—Amarillo; state, 2-yr.; 1929; Dr. George T. Miller	175	5,952	1,033	8,005
Amber University—Garland; private, 4-yr.; 1971; Dr. Douglas W. Warner	75	1,498	1,074	...
Angelina College—Lufkin; state, 2-yr.; 1968; Dr. Jack W. Hudgins.	110	3,145	1,800	1,900
Angelo State University—San Angelo (See **Texas State University System**)				
*****Arlington Baptist College**—Arlington; Baptist; 1939 (as Bible Baptist Seminary; changed to present name in 1965); Dr. Wayne Martin	15	171	49	...
Austin College—Sherman; Presbyterian USA, 2-yr.; 1849; Dr. Harry E. Smith	94	1,257	127	450
Austin Community College—Austin; state/municipal, 2-yr.; 1973; Dr. Dan Angel	1,339	24,082	19,302	3,079
Austin Presbyterian Theological Seminary—Austin; private (Presbyterian); 3-yr.; 1902 (successor to **Austin School of Theology,** est. 1884); Dr. Jack L. Stotts	20	242	78	190
Baptist Missionary Association Theological Seminary—Jacksonville; Baptist Missionary; 4-yr.; 1955 (as **North American Theological Seminary**); Dr. Philip R. Bryan	14	73	13	4
Baylor College of Dentistry—Dallas; private, 4-yr. professional; 1905; Dr. Dominick P. DePaola	204	427	257	...
Baylor College of Medicine—Houston; private (Baptist until 1969); professional; 1903 (in Dallas, moved to Houston in 1943); Dr. William T. Butler	3,087	2,297	...	...
Baylor University School of Nursing—Waco; Baptist, 4-yr.; 1950; Phyllis Karns, Ph.D., R.N., Dean	27	175	...	...
Baylor University—Waco; Baptist, 4-yr.; 1845 (at Independence; merged with **Waco University** in 1887 and moved to Waco); Dr. Herbert H. Reynolds	611	12,019	4,797	470
Bee County College—Beeville; state, 2-yr.; 1966; Dr. Norman E. Wallace	125	2,250	1,914	300
Blinn College—Brenham; state, 2-yr.; 1883 (as academy; junior college, 1927); Dr. Walter C. Schwartz	272	7,098	6,416	...
Brazosport College—Lake Jackson; state, 2-yr.; 1967; Dr. John Grable	57	3,850	1,200	2,840
Brookhaven College—Farmers Branch (See **Dallas County Community College District**)				
Cedar Valley College—Lancaster (See **Dallas County Community College District**)				
Central Texas College—Killeen; state, 2-yr.; 1967; Dr. James R. Anderson.	261	5,303	8,047	1,594
Cisco Junior College—Cisco; state, 2-yr.; 1909 (as private institution; became state school in 1939); Dr. Roger C. Schustereit	57	2,100	893	250
Clarendon College— Clarendon; state, 2-yr.; 1898 (as church school; 1927 became state school); Jerry D. Stockton	31	1,156	713	177

Name of Institution; Location; Ownership; 2-yr., 4-yr., Upper Level; Date of Founding; President	Number in Faculty	Enrollment Regular Term 1990-01	Enrollment Summer Session 1990	Extension or Continuing Ed.
College of the Mainland—Texas City; state/local, 2-yr.; 1966; Dr. Larry L. Stanley	370	3,763	3,157	4,500
Collin County Community College—McKinney; state/local, 2-yr.; 1985; Dr. John H. Anthony	325	9,091	6,870	3,050
Concordia Lutheran College—Austin; Lutheran (Missouri), 4-yr.; 1926; Dr. Ray F. Martens	34	682	103	...
Cooke County College—Gainesville; state, 2-yr.; 1924 (as Gainesville Junior College; name changed in 1960); Dr. Luther Bud Joyner	150	3,500	750	1,500
Corpus Christi State University—Corpus Christi (See Texas A&M University System)	...			
Dallas Baptist University—Dallas; Southern Baptist, 4-yr.; 1898 (as Decatur Baptist College; moved to Dallas and name changed in 1965); Dr. Gary Cook	141	2,333	1,680	1,245
Dallas Christian College—Dallas; Church of Christ, 4-yr.; 1950; Gene R. Shepherd	15	99	...	...
DALLAS COUNTY COMMUNITY COLLEGE DISTRICT—Lawrence W. Tyree, Chancellor				
Brookhaven College—Farmers Branch; community, 2-yr.; 1978; Acting Pres., Dr. Larry Darlage	‡425	9,000	6,600	10,000
*Cedar Valley College—Lancaster; community, 2-yr., 1977; Dr. Floyd S. Elkins	150	3,069	1,000	3,000
Eastfield College—Mesquite; community, 2-yr.; 1970; Dr. Justus D. Sundermann	‡585	9,769	6,063	5,200
El Centro College—Dallas; community, 2-yr.; 1966; Dr. Wright L. Lassiter Jr.	‡495	5,784	3,985	4,102
Mountain View College—Dallas; community, 2-yr; Dr. William H. Jordan	‡193	6,318	4,805	2,500
North Lake College—Irving; community, 2-yr.; 1977; Dr. Jim Horton	450	6,556	4,015	4,471
Richland College—Dallas; community, 2-yr; 1972; Dr. Stephen K. Mittelstet	‡641	11,092	10,712	8,000
Dallas Theological Seminary—Dallas; private, graduate; 1924; Dr. Donald K. Campbell	70	1,374	606	59
Del Mar College—Corpus Christi; state, 2-yr.; 1935; Dr. B.R. Venters	675	10,000	...	15,000
Eastfield College—Mesquite (See Dallas County Community College District)				
East Texas Baptist University—Marshall; Baptist, 4-yr.; 1913 (as College of Marshall; changed to East Texas Baptist College in 1944; became university in 1984); Dr. Robert E. Craig	64	924	...	...
East Texas State University—Commerce; state, 4-yr.; 1889 (as East Texas Normal College; renamed East Texas State Teachers College in 1923; "Teachers" dropped in 1957 and university status conferred in 1965); Dr. Jerry D. Morris	290	7,979	7,872	...
East Texas State University at Texarkana—Texarkana; state, upper-level; 1971; Dr. John F. Moss	39	1,287	1,109	...
East Texas State University Commuter Facility—Garland; state, extension facility; 2-yr.; Jerry Morris	9	2,000	...	1,628
El Centro College—Dallas (See Dallas County Community College District)				
*El Paso Community College District—El Paso; state, 2-yr.; 1969; three campuses: Rio Grande, TransMountain and Valle Verde; Robert Shepack	880	13,833	6,878	4,738
*Episcopal Theological Seminary of the Southwest—Austin; Episcopal; 1952; Very Rev. Durstan R. McDonald, Provost	15	71	25	...
Frank Phillips College—Borger; state; 1948; Dr. Vance W. Gipson	‡78	964	426	...
Galveston College—Galveston; state/local, 2-yr.; 1967; Dr. Marc Nigliazzo	76	2,115	1,612	1,000
Grayson County College—Denison; state, 2-yr.; 1965; Dr. Jim M. Williams	110	3,500	3,100	2,500
Hardin-Simmons University—Abilene; Southern Baptist, 4-yr.; 1891 (as Simmons College; changed to Simmons University in 1925; changed to present name in 1934); Dr. Jesse C. Fletcher	151	1,930	926	100
Hill College—Hillsboro; state, 2-yr.; 1923 (as Hillsboro Junior College; name changed in 1962); Dr. W.R. Auvenshine	60	1,650	752	200
Houston Baptist University—Houston; Baptist, 4-yr.; 1960; Dr. E.D. Hodo	120	2,252	1,136	546
Houston Community College—Houston; state, 2-yr.; 1971; Dr. Charles A. Green, Chancellor	557	30,000	27,425	39,127
Howard College—Big Spring; state, 2-yr.; 1945; Dr. Bob E. Riley	150	2,500	966	500
Howard Payne University—Brownwood; Southern Baptist, 4-yr.; 1889; Dr. Don Newbury	92	1,390	507	53
*Huston-Tillotson College—Austin; Methodist/Church of Christ; 1875; Dr. Joseph T. McMillan Jr.	46	520	213	...
*Incarnate Word College—San Antonio; 1881, 4-yr.; Louis J. Agenese Jr.	140	2,240	831	...
International Bible College—San Antonio; private, 4-yr.; 1944; Rev. David B. Coote	10	135	...	...
Jacksonville College—Jacksonville; Missionary Baptist, 2-yr.; 1899; Edwin Crank	30	261	129	18
Jarvis Christian College—Hawkins; Christian Church, 4-yr.; 1912; Dr. Sebetha Jenkins	55	600	...	...
Kilgore College—Kilgore; state, 2-yr.; 1935; Dr. B.E. Woodruff	185	4,443	2,560	2,467
LAMAR UNIVERSITY SYSTEM—Dr. George McLaughlin, Chancellor				
Lamar University - Beaumont—Beaumont; state, 4-yr.; 1923 (as South Park Junior College; name changed to Lamar College, 1932; name changed to Lamar State College of Technology in 1951; present name since 1971); Dr. Billy J. Franklin	597	10,196	4,939	1,735
Lamar University - Orange—Orange; state, 2-yr.; 1969; Dr. Steve Maradian	65	1,283	870	72
Lamar University - Port Arthur—Port Arthur; state, 2-yr.; 1909 (as Port Arthur College; became part of Lamar University in 1975); Dr. Sam Monroe	101	2,052	650	235
Laredo Junior College—Laredo; municipal, 2-yr.; 1946; Dr. Roger L. Worsley	300	5,125	3,569	2,453
Laredo State University—Laredo (See Texas A&M University System)				
LeTourneau University—Longview; private, 4-yr.; 1946 (as LeTourneau Technical Institute; became 4-yr. college in 1961); Dr. Alvin O. Austin	61	1,026	274	...
*Lee College—Baytown; state; 1934; Dr. Vivian B. Blevins	216	5,100	2,350	2,835
Lon Morris College—Jacksonville; Methodist, 2-yr.; 1854 (as Danville Academy; name in 1873 to Alexander Institute at Kilgore; present name since 1923); Dr. W. Faulk Landrum	33	375	80	...

Name of Institution; Location; Ownership; 2-yr., 4-yr., Upper Level; Date of Founding; President	Number in Faculty	Enrollment Regular Term 1990-01	Summer Session 1990	Extension or Continuing Ed.
Lubbock Christian University—Lubbock; Church of Christ, 4-yr.; 1957; Dr. Steven S. Lemley	100	1,035	299	...
McLennan Community College—Waco; state, 2-yr.; 1965; Dr. Dennis Michaelis	165	5,750	5,240	2,950
McMurry University—Abilene; Methodist, 4-yr.; 1923; Dr. Thomas K. Kim	75	1,633	729	...
Midland College—Midland; state, 2-yr.; 1972; Dr. Jess H. Parrish	‡220	4,005	2,681	3,000
Midwestern State University—Wichita Falls; state, 4-yr.; 1922; Dr. Louis J. Rodriguez	155	5,508	3,973	1,981
Mountain View College—Dallas (See Dallas County Community College District)				
Navarro College—Corsicana; state, 2-yr.; 1946; Dr. Gerald E. Burson	165	2,828	...	5,500
Northeast Texas Community College—Mount Pleasant; state, 2-yr.; 1984; Mike Bruner	‡85	1,782	1,013	702
North Harris County College—Houston; three campuses: East, South and West; state, 2-yr.; 1972; Dr. John E. Pickelman, Chancellor	717	15,826	...	11,822
North Lake College—Irving (See Dallas County Community College District)				
*Northwood Institute—Cedar Hill;private; 1966; Dean John Castle	13	205	27	210
Oblate School of Theology—San Antonio; Roman Catholic, 4-yr.; 1903 (in present location since 1929; formerly DeMazenod Sholasticate); Rev. Patrick Guidon, O.M.I.	21	210	50	...
*Odessa College—Odessa; state; 1946; Dr. Philip T. Speegle	136	4,868	2,396	18,993
Our Lady of the Lake University of San Antonio—San Antonio; Catholic, 4-yr.; 1896 (as academy for girls; became senior college in 1911; became university in 1975); Sister Elizabeth Anne Sueltenfuss	‡157	2,693	929	500
Palo Alto College—San Antonio (See Alamo Community College District)				
Panola College—Carthage; state, 2-yr.; 1947 (as Panola Junior College; name changed, 1988); Dr. Gary McDaniel	51	1,568	745	308
Paris Junior College—Paris; state, 2-yr.; 1924; Bobby R. Walters	‡117	2,326	1,481	1,630
Paul Quinn College—Dallas; African Methodist Episcopal, 4-yr.; 1872 (in Waco; moved to Dallas in 1990); Dr. Warren W. Morgan	96	1,020	...	...
Prairie View A&M University—Prairie View (See Texas A&M University System)				
Ranger Junior College—Ranger; state, 2-yr.; 1926; Dr. Joe Mills	50	849	516	...
Rice University—Houston; private, 4-yr.; 1912 (as Rice Institute; name changed to present form in 1960); Dr. George Rupp	520	4,000	...	3,305
Richland College—Dallas (See Dallas County Community College District)				
Rio Grande Bible Institute and Language School—Edinburg; private, 4-yr.; 1946; Dr. Gordon E. Johnson	30	184	20	...
St. Edward's University—Austin; Roman Catholic, 4-yr.; 1885; Dr. Patricia A. Hayes	188	3,086	603	...
St. Mary's University—San Antonio; Roman Catholic, 4-yr.; 1852; Rev. John Moder, S.M.	‡219	4,045	...	...
St. Philip's College—San Antonio (See Alamo Community College District)				
Sam Houston State University—Huntsville (See Texas State University System)				
San Antonio College—San Antonio (See Alamo Community College District)				
San Jacinto College District—Thomas Sewell, Chancellor				
*San Jacinto College, Central Campus—Pasadena; state, 2-yr.; 1961; Dr. Monte Blue	439	9,329	3,629	...
San Jacinto College-North Campus—Houston; state, 2-yr.; 1974; Dr. Ed Lehr	96	3,778	2,057	1,390
San Jacinto College-South Campus—Houston; state, 2-yr.; 1979; Dr. Parker Williams	222	5,068	...	1,906
Schreiner College—Kerrville; Presbyterian, 4-yr.; 1917; Dr. Sam Junkin	50	600	86	...
South Plains College—Levelland; state, 2-yr.; 1958; Dr. Marvin L. Baker	285	5,152	2,593	2,240
South Texas College of Law—Houston; private, 3-yr.; 1923; Dr. William L. Wilks	‡75	1,363	940	3,000
Southern Methodist University—Dallas; Methodist, 4-yr.; 1911; Dr. A. Kenneth Pye	477	8,798	3,562	205fte's
Southwest Collegiate Institute for the Deaf—Big Spring; state, 2-yr.; 1980; Dr. Ron Brasel	25	125	20	...
Southwest Texas Junior College—Uvalde; state, 2-yr.; 1946; Dr. Billy Word	70	2,658	1,413	...
Southwest Texas State University—San Marcos (see Texas State University System)				
Southwestern Adventist College—Keene; Seventh-Day Adventist, 4-yr.; 1893 (as Keene Industrial Academy; became Southwestern Junior College, then changed to Southwestern Union College in 1963); Dr. Marvin Anderson	55	797	309	197
Southwestern Assemblies of God College—Waxahachie; Assemblies of God, 4-yr.; 1927 (in Enid, Okla., as Southwestern Bible School; moved to Fort Worth and merged with South Central Bible Institute in 1941; moved to Waxahachie as Southwestern Bible Institute in 1943; present name since 1963); Dr. Delmer R. Guynes.	28	686	172	221
Southwestern Baptist Theological Seminary—Fort Worth; Southern Baptist, 4-yr.; 1908; Dr. Russell H. Dilday	‡180	3,740	1,300	1,179
Southwestern Christian College—Terrell; Church of Christ, 4-yr.; 1948 (as Southern Bible Institute in Fort Worth; moved to Terrell and changed name to present form in 1950); Dr. Jack Evans Sr.	18	235	...	...
Southwestern University—Georgetown; Methodist, 4-yr.; 1840 (Southwestern University was a merger of Rutersville (1840), Wesleyan (1846) and McKenzie (1841) colleges and Soule University (1855). First named Texas University; chartered under present name in 1875); Dr. Roy B. Shilling Jr.	128	1,239	212	...
Stephen F. Austin State University—Nacogdoches (See Texas State University System)				
Sul Ross State University—Alpine (See Texas State University System)				
Sul Ross State University Uvalde Study Center—Uvalde (See Texas State University System)				
Tarleton State University—Stephenville (See Texas A&M University System)				
Tarrant Co. Junior College—Fort Worth; community, 2-yr.; 1965; three campuses: Northeast, Northwest and South; C.A. Roberson, Chancellor	1,093	27,999	10,678	14,010
Temple Junior College—Temple; state, 2-yr.; 1926; Dr. Marvin R. Felder	78	2,350	1,840	2,100
Texarkana College—Texarkana; state, 2-yr.; 1927; Dr. Carl M. Nelson	199	4,500	2,708	3,500
Texas A&I University—Kingsville (See Texas A&M University System)				

Name of Institution; Location; Ownership; 2-yr., 4-yr., Upper Level; Date of Founding; President	Number in Faculty	Enrollment Regular Term 1990-01	Summer Session 1990	Extension or Continuing Ed.
TEXAS A&M UNIVERSITY SYSTEM—Perry L. Adkisson, Chancellor				
Corpus Christi State University—Corpus Christi; state, upper-level; 1973; Dr. Robert R. Furgason	150	3,815	4,248	. . .
Laredo State University—Laredo; state, 2-yr; 1969; Dr. Leo Sayavedra	‡60	1,273	959	. . .
Prairie View A&M University—Prairie View; state, 4-yr.; 1876 (as **Alta Vista Agricultural College**; name changed to **Prairie View State Normal School** in 1879; called **Prairie View University** by 1947, when it was changed to **Prairie View Agricultural and Mechanical College** as a branch of the **Texas A&M University System**; present name since 1973); Dr. Julius W. Becton Jr.	304	4,954	2,257	. . .
Tarleton State University—Stephenville; state, 4-yr.; 1899 (as **John Tarleton College**; taken over by state in 1917 as **John Tarleton Agricultural College**; changed 1949 to **Tarleton State College**; present name since 1973); Dr. Dennis McCabe (Interim)	302	6,251	4,349	2,500
Texas A&I University—Kingsville; state, 4-yr.; 1925 (as **South Texas Teachers College**; name changed to **Texas College of Arts and Industries** in 1967; to present name in 1967; made part of **University of South Texas System** in 1977); Dr. Manuel L. Ibanez	362	6,014	6,343	887
Texas A&M University—College Station; state, 4-yr.; 1876 (as **Agricultural and Mechanical College of Texas**; present name since 1963); Dr. William H. Mobley.	2,200	41,171	16,116	. . .
Texas A&M University College of Medicine—College Station; state, 4-yr.; 1976; Dr. Richard A. DeVaul, Dean	638	182	. . .	. . .
Texas A&M University College of Veterinary Medicine—College Station; state, 4-yr.; 1916; Dr. John A. Shadduck, Dean	175	1,700	400	188
Texas A&M University at Galveston—Galveston; state, 4-yr.; 1962 (as **Texas Maritime Academy**; changed to **Moody College of Marine Sciences and Maritime Resources** and raised to 4-yr. college in 1971; changed again to present name); Dr. William Merrell .	60	1,076	435	50
West Texas State University—Canyon; state, 4-yr.; 1910 (as **West Texas State Normal College**; became **West Texas State Teachers College** in 1923; in 1949 became **West Texas State College**; changed to present form in 1949); Dr. Barry B. Thompson	355	6,193	4,044	245
Texas Baptist Institute and Seminary—Henderson; Missionary Baptist, 4-yr.; 1948; Dr. Ray O. Brooks	14	67	. . .	. . .
Texas Christian University—Fort Worth; Disciples of Christ, 4-yr; 1873 (as **Add-Ran College** at Thorp Spring; name changed to **Add-Ran Christian University** 1890; moved to Waco 1895; present name since 1902; moved to Fort Worth 1910); Dr. William E. Tucker, Chancellor	321	6,500	2,300	156
Texas College—Tyler; Christian Methodist Episcopal, 4-yr; 1894; Dr. Maurice Cherry. .	33	470	70	. . .
Texas College of Osteopathic Med.—Fort Worth; state, 4-yr.; 1966 (as private college; came under direction of **North Texas State University,** now **Univ. of North Texas,** in 1975); Dr. David M. Richards	150	380	. . .	. . .
Texas Lutheran College—Seguin; Lutheran, 4-yr.; 1891; Dr. Charles Oestreich	80	1,265	248	117
Texas Southern University—Houston; state, 4-yr.; 1926 (as **Houston Colored Junior College**; upper level added and name changed to **Houston College for Negroes** in mid-1930s; became **Texas State University for Negroes** in 1947; present name since 1951); Dr. William H. Harris.	‡514	9,441	1,903	. . .
Texas Southmost College—Brownsville; state, 2-yr.; 1926 (as **Brownsville Junior College**; name changed in 1949); Dr. Juliet V. Garcia	155	5,850	2,300	861
TEXAS STATE TECHNICAL COLLEGE SYSTEM—Dr. Cecil Groves, Chancellor				
Texas State Technical Institute-Amarillo—Amarillo; state, 2-yr.; 1970; Dr. Ron DeSpain, Campus President.	72	657	524	1,319
Texas State Technical Institute-Harlingen—Harlingen; state, 2-yr.; 1967; Dr. J. Gilbert Leal, Campus Pres.	162	3,000	2,000	5,000
Texas State Technical Institute-Marshall—Marshall; state, 2-yr.; (authorized by 72nd Legislature, 1991);	. . .	. . .	. . .	. . .
Texas State Technical Institute-Sweetwater— Sweetwater; state, 2-yr.; 1971; Dr. Clay Johnson, Campus President.	100	800	. . .	. . .
Texas State Technical Institute- Waco—Waco; state, 2-yr.; 1965 (as **James Connally Technical Institute**; name changed in 1969); Dr. Don E. Goodwin, Campus Pres.	354	3,803	2,651	272
TEXAS STATE UNIVERSITY SYSTEM—Lamar G. Urbanovsky, Executive Director				
Angelo State—San Angelo; state, 4-yr.; Dr. Lloyd D. Vincent	204	6,298	2,653	372
Sam Houston State University—Huntsville; state, 4-yr.; 1879; Dr. Martin J. Anisman . . .	564	12,738	9,770	7,766
Southwest Texas State University—San Marcos; state, 4-yr.; 1903 (as **Southwest Texas Normal School**; name changed in 1918 to **Southwest Texas State Normal College,** in 1923 to **Southwest Texas State Teachers College,** in 1959 to **Southwest Texas State College,** and in 1969 to present form); Dr. Jerome H. Supple	901	20,944	9,100	. . .
Sul Ross State University—Alpine; state, 4-yr.; 1940 (as **Sul Ross State Normal College**; changed to **Sul Ross State Teachers College** in 1923; to **Sul Ross State College** in 1949; and to present name in 1969); Dr. R. Vic Morgan	95	2,273	2,581	. . .
Sul Ross State University Uvalde Study Center—Uvalde; state, upper-level; 1973; Dr. Frank W. Abbott, Dean	17	477	329	. . .
Texas Tech University—Lubbock; state, 4-yr.; 1923 (as **Texas Technological College**; present name since 1969); Dr. Robert W. Lawless	1,666	25,363	9,610	29,413
Texas Tech University Health Sciences Center—Lubbock; state, professional; 1969; Dr. Robert W. Lawless.	488	894	477	2,657
Texas Wesleyan University—Fort Worth; United Methodist, 4-yr.; 1891 (as college; present name since 1989); Dr. W.L. Hailey, Interim Pres.	73	1,429	. . .	105

Name of Institution; Location; Ownership; 2-yr., 4-yr., Upper Level; Date of Founding; President	Number in Faculty	Enrollment Regular Term 1990-01	Summer Session 1990	Extension or Continuing Ed.
Texas Woman's University—Denton; state, 4-yr.; 1901 (as **College of Industrial Arts;** name changed to **Texas State College for Women,** 1934; present name since 1957); Dr. Shirley S. Chater	400	9,850	9,425	...
Trinity University—San Antonio; Presbyterian, 4-yr.; 1869 (at Tehuacana; moved to Waxahachie, 1902; moved to San Antonio, 1942); Dr. Ronald K. Calgaard	234	2,538	321	...
Trinity Valley Community College—Athens; state, 2-yr.; 1946 (originally **Henderson County Junior College**); Dr. Ronald C. Baugh	127	4,460	2,059	3,210
Tyler Junior College—Tyler; state, 2-yr.; 1926; Dr. Raymond M. Hawkins	200	8,000	3,000	10,000
University of Central Texas—Killeen; private, 4-yr.; 1973 (originally **American Technological University;** name changed, 1989); Dr. L. Harlan Ford	39	539	495	...
*****University of Dallas**—Irving; Catholic; 1956; Dr. Robert A. Sasseen	182	2,649	1,250	225
UNIVERSITY OF HOUSTON SYSTEM—Marguerite Ross Barnett, President				
University of Houston—Houston; state, 4-yr.; 1927; Dr. Marguerite Ross Barnett	‡1,988	33,117	14,000	2,000
University of Houston-Clear Lake—Houston; state, upper level; 1974; Dr. Thomas M. Stauffer	880	7,560	4,054	4,000
University of Houston-Downtown—Houston; state, 4-yr.; 1948 (as **South Texas College;** made part of University of Houston in 1974); (Vacancy)	347	8,702	3,294	1,550
University of Houston-Victoria—Victoria; state, upper-level; 1973; Dr. Glenn A. Goerke	72	1,164	1,108	783
University of Mary Hardin-Baylor—Belton; Southern Baptist, 4-yr.; 1845; Dr. Bobby E. Parker	‡82	1,808	750	...
University of North Texas—Denton; state, 4-yr.; 1890 (as **North Texas Normal College;** name changed in 1923 to **North Texas State Teachers College;** in 1949 to **North Texas State College;** became a university in 1961; present name since 1988); Dr. Alfred F. Hurley, Chancellor	†	27,100	12,070	...
University of St. Thomas—Houston; private, 4-yr.; 1947; Dr. Joseph M. McFadden	148	1,964	865	...
UNIVERSITY OF TEXAS SYSTEM—Hans Mark, Chancellor				
University of Texas at Arlington—Arlington; state, 4-yr.; 1895 (as **Arlington College;** in 1917, changed to state institution and renamed **Grubbs Vocational College;** 1923 changed to **North Texas Agricultural and Mechanical College;** in 1949 changed to **Arlington State College;** present name since 1967); (Vacancy)	1,514	24,783	12,627	5,776
University of Texas at Austin—Austin; state, 4-yr.; 1883; Dr. William H. Cunningham	2,044	49,617	20,672	...
University of Texas at Brownsville—Brownsville; state, 2-yr.; 1973 (as branch of **Pan American College;** changed to **The University of Texas-Pan American-Brownsville;** present name since Sept. 1991); Dr. Homer J. Pena	80	1,450	...	...
University of Texas at Dallas—Richardson; state, 4-yr.; 1961 (as **Graduate Research Center of the Southwest;** changed to **Southwest Center for Advanced Studies** in 1967; joined U.T. System and present name adopted in 1969; 4-yr. university since 1975); Dr. Robert H. Rutford	206	8,700	5,625	9,147
University of Texas at El Paso—El Paso; state, 4-yr.; 1913 (as **Texas College of Mines and Metallurgy;** changed to **Texas Western College of U.T.** in 1949; present name since 1967); Dr. Diana Natalicio	729	16,524	7,928	2,354
University of Texas at San Antonio—San Antonio; state, 4-yr.; 1969; Dr. Samuel Kirkpatrick	1,000	15,489	7,525	...
University of Texas at Tyler—Tyler; state, upper-level; 1971 (as **Tyler State College;** became **Texas Eastern University** in 1975; joined U.T. System in 1979); Dr. George F. Hamm	‡221	3,725	2,664	863
University of Texas of the Permian Basin—Odessa; state, 4-yr.; 1973 (as 2-yr. institution; expanded to 4-yr., Sept. 1991); Dr. Duane Leach	63	2,046	1,029	14
University of Texas-Pan American—Edinburg; state, 4-yr.; 1927 (as **Edinburg Junior College;** changed to **Pan American College** and made 4-yr. institution, 1952; became **Pan American University** in 1971; present name since 1991); Dr. Miguel A. Nevarez	400	12,200	6,600	...
§UNIVERSITY OF TEXAS HEALTH SCIENCE CENTER AT HOUSTON—Dr. David Lowe, President	1,026	3,036	1,632	13,405
Established 1972; consists of following divisions (year of founding): Dental Branch (1905); Graduate School of Biomedical Sciences (1963); Medical School (1970); School of Allied Health Sciences (1973); School of Nursing (1972); School of Public Health (1967); Division of Continuing Education (1958).				
§UNIVERSITY OF TEXAS HEALTH SCIENCE CENTER AT SAN ANTONIO—Dr. John P. Howe III, President	‡1,090	2,362	...	...
Established 1968; consists of following divisions (year of founding): Dental School (1970); Graduate School of Biomedical Sciences (1970); Health Science Center (1972); Medical School (1959 as South Texas Medical School of University of Texas; 1966 name changed to present form); School of Allied Health Sciences (1976); School of Nursing (1969).				
§UNIVERSITY OF TEXAS MEDICAL BRANCH AT GALVESTON—Dr. Thomas N. James, President	800	2,300	...	...
Established 1890; consists of following divisions (year of founding): Graduate School of Biomedical Sciences (1952); Medical School (1891); School of Allied Health Sciences (1968); School of Nursing (1890).				
§UNIVERSITY OF TEXAS SOUTHWESTERN MEDICAL CENTER AT DALLAS—Dr. Kern Wildenthal	2,959	2,661	...	...

Name of Institution; Location; Ownership; 2-yr., 4-yr., Upper Level; Date of Founding; President	Number in Faculty	Regular Term 1990-01	Summer Session 1990	Extension or Continuing Ed.
		Enrollment		

Established 1943 (as private institution; became **Southwestern Medical College of U.T.** 1948; in 1967 became **U.T. Southwestern Medical School at Dallas**; made part of **U.T. Health Science Center at Dallas** in 1972; name changed again to present form); consists of following divisions (year of founding): Graduate School of Biomedical Sciences (1947); School of Allied Health Sciences (1968); Southwestern Medical School (1943).

§¶**UNIVERSITY OF TEXAS SYSTEM CANCER CENTER**—Dr. Charles A. Le-Maistre, President	585	740	. . .	. . .
Consists of following divisions (year of founding): **M.D. Anderson Hospital and Tumor Institute,** Houston (1941); **Science Park,** Bastrop (1971).				
Vernon Regional Junior College—Vernon; state, 2-yr.; 1972; Dr. Wade Kirk	46	1,862	1,100	7,490
Victoria College—Victoria; state, 2-yr.; 1925; Dr. Jimmy Goodson	85	3,328	1,397	330
Wayland Baptist University—Plainview; Southern Baptist, 4-yr.; 1910; Dr. Lanny Hall . .	‡79	2,082	1,634	180
Weatherford College—Weatherford; state, 2-yr.; 1869 (as branch of Southwestern University; 1922, became denominational junior college; changed to municipal junior college, 1949); Dr. E.W. Mince	‡124	2,097	1,491	249
Western Texas College—Snyder; state, 2-yr.; 1969; Dr. Harry Krenek	55	1,100	860	730
West Texas State University—Canyon (See **Texas A&M University System**)				
Wharton County Junior College—Wharton; state, 2-yr.; 1946; Dr. Elbert C. Hutchins. . . .	120	3,000	1,000	3,000
Wiley College—Marshall; Methodist, 4-yr.; 1873; Dr. David L. Beckley	27	417	. . .	. . .

*No reply received to questionnaire. Information repeated from 1990-91 Texas Almanac.
†This information not furnished by institution.
‡Includes part-time instructors.
§Includes faculty and enrollment at all branches or divisions.
¶Teaching Hospital and Research Institute.

Texas Chambers of Commerce

The following list of chambers of commerce was furnished to the Texas Almanac by East Texas Tourism.

Abernathy—Abernathy C of C, Box 539 (79311).
Abilene—Abilene C of C, Box 2281 (79604).
Albany—Albany C of C, Box 536 (76430-0185).
Alice—Alice C of C, Box 1609 (78333).
Allen—Allen C of C, P.O. Box 822 (75002).
Alpine—Alpine C of C, Box 209 (79831).
Alvin—Alvin-Manvel C of C, Box 2082 (77511-2028).
Amarillo—Amarillo C of C, Box 9480 (79105).
Anahuac—Anahuac Area C of C, P.O. Box R (77514).
Andrews—Andrews County C of C, 700 W. Broadway (79714).
Angleton—Greater Angleton C of C, Box 1356 (77515).
Anson—Anson C of C, Box 351 (79501).
Aransas Pass—Aransas Pass C of C, 452 Cleveland Blvd. (78336).
Archer City—Archer County C of C, Box 877 (76351).
Arlington—Arlington C of C, Box 607 (76004-1486).
Arp—Arp Area C of C, Box 146 (75750).
Athens—Athens C of C, Box 2600 (75751).
Atlanta—Atlanta C of C, P.O. Box 29 (75551).
Austin—Austin Conv. & Visitors Bureau, P.O. Box 1967 (78767-1967).
Azle—Azle C of C, Box 598 (76020).
Baird—Baird C of C, Box 846 (79504).
Balch Springs—Balch Springs C of C, Box 80095 (75180).
Ballinger—Ballinger C of C, Box 577 (76821).
Bandera—Bandera County C of C, Box 171 (78003).
Bartlett—Bartlett Area C of C, Box 564 (76511).
Bastrop—Bastrop C of C, Box 681 (78602).
Bay City—Bay City C of C, Box 768 (77404-0768).
Baytown—Baytown C of C, Box 330 (77522).
Beaumont—Beaumont C of C, Box 3150 (77704).
Bedford—Hurst-Euless-Bedford C of C, Box 969 (76022).
Beeville—Bee County C of C, Box 4099 (78104).
Bellaire—Bellaire-S.W. Houston C of C, Box 788 (77401).
Bellmead—Bellmead C of C, P.O. Box 4615 (76705).
Bellville—Bellville C of C, Box 670 (77418).
Belton—Belton Area C of C, Box 659 (76513).
Big Lake—Big Lake C of C, Box 905 (76932).
Big Spring—Big Spring C of C, Box 1391 (79721-1391).
Bishop—Bishop C of C, 115 S. Ash (78343).
Blanco—Blanco C of C, Box 626 (78606).
Boerne—Greater Boerne C of C, 1209 S. Main (78006).

Bonham—Bonham C of C, 510 N. Main (75418).
Borger—Borger C of C, Box 490 (79008-0490).
Bowie—Bowie C of C, 115 E. Tarrant (76230).
Brackettville—Kinney County C of C, Box 386 (78832).
Brady—Brady C of C, 101 E. 1st (76825).
Brazosport—Brazosport C of C, Box 2470 (77541).
Breckenridge—Breckenridge C of C, Box 1466 (76024).
Brenham—Washington County C of C, 314 S. Austin (77833).
Bridge City—Bridge City C of C, 150 W. Roundbunch (77611).
Bridgeport—Bridgeport C of C, Box 1104 (76026).
Brownfield—Brownfield C of C, Box 152 (79316).
Brownsville—Brownsville C of C, Box 752 (78520).
Brownwood—Brownwood C of C, Box 880 (76801).
Bryan—Bryan-College Station C of C, Box 726 (77806).
Buchanan Dam—Lake Buchanan C of C, Box 282 (78609).
Buffalo—Buffalo C of C, Box 207 (75831).
Burkburnett—Burkburnett C of C, 412 N. Avenue C (76354).
Burleson—Burleson C of C, Box 9 (76028).
Burnet—Burnet C of C, Drawer M (78611).
Burton—Burton C of C, Rt. 1, Box 23 (77835).
Caldwell—Caldwell C of C, Box 126 (77836-0126).
Calvert—Calvert C of C, Box 132 (77837).
Cameron—Cameron C of C, Drawer 432 (76520).
Camp Wood—Nueces Canyon C of C, Box 369 (78833).
Canadian—Canadian-Hemphill C of C, Box 365 (79014).
Canton—Canton C of C, 170 E. Tyler (75103).
Canyon—Canyon C of C, Box 8 (79015).
Carrizo Springs—Dimmit County C of C, 107 Nopal St. (78834).
Carrollton—Metrocrest C of C, 1204 Metro Crest Dr. (75006-5735).
Carthage—Carthage C of C, Box 207 (75633).
Castroville—Castroville C of C, Box 572 (78009).
Cedar Hill—Cedar Hill C of C, Box 355 (75104).
Center—Shelby County C of C, 321 Shelbyville (75935).
Centerville—Centerville C of C, Box 422 (75833).
Childress—Childress C of C, Box 35 (79201).
Cisco—Cisco C of C, 309 Conrad Hilton (76437).

Clarendon—Clarendon-Donley County C of C, Box 730 (79226).
Clarksville—Clarksville C of C, 101 N. Locust (75426).
Claude—Armstrong County C of C, Box 328 (79109).
Cleburne—Cleburne C of C, Box 701 (76033-0701).
Cleveland—Greater Cleveland C of C, Box 1733 (77328).
Clifton—Clifton C of C, Box 104 (76634).
Clyde—Clyde C of C, Box 257 (79510).
Coldspring—Coldspring C of C, P.O. Box 980 (77331).
Coleman—Coleman C of C, Box 796 (76834).
Colleyville—Colleyville Area C of C, Box 445 (76034).
Colorado City—Colorado City C of C, Box 242 (79512).
Columbus—Columbus Area C of C, Box 185 (78934).
Comanche—Comanche C of C, Box 65 (76442).
Comfort—Comfort C of C, Box 777 (78013).
Commerce—Commerce C of C, Box 290 (75428).
Conroe—Conroe C of C, Drawer 2347 (77305).
Cooper—Delta County C of C, Box 457 (78432).
Copperas Cove—Copperas Cove C of C, 311 S. First St. (76522).
Corpus Christi—Corpus Christi C of C, Box 640 (78403).
Corsicana—Corsicana Area C of C, Box 426 (75110).
Cotulla—Cotulla-La Salle C of C, 112 N. Front St. (78014).
Crane—Crane County C of C, 409 S. Gaston (79731).
Crockett—Houston County C of C, Box 307 (75835).
Crosby—Crosby Huffman C of C, Box 452 (77532).
Crosbyton—Crosbyton C of C, 115 S. Ayrshire (79322).
Crowley—Crowley C of C, Box 299 (76036).
Crystal Beach—Bolivar Peninsula C of C, P.O. Box 1170 (77650).
Crystal City—Zavala County C of C, P.O. Box 569 (78839).
Cuero—Cuero C of C, 103 N. Esplanade (77954).
Daingerfield—Daingerfield C of C, 208 Jefferson (75638).
Dalhart—Dalhart Area C of C, Box 967 (79022).
Dallas—Greater Dallas C of C, 1201 Elm, Ste. 2000 (75270).
DeKalb—DeKalb C of C, P.O. Box 219 (75559).
DeSoto—DeSoto C of C, 1001 E. Pleasant Run (75115).
Decatur—Decatur C of C, Box 474 (76234).
Deer Park—Deer Park C of C, 110 Center (77536).
Del Rio—Del Rio C of C, 1915 Ave. F (78840).
Dell City—Dell Valley C of C, Box 709 (79837).
Denison—Denison Area C of C, Box 325 (75020).
Denton—Denton C of C, P.O. Box P (76202-1719).
Denver City—Denver City C of C, 104 W. 3rd St. (79323-3108).
Devine—Greater Devine C of C, Box 443 (78016-0443).
Dickinson—North Galveston County C of C, Box 426 (77539).
Dimmitt—Dimmitt C of C, 115 W. Bedford (79027).
Donna—Donna C of C, 129 S. 8th (78537).
Dublin—Dublin C of C, 213 E. Blackjack (76446-1203).
Dumas—Moore County and Dumas C of C, Box 735 (79029).
Duncanville—Duncanville C of C, Box 380036 (75138).
Eagle Lake—Eagle Lake C of C, Box 216 (77434).
Eagle Pass—Eagle Pass C of C, Box 1188 (78853-1188).
Early—Early C of C, P.O. Box 3010 (76803).
Earth—Earth C of C, Box 496 (79031).
Eastland—Eastland C of C, 102 S. Seaman (76448).
Eden—Eden C of C, Box 367 (76837).
Edgewood—Edgewood C of C, Box 724 (75117).
Edinburg—Edinburg C of C, Box 85 (78540).
Edna—Jackson County C of C, Box 788 (77957).
El Campo—El Campo C of C, Box 446 (77437).
El Paso—El Paso C of C, Box 9738 (79901).
Electra—Electra C of C, 112 W. Cleveland (76360).
Elgin—Elgin C of C, Box 408 (78621).
Emory—Emory C of C, (75440).
Ennis—Ennis Area C of C, Box 1177 (75120).
Eustace—Eustace Area C of C, Box 333 (75124).
Fairfield—Fairfield C of C, Box 956 (75840).
Falfurrias—Falfurrias C of C, Box 476 (78355).
Falls City—Falls City C of C, Box 289 (78113).
Farmers Branch—Farmers Branch C of C, 4100 McEwen, #174 (75244).
Farmersville—Farmersville C of C, Box 366 (75031).
Farwell—Farwell C of C, Box 117 (79325).
Flatonia—Flatonia C of C, Box 651 (78941).
Florence—Florence C of C, Box 201 (76527).
Floresville—Floresville C of C, Box 220 (78114).
Flower Mound—Flower Mound C of C, 3648 Long Prairie Rd (75028).

Floydada—Floydada C of C, Box 147 (79235-0147).
Forney—Forney Area C of C, P.O. Box 570 (75126-0570).
Fort Davis—Fort Davis C of C, Box 378 (79734).
Fort Stockton—Fort Stockton C of C, Box C (79735).
Fort Worth—Fort Worth C of C, 777 Taylor, Ste. 900 (76102-4997).
Franklin—Franklin C of C, Box 126 (77856).
Fredericksburg—Fredericksburg C of C, Box 506 (78624-0506).
Freer—Freer C of C, Box 717 (78357).
Friendswood—Friendswood C of C, Box 11 (77546).
Friona—Friona C of C, Box 905 (79035).
Frisco—Frisco C of C, Box 1074 (75034).
Gainesville—Gainesville Area C of C, Box 518 (76240).
Galena Park—Galena Park C of C, Box 427 (77547).
Galveston—Galveston C of C, 621 Moody, Ste. 300 (77550).
Garland—Garland C of C, Box 460939 (75046-0939).
Gatesville—Gatesville C of C, Box 206 (76528).
Georgetown—Georgetown C of C, Box 346 (78627).
Giddings—Giddings C of C, Box 180 (78942).
Gilmer—Upshur County C of C, Box 854 (75644-0854).
Gladewater—Gladewater C of C, Box 1409 (75647).
Glen Rose—Glen Rose-Somervell County C of C, Box 605 (76043).
Goldthwaite—Mills County C of C, P.O. Box 308 (76844).
Goliad—Goliad County C of C, Box 606 (77963).
Gonzales—Gonzales C of C, Box 134 (78629-0134).
Gorman—Gorman C of C, Box 266 (76454).
Graham—Graham C of C, Box 299 (76046).
Granbury—Lake Granbury Area C of C, Box 277 (76048).
Grand Prairie—Grand Prairie C of C, Box 531227 (75053-1227).
Grand Saline—Grand Saline C of C, P.O. Box R (75140).
Grandfalls—Grandfalls C of C, Box 269 (79742).
Grapevine—Grapevine C of C, Box 368 (76051-0368).
Greenville—Greenville C of C, Box 1055 (75403).
Groesbeck—Groesbeck C of C, Box 326 (76642-0326).
Groves—Groves C of C, 4399 Main Ave. (77619).
Groveton—Groveton C of C, Box 366 (75845-0366).
Hale Center—Hale Center C of C, Box 487 (79401-0487).
Hallettsville—Hallettsville C of C, Box 313 (77964).
Hallsville—Hallsville Area C of C, Box 535 (75650).
Haltom City—Northeast Tarrant County C of C, 5001 Denton Hwy. (76117).
Hamilton—Hamilton C of C, Box 429 (76531).
Hamlin—Hamlin C of C, Box 402 (79520-0402).
Harlingen—Harlingen Area C of C, Box 189 (78551).
Haskell—Haskell C of C, 112 1/2 N. Ave. E (79521).
Hawkins—Greater Hawkins C of C, Box 345 (75765).
Hearne—Hearne C of C, Box 713 (77859).
Hebbronville—Hebbronville C of C, 210 N. Smith (78361).
Hemphill—Sabine County C of C, Box 717 (75948).
Hempstead—Hempstead C of C, Box 921 (77445).
Henderson—Rusk County C of C, Box 432 (75653-0432).
Henrietta—Henrietta & Clay County C of C, Box 75 (76365).
Hereford—Deaf Smith County C of C, Box 192 (79045).
Hewitt—Greater Hewitt C of C, P.O. Box 661 (76643).
Hidalgo—Hidalgo C of C, 611 E. Coma (78557).
Hillsboro—Hillsboro C of C, Box 358 (76645).
Hitchcock—Hitchcock C of C, Box 389 (77563).
Hondo—Hondo C of C, Box 126 (78861).
Honey Grove—Honey Grove C of C, 808 N. 8th St. (75446).
Houston—Houston C of C, 1100 Milam Bldg. (77002).
Howe—Howe C of C, P.O. Box 250 (75059-0250).
Hughes Springs—Hughes Springs C of C, Box 218 (75656).
Humble—Humble Area C of C, Box 3337 (77347-3337).
Huntsville—Huntsville-Walker County C of C, Box 538 (77342-0538).
Hutchins—Hutchins C of C, Box 561 (75141).
Ingleside—Ingleside C of C, Box 686 (78362).
Iowa Park—Iowa Park C of C, Box 416 (76367).
Iraan—Iraan C of C, Box 153 (79744).
Irving—Irving C of C, 3333 N. MacArthur, (75062).
Italy—Italy C of C, Box 409 (76651).
Jacksboro—Jacksboro C of C, Box 606 (76056).
Jacksonville—Jacksonville C of C, Box 1231 (75766).
Jasper—Jasper C of C, Box 638 (75951).

Jefferson—Marion County C of C, 116 W. Austin (75657).
Jewett—Jewett C of C, Box 220 (75846).
Joshua—Joshua C of C, P.O. Box 1292 (76058).
Jourdanton—Jourdanton Community C of C, Box 747 (78026).
Junction—Kimble County C of C, 402 Main (76849).
Karnes City—Karnes City Community C of C, 314 E. Calvert (78118).
Katy—Greater Katy C of C, 6701 Hwy. Blvd.,#100 (77493).
Kaufman—Kaufman C of C, 112 S. Washington (75142).
Keller—Greater Keller C of C, Box 761 (76248).
Kemp—Kemp C of C, Box 484 (75143).
Kenedy—Kenedy C of C, Box 1929 (78119).
Kennedale—C of C, (76060-9988).
Kerens—Kerens C of C, Box 117 (75144).
Kermit—Kermit C of C, 112 N. Poplar (79745).
Kerrville—Kerrville Area C of C, 1200 Sidney Baker (78028).
Kilgore—Kilgore C of C, Box 1582 (75662).
Kilgore—C of C, (75662).
Killeen—Greater Killeen C of C, Box 548 (76540).
Kingsland—Kingsland-Lake LBJ C of C, Box 465 (78639).
Kingsville—Kingsville C of C, Box 1030 (78363).
Kirbyville—Kirbyville C of C, Box 417 (75956).
Knox City—Knox City C of C, Box 91 (79529).
Kountze—Kountze C of C, Box 878 (77625).
La Grange—La Grange Area C of C, 163 W. La Fayette (78945).
La Marque—La Marque C of C, P.O. Box 387 (77568).
La Porte—La Porte-Bayshore C of C, Box 996 (77571-0996).
Ladonia—Ladonia C of C, Box 44 (75449).
Lake Dallas—Lake Cities C of C, Box 1028 (75065).
Lamesa—Lamesa Area C of C, P.O Drawer J (79331).
Lampasas—Lampasas County C of C, Box 627 (76550-0627).
Lancaster—Lancaster C of C, Box 1100 (75146).
Laredo—Laredo C of C, Box 790 (78042-0790).
Leakey—Frio Canyon C of C, Box 743 (78873).
Leonard—Leonard C of C, Box 157 (75452).
Levelland—Levelland Area C of C, 1101 Avenue H (79336).
Lewisville—Lewisville C of C, Box 416 (75067).
Lexington—Lexington C of C, Box 562 (78947).
Liberty—Liberty-Dayton Area C of C, Box 1270 (77575).
Lindale—Lindale C of C, P.O. Box 670 (75771).
Linden—Linden C of C, Box 429 (75563).
Littlefield—Littlefield C of C, Box 507 (79339).
Livingston—Polk County C of C, 516 W. Church (77351).
Llano—Llano County C of C, 700 Bessmer Avenue (78643).
Lockhart—Lockhart C of C, P.O. Box 840 (78644).
Lockney—Lockney C of C, Box 85 (79241).
Lone Star—Lone Star C of C, Box 505 (75668-0505).
Longview—Longview C of C, Box 472 (75606-0472).
Louise—Louise-Hillje C of C, Box 156 (77455).
Lubbock—Lubbock C of C, Box 561 (79408).
Lueders—Lueders C of C, Box 158 (79533).
Lufkin—Angelina County C of C, Box 1606 (75901).
Luling—Luling C of C, Drawer 710 (78648).
Lumberton—Lumberton C of C, Box 8574 (77711).
Lytle—Greater Lytle C of C, Box 640 (78052-0640).
Mabank—Mabank C of C, Box 201 (75147).
Madisonville—Madison County C of C, 118 S. Elm St. (77864).
Malakoff—Malakoff Area C of C, Box 1042 (75148).
Mansfield—Mansfield C of C, Box 363 (76063).
Marathon—Marathon C of C, P.O. Box 163 (79842).
Marble Falls—Marble Falls-Lake LBJ C of C, Box 801 Hwy. 281 (78654).
Marfa—Marfa C of C, Box 635 (79843).
Marlin—Marlin C of C, Box 369 (76661).
Marshall—Greater Marshall C of C, Box 520 (75670).
Mart—Mart C of C, Box 59 (76664).
Mason—Mason C of C, Box 156 (78656).
Mathis—Lake Corpus Christi C of C, Box 195 (78368).
McAllen—McAllen C of C, Box 790 (78502-0790).
McCamey—McCamey C of C, Box 906 (79752).
McGregor—McGregor C of C, 303 S. Main St. (76657).
McKinney—McKinney C of C, Box 621 (75069).
Melissa—Melissa C of C, (75071).
Memphis—Memphis C of C, 113 S. 6th (79245).

Travel Assistance

The Texas Department of Highways and Public Transportation operates a broad tourist assistance program. Texans or visitors to the state can get information on travel planning, travel literature, and emergency road conditions from the department's hotline. That telephone number is 1-800-452-9292.

The information program is operated by the department's Travel and Information Division.

Menard—Menard C of C, Box 64 (76859).
Mercedes—Mercedes C of C, Box 37 (78570).
Merkel—Merkel C of C, Box 536 (79536).
Mesquite—Mesquite C of C, Box 850115 (75185-0115).
Mexia—Mexia Area C of C, Drawer 352 (76667).
Miami—Miami C of C, Box 456 (79059).
Midland—Midland C of C, Box 1890 (79701).
Midlothian—Midlothian C of C, Box 609 (76065).
Mineola—Mineola C of C, Box 68 (75773-0068).
Mineral Wells—Mineral Wells C of C, Box 1408 (76067).
Mission—Mission C of C, Box 431 (78572-0431).
Monahans—Monahans C of C, Box 1040 (79756).
Mont Belvieu—West Chambers County C of C, P.O. Drawer 750 (77580).
Montgomery—West Montgomery County C of C, Box 1 (77356).
Moody—Moody C of C, Box 419 (76557).
Morton—Morton Area C of C, 106 S.W. 1st St. (79346).
Moulton—Moulton C of C, Box 482 (77975).
Mount Pleasant—Mount Pleasant-Titus County C of C, P.O. Box 237 (75455).
Mount Vernon—Franklin County C of C, Box 554 (75457).
Muenster—Muenster C of C, P.O. Box 479 (76252).
Muleshoe—Muleshoe C of C, Box 356 (79347-0356).
Munday—Munday C of C, Drawer L (76371).
Nacogdoches—Nacogdoches County C of C, Drawer 1918 (75963-1918).
Naples—Naples C of C, Box 550 (75568).
Navasota—Grimes County C of C, Box 530 (77868).
Nederland—Nederland C of C, Box 891 (77627).
New Boston—New Boston C of C, 109 N. Ellis (75570).
New Braunfels—Greater New Braunfels C of C, Box 311417 (78131-1417).
New Caney—East Montgomery County C of C, Box 967 (77357).
Newton—Newton County C of C, Drawer 65 (75966).
Nixon—Nixon Area C of C, P.O. Box 56 (78140).
Nocona—Nocona C of C, Box 27 (76255).
Normangee—Normangee C of C, Box 436 (77871).
Oakwood—Oakwood C of C, Box 225 (75855).
Odessa—Odessa C of C, Box 3626 (79760).
Olney—Olney C of C, 108 E. Main (76374).
Olton—Olton C of C, Box 487 (79604).
Omaha—Omaha C of C, Box 816 (75571).
Onalaska—Onalaska C of C, Box 610 (77360).
Orange—Greater Orange Area C of C, Box 218 (77630-5620).
Overton—Overton C of C, Box 6 (75684).
Ozona—Ozona C of C, Box 1135 (76943-1135).
Paducah—Paducah C of C, Box 863 (79248).
Palacios—Palacios C of C, Box 774 (77465).
Palestine—Palestine C of C, P.O. Box I (75802).
Pampa—Pampa C of C, Box 1942 (79066-1942).
Panhandle—Panhandle C of C, Box 1021 (79068).
Paris—Lamar County C of C, Box 1096 (75461).
Pasadena—Pasadena C of C, 4334 Fairmont Pkwy. (77504).
Pearland—Pearland-Hobby Area C of C, 3501 Liberty Dr. (77581).
Pearsall—Pearsall C of C, 317 S. Oak St. (78061).
Pecos—Pecos C of C, Box 27 (79772-0027).
Perryton—Perryton-Ochiltree C of C, Drawer 789 (79070).
Pharr—Pharr C of C, P.O. Box 1341 (78577-1341).
Pilot Point—Pilot Point C of C, Box 497 (76258).
Pittsburg—Camp County C of C, 202 Jefferson (75686).
Plainview—Plainview C of C, Box 340 (79072).

Plano—Plano C of C, 1200 E. 15th (75074).
Pleasanton—Pleasanton C of C, Box 153 (78064).
Pointblank—North San Jacinto Chamber C of C, P.O. Box 525 (77364).
Port Aransas—Port Aransas C of C, Box 356 (78373).
Port Arthur—Greater Port Arthur C of C, 4749 Twin City Hwy. (77642).
Port Isabel—C of C, (78578).
Port Lavaca—Port Lavaca-Calhoun County C of C, Box 528 (77979).
Port Mansfield—Port Mansfield C of C, Box O (78598).
Port Neches—Port Neches C of C, 1207 Port Neches Ave (77651).
Port O'Connor—Port O'Connor C of C, Box 701 (79982-0701).
Portland—C of C, (78374).
Post—Post C of C, P.O. Box 610 (79356).
Poth—Poth C of C, Box 328 (78147).
Premont—Premont C of C, Box 706 (78375).
Princeton—Princeton C of C, Box 189 (75077).
Prosper—Prosper C of C, P.O. Box 777 (75078).
Quanah—Quanah C of C, Box 158 (79252).
Quinlan—Quinlan Area C of C, P.O. Box 1722 (75474).
Quitman—Quitman C of C, Box 426 (75783).
Ralls—Ralls C of C, Box 807 (79357-0806).
Ranger—Ranger C of C, Box 57 (76470).
Raymondville—Raymondville C of C, Box 746 (78580).
Refugio—Refugio County C of C, Box 127 (78377).
Richardson—Richardson C of C, 411 Belle Grove Dr. (75080).
Rising Star—Rising Star C of C, Box 189 (76471-0189).
Robstown—Robstown C of C, Box 111 (78380).
Rockdale—Rockdale C of C, 100 E. Cameron (76567).
Rockport—Rockport-Fulton Area C of C, Box 1055 (78382).
Rocksprings—Edwards County C of C, Box 267 (78880).
Rockwall—Rockwall C of C, Box 92 (75087).
Rosebud—Rosebud C of C, Box 369 (76570).
Rosenberg—Rosenberg-Richmond C of C, 4120 Ave. H (77471).
Rotan—Rotan C of C, P.O. Box 275 (79546).
Round Rock—Round Rock C of C, 212 E. Main (78664).
Rowlett—Rowlett C of C, P.O. Box 610 (75088).
Royse City—Royse City C of C, Box 547 (75089).
Rule—Rule C of C, Box 607 (79547).
Rusk—Rusk C of C, Box 67 (75785).
Sabinal—Sabinal C of C, Box 55 (78881).
Saginaw—Saginaw C of C, P.O. Box 7989 (76179).
Saint Jo—Saint Jo C of C, Rt. 1, Box 204B (76265).
Salado—Salado C of C, Box 81 (76571).
San Angelo—San Angelo C of C, 500 Rio Concho Dr. (76903).
San Antonio—Greater San Antonio C of C, Box 1628 (78296).
San Augustine—San Augustine County C of C, 134 W. Columbia (75972).
San Benito—San Benito Area C of C, P.O. Box 1623 (78586).
San Diego—San Diego C of C, P.O. Box 849 (78384).
San Marcos—San Marcos C of C, Box 2310 (78667-2310).
San Saba—San Saba County C of C, Courthouse (76877).
Sanger—Sanger Area C of C, Box 537 (76266).
Santa Anna—Santa Anna C of C, Box 275 (76878).
Santa Fe—Santa Fe C of C, P.O. Box 681 (77510).
Schulenburg—Schulenburg C of C, Box 65 (78956).
Seagoville—Seagoville C of C, 107 Hall Road (75159).
Seagraves—Seagraves-Loop Area C of C, Box 1257 (79359-1257).
Sealy—Sealy C of C, Box 586 (77474).
Seguin—Seguin & Guadalupe County C of C, Box 710 (78156).
Seminole—Seminole C of C, Box 1198 (79360).
Seven Points—Cedar Creek Lake C of C, Box 100 (75143).
Seymour—Seymour C of C, Box 1379 (76380).
Shamrock—Shamrock C of C, Box 588 (79079-0588).
Shepherd—Greater Shepherd C of C, Box 520 (77371).
Sherman—Sherman Area C of C, Box 1029 (75091-1029).
Shiner—Shiner C of C, Box 221 (77984).
Silsbee—Silsbee C of C, 835 Hwy. 96 South (77656).
Sinton—Sinton C of C, Box 217 (78387).
Slaton—Slaton C of C, Box 400 (79364-0400).

Smithville—Smithville C of C, Box 716 (78957).
Snyder—Snyder C of C, Drawer CC (79549).
Somerville—Somerville C of C, Box 352 (77836).
Sonora—Sonora C of C, Box 1172 (76950).
Southlake—C of C, (76092).
Spearman—Spearman C of C, Box 161 (79081-0161).
Stamford—Stamford C of C, Box 1206 (79553).
Stanton—Stanton C of C, Box 615 (79782).
Stephenville—Stephenville C of C, Box 306 (76401).
Stockdale—Stockdale C of C, Box 366 (78160).
Stonewall—Stonewall C of C, Box 1 (78671).
Stratford—Stratford C of C, Box 570 (79084).
Sudan—Sudan C of C, P.O. Box 224 (79371).
Sugar Land—Fort Bend C of C, 445 Commerce Green (77478).
Sulphur Springs—Hopkins County C of C, Box 347 (75482).
Sweeny—Sweeny C of C, Box 338 (77480).
Sweetwater—Sweetwater C of C, Box 1148 (79556).
Taft—Taft C of C, Box 65 (78390).
Tahoka—Tahoka C of C, Box 777 (79373).
Taylor—Taylor C of C, Box 231 (76574).
Teague—Teague C of C, 316 Main, Ste. 103 (75860).
Temple—Temple C of C, Box 158 (75603-0158).
Terrell—Terrell C of C, Box 97 (75160).
Texarkana—Texarkana C of C, Box 1468 (75504).
Texas City—Texas City-LaMarque C of C, Box 3330 (77592-3330).
The Colony—The Colony C of C, P.O. Box 296006 (75056).
The Woodlands—S. Montgomery County-Woodlands C of C, 1400 Woodloch Forest (77380).
Thorndale—Thorndale C of C, Box 666 (76577).
Three Rivers—Three Rivers C of C, P.O. Drawer 1648 (78071).
Throckmorton—Throckmorton C of C, Box 711 (76083).
Timpson—Timpson C of C, Box 400 (75975).
Tomball—Tomball Area C of C, Box 516 (77375).
Trinity—Trinity Peninsula C of C, Box 549 (75862).
Troup—Troup C of C, Box 336 (75789).
Tulia—Tulia C of C, Box 267 (79088).
Tyler—Tyler Area C of C, Box 390 (75710).
Universal City—Randolph Metrocom C of C, 2060 Universal City (78148-3499).
Uvalde—Uvalde C of C, Box 706 (78802-0706).
Van—Van C of C, Box 55 (75790).
Van Alstyne—Van Alstyne C of C, Box 698 (75095).
Van Horn—Van Horn C of C, Box 762 (79855).
Vernon—Vernon C of C, Box 1538 (76384).
Victoria—Victoria C of C, Box 2465 (77902).
Vidor—Vidor C of C, Box 413 (77662).
Waco—Waco C of C, Box 1220 (76703).
Waller—Waller C of C, 31315 FM 2920, #7 (77484).
Waxahachie—Waxahachie C of C, Box 187 (75165).
Weatherford—Weatherford C of C, Box 310 (76086).
Weimar—Weimar C of C, Box 90 (78962).
Wellington—Collingsworth C of C, P.O. Box 267 (79095).
Weslaco—Weslaco C of C, Box 8488 (78596).
West—West C of C, Box 123 (76691).
West Columbia—West Columbia C of C, Box 837 (77486).
West Tawakoni—C of C, (75474).
Wharton—Wharton C of C, Box 868 (77488).
Wheeler—Wheeler C of C, Box 221 (79096).
White Oak—White Oak C of C, P.O. Box 235 (75693).
White Settlement—White Settlement Area C of C, Box 150461 (76108).
Whitesboro—Whitesboro C of C, 101 W. Main (76273).
Whitewright—Whitewright C of C, Box 189 (75491).
Whitney—Whitney C of C, Box 604 (76692).
Wichita Falls—Wichita Falls C of C, Box 1860 (76307-1860).
Willis—Willis Area C of C, Box 1379 (77378).
Wills Point—Wills Point C of C, Box 217 (75169).
Wimberley—Wimberley C of C, Box 12 (78676).
Wink—Wink C of C, Box 397 (79789).
Winnie—Winnie Area C of C, Box 147 (77665).
Winnsboro—Winnsboro C of C, 201 W. Broadway (75494).
Winters—Winters Area C of C, Box 698 (79567).
Wolfe City—Wolfe City C of C, Box 8 (75496).
Wolfforth—Wolfforth C of C, Box 35 (79382).
Woodville—Tyler County C of C, 201 N. Magnolia St. (75979).
Wylie—Wylie Area C of C, Box 918 (75098).
Yoakum—Yoakum C of C, Box 591 (77995).
Yorktown—Yorktown C of C, Box 488 (78164).
Zapata—Zapata County C of C, Box 1028 (78076).

Culture

The Arts In Texas

The following information on the fine arts in Texas was prepared for the Texas Almanac by the staff of the Texas Commission on the Arts.

Culture in Texas, as in any market, is a mixture of activity generated by both the commercial and the non-profit sectors.

The commercial sector encompasses Texas-based profit-making businesses including commercial recording artists (such as the legendary Willie Nelson), nightclubs, record companies, private galleries, assorted boutiques which carry fine art collectibles and private dance and music halls. In addition, Texas is becoming an important media center, with Texas-based publications, television and film companies gaining national recognition.

Texas also has extensive cultural resources offered by non-profit organizations that are engaged in charitable, educational and/or humanitarian activities.

The Texas Legislature has authorized six state agencies to administer cultural services and funds for the public good. The agencies, listed below, fall under the auspices of the Texas Legislature's Cultural and Historical Resources Committee. They are:

State Antiquities Committee, Box 12276, Austin 78711; **Texas Commission on the Arts,** Box 13406, Capitol Sta., Austin 78711; **Texas Film Commission,** Texas Department of Commerce, Box 12428, Austin 78711; **Texas Historical Commission,** Box 12276, Austin 78711; **Texas State Library and Archives Commission,** Box 12927, Austin 78711; and the **State Preservation Board,** Box 13286, Austin 78711.

Although not a state agency, another organization that provides cultural services to the citizens of Texas is the **Texas Committee on the Humanities,** 1604 Nueces, Austin 78701.

The **Texas Commission on the Arts** was established in 1965 to develop a receptive climate for the arts in Texas, to attract outstanding artists to Texas, to serve as a source of arts information to state government and Texas at large and to expand and enhance the cultural opportunities for all Texans. The commission accomplishes these goals by providing financial, informational and technical assistance.

The Texas Commission on the Arts provides services and financial assistance to a wide range of non-profit arts organizations. Its clientele includes theaters (professional, civic, children's, ethnic), media (radio, television, film, publications), festivals, music (folk, symphonic, chamber, choral, jazz, opera and new music), visual arts (sculpture, crafts, photography, painting, environmental), dance (modern, ballet, folkloric), schools, presenters of cultural events and services organizations.

Some of Texas' major non-profit arts institutions — orchestras, museums, dance companies, theaters and cultural centers — are listed below. These and others can also be found under the subhead, "Recreation," in the county reports.

Addison—Addison Centre Theatre, Box 933 (75001).

Amarillo—Amarillo Symphony Orchestra, Box 2552 (79105); Lone Star Ballet, Box 1133 (79178).

Austin—Austin Symphony Orchestra, 1101 Red River (78701); Ballet Austin, 3002 Guadalupe (78705); Laguna Gloria Art Museum, Box 5568 (78763); Paramount Theatre for the Performing Arts, Box 1205 (78767).

Beaumont—Beaumont Art Museum, 1111 9th St. (77702).

Corpus Christi—Art Museum of South Texas, 1902 N. Shoreline Dr. (78401); Corpus Christi Ballet, 5610 Everhart (78469).

Corsicana—Corsicana Community Playhouse, Box 2224 (75110).

Dallas — Dallas Opera, 1925 Elm (75201); Dallas Museum of Art, 1717 N. Harwood (75201); Dallas Symphony Orchestra, Box 26207 (75226); Dallas Theatre Center, 3636 Turtle Creek Blvd. (75219); Shakespeare Festival, 3630 Harry Hines (75210); Theatre Three, 2800 Routh (75201).

El Paso—El Paso Museum Of Arts, 1211 Montana Ave. (79902); El Paso Symphony Orchestra, Box 180 (79942).

Fort Worth—Amon Carter Museum Of Western Art, Box 2365 (76101); Museum of Modern Art, 1309 Montgomery (76107); Fort Worth Ballet Assn., 6845 Green Oaks Rd. (76116); Fort Worth Opera, 3505 W. Lancaster (76107); Fort Worth Symphony Orchestra, 4401 Trail Lake Dr. (76109); Kimbell Art Museum, Box 9440 (76107); Stage West, Box 2587 (76113); Van Cliburn Foundation, 2525 Ridgmar Blvd. (76116).

Houston — Alley Theatre, 615 Texas (77002); Contemporary Arts Museum, 5216 Montrose Blvd. (77006); Houston Ballet Foundation, Box 130487 (77219); Houston Grand Opera, 510 Preston, #500 (77002); Houston Museum of Fine Arts, Box 6826 (77265); Houston Symphony Orchestra, 615 Louisiana (77002); Texas Opera Theatre, 510 Preston, #440 (77002); Theatre Under the Stars, 4235 San Felipe (77027).

Midland/Odessa — Midland/Odessa Symphony and Chorale, Box 60658 (79711).

Round Top — James Dick Foundation for the Performing Arts, Box 89 (78954).

San Antonio — Carver Cultural Center, 226 N. Hackberry (78202); Guadalupe Cultural Arts Center, 1300 Guadalupe (78207); McNay Art Institute, Box 6069 (78209); San Antonio Art Institute, Box 6069 (78209); San Antonio Museum Association, Box 2601 (78299-2601); San Antonio Performing Arts Assn., 110 Broadway, Ste. 230 (78205); San Antonio Symphony Orchestra, 109 Lexington Ave., Ste. 207 (78205); Southwest Craft Center, 300 Augusta (78205).

The **Texas Arts Council,** 3939 Bee Caves Rd., Ste. 1A, Austin 78746, promotes, develops and supports local arts agencies. Listed below are the members as of mid-1987:

Abilene—Abilene Cultural Affairs Council, Box 2281 (79604).

Albany—The Old Jail Art Center, Rt. 1, Box 1 (76430).

Amarillo—Amarillo Arts Committee, 1000 S. Polk (79101).

Andrews—Andrews Cultural Affairs Committee, 800 NW 12th Place (79714).

Arlington—Arlington Fine Arts Council, Box 13741 (76013).

Austin—Cultural Arts Program — PARD, Box 1088 (78767).

Beaumont, Orange and Port Arthur—Southeast Texas Arts Council, Box 3925, Beaumont (77704).

Bellaire—Arts Council of Bellaire, Box 862 (77401).

Big Spring—Big Spring Cultural Affairs Council, Box 1391 (79720).

Bonham—FUN, Inc., Box 740 (75418).

Borger—Magic Plains Arts Council, 1314 Lancelot (79007).

Brackettville—Old Quarry Society for the Performing Arts, Box 813 (78832).

Breckenridge—Breckenridge Fine Arts Center, Box 549 (76024).

Brenham—Arts Council of Washington County, 701 Milroy St. (77833).

Brownwood — Cultural Affairs Commission, Box 880 (76801).

Burkburnett—Burkburnett Arts Council, Box 652 (76354).

Carrizo Springs—Arts Council of Dimmit County, 414 Pena (78834).

Clifton—Bosque Conservatory of Fine Arts, Box 373 (76634).

College Station—Arts Council of Brazos Valley, 111 University Dr., Ste. 217 (77840).

Columbus—Live Oak Art Club, Box 835 (78934).

Corpus Christi—Corpus Christi Arts Council, 1521 N. Chaparral (78401).

Corsicana—Navarro Council of the Arts, Box 2224 (75110).

Dalhart—Dalhart Fine Arts Assn., 1102 Denver (79022).

Dallas—Division of Cultural Affairs, Majestic Theatre, 1925 Elm, Ste. 600 (75201).

Del Rio—Del Rio Council for the Arts, Box 178 (78841).

Denison—Denison Arts Council, Box 325 (75020).

Denton—Greater Denton Arts Council, 207 S. Bell (76201).

DeSoto—DeSoto Council of Cultural Arts, 1214 Wellington (75116).

Dumas—Quality of Life Committee, 201 S. Bliss (79029).

Duncanville—Duncanville Regional Arts Assn., Box 381014 (75138).

Eagle Pass—Arts Council of Eagle Pass, 1910 Olive (78852).

El Paso—El Paso Arts Alliance, 333 E. Missouri (79901); El Paso Arts Resources Department, City of El Paso, 2 Civic Center Plaza (79901).

Floydada—Floyd County Arts Assn., Box 73 (79235).

Fort Worth—Arts Council of Fort Worth, One Tandy Center, Ste. 150 (76102).

Friendswood—Friendswood Fine Arts Council, Box 1600 (77546).

Gainesville—Cooke County Arts Council, Box 251 (76240).

Garland—Garland Center for the Performing Arts, Box 469002 (75040).

Granbury—Hood County Arts Council, Box 595 (76048).

Grand Prairie—Grand Prairie Arts Council, Box 1613 (75053).

Harlingen—Harlingen Cultural Arts Center Council, Box 609 (78551).

Hearne—Robertson County Arts Council, Box 203 (77859).

Houston—Cultural Arts Council of Houston, 1950 W. Gray, Ste. 6 (77019).

Huntsville—Huntsville Arts Commission, 1212 Ave. M (77340).

Hurst/Euless/Bedford—Trinity Arts Council, Box 18345, Fort Worth (76118).

Irving—City of Irving Arts Board, 3333 N. McArthur, Ste. 300 (75062); Irving Cultural Affairs Council, same address.

Jacksonville—Jacksonville Council on the Arts, Box 1231 (75766).

Killeen—Vive les Artes Societe, Box 321 (76540).

Lake Jackson—Brazosport Fine Arts Council, 400 College Dr. (77566).

Laredo—Laredo Council for the Arts, Box 790 (78040).

Levelland—Levelland Fine Arts Council, Box 8084 (79338).

Lewisville—Lewisville Cultural Arts Council, Box 416 (75067).

Liberty Hill—Liberty Hill Cultural Affairs Council, Box 158 (78642).

Littlefield—Lamb County Council for the Arts, Box 507 (79339).

Longview—Longview Arts Council, Box 1133 (75606).

Lubbock—Lubbock Cultural Affairs Council, Box 561 (79408).

Lufkin—Angelina County Cultural Affairs Council, Box 1606 (79501).

Marshall—Marshall Regional Arts Council, Box 520 (75671).

Mesquite—Mesquite Arts Council, Box 2104 (75149).

Midland—Midland Arts Assembly, Box 3494 (79702).

Monahans—Ward County Activities Council, 400 E. Fourth (79756).

New Braunfels—Greater New Braunfels Arts Council, Box 1171 (78130).

Odessa—Odessa Cultural Council, Box 7195 (79760).

Orange—(See Beaumont).

Pampa—Pampa Fine Arts Assn., Box 818 (79066).

Paris—Paris Arts Development Council, Box 1096 (75460).

Pasadena—Pasadena Area Cultural Arts Council, Box 3412 (77501).

Pittsburg—Pittsburg/Camp County Arts Council, Box 72 (75686).

Plainview—Plainview Cultural Council, Box 627 (79072).

Plano—Plano Cultural Arts Council, 1076 Collin Creek Mall, 811 N. Central Expwy. (75075).

Port Arthur—(See Beaumont).

Port Lavaca—Calhoun County Arts Council, Box 31 (77979).

Post—Caprock Cultural Assn., Box 37 (79356).

Richardson—Richardson Arts Commission, 411 W. Arapaho (75080).

San Angelo—San Angelo Cultural Affairs Council, Box 2477 (76902).

San Antonio—Arts Council of San Antonio, 227 S. Presa (78205).

Schulenburg—Backstage Inc. Arts Council, Box 66 (78956).

Seagoville—Seagoville Fine Arts Council, Rt. 2, Box 68 (75159).

Sealy—Friends of Arts and Culture in Sealy, Box 1124 (77474).

Sherman—Council for the Arts, Box 1029 (75090).

Snyder—Snyder Cultural Affairs Committee, 2715 48th (79549).

Stephenville—Cross Timbers Fine Arts Council, Box 1172 (76401).

Sugar Land—Fort Bend Arts Council, Sugar Creek Nat'l. Bank, One Sugar Creek Blvd. (77478).

Sweetwater—Sweetwater Cultural Affairs Comm., Box 450 (79556).

Temple—Temple Cultural Activities Center, Box 3292 (76501).

Terrell—Cultural Arts of Terrell, Box 744 (75160).

Texarkana—Texarkana Regional Arts & Humanities Council, Box 1171 (75504).

The Woodlands—The Woodlands Living Arts Council, Box 7411 (77387).

Uvalde—Uvalde Arts Council, Box 1451 (78801).

Vernon—Vernon Council of the Arts, 4107 Bismark (76384).

Victoria—Cultural Council of Victoria, Box 1758 (77902).

Waco—Greater Waco Council for the Arts, 2518 Wooddale Cir. (76710).

Waxahachie—Waxahachie Arts Council, 216 Pensacola Dr. (75165).

Weatherford—Weatherford Performing Arts Council, 801 W. Spring (76086).

West Houston—West Houston Cultural Arts Council, 13302 Alchester Ln. (77079).

Wichita Falls—Wichita Falls Arts Commission, 3702 Cedar Lane (76308).

Texas State Artists

A committee of the Legislature, consisting of three Representatives and three Senators, names the Texas State Artists and alternates. The Legislative Reference Library, Austin, supplied this list.

1971-1972 Joe Ruiz Grandee, Arlington; no alternate.

1972-1973 Melvin C. Warren, Clifton; no alternate.

1973-1974 Ronald Thomason, Weatherford; A. C. Gentry Jr., Tyler, alternate.

1974-1975 Jo Rader Roberts, Dripping Springs; Bette Lou Voorhis, Austin, alternate.

1975-1976 Jack White, New Braunfels; no alternate.

1976-1977 James Boren, Clifton; Kenneth Wyatt, Lubbock, alternate.

July 4, 1975-July 4, 1976 Robert Summers, Glen Rose, Bicentennial Artist.

1977-1978 Edward "Buck" Shiwetz, DeWitt Co.; Renne Hughes, Tarrant Co., alternate.

1978-1979 Jack Cowan, Rockport; Gary Henry, Palo Pinto Co., and Joyce Tally, Caldwell Co., alternates.

1979-1980 Dalhart Windberg, Travis Co.; Grant Lathe, Canyon Lake, alternate.

1980-1981 Harry Ahysen, Huntsville; Jim Reno, Simonton, alternate.

1981-1982 Jerry Newman, Beaumont; Raul Gutierrez, San Antonio, alternate.

1982-1983 Dr. James H. Johnson, Bryan; Armando Hinojosa, Laredo, alternate.

1983-1984 Raul Gutierrez, San Antonio; James Eddleman, Lubbock, alternate.

1984-1985 Covelle Jones, Lubbock; Ragan Gennusa, Austin, alternate.

1986-1987 Ragan Gennusa, Dripping Springs; Chuck DeHaan, Graford, alternate.

1987-1988 Neil Caldwell, Angleton; Rey Gaytan, Austin, alternate.

1988-1989 Rey Gaytan, Austin.

1989-1990 Mondel Rogers, Sweetwater.

(Note: There was no state artist from June 1, 1985 to October 1, 1986.)

Public Libraries

The following information on Texas public libraries was furnished by Richard E. Getz of the Library Development Division, Texas State Library, Austin.

Texas public libraries continue to improve in their efforts to meet the educational, informational and recreational needs of the state's citizens. Perhaps no other public-supported institution directly serves as many Texans, young and old, as does the public library. Statistics for 1989, the latest available, reported to the Texas State Library by 474 public libraries across Texas bear out this fact. They show:

• A total of 15,526,299 Texans are served by public libraries, or 91 percent of the state's population.

• A total of 63,959,816 library materials were checked out to Texans, a figure equivalent to 4.12 items for every person in the state. These materials include books, records, cassettes, magazines, 16mm films, videocassettes and art prints.

• A total of 12,679,179 reference questions were asked by library users, both in person and over the telephone.

• A total of 3,985,044 persons attended programs at the library, including "story hour" programs and summer reading club programs for children, as well as cultural, entertainment and education programs for adults.

The growth in services to library users has continued over the past five years. From 1985 to 1989 circulation of library materials increased by 23 percent; the number of reference questions handled by library reference staffs increased by 18 percent; and the number of persons visiting the library increased 66 percent to 32,258,145.

All of these services were provided by public libraries in 1989 with very modest support from tax sources. Total city, county and school district tax support of public libraries amounted to only $8.80 per capita, less than one-half the price of many paperback books. The State of Texas expended approximately 34 cents per capita to finance 10 cooperative public library systems, which undertook various projects to develop and improve public library services. A breakdown of public library funding for 1989 follows:

Source	Amount	Percent
Cities	$109,544,347	72.3
Counties	26,603,022	17.6
School districts	558,050	.4
State	5,435,757	3.6
Federal	3,098,349	2.0
Other (Private, etc.)	6,187,273	4.1
Total	$151,426,798	100.0

There are considerable data that suggest that this level of support is inadequate to meet the needs of Texas citizens for public library services. Out of the 474 libraries reporting for 1989 to the Texas State Library, 32 failed to meet the minimum standards for adequacy of budget, staff, book collection and hours of operation set by the state. Statistics for these 32 libraries show that the typical library in this category serves under 10,000 population, has a per capita budget from local tax sources of about 25 percent of the state average, has a total budget from all sources of less than one-third of the state average, and is administered by one person working part-time.

Clearly, much remains to be done, particularly in less populated areas of the state, to bring library services up to adequate standards. Thirteen counties are without a public library, while 1.18 million others live in areas of the state without library service. Libraries in urban areas face a different, but no less critical, problem of coping with rapid population growth and consequent demands for service by new residents. As the major Texas cities grow in size and population, there is a need for new library facilities in outlying suburban areas, along with new library collections and staff to provide service at these facilities.

The following table lists all 474 public libraries in Texas, along with statistics on two of the most important services provided to Texas citizens: circulation of library materials (books as well as audio-visual and other materials), and reference questions asked at the library, as well as over the telephone. A zero (0) indicates that the library is unable to provide the information. "NA" means not applicable.

Texas Library Activity, 1990

County, No. Libraries/ Libraries	Materials Circulated	Inquiries Answered
Anderson, 2	147,336	1,576
Frankston	9,291	1,576
Palestine	138,045	0
Andrews, 1	47,868	3,384
Andrews	47,868	3,384
Angelina, 2	138,736	12,352
Diboll	41,702	1,820
Lufkin	97,034	10,532
Aransas, 1	71,970	1,867
Rockport	71,970	1,867
Archer, 1	11,560	550
Archer City	11,560	550
Armstrong, 1	1,292	0
Claude	1,292	0
Atascosa, 5	89,144	9,018
Charlotte	4,891	0
Jourdanton	17,613	2,434
Lytle	24,410	356
Pleasanton	33,130	5,500
Poteet	9,100	728
Austin, 3	86,842	2,679
Bellville	49,364	1,460
Sealy	22,157	982
Wallis	15,321	237
Bailey, 1	42,731	1,100
Muleshoe	42,731	1,100
Bandera, 1	23,724	552
Bandera	23,724	552
Bastrop, 3	110,046	9,675
Bastrop	56,208	2,001
Elgin	7,168	466
Smithville	46,670	7,208
Baylor, 1	14,260	4,500
Seymour	14,260	4,500
Bee, 1	51,940	120
Beeville	51,940	120

County, No. Libraries/ Libraries	Materials Circulated	Inquiries Answered
Bell, 7	399,050	56,310
Bartlett	9,668	1,525
Belton	44,334	2,684
Harker Heights	31,050	5,600
Killeen	121,016	21,985
Morgan's Point	1,476	0
Saledo	1,135	8
Temple	190,371	24,508
Bexar, 3	3,657,422	6,398
Leon Valley	38,118	3,012
San Antonio	3,580,688	0
Universal City	38,616	3,386
Blanco, 2	16,100	318
Blanco	6,888	125
Johnson City	9,212	193
Borden, 0	NA	NA
Bosque, 0	NA	NA
Bowie, 2	200,493	11,137
New Boston	16,341	529
Texarkana	184,152	10,608
Brazoria, 1	1,028,516	39,018
Angleton	1,028,516	39,018
Brazos, 1	386,802	29,308
Bryan	386,802	29,308
Brewster, 1	52,168	2,648
Alpine	52,168	2,648
Briscoe, 1	690	25
Silverton	690	25
Brooks, 1	91,568	3,185
Falfurrias	91,568	3,185
Brown, 1	93,443	0
Brownwood	93,443	0
Burleson, 1	18,411	416
Caldwell	18,411	416
Burnet, 1	169,772	27,625
Burnet	169,772	27,625

County, No. Libraries/ Libraries	Materials Circulated	Inquiries Answered
Caldwell, 2	76,278	2,189
Lockhart	36,882	1,040
Luling	39,396	1,149
Calhoun, 1	70,731	2,141
Port Lavaca	70,731	2,141
Callahan, 3	24,452	920
Baird	3,578	100
Clyde	11,140	120
Cross Plains	9,734	700
Cameron, 8	371,127	37,723
Brownsville	68,814	10,199
Harlingen	166,757	10,020
La Feria	17,618	2,628
Laguna Vista	2,006	0
Los Fresnos	24,259	58
Port Isabel	12,888	6,925
Rio Hondo	6,725	177
San Benito	72,060	7,716
Camp, 1	31,207	1,300
Pittsburg	31,207	1,300
Carson, 1	58,943	4,943
Panhandle	58,943	4,943
Cass, 1	20,223	1,200
Atlanta	20,223	1,200
Castro, 1	101,162	1,420
Dimmitt	101,162	1,420
Chambers, 1	114,074	6,894
Anahuac	114,074	6,894
Cherokee, 2	96,537	4,072
Jacksonville	80,737	3,297
Rusk	15,800	775
Childress, 1	27,361	2,985
Childress	27,361	2,985
Clay, 1	44,292	678
Henrietta	44,292	678
Cochran, 1	6,646	50
Morton	6,646	50
Coke, 1	7,634	200
Robert Lee	7,634	200
Coleman, 2	19,018	1,967
Coleman	19,018	1,967
Santa Anna	0	
Collin, 5	1,168,186	123,884
Allen	86,701	5,000
Farmersville	15,056	1,104
McKinney	134,627	31,533
Plano	898,209	85,072
Wylie	33,593	1,175
Collingsworth, 1	15,744	208
Wellington	15,744	208
Colorado, 4	86,073	4,898
Columbus	42,694	2,720
Eagle Lake	23,608	1,500
Sheridan	1,769	0
Weimar	18,002	678
Comal, 3	197,426	7,988
Bulverde	4,905	1,074
Canyon Lake	21,394	227
New Braunfels	171,127	6,687
Comanche, 2	28,644	5,104
Comanche	21,900	4,504
DeLeon	6,744	600
Concho, 2	7,647	91
Eden	6,498	79
Paint Rock	1,149	12
Cooke, 2	120,152	8,482
Gainesville	102,933	8,118
Muenster	17,219	364
Coryell, 2	155,994	5,568
Copperas Cove	117,625	3,748
Gatesville	38,369	1,820
Cottle, 1	6,625	10
Paducah	6,625	10
Crane, 1	26,000	2,000
Crane	26,000	2,000
Crockett, 1	18,551	345
Ozona	18,551	345
Crosby, 1	31,525	964
Crosbyton	31,525	964
Culberson, 1	15,677	814
Van Horn	15,677	814
Dallam, 1	20,828	1,200
Dalhart	20,828	1,200
Dallas, 22	8,763,261	2,409,024
Balch Springs	45,597	306
Carrollton	457,208	50,200
Cedar Hill	73,779	0
Coppell	118,871	5,270
Dallas	4,364,027	1,725,886
Dallas County	90,144	13,655
DeSoto	120,285	43,413
Duncanville	187,481	18,191
Farmers Branch	229,011	0
Garland	751,854	189,454
Grand Prairie	297,334	20,799
Highland Park	113,388	943
Hutchins	14,360	570
Irving	779,032	153,944
Lancaster	63,950	10,333
Mesquite	366,069	86,070
Richardson	538,118	86,640
Rowlett	78,332	1,250
Sachse	26,039	0
Seagoville	18,384	0
Sunnyvale	14,958	0
Wilmer	15,040	2,100
Dawson, 1	84,087	0
Lamesa	84,087	0
DeWitt, 3	51,333	5,840
Cuero	19,812	120
Yoakum	21,764	5,200
Yorktown	9,757	520
Deaf Smith, 1	86,970	1,368
Hereford	86,970	1,368
Delta, 1	21,485	1,227
Cooper	21,485	1,227
Denton, 11	785,586	45,667
Aubrey	6,203	1,440
Denton	424,297	20,936
Flower Mound	43,899	2,600
Justin	1,613	0
Krum	5,463	97
Lake Dallas	27,265	1,232
Lewisville	153,931	7,421
Pilot Point	31,321	1,526
Roanoke	5,611	185
Sanger	11,299	230
The Colony	74,684	10,000
Dickens, 0	0	0
Dimmit, 1	23,582	1,596
Carrizo Springs	23,582	1,596
Donley, 1	20,332	0
Clarendon	20,332	0
Duval, 0	NA	NA
Eastland, 4	16,283	1,186
Cisco	4,568	250
Eastland	10,715	936
Gorman	0	0
Ranger	1,000	0
Ector, 1	554,447	36,992
Odessa	554,447	36,992
Edwards, 1	8,818	49
Barksdale	8,818	49
Ellis, 4	288,394	5,524
Ennis	66,467	1,096
Ferris	11,448	100
Midlothian	26,586	575
Waxahachie	183,893	3,753
El Paso, 2	1,294,915	107,423
El Paso	1,243,786	101,223
Fabens	51,129	6,200
Erath, 2	71,218	2,626
Dublin	4,667	126
Stephenville	66,551	2,500
Falls, 1	12,175	728
Marlin	12,175	728
Fannin, 3	83,034	15,100
Bonham	59,971	15,000
Honey Grove	16,769	100
Leonard	6,294	0
Fayette, 3	56,651	1,335
Flatonia	2,900	35
La Grange	33,787	300
Schulenburg	19,964	1,000
Fisher, 1	7,323	404
Rotan	7,323	404
Floyd, 1	18,107	1,500
Floydada	18,107	1,500
Foard, 1	16,725	378
Crowell	16,725	378
Fort Bend, 1	729,854	71,287
Richmond	729,854	71,287
Franklin, 1	42,404	1,750
Mount Vernon	42,404	1,750

County, No. Libraries/ Libraries	Materials Circulated	Inquiries Answered
Freestone, 2.	95,586	9,429
Fairfield	39,385	2,100
Teague	56,201	7,329
Frio, 1	39,120	1,850
Pearsall	39,120	1,850
Gaines, 1	36,435	3,459
Seminole	36,435	3,459
Galveston, 8.	990,032	83,248
Dickinson	53,512	2,138
Friendswood	135,728	7,267
Galveston	285,236	37,117
Hitchcock	22,136	4,675
La Marque	50,032	2,537
League City	202,142	15,155
Santa Fe	32,988	450
Texas City	208,258	13,909
Garza, 1	14,747	780
Post	14,747	780
Gillespie, 1.	120,653	9,504
Fredericksburg	120,653	9,504
Glasscock, 0.	NA	NA
Goliad, 1	14,924	315
Goliad	14,924	315
Gonzales, 2	2,870	61
Gonzales	0	0
Smiley	2,870	61
Gray, 2	126,831	12,260
McLean	15,633	300
Pampa	111,198	11,960
Grayson, 6	475,791	42,250
Denison	164,200	24,426
Howe	28,172	15,840
Sherman	232,677	1,267
Van Alstyne	17,702	56
Whitesboro	18,004	661
Whitewright	15,036	0
Gregg, 3	354,341	64,030
Gladewater	51,121	1,204
Kilgore	57,487	3,514
Longview	245,733	59,312
Grimes, 1.	41,983	1,500
Navasota	41,983	1,500
Guadalupe, 2	159,514	17,409
Schertz	57,155	6,450
Seguin	102,359	10,959
Hale, 4	100,010	15,573
Abernathy	7,320	390
Hale Center	12,513	148
Petersburg	6,382	35
Plainview	73,795	15,000
Hall, 2	18,118	3,674
Memphis	18,118	3,674
Turkey	0	0
Hamilton, 1	21,116	95
Hamilton	21,116	95
Hansford, 2	29,496	1,601
Gruver	7,247	200
Spearman	22,249	1,401
Hardeman, 1	13,500	300
Quanah	13,500	300
Hardin, 3	107,265	6,188
Kountze	29,495	1,799
Silsbee	64,602	4,354
Sour Lake	13,168	35
Harris, 6	11,744,705	3,951,446
Baytown	656,580	22,163
Bellaire	146,517	7,484
Deer Park	166,427	2,825
Houston	6,304,414	3,495,423
Houston/HCPL	4,021,323	388,795
Pasadena	449,444	34,756
Harrison, 1.	119,710	0
Marshall	119,710	0
Hartley, 0.	NA	NA
Haskell, 1.	20,900	0
Haskell	20,900	0
Hays, 5.	234,176	21,525
Buda	12,543	950
Dripping Springs	7,920	258
Kyle	13,583	606
San Marcos	188,842	19,711
Wimberley	11,288	0
Hemphill, 1	51,513	1,991
Canadian	51,513	1,991
Henderson, 2	139,591	3,120
Athens	104,199	0
Malakoff	35,392	3,120

County, No. Libraries/ Libraries	Materials Circulated	Inquiries Answered
Hidalgo, 9	1,166,492	375,008
Alamo	27,888	6,383
Donna	59,798	19,396
Edinburg	133,115	11,867
Elsa	37,917	1,991
McAllen	516,937	247,367
Mercedes	52,225	3,851
Mission	97,921	59,611
Pharr	80,416	17,784
Weslaco	160,275	6,758
Hill, 3.	46,650	16,649
Hillsboro	33,274	16,000
Mount Calm	4,446	0
Whitney	8,930	649
Hockley, 1	66,781	2,100
Levelland	66,781	2,100
Hood, 1	73,000	7,800
Granbury	73,000	7,800
Hopkins, 1	47,991	0
Sulphur Springs	47,991	0
Houston, 1	52,295	2,406
Crockett	52,295	2,406
Howard, 1	121,881	11,000
Big Spring	121,881	11,000
Hudspeth, 2	16,051	600
Dell City	9,895	150
Fort Hancock	6,156	450
Hunt, 4.	122,743	15,293
Commerce	20,500	800
Greenville	77,793	13,045
West Tawakoni	17,639	1,180
Wolfe City	6,811	268
Hutchinson, 1	104,796	3,266
Borger	104,796	3,266
Irion, 0.	NA	NA
Jack, 1.	20,123	480
Jacksboro	20,123	480
Jackson, 1	49,206	739
Edna	49,206	739
Jasper, 3	107,432	2,907
Buna	26,092	83
Jasper	49,576	1,082
Kirbyville	31,764	1,742
Jeff Davis, 1.	16,588	71
Fort Davis	16,588	71
Jefferson, 6	907,335	95,092
Beaumont	350,127	63,868
Beaumont/JCL	78,910	2,098
Groves	56,286	5,179
Nederland	105,023	2,667
Port Arthur	243,490	17,225
Port Neches	73,499	4,055
Jim Hogg, 1	10,468	676
Hebbronville	10,468	676
Jim Wells, 1	202,472	7,072
Alice	202,472	7,072
Johnson, 3	319,694	49,745
Alvarado	8,959	225
Burleson	115,157	12,500
Cleburne	195,578	37,020
Jones, 2	12,539	413
Anson	4,169	263
Stamford	8,370	150
Karnes, 4	149,898	3,234
Falls City	22,647	612
Karnes City	48,655	1,610
Kenedy	55,495	632
Runge	23,101	380
Kaufman, 2	237,213	6,467
Kaufman	24,690	3,996
Terrell	212,523	2,471
Kendall, 3	79,150	4,688
Boerne	62,195	3,298
Comfort	13,863	1,350
Kendalia	3,092	40
Kenedy, 0	NA	NA
Kent, 1.	7,853	180
Jayton	7,853	180
Kerr, 1.	211,374	30,383
Kerrville	211,374	30,383
Kimble, 1.	19,045	1,212
Junction	19,045	1,212
King, 1.	905	139
Guthrie	905	139
Kinney, 1.	22,430	68
Brackettville	22,430	68
Kleberg, 1	114,063	1,940
Kingsville	114,063	1,940

County, No. Libraries/ Libraries	Materials Circulated	Inquiries Answered
Knox, 1	9,422	436
Munday	9,422	436
La Salle, 1	10,940	312
Cotulla	10,940	312
Lamar, 1	128,608	22,450
Paris	128,608	22,450
Lamb, 1	41,038	1,830
Littlefield	41,038	1,830
Lampasas, 1	39,957	2,491
Lampasas	39,957	2,491
Lavaca, 1	38,963	1,956
Hallettsville	38,963	1,956
Lee, 1	29,985	43
Giddings	29,985	43
Leon, 2	3,000	5
Buffalo	3,000	5
Centerville	0	0
Liberty, 3	165,253	11,136
Cleveland	35,220	3,120
Dayton	44,906	4,788
Liberty	85,127	3,228
Limestone, 2	51,199	1,772
Groesbeck	22,696	1,209
Mexia	28,503	563
Lipscomb, 2	15,892	536
Booker	10,521	5
Higgins	5,371	531
Live Oak, 1	65,309	5,576
George West	65,309	5,576
Llano, 1	103,172	2,273
Llano	103,172	2,273
Loving, 0	NA	NA
Lubbock, 4	584,146	38,469
Idalou	11,483	0
Lubbock	554,793	37,999
Slaton	15,192	384
Wolfforth	2,678	85
Lynn, 1	5,813	175
Tahoka	5,813	175
Madison, 1	22,095	1,354
Madisonville	22,095	1,354
Marion, 1	0	0
Jefferson	0	0
Martin, 1	8,456	0
Stanton	8,456	0
Mason, 1	13,444	452
Mason	13,444	452
Matagorda, 2	114,336	8,800
Bay City	76,818	5,200
Palacios	37,518	3,600
Maverick, 2	53,955	314
Eagle Pass	46,468	35
Quemado	7,487	279
McCulloch, 1	43,452	1,230
Brady	43,452	1,230
McLennan, 4	633,280	111,890
Hewitt	13,457	675
McGregor	9,450	5
Waco	594,859	111,009
West	15,514	201
McMullen, 0	NA	NA
Medina, 3	61,142	6,711
Castroville	22,228	2,596
Devine	15,783	2,813
Hondo	23,131	1,302
Menard, 1	16,027	1,150
Menard	16,027	1,150
Midland, 1	456,467	49,365
Midland	456,467	49,365
Milam, 2	48,448	2,436
Cameron	21,678	231
Rockdale	26,770	2,205
Mills, 0	NA	NA
Mitchell, 1	30,988	1,250
Colorado City	30,988	1,250
Montague, 2	79,122	2,300
Bowie	66,085	0
Nocona	13,037	2,300
Montgomery, 3	558,422	112,069
Conroe	503,411	101,467
Splendora	44,271	9,012
Willis	10,740	1,590
Moore, 1	71,836	3,333
Dumas	71,836	3,333
Morris, 1	25,745	290
Daingerfield	25,745	290

County, No. Libraries/ Libraries	Materials Circulated	Inquiries Answered
Motley, 1	9,066	155
Matador	9,066	155
Nacogdoches, 1	130,180	5,000
Nacogdoches	130,180	5,000
Navarro, 1	159,971	12,049
Corsicana	159,971	12,049
Newton, 1	9,049	260
Newton	9,049	260
Nolan, 1	92,681	7,379
Sweetwater	92,681	7,379
Nueces, 2	1,009,309	523,990
Corpus Christi	965,024	522,850
Port Aransas	44,285	1,140
Ochiltree, 1	66,290	2,285
Perryton	66,290	2,285
Oldham, 1	3,670	5
Vega	3,670	5
Orange, 2	267,984	15,473
Orange	193,221	11,661
Vidor	74,763	3,812
Palo Pinto, 1	98,467	7,666
Mineral Wells	98,467	7,666
Panola, 1	65,970	10,885
Carthage	65,970	10,885
Parker, 2	187,568	8,823
Springtown	5,359	0
Weatherford	182,209	8,823
Parmer, 1	26,323	872
Friona	25,323	872
Pecos, 3	134,080	19,700
Fort Stockton	115,600	19,400
Imperial	7,000	300
Irann	11,480	0
Polk, 2	94,745	7,843
Corrigan	29,886	5,077
Livingston	64,859	2,766
Potter, 1	1,209,154	512,378
Amarillo	1,209,154	512,378
Presidio, 2	35,630	728
Marfa	28,667	720
Presidio	6,963	
Rains, 1	19,177	955
Emory	19,177	955
Randall, 1	31,479	246
Canyon	31,479	246
Reagan, 1	22,061	1,000
Big Lake	22,061	1,000
Real, 0	NA	NA
Red River, 1	27,558	520
Clarksville	27,558	520
Reeves, 0	NA	NA
Refugio, 1	26,703	837
Refugio	26,703	837
Roberts, 1	3,501	4
Miami	3,501	4
Robertson, 2	16,690	102
Franklin	5,000	0
Hearne	11,690	102
Rockwall, 1	53,014	2,104
Rockwall	53,014	2,104
Runnels, 2	36,521	657
Ballinger	20,249	273
Winters	16,272	384
Rusk, 1	165,301	34,937
Henderson	165,301	34,937
Sabine, 1	27,782	217
Pineland	27,782	217
San Augustine, 1	29,566	624
San Augustine	29,566	624
San Jacinto, 2	35,198	739
Coldspring	12,494	0
Shepherd	22,704	739
San Patricio, 7	205,950	15,745
Aransas Pass	32,934	5,385
Ingleside	24,103	2,043
Mathis	11,854	86
Odem	2,988	386
Portland	76,168	3,790
Sinton	27,315	1,085
Taft	30,588	2,970
San Saba, 1	15,396	65
San Saba	15,396	65
Schleicher, 1	7,641	328
Eldorado	7,641	328
Scurry, 1	97,363	4,150
Snyder	97,363	4,150

County, No. Libraries/ Libraries	Materials Circulated	Inquiries Answered
Shackelford, 1	0	0
Albany	0	0
Shelby, 1	20,546	699
Center	20,546	699
Sherman, 1	8,146	981
Stratford	8,146	981
Smith, 2	267,088	15,498
Tyler	259,188	15,498
Whitehouse	7,900	0
Somervell, 1	21,766	780
Glen Rose	21,766	780
Starr, 1	0	0
Rio GrandeCity	0	0
Stephens, 1	14,360	3,524
Breckenridge	14,360	3,524
Sterling, 0	NA	NA
Stonewall, 1	15,476	507
Aspermont	15,476	507
Sutton, 1	8,508	0
Sonora	8,508	0
Swisher, 1	25,283	1,348
Tulia	25,283	1,348
Tarrant, 20	6,702,516	2,163,238
Arlington	1,238,631	953,802
Azle	67,067	2,528
Bedford	411,267	29,598
Crowley	1,177	200
Euless	158,510	42,454
Everman	4,093	321
Forest Hill	3,532	364
Fort Worth	3,356,148	992,308
Grapevine	285,113	4,571
HaltomCity	101,818	1,032
Hurst	305,600	37,476
Keller	51,336	2,600
Lake Worth	19,331	0
Mansfield	65,480	20,485
North Richland Hills	320,379	43,503
Richland Hills	73,399	6,685
River Oaks	53,502	297
Saginaw	33,460	2,006
Watauga	49,810	15,240
White Settlement	102,863	7,768
Taylor, 1	397,534	198,510
Abilene	397,534	198,510
Terrell, 1	25,600	0
Sanderson	25,600	0
Terry, 1	68,790	3,214
Brownfield	68,790	3,214
Throckmorton, 0	NA	NA
Titus, 1	62,092	2,600
Mount Pleasant	62,092	2,600
Tom Green, 1	580,756	36,966
San Angelo	580,756	36,966
Travis, 4	2,461,301	323,055
Austin	2,393,572	321,705
Austin/Westbank	35,836	1,350
Lake Travis	10,075	0
Pflugerville	21,818	0
Trinity, 2	39,563	708
Groveton	6,392	180
Trinity	33,171	528
Tyler, 1	100,153	24,204
Woodville	100,153	24,204
Upshur, 1	51,234	3,374
Gilmer	51,234	3,374
Upton, 2	39,114	3,010
McCamey	22,807	2,450
Rankin	16,307	560
Uvalde, 1	78,430	2,789
Uvalde	78,430	2,789
Val Verde, 1	111,032	7,230
Del Rio	111,032	7,230
Van Zandt, 2	79,161	2,624
Canton	55,130	2,000
Grand Saline	24,031	624
Victoria, 1	363,324	82,482
Victoria	363,324	82,482
Walker, 2	58,001	27,955
Huntsville	56,736	27,905
New Waverly	1,265	50
Waller, 1	42,037	5,616
Hempstead	42,037	5,616
Ward, 1	101,110	1,623
Monahans	101,110	1,623
Washington, 1	87,500	2,400
Brenham	87,500	2,400
Webb, 1	83,718	2,195
Laredo	83,718	2,195
Wharton, 1	238,528	16,796
Wharton	238,528	16,796
Wheeler, 2	28,899	1,325
Shamrock	18,811	1,096
Wheeler	10,088	229
Wichita, 4	365,119	16,621
Burkburnett	36,592	4,943
Electra	11,119	1,750
Iowa Park	34,637	1,325
Wichita Falls	282,771	8,603
Wilbarger, 1	54,491	1,983
Vernon	54,491	1,983
Willacy, 1	47,000	4,000
Raymondville	47,000	4,000
Williamson, 6	373,863	26,440
Cedar Park	32,287	750
Florence	6,600	500
Georgetown	105,799	6,300
Leander	5,721	690
Round Rock	184,556	13,200
Taylor	38,900	5,000
Wilson, 1	59,121	7,488
Floresville	59,121	7,488
Winkler, 1	32,337	4,896
Kermit	32,337	4,896
Wise, 6	130,533	6,589
Alvord	5,074	402
Boyd	3,845	64
Bridgeport	59,363	5,950
Chico	5,031	135
Decatur	55,026	0
Newark	2,194	38
Wood, 3	74,964	3,258
Hawkins	4,040	100
Quitman	28,955	608
Winnsboro	41,969	2,550
Yoakum, 2	96,817	12,324
Denver City	81,340	6,500
Plains	15,477	5,824
Young, 2	164,205	11,904
Graham	111,070	5,300
Olney	53,135	6,604
Zapata, 1	85,373	975
Zapata	85,373	975
Zavala, 1	7,457	87
Crystal City	7,457	87

Texas Institute of Letters

Since 1939, the **Texas Institute of Letters** has chosen each year outstanding books which are either by Texans or about Texas subjects. Awards have been made for fiction, nonfiction, Southwest history, general information, children's books, poetry and book design. These awards for recent years are listed below:

Year—Author / Title
1985 Elizabeth W. and Robert A. Fernea.... The Arab World: Personal Encounters
Larry McMurtry............ Lonesome Dove
Darwin Payne................ Owen Wister
Reginald Gibbons.......... Mr. Walsh's Mare
Paula Paul ... Sarah, Sissy Weed and the Ships of the Desert
C. W. Smith................. Uncle Dad
Andrew Hudgins........ Saints and Strangers
Walter McDonald .... Witching on Hardscrabble
Book Design Award: Walter Horton ... "Dallas Architecture," published by Texas Monthly Press

Year—Author / Title
1986 William H. and William N. Goetzmann . The West of the Imagination
Rosalind Wright .... Veracruz
Alfred W. Crosby... Ecological Imperialism: The Biological Expansion of Europe, 900-1900
Gail Galloway Adams .... Inside Dope
Edward Hirsch .... Wild Gratitude
Brenda Bell................ Life After Death
Book Design Award: George Lenox and Omega Clay ... "The Panoramic Photography of Eugene O. Goldbeck," written by Clyde Burleson and Jessica Hickman.
The special Barbara McCombs/Lon Tinkle Award for continuing excellence in Texas Letters: Elmer Kelton, San Angelo.

1987 Beverly Lowry............ The Perfect Sonya
Kenneth B. Ragsdale........ The Year America

Poets Laureate

The Texas Legislature designates Texas Poets Laureate and alternates. The Poetry Society of Texas and the Secretary of the Senate's office, Austin, supplied this list for recent years.

Tommy Tune

Texas Native Wins Two More Tonys

Texas native Tommy Tune was honored with a 1991 Tony for Best Director of a Musical and another for Best Choreography at the 45th annual Tony Awards. The two Tonys, which honored Tune for his work on the hit Broadway musical, *The Will Rogers Follies*, were numbers eight and nine for the 52-year-old former Houstonian. Last year, Tune won twin Tony Awards for the same categories for the musical, *Grand Hotel*. He is the first person to win both awards in consecutive seasons.

Tony Awards, Broadway's highest accolades, are presented annually by the American Theatre Wing. Tune has won more Tonys in more different categories than any other person.

The Will Rogers Follies, which has been described as "an all-American extravaganza complete with rope tricks, a dog act and long-legged Ziegfeld dancers," won a total of six Tonys. The award ceremony was held at the Minskoff Theater in New York on June 2, 1991.

Tune, who was born in Wichita Falls in 1939, has been involved in dancing almost all his life. During his boyhood in Houston, he organized patio revues in his backyard. At the age of five, Tune's mother enrolled him in a tap and tumbling class. When Tune got to high school, he signed up for drama class. And when a friend took him to see his first professional musical, *The King and I*, he knew he had found what he wanted to do for the rest of his life.

Tune attended Lon Morris Junior College in Jacksonville for two years, then earned a degree in drama from The University of Texas at Austin. "My dream," says the Texas-tall Tune, "was to dance in the chorus of a Broadway show. I didn't know that chorus boys don't come 6 foot 6." After bouncing from New York to the West Coast and back, Tune made his Broadway debut in *Baker Street* in 1965.

In 1974, Tune won his first Tony as Best Supporting Actor in a Musical for his role in *Seesaw*. Subsequent Tonys included Best Choreography in 1980 for the Broadway production of the London hit, *A Day in Hollywood/A Night in the Ukraine*; Best Director of a Musical for *Nine* in 1982; and double Tonys, for Best Actor in a Musical and Best Choreography, for *My One and Only* in 1983.

Tune has also appeared in, choreographed or directed *A Joyful Noise*, *How Now, Dow Jones*, *Stepping Out*, and *Best Little Whorehouse in Texas*.

A History of the Mystery

This article was written by Mike Kingston, editor of the Texas Almanac.

There are few intellectual or literary endeavors in which Texas has not lagged behind both the nation and the other parts of the world. Development of mystery or detective fiction is no different.

A rich heritage of bad guys and shining heros already existed before Texas writers got into the swim of the mystery market. Edward Anderson with his 1937 novel, *Thieves Like Us,* and Jim Thompson with several non-fiction crime stories broke ground for mystery writers in the Texas of the 1930s. But the genre did not take root.

One reason, of course, is the lack of a professional literary tradition in Texas at the time. J. Frank Dobie and Walter Prescott Webb were by example making writing a serious profession.

Dr. James Ward Lee, chair of the English Department at the University of North Texas, also sees Texans' image of themselves as a barrier. In an unpublished paper, he notes that the cynicism that fueled the growth of mystery fiction elsewhere in the nation in the 1930s didn't reach Texas until later. Although most Texans lived in metropolitan areas in the 1940s, they did not perceive Texas as an urban state until the 1970s or later. Texas writing remained strongly romantic and even naive, stuck in a cultural time warp dating to about 1840. Aspiring writers in Texas either embraced the romanticism dear to the state's intelligencia or left for less repressive climes to pursue their art.

Three pioneers in mystery-crime writing in Texas were Edward Anderson, Jim Thompson and James Atlee Phillips, writing as Philip Atlee. Anderson's 1930s novel, *Thieves Like Us,* was made into a movie, and Thompson wrote several crime novels. Phillips, under his pseudonym, published 29 novels and won an Edgar Award from the Mystery Writers of America in 1970 for *The White Wolverine Contract.*

Crime literature is a relatively recent addition to the literary scene. One reason is simple: Detective stories cannot be written when there are no detectives. And it was not until the early 19th century that large police departments began to adopt specialized investigatory techniques. The word "detective" dates from the mid-1840s, but even then it did not come into common usage until the 1870s.

When crime writing came into vogue, plots were set mostly in cities, like Paris or London, with large police departments. In some early writing, the criminals were the heroes.

Mystery writing has celebrated its 150th birthday, dating in America to the publication of Edgar Allan Poe's *Murders in the Rue Morgue* in 1841, which, by the way, was set in Paris. He followed in the next four years with two other mysteries, *Marie Roget* and *The Purloined Letter,* and several short stories.

Crime writing got an earlier start in Europe. Francois Eugene Vidocq in 1829 published his *Memoirs,* purporting to be the story of his career beginning as a petty thief developing through a phase as police informer to finally head the Paris police agency. The criminal, in this case, was the hero. Though many authorities think Vidocq's tale should be classified as fiction, it's still considered non-fiction.

William Godwin introduced British readers to a form of the mystery in 1794 with *The Adventures of Caleb Williams.* Godwin, father of Mary Shelly, creator of *Frankenstein* and the horror genre, is considered father of the British mystery story. He wrote from the uncommon view at the time that the criminal justice system was corrupt, as was the rule of law. Mystery and crime fiction usually is very conservative in that it re-emphasizes in the end the righteousness of the existing rule of law, much as modern horror fiction does. A sharp sense of right and wrong was preserved.

Arthur Conan Doyle entered the field in the 1890s, earning distinction as the father of crime literature.

On the American side of the Atlantic, Anna Katharine Green's *The Leavenworth Case* published in 1878 was the next step in development of crime fiction.

The English country house murder mystery gained early popularity, divorcing itself from the rugged urban slums and presenting to readers a homogenized killing with little blood or violence. The plot and intrigue were paramount in these stories, and the murder itself somewhat incidental.

Crime fiction began in the short-story form and lengthened into full-novel length. It gained popularity in dime novels in the early part of the 20th century, and after World War I in the United States, the hard-boiled detective became standard fare in pulp magazines. Raymond Chandler and Dashiell Hammett both started in these outlets. And the American crime story broke completely with its European counterparts by featuring a tough man of action. The neat, orderly murder of the English country house was out, and bloody, gory murder was put back on the streets and in dark alleys in the hands of thugs and punks where it belonged.

The new detective operated barely within the law himself, and before the final shot echoed, a rough justice was meted out. This operator knew the ins and outs of the justice system and usually did not like what he saw. If shortcuts were necessary to assure the bad guy got his due, so be it. Usually, mysteries were set on either the East or West Coasts and occasionally in Chicago.

In the 1950s, the police procedural came of age, changing the focus of the mystery story. Originally, the writer gave mystery readers clues, so they could pit their skills with the protagonist and try to solve the crime. This competition ended with the police procedural, for it took the reader inside the law-enforcement agency. Descriptions of the internal operations of the agency became paramount.

Since the 1960s the mystery genre has spawned subgenre in multiple directions. Detectives now are not limited to the 1930s stereotype tough guy. They range from teen-age girls to gray-haired grandmothers, from young boys to elderly rabbis. Detectives can come from either sex or sexual preferences. Usually they are brighter than a few decades ago, if perhaps not as moral, and often they have mastered aspects of our new high-tech age.

All successful mysteries, novel-length or short story, have a few common characteristics. They play fair by giving the reader the clues from which to solve the mystery, and they are written to entertain the reader. Action usually outweighs character development, and the writer never, never preaches morals or ethics to the reader.

To paraphrase one crime writer of note: Once the clues have been examined and evaluated, what remains should be a good story, well told.

Texas' Mystery Writers

Death can come subtly as a delicate mist from an aerosol container or as brutally as a flint projectile point gouging through the ribs and heart muscle. It can be crass, from a gun shot, or as quietly lethal as an unexpected drug overdose.

However a victim is dispatched by mystery writers who practice their craft in Texas, one can be sure that an engaging story will follow. Those writers who call the state home — and some who have been raised here and left — can craft a story to entertain the most discerning reader with the best practitioners of the genre.

Patricia Highsmith

Perhaps the best known of Texas' mystery writers is an expatriate, Patricia Highsmith, who left Fort Worth years ago for England. Her work appears on both sides of the Atlantic, assigned to the mystery genre in the United States and to literary status in France.

Highsmith's writing is of the highest quality, eschewing bloody violence and action for chilling psychological suspense.

As a group, mystery writers have abandoned the pastoral theme that mesmerizes so many creative

David Lindsey

writers in Texas. Even speculative fiction writers in Texas (horror, science fiction and fantasy) tend to set stories in rural areas. With a few exceptions, mystery writers stick to the city, and in the process, give readers some of the better insights into urban Texas, although at the seamy side. Mystery writers fill some of the void in the state's urban fiction.

There is no head-count available on the number of people writing mysteries in Texas. The Southwest Chapter of the Mystery Writers of America has 95 members in three states and meets monthly in Houston. That is one indication of the professional interest in mystery writing.

David Lindsey

Texas mystery writers come from varied backgrounds, and most found their way into mystery writing by reading mysteries.

An exception is David Lindsey of Austin, one of the top, if not the best, of the current generation of Texas mystery writers. Though raised in Silver, a tiny community in Coke County near San Angelo, he is not attracted to the pastoral theme. It's simply not part of his experience.

Lindsey took a degree from the University of North Texas (then North Texas State University) and entered publishing for a time. In 1980, at age 35, he decided to try his hand at writing fiction. With a wife and two children to support, he couldn't make a mistake, and from his knowledge of publishing, he knew mysteries sold.

Trouble was, Lindsey was not a mystery reader. So he purchased a dozen or so mysteries to get an idea of the market and the latitude. His first book, *Red Death, Black Gold*, was a formulaic action adventure story set in San Antonio. The format was not satisfying, for it ignored character development and plot.

To add realism to his next books, Lindsey initiated a relationship with the homicide division of the Houston Police Department that has lasted a decade. Association with the detectives and traumatic visits to actual murder scenes filled the writer with a sense of horror. But the experience also aroused an obsession to understand how a human being could inflict such violence on another.

Lindsey took care to impart the physical nature of violent death in his next two novels, *In a Cold Mind* and *Heat From Another Sun*. He won praise from fellow writers for bringing realism to readers, but critics charged him with use of gratuitous violence.

Violence is not pleasant, Lindsey observes, and he will not depict it as such, no matter what the critics say. "It's a shame to treat violence as entertainment," he says. But the nightly dose of sterile violence on TV distorts the true nature of the action.

In his first four novels based in Houston, Lindsey developed the character of Stuart Haydon, a millionaire cop, but in *Mercy*, he switched to a female protagonist in officer Carmen Palma.

Lindsey's focus also has changed from concentration on investigatory techniques to studying the psychology of the killer, the victim's family and friends and the investigators.

Being tagged as a mystery writer is limiting, Lindsey complains. He sees his latest work as more mainstream fiction, although in a mystery format. In the future, he probably will move toward mainstream writing. But he feels that writers are at a disadvantage for they serve their apprenticeships in public with their mistakes in plain view. Nevertheless, Lindsey's work gives readers a view of urban life in Texas that usually isn't portrayed and mixes in a good story to boot.

Joan Lowrey Nixon

Joan Lowrey Nixon became a juvenile mystery writer through a committee decision. Sort of. Just after moving to Texas in 1960, she attended a writers' workshop and heard two speakers discuss juvenile writing.

She told her four young children about the sessions, asking what type of juvenile writing she should try. Later in the day, sixth-grader Kathleen and second-grader Eileen said their mother should write mysteries and put her daughters in them.

Seventy-eight juvenile books later, Mrs. Nixon has three Edgars (mystery writers' equivalent to an Oscar) to her credit and a busy writing schedule stretching into the future.

Writing juvenile mysteries is no different from challenging the adult market; the stories must be entertaining. And, of course, there must be a mystery involved. Mrs. Lowrey gives her protagonist a personal problem to solve and creates a challenging mystery to be solved. The major differences in writing for the younger readers are the length of the work, which is shorter (less than 50,000 words), and avoiding the taboos against gore and too much violence. Common sense helps to get around these, she says.

All but one of her mysteries have been set in Texas, although she changes locales. Each novel has a different set of characters. Her young adult novels usually feature a female protagonist, though in her writing for intermediate readers (ages 8-12), she has used males as main characters. The reason is simple: She has better understanding of young girls than boys. For each book, she checks with police in the locale where the story will take place. Police procedures vary, and she wants to make the books as authentic as possible. She's visited county jails for background on the chance that a character might end up incarcerated.

No attempt is made to put a moral in the novels, but if a theme can be identified it is probably one of hope. The Houston writer tries to make the young readers feel good about themselves.

Mrs. Lowrey's books that won Edgars are *The Kidnapping of Christina Lattimore* in 1980, *The Seance* in 1981 and *The Other Side of Dark* in 1986. And while these honors are important, Mrs. Lowrey perhaps most treasures letters from youngsters who have been introduced to books and reading through her work. One 15-year-old girl wrote, for example, that she had never read a book until picking up one of Mrs. Lowrey's mysteries and now she wanted to read everything the author had written.

Writers like Mrs. Lowrey attract the young readers today and prepare the audience for mystery writers in the future.

A.W. Gray

Like many people, A.W. "Bill" Gray always wanted to write but never had time. When time became available, he took full advantage of it — in prison.

Raised in Highland Park and a graduate of Southern Methodist University, Gray was an extremely successful insurance agent. But he ran afoul of federal law while operating a bonding company in the early 1980s and was sentenced to seven years in prison. (Gray contends he did nothing illegal.) From 1984-87 he was an inmate in the federal correctional institution in Big Spring.

Gray spent his first year in prison moping in the corner, separating himself from other inmates. Then he got acquainted with several of them and used their experiences in his books.

The writer could have been the subject of a book himself, for in his younger years he played professional poker and also knocked around with Lee Trevino before the golfer hit it big on the pro golf tour.

While in prison, Gray wrote and sold four novels, despite less than ideal working conditions. Each page of copy was written in longhand and then typed on a typewriter reserved for preparing legal documents. He produced about one page of finished copy a day.

Nevertheless, he polished his writing skills and developed a market for his work.

In two of his novels, *Size* and *A Man Off Sides*, his protagonists are on the wrong side of the law. He also has developed the character, Bino Phillips, a former SMU basketball player who practices law in Dallas, as the protagonist in two novels, *Bino* and *In Defense of Judges*.

Gray says his books are not mysteries, but crime fiction, the distinction being that there is no "mystery" in store as it unfolds. He concentrates on character development, believing that the reader must like the protagonist and identify with him to a degree. On the other hand, readers also must feel some revulsion for the bad guy, otherwise there is not enough emotion when the good guy triumphs.

Mystery or crime fiction probably will remain Gray's staple product, although he has written two horror novels that were published under a pseudonym.

No attempt is made to deliver a message in his books, but Gray's characters, particularly in *Size* and *A Man Off Sides*, have reservations about the criminal justice system. For people on the wrong side of the law, Gray feels, this is a realistic attitude. Gray himself feels he was mistreated by the system and had not committed a crime. Consequently, he has little regard for federal DAs or FBI agents, although, ironically enough, his brother is with the FBI.

Most of the incidents in Gray's books come from actual events garnered from the lives of people, especially fellow inmates at Big Spring, the author has known.

Gray's novels are entertaining and satisfying to readers, and they reflect a point of view that's unique in Texas fiction. Again, they also provide insight into the workings of an important element of urban society — the criminal justice system — that gets too little critical scrutiny.

Jay Brandon

Jay Brandon's *Fade the Heat*, his fourth published novel, was nominated for an Edgar Award in fiction in 1991. It was the high point in a writing career that began in the fifth grade in San Antonio for the former Bexar County assistant prosecuting attorney.

"It seemed like the logical thing to do to want to write," Brandon says. So he composed short stories at age 10 that he later read to his fifth-grade classmates. The following year, he turned the reading over to another youngster while he continued to compose stories.

After receiving a BA in English at the University of Texas at Austin in 1975, Brandon attended a writing seminar at Johns Hopkins University. He later received a law degree from the University of Houston and worked for the Court of Criminal Appeals in Austin and for the district attorney in Bexar County. He wrote five novels before getting one published. But since 1985, he has published four novels, *Deadbolt, Tripwire, Predator's Waltz,* and *Fade the Heat.* The latter book also was released as an audio-cassette presentation.

Unlike Lindsey or Gray, Brandon does a detailed outline of his novels in advance. "I work hard on plots because they are the most difficult part for me," he says. Characterization is done during the writing phase, and it is the easiest part of the work. Also unlike many writers, Brandon does not do much rewriting. "It depends on the editor," he says. On his first book, rewriting was a major task. But on his last one, he rewrote only three pages at the editor's request.

Though writing about the criminal justice system in which he has worked, most of his ideas came before he was an assistant prosecutor. He started writing *Fade the Heat* before joining the Bexar County DA's staff. After some time on the job, Brandon used his experience to add some legal background to the book that, he says, should impart a sense of outrage at the criminal-justice system.

Although a sequel to *Fade the Heat* is in the works, Brandon would like to move to another genre. One appealing project would be a multi-generational book spanning the history of a family. Horror fiction also interests him. "I've never read a truly scary ghost story, and I'd like to try one," Brandon says.

Brandon has set stories in Houston and in San Antonio, providing insight into life in these urban areas, along with some riveting stories.

Richard Abshire

Richard Abshire of Dallas is one of several former street cops trying their hands at mystery writing. Abshire has co-authored two novels, *Gant* and *The Shaman Tree*, with William Clair, a retired Dallas police officer. In addition, he has written two novels with Jack Kyle as his protagonist, *Dallas Drop* and *Turnaround Jack.*

A native of Paris, Lamar County, Abshire began writing about the time he learned to read, which was

A. W. Gray

before he started to school. "I was the kid who was always writing school plays," he says.

As soon as he turned 21, in 1967, he joined the Dallas Police Department, where he stayed for 12 years. During that time he completed work on a BA in criminal justice from Sam Houston State University and an MA in liberal arts from Southern Methodist University.

His first published work was a nonfiction series on crime that ran in the "Dallas Observer."

Neither as a single author nor as a coauthor does Abshire regularly produce copy. "I wish I could say I produced three pages of finished copy a day like a good guy, but I don't," he confesses.

And he does not do a detailed outline either. He writes a synopsis, which he uses for chapter leads. Sometimes he does not know who will be the bad guy when he starts out. Too much planning can limit the flow of the action, he feels.

After considerable thought is given to an idea, he can bang out the story in a short time. (Once he and Clair produced 450 pages of copy in five days.) Then comes the rewriting. "That's when I do my best writing, during rewrite," he says.

Character development is the most important part of writing for Abshire. And he likes to put protagonists in situations in which their options are limited. "That's when a person's character is revealed," Abshire says. "It's easy to make the right, or moral, choices when everything is going well." In the Kyle novels, the theme is betrayal, for Kyle deals with a series of characters, including his ex-wife and a former boss, who can't be trusted.

Watching Abshire write might be fun. He reads his dialogue aloud, portraying whatever characters are involved to ensure realism in the conversation. "Sometimes this performance gets quite animated," he laughs.

The characters are composed from real life, usually a mixture of two or more people Abshire has known.

Another Jack Kyle novel is complete. Abshire would like to do a multi-generational novel on the idea of evil. He has in mind setting one in his hometown of Paris and building the story around a lynching in the 1930s.

For this former police officer, crime has begun to pay.

Bill Crider

The mystery-writing bug bit Bill Crider early and deep. As a youngster, he broke in on the Hardy Boys, Nancy Drew and other fiction of that ilk, even trying his hand on his first fiction at age 10. That tale of a man being eaten by rats never got finished. From that beginning, Crider began to take a serious and abiding interest in mysteries. His doctoral dissertation, for example, was on private-eye novels.

And the interest also been translated into some success as a professional writer. Crider has 10 novels sold, mostly his popular Sheriff Dan Rhodes series, and has plans for several more.

Kinky Friedman

Mysteries retain their popularity for many reasons, but one is the basically conservative nature of the stories. "Justice is usually done," Crider notes, "and the guilty are punished. That doesn't always get done in real life."

A professor of English at Alvin Community College, Crider still enjoys mystery novels, along with his other tastes in reading. Mysteries, he thinks, are usually well-written and entertaining. As important as the story is the way the novel is written in his mind, the writing style, character development, background. Mystery writers cover these bases pretty well.

Unlike most other Texas mystery writers, Crider's protagonist, Sheriff Rhodes, plies his trade in a rural area. Murder in Rhodes' county is still rare enough to excite comment and concern. But as in much of today's rural Texas, the problems of the big cities are finding their way to the state's less populated areas. Drug abuse, major theft and other crimes usually associated with urban areas are more frequently impinging on the pastoral primness of rural areas.

This, too, is a segment of Texas life that often is overlooked in fiction. But Crider is not selling social message or morality. The point of a mystery first and foremost is to entertain. Moralizing is "the last thing I would think about," Crider says.

Among the trends Crider sees developing is the growing popularity of the regional novel. Tony Hillerman led the way with his series of mysteries built around the Navajo culture in the Southwest.

A past president of the Southwest Chapter of the Mystery Writers of America, Crider sees a bright future for the genre in coming years.

D.R. Meredith

"It was a dark and snowy night. . ." might be the opening paragraph of a description of the mystery-writing career of Doris "D.R." Meredith of Amarillo. She has two series of books based on small-town characters that are popular with readers, The Sheriff and lawyer-detective John Lloyd Branson.

During the cold, cold winter of 1977 in the Texas Panhandle, the homebound Mrs. Meredith read scads of mystery novels, not a few of which were devoured while awaiting her new daughter's 2 a.m. feeding. At her husband's urging, she tried her hand at a mystery, filling several spiral notebooks with the hand-written text. Then the manuscript was put in a drawer and forgotten.

A conversation with a publisher at a Western Writers of America meeting in Albuquerque kindled Mrs. Meredith's interest in selling the book. The manuscript was retrieved from the drawer, partially rewritten, typed and sold. The book, The Sheriff and the Panhandle Murders was published in 1984, the first of four in the series.

Characterization is the most important part of writing, Mrs. Meredith believes. If readers do not care about the characters, it will not be a memorable book. She understands this is not a consensus view, but "that's why you see so many different types of novel."

Writing has been an obsession of Mrs. Meredith since her childhood in Cushing, Okla. She received a degree in English from the University of Oklahoma and had done post-graduate work at the University of North Texas and at West Texas State University.

Much of Mrs. Meredith's writing concerns rural Texas, but she does venture into mid-sized Amarillo, as she did in the 1990 John Lloyd Branson novel, The Masquerade Murders, concerning the serial killer of prostitutes. Readers have liked the approach she took that the serial killer was not insane but made a conscious choice to murder the call girls, Mrs. Meredith says.

Background and authenticity of setting are important for the writer, and she likes to write tales with archaeological backgrounds. That shows in novels like The Folsom Man Murders, in which the victim is dispatched with a dart launched from an atlatl, a prehistoric throwing stick.

Mysteries are the staple of Mrs. Meredith's writing career, but she also does historical novels, two of which under contract deal with the life of a woman on the Panhandle frontier in the 19th century.

The "dark and snowy nights" of the mean winter of 1977 are long gone, but D.R. Meredith's career is moving right along in the sunshine of success.

Carole Nelson Douglas

Realism. Authenticity. These are not words that enter into discussions of works by Carole Nelson Douglas, for she has dipped into the fantasy genre for many of her 21 novels.

But the immigrant to Fort Worth from St. Paul, Minn., tried her hand at mystery writing in 1990 and came up with a winner, Good Night, Mr. Holmes.

Sherlock Holmes' fans will recognize the four-word title as one of the more famous quotes from A Scandal in Bohemia in which Irene Adler, opera singer-actress, has outsmarted Mr. Holmes. She was the only woman and one of precious few other characters to do so.

In the neo-Holmesian literature Irene is usually resurrected as a love interest of Holmes. And most of this genre has been written by men, who create weak women that suffer from brain fever, "whatever that is," Mrs. Douglas quips.

So Good Night, Mr. Holmes develops Irene as a formidable character, Holmes' equal as an investigator. Irene even has her Watsonesque chronicler in Penelope "Nell" Huxleigh.

Mrs. Douglas began writing in high school and wrote most of a novel in college. But she set it aside to begin an award-winning career as a journalist in St. Paul. After a decade on the newspaper, she resurrected the novel, finished it and with a bit of luck sold it in 1977.

She was successful enough over the next seven years to finally be able to quit her job and devote full time to writing. Her prodigious output in genres ranging from fantasy to romance to mainstream and historical was necessary. "To be a working writer, you have to be prolific, unless you make the bestseller list," Mrs. Douglas explains.

Fantasy has been the most difficult genre for the writer. "You make up the world and have to be cognizant of where each character is and why throughout the book. While working on fantasy you get into almost an altered state," she says.

There was no altered state in Good Night, Mr. Holmes, just a satisfying re-creation of Victorian London and a style that Dr. Watson could not have improved.

A sequel, Good Morning, Mr. Holmes, was released in the summer of 1991 and proved to be another delightful story in the Holmes-Adler tradition.

Mrs. Douglas and her husband moved to Texas from Minnesota in 1984. Friends pointed out that Texas was much, much warmer than their home state. "But we pointed out that you don't have to shovel sweat," Mrs. Douglas quips.

Kinky Friedman

Easily the most colorful of Texas' mystery writers is Kinky Friedman, former country singer, failed politician and hip private detective in New York City.

Friedman toured with his musical group, the Texas Jewboys, in the 1970s, but he turned to writing mysteries in the 1980s. He was in search of a lifestyle that didn't require his presence.

A native Texan, Friedman cashed in on publicity he received for saving a victim from an armed robber in New York City. Within months, his first novel, Greenwich Killing Time, was on the market. When the manuscript was turned down by 17 publishers, Friedman quips, he knew he had a winner.

At a pace of about one a year, four more Friedman mysteries, each featuring himself as the protagonist, have found willing readers. All were written on a ranch in Kerr County in Friedman's green wooden trailer with only three cats and a pet armadillo as company.

Story-telling came early to Friedman, who while in his teens enthralled participants at the family's boys' camp. The writing came much later.

The best part of Friedman's books is the hip dialogue between himself as protagonist and other characters and the wry commentary based on street smarts that sprinkle the book.

And there are little tidbits that send trivia buffs into ecstasy. For example, in his latest book, *Musical Chairs*, Friedman points out that the figure of Abraham Lincoln in the memorial in Washington is signing the letters "A" and "L" in sign language. True? Yep, says Friedman, information courtesy his friends at the Gallaudet University, a school for the deaf.

While Friedman's books are entertaining in the first degree, they sometimes lack the structure of a classic mystery. As he told one interviewer, "If you get a plot in a Kinky book you should consider it gravy."

There have been some discussions of taking the books to a television series, starring, of course, the Kinkster himself.

Friedman also is moving into non-fiction writing, something of a reversal of the usual career development. He has had articles in *The New York Times* and did an article for *Rolling Stone* on Willie Nelson.

If Friedman moves away from mystery writing, it will be a major loss for readers who like continuous belly laughs while winding their way through the bodies and intrigue of a good whodunit.

Other Notables

It is impossible in a short survey of mystery writers in and of Texas to cover all deserving authors. In addition to those already reviewed, here is a short list of others who have had novels published.

The late **Edward Mathis** produced a sizable body of quality work in his Dan Roman series. Most of the novels are set in the mid-cities area between Fort Worth and Dallas, although some have been moved to rural areas. The works are entertaining, and his death deprived mystery lovers of his remarkable talents.

As earlier mentioned, today's mystery writers in Texas often provide the only insight into urban areas that is available in fiction in the state. **Jesse Sublett** of Austin is a major contributor to background on a segment of the state's culture. A rock musician himself, Sublett has set two mysteries, *The Rock Critic Murders* and *Tough Baby*, in the subculture of the Austin music world. The protagonist is a drummer in rock bands, and the development of both novels is laced with views into this world. First-rate stuff.

Susan Baker of Galveston took a former probation officer and stuck her center stage in Baker's first novel, appropriately named, *My First Murder*. The setting ranges from second-rate Galveston restaurants to the posh neighborhoods of Arlington to East Fort Worth. Really a neat read, particularly for a first effort.

A series of apparently unrelated killings sets off the story in *You'll Hear From Us* by **Marilyn Cooley** and **James Edward Gunn**. Gunn is a former member of a SWAT team in the Houston Police Department. And this complex mystery, set in Houston, is another good first novel.

Margot Fraser of Odessa debuted in the mystery field with *The Laying Out of Gussie Hoot* that arguably is a mainstream novel in thin disguise. The killers of Gussie Hoot are known from early on, but the real detective work comes in laying bare the character of the victim. Mystery aside, Ms. Fraser's novel is an excellent study of the phenomenon of the ruling dowager in rural Texas. An excellent read.

Mystery writing got a very late start in Texas, but it is obvious by the quality of writing and the number of aspiring writers that the state is catching up fast.

Mostly Murder

Most Texans don't like murder. Not the real thing anyway, despite what the state's crime statistics might suggest. Fictional murder, however, is another matter. Quite another. Mysteries are among the state's best-selling novels. And most have a corpse or two scattered around to focus the reader's attention.

Barbara Unger learned that lesson early on, first as a book store owner and later as the publisher of the popular quarterly tabloid, **Mostly Murder**.

Mystery readers hunger for information about the genre they love. Not just information on the novels, either. They want to know about the mystery writers and about the stuff that mysteries are made of — police procedures, forensics, instruments of dispatch, the whole caboodle.

When she first acquired an interest in the House of Books, a popular North Dallas bookery, in the early '80s, Ms. Unger increased the size of the mystery section. She liked mysteries and knew others did, too. To further enhance interest, she organized a monthly Mystery Lovers Book Club, where authors and people involved in real-life crime fighting regaled readers with tales of their crafts. The club was a popular feature at the book store.

In 1988, however, the store fell victim to Texas' waning economy, and Ms. Unger turned her energies full time to piquing mystery fans' interest. The first issue of **Mostly Murder** appeared in book stores and libraries in January 1990 and was well-received.

Tons of mysteries are among the 50,000 books published in the United States each year. The success of each often depends on the amount of publicity the book and author receive. Authors published by small presses are at a disadvantage, for they often must promote their works alone, unaided by a substantial budget from the publisher.

For one edition alone in 1990, Ms. Unger received 140 review copies of books. From that group, she ran 40 reviews, a number she tries to maintain in each edition. There are other features, including backlists of mysteries, reviews of video and audio renderings of mysteries, and articles by authors.

Reviewers are not paid for their work. This practice, followed in the trade, made Ms. Unger uncomfortable at first. But she found that authors like to review books and write articles to keep their names before the public. Other reviewers also contribute for the love of the chase through the fictional crimes.

People like mysteries because they like to solve puzzles, Ms. Unger thinks. They also like to see the criminals get their due, a result frequently missing in real-life crime. So in this degree, mysteries reflect public attitudes toward crime and criminals.

Sub-genres of the mystery novel have proliferated over the years since Raymond Chandler gave readers the tough-guy private investigator and "put murder back in the streets where it belonged" in the 1930s. Police procedurals have proved popular in recent years, and with the feminist movement, there has been an influx of tough-gal private eyes. Ms. Unger sees the emergence of another figure, the older woman as detective and protagonist. Not copies of Agatha Christie's Miss Marple, but intelligent, active — both sexually and socially — gray-haired detectives.

Other writers speak to social issues as well as provide entertainment. David L. Lindsay, perhaps Texas' best mystery writer, recently laid out the problem of female child abuse in his novel, *Mercy*, which centered on female homosexual sado-masochism.

The criminal justice system gets a thorough airing in the works of A.W. "Bill" Gray, who has directed attention to the cynicism and the resulting injustice in the justice system; Jay Brandon, a former prosecutor, taps the same thesis, but from a different perspective. Former police officers, Richard Abshire and William Clair of Dallas and James Edward Gunn of Houston, contribute through their fiction the law-enforcement officers' views.

Even when the authors, like D. R. Meredith of Amarillo or Bill Crider of Alvin, locate their protagonists outside the urban areas, relevant social issues are touched upon. Ms. Meredith recently dealt with control of water pollution in a novel, and Crider used a transvestite as an antagonist. Neither issue is the traditional fare of Texas literature.

But these themes are not preachy. Texas' mystery writers are true to the golden rule of the genre: entertain the reader. Anything else that happens along the way is gravy. And Ms. Unger's **Mostly Murder** helps Texans keep track of how the state's authors and others from around the country are doing.

Major Film Projects Hit New High

Information for the following article was supplied by the Texas Film Commission of the Texas Department of Commerce.

The number of major film projects filmed at least partially in Texas hit a new high in 1989, followed by the second-highest year in 1990. The 32 projects filmed in Texas in 1989 had gross production budgets of $116,400,000, while the 31 filmed in 1990 had budgets of $42,855,000. Usually, 50 percent of a project's production budget is spent in the host community.

Major projects include feature films and television movies, specials and series. Not included in these totals are television commercials, industrial films, documentaries, music videos or other film/video projects. Revenues from these non-entertainment productions are estimated at $100-125 million annually.

Movie projects shot in Texas in 1989 included 19 feature movies, eight TV movies, five TV series and one TV special. Among the feature films were **Texasville,** shot near Wichita Falls and Archer City and starring Cybill Shepherd, Timothy Bottoms, Jeff Bridges, Randy Quaid, Annie Potts, and Cloris Leachman; **Problem Child,** filmed in Mesquite and Dallas, starring John Ritter and Jack Warden; **Daddy's Dyin', Who's Got the Will,** using locations around Denton, Ponder, Waxahachie, Maypearl and Arlington, and featuring Beverly D'Angelo, Keith Carradine, Tess Harper and Beau Bridges; and **RoboCop 2,** with Peter Weller and Nancy Allen, made in Houston.

TV movies included **Fire and Rain,** made in Dallas with Angie Dickinson and Charles Haid, and **Pair of Aces,** shot in the Austin area and starring Kris Kristofferson, Willie Nelson and Rip Torn. Television specials were led by the filming of the 15th season of the C&W music series, **Austin City Limits,** featuring, among others, Stevie Ray Vaughn, Lyle Lovett, Waylon Jennings, Michelle Shocked, George Jones and Beausoleil.

Feature movies shot in Texas in 1990 included **Ballad of the Sad Cafe,** filmed around Spicewood and starring Vanessa Redgrave, Rod Steiger and Keith Carradine and **Hard Promises,** shot in Lockhart, Austin and Pflugerville featuring Sissy Spacek and William Petersen.

Among 1990's TV movies were **A Killing in a Small Town,** starring Barbara Hershey, Hal Holbrook and Brian Dennehy shot on location in Plano, McKinney and Dallas, and **In Broad Daylight,** filmed in Elgin, Coupland and Bastrop, and starring Brian Dennehy and Cloris Leachman. The filming of **Austin City Limits** continued, featuring Sara Hickman, Cowboy Junkies, Joe Ely, Highway 101 and Kelly Willis. In all, there were 11 feature movies made in Texas in 1990, as well as five TV movies, 10 TV series and five TV specials.

TFC Brings Film Making to Texas

The **Texas Film Commission (TFC),** a department of the Texas Department of Commerce, was established in 1971 to assist film producers find the locations, facilities and personnel needed to make films and videos in the Lone Star State. In a 1986 survey of Hollywood producers conducted by a California State Senate Select Committee, the TFC was called the "most effective" of the 120 state and city film commissions in existence at that time.

In the 20 years since it was formed, the TFC has spent a total of $3,861,859 in assisting almost 400 film projects with gross production budgets of just over $1 billion. Typically, 50 percent of a project's budget is spent in the host community, so about $500 million was spent in Texas.

Services offered to film producers by the TFC include locations research and selection; key contact information for local, state and federal government entities, private businesses and citizens; and preproduction consultation and information on crew availability, equipment rental, facilities, transportation, housing, weather and Texas state laws that pertain to filmmaking.

Originally established as a division of the Gover-

nor's Office, the Film Commission became a division of the Texas Economic Development Commission in Sept. 1985, then was transferred to the Texas Department of Commerce in Sept. 1987.

Below is a table showing the number of major productions assisted by the TFC and the gross budgets of those projects. Not included are the many TV commercials, industrial films, documentaries, music videos and other film/video projects that are filmed in Texas each year.

Year	Number of Projects	Gross Budgets
1971-1979	119	$178,200,000
1980	22	99,500,000
1981	18	55,000,000
1982	13	45,700,000
1983	30	114,100,000
1984	30	89,900,000
1985	27	56,700,000
1986	28	102,100,000
1987	24	66,300,000
1988	24	92,500,000
1989	32	116,400,000
1990	31	42,855,000
Totals	398	$1,059,255,000

Film Commissions in Texas

In addition to the following film commissions, which were operating in Texas as of early summer, 1991, many chambers of commerce and convention and visitors' bureaus have employees who specialize in assisting film companies:

Texas Film Commission
Texas Dept. of Commerce
Box 12728
Austin 78711
(512) 469-9111
FAX 512-320-9626

Amarillo Film Office
P.O. Box 9480
Amarillo 79105
(806) 374-1497
(806) 692-1338

Austin Film Liaison
P.O. Box 1088
Austin 78767
(512) 499-2404
FAX (512) 499-6385

El Paso Film Commission
1 Civic Center Plaza
El Paso 79901
(915) 534-0698
FAX (915) 532-2963

Houston Film Commission
3300 Main Street
Houston 77002
(713) 523-5050
WATS (800) 231-7799
FAX (713) 524-5376

Irving Film Commission
1 Dallas Communications Complex
LB 119
6301 N. O'Connor
Irving 75039-3510
(214) 869-0303
WATS (800) 2-IRVING

Film Commission of North Texas
3 Dallas Communications Complex
Lock Box N-57
6311 N. O'Connor Rd.
Irving 75039
(214) 869-7657

San Antonio Film Commission
Box 2277
San Antonio 78298
(512) 270-8700
WATS (800) 447-3372
FAX (512) 270-8782

A Brief History of Spain

Acknowledgements

For 300 years of its recorded history, Texas was a large, undeveloped part of the Spanish empire. On the 500th anniversary of Christopher Columbus' contact with the New World, it is appropriate to review the history of Spain to appreciate the role it played in European history during this span. This brief history was written by Mike Kingston, editor of the Texas Almanac. He wishes to express appreciation to Dr. Carolyn Boyd of the University of Texas at Austin and Dr. Donald Chipman of the University of North Texas in Denton for their help in writing this history. Any errors of fact or interpretation are the author's alone.

Prehistoric Spain

Geographical diversity in Spain is so great that it has been called a continent unto itself. Certainly through much of the nation's history, the massive Pyrenees mountains along its northern border with France have served as a barrier, blocking Spain's active participation in the affairs of the rest of Europe.

The interior of the peninsula also is crisscrossed by mountain ranges, broken by river systems and plains. Four of the region's five major rivers — the Duero, Tajo, Guadiana and Guadalquivir — flow westward to the Atlantic. Only the Ebro, in the northeastern corner of Spain, drains to the Mediterranean. Climates vary from the semitropical along the southern and southeastern shores to cooler and more arid in the mountains and on the plains.

Earliest evidence indicates Spain was a crossroads for diverse cultures and a center of improvisation and creativity.

The earliest inhabitants were traditional hunter-gatherers who found the mountainous and well-forested land friendly and productive. Some of humankind's first scientific advances may have taken place on the southern plains of the Iberian peninsula. Chert and quartz fragments found in strata dating to 17,000 years ago have such a similarity to American Indian arrowheads that, if found in a North American context, would be identified as such. If these artifacts are projectile points, Spain may have been a site of development of the bow-and-arrow. The earliest evidence of ancient water-preserved arrow shafts turned up in Denmark and dated at 10,000 years old. Bows, dating to 8,000 years, also are found in Denmark.

Equally impressive is the Paleolithic rock art found in a cave in the foothills of the Cantabrian mountains of northern Spain on the Bay of Biscay. The celebrated Grand Gallery at Altamira was discovered in the summer of 1879 by a Spanish nobleman, Don Marcelino de Sautuola, and his daughter, Maria. An enthusiastic antiquarian, Sautuola busily searched for pottery shards and other artifacts in the newly discovered cave. His daughter looked at the ceiling of the three- to five-foot high chamber and found a series of paintings of various animals. So modern was the style of the illustrations that some scientists immediately labeled them fakes. Sautuola suffered from the allegations of fraud. Only after similar cave paintings were discovered in France following his death was the Spaniard cleared of charges of deception. This early art has been judged to be 15,000 years old.

Not far from Altamira at the El Juyo cave, archaeologists have discovered what is considered to be the oldest religious shrine on record. The 14,000-year-old sanctuary is 118 square feet and appears to have been constructed with the work of many people. It has features not needed for everyday living, and it is associated with a supernatural being, in this case a crudely carved head bearing both manlike and beast-like features. It is appropriate that a land such as Spain, so much of whose modern history has been centered around religion, should be the home of such an ancient shrine.

Like Ireland, England and other European countries, Spain has a series of megalithic monuments that have archaeologists speculating as to their purpose and importance. Some cobbled tombs and massive stone structures have been dated to 4500 B.C. Dolmens — two or more huge stones supporting a horizontal stone roof — are found in the Basque region of the western Pyrenees, and these have been dated to between 4000-2000 B.C.

The purpose of these structures is unknown. Some authorities suggest they were burial sites or religious monuments. Or perhaps boundary markers noting the limits of tribal lands. Similarly, the dolmens could have been used for burial or as dwellings for sheep herders during the summer.

Megaliths fascinate investigators and laymen. In the 19th century, some structures were thought to have been imported to the Western Mediterranean by Near Eastern traders. But some Iberian megaliths are now dated older than those in the eastern Mediterranean. Current thought is that the Spanish megaliths were built by indigenous peoples. The stone monuments can be found at 19 sites on the peninsula. Still unanswered is the major question: For what reason?

During the last Ice Age about 10,000 years ago when sea levels were much lower, the people known today as Iberians crossed at the Strait of Gibraltar from North Africa to populate much of central and eastern Spain.

Expansion of the economy began early. Stock raising developed, with sheep initially raised for milk, fertilizer and mutton. Evidence of wooly breeds of sheep does not show up until after 800 B.C.

Simple irrigation of crops began in the river valleys of southeast Spain about 2200 B.C.

Mining came to mineral-rich southern Spain early in the second millennium B.C., probably on the Rio Tinto, north of present-day Huelva.

About 1200 B.C. archaeological evidence suggests a major change took place in the ancient economy with a move of inhabitants from caves to river valleys with the apparent intention to farm larger plots of land. Positions were taken on high ground near the best lands, and defensive installations were established. Farming was a viable supplement or alternative to hunting and gathering. Meat spoiled soon after a kill, but grains could be kept edible for 20 years. Grain silos are the first large food storage units to be found on the Mesetas (plains).

Large-scale farming also took a technological revolution. Plough teams replaced hoes, which were so efficient for cultivating smaller plots of land in river bottoms. The new farming technique required deep plowing accomplished only with draft animals. Farm implements, however, continued to be fashioned from stone until Phoenician traders brought metal-working technology to the peninsula after the mid-9th century B.C.

Metal was scarce during this period, but nevertheless, the Iberians were quite good artisans. Gold torques found in a pot near Badajoz have been linked in quality to similar jewelry made in Ireland. Indeed some could have been made in Ireland, indicating there was some early trading.

Between 1000-600 B.C., two waves of Celtic peoples entered the peninsula. The first came across the northwest Pyrenees and established themselves in the northwestern peninsula. A second influx four hundred years later made its way into the central portion of the land, where they mixed with the Iberians to form the Celtiberian race that proved formidable adversaries to future invaders.

Another major change in the lives of peninsula inhabitants came with the opening of trade by the Phoenicians in the late 9th and early 8th centuries B.C. Archaeological evidence does not support the classical historical tradition dating arrival of these eastern traders at 1100 B.C. The first evidence of the Phoenician presence comes about 800 B.C. Mineral wealth was the first major attraction to traders. A base was established at Gadir (modern Cadiz), and trading posts were built along the coast and up the Guadalquivir River. The silver mines of the kingdom of Tartessos could be exploited from these colonies.

Phoenician families with ties to the homeland colonized these posts, and the traders operated within two major systems. First, one route ranged from Gadir to Ireland and northwestern Europe. The second developed through colonization of the Spanish coast, where factories were established to manufacture trade goods, like iron objects, cloth, dyes and foodstuffs, for the Phoenicians. About the same time these systems were developed, the Phoenicians also established an emporium, or trade center, in North Africa that was to play a major role in early Spanish history. The princess Dido founded the city of Carthage, the Phoenician word for "New City," a little before 800 B.C. A century later the small port became a major stopover for maritime trade between Spain and the Levant.

Until Assyria's defeat by the Babylonians in 612 B.C., Phoenicians had an exclusive contract to provide Assyrians with raw materials. After Nebuchadnezzar defeated the Assyrians at Tyre, the trade relation was destroyed, and the Phoenicians' role in Spain declined rapidly.

Through the Phoenicians, however, early Spain began the process of "orientalization" with adoption of eastern Mediterranean fashions, cultural values and technologies. After 775 B.C., iron-working, large-scale silver mining, wheel-made pottery, cast-bronze figures, a realistic art style and a host of new religions were adopted in Spain after Phoenician introduction.

Asian Greeks joined the trade in the 7th century B.C., opening a route along the northern Mediterranean. Colonies were established at Emporion about 575 B.C. from Massilia (modern Marseilles) and later at Rhode. Both are on the northeast coast of Catalonia. Greek pottery has been excavated from these sites, and after 470 B.C. Greek coins are found.

The greatest Greek prosperity in Spain probably fell between 450-350 B.C., from which period great quantities of pottery are found. The first coins in Spain were produced at these two Greek colonies after 470 B.C., and the Greeks were the sole issuing agent for coinage for the next 240 years.

The coins were small and unacceptable for large transactions. But they reflected the Greeks' pride of citizenship and were a tribute to the cities' Helenicity.

Classical mentality was unabashedly acquisitive, not productive. People wanted to gain riches to live the good life, not to create capital. Wealth, quite simply, was necessary for one to live well.

With Phoenicia's downfall, Carthage assumed the leadership of the Semitic peoples in the western Mediterranean. Evidence of destruction of inland settlements in the mid-4th century indicates the Carthaginians attempted to push their influence inland. In 348 B.C. Carthage and Rome signed an agreement designating spheres of influence, and one indication of Carthage's dominance in Spain came with the Greeks adopting the Punic measuring system in 290 B.C.

Carthage's defeat by Rome in the First Punic War, which began in 264 B.C., destroyed its navy, and the decline of the trading nation began. Hamilcar, who saved Carthage from the Revolt of the Mercenaries in 241-238 B.C. when the city could not pay its hired army, became commander in chief of the Punic forces. A bitter enemy of Rome, he saw the subjugation of the Iberian peninsula as a way to build trade, to pay off the indemnity to Rome and to set up a staging area for an eventual invasion of Rome. His son, Hannibal, age nine, accompanied him to Spain.

Hamilcar was successful in spreading Carthaginian control over the southern and eastern peninsula, subjugating the Iberian and Celtic tribes. When he died in battle in 229 B.C., another son, Hasdrubal, continued the war until his assassination in 221 B.C. At that time, the army elected 26-year-old Hannibal as its commander in chief.

In violation of its treaty with Carthage, Rome placed the city of Sagunto, near modern Valencia, under its protection. When several pro-Carthaginian leaders were killed, Hannibal besieged the city and eventually destroyed it. The action started the Second Punic War. Rome invaded Spain, but Hannibal began his trek to Italy, leaving his brother Hasdrubal to fight the Roman legions.

In April 218 B.C., Hannibal left New Carthage, ignored the Rome-designated barrier of the Ebro River, crossed the Pyrenees to the Rhone River and then negotiated the Alps to the area of Turin in northern Italy. Victories came quickly and early for the young Carthaginian general. But he eventually became bogged down in Italy.

In Spain, his brother had serious problems with the poorly led Roman army, prohibiting him from joining Hannibal to press the invasion of Rome.

Scipio was selected to head the Roman forces in Spain in 210 B.C., and he set out to destroy the main Punic base at New Carthage. Finally, Hasdrubal's forces were routed, Scipio captured Gadir, and then, crossing the Strait of Gibraltar, Scipio attacked Carthage itself.

Hannibal returned to Carthage in 201 B.C., and the city fell to Scipio a year later, ending the war.

Carthaginian influence in Spain ended with Rome's victory over Gadir (Cadiz) in 206 B.C., which established Roman dominance over the Spanish coast, if not the hinterlands. Rome began pacification of Iberia by colonizing the area at Italica, near Seville, with Roman army veterans.

Under the eastern Mediterranean influence, Spaniards became great urbanists, beginning with the establishment in 600 B.C. of Ullastret, just south of Emporion. By 200 B.C., a visitor to Spain would have been surprised by the number of towns that cropped up. This trend reflected a sophisticated understanding of organization and delegation of power, for each town needed a favorable ecological base, advanced agriculture and technology, and complex social organization.

Though the strips of the eastern and southern coasts of Spain were settled, civilized and cosmopolitan, the remainder of the country was not. That became a challenge for the Romans during the next 200 years: to turn this wild, mineral-rich country into a productive province. They succeeded admirably.

Transition

Spain was a mixed blessing for Rome. Its precious metals, minerals and agriculturally productive land were welcomed. But inhabitants were another matter. Warlike and independent, they caused Roman administrators no end of trouble for the first two centuries of occupation.

The cosmopolitan eastern periphery of the peninsula quickly embraced Rome, as did mining and agricultural areas. Fisheries rivaled agriculture in antiquity and profit, and other exports included wine, honey, oil, linen and horses. Much of Spain, however, was under tenuous control. Among the benefits of Roman occupation were construction of 13,000 miles of roads that aided commerce, as well as expedited military suppression of rebels. About 134 B.C. warlike natives finally were subjugated, bringing peace to the provinces. (Initially, Spain was divided into two provinces. After 14 B.C., there were three, and there were as many as six under later Roman administration.)

Spaniards profited little from the country's minerals. Mining was controlled by the Roman government, and profits left the peninsula. Roman citizenship, with its legal advantages, had to be earned. Under Julius Caesar, army veterans were given land to settle to serve as examples of good citizens for their neighbors and to provide a loyal militia.

Rome's imprint lingers throughout Spain. Mosaics dating from Roman times are preserved in a courtyard of Malaga's Museo de Bellas Artes near the downtown cathedral. Dallas Morning News Photo.

Most Roman rulers simply exploited the land and resources, but maintaining peace was probably more expensive than in other provinces.

Julius Caesar died before instituting broader reforms. Augustus, however, made Spain a full participant in the Roman world. Roman citizenship was extended to many inhabitants, and Spaniards occasionally were brought into the government. Life under the Romans was quiet. By the millennium, only one legion was stationed in the peninsula, and Spanish legions were garrisoned in other areas, notably England.

Roman administration did not prepare Spaniards citizens for self-government. Those with administrative talent were whisked off to Rome, while administrators were imported from Rome. Nevertheless, Romans from Spain rose to the highest ranks of government, such as the emperor Trajan. Most of the artists, philosophers and administrators from Spain, however, were children of Roman officials, not native Spaniards.

Christianity came to the peninsula in the 2nd century — if not earlier as indicated by the legend of Saint James' visit — and permeated society by the 3rd century. As in other Roman provinces, apathy took root in Spain. The Roman grip on the province slipped away unnoticed, replaced by Germanic barbarians. By the early 5th century, only Roman institutions remained. Barbarian Alans, Vandals and Suevi entered Spain for a time, but the Visigoths, the most Romanized of the German tribes, eventually ousted them.

Visigoths, like others on the edge of the empire, thought of themselves as Romans. However, they excelled the Hispanic population only in the application of force. Culturally and economically, the natives were more advanced.

From the late 5th century to the early 8th century, the Visigoths ruled Spain, though they were a minority. Initially religion generated friction. Visigoths were Arian Christians, accepting Jesus as a good man or prophet, not as one with God. Native Hispanics were Trinitarians. When Recared assumed the Visigothic throne in 589 A.D., he, with several Arian bishops, converted to Roman Catholicism. Thereafter, the Hispanic church under the Visigoths became the most vigorous and best educated in Latin Christendom.

Spain was a center for Jewish immigration, and under the Visigoths, persecution of Jews was widespread. In the early 7th century, 80,000 Jews were forcibly converted to Christianity, and many who resisted baptism were tortured, killed or had property confiscated.

Byzantine Emperor Justinian aspired to resurrect the Roman empire. For 70 years in the late 6th century, he occupied a foothold in southeastern Spain and the Balearic Islands. Further expansion into other former Roman land was not accomplished.

Visigoths in Spain failed to adopt a hereditary monarchy. Military skill was the major criterion for Visigothic kingship. The king had to be a visible and successful warrior. Each turnover in leadership could be — and often was — contested by arms, and each administration suffered connivance and intrigue. In one such transition, North African Arabs conquered the region and established a rule that lasted almost 800 years.

The Arab Invasion

In 711, an emancipated Berber slave, Tariq, landed at Gibraltar with 7,000 men and raided for booty. Resistance was so light, the small army essentially captured the Hispanic peninsula, moving almost as far north as the Pyrenees within three years.

While there were sorties into France, the Arabs showed little interest in gaining a foothold in northern Europe past the Pyrenees. Charles Martel defeated an Arab army at Poitiers in 732 to discourage further forays north of the mountains. In 756, Abdul Rahman, the only survivor of the once-powerful Arab Umayyad dynasty, established a strong central government on the peninsula, and over the next two centuries, the Moorish culture of Spain reached its zenith.

Muslim Spain, called al-Andalus, became the most civilized and materially advanced area of Western Europe. Cordoba, a southern Spanish city with dozens of libraries and 900 public baths, emerged as the most splendid city on the continent.

Because Visigothic rule was harsh, many in Spain welcomed the new regime. Jews, in particular, fared better under Muslims, establishing centers of learning in Spain, as well as contributing to the country's rising cultural level.

Christians and Jews were not required to give up their religion, since, under Islam, both were considered "people of the book," having received divine revelation from their shared sacred writings. Conversions were not encouraged, since Muslims were not required to pay taxes. Non-Muslims paid a head tax, and mass conversions would have strained government finances. The first Moorish invaders did not bring women to Spain, and they soon intermarried with the native population. Succeeding generations more quickly adopted the Islamic religion, though Christianity and Judaism remained viable. Christians who adopted the Arab language and manner of dress were called *Mozarabs*.

The Umayyads fended off challenges to their rule, defeating attempted invasions by the Vikings in the 10th century. Spain was the only European country not to fall victim to these seafaring warriors.

Despite replacement of the caliphate of Cordoba with small kingdoms called *taifas* in the 11th century and successive invasions by the Almoravids in the 12th century and the Almohads in the 13th century, the cultural level of Islamic Spain remained high. Though these new rulers from North Africa were more warlike, support for arts and sciences remained high. Translation centers at Toledo and Cordoba brought ancient Greek science and philosophy to Europe through Spain. Writings of Aristotle and Plato were re-introduced and contributed to the development in European science. Arab scientists added their original work to supplement the ancient masters to advance modern science.

The Reconquista

Rise of the *taifas* destroyed any cohesion of government in Spain, though the Umayyad intellectual tradition remained. But the small Christian states of northern Spain gained an opportunity to organize and to pursue what became the *Reconquista*. Led by the hardy men of the Basque and Cantabrian mountains, Spanish Christians began slowly to regain the land conquered by the Arabs.

While feudalism made inroads in northern Europe, the monarchy remained strong among Spanish Christians from the Visigoth tradition. Their king had to be a good warrior, and vassals paid him homage. Resistance to the invaders began in the small states of Asturias and Leon, and slowly the Christians regained lost territory.

During the 11th century, the states of Castile and Aragon emerged. Conquered land was distributed by the kings. Often settlers had to be encouraged to move into the newly regained territory. Special privileges and rights — called *fueros* — were granted to settlers as inducements for settlement on the expanding frontier. As in all frontier societies, these hardy individuals were fiercely independent, a trait that caused future rulers many difficulties. Dealing with the various classes of society — nobility, church and towns — brought a form of representative government to Spain, long before it appeared elsewhere in Europe. The first cortes, or parliament, was established in Aragon in 1162, antedating its English counterpart by more than 130 years. Democratically elected town councils sat in Leon and Castile about 1220. Unfortunately, these forerunners to modern representative government did not survive the assault by a centralized monarchy in future centuries.

Five principal Hispanaic kingdoms, Leon, Navarre, Aragon, Catalonia and Castile, eventually took part in the Reconquest, with Castile becoming the strongest. The kingdom gained its name — "land of castles" — from the practice of fortifying each new frontier as the Reconquest expanded the boundaries of Spain southward. Many such fortresses dotted Castile.

Through the long Reconquest many elements of Spanish culture evolved. Acquisition of land through military support and valor was among these. Indeed, through the centuries, glory gained through military action became a central characteristic, serving Spain well during times of struggle, but distorting the culture in peacetime by holding in contempt such activities as manual labor, commerce and other enterprise.

Under the Visigoths, the Hispanic peninsula was considered a single entity. As the Reconquest progressed, a splintering took place. Aragon emerged as a confederation of small states, and its king ruled under many legal restraints. Alfonso VII was the last emperor of "Castile and all of Spain," dividing the kingdom among his sons at his death. Castile was separated from Leon during this process.

Religion was a major force in the Hispanic society, the unifying element under which northern Spain completed the Reconquest.

In 813 in northwestern Spain, an impressive tomb was discovered that legend said contained the remains of St. James, the brother of Jesus. The saint, it was said, visited Spain in the 1st century, and upon his death, his body was brought back to the peninsula for burial. The cult of St. James, or Santiago, grew when the figure of the saint was seen fighting alongside Spanish troops against the Muslims. The shrine of Santiago de Compostela became a popular destination for European pilgrims and drew attention to the Moorish occupation of Spain. Knights from across the continent, especially France, journeyed to Spain to join in the holy war. Santiago, Matamoros (St. James, Slayer of Moors), became the patron saint of Spain and served as a rallying point around which the Reconquest progressed. Spain, then, adopted a Moorish tactic, operating under an aggressive religious faith.

In the late 10th century, as the rest of the Christian world embarked on an era of Crusades against the Arabs (and sometimes the Eastern Christian world, as well), Christian kingdoms stepped up efforts to regain their peninsula from the infidel.

Religious piety took many forms. Monasticism was strong, and several military orders were organized to pursue the Reconquest. But religion also had a dark side. A precursor of the Inquisition occurred early in 1197 when Pedro II of Aragon ordered all heretics out of the country upon pain of death by fire.

The Reconquest began in 722 with the battle of Covadonga and ended in 1492 with the final defeat of Granada. It did not proceed at an even pace throughout the period. Between the beginning and end, Christian forces often were diverted to fight each other, as were Muslim armies, and on occasion, Christian would join Muslim to fight other Muslims or other Christians.

Moorish military domination of the peninsula ended with the battle of Las Navas de Tolosa in 1212, when Alfonso VIII of Castile led an army manned from Castile, Navarre, Aragon and Portugal. The Spaniards gained the advantage of high ground over the Moors when a shepherd directed them through a hidden pass marked with a cow's skull. (The shepherd received such recognition for the act that he adopted the symbol "head of cow" as his family name — Cabeza de Vaca — and a descendant, Alvar Nunez Cabeza de Vaca, in the early 16th century was one of the first Spaniards to explore the interior of Texas.)

Other old Spanish cities soon were recaptured. Cordoba was retaken in 1236, Valencia in 1238, and Seville in 1248. Only Granada remained in Moorish hands, and it was required to pay heavy tribute until it, too, fell a century and a half later.

Meanwhile, Spain was in the mainstream of European activity. Catalonia, a northeastern province on the Mediterranean Sea, led in the development of banking and finance and operated within the European monetary system. It was the first of the Hispanic states to establish overseas colonies, locating in the "Latin" duchy of Athens in Greece between 1309 and 1388. Concepts such as viceroyalty (a personal representative of the king) and *encomienda* (a labor-distribution system) that eventually were used in the New World were pioneered by the Catalans.

Barcelona's shipyards vied with others in Europe in building the finest ships available. The sciences of astronomy and math were used to improve navigation, and Catalan mariners contributed to the continent's explorations. The plague of the mid-14th century severely damaged Catalonia's economy — as it did most port cities — and struck a blow from which the kingdom recovered slowly.

Early in the Reconquest, Muslims usually left an area conquered by the Christians. Later in the operation, however, they would stay in their homeland, and as the Reconquest was completed, Spain became a pluralistic society with Christians, Jews and Muslims living and working together. Indeed, much of the economy was in the hands of the Jews and much of the skilled and unskilled labor was done by Muslims.

Trade fairs, which controlled international trade and finance in the Middle Ages, were held at several locations in Spain each year.

During the latter days of the Reconquest, Alfonso X (1252-1284) placed a premium on culture. Scholars from across Europe came to Toledo to study. The Greek classics, which had been translated into Arabic, were again translated into Latin, and in that form were made known to the rest of Europe.

Universities had been established in Palencia in 1212 (and later moved to Valladolid) and in Salamanca in 1243.

In the 14th century, Spain's economy developed around sheep-raising, textile industries and some manufacturing. Agriculture was dealt a serious blow with the development of the Mesta, an organization of sheep and cattle raisers, initially in Castile. Often grazing rights were given priority over crops to the detriment of agriculture. But the livestock owners paid more taxes and paid them regularly, giving them greater stroke with authorities.

Castles are a common sight in Castile, which draws its name from the prominence of the structures across its countryside. Most were built during the Reconquista as land was regained from the Muslims. Photo courtesy of the Spanish National Tourist Office.

Spain remained the easiest country in Europe for an individual to advance in social class, for caste and honor were the result of military prowess. Beginning in the 14th century, manual labor came to be viewed as a loss of caste, as did commerce and entrepreneurism in later decades.

As Muslims were defeated and the Spanish states exercised more control over the peninsula, religious toleration declined.

Midway in the 14th century, Spain was struck by the plague, and the economy began to decline. On Ash Wednesday in 1391, an anti-Jewish riot broke out in the Seville, and the Jewish quarter of the city was burned to the ground. The riots spread to other cities, as crowds blamed Jews for many of their problems. Mass conversions were demanded, and for the first time, many Jews complied, abandoning the age-old faith of their fathers. Sources do not agree, and estimates vary wildly, but it is thought that half the peninsula's 200,000 Jews converted, sincerely or otherwise, by the early 15th century. But the evolving religious problems were not solved.

As the 15th century wound down, a marriage between royalty of two Spanish kingdoms forged a united crown and set the peninsula on course for its Golden Age.

The Catholic Sovereigns

Ferdinand and Isabella did not, as is often thought, create a modern state in Spain during their long rule. Their accomplishment was to streamline government, to reduce the power of the nobility and the towns, to improve tax collections, and to reform the Spanish church. And most important, for the first time in centuries, during their reign the crown of Spain was unified.

Under no circumstances, however, did they impose absolutism on the Spanish people. That was left to the Habsburgs. During the late 14th and early 15th centuries, the power of the nobles and the towns was too great for the crown to maneuver freely.

The marriage of Ferdinand and Isabella was one of political necessity. Isabella needed a king to help assert her claim to the crown of Castile, and Ferdinand's father, Juan, required an ally to thwart France's design on his kingdom.

In 1469, the pair wed, but the crowns of the two kingdoms were not formally unified until the death of Ferdinand's father in 1474. There was no joining of institutions, however; each kingdom on the peninsula remained independent, though they shared a common sovereign. The laws of each jurisdiction were observed by the crown. Unofficially, the new sovereigns had spheres of interest. Ferdinand concentrated on foreign affairs and proved so astute that Machiavelli use him as his model for a perfect Renaissance prince in his work, The Prince. Meanwhile, Isabella was concerned with domestic and religious issues.

Early in their reign, Ferdinand and Isabella convinced Pope Sixtus IV to establish an inquisition in Spain to combat heresy. A papal inquisition had operated in Rome in the 12th and 13th centuries. But Ferdinand and Isabella also received papal approval to appoint officials to the Spanish Inquisition, which was to be an office of the state.

Spain was unique among the European nations in that its population included many Jews and Muslims. A forced conversion of Jews — called "conversos" — in the late 14th century produced many nominal Christians, but some conversos only paid lip service to Christianity in public and practiced Judaism in private. These latter conversos — also called "New Christians" — were considered heretics and were the initial target of the Inquisition.

Heresy was at least a two-dimensional problem: First, most Spaniards believed the nation was chosen by God and was following a grand divine design. Any deviation from the principles of the church could bring God's displeasure down on them, either individually or as a nation. Secondly, when a state religion was embraced by a sovereign, heresy also became treason. None of the circumstances created by even the presence of heretics was acceptable. So for most of its 350-year history, the Spanish Inquisition was popular with the faithful, regardless of the criticism it received.

Also, the Inquisition was the first government institution with peninsula-wide authority, and the social position of the accused was of no concern.

The reign of Ferdinand and Isabella launched Spain into its golden age and into prominence in world history. Known as the Catholic Sovereigns for their support of the church, they began the task of unifying the Hispanic peninsula. Ferdinand picture from Culver Pictures; Isabella from Associated Press.

Nobility or peasant, merchant or clergy. All were equal before the inquisitors. The institution became a convenient political tool, as well as a watchdog over standards in belief. The principle of political and religious unity established in Spain in the 15th century became the standard for Europe in the 16th century. Foreigners often were unable to understand the popularity of the Inquisition among the Spanish faithful. Judged by the standards of the times, the Spanish Inquisition was neither cruel nor unjust though it appears brutal and bigoted by today's standards of justice.

In 1480, Ferdinand and Isabella renewed the *Reconquista*, which had been in abeyance since the late 13th century. Only the small kingdom of Granada bordering only on Castile remained under Muslim control, and it had paid tribute to the crown for more than a century.

Early in their reign, Ferdinand and Isabella had to deal with the nobility and the towns. Over the centuries, both groups had been given special rights and privileges in return for services to their kings, and these rights were fiercely defended by both groups. Unlike other areas in Europe, many Spanish towns had their own charters and operated independently of nearby nobles. Elsewhere in Europe, towns often were controlled by the nobility as part of their estate. More than 12,000 towns, villas and hamlets existed in Spain at the beginning of the 16th century.

To restore order in the countryside, the crown supported establishment of the Hermandad, an organization of towns that financed an armed force to combat lawless raids near cities. The Hermandad restored order and balanced the military threat of the nobility.

Political control of the towns also was restored. The office of corregidor was established in important municipalities to represent the crown's interests, particularly in tax collections.

Between 1482 and 1498, the Cortes of Castile was not called to meet. This representative body was not abolished, but subordinated to the crown. Its role was reduced to ratification of action by the crown. But the royal authority was not equal in all kingdoms. Isabella could levy indirect taxes, which she did, without approval of the Cortes in Castile, and thereby weakened the representative body. Ferdinand had to politick Aragon's Cortes for authorization of extra revenues.

Government administration was modernized. Ferdinand and Isabella replaced members of the nobility with highly qualified laymen. This and other reforms resulted in tax collections increasing thirty-fold between 1474 and 1504.

Support of religion by Ferdinand and Isabella did not mean subordination to the papacy. The Spanish church, with its vast revenues, supported much of the *Reconquista*. Ferdinand and Isabella also received permission to levy a special assessment to support the final conquest of Granada. In addition, they obtained the right of approval of papal appointments in Granada, an authority later extended to the New World colonies.

A devout Roman Catholic, Isabella was concerned about the state of the Spanish church. Clergy were poorly educated, and many lived in concubinage. Simony was widespread, and morals generally were low. The queen convinced church officials to allow her confessor (and later Cardinal) Ximenez de Cisneros to reform the mendicant orders, beginning with his own, the Franciscans. Through this and other church reforms, Spanish Catholics anticipated the complaints that gave rise to the 16th century Reformation else-

where in Europe and allowed Spain to stand aloof from the chaos and violence that marked the middle of the century. The reformed Spanish church emerged as an example for other churches in Europe.

1492 was a banner year in Spanish history. Christopher Columbus, with royal backing, established contact with the New World, and four years later, Pope Alexander VI divided the holdings in the western sea between Portugal and Spain. Spain's papal charge was to defeat the enemies of the church and to spread Christianity, a responsibility the nation vigorously pursued.

Politically, two other events surpassed the discovery in immediate importance. First, Granada fell to the armies of Ferdinand and Isabella, making Spain the only Christian nation to regain its territory and restore its previous religion after falling to the forces of Islam. The great energies and ambitions that drove the *Reconquista* within a generation would be turned toward the conquest of the land and souls of the native Americans across the Atlantic.

Further, the Jews were finally expelled from Spain, following the action of England and France in previous years. While the move promoted religious unity, it proved disastrous in later years, for the Jews were the only segment of the Spanish population with the practical experience to manage the complex financial problems that were to cripple the peninsula in the decades to come.

Also, a Spaniard became pope, Alexander VI, the same year, and a Spanish grammar was published in 1492, the first standardization of language taken by any European country.

Pope Alexander VI recognized the contributions of Ferdinand and Isabella to the church in 1496 when he first called them the "Catholic sovereigns."

During their reign, Ferdinand and Isabella had set the stage for what has been termed Spain's "golden age." The nation's army became paramount on the battlefields of Europe and in the Americas; the church's leadership often was directed by Spanish faithful; the intellectuals of the nation provided leadership in literature and science. But there was an Achilles' heel, unrecognized at the time: Ferdinand's arranged political marriages of their children, initially considered so astute, proved both a boon and a curse. The Spanish nation was soon to be caught up in the struggles, intrigues and ambitions of one of Europe's most powerful dynastic families, the Habsburgs.

Ferdinand and Isabella's daughter, Joanna, was married to Philip the Fair of Flanders, grandson of Maximilian, a Habsburg and Holy Roman Emperor. Upon the death of Isabella in 1504, attempts were made to place Joanna on the Castilian throne. But she was obviously mentally ill, and her father, Ferdinand, became regent as was provided in Isabella's will. For a brief time, her husband, Philip, attempted to rule, but he died in 1506. She was incapacitated by grief, and Ferdinand returned as regent, serving until his death.

Joanna's son, Charles, was only 16 at the time, and had never set foot on Spanish soil. But he was named king. Cardinal Ximenez de Cisneros, Isabella's former confessor, sat as regent between the time of Ferdinand's death in January 1516 and Charles' arrival in Spain to assume the throne of Castile in September 1517.

A turbulent, uncertain period followed Charles to the throne, but Spain already had embarked on its golden century in which it was to attain the highest pinnacle of power in the Western world.

Charles V of Flanders (also Charles I of Spain), the grandson of Ferdinand and Isabella, led Spain away from its provincialism and into a role of leadership of 16th century Europe. Picture from Culver Pictures.

Charles V

Spain became a major player on the European stage with the ascension of Charles V to the head of government in 1517. His entry was inauspicious. The 16-year-old grandson of Ferdinand and Isabella was a native of Flanders. He spoke no Spanish and had no Spanish advisers upon taking the throne.

(Charles' European title will be used in this article; in Spain's succession, he is Charles I.)

More responsibility soon rested on his shoulders and eventually on Spain. His paternal grandfather, Maximilian, was the Holy Roman Emperor. Upon his death, the title and responsibilities fell upon Charles V who politicked the title and authority from his brother, Ferdinand, of Austria.

(The Habsburg family was founded by Guntran the Rich in 950 and named for its ancestral seat, Habsburg, or Habichtsburg, or "Hawks Castle." For a time, the family split, but it was reunited in the early 15th century. Several members had led the Holy Roman Empire, which was formed in 800 to resuscitate the "Empire of the West." The empire lost power in the 13th century and finally was dissolved in 1806 when it was feared that Napoleon I might annex the title.)

Spain was uniquely prepared for leadership of the Holy Roman Empire, once Charles V matured in his leadership. Under Ferdinand and Isabella, Spain had become perhaps the best educated country in Europe. Beginning with six universities in 1450, 27 more were opened in the next 150 years. The schools accepted men and women, and women were allowed to lecture in the universities. The printing press also came to Spain in the late 15th century. Before 1500, 725 books were published in 25 towns, far exceeding the 358 printed in England in the same period. Each town with more than 2,000 population had a Latin school of some type, and an estimated five percent of the population was university trained.

With the reform of the Spanish church under Ferdinand and Isabella, Bible study gained importance. In 1517, the first of six volumes of the "Polyglot Bible of Alcala," the initial critical edition of the Holy Bible, was published. Ironically, this publication came the same year that Martin Luther nailed his 95 theses condemning indulgences — abuses and theory — to the church door in Wittenberg. Biblical scholars studied original manuscripts in Hebrew, Chaldean, Greek and Latin in preparing the critical work, with the support of Cardinal Ximenez de Cisneros. And for a brief time (1527-32), Spain was the center of Erasmianism, the humanistic movement that suggested the church should be as interested in human affairs as in heavenly concerns, thus providing an impetus for the Reformation.

As Charles V matured, his appreciation of the talents of his Hispanic subjects deepened, and many became prominent advisers in his administration. Spaniards responded with growing respect and affection for their sovereign, sharing many of his goals and aspirations. Spain was a major player in the game of European politics for the first time, and Spaniards rather liked the limelight.

The king's popularity was enhanced by the economic boom that accompanied his reign. Sales were enormous at Spain's three major trade fairs, Medina del Campo, Villalon, and Medina del Rio Seco. Employment in the silk industry soared. Wool was gobbled up by foreign merchants. On the other hand, Spain, under Charles V, did not impose mercantilist demands on its American colonies, though trade often was restricted to Castile. (England, for example, required its American colonies to buy only goods manufactured in the mother country.) Demands for goods from Spain's American colonies strained the country's industrial capacity (and, indeed, were blamed for the price rise that soon buffeted Spain). Spain's colonies initially showed little interest in starting their own industries to supply their needs, concentrating, instead, on conquest, exploration for precious metals and mining.

The first crisis in Charles' reign came when he left Spain in 1519 to secure the title of Holy Roman Emperor. Cardinal Adrian, as regent, encountered problems when the cities balked at higher assessments for support of the government. Expenses rose when the state provided for defense of newly reconquered Granada, and Charles also required additional revenues for the general operation of government. The etiquette of the court of Burgundy, ostentatious and expensive, also was brought to Spain by Charles. The rituals were designed to impress participants with the power and grandeur of the king and to set the rigid social caste system of the king's servants and subjects. By 1520, the country verged on bankruptcy, and beginning with Toledo, many cities rejected the crown's demands for additional money and took up arms.

Ferdinand and Isabella had sided with the cities in disputes with the nobility in the late 15th century, but Charles' officials got cooperation from the nobility in putting down the so-called "Revolt of the Comuneros," which ended in 1524. If the towns had won the power struggle, Castile could have become Europe's first constitutional monarchy; instead, the revolt pushed the country further toward absolutism.

Financial problems multiplied throughout Charles' reign, as Castile was asked to finance the many wars he fought with France, Protestants in Germany and the Netherlands, and the Turks. As Holy Roman Emperor, Charles envisioned the unity of Europe under a single monarchy — and a single church — as his goal, as well as defense of the realm against the infidel Turks. This view, however, did not stop him from unleashing an unpaid, hungry, angry army on Rome in 1526, which subjected the holy city to the most terrible sack in its troubled history. With the many lands under his sovereignty, Charles V controlled more European territory than any leader between Charlemagne and Napoleon.

The modern concept of budgeting revenues had not evolved. Funds were borrowed at interest rates of 30 percent or more with income from various levies pledged to the retirement of the debt. Genoese bankers provided many loans, and the government sold bonds, called *juros*, to the nobility. Finances continued to be strained even after precious metals from the American colonies began to arrive about mid-century. The Aztecs and Incas were conquered early in Charles' reign, and the Spanish empire in the New World expanded aggressively. Seville became the center for American colonial trade, and commerce was controlled by the *Casa de Contractacion* (House of Trade), which after 1503 supervised trade, operated a school of navigation and collected tariffs. Between 1525-1538, all of Charles' dominions were allowed to trade with the colonies, but thereafter the monopoly was returned to Castile. But Charles simply spent more revenue than came in, and the financial burden was not distributed evenly across the empire. Castile, which assumed the responsibility of developing the colonies, carried the heaviest financial burden by far.

Charles' style of rule was casual. Each country in his domain had a viceroy, and the king travelled almost constantly, never staying in one jurisdiction for long at a time. A councillor form of government was developing, with advisory councils aiding Charles in various areas of interest.

Decline of segments of agriculture contributed to the financial problems. Livestock raisers, organized in the Mesta, prospered and the sheepmen paid a significant share of taxes. Spain suffered a famine in 1506 and imported wheat. After 1520, wheat imports were necessary to meet domestic and colonial demands, and the practice grew throughout the century. The decline of agriculture in the 16th century contributed to a population shift from the north of Castile to Seville in the south, where more economic opportunities existed. Agriculture also required manual labor, which citizens of the peninsula were beginning to consider beneath their dignity. Travelers reported that northern Castile appeared to be abandoned, a vast, empty land.

Importation of other goods also expanded when Spanish industry failed to meet the demands from the colonies. A price spiral stemming from the importation of bullion from the New World drove up wages to effectively reduce Spanish industry's ability to compete with other countries. Since the clergy and the nobility paid no taxes, the king's demands for more revenues fell heavily on industry and on small farmers, further aggravating their problems. (The church, it should be noted, also paid taxes as an institution; only the clergy was exempt from direct taxation.) Only the iron industry in the Basque provinces in the north and the textile manufacturers in Castile prospered. Among other problems elsewhere in the country, craft guilds were supported by the government and blocked modernization by imposing antiquated production methods on some industries. This further weakened the ability of Spanish industry to compete in the world market. One study in the 16th century found that Spain's imports were eight times the levels of its exports, a huge trade deficit by any standard or in any age.

While export of material goods faltered, Spain's distribution of religion was a spectacular success. Under terms of the papal bull that divided the New World between Spain and Portugal, the crown of Castile was charged with spreading the faith, and no missionary, priest or friar entered the New World without permission of the crown. A revitalized Spanish church generated many friars with exceptional evangelical skills. In the 13th century, a Castilian friar, Santo Domingo de Guzman, organized preaching friars into the Dominican order to spread the faith. While the Dominicans were well-known for their role in the operation of the Inquisition, they also spearheaded the evangelical movement of the church in the New World, along with Franciscans and Augustinians. Within a generation, they had accomplished the so-called spiritual conquest of New Spain and other New World provinces. (Later these mendicant orders were joined by another, the Jesuits, also conceived by a Spaniard, Ignatius of Loyola, during the religious fervor that resulted from the Spanish reformation of the church.)

Exploration of the periphery of existing Spanish colonies continued. But the incursions by Coronado in 1541 and by DeSoto in 1539 — both of which covered parts of Texas — were among the last military explorations in the New World.

Concern developed about the harsh and violent tactics of the conquistadors in conquering the native peoples and about their treatment once subjugated. Bartolome de las Casas, a friar who came to the New World as a conqueror and left as a defender of the Indians, raised a loud and learned voice against the military policy. Indeed, even the status of the natives as reasoning, rational beings of equal standing with the "civilized" Spaniards was debated. While de las Casas relied on learning and years of practical experience in working with the native Americans, his principal antagonist, Sepulveda, knew nothing of the natives, but quite a bit about Aristotle, whose theory on "natural slavery" — some people are born to serve; others to be masters — was applied to the natives of New Spain. Charles V in 1550 suspended expeditions in the New World until the questions of status and treatment of the natives were resolved. Much later, natives were recognized as humans, if somewhat innocent by European standards, and the "pacification" of the New World was placed in the hands of the missionaries, with the military used only for protection, as was the case throughout the history of Texas.

In Spain, the Inquisition continued its quest for heretics throughout the kingdoms with the hearty support of Charles, but the institution did not successfully extend its heavy hand to other parts of his domain. Actually, Charles cracked down on Protestants in Germany and the Netherlands only when they became political rebels, as well as religious dissenters. Then he embarked on bloody wars that added to Spain's financial problems. It has been estimated that Charles regularly spent about twice as much as was taken in, and government finance became a major preoccupation for his ministers and for Genoese bankers who came to Spain. When he abdicated, his son, Philip II, received a 20 million ducat debt as a legacy.

Charles V expanded Spaniards' narrow provincialism to a cosmopolitan scope. Spaniards took a more direct hand in the great events of the day in Europe. Confident, well-educated, aggressive, even arrogant, Spain operated with confidence, if not always with wisdom.

Despite the Spanish attitude, Charles was not successful in bringing all of Europe under his reign. The Bourbons of France opposed his every step, and the Protestants rejected the Catholic rule. Despite Charles' piety, relations with Rome often were stormy. The nobility in the Netherlands and in Germany also used the religious ferment to attempt to reassert their dwindling medieval privileges. Charles was at war with France almost continually throughout his reign, attempting to control southern France and then defending Spanish interests in northern Italy against French incursions. In the German states he managed to help his brother subdue the Protestants, but Charles' army fell victim to treachery by a trusted ally, Maurice of Saxony, and limped home defeated.

Charles married Isabel of Portugal, and they had one son to survive infancy, Philip II, who became the greatest of the Spanish monarchs. From birth, young Philip trained for international leadership, and he had an advantage with the Spanish people that his father never enjoyed: He was a native Spaniard and truly loved the country.

Charles V was the first of the kings of the golden age, as Spaniards call the 16th century. He aspired to great goals and was partially successful. If he was slow and unsure of his policy in the New World, it must be remembered that he was among the first to grapple with the many problems of colonial administration on a worldwide basis. For the most part, however, his concerns were with his grand design for Europe, a goal never achieved.

Philip II

Philip II was only 29 years old when in 1556 Charles V abdicated. No sovereign was better prepared for the responsibility. From birth, Philip was trained to rule. Formal education was complemented with daily discussions with his father on policy and government. Beginning with Milan in 1540, the young heir apparent assumed responsibility for parts of the empire. Next, he was invested with the government of Naples and Sicily in 1554, and the Netherlands in 1555, before becoming King of Spain in 1556.

The new sovereign in 1554 married Mary Tudor, the Roman Catholic queen of England. Spaniards and Englishmen shared a mutual distrust, and Philip learned to ingratiate himself with these foreigners.

Under Mary, the English Parliament rescinded all anti-Catholic legislation, and she brutally crushed several abortive anti-Catholic uprisings. Philip, through this turmoil, counseled caution and moderation.

During his term at the English court, Philip became friendly with Elizabeth Tudor, a Protestant, who became queen on the death of Mary, her stepsister, in 1558. He later proposed to Elizabeth, but received no answer. So he married Isabel of Portugal.

France went to war with Spain when Philip took the throne. Surrounded by Spanish territory, the French feared the ambitions of the Spanish crown. But Philip inherited big financial problems. And in 1557, Spain declared virtual bankruptcy, causing a major financial panic. Government bonds, issued in lieu of silver payments, quickly depreciated in value. Lenders also raised interest rates on future loans, aggravating the problem. Despite defeating France on the battlefield, Philip had to agree to the Treaty of Cateau-Cambresis in 1559 when his money ran out.

Philip has been pictured as a cold, calculating, mindlessly ambitious king, intent on expanding the Spanish empire and his personal power by any method necessary. Critics harp on the inefficiency of the colonial system, and interminable delays in the decision-making process.

Much of Philip's energy was devoted to financing government. When he took office in 1556, all the country's revenues through 1561 had been pledged. In the 1570s, when he was fighting the Dutch and the Ottoman Empire on two fronts, he was spending double the average income. Few will blame Philip for showing interest in attempts by an alchemist to turn base metals into gold or silver.

Hopes rose that Spain's mineral wealth, legendary in prehistoric and Roman times, might solve the money problem. Silver was discovered at Guadalcanal, north of Seville, in 1555. But the deposit played out far too soon to help the hard-pressed sovereign.

Practically every revenue-generating device known to government of the day was tried. Government offices were sold to the highest bidder, with an unspoken understanding that officials were to skim a little cream from the top of revenues. Religious offices also were marketed, as were titles of nobility.

The bloom also faded from the Spanish economy, which prospered during the reign of Charles V. But several policy mistakes haunted the realm. Social status, honor and purity of blood became paramount values in Spanish society. No taint of Jewish or Muslim ancestors could be tolerated, although many distinguished Spanish families had just that background, thanks to the forced religious conversions of the previous two centuries. Commerce and manual labor were not considered proper enterprises for ambitious

The Armadas

Europe in the 16th century was ruled by a small clique of families led by the Habsburgs who controlled Spain and the Holy Roman Empire. Philip II's father, Charles V of Flanders (and Charles I of Spain) was the first Habsburg to hold the Spanish throne. The closeness of the leadership made many figures familiar with their adversaries.

Philip II, as the pivotal figure in the last half of the 16th century, had many former friends opposing him. There was William of Orange, leader of the Protestant resistance in the Netherlands. William, born a Lutheran, converted to Catholicism at the insistence of Charles V. The future rebel was a member of the court and a close friend of Philip during their youth.

William rejoined the Protestants when they revolted against Charles and was a continual problem until Philip II, on the sixth attempt, had him assassinated in 1584.

Queen Elizabeth of England was of the same mold. She and Philip II were friends while he was married to her half sister, Mary I of England, and he was king of England. When Elizabeth, a Protestant, gained the throne upon Mary's early death, Philip II proposed marriage. When Elizabeth delayed a response, the Spanish king turned to another bride. Each respected the other during their reigns, though their relationship was marked by mutual animosity.

In 1585, events came to a head. The fight in the Netherlands drained Spanish men and resources. Under Alexander Farnese, Duke of Parma, a subtle politician and a great military tactician, Spanish forces began to regain territory from insurgents. But Elizabeth, who had been providing minor financial aid, sent 5,000 foot soldiers and 1,000 cavalry under Robert, Earl of Leicester, one of her top advisers and military leaders, to aid the Protestant rebels.

Additionally, Francis Drake and other English sea dogs raided the Spanish Main with alarming success, diverting silver from the New World colonies slated to finance Spain's European enterprises.

Capping the series of events, Elizabeth sentenced the Catholic, Mary, Queen of Scots, her cousin and

next in line for the English throne in event of Elizabeth's death, to death after imprisoning her for many years. Mary was tried for her role in a plot to kill Elizabeth. In her will of 1577, Mary gave Philip II her rights to the English throne.

Based on these provocations, Philip II acted. In 1585, the Marquis de Santa Cruz suggested attacking England with a huge armada of 500 ships. Parma, who commanded the finest fighting force in Europe at the time, proposed invading England across the English Channel from the Netherlands. Spain's finances at the time ruled out either plan.

As Elizabeth became bolder, Philip II resurrected the plans into a single operation on a reduced scale. Santa Cruz would assemble the armada, while Parma prepared troops and transportation for the invasion. As conceived by Philip II, the two forces would rendezvous somewhere in the channel, the armada would protect the troop crossing, and Catholics in England would joyously revolt against their Protestant queen.

In 1586, Santa Cruz and Parma began preparations to put the plan into action. Logistics were forbidding. At no time in history had a nation attempted to assemble such a group of ships, outfit it with food and weapons, and coordinate its movements. Santa Cruz faced serious provisioning problems and several times postponed the departure of the armada. Ships were drawn from across the Spanish empire and from other sources. Mediterranean ships, usually of shallower draft and more lightly built than the ocean-faring ships of the Atlantic fleet, were pressed into service.

Philip II had annexed Portugal in 1581, and, with Portugal's navy added to his own, had an impressive fleet at his disposal. Santa Cruz initially wanted 500 ships, but had to settle for less than one-third of that number. As 1588 opened, Philip II was anxious for the armada to take to the sea. In February, Santa Cruz died. Don Alonso Perez, the Duke of Medina Sidonia, was chosen as his replacement. After an impassioned protest of his inability to direct an operation of such magnitude, Medina Sidonia accepted. He was one of

Continued on Next Page

Spaniards. Avenues, other than the military, that were approved and available included service in the church, in colonial administration or in the royal government.

Unlike other European countries, Spain developed no sizable stable middle-class. Once an entrepreneur acquired sufficient wealth, he purchased a title and/or land and withdrew from commerce. Government bonds, so necessary to finance the needs of the crown, attracted money that should have been reinvested in the nation's economy. Most of the crown's share of precious metals mined in the Americas lingered in Spain only long enough to be rerouted to some other European financial center. Colonial revenue ranged from 11 percent of the crown's income in 1554 to 20 percent in 1598. It was never any larger than the income from church sources and much less than extracted from the citizens of Castile. As time went on, a larger percent of the American revenue stayed in the colonies for administration and for public works. Little of the newly generated wealth was pumped into the nation's economic life, and Spain missed the opportunity to build a stable, efficient economic base.

The church and the nobility controlled most of Spain's productive land, and much of the holdings were not used efficiently. Agricultural production increased only by cultivating more land, not from innovation or improved farming techniques.

So the Spanish empire limped on, a marvel of resiliency in a Europe almost totally aligned against it.

Philip II took his role in government seriously. He felt personally responsible to God for the well-being of each of his subjects. Every effort was made to operate the government within the moral teachings of the church, though it is ironical that the Spanish crown's interpretation of these teachings often coincided with the demands of practical politics.

One example of this concern came in 1573 when Spanish colonial policy was changed to allow priests to lead in the pacification of newly contacted natives in the American colonies. The harsh, brutal military tactics that conquered most of the colonies was abandoned, and the army was only to provide protection for the missionaries. Under this policy, the missions of Texas were established in the 18th century.

Although governing with the aid of seven departments, Philip personally made every decision — every one! — whether a minor household matter or a major military strategy. He read and annotated every dispatch and report in his government and then discussed the issues with pertinent advisers. Obviously, the process was time-consuming, and distance compounded the time needed for a decision. Critics quipped that if Spain's bureaucrats administered death, everyone would live to a ripe old age.

From a modern perspective, the administration was inefficient. But Philip II — and to a lesser extent his father, Charles V — was pioneering the first colonial system of worldwide proportions. Indeed, Spain was uniquely qualified for the task, for kingdoms of that country had for centuries operated colonies on a smaller scale. In the 12th century, Catalonia colonized parts of Greece and Sicily and pioneered the use of viceroys as the king's representatives in these territories. Just prior to Columbus' contact with the New World, Spain subjugated the Canary Islands and gained experience in dealing with people of a different, less cosmopolitan culture. (Indeed, with Jewish and Muslim subjects, Spain for a time had been Europe's only multiracial, multicultural country.)

Various land policies used in the New World — such as the *encomienda* in which natives' labor was given Spanish subjects in reward for military contributions — were developed during the *Reconquista*.

Despite the system's many and obvious shortcomings, Spain did control its American colonies for more than 300 years, while England, with far less territory colonized in North America, lost control of its colonies in less than half that time.

While treaties and truces gave Spain some respite from war early in Philip's reign, events in the last half of the 16th century brought turmoil and disaster.

From Previous Page

the wealthiest Spaniards of the day and probably the best administrator, although his military experience at sea was limited.

Once men and materiel were gathered on board ship, it was imperative for the armada to depart, lest food and water spoil and disease break out among the cooped-up personnel. Medina Sidonia took the armada to sea on May 30, and it immediately ran into inclement weather that was to dog the operation until the end.

One hundred and thirty seven ships sailed that day, 109 of them fighting ships and the others supply vessels. More than 1,000 cannons were on board. The ships were manned by 8,000 sailors, and 19,000 soldiers were carried, partly to fight sea battles and partly to reinforce Parma's invasion troops.

By July 18, the armada was ten miles off the coast of Plymouth. Medina Sidonia's instructions from King Philip II were to engage the enemy if attacked, but not to seek out the enemy. The primary goal was to defend Parma's troops as they crossed the channel near Margate. That night the English coastline was ablaze with bonfires, lighted to warn of the long-awaited coming of the Spanish armada.

Much has been made of the strategy of the English and Spanish ships that faced one another in the channel for the next two weeks.

Spanish ships were slower and more heavily loaded than the English, for they fought with a philosophy of land-bound warriors. Their strategy, which had been successful, was to move in close to the enemy ships, catch them with grappling hooks, and board them. Hence, the large complement of soldiers on board. The ships also were constructed with boarding operations in mind. Large "castles" were placed on the fore and aft on the ship to facilitate boarding an enemy ship that is more easily jumped down upon than climbed up onto in combat.

The heavy guns carried by the Spanish ships were accurate only at close range, for they were used just prior to the boarding operations to soften up the enemy.

On the other hand, the English were evolving a new method of sea warfare that would eventually dominate ocean fighting in later generations. But it was not perfected in 1588.

First of all, many of the English ships were longer and sat lower in the water than their Spanish counterparts. They carried as many guns — but of longer range — as the Spanish, and the English ships were not as heavily laden with men, supplies and materiel. Their evolving strategy was to bludgeon enemy ships with long-range artillery, attempting to sink, not capture, the craft. Under no circumstances did the English commanders want to get close enough to the Spanish ships to board. They were lost if they did.

So for more than two weeks, the two forces sparred and battled almost the length of the channel. The English battered the Spanish ships from afar, causing considerable damage to some, but sinking none. Most of the ships lost by the armada in the channel were damaged in accidents or by sabotage. The sleeker, faster English ships adroitly kept their distance, greatly frustrating the Spanish. Introduced by the English Admiral Charles Howard was the line of fire, which later became a standard naval tactic. English ships in a line would pass a Spanish ship, unloading rapid broadsides on the enemy. The tactic wreaked havoc on ships and morale.

On only two days during the conflict did the Spanish have the wind advantage, and on both occasions, the English avoided Spanish attempts to board.

The major breakdown in Spanish strategy came when Parma was unprepared to cross the channel. Many of the flat-bottomed barges built for the operation were unseaworthy and his problems were compounded by a Dutch blockade of the shallows along the coast of the channel. Without aid from the fleet, he could not have left port, and the fleet had no shallow-draft ships to help him. A breakdown in communications was the final nail in the coffin of the grand scheme.

On July 29, the English finally defeated the Spanish off the coast of Graveline, Flanders, but they were stopped from sinking it by a heavy rain squall that struck in the late afternoon. The following morning, a

Continued on Next Page

Muslims in southern Spain revolted against the bad treatment by the central government and received help from religious allies in North Africa. Philip put his illegitimate half brother (on his father's side), Don John of Austria, in command of Spanish forces to put down the revolt in 1570.

For several years, the Turks controlled the Mediterranean, making life miserable for traders in both ends of the sea. After his success with the Muslims in Spain, Don John was given command in 1571 of a multi-national naval force sent to deal with the Turks. At Lepanto, a well-protected bay within the Gulf of Patras on the Adriatic Sea, a Spanish-led armada defeated the Turks in October 1571, ending their dominance of the Mediterranean. Don John later took command of troops in the Netherlands where Protestants fought a determined war with the Spanish monarch. John died of disease during this duty.

Even during the turmoil, Philip pursued a project close to his heart: the construction of Escorial, a combination palace and monastery, near Madrid, the capital of Spain after 1561. From 1563-1584, work continued on the edifice, despite the crown's nagging financial problems.

Interest rates rose to 30-40 percent after the bankruptcy of 1557, and in 1577, Philip again shook up lenders by suspending payments on all loans made after 1560. He was then able to negotiate lower interest rates, which eased financial pressures for another 20 years.

A long-standing truce in the Netherlands broke down after Protestants looted or destroyed 400 churches and monasteries in 1566. The next year, the battle was engaged in earnest, and the war lasted until the Dutch finally won in the mid-17th century.

In 1581, Philip, claiming the throne as the son of a Portuguese princess, was confirmed as sovereign by the kingdom's cortes, reuniting the Hispanic peninsula for the first time in nine centuries. It also was the merger of the world's two largest colonial powers. And, the combined sea forces of the two countries gave the united peninsula the largest navy in the world.

Philip II, groomed from birth for leadership, is considered Spain's greatest king. Associated Press Picture.

Philip tolerated Elizabeth I, even when her ships were pirating Spanish vessels in the Caribbean. But she went too far in 1585 by sending troops, as well as money, to the Netherlands to aid the Dutch against the Spanish.

Almost immediately, Philip began to plot the Invincible Armada (See the feature, **The Armada**, below).

Defeat of the Armada of 1588 was a turning point in Spanish history. Until then, it appeared the Spanish were God's newly chosen people. Invincible at war, creative in verse and prose, among the most pious people in Christendom, they were blessed in all activities. They were indeed pursuing God's will, and He was rewarding them. The Armada's defeat broke this spell. The country did not fall apart; it was too powerful and confident. But small self-doubts began to crack the veneer of the Spanish.

At Escorial, Philip toiled away, reading every report, making thoughtful and prayerful decisions, and running up a staggering debt. By the time he turned the reins of government over to his son, Philip III, debt stood at 100 million ducats, five times the size it had been a half-century earlier when Charles V abdicated.

Spain remained potent and powerful and confident. But the seeds of its destruction were sown and awaiting only another round of deficit spending to flourish.

From Previous Page

fresh wind took the Spanish northward, and Medina Sidonia opted to return to Spain via a route around Scotland and Ireland, rather than try to return through the English Channel. Since the armada had been unable to succeed in its primary task of invading England, Medina Sidonia thought it better to save the ships and not risk further encounters.

In retrospect, the decision was bad. None of the Spanish had experience in the stormy North Sea, nor were they familiar with the coasts of the outlying islands, Scotland or Ireland. Weather was the worst enemy, surpassing the hostility of the English, Scots or Irish. More Spanish ships and lives were lost in the voyage home than in the campaign through the channel. Fewer than 70 ships returned to Spanish ports over the next three months.

Medina Sidonia set a course well west of the Irish coast. None of the ships following the course were wrecked, although some sank from damages sustained in battle or from battering the high winds and heavy seas.

Twenty-six ships wrecked on the Irish coast where bandits may have enticed vessels onto the rocky shores with bonfires. Of 6,000 men on these boats, only 750 returned to Spain. Piracy and salvage were ways of life on the coast, and many survivors were killed by the Irish for their clothes, money and other valuables.

Authorities also executed some 1,500 survivors. English control of Ireland was tenuous, and the threat of seasoned Spanish troops aiding an Irish revolt terrified officials. Richard Brigham, governor of Connacht, alone meted out summary justice to survivors of a half-dozen ships.

On the other hand, some Irish clans welcomed the survivors and saw to their safety. In come cases, the Spaniards were transported across the country and put on boats to Scotland.

Even after the disaster of the armada, Spain had the strongest navy in the world. Philip II immediately began construction of new fighting ships, and Spanish officers reviewed the battle tactics. In coming years, Spain managed to improve protection of its vital treasure fleets traveling from the New World each year.

On the continent, England continued to support Protestant rebels. In 1596, the English again sacked the Port of Cadiz and held the facility for two weeks. A treasure fleet was lost, playing havoc with Philip II's finances. With national pride and finance shocked, preparations began for another armada. Don Martin de Padilla Manrique commanded, but his luck was bad. King Philip ignored warnings of bad weather in the channel in November and launched the fleet on Oct. 24. Four days after leaving Lisbon, bad weather scattered the fleet, destroying 32 fighting ships and drowning 3,000 men.

The following year, another armada was launched in an operation that was the best kept secret of the 16th century. Falmouth was the objective, a port where troops could be landed. England was caught totally unaware, and some reports tell of Spanish troops actually taking and holding positions for two days near Falmouth. But another fall storm scattered the fleet, and when support failed to arrive, the troops left. This story is discounted by many historians because English records don't speak of it.

Ireland and Spain share a special feeling, both bitter enemies of England with a common, intense devotion to Roman Catholicism. In 1596, Hugh O'Neill Earl of Tyrone, began urging Philip II to invade Ireland and aid in a rebellion against Elizabeth. Under her reign, England began a systematic destruction of the Celtic culture of Ireland.

When Philip II died on Sept. 13, 1598, his son, Philip III, took the throne. When Tyrone started a rebellion, immediate preparations began for an invasion of Ireland. Plans were to land troops, which would be periodically supplied by sea. No plans were made for a Spanish naval presence.

Troops were landed, but the Irish rebels were unreliable. Eventually a truce was called, and the Spanish returned home. In 1604, the hostilities between England and Spain ended. Spanish hegemony in Europe was intact for another four decades, but its monopoly in the Caribbean was ended. Spanish sea power was unable to defeat a determined English defense and the weather.

The Long Decline

Spain's decline as the leading world power in the 17th century was not precipitous, though it became apparent to friends and foes alike as the century wore on.

Philip II died in 1598, leaving his son, Philip III, with a mountain of debt and hostile nations at all borders. War had exhausted the nation.

Philip III — sometimes called the "laziest" king of Spain ever — had none of his father's strength of character or his dedication to his subjects and their government. Where Philip II personally conducted the business of government from Escorial, his son turned the reins of power over to his favorite, or first minister, Marquis of Denia, Duke of Lerma, whose early successes later were buried beneath failure and scandal. Lerma extricated Spain from its difficulties with the Netherlands with an unfavorable 12-year truce. Upon the ascension of James I after the death of Elizabeth I in 1603, Spain's relations with England improved immediately and remained cordial.

To overcome some of the financial problems, Philip III debased the money supply with the introduction of copper coinage. In 1609, he expelled the Moriscos (converted Muslims) to the detriment of large parts of Spain where they provided the manual labor and technical expertise to keep the economy running.

Religion and intellectual life were in a slow decline. Philip II in 1559 had banned Spaniards from studying in foreign universities, where heretical ideas (heretical to Spain, at least) were rampant. This isolation took its toll on the creativity of Spaniards, and additionally, the Inquisition, by enforcing a narrowness of thought in a vain attempt to freeze a moment of the nation's culture in time, reduced the energy of the clergy and led to its decline during the century, although its numbers increased.

At the same time, the church benefited from inspired leadership during the century. Three Spaniards, St. Theresa, who had replaced Santiago as Spain's patron five years earlier, St. Ignatius of Loyola, and St. Francis Xavier were canonized.

Lerma fell from power in 1618, disgraced by scandal and suffering from policy failures. In the same year, Spain entered the Thirty Years' War, a series of conflicts mostly involving religion, that lasted until 1648. Philip III died three years later, succeeded by his 16-year-old son, Philip IV.

Philip IV relied on his favorite, Don Gaspar de Guzman, the Count-Duke of Olivares, to run the government. Their relationship, however, was much closer than that of Lerma and Philip III, for Olivares prompted the king to assume a leading role in the government. Olivares properly saw that the decentralized administration of Spain, with poor tax collection and begrudging cooperation from the member kingdoms, was weak. But Olivares' attempted centralization did little to improve government and actually provoked secession by Catalonia in 1640 and by Portugal a year later. Catalonia later returned to the fold; Portugal did not. In the Treaty of Munster, which ended the Thirty Years' War in 1648, Spain recognized the independence of the Netherlands.

Foreign trade declined through most of the century, and the drop in colonial trade did not end until mid-century. Previously the colonial trade was based on mining and Castilian agriculture. As the colonies expanded away from mining into agriculture, trade demands changed, and Spain's industry could not meet the demand. Consequently, Spain's financial condition was never stable. In 1627, payments to bankers again were suspended in another of the so-called bankruptcies — actually a conversion of debt, for bankers were given juros, or government bonds, in lieu of payment in silver — that the government faced about every 20 years. A year later, the American treasure fleet was captured, depriving the government of anticipated revenue and further complicating its finances.

Upon Olivares' death in 1645, Philip IV took personal control of the government, operating more in the style of his grandfather, Philip II, although without the positive results. Philip IV was not successful. Only slowly did the kingdom begin to regain confidence. The intellectual decline of the nation lapsed it behind the northwestern European states. In a period when the intricacies of commerce and the virtue of hard manual work were extolled in developing nations, Spaniards maintained a devotion to militarism and a disdain of manual labor. Economically, scientifically and intellectually, Spain fell irrevocably behind its European rivals. And the spirit of the people also suffered a serious erosion of the self-confidence that was masked by arrogance throughout the Golden Age of the previous century.

Philip III devoted much time to the pleasures of court, as did his son, Philip IV for a time. At one point, Philip IV asked Mother Maria de Jesus de Agreda, mother superior of a convent and a confidant, to have her nuns do penance for his sins. Though Mother Maria pointed out it was customary for the penitent to do the penance for himself, the request stood. (Mother Maria is the famous "Woman in Blue" who is said to have preached to Texas Indians in the 18th century through so-called bilocation, without leaving Spain.)

In 1625, Castile's Cortes complained that 9,000 monasteries were operated in the province (and probably as many convents) involving up to 200,000 clergy. The church became a refuge for the lesser sons of the nobility, and an acceptable career for other Spaniards during the century.

Despite Spain's many problems, it maintained and expanded a worldwide empire in the 17th century. For example, Santa Fe, N.M., and Jamestown, Va., were established within a few years of each other. But Santa Fe was the 200th town established by the Spanish in the New World, while Jamestown became Great Britain's first permanent settlement. Often Spain has been criticized for the inefficient operation of its colonial system. But Spain actually was the first of the great colonial powers and had no experience upon which to base policy. It is amazing not that Spain was so inefficient, but that it did so well and lasted so much longer than anyone thought possible.

Charles II followed his father, Philip IV, to the throne in 1665 at the age of four. His reign, the last of the Habsburg line in Spain that began more than a century earlier, was distinguished only as the golden age of the privileged classes. Charles died in 1700 with no successor, and he willed the throne to his grandnephew, Philip of Anjou, who was the grandson of Louis XIV of France. Fearing a union of the two powers, Great Britain, the Netherlands, Austria, Prussia and most of the German states entered into a coalition against France and Spain in 1701. The war — called the War of Spanish Succession — lasted until 1713, when Philip V won recognition of his claim to the Spanish throne, but gave up any claim to the throne of France.

Philip V was the first of the Bourbon dynasty that was to perk Spain's spirit and to almost return it to the pinnacle of European leadership before disaster again overtook the nation.

Resurgence

Spain reached the nadir of its decline under Charles II, but the seeds of recovery also were sown. Catalonia began an economic recovery in the last decades of the 17th century, though Castile remained mired in a morass of bad planning and poor citizen morale.

Once Philip V, a Bourbon, attained power and settled with his enemies, he undertook the task of modernizing and centralizing Spain's government. When the reorganization was complete, Spain, for the first time since the days of the Roman occupation, was under a single administration. France was the model. Catalonians rebelled against the changes, and they suffered for a generation after Philip put down the revolt.

For 20 years before his death in 1746, Philip V was intermittently insane. Two sons died after succeeding him on the throne. Luis I served less than a year before his death in 1724, and Philip reassumed the throne. Fernando VI followed his father to the throne in 1746.

Fernando suffered from a mental disability similar to his father's during his reign from 1746 to 1759. Nevertheless, Fernando's major accomplishment was to keep Spain at peace for more than a decade.

Charles III, son of Philip V and Isabel Farnese, succeeded Fernando VI. Charles served an apprenticeship as king of Naples, never expecting an opportunity to rule Spain because of the two older stepbrothers.

The new sovereign began a revival of Spain through changes in government and improvement in education. He upgraded the caliber of men appointed to positions in the church and in colonial administration. Jose de Galvez, one of the many professional men employed by the king, became famous in Texas history through his survey of the Spanish presidios across the northern boundary of New Spain. Upon Galvez' recommendations, several presidios in Texas were closed and part of the population relocated.

Charles III joined France against Great Britain for the final two years of the Seven Years' War. When Britain won in 1763, Spain lost Uruguay and Florida but gained the Louisiana Territory from France. (For Texas this was a bad turn of events. The region's role had been that of a frontier area, and it thereby got attention from colonial administration. With Spain's eastern colonial boundary moving to the Mississippi River, Texas was simply a big open region meriting little attention. During this period, the capital of Texas actually was located at Los Adaes presidio, near present-day Natchitoches, La.)

To solve economic problems, Charles III established factories in the interior of Spain and convinced the craft guilds to loosen restrictions on young workers. Internal tariffs were reduced or eliminated. Agricultural reform was attempted for the first time in history during the 1760s, and food production increased when additional land was placed in production.

Spaniards accepted the monarchist paternalism of their government, and agitation for representative government on the peninsula did not begin until late in the century. The Enlightenment was slow in coming to Spain, but its ideas received support by a small, but influential, minority. Most Spaniards and the king still supported the work of the Inquisition, which punished more than 10,000 people during Philip V's 45-year reign. The Enlightenment also reached the colonies during Charles' reign and set the stage for a colonial revolt in the following century.

Food riots broke out in major Spanish cities in 1766 and caught the crown's attention. Changes were made. But blame for the riots had to be assessed, and the scapegoat turned out to be the Jesuits. The religious order was banished from the Spanish empire in 1767, affecting about 10,000 clergy. Later the order was reinstated and then banished again.

Under Charles, Spain played a significant, if not well-known, role in the American revolution. Charles did not commit troops, but Spain controlled the Mississippi valley and kept the British occupied in Florida. Additionally, the crown instructed Spanish officials, like Bernardo de Galvez, Jose's nephew, to cooperate with the Americans. Galvez saw that cattle from Texas were driven to the Mississippi to feed revolutionaries. By tying up British troops in Florida, Spain prevented Great Britain from giving its full attention to the uprising in the northern American colonies.

Charles' drive to make Spain more rational, more orderly, better educated and more productive was rewarded by a growing prosperity in the late 18th century. In the American colonies, an expanding creole class established itself as a society that could stand without Spain. During Charles' reign, there were an estimated 17 million Spanish subjects in the Americas, while the population of the peninsula was about 10 million. The tail was wagging the dog, and the seeds of revolt were sowed.

At his death in 1788, Charles' Spain was still backward, compared to its European contemporaries, but it was doing much better, having regained respect in international affairs. The nation had enjoyed the most enlightened and most prosperous reign of a king in modern Spanish history. Historians rank Charles III second only to Philip II in Spanish history.

Unfortunately, Spain's luck did not last long, for disaster was just a few decades away.

Divorce

The reigns of the two successors to Charles III were periods of chaos and dismemberment within the once powerful Spanish empire.

Charles IV, who succeeded his father in 1788, was a weak sovereign and fearful of political forces unleashed by the French Revolution. When Louis XVI of France was executed in 1792, Don Manual Godoy was chosen by Charles to lead the Spanish army against the new republic. France fought back with surprising energy and success, and by 1795 occupied towns in northern Spain and forced a truce. At the same time, Spain was in almost permanent war against the British. In 1796, France and Spain aligned against Britain, and two years later, Spain went to war with Portugal, Britain's closes ally on the continent. By 1808, these wars had run their courses, and Spain remained friendly with France, hoping to protect its American colonies.

Ferdinand VII took the throne on the abdication of his father, Charles IV, in 1808. Ferdinand was a weak leader, and on a visit to France, Napoleon made Ferdinand and his father renounce their claims to the Spanish throne. Napoleon then proclaimed his brother, Joseph, king of Spain.

When Joseph entered Spain, accompanied by French troops, the first true people's revolution in European history commenced. Spain's lower classes took to the offense with a guerrilla campaign that harassed the invaders, and the nobility and upper classes served in the regular army. By 1813, with help from the British and the Portuguese, the French and King Joseph were driven from Spain. The nation's infrastructure had been badly damaged and hard economic times were ahead.

Turmoil buffeted Spain. A representative cortes was organized by townspeople from across Spain and met in Cadiz in 1812. The liberals wrote a constitution setting up a monarchy answering to the people. While the American colonies were recognized as part of Spain, they were not given proper representation. Fears of the Spanish colonial Americans that they would have little role in the Spanish government were confirmed. Revolutions erupted throughout the colonies. Father Miguel Hidalgo had fired Mexicans' imagination with his revolt in Dolores in 1810. (In 1813, the so-called Green Flag Rebellion was staged in Texas, only to be put down by the Spanish army.)

The Spanish Americans were right. The colonies were only on the verge of the consciousness of Spaniards, who could not understand why the Americans would abandon the many benefits of Spanish rule. The attitude never changed, and Spaniards often thought that the people of the Americas never really wanted to withdraw from the empire.

Fernando returned to Spain in 1814 and declared the constitution null and void, being unwilling to abandon the crown's absolutism.

Spain was in constant political flux between 1811-1820, but no matter who was in charge, there was little change in the policy toward the colonies. In this period, 30 military expeditions were organized and sent to the colonies. More than 47,000 men and officers left the peninsula. Spaniards could not imagine why the colonists were dissatisfied with their lot in the empire and would not accept their legitimate desire for self-government.

Shortly before the empire crumbled in the Americas, Spanish officials tried to implement policies to attract settlers to its vast underpopulated lands in North America. A former Spanish subject, Moses Austin, received approval to bring 300 families into the land. But Mexico achieved independence before Austin could bring people in. His son, Stephen F. Austin, took up the project after his father's death and made his way into North American history as one of the greatest early pioneers.

Mexico broke away from the Spanish empire in 1821, and with the divorce, Texas slipped from under the Spanish yoke. Spain moved on to more troubled times, but the first of the great colonial empires had left its mark on the land and the people of Texas extending even until today.

Bibliography
For "A Brief History of Spain"

Aveling, J.C.H., **The Jesuits;** Stein and Day, New York, 1981.

Beeching, Jack, **The Galleys of Lepanto;** Charles Scribner's Sons, New York, 1982.

Boxer, C.R., **The Church Militant and Iberian Expansion,** 1440-1770; The Johns Hopkins University Press, Baltimore, 1978.

Braudel, Fernand, **The Mediterranean and the Mediterranean World in the Age of Philip II, Vols. I & II;** Harper Calophon Books, Harper & Row, New York (English translation), 1972.

Castro, Americo, **The Spaniards: An Introduction to Their History;** University of California Press, Berkeley and Los Angeles, 1971.

Chudoba, Bohdan, **Spain and the Empire,** 1519-1643; Octagon Books, A Division of Farrar, Straus, Giroux, New York, 1977 (1952 reprint).

Clendinnen, Inga, **Ambivalent Conquests: Maya and Spaniard in Yucatan,** 1517-1570; Cambridge University Press, Cambridge, 1987.

Collins, Roger, **The Basques;** Basil Blackwell Ltd., Oxford, UK, 1986.

Collins, Roger, **Early Medieval Spain: Unity in Diversity,** 400-1000; St. Martin's Press, New York, 1983.

Cook, M.A., ed., **A History of the Ottoman Empire to** 1730; Cambridge University Press, Cambridge, 1976 (1980 reprint).

Costeloe, Michael P., **Response to Revolution: Imperial Spain and the Spanish American Revolutions,** 1810-1840; Cambridge University Press, Cambridge, 1986.

Crow, John A., **The Epic of Latin America (3rd Edition);** University of California Press, Berkeley and Los Angeles, 1980.

Crow, John A., **Spain: The Root and the Flower;** University of California Press, Berkeley and Los Angeles, 1962, 1975, 1986.

Davies, R. Trevor, **The Golden Century of Spain, 1501-1621;** Greenwood Press, Westport, Conn., 1984 (1937 reprint).

Defourneaux, Marcelin, **Daily Life in Spain in the Golden Age;** Stanford University Press, Stanford, Calif., 1966.

Durant, Will, **The Reformation: The Story of Civilization;** Simon and Schuster, New York, 1957.

Elliott, J.H., **Imperial Spain,** 1469-1716; New American Library, New York and Scarborough, Ont., (no date).

Elliott, J.H., **Spain and Its World,** 1500-1700; Yale University Press, New Haven, 1989.

Elliott, J.H., **The Count-Duke of Olivares: The Statesman in an Age of Decline;** Yale University Press, New Haven, 1986.

Elton, G.R., **The Reformation: The New Cambridge Modern History;** Cambridge University Press, Cambridge, 1958.

Fallon, Niall, **The Armada in Ireland;** Wesleyan University Press, Middleton, Conn., 1978.

Fernandez-Armesto, Felipe, **The Spanish Armada: The Experience of War in 1588;** Oxford University Press, New York, 1988.

Goldstein, Thomas, **Dawn of Modern Science: From the Arabs to Leonardo da Vinci;** Houghton Mifflin Co., Boston, 1980.

Goodman, David C., **Power and Penury: Government, technology and science in Philip II's Spain;** Cambridge University Press, New York and Cambridge, 1988.

Graham, Winston, **The Spanish Armadas;** Doubleday & Co., Inc., New York, 1972.

Haliczer, Stephen, **The Comuneros of Castile: The Forging of a Revolution,** 1475-1521; University of Wisconsin Press, Madison, 1981.

Hanke, Lewis, **Aristotle and the American Indians: A Study in Race Prejudice in the Modern World;** University of Indiana Press, Bloomington and London, 1970 (1959 reprint).

Harrison, Richard J., **Spain at the Dawn of History: Iberians, Phoenicians and Greeks;** Thames and Hudson, Ltd., London, 1988.

Hauben, Paul J., ed., **The Spanish Inquisition: A Crucible of National Values;** John Wiley and Sons, Inc., New York, 1969.

Hay, Denys, ed., **The Renaissance,** 1493-1520: New Cambridge Modern History; Cambridge University Press, Cambridge.

Howarth, David, **The Voyage of the Armada: The Spanish Story;** Penguin Books, New York, 1982.

Hull, Anthony H., **Charles III and the Revival of Spain;** University Press of America, Washington, D.C., 1980.

Hume, Martin A.S. (edited with notes by Henry Ketcham), **Philip II of Spain;** Haskell House Publishers Ltd., New York, 1969 (1897 reprint).

Kaman, Henry, **Spain,** 1469-1714: A Society in Conflict; Longman Group Ltd., Essex, England, 1983.

Lalaguna, Juan, **A Traveller's History of Spain;** Interlink Books, Brooklyn, 1990.

Lea, Henry Charles, **The Moriscos of Spain: Their Conversion and Expulsion;** Haskell House Publlishers Ltd., New York, 1968 (reprint 1901).

Lewis, Bernard, **The Muslim Discovery of Europe;** W.W. Norton & Co., New York, 1982.

Lunenfeld, Mavin, **The Council of the Santa Hermandad: A Study of the Pacification Forces of Ferdinand and Isabella;** University of Miami Press, Coral Gables, Fla., 1970.

Lynch, John, **Spain Under the Habsburgs, Vols. I & II;** New York University Press, New York, 1984.

Mansfield, Peter, **The Arab World: A Comprehensive History;** Thomas Y. Crowell Co., New York, 1976.

Mattingly, Garrett, **The Armada;** Houghton Mifflin Co., Boston, 1959.

Meinig, D.W., **The Shaping of America: A Geological Perspective on 500 Years of History, Vol. I;** Yale University Press, New Haven and London, 1986.

Moscati, Sabatino, Director, **The Phoenicians;** Abbeville Press, New York, 1988.

Nowell, Charles E., **The Great Discoveries and the First Colonial Empires;** Greenwood Press, Westport, Conn., 1982 (reprint 1954).

O'Callaghan, Joseph F., **A History of Medieval Spain;** Cornell University Press, Ithaca, N.Y., and London, England, 1975.

Pardo, Antonio (translated by David Macrae), **The World of Ancient Spain;** Minerva, S.A., Geneve, 1976.

Parry, J.H., **The Spanish Seaborne Empire;** University of California Press, Berkeley, 1966 (1990 paperback).

Parry, J.H., **The Age of Reconnaissance: Discovery, Exploration and Settlement 1450-1650;** University of California Press, Berkeley and Los Angeles, 1963.

Payne, Stanley, **A History of Spain and Portugal, Vols. I & II;** University of Wisconsin Press, Madison, 1973.

Payne, Stanley, **Spanish Catholicism: An Historical Overview;** The University of Wisconsin Press, Madison, 1984.

Peters, Edward, **Inquisition;** The Free Press, A Division of Macmillan, Inc., New York, 1988.

Pfeiffer, John E., **The Creative Explosion: An Inquiry Into the Origins of Art and Religion;** Harper & Row, New York, 1982.

Ranke, Leopold, **The Ottoman and the Spanish Empires, in the Sixteenth and Seventeenth Centuries;** Whittake and Co., London, 1975 (1843 reprint).

Renfrew, Colin, ed., **The Megalithic Monuments of Western Europe;** Thames and Hudson, Ltd., London, 1981.

Roth, Cecil, **The Spanish Inquisition;** Norton Library, W.W. Norton & Co., New York, 1967 (1937 reprint).

Soren, David; Aicha Ben Abed Ben Khader and Hedi Slim, **Carthage: Uncovering the Mysteries and Splendors of Ancient Tunisia;** Simon and Schuster, New York, 1990.

Sutherland, C.H.V., **The Romans in Spain;** Greenwood Press, Westport, Conn., 1982 (reprint).

Veliz, Claudio, **The Centralist Tradition of Latin America;** Princeton University Press, Princeton, N.J., 1980.

Webber, Carolyn, and Aaron Wildavsky, **A History of Taxation and Expenditure in the Western World;** Simon and Schuster, New York, 1986.

"Weather Highlights" from Page 113.

County. Tornadoes touched down in Hillsboro and Belton, Hill and Bell Counties, causing heavy damage to barns and sheds. More than 4 inches of rain accumulated in 90 minutes in Garland, Dallas County, causing extensive flash flooding. One fatality occurred when a man was swept off the roadway. Total damage estimates from flash flooding in Dallas County were $7.6 million.

April 24-26, 1990: Severe thunderstorms hit many areas of Texas during the three-day period. Three tornadoes touched down in Parker County causing damage to several homes. Winds were estimated at 80 mph in Alvord, Wise County. Meanwhile, 15 inches-18 inches of rainfall were reported in Comanche and Brown Counties. Two fatalities due to flash flooding occurred in Brownwood, Brown County. On the 26th, 3-inch rainfalls in the Dallas and Houston metro areas caused severe flooding, while wind gusts of 112 mph were reported at Laughlin Air Force Base, Val Verde County. In Caldwell, Burleson County, 13.04 inches of rain fell in 10 hours. Flash flooding killed three people in Sunray, Moore County, when their car was washed off the highway. In Hood County homes were reportedly flooded to a depth of greater than 4 feet. The largest official rainfall reported on the 25th-26th was 14.96 inches at De Leon, Comanche County.

April 27, 1990: Another outbreak of severe thunderstorms moved across the state bringing funnel clouds and one tornado near College Station, Brazos County, and spawning at least four more tornadoes near Houston, Harris County. Two tornadoes were seen in Limestone County while baseball-sized hail fell in Mexia. Parker County was declared a disaster area by Gov. Clements because of an oil spill, tornado, and flooding that all occurred during the month. An estimated $20 million in damage from the storms were reported in Houston.

May 1990: The pattern of heavy rainfall events that started in late April continued into May throughout most of North Central and East Texas, causing extensive flooding along the Red River and Trinity River, as well as many other smaller creeks and rivers. Three fatalities occurred in Tarrant County when swift flowing waters swept cars off roadways. Overall, 12 people were killed because of rising flood waters. The Trinity River set a new depth record of 19.9 feet at Liberty, Liberty County, breaking the previous record of 29.3 feet in 1908. In Houston County, 50,000 acres of land were under water, as was land in many other counties in East Texas. The 1,200 oyster fishermen in and around Galveston Bay lost an estimated $12 million. Total damage to agriculture and land alone was estimated to be near $700 million, with total damage probably topping $1 billion. Over 50 counties were declared disaster areas, making the floods of 1990 some of the most severe in Texas' history.

August 15-31, 1990: A ridge of high pressure became stationary over the state on the 15th, allowing hot, dry air from Mexico to push maximum temperatures over 100 degrees F at many locations. By the 22nd, the entire state, except for the Upper Coast, had maximum temperatures between 95 degrees F and 105 degrees F. Waco, McLennan County, was the hot spot for the state, with an average maximum temperature of 100.1 degrees F for the month. Waco also set five record high maximum temperatures, including a 109 degrees F reading on the 31st.

September 16-18, 1990: A cluster of heavy thunderstorms remained nearly stationary over portions of the Edwards Plateau from the evening of the 16th to the early morning hours of the 18th. Total rainfall amounts ranged from 4 inches-7 inches. Oak Creek Lake, Coke County, received 6.31 inches. Sonora, Sutton County, received 6.35 inches, and the Duncan Wilson Ranch, Schleicher County, recorded 5.21 inches. Many secondary roads and low-water crossings were impassable due to flash flooding.

December 21-24, 1990: The arrival of cold, arctic air in Texas on the 21st caused temperature drops of 40 degrees F — 50 degrees at many locations. In fact, some single-hour temperature drops of 15 degrees F — 20 degrees F were not uncommon. Numerous minimum temperature records were broken on the 23rd, including a -6 degrees F minimum at Amarillo, Potter County. The lowest minimum was -12 degrees F at Bravo, Hartley County. Thirteen deaths were caused by icy road conditions resulting from the freezing rain and snow accompanying the cold air outbreak.

"Destructive Weather" from Page 116.

been blown away. Celia caused 11 deaths in Texas, at least 466 injuries, and total property and crop damage in Texas estimated at $453,773,000. Hurricane Celia crossed the Texas coastline midway between Corpus Christi and Aransas Pass about 3:30 p.m. CST on Aug. 3. Hardest hit was the metropolitan area of Corpus Christi, including Robstown, Aransas Pass, Port Aransas and small towns on the north side of Corpus Christi Bay.

June 12-13, 1973: **Rainstorm.** Southeastern Texas. Ten drowned. Over $50 million in property and crop damage. From 10-15 inches of rain recorded.

Nov. 23-24, 1974: **Flash Flooding.** Central Texas. Over $1 million in property damage. Thirteen people killed, ten in Travis County.

June 15, 1976: **Rainstorm.** Harris County. Rains in excess of 13 inches caused damage estimated at near $25 million. Eight deaths were storm-related, including three drownings.

Aug. 1-4, 1978: **Heavy Rains, Flooding.** Edwards Plateau, Low Rolling Plains. Remnants of **Tropical Storm Amelia** caused some of the worst flooding of this century. As much as 30 inches of rain fell near **Albany** in Shackelford County, where six drownings were reported. **Bandera, Kerr, Kendall** and **Gillespie counties** were hit hard, as 27 people drowned and the damage total was at least $50 million.

Dec. 30-31, 1978: **Ice Storm.** North Central Texas. Possibly the **worst ice storm** in 30 years hit Dallas County particularly hard. Damage estimates reached $14 million, and six deaths were storm-related.

April 10, 1979: The worst single **tornado** in Texas' history hit **Wichita Falls.** Earlier on the same day, several tornadoes hit farther west. The destruction in Wichita Falls resulted in 42 dead, 1,740 injured, over 3,000 homes destroyed and damage of approximately $400 million. An estimated 20,000 persons were left homeless by this storm.

In all, the tornadoes on April 10 killed 53 people, injured 1,812 and caused over $500 million damages.

May 24-25, 1981: Severe **flooding** in **Austin** claimed 13 lives, injured about 100 and caused $40 million in damages. Up to 5.5 inches of rain fell in one hour just west of the city.

April 2, 1982: A **tornado** outbreak in Northeast Texas. The most severe **tornado struck Paris;** 10 people were killed, 170 injured and 1,000 left homeless. Over $50 million in damages resulted. A total of 7 tornadoes that day left 11 dead and 174 injured.

Aug. 15-21, 1983: **Hurricane Alicia** was the first hurricane to make landfall in the continental U.S. in three years (Aug. 18), and one of the costliest in Texas history ($3 billion). Alicia caused widespread damage to a large section of Southeast Texas, including coastal areas near **Galveston** and the entire **Houston** area. Alicia spawned 22 tornadoes, and highest winds were estimated near 130 mph. In all, 18 people in South Texas were killed and 1,800 injured as a result of the tropical storm.

Storms in 1985 and 1986 can be found in Weather Highlights for those years.

Jan. 12-13, 1985: A record-breaking snowstorm struck West and South Central Texas with up to 15 inches of snow that fell at many locations between San Antonio and the Rio Grande. San Antonio recorded 13.2 inches of snow for Jan. 12 (the greatest in a day) and 13.5 inches for the two-day total. Eagle Pass reported 14.5 inches of snow.

June 26, 1986: Hurricane Bonnie made landfall between High Island and Sabine Pass around 3:45 a.m. The highest wind measured in the area was a gust to 97 m.p.h., which was recorded at the Sea Rim State Park. As much as 13 inches of rain fell in Ace in southern Polk County. There were several reports of funnel clouds, but no confirmed tornadoes. While the storm caused no major structural damage, there was widespread minor damage. Numerous injuries were reported.

May 22, 1987: A strong, multiple-vortex tornado struck the town of Saragosa (Reeves Co.), essentially wiping it off the map. Of the town's 183 inhabitants, 30 were killed and 121 were injured. 85% of the town's structures were completely destroyed, while total damage topped $1.3 million.

September 16-18, 1988: Hurricane Gilbert struck 125 miles south of Brownsville, Cameron County, bringing tides of 3 feet-6 feet above average, rainfalls of 6 inches-10 inches, and at least 29 tornadoes. Total damage associated with Gilbert in Texas was estimated at $3 million-$5 million. The only death attributed to the storm was a woman who was killed by a tornado spawned by remnants of Gilbert in the San Antonio area.

"Tornadoes" from Page 116.

any hour of the day, they occur with greatest frequency during the late spring and early summer months, and between the hours of 4 p.m. and 8 p.m. In the period 1951-1986, nearly 62 per cent of all Texas tornadoes occurred within the 3-month period of April, May and June. Slightly more than one-fourth of the total occurred in May.

Partly due to the state's size, more tornadoes have been recorded in Texas than in any other state. Between 1951 and 1988, 4,465 funnel clouds reached the ground, thus becoming tornadoes. In the density of tornadoes, Texas ranks eleventh among the 50 states, with an average of 4.4 tornadoes per 10,000 square miles per year during this period.

The greatest outbreak of tornadoes on record in Texas was associated with **Hurricane Beulah** in September, 1967; 115 tornadoes, all in Texas, are known to have occurred with this great hurricane within a 5-day period, Sept. 19-23. Sixty-seven occurred on Sept. 20, a Texas record for a single day. As a result of Hurricane Beulah, September 1967, had 124 tornadoes, a Texas record for a single month. The greatest number in Texas in a single year was 232, also in 1967. The second-highest number in a single year was in 1982, when 203 tornadoes occurred in Texas, 123 of them in May, making it the worst outbreak of spring tornadoes in Texas.

An accompanying table, compiled by Environmental Data Service, National Oceanic and Atmospheric Administration, lists tornado occurrences in Texas, by months, for the period 1951-1988.

Texas' Record Cold Wave

The "Winter of '99" was long remembered by Texans. It brought the most intense cold wave on record throughout the state on Feb. 11-12-13, 1899.

Minimum temperatures ranged from 6 to 23 degrees below zero over the northern portion of the state to about 12 above over the southern portion. Lowest temperatures occurred on the morning of Feb. 12 except at a few locations where the minimum was observed the next day. The Weather Bureau Office at Galveston recorded a temperature of 7.5 degrees, the lowest of record since the opening of this station in 1871. The next morning, Galveston Bay was covered over with thin ice except in the main channel or tide current. The lowest temperature ever recorded in Texas (−23 degrees) occurred at Tulia on Feb. 12 — a record which was later equalled at Seminole on Feb. 8, 1933.

Winter weather hit Texas early in February, 1899. Cold Polar Canadian air entered Texas Feb. 4, reaching Central Texas on Feb. 6. Temperatures moderated a little, in advance of a second surge of cold air that entered the Texas Panhandle during the early morning of Feb. 8. As this mass of cold air reached Brownsville at about 6 a.m. on Feb. 10, the third and most frigid mass of Polar Canadian air was poised over Alberta and Saskatchewan ready to plunge southward. This chilling outbreak reached Texas very early in the morning of Feb. 11, and by 7 a.m. the next day, was centered over portions of Northwest Texas, Oklahoma and Kansas. By now, the leading edge of the air mass had plunged as far south as the Isthmus of Tehuantepec in southern Mexico. By Feb. 13, the air mass was centered over the Texas coast, while the cold front (the leading edge of the air mass) had reached San Salvador in Central America. The highest barometric pressure (reduced to sea level) recorded in Texas during the cold wave was 31.06 inches of mercury (1051.8 millibars) at Abilene. At Galveston, the highest barometric pressure recorded was 30.73 inches (1040.6 millibars).

Texas Droughts, 1892-1990

The following table shows the duration and extent of Texas droughts by climatic division, 1892-1990. For this purpose, droughts are arbitrarily defined as when the division has less than 75 per cent of the 1931-1960 average precipitation. The 1931-1960 average precipitation is shown at the bottom of the table for each division, in inches. A short table that follows shows the frequency of droughts in each area and the total years of droughts in the area. Recent years have brought less

than 75 per cent of average precipitation for 5 Texas divisions. In 1988, the Edwards Plateau, South Central, Upper Coast, and Southern divisions received less than 75 per cent of average rain fall. In 1989, the Edwards Plateau and Southern divisions were joined by the Lower Rio Grande Valley with less than 75 per cent of average precipitation. In 1990, the Lower Rio Grande Valley continued to be dry, receiving 73 per cent of the average precipitation.

Year	High Plains	Low Rolling Plains	North Central	East Texas	Trans-Pecos	Edwards Plateau	South Central	Upper Coast	Southern	Lower Valley
1892					68			73		
1893			67	70		49	56	64	53	59
1894					68					
1897							73		72	
1898									69	51
1901		71	70			60	62	70	44	
1902									65	73
1907										65
1909			72	68	67	74	70			
1910	59	59	64	69	43	65	69	74	59	
1911										70
1916		73		74	70		73	69		
1917	58	50	63	59	44	46	42	50	32	48
1920										71
1921					72					73
1922					68					
1924			73	73		71		72		
1925			72				72			
1927								74		74
1933	72				62	68				
1934	66				46	69				
1937									72	
1939						69				72
1943			72							
1948			73	74	62		73	67		
1950						68			74	64
1951					61	53				
1952	68	66			73				56	70
1953	69				49	73				
1954	70	71	68	73		50	50	57	71	
1956	51	57	61	68	44	43	55	62	53	53
1962						68			67	65
1963			63	68		65	61	73		
1964	74				69					63
1970	65	63				72				
1988						67	62	67	68	
1989						72			66	64
1990										73

1931-1960 Normal (inches) — 18.51, 22.99, 32.93, 45.96, 12.03, 25.91, 33.24, 46.19, 22.33, 24.27.

1941-1970 Normal (inches) — 18.59, 23.18, 32.94, 45.37, 11.57, 23.94, 33.03, 46.43, 21.95, 23.44.

1951-1980 Normal (inches) — 17.73, 22.80, 32.14, 44.65, 11.65, 23.52, 34.03, 45.93, 22.91, 24.73.

1961-1990 Normal (inches) — 18.88, 23.77, 33.99, 45.67, 13.01, 24.00, 34.49, 47.63.

DROUGHT FREQUENCY

This table shows the number of years of drought and the number of separate droughts. For example, the High Plains has had 10 drought years, consisting of five 1-year droughts, one 2-year drought and one 3-year drought, for a total of seven droughts.

Years										
1	5	6	8	6	5	8	11	9	10	13
2	1	1	2	2	4	4	2	2	2	1
3	1				1					
Total Droughts	7	7	10	8	10	12	13	11	12	14
Drought Years	10	8	12	10	16	16	15	13	14	15

Get the Feel of Texas Weather

Windchill Chart

Estimated Wind Speed MPH	ACTUAL THERMOMETER READING(°F)						
	50	40	30	20	10	0	−10
	APPARENT TEMPERATURE (°F)						
Calm	50	40	30	20	10	0	−10
5	48.3	38.0	27.8	17.5	7.1	−3.2	−13.5
10	44.6	33.5	22.5	11.5	0.5	−10.5	−21.4
15	41.3	29.6	18.0	6.3	−5.3	−16.7	−28.1
20	38.5	26.2	14.0	1.8	−10.4	−22.3	−34.2
25	36.1	23.3	10.6	−2.1	−14.8	−27.2	−39.5
30	34.1	20.9	7.8	−5.3	−18.3	−31.0	−43.7
40	30.9	17.1	3.2	−10.6	−24.0	−37.4	−50.7

The table above was devised by Dr. Robert G. Steadman, Texas Tech University, and was furnished to the Texas Almanac by the National Oceanic and Atmospheric Administration.

How Hot Does It Feel?

In the 40-year period from 1936 to 1975, nearly 20,000 people were killed in the United States by the effects of excessive heat. The overall effect of excessive heat on the body is known as heat stress. Important factors contributing to heat stress are: (1) air temperature; (2) humidity; (3) air movement; (4) radiant heat from incoming solar radiation (insolation), bright lights, stove or other source; (5) atmospheric pressure; (6) physiological factors which vary among people; (7) physical activity; and (8) clothing.

Of the above factors, temperature and humidity can be controlled by air conditioning. Air movement may be controlled by fans; even a slight breeze is usually effective in reducing heat stress in hot, muggy weather. However, at very high temperatures (above normal body temperature of about 98.6° F.), winds above 10 miles per hour can increase heat stress in a shaded area by adding more heat to the body, whereas when the body is exposed to direct sunlight the effect of wind is nearly always to reduce heat stress. Radiant heating can be mitigated by shielding or by moving away from the source (for example, seeking shade). Atmospheric pressure is not usually a significant factor; however, at very high elevations, decreased pressure (and therefore decreased air supply) can contribute to heat exhaustion.

General Heat Stress Index

Danger Category	Apparent Temperature (°F)	Heat Syndrome
1. Caution	80°-90°	Fatigue possible with prolonged exposure and physical activity.
2. Extreme Caution	90°-105°	Sunstroke, heat cramps and heat exhaustion possible with prolonged exposure and physical activity.
3. Danger	105°-130°	Sunstroke, heat cramps or heat exhaustion likely. Heatstroke possible with prolonged exposure and physical activity.
4. Extreme Danger	Greater Than 130°	Heatstroke or sunstroke imminent.

NOTE: Degree of heat stress may vary with age, health and body characteristics.

How Cold Does It Feel?

Many factors enter into the feeling of coolness or extreme cold, the temperature and wind speed being most important. The following simplified table is based upon more complex "Wind-Chill" indexes available from the National Oceanic and Atmospheric Administration (National Weather Service).

Thermometer readings are listed in the figures across the top of the chart; the wind speeds are shown down the left side. To determine how chilly it really feels, get the proper column for each. Note the figure where they cross.

Thus, a 20-degree temperature with a 20-mile-an-hour wind is equal in chill to 1.8 degrees above zero. A temperature of 10 degrees with a 15 mph wind is equal to 5.3 degrees below.

A 10-mile-an-hour wind sets twigs dancing in the trees. A 25-mile-an-hour wind sets big branches moving, and if the temperature is even cool, it sets teeth chattering.

A chill effect of anything below 25 below zero creates the danger of freezing for persons not properly clothed.

Heat Discomfort Chart

Actual Thermometer Reading (°F)	RELATIVE HUMIDITY(%)										
	0	10	20	30	40	50	60	70	80	90	100
	APPARENT TEMPERATURE (°F)										
70	64.8	65.6	66.4	67.3	68.1	68.8	69.6	70.4	71.1	71.8	72.5
75	70.1	71.2	72.1	73.0	73.7	74.6	75.3	76.1	77.1	78.2	79.2
80	75.6	76.6	77.5	78.4	79.4	80.5	81.7	83.0	84.7	86.4	88.3
85	79.9	81.0	82.2	83.6	85.0	86.7	88.7	91.0	93.7	96.8	100.6
90	84.0	85.5	87.1	89.0	91.2	94.1	97.0	101.0	105.4	110.8	
95	88.0	90.0	92.4	95.3	98.4	102.6	107.4	113.9			
100	91.8	94.6	97.8	101.7	106.6	112.7	120.4				
	RELATIVE HUMIDITY (%)										
	0	5	10	15	20	25	30	35	40	45	50
105	95.8	97.5	99.4	101.5	103.8	106.4	109.3	112.4	116.5	121.1	126.0
110	99.7	101.9	104.2	107.0	110.3	113.8	118.0	121.8	128.6		
115	103.6	106.4	109.6	113.3	117.6	122.6	128.4				
120	107.4	111.1	115.2	120.1	125.7	132.2					

The table above was devised by Dr. Robert G. Steadman, Texas Tech University, and was furnished to the Texas Almanac by NOAA.

Non-Agricultural Employment, 1990
Cont. from Page 530.

Industry	Dec. 1989 (000)	Dec. 1990 (000)	Change For Year (000)
Health Services.......	459.9	482.7	22.8
Educational Services ..	86.2	87.5	1.3
Engineering & Mgmt. Service......	149.0	152.2	3.2
Other Services & Misc.	302.9	311.6	8.7
Total Government......	1,232.5	1,302.0	69.5
Federal Government ..	199.6	199.0	—0.6
State Government	251.2	284.1	32.9
Local Government	781.7	818.9	37.2

*Estimated number of nonagricultural jobs in Texas without reference to place of residence of workers. Estimates of TEC made in cooperation with Bureau of Labor Statistics, U.S. Department of Labor.

Unseasonable rains in May 1990 flooded many residential areas in North Texas, like this Rochester Park neighborhood in Dallas. Dallas Morning News Photo.

Precipitation (Inches) 1989

	High Plains	Low Rolling Plains	North Central	East Texas	Trans-Pecos	Edwards Plateau	South Central	Upper Coast	Southern	Lower Valley
Jan	0.39	0.77	2.67	5.35	0.29	2.07	4.71	6.47	1.45	1.20
Feb	0.82	2.04	3.68	3.71	1.34	2.52	0.66	0.76	0.46	0.34
Mar	0.65	1.00	3.22	6.04	0.25	1.54	1.97	2.71	0.58	0.08
Apr	0.18	0.51	1.48	2.24	0.12	0.71	2.26	1.55	2.32	2.39
May	2.78	3.81	8.23	8.69	0.90	2.81	2.92	6.69	0.48	0.44
Jun	4.94	5.36	7.81	9.00	0.80	2.45	4.51	12.61	2.03	2.38
Jul	1.65	0.82	2.34	4.22	0.84	0.60	1.29	4.18	0.71	2.14
Aug	3.52	2.38	2.57	1.98	2.77	1.15	1.58	4.68	1.70	1.34
Sep	2.52	3.91	2.70	1.79	1.33	1.56	1.44	1.62	1.63	1.41
Oct	0.24	0.60	1.52	2.33	0.33	2.10	2.22	2.73	1.62	1.14
Nov	0.01	0.05	0.54	1.37	0.12	0.93	2.03	2.69	0.71	0.55
Dec	0.36	0.30	0.43	1.53	0.17	0.31	0.76	1.04	1.09	2.17
Ann	18.06	21.55	37.19	48.25	9.26	18.75	26.35	47.73	14.78	15.58

Precipitation (Inches) 1990

	High Plains	Low Rolling Plains	North Central	East Texas	Trans-Pecos	Edwards Plateau	South Central	Upper Coast	Southern	Lower Valley
Jan	0.90	1.45	3.43	7.56	0.17	0.71	1.51	4.99	0.65	0.47
Feb	1.50	2.41	3.90	4.23	0.49	2.35	3.11	3.49	2.29	1.53
Mar	1.25	2.47	5.51	7.19	0.73	2.41	3.57	5.31	2.41	1.33
Apr	1.77	4.27	6.90	4.65	0.73	3.41	3.55	4.48	3.35	2.51
May	1.29	3.21	6.10	7.78	0.52	3.31	2.19	3.97	1.66	2.40
Jun	0.61	1.86	1.83	2.90	0.29	0.45	0.64	1.92	0.12	0.62
July	2.54	3.61	3.02	2.79	3.95	5.89	5.69	5.36	5.88	0.94
Aug	2.14	2.30	2.16	1.77	3.42	1.58	0.90	1.52	1.63	1.55
Sept	2.73	3.43	3.34	4.34	4.35	4.60	3.36	4.56	3.21	3.67
Oct	0.76	1.29	2.65	4.50	2.20	2.50	2.28	2.98	1.60	1.22
Nov	0.95	2.20	3.91	5.54	0.59	1.78	2.06	2.87	1.76	0.91
Dec	0.34	0.81	1.41	3.92	0.39	0.30	0.84	2.59	0.12	0.58
Ann	16.78	29.31	44.16	57.17	17.83	29.29	29.70	44.04	24.68	17.73

Temperatures 1989

	High Plains	Low Rolling Plains	North Central	East Texas	Trans-Pecos	Edwards Plateau	South Central	Upper Coast	Southern	Lower Valley
Jan	41.5	46.6	49.0	51.2	46.7	50.2	56.8	58.2	59.4	65.0
Feb	35.5	37.6	41.9	45.0	49.4	46.5	52.2	52.5	56.4	60.2
Mar	51.9	55.2	55.6	56.9	58.7	58.1	61.6	60.9	65.3	67.7
Apr	61.2	65.2	65.7	65.5	68.0	67.4	69.5	78.7	73.1	74.4
May	68.9	73.2	73.6	73.3	76.0	77.5	79.2	77.7	83.9	82.7
Jun	71.4	75.2	76.3	76.4	80.3	79.3	81.4	80.0	85.4	84.4
Jul	77.7	82.2	81.5	80.1	81.8	83.4	83.8	82.3	86.9	85.0
Aug	76.1	80.7	80.9	80.3	79.2	81.9	83.4	81.9	85.9	85.1
Sep	67.0	71.3	73.2	73.6	72.7	74.1	77.8	77.2	80.4	81.2
Oct	61.0	66.0	67.7	67.1	65.6	67.5	71.3	71.1	73.8	75.0
Nov	48.7	53.9	57.1	58.6	54.7	57.2	63.2	63.9	65.5	70.1
Dec	32.6	35.9	38.0	39.7	41.3	40.1	44.4	45.3	46.7	49.9
Ann	57.8	61.9	63.4	64.0	64.5	65.3	68.7	68.3	71.9	73.4

Temperatures 1990

	High Plains	Low Rolling Plains	North Central	East Texas	Trans-Pecos	Edwards Plateau	South Central	Upper Coast	Southern	Lower Valley
Jan	40.0	47.0	50.9	52.0	46.7	51.0	57.3	57.3	59.3	63.4
Feb	43.1	49.8	52.7	55.1	50.6	54.4	60.0	60.3	62.6	66.1
Mar	48.1	53.6	56.8	59.0	56.7	57.7	62.6	63.4	65.1	69.4
Apr	57.7	61.4	63.6	64.8	65.9	65.4	69.4	69.1	72.1	75.1
May	64.9	70.3	72.3	72.4	73.3	73.8	78.2	77.5	80.7	80.9
Jun	80.9	83.7	83.0	81.6	85.2	84.7	85.2	83.9	88.1	85.6
July	76.2	79.8	81.3	81.0	78.2	79.7	82.5	82.1	84.4	84.4
Aug	76.0	80.4	82.9	82.8	76.0	80.2	84.6	84.1	85.3	85.7
Sept	72.0	76.4	78.4	78.6	73.1	76.2	80.2	80.0	81.1	81.8
Oct	58.4	62.9	65.2	64.9	63.1	64.8	69.6	69.1	71.9	75.0
Nov	50.3	55.7	59.3	59.7	55.7	58.5	64.5	64.4	66.3	70.4
Dec	35.3	40.2	43.8	46.9	46.0	47.0	53.3	54.7	56.6	60.9
Ann	58.6	63.4	65.9	66.6	64.2	66.1	70.6	70.5	72.8	74.9

Texas Mineral Production

Texas has maintained its role as one of the leading mining states in the nation, ranking **fourth nationally in 1990 in total mineral output.** It is also a top petroleum-producing state.

Petroleum products were by far the largest money producers. According to Texas Mid-Continent Oil and Gas Association, 672 million barrels of crude oil and condensate were produced at a value of $15 billion in 1990. There were 5.6 trillion cubic feet of natural gas produced at a value of $8.1 billion in 1989.

Coal production in the state continued to increase. Lignite is by far the most common coal produced, and it is used by 11 plants for the production of steam-generated electricity. The Bureau of Economic Geology at the University of Texas in Austin estimates 23 billion tons of lignite reserves. Economically recoverable reserves of strippable lignite are estimated at 9 billion to 11 billion

tons. Two small bituminous coal operations supply fuel for cement operations in Webb County, but their production is negligible.

Cement was the top-valued construction material, according to the Bureau of Mines, generating $353.8 million in revenue from 8,000,000 short tons produced. Texas also retained its position as a leading **stone**-producing state with 12,800,000 short tons produced valued at $285.7 million. **Sand and gravel** shipments of 58,000,000 short tons were valued at $210.7 million.

In addition, Texas was the leading state in the production of Frasch **sulfur,** shipping 2,240,000 metric tons. But the value was not reported to protect producers' proprietary data.

Total **nonfuel mineral production** for the state in 1990 was more than $1.5 billion, according to the Bureau of Mines, substantially more than in 1989 (see table).

Oil and Gas in Texas, 1991
This article is by Jay Cassel of Texas Mid-Continent Oil and Gas Association.

Texas crude oil and natural gas production in 1990 was valued at approximately $22.5 billion — with accompanying severance and industry corporate franchise taxes helping to underwrite state government and royalty payments and property taxes adding to the overall economic health of Texas. But, despite this impressive figure, these are not particularly good times for the industry — in Texas or in this country.

Domestic oil production and reserves fell to their lowest levels in five years in 1990, and these developments were mirrored in Texas. Crude oil production fell for the 12th consecutive year while reserves continued in a five-year slide.

As has been pointed out here before, the reserves decline is due in large part to the fact that no major oil field — one with reserves of 100 million barrels or more — has been discovered in the state since 1971.

However, both the reserves and the production de-

clines are due to yet an even more important factor: price; last year's average price for a barrel of Texas crude was $22.39 — up from $17.84 in 1989 and the highest since the $26.92 level of 1985. However, the average price of oil in 1991 — about $20.50 — adjusted for inflation is lower than it was in 1974.

Moreover, while oil prices have not been at a level sufficient to stimulate extensive drilling for new supplies, current natural gas prices are at a critically low level. The price for 1,000-feet of natural gas (an Mcf) has been averaging only $1.45 for the past five years, not high enough to encourage drilling nor the production of supplies already discovered.

To put this problem in relative and understandable terms, it should be noted that on a British Thermal Unit (BTU) equivalency basis, an Mcf of natural gas should have the value of one-sixth of a 42-gallon barrel of oil. Yet, last year in Texas, the ratio between the already noted prices of these commodities was one to 15, with gas on the short side.

The Texas petroleum industry in 1991 is being affected by two factors that are having a worldwide effect — an oversupply of oil, with most of it coming from Organization of Petroleum Exporting Countries (OPEC), and the expectation of only a modest one per cent per year increase in demand over the next decade. This means that no significant change in oil prices — or gas prices — should be expected during that period.

Texas Oil History

Indians found oil seeping from the soils of Texas long before the first Europeans arrived. They told explorers that the fluid had medicinal values. The first record of Europeans using crude oil, however, was the caulking of boats in 1543 by survivors of the DeSoto expedition near Sabine Pass.

Melrose, in Nacogdoches County, was the site in 1866 of the first drilled well to produce oil in Texas. The driller was Lyne T. Barret (whose name has been spelled several ways by historians). Barret used an auger, fastened to a pipe and rotated by a cogwheel driven by a steam engine—a basic principle of rotary drilling that has been used since, although with much improvement.

In 1867 Amory (Emory) Starr and Peyton F. Edwards brought in a well at Oil Springs, in the same area. Other wells followed and Nacogdoches County was the site of Texas' first commercial oil field, pipeline and effort to refine crude. Several thousand barrels of oil were produced there during these years.

Other oil was found in crudely dug wells in Texas, principally in Bexar County, in the latter years of the 19th century. But it was not until June 9, 1894, that Texas had a major discovery. This occurred in the drilling of a water well for the City of Corsicana. Oil caused that well to be abandoned, but a company formed in 1895 drilled several producing wells. The first well-equipped refinery in Texas was built and this plant usually is called the state's first refinery, despite the earlier effort at Nacogdoches. Discovery of the Powell Field near Corsicana followed in 1900.

Spindletop, 1901

Jan. 10, 1901, is the most famous date in Texas petroleum history. This is the date that the great gusher erupted in the oil well being drilled at Spindletop, near Beaumont, by a mining engineer, Capt. A. F. Lucas. Thousands of barrels of oil flowed before the well could be capped. This was the first salt dome oil discovery. It created a sensation throughout the world, and encouraged exploration and drilling in Texas that has continued since.

Texas oil production increased from 836,039 barrels in 1900 to 4,393,658 in 1901; and in 1902 Spindletop alone produced 17,421,000 barrels, or 94 per cent of the state's production. Prices dropped to 3c a barrel, an all-time low.

A water-well drilling outfit on the W. T. Waggoner Ranch in Wichita County hit oil, bringing in the Electra Field in 1911. In 1917, came the discovery of the Ranger Field in Eastland County. The Burkburnett Field in Wichita County was discovered in 1919.

Oil discoveries brought a short era of swindling with oil stock promotion and selling on a nationwide scale. It ended after a series of trials in a federal court.

The Mexia Field in Limestone County was discovered in 1920, and the second Powell Field in Navarro County in 1924.

Another great area opened in 1921 with discovery of oil in the Panhandle, a field which developed rapidly with sensational oil and gas discoveries in Hutchinson and contiguous counties and the booming of Borger.

The Luling Field was opened in 1922 and 1925 saw the comeback of Spindletop with a production larger than that of the original field. Other fields opened in this period included Big Lake, 1923; Wortham, 1924-25 and Yates, 1926.

In 1925 Howard County was opened for production. Winkler in West Texas and Raccoon Bend, Austin County, were opened in 1927. Sugar Land was the most important Texas oil development in 1928. The Darst Creek Field was opened in 1929. In the same year, new records of productive sand thickness were set for the industry at Van, Van Zandt County. Pettus was another contribution of 1929 in Bee County.

East Texas Field

The East Texas field, biggest of them all, was discovered near Turnertown and Joinerville, Rusk County, by veteran wildcatter C. M. (Dad) Joiner, in October 1930. The success of this well—drilled on land condemned many times by geologists of the major companies—was followed by the biggest leasing campaign in history. The field soon was extended to Kilgore, Longview and northward.

The East Texas field brought a large overproduction and a rapid sinking of the price. Private attempts were made to prorate production, but without much

Texas Oil and Gas Production, Amount and Value

Source: Railroad Commission and Texas Mid-Continent Oil and Gas Association

Year	Crude Oil & Condensate Production (thousand bbls.)	Value (Add 000)	Average Price Per Barrel	Natural Gas Production (million cu. ft.)	Value (Add 000)	Average Price (Cents Per MCF)	Year	Crude Oil & Condensate Production (thousand bbls.)	Value (Add 000)	Average Price Per Barrel	Natural Gas Production (million cu. ft.)	Value (Add 000)	Average Price (Cents Per MCF)
1915	24,943	$13,027	$.52	13,324	$2,594	19.5	1975	1,221,929	9,336,570	7.64	7,485,764	3,885,112	51.9
1920	96,868	313,781	3.24	37,063	7,042	19.0	1976	1,189,523	10,217,702	8.59	7,191,859	5,163,755	71.8
1925	144,648	262,270	1.81	134,872	7,040	5.2	1977	1,137,880	9,986,002	8.78	7,051,027	6,367,077	90.3
1930	290,457	288,410	.99	517,880	18,488	3.6	1978	1,074,050	9,980,333	9.29	6,548,184	6,515,443	99.5
1935	392,666	367,820	.94	642,366	13,233	2.1	*1979	1,018,094	12,715,994	12.49	7,174,623	8,509,103	118.6
1940	493,209	494,000	1.00	1,063,538	19,356	1.8	1980	977,436	21,259,233	21.75	7,115,889	10,673,834	150.0
1945	754,710	914,410	1.21	1,711,401	44,839	2.6	1981	945,132	32,692,116	34.59	7,050,207	12,598,712	178.7
1950	829,874	2,147,160	2.59	3,126,402	146,941	4.7	1982	923,868	29,074,126	31.47	6,497,678	13,567,151	208.8
1955	1,053,297	2,989,330	2.84	4,730,798	378,464	8.0	1983	876,205	22,947,814	26.19	5,643,183	14,672,275	260.0
1960	927,479	2,748,735	2.96	5,892,704	665,876	11.3	1984	874,079	25,138,520	28.76	5,864,224	13,487,715	230.0
1965	1,000,749	2,962,119	2.96	6,636,555	858,396	12.9	1985	860,300	23,159,286	26.92	5,805,098	12,665,114	218.0
1970	1,249,697	4,104,005	3.28	8,357,716	1,203,511	14.4	1986	813,620	11,976,488	14.72	5,663,491	8,778,410	155.0
1971	1,222,926	4,261,775	3.48	8,550,705	1,376,664	16.1	1987	754,213	11,321,345	17.53	5,516,224	7,612,389	138.0
1972	1,301,685	4,536,077	3.48	8,657,840	1,419,886	16.4	1988	727,928	10,729,660	14.74	5,702,643	7,983,700	140.0
1973	1,294,671	5,157,623	3.98	8,513,850	1,735,221	20.4	1989	679,575	12,123,624	17.84	5,595,190	8,113,026	145.0
1974	1,262,126	8,773,003	6.95	8,170,798	2,541,118	31.1	1990	672,081	15,047,902	22.39	NA	NA	NA

*Beginning in 1979 data are from Department of Energy and Texas State Comptroller of Public Accounts.

Note: The production figures of natural gas differ from those found in table entitled "Ultimate Disposition of Texas Natural Gas," which are provided by the Railroad Commission. DOE figures do not include gas that is vented or flared or used for pressure maintenance and repressuring, but do include non-hydrocarbon gases.

success. On Aug. 17, 1931, **Gov. Ross S. Sterling** ordered the National Guard into the field, which he placed under martial law. This drastic action was taken after the Texas Railroad Commission had been enjoined from enforcing production restrictions. After the complete shutdown, the Texas Legislature enacted legal proration, the system of regulation still utilized.

The most significant subsequent oil discoveries in Texas were those in West Texas, following a discovery well in Scurry County, Nov. 21, 1948, and later major developments in that region. Many of the leading Texas counties in minerals value are in that section.

Major Fields

Texas fields with estimated ultimate recovery of 100 million barrels of oil or more are in the following list, which gives the name of the field, county and discovery date. Data furnished by **Oil and Gas Journal.**

Panhandle, Carson-Collingsworth-Gray-Hutchinson-Moore-Potter-Wheeler, 1910; **Thompson** (all fields), Fort Bend, 1921; **Howard-Glasscock,** Howard, 1925; **Iatan East,** Howard, 1926; **Yates,** Pecos, 1926; **Waddell,** Crane, 1927; **Van,** Van Zandt, 1929; **Ward Estes North,** Ward, 1929; **Cowden North,** Ector, 1930; **East Texas,** Gregg-Rusk, 1930; **Sand Hills,** Crane, 1930; **Conroe,** Montgomery, 1931; **Tom O'Connor,** Refugio, 1931; **Cowden South,** Ector, 1932; **Greta** (all fields), Refugio, 1933; **Tomball,** Harris, 1933; **Means** (all fields), Andrews-Gaines, 1934; **Anahuac,** Chambers, 1935; **Goldsmith** (all fields), Ector, 1935; **Hastings,** Brazoria, 1935; **Magnet Withers** (all fields), Wharton, 1936; **Seminole** (all fields), Gaines, 1936; **Webster,** Harris, 1936; **Jordan,** Crane-Ector, 1937; **Slaughter,** Cochran, 1937; **Wasson** (all fields), Gaines, 1937; **Dune,** Crane, 1938; **West Ranch,** Jackson, 1938; **Keystone,** Winkler, 1939; **Diamond M,** Scurry, 1940; **Hawkins,** Wood, 1940; **Fullerton** (all fields), Andrews, 1941; **McElroy,** Crane, 1941; **Oyster Bayou,** Chambers, 1941; **Welch,** Dawson, 1941; **Quitman** (all fields), Wood, 1942; **Anton-Irish,** Hale, 1944; **TXL** (all fields), Ector, 1944; **Block 31,** Crane, 1945; **Levelland,** Cochran-Hockley, 1945; **Midland Farms** (all fields), Andrews; 1945; **Andector,** Ector, 1946; **Dollarhide,** Andrews, 1947; **Kelly-Snyder,** Scurry, 1948; **Cogdell Area,** Scurry, 1949; **Prentice,** Yoakum, 1950; **Salt Creek,** Kent, 1950; **Spraberry Trend,** Glasscock-Midland, 1952; **Lake Pasture,** Refugio, 1953; **Neches,** Anderson-Cherokee, 1953; **Fairway,** Anderson-Henderson, 1960; **Giddings,** Lee-Fayette-Burleson, 1971.

Receipts By Texas From Tidelands
(Source: General Land Office)

The following table shows receipts from tidelands in the Gulf of Mexico by the Texas General Land Office to Aug. 31, 1990. It does not include revenue from bays and other submerged area owned by Texas.

From	To	Total	Bonus	Rental	Royalty	Lease*
6- 9-1922	9-28-1945	$924,363.81	$814,055.70	$61,973.75	$48,334.36	...
9-29-1945	6-23-1947	296,400.30	272,700.00	7,680.00	16,020.30	...
6-24-1947	6- 5-1950	7,695,552.22	7,231,755.48	377,355.00	86,441.74	...
6- 6-1950	5-22-1953	55,095.04	—	9,176.00	45,919.04	...
5-23-1953	6-30-1958	54,264,553.11	49,788,639.03	3,852,726.98	623,187.10	...
7- 1-1958	8-31-1959	771,064.75	—	143,857.00	627,207.75	...
9- 1-1959	8-31-1960	983,335.32	257,900.00	98,226.00	627,209.32	...
9- 1-1960	8-31-1961	3,890,800.15	3,228,639.51	68,578.00	593,582.64	...
9- 1-1961	8-31-1962	1,121,925.09	297,129.88	127,105.00	697,690.21	...
9- 1-1962	8-31-1963	3,575,888.64	2,617,057.14	177,174.91	781,656.59	...
9- 1-1963	8-31-1964	3,656,236.75	2,435,244.36	525,315.00	695,677.39	...
9- 1-1964	8-31-1965	54,654,576.96	53,114,943.63	755,050.12	784,583.21	...
9- 1-1965	8-31-1966	22,148,825.44	18,223,357.84	3,163,475.00	761,992.60	...
9- 1-1966	8-31-1967	8,469,680.86	3,641,414.96	3,711,092.65	1,117,173.25	...
9- 1-1967	8-31-1968	6,305,851.00	1,251,852.50	2,683,732.50	2,370,266.00	...
9- 1-1968	8-31-1969	6,372,268.28	1,838,118.33	1,491,592.50	3,042,557.45	...
9- 1-1969	8-31-1970	10,311,030.48	5,994,666.32	618,362.50	3,698,001.66	...
9- 1-1970	8-31-1971	9,969,629.17	4,326,120.11	726,294.15	4,917,214.91	...
9- 1-1971	8-31-1972	7,558,327.21	1,360,212.64	963,367.60	5,234,746.97	...
9- 1-1972	8-31-1973	9,267,975.68	3,701,737.30	920,121.60	4,646,116.78	...
9- 1-1973	8-31-1974	41,717,670.04	32,981,619.28	1,065,516.60	7,670,534.16	...
9- 1-1974	8-31-1975	27,321,536.62	5,319,762.85	2,935,295.60	19,066,478.17	...
9- 1-1975	8-31-1976	38,747,074.09	6,197,853.00	3,222,535.84	29,326,685.25	...
9- 1-1976	8-31-1977	84,196,228.27	41,343,114.81	2,404,988.80	40,448,124.66	...
9- 1-1977	8-31-1978	118,266,812.05	49,807,750.45	4,775,509.92	63,683,551.68	...
9- 1-1978	8-31-1979	100,410,268.68	34,578,340.94	7,318,748.40	58,513,179.34	...
9- 1-1979	8-31-1980	200,263,803.03	34,733,270.02	10,293,153.80	155,237,379.21	...
9- 1-1980	8-31-1981	219,126,876.54	37,467,196.97	13,100,484.25	168,559,195.32	...
9- 1-1981	8-31-1982	250,824,581.69	27,529,516.33	14,214,478.97	209,080,586.39	...
9- 1-1982	8-31-1983	165,197,734.83	10,180,696.40	12,007,476.70	143,009,561.73	...
9- 1-1983	8-31-1984	152,755,934.29	32,864,122.19	8,573,996.87	111,317,815.23	...
9- 1-1984	8-31-1985	140,568,090.79	32,650,127.75	6,837,603.70	101,073,959.34	...
9- 1-1985	8-31-1986	†88,736,086.55	6,365,426.23	4,241,892.75	78,289,592.27	$427,606,859.83
9- 1-1986	8-31-1987	†50,812,221.85	4,186,561.63	1,933,752.50	44,691,907.22	9,254,349.70
9- 1-1987	8-31-1988	†44,080,535.71	14,195,274.28	1,817,058.90	28,068,202.53	12,794,533.51
9- 1-1988	8-31-1989	†49,447,445.51	12,995,892.74	1,290,984.37	35,160,568.40	12,345,934.53
9- 1-1989	8-31-1990	†49,315,436.47	7,708,449.54	1,275,449.87	40,331,537.06	19,371,915.04
Total		†$2,034,236,141.47	$551,500,520.14	$117,791,184.10	$1,364,944,437.23	$481,373,592.61
Recapitulation:						
Inside three-mile line ...		363,561,724.12	134,727,878.89	32,858,636.27	195,975,208.96	0
Between three-mile line and three marine-league line..		1,667,849,051.77	414,120,556.86	84,759,266.64	1,168,969,228.27	0
Outside three marine-league line		†2,825,365.58	2,652,084.39	173,281.19	0	481,373,592.61
Totals		†$2,034,236,141.47	$551,500,520.14	$117,791,184.10	$1,364,944,437.23	$481,373,592.61

Totals including revenue in "Lease" column: Total mineral leases: $2,515,609,734.08
Total outside 3-marine league limit: 484,198,958.19

*Revenue from continental shelf settlement with federal government under Public Law 99-272 (for fuller explanation, see article, "History of Texas Public Lands" in Politics and Government section).

†Does not include amounts in "Lease" column.

History of Texas Drilling
Source: Oil and Gas Journal
and American Petroleum Institute.

	Wells Completed	Oil Wells	Gas Wells	Stratigraphic & Core Tests	Service Wells	Dry Holes	Percent Dry
1889-1900*	97	71	2			24	24.7
1901-1910*	692	462	9			221	32.0
1911-1920*	2,451	1,682	66			703	28.7
1921-1930*	6,352	3,745	306			2,301	36.2
1931-1940*	9,915	7,404	288	...	...	2,224	22.9
1941-1950*	9,147	5,767	457	...	44	2,901	32.5
1951-1960*	18,439	10,838	814	...	155	6,632	36.0
1961-1970*	11,595	5,798	1,115	367	393	4,121	35.8
1971	7,728	3,880	810	8	449	2,581	33.4
1972	8,088	3,963	943	8	414	2,760	34.1
1973	8,494	3,686	1,475	34	362	2,937	34.6
1974	9,808	4,402	1,843	19	260	3,284	33.5
1975	12,483	6,074	2,135	36	361	3,877	31.1
1976	12,740	5,779	2,443	45	285	4,188	32.9
1977	14,759	6,533	3,064	37	443	4,682	31.7
1978	15,037	6,086	3,292	26	415	5,218	34.7
1979	16,149	6,765	3,609	35	515	5,225	32.4
1980	19,253	9,668	3,684	10	546	5,345	27.8
1981	23,940	13,052	3,807	2	368	6,711	28.0
1982	26,849	13,851	4,345	4	692	7,957	29.6
1983	24,616	13,102	3,317	...	652	7,545	30.6
1984	26,134	14,591	3,242	17	678	7,606	29.1
1985	18,882	11,206	2,215	...	666	5,461	28.9
1986	11,425	6,141	1,326	2	345	3,958	34.6
1987	10,797	5,504	1,589	...	365	3,704	34.3
1988	9,106	6,441	2,665	...	...	3,155	...
1989	7,674	4,914	2,760	...	...	2,380	...
†1990	8,487	5,593	2,894	...	...	2,744	...
Total	938,930	509,031	82,030	1,385	13,516	282,625	...

*Annual Averages.
†Preliminary.

Rigs Actually Making Hole
Source: Baker Hughes, Inc.

Year	Average
1978	855
1979	770.2
1980	987.7
1981	1,317.0
1982	989.6
1983	798
1984	850.1
1985	677
1986	311
1987	293
1988	281
1989	265
1990	349

Texas Natural Gas Production and Initial Disposition—1989
Source: Railroad Commission of Texas
(All Gas Volumes in Thousands Cubic Feet)

GAS WELL GAS
Number of Wells, December—46,248

	Volume
Total Production	4,210,017,599
Disposition:	
Fuel System & Lease Use	48,184,151
Gas Lift	7,148,691
Pressure Maintenance and Repressuring	71,319
Transmission Lines	1,479,951,397
Processing Plants	2,642,079,709
Carbon Black Plants	659,800
Vented or Flared	1,052,739
Extraction Loss (lease)	30,869,793

CASINGHEAD GAS
Number of Wells, December—184,699

	Volume
Total Production	1,308,456,980
Disposition:	
Fuel System and Lease Use	40,046,650
Pressure Maintenance and Repressuring	3,720,148
Transmission Lines	70,115,624
Processing Plants	1,494,888,636
Carbon Black Plants	630,967
Vented or Flared	13,138,745

Ultimate Disposition of Texas Natural Gas—1989
Source: Railroad Commission of Texas
(All Gas Volumes in Thousands Cubic Feet)

	Volume	Percent of Total
Total Production	5,518,474,579	100.00
Disposition:		
Plant Fuel & Lease Use	378,174,204	6.85
Pressure Maintenance and Repressuring	339,702,390	6.16
Transmission Lines	3,988,510,956	72.29
Cycled	113,491,811	2.05
Carbon Black	2,691,522	.05
Underground Storage	104,678,119	1.90
Vented or Flared	29,933,007	.54
Plant Meter Difference	31,706,178	.57
Acid Gas H2S & CO2	159,982,212	2.89
*Extraction Loss	369,604,180	6.70

*Shrinkage in volume due to removal of liquified hydrocarbons.

Texas Natural Gas Reserves
Source: Committee on Natural Gas Reserves, American Gas Association and Department of Energy
(Millions of Cubic Feet)

Year	Proved Reserves	Percent Annual Change	Year	Proved Reserves	Percent Annual Change	Year	Proved Reserves	Percent Annual Change
1945	78,306,676	—	1962	119,503,798	−0.3	*1979	53,021,000	−.02
1946	86,343,459	10.3	1963	117,809,376	−1.4	*1980	50,287,000	−.05
1947	90,025,566	4.2	1964	118,855,055	0.9	*1981	50,469,000	†
1948	95,708,553	6.3	1965	120,616,760	1.5	1982	49,757,000	†
1949	99,170,403	3.6	1966	123,609,326	2.5	1983	50,052,000	†
1950	102,404,077	3.3	1967	125,415,064	1.5	1984	49,883,000	†
1951	105,653,229	3.2	1968	119,001,106	−5.1	1985	49,035,000	†
1952	105,732,763	0.1	1969	112,392,622	−5.6	1986	40,574,000	−17.3
1953	106,529,626	0.8	1970	106,352,993	−5.4	1987	38,711,000	−4.6
1954	105,129,062	−1.3	1971	101,472,108	−4.6	1988	38,200,000	−1
1955	108,287,548	3.0	1972	95,042,043	−6.3	1989	38,400,000	†
1956	112,728,750	4.1	1973	84,936,502	−10.6			
1957	113,084,518	0.3	1974	78,540,717	−7.5	*These Department of Energy figures differ from preceding American Petroleum Institute figures.		
1958	115,045,743	1.7	1975	71,036,854	−9.6			
1959	120,475,783	4.7	1976	64,651,410	−9.0	†Percentage less than one percent.		
1960	119,489,393	−0.8	1977	62,157,836	−3.8			
1961	119,838,711	0.3	1978	54,600,235	−12.2			

Texas Oil Production by Counties

Source: Compiled by the Texas Mid-Continent Oil & Gas Association

This table shows the year of oil or gas discovery in each county, oil production in 1989 and 1990 and total oil production from date of discovery to Jan. 1, 1991.

County	Year of Discovery	Crude Production* 1989	Crude Production* 1990	Total Prdn. to Jan. 1, 1991 (bbls.)
Anderson	1929	1,840,621	1,697,248	282,654,359
Andrews	1930	37,688,654	37,933,471	2,372,071,257
Angelina	1936	12,276	8,791	422,642
Aransas	1936	469,105	498,703	77,457,256
Archer	1911	2,814,915	2,850,546	467,949,460
Atascosa	1917	1,354,496	1,236,387	138,595,610
Austin	1915	558,603	576,034	108,606,313
Bastrop	1913	610,802	484,328	12,771,864
Baylor	1924	294,963	313,912	55,139,246
Bee	1930	814,025	819,327	99,091,271
Bell	1980	0	0	446
Bexar	1889	640,716	550,793	32,548,292
Borden	1949	5,679,658	5,936,981	340,003,250
Bowie	1944	341,147	310,383	3,130,446
Brazoria	1902	4,682,742	4,266,230	1,226,258,666
Brazos	1942	7,966,816	4,078,458	73,427,789
Brewster	1969	0	0	56
Briscoe	1982	0	0	3,554
Brooks	1936	812,996	831,556	153,760,129
Brown	1917	497,768	349,461	50,561,288
Burleson	1938	4,848,406	6,771,993	108,246,164
Caldwell	1922	1,634,279	1,509,757	266,306,368
Calhoun	1935	1,272,082	1,179,390	92,679,999
Callahan	1923	1,038,737	1,028,803	79,523,155
Cameron	1944	2,937	3,505	434,009
Camp	1940	462,223	449,404	22,857,932
Carson	1921	746,955	701,667	172,852,364
Cass	1935	1,109,786	1,025,738	105,320,542
Chambers	1916	3,891,605	3,323,530	878,731,416
Cherokee	1926	904,436	788,124	64,761,520
Childress	1961	17,651	13,596	1,346,966
Clay	1902	1,750,379	1,598,537	188,276,011
Cochran	1936	7,726,652	8,265,969	428,357,278
Coke	1942	1,485,523	1,331,036	209,281,131
Coleman	1902	658,997	722,089	88,597,171
Collin	1963	0	0	53,000
Collingsworth	1936	8,923	8,595	1,169,450
Colorado	1932	903,779	886,961	31,523,143
Comanche	1918	29,168	30,820	5,764,906
Concho	1940	387,567	1,408,057	8,948,477
Cooke	1926	2,909,276	2,382,207	360,386,815
Coryell	1964	0	0	1,100
Cottle	1955	163,970	135,489	3,281,360
Crane	1926	19,026,673	19,341,195	1,552,323,778
Crockett	1925	3,964,980	3,968,151	311,095,793
Crosby	1955	751,803	734,261	14,122,316
Culberson	1953	432,240	409,238	21,542,023
Dallam	1954	0	0	0
Dallas	1986	0	0	231
Dawson	1937	6,543,433	6,549,321	294,809,170
Delta	1984	736	136	63,790
Denton	1937	15,891	15,855	3,346,233
DeWitt	1930	658,027	678,944	61,129,760
Dickens	1953	322,953	432,756	5,597,737
Dimmit	1943	1,842,148	3,737,154	86,581,411
Donley	1967	0	0	0
Duval	1905	3,102,903	2,880,493	557,709,493
Eastland	1917	1,106,053	1,019,051	149,206,256
Ector	1926	38,060,086	35,897,269	2,726,524,140
Edwards	1946	4,997	4,371	418,324
Ellis	1953	8,858	7,210	794,363
Erath	1917	18,534	15,000	1,978,474
Falls	1937	18,731	16,127	742,878
Fannin	1980	0	0	13,281
Fayette	1943	2,768,179	2,588,567	62,917,223
Fisher	1928	2,472,930	2,265,676	230,887,287
Floyd	1952	3,254	3,092	123,510
Foard	1929	386,204	347,087	20,816,157
Fort Bend	1919	4,784,157	4,139,260	647,165,432
Franklin	1936	1,422,085	1,356,543	167,469,674
Freestone	1916	645,002	598,524	40,437,917
Frio	1934	2,034,909	9,893,130	106,929,198
Gaines	1936	42,686,616	42,810,261	1,670,602,104
Galveston	1922	1,871,571	1,838,966	429,457,498
Garza	1926	6,765,979	7,203,639	250,618,823
Glasscock	1925	5,145,443	4,993,973	192,582,834
Goliad	1930	744,097	782,542	73,556,080
Gonzales	1902	988,189	1,709,920	29,012,335
Gray	1925	3,023,914	2,782,973	642,556,026
Grayson	1930	2,445,008	2,355,532	231,380,753
Gregg	1931	30,025,022	29,265,112	3,079,362,443
Grimes	1952	390,479	321,841	6,229,116
Guadalupe	1922	1,122,588	1,195,488	188,051,203
Hale	1946	2,148,363	1,941,352	148,177,329
Hamilton	1938	2,148	2,067	129,172
Hansford	1937	463,833	410,851	34,928,925
Hardeman	1944	2,915,188	2,991,016	46,854,172
Hardin	1893	3,573,864	3,184,560	411,198,902
Harris	1905	6,809,524	5,897,161	1,324,111,994
Harrison	1928	1,383,893	1,380,368	74,449,012
Hartley	1937	360,569	356,107	2,814,622
Haskell	1929	1,072,408	1,045,694	106,357,516
Hays	1956	0	0	79
Hemphill	1955	788,620	725,955	28,438,448
Henderson	1934	1,810,203	1,635,113	157,092,316
Hidalgo	1934	2,170,030	2,259,914	61,423,073
Hill	1949	3,286	2,436	52,301
Hockley	1937	31,780,744	28,967,940	1,280,032,618
Hood	1958	4,235	6,212	81,294
Hopkins	1936	886,850	792,799	82,330,403
Houston	1934	894,278	809,916	45,429,762
Howard	1925	10,805,535	10,971,421	694,930,307
Hunt	1942	3,720	3,014	1,864,979
Hutchinson	1923	1,885,429	1,881,897	510,458,445
Irion	1928	2,642,604	2,789,406	67,683,641
Jack	1923	1,941,909	1,853,791	187,527,154
Jackson	1934	4,008,549	3,599,439	656,164,692
Jasper	1928	991,557	835,816	20,856,587
Jeff Davis	1980	0	0	20,866
Jefferson	1901	3,443,205	3,082,585	496,553,807
Jim Hogg	1922	881,597	816,713	106,003,324
Jim Wells	1933	853,675	739,903	457,243,288
Johnson	1962	0	0	194,000
Jones	1926	1,356,841	1,329,411	206,770,955
Karnes	1930	744,301	738,399	101,005,251
Kaufman	1948	234,737	241,866	22,839,479
Kenedy	1947	634,589	646,446	31,800,494
Kent	1946	11,947,948	11,384,262	448,438,235
Kerr	1982	4,580	2,833	63,232
Kimble	1939	2,061	1,710	86,788
King	1943	7,215,951	8,720,652	114,402,614
Kinney	1960	0	0	402
Kleberg	1926	1,294,272	1,225,284	325,430,823
Knox	1946	1,036,189	888,075	55,880,875
Lamb	1945	479,910	518,917	27,801,368
Lampasas	1985	0	0	111
La Salle	1940	356,170	1,983,446	17,108,997
Lavaca	1941	687,003	736,258	21,370,648
Lee	1939	3,544,235	3,145,129	85,676,464
Leon	1936	2,856,984	2,745,469	36,287,593
Liberty	1905	2,730,394	2,834,143	495,721,101
Limestone	1920	269,404	257,053	116,103,071
Lipscomb	1956	1,402,967	1,461,072	48,772,807
Live Oak	1931	1,532,368	1,465,250	70,279,660
Llano	1978	0	0	647
Loving	1925	1,848,609	1,960,670	90,225,617
Lubbock	1941	2,571,260	2,569,479	41,724,559
Lynn	1950	491,506	507,340	15,313,725
McCulloch	1938	6,939	6,365	177,589
McLennan	1902	4,397	3,164	300,671
McMullen	1919	4,216,359	3,536,682	78,944,006
Madison	1946	920,337	854,517	24,201,538
Marion	1910	484,805	542,265	51,853,150
Martin	1945	7,883,813	7,632,191	227,421,148
Matagorda	1904	1,604,860	1,552,471	261,222,755
Maverick	1929	1,269,344	1,261,140	36,900,372
Medina	1901	197,241	194,676	9,167,767
Menard	1941	141,976	143,331	5,690,298
Midland	1945	8,980,061	8,693,311	455,926,141
Milam	1921	287,500	265,284	11,679,067
Mills	1982	0	0	28,122
Mitchell	1920	5,141,631	4,889,206	176,890,644
Montague	1924	2,210,797	2,242,457	267,218,912
Montgomery	1931	3,424,512	2,737,044	751,443,635

County	Year of Discovery	Crude Production* 1989	1990	Total Prdn. to Jan. 1, 1991 (bbls.)
Moore	1936	725,749	795,188	24,292,408
Motley	1957	306,523	304,465	9,439,325
Nacogdoches	1866	87,308	76,344	2,845,929
Navarro	1895	761,515	719,488	212,529,223
Newton	1937	734,768	889,501	43,135,081
Nolan	1939	2,105,517	1,965,322	172,175,793
Nueces	1930	2,808,969	2,512,933	539,153,603
Ochiltree	1951	1,715,828	1,505,450	141,783,547
Oldham	1957	282,900	325,071	11,606,094
Orange	1913	2,033,603	2,143,477	130,546,982
Palo Pinto	1902	367,321	313,386	17,874,218
Panola	1917	1,514,509	1,855,514	64,366,328
Parker	1942	53,556	46,018	2,627,228
Parmer	1963	0	0	144,000
Pecos	1926	31,994,122	26,655,910	1,505,423,527
Polk	1930	1,265,987	1,256,622	96,404,603
Potter	1925	220,290	198,099	6,351,486
Presidio	1980	0	0	1,873
Rains	1955	0	0	148,763
Reagan	1923	6,693,374	6,322,947	422,210,361
Red River	1951	438,590	252,956	2,362,681
Reeves	1939	1,448,665	1,455,038	64,529,175
Refugio	1928	10,164,904	9,066,016	1,244,551,370
Roberts	1945	519,802	476,625	40,126,321
Robertson	1944	71,225	54,465	1,719,074
Runnels	1927	1,450,701	1,237,874	135,884,259
Rusk	1930	8,444,318	7,690,643	1,766,118,575
Sabine	1981	24,574	50,404	928,068
San Augustine	1947	43	0	18,015
San Jacinto	1940	146,849	259,951	22,095,332
San Patricio	1930	2,077,867	1,788,300	468,841,425
San Saba	1982	0	0	32,362
Schleicher	1937	926,425	845,091	79,313,012
Scurry	1923	15,769,722	13,825,698	1,825,516,736
Shackelford	1910	1,624,190	1,615,420	165,375,193
Shelby	1917	135,348	97,368	1,629,764
Sherman	1938	755,608	931,657	5,139,600
Smith	1931	3,711,727	3,469,311	238,271,968
Somervell	1978	0	0	119
Starr	1929	1,864,460	2,323,818	265,609,901
Stephens	1916	6,023,857	5,601,323	286,547,844
Sterling	1947	2,243,461	2,455,579	65,239,511

County	Year of Discovery	Crude Production* 1989	1990	Total Prdn. to Jan. 1, 1991 (bbls.)
Stonewall	1938	4,596,835	6,081,167	226,088,686
Sutton	1948	142,784	129,419	6,255,112
Swisher	1981	0	0	6
Tarrant	1969	0	10	10
Taylor	1929	1,123,880	1,046,387	124,010,720
Terrell	1952	95,679	91,124	3,549,508
Terry	1940	7,822,520	8,502,823	363,142,997
Throckmorton	1924	1,791,159	1,853,451	110,361,187
Titus	1936	1,580,712	1,533,718	200,992,567
Tom Green	1940	1,636,548	1,608,313	79,021,937
Travis	1934	1,878	2,653	709,419
Trinity	1946	22,222	63,943	158,963
Tyler	1937	369,967	431,232	33,618,537
Upshur	1931	555,072	506,967	277,251,894
Upton	1925	10,151,864	9,397,606	678,625,929
Uvalde	1950	0	0	1,814
Val Verde	1935	408	533	116,915
Van Zandt	1929	3,044,638	3,111,431	522,124,566
Victoria	1931	1,482,475	1,357,849	237,459,273
Walker	1934	5,982	7,888	385,669
Waller	1934	204,947	198,464	19,425,717
Ward	1928	7,580,075	7,986,094	668,714,766
Washington	1915	352,412	292,009	19,734,745
Webb	1921	3,004,635	2,583,994	127,432,240
Wharton	1925	4,798,088	4,787,301	303,404,400
Wheeler	1921	1,617,525	1,438,717	90,395,126
Wichita	1910	4,082,537	4,154,097	787,436,583
Wilbarger	1915	1,276,930	1,218,501	252,208,159
Willacy	1936	1,339,192	1,197,550	103,325,286
Williamson	1915	15,000	13,301	9,388,875
Wilson	1941	1,838,222	1,973,734	37,111,256
Winkler	1926	5,927,753	5,420,504	1,007,580,088
Wise	1942	1,355,533	1,282,080	87,708,141
Wood	1941	11,607,119	11,138,805	1,097,156,513
Yoakum	1936	34,652,028	32,858,005	1,664,036,581
Young	1917	3,430,775	3,190,912	280,666,940
Zapata	1919	380,501	445,503	43,036,871
Zavala	1937	992,310	7,424,941	27,806,651

State Totals: 1989, 679,575,353; 1990, 672,081,492; 1991, 53,780,245,018.

*Includes condensate production.

Nonpetroleum Minerals

The nonpetroleum minerals that occur in Texas constitute a long list. Some are currently mined; some may have a potential for future development; some are minor occurrences only. Although overshadowed by the petroleum, natural gas and natural gas liquids that are produced in the state, many of the nonpetroleum minerals are, nonetheless, important to the economy.

In 1990, they were valued at approximately $1.6 billion. Texas is annually among the nation's leading states in value of nonpetroleum mineral production. In 1990, Texas ranked fourth nationally in total mineral output.

Locations of the resource areas of many nonpetroleum minerals are shown on a "Mineral Resources of Texas" map issued by the Bureau of Economic Geology of The University of Texas at Austin. Also available for purchase from the Bureau is a computer-generated, detailed listing of Texas nonpetroleum mineral producers.

The Bureau of Economic Geology, which functions as the state geological survey of Texas, revised the following information about nonpetroleum minerals for this edition of the Texas Almanac. Publications of the bureau, on file in many libraries, contain more detailed information. A catalog of Bureau publications is available free on request from the Bureau (University Station, Box X, Austin, TX 78713-7508; telephone 512 471-1534).

Texas' nonpetroleum minerals are as follows:

ALUMINUM — No aluminum ores are mined in Texas, but three Texas plants process aluminum materials in one or more ways. Plants in San Patricio and Calhoun counties produce aluminum oxide (alumina) from imported raw ore (bauxite), and a plant in Milam County reduces the oxide to aluminum.

ASBESTOS — Small occurrences of amphibole-type asbestos have been found in the state. In West Texas, richterite, a white, long-fibered amphibole, is associated with some of the talc deposits northwest of Allamoore in Hudspeth County. Another type, tremolite, has been found in the Llano Uplift of Central Texas where it is associated with serpentinite in eastern Gillespie and western Blanco County. No asbestos is mined in Texas.

ASPHALT (Native) — Asphalt-bearing Cretaceous limestones crop out in Burnet, Kinney, Pecos, Reeves, Uvalde and other counties. The most significant deposit is in southwestern Uvalde County where asphalt occurs naturally in the pore spaces of the Anacacho Limestone. The material is quarried and used extensively as road-paving material. Asphalt-bearing sandstones occur in Anderson, Angelina, Cooke, Jasper, Maverick, Montague, Nacogdoches, Uvalde, Zavala and other counties.

BARITE — Deposits of a heavy, nonmetallic mineral, barite (barium sulphate) have been found in many localities, including Baylor, Brown, Brewster, Culberson, Gillespie, Howard, Hudspeth, Jeff Davis, Kinney, Llano, Live Oak, Taylor, Val Verde and Webb counties. During the 1960s, there was small, intermittent production in the **Seven Heart Gap** area of the **Apache Mountains** in Culberson County, where barite was mined from open pits. Most of the deposits are known to be relatively small, but the Webb County deposit has not been evaluated. Grinding plants, which prepare barite mined outside of Texas for use chiefly as a weighting agent in well-drilling muds and as a filler, are located in Brownsville, Corpus Christi, El Paso, Galena Park, Galveston, and Houston.

BASALT (TRAP ROCK) — Masses of basalt — a hard, dark-colored, fine-grained igneous rock — crop out in Kinney, Travis, Uvalde and several other counties along the Balcones Fault Zone, and also in the Trans-Pecos area of West Texas. Basalt is quarried near Knippa in Uvalde County for use as road-building material, railroad ballast and other aggregate.

BENTONITE (see **Clay**).

BERYLLIUM — Occurrences of beryllium minerals at several Trans-Pecos localities have been recognized for several years. Evaluation and development of a beryllium prospect near Sierra Blanca in Hudspeth County, a portion of which is on state-owned land, is now underway. Behoite and other beryllium minerals are associated with fluorspar at this site.

BRINE (see also **Salt, Sodium Sulphate**) — Many wells in

Nonfuel Mineral Production and Value, 1988, 1989 and 1990

Source: U.S. Bureau of Mines

(Production measured by mine shipments, sales or marketable production, including consumption by producer.)

Mineral	1988 Produc-tion	1988 Value (add 000)	1989 Produc-tion	1989 Value (add 000)	*1990 Produc-tion	*1990 Value (add 000)
Cement:						
Masonry, thousand short tons	136	$10,800	133	$10,735	145	$11,750
Portland, thousand short tons	7,000	292,256	7,200	286,236	8,000	320,000
††Clays, metric tons	2,714,451	17,468	2,276,629	15,962	2,537,031	17,966
Gemstones	†	340	†	**	†	**
Gypsum, thousand short tons	1,943	15,790	1,993	17,044	2,036	17,932
Lime, thousand short tons	1,192	55,935	1,304	60,829	1,297	60,505
Salt, thousand short tons	7,802	62,925	7,856	69,934	7,852	79,464
Sand and gravel:						
Construction, thousand short tons	50,370	171,167	§43,900	§155,800	58,000	210,700
Industrial, thousand short tons	1,631	26,645	1,661	29,107	1,700	29,400
Stone:						
Crushed, thousand short tons	§82,000	§271,300	76,823	252,982	82,800	285,700
Dimension, short tons	§66,354	§8,310	81,268	12,449	84,500	12,600
Sulphur (Frasch), thousand metric tons	2,622	**	2,446	**	2,240	**
Talc and pyrophyllite, metric tons	236,730	4,466	241,777	4,564	**	**
‡Undistributed	...	531,416	...	546,812	...	509,648
Total Texas Values	...	$1,468,818	...	$1,462,454	...	$1,555,665

*Preliminary. †Not available.
‡Includes clays (ball clay, kaolin), helium, (crude, grade A), iron ore, magnesium compounds, magnesium metal, sodium, sulfate (natural), and values indicated by symbol **.
§Estimated.
**Data withheld to avoid disclosing proprietary data; value included with Undistributed.
††Excludes certain clays; kind and value included in Undistributed.

Texas produce brine by solution mining of subsurface salt deposits, mostly in West Texas counties such as Andrews, Crane, Ector, Loving, Midland, Pecos, Reeves, Ward and other West Texas counties. These wells in the Permian basin dissolve salt from the Salado Formation, an enormous salt deposit that extends in the subsurface from north of Big Bend northward to Kansas, has an east-west width of 150 to 200 miles, and may have several hundred feet of net salt thickness. The majority of the brine is used in the petroleum industry, but it also is used in water softening, the chemical industry and other uses.

Three Gulf Coast counties, Fort Bend, Duval and Jefferson, have brine stations that produce from salt domes.

BUILDING STONE (DIMENSION STONE) — Granite and **limestone** currently are quarried for use as dimension stone. The granite quarries are located in Burnet, Gillespie, Llano and Mason counties; the limestone quarries are in Shackelford and Williamson counties. Past production of limestone for use as dimension stone has been reported in Burnet, Gillespie, Jones, Tarrant, Travis and several other counties. There has also been production of **sandstone** in various counties for use as dimension stone.

CEMENT MATERIALS — Cement is currently manufactured at 13 plants in Bexar, Comal, Dallas, Ector, Ellis, Hays, McLennan, Nolan, and Potter counties. Many of these plants utilize Cretaceous limestones and shales or clays as raw materials for the cement. On the Texas High Plains, a cement plant near Amarillo uses impure **caliche** as the chief raw material. **Iron oxide**, also a constituent of cement, is available from the iron ore deposits of East Texas and from smelter slag. **Gypsum**, added to the cement as a retarder, is found chiefly in North Central Texas, Central Texas and the Trans-Pecos area.

CHROMIUM — Chromite-bearing rock has been found in several small deposits around the margin of the Coal Creek serpentinite mass in northeastern Gillespie County and northwestern Blanco County. Exploration has not revealed significant deposits.

CLAYS — Texas has an abundance and variety of ceramic and nonceramic clays and is one of the country's leading producers of clay products.

Almost any kind of clay, ranging from common clay used to make ordinary brick and tile to clays suitable for manufacture of specialty whitewares, can be used for ceramic purposes. Fire clay suitable for use as refractories occurs chiefly in East and North Central Texas; ball clay, a high-quality plastic ceramic clay, is found locally in East Texas.

Ceramic clay suitable for quality structural clay products such as structural building brick, paving brick and drain tile is especially abundant in East and North Central Texas. Common clay suitable for use in the manufacture of cement and ordinary brick is found in most counties of the state. Many of the Texas clays will expand or bloat upon rapid firing and are suitable for the manufacture of lightweight aggregate, which is used mainly in concrete blocks and highway surfacing.

Nonceramic clays are utilized without firing. They are used primarily as bleaching and adsorbent clays, fillers, coaters, additives, bonding clays, drilling muds, catalysts and potentially as sources of alumina. Most of the nonceramic clays in Texas are **bentonites** and **fuller's earth**. These occur extensively in the Coastal Plain and locally in the High Plains and Big Bend areas. **Kaolin clays** in parts of East Texas are potential sources of such nonceramic products as paper coaters and fillers, rubber fillers and drilling agents. Relatively high in alumina, these clays also are a potential source of metallic aluminum.

COAL (see also **Lignite**) — **Bituminous coal**, which occurs in North Central, South and West Texas, was a significant energy source in Texas prior to the large-scale development of oil and gas. During the period from 1895 to 1943, Texas mines produced more than 25 million tons of coal. The mines were inactive for many years, but the renewed interest in coal as a major energy source prompted a revaluation of Texas' coal deposits. In the late 1970s, bituminous coal production resumed in the state on a limited scale when mines were opened in Coleman, Erath and Webb counties.

Much of the state's bituminous coal occurs in North Central Texas. Deposits are found there in Pennsylvanian rocks within a large area that includes Coleman, Eastland, Erath, Jack, McCulloch, Montague, Palo Pinto, Parker, Throckmorton, Wise, Young and other counties. Before the general availability of oil and gas, underground coal mines near **Thurber, Bridgeport, Newcastle, Strawn** and other points annually produced significant coal tonnages. Preliminary evaluations indicate substantial amounts of coal may remain in the North Central Texas area. The coal seams there are generally no more than 30 inches thick and are commonly covered by well-consolidated overburden. Ash and sulphur content are high. Beginning in 1979, two bituminous coal mine operations in North Central Texas — one in southern Coleman County and one in northwestern Erath County — produced coal to be used as fuel by the cement industry. Neither mine is currently operating.

In South Texas, bituminous coal occurs in the Eagle Pass district of Maverick County, and bituminous **cannel coal** is present in the Santo Tomas district of Webb County. The Eagle Pass area was a leading coal-producing district in Texas during the late 1800s and early 1900s. The bituminous coal in that area, which occurs in the Upper Cretaceous Olmos Formation, has a high ash content and a moderate moisture and sulphur content. According to reports, Maverick County coal beds range from four to seven feet thick.

The cannel coals of western Webb County occur near the Rio Grande in middle Eocene strata. They were mined for more than 50 years and used primarily as a boiler fuel. Mining ceased from 1939 until 1978, when a surface mine was opened 30 miles northwest of Laredo to produce cannel coal for use as fuel in the cement industry and for export. An additional mine has since been opened in that county. Tests show that the coals of the Webb County Santo Tomas district have a high hydrogen content and yield significant amounts of gas and oil when distilled. They also have a high sulphur content. A potential use might be as a source of various petrochemical products.

Coal deposits in the Trans-Pecos country of West Texas include those in the Cretaceous rocks of the **Terlingua** area of Brewster County, the Eagle Spring area of Hudspeth County and the San Carlos area of Presidio County. The coal deposits in these areas are believed to have relatively little potential for development as a fuel. They have been sold in the past as a soil amendment (see Leonardite).

COPPER — Copper minerals have been found in the Trans-Pecos area of West Texas, in the Llano Uplift area of Central Texas and in redbed deposits of North Texas. No copper has been mined in Texas during recent years, and the total copper produced in the state has been relatively small. Past attempts to mine the North Texas and Llano Uplift copper deposits resulted in small shipments, but practically all the copper production in the state has been from the **Van Horn-Allamoore** district of Culberson and Hudspeth Counties in the Trans-Pecos area. Chief output was from the **Hazel copper-silver mine** of Culberson County that yielded over 1 million pounds of copper during 1891-1947. Copper ores and concentrates from outside of Texas are processed at smelters in El Paso and Amarillo.

CRUSHED STONE — Texas is among the leading states in the production of crushed stone. Most production consists of **limestone**; other kinds of crushed stone produced in the state include **basalt** (**trap rock**), **dolomite**, **granite**, **marble**, **rhyolite**, **sandstone** and **serpentinite**. Large tonnages of crushed stone are used as aggregate in concrete, as road material and in the manufacture of cement and lime. Some is used as riprap, terrazzo, roofing chips, filter material, fillers and for other purposes.

DIATOMITE (DIATOMACEOUS EARTH) — Diatomite is a very lightweight siliceous material consisting of the remains of microscopic aquatic plants (diatoms). It is used chiefly as a filter and filler; other uses are for thermal insulation, as an abrasive, as an insecticide carrier and as a lightweight aggregate, and for other purposes. The diatomite was deposited in shallow fresh-water lakes that were present in the High Plains during portions of the Pliocene and Pleistocene epochs. Deposits have been found in Armstrong, Crosby, Dickens, Ector, Hartley and Lamb counties. No diatomite is mined in Texas.

DOLOMITE ROCK — Dolomite rock, which consists largely of the mineral dolomite (calcium-magnesium carbonate), commonly is associated with **limestone** in Texas. Areas in which dolomite rock occurs include Central Texas, the Callahan Divide and parts of the Edwards Plateau, High Plains and West Texas. Some of the principal deposits of dolomite rock are found in Bell, Brown, Burnet, Comanche, Edwards, El Paso, Gillespie, Lampasas, Mills, Nolan, Taylor and Williamson counties. Dolomite rock can be used as **crushed stone** (although much of Texas dolomite is soft and not a good aggregate material), in the manufacture of lime and as a source of **magnesium**.

FELDSPAR — Large crystals and crystal fragments of feldspar minerals occur in the Precambrian pegmatite rocks that crop out in the Llano Uplift area of Central Texas — including Blanco, Burnet, Gillespie, Llano and Mason counties — and in the Van Horn area of Culberson and Hudspeth counties in West Texas. Feldspar has been mined in Llano County for use as roofing granules and as a ceramic material but is not currently mined anywhere within the state.

FLUORSPAR — The mineral fluorite (calcium fluoride), which is known commercially as fluorspar, occurs both in Central and West Texas. In Central Texas, the deposits that have been found in Burnet, Gillespie and Mason Counties are not considered adequate to sustain mining operations. In West Texas, deposits have been found in Brewster, El Paso, Hudspeth, Jeff Davis and Presidio counties. Fluorspar has been mined in the **Christmas Mountains** of Brewster County and processed in Marathon. Former West Texas mining activity in the **Eagle Mountains district** of Hudspeth County resulted in the production of approximately 15,000 short tons of fluorspar during the peak years of 1942-1950. No production has been reported in Hudspeth County since that period. Imported fluorspar is processed in Brownsville, Eagle Pass, El Paso and Houston. Fluorspar is used in the steel, chemical, aluminum, magnesium, ceramics and glass industries and for various other purposes.

FULLER'S EARTH (see **Clay**).

GOLD — No major deposits of gold are known in Texas. Small amounts have been found in the Llano Uplift region of Central Texas and in West Texas; minor occurrences have been reported on the Edwards Plateau and the Gulf Coastal Plain of Texas. Nearly all of the gold produced in the state came as a by-product of silver and lead mining at **Presidio mine**, near **Shafter**, in Presidio County. Additional small quantities were produced as a by-product of copper mining in Culberson County and from residual soils developed from gold-bearing quartz stringers in metamorphic rocks in Llano County. No gold mining has been reported in Texas since 1952. Total gold production in the state, 1889-

1952, amounted to more than 8,419 troy ounces according to U.S. Bureau of Mines figures. Most of the production — at least 73 percent and probably more — came from the Presidio mine.

GRANITE — Granites in shades of red and gray and related intrusive igneous rocks occur in the Llano Uplift of Central Texas and in the Trans-Pecos country of West Texas. Deposits are found in Blanco, Brewster, Burnet, El Paso, Gillespie, Hudspeth, Llano, McCulloch, Mason, Presidio and other counties. Quarries in Burnet, Gillespie, Llano and Mason counties produce Precambrian granite for a variety of uses as **dimension stone** and **crushed stone**.

GRAPHITE — Graphite, a soft, dark-gray mineral, is a form of very high-grade carbon. It occurs in Precambrian schist rocks of the Llano Uplift of Central Texas, notably in Burnet and Llano counties. Crystalline-flake graphite ore formerly was mined from open pits in the Clear Creek area of western Burnet County and processed at a plant near the mine. The mill now occasionally grinds imported material. Uses of natural crystalline graphite are refractories, steel production, pencil leads, lubricants, foundry facings and crucibles and for other purposes.

GRINDING PEBBLES (ABRASIVE STONES) — Flint pebbles, suitable for use in tube-mill grinding, are found in the Gulf Coastal Plain where they occur in gravel deposits along rivers and in upland areas. Grinding pebbles are produced from Frio River terrace deposits near the McMullen-Live Oak county line, but the area is now part of the Choke Canyon Reservoir area.

GYPSUM — Gypsum is widely distributed in Texas. Chief deposits are bedded gypsum in the area east of the High Plains, in the Trans-Pecos country and in Central Texas. It also occurs in salt dome caprocks of the Gulf Coast. The massive, granular variety known as rock gypsum is the kind most commonly used by industry. Other varieties include **alabaster**, **satin spar** and **selenite**.

Gypsum is one of the important industrial minerals in Texas. Bedded gypsum is produced from surface mines in Culberson, Fisher, Gillespie, Hardeman, Hudspeth, Kimble, Nolan and Stonewall counties. Gypsum was formerly mined at **Gyp Hill salt dome** in Brooks County and at **Hockley salt dome** in Harris County. Most of the gypsum is calcined and used in the manufacture of gypsum wallboard, plaster, joint compounds and other construction products. Crude gypsum is used chiefly as a retarder in portland cement and as a soil conditioner.

HELIUM — Texas is a leading producer of this very light, nonflammable, chemically inert gas. Helium is extracted from natural gas of the Panhandle area at the U.S. Bureau of Mines Exell plant near Masterson in Moore County and at two privately owned plants in Moore and Hansford counties. As a conservation measure, the Bureau of Mines injects the helium that is not sold when the gas is produced into the Cliffside gas field near Amarillo for storage. Helium is used in cryogenics, welding, pressurizing and purging, leak detection, synthetic breathing mixtures and for other purposes.

IRON — Iron oxide (limonite, goethite and hematite) and iron carbonate (siderite) deposits occur widely in East Texas, notably in Cass, Cherokee, Marion and Morris counties, and also in Anderson, Camp, Harrison, Henderson, Nac-ogdoches, Smith, Upshur and other counties. **Magnetite** (magnetic, black iron oxide) occurs in Central Texas, including a deposit at **Iron Mountain** in Llano County. **Hematite** occurs in the Trans-Pecos area and in the Llano Uplift of Central Texas. The extensive deposits of **glauconite** (a complex silicate containing iron) that occur in East Texas and the hematitic and goethitic Cambrian sandstone that crops out in the northwestern Llano Uplift region are potential sources of low-grade iron ore.

Limonite and other East Texas iron ores are mined from open pits in Cherokee and Henderson counties for use in the preparation of **portland cement**, as a weighting agent in well-drilling fluids, as an animal feed supplement and for other purposes. East Texas iron ores also were mined in the past for use in the iron-steel industry.

KAOLIN (see **Clay**).

LEAD AND ZINC — The lead mineral **galena** (lead sulphide) commonly is associated with zinc and silver. It formerly was produced as a by-product of West Texas silver mining, chiefly from the **Presidio mine** at **Shafter** in Presidio County, although lesser amounts were obtained at several other mines and prospects. Deposits of galena also are known to occur in Blanco, Brewster, Burnet, Gillespie and Hudspeth counties.

Zinc, primarily from the mineral sphalerite (zinc sulphide), was produced chiefly from the **Bonanza** and **Alice Ray mines** in the **Quitman Mountains** of Hudspeth County. In addition, small production was reported from several other areas, including the **Chinati** and **Montezuma mines** of Presidio County and the **Buck Prospect** in the **Apache Mountains** of Culberson County. Zinc mineralization also occurs in association with the lead deposits in Cambrian rocks of Central Texas.

LEONARDITE — Deposits of weathered (oxidized) low-Btu value bituminous coals, generally referred to as "leonardite," occur in Brewster County. The name leonardite is used for a mixture of chemical compounds that is high in humic acids. In the past, material from these deposits was sold as soil conditioner. Other uses of leonardite include modification of viscosity of drill fluids and as sorbants in water-treatment.

LIGHTWEIGHT AGGREGATE (see **Clay, Diatomite, Perlite, Vermiculite**).

LIGNITE — Lignite, a low-rank coal, is found in belts of Tertiary Eocene strata that extend across the Texas Gulf Coastal Plain from the Rio Grande in South Texas to the Arkansas and Louisiana borders in East Texas. The largest resources and best grades (approximately 6,500 BTU/pound) of lignite occur in the Wilcox Group of strata north of the Colorado River in East and Central Texas.

The near-surface lignite resources, occurring at depths of less than 200 feet in seams of three feet or thicker, are estimated at 23 billion short tons. Recoverable reserves of strippable lignite — those that can be economically mined under current conditions of price and technology — are estimated to be 9 billion to 11 billion short tons.

Additional lignite resources of the Texas Gulf Coastal Plain occur as deep-basin deposits. Deep basin resources, those that occur at depths of 200 to 2,000 feet in seams of five feet or thicker, are comparable in magnitude to near-surface resources. The deep-basin lignites are a potential energy resource that conceivably could be utilized by in situ (in place) recovery methods such as underground gasification.

As with bituminous coal, lignite production was significant prior to the general availability of oil and gas. Remnants of old underground mines are common throughout the area of lignite occurrence. Large reserves of strippable lignite have again attracted the attention of energy suppliers, and Texas is now the nation's 6th leading producer of coal, 99 percent of it lignite. Eleven large strip mines are now producing lignite that is burned for mine-mouth electric power generation, and additional mines are planned. One of the currently operating mines is located in Milam County, where part of the electric power is used for alumina reduction. Other mines are in Atascosa, Bastrop, Freestone, Grimes, Harrison, Limestone, Rusk, Panola, Titus and Hopkins counties, where the electricity generated supplies municipal, domestic and industrial needs. Another Harrison County strip mine produces lignite that is used to make activated carbon.

LIME MATERIAL — Limestones, which are abundant in some areas of Texas, are heated to produce lime (calcium oxide) at a number of plants in the state. High magnesium limestone and dolomite are used to prepare lime at a plant in Burnet County. Other lime plants are located in Bexar, Bosque, Comal, Hill, Johnson and Travis counties. Lime production captive to the kiln's operator occurs in several Texas counties. Lime is used in soil stabilization, water purification, paper and pulp manufacture, metallurgy, sugar refining, agriculture, construction, removal of sulfur from stack gases and for many other purposes.

LIMESTONE (see also **Building Stone**) — Texas is one of the nation's leading producers of limestone, which is quarried in more than 60 counties. Limestone occurs in nearly all areas of the state with the exception of most of the Gulf Coastal Plain and High Plains. Although some of the limestone is quarried for use as dimension stone, most of the output is crushed for uses such as bulk building materials (crushed stone, road base, concrete aggregate), chemical raw materials, fillers or extenders, lime and **portland cement** raw materials, **agricultural limestone** and removal of sulfur from stack gases.

MAGNESITE — Small deposits of magnesite (natural magnesium carbonate) have been found in Precambrian rocks in Llano and Mason counties of Central Texas. There formerly was small-scale mining of magnesite in the area — some of the material was used as **agricultural stone** and as **terrazzo chips**. Magnesite also can be calcined to form magnesia, which is used in metallurgical furnace refractories and other products.

MAGNESIUM — On the Texas Gulf Coast in Brazoria County, **magnesium chloride** is extracted from sea water at a plant in Freeport and used to produce magnesium compounds and magnesium metal. During World War II, high-magnesium Ellenburger **dolomite** rock from Burnet County was used as magnesium ore at a plant near Austin.

MANGANESE — Deposits of manganese minerals, such as braunite, hollandite and pyrolusite, have been found in several areas, including Jeff Davis, Llano, Mason, Presidio and Val Verde counties. Known deposits are not large. Small shipments have been made from Jeff Davis, Mason and Val Verde counties, but no manganese mining has been reported in Texas since 1954.

MARBLE — Metamorphic and sedimentary marbles suitable for monument and building stone are found in the Llano Uplift and nearby areas of Central Texas and the Trans-Pecos area of West Texas. Gray, white, black, greenish black, light green, brown and cream-colored marbles occur in Central Texas in Burnet, Gillespie, Llano and Mason counties. West Texas metamorphic marbles include the bluish-white and the black marbles found southwest of Alpine in Brewster County and the white marble from **Marble Canyon** north of Van Horn in Culberson Coun-

ty. Marble can be used as **dimension stone, terrazzo** and roofing aggregate and for other purposes.

MERCURY (QUICKSILVER) — Mercury minerals, chiefly **cinnabar,** occur in the Terlingua district and nearby districts of southern Brewster and southeastern Presidio counties. Mining began there about 1894, and from 1905 to 1935, Texas was one of the nation's leading producers of quicksilver. Following World War II, a sharp drop in demand and price, along with depletion of developed ore reserves, caused abandonment of all the Texas mercury mines.

With a rise in the price, sporadic mining took place between 1951-1960. In 1965, when the price of mercury moved to a record high, renewed interest in the Texas mercury districts resulted in the reopening of several mines and the discovery of new ore reserves. By April 1972, however, the price had declined and the mines have reported no production since 1973.

MICA — Large crystals of flexible, transparent mica minerals in igneous pegmatite rocks and mica flakes in metamorphic schist rocks are found in the Llano area of Central Texas and the Van Horn area of West Texas. Most Central Texas deposits do not meet specifications for sheet mica, and although several attempts have been made to produce West Texas sheet mica in Culberson and Hudspeth counties, sustained production has not been achieved. A mica quarry operated for a short time in the early 1980s in the **Van Horn** area of Culberson and Hudspeth counties to mine mica schist for use as an additive in rotary drilling fluids.

MOLYBDENUM — Small occurrences of molybdenite have been found in Burnet and Llano counties, and wulfenite, another molybdenum mineral, has been noted in rocks in the Quitman Mountains of Hudspeth County. Molybdenum minerals also occur at Cave Peak north of Van Horn in Culberson County, in the **Altuda Mountain** area of northwestern Brewster County and in association with **uranium ores** of the Gulf Coastal Plain.

PEAT — This spongy organic substance forms in bogs from plant remains. It has been found in the Gulf Coastal Plain in several localities including Gonzales, Guadalupe, Lee, Milam, Polk and San Jacinto counties. There has been intermittent, small-scale production of some of the peat for use as a soil conditioner.

PERLITE — Perlite, a glassy igneous rock, expands to a lightweight, porous mass when heated. It can be used as a lightweight aggregate, filter aid, horticultural aggregate and for other purposes. Perlite occurs in Presidio County, where it has been mined in the **Pinto Canyon** area north of the **Chinati Mountains.** No perlite is currently mined in Texas, but perlite mined outside of Texas is expanded at plants in Bexar, Dallas, El Paso, Guadalupe, Harris and Nolan counties.

PHOSPHATE — Rock phosphate is present in Paleozoic rocks in several areas of Brewster and Presidio counties in West Texas and in Central Texas, but the known deposits are not large. In Northeast Texas, sedimentary rock phosphate occurs in thin conglom-eratic lenses in Upper Cretaceous and Tertiary rock units; possibly some of these low-grade phosphorites could be processed on a small scale for local use as a fertilizer. Imported phosphate rock is processed at a plant in Brownsville.

POTASH — The potassium mineral **polyhalite** is widely distributed in the subsurface Permian Basin of West Texas and has been found in many wells in that area. During 1927-1931, the federal government drilled a series of potash-test wells in Crane, Crockett, Ector, Glasscock, Loving, Reagan, Upton and Winkler counties. In addition to polyhalite, which was found in all of the counties, these wells revealed the presence of the potassium minerals **carnallite** and **sylvite** in Loving County and carnallite in Winkler County. The known Texas potash deposits are not as rich as those in the New Mexico portion of the Permian Basin and have not been developed.

PUMICITE (VOLCANIC ASH) — Deposits of volcanic ash occur in Brazos, Fayette, Gonzales, Karnes, Polk, Starr and other counties of the Texas Coastal Plain. Deposits also have been found in the Trans-Pecos area, High Plains and in several counties east of the High Plains. Volcanic ash is used to prepare pozzolan cement, cleansing and scouring compounds and soaps and sweeping compounds; as a carrier for insecticides, and for other purposes. It has been mined in Dickens, Lynn, Scurry, Starr and other counties.

QUICKSILVER (see **Mercury**).

RARE-EARTH ELEMENTS AND METALS — "Rare-earth elements" is commonly applied to elements of the lanthanide group (atomic numbers 57 through 71) plus **yttrium.** Yttrium, atomic number 39 and not a member of the lanthanide group, is included as a rare-earth element because it has similar properties to members of that group and usually occurs in nature with them. The metals **thorium** and **scandium** are sometimes termed "rare metals" because their occurence is often associated with the rare-earth elements.

The marjority of rare-earth elements are consumed as catalysts in petroleum cracking and other chemical industries. Rare earths are widely used in the glass industry for tableware, specialty glasses, optics and fiber optics. **Cerium oxide** has growing use as a polishing compound for glass, gem-stones, cathode-ray tube faceplates, and other polishing. Rare earths are alloyed with various metals to produce materials used in the aeronautic, space and electronics industries. Addition of rare-earth elements may improve resistance to metal fatigue at high temperatures, reduce potential for corrosion, and selectively increase conductivity and magnetism of the metal.

Various members of this group, including thorium, have anomalous concentrations in the rhyolitic and related igneous rocks of the Quitman Mountains and the Sierra Blanca area of Trans-Pecos.

SALT (SODIUM CHLORIDE) (see also **BRINES**) — Salt resources of Texas are virtually inexhaustible. Enormous deposits occur in the subsurface Permian Basin of West Texas and in the salt domes of the Gulf Coastal Plain. Salt also is found in the alkali playa lakes of the High Plains, the alkali flats or **salt lakes** in the Salt Basin of Culberson and Hudspeth counties and along some of the bays and lagoons of the South Texas Gulf Coast.

Texas is one of the leading salt-producing states. **Rock salt** is obtained from underground mines in salt domes at **Grand Saline** in Van Zandt County. Approximately one-third of the salt produced in the state is from rock salt; most of the salt is produced by solution mining as brines from wells drilled into the underground salt deposits.

SAND, INDUSTRIAL — Sands used for special purposes, due to high silica content or to unique physical properties, command higher prices than common sand. Industrial sands in Texas occur mainly in the Central Gulf Coastal Plain and in North Central Texas. They include abrasive, blast, chemical, engine, filtration, foundry, glass, hydraulic-fracturing (propant), molding and pottery sands. Recent production of industrial sands has been from Atascosa, Colorado, Hardin, Harris, Liberty, Limestone, McCulloch, Newton, Smith, Somervell and Upshur counties.

SAND AND GRAVEL (CONSTRUCTION) — Sand and gravel are among the most extensively utilized resources in Texas. Principal occurrence is along the major streams and in stream terraces. Sand and gravel are important bulk construction materials, used as railroad ballast, base materials and for other purposes.

SANDSTONE — Sandstones of a variety of colors and textures are widely distributed in a number of geologic formations in Texas. Some of the sandstones have been quarried for use as dimension stone in El Paso, Parker, Terrell, Ward and other counties. Crushed sandstone is produced in Freestone, Gaines, Jasper, McMullen, Motley and other counties for use as road-building material, **terrazzo stone** and aggregate.

SERPENTINITE — Several masses of serpentinite, which formed from the alteration of basic igneous rocks, are associated with other Precambrian metamorphic rocks of the Llano Uplift. The largest deposit is the Coal Creek serpentinite mass in northern Blanco and Gillespie counties from which **terrazzo chips** have been produced. Other deposits are present in Gillespie and Llano counties. (The features that are associated with surface and subsurface Cretaceous rocks in several counties in or near the Balcones Fault Zone and that are commonly known as "serpentine plugs" are not serpentine at all, but are altered igneous volcanic necks and pipes and mounds of altered volcanic ash — palagonite — that accumulated around the former submarine volcanic pipes.)

SHELL — **Oyster shells** and other shells in shallow coastal waters and in deposits along the Texas Gulf Coast have been produced in the past chiefly by dredging. They were used to a limited extent as raw material in the manufacture of **cement**, as **concrete aggregate** and road base, and for other purposes. No shell has been produced in Texas since 1981.

SILVER — During the period 1885-1952, the production of silver in Texas, as reported by the U.S. Bureau of Mines, totaled about 33 million troy ounces. For about 70 years, silver was the most consistently produced metal in Texas, although always in moderate quantities. All of the production came from the Trans-Pecos country of West Texas, where the silver was mined in Brewster County (**Altuda Mountain**), Culberson and Hudspeth counties (**Van Horn Mountains** and **Van Horn-Allamoore districts**), Hudspeth County (**Quitman Mountains** and **Eagle Mountains**) and Presidio County (**Chinati Mountains** area, **Loma Plata mine** and **Shafter district**). Chief producer was the **Presidio mine** in the Shafter district, which began operations in the late 1800s, and, through September 1942, produced more than 30 million ounces of silver — more than 92 percent of Texas' total silver production. Water in the lower mine levels, lean ores and low price of silver resulted in the closing of the mine in 1942. Another important silver producer was the **Hazel copper-silver mine** in the **Van Horn-Allamoore district** in Culberson County, which accounted for more than 2 million ounces.

An increase in the price of silver in the late 1970s stimulated prospecting for new reserves, and exploration began near the old **Presidio mine**, near the old **Plata Verde mine** in the **Van Horn Mountains district**, at the **Bonanza mine** in the **Quitman Mountains district** and at the old **Hazel mine**. A decline in the price of silver in the early 1980s, however, resulted in reduction of exploration and mine development in the region. There is no current exploration in these areas.

SOAPSTONE (see **Talc** and **Soapstone**).

SODIUM SULFATE (SALT CAKE) — Sodium sulfate minerals occur in salt beds and brines of the alkali playa lakes of the High Plains in West Texas. In some lakes, the sodium sulfate minerals are present in deposits a few feet beneath the lakebeds. Sodium sulfate also is found in underground brines in the Permian Basin. Current production is from brines and dry salt beds at alkali lakes in Gaines and Terry counties. Past production was reported in Lynn and Ward counties. Sodium sulfate was used chiefly by the detergent and paper and pulp industries. Other uses are in the preparation of glass and other products.

STONE (see **Building Stone; Crushed Stone**).

STRONTIUM — Deposits of the mineral celestite (strontium sulfate) have been found in a number of places, including localities in Brown, Coke, Comanche, Fisher, Lampasas, Mills, Nolan, Real, Taylor, Travis and Williamson counties. Most of the occurrences are very minor, and none is currently produced in the state.

SULFUR — Texas is one of the world's principal sulfur-producing areas. The sulfur is mined from deposits of native sulfur, and it is extracted from sour (sulfur-bearing) natural gas and petroleum. Recovered sulfur is a growing industry and accounted for approximately 60 percent of all 1987 sulfur production in the United States, but only approximately 40 percent of Texas production. Native sulfur is found in large deposits in the caprock of some of the salt domes along the Texas Gulf Coast and in some of the surface and subsurface Permian strata of West Texas, notably in Culberson and Pecos counties. Native sulfur obtained from the underground deposits is known as Frasch sulfur, so-called because of Herman Frasch, the chemist who devised the method of drilling wells into the deposits, melting the sulfur with superheated water and forcing the molten sulfur to the surface. Most of the production now goes to the users in molten form.

Frasch sulfur is produced from only one Gulf Coast salt dome in Wharton County and from West Texas underground Permian strata in Culberson County. Operations at several Gulf Coast domes have been closed in recent years. During the 1940s, acidic sulfur earth was produced in the **Rustler Springs district** in Culberson County for use as a fertilizer and soil conditioner. Sulfur is recovered from sour natural gas and petroleum at plants in numerous Texas counties. Sulfur is used in the preparation of fertilizers and organic and inorganic chemicals, in petroleum refining and for many other purposes.

TALC AND SOAPSTONE — Deposits of talc and soapstone are found in the Precambrian metamorphic rocks of the **Allamoore area** of eastern Hudspeth and western Culberson counties. Soapstone, containing **talc**, occurs in the Precambrian metamorphic rocks of the Llano Uplift area, notably in Blanco, Gillespie and Llano counties. Current production is from surface mines in the Allamoore area. Talc is used in ceramic, roofing, paint, paper, plastic, synthetic rubber and other products.

TIN — Tin minerals have been found in El Paso and Mason Counties. Small quantities were produced during the early 1900s from the **Franklin Mountains** north of El Paso. **Cassiterite** (tin dioxide) occurrences in Mason County are believed to be very minor. The only **tin smelter** in the United States, built at Texas City by the federal government during World War II and later sold to a private company, processes tin concentrates from ores mined outside of Texas, tin residues and secondary tin-bearing materials.

TITANIUM — The titanium mineral rutile has been found in small amounts at the Mueller prospect in Jeff Davis County. Another titanium mineral, ilmenite, occurs in sandstones in Burleson, Fayette, Lee, Starr and several other counties. Deposits that would be considered commercial under present conditions have not been found.

TRAP ROCK (see **Basalt**).

TUNGSTEN — The tungsten mineral scheelite has been found in small deposits in Gillespie and Llano counties and in the **Quitman Mountains** in Hudspeth County. Small deposits of other tungsten minerals have been prospected in the **Cave Peak** area north of Van Horn in Culberson County.

URANIUM — Uranium deposits were discovered in the Texas Coastal Plain in 1954 when abnormal radioactivity was detected in the Karnes County area. A number of uranium deposits have since been discovered within a belt of strata extending more than 250 miles from the middle Coastal Plain southwestward to the Rio Grande.

Various uranium minerals also have been found in other areas of Texas, including the Trans-Pecos, the Llano Uplift and the High Plains. With the exception of small shipments from the High Plains during the 1950s, all the uranium production in Texas has been from the Coastal Plain. Uranium has been obtained from surface mines extending from northern Live Oak County, southeastern Atascosa County, across northern Karnes County and into southern Gonzales County. All mines are now reclaimed.

All current uranium production is by in-situ leaching, brought to the surface through wells, and stripped from the solution at several Coastal Plain recovery operations. Decreased demand and price of uranium since 1980 has brought a sharp decline in operations in Texas.

VERMICULITE — Vermiculite, a mica-like mineral that expands when heated, occurs in Burnet, Gillespie, Llano, Mason and other counties in the Llano region. It has been produced at a surface mine in Llano County. Vermiculite, mined outside of Texas, is exfoliated (expanded) at plants in Dallas, Houston and San Antonio. Exfoliated vermiculite is used for lightweight concrete aggregate, horticulture, insulation and other purposes.

VOLCANIC ASH (see **Pumicite**).

ZEOLITES — The zeolite minerals clinoptilolite and analcime occur in Tertiary lavas and tuffs in Brewster, Jeff Davis and Presidio counties, in West Texas. Clinoptilolite also is found associated with Tertiary tuffs in the southern Texas Coastal Plain, including deposits in Karnes, McMullen and Webb counties, and currently is produced in McMullen County. Zeolites, sometimes called "molecular sieves," can be used in ion-exchange processes to reduce pollution, as a catalyst in oil cracking, in obtaining high-purity oxygen and nitrogen from air, in water purification and for many other purposes.

ZINC (see **Lead** and **Zinc**).

Utilities in Texas

Because of its large size, population and economic activity, Texas ranks high among the states in the scope of its utilities. It was one of the first states to utilize the telegraph and telephone extensively. A history of telephones in Texas appeared in the 1972-73 Texas Almanac, and other editions record much of the development of utilities.
The following information was prepared through the cooperation of utility firms and their trade associations.

Telephones

Texas had 8,863,719 telephone lines in service on Dec. 31, 1990, served by 58 local-exchange companies. In addition to local service, those companies also provide approximately one-third of the intrastate long distance service in Texas. AT&T and some 154 other competitive carriers provide most of the intrastate and all of the interstate long distance service enjoyed by Texans. Southwestern Bell Corporation — which through its telephone company subsidiary also serves Arkansas, Kansas, New Mexico and Oklahoma — became a separate entity Jan. 1, 1984, the date of divestiture of the Bell System, and is no longer associated with AT&T.

The largest subsidiary of the corporation is Southwestern Bell Telphone Company, which provides local telephone access service to some 9 million customers in five states, including Texas.

The Texas Division of Southwestern Bell Telephone was created in 1984, with Dallas selected as its headquarters city.

The Texas Division of Southwestern Bell Telephone serves more than 6.9 million customers in 530 Texas communities. With some 30,558 employees, Southwestern Bell remains one of the largest non-governmental employers in the state.

Southwestern Bell handles over 87 million local calls, and provides access for an additional 6 million direct-dialed long distance calls each day. The company serves Texas with over one million miles of copper and fiber optic cable.

By the end of 1990, the Texas telephone industry had made a total plant investment of $18,507,427,750. The industry's 37,690 employees are paid wages of $1,388,037,264. annually. Telephone companies in Texas pay state and local taxes of $535 million and federal income taxes of $316 million.

Major independent telephone companies in Texas and their total access lines as of Dec. 31, 1990 were: GTE Southwest, with 1,204,791 lines; Contel of Texas, with 167,-801 lines; Central Telephone Co. of Texas, with 127,393 lines; United Telephone Co. of Texas, with 110,750 lines; and Lufkin-Conroe Telephone Exchange, with 63,717. (Because telephone customers can now own the wiring within their premises, as well as all the equipment inside, the industry no longer counts total telephones they serve. Access lines reflect the number of connections the companies provide, and does not equate to number of customers.)

The 58 independent telephone companies in Texas include 24 telephone cooperatives, subscriber-owned systems serving more than 100,850 access lines through 204 exchanges in the state. While the Bell System companies serve approximately 80 percent of all Texans, the independent companies serve more than half of the state's 250,000 square miles of certified service territory.

In the Houston metro area, Southwestern Bell and five independent telephone companies cooperate to serve 1,300,000 customers, possibly the largest in the nation. On the other hand, **Big Bend Telephone Co.** in West Texas serves about 3,145 subscribers in a service area of 19,000 square miles — roughly equal to the states of Connecticut, Delaware, Massachusetts and Rhode Island combined.

The following table shows the number of telephone access lines on Dec. 31, 1990, in the calling scope of many of Texas' principal cities. Some of the larger cities and towns not shown are included in the metropolitan exchanges of Dallas, Houston, Fort Worth and San Antonio.

Abilene	57,783
Amarillo	93,803
Arlington	111,030
Austin (Metro)	413,723
Bay City	12,077
Beaumont	66,194
Brownsville-Harlingen	75,349
Cleburne	18,695
Corpus Christi (Metro)	132,239
Corsicana	13,347
Dallas	1,037,132
El Paso	232,969
Fort Worth	528,724
Galveston	41,116
Greenville	14,229
Houston	1,553,151
Laredo	48,414
Longview	52,393
Lubbock	116,571
McAllen-Edinburg	61,938
McKinney	14,824
Midland	58,128
Mineral Wells	8,734
Odessa	56,308
Paris	18,812
Port Arthur	32,145
San Antonio Metro	593,482
Temple	27,020
Texas City	14,711
Tyler	62,013
Vernon	6,561
Victoria	34,678
Waco	91,433
Wichita Falls	53,020

Electric Utilities

In 1990, utilities serving customers in Texas reported 133 electric power plants (15 not in Texas) with a **total generating capability** of about 66,711 megawatts.

Some of the 133 power plants have several units. For about 335 generating units in Texas, plus 37 outside of Texas, the total capability in 1990 was reported as 62 percent natural gas fueled, 30 percent coal and lignite fueled, 7 percent nuclear fueled and 1 percent hydroelectric and other. In addition, about 3,200 megawatts of cogeneration capability was reportedly in operation in Texas.

The nine major investor-owned electric utility companies operating in Texas are: Central Power & Light, El Paso Electric Co., Gulf States Utilities Co., Houston Lighting and Power Co., Southwestern Electric Power Co., Southwestern Public Service Co., Texas-New Mexico Power Co., TU Electric and West Texas Utilities Co.

Also supplying electric power to Texas customers are municipally owned systems, rural electric cooperatives and state and federally financed projects.

As 1991 began, these investor-owned companies had a total investment in plants and facilities to serve Texas customers of about $43.7 billion.

Location of the **first power plant** in Texas is uncertain. Some authorities believe a plant that began operation on Dec. 17, 1882, in Houston was first; others credit

Galveston with the first plant. Either of these would be among the first in the United States, since the initial American plant started in New York City in the summer of 1882.

As late as 1910, Texas electrical operations were mainly limited to isolated municipal and individually owned plants. In 1912 **Texas Power & Light Co.** started building Texas' **first high-voltage transmission line.** It extended from Waco to Fort Worth, with a branch from Hillsboro through Waxahachie to Ferris, where it branched north to Trinity Heights (Dallas) and south to Corsicana.

Rural electrification began after the first transmission lines were constructed. By the early 1930s some 48,-000 rural families were receiving service.

Gas Utilities

Approximately 298 investor-owned gas companies in Texas are classified as gas utilities and come under the regulatory jurisdiction of the Texas Railroad Commission. Approximately 184 of these companies reported **gas operating revenue** of $7 billion in 1989, with **operating expenses** of $6.4 billion.

In 1989, fixed investment for distribution facilities in Texas was $1.66 billion and for transmission facilities, $4.7 billion. Investment in Texas plants in service totaled $7.66 billion. There were 55 investor-owned and 86 municipally owned distribution systems in operation in 1989 serving approximately 1,013 Texas cities.

The eight largest distribution systems — six private and two municipal — served 95 percent of all residential customers. In 1989, there were approximately 3.2 million residential customers, 274,185 small commercial and industrial users, 542 large industrial customers and 9,196 other gas utility customers. The breakdown of distribution sales to these customers was: 67 Mcf per residential customer, 598 Mcf per commercial customer, 115,923 Mcf per industrial customer and 5,234 Mcf for customers in the "other" category. Distribution sales amounted to 487.6 billion cubic feet in 1989.

In addition to industrial sales made by distribution companies, transmission companies reported pipeline-to-industry sales of 1.42 trillion cubic feet and revenue from these sales of $3.1 billion.

In 1989, the average annual residential gas bill in the U.S. was $534. The average annual bill in Texas for the same year was $385, down $28 from the previous year. The State of Texas collected $8 million in **gross receipts taxes** from gas utilities in fiscal year 1989.

There were 46,792 producing gas wells in the state at the end of 1989, down 3,796 from the previous year. New gas well completions during 1989 numbered 1,435, down 71 from 1989.

Texas had a total of 136,427 miles of **natural gas pipelines** in operation in 1989, including 20,610 miles of **field and gathering lines,** 46,337 miles of **transmission lines** and 69,480 miles of **distribution lines.**

Estimated proved **gas reserves** in the state amounted to 38.38 trillion cubic feet in 1989. Gross production of natural gas, including **casinghead gas,** in 1989 was 4.57 trillion cubic feet. At year end in 1989, 22 underground storage reservoirs in the state contained 407.8 billion cubic feet of gas.

Electric Cooperatives

The 76 electric distribution cooperatives operating in Texas were serving over 1.075 million rural connections by the end of 1990. The systems, plus two of Texas' three generation and transmission (G&T) cooperatives, were operating more than 257,000 miles of lines extending into all but nine of the 254 counties in Texas. Power produced by the third G&T is relayed through non-cooperatively owned lines to the distribution co-operatives' load centers. Seven additional G&T cooperative federations have no operating facilities but represent their respective member cooperatives in their relations with regulatory bodies and their wholesale power suppliers. Five of the seven have personnel. Altogether, the 76 distribution and five staffed G&Ts employ over 5,550 persons. Average number of consumer units served by the 76 distribution cooperatives, per mile of line: 4.18.

Civic Organizations

Listed below are privately supported civic, commercial and other non-profit Texas organizations that provided information on questionnaires sent to them by the Texas Almanac. Organizations that did not return questionnaires by June 1, 1991, are not included. These are mostly statewide organizations, but in some cases regional organizations are included. Listing is alphabetical by the keyword in the title; i.e., Texas Egg Council is found under "Egg."

AFL-CIO, Texas—Pres., Joe D. Gunn. Office Address: Box 12727, Austin 78711.

Advertising & Magazine Publishing, Texas Council of—Exec. Dir., Marsha Cook; Pres., Larry Spiegel, 10000 N. Central Expy., #1200, Dallas 75231. Office Address: 1104 West Avenue, #101, Austin 78701.

Aglime & Fertilizer Assn., Texas-Louisiana—Assn. Coordinator, Dana Tucker. Office Address: Box 891, Georgetown 78627.

Agricultural Organizations

Agricultural Agents Assn., Texas County—Pres., Glenn Huddleston, County Courthouse, Palestine 75801.

Agricultural Aviation Assn., Texas—Exec. Dir., Joe McCullough; Pres., Bill Nunley, Box 163, Batesville 78829. Office Address: 1033 La Posada Dr., #220, Austin 78752.

Agricultural Consultants, Texas Assn. of—Exec. Dir., Joe McCullough; Pres., Glenn Crane, Rt. 2, Box 225-I, East Bernard 77435. Office Address: 1033 La Posada Dr., #220, Austin 78752.

Agricultural Cooperative Council, Texas—Exec. Vice Pres., Billy L. Conner; Pres., Keith Streety, Rt. 1, Box 286, Levelland 79336. Office Address: Box 9527, Austin 78766.

Agricultural Teachers Assn. of Texas, Vocational—Exec. Dir., Guy Finstad; Pres., Bruce Smith, 805 Hastings, Dumas 79029. Office Address: 614 E. 12th St., Austin 78701.

Alcoholism and Drug Abuse Counselors, Texas Assn. of—Exec. Dir., Joe McCullough; Pres., Al Conlan, 1500-B Norwood, #208, Hurst 76054. Office Address: 1033 La Posada Dr., #220, Austin 78752.

Aloe Science Council, International—Exec. Dir., Don McCullough; Pres., Ray Henry, 1101 Rio Hondo, Harlingen 78550. Office Address: 1033 La Posada Dr., #220, Austin 78752.

American Legion, Dept. of Texas—Dept. Adj., Jim D. Lemley; Cmdr., Derek G. Shultz, 3501 Tanglewood Dr., Bryan 77802. Office Address: Box 789, Austin 78767.

Anesthesiologists, Texas Society of—Exec. Sec., Ann Becker; Pres., Dr. Asa C. Lockhart. Office Address: 1905 N. Lamar Blvd., #107, Austin 78705.

Apparel Mfrs. Assn., Southwest Division of —Exec. Dir., Cincie Drieth; Pres., Shirley Bradford, 4848 Military Pkwy., Dallas 75223. Office Address: Box 585931, Dallas 75258.

Archaeological Associations

Central Texas Arch. Society—Pres., Dr. John Fox, 7830 Delhi Rd., Waco 76712. Office Address: 4229 Mitchell Rd., Waco 76710. **El Paso Arch. Society**—Pres., Joe Guinn, 5000 Alabama, #31, El Paso 79930. Office Address: Box 4345, El Paso 79914.

Houston Arch. Society—Pres., Elisa G. Phelps, 704 Marshall, Houston 77006. Office Address: Box 6751, Houston 77265.

Midland Archeological Society—Pres., Teddy Stickney. Office Address: Box 4224, Midland 79704.

Nautical Archaeology, Institute of—Exec. Dir., Robert K. Vincent Jr. Office Address: Drawer HG, College Station 77841-5137.

Panhandle Archeological Society—Pres., Reba Jones, 2319 Judy, Amarillo 79106. Office Address: Box 814, Amarillo 79105.

Southern Texas Arch. Assn.—Exec. Dir., C. K. Chandler; Pres., Ray Blackburn, 12530 Enfield Dr., San Antonio 78232. Office Address: 123 Crestline, San Antonio 78201.

Architects, American Inst. (Dallas Chapter)—Exec. Dir., Gloria Wise; Pres., Brent Byers, 501 Elm, Ste. 500, Dallas 75202. Office Address: 2811 McKinney, Ste. 20, LB 104, Dallas 75204.

Architects, Texas Society of—Exec. Dir., David Lancaster; Pres., Bill D. Smith, 5910 N. Central Expy., #1200, Dallas 75206. Office Address: 114 W. 7th St., #1400, Austin 78701.

Art Education Assn., Texas—Exec. Dir., Judy Shimp; Pres., Cindy Broderick, 2511 Old Gate Rd., San Antonio 78230. Office Address: 4020 McEwen, #105, Dallas 75244-5019.

Arts, Texas Assn. for the Promotion of the—Pres., Peter Marzio, Box 6826, Houston 77265. Office Address: 1300 S. Mahon, Tyler 75701.

Asparagus Growers Assn., Texas—Exec. Dir., Diana Barnes, 104 Scottie Dr., Boerne 78006; Pres., Barbara Hopson. Office Address: Box 90926, Austin 78709-0926.

Assessing Officers, Texas Assn. of—Exec. Dir., Patrick T. Miller; Pres., Harold Hagan, Harris CAD, Box 920975, Houston 77292. Office Address: 8303 N. MoPac Expy., #245-C, Austin 78759-8370.

Association Executives, Texas Society of—Chmn. of Bd., Robert Floyd; Pres., Marilyn Monroe, 2550 S. IH-35, #200, Austin 78704. Office Address: Box 1669, Austin 78767.

Austin College Alumni Assn.—Exec. Dir., Randy Hudson; Pres., Glo Stegall, 6204 S. 86th E. Ave., #L, Tulsa, OK 74133. Office Address: Ste. 6G, Box 1177, Sherman 75091-1177.

Automotive Service Association—Pres., G. W. Merwin III; Chmn., Gary Spear, 1212 Calle de Comerico, Santa Fe, NM 87501. Office Address: Box 929, Bedford 76095.

Automotive Wholesalers of Texas—Pres. & CEO, Robert A. Stluka Jr. Office Address: Box 17397, Austin 78760.

Auto and Truck Parts Assn., Texas—Exec. Dir., Mike T. Marks; Pres., David Crane. Office Address: 1601 Rio Grande, #440, Austin 78701.

Bankers Assn. of Texas, Independent—Exec. Dir., Christopher L. Williston; Pres., B.A. Donelson, Box 48, Stratford 79084. Office Address: 400 W. 15th, #700, Austin 78701.

Bankers Association, Texas—Pres., Robert E. Harris; Chmn., Shelley H. Collier Jr., 2424 N. 10th, McAllen 78502. Office Address: 203 W. 10th, Austin 78701.

Baptist General Convention of Texas—Exec. Dir., William M. Pinson Jr.; Pres., Phil Lineberger, 701 W. Beltline Rd, Richardson 75080. Office Address: 333 N. Washington, Dallas 75246-1798.

Bar of Texas, State—Exec. Dir., Karen R. Johnson; Pres., James N. Parsons III, Drawer 2210, Palestine 75802. Office Address: Box 12487, Austin 78711.

Baylor Alumni Assn.—Exec. Vice Pres., James F. Cole; Pres., Ray Burchette Jr., 5814 Westmont, Austin 78731. Office Address: BU Box 97116, Waco 76798-7116.

Big Bend Natural History Assn.—Exec. Dir., Rick L. LoBello; Chmn., Jack Skiles, Box 164, Langtry 78871. Office Address: Box 68, Big Bend National Park 79834.

Birds of Prey Center, Dallas—Pres., Dennis D. Smith, 7109 Winterberry, Dallas 75249. Office ADdress, 7575 Wheatland Rd., Dallas 75249.

Blueberry Growers Assn., Texas—Assn. Coordinator, Dana Tucker. Office Address: Box 891, Georgetown 78627.

B'nai B'rith Women (Southwest Region)—Reg. Dir., Elaine L. Altschuler; Chmn., Barbara Rabinowitz, 12310 Wrenthorpe, Houston 77031. Office Address: 4660 Beechnut, #246, Houston 77096.

Boating Trades Assn. of Texas—Pres., Ken Lovell. Office Address: 3811 Turtle Creek Blvd., #950, Dallas 75219-4419.

Bowling Proprietors' Assn. of America—Exec. Dir., V. A. Wapensky; Pres., Walter J. Hall, 1112 N. Rolling Rd., Baltimore 21228. Office Address: 615 Six Flags Drive, Arlington 76011.

Brahman Breeders Assn., American—Exec. Vice Pres., Wendell E. Schronk; Pres., Ed Cullers, Box 145, Hungerford 77448. Office Address: 1313 La Concha Ln., Houston 77054.

Brangus Breeders Assn., Texas—Exec. Admin., Joe Patterson; Pres., Jim Jones, 2202 Timberloch, #107, The Woodlands 77380. Office Address: Box 690750, San Antonio 78269-0750.

Broiler Council, Texas(See **Poultry Associations**))

Business, Texas Assn. of—Exec. Officer, H. Dane Harris; Chmn., Paul W. Kerr, Box 6107, Temple 76503. Office Address: 1209 Nueces, Austin 78701.

Business, Natl. Federation of Independent—State Dir., Robert S. Howden. Office Address: 815 Brazos, #900, Austin 78701.

Cancer Society, American (Texas Div., Inc.)—Exec. Vice Pres., Jack M. Hardison; Pres., Dr. Charles E. Oswalt III, 820 Montgomery Rd., Graham 76046. Office

Address: 2433 Ridgepoint Dr., Austin 78754.

Cave Management Assn., Texas—Executive Director, Mike Walsh; Pres., Jack Ralph, 545 Loop Dr., Seguin 78155. Office Address: Box 310732, New Braunfels 78131.

Cerebral Palsy Assn. of Texas, Inc. United—Exec. Dir., Patricia Anderson; Pres., Nancy Pontigo. Office Address: 900 Congress Ave., #220, Austin 78701.

Chambers of Commerce Executives, Texas—Exec. Dir., Linda Bowman; Pres., Tracey S. Wheeler, #2 West Texas Ave., Baytown 77520. Office Address: 900 Congress, #501, Austin 78701-2447.

Chamber of Commerce, Rio Grande Valley—Pres. & CEO, Bill Summers. Office Address: Box 1499, Weslaco 78596.

Chamber of Commerce, Texas—Pres., Larry S. Milner; Chmn. & CEO, Don Jordan, Box 4567, Houston 77210. Office Address: 900 Congress, #501, Austin 78701-2447.

Christian Church (Disciples of Christ) in the SW—Regional Minister & Pres., M. Margaret Harrison; Pres., Rev. Fred Banda, 1180 Junction Hwy., Kerrville 78028. Office Address: 2909 Lubbock, Fort Worth 76109.

Christmas Tree Growers Assn., Texas—Exec. Sec.-Treas., Al Buehring; Pres., Jim Everett. Office Address: 424 American Bank Plaza, Corpus Christi 78475-1297.

Churches, Texas Conference of—Exec. Dir., Rev. Dr. Frank H. Dietz; Pres., Bishop Charles Grahmann, Box 190507, Dallas 75219. Office Address: 2704 Rio Grande, Apt. 9, Austin 78705-4089.

Circulation Management Assn., Texas—Exec. Dir., Faires Kuykendall; Pres., Franklin Rodriguez, Box 2171, San Antonio 78297. Office Address: 2427 St. Gregory Ct., Arlington 76013.

Civil Air Patrol (Texas Wing)—Wing Cmdr., Col. G.H. Parker, 12122 Palmton, Houston 77034. Wing Vice Cmdr., Jim Zoeller, 1205 Lansdowne, Arlington 76012. Office Address: Bldg. 4212, Bergstrom AFB 78743.

Communication Assn., International—Exec. Dir., Robert L. Cox; Pres., Jay G. Blumler, Center for TV Research, U. of Leeds, Leeds, YORKS LS2 9JT UK. Office Address: Box 9589, Austin 78766.

Contractors Organizations

Air Conditioning Con. Assn., Texas— Pres., James Chapline. Office Address: 3470 Ella Blvd., Houston 77018.

Drilled Shaft Con. Inc., Assn. of—Exec. Dir., Scot Litke; Pres., Alan Macnab, 5820 Main, #612, Williamsville, NY 14221. Office Address: Box 280379, Dallas 75228.

General Con. of Texas, Highway, Heavy, Utility and Industrial—Exec. Dir., Thomas L. Johnson; Pres., Zack Burkett III, Box 40, Graham 76046. Office Address: Box 2185, Austin 78768.

Mechanical Con. Assn. of Texas—Exec. Dir., Roy Bohrer; Pres., Glenn Randle, Box 2689, Austin 78768. Office Address: 1033 La Posada Dr., #220, Austin 78752.

Painting & Decorating Con., Texas Council of—Exec. Dir., Mike T. Marks; Pres., Jack Thomas III. Office Address: 1601 Rio Grande, #440, Austin 78701.

Plumbing, Heating and Cooling Con. of Texas—Exec. Dir., Mike T. Marks; Pres., Travis Blair. Office Address: 1601 Rio Grande, #440, Austin 78701.

Roofing Con. Assn. of Texas—Exec. Dir., Roy K. Bohrer; Pres., Harry Bruton, Box 8794, Corpus Christi 78412. Office Address: 1033 La Posada Dr., #220, Austin 78752.

Corrections Assn., Texas—Exec. Dir., Roy Borer; Pres., Chris A. Mealy, 8050 Airport Rd., Ste. E, Georgetown 78628. Office Address: 1033 La Posada Dr., #220, Austin 78752.

Cotton Organizations

Cotton Ginners Assn., Texas—Exec. Vice Pres., Tony D. Williams; Pres., Gene Beck, Rt. 10, Box 264, Lubbock 79404. Office Address: 400 W. 15th, #1210, Austin 78701.

Cotton Growers Co-operative Assn., Texas—Exec. Dir., A. E. Schmidt; Pres., Paul Underwood, Box 391, Taylor 76574. Office Address: 2303 Lillie Lane, Taylor 76574.

Cotton Growers, Inc., Plains—Exec. Vice Pres., Donald A. Johnson; Pres., J. Larry Nelson, Box 37, Edmonson 79032. Office Address: 4510 Englewood, Lubbock 79414.

Cotton Growers Assn., Rolling Plains—Exec. Dir., Mark Lundgren, Rt. 1, Avoca 79503; Pres., Larry Schwarz, Camp Spring Rd., Snyder 79549. Office Address: Box 1108, Stamford 79553.

Counseling and Development, Texas Assn. for—Exec. Sec., Charlotte McKay; Pres., Marilyn Finer-Collins, 5200 Wesleyan #A-114, Houston 77005. Office Address: 316 W. 12th, #402, Austin 78701.

Counties, Texas Assn. of—Exec. Dir., Sam D. Seale; Pres., Carl Duncan, 900 Austin, Portland 78374. Office Address: 1204 San Antonio, Austin 78768.

Court Reporters Assn., Texas—Exec. Dir., Christopher Boyd, 1315 Harriet Court, Austin 78756; Pres., Dan Stunkard. Office Address: 4020 McEwen, #105, Dallas 75244-5019.

Credit Union League and Affiliates, Texas—Pres., John D. Dunagan. Office Address: Box 655147, Dallas 75265.

Dancing, Texas Assn of Teachers of—Exec. Dir., Laine Johns; Pres., Julia C. Robertson. Office Address: Box 530676, Grand Prairie 75053.

Daughters Organizations

American Colonists, Texas Society of Daughters of— Pres., Mrs. Mary Collie Cooper, 740 Garden Acres, College Station 77802.

Colonial Wars, Texas Society Daughters of—Pres., Mrs. Kenneth L. Wickett, 2461 Ridgmar Plaza, Fort Worth 76116.

1812, Texas Society, United States Daughters of— Pres., Mrs. W.M. Choat, 412 Oak Dr., Lake Jackson 77566.

Republic of Texas, Daughters of the—Pres., Betty Burr, Nacogdoches. Office Address: 5758 Balcones Drive, Suite 201, Austin 78731.

Dermatological Society, Texas—Admin. Coord., Paula J. Rigling; Pres., Dr. Ed Spencer. Office Address: 1801 N. Lamar Blvd., Austin 78701.

Diabetes Assn., Inc., American (Texas Affiliate)— Exec. Vice Pres., Phillip L. Fry; Pres., Dr. Jaime A. Davidson. Office Address: 8140 No. Mopac, Bldg. 1, #130, Austin 78759.

Diabetes and Endocrine Assn., Texas—Exec. Sec., Dr. Veronica K. Piziak; Pres., Dr. Richard Berger, 5200 Meadowcreek, #2046, Dallas 75248. Office Address: 2401 S. 31st St., Temple 76508.

Dietetic Assn., Texas—Exec. Dir., Don R. McCullough; Pres., Kathy Masters, Houston. Office Address: 1033 La Posada Dr., #220, Austin 78752.

Donkey and Mule Society, Inc., American—Member Svcs. Officer, Betsy Hutchins; Pres., Paul A. Hutchins. Office Address: 2901 N. Elm, Denton 76201.

Dulcimer Society, Lone Star State—Pres., Linda Thompson. Office Address: 1517 Laurelwood, Denton 76201.

Earth Scientists, Society of Independent Professional—Exec. Sec., Diane M. Finstrom; Jon F. Cobb, 4625 Greenville, #306, Dallas 75206. Office Address: 4925 Greenville, #170, Dallas 75206.

Egg Council, Texas—Exec. Vice Pres., James Grimm; Pres., Ernest Mahard, Box 248, Prosper 75078. Office Address: Box 9589, Austin 78766.

Electronics Assn., Inc., Texas—Exec. Sec., Polly Thompson; Pres., Larry Parnell, 3520 Fairmont Pkwy., Pasadena 77504. Office Address: 2708 W. Berry, Fort Worth 76109.

Emu Assn., American—Exec. Dir., Don McCullough; Pres., Al Jodoin, Box 1334, Whitney 76692. Office Address: 1033 La Posada Dr., #220, Austin 78752.

Engineers Council of Texas, Consulting— Exec. Dir., J. P. Word; Pres., Wilton N. Hammond, c/o Carter & Burgess, Fort Worth. Office Address: 400 W. 15th, #820, Austin 78701.

Faculty Assn., Texas—Dir., Charles Zucker; Pres., Harb Hayre, Electrical Engineering, Univ. of Houston, Houston 77004. Office Address: 316 W. 12th, Austin 78701.

Fair Assn., East Texas—Mgr., Bob Murdoch; Pres., Herbert C. Buie. Office Address: 411 W. Front, Tyler 75702.

Fair of Texas, State—Gen. Mgr., Errol McKoy; Chmn., David G. Fox. Office Address: Box 150009, Dallas 75315.

Fairs and Expositions, Texas Assn. of—Sec.-Treas., Frances R. Cooper; Pres., Don Thorn, Box 4812, Odessa 79762. Office Address: Box 577, Santa Rosa 78593.

Farm Bureau, Texas—Exec. Dir., Vernie R. Glasson III; Pres., S.M. True Jr. Office Address: Box 2689, Waco 76702-2689.

Farm and Ranch Club, East Texas—Sec.-Treas., Bob Murdock; Pres., Ted Conover. Office Address: 411 W. Front, Tyler 75702.

Farmers of America, Texas Assn. of Future—Exec. Sec., Rebecca L. McClinton; Pres., Matt Owen. Office Address: Box 13064, Austin 78711.

Farmers Union, Texas—Pres., Joe Rankin, Rt. 1, Box 70, Ralls 79357. Office Address: Box 7276, Waco 76714.

Fashion Assn., Inc., American—Exec. Admin., Bette Hamilton; Pres., Kenneth R. Feagins. Office Address: 2300 Stemmons, A.M. Box 586454, Dallas 75258.

Fertilizer Conference, Southwest—Exec. Dir., Joe McCullough; Pres., John Duffy, Box 388, Yazoo City, MI 39194. Office Address: 1033 La Posada Dr., #220, Austin 78752.

Folklore Society, Texas—Sec.-Editor, F. E. Abernethy; Pres., Jeri Tanner, 5405 15th, Lubbock 79416. Office Address: Box 13007, SFA Station, Nacogdoches 75962-3007.

Food Processors Assn., Texas—Exec. Dir., Al B. Wagner Jr.; Pres., Ronald DeVoe, Box 1867, Fort Worth 76101. Office Address: Box 341, College Station 77841.

Forage and Grassland Council, Texas—Exec. Dir., Dana Tucker. Office Address: Box 891, Georgetown 78627.

Foresters, Texas Society of American—Business Mgr., Mahlon Hammetter; Pres., Ernie Smith, 4126 Old Tyler Rd., Nacogdoches 75961. Office Address: Box 150555, Lufkin 75915.

Fruit Growers Assn., Texas—Exec. Sec., Norman Winter. Office Address: 4348 Carter Creek, #101, Bryan 77802.

Funeral Directors Assn., Texas—Exec. Dir., John W. Coker; Pres., Robert R. Smiley, 204 E. Front, Corrigan 75939. Office Address: 1513 S. IH-35, Austin 78741.

Genealogical Society, Texas State—Pres., Marynell Bryant, Rt. 4, Box 56, Sulphur Springs 75482.

Geological Society, West Texas—Exec. Dir., Marie D. Bellomy; Pres., J. Scott Alcorn, Box 4297, Midland 79702. Office Address: 119 N. Colorado, #109, Midland 79701.

Ginners Assn., Texas Independent—Exec. Vice Pres., Sharon Hull; Pres., Ron Craft, Rt. 1, Plains 79355. Office Address: 1300 Guadalupe, #200, Austin 78701.

Grain and Feed Assn., Texas—Exec. Vice Pres., Darrell Ketchum; Pres., Jack Hamil, Friona. Office Address: 1107 Sinclair Bldg., Fort Worth 76102.

Grange, Texas State—Exec. Dir., James H. Kiles; Pres., C.J. Lampman, 10901 FM 1560 N, #4, San Antonio 78254. Office Address: HC-13, Box 6A, Fredericksburg 78624.

Grape Growers Assn., Texas—Exec. Dir., Roy K. Bohrer; Pres., Roy Renfro, Rt. 1, Box 11A, Pottsboro 75076. Office Address: 1033 La Posada Dr., #220, Austin 78752.

Grocers Assn., D-FW—Exec. Dir., Valerie A. Schenewerk; Pres., Bud McCaghren, Box 764283, DAllas 75376-4283. Office Address: 3001 LBJ Fwy., #133, Dallas 75234.

Hawking Assn., Texas—Sec.-Treas., Bill Foster; Pres., Robert Hilton, 5033 Leameadow, Garland 75043. Office Address: 1503 Grantbrook Lane, Dallas 75228.

Healthcare Environmental Services, Texas Soc. for— Exec. Dir., Terry Townsend; Pres., Joe Zamora. Office Address: Box 15587, Austin 78761.

Healthcare Facilities Management, Texas Assn. of— Exec. Dir., Terry Townsend; Pres., Don Fitz. Office Address: Box 15587, Austin 78761.

Healthcare Human Resources Admin., Texas Society—Exec. Dir., Terry Townsend; Pres., Janice Jessen, 1215 E. Court, Seguin 78155. Office Address: Box 15587, Austin 78761.

Heart Assn., American, Texas Affiliate—Exec. Vice Pres., Wyndell C. Rivers; Pres., Dr. Gregory J. Phillips, Fort Worth. Office Address: 1700 Rutherford Lane, Austin 78754.

Highway 67 Assn., U.S.—Sec.-Treas., George R. Jordan; Pres., Bill Rainey, Box 576, Cleburne 76031. Office Address: 401 Rio Concho Dr., #703, San Angelo 76903.

History/Historical Organizations

Baptist Historical Society, Texas—Sec.-Treas., Robert Phillips; Pres., C. W. Bess, 420 Craig Circle, Lewisville 75067. Office Address: Box 22000, Fort Worth 76122-4490.

Catholic Historical Society, Texas—Exec. Officer, Br. Richard Daly; Pres., Dr. Frances Panchok, 11709 Joan of Arc, Houston 77024. Office Address: 3001 S. Congress, Austin 78704.

East Texas Historical Assn.—Exec. Dir., Archie P. McDonald; Pres., Ron Hufford, Box 1488, Lufkin 75901. Office Address: Box 6223, SFA Station, Nacogdoches 75962.

El Paso County Historical Society, —Pres., Richmond

L. McCarty, 4220 Canterbury Dr., El Paso 79902. Office Address: Box 28, El Paso 79940.

Foundation, Texas Historical —Exec. Dir., Jackie Browning Stocker; Pres., Elizabeth Susser, 225 Wilshire Pl., Corpus Christi 78411. Office Address: 1821 Westlake, #102, College Station 77843-3137.

Jewish Historical Society, Texas —Exec. Sec., Jan Hart; Pres., Fay Brachman, 3720 Autumn Dr., Fort Worth 76109. Office Address: Box 10193, Austin 78766-0193.

Oral History Assn., Texas—Sec./Treas., Lois E. Myers. Office Address: BU Box 97271, Baylor U., Waco 76798-7271.

Panhandle Plains Historical Society—Dir., D. Ryan Smith; Pres., Jim Hubbard, Box 436, Claude 79019. Office Address: Box 967, W.T. Station, Canyon 79016.

Permian Historical Society—Pres., Lorene Barbee, Rt. 3, Box 308, Big Spring 79720. Office Address: 4901 E. University, Odessa 79762-8301.

Texas State Historical Assn.—Exec. Dir., Ron Tyler; Pres., Max S. Lale, Fort Worth and Marshall. Office Address: 2.306 Sid Richardson Hall, Austin 78712.

West Texas Historical Assn.—Exec. Dir., B. W. Aston; Pres., Earl Elam, 407 N. Cockrell, Alpine 79830. Office Address: Box 152, HSU, Abilene 79698.

Home Economics Assn., Texas—Exec. Sec., Kim Kamin; Pres., Lillian Chenoweth. Office Address: Box 831, Hurst 76053.

Homefurnishings Assn., Southwest—Exec. Dir., Al Stillmen. Office Address: Box 581207, Dallas 75258.

Horse Organizations

Appaloosa Horse Club, Texas —Exec. Sec., Dawna Harwell; Pres., W.O. Wetzel, Rt. 1, Box 294, Streetman 75859. Office Address: Box 557, Cedar Hill 75104.

Cutting Horse Assn., National—Exec. Dir., Don Landry; Pres., Dennie Dunn, Box 588, Azle 76020. Office Address: 4704 Hwy. 377 So., Fort Worth 76116-8805.

Paint Horse Assn., American—Exec. Sec., Ed Roberts; Pres., Guy Walker, Box 41, Laurel, MS 39441. Office Address: Box 961023, Fort Worth 76161-0023.

Quarter Horse Assn., American—Exec. Vice Pres., Ronald Blackwell; Pres., Jim Barton, Road 1, Box 18, Greene, NY 13778. Office Address: 2701 I-40 East, Amarillo 79168.

Horticultural Society, Texas State— Exec. Vice Pres., Norman Winter. Office Address: 4348 Carter Creek, #101, Bryan 77802.

Hospital Associations

Hospital Assn., Texas—Pres., Terry Townsend; Chmn., Doug Hawthorne. Office Address: Box 15587, Austin 78761.

Hospital Auxiliaries, Texas Assn. of—Exec. Dir., Terry Townsend; Pres., Margaret Hall. Office Address: Box 15587, Austin 78761.

Central Service Personnel, Texas Society of— Exec. Dir., Terry Townsend; Pres., Betty Strickland. Office Address: Box 15587, Austin 78761.

Educators, Texas Society for Hospital—Exec. Dir., Terry Townsend; Pres., Dianne deMoville, 3501 Knickerbocker Rd., San Angelo 76904. Office Address: Box 15587, Austin 78761.

Financial Administration, Texas Assn. of—Exec. Dir., Terry Townsend; Pres., Alan Levine, 1301 Pennsylvania, Fort Worth 76104. Office Address: Box 15587, Austin 78761.

Infection Control Practitioners, Texas Society of— Exec. Dir., Terry Townsend; Pres., Sue Sebazco. Office Address: Box 15587, Austin 78761.

Medical Staff Services, Texas Society for—Exec. Dir., Terry Townsend; Pres., Lynne Humphrey. Office Address: Box 15587, Austin 78761.

Nurse Executives, Texas Organization of—Exec. Dir., Terry Townsend; Pres., Geraldine McFadden. Office

---

Address: Box 15587, Austin 78761.

Patient Representatives, Texas Society of—Exec. Dir., Terry Townsend; Pres., Ben Welmaker, 919 E. 32nd, Austin 78705. Office Address: Box 15587, Austin 78761.

Public Relations, Texas Society for Hospital—Exec. Dir., Terry Townsend; Pres., Debby V. Rektorik, Box 1110, Weslaco 78596. Office Address: Box 15587, Austin 78761.

Purchasing & Materials Mgmt., Texas Soc. of Hospital—Exec. Dir., Terry Townsend; Pres., Gary Taylor. Office Address: Box 15587, Austin 78761.

Quality Assurance, Texas Society for—Exec. Dir., Terry Townsend; Pres., Patsy Smith, 9440 Poppy Dr., Dallas 75218. Office Address: Box 15587, Austin 78761.

Social Work Directors, Texas Society for—Exec. Dir., Terry Townsend; Pres., Wayne L. Dorris, 1515 Holcombe Blvd., Box 103, Houston 77030. Office Address: Box 15587, Austin 78761.

Trustees, Texas Hospital—Exec. Dir., Terry Townsend; Pres., A. E. Fogle Jr., Box 3594, Abilene 79604. Office Address: Box 15587, Austin 78761.

Volunteer Services, Texas Assn., Directors of— Exec. Dir., Terry Townsend; Pres., Linda Branson. Office Address: Box 15587, Austin 78761.

Hotel Assn. of Texas, Historic—Exec. Dir., Laney Bristol; Pres., Loretta Schmidt. Office Address: 501 W. Main, Fredericksburg 78624.

Insurance Agents of Texas, Independent—Exec. Dir., Ernest N. Stromberger; Pres., Matt Berry, 1615 Guadalupe, Austin 78767. Office Address: Box 1663, Austin 78767.

Interior Design, Texas Assn. for (TAID)—Exec. Dir., Ms. Lazan Mathews; Pres., Cathy L. Hendricks, 13750 Hwy. 281 N., Ste. 380, San Antonio 78232. Office Address: Box 815, Austin 78767-0815.

Interior Designers, Texas Chapter of American Soc.— State Admin., Sherri Hendrix; Pres., James J. Marstiller. Office Address: 1909-C Hi Line Drive, Dallas 75207.

Jewelers Assn., Inc., Texas—Office Address: 504 W. 12th, Austin 78701.

Keep Texas Beautiful, Inc.—Exec. Dir., William Yenne; Pres., SueAnn Wade-Crouse. Office Address: Box 2251, Austin 78768.

Knights of Pythias, Grand Lodge of Texas—Exec. Off., John H. Ellis Jr.; Grand Chancellor, John L. Bates, 212 N. 6th, Waco 76701. Office Address: Box 150002, Longview 75615.

Knights of the Order of San Jacinto—Exec. Sec., Maydee J. Scurlock; Knight-Cmdr., Joe E. Ericson, 1614 Redbud, Nacogdoches 75961; Secy.-Treas., T. Talmage Main Jr., 4564 Arcady, Dallas 75205. Office Address: 5942 Abrams Rd., #222, Dallas 75231.

Land Title Assn., Texas—Exec. Dir., Cathy Lancaster; Pres., Larry Molinare. Office Address: 220 W. 7th, #201, Austin 78701.

Lawyers Assn., Texas Young—Dir., Karen Judson; Pres., Kirk P. Watson, Box 1802, Austin 78767. Office Address: 1414 Colorado, #501, Austin 78701.

Legal Reserve Officials Assn., Texas—Exec. Dir., Greg Talley; Pres., Jack Williamson, Box 8157, Dallas 75205. Office Address: Box 12576, Capitol Sta., Austin 78711.

Letters, Texas Institute of—Sec.-Treas., James Hoggard; Pres., Robert Flynn, 101 Cliffside, San Antonio 78231. Office Address: Box 9032, Wichita Falls 76308.

Livestock Trailer Manufacturers, Nat'l Assn. of— Exec. Dir., Don McCullough; Pres., Ron Jackson, Box 646, Madill, OK 73446. Office Address: 1033 La Posada Dr., #220, Austin 78752.

Lung Assn. of Texas, American—Managing Dir., Edward Carter; Chmn. of Board, Dr. Gary D. Harris, 7402 Bridgewater, San Antonio 78209. Office Address: Box 26460, Austin 78755-0460.

Manufactured Housing Assn., Texas—Pres., William L. Ehrle Sr. Office Address: 2215 E. Anderson Lane, Austin 78752.

Medical Assn. Auxiliary, Texas—Exec. Dir., Amy Wilson; Pres., Cyndy Hudgins, Dallas. Office Address: 401 W. 15th, Austin 78701.

Medical Assn., Texas Veterinary—Exec. Dir., Donald M. Ward; Pres., Lloyd N. Fiedler, 6550 N. Lemmon Ave., Dallas 75209-4599. Office Address: 6633 Hwy. 290 E, #201, Austin 78723-1157.

Mental Health Assn. in Texas—Exec. Dir., Stella C. Mullins; Pres., Rusty Kelley, Suite. 1100, Austin 78701. Office Address: 8401 Shoal Creek Blvd., Austin 78758-7544.

Military Order of the World Wars—Chief Admin. Officer, Lt. Gen. C. M. Talbott; Pres., Capt. Dwight F. Copley, 16776 Bernardo Center Dr., #110B, San Diego, CA 92128. Office Address: 435 N. Lee, Alexandria 22314.

Motorcycle Dealers Assn., Texas—Exec. Dir., Mike T. Marks; Pres., Gene Brady. Office Address: 1601 Rio Grande, #440, Austin 78701.

Motor Transportation Assn., Texas—Pres., Robert A. Floyd; Pres., Sam Bishop, Box 33940, San Antonio 78265. Office Address: 700 E. 11th, Austin 78701.

Municipal Advisory Council of Texas—Exec. Dir., Danny Burger; Chmn. of Board, Ross A. Moring, Box 655415, Dallas 75265. Office Address: Box 2177, Austin 78768-2177.

Municipal Clerks Assn., Texas—Exec. Dir., Dorothy Byrd; Pres., Ranette Boyd, City Hall, Lubbock 79424. Office Address: 1400 Kendolph, Denton 76205.

Music Educators Assn., Inc., Texas—Exec. Dir., Bill Cormack; Pres., Scott Taylor, 13221 Kerr Place, Dallas 75244. Office Address: Box 49469, Austin 78765-9469.

National Guard Assn. of Texas—Exec. Dir., Lewis O. King; Pres., Maj. C. Terry Granade, 3706 Crawford, Austin 78731. Office Address: Box 10045, Austin 78766.

Nature Conservancy, Texas—State Dir., David Braun; Pres., Thomas W. Rollins, 711 Navarro, #410, San Antonio 78205-1721. Office Address: Box 1440, San Antonio 78295-1440.

Newspaper Assn., Texas Daily—Exec. Vice Pres., Philip A. Berkebile; Pres., Lissa Walls, 1050 Wilcrest, Houston 77042. Office Address: 98 San Jacinto Blvd., #1250, Austin 78701.

Nuclear Medicine, Texas Assn. of Physicians in—Admin. Coord., Paula J. Rigling; Pres., Dr. Bill Byrd. Office Address: 1801 N. Lamar Blvd., Austin 78701.

Nurserymen, Texas Assn. of—Pres., Ed Edmondson; Chmn., Grady Wadsworth, DSR Box 73, El Campo 77437. Office Address: 7730 S. IH-35, Austin 78745-6621.

Nursing, Texas League for—Exec. Sec., Patty Roberts; Pres., Nannette L. Goddard, 16800 Imperial Valley, #220, Houston 77060. Office Address: 11607 Wiginton Drive, Austin 78758.

Oil and Gas Assn., Texas Mid-Continent—Exec. Dir., Robert L. Looney. Office Address: 1115 San Jacinto Blvd., #275, Austin 78701-1906.

Oil and Gas Assn., North Texas—Exec. Vice Pres., Joseph A. Aboussie; Pres., Gary Shores, Box 1830, Wichita Falls 76307. Office Address: 726 Scott, #801, Wichita Falls 76301.

Optometric Assn., Texas—Exec. Dir., BJ Avery; Pres., Wallace Ryne, 931 E. Main, Uvalde 78801. Office Address: 1016 La Posada, #174, Austin 78752.

Paper & Allied Products Assn., Southwest (SWPAPA)—Exec. Dir., Banks Miller; Pres., Joe Evans. Office Address: Box 610250, Austin 78761.

Paperweight Collectors Asso.—Chmn., Harvey Jones; Pres., Joyce Glore, 1631 Aquarena Springs Dr., #408, San Marcos 78666. Office Address: Box 12762, Austin 78711.

Parents and Teachers, Texas Congress of (PTA)—Exec. Dir., John C. Schneider; Pres., Shirley Igo. Office Address: 408 W. 11th, Austin 78701.

Parliamentarians, Texas State Assn. of—Exec. Dir., Donna Reed; Pres., Jayne Brainard, Amarillo. Office Address: 9318 Faircrest, Dallas 75238.

Pathologists, Texas Society of, Inc.—Admin. Coord., Paula J. Rigling; Pres., Dr. Robert F. Peterson. Office Address: 1801 N. Lamar Blvd., Austin 78701.

Peanut Growers' Assn., Southwest—Exec. Dir., Ross Wilson. Office Address: Box 338, Gorman 76454.

Pecan Growers Assn., Texas—Office Address: 4348 Carter Creek, #101, Bryan 77802.

Pest Control Assn., Inc., Texas—Exec. Dir., Carter Cook; Pres., Clay Stroope, Box 4305, Austin 78765. Office Address: 1033 La Posada Dr., #220, Austin 78752-3824.

Pharmaceutical Assn., Texas—Exec. Dir., Paul F. Davis; Pres., Ronald C. Edwards, 15415 Katy Freeway, #800, Houston 77094. Office Address: Box 14709, Austin 78761.

Physical Therapy Assn., Texas—Exec. Dir., Diane Carminati; Pres., Jerry Hurt, Box 36293, Houston 77236. Office Address: 400 W. 15th, #805, Austin 78701-1647.

Physicians, Texas Academy of Family—Exec. Dir., Jim White; Pres., Dr. C. Timothy Lambert, 10420 Montwood, Ste. H, El Paso 79935. Office Address: Box 9802, #677, Austin 78766.

Plant Society of Texas, Native—Exec. Dir., Dana Tucker. Office Address: Box 891, Georgetown 78627.

Plant Food Institute, Texas—Exec. Dir., Joe McCullough; Pres., C. W. Wright, Rt. 2, Box 238-A, Robstown 78380. Office Address: 1033 La Posada Dr., #220, Austin 78752.

Poetry Society of Texas—Asst. Corresp. Sec., Faye

**Carr Adams; Pres., Dan Stodghill. Office Address: 4244 Skillman, Dallas 75206.

Police Assn., Texas—Exec. Dir., Glenn E. Simmons, Jr.; Pres., Jerry Neal, 609 S. Pierce, Amarillo 79101. Office Address: Box 4247, Austin 78765.

Poultry Associations

Broiler Council, Texas—Exec. Vice Pres., James Grimm; Pres., Mitch Menefee, Box 648, Carthage 75633. Office Address: Box 9589, Austin 78766.

Poultry Assn., Texas Allied—Exec. Vice Pres., James Grimm; Pres., E. E. Griffin, Box 834, Springhill, LA 71075. Office Address: Box 9589, Austin 78766.

Poultry Federation, Texas—Exec. Vice Pres., James Grimm; Pres., William Abbott, Box 648, Carthage 75633. Office Address: Box 9589, Austin 78766.

Poultry Improvement Assn., Texas—Exec. Vice Pres., James Grimm; Pres., Jerry Autry, Box 3039, Bryan 77805. Office Address: Box 9589, Austin 78766.

Prairies Assn. of Texas, Native—Pres., Lea Stone, 301 Nature Center, Austin 78746. Office Address: Box 331376, Fort Worth 76163.

Preservation Texas Alliance—Pres., Jill H. Souter, 350 Wildrose, San Antonio 78209. Officve Address: Box 12892, Austin 78711.

Press Organizations

Press Assn., Texas High School—Dir., Mary K. Sparks. Office Address: Box 23866, Denton 76204.

Press Assn., Texas—Exec. Vice Pres., Lyndell Williams; Pres., Mary Judson, Box 1116, Port Aransas 78373. Office Address: 718 W. 5th, Austin 78701.

Press Assn., West Texas—Exec. Dir., Barbara Kelly; Pres., Rick Craig, Box 339, Hamlin 79520. Office Address: 2502 Ivanhoe, Abilene 79605-6216.

Prevent Blindness, Texas Society to (Dallas Branch)—Exec. Dir., Mary Morris; Pres., Lynda Coumelis. Office Address: 3610 Fairmount St., Dallas 75219.

Producers and Royalty Owners Assn., Texas Independent—Office Address: 1910 InterFirst Tower, Austin 78701.

Property Tax Professionals, Texas Assn. of—Exec. Dir., Don McCullough; Pres., R. E. McElroy, 3609 Smith-Barry Rd., #100, Arlington 76013. Office Address: 1033 La Posada Dr., #220, Austin 78752.

Public Employees Assn., Texas—Exec. Dir., Lane A. Zivley; Pres., Robert J. Ehrhardt. Office Address: Drawer 12217, Capitol Sta., Austin 78711.

Publishers of Texas, Book—Exec. Dir., Pam Lange; Pres., John F. Stetter, Texas A&M University Press, Drawer C, College Station 77843. Office Address: 3404 S. Ravinia, Dallas 75233.

Ranching Heritage Association—Exec. Gen. Mgr. & VP, Alvin G. Davis; Pres., John R. Anderson, Box 136, Gail 79738. Office Address: Box 4040, Lubbock 79409.

Range Management, Texas Section of Society for—Pres., Fred C. Bryant, 7605 Detroit Ave., Lubbock 79423.; Exec. Vice Pres., Peter V. Jackson, 1839 York St., Denver, CO 80206.

Recreational Vehicle Assn., Texas—Exec. Dir., Jamie Thompson, 11243 Pinehurst, AUstin 78747; Pres., William D. Pearson, 731 Rim Rock, Kerrville 78028. Office Address: 3355 Bee Cave Rd., #104, Austin 78746.

Research League, Texas—Pres., Gary E. Wood; Chmn., J. Sam Winters, Box 1148, Austin 78767. Office Address: Box 12456, Austin 78711-2456.

Retailers Assn., Texas—Pres., Michael R. Moore; Chmn.,Glen Stranahan, 1000 E. 41st, Austin 78765. Office Address: 504 W. 12th, Austin 78701.

Savings and Loan League, Texas—Pres., Tom S. King. Office Address: 408 W. 14th, Austin 78701.

School Boards, Texas Association of—Exec. Dir., Billy D. Walker; Pres., Patti Clapp. Office Address: Box 400, Austin 78767-0400.

School Food Service Assn., Texas—Exec. Dir., Carole Pfennig; Pres., Barbara Clark, 1206 W. Arkansas, Arlington 76015. Office Address: 7701 N. Lamar, #518, Austin 78752.

Secretaries Assn., Texas Educational—Exe. Dir., Lois M. Stover; Pres., Marilyn James, 9706 Chimney Rock, Houston 77096-4104. Office Address: Box 1565, Austin 78767.

Sheep Breeders Assn., American Rambouillet—Sec., Jo Ann Custer; Pres., Thomas V. Boyer, 2250 Chalk Creek, Coalville, UT 84017. Office Address: 2709 Sherwood Way, San Angelo 76901.

Sheriffs' Assn. of Texas, Inc.—Exec. Dir., Gordon

Johnson; Pres., Jack Harwell, 219 N. 6th, Waco 76701. Office Address: Box 4488, Austin 78765.

Shrimp Assn., Texas—Exec. Dir., Lucy Gibbs; Pres., Harris Lasseigne, Star Rte., Box 17, Brownsville 78521. Office Address: 2101 S. IH-35, #107, Austin 78741.

Shrine Assn., Texas—Sec.-Treas., W. A. Spoonts; Pres., Nolan H. Flowers, 2701 N. 42nd, Waco 76710. Office Address: Box 1950, Wichita Falls 76307.

Sign Manufacturers Assn., Texas—Exec. Dir., Marcie Funchess; Pres., Gary Cox, Box 1832, Amarillo 79105. Office Address: 2301-C Central Dr., #411, Bedford 76021.

Skeet Shooters Assn., Texas—Pres., Gene D. Jackson. Office Address: Box 830530, Richardson 75083-0530.

Skeet Shooting Assn., National—Exec. Dir., Mike Hampton; Pres., Walter C. Badorek, 4238 Onyx, Klamath Falls, OR 97603. Office Address: Box 680007, San Antonio 78268-0007.

Social Workers, Texas Chapter of the Natl Assn. of—Exec. Dir., Susan Negreen; Pres., Sandra A. Lopez, 5311 Kirby Dr., #217, Houston 77005. Office Address: 810 W. 11th, Austin 78701.

Soil & Water Conservation Districts, Assn. of Tex.—Exec. Dir., Robert G. Buckley; Pres., Charles D. Clark, Box 126, Menard 76859. Office Address: Box 658, Temple 76503.

Sons Organizations

American Revolution, Sons of the (Texas Society)—Exec. Dir., Frank A. Gibson; Pres., Col. E. Graham Martin, 1207 Horseshoe Lane, Lindale 75771. Office Address: Box 27288, Austin 78755.

Confederate Veterans, Sons of (Texas Division)—Cmdr., James N. Vogler Jr., 8506 Braesdale Lane, Houston 77071. Office Address: Box 619, Hillsboro 76645.

Hermann in the State of Texas, Grand Lodge of the Sons of—Grand Pres., Leroy Muehlstein. Office Address: 515 S. St. Mary's, San Antonio 78205.

Republic of Texas, Sons of the—Exec. Secy., Maydee J. Scurlock; Pres.-Gen., Sam Houston IV, 711 Dominion, Katy 77450. Office Address: 5942 Abrams Road, #222, Dallas 75231.

Revolution in the State of Texas, Sons of—Exec. Dir., Thomas Bresnehen; Pres., Kenneth E. Ingram, 3119 Colony Dr., San Antonio 78230. Office Address: 3207 Top Hill Rd., San Antonio 78209.

Southern Methodist University—Interim Exec. Dir., Carol M. Lorton; Robert H. Thomas. Office Address: 3000 Daniel, Dallas 75205.

Soybean Assn., Texas—Exec. Dir., D. Trent Roberts; Pres., Worth Matteson III, RR 3, Box 119-B, DeKalb 75559-9431. Office Address: 1501 N. Pierce, #110, Little Rock, AR 72207.

Speech-Language-Hearing Assn., Texas—Exec. Dir., Banks Miller; Pres., Cherry Wright. Office Address: Box 610250, Austin 78761.

Sportsmen Conservationists of—Exec. Dir., Alan Allen; Pres., Michaux Nash Jr., Box 28816, Dallas 75288. Office Address: 807 Brazos, #311, Austin 78701.

Surgeons, American College of—Exec. Off., John Preskitt; Pres., Jay Hoppenstein, 8220 Walnut Hill Ln., Dallas 75231. Office Address: 3409 Worth, 420 Sammons, Dallas 75246.

Surveyors, Texas Society of Professional—Exec. Dir., Don R. McCullough; Pres., Amil Baker Jr., 11003 Wye Dr., San Antonio 78217. Office Address: 1033 La Posada Dr., #220, Austin 78752.

Taxpayers, Inc., Texas Assn. of—Exec. Vice Pres., William Allaway; Pres., William Renfro. Office Address: 400 W. 15th, #400, Austin 78701.

Teachers Organizations
(See also **Faculty**)

Teachers, Texas Federation of—Pres., John Cole. Office Address: Box 776, Austin 78767.

Teachers Assn., Texas State—Exec. Dir., David A. Bongiolatti; Pres., Olivia Besteiro. Office Address: 316 W. 12th, Austin 78701.

Teachers of English, Texas Joint Council of—Pres., Barbara A. Teer; Pres., Ginna Rhodes, Box 473, Santa Teresa, NM 88008. Office Address: 909 Elms Rd., Killeen 76542.

Teachers, Texas Junior College—Exec. Sec., Charles L. Burnside; Pres., Steve Dutton, Box 447, Amarillo 79178. Office Address: 7748 Highway 290 West, #310, Austin 78736.

Telephone Pioneers of America, Lone Star Chap. 22—Exec. Dir., Mary Frances Zaby; Pres., John Buhl, One Bell Plaza, #3235, Dallas 75202. Office Address: One Bell Plaza, #924, Dallas 75202.

Thoracic Society, Texas (Med. Sec. of Amer. Lung A—Chapter Admin., Linda Nichols; Pres., Stephen G. Jenkinson, M.D.. Office Address: Box 26460, Austin 78755-0460.

Towing Association, Lone Star State—Pres., Hank Mahoney Jr. Office Address: 2726 Bissonet, Houston 77005.

Travel Industry Assn., Texas—Exec. Dir., Vic Heller. Office Address: 900 Congress Ave., #405, Austin 78701.

Travelers Protective Assn. of America, Texas Div.—Exec. Dir., Nathan L. Hutson. Office Address: 2612 W. Waco Dr., Waco 76707.

Tribal American Network, Inc.—Pres., Frank McLemore. Office Address: Box 140343, Dallas 75214-0343.

Turf Irrigation Assn., Texas—Exec. Dir., Roy K. Bohrer; Pres., Delancey Spain, 1813 Wedgewood, Grand Prairie 75050. Office Address: 1033 La Posada Dr., #220, Austin 78752.

Turkey Federation, Texas—Exec. Vice Pres., James Grimm; Pres., Herb Chafin, Box 1288, Temple 76503. Office Address: Box 9589, Austin 78766.

University Presidents & Chancellors, Council of Public—Exec. Dir., Wanda J. Mills; Chmn., Billy Franklin, Lamar Univ., 4400 Martin Luther King, Beaumont 77710. Office Address: 2609 Coatbridge, Austin 78745-3423.

Urological Society, Texas—Admin. Coord., Paula J. Rigling; Pres., Dr. Donald L. McKay. Office Address: 1801 N. Lamar Blvd., Austin 78701.

Veterans of Foreign Wars of the United States (Dept. of Texas)—Exec. Dir., Glen M. Gardner Jr.; Cmdr., Charles S. Pearson. Office Address: 8503 N. IH-35, Austin 78753.

War of 1812 in State of Texas, General Soc. of the—Sec.-Treas., Thomas F. Bresnehen; Pres., David Yielding, 1614 Antelope Tr., Harker Heights 76543. Office Address: 3207 Top Hill Road, San Antonio 78209.

Wars in Texas, Society of Colonial—Exec. Dir., Thomas F. Bresnehen; Pres., Paul W. Adams Jr., 2919 Chisholm Trail, San Antonio 78217. Office Address: 3207 Top Hill Road, San Antonio 78209.

Water Conservation Assn., Texas—Exec. Dir., Leroy Goodson; Pres., Robert J. Huston, 1910 Stoneridge Terrace, Austin 78746. Office Address: 206 San Jacinto Bldg., Austin 78701.

Wildlife Assn., Exotic—Exec. Dir., Chick Rives; Pres., Joe Green, Star Rt. HC89-525, Eden 76837. Office Address: 216 Highway 27 West, Ingram 78025.

Women Voters of Texas, League of—Exec. Dir., Joann Lovelace; Pres., Evelyn Bonavita. Office Address: 1212 Guadalupe, #107, Austin 78701.

Women's Clubs, Texas Federation of—Exec. Sec., Margie L. Brown; Pres., Dorothy M. Boutwell. Office Address: 2312 San Gabriel, Austin 78705.

Writers Assn., Texas Outdoor—Exec. Dir., Paul Hope; Pres., Dell Toedt, 7630 Blue Mist Mountain Dr., San Antonio 78255. Office Address: 1415 Northridge, Austin 78723.

Advertisers' Index

INDEX